The Concise New Partridge Dictionary of Slang and Unconventional English

The *Concise New Partridge* presents, for the first time, all the slang terms from the *New Partridge Dictionary of Slang and Unconventional English* in a single volume.

With over 60,000 entries from around the English-speaking world, the *Concise* gives you the language of beats, hipsters, Teddy Boys, mods and rockers, hippies, pimps, druggies, whores, punks, skinheads, ravers, surfers, Valley girls, dudes, pill-popping truck drivers, hackers, rappers and more.

The *Concise New Partridge* is a spectacular resource infused with humour and learning – it's rude, it's delightful, and it's a prize for anyone with a love of language.

The Concise New Partridge Dictionary of Slang and Unconventional English

Tom Dalzell (Senior Editor)

and

Terry Victor (Editor)

Routledge
Taylor & Francis Group

LONDON AND NEW YORK

First published 2008 by Routledge
2 Park Square, Milton Park, Abingdon, Oxon OX14 4RN
Simultaneously published in the USA and Canada
by Routledge
270 Madison Ave, New York, NY 10016

Routledge is an imprint of the Taylor & Francis Group, an informa business

© 2006, 2008 new editorial matter and selection, Tom Dalzell and Terry Victor;
material taken from *The Dictionary of Slang and Unconventional English*,
8th edition (first published 1984), E. Partridge and P. Beale estates

Typeset in India by Alden Prepress Services Private Limited, Chennai, TN
Printed and bound in Great Britain by Bell & Bain Ltd, Glasgow

British Library Cataloguing in Publication Data
A catalogue record for this book is available from the British Library

Library of Congress Cataloging in Publication Data

Partridge, Eric, 1894–1979.
The concise new Partridge dictionary of slang and unconventional English/
[edited by] Tom Dalzell, Terry Victor.
p. cm.
Rev. ed of: Dictionary of Slang and Unconventional English, 8th ed.,1984, by E. Partridge
and edited by P. Beale.
"2006 new editorial matter and selection, Tom Dalzell and Terry Victor;
material taken from The Dictionary of Slang and Unconventional English,
8th edition (first published 1984), E. Partridge and P. Beale estates" – T.p. verso.
1. English language – Slang – Dictionaries. I. Dalzell, Tom, 1951- II. Victor, Terry. III. Partridge, Eric,
1894–1979. Dictionary of slang and unconventional English. IV. Title. V. Title: Dictionary of slang and
unconventional English. VI. Title: New Partridge dictionary of slang and unconventional English.
PE3721.P3 2007
427'.09 – dc22
2007028776

ISBN10: 0-415-212-59-6 (hbk)
ISBN10: 0-203-96211-7 (ebk)

ISBN13: 978-0415-21259-5 (hbk)
ISBN13: 978-0203-96211-4 (ebk)

CONTENTS

CONTENTS

Entries A to Z

CONTRIBUTORS

Dr Richard Allsopp, a native of Guyana, is Director of the Caribbean Lexicography Project and former Reader in English Language and Linguistics, University of the West Indies, Cave Hill, Barbados. He edited the *Dictionary of Caribbean English Usage*.

Dr Dianne Bardsley is Manager of the New Zealand Dictionary Centre at Victoria University of Wellington. Her PhD involved the compilation and analysis of a rural New Zealand English lexicon from the years 1842–2002. She was contributing editor for the *New Zealand Oxford Dictionary* and is currently leading several New Zealand lexicography research projects.

James Lambert has worked primarily in Australian English, specialising in slang in general and Australian slang in particular. He was assistant editor of *The Macquarie Dictionary of New Words* and general editor of *The Macquarie Book of Slang* and *The Macquarie Slang Dictionary*.

John Loftus manages the online archive at www.hiberno english.com. He was a senior research assistant on *A Dictionary of Hiberno-English*.

Lewis Poteet is a leading Canadian authority on slang and dialect. He has written extensively about language in Canada's maritime provinces and edited *Car & Motorcycle Slang, Hockey Talk, Plane Talk, Car Talk* and *Cop Talk*.

John Williams served as a consulting lexicographer on this project. He has been contributing to general language dictionaries, both monolingual and bilingual, for more than 20 years. He is the author of three children's dictionaries, as well as several articles on the practice of lexicography.

PREFACE

Eric Partridge made a deep and enduring contribution to the study and understanding of slang. In the eight editions of *The Dictionary of Slang and Unconventional English* published between 1937 and 1984, Partridge recorded and defined the slang and unconventional English of Great Britain, and to a lesser extent her dominions, from the 1600s to the 1970s. For the years up to 1890, Partridge was by his own admission quite reliant on Farmer and Henley's *Slang and its Analogues*, which he used as an 'expansible framework'. When it came to the slang for the years 1890 to 1945, Partridge was original and brilliant, especially in his treatment of underworld and military slang. His attitude towards language was scholarly and fun-loving, scientific and idiosyncratic. His body of work, scholarship and dignity of approach led the way and set the standard for every other English-language slang lexicographer of the twentieth century.

Our respect for Partridge has not blinded us to the features of his work that have drawn criticism over the years. His protocol for alphabetising was quirky. His dating was often problematic. His etymologies at times strayed from the plausible to the fanciful. His classification by register (slang, cant, jocular, vulgar, coarse, high, low, etc.) was intensely subjective and not particularly useful. Furthermore, his early decision to exclude American slang created increasingly difficult problems for him as the years passed and the influence of American slang grew. Lastly, Partridge grew to lose the ability to relate to the vocabulary he was recording. In 1937, Partridge was a man of his time, but the same could no longer be said in 1960. There is a profound relationship between language and culture, and neither Partridge nor Paul Beale, editor of the 8th edition, seem to have assimilated the cultural changes that began at the end of World War 2. This left them without the cultural knowledge needed to understand the language that they were recording. Their lack of cultural understanding accelerated with time, and this is sadly reflected in the later entries. Beatniks and drug addicts, and their slang, baffled Partridge and Beale, who lacked either the personal experience or historical perspective needed to understand underlying countercultures.

Partridge himself observed, 'More than almost any other kind of book, a dictionary constantly needs to be revised; especially, of course, if it deals with the current form of a language and therefore has to be kept up to date'. With *The New Partridge Dictionary of Slang and Unconventional English* we tried to do just that. We picked up where Partridge left off, recording the slang and unconventional English of the English-speaking world since World War 2 with the same scholarship and joy in language that characterised Partridge's work. We are not, and cannot be, Partridge: but we can strive to be proud heirs of Partridge and to speak with a voice that Partridge would recognise as an echo of his own. We have worked hard to continue the Partridge tradition, observing high standards of lexicography while producing an accessible work informed by, and infused with, the humour, mischief

and energy that are endemic to slang. This Concise version of the New Partridge contains every entry in New Partridge as well as several hundred new words that have come into the slang lexicon since 2005. The Concise is presented without the hundreds of thousands of citations in the New Partridge, creating an affordable alternative to our update of Partridge. Lastly, we improved dating information given on hundreds of headwords.

Criteria for inclusion

We use three criteria for including a term or phrase in this dictionary. We include (1) slang and unconventional English, (2) used anywhere in the English-speaking world and (3) after 1945.

Rather than focus too intently on a precise definition of slang or on whether a given entry is slang, jargon or colloquial English, we take full advantage of the wide net cast by Partridge when he chose to record 'slang and unconventional English' instead of just slang, which is, after all, without any settled test of purity. We have considered for inclusion all unconventional English that has been used with the purpose or effect of either lowering the formality of communication and reducing solemnity and/or identifying status or group and putting oneself in tune with one's company. A term recorded here might be slang, slangy jargon, a colloquialism, an acronym, an initialism, a vulgarism or a catchphrase. In all instances, an entry imparts a message beyond the text and literal meaning. This approach is especially useful when dealing with world slang and unconventional English. A broader range has permitted inclusion of many Caribbean entries, for instance, which merit inclusion but might not meet a stringent pure-slang-only test. Our only real deviation from Partridge's inclusion criteria is a much diminished body of nicknames. The regiment nicknames that populate Partridge's work no longer fulfil the language function that they did in the United Kingdom of Partridge's day.

If there was a question as to whether a potential entry fell within the target register, we erred on the side of inclusion. We generally chose to include poorly attested words, presenting the entry and our evidence of usage to the reader who is free to determine if a candidate passes probation.

Partridge limited his dictionary to Great Britain and her dominions. We elected the broader universe of the English-speaking world. Globalisation has affected many facets of life, not the least of which is our language. There are words that are uniquely Australian, American or British, but it is impossible to ignore or deny the extent of cross-pollination that exists between cultures as regards slang. We were aided in our global gathering by indigenous contributors from Australia, Canada, the Caribbean, Ireland and New Zealand. We also include pidgin, Creolised English and borrowed foreign terms used by English-speakers in primarily English-language conversation. We include slang and unconventional English heard and used at any time after 1945. We chose the end of the war in 1945 as our starting point primarily because it marked the beginning of a series of profound cultural changes that produced the lexicon of modern and contemporary slang. The cultural transformations since 1945 are mind-boggling. Television, computers, drugs, music, unpopular wars, youth movements, changing racial sensitivities and attitudes towards sex and sexuality are all substantial factors that have shaped culture and language.

No term is excluded on the grounds that it might be considered offensive as a racial, ethnic, religious, sexual or any kind of slur. This dictionary contains many entries and citations that will, and should, offend. To exclude a term or citation because it is offensive is to deny the fact that it is used: we are not prescriptivists and this is simply not our job. At the same time, we try to avoid definitions or editorial comment that might offend.

We were tempted, but finally chose not to include an appendix of gestures, although many serve the same function as slang. Examples include the impudent middle finger, Ralph Cramden's Raccoon greeting and handshake, the elaborate mimes that signal 'jerk-off' or 'dickhead', Johnny Carson's golf swing, Vic Reeves' lascivious thigh rubbing and Arsenio Hall's finger-tip-touch greeting. Neither did we include an appendix of computer language such as emoticons or leet speak, although we have included throughout several of the more prominent examples of Internet and text messaging shorthand that have become known outside the small circle of initial users.

We tried but in the end decided not to include the word/word phenomenon ('Is she your *friend* friend or friend friend?') or the word/word/word construction ('The most important three things in real estate are location, location, location'). We could not include the obvious pregnant silence that suggests 'fuck' ('What the **** do you think you're doing?'). We shied away from the lexicalised animal noises that often work their way into informal conversation, such as a cat noise when someone is behaving nastily. We similarly did not include musical phrases that have become part of our spoken vocabulary, such as the four-note theme of *The Twilight Zone* which is used to imply an uncanny weirdness in any coincidence, or melodramatic hummed violin music that serves as vocal commentary on any piteous tale.

Using *The Concise New Partridge*

We hope that our presentation is self-evident and that it requires little explanation. We use only a few abbreviations and none of the stylistic conceits near and dear to the hearts of lexicographers.

Headwords

We use indigenous spelling for headwords. This is especially relevant in the case of the UK **arse** and US **ass**. For Yiddish words, we use Leo Rosten's spelling, which favours 'sh-' over 'sch-'. An initialism is shown in upper case without full stops (for example, **BLT**), except that acronyms (pronounced like individual lexical items) are lower case (for example, **snafu**).

Including every variant spelling of a headword seemed neither practical nor helpful to the reader. For the spelling of headwords, we chose the form found in standard dictionaries or the most common forms, ignoring

uncommon variants as well as common hyphenation variants of compounds and words ending in 'ie' or 'y'. For this reason, citations may show variant spellings not found in the headword.

Placement of phrases

As a general rule, phrases are placed under their first significant word. However, some invariant phrases are listed as headwords; for example, a stock greeting, stock reply or catchphrase. Terms that involve a single concept are grouped together as phrases under the common headword; for example, **burn rubber**, **lay rubber** and **peel rubber** are all listed as phrases under the headword **rubber**.

Definition

In dealing with slang from all seven continents, we encountered more than a few culture-specific terms. For such terms, we identify the domain or geographic location of the term's usage. We use conventional English in the definitions, turning to slang only when it is both substantially more economical than the use of conventional English and is readily understood by the average reader.

Gloss

The voice and tone of *The New Partridge Dictionary of Slang and Unconventional English* is most obvious in the gloss: the brief explanations that Partridge used for 'editorial comment' or 'further elucidation'. Partridge warned against using the gloss to show what clever and learned fellows we are – a warning that we heed to the very limited extent it could apply to us. We chose to discontinue Partridge's classification by register.

Country of origin

As is the case with dating, further research will undoubtedly produce a shift in the country of origin for a number of entries. We resolutely avoided guesswork and informed opinion.

Dating

Even Beale, who as editor of the 8th edition was the direct inheritor of Partridge's trust, noted that Partridge's dating 'must be treated with caution'. We recognise that the accurate dating of slang is far more difficult than dating conventional language. Virtually every word in our lexicon is spoken before it is written, and this is especially true of unconventional terms. The recent proliferation of electronic databases and powerful search engines will undoubtedly permit the antedating of many of the entries. Individualised dating research, such as Allen Walker's hunt for the origin of 'OK' or Barry Popik's exhaustive work on terms such as 'hot dog', produces dramatic antedatings: we could not undertake this level of detailed research for every entry.

Conclusion

In the preface to his 1755 *Dictionary of the English Language*, Samuel Johnson noted that 'A large work is difficult because it is large,' and that 'Every writer of a long work commits errors'. In addition to improvements in our dating of terms and identification of the country of origin, it is inevitable that some of our definitions are incorrect or misleading, especially where the sense is subtle and fleeting, defying paraphrasing, or where kindred senses are interwoven. It is also inevitable that some quotations are included in a mistaken sense. For these errors, we apologise in advance.

We carry the flame for words that are usually judged only by the ill-regarded company they keep. Just as Partridge did for the sixteenth century beggars and rakes, for whores of the eighteenth century, and for the armed services of the two world wars, we try to do for the slang users of the last 60 years. We embrace the language of beats, hipsters, Teddy Boys, mods and rockers, hippies, pimps, druggies, whores, punks, skinheads, ravers, surfers, Valley Girls, dudes, pill-popping truck drivers, hackers, rappers and more. We have tried to do what Partridge saw as necessary, which was simply to keep up to date.

Tom Dalzell, Berkeley, California
Terry Victor, Caerwent, South Wales
Spring 2005
Re-edited for the Concise edition in the spring of 2007

ACKNOWLEDGEMENTS

Our debt to Sophie Oliver defies description. With good humour and a saintly tolerance for our so-called wit and attempts to corrupt, she herded this project through from a glimmer in the eye to print on the page.

We bow to and thank the following who helped along the way: Mary Ann Kernan, who was charged with putting this project together in 1999 and 2000; John Williams, who must be credited for all that is right about our lexicography and excused for anything that is not; Robert Hay and Mike Tarry of Alden for their unending work on the database and cheerful handling of every problem we could throw at them; Claire L'Enfant; James Folan for rescuing us in the content edit phase; Louise Hake for her cheerful determination in the editing and production phases; our fine copy editors Sandra Anderson, Howard Sargeant and Laura Wedgeworth; and Aine Duffy for her enthusiastically scurrilous vision of the whole project as it developed.

Finally, we thank Oxford University Press for providing us with access to the 'Oxford English Dictionary Online', a brilliant online presentation of the *Oxford English Dictionary*, one of the leading sources for dating.

Tom Dalzell and Terry Victor

This dictionary would never have seen the light of day without the time and support given to me by my family – Cathy most notably, also Jake, Julia, Rosalie and Charlotte. I thank and owe you big-time, major league and humongously. Who knew it would take so much? In their own ways, and from a distance, my parents guided. Audrey, Emily and Reggae started the project with me but did not stay for the end.

I also thank: my slang mentors Paul Dickson and Madeline Kripke (and better mentors you could not hope for); Archie Green, who saved Peter Tamony's work for posterity and encouraged me throughout this project; Jesse Sheidlower, Jonathon Green and Susan Ford, slang lexicographers, friends and comrades in words; Dr Lisa Winer for her voluminous and fine work on the slang of Trinidad and Tobago; Jan Tent for his excellent collection of Fijian slang; Dr Jerry Zientara, the learned and helpful librarian at the Institute for Advanced Study of Human Sexuality in San Francisco, which kindly opened its incomparable library to me; Tom Miller, Bill Stolz, John Konzal and Patricia Walker, archivists at the Western Historical Manuscript Collection, University of Missouri at Columbia, for their help and insights during my work with the Peter Tamony archives; the Hon. Sir Colville Young for leading me to Richard Allsopp; Jim Holliday for his help on the slang of pornography; Jennifer Goldstein for her help on the slang of sex dancers; Richard Perlman for his patient and Zen-like technological help; Angela Jacobson, Elizabeth McInnis and Caitlan Perlman, who helped as

readers; Mr Baldwin, Mr Muir, Mr Lee, Dr Robert Regan and Dr Gordon Kelly for the English and popular culture they taught me.

I thank my fellow language writers and lexicographers who were generous in their encouragement, advice and assistance: Reinhold Aman, a brave and brilliant pioneer, the late Robert Chapman, Gerald Cohen, Trevor Cralle, Jim Crotty, Connie Eble, Jonathan Lighter, Edward MacNeal, Geoffrey Nunberg, Judi Sanders, Leslie Savan and Oliver Trager.

Our Australian contributor, James Lambert, was given recourse to the various databases of the Macquarie Library Pty Ltd, who publish synchronic dictionaries for the Australian and Asian markets, and for these vast resources we are grateful.

Lastly, I acknowledge Terry Victor. The demands of this project have only strengthened our friendship.

Tom Dalzell

My wife, Liz, deserves a dictionary entry of her own as a definition of tolerance, patience and encouragement way beyond conventional expectations. In the wider world, my sister and family added to both my library and vocabulary; and my other family, now in Spain, even went so far as to put a christening on hold until a deadline had been met, as well as allowing me access to the playground language of our time. I must also thank Gerri Smith for her tolerant understanding that I could not be in two places at once.

Serendipity brought me to Tom Dalzell and through him I have had the advantage and benefit of all of the influences and providers of expertise that he names above, especially Jonathon Green. In addition to those named I am grateful for the knowledgeable encouragement of Michael Quinion and David Crystal; and, in matters polari, Paul Baker.

For particular contributions I would like to thank: Flight Lieutenant Andrew Resoli; Lisa and Tim Hale; David Morrison; some of the inmates at HMP High Down in the summer of 2002; Antonio Lillo for his work on rhyming slang; various magazine editors and journalists who addressed so many of my queries of modern usage; and, for a splendid collection of cocaine-related slang, a certain group of musicians (whose management would prefer that they remain anonymous). I also enjoyed the advantage of the correspondence that the Partridge and Beale 8th edition still attracts: I am grateful to all who wrote in, and I look forward to seeing more contributions at *www.partridge-slang.com*.

Above all, I must make mention of two people: Eric Partridge, who is my hero, and Tom Dalzell, who is my friend.

Terry Victor

OBSERVATIONS ON SLANG AND UNCONVENTIONAL ENGLISH

Some notes on the challenges of lexicography, drawn entirely from the writings of Eric Partridge (1894–1979)

Partridge wrote widely on matters concerning the English language. He did not, by any means, restrict his interest to matters slang and unconventional; however, it is his work in this area that had, and continues to have, the greatest impact, and on which his reputation is most celebrated. He wrote more than forty books in his lifetime, considering such diverse topics as abbreviations, American tramp and underworld slang, British and American English since 1900, comic alphabets, English and American Christian names, Shakespeare's bawdy, usage and abusage, and he contributed to many, many more. It is so substantial a body of work that any list short of a full bibliography will inevitably do his great achievement a disservice. He was a philologist, etymologist, lexicographer, essayist and dictionary-maker; he is a legend and an inspiration.

The flavour, and wisdom, of Partridge's work is gathered in the quotations that follow, loosely grouped by subject, and presented under sub-headings that make new use of a selection of his book and article titles.

Slang Today and Yesterday

From about 1850, slang has been the accepted term for 'illegitimate' colloquial speech: but since then, especially among the lower classes, 'lingo' has been a synonym, and so also, chiefly among the cultured and the pretentious, has 'argot'. Now 'argot', being merely the French for 'slang', has no business to be used thus – it can rightly be applied only to French slang of French cant: and 'lingo' properly means a simplified language that, like Beach-la-Mar and Pidgin-English, represents a distortion of (say) English by coloured peoples speaking English indeed but adapting it to their own phonetics and grammar. 'Jargon' – originally as in Chaucer, used of the warbling of birds – has long been employed loosely and synonymously for slang, but it should be reserved for the technicalities of science, the professions and the trades: though, for such technicalities, 'shop' is an equally good word.[1]

[S]lang is much rather a spoken than a literary language. It originates, nearly always, in speech.[1]

Slang is easy enough to use, but very hard to write about with the facile convincingness that a subject apparently so simple would, at first sight, seem to demand. But the simplest things are the hardest to define, certainly the hardest to discuss, for it is usually at first sight only that their simplicity is what strikes one the most forcibly. And slang, after all, is a peculiar kind of vagabond language, always hanging on the outskirts of legitimate speech, but continually straying or forcing its way into the most respectable company.[2]

Language in general and every kind of language belongs to everyone who wishes to use it.[3]

Slang, being the quintessence of colloquial speech, must always be related to convenience rather than scientific laws, grammatical rules and philosophical ideals. As it originates, so it flourishes best, in colloquial speech.[1]

Slang may and often does fill a gap in accepted language.[1]

Words, Words, Words!

Every group or association, from a pair of lovers to a secret society however large, feels, at some time or other, the need to defend itself against outsiders, and therefore creates a slang designed to conceal its thoughts: and the greater the need for secrecy, the more extensive and complete is the slang[.][1]

The specialization that characterizes every vocation leads naturally to a specialized vocabulary, to the invention of new words or the re-charging of old words. Such special words and phrases become slang only when they are used outside their vocational group and then only if they change their meaning or are applied in other ways [...] But, whatever the source, personality and one's surroundings (social or occupational) are the two co-efficients, the two chief factors, the determining causes of the nature of slang, as they are of language in general and of style.[1]

One kind of *eyewash*, the army's innumerable 'states' and 'returns' was known as *bumf*, short for *bum-fodder*: the abbreviation was common in English public schools from before 1900; the full term for toilet-paper dates back to the seventeenth century, when it was coined by Urquhart, the translator of Rabelais; Urquhart is one of the most prolific originators of the obscenities and vulgarities of our language, and with him rank Shakespeare and Burns.[4]

In English, the ideas most fertile in synonyms are those of drinking, drunkenness, money, and the sexual organs and act.[1]

Many slang words, indeed, are drawn from pleasurable activities (games, sports, entertainments), from the joy of life, from a gay abandon: for this reason it has been wittily called 'language on a picnic'.[1]

Common to – indeed, very common in – the jazzman's and the Beatnik's vocabulary is the noun pad, whence the entirely Beatnik pad me, a cat's invitation to a chick to share his room and bed. [...] The Beatniks got it from the jazzmen who got it from the American underworld who got it from the British underworld (pad, a bed) who got it from Standard English of the sixteenth–eighteenth centuries (pad, a bundle of straw to lie on).[5]

The metaphors and allusions [in slang] are generally connected with some temporary phase, some ephemeral vogue, some unimportant incident; if the origin is not nailed down at the time, it is rarely recoverable.[1]

[B]orrowings from foreign languages produce slang; and every language borrows. Borrowings, indeed, have a way of seeming slangy or of being welcomed by slang before standard speech takes them into its sanctum.[1]

War always produces a rich crop of slang.[6]

[W]ar (much as we may hate to admit the fact), because, in all wars, both soldiers and sailors and, since 1914, airmen and civilians as well, have imported or adopted or invented hundreds of words, terms, phrases, this linguistic aspect ranking as, if we except the unexceptable 'climate of courage,' the only good result of war.[7]

Human characteristics, such as a love of mystery and a confidential air (a lazy freemasonry), vanity, the imp of perversity that lurks in every heart, the impulse to rebellion, and that irrepressible spirit of adventure which, when deprived of its proper outlook in action, perforce contents itself with verbal audacity (the adventure of speech): these and others are at the root of slang[.][1]

Here, There and Everywhere

When we come to slang and familiar speech generally, we come to that department of the vocabulary in which British and American differences are naturally greater than anywhere else, just as they are greater in the colloquial language generally than in the literary.[8]

American slang is more volatile than English and it tends, also, to have more synonyms, but a greater number of those synonyms are butterflies of a day; English synonyms are used more for variety than from weariness or a desire to startle. American slang is apt to be more brutal than English[.][1]

Canada also has an extensive and picturesque objective slang, but that slang is 80 per cent American, with the remainder rather more English than native-Canadian[...] it is linguistically unfair to condemn it for being so much indebted to its near and 'pushing' neighbour[.][1]

Australian speech and writing have, from the outset, tended to be unconventional [...] The unconventionality is linguistic.[9]

The truth is that South African slang, as distinct from indispensable Africanderisms, is not intrinsically so vivid, humorous, witty, or divinely earthy as Canadian and Australian slang, nor is it nearly so extensive, nor has it, except during the Boer War, succeeded in imposing itself upon English slang, much less upon Standard English[.][1]

New Zealand is like South Africa in that its population is too small to have much influenced the language of the mother country whether in Standard or in unconventional English.[1]

Usage and Abusage

Some of the upstart qualities [of slang] and part of the aesthetic (as opposed to the moral) impropriety spring from the four features present in all slang, whatever the period and whatever the country: the search for novelty; volatility and light-headedness as well as light-heartedness; ephemerality; the sway of fashion. In the standard speech and still more in slang we note that the motive behind figurative expressions and all neologisms is the desire to escape from the old accepted phrase: the desire for novelty operates more freely, audaciously, and rapidly in slang – that is the only difference. [...O]f the numerous slang words taken up by the masses and the classes, most have only a short life, and that when they die, unhonoured and unsung, they are almost immediately replaced by novelties equally transitory: the word is dead, long live the word! [...S]lang, as to the greater part of its vocabulary and especially as to its cuckoo-calling phrases and it's parrot-sayings, is evanescent; it is the residuum that, racy and expressive, makes the study of slang revelatory of the pulsing life of the language.[1]

[S]lang is indicative not only of man's earthiness but of his indomitable spirit: it sets him in his proper place: relates a man to his fellows, to his world and the world, and to the universe.[10]

And slang is employed for one (or two or more) of thirteen reasons:

1   In sheer high spirits; 'just for the fun of the thing'.
2   As an exercise in wit or humour.
3   To be 'different' – to be novel.
4   To be picturesque.
5   To be startling; to startle.
6   To escape from cliché's and long-windedness.
7   To enrich the language.
8   To give solidity and concreteness to the abstract and the idealistic, and nearness to the

9   To reduce solemnity, pain, tragedy.
10   To put oneself in tune with one's company.
11   To induce friendliness or intimacy.
12   To show that one belongs to a certain school, trade or profession, intellectual set or social class. In short to be in the fashion – or to prove that someone else isn't.
13   To be secret – not understood by those around one.[11]

But no real stylist, no-one capable of good speaking or good writing, is likely to be harmed by the occasional employment of slang; provided that he is conscious of the fact, he can employ it both frequently and freely without stultifying his mind, impoverishing his vocabulary, or vitiating the taste and the skill that he brings to the using of that vocabulary. Except in formal and dignified writing and in professional speaking, a vivid and extensive slang is perhaps preferable to a jejune and meagre vocabulary of standard English; on the other hand, it will hardly be denied that, whether in writing or speech, a sound though restricted vocabulary of standard English is preferable to an equally small vocabulary of slang, however vivid may be that slang.[1]

The Gentle Art of Lexicography

I began early in life: and it is the course of my life which, allied to a natural propensity to original sin, has made a lexicographer out of me.[12]

For most of us, a dictionary is hardly a book to read; a good dictionary, however, is a book to browse in. Some dictionaries are so well written that one just goes on and on. To write such a dictionary has always been my ambition.[12]

Slang [etymology/lexicography] demands a mind constantly on the *qui vive*; an ear constantly keyed to the nuances of everyday speech, whether among scholars or professional men or craftsmen or labourers; a very wide reading of all kinds of books.[13]

I have read much that is hopelessly inferior, hopelessly mediocre; and much that, although interesting, is yet devoid of literary value. But ever since my taste acquired a standard, I have been able to extract some profit from even the most trashy book.[14]

There is far more imagination and enthusiasm in the making of a good dictionary than in the average novel.[15]

Words at War: Words at Peace

For over a century, there have been protests against the use of slang and controversies on the relation of slang to the literary language or, as it is now usually called, Standard English. Purists have risen in their wrath and conservatives in their dignity to defend the Bastille of linguistic purity against the revolutionary rabble. The very vehemence of the

attack and the very sturdinessof the defence have ensured that only the fittest survive to gain entrance to the citadel, there establish themselves, and then become conservatives and purists in their turn.[16]

Any term that prevents us from thinking, any term that we employ to spare us from searching for the right word, is a verbal narcotic. As though there weren't too many narcotics already...[17]

Words are very important things; at the lowest estimate, they are indispensable counters of communication.[18]

Notes/bibliography

1   *Slang Today and Yesterday*, 1933: George Routledge & Sons, London
2   *Slang Today and Yesterday*, 1933, quoting Greenough and Kittredge, *Words and their Ways in English Speech*, 1902: George Routledge & Sons, London
3   'The Lexicography of Cant', *American Speech*, Volume 26, Issue 2, May 1951: The American Dialect Society, Durham, North Carolina
4   'Byways of Soldier Slang' in *A Martial Medley*, 1931: Scholartis Press, London
5   'A Square Digs Beatnik', August 1959. Originally published for private circulation Christmas 1959/New Year 1960. Collected in *A Charm of Words*, 1960: Hamish Hamilton, London
6   'Words Get Their Wings', originally published in *Chamber's Journal*, July-August 1945. Collected in *Words at War: Words at Peace*, 1948: Frederick Muller, London
7   'Introduction' in *Dictionary of New Words*, Mary Reifer, 1957: Peter Owen, London
8   *British and American English Since 1900*, co-authored with John W. Clark, 1951: Andrew Dakers, London
9   'Australian English' in *A Charm of Words*, 1960: Hamish Hamilton, London
10   *Usage & Abusage*, 1947: Hamish Hamilton, London [originally published in the US in 1942]
11   *The World of Words*, 2nd edition, 1939: Hamish Hamilton, London [reduced by Eric Partridge from a fuller consideration in *Slang Today and Yesterday*, 1933, and based on the work of M. Alfredo Niceforo, *Le Génie de l'Argot*, 1912]
12   *The Gentle Art of Lexicography*, 1963: André Deutsch, London
13   *Adventuring Among Words*, 1961: André Deutsch, London
14   *Journey to the Edge of Morning*, ©1946, reprinted 1969: Books for Libraries Press, New York
15   As Corrie Denison, a pseudonymous epigraph to *A Classical Dictionary of the Vulgar Tongue* by Captain Francis Grose (3rd edition, 1796), edited by Eric Partridge, 1931: Scholartis Press, London
16   *Here, There and Everywhere*, 1950: Hamish Hamilton, London
17   'Verbal Narcotics', originally published in *Good Housekeeping* magazine, June 1949. Collected in *From Sanskrit to Brazil*, 1952: Hamish Hamilton, London
18   'Words in Vogue: Words of Power', 1942: collected in *Words at War: Words at Peace*, 1948: Frederick Muller, London

Aa

A *noun* **1** amphetamine *US, 1967*. **2** LSD. An abbreviation of ACID *US, 1977*. **3** in a deck of playing cards, an ace *US, 1988*. ▶ **get A into G; get your A into G** to stop idling; to apply yourself to an activity; to start doing something useful. Euphemistic for GET YOUR ARSE IN GEAR *NEW ZEALAND, 2002*

A *adjective* **1** reserved for the best; the best *US, 1945*. **2** anal *US, 1997*

a2m *noun* a scene in a pornographic film in which an object or body part is withdrawn from a rectum and taken into a mouth without either washing or editing. Shorthand for 'ass-to-mouth' *US, 1997*

A3 anytime, anyplace, anywhere. An abbreviation used in text messaging *UK, 2003*

AAA *noun* an amphetamine tablet. In the US, the AAA is the national automobile club, which, like an amphetamine tablet, helps you get from one place to another *US, 1993*

A and A *noun* in the military, a leave for rest and recreation. A jocular abbreviation of 'ass and alcohol' *US, 1966*

A and B *noun* assault and battery *US, 1986*

aap; arp *noun* a marijuana cigarette. From Afrikaans for 'monkey' *SOUTH AFRICA, 1946*

aardvark *noun* an F-111 combat aircraft or any aircraft that is awkward-looking or difficult to fly. Vietnam war usage *US, 1963*

ab *noun* an abscess, especially as a result of injecting drugs *US, 1952*

AB *noun* **1** the Aryan Brotherhood, a white prison gang in the US *US, 1990*. **2** the bleed period of the menstrual cycle. An abbreviation of 'Annie Brown' *NEW ZEALAND, 1996*

ABA *noun* a traveller's cheque *US, 1985*

abb *adjective* abnormal *US, 1991*

abba-dabba *noun* chatter, gossip. Undoubtedly originated with the song 'The Aba-Daba Honeymoon', written in 1913 and re-released with great success by Larry Clinton and His Orchestra in March 1948, in which 'abba-dabba' is the chatter of monkeys *US, 1961*

abba-dabba *adjective* dark-skinned, especially Arabic *US, 1975*

abbed *adjective* having well-defined abdominal muscles *UK, 2002*

abbey *noun* a swindler who impersonates a priest *US, 1950*. ▶ **on the abbey** engaged in a swindle involving clergy impersonation *US, 1992*

abbott *noun* a capsule of pentobarbital sodium (trade name Nembutal™), a central nervous system depressant. From the name of the manufacturer *US, 1971*

Abby Singer *noun* in television and film making, the next-to-last shot of the day. Singer was active in US television from the early 1950s until the late 1980s; his name became an eponym when he was an Assistant Director in the 1950s *US, 1990*

ABC *noun* **1** an American-born Chinese *US, 1984*. **2** in poker, the ace, two and three *US, 1988*

ABC *adjective* of a piece of chewing gum, *a*lready *b*een *c*hewed. Childish usage *US, 2004*

ABC ad *noun* a newspaper advertisement listing shows in alphabetical order *US, 1973*

ABC class *noun* the entry grade in a primary school *TRINIDAD AND TOBAGO, 2003*

ABCing you used as a farewell. Intended as a clever variant of 'I'll be seeing you' *US, 1947*

ABC's *noun* underwear *US, 1949*

ABC-ya used as a farewell. Intended as a clever variant of 'I'll be seeing you' *US, 2002*

abdabs; habdabs; screaming abdabs *noun* a condition of anxiety, uneasiness, nervousness; also, but rarely, *delirium tremens* or a state of enraged frustration. Always following 'the', usually now phrased (to give someone) the screaming abdabs *UK, 1946*

abdicate *verb* to vacate a public toilet upon orders of a homosexual-rousting attendant. The royal imagery is derived from the homosexual as QUEEN *US, 1941*

Abdul *noun* **1** used as a term of address for any Turkish soldier. World War 1 coinage *UK, 1925*. **2** any male Arab. Gulf war usage *US, 1991*

Abe *noun* **1** a five-dollar note. An abbreviation of ABE LINCOLN *US, 1945*. **2** any Jewish male. Also variant 'Abie'. From the archetypal Jewish name: Abraham *US, 1914*

A bean *noun* a capsule of MDMA, the recreational drug best known as ecstasy *UK, 2003*

Abe Lincoln *noun* a five-dollar note. The note bears an engraving of President Lincoln *US, 1966*

Aber *nickname* Aberdare, Abergavenny, Aberystwyth or any town so constructed. From Welsh for 'where two waters meet' *UK: WALES, 2001*

abercrombie *noun* **1** a person devoted to prep-school fashions and style *US, 2004*. **2** someone who strives at creating the impression of knowing all *US, 1945*

abfab *adjective* *ab*solutely *fab*ulous. Originally the slang of Australian teenagers. From early 1990s in the UK it has been the widely familiar short-form of popular television situation comedy *Absolutely Fabulous* *AUSTRALIA, 1965*

Abigail *noun* a staid, traditional, middle-aged homosexual man *US, 1972*

able *adjective* strong, capable, courageous. In general speech, this word is usually followed by 'to do [something]', but the Canadian use tends to follow the otherwise obsolete pattern of letting it stand alone or with an intensifier *CANADA, 1980*. ▶ **can't spell able** be unable to do what you are told to do *BARBADOS, 1996*

Able Dog *noun* the propeller-driven Douglas AD Skyraider. Based on the letters A and D in phonetic alphabet. The Skyraider was manufactured between 1946 and 1957; it saw service in Korea and Vietnam *US, 1961*

able Grable *noun* a sexually attractive girl *US, 1945*

abo *noun* an Australian Aboriginal. An abbreviation of 'aborigine' blended with the '-o' suffix. Now a strongly taboo word, formerly in frequent use by white people, and viewed by them as less marked than other terms such as 'boong' or 'coon'. It was even used in names for products, businesses, etc *AUSTRALIA, 1906*

abo *adjective* Australian Aboriginal; of, or pertaining to, Australian Aboriginals *AUSTRALIA, 1911*

aboard *adverb* present, part of an enterprise *US, 1957*. ▶ **go aboard of someone** to act vigorously and aggressively, to attack, or scold vigorously *CANADA, 1980*

A-bomb; atom bomb *noun* marijuana combined in a cigarette with cocaine, heroin or opium. The addition of narcotic enhancements to a BOMB (a marijuana cigarette) is signified by the 'A' *US, 1969*

A-bombed *adjective* under the influence of amphetamines *US, 1975*

A-bone *noun* a Model A Ford car, first built in 1927 *US, 1951*

aboot *preposition* used as a humorous attempt to duplicate a Canadian saying 'about' *US, 1995*

abort *verb* to defecate after being the passive partner in anal sex *US, 1972*

abortion *noun* a misfortune; an ugly person or thing *US, 1943*

about-face *noun* a 180-degree turn executed while driving fast *US, 1965*

about it; 'bout it *adjective* in favour of something *US, 2001*

about right *adjective* correct, adequate *UK, 1850*

above board *adjective* entirely honest. From card playing *UK, 1616*

above par *adjective* **1** in excellent health or spirits. Originates from describing stocks and shares as above face value *UK, 1937*. **2** mildly drunk. By extension from the previous sense *UK, 1984*

abracadabra, please and thank you used as a humorous embellishment of 'please'. A signature line from the *Captain Kangaroo* children's television show (CBS, 1944–84). Repeated with referential humour *US, 1944*

Abraham Lincoln; Abie Lincoln *adjective* disgusting, contemptible. Glasgow rhyming slang for STINKING *UK, 1988*

Abrahampstead *nickname* Hampstead, an area of north London with a large Jewish population. A combination with the archetypal Jewish name Abraham *UK, 1981*

abs *noun* the abdominal muscles *US, 1956*

absobloodylutely *adverb* absolutely, utterly. First recorded as 'absoballylutely' *UK, 1914*

absofuckinglutely *adverb* absolutely *UK, 1921*

absolutely! used for registering complete agreement *UK, 1937*

Absolutely, Mr Gallagher. Positively, Mr Shean. used for a humorous assent. From the Vaudeville team of Gallagher and Shean *US, 1922*

absotively; absitively *adverb* certainly. A jocular blend of 'positively' and 'absolutely' *US, 1926*

Abyssinian polo *noun* a game of dice *US, 1962*

Abyssinian tea *noun* khat, a natural stimulant grown in Kenya, Ethiopia and Somalia *UK, 2004*

Ac *noun* an Acura car *US, 2002*

AC/DC; AC-DC *noun* in gay society, a couple *UK, 2002*

AC/DC; AC-DC *adjective* bisexual. A pun on electricity's AC (alternating current) and DC (direct current) *US, 1960*

ACAB *all coppers are bastards*. An initialism, a philosophy, a tattoo *UK, 1996*

academy *noun* a jail or prison *US, 1949*

Academy Award *noun* recognition of excelling in a field *US, 1958*

Academy Award *adjective* **1** excellent *US, 1958*. **2** histrionic *AUSTRALIA, 1966*

Academy Award winning *adjective* histrionic *AUSTRALIA, 1987*

Acapulco *noun* marijuana from southwest Mexico. A shortened form of ACAPULCO GOLD *US, 1970*

Acapulco gold *noun* golden-leafed marijuana from southwest Mexico. A popular, well-known strain of cannabis. The song 'Acapulco Gold' by the Rainy Daze was released in 1967 and had just begun its climb on the pop charts when programme directors figured out what it was about and pulled it off play lists *US, 1965*

acca; acker *noun* an academic whose work serves the marketplace rather than the intellect; hence a particularly sterile piece of academic writing. An abbreviation punning on OCKER (a coarse Australian) *AUSTRALIA, 1977*

accelerator *noun* **1** an amphetamine tablet *US, 1993*. **2** an arsonist *US, 1992*

accessory *noun* a boyfriend or girlfriend *US, 1992*

accibounce *noun* a minor collision or accident *TRINIDAD AND TOBAGO, 2003*

accident *noun* a murder that cannot be proved as such *US, 1964*

accidentally on purpose *adverb* apparently accidental yet deliberately done, especially with hidden malicious purpose *US, 1887*

accommodation arrest *noun* a pre-arranged, consensual raid of an illegal gambling operation, designed to give the appearance of strict enforcement of laws *US, 1961*

according to Hoyle *adverb* in keeping with established rules and norms. After Edmond Hoyle (1672–1769), who codified the rules for many games *US, 1904*

accordion act *noun* collapsing under pressure *US, 1989*

accordion war *noun* US tactics during the Korean war: accordion-like movements up and down Korea by land forces *US, 1982*

account executive *noun* a pimp who procures and profits from high-price prostitutes *US, 1972*

accrue *verb* ▶ **accrue chocolate** to behave towards officers in an obsequious, sycophantic manner. Royal Navy usage; a play on BROWN-NOSE (to behave obsequiously, etc.) *UK, 1929*

accumulator *noun* a type of bet where the amount won on one event becomes the stake for the next event; a bettor who operates in such a manner *UK, 1889*

ace *noun* **1** a very close friend *US, 1932*. **2** used as a form of address *UK, 1919*. **3** a good and reliable friend *US, 1941*. **4** one dollar *US, 1900*. **5** one hundred dollars *US, 1974*. **6** one-eighth of an ounce of a drug *US, 1989*. **7** phencyclidine, the recreational drug known as PCP or angel dust *US, 1981*. **8** in dice games, a rolled one *US, 1999*. **9** an important or notable CB user. Citizens' band radio slang *US, 1976*. **10** a prison sentence of one year *US, 1927*. **11** in the theatre, a one-night engagement *US, 1981*. **12** in pool, the number one ball *US, 1878*. **13** a table for one at a restaurant *US, 1961*. **14** a single rotten fruit *UK, 1963*. **15** in lunch counter usage, a grilled cheese sandwich *US, 1975*. **16** the grade 'A' *US, 1964*. ▶ **ace in the hole** an undisclosed resource *US, 1908*. ▶ **ace up your sleeve** a resource that is yet to be revealed. From the popular belief that card cheats hide cards up their sleeves *US, 1927*. ▶ **on your ace** alone; by yourself *AUSTRALIA, 1904*

ace *verb* **1** to outsmart someone *US, 1929*. **2** to work your way somewhere, to engineer something *US, 1929*. **3** to do well in an examination *US, 1957*. **4** to kill someone *US, 1975*

ace *adjective* exceptional, expert, excellent *US, 1930*

ace boon coon; ace boon poon *noun* a very close friend *US, 1958*

ace boy *noun* a very good male friend *BERMUDA, 1985*

ace cool *noun* a very close and trusted friend *US, 1988*

ace-deuce *noun* **1** a fellow prisoner upon whom you rely without question *US, 1989*. **2** your best friend *BELIZE, 1996*

ace-deuce *verb* in craps, to sustain a heavy loss *US, 1987*

ace-deuce *adjective* **1** cross-eyed *US, 1955*. **2** riding a racehorse with the right stirrup higher than the left *US, 1948*

ace-deuce *adverb* on an angle, with one side higher than the other *US, 1948*

ace-douche *noun* in craps, a first roll of three. 'Douche' is an intentional corruption of 'deuce'; a come-out roll of three loses *US, 1999*

ace high; aces high *adjective* the very best. From poker *US, 1896*

ace in *verb* **1** to manipulate someone or something into a situation *US, 1971*. **2** to become associated with a group and work your way into it *US, 1992*

acelerante *noun* an amphetamine or central nervous system stimulant. Borrowed Spanish used by English-speakers *US, 1992*

ace man *noun* a youth gang's top fighter *US, 1953*

ace note *noun* a one-dollar note *US, 1929*

ace of spades *noun* the vulva *US, 1960*

ace on *adjective* skilled at *BAHAMAS, 1982*

ace out *verb* **1** to fool someone; to swindle someone *US, 1933*. **2** to exclude someone *US, 1964*. **3** in poker, to win a hand by bluffing while holding a relatively low-value hand *US, 1983*

ace over apex *adverb* head over heels *US, 1960*

aces *noun* in poker, a hand with a pair of aces *US, 1987*. ▶ **aces in both places** in craps, a roll of two *US, 1999*

aces *adjective* excellent *US, 1901*

acey-deucey *noun* **1** in backgammon, a variant rule under which the game is started in positions other than the standard layout *US, 1944*. **2** a bisexual. A probable elaboration of AC/DC *US, 1980*

acey-deucey *verb* (used of a jockey) to ride with the inside stirrup lower than the outside stirrup. A riding style popularised by legendary jockey Eddie Acaro *US, 1948*

acey-deucy *noun* in craps, a roll of a one and a two *US, 1974*

acey-deucy *adjective* bisexual. A probable elaboration of AC/DC *US, 1972*

achiever *noun* a devoted fan of the film *The Big Lebowski*. In the film, the rich Lebowski sponsors a programme named the 'Little Lebowski Urban Achievers' *US, 2004*

Achnard *noun* a taxi driver. New York police slang, corrupting 'Ahmed' as an allusion to the preponderance of immigrants among New York's taxi-driving workforce *US, 1997*

acid *noun* **1** LSD *US, 1965*. **2** rum *BARBADOS, 1965*. **3** by extension, any alcoholic beverage *TRINIDAD AND TOBAGO, 2003*. **4** impudence, heavy sarcasm. Especially in the phrase 'come the old acid' *UK, 1962*. ▶ **put the acid on 1** to pressure someone; to put someone to the test. From 'acid test' *AUSTRALIA, 1906*. **2** to pressure someone sexually *AUSTRALIA, 1939*

acid freak *noun* a habitual user of LSD *US, 1966*

acid funk *noun* a depression brought on by LSD use *US, 1971*

acid head *noun* a habitual user of LSD *US, 1966*

acid house *noun* a mesmeric dance music genre characterised by electronic 'squelching' sounds. An artistic and lexicographic extension of HOUSE (MUSIC) *US, 1988*

acid jazz *noun* a dance music genre *UK, 1999*

acid mung *noun* the sensation while under the influence of LSD of having an oily face *US, 1971*

acido *noun* LSD *US, 1971*

acid rock *noun* a genre of rock music. Folk etymology claims the music to be inspired by the altered states of conciousness induced by ACID (the hallucinogenic drug LSD); certainly this was a commercial style of music being marketed to the mass audience when high-profile musicians were experimenting with LSD *US, 1966*

acid test *noun* an event organised to maximise the hallucinatory experiences of LSD. Ken Kesey and the Merry Pranksters organised acid tests in Palo Alto, Portland (Oregon), Los Angeles and Mexico in 1966 *US, 1966*

acidy *adjective* psychedelic. From ACID (LSD) *UK, 1998*

acieeed!; aceeed! called out to register a delight in, and identification with, club dance music. Three 'e's seem to be a constant in the various spellings that attempt to capture the fervour generated by early acid house culture *UK, 1999*

ack *noun* **1** a pimple *US, 1968*. **2** in computer programming, a message sent from one system or program to another, acknowledging receipt of a previous message *US, 1986*

ack *verb* **1** to acknowledge a letter, etc. Clerical usage, originally Civil Service *UK, 1984*. **2** in computer programming, to acknowledge receipt of a message *UK, 1986*

ack-ack *noun* anti-aircraft artillery. An initialism, using the phonetic alphabet that was current until 1941. Usage survived the new alphabet rather than being amended to 'able able' *US, 1926*

ack-ack *verb* to shoot someone or something *US, 1947*

ackamarackus; ackamaracka *noun* fanciful speech intended to deceive *US, 1933*

ack emma *noun* the morning. Military origins, from the phonetic alphabet: ack (A) current 1904–41, emma (M) 1904–27 *UK, 1890*

acker; akka; ackers *noun* money in any form. Originally military usage for the (Egyptian) piastre, probably from Arabic *fakka* (small change) *UK, 1937* ▷*see:* ACCA

Acker Bilk *noun* milk. Rhyming slang, based on West Country jazz musician Acker Bilk (b.1929) *UK, 1992*

ackle *verb* to fit or function properly *UK, 1961*

ack Willy; ack Willie *adjective* absent without leave. In World War 2 military use; signalese for AWOL, the official abbreviation *AUSTRALIA, 1942*

acme wringer *noun* the finger. Glasgow rhyming slang *UK, 1988*

acne *noun* a rough road-surface *US, 1976*

acorn *noun* in a casino, a generous tipper *US, 1984*

acorns *noun* the testicles *US, 1975*

acorn shell *noun* a condom *UK, 1990s*

acquire *verb* to steal something. Ironic use of the conventional sense *UK, 1937*

acre; acher *noun* the backside *AUSTRALIA, 1938*

across *preposition* ▶ **across the bridge to Dartmouth** mentally ill, institutionalised. In the twin cities of Halifax and Dartmouth, Nova Scotia, the Nova Scotia Hospital, the institution for the mentally unstable, is in the latter *CANADA, 1999*

across the board *noun* in horse racing, a bet that a horse will win, place (finish second), or show (finish third) *US, 1964*

across the ditch *noun* Australia *NEW ZEALAND, 1998*

across the pavement *adverb* (of criminal activity) in a street situation *UK, 1977*

act *noun* the disguise and staged personality assumed by an expert card counter playing blackjack in a casino in the hope of avoiding detection and ejection *US, 1991*. ▶ **get in on the act; be in on the act** to become, or be, involved in another's activity *US, 1947*. ▶ **get into the act** to take part. If not coined by, popularised as part of the catchphrase 'everybody wants to get into the act' by comedian Jimmy Durante on the radio in the 1940s *US, 1946*. ▶ **get your act together; get it together** to take control of your personal condition; to get your mind and emotions under control; to become organised. A variation of 'pull yourself together' *US, 1973*. ▶ **hard act to follow; tough act to follow** something or someone who cannot be easily outdone *US, 1963*. ▶ **put on an act** to give an exaggerated performance; to indulge in histrionics *AUSTRALIA, 1944*

act *verb* ▶ **act as if** in twelve-step recovery programmes such as Alcoholics Anonymous, used as a slogan for new participants in the programme *US, 1998*. ▶ **act cute** to behave in an annoyingly adorable fashion *SINGAPORE, 2002*. ▶ **act the angora** to play the fool. The angora goat supplies this variation of ACT THE GOAT *AUSTRALIA, 1942*. ▶ **act the goat** to play the fool *AUSTRALIA, 1940*. ▶ **act the maggot** to play the fool *IRELAND, 2003*. ▶ **act your age not your shoesize** to behave in a manner appropriate to your years. A humorous extension of 'act your age' *US, 1986*

act-ass *noun* a show-off; a braggart *US, 1970*

acting Jack *noun* **1** a lance sergeant. Korean war usage *US, 1917*. **2** a soldier temporarily appointed to higher rank, especially to serve as a platoon leader in basic training *US, 1942*

action *noun* **1** sexual activity *US, 1956*. **2** activity, especially of the kind to arouse interest or excitement. Often in the greetings 'where's the action?' and 'what's the action?' *US, 1964*. **3** betting, gambling *US, 1885*. **4** the amount that a gambler is willing to bet *US, 1991*. **5** in pool, a game played with wagers *US, 1990*. **6** in pool, spin imparted on the cue ball to affect the course of the object ball or the cue ball after striking the object ball *US, 1913*. **7** a political act, often confrontational or violent *US, 1971*. ▶ **piece of the action; share of the action** an involvement in an activity; a share in the profits of something *US, 1957*

action *suffix* used for emphasis of the noun to which it is suffixed, without change in meaning. For example, 'I'm ready for some Chinese food action' *US, 1982*

action beaver *noun* a film featuring full nudity and sexual activity short of intercourse *US, 1974*

action faction *noun* a subset of the political left that advocated forceful, confrontational tactics *US, 1968*

action player *noun* a gambler who bets heavily, frequently and flamboyantly *US, 2003*

action room *noun* **1** a poolhall where betting is common *US, 1972*. **2** a place where betting and gambling take place *US, 1972*

active citizens *noun* fleas, bedbugs or body lice *US, 1949*

actor *noun* **1** a liar, a bluffer. Criminal usage *UK, 1950*. **2** a troublemaker *US, 1964*

actor-proof *adjective* denoting a part in a play or performance so well written that no amount of bad acting can ruin it *US, 1973*

actor's Bible *noun* *Variety* magazine *US, 1981*

actor's reach *noun* a seemingly sincere effort to pay for your meal when eating in a group at a restaurant, masking a secret hope that someone else will pay. Based on the stereotype of the actor as starving artist, timing his reach for his wallet to produce a demur from someone else at the table who has already reached for their wallet to pay *US, 1999*

actual *noun* in the Vietnam war, a unit commander *US, 1991*

actuary *noun* in an illegal betting operation, an oddsmaker *US, 1971*

AD *noun* a drug addict. Either a straightforward abbreviation of 'addict' or, as has been seriously suggested, an initialism of 'drug addict' reversed to avoid confusion with a District Attorney *US, 1970*

adafookman! used in black criminal society as an all-purpose protestation of innocence, e.g. 'have I?', 'I didn't!'. A phonetic slovening of 'have I fuck, man!' *UK, 2002*

Ada from Decatur; Ada Ross, the Stable Hoss *noun* in a game of dice, a roll of eight. A homophonic evolution of 'eighter' *US, 1918*

Ad Alley *nickname* the advertising industry, especially that located in New York and commonly known in the US as 'Madison Avenue' after the New York street where many advertising agencies had their offices *US, 1952*

Adam *noun* **1** MDMA, the recreational drug best known as ecstasy. An anagram *US, 1985*. **2** a partner in a criminal enterprise *UK, 1797*. **3** a homosexual's first sexual partner. From Adam as the biblical first man *US, 1972*. ▶ **not know someone from Adam** to be ignorant about an identification *UK, 1784*

Adam and Eve *noun* a pill of MDEA and MDMA, the recreational drugs best known as ecstasy. A combination of ADAM (MDMA) and the obvious partner; note MADMAN and MADWOMAN as synonyms for MDMA and MDEA repectively *UK, 1996*

Adam and Eve; adam *verb* **1** to believe. Rhyming slang. Franklyn suggests it ante-dates 1914; *the Oxford English Dictionary* finds the earliest citation at 1925 *UK*. **2** to leave, especially in a hurried manner *UK, 1998*

Adam and Eve on a raft *noun* two eggs on toast. Restaurant slang *US, 1909*

Adam Ants *noun* pants. Rhyming slang for UK underwear not US trousers; formed on Adam Ant, the stage name of singer and actor Stuart Goddard (b.1954) *UK, 2003*

adamatical *adjective* naked. Without a conventional fig leaf *UK, 1961*

Adam's off-ox *noun* a complete stranger. Used in the expression 'he wouldn't know me from Adam's off-ox' *US, 1983*

adbuster *noun* in anticorporate activism, the non-specific description for those involved in cultural subversion *CANADA, 1989*

adbusting *noun* in anticorporate activism, the act of subverting brand advertising, usually by parody or mockery *US, 2000*

addick *noun* an addict. A misspelling that reflects pronunciation *US, 1997*

addict *noun* a victim of a confidence swindle who repeatedly invests in the crooked enterprise, hoping that his investment will pay off *US, 1985*. ▶ **addict waiting to happen** in twelve-step recovery programmes such as Alcoholics Anonymous, used for describing the childhood of addicts of the future *US, 1998*

additood *noun* a confrontational manner. The English version of Americanised pronunciation, adopting the US slang sense of 'attitude' *UK, 1990s*

addy *noun* an address *US, 2002*

A-deck *noun* a prison cell used for solitary confinement *US, 1984*

adger *verb* in computing, to make an avoidable mistake *US, 1991*

adidas *noun* a prison training instructor. From the similarity between the stripes on an instructor's uniform and the logo-styling on Adidas™ sports equipment *UK, 1996*

adios amoebas used as a humorous farewell. The 'amoebas' is an intentional butchering of *amigos US, 1988*

adios motherfucker used as a farewell. Jocular or defiant; sometimes abbreviated to AMF *US, 1986*

Adirondack steak; Adirondack goat *noun* game, especially venison, killed out of season *US, 1954*

adjectival *adjective* used as a euphemistic substitute for any intensifying adjective that may be considered unsuitable *UK, 1910*

adjuster *noun* a hammer *US, 1990*

adjust the stick! used as a humorous admonition to casino employees at a craps table when the players are losing *US, 1983*

ad-lib *verb* to date indiscriminately *US, 1960*

ad man *noun* **1** a prisoner who is friendly or aligned with the prison administration *US, 1976*. **2** a swindler who sells advertising space in a non-existent publication or a publication with whom he has no association *US, 1992*

Admiral Browning *noun* in the navy, human excrement *UK, 1961*

admiral's mate *noun* in the Royal Navy, a boasting know-all rating *UK, 1962*

admiral's watch *noun* a good night's sleep *US, 1949*

admiralty brown *noun* toilet paper. Originally Royal Australian Navy usage *AUSTRALIA, 1961*

admish *noun* the admission price of a performance *US, 1981*

a-double-scribble *noun* used as a euphemism for 'ass' in any of its senses *US, 1996*

Adrian Quist *adjective* drunk. Rhyming slang for PISSED; formed on the name of the Australian tennis player, 1913–91 *AUSTRALIA, 1978*

adrift *adjective* **1** absent without leave; missing. Originally nautical usage *US, 1841*. **2** confused *UK, 1962*

adult baby *noun* a person, often a prostitute's client, whose sexual needs are manifested in a desire to be dressed and treated as an infant *UK, 1995*

advance *verb* ▶ **advance the spark** to prepare *US, 1945*

advertise *verb* **1** to signal your intentions unwittingly but plainly *US, 1931*. **2** to dress or behave in a sexually provocative manner; to pluck and pencil the eyebrows. Gay use, on the premise that it pays to advertise *US, 1972*. **3** in poker, to bluff in a manner that is intended to be caught, all in anticipation of a later bluff *US, 1949*. **4** in gin, to discard in a manner that is designed to lure a desired card from an opponent *US, 1971*. **5** to activate the siren and/or flashing lights of a police car *US, 1976*

advertised *noun* ▶ **on the advertised** on the railways, on time *US, 1975*

adzine *noun* a single-interest fan magazine containing only advertising *US, 1982*

aerated; aeriated *adjective* excited, angry *UK, 1984*

aerial *adjective* used as a modifier for any sexual position where at least one participant is off the ground *US, 1995*

Aesop *noun* in poker, any player who tells stories while playing *US, 1996*

af; aff *noun* an African. Derogatory *SOUTH AFRICA, 1976*

A-factor *noun* the 'Antarctic factor', which explains any and all unexpected and added difficulties encountered *ANTARCTICA, 1988*

AFAIC used as shorthand in Internet discussion groups and text messages to mean 'as far as I'm concerned' *US, 2002*

AFF *noun* an attraction to South Asian females. An abbreviation of 'Asian female fetish' *US, 1997*

affirmative yes. Used with irony, mocking a military response *US, 1976*

affy bud *noun* a type of marijuana that originates in Afghanistan *UK, 2004*

afgay *noun* a homosexual. See: AGFAY *US, 1972*

Afghan *noun* any Afghan, Pakistani or other central Asian who immigrated to Australia in the C19 to work as camel-drivers in desert regions. Formerly generally regarded with suspicion and contempt by white Australians, which accounts for the fossilisation of the term in various derogatory phrases; the occupation has long since disappeared *AUSTRALIA, 1869*

Afghani *noun* hashish oil from Afghanistan. Although Afghanistan is best known for its heroin, hashish is a second important export *US, 1992*

Afghani black; Afghani pollen *noun* varieties of hashish from Afghanistan *UK, 2003*

AFK used as shorthand in Internet discussion groups and text messages to mean 'away from keyboard' *US, 2002*

Afkansastan *noun* Afghan marijuana grown in Kansas *US, 2001*

afloat *adjective* drunk *US, 1809*

AFO *nickname* the Arellano-Felix Organization, a criminal enterprise that functioned as a transportation subcontractor for the heroin trade into the US *US, 1998*

afoot or ahossback *adjective* unsure of the direction you are going to take *US, 1895*

A for effort *noun* praise for the work involved, if not for the result of the work. From a trend in US schools to grade children both on the basis of achievement and on the basis of effort expended. Faint praise as often as not *US, 1948*

Africa hot *adjective* extremely hot *US, 1992*

African *noun* **1** a manufactured cigarette (not hand-rolled) *AUSTRALIA, 1959*. **2** a type of marijuana claimed to have been grown in Africa *UK, 2003*. **3** in American casinos, a black betting chip worth $100 *US, 1983*

African black *noun* a potent type of marijuana, presumed to be from Africa, possibly Morocco *US, 1970*

African bush *noun* marijuana *US, 1979*

African dominoes *noun* dice *US, 1919*

African golf *noun* the game of craps *US, 1919*

African grape *noun* a watermelon. Based on the stereotypical association between rural black people and a love of watermelon *US, 1980*

African guff-guff *noun* a non-existent disease suffered by soldiers *US, 1947*

African plum *noun* a watermelon *US, 1973*

African queen *noun* a white homosexual man who finds black men attractive. Punning on the Bogart film *US, 1979*

African salad *noun* khat, a natural stimulant grown in Kenya, Ethiopia and Somalia *UK, 2004*

African toothache *noun* any sexually transmitted infection *US, 1964*

African Woodbine *noun* a marijuana cigarette. Woodbine™ was a well-known brand of cheaper cigarette *UK, 1975*

Afro *noun* a bushy, frizzy hairstyle embraced by black people as a gesture of resistance in the 1960s *US, 1966*

afromobile *noun* a wicker pedicab *US, 1939*

Afro pick *noun* a gap-toothed comb used for an Afro hairstyle *US, 1986*

afterbirth *noun* rhubarb *AUSTRALIA, 1943*

afterburner *noun* a linear amplifier for a citizens' band radio *US, 1976*

afterclaps *noun* consequences *BELIZE, 1996*

after-hours *adjective* open after bars and nightclubs close at 2am *US, 1947*

afterlater *adverb* later *US, 1997*

after-nine *noun* a black male homosexual who pretends to be heterosexual during working hours *SOUTH AFRICA, 2000*

afternoon *noun* the buttocks, especially large female buttocks *BARBADOS, 1996*

afternoon farmer *noun* a lazy and unsuccessful farmer *CANADA, 1960*

afters *noun* **1** the dessert course of a meal. Originally military usage *UK, 1909*. **2** drinks, or a session of drinking, served in a public house after licensing hours *UK, 2000*. **3** the after-effects of too much alcohol *IRELAND, 1997*. **4** further fighting after a fight appears to have ended *UK, 1974*

after tears *noun* a post-funeral celebration. Scamto youth street slang (South African townships) *SOUTH AFRICA, 2005*

afterthought *noun* an unplanned pregnancy; the child of an unplanned pregnancy *UK, 1914*

after you, Claude – no, after you, Cecil used to depict a lack of aggression or unnecessary good manners. A catchphrase regularly delivered by Jack Train and Horace Percival in the BBC radio comedy *ITMA*, 1939–49. Contemporary usage has been widely applied to sports such as cricket, hockey, football and motor-racing, and also to first-past-the-post electoral systems *UK, 1939*

after you with the trough! used in response to someone's belching. A unsubtle implication that the belcher is a pig who has eaten too much. Mainly northern England *UK, 1977*

ag *adjective* angry. An abbreviation of 'aggravated' *US, 2000*

AG *adjective* all good *US, 1997*

ag used as an all-purpose intensifier. Pronounced like the German *ach*. Can precede any sentence for various effects, such as the more neutral, 'Ag, I don't know'. Used by some people as a stand-alone expletive *SOUTH AFRICA, 1833*

ag; agg *noun* trouble; problems; a nuisance. A further reduction of AGGRO (aggravation) *UK, 1996*

again! used for expressing strong approval *ANTIGUA AND BARBUDA, 1996*

against the law *adjective* (used of a woman) extraordinarily beautiful *US, 1997*

against the wall *adjective* said of a confidence swindle which is perpetrated without a fake office, extras, props, etc *US, 1940*

A-game *noun* in a casino or cardroom, the poker game with the highest stakes *US, 1949*

Aga saga *noun* a genre of popular novel-writing, plotting comfortable, domestic and emotional middle-class lives. Based on Aga stoves which are recognised as an appropriate social symbol or aspiration *UK, 1992*

agate *noun* **1** a marble in the slang sense of sanity *US, 1951*. **2** a small penis *US, 1967*

agates *noun* the testicles *US, 1941*

A-gay *noun* a prominent, sought-after homosexual man *US, 1982*

age *noun* **1** length of service for an employer; seniority *US, 1946*. **2** in poker and other card games, the person to the immediate left of the dealer *US, 1963*

-age *suffix* used as an embellishment without meaning at the end of nouns. The suffix got a second wind with the US television series *Buffy The Vampire Slayer US, 1981*

ageable *adjective* very old *TRINIDAD AND TOBAGO, 2003*

age before beauty used as a mock courtesy when allowing someone to precede you *UK, 1977*

age card *noun* proof of legal age *US, 1968*

agent *noun* **1** the operator of a rigged carnival game *US, 1985*. **2** in casino gambling, a confederate of a cheat *US, 1996*

Agent Scully *noun* oral sex. A reference to the name of the female lead in the *X-Files* television series, punning on her name and SKULL (oral sex) *US, 2001*

agfay *noun* a homosexual man. Pig Latin for FAG *US, 1942*

agged *adjective* angry, aggravated *US, 1998*

aggie *noun* **1** an aggressive, domineering male. From the conventional 'aggressive' *US, 1968*. **2** during the Korean war, any young Korean *US, 1951*. **3** agoraphobia *UK, 1980*. **4** a farm tool, especially a hoe *US, 1972*

aggie *adjective* angry, agitated *US, 2002*

aggie overdrive *noun* in trucking, coasting in neutral gear *US, 1976*

Aggie Weston's; Aggie's *nickname* a hostel for sailors provided by the charity RSR (Dame Agnes Weston's Royal Sailors Rests). Co-founded in 1876 by Agnes Weston (1840–1918) to try and save sailors from 'booze and brothels' and still trying. Grateful sailors used to call Weston-Super-Mare in the southwest of England 'Aggie-on-horseback' *UK, 1962*

aggravation *noun* (of police or criminals) an act of harrassment. Metropolitan Police slang *UK, 1970*

aggressive *adjective* used as a coded euphemism for 'dominant' in sadomasochistic sex *US, 1986*

aggro *noun* **1** trouble, strife; problems; a nuisance. Abbreviated from 'aggravation' *UK, 1969*. **2** aggression *AUSTRALIA, 1982*

aggro *adjective* aggressively angry *AUSTRALIA, 1986*

aginner *noun* a person morally opposed to carnivals and the circus *US, 1981*

agitate *verb* ▶ **agitate the gravel** to leave. Teen slang *US, 1958*

agitprop *noun* agitation and propaganda as an unfocused political tactic; a fashionable genre of theatre arts with a (usually) left-wing political agenda. Adopted from the name given to a department of the Central Committee of the Russian Communist Party responsible for agitation and propaganda on behalf of communist ideals; a conflation of *agitatsiya* and *propaganda* *UK, 1934*

aglish *adjective* nauseated; sick to one's stomach. Used around the Lunenburg area in Nova Scotia, where many German settlers still adapt old expressions *CANADA, 1999*

-a go-go *suffix* all over the place, in a mess; on the go. In the manner of GO-GO (a disco), hence dancing applied figuratively *UK, 1986*

agonies *noun* the physical and psychological pain suffered when withdrawing from drug addiction *US, 1992*

agonised button *noun* on military uniforms, an anodised aluminium (Staybrite) button. Anodised (electro-plated) aluminium replaced brass and white metal as the main metal for British Other Ranks military insignia from about 1950 onwards *UK, 1984*

agony *noun* ▶ **pile on the agony; pile up the agony; put on the agony** to exaggerate, to show-off. Originally theatrical usage *US, 1837*

agony aunt; agony auntie *noun* a newspaper or magazine columnist who advises readers on questions of a personal nature; hence an adviser or counsellor on intimate problems *UK, 1975*

agony column *noun* a newspaper or magazine feature of readers' letters seeking help for personal problems with replies from a columnist or agony aunt *UK, 1975*

a good craftsman never blames his tools used for dismissing an attempt by someone to blame a mistake on a piece of equipment or something within their control *US, 1997*

agricultural *adjective* in cricket, describes a simple, slogging shot off a sweeping bat *UK, 1982*

A-head *noun* **1** an amphetamine abuser *US, 1971*. **2** a frequent user of LSD *US, 1971*

ahhh, Rooshan used as a youth-to-youth greeting. A short-lived fad greeting associated with bebop jazz *US, 1949*

a-hole *noun* **1** the anus. A' as in ASS of ARSE *US, 1942*. **2** by extension, a despised person *US, 1942*

-aholic; -oholic; -holic *suffix* an addict of, or addicted to, the prefixed thing or activity. Usage may be literal or figurative. From 'alcoholic' (a person addicted to alcohol); the first widely recognised extended usage was 'workaholic' (1968) *US, 1964*

ail; aiii! yes! Popularised in the UK in the late 1990s by Ali G (comedian Sacha Baron-Cohen) *UK, 2002*

AIF *adjective* deaf. Rhyming slang, from Australian *Imperial Forces* *AUSTRALIA, 1973*

a-ight used for expressing agreement or affirmation *US, 1995*

aim *verb* ▶ **aim Archie at the armitage** (of a male) to urinate. *Armitage* Shanks are manufacturers of toilet furniture *AUSTRALIA, 1971*

aimie *noun* an amphetamine *UK, 2003*

ain't; aint *verb* replaces am not, are not, is not, has not, have not. A widely used solecism *UK, 1710*

ain't buyin' it! I don't believe you *US, 1990*

ain't havin' it! it is not allowed *US, 1990*

ain't love grand! used for registering the pleasure of being in love or, ironically, the opposite *US, 1977*

ain't no joke! I am serious! *US, 1990*

ain't no shame in my game used for expressing a lack of shame when engaged in an activity that might shame others *US, 2002*

ain't no thang; ain't no big thang used for dismissing something as not problematic *US, 1985*

ain't that a bite! isn't that too bad! Teen slang *US, 1951*

ain't the beer cold! used for conveying that all is well in the world. Popularised by baseball radio announcer Chuck Thompson, who used the phrase as the title of his autobiography. Repeated with referential humour *US, 1982*

ain't with that I do not agree or consent *US, 1990*

ain't you got no couf? where are your manners, dress sense, etc? Military; a pun on 'uncouth' *UK, 1984*

AIO *noun* a college student who does not belong to a fraternity *US, 1968*

AIP *noun* heroin from Afghanistan, Iran and/or Pakistan *US, 1982*

air *noun* **1** a jump while snowboarding *US, 1996*. **2** in foot-propelled scootering, a jump *UK, 2000*. **3** air support, air power, bombing. Vietnam war usage *US, 1991*. **4** in the pornography industry, an ejaculation that cannot be seen leaving the penis and travelling through the air. In a situation which calls for visual proof of the ejaculation, air is not good *US, 1995*. **5** air brakes on a truck or railway carriage *US, 1897*. **6** the mood created by a person or persons. There is 'good air' and there is 'bad air' *US, 1988*. ▶ **get air** to be ignored *UK, 2005*. ▶ **in the air** (used of the flank of an army) unprotected by natural or man-man obstacles *US, 1982*. ▶ **leave in the air** to abandon someone without support *UK, 1948*. ▶ **turn the air blue; make the air turn blue** to use obscene or blasphemous language *UK, 1890*. ▶ **up in the air** (used of a pair in a game of poker) formed with help from the communal face-up cards *US, 1992*

air *verb* ▶ **air your belly** to vomit *US, 2000*

air artist *noun* a railway engineer skilled at the use of air brakes *US, 1977*

airbag *noun* a person who talks too much *US, 2004*

airbags *noun* the lungs *US, 1945*

air ball *noun* **1** in pinball, a ball that is lost out of play without having been flipped *US, 1977*. **2** in pool, a shot in which the cue ball does not hit any other ball *US, 1993*

air bandit *noun* a gambling cheat *US, 1969*

air barrel *noun* in pool, that which backs a bet made without money to back the bet. A BARREL is a betting unit; an 'air barrel' is thus an illusory betting unit *US, 1990*

air biscuit *noun* a fart *US, 2001*

air-conditioned *adjective* sexually frigid *UK, 1983*

air dance *noun* capital punishment by hanging. A specific dance name is sometimes substituted for 'dance', such as 'air polka' *US, 1982*

air-dash *verb* to travel in an aircraft (a degree of urgency is implied) *2001*

airedale *noun* **1** a Wall Street gentleman. An extension of the symbol of the Airedale as an aristocratic dog *US, 1925*. **2** a navy pilot *US, 1942*. **3** a plane handler on an aircraft carrier *US, 1943*

air giver *noun* a railway brakeman *US, 1977*

air guitar *noun* an imagined guitar used to mimic a rock guitar player *US, 1982*

airhead *noun* **1** a person who is not inclined to think, not equipped to think, or both *US, 1972*

air hog *noun* in the language of hang gliding, the flier in a group who stays in the air longest *US, 1992*

airie *noun* an aeroplane. In Glasgow, a shortening of the local pronunciation 'airieplane' *UK: SCOTLAND, 1985*

airish *adjective* **1** cold *US, 1985*. **2** arrogant, showing off *US, 1943*

air jammer *noun* a railway worker who connects airhoses and air signals on a train *US, 1977*

Air Jesus; Air Hebrews *noun* sandals. Alluding to Nike Air Jordan™ sports shoes *US, 1992*

air junkie *noun* in the language of hang gliding, a devoted, obsessed flier *US, 1992*

air-kiss *verb* to go through the motions of kissing but deliberately fail to make contact with the person who would normally be kissed *UK, 1985*

airlock *verb* to speak. C. I. Macafee glosses as 'from the cut-out in a diesel engine if air enters the fuel system' in *A Concise Ulster Dictionary*, 1996 *UK: NORTHERN IRELAND, 1996*

airlocked *adjective* extremely drunk *UK: NORTHERN IRELAND, 1996*

airmail *noun* **1** rubbish thrown from the upper windows of a building to the courtyard below *US, 1952*. **2** objects thrown by prisoners down onto guards or other prisoners below *US, 1992*

airmail *verb* to throw rubbish from the upper windows of a building to the courtyard below *US, 1968*

air monkey *noun* a railway air-brake repairman *US, 1946*

air off *verb* to talk loudly *TRINIDAD AND TOBAGO, 1960*

airplane *noun* **1** a device used for holding a marijuana cigarette that has burnt down to the stub. An abbreviation of the fuller JEFFERSON AIRPLANE *US, 1970*. **2** marijuana *UK, 1998*

airplane *verb* to inhale through the nose the smoke of the stub of a marijuana cigarette *US, 1970*

airplane blonde; aeroplane blonde *noun* a brunette, usually a woman, with dyed blonde hair. Jocular, implying the punchline 'blonde up top but you know there's a black box somewhere' *UK, 1999*

airplane driver *noun* a fighter pilot. Gulf war usage *US, 1992*

airplane rule *noun* in computing, the belief that simplicity is a virtue *US, 1991*

air ride *noun* a car with pneumatic shock absorbers *US, 1975*

airs *noun* a pair of Nike Air Jordan™ trainers (sneakers) *US, 1990*

airs and graces *noun* braces; suspenders. Rhyming slang, surviving earlier senses 'Epsom Races' and 'faces' *UK, 1960*

air shot *noun* an act of sexual intercourse that stops short of orgasm. Royal Navy slang, from 'torpedo drill' *UK, 1979*

air sucker *noun* a jet aeroplane *US, 1963*

air-to-mud *adjective* (used of shots fired or bombs dropped) from the air to the ground *US, 1991*

air tragic *noun* air traffic control. In Royal Air Force use *UK, 2002*

airy *adjective* marijuana-intoxicated *US, 1949*

airy a none. As used in Nova Scotia's South Shore, this expression is a form of the archaic 'ne'er a' or a short form of 'never a' *CANADA, 1999*

airy-fairy *noun* a member of the RNAS (Royal Naval Air Service) later the Fleet Air Arm *UK, 1979*

airy-fairy *adjective* delicate, fanciful; insubstantial, trivial *UK, 1869*

aitch *noun* **1** hell. A euphemism *US, 1950*. **2** heroin *US, 1945*

ai te guacho I'll see you later. 'Guacho' pronounced 'watch-o,' a pure invention. Border Spanish used in English conversation by Mexican-Americans *US, 1950*

AJ *noun* an 'acting jack', or an acting noncommissioned officer *US, 1991*

ajax *noun* **1** in hold 'em poker, an ace and a jack as the first two cards dealt to a particular player. Punning on the brand name of a cleaning agent *US, 1981*. **2** any youth gang member under the age of 16. A borrowing from the slogan for Ajax™ cleaner – 'comes out clean' – and the fact that a juvenile offender will be treated far less harshly than an adult *US, 1993*

ajax *adjective* **1** nearby. Possibly derived from 'adjacent' *UK, 2002*. **2** clean. An allusion to the branded cleaning product *US, 2002*

AK *noun* **1** a sycophant *US, 1939*. **2** a mean and nasty old man. An abbreviation of the Yiddish ALTER KOCKER *US, 1942*. **3** an AK-47 semi-automatic rifle *US, 1990*

AK *verb* to curry favour by obsequious behaviour. An abbreviation of 'ass-kiss' *US, 1939*

AK47 *noun* a variety of marijuana. From the automatic weapon designed by Mikhail Kalashnikov, *2002*

AKA *noun* an alias. An acronym of 'also known as'; from police jargon *US, 1955*. ► **go AKA** to assume an alias *US, 1983*

AK amp *noun* an amputation at the knee. Vietnam war medic usage *US, 1990*

akey-okey *adjective* satisfactory *US, 1960*

aks *verb* to ask. A familiar mispronunciation, especially in black and youth usage *UK, 2005*

AL *adjective* not to be believed. An abbreviation of 'always lying' *US, 1995*

ala-ala's *noun* the testicles. Hawaiian youth usage *US, 1981*

Alabama wool *noun* cotton *US, 1958*

a-la-beff *noun* vaginal intercourse, the woman on hands and knees and the man entering her from behind. An allusion to the mating of cattle and the French *boeuf* *TRINIDAD AND TOBAGO, 1980*

Aladdin's cave *noun* the location of a successful thief's ill-gotten gains. Metropolitan Police slang. After the tale of Aladdin in *The Arabian Nights* *UK, 1970*

alambrista *noun* a Mexican illegally present in the US. Border Spanish used in English conversation by Mexican-Americans; from the Spanish for 'wire' *US, 1974*

Alameda *noun* in bar dice games, a roll that produces no points for the player. Alameda is an island city just west of Oakland. In Alameda, a worthless hand is called a 'Milpitas', alluding to a small and relatively poor city just north of San Jose *US, 1971*

alamo used for registering a strong sexual interest in someone. Derives from the initial letters of 'lick me out' *UK, 2002*

Alamo Hilton *nickname* a heavily fortified bunker beneath the Khe Sanh base in South Vietnam during the Vietnam war *US, 1990*

Alan Whickers; Alans *noun* knickers. Rhyming slang, formed from the name of reporter, broadcaster and television personality Alan Whicker (b.1925), who first came to prominence in the late 1950s *UK, 2003*

Alaska hand *noun* in hold 'em poker, a king and a three as the first two cards dealt to a particular player. Built from the synonymous KING CRAB, which is found in Alaska *US, 1981*

Alaskamo *noun* an American Indian from Alaska *US, 1963*

Alaska strawberries *noun* beans *US, 1991*

Alaska time *noun* used for explaining tardiness *US, 1976*

Alaska turkey *noun* salmon *US, 1948*

Alaska tuxedo *noun* a wool work suit *US, 1965*

Alb *noun* an Albanian *UK, 1945*

albatross *noun* **1** a very sick, incurable hospital patient, lingering near death *US, 1985*. **2** a Grumman HU-16 amphibian aircraft, best known as a rescue aircraft during the Korean and Vietnam wars *US, 1991*. **3** cooked chicken. Royal Navy use; presumably inspired by Coleridge's 'The Rime of the Ancient Mariner' *UK, 1995*

Alberta Clipper *noun* a cold weather system that blows from the Canadian Rocky Mountains eastward. A winter phenomenon, with wind and usually snow *CANADA, 1999*

Albert County tartan; Albert County dress tartan *noun* a plaid wool shirt, as used by woodsmen. Albert County is in the Moncton, New Brunswick, area *CANADA, 1993*

albino *noun* in pool, the white cue ball *US, 1988*

albino grass *noun* snow fallen on a Vancouver, British Columbia, lawn *CANADA, 2002*

Alcan *nickname* the Alaska-Canada Highway *US, 1975*

Al Capone *noun* heroin *UK, 2002*

alcho *noun* an alcoholic *UK, 1996*

alco; alko *noun* an alcoholic *AUSTRALIA, 1965*

alcoholiday *noun* a holiday or festive period that is spent drinking alcohol *GUYANA, 1975*

alcohol rub *noun* a cocktail party *US, 1968*

alderman *noun* **1** in the circus and carnival, an office worker who informs on his fellow workers *US, 1981*. **2** a big paunch. Referring to the supposed physique and appetite of local elected officials *US, 1933*

al desko *adverb* (used of a meal) consumed at your desk at work. A play on *al fresco US, 1981*

alec; aleck; alick *noun* an idiot. Shortening of SMART ALEC *AUSTRALIA, 1919*

aled up *adjective* under the influence of beer *UK, 1996*

aletank *noun* a heavy drinker. A modern variant of the earlier, now obsolete 'alecan' (a heavy drinker) *UK, 2002*

a-levels *noun* anal sex, especially when advertised as a service offered by a prostitute. A play on the name given to 'advanced-level' examinations in the British education system *UK, 2003*

Alexander *noun* a telephone. From Alexander Graham Bell, 1847–1922, Scottish-born inventor of the telephone *UK, 1999*

Alf *noun* an ordinary uneducated, unsophisticated Australian male. Counterpart of the ROY *AUSTRALIA, 1960*

alfalfa *noun* **1** money. Circus and carnival usage *US, 1917*. **2** marijuana *US, 1995*

alias man *noun* a confidence swindler *JAMAICA, 1961*

alibi *noun* **1** in a rigged carnival game, the reason given by the game operator to disqualify a legitimate win *US, 1985*. **2** in sports, an excuse for not performing well. In 1914, sports writer Ring Lardner created the character Alibi Ike, who always had an excuse for not playing well *US, 1914*. **3** a weak excuse. A watered-down version of the conventional use *US, 1899*

alibi day *noun* payday. Used in logging camps, suggesting that loggers suddenly develop illnesses and injuries that prevent them from working when they have cash in hand *US, 1958*

alibi ghee *noun* a person who can be counted upon to provide an alibi for a criminal *US, 1950*

alibi Ike *noun* any criminal who regularly asserts alibis when questioned about a crime *US, 1915*

Alice *noun* **1** LSD. A phonetic pun on the first two letters of LSD, influenced by Lewis Carroll's *Alice's Adventures in Wonderland*, 1865, and *Through the Looking-Glass and What Alice Found There*, 1871, which were considered inspirational works by the hippy subculture of the late 1960s. The obvious reference, but not a citation of usage, is Jefferson Airplane's 'White Rabbit', 1969 *US, 1972*. **2** a military backpack *US, 1988*. ▶ **to have Alice** to experience the bleed period of the menstrual cycle *US, 1968*

Alice *nickname* Alice Springs. Early use is always preceded by 'the' *AUSTRALIA, 1901*

Alice B. Toklas brownies *noun* chocolate brownies laced with marijuana or hashish. Toklas' original 1954 recipe, which was for fudge, not brownies, carried the caution: 'Should be eaten with care. Two pieces are quite sufficient' *US, 1969*

alickadoo *noun* a rugby club official or committee member. Possibly from a book by Alec Kadoo *IRELAND, 1997*

alien *noun* in casino gambling, a betting chip from another casino *US, 1983*

Alimony Gallery *noun* ex-wives of players at an exhibition game by celebrity filmmakers *CANADA, 2002*

A-list *noun* used for denoting all that is associated with the greatest contemporary fame and celebrity. In conventional media jargon the A-list is a notional social elite of those who are considered prestigious enough to add top-value to a guest list *US, 1984*

alive *adjective* **1** said of a multiple-race bet in horse racing in which the first or early legs of the bet have been won *AUSTRALIA, 1989*. **2** in horse racing, said of a horse subject to heavy betting *US, 1990*

alize *noun* any alcoholic beverage *US, 2002*

alko *noun* ▷*see:* ALCO

alky; alkie *noun* **1** an alcoholic *US, 1952*. **2** alcohol, especially methyl alcohol *US, 1844*. **3** methanol used as fuel for racing cars *US, 1970*

alkyed *adjective* drunk *US, 1970*

alky tank *noun* a holding cell in a jail reserved for drunk prisoners *US, 1962*

all *adverb* **1** very, *1994*. **2** so *US, 1997*

all ▶ **be all** used as a quotative device to report a conversation *US, 1992*

all about *adjective* **1** alert, efficient. Mostly Royal Navy use *UK, 1946*. **2** interested in *US, 1999*

all alone *adjective* in horse racing, leading a race by several lengths *US, 1951*

All-American *nickname* the 82nd Airborne Division. Taken from the two A's on the division's patch. There were many double-A variants, such as 'All-African', 'Alcoholics Anonymous', and 'Almost Airborne', but 'All-American' was the most common *US, 1991*

all-American drug *noun* cocaine *US, 1998*

all and everyone *noun* every single person *TRINIDAD AND TOBAGO, 1973*

all a penny *adjective* inexpensive and plentiful *BARBADOS, 1978*

All Black *nickname* a member of the New Zealand international men's rugby team *NEW ZEALAND, 1986*

all chiefs and no Indians; too many chiefs and not enough Indians a situation in which too many people are giving orders and too few are available to obey; a top-heavy command structure. Military coinage, meaning all officers not other ranks. *US, 1972*

all-clear *noun* authorisation, official approval. From the earlier and continuing use as a signal that a danger has passed *UK, 1936*

all coppers are bastards; all coppers are cunts serves as a catchphrase among certain sections of society. From, or possibly the inspiration for, a chanted jingle: 'I'll sing you a song / And it wont take long (or: It's not very long) / All coppers are bastards.' *UK, 1945*

all dat *noun* everything. Popularised in the UK in the late 1990s by Ali G (comedian Sacha Baron-Cohen) *UK, 2003*

all day *adjective* **1** in bar dice games involving up to three rolls, taking all three rolls to make the player's hand *US, 1976*. **2** in craps, said of a bet that is in effect until the shooter rolls his point or a seven *US, 1983*

all day and night *noun* a life prison sentence *US, 1976*

all day from a quarter *noun* a jail sentence of 25 years to life *US, 1992*

all-day sucker *noun* a large lollipop that takes a long time to consume *AUSTRALIA, 1939*

all down the line *adverb* in every way, completely, at every opportunity *UK, 1976*

allergic *adjective* having a dislike for someone or something. Generally jocular usage *UK, 1937*

alley *noun* **1** a fictional place characterised by the preceding thing or activity *US, 1954*. **2** in horse racing, a stall in the starting barrier *AUSTRALIA, 1982*. **3** on the railways, the track visible ahead of a train *US, 1975*. **4** a walkway between rows of prison cells *US, 1992*. **5** a playing marble *AUSTRALIA, 1934*. ▶ **make your alley good** to improve your situation; to redeem yourself in the eyes of others *AUSTRALIA, 1924*. ▶ **up your alley** apt to your style or taste *US, 1924*

alley apple *noun* **1** a brick or cobblestone *US, 1927*. **2** horse manure; a piece of faeces; excrement *US, 1960*

alley bourbon *noun* strong, illegally manufactured whisky *US, 1999*

alley cat *noun* **1** a sexually promiscuous person, especially a woman *UK, 1926*. **2** a young person who idles on a street corner *US, 1945*. **3** a person who survives on begged or stolen pickings *GUYANA, 1996*

alley cleaner *noun* a handgun *US, 1957*

alley craps *noun* a spontaneous, loosely organised, private game of craps, rarely played in an alley *US, 1977*

alley juice *noun* denatured alcohol (ethyl alcohol) to which a poisonous substance has been added to make it unfit for consumption *US, 1992*

alley-oop *noun* in snowboarding, a 360-degree turn in the direction of the back of the board *CANADA, 1996*

alley-scoring *noun* the recyling of food, furniture or anything else left in the rubbish *US, 1997*

alley up *verb* to pay off a debt *NEW ZEALAND, 2002*

alley-wise *adjective* sophisticated in the ways of the world *US, 1974*

allez-oop! used to accompany the action when lifting a child, or boosting someone over or onto something. Originally used by circus acrobats. A combination of French *allez* (to go) with a Franglais version of 'up' *UK, 1931*

all fall down used for describing a catastrophe or chaos *GRENADA, 1996*

all fart and no shit *adjective* said of a person who makes empty promises *UK, 1989*

all-fired *adjective* used as an intensifier. Perhaps a euphemism for 'hell-fired', as are INFERNAL, DAMNED, etc *US, 1845*

all gas and gaiters *adjective* used as a derisory description of bishops and other church dignitaries; pompous nonsense. Originally 'All is gas and gaiters', Charles Dickens, *Nicholas Nickleby*, 1838–39. Repopularised as a useful catchphrase by the BBC situation comedy *All Gas and Gaiters*, 1967–71 *UK, 1967*

all get-out *noun* a high degree of something *US, 1884*

all gong and no dinner *adjective* all talk and no action *UK, 1981*

all hands *adjective* sexually aggressive *US, 1963*

all het up *adjective* ▷*see:* HET UP

alligation *noun* the charring of burnt wood *US, 1955*

alligator *noun* **1** an enthusiastic fan of swing jazz *US, 1936*. **2** any unpleasant and difficult task *US, 1990*. **3** a circus performer's wife *US, 1981*. **4** in electric line work, an insulated line tool known formally as a 'tie stick' *US, 1980*. **5** in television and film making, a clamp used to attach lighting *US, 1987*

alligator *verb* (of a painting) to crack *US, 1955*

alligator see you later. Rhyming slang, inspired or influenced by 'See you later, alligator / In a while, crocodile.' (Bill Haley & the Comets, 'See you later, Alligator', 1956.) *UK, 1960*

Alligator Alley *nickname* Interstate Highway 75, which connects Naples and Fort Lauderdale, Florida. So named because it crosses the heart of what had been an impenetrable wilderness, the Florida Everglades. The name is thought to have been coined by the American Automobile Association in 1966 to express supreme disdain for what it considered to be an unsafe toll road *US, 1966*

alligator bait *noun* **1** a black person *US, 1901*. **2** bad food, especially fried liver *US, 1926*

alligator boot *noun* a railwayman's work-boot damaged by diesel oil so that the uppers have parted from the sides. From the appearance of the flapping leather *UK, 1970*

alligator burns *noun* charrings on burnt wood in the form of scales that resemble an alligator's hide *US, 1981*

alligator mouth *noun* a braggart; a verbal bully *US, 1961*

alligator skins *noun* paper money *US, 1949*

all in *adjective* **1** exhausted, tired out. A term coined in the Stock Exchange where it was used to describe a depressed market *UK, 1903*. **2** said of a poker player who has bet their entire remaining bankroll *US, 1979*

all jam and Jerusalem *adjective* applied derisively to the Women's Institute. A catchphrase, probably dating from the 1920s, that targets the two widely-known details of WI lore: jam-making and the anthemic use of William Blake's hymn 'Jerusalem' *UK, 1977*

all jokes and no tokes *adjective* used by casino employees to describe poor tipping by gamblers *US, 1983*

all like ▶ **be all like** used as a quotative device, combining two other devices for 'to say' *US, 1997*

all man jack *noun* everybody who is involved *TRINIDAD AND TOBAGO, 1973*

all mouth *adjective* boastful; unable to back up words with deeds *BARBADOS, 1996*

all mouth and no trousers *adjective* all talk and no substance *UK, 1977*

all-nighter *noun* **1** an engagement between a prostitute and customer that lasts all night; a prostitute's client who pays to stay all night. Also known as an 'all-night' *UK, 1960*. **2** any task worked on all night long, especially to meet a deadline for the following day *AUSTRALIA, 1966*. **3** a person who stays in jail all night after being arrested *US, 1992*

all-night money *noun* a prostitute's charge for spending the night with a customer *US, 1992*

all of a doodah *adjective* nervous, dithering with excitement *UK, 1952*

all of a tiswas; all of a tizwas; all of a tizzy *adjective* in a state of panic or excited confusion. Probably a Royal Air Force coinage; from TIZZ; TIZZY (a state of panic), contriving what appears to be an etymology by amending the source-word to 'tiswas', a combination of 'it is' and 'was', suggesting a play on the earlier colloquial phrase 'not know whether you are coming or going' (to be in a state of confusion) *UK, 1984*

all on *adjective* prepared for violence *NEW ZEALAND, 1999*

all on top! that's untrue! Criminal use, probably from the 1920s or 30s; what's 'on top' is in addition to the truth *UK, 1984*

all-out *adjective* very drunk *GUYANA, 1952*

all over bar the shouting *adjective* finished for all intents and purposes *UK, 1842*

all over it *adjective* in complete control *US, 2002*

all over the place like a madwoman's knitting *adjective* in chaos, in utter disarray. Several variants including 'all over the place like a madwoman's custard / lunch-box / shit'. An elaboration of conventional and unconventional senses of 'all over the place' *AUSTRALIA, 1953*

all over the shop *adjective* confused, in disarray; everywhere *UK, 1874*

all over you like a rash *adjective* making determined advances of an intimate or personal nature *UK, 1999*

allow *verb* to be lenient towards someone, to let someone off lightly. Predominantly black usage *UK, 2002*

all piss and wind *adjective* prone to boasting *NEW ZEALAND, 2002*

all pissed-up and nothing to show *adjective* used of someone who has spent or, more precisely, drunk all his wages or winnings. A variation, probably from the 1920s, in the manner of 'all dressed up and nowhere to go' *UK, 1961*

all quiet on the Western Front *adjective* used to describe a situation in which not much is happening. From a World War 1 communiqué that became a satirical catchphrase; now generalised, probably influenced by the 1929 novel by Erich Maria Remarque and the 1930 film so titled. In the US, the phrase replaced the Civil War-era 'all quiet on the Potomac' *UK, 2003*

all reet *adjective* good; all right *US, 1946*

all right *adjective* in possession of drugs *US, 1971*

all right used as a greeting among prisoners *US, 1992*

all right for some! used for registering envy of another's advantages or luck *UK, 1969*

all rooters and no shooters used at casino craps tables for encouraging a player to take a turn as a shooter *US, 1983*

all rootie used as an expression of agreement or satisfaction. Especially popular after Little Richard's 1955 hit song 'Tutti Frutti' *US, 1957*

all round the option *adverb* all over the place, everywhere *UK, 1957*

all show and no go *adjective* used for describing someone who cannot back appearances with action *US, 2000*

all singing all dancing *adjective* configured or equipped with all possible enhancements. Especially of financial and IT products, but originally from the advertising matter for *Broadway Melody*, 1929, the first Hollywood musical *US, 1929*

all star *noun* a drug user who abuses many different drugs *US, 1992*

all systems go *noun* a state of readiness. Often humorous; adopted from the jargon of space exploration *US, 1974*

all that *noun* sexual activity. A shortening of the conventional, already partially euphemistic 'all that sort of thing' *UK, 1970*

all that *adjective* superlative, very good *US, 1991*

all that and a bag of chips! *noun* used for expressing strong approval *US, 1997*

all that and then some *noun* everything *US, 1998*

all the best good bye. By ellipsis from conventional 'all the best of luck/fortune', etc *UK, 1968*

all the better for seeing you used as a 'witty' riposte to the greeting: 'How are you?'. A catchphrase *UK, 1977*

all the eighths *noun* a seven-eighths point movement in a stock price *US, 1988*

all the fives *noun* fifty-five. In Bingo, House or Tombola, the formula 'all the' announces a double number. Varies numerically, from 'all the twos' (22) to 'all the eights' (88). Recorded by Laurie Atkinson around 1950 *UK, 1943*

all the go *adjective* in the height of fashion *UK, 1793*

all there *adjective* **1** sane *UK, 1864*. **2** alert, aware, sharp *UK, 1880*

all the same khaki pants used for expressing the sentiment that there is no difference between the matters in question. Khaki trousers are the regular schoolboy uniform, eliminating personal, social or class difference *TRINIDAD AND TOBAGO, 1996*

all the way *adjective* in the military, destined for leadership *US, 1982*

all the way *adverb* to a championship *US, 1959*

all the way live *adjective* excellent, superlative *US, 1982*

all the world and his dog *noun* everybody. A humorous variation of ALL THE WORLD AND HIS WIFE *AUSTRALIA, 1984*

all the world and his wife *noun* everybody. Generally with a sense of hyperbole *UK, 1738*

all-time *adjective* excellent *US, 1964*

all-timer's disease *noun* used by surfers humorously to describe a person's proclivity to exaggerate when recounting surf conditions or their accomplishments *US, 1991*

all tits and teeth *adjective* used for describing a woman who makes the most of a distracting smile and breasts *UK, 1967*

all to buggery *adjective* awry, bungled, utterly confused, unsatisfactory, mixed-up *UK, 1984*

all to cock *adjective* awry, bungled, utterly confused, unsatisfactory, mixed-up *UK, 1948*

all to hell *adjective* utterly ruined *US, 1968*

all two *adjective* both *BARBADOS, 1975*

all up *adjective* **1** (of things) exhausted, fruitless, ruined; (of people) bankrupt, defeated, doomed to die. Especially in the phrase 'all up with' *UK, 1818*. **2** (of betting) with the winnings of one bet forming the stake of the next *AUSTRALIA, 1933*

allus *adverb* always *UK, 1852*

all vanilla *noun* in poker, a spade flush *US, 1948*

all wind and piss; all wind and water *adjective* boastful; not backing up words with action *UK, 1961*

all wool and a yard wide *adjective* excellent, reliable *US, 1882*

alma mater *noun* a prison where a criminal has served time. From Latin for 'fostering mother'; adopted with obvious irony from its English school or university use, first recorded in 1718 *US, 1949*

almighty *adjective* great; impressive *UK, 1824*

almond rock *noun* **1** a frock, a dress. Rhyming slang *UK, 1979*. **2** the penis. Obsolete rhyming slang for COCK. Also shortened to 'almond' *UK, 1969*

almond rocks; almonds; rocks *noun* socks. Rhyming slang, based on a confection popular from the mid-C19, can be presumed therefore to be late C19 in origin. In the mid-C20 it was popularly abbreviated to 'almonds'; later use seems to favour 'rocks', i.e. 'cotton rocks'. A specialised military variation arising during World War 1 was 'army rocks' *UK, 1979*

Aloha Airlines *nickname* an aviation unit attached to the 25th Infantry Division during the Vietnam war *US, 1991*

alone player *noun* a card cheat who works alone *US, 1961*

Al Pacino *noun* a cappuccino coffee. Rhyming slang, formed from the name of the US film actor (b.1940) *UK, 2003*

alpha *adjective* used for intensifying a personal insult. From conventional usage indicating a premier example *UK, 2005*

alphabet city *nickname* an imprecisely defined area on the lower east side of Manhattan, near Avenues A, B, C and D *US, 1980*

Alphonse *noun* **1** a pimp. Rhyming slang for PONCE *UK, 1943*. **2** a homosexual. Rhyming slang for PONCE (an effeminate male) *UK, 2003*

alpine snow *noun* cocaine ingested off a woman's breasts *UK, 2001*

alpine stick *noun* an oversized frankfurter *NEW ZEALAND, 1984*

Alpo *noun* sausage topping for a pizza. An allusion to a branded dog food *US, 1996*

alrightnik *noun* a person who has succeeded in material terms *US, 1968*

alrighty! used for expressing agreement or satisfaction *AUSTRALIA, 1997*

also-ran *noun* anyone not performing very well. Originally applied in horse racing to any horse placed fourth or worse and thus not winning any money on the race *US, 1896*

altar *noun* a toilet *US, 1962*

altered *adjective* very drunk. A suggestion of a completely altered state of perception *US, 1991*

alter ego *noun* a false identification card that permits a minor to be served alcohol *US, 1990*

alter kocker; alte kaker *noun* a mean and nasty old man. Yiddish for German for 'old shitter' *US, 1968*

altogether *noun* ▶ **the altogether** complete nudity *UK, 1894*

alum; alumn *noun* an alumnus or alumna *US, 1934*

aluminium cookie *noun* a compact disc (CD) *UK, 2002*

aluminium crow *nickname* a CF-100 Canuck jet fighter aircraft. The aircraft first flew in 1950, and is also known as LEAD SLED and THE CLUNK *CANADA, 1950*

aluminum *noun* ▶ **the aluminum** in horse racing, the inside rail *AUSTRALIA, 1989*

aluminum overcast *noun* any very large military aircraft *US, 1961*

Alvin *noun* a naive, easily-cheated person. Circus and carnival usage *US, 1949*

always late in take off, always late in arrival *nickname* the Italian airline Alitalia. Most airlines seem to attract jocular nicknames. This is one of the more memorable *2002*

Alzheimer's avenue *noun* an area in a hospital or nursing home frequented by memory-impaired patients *AUSTRALIA, 1987*

am *noun* an amateur *UK, 2000*

amateur half-hour; amateur hour *noun* a poorly organised event *US, 1939*

amateur night *noun* **1** New Year's Eve. Just as amateur Christians attend church only twice a year, or amateur Jews attend services only twice a year, amateur drunks only drink to oblivion once a year *US, 1977*. **2** a night when the tips left by a restaurant's customers are low *US, 1995*. **3** sex with a chance acquaintance who is not a prostitute *US, 1960*

amazer machine; amazer *noun* in trucking, a police radar unit used for measuring vehicle speed *US, 1976*

Amazon *noun* a tall, strong, sexually attractive woman *US, 1954*

Amazon Annie *nickname* a cannon designed to fire atomic shells *US, 1958*

ambassador *noun* a representative of a drug dealer *US, 1997*

amber *noun* beer. In constructions such as 'quaff an amber' *NEW ZEALAND, 1959*

amber fluid *noun* beer *AUSTRALIA, 1906*

amber gambler *noun* a motorist who speeds up through a yellow light *NEW ZEALAND, 1979*

ambidextrous *adjective* bisexual. A pun on the ability to use either hand *US, 1966*

ambisextrous *adjective* bisexual. A pun that puts sex in 'ambidextrous' *US, 1926*

Ambitious City *nickname* Hamilton, Ontario. Hamilton has thrived through steel and car assembly, benefiting by the Auto Pact between the US and Canada *CANADA, 1965*

ambo *noun* **1** an ambulance *AUSTRALIA, 1996*. **2** an ambulance driver. Commonly heard in New Zealand *AUSTRALIA, 1998*

ambov *noun* in prison use, the Association of Members of Boards of Visitors; a member of the association. An initialism *UK, 1996*

ambulance *noun* a brakevan (caboose) *US, 1977*

ambulance chaser *noun* a disreputable solicitor, especially one who arrives or has an agent arrive at the scene of a disaster to seek clients from among the victims; in UK usage since the 1990s, solicitors who advertise on television for 'no-win no-fee' clients. From the image of following an ambulance to an accident *US, 1896*

ambush academy *noun* during the Vietnam war, training in jungle warfare, especially of the unconventional sort *US, 1991*

ambush alley *nickname* the section of Route 19 between An Keh and the base of the Mang Giang Pass, South Vietnam. So named by truckers after countless Vietcong ambushes, borrowed from the Korean war (1952) where the term was used for any dangerous road *US, 1965*

am dram *adjective* amateur dramatic; hence, exaggerated, unsubtle, histrionic *UK, 1985*

amebiate *verb* to get drunk *US, 1966*

ameche *noun* a telephone. From actor Don Ameche's performance as Alexander Graham Bell in a 1939 film *US, 1941*

amen! used for expressing strong approval *US, 1934*

amen corner *noun* the front rows of pews in a church where the most devout sit, approving the words of the preacher with shouts of 'Amen!' *US, 1860*

Americalley *nickname* in Vietnam, the 23rd Infantry Division, which played a key role in the massacre of Vietnamese civilians at My Lai. The 23rd was formally named the Americal Division. The 'calley' variant referred to a key participant in My Lai *US, 1991*

American Airlines *noun* in hold 'em poker, the ace of diamonds and ace of hearts as the first two cards dealt to a player. From the initials AA *US, 1981*

American taxpayer *noun* any violator of routine traffic laws. From the vociferous indignation voiced when stopped by a police officer *US, 1962*

American tweezers *noun* any specialty tool used by a burglar *US, 1982*

American Wake *noun* a farewell party for those emigrating to America in the late C19 and early C20 *IRELAND, 1997*

American way *noun* relatively peaceful co-existence by rival organised crime families *US, 1992*

Amerika; Amerikkka *noun* the United States. A spelling favoured by the political counterculture in the late 1960s and early 1970s; in the second form, 'kkk' signifies the white supremacist Ku Klux Klan. Rap artist Ice Cube's 1990 album 'AmeriKKKa's Most Wanted' gave the KKK spelling high-profile exposure *US, 1969*

Amerikan *adjective* American *US, 1969*

Amerikill *nickname* the 23rd Infantry Division. Derogatory *US, 1991*

AMF used as a farewell. From ADIOS MOTHERFUCKER *US, 1963*

amidships *adverb* (used of a blow to the abdomen) across the central area of the body. From the naval term for the middle of a ship *UK, 1937*

a mighty roar went up from the crowd used as a humorous comment on a lack of response to a joke or comment. Coined by Keith Olberman on ESPN 'to describe players or fans who do not seem to be as happy as they should be following a home run, touchdown, or victory' *US, 1997*

amigo *noun* used as a term of address. Spanish for 'friend' *US, 1974*

Amish golf *noun* croquet. An allusion to the perceived joy that the Amish people take in playing croquet *US, 1969*

Amityville; 'Ville *nickname* Detroit, Michigan, US. Coinage is claimed by rap-artist Eminem, after the 1979 film *The Amityville Horror US, 2000*

ammo *noun* **1** ammunition, actual or figurative *US, 1911*. **2** cash *US, 2003*

ammunition *noun* **1** a gambler's bankroll *US, 1983*. **2** a tampon or sanitary towel; tampons or sanitary towels *UK, 1984*

amoeba *noun* **1** phencyclidine, the recreational drug known as PCP or angel dust *US, 1994*. **2** a Commodore Amiga™ personal computer *US, 1991*

amonia *noun* pneumonia *BAHAMAS, 1982*

Amos and Andy *noun* brandy; shandy. Rhyming slang, based on a US radio comedy that ran from 1928–43 *UK, 1974*

amp *noun* **1** an ampoule (a glass vessel of drugs intended for hypodermic injection) *UK, 1968*. **2** an ampoule of methadone, used to break a heroin addiction *UK, 1985*. **3** amphetamine, *2004*. **4** an amplifier, especially one for electric instruments *US, 1967*. **5** an amputation; an amputee. Medical slang *US, 1942*

amped *adjective* **1** under the influence of a central nervous system stimulant, usually amphetamines or methamphetamine *US, 1972*. **2** ready for anything, very excited, psyched up *US, 1986*. **3** (used of a music system) equipped with powerful amplifiers *US, 1995*. **4** silent *US, 1993*

amper *noun* an ampersand (&) *US, 1991*

amphet *noun* amphetamine *US, 1982*

amphoterrible *nickname* the antifungal drug Amphotericin B. A nickname based on the drug's severe side effects *US, 1994*

amp joint *noun* marijuana and amphetamine (or possibly another drug) mixed and rolled for smoking in a cigarette *UK, 1998*

Am Sam *nickname* American Samoa *US, 1982*

amscray *verb* to leave. Pig Latin version of 'scram' *US, 1934*

-amundo *suffix* used as a humorous mechanism to form a slang equivalent. Popularised by the Fonz (Henry Winkler) on the US television programme *Happy Days*, set in the 1950s, which aired from 1974 until 1984 *US, 1992*

AMW *noun* a vacuous female celebrity or hanger-on. An abbreviation of 'actress, model, whatever' *US, 1988*

amy; amie *noun* amyl nitrite; an ampoule of amyl nitrite *US, 1966*

amyl *noun* amyl nitrate or butyl nitrate, when taken recreationally or to enhance sexual arousal *US, 1971*

amyl house *noun* a dance music genre *UK, 1996*

anal *noun* anal sex. A brief search of the Internet reveals an overwhelming and mainly heterosexual use of 'anal' in this sense *US, 2000*

anal & oral *noun* anal sex and oral sex, when advertised as services offered by a prostitute *UK, 2003*

anal amigo *noun* a male homosexual *UK, 2003*

anal groundsman *noun* a homosexual man *UK, 1983*

analog *adjective* in computing, pertaining to the world outside the Internet. A figurative extension of a technical term *US, 1997*

anchor *noun* **1** a brake. Originally truck driver usage, and then widespread *UK, 1936*. **2** a younger brother or sister. A younger sibling is likely to hold you back or prevent you from going out with your friends *UK, 2003*. **3** an examination that has been postponed *US, 1955*.

4 a parachutist who hesitates before jumping *UK, 1943*. **5** a brakevan (caboose) *US, 1977*. **6** a pick-axe *UK, 1863*

anchor *verb* **1** to stay put, to remain *US, 1906*. **2** to wait *US, 1990*. **3** to the apply the brakes of a car or truck *US, 1946*

anchored *adjective* married *US, 1949*

anchor ice *noun* ice formed along the bottom of bodies of water. This northern phenomenon is also known as 'ground ice' *CANADA, 1945*

anchor man *noun* in casino blackjack, the gambler immediately to the dealer's right *US, 1985*

ancient *adjective* unfashionable, out of style *US, 2004*

ancient Mary *noun* an AM radio *US, 1976*

and a half used for intensifying the preceding noun *UK, 1832*

and all that 1 used for intensifying *US, 1992*. **2** et cetera *UK, 1931*

and all that caper et cetera *UK, 1964*

and all that jazz and so on. From JAZZ (nonsense) *US, 1959*

and a merry Christmas to you too! used ironically in response to a disparagement or an insult *UK, 1976*

and and and so on, etc *UK, 1984*

and away we go! used as a humorous signal that something has just started. A signature line of comedian Jackie Gleason *US, 1954*

and co and the rest of them (of people or things with something in common) *UK, 1757*

Anderson cart *noun* a cart made from a cut-down car and pulled by horses, during the 1930s depression; later, any car that ran out of petrol or broke down *CANADA, 1987*

Andes candy *noun* cocaine. A near reduplication based on the cocoa grown in the Andes Mountains *US, 1990*

and everything used for completing a list or a thought. If anything less sincere than synonymous *et cetera UK, 1984*

and like it! used in anticipation of a grousing reponse to an order. Naval use *UK, 1943*

and like that et cetera; and so on *US, 1977*

and monkeys might fly out of my butt used as a reflection of the high unlikelihood of something happening *US, 1992*

andro *adjective* androgynous *US, 1999*

android *noun* a patient with no normal laboratory values *US, 1994*

and so it goes used as an ironic affirmation. The signature sign-off of television journalist Linda Ellerbee, with homage to Kurt Vonnegut's use of 'so it goes'. Repeated with referential humour *US, 1992*

and that et cetera; and that sort of thing. Also widely used in Australia *UK, 1821*

and that ain't hay used for humorous assertion that the topic of discussion is no small thing. Both Abbot and Costello in the film *It Ain't Hay* and Mickey Rooney in *Girl Crazy* used the phrase in high-profile ways in 1943. It stayed popular for most of the decade *US, 1943*

and that's the truth! used as a humorous affirmation of what you have just said. A signature line of the Edith Ann character played by Lily Tomlin on the television comedy programme *Rowan and Martin's Laugh-In* (NBC, 1968–73). Repeated with referential humour *US, 1968*

and that's the way it is! used as a humorous affirmation. The signature sign-off of television newsman Walter Cronkite, who ended his nightly newscast thus from 1962 until 1981. Repeated with referential humour, often imitating the lilt and bass of Cronkite's voice *US, 1962*

and then some and more; and much more. Probably an elaboration of C18 Scots 'and some' *US, 1908*

and there was much rejoicing used as a humorous comment on a favourable reaction. Popularised in the US by Keith Olberman of ESPN, borrowed from *Monty Python and the Holy Grail US, 1975*

and will! used for expressing a commitment to do something *US, 1947*

Andy Capp's Commandos *nickname* the Army Catering Corps, the ACC. A humorous elaboration of the official military abbreviation. Andy Capp is the workshy hero of a long-running cartoon strip *UK, 1995*

Andy Gump *noun* the surgical removal of the mandible in the treatment of jaw cancer. The post-operative patient looks like they have no chin, resembling the comic strip character *US, 1980*

Andy Gump chin *noun* a receding chin *US, 1970*

and you know that! used for expressing approval or praise *US, 1992*

and you too!; and you! used as a sharp rejoinder to an insult *UK, 1961*

Andy Pandy *noun* **1** an effeminate man, heterosexual or homosexual. From a BBC television puppet who first appeared in 1950 *UK, 1983*. **2** a brandy. Rhyming slang *UK, 2000*

Andy Rooney *noun* in poker, any player, usually short, who is inclined to complain. An allusion to the US television journalist's stature *US, 1996*

ANFO *noun* any nuisance of foreign origin. Acronym in use during the 1970s by the British Army in Northern Ireland, borrowing the initials from *Ammonium Nitrate Fuel Oil*, a type of explosive *UK, 1984*

angel *noun* **1** an outside investor, especially one who backs a theatrical production. Theatrical origins *US, 1891*. **2** a male homosexual. Originally referred to the passive partner, but later to any homosexual *US, 1927*. **3** a nurse. In the UK *Angels* was a BBC television drama series about nurses broadcast 1975–83 *US, 1991*. **4** cocaine *AUSTRALIA, 1942*. **5** in aviation, a 1000-foot increment of altitude *UK, 1943*. **6** in air combat, a misleading image or blind spot *US, 1998*

Angel *noun* **1** a member of the Hell's Angels motorcyle gang *US, 1965*

angel cake *noun* an attractive girl *US, 1962*

angel dust *noun* **1** phencyclidine, the recreational drug also known as PCP. Originally a veterinary anaesthetic, it became a popular recreational drug regarded as a cheaper substitute for other illicit drugs *US, 1970*. **2** money borrowed informally from a friend *US, 1976*

angel face *noun* an effeminate man *US, 1949*

angel food *noun* a member of the US Air Force as an object of homosexual desire *US, 1988*

angel gear *noun* neutral gear while coasting down a hill *NEW ZEALAND, 1989*

angel hair *noun* phencyclidine, the recreational drug known as PCP or angel dust *US, 1994*

angelina sorority *noun* the world of the young homosexual male *US, 1972*

angel kiss *noun* a freckle *US, 1972*

angel mist *noun* phencyclidine, the recreational drug known as PCP or angel dust *US, 1994*

angel puss *noun* used as an endearing term of address *US, 1936*

Angel's bible *noun* a Harley-Davidson motorcycle manual *US, 1992*

angels in a sky *noun* LSD *UK, 2003*

angel's kiss *noun* a night breeze. Korean war usage *US, 1961*

angel's seat *noun* the cupola on top of a brakevan (caboose) *US, 1946*

angel teat *noun* a whisky with a rich bouquet *US, 1945*

angel track *noun* an armoured personnel carrier used as an aid station *US, 1971*

angel with a dirty face *noun* a male homosexual who due to caution or fear has yet to act upon his desire. After the 1938 Warner Brothers film *Angels With Dirty Faces US, 1941*

Angie *noun* cocaine *US, 1994*

angishore *noun* ▷*see:* HANGASHORE

angle *noun* a scheme, especially an illegal one *US, 1920*

angle shooter *noun* a poker player who exploits other players by bending the rules of the game *US, 1982*

Anglo *noun* **1** a white person. The term was brought to the mainstream by Mexican-Americans in the southwestern US *US, 1943*. **2** an Anglo-Australian. Used as a derogatory term by people from a Mediterranean or Middle Eastern background, opposing the term 'wog' *AUSTRALIA, 1982*

Anglo *adjective* of or pertaining to Anglo-Australians *AUSTRALIA, 1982*

Anglo-Banglo *adjective* of Anglo-Indian birth *UK, 1984*

Angola black; Angola *noun* a potent marijuana from East Africa *US, 1982*

angora *noun* in horse racing, the totalisator. Rhyming slang, from 'tote' to 'angora goat' to 'angora' *AUSTRALIA, 1989*

angry *adjective* (used of a penis) sexually aroused, erect *US, 1970*

angry nine *nickname* during the Korean war, an AN/GRC-9 radio *US, 1994*

angryphone *noun* an anglophone (a native English speaker in Quebec) *CANADA, 2002*

animal *noun* **1** a person displaying vulgar manners, attitudes, etc; a despicable human being; a brute *AUSTRALIA, 1892*. **2** in American football, an extremely physical player *US, 1978*. **3** used among musicians as a nickname for a drummer. From the character/puppet/musician 'Animal' (legendarily, based on Keith Moon, 1946–78, the original drummer with The Who) who appeared in *The Muppet Show*, from 1976, and in subsequent film and television Muppet projects *UK, 1976*. **4** an aggressive approach to surfing *AUSTRALIA, 1985*. **5** in prison, a sex offender. Contemptuous *UK, 1996*. **6** a thing of a given sort *UK, 1922*. **7** LSD *US, 1994*. **8** amyl nitrate *UK, 2002*. **9** in the Vietnam war, a gang-rigged set of claymore mines *US, 1983*. **10** a furpiece *US, 1959*. ▶ **go animal** to act wildly, without inhibition *US, 1968*

animal! used for expressing approval *UK, 2003*

animal car *noun* a brakevan (caboose) *US, 1938*

animal run *noun* the wild behaviour of some military personnel on shore leave *UK, 1987*

Animals of the Army *nickname* during the Vietnam war, used as a name for the Airborne Rangers *US, 1984*

animal trainer *noun* a person who engages in sexual activity with animals *US, 1978*

animal zoo *noun* a rowdy college fraternity *US, 1967*

anime *noun* a type of Japanese animation, often adapted to sexual themes *JAPAN, 1991*

ankle *noun* a woman *US, 1942*

ankle *verb* **1** to walk; to travel *US, 1926*. **2** in television and film making, to disassociate yourself from a project *US, 1990*. ▶ **ankle a show** to walk out of a performance *US, 1973*

ankle-biter *noun* **1** a petty, narrow-minded bureaucrat *US, 1990*. **2** a child. Also 'knee biter'. Humorous, not particularly kind to children *US, 1963*

ankle bracelets *noun* the < and > characters on a computer keyboard *US, 1991*

ankled *adjective* drunk. A Bristol usage *UK, 2002*

ankle express *noun* walking *US, 1919*

ankle-slapper *noun* a small wave *US, 1991*

anklets *noun* leg irons *US, 1950*

Annabel Giles; annabels *noun* haemorrhoids. Rhyming slang for 'piles', formed from the name of the UK television presenter (b.1960) *UK, 2003*

annex *verb* to steal *US, 1845*

Annie from Arkansas *noun* in craps, an eight *US, 1993*

Annie Rooney *noun* an outburst of bad temper *UK, 1988*

Annie's alley *noun* the vagina. Attested by a police matron at the San Francisco Women's Detention Center in April 1949; a woman prisoner was thought to be concealing $13.00 'in Annie's Alley' *US, 1949*

annihilated *adjective* drunk *US, 1975*

annish *noun* an anniversary issue of a single-interest fan magazine *US, 1982*

anoint *verb* to whip someone *US, 1962*

anorak *noun* **1** a studious and obsessive hobbyist widely characterised as boring and unfashionable. From the stereotypical wardrobe of certain groups of hobbyists such as trainspotters *UK, 1991*. **2** by extension, a person who is socially inept and therefore unable to be, or not interested in becoming, part of a peer group *UK, 1999*

anoraky *adjective* studious and obsessive *UK, 2001*

A N Other *noun* used in speech as an all-purpose formula for an unknown identity. A written convention that has taken on a life of its own *UK, 2003*

another country heard from used for humorously acknowledging that someone who had previously been silent has spoken up *US, 1970*

another day, another dollar a humorous expression of a day-by-day philosophy of life *US, 1939*

anothery *noun* another, especially another drink of beer *AUSTRALIA, 1963*

answer *noun* a rap artist's response to another's song *US, 1995*

answer *verb* to score soon after an opponent has scored *US, 1979*

answer record *noun* a rap song released in response to another song *US, 1995*

Antarctica monster *noun* fire *ANTARCTICA, 1977*

Antartic 10 *noun* any moderately good-looking person of the sex that attracts you. The humour lies in the fact that a 'ten' in Antarctica would be a 'five' anywhere else *ANTARCTICA, 1991*

ante *noun* the money required to begin a project *US, 1895*

anteater *noun* **1** in trucking, a short-nosed C-model Mack tractor *US, 1971*. **2** an uncircumcised penis *US, 1970*

antenna platoon *noun* during the Vietnam war, a platoon with an unusually large number of radios assigned to it *US, 1989*

ante up *verb* to provide money for a project *US, 1865*

anthem *noun* in contemporary dance music and club culture of the 1980s, 90s and on, any song that fills the dance floor and gets clubbers singing along *UK, 2003*

anti-frantic *adjective* calm, collected *US, 1983*

antifreeze *noun* **1** alcohol *US, 1953*. **2** heroin *US, 1994*

anti-proliferation device *noun* a condom *UK, 1998*

antique HP *noun* an old homosexual man. HP is an abbreviation of HOMEE-PALONE (a man) *UK, 2002*

antsy *adjective* agitated, anxious *US, 1950*

antwacky *adjective* old-fashioned, especially of clothes. Liverpool use; possibly from 'antiquey' *UK, 2002*

anus bandit *noun* a predatory male homosexual *US, 1962*

anxious *adjective* good *US, 1944*

anybody in there? do you have any intelligence? *AUSTRALIA, 1995*

anyhoo *adverb* anyhow. A deliberate mispronunciation *US, 1946*

any kine *noun* anything. Hawaiian youth usage *US, 1981*

any more for any more? does anyone want more food?; also used to announce a final opportunity to purchase something *UK, 1977*

any old how *adverb* **1** in an untidy or disordered state *UK, 1933*. **2** in any case, anyway *UK, 1958*

anyone can cook *nickname* the Army Catering Corps, the ACC. A humorous elaboration of the official military abbreviation *UK, 1995*

anyone for tennis? used for humorously suggesting an activity. Seen as quintessentially British and enormously witty in its many variant forms *US, 1951*

anyroad anyway. Also used as an adverb. Northern dialect, widely familiar from television programmes such as *Coronation Street UK, 1896*

anything for a laugh serves as a justification for doing something because you have no choice in the matter. Often rueful *UK, 1969*

anything for a quiet wife a catchphrase that means exactly what it says. A jocular perversion of the proverbial saying 'anything for a quiet life' *UK, 1977*

any-to-come *noun* in gambling, a type of conditional bet in which all or part of a winning is returned on another bet. May be abbreviated as ATC *UK, 2001*

Anytown USA; Anytown *noun* a notional American town that represents the appearance or values of stereotypical small-town America *UK, 1992*

anywhere *adverb* in possession of drugs *US, 1946.* ▶ **not get anywhere** to fail to reach your goal, to not succeed in achieving your object *US, 1932*

Anzac biscuit; Anzac *noun* a popular biscuit made with oats, sugar, flour and golden syrup *AUSTRALIA, 1923*

A-OK *adjective* completely acceptable. US Navy Captain Alan G. Shepard was widely credited for introducing the term to the general public during the first US space flight. Shepard later denied ever having said 'A-OK', insisting that he had been spelling out awkward – 'AWK' *US, 1959*

A-one; A-1 *adjective* excellent, first-class. Originally of ships, then of persons and things *US, 1846*

AOS used for suggesting that there are no good options in a particular situation. An abbreviation of 'all options suck' or 'all options stink' *US, 2001*

a over k *adverb* knocked upside down. An abbreviation of 'arse over kite' *NEW ZEALAND, 1998*

a over t *adverb* head over heels. An abbreviation of ARSE OVER TIT *UK, 1984*

Apache *noun* Fentanyl, a synthetic narcotic analgesic that is used as a recreational drug *UK, 2004*

Apache land *noun* a rough or dangerous urban area *UK: SCOTLAND, 1988*

apartment *noun* a prison cell *US, 1949*

apartment girl *noun* a prostitute who works out of her own apartment or comes to a customer's apartment *US, 1992*

apartment house *noun* in bar dice games, a roll from the cup in which some dice are stacked on top of others, invalidating the roll *US, 1971*

APB *noun* in police work, an all points bulletin, broadcast to all who are listening *US, 1957*

apcray *noun* nonsense; rubbish. A Pig Latin version of CRAP *US, 1937*

ape *noun* in the entertainment industry, a technical member of a film crew *US, 1970*

ape *adjective* crazed, frenzied, demonstrating rage or delight. Based on the behaviour of apes in films – not in real life *US, 1955.* ▶ **go ape** to lose control; to react unrestrainedly *AUSTRALIA, 1988*

ape bars *noun* high handlebars on a customised motorcycle *US, 1966*

ape drape *noun* a hair style in which the hair is worn short at the front and long at the back. Most commonly known as a 'mullet' *US, 1995*

ape hangers *noun* high handlebars on a customised motorcycle. A term based on the visual aspect, with the handlebars forcing an ape-like pose *US, 1965*

apeshit *adjective* ▶ **go apeshit** to lose control; to go crazy *US, 1951*

apeth *noun* ▷*see:* HA'P'ORTH

ape wagon *noun* a brakevan (caboose) *US, 1977*

aphrodite *noun* a nightgown. Rhyming slang for 'nightie' *NEW ZEALAND, 1875*

A-pie *noun* apple pie *US, 1967*

A-plug *noun* a plug inserted in the rectum as part of a sadomasochistic encounter. An abbreviation for 'ass-plug' *US, 1979*

apoplectic *adjective* behaving in a violently temperamental manner. From the symptoms of apoplexy *UK, 1984*

apostles *noun* ▶ **the apostles** in craps, a roll of twelve *US, 1999*

app *noun* an application *UK, 1996*

appalling *adjective* objectionable, ugly, etc. An example of overused society and middle-class hyperbole *UK, 1937*

apparatchik *noun* an office worker in a support role *US, 1974*

appie *noun* an appendectomy patient *US, 1985*

applause *noun* a sexually transmitted infection, especially gonorrhea. An excruciating pun on CLAP *US, 1990*

apple *noun* **1** a person. Usually heard with a qualifying adjective such as 'bad' or 'rotten' *US, 1887.* **2** the gullible victim of a confidence swindle *US, 1992.* **3** a native American Indian who curries favour with the white establishment by embracing white cultural values. A variation on a theme – red on the outside, white on the inside *US, 1980.* **4** a particular type of MDMA, the recreational drug best known as ecstasy. Sometimes embellished to 'apple E' or 'green apple' *UK, 1996.* **5** a capsule of secobarbital sodium (trade name Seconal™), a central nervous system depressant *US, 1980.* **6** a self-propelled barracks barge. From the ship's official designation as an 'APL' *US, 1971.* **7** the vagina *US, 1980.* **8** a one-hundred dollar note *NEW ZEALAND, 1998.* **9** the heart. An abbreviation of 'apple tart', and by rhyming slang to 'heart' *NEW ZEALAND, 1989.* **10** a citizens' band radio enthusiast of unlimited zeal *US, 1976*

Apple *noun* ▶ **The Apple** New York City *US, 1938* ▷*see:* BIG APPLE

apple and pip *verb* **1** to sip. Rhyming slang *UK, 1972.* **2** to urinate. Rhyming slang, formed on back-slang 'sip'/PISS. Also used in a noun sense *UK, 1960*

apple box *noun* in the television and film industries, any device used to raise an actor or object to the desired height *US, 1977*

apple-catchers *noun* a type of roomy underpants *AUSTRALIA, 1965*

apple core; apple *noun* twenty pounds; in betting, odds of 20–1. Rhyming slang for SCORE *UK, 1974*

apple fritter; apple *noun* bitter (beer). Rhyming slang *UK, 2002*

applehead *noun* a dull, stupid person *US, 1951*

Apple Isle; Apple Island *noun* Tasmania. The island state is noted for is apple-growing industry *AUSTRALIA, 1906*

apple jacks *noun* pieces of crack cocaine. From a resemblance to a popular breakfast cereal *US, 1994*

apple-knocker *noun* **1** a rustic, especially a naive one *US, 1919.* **2** an outdoor toilet. From the image of apples dropping onto the outhouse roof *US, 1975*

apple orchard *noun* a location where police wait parked, certain that they will soon witness a driving infraction *US, 1970*

apple pie order *noun* complete and perfect order *US, 1975*

apple pips *noun* the lips. Rhyming slang *UK, 1960*

apple-polisher *noun* a person who shamelessly curries favour from those above him. Several variant forms are attested *US, 1927*

apples *noun* the female breasts *US, 1942*

apples *adjective* **1** satisfactory, good. Possibly rhyming slang for 'apples and rice', 'nice' *AUSTRALIA, 1943.* **2** in good shape or condition *NEW ZEALAND, 1998*

apples and pears; apples *noun* stairs. Rhyming slang *UK, 1857*

apple tart; apple *noun* a fart. Rhyming slang *UK, 2003*

apple up *verb* to become frightened *US, 1966*

apple z *verb* to undo something. A figurative use of the 'undo last command' function on an Apple Macintosh™ computer *US, 2003*

application *noun* ▶ **take an application** (used of a pimp) to probe the psyche of a woman who is a candidate to come to work for you *US, 1972*

apprentice *noun* in horse racing, a jockey who has ridden for less than a year *US, 1947*

appro *noun* ▶ **on appro** on approval *UK, 1874*

appropriate *verb* to steal something. Ironic military use *US, 1960*

appy *noun* an appendectomy *US, 1994*

apricots *noun* the testicles *UK, 1985*

April fool *noun* **1** a tool. Rhyming slang, originally meaning a burglar's tool then in more general use as a workman's tool *UK, 1960*. **2** a weapon such as a handgun, knife, etc. Rhyming slang; a narrower sense of the much earlier 'tool' *UK, 2002*. **3** a stool, usually a bar stool. Rhyming slang *UK, 1960*

April in Paris; April *noun* the backside, the buttocks. Rhyming slang for ARIS *UK, 1998*

April shower *noun* a flower. Rhyming slang *UK, 1960*

April showers *noun* beer by Flower & Sons, 'Flower's'. Rhyming slang *UK, 1992*

apron *noun* **1** a woman or wife *US, 1970*. **2** the gross daily receipts from a carnival concession *US, 1990*. ▶ **out of the apron** (used of gambling in a casino) using money borrowed from the casino *US, 1982*

aqua; acqua *noun* water. From and synonymous with Latin *aqua* via Italian *acqua UK, 2002*

aqua boot *verb* to vomit into the ocean *US, 1991*

A-rab *noun* an Arab. Not flattering, but more oafish than derogatory. The slang sense of the word is gained strictly through pronunciation – a long first 'A', two drawn out syllables, and a light twang with the second. In his 1962 rock/novelty record 'Ahab the Arab', Ray Stevens gave a loud public voice to this pronunciation *US, 1972*

Arab *noun* **1** used as a term of mild abuse. There is no racist intent in this term, deriving as it does from 'street Arab' an obsolete term for a homeless child *UK: SCOTLAND, 1985*. **2** a dolt *BERMUDA, 1985*. **3** a street peddler selling fruit or vegetables. Originates from Baltimore *US, 1935*

Arab lover *noun* a driver who obeys the fifty-five miles an hour speed limit. A term coined during the Arab oil embargo of the early 1970s *US, 1976*

arbitrary *adjective* insignificant, unimportant. Nowhere near as popular as its conventional cousin RANDOM *US, 1986*

arc *verb* in computing, to archive something *US, 1997*

arc around *verb* to engage in enthusiastic and energetic, if meaningless and aimless, activity. US naval aviator usage *US, 1986*

ARC girl *noun* a female representative of the American Red Cross. Vietnam war usage *US, 1968*

Archbish *noun* an Archbishop *UK, 1994*

Archie *noun* **1** the notional cause of confusion. As in 'Archie buck them up' or 'Archie fuck them up'; from the late 1960s Jamaican hit record 'Archie Buck Them Up' by Lord Creator *TRINIDAD AND TOBAGO, 2003*. **2** a young and untrained farm hand *NEW ZEALAND, 1946*

architect *noun* in poker, a player who bets heavily. So called because his betting builds the pool of bets *US, 1988*

arctic *adjective* **1** cold *US, 1989*. **2** in poker, said of a very poor hand or series of very poor hands *US, 1996*

Arctic explorer *noun* a user of heroin and/or cocaine *US, 1959*

arena rat *noun* **1** a young person who hangs around a skating arena *CANADA, 1957*. **2** a woman who invites sexual relations with professional wrestlers *US, 1990*

are you for real? used for humorously questioning a person's sincerity *US, 1949*

are you kidding? you must be joking!; are you serious? Derisive, ironic and more of an exclamation than a question. *US, 1984*

are you looking at me? used as a belligerent challenge to a stranger *US, 1994*

are you ready to throw down? used as a call soliciting a response ('yes, we are') at a party *US, 2002*

are you stupid or French? used for expressing a dim opinion of someone's intellectual firepower *CANADA, 2002*

arf *noun* half. Written as it's said *UK, 1854*

arg *noun* in computing, an argument *US, 1981*

Argentina *noun* ▶ **do an Argentina** to go missing presumed dead *UK, 2003*

Argie *noun* an Argentinian. This abbreviation is not recorded until the Anglo-Argentine conflict for the Falklands/Malvinas in 1982 *UK, 1982*

argle-bargle *noun* the sound made by seabirds. This Nova Scotia expression seems to imitate the sound it describes *CANADA, 1988*

argue *verb* ▶ **argue the toss** to argue over something already decided *UK, 1925*

argy-bargy *noun* an argument, quarrelling. Also sometimes known as 'argle-bargle' *UK, 1887*

argy-bargy *verb* to argue. From the noun *UK, 1888*

Aries *noun* heroin *US, 1994*

aris *noun* **1** the backside, the buttocks; the anus. Rhyming slang from ARISTOTLE – BOTTLE – BOTTLE AND GLASS – ARSE. Also variants 'arris' and 'harris' *UK, 1979*. **2** a bottle. Also variant form 'aras' *AUSTRALIA, 1966*

ari-stock-rat *noun* a Canadian person of mixed Indian and French ancestry. The pride behind the insult in 'aristocrat' has been justified by the honouring of Louis Riel, who led a Metis rebellion during the settling of the Canadian West *CANADA, 1962*

Aristotle *noun* a bottle. Rhyming slang *AUSTRALIA, 1897*

Aristotle's lantern *noun* a sea urchin *CANADA, 1990*

Arizona *noun* buttermilk. Because a waitress thinks any man drinking buttermilk ought to be in Arizona for his health *US, 1946*

Arizona stop *noun* a rolling stop at a traffic signal or stop sign *US, 1962*

Arizona Territory *noun* an area southwest of Da Nang, South Vietnam, with imprecise boundaries and a strong Vietcong presence *US, 1991*

arji *noun* marijuana *US, 2001*

ark *noun* a dance hall *US, 1953*

Arkansas credit card *noun* a hose used to syphon petrol from another car *US, 1976*

Arkansas fire extinguisher *noun* a chamberpot *US, 1958*

Arkansas flush *noun* in poker, a worthless hand consisting of four cards in one suit and a fifth in another *US, 1950*

Arkansas gravel; Arkansas pavement *noun* small trees used as a makeshift bridge over a mud hole *US, 1954*

Arkansas toad stabber *noun* a sharp knife *US, 1994*

Arkansas toothpick *noun* a hunting knife *US, 1836*

Arkansas traveler; Arkansas special *noun* any unimportant railway line *US, 1950*

Arkansas wedding cake *noun* cornbread *US, 1958*

Arky; Arkie *noun* a resident of Arkansas; an unsophisticated rustic from the south central US. Often used with contempt *US, 1927*

arm *noun* **1** a police officer *US, 1956*. **2** the penis *US, 1972*. ▶ **off the arm** in food and beverage servers' argot, served without a tray *US, 1950*. ▶ **on the arm** without charge *US, 1926*. ▶ **put the arm on** to pressurise with criminal intent, to extort, to blackmail, to threaten; to arrest *US, 1943*. ▶ **under the arm** no good, inferior; loathsome *UK, 1958*. ▶ **up the arm** in betting, odds of 11 – 8. From the TICK-TACK signal used by bookmakers *UK, 1991*

arm and a leg *noun* **1** a high cost *UK, 1956*. **2** a prison sentence of five to ten years *US, 1991*

arm candy *noun* **1** someone good-looking enough for you to be seen out with *US, 1992*. **2** recreational drugs that are injected into the arm *UK, 2002*

armchair *adjective* removed from the action; said of an observer who acts as if he is a participant *US, 1955*

armchair general *noun* a person whose opinions are entirely unsupported by experience *US, 1960*

armchair ride *noun* in horse racing, an easy victory *US, 1976*

Armenian chrome *noun* aluminium paint *US, 1961*

arm hole *noun* the armpit *BAHAMAS, 1982*

armo *noun* armed robbery. Prison slang *NEW ZEALAND, 1999*

armor *noun* a female's figure *US, 1997*. ► **in the armor** (used of beer) in a can *US, 1967*

armpiece *noun* an attractive woman chosen as a social companion for the impression she makes on others *US, 1983*

armpit *noun* **1** a highly undesirable town or place *US, 1968*. **2** an obnoxious, unfriendly person *US, 1968*

armpit of the world; armpit of the universe *noun* the worst place *US, 1968*

arms *noun* ► **get your arms around** to grasp the meaning of *US, 1989*

armshouse *noun* a gang fight. Urban youth slang, probably from a use of firearms in such conflicts *UK, 2005*

arm-stretcher *noun* a heavy suitcase *US, 1992*

armstrong *adjective* done by hand, necessitating arm strength rather than mechanical leverage *CANADA, 1963*

armstrong method *noun* the technique of using hand and arm strength to get a job done *CANADA, 1987*

arm trophy *noun* a stunning and sexually appealing companion, valued for the prestige attached to their presence *US, 1994*

army *noun* a large bankroll. Alluding to the green of currency and military uniforms *US, 1990*

army banjo *noun* a shovel or other entrenching tool *US, 1991*

army brat *noun* a person who grew up the child of a career member of the army *US, 1931*

army craps *noun* a game of craps in which the shooter serves as the banker *US, 1984*

Army Criminal Corps *nickname* the Army Catering Corps, the ACC. An elaboration of the official military abbreviation *US, 1995*

army game *noun* any game of chance played in an aggressive and/or dishonest fashion *US, 1890*

army marbles *noun* dice. From the view that soldiers are fond of dice games *US, 1963*

army odds *noun* in a dice game, the true odds, not approximate odds often used in street games *US, 1962*

Army Peace Corps *noun* the US Army Special Forces. Highly trained killers, so an ironic term *US, 1990*

army roll *noun* a controlled roll of the dice by a skilled cheat in a game of craps *US, 1963*

army tank *noun* an American serviceman. Rhyming slang for YANK. Recorded among Australian prisoners-of-war in the Far East *AUSTRALIA, 1945*

arnold *noun* pork *JAMAICA, 1988*

aroha job *noun* a job done out of friendship without charge or at reduced rates. From the Maori word for 'love' *NEW ZEALAND, 1985*

aroma *noun* amyl nitrite or butyl nitrite *US, 1980*

aroma of man *noun* an ampoule of amyl nitrite. Originally a brand name; later used generically *US, 1992*

-aroo *suffix* used as a festive if meaningless embellishment of a noun *US, 1941*

-arooni *suffix* used as a meaningless embellishment of a word. A highly affected style of speaking invented and marketed with limited success by jazz musician Slim Gaillard *US, 1946*

around the world *noun* **1** the oral stimulation of all parts of a partner's body *US, 1951*. **2** in Keno, a bet made on the numbers found in the eight corners of a Keno ticket – 1, 10, 31, 40, 41, 50, 71 and 80 *US, 1969*

arrest-me-red *noun* a bright red colour of paint on a car, bound to attract the attention and interest of law enforcement *US, 1992*

arrow *noun* an amphetamine tablet *US, 1993*. ► **bust an arrow; blow an arrow** in a carnival or small circus, to become lost when travelling from one town to another. In the past, advance men would paste arrows along the roadside to show the way to the next stop; if you missed an arrow, you got lost *US, 1973*. ► **like an arrow** in poker, said of a sequence of five cards conventionally known as a 'straight' *US, 1988*

arrow *verb* to assign a task to someone *SINGAPORE, 2002*

arrow of desire *noun* the penis. A poetic image drawn from William Blake's 'Jerusalem', 1808 *UK, 2003*

'Arry's gators Thank you. A play on Japanese *arrigato* (thank you) *AUSTRALIA, 1958*

arse *noun* **1** the posterior, the buttocks. In conventional usage from Old English until early C18, at which time it was deemed impolite language and began a celebrated existence in slang, rarely appearing in print with all four letters in place. It was not until 1860 that the American ASS appeared. The spelling in Australia is 'arse', but pronounced with a long 'a' and no 'r'. Since the 1980s there has been some encroachment of the American 'ass', but this is still strongly associated with the US *UK, c1000*. **2** the base, the bottom; the tail end; the seat of a pair of trousers *AUSTRALIA, 1945*. **3** yourself; your body or person *UK, 1979*. **4** a fool; a despicable person *AUSTRALIA, 1944*. **5** boldness, gall, gumption, impudence; hence, luck as a result of this *AUSTRALIA, 1958*. **6** dismissal, especially from a job; rejection. Generally with verbs 'give' and 'get' *AUSTRALIA, 1955*. ► **ask me arse** used when refusing to cooperate or when withholding information. Other variations used are: 'ask me bollix', 'ask me sack', 'ask me left one'. ('Me' is a common Hiberno-English pronunciation for 'my'.) *IRELAND, 1991*. ► **get off your arse; get off your ass** to start doing something. Often in the imperative *UK, 1979*. ► **get your arse in gear** to start making an effort *UK, 2000*. ► **make an arse of** to make a mess of something; to botch something *UK: SCOTLAND, 1996*. ► **not know your arse from a hole in the ground** to be completely ignorant (of a given subject) *UK, 1982*. ► **not know your arse from your elbow** to be ignorant *UK, 1930*. ► **on your arse** in dire straits, especially financial *US, 1917*. ► **out on your arse** ejected, evicted, expelled. A variation of 'out on your ear' *UK, 1998*. ► **put on the arse bit** to indignantly tell someone what you think of him or her *AUSTRALIA, 1975*. ► **take it up the arse** to submit to a more powerful force *UK, 2000*. ► **the arse drops out of; the arse falls out of** (of a financial venture) to fail dismally *AUSTRALIA, 1969*. ► **up someone's arse** very close behind, in close proximity *UK, 1997*. ► **up your own arse** very self-involved *UK, 2000*. ► **you couldn't find your arse with both hands** you are stupid *UK, 1999*. ► **your arse is nippin buttons** you are nervous, you are full of trepidation *UK: SCOTLAND, 1988*. ► **your arse off** to a great degree; vigorously. Used to intensify verb meanings, thus 'to work your arse off' means 'to work hard'; very common with the verb 'work' and the verb 'fuck' and its synonyms *UK, 1972*

arse *verb* **1** to make a mess of something, to botch something *UK: SCOTLAND, 1996*. **2** to eat something greedily, to consume something quickly *UK: SCOTLAND, 1996*. **3** of a vehicle, to reverse *UK, 1959*

arse *adjective* inferior, shoddy, valueless, unpleasant, disliked for whatever reason *UK, 2002*

arse about *adjective* back to front *AUSTRALIA, 1979*

arse about; arse around *verb* to idle, to fool about *UK, 1664*

arse about face *adjective* back to front *UK, 1984*

arse all *noun* nothing, nothing at all. On the model of FUCK ALL (nothing) *UK, 2002*

arse bandido *noun* a male homosexual, especially the active partner in anal sex. Derogatory *UK, 2001*

arse biscuit *noun* a fart. A variation of AIR BISCUIT *UK, 2003*

arse cleavage; arsehole cleavage *noun* the cleft between the buttocks when partially displayed above a slipped-down trouser waistband *UK, 2002*

arse crawler *noun* a sycophant. Often reduced to CRAWLER *UK, 1937*

arse cress *noun* the hair surrounding the anus *UK, 2002*

arsed *adjective* bothered; worried. Popularised since the mid-1990s by television situation comedy *The Royle Family UK, 1999*

-arsed; -arse *suffix* used to intensify a characteristic *UK, 2000*

arse end; a-end *noun* **1** the back or tail end *AUSTRALIA, 1955*. **2** the end, the final part *UK, 1942*

arse-first *adverb* back-to-front *AUSTRALIA, 1962*

arsefuck *verb* to engage in anal sex *AUSTRALIA, 1998*

arse fucker *noun* a male who takes the active role in anal sex
AUSTRALIA, 1996

arse grapes *noun* haemorrhoids *UK, 1997*

arsehole *noun* **1** the anus. Literally the hole in the ARSE (buttocks, posterior); use ranges from the anatomically correct e.g. 'itchy arsehole' to the barely feasible or figurative suggestions associated with 'stick it up your arsehole' *UK, 1400*. **2** by extension, a despised person. Widely used in the UK and Australia, it is a stronger term than ASSHOLE, the US equivalent from which it derives *UK, 1977*. **3** courage, nerve *UK, 2001*. ▶ **get the arsehole with someone; have the arsehole with someone** to become, or be, annoyed with someone *UK, 2002*

arsehole *verb* **1** to dismiss someone, especially from employment; to reject someone *AUSTRALIA, 1950*. **2** to go, to leave *UK, 1982*

arsehole crawler *noun* a sycophant. An extension of ARSE CRAWLER, often reduced to CRAWLER *UK, 1961*

arsehole creeper *noun* a sycophant. A variation of ARSEHOLE CRAWLER *UK, 1984*

arseholed *adjective* very drunk *UK, 1984*

arsehole lucky *adjective* extremely lucky *UK, 1999*

arsehole mouth *noun* tightly pursed lips *UK, 2005*

arseholes *noun* ▶ **give someone arseholes** to attack someone with vigour *NEW ZEALAND, 1968*

arseholes! used as a general exclamation of rejection, frustration or criticism. Occasionally extended as 'arseholes to you' *UK, 1937*

arsehole street *noun* an unpleasant place to be; serious trouble. You can be 'in' or 'up' arsehole street *UK, 1984*

arse-holing *adjective* used as an intensifier *UK, 1966*

arse in a sling *noun* a state of defeat or depression. Usually phrased 'have (get) your arse in a sling' or 'your arse is in a sling'. From the obsolete 'eye in a sling' *UK, 1967*

arse-lick *verb* to behave in a sycophantic manner *UK, 1968*

arse-licker *noun* a sycophant *UK, 1938*

arse-licking; ass-licking *adjective* obsequious *UK, 1912*

arse like a wizard's sleeve *noun* an unusually loose rectum and anus *UK, 2002*

arse luck *noun* very bad luck indeed *SINGAPORE, 2002*

Arsenal *noun* ▶ **Arsenal are playing at home; Arsenal are at home** the bleed period of the menstrual cycle. A euphemism based on the colour of blood. Arsenal, a London football team, play in red shirts; as other teams also play in red this is probably also a pun on arse 'n' all (the genitals) *UK, 2000*

arseness *noun* annoying stupidity *TRINIDAD AND TOBAGO, 1979*

arsenut *noun* a small, hardened lump of excrement that clings to the hair around the anus *UK, 2003*

arse over bollocks *adverb* head over heels. A variation of ARSE OVER TIT *UK, 1998*

arse over head *adverb* head over heels *AUSTRALIA, 1962*

arse over tit *adverb* head over heels *UK, 1922*

arse over turtle *adverb* head over heels *AUSTRALIA, 1955*

arse paper *noun* any person or thing of limited use *NEW ZEALAND, 1998*

arse-polishing *noun* any office job. In military use *UK, 1949*

arsetronaut *noun* a male homosexual. An allusion to anal sex *NEW ZEALAND, 2002*

arse up *verb* to bungle something, to make a mess of something. First recorded in adjectival or adverbial form as 'arse up with care' in 1937 *UK, 1937*

arse-up *adjective* dead, finished, out of operation *UK, 2001*

arse-up *adverb* upside down *AUSTRALIA, 1994*

arse upwards *adverb* back to front; upside down *UK, 1984*

arseways *adverb* incorrectly done, wrongly positioned *IRELAND, 1992*

arsewise *adjective* absurd, foolish, mistaken, wrong *UK, 1962*

arsey *adjective* **1** lucky. From TIN ARSE *AUSTRALIA, 1950*. **2** moody. Also variant 'arsy' *UK, 1997*

arsey boo *adjective* chaotic, unorganised *NEW ZEALAND, 1988*

arsy-varsy; arsy-versy *adverb* back-to-front; upside-down; perversely *UK, 1539*

arsy-versy *adjective* homosexual. From ARSY-VARSY (perversely) playing on ARSE (the bottom) as a stereotypical object of homosexual attraction. *The Sunday Times*, 22nd August 1976, published a letter that preferred the use of GAY to 'arsy-versy' *UK, 1976*

Artful Dodger *noun* the penis. Rhyming slang for TODGER, formed from a light-fingered character in Charles Dickens' *Oliver Twist UK, 2003*

Artful Dodger *nickname* Roger Staubach (b 1942), a dominant quarterback at the college and professional levels in the 1960s and 70s. A two-for-one nickname, rhyming 'Dodger' with 'Roger' and alluding to the Dickens character *US, 1963*

Arthur *noun* arthritis. Used by North Sea trawlermen *UK, 1974*

Arthur Ashe; Arthur *noun* cash. Rhyming slang, based on the name of tennis champion Arthur Ashe, 1943–93 *UK, 1992*

Arthur Bliss *noun* an act of urination. Rhyming slang for PISS, formed from classical composer Sir Arthur Bliss, 1891–1975 *UK, 2003*

Arthur Duffy *noun* ▶ **take it on the Arthur Duffy** to leave quickly. A sprinter, in 1902 Duffy was the first to run the 100-yard dash in 9.6 seconds; he later wrote a sports column for the *Boston Post US, 1905*

Arthur Fowler *noun* a fart. Rhyming slang for GROWLER; Arthur Fowler was a character who appeared in BBC television soap opera *EastEnders UK, 2003*

Arthur Lowe; Arthur *noun* no. Glasgow rhyming slang, formed from the name of the English actor, 1915–82, who is fondly remembered for *Dad's Army*, 1968–77 *UK: SCOTLAND, 1988*

artic *noun* an articulated lorry *UK, 1951*

artichoke *noun* LSD. From the code name for the drug devised by the Central Intelligence Agency during its early experimentation with the drug *US, 2001*

article *noun* a person, usually of a type denoted. Jocular, derogatory *UK, 1811*

artificial *noun* an object the name of which escapes the speaker at the moment *BARBADOS, 1965*

artillery *noun* **1** guns *US, 1822*. **2** in boxing, heavy blows *US, 1954*. **3** in other sports, something accomplished from a distance *US, 1957*. **4** the equipment needed to inject a drug *US, 1915*. **5** strict discipline; a greater power *US, 1954*. **6** baked beans, or any food producing flatulence *US, 1916*

artillery ears *noun* partial deafness caused by exposure to the loud noise of the artillery *US, 1982*

artish *noun* an issue of a single-interest fan magazine containing mostly illustrations *US, 1982*

artist *noun* **1** a person who is proficient at the activity that precedes *AUSTRALIA, 1889*. **2** a person who is devoted to, or especially proficient in, a reprehensible activity *US, 1890*

artist for the government *noun* a person who draws unemployment insurance payments *CANADA, 1993*

arts *noun* ▶ **the arts** martial arts *BERMUDA, 1985*

artsy *adjective* artistic in a pretentious, vulgar way *UK, 1955*

artsy-craftsy *adjective* pretentiously artistic but not notably useful or comfortable *UK, 1902*

artsy-fartsy *adjective* excessively arty *US, 1964*

arty *noun* artillery *US, 1864*

arty-farty *adjective* pretentious, artificially cultural *US, 1967*

arty roller *noun* a collar. Rhyming slang *AUSTRALIA, 1945*

arva; harva *noun* sexual intercourse. Derives from Romany *charva* (to interfere with). Anal intercourse is the FULL HARVA *UK, 2002*

Arvin noun any South Vietnamese soldier. The South Vietnamese Army was known as the ARVN (*Army of the Republic of Viet Nam*); it took one vowel and very little imagination to get to Arvin US, 1966

ARVN attitude noun cowardice. Not particularly kind to the South Vietnamese Army (ARVN) US, 1991

arvo noun afternoon. From the first syllable of 'afternoon' (with voicing of the 'f') and-o suffix. Extremely common colloquially, usually in the phrase 'this arvo', giving rise to the common reanalysis 'the sarvo'. Other forms, rare in print, are 'afto', the simple 'arve' and also 'aftie' and 'arvie' AUSTRALIA, 1927

as as can be AUSTRALIA, 1996

as all get out as can be AUSTRALIA, 1964

asap; ASAP 1 *as soon as* possible. Originally military; either spoken as an acronym spelt out and stressed or vocalised as 'a-sap' in the US, 'assap' in the UK US, 1955. **2** *as slowly as* possible. Facetious, bitter variant on 'as soon as possible' CANADA, 2002

asbestos pants noun in poker, used for describing what a player on a very good streak of luck needs US, 1988

A-sex noun sex experienced while under the influence of amphetamine US, 1975

ash noun marijuana. The dropped 'h' of the London accent causes a punning variant on HASH UK, 1990s

ash verb to drop cigarette ash AUSTRALIA, 1930

ashcan noun **1** a depth charge US, 1918. **2** a small, powerful, cylindrical firecracker US, 1970. **3** in the television and film industries, an arc light roughly shaped like a rubbish bin US, 1942

Ashcan City nickname during the Korean war, a US Army processing centre eight miles from Inchon. From ASCOM (*Army Service Command*) to 'Ascom City' to 'Ashcan City' US, 1994

ash cash noun a fee paid to doctors for signing a cremation form. Medical slang UK, 2001

as he has to be adverb used as an intensifier. Follows an adjective, such as 'fine as he has to be' US, 1997

ashes noun marijuana US, 1977. ► **get your ashes hauled** to be brought to ejaculation US, 1906

ashtray noun the desert. Gulf war usage US, 1991

Asian moll noun a prostitute with an Asian customer base US, 1982

Asian two-step noun any highly venomous snake encountered in the jungles of Southeast Asia. From the belief that the venom will kill the victim within two steps of the bite US, 1966

Asiatic adjective deranged US, 1955

Asia West nickname Richmond, a town in British Columbia CANADA, 2002

as if! used as a humorous expression of extreme scepticism US, 1981

ask noun **1** a request. Generally in the collocation 'big ask' AUSTRALIA, 1994. **2** the asking price for a racehorse. A horse with a 'big ask' is deemed by the speaker to be over-priced AUSTRALIA, 1989

ask verb ► **ask for six and go airborne** to request the rotation travel allowance of six cents a mile in order to fly home US, 1991. ► **ask the question** to ask someone to have sex GUYANA, 1996. ► **ask what you have to sell** to invite sex BARBADOS, 1996

ask yourself! be reasonable! AUSTRALIA, 1942

as like as not adverb ▷see: LIKE AS NOT

as my pappy would say... used as a humorous introduction or segue. A signature line from *Maverick*, an early and popular television Western (ABC, 1957–62). Repeated with referential humour US, 1957

asparagus noun **1** a boy's penis. From the language of child pornography US, 2003. **2** in horse racing, a bettor who arrives at the track with an armful of racing forms. From the observation that the bettor 'has more tips than a tin of asparagus' AUSTRALIA, 1989

aspendicitis noun a notional medical condition of a symptomatic need to spend money. A humorous diagnosis, playing on 'spend' and 'appendicitis'. The earliest use is as the title of a 1961 jazz composition by Peter Schickele US, 1961

asphalt eater noun a drag racer who performs well US, 1964

asphalt jungle noun a large city. The title of a 1949 book by W. R. Burnett as well as an ABC television series starring Jack Warden in 1961 US, 1920

asphalt pilot noun a truck driver US, 1976

aspirin smoke noun a cigarette adulterated with crushed aspirin, providing a drug-like effect US, 1992

aspro noun ▷see: ASS PRO

ass noun **1** the buttocks, the posterior US, 1853. **2** the vagina UK, 1684. **3** sex; a person as a sexual object US, 1910. **4** the self; a person US, 1945. **5** a fool. From the level of intelligence stereotypically credited to the animal UK, 1578. ► **ass on fire** said of a person who is either angry or rushed US, 1983. ► **bring ass to kick ass** to have the courage needed to fight someone US, 1990. ► **bust your ass** to hurry, to exert yourself; to work extermely hard US, 1941. ► **case of the ass** anger; frustration. Vietnam war usage US, 1968. ► **eat someone's ass out** to berate someone US, 1996. ► **in ass** in trouble TRINIDAD AND TOBAGO, 1980. ► **take it in the ass** to take the passive role in anal intercourse US, 1983. ► **up your ass!; up your arse!** an expression of contempt, rejection or derision US, 1956. ► **your ass is grass** used for conveying the state of being in great trouble US, 1956. ► **your ass off** greatly intensifies the effort made in doing something US, 1946

ass verb to engage in prostitution US, 1991

ass adjective terrible, bad US, 1992

-ass; -assed suffix used as an intensifier for the preceding adjective or adverb US, 1903

ass-and-trash noun during the Vietnam war, people and cargo to be transported by aeroplane US, 1983

ass-ass verb to humiliate yourself US, 2002

ass backwards adverb in reverse order US, 1942

ass bandit; arse bandit; asshole bandit noun a male homosexual, especially the active partner in anal sex. Usually derogatory; combines ASS with 'bandit' – or 'brigand', conventionally a generally romantic image of a villain who will take what he wants US, 1968

ass bite noun harsh criticism US, 1973

ass-blow verb to lick, suck and tongue another's anus US, 1941

ass bucket noun a despised person US, 1953

ass burglar noun the active partner in anal sex; more generally, a male homosexual US, 1979

ass cache noun a supply of drugs hidden in the rectum US, 1992

ass chewing noun a harsh reprimand or scold US, 1954

ass cunt noun the anus. Analogised to a vagina US, 1974

assed out adjective in severe trouble US, 1993

ass end noun the least desirable part of anything US, 1947

ass ends noun the differentials of a truck tractor US, 1961

ass English noun the body movements and incantations of a dice shooter who believes that he can control the roll of the dice US, 1950

assets noun the genitals, especially the male genitals UK, 1998

ass fuck noun **1** anal sex US, 1940. **2** a despicable person US, 2001

ass-fuck verb to engage in anal sex, especially in the active role US, 1940

ass fucker noun the active partner in anal sex US, 1979

ass fucking noun anal sex US, 1970

ass gasket noun a disposable paper toilet seat cover US, 1994

ass hammer noun a motorcycle US, 1975

asshole noun **1** the anus US, 1935. **2** a fool; a person held in contempt US, 1933. **3** in logging and power line work, a kink in a cable US, 1959. ► **from asshole to appetite** all over, in all parts US, 1964. ► **your asshole's sucking wind** you are talking nonsense US, 1961

asshole bandit noun ▷see: ASS BANDIT

asshole buddy noun a very close friend US, 1945

asshole naked *adjective* completely naked *US, 1969*

asshole of creation *noun* a remote, desolate place *US, 1964*

asshole of the world; arsehole of the world *noun* the most despised place, area or location. Other embellishments include 'arsehole of the universe' or 'of the nation' *US, 1949*

assholes *noun* ▶ **assholes and elbows** said of a chaotic situation *US, 1987*

asshole to belly button *adjective* said of people pressed close together, one behind the other *US, 1973*

ass hound *noun* a man who obsessively engages in the pursuit of women for sex *US, 1952*

assified *adjective* **1** foolish *BARBADOS, 1965.* **2** pompous *GUYANA, 1996*

ass in a sling in deep trouble *US, 1990*

ass-in-the-grass test *noun* a rough approximation of the percentage of troops actually in combat at a given moment. Used in the Vietnam war *US, 1990*

assishness *noun* pure stupidity *TRINIDAD AND TOBAGO, 2003*

ass kickers *noun* heavy work shoes or boots *US, 1996*

ass-kiss *verb* to behave in an ingratiatingly sycophantic manner *US, 1961*

ass-kisser; arse-kisser *noun* a sycophant. Combines ARSE/ASS (the buttocks) with conventional 'kisser'. As a demonstration of subservience the image is much older than the term; it can be seen in C16 woodcuts of devil-worshippers lifting the goat's tail to plant their kisses *US, 1766*

ass-kissing *noun* sycophantic or ingratiating behaviour *US, 1942*

ass-kissing *adjective* sycophantic *US, 1942*

ass-licking *adjective* ▷*see:* ARSE-LICKING

ass man; arse man *noun* a man who considers that the (suggestive) appearance of a woman's posterior provides the supreme initial sexual attraction *US, 1972*

ass munch *noun* a person who is easily despised *US, 1996*

assmuncher *noun* a despised person *US, 2003*

as soon as *adverb* as soon as possible. A shortening of the conventional phrase *UK, 2000*

ass out *verb* to make a fool of yourself *CANADA, 2002*

ass-out *adverb* extremely *US, 1995*

ass over tea kettle; ass over tea cups *adverb* head over heels *US, 1948*

ass peddler *noun* a male prostitute *US, 1979*

ass pro; asspro; aspro *noun* a male homosexual prostitute. A combination of ASS and 'pro(stitute)', but note Aspro™ the branded analgesic *AUSTRALIA, 1955*

ass queen *noun* a homosexual man who is particularly attracted to other men's buttocks *US, 1978*

ass ripper *noun* a difficult course or test *US, 1968*

ass's gallop *noun* a brief period of time *IRELAND, 2003*

ass time *noun* time wasted sitting around *US, 1994*

assume *verb* ▶ **assume the angle; assume the position** to kneel for punishment doled out as part of a hazing ritual *US, 1940*

asswipe; arsewipe *noun* **1** toilet paper *US, 1958.* **2** by extension, a despicable or offensive person *US, 1952*

A-state *nickname* Arkansas *US, 2002*

asterisks *noun* used as an all-purpose euphemism for any potentially offensive noun, singular or plural. From the publishers' convention of replacing offensive words or parts of words with an * for each missing letter *UK, 2003*

as the feller says used for introducing a statement which the speaker does not necessarily accept *US, 1975*

as the skua flies in a straight line. Antarctica's adaptation of the common 'as the crow flies', using instead the South Pole's predatory gull as the bird in question *ANTARCTICA, 1936*

Astor's pet horse *noun* used in comparisons with a person, especially a woman, who is over-dressed *US, 1950*

astronaut *noun* the buttocks or anus *US, 2003*

astro turf *noun* marijuana *UK, 2003*

as you do as you do (but perhaps shouldn't). A conversational interjection used to make a comic admission of some odd behaviour *AUSTRALIA, 1996*

as you were used for the retraction of a preceding statement. From the military drill command *UK, 1864*

atari *noun* crack cocaine *US, 1993*

A-Team *noun* the basic functional unit of the US Special Forces in Vietnam, consisting of 10 to 12 trained commandos *US, 1990*

ate out *adjective* (of trousers) worn, baggy, saggy *US, 2002*

ate up *adjective* **1** in the US Air Force, dedicated to service *US, 1998.* **2** in the US Army, confused, dim *US, 1998*

Athenian *noun* in homosexual usage, an anal sex enthusiast *US, 1987*

-athon *suffix* used to create a word suggesting the root word activity carried on for a long period of time. From 'marathon' *US, 1934*

at it *adjective* **1** engaged in criminal activity *UK, 1970.* **2** engaged in sexual intercourse *AUSTRALIA, 1972*

ATL *nickname* Atlanta, Georgia *US, 2002*

ATM *noun* a generous person. From the most common US name for a bank's *a*utomatic *t*eller *m*achine *US, 1997*

a toda madre! excellent! Border Spanish used in English conversation by Mexican-Americans *US, 1974*

atom bomb *noun* ▷*see:* A-BOMB

atom-bombo *noun* a cheap but very potent wine. A play on the power of the atom bomb, intensifying BOMBO (a fortified wine) *AUSTRALIA, 1953*

atomic *noun* a cigar-sized marijuana cigarette *US, 1953*

atomic *adjective* (of a drug) very-powerful *US, 1971*

A-town *nickname* Atlanta, Georgia *US, 1995*

atshitshi *noun* marijuana. disguised by using a variant of 'secret language' Pig Latin *SOUTH AFRICA, 1977*

attaboy *noun* praise, especially from a boss *US, 1970*

attack *noun* ▶ **attack of the slows** in horse racing, an imaginary illness that plagues a horse midway through a race *US, 1951*

attagirl! used for encouraging a female *US, 1924*

attention *noun* ▶ **jump to attention; spring to attention** to achieve an erection. From military drill, in use after World War 2 *UK, 1984*

attic *noun* a drug addict. A phonetic corruption *US, 1992*

attic hand *noun* in oil drilling, the worker who handles the drill pipe *US, 1954*

attitude *noun* **1** aggressive or antagonistic behaviour *US, 1975.* **2** an air of detached superiority *US, 1994*

attitude adjustment *noun* a change in outlook produced by alcohol, threats or other inducements *US, 1984*

attitude arrest *noun* an arrest motivated by the subject's lack of respect towards the arresting police officer *US, 1992*

attitude test *noun* the extremely subjective criteria used by a traffic police officer in deciding whether to issue a traffic ticket or let the offending driver off with a warning *US, 1984*

atto- *prefix* used as a diminishing intensifier. Literally meaning 'ten to the power of negative eighteen' *US, 1997*

au contraire *adverb* to the contrary. French used by those who speak no French; adds a camp tone *US, 1955*

auction gale *noun* an equinoctial gale. 'Auction' echoes the sound of 'equinoctial' *CANADA, 1999*

Audi *noun* ▶ **to be audi** to leave *US, 1992*

Audi 5000 *adjective* already gone *US, 1998*

Audi 5000! goodbye. Playing on 'Audi' and 'out of here' *US, 1991*

Audie *nickname* the voice that announced the time on telephone time services *US, 1955*

auger in *verb* to crash an aeroplane *US, 1957*

augustus *noun* a male homosexual. A roundabout allusion to anal intercourse; Augustus Gloop is a character in *Charlie and the Chocolate Factory*, Roald Dahl, filmed as Willie *Wonka and the Chocolate Factory*, 1971. At the climax of the story Augustus is sucked up a chocolate pipe *UK, 2002*

auld lang syne *noun* mutual, simultaneous oral sex between two people. Rhyming slang for 69 formed from the song that people enjoy once a year. *UK, 2003*

auld wan *noun* ▷*see:* OUL ONE

au naturel *adjective* naked. French used by those who speak no French; informal, jocular, affected *US, 1967*

aunt *noun* the manager of a brothel *UK, 1606*

Aunt Bettie *noun* an overly cautious person *US, 1945*

Aunt Ella *noun* an umbrella. Rhyming slang *UK, 1960*

Aunt Emma *noun* **1** used as a personification of a matronly aunt *US, 1947*. **2** in croquet, a cautious, conservative, dull player *US, 1977*

Aunt Fanny *nickname* the Federal Communications Commission *US, 1976*

Aunt Flo *noun* the bleed period of the menstrual cycle *US, 1954*

Aunt Flo from Red River *noun* the bleed period of the menstrual cycle *CANADA, 2001*

Aunt Haggie's children *noun* any stupid, lazy, despised people *BERMUDA, 1985*

Aunt Hazel *noun* marijuana *US, 2001*

auntie *noun* **1** an older, effeminate male homosexual. A tad cruel, if not derogatory *US, 1930*. **2** a disoriented unlambed ewe that thinks she has lambed and steals the lamb of another *NEW ZEALAND, 1999*. **3** the bleed period of the menstrual cycle. Also variant 'aunty' *NORFOLK ISLAND, 1992*

Auntie; Aunty *nickname* the British Broadcasting Corporation *UK, 1962*

Auntie Ena *noun* a cleaner. Rhyming slang *UK, 1992*

Auntie Lily *adjective* silly. Rhyming slang *UK, 1945*

auntie man *noun* **1** a man who is completely dominated by his wife *TRINIDAD AND TOBAGO, 2003*. **2** an effeminate man, especially a homosexual *GUYANA, 1996*

Auntie Nellie; Aunty Nelly *noun* the belly. Rhyming slang; sometimes shortened to 'aunty' *UK, 1961*

Auntie Wicky *nickname* Queen Victoria *BAHAMAS, 1982*

Aunt Jane's room *noun* an outdoor toilet *US, 1939*

Aunt Jemima *noun* a black woman who seeks approval from white people by obsequious behaviour. Ironically, singer/actor Ethel Ernestine Harper, who portrayed Aunt Jemima in pancake commercials from 1948 until 1966, was by all accounts anything but the stereotypical subservient black woman *US, 1966*

Aunt Julia *noun* communist propaganda. Possibly from a code word passed to Communist stevedores on waterfronts to indicate the shipment of communist printed material is aboard ship' *US, 1953*

Aunt Maggie *noun* ▶ **out Aunt Maggie's window** (used of a homerun) out of the ballpark *US, 1962*

Aunt Mary *noun* marijuana. MARY is a familiar pun on 'marijuana' *US, 1959*

Aunt Nell *noun* the ear. Usually as a plural *UK, 2002*

Aunt Nell *verb* to listen. Often an imperative *UK, 1992*

Aunt Nelly fake *noun* an earring. A combination of AUNT NELL (the ear) and 'fake' (an artificial thing); usually as a plural *UK, 1997*

Aunt Nora *noun* cocaine *US, 1994*

Aunt Ruby *noun* the bleed period of the menstrual cycle *US, 2002*

Aunt Thomasina *noun* **1** a black woman who curries favour with white people by obsequious behaviour. An echo of the much more commonly heard UNCLE TOM *US, 1963*. **2** a woman who does not support feminism *US, 1970*

Aunt Tillie; Aunt Tilly *noun* **1** used as the personification of a fussy old maid *US, 1960*. **2** the bleed period of the menstrual cycle *US, 1999*

Aunt Tom *noun* a woman who does not support the goals of feminism. An attempt to link semantically the struggle of women with the struggle of black slaves by borrowing from the well-known UNCLE TOM *US, 1968*

Aunty Nelly *noun* ▷*see:* AUNTIE AND VARIANTS

aurora borealis *noun* phencyclidine, the recreational drug known as PCP or angel dust *US, 1977*

Aussie *noun* **1** Australia. From *Australia* and '-ie' suffix. Pronounced 'ozzie', not 'ossie', the common mistake made by north Americans. Generally used positively with a sense of national pride in all meanings *AUSTRALIA, 1915*. **2** an Australian. Originally used of Australian soldiers in World War 1 *AUSTRALIA, 1918*. **3** Australian English *AUSTRALIA, 1945*. **4** the Australian dollar *AUSTRALIA, 1956*

Aussie *adjective* Australian *AUSTRALIA, 1915*

Aussie haka; Australian haka *noun* a gesture showing that you have no money to pay for the next round of drinks at a pub *NEW ZEALAND, 1998*

Aussie kiss *noun* oral-genital stimulation. Described as 'similar to a French Kiss, but given down under' *UK, 2002*

Aussie steak *noun* mutton *US, 1947*

Australia *noun* an ounce of marijuana or other drug. Punning the abbreviation 'oz' (ounce) with the familiar diminutive 'Oz' (Australia) *UK, 2003*

Australian *noun* **1** Australian English. Jocularly seen as a separate language from British English, or other varieties of English *AUSTRALIA, 1902*. **2** a practitioner of mouth-to-anus sex. From a somewhat forced 'down under' joke *US, 1979*

Australian days *noun* night-work *UK, 1970*

Australian salute *noun* a hand-movement brushing flies away from the face *AUSTRALIA, 1972*

Australian yo *noun* in craps, a roll of three. A roll of three is rarely a good thing, and is usually best face-down; if a three is face-down, an eleven is face-up. Eleven is 'yo', with the three thus 'down-under the yo' *US, 1999*

Austrian Oak *nickname* ▷*see:* OAK

auto *adjective* automatic. A colloquial abbreviation *US, 1995*

autocutie *noun* an attractive but incompetent television presenter. A compound of 'autocue' and CUTIE (an attractive young woman) *UK, 2003*

auto-getem *noun* automatic weapons fire. Broken down – 'automatic fire gets 'em' *US, 1972*

automagically *adverb* in computing, in an automatic but explanation-defying complicated fashion *US, 1981*

automatic tongue-wiper *noun* a sycophant or toady *US, 1977*

automaton *noun* in poker, a player who bets and plays in an extremely predictable manner *US, 1996*

autumn leaves *noun* in horse racing, a steeplechase jockey who has suffered a series of falls. A shameless pun *AUSTRALIA, 1989*

Av *nickname* Telegraph Avenue, Berkeley, California *US, 1966*

Ava Gardner *adjective* avant-garde *UK, 1983*

Avenue *noun* ▶ **the Avenue 1** Fifth Avenue in New York. In gay use. Fifth Avenue was, in the 1940s and 50s, favoured by homosexual prostitutes *US, 1940s to 50s*. **2** Telegraph Avenue, Berkeley, Calfiornia *US, 1966*

average *adjective* mediocre; not the best; just plain dreadful *AUSTRALIA, 1981*

avgas *noun* jet fuel *US, 1990*

aviator *noun* in trucking, a driver who drives very fast *US, 1971*

awake *adjective* sexually aroused *US, 1985*

awake to aware of a secret plan, trick, deception or the like; aware of a person's deceitful character or hidden agenda. Now generally A WAKE-UP TO *AUSTRALIA, 1954*

a wake-up *adjective* alert; knowing; wise to. There is some confusion about whether this idiom should be construed nominally with 'a' being the article and 'wake-up' being a noun, meaning 'an alert person, a person who knows what's what', or adjectivally as defined here. The earliest evidence (from 1916) supports the noun theory, but since the 1940s it has become impossible to definitely determine the part of speech in print as it is found spelt variously as 'a wake-up', 'a wakeup', 'awake up' and 'awake-up'. The fact that the plural form 'wake-ups' is only attested by a solitary citation from 1943 suggests that it is now conceived of as an adjectival phrase however it may be spelt *AUSTRALIA, 1916*

a wake-up to aware of a secret plan, trick, deception or the like; aware of a person's deceitful character or hidden agenda *AUSTRALIA, 1944*

away *adjective* **1** in prison. Euphemistic *UK, 1909*. **2** overseas *BARBADOS, 1965*. **3** crazy *UK: SCOTLAND, 1988*. **4** in bar dice games, counting for nothing. A call of 'aces away' would mean that rolls of one have no point value *US, 1976*

away laughing *adjective* in a good position, especially when embarking on a new venture *NEW ZEALAND, 1965*

awesome *adjective* great, excellent. An informal variation of the conventional sense *US, 1975*

awfuck disease *noun* the sense of dread that you feel the morning after doing something that you, upon reflection, wished you had not done. Used in jokes more than in real life, with the punch-line a variation on 'Aw fuck, why did I do that?' *US, 2001*

awful *adverb* very *UK, 1818*

awkward squad *noun* collectively, people who do not, or will not, conform; a notional grouping of people who are 'difficult' *UK, 1796*

AWOL; awol *adjective* missing. Military coinage, from ' *a*bsent *w*ithout *l*eave'; now widely applied, both as initialism or acronym, to most circumstances where permission for absence would be required *UK, 1920*

AWOL bag *noun* in the Korea and Vietnam wars, an overnight bag *US, 1956*

ax; axe *noun* **1** a musical instrument, especially an electric guitar. Originally used in jazz circles for any instrument, particularly a saxophone or trumpet, instruments on which 'chops' (musical figures) are played; surely 'axe' was coined as a pun. The word itself suggests a chopper, a tool that you can carry over your shoulder – to many jazz and, subsequently, rock musicians, their instrument is exactly that *US, 1955*. **2** any sharp-edged weapon *US, 1950*. **3** a knife used or intended for use as a weapon *US, 1972*

4 dismissal from employment. Usually heard in the phrases 'get the axe' or 'give the axe' *US, 1883*. **5** in a gambling operation, the house's cut of the bets *US, 1974*. **6** the lip of a wave *US, 1991*. ▶ **get the axe** in surfing, to be knocked off your board by a wave *US, 1957*

axe god *noun* a popular electric-guitar player who inspires hero-worship with his musical technique. Based on AXE (a guitar). The graffito 'Clapton is God', deifying the popular guitarist Eric Clapton (b.1945), was widespread in the late 1960s *UK, 1999*

axe handle *noun* an imprecise unit of measurement, especially when applied to the breadth of a man's shoulders or woman's buttocks *US, 1947*

axe handle party *noun* a riot or brawl *US, 110*

axe hero *noun* a popular electric-guitar player who inspires hero-worship with his musical technique. Based on AXE (a guitar) *UK, 1996*

axe man *noun* **1** an electric guitarist; rarely, any musician. Based on AXE (a guitar or any instrument) *UK, 1976*. **2** a person who decides when a company will discharge an employee *TRINIDAD AND TOBAGO, 1975*

axe-wound *noun* the vagina *UK, 2003*

axle grease *noun* **1** money. Probably because 'it makes the wheels go round' *AUSTRALIA, 1943*. **2** any particularly thick and sticky hair pomade. Known and used in the UK, US and Australia *AUSTRALIA, 1943*

aye, doogie aye used for expressing disbelief in whatever you have just been told. An elaboration of 'aye' (yes) spoken with irony heavy enough to mean 'no'. Several variations including: 'aye Hawkeye', 'aye, hooch-aye'; 'aye, Popeye' and 'aye, that eye' *UK: SCOTLAND, 1988*

ayemer *noun* (from television) a morning show. This term is thought to have been imported into Canada, from the US *Variety* magazine *CANADA, 2002*

'ay is for 'orses; hay is for horses used as a disdainful rejoinder when someone says 'eh?' or 'hey!'. This, the oldest of all catchphrases, is recorded in Swift's 'Polite Conversations', 1738 *UK, 1738*

ayo used as a greeting *US, 1995*

Ayrton Senna *noun* a ten pound note. Rhyming slang for 'tenner'; formed from Brazilian Formula-One racing driver Ayrton Senna da Silva, 1963–1994 *UK, 2004*

Aztec hop; Aztec revenge; Aztec two-step *noun* diarrhoea suffered by tourists in Mexico *US, 1953*

azz *noun* the buttocks. A variation of ASS *US, 2002*

Bb

B *noun* **1** Benzedrine™ (amphetamine sulphate), a central nervous system stimulant *US, 1986*. **2** a matchbox full of marijuana *US, 1971*. **3** a buddy, a brother; used as an address for a fellow black man; used as an address for a fellow of either sex. Initialism *US, 1995*. **4** a bastard *AUSTRALIA, 1921*. **5** a Cadillac Brougham car *US, 1980*. ▶ **put the B on** to ask for money for sex after giving the appearance of being seduced *US, 1954*

B *adjective* **1** used as an intensifier. A euphemistic abbreviation of BLOODY or BASTARD, sometimes shown in print with leader dots or asterisks representing the missing letters *UK, 1926*. **2** (used of a film) second-tier in terms of actors and budget *US, 1946*. **3** in the written shorthand of the Internet and text message, fulfilling the masculine role in a homosexual (male or female) relationship. Short for BUTCH *UK, 2004*

B1 *noun* ▶ **do a B1; do a bee wan** to go somewhere else, to change direction. This derives from the bureaucracy that governs unemployment benefit; if you are in need of immediate support when you first register unemployed you will be issued with a form B1 (an application for Income Support) which is administered at a different location *UK: SCOTLAND, 1988*

B2B *adjective* (used of a business transaction) between two businesses *US, 1999*

B-40 *noun* a cigar laced with marijuana and dipped in malt liquor. Possibly named for the appearance and/or effects of the B-40 grenade launcher used by the Viet Cong during the Vietnam war *US, 1998*

B-52 *noun* a powerful amphetamine tablet *US, 1993*

BA *noun* **1** nothing whatsoever. A euphemistic abbreviation of BUGGER ALL, often elaborated as SWEET BA *UK, 1961*. **2** a bare ass. Usually in the context of exposing the buttocks to shock or amuse *US, 1970*. ▶ **hang a BA** to expose your bare ass *US, 1970*

baadass; baaadasss *adjective* very bad, very dangerous *US, 1971*

baba-bing; ba-da-bring ▷*see:* BADDA BING

babbler *noun* a sheep camp-cook. An abbreviation of the rhyming slang BABBLING BROOK *NEW ZEALAND, 1919*

babbling *noun* cooking. After BABBLING BROOK (a cook). There is no record of 'babble' (to cook) but its existence is surely implied *US, 1962*

babbling brook *noun* **1** a gossip, a chatty person *US, 1913*. **2** a cook. Rhyming slang. In early use very common among shearers, stockmen and soldiers *AUSTRALIA, 1904*. **3** a criminal. Rhyming slang for 'crook'. Can be shortened to 'babbler'. *AUSTRALIA, 1919*

babbo *noun* a naive, law-abiding citizen *US, 1992*

babe *noun* **1** an attractive young woman *US, 1905*. **2** an attractive young male *US, 1973*. **3** used as a term of address *US, 1906*

babe alert *noun* a notification that there are attractive people nearby *AUSTRALIA, 1996*

babelicious *adjective* extremely sexually attractive. Coined by Mike Myers on the US television programme *Saturday Night Live* and popularised by the film *Wayne's World*, 1992 *US, 1992*

Babe Ruth *noun* the truth. Prison rhyming slang *NEW ZEALAND, 1999*

babes *noun* used as a term of singular address, both general and affectionate *UK, 1997*. ▶ **the babes; the wee babes** used as an expression of appreciation: excellent, good, exactly as required. Glasgow slang. This may well be a product of rhyming slang formed on 'Babes in the Wood'(good) *UK: SCOTLAND, 1988*

babes, parties, tunes used as a humorous assessment of what is important in life. The 'Wayne's World' skits on *Saturday Night Live* in the 1990s used the mock-Latin motto 'babum, partium, tuneum'. The English 'translation' is repeated with referential humour *US, 1994*

babies *noun* dice *US, 1974*

babo *noun* nalorphine, a morphine derivative that acts to reverse the effects of morphine and other narcotics *US, 1967*

baboo *noun* an Indian man. A term of respect within the culture; a term of disrespect when used by outsiders *TRINIDAD AND TOBAGO, 1914*

baboon butt *noun* the red, sore buttocks of someone riding as a passenger on a motorcycle *US, 1988*

babu *noun* an East Indian. Also recorded in the Fiji Islands *JAMAICA, 1921*

baby *noun* **1** used as a friendly term of address *US, 1921*. **2** a sweetheart, a girlfriend *US, 1839*. **3** a prostitute's customer *US, 1957*. **4** a young, inexperienced male homosexual *US, 1954*. **5** a young performer new to the pornography industry who looks even younger than he or she is *US, 1995*. **6** in horse racing, a two-year-old horse *US, 1976*. **7** in professional wrestling, a wrestler or other participant designed to be an audience favourite. A shortened BABYFACE *US, 1999*. **8** in the film industry, a screenplay *US, 1994*. **9** an impressive, large object *US, 1907*. **10** marijuana *US, 1960*. **11** a puma or cougar. Circus and hunting usage *US, 1946*. **12** in the television and film industries, a focused 500 watt light source *US, 1960*. **13** in poker, a 2, 3, 4 or 5 *US, 1979*. ▶ **in baby** pregnant *TRINIDAD AND TOBAGO, 1942*

baby 007 *noun* in the Vietnam war, an investigative agent from the Army Criminal Investigation Division, most likely working undercover to identify drug users *US, 1991*

baby ass *noun* someone who is babyish. Teen slang *US, 2003*

baby batter *noun* semen *US, 1997*

baby Benz *noun* a Mercedes 190 *US, 1989*

baby bhang *noun* marijuana *US, 1979*

baby blue *noun* a tablet of Viagra, an erection-inducing drug taken recreationally for performance enhancement *US, 2002*

baby blues *noun* **1** capsules of the synthetic opiate oxycodone used recreationally *US, 2003*. **2** blue eyes *US, 1957*. **3** post-natal depression *UK, 1979*

baby bonus *noun* the Canadian family allowance. Also used in Australia *CANADA, 1957*

baby boomer *noun* a person born roughly between 1945 and 1955. After World War 2, America and Europe saw a boom in the birthrate *US, 1974*

baby buggy *noun* **1** a Mini Metro car. Citizens' band radio slang *UK, 1981*. **2** a convertible Volkswagen Beetle *US, 1992*

baby bumper *noun* a child molester *US, 1992*

baby burglar *noun* a young thief *UK, 1996*

babycakes *noun* used as a term of endearment *US, 1967*

baby catcher *noun* an obstetrician. From an earlier (1937) sense of 'midwife' *US, 1970*

baby discovers! used as a melodramatic reaction to another's surprise *US, 1972*

baby doll *noun* any central nervous system stimulant *US, 1955*

baby dolls *noun* pyjamas for girls consisting of a baggy top and a short trouser bottom *UK, 1957*

babydyke *noun* a young or inexperienced lesbian *US, 1999*

babyface *noun* **1** in professional wrestling, the wrestler designed by the promoters to be the audience favourite in a match *US, 1958*. **2** by extension, any figure in the professional wrestling industry designed to be cheered or liked by the fans *US, 1999*. **3** an attractive young woman. Reported by a Jamaican inmate in a UK prison, August 2002 *JAMAICA, 2002*

baby father; baby daddy *noun* a woman's boyfriend, live-in lover or unmarried partner, especially when the father of her child *JAMAICA, 1987*

baby femme *adjective* (used of a fashion style) suggesting both youthful innocence and sexual abandon *US*, *1995*

babyflot *noun* a Russian airline created by the breakup of Aeroflot in 1991 *CANADA*, *2002*

baby food *noun* semen *US*, *1972*

baby fucker *noun* a child molester *US*, *1985*

baby gangster *noun* a young member of a youth gang *US*, *1989*

baby grand *noun* five hundred dollars. Punning on the piano size and a 'grand' as $1000 *US*, *1963*

baby gun *noun* a short, bullet-shaped surf board designed for big-wave conditions *US*, *1970*

baby habit *noun* the irregular, unaddicted use of a drug *US*, *1992*

baby hero *noun* in the Vietnam war, a brave soldier *US*, *1991*

Baby Huey *noun* a military helicopter. An embellishment of the more common and simpler HUEY, alluding here to a comic strip character *US*, *1969*

baby legs *noun* in television and film making, a low-legged tripod for supporting lights *US*, *1987*

baby life *noun* a prison sentence of at least ten years *US*, *2002*

baby lifter *noun* a brakeman on a passenger train *US*, *1946*

Babylon *noun* **1** the white establishment; a symbol of all that is corrupt and evil. From the mystical 'Babylon of the Apocalypse' *JAMAICA*, *1943*. **2** by extension, the United States *US*, *1972*. **3** the police *JAMAICA*, *1996*

Babylonian *noun* a white person *US*, *2004*

babylons *noun* the female breasts *UK*, *2001*

baby mix *noun* short kava drinking sessions, especially on a night before work. Kava is a tranquillising herbal beverage. Recorded by Jan Tent *FIJI*, *1997*

baby moon *noun* in hot rodding, a small, chrome convex wheel cover *US*, *1993*

baby mother *noun* an unmarried mother *JAMAICA*, *1989*

baby needs a pair of shoes! used for summoning good luck while rolling the dice in craps *US*, *2003*

baby pro *noun* a very, very young prostitute *US*, *1961*

baby race *noun* in horse racing, a relatively short race for two-year-old horses *US*, *1976*

baby raper *noun* a child molester *US*, *1961*

baby rip *noun* a small current travelling seaward from shore. An abbreviation of 'rip tide' or 'rip current' *US*, *1990*

baby-san *noun* **1** an East Asian child; a young woman. Coined during the US occupation of Japan, used frequently in Vietnam *US*, *1954*. **2** by extension, used by Vietnamese prostitutes to refer to a virgin and by US troops to refer to an inexperienced, untested soldier *US*, *1990*

baby scratch *noun* the most basic technique of manipulating a vinyl record to create new music *US*, *2002*

baby shit *noun* mustard. A Vietnam contribution to the time-honoured and considerable lexicon of derogatory references to food in the armed forces *US*, *1972*

babysit *verb* **1** to guide a person through an LSD or other hallucinatory drug experience *US*, *1968*. **2** to act as a mentor or protector for newly arrived prisoners *US*, *1984*. **3** to date someone who is substantially younger than you *US*, *1990*

babysitter *noun* in a fleet, a destroyer accompanying an aircraft carrier *US*, *1965*

baby's leg *noun* any food, sweet or savoury, that is presented as a pastry roll. School and services use; from the appearance and, surely, a reflection on institutional catering *UK*, *1935*

baby slit *noun* a tablet of MDMA, the recreational drug best known as ecstasy. Possibly, a euphemistic rendering of 'little cunt' (a small thing) *UK*, *2003*

baby snatcher *noun* an adult who is sexually attracted to children or adolescents *UK*, *1927*

baby stealer *noun* a male or female lover of a much younger or very young person; an older person who prefers such relationships *UK*, *1937*

baby strainer *noun* a condom *UK*, *1998*

baby T *noun* crack cocaine *US*, *1994*

baca *noun* tobacco *NORFOLK ISLAND*, *1992*

bacalao *noun* the unwashed vagina. From the Spanish for 'codfish' *JAMAICA*, *1996*

baccy; bacco; bacca *noun* tobacco *UK*, *1792*

bach *noun* a vacation cottage *NEW ZEALAND*, *1984*

bachelor *noun* in police work, an officer who works best alone *US*, *1992*

bachelor pad *noun* the apartment of a young, single, urbane, sophisticated man *US*, *1976*

bachelors' hall *noun* a residence of unmarried men, originally from a Hudson's Bay trading post building for clerks *UK*, *1746*

bachy; batchy *noun* **1** a room where a man lives alone or brings women for sex *GUYANA*, *1996*. **2** a small house occupied by a single man *TRINIDAD AND TOBAGO*, *2003*

back *noun* **1** an illegal gambling operation. An abbreviation of 'back office' *US*, *1973*. **2** a drink taken immediately after another, a 'chaser' *US*, *1982*. **3** the musical accompaniment which a jazz band gives a soloist *US*, *1970*. **4** support, help *US*, *1989*. **5** the buttocks *US*, *1993*. **6** potency; virility *GUYANA*, *1996*. ▶ **get off someone's back** to cease annoying, aggravating, nagging or criticising someone. Often in the exasperated imperative 'Get off my back!' *UK*, *1961*. ▶ **get on someone's back** to annoy, aggravate, nag or criticise someone *AUSTRALIA*, *1959*. ▶ **get someone's back; have someone's back** to defend or protect someone *US*, *1990*. ▶ **it's got a back to it** used of an article that is being lent, stressing that the loaned article must be returned. A catchphrase mainly in London use *UK*, *1961*. ▶ **like the back of a bus; like the back end of a bus** ugly, unattractive *UK*, *1959*. ▶ **on your back 1** (of a woman) working as a prostitute *AUSTRALIA*, *1968*. **2** (of a woman) engaged in sexual intercourse *AUSTRALIA*, *1979*. **3** penniless. An Australian variant, 'on the back of your arse', is first recorded in 1961 *UK*, *1937*

back *verb* to carry something on your back *BAHAMAS*, *1982*. ▶ **back a tail** to engage in anal sex *AUSTRALIA*, *1973*. ▶ **back and fill** to vacillate. Nautical imagery, from the term for handling sails to catch and then spill the wind *US*, *1975*. ▶ **back off the course** to bet a large amount on something *AUSTRALIA*, *1965*. ▶ **back off the map** to bet a large amount on something *AUSTRALIA*, *1975*

back-ah-yard *noun* in the Caribbean, the West Indies, used for expressing the general concept of home. West Indian and UK black; literally 'back [at] our YARD', *UK*, *1977*

backanahan *adjective* untrustworthy, underhanded *BELIZE*, *1996*

back and belly *noun* a very thin person, especially a woman *GUYANA*, *1996*

back and belly *adverb* entirely, completely *TRINIDAD AND TOBAGO*, *2003*

back-and-forth *noun* conversation *US*, *1976*

backasswards *adverb* in the wrong order *US*, *1951*

backblocker *noun* a resident of a remote area, especially the area beyond the river gorges in Canterbury and Otago, New Zealand *NEW ZEALAND*, *1910*

backblocks *noun* remote and sparsely populated land beyond the outskirts of a town or city *AUSTRALIA*, *1879*

back bottom *noun* the rump or posterior. Used as a counterpart to FRONT BOTTOM *AUSTRALIA*, *2001*

backbreaker *noun* LSD combined with strychnine *UK*, *1998*

backcap *noun* an answer *US*, *1945*

backchat *noun* **1** impudent replies; answering back in an insolent manner. Originally military *UK*, *1901*. **2** sexual badinage; verbal flirting *AUSTRALIA*, *1963*

backchat *verb* to answer back in an insolent manner *AUSTRALIA*, *1919*

back dex *noun* amphetamines *UK*, *2003*

back door; backdoor *noun* **1** the anus and rectum *UK, 1694.* **2** in sports, the advancement of a team in a playoff situation as a result of the actions of another team *US, 1952.* **3** in a group motorcycle ride, the last rider in the group, usually the most experienced; the final citizens' band radio user in a convoy *US, 1976.* **4** a surreptitious way of entering a protected system or website, made possible by a weakness in the system *US, 1990.* ► **go out the back door** to back down from a confrontation *US, 1981*

back-door; backdoor *verb* **1** to commit adultery *US, 1982.* **2** in surfing, to start a ride behind the peak of a wave *US, 1980.* **3** to bypass something; to exclude something *CANADA, 1993*

back-door; backdoor *adjective* **1** adulterous *US, 1947.* **2** in poker, describing an unexpected hand produced by drawing *US, 1979*

back-door alcoholic *noun* an alcoholic who admits his alcoholism and joins a twelve-step recovery programme for addicts after initially characterising himself as an enabler of another alcoholic *US, 1998*

backdoor artist *noun* a swindler, especially a drug user who deceives other drug users *US, 1992*

backdoor Betty *noun* a woman who enjoys anal sex *US, 2000*

back-door bust *noun* an arrest for one crime, usually major, after a detention or arrest for another, usually minor *US, 1992*

back door closed *adjective* describes a convoy when the final vehicle is looking out for any police interest. Citizen band radio slang *US, 1976*

backdooring *noun* anal intercourse *UK, 1997*

backdoor parole; backgate parole *noun* death while serving a prison sentence. A black joke *US, 1929*

backdoor pensioner *noun* a sheep dog who is past his working days. The term implies an honourable retirement. A dog of similar years but just a 'bit of an old pooch' would be more likely referred to as a POT-LICKER *NEW ZEALAND, 1981*

back door trots *noun* diarrhoea *UK, 1801*

back-double *noun* a back street, a side road *UK, 1932*

back down *verb* in betting on horse racing, to force the odds on a horse lower through heavy betting *US, 1951*

back 'em down *verb* in trucking, to reduce speed *US, 1976*

backer *noun* a person who is a frequent participant in anal sex *TRINIDAD AND TOBAGO, 2003*

backfield *noun* the supporting members of a criminal group *US, 1970*

backfire *verb* to fart *UK, 1998*

backflash *noun* in pinball, the painted glass panel at the front of the machine. Conventionally known as the 'backglass' *US, 1977*

back flip *verb* in pinball, to flip the ball to the same side of the playing field as the flipper *US, 1977*

back forty *noun* a large, remote piece of land; a backyard. Originally a reference to a farmer's most distant 40-acre parcel; the usage generalised and then became humorous *US, 1950*

back-forty accent *noun* country speech *CANADA, 1958*

back gate exit *noun* death while in prison *US, 1992*

backhand *adjective* in surfing, with your back to the wave *AUSTRALIA, 1985*

backhander *noun* a bribe; a gratuity given surreptitiously *UK, 1971*

back haul *noun* on the railways, a return trip *US, 1977*

backhouse *noun* an outside toilet, especially without plumbing *US, 1984*

backhouse flush *noun* in poker, a very poor hand. From 'backhouse' (an outside toilet) *US, 1984*

backie *noun* **1** an act of using someone's bent back as a platform to climb a wall or get over an obstacle *UK: SCOTLAND, 1985.* **2** a ride, as passenger, on the back of a bicycle *UK: SCOTLAND, 1985*

backings *noun* in the illegal production of alcohol, low-proof distillate not potent enough to be considered whisky *US, 1974*

back in the day *adverb* at a time in the past that evokes a feel of nostalgia, real or conjured *US, 1988*

back in the saddle; back in the saddle again *adjective* experiencing the bleed period of the menstrual cycle *US, 1954*

back in the teapot, doormouse! used as an admonition to a child to be quiet *CANADA, 2002*

backjunk *noun* a big piece of wood at the back of a fire. Better known in the US as a 'backlog', the name of the 'backjunk' comes from the pronunciation of 'chunk' as 'junk' *CANADA, 1958*

back light *noun* the rear window of a car *US, 1959*

back line *noun* the wall of amplifiers and speakers behind a rock band in concert *US, 1985*

backline *verb* in casino blackjack, to place a bet in another player's square *US, 1996*

backlip *noun* impertinence, talking back *US, 1959*

back-me-up *noun* a friend who can be counted on for support in a confrontation *US, 1984*

back number *noun* a person who is hopelessly out of date *US, 1960*

back of beyond *noun* a remote area *AUSTRALIA, 1879*

back of Bourke *noun* a remote area. Bourke is a county centre in central New South Wales *AUSTRALIA, 1896*

back of the yards *noun* a neighbourhood in Chicago around and behind the now defunct Union Stockyards *US, 1982*

back-o-wall *noun* any slum. Originally applied to the slums of west Kingston, Jamaica *JAMAICA, 1978*

back pack *noun* a gang insignia tattooed on a gang member's back *US, 1992*

back passage *noun* the rectum. Euphemistic *UK, 1960*

back-pasture hauler *noun* in trucking, a driver who prefers back roads and smaller motorways *US, 1971*

back porch *noun* a late position in a hand of poker *US, 1996*

back-porch nigger *noun* an obsequious, fawning black person *US, 1971*

back rack *noun* in pinball, the part of the machine that rises as a panel at the front of the machine. Conventionally known as a 'lightbox' *US, 1977*

backra fire *noun* electricity *GUYANA, 1996*

backra-Johnny *noun* a poor white person *BARBADOS, 1996*

backroom boy *noun* a scientific technician, especially if engaged in research that may be secret. Usually used in the plural *UK, 1943*

backroom job *noun* a tattoo on a part of the body that is usually clothed *US, 1997*

back row *noun* a prison cell used for solitary confinement *US, 1984*

backs *noun* money, especially counterfeit money. Probably an abbreviation of GREENBACK *US, 1945*

back-sack-and-crack-wax *noun* a male depilatory treatment. 'Sack' is sometimes spelt, more correctly, 'sac', from scrotal sac, and 'n' is occasionally used for 'and' *UK, 2003*

back-sass *noun* impudent talking back to an elder *US, 1968*

back-sass *verb* to talk back impudently *US, 1950*

back-scratch *verb* to remove from a tank enemy soldiers who have climbed onto it, usually by directing light-weapon fire onto the tank *US, 1991*

back-scuttle *verb* to play the active role in sex, anal or vaginal, from behind *US, 1885*

back seat *noun* in poker, any of the positions farther from the dealer than the third player to his left *US, 1973.* ► **in the back seat** ignored, forgotten. Building on the CAR (clique) metaphor *US, 1998.* ► **take a back seat** to be or become less important than someone or something else *US, 1902*

backshow *noun* in gambling on broadcast racing, any betting before the current show price *UK, 2001*

backside *noun* ► **while your backside points to the ground** while you are alive *AUSTRALIA, 1992*

backside! used for expressing strong scepticism *AUSTRALIA, 1971*

backside furrit; backside forward *adverb* thoroughly, inside out *UK: SCOTLAND, 1988*

back-slack *verb* to talk back *NEW ZEALAND, 1929*

backslap *noun* a celebratory event of mutual congratulation. From conventional 'backslapping' *AUSTRALIA, 2002*

backslide *noun* in trucking, a return trip *US, 1976*

backspace and overstrike! in computing, used for expressing alarm about a mistake that has just been made *US, 1991*

back stairs *noun* the anus and rectum considered as a sexual passage. Euphemistic or humorous simile for 'the back way up' *UK, 2001*

backstop *noun* 1 in baseball, the catcher *US, 1887*. 2 by extension, a person who provides a second line of defence in a venture *AUSTRALIA, 1944*

backstop *verb* to act as a backstop *AUSTRALIA, 1955*

backstory *noun* history, previous experience. Adopted into wider usage from screen-acting jargon where it is used to describe what has happened before the story starts *UK, 2000*

backs to the wall! used as a humorous catchphrase to acknowledge the presence of a male homosexual. Homophobic; suggesting a fear of anal sex/rape *UK, 2003*

backstreet boy *noun* a young man dressed in the trendiest of clothes with the trendiest of haircuts. Not a compliment; an allusion to a band of the late 1990s that was thought to value style to the exclusion of substance *US, 2001*

backstroke *noun* in trucking, a return trip *US, 1976*

back-talk *noun* insolent answering back *AUSTRALIA, 1950*

back-talk *verb* to answer back with impudence *UK, 1887*

back teeth *noun* ▶ **to the back teeth** to capacity; totally; completely *AUSTRALIA, 1933*

back teeth are floating used for describing an extreme need to urinate *US, 1923*

back the card to bet on every race at a meeting *AUSTRALIA, 1971*

back time *noun* 1 in the Vietnam war, rear-area or non-combat duty *US, 1991*. 2 the portion of a prison sentence not served at the time of parole, which must be served if parole is violated *US, 1992*. 3 all time spent incarcerated before sentencing *US, 1992*

back to *preposition* used in the names of reunion parties *AUSTRALIA, 1925*

back-to-back *noun* heroin then crack used in sequence *US, 1994*

back-to-back *adjective* consecutive. Usually used in a sports context. If there is a third consecutive event, the term is simply expanded to 'back-to-back-to-back' *US, 1952*

back to hacking used as a farewell, by computer enthusiast to computer enthusiast *US, 1983*

back to the drawing board! used after the failure of an endeavour *US, 1965*

back to the salt mines!; back to the mines! back to work! An ironic reference to hard labour in the Siberian salt mines *US, 1933*

back track *verb* when injecting a drug, to draw blood up into the syringe to mix with the drug that is being injected *US, 1992*

back-up *noun* 1 a person supporting another in a fight *AUSTRALIA, 1975*. 2 a second helping of food *AUSTRALIA, 1929*. 3 serial sex between one person and many others, usually consensual *AUSTRALIA, 1965*. 4 the path from the death cell to the death chamber in prison *US, 1992*

backups *noun* extremely bright lights on the rear of a car used to blind would-be kidnappers or terrorists *US, 1992*

backward in coming forward *adjective* reluctant to do something, modest, shy. More often phrased as 'not backward in coming forward' *UK, 1830*

backwards *noun* any central nervous system depressant *US, 1966*

back-warmer *noun* a female motorcyle passenger. Biker (motorcycle) usage *US, 2002*

backwash *noun* answering back in an insolent manner *AUSTRALIA, 1969*

backwashing *noun* after injecting a drug, the drawing of blood back into the syringe, with the intention of collecting any drug residue, and reinjecting the resultant mix *UK, 2003*

backwater *noun* in trucking, back roads or small motorways *US, 1976*

backwhack *noun* the back-slash key (\\) on a computer keyboard *US, 1991*

back wheel *noun* in horse racing, the second bet in a two-part bet *US, 1994*

back wheels *noun* the testicles *UK, 1998*

backyard *noun* 1 the buttocks *US, 1972*. 2 the anus *US, 1967*. 3 in a circus, the performers as a group distinguished from the administrative and support staff *US, 1960*. 4 the road visible behind you *US, 1976*

backyard butchery *noun* an amateur's modification of a surfboard, obviating the design features of the manufacturer *AUSTRALIA, 2003*

backyarder *noun* a surfboard built by or modified by an amateur *AUSTRALIA, 2004*

bacon *noun* 1 the police; a police officer. From PIG (a policeman). During the late 1960s and early 70s, a favoured chant of the radical left youth movement in the US was 'Today's pig, tomorrow's bacon!' *US, 1974*. 2 money *US, 1946*. 3 the buttocks *BAHAMAS, 1982*. ▶ **bring home the bacon** to succeed as a wage earner, supporting one's family; to achieve success; to succeed in a given undertaking. Generally thought to echo the ancient tradition in Dunmow, England, of presenting a flitch of bacon to a happily married couple but originates in the US country-fair 'sport' of catching a greased pig. The phrase was popularised, if not invented, by the mother of Joe Gans, a black lightweight boxer *US, 1909*. ▶ **save someone's bacon** to rescue someone financially *UK, 1654*

bacon and eggs *noun* 1 the legs. Rhyming slang *AUSTRALIA, 1942*. 2 a black person who is partly or completely albino *TRINIDAD AND TOBAGO, 2003*

bacon assegai *noun* the penis and testicles *UK, 1983*

bacon bits *noun* the breasts. Rhyming slang for TIT(S) *UK, 2003*

bacon bonce *noun* 1 a slow-witted person *UK, 1958*. 2 a sex offender. Rhyming slang for NONCE *UK, 1996*. 3 a bald or balding man *UK, 1984*

bacon getter *noun* a handgun, especially a single-action revolver *US, 1957*

bacon rashers *noun* the vagina *UK, 2001*

bad *noun* 1 fault *US, 1999*. 2 crack cocaine *US, 1994*. ▶ **get in bad with** to get in trouble or disfavour with someone or some agency of authority *UK, 1928*

bad *adjective* 1 good; tough *US, 1897*. 2 in computing, broken as designed *US, 1991*

bad ass *noun* a tough, fearless person *US, 1956*

bad-ass *adjective* excellent; worthy of respect, tough. Originally black usage but now more widely known *US, 1955*

Bad-Ass Billy *nickname* Brigadeer General William R. Bond of the 199th Light Infantry Brigade, killed by a sniper's bullet about 70 miles northeast of Saigon on 1st April 1980 *US, 1999*

bad-bad *adjective* very bad *BAHAMAS, 1982*

bad beat *noun* in poker, a disappointing loss, either with a good hand or a big bet *US, 1982*

bad belly *noun* an upset stomach *BAHAMAS, 1982*

bad boy *noun* 1 something that is impressive *US, 1974*. 2 a rascal, a misfit *US, 1948*. 3 a violent, tough young criminal *BARBADOS, 1976*

bad bundle *noun* inferior-quality heroin *US, 1971*

bad butch *noun* an aggressive, 'mannish' lesbian *US, 1967*

bad buzz *noun* an unpleasant event *CANADA, 1993*

bad cop *noun* in a pair of police, the partner who plays the aggressive and hard-nosed role during an interrogation *US, 1991*

badda bing; bada-bing; ba-da-bing used as an embellishing intensifier. The variations are nearly endless *US, 1972*

bad dad *noun* a person whose opinion of his own toughness exceeds the rest of the world's estimation *US, 1973*

baddap! *verb* to be shot. Echoic of gun fire *UK, 1994*

badden *verb* to become intoxicated on drugs or alcohol *TRINIDAD AND TOBAGO, 2003*

baddest *adjective* toughest; most admired. The unconventional superlative of 'bad' in the 'bad-as-good' sense of the word *US, 1938*

baddie *noun* 1 a villain, especially in works of fiction. A childish epithet for a staple character of popular mass-entertainment, also used 'ironically' in law-enforcement. Also variant 'baddy' *US, 1937*. 2 an unwell feeling *UK: SCOTLAND, 1988*. 3 a slight wound, such as a graze or cut. Nursery and childish usage *UK, 1993*

bad dog *noun* an unpaid debt *AUSTRALIA, 1953*

bad eye *noun* a spell or curse caused by looking with envy or insincere goodwill *TRINIDAD AND TOBAGO, 1972*

badeye *verb* to glare, to stare with menace *US, 1990*

bad food *noun* food or drink made with ingredients believed to instill sexual fidelity or attraction *BARBADOS, 1996*

badge *noun* 1 a police officer *US, 1925*. 2 a prison guard *US, 1992*. 3 a small amount of a drug relative to the amount paid *US, 1971*

badge *verb* to show a police badge, especially as part of a psychological ploy to elicit information *US, 1970*

badge bandit *noun* a police officer, especially a motorcycle police officer *US, 1960*

badger *noun* in horse racing, an inexpensive horse that qualifies its owner for race track privileges *US, 1976*

badger game *noun* a swindle in which a prostitute lures a customer or victim to a room where he is robbed by a confederate of the prostitute, often posing to be her husband *US, 1909*

badger-gassing *noun* an act or instance of farting, or its malodorous after-effect. After a controversial means of exterminating badgers *UK, 2003*

badger scratching *noun* the act of fondling a woman's vagina *UK, 2002*

badger's nadgers *noun* anything considered to be the finest, the most excellent, the best. Formed on NADGERS (the testicles), this is further variation on the DOG'S BOLLOCKS and MUTT'S NUTS theme; usage noted, most significantly, on a greeting card being sold by a high street chain, January 2004 *UK, 2004*

bad go *noun* a small amount of a drug relative to the price paid *US, 1971*

bad guy *noun* a criminal. Originally children's vocabulary from watching Western films. Perhaps orginating in the mid-1960s *US, 1977*

bad hair day *noun* a day on which your hair is especially unruly; hence, a day on which nothing goes to plan *US, 1991*

bad hat *noun* 1 someone who can be counted on to misbehave *US, 1914*. 2 a pimp *US, 1997*

bad head *noun* a violent, tough young criminal *BELIZE, 1996*

bad idea jeans *noun* the notional clothing worn by someone who has displayed an utter lack of common sense. From a skit on *Saturday Night Live US, 1994*

bad John *noun* any man who is violence-prone. An allusion to John 'Bad John' Archer, a criminal who figured prominently in early C20 life *TRINIDAD AND TOBAGO, 1935*

bad looker *noun* an ugly person. Used with a negative *AUSTRALIA, 1959*

badly *adverb* wonderfully, excellently; very *UK, 2004*

badly packed kebab *noun* the vagina. A visual similarity to the dish eaten late at night, when half-drunk *UK, 2002*

badmarsh *adjective* of bad character, disreputable. From Hindustani *badmásh* (a bad character or disreputable person) *UK, 2006*

bad medicine *noun* a person or thing that promises trouble. An imitation of the speech of native American Indians *US, 1920*

bad mind *noun* malice *TRINIDAD AND TOBAGO, 1979*

bad motherfucker *noun* a fearless, tough person *US, 1972*

bad mouth *noun* a curse, a put-down *US, 1960*

badmouth *verb* to insult someone, to disparage someone *US, 1941*

badness *noun* something that is very good *US, 1986*

bad news *noun* 1 a person who is better avoided *UK, 1946*. 2 something, abstract or actual, that is unpleasant or contemptible *US, 1917*. 3 the M-48 'Patton' tank, designed for combat in Europe against Soviet tanks, then the mainstay of the US Army and Marines in Vietnam *US, 1991*. 4 in drag racing, a car that performs very well *US, 1965*

bad nigger *noun* a tough, fearless, respect-commanding black person. A term of praise *US, 1965*

bad-o *adjective* excellent *US, 1991*

badonkadonk *noun* large, shapely buttocks. From the Comedy Central television programme *Crankyankers US, 2004*

bad on you! shame on you! Recorded by Jan Trent in 1997 *FIJI, 1997*

bad paper *noun* 1 a discharge from the military other than an honourable discharge, such as the UD (undesirable discharge) or resignations for the good of the service *US, 1971*. 2 counterfeit money or securities *US, 1981*

bad-pay *adjective* slow in paying a debt or obligation *GRENADA, 1976*

bad penny *noun* an unreliable or untrustworthy person; someone of little or no worth. A figurative sense from debased coinage; orginally 'bad ha'penny' before inflation *UK, 1937*

bad rack *noun* at a casino, a list of customers who are poor credit risks *US, 1974*

bad rock *noun* cocaine; crack cocaine *UK, 2003*

bads *noun* the depression following the use of hallucinogens or amphetamines *US, 1970*

bad scene *noun* an unpleasant situation; a depressing experience *US, 1966*

bad scran *noun* bad luck *IRELAND, 1989*

bad seed *noun* 1 peyote; heroin *US, 1969*. 2 mescaline, the hallucinogenic alkaloid of peyote *US, 2001*. 3 marijuana *UK, 1998*

bad shit *noun* high quality drugs, especially marijuana *1996*

bad sick *noun* any sexually transmitted infection *ANTIGUA AND BARBUDA, 1996*

bad-talk *verb* to disparage someone or something *BAHAMAS, 1982*

bad thing *noun* an inherently bad idea. From *1066 and All That,* the history parody in which Sellar and Yeatman created the 'bad thing' device: 'Indeed, he had begun badly as a Bad Prince, having attempted to answer the Irish Question by pulling the beards of the aged Irish chiefs, which was a Bad Thing and the wrong answer' *US, 1931*

bad time *noun* 1 time served in prison that does not count towards the overall sentence; time served in a military stockade that does not count towards the overall period of service *US, 1968*. 2 a jail or prison sentence for a petty, avoidable offence *US, 1977*. 3 the bleed period of the menstrual cycle *US, 1954*

bad trip *noun* an unpleasant, frightening or unnerving experience with LSD *US, 1966*

bad trot *noun* a losing streak; a period of heavy or sustained losses *AUSTRALIA, 1936*

bafan *noun* a clumsy person. From 'baff-hand' (a cripple) *JAMAICA, 1956*

baff *verb* to vomit *US, 1968*

bafflegab *noun* verbose language that is difficult to penetrate and impossible to understand. The term, by all accounts, was coined by Milton A. Smith of the United States Chamber of Commerce. Smith defined the term as 'Multiloquence characterized by consummate interfusion of circumlocution or periphrasis, inscrutability, incognizability, and other familiar manifestations of abstruse expatiation commonly utilized for promulgations implementing procrustean determinations by governmental bodies' *US, 1952*

bag *noun* 1 an interest *US, 1964*. 2 a way of doing things *US, 1962*. 3 an unattractive young woman *AUSTRALIA, 1965*. 4 a police uniform *US, 1944*. 5 duty as a uniformed police officer *US, 1973*. 6 a breathalyser.

From 'breathalyser bag' *UK, 1967*. **7** the scrotum *US, 1938*. **8** a sexually promiscuous woman or a prostitute *US, 1893*. **9** a condom *US, 1922*. **10** a diaphragm *US, 1964*. **11** a collection raised in a single effort. Figurative application of the game-bag in which hunters gather their kill *UK, 1900*. **12** a large score made by a player *AUSTRALIA, 1986*. **13** a package of drugs *US, 1952*. **14** a small paper packet or plastic bag containing heroin; thus a standardised measure of heroin, either by cost or volume. Also variant 'bagel' *US, 1952*. **15** heroin. Adopted by drug-users from the sense of 'bag' meaning 'an interest or way of doing things' *UK, 2001*. **16** a parachute. Originally Royal Air Force usage, then the army also *UK, 1943*. **17** a fuel tank on an aeroplane *US, 1991*. **18** a member of a college fraternity. An abbreviation of BAGGER, itself an abbreviation of FRATTY BAGGER *US, 1998*. **19** bed *US, 1969*. ▶ **bag of snakes** a business acquisition full of bad surprises *US, 1991*. ▶ **get a bag!** learn how to catch! In cricket used as a derisive retort to a fielder who drops an easy catch *AUSTRALIA, 1986*. ▶ **in the bag 1** drunk *US, 1940*. **2** as good as done *US, 1921*. **3** corrupted, bribed, beholden to someone else *US, 1926*. **4** (of a horse) not being run on its merits; being run to lose; (of a jockey) not riding to win. Literally, the money that has been bet on the horse will stay in the bookmaker's bag *AUSTRALIA, 1903*. ▶ **on someone's bag** in golf, working as a caddie *US, 2000*. ▶ **out of the bag** unexpectedly good *AUSTRALIA, 1954*

bag *verb* **1** to arrest someone *UK, 1824*. **2** to catch, capture or obtain something for yourself *US, 1861*. **3** to shoot down a plane. A hunting allusion in Royal Air Force use *UK, 1943*. **4** in sport, to score a specified number of goals or points *AUSTRALIA, 2000*. **5** to disregard, dismiss or stop something. Figurative use of throwing rubbish in a rubbish bag *US, 1988*. **6** to cancel a social engagement. The *Dictionary of American Regional English* lists a related meaning: 'to feign illness in order to avoid one's responsibilities' from 1967 *CANADA, 2002*. **7** to abandon or leave a place or thing *US, 1962*. **8** to criticise or denigrate someone or something *AUSTRALIA, 1969*. **9** to dismiss from employment. A variation of SACK *UK: SCOTLAND, 1988*. **10** to bribe someone; to arrange an outcome *US, 1948*. **11** to impregnate *US, 1949*. **12** to hang in loose folds. Especially applied to trousers out of shape at the knees *UK, 1824*. **13** to use a resuscitation bag. Medical use *UK, 1980*. **14** to sleep, to doze *US, 1994*. **15** to leave. Hawaiian youth usage *US, 1981*. ▶ **bag and tag 1** to place a dead soldier in a body bag and identify the soldier with a tag on the outside of the body bag *US, 1991*. **2** (used of a prison guard) to count and account for prisoners during scheduled count times *US, 2002*. **3** to apprehend someone and take them into police custody *AUSTRALIA, 2001*. ▶ **bag ass** to leave, especially in a hurry *US, 1972*. ▶ **bag beaver** to have sex with a woman. Combining hunting and sexual metaphors *US, 1994*. ▶ **bag your head** to stop talking *US, 1962*

-bag *suffix* when in combination with an undesirable thing, used to label a person who epitomises the unpleasant quality. Michael Munro in *The Patter, Another Blast* (1988) offers the examples 'crap-bag' (a coward), GROTBAG (a dirty person) and 'stum-bag' (an idiot) *UK, 1988*

bagaga; bagadga *noun* the penis. Probably from Italian '*bagagli*' (luggage) *US, 1963*

bag and baggage used for conveying to a prisoner that he is to be released from jail *US, 1977*

bag biter *noun* in computing, something or someone that does not work well *US, 1981*

bag boy *noun* a bookmaker *AUSTRALIA, 1945*

bag case *noun* a fatally injured motorist, especially one with gruesome injuries *US, 1962*

bag-chaser *noun* a drug user who is obsessed with getting drugs *US, 1989*

bag drag *noun* in Antarctica, the act of dragging your luggage for a pre-flight weigh-in *ANTARCTICA, 1996*

bagel *noun* **1** a Jewish person. Usually playful rather than derogatory *US, 1955*. **2** a tyre *US, 1977*. **3** a fool *UK, 1996*

bagel *verb* in a sporting event, to defeat your opponent without letting your opponent score. It is claimed that the usage was coined by tennis player Eddie Dibbs and popularised by tennis writer and broadcaster Bud Collins *US, 1976*

bagel bumper *noun* a lesbian. Based on a visual similarity between the vagina and a bagel *UK, 2003*

bagel face *noun* a Jewish person. Derogatory *US, 1979*

bag-follower *noun* an attractive woman who carries packets of heroin for a heroin dealer while bestowing status upon him with her good looks *US, 1978*

bag full of shit *noun* an utterly contemptible person *UK, 1998*

bagful of busted arseholes *noun* the epitome of ugliness or feeling poorly *NEW ZEALAND, 1998*

baggage *noun* **1** a boyfriend, agent or other male who accompanies a female pornography performer to the set. Not flattering *US, 1995*. **2** a non-playing observer of a card or dice game *US, 1950*

baggage smasher *noun* a baggage handler *US, 1968*

bagged *adjective* **1** fixed, corrupted, bribed *US, 1942*. **2** drunk *US, 1953*

bagger *noun* **1** a poker player who does not bet aggressively when holding a good hand until late in the hand *US, 1966*. **2** a boy who wears his trousers so low that his boxer shorts hang out above his belt line *US, 1986*. **3** someone who talks, dresses and projects an East Coast, prep-school persona; a member of a college fraternity *US, 1980*. **4** someone who plays footbag *US, 1997*

baggers *noun* baggy shorts or swimming trunks *AUSTRALIA, 1963*

baggie *noun* **1** a plastic bag filled with a variable amount of loose marijuana. From the trademarked name of a brand of plastic sandwich bags *US, 1980*. **2** a condom *US, 1971*

baggies *noun* loose trousers or shorts, especially loose-fitting shorts or swimming trunks popularised by surfers. Trousers have been called BAGS on and off since the mid-C19; 'baggies' derives from the baggy fit *US, 1963*

bagging *noun* denigration *AUSTRALIA, 1986*

bag guy *noun* a toy balloon vendor *US, 1949*

baggy *adjective* a loose fashion briefly popular with ravers; the baggy trouser style continued to be popular with UK skateboarders *UK, 1993*

baggy arse *noun* an inexperienced, naive prison guard *AUSTRALIA, 1987*

baggy-arse; baggy-arsed *adjective* (of a soldier) substandard, second-rate, shoddy *AUSTRALIA, 1953*

baggy green cap *noun* the cap worn by Australian test cricketers. Also simply the 'baggy green', and hence, 'to wear the baggy green' – meaning 'to represent Australia in test cricket' *AUSTRALIA, 1995*

Baghdad Betty *nickname* during the US war against Iraq in 1991, a female Iraqi disc jockey who broadcast propaganda to US troops *US, 1991*

Baghdad Boys *noun* during the Gulf war, reporters from the Cable News Network *US, 1991*

baghead *noun* a habitual cocaine or heroin user. From BAG (drugs) combined with HEAD (a user) *UK, 1996*

bag job *noun* **1** a cheating scheme involving a casino employee as a confederate *US, 1950*. **2** a burglary, especially when committed by law enforcement or intelligence agents looking for information *US, 1971*

bag lady *noun* **1** a destitute woman who wanders the streets with her possessions in shopping bags *US, 1972*. **2** a condom *UK, 1998*

bagman *noun* **1** a person who collects, makes or holds illegal payments *US, 1935*. **2** a bookmaker *AUSTRALIA, 1956*. **3** a bookmaker's clerk *AUSTRALIA, 1973*. **4** in the circus or carnival, a person who makes change for customers, often cheating them *US, 1980*. **5** a member of a shoplifting team who carries away the stolen goods *AUSTRALIA, 1975*. **6** a drug dealer; a person in possession of drugs *US, 1970*. **7** an itinerant man carrying his possessions in a bag; a swagman *AUSTRALIA, 1866*

Bagman's Gazette *noun* an imaginary publication that is cited as a source of rumours *AUSTRALIA, 1959*

Bagmen's Union *noun* a fictitious union to which itinerant travellers belonged during the Depression *AUSTRALIA, 1954*

bag of arse *noun* anything inferior *UK, 2002*

bag of bones *noun* **1** a skinny person or animal *AUSTRALIA, 1903*. **2** a 'bush pilot' aeroplane *CANADA, 1984*

bag of coke *noun* a man. Rhyming slang for a **BLOKE**; variation of BUSHEL OF COKE *AUSTRALIA, 1976*

bag off *verb* to form an intitial liaison with someone sexually attractive, especially with a view to greater intimacy *UK, 2002*

bag of flour *noun* a bathroom shower. Rhyming slang *UK, 1980*

bag of fruit *noun* a suit. Rhyming slang *AUSTRALIA, 1924*

bag of nails *noun* a state of confusion *AUSTRALIA, 1942*

bag of shit *noun* **1** a despicable person *AUSTRALIA, 1970*. **2** anything of poor quality *UK, 1995*

bag of shit tied up with string *noun* a clumsy, shapeless or scruffy person. Probably military in origin; usually in phrases such as 'looks like a bag of shit tied up with string' *UK, 1984*

bag of snakes *noun* a lively young woman *AUSTRALIA, 1984*

bag of tricks *noun* ▷*see:* BOX OF TRICKS

bag of yeast *noun* a priest. Rhyming slang *AUSTRALIA, 1971*

bag on; bag *verb* to insult someone in a competitive, quasi-friendly spirit *US, 1993*

bag-o-wire *noun* an informer or betrayer *JAMAICA, 1982*

bagpipe *verb* to stimulate the penis to orgasm under the armpit of a lover. Homosexual use *UK, 1904*

bags *noun* **1** a great amount *UK, 1931*. **2** loose fitting trousers. There have been 'bum-bags', 1860, 'howling bags' (with a loud pattern), 1850–90, and 'go-to-meeting bags' (best clothes), 1870–1910. 'Oxford bags', a very wide-legged cut, were introduced in the early 1920s and are still known *UK, 1853*. **3** a mess; a botched enterprise *IRELAND, 2004*. ▶ **make a bags of** make a mess of something *IRELAND, 1998*

bags *verb* to claim rights to something; to reserve something *AUSTRALIA, 1944*

bags!; bagsy!; bagsey! used to claim possession or authority. Mainly juvenile; may be structured as a verb *UK, 1897*

bag-shanty *noun* a brothel. Royal Navy use; a combination of BAG (a promiscuous woman) and conventional 'shanty' (a hut) *UK, 1890*

bagsing *noun* the act of claiming priority rights to something; reserving something *AUSTRALIA, 2003*

bagswinger *noun* a bookmaker's clerk *AUSTRALIA, 1977*

bag up *verb* **1** to put a condom on a penis. Also variant 'bag it up' *UK, 2002*. **2** to divide a powdered drug into bags preparatory to selling it *US, 1989*. **3** of a fizzy drink, to fill the stomach with gas *UK: SCOTLAND, 1988*. **4** to laugh *US, 1989*

Bahama ham *noun* the conch *BAHAMAS, 1982*

Bahama hooter *noun* a marijuana cigarette *US, 1992*

bahookie *noun* the buttocks; the anus *UK, 1985*

bail *verb* **1** to leave a relationship or situation *US, 1977*. **2** to fall while skateboarding *US, 1984*. **3** in mountain biking, to jump off a bicycle in order to avoid an accident *US, 1996*. **4** in foot-propelled scootering, to abandon a scooter in mid-jump *UK, 2000*. **5** to land inelegantly or badly when completing a snowboarding jump *US, 1995*

bail bandit *noun* a person who commits a crime while out on bail *UK, 2002*

bailing-wire artist *noun* on the railways, a creative but incompetent mechanic *US, 1977*

bail out *verb* **1** to jump off a surfboard when you are about to be knocked off the board by a wave *US, 1964*. **2** in skateboarding, to fall badly *UK, 2003*

bail up *verb* **1** to hold someone up; to rob someone by holding up. In common use by bushrangers during the colonial period. Transferred sense from 'bail up' (to place a dairy cow into a bail for milking), from 'bail' (a frame for securing a cow's head). It could also be used intransitively to mean 'to submit to being held up and robbed'. Now only used in historical novels *AUSTRALIA, 1838*. **2** to

hold someone at bay; to corner someone *AUSTRALIA, 1841*. **3** to stop someone for a conversation *AUSTRALIA, 1998*

bail up! stand and deliver! *AUSTRALIA, 1842*

bait *noun* **1** in poker, a small bet that is hoped will lure another player into a larger bet *US, 1967*. **2** in shuffleboard, a shot made to entice the opponent to try to go after the disc *US, 1967*. **3** a person who attracts a specified type or category of attention *US, 1942*. **4** a small meal *US, 1958*. **5** in prison, credit, especially on the purchase of drink, drugs or tobacco *UK, 1996*

bait *verb* in gin, to discard a card in a manner that is designed to lure a desired card from an opponent *US, 1971*. ▶ **bait the hole** in American football, to feign a running play in order to draw defenders towards the line and block them there *US, 1984*

bait can *noun* a worker's lunch box *US, 1985*

bait money *noun* cash with pre-recorded serial numbers set aside by a bank to be included in money given to a robber *US, 1992*

Baja bug *noun* a Volkswagen Beetle modified for surfer use. 'Baja' is a reference to Baja California, the Mexican state immediately south of California *US, 1991*

bake *noun* **1** a verbal assault, a roasting *AUSTRALIA, 1975*. **2** a complete and hopeless outcast. An abbreviation of Bakersfield, a city at the south end of California's San Joaquin Valley, 'the other side of nowhere' to the surfers who use this term *US, 1991*. **3** illegal drugs manufactured in an illegal laboratory *NEW ZEALAND, 1986*

bake *verb* to manufacture illegal drugs in a laboratory *NEW ZEALAND, 1986*. ▶ **bake biscuits** to record and produce a phonograph record *US, 1959*

baked *adjective* drug-intoxicated, especially by marijuana *US, 1978*

baked-bean *noun* a sexual interlude. Rhyming slang for SCENE *UK, 2000*

baked beans *noun* jeans. Prisoners' rhyming slang *UK, 2001*

baked potato *noun* a drug-user who watches television while intoxicated. A play on COUCH POTATO (a habitual idler/television watcher) formed on BAKED (intoxicated) *US, 1996*

baked wind pills *noun* beans *CANADA, 1998*

baker *noun* **1** the electric chair *US, 1950*. **2** a marijuana smoker *US, 1997*. **3** a grade of 'B' in academic work *US, 1968*

Baker flying *adjective* experiencing the bleed period of the menstrual cycle. In the navy, a red Quartermaster B (Baker in the phonetic alphabet) flag is flown to signify 'Danger' and 'Keep out', providing several theories for application to menstruation *US, 1960*

Bakerloo *noun* in cricket, a batsman who is playing down the wrong line. A jocular reference to the Bakerloo line on London's underground system *UK, 2003*

baker's fog *noun* in the Maritime Provinces, regular sliced white bread *CANADA, 1998*

bakey; bakie *noun* a baked potato *UK, 1943*

bakkie *noun* a utility vehicle used in South Africa *SOUTH AFRICA, 2000*

baksis *noun* a small extra added to a purchase by a vendor in the hope of encouraging return business *GUYANA, 1996*

balance *verb* ▶ **balance the books** in an illegal betting operation, to place bets with other operations when betting is too heavy on one proposition *US, 1979*

Balconville *nickname* the Point St Charles area of Montreal. One of two nicknames for this neighborhood (the other is 'The Pointe') because most dwellings have a balcony on which people sit a lot. Bilingual and harmonious, its mixture of French and English is noted in the word itself, which is partly from each language. It is the title of a 1980 play by David Fennario *CANADA, 1980*

balcony *noun* the female breasts *US, 1964*

bald head *noun* to a Rastafarian, any non-Rastafarian *JAMAICA, 1976*

bald-headed *adjective* (used of a rotary bit in oil drilling) worn out *US, 1954*

bald-headed mouse *noun* the penis *UK, 2003*

bald-headed prairie *noun* treeless and shrubless plains *CANADA, 2002*

baldheaded row *noun* the front row of a burlesque or strip show *US,* *1887*

bald-tyre bandit *noun* a police officer detailed to traffic duty *UK, 1977*

Baldwin *noun* a handsome man. From the family of handsome actor brothers *US, 1995*

baldy *noun* **1** a worn tyre; in the US, especially in hot rodding and drag racing *US, 1965*. **2** a Hereford cow. This breed of cattle has a white face or head *AUSTRALIA, 1887*. **3** the white-headed pigeon, endemic to Australia *AUSTRALIA, 1969*. **4** an artist's model denuded of pubic hair *UK, 1984*

baldy *adjective* (of a tyre) with a worn tread *AUSTRALIA, 1979*

baldy! refuse! A children's catchword *NEW ZEALAND, 1942*

baldy lad *noun* the penis *UK, 2001*

bale *noun* **1** marijuana compressed into a large bale similar to a bale of hay *US, 1971*. **2** any quantity of marijuana *US, 2001*

bale *verb* ▶ **bale the kale** to win a lot of money gambling. From KALE (money) *US, 1962*

bale of hay *noun* a male homosexual. Rhyming slang for GAY *UK, 2003*

bale of straw *noun* a blonde white woman *US, 1928*

Bali belly *noun* any gastro-intestinal infection obtained when holidaying in Bali, Indonesia or other areas of Southeast Asia *AUSTRALIA, 1984*

balk *verb* **1** to cover up *AUSTRALIA, 1975*. **2** in poker, to hesitate when it is your turn to bet in the hope of seeing whether players who follow you are prepared to call the bet *US, 1996*

ball *noun* **1** a thoroughly good time *US, 1932*. **2** an act of sexual intercourse *US, 1970*. **3** a single scoop of ice-cream *US, 1960*. **4** crack cocaine *US, 1994*. **5** black-tar heroin *UK, 2002*. **6** one dollar. Mainly prison slang *US, 1895*. ▶ **on the ball** alert to any opportunity *UK, 1967*. ▶ **out on a ball; be riding a ball** (used of a customer trading in a car) believing that your old car is worth more than it is *US, 1980*. ▶ **that's the way the ball bounces** that's how things turn out *US, 1952*. ▶ **the ball is in your court** it is your turn; it is your decision. A variation of the conventional phrase 'the ball is with you' *UK, 1963*

ball *verb* **1** to have sex *US, 1952*. **2** to fondle a man's penis *US, 1968*. **3** to thoroughly enjoy yourself *US, 1942*. **4** to go or take something somewhere very quickly *US, 1939*. **5** to insert amphetamine or methamphetamine in the vagina before sexual intercourse *US, 1971*. **6** to secrete and smuggle cocaine in the vagina *UK, 2002*. ▶ **ball the jack** to travel very quickly *US, 1913*

-ball *suffix* combines with an unpleasant substance to create a contemptible person *UK, 1970*

balla *noun* a man with a lot of money *US, 1999*

ballad *noun* a love letter *US, 1960*

ballahoo and all the crew *noun* everybody *TRINIDAD AND TOBAGO, 1996*

ball and chain *noun* a man's wife *US, 1921*

ballast scorcher *noun* a fast-riding railway engineer *US, 1946*

ballbag *noun* **1** the scrotum *AUSTRALIA, 1985*. **2** an athletic supporter *US, 1968*

ball blinder *noun* a condom. An image of something that debilitates BALLS (the testicles) *UK, 1998*

ballbreaker *noun* **1** a difficult task, a boring situation; any circumstance that saps your spirit. The prosaic etymology leads to any task that strains the testicles; more likely that 'balls' represent power or spirit in this context *US, 1942*. **2** a powerful, assertive woman; someone who demands or actively exacts a difficult requirement. Taking 'balls' to mean 'power and spirit', this extends from the previous sense *US, 1944*

ball-busting *adjective* harassing, dominating, controlling *US, 1954*

ball-cutter *noun* a person who belittles and demeans others *US, 1962*

baller *noun* **1** a drug dealer, usually of crack cocaine *US, 2001*. **2** an attractive male *US, 2002*. **3** a member of a youth gang who is prospering financially *US, 1995*

ballet master *noun* on the railways, the supervisor of track crews. An extension of the track worker as a GANDY DANCER *US, 1977*

balley *noun* a free show outside a carnival attraction, intended to create interest in paying to see the act inside *US, 1985*

ballgame *noun* **1** a state of affairs, especially if challenging. Sporting imagery *US, 1930*. **2** during the Vietnam war, an exhange of fire or firefight with the enemy *US, 1991*. ▶ **a whole new ballgame** a completely different set of circumstances *US, 1968*

ballhead *noun* a white New Zealander *NEW ZEALAND, 1989*

ball hop *noun* a deliberate fabrication, an unsupported rumour. Gaelic *IRELAND, 2001*

ballhuggers *noun* **1** very tight trousers. Hawaiian youth usage *US, 1982*. **2** a pair of men's close-fitting and revealing nylon swimming trunks *AUSTRALIA, 2003*

ballie *noun* an old man; any old person, especially your parent. From the Afrikaans *ou bal SOUTH AFRICA, 2004*

ball in hand *noun* in pool, the right to shoot from anywhere behind the headstring after another player has hit the cue ball into a pocket *UK, 1807*

ballistic *adjective* extremely angry; out of control. Originally applied to an out-of-control missile *US, 1985*

ballistics *noun* graphic, aggressive rap lyrics *US, 1991*

ballocky; bollocky; bollicky *adjective* naked. Often combined with 'naked', compare with BOLLOCK NAKED and STARK BOLLOCK NAKED *UK, 1961*

ball of chalk *noun* a walk. Rhyming slang, sometimes condensed to a simple 'ball' *UK, 1936*

ball-off *noun* an act of male masturbation *UK, 1961*

ball off *verb* (of a male) to masturbate *UK, 1961*

ball of fire *noun* a dynamic and energetic person *US, 1900*

ball of malt *noun* a large glass of whiskey *IRELAND, 2001*

ball of muscle *noun* **1** a powerfully built, fit and healthy person or animal *AUSTRALIA, 1914*. **2** a person with a great deal of energy *NEW ZEALAND, 1984*

ball of wax *noun* a complete set of facts or situation *US, 1953*

balloon *noun* **1** a lieutenant. Coined in Korea *US, 1951*. **2** used as a humorous synonym of 'platoon' *US, 1967*. **3** a woman's breast. Usually in the plural *US, 1962*. **4** a condom *US, 1966*. **5** a small amount of heroin, whether or not it is actually in a balloon *US, 1967*. **6** a heroin dealer *UK, 2002*. **7** a foolish, talkative person. Because they are 'full of hot air' *UK: NORTHERN IRELAND, 1996*. **8** a dollar *US, 1973*. ▶ **the balloon goes up** something happens. Used especially in the past tense in phrases like 'when did the balloon go up?' and 'the balloon went up at 6 o'clock', often when the event referred to was some kind of trouble. Military in origin, probably World War 1, from the raising of an observation balloon just before an attack *UK, 1924*

balloon *verb* to dramatically and constantly change your shape in order not to present a predictable target. Military *UK, 1995*

balloon car; balloon *noun* a *saloon* bar. Rhyming slang *UK, 1960*

balloon foot *noun* a slow driver *US, 1993*

balloon head *noun* an empty-headed, dim-witted dolt. Sometimes contracted to 'balloon' *US, 1931*

balloon juice *noun* **1** empty talk. A play on the 'hot air' typically found inside balloons *US, 1900*. **2** a sweet, bright coloured fruit-based drink *BARBADOS, 1965*

balloon knot *noun* the anus. Visual imagery *UK, 1998*

balloon tyres *noun* dark bags beneath an actor's eyes *UK, 1952*

ballpark *noun* an approximate range *US, 1957*

ballroom *noun* a singles bar with a reputation for easy sexual conquests *US, 1985*

ballroom blitz *noun* the breasts. Rhyming slang for TIT(S), formed from the title of a 1973 song that was successful for The Sweet *UK, 2003*

balls *noun* **1** the testicles. From the shape *UK, 1325*. **2** courage, daring *UK, 1893*. **3** strength, substance *UK, 1981*. **4** nonsense *UK, 1857*. ▶ **all balls** nonsense. An elaboration of BALLS *UK, 1937*. ▶ **as balls** used as an intensifier *US, 1988*. ▶ **balls in a vice** at an extreme disadvantage, overpowered *US, 1987*. ▶ **balls like a Scoutmaster** great courage or sexual prowess. Based on the image of a Boy Scout leader as a paedophile *NEW ZEALAND, 1999*. ▶ **bust your balls; break your balls** to work to your fullest capability; to try your hardest *US, 1944*. ▶ **by the twenty-four swinging balls of the twelve apostles!** used as a register of anger and despair *US, 2001*. ▶ **don't get your balls in a knot** do not become agitated *AUSTRALIA, 1979*. ▶ **get your balls in an uproar** to become unduly excited. Of military origin *CANADA, 1961*. ▶ **have someone's balls for a necktie** to punish someone severely. Generally in a future tense *UK, 1973*. ▶ **have your balls torn off** to be severely reprimanded *UK, 1977*. ▶ **lay your balls on the chopping-block** to take responsibility (for an action or opinion) and thereby risk humiliation or rejection *UK, 2001*. ▶ **make a balls of** to spoil something, to make a mess of something. From BALLS (nonsense) *UK, 1889*. ▶ **to have someone by the balls** to exert complete control over someone; to have complete power over someone *US, 1918*

balls *verb* to secrete objects in a man's underpants, nestling whatever you wish to keep hidden around the testicles (balls) *UK, 1997*

balls! used as an all-purpose expletive. A figurative use of 'balls'='testicles' *UK, 1957*

balls-achingly *adverb* tediously *UK, 1972*

ballsack *noun* a skimpy bathing suit for a man *US, 1997*

balls-and-all *adjective* with complete commitment *AUSTRALIA, 2001*

balls-ass naked *adjective* completely naked *US, 1958*

ballsed-up *adjective* ruined, wrecked, messed up *AUSTRALIA, 1986*

balls-out *adverb* at full speed *US, 1945*

balls-to-the-walls *adjective* unrestrained, full-out *US, 1967*

balls to you! registers an impatient dismissal of anything specified. Variants include 'balls to that', and 'balls to X' *UK, 1923*

balls-up *noun* a mess, a muddle, a mistake *UK, 1934*

balls up *verb* to make a mistake; to err; to mess something up *AUSTRALIA, 1969*

ballsy *adjective* gutsy, courageous *US, 1935*

ball team; baseball team *noun* a group of gambling cheats who work in casinos *US, 1987*

ball tearer *noun* **1** something extraordinary *AUSTRALIA, 1974*. **2** a violent person *AUSTRALIA, 1973*. **3** a difficult, physically demanding task. A military variation of BALLBREAKER *AUSTRALIA, 1984*

ball up *verb* to ruin something *AUSTRALIA, 1982*

bally; bally act; ballyhoo *noun* any method used to draw a crowd; a small, free performance given outside a place of entertainment in the hope of drawing customers inside. Circus and carnival usage *US, 1901*

bally *adjective* **1** used as a euphemism for 'bloody' *UK, 1885*. **2** very angry. Probably by ellipsis from 'bally mad' *UK, 1997*

ballyhoo *verb* to draw a crowd *US, 1965*

balm *verb* to embalm a body *BAHAMAS, 1980*

Balmain basket weaver *noun* a trendy, leftist member of the middle class. Derogatory; after the affluent Sydney suburb of Balmain *AUSTRALIA, 1986*

Balmain basket-weaving *adjective* characteristic of a Balmain basket weaver *AUSTRALIA, 1992*

Balmaniac *noun* a person from the affluent Sydney suburb of Balmain. Recorded as 'Balmain footballers' by Baker, 1943 *AUSTRALIA, 1969*

balmy *adjective* drunk *US, 1850*

balmy breeze; breeze *noun* cheese. Rhyming slang *UK, 1961*

baloney *noun* **1** utter nonsense *US, 1922*. **2** the penis *US, 1928*. **3** a die that has been flattened on several edges to favour one surface *US, 1974*. **4** electric cable. Electric line industry usage *US, 1980*

baloney pony *noun* the penis *US, 2002*. ▶ **ride the baloney pony** to have sex *US, 2001*

baloobas *noun* the breasts *AUSTRALIA, 1988*

balot; ballot *noun* opium; heroin *US, 1986*

balsa boy *noun* a male pornography performer who has trouble maintaining an erection. One of many WOOD images *US, 1995*

Balt *noun* an immigrant of Eastern European extraction; any European immigrant to Australia during the immediate post-World War 2 period. Derogatory; common in the 1940–50s when it was often applied indiscriminately to any European migrant *AUSTRALIA, 1963*

Balti belt *noun* any area with a conglomeration of Indian restaurants; especially Birmingham's Sparkhill and Sparkbrook districts. Named for the area's preponderance of restaurants and takeaways offering Indian and Pakistani cuisine. (Balti is a kind of curry cooked and served in the pot after which it is named) *UK, 2003*

Balto *nickname* Baltimore, Maryland *US, 1981*

bam *noun* **1** a pill or capsule of amphetamines. An abbreviation of 'bambita' *US, 1970*. **2** a pill containing both a barbiturate and an amphetamine *UK, 1983*. **3** a central nervous system depressant *UK, 2003*. **4** a cigarette made with poor quality marijuana *US, 1952*. **5** a violent individual *UK, 2000*. **6** a female member of the US Marine Corps. A 'broad-assed marine'. Gulf war usage *US, 1991* ▷*see:* **BAMPOT; BAMSTICK**

bama *noun* a conventional person, profoundly out of touch with current trends *US, 1970*

bama chukker *noun* a poor southern white *US, 1966*

bamalacha rambler *noun* a marijuana smoker *US, 1959*

bamalam *noun* marijuana. Variation of BAMALACHA *US, 1973*

bambalacha; bamba; bammy *noun* marijuana *US, 1938*

bambalacha rancher *noun* a marijuana user, possibly a grower *US, 1959*

bam-bam *noun* the buttocks *TRINIDAD AND TOBAGO, 2003*

bambino *noun* **1** a child. Italian used by English-speakers with no knowledge of Italian *ITALY, 1995*. **2** an amphetamine or other central nervous system stimulant *US, 1992*

bambi-sexual *noun* a homosexual whose sexual activity is characterised by kisses, caresses and emotion. Punning on the gentle deer Bambi, hero of the novel by Felix Salten and the film by Disney *US, 1985*

bamboo *noun* ▶ **in the bamboo** neglected, forgotten *TRINIDAD AND TOBAGO, 1987*

bamboo manicure *noun* torture using bamboo splinters forced under the fingernails. Korean and then Vietnam war usage *US, 1982*

bamboo telegraph *noun* the spreading of gossip or rumours in a jungle. Vietnam war usage *US, 1929*

bamboo wedding *noun* a marriage with Hindu rites *GUYANA, 1996*

bamboozle *verb* to deceive someone, to swindle someone. Arguably conventional English but with a slangy ring nevertheless *UK, 1703*

bambs *noun* central nervous system depressants *UK, 1998*

Bambu *noun* any cigarette rolling papers. The brand name of the rolling papers favoured by marijuana-smoking Beats of the 1950s, often used in a generic, eponymous sense *US, 1977*

bamf! **1** in computing, a notional sound during a magical transformation in a multi-user dungeon. Also an acronym produced from 'bad-ass motherfucker' *US, 1991*. **2** used as Internet shorthand to mean 'I am leaving this discussion'. A sound effect from the X-Men comic books *US, 1997*

bammer *noun* **1** weak, low grade marijuana *US, 1997*. **2** not genuine or of poor quality. Derives, perhaps, from BUMMER (a disappointing or depressing event) *US, 1993*

bammie *noun* a commerically manufactured cigarette adulterated with marijuana *UK, 1983*

bampot; bamstick; bam *noun* a fool; an eccentric; a madman *UK, 1911*

bamsie *noun* the buttocks *BARBADOS, 1996*

bamsie fly *noun* a pest, a nuisance *TRINIDAD AND TOBAGO, 1996*

bamsie man *noun* a male homosexual *TRINIDAD AND TOBAGO, 1996*

ban *noun* a banana. Greengrocer's familiar abbreviation, usually in the plural *UK, 1984*

banana *noun* **1** an Asian-American who rejects his Asian heritage and seeks to blend into the dominant white culture. Like a banana, the person described is yellow on the outside, white on the inside *US, 1970*. **2** a Hong Kong Chinese of European or American parentage or aspirations *HONG KONG, 1997*. **3** a New Zealand-born Chinese person *NEW ZEALAND, 1998*. **4** a person of mixed race, with both black and white ancestors *US, 1945*. **5** a hospital patient suffering from jaundice *US, 1983*. **6** in American casinos, a £20 chip. From the yellow colour *US, 1985*. **7** the penis *US, 1916*. **8** a parenthesis sign (or) on a computer keyboard *US, 1991*. **9** the convex curvature of the bottom of a surfboard *US, 1965*. **10** a comic in a burlesque show *US, 1953*. **11** a crazy or foolish person *US, 1919*. **12** a dollar *US, 1970*. **13** an Australian £1 note *AUSTRALIA, 1953*.
▶ **off your banana** mentally unstable, crazy *UK, 1999*

banana *verb* in television and film making, to walk in a slight curve in front of the camera to preserve focus *US, 1990*

banana-balancer *noun* an officer's steward or cabin-hand *AUSTRALIA, 1960*

banana belt *nickname* **1** southeastern Alaska *US, 1937*. **2** the South Orkney Islands and South Georgia, warm only in comparison with the harsh cold of Antarctica. The term has been applied to a relatively less cold area in a cold region since 1898 *ANTARCTICA, 1958*

bananabender *noun* a person from Queensland. The Australian state of Queensland has a large banana industry *AUSTRALIA, 1964*

banana boy *noun* a young white man brought up in the Anglo-Saxon tradition of Natal, later KwaZulu-Natal; hence a sportsman who is resident in KwaZulu-Natal *SOUTH AFRICA, 1956*

banana clip *noun* the curved magazine or clip for a US Army carbine *US, 1968*

banana farm *noun* an asylum for the insane. Used among Britons in tropical or semi-tropical countries *UK, 1976*

banana hammock *noun* a brief male bikini *US, 1997*

banana jockey *noun* any person who hangs on to the side of a truck driving a load of bananas to town *GRENADA, 1996*

Bananaland *nickname* the state of Queensland. Named after the banana industry there *AUSTRALIA, 1880*

Bananalander *noun* a person from Queensland *AUSTRALIA, 1887*

banana oil *noun* nonsense; persuasive talk *US, 1924*

banana peels *noun* surplus military tyres that are worn smooth and hence useless *US, 1992*

banana race *noun* a fixed horse race *US, 1967*

bananas *adjective* madly excited; mad; behaving oddly. Derives from BANANA OIL (nonsense), which abbreviates as 'bananas'; 'to become mad' is 'to go bananas' *US, 1957*

banana shot *noun* in pool, a shot at an object ball near a cushion, with spin imparted such that the cue ball follows through after striking the object ball and comes to rest after bouncing off the cushion *US, 1993*

banana skin *noun* a potential if trivial danger that is easily avoided when not overlooked *UK, 1907*

bananas on bananas *noun* too much of something, even a good something *US, 1977*

banana split *noun* **1** amyl nitrite; an ampoule of amyl nitrite. A reference to the banana-like smell of the drug vapours *US, 1968*. **2** a variety of MDMA, the recreational drug best known as ecstasy. From the logo pressed into the pill; after the cult children's television programme *The Banana Splits* (originally broadcast 1968–70) *UK, 2002*

banana splits *noun* diarrhoea. Rhyming slang for THE SHITS *UK, 2003*

banana tree *noun* the penis *UK, 1973*

banana van *noun* a flatbed railway carriage that sags in the middle *UK, 1966*

banana wagon *noun* a low handcart used for transporting aeroplane parts *US, 1955*

banana wing *noun* in motor racing, an aerodynamic wing shape *US, 1908*

banana with cheese *noun* marijuana and freebase cocaine combined for smoking *US, 1979*

banano *noun* marijuana *UK, 2003*

band *noun* in prison, a riot squad *US, 1976*

bandaged up *adjective* in trucking, said of a truck with any improvised winter front *US, 1971*

bandage factory *noun* a hospital *US, 1941*

band-aid *noun* **1** in trucking, an improvised winter fronting for a truck *US, 1971*. **2** a medic. During the Vietnam war, a radio call for a 'band-aid' was a call for a medic *US, 1991*

B and B gang *noun* on the railways, a building and bridge crew *US, 1977*

band box *noun* a county jail *US, 1992*

band chick *noun* a woman who is attracted to, and makes herself available to, musicians. An early term for what would come to be known as a 'groupie' *US, 1961*

B and D *adjective* bad and dangerous *US, 1993*

B and D; B/D *noun* bondage and domination (or discipline) as sexual activites *US, 1974*

B and E *noun* burglary. From the initials for 'breaking and entering' *US, 1965*

Band House *nickname* the Chicago House of Corrections *US, 1946*

bandicoot *noun* ▶ **as a bandicoot** completely as specified; extremely so *AUSTRALIA, 1845*. ▶ **like a bandicoot on a burnt ridge** lonely and forlorn *AUSTRALIA, 1901*

bandicoot *verb* to dig out a subsoil crop, especially potatoes, without disturbing the plant *in situ*, usually surreptitiously *AUSTRALIA, 1896*

band in the box *noun* pox. Rhyming slang *UK, 1971*

bandit *noun* **1** a petty thief, usually preceded by the object of the crime. Ironic *UK, 1977*. **2** an obvious homosexual. An abbreviation of ARSE/ASS BANDIT *UK, 2001*. **3** a hostile aircraft *US, 1942*. **4** an unsolved construction problem *US, 1961*

bandit odds *noun* betting odds that strongly, if secretly, favour one betting position *US, 1977*

bandit territory *noun* in Metropolitan Police slang, the Home Counties areas fringing London that are policed by other forces *UK, 1999*

band moll *noun* a woman who makes herself sexually available to the members of a rock group; a groupie *AUSTRALIA, 1969*

band of hope; bander *noun* soap. Rhyming slang, based on the name of a temperance organisation founded in Leeds in 1847. The truncated variation is recorded in Australia by Sidney J. Baker in 1943 *UK, 1938*

B and S *noun* brandy and soda. A popular drinker's abbreviation *UK, 1868*

bandwidth *noun* attention span. A borrowing of a technical term with a technical meaning (the volume of information that can be handled within a time unit) for a humorous, broader usage *US, 1991*

bandy *noun* a bandicoot *AUSTRALIA, 1953*

Bandywallop *noun* an imaginary remote town *AUSTRALIA, 1958*

bang *noun* **1** an instance of sexual intercourse *UK, 1691*. **2** pleasure, enjoyment *US, 1929*. **3** a person judged on their sexual performance *UK, 1937*. **4** a popular schoolgirl *UK, 1971*. **5** an injection of a narcotic *US, 1922*. **6** the sudden effect of a drug *US, 1948*. **7** marijuana *US, 1993*. **8** a swallow of alcohol *UK, 2001*. **9** an attempt. Usually in the form 'to have a bang (at)' *UK, 1948*. **10** an exclamation point (!). From the slang of printers to the slang of computer enthusiasts *US, 1931*

bang *verb* **1** to have sex *UK, 1720*. **2** to stimulate a woman's vagina by introducing and withdrawing a finger in rapid order *US, 1971*. **3** to inhale or to inject a drug intraveneously *US, 1926*. **4** to swallow a tablet *UK, 2001*. **5** to engage in youth gang criminal activity *US, 1986*.

6 (of dance music) to have a danceable beat *AUSTRALIA, 2001*. **7** to make a turn *US, 1969*. ▶ **bang balls** to have a plan backfire *SINGAPORE, 2002*. ▶ **bang goes that** used for suggesting that something has come to an end *NEW ZEALAND, 1998*. ▶ **bang heads** to fight *US, 1968*. ▶ **bang like a dunny door; bang like a hammer on a nail** to be an exceptional sexual partner. Many variations, including 'bang like a rattlesnake', 'bang like a shithouse door in a gale' and 'bang like a shithouse rat' *AUSTRALIA, 1968*. ▶ **bang the crap out of** of a male, to exhaust a sex-partner by vigorous sexual activity. An intensification of BANG (to have sex) on the model of 'beat the crap out of' (to thrash) *UK, 2003*

bang *adverb* very much, extremely *UK, 2000*

bangarang; banggarang *noun* an uproar, a riot *JAMAICA, 1943*

bang-bang *noun* the penis *BAHAMAS, 1982*

bang belly *noun* **1** a Newfoundland boiled pudding made of flour, molasses, soda and seal-fat or suet *CANADA, 1960*. **2** the protruding stomach of a child *JAMAICA, 1996*

bang bottle *noun* a condom *UK, 1990s*

Bang-clap *nickname* Bangkok, Thailand. During the Vietnam war, Bangkok was a rest and recreation destination, with plenty of sex and almost as much venereal disease *US, 1991*

banged *adjective* intoxicated on a drug, especially marijuana *US, 1980*

banged up *adjective* **1** specifically, being locked in a police or prison cell; generally, imprisoned. The image of a cell door having been *banged* shut. Closely following the verb sense which is first recorded in 1950 *UK, 1990*. **2** pregnant *NEW ZEALAND, 2002*

banger *noun* **1** a sausage. Perhaps from the resemblance to a bludgeon *UK, 1919*. **2** a firework producing a loud bang *UK, 1959*. **3** a detonator *UK, 1966*. **4** a near-derelict motor vehicle, usually a car or van. From the back-firing of a worn-out or poorly-maintained engine *UK, 1962*. **5** a cylinder in a car engine. Usually prefaced with a numeral *UK, 1970*. **6** a fender, especially a front fender *US, 1976*. **7** a boxer who relies on brute strength and aggressive tactics *US, 1968*. **8** in hot rodding and motor racing, a collision *US, 1933*. **9** a gang member. Shortened form of GANGBANGER. *US, 1985*. **10** a heavy metal music enthusiast who dances with zeal *US, 2001*. **11** a hypodermic needle and syringe *US, 1986*. **12** a kiss, especially one that is forcefully delivered *UK, 1898*. **13** in pool, an unskilled if forceful player *US, 1990*. **14** a billiard ball. Usually in the plural, extended from the sense as 'testicle' *UK, 1984*. **15** in the casino game Keno, the punch tool used to make holes in tickets showing the numbers bet on *US, 1978*

bangers *noun* the testicles *UK, 1961*

Bangers *nickname* Bangkok *AUSTRALIA, 1985*

bangers and mash *noun* an act of urination. Rhyming slang for SLASH, formed from one of the great dishes of British cuisine *UK, 2003*

bang gotcher *noun* any film of the Western genre. From children's recreation of the cowboy action in such films: firing toy (or pretend) guns, crying 'Bang! Got you!' so their play-enemies don't miss the point *AUSTRALIA, 1953*

banging *adjective* **1** drug-intoxicated *UK, 2003*. **2** wonderful, great, excellent. Originally recorded by Francis Grose in 1788 and possibly anticipated two centuries earlier; in the 1990s 'banging' enjoyed the wide popularity of a new coinage. Also variant 'bangin' *UK, 1997*

banging-off *noun* sexual intercourse. Royal Navy use *UK, 1984*

Bangla *noun* a Bangladeshi *SINGAPORE, 2002*

bang on *verb* **1** to talk lengthily and repetitiously about a particular topic *UK, 1959*. **2** in computing, to subject a piece of equipment or a new program to a stress test *US, 1991*

bang on *adverb* exactly, correct. Coined by World War 2 Royal Air Force bomber crews for 'bang on the target'; adopted into civilian usage as soon as the war was over *UK, 1943*

bang on it *adjective* drunk or drug-intoxicated *UK, 2003*

bang on the latch *noun* a last drink after closing time *IRELAND, 2003*

bang on the money *adjective* absolutely correct, exact *UK, 1994*

bang out *verb* **1** to manufacture or produce something, especially without care; to distribute something *UK, 2000*. **2** to eject from a

fighter plane *UK, 1991*. **3** when freefalling from a plane, to spread your body into a wide shape *UK, 1995*

bang out of order *adjective* ▷*see:* OUT OF ORDER

bang shift *noun* a quick, forceful gear shift while racing *US, 1965*

bang-shoot *noun* any thing, matter or business at issue at the moment. A playful variation of SHEBANG and SHOOTING MATCH; usually heard as 'the whole bang-shoot' *UK, 1984*

bangster *noun* a needle-using drug addict *US, 1950*

bang stick *noun* a firearm *UK, 1961*

bangtail *noun* **1** one of several inferior kinds of horse; a racehorse. From the practice of bobbing the horse's tail *US, 1921*. **2** a return-address envelope sent with a bill, containing a product offer on a detachable portion of the envelope flap *US, 1986*

bang to rights *adjective* **1** denoting an absolute certainty that fully justifies arrest on a criminal charge, as when caught red-handed. Intensifies 'to rights' (fairly, legally) *UK, 1904*. **2** by extension, describing a satisfactory state of affairs *UK, 1962*

bang-up *noun* a period during which a prisoner is locked in a cell. From the verb *UK, 2002*

bang up *verb* **1** to inject a drug *UK, 1982*. **2** to prepare marijuana as a cigarette *UK, 2000*. **3** in prison, to lock someone or be locked into a cell *UK, 1950*. **4** to end a poker game *US, 1979*

bang-up *adjective* excellent; first-rate *IRELAND, 1821*

banjax *verb* to batter, to beat, to destroy someone or something *IRELAND, 1939*

banjaxed *adjective* **1** not in working order. Given fresh impetus in the UK in the 1970s by popular broadcaster Terry Wogan, possibly from the phonetic similarity to the then unacceptable BOLLOCKSED *IRELAND, 1939*. **2** drunk. Playing on the sense 'not in working order', SMASHED *UK, 2002*

banjo *noun* **1** a generously proportioned sandwich or filled roll. In military use in forms such as an 'egg banjo' or a 'chip banjo' *UK, 1961*. **2** in prison, any food that has been acquired by illicit means *UK, 1950*. **3** a shovel *UK, 1918*. **4** the rear end of a car or truck *US, 1971*. **5** in rugby, a head-high tackle *NEW ZEALAND, 1998*

banjo *verb* **1** to beat someone. From BANJAX (to batter) *UK, 1982*. **2** to murder someone *UK, 1999*. **3** to force open a door or window *UK, 1981*

banjoed *adjective* broken down, battered. From BANJO (to beat), ultimately from BANJAX (to destroy) *UK, 1987*

banjo player *noun* a born-and-(in-)bred country-dweller. Probably inspired by 'Duelling Banjos', a musical sequence in the film *Deliverance*, 1972, in which the guitar symbolises urban America and the banjo represents an impoverished rural existence *UK, 2001*

bank *noun* **1** money; wealth *US, 1991*. **2** a sum of money ready for immediate use, especially for gambling *AUSTRALIA, 1919*. **3** a person who finances a gambling enterprise *US, 1964*. **4** a prison cell for solitary confinement *US, 1962*. **5** a toilet *US, 1995*. ▶ **on the bank** subsisting on bank loans *AUSTRALIA, 1955*. ▶ **take it to the bank; put it in the bank** to be very sure of a fact *US, 1977*

bank *verb* **1** to enjoy yourself on an outing on a bank holiday *BARBADOS, 1965*. **2** to prove someone guilty of a crime *US, 1992*. **3** to surround someone to beat them *US, 1997*

bank bandit *noun* a barbiturate capsule or other central nervous system depressant. Possibly from the calming effect that enables criminals to overcome nerves *US, 1992*

banked out *adjective* rich *US, 2002*

banker *noun* **1** a usurer, an illegal lender of money *US, 1988*. **2** a criminal who controls a stock of forged currency notes *UK, 1966*. **3** a person with a large sum of gambling money *AUSTRALIA, 1979*. **4** the operator of an illegal numbers racket or lottery *US, 1959*. **5** in a functionally compartmentalised illegal drug operation, the person who receives payment for drugs bought *US, 1987*. **6** a creek, river, etc, full to overflowing *AUSTRALIA, 1848* ▷*see:* MERCHANT BANKER

banker's bit *noun* a prison sentence of five to ten years. A common sentence for bankers caught commiting fraud *US, 1950*

banker's row *noun* a line of side-by-side high-yield gold seams *CANADA, 1952*

banker's set *noun* in dominoes, the 3–2 piece. So named because opponents cannot score on it *US, 1959*

banking *noun* masturbation. From BARCLAY'S BANK for WANK *UK, 1983*

bank off *verb* to place a prisoner in a punishment cell *US, 1981*

bank repairs *noun* a lack of financing *US, 1954*

bankroll *verb* to finance a project. The image of a roll of banknotes *US, 1928*

bank shot *noun* a delayed fuse shell fired by a tank in such a manner as to bounce off an object and around a corner to explode at or near the target. Borrowed from any number of sports and games. Vietnam war usage *US, 1990*

bank teller job *noun* in horse racing, a bet on the surest of sure things. So certain is the bettor of winning that he could safely borrow money from a bank one day, bet it that afternoon, and pay it back the next day *AUSTRALIA, 1989*

bank up *verb* to save money *BAHAMAS, 1982*

banter *noun* slang. By extension from its conventional senses *UK, 2000*

banyan *noun* a picnic on a beach, when organised from a naval vessel *UK, 1987*

banzai *noun* in drag racing, a complete effort *US, 1965*

banzai! used as an expression of joy and excitement *US, 1985*

bap *noun* a sophisticated and privileged Black American woman. An acronym, on the model of JAP (a Jewish-American Princess) *US, 2001*

bap *verb* to shoot someone or something *US, 1966*

baparazzi *noun* press photographers who specialise in catching their subjects topless. A play on BAPS (the breasts) and 'paparazzi' *UK, 2003*

baphead *noun* a fool. Black and urban youth slang *UK, 2001*

bappo *noun* a baptist *AUSTRALIA, 1953*

baps *noun* the female breasts. After the small soft bread rolls *AUSTRALIA, 1992*

baptism of fire *noun* an inexperienced soldier's first combat experience *US, 1990*

Baptist bag *noun* a brown paper bag in which a bottle of beer can be concealed *US, 1992*

bar *noun* **1** a pound. Directly from Romany *bar*, ultimately Romany *bauro* (heavy or big); usually in the phrase 'half a bar' (until decimalisation in 1971: ten shillings; post-decimalisation: 50p) although inflation seems to have had an effect *UK, 1911*. **2** one million dollars *US, 1997*. **3** a package of heroin *US, 1978*. **4** a block of cannabis resin weighing approximately a kilogram *US, 1967*. **5** used as a name for any variable object *US, 1983*. **6** an erection. Especially used in the form 'have a bar' *UK, 1961*. ▶ **not stand a bar of; not have a bar of** to detest, deny or reject someone or something, to be unable to tolerate someone or something *AUSTRALIA, 1933*

bar *verb* **1** (especially in Queensland) to claim something as your right; to reserve something *AUSTRALIA, 1971*. **2** to give somebody a ride on the bars or your bicycle *NEW ZEALAND, 1959*

bar *adjective* a 'minus' attached to a grade *US, 1968*

bar *preposition* in betting, used for indicating the number of horses excluded from the offered odds *UK, 1860*

bar! used as a call in children's games, chiefly in Queensland and New South Wales, to indicate that one is safe from being caught or tagged *AUSTRALIA, 2003*

barb *noun* **1** a barbiturate *US, 1966*. **2** a college student who is not a fraternity member. The fraternity system is known as the 'Greek society', and in Greek a 'barbarian' was any non-Greek *US, 1900*

Barbara Hutton *noun* in hold 'em poker, a five and ten as the first two cards dealt to a player. Hutton (1913–1979) was heiress to the Woolworth fortune; Woolworth was the foremost five and ten cent store in America *US, 1981*

barbecue *noun* **1** a self-immolation. The term enjoyed a brief and gruesome popularity in the early 1960s *US, 1963*. **2** the burning of a prisoner locked in a cell *US, 1992*. **3** a napalm bombing *US, 1968*. **4** radiation treatment. Medical slang *US, 1994*. **5** a fatal overdose of narcotics *US, 1992*. **6** an attractive girl or woman *US, 1938*

barbecue *verb* to put someone to death by electrocution *US, 1990*

barbed wire *nickname* Castlemaine XXXX beer. From the resemblance of the four X's *AUSTRALIA, 1983*

barbed wire city *noun* a military stockade *US, 1964*

barber *noun* **1** a thief who operates by stealth. Derives from the thief's ability to 'cut and trim' *AUSTRALIA, 1938*. **2** in pool, a close miss, usually made intentionally to avoid a scratch *US, 1993*

Barber *noun* ▶ **the Barber** the Greymouth wind coming across and off the Mawhera River *NEW ZEALAND, 1998*

barber *verb* **1** to rob hotel rooms *AUSTRALIA, 1950*. **2** to talk; to gossip. Derives from a stereotypical barber's inconsequential but incessant chatter with a chair-bound customer *US, 1938*

barber chair *noun* in logging, the stump left from a poorly cut tree, which in falling leaves an upright large splinter *US, 1941*

barber pole *noun* in casino gambling, a bet comprised of various coloured chips *US, 1980*

barber shop *noun* in trucking, a bridge with a low clearance. Citizens' band radio slang *US, 1977*

barbidex *noun* a combination of central nervous system stimulants and depressants *US, 1992*

barbie *noun* **1** a barbecue *AUSTRALIA, 1976*. **2** an outdoor party centred around food cooked on a barbecue *AUSTRALIA, 1981*

Barbie; Barbie Doll *noun* **1** an idealised woman, one who conforms to the role-model of the blonde-haired, blue-eyed plastic doll. A generally derisory usage; from Barbie™, a manufactured doll originally intended for young girls, which has become a cultural symbol. Also variant 'Barbie Girl' *US, 1976*. **2** a barbiturate capsule *US, 1979*

barbied *adjective* used of a woman who has become subservient to a man. From BARBIE DOLL, an idealised concept of womanhood manufactured and marketed by Mattel *UK, 1996*

Barclaycard *noun* a sawn-off shotgun used to shoot doors off their hinges. From the credit card's advertising slogan 'A Barclaycard gets you anywhere' *UK, 1995*

Barclay's Bank; barclay *noun* of a male, an act of masturbation. Rhyming slang for WANK (masturbation); probably, according to most authorities, in use since the 1930s *UK, 1980*

Barcoo buster *noun* a westerly gale in mid- or south Queensland. The Barcoo Shire is one of the most isolated areas in Australia *AUSTRALIA, 1943*

Barcoo rot *noun* a type of scurvy caused by a lack of fresh food *AUSTRALIA, 1870*

Barcoo spews *noun* a gastric disorder characterised by vomiting. Named after a river in Queensland *AUSTRALIA, 1901*

bare *adverb* very; many *UK, 2005*

bare-ass; bare-assed *adjective* naked *UK, 1562*

bareback *verb* **1** to engage in sex without a condom *US, 1970*. **2** to surf without a wetsuit *US, 1991*

bareback *adjective* in trucking, said of a tractor without a trailer *US, 1942*

bareback *adverb* (used of sex) without a condom *US, 1960*

bareback rider *noun* a man who has sex without using a condom *US, 1960*

barefoot *adjective* **1** (of sex) without a condom *US, 1963*. **2** (of a car or truck) lacking one or more tyres *US, 1941*. **3** (of a citizens' band radio) operating without a power booster *US, 1976*. **4** in craps, said of a bet on the pass line without odds taken *US, 1983*

barefooted *adjective* (of a drink) undiluted *US, 1847*

barefoot pilgrim *noun* in the used car business, a naive, trusting, unsophisticated customer *US, 1968*

barefoot rice *noun* plain rice *BAHAMAS, 1982*

bare metal *noun* a new computer which is not equipped with even an operating system *US, 1991*

bare-pole *adjective* naked *CANADA, 1988*

bares *noun* the bare fists *US, 1972*

barf *noun* beef US, 1996

barf *verb* **1** to vomit US, 1958. **2** in computing, to fail to operate US, 1983. **3** in hot rodding and drag racing, to damage something completely or partially, leaving parts scattered US, 1993

barfbag *noun* **1** a bag provided for airsick air passengers, to use for vomiting US, 1966. **2** by extension, a despicable person US, 1973

barf, beer and a cigar *noun* a fighter pilot's breakfast US, 1986

barf buddy *noun* a drinking companion US, 1977

barfic *noun* an unartistic computer graphic created with keyboard characters US, 1995

bar-fly *noun* a too-frequent frequenter of bars and saloons US, 1906

barf me out! used for expressing disgust US, 1982

barfola used as a general-purpose, all-round expression of disgust US, 1985

barf whiff *noun* the odour of vomit US, 1991

barfy *adjective* unpleasant, disgusting US, 1957

bargain *noun* a stroke of good luck US, 1990

bargain day *noun* in a criminal proceeding, the final day before trial when the prosecuting attorney will accept a lesser guilty plea US, 1992

barge *noun* **1** any large car. A nautical comparison similar to the more generic BOAT US, 1968. **2** a large, unwieldy surfboard US, 1963. **3** a large vagina US, 1972

barge *verb* to come; to go; to leave; to arrive; to move US, 1929

barge in *verb* to intrude, to interfere, especially if rudely or clumsily UK, 1923

barge pole *noun* a large penis US, 1967

bar girl *noun* a female prostitute who works in a bar AUSTRALIA, 1988

bargoo *noun* a mixture of meat and vegetables cooked together in a boiling kettle CANADA, 1986

bargoon *adjective* cheap; at an unusually low price CANADA, 2002

bar-hop *verb* to move in a group from one bar to another, stopping at each for a drink or two US, 1948

bari *noun* a baritone saxophone US, 1955

baries *noun* bare feet UK: SCOTLAND, 1985

bark *noun* **1** the skin UK, 1758. **2** money US, 1973. **3** a cough UK, 1937

bark *verb* **1** to cough UK, 1937. **2** to brag US, 1968. **3** to tell a lie US, 1997.
▶ **bark the tires** to produce a chirping sound from the tyres on the road while shifting gears US, 1992

barker *noun* **1** a person who stands at the door of a business calling out to people passing by, trying to lure them into the business UK, 1699. **2** an unsophisticated master of ceremonies US, 1986. **3** an antique dealer's assistant UK, 2003. **4** in craps played in a casino, the stickman. The stickman controls the pace of the game and engages in steady banter with the players US, 1983. **5** a dog UK, 1980. **6** a person with a nasty cough. From the verb BARK UK, 1937. **7** a singer US, 1973. **8** a handgun US, 1814

barkers *noun* shoes. An extension of the much more commonly used DOGS (shoes) US, 1929

barker's egg *noun* a piece of dog excrement AUSTRALIA, 1985

barkey; barkie; barky *noun* a sailor. The term appears to derive from Italian *barca* (a boat), perhaps from 'barque' UK, 2002

barking *adjective* raving mad. Derives, in some way, from the behaviour of a mad, rabid or over-excited dog UK, 1968

barking cockroach *noun* the notional creature blamed when someone in a crowd farts BERMUDA, 1985

barking dogs *noun* tired feet US, 1960

barking spider *noun* the notional creature blamed when someone in a crowd farts US, 1989

Bar-L *noun* ▶ **the Bar-L** HM Prison Barlinnie in the East End of Glasgow UK: SCOTLAND, 1985

barley *noun* beer US, 1972

barley! used as a call in children's games. Perhaps from French *parlez* (to parley). Used to indicate that one is safe from being caught or tagged. Some jocular use by adults UK, 1814

barley mo' *noun* a moment. An elaboration of MO, formed on Barley Mow, a popular pub name UK, 2005

barley pop *noun* beer US, 1976

barley water *noun* beer US, 1966

Barlinnie drumstick *noun* a weapon improvised from a length of lead pipe and a few nails. Barlinnie is a Glasgow prison UK: SCOTLAND, 1976

barmpot *noun* a person who is deranged, crazy or eccentric. A fusion of BARMY and POTTY, ultimately from *barm* (a dialect term for 'yeast') UK, 1951

barmy *noun* a mad or eccentric person. Derives from *barm*, a dialect term for 'yeast'. An early source remarks 'frothing like barm hence, full of ferment, flighty, empty-headed'. It is probably relevant to note also the lunatic asylum built in 1828 at Barming Heath, Kent (now the site of Maidstone Hospital) UK, 2001

barmy *adjective* mad; eccentric UK, 1851

Barmy Army *nickname* fans of the England cricket team UK, 1996

barmy wagon *noun* an ambulance used for the secure transport of the insane. From BARMY (a mad or eccentric person) UK, 1959

barn *noun* **1** in trucking, a truck garage US, 1976. **2** in poker, a hand consisting of three cards of the same suit and a pair. Conventionally known as a 'full house' US, 1988

Barnaby Rudge; barnaby *noun* a judge. Rhyming slang, formed on the title of the Dicken's novel UK, 1960

barnburner *noun* **1** an exciting idea, event or thing US, 1934. **2** a member of the Royal Canadian Mounted Police. From an unfortunate miscalculation of force in the 1970s that led to the burning of a barn where separatists met with American Black Panthers CANADA, 1979

barnburner wizard *noun* a high-achieving salesman US, 1974

Barn dance *noun* the chaotic movement of pedestrians as soon as traffic signals permit. From the name of Henry Barnes, New York's traffic commissioner in the 1960s AUSTRALIA, 1984

barndance card *noun* a debriefing after combat US, 1992

barn disease *noun* the many woes found in a motorcycle that has been left idle for several years. Biker (motorcycle) usage US, 2001

barn door *noun* **1** the fly on a pair of trousers. Used in the euphemistic warning: 'Your barn door is open' US, 1950. **2** any target that is too large to miss UK, 1679. **3** an extremely large halibut. Alaskan and Canadian usage CANADA, 1989. **4** in stage lighting, and the television and film industries, blinders used to focus a studio lamp. Conventionally known as a 'variable mask' US, 1960. **5** a type of fuel injection system US, 1965

barnet *noun* the head. From BARNET FAIR (the hair) UK, 1994

barnet fair; barnet *noun* the hair. Rhyming slang, usually compressed to 'barnet'. Barnet Fair, itself, had ceased be a major event at least 50 years before this slang was coined UK, 1857

barney *noun* **1** a fight or argument. From British dialect AUSTRALIA, 1858. **2** a police officer US, 1976. **3** an unattractive, unpopular young man US, 1987. **4** a new Internet user whose interest will soon lapse US, 1997. **5** in the television and film industries, a noise-reducing pad placed over a camera US, 1977

barney *verb* **1** to argue about something AUSTRALIA, 1942. **2** to travel in high style US, 1949

Barneyano *noun* speech or writing in a mode of satirical truth, without avoiding anything CANADA, 2002

Barney moke *noun* an act of sexual intercourse. Rhyming slang for POKE; a suggestive contrast with BARNEY (an argument). Sometimes shortened to 'Barney'. From an earlier pickpockets' use of the rhyme for 'poke' (a bag or pocket) UK, 1984

Barney's brig *noun* the essence of disorder. The full expression includes 'both main tacks over the foreyard', showing the nautical origins if not explaining who Barney was US, 1975

Barney's bull *noun* a condition, especially a worthless or negative state. Originally 'to be like Barney's bull' meant 'extremely fatigued or distressed'; Partridge noted the range extended as: 'bitched, buggered, and bewildered like Barney's bull'; 'well fucked and far from home like Barney's bull' and 'all behind like Barney's bull'. In 2003 a quick search of the Internet revealed: 'buggered like Barney's bull' from the northeast UK; 'more mixed up than Barney's Bull' from western Canada, of Scots-Irish descent; 'get into more trouble than Barney's bull' from Australia; and 'mad as Barney's bull' *UK, 1908*

barnie *noun* a big fight or punch-up *SOUTH AFRICA*

barn money *noun* in horse racing, money bet by purportedly informed track insiders *US, 1994*

barnstorm *verb* to travel from town to town, performing, competing or campaigning *US, 1888*

barnyard expression; barnyard language *noun* profanity *US, 1968*

barnyard golf *noun* the game of horseshoe pitching *US, 1925*

barnyard hen *noun* a prostitute not favoured by her pimp *US, 1957*

barnyard polka *noun* the elaborate, careful walk of a person trying not to step in cow manure *CANADA, 1987*

bar of chocolate *noun* praise, especially when given by senior officers. Royal Navy, usually phrased as 'get a bar of chocolate' *UK, 1962*

bar of soap *noun* 1 marijuana. Rhyming slang for DOPE; a bar of cannabis may coincidentally resemble a bar of soap (see: SOAP BAR), but the usage is simply a convenient rhyme. Rhyming slang often clips, here giving BAR an alternate etymology *US, 1940*. 2 in dominoes, the double blank *US, 1959*

baron *noun* in prison, a powerful criminal whose influence is built on illegal trading in drugs, tobacco, phone cards or money. From the conventional sense of 'baron' (a man of power and influence) *UK, 1950*. ▶ **on the baron** free. Royal Navy usage *UK, 1962*

barossa *noun* a girl. Rhyming slang for Barossa Pearl (a popular white wine). *AUSTRALIA, 1980*

barouche; cabouche *noun* a car; a taxi *UK, 1992*

barra *noun* a barrumundi *AUSTRALIA, 1900*

barrack *verb* 1 to ridicule someone; to jeer at someone. Probably from Northern Ireland dialect sense 'to brag or boast' *AUSTRALIA, 1878*. 2 in sport, to cheer for a team; to support a person or team; hence, to cheer on a person. The usual meaning since 1945 *AUSTRALIA, 1890*

barracker *noun* in sport, a person who 'barracks' for a team; a supporter *AUSTRALIA, 1889*

barrack-room lawyer; barrack-lawyer *noun* anyone unqualified who argues knowledge of rules, regulations or law, especially in a petty confrontation with authority; hence a generally argumentative person of the 'I know better than you'-type. Originally military *UK, 1943*

barracouter *noun* a Tasmanian *AUSTRALIA, 1966*

barracuda *noun* an aggressive, unprincipled person *US, 1957*

barrel *noun* 1 a tablet of LSD. Usually in the plural *US, 1971*. 2 a perfect wave breaking *US, 1991*. 3 a cylinder in an car engine *US, 1948*. 4 in pool, a betting unit *US, 1990*. ▶ **have someone over a barrel** to have someone at a disadvantage *US, 1939*. ▶ **in the barrel** in prison, especially in solitary confinement *US, 1992*. ▶ **right into your barrel; right up your barrel** decidedly your concern, interest, business *AUSTRALIA, 1942*

barrel *verb* 1 to knock someone over; to flatten someone; also, to beat up someone, to punch someone, to deliver a blow *AUSTRALIA, 1969*. 2 to scold someone. Prison usage *NEW ZEALAND, 1999*. 3 to hold someone at bay; to corner someone *AUSTRALIA, 1982*. 4 to drive at great speed *AUSTRALIA, 1977*

barrel-ass; barrel *verb* to move rapidly, generally oblivious to any obstacles *US, 1930*

barrel-back with barn doors *noun* a 1946 Ford Monarch. The 'barn doors' refer to the car's wood trim *US, 1992*

barreled out *adjective* in pool, depleted of money to bet *US, 1980*

barrel fever *noun* delirium tremens suffered by an alcoholic *US, 1949*

barrelhouse *noun* some combination of brothel, bar and rooming house *US, 1883*

barrel roll *noun* the US air campaign conducted over northern Laos in support of the Royal Lao Government, against the Pathet Lao and North Vietnamese forces *US, 1991*

barrier rogue *noun* a racehorse that is agitated by the starting barrier *AUSTRALIA, 1982*

barrier-to-box *noun* in horse racing, the entire length of the race *AUSTRALIA, 1989*

barrio *noun* a disadvantaged neighbourhood. Liverpool usage; adopted from conventional 'barrio' (a Spanish speaking neighbourhood in a US city) to give a romantic identity to an urban locality *UK, 2002*

barrow *noun* ▶ **on my barrow** giving me trouble *UK, 1956* ▷ *see:* BORROW PIT

barrow wheel *noun* a cast-metal spoked wheel *UK, 1984*

barry *noun* 1 a youth who drives up and down a Fenland village street with very loud music blaring from the car's sound-system and, apparently, a hoe sticking out of the boot. Local teen slang, probably originally mocking an actual boy called Barry *UK: ENGLAND, 2004*. 2 something shockingly bad *AUSTRALIA, 1997*

barry *adjective* good, excellent, wonderful. Edinburgh slang, widely used in Irvine Welsh, *Trainspotting*, 1993, but not in the film *UK: SCOTLAND, 1993*

Barry Crocker *noun* something shockingly bad. Rhyming slang for SHOCKER. After Barry Crocker, born 1935, Australian singer and actor who, amongst other things, starred in the title role of the Barry McKenzie films of the 1970s, based on the slang-rich cartoon script by Barry Humphries originally published in *Private Eye* in the 1960s *AUSTRALIA, 1997*

Barry McGuigan; Barry *noun* a notable defecation. Rhyming slang for 'big 'un', formed from the name of the bantam/featherweight boxer from Northern Ireland (b.1961) *UK, 2003*

barry up *verb* to enhance an (old) car in a manner designed to be noticed. The identity of the Barry honoured with this coinage is unknown *UK, 2005*

Barry White; Barry *noun* 1 excrement; hence rubbish. Contemporary rhyming slang for SHITE, based on the name of soul singer Barry White, 1944–2003 *UK, 2002*. 2 a fright. Popney rhyming slang, based on the name of soul singer Barry White, 1944–2003. Popney was contrived for www.music365.co.uk, an Internet music site *UK, 2001*

Barry White; Barry *adjective* inferior; shoddy *UK, 2003*

Barry-Whiter *noun* an event that lasts all night, especially a drinking spree or a rave. Rhyming slang for 'all-nighter'; based on the name of US singer Barry White, 1944–2003. Remembered by Jonathan Telfer, *Writers News*, 2003 *UK, 2003*

barse-ackwards *adjective* end-first *US, 1975*

bar steward *noun* a bastard. A jocular euphemism; although well known previously, widely popularised in the late 1990s as an advertising strapline for Heineken Export lager: 'From your smooth-talking bar steward' *UK, 1961*

bar stool *noun* 1 a vehicle which is never or rarely driven *US, 1992*. 2 used as a euphemism for 'bastard'. Jocular *UK, 1999*

bart *noun* a criminally-inclined youth, especially a youth gang member *US, 1963*

barter *verb* (among young women in Montreal) to trade sexual favours for desired gifts *CANADA, 2002*

Bart's *nickname* St Bartholomew's Hospital, London *UK, 1937*

Bart Simpson *noun* 1 a type of LSD identified by an icon of the cartoon hero. Bart Simpson, an animated character, was created by Matt Groening in 1987 *UK, 1996*. 2 a variety of MDMA, the recreational drug best known as ecstasy, identified by the embossed motif *UK, 2002*. 3 heroin *UK, 2002*

bar up *verb* 1 to get an erection *AUSTRALIA, 1983*. 2 to become excited *US, 1996*

bas *noun* a *bas*tard, generally in its slang sense. Pronounced, and occasionally written 'bahss' or 'bass' in accordance with the full pronunciation of 'bastard' *UK, 1977*

Basco *noun* a person of Basque extraction *CANADA, 1963*

base *noun* **1** freebase cocaine; basic cocaine from which the hydrochloride has been removed *US, 1982*. **2** an amphetamine, *2001*

base *verb* **1** to smoke freebase cocaine *US, 1987*. **2** to argue *US, 1990*. **3** to verbally attack someone using sarcasm to convey an accurate if cruel appraisal of them. An abbreviation of 'de*base*' *US, 1997*

baseball *noun* **1** homosexual activity. Back formation from the use of PITCH and CATCH as terms meaning 'to have the active and passive roles in homosexual sex' *US, 1989*. **2** a defensive fragmentation hand grenade that explodes on impact, used in Vietnam. Shaped and sized like a baseball *US, 1991*. **3** in horse racing, a bet on one horse in one race and all horses in another *US, 1976*. **4** crack cocaine *UK, 1998*

Baseball Annie *noun* a woman who makes herself available sexually to professional baseball players *US, 1949*

baseball bat *noun* the penis *AUSTRALIA, 1999*

baseball bum *noun* in craps, the number nine *US, 1949*

baseballer *noun* a drug user who smokes freebase cocaine *US, 1992*

baseball whiskers *noun* a sparsely bearded face *US, 1952*

base bludger *noun* a member of the services who is stationed at the base. Derogatory *AUSTRALIA, 1948*

base camp commando; base camp desk jockey *noun* somebody with bellicose opinions about the way the war should be conducted but no intention of leaving their post away from combat to do it. Vietnam war usage *US, 1986*

base crazies *noun* obsessive searching behaviour experienced by crack cocaine users *US, 1989*

base crazy *noun* a drug user who searches on hands and knees for cocaine or crack cocaine *UK, 2002*

base dealer *noun* a card cheat who deals from the bottom of a deck *US, 1993*

based out *adjective* used of a crack or freebase addict who is unable to control usage *UK, 2002*

base gallery *noun* a room or building where freebase cocaine users pay to enter and then buy and smoke freebase cocaine. An extension of 'shooting gallery' *US, 1992*

base head *noun* a regular smoker of freebase cocaine *US, 1986*

base house *noun* a house or apartment where freebase cocaine is sold. A term and concept that all but vanished with the advent of crack cocaine in the mid-1980s *US, 1992*

baseman *noun* a drug user who smokes freebase cocaine *US, 1992*

basement *noun* channel one on a citizens' band radio *US, 1976*. ▶ **in the basement** in stud poker, dealt facing down *US, 1988*

base out *verb* to idle *BELIZE, 1996*

baser *noun* a user of freebase cocaine *US, 1989*

bases loaded *noun* in craps, bets placed on every possible combination *US, 1974*

base wallah *noun* a member of the services who is stationed at the base. Derogatory *AUSTRALIA, 1919*

base walloper *noun* a military officer serving at a rear echelon base *NEW ZEALAND, 2002*

bash *noun* **1** an attempt, try, go *UK, 1939*. **2** a party *UK, 1901*. **3** a drag racing event *US, 1960s to 70s*. **4** a long cycle ride, especially if fast and arduous. 'The Brighton Bash' is from London to Brighton and back *UK, 1961*. **5** a route march, as in '5-mile-bash', etc. Military usage *UK, 1984*. **6** an act of sexual intercourse *UK, 1979*. **7** a person judged on their sexual performance *AUSTRALIA, 1967*. **8** marijuana. A possible pun on BANG (marijuana) or misspelling of BUSH (marijuana) *US, 1971*. **9** a dent put into a felt hat to make it look better, especially an Australian Army slouch hat *AUSTRALIA, 1954*. ▶ **on the bash** to be working as a prostitute *UK, 1936*

bash *verb* **1** to criticise someone or something. Often combined as a suffix with the object of criticism *UK, 1963*. **2** to hit someone *UK, 1790*.

3 while surfing, to slam into a wave *US, 1991*. **4** to work as a prostitute *UK, 1961*. **5** to eat with great fervour *US, 1945*. **6** to indulge in heavy drinking *AUSTRALIA, 1947*. ▶ **bash ears** to talk on the telephone. Teen slang *US, 1951*. ▶ **bash one out** (of a male) to masturbate *UK, 2002*. ▶ **bash someone's ear** to talk to someone at length *AUSTRALIA, 1965*. ▶ **bash the bishop** (of a male) to masturbate. Based on a perceived resemblance between the erect penis and a conventional chess piece or, possibly, the helmet and an episcopal mitre; bishops may also be 'banged', 'battered', 'beaten', 'buffed', 'captured', 'flipped', 'flogged' and 'murdered'; notwithstanding, the bishop has also inspired punning variants: 'cardinals', 'obsolete jesuits', 'pope', 'priests' and 'one-eyed monk' *UK, 1961*. ▶ **bash the bottle** to drink alcohol to excess *AUSTRALIA, 1971*. ▶ **bash the spine** to sleep *AUSTRALIA, 1945*. ▶ **bash wheels** in the usage of youthful model road racers (slot car racers), to race *US, 1997*

basha; basher *noun* a makeshift temporary shelter. Originally Assamese for a 'bamboo hut'; acquired by the military and now in use among the UK homeless *UK, 1961*

bash artist *noun* a person prone to fighting *NEW ZEALAND, 1998*

bash down *verb* to record a song in one take *UK, 1983*

bashed *adjective* drunk *US, 1982*

basher *noun* **1** in trainspotting, an enthusiast who will travel for as far as is possible in the train behind a specific locomotive *UK, 2003*. **2** a prize-fighter; a thug *UK, 1937*. **3** a physical training instructor. Military *UK, 1943*. **4** a fast, reckless skier *US, 1963*. **5** in the television and film industries, a simple 500 watt flood light *US, 1960*

bashie *noun* an impromptu party *GRENADA, 1996*

bashing *noun* **1** heavy losses. Usually as 'get a bashing' or 'take a bashing' *UK, 1948*. **2** a beating-up; a beating *UK, 1958*

-bashing *suffix* vigorous compulsory activity. Military, in combination with an appropriate noun: SPUD-BASHING (potato peeling) and SQUARE-BASHING (military parade-drill) *UK, 1943*

bash it up you! go away! stop bothering me! *AUSTRALIA, 1953*

bashment *noun* a dance party; a form of reggae music *BARBADOS, 1996*

bash up *verb* **1** to thrash someone, to beat someone up *UK, 1954*. **2** to construct something with haste and a lack of care *NEW ZEALAND, 1999*

bashy *adjective* excellent, best. Urban youth slang *UK, 2005*

basie; basey *noun* **1** a person living on a military base *US, 1993*. **2** an Antarctica expeditioner. A South African contribution to South Pole slang *ANTARCTICA, 1964*

Basil Boli; Basil *noun* excrement; an act of excretion. Modern rhyming slang for TOLEY (a turd), based on French footballer Basil Boli who played for Glasgow Rangers and was not highly regarded by the fans *UK: SCOTLAND, 2002*

Basil Brush *noun* **1** marijuana. From the herb 'basil', thus punning on WEED (marijuana), elaborated as the name of a elevision puppet; at times shortened to a simple 'basil' *UK, 1996*. **2** the vaginal infection *Candida albicans*, commonly called thrush. Contemporary rhyming slang, based on a puppet fox with a distinctive laugh (Boom! Boom!), popular on children's television in the 1960s and 70s *UK, 2002*

Basil Fawlty *noun* a balti (a type of curried dish). Rhyming slang *UK, 2003*

basinful *noun* as much as you can tolerate *UK, 1935*

basing gallery *noun* a room, apartment or house where cocaine is smoked in freebase form *US, 1995*

basin of gravy; basin *noun* a baby. Imperfectly formed rhyming slang *UK, 1961*

baskervilles *noun* a police-informer or someone who has assisted the police in some other way in the making of an arrest. A play on DOG, referring to *The Hound of the Baskervilles* by Arthur Conan Doyle, 1902 *AUSTRALIA, 1973*

basket *noun* **1** a despicable person; used as a euphemism for 'bastard' *UK, 1936*. **2** the male genitals as seen through tight trousers *US, 1941*. **3** a woman's labia *US, 1949*. **4** an elderly woman. Disrespectful; possibly deriving from a play on OLD BAG *UK, 1984*. **5** in roulette, a bet on zero, double zero and two. Sometimes expanded to 'basket bet' *US, 1983*

basket! used for expressing great frustration *SINGAPORE, 2002*

basketball *noun* **1** in Vietnam, an aircraft mission to illuminate the terrain below *US, 1991*. **2** a 250 mg capsule of Placidyl™ (ethchlorvynol), a hypnotic drug *US, 1992*

basket case *noun* **1** a person who is emotionally debilitated *US, 1952*. **2** any dysfunctional organisation or entity *UK, 1973*

basket days *noun* days of good weather *US, 1965*

basketful of meat *noun* a large penis. From BASKET *US, 1941*

basket head *noun* a Vietnamese peasant. Alluding to the straw hats worn by many *US, 1991*

basket of snakes *noun* in a car, an exhaust system with individual headers that intertwine *US, 1965*

baskets *noun* the female breasts *US, 1968*

basket shopping *noun* the practice of observing the crotch of a clothed male to gauge the size of his penis. Also known as 'basket watching' *US, 1964*

basketweave *nickname* Highway 401 (the Trans-Canada) across Toronto *CANADA, 2002*

basket weaver *noun* **1** a homosexual male who wears tight trousers, thus displaying the countour of his genitals *US, 1960s*. **2** an advocate of simple values and an unsophisticated lifestyle. Derogatory *AUSTRALIA, 2003*

basking shark *noun* a Citroen DS or Citroen ID car. Car dealers' slang; from the shape and appearance *UK, 1981*

Basra belly *noun* diarrhoea experienced by travellers in the Middle East *US, 1976*

bass *noun* **1** one fifth of a gallon of alcohol *US, 1975*. **2** a defiant, tough person. An abbreviation of BAD ASS *US, 2002*

bassackwards *adjective* in the wrong order. An intentionally jumbled ASS BACKWARDS. US quotation expert Fred Shapiro recently found the term used by Abraham Lincoln in 1865, a substantial antedating *US, 1865*

bastard *noun* **1** a despised or disrespected person; a derogatory insult or challenging form of address to someone considered objectionable. Originally, 'a person born out of wedlock', the value of the insult has survived since C16 and ignored the current social acceptance of illegitimate status *UK, 1598*. **2** a fellow, a man. With reduction, from partial to almost full, of the negative sense *US, 1861*. **3** used as a term of endearment. Affectionate usage with no pejorative connotation; whilst by no means exclusive to Australia in this sense, it is almost the defining Australian cliché; on a par with 'G'day'. Recorded in New Zealand: 'You are a right bastard, aren't you?' *AUSTRALIA, 1882*. **4** a thing, especially one causing problems or distress *AUSTRALIA, 1915*. ▶ **as a bastard** used to intensify a personal quality or condition *UK, 2002*. ▶ **happy as a bastard on Father's Day** extremely unhappy. The idea is that a bastard does not knows their father and so cannot celebrate on Father's Day *AUSTRALIA, 1962*. ▶ **like a bastard** used to intensify a personal quality or condition *AUSTRALIA, 1962*. ▶ **lonely as a bastard on father's day** extremely lonely *AUSTRALIA, 1981*

bastard *adjective* bad, unpleasant; used as an intensifier *UK, 1982*

-bastard- *infix* used as an intensifier *UK, 2000*

bastard amber *noun* a colour of lighting gel for the theatre *CANADA, 2001*

bastard from the bush *noun* a person from the country who comes to the city and behaves in an unmannerly way. From a bawdy ballad so titled, based on the poem 'The Captain of the Push' (1892) by Henry Lawson *AUSTRALIA, 1962*

bastardisation *noun* debasing and cruel initiation rights; hazing *AUSTRALIA, 1964*

bastardise *verb* to create a single motor vehicle from two others, especially with criminal intent *UK, 1996*

bastardry *noun* despicable behaviour; cruel punishment *AUSTRALIA, 1945*

bastardy *adjective* used as an intensifier. Elaboration of BASTARD *UK, 2000*

bastartin *adjective* used as an intensifier. Glasgow slang, probably formed on BASTARD *UK: SCOTLAND, 1988*

basted *adjective* drunk *US, 1928*

Bastille *noun* **1** the local police station *AUSTRALIA, 1965*. **2** HMP Strangeways during the prison riot of April 1990. Earlier, generalised sense as 'a prison' has given way to this specific, often nostalgic use *UK, 1996*

basuco; bazuko *noun* coca paste, the basic ingredient in the manufacturing process of cocaine; hence, cocaine *US, 1984*

bat *noun* **1** a foolish or eccentric person *US, 1894*. **2** an ugly woman *US, 1972*. **3** an extended period of drunkenness *CANADA, 1977*. **4** a drinking binge *US, 1846*. **5** a fat marijuana cigarette. Pun on 'baseball *bat*' as STICK *US, 1975*. **6** a shoe; a slipper. Variant spellings are 'batt' and 'bate' *UK, 1992*. **7** male mastubation *AUSTRALIA, 1985*. **8** in horse racing, the whip used by the jockey *US, 1951*. ▶ **at bat** said of an appearance before a judge, magistrate or parole board *US, 1967*. ▶ **like a bat out of hell** at great speed *US, 1909*. ▶ **off the bat** immediately, swiftly. From the speed that a ball moves when struck by a bat *US, 1907*. ▶ **off your own bat** without assistance, independently. Usage inspired by cricket *UK, 1845*. ▶ **on the bat** to be working as a prostitute. Extended from an obsolete use of 'bat' (a prostitute) *UK, 1984*

bat *verb* to dance on a stage. Also spelled 'batt' or 'bate' *UK, 2002*. ▶ **bat on a sticky wicket 1** to contend with great difficulties. From the game of cricket; the ball bounces unpredictably on a pitch that is drying out *UK, 1952*. **2** to have sex with a woman who has recently had sex with another man or other men *AUSTRALIA, 1985*. ▶ **bat the breeze** to talk, chat or gossip *US, 1941*

bat and balls *noun* the male genitals with the penis erect *UK, 2003*

bat and wicket *noun* a ticket. Rhyming slang, sometimes shortened to 'bat' *UK, 1931*

bat away *verb* in a carnival, to operate swindles aggressively and without fear of arrest. A term borrowed from the game of baseball *US, 1985*

bat-bat *noun* the buttocks *ANTIGUA AND BARBUDA, 1996*

batch *noun* an ejaculation's worth of semen *US, 1973*

batch; bach *verb* to live as a bachelor *US, 1862*

batcher *noun* someone who lives alone. From earlier 'bach', 'batch' (to live alone); ultimately from 'bachelor' *AUSTRALIA, 1943*

batch kick *noun* in the usage of pickpockets, the hip pocket *US, 1949*

Bates; John Bates; Mr Bates *noun* a gullible victim of a swindle *US, 1908*

bath *noun* **1** a heavy loss in a business or betting proposition *US, 1936*. **2** in television and film making, any of the chemical mixtures used to develop film *US, 1987*. ▶ **be in anything except a bath** to not wash oneself very often; to have poor personal hygiene *AUSTRALIA, 1932*

bath dodger *noun* an English person. In Australian folklore the English are noted as stinting on personal hygiene *AUSTRALIA, 1987*

bathers *noun* a swimming suit *AUSTRALIA, 1930*

bat house *noun* **1** a brothel. A combination of CATHOUSE (a brothel) and ON THE BAT (to be working as a prostitute) *AUSTRALIA, 1941*. **2** a mental hospital *US, 1962*

bathroom locks *noun* long, combed, styled, braided dreadlocks *JAMAICA, 1979*

baths *noun* Turkish baths where the main attraction is sex between homosexual men *US, 1968*

bathtub *noun* **1** a sedan convertible with two cross seats. Conventionally known as a 'touring car' *US, 1954*. **2** a motorcycle sidecar *US, 1960*

bathtub curve *noun* in computing, used as a description of a notional graph of the predicted failure rate of a piece of electronic equipment. Evoking a cross-section of a bathtub as the graph – briefly high, long low, high again at the end *US, 1991*

bathtub gin *noun* homemade alcohol, perhaps approximating gin *US, 1974*

bathtub speed *noun* methcathinone *US, 1998*

bati-man *noun* a homosexual *JAMAICA, 1955*

Batman *noun* **1** a variety of MDMA, the recreational drug best known as ecstasy, identified by the embossed Batman motif *UK, 2002*. **2** a variety of LSD identified by the printed bat-logo *UK, 1996*. **3** cocaine *UK, 2002*. **4** heroin *UK, 2002*

bat out *verb* on the railways, to switch cars quickly and expertly *US, 1977*

bat pad *noun* in cricket, a fielder positioned close to the facing bat *AUSTRALIA, 1989*

batphone *noun* a police radio; the police personal radio system. Inspired by comic book crimefighter Batman's utility belt *UK, 1977*

bats *noun* a deck-landing officer on an aircraft-carrier. From the signalling 'bats' the officer carries *UK, 1962*. ▶ **have bats in the belfry** to be mad or eccentric *UK, 1911*

bats *adjective* crazy; very eccentric; mad, to any degree. From the phrase HAVE BATS IN THE BELFRY *UK, 1911*

batsh *noun* in caving and pot-holing, bat excreta. A shortening of 'bat shit' *UK, 2004*

batshit *adjective* crazy, out of control, angry *US, 1970*

batten *verb* (of a man) to live off the earnings of a prostitute. In the structure 'batten on someone' *AUSTRALIA, 1964*

batter *noun* a board used to cover a window before a hurricane or storm *BAHAMAS, 1982*. ▶ **on the batter 1** engaging in a self-indulgent variety of drinks, drugs and other recreational excesses *UK, 1839*. **2** on the run from the police *UK, 1984*. **3** to be working as a prostitute. Variation of ON THE BAT *UK, 1890*

batter *verb* to beg on the street *US, 1950*

battered *adjective* drunk. From an earlier sense as 'debauched' *UK, 2002*

battery *noun* a concealed device for giving an electric shock to a horse in a race *AUSTRALIA, 1936*. ▶ **get your battery charged** to have sex *US, 1935*

battery *verb* to knock; to hit; to knock down. From Italian *battere UK, 2002*

battery acid *noun* **1** coffee. Originally military usage *US, 1941*. **2** grapefruit juice or sour lemonade *US, 1945*. **3** LSD. An elaboration of ACID (LSD) *UK, 1998*

battery girl *noun* a prostitute who is subject to a controlling supply of drugs, etc, and consequently is managed and kept in a similar way to a battery hen *UK, 1968*

batting and bowling *noun* bisexual sexual activity *UK, 1984*

battle *noun* **1** in a betting operation, the eternal plus-and-minus relationship between bettors and the betting operation *AUSTRALIA, 1989*. **2** an unattractive woman *US, 1948*. ▶ **on the battle** working as a prostitute *AUSTRALIA, 1944*

battle *verb* **1** to breakdance competitively with the object of demonstrating the most individual style. Conventional 'battle' (a violent struggle) adopted for this non-violent clash *US, 1999*. **2** to compete in a public demonstration of DJ skills or to establish a sound-system's superiority; to compete in rap performance; to compete in graffiti skills *US, 2000*. **3** to attack someone verbally *US, 1998*. **4** to struggle for a living; to work hard despite troubles and exhibit courage in doing so *AUSTRALIA, 1895*. **5** to have sex; to impregnate someone *NEW ZEALAND, 1998*. **6** to work as a prostitute *AUSTRALIA, 1898*. **7** to attempt to make a living at the racecourse, either by running or gambling on horses *AUSTRALIA, 1895*. ▶ **battle the iron men** in horse racing, to bet using pari-mutuel machines *US, 1951*

battleaxe; battleax *noun* an old or elderly woman who is variously characterised as resentful, vociferous, thoroughly unpleasant, usually arrogant and no beauty *US, 1896*

battle cruiser; battle *noun* **1** a public house. Rhyming slang for BOOZER, sometimes expanded to 'battle and cruiser' *UK, 1960*. **2** an aggressive, 'mannish' lesbian *US, 1982*. **3** a formidable older woman. As with BATTLESHIP this seems to play on OLD BAT, but possibly with a rhyming slang influence: 'battle-cruiser' from BRUISER (a rugged physical specimen) *UK, 1984*

Battle of Hastings *adjective* history, in the past. The one historical date that most of the UK remembers *UK, 2002*

battle of the bulge *noun* an effort to lose weight *US, 1956*

battler *noun* **1** a person who struggles to make a living; a person who 'battles' *AUSTRALIA, 1896*. **2** a gambler who tries to make a living by gambling; a habitual punter who is always struggling; also, a struggling horse owner-trainer *AUSTRALIA, 1895*. **3** a prostitute, especially a self-managed prostitute *AUSTRALIA, 1898*. **4** in horse racing, someone who is just barely making a living from the sport or from betting on the sport *AUSTRALIA, 1989*

battle scar *noun* a bruise on the skin caused by sucking. Hawaiian youth usage *US, 1982*

battleship *noun* **1** a powerful and domineering woman. An extension of OLD BAT, playing on the physical similarities between an ironclad and a formidable woman *US, 1931*. **2** a railway coal tender *US, 1946*

battle wagon *noun* **1** a battleship. Royal Navy origins, then Royal Air Force *UK, 1943*. **2** an expensive car. Army usage *UK, 1943*

battle weapon *noun* a specially produced vinyl recording of hip-hop samples, used to 'scratch' (manipulate the sounds into an overall soundscape) and to 'battle' (compete with one another DJ). DJ and hip-hop use *US, 2002*

battling *adjective* struggling to eke out a living; going through hard times *AUSTRALIA, 1895*

batty *noun* **1** homosexuality. Reduced from BATTY BOY (a homosexual); ultimately 'batty' (a bottom) is West Indian, hence UK black *UK, 2000*. **2** the buttocks. Also variant 'bati' *JAMAICA, 1935*

batty *adjective* eccentric, odd, insane *US, 1903*

batty boy; batty bwai; batty bwoy *noun* a homosexual. Combines BATTY (the buttocks) with 'a youth'; from West Indies into wider UK usage popularised in the 1990s by comedian Ali G (Sacha Baron-Cohen) *UK, 1992*

battyfang *verb* to hit, beat, bite or maul someone. From earlier conventional 'batterfang' (to batter) *UK, 1909*

batty hole *noun* **1** the anus *BAHAMAS, 1982*. **2** a despised person. By extension from BATTY HOLE (the anus) *UK, 2006*

batty man *noun* a male homosexual *ANTIGUA AND BARBUDA, 1977*

batty rider(s) *noun* a very short and skimpy skirt or fashion shorts worn to expose as much as they conceal. From BATTY (the buttocks) *JAMAICA, 1994*

batty wash *noun* the act of licking an anus with the tongue. West Indies origins *UK, 2000*

batwank *noun* nonsense *UK, 1997*

batwings *noun* in the language of parachuting, surfaces applied to the arms and body to slow the rate of descent *US, 1978*

baw *noun* a ball. A Glasgow word, spelt as the local pronunciation *UK: SCOTLAND, 1996*

bawbag *noun* a despicable man. A Glasgow variation of BALLBAG (the scrotum), by analogy with SCROAT (a despicable man) *UK: SCOTLAND, 2002*

bawdy basket *noun* a woman with a sexually transmitted infection *US, 1973*

baw hair *noun* a pubic hair used as the narrowest possible measurement. Derives from BAWS (the testicles) *UK: SCOTLAND, 1988*

bawl *verb* to speak with enthusiasm, especially if complaining *GRENADA, 1977*

bawl out; ball out *verb* to reprimand someone *US, 1899*

baws *noun* the testicles. Glasgow slang, extended from BAW (a ball) *UK: SCOTLAND, 1988*

bay *noun* ▶ **over the bay** drunk *US, 1787*. ▶ **the bay** Long Bay Gaol, Sydney *AUSTRALIA, 1942*

bay and a gray *noun* in poker, a bet involving a red chip (the bay) and a white chip (the gray) *US, 1951*

bayonet *noun* a hypodermic needle *US, 1986*. ▶ **take the bayonet course** to participate in bismuth subcarbonate and neoarsphenamine therapy for syphilis *US, 1981*

bayonet drill *noun* sexual intercourse *US, 1964*

Bay State *noun* any standard medical syringe. Drug addict usage *US,
1973*

Bay Street barber *noun* a greedy investment broker who skims
large amounts off every transaction as a management fee *CANADA,
2002*

Bay Street boys *noun* the class of politically powerful white Nassau
merchants *BAHAMAS, 1982*

bay window *noun* a protruding stomach *US, 1889*

baywop *noun* an outport Newfoundlander. 'Wop' in this use is a
Newfoundland pronunciation of 'wasp' *CANADA, 1979*

bazillion *noun* a mythical very large number *US, 2001*

bazongas; bazoongas; bazonkas *noun* the female breasts.
Probably a variation of BAZOOKAS *US, 1972*

bazoo *noun* **1** the mouth *US, 1877*. **2** an old car, usually treasured
regardless of its condition. French-Canadian, adapted by English-
speakers *CANADA, 1992*

bazooka *noun* **1** the penis. The penis as a weapon imagery, here
based on the 'bazooker' anti-tank rocket launcher; sometimes
embellished to 'bazooka shooter' *US, 1984*. **2** a high-powered car *US,
1959*. **3** an extra-large, potent marijuana cigarette laced with
cocaine. Either from the similarity in physical shape and figurative
power to the type of artillery shell used by a bazooka anti-tank
weapon, or form (Colombian Spanish) *bazuco*, a cocaine derivative
made from coca paste *US, 1984*. **4** cocaine; crack cocaine. The
metaphor of a portable rocket-launcher, possibly a variation of
BASUCO *UK, 2003*. **5** in television and film making, a light support
used on a catwalk *US, 1990*

bazooka'd *adjective* drunk *UK: SCOTLAND, 1988*

bazookas *noun* the female breasts. Perhaps from the shape of the
shell fired by a bazooka anti-tank weapon, probably influenced by
conventional 'bosom' *UK, 1963*

bazoomas; bazoombas *noun* the female breasts. An elaboration of
BAZOOMS that echoes the shape of BAZOOKAS *UK, 1984*

bazooms *noun* the female breasts. Originally a corruption of 'bosom'
with the same sense, then evolved to mean 'breasts' *US, 1936*

bazooties *noun* the female breasts *US, 1997*

bazoo wagon *noun* a brakevan (caboose) *US, 1977*

bazuca *noun* the residue of smoked freebase cocaine, itself mixed
with tobacco and smoked *US, 1984*

bazulco *noun* cocaine *UK, 2002*

bazz *noun* pubic hair *IRELAND, 1999*

bazza *noun* a stereotypically uncultured and uneducated urban
youth. An informal variant of the name Barry *UK, 2005*

Bazza; Bazzer *noun* used as a common nickname for people
named Barry *AUSTRALIA, 1971*

Bazzaland *nickname* Australia. A tribute to the cultural influence of
Barry (Bazza) McKenzie, a cartoon character created by Barry
Humphries (b.1934) *AUSTRALIA, 1973*

bazzer *noun* **1** an exciting event or situation *UK, 1983*. **2** a haircut
IRELAND, 1983

bazz-off *noun* a respite from doing something *IRELAND, 1960*

BB *noun* **1** in baseball, a fastball. A pitch thrown so fast that it seems
as small as a BB pellet to the batter *US, 1970*. **2** any smart person,
especially a professor. An abbreviation of 'big brains' *US, 1947*. **3** a
male homosexual. An abbreviation of BUM BOY *UK, 1961*

BB *adjective* in sports betting, said of consecutive wagers. An
initialising of 'back-to-back' *US, 1973*

BBA *noun* a woman with large buttocks. An abbreviation of 'broads
with big asses' *US, 1968*

BBC *noun* British born Chinese *UK, 1998*

BBFN used as shorthand in Internet discussion groups and text
messages to mean 'bye-bye for now' *US, 2002*

BBL used in computer message shorthand to mean 'be back later'
US, 1991

B board *noun* an electronic newsgroup. A contraction of 'bulletin
board' *US, 1991*

B bomb *noun* an amphetamine inhaler. Withdrawn from the market
by Smith Kline & French in 1949 after widespread abuse. A wad of
Benzedrine-soaked cotton found in an asthma inhaler would be
removed, immersed in a drink until drug and drink form a single
intoxicating solution, reputedly 100 times stronger than a single
Benzedrine tablet *US, 1969*

B-boy *noun* **1** a breakdancer; later, anyone involved in hip-hop
culture *US, 1981*. **2** a streetwise young black man. By extension from
the previous sense *US, 1981*. **3** a *buddy*, a *brother*; used as a form of
address. The initialism 'b' muddled with 'B-boy' (a young
streetwise black male) *US, 1992*

BBW *noun* a fat woman. An abbreviation of 'big, beautiful woman'; a
fetish with a large male following *US, 1988*

BC *noun* contraception; birth control *US, 1985*

B cat *noun* an ostentatiously homosexual male prisoner. From the
official categorisation by California prison authorities *US, 1989*

BC bud *noun* high grade marijuana from British Columbia *CANADA,
2003*

BCD *noun* military eyeglasses. Because they are so unattractive, they
are deemed 'birth control devices'. Also variant BCG (birth control
goggles) *US, 1991*

BC Kush *noun* a local variety of marijuana in British Columbia
CANADA, 2002

BC Lounge *noun* a Burger Chef fast-food franchise restaurant *US, 1979*

BCNU used in computer message shorthand to mean 'be seeing
you' *US, 1991*

BD *noun* a syringe. An allusion to Becton-Dickison, a medical
supplies manufacturer *US, 1982*

BDF *noun* a big, strong, dumb brute. New York police slang; an
abbreviation of 'big dumb fuck' *US, 1997*

B dog *noun* used as a term of address between members of the
Bloods gang *US, 1998*

BDSM; SM *noun* bondage, domination, sadism and masochism or
sado-masochism, unified as a sexual subculture *US, 1969*

be *verb* are. Generally dialect but recorded here as an urban black
use *UK, 2003*. ▶ **be in it** to take part in something *AUSTRALIA, 1928*.
▶ **be on** to watch something; to observe something *AUSTRALIA, 1906*

beach *noun* in prison, a shower room *US, 1992*. ▶ **on the beach 1** in
a fishing community, where people who do not fish are. Though
cynical, this division of maritime humans describes the division in
most fishing villages in Nova Scotia: people are divided between
those who go fishing and those who work at fish plants, are
housewives or farmers *CANADA, 1975*. **2** out of work *US, 1899*. ▶ **the
beach** Saudi Arabia. Gulf war usage *US, 1991*

Beach *noun* ▶ **the Beach** Miami Beach, Florida *US, 1993*

beach *verb* **1** to kick a ball very high *BARBADOS, 1965*. **2** in trucking, to
bring a truck to a stop in a parking place *US, 1971*

beach-bash *verb* to lie on the sand, especially when exercised in
romantic manoeuvres. Jocular variation on SQUARE-BASHING
(military drill) *AUSTRALIA, 1953*

beach bomber *noun* a bicycle modified for riding on the sand *US,
1991*

beach boy *noun* **1** a young male who spends a great deal of time at
the beach *US, 1965*. **2** a handsome, young black man who takes
white female tourists as lovers *BARBADOS, 1996*

beach bum *noun* someone whose devotion to spending a lifetime at
the beach has left them destitute and an outcast *US, 1965*

beach bunny *noun* a young female who spends a great deal of time
at the beach, surfing or associating with surfers *US, 1963*

beach chick *noun* a young woman living a Bohemian lifestyle near
the beach in the 1950s. Peter Tamony described the term as
follows: 'Originally applied to girls who lived at Stinson Beach
[north of San Francisco] who were bisexual. By those unfamiliar
with its background, and both ways implication, it has been

extended to any girl who associated with the so-called Beat Generation inhabitants of North Beach in San Francisco' *US, 1958*

beached whale *noun* an obese hospital patient *US, 1994*

beach head *noun* a person who spends a great deal of time at the beach *US, 1991*

beach pig *noun* a police officer assigned to a beach patrol *US, 1991*

beach rat *noun* a person who spends a great deal of time at the beach *US, 1990*

bead counter *noun* a Roman Catholic; a worshipper in any religion that uses strung beads (the rosary, 'worry beads', the Nenju, the mala etc) within its practice *UK, 1809*

bead jiggler *noun* a Roman Catholic. After rosary beads *US, 1966*

bead rattler *noun* a Roman Catholic. After rosary beads *UK, 2000*

beady *noun* the eye. From the conventional cliché, 'beady eye' *US, 1978*

beagle *noun* **1** a sausage *US, 1927*. **2** a racehorse *US, 1923*

be a good bunny used as a farewell. A catchphrase television sign-off on *The Wendy Barrie Show* (1949–1950), a celebrity-based programme. Repeated with referential humour *US, 1949*

beak *noun* **1** the nose *UK, 1715*. **2** cocaine. From the previous sense; a reference to the manner in which the drug is taken *UK, 2001*. **3** in horse racing, a bet that a horse will win. Extended from the sense as a 'nose', suggesting that the horse will win by a 'nose' *US, 1951*. **4** a magistrate. Widely used by those who have occasion to be 'up before the beak' *UK, 1749*. **5** a schoolteacher. A dated usage that has survived thanks to Billy Bunter and other schoolboy literature *UK, 1888*

beak baby *noun* a cocaine-user, especially female. An alliterative extension of BEAK (cocaine) *UK, 2001*

beaked *adjective* cocaine-intoxicated. From BEAK (cocaine) *UK, 2002*

beaker *noun* a scientist. Presumably after the character Beaker on the television programme *The Muppets*. Dr. Beaker was also the name of a character in the cult-favourite show *Supercar* (1961–1962), but the slang term was more likely derived from the later popular children's show. *ANTARCTICA, 1990*

beakerdom *noun* the world of science and scientists. Extends from BEAKER (a scientist) *ANTARCTICA, 1996*

beak lunch *noun* cocaine used around the middle of the day *UK, 2002*

beak up *verb* to use cocaine. From BEAK (the nose) *US, 1991*

be-all and end-all *noun* the most important thing *UK, 1854*

beam *noun* **1** the backside, rump *AUSTRALIA, 1945*. **2** a good person *US, 1945*. **3** cocaine *UK, 2003*. ► **off the beam** incorrect *US, 1945*. ► **on the beam 1** good; to the point; balanced *US, 1941*. **2** intoxicated on marijuana. Later to take on a far greater place in the lexicon of crack cocaine *US, 1970*

'Beam *noun* a Sunbeam motorcycle (in production from 1912–57) *UK, 1979*

beam *verb* **1** in computing, to transfer a file electronically. From the terminology of the original *Star Trek* television series *US, 1991*. **2** (used of a female) to experience erect nipples. Related to describing such a female as having her HIGH BEAMS on *US, 2003*

beamer *noun* **1** a smile. From conventional 'beam' (to smile broadly) *UK, 2001*. **2** a deep blush *UK: SCOTLAND, 1985*. **3** in cricket, a fast ball that is bowled at the batsman's head *UK, 1961*. **4** a crack cocaine user. From BEAM UP (TO SCOTTY) (to smoke crack cocaine) *US, 1992*

beamers; beemers *noun* crack cocaine. After BEAMER (a crake cocaine user) *US, 1988*

beam me up, Scotty used for a humorous suggestion that one would be better off somewhere else due to the lack of intelligent life here. From the short-lived *Star Trek* television series (1966–1969) which has enjoyed an eternal after-life *US, 1985*

beams *noun* the eyes *UK, 2002*

beam up to Scotty; beam up; beam *verb* to smoke crack cocaine and become cocaine-intoxicated. From the pop phrase 'Beam me up, Scotty' used repeatedly on the first generation of *Star Trek* television programmes from 1966 to 69 *US, 1986*

beamy *adjective* wide. Originally 'broad in the beam', then shortened and applied to a ship's width, and then by extension to other objects and to people, especially those wide in the seat *US, 1961*

bean *noun* **1** anything at all; very little *US, 1833*. **2** a dollar *US, 1902*. **3** a coin *UK, 1799*. **4** in American casinos, a $1 betting chip *US, 1967*. **5** a man, a fellow, especially as a form of address. Often embellished to 'old bean' *UK, 1917*. **6** a Mexican, Mexican-American or Latin American *US, 1949*. **7** a capsule or tablet of Benzedrine™ (amphetamine sulphate), a central nervous system stimulant *US, 1967*. **8** a capsule of a central nervous system depressant *UK, 2003*. **9** a capsule of MDMA, the recreational drug best known as ecstasy *US, 2000*. **10** the head *US, 1905*. **11** the hymen *US, 1950*. **12** the penis *US, 1967*. **13** the clitoris *UK, 2001*

Bean *nickname* Coleman Hawkins, jazz tenor saxophonist (1901–69). A signature tune of the Coleman Hawkins Orchestra was his 1940 composition 'Bouncing With Bean' *US, 1940*

bean *verb* to hit someone on the head *US, 1910*

bean book *noun* a worker's book of meal coupons *US, 1954*

bean-choker *noun* a Mexican or Mexican-American *US, 1980*

bean chute; bean slot *noun* the opening in a solid prison cell door through which food is passed to the prisoner within *US, 1998*

bean-counter *noun* an accountant *US, 1975*

bean-eater *noun* **1** a Mexican, Mexican-American or Latin-American *US, 1919*. **2** an Argentinian *UK, 1982*

beaned up *adjective* under the influence of Benzedrine™ (amphetamine sulphate), a central nervous system stimulant *US, 1971*

beaner *noun* **1** a Mexican or Mexican-American. Derogatory, from the association of beans with the Mexican diet *US, 1965*. **2** in the universe created by the Firesign Theatre (and accepted by the late 1960s popular culture), one of the five lifestyles of man, characterised by an obsession with colour televisions and rubbish piled up outside homes. Described in Firesign Theater's 'Big Book of Plays' *US, 1996*

beanery *noun* a low-cost, low-quality restaurant *US, 1887*

bean feast *noun* any form of festive occasion or jollification. Originally an annual feast given by employers *UK, 1805*

bean-flicker *noun* a lesbian. A reference to clitoral stimulation *UK, 2002*

bean head *noun* an amphetamine addict *US, 1992*

bean house bull *noun* gossip or tall tales told at a truck stop *US, 1976*

beanie *noun* **1** in Vietnam, a member of the US Special Forces. A shortened form of 'Green Beanies', itself word play based on 'Green Berets' *US, 1991*. **2** a police nightstick *US, 1952*. **3** breaking and entering. A pronunciation of the common B AND E *CANADA, 2000*. **4** an attractive girl. Perhaps as an allusion to Beanie Babies™ dolls *UK, 2004*

beanie light *noun* a flashing, rotating light on an emergency vehicle *US, 1969*

beanies *noun* tablets of any prescription drug taken recreationally, especially when the appearance resembles a kind of bean *UK, 1999*

beanies and weenies *noun* c-rations of hot dogs with beans. Vietnam war usage *US, 1990*

bean juice *noun* tomato sauce that canned baked beans are preserved in, and served with *UK, 1999*

beanmobile *noun* a car embellished with bright colours, chrome and other accessories associated with Mexican-American car enthusiasts *US, 1981*

beano *noun* **1** a Mexican, Mexican-American or Latin American *US, 1978*. **2** a meal; a feast *UK, 1914*

bean oil *noun* in motor racing, Castrol R™ oil. Castrol R™ is made from castor bean oil *US, 1992*

bean patch *nickname* during the Korean war, an assembly area on the northern outskirts of Masan, a seaport about 40 miles west of Pusan *US, 1982*

beanpole *noun* a tall, thin person *US, 1837*

bean queen *noun* a homosexual who prefers Latin Americans as sexual partners but is not Latin American themselves *US, 1988*

bean rag *noun* a red flag raised on a ship during mealtime *US, 1960*

beans *noun* **1** sexual satisfaction. The metaphor is of a meal that 'fills you up' *UK, 1997*. **2** a meal. Coined in World War 2, still popular in Vietnam *US, 1942*. **3** the lunch break during a working day *US, 1946*. **4** crack cocaine *UK, 2003*. **5** horsepower *US, 1965*. **6** a small amount of money; money *UK, 1893*

beans and baby dicks *noun* in the Vietnam war, beans and hot dogs *US, 1991*

beans and motherfuckers *noun* in the Vietnam war, lima beans and ham, one of the least popular c-rations *US, 1990*

bean sheet *noun* on the railways, a time card or time sheet *US, 1977*

bean-stealer *noun* in the Royal Air Force, a married man who lives in the mess *UK, 1984*

bean store *noun* a roadside restaurant or motorway truck stop restaurant *US, 1976*

bean time *noun* time for a meal *US, 1984*

Beantown; Bean Town *nickname* Boston, Massachusetts. Because Boston is known for its baked beans *US, 1901*

bean up *verb* to take amphetamines *US, 1976*

bean wagon *noun* a no-frills lunch counter *US, 1960*

beany *noun* a green polyster baseball cap issued to US soldiers since 1962, known officially as the Army Utility Cap *US, 1990*

bear *noun* **1** in the US, a motorway patrol officer or state trooper; a police officer in the UK. Shortened from SMOKEY THE BEAR *US, 1975*. **2** a hairy and stocky man, of a type beloved by some homosexuals *US, 1994*. **3** a boisterous, rowdy or aggressive young man, especially in the context of heavy drinking *UK: SCOTLAND, 1985*. **4** a building-site or oil-rig worker *UK: SCOTLAND, 1996*. **5** an unattractive woman *US, 1982*. **6** a cautious and conservative poker player *US, 1988*. **7** a difficult task or situation *US, 1966*

Bear *nickname* US General H. Norman Schwarzkopf (b.1934), commander of the US forces during the Gulf war *US, 1991*

bear cage *noun* a police station. A logical extension of BEAR (the police) *US, 1976*

bear cat *noun* on the railways, a demanding and disliked foreman *US, 1977*

beard *noun* **1** a person used to mask the identity of the actual controlling agent; a person who escorts another to a social function in order to mask the identity of one or the other's lover or sexual orientation. Originally from gambling, referring to a front for betting *US, 1956*. **2** in gambling, a person who bets for someone else, especially for a cheat *US, 1962*. **3** a broker who buys up stock quietly and secretly for bidders in a corporate takeover who hope to disguise their intentions *US, 1988*. **4** an intellectual or academic. Unkind if not derisive *US, 1927*. **5** a male member of an Orthodox Jewish group *US, 1967*. **6** an 'older' surfer. In the youth culture of surfing, 'old' is a relative term *US, 1991*

beard *verb* to serve as a beard for someone *US, 1971*

bearded clam *noun* the vulva. Combines FISH with visual imagery *US, 1965*

bearded lady *noun* the vulva *US, 1967*

beardie; beardy *noun* **1** an act of rubbing a stubbly face against a smooth one *UK, 1985*. **2** a bearded person *UK, 1941*

beardie-weirdie *noun* a bearded person. Disparaging *UK: SCOTLAND, 2001*

beard jammer *noun* the manager of a brothel *US, 1962*

beard man *noun* a Rastafarian *JAMAICA, 1952*

beardsman *noun* a Rastafarian with shaved or trimmed hair *JAMAICA, 1985*

beard-stroking *noun* serious consideration of something, deep thought *UK, 2003*

beard-stroking *adjective* intellectual or boring or both *UK, 2003*

bear grease *noun* in electric line work, any gel used as an electric contact aid *US, 1980*

bearings *noun* the stomach. Suggested derivations all seem based on the body as a machine. However, it is possible that this is from a sense of disorientation after vomiting, thus confusing the losing of the contents of your stomach with a loss of bearings *AUSTRALIA, 1943*. ▶ **too many bearings on it** a situation too complicated to explain. This phrase uses a nautical term for location-finding, 'bearings' (i.e. from a compass), metaphorically *CANADA, 1999*

bearing up used in response to a personal enquiry such as 'how are you?' or 'how's things?' *UK, 1984*

bear insurance *noun* a gun, the bigger the better the insurance *US, 1965*

bear in the air *noun* a police helicopter. This travelled from citizens' band radio slang into a still-surviving, wider usage *US, 1976*

bearish *adjective* (of a man) large and hairy *AUSTRALIA, 1994*

bear joint *noun* in a carnival, a game in which stuffed teddy bears are the prize *US, 1960*

bear meat *noun* a speeding vehicle without the benefit of citizens' band radio communications. Easy prey for BEAR (the police) *US, 1976*

bear paw *noun* **1** round-footed snowshoes worn while doing chores *US, 1993*. **2** the badge necessary to get into the inner area of the 2002 G8 summit meeting in Alberta *CANADA, 2002*

bear pit *noun* an auditorium, or other arena, peopled with a rowdy, challenging, even confrontational audience. From the late night audiences at the Edinburgh Festival's Fringe Club *UK, 1996*

bear's paw *noun* a saw. Rhyming slang. Noted by Ray Puxley in 1992 as 'a seldom heard term for a carpenter's tool' *UK, 1934*

bear trap *noun* **1** in the Canadian Navy, a helicopter haul-down and securing device *CANADA, 1995*. **2** the clutch on a Laverda motorcycle. Named after the amount of effort required to pull the clutch lever in *US, 1992*. **3** in television and film making, a strong clamp used for attaching lights to rigging *US, 1987*. **4** a police radar-trap for speeding motorists *US, 1976*

Bear Whiz Beer *noun* an inferior beer. A popular beverage in Firesign Theater skits; its motto is the stunning 'It's in the water! That's why it's yellow!' *US, 1993*

beast *noun* **1** a very unattractive woman, especially if sexually proactive *US, 1942*. **2** a sexually available female *US, 1955*. **3** in prison, a sex offender, a convicted paedophile *UK, 1996*. **4** anything excellent *UK, 1996*. **5** the penis *US, 2001*. **6** a white person; a white US soldier in Vietnam. Used by US soldiers of colour in Vietnam *US, 1991*. **7** heroin; heroin addiction *US, 1958*. **8** LSD *US, 1967*. **9** Milwaukee's Best™, an inexpensive beer favoured by cash-strapped youth. Appropriately, Milwaukee's Best Light is simply 'Beast Light' *US, 1987*. **10** a large, fast car *US, 1951*. **11** a car with a raised front end *US, 1980*. **12** an expensive and powerful citizens' band radio *US, 1976*. ▶ **as a beast** used as an intensifier *US, 2003*. ▶ **the beast** the police; any figure of authority or oppression. West Indian, hence UK black *UK, 1993*

beast *verb* to have anal sex *UK, 1999*. ▶ **get beasted in** to eat with great enthusiasm *UK: SCOTLAND, 1985*

beast about *verb* to treat someone with a harsh physicality *UK, 1995*

beastbwai; beast boy *noun* the police; any figure of authority or oppression. Combines THE BEAST (the police, etc.) with BWAI (boy, a youth in UK black/West Indian gang culture) *UK, 1994*

beastie *noun* **1** used as an endearing form of 'beast'; also, in a jocular sense, of an insect. Mainly Scottish *UK, 1864*. **2** an attractive woman. Objectifying a woman as an animal, much the same as 'filly' *UK, 1984*

beasting *noun* from a male perspective, an act of sexual intercourse. Possibly inspired by the BEAST WITH TWO BACKS *UK, 2003*

beastly *adjective* **1** bad (to whatever degree), unpleasant, horrid. Usage considered to be dated, childish or upper-class *UK, 1611*. **2** excellent *US, 1953*. **3** excessive *US, 2000*

beastly *adverb* badly, unpleasantly, very, excessively. Stereotypically upper-class usage *UK, 1844*

beast with two backs *noun* vaginal, face-to-face sexual intercourse between a heterosexual couple; sex between two people. From Shakespeare *UK, 1604*

beasty *noun* a repulsive, disgusting person *US, 1985*

beasty *adjective* repulsive, disgusting *US, 1982*

beat *noun* **1** a regular route or locale (of a prostitute or police officer) *UK, 1721*. **2** a member of the 1950s youth counterculture *US, 1961*. **3** in horse racing, an unfortunate defeat *US, 1976*. **4** a crime which has not been solved *US, 1992*. **5** in television and film making, the main storyline *US, 1990*. **6** a car *US, 1947*

beat *verb* **1** to cheat, to swindle, to steal *US, 1849*. **2** to defy someone's understanding *UK, 1882*. ▶ **beat about the bush; beat around the bush 1** (of a female) to masturbate. Wordplay on 'beat' (used in many terms of male masturbation) and BUSH (the pubic hair), in some way reversing the familiar meaning of 'beat around the bush' (to avoid coming to a point) *UK, 1991*. **2** to avoid coming to the point of a discussion. A term that has its origin in the hunting of birds *UK, 1659*. ▶ **beat feet** to leave *US, 1944*. ▶ **beat hollow** to outdo someone utterly and completely *BARBADOS, 1996*. ▶ **beat it 1** to leave quickly *US, 1878*. **2** (of a male) to masturbate *US, 1995*. ▶ **beat off with a stick** to get more than enough sexual offers *AUSTRALIA, 1999*. ▶ **beat the band** to surpass everything *US, 1897*. ▶ **beat the board** in poker, to hold the best hand showing *US, 1963*. ▶ **beat the bushes 1** in horse racing, to race a horse in minor circuits, where the horse can be a big fish in a little pond *US, 1951*. **2** to drive in the lead position of a group of trucks travelling together on a motorway *US, 1976*. ▶ **beat the clock 1** to finish a task before the prescribed time. In the UK orginally military, perhaps from an American parlour game. From the late 1950s-60s, it was used as the title of a gameshow segment in the television variety programme *Sunday Night at the London Palladium*, *UK, 1961*. **2** to return alive from an SAS mission *UK, 1980*. ▶ **beat the cotton** to soak and then pound used cottons, used to strain drug doses, in an attempt to leach out enough heroin for another dose *US, 1989*. ▶ **beat the Dutch** to astonish or frustrate someone *US, 1775*. ▶ **beat the eightball** to use heroin *US, 1971*. ▶ **beat the favorite** in horse racing, to place a small bet on a horse with long odds to win rather than betting on the horse favoured to win *US, 1951*. ▶ **beat the gun** (of an engaged couple) to have sex, especially if the fiancée falls pregnant. The sporting imagery of being under starter's orders *AUSTRALIA, 1984*. ▶ **beat the man** to sleep. Prison usage suggesting that in sleep one escapes domination by prison authorities. *US, 1990*. ▶ **beat the priest and take his gown; beat the priest** to do that which you should not do in an open, notorious and brazen fashion *GRENADA, 1978*. ▶ **beat the pup** (of a male) to masturbate *US, 1950*. ▶ **beat the rap** to withstand harsh interrogation *UK, 1996*. ▶ **beat the snot out of** to thrash someone soundly, to beat someone up *US, 1989*. ▶ **beat the starter** (of an engaged couple) to have sex, especially if the fiancée falls pregnant. Sporting imagery, racing ahead while still under starter's orders *UK, 1984*. ▶ **beat your baloney** (of a male) to masturbate *US, 1969*. ▶ **beat your bishop** (of a male) to masturbate *US, 1916*. ▶ **beat your chops; beat up your chops** to talk *US, 1945*. ▶ **beat your face** to perform push-ups *US, 1998*. ▶ **beat your gums; beat up your gums** to talk without purpose or without effect *US, 1945*. ▶ **beat your meat; beat the meat** (of a male) to masturbate *US, 1936*. ▶ **beat yourself up** to be harshly self-critical, to struggle with your conscience *UK, 2003*. ▶ **can't beat it in the Navy** used for expressing admiration of a boat-handling job. Among Canadian east coast fishermen, with the tradition of navy techniques very strong, this term expresses high praise *CANADA, 1908*

beat *adjective* **1** world-weary, spiritual, jaded, intellectual *US, 1947*. **2** utterly tired *UK, 1821*

beat artist *noun* a swindler *US, 1989*

beat bag *noun* a bag of drugs that is heavily adulterated or is completely counterfeit *US, 1993*

beatdown *noun* a physical beating; hence figuratively, a defeat *US, 1995*

beater *noun* **1** an older car, usually not in good condition, used for day-to-day driving *US, 1990*. **2** a drumstick *BAHAMAS, 1975*

beat for *adjective* lacking *US, 1973*

beat generation *noun* the alienated class of young Americans who came of age in the mid-1940s and then embraced an alternative lifestyle and values in the 1950s *US, 1950*

beating *noun* a violent ache *BARBADOS, 1965*

beat loot *noun* a pittance; a small amount of money *US, 1973*

beatnik *noun* a follower of the beat generation (avant-garde 'visionaries, rebels and hipsters') derided and defined by stereotypical appearance (black beret for men, black tights for women) and lifestyle choices (Charlie Parker's jazz, marijuana, performance poetry, etc). Coined in 1958 (the first popular, non-Russian use of the suffix -NIK) by San Francisco newspaper columnist Herb Caen, extended from BEAT (a member of the 1950s youth counterculture) and a pun on the FAR OUT example of 'sputnik' (a Russian satellite launched in 1959) *US, 1958*

beat off *verb* (of a male) to masturbate *US, 1962*

beat out *verb* to strip someone of their membership in a youth gang, accomplished by a ritualistic beating *US, 1995*

beat pad *noun* an establishment where poor quality marijuana is sold *US, 1960*

Beatrix Potter; Beatrix *noun* an ugly woman. Possibly rhyming slang for ROTTER based on the name of author and illustrator Beatrix Potter (1866–1943) *UK, 2002*

beat sheet *noun* **1** in television and film making, a short summary of a story *US, 1990*. **2** a pornographic magazine *US, 1997*

Beattie and Babs *noun* pubic lice, crab-lice. Rhyming slang for CRABS based on an early C20 music hall act who are, unfortunately, best remembered by this term *UK, 1960*

beat-up *adjective* shoddy, shabby, worn out *US, 1946*

beau *noun* used as a term of address between young males *US, 1954*

beaut *noun* **1** a beauty, an impressive person or thing *US, 1895*. **2** a potent amphetamine capsule. An abbreviation of BLACK BEAUTY *US, 1992*

beaut *adjective* excellent, terrific, wonderful, splendid *AUSTRALIA, 1918*

beaut *adverb* excellently, splendidly *AUSTRALIA, 1969*

beaut! used for expressing strong admiration *AUSTRALIA, 1953*

beauteous maximus *noun* something that is excellent. Mock Latin *US, 1993*

beautiful *adjective* in the counterculture of the 1960s and 70s, used as an all-purpose adjective of approval. A vague but central word of the hippie era, suggesting passivity, appreciation for nature, kindness, etc *US, 1961*

beautiful! **1** used for expressing enthusiastic agreement *US, 1975*. **2** used, with heavy irony, as a register of disappointment *UK, 2005*

beautiful and; lovely and *adjective* satisfactory; nice. Always followed by another adjective for which this serves as an intensifier. Examples: 'I hit it beautiful and hard'; 'The water was lovely and hot' *UK, 1939*

beautiful boulders *noun* crack cocaine, *2003*

beautiful people *noun* the cream of society's crop; the wealthy, fashionable people of high society and the arts, especially those celebrated as trendsetters *US, 1964*

beautifuls; boofuls *noun* beautiful, as a form of address; the latter is addressed to babies or those behaving so and thus characterised as babies *UK, 1984*

beauty *noun* **1** something excellent; a splendid example of something *AUSTRALIA, 1852*. **2** used as an affectionate form of address *UK: WALES, 2000*. **3** an amphetamine. A shortened BLACK BEAUTY *US, 1993*

beauty *adjective* excellent *NEW ZEALAND, 1963*

beauty! **1** used for registering great approval. Also spelt 'bewdy' to represent Australian pronunciation. *AUSTRALIA, 1952*. **2** thank you! *AUSTRALIA, 1968*

beauty bolt *noun* in the used car business, a new and shiny bolt intended to give the impression of a complete engine rebuild *US, 1997*

beauty farm *noun* a resort with a focus on improving appearances
US, 1972

beauty parlor *noun* a brothel *US, 1949*

beaver *noun* **1** a woman's pubic region; a woman as a sex object;
sex with a woman. Although recorded at least as early as 1927,
'beaver' did not come into its own until the mid-1960s, with an
explosion of films featuring full frontal female nudity but no sexual
activity and titles punning on 'beaver' – *Bald Beaver, Beaver Works
in the Bush Country, Hair Raising Beaver, Fine Feathered Beavers,
Leave it to Beavers*, and so on. As published sexual material got
more graphic, so did the association of the term. Despite the
highly sexual origin of the term, it was used by truck drivers with a
slightly naughty innocence to refer to women *US, 1927.* **2** a
pornographic film *US, 1969.* **3** a beard *US, 1871.* **4** a top hat *BARBADOS,
1965.* **5** a white police helmet *BARBADOS, 1982.* **6** a police officer *US, 1961*

beaver away *verb* to work industriously. From the characteristic
behaviour of the beaver *UK, 1946*

beaver bait *noun* money *US, 1976*

beaver bear *noun* a policewoman. Combines BEAVER (a woman) with
BEAR (the police) *US, 1976*

beaver biscuits! used for expressing disapproval. A signature line of
Colonel Sherman Potter on *M*A*S*H* (CBS, 1972–83). Repeated
with referential humour *US, 1972*

beaver cleaver *noun* a womaniser; the penis. It opens or splits the
BEAVER (a woman or the vagina) *UK, 1981*

beaver creek *noun* ▶ **have a bite at beaver creek** to perform
oral sex on a woman *US, 2001*

beaver-eater *noun* a person who performs oral sex on a woman. In
a brilliant sexually charged pun, Vladamir Nabokov in *Lolita* wrote
of 'the Palace Sentries, or Scarlet Guards, or Beaver Eaters, or
whatever they are called', creating misdirected confusion with
'Beef Eaters' but leaving no doubt as to the sexual nature of his
malapropism *US, 1955*

beaver fever *noun* an obsession with women and sex *US, 1997*

beaver film *noun* a mildly pornographic film, featuring full frontal
nudity *US, 1969*

beaver flick *noun* a pornographic film *US, 1970*

beaver leaver *noun* a male homosexual. Rhymed on BEAVER (the
vagina) to suggest no interest in the female sex *US, 2003*

beaver loop *noun* a repeating video featuring female frontal nudity
US, 1971

beaver magazine *noun* a magazine featuring photographs of nude
women, focused on their genitals, usually not engaged in sex *US,
1967*

beaver movie *noun* a film featuring female frontal nudity *US, 1971*

beaver patrol *noun* girl-watching *US, 1967*

beaver picture *noun* a film, the main attraction of which is a
number of shots of women's genitals; a photograph of a woman's
genitals *US, 1969*

beaver pie *noun* the female genitals, especially as the object of
sucking and licking *UK, 1983*

beaver-shooting *noun* a concerted voyeuristic effort to find women
whose genitals or pubic hair can be seen *US, 1970*

beaver shot *noun* a photograph or filming of a woman's genitals. In
the early 1960s LA-based band The Periscopes recorded a
rock'n'roll tune called 'Beaver Shot' which was banned from the
radio after two plays *US, 1970*

beaver tail *noun* **1** a quick-baked or quick-fried sweet bread *CANADA,
1998.* **2** a design configuration on a shotgun *US, 1981*

beaver-with-stick *noun* full frontal male nudity *US, 1977*

be-back *noun* in the used car business, a potential customer who
has visited the car lot, inspected the cars for sale, left, and then
returned to negotiate *US, 1959*

bebe *noun* crack cocaine *US, 1994*

bebop *verb* to take part in gang fights *US, 1965*

be careful, Matt! used as a humorous caution. A signature line of
Miss Kitty Russell (portrayed by Amanda Blake) to Marshall Matt
Dillon on the television Western *Gunsmoke* (CBS, 1955–75).
Repeated with referential humour *US, 1955*

Becks and Posh *noun* food. Rhyming slang for NOSH, formed from
the nicknames of footballer David Beckham and his wife, singer
Victoria Beckham *UK, 2003*

becky *noun* in electric line work, a cable sling *US, 1980*

be cool used as a farewell *US, 1984*

bed *noun* the playing surface of a pool table *US, 1990.* ▶ **get into
bed with** in business or politics, to merge with, to become a
partner of, to start a venture with *UK, 1977.* ▶ **put to bed** to
complete a piece of work. Office jargon that now infects every
workplace; an extension of the figurative sense used by printers *UK,
2005*

bed *verb* to have sex with someone *UK, 1548*

bed and breakfast *noun* a very short prison sentence *UK, 1996*

bedbait *noun* a sexually alluring young woman or young man *UK, 1963*

bed blocker *noun* a patient who has an extended stay in hospital
CANADA, 1986

bedbug *noun* **1** a Pullman porter *US, 1940.* **2** a person who is
somewhere between amusingly eccentric and alarmingly disturbed
US, 1832. **3** a Volkswagen camper van *UK, 1981*

bedbug hauler *noun* a removal van driver *US, 1971*

bedbug row; bedbug alley *noun* a poor, crime-ridden area in a city
US, 1969

bed-check Charlie *noun* a pilot flying night air raids against US
troops. Korean war usage *US, 1964*

bedden *verb* ▶ **bedden your head** to become drunk or drug-
intoxicated *TRINIDAD AND TOBAGO, 1979*

beddie-weddie *noun* bed. Children's vocabulary borrowed by adults
US, 1945

beddy *noun* **1** in circus and carnival usage, the place where a person
spends the winter or off-season *US, 1981.* **2** a promiscuous girl *US, 1989*

beddy-bye; beddy byes; beddie-byes *noun* sleep or bed. A
nursery term, used for effect elsewhere *UK, 1906*

bed flute *noun* the penis *AUSTRALIA, 1992*

Bedfordshire *noun* a bed; bed. A humorous extension from the
name of an English county *UK, 1665*

bed-hop *verb* to habitually have casual sex *US, 1974*

bed-hopper *noun* a person who lives a sexually promiscuous life
AUSTRALIA, 1972

bed house *noun* **1** a brothel *US, 1973.* **2** a brakevan (caboose) *US, 1977*

bedlamer *noun* in Newfoundland, a young seal; also a young boy.
The term comes either from the noise they make, or, according to
some sources, the French *bête de la mer* (beast of the sea) *CANADA,
1959*

Bedouin Bob *noun* any Saudi; any desert nomad. Gulf war usage *US,
1991*

Bedourie shower *noun* a dust storm. Bedourie is an inland town in
Queensland. The name Bedourie is taken from an Aborigine word
for 'dust storm'. Other locations similarly used by nature, weather
and irony: Bourke, Bogan, Cobar, Darling, Wilcannia and Wimmera
AUSTRALIA, 1945

bedpan commando *noun* a medic in the Medical Corps in Vietnam
US, 1991

Bedrock *noun* a common name for US armed forces camps during
the Persian Gulf war. An allusion to the prehistoric town on the
cartoon television series *The Flintstones* (ABC, 1960–66), home to
quarry worker Fred Flintstone and his wife Wilma *US, 1990*

bed rock *verb* in low riding, to rock the bed of a truck from side to
side using hydraulic pumps *US, 1992*

bedroom *noun* any place where homosexual men can have sex *UK,
2002*

bedroom eyes *noun* a sensual face and eyes that convey desire *US,*
1947

Beds *noun* Bedfordshire. A spoken form of the conventional written
abbreviation, considered colloquial when used in speech as a
genuine equivalent of the original name *UK, 1937*

bed-sit jungle *noun* an urban area where a bed-sitter is usually available as rented accommodation; the generality of life in rented
bed-sit accommodation *UK, 2001*

bed-sitter; bedsit *noun* a single-room combining bedroom and
living accommodation; a bed-sitting room *UK, 1927*

bed-sitter-land *noun* an urban area where a bed-sitter is commonly
available as rented accommodation; the generality of life in rented
bedsit accommodation *UK, 1968*

Bed-Stuy *nickname* the Bedford-Stuyvesant neighbourhood of New
York City. The area is the epitome of urban American poverty *US,*
1997

bedworthy *adjective* sexually desirable *UK, 1936*

bee *noun* **1** a drug addiction. Also known as 'a bee that stings' *US,*
1960. **2** a barbiturate or other central nervous system depressant,
especially Nembutal. A Nembutal capsule is commonly known as
a YELLOW JACKET, hence the 'bee' *US, 1963*. **3** in a deck of playing
cards, a joker, especially when the deck is made by the playing
card manufacturer Bee *US, 1988*. ▶ **get a bee up your arse; have
a bee up your arse** to be in a restless or anxious condition; to
be obsessed by a notion. A variation on 'a bee in the bonnet' *UK,*
1990s. ▶ **put the bee on** to swindle someone *US, 1949*

bee *verb* to beg *US, 1962*

bee *adjective* bloody (an intensifier). A rendering of the initial letter
for euphemism's sake *UK, 1926*

be easy! relax! *US, 2003*

Beeb *nickname* the BBC (British Broadcasting Corporation) *UK, 1967*

bee-bee *noun* crack cocaine *US, 1993*

bee-bopper *noun* a person who is trying too hard to be something
that they are not – fashionable, trendy, up-to-date *US, 1987*

beech *verb* during the period 1963–65, to permanently close down
a section of railway or a railway station. After Richard Beeching,
1913–85, chairman of the British Rail Board 1963–65, at the end
of which time he was made a Life Peer, author of the 'Beeching
Report' that prescribed a substantial contraction of the UK's rail
networks *UK, 1964*

beechams *noun* ▶ **the beechams** the police. Rhyming slang, from
Beecham's Pill™, a branded medication to THE BILL (the police) *UK,*
1992

Beecham's pill *noun* **1** a fool, an idiot. Rhyming slang for DILL (a
fool). From the proprietary name of a laxative formerly popular as
a cure-all *AUSTRALIA, 1950*. **2** a photographic still. Rhyming slang *UK,*
1971. **3** a theatrical bill; an advertising poster. Rhyming slang *UK, 1992*

Beecham's pills *noun* the testicles. An extension of PILLS with a
commercial formula *UK, 1980*

bee cocky *noun* a bee farmer; an apiarist *AUSTRALIA, 1956*

beedi; beadi; bidi; biri *noun* a small, high nicotine-content, cigarette made of tobacco dust poured into a small tube of rolled leaf
tied with a cotton thread, often flavoured with strawberry, vanilla,
mint, chocolate, mango, pineapple, grape, licorice, cherry, etc. The
word is of Hindi origins. Popular brands are Mangalore, Kailas, Shiv
Sagar and Irie *UK, 2003*

beedler *noun* a hard-driving work foreman or supervisor *US, 1946*

beef *noun* **1** a complaint, an argument, a fight *US, 1899*. **2** conflict,
feuding. A wider use of the previous sense *US, 2002*. **3** an arrest or
criminal charge *US, 1928*. **4** in prison, a written reprimand *US, 1967*.
5 the vagina; an attractive and sexual woman *BARBADOS, 1982*. **6** the
penis *US, 2001*. **7** in homosexual society, a masculine man or a
member of the armed forces whatever his gender-preference *US,*
1972. **8** in the navy, a male homosexual *UK, 1962*. **9** a dramatic and
unintended ending of a surf ride *US, 1991*. **10** a backwards fall off a
skateboard *US, 1997*. ▶ **put some beef into it** to try hard, to work
hard, to make an effort *UK, 1961*

beef *verb* **1** to complain. From an earlier sense: to shout *US, 1866*. **2** to
have sex *US, 1975*. **3** in prison, to issue a disciplinary reprimand *US,*
1967

beef *adjective* **1** aggressive, violent, hostile *US, 2002*. **2** homosexual.
Navy usage *UK, 1962*

beef! in the youth trend for 'souped-up' motor-scootering, used for
registering approval of the achievements of a daring, risk-taking
rider *UK, 2004*

Beefa *nickname* the Balearic island of Ibiza *UK, 2002*

beef and shrapnel *noun* in the Vietnam war, a meal of beef and
potatoes *US, 1991*

beef-a-roni *noun* a muscular, handsome male. Punning with the
name of a food product and the many meat images involved in
sexual slang *US, 1985*

beef bayonet *noun* the penis *AUSTRALIA, 1971*

beef bugle *noun* the penis, especially as an object of oral sex
AUSTRALIA, 1971

beefcake *noun* **1** artistic or photographic depictions of nude or
partially nude muscular men. The gender equivalent of CHEESECAKE
US, 1949. **2** a muscular man *US, 1949*

beef curtains *noun* the labia *US, 1998*

beefer *noun* **1** a constant and tiresome complainer *US, 1950*. **2** a male
homosexual. Royal Navy use *UK, 1982*

beef-heart; beef *verb* to fart. Also used as a noun. Rhyming slang;
perhaps related to obsolete non-rhyming sense: a 'bean' *UK, 1960*

beef injection; hot beef injection *noun* sexual intercourse *US, 1968*

beef it *verb* in motorcycle racing, to fall to the ground and suffer a
severe scrape *US, 1992*

beef of the sea *noun* the loggerhead turtle *BARBADOS, 1982*

beef squad *noun* a group of thugs hired by management to help
break a strike *US, 1956*

beefsteak eye *noun* a black eye. From the folk remedy of covering
the blackened eye with a raw steak *US, 1950*

beef torpedo *noun* the penis *UK, 1983*

beef trust *noun* **1** in sports, a group of large athletes *US, 1928*. **2** a
chorus of large women who entertain men *US, 1931*

beef up *verb* to enhance someone or something, to strengthen
someone or something *US, 1944*

beefy *adjective* (used of a shot in croquet) long and hard *US, 1977*

beehive *noun* **1** a five pound note. Rhyming slang, playing on BEES
AND HONEY (money) *UK, 1962*. **2** in trucking, any large truck stop
offering a full range of services *US, 1976*. **3** an office in a railway yard
US, 1946

Beehive *noun* ▶ **the Beehive** New Zealand's Parliament buildings.
Designed by Sir Basil Spence, the building's domes are evocative
of a beehive *NEW ZEALAND, 1981*

beehive burner *noun* a combustion chamber to burn waste wood
from sawmills *CANADA, 1989*

beehive it *verb* to leave hurriedly. Vietnam war use *US, 1991*

beehive round *noun* an artillery shell that scatters small nails with
fins instead of shrapnel, first used in Vietnam in 1964 *US, 1991*

beeitch *noun* used as a synonym of 'bitch', especially as a term for a
woman *US, 1993*

beekie *noun* during a labour dispute or organising drive, a company
spy *US, 1949*

beel *noun* a car *VIRGIN ISLANDS US, 1996*

Beemer; Beamer; Beamie *noun* a BMW car *US, 1982*

Bee More *nickname* Baltimore, Maryland *US, 1989*

been *verb* ▶ **been around** sexually experienced *US, 1979*. ▶ **been
there** said of a person with whom the speaker has had sex *FIJI,*
1996. ▶ **been there, doing that** experiencing the bleed period of
the menstrual cycle. The 'been there' part offers consolation to
those who recently were on it or had cramps previously, while the
'doing that' part refers to the fact that you are on your period

currently *US, 2001*. ▶ **been there, done that** used as a laconic, world-weary dismissal of another's suggestion *AUSTRALIA, 1975*.
▶ **been there, done that, bought the tee-shirt** used as a laconic, world-weary dismissal of another's suggestion. An elaboration of BEEN THERE, DONE THAT *UK, 2000*

been-there medal *noun* the Vietnam Campaign Service Medal *US, 1991*

been-to *noun* a west African, especially a Ghanaian or Nigerian, who has 'been to' England, usually for study, and whose social status has thereby been enhanced; a British academic who has 'been to' any one of the more prestigious US universities *UK, 1982*

beep *noun* an effeminate man, especially a homosexual *JAMAICA, 1995*

beep beep! pay attention! *US, 1961*

beeper *noun* **1** the telephone *US, 1968*. **2** an electronic paging device *US, 1970*

beer *noun* **1** in the illegal production of alcohol, fermented grain or sugar mash *US, 1887*. **2** the chest. Rhyming slang, from the slogan 'beer is best' *UK, 1980*. ▶ **on the beer** engaged in a drinking session *UK, 1909*

beer barn *noun* a tavern *NEW ZEALAND, 1976*

beer belly *noun* the protruding stomach of an excessive beer drinker *US, 1960*

beer blast *noun* a party organised around the consumption of beer *US, 1967*

beer bottle glasses *noun* thick eye glasses *US, 1984*

beer bummer *noun* a person who cadges drinks from others *NEW ZEALAND, 1906*

beer bust *noun* a party organised around the consumption of beer *US, 1913*

beer can *noun* any small car that would easily get crushed in a significant accident *US, 1992*

beer can grenade *noun* a crude hand grenade fashioned by the Viet Cong, packed inside a beer can *US, 1990*

beer chit *noun* money. In Royal Air Force use *UK, 2002*

beer coat *noun* a warm feeling, or one of imperviousness to weather conditions, that prevails after drinking. From private correspondence, 2002 *NEW ZEALAND, 2002*

beer compass *noun* the homing instinct that remains active when drunk *UK, 2002*

beer cozy *noun* a styrofoam or plastic cylinder that slips over a beer can, serving as insulation *US, 2000*

beered; beered out *adjective* drunk on beer *US, 1930*

beer flat *noun* an apartment where beer is sold privately and illegally *US, 1980*

beer goggles *noun* a drink-induced clouding of visual perception that enhances the sexual allure of previously unappealing companions *US, 1987*

beer goitre *noun* the protruding stomach of a serious beer drinker *NEW ZEALAND, 1998*

beer gut *noun* the protruding stomach of an excessive beer drinker *AUSTRALIA, 1967*

beer-gutted *adjective* (of men) having a protruding stomach from drinking beer excessively *AUSTRALIA, 1987*

beer high grade *noun* cash from rich gold-prospecting seams *CANADA, 1963*

beer me! please give me another beer! *US, 1986*

beernoculars *noun* your vision and judgment after drinking too many beers *US, 1986*

beer o'clock *noun* quitting time on a job *NEW ZEALAND, 2000*

beer parlour *noun* a room in a hotel licensed to sell beer. Originally named to distinguish them from taverns, they have been more recently licensed to serve men and women *CANADA, 1965*

beer run *noun* a trip to a store to buy beer for a party *US, 1971*

beer sandwich *noun* a lunch consisting of beer, beer and more beer *NEW ZEALAND, 1998*

beer scooter *noun* the ability to return home when too drunk to, afterwards, remember the journey *UK, 1999*

beer spanner *noun* a bottle opener. Royal Air Force use *UK, 1984*

beer-thirty *noun* a fictional time of day, suggesting that a beer is overdue *US, 1980*

beer-up *noun* a session of beer drinking *AUSTRALIA, 1919*

beer up *verb* to drink a great deal of beer *US, 1960*

beer vouchers *noun* money *UK, 2002*

bees and honey *noun* money. Rhyming slang *UK, 1892*

bee shit *noun* honey. From the mistaken belief that bees defecate honey *US, 1984*

bee's knees *noun* the acme of perfection, the best. Always preceded by 'the'; a favourite construction of the flapper of the 1920s *AUSTRALIA, 1905*

bee stings *noun* small female breasts *US, 1964*

beeswax *noun* **1** business, in the senses 'mind your own business' and 'none of your business' *US, 1934*. **2** income tax; betting tax. Rhyming slang, cleverly punning 'bees' (BEES AND HONEY, 'money') and, possibly, 'whack(s)' for 'the taxman's portion' *UK, 1989*

bees wingers *noun* the fingers. Rhyming slang *UK, 1980*

beetle *noun* **1** in horse racing, a poorly performing horse *US, 1915*. **2** a female. Circus and carnival usage *US, 1931*

Beetle *nickname* the original Volkswagen car and later models of a similar shape. Derives from the shape of the car, first imported to the US in 1949; by 1960 the nickname was in worldwide usage and by Volkswagen's advertisers by the 1970s. In 1998 the manufacturers unveiled the 'New Beetle' *US, 1960*

beetle-crusher; beetle-stomper *noun* a soldier in the infantry *UK, 1889*

beetle-crushers *noun* heavy boots, especially 'Doc Martens'. In *The Lore and Language of Schoolchildren*, 1959, Iona and Peter Opie record 'beetle-crushers' as 'big-feet or the nickname for someone so-blessed' *UK, 1996*

beevo *noun* an alcoholic beverage *US, 1977*

Bee Wee *nickname* British West Indian Airways *TRINIDAD AND TOBAGO, 1980*

beeyatch *noun* used as an emphatic variation of 'bitch', especially when used to a woman or as exclamation *US, 2001*

beeze *noun* the penis *UK, 1976*

beezer *noun* **1** the nose *US, 1908*. **2** in horse racing, a horse's nose *US, 1951*. **3** a pedigree Ibizan hound *US, 2000*

beezer *adjective* excellent; most attractive. *UK, 1961*

Beezer; Beeza *noun* a BSA motorcyle, in production since 1909; also a BSA car. The company name is actually an initialism of *Birmingham Small Arms*. BSA owners claim that the initials in fact stand for '*Bastard Stalled Again*' or '*Bolts Scattered All Over*' *UK, 1961*

befok *adjective* crazy, angry, lacking emotional control. From the Afrikaans for 'fucked up' *SOUTH AFRICA, 1979*

before-days *adverb* in the past *BARBADOS, 1982*

before time *adverb* long ago. Hawaiian youth usage *US, 1982*

befuggered *adjective* drunk. A conflation of BUGGERED and FUCKED *UK, 2002*

beg *noun* in a telephone solicitation, the actual plea to purchase that which is being sold *US, 1959*. ▶ **on the beg** begging, scrounging *UK, 1988*

beg *verb* ▶ **go begging** to be spare and available *UK, 2004*

begerk *noun* male masturbation. Oil rig workers use the term to refer to a 'big jerk' *AUSTRALIA, 1985*

beggar *noun* **1** a person, usually a man or boy. Euphemistic for BUGGER; sometimes spelt 'begger' *UK, 1833*. **2** an unpleasant, very dangerous or difficult thing, project, episode or circumstance; a nuisance. Euphemistic for BUGGER *UK, 1937*

beggar used as a euphemistic replacement for 'bugger' in all expletive phrases and exclamations *UK, 1937*

beggar boy's arse; beggar boy's ass *noun* money. Rhyming slang for BRASS (money) *UK, 1960*

beggar my neighbour *noun* the dole. Rhyming slang for the LABOUR (Exchange); usually follows 'on the' as in 'on the labour'. (to be drawing unemployment benefit). Sometimes shortened to 'beggar' *UK, 1960*

beggar's lagging; tramp's lagging *noun* a prison sentence of 90 days *UK, 1950*

beggered *adjective* tired. A euphemism for BUGGERED UP *NEW ZEALAND, 1984*

be good to yourself used with humour as a farewell. A catchphrase television sign-off on *The Don McNeil television Club* (ABC, 1950–51). Repeated with referential humour *US, 1950*

begorrah!; begorah!; begor! by God! Originally a genuine euphemism, latterly a cliché ascribed to stereotypical Irish *IRELAND, 1839*

beg your pardon *noun* a garden. Rhyming slang. Probably a post-World War 2 coinage on the grounds that pre-war Cockneys had 'yards' not 'gardens' *UK, 1961*

behavior report *noun* a letter home from a military recruit to his girlfriend *US, 1945*

behind *noun* the buttocks *UK, 1786*

behind *adjective* **1** imprisoned *US, 1961*. **2** committed, dedicated *US, 1968*

behind *preposition* **1** (of a drug) under the influence of *US, 1967*. **2** as a result of *US, 1957*

behind-the-behind *noun* anal sex *US, 1967*

behind the bridge *adverb* in any ghetto or slum. Originally a reference to the slums of Port of Spain at the back of the East Dry River *TRINIDAD AND TOBAGO, 1992*

behind the door *adverb* locked in a prison cell *UK, 1996*

behind the door when brains were given out stupid *AUSTRALIA, 1969*

behind with the rent *adjective* homosexual. Extended from a pun on 'buttocks' and 'behind' *UK, 2000*

beige *noun* a light-skinned black person *US, 1945*

beige *verb* to chemically darken cocaine to give it the appearance of a purity that it does not possess *US, 1989*

beige *adjective* bland, boring *US, 1982*

beige frame *noun* a light-skinned black woman *US, 1953*

beiging *noun* a chemical process to change the colour of cocaine and enhance its commercial possibilities, *2002*

be-in *noun* an organised gathering for the celebration of counterculture lifestyles and values. Originally applied to an event in San Francisco in January 1967, and then to similar events elsewhere. Organisers ('inspirers') of that event wrote: 'When the Berkeley political activists and the love generation of the Haight Ashbury and thousands of young men and women from every state in the nation embrace at the gathering of the tribes for a Human Be-In at polo field in Golden Gate Park the spiritual revolution will be manifest and proven' *US, 1967*

bejabbers; bejabers *noun* used as a jocular euphemism for 'bejesus' *US, 1959*

bejesus; bejasus *noun* used as a mild expletive. An ameliorated 'Jesus', originally recorded in 1908 but not widely used until the 1930s *US, 1908*

bejiminy *noun* used as a mild expletive *US, 1946*

bejonkers *noun* the female breasts *AUSTRALIA, 1988*

Bela and Boris *noun* in hold 'em poker, the two of clubs and the two of spades. An allusion to Bela Lugosi and Boris Korloff of horror film fame, with a nod to the horror that they visit upon a hand in hold 'em poker *US, 1996*

belasian *noun* a drunk, *bell*igerent *Asian US, 2003*

belch *noun* a complaint. Circus and carnival usage *US, 1981*

belch *verb* to act as a police informer *US, 1901*

belcher *noun* **1** the mouth *US, 1950*. **2** a police informer *US, 1956*

Belgian lace *noun* a pattern of white foam from the frothing head of beer that remains in an empty glass *UK, 2002*

believe 1 used for registering agreement *UK, 2005*. **2** used as an assertion of sincerity. A shortening of phrases like 'you can believe me', 'you must believe what I say', etc. Recorded in use among young, urban blacks *UK, 1999*

believer *noun* **1** in trucking, a driver who follows all laws and company rules *US, 1971*. **2** a dead enemy soldier. Vietnam war use *US, 1991*

be like used as a meaningless response to a greeting *US, 1980*

Belinda Carlisles *noun* haemorrhoids. Rhyming slang for 'piles', formed from the name of US singer Belinda Carlisle (b.1958) *UK, 2003*

bell *noun* **1** the head of the penis. From the shape *UK, 2001*. **2** the clitoris *AUSTRALIA, 1988*. **3** a telephone call. Teen slang *US, 1951*. ► **give someone a bell** to telephone someone. From the ringing bell of original telephones *UK, 1982*. ► **on a bell** in television and film making, shooting a scene. From the bell used on location to signal that shooting is about to begin *US, 1990*

bell *verb* to telephone someone. An allusion to Alexander Graham Bell, telephone pioneer, and/or to the bell that rang on early telephones *US, 1973*

belladonna *noun* an extremely potent hybrid marijuana. *Bella donna* is Italian for 'beautiful woman'. This plant, a hybrid of SUPERSKUNK, shares its name with *Atropa belladonna*, the poisonous deadly nightshade *UK, 2001*

bell cow *noun* in marketing, a popular, high-profit item *US, 1986*

belle *noun* a young and effeminate male homosexual *US, 1940*

bell end *noun* the head of the penis. From the shape *UK, 1973*

bellhop *noun* a member of the US Marine Corps. An abbreviated form of the longer SEAGOING BELL HOP, which teases the marines for their uniforms *US, 1929*

bellied *adjective* drunk *UK, 2003*

bellows *noun* the lungs *US, 1843*

bell-ringer *noun* any door-to-door salesman or canvasser *US, 1960*

bell rope *noun* the penis *US, 1969*

bells *noun* bell-bottomed trousers. Naval origins *UK, 1948*

bells! used for expressing approval *US, 1948*

bells and whistles *noun* **1** entertaining features that are not necessary to a computer program *US, 1983*. **2** extra features designed by underwriters to attract investors in a bond issue *US, 1988*

Bell Telephone hour *noun* a session of torture in which US soldiers used the electricity from field telephones to shock suspected Viet Cong. The term suggests a television programme, not genital-oriented electric torture *US, 1991*

belly *noun* **1** a fat person *US, 1997*. **2** the swell in a thicker-than-normal surfboard *US, 1963*. **3** a stomach ache *BARBADOS, 1965*. **4** pregnancy *BARBADOS, 1982*

belly *verb* ► **belly the wall** to stand facing a wall for inspection by prison guards *US, 1950*

bellyache *noun* any small-town newspaper *US, 1975*

bellyache *verb* to complain *US, 1881*

bellyacher *noun* a complainer *US, 1930*

belly and back *adverb* completely; without mercy *GUYANA, 1996*

belly board *noun* in television and film making, a low camera platform *US, 1990*

bellybump *verb* **1** to jostle; to shove; to rough up *US, 1961*. **2** to ride a sled face-down *US, 1912*

bellybuster *noun* **1** a stomach-first dive into the water *AUSTRALIA, 1941*. **2** a greasy hamburger or other food likely to provoke indigestion *US, 1981*

belly button *noun* **1** the navel. More naïve than childish; derives from the appearance of an umbilical knot *US, 1877*. **2** a bullet hole *UK, 2001*

belly fiddle *noun* a guitar *US, 1970*

belly flop *noun* a dive into the water stomach first, intentionally or not *US, 1895*

belly flopper *noun* **1** a poorly executed dive resulting in a painful impact on the water surface with the belly *AUSTRALIA, 1941*. **2** a rifleman shooting from a prone position *US, 1957*

bellyful *noun* as much as you can tolerate; more than enough *UK, 1687*

belly full and behind drunk *adjective* too full with food and drink to act *BARBADOS, 1996*

belly fummux *noun* stomach pains *IRELAND, 1996*

belly gas *noun* air injected into the abdominal cavity to raise the diaphragm *US, 1961*

belly gun *noun* a handgun *US, 1926*

belly habit *noun* **1** severe stomach cramping suffered during withdrawal from a drug addiction *US, 1970*. **2** a drug addiction, especially to an opiate *US, 1992*

belly hit *noun* in poker, a card drawn that completes an inside straight *US, 1951*

bellyologist *noun* a person who eats too much *BARBADOS, 1965*

belly pad *noun* a pancake *US, 1958*

belly queen *noun* a male homosexual who prefers face-to-face intercourse *US, 1965*

belly ride *noun* sexual intercourse *US, 1993*

bellyrubber *noun* a slow song in which partners dance close to each other *US, 1992*

belly rubbing *noun* dancing *UK, 1977*

belly-stick; stick *noun* in a confidence swindle involving fixed gambling, a confederate who appears to win consistently *US, 1940*

belly tanker *noun* in drag racing, a car made out of salvaged aeroplane fuel tanks for lake bed racing *US, 1992*

belly up *verb* to approach and stand against something, usually a bar *US, 1907*

belly-up *adjective* bankrupt, out of business; dead *US, 1920*

bellywash *noun* a soft drink, soda. Originally applied to a weak drink, and then to soda *US, 1926*

belly whacker *noun* a poorly executed dive resulting in a painful impact on the water surface with the belly *AUSTRALIA, 2003*

belly-whop *verb* in sledding, to dive stomach-first onto the sled *US, 1955*

belly woman *noun* a pregnant woman *JAMAICA, 1834*

belly works *noun* diarrhoea *GUYANA, 1996*

below par *adjective* in poor health or spirits. From describing stocks and shares as below face value *UK, 1937*

below the radar *adverb* keeping a low profile; unperceived *US, 1990*

below the zone *adverb* (used of a military promotion) unexpectedly early. Vietnam war usage *US, 1989*

belt *noun* **1** a hit; a punch *UK, 1937*. **2** a gulp, especially of strong alcohol *US, 1922*. **3** the first, strong effect of a drug *US, 1948*. **4** a prostitute; any woman regarded as a sex-object. The earlier sense of 'prostitute' seems to have been spread from the Australian to the British forces during World War 2 and, in so doing, broadened its intention *AUSTRALIA, 1945*. ▶ **below the belt** unfair, unsportsmanlike. From the language of boxing, where a blow below the belt is prohibited *UK, 1890*. ▶ **under your belt** personal experience of something. From an earlier use, of food in your stomach *UK, 1958*

belt *verb* to hit someone or something. From earlier sense: to hit with a belt *UK, 1838*

belta *adjective* good, excellent *UK, 2003*

belt along; belt *verb* to move at great speed. Originally Gloucestershire dialect *UK, 1890*

belt buckle polisher *noun* a song suited for slow dancing *US, 1984*

belt down; belt *verb* to rain heavily *UK, 1984*

belted *adjective* drunk or drug-intoxicated *US, 1970*

belter *noun* **1** a thrilling event; a wonderful thing *UK, 1983*. **2** a song that can be sung with great vigour; a type of singer that has a vigorous approach to a song *UK, 1984*

belting *noun* a beating whether punitive or pugilistic *UK, 1825*

belting *adjective* excellent *UK, 2002*

belt out *verb* to sing or play a musical instrument with great vigour *UK, 1953*

belts and boards *noun* accoutrements for a Royal Canadian Air Force officer's uniform on formal ceremonial occasions *CANADA, 1995*

belt up! be quiet! *UK, 1949*

Beltway commando *noun* any military bureaucrat working in Washington D.C. Gulf war usage *US, 1991*

be lucky goodbye. Cockney, maybe MOCKNEY *UK, 1974*

Belushi *noun* a combination of cocaine and heroin. In memory of the SPEEDBALL mix that killed film actor John Belushi, 1949–82 *US, 1998*

Belyando spruce; Belyando sprue *noun* marijuana from the Belyando area of Queensland *AUSTRALIA, 1977*

be my guest! do as you wish; you are welcome to have whatever has been asked for *US, 1955*

ben *noun* **1** a lavatory. Rhyming slang for 'Benghazi', KARZY (a lavatory); from the Libyan seaport and probably originating in the desert campaign of World War 2 *UK, 1992*. **2** benzodiazepine, an anti-depressant, especially Valium™. Also referred to as 'benzo', *1996*

Ben; Bennie; Benjamin *noun* Benzedrine™ (amphetamine sulphate), or another central nervous system stimulant. Truckers often personify stimulants, referring to 'my good friend Benjamin' or saying 'better let Bennie drive' *US, 1971*

benar *adjective* better. Originally C16, conjugated as BENE (good), '*benar, benat* ' (best); the 'best' sense is now obsolete but 'good' and 'better' survived in the affected surroundings of polari *UK, 2002*

bench *noun* **1** an athletic's team coaching staff and reserve players, collectively *US, 1962*. **2** a youth gang *US, 1951*. ▶ **ride the bench; warm the bench** to sit on the sidelines of an athletic contest as a substitute player *US, 1911*

bench *verb* **1** to remove someone from competition. Originally a sports term – the player literally returned to the bench during a game. Later applied to a variety of situations *US, 1917*. **2** to reprimand someone *US, 1997*

bench boy *noun* an athlete who never makes the starting lineup and thus spends most of the time during games sitting on the team bench *US, 1999*

bench jockey *noun* in a team sport, a substitute player, especially one who makes his opinion known from the bench *US, 1939*

bench race *verb* to talk about drag racing without actually doing it *US, 1960s to 70s*

benchwarmer *noun* a substitute player on a sports team *US, 1905*

bend *noun* **1** a spree, especially involving hard drinking; hence, a drug-induced hallucinogenic experience *UK, 1979*. **2** money *US, 1973*

bend *verb* **1** to deliberately slur or distort a musical note *US, 1960*. **2** to fraudulently affect the outcome of a sporting event; to bribe or by other means corrupt authority *UK, 1864*. **3** to take part in a gang fight *US, 1993*. ▶ **bend the elbow** to enjoy a few drinks *NEW ZEALAND, 1994*. ▶ **bend the iron; bend the rust; bend the rail** to change the position of a railway point *US, 1946*

bended knees *noun* cheese. Rhyming slang, sometimes shortened to 'bended'; noted in use amongst tramps *UK, 1960*

bender *noun* **1** a prolonged session of hard drinking *US, 1845*. **2** a male homosexual who plays the passive role in anal sex; a homosexual *US, 1965*. **3** a stolen car *US, 1992*. **4** any bending joint in the body, such as the elbow or knee *US, 1973*. **5** a Roman Catholic *NEW*

ZEALAND, *1998*. **6** a suspended prison sentence *UK, 1996*. **7** a hammer *US, 1980*

bender mender *noun* a hangover cure, especially a stiff drink. Elaborated on BENDER (a prolonged session of hard drinking) *UK: SCOTLAND, 1988*

bending drill *noun* an act of defecation in the open-air. Military use, originating with the British army in North Africa during World War 2 *UK, 1945*

bend over *verb* to submit; to give in to someone. An image that suggests bending over is 'to be buggered' *US, 1960s*

bend over, brown eyes used as a humorous instruction to a patient about to undergo a rectal examination *US, 1989*

bends and motherfuckers *noun* the squat-thrust exercise drill. Vietnam war usage. In gentler times, known as a 'burpee' *US, 1991*

bend up *verb* to encourage or enable another's intoxication *UK, 1999*

bene; ben; bien *adjective* good. Originally C16, adapted from Italian *bene*, possibly Latin *bonus* (good) *UK, 2002*

benefit *noun* any hardship or unpleasant feature of army life. Used with obvious irony *US, 1968*

Ben Franklin *noun* a $100 note. From the engraving on the note *US, 1990*

Bengal lancer *noun* an opportunist, especially one who takes risks in pursuit of criminal gain. Glasgow rhyming slang for CHANCER *UK, 2005*

be nice! used by US troops in Vietnam when caught by surprise or provoked by another *US, 1982*

benies *noun* benefits *US, 1970*

Benjie; Benji *noun* a $100 note. From the portrait of Benjamin Franklin on the note *US, 1985*

benjo *noun* a toilet. From Japanese *AUSTRALIA, 1988*

Bennett buggy *noun* a car converted to a four-wheel, horse-drawn carriage by removal of the engine, drive train and windshield (in depression times); later, any broken-down car *CANADA, 1987*

Ben Nevis *noun* a long prison sentence. Prison slang, reported in private correspondence by a serving prisoner in January 2002. Ben Nevis is Britain's highest mountain to climb *UK, 2002*

bennie *noun* a female prostitute's customer who prefers to perform oral sex on the prostitute *US, 1964*

bennie God *noun* the sun *US, 1965*

bennie machine *noun* a reflector used while sunbathing *US, 1965*

bennies *noun* **1** sun rays. A shortened form of 'beneficial' *US, 1965*. **2** during the Vietnam war, basic comforts. A shortened form of 'benefits' *US, 1976*

benny *noun* **1** a Falkland Islander *UK, 1982*. **2** an amphetamine, especially Benzedrine™ (amphetamine sulphate), a central nervous system stimulant *US, 1945*. **3** a Benzedrine™ inhaler *US, 1970*. **4** a Benson & Hedges cigarette *UK, 1996*. **5** in Vancouver Island, an order of Eggs Benedict *CANADA, 2002*. **6** an overcoat *UK, 1812*. **7** a Ben Sherman shirt, a fashion item given iconic status by skinheads *UK, 2001*. **8** a sports fan who looks back at a basketball game and analyses what might have been. Synonymous with 'Monday Morning Quarterback' except basketball people like to call them 'Bennys''. Probably from the image of men in overcoats *US, 1946*. **9** a person who looks and talks the part of a surfer but does not actually surf *US, 1991*. ► **get a benny on** to lose your temper *UK, 1997*

benny blue *noun* in craps, a roll of seven when shooting for your point. From the call, 'Benny blue, you're all through!' *US, 1985*

benny boost *noun* a shoplifting technique involving the use of an oversized, specially equipped overcoat *US, 1992*

Benny boy *noun* a young transvestite prostitute found in Manila and other Southeast Asian cities *PHILIPPINES, 1967*

benny chaser *noun* coffee consumed with Benzedrine™ (amphetamine sulphate), a central nervous system stimulant. Used with humour by truckers who rely on different forms of stimulation to stay awake for long periods *US, 1971*

benny house *noun* a primarily heterosexual brothel that will upon request procure a male sexual partner for a male client *US, 1965*

Benny Mason; Mr Mason *noun* marijuana that is so potent that it must be stored in a pot or mason jar (a glass jar for preserving food) to contain the smell *US, 1992*

benny suggs *noun* good ideas. Military; from 'beneficial *suggestions*' *UK, 1995*

benny worker *noun* a thief who uses an overcoat to hide his movements or goods *US, 1949*

beno *adjective* used as a humorous description of a woman's condition while experiencing the bleed period of the menstrual cycle. From the pronunciation – 'There will *be no* fun tonight' *US, 1954*

benson *noun* a toady, a sycophant. Apparently derived from the name of the butler character in US television situation comedy *Soap*, 1978–82, and its concurrent spin-off *Benson*, 1979–86 *UK: SCOTLAND, 1996*

bent *noun* a homosexual *UK, 1957*

bent *adjective* **1** stolen *US, 1930*. **2** corrupt, crooked, criminal. The opposite of STRAIGHT (honest/conventional) *UK, 1914*. **3** unfaithful *UK, 1958*. **4** sexually deviant *UK, 1957*. **5** homosexual *UK, 1959*. **6** drunk or drug-intoxicated *US, 1833*. **7** ill-humoured; grouchy *US, 1965*. **8** spoiled, broken, out-of-order *UK, 1930*. **9** suffering from decompression sickness *UK, 1984*. ► **bent as a butcher's hook** very corrupt, incontrovertibly criminal *UK, 1977*. ► **bent as a nine-bob note** **1** corrupt, crooked. In pre-decimalisation currency, ten-bob (ten shillings) was the only currency note for less than a pound value; a nine-bob note would have been an obvious forgery *UK, 2000*. **2** ostentatiously homosexual. A sterling elaboration of BENT *UK, 2000*. ► **bent as arseholes** corrupt, crooked *UK, 1998*

bent and greased *adjective* prepared to be taken advantage of. The sexual allusion is difficult to miss *US, 1994*

bent eight *noun* an eight-cylinder V engine *US, 1948*

bent stovebolt *noun* in drag racing and hot rodding, a Chevrolet V-8 engine *US, 1968*

Bent Whore *nickname* Bien Hoa, South Vietnam, site of an American air base during the Vietnam war *US, 1991*

benz *noun* a tablet of Benzedrine™ (amphetamine sulphate), a central nervous system stimulant *US, 1969*

Benz *nickname* a Mercedes-Benz car *US, 1990*

Benzedrina *noun* in homosexual usage, a personification of Benzedrine™ (amphetamine sulphate), a central nervous system stimulant *US, 1980*

Benzo *noun* a Mercedes-Benz car *US, 1986*

bequeenum *adjective* homosexual *UK, 2003*

Berb *noun* a social outcast *US, 1993*

Berdoo; San Berdoo; San Berdu *nickname* San Bernadino, California, east of Los Angeles *US, 1914*

bergwind *noun* a warm offshore breeze *SOUTH AFRICA, 1876*

bergy bit *noun* a small iceberg *UK, 1906*

bergy seltzer *noun* a fizzing produced in an iceberg when trapped air is released *ANTARCTICA, 2000*

berk; birk; burk; burke *noun* a fool. Almost certainly a reduction of the rhyming slang BERKSHIRE HUNT or BERKELEY HUNT (a CUNT) yet so widely used that the original sense has almost been lost; there is a suggestion that 'berk' may be a diminution of BERKELEYS (the female breasts), thus TIT (a fool) *UK, 1936*

Berkeley Quality Software *noun* any computer program that is incomplete or incorrect *US, 1991*

berkeleys *noun* the female breasts. From Romany *berk* (a breast) *UK, 1984*

berkers *adjective* angry, emotionally unstable. From 'berserk' *NEW ZEALAND, 1998*

berko *adjective* berserk; crazy *AUSTRALIA, 1961*

Berks *noun* Berkshire. A spoken form of the conventional written abbreviation, considered colloquial when used in speech as a genuine equivalent of the original name *UK, 1937*

Berkshire hunt; Berkeley hunt *noun* **1** a fool. Rhyming slang for CUNT, generally in the reduced form BERK. Also variant 'Birchington hunt' *UK, 1937*. **2** the vagina. Rhyming slang for CUNT. Also variant 'Birchington hunt' *UK, 1937*

berky *noun* a complete loss of temper and emotional stability *NEW ZEALAND, 1985*

berley *noun* in fishing, any material added to water in order to attract fish. Origin unknown *AUSTRALIA, 1874*

berley *verb* to place berley in the water to attract fish *AUSTRALIA, 1852*

Berlin Wall *noun* a testicle. Rhyming slang for 'ball', generally in the plural (BALLS) *UK, 2003*

Bermuda crescent *noun* a semi-circle of dance floor in front of a stage that remains empty when a band is playing. A joke on the Bermuda Triangle, a vast three-sided area of the Atlantic with angles at Bermuda, Puerto Rico and Fort Lauderdale, Florida, where ships and planes apparently disappear *UK, 1999*

Bermuda time *adverb* late *BERMUDA, 1985*

Bermuda triangle *noun* the vagina *UK, 2001*

Bernard Langered *adjective* drunk. An elaboration of LANGERED (drunk), playing on the name of German golfer Bernhard Langer (b.1957), possibly as an ironic swipe at his 'born-again' Christianity *UK, 2002*

Berni; Bernice; Bernie *noun* cocaine *US, 1933*

Bernie *noun* one million pounds. A jibe at Formula One motor racing tycoon Bernie Ecclestone who had his £1,000,000 donation to the Labour Party returned for reasons of political expediency 2002 *UK, 2002*

Bernie's flakes; Bernie's gold dust *noun* cocaine *UK, 2002*

berries *noun* **1** crystalised cocaine *US, 1949*. **2** anything considered to be the finest, the most excellent, the best. Probably a figurative use of THE BERRIES (testicles) in the same way that BOLLOCKS carries both senses. Also variant 'the berrs' *UK: SCOTLAND, 1974*

berry *noun* **1** a dollar *US, 1916*. **2** crack cocaine *US, 1993*

berry *verb* to communicate via instant wireless messaging *CANADA, 2002*

berry sugar *noun* extra fine granulated sugar *CANADA, 2002*

Bert *nickname* ▷ *see:* FAT ALBERT

berth *noun* a job working on a fishing boat. Originally, when fishing was done from dories, a 'berth' was a specific spot on one side of the dory where a fisherman was to row and work lines. It has come to mean any job on a fishing boat *CANADA, 1999*

Bertie *noun* ▶ **do a Bertie** to become an important informer. Police slang; after Bertie Smalls, a notorious or legendary (depending on your point of view) small-time robber turned police informer who, in 1973, became the original SUPERGRASS *UK, 1999*

be seeing you goodbye. 'Be seeing you' gained a sinister, threatening edge in 1967 when used in cult television series *The Prisoner UK, 1937*

Bess *noun* used as a term of address among male homosexuals *US, 1965*

bessie *noun* **1** the penis *US, 1973*. **2** a best-friend. Pronounced 'bezzie', used by teenagers *UK, 2003*

best *noun* a stroke of a cane, or 'the slipper' applied as corporal punishment. For some reason six was always the most popular number of deliveries ('six of the best') but the term varies to account for the punisher's preference. Corporal punishment has not been permitted in UK schools since the later C20 *UK, 1912*. ▶ **one of the best** a good man, a good companion *UK, 1937*

best *verb* should *US, 1973*. ▶ **give (a number) of the best** to give (so many) belts with a cane *AUSTRALIA, 1965*

best-best *adjective* the very best *BARBADOS, 1982*

best bet *noun* the most advantageous option *UK, 1941*

best bib and tucker *noun* your best clothes. Originally of an article worn by women and girls, in more generalised use by mid-C19 *UK, 1747*

best blue; best BD *noun* the better of an airman's or a soldier's two issued uniforms. BD is *battledress*'. In use throughout World War 2 and National Service, 1939–62 *UK, 1939*

best boy *noun* in television and film making, the electrician's assistant *US, 1937*

bestest *adjective* best. A solecism; childish, occasionally jocular or as an endearment *UK, 1905*

best friend *noun* your penis *AUSTRALIA, 1992*

best girl *noun* a fiancée, a wife or a special girlfriend *US, 1887*

be's that way used as a world-weary but wise acknowledgement that what is, is *US, 1968*

best of British luck!; best of British! used as an offer of good wishes, sometimes sincerely but generally with such heavy irony that the opposite is intended and inferred. Military coinage, in general use by 1960 *UK, 1940s*

best piece *noun* a girlfriend or wife *US, 1971*

best seller *noun* a Ford Cortina car. Citizens' band radio slang, presumably inspired by Ford's sales figures at the time of coinage *UK, 1981*

bet *verb* ▶ **bet a pound to a piece of shit** used as a statement of absolute certainty. Usually construed positively as 'I will' or 'would bet'; occasional and earlier use may be negative *UK, 1937*. ▶ **bet like the Watsons** to bet heavily on horses. After legendary Australian gamblers *AUSTRALIA, 1949*. ▶ **bet London to a brick** used as a statement of absolute certainty *AUSTRALIA, 1945*. ▶ **bet on a horse** to be addicted to heroin or morphine *US, 1992*. ▶ **bet on the blue** to gamble on credit *AUSTRALIA, 1949*. ▶ **bet on the coat** to place a dummy bet with a bookmaker to encourage genuine interest in a bet *AUSTRALIA, 1949*. ▶ **bet the dog** in bar dice games, to bet the total amount of the pot *US, 1971*. ▶ **bet the ranch; bet the farm** to be absolutely certain about something *US, 1981*. ▶ **bet until your nose bleeds** in horse racing, to bet all of your resources on a sure thing *AUSTRALIA, 1989*. ▶ **want to bet on it?** a catchphrase used, with *bet* emphasised, as a challenging expression of doubt *UK, 1971*

bet! used for expressing approval *US, 1987*

beta *noun* **1** a test or probationary stage. Borrowed from the technical process of external testing of a product *US, 1991*. **2** the grade 'B' in academic work *US, 1968*

betcha! used as a statement of certainty. A phonetic blending of 'bet you' or an elision of BET YOUR ASS/BOOTS/LIFE, etc *UK, 1964*

bet-down *adjective* very ugly *IRELAND, 2001*

be the ... used as a command. Mockingly, from Zen philosophy, as in 'Driver, be the fast lane'. *US, 1984*

be there, aloha used as a farewell. Repopularised by ESPN's Keith Olberman, borrowed from the television programme *Hawaii 5-0 US, 1978*

be there or be square if you do not attend an event thus advertised you will risk being thought unfashionable. A popular catchphrase or slogan *UK, 1960*

betise *noun* an ill-timed remark. The term comes from French *CANADA, 2002*

bet on top *noun* a bogus bet laid by a bookmaker's confederate to encourage genuine interest in a particular gamble. The bookmaker's clerk will place the bet 'on top' (not in the body) of the betting book *UK, 1961*

Bette *noun* a person who looks better from a distance. After singer Bette Midler who recorded the song 'From a Distance', 1990 *UK, 2004*

better half *noun* a wife. A jocular usage that, over time, has also referred to 'a husband', 'a close friend' and 'a man's soul' *UK, 1580*

better idea *noun* in car repair shops, used to describe any of several ill-advised equipment developments by Ford. Derived from a Ford advertising slogan – 'Ford has a better idea' *US, 1992*

better living through chemistry used as a humorous endorsement of mind-altering recreational drug use. Borrowed from an advertising slogan of DuPont Chemicals *US, 1970*

better than a poke in the eye with a sharp stick describes an event or circumstance that is of minimal desirability. A 'burnt stick' or a 'blunt stick' allow further variation of the basic formula *AUSTRALIA, 1974*

betting ring *noun* the area at a racecourse devoted to betting *AUSTRALIA, 1966*

betting shop *noun* an illegal establishment for betting *AUSTRALIA, 1956*

betting tool *noun* in horse racing, a horse that consistently wins *US, 1960*

Betty *noun* **1** an attractive female *US, 1988.* **2** an old woman. Probably after Betty Hoskins (b.1922), well known to audiences of Graham Norton's television programmes since 1998 *UK, 2003*

betty bracelets *noun* police *UK, 1993*

Betty Coed *noun* the stereotypical female high school or college student *US, 1961*

Betty Crocker *noun* used by combat troops in Vietnam to describe their peers not in combat, especially those in Saigon. Betty Crocker is the mythical yet trademarked American homemaker created in 1921 by the Washburn Crosby Company, forerunner to General Mills Incorporated. One of many terms coined in Vietnam *US, 1969*

Betty Grable *noun* **1** sable. Rhyming slang in criminal use, based on the name of film actress Betty Grable (1916–73) *UK, 1956.* **2** a table. Rhyming slang, based on the name of film actress Betty Grable (1916–73). Also shortened to 'betty' *UK, 1992*

between pictures *adjective* out of work, unemployed. A euphemism, true in the entertainment industry, jocular elsewhere *US, 1954*

between you and me and the gate-post; between you and me and the bedpost between ourselves. Conjuring the image of a confidence passed over a garden gate. The 'bedpost', a still-used variation, allows for more intimate intercourse *UK, 1832*

bet your ass used as a statement of absolute certainty *US, 1928*

bet your boots used as a statement of absolute certainty *US, 1856*

bet your bottom dollar used as a statement of absolute certainty *US, 1935*

bet your hat used as a statement of absolute certainty *US, 1879*

bet your life used as a statement of absolute certainty *US, 1852*

Beulah land *noun* heaven. From the book of Isaiah, 62:4 *US, 1939*

bevels *noun* dice that have been altered by rounding off the sides slightly so as to produce a desired point *US, 1963*

beverada; bevois *noun* **1** a drink, especially beer. Affected variations of BEVVY *UK, 2002.* **2** a public house. An affected variation of BEVVY CASEY *UK, 2002*

Beverley Pills *noun* the prescription drug Vicodin™ when taken recreationally *US, 2002*

bevie homie *noun* a heavy drinker *UK, 1953*

Bevin *noun* in the mining industry, a shift spent at home as a result of mechanical breakdown. After Ernest Bevin, 1881–1951, statesman and creator of the Transport and General Workers Union. This term, like most of the UK's mining industry, has not survived the intervening years *UK, 1970*

bevo *noun* any alcoholic beverage *US, 2003*

bevvied; bevvied up *adjective* drunk. From BEVVY (an alcoholic drink) *UK, 1960*

bevvy *verb* to drink alcohol *UK, 1934*

bevvy; bevie *noun* ► **on the bevvy; on the bevie** to be drinking, especially for a period of time dedicated to drunkenness *UK, 1953*

bevvy; bevie; bevv *noun* **1** an alcoholic drink, especially beer. Possibly from the circus term 'bevie' (a public house), or an abbreviation of 'beverage'; both derive from C15 'bever ' (drink), and ultimately from Latin *bibere UK, 1889*

bevvy casey; bevie casey *noun* a public house. A combination of BEVVY (an alcoholic drink) and, ultimately, Italian *casa* (house) *UK, MID-C19*

bevvy omee *noun* a drunkard. A combination of BEVVY (an alcoholic drink) and OMEE (a man) *UK, 1937*

bevvy-up *noun* a drinking session *UK, 1962*

bevvy up *verb* to drink alcohol. An elaboration of BEVVY *UK, 1970*

bewitched, bothered and bewildered *adjective* confused. The title of a song from the 1940 show *Pal Joey*, lyrics by Lorenz Hart, music by Richard Rodgers *US, 1950*

Bexley Heath; bexleys *noun* the teeth. Rhyming slang, based on a convenient area of Greater London *UK, 1992*

beyond *adjective* outstanding, amazing, extraordinary *US, 1999*

beyond *adverb* in England *IRELAND, 1997*

bezazz; bizzazz *noun* glamour, sparkle, energy, excitement. A variation, if not a misspelling, of PIZZAZZ *US, 1970*

bezel *noun* any car part *US, 1959*

bezzie *adjective* best *UK, 2005*

BF; bee eff *noun* a bloody fool. A euphemistic abbreviation *UK, 1960*

BFD *noun* a big fucking *deal*. Sometimes euphemised from 'fucking' to 'fat' *US, 1966*

BFE *noun* any remote location. An abbreviation of BUMFUCK, EGYPT *US, 1989*

BFI *noun* **1** in computer technology, an approach relying on *brute force* and *ignorance* rather than elegant analysis *US, 1986.* **2** a massive heart attack or stroke; a *big fucking infarct US, 1994*

B flat *adjective* fat. Rhyming slang *UK, 2002*

BFN *noun* an extremely remote place. An abbreviation of BUTT FUCKING NOWHERE *US, 2002*

BFU *adjective* big, fat and ugly *US, 1996*

BG *noun* a young member of a youth gang. An abbreviation of baby gangster *US, 1995*

B game *noun* in a gambling establishment or cardroom, the table with the second highest betting limit *US, 1988*

BGF the *Black Guerilla Family*, a black prison gang *US, 2000*

B girl *noun* **1** a woman who works in a bar, encouraging customers through flirtation to buy drinks, both for themselves and for her *US, 1936.* **2** a young woman involved in early hip-hop. From 'break girl' *US, 2000*

BH! used in anger, astonishment, disappointment and frustration. A euphemistic abbreviation of BLOODY HELL! *UK, 1928*

bhang *noun* **1** marijuana, usually presumed to be from India. Urdu for *cannabis indica* (Indian hemp), also used for a marijuana tea. Known in various forms since 1598, modern usage and variant spelling, 'bang', probably begins with hippies *INDIA, 1948.* **2** a mixture of marijuana pollen and ghee for smoking *UK, 2002*

bhang lassi *noun* yoghurt and marijuana combined in a drink *INDIA, 2003*

B head *noun* a barbiturate user or addict *US, 1979*

bhoy *noun* an Irishman involved in crime or political violence, especially as 'the Bhoys'. Irish pronunciation of 'boy' *UK: NORTHERN IRELAND, 2001*

bi *noun* a *bi*sexual person *US, 1956*

bi *adjective* *bi*sexual *US, 1956*

bianc; beone; beyonek; beyong *noun* a shilling. From Italian *bianco* (white) for the silver of the coin; these variations survived in theatrical and gay society from mid-C19 until UK decimalisation in 1971 *UK, 2002*

Bianca blast *noun* oral sex performed with a mouth full of Bianca mouth wash *US, 1993*

bib *noun* **1** in horse racing, a horse's nose or head as a measure of a close finish *AUSTRALIA, 1989.* **2** a tablet of MDMA, the recreational drug best known as ecstasy *UK, 2003.* ► **push your bib in; put your bib in; stick your bib in** to interfere *AUSTRALIA, 1959*

bib *verb* to sound a horn. A variation of conventional 'beep' *UK, 2004*

bibby *noun* **1** a native woman or girl. A new spelling for obsolete Anglo-Indian 'bebee' *UK, 1975.* **2** mucus *BARBADOS, 1982*

bibby-dibby *adjective* petty, trivial, worthless *JAMAICA, 2003*

bibi *adjective* bisexual *UK, 2002*

Bible *noun* **1** the truth *US, 1948*. **2** a fundamental source book, if not the most authoritative reference book in a given field *US, 1893*. **3** on the railways, the book of company rules *US, 1946*. **4** in trucking, the Interstate Commerce Commission's book of regulations governing trucking *US, 1971*. **5** the Harley-Davidson repair manual. Biker (motorcycle) usage *US, 2001*. **6** in a unionised work environment, the union contract *US, 1963*. **7** in circus and carnival usage, a programme or souvenir magazine *US, 1981*. **8** in the circus or carnival, *The Billboard*, a business newspaper *US, 1980*. ▶ **the Bible** *Glass's Guide to Used Car Prices*, first published in 1933. A specialist use for the motor trade *UK, 1981*

bibleback *noun* **1** a prisoner who has turned to religion, sincerely or not *US, 1972*. **2** in the circus or carnival, a folding plank used for grandstands *US, 1980*

Bible-basher; Bible-thumper *noun* an evangelical Christian *US, 1885*

bible-bashing *adjective* Christian, especially zealously so *AUSTRALIA, 1975*

Bible belt *noun* **1** rural America, especially in the south, where fundamentalist Christians dominate the culture *US, 1924*. **2** the political interests and constituency of the (Christian) religious right *UK, 2001*. **3** any area with a fundamentalist Christian majority *UK, 2001*

Bible belter *noun* a person from the rural mid-western or southern US. Implies ignorance, gullibility and backwardness *US, 1978*

Bible bunny *noun* a Christian who is filled with spiritual joy *US, 1998*

Bible puncher *noun* in the armed services, a chaplain. Not recorded until 1961 but suggested by BIBLE-PUNCHING, 1937 *UK, 1961*

Bible-punching *noun* a sermon, a religious talk. Also, now more usually, used as an adjective *UK, 1937*

Bible run *noun* in television and film making, a weekly print-out of all production expenses *US, 1990*

Biblical neckline; Biblical top *noun* a low-cut neckline on an item of ladies' wear that reveals generous amounts of cleavage, or more. A pun on 'Lo and behold!'. Possibly Australian in origin and, when noted in 1984, was thought to have slipped into disuse by the mid-1960s. It is currently alive and well in the UK in comedian's patter: 'I see you're wearing your biblical top tonight … Lo and behold! And, yea, I can see the promised land. And, hallelujah! – there is milk and honey! One on each tap' *UK, 1984*

bic *verb* to understand. Vietnam war usage; a corrupted *biet*, Vietnamese for 'understand' *US, 1991*

bicarb *noun* bicarbonate of soda *US, 1922*

bice; byce *noun* two, especially £2. From French *bis* (twice) *UK, 1937*

bice and a roht; bice and a half *noun* in betting, odds of 5–2. The literal sense is 'two and a half'; in betting odds the '–1' is usually implied. From BICE (two) *UK, 1937*

bicho *noun* the penis *US, 1976*

bicky; bikky *noun* a biscuit *UK, 1886*

bicoastal *adjective* pertaining to the west and east coasts of the US. Almost always used with a sense of mocking, hyper-formality *US, 1984*

bi-curious *adjective* interested in experimenting with bisexuality *US, 1990*

bicycle *noun* **1** a sexually promiscuous female *UK, 1989*. **2** a bisexual *US, 1978*. **3** in lowball poker, the lowest possible straight *US, 1981*. **4** in electric line work, a chain drill used for drilling holes *US, 1980*. ▶ **on your bicycle** in boxing, staying away from the opponent's punches by back pedalling *US, 1936*

bicycle *verb* **1** in television and film making, to work on multiple projects simultaneously. In the days of silent films, to show a film at several different theatres required transporting it from one theatre to another, often by bicycle *US, 1977*. **2** to ride a surfboard with a wide stance *US, 1977*

bicycle pump *noun* a large syringe. Korean war usage *US, 1961*

bid *noun* an old woman, especially one who complains or fusses. A shortening of BIDDY *UK, 1984*

biddims *noun* trousers that are too short and narrow *BARBADOS, 1996*

biddle move *noun* a manoeuvre by a cheat or a conjuror that moves a selected playing card to the bottom of the deck *UK, 2003*

biddy *noun* an old woman, usually one prone to complain and fuss. The dominant sense of the term in the US, with the older sense of a 'young woman' unknown *US, 1938*

bidness *noun* business. A Texas corrupted pronunciation of a Texas activity *US, 1984*

biff *noun* **1** a blow, a hit, a whack *US, 1847*. **2** fighting, especially fighting on a sporting field *AUSTRALIA, 1970*. **3** in mountain biking, a crash *US, 1996*. **4** in pinball, a forceful hit with the flipper *US, 1977*. **5** the vagina, the vulva *UK, 1997*. **6** a person deformed to some degree by spina bifida. An offensive term used by schoolchildren *UK, 2003*. **7** a toilet *US, 1942*

biff *verb* **1** to hit someone or something *UK, 1888*. **2** to throw something *NEW ZEALAND, 1964*. **3** in computing, to inform someone of incoming mail *US, 1991*. **4** to fail *US, 1997*

biffa *adjective* very ugly. Probably derives from US BIFFER (an unattractive woman); however UK theories abound, including: 'Biffo the Bear' in the Beano comic from 1948, simply known as 'Biffo' by the 1990s; 'Biffa Bacon' in the later *Viz* comic; and the familiar company name, 'Biffa Waste Services' *UK, 2003*

biffer *noun* **1** someone with a reputation as a hard hitter, especially in sports *UK, 2003*. **2** any implement used for hitting, whether designed for such a purpose or improvised *UK, 2003*. **3** an unattractive woman *US, 1932*

biffoe *noun* a rude and obnoxious person *UK, 1983*

biffy *noun* a toilet *US, 1942*

biffy *adjective* drunk *UK, 1961*

bifta *noun* **1** a marijuana cigarette; sufficient marijuana to make a cigarette. Also Variant spellings 'biftah' or 'bifter' *UK, 1996*. **2** a cigarette. Sometimes shortened to 'bif'. *UK, 1996*

big *verb* to impregnate someone *US, 1917*

big *adjective* **1** generous. Often ironic, especially in the phrase 'that's big of you' *US, 1934*. **2** in darts, the larger of two sections of a number on the dartboard. For example, the larger 6 section would be 'big six' *US, 1980*. ▶ **like a big dog** to an extreme *US, 1987*. ▶ **the big dish** a big win. Australian gambling slang *AUSTRALIA, 1949*. ▶ **too big for your boots** conceited, self-important *UK, 1879*

big *adverb* very successfully; to a great degree. Especially in the phrase GO OVER BIG *US, 1893*. ▶ **go over big** to achieve great success *US, 1962*

Big A *noun* **1** AIDS *US, 1992*. **2** in poker, an ace, especially when it is the deciding card in a hand *US, 1988*. ▶ **give someone the Big A** to dismiss, reject or sack someone. The 'big A' is a euphemism for 'arse' *AUSTRALIA, 1976*

Big A *nickname* **1** Eddie Arcaro (1916–1917), dominant jockey in American horse racing from 1933 until 1962, one of only two jockeys to win the Kentucky Derby five times. The 'Big' sobriquet supplied a dose of irony when applied to a man who stood 5' 2" and weighed 114 pounds *US, 1937*. **2** the Aqueduct Race Track in Westbury, New York *US, 1959*. **3** the US federal penitentiary in Atlanta, Georgia *US, 1982*

big air *noun* an impressive distance between a snowboarder and the snow *US, 1994*

big an heavies *noun* Benson & Hedges™ cigarettes *UK: SCOTLAND, 1988*

big apple *noun* a cap with a big visor. In vogue during the 'Superfly' era of the early 1970s *US, 1970*

Big Apple *nickname* New York. Slang etymologists Gerald Cohen and Barry Popik have researched the origins of the term extensively, destroying along the way a number of popular yet false etymologies. Cohen and Popik trace the first printed use of the term to New York sportswriter John J. Fitzgerald, who heard the term used by black racetrack stable hands *US, 1921*

big-arsed *adjective* big *UK, 2000*

big-ass *adjective* very large *US, 1957*

big-ass bird *noun* the Boeing B-17 military aircraft *US, 1961*

big-assed *adjective* large US, 1945

Big B *nickname* Berlin US, 1944

big bag *noun* a large bag of heroin; heroin US, 1969

big ball *noun* **1** in pool, an object ball that can be hit either directly or on the rebound off a cushion. Because there are two ways to hit it, it is a bigger target, hence a 'big ball' US, 1913. **2** in bowling, a roll that forcefully hooks into the standing pins US, 1962

big baller *noun* a big spender US, 2001

big banger *noun* a motorcyle with a large one-cylinder engine US, 1965

big beast *noun* an important, powerful person UK, 2000

big belly *noun* a B-52 bomber US, 1986

Big Ben *noun* **1** ten; ten pounds. Rhyming slang UK, 1960. **2** the new, large design hundred-dollar note minted in the late 1990s. The 'Ben' is an allusion to Benjamin Franklin, the C18 slang lexicographer whose portrait graces the note US, 1996. **3** Benzedrine™ (amphetamine sulphate), a central nervous system stimulant US, 1966. **4** in craps, a roll of ten. Rhyming slang US, 1999. **5** a prison siren that announces an escape or riot US, 1950. **6** the penis. A visual pun from the London landmark UK, 2001

Big Ben *nickname* the USS Franklin (heavily damaged off Japan on 19th March 1945, repaired and mothballed); the USS Bennington (commissioned in 1944, decommissioned in 1970). The Bennington was featured in the opening scene of the CBS television programme *Navy Log* in 1956 and 1957 US, 1954

Big Bertha *noun* an over-sized slot machine used as a promotion for hotel guests and to lure prospective gamblers into a casino US, 1984

Big Bertha *nickname* the Ringling Brothers, Barnum and Bailey Circus US, 1973

big bikkies *noun* a large amount of money. From BICKY, a diminiutive form of 'biscuit' NEW ZEALAND, 1980

big bill *noun* a $100 note US, 1961

big bird *noun* a long prison sentence. A play on BIRD (LIME) (time served in prison) and 'Big Bird' a large puppet featured on *Sesame Street*, a children's television programme since 1969 UK, 2000

Big Bird *noun* in homosexual usage, a man with a large penis. An allusion to a character on the children's television programme *Sesame Street* US, 1980

big bitch *noun* the prison sentence given to habitual criminals US, 1962

big bloke *noun* cocaine US, 1959

big blow *noun* a hurricane. Used by Australian fishermen and sailors AUSTRALIA, 1944

Big Blue 82 *noun* a 12,540-pound BLU-82 bomb. A vicious anti-personnel weapon, developed for vegetation clearing in Vietnam, used again in the Persian Gulf war and Afghanistan US, 1991

big blue bin *noun* the outdoors, when surplus grain is stored there CANADA, 1987

big-boobed *adjective* of a female, having generously proportioned breasts US, 1970

big book *noun* in twelve-step recovery programmes such as Alcoholics Anonymous, the book *Alcoholics Anonymous*, first published in 1939 and still the central document of the recovery movement US, 1998

Big Bopper *nickname* J. P. Richardson (1930–59), a Texas disc jockey in the early years of rock and roll whose hit recording of 'Chantilly Lace' propelled him into performing stardom, which in turn placed him on the small aeroplane 'American Pie' that carried Buddy Holly and him to their death UK, 1982

big boss *noun* heroin US, 1972

big box *noun* a large chain of shops featuring a single type of merchandise US, 1993

big boy *noun* **1** a tank. Vietnam war usage. The bigger the tank and the more weapons mounted on the tank, the more likely it was to be called a 'big boy' US, 1968. **2** a marijuana cigarette UK, 1999

big brother *noun* **1** the penis, especially a large penis US, 1965. **2** the erect penis US, 1967

Big Brother *noun* used as the personification of all-encompassing government authority. From George Orwell's 1949 novel *1984* UK, 1949

big brown eye *noun* the female breast US, 1971

big brownies *noun* MDMA, the recreational drug best known as ecstasy. A variation of BROWNIE (amphetamine or MDMA) that distinguishes SPEED from ECSTASY UK, 1998

big bud *noun* a very popular variety of marijuana with heavy buds UK, 2004

Big C *noun* **1** cancer US, 1964. **2** cocaine US, 1959. **3** commitment to a relationship seen as something to be feared or avoided UK, 2003. **4** in citizens' band radio slang, applied to many UK towns beginning with C, specifically Caernarfon, Carlisle, Chichester or Chippenham. This logic is continued throughout the alphabet, e.g. 'big B by the sea' (Brighton), 'big D' (Dorchester), 'big W' (Worthing); also, villages beginning with C become 'little C' or, in Scotland, 'wee C' UK, 1981. **5** a female as an sexual object. A hint of CUNT US, 1963. **6** a railway conductor US, 1968

big cage *noun* a prison US, 1949

big car, small dick; BCSD used for insulting someone who has a large or expensive car. Used proverbially: a car is a phallic symbol UK, 1999

big casino *noun* **1** the best that you can do; your greatest resource US, 1922. **2** cancer US, 1951. **3** any sexually transmitted infection US, 1948. **4** capital punishment, the death penalty US, 1960

big cat *noun* **1** a Jaguar car UK, 1981. **2** in poker, a hand comprised of five cards between eight and king and no pairs among them. Also known as 'big tiger' US, 1963

big Charlie *noun* **1** a CH-3C helicopter used during the Vietnam war for counterinsurgency airlifts US, 1985. **2** an important white man US, 1968

big cheese *noun* the most important person in a given organisation or enterprise US, 1914

big chicken dinner *noun* a bad conduct discharge. Playing with initials: armed forces usage US, 1991

big chief *noun* the hallucinogenic drug, mescaline US, 1971

big conk, big cock used as a summary of the folk wisdom that there is correlation between the size of a man's nose and the size of his penis UK, 1961

Big D *noun* **1** death US, 1977. **2** LSD US, 1966. **3** the penis. D as in DICK US, 1998

big D *nickname* **1** Dallas, Texas US, 1930. **2** Detroit, Michigan US, 1961. **3** Denver, Colorado US, 1967

big dad *noun* a senior drill instructor. Vietnam war usage US, 1991

big daddy *noun* **1** an immense wave US, 1977. **2** an important and influential man US, 1948

Big Daddy *nickname* **1** Jesse Unruh (1922–1987), a Democratic politican of great influence in California US, 1962. **2** Ed Roth (1932–2001), the hot rod artist most famous for creating the Rat Fink character in the early 1960s US, 1968. **3** Don Garlits (b.1932), the dominant drag racing driver in the US from the early 1960s to 70s US, 1965. **4** the Federal Communications Commission US, 1976

big dago *noun* a sandwich made on Italian bread US, 1960

big dance in Newark *noun* in circus and carnival usage, a jocular explanation for a small audience US, 1981

big day *noun* visiting day in prison US, 1949

big dead one *nickname* later in the Vietnam war, the First Infantry Division. A sad play on BIG RED ONE after heavy attrition through casualties US, 1991

big deal *noun* a major issue; often ironic, occasionally as an exclamation, used to dismiss such an issue as of little or no importance US, 1943

big Dick *noun* **1** in craps, a roll of ten. Often embellished to 'big Dick from Boston', 'big Dick from Battle Creek', and 'big Dick the ladies' friend'. Gambling slang authority, the late Thomas Clark, theorised that 'dick' came from the French *dix*. Another popular folk etymology is that the original Big Dick was Boston dice cheater Richard Mantell who was shot to death as he switched dice while trying to shoot a ten. The addition of 'the ladies' friend' leaves little doubt as to the most probable etymology – ten inches would indeed be big *US, 1904*. **2** a 14-inch rocket *US, 1946*

Big Dig *noun* a massive public works project in Boston, Massachusetts, replacing an existing six-lane central arterial motorway with an eight-to-ten lane underground expressway directly beneath the existing road *US, 1988*

big ditch *nickname* the Atlantic Ocean. A refinement of DITCH *US, 1909*

big dog *noun* in poker, a hand comprised of five cards between nine and ace and no pairs among them *US, 1963*

big dollar *noun* a great deal of money in any currency *UK, 2000*

big drink *noun* an ocean, especially the Atlantic Ocean. The term was first used to mean the Mississippi River; by the time it was applied to the ocean, the river sense had receded *US, 1883*

big drive *noun* a powerful injection of a drug *US, 1949*

big duck *noun* in trucking, a Republic moving van *US, 1976*

big duke *noun* in poker, especially hold 'em poker, a strong hand *US, 1981*

Big E *noun* **1** a dismissal, a rejection. The first letter of ELBOW (a dismissal) *UK, 1982*. **2** a railway engineer *US, 1977*

Big E *nickname* the USS Enterprise. Two aircraft carriers carried the name Enterprise and the nickname 'Big E', the first commissioned in 1936 and the second in 1961 *US, 1942*

big ears *noun* in the language of paragliding, an intentional collapsing of both tips of the wing to increase speed *US, 1992*

Big Easy *nickname* New Orleans, Louisiana *US, 1970*

big eat; big heaps *noun* a feast; a great meal *TRISTAN DA CUNHA, 1964*

big eight *noun* in poker, four twos. A borrowing from the game of craps *US, 1988*

big eights; big 8's good wishes *US, 1976*

big enchilada *noun* the supreme leader. A term coined and popularised by the Nixon White House during the Watergate scandal *US, 1973*

big end *noun* **1** in drag racing, the end of the quarter-mile race course where highest speeds are attained *US, 1960s to 70s*. **2** top speed. Biker (motorcycle) usage *US, 2001*

big-endian *adjective* in computing, denoting computer architecture in which the most significant byte is found in the lowest address *US, 1991*

big eye *noun* **1** a high-powered telescope, especially the one located on Palomar Mountain, California *US, 1949*. **2** a Lockheed EC-121 Warning Star aircraft. Deployed in Vietnam to provide early warning and communication relay; later redesignated the COLLEGE EYE *US, 1991*. **3** insomnia. A common condition in Antarctica because of the wild swings in daylight hours *ANTARCTICA, 1959*. **4** avarice *BAHAMAS, 1982*

big F the word 'fuck', in all uses *INDIA, 2002*

big fat *noun* a large marijuana cigarette *UK, 2001*

big fat one *noun* a large marijuana cigarette *UK, 2001*

big-feeling *adjective* inordinately proud *CANADA, 1988*

big fella *noun* the penis. An obvious, perhaps boastful, variation of OLD FELLOW *UK, 2001*

big fellow *noun* a law enforcement official of the US federal government *US, 1974*

big fish *noun* a very important person or thing *US, 1836*

big fish, little fish, cardboard box *noun* the hand movements that characterised techno-style dancing in the early 1990s *UK, 2001*

big flake *noun* cocaine *UK, 1998*

big foot *noun* **1** a prominent, highly visible journalist or columnist, especially one covering politics *US, 1980*. **2** an inflammation of the foot *JAMAICA, 2003*

big foot country *noun* the deep, rural south of the US *US, 1974*

big fours; big 4's yes, emphatically. Citizens' band radio slang *US, 1976*

big friend *noun* a bomber aircraft *US, 1946*

big fucking deal *noun* a major issue. An elaboration of BIG DEAL. Often used to dismiss something as not being a major issue *US, 1977*

big full *noun* in poker, a hand consisting of three aces and two kings. This hand represents the best possible variation of the hand conventionally known as a 'full house' *US, 1978*

big G *noun* God *US, 1981*

big general *noun* in a bar dice game, a first roll showing five dice of the same denomination *US, 1974*

Big George *noun* a twenty-five cent piece *US, 1973*

biggie *noun* **1** a big deal; something of consequence or difficulty. Often in the negative: 'no biggie' *US, 1945*. **2** an important person *US, 1926*. **3** a big-name actor who can be counted on to draw a large audience *US, 1926*. **4** an act of defecation. Children's vocabulary *NEW ZEALAND, 1994*. **5** marijuana *UK, 2003*. **6** a 26-ounce bottle of rum *GUYANA, 1978*

big girl *noun* an effeminate, weak and/or cowardly male *AUSTRALIA, 1986*

big girl's blouse *noun* an effeminate, weak and/or cowardly male *UK, 1969*

big girls' board *noun* the London variety of dartboard. Used with derision by Manchester board players *UK, 1980*

biggity *adverb* in a haughty, arrogant or conceited way *US, 1880*

big green *noun* in sporting and music events, corporate sponsors *US, 1992*

biggums *adjective* overweight *US, 1994*

big gun *noun* a large surfboard designed for big-wave conditions *AUSTRALIA, 1963*

biggun *noun* anything big. A shortening of 'big one'; either deliberately jocular or matter-of-factly *UK, 1971*

Big H *noun* heroin *US, 1953*

big hair *noun* an extravagant, large-sized hairdo *US, 1978*

Big Harry *noun* heroin. An elaboration of HARRY (heroin) on the model of BIG H (heroin) *US, 1975*

big hat *noun* a local state trooper. From the wide-brimmed hats formerly worn by many state troopers *US, 1967*

big hat, no cattle used for describing someone who appears the part but has no substance *US, 1977*

big head *noun* **1** a conceited, arrogant or haughty person *US, 1846*. **2** arrogance, excessive pride *US, 1992*

big-headed *adjective* conceited, arrogant, haughty *US, 1967*

big heaps *noun* a large meal *ANTARCTICA, 1964*

big hit *verb* to defecate. Rhyming slang for SHIT *AUSTRALIA, 1960*

big hitter *noun* **1** an important, influential or powerful person. From the sporting sense *UK, 2002*. **2** a sportsperson who strikes a ball especially hard with a bat, club or racket, etc *UK, 2002*

big hole *noun* **1** the emergency stop position on a railway air brake *US, 1931*. **2** in trucking, the position of the gear shift with the most gear combinations *US, 1942*

big hook *noun* a wrecking crane *US, 1929*

big house *noun* **1** a prison. Usually follows 'the' *US, 1913*. **2** a crown court *UK, 1996*. **3** a mental hospital; any large, impersonal, threatening institution. Extended from an earlier usage (a workhouse) *UK, 1984*

Big House *noun* ▶ **the Big House** New Scotland Yard *UK, 2001*

big Huey; big Huey Long *noun* a long prison sentence. An allusion to Huey Long, former governor of Louisiana reputed to have advocated harsh prison sentences *NEW ZEALAND, 1999*

big idea *noun* a bad idea *US, 1960*

Big Inch *nickname* a pipeline from east Texas to the northeast states, built 1942–43. The success of the project – and its naughty-sounding nickname – gave birth to the 'Little Big Inch' (Texas to New Jersey, 1943–44) and 'Big Inch-by-Inch' (Edmonton to British Columbia, 1951–53) *US, 1947*

big iron *noun* **1** a large car *US, 1975.* **2** a large, powerful, fast, expensive computer *US, 1991*

Big J *nickname* Juarez, Mexico *US, 1970*

big jobs *noun* an act of defecation; excrement. Thus 'to do big jobs'; childish *UK, 1971*

Big Joe *noun* a novice, especially a military recruit *US, 1947*

Big Joe from Boston *noun* in craps, a ten *US, 1957*

big John *noun* a police officer, the police; used mainly by black teenagers *US, 1980*

Big John *nickname* the John Hancock Center, Chicago, Illinois *US, 1997*

big juicer *noun* a powerful, all-night AM radio station *US, 1976*

Big K *nickname* Korea *US, 1970*

big kahuna *noun* a top leader. From a Hawaiian term for 'priest' or 'wise man' *US, 1990*

Big L *noun* **1** love *US, 1987.* **2** a loser *US, 1984*

Big L *nickname* **1** Lubbock, Texas *US, 1976.* **2** the federal penitentiary in Leavenworth, Kansas *US, 1970.* **3** the offshore 'pirate' radio station, Radio London, that broadcast off the Essex coast from 1964 until it was forced off the air on 14th August 1967 *UK, 2004*

big-league *verb* to associate with important, influential, connected or rich people *US, 1999*

big-league *adjective* powerful, influential, important *US, 1919*

big leagues *noun* a high level in any field. Also used in the singular *US, 1941*

big legs *noun* a generous spender *US, 1987*

Big M *noun* **1** morphine *US, 1959.* **2** a million pounds. Dates from a time in the C20 when a million pounds was less commonplace *UK, 1978.* **3** marriage *US, 1966*

Big M *nickname* Memphis, Tennessee *US, 1976*

Big Mac *noun* a large area of grazed skin. Skateboarders' slang; from the similarity of appearance to a branded hamburger *UK, 1998*

big mama *noun* the ocean *US, 1991*

Big Man *noun* God *UK, 2002*

big man on campus *noun* a socially prominent student. Initially used with respect, but often in later years with irony, if not scorn *US, 1930s to 70s*

big meeting in the sky *noun* heaven as characterised by those who are part of twelve-step recovery programmes such as Alcoholics Anonymous *US, 1998*

Big Mo *nickname* the USS Missouri *US, 1945*

big mother *noun* a Sikorsky SH-3 helicopter used by the US Navy in Vietnam for search and rescue missions *US, 1990*

big mouth *noun* an indiscreet, boastful or overly verbose person; a quality of indiscreet talkativeness *US, 1889*

big mover *noun* a person who is, either consistently or on a specific occasion, highly successful *AUSTRALIA, 1969*

Big Muddy *nickname* **1** the Mississippi River *US, 1846.* **2** the Missouri River *US, 1825*

big nickel *noun* five hundred dollars *US, 1961*

big noise *noun* **1** an important and influential person *US, 1906.* **2** in poker, the alpha player at a table *US, 1996*

big-note *verb* in betting, to exaggerate your status or bankroll *AUSTRALIA, 1989*

big-noter *noun* a zealous horse racing fan *AUSTRALIA, 1967*

big-note yourself *verb* to overstate your importance *AUSTRALIA, 1953*

bignum *noun* any very large number, especially if greater than 2,147,483,648 *US, 1983*

big number *noun* in drag racing, 200 miles per hour, first officially recorded on 12th July, 1964 *US, 1968*

big NUMBER-oh *noun* a birthday ending with a zero, especially 30, 40 and 50. For instance, 50 is the 'big-five-oh', *US, 1980*

Big O *noun* **1** an orgasm *US, 1968.* **2** opium; heroin *US, 1957.* **3** a railway conductor. From the labour organisation name 'Order of Railroad Conductors' *US, 1930*

Big O *nickname* **1** Okinawa, Japan *US, 1972.* **2** Omaha, Nebraska *US, 1976*

big on *adjective* especially enthusiastic about something; considering something to be particularly important *US, 1864*

big one *noun* **1** one hundred dollars *US, 1961.* **2** one million dollars *US, 1967.* **3** one thousand dollars *US, 1863.* **4** in prison, one pound (£1) *UK, 2000.* **5** World War 2 *US, 1971.* **6** in horse racing, the race on a given day with the highest prize money *AUSTRALIA, 1989.* **7** the Ringling Brothers, Barnum and Bailey circus *US, 1973.* **8** a substantial lie *UK, 1984*

big orange pill *noun* during the war in Vietnam, the anti-malarial pill taken once a week in addition to the daily medication. Chloroquine-primaquine was taken weekly in the form of a large, orange-coloured pill *US, 1991*

bigot *noun* in computing, a person who is irrationally attached to a particular operating system or computer language *US, 1991*

big ouch *noun* a serious injury *US, 1962*

big outpatient department in the sky *noun* death *US, 1989*

Big Owe *nickname* the Olympic Stadium in Montreal, built for the 1976 Games *CANADA, 2002*

big ox *noun* on the railways, a freight train conductor *US, 1977*

big pond *noun* **1** the Atlantic Ocean. An ironic understatement of the distance between the UK and the US; 'great pond', an earlier variation, is recorded from 1641 *US, 1833.* **2** during the Vietnam war, the Pacific Ocean. Playing on the use of the term since the 1830s to refer to the Atlantic Ocean *US, 1991*

big PX in the sky *noun* death. Vietnam war usage, grim humour based on many cheerful euphemisms for death as a 'big [fill in the blank] in the sky' *US, 1991*

Big Q *nickname* the San Quentin State Prison, California. Just north of San Francisco, San Quentin houses California's death chamber *US, 1961*

big quid *noun* a great deal of money. Pre-1966, a 'quid' was a one-pound note; its usage did not change with the change to Australian dollars, referring to money in general *AUSTRALIA, 1989*

Big R *noun* **1** during the Korean war, rotation home. Distinguished from the conventional R AND R (rest and recreation) *US, 1960.* **2** in trucking, a Roadway Express truck *US, 1976*

big red *noun* **1** secobarbitol, a sedative-hypnotic drug marketed under the brand name Seconal™ *US, 2001.* **2** adriamycin, an extremely toxic agent used in chemotherapy *US, 1994.* **3** in craps, a one-roll bet on a seven. If the shooter rolls a seven, he loses; 'big red' thus serves as a diplomatic way to bet that the shooter will lose on the next roll *US, 1981.* **4** the desert sun *US, 1991*

Big Red One *nickname* the First Infantry Division, US Army. The Division's patch is a big red number one *US, 1970*

big red wrench *noun* in hot rodding and motor racing, an oxyacetylene cutting torch *US, 1993*

big rig *noun* a large tractor trailer with eighteen or more wheels *US, 1986*

Big Rock *nickname* the US federal penitentiary on Alcatraz Island, San Francisco Bay *US, 1970*

big rush *noun* cocaine *UK, 1998*

bigs *noun* **1** in pool, the striped balls numbered 9 to 15 *US, 1990.* **2** cigarettes *US, 1997*

bigs-and-littles *noun* in hot rodding, the combination of large rear tyres and small front tyres *US, 1993*

big shit *noun* **1** an important person, if only in their own eyes *US, 1934.* **2** an important event or thing *US, 1960*

big shot *noun* an important and influential person *US, 1927*

big shotgun noun a 106 mm recoilless rifle, developed during the Korean war and used extensively by the US Marines in Vietnam US, 1991

big-six talk noun talk unsupported by action US, 1990

big sleep noun death; capital punishment US, 1951

big slick noun in hold 'em poker, an ace and a king as the first two cards dealt to a player US, 1981

Big Smoke noun **1** any large city or town. Originally Australian Aboriginal pidgin AUSTRALIA, 1848. **2** any city in British Columbia CANADA, 1989

Big Smoke nickname **1** the city of Sydney AUSTRALIA, 1959. **2** Pittsburgh, Pennsylvania US, 1930

big snip noun a vasectomy CANADA, 2002

big spark noun an electric shock administered in a hospital to a patient whose heart has failed in an attempt to revive the heart US, 1994

big spit; long spit noun the act of vomiting; vomit AUSTRALIA, 1967. ▶ **go for the big spit** to vomit AUSTRALIA, 1964

big stick noun the large aerial ladder used by firefighters US, 1963

big stuff noun **1** any very important or influential person US, 1911. **2** artillery, artillery fire. Vietnam war usage US, 1991

big-style adverb very much; completely, absolutely UK, 1999

big tender noun a scene in a pornographic film when the participants hug each other US, 1991

big-ticket adjective expensive; representing a major purchase US, 1945

big time noun **1** the highest level of achievement in a field. Originally theatrical US, 1910. **2** a long sentence to state prison US, 1939. **3** heroin US, 1971. ▶ **get big time** to put on airs, to assume a 'posh' accent. Used by a Midlands professional man, in a BBC Radio 4 programme on class distinction, 4th February 1980 UK, 1980

big-time verb to show off US, 1957

big time adverb very much, entirely, utterly. The term got a big boost in the US during the 2000 presidential election when Republican vice-presidential candidate Dick Cheney concurred with candidate Bush's assessment of a New York Times reporter as a 'major-league asshole' by mumbling 'Yeah, big time' at a campaign stop in Naperville, Illinois, on 4th September. A live microphone picked up the insults, giving 'big time' its fifteen minutes of fame US, 1957

Big Tom noun in a carnival ball-throwing game, a big stuffed cat target that has been weighted and is thus hard to knock down US, 1981

big top noun a prison, especially a maximum-security state prison US, 1955

Big T-Owe nickname the sports stadium in downtown Toronto, which loses money CANADA, 2002

big train noun in horse racing, a great racehorse US, 1951

big trip noun a holiday to Britain and Europe. For many Australians such a holiday is only taken once in a lifetime AUSTRALIA, 1978

big truck adjective of lesbians, 'manly', masculine. Probably inspired by DIESEL (a 'manly' lesbian) UK, 2003

big Turk noun an ostrich. Circus and carnival usage US, 1981

big twenty noun a 20-year career in the armed forces US, 1991

big twist noun an occasion for celebration; an outstanding success AUSTRALIA, 1959

Big Two nickname World War 2 US, 1961

big up noun **1** very positive agreement UK, 2002. **2** a socially prominent person BARBADOS, 1996

big up verb to boost, to promote something, to show off; to praise something UK, 1994

big-up adjective pregnant BAHAMAS, 1995

Big V noun a vasectomy CANADA, 2002

Big V nickname Vietnam US, 1972

big wheel noun a prominent, powerful and important person US, 1942

big white chief; great white chief noun your boss; a person of importance in a superior or most superior position. A casually racist, supposedly jocular usage, modelled on Native American Indian speech UK, 1937

big white telephone noun the toilet bowl when vomiting into it AUSTRALIA, 1985

big whoop! used to mock the importance of what has just been said US, 1981

bigwig noun a person of high rank or position or money UK, 1731

big win noun complete luck US, 1991

big yard noun the main yard in a prison where the general population mingles for recreation US, 1987

bijou adjective small, as a positive characteristic. Adopted from French bijou (small); used widely of houses and other buildings, and with greater variation in homosexual society UK, 1860

bijoux noun jewels. Directly from French bijoux UK, 1992

bike noun **1** a promiscuous woman. Suggests 'easy availability for a ride'. Often in compound as 'office bike', 'school bike', 'town bike', 'village bike', etc.; occasionally, if reputation demands, 'the bike' AUSTRALIA, 1945. **2** a motorcycle police officer US, 1958. **3** in harness racing, a two-wheeled horse drawn vehicle for one person, used for training or for racing US, 1994. **4** in lowball poker, a sequence from five down to ace US, 1978

bike chemist noun a person who uses his knowledge of chemistry to manufacture illegal drugs US, 1992

bike doc noun in mountain biking, a bicycle mechanic US, 1992

biker noun a person who rides a motorbike. In Australia generally used as distinct from 'bikie' (a member of a motorcycle gang) US, 1968

bike space noun the vagina. From the phrase 'I know WHERE I'D LIKE TO PARK MY BIKE', said by a man considering a woman as a sexual object UK, 2001

bikie noun a member of a motorcyle gang AUSTRALIA, 1967

bikie chick noun a female member, or associate of a member, of a motorcycle gang AUSTRALIA, 1994

bikini bar noun a sex club where the dancer strips down to her bikini US, 1988

bikini wax noun an application of hot wax to remove a woman's pubic hair US, 1982

bilged adjective worn out, tired US, 1968

bilingual adjective bisexual US, 1964

bill noun **1** a dollar US, 1915. **2** one hundred dollars US, 1929. **3** the nose US, 1952 ▷ see: BILLY WHIZZ. ▶ **do a bill** to spend one hundred dollars US, 1974. ▶ **the bill** the police. Abbreviated from OLD BILL; can also be used of a single police-officer in the sense of representing the whole organisation. Widespread usage popularised since 1985 by UK television police drama The Bill UK, 1969 ▷ see: OLD BILL

Bill! used as a warning that police are near US, 1998

billabong noun ▶ **on the billabong** unemployed and camped by a waterhole, especially in Western Australia and the Northern Territories AUSTRALIA, 1978

billabonger noun an unemployed, homeless person who camps by a waterhole, especially in Western Australia and the Northern Territories AUSTRALIA, 1978

billards noun the testicles AUSTRALIA, 1988

Bill Blass noun crack cocaine. Quite why the name of American fashion designer Bill Blass (1920–99) should be used for this drug is uncertain US, 1998

Bill Clinton noun an act of oral sex on a man. In the late 1990s the US Presidency of William Jefferson Clinton (b.1946) was nearly brought down by a sex scandal that involved the President with Whitehouse intern Monica Lewinsky. Bill Clinton denied 'sexual relations with that woman' but eventually admitted that fellatio had occurred and 'a relationship with Miss Lewinsky that was not appropriate' US, 1999

Bill Daley *noun* ▶ **on the Bill Daley** in horse racing, having taken the lead at the start of the race and held it for the entire race *US, 1932*

billfold biopsy *noun* a hospital's analysis of the ability of a patient seeking admission to pay their bill *US, 1986*

Bill from the Hill *nickname* the Notting Hill police. An elaboration of THE BILL (the police) *UK, 1996*

Billie Hoke *noun* cocaine. A personification based on COKE *US, 1959*

billies; billys *noun* money *US, 1982*

bills *noun* **1** money *US, 1997*. **2** the game of pool *US, 1993*

bill shop *noun* a police station. From THE BILL (the police) *UK, 1977*

bill stickers *noun* underpants. Rhyming slang for 'knickers', sometimes shortened to 'bills' *UK, 1992*

Bill Wyman; bill; wyman *noun* the hymen. Rhyming slang, based on the name of Rolling Stone bassist Bill Wyman (b.1936) *UK, 2002*

billy *noun* **1** a metal pail with a handle used for boiling water, making tea, cooking, etc, over a fire when camping or in the bush. A quintessential item of the Australian bush. Scottish English had (c.1828 *Scottish National Dictionary*) 'billy-pot' as 'a cooking utensil' and this is probably the origin. Not, as variously conjectured, from French *bouilli* 'boiled', nor Wiradjuri (an eastern Australian Aboriginal language) *billa* 'water', nor the proper name Billy *AUSTRALIA, 1849*. **2** a police officer's blackjack or club, a truncheon *US, 1850*. **3** a warning signal *IRELAND, 1976*. **4** a bong (a water-pipe) for smoking marijuana. A play on 'billabong' (a water hole) *AUSTRALIA, 1988* ▷*see:* BILLY WHIZZ. ▶ **boil the billy** to stop for a break and make tea in a billy. Occasionally used to mean to make tea not in a billy but an electric kettle or the like *AUSTRALIA, 1867*

Billy Bowleg *noun* the personification of a Seminole Indian *US, 1982*

Billy-boy; billy *nickname* a Protestant, especially a supporter of Glasgow Rangers football club. This goes back to William of Orange, and is now most familiar from the song (to the tune of 'Marching Through Georgia') which is used as a football battle-hymn: 'Hurrah! Hurrah! We are the Billy Boys; / Hurrah! Hurrah! We make a lot of noise; / We're up to here, we never fear – we all are Billy's sons, / We are the Glasgow Billy Boys. / We belong to Glasgow, we're Orange and we're true / Scotland is our country, our colours white and blue, / We're Protestants and proud of it , we're known near and far, / Glasgow Billy Boys they call us.' *UK: SCOTLAND, 1935*

Billy Bragg; billy *noun* **1** an act of sexual intercourse. Rhyming slang for SHAG, formed from the name of the UK singer and political activist (b.1957) *UK, 2003*. **2** stolen goods. Rhyming slang for SWAG, formed from the name of the UK singer and political activist (b.1957) *UK, 2004*

Billy Bunter; billy *noun* **1** a customer, especially of discreet or illegal services. Rhyming slang for PUNTER; from the fictional schoolboy created by Frank Richards (Charles Hamilton 1876–1961) *UK, 1992*. **2** a shunter. Hauliers' rhyming slang *UK, 1951*

Billy Button *noun* any foolish person who works without assurances that he will be paid for his work *VIRGIN ISLANDS, U.S., 1996*

billy can *noun* **1** a can used for making coffee *AUSTRALIA, 1885*. **2** a metal pail with a handle used for boiling water, making tea, cooking etc, over a fire when camping or in the bush *AUSTRALIA, 1870*

billy cart *noun* a child's toy racing cart. From 'billy' as 'a male goat', originally billycarts were hitched to goats and raced *AUSTRALIA, 1923*

Billy Fury *noun* a jury. Rhyming slang, formed from the name of the popular UK singer, 1940–83 *UK, 2004*

billy goat *noun* **1** a tufted beard. From the similarity between the wearer's facial hair and that of a male goat *UK, 1882*. **2** in horse racing, the totalisator. Rhyming slang for 'tote' *AUSTRALIA, 1989*. **3** in trucking, the 318 horsepower Detroit diesel engine *US, 1971*

Billy Guyatt *noun* a diet. Rhyming slang, sometimes shortened to 'Billy' *AUSTRALIA, 1989*

billy lid *noun* a kid. Rhyming slang *AUSTRALIA, 1988*

Billy No-Bird *noun* a man who is characteristically without a girlfriend *UK, 2001*

Billy No-Mates *noun* a friendless person *UK, 2003*

billyo *noun* ▶ **like billyo** at great speed *UK, 1885*. ▶ **to billyo** to hell; to blazes *AUSTRALIA, 1939*

Billy Ocean *noun* suntan lotion. Rhyming slang, formed from the name of popular Trinidad-born singer (b.1950) *UK, 2003*

billys *noun* ▷*see:* BILLIES

Billy's Slough *nickname* a town named Williams Lake in British Columbia *CANADA, 1989*

billy tea *noun* tea made in a billy *AUSTRALIA, 1890*

Billy Whizz; Billy Whiz; billy; bill *noun* an amphetamine. WHIZZ (amphetamine) disguised as cartoon strip character Billy Whizz, whose adventures started in the *Beano* in 1964 *UK, 1985*

billy willy *noun* a symptomatic reduction in the size of a penis caused by amphetamine use. A combination of BILLY (WHIZZ) (amphetamine) and WILLY (the penis) *UK, 2003*

bim *noun* **1** a shortened form of 'bimbo' *US, 1925*. **2** a police officer *US, 1971*

Bim and Bam *noun* two inseparable friends *TRINIDAD AND TOBAGO, 1987*

bimbette *noun* a young, mindless, attractive woman. A diminuitive of the more widely known BIMBO *US, 1982*

bimble *verb* to wander without purpose. A variation of 'bumble' (to idle), perhaps with reference to BIMBO ('a dupe', hence 'mindless') *UK, 1987*

bimbo *noun* **1** a well-built, attractive, somewhat dim woman. An offensive term *US, 1920*. **2** a dupe *UK, 2002*

bimph *noun* toilet paper. A variation on 'bumph' (paperwork) which is derived from BUM FODDER *UK, 2002*

bin *noun* **1** a pocket *UK, 1936*. **2** a hospital or other institution for the treatment of psychiatric problems and mental illness. Abbreviation of LOONY BIN *UK, 1938*. **3** a cell in a prison or a police station *UK, 1977*. ▶ **the bins** a Goodwill Industry's used clothing store, where used clothing is sold by the pound *US, 1997*

bin *verb* **1** to throw something away. Reduced from the sense 'to throw in the rubbish bin' *UK, 1991*. **2** to finish with a friend or a lover. From the sense 'to throw away' *UK, 2001*. **3** to dismiss someone or something; to abandon someone or something *UK, 1995*

bind *noun* a bore, a nuisance. Originally Royal Air Force use *UK, 1930*

binders *noun* brakes. Used in many contexts, from military transport to trains to drag racing *UK, 1942*

bindi-eye; bindii *noun* any of various native spiny Australian plants; also, the introduced South American plant, *Solvia sessilis*, a common lawn weed having sharp prickles; hence, one of these prickles. The word comes from the Australian Aboriginal languages Kamilaroi and Yuwaalaraay *AUSTRALIA, 1896*

bindle *noun* **1** heroin. From an earlier sense a (portion of drugs) *UK, 2003*. **2** a portion or packet of drugs. After an obsolete term for 'a vagrant's bundle' *US, 1934*

bindle stiff *noun* a migratory worker; a tramp *US, 1897*

bine *noun* a cigarette; an act of smoking a cigarette. Shortened from the brand name Woodbine™ but used generically *UK, 1975*

bing *noun* **1** jail, especially solitary confinement in jail *US, 1932*. **2** an injection with a hypodermic needle and syringe *US, 1918*. **3** crack cocaine; a piece of crack cocaine *US, 1994*

bing! used as a sound effect for something that happens instantly. Probably echoic of a bell *UK, 2001*

binge *noun* a period of heavy drinking or drug-taking; a drinking spree. From dialect sense 'to soak' *UK, 1854*

binge *verb* **1** to eat or drink to excess *UK, 1854*. **2** to use crack cocaine heavily. From the sense 'to drink heavily' *UK, 1998*

binger *noun* **1** a deep inhalation of marijuana smoke filtered through a water-pipe *US, 1998*. **2** a drug addict, especially of crack cocaine. Extended from BINGE (to heavily use crack cocaine) *UK, 1998*. **3** a losing bet. Glasgow slang *UK: SCOTLAND, 1985*

bingey; bingy; binghi; binjey *noun* the stomach, the belly. Of Aboriginal origin *AUSTRALIA, 1926*

bingle *noun* **1** a motor accident causing only minor damage and not resulting in injury *AUSTRALIA, 1970*. **2** a dent or crack in a surfboard *AUSTRALIA, 1966*

bingo *noun* **1** a cheap wine. The exclamation 'bingo' alludes to the sudden effect of the drink *CANADA, 1963*. **2** a prison riot *US, 1992*

bingo *verb* to inject a drug intravenously *US, 1992*

bingo *adjective* (of a plane's fuel tank) with just enough fuel to reach home base *US, 1956*

bingo! used for emphasis or for registering pleasurable surprise, success, excitement *UK, 1927*

bingo boy *noun* a young alcoholic *US, 1946*

bingo wing *noun* a pendulous spread of flabby upper arm that is characteristic of some older women *UK, 2002*

bings *noun* crack cocaine *UK, 1998*

binky *noun* **1** a baby's dummy (pacifier) that a heroin user has converted into a squeeze bulb for injecting a dose of heroin through an eye dropper and needle into the vein. From the common childrens' nickname for a dummy *US, 1989*. **2** marijuana; a marijuana cigarette *UK, 2003*

binocs *noun* binoculars *US, 1943*

bin off *verb* to set something aside, to discard something. Teen slang *UK, 2002*

binos *noun* binoculars *US, 1976*

bin rat *noun* a supply clerk in the Royal Canadian Air Force *CANADA, 1995*

bins *noun* a pair of spectacles, glasses; binoculars; hence, the eyes. Abbreviated from 'binoculars'; also variant 'binns' *UK, 1958*

bint *noun* **1** a girlfriend, a young woman. From Arabic *bint* (a daughter), often combined with a critcal adjective to derogatory effect *UK, 1855*. **2** a promiscuous woman. Derogatory *UK, 1855*

bio *noun* a biography *US, 1947*

bio *adjective* excellent *US, 1984*

bio break *noun* a visit to the toilet. A euphemism popular with the more jargon-friendly computer-users, *1998*

biog *noun* a biography *US, 1942*

biologist *noun* a person whose interest in companionship is primarily sexual *US, 1973*

biopic *noun* a biographical film *US, 1951*

bip *noun* the head; the brain *US, 1947*

bip *verb* **1** to break into a house while the housewife is outside hanging laundry on the line to dry. An abbreviation of SCALLYBIP *US, 1972*. **2** to simultaneously take heroin and cocaine into the body through the nose, *2002*

bipe *verb* to break and enter the dwelling of another while they sleep, with the intent of stealing *US, 1990*

bippy *noun* used as a jocular euphemism for 'ass'. Coined and popularised by Rowan and Martin on the television programme *Laugh-In* (NBC,1968–73); a wildly popular word for several years, the key word in the title of the 1969 Rowan and Martin film *The Maltese Bippy*, and then abandoned on the junk heap of slang *US, 1967*

bird *noun* **1** a young woman; a sweetheart. First used in C14; not considered a slang term until C19 when it also meant 'a prostitute' (obsolete by 1920). Primarily a British term, but briefly popular in the US in the late 1960s *UK, 1838*. **2** the vagina *US, 1963*. **3** an ordinary fellow. Also known as an 'old bird' *US, 1839*. **4** the penis *US, 1969*. **5** a homosexual man *US, 1956*. **6** a 25-cent piece *US, 1949*. **7** a surfer who uses any bird or wings as his surfboard logo *US, 1988*. **8** a police informer. From the sense of STOOL PIGEON and SING *CANADA, 2002*. **9** a certainty. A shortening of DEAD BIRD *AUSTRALIA, 1941*. **10** in horse racing, a horse that as seen as likely to win a race *AUSTRALIA, 1989*. **11** a twenty-five cent betting token *US, 1974*. **12** a gesture of the middle finger, meaning 'fuck you' *US, 1961*. **13** an amphetamine tablet *US, 1992*. **14** a kilogram of cocaine *US, 2002*. **15** Wild Turkey™ whisky *US, 1984*. **16** an aeroplane *US, 1918*. **17** a helicopter *US, 2001*. **18** a Ford Thunderbird car *US, 1976*. **19** a Pontiac

Firebird car *US, 1976* ▷*see:* BIRD LIME. ▶ **for the birds 1** no good, shoddy *US, 1944*. **2** trivial; not worthy of intelligent interest *US, 1951*. ▶ **out of your bird** insane *UK, 2001*. ▶ **the bird 1** negative criticism. Originally theatrical; now usually phrased 'get the bird' or 'give the bird' *UK, 1884*. **2** a vocal demonstration of complete disapproval *UK, 1952*

Bird *nickname* Charlie Parker (1920–1955), the jazz legend credited as an originator of bebop, the jazz style that followed the big band swing era *US, 1946*

bird bandit *noun* a womaniser *UK, 1984*

birdbath *noun* **1** a cursory washing of the body using little water *US, 1953*. **2** the area in a military motor pool where vehicles are washed. Coined in Vietnam *US, 1980*

birdbrain *noun* a human who gives the impression of possessing a bird-size brain; a fool *US, 1933*

bird-brained *adjective* foolish; not-clever-enough; stupid *UK, 1922*

birdcage *noun* **1** the anus *US, 1972*. **2** a used car lot, especially one surrounded by chicken wire *NEW ZEALAND, 1998*. **3** a mounting enclosure at a racecourse. So named as it is often surrounded by a wire mesh fence *AUSTRALIA, 1893*. **4** in harness racing, the enclosure where horses are paraded before events *US, 1997*. **5** an air control tower *US, 1965*. **6** a railway lantern *US, 1945*. **7** a Volvo car *UK, 1981*. **8** in motor racing, a chassis made of many small pieces of tubing or a tubular roll bar structure *US, 1965*. **9** a box used for storing dice *US, 1962*

Birdcages *noun* ▶ **the Birdcages** the first legislative buildings in Victoria, British Columbia. So described because of their gimcrack architectural elaboration; now all obliterated. *CANADA, 1968*

bird circuit *noun* a prolonged group tour of gay bars; the bars themselves *US, 1956*

bird colonel; full-bird colonel *noun* in the US Army, a full colonel. From the eagle insignia *US, 1946*

bird course *noun* an easy course in university *CANADA, 2002*

bird dog *noun* **1** a scout *US, 1929*. **2** in professional sports, a talent scout or a scout's associates who let him know about players who may be prospects for professional play *US, 1950*. **3** a person who provides information about potential victims to a thief or group of thieves *US, 1977*. **4** a person who solicits players for gambling, whether in a casino or a private poker game *US, 1949*. **5** in the used car business, either a customer who has been referred to a salesman or the person doing the referring *US, 1975*. **6** in a two-car police speed-monitoring unit, the car that chases down speeding cars or trucks based on radar readings in the second car *US, 1971*. **7** a navigational device in planes that points in the direction of a radio signal *US, 1956*

bird-dog *verb* **1** to flirt with another's date *US, 1941*. **2** to look for, find and return with someone or something *US, 1948*

bird egg *noun* an amphetamine tablet *US, 1993*

bird feeder *noun* in trucking, the air-intake pipe *US, 1971*

bird food *noun* inferior quality marijuana *US, 2001*

bird head *noun* a type of LSD *UK, 2003*

bird house *noun* a jail or prison *US, 1949*

birdie *noun* **1** a passive, effeminate male homosexual *US, 1921*. **2** a bird, especially a small bird. Childish *UK, 1792*. **3** an aircraft. Used by the Australian Army in Korea, 1951–53 *AUSTRALIA, 1958*

birdie powder *noun* any powdered drug, such as heroin or cocaine *US, 1992*

bird in a cage *noun* the rank of Specialist 5 in the US Army. From the eagle under a curved stripe on the chevron *US, 1968*

bird lime; bird *noun* **1** a sentence of imprisonment. Rhyming slang for TIME. The abbreviation is used especially in 'do bird' (to serve a prison sentence) *UK, 1857*. **2** by extension, a personal history of imprisonment. Rhyming slang for TIME *UK, 1857*

birdman *noun* a prisoner. A combination of BIRD (LIME) (a prison sentence) and 'man', playing on famous convict 'the Birdman of Alcatraz' *UK, 1996*

bird nest *noun* a person's room, apartment or house *US, 1973*

bird of paradise *noun* the US armed forces insignia designating honourable discharge *US, 1946*

bird sanctuary *noun* any institution where traffic violators who are under pursuit are free from further pursuit once they pass the gates *US, 1962*

birdseed *noun* **1** nonsense *US, 1909*. **2** a small amount of money *US, 1982*

bird's eye *noun* a small dose of heroin *US, 1973*

bird shit *noun* a paratrooper. From the jocular tease that only two things fall from the sky, paratroopers and bird shit *US, 1991*

bird's nest *noun* **1** pubic hair that can be seen to extend from the crotch to the navel; pubic hair. Homosexual use; tangled imagery *US, 1972*. **2** in the Royal Navy, a WRNS' cabin. A member of the *Women's Royal Naval Service* is popularly known as a Wren, hence this pun; remembered from World War 2 but not recorded until 1984 *UK, 1984*. **3** the chest, especially (of a man) if hairy. Rhyming slang, but also partly from the imagery. *UK, 1970*. **4** a hole in the upholstery of the driver's seat of a car from long use and too much weight *US, 1992*

bird speed *adverb* extremely fast *BARBADOS, 1965*

bird-turd *verb* to disparage someone or something; to speak with a lack of sincerity. A close relation of CHICKENSHIT *US, 1947*

bird watcher *noun* a man given to the practice of watching girls go by. A pun on BIRD (a young woman) *UK, 1984*

bird watching *noun* (used of young males) looking sensually and whistling at passing young women *TRINIDAD AND TOBAGO, 1995*

birdwood *noun* a cigarette *US, 1944*

birdyback *noun* containers or trailers shipped by air. A poor borrowing from PIGGYBACK *US, 2003*

biri *noun* ▷see: BEEDI

birk *noun* a mentally slow person *US, 1976* ▷see: BERK

birling *adjective* drunk. From Scottish dialect *birl* (to spin) *UK: SCOTLAND, 1988*

biro *noun* a ballpoint pen used as an improvised means of injecting drugs. From the conventional generic sense of 'biro' as a 'ballpoint pen' *UK, 1996*

birth control engine *noun* a large locomotive which could burn up to five tons of coal per shift. Firing them up in the early morning was said to make a man impotent for weeks *UK, 1970*

birthday card *noun* in poker, the one card needed and drawn to complete an unlikely good hand *US, 1996*

birthday present *noun* in tiddlywinks, a stroke of good luck *US, 1977*

birthdays *noun* ▶ **think all your birthdays have come at once** to be overjoyed or overwhelmed, especially from something unexpected *AUSTRALIA, 1957*

birthday suit *noun* a state of nudity *UK, 1771*

biscuit *noun* **1** a good-looking member of whatever sex attracts you *US, 1990*. **2** a promiscuous woman *US, 1993*. **3** the buttocks *US, 1950*. **4** the head *US, 1934*. **5** a watch *US, 1905*. **6** a phonograph record *US, 1950*. **7** in the context of live rock and roll, a deep bass note when it is felt as well as heard. A term especially but not exclusively applied to the bass playing of Phil Lesh of the Grateful Dead *US, 1997*. **8** a white tablet of methadone, a synthetic narcotic used to treat heroin addicts *US, 1972*. **9** fifty rocks of crack cocaine *US, 2003*. **10** a tablet of MDMA, the recreational drug best known as ecstasy *UK, 2002*. **11** the hallucinogenic drug, peyote *US, 1992*. **12** a handgun *US, 1946*. **13** a black prisoner *US, 1976*. **14** a can of c-rations. Vietnam war usage *US, 1991*. **15** used as a euphemism for 'bitch' *US, 1999*. **16** a fool, an idiot *SOUTH AFRICA, 2004*

biscuit *adjective* easy *US, 1997*

biscuit bitch *noun* a female Red Cross volunteer. Vietnam war usage; less common than the more popular DOUGHNUT DOLLY *US, 1983*

biscuit box *noun* a Ford Transit van, or other vehicle of similar style. When struck, an unladen van has a similar tonal quality to an empty biscuit tin *UK, 1981*

biscuit class *noun* economy class air travel on a small route. A playful allusion to 'business class' travel and the biscuits given to economy class passengers *NEW ZEALAND, 1987*

Biscuit Foot McKinnon *nickname* used as a nickname for a stereotypical Cape Bretoner. Because of the large Scottish settlement of this part of Nova Scotia, many people have the same last name: MacDonald, McKinnon, and so forth. Nicknames are common to distinguish family members with the same first name, too. *CANADA, 1999*

biscuits *noun* **1** money *US, 1977*. **2** crack cocaine. From BISCUIT (a measure of crack) *UK, 2003*

biscuits and cheese *noun* the knees. Rhyming slang, remembered in use during World War 2, sometimes shortened to 'biscuits' *UK, 1960*

biscuit snatcher *noun* the hand; a finger *US, 1953*

bi-sex *noun* bisexual sex *UK, 2003*

bish *noun* a bishop *UK, 1937*

bish, bash, bosh; bish-bash-bosh *adjective* rough and ready; also used in a semi-exclamatory sense as an echoic representation of anything swiftly expedited *UK, 2000*

bishop *noun* **1** the penis. Used in a variety of expressions that refer to male masturbation *US, 1916*. **2** a private investigator *UK, 1972*

bishop's bash *noun* of a male, the act of masturbation. From the verbal idiom BASH THE BISHOP *UK, 2005*

bissom; besom *noun* a slovenly woman. Dialect *UK: SCOTLAND, 1911*

bisto *noun* a fart. From the advertising slogan 'Aaah Bisto...' savouring the aroma of a branded gravy *UK, 2004*

bit *noun* **1** a prison sentence *US, 1866*. **2** an interest; an affected mannerism; a role *US, 1955*. **3** a woman, especially when regarded sexually *UK, 1923*. **4** sexual intercourse *AUSTRALIA, 1945*. **5** an activity *US, 1968*. **6** used as a meaningless embellishment of the preceding noun, as in 'Let's do the lunch bit' *US, 1955*. **7** twelve and a half cents *US, 1821*. **8** twelve dollars and fifty cents *US, 1929*. **9** your home or home area *UK: SCOTLAND, 1988*. **10** a bullet *UK, 2001*. ▶ **champ at the bit; chomp at the bit** to be enthusiastically eager. From a horse's characteristic behaviour *UK, 1645*. ▶ **pull a bit** to serve a prison sentence *US, 1969*. ▶ **take the bit out of** to exhaust someone *UK: SCOTLAND, 1988*. ▶ **wee red bit** the glowing end of a cigarette, especially when used as a means of lighting another cigarette *UK: SCOTLAND, 1988*

bita *noun* a bit of. Reflecting a lazy pronunciation *UK, 1999*

bitaine *noun* a prostitute *UK, 2002*

bit bashing *noun* low level, tedious computer programming *US, 1991*

bit bucket *noun* in computing, the mythical place where lost information goes *US, 1983*

bitch *noun* **1** a woman. Although Grose considered it 'the most offensive appellation that can be given to an English woman,' it is used in this sense with no derogatory intent; it is dismissive or patronising, based on gender rather than the unpleasant and lewd characteristics of earlier and concurrent usages. Comedian Richard Blackwood (b.1972) used 'bitch' in this sense, referring to Queen Elizabeth II, during an edition of BBC television's *Have I Got News For You* in October 2000. Six viewers complained to the Broadcasting Standards Commission. The BBC argued 'Richard Blackwood was using the term as it is currently used, for example, in British and American Rap Music simply to mean "woman", and not as a term of abuse'. The complaints were not upheld *UK, 1713*. **2** a despicable woman *UK, 1400*. **3** the person taking the passive role in a male homosexual relationship; a feminine or weak man *US, 1923*. **4** a sexual submissive of either gender in a sado-masochistic relationship. Generally attached to a possessive pronoun *UK, 2002*. **5** a remarkable person or thing *US, 1943*. **6** something that is difficult or unpleasant *UK, 1814*. **7** in the youth trend for 'souped-up' motor-scootering, a driver's scooter *UK, 2004*. **8** in a deck of playing cards, any queen; in the game of hearts, the queen of spades *US, 1900*. **9** in chess, the queen *US, 1971*. **10** a complaint; an extended period of complaining *US, 1945*. **11** a crude candle *CANADA, 1961*. **12** a u-turn *US, 2000*. **13** the middle position of the back seat of a car *US,*

1989. ▶ **put the bitch on someone** to file criminal charges accusing someone of being a habitual criminal *US, 1972*

bitch *verb* **1** to complain *US, 1918.* **2** to inform on someone *UK, 2000.* **3** to identify and punish someone as a habitual criminal *US, 1976.* **4** to ruin something *UK, 1823*

bitch about *verb* to be unreliable and troublesome; to change or renegotiate arrangements *UK, 1959*

bitch-ass *adjective* weak, effeminate *US, 2002*

bitch-ass nigga *noun* a weak or effeminate black male *US, 1995*

bitch bar *noun* anything that serves as a hand grip for a motorcycle passenger. Biker (motorcycle) usage, alluding to a female passenger *US, 2000*

bitch basket *noun* a Volkswagen Cabriolet *US, 1997*

bitch bath *noun* a cleaning of the body using little water, powder or other odour-masking agents *US, 1953*

bitch blow *noun* a violent blow *BAHAMAS, 1982*

bitch box *noun* a public address loudspeaker system *US, 1945*

bitchcakes *adjective* aggressive *US, 2004*

bitchen; bitching *adjective* excellent *US, 1957*

bitchen twitchen *adjective* excellent *US, 1982*

bitcher *noun* a habitual criminal *US, 1963*

bitches' Christmas *noun* Halloween. A glorious homosexual holiday, erotic and exotic *US, 1964*

bitch fight *noun* a quarrel between ostentatiously effeminate male homosexuals *US, 1964*

bitch fit *noun* a temper tantrum *US, 1969*

bitch hook *noun* an all-purpose quick-release hook for use with a tractor and chain *CANADA, 1992*

Bitchin' Betty *noun* in the Canadian Air Force, an automatic audible vocal warning system of danger *CANADA, 1995*

bitching *noun* the act of complaining about or disparaging someone or something. From the verb BITCH (to complain) *US, 1953*

bitching *adjective* used as a negative intensifier. An abbreviation of 'son-of-a-bitching' *US, 1928*

bitching week *noun* on an Atlantic weather ship, the third week of a four week tour of station. Derives from BITCH (to complain) as this is the time when tempers are shortest *1963*

bitch kitty *noun* an excellent instance of, or example of, something *US, 1944*

bitch lamp *noun* an improvised lamp *US, 1960*

bitch money *noun* earnings from prostitution and pimping *UK, 2001*

bitch off *verb* to irritate someone *US, 1975*

bitch on wheels *noun* a person, especially a woman, with a truly nasty disposition *US, 1966*

bitch out *verb* to criticise someone harshly *US, 1986*

bitch pad *noun* a small seat mounted behind the regular seat on a motorcycle *US, 1992*

bitch pie *noun* a pizza with pepperoni, mushroom and sausage. The initials of the toppings – PMS – suggest a cranky woman *US, 1996*

bitch piss *noun* bottled alcopop (branded alcoholic beverage with the characteristics of a soft drink) or other alcoholic drinks deemed to be for feminine consumption *UK, 2002*

bitch session *noun* a group airing of complaints *US, 1960*

bitch slap *verb* **1** to slap someone full across the face *US, 1995.* **2** by extension, to soundly defeat or better someone or something *US, 2002*

bitchsplitter *noun* the penis. Used on-air in the telling of a joke by syndicated US broadcaster Mancow Muller, adopted as a name by a Canadian death metal band *US, 2003*

bitch tits *nickname* an overweight male *UK, 2005*

bitch up *verb* to spoil or ruin something *BARBADOS, 1965*

bitch with a capital C *noun* a truly hideous person. A suggestion of CUNT *US, 2003*

bitchy *adjective* malicious, spiteful *US, 1925*

bite *noun* **1** a small meal or a snack *US, 1899.* **2** the portion of the money bet by gamblers taken as the share for the establishment sponsoring the gambling *US, 1988.* **3** a price *US, 1958.* **4** in motor racing, traction between the tyres and track *US, 1970.* **5** something that is very disagreeable *US, 1951.* ▶ **put the bite on** to extort *AUSTRALIA, 1919*

bite *verb* **1** to copy or steal another person's style, especially to copy a breakdancing move, or to plagiarise a rap lyric *US, 1979.* **2** to ask someone for a loan of money *AUSTRALIA, 1912.* **3** to be taken in, to be duped. A figurative use of the literal 'take the bait' *UK, 1987.* **4** to be unfair or extremely distasteful *US, 1971.* **5** to itch *BARBADOS, 1965.* **6** to flex, and thus contract, the sphincter during anal sex *US, 1972.* ▶ **bite feathers** to lie on your stomach, especially in antici- pation of anal sex *US, 1964.* ▶ **bite it** to die *US, 1977.* ▶ **bite off more than you can chew** to be unable to complete a task that is too great for your ambitions *US, 1878.* ▶ **bite the bag** in computing, to fail, especially in a dramatic fashion *US, 1983.* ▶ **bite the big one** to die *US, 1979.* ▶ **bite the brown** to perform mouth-to-anus sex *US, 1972.* ▶ **bite the dust** to go down in defeat *US, 1982.* ▶ **bite the pillow** to take the recipient role in anal sex *AUSTRALIA, 1987.* ▶ **bite to the bone** to punish someone with all the severity allowed under the law *US, 1962.* ▶ **bite your lips** to smoke a marijuana cigarette *US, 1959*

bite and a button *noun* a negligible price *UK, 2003*

bite in the britches *noun* in trucking, a speeding ticket *US, 1976*

biter *noun* **1** a copier of breakdance moves; a plagiarist of rap lyrics *US, 1999.* **2** the vagina *US, 1998.* **3** a tooth *US, 1946*

bit hurt *noun* the agony of withdrawal from a drug addiction *US, 1990*

bit much *noun* used to describe, or in response to, anything that is excessive, too demanding, arrogant, objectionable, etc *UK, 1974*

bit 'na half people *noun* a family that is just above the poverty line. In colonial British Guiana currency, a 'bit' was a silver coin valued at 8 cents; 12 cents was a popular retail food-price marker for items of poor fare in markets *GUYANA, 1996*

bit of *noun* used to stress an affection or sympathy for the noun it describes *UK, 1808*

bit of a bugger *noun* a nuisance; a difficulty *UK, 2003*

bit of alright; bit of all right *noun* **1** a sexually attractive person *UK, 1898.* **2** something excellent, especially an unexpected treat or a stroke of good luck. Sometimes also a 'little bit of all right' *UK, 1907*

bit of black *noun* a black person objectified sexually *UK, 1974*

bit of bod *noun* the body as an object of sexual interest *UK, 1970*

bit of Braille *noun* **1** sexual fondling and groping. The Braille alphabet is read with fingertips – hence the image of feeling and touching *AUSTRALIA, 1984.* **2** a racing tip. Designed for the blind, the Braille alphabet is read by feeling; in horse racing gamblers mainly decide on bets by 'reading' form or because they have 'a feeling' *AUSTRALIA, 1961*

bit of brush *noun* a woman regarded and categorised as a sexual object; the act of sex *AUSTRALIA, 1965*

bit of bum *noun* from a male perspective, sex with another person; the person so desired objectified in a purely sexual context *UK, 1984*

bit of crackling *noun* a woman regarded as a sexual object *UK, 1949*

bit of cunt *noun* a woman regarded and categorised as a sex object; an act of sexual intercourse *UK, 1984*

bit of dirt *noun* a farm *NEW ZEALAND, 1987*

bit of ebony *noun* a black woman regarded as a sexual category *UK, 1984*

bit of elastic *noun* the penis *UK, 1999*

bit of fluff *noun* a woman, especially when regarded sexually *UK, 1847*

bit of hard *noun* **1** an erection *UK, 1978.* **2** in homosexual sexual relations, a male partner *UK, 2002*

bit of hod *noun* a promiscuous, or potentially promiscuous, girl *UK, 1963*

bit of kit *noun* an item of equipment, especially mechanical or electrical *UK, 2000*

bit of mess *noun* a prostitute's lover who is neither ponce nor client *UK, 1977*

bit of nonsense *noun* an easily achieved criminal act *UK, 1968*

bit of posh *noun* an upper-class or socially superior young woman regarded as a sexual object *UK, 1977*

bit of rough *noun* a male lover, categorised as of a lower social status, or a rougher background than the partner. The relationship defined may be homo- or heterosexual. Original usage described a female but from the mid-C20 the male predominates *UK, 1985*

bit of skin *noun* a woman viewed as a sex object *AUSTRALIA, 1962*

bit of skirt *noun* a woman viewed as a sex object *AUSTRALIA, 1904*

bit of slap and tickle *noun* **1** kissing and cuddling; sexual petting which may be considered as foreplay by one participant *UK, 1984*. **2** sexual intercourse. An extension of the previous sense *UK, 1984*

bit of spare *noun* anyone providing sexual favours, even on a short-term or occasional basis; an unattached woman, especially at a club, party or any place where men may be expected to look for a sexual companion or conquest. 'Bit of' plus conventional use of 'spare' (available) *UK, 1977*

bit of stray *noun* a casual sexual acquaintance, usually female *UK, 2001*

bit of tail *noun* **1** a woman regarded as a sexual object *UK, 1984*. **2** an act of anal intercourse; an act of sexual intercourse where the male partner enters the female from behind *UK, 1984*

bit of the other *noun* sexual intercourse *UK, 1984*

bit of tickle *noun* a woman regarded as a sexual object; sexual intercourse *UK, 1984*

bit of tit *noun* a woman regarded as a sexual object; sex with a woman *UK, 1984*

bit of work *noun* a crime; a robbery *UK, 1996*

bit on the side *noun* a secret lover in addition to your regular partner; a love affair; extra-marital sex *UK, 1977*

bits *noun* **1** the male genitals. Sympathetically of a baby boy, jocularly of a man *UK, 1976*. **2** in betting, odds of 11–10 *UK, 1991*. ▶ **in bits** emotionally distraught; tearful *UK, 1999*. ▶ **to bits** (of a specified emotion) extremely *UK, 1964*

bits and bats *noun* knick-knacks *UK, 1961*

bits and bobs *noun* miscellaneous small articles *UK, 1896*

bits and tits *noun* the controls *AUSTRALIA, 1962*

bits of kids *noun* youngsters *UK, 1999*

bits on the ear'ole *noun* in betting, odds of 13–8. From the TICK-TACK signal used by bookmakers, an elaboration of EAR'OLE (6–4) *UK, 1991*

bit spit *noun* any electronic communication *US, 1997*

bitsy *adjective* small, tiny *US, 1905*

bitter-mouth *verb* to speak harshly *US, 1947*

bit twiddler *noun* a computer operator *US, 1974*

bitty *noun* a girl *US, 1962*

bitty *adjective* tiny. A corruption and shortening of ITSY-BITSY *US, 1905*

bitty box *noun* a small computer, especially a single-tasking-only machine *US, 1991*

bitumen blonde *noun* an Aboriginal woman *AUSTRALIA, 1985*

bitzer; bitser; bitza *noun* a dog of mixed breed. A shortening of the phrase 'bits of this and bits of that' *AUSTRALIA, 1936*

biz; bizz *noun* **1** business *US, 1861*. **2** the syringe and other equipment used by intravenous drug users *US, 1949*. **3** a small amount of a drug *US, 1971*. ▶ **do the bizz** to engage in sexual activity *IRELAND, 1995*. ▶ **in the biz bag** in trouble with police management *US, 1994*. ▶ **the biz** the 'profession', loosely the entertainment, theatre or film making business. An industry coinage that lends dignity to the least secure of employment paths *UK, 1961*

bizarro *noun* a bizarre person. Influenced by, if not directly descended from, 'Bizarro' a comic-book villain who first challenged Superman in the late 1950s *US, 1980*

bizarro *adjective* bizarre *US, 1971*

biznatch; biznitch *noun* used as a euphemism for 'bitch' in any sense. From rapper JayZ *US, 2002*

bizotic *adjective* unexpected, out of the ordinary *US, 1984*

bizzazz *noun* ▷*see:* BEZAZZ

bizzies; busies *noun* the police. From the plural of BUSY (a detective, a CID officer), but all distiction of rank is lost *UK, 1948*

bizzing *noun* sliding on an icy road while hanging onto the rear bumper of a car. A verbal noun with no recorded use of 'bizz' as a verb *US, 1969*

bizzle *noun* a brother, in the sense as male companion, especially in the phrase 'fa' shizzle my bizzle' (emphatically yes). A hip-hop, urban black coinage, formed as a rhyming reduplication of SHIZZLE (sure, yes), after 'fa' shizzle my nizzle' (yes my nigger). London rapper Maxwell Ansah recorded under the name Lethal Bizzle in 2002 *US, 2002*

bizzo *noun* **1** business *AUSTRALIA, 1969*. **2** an ill-tempered woman. A corruption or evolution of 'bitch' *US, 2001*

bizzurd *adjective* bizarre and absurd. Derived by ellipsis. Hip-hop, urban slang; noted in connection with a legal dispute over rap lyrics by *BBC News*, 6th June 2003. *UK, 2003*

bizzy *noun* ▷*see:* BUSY

BJ; bj *noun* an act of oral sex, a blow job *US, 1949*

B joint *noun* a bar where women coax customers to buy drinks *US, 1993*

BJs *noun* crack cocaine *UK, 2003*

BK Lounge *noun* a Burger King™ fast food restaurant. Mocking attribution of class *US, 1985*

BK's *noun* British Knight™ shoes. Favoured by members of the Crips youth gang, for whom the initials also stand for 'Blood Killer' *US, 2000*

blab *verb* to inform on someone, to reveal something while speaking *UK, 1583*

blabber *noun* a very talkative hospital patient *US, 1994*

black *noun* **1** hashish. An all-purpose abbreviation for strains of dark-coloured cannabis resin, e.g. PAKISTANI BLACK *US, 1975*. **2** a black amphetamine capsule *UK, 2003*. **3** night *US, 1947*. **4** in American casinos, a $100 chip *US, 1980*. ▶ **in the black** financially solvent. From the pre-computer practice of recording credit items in black ink *US, 1928*. ▶ **on the black** engaged in black-market activities *UK, 1961*. ▶ **the black 1** blackmail; the information held by a blackmailer. Hence, 'put the black on' (to blackmail) *UK, 1970*. **2** the black market. During the war in Vietnam, the term referred specifically to the black market which flourished on Le Loi Street, Saigon *UK, 1961*

black *verb* to blackmail someone. An abbreviation of the conventional activity *UK, 1928*

black *adjective* **1** secret *US, 1965*. **2** extremely crowded *IRELAND, 1998*. ▶ **it's a black thing; it's a black thang** used for identifying a behaviour or sensibility that is associated with black people *US, 1993*

black acid *noun* LSD *US, 1970*

black action *noun* casino betting in $100 increments *US, 1991*

blackamoor *noun* a black Angus or Friesian cow *NEW ZEALAND, 1956*

Black and Decker *noun* the penis. Rhyming slang for PECKER (the penis). In its many slang manifestations the penis appears as all kind of tools, here it is formed on a manufacturer of power tools *UK, 1998*

black and tan *noun* **1** a drink of porter or stout mixed equally with ale (pale or brown) *UK, 1889*. **2** a capsule of Durophet™, trade name for a combination of central nervous system stimulants and depressants *UK, 1978*

black and tan *adjective* catering to both black and white customers *US, 1887*

black and white *noun* **1** a police car. From the traditional colours of police cars in the US *US, 1958*. **2** an amphetamine capsule, especially Durophet™. From the colours of the capsule *UK, 1978*. **3** a capsule containing both a central nervous system stimulant and a barbiturate *US, 1971*. **4** a soda fountain drink made with chocolate syrup, seltzer and vanilla ice-cream *US, 1947*. **5** night. Rhyming slang, always spoken in full *UK, 1937*

black and white fever *noun* an aversion to police *US, 1970*

black and white minstrel *noun* an amphetamine tablet (Durophet™). An elaboration of BLACK AND WHITE, used especially in the plural, based on *The Black and White Minstrel Show*, a 1960s television programme *UK, 1996*

black and whites *noun* the black trousers or skirt and white shirt worn by American casino dealers *US, 1961*

black and white taxi *noun* a police car *US, 1962*

black art *noun* in computing, an array of techniques developed and discovered for a particular system or application *US, 1991*

black ash *noun* marijuana. London pronunciation of 'black hash' *UK, 1991*

black ass *noun* a car without working rear lights *US, 1962*

black as the ace of spades *adjective* utterly black or, of skin, deeply black *US, 1882*

black bag *noun* a brown-haired prostitute *US, 1960*

black bag job *noun* a burglary, especially one committed by law enforcement or intelligence agents *US, 1966*

black Bart *noun* dark hashish. A generic term for 'marijuana'; connotes a romantic view of the drug's illegal status by association with the C19 US outlaw *UK, 1998*

black beauty *noun* **1** a black amphetamine capsule *US, 1969*. **2** a capsule containing both barbiturate and amphetamine *US, 1973*

black belt *noun* **1** a neighbourhood of black families that circles a city or area *US, 1951*. **2** in the US Army, a senior drill instructor. Not a reference to martial arts, simply to the uniform. Vietnam war usage *US, 1991*

black bess yes. Rhyming slang *UK, 1992*

black Betty *noun* a van for transporting prisoners *US, 1965*

blackbird *noun* **1** a black person. A US mass murderer believed that among the secret messages hidden in the music of the Beatles were references to a coming black uprising in the song 'Blackbird' *US, 1832*. **2** an unmarked military aircraft, such as a C-123 or C-130. Used by the Studies and Observations Group (SOG) in Vietnam, the highly secret, elite, unconventional warfare component of the US military presence in Southeast Asia *US, 1991*. **3** an amphetamine capsule *US, 1972*. **4** LSD *UK, 2003*

black blizzard *noun* a black prairie soil dust storm *CANADA, 1962*

black Bombay *noun* hashish, potent and dark in colour *US, 1993*

black bomber; bomber *noun* any central nervous system stimulant, especially a capsule of diethylpropion (Durophet™), an amphetamine-like stimulant *UK, 1963*

black book *noun* **1** a corporation's plan for battling a hostile takeover *US, 1988*. **2** in a casino, a list of persons to be excluded from the casino *US, 1991*. **3** a graffiti artist's notebook containing ideas, outlines, sketches and plans for future graffiti pieces *US, 1997*

black bottom *noun* a neighbourhood where most of the population are poor black people *US, 1915*

black box *noun* **1** in an aeroplane, the container and equipment used for the automatic recording of all flight data and cockpit conversation. A specialised use of Royal Air Force slang *UK, 1964*. **2** the notional container in which proprietary technical information is secured in dealings over industrial property rights *US, 1974*. **3** any high technical piece of electronics equipment *US, 1945*. **4** a hearse *UK, 1981*. **5** a linear amplifier for a citizens' band radio. Sometimes embellished as 'little black box' *US, 1976*

black Cadillac *noun* an amphetamine capsule *US, 1980*

black cap *nickname* a member of the New Zealand international men's cricket team *NEW ZEALAND, 2000*

black Christmas *noun* a snow-free Christmas. A forced allusion to the famous 'White Christmas' *US, 1938*

black-coated worker; black-coated workman; little black worker *noun* a prune. From the appearance and the work done during the digestive process. Remembered, in 1970, as being used by Lord Hill 'The Radio Doctor' during World War 2. Noted in Manchester in *Daltonian*, December 1946, then generally in the Midlands and London *UK, 1946*

black crow *noun* during the Vietnam war, a long-range ignition detector. Highly effective from the air in locating enemy convoys; used in conjunction with a beacon tracking system *US, 1991*

black-dog *adjective* melancholic, depressed *UK, 1826*

black domina *noun* dark hashish. An allusion to the sexual domination of a black mistress *UK, 2002*

black dot *noun* a type of LSD. From the appearance *UK, 1996*

black eagle *noun* heroin *UK, 2003*

black-enamelled *adjective* dark-skinned. Military, intended as jocular *UK, 1984*

blacketeer *noun* a black market racketeer. A World War 2 coinage, possibly journalistic *AUSTRALIA, 1953*

blackfellow's delight *noun* rum. A disparaging view of Aboriginal Australians' drinking habits *AUSTRALIA, 1953*

black fever *noun* sexual attraction felt by a white person for black people *US, 1977*

black forest *noun* the female genitals. This pet name for a vagina describes its location in a straightforward simile for the pubic hair, ostensibly punning on the *Schwarzwald* region of southwest Germany. Derived possibly as a reference to Black Forest gateaux (sticky, chocolatey, cherry-laden cakes; a cultural-icon in the UK since the 1970s), the cake imagery suggesting an oral-sex dimension to the usage. Also note 'A Walk In The Black Forest' by Horst Jankowski, a popular instrumental recording in the 1960s; a satisfying metaphor for sexual activity *UK, 2001*

black Friday *noun* the day after Thanksgiving *US, 1975*

black gang *noun* **1** collectively, a ship's engineer's department *US, 1895*. **2** an aviation mechanics team. The source of the term is likely to be their black overalls *CANADA, 1997*

black ganja *noun* hashish, dark in colour. The term is heard and seen with all the possible variant spellings of GANJA found at that entry *US, 1978*

black gold *noun* **1** oil. An outsiders' term, not used by those in the business *US, 1910*. **2** highly potent marijuana. Derived from the previous sense, punning on the richness and the colour of the hashish *US, 1946*. **3** distilled, concentrated heroin *US, 1987*

Black Hand *noun* a secret criminal organisation composed of first-generation Italian immigrants to the US *US, 1898*

black hash *noun* hashish mixed and darkened with opium *US, 1975*

black hat *noun* **1** in a drama, or in life viewed as a drama, the villain *US, 1964*. **2** a computer hacker with no honourable purpose. Sometimes embellished to 'black hat hacker' *US, 2001*. **3** a member of Pathfinder platoon, dropped behind enemy lines to make deep reconnaissance patrols and to establish landing zones for the initial helicopter waves *US, 1982*. **4** a US Army drill instructor *US, 1986*

blackhead *noun* a black person. Derogatory, unless ironically self-descriptive. Otherwise a 'blackhead' is a skin blemish *UK, 2000*

black heart *noun* depression *UK, 1996*

black hole *noun* **1** the vagina. Originally a reference to 'the black pit of hell'. Now a 'black hole' is widely known to be a celestial phenomenon into which anything may be sucked to disappear without trace *UK, 2001*. **2** in computing, the notional place where e-mail that is sent but not received disappears *US, 1991*

black horse *nickname* the US Army's 11th Armored Cavalry Regiment. So named because of the Regiment's insignia *US, 1991*

black-is-white *adverb* completely, thoroughly. Collected by Richard Allsopp *TRINIDAD AND TOBAGO, 1998*

black jack *noun* **1** the penis of a black man. Homosexual usage *US, 1965*. **2** a fifty-ton Santa Fe Railroad coal hopper *US, 1977*

Black Jack *nickname* **1** black-labelled Jack Daniels™ whisky *US, 1982*. **2** US General John J. Pershing (1860–1948) *US, 1951*

blackjack mission *noun* during the war in Vietnam, an operation carried out by a mobile strike force. The mobile strike forces were light infantry battalions equipped and trained to operate in remote areas without any significant logistical requirements or support *US, 1991*

Black Jeff *noun* a wasp *BAHAMAS, 1982*

black light *noun* an ultraviolet light, under which fluorescent paint glows *US, 1971*

Black Lions *nickname* a navy fighter squadron formally identified as VF-213, commissioned in 1955 *US, 1990*

black magic *noun* **1** the M-16 rifle, the standard rifle used by US troops in Vietnam after 1966 *US, 1991*. **2** in computing, a technique that works without any apparent reason for its success *US, 1991*

Black Magic box *noun* a police van. Plays on BLACK MARIA (a police van) and Black Magic™ chocolates *UK, 1981*

black man kissed her *noun* a sister. Rhyming slang from the early part of C20 which appears to have all but died out by 1948 when Carribean immigration began in earnest and revived usage. Noted as coming back into currency by 1960 *UK, 1960*

black man's wheels *noun* a BMW car *UK, 1999*

Black Maria *noun* **1** a police wagon or van for transporting those who have been arrested. The etymology is uncertain beyond the colour black *US, 1843*. **2** in a deck of cards, the queen of spades *US, 1988*. **3** highly potent marijuana *UK, 2001*

black marketeer *noun* an unlicensed bookmaker quoting his own prices and odds *AUSTRALIA, 1953*

black micro *noun* a variety of LSD in tablet form *UK, 1996*

black mo; black moat; black mote *noun* highly potent, dark coloured marijuana resin *US, 1972*

black molly *noun* **1** a black amphetamine capsule *US, 1970*. **2** a barbiturate capsule *US, 1973*

Black Monday *noun* **1** 28th May 1962. The date of a dramatic stock market crash *US, 1962*. **2** 19th October 1987. The date of the greatest single-day stock market crash in the US since the Depression *US, 1987*

black money *noun* cash that is not accounted for in the financial records of a business *US, 1963*

black oil *noun* hashish oil *UK, 1977*

black on black *noun* a car with a black exterior and black upholstery. Black teen slang *US, 1980*

black-out *noun* a very dark-skinned black person *US, 1947*

black pearl *noun* heroin *US, 1994*

black pen *noun* a parole report *UK, 1996*

black peter *noun* in prison, a punishment cell. An elaboration of 'peter' (a cell) *AUSTRALIA, 1953*

black pill *noun* a pill of opium; heroin *US, 1969*

Blackpool rock *noun* the penis. Rhyming slang for COCK; a visual pun on a long pink sweet that is made to be sucked. Similarly sweet references to the male anatomy can be found at ALMONDROCK, BRIGHTON ROCK and STICK OF ROCK. Probably inspired or influenced by the innuendo-laden song 'With My Little Stick of Blackpool Rock' by George Formby, 1937 *UK, 1992*

black powder *noun* ground hashish and opium. An explosive mixture named after an early form of gunpowder *US, 2001*

black power *nickname* a Maori gang or member of the gang *NEW ZEALAND, 1978*

black Protestant *noun* **1** used as a term of contempt for Protestants in Ireland. This term appears to have become diluted over the years *IRELAND, 2001*. **2** a non-observant Protestant or one prejudiced against Roman Catholics *US, 1969*

black rain *noun* rain that has been contaminated by smoke from oil field fires. Gulf war usage *US, 1991*

Black Rats *nickname* the Traffic Division of the Metropolitan Police based at New Scotland Yard *UK, 1999*

black rock *noun* crack cocaine. An elaboration of ROCK (crack cocaine) which has more to do with the drug's reputation than colour, *2003*

black rover *noun* a Metropolitan Police warrant card. This card authorises free travel throughout the London Transport system and thus plays on a London Transport Red Rover ticket which allowed the purchaser unlimited travel *UK, 2002*

black Russian *noun* **1** blackened opium *US, 1969*. **2** dark hashish *US, 1969*. **3** marijuana resin mixed with opium *US, 2001*

black shoe *noun* an officer in the US Navy other than an aviator. Aviation officers wore brown shoes *US, 1950*

blacksmith *noun* an incompetent sheep station cook *NEW ZEALAND, 1941*

black snake *noun* a freight train composed entirely of coal tenders *US, 1938*

Black Sox *nickname* the New Zealand international men's softball team *NEW ZEALAND, 2000*

black star *noun* a type of LSD *UK, 1998*

blackstick *noun* a clarinet *US, 1937*

black stranger *noun* a complete stranger *IRELAND, 1962*

Black Street *noun* the notional location of a clinic treating those with sexually transmitted infections. Euphemistic *UK: SCOTLAND, 1988*

black stuff *noun* opium; heroin *US, 1936*

blackstuff *noun* tarmacadam *UK, 1982*

black stuff *nickname* Guinness *IRELAND, 2000*

Black Stump *noun* used as an imaginary marker for a remote place. Often used in phrases such as 'this side of the black stump', 'out near the Black Stump', 'the other side of the Black Stump' or 'beyond the Black Stump'. From a fire-blackened tree stump used as a marker for navigation in the country *AUSTRALIA, 1957*

black sunshine *noun* LSD *UK, 1998*

black tabs *noun* a type of LSD *US, 1982*

black tar *noun* crude, impure, potent heroin from Mexico *US, 1986*

black tar blanco *noun* heroin *UK, 2002*

black tide *noun* an oil slick on the ocean surface *US, 1991*

black-tie *adjective* **1** calling for formal dress *UK, 1933*. **2** said of an event in Antarctica in which those in attendance are not wearing red clothes issued by the US National Science Foundation *ANTARCTICA, 1991*

black type *noun* in horse racing, a horse that has won or been placed in a stakes race. Bold face type is used in a sales catalogue to identify horses that have won or been placed *US, 1997*

Blackus *noun* used as a term of address for a dark-skinned person *BAHAMAS, 1982*

black velvet *noun* **1** sexual relations with Aboriginal or other dark-skinned women *AUSTRALIA, 1899*. **2** a black woman's vagina *US, 1967*. **3** a drink of stout mixed with champagne. From the colour and texture. An economical variation is poor man's velvet (stout and cider); sometimes shortened to 'blackers' *UK, 1937*

black water *noun* **1** coffee, especially when weak *US, 1850*. **2** sewage. Euphemism used in recreational vehicle camping *US, 1993*

black whack *noun* phencyclidine, the recreational drug known as PCP or angel dust *US, 1994*

black widow *noun* **1** a black amphetamine capsule; Benzedrine™ (amphetamine sulphate), a central nervous system stimulant *US, 1972*. **2** a capsule containing both barbiturate and amphetamine *US, 1973*. **3** an M-16 rifle equipped with a night scope *US, 1991*. **4** a limited edition, fuel-injected 1957 Chevrolet 150 sedan, built strictly for racing but then banned from stock car racing *US, 1992*

black wings *noun* oral sex with a black woman *US, 2000*

blacky; blackie *noun* a black person. Derogatory, but not necessarily deliberately so *UK, 1815*

blacky carbon *noun* in drag racing, petrol *US, 1965*

blacky-white; blackie-white *noun* an Anglo-Indian half-caste *INDIA, 1977*

bladder *noun* **1** a balloon. Circus and carnival usage *US, 1981*. **2** a collapsible drum for holding liquids *US, 1991*. **3** a local newspaper. Derives from a less-than-favourable description of its contents *UK, 1970*

bladder bird *noun* a tanker aircraft used for aerial bulk fuel delivery. Vietnam war usage *US, 1991*

bladder boat *noun* an inflatable rubber boat. Vietnam war usage *US, 1991*

bladder-buster *noun* a very large beverage container *US, 1997*

bladdered *adjective* very drunk *UK, 1997*

blade *noun* **1** a knife *US, 1896*. **2** a surgeon *US, 1974*. **3** a man *US, 1948*. **4** a Cadillac car, especially a Coupe de Ville or Fleetwood. Black teen slang *US, 1980*. **5** a type of expensive chrome car wheel rim *US, 1998*. **6** a moped *BERMUDA, 1985*. **7** a dollar *US, 2002*

blade *verb* to skate on rollerblades *US, 1997*

blader *noun* a rollerblader *US, 1989*

blade-runner *noun* someone who transports stolen goods or contraband. Taken from the science-fiction film *Blade Runner*, 1982, based on Philip K. Dick's cyberpunk novel *Do Androids Dream of Electric Sheep?*, 1968 *UK, 2001*

blading *noun* the act of using rollerblades *US, 1995*

blag *noun* **1** a robbery, especially an armed robbery; a bank or post-office robbery. Probably an abbreviation of 'blackguard' *UK, 1885*. **2** a piece of persuasive bluff *UK, 1962*. **3** used as a term of abuse. Usage appears restricted to northern grammar schools deriving, perhaps, from a shortening of 'blaggard' (a blackguard) *UK, 1963*

blag *verb* **1** to hoax or deceive someone; to bluff someone; to persuade someone; to wheedle something; to scrounge something. From French *blaguer* (to joke), possibly informed by conventional English 'blaggard' *UK, 1958*. **2** to successfully persuade another person into having sex with you *UK, 2002*. **3** to rob something, especially with violence *UK, 1933*

blagard *verb* to talk profanely or obscenely. According to one source, this term is in use with this meaning in Nova Scotia's South Shore. It derives from the French *blague* (chaff, humbug, hoax, fib) but may also derive from an English gang of blacking boys and torch-carriers in London known for their scurrilous language. In the form 'blackguarding', it is in use in parts of the US with the same meaning as in Nova Scotia *CANADA, 1988*

blagger *noun* **1** a robber who will use violence as necessary. In *The Lag's Lexicon*, 1950, Paul Tempest noted the term was 'used very occasionally'; during the 1970s usage proliferated through the agency of television programmes like *The Sweeney* *UK, 1950*. **2** a persuasive person who is employed to attract customers *UK, 1963*. **3** a persuasive criminal, a confidence trickster *UK, 1966*

blagging *noun* a robbery, especially with violence. Derives, possibly, from 'blackguard' *UK, 1933*

blag merchant *noun* a pay-roll bandit, an armed robber. Combines BLAG (a robbery with violence) with the colloquial use of 'merchant' (a man) *UK, 2000*

blah *verb* to say empty and meaningless things, to talk without saying anything worth saying *UK, 2004*

blah *adjective* without energy, without spark, unmotivated *US, 1922*

blah; blah blah; blah blah blah *noun* empty and meaningless talk; so on and so forth; used for implying that what is being said is not worth the saying or has been said too often already. Echoic of nonsense speech, possibly German *blech* (nonsense); synonymous with RHUBARB (nonsense) which may also be repeated two or three times for emphasis *UK, 1918*

blahs *noun* a minor illness; a feeling of ennui *US, 1968*

blair; blare *verb* to criticise, humiliate or mock someone or something. Possibly from conventional 'blare' (to shout); probably predates Tony Blair's rise to political and media prominence, although current usage is certainly informed by his Prime Ministership *UK, 1998*

blak *noun* black. Fashionable misspelling *UK, 2002*

blam *verb* to slam loudly *BARBADOS, 1965*

blamed; blame *adjective* used as a euphemistic intensifier replacing 'damned'. An equivalent to BLINKING *US, 1944*

blancas *noun* amphetamines or other central nervous system stimulants. Border Spanish used in English conversation by Mexican-Americans; from the Spanish for 'white' *US, 1967*

blanco *noun* heroin; cocaine. Spanish for 'white' *US, 1973*

blank *noun* **1** a packet of non-narcotic white powder sold as narcotics *US, 1966*. **2** a worthless person or thing *US, 1950*. **3** in a carnival, a bad day, a bad engagement or a bad customer *US, 1985*. **4** in poker, a useless card in the dealt hand *US, 1992*. **5** the top of a skateboard *US, 1976*. **6** a refusal of parole *US, 1996*. **7** a tablet of Aspirin *US, 1990*.
▸ **give someone the blank** to ignore someone *UK, 1999*

blank *verb* **1** to ignore someone. Any response is 'blanked out' *UK, 1977*. **2** to forget something *UK, 1996*. **3** to erase something. An abbreviated variation of the conventional 'blank out' *UK, 1981*

blank; blankety; blankety-blank used as a self-censored deletion of an expletive, regardless of part of speech. Written more often than spoken, but not without uses in speech *UK, 1854*

blank canvas *noun* the body of a person who is about to get their first tattoo *US, 1997*

blanket *noun* **1** a cigarette paper *US, 1925*. **2** a marijuana cigarette. Perhaps because it is shaped like a *blanket* roll *US, 1935*. **3** any sandwich *US, 1960*. **4** an overcoat; a top coat *US, 1925*. **5** in the US military, a beret *US, 1992*. **6** in trucking, a parking lot *US, 1976*. ▸ **on the blanket 1** used of prisoners who refuse to wear a uniform as a means of protest and are thereby wrapped in a blanket. Originating with republican prisoners making a political protest in the Maze Prison in Belfast in the mid-1970s *UK, 1979*. **2** (of an Indian) used for describing someone who has been aggressive but has stopped *CANADA, 1959*

blanket-ass *noun* a native American Indian. Derogatory *US, 1973*

blanket craps *noun* an informal game of craps with the shooter acting as banker *US, 1977*

blanket drill *noun* sex in bed *US, 1964*

blanket finish *noun* in horse racing, a close finish between several horses. So called because the horses contending for the lead could all be covered by a single figurative blanket *US, 1951*

blanket game *noun* in the circus or carnival, a private gambling game for employees only, played on a blanket *UK, 1980*

blanket harbour *noun* bed *CANADA, 1998*

blanket party *noun* a ritual in which the offending person is covered with a blanket, which prevents identification of the wrong-doers, and then beaten *US, 1969*

blanket roll *noun* a controlled roll of the dice by a skilled cheat, best made on a blanket spread on the ground *US, 1950*

blankety; blankety-blank ▷*see:* BLANK

blarney *noun* **1** honeyed flattery, pleasant talk that seeks to deceive; hence plausible nonsense. A fine example can be found at *www.blarneycastle.ie* in the gentle assertion that 'the term "Blarney" was introduced into the English language by Elizabeth I of England[.]' *IRELAND, 1766*. **2** an Irish accent. The Blarney stone is incorporated into the battlements of Blarney Castle – eight miles north of Cork city in southern Ireland. Familiar legend holds the promise that whoever kisses this stone will receive the gift of eloquence, hence 'blarney' (pleasant talk), here considered to be speech with an Irish lilt *UK, 2000*

blarney *verb* to talk flatteringly or persuasively *UK, 1803*

blarneying *adjective* of a manner of speech, persuasive, flattering *US, 1869*

blarry *adjective* ▷*see:* BLERRY

blart *verb* to talk compulsively, especially about emotional upheaval. A combination of conventional 'blurt' and BLAB (to talk) or **blub** (to cry) *UK, 2001*

blasé blasé and so on and so on. An embellishment of the more expected BLAH BLAH BLAH *US, 2002*

blasé queen *noun* a characteristically up-market homosexual male *UK, 2002*

blast *noun* **1** an extremely enjoyable time *US, 1950*. **2** a party, especially a loud and raucous one *UK, 1959*. **3** an injection of a drug *US, 1952*.

4 cocaine; any drug with a powerful effect *US, 1992*. **5** a taste or a portion, especially of alcoholic drink *US, 1988*. **6** a parachute jump. Vietnam war usage *US, 1991*. **7** an escape *US, 1970*. **8** a stern admonishment; a severe rebuke *US, 1874*

blast *verb* **1** to use a drug, especially to smoke marijuana *US, 1943*. **2** to criticise someone or something severely. Mainly journalistic *UK, 1953*. **3** to reprimand someone *UK, 1984*

blast! used for expressing disgust or dismay *UK, 1634*

blasted *adjective* **1** cursed, damned; often used as a euphemism for 'bloody' *UK, 1750*. **2** highly intoxicated on any drug or alcohol *US, 1928*

blaster *noun* **1** a gun, especially a pistol *US, 1964*. **2** a powerful, hard-breaking wave *US, 1964*

blast from the past *noun* a song that was popular in the past and is still popular with those who were young when the song was popular *US, 1965*

blasting oil *noun* nitroglycerin, used by criminals to blast open safes *US, 1949*

blast off *verb* **1** to leave. Borrowed with great fervour from the language of space travel *US, 1954*. **2** to use and become intoxicated by a drug *US, 1961*. **3** of a car, especially a racing car, to drive off at speed. Uses a rocket launch as a metaphor *AUSTRALIA, 1984*

blast party *noun* a gathering of marijuana smokers *US, 1958*

blasty *adjective* in Newfoundland, used of a dead, dry branch, good for kindling *CANADA, 1980*

blat *noun* a short journey, usually for pleasure. Used by late 1980s-early 90s counterculture travellers *UK, 1999*

blat *verb* to fire a gun. Probably derived from a comic strip representation of a weapon in action: 'Blat! Blat! Blat!' *UK, 1995*

blatant *adjective* excellent. Recorded in use among young urban blacks *UK, 1999*

blathered *adjective* drunk. From the dialect word *blather* (to talk nonsense) *UK, 2002*

blatherskite; bletherskite; bletherskate *noun* a person who talks too much or too offensively. Originally Scottish dialect *US, 1791*

blats *noun* cash, money. In Royal Air Force use *UK, 2002*

blatted *adjective* drunk *UK, 2003*

blaxploitation *noun* the exploitation of black culture and imagery for commercial gain, especially in films *US, 1971*

blaze *noun* **1** in a card game with five cards per hand, a hand with five face cards *US, 1962*. **2** in a deck of playing cards, a face card *US, 1987*. **3** marijuana *US, 1998*

blaze *verb* **1** to leave *US, 1983*. **2** to move quickly *US, 1996*. **3** to have sex *US, 1997*. **4** to light a marijuana cigarette or other drug-smoking conveyance. Also expressed as to 'blaze up' *US, 1985*

blazed *adjective* drug-intoxicated *UK, 1998*

blaze full *noun* in poker, a hand consisting of three cards of one face card rank and a pair of another. The 'full' is drawn from the conventional name for the hand, a 'full house' *US, 1968*

blazer *noun* a big diamond *US, 1949*

blazes *noun* the flames of hell. Used in comparisons and as a euphemism for 'hell' *UK, 1818*

blazing *adjective* exceptionally attractive *UK, 1864*

blazing *adverb* used as an intensifier. Generally euphemistic for BLOODY *US, 1855*

bleach *verb* **1** to spend an extended period of days and nights in nightclubs *UK, 2000*. **2** to soak and flush a hypodermic needle and syringe with bleach to prevent transmission of HIV *US, 1989*. **3** to lie awake at night with a sense of impending doom *JAMAICA, 2003*

bleacher bum *noun* **1** a loud, rowdy sports fan who favours the inexpensive bleacher seats *US, 1981*. **2** a fan of the Chicago Cubs professional baseball team *US, 1998*

bleach tabs *noun* sterilising tablets issued to drug addicts *UK, 1996*

bleat *noun* **1** in prison, a petition to the Home Secretary *UK, 1950*. **2** a feeble complaint *UK, 1916*

bleat *verb* **1** to complain *US, 1985*. **2** to repeatedly deny guilt *UK, 1996*

bleed *noun* in pinball, a ball that leaves play having scored few points *US, 1979*

bleed *verb* **1** to extort money from someone *UK, 1680*. **2** to dilute a drug *US, 1992*. **3** to be showing lipstick on your face or clothes *US, 1968*. ▶ **bleed someone dry; bleed someone white** to drain a person or other resource of all money or value. The image of draining a life's blood *UK, 1982*

bleeder *noun* **1** a person *UK, 1887*. **2** a contemptible person *UK, 1887*. **3** a casino employee or executive who worries extensively about money being lost to gamblers *US, 1974*. **4** in poker, a player who methodically if undramatically drains money from the game by conservative, steady play *US, 1988*. **5** a boxer who is prone to bleeding *US, 1975*

bleeding *adjective* used as an intensifier. Originally replaced BLOODY, then used in its own right or as a substitute for less acceptable intensifiers; not necessarily intended as euphemistic *UK, 1858*

bleeding *adverb* used as an intensifier *UK, 1884*

bleeding deacon *noun* a person with an over-inflated sense of self-importance to an organisation. Usually used in the context of self-help recovery groups such as Alcoholics Anonymous *US, 1988*

bleeding edge *noun* the absolute forefront of technology. A punning combination of 'leading edge' and 'cutting edge' *US, 2000*

bleeding heart *adjective* sensitive to the plight of others, anguished. Disparaging, often as 'bleeding heart liberal' *UK, 1958*

bleeding obvious *noun* anything that really shouldn't need saying. Usually construed as *the* bleeding obvious. In 2003 the British satirical website 'University of the Bleeding Obvious' was one of the most popular comedy sites on the Internet *AUSTRALIA, 1996*

bleeding spot *noun* an oil leak on an asphalt road *US, 1962*

bleeding well *adverb* certainly, definitely *UK, 1884*

bleep *verb* to superimpose an electronic noise over expletives in a television or radio broadcast *US, 1966*

bleep used as a euphemistic replacement for an expletive, regardless of part of speech *US, 1968*

bleezin *adjective* drunk *UK, 2002*

blem *noun* a pimple. A shortened form of the conventional English 'blemish' *US, 1968*

blench *adjective* used approvingly to describe a muscular person *UK, 2005*

Blenheimers *noun* memory loss due to wine consumption. Named after a wine brand *NEW ZEALAND, 1998*

blerry; blarry; blirry *adjective* used as an intensifier. A variation of BLOODY reflecting Afrikaans pronunciation *SOUTH AFRICA, 1920*

blert *noun* a fool. Liverpool usage *UK, 2002*

bless *verb* to approve the forwarding of a proposed action. Military usage *US, 1986*

bless used ironically, as if patronising a child. An abbreviation of the prayer: 'God bless', often preceded with a cod-sympathetic 'aah!' *UK, 1999*

blessed sacrament *noun* marijuana *US, 2001*

blessing *noun* a harsh rebuke *BAHAMAS, 1982*

bless your cotton socks; bless your little cotton socks used for registering gratitude or affection. A catchphrase favoured by the middle-classes. Considered to be archaic when first recorded however the phrase has survived into C21 *UK, 1961*

bless your pea-pickin' hearts used for expressing thanks. A catchphrase television sign-off on *The Ernie Ford Show* (NBC, 1956–61), a music variety programme. Repeated with referential humour *US, 1956*

bletch! used as an all-purpose, potent expression of disgust. From the German *brechen* (to vomit) *US, 1981*

bletcherous *adjective* in computing, poorly designed, dysfunctional *US, 1981*

blew-it *noun* a Buick car *US, 1997*

blighter *noun* **1** a despicable male *UK, 1896*. **2** a man. From jocular use of the previous sense *UK, 1904*

Blighty *nickname* Britain; England. Originally military, from Hindustani *bilayati* and Arabic *wilayati* (foreign, especially European) *UK, 1915*

bliksem *noun* a despicable person, a contemptible fool. From Afrikaans *bliksem* (lightning) *SOUTH AFRICA, 1950*

bliksem *verb* to smack, punch or beat up. Probably a reduction of the earlier South African 'to donner the bliksem out of' (to beat the lights out of) *SOUTH AFRICA, 2004*

blim *noun* a small crumb of cannabis resin *UK, 1996*

blim burn *noun* a scorch mark or a tiny burn-hole as a result, when smoking hashish, of burning particles; a small burning cinder of cannabis resin *UK, 2003*

blim burn *verb* to mark or burn something with a blim burn *UK, 2004*

blimey!; blime! used for registering surprise or shock. An abbreviation of COR BLIMEY! (God blind me!) *UK, 1889*

blimey O'Riley!; blimey O'Reilly! used for registering surprise *UK, 1987*

blimmin'; blimmin' well *adjective* used as a euphemistic intensifier. Possibly derived from BLIMEY! or BLOOMING *UK, 1984*

blimp *noun* **1** in necrophile usage, a corpse with a distended abdomen *US, 1987*. **2** an obese person *US, 1934*. **3** in the television and film industries, a camera's sound-proofing housing *US, 1977*. **4** a bus *US, 1990*. **5** a private inter-personal signal *UK, 2000*

blimpish *adjective* very conservative or reactionary. After Colonel Blimp, a reactionary man *UK, 1938*

blimp out; blimp up *verb* to put on weight, especially if such growth is rapid or dramatic. From the shape of a conventional 'blimp' *US, 1979*

blind *noun* **1** a legitimate business used to conceal an illegal one *US, 1929*. **2** an area in prison where guards cannot easily see what is going on *US, 1989*. **3** a baggage carriage, usually immediately behind the engine of a passenger train *US, 1893*. **4** a wallet or purse. Pickpocket use *UK, 1977*. ▶ **make the blind see** to perform oral sex on an uncircumcised man *US, 1981*

blind *verb* to curse, to swear. The meaning survives in EFF AND BLIND *UK, 1943*. ▶ **blind by science** to defeat brawn with brains. According to one source 'it arose when the scientific boxers began, ca. 1880, to defeat the old bruisers' *AUSTRALIA, 1937*. ▶ **blind with science** to confuse or convince someone by superior, inventive or nonsensical argument, explanation or vocabulary. Synonymous variation of earlier 'dazzle with science' *UK, 1948*

blind *adjective* **1** an intensifier, a euphemism for 'bloody' or 'bleeding' *UK, 1959*. **2** very drunk *UK, 1630*. **3** highly drug-intoxicated. From an earlier alcohol sense *US, 1952*. **4** (used of a car) stripped of headlights *US, 1977*. **5** (used of a bet) placed before seeing the cards being bet on *US, 1963*. **6** uncircumcised *US, 1925*. **7** nasty, cruel *SOUTH AFRICA, 2004*. ▶ **like blind cobbler's thumbs** describes thickly swollen nipples *UK, 2001*. ▶ **not take a blind bit of notice** to utterly ignore or disregard someone or something, to be oblivious to someone or something *UK, 1961*

blind bat *noun* an AC-130 aircraft used for night flare missions in Vietnam between 1964 and 1970. Bats are not, of course, blind; they see at night *US, 1971*

blind blast *noun* a parachute jump at night in enemy territory. Vietnam war usage *US, 1991*

blind country *noun* closed-in country of the colourless type and of little worth *AUSTRALIA, 1959*

blind drunk *adjective* very drunk *UK, 1959*

blinded *adjective* drunk *US, 1984*

blinder *noun* anything excellent, or something excellently well-performed. From the 'dazzling' nature of anything so-called *UK, 1950*

blind fence *noun* a person who unknowingly buys stolen goods *US, 1949*

Blind Freddy; Blind Freddie *noun* an imaginary blind man. Used as a type for an inability to see the obvious. The existence of a real person nicknamed 'Blind Freddy' has not been confirmed *AUSTRALIA, 1946*

blinding *adjective* great, excellent, terrific, etc *UK, 1985*

blindingly *adverb* excellently, wonderfully, stupendously *UK, 1999*

blindjaret *noun* a cigarette *JAMAICA, 1985*

blind link *noun* on the Internet, a link that is misleading or false, taking you somewhere other than where you expect to go. Common on pornography websites *US, 2000*

blindman's buff *noun* snuff. Rhyming slang, noted by Red Daniells, 1980 *UK, 1980*

blindman's snow *noun* a late spring snowfall, supposed to have curative properties for the eyes and feet *CANADA, 1988*

blind mullet *noun* a piece of excrement floating in the water *AUSTRALIA, 1987*

blind pig *noun* **1** a speakeasy, where alcohol is served illegally *US, 1886*. **2** in poker, an unskilled but lucky player. From the adage that even a blind pig will find an acorn over time *US, 1996*

blind pigeon *noun* stuffed cabbage *US, 1997*

blinds *noun* **1** dark glasses *BERMUDA, 1985*. **2** among bus-spotters, a bus's roller display of desinations *US, 2003*

blindside *verb* to hit or attack someone without warning. Originally a term from American football, and then extended as a metaphor *US, 1968*

blind tiger *noun* an illegal drinking establishment *US, 1909*

blindza *noun* money *BARBADOS, 1984*

bling *noun* a vulgar or ludicrously ostentatious display of wealth *US, 2003*

bling-bling *noun* **1** wealth, especially as manifested in expensive, if tasteless, jewellery. Coined by hip-hop rapper B.G. and appearing in his 1999 'Chopper City in the Ghetto' *US, 1999*. **2** ostentation. A generalised sense that derives from the previous sense *UK, 2003*

bling-bling *verb* to be successful, especially in hip-hop; hence, to be ostentatious; to make money *US, 2003*

bling-blinger *noun* a successful or established member of the hip-hop community. From the BLING-BLING worn as an ostentatious symbol of status *US, 2000*

blinged; blinged out *adjective* ostentatious; expensively bejewelled, especially if a tasteless display. From BLING-BLING (ostentatious jewellery) *US, 2000*

blinging *adjective* ostentatious and expensive. Derives from BLING-BLING (ostentatious jewellery) *UK, 2003*

bling it up *verb* to have an ostentatiously expensive lifestyle; to temporarily lead such a life. Extended from BLING-BLING (wealth, tasteless ostentation) *UK, 2003*

Blinglish *noun* a slang and black patois-rich form of English, especially when used by white urban youths. Extended from BLING *UK, 2005*

bling-tastic *adjective* extravagantly ostentatious *UK, 2002*

blink *noun* a hiding place *US, 1949*. ▶ **on the blink 1** broken, not functioning *US, 1899*. **2** without funds *US, 1949*

blink *verb* to miss seeing a fight, attack or other cause of excitement *US, 1976*

blinkenlights *noun* diagnostic lights on the front panel of a computer *US, 1991*

blinker *noun* **1** a quadriplegic. Vietnam war gallows humour, suggesting that a quadriplegic is capable only of blinking his eyes *US, 1980*. **2** an eye *UK, 1809*. **3** a police helicopter *US, 1980*

blinkey *noun* **1** a vehicle with one headlight not working *US, 1976*. **2** a timing light at the finish line of a drag strip *US, 1968*

blink-eyed *adjective* cross-eyed *US, 1969*

blinking *adjective* used as a mild intensifier; a euphemisim for 'bleeding'. The term probably derives from 'blank', an obsolete euphemism for DAMNED which stresses the fact of euphemism – the blank space – as much as the object of intensification *UK, 1914*

blinkus of the thinkus *noun* a momentary loss of concentration *US, 1971*

blinky *noun* **1** a person with poor or no eyesight *US, 1922.* **2** freebase cocaine *US, 1992*

blinky *adjective* agitated, upset *US, 1992*

blip *noun* **1** a temporary effect, especially one that is unwanted *UK, 1975.* **2** a minor fluctuation, usually upward, in the stock market or other measures of corporate fortunes *US, 1988.* **3** a source of surprise *US, 1947.* **4** a nickel (five-cent piece) *US, 1935*

blip *verb* **1** to send a message by e-mail *UK, 2002.* **2** in hot rodding or drag racing, to throttle up quickly and then release, momentarily increasing the revolutions per minute *US, 1965*

blip *adjective* classy *US, 1948*

blip jockey *noun* a person who monitors electronic equipment *US, 1960*

blippy *adjective* used as a euphemism roughly meaning 'damned' *US, 1974*

bliss *noun* any drug that is smoked, especially a mixture of heroin, methamphetamine and MDMA, the recreational drug best known as ecstasy *US, 1996*

bliss cup *noun* in the usage of counterculturalists associated with the Rainbow Nation gatherings, a homemade cup or bowl for eating and drinking *US, 1997*

bliss out *verb* to become ecstatic. Used in a derogatory fashion, usually when applied to religious or cult zealots *US, 1973*

B list; C list *noun* used for denoting all that is associated with a level of fame and celebrity that is not quite paramount. In conventional media jargon the A-LIST is a notional social elite of those who are considered prestigious enough to add top-value to a guest list. The B-list and C-list are the lesser ranks of the well-known and media-friendly who nevertheless get invited to events by those who market the cult of celebrity *US, 1928*

blisted *adjective* intoxicated by drug smoking *US, 1995*

blister *noun* **1** a bump placed on a playing card by pressing it against a small sharp object, used by card cheats to identify the value of the card *US, 1991.* **2** a fine attached to a window of a vehicle for a parking infringement *AUSTRALIA, 1971.* **3** an unpleasant, obnoxious person *UK, 1806.* **4** a prostitute *US, 1905*

blister *verb* to attack someone; to attack someone verbally *AUSTRALIA, 1968*

blisterfoot *noun* an infantry soldier *US, 1945*

blister work *noun* extortion *US, 1950*

blisty *adjective* windy, cold, not suitable for surfing *US, 1991*

blithering *adjective* contemptible; used as an negative intensifier *UK, 1889*

blitz *noun* an intensive campaign; a concentrated effort. After German *blitz* (understood in English as 'all-out offensive warfare') *US, 1940*

blitz *verb* **1** to intensively campaign for and achieve maximum public awareness. From German *blitzkrieg* (a lightning war) *UK, 2002.* **2** to defeat someone soundly *US, 1940.* **3** in horse racing, to win convincingly *AUSTRALIA, 1989.* **4** in tiddlywinks, to pot all six winks of one colour before the 20-minute time-limit has elapsed and thus score an easy victory *US, 1980.* **5** in gin, to win and leave an opponent scoreless *US, 1971.* **6** in bar dice games, to bet the total amount of the pot *US, 1971*

blitz buggy *noun* a car. Teen slang *US, 1941*

blitzed *adjective* drunk or drug-intoxicated *US, 1966*

blitzkrieged *adjective* suddenly drunk *US, 1974*

blivet *noun* **1** an obnoxious person, especially with bad hygiene *US, 1949.* **2** in computing, a problem which cannot be solved or any impossibility *US, 1991*

blizz *noun* a blizzard *ANTARCTICA, 1911*

blizz *verb* to blow a blizzard *ANTARCTICA, 1911*

blizzard *noun* **1** poor television reception characterised by flickering white dots *US, 1952.* **2** the cloud of thick, white smoke produced when smoking freebase cocaine *US, 1992.* **3** cocaine. A play on SNOW (cocaine) *UK, 2003*

blizzard head *noun* in the early days of black and white television, a blonde. So called because a blonde's hair takes up all the light in the picture *US, 1948*

blizzed in *adjective* confined indoors by harsh weather conditions *ANTARCTICA, 1951*

blizzy *adjective* snowy *ANTARCTICA, 1996*

blo *noun* cocaine *US, 1993*

bloater *noun* **1** a fat person. From 'bloat' (to swell), influenced by the 'bloater fish'. There is some evidence of a similar usage in the late C19, and, again, in mid-C20 in South Africa where the sense is 'gross and ugly' *UK, 2001.* **2** a dead sheep or cow *NEW ZEALAND, 2000*

blob *noun* **1** in cricket, a batsman's innings score of no runs. From the image of a zero shown beneath the batsman's name on the scoresheet *UK, 1889.* **2** a mistake. From the previous sense *UK, 1903.* **3** a fool *AUSTRALIA, 1916.* **4** the bleed period of the menstrual cycle *UK, 2000.* **5** a gonorrhoeal ulcer *UK, 1961.* ► **on blob; on the blob** in the bleed-period of the menstrual cycle. The image of blobs of blood *US, 2000*

blob *verb* **1** to suffer from a sexually transmitted infection. Literally, 'to drip', but after BLOB (a gonorrhoeal ulcer) *UK, 1984.* **2** to make a mistake *UK, 1999*

blobby *adjective* used for describing uneven stage lighting *UK, 1952*

blob hammock *noun* a sanitary towel. Combines BLOB (the bleed period of the menstrual cycle) with the image of a hammock, also seen in WEE HAMMOCK *UK, 2002*

blob out *verb* to relax completely. Commonly used in conversation since the 1980s *NEW ZEALAND, 2003*

block *noun* **1** a prison segregation unit *UK, 1996.* **2** prison *US, 1983.* **3** marijuana or hashish compressed in a block *UK, 2000.* **4** a measured quantity of morphine *UK, 1992.* **5** a ban, an embargo. Used in phrases like PUT A BLOCK ON and PUT THE BLOCK ON *UK, 1970.* **6** used as a retort after being insulted *US, 1992.* **7** a watch. Circus and carnival usage *US, 1972.* ► **do your block; do the block** to lose control; to lose your temper *AUSTRALIA, 1907.* ► **knock someone's block off** used as a threat of personal violence *UK, 1984.* ► **on the block 1** engaged in prostitution on the street *US, 1941.* **2** subjected to serial rape *NEW ZEALAND, 1973.* ► **put a block on; put the block on 1** to veto, ban, or embargo something. Literally, to apply 'a block' (a ban) *UK, 1961.* **2** in prison, to reinforce the regulations *UK, 1996.* ► **use your block** to act wisely *AUSTRALIA, 1959*

block *verb* **1** to sodomise someone or subject them to serial rape *NEW ZEALAND, 1978.* **2** to fool someone *AUSTRALIA, 1955*

block! used as the riposte to 'face!', thus preventing notional embarrassment. Youth slang *US, 1997*

blockaides *noun* condoms. Coined in response to AIDS *UK, 1998*

block and tackle *noun* illegally manufactured whisky *US, 1974*

block boy *noun* a youth who spends his abundant free time idling on a street corner, looking or hoping for trouble *US, 1970*

blockbuster *noun* **1** a capsule of pentobarbital sodium (trade name Nembutal™), a central nervous system depressant. Sometimes shortened to 'buster' *US, 1970.* **2** a heavy bomb powerful enough to flatten a city block; hence anything that makes a considerable impact. Initially used by the Royal Air Force; since the 1960s generally applied as journalistic or marketing terms for films, novels, etc *US, 1942.* **3** a .357 Magnum bullet *US, 1962*

blocked *adjective* drunk or drug-intoxicated, especially by amphetamine, barbiturate or marijuana. The experiencing of real life is *blocked* out *US, 1956*

blocker *noun* **1** a confederate who shields a casino cheat from being seen as he robs a slot machine *US, 1984.* **2** a member of a shoplifting team who distracts attention and blocks pursuit *UK, 1996*

blockhead *noun* **1** a stupid fool, an idiot. Originally 'a wooden base for hats or wigs', hence 'wooden-*headed*' *UK, 1549.* **2** a drunken yob. This usage was coined by Ian Dury in the song 'Blockheads', which offered the lyrical definition: '"pissed up" gangs of lads' *UK, 1977.* **3** a marijuana user. A combination of BLOCK (marijuana) and HEAD (a user) *UK, 2001.* **4** a railway brakeman *US, 1977*

block hustle *noun* a small-scale swindle *US, 1997*

blockie *noun* **1** a farmer on a small block of land. Sometimes heard as 'blocker' *AUSTRALIA, 1944*. **2** in Queensland, Victoria and Tasmania, a circuit of a street block in a vehicle done, especially repeatedly, for entertainment *AUSTRALIA, 2003*

blocking *noun* serial sex between one person and multiple partners, consensual or not, heterosexual or homosexual *NEW ZEALAND, 1998*

block-rockin' *adjective* expressive of greatness with regard to hip-hop and club culture. Extends 'rockin' as a general term of approval with the punning suggestion that whatever is so described has the power to rock a city block *US, 2000*

blocks *noun* dice *US, 1962*. ▶ **put the blocks to someone** to have sex with someone *US, 1888*. ▶ **up on blocks** in the bleed period of the menstrual cycle. A mechanical image of an out of service car being up on blocks for repair *UK, 2002*

block-up *adjective* marijuana-intoxicated *UK, 2002*

blog *noun* a regularly updated Internet webpage of links to interesting news stories or websites annotated with personal commentary. An abbreviation of 'we*blog*' *US, 1999*

blog *verb* to create or update a weblog *US, 2000*

blogger *noun* a person who maintains a weblog *US, 2000*

blogosphere *noun* the areas of interest that preoccupy those who create or pay attention to blogs [web logs] *UK, 2002*

bloke *noun* **1** a man; a fellow. Generally used in a neutral sense, but also commonly in a positive sense connoting a 'decent, down-to-earth, unpretentious man', especially in the phrase 'good bloke'. There has been a recent trend, since the 1990s, to also use 'bloke' negatively to mean a 'male chauvinist' *UK, 1829*. **2** a boyfriend *AUSTRALIA, 1908*. **3** a homosexual man's boyfriend or partner. Originally recorded as a navy usage *UK, 1937*. **4** a male animal *AUSTRALIA, 1982*. **5** a person of any gender. A rare usage *AUSTRALIA, 1988*

bloke car *noun* a sports car on the downslope of its career sold to American pilots stationed in the United Kingdom *UK, 1992*

bloker *noun* a cocaine user *US, 1992*

blokey *noun* a man. An elaboration of BLOKE *UK, 2000*

blokey *adjective* (of a man) chauvinistic; masculine in a negative way *AUSTRALIA, 1992*

blokeyness; blokiness *noun* the state of being blokey *AUSTRALIA, 1994*

blokish; blokeish *adjective* describes men's behaviour that is straightforwardly, perhaps stereotypically, 'masculine' *UK, 1957*

blonde *noun* **1** coffee with cream *US, 1952*. **2** golden-leafed marijuana *UK, 2003*

blonde *adjective* foolish, daft, silly. Teen slang, from the stereotypical attributes ascribed to blondes *UK, 2003*

blonde and sweet *adjective* (used of coffee) with cream and sugar *US, 1945*

blonde from the coast *noun* a pale, light-coloured marijuana with claims by sellers that it comes from Colombia *US, 1976*

blondie; blondy *noun* a blonde-haired person; when spelt with a capital B, a nickname for such a person. Famously in the cartoon strip *Blondie* by Chic Young, from 1930, although unlikely to have been coined by him. Adopted in 1974 by the pop group Blondie *US, 1948*

blonk *noun* an incompetent, inept, boring person *AUSTRALIA, 1985*

bloober *noun* a female breast *US, 1954*

bloochie *noun* any cumbersome object. From Polish immigrant speech *US, 1982*

blood *noun* **1** a black person *US, 1965*. **2** used as a general form of address regardless of race, signalling friendliness. From the previous sense; sometimes spelt 'blud' *UK, 2002*. **3** wine *US, 1959*. **4** pizza sauce *US, 1996*. **5** tomato juice *US, 1936*. ▶ **make someone's blood boil** to infuriate someone *UK, 1848*. ▶ **your blood is worth bottling** you are wonderful *AUSTRALIA, 1958*

blood! used for expressing strong disapproval *JAMAICA, 1978*

blood alley *noun* an unsafe stretch of a road *US, 1978*

blood bank *noun* **1** a hospital *UK, 1981*. **2** a finance company *US, 1975*

blood box *noun* an ambulance *US, 1976*

blood bread *noun* payment for donating blood *US, 1971*

blood chit *noun* a written notice in several languages, carried by members of the American armed forces, identifying the person as American and promising a reward for help in evading the enemy. The US Department of Defense Policy on Blood Chits states that the chits 'are a tool used by an evader or escapee after all other measures of independent evasion and escape have failed and the evader(s) considers assistance vital to survival. Upon receiving assistance, the evader or escapee provides the assistor with the blood chit number. The blood chit represents an obligation of the U.S. Government to compensate the claimant, or his immediate family if the claimant is deceased, for services rendered to DoD personnel.' The version used in the Vietnam war had the plea for 'assistance in obtaining food, shelter and protection' in English, Burmese, Chinese, Thai, Laotian, Cambodian, Vietnamese, Malayan, Indonesian, Tagalog, Visayan, French and Dutch *US, 1941*

bloodclaat; bloodclot; blood clot *noun* a contemptible person. West Indian, hence UK black patois; literally a 'sanitary towel', applied figuratively *JAMAICA, 1994*

blood clart *adjective* used as a negative intensifier. Black urban youth slang, of Jamaican origins *UK, 2006*

blood cloth *noun* an improvised sanitary towel *ANTIGUA AND BARBUDA, 1996*

blood factory *noun* a hospital *UK, 2000*

bloodhound *verb* to track someone down *US, 1963*

blood house *noun* **1** a tavern with a reputation for brawling *NEW ZEALAND, 1999*. **2** a public hotel, especially a rough one *AUSTRALIA, 1952*

blood in *verb* in prison, to establish your credentials for toughness by slashing another prisoner *US, 2000*

blood in, blood out used for expressing the rules for entering (to kill) and leaving (to be killed) a prison gang *US, 2000*

bloodman *noun* a person who is at any moment capable of physical violence *US, 2002*

blood money *noun* in gambling, money that is won after long, hard work *US, 1979*

blood nose *noun* a nose that is bleeding, as from a punch *AUSTRALIA, 1960*

bloodnut *noun* a red-haired person *AUSTRALIA, 1998*

blood poker *noun* poker played as business with no social trappings *US, 1988*

blood simple *adjective* crazed by violence *US, 1994*

blood stripe *noun* a military promotion that is made possible only by the demotion of another unit member *US, 1968*

bloodwagon *noun* an ambulance *UK, 1922*

blood weapon *noun* a weapon captured from an enemy soldier, especially a soldier killed by the man taking the weapon *US, 1990*

blood wings *noun* the first set of parachute insignia that a paratrooper receives upon qualification at different levels of expertise *US, 1989*

Bloody *noun* a Bloody Mary drink, made with vodka and tomato juice *US, 1978*

bloody *adjective* **1** used as an intensifier; damned. After the adverbial use. Popular belief holds 'bloody' to be blasphemous and derives it as a contraction of 'by our lady' however there are no grounds to support this contention. Life's blood itself must be the significant source. In the UK the most famous use is probably 'Not bloody likely!' in the play *Pygmalion* by George Bernard Shaw, which shocked London audiences when first performed in 1916. The high frequency with which this term was used in Australia, especially in colonial times, has led to the appellation 'the Great Australian Adjective'. In 1847, a commentator noted that a bullock-driver (proverbially great swearers) used the term 25 times in a quarter-hour period, and thus calculated that he would have said 'this disgusting word' no less than 18,200,000 times in the course of 50 years (*Australian National Dictionary*). Though formerly ranked amongst the strongest taboo terms among polite speakers, and not permitted in print, it was evidently part of daily speech for many working class people. Now still commonly used in informal contexts. Taboo-wise its place has been taken by the synonymous FUCKING. Writing in 1942, one Australian commentator observed 'that "bloody" was no longer the main Australian adjective', *UK, 1676*. **2** unpleasant; unpleasantly difficult *UK, 1934*

bloody *adverb* exceedingly *UK, 1676*

-bloody- *infix* damned *AUSTRALIA, 1945*

bloody cunt hat *noun* a narrow green cap worn by English Army officers *UK, 1980*

bloody hell!; bee aitch; BH used for registering shock, surprise, exasperation, etc. Combines BLOODY (an intensifier) with HELL (used in oaths) to create an expletive so familiar that it is often pronounced as one word. Occasionally abbreviated to euphemistic initials *UK, 1955*

Bloody Mary *noun* **1** a drink made of vodka and tomato juice, and, optionally, Tabasco or Worcester Sauce. From the colour; ultimately a pun on the nickname of Queen Mary, 1516–1558 *UK, 1956*. **2** the bleed period of a woman's menstrual cycle *US, 1968*

bloody oath! used to register (enthusiastic) agreement *AUSTRALIA, 1848*

bloody well *adverb* definitely, certainly. A British slang expression used in English parts of its former colonies; extended from the adverbial sense of BLOODY *AUSTRALIA, 1904*

blooey *adjective* ▶ **go blooey** to go out of business; to break down completely *US, 1910*

blooker *noun* an M79 grenade launcher. Vietnam war usage. It is a single-shot, break-open, breech-loading, shoulder-fired weapon *US, 1973*

bloomer *noun* **1** a mistake *UK, 1889*. **2** in the circus or carnival, a complete lack of business *UK, 1904*. **3** in horse racing, a horse that performs well early in the morning during the workout but not in a race later in the day *US, 1951*. **4** an empty wallet, purse or safe *US, 1949*

bloomer boy *noun* a paratrooper *US, 1948*

Bloomie's *nickname* the Bloomingdale's department store, especially the original store located on Third Avenue between 59th and 60th Streets, New York *US, 1977*

blooming *adjective* a mild intensifier, a euphemism for 'bleeding'. Usage popularised in the 1880s by music hall singer Alfred 'The Great' Vance *UK, 1879*

blooming well *adverb* used as an intensifier *UK, 1959*

bloop *noun* in the television and film industries, a device used on the junction of a photographic sound track to eliminate any audio cue that there is a splice in the film *US, 1960*

blooper *noun* **1** an error, especially a humiliating and/or humorous one *US, 1947*. **2** in television, radio or film making, an unintentionally funny misspoken line *US, 1926*. **3** an M79 grenade launcher. Vietnam war usage. It is a single-shot, break-open, breech-loading, shoulder-fired weapon *US, 1978*

blooper ball *noun* **1** slow-pitch softball *US, 1981*. **2** a grenade used in an M-79 grenade launcher *US, 1982*

bloop tube; bloop gun *noun* an M79 grenade launcher. Vietnam war usage. It is a single-shot, break-open, breech-loading, shoulder-fired weapon *US, 1971*

blooter *noun* a task that is quickly and sloppily performed *UK: SCOTLAND, 1988*

blooter *verb* **1** to incapacitate someone with a violent blow *UK: SCOTLAND, 2003*. **2** to do something to excess *UK: SCOTLAND, 1988*. **3** to drink heavily *UK: SCOTLAND, 1988*

blootered *adjective* drunk. Possibly from Scottish *bluiter* (to talk foolishly), or a corruption of PLOOTERED (drunk) *UK, 1911*

bloozer *noun* an utter sentimentalist *UK, 1985*

blossom *noun* a facial blemish *US, 1942*

blot *noun* the anus or backside. From conventional 'blot' (a dark patch) *AUSTRALIA, 1945*

blot *verb* ▶ **blot the copybook** in horse racing, to fail dramatically and completely *AUSTRALIA, 1989*. ▶ **blot your copy book** to make a mistake, or to make a bad impression, or to spoil your record. A figurative use of school imagery *UK, 1937*

blotch *noun* food. Anglo-Irish *, 1958*

blotch *verb* to stain your underwear when what had seemed like flatulence was something more *US, 1989*

blotter *noun* **1** a tiny piece of absorbent paper impregnated with LSD and ingested as such *US, 1971*. **2** cocaine *UK, 2003*. **3** the record of arrests held at a police station *US, 1970*

blotter cube *noun* a type of LSD *UK, 2003*

blotting paper *noun* food eaten to mollify the effects of alcohol when on a binge *AUSTRALIA, 1960*

blotto *adjective* very drunk; in a drunken stupor. Possibly from the absorbent quality of blotting paper, or from a conventional mid-C19 usage of 'blotted' as 'blurred' *UK, 1917*

blottoed *adjective* drunk *UK, 2002*

blouse *noun* **1** a woman, especially a business woman *UK, 1997*. **2** an overly effeminate male; a weak man *AUSTRALIA, 2003*. **3** in card playing, a singleton. Sometimes embellished to 'blousey suit' *UK, 1961*

bloused *adjective* in card playing, to have been dealt a singleton. From BLOUSE *AUSTRALIA, 1961*

blow *noun* **1** cocaine *US, 1971*. **2** heroin *US, 2002*. **3** a dose of a drug, especially a dose of cocaine to be snorted *US, 1953*. **4** marijuana *UK, 1996*. **5** a cigarette; a smoke *UK, 1936*. **6** a rest from work. From the sense as 'smoking tobacco', traditionally done on a break *AUSTRALIA, 1910*. **7** a breath of fresh air, a 'breather', especially in the phrase 'get a blow' *UK, 1849*. **8** an act of oral sex performed on a man. A contraction of BLOW JOB *US, 1946*. **9** a high wind; a strong storm; a cyclone *AUSTRALIA, 1935*. **10** in horse racing, a lengthening of the odds being offered *AUSTRALIA, 1988*. **11** a confidence swindle involving the claimed ability to change the denomination on currency *US, 1957*. ▶ **have a blow 1** to sniff glue *NEW ZEALAND, 1998*. **2** of musicians, to make music *UK, 1984*

blow *verb* **1** to smoke, especially to smoke marijuana. Originally 'to smoke a pipe or cigar', now drugs use only. Usage often specifies marijuana thus 'blow SHIT', 'blow a STICK', etc *US, 1772*. **2** to register on a blood alcohol breath testing device *US, 1978*. **3** to perform oral sex *US, 1930*. **4** to masturbate *UK, 1978*. **5** to orgasm; to ejaculate *AUSTRALIA, 1952*. **6** to open something with explosives *UK, 1602*. **7** to inform, to betray someone; to tell tales. Originally a conventional usage but progressed in status to slang in the mid-C17 *UK, 1575*. **8** to boast *AUSTRALIA, 1858*. **9** to spoil something, to destroy something *US, 1899*. **10** to waste an opportunity, to bungle *US, 1907*. **11** to dismiss something, as of no importance; to damn something. Semi-exclamatory; euphemistic *UK, 1835*. **12** to be useless, unpopular, distasteful. Often in the context of an exclamation such as 'That blows!' *US, 1997*. **13** to spend money, especially in a lavish or wasteful manner *UK, 1874*. **14** to leave *US, 1898*. **15** to play a musical instrument. Used with all instruments, not just those requiring wind *US, 1949*. **16** used as a mild replacement for 'damn' *UK, 1781*. **17** to lengthen the odds offered on a horse or greyhound; (of a horse or greyhound) to have its odds lengthen *AUSTRALIA, 1975*. ▶ **blow a gasket** to lose your temper completely *US, 1949*. ▶ **blow a hype** to become overexcited *US, 1986*. ▶ **blow a load** to ejaculate *US, 1995*. ▶ **blow a nut** to ejaculate *US, 1994*. ▶ **blow a shot** while trying to inject a drug, to miss the vein or otherwise waste the drug *US, 1966*. ▶ **blow a tank** to use an explosive charge to open a safe *NEW ZEALAND, 1998*. ▶ **blow a vein** while injecting a drug, to cause a vein to collapse *US, 1974*. ▶ **blow and go** to vent air before an ascent to the surface while outside a submarine *US, 1991*. ▶ **blow beets** to vomit *US, 1968*. ▶ **blow chow** to vomit *US, 1988*. ▶ **blow chunks** to vomit *US, 1992*. ▶ **blow dinner** to vomit *US, 1968*. ▶ **blow down someone's ear** to whisper to someone *UK, 1938*. ▶ **blow dust** to shoot a gun *US, 2001*. ▶ **blow grits** to vomit *US, 1979*. ▶ **blow his poke** (of a fish) to regurgitate its stomach. The word 'poke' is a very old English word for 'bag' *CANADA, 1982*. ▶ **blow lunch** to vomit *US, 1965*. ▶ **blow pies** to vomit *US, 2003*. ▶ **blow smoke 1** to brag *US, 1946*. **2** to inhale crack cocaine smoke *UK, 1998*. ▶ **blow someone's mind 1** to amaze

someone; to surprise someone; to shock someone. A figurative sense, extended from the sense as a 'hallucinogenic experience' *US, 1965*. **2** to render someone unable to comprehend *US, 1961*.
▶ **blow someone's top 1** to render someone unable to comprehend *US, 1961*. **2** to induce psychosis in someone *US, 1946*.
▶ **blow the brains out** to install a sun roof on a car *US, 1997*.
▶ **blow the cobwebs away** to take some fresh air or exercise and so become revivified *UK, 2003*. ▶ **blow the gaff** to reveal a secret, to inform *UK, 1812*. ▶ **blow the lid off** (of a secret plan or a hidden state-of-affairs) to publicly reveal something, especially to expose it in a spectacular way *US, 1928*. ▶ **blow the rag** to deploy a reserve parachute when the main parachute fails to deploy *US, 1991*. ▶ **blow the whistle** to inform against an activity or crime and by so doing cause the subject of such complaint to cease *UK, 1934*. ▶ **blow this cookie stand** to leave *US, 1977*. ▶ **blow this disco** to leave *US, 1994*. ▶ **blow this popsicle stand** to leave *US, 1986*. ▶ **blow this taco stand** to leave *US, 1988*. ▶ **blow this trap** to leave *US, 1958*. ▶ **blow tubes** to smoke marijuana filtered through glass tubes *US, 1991*. ▶ **blow your bags** to boast. Possibly from 'bagpipes', in a similar way to the conventional 'blow your own trumpet' *AUSTRALIA, 1961*. ▶ **blow your beans** to ejaculate *AUSTRALIA, 1985*. ▶ **blow your bowel bugle** to fart *UK, 1978*. ▶ **blow your cap** to become uncontrollable with anger or excitement. Beatniks' variation on BLOW YOUR TOP *UK, 1984*. ▶ **blow your cookies** to ejaculate *UK, 2000*. ▶ **blow your cool** to become very angry, excited, nervous, etc. Since the mid-1950s it has been uncool in youth and counterculture to demonstrate too much emotion *US, 1961*. ▶ **blow your dust** to ejaculate *UK, 1978*. ▶ **blow your jets** to become angry *US, 1960*. ▶ **blow your lid** to lose your control emotionally; to become angry *US, 1935*. ▶ **blow your lump** to completely lose your emotional composure *US, 1951*. ▶ **blow your mind 1** to have a hallucinogenic experience; to experience a pyschotic break as a result of drug use *US, 1965*. **2** to lose your mind, to go crazy, to render unable to comprehend *US, 1965*. ▶ **blow your roof** to smoke marijuana *US, 1950*. ▶ **blow your stack** to lose your temper *US, 1947*. ▶ **blow your top 1** to explode with anger *UK, 1928*. **2** to lose your mind, to go crazy *US, 1961*. **3** to lose emotional control *US, 1946*. **4** to engage in inconsequential conversation *US, 1947*. ▶ **blow your wheels** to act without restraint *US, 1955*. ▶ **blow your wig** to lose emotional control; to become angry *US, 1952*. ▶ **blow z's** to sleep. Vietnam war usage *US, 1991*

blow!; blow it!; blow you! used as a non-profane oath *UK, 1823*

blow away *verb* **1** to kill someone, usually with a gun *US, 1913*. **2** to impress or astonish someone; hence, to be impressed or astonished *US, 1975*

blowback *noun* a method of smoking marijuana that requires two people: one takes the lit end of a joint into the mouth and blows, thus forcing the smoke into the lungs of the inhaler at the usual end; hence, any improvised method of forcing marijuana smoke for another to inhale; an act of inhaling exhaled marijuana smoke by simply placing your lips close to the exhaler's *UK, 1996*

blow back *verb* in gambling, to lose all or most of your winnings *US, 1990*

blow bath *noun* during the war in Vietnam, a bath, massage and sex *US, 1969*

blow blue *verb* to inhale powdered cocaine *UK, 1998*

blowboy *noun* a male homosexual *US, 1935*

blowby *noun* in a car or truck, exhaust gases and carbon particles that enter the crankcase instead of being diverted into the exhaust system. So named because the particles and gases 'blow by' the piston rings *US, 1960*

blow dart *noun* a hypodermic needle used to inject drugs *US, 1971*

blow down *verb* to shoot and kill someone *US, 1871*

blower *noun* **1** a telephone. Carried over from the 'speaking tube' which was blown through to alert the receiver; has also been applied to the telegraph system when used for the transmission of racing results. During World War 2, and for some time after, applied to a public address system *UK, 1922*. **2** someone who succeeds at failing most of what they attempt. A noun formation from BLOW as a verb (to be useless) *US, 1993*. **3** a respirator *US, 1994*.

4 in a jazz band, a soloist *US, 1960*. **5** a handkerchief *US, 1960*. **6** a marijuana smoker *US, 1949*. **7** a party *US, 2001*. **8** a pistol *US, 1976*. **9** in hot rodding and drag racing, a supercharger *US, 1948*

blowhard *noun* a boaster, a braggart *US, 1857*

blowhole *noun* **1** the mouth *US, 1950*. **2** the anus *US, 1947*

blowie *noun* **1** an act of oral sex on a man. An abbreviated BLOW JOB *AUSTRALIA, 1999*. **2** a blowfly *AUSTRALIA, 1916*

blow-in *noun* **1** the arrival in prison of a new prisoner *US, 1949*. **2** a new arrival; a person who has dropped in *AUSTRALIA, 1937*

blow in *verb* to arrive *US, 1882*

blowing smoke *noun* marijuana *UK, 1998*

blow it! ▷*see:* BLOW!

blow job *noun* **1** an act of oral sex performed on a man, or, occasionally, a woman *US, 1942*. **2** a favourable film review *US, 1997*. **3** a safe robbery in which explosives are used to gain access to the safe *US, 1973*. **4** a jet aircraft. Royal Air Force use. A jocular application of the sexual sense (oral sex) but also in comparison to a piston-driven engine *UK, 1984*

blowman *noun* a member of a youth gang designated as a shooter *US, 1979*

blow me down! used as an expression of surprise *UK, 1928*

blow monkey *noun* a person with a strong interest in performing oral sex and/or using cocaine *US, 1997*

blown *adjective* **1** drunk or drug-intoxicated *US, 1980*. **2** of a blood vein, collapsed *US, 1989*. **3** in hot rodding and drag racing, using a supercharger; of any car, but especially a racing car, supercharged *US, 1948*

blown away *adjective* drunk or drug-intoxicated *US, 1981*

blown in *adjective* of a car, partially resprayed. Used by the motor trade *UK, 1968*

blown out *adjective* **1** said of choppy ocean conditions unfavourable for surfing *US, 1963*. **2** among London taxi drivers, having failed to get a final fare-paying passenger *UK, 1939*. **3** drug-intoxicated *US, 1972*

blow-off *noun* **1** the end of a circus performance; the final performance in a circus engagement *US, 1913*. **2** in the circus or carnival, the crowd leaving a performance *US, 1980*. **3** oral sex performed on a man *US, 1972*. **4** the moment in a confidence swindle when the victim is left to discover his loss *US, 1969*

blow off *verb* **1** to fart *UK, 1984*. **2** (of a male) to orgasm, ejaculate *AUSTRALIA, 1971*. **3** to scold someone *AUSTRALIA, 1947*. **4** to ignore, to dismiss someone *US, 1965*. **5** to fail to attend *US, 1986*. **6** in hot rodding, to win a race *US, 1965*

blow-off number *noun* a wrong telephone number deliberately given to an unwanted suitor. From BLOW OFF (to dismiss). Coined for US television comedy *Seinfeld*, 1993–98 *US, 1997*

blow out *noun* **1** a heavy meal *UK, 1924*. **2** a party or meal unlimited by normal rules of conduct *US, 1815*. **3** in horse racing, a short but intense workout several days before a race *US, 1968*. **4** crack cocaine *UK, 1998*. **5** an utter failure *US, 1938*. ▶ **give someone the blowout** to rid yourself of someone *US, 1979*

blow out *verb* **1** (of a police case) to fail. Metropolitan Police slang. Figurative use of 'blow out' (a pneumatic tyre puncturing suddenly) *UK, 1970*. **2** to reject an agreement or responsibility. More often elaborated as BLOW OUT OF THE WATER *UK, 1984*. **3** to manufacture drugs *UK, 2001*. **4** to lengthen the odds offered on a horse or greyhound; to have its odds lengthen *AUSTRALIA, 1911*. ▶ **blow out of the water** to reject something absolutely, especially when applied to an agreement or responsibility *UK, 2002*

blows *noun* heroin *UK, 2002*

blowsing *noun* the sniffing of glue or other industrial solvents *UK, 1982*

blow that for a joke! used for a complete rejection *NEW ZEALAND, 1998*

blow through *verb* **1** to leave *AUSTRALIA, 1950*. **2** to give information over the telephone. To use the BLOWER (a telephone) *UK, 1970*

blow torch *noun* **1** in military aviation, a jet fighter *US, 1950*. **2** in drag racing, a car powered by a jet engine *US, 1965*

Blowtorch Bob; Blowtorch *nickname* Robert William Komer, a Lieutenant Colonel in the US Army and a CIA operative in Vietnam from 1967 to 70. It is said that the nickname was coined by US Ambassador to Vietnam Henry Cabot Lodge, who likened arguing with Komer to having a blowtorch aimed at the seat of your trousers *US, 1991*

blow-up *noun* **1** an emotionally intense quarrel that soon blows over. From the explosive quality of such conflicts *UK, 1809*. **2** a corpse that has exploded from a build-up of internal gas *US, 1962*

blow up *verb* **1** to lose your temper *UK, 1871*. **2** in an endurance sport, especially cycling, to reach a point of utter exhaustion *US, 2001*. **3** to quit a job without notice *US, 1946*. **4** to inform against someone. A variation of BLOW THE WHISTLE *UK, 1982*. **5** (used of a telephone, especially a mobile phone) to ring *US, 2002*. **6** to receive repeated electronic pages *US, 2001*. **7** (used of a racehorse) to breath hard after a race *US, 1997*

blow you! ▷*see:* BLOW!

blow-your-mind roulette *noun* a drug activity in which a variety of pills are mixed together and individuals take a random selection of pills from the mix *US, 1970*

BLT *noun* **1** a bacon, lettuce and tomato sandwich *US, 1952*. **2** a police officer looking for trouble. From BACON (a police officer). Punning on the common usage as a 'bacon, lettuce and tomato sandwich' *CANADA, 2002*

blubber *noun* **1** a fat person *US, 1997*. **2** the act of using the thumb and forefinger to pinch another's cheeck *US, 1950*

blubberbag *noun* a rubber petrol or fuel-oil transport tank *CANADA, 1964*

blubberbutt *noun* an obese person *US, 1952*

blubbers *noun* the female breasts *US, 1949*

bludge *noun* **1** an easy job, requiring little work *AUSTRALIA, 1943*. **2** a respite from work or duty *AUSTRALIA, 1957*. **3** an instance of taking it easy on a job *AUSTRALIA, 1957*. **4** an act of borrowing or sponging *NEW ZEALAND, 1974*

bludge *verb* **1** to live off another's hospitality. A back formation from bludger . Usually with 'on', though since the 1960s also with 'off' *AUSTRALIA, 1899*. **2** to borrow something; to cadge something *NEW ZEALAND, 1945*. **3** to relax, especially when there is work to be done *AUSTRALIA, 1942*

bludger *noun* **1** a pimp; a man who lives off the earnings of a prostitute. This is the earliest sense of this word and derives from the obsolete British and early Australian slang 'bludgeoner' (a pimp who uses a bludgeon to rob people visiting his prostitute. They were also called 'stick slingers'. By 1900 the sense 'pimp' was well established. The strongly negative sense of sponging off others derives from the fundamental nature of the pimp *AUSTRALIA, 1898*. **2** a lazy person who does not do their fair share of work; a person who lives off another's hospitality *AUSTRALIA, 1900*. **3** a despicable person *AUSTRALIA, 1906*. **4** a stingy person who borrows rather than buys *AUSTRALIA, 1972*. **5** any person. Often in the phrase 'poor bludger' (a sorry individual) *AUSTRALIA, 1969*. **6** used jocularly or affectionately as a term of address to friends *AUSTRALIA, 1960*. **7** something which causes aggravation *AUSTRALIA, 1992*

bludging *noun* used as the verbal noun of bludge *AUSTRALIA, 1984*

bludging *adjective* lazy *AUSTRALIA, 1948*

blue *noun* **1** methylated spirits as an alcoholic drink. From the colour of the fluid *UK, 1966*. **2** an amphetamine tablet. From the colour of the tablet *UK, 1992*. **3** a barbiturate capsule *US, 1969*. **4** a capsule of Drinamyl™, a combination of dexamphetamine sulphate and amylobarbitone. A favourite drug of abuse for mid-1960s Mods *UK, 1985*. **5** crack cocaine *UK, 2003*. **6** cocaine *US, 1945*. **7** Foster's beer *AUSTRALIA, 1988*. **8** an argument, dispute *AUSTRALIA, 1961*. **9** a fight, a brawl *AUSTRALIA, 1943*. **10** an error, a mistake *AUSTRALIA, 1941*. **11** a police officer *UK, 1844*. **12** a trusted prisoner with special privileges and responsibilities *NEW ZEALAND, 1989*. **13** boy, as an affectionate or possessive form of address; a young male homosexual. Gay slang, current in UK prisons February 2002; possibly from the nursery rhyme 'Little Boy Blue come blow on your horn', punning on HORN (an erection) *UK, 2002*. **14** a black man. A shortened BLUE BOY *US, 1964*. **15** a work protest *NEW ZEALAND, 2001*. ▶ **on the blue** (used

of a bet) on credit *AUSTRALIA, 1989*. ▶ **out of the blue** unexpectedly, suddenly and surprisingly *US, 1910*. ▶ **under the blue** said of a rigged carnival game being operated with police protection *US, 1985*

blue *verb* **1** to squander money. A possible variant of BLOW *UK, 1846*. **2** of a bookmaker, to lose on a race *UK, 1937*. **3** to fight *AUSTRALIA, 1962*. **4** to arrest someone. Allusion to the BOYS IN BLUE (the police) *UK, 1997*. **5** in horse racing, to commit an error of judgment *AUSTRALIA, 1989*

blue *adjective* **1** depressed, sad *UK, 1821*. **2** sexually explicit, porno-graphic *UK, 1864*. ▶ **all blue** in poker, a flush consisting of clubs or spades *US, 1967*

blue acid *noun* LSD. Named because of its colour when dripped onto sugar or blotting paper, or from the colour of a hallucination *US, 1969*

blue almonds *noun* a recreational drug cocktail of Viagra™, an erection-inducing drug taken recreationally for performance enhancement, and MDMA, the recreational drug best known as ecstasy. Apparently in popular use amongst lesbians in Sydney *AUSTRALIA, 2003*

blue and clear *noun* an amphetamine tablet *US, 1993*

blue and white *noun* a police car. A variation on BLACK AND WHITE *US, 1974*

blue angel *noun* a tablet of Amytal™, a central nervous system depressant *US, 1967*

blue-arsed fly *noun* used as an example of something in a state of agitation or frenzied activity *AUSTRALIA, 1955*

blue baby *noun* a capsule of the synthetic opiate oxycodone used recreationally *US, 2003*

blue bag *noun* **1** a police uniform *US, 1973*. **2** heroin *UK, 2002*

blue balls *noun* **1** a pain in the testicles caused by long periods of sexual arousal without release. Also South African variant 'blou balles' *US, 1916*. **2** any sexually transmitted infection *US, 1912*

blue band *noun* a capsule of Carbitral™, a central nervous system depressant. On 27th August 1967, Brian Epstein, manager of the Beatles, was found dead from an overdose of Carbitral *US, 1971*

blue bark *noun* a pass for a military person travelling home for a family member's funeral *CANADA, 1995*

blue barrel *noun* a blue, barrel-shaped tablet of LSD *US, 1971*

blueberry *noun* **1** marijuana with blue-coloured buds and a 'fruity' flavour; especially a locally grown variety in British Columbia *CANADA, 2002*. **2** a resident of the Lac-St-Jean area, Quebec. The most famous and widespread use of this word (which comes from the large blueberry crop grown in the area) was the nickname of Howie Morenz, Canadiens hockey player, known as the 'Bionic Blueberry' *CANADA, 2001*

blueberry grunt *noun* in Nova Scotia, a deep-dish blueberry pie *CANADA, 1995*

bluebird *noun* a capsule of amobarbital sodium (trade name Amytal™), a central nervous system depresssant *US, 1953*

bluebirds *noun* waves on the horizon, seen from near the shore *US, 1964*

blue blazes *noun* used as a euphemism for 'the hell' *AUSTRALIA, 1932*

blue bloater *noun* **1** a hospital patient suffering from chronic bronchitis. The blue colouring is from lack of oxygen; the bloating is from the lungs as they retain water *US, 1994*. **2** an overweight patient suffering from emphysema *US, 1973*

blue bomber *noun* a central nervous system stimulant *UK, 1966*

blue book *noun* **1** in horse racing, a sheet showing the contenders in a day's races, the odds on the horses and the handicapping *US, 1951*. **2** a test in school or university. From the examination booklets bound in light blue paper used in many US schools and universities *US, 1951*

bluebottle *noun* **1** a police officer. A singular occurence in Shakespeare's *Henry IV Part 1*, 1597, then unrecorded until 1846 *UK, 1846*. **2** a Ministry of Defence uniformed warden *UK, 1969*. **3** a Portugese man-of-war *US, 1991*

blue box *noun* **1** a homemade electronic tone generator used for manipulating and defrauding telephone networks. Generic, possibly after the colour of the first model *US, 1974*. **2** a police van used for transporting prisoners *US, 1976*

blue boy *noun* **1** an amphetamine tablet *US, 1952*. **2** a black man *US, 1967*. **3** a police officer. From the traditional blue uniform *UK, 1883*

blue bullet *noun* a capsule of amobarbital sodium (trade name Amytal™), a central nervous system depressant *US, 1977*

blue can *noun* a can of Foster's beer *AUSTRALIA, 2003*

blue cap *noun* a military prison staff member. From the blue-topped cap worn as a part of the uniform *UK, 1979*

blue chair *noun* LSD. Possibly a variation of BLUE CHEER (LSD) *US, 1975*

blue cheer *noun* a type of LSD (usually mixed with Methedrine™) supplied in blue pills or capsules. From Blue Cheer™, a branded detergent *US, 1970*

blue cheese *noun* hashish *US, 1992*

blue-chip *adjective* of the highest quality. A term that spread from poker (the blue chip is the highest value) to stocks to general usage *US, 1904*

blue-chipper *noun* an excellent student athlete with potential for playing professionally *US, 1984*

blue-clue caper *noun* a scheme by one police officer to cause harm to another police officer *US, 1983*

bluecoat *noun* a police officer *US, 1976*

blue collar *adjective* belonging to or characteristic of the working class *US, 1950*

blue de Hue *noun* marijuana from Vietnam. Misspelt and mispronounced, 'blue' sounds like the past tense of BLOW (marijuana) and the Vietnamese city of 'Hue' does not rhyme with 'blue', except in this instance *US, 1982*

blue devil *noun* a capsule of amobarbital sodium (trade name Amytal™), a central nervous system depressant *US, 1967*

blue doll *noun* a capsule of amobarbital sodium (trade name Amytal™), a central nervous system depressant *US, 1977*

blue duck *noun* **1** a failure, a flop *AUSTRALIA, 1895*. **2** rain or fog *NEW ZEALAND, 1951*

blue duppy *noun* a bruise, especially one produced by a cricket ball *BARBADOS, 1965*

blue-eyed boy *noun* a person who is unreasonably favoured. Derogatory *UK, 1924*

blue-eyed devil *noun* a white person *US, 1972*

blue-eyed Indian *noun* in trucking, a truck owned by the Navajo Freight Lines *US, 1976*

blue eyes *noun* a pupil favoured by a teacher. From conventional BLUE-EYED BOY *UK, 1974*

blue fever *noun* any sexually transmitted infection. Navy 'lower decks' usage *UK, 1961*

blue fit *noun* a state of shock *NEW ZEALAND, 1946*

blue flags *noun* LSD *US, 1976*

blue-flame *verb* to ignite a fart *AUSTRALIA, 1992*

blue flamer *noun* a zealot *US, 1991*

blue flu *noun* an organised work stoppage in which all the affected workers call in sick the same day *US, 1967*

blue flue boat *noun* a ship of the Blue Funnel Line ('Blue Flue Line'). Recorded as a 'Blue-Funneller' in 1929 and not recorded in this form until 1984; the shipping line ceased to exist in 1986 *UK, 1984*

blue foot *noun* **1** a prostitute. David Powis suggests that this is possibly of West Indian origin. In 1940s Jamaica 'a bluefoot man' is an 'outsider' *UK, 1977*. **2** a white prisoner. Used by black prisoners *UK, 1996*

blue funk *noun* a state of extreme fear *UK, 1861*

bluegill *noun* the penis *US, 1990*

bluegrass *verb* to commit someone to the Lexington (Kentucky) Federal Narcotics Hospital. Kentucky's nickname is 'the Bluegrass State' *US, 1953*

blue hair *noun* an older person, especially an older woman *US, 1981*

blue happiness *noun* liquid morphine *US, 1989*

blue haze *noun* the sense of euphoria and distance produced by a large dose of alprazolam (trade name Xanax™), a benzodiazepine used for short term relief of symptoms of anxiety *US, 1993*

blue heaven *noun* **1** sodium amytal, a barbiturate *US, 1954*. **2** LSD. Named because of the colour of the drug when dripped onto sugar or blotting paper, or possibly from the colour of a hallucination *US, 1977*

blue hero *noun* heroin *UK, 2003*

blue ice *noun* frozen toilet waste from an aircraft which melts off and falls *US, 1982*

blue in the armor *noun* a can of Pabst Blue Ribbon beer *US, 1967*

bluejack *verb* to send an anonymous one-way message to a mobile phone enabled with 'Bluetooth' radio technology *UK, 2004*

blue jay *noun* a capsule of sodium amytal, a compound used as a sedative and hypnotic *US, 1953*

blue job *noun* any member of an official service that wears a blue uniform (police, Royal Navy, Royal Air Force, etc) *UK, 1943*

blue John *noun* strong, homemade whisky *US, 1986*

blue juice *noun* a powerful wave *US, 1991*

blue lady *noun* methylated spirits *NEW ZEALAND, 1988*

blue lamp disco *noun* a police car with flashing lights *UK, 1981*

blue light *noun* a marked police car *US, 1976*

blue line *noun* a river. From the designation of a river on a map *US, 1976*

blue line sweep *noun* a military operation on a river or stream. In Vietnam military jargon, a 'blue feature' was a body of water and a 'blue line' was a stream or river as depicted on a map *US, 1991*

Blue Max *nickname* **1** the Congressional Medal of Honor *US, 1988*. **2** a gunship of the First Air Cavalry Division, one of only two aerial rocket artillery battalions in the US Army's history. Vietnam war usage *US, 1991*

blue meanie *noun* Copelandia cyancens or Panaeolus cyanescens: a mushroom with potent psychactive properties *NEW ZEALAND, 1991*

blue meanies *noun* the police or other enforcement authorities; a section of society with an anti-freedom point of view. From so-named predatory characters in the 1968 Beatles' cartoon film *The Yellow Submarine US, 1969*

blue microdot *noun* a type of LSD *UK, 1998*

blue mist *noun* LSD. Named because of the colour of the drug when dripped onto sugar or blotting paper, or possibly from the colour of a hallucination. *US, 1974*

blue molly *noun* an amphetamine capsule *UK, 2003*

blue moons *noun* **1** a type of LSD. Identified by blue moon pictures on blotting paper TAB(S) (tablets) of ACID, a boastful comparison to the rare quality of a 'blue moon' *UK, 2003*. **2** marijuana with a blue-coloured leaf *UK, 2002*

blue movie *noun* a sexually themed or pornographic film *US, 1957*

blue murder *noun* cries of terror or alarm; a great noise. Generally in combination, e.g. 'cry blue murder', 'howl', 'scream', 'yell', etc *UK, 1859*

blue mystic *noun* a powerful psychedelic drug in pill or powder form *US, 2001*

blue nitro *noun* the recreational drug GHB *US, 1998*

bluenose *noun* a Nova Scotian. This persistent nickname for residents of the province has several suggested origins, starting of course with the colour the nose turns in cold weather on a fishing boat, as well as the fame of a privateer from the province which had a blue cannon in the prow *CANADA, 1785*

blue-nosed *adjective* excessively moral, puritanical, repressed *US, 1890*

blue-on-blue *noun* **1** in battle, fire unintentionally directed at friendly forces *US, 1991*. **2** clear blue sky and a calm blue sea *US, 1986*

blue one *noun* in carnival usage, poor location or slow business for a concession stand *US, 1981*

blue pages *noun* in television and film making, additions to a script after production has started *US, 1990*

blue-pencil *verb* to censor something. From the traditional colour of an editor's pencil *US, 1888*

blue pill *noun* a very powerful handgun *US, 1957*

blueprint *verb* in drag racing, to bring an engine precisely to its tolerance for racing *US, 2004*

blue room *noun* **1** a toilet. Usually applied to a portable toilet on a construction site *US, 1965*. **2** a cell used for solitary confinement *US, 1976*. **3** any room in a police station or jail where rough interrogations take place *US, 1992*

blues *noun* **1** a deeply felt sense of sadness, rejection or depression. Shortened from the 'blue devils' *UK, 1741*. **2** methylated spirits as an alcoholic drink. From its colour *UK, 1966*. **3** an illegal drinking house, especially one where music is also provided *UK, 1977*. **4** in the army, a dress uniform; in the navy, a walking out uniform *UK, 1948*. **5** a formal blue dress uniform of the US Marines *US, 1991*. **6** jeans worn by convicts *UK, 1996*. **7** unreserved bleacher seats in a circus *US, 1980*. **8** money. From blue gambling chips *US, 1976*

blue sage; blue saze *noun* a variety of marijuana with a blue tint. It is likely that 'saze' is a misspelling or mispronunciation. Also known as BLUE MOONS *US, 1943*

blues and twos *noun* police emergency response vehicles. UK police cars have *blue* flashing lights and *two*-tone sirens, thus when a police vehicle is attending an emergency with all its alarms blazing and wailing it is said to be using 'blues and twos', and hence the derivation of this term *UK, 2001*

blue shirt *noun* an active firefighter, as distinguished from an officer *US, 1954*

blue sky *noun* **1** worthless securities; a pleasant appearance with difficulties ignored *US, 1906*. **2** heroin *US, 1987*

blue sky blonde *noun* highly potent marijuana from Columbia *US, 1982*

blues man *noun* a methylated spirits drinker *UK, 1966*

bluesnarf *verb* to steal personal information from a mobile phone enabled with Bluetooth™ radio technology. A compound of the *Blue*tooth brand and SNARF (to take, to grab) *UK, 2004*

Blue Spader *nickname* a soldier of the 1st Battalion, 26th Infantry, 2nd Brigade, 1st Infantry Division. From the blue spade on the insignia. Served in World War 2, Berlin, Vietnam from 1965 until 1970, Bosnia, Macedonia and Kosovo *US, 1991*

blue spot *noun* a spotlight with a blue filter, sometimes required by law during striptease shows *US, 1986*

blue star *noun* a type of LSD identified by a printed blue star *UK, 1998*

blue steeler *noun* a particularly erect erection *US, 1997*

blue streak *noun* an emphatic and vigorous degree. Used to modify 'talk' or variations on talking *US, 1830*

bluesuit *noun* a uniformed police officer *US, 1970*

bluesuiter *noun* a member of the US Air Force *US, 1963*

blue swimmer *noun* a ten dollar note. From the resemblance of the colour of the note to the 'blue swimmer' crab *AUSTRALIA, 2003*

blue ticket *noun* **1** a one-way train or bus ticket given by the police to criminals whose presence in town is no longer deemed acceptable *US, 1993*. **2** a discharge from the US armed services as 'unsuitable for military service' *US, 1991*. **3** a one-way ticket out of Alaska *US, 1993*

blue tip *noun* a capsule of amobarbital sodium (trade name Amytal™), a central nervous system depressant *US, 1977*

blue tongue *noun* an unskilled worker. After the blue-tongued lizard *AUSTRALIA, 1943*

blue veiner *noun* a rigid erection *US, 1975*

blue velvet *noun* a combination of cough syrups, especially codeine-based syrups, used as a weak heroin substitute *US, 1994*

blue vex *adjective* extremely angry *BARBADOS, 1990*

blue vials *noun* LSD *UK, 1998*

blue-water man *noun* a sailor experienced in ocean sailing *US, 1975*

blue water Navy *noun* during the war in Vietnam, a ship that was part of the US Navy presence off the coast of Vietnam *US, 1948*

bluey *noun* **1** a capsule of Drinamyl™, a combination of amphetamine and barbiturate *UK, 1963*. **2** a methylated spirit drinker. From the colour of the spirit *UK, 1961*. **3** a five pound note (£5). From the colour *UK, 1982*. **4** an airmail letter. Gulf war usage *UK, 1991*. **5** a blue blanket as used by itinerants for carrying possessions; a swag *AUSTRALIA, 1878*. **6** a summons. In late C19 called 'a piece of blue paper' *AUSTRALIA, 1909*. **7** a portable gas stove used by Royal Marines in Northern Ireland *UK, 1984*. **8** a pornographic film *AUSTRALIA, 1985*

Bluey *noun* used as a nickname for a red-haired person. Ironic in origin *AUSTRALIA, 1906*

blueys *noun* denim trousers, jeans *AUSTRALIA, 1917*

bluff *noun* a lesbian who enjoys both the active and passive role in sex *US, 1970*

blunderturd *noun* a Triumph 'Thunderbird' motorcycle *UK, 1984*

blunjie; blunjy *adjective* yielding, squashy. Given some currency in the 1950s by surreal radio comedy *The Goons UK, 1984*

blunk *adjective* in a state of intoxication that is the result of drink and drugs. An elision of any word for 'intoxicated' that begins 'bl' and 'drunk' *UK, 1984*

blunt *noun* **1** marijuana rolled and smoked in a hollowed out cigar. Generic usage but originally made with a Phillies Blunt™ *US, 1988*. **2** a mixture of marijuana and cocaine *US, 2003*. **3** a capsule of Seconal™ or other barbiturate in a black capsule *US, 1980*. **4** cocaine *UK, 2003*. **5** a hypodermic syringe *US, 1980*. **6** a knife *US, 1971*. **7** a coin. Circus and carnival usage *UK, 1708*

blunted *adjective* marijuana-intoxicated *US, 1993*

blunted up *adjective* marijuana-intoxicated *UK, 2001*

blunt end *noun* the stern of a ship. Used by 'landlubbers', often jocular *UK, 1961*

bluntie *noun* marijuana rolled and smoked in a hollowed out cigar *US, 1997*

blunt nib; blunt *noun* a reporter. Press photographers' slang *UK, 2004*

blur *noun* someone who is lost in his own world. Intensified at times as 'blur like fuck' *SINGAPORE, 2002*

blurt *noun* the vagina. In conventional English 'blurt' (to puff with scorn) involves compressing and opening lips. The imagery, perhaps, explains the etymology *UK, 2001*

blurter *noun* the anus *NEW ZEALAND, 1998*

blute *noun* newspapers cut and folded to look like currency *US, 1992*

bluttered *adjective* drunk. Possibly a variation of BLOOTERED *UK, 2002*

bly *noun* an oxy-acetylene blow torch. Criminal use *UK, 1996*

BM *noun* a BMW car. Further abbreviated from BEEMER rather than directly from the BMW brand name; the car is a status-symbol, and seeking to sound evermore casual about its name is simple snobbery *UK, 1999*

BMO *noun* used by US troops in the war against Iraq to describe Saudi women. Initialism of 'black moving objects' *US, 1991*

BMOC *noun* a popular and visible college boy. A 'big man on campus' *US, 1934*

BMQ *noun* a homosexual male who hides his sexuality. A 'black market queen'. *UK, 2002*

BMT *noun* habitual lateness. Initialism of 'black man's (or men's) time', based on a stereotypical characteristic *UK, 2000*

BMW *noun* from a British Indian (Hindu) perspective, a person who is categorised as black, Muslim or white *UK, 2006*

BNF *noun* a science fiction fan well known by other fans. A 'big-name fan' *US, 1982*

bo *noun* **1** a man, a companion; often used as a form of address. From the nickname Beau, or abbreviated from 'boy'. Originally English but now US. UK cryptic crosswords often rely on the clue 'an American' to signal the letters 'bo' *UK, 1729.* **2** a hobo. A reality and term that only barely lingered into the 1950s *US, 1899.* **3** marijuana *US, 1975*

BO *noun* body odour. An initialism coined for soap advertisements; made even more infamous by the comic strip villain B.O. Plenty in *Dick Tracy US, 1931*

bo *adjective* excellent, fashionable, trendy *US, 1963*

BO! go away! A euphemistic abbreviation of BUGGER OFF *UK, 1984*

bo!; boh! used as an expression of approval. As in the phrase 'Bo Yakasha!' used by cult comic figure Ali G (Sacha Baron-Cohen) *UK, 2000*

board *noun* **1** a surfboard *US, 1963.* **2** in a game of poker in which some cards are dealt face-up, all face-up cards collectively *US, 1992.* ▶ **off the board** in horse racing, said of odds greater than 99–1 *US, 1976.* ▶ **on board** on the railways, on duty, at work *US, 1977.* ▶ **take off the board** in sports betting, to fail to establish a pointspread on a game or event *US, 1975*

board *verb* ▶ **board with Aunt Polly** to draw disability insurance. A logging term *US, 1931*

board cord *noun* a line attached at one end to a surfer and at the other to the surfboard *US, 1977*

boarded up *adjective* in prison, wearing an improvised armour, such as magazines inserted under clothing, to protect yourself from attack by other prisoners *UK, 1996*

boardie *noun* a surfer *NEW ZEALAND, 1999*

boardies *noun* baggy surfing shorts *AUSTRALIA, 1979*

boarding house *noun* a jail *US, 1942*

boarding house reach *noun* an effort by a diner to reach for a serving plate rather than ask for it to be passed *US, 1906*

board jock; board sock *noun* a protective surfboard cover *US, 1977*

board knees *noun* lumps on a surfer's knees from prolonged hours kneeling on a surfboard *AUSTRALIA, 1963*

Board of Trade duff *noun* tinned pudding. Merchant Navy use *UK, 1979*

boards *noun* **1** the stage; live theatre. Always after the definite article *UK, 1768.* **2** skis. Probably from the fact that early homemade skis were sometimes shaped from planks *CANADA, 1989.* ▶ **on the boards** in solitary confinement *US, 1976*

board shorts *noun* almost knee-length shorts favoured by surfboarders *AUSTRALIA, 1963*

boardwalk oyster *noun* a used condom. From the appearance and location of discovery *UK, 1998*

boar's nest *noun* in oil drilling, any poorly planned, makeshift arrangement of equipment *US, 1954*

boast *verb* **1** to brag as a part of a rap performance *US, 2000.* **2** to smoke marijuana *US, 1997*

boasty *adjective* arrogant *BAHAMAS, 1982*

boat *noun* **1** a car, especially a large car *US, 1914.* **2** a prison transfer; a group of prisoners being transferred; the bus used to transfer them *US, 1956.* **3** a non-prostitute who flaunts her sexual availability to hotel customers *UK, 2005.* **4** phencyclidine, the recreational drug known as PCP or angel dust. A shortened form of LOVE BOAT *US, 1984.* **5** heroin *US, 1993.* **6** a combination of marijuana and phencyclidine, the recreational drug known as PCP or angel dust *UK, 2003.* **7** in poker, a hand consisting of three of a kind and a pair. Conventionally known as a 'full house' *US, 1981.* ▶ **off the boat** said of immigrants, especially black people *UK, 2001*

boat anchor *noun* a crippled or useless piece of computer equipment; by extension, a useless person *US, 1991*

boat and oar *noun* a whore. Rhyming slang *UK, 2003*

boat girl *noun* a prostitute plying her trade on the docks *NEW ZEALAND, 1978*

boatie *noun* the operator of a small motorboat *NEW ZEALAND, 1972*

boat in a moat *noun* a casino that must, as a result of gambling laws, float *US, 2003*

boatload *noun* a large amount *UK, 1999*

boat people *noun* people who arrive at casinos on bus excursion trips *US, 1994*

boat race *noun* **1** a fixed horse race or other competition *US, 1917.* **2** the face. Rhyming slang, probably in use from the late 1940s. Often shortened to 'boat' *UK, 1958*

boats *noun* shoes or feet, especially large ones *US, 1956*

boat tail *noun* an Alfa Romeo Spyder convertible. The rear end comes to a point, not unlike a boat *US, 1992*

bob *noun* **1** a shilling; a non-specific amount of money. Obsolete since decimalisation in 1971, except in phrases like QUEER AS A NINE BOB NOTE and abstract representations of money such as 'a few bob' (an undefined sum of money) *UK, 1789.* **2** a dollar *US, 1930.* **3** marijuana. Very likely derived from Bob Marley, a highly visible marijuana lover. A long list of derivatives play with the term – 'see bob', 'talk with bob', 'bob's on the phone' – and serve as a code for discussing marijuana and its use *US, 1997.* **4** a marijuana cigarette. Other possible derivations include BOB HOPE and BOBO BUSH *US, 1998.* **5** crack cocaine. An abbreviation of BOBO *UK, 1998.* **6** in hot rodding and drag racing, to cut or shorten a fender *US, 1966.* **7** a shoplifter *US, 1962*

bob *verb* to perform oral sex on a man *US, 1995.* ▶ **bob for apples** to remove impacted faeces by hand *US, 1989*

bob *adjective* pleasant. Survives in the phrase 'all is bob' and the variant 'on bob' *UK, 1721*

Bob *adjective* used by US troops in the war against Iraq as an adjective for all things Saudi *US, 1991*

Bob and Dick *noun* the penis. Rhyming slang for PRICK (the penis) *UK, 1974*

Bob and Dick; Bob, Harry and Dick *adjective* sick. Rhyming slang; from the people who brought you TOM AND DICK; TOM, HARRY AND DICK *UK, 1868*

bobber *noun* a person who has died by drowning or has fallen into the water *US, 1987*

bobbers *noun* **1** the female breasts *UK, 1968.* **2** pieces of cork hung as a fringe around a hat's brim to keep flies away *AUSTRALIA, 1942*

bobbins *noun* nonsense *UK, 2005*

bobble *verb* (used of a racehorse) to stumble or break stride in a clumsy manner *US, 1976*

bobble bumper *noun* in pinball, a bumper that scores and kicks the ball on contact *US, 1977*

bobble twanger *noun* a lesbian. In Royal Air Force use *UK, 2002*

Bobbsey Twins *noun* **1** used as a representation of either innocence or a strong resemblance. From a popular series of 72 children's books created by Edward Stratemeyer in 1904 and written under the name of Laura Lee Hope by writers under contract to Stratemeyer *US, 1969.* **2** two girls who regularly double-date *US, 1968*

bobby *noun* **1** a police officer. A familiar abbreviation of the name Robert honouring Mr, later Sir, Robert Peel, who is credited with the founding of the Metropolitan Police in 1829 *UK, 1844.* **2** during the Korean war, the Soviet BA-64 light armored car used by North Korea *US, 1952*

bobby *verb* to serve as a police officer *UK, 1967*

bobby dangler *noun* the penis. A play on BOBBY-DAZZLER *CANADA, 1971*

bobby-dazzler *noun* something or someone wonderful, exciting, magnificent *UK, 1866*

Bobby Moore; bobby *noun* **1** a door. Rhyming slang, based on the name of the footballer who was England's 1966 World Cup winning captain *UK, 1998.* **2** the state of affairs, the current situation. Rhyming slang for THE SCORE (the current situation) *UK, 1996*

bobbysoxer *noun* a teenage girl. 'Bobby socks' (ankle-high white socks, first recorded in 1927) as a generational trademark for American teenagers arrived on the national scene in June 1937, with a cover photograph in *Life* magazine. After 'the socks' came 'the soxer'. The 'bobby' is most likely constructed on 'to bob' (to cut or shorten) US, 1944

bobette noun a London Metropolitan Woman Police Officer. A feminised variation of BOBBY (a policeman) UK, 1999

bobfoc noun a girl with a beautiful body but an ugly face. Acronym formed from *Body Off* Baywatch, *Face off* Crimewatch, two television programmes – one fiction, one factual – which represent (apparently) the extremes of human appearance UK, 2002

Bob Hope noun marijuana. Abbreviates to BOB. British-born American entertainer Bob Hope (1903–2003) is not associated with drugs except as a rhyme for DOPE UK, 1992

bob job noun a reduction in size achieved by cutting US, 1954

Bob Marley noun cocaine. Rhyming slang for CHARLIE (cocaine); after reggae musician Bob Marley (1945–1981), a Rastafarian UK, 2001

bobo noun 1 a person who enjoys the trappings of success but nevertheless espouses countercultural values. From 'bourgeois bohemian', but surely too close to a clown's name to be a coincidence US, 2000. 2 a fool JAMAICA, 1943. 3 the vagina BAHAMAS, 1982. 4 the buttocks US, 1974. 5 crack cocaine. Possibly playing on BEBE UK, 1998. 6 prison-issued canvas shoes US, 2002

bobo bush noun marijuana US, 1936

Bobo Johnny noun any naive, gullible person SAINT KITTS AND NEVIS, 1969

Bob Squash noun an area of a public lavatory where hands are washed. Rhyming slang for 'wash'; originally, during World War 1, 'to wash'; thereafter used by pickpockets as 'on the bob' (stealing from the jackets of people washing their hands) UK, 1961

bobsy-die noun a commotion or fuss. A variation on the British dialect *bob-a-dying* NEW ZEALAND, 1935

Bob's your uncle everything is all right. Most commentators offer the relationship between Prime Minister Robert Gascoyne-Cecil, 3rd Marquis of Salisbury (1830–1903) and his nephew Arthur Balfour (1848–1930) as the source of the phrase; the former (Uncle Bob), in 1887, controversially (allegedly nepotistically) appointed the latter as secretary for Ireland. This idiom, very familiar in the UK, is all but unknown in the US so that when Jann Turner-Lord published *A Dictionary of Slang for British Mystery Fans* in 1992 it was entitled *Bob's Your Uncle* UK, 1937

bobtail noun 1 in poker, four fifths of a straight that can be completed at either end US, 1865. 2 on the railways, a switching engine US, 1977

bobtail verb in trucking, to drive a tractor without a trailer US, 1946

Bob White noun in trucking, a flap valve on the smokestack US, 1971

bod noun 1 person. An abbreviation of 'body' UK, 1935. 2 the body, as in physique UK, 1933. 3 an aeroplane passenger. Flight crew use UK, 1960

bodacious adjective amazing, impressive. A C19 word from the American frontier, rediscovered by the late C20 young. The term 'bodacious tatas' as descriptive of 'magnificent breasts' was made widely popular by the 1982 film *Officer and a Gentleman*. In Australia, popularised by radio announcer Doug Mulray US, 1843

bo-deen noun a police officer US, 2001

bodega noun a shop. An affected acquisition, directly from Spanish UK, 2002

bodewash noun dry buffalo dung. The word is an adaptation of the French *bois de vache* (cow wood) CANADA, 1953

bodger noun in the building trade, any inferior tradesman (such as a builder, electrician, mechanic or plumber) who is able to patch and mend, and is, perhaps, unqualified; on a building site, the jack-of-all-trades worker who fixes minor problems. A dialect word first recorded in 1552 UK

bodger adjective fake; false AUSTRALIA, 1950

bodgie noun 1 anything worthless. Also variant 'bodgey' AUSTRALIA, 1953. 2 a male member of an urban youth subculture of the 1950s. Now only historical use. 'Bodgies' were noted for a peculiar style of dress (shocking for its day) that was in conscious imitation of American youth, including tight trousers, jackets, no ties and having slicked back hair with large sideburns. Their female

counterparts were 'widgies'. This group was the subject of numerous alarmist media reports about youth deliquency. In origin the term must be related to other senses of 'bodgie/bodger', but exactly how is unclear. One theory, that it is a nominal use of 'bodgie' as 'counterfeit', referring to clothing made from poor quality cloth passed off as American material, is unsubstantiated by any early evidence AUSTRALIA, 1954. 3 a young swing jazz enthusiast US, 1952

bodgied up adjective dressed up in a pretentious manner AUSTRALIA, 1972

bodgy; bodgie verb to conceal someone or something AUSTRALIA, 1968

bodgy; bodgie adjective 1 false, counterfeit, phoney, sham. Appearing simultaneously with the synonymous 'bodger', these terms must derive from British dialect *bodge* (to make or mend clumsily or poorly), a variant of 'botch'. Recorded earliest in prison and underworld use it perhaps referred originally to a poorly done quota of work that prisoners had to submit daily AUSTRALIA, 1944. 2 poorly made or executed; worthless, hopeless AUSTRALIA, 1944

bodice-ripper noun a sexually themed romantic/historical novel aimed at an adult female audience US, 1980

bodied adjective (used of a female) well built US, 1947

bodilicious noun an attractive physique. A compounding of 'body' and 'delicious', perhaps intended as a gentle pun on BODACIOUS. Recorded in contemporary gay culture as an 'edible body' UK, 2003

body noun 1 a person, especially if under suspicion or arrest; a person to be framed for a crime. Police and criminal usage UK, 1970. 2 a prisoner. Prison officers' use UK, 1996. 3 in the usage of showgirls, a man US, 1981

body verb to kill someone US, 1999

body armour noun a condom UK, 1998

body by Fisher noun a woman with an attractive body. An allusion to an advertising slogan of the General Motors Corporation, boasting of the superiority of a car 'body by Fisher' US, 1949

body cheese noun any buildup of body cells such as ear wax or eye secretions US, 1988

body contact squad noun Korean soldiers who acted as suicide bombers US, 1982

body knocker noun a person who works in a car body repair shop US, 1993

body lotion noun a drink. Citizens' band radio slang UK, 1981

body packer noun a person who smuggles drugs inside their body US, 1997

body popping noun an urban dance-style incorporating robotic movements US, 1984

body queen noun a homosexual man attracted to men with muscular bodies US, 1970

body rain noun corporate executives in search of employment after a takeover, merger or business failure. A macabre image recalling the suicides by jumping associated with the market crash of 1929 US, 1988

body shop noun a bar catering to an unmarried clientele with sexual agendas US, 1970

body shot noun a ritual in which a person licks salt off someone else, drinks a shot of tequila and then sucks on a lemon in the other's mouth US, 2001

body snatcher noun 1 a morgue employee who retrieves and transports corpses to the morgue US, 1993. 2 someone who steals another's date US, 1955. 3 a person who selects prime farm stock for butchering NEW ZEALAND, 2002

body swerve noun any deliberate act of avoiding someone or something. From football terminology into general parlance UK: SCOTLAND, 1985

body-swerve verb to avoid something UK: SCOTLAND, 1992

body time noun in casinos, the amount of time a player, whose playing time is being tracked, spends gambling US, 1996

body-to-body *noun* a sexual service offered in some massage parlours in which a girl will massage her client with her body *UK, 2003*

body womping *noun* body surfing *US, 1987*

boerewors curtain *noun* the invisible line marking the beginning of South African suburbs where Afrikaans people dwell *SOUTH AFRICA, 1996*

boerie *noun* the penis. From the Afrikaans for 'farm sausage' *SOUTH AFRICA, 2005*

bof *noun* **1** an old or older person who is rated as uninteresting. An acronym formed on *boring old fart UK, 2005.* **2** a record album consisting of the 'best of' the artist's previous recordings *US, 1982*

boff *noun* **1** a hearty laugh *US, 1945.* **2** sex; an act of sexual intercourse *US, 1956*

boff *verb* **1** to have sex *US, 1937.* **2** to kiss and caress *US, 1968.* **3** to make a mistake, to do something wrong. Possibly euphemistic; sometimes 'boff up'. School children's slang *UK, 1977.* **4** to vomit *US, 1993*

boffed *adjective* drunk *US, 1984*

boffin *noun* a scientist; a forensic expert *UK, 1945*

boffo *noun* **1** a great joke *US, 1968.* **2** a one-year prison sentence *US, 1930*

boffo *adjective* very impressive, popular, successful. Originally theatrical when it was often used of a comedic success, and in which sense it probably derives from 'buffo' (a comic actor; comic) *US, 1949*

boffola *noun* **1** a hearty laugh; a joke that produces a hearty laugh *US, 1946.* **2** a smash hit, a success *US, 1947*

bog *noun* **1** a lavatory. Abbreviated from obsolete 'bog house'. Often follows 'the' and often in the plural *UK, 1789.* **2** an act of defecation *AUSTRALIA, 1932.* **3** a police station *UK, 1962.* **4** in Western Australia, an unrefined and loutish person from a lower socio-economic area *AUSTRALIA, 1997.* **5** a type of putty used to fill dents in the bodywork of vehicles *AUSTRALIA, 1989*

bog *verb* **1** to defecate *UK, 1982.* **2** (used of a motorcycle engine) to lose power and slow down *US, 1973*

bogan *noun* an unrefined and loutish person from a lower socio-economic area. The term gives rise to any number of derivatives, such as 'boganhood', 'boganism', 'boganity' and 'Bogansville' (the notional home of bogans) *AUSTRALIA, 1987*

bogan *adjective* of or relating to a bogan *AUSTRALIA, 1988*

Bogan shower *noun* a dust storm. Bogan is an inland town in New South Wales. Other locations similarly used by nature, weather and irony: Bedourie, Bourke, Cobar, Darling, Wilcannia and Wimmera *AUSTRALIA, 1945*

bogart *noun* a bully. From the verb 'to bogart'; a critical view of out-of-fashion film 'tough guy' behaviour personified by film actor Humphrey Bogart *US, 1994*

bogart *verb* **1** to bully. As 'tough guy' films and the forceful characters portrayed by actors like Humphrey Bogart went out fashion, so the usage moved from admiring to critical. Also variant 'bogard' *US, 1966.* **2** to selfishly keep possession of something that you are expected to return or forward, especially drugs. After the alleged meanness of film actor Humphrey Bogart (1899–1957), or, perhaps, from the way he would keep a cigarette dangling from his lips. Sometimes spelt 'bogard' or 'bogarde' *US, 1957.* **3** to overdose on drugs *UK, 1996*

bog bird *noun* a woman who is willing to have sex in a public lavatory *UK, 2003*

bogey *noun* **1** a uniformed police officer; a police detective. From 'bogey-man' (a terrifying creature), ultimately from 'old bogey' (the devil); alternatively spelt 'bogie' or 'bogy' *UK, 1924.* **2** an unidentified aircraft, presumed to be hostile until identified as friendly. Coined in World War 2 and used since *US, 1943.* **3** in betting, the outstanding loser in any book *UK, 1991.* **4** a small lump of dried nasal mucus. Variant spellings include 'bogy' and 'bogie' *UK, 1937.* **5** a wash taken in a creek, dam, etc, especially after a day's work *AUSTRALIA, 1874.* **6** a child's steerable cart constructed from pram wheels and odds and ends of wood *UK: SCOTLAND, 1985.* **7** in trucking,

a set of two axles *US, 1986.* **8** a stalemate, a deadlock *UK: SCOTLAND, 1985*

Bogey *nickname* Humphrey Bogart (1899–1957), American actor *US, 1972*

bogey *verb* to swim and wash in a creek, damn, etc, especially after a day's work; (of working dogs) to take a dip in a body of water to cool down and as a break from work. From Dharug, the extinct Australian Aboriginal language of the Sydney region *AUSTRALIA, 1788*

bogey *adjective* fraudulent, bogus *US, 1977*

bog-eyed *adjective* bleary-eyed as the result of too much drink or too little sleep, or both *UK, 1999*

bogger *noun* a person from or living in a rural part of Ireland especially anyone not living in Dublin. This term makes use of the suffix -ER, especially common in Dublin Hiberno-English *IRELAND, 1997*

boggie *noun* a hippy who is resistant to change, or too drug-intoxicated to be a part of any activity. Coinage credited to counterculture artist Edward Barker, 1970 *UK*

boggie bear *noun* an ugly person *US, 1947*

boggie board *noun* a small, foam board surfed in a prone position *AUSTRALIA, 1985*

bogging *adjective* filthy *UK: SCOTLAND, 1985*

bogie man *noun* a worker who repairs railway rolling stock. A pun on a devilish creature and a conventional piece of under-carriage *UK, 1970*

bog-in *noun* a hearty meal. After the verb sense *AUSTRALIA, 1954*

bog in *verb* to eat voraciously *AUSTRALIA, 1917*

bog lap *noun* in Western Australia, a circuit of a street block in a vehicle done, especially repeatedly, for entertainment *AUSTRALIA, 1996*

bogman *noun* anyone who does not live in a city or a town *IRELAND, 1992*

Bogners *noun* blue jeans worn when skiing. Alluding to the stylish stretch trousers manufactured by the German Bogner firm *US, 1963*

bogof *noun* a retail special offer: *Buy One Get One Free UK, 2003*

bog off *verb* to go, to depart; generally used as a euphemistic imperative. Originally Royal Air Force, possibly from 'take-off' (in an aircraft), to 'leave the earth (bog) behind' *UK, 1996*

bogosity *noun* the degree to which anything can be described as wrong or in error. Computer hacker slang from BOGUS (wrong) *US, 1981*

bog out *verb* to become intoxicated on drugs *US, 1998*

bog-standard *adjective* ordinary, normal, usual *AUSTRALIA, 1983*

bog-trotter *noun* an Irish person. From the nature of Eire's terrain *UK, 1682*

bog-trotting *adjective* Irish. From BOG-TROTTER (an Irish person) *UK, 1997*

bogue *noun* a cigarette *US, 1994*

bogue *verb* **1** to smoke a cigarette. A part-of-speech shift derived from Humphrey Bogart, cigarette-smoking icon *US, 1983.* **2** to depress someone *US, 1986*

bogue *adjective* wrong; sick. From BOGUS; sometimes seen spelt as 'boag' *US, 1960*

bogue out *verb* in computing, to become non-functional suddenly and without warning *US, 1983*

bog up *verb* to make a mess of something, to do something incompetently. Originally military; likely to derive from BOG (a lavatory) and all that implies, but at the same time euphemistic and tending towards BUGGER UP *UK, 1948*

bogus *noun* counterfeit money *US, 1798*

bogus *adjective* **1** disagreeable, offensive; wrong *US, 1876.* **2** in computing, non-functional, useless, false or incorrect *US, 1981*

bogus beef *noun* idle, insincere conversation *US, 1947*

bogwash *verb* to force a person's head into the toilet bowl, and flush. From BOG (a lavatory) *UK, 1996*

bogwoppit *noun* an ugly woman. In Royal Air Force use *UK, 2002*

bohawk *noun* a member of the Bohemian counterculture *US, 1952*

bohd *noun* **1** marijuana *UK, 1998*. **2** phencyclidine, the recreational drug known as PCP or angel dust. Possibly a mispronunciation of BOAT *UK, 2001*

boho *noun* a Bohemian, in the sense of an unconventional person *US, 1958*

boho *adjective* unconventional, bohemian *US, 1958*

bohunk *noun* **1** a Czechoslovakian immigrant *US, 1903*. **2** a ill-mannered, loutish person *US, 1919*

boil *noun* in surfing, a turbulence or disturbance on a developing wave *US, 1980*. ▶ **off the boil** having lost your form and luck *AUSTRALIA, 1989*

boil *verb* ▶ **boil it till it assholes** to continue to heat maple sap until it forms vortexes, indicating that it is nearing the candy stage *CANADA, 1992*. ▶ **boil the hides** in drag racing, to smoke a car's tyres *US, 1965*

boil down *verb* to reduce something to its essence. A figurative use of the conventional sense *UK, 1880*

boiled *noun* a boiling hot solution of sugar and water used as an offensive weapon *UK, 1996*

boiled *adjective* **1** very drunk *US, 1884*. **2** angry *US, 1929*

boiled owl *noun* **1** used as a representation of the ultimate drunkard *US, 1864*. **2** the last thing in the world that you would want to eat *US, 1975*

boiler *noun* **1** a woman considered by most to be devoid of, or past the age of, sexual appeal. Flesh considered as chicken meat: a 'boiler' is no longer a fresh and tasty chick but a tough old bird *UK, 1962*. **2** an unskilled cook. Proficient only at boiling meals *US, 1975*. **3** the stomach *US, 1886*. **4** the vagina *UK, 1985*

boilermaker *noun* **1** a shot of whisky followed by a glass of beer; a beer and whisky combined *US, 1942*. **2** a pint of beer that is an equal mixture of draught mild and bottled brown ale; a salted beer *UK, 1961*

boiler room *noun* an office used in an elaborate swindle *US, 1931*

boiler water *noun* whisky *US, 1977*

boiling *adjective* extremely hot. A familiar exaggeration *UK, 1930*

boilover *noun* in horse racing, an unexpected win by a long shot; a loss by the favourite *AUSTRALIA, 1871*

boil-up *noun* a trail stop for tea and rest *CANADA, 1998*

boing *verb* while snowboarding, to bounce off something *US, 1990*

boing! used as a jocular catchphrase that indicates a sexual interest or readiness. Sometimes embellished to 'Boing! said Zebedee'. Coincidental to the original US catchphrase, this began with the UK translation/adaptation, by Eric Thomson, 1929–84, of French animated children's television programme *Le Manège Enchanté* into *The Magic Roundabout*, BBC 1963–71 and 1974–77. Zebedee was a spring-mounted character, best remembered as making his entrances and exits to a narrated 'Boing!' and signalling the end of each episode by announcing that it was time for bed. Popularised in the UK with the recording of a stand-up comedy routine by Jasper Carrott *US, 1948*

bo-ing! used for humorously expressing approval or delight. Teen slang *US, 1955*

boink *noun* an in-person meeting of participants in an Internet discussion group *US, 1995*

boink *verb* to have sex with someone *US, 1897*

Bo Jimmy *noun* marijuana *US, 1992*

bok *noun* an eager person *SOUTH AFRICA, 1978*

Bok *noun* a sportsman or woman in a team that represents South Africa in international competition, a 'Spring*bok*' *SOUTH AFRICA, 1972*

bok *adjective* keen for something interesting *SOUTH AFRICA, 1975*

boke; boak *noun* nausea; a need to vomit; vomiting *UK, 1911*

boke; boak *verb* to vomit; to induce vomiting *UK, 1911*

boker *noun* an unsophisticated rustic *US, 1968*

bokkie; bok *noun* a lover, especially as an endearment *SOUTH AFRICA, 1959*

boko *noun* the nose *US, 1859*

bold *adjective* **1** used to suggest homosexuality or of the stereotypical characteristics associated with gay men. This usage was originated and made familiar by the BBC radio comedy *Round The Horne*, 1965–9 *UK, 1967*. **2** successful, excellent *US, 1965*

bold-as-brass; as bold as brass *adjective* audacious, extremely impudent *UK, 1789*

Bolivian marching powder *noun* cocaine *US, 1984*

bollards *noun* the testicles. A play on BOLLOCKS *UK, 2003*

bollicky; bollocky *adjective* (of either sex) totally naked. Literally, 'with the bollocks exposed' *AUSTRALIA, 1950*

bollix *noun* **1** nonsense talk. The spelling reflects Hiberno-English pronunciation of BOLLOCKS *IRELAND, 1996*. **2** a contemptible person. Variant spelling of BOLLOCKS *IRELAND, 2000*

bollix *verb* to bungle something, to ruin something *US, 1937*

bollixing *adjective* used as a negative intensifier *US, 1954*

bollo *noun* nonsense. A shortening of BOLLOCKS *UK, 2003*

bollock *noun* **1** a ball (a society dance). A pun on BALL(S) (a testicle/testicles) *UK, 1982*. **2** a chronic failure, a mess *UK, 2001*

bollock; ballock *verb* to reprimand someone, to admonish someone, to scold someone *UK, 1938*

bollockache *noun* an unnecessary or annoying cause of weariness *UK, 1998*

bollockchops *noun* a stupid person, an idiot; used as a ribald form of address *UK, 1991*

bollocking *adjective* used as an intensifier, especially in a negative context *UK, 2000*

bollocking; ballocking *noun* a telling-off, a scolding. From BOLLOCK (to reprimand, to scold) *UK, 1938*

bollockless *adjective* cowardly, lacking in courage. A lack of BOLLOCKS (the testicles, hence 'manly' qualities) *UK, 2000*

bollock naked *adjective* totally naked *UK, 1922*

bollocko *adjective* naked. Abbreviated from STARK BOLLOCK NAKED *UK, 2001*

bollocks *adjective* nonsensical *UK, 1996*

bollocks! used as an all purpose expletive. Figurative use of 'testicles' *UK, 1969*

bollocks; ballocks *noun* **1** the testicles. Rarely singular *UK, 1744*. **2** nonsense. The 1977 album 'Never Mind The Bollocks Here's The Sex Pistols' brought 'bollocks' to shop windows across the UK. At the time there was outrage but a quarter of a century later the word is now commonplace *UK, 1919*. **3** anything considered to be the finest, the most excellent, the best. An abbreviated form of DOG'S BOLLOCKS; usually after 'the' *UK, 2000*. **4** nerve, courage. BOLLOCKS (testicles) and bravery are both symbols of masculinity, one must therefore equal the other *UK, 1995*. **5** trouble, conflict *UK, 2001*. **6** a despicable contemptible person *UK, 2003* ▷ *see:* DOG'S BOLLOCKS. **7** fools. The singular fool may well be a bollock or bollocks *UK, 2006*. ▶ **do your bollocks 1** to become enraged, to lose your temper *UK, 1999*. **2** to lose all your money gambling *UK, 2000*. ▶ **go to bollocks** to be forgotten *UK, 1995*. ▶ **will it bollocks** used rhetorically to register doubt and disbelief *UK, 2000*

bollocks about; ballocks about *verb* to play the fool *UK, 1961*

bollocksed; ballocks'd *adjective* **1** ruined, thwarted *UK, 1961*. **2** damned *UK, 1997*. **3** drunk *UK, 2003*

bollocks on *verb* to talk nonsense. From BOLLOCKS (nonsense) *UK, 2000*

bollocky *adjective* used as an intensifier. On the model of BLOODY *UK, 1992* ▷ *see:* BALLOCKY, BOLLICKY

bolloxed *adjective* **1** unwell *UK, 1998*. **2** drunk. A variation of BOLLOCKSED *US, 1986*

boll weevil *noun* **1** in oil drilling, an inexperienced worker *US, 1954*. **2** a novice trucker *US, 1971*

Bolly *nickname* *Bolli*nger, a branded champagne *UK, 2001*

Bollywood *nickname* the film industry in Bombay *INDIA, 1989*

bolo *noun* **1** in boxing, an uppercut *US, 1950*. **2** a directive to be on the look-out for something *US, 1986*. **3** a friend. Described as a 'hippy term' *UK, 1977*. **4** a traveller to Antarctica who is jaded and exhausted from having been there too long *ANTARCTICA, 2003*. **5** crack cocaine. Spanish *US, 1994*. **6** an unknown, sinister male *US, 2002*

bolo badge *noun* a Purple Heart military decoration for battle wounds, especially those suffered in a foolish action *US, 1968*

bolohead *noun* a bald person *US, 1981*

bolo shot *noun* in handball, any shot hit with the fist *US, 1977*

bolshie; bolshy *noun* a Bolshevik *US, 1919*

bolshie; bolshy *adjective* obstructive, unco-operative, deliberately difficult. From 'Bolshevik', but without political significance *UK, 1918*

bolt *noun* **1** an escape, a flight *AUSTRALIA, 1915*. **2** phencyclidine, the recreational drug known as PCP or angel dust *US, 1986*. **3** a blemish; a pimple *US, 1969*

bolt *verb* **1** to leave *US, 1845*. **2** to escape from prison or custody *UK, 1811*. **3** in poker, to withdraw from a hand *US, 1988*

bolter *noun* **1** a landing on an aircraft carrier in which the plane misses the arresting mechanisms *US, 2002*. **2** an unexpected selection for a sports team, a board or political team *NEW ZEALAND, 1995*. **3** in horse racing, a winning horse with long odds *AUSTRALIA, 1989*

bolts *noun* a tattooed depiction of lightning bolts, symbolising a prisoner's association with a white pride prison gang *US, 1989*

bolts and jolts *noun* a combination of central nervous system stimulants and depressants *US, 1946*

bolts and nuts *adjective* mentally unstable; crazy *US, 1984*

bomb *noun* **1** a great deal of money *UK, 1958*. **2** a marijuana cigarette, especially a large one *US, 1951*. **3** high potency, relatively pure heroin *US, 1960*. **4** crack cocaine *US, 1994*. **5** potent heroin *US, 1969*. **6** a dose of sedative, especially one administered to dope a racehorse; a sedative pill *AUSTRALIA, 1950*. **7** in a horse race, a winning horse that ran with very high odds *US, 2002*. **8** a forceful blow with the fist *US, 1949*. **9** in tiddlywinks, a long-distance shot *US, 1977*. **10** a skateboarding manoeuvre in which the rider crouches and holds the sides of the board as the board leaves the ground *US, 1976*. **11** a fast car. Teen slang *US, 1953*. **12** a dilapidated motor vehicle *AUSTRALIA, 1950*. **13** an improvised water-heating device in prison *NEW ZEALAND, 1982*. **14** a dismal failure, especially in show business *US, 1952*. **15** an unexpected bass drum accent *US, 1955*. ▶ **go like a bomb; go down a bomb** to be very successful and exciting *UK, 1967*. ▶ **make a bomb** to become rich, to make a large profit. From BOMB (a great deal of money) *UK, 1958*. ▶ **the bomb; da bomb** the very best, something that is very good *US, 1973*

bomb *verb* **1** to place graffiti with an emphasis on quantity, not quality *US, 2000*. **2** to swallow a quantity of a powdered drug and its cigarette-paper wrapping *UK, 2000*. **3** in horse-racing, to dope a horse *AUSTRALIA, 1953*. **4** to run or drive at speed *UK, 1978*. **5** in mountain biking, to travel fast downhill *US, 1992*. **6** to train intensely, alternating heavy weights with light weights *US, 1984*. **7** in tiddlywinks, to play a wink at a pile of winks with destructive intent *UK, 1980*. **8** to fail dramatically; to flop. Originally theatrical *US, 1958*. **9** in computing, to cease to function completely and suddenly *US, 1991*. ▶ **get bombed** to be overcome by a wave while surfing *US, 1965*

bomb *adjective* dilapidated *AUSTRALIA, 1979*

bomba *noun* a vintage car that has been restored *US, 1995*

Bombay bloomers *noun* baggy, loose-fitting shorts *US, 2002*

Bombay Welsh *noun* English as spoken by Indians and Anglo-Indians. From the similarity in lilting cadences of speech between the broadest Indian and Welsh accents. It is interesting to note that an English person attempting a Welsh accent often sounds Indian, particularly to Welsh ears *UK, 1984*

bomb doors *noun* the vagina *UK, 2001*

bombed *adjective* extremely drunk or drug-intoxicated *US, 1956*

bombed out *adjective* **1** extremely marijuana-intoxicated *US, 1999*. **2** crazy *UK, 1987*. **3** (of a motor) worn out. The result when a car is made to BOMB (to drive flat-out) too often *UK, 2001*

bomber *noun* **1** a graffiti artist *US, 1997*. **2** an extra large, thick or potent marijuana cigarette. Named as an allusion to size and shape *US, 1949*. **3** a tablet or capsule of amphetamine or barbiturate, hence a generic name for amphetamine or barbiturate in any form *US, 1950*. **4** a hard-hitting, aggressive boxer *US, 1937*. **5** a powerful, hard-breaking wave *US, 1964*. **6** an old, battered car, especially one used in a demolition derby contest *US, 1977*. **7** a person with poor fashion sense *US, 1997*. **8** a sixteen-ton oil-carrying wagon *UK, 1970* ▷*see:* **BLACK BOMBER**

bomb farm *noun* an area on a military base where bombs are stored *US, 1991*

bomb-happy *adjective* with nerves gone through exposure to bombing *UK, 1944*

bombida *noun* a mixture of heroin and cocaine. From the Spanish, literal translation 'little bomb' *US, 1975*

bombido *noun* **1** injectable Benzedrine™ (amphetamine sulphate), a central nervous system stimulant *US, 1982*. **2** heroin *UK, 2002*

bombie; bommie *noun* a hazardous submerged off-shore reef over which waves break. From *bombora*, from an Australian Aboriginal language *AUSTRALIA, 1949*

bombilla *noun* an ampoule filled with a drug *US, 1998*

bombing *adjective* in foot-propelled scootering, at great speed *UK, 2000*

bombita; bombito *noun* a tablet of amphetamine sulphate (Dexedrine™), a central nervous system stimulant *US, 1966*

bomb line *noun* during the Korean war, the line beyond which bombing was deemed safe *US, 1986*

bombo *noun* cheap and poor quality wine or stronger alcoholic drink *AUSTRALIA, 1942*

bomboara *noun* a large wave that breaks seaward of the normal surf line *AUSTRALIA, 1965*

bombosity *noun* the buttocks *US, 1932*

bomb-out *noun* in competitive surfing, early elimination *US, 1988*

bomb out *verb* **1** to fail to appear as expected *UK, 1979*. **2** to reject someone *UK, 1985*. **3** to knock a surfer off a surfboard *US, 1964*

bomb-proof *adjective* having an impregnable excuse to avoid selection or responsibility for a(n) (unpleasant) task; invulnerable. Military use; remembered as 1950s, but possibly earlier *UK, 1984*

bombs *noun* the female breasts *US, 1968*

bombs away *noun* heroin *UK, 2002*

bombshell *noun* **1** a sudden or great surprise. Often in the phrase 'drop a bombshell' *UK, 1860*. **2** a woman who is astonishingly attractive *US, 1933*

bomb up *verb* while hunting, to fire a flurry of loosely aimed shots at a herd *NEW ZEALAND, 1984*

Bom-de-Bom *noun* Ba Muoi Ba beer, a staple in Saigon during the Vietnam war *US, 1990*

bomfog *noun* dense and verbose language. When Governor Nelson Rockefeller campaigned for the Republican nomination for president in 1964, he tended to end speeches with a reference to the 'brotherhood of man under the fatherhood of God', a phrase which compacts into the acronym BOMFOG. Reporters covering the campaign began to refer to the end of his speeches as BOMFOG. The term survived and eventually took on a more general, less flattering meaning *US, 1965*

bommie *noun* a huge wave. An abbreviation of *bombara*, from an Australian Aboriginal language *AUSTRALIA, 1991* ▷*see:* **BOMBIE**

bona; bonar *adjective* good, pleasant, agreeable. Theatrical origins from Latin *bonum* and Italian *buono* (good) *UK, 1875*

bonafide *noun* the significant other in your emotional life. Latin for 'good faith'. Black usage *UK, 1994*

bona vardering *adjective* attractive. A combination of 'bona' (good) and 'varda' (to look) thus 'good looking' *UK, 1997*

bonce *noun* the head. Originally adopted by schoolboys from the name given to a large marble, in a jocular reference to the shape *UK, 1889*

bondage *noun* indebtedness *US, 1945*

bondage pie *noun* a pizza with sausage and mushroom topping. The initials of the toppings – S and M – suggest bondage *US, 1996*

Bondi cigar *noun* in Sydney, a piece of excrement floating in the surf. So-named from the notoriety of a sewerage outlet near Bondi beach *AUSTRALIA, 1996*

Bondi tram; Bondi bus *noun* used as an example of something that moves quickly. The actual tram apparently went out of business in 1960 *AUSTRALIA, 1959*

Bondo mechanic *noun* a body shop worker who relies too heavily upon large amounts of body putty and too little upon finesse or craft *US, 1992*

bondook *noun* a weapon. Gulf war usage *UK, 1991*

bone *noun* **1** the penis, especially when erect *US, 1916*. **2** the active participant in homosexual sex *US, 2001*. **3** the middle finger raised in a gesture meaning, roughly, 'fuck you' *US, 1957*. **4** a marijuana cigarette; hence, marijuana. A visual pun *US, 1978*. **5** a tobacco cigarette. A visual pun *US, 1992*. **6** a measurement of crack cocaine sold for $50 dollars *US, 2003*. **7** heroin *US, 1993*. **8** a dollar *US, 1889*. **9** one thousand dollars *US, 1988*. **10** a trombone *US, 1918*. **11** an irritation; an annoyance; an aggravation. A figurative extension of a 'bone in the throat' *US, 1944*. **12** a domino. Usually in the plural *US, 1959*. **13** in private poker games or other private gambling, a white betting chip *US, 1866*. **14** a black person *US, 1992*. **15** in baseball, an error in judgment. An abbreviation of 'bonehead play' or BONER *US, 1915*

bone *verb* **1** to have sex from the male point of view *US, 1971*. **2** to interrogate a suspect. Police and criminal use; probably from earlier sense (to seize, to arrest) *UK, 1966*. **3** in mountain biking, to strike the nose of your seat with your buttocks *US, 1992*. **4** to study intensely *US, 1859*

bone *adjective* tasteless, unfortunate, inferior *UK, 1995*

bone banger; bone crusher *noun* an orthopaedist *US, 1994*

bone blanket; bone bonnet *noun* a condom. Contrived to wrap the BONE (an erection) *UK, 1998*

bone box *noun* the mouth. Obsolete teen slang *CANADA, 1946*

bonecrusher *noun* **1** in trucking, a truck that rides very roughly *US, 1971*. **2** crack cocaine *US, 1998*

bonecrushers *noun* the very painful symptoms of withdrawal from drug addiction *US, 1990*

boned *adjective* **1** tipsy *UK, 1949*. **2** having been hit hard on the head *UK, 1977*

bone dance *noun* sex *US, 1988*

bone dome *noun* a protective helmet; a crash helmet. Originally aviators' usage (1930s), subsequently used by motorcyclists (1950s) and cyclists (1980s) *UK, 1984*

bonehead *noun* **1** an idiot *US, 1908*. **2** a bald-headed person; a skinhead; hence an extreme skinhead haircut *UK, 1981*

bone hog *noun* a sexually active female, especially one who enjoys performing oral sex on men *US, 2003*

bone-on *noun* an erection *US, 1927*

bone orchard *noun* a cemetery *UK, 1982*

bone out *verb* **1** to back down from a confrontation; to run away from danger *US, 1993*. **2** to leave quickly *US, 1993*. **3** while snowboarding, to hold your leg straight during a manoeuvre in the air *US, 1990*

bone queen *noun* a male homosexual who favours performing oral sex *US, 1964*

boner *noun* **1** a blunder *US, 1912*. **2** an erection. The supposed bone-like quality of an erect penis, with which you BONE (have sex) *US, 1961*. **3** an old or poor-quality steer, slaughtered for mince or sausage *NEW ZEALAND, 1963*

boneroo *noun* high quality drugs *US, 1992*

bones *noun* **1** dice. The term has journeyed from colloquial to standard English and now to slang *UK, 1400*. **2** heroin *US, 1984*. **3** crack cocaine *UK, 2003*. **4** the basic facts of something *UK, 1999*. **5** an orthopaedist *US, 1892*. **6** spare ribs *US, 1990*. ▶ **make your bones 1** to establish yourself as a fully fledged member of a crime organisation, usually by carrying out an execution-style murder *US, 1972*. **2** by extension, to establish yourself as an equal in a group setting *US, 1996*. ▶ **on your bones** destitute or almost so. An image of emaciation *UK, 1924*. ▶ **the bones** the boyfriend *UK, 2002*

bone shack *noun* any place where a couple have sex *US, 1997*

boneshaker *noun* **1** a bicycle. Coined as a literal description of early bicycles, and remains in use despite technological advances *US, 1871*. **2** a rigid-frame motorcyle, especially a rigid-frame Harley-Davidson *US, 1962*

bone up *verb* to study, especially at the last minute. An American outgrowth of the C18 'bone' with the same meaning *US, 1918*

bone works *noun* rough treatment *US, 1970*

boney *adjective* genuine, satisfactory. An alteration of '*bona*fide' *UK, 1996*

boneyard *noun* **1** a cemetery *US, 1866*. **2** in various industrial settings, the site for dumping broken vehicles and equipment which can be cannibalised for parts *US, 1913*. **3** in dominoes, the pile of unusued tiles *US, 1897*. **4** the area off a beach where waves break *US, 1965*. **5** a conjugal visit in prison *US, 1989*

boneyize *verb* to lay claim to something *CANADA, 1989*

boney maroney *noun* a very thin person. In various spellings, but surely originating in the rock'n'roll lyric from the 1957 song by Larry Williams *US, 1957*

bone you! bone ya! used as an all-purpose, defiant insult *US, 1963*

bonfire *noun* **1** in firefighter usage, a multiple-alarm fire *US, 1954*. **2** a burning cigarette stub *US, 1945*

bong *verb* to drink beer directly from a keg, using a hose and funnel *US, 1982*

bong; bhong *noun* **1** a pipe with a water-filled bowl through which marijuana or crack cocaine smoke is drawn for inhalation *US, 1971*. **2** a bong's worth of marijuana *AUSTRALIA, 1987*. **3** a Maori or Pacific Islander *NEW ZEALAND, 1984*

bong; bung *adjective* dead. From Aborigine *bong* (dead) *AUSTRALIA, 1857*

bong brain *noun* a marijuana addict *AUSTRALIA, 1987*

bong land *noun* a state of marijuana intoxication. Extended from BONG (a water-pipe, used for smoking marijuana) *UK, 2002*

bongo *noun* **1** a marijuana cigarette *UK, 1983*. **2** in skateboarding, a fall or the wounds resulting from a fall *US, 1976*

bongo mag *noun* a pornographic magazine *UK, 2002*

bong on *verb* to smoke marijuana. Often seen as a graffiti'd credo *AUSTRALIA, 1988*

bong up *verb* to become intoxicated by inhaling marijuana through a water-filled pipe *UK, 1996*

bonhunkus *noun* the buttocks *US, 1941*

boning tool *noun* the penis. Combines 'boning' (sexual intercourse) with a pun on 'tool' (an implement suited to a given task/the penis) *US, 2001*

bonish *adjective* covetous *CANADA, 1987*

bonita *noun* **1** heroin *UK, 2002*. **2** milk sugar (lactose) used to dilute heroin. Mexican Spanish *US, 1973*

bonk *noun* sexual intercourse. A light-hearted, almost euphemistic term; probably from 'bonk' (a noise) playing on BANG *UK, 1984*

bonk *verb* **1** to hit someone or something with, or against, something hard *UK, 1931*. **2** to have sex *UK, 1975*. **3** in an endurance sport, especially cycling, to reach a point of utter exhaustion *US, 1979*. **4** to bounce a snowboard off a non-snow platform. From the noise of the contact between board and DEATH BOX *US, 1995*

bonkbuster *noun* a type of popular novel containing frequent, explicit sexual encounters *UK, 1988*

bonker board *noun* a large, cumbersome, old-fashioned surfboard *AUSTRALIA, 1996*

bonkers *noun* the female breasts. An elision of BAZONKAS *US, 1995*

bonkers *adjective* crazy *UK, 1957*

bonkers *adverb* crazy *UK, 1957*

bonkers as conkers *adjective* crazy, mad, very eccentric. An elaboration of BONKERS *UK, 2003*

bonneroo; bonaroo *adjective* good, smart, sharp. Largely, if not exclusively, prison slang *US, 1926*

bonnet *noun* in motor racing, a safety helmet *US, 1993*

bonnie *noun* a Triumph Bonneville motorcyle *US, 1976*

Bonnie Dick *nickname* the USS Bonhomme Richard. An aircraft carrier named after Capt. John Paul Jones' famous ship in the American Revolution *US, 1955*

Bonny Prince *noun* cocaine. A disguising of CHARLIE (cocaine) using the name of 'Bonny (or Bonnie) Prince Charlie', Charles Edward Stuart, 1720–88 *UK, 2002*

bonspiel *noun* a curling tournament *CANADA, 2001*

bontoger; bontogeriro; bontoser *adjective* excellent, admirable. Elaborations of BONZER (excellent) *AUSTRALIA, 1904*

bonus! used for expressing delight and/or approval *US, 1997*

bonus baby *noun* an amateur athlete who signs a professional contract with a large signing bonus *US, 1962*

bony-bony *adjective* very thin *NORFOLK ISLAND, 1992*

bonzer; bonza *noun* someone or something that is excellent *AUSTRALIA, 1904*

bonzer; bonza *adjective* excellent, terrific, wonderful, fabulous, good. This word is the only surviving member of a set of synonymous terms that all appeared in the first decade of C20, the others being 'bontosher', 'boshter' and 'bosker'. It is claimed that these were all corruptions of an original term that was a compound of the French words *bon* (good) and *toujours* (always) *AUSTRALIA, 1904*

bonzer; bonza *adverb* excellently; brilliantly; well *AUSTRALIA, 1914*

bonzo *noun* a chance *UK, 1999*

bonzo *adjective* crazy *US, 1979*

boo *noun* **1** marijuana *US, 1959*. **2** a sexual partner or lover *US, 1997*. **3** an attractive young person *US, 1968*. **4** used as a term of endearment *US, 2004*. **5** an unlexicalised verbalisation of disapproval *UK, 1801*. **6** a sulk. Adapted from BOOHOO (a childish vocalisation of sobbing) *UK, 2001*. **7** bird or lizard droppings *BARBADOS, 1998*. **8** anything at all. Usually heard in the warning – 'don't say boo' *US, 1883*. **9** nasal mucus *BAHAMAS, 1982*

boo *verb* in contemporary dance culture, to give an unlexicalised verbalisation of approval. A deliberate reversal of the negative sense *UK, 2003*. to sob loudly. A shortened form of BOOHOO *UK, 2005*

boo *adjective* excellent. Youth usage *US, 1952*

booay; boohai *noun* a remote area. Probably a corruption of the Maori placename, Puhoi *NEW ZEALAND, 1963*

boob *noun* **1** a fool. Almost certainly from C16 'booby', meaning a 'stupid fellow' *US, 1907*. **2** the female breast. From synonymous 'bub'. Generally used in the plural *US, 1931*. **3** jail. Could date as far back as the 1880s, which is feasible since 'booby hatch', from which 'boob' is ultimately derived, dates back as far as 1859 in the US *US, 1908*. **4** a blunder, a *faux pas US, 1934*

boob *verb* **1** to blunder *UK, 1935*. **2** to perform poorly, to botch something *US, 1919*

boob box *noun* a television; television *US, 1968*

boob gear *noun* prison clothing *NEW ZEALAND, 1999*

boob gun *noun* an improvised tattoo machine *NEW ZEALAND, 1999*

boob happy *adjective* mentally unbalanced as the result of being imprisoned. Derives from BOOB (a jail) and the suffix -HAPPY (mentally unbalanced) *AUSTRALIA, 1968*

boob head *noun* a prisoner *NEW ZEALAND, 1994*

boobie *noun* used as an endearing term of address. Popularised by comic Jerry Lewis in the mid-1950s; mock Yiddish *US, 1960* ▷ *see:* BOOBY

boo-bird *noun* a sports fan who constantly and loudly boos during a game *US, 1948*

boobitas; boobititas *noun* small female breasts. A borrowed use of the Spanish diminuitive *US, 1963*

boob job *noun* surgery to alter a woman's breast size *US, 1986*

boo-boo *noun* **1** an error. Children's vocabulary *US, 1953*. **2** a bruise or scrape *US, 1954*. **3** the human posterior. A childish reduplication of 'bottom' *UK, 1964*. **4** any vexatious flying insect *BAHAMAS, 1982*

boo boo bama *noun* marijuana *UK, 2003*

boo-boos *noun* the testicles *US, 1951*

boob rat *noun* a prisoner who is always returning to prison. Derives from BOOB (a jail) *AUSTRALIA, 1967*

boobs *noun* in poker, a pair of queens *US, 1988*

boob sling *noun* a brassiere *US, 1968*

boob talk *noun* any secret or coded language used in prison. Derives from BOOB (a jail) *AUSTRALIA, 1993*

boob tat *noun* a tattoo acquired in prison *US, 1998*

boob tube *noun* **1** television. First came THE TUBE, and then the obvious reduplication *US, 1963*. **2** in women's fashion, a strapless top made of stretchable material. Sometimes also called a 'booby tubey' *UK, 1978*

boob weed; boob tobacco *noun* prison-issue tobacco. Derives from BOOB (a jail) and WEED (tobacco) *AUSTRALIA, 1967*

booby *adjective* foolish *US, 1958*

booby; boobie *noun* **1** a female breast *US, 1916*. **2** nasal mucus *BAHAMAS, 1982*

booby hatch *noun* a mental hospital *US, 1896*

booby prize *noun* a reward for stupidity, often given humorously to whoever comes last in a contest. Elaborated on BOOBY (foolish) *US, 1889*

booby trap *noun* a dishonest carnival game *US, 1950*

boochie *noun* a Japanese person *US, 1950*

boo-coo; boo koo *noun* a large number; a lot *US, 1918*

boo-coo; boo koo *adjective* a large number of; a lot of *US, 1986*

boodle *noun* **1** profits appropriated quietly, and usually illegally *US, 1858*. **2** a fake bankroll used in confidence swindles *US, 1985*. **3** a package of snacks *US, 1900*

booed and hissed *adjective* drunk. Rhyming slang for PISSED (drunk) *UK, 1980*

boof *verb* to hide prison contraband in your rectum *US, 2000*

boofhead *noun* a person with an oversized head; hence, a fool, idiot, dimwit. The term dates back to the 1930s and first appears in print in 1941. Popularised by Boofhead, a cartoon character appearing in the Sydney *Mirror* in the 1940s. Probably a contraction of earlier British and Australian 'bufflehead'. The suggestion that it is from British dialect *boof* (stupid) is chronologically improbable *AUSTRALIA, 1945*

boof-headed *adjective* fat-headed; stupid *AUSTRALIA, 1965*

boofy *adjective* (of a male) brawny, overtly masculine and a bit stupid *AUSTRALIA, 1992*

boog *noun* a black person. Offensive *US, 1937*

boogaloo *noun* **1** basic rock 'n' roll music; in a broader sense, the spirit of rock 'n' roll. Originally 1965, and conventionally, 'a dance performed to rock 'n' roll music' *US, 2003*. **2** a black person *US, 1970*

boogaloo *adjective* drunk *UK, 2002*

booger *noun* **1** a glob of nasal mucus *US, 1891*. **2** cocaine *US, 1997*. **3** a fellow; a rascal *UK, 1708*. **4** the vagina; and so, woman as sexual object *US, 1959*. **5** a technician in avionics *CANADA, 1995*

booger drag *noun* a man dressed as a woman, but revealing his masculinity by not shaving his face, arms and/or legs *US, 1997*

booger-picker *noun* a long-shafted tool used to remove oil seals and install windshields *US, 1992*

booger wire *noun* in electric line work, a neutral wire *US, 1980*

boogie *noun* **1** a black person. Offensive *US, 1923*. **2** the vagina *US, 1969*. **3** syphilis, especially in its second stage *US, 1982*

boogie *verb* **1** to dance, especially with abandon *US, 1947*. **2** to go, especially in a hurry *US, 1970*. **3** to have sex *US, 1960*

boogie box *noun* a large portable stereo system associated, stereotypically, with black youth culture *US, 1987*

boogie-joogie *verb* to fool around *US, 1968*

boogie man; boogy man *noun* a mythical demon, used to frighten children *US, 1905*

boogie pack *noun* a pocket-sized portable cassette-player with lightweight headphones *UK, 1982*

boogie party *noun* a party held to raise money to pay the rent *US, 1982*

boohonged *adjective* drunk *UK, 2003*

boohoo *verb* to cry loudly *UK, 1840*

boo hoo used ironically for pretending sorrow. Echoic of genuine weeping *UK, 2001*

boojie *noun* a middle-class person. A refinement of 'bourgeois' and not used with kindness *US, 1970*

book *noun* **1** in horse racing, the schedule of a jockey's riding assignments *US, 1976*. **2** a betting operation *US, 1917*. **3** in sports, the collective, conventional wisdom in a given situation *US, 1985*. **4** collectively, the mares bred with a single stallion in a year *US, 1997*. **5** ten thousand doses of LSD soaked into paper *US, 1999*. **6** one pound of drugs *US, 1976*. **7** half a kilogram of drugs *US, 1976*. **8** a hard-working, focused, serious student *US, 1968*. ▶ **do the book (and cover)** to serve a life sentence in prison *US, 1976*. ▶ **get the book 1** in prison, to be reprimanded *UK, 1996*. **2** to become religious. The book is the *Bible* but other works could apply equally well *UK, 1996*. ▶ **make book** to bet *US, 1962*. ▶ **on the book 1** used of a high-security prisoner who must constantly be identified by a small official book and photograph *UK, 1996*. **2** in the theatre, working as a prompter. The book in question is a play's text *UK, 1964*. **3** on credit *UK, 1984*. ▶ **the book** the unwritten code of style and conduct observed by pimps *US, 1972*. ▶ **throw the book at; give the book** to sentence someone to a maximum penalty allowed by law *US, 1908*

book *verb* **1** to study *US, 1968*. **2** to realise; to see and understand *UK, 1970*. **3** to assume something *UK, 1999*. **4** to depart, usually hurriedly *US, 1974*. ▶ **book a party of two** to arrange for oral sex to be performed on two male prisoners *US, 1989*. ▶ **book the action** to accept a bet *US, 1980*. ▶ **book your seat** to pad the seat of your trousers with newspaper or a book before going to be caned. Schoolboy usage, post World War 2 until the 1970s when corporal punishment was outlawed *US, 1961*

book *adjective* acceptable, agreeable. Derives from texting, in particular from the predictive text facility: when attempting to text the word COOL the word 'book' may be offered *UK, 2005*

book-beater *noun* a serious, hard-working student *US, 1945*

book 'em, Danno used for humorous suggestion that somebody has been caught in an improper act. From the US television series *Hawaii Five-O* (1968–1980), in which Detective Steve McGarrett would order Detective 'Danno' Williams to arrest a suspect *US, 1968*

bookend *verb* in twelve-step recovery programmes such as Alcoholics Anonymous, to speak with a fellow recovering addict both before and after confronting a difficult situation *US, 1998*

booket *noun* a woman who receives a cunnilinguist's attention. West Indian patois for 'bucket' *UK, 2002*

book gook *noun* a diligent, socially inept student. Teen Slang *US, 1951*

bookie *noun* a bookmaker. Sometimes spelt 'booky' *UK, 1885*

bookie's chance *noun* in horse racing, a horse with high odds (12–1 or higher) that bookmakers deem the favourite *AUSTRALIA, 1989*

bookman *noun* a prisoner serving a life sentence *US, 1949*

books *noun* **1** used as a figurative description of membership in a criminal organisation *US, 1964*. **2** employment documents that are returned to a dismissed worker *UK: SCOTLAND, 1988*. ▶ **do books** to steal or forge official benefit books, such as child benefit *UK, 1996*

▶ **in someone's bad books** in disfavour *UK, 1861*.
▶ **in someone's good books** in favour *UK, 1839*

book up *verb* to study *US, 1975*

boola-boola *adjective* characterised by extreme boosterism and spirited support of an institution. The song 'Boola Boola' has been one of Yale University's football fight songs since 1901 when it was written by Allan M. Hirsh, who explained the meaning of the word as follows: 'It is interesting to note that many people have asked us what the word "Boola" meant, and we said it was Hawaiian and meant a joy cry. We stuck to this for several years until someone came along and pointed out to us that there was no B in the Hawaiian language and therefore Boola could not possibly be Hawaiian. So the fact remains that we do not know what it means, except that it was euphonious and easy to sing and to our young ears sounded good'. The song was an 'adaptation' of an 1898 'La Hoola Boola' performed by Bob Cole and Billy Johnson *US, 1900*

boolhipper *noun* a black leather jacket with a belt in the back *US, 1970*

boolum *noun* a boaster or an intimidating braggart. From the Irish *buaileam sciath IRELAND, 2000*

boom *noun* **1** potent marijuana *US, 1946*. **2** fake crack cocaine *US, 2001*. **3** the erect penis *US, 1958*

boom *adjective* fashionable, pleasing *CANADA, 1993*

boom! used for expressing enthusiasm *US, 2002*

boom and zoom; b and z *verb* in air combat, to use a relative altitude advantage to attack an opponent (to boom) and then return to a superior position out of danger (to zoom) *US, 1986*

boombastic *adjective* excellent; also (of music) resounding. Elaboration of conventional 'boom' (a booming sound) or BOOM (pleasing), informed by BOOM (marijuana) *CANADA, 1991*

boom-boom *noun* **1** sex. From Asian pidgin. Major use in Vietnam during the war *US, 1964*. **2** the buttocks *BAHAMAS, 1982*. **3** an act of defecation. Children's bathroom vocabulary *US, 1960*. **4** live music *US, 2003*. **5** a pistol *US, 1945*. **6** a cowboy or Western film *US, 1947*

boom-boom *verb* to copulate *US, 1971*

boom boom! used for signalling or accompanying the punch-line of a joke, especially a bad or corny joke. Coined as a catchphrase for children's television puppet Basil Brush, first seen in 1963 *UK, 1963*

boom-boom girl *noun* a prostitute. Vietnam usage *US, 1966*

boom-boom house; boom-boom parlor *noun* a brothel *US, 1966*

boom-booms-a-gogo *noun* a unit of quad-fifty machine guns. Korean war usage *US, 1982*

boom box *noun* a large, portable radio and tape player *US, 1981*

boom boy *noun* a marijuana user *US, 1992*

boom bye; boom bwoy *noun* a homosexual male. Jamaican patois rendering of BUM BOY *JAMAICA, 2002*

boomer *noun* **1** a large example of something *AUSTRALIA, 1843*. **2** a large kangaroo *AUSTRALIA, 1830*. **3** a powerful, hard-breaking wave *AUSTRALIA, 1942*. **4** a nuclear submarine armed with missiles *US, 1976*. **5** a member of the baby boom generation, born between roughly 1945 and 1955 *US, 1982*. **6** a worker who travels from job to job *US, 1893*. **7** during aerial refuelling, the boom operator on the fuelling plane *US, 1986*. **8** in trucking, a binder used to tie down a load *US, 1971*

boomer! excellent! *AUSTRALIA, 1998*

boomerang *noun* **1** a young person who moves back in with their parents after moving out *US, 1997*. **2** a repeat offender, a recidivist *US, 2002*. **3** a plane flight that returns without reaching its destination because of poor weather *ANTARCTICA, 1994*. **4** a man with more than one girlfriend. In West Indian and UK black use *UK, 2002*. **5** in television and film making, a device that holds a filter in front of a light *US, 1987*

boomerang *verb* to return to prison shortly after being released *US, 1992*

boomers *noun* LSD *UK, 2004*

booming *adjective* excellent *US, 1990*

boom out *verb* to go to the US to work *CANADA, 2002*

boomps-a-daisy! used as a childish catchphrase or light-hearted response to trivialise a minor physical accident. Blending WHOOPS-A-DAISY! with 'bump'. 'Hands, Knees and Boomps-a-Daisy!' was a popular song and 'The Boomps-a-Daisy' a popular dance in the 1930s *UK, 1961*

booms *noun* drums *US, 1960*

boom squad *noun* the group of prison guards who are used to quell disturbances *US, 2000*

boom wagon *noun* in trucking, a truck hauling dynamite *US, 1942*

boomy *adjective* emphasising low frequencies, producing poorly defined sound. Used in television and film making *US, 1987*

boon *noun* a black person. Possibly reduced from BOON COON (a good friend) *US, 1967*

boon *adjective* close, intimate *US, 1969*

boona *noun* ▶ **give it the full boona** to hold nothing back. From *boona*, an Indian dish which, when served in some Glasgow Indian restaurants, is available as a 'half boona' or a 'full boona' *UK: SCOTLAND, 1988*

boon coon *noun* a very close friend *US, 1958*

boondagger *noun* a lesbian with overtly masculine mannerisms and affectations *US, 1972*

boondie *noun* **1** in Western Australia, a rock. Probably from an Australian Aboriginal language *AUSTRALIA, 2002*. **2** in Western Australia, a piece of conglomerated sand used by children to throw at one another in play *AUSTRALIA, 1952*

boondock *verb* **1** in trucking, to drive on back roads, avoiding major motorways *US, 1971*. **2** to drive off-road through a remote area *US, 1993*. **3** in tiddlywinks, to send an opponent's wink a long way away, especially out of the playing area. After US BOONDOCKS (an isolated region) *UK, 1980*. **4** in tiddlywinks, to shoot from a position far from the action *US, 1977*

boondocker *noun* a party held in the country *US, 1966*

boondockers *noun* marine-issued combat boots *US, 1942*

boondocks *noun* the remote end of nowhere *US, 1909*

boondoggle *noun* a business trip or venture designed for the enjoyment of those involved, not for its stated purpose *US, 1935*

booner *noun* **1** a talent scout. An allusion to American frontier pioneer Daniel Boone *US, 1981*. **2** an unrefined and loutish person from a lower socio-economic area *AUSTRALIA, 1996*

boong *noun* an Aboriginal person; hence, any other dark-skinned person. From the Australian Aboriginal language Wemba, meaning 'person'. Used disparagingly by white people. Now strongly taboo *AUSTRALIA, 1924*

boonga *noun* a Pacific Islander or any other dark-skinned person *NEW ZEALAND, 1957*

boong moll *noun* a prostitute who serves dark-skinned men. A combination of BOONG (an Aboriginal or dark-skinned man) and MOLL (a prostitute) *AUSTRALIA, 1953*

boongy *noun* the buttocks *BAHAMAS, 1995*

boonie hat *noun* a fatigue hat, made of cotton canvas with a brim around, that kept the sun and rain off the heads of American soldiers in Vietnam *US, 1972*

boonie rat *noun* a soldier serving in the jungle or other remote area *US, 1967*

boonies *noun* a remote rural area. An abbreviation of BOONDOCKS *US, 1956*

booooo! an exclamation of approval. The difference with 'boo' (an unlexicalised verbalisation of disapproval) is essentially one of intention *UK, 2005*

booorrring *adjective* very boring. Slang by drawn out pronunciation. From popular entertainment *US, 1981*

boo out *verb* to leave *US, 1959*

boops *noun* a man who supports a woman with whom he lives without the benefit of marriage *JAMAICA, 2003*

boopsie *noun* a woman supported by a man with whom she lives without the benefit of marriage *JAMAICA, 1996*

boo-reefer *noun* marijuana *US, 1972*

booshway *noun* the boss. A slurring of the French *bourgeois CANADA, 1952*

boost *noun* **1** a theft, especially a car theft *US, 1995*. **2** in poker, an increased or raised bet *US, 1988*. **3** a background player in a large confidence swindle *US, 1985*. **4** crack cocaine *UK, 2003*. ▶ **on the boost** engaged in shoplifting *US, 1962*

boost *verb* **1** to steal, especially (in the US) to steal a car or to shoplift *US, 1928*. **2** to illegally open a lock using force, skill or technology. From the sense 'to steal' *UK, 2001*. **3** in poker, to increase the amount bet on a hand *US, 1967*. **4** to inject a drug intravenously *US, 1998*. ▶ **boost one** to defecate *US, 1992*

booster *noun* **1** a thief, especially a shoplifter or car thief *US, 1908*. **2** a full-time, career thief *US, 1977*. **3** a criminal who specialises in selling stolen goods *US, 1985*. **4** a confederate of a cheat who lures players to a card game, carnival concession or other game of chance *US, 1906*. **5** an additional dose of a drug taken to prolong intoxication *US, 1970*

booster fold *noun* a special inside jacket pocket used by shoplifters *US, 1972*

booster pill *noun* a central nervous system stimulant *US, 1971*

booster stick *noun* a tobacco cigarette that has been enhanced with marijuana or marijuana extract *US, 1973*

boosting ben *noun* a special overcoat used by shoplifters *US, 1950*

boosting bloomers; booster bloomers *noun* underwear designed for concealing merchandise that has been shoplifted *US, 1972*

boot *noun* **1** dismissal from employment or other engagement. The image of being kicked away *UK, 1881*. **2** a black person *US, 1954*. **3** a newly enlisted or drafted recruit in the armed services, especially the marines *US, 1911*. **4** in the US Army, a second lieutenant *US, 1966*. **5** amusement or pleasure *US, 1979*. **6** a bootleg product *US, 1999*. **7** while injecting a drug intravenously, the drawing of blood into the syringe to mix with the drug *US, 1987*. **8** any central nervous system depressant *US, 1992*. **9** a bag of heroin *UK, 1996*. **10** a cigarette *US, 1996*. **11** a woman, especially an unattractive woman *UK, 1983*. **12** an error, especially in sports *US, 1913*. **13** a cash incentive designed to improve a business deal *US, 1997*. **14** a linear amplifier for a citizens' band radio *US, 1976*. **15** a condom *US, 1966*. **16** in television and film making, a tripod cover *US, 1987* ▷*see:* OLD BOOT. ▶ **stick the boot in; put the boot in** to kick a prostrate foe; hence, figurative usage 'to kick someone when they're down'; (political and commercial) to take an unnecessary advantage, to betray someone. In widespread usage since mid-C20; the figurative sense has been known from the mid-1960s *UK, 1916*. ▶ **the boot is on the other foot; the boot is on the other leg** the balance of power or responsibility has shifted to the opposing party *UK, 1866*

boot *verb* **1** while injecting a drug, to draw blood into the syringe, diluting the drug dose so as to prolong the effect of the injection *US, 1952*. **2** to kick something, literally or in the slang sense of 'breaking a habit' *US, 1877*. **3** to dismiss someone from employment *UK, 1988*. **4** to walk; to patrol on foot. Vietnam war usage *US, 1905*. **5** in horse racing, to spur or kick a horse during a race *US, 1951*. **6** in a game, to misplay a ball *US, 1976*. **7** to vomit *US, 1971*. **8** in Alberta, to purchase alcohol or tobacco illegally for a minor *CANADA, 2001*. ▶ **boot and rally** to continue drinking after vomiting *US, 1989*. ▶ **boot the gong** to smoke marijuana. A play on KICK THE GONG where GONG is 'opium' *UK, 1998*

bootalize *verb* to have sex *BAHAMAS, 1982*

boot-and-shoe *adjective* (used of a drug addict) desperately addicted *US, 1936*

bootboy *noun* a member of the youth fashion and gang movement that was synonymous with and then succeeded the skinheads. Characterised by heavy lace-up boots (Doc Martens), tidy hair and smart utilitarian wear; as a group, boot boys are associated with aggressive behaviour, especially football hooliganism *UK, 1972*

booted *adjective* intoxicated by marijuana, or another narcotic drug *US, 1995*

booter *noun* a jockey with an inclination to spur his mount incessantly *US*, *1959*

booth *noun* a room, especially a bedroom *UK*, *2002*

booth bimbo; booth bunny *noun* an attractive, well-built, sometimes scantily clad woman hired to work in a company's booth during a trade show *US*, *1989*

booties *noun* **1** rubber surf boots *US*, *1987*. **2** in electric line work, meter clip insulators *US*, *1980*. **3** boots, especially knitted boots for a baby *US*, *1965*

boot it!; boot it baby! used as an exhortation to continue *US*, *1968*

bootlace *noun* ▶ **not be someone's bootlace** to not come close to equalling another's achievements *AUSTRALIA*, *1959*

bootleg *noun* **1** a pirated and illegally marketed recording. In the 1960s and 70s only dedicated music fans were really aware of such product. The bootlegs of Bob Dylan's music easily outnumbered his official releases so, in 1991, his record company began to release 'The Bootleg Series'. As ever, other artists followed where Dylan led. Alas many use it as an excuse to release material that may otherwise not be of sufficient quality. 'Bootleg' has always implied a lesser quality of recording, now it's official *UK*, *1951*. **2** illegally manufactured alcohol *US*, *1898*

bootleg *verb* **1** to manufacture or provide something illegally *US*, *1928*. **2** to manufacture or distribute illegal alcohol *US*, *1922*. **3** in roller derby, to deviate from the scripted game plan *US*, *1999*

bootleg *adjective* **1** smuggled; illegally copied; unofficial; counterfeit. Derives from the practice of carrying a flat bottle of alcohol hidden in a boot leg *US*, *1889*. **2** imitation *US*, *1893*. **3** inferior, shoddy *US*, *2002*. **4** (used of an action paper) unofficial, advance *US*, *1986*

bootlegger *noun* a manufacturer or a dealer in illegally manufactured alcohol *US*, *1890*

bootlegger turn *noun* a 180-degree turn executed while driving fast accomplished by a combination of spinning the wheel, shifting down the gears and accelerating *US*, *1955*

bootleg tool *noun* a tool that is used by workers despite the fact that it has not been approved by tooling inspectors *US*, *1955*

bootlick *verb* to seek favour through obsequious behaviour *US*, *1845*

bootlicker *noun* a person who seeks favour through obsequious behaviour *US*, *1848*

boot mooch *noun* a person who is always asking others for a cigarette *US*, *1996*

bootneck; bootie *noun* a Royal Marine *UK*, *1925*

boot party *noun* a senseless beating, initiated for the sheer joy of the beating *CANADA*, *2002*

boot pie *noun* a series of kicks delivered in a scuffle *UK*, *1983*

boot rest *noun* an accelerator pedal *US*, *1976*

boots *noun* a tyre *US*, *1948*. ▶ **put the boots to 1** to have sex with someone *US*, *1933*. **2** to kick someone, especially when they are on the ground *US*, *1894*

-boots *suffix* a person, when combined with a trait. Found in terms such as BOSSY-BOOTS, 'lazy-boots', SLY-BOOTS and 'smooth-boots' *UK*, *1599*

boots and all *adverb* enthusiastically, in a totally committed way *AUSTRALIA*, *1953*

boots and socks *noun* syphilis; hence any sexually transmitted infection. Rhyming slang for POX *UK*, *2003*

boot scoot *verb* to dance side-by-side in a line to country and western music *US*, *1991*

bootstraps *noun* ▶ **pull yourself up by your bootstraps; raise yourself by your own bootstraps** to try harder, to improve yourself within a given area *UK*, *1936*

boot suppository *noun* any strong measure taken to encourage an obnoxious patient to leave a hospital. An image based on a 'kick in the ass' *US*, *1994*

bootsy *noun* in a small hotel, a boots (the servant who was employed to clean guest shoes) also working as a porter. In 1957, *The Army Game*, a television situation comedy, introduced a

character called Bootsy; this workshy character, played by Alfie Bass (1921–87), proved so popular that *Bootsy and Snudge*, a spin-off, was aired. The elaboration of conventional 'boots' was not a great leap *UK*, *1966*

bootsy *adjective* bad, unpleasant *US*, *2003*

boot up *verb* to prepare for a fight *US*, *1998*

booty *adjective* unpleasant; unattractive *US*, *1997*

booty; bootie *noun* **1** the buttocks *US*, *1928*. **2** the vagina *US*, *1925*

booty bandit *noun* an aggressive, predatory male homosexual *US*, *1962*

booty bump *verb* to ingest drugs, usually methamphetamine, diluted in an enema *US*, *2002*

booty call *noun* a date made for the sole purpose of engaging in sex *US*, *1997*

booty cheddar *noun* nonsense *US*, *2003*

booty-dance *verb* to shake the buttocks *US*, *2003*

booty drought *noun* a sustained lack of sex *US*, *1989*

booty juice *noun* the drug MDMA, the recreational drug best known as ecstasy, dissolved in any liquid *US*, *1997*

bootylicious *adjective* sexually attractive, especially with reference to the buttocks. A compound of BOOTY (the buttocks) and 'delicious' *US*, *2001*

boo-yah!; booyaka!; boo-yakka! used for registering delight. Echoic of gun use. West Indian and UK black *UK*, *1994*

booyakasha!; boyakasha! used for registering delight. An elaboration of BOO-YAKKA!; similarly echoic of gun use. Popularised in the UK in the late 1990s by Ali G (comedian Sacha Baron-Cohen) *UK*, *2001*

boo-yakka *verb* to shoot. Onomatopoeic *UK*, *1994*

booze *noun* **1** alcoholic drink of any kind. In Australia generally referring to beer *UK*, *1859*. **2** a drinking-bout; drinking *UK*, *1864*. ▶ **on the booze** engaged in a period of hard drinking *NEW ZEALAND*, *1850*

booze *verb* to drink alcohol, especially immoderately *UK*, *1325*

booze artist *noun* a habitual drinker; an alcoholic *AUSTRALIA*, *1940*

booze bag *noun* a blood alcohol measuring device of the early-type that required a suspected drinker to blow into a bag *UK*, *1969*

booze balloon *noun* a heavy drinker's protruding stomach *US*, *1979*

booze belly *noun* the protruding stomach of a drunkard *US*, *1970*

booze cruise *noun* **1** a return Channel-crossing from England to France for the purpose of buying and importing cheaper (less heavily taxed) alcohol *US*, *1979*. **2** in Scotland, a pleasure cruise on the Clyde, or on a loch or canal, during which the main pleasure and purpose is heavy drinking *UK: SCOTLAND*, *1996*. **3** a drive while drinking *US*, *1992*

boozed; boozed up *adjective* drunk. First recorded by amateur slang lexicographer Benjamin Franklin in 1737; obsolete, perhaps, but not forgotten *US*, *1737*

boozehound *noun* an alcoholic *US*, *1911*

boozer *noun* **1** a drinker of alcohol; a habitual drinker; an alcoholic *UK*, *1606*. **2** a place where alcohol is served; a public house or bar *UK*, *1895*

boozeroo *noun* **1** a drinking spree or party *NEW ZEALAND*, *1908*. **2** a pub *NEW ZEALAND*, *1963*

booze-rooster *noun* a heavy drinker *US*, *1962*

booze snooze *noun* a nap taken in anticipation of a night of drinking *US*, *2004*

booze-up *noun* a drinking bout *UK*, *1947*

boozle *noun* sexual intercourse *UK*, *1960*

boozorium *noun* a bar-room, especially in a hotel *CANADA*, *1975*

boozy *noun* a drunkard *IRELAND*, *1977*

boozy *adjective* mildly drunk *UK*, *1536*

bop *noun* **1** a dance; any dance to popular music. Derives from bebop (a jazz genre first recorded in 1945) *UK*, *2001*. **2** a dance party

US, 1973. **3** liveliness, spirit, rhythm *US, 1997.* **4** a blow; a punch *US, 1932.* **5** a member of a youth gang *US, 1958.* **6** nonsense *US, 1973.* **7** phencyclidine, the recreational drug known as PCP or angel dust *US, 1995*

bop *verb* **1** to dance to popular or rock music. Abbreviated and adapted from bebop (a jazz genre first recorded in 1945) *UK, 1978.* **2** to move with rhythm *US, 1959.* **3** to have sex with someone *US, 1974.* **4** to engage in gang fighting *US, 1950.* **5** to hit someone, to beat someone *UK, 1928.* **6** to murder someone *UK, 1999.* **7** in team gambling, to move to a card table identified by a confederate counting cards there to be primed for better-than-average odds *US, 1985.* **8** to leave. Black urban youth slang *US, 2006.* ▶ **bop the baloney** (of a male) to masturbate *US, 1983*

bo peep *noun* a look or polite search *AUSTRALIA, 1941*

Bo Peep; Little Bo Peep *noun* sleep; a sleep. Rhyming slang, formed from the name of a nursery rhyme character (who should have been counting sheep) *UK, 1960*

bop glasses *noun* horn-rimmed eye glasses. From the style favoured by bop jazz musicians *US, 1958*

bop 'n slop *verb* to lose your inhibitions and enjoy yourself at a party *US, 1968*

bop off *verb* to leave *US, 1959*

bopper *noun* **1** a fighter, especially a gang fighter *US, 1958.* **2** a song in the style of bebop jazz *US, 1965*

boppers *noun* shoes *US, 1975*

boppy *adjective* affected gang mannerisms *US, 1967*

boracic *noun* smooth, insincere talk *UK, 1950*

boracic lint; boracic; brassic; brassick *adjective* having little or no money, penniless. Rhyming slang for **SKINT** (penniless) *UK, 1959*

Borax *noun* any low quality retail merchandise that is impressive on first glance *US, 1929*

border *noun* **1** a capsule of a noncommercial barbiturate compound *US, 1971.* **2** a woman's pubic hair. A cultivated variation of the **GARDEN** theme *UK, 2001*

border work *noun* subtle markings on the printed edge of the back of a playing card for identification of the card by a cheat *US, 1988*

bore *verb* ▶ **bore the pants off** to bore someone utterly *UK, 1954.* ▶ **bore the twat off** to bore someone utterly *UK, 1993*

bore it up *verb* to attack someone; to harangue or verbally abuse someone *AUSTRALIA, 1951*

borer *noun* a knife *UK, 2002*

boress *noun* a practical joke *US, 1958*

Boris Becker *noun* the penis. Rhyming slang for **PECKER**, formed from the name of the German tennis player (b.1967) *UK, 2003*

born-again *noun* a devout, conservative Christian who professes to have been born again in a religious sense. Often uttered without sympathy *US, 1986*

born-again *adjective* used derisively to describe anyone who expediently and enthusiastically adopts, or is re-associated with, an earlier belief or stance. A satirical adoption of a fundamental Christian tenet *US, 1977*

born in a trunk *adjective* born into a family in show business *US, 1981*

Boro *noun* a Marlboro™ cigarette *US, 1996*

boro-boros *noun* old clothes worn for dirty tasks. Hawaiian youth usage *US, 1981*

borrow *noun* an act of borrowing. Especially in the phrase 'can I have a borrow?' *UK, 1999.* ▶ **on the borrow** on the scrounge, cadging *UK, 1937*

borrow *verb* **1** to steal *US, 1821.* **2** to arrest someone. Metropolitan Police slang; a narrow sense of conventional 'borrow' (to take temporary possession) *UK, 1970*

Borrowers *noun* ▶ **the Borrowers** the UK armed forces. This nickname, used by the US armed forces of their UK allies, mocks the paucity of basic supplies such as toilet paper that force the UK troops to beg from their American neighbours. Probably

influenced by *The Borrowers*, Mary Norton, 1952, and the 1998 Hollywood film version *US, 2003*

borrow pit; barrow; bar pit *noun* in rural western Canada, the pit from which earth is being removed for construction purposes *CANADA, 1987*

borsch! used for expressing disgust *US, 1968*

Borscht Belt *noun* a group of resort hotels in the Catskill Mountains of the eastern US with a primarily Jewish clientele. Alluding to the cold beet soup 'borscht' because of the eastern European heritage of many of the Jewish guests *US, 1941*

Borscht circuit *noun* the Borscht belt *US, 1936*

bory *adjective* **1** big, large. English gypsy use, from Romany *bawro UK, 2000.* **2** pregnant. English gypsy use, from the previous sense *UK, 2000*

bo selecta! used in approval of a dance music DJ's performance or technique. *Bo Selecta!* was used as the title of a Channel 4 television comedy programme first broadcast in 2002 *UK, 1999*

bosh *noun* nonsense *UK, 1834*

bosh *verb* **1** to swallow drugs, especially in tablet-form; to inhale drug-smoke *UK, 1996.* **2** to put an end to something. An extension of 'put the **KIBOSH** to' *US, 1997*

bosh *adjective* performed quickly and without great thought *UK, 2000*

bosh! used for registering a humorous victory or triumphant action. Echoic of a comedy sound effect *UK, 1998*

bosker *adjective* splendid *AUSTRALIA, 1904*

boso *noun* used as a term of address to a male whom the speaker deems socially superior *FIJI, 1993*

boson *noun* in computing, an imaginary concept, the smallest possible unit measuring the bogus content of something *US, 1997*

boss *noun* **1** used as an informal address or reference to the officer in command *UK, 1987.* **2** the commanding officer *AUSTRALIA, 1988.* **3** a marine drill instructor *US, 1991.* **4** a prison guard or official *US, 1970.* **5** the owner or man in charge of a large rural property *AUSTRALIA, 1902.* **6** the best *US, 1878.* **7** in poker, the best hand at a given moment *US, 1990.* **8** pure heroin *US, 1961.* **9** the penis. Either a male coinage or heavily ironic *US, 2001.* **10** in carnival usage, a person whom thieves use to estimate the value of articles that they have stolen *US, 1981.* ▶ **the boss** your wife. Jocular, probably *AUSTRALIA, 1984*

Boss *noun* ▶ **the Boss** songwriter and musician Bruce Springsteen (b.1949) *US, 1980*

boss *adjective* very good, excellent. The word was around for 70 years before taking off; it was popular beyond description in 1965 and 1966 *US, 1873*

boss used as a sentence-ending intensifier *SINGAPORE, 2002*

boss Charley *noun* a white person or white people collectively *US, 1967*

boss cocky *noun* **1** an owner of a rural property who employs labour *AUSTRALIA, 1879.* **2** a self-important person in authority; one who lords it over others *AUSTRALIA, 1902*

boss-eyed *adjective* **1** having only one eye; having only one good eye; having a squint, cross-eyed *UK, 1860.* **2** lopsided, skewed; wrong *UK, 1898*

boss game *noun* a highly developed, status-conscious sense of style *US, 1975*

boss (her) *verb* in trucking, to back a tractor and trailer into position *US, 1971*

boss hoss *noun* an admired, popular man *US, 1968*

bossin' *adjective* excellent. Youth slang *UK, 2000*

bossman *noun* a male leader. Elaboration of **BOSS** *US, 1934*

Bosstown *nickname* Boston, Massachusetts. The nickname and the presumed rock and roll genre of the 'Bosstown Sound' were largely the artificial engineerings of a record company executive trying to convince the record-buying world that groups such as Ultimate Spinach, Bagatelle, Beacon Street Union and Earth Opera were worth their record-buying dollars *US, 1982*

bossy-boots *noun* a domineering person *UK, 1983*

Boston coffee *noun* **1** tea. A historical allusion to the Boston Tea Party *US, 1960*. **2** coffee with a lot of cream or milk *US, 1958*

Boston Glob *nickname* the *Boston Globe* newspaper *US, 1981*

Boston marriage *noun* an arrangement in which two women live together in an outwardly platonic relationship *US, 2001*

Boston quarter *noun* a tip of five or ten cents. A jab at the parsimony of New Englanders *US, 1942*

Boston screwdriver *noun* a hammer *US, 1969*

Boston States *noun* New England, from the Maritime Provinces perspective *CANADA, 1948*

Boston tea party *noun* a sexual fetish in which the sadist defecates or urinates on the masochist *US, 1967*

bot *noun* **1** the buttocks, the *bottom*. Also spelt 'bott' *UK, 1961*. **2** an on-line software agent that performs a specified task. Short for 'robot' *US, 1996*. **3** a habitual cadger. From the sense as 'a parasitic worm, a maggot' *AUSTRALIA, 1916*

bot *verb* to cadge something *AUSTRALIA, 1921*

-bot *suffix* used in combination with a noun or abbreviated noun to create a robotic entity or creature with mechanical characteristics. From 'robot' *US, 1978*

botanist *noun* a physician who views his patients as having plant-level intelligence *US, 1978*

Botany Bay *verb* to run away. Rhyming slang. Botany Bay was the name given to the original penal settlement in Australia *AUSTRALIA, 1945*

Botch *nickname* the Canadian Basic Officer Training Course *CANADA, 1995*

bother *noun* trouble *UK, 1834*

bother *verb* ▶ **bother your arse; bother your shirt; bother your bunnit; bother your puff** to make an effort. Glasgow slang *UK: SCOTLAND, 1985*

bother!; bother it! used for registering annoyance *UK, 1840*

botheration *noun* annoyance; nuisance. Often used as an exclamation of annoyance *UK, 1797*

bothered! used sarcastically for expressing a lack of care or interest in something that has just been spoken of *UK, 1937*

both-eye principle *noun* the careful surveillance of company operations, in a large family business *CANADA, 2002*

both ways *noun* **1** a wager that a selected horse, dog, etc will finish a race in the first three. Also heard as 'each way' *UK, 1869*. **2** a bet in craps both that the shooter will win and that the shooter will lose. In craps, gamblers can bet that the shooter will win, that he will lose, or both *US, 1950*. ▶ **go both ways** **1** to be willing to play both the active and passive role in homosexual sex *US, 1972*. **2** to be bisexual *US, 1988*

botray *noun* crack cocaine *UK, 1998*

Botties; Botanicals *nickname* the Royal Botanical Gardens in Sydney, Australia *AUSTRALIA, 1981*

bottle *noun* **1** courage, nerve, spirits. A figurative sense of the rhyming slang BOTTLE AND GLASS, (ARSE). If you lose your nerve you are said to 'lose your bottle' (to lose control of your arse), literally 'to defecate uncontrollably as a result of fear' *UK, 1958*. **2** a dose of crack cocaine, whether or not it is actually in a small bottle *US, 1992*. **3** a small container of amphetamine or methamphetamine in liquid form *US, 1980*. **4** in betting, odds of 2–1 *UK, 1991*. **5** in electric and telephone line work, any glass insulator *US, 1980*. ▶ **on the bottle** engaged as a pickpocket. From rhyming slang BOTTLE OF FIZZ for THE WHIZ and thus a direct translation from ON THE WHIZ *UK, 2003*. ▶ **the bottle, big house, or box** in twelve-step recovery programmes such as Alcoholics Anonymous, used as a description of the three options for an addict who does not recover from their addiction – a return to drinking, prison and death *US, 1998*

bottle *verb* **1** to attack someone with a bottle, especially in the face *UK, 1984*. **2** to lose your nerve, to back down. A contraction of BOTTLE OUT, a contradiction of BOTTLE (nerve). Often in the expression 'bottle it' *UK, 1999*. **3** to have anal sex, especially with a woman. From rhyming slang BOTTLE AND GLASS (ARSE) *UK, 1961*. **4** of a

man, to have sex with a woman; to impregnate a woman *UK, 1961*. **5** to lick someone's anus. Homosexual use; from rhyming slang BOTTLE AND GLASS (ARSE) *UK, 1984*. **6** to smell badly, to stink *UK, 1979*. **7** in prison, to conceal articles such as drugs or money in the rectum. From rhyming slang BOTTLE AND GLASS (ARSE) *UK, 1996*

bottle and glass *noun* **1** quality; elegant behaviour. Rhyming slang for CLASS, usually as a negative *UK, 1959*. **2** the backside; the anus. Can be shortened to 'bottle'. Rhyming slang for ARSE. This rhyme extends to APRIL IN PARIS *UK, 1930*

bottle and a half *noun* in betting, odds of 5–2. In bookmaker slang BOTTLE is 2–1, here the addition of a half increases the odds to 2½-1 or 5–2. *UK, 1991*

bottle and stopper *noun* a police officer. Rhyming slang for COPPER. Sometimes shortened to 'bottle' *US, 1928*

bottle baby *noun* an alcoholic *US, 1925*

bottle blonde *noun* a person whose blonde hair is the result of bleach, not nature *US, 1972*

bottle-cap colonel *noun* a lieutenant colonel in the US Army. Vietnam war usage. From the insignia *US, 1986*

bottle club *noun* a business disguised as a club in an attempt to circumvent alcohol laws *US, 1951*

bottle dealer *noun* a drug dealer who sells pills in large quantities *US, 1971*

bottle-fed *adjective* said of a car engine that is being tested with petrol fed from a bottle through a rubber hose *US, 1992*

bottle man *noun* a drunkard *US, 1944*

bottle merchant; bottler *noun* a coward, someone who loses nerve. From BOTTLE (nerve) and BOTTLE OUT (to lose your nerve) *UK, 2000*

bottleneck *noun* **1** a style of guitar playing in which a smooth piece of metal or glass is moved smoothly up and down the fretboard creating a glissando effect. The original device was, in fact, the neck of a bottle worn over the finger *US, 1973*. **2** a marijuana pipe made from the neck of a beer or soft drink bottle *SOUTH AFRICA, 2004*

bottle of beer *noun* the ear. Rhyming slang, always used in full *UK, 1961*

bottle of fizz *verb* to work as a pickpocket; to steal something quickly as an opportunity arises. Rhyming slang for THE WHIZZ (pickpocketing) *UK, 1938*

bottle of scent *noun* a male homosexual. Rhyming slang for BENT *UK, 2003*

bottle of water *noun* a daughter. Rhyming slang *UK, 1961*

bottle-oh *noun* a person who collects and sells used bottles *AUSTRALIA, 1898*

bottle out *verb* to lose your nerve. From BOTTLE (nerve), a contraction of 'bottle fallen out' *UK, 1979*

bottler *noun* **1** a man who takes the active role in anal sex. Extended from the verb BOTTLE. (to have anal sex) *UK, 1961*. **2** someone or something that is excellent. Origin unknown *AUSTRALIA, 1855*. **3** a collector of money for a street-entertainer. Used by showmen and buskers *UK, 1935* ▷*see:* BOTTLE MERCHANT

bottler; bottling *adjective* superlatively good, excellent *AUSTRALIA, 1959*

bottletop *noun* something gained; a thing of some value. Rhyming slang on COP (to obtain) but used as a noun; sometimes abbreviated to 'bottle' *UK, 1974*

bottle top *verb* to catch, gain or understand something. Rhyming slang on various senses of the verb COP. Sometimes heard as an abbreviated 'bottle' *UK, 1974*

bottle to the field *noun* in racing, bookmaker's odds of 2–1 *UK, 1967*

bottle up *verb* to repress or contain your feelings *UK, 1853*

bottle up and go *verb* to leave *US, 1947*

bottley *adjective* nervous. From BOTTLE (courage, nerve, spirits) *UK, 2000*

bottom *noun* **1** the buttocks. A colloquial usage, delightfully defined in the *Oxford English Dictionary* as follows: 'The sitting part of a man, the posteriors, the seat' *UK, 1699*. **2** the submissive partner in a homosexual or sado-masochistic relationship *US, 1961*

Bottom *nickname* Miami, Florida *US, 1991*

bottom bitch *noun* the pimp's favourite of the prostitutes working for him; the leader of the prostitutes *US, 1967*

bottom burp; botty burp; burp; botty banger *noun* a fart *UK, 1984*

bottom dollar *noun* your last dollar. Heard in the context of betting your 'bottom dollar' *US, 1954*

bottom end *noun* in drag racing, the portion of the track just after the starting line *US, 1960*

bottom feeder *noun* **1** a despised person of low-status who grasps any opportunity or means of survival. An allusion to the underwater lifestyle of certain fish *US, 1980*. **2** in poker, a low-betting player who tries to eke out meagre winnings against unskilled players *US, 1996*

bottom fisher *noun* a stock investor looking for stocks with a poor recent showing *US, 1988*

bottom girl *noun* the pimp's favourite of the prostitutes working for him; the leader of the prostitutes *US, 1973*

bottom line *noun* the final analysis *US, 1967*

bottom man *noun* the passive partner in a homosexual relationship *US, 1972*

bottoms *noun* **1** dice that have been marked to have two identical faces *US, 1962*. **2** the worst *US, 1955*

bottom's up *noun* a common position for anal and/or vaginal sex, in which the passive partner lies on their stomach *US, 1960*

bottoms up! used as a toast. From drinking by upturning a glass or a bottle *UK, 1917*

bottom weight a minimum amount *UK, 1962*

bottom woman *noun* the pimp's favourite of the prostitutes working for him; the leader of the prostitutes *US, 1969*

Botts' dots *noun* small bumps delineating lanes on motorways *US, 1971*

botty; bottie *noun* the human bottom. Originally of a baby's or child's posterior; now less specific but usage is generally childish *UK, 1874*

botzelbaum pie *noun* an upside-down pie. Used in Mennonite Waterloo County, Ontario *CANADA, 2001*

boubou *noun* crack cocaine. A possible play on BEBE, BOULYA or BOULDER (crack cocaine) *UK, 1998*

boucher *noun* in Franco-Ontario, a fiddle player. *Boucher* is French for 'butcher', and is applied to fiddle playing from the fact that the player 'saws and saws' to make music *CANADA, 1969*

boudoir *noun* an army tent *US, 1945*

bougie; bouji *adjective* bourgeois *US, 1975*

boulder; boulders *noun* crack cocaine; a piece of crack cocaine. Built on the ROCK metaphor *US, 1998*

boulder baby *noun* a crack cocaine addict. From the ROCK metaphor *US, 2002*

boulder-holder; over-the-shoulder boulder-holder *noun* a brassiere *UK, 1970*

boulevard *noun* **1** a long, straight hallway *US, 1965*. **2** in trucking, a major motorway *US, 1986*

boulevard boy *noun* a young male prostitute in an urban setting *US, 1987*

boulya *noun* crack cocaine. A possible play on BOULDER (crack cocaine) *UK, 1998*

bounce *noun* **1** a brainstorming session *US, 1984*. **2** a jail or prison sentence *US, 1957*. **3** an air-to-air attack *US, 1943*. **4** in horse racing, a poorly run race followed by a well-run race *US, 1997*. ▶ **on the bounce** consecutively, one after the other *UK, 2001*. ▶ **the bounce** bouncers, door-security, collectively *UK, 2005*

bounce *verb* **1** to maintain order in a bar or nightclub, ejecting people from the premises if necessary *US, 1874*. **2** (of a cheque) to be returned as worthless by the bank with which it has been drawn *US, 1936*. **3** to leave *US, 1996*. **4** (used of a message sent electronically) to return to the sender, undeliverable as addressed

US, 1991. **5** to pay; to provide without charge *US, 1970*. **6** to activate a car's suspension system so as to cause the car to bounce up and down *US, 1980*

bounce back *noun* the return of an overdraft *US, 1949*

bounce back *verb* to recover or return from a setback *UK, 1950*

bouncer *noun* **1** a person, usually a strong man, employed to maintain and restore order in a bar, restaurant, club or performance. In the UK, 'bouncers' collectively are THE BOUNCE. *US, 1883*. **2** the female breast. Obvious imagery and, equally obvious, usually in the plural *UK, 1972*. **3** a brakevan (caboose) *US, 1946*

bounce shot *noun* in a dice game, a type of controlled shot by a skilled cheat *US, 1950*

bouncing Betty *noun* a land-mine first used in World War 2, prevalent in Vietnam, that bounces waist-high and then sprays shrapnel when triggered *US, 1943*

bouncing powder *noun* cocaine *US, 1971*

bouncy-bouncy *noun* sexual intercourse *US, 1960*

bounder *noun* someone whose manners or company are unacceptable; hence a vulgar and unwelcome pretender to polite society; a nuisance. Survives in ironic usage, often applied to inanimate objects *UK, 1889*

boungy; bungy *noun* the anus *BAHAMAS, 1982*

bounty *noun* a black person who sides with the white authorities. Derives from 'Bounty', a chocolate and coconut confection that is brown on the outside and white on the inside *UK, 1996*

Bounty bar *noun* an Indian person who is considered to have exchanged heritage and community values for acceptance by white society. After the chocolate coated coconut branded confectionery. British Indian (Hindi) urban slang. *UK, 2006*

bouquet straight *noun* in poker, a sequenced hand comprised of all red or all black suits, but not a flush. It looks impressive, but is worth no more than any non-flush straight *US, 1996*

bourbon bibber *noun* an oil worker from Kentucky *US, 1954*

Bourke shower *noun* a dust storm. Bourke is an inland town in New South Wales. Other locations similarly used by nature, weather and irony: Bedourie, Bogan, Cobar, Darling, Wilcannia and Wimmera *AUSTRALIA, 1945*

Bournville Boulevard *noun* the anus, the rectum. Cadbury's chocolate is made in Bournville, in Birmingham; a UK version of HERSHEY HIGHWAY *UK, 1997*

Boutros Boutros Ghali; boutros *noun* cocaine. Rhyming slang for CHARLIE (cocaine), formed on the name of the Secretary General of the United Nations, 1992–1996 *UK, 2003*

bovina *noun* in homosexual usage, a woman, especially one with large breasts *US, 1980*

bovver *noun* trouble, fighting, violent behaviour, especially when associated with skinhead culture. From a London pronunciation of 'bother' *UK, 1969*

bovver boot *noun* a heavy-duty boot used as a kicking-weapon, stereotypically worn by a skinhead *UK, 1969*

bovver boy *noun* a member of a hooligan gang, generally characterised as a skinhead, and therefore associated with extreme right-wing, racist violence. Extended from BOVVER (trouble) and very rarely seen in the singular *UK, 1970*

bow *noun* the elbow. Elbows used to establish position are a key part of the anatomy in basketball *US, 1980*. ▶ **on the bow** gratis; scrounging. From an earlier, related sense (without paying) *UK, 1938*

bow *verb* to perform an act of oral sex. From the conventional sense (bending at the waist) *JAMAICA, 1995*

bow and arrow *noun* **1** a native American Indian; Indian ancestry *US, 1930*. **2** a sparrow. Cockney rhyming slang *UK, 1931*

bow-and-arrow *adjective* not armed with a pistol *US, 1984*

bow and quiver *noun* the liver, especially in contexts of irritability or liverishness. Rhyming slang *UK, 1961*

bow-cat *noun* a man who fellates. A combination of BOW (oral sex) and CAT (a man) *JAMAICA, 1995*

bower bird *noun* an avid collector of many and various things. From the mating habit of certain male bower birds which collect coloured items to make a display for females *AUSTRALIA, 1926*

bowl *noun* **1** a pipe for smoking marijuana, hashish or crack cocaine *US, 1974.* **2** an approximate measure of marijuana, between one thirtysecond and one sixteenth of an ounce. The amount needed to fill a pipe *US, 1972.* **3** in cricket, a period of bowling *UK, 1961*

bowl basher *noun* the active male in anal sex *AUSTRALIA, 1985*

bowl brandy *noun* faeces, excrement *UK, 2002*

bowlegged *adjective* (of prison sentences) concurrent *US, 1990*

bowler *noun* an ugly girl. Uncertain origin, possibly from 'bow', abbreviated from BOW-WOW, with the suffix -ER *IRELAND, 2003*

bowling green *noun* a fast stretch of railway line *UK, 1970*

bowl it around *verb* to strut and posture in an unsubtly masculine way. Teen slang *UK, 2003*

bowlodrome *noun* a bowling alley *US, 1953*

bowlster *noun* a bowler *US, 1953*

bows *noun* ▶ **take bows** to falsely take credit for something *US, 1997*

bowser *noun* **1** a dog *US, 1965.* **2** by extension, an ugly person *US, 1978.* **3** a petrol pump *AUSTRALIA, 1918*

bowser bag *noun* a container used by restaurants to package unfinished meals to be taken home by diners. A variation on the more common DOGGY BAG *US, 1965*

bowsie *noun* a disreputable drunkard, a lout, a quarrelsome drunkard *IRELAND, 1990*

bowsprit *noun* an erect penis. It does not take much imagination to see the comparison *UK, 1741*

bow tie *noun* **1** a married woman's lover *NEW ZEALAND, 1948.* **2** a Chevrolet car *US, 1993*

bow-wow *noun* a 'dog', literally and in its slang senses *US, 1935*

box *noun* **1** the vagina; a woman *UK, 1605.* **2** the posterior, the buttocks. Originally black, then gay usage *US, 1965.* **3** a jail or prison. Usually heard as 'the box' *US, 1995.* **4** a secure prison cubicle for a one-to-one visit *UK, 1978.* **5** a cell used for solitary confinement *US, 1976.* **6** a safe *US, 1902.* **7** in a court of law, the witness box *AUSTRALIA, 1973.* **8** approximately 20 one-kilogram plates of pressed hashish *CANADA, 2002.* **9** a small amount of marijuana, approximately enough to fill a matchbox *US, 1967.* **10** a guitar. May also refer to a banjo *US, 1911.* **11** a piano *US, 1908.* **12** a record player *UK, 1924.* **13** a large, portable radio and tape player. A shortened GHETTO BOX *US, 1985.* **14** television. Usually after 'the' *US, 1950.* **15** a polygraph machine *US, 1997.* **16** an old and inferior car *US, 1973.* **17** a new car showroom *US, 1989.* **18** a coffin *UK, 1864.* **19** in bar dice games, a leather or vinyl cup used to shake dice before spilling them out *US, 1976.* **20** in horse racing, a combination bet that covers many different possible outcomes *US, 2001.* **21** in horse racing, a horse stall *AUSTRALIA, 1989.* **22** a pool table, especially a large one *US, 1990.* **23** in the sport of fencing, an electric recording apparatus *UK, 1988.* **24** a reinforced item of underwear designed to protect a sportsman's genitals *UK, 1961.* **25** a person who is profoundly out of touch with current trends. A three-dimensional SQUARE *US, 1976.* **26** in the Royal Air Force, an aircraft cockpit simulator *UK, 1984.* **27** in the Vietnam war, an aerial target zone approximately 5/8 of a mile wide by 2 miles long *US, 1988.* **28** a submarine's main battery *UK, 1979.* ▶ **in the box 1** engaged in vaginal sex *US, 1972.* **2** dealing drugs *US, 1997.* ▶ **off your box; out of your box 1** drunk or drug-intoxicated *UK, 1981.* **2** mentally disturbed; behaving erratically. Perhaps an allusion to the Greek myth of Pandora's box and the evils it contained *UK, 2000.* ▶ **out of the box** in motor racing, exactly as produced by the manufacturer, without any modifications *US, 1993.* ▶ **put someone in the box** to kill someone *US, 2000.* ▶ **take a box** to defecate *IRELAND, 1995.* ▶ **take someone out of the box** to kill someone *US, 1995*

box *verb* **1** to confirm the death of a hospital patient *US, 1977.* **2** to die *US, 1994.* **3** in an illegal lottery, to bet on a group of related numbers rather than a single number *US, 1974.* **4** to make a mistake; to muddle things. Originally referred to mixing flocks of sheep *AUSTRALIA, 1873.* ▶ **box clever** to use your wits; to behave shrewdly *UK, 1936.* ▶ **box the fox** to steal apples. Origin obscure *IRELAND,*

1976. ▶ **couldn't box chocolates; couldn't box kippers** to be a poor quality boxer. Punning on conventional senses of 'box' *UK, 1936.*

Box 100 *noun* the notional repository for information given to police by informants *US, 1979*

box bag *noun* the amount of marijuana (the bag) which can be bought for a carton of cigarettes (the box) *US, 1992*

box boy *noun* a DJ's assistant who has the responsibility for the DJ's boxes of records *UK, 2001*

boxcar *noun* **1** any four-engine bomber *US, 1946.* **2** a prison cell *US, 1982.* **3** an amphetamine or central nervous system stimulant *US, 1992*

boxcar numbers *noun* a lot of money *US, 1950*

boxcars *noun* **1** in horse racing, high odds. From the high numbers used to identify railway carriages *US, 1934.* **2** in a game of dice, a roll of two sixes *US, 1949.* **3** in poker, a pair of sixes or three sixes. A borrowing from the game of craps *US, 1988.* **4** any large number; a long prison sentence *US, 1950*

boxcar tourist *noun* a hobo travelling by freight train *US, 1946*

boxed *adjective* **1** marijuana-intoxicated *US, 1958.* **2** muscular, well-toned *US, 1997.* **3** incarcerated *US, 1970*

boxer *noun* **1** an urban youth with a large and loud portable radio and tape player *UK, 1983.* **2** a person running a game of two-up *AUSTRALIA, 1911.* **3** a railway boxcar *US, 1977*

boxes *noun* in craps, a roll of two fours *US, 1983*

Box Five; Box Six; Box *nickname* the UK secret intelligence services *UK, 2002*

boxfresh *adjective* of shoes, especially trainers, unworn *UK, 2003*

boxie *noun* a person with bleached blond hair *US, 1987*

boxies *noun* men's boxer shorts, *2001*

boxing glove *noun* a condom. Playing on BOX (the vagina; the male genitals; sexual intercourse), with GLOVE (a condom) *UK, 1998*

boxing Josh *noun* masturbation *BAHAMAS, 1982*

box-it *noun* a mixture of cheap wine and cider *UK, 1982*

box-kicker *noun* a supply clerk in the US Marines *US, 1998*

boxla *noun* box lacrosse. Lacrosse, an Indian game, was played practically without side boundaries and with goals as much as a half mile apart. Box lacrosse introduced side boards and a playing surface the size of a hockey rink *CANADA, 1958*

box lunch; box lunch at the Y *noun* oral sex on a woman. The character Y resembles a woman's groin; plays on BOX (the vagina) *US, 1964*

box man *noun* a criminal who specialises in breaking into safes *US, 1902*

box of birds; box of ducks *noun* a state of great contentment *NEW ZEALAND, 1943*

box of fruit; bowl of fruit *noun* a suit. Rhyming slang *NEW ZEALAND, 1963*

box of L *noun* a box of 100 ampoules containing methamphetamine hydrochloride (trade name Methedrine™), a central nervous system stimulant *US, 1973*

box of sharks *noun* used for expressing great surprise, in phrases such as: 'she nearly gave birth to a box of sharks' *CANADA, 1984*

box of tricks; bag of tricks *noun* a tool box, or any similar receptacle; a notional repertoire of tools and skills needed for any purpose *UK, 1953*

box-on *noun* a fight, a struggle *AUSTRALIA, 1919*

box on *verb* to continue fighting; to persevere with anything important or strenuous *AUSTRALIA, 1919*

box on wheels *noun* a hearse *US, 1976*

box screw *noun* a bank guard *US, 1949*

box seat *noun* the most advantageous area off a beach for a surfer to catch a wave *AUSTRALIA, 1965*

box shot *noun* in a dice game in which the dice are rolled from a cup, a controlled shot *US, 1950*

box slugger *noun* a criminal specialising in breaking into safes *US,
1970*

box someone's ears *verb* to hit someone round the head *UK, 1601*

box tool *noun* any tool used for breaking into a safe *US, 1972*

box-up *noun* a mix-up, a confusion. Also used a verb and, as 'boxed-
up', an adjective *AUSTRALIA, 1945*

boy *noun* **1** heroin *US, 1953*. **2** the penis *IRELAND, 1992*. **3** a male friend.
Connotes affection and loyalty *US, 1997*. **4** a homosexual male
prostitute *US, 1971*. **5** a lesbian *US, 1997*. **6** a boxer or wrestler *US, 1977*.
7 in a deck of playing cards, a jack or knave *US, 1967*. **8** in horse
racing, a jockey *US, 1951*. **9** a dollar; money *UK, 1780*

boy beaver *noun* the male sex organs and pubic hair *US, 1987*

boychik *noun* a boy or young man. Also variant 'boychick'. As is the
case with most diminuitives, used with affection; coined by
Yiddish speakers in America *US, 1951*

boyf *noun* a boyfriend *UK, 2003*

boy-gal *noun* a male homosexual *US, 1990*

boy-girl *noun* a young, effeminate, male homosexual *US, 1952*

boy-hole *noun* a young and passive homosexual male. Sexual
objectification *US, 1997*

boy in the boat *noun* the clitoris *US, 1916*

boykie; boytjie *noun* a boy, a youth; used as an admiring form of
address to a man. An Anglo-Afrikaans diminutive of 'boy' *SOUTH
AFRICA, 1974*

boyno hello *UK, 2002*

boyo *noun* **1** used as a good-humoured form of address to a man.
An elaboration of 'boy', stereotypically Irish or Welsh *IRELAND, 1898*.
2 a Welsh man. Somewhat patronising; after what is thought to be
a stereotypically Welsh form of address *UK, 1953*

boyo *adjective* mildly pornographic, featuring naked men *US, 1970*

boy! oh boy! used for registering shock, surprise, satisfaction, etc;
also used to emphasise or draw attention to the statement that
follows *US, 1917*

boys *noun* **1** the male genitals. From *Seinfeld* (NBC, 1990–98). Both
Seinfeld and his wacky neighbour Kramer (Michael Richards)
referred to their genitals as 'my boys'. Repeated with referential
humour *US, 1998*. **2** a group of homosexual male friends; collectively,
the male homosexual community *US, 1972*. **3** racketeers *US, 1979*.
4 used by professional wrestlers to refer to other professional
wrestlers *US, 1990*. **5** sledge dogs *ANTARCTICA, 1966*. ▶ **do the boys** to
engage in homosexual activity *US, 2002*

boys and girls *noun* heroin and cocaine, mixed and injected
together *US, 1993*

boy scout *noun* **1** a state trooper *US, 1973*. **2** a person who is
extremely, and usually distressingly, sincere *US, 1997*

boyshape *noun* a boyfriend. Teen slang *UK, 2003*

boysie *noun* used as a term of address to a boy or man *AUSTRALIA, 1929*

boys in blue *noun* the police; sailors; US Federal troops. Rarely, if
ever, occurs in the singular. Derives from the colour of the uniform; sometimes heard as 'men in blue' or 'gentlemen in blue'
UK, 1851

boys of Baghdad *noun* during the Gulf war, reporters for the Cable
News Network *US, 1991*

boys on the hill *noun* the members of New Zealand's parliament
NEW ZEALAND, 1984

Boy's Town *noun* a city neighbourhood dominated by homosexual
men. A play on Father Flanagan's Boys Home, a home for delinquent and homeless boys in Omaha, Nebraska *US, 1984*

boys' toy; big boys' toy *noun* any automotive, mechanical or electronic piece of technology designed to appeal to men, especially
an unnecessary one; a gadget *UK, 2000*

boy toy *noun* a young, attractive woman or man who is the object
of sexual desire of their elders, homosexual or heterosexual *US, 1989*

boy wonder *noun* a man not held in high esteem. An ironic usage
AUSTRALIA, 1954

bozack *noun* **1** sex. Usually heard as 'do the bozack' *US, 1989*. **2** the
penis; the entire male genitalia. Sometimes shortened to 'zack' *US,
1990*

bozo *noun* **1** a buffoon. In the US, the older sense of 'bozo' as 'a
fellow' was supplanted by the figure Bozo the Clown, who first
appeared on record in 1946 and then became a fixture on local
television programmes throughout the US beginning in 1949 *US,
1916*. **2** heroin *UK, 1998*. **3** an ounce of heroin *US, 1992*

bozotic *adjective* in computing, ridiculous *US, 1991*

BP *noun* **1** in blackjack counting teams, the player who places the
large bets based on cues from other members of the team who
have been counting cards at a particular table. An intialism for 'big
player' *US, 1991*. **2** in American casinos, a serious gambler. The
initials stand for 'big player' *US, 1985*. **3** a young prostitute. An
abbreviation of 'baby pro' *US, 1971*

BPOM *noun* in homosexual shorthand usage, a man with a large
penis, a *big piece of meat US, 1979*

BPS *noun* a wooden stick used by police for probing a corpse. New
York police slang; an abbreviation of 'brain-picking stick' *US, 1997*

BQ *noun* a male homosexual who favours anal sex. An abbrerviation
of BROWNIE QUEEN *US, 1964*

BR *noun* **1** a bankroll *US, 1915*. **2** money. From the term 'bankroll' *US,
1915*. **3** in carnival usage, any hyperbolic story. An extension of the
'bankroll' sense, the roll of money used by the operator of a rigged
game to distract and divert the attention of a player from how the
game is rigged *US, 1985*. **4** Banana Republic™, a chain of shops
selling casual clothing *US, 1997*

bra *noun* used for addressing a friend. Phonetic abbreviation of
BROTHER (a fellow) *UK, 1968*

brace *verb* to apprehend someone; to arrest someone; to accost
someone *US, 1889*

brace and bit; brace *noun* **1** the equipment needed to prepare and
inject a drug. Rhyming slang, from OUTFIT *NEW ZEALAND, 1999*. **2** the
female breast. Rhyming slang for TIT; usually in the plural.
Sometimes shortened to 'brace' *US, 1928*. **3** an act of defecation.
Rhyming slang for SHIT. Sometimes shortened to 'brace' *UK, 2003*

brace face *noun* any person wearing an orthodontic brace *US, 1991*

bracelet play *noun* in poker, an exceptionally crafty play. An allusion
to the 'bracelet prize' in the World Series of Poker *US, 1996*

bracelets *noun* handcuffs *UK, 1661*

bracer *noun* any strong alcoholic drink *US, 1830*

brace-up *noun* a prison- or police-cell *UK, 1974*

brace work *noun* poorly executed markings on the back of cards by
card cheats *US, 1961*

bra chute *noun* a type of parachute malfunction *US, 1982*

bracket *noun* an unspecified part of the body. Usually as part of a
threat; 'a punch up the bracket'; probably coined by scriptwriters
Ray Galton and Alan Simpson *UK, 1984*

Bradman pills *noun* in horse racing, diuretic pills used by jockeys to
lose weight. An allusion to cricket legend Donald Bradman; if you
take enough diuretics, you will make a hundred runs before lunch
AUSTRALIA, 1989

Brad Pitt; brad *noun* an act of defecation. Rhyming slang for SHIT
formed on the name of American film-actor Brad Pitt (b.1963) *UK,
1998*

brads *noun* money *UK, 1812*

Brady *noun* a theatre seat reserved for a friend of the theatre
management. An allusion to William Brady (1863–1950), American
impresario *US, 1981*

braff *adjective* worthless *UK, 2005*

braggadocious; bragadocious *adjective* boastful *US, 1956*

brag-rag *noun* a military decoration in the form of a ribbon *US, 1960*

brah *noun* used as a term of address, young surfing male to young
surfing male. A surfer's 'brother' *US, 1981*

brahma; Brahma *noun* a pleasing thing. From Hindu mythology
Brahmâ, the creator *UK, 1977*

Brahms and Liszt; Brahms *adjective* drunk. Rhyming slang for PISSED (drunk) *UK, 1978*

braid *noun* a prison warden or other official *US, 1950*

brain *noun* **1** oral sex performed on a male. An extension of HEAD *US, 1998*. **2** a smart person *UK, 1914*. **3** a dumb person *US, 1981*. **4** the penis. Derisive usage *US, 2001*. ▶ **get something or someone on the brain** to become obsessed by something or someone *UK, 1989*. ▶ **out of your brain** drunk or drug-intoxicated *UK, 1973*

brain *verb* to hit someone on the head *US, 1938*

brain bag *noun* in trucking, anything used by a trucker to store maps, permits, and other paperwork *US, 1971*

brain bender *noun* a strenuous, rowdy party *US, 1966*

brain bleach *noun* LSD. A variation on the conventional 'brainwash' *UK, 2001*

brain-boshing *adjective* intoxicating. Extending from BOSH (to take pills) *UK, 2002*

brain box *noun* **1** the head; the mind *UK, 1823*. **2** a person of above average intelligence *UK, 2000*

brain boy *noun* in oil drilling, an engineer *US, 1954*

brain bucket *noun* a safety helmet. Coined in the US Air Force, adapted to drag racing and then to a variety of sports *US, 1955*

brain burner *noun* an intravenous injection of amphetamine or methamphetamine *US, 1992*

brain candy *noun* an insignificant entertainment or diversion as opposed to something that requires thought *US, 1981*

brain cramp *noun* a mental error *US, 1982*

brain damage *noun* heroin *UK, 1998*

brain-damaged *adjective* in computing, clearly wrong *US, 1983*

brain derby *noun* a test or examination *US, 1961*

brain donor *noun* an idiot. The image of an empty head. *UK, 1981*

brain drain *noun* **1** the large-scale migration of talented and intelligent people from and/or to somewhere. According to William Safire, probably coined in 1963 to describe the exodus of British scientists to the US *UK, 1963*. **2** forensic scientists; a forensic science department. Police term, used ironically *UK, 1971*

brain fade *noun* a momentary mental lapse *US, 1980*

brain fart; mind fart *noun* a temporary mental lapse. Probably a jocular derivation from BRAINSTORM *US, 1983*

brain freeze *noun* a searing headache experienced when eating frozen food or drinks *US, 1993*

brainfucker *noun* an idea that is difficult to comprehend *UK, 2002*

brainiac *noun* a very intelligent person *US, 1986*

brainless *adjective* **1** very drunk *UK: SCOTLAND, 1985*. **2** good, excellent *UK, 2002*

brain pill *noun* an amphetamine tablet *UK, 2003*

brain plate *noun* on the railways, a conductor's cap badge *US, 1975*

brains *noun* **1** oral sex. In the progression of HEAD to 'skull' to 'brains' *US, 2000*. **2** a railway conductor. Often after 'the' *US, 1946*

brain screw *noun* a prison psychological counsellor *US, 1951*

brainstorm *noun* a sudden, good idea *US, 1925*

brain surgeon *noun* **1** a poker player who over-analyses every situation *US, 1982*

brain surgery *noun* any difficult, demanding work. Used in contrast to the job at hand *US, 1980*

brain tickler *noun* a tablet or capsule of amphetamine *UK, 1998*

brain train *noun* a school bus *US, 1976*

brain trust *noun* a group of expert advisors. Although found at least as early as 1910, not popularised until 1933 in association with US President Franklin Roosevelt's advisors *US, 1910*

brainwash *verb* to convince someone systematically and in a manipulative manner that something they do not believe is true. Although the term was coined to describe the actions of authoritarian, Soviet-bloc regimes, probably the most famous use of 'brainwash' in the US was by George Romney, candidate for the Republican presidential nomination in 1968, who claimed that he had been brainwashed to support the US war against Vietnam *US, 1951*

brainy *adjective* intelligent, clever *UK, 1845*

brake fluid *noun* any medication used to sedate an unruly prisoner *US, 1991*

brake pads *noun* the condition that exists when a tight-fitting pair of trousers, shorts, bathing suit or other garment forms a wedge between a woman's labia, accentuating their shape. A visual image *US, 2002*

braker *noun* a railway brakeman *US, 1977*

brakie *noun* a brakeman on a freight train *US, 1887*

bram *noun* a small party with dancing *BARBADOS, 1965*

Brambladesh; Bramistan *nickname* the Brampton region of Toronto *CANADA, 2002*

brammer *adjective* excellent, outstandingly good. Derives from BRAHMA (something good) *UK, 1987*

branch *noun* a match *US, 1973*

Brancher *nickname* a member of the Special Branch of the Irish police force *IRELAND, 1997*

branch out *verb* to become fat *AUSTRALIA, 1953*

Brandon Block *noun* the penis; a fool. Rhyming slang for COCK; formed from the name of a London-born dance music DJ *UK, 2003*

brand X *noun* **1** marijuana *US, 1980*. **2** a marijuana cigarette *US, 1992*. **3** in trucking, a small and unknown trucking company *US, 1976*

brandy *noun* lubricant applied to the anus in preparation for anal sex *UK, 2002*

brandy and rum; brandy *noun* the buttocks, the posterior. Rhyming slang for BUM *UK, 1993*

brandy latch *noun* a toilet. A combination of BRANDY (AND RUM) (the posterior) and 'latch' (a lock) *UK, 2002*

brandy snap *noun* a slap. Rhyming slang *UK, 2003*

brannigan *noun* a brawl, literal or figurative *US, 1940*

brap *adjective* excellent *UK, 2005*

brap! brap!; brap! brap! brap! used for expressing pleasurable excitement *UK, 2005*

brasco *noun* a toilet. Origin unknown. *AUSTRALIA, 1955*

brass *noun* **1** in the military, high-ranking officers as a collective entity *US, 1864*. **2** money, cash *UK, 1598*. **3** in carnival usage, fake jewellery *US, 1981*. **4** brass knuckles *US, 1980* ▷*see:* BRASS NAIL, TOP BRASS

brass *verb* to rob a person of their money by deception; to con someone *AUSTRALIA, 1939*. ▶ **brass it out** to brazen it out. From the conventional use of 'brass' (effrontery or impudence) *UK, 1969*

brass *adjective* fashionable, smart *UK, 1968*

brass band *noun* **1** the hand. Rhyming slang *UK, 1952*. **2** a back-up military unit sent to help a small, outnumbered unit *US, 1991*

brass buttons *noun* a police officer; the police in general *US, 1974*

brass collar *noun* railway management *US, 1977*

brassed off; brassed *adjective* disgruntled. Originally military slang *UK, 1942*

brasser; brazzer *noun* a female of dubious sexual morals *IRELAND, 1991*

brass fart *noun* a thing of negligible value. Probably a convenient shortening of BRASS FARTHING *UK, 1996*

brass farthing *noun* a trivial sum of money, or less *UK, 1642*

brass-happy *adjective* extremely anxious to be promoted within the officer corps *US, 1946*

brass house *noun* a brothel, a whorehouse. Where a BRASS (NAIL) (a prostitute) works *UK, 2001*

brassies *noun* brass knuckles *US, 1949*

brass man *noun* a confidence trickster. From earlier 'brass' (a horse-racing confidence trick) *AUSTRALIA, 1953*

brass monkey *noun* used in a number of figures of speech, especially as a basis for comparison *US, 1857*

brass-monkey *adjective* (of weather) bitterly cold. May be of nautical origin but the popular etymology involving powder monkeys and cannon balls remains unproven. Usually as 'brass-monkeys' or 'brass-monkey weather'; from the phrase 'cold enough to freeze the balls off a brass monkey' *UK, 1857*

brass nail; brass *noun* a prostitute. Rhyming slang for TAIL (a woman sexually objectified), also punning on something you buy 'to bang' *UK, 1933*

brass razoo *noun* a small amount of money *AUSTRALIA, 1941*

brass ring *noun* an elusive but valuable prize *US, early 1950s*

brass tacks *noun* the basic facts; the basic reality. Rhyming slang for 'facts' *US, 1895*

brass up *verb* 1 to pay money *UK, 1898*. 2 to rebuke someone *BARBADOS, 1965*

brassy *adjective* (of a woman) ostentatious, cheap but flashy; prostitute-like. A variation of an earlier, obsolete sense (impudent and shameless); probably from BRASS (NAIL) (a prostitute), but note the bright appearance of polished brass, a relatively cheap metal *UK, 1937*

brat *noun* 1 a child, especially a troublesome junior; a baby. Possibly from Scottish dialect *bratchart UK, 1505*. 2 a young and/or weak man used as a passive homosexual partner, especially in prison *US, 1961*

brat pack *nickname* a group of young film actors who played roles in John Hughes films of the 1980s. Frequently mentioned as members of the group included Anthony Michael Hall, Emilio Estevez, Charlie Sheen, Judd Nelson, Molly Ringold, Rob Lowe and Ally Sheedy. A play on the Sinatra-centric Rat Pack of the 1950s and 60s *US, 1985*

bravo *noun* a soldier in the US infantry. Vietnam war coinage and usage *US, 1980*

bravo delta *noun* a nonfunctioning piece of hardware. A phonetic-alphabet euphemism for 'broke dick' *US, 1988*

brawl *noun* a rowdy party *US, 1927*

brazil *verb* to decline to pay interest on an existing loan *CANADA, 1989*

Brazilian landing strip; Brazilian *noun* the trimming of a woman's pubic hair such that only a narrow strip remains; the result thereof *US, 2001*

Brazil water *noun* coffee *US, 1949*

BRB used in computer message shorthand to mean 'be right back' *US, 1991*

brea *noun* heroin *UK, 2003*

breach *noun* ▶ **in the breach** in poker, first to act in a given situation *US, 1988*

bread *noun* 1 money. The term was used at least as early as the 1930s, but it did not gain wide acceptance until the 1960s *US, 1935*. 2 ship's biscuits *TRISTAN DA CUNHA, 1910*

bread and bread *noun* a homosexual couple; more generally, any dull combination of two similar things *UK, 1984*

bread and butter *noun* 1 a livelihood, the means of living; a basic, motivating interest *UK, 1837*. 2 used by bookmakers to describe bets by inexperienced, unskilled bettors *AUSTRALIA, 1989*. 3 a crazy person. Rhyming slang for NUTTER *UK, 1992*

bread and butter! used as a charm when two people who are walking side-by-side are momentarily separated by a person or object *US, 1939*

bread and cheese *verb* to sneeze. Rhyming slang also used as a noun *UK, 1938*

bread and jam *noun* a tram *AUSTRALIA, 1902*

bread and lard *adjective* hard *UK, 1961*

bread and point *noun* a meagre meal, mainly bread. Another surviving, related expression is 'bread and pullet' or 'pull-it' *CANADA, 1987*

breadbasket *noun* the stomach *UK, 1785*

bread box *noun* 1 the stomach. A lesser-known cousin of BREADBASKET *US, 1919*. 2 a safe that is easily broken into *US, 1949*

breaded *adjective* wealthy. Formed on BREAD [money] *UK, 2005*

breadfruit swopper *noun* a conventional if cheap person *BARBADOS, 1965*

bread hooks *noun* the fingers, the hands *CANADA, 1973*

bread knife *noun* a wife. Rhyming slang *UK, 2003*

breads *noun* money *BAHAMAS, 1982*

breadwinner *noun* the person responsible for supporting a family. Drawn from BREAD (money) *UK, 1821*

break *noun* 1 in hip-hop culture, an instrumental section from any recorded source that is mixed with other similar selections to make a new piece of music *US, 1993*. 2 a piece of luck, good unless otherwise qualified, e.g. 'bad break' *US, 1926*. 3 a break-in, or illicit entry, into a building *UK, 1959*

break *verb* 1 to escape from prison *UK, 1996*. 2 in blackjack, to exceed 21 points, losing the hand *US, 1991*. 3 to run away *US, 1993*. 4 in theatrical use, to stop work during or at the end of rehearsal, e.g. 'the cast broke for tea' *UK, 1984*. 5 of money, to change a coin or a note into coins or notes of smaller denominations *UK, 1844*. 6 to steal something *US, 2003*. 7 to do something to excess *US, 1989*. ▶ **break bad** to act in a threatening, menacing manner *US, 1997*. ▶ **break camp** to leave. Military or Western overtones *US, 1986*. ▶ **break fives** to shake hands *BARBADOS, 1965*. ▶ **break his (or her) cherry** (used of a racehorse) to win the first race in a racing career *US, 1951*. ▶ **break ill** to make a mistake, to blunder *US, 1989*. ▶ **break it big** to win a great deal of money *AUSTRALIA, 1954*. ▶ **break it down** to stop, to cease; as an imperative, stop talking! *AUSTRALIA, 1944*. ▶ **break luck** (of a prostitute) to have sex with the first customer of the day or night *US, 1969*. ▶ **break out into assholes** to become deeply frightened *US, 1964*. ▶ **break out the rag** to lose your temper after losing a game *US, 1971*. ▶ **break someone's balls** to harrass, to nag someone *US, 1970*. ▶ **break someone's chops** to give someone a hard time, to harass someone *US, 1953*. ▶ **break starch** to put on a fresh uniform *US, 1968*. ▶ **break stick in ears** to ignore advice or counsel *GRENADA, 2002*. ▶ **break tape** to fire your weapon. Vietnam war usage *US, 1991*. ▶ **break the bank** to divide the winnings up among members of a blackjack counting team *US, 1991*. ▶ **break the house** in gambling, especially an illegal gambling enterprise, to win a great deal of money from the house *US, 1989*. ▶ **break the night** to stay up all night *US, 1989*. ▶ **break the seal** to urinate for the first time in a serious bout of drinking. Subsequent visits to the toilet will occur with urgent regularity after 'breaking the seal' *UK, 2002*. ▶ **break the sound barrier** to fart. Probably dating to the late 1960s when the test-flights of supersonic airliner Concorde first made the potential simile widely-known *CANADA, 1984*. ▶ **break watches** (of a racehorse) to run very fast during a morning workout *US, 1951*. ▶ **break weak** to back down from a confrontation *US, 1992*. ▶ **break wide** to leave *US, 1992*. ▶ **break wind** 1 to fart *UK, 1606*. 2 to drive in the lead position in a group of trucks travelling along a motorway together. Citizens' band radio usage *US, 1977*

breakage *noun* in horse racing pari-mutuel betting, the change left over after paying off bets to the nearest nickel, dime or dollar *US, 1947*

break a leg! to an actor, good luck! Theatrical superstition considers a wish of good luck to be tempting fate. Folk-etymology offers the example of American actor John Wilkes Booth who assassinated President Abraham Lincoln. The assassin jumped on stage and broke his leg. Unlikely. It is remembered in use in the 1930s, and is suspected to be of English origin; it is certainly widely used in the UK *US, 1973*

breakaway *noun* 1 any piece of equipment or clothing that will tear free from a police officer's body during a fight *US, 1962*. 2 in television and film making, a prop designed to break easily upon impact *US, 1990*

breakbeat *noun* in contemporary dance culture, a sampled beat that is looped to create a rhythmic pattern; hence, a musical style *US, 1988*

breakdancer; breaker *noun* a dancer who finds expression in the rhythms of hip-hop music *US, 1984*

breakdancing *noun* an energetic dance improvised to the rhythms of hip-hop; often danced competitively. The origin of hip-hop is credited to New York DJ Kool Herc who mixed in rhythmic 'breakdown parts' which dancers then interpreted *US, 1983*

breakdown *noun* **1** a shotgun *US, 1994*. **2** a noisy, rowdy party *JAMAICA, 1996*

break down *verb* to explain something *US, 1965*

breaker *noun* **1** a citizens' band radio user. Usage extended from the announcement of a citizens' band radio user's presence on a waveband *US, 1976*. **2** in horse racing, a horse that starts a race with a great burst of speed *US, 1982*

breaker!; break! used for announcing your presence on citizens' band radio. Literally announcing someone who wishes to 'break-in' to the airwaves, often formulated with information on direction, radio channel, road number or type of contact sought *US, 1976*

breakers *noun* in certain games of poker, cards that qualify a player to open betting *US, 1988*

breakers ahead! used as a general purpose warning of impending problems. Of obvious nautical origin, from the cry of the masthead lookout *US, 1963*

breakfast burrito *noun* the penis *UK, 2003*

breakfast club *noun* a nightclub operating after other clubs close at 2am, staying open until the early morning when breakfast is served *US, 1954*

breakfast of champions *noun* **1** simultaneous, mutual oral sex *AUSTRALIA, 1985*. **2** crack cocaine. A new, ironic application for the slogan used by Wheaties™ since the 1930s; adopted as the title of a 1973 novel by Kurt Vonnegut Jr, and released as a film in 1999 *UK, 1998*. **3** beer *US, 1976*

breakfast of losers *noun* methaqualone, the recreational drug best known as Quaaludes™. Punning on the slogan of a popular cereal brand – 'breakfast of champions' *US, 1987*

breakfast time *noun* ▶ **to breakfast time** to eternity *AUSTRALIA, 1969*

breaking *noun* break dancing, especially its gymnastic and acrobatic aspect *US, 1984*

break in the weather *noun* in betting on horse racing, a change of luck *AUSTRALIA, 1989*

break into *verb* to achieve an entrance into an occupation or activity *US, 1899*

break it off! give me your money! *US, 1997*

break loose *verb* in drag racing, to lose traction and spin the wheels without moving *US, 1970*

break-luck *noun* a prostitute's first customer of the day *US, 1993*

break man *noun* a prison guard who orchestrates the opening of cells in the morning *US, 1977*

break out *verb* to leave *US, 1997*

breakup *noun* in Alaska, the season between winter and summer *US, 1904*

break up *verb* to cause someone to laugh uproariously *US, 1895*

break your duck *verb* to do something for the first time. A figurative application of the cricketing term (to score at least one run) *UK, 1998*

breast check *noun* a walk through a crowd in search of attractive female breasts *US, 1995*

breast job *noun* surgery to alter a woman's breast size *US, 2002*

breathe *noun* in poker, to pass without betting *US, 1988*

breather *noun* **1** in sports, a game against a weak opponent. From the conventional sense (a rest) *US, 1945*. **2** the nose *US, 1973*. **3** a person who derives sexual pleasure from telephoning someone and breathing heavily when they answer the phone *US, 1986*. **4** in trucking, the air intake pipe *US, 1971*

breather crimp *noun* a virtually undetectable bend or crease put onto a playing card by a cheat or a conjuror *2003*

Breather U *noun* any college with a poor sports programme. Humourous to those who attach importance to a college's sports programme *US, 1988*

breath of God *noun* crack cocaine *US, 1997*

breck *noun* breakfast *US, 1983*

brecko *noun* breakfast *AUSTRALIA, 1983*

bredda *noun* **1** a brother, a fellow black person. Phonetic spelling of West Indian pronunciation. West Indian and UK black *1992*. **2** a boy *JAMAICA, 2000*

bredgie *noun* a friend. Originally black usage, now youth slang *UK, 2002*

bredren; bredrin *noun* a man's friend; friends; a fellow youth gang member. Conventional 'brethren' ('brothers', with religious and political overtones) adopted for everyday use by the West Indian and UK black communities *UK, 1994*

bree *noun* a young woman *US, 1992*

breed *noun* **1** a person of mixed ancestry, Indian and non-Indian *CANADA, 1956*. **2** a person who is not white *US, 1992*

breed *verb* ▶ **breed a scab** to create trouble *US, 1941*

breeder *noun* **1** from the homosexual point of view, a heterosexual. Usually used as an insult *US, 1979*. **2** any food that is believed to render a man potent and fecund *JAMAICA, 2003*

breeze *noun* **1** something that is achieved easily and quickly *US, 1928*. **2** in horse racing, an easy pace during a workout or race *US, 1951*. **3** an escape from prison *US, 1948*. **4** a prison sentence that is nearly completed *US, 1962*. **5** a calm, collected person *US, 1992*. **6** the air used in air brakes *US, 1939*. **7** (of a car) power *US, 1955*. **8** used as a term of address *US, 1966* ▷ *see:* **BALMY BREEZE**

breeze *verb* **1** to move or go quickly; to move or go casually or without effort. Generally before 'along','in', 'off', 'through', etc *US, 1907*. **2** to succeed in achieving something without making a great effort *UK, 2004*. **3** to escape; to go *US, 1913*. **4** in pool, to only barely glance the object ball with the cue ball *US, 1990*

breeze off *verb* to stop working and relax in the shade *BELIZE, 1996*

breezer *noun* **1** a fart *AUSTRALIA, 1973*. **2** a despised person *UK, 2003*

breezeway *noun* the area in a prison where the most derelict of the convicts gather *US, 1984*

breezy *noun* a young woman *US, 2004*

breid and watter *noun* talk, speechifying. Glasgow rhyming slang for PATTER, on the Scottish pronunciation of 'bread and water' *UK, 1988*

brekker; brekkers *noun* breakfast *UK, 1889*

brekkie; brekky *noun* breakfast. Childish *UK, 1904*

Brenda Bracelets; Brenda *noun* a police officer; the police. An example of CAMP trans-gender assignment, in this case as an alliterative play on BRACELETS (handcuffs) as stereotypical police equipment *UK, 1992*

Brenda Frickers *noun* knickers. Rhyming slang, formed on the name of the Irish actress (b.1945), best known for her film work *UK, 2003*

Brenda skunk; Brenda *noun* a hybrid variety of potent marijuana *2002*

brer *noun* a fellow black man. Old contraction of 'brother' *UK, 2000*

bressles *noun* pubic hair *NORFOLK ISLAND, 1992*

brew *noun* **1** beer; a glass, bottle or can of beer *US, 1907*. **2** a cup, mug or pot of tea. Tea is *brewed* by immersing tea leaves (loose or bagged) in boiling water *AUSTRALIA, 1905*. **3** an illicitly made alcoholic beverage *AUSTRALIA, 1950*. **4** a stew *AUSTRALIA, 1957*. **5** used as a male-to-male term of address *BERMUDA, 1985*. **6** a Jewish person. An abbreviation of 'Hebrew' *US, 1997* ▷ *see:* **BURROO**

brew *verb* to make and heat an injectable solution of heroin and water *UK, 1996*

brewdog *noun* a can of beer *US, 1988*

brewed *adjective* drunk US, 1986

brewer *noun* a prostitute who will allow sexual intercourse without a condom UK, 1997

brewer's droop *noun* a temporary inability to achieve an erect penis caused by drinking too much alcohol, especially beer AUSTRALIA, 1970

brewha *noun* a glass, bottle or can of beer US, 2001

brewski; brewsky *noun* beer; a serving of beer. Mock Polish US, 1978

brewster *noun* a beer US, 1986

Brewster's *noun* a great deal of money; a fortune. A reference to *Brewster's Millions*, 1945, remade 1985, a comedy flim about huge amounts of money UK, 2001

brew up *verb* to make tea UK, 1916

briar *noun* a hacksaw blade US, 1950

briar patch *noun* a female's pubic hair US, 1967

bribe *noun* in marketing, the initial, attractive offer to join a book or music club US, 1986

brick *noun* **1** a good man. A term of approval UK, 1840. **2** someone with exceptionally good credit US, 2001. **3** a person lacking social skills US, 1968. **4** a profit made fraudulently UK, 1979. **5** a sentence of ten years in jail AUSTRALIA, 1944. **6** a street tough person AUSTRALIA, 1840. **7** a die that has been shaved on one face US, 1950. **8** in poker, a drawn card that fails to improve the hand US, 1996. **9** ten cartons of stolen cigarettes US, 1982. **10** a carton of cigarettes US, 1906. **11** a kilogram of, usually compressed, marijuana, or, less commonly, another drug US, 1967. **12** marijuana. From the sense as a measurement of the drug UK, 1996. **13** crack cocaine US, 2003. **14** an Australian ten pound note; the sum of ten pounds. From the colour of the note. After the introduction of decimal currency in 1966 the meaning changed to either 'twenty dollars' (an equivalent value) or, most commonly, 'ten dollars' (numerically the same). Neither of the new notes were brick coloured and the term has all but died out AUSTRALIA, 1914. **15** a pound sterling (£1) UK: SCOTLAND, 1988. **16** a four-man infantry patrol. Used by the British Army in Northern Ireland UK, 1995. **17** an abandoned, partially consumed can or bottle of beer US, 2002

brick *nickname* the British Columbia Resources Investment Corporation. A near-abbreviation CANADA, 1979

brick *verb* **1** to have sex leaning against a brick wall for balance and purchase UK, 2001. **2** to cheat or defraud someone UK, 1979. **3** to fail to deliver as promised US, 1993. **4** to hurl bricks, rocks or other hard objects. A word commonly used in the 1960s in American cities during events called 'riots' by the dominant power and 'uprisings' by leftists US, 1972. **5** to miss a shot; to fail US, 2001. ▶ **brick your pants** to soil your underwear as a result of fear; to be very afraid UK, 2005

bricked *adjective* **1** drug-intoxicated US, 1992. **2** in a court of law, having an unsigned police statement used against you AUSTRALIA, 1977

bricker *verb* to steal; to shoplift UK, 1970

brick gum *noun* heroin UK, 1998

brickhouse *noun* in poker, a full house that is not the best hand. An allusion built on 'brick' as a 'useless card' US, 1996

brick it *verb* to be very nervous or worried; to be thoroughly frightened. Variation of SHIT IT UK, 1996

bricks *noun* in prison, the world outside the prison walls US, 1976. ▶ **hit the bricks 1** to leave, especially to leave prison US, 1931. **2** to go on strike; to be on strike. Also variants 'on the bricks' or 'pound the bricks' US, 1938. ▶ **to the bricks** extremely, utterly, completely US, 1928

bricks and clicks *noun* a business that combines trading from traditional business premises with e-commerce and Internet-only custom UK, 2000

bricks and mortar *noun* **1** a house; houses, property. Usually in phrases like 'his money's in bricks and mortar' UK, 1855. **2** a daughter. Rhyming slang UK, 1960

brick shithouse *noun* a woman, or rarely a homosexual man, with a curvaceous figure; a powerfully built man. Sometimes euphemised to a simple 'house' US, 1928

bricktop *noun* a red-haired person US, 1856

Bricktop *nickname* Ada Smith de Conge, a singer, actress and Paris nightclub hostess (died 1984) US, 1952

brickweed *noun* marijuana that has been compressed into a brick for transportation UK, 2004

bricky; brickie *noun* a bricklayer UK, 1880

Brickyard *nickname* the Indianapolis speedway. The speedway was once faced with bricks US, 1958

bridal suite *noun* **1** a two-man prison cell. A frank allusion to homosexual sex in prison NEW ZEALAND, 1999. **2** a room where police assigned the late night shift can sleep US, 1994

bride *noun* **1** a model of good behaviour BARBADOS, 1965. **2** a prostitute UK, 1981

bride's nightie *noun* ▶ **like a bride's nightie** used as the epitome of quickness AUSTRALIA, 1984

bride's slide *noun* in backgammon, the customary play with a first roll of 6–5: moving a back man 11 points US, 1976

bridge *noun* **1** a holder for a marijuana cigarette. A common term in the 1950s, largely supplanted by ROACH CLIP in the 1960s US, 1955. **2** a slightly curved playing card, altered by a cheat to manipulate the cutting of a deck US, 1991. **3** a pickpocket who reaches around the victim to pick their pocket US, 1949. **4** a group of four in a restaurant or soda fountain. An allusion to a bridge party US, 1967. ▶ **under the bridge** in a smuggling operation, across a border US, 1956

bridge and tunnel *adjective* said of a resident of New Jersey who commutes to New York. Disparaging US, 1984

bridge bender *noun* a motor vehicle manufactured by Vauxhall UK, 1981

bridge jumper *noun* in horse racing, a person who regularly bets on favourites and is distraught if the favourite does not win US, 1951

bridge monkey; bridge stiff *noun* on the railways, a bridge construction worker US, 1977

Bridge of Sighs *nickname* an overpass connecting the New York City jail with the criminal court building. A borrowing from Venice's Ponte de Sospiri, romanticised by Lord Byron US, 1955

bridges *noun* bridge tolls for which a truck driver is paid in advance or reimbursed US, 1963

brief *noun* **1** a solicitor, a barrister or other legal representative of an accused person. From an earlier sense (the legal case presented to a barrister) UK, 1977. **2** a warrant to search or arrest someone; a Metropolitan Police warrant-card UK, 1970. **3** a ticket for any purpose UK, 1937. **4** a playing card that has been trimmed slightly so that a cheat can locate it within a deck by feel UK, 1988

brig *noun* a Brigadier; also, until the rank was abolished, a Brigadier General. Military UK, 1899

briggity *adjective* arrogant, vain, stubborn US, 1884

bright *noun* **1** morning US, 1941. **2** a light-complexioned black person US, 1976

bright *adjective* (of skin) light-coloured BAHAMAS, 1982

bright and frisky; bright 'n' frisky; Brighton *noun* whisky. Rhyming slang, probably as a deliberate variation of the earlier 'gay and frisky' reflecting the shift in the meaning of 'gay'; it is interesting to note therefore that the contraction 'Brighton' also has rhyming slang noun and adjective senses (homosexual), and that Brighton is regarded as one of the UK's centres of homosexual culture UK, 1969

bright disease *noun* the condition of knowing too much for your own good US, 1953

bright-eyed and bushy-tailed *adjective* alert and enthusiastic, lively US, 1942

bright eyes *noun* **1** a lookout during a criminal venture US, 1956. **2** the high beam setting on headlights US, 1977

brightlight team *noun* in Vietnam, a small group from the special forces sent to rescue American prisoners of war US, 1981

Brighton bucket *noun* ▶ **like a Brighton bucket** without recognising someone when you pass them in the street. An image of the pitch buckets on a conveyor system at the Brighton pier, passing each other on belts *TRINIDAD AND TOBAGO, 1987*

Brighton pier *verb* to disappear. Rhyming slang *UK, 1998*

Brighton pier; brighton *adjective* (especially of a man) homosexual. Rhyming slang for QUEER (homosexual). Earlier use of the same rhyme meant 'unwell' or 'peculiar', the meaning shifting with the sense of 'queer'; possibly also influenced by the reputation of Brighton as a centre for gay society and culture *UK, 1960*

Brighton rock *noun* the penis. Rhyming slang for COCK, and a visual pun on a long pink sweet that is made to be sucked. Similarly sweet references to the male anatomy can be found at ALMOND ROCK, BLACKPOOL ROCK and STICK OF ROCK *UK, 1992*

brights *noun* white socks *US, 1969*

Bright's Disease *nickname* Bright's Wine™, a brand of cheap wine, grown and processed in Niagara, Ontario *CANADA, 2001*

bright spark *noun* a cheerful, energetic person *NEW ZEALAND, 2002*

bright spot *noun* in oil drilling, an area that has indications of a productive field *US, 1997*

bright, white and dead white *adjective* ▷ *see:* LIGHT, BRIGHT, DAMN NEAR WHITE

brighty *adjective* very smart *US, 1945*

brig rat *noun* a prisoner *US, 1942*

brill; brills *adjective* excellent, marvellous. An abbreviation of 'brilliant'; also used as exclamation. Military usage possibly predates modern slang by several decades *UK, 1979*

brilliant *adjective* wonderful, excellent *UK, 1979*

brim *noun* **1** any hat *US, 1965.* **2** a straw hat *BAHAMAS, 1982*

brims *noun* identical hats worn by members of a youth gang *US, 1982*

brimson *noun* a braggart; a fantasist. English gypsy use *UK, 2000*

bring *verb* to compel someone to do something. *US, 1972.* ▶ **bring it in** in poker, to make the first bet of a hand *US, 1990.* ▶ **bring it on** used for challenging an opponent to begin a competition *US, 1998.* ▶ **bring pee** to frighten someone severely. Vietnam war usage *US, 1966.* ▶ **bring smoke 1** to call for an artillery barrage *US, 1990.* **2** by extension, to reprimand someone in harsh, profane tones *US, 1968.* ▶ **bring someone to book** to bring someone to account; to cause someone to face authority, investigation or judgement *UK, 1804*

bring-a-plate *adjective* (of a party or the like) partially self-catered *AUSTRALIA, 1979*

bringdown *noun* an event or person that discourages or depresses you *US, 1939*

bring down *verb* to depress someone, to deflate someone *US, 1935*

bring it away *verb* to effect an abortion. The 'it' in question is the foetus *UK, 1984*

bring it, don't sing it! used to invite action instead of words *US, 1998*

bring off *verb* **1** to achieve an intended outcome, to be successful in making something happen *UK, 1928.* **2** to induce and achieve an orgasm *UK, 1984*

bring on *verb* to excite someone sexually *UK, 1961*

bring on the dancing girls! a facetious call for an exciting spectacle that is used as a register of boredom *UK, 1984*

bring out *verb* to introduce someone to homosexuality, to awaken in someone their homosexuality *US, 1941*

bring up *verb* **1** to vomit *UK, 1719.* **2** to try someone on a criminal charge *US, 1823*

brinny *noun* a stone, especially a small stone or pebble that is used for throwing. Probably from an Australian Aboriginal language *AUSTRALIA, 1943*

Bris; Brissie; Brizzie *noun* Brisbane *AUSTRALIA, 1945*

Brish *adjective* British. From a drunken slurring; especially in Sydney *AUSTRALIA, 1951*

brisket *noun* the female breast. A butcher's pun describing the cut of breast meat next to the ribs *UK, 1979*

bristol *noun* in tiddlywinks, a shot that moves both the player's wink and an opponent's, the manoeuvre starting and finishing with the player's wink sitting on the opponent's. The manoeuvre, dating from the 1960s, is credited eponymously to Bristol University Tiddlywinks Society *UK, 1980*

Bristol City; bristol *noun* the female breast. Rhyming slang: *Bristol City* Football Club and TITTY (a breast); supported by an alliterative connection between 'breast' and 'brist'; usually in the plural *UK, 1960*

Bris-vegas *nickname* Brisbane *AUSTRALIA, 2003*

Brit *noun* a Briton *UK, 1901*

Brit *adjective* British. An abbreviation, usually as a prefix. Usages include: Britflick (a UK film), Britlit (new UK writing) and *britpulp!* (an anthology of short-stories) *AUSTRALIA, 1971*

britch *noun* a side trouser pocket *US, 1950*

britches *noun* in Newfoundland, the sac of codfish eggs found in the pregnant female *CANADA, 1975*

Brit hop *noun* British hip-hop *UK, 1999*

British disease *noun* a strike or work stoppage *NEW ZEALAND, 1984*

British Standard Handful *noun* the average female breast. A play on standards established by the British Standards Institute *UK, 1977*

Britland *nickname* Britain *UK, 2002*

Britney Spear; britney *noun* a year. Rhyming slang, formed on the name of popular US entertainer Britney Spears *UK, 2004*

Britney Spears; Britneys *noun* beers. Popney rhyming slang, based on the name of popular entertainer Britney Spears (born 1981). Popney was contrived for *www.music365.co.uk*, an Internet music site *UK, 2001*

Britpop *noun* a loose categorisation of contemporary *British popular* music *UK, 1999*

brittle *adjective* (used of a computer program) functional, but easily rendered dysfunctional by changes or external stimuli which should not have the effect they have *US, 1991*

Brixton briefcase *noun* a large portable stereo system associated, stereotypically, with black youth culture *UK, 1990*

bro *noun* a *brother*, in the sense of a fellow in a given situation or condition; especially of a fellow black; also of a fellow student in UK public school usage *US, 1957*

broach *verb* to inject an illegal drug *US, 1992*

broad *noun* **1** a woman. Somewhere between derogatory and so old-fashioned as to be charming in a hopeless way *US, 1911.* **2** a male homosexual who plays the passive sexual role *US, 1984.* **3** in a deck of playing cards, a queen *UK, 1781.* **4** an identity card; any paper of identification, insurance book, etc *UK, 1950.* **5** a credit card. Extended from the previous sense *UK, 1977*

broadcast *verb* to engage in conversation *US, 1959*

broadie *noun* **1** a woman. A slightly embellished BROAD *US, 1932.* **2** the movement of a surfer across the face of a wave *SOUTH AFRICA, 1965*

broad joint *noun* a bar where prostitutes are available along with the drinks *US, 1956*

broads *noun* playing cards *UK, 1781*

broadski *noun* a woman *US, 1967*

broad squad *noun* in prison, a group of homosexual men *US, 1990*

broad tosser *noun* the operator of a three-card monte game swindle *US, 1980*

Broadway *noun* in poker, a five-card sequence ending with an ace as the highest card of the sequence *US, 1988*

Broadway Arab *noun* a Jewish person *US, 1946*

broccoli *noun* marijuana *US, 1969*

brockly *adjective* muscular. A vegetable pun, alluding to professional wrestler Brock Lesnar *US, 2003*

Brodie; Brody *noun* **1** a fall or leap from a great height. An allusion to Steve Brodie, a New York bookmaker who in 1886 claimed to have survived a leap from the Brooklyn Bridge and then opened a tavern which succeeded as a result of the publicity surrounding his claimed leap *US, 1899*. **2** a feigned drug withdrawal spasm *US, 1936*. **3** a failure to perform as expected *CANADA, 1976*. **4** a play that is a complete failure *US, 1973*. **5** a skid, usually controlled *US, 1953*

broform *noun* a retail discount given to friends. Snowboarder's slang; conflates BRO (a friend) with 'proform' (a discount given to professionals) *US, 1995*

brogans *noun* heavy work shoes. From the Gaelic. During the US Civil War, the sturdy and durable leather shoes issued to infantrymen were nicknamed Brogans or Jefferson Booties *US, 1835*

broges *noun* work shoes. An abbreviation of BROGANS *US, 1990*

bro-ing *noun* in market research, the testing of fashion prototypes in inner-city, predominantly black neighbourhoods. From BRO (a fellow black) in a sense that categorises a target customer *US, 2001*

broja *noun* heroin. *2002*

brok *verb* to depart, to leave. Urban youth slang, probably derived from conventional 'break' in a similar sense to SPLIT *UK, 2006*

broke *adjective* having little or no money, bankrupt. A variant of conventional 'broken' used in this sense from C16 *UK, 1661*. ▶ **go for broke** to make the utmost effort to achieve a desired end *US, 1951*

broke dick *noun* a nonfunctioning piece of hardware *US, 1988*

broke-down *noun* a brawl *BAHAMAS, 1995*

broke money *noun* a small amount of money given to a gambler who has lost his entire bankroll *US, 1950*

broken *adjective* **1** in the bleed period of the menstrual cycle *US, 2001*. **2** depressed, acting oddly *US, 1981*

broken arrow *noun* **1** an accident involving nuclear weapons *US, 1980*. **2** in computing, an error code on line 25 of a 3270 terminal *US, 1991*

broken arse *noun* a person who has been completely subjugated. Prison usage *NEW ZEALAND, 1999*

broken knuckles *noun* sleeping quarters on a train *US, 1946*

broken rail *noun* an older, physically run-down railway worker *US, 1977*

broken wrist *noun* an effeminate male homosexual *US, 1968*

broker *noun* a drug dealer *US, 1962*

broket *noun* on a computer keyboard, the characters <and>. A contraction of 'broken bracket' *US, 1983*

brolly *noun* an umbrella *UK, 1874*

broly *adjective* conforming to surfer etiquette *US, 1991*

bro-man *noun* used as a male-to-male term of address *BAHAMAS, 1982*

bronc *noun* in oil drilling, an inexperienced driller *US, 1954*

bronch *verb* to use a bronchoscope. Medical use *UK, 1980*

bronco *noun* a young male recently initiated into homosexual sex *US, 1967*

bronc stomper *noun* a cowboy who specialises in the breaking of horses, i.e. getting them to accept bridle, bit and saddle *CANADA, 1954*

bronski *verb* to sandwich a face between female breasts *US, 1995*

Bronson *noun* cocaine. From the infamous UK criminal Charlie Bronson (b.1952), with CHARLIE leading to 'cocaine' *UK, 2001*

Bronx Bull *nickname* Jake LaMotta (b.1921), a middleweight boxer who fiercely made his presence felt in the ring in the 1940s and 1950s *US, 1952*

Bronx cheer *noun* a combination of booing and a derisory farting noise, expressing disgust *US, 1922*

bronze; bronza; bronzer; bronzo *noun* the anus; the buttocks. Probably derives as a shade of brown *AUSTRALIA, 1953*

bronze John *noun* the sun *US, 1954*

Bronzeville *noun* a city neighbourhood with a largely black population *US, 1950*

bronze-wing *noun* a person of part-Aboriginal and part white descent. From the colour of a bronze-wing pigeon *AUSTRALIA, 1956*

bronzie; branzy *noun* a sun tan; bronzed skin *UK, 1987*

bronzie machine *noun* a tanning machine *UK, 2002*

broo *noun* the employment exchange; unemployment benefit. The Scots shortened form of 'bureau' *UK, 1998*

Brookolino *nickname* Brooklyn, New York *US, 1982*

broom *noun* **1** the person who is assigned to or takes it upon himself to keep a workplace neat. Sometimes embellished to 'broom man' *US, 1973*. **2** a hat *US, 1960*

broom *verb* **1** to travel *UK, 1921*. **2** to run away, to leave *UK, 1821*

broomie *noun* in sheep-shearing, a person employed to keep the shearing floor swept clean. Extended from a conventional 'broom'; also known and used by New Zealand sheep-shearers *AUSTRALIA, 1895*

broom stack *noun* a truck exhaust stack that is flaming or smoking *US, 1961*

broomstick *noun* in electric line work, a phase spacer used for keeping phases from contacting each other midspan *US, 1980*

broosted *adjective* rich; having achieved great wealth. Extended from BREWSTER'S (a great deal of money) *UK, 2002*

bros before hoes used as a rallying cry for the precedence of male friendship over relationships with females. Sometimes seen as the abbreviation BBH *US, 2004*

broski; browski *noun* used as a male-to-male term of address. Doing to BRO what was done to BREW *US, 1997*

brothel creeper *noun* a patron of brothels *US, 1977*

brothel creepers *noun* suede-topped, crepe-soled shoes, either of the style also known as desert boots or the thick-soled variety favoured by Teddy Boys. Originally military, from World War 2; the etymology appears to be obvious, certainly the early types of these shoes allowed for silent movement *UK, 1954*

brothel spout *noun* a prostitute who is physically and emotionally worn out by her work *US, 1993*

brother *noun* **1** a black man *US, 1910*. **2** a fellow member of a countercultural or underground political movement *US, 1968*. **3** in carnival usage, a woman's husband or lover *US, 1981*. **4** heroin. A rare variant on the common BOY *US, 1990*

Brother Andre's Last Erection *nickname* the Oratory near the top of the mountain in Montreal. Brother Andre was a poor priest whose charisma made him widely known in Quebec as a healer; he raised funds to build the mammoth St Joseph's Oratory, and slept in an anteroom as caretaker *CANADA, 1990*

brother Ben *noun* Benzedrine™ (amphetamine sulphate), a central nervous system stimulant, or another central nervous system stimulant *US, 1971*

Brother Jonathan *nickname* the United States *CANADA, 1962*

brother man *noun* used as a term of address to establish solidarity, among black men *US, 1974*

broth of a boy *noun* a boy or man who represents the absolute quintessence of what a boy or man should be. The earliest recorded instance is in Byron's *Don Juan*, 1822; however modern usage is mainly Irish *UK, 1822*

brought down *adjective* in a sad or suddenly depressed state of mind, especially after drug use *US, 1946*

brown *noun* **1** the anus and/or rectum *US, 1916*. **2** faeces *IRELAND, 1991*. **3** anal sex; an act of anal intercourse *UK, 1894*. **4** heroin, especially if only partially refined *US, 1962*. **5** darker coloured hashish *US, 1981*. **6** an amphetamine tablet *US, 1972*

brown *verb* **1** to perform anal sex upon someone *US, 1933*. **2** to force others to behave in an obsequious, sycophantic manner *UK, 1998*

brown *adjective* **1** (of behaviour) obsequious, sycophantic. As in BROWN NOSE (a sycophant); extends from an image of submissive homage to another's backside *UK: SCOTLAND, 1988*. **2** used for describing sexual activities involving excrement *UK, 2002*. **3** (of a person's skin colour) white *JAMAICA, 2003*

brown Abe *noun* a US penny. From the engraving of President Abraham Lincoln on the coin *US, 1945*

brown acid *noun* a type of LSD. At the Woodstock festival in August 1969, there were several public address announcements recording the 'brown acid' that was 'not specifically good' *US, 1969*

brown ankles *noun* an utter sycophant. An ordinary sycophant is a BROWN NOSE; the toady here is even further ensconced in the nether regions *NEW ZEALAND, 1976*

brown-back *noun* a ten-shilling note. From the colour of the note; such currency was in use between 1928–40 and again from 1948–70 and withdrawn from circulation with the onset of decimalisation in 1971 *UK, 1961*

brown bag *noun* an unmarked police car *US, 1976*

brown-bag *verb* to carry lunch to work, especially in a brown paper lunch bag *US, 1968*

brown bagger *noun* a married person. From the image of bringing lunch packed in a brown bag to work; originally military usage *US, 1947*

brown bar *noun* in the US Army, a second lieutenant. The single brass bar worn by the second lieutenant was camouflaged in the field and became a single brown bar *US, 1977*

brown bomb *noun* a laxative *US, 1990*

brown bomber *noun* **1** a large laxative pill, favoured by military medics since World War 2 *US, 1941*. **2** a type of LSD. From the colour of the capsule *UK, 1998*

brown boot Army *noun* the army as it once was *US, 1968*

brown bottle *noun* beer *US, 1976*

brown bottled *adjective* drunk on beer *UK, 1981*

brown bottle shop *noun* a pub *UK, 1981*

brown boy *noun* a male who derives sexual pleasure from eating the faeces of others *US, 1971*

brown bread *adjective* dead. Rhyming slang *UK, 1979*

Brown Brothers *noun* the black community *UK, 1998*

brown bucket *noun* the rectum and/or anus *US, 1949*

brown coat *noun* in prison or borstal, a prisoner on remand or awaiting deportation. From the colour of the uniform which differentiates this type of prisoner from the majority of inmates who were, at the time of use, dressed in grey *UK, 1950*

brown cow *noun* an alcoholic drink made from coffee liqueur and cream or milk. It is identified in Tom Dalzell's *The Slang of Sin* as a 'barrel of beer' *CANADA, 1998*

brown crown *noun* a notional sign of one who has failed miserably *US, 1966*

brown crystal *noun* heroin *UK, 1998*

brown derby *noun* during the Vietnam war, a hot meal that was flown to the troops in the field *US, 1991*

brown dots *noun* a type of LSD *US, 1975*

brown downtown *noun* brown heroin *US, 1992*

browned off *adjective* **1** bored or fed-up with something or something *UK, 1938*. **2** depressed, angry *US, 1950*

brown eye *noun* the anus *US, 1954*

brown-eyed cyclops *noun* the anus. In Greek mythology the Cyclops were one-eyed giants; the imagery employed here is clear *UK, 2002*

brown eyes *noun* the female breasts, especially the nipples *US, 1932*

Brown family *noun* collectively, all passive participants in anal sex *US, 1950*

brown-hatter *noun* a homosexual man *UK, 1950*

brown helmet *noun* a notional sign of one who has been rejected in romance *US, 1968*

brownie *noun* **1** the anus *US, 1927*. **2** a sycophant. An abbreviation of BROWN NOSER *US, 1993*. **3** a homosexual, especially one of wealth or position *US, 1916*. **4** a notation of bad conduct or poor work performance; a demerit *US, 1910*. **5** a black person. Coincidental to the US sense (a brown-skinned Asian) *UK, 2002*. **6** a traffic police officer *US, 1987*. **7** a police radar unit used for measuring vehicle speed. An allusion to the camera brand, a metaphor for radar *US, 1976*. **8** in trucking, a three-speed auxiliary gearbox. Originally manufactured by the Brownolite Transmission Company, hence the diminutive *US, 1971*. **9** marijuana *US, 1966*. **10** any amphetamine; MDMA, the recreational drug best known as ecstasy. Originally 'amphetamines', from the colour; hence, via confused recreational drug-users, 'ecstasy' *UK, 2001*. **11** an empty beer bottle *NEW ZEALAND, 1979*

brownie point *noun* an imaginary award or credit for a good deed *US, 1953*

brownie queen *noun* a male homosexual who enjoys the passive role in anal sex *US, 1968*

brownies *noun* **1** the female breasts, especially the nipples *US, 1982*. **2** dice that have had their spots altered for cheating. More commonly known as 'busters', which leads to the cartoon character 'Buster Brown', which leads to 'Brown' *US, 1950*

Browning Sister *noun* a male homosexual. From BROWN (anal sex). A term used in the 1940s *US, 1941*

brown job *noun* **1** a soldier. From the khaki uniform *UK, 1943*. **2** oral-anal sex *US, 1971*

brown list *noun* an imagined list of those in disfavour. A euphemistic SHIT LIST *UK, 1998*

brown lover *noun* a person with a fetishistic love of excrement *US, 1996*

brownmouth *noun* a talkative fool *IRELAND, 1991*

brown-nose *verb* to curry favour in a sycophantic fashion *US, 1938*

brown nose; brown noser *noun* a toady; a sycophant. Originally military *US, 1938*

Brown Nurses *nickname* Our Lady's Nurses (for the Poor), a Catholic organisation founded in 1913. From the brown uniform *AUSTRALIA, 1984*

brown one; brown 'un *noun* on the railways, a distant signal *UK, 1970*

brownout *noun* a near but not complete loss of consciousness. Not quite a 'blackout' *US, 1992*

brown paper *noun* **1** a sycophant. A logical extension of ASSWIPE *US, 1968*. **2** a caper in the sense of an occupation or racket. Rhyming slang *UK, 1974*

brown-paper roll *noun* a cigarette hand-rolled in brown paper *BAHAMAS, 1982*

brown rhine; brown rine *noun* heroin. From the colour and a pronunciation of 'heroin' *US, 1953*

browns *noun* the uniform issued to a prisoner on remand or awaiting deportation in borstals and detention centres. From the colour *UK, 1978*

brown shoes *noun* a person who does not use drugs *US, 1970*

brown shower *noun* an act of defecation as part of sadomasochistic sex play *UK, 2003*

brown slime *noun* a mixture of cola syrup and nutmeg, used as a substitute for drugs by the truly desperate *US, 1992*

brown stuff *noun* opium *US, 1950*

brown sugar *noun* **1** grainy, poor quality heroin *US, 1971*. **2** a black woman, especially a beautiful one. Originally black use only, from the skin colour and a suggestion of sweetness *US, 1971*. **3** by extension, a sexually desirable black man. Adopted by black women *US, 1996*. **4** a coarse, unrefined person *AUSTRALIA, 1989*

brown tape *noun* heroin *UK, 2002*

brown tongue *noun* an informer. The disdainful image of an informer licking the anus of authority *UK, 1996*

brown trousers *noun* extreme nervousness, fear. From the state of your trousers after an involuntary fear-induced evacuation *UK, 2005*

brown trout *noun* faeces, when thrown by prisoners from their cells onto guards *US, 1992*

brown underpants *noun* used as a symbol of extreme fear or cowardice. An image of soiled underwear *UK, 1998*

brown water navy *noun* during the Vietnam war, the US Navy presence on rivers and deltas *US, 1961*

brown windsor *noun* ▷*see:* WINDSOR CASTLE

brown wings *noun* experience of anal intercourse, or anal-oral sexual contact, considered as an achievement. Originally Hell's Angel usage; 'brown' (the colour associated with the anus) plus 'wings' (badge of honour) *US, 1971*

Bruce *noun* used as a stereotype of an effeminate male homosexual *US, 1973*

Bruce Lee *noun* an erect nipple. Clever but misinformed pun on San Francisco-born martial arts film actor Bruce Lee as a HARD (muscular) NIP (a Japanese person); in fact Bruce Lee (1940–73) was a native of Hong Kong, not Japan *UK, 2002*

bruck *noun* in western Canada, a combination bus and truck *CANADA, 1961*

bruckins *noun* a noisy, rowdy party *JAMAICA, 1996*

bruck-up *verb* to beat up. British Indian (Hindi) urban youth slang *UK, 2006*

brud *noun* used as a friendly term of address *NORFOLK ISLAND, 1992*

bruiser *noun* **1** a rugged physical specimen; a thug *UK, 1742*. **2** a club used for beating sediment out of sponges *BAHAMAS, 1982*

brukdown *noun* a noisy, rowdy party *BELIZE, 1996*

bruk up *verb* to thrash someone, to beat someone up. Early C21 black youth usage; an elision of 'break up' and FUCK UP (to destroy) *UK, 2002*

brumby *noun* a feral horse. Origin unknown. Various conjectures, such as an eponymous Major Brumby, or that an Aboriginal language is the source, are based on no solid evidence *AUSTRALIA, 1880*

brummy; brummie *adjective* from Birmingham, England. Both the city of Birmingham and its inhabitants can be called 'Brum'. From Brummagem; the local spelling was a phonetic reflection of the local pronunciation: 'Brummagem' = Bromwichham (after Bromwich), in turn a corruption of Brimidgeham, the old form of Birmingham. Brummagem has an obsolete sense as 'counterfeit, inferior or fake' (of coins, antiques, etc.) as Birmingham was a centre of manufacture for such articles in the C17 and C18. Also, since 1954, used as a noun *UK, 2001*

brush *noun* **1** female pubic hair *AUSTRALIA, 1941*. **2** a moustache *US, 1824*. **3** an intravenous injection of an illegal drug *US, 1992*. **4** a person who organises the seating for card players *UK, 2003*. **5** a technique for introducing altered dice into a game as the dice are passed from player to shooter. Also known as a 'brush-off' *US, 1950*

brush *verb* to introduce marked cards or loaded dice into a game *US, 1993*. ▶ **brush your teeth and comb your hair** in trucking, to slow down to the legal speed limit because of the presence of police ahead *US, 1976*

brush ape *noun* an unsophisticated rustic *US, 1920*

brusher; brushman *noun* a casino employee who tries to lure casino visitors into playing poker *US, 1988*

brush-off *noun* a rejection *US, 1938*

Brussels sprout; brussel *noun* **1** a Boy Scout, a Scout. Rhyming slang, since about 1910 *UK, 1960*. **2** a tout, either of the ticket or racing tipster variety. Rhyming slang *UK, 1992*

brutal *adjective* **1** extremely good, intense *US, 1964*. **2** terrible, very bad *US, 1983*

brutally *adverb* very *US, 1995*

brute *noun* **1** any large vehicle or vessel that is difficult to handle *US, 1860*. **2** in the television and film industries, a large spotlight used to simulate sunlight *US, 1960*

brute force *noun* in computing, a simplistic and unsophisticated programming style *US, 1991*

brute force and ignorance *noun* physicality applied without thought; also, a deliberate disregard for tact or delicacy. A catchphrase that means exactly what it says, usually jocular *UK, 1930*

bruv *noun* a brother; a friend; used as a friendly form of address from one man to another. A phonetic abbreviation *UK, 2000*

bruz *noun* used as a term of address, man to man *US, 1958*

BS *noun* bullshit, in all its senses. A euphemism accepted in polite society *US, 1900*

BS and bells *noun* in firefighter usage, a long period with activity *US, 1954*

BSH *noun* the average female breast. An abbreviation of BRITISH STANDARD HANDFUL, a play on BSI standards set by the British Standards Institute *UK, 1977*

B-squared *noun* a brassiere. Schoolgirl slang, presumably also written B^2 *UK, 1971*

BT *noun* **1** the posterior, the buttocks. By elision, a euphemism for 'bottom' *UK: SCOTLAND, 1998*. **2** an inhalation of marijuana smoke filtered through a water-pipe. An abbreviation of 'bong toke' *US, 1997*

BT Baracus *noun* a child who lives in a house without a phone; subsequently a child without a mobile phone. Derives from a reliance on BT (British Telecom) and a play on the character BA Baracus played by Mr T in the television adventure series *The A Team*, 1984–88 *UK, 2004*

BTI *noun* television interference with a citizens' band signal. An abbreviation of 'boob tube interference' *US, 1976*

BTM *noun* the posterior, the buttocks. A domestic euphemism for 'bottom' *UK, 1937*

BTO *noun* an influential and admired person. A 'big-time operator' – not without overtones of smarminess *US, 1944*

BTW used in computer message shorthand to mean 'by the way' *US, 1991*

BU *noun* sexual attraction. An abbreviation of 'biological urge' *US, 1934*

Bu; the Bu; Mother Bu *nickname* Malibu, California *US, 1991*

BUAG *noun* a simple drawing made with computer characters. A 'big ugly ASCII graphic' *US, 1995*

bub *noun* **1** used as a term of address, usually to a stranger and usually in a condescending tone *US, 1839*. **2** the female breast *UK, 1826*. **3** a baby *AUSTRALIA, 1992*. **4** a blue flashing police car light *US, 1987*

bubba *noun* **1** a stereotypical white, southern male *US, 1982*. **2** a friend, especially as a term of address. A variation of BROTHER *US, 1983*. **3** marijuana *US, 1997*

bubbie circus *noun* a chorus line or other display of multiple women with large breasts *US, 1967*

bubbies and cunt *noun* a poor woman's dowry *US, 1967*

bubblate *verb* to idle, to pass time with friends *US, 2004*

bubble *noun* **1** an informer. From rhyming slang BUBBLE AND SQUEAK (to inform) *UK, 1996*. **2** a glass-enclosed control panel on a vehicle of any sort *US, 1983*. **3** an aeroplane cockpit *US, 1986*. **4** in motor racing, a clear plastic dome that covers the driver *US, 1965*. **5** in the television and film industries, an incandescent electric light bulb *US, 1960*. **6** a specialisation *US, 1997*. **7** an instance of weeping *UK: SCOTLAND, 1985*. ▶ **on the bubble 1** engaged in swindling as a career *US, 1997*. **2** in motor racing, in one of the lower spots in the qualifying stage of an event, subject to being displaced by a better performance of another car *US, 1993*. **3** in motor racing, the most favourable starting position (the pole position) *US, 1948*

bubble *verb* **1** to weep *UK: SCOTLAND, 1985*. **2** to kill someone by injecting air into their veins *US, 1982*

bubble and squeak *noun* **1** an act of urination. Rhyming slang for LEAK *AUSTRALIA, 2002*. **2** a week. Rhyming slang *UK, 1979*. **3** a Greek. Rhyming slang; derogatory. Can be shortened to 'bubble', or used in the plural form 'bubbles and squeaks' to refer to Greeks and Cypriots, collectively *UK, 1938*

bubble and squeak; bubble; bubble up *verb* to inform on someone. The original rhyming slang meaning was 'to speak'; hence 'to speak about', 'to inform' *UK, 1961*

Bubbleberry *noun* in British Columbia, a hybrid variety of marijuana *CANADA, 2002*

bubble brain *noun* a distracted, unfocused person *US, 1981*

bubble-burner *noun* in trucking, an engine run on propane gas *US, 1971*

bubble chaser *noun* a bombardier on a bomber aircraft. A reference to the bubbles in the levelling device used *US, 1945*

bubble dance *verb* to wash dishes *US, 1947*

bubble-dancer *noun* a person employed as a dishwasher *US, 1960*

bubblegum *noun* **1** the posterior, the buttocks, especially of a curvaceous woman. Rhyming slang for BUM *UK, 1998*. **2** cocaine; crack cocaine. Probably a play on Bazooka™, a branded bubble-gum, and BAZOOKA (cocaine; crack) *UK, 1998*. **3** a hybrid marijuana with a sweet 'pink' taste *UK, 2002*

bubblegum *adjective* unimaginative, highly commercial, insincere. Usually used to describe music *US, 1963*

bubble gum machine *noun* **1** a vehicle with flashing lights especially a police car. Sometimes shortened to 'bubble machine' *US, 1968*. **2** the H-13 army helicopter. Vietnam war usage *US, 1968*

bubblegummer *noun* a pre-teenager or young teenager *US, 1970*

bubblehead *noun* **1** a person whose thinking is not grounded in reality *US, 1945*. **2** a submariner *US, 1986*

bubbler *noun* a water tank or cooler. Korean war usage. Also heard in New South Wales and Queensland *US, 1961*

bubble team *noun* a sports team that might or might not make a play-off or be invited to a tournament *US, 1989*

bubble-top *noun* an OH-13 Sioux helicopter, used for observation, reconnaissance, and medical evacuation in the Korean war and the early years of the war in Vietnam. So named because of the distinctive plexiglas canopy *US, 1984*

bubble trouble *noun* a flat tyre or other tyre problem *US, 1976*

bubbling *adjective* (of an event) beginning to get exciting *US, 2002*

bubbling bundle of barometric brilliance *noun* used as the introduction for Bobbie the weather girl on AFVN television, Saigon, during the Vietnam war. Officially she served as a secretary for the US Agency for International Aid in Saigon from 1967 to 1969. Her unpaid weather broadcasts, which always ended with the benediction of wishing 'everyone a pleasant evening weather-wise and good wishes for other-wise,' were greatly appreciated by the men in the field *US, 1990*

bubbly *noun* champagne *UK, 1920*

bubbly *adjective* **1** cheerful, full of spirit *US, 1939*. **2** tearful, sulky *UK: SCOTLAND, 1985*. **3** (used of the ocean) rough *TRISTAN DA CUNHA, 1993*

bubby *noun* the female breast. Usually in the plural *UK, 1655*

bubonic *noun* potent marijuana *US, 2001*

bubonic *adjective* potent, extreme, intense *US, 1993*

buccaneer *noun* a homosexual. Rhyming slang for QUEER *UK, 1998*

buccaneer *adjective* homosexual. Rhyming slang for QUEER *UK, 1998*

buck *noun* **1** a dollar. Originally US but applied in Hong Kong and other countries where dollars are the unit of currency *US, 1856*. **2** one hundred dollars; a bet of one hundred dollars *US, 1973*. **3** in motor racing, 100 miles per hour *US, 1993*. **4** a young black man. Overtly racist; an unfortunate favourite term of US President Ronald Reagan when speaking unscripted *US, 1835*. **5** used as a term of address. The racist implications of the word from the US are not present in the Bahamas *BAHAMAS, 1982*. **6** a male Australian Aboriginal. Now only in racist or historical use *AUSTRALIA, 1870*. **7** a male homosexual *US, 1984*. **8** a criminal; a hoodlum; a young ruffian. Originally Liverpool use, where it survives *UK, 2001*. **9** a type of homemade alcoholic drink *US, 1991*. **10** an attempt *NEW ZEALAND, 1941*. **11** in prison, a sit-down strike by the prisoners *US, 1972*. **12** a used car that is in very poor condition *US, 1980*. ▶ **pass the buck** to avoid responsibility by shifting the onus to someone else. Deriving from the game of poker *US, 1912*. ▶ **the buck stops here** the ultimate responsibility for whatever may be avoided by others is accepted here, or by me, or by this office. A popular catchphrase, originally coined in 1952 by US president Harry S. Truman who had it as a personal motto and displayed on his desk, just in case he forgot *US, 1952*

buck *verb* **1** to fight your way through a difficult surfing situation *US, 1965*. **2** in electric line work, to lower voltage *US, 1980* ▷*see:* BUCK IT. ▶ **buck the clock; buck the calendar** in oil drilling, to work hard in the hope of finishing a job by quitting time *US, 1954*. ▶ **buck the tiger** to play faro, a game of chance that was extremely popular in the C19 and only rarely seen in modern times *US, 1849*

buck *adjective* newly promoted, inexperienced. Military; a back-formation from now conventional 'buck private', also ranked in such company as 'buck sergeant' and 'buck general' *US, 1917*

buck and doe *noun* snow. Rhyming slang, generally as a complete rhyme on 'fuckin' snow' *UK, 1992*

buckaroo; buckeroo *noun* a proud, manly man of the Western sort, likely a cowboy *US, 1827*

buck cop *noun* a new constable in the Royal Canadian Mounted Police *CANADA, 1953*

bucker *noun* a lumberman who works on felled trees *CANADA, 1989*

buckeroo *noun* one dollar. An embellishment of BUCK *US, 1942*

bucket *noun* **1** a jail *US, 1894*. **2** a cell used for solitary confinement *US, 1989*. **3** the vagina *UK, 2001*. **4** the buttocks; the anus *US, 1938*. **5** a car *US, 1939*. **6** a small car *US, 2000*. **7** a truck with a non-roofed container *UK, 1981*. **8** in hot rodding, the body of a roadster, especially one from the 1920s *US, 1965*. **9** an engine cylinder *US, 1971*. **10** in pool, a pocket that appears receptive to balls dropping *US, 1988*. **11** an impressive quantity of alcoholic drinks. From the original sense (a single glass of spirits) *UK, 1985*. ▶ **have a bucketfull** said of a racehorse that has been fed heavily before a race to decrease its chances of winning *US, 1951*

bucket *verb* **1** to denigrate someone or something *AUSTRALIA, 1974*. **2** to throw something out, to throw something in the bin *UK: SCOTLAND, 1988*

bucket-a-drop *adverb* (of rain) falling heavily *GRENADA, 1996*

bucket and pail; bucket *noun* a jail. Rhyming slang *US, 1894*

bucket bong; bucket *noun* a water-pipe improvised using a bucket of water and a plastic bottle used for smoking marijuana. A combination of conventional 'bucket' and BONG (a water-pipe) *AUSTRALIA, 1994*

bucket gunner *noun* in carnival usage, a person who from a hidden location operates the mechanisms that determine a game's outcome *US, 1981*

bucket head *noun* a socially inept person *US, 1906*

bucket job *noun* an intentional loss in an athletic contest *US, 1955*

bucketload *noun* a great amount *UK, 1994*

bucket mouth *noun* in trucking, a trucker who monopolises conversation on the citizens' band radio *US, 1976*

bucket of blood *noun* a bar or dance hall where hard drinking and hard fighting go hand in hand *US, 1915*

bucket of bolts *noun* a dilapidated car, truck, boat or plane *US, 1942*

bucket of steam *noun* a mythical task for a newly hired helper on a job *US, 1963*

bucket shop *noun* an investment office that swindles its clients *US, 1879*

bucket worker *noun* a swindler *US, 1949*

buck fever *noun* in shuffleboard, the anxiety often experienced on the last shot *US, 1967*

buck for *verb* to energetically strive towards promotion, honours or some other target of personal ambition or recognition *UK, 1979*

buck general *noun* a brigadier general *US, 1947*

buck it; buck *verb* in craps, to roll a number that has previously been rolled *US, 1974*

buckle *verb* ▶ **buckle for your dust** in the Vietnam war, to fight with spirit and determination, thus winning the respect of fellow soldiers *US, 1991*

buckle bunny *noun* a woman who seeks short-term sexual liaisons with rodeo cowboys *US, 1978*

bucklebuster *noun* a line in a performance that is guaranteed to produce loud laughter *US, 1973*

buckled *adjective* **1** ugly *US, 1993.* **2** drunk *UK, 2002*

buckle my shoe *noun* a Jewish person. Most rhyming slang for 'Jew' uses 'two'; this term takes a traditional nursery-rhyme: 'one, two / buckle my shoe' *UK, 1977*

Buckley's chance; Buckley's hope; Buckley's *noun* no chance at all. Thought to be named after William Buckley, an escaped convict, but the fact that he evaded capture by living with Aboriginals for 32 years would rather imply that Buckley's chance should be very good. The ironic phrase 'You've got two chances: Buckley's and none!' is perhaps punningly connected with the name of a former Melbourne firm 'Buckley and Nunn' *AUSTRALIA, 1895*

bucko *noun* **1** a man, especially an unrefined or crude man *US, 1883.* **2** used as a term of address to a man. Slightly derisive, or at least kidding. From the C19 sense (a blustering bully) *UK, 1890*

buck-passer *noun* anyone who avoids a personal responsibilty by shifting the onus onto someone else. From PASS THE BUCK *US, 1933*

buck-passing *noun* an avoidance of responsibility by shifting the onus to someone else. From PASS THE BUCK *US, 1933*

buckra *noun* a white person *US, 1787*

buck rat *noun* the epitome of physical fitness *NEW ZEALAND, 1958*

Buck Rogers gun *noun* an M-3 Tommy gun *US, 1947*

bucks *noun* ▶ **the bucks** a lot of money *US, 1992*

Bucks *noun* Buckinghamshire. A spoken form of the conventional written abbreviation, considered colloquial when used in speech as a genuine equivalent of the original name *UK, 1937*

buckshee *noun* something above a usual amount that is given for free. Originally from the British Army in Egypt and India, ultimately from Persian. Occasionally used in the plural. Variant spellings include 'bucksheesh', 'buckshish', 'backsheesh', 'backshish', 'bakshee', 'baksheesh' and 'bakshish' *UK, 1916*

buckshee *adjective* **1** free, spare, extra *UK, 1916.* **2** worthless *CANADA, 1995.* **3** of a local non-commissioned officer, with rank but no additional pay *AUSTRALIA, 1959*

buck slip *noun* a form used for intra-office handwritten communications; officially a Routing and Transmittal Slip, Optional Form 41 *US, 1986*

buck's party *noun* a party or outing that is exclusively male; now especially an all-male pre-wedding party thrown for the groom *AUSTRALIA, 1918*

bucks up *adjective* in drag racing, winning and making money *US, 1968*

buckwheat *noun* **1** an unsophisticated rustic *US, 1866.* **2** a black male *US, 1978*

buckwheat farmer *noun* an unsuccessful, incompetent farmer *CANADA, 1944*

buckwheats *noun* **1** abuse, persecution *US, 1942.* **2** diminution of power or standing in an organised crime enterprise *US, 1964*

buck willy *adjective* uninhibited, rowdy, drunk *US, 2002*

bucky *noun* **1** a shotgun *US, 1995.* **2** a home-made gun *JAMAICA, 2000*

bud *noun* **1** the flower of the marijuana plant; hence marijuana *US, 1978.* **2** a girl *US, 1965.* **3** the female nipple *US, 1990.* **4** a friend, a buddy *US, 1935.* **5** used as a term of address, usually male-to-male *UK, 1614.* **6** the penis *BAHAMAS, 1982*

Bud *noun* Budweiser™ beer; a Budweiser™ beer *US, 2000*

bud *verb* to subject a boy to his first homosexual experience *UK, 1987*

budded; budded out *adjective* intoxicated on marijuana *US, 1997*

buddha *noun* **1** a type of LSD identified by a representation of Buddha *UK, 2004.* **2** a marijuana cigarette embellished with crack cocaine *US, 1989.* **3** potent marijuana, usually of Asian origin. Also spelt 'buddah' or 'buda' *US, 1988*

buddhaed *adjective* intoxicated on marijuana *US, 1997*

Buddha grass *noun* marijuana. Vietnam war usage *US, 1975*

Buddhahead *noun* a Japanese person. Offensive *US, 1945*

Buddha stick *noun* marijuana from Thailand packaged for transport and sale on a small stick *US, 1982*

Buddha zone *noun* death; the afterlife. Vietnam war usage; just a bit cynical *US, 1991*

Buddhist priest! used as a mock profanity to express surprise, disgust or annoyance during the war in Vietnam. A region-appropriate evolution of JUDAS PRIEST! *US, 1991*

buddy *noun* **1** a companion, a friend. A colloquial usage that is probably derived from 'brother' *US, 1850.* **2** a fellow citizens' band radio user. Citizens' band radio slang, adopted from the more general sense as 'a fellow, a man'; often used as 'good buddy' *US, 1976.* **3** in homosexual culture, a good friend who may or may not be a lover *US, 1972.* **4** a volunteer companion to a person with AIDS *US, 1984.* **5** a marijuana cigarette *US, 1991.* **6** a beer *US, 1994*

buddy-buddy *adjective* friendly *US, 1944*

buddy check *noun* a last-minute inspection of a parachutist's gear by his jump partner *US, 2000*

buddy-fuck *verb* (of a male) to steal a friend's date *US, 1966*

buddy gee *noun* a close friend *US, 1973*

Buddy Holly *noun* money. Rhyming slang for LOLLY, formed from the name of the US singer, 1936 – 59 *UK, 2004*

buddy poker *noun* a game of poker in which two friends are playing as partners, but not in collusion *US, 1968*

buddyro; buddyroo *noun* a pal; used as a term of address for a friend *US, 1951*

buddy system *noun* during the Korean war, a plan teaming American and Korean soldiers in the hope of providing one-on-one mentoring and training *US, 1968*

buddy window *noun* a hole between private video booths in a pornography arcade designed for sexual contact where none is officially permitted *US, 1996*

budge *noun* in the language of pickpockets, the front trouser pocket *US, 1949*

budget *adjective* below expectations, disappointing *US, 1986*

budgie *noun* **1** a budgerigar, a small parrot native to inland Australia and a common cage bird *AUSTRALIA, 1935.* **2** a talkative man, especially one of small stature; a small-time police-informer. From a passing similarity to a budgerigar's characteristics. The television drama *Budgie*, 1971 – 72, starred Adam Faith as the epitome of all of the above definition. It is difficult to tell whether the television programme created or popularised this usage *UK, 1977.* **3** the time. Used by miners, usually in the form of a question *UK, 1970.* **4** a hippie who moved back to the land in Slocan Valley, British Columbia *CANADA, 1989*

budgie-smugglers *noun* a pair of men's close-fitting and revealing nylon swimming trunks *AUSTRALIA, 2002*

budgie's tongue *noun* the clitoris, especially when erect. From the visual similarity *UK, 2002*

budgy *adjective* chubby *US, 1971*

bud head *noun* **1** a beer drinker. Not confined to drinkers of Budweiser™ beer *US, 1972.* **2** a frequent marijuana user *US, 1997*

budli-budli *noun* **1** anal sex. From Urdu *badli* (to change) *INDIA, 1961.* **2** a homosexual man *UK, 1998*

bud mud *noun* diarrhoea from drinking too much beer. An allusion to Budweiser™ beer *US, 1997*

buds *noun* **1** small female breasts *US, 1967.* **2** marijuana, especially the most psychoactive part of the plant. Also spelled 'budz' *US, 1997*

bud sesh *noun* an informal gathering for the social consumption of marijuana. Punning on BUDDY/BUD plus 'session' *US, 2005*

budsky *noun* used as a term of address. A meaninglessly decorative 'buddy' *US, 1984*

Budweiser crest; Budweiser label *noun* the emblem of the Navy SEALS (the sea, air and land team) *US, 1992*

buf; buff *noun* any large military aircraft like a Grumman A-6, a Boeing B-52, and a Sikorsky CH-33, especially the B-52

Stratofortress. An abbreviation of 'big ugly fat fucker' or, in polite company, 'fellow' *US*, *1968*

BUFE; buffy *noun* a ceramic elephant, ubiquitous in souvenir shops in Vietnam during the war. An initialism and acronym created from 'big ugly fucking elephant' *US*, *1973*

buff *noun* **1** an enthusiast, especially a knowledgable enthusiast, a specialist. Originally 'an enthusiast about going to fires', Webster, 1934, from the buff uniform of New York's volunteer firemen. The sense has gradually generalised until the field of interest has, in all cases, to be specified *US*, *1903*. **2** a fart. Echoic *UK*, *1965*. **3** a workout with weights *US*, *1989*. **4** a water buffalo *US*, *1977*. ▶ **in the buff** naked *UK*, *1602*

buff *verb* **1** to erase graffiti *US*, *1995*. **2** in hospital usage, to make notations in a patient's chart that makes the patient look better than they are and ready for the next stage of their care *US*, *1994*. ▶ **buff the banana** (of a male) to masturbate *US*, *2001*

buff *adjective* **1** handsome, excellent *US*, *1982*. **2** (of a young woman) sexually attractive. Current in south London *UK*, *2003*. **3** (used of a body) well-toned, well-exercised *US*, *1982*

buffalo *noun* **1** an American Indian male with especially long hair *US*, *1963*. **2** a five-cent piece. From the engraving on the coin *US*, *1945*. **3** the CV-7, a military transport aircraft built by DeHavilland Aircraft of Canada *US*, *1991*

buffalo *verb* to confuse someone, to intimidate someone *US*, *1960*

buffalo bagels! used for expressing disapproval. A signature line of Colonel Sherman Potter on *M*A*S*H* (CBS, 1972–83). Repeated with referential humour *US*, *1972*

buffalo gun *noun* a large calibre gun. Korean war usage *US*, *1989*

buffarilla *noun* an ugly girl. A blend of 'buffalo' and 'gorilla' *US*, *1968*

buff book *noun* a magazine catering to enthusiasts of a particular hobby or pastime *US*, *1993*

buffed; buffed up *adjective* muscular; in very good physical condition *US*, *1995*

buffer *noun* **1** a pleasant, foolish old man; a man. From French *bouffon* (a jester). As 'buffer' since 1749 but in the latter-half of C20 it seems to survive only as 'old buffer'. Modern usage implies a tolerant attitude to the subject *UK*, *1749*. **2** in the world of crack cocaine users, a woman who will perform oral sex in exchange for crack cocaine or the money to buy it *US*, *1992*

buffers *noun* the female breasts *US*, *1964*

buffet flat *noun* a party held to raise rent money *US*, *1982*

buff up *verb* to engage in strenuous exercise with a goal of body conditioning *US*, *2000*

bufu *noun* a male homosexual. An abbreviation of **BUTTFUCKER** *US*, *1982*

bug *noun* **1** a hidden microphone or listening device *US*, *1956*. **2** in the television and film industries, a small earphone used by a sound mixer *US*, *1977*. **3** any unspecified virus *UK*, *1919*. **4** a malfunction in design, especially of a computer or computer software *US*, *1878*. **5** a sociopathic criminal *US*, *1987*. **6** a burglar alarm *US*, *1926*. **7** an illegal numbers lottery *US*, *1963*. **8** in poker, a joker played as an ace or a wild card to complete a flush or straight *US*, *1967*. **9** an enthusiastic interest; a popular craze *UK*, *1902*. **10** a Bugatti sports car *US*, *1965*. **11** a Volkswagen car. A VW **BEETLE** is the eponymous hero of the Disney film *The Love Bug*, 1969 *US*, *1976*. **12** a chameleon. Circus and carnival slang *US*, *1973*. **13** in horse racing, a weight handicap *US*, *1941*. **14** in electric line work, a transformer *US*, *1980*. **15** a torch. Circus and carnival usage *US*, *1980*. ▶ **have a bug up your ass** to be annoyed or angry *US*, *1949*. ▶ **put a bug in someone's ear** to hint at something *US*, *1905*. ▶ **the bug** malaria *US*, *1947*

Bug *nickname* the Green Hornet Tavern in Pointe Claire, Quebec *CANADA*, *2002*

bug *verb* **1** to bother someone, to annoy someone *US*, *1947*. **2** to panic, to be anxious *US*, *1988*. **3** to watch something *US*, *1952*. **4** to talk and act in a disassociated, irrational way while under the influence of crack cocaine *US*, *1992*. **5** to confine someone in a psychiatric ward *US*, *1992*. **6** to arm something with an alarm *US*, *1919*. **7** to attach or install a listening device *US*, *1919*. **8** among vagrant alcoholics, to attack someone with bricks, bottles and boots *UK*, *1966*. **9** to dance *US*, *1968*

bugaboo *noun* an imagined object of terror *UK*, *1740*

bugaboos *noun* nasal mucus *BARBADOS*, *1965*

bugas *noun* a pair of trainers (sneakers) *JAMAICA*, *1998*

bug bag *noun* a sleeping bag *CANADA*, *1957*

bug boy *noun* in horse racing, a jockey who has not yet won a race and who is given a five-pound weight allowance. Because of the 'bug' or asterisk denoting the jockey's status in the racing programme *US*, *1968*

bug buster *noun* a physician specialising in infectious diseases *US*, *1985*

bug catcher *noun* in drag racing, an air scoop that forces air into the carburettor *US*, *1970*

bug collectors *noun* in motorcycle racing, unbreakable goggles *US*, *1973*

bug doctor *noun* a psychiatrist *US*, *1951*

bug dope *noun* insect repellant *US*, *1993*

bug eye *noun* **1** in television and film-making, a fisheye lens *US*, *1987*. **2** an Austin-Healy Sprite *US*, *1992*

bug flea *noun* an epidemiologist specialising in infectious diseases *US*, *1994*

bugfuck *adjective* deranged, out of control *US*, *1994*

buggalugs *noun* used as a term of address. A variation of **BUGGERLUGS** *NEW ZEALAND*, *2002*

bugged *adjective* **1** angry *US*, *1956*. **2** mentally unbalanced, crazy. Often used as 'bugged-out' *UK*, *2001*. **3** covered with sores and abscesses from septic injection of a narcotic. Drug addicts' use *UK*, *1978*

bugged up *adjective* anxious, nervous *US*, *1949*

bugger *noun* **1** a person who takes part in anal sex. A perfectly correct usage in legalese, otherwise considered vulgar *UK*, *1555*. **2** a disagreeable person; often used as a term of abuse *UK*, *1719*. **3** a person, a regular fellow *UK*, *1830*. **4** an unpleasant, very difficult or dangerous thing, project, episode, circumstance; a nuisance *UK*, *1918*. ▶ **give a bugger** to care, generally in a negative context *UK*, *1922*

bugger *verb* **1** to play the active role in anal sex *UK*, *1598*. **2** to bungle something, to ruin something *US*, *1847*. ▶ **be buggered** used for dismissing the sense of a word repeated from a preceding statement *UK*, *2001*

bugger! used as an expletive *UK*, *1923*

bugger about; bugger around *verb* **1** to waste time *UK*, *1923*. **2** to meander, to wander pointlessly around *UK*, *1923*. **3** to inconvenience or make difficulties for someone *UK*, *1957*. **4** to be unfaithful to your wife, or husband, etc. Whilst the act may well remain the same the sense here is not to commit adultery with someone but, rather, is defined in terms of the person spurned *CANADA*, *1980*. **5** to fiddle with something or someone; to caress or interfere with someone *UK*, *1937*

bugger all; sweet bugger all *noun* nothing whatsoever *UK*, *1918*

buggerama! used for expressing self-deprecating distress *NEW ZEALAND*, *1998*

buggeration! used as an expletive. An elaboration of **BUGGER!** *UK*, *1988*

buggeration factor *noun* any unforeseen hazard that complicates a proposed course of action. Originally military *UK*, *1981*

bugger-bafflers *noun* side-vents at the bottom rear of a man's jacket. Tailors' usage *UK*, *1971*

buggered *adjective* **1** damned *UK*, *1937*. **2** very drunk *UK*, *2005* ▷*see:* **BUGGERED UP; BUGGERED**

buggered if I know! used as a profession of absolute ignorance *UK*, *1984*

buggered up; buggered *adjective* exhausted, broken *UK*, *1923*

bugger for *noun* a person who is energetically committed to a subject *noun*, e.g. 'a bugger for work', 'a bugger for women' *UK*, *1970*

bugger-grips; bugger's grips *noun* side-whiskers, especially when generously proportioned. Originally naval; the image is of a convenient pair of grips for a sodomiser to hold on to during anal sex *UK, 1967*

bugger-in-a-bag *noun* around Cascapedia Bay, a fruit pudding in an oiled, floured bag to make it waterproof *CANADA, 1998*

buggerise about; buggerise around *verb* to fool about *AUSTRALIA, 1953*

bugger it! used as an expletive. A variation of BUGGER! *UK, 1961*

buggerlugs *noun* used as a form of friendly address. Originally nautical, used between men *UK, 1934*

bugger me! used as an expletive *UK, 1981*

bugger me backwards! used for registering surprise or exasperation. An elaboration on BUGGER ME! *UK, 2000*

bugger me dead! used for registering surprise *AUSTRALIA, 1971*

bugger me gently! used for registering surprise. In the late 1980s and early 90s, this exclamation was very much associated with the character Lizzie Birdsworth in the Australian television drama series, *Prisoner Cell Block H UK, 1984*

bugger off *verb* to leave, to go *UK, 1922*

bugger sideways *verb* to defeat someone, to confound someone. Often used as a personal exclamation: 'bugger me sideways!' *UK, 2002*

bugger sugar *noun* cocaine *UK, 2003*

bugger that for a joke! used as an expression of disbelief *NEW ZEALAND, 1949*

bugger this for a game of soldiers!; bugger that for a game of soldiers! 'no chance'; used as an emphatic dismissal of any activity or notion that you have no wish to subscribe to. A variation of SOD THIS FOR A GAME OF SOLDIERS!, FUCK THIS FOR A GAME OF SOLDIERS!, etc *UK, 1998*

bugger up *verb* to spoil something; to ruin something; to exhaust something *UK, 1937*

buggery *noun* hell. A substitute for 'hell' in strong phrases of rejection, ruination and disapproval. Used in phrases such as 'like buggery' (vigorously: 1937), 'go to buggery!' (go away!: 1966) or 'is it buggery!' (not likely!: 1984) *UK, 1898.* ▶ **to buggery; all to buggery** in a state of ruination or destruction *UK, 1923.* ▶ **will I buggery!** used as an expression of strong disagreement. Often applied in the third person: 'will he buggery!', 'will they buggery!' *UK, 1961*

buggery *adjective* used as an intensifier. On the model of BLOODY *UK, 1992*

buggery bollocks! used for registering annoyance *UK, 1992*

bugger you! used for registering anger towards someone *UK, 1887*

bugging *noun* an instance of attacking someone with violence *UK, 1966*

bugging *adjective* **1** disappointed, let down *US, 1996.* **2** crazy *US, 1995*

buggy *noun* **1** a car. Unavoidably, if not deliberately, folksy *US, 1926.* **2** a brakevan (caboose) *US, 1899*

buggy *adjective* silly, insane, or inbetween *US, 1902*

buggy whip *noun* a long radio antenna on a car or truck *US, 1962*

bug hole *noun* a run-down, disreputable theatre *US, 1952*

bughouse *noun* a mental hospital *US, 1899*

bughouse *adjective* insane, mad *US, 1894*

bug joint *noun* a premises that is infested with insects *UK, 1966*

bug juice *noun* **1** an insect repellant. The term was coined in World War 2 and has been used since. In Vietnam, there was no shortage of bugs or 'bug juice', which was also used to light fires, clean weapons and heat cans of c-rations *US, 1944.* **2** Kool-Aid™ (a fruit drink made from a powder to which you add water), or a sugary, powdered, artificially flavoured Kool-Aid-like drink. Coined in World War 2, popular in Vietnam, and the title and subject of a rousing Girl Scout song sung to the tune of 'On Top of Old Smokey' *US, 1946.* **3** medication given to those with mental disorders *US, 2002.* **4** any antibiotic *US, 1985.* **5** an opiate or other depressant used as knock-out drops *US, 1949.* **6** cheap alcohol. Originally just meaning

'whisky' but, over time, less discerning *US, 1863.* **7** in aviation, propeller de-icing fluid. US Air Force use *US, 1945.* **8** tear gas *US, 1950*

bugle *noun* **1** the nose *US, 1865.* **2** cocaine. Adapted from the previous sense, which is the favoured point of entry for most cocaine *UK, 1997.* **3** the erect penis *IRELAND, 1991*

bug off; bugg off *verb* to go away. A broadcastable euphemism for BUGGER OFF *UK, 1976*

bug-out *noun* **1** any hasty retreat; a dramatic evasive manoeuvre used by fighter pilots *US, 1957.* **2** a lively, wild time *US, 1995*

bug out *verb* **1** to flee *US, 1950.* **2** to go insane *US, 1961*

bugout unit *noun* a military unit with a reputation for running under fire. Korean war usage *US, 1982*

bug rake *noun* a comb. Juvenile; certainly since the 1950s, probably earlier *UK, 1983*

bug roost *noun* a hotel catering to oil field workers *US, 1954*

bug run *noun* a parting in the hair *UK, 1948*

bugs *noun* biology. School use *UK, 1963*

bugs *adjective* crazy *US, 1903*

Bugs Bunny *adjective* funny. Prison rhyming slang *NEW ZEALAND, 1997*

Bugs Bunny; bugs; bugsy *noun* money. Rhyming slang, based on the name of the Warner Brothers' animated cartoon character *AUSTRALIA, 1989*

bug ship *noun* during the Vietnam war, a Bell UH-1H Huey helicopter converted to spray the chemical defoliant Agent Orange *US, 1991*

bugsmasher *noun* a Beech C-47 Expeditor, a military transport plane used from World War 2 until early in the Vietnam war *US, 1991*

bug splat *noun* the limited devastation of targeted bombing *US, 2003*

bug test *noun* a psychological fitness test *US, 1992*

bug torch *noun* a railway lantern *US, 1975*

buh-bye goodbye. From a *Saturday Night Live* skit teasing the formulaic way in which flight attendants wish farewell to air passengers as they leave the plane *US, 1996*

build *verb* **1** to serve time in prison *US, 1967.* **2** to construct a marijuana cigarette. A variant is 'build up' *UK, 1994.* ▶ **build a fire** to operate a diesel truck at top speed *US, 1971.* ▶ **build that bridge** to get over something that took place in the past *US, 1995*

builder *noun* a bodybuilder *US, 1984*

building *noun* ▶ **on the building** in the building trade *UK, 1959*

build-up *noun* in horse racing, betting at the track designed to increase the odds on a bet made away from the track *US, 1960*

bukkake *noun* a photograph or video depicting multiple men ejaculating onto a single woman. Japanese slang meaning 'splash', used by English-speakers with no further knowledge of Japanese; a popular fetish in the US and UK. The prototype video shows a pretty young girl kneeling at the centre of a room with many men (up to several hundred) masturbating off camera and ejaculating on her with no further sexual contact *US, 2000*

bukuso'clock *noun* in the evening *SOUTH AFRICA, 2003*

bulb *noun* the core of a capsule of drugs *US, 1971*

bulb snatcher *noun* an electrician, especially one engaged in bulb replacement *US, 1974*

bulge *noun* **1** the male genitals, especially as may be hinted at or imagined when dressed *UK, 2002.* **2** a lead. Sports usage, describing team standings *US, 1951*

bulk *noun* ▶ **in bulk; in baulk; in balk** unable to do anything, especially as a result of laughter; disabled. From 'baulk' (an area of a snooker or billiards table) suggesting 'out of play' *UK, 1937*

bulk *adjective* large in amount or quantity *AUSTRALIA, 1977*

bulk *adverb* many; much, *1987*

bulkhead *verb* to speak disparagingly in a voice intended to be overheard *US, 1863*

bulkie *noun* in Boston, a sandwich roll *US, 1997*

bull *noun* **1** nonsense. An abbreviation of BULLSHIT *US, 1902.* **2** a police officer, especially a detective; a prison guard *US, 1893.* **3** an aggressive, mannish lesbian *US, 1967.* **4** in prison, a person who can withstand physical hardship *US, 1990.* **5** a wharf labourer unfairly favoured for employment *AUSTRALIA, 1957.* **6** an aggressive poker bettor *US, 1988.* **7** in the circus, an elephant, male or female *US, 1921.* **8** a battle tank *US, 1976.* **9** in a deck of playing cards, an ace *US, 1963* ▷*see:* BULLDYKE

bull *verb* **1** to polish something, especially boots; hence, to clean a uniform, kit or quarters. A variant is 'bull up'. Services usage since 1950, possibly earlier *UK, 1950.* **2** to lie; to pretend; to distort the truth or exaggerate; to tell tall stories *AUSTRALIA, 1954.* **3** to take the active role in homosexual anal sex; to be a homosexual *BARBADOS, 1987.* **4** in poker, to bluff repeatedly, betting in amounts designed to drive other players out of hands simply by virtue of the size of the bet *US, 1963*

bull *adjective* when describing a military rank, full. Korean war usage *US, 1973*

bull! used as an expression of utter disbelief, often surprised or contemptuous disbelief. A euphemistic shortening of BULLSHIT *AUSTRALIA, 1964*

Bullamakanka *noun* an imaginary remote place *AUSTRALIA, 1953*

bull and cow *noun* an argument, a disturbance. Rhyming slang for 'row' *UK, 1859*

bull and pants *noun* trousers. Rhyming slang for 'pants' *AUSTRALIA, 1961*

bull artist *noun* a person who habitually lies or exaggerates *US, 1918*

bullcrap *noun* nonsense. A slightly euphemised BULLSHIT *US, 1935*

bulldag *verb* to perform oral sex on a woman *US, 1954*

bulldagger *noun* a lesbian with masculine affectations and mannerisms. A variant of BULLDYKE *US, 1929*

bull derm *noun* any low grade of tobacco issued by the state to prisoners. A corruption of Bull Durham™, an RJ Reynolds tobacco brand *US, 2001*

bulldog *noun* **1** the earliest edition of a morning newspaper *US, 1986.* **2** a Mack™ truck. From the company's logo *US, 1971.* **3** in electric line work, a wire grip used for holding a conductor under tension *US, 1980*

bulldog *verb* **1** to turn a safe upside down and use an explosive to open it from the bottom *US, 1949.* **2** (used of a professional insider in horse racing) to falsely claim to have given good information in a completed race *US, 1968.* **3** in the illegal production of alcohol, to sweat whisky out of used barrel staves *US, 1974.* **4** to intimidate someone verbally and/or physically *US, 1992*

bulldog nose *noun* a severe case of gonorrhea. A truly hideous image *US, 1967*

bulldoze *verb* to coerce, to bully or to intimidate someone, especially to further political ends. By back-formation from conventional 'bulldozer' (a heavy caterpillar tractor for removing obstacles) *US, 1876*

bulldozer *noun* a poker player whose aggressive betting is not contingent upon holding a good hand *US, 1988*

bull dust *noun* nonsense, rubbish. A euphemism for BULLSHIT, but based on the Australian English term 'bulldust' (fine powdery dirt or sand as found in a stockyard) *AUSTRALIA, 1951*

bulldust *verb* to lie; to pretend; to distort the truth or exaggerate; to tell tall stories *AUSTRALIA, 1967*

bulldyke; bulldike; bull *noun* a lesbian with masculine affectations and mannerisms *US, 1931*

bulldyker; bulldiker *noun* a lesbian with masculine affectations and mannerisms. A variant of BULLDYKE *US, 1906*

buller *noun* a male homosexual *BARBADOS, 1996*

bullet *noun* **1** one year of a prison sentence *US, 1967.* **2** in cards, an ace *US, 1807.* **3** a portion of marijuana wrapped in plastic or tinfoil *NEW ZEALAND, 1979.* **4** a quart bottle of beer, especially of Budweiser™ beer *US, 1967.* **5** a capsule of secobarbital sodium (trade name Seconal™), a central nervous system depressant *US, 1972.* **6** a device that delivers a measured quantity of powdered drug for inhalation *UK, 1999.* **7** a narcotic suppository *US, 1984.* **8** a rivet *US, 1960.* **9** a short surfboard with a rounded nose *US, 1991.* **10** in skateboarding, a riding position: crouching low on the board with arms outstretched *US, 1976.* **11** a single spurt of semen during male ejaculation. Plays on SHOOT (to ejaculate) *US, 1966.* **12** dismissal from employment *UK, 1841.* **13** a rejection letter *US, 1982.* ▶ **put a bullet in Rover** to stop talking and start listening *US, 1992.* ▶ **with a bullet** advancing up the popular music charts. From the typographical symbol that indicates the tune's progress *US, 1980*

bullet bag *noun* a condom. Combines BULLET (an ejaculation of semen) with a suitable carrier/container *UK, 1998*

bullet lane *noun* the passing lane on a motorway *US, 1976*

bulletproof *adjective* **1** invulnerable, irrefutable *UK, 1961.* **2** in computing, able to withstand any change or external stimulus *US, 1991*

bullet-stopper *noun* a soldier in the infantry *US, 1998*

bull feathers *noun* nonsense. A euphemism for BULLSHIT *US, 1971*

bullfighter *noun* an empty railway carriage *US, 1946*

bull fries *noun* the cooked testicles of castrated bulls. More commonly known in the US as 'prairie oysters' *CANADA, 1987*

bullfrog *verb* in craps, to make a bet on a single roll of the dice *US, 1983*

bullfucker *noun* a liar; used as a friendly form of address to a fellow. Blends BULLSHITTER (a liar) and MOTHERFUCKER (a person) *US, 1979*

bull gang *noun* a large work crew, especially of unskilled workers *US, 1954*

bull goose *noun* **1** a railway yardmaster *US, 1977.* **2** by extension, the person in charge of any situation *US, 1932*

bullhead *noun* an extremely large penis *US, 1973*

bull horrors *noun* the terror of the police felt by a drug addict *US, 1927*

bullia capital *noun* crack cocaine *UK, 1998*

bulling *adjective* **1** very good *US, 1953.* **2** enraged *IRELAND, 1998*

bullion *noun* crack cocaine *UK, 1998*

bull it through *verb* to accomplish something by sheer strength rather than by skill and planning, especially of an outdoor task *CANADA, 1961*

bull jive *noun* **1** insincere talk *US, 1971.* **2** marijuana that has been adulterated with catnip or another leaf-like substance *US, 1973*

bull juice *noun* condensed milk. Mainly nautical use *UK, 1961*

bull-moose *noun* a huge, powerful man; hence, a foreman *US, c.1940*

bull night *noun* an evening on which recruits and trainees are confined to barracks to prepare for an inspection the following day. Military, based on BULL (to polish, to clean) *UK, 1984*

bull nun *noun* a monk *CANADA, 1960*

bullo *noun* nonsense. An elaboration of BULL *AUSTRALIA, 1942*

bullock *verb* **1** to work tirelessly. Adopting the characteristic from the beast *AUSTRALIA, 1875.* **2** to use an inner strength and determination in order to get your way or follow your ambition. A figurative use of the previous sense *AUSTRALIA, 1930*

bullocking *adjective* strong and aggressive in attack. From an earlier sense of the word (hard physical work) *NEW ZEALAND, 1959*

bullock's blood *noun* a drink of rum mixed in strong ale *UK, 1949*

bullocky *noun* beef. Pidgin *AUSTRALIA, 1839*

bull of the woods *noun* **1** a college official such as a dean *US, 1947.* **2** in oil drilling, an important company official *US, 1954.* **3** on the railways, a carriage shop foreman *US, 1968*

bullpen *noun* **1** a holding cell in a courtroom or a jail *US, 1880.* **2** an open area in an office with desks *US, 1983.* **3** in a nightclub, chairs without tables for patrons who want only to listen to the music *US, 1956.* **4** a room where a work crew congregates *US, 1946*

bull prick *noun* in oil drilling, an elevator pin *US, 1954*

bullpup *noun* **1** a target pistol, especially one with an elaborate stock *US, 1957*. **2** the air-to-ground missile (AGM) carried on fighter jets *US, 1991*

bull ring *noun* **1** a strongly-muscled anus; in terms of anal intercourse, a virgin anus. Homosexual use *UK, 2003*. **2** in motor racing, an oval track *US, 1965*. **3** in horse racing, a small track *US, 1976*

bullring camp *noun* a homosexual male brothel *UK, 1987*

bullringer *noun* on the railways, a yard pointsman *US, 1990*

bulls *noun* nonsense. A shortening of BULLSHIT *AUSTRALIA, 1969*

bull-scare *verb* (used of the police) to frighten or intimidate someone without arresting them *US, 1971*

bull session *noun* an informal group discussion *US, 1919*

bull's eye *noun* **1** a powerful, focused torch *US, 1992*. **2** fifty pounds (£50). From the score at darts *UK, 1997*

bullsh *noun* nonsense, rubbish. A euphemistic shortening of BULLSHIT *AUSTRALIA, 1919*

bullshipper *noun* an oilfield worker from Oklahoma *US, 1954*

bullshit *noun* nonsense *US, 1914*

bullshit *verb* to deceive someone, to fool someone *US, 1937*

bullshit! nonsense!, rubbish! *AUSTRALIA, 1985*

bullshit artist *noun* a person who habitually lies or exaggerates *US, 1942*

bullshit-ass *adjective* rubbishy, awful. Combines bullshit (nonsense) with -ASS (an intensifier for the preceding adjective) *US, 2002*

bullshit baffles brains used to describe the defeat of logic by a convincing argument. Originally military, probably from World War 2, this catchphrase even gave rise to the Pig Latin *excrementum vincit cerebellum* *UK, 1995*

bullshit black *noun* the flat black paint often found on a used car's chassis *US, 1962*

bullshit bomber *noun* a plane used in a propaganda-dropping operation *US, 1980*

bullshit rich *adjective* very rich. A gem from the slang of miners *US, 1994*

Bullshit Tax *nickname* the Canadian Blended Sales Tax (BST), as the Goods and Services Tax was known at first in the Maritime provinces. The introduction of this national tax in 1990 provoked protests, and the parody of the acronym BST in the Maritimes actually caused the government to change it to the HST (Harmonized Sales Tax) *CANADA, 1990*

bullshitter *noun* a liar, a braggart, a bluffer *US, 1933*

Bullshit Towers *noun* the control tower of an aerodrome *CANADA, 1995*

bullskate *verb* to pretend, to deceive someone, to brag. A euphemism for BULLSHIT *US, 1947*

bull's nose *noun* on the railways, a goods wagon coupler *US, 1975*

bull's wool *noun* any stolen goods *US, 1945*

bullsworth *noun* in circus usage, a lie *US, 1981*

bully *noun* a bulldozer *NEW ZEALAND, 1981*

bully *adjective* excellent *UK, 1599*

bully beef *noun* a senior prison-officer; a prison officer. Rhyming slang for 'chief' *UK, 1958*

bully beef *adjective* deaf. Rhyming slang, depending on Scottish pronunciation *UK, 1961*

bully club *noun* a police baton *US, 1963*

bully for you! excellent; good for you! Originally sincere, now ironic or jocular *US, c.1788*

bullyon *noun* cannabis resin and herbal marijuana. A misspelling of 'bouillon', a thin clear soup similar in appearance to marijuana tea, commercially available as small cubes which resemble blocks of HASH *UK, 2003*

bully stick *noun* a police baton *US, 1990*

bullywhack *verb* to lie or at least exaggerate *CANADA, 1987*

bulrush *noun* a paint brush. Rhyming slang *UK, 1998*

buly *noun* an ambulance *UK, 1988*

bum *noun* **1** the buttocks; occasionally and specifically, the anus, the rectum. A good Middle English word that survived in conventional usage until the late C18. The etymology is very uncertain; possibly from Italian *bum* (the sound of an explosion), and it is suggested (elsewhere) that 'bum' is echoic of buttocks slapping a flat surface. What is certain is that it is now in semi-conventional currency. It is not an abbreviation of BOTTOM which is a much later coinage *UK, 1387*. **2** a bag in which classified documents which are to be destroyed are placed *US, 1986*. **3** a lazy person; a beggar; a vagrant *US, 1864*. **4** a boaster, a braggart *UK: SCOTLAND, 1985*. ▶ **give your bum an airing** to use the lavatory *UK, 1984*. ▶ **on the bum 1** living as a beggar *US, 1907*. **2** (of machinery) not working, broken, not operating correctly *CANADA, 1961*. ▶ **take it up the bum** to take the passive role in anal intercourse *UK, 2003*

bum *verb* **1** to engage in anal intercourse. From BUM (the buttocks, the bottom); possibly playing on the phrase 'bum a fag' (to scrounge a cigarette) which can be understood to mean 'sodomise a gay man' *UK, 1999*. **2** to beg; to borrow something without the expectation of returning it *US, 1857*. **3** to feel poorly or depressed *US, 1989*. **4** to have a bad experience with a hallucinogenic drug *US, 1972*. **5** in computing, to improve something by removing or rearranging it *US, 1983*. **6** to wander, to idle, to live as a vagrant *AUSTRALIA, 1933*. **7** to boast, to brag. Also used as 'bum up' *UK, 1937*. ▶ **bum your chaff; bum your chat; bum your load** to tell a tall story to impress or convince someone *UK, 1937*

bum *adjective* **1** injured, damaged, faulty *US, 1902*. **2** inferior, bad, of poor-quality *US, 1859*

bum about; bum around *verb* to wander or live idly *US, 1926*

bumba; bumbo *noun* the anus or vagina *JAMAICA, 1980*

bum bandit *noun* a male homosexual *UK, 1983*

bum-beef *verb* to frame an innocent person *US, 1968*

bum bend *noun* an unpleasant experience under the influence of a hallucinogen *US, 1971*

bumbershoot *noun* an umbrella *US, 1896*

bumble bee *noun* **1** a motor cycle, especially a two-stroke model. Citizens' band radio slang, after the US sense (1976) as a 'two-stroke/two-cycle engine'; in both cases an allusion to the sound of the motor *UK, 1981*. **2** any two-cycle engine *US, 1971*. **3** an amphetamine tablet *US, 1980*

bumbled up *adjective* drunk to the point of passing out *US, 1968*

bumblee *noun* **1** a small car not built in the US. Dismissive, vaguely jingoistic; of the era when American-made cars dominated the market in the US but the influx of foreign-made cars had begun *US, 1968*. **2** in Passaic, New Jersey, a police officer *US, 2000*

Bumblefuck *noun* any remote, small town *US, 1989*

bumblepuppy *noun* in poker, an inexperienced and/or unskilled player. Originally from the game of whist *UK, 1884*

bumbo *noun* whisky *AUSTRALIA, 1942* ▷*see:* BUMBA

bumboclot; bumboclaat; bamb'clat; bumbaclaat *noun* **1** a sanitary towel; a cloth for wiping faeces. West Indian and UK black patois, literally 'bottom-cloth'. There is a, possibly disingenuous, belief amongst some Jamaicans that Bumbo was a king of Africa *JAMAICA, 1980*. **2** used as direct abuse or as an intensifier. West Indian and UK black patois. Can also be used as an exclamation to register shock, surprise or anger *UK, 1994*

bum boy *noun* **1** a homosexual male, especially a youthful, sexually inexperienced male who is the object of an older homosexual's desire *UK, 1929*. **2** a sycophant *UK, 1929*

bumbrella *noun* an umbrella *US, 1896*

bum bud *noun* inferior marijuana *US, 1993*

bum-bum *noun* the buttocks *TRINIDAD AND TOBAGO, 2003*

bum-bust *verb* to arrest someone on false or non-existent charges *US, 1977*

bumbye; bumbai *adverb* sometime soon. Hawaiian youth usage *US, 1981*

bum chum *noun* a passive homosexual male *AUSTRALIA, 1972*

bum crumb *noun* a small lump of excrement that clings to the anal hair *UK, 2003*

bum dough *noun* counterfeit money *US, 1992*

bumf; bumph *noun* **1** paperwork; official papers. An abbreviation of BUM FODDER (toilet paper) *UK, 1889*. **2** toilet paper. An abbreviation of BUM FODDER. The elaboration, 'bog bumf', not recorded until 1984, is tautological but pleasingly alliterative. *UK, 1889*

bum-face *noun* used as a derogatory form of address *UK, 1972*

bum-fluff *noun* **1** the soft facial hair of an adolescent boy. The image of sparsely spread hair on a backside *UK, 1949*. **2** empty talk; nonsense *AUSTRALIA, 1945*. **3** a contemptible man, especially one who is younger than, or of junior status to, the speaker *UK, 2000*

bum-flufferies *noun* details; the small print. An extension of BUMF (paperwork) but note BUM-FLUFF (nonsense) *UK, 2001*

bum fodder *noun* toilet paper. Around 1660 an anonymous author, now presumed to be Alexander Brome (1620–66), wrote 'Bummfoder: or Waste-Paper Proper to Wipe the Nations Rump with' *UK, 1660*

bum freezer *noun* a short coat *UK, 1932*

bum fuck *noun* a digital massage of the prostate via the anus and rectum as a diagnostic and therapeutic procedure *UK, 1961*

bumfuck *verb* to have anal intercourse, to sodomise someone. Combines BUM (the posterior) with FUCK (to have sex) *US, 1866*

Bumfuck, Egypt *noun* a mythical town that is the epitome of remoteness. With variants *US, 1972*

bum fun *noun* an intimate fondling of another's bottom *UK, 2000*

bum gravy *noun* liquid excreta, diarrhoea *UK, 2002*

bum-hole *adjective* inferior, bad *UK, 1984*

bumhole; bum-hole *noun* the anus. Logically follows BUM (the posterior) *UK, 1979*

bum jacket *noun* a short, everyday jacket *US, 1967*

bum-kicked *adjective* depressed *US, 1974*

bum-knuckle *noun* the coccyx; hence, also used as a generalised insult *UK, 2003*

bumlicker *noun* a sycophant, a toady. Combines BUM (the buttocks, the anus) with 'someone who licks'; as a demonstration of subservience this image is far older than the term and can be seen in C16 woodblocks of devil-worshippers pledging their service to the hindquarters of a goat *UK, 2000*

bum lift *noun* a procedure in cosmetic surgery to firm up the buttocks *UK, 1992*

bum man *noun* a man who is especially fond of female buttocks *NEW ZEALAND, 1998*

bummed *adjective* depressed, irritated *US, 1973*

bummer *noun* **1** a male homosexual. Also known as a 'bummer boy' *UK, 1967*. **2** a disappointing or depressing event *US, 1965*. **3** a bad experience with LSD or another hallucinogen *US, 1966*. **4** a beggar, a tramp, a bum *US, 1855*

bummy *noun* a transient, penniless, dirty person *US, 1923*

bummy *verb* to intimidate someone. Current among UK Yardies and other West Indian communities *JAMAICA, 2000*

bummy *adjective* dirty, wretched *US, 1896*

bummy-ass *adjective* low, disreputable, shoddy *US, 1990*

bum-numbing *adjective* used to describe any tedious activity that keeps a participant seated until the posterior has lost any sense of feeling *UK, 1976*

bum of the month *noun* a person identified as a poor performer. A term coined in connection with heavyweight boxer Joe Louis, who fought against a series of unworthy contenders *US, 1970*

bum out *verb* to depress someone; to disappoint someone *US, 1970*

bump *noun* **1** in a striptease or other sexual dance, a forceful pelvic thrust *US, 1931*. **2** in professional wrestling, a fall to the mat or floor, embellished with grunts, shakes and body spasms that create the impression that the opponent has truly hurt the victim *US, 2000*. **3** a dose of cocaine *UK, 1996*. **4** a single dose of the recreational drug

ketamine *US, 1995*. **5** a single dose of crystalised methadrine *US, 1985*. **6** crack cocaine; also counterfeit crack cocaine *UK, 1998*. **7** a fatal overdose of a drug. A nuance of the sense as 'a single dose of a drug', possibly influenced by the sense 'to kill' *UK, 2001*. **8** an assassination; a murder *US, 1919*. **9** in poker, an increase in the bet on a hand *US, 1988*. **10** in betting, a doubling of the bet in effect *US, 1986*. **11** a promotion in pay or responsibility *US, 1949*. **12** in computing, an increment *US, 1991*. **13** in volleyball, an underhand forearm pass to a team mate *US, 1985*. ▶ **the bump** dismissal from employment *UK: SCOTLAND, 1988*

bump *verb* **1** to kill someone *US, 1914*. **2** (of a prisoner) to let it be known that a debt owed to another inmate cannot be repaid *UK, 1996*. **3** to give an employee a promotion *US, 1957*. **4** to slide a large stack of gambling chips up next to a player's bet to size the amount of chips for a payoff *US, 1991*. **5** in poker, to increase another player's bet *US, 1961*. **6** to talk a customer into a higher price *US, 1980*. **7** to defraud someone, to swindle someone *UK, 1988*. **8** in professional wrestling, to fall to the mat in feigned pain *US, 1999*. **9** to boost a state of drug intoxication *UK, 1998*. **10** in a striptease or other sexual dance, to thrust the hips forward as if copulating *US, 1936*. **11** in hot rodding and low riding, to drive slowly in a lowered vehicle, especially one with a hydraulic suspension system that will bounce the car up and down *US, 1993*. **12** to develop breasts *BAHAMAS, 1982*. **13** to play music loudly *US, 1998*. ▶ **bump fuzz** (used of a female) to have sex with another woman *US, 1997*. ▶ **bump gums** to speak without saying much *US, 1945*. ▶ **bump heads** to fight *US, 1971*. ▶ **bump pussies; bump donuts; bump fur** (used of lesbians) to have sex, especially by engaging in vulva-to-vulva friction *US, 1967*. ▶ **bump the blanket** to masturbate in bed *UK, 2000*. ▶ **bump titties** to fight *US, 1985*. ▶ **bump uglies** to have sex *US, 1989*

bump and bore *verb* (of a racehorse) to veer off course and bump into an opponent *US, 2003*

Bump City *nickname* Oakland, California. The title of a 1972 record album by the group Tower of Power, as well as a 1979 book by John Krich *US, 1972*

bumper *noun* **1** the buttocks *US, 1963*. **2** the female breast. Generally in the plural *US, 1947*. **3** a person who enjoys performing oral sex on women *US, 1950*. **4** a lesbian *US, 1982*. **5** in pool, the cushion on the side of the table *US, 1990*. **6** in horse racing, a (National Hunt) flat race *UK, 1965*. **7** any alcholic beverage *BERMUDA, 1985*. **8** crack cocaine *UK, 2003*. **9** a cigarette butt *AUSTRALIA, 1899*

bumper *verb* **1** to make a whole cigarette from collected butts. From BUMPER (a cigarette butt) *AUSTRALIA, 1968*. **2** to extinguish a cigarette and save the butt for smoking later. From BUMPER (a cigarette butt) *AUSTRALIA, 1978*

bumper *adjective* especially large or enlarged *UK, 1759*

bumper jumper *noun* a vehicle that is too close behind another. Citizens' band radio slang *UK, 1981*

bumper kit *noun* the female buttocks *US, 1995*

bumper shine *verb* ▷*see:* BUM SHINE

bumper-shooter *noun* someone who picks up cigarette ends *AUSTRALIA, 1953*

bumper tag *noun* **1** a slight collision between cars, especially a rear end collision *US, 1980*. **2** in pool, a shot that is made off two cushions on the side of the table. Punning on a term commonly used to describe a traffic jam *US, 1990*

bumper-to-bumper *adjective* (used of car traffic) moving slowly and close together *US, 1938*

bumper-up; bumper-upper *noun* a prostitute's handyman *AUSTRALIA, 1953*

bumping *adjective* excellent *US, 1985*

bump list *noun* a list of murder targets *US, 1963*

bumpman *noun* in a pickpocket team, a confederate who bumps and distracts the targeted victim *US, 1940*

bump off *verb* to kill someone *US, 1907*

bumps *noun* **1** cocaine. From BUMP (a dose of cocaine) *US, 1997*. **2** loud bass notes as amplified on a stereo *US, 1997*

bump shop *noun* a car body repair shop *US, 1978*

bump spot *noun* in drag racing, the elapsed time of the driver in the final spot of the qualifying field, subject to being displaced by a better performance of a car yet to qualify *US, 1968*

bump stick *noun* in drag racing, a camshaft *US, 1968*

bum puncher *noun* a male taking the active role in anal sex, especially when finesse is not an issue *AUSTRALIA, 1985*

bump up *verb* to increase something *UK, 1940*

bumpy *noun* the buttocks *BERMUDA, 1985*

bum rap *noun* **1** an unfair or false accusation or reputation *US, 1952*. **2** a false criminal accusation; an unfair conviction *US, 1926*

bum-rap *verb* to arrest someone without proof of guilt *US, 1947*

bum robber *noun* a male homosexual. An exact synonym of ASS/ARSE BANDIT *UK, 1972*

bum-rush *verb* to swarm someone; to attack someone *US, 1987*

bumscare *verb* to drop your trousers, bend over and expose your buttocks *AUSTRALIA, 1985*

bum shine; bumper shine *verb* to hang onto the rear bumper of a car and slide behind it in icy weather *CANADA, 1987*

bumsicle *noun* a hypothermic alcoholic *US, 1994*

bums-on-seats *noun* a theatrical audience seen as a source of income *UK, 1982*

bum steer *noun* a piece of bad advice. A combination of BUM (inferior) and obsolete, except in this connection, 'steer' (direction) *US, 1924*

bumsters *noun* trousers designed to be worn very low on the hips. A play on the more familiar 'hipsters' and BUM (the buttocks) *UK, 2003*

bumsucker *noun* a sycophant *UK, 1950*

bum-sucking *adjective* sycophantic *UK, 1949*

bum tag *noun* a piece of faecal matter in the hair about the anus *UK, 1961*

bum trip *noun* **1** a bad experience with LSD or another hallucinogen *US, 1966*. **2** any bad experience *US, 1965*

bum tripper *noun* a person experiencing a psychotic break while using a hallucinogenic drug *US, 1967*

bumwad *noun* toilet paper, or any material used in place of toilet paper *US, 1896*

bum-waggle *verb* to power-walk. From the exaggerated motions of those who practise the sport *AUSTRALIA, 1984*

bum warmer *noun* a car coat *US, 1961*

bun *noun* **1** the vagina *US, 1970*. **2** a woman who has sexual intercourse with multiple male partners *AUSTRALIA, 2003*. **3** marijuana *UK, 1998*. **4** the head *NEW ZEALAND, 1984*. ► **do your bun** to lose your temper *NEW ZEALAND, 1960*. ► **have a bun on** to be drunk *US, 1960*

bun *verb* to take the active role in anal sex *AUSTRALIA, 1992*

bun bandit *noun* the active male in male-on-male anal sex *US, 1964*

bun-biter *noun* a sycophant or toady. School usage *US, 1961*

bun boy *noun* **1** a male homosexual prostitute whose prominent feature is his buttocks *US, 1983*. **2** a sycophantic assistant *US, 1988*

bunce *verb* to overcharge someone, especially if obviously rich or eager *UK, 1979*

bunce; bunts; bunse *noun* money; profit; extras. Possibly a corruption of 'bonus' *UK, 1812*

bunce up *verb* to pool your financial resources *UK: NORTHERN IRELAND, 1996*

bunch *noun* a non-specific amount of something *US, 1996*. ► **the bunch** in a race, the main body of competitors. A specialised variation of the conventional sense (a group of people) *UK, 1961*

bunch *verb* **1** to gather a deck of playing cards to shuffle *US, 1988*. **2** to quit a job *US, 1927*

bunched *adjective* physically exhausted *IRELAND, 1989*

bunch of bananas *noun* in a car, an exhaust system with individual headers that intertwine *US, 1965*

bunch of bastards *noun* a tangled rope. Naval origins *UK, 1961*

bunch of fives *noun* the fist; a punch; a series of blows delivered with the fist *UK, 1821*

bunch of flowers *noun* in horse racing, used by jockeys to describe a very small tip, or no tip at all, from an owner after winning a race *AUSTRALIA, 1989*

bunch of grapes *noun* a large mess of knots in a fishing line *AUSTRALIA, 1982*

bunch punch *noun* **1** sex involving multiple males and a single female *US, 1975*. **2** by extension, any chaotic situation in which it is not clear who is doing what to whom *US, 1975*

bunco *noun* **1** fraud; an act of fraud, especially a swindle by means of card-trickery; a confidence trick *US, 1914*. **2** a squad of police assigned to confidence swindles *US, 1947*

bunco *verb* to swindle someone, to cheat someone *US, 1875*

bunco artist *noun* a professional swindler *US, 1945*

bunco booter *noun* an infrequent smoker *US, 1996*

bundie *noun* a hamburger bun *IRELAND, 1991*

bundle *noun* **1** a good deal of money. From an earlier sense (a roll of money) *US, 1903*. **2** a long prison sentence *US, 1950*. **3** a bundle of packets of heroin; heroin *US, 1986*. **4** a sexually appealing woman *US, 1993*. **5** a fight *US, 1937*. ► **go a bundle on** to highly regard someone or something *UK, 1957*

bundle *verb* **1** to fight *UK, 1958*. **2** to make someone incapable of action *US, 1976*

bundle buggy *noun* a small delivery truck *US, 1971*

bundle of socks *noun* the head. Rhyming slang for 'thinkbox' *AUSTRALIA, 1945*

bundu *noun* wilderness, desert; the bush, the jungle; the countryside. Etymology unknown; possibly derived from the shona word for 'grassland'. Possibly adopted into British Military use during the campaign against the Mau-Mau in Kenya in the early 1950s; in 1984, the variant 'bundoo' was recorded in use by the British military in Northern Ireland *SOUTH AFRICA, 1939*

bunfight *noun* a tea party. A 'bun' is a 'sticky cake', and this describes what happens when a children's tea party gets out of hand *UK, 2001*

bun floss *noun* a thong-backed bikini bottom *US, 1991*

bung *noun* **1** a bribe *UK, 1950*. **2** a tip, a gratuity. Glasgow slang *UK, 1985*. **3** the anus *UK, 1788*. ► **on the bung** being in regular receipt of bribes, or receiving benefits in exchange for bribery *UK, 2001*

bung *verb* **1** to throw; to put; to send, especially with use of force *UK, 1825*. **2** to tip; to pay a financial gratuity *UK, 1958*. **3** to bribe someone *UK, 1950*. **4** to pay protection money to someone in authority. A specialisation of the previous sense *UK, 1968*. **5** to hit someone *UK, 1984*. ► **bung it on** to behave pretentiously; to give oneself airs and graces *AUSTRALIA, 1942*. ► **bung on an act** to give an exaggerated performance; to indulge in histrionics *AUSTRALIA, 1962*. ► **bung on side** to behave pretentiously; to give oneself airs and graces *AUSTRALIA, 1967*. ► **bung on the bull** to behave pretentiously *AUSTRALIA, 1973*

bung *adjective* broken, ruined, wrecked. Originally Aboriginal pidgin English meaning 'dead', from the Australian Aboriginal language Jagara *AUSTRALIA, 1897* ▷*see:* BONG. ► **go bung** to fail *AUSTRALIA, 1885*

bungalow *noun* a dormitory room *US, 1992*

bunged *adjective* tipsy *SOUTH AFRICA, 1946*

bunger *noun* **1** a bruised and discoloured eye *US, 1949*. **2** an exploding firework *AUSTRALIA, 1929*. **3** a cigarette *AUSTRALIA, 1995*

bung-full *adjective* absolutely full, especially as a result of eating and drinking. Full up to the point where a stopper should be necessary to contain it all *UK, 1984*

bunghole *noun* **1** the anus *UK, 1611*. **2** by extension, a despicable, unlikeable person *US, 1968*. **3** a pastry treat made from leftover pie dough spread with brown sugar, cinnamon and butter *CANADA, 1992*. **4** cheese *AUSTRALIA, 1919*

bunghole *verb* to sodomise someone. From the noun BUNGHOLE (the anus) *US, 1939*

bungi *verb* to have anal sex CANADA, 2002

bungie *noun* a mildly left-wing white student in South Africa during the struggle against apartheid SOUTH AFRICA, 1996

bungie-hole *verb* to sodomise someone. A variation of BUNGHOLE US, 1997

bung navel *noun* a protruding navel BARBADOS, 2003

bungo *noun* a very black, ugly and stupid rustic JAMAICA, 1979

bung on *verb* **1** to put on an article of clothing, especially carelessly. From BUNG (to throw, to put) UK, 1984. **2** to stage a party, event, etc AUSTRALIA, 1972

bungo-toughy *noun* a young child who behaves poorly; a little ruffian GUYANA, 1996

bunhead *noun* a dolt; an outcast US, 1988

bun-huggers *noun* tight-fitting trousers US, 1964

bunjee; bunjie; bungee *noun* an India-rubber eraser; India rubber. More familiar in later use as 'elasticated rope' and, since 1979, in an extreme sports context (bungee jumping) UK, 1928

bunk *noun* **1** nonsense US, 1900. **2** a weak drug, especially heroin US, 1992. **3** a hiding place US, 1950. **4** a prisoner's cell or the area immediately around his bed in a dormitory setting US, 1998. ▶ **do a bunk; pull a bunk** to abscond, to run away UK, 1870

bunk *verb* **1** to abscond or play truant, usually from school or work. Also to 'bunk off' UK, 1934. **2** to sleep, to stay the night. Introduces a military or Western feel US, 1840. **3** to travel without a ticket UK, 1996. **4** to carry a passenger on the cross-bar of a bicycle AUSTRALIA, 1959. **5** to hide something US, 1950

bunk *adjective* worthless US, 1990

bunker *noun* **1** anal sex US, 1949. **2** a premises used by a criminal gang as a base from which to conduct violent robberies UK, 1982

bunkered *adjective* in a situation from which it is difficult to escape. A figurative application of golfing terminology UK, 1894

bunk fatigue *noun* sleep US, 1915

bunk fee *noun* the amount charged to smoke opium in an opium den US, 1992

bunk flying *noun* dramatic, on-the-ground discussions of flying exploits US, 1933

bunk in *verb* to sneak into an entertainment venue without paying. Schoolboy reversal of 'bunk off' UK, 2000

bunk patrol *noun* a nap while off duty. Mounted Police usage CANADA, 1953

bunkum *noun* nonsense. In or around 1820 the Congressman representing Buncombe County in North Carolina, USA, in seeking to impress his constituents, made a pointless speech to Congress; over time 'Buncombe' became 'bunkum' US, 1862

bunk-up *noun* **1** an act of sexual intercourse. Originally military, post-World War 2 UK, 1958. **2** a lifting-up as assistance in climbing or reaching AUSTRALIA, 1919

bunky *noun* in jail or prison, a cellmate US, 1858

bunnit *noun* ▶ **do your bunnit** to lose your temper. Glasgow slang UK, 1985

bunny *noun* **1** a Playboy Club hostess; a nightclub hostess dressed in a costume that is representative of a rabbit. A shortening of the official job-description: Bunny Girl US, 1960. **2** a woman blessed with few if any sexual inhibitions US, 1971. **3** a female surfer or a male surfer's girlfriend US, 1936. **4** a homosexual male prostitute US, 1967. **5** the rectum US, 1977. **6** a conversation UK, 1958. **7** a person who talks too much, especially stupidly UK, 1954. **8** a fool, a dupe AUSTRALIA, 1943. **9** a pilotman UK, 1970. **10** in shuffleboard, the disc on a number representing the winning score US, 1967. **11** in the sport of field archery, a 15 cm target face. Derives from the small face of a 'bunny' (rabbit) which, along with faces of other small creatures, is used as a target UK, 1988

bunny *verb* to talk, to chat. The childish word for a 'rabbit' replaces the rhyming slang RABBIT AND PORK; RABBIT (to talk) UK, 1958

bunny boiler *noun* an obsessive, possessive woman. From the action in the film *Fatal Attraction*, 1987, in which actress Glenn Close put the fear of God into adulterous men UK, 2002

bunny boilery *adjective* of a woman scorned, unhealthily obsessed with her (ex-)lover. From BUNNY BOILER UK, 2003

bunny book *noun* a sexually explicit magazine. From the Playboy bunny. US, 1967

bunny boot *noun* a large white felt boot, now usually made of rubber with an inflatable air layer for insulation US, 1954

bunny cap *noun* a fur-lined pile cap. Vietnam war usage US, 1968

bunny chow *noun* a hot Indian or Malay curry served in a hollowed out loaf of bread. Created and coined by Hindi Indians in Durban SOUTH AFRICA, 2001

bunny dip *noun* a method of serving bar customers drinks calculated to keep a woman's breasts from spilling out from a low-cut, tight bodice. A technique perfected by and taught to Playboy Bunnies US, 1985

bunny fuck *verb* to have sex quickly, if not frantically US, 1971

bunny hole *noun* an excavation in a fox hole to provide protection from a mortar attack. Korean war usage US, 1957

bunny hop *noun* the act of bouncing both wheels of a bicycle off the ground into the air US, 1953

bunny hug *noun* a girl's hooded sweatshirt. Especially in Saskatchewan, where it gets very cold in winter, this term is used for a key warm layer of clothing CANADA, 2004

bunny suit *noun* a thick flight suit worn by an aircrew member over an anti-gravity suit US, 1966

buns *noun* **1** the buttocks US, 1877. **2** the feet US, 1973

bunt *noun* the buttocks. A blend of 'buttocks' and 'cunt' US, 1967

bunter *noun* a prostitute US, 1973

bunty *noun* **1** semen UK, 2000. **2** an affectionate term for a small person, especially a small middle-aged woman. From Scottish/Irish dialect UK, 1977

buoy *noun* a surfer who lingers in the water, rarely catching a wave US, 1991

bupkes; bupkis *noun* nothing – used for expressing scorn at something deemed foolish or trivial. From the Russian for 'beans' US, 1942

bupp *verb* to strike your head against something BARBADOS, 1965

buppie; buppy; bumpie *noun* a (young) black urban professional; a (young) black upwardly mobile professional. A socio-economic acronym on the model of YUPPIE; as forced as 'yuppie' seemed natural and only a marginal term in the vernacular US, 1986

buppies *noun* bread and butter; a slice of bread and butter. After earlier variations: 'bupper', 'buppie', 'bups', 'bupsie'; derived by infantile reduction UK, 1978

'burb *noun* a suburb. Often in the plural US, 1971

burble *verb* in computing, to post an inflammatory message that displays the person's complete ignorance on the subject in question. From Lewis Carroll's 1871 *Through the Looking Glass*, in which the Jabberwock 'burbled' (spoke in a murmuring or rambling manner) US, 1991

bureau-drawer special *noun* a small, inexpensive handgun US, 1962

burg *noun* **1** a city or town US, 1835. **2** a burglary US, 1983

burger *noun* **1** a variety of MDMA, the recreational drug best known as ecstasy UK, 1996. **2** a shapeless, uneven wave. An abbreviation of MUSHBURGER US, 1991. **3** a scrape or raw bruise suffered while skateboarding US, 1976

burglar *noun* **1** a prison officer doing a surprise cell-search, especially of an officer who is considered an expert in this business. Heavily ironic UK, 1980. **2** the operator of a dishonest carnival game US, 1950

buried *adjective* **1** of food, canned JAMAICA, 1979. **2** in new car sales, owing more on a loan than the car securing the loan is worth US, 1975

buried treasure *noun* in computing, an unexpected and usually poorly written piece of code found in a program *US, 1991*

burk *verb* to vomit *US, 1960*

burk; burke *noun* ▷*see:* BERK

burl *noun* **1** an attempt, try or go at anything *AUSTRALIA, 1917.* **2** in horse racing, odds of 5–1. Rhyming slang, abbreviated from 'Burl Ives' for 'fives' *AUSTRALIA, 1989*

burlap *noun* dismissal from employment. An elaboration of the more common term, 'getting the SACK' *US, 1951*

burley; burly *noun* burlesque *US, 1934*

burleycue *noun* burlesque *US, 1923*

burlin *adjective* drunk *UK, 2002*

Burlington hunt *noun* **1** the vagina. Rhyming slang for CUNT. A lesser-known variation of Berkshire hunt and Berkeley hunt *UK, 1960.* **2** a fool. Rhyming slang for CUNT *UK, 1960*

burly *noun* **1** something which is not easily accomplished *US, 1993.* **2** in foot-propelled scootering, a difficult trick or stunt which has pain or injury as the price of failure; a scooter-rider who specialises in such tricks *UK, 2000*

burly *adjective* **1** intimidating. A surfer term used to describe a wave, brought into broader youth usage *US, 1993.* **2** very cold *US, 1991*

burly show *noun* in carnival usage, a burlesque show *US, 1981*

BURMA written on an envelope, or at the foot of a lover's letter as lovers' code for '*be undressed (or upstairs) and ready my angel*'. Widely-known, and well-used by servicemen. Now a part of the coded vocabulary of texting *UK, 1960*

Burmese Fuckin' Incredible *noun* a variety of marijuana seed from British Columbia *CANADA, 2002*

burn *noun* **1** tobacco; a cigarette *AUSTRALIA, 1960.* **2** a swindle *US, 1960.* **3** an exhibition, a display. From BURN (to spray graffiti) *US, 2002.* **4** a thrill-seeking act of fast driving *AUSTRALIA, 1965.* **5** the initial flooding of sensations after injecting heroin *US, 1973.* **6** a caustic chemical treatment of the skin *US, 1997*

burn *verb* **1** to put someone to death by electrocution *US, 1927.* **2** to kill someone *US, 1933.* **3** to shoot a gun at someone, either just grazing them or making them jump to avoid being hit *US, 1953.* **4** to cheat, swindle someone *UK, 1698.* **5** to put someone under an unfair obligation *UK, 1997.* **6** to expose the identity of a person or place *US, 1959.* **7** to completely cover another graffiti artist's work with your own *US, 1995.* **8** in private dice games, to stop the dice while rolling, either as a superstition or to check for cheating *US, 1950.* **9** while playing blackjack, to place an unplayed card into the discard card holder *US, 1982.* **10** to smoke marijuana *US, 1964.* **11** to infect someone with a sexually transmitted disease *US, 1967.* ▶ **burn an Indian** to smoke marijuana *US, 1992.* ▶ **burn logs** to smoke marijuana *UK, 2001.* ▶ **burn paint** (used of a car or truck) to be engulfed in flames *US, 1977.* ▶ **burn someone's butt** to annoy, to irritate someone *US, 2001.* ▶ **burn the breeze** to drive fast *US, 1971.* ▶ **burn the lot** (used of a carnival) to cheat a town so badly that no carnival will be able to come to that town for some time *US, 1989.* ▶ **burn the main line** to inject a drug intravenously *UK, 1998.* ▶ **burn the road up** to leave *US, 2002.* ▶ **burn the yellow** to race through a yellow traffic light. Used in Montreal, translated and borrowed from the French *CANADA, 1992.* ▶ **burn up the wires** to spend a great deal of time on the telephone. Originally a term applying to the telegraph. As telephones become increasingly independent of wires, it will be interesting to see if the phrase survives *US, 1954.* ▶ **enough money to burn a wet mule** a great deal of money. Slang synonyms for 'money' are found in variants of the phrase *US, 1895*

burn and smoulder *noun* the shoulder. Rhyming slang, perhaps in reference to a sunburnt shoulder *UK, 1992*

burn artist *noun* a cheat, a conman, especially in dealings with drugs *US, 1968*

burn, bash, bury used as the rubbish disposal creed of Australian troops in Vietnam *AUSTRALIA, 1990*

burn cards *noun* in blackjack played in casinos, a few cards taken from the top of a newly shuffled pack and discarded *US, 1980*

burn down *verb* **1** to overuse and thus ruin something *US, 1953.* **2** to shoot and kill someone *US, 1932*

burned out; burnt out *adjective* **1** recovering from drug dependence *UK, 1978.* **2** exhausted beyond mental or physical capacity *US, 1980*

burner *noun* **1** a criminal who specialises in breaking into safes using an acetylene torch *US, 1950.* **2** a handgun *US, 1926.* **3** a very fast runner *US, 1978.* **4** an extraordinary person *US, 1952.* **5** a marijuana smoker *US, 1985.* **6** a drug addiction *US, 1992.* **7** a complete piece of graffiti art *US, 1997*

Burnese; burnie *noun* cocaine. A variation on Berni, Bernice or Bernie *US, 1933*

burn head *noun* any Rastafarian who defies the norms and shaves *JAMAICA, 1980*

burnie *noun* a partially smoked marijuana cigarette *US, 1952*

burning and turning *adjective* of a helicopter, with engine running and blades rotating *UK, 1978*

burn off *verb* to drive very fast, especially if showing off *AUSTRALIA, 1984*

burnout *noun* **1** a person whose mental capacity has been diminished by extended drug or alcohol use *US, 1973.* **2** an uninhabitable, ruined tenement, whether it has been burnt or not *US, 1987.* **3** in drag racing, the pre-race spinning of the car's rear tyres to clean and heat the tyres, producing crowd-pleasing smoke and noise *US, 1988.* **4** in the youth trend for 'souped-up' motor-scootering, any achievement of a daring, risk-taking rider *UK, 2004*

burn out *verb* to make a fire in a prisoner's cell as retaliation for real or perceived cooperation with prison authorities *US, 1974*

burnout box *noun* in drag racing, the area where tyres are heated and cleaned before a race *US, 1993*

burn rubber! leave me alone! *US, 1996*

burnt *adjective* exhausted *US, 1995*

burnt cheese *noun* a fart *AUSTRALIA, 1998*

burnt cinder; burnt *noun* a window. Cockney rhyming slang, relying on the accent for an accurate rhyme *UK, 1958*

burnt end *noun* in bowls, a stage of play that has to be replayed when the jack is driven out of bounds *UK, 1990*

burn-through *noun* the process of cleaning tyres on a dragster with bleach poured on the ground over which the tyres are spun *US, 1970*

burnt money *noun* a bet in a dice game lost because of a rule violation *US, 1997*

burnt offering *noun* overcooked food, especially meat. Adopted, ironically, from the conventional religious sense *UK, 1937*

burn-up *noun* the act of racing or riding fast on a motorcycle. To 'burn-up' the tyre-rubber and leave scorch-marks on the road *UK, 1971*

burn up *verb* to fall silent; to stop talking. Often as an imperative *AUSTRALIA, 1971*

burp *noun* **1** an act of vomiting; vomit *AUSTRALIA, 1967.* **2** a belch. Echoic *US, 1932.* **3** any alcoholic beverage *BERMUDA, 1985* ▷*see:* BOTTOM BURP

burp *verb* to belch; to cause a baby to belch. The variant spelling, 'birp', has been recorded *US, 1932.* ▶ **burp the worm** (of a male) to masturbate *US, 2001*

burp gun *noun* a submachine gun *US, 1946*

burp 'n' blow *noun* an act of burping into your cupped hands then blowing the retained air at a chosen victim *UK, 2004*

burqa *noun* an out-of-style fashion garment. The conventional 'burqa' is a complete head and body shroud worn by women in the strictest Muslim societies. This teenspeak reflects the end of fundamentalist Taliban rule in Afghanistan *US, 2002*

burr *noun* the recurring operating expenses in a circus or carnival *US, 1980*

burrhead *noun* a black person *US, 1902*

burrito *adjective* cold. From 'brrrr' as a vocalisation of feeling cold *US, 1997*

burrito bag *noun* a mesh restraint used by police to contain a violent person *US, 1997*

burrito poncho *noun* a condom *UK, 1998*

burro *noun* a racehorse that does not perform well *US, 1947*

burroo; brew; buro *noun* an unemployment exchange; the Department of Social Security. From a Glasgow pronunciation of 'bureau' as in 'Employment Bureau' *UK, 1937*

burrower *noun* a researcher. Security service jargon *UK, 1977*

burr under your saddle blanket *noun* an unexplained irritability *CANADA, 1987*

burr up your ass *noun* a person with a displeased focus on something *US, 1960*

burst *noun* **1** a period of re-enlistment in the military. A 'burst of six' would thus be re-enlistment for six years *US, 1968*. **2** a drinking binge *NEW ZEALAND, 1998*

burst *verb* **1** to strike someone violently. This usage is common all over Ireland, and is used in a rhetorical sense, rather than literally *IRELAND, 1987*. **2** to pay for something that costs relatively little with a banknote. Literally 'to burst the completeness of the banknote'; a variation of conventional 'break' *UK, 1988*. **3** to ejaculate *BAHAMAS, 1971*. ▶ **burst out in fairy lights** to show an expected level of enthusiasm *UK: SCOTLAND, 1996*

burster; buster *noun* anything of superior size or astounding nature *US, 1831*

bursting at the seams *adjective* overfull *UK, 1962*

Burton-on-Trent; Burton *noun* rent. Rhyming slang, based on an East Midlands' town *UK, 1932*

Burton-on-Trent; Burton *adjective* homosexual. Rhyming slang for BENT (homosexual) *UK, 1996*

burwash *noun* a swindle, for fun or profit *UK, 1983*

bury *verb* **1** to sentence a criminal to a long or life term in prison *US, 1904*. **2** in casino gambling, to place a card in the middle of a deck or in the discard pile *US, 1991*. ▶ **bury the stiffy** from a male perspective, to have sex *US, 1994*. ▶ **bury the tach** to rev an engine up beyond what would be considered a prudent revolutions per minute level. The tachometer measures the revolutions per minute *US, 1992*

bus *noun* **1** an ambulance *US, 1992*. **2** a wheelbarrow *TRISTAN DA CUNHA, 1906*. **3** a plane *UK, 1913*. **4** a car *UK, 1921*. **5** a large touring motorcycle. Biker (motorcycle) usage *US, 2003*. ▶ **more bus than Battoo** big-breasted. Battoo is the owner of a bus company *TRINIDAD AND TOBAGO, 2003*. ▶ **on the bus** part of a countercultural movement. From the language of Ken Kesey, Neal Cassady and the Merry Pranksters *US, 1994*

bus *verb* to shoot a gun at someone *US, 1995*. ▶ **bus one** to leave *US, 1993*

bus and tram *noun* jam. Rhyming slang, possibly punning on the constituent parts of a traffic jam *UK, 1978*

bus and truck *adjective* said of a travelling show, with the cast and crew travelling by bus, with the props and wardrobe in a truck *US, 1973*

bus driver *noun* **1** in poker, the player in a given hand who controls the betting *US, 1996*. **2** a pilot, especially the pilot of a military transport aircraft *US, 1944*

buse *verb* to swear at someone. An abbreviation of 'abuse' *BARBADOS, 1965*

bus face *noun* the worn-out look gained from sleeping on a bus overnight *US, 1997*

bush *noun* **1** pubic hair, especially a woman's pubic hair. A source for endless punning during the US presidential election of 2000; President Bush Jr's lack of *gravitas* opened him up to 'bush' puns to an extent that his father did not have to endure *UK, 1650*. **2** a sexually active female *US, 1966*. **3** a bushy hairstyle, especially on a black person *US, 1972*. **4** marijuana *US, 1951*. **5** cocaine *US, 1998*. **6** the woods *US, 1997*. **7** the suburbs. An urban sneer; from the conventional Australian sense of 'bush' (country in its natural state) *AUSTRALIA, 1942*. ▶ **go bush** to move to or visit the county *AUSTRALIA, 1916*. ▶ **take the bush; take to the bush** to escape; to run wild;

to leave the town for the country. Originally of escaping convicts; but also carrying the sense of an Aborigine returning to traditional life *AUSTRALIA, 1804*

Bush *nickname* Flatbush, Brooklyn, New York *US, 1995*

bush *verb* **1** to ambush someone *US, 1947*. **2** in the used car business, to extract through any of a series of questionably ethical means more from a customer than originally contemplated by the customer *US, 1953*. **3** to deceive someone *US, 1971*

bush *adjective* **1** second-rate, amateurish *US, 1959*. **2** rough and ready *AUSTRALIA, 1969*

bush Baptist *noun* a religious zealot lacking formal theological training *US, 1967*

bush-bash *verb* to forge a path through scrubland; to travel through virgin bush *AUSTRALIA, 1967*

bush basher *noun* a person who forges a new pathway through scrubland *AUSTRALIA, 1971*

bush blaster *noun* the penis *US, 2001*

bush bunny *noun* a woman from a remote area; a naive, unsophisticated woman *FIJI, 2004*

bush captial *nickname* Canberra, the capital city of Australia. So-called because it was a new city built in the 'bush' (countryside) halfway between the two major cities of Sydney and Melbourne *AUSTRALIA, 1906*

bush child *noun* an illegitimate child *CAYMAN ISLANDS, 1985*

bush dance *noun* an Australian-style country dance *AUSTRALIA, 1983*

bush dinner *noun* oral sex on a woman *US, 1967*

bus head *noun* hair that is in complete disarray after a long bus ride *US, 1988*

bushed *adjective* **1** very tired *US, 1879*. **2** showing adverse psychological effects from having to live in bad weather. Confinement and isolation, especially in the north of North America, give this widely used term a special meaning, different from 'going native' *CANADA, 1952*. **3** lost in bushland *AUSTRALIA, 1844*. **4** lost, but not in the bush *AUSTRALIA, 1963*

bushel *noun* **1** in trucking, a load of half a ton *US, 1976*. **2** the neck, the throat. The full form is 'bushel and peck'. Rhyming slang, based on imperial units of volume *UK, 1979*

bushel-cunted *adjective* possessing a slack and distended vagina *US, 1980*

bushel of coke *noun* a man. Rhyming slang for a BLOKE *UK, 1960*

bushes *noun* any place where sexual activity takes place, whether or not an actual bush is involved *US, 1975*

bushfire *noun* used as a comparison for something that is exceedingly fast *AUSTRALIA, 1962*

bushfire blonde *noun* a red-headed woman *AUSTRALIA, 1943*

bush gang *noun* a prison work gang working without the traditional chains *CANADA, 1987*

bush herb *noun* unremarkable marijuana *UK, 1994*

bushie *noun* **1** a rough, tough, unattractive or otherwise unappealing woman. From BUSHPIG *AUSTRALIA, 1987*. **2** a person who lives in the bush. Can be used negatively to mean a 'country bumpkin', or positively to refer to someone skilled at surviving in the harsh conditions of the Australian outback *AUSTRALIA, 1887*

Bushie *noun* a supporter or a member of the administration of US President George W. Bush *US, 2002*

Bush is another word for cunt used as a slogan that registers absolute contempt for US President George W. Bush. Punning on the sense of BUSH as pubic hair and CUNT (the vagina) as 'despicable individual' *US, 2003*

bush lawyer *noun* a person with some knowledge of law but no actual qualifications *AUSTRALIA, 1835*

bush-league *adjective* petty, mediocre, trivial, inconsequential, second-rate *US, 1908*

bush light *noun* in the pornography industry, a light used to illuminate the genitals of the performers *US, 1995*

bushline *noun* ▶ **put out the bushline on the ice** in Cape Breton, to set out the small evergreen trees on solid ice to mark a trail for skating or skimobiling on a road. The term, by extension, seems to apply to a variety of metaphorical situations, involving fitness CANADA, 2000

bush mag *noun* a magazine featuring photographs of naked women, focusing on their pubic hair and vulvas US, 1972

bushman's breakfast *noun* a yawn, a stretch, urinating and a look around, or some variation thereof NEW ZEALAND, 1998

bushman's clock *noun* a kookaburra, a native Australian bird with a loud laughing territorial call frequently heard at dawn and dusk AUSTRALIA, 1846

bushman's hanky *noun* the act of blowing nasal mucus from one nostril while holding the other closed AUSTRALIA, 1996

bush mechanic *noun* a mechanic with no formal training and, often, no special skill BAHAMAS, 1982

Bush-muncher *noun* a proponent of US President George W. Bush's points of view. Derogatory; a play on BUSH (the pubic hair, hence the vagina) and CARPET-MUNCHER (a cunnilinguist), which leads to an obvious parallel with ARSE/ASS-LICKER (an obsequious sycophant) US, 2003

bush orchestra *noun* a morning chorus of indigenous New Zealand song birds NEW ZEALAND, 1982

bush pad *noun* a motorcycle's passenger seat. Biker (motorcycle) usage, coarsely identifying a woman passenger in terms of her genitals US, 2003

bush parole *noun* escape from prison US, 1960

bush patrol *noun* sex with a woman. The BUSH in question here is the woman's pubic hair US, 1964

bushpig *noun* a rough, tough, unattractive or otherwise unappealing woman AUSTRALIA, 1985

bush-pop *verb* (of cowboys) to ride in the bush to round up cows CANADA, 1964

bushranger *noun* a person who commits petty crime; a swindler or cheat. Figurative use of the usual sense as 'an escaped convict who lives by highway robbery', common during Australia's colonial era AUSTRALIA, 1855

bush shave *noun* a shave without the benefit of water or shaving cream US, 1990

bush telegraph *noun* an information network utilising word of mouth; the grapevine AUSTRALIA, 1962

bush time *noun* during the Vietnam war, the amount of time spent in combat US, 1987

bush tucker *noun* food consisting of native Australian flora and fauna. Originally used to refer to food making up the diet of Australian Aboriginals, nowadays also for items of restaurant cuisine AUSTRALIA, 1895

Bush Week *noun* a putative week during which country folk visit the city and the normal rules of society are laid aside. Always in the formulaic rhetorical question 'What do you think this is? Bush Week?' AUSTRALIA, 1919

bushwhacker *noun* **1** an outlaw who attacks by ambush US, 1926. **2** a rapist. Playing on the sexual meaning of BUSH US, 1976. **3** a man who enjoys sex in park bushes US, 1966. **4** a person from the country; a country bumpkin US, 1809

bush whiskey *noun* strong, homemade whisky US, 1999

Bushy Park *noun* **1** a lark, a spree. Rhyming slang, formed on the name of a park close to Hampton Court UK, 1859. **2** a woman's pubic hair. By extension, the shortened form 'bushy' is a pet name for 'the vagina', deriving from BUSH (pubic hair); possibly a play on the outer London beauty spot Bushey Park, source of the similar, now obsolete C19 phrase 'take a turn in Bushey Park' (to have sex) US, 1980

business *noun* **1** sex with a prostitute; prostitution. From a sense, originating in C17, as 'sexual intercourse'; in 1630 the described cost was 'one hundred crownes' UK, 1911. **2** the genitals, male or female US, 1949. **3** a syringe employed by intravenous drug users US, 1949. **4** the actual cheating move of a card cheat US, 1973. **5** used as a deliberately vague reference to any matter that is of concern or under consideration; later use tends to describe the matter (in phrases such as 'a bad business') without being any more specific UK, 1605. **6** when combined with an indefinite intensifier in phrases such as 'what a business', 'quite a business', etc, something unexpectedly difficult to do or get UK, 1843. ▶ **do business 1** to engage in an illegal activity such as bribery US, 1984. **2** in pool, to intentionally lose a game or other competition US, 1989. **3** in horse racing, to cooperate in the fixing of a race US, 1951. ▶ **do the business** to settle the matter UK, 1823. ▶ **do your business** to defecate UK, 1645. ▶ **give someone the business; do the business** to have sex US, 1942. ▶ **on the business** engaged in prostitution UK, 1961. ▶ **the business 1** the finest, the most perfect, the most complete; anything particularly good UK, 1982. **2** prostitution US, 1952

business end the operative part of something, the part that matters UK, 1878

business girl *noun* a prostitute UK, 1888

businessman *noun* **1** any official or witness who will accept a bribe US, 1950. **2** in horse racing, a jockey who may be persuaded to lose a race intentionally US, 1951

businessman's special; businessman's lunch *noun* DMT (dimethyltryptamine), a powerful but short-lasting hallucinogen. An allusion to the fact that it can be taken, experienced and recovered from in short order US, 1967

bus jockey *noun* a bus driver US, 1954

busk *verb* to work as a street entertainer. The earlier sense from which this derives means 'to offer goods and entertainment for sale in bars' US, 1920

busker *noun* an itinerant purveyor of entertainment to passers-by in the street, or on the London Underground, or other informal locations. Possibly from 'buskin', a short boot worn by entertainers from C16–19 UK, 1859

bussie *noun* a bus driver. Common among professional baseball players in the days when bus travel dominated travel between cities US, 1967

bust *noun* **1** a police raid, especially for suspected drug offences US, 1938. **2** an arrest US, 1953. **3** a burglary UK, 1857. **4** a complete failure US, 1842. **5** in poker, a worthless hand US, 1963

bust *verb* **1** to arrest someone US, 1940. **2** to catch someone with evidence of guilt; to report on someone US, 1960. **3** to reduce someone in rank or standing US, 1878. **4** to inform the police; in later use especially, to inform the police about illicit drugs UK, 1859. **5** to inform on a fellow prisoner UK, 1980. **6** to insult someone US, 1985. **7** to praise and promote something US, 1997. **8** to give someone something, to lend someone something US, 1990. **9** in pontoon (blackjack, vingt-et-un), to exceed 21 points UK, 1939. **10** in pool, to break to start a game US, 1990. **11** when driving, to turn in a new direction US, 1993. **12** in the used car business, to reduce a car in price US, 1975. **13** to smoke a marijuana cigarette US, 1998. ▶ **bust a box** to break into a safe US, 1966. ▶ **bust a cap 1** to shoot a gun US, 1965. **2** to use drugs US, 1971. ▶ **bust a few** to surf US, 1997. ▶ **bust a grape** in prison, to commit a foolish act as a result of a sense of intense desperation US, 1990. ▶ **bust a gut** to make a great effort. Originally a dialect term UK, 1912. ▶ **bust a move 1** to make a move; to take action; to dance US, 1984. **2** to move quickly US, 1991. ▶ **bust a stop sign** to ignore a stop sign US, 1973. ▶ **bust a trick** in foot-propelled scootering, to achieve success in a difficult manoeuvre UK, 2000. ▶ **bust jungle** to break through a jungle with a tank or armoured carrier. Vietnam war usage US, 1977. ▶ **bust laugh** to laugh out loud. Hawaiian youth usage US, 1982. ▶ **bust someone's balls** to tease someone relentlessly, provoking their anger US, 1955. ▶ **bust someone's drawers** to have sex, seen as a conquest US, 1990. ▶ **bust suds** to wash dishes US, 1971. ▶ **bust the mainline** to inject a drug into a vein US, 1938. ▶ **bust the rut; bust a rut** to blaze a trail. From the Northern Territory AUSTRALIA, 1951. ▶ **bust your boiler** to over-exert yourself NEW ZEALAND, 1946. ▶ **bust your buns** to exert yourself; to try hard US, 1964. ▶ **bust your chops** to harass or provoke someone US, 1953. ▶ **bust your conk** to feel very happy, especially under the influence of a drug US, 1973. ▶ **bust your guts out** to over-exert yourself *NEW ZEALAND, 1959.* ▶ **bust your hump** to work extremely hard *UK, 2001.* ▶ **bust your nut** to experience an orgasm *US, 1964*

bust *adjective* without funds *US, 1990*

busta *noun* **1** a person who informs on another *US, 2000.* **2** a social outcast *US, 1998*

bust developer *noun* a singer who performs during a striptease act *US, 1981*

busted *adjective* **1** without, or very short of, money; bankrupt, ruined *US, 1837.* **2** ugly *US, 2002*

buster *noun* **1** pleasure, especially sexual pleasure *US, 1973.* **2** something that is excellent *US, 1973.* **3** used as a term of address. Lends a self-conscious, old-fashioned tone *US, 1866.* **4** a fool *US, 1995.* **5** in circus usage, a bad fall. An allusion to comic actor Joseph 'Buster' Keaton *US, 1981.* **6** a heavy fall from a horse *AUSTRALIA, 1878.* **7** a firecracker *US, 1952.* **8** a hard roll of bread. Trawlermen's term *UK, 1969.* **9** any of several tools used by burglars or as weapons *US, 1949.* **10** in poker, a card that does not improve a hand *US, 1961.* **11** a shoplifter *CANADA, 1984.* **12** a strong wind from the south. A shortening of SOUTHERLY BUSTER *AUSTRALIA, 1873.* **13** on a plane, full power *US, 1991* ▷ *see:* BURSTER

busters *noun* dice that have had their spots altered to aid cheating *US, 1962*

bust hand *noun* in bar dice games, a roll that produces no points for the player *US, 1971*

bust-head *noun* potent whisky or beer, especially if manufactured illegally *US, 1857*

bus therapy *noun* keeping a problem prisoner in transit in prison transport between prisons *US, 1996*

busticate *verb* **1** to break *US, 1916.* **2** to leave *US, 2002*

bus ticket *noun* a transfer from one prison to another *US, 1989*

bust in *verb* in a dice cheating scheme, to introduce altered dice into a game *US, 1963*

bustle-punching *noun* frottage; an act of unwanted intimacy, usually in a crowded place, when a man rubs his penis against the hindquarters of an unsuspecting woman *UK, 1977*

bustle rack *noun* on a tank, welded pipe framework on the turret used as a sort of roof rack, storing food, drinks and supplies *US, 1991*

bust off *verb* to experience orgasm. Derives from BUST YOUR NUT *US, 1996*

bust on *verb* **1** to criticise someone, to tease someone *US, 1986.* **2** to shoot someone *US, 2001*

bust-out *noun* a bankruptcy forced upon a business by organised crime, usually a lending enterprise owed money by the head of the business *US, 1988*

bust out *verb* **1** to take over a legitimate business, exploit its credit to the maximum, and then liquidate all assets *US, 1962.* **2** in a dice cheating scheme, to remove altered dice from a game and reintroduce the legitimate dice *US, 1963*

bust-out *adjective* **1** in gambling, dishonest or part of a cheating scheme *US, 1937.* **2** without money, broke *US, 1965*

bust-out joint *noun* a casino or gambling establishment that cheats gamblers *US, 1979*

bust-out man *noun* in a dice cheating scheme, the confederate whose special skill is the switching of tampered dice with the legitimate dice *US, 1950*

bust-out mob *noun* a group of confederates gambling with altered dice *US, 1972*

bust-up *noun* an altercation; a serious argument or disagreement. From the earlier sense (an explosion) *UK, 1899*

busty substances *noun* the female breasts. A jocular coinage by comedian Peter Cook *UK, 1966*

bus' up *verb* to wreak havoc. Hawaiian youth usage *US, 1981*

bus-whargus *adjective* extremely ugly *NORFOLK ISLAND, 1992*

busy *adjective* **1** actively searching for, or engaged in, a sexual liaison. Homosexual usage *US, 1965.* **2** (used of a card in poker) producing a

pair or otherwise improving a hand *US, 1988.* ▶ **get busy 1** to have sex *US, 1989.* **2** to rob someone *US, 1987*

busy; bizzy; busie *noun* police; a police officer, originally a detective. From earlier 'busy fellow' – a suggestion that plain clothes officers are busy while their uniformed colleagues 'plod' *UK, 1904*

busy as a one-armed paper-hanger in a gale *adjective* extremely busy. First recorded in the US and New Zealand, but also known in Canada where it may be lengthened by 'with the itch', and in Australia and UK with the elaboration 'with crabs' or 'with the crabs' *US, 1939*

busy bee *noun* phencyclidine, the recreational drug known as PCP or angel dust *US, 1994*

busylickum *noun* a nosey person *BARBADOS, 1965*

but *noun* a halibut. Trawlermen's use *UK, 1980*

but *adverb* though, however. Used at the end of a statement. This is one feature of Australian English that parents and teachers have long sought to wipe out via the correction of any youth saying it. Typically the argument 'you can't end a sentence with a preposition/conjunction' is put forward, but clearly 'but' is an adverb here, modifying the verb of the statement (not to mention highlighting the grammatical ignorance of the would-be corrector). Speakers of US and British English are often confused when first meeting this regionalism, and will patiently wait for the continuation of the sentence following what they hear as a conjunction – 'it isn't coming, but!'. The first undeniable example dates to 1938, and it was common by the 1950s. Also heard among Hawaiian youth *AUSTRALIA, 1938*

but *conjunction* **1** used for expressing surprise or recognition of something unexpected *UK, 1846.* **2** used for emphasizing the following word or words *UK, 1887*

butch *noun* **1** the person fulfilling the masculine role in a homosexual relationship *US, 1954.* **2** a very short haircut *US, 1982*

butch *adjective* **1** overtly masculine *US, 1936.* **2** fulfilling the masculine role in a male or female homosexual relationship. Originally applied to male and female homosexuals, but later predominantly to lesbians *US, 1941.* **3** heterosexual *US, 1949.* **4** unafraid, unabashed. A nuance of the 'overtly masculine' sense used in contemporary gay society *UK, 2003*

butch broad *noun* an aggressive lesbian with masculine affectations *US, 1966*

butch dike *noun* an aggressive, mannish lesbian *US, 1969*

butcher *noun* **1** a beer glass of 170 ml capacity; also, a serving in one of these glasses. Used only in the state of South Australia, the 'butcher' was originally a long thin glass holding over a pint; the size has gradually diminished over the years. Said by some to be derived from the German *becher* (C19 South Australia had a large German migrant community), but this doesn't sound remotely like 'butcher'. Other folk etymologies about butchers requiring a certain type of beer glass abound *AUSTRALIA, 1889.* **2** a surgeon *US, 1849.* **3** a medical student. Used by undergraduates of the University of Sydney *AUSTRALIA, 1984.* **4** a prison dentist *UK, 1996.* **5** a prison guard captain *US, 1983.* **6** in a pack of playing cards, a king *UK, 1937*

Butcher Brigade *nickname* the 11th Infantry Brigade of the Americal Division, US Army. So named after the Brigade's role in the massacre at My Lai became known *US, 1991*

butcher charts *noun* large pieces of paper used during a briefing or brainstorming session. Named because the paper used is similar to the paper used by butchers to wrap meat *US, 1986*

butcher's apron *nickname* the ribbon of the United Nations' medal for active service in Korea. From the narrow vertical white stripes and washed-out blue background. The nickname was already current in 1954 *UK, 1954*

butcher's hook; butcher's *noun* a look. Rhyming slang *UK, 1936*

butcher's hook; butcher's *adjective* ▶ **go butcher's hook** to get angry or upset *AUSTRALIA, 1918.* sick, ill, unwell. Rhyming slang for CROOK *AUSTRALIA, 1967*

butcher shop *noun* a hospital casualty department or operating room *US, 1918*

butcher's overall *noun* a surgeon's white protective overall. Royal Navy use *UK, 1964*

butch it up *verb* to act in an aggressive, manly manner. Homosexual usage, male and female *US, 1963*

butch kick *noun* in the usage of pickpockets, a hip pocket *US, 1949*

butch number *noun* a manly homosexual man desired by others as a partner in sex *US, 1967*

butch out *verb* (used of a woman) to affect a mannish appearance *US, 1999*

butch pad *noun* an apartment or house where lesbians congregate *US, 1973*

butch queen *noun* a decidedly masculine male homosexual *US, 1966*

butch trade *noun* a seemingly heterosexual man who consents to homosexual sex in the male role, receiving orally or giving anally *US, 1970*

butchy *adjective* overtly masculine in affectation and mannerisms *US, 1956*

bute *noun* butazolodin, a pain-killer *UK, 1981*

but, I digress used as a humorous end to a wandering thought. A catchphrase attrbitued to author Max Shulman in cigarette advertisements of the 1950s *US, 1961*

butler *noun* crack cocaine *UK, 2003*

butler's revenge *noun* an inaudible fart. A public school coinage, commenting on the dignified restraint of senior male servants; *not an eponym UK, 1984*

but mine is worth... used as a bragging description of a BMW car *CANADA, 2002*

butt *noun* **1** the buttocks, the posterior; used in many senses and phrases as a replacement for 'arse' or 'ass' *UK, 1720*. **2** by extension, the tail end of anything *US, 1970*. **3** the tail end of a prison sentence *US, 1949*. **4** a cigarette *US, 1902*

butt *verb* in tiddlywinks, to knock a wink off a pile *US, 1977*

butt *adverb* very *US, 1990*

butt board *verb* to ride a skateboard sitting down *US, 1997*

butt boy *noun* a sycophant; a toady *US, 1950*

butt can *noun* any improvised ashtray *US, 1968*

butt-check *verb* in snowboarding, to maintain balance by making brief contact between buttocks and snow *UK, 2002*

butt drop *noun* a backwards fall while snowboarding *US, 1990*

butt end *noun* the discarded end of a cigarette or marijuana cigarette *UK, 2000*

buttendski *noun* the buttocks *NEW ZEALAND, 1998*

butter *noun* **1** insincerity *US, 1945*. **2** crack cocaine *US, 1998*

butter; butters *adjective* ugly, unattractive. Perhaps a play on BUTT UGLY. Current in south London *UK, 1998*

butter-and-egg man *noun* an unsophisticated free spender. Coined by 1920s nightclub performer Texas Guinan for a shy, middle-aged man so flattered by her friendliness that he paid the steep cover charge for every guest in the house and pressed $50 notes on all the entertainers. When he said he was in the dairy business, she introduced him as 'the big butter-and-egg man' *US, 1924*

butter and eggs *noun* an illegal lottery. Most commonly known as a NUMBERS game *US, 1973*

butterball *noun* **1** a fat person or animal *US, 1941*. **2** an idiot *UK, 1981*

butterbar *noun* a second lieutenant in the US Army. Vietnam coinage, from the gold-bar insignia. *US, 1973*

butterbox *adjective* (of a man) effeminate. From an earlier sense (fop) *UK, 1971*

butter boy *noun* a very young police officer. After an earlier senses as 'novice' applied to sailors and taxi drivers *UK, 1977*

buttered bread *adjective* dead. Rhyming slang *UK, 1998*

buttered bun *noun* a prostitute, or, less specifically any woman, who has already had sex with several customers/men; sex with this woman. Also heard in the plural *UK, 1699*

butter-fingered *adjective* prone to dropping things *UK, 1615*

butterfingers *noun* a clumsy person, prone to dropping things. After the adjective *UK, 1837*

butterflies in your stomach; butterflies *noun* the feeling of queasiness that accompanies fear or nervousness. The fluttering of butterflies as a metaphor for the unsettled sensations of trepidation *US, 1940*

butter flower *noun* marijuana. From the appearance of cannabis resin *US, 1971*

butterfly *noun* **1** a person who is romantically fickle *US, 1947*. **2** a note thrown from a train to a repair crew *US, 1946*. **3** in electric line work, a conductor take-up reel *US, 1980*. **4** in television and film-making, a large screen used to direct or diffuse light *US, 1987*

butterfly *verb* **1** to engage in promiscuous sex *US, 1946*. **2** in the gambling game two-up, to toss the coins so that they flutter in the air and appear to be actually spinning. The object of butterflying is to make the coins fall the way the tosser wishes and is consequently illegal in the game *AUSTRALIA, 1949*. **3** to leave someone *US, 1991*

butterfly kiss *noun* an intimate caress made by fluttering eyelashes over a partner's skin *UK, 1871*

butterfly wheel *noun* in drag racing, a bifurcated steering wheel shaped like two opposing butterfly wings *US, 2002*

butterhead *noun* a stupid person, especially a stupid black person *US, 1963*

buttering-up *noun* an act of persuasive flattery *UK, 1819*

butter legs *noun* a promiscuous woman. Because, like butter, her legs are 'easy to spread' *AUSTRALIA, 1985*

buttermilk *noun* beer *US, 1977*

butter up *verb* to flatter someone with an intent to persuade them *UK, 1819*

butter would not melt in someone's mouth an appearance of innocence. Usually contemptuous in the phrase 'as if butter would not melt in his/her mouth' occasionally shortened to 'butter would not melt' *UK, 1530*

butt floss *noun* a thong or string bikini with only a slender piece of fabric passing between the cheeks of the buttocks *US, 1991*

butt-fuck *verb* **1** to copulate anally *US, 1968*. **2** to light one cigarette with the burning butt of another *US, 2001*. **3** since the Vietnam war, to attack from the rear *US, 1991*

buttfucker *noun* a homosexual male *US, 1997*

butt fucking *noun* anal sex *US, 1999*

Butt Fucking Nowhere *noun* any remote place *US, 2002*

butt hair *noun* a parting down the centre of the head *US, 1991*

butthead *noun* a generally unlikeable, disagreeable, dim-witted person *US, 1973*

butthole *noun* **1** the anus *US, 1951*. **2** by extension, a despicable or offensive person *US, 1962*

buttie *noun* a walk in the company of a friend. Possibly extended from 'butty/buttie' (a friend) *UK: SCOTLAND, 1988*

butt in *verb* to intrude into another's business or conversation *US, 1899*

buttinski; buttinsky a meddler; a person who interferes in the affairs of others *US, 1902*

buttkiss *noun* nothing at all. Variation of BUPKES; BUPKIS *US, 1997*

butt kit *noun* an ashtray *US, 1958*

buttlegger *noun* a person who smuggles cigarettes from states with low or no cigarette taxes to states with high cigarette taxes *US, 1976*

buttlegging *noun* the smuggling of cigarettes from states with low or no cigarette taxes to states with high taxes *US, 1977*

buttload *noun* a large amount *US, 1991*

buttly *adjective* very ugly. A blend of 'butt' and 'ugly' *US, 1989*

buttmunch *noun* a contemptible person *US, 1996*

button *noun* **1** a police badge *US, 1929*. **2** by extension, a police officer *US, 1953*. **3** a person who acts as lookout *US, 1992*. **4** in organised crime, a person who kills on the orders from above. Sometimes expanded as 'button man' or 'button guy' *US, 1966*. **5** a small quantity of an item to be smuggled *US, 1956*. **6** the edible, psychoactive portion of a peyote cactus *US, 1953*. **7** opium *UK, 1996*. **8** a tablet of Mandrax™, a branded tranquillizer *SOUTH AFRICA, 2002*. **9** the clitoris *UK, 1900*. **10** the chin. Boxing jargon, usually in the phrase 'on the button', describing a blow right on the chin *US, 1920*. **11** in poker, a marker on the table that signifies the dealer; the dealer *UK, 2003*. **12** a Chrysler car equipped with push-button automatic transmission *US, 1968*. **13** in the television industry, a dramatic or funny climax to a scene *US, 1990*. ▶ **not have a button** to have no money *IRELAND, 1992*. ▶ **on the button** exactly; precisely. Possibly from boxing jargon, 'on the BUTTON' (on the chin) *US, 1903*

button *verb* ▶ **button your lip; button your lips; button your face; button it; button up** to stop talking. Often as an injunction or exclamation. Used since 1836; and 'button it' first recorded in 1980 *US, 1947*

button B *adjective* very short of money. From the 1920s until the 60s, in a UK telephone box you would press button B to get your money back, hence this pun on 'pressed for money' *UK, 1961*

button-dicked *adjective* possessing a small penis *US, 1994*

buttoned up *adjective* **1** of a reserved or uncommunicative nature. A figurative image *UK, 1936*. **2** silent, refusing to answer questions. In line with the injunction to BUTTON YOUR LIP *UK, 1959*. **3** (of persons) alert, well-prepared *UK, 1967*. **4** (of a plan or a situation) successfully organised or well-prepared. A variant is 'buttoned' *UK, 1940*

button-hole *noun* a *button-hole* flower; a bouquet *UK, 1879*

buttonhole maker *noun* a person who has only females as children *US, 1954*

button mob *noun* uniformed police officers, especially in large numbers when present at a political demonstration or similar gathering. Used by those in whom the police seem interested *UK, 1977*

buttons *noun* **1** a page (a domestic servant). Survives mainly as Buttons, a character in the pantomime of *Cinderella UK, 1848*. **2** a messenger *US, 1962*

button up *verb* to close completely *US, 1941*

butt out *verb* to extricate yourself from the interference in which you are engaging. Generally as an imperative *US, 1906*

butt plant *noun* a backwards fall while snowboarding *US, 1993*

butt plate *noun* used as a friendly if derisive term by the marines to describe the army infantry, and by the army infantry to describe the marines. In the literal sense, a 'butt plate' is the metal or rubber covering of the end of the stock on a rifle *US, 1991*

butt plug *noun* **1** a device that is inserted into the anus during sex, sometimes to retain an enema and sometimes simply for the sensation *US, 1989*. **2** an offensive, unlikeable person *US, 1993*

buttrose *adjective* very bad *US, 2002*

butt slut *noun* a male homosexual who takes a passive sexual role *US, 1992*

butt tuck *noun* cosmetic surgery reducing and lifting the buttocks *US, 1984*

butt-twitcher *adjective* revealing the shape of the wearer's buttocks *US, 1951*

butt ugly *adjective* very ugly *US, 1986*

buttwipe *noun* **1** toilet paper *US, 1971*. **2** a despicable or offensive person *US, 1991*

butty *noun* **1** a sandwich. Also spelt 'buttie'. Originally used in northern England, especially Liverpool, as a dialect elision of 'buttery'; now widespread, especially as 'jam butty', 'chip butty', etc *UK, 1855*. **2** a non-powered, towed canal boat that is part of a working pair. Also known as a 'butty boat' *UK, 1944*. **3** a friend, a workmate; also used as a form of address. Variants are 'butt' and 'buttie'. Either from mining where 'butty' was 'a middleman', or from Romany *booty-pal* (a fellow workman) or, most probably,

Warwickshire dialect *butty* (a fellow servant or labourer). Modern use may be influenced by BUDDY *UK, 1859*

buttyboy *noun* a friend; a workmate; also used as a form of address. An elaboration of BUTTY *UK: WALES, 2002*

butu *noun* heroin *UK, 1998*

buturakie *verb* to jump on a person in order to rob them or beat them up. From Fijian *buturaka*, the equivalent of perhaps playing on STICK/PUT THE BOOT IN. Picked up from Fijian sailors on the waterfronts of Sydney and Auckland *AUSTRALIA, 1958*

but why? used humorously with varying meanings. For example, a teacher might ask the class to pass in their homework, whereupon at least one member of the class will mutter, 'But why?' *US, 1963*

buvare *noun* anything drinkable. Originally C19 theatrical slang *UK, 2002*

buy *noun* **1** a purchase of illicit merchandise, especially drugs *US, 1906*. **2** a purchase *AUSTRALIA, 1987*

buy *verb* **1** to gamble on a result higher than the bookmaker's favoured spread *UK, 2001*. **2** to accept a fiction as truth *UK, 2000*. **3** in poker, to draw a card or cards after the initial deal *US, 1967*. ▶ **buy a homestead** to be thrown from your horse *CANADA, 1987*. ▶ **buy a pot** in poker, to win a hand by betting so excessively as to drive all other players from the hand *US, 1963*. ▶ **buy a pup** to be the victim of a swindle *UK, 1996*. ▶ **buy a suit** to kill someone. Referring to funeral attire *US, 1997*. ▶ **buy an orchard** in trucking, to drive off the road into trees or brush *US, 1971*. ▶ **buy some new shoes** to flee while released from custody on bail *US, 1949*. ▶ **buy someone a suit** to bribe someone *US, 1984*. ▶ **buy the dick** to die *US, 1971*. ▶ **buy the farm** to die *US, 1958*. ▶ **buy the rack** in horse racing, to bet on every possible combination of winners in a Daily Double bet *US, 1947*. ▶ **buy the ranch** to die. A primary euphemism used by US soldiers in Vietnam *US, 1976*

buy-and-bust *noun* a police operation in which an undercover officer buys an illegal drug and then immediately arrests the seller *US, 2000*

buy-down *noun* a bribe paid to a police officer to release a criminal or to reduce the severity of the charges against him *US, 2001*

buyer *noun* a gambler who bets on a result higher than the bookmaker's favoured spread *UK, 2001*

buy-I *noun* an East Indian. An English adaptation of the Hindi *Niyabingi* (merchant) *JAMAICA, 1979*

buying-and-selling cord *noun* a rough measure of wood depending on the bargaining skill of the buyer and seller. When you're buying, it's more; when you're selling, it's less *CANADA, 2001*

buy into *verb* to involve yourself in something, to believe in something. Originally a gambling term, 'to buy into a game' *AUSTRALIA, 1943*

buy it *verb* **1** to accept an answer or punch-line; especially in the catchphrase that signals resignation: 'I'll buy it' *UK, 1937*. **2** to die; to become a casualty. World War 1 and 2 *UK, 1825*

buy money *noun* the money used to buy contraband *US, 1981*

buy-up *noun* in prison, a purchase of groceries, toiletries, etc, made by prisoners. 'Buy-ups' are restricted to a certain small amount for each prisoner, often consisting of wages earned for prison work *AUSTRALIA, 1944*

Buzby *noun* British Post Office Telephones, subsequently British Telecom, the authority controlling the use of citizens' band radio in the UK. Citizens' band radio slang; the name of the cartoon bird created in the late 1970s to market British Post Office Telephones; in turn a play on BUZZ (a telephone call) *UK, 1981*

buzz *noun* **1** a rumour; gossip; news *UK, 1821*. **2** an immediate sensation of a drug or alcohol *US, 1849*. **3** a thrilling sensation *US, 1937*. **4** a telephone call *US, 1930*. **5** a police car *US, 1973*. **6** x-ray therapy *US, 1994*

buzz *verb* **1** to telephone someone; to summon someone by buzzer *US, 1929*. **2** to call for someone *US, 1946*. **3** to leave. A variant is 'buzz off' *UK, 1914*. **4** to kiss someone *US, 1945*. **5** to feel pleasurable sensations resulting from drug use *UK, 1992*. **6** to engage in solvent abuse *UK: SCOTLAND, 1985*. **7** to pick pockets *UK, 1812*. **8** to snatch a woman's purse *US, 1950*. **9** to fly very close to an object *US, 1944*.

10 (used of a computer program or operation) to run without any sign of progress *US, 1981*. **11** to activate a remote device unlocking a door. From the buzzing sound the device often makes *US, 1997*. **12** to anger someone; to alienate someone; to annoy *US, 1952*. **13** of music, to become lively and energetic *UK, 1972*. ▶ **be buzzing** to be happening. A criminal context *US, 1941*. ▶ **buzz around the barrel** to eat a snack *US, 1960*

buzzard *noun* the eagle insignia of a full colonel or the Women's Army Corps *US, 1931*

buzzard's roost *noun* **1** the office in a railway yard *US, 1977*. **2** the highest seats in a cinema balcony *US, 1920*

buzz bomb *noun* a person rendered emotionally unstable due to long incarceration *US, 1976*

buzz boy *noun* a fighter pilot *US, 1944*

buzzcocks *noun* people, a general term of address. An extention of COCK (a male-to-male term of address). 'Get a buzz, cock', allegedly the final words of a magazine review for 1970s UK television drama series *Rock Follies*, adopted as the name of Manchester punk band The Buzzcocks. In the mid-1990s BBC television screened a new music panel game that should have been called *Never Mind The Bollocks*, after the Sex Pistols' 1977 album. To avoid causing offence the programme makers substituted 'Buzzcocks' for 'Bollocks' and the programme's continuing success inspired this new, heavily ironic usage which, probably by chance, echoes the original sense *UK, 2001*

buzz-crusher *noun* anything or anyone who dampens your sense of euphoria *US, 1988*

buzz-cut *noun* a very short haircut; a person with a very short haircut. Perhaps from the sound of the electric clippers *US, 1977*

buzzed *adjective* **1** drunk *US, 1952*. **2** drug-intoxicated. From the previous sense *US, 1972*

buzzed up *adjective* drug-intoxicated *UK, 2000*

buzzer *noun* **1** a badge *US, 1914*. **2** a burglar alarm *US, 1949*. **3** a door-bell *US, 1934*. **4** in a hospital casualty department, a defibrillator paddle *US, 1994*. **5** in horse racing, a battery-powered device used illegally by a jockey to shock a horse during a race *US, 1942*

buzzing *adjective* **1** drunk *US, 2003*. **2** manic, hyperactive *US, 1994*

buzzing your tits off *adjective* very drug-intoxicated *UK, 2003*

buzz job *noun* the flying of an aircraft low to the ground to impress or scare those on the ground *US, 1943*

buzz ticket *noun* a dole card required to sign on as unemployed in order to receive benefit. The dole is seen here as money to be spent on drugs to get a 'buzz' (a pleasurable sensation); the whole puns on 'bus ticket' *UK, 1997*

buzztrack *noun* in the television and film industries, a sound track without modulations *US, 1960*

buzzword; buzz-phrase *noun* a currently fashionable word or expression, especially a borrowing from jargon or technology that is used to impress rather than inform and is thus rendered essentially meaningless *US, 1946*

BW *noun* an obese hospital patient. An abbreviation of BEACHED WHALE *US, 1994*

BW *nickname* the Black Warriors prison gang *US, 2000*

bwai *noun* a black youth involved in gang culture. West Indian pronunciation of 'boy' *UK, 1994*

BWOC *noun* a popular and visible college girl; a big woman on campus *US, 1947*

BY *adjective* (of a telephone line) busy *US, 1968*

by any means necessary; by whatever means necessary used as a slogan by the radical political left of the 1960s to reflect a belief that the end justifies the means, up to and including violent action *US, 1970*

by Christchurch! used as an oath. A euphemistic avoidance of blasphemy, used in New Zealand (by reference to Christchurch, Canterbury Province) and in the UK (Christchurch, Dorset) *UK, 1984*

by crikey! used as a euphemism for 'by christ!' *AUSTRALIA, 1901*

by cripes! used as a euphemism for 'by Christ!' *AUSTRALIA, 1902*

bye-bye; bye-byes *noun* sleep. From an earlier use as a soothing sound used to lull a child to sleep, perhaps from a shortening of 'lullaby' *UK, 1867*

bye Felicia! used for inviting someone to leave. From the film *Friday US, 2004*

bye now goodbye *UK, 1967*

by George! used as a mild exclamation or oath. Derives from St George, the patron saint of England *UK, 1598*

by George, one of these days I gotta straighten up that closet! used as a humorous commentary on a cluttered mess. A signature line from the comedy *Fibber McGree and Moll* (radio 1935–1957, television 1959–1960). Repeated with referential humour *US, 1958*

by golly! used as a euphemism for 'by God!' *US, 1833*

by guess and by gosh *adjective* without planning, relying on serendipity *US, 1914*

by gum! used euphemistically for 'by God'. Northern English usage *UK, 1960*

by heck! used as an exclamation of surprise, indignation, etc; also as a means of stressing what follows. Northern English usage *US, 1922*

by here; by there *adverb* here; there. A south Walian form probably based on the rhythm or sound of the original Welsh *yma* (here) and *yno* (there) *UK, 1985*

by himself in the box used as a stock answer to describe a racehorse's lineage if it is either unknown or none of the asker's business *AUSTRALIA, 1989*

by hokey! used for expressing great surprise *NEW ZEALAND, 2001*

by jumbo! used as a substitute for an oath *US, 1959*

by me in poker, used for expressing a player's decision not to bet *US, 1988*

BYO a request that guests 'bring your own' *US, 1968*

BYOB used in invitations as an instruction to bring your own booze or bottle *US, 1968*

BYOG an invitation to bring your own grog to a party *NEW ZEALAND, 1976*

byplay *noun* a device on a dishonest carnival game that can be activated to let players win *US, 1950*

bysie-bye goodbye. An elaboration of 'bye' *UK, 1984*

by the centre!; by the left! used as an emphatic register of shock, surprise, etc. Adopted, originally by the military, from military drill commands *UK, 1971*

by the holy old dynamiting Jesus! used as an extreme oath in Nova Scotia *CANADA, 1988*

by the holy old twist used as an oath. Many Nova Scotia oaths refer to Christ and go back to the Elizabethan style of sacrilegious, elaborate expressions (e.g. the twisted body on the cross echoes 'sblood' (God's blood) and 'sbody' (God's body) *CANADA, 1988*

by-the-hour hotel; by-the-hour motel *noun* a motel or hotel used by prostitutes where it is possible to rent a room in short increments *US, 1992*

by the lord liftin' Jesus! one of many elaborate Nova Scotian sacrilegious oaths *CANADA, 1988*

by the rattly-eyed Jesus! in Nova Scotia, used as an oath *CANADA, 1999*

Cc

C *noun* **1** the Viet Cong; a member of the Viet Cong *US, 1966*. **2** cocaine *US, 1921*. **3** amphetamines. Heard as 'the C' *UK, 2003*. **4** methcathinone. Heard as 'the C' *US, 2003*. **5** a woman viewed as a sexual object. An abbreviation of CUNT *US, 1976*. **6** a CBE (Commander of the Order of the British Empire). Civil servant usage; suggestive of a casual familiarity with the honour *UK, 1961*. **7** contraception *US, 1997*. **8** one hundred dollars *US, 1839*. **9** in poker, the third player to the left of the dealer *US, 1988*. **10** the commission charged by a bookmaker *US, 1960*

C-47 *noun* a clothes peg. Used by television and film crews, mocking the formality of the official jargon of their craft *US, 2003*

cab *noun* ► **take a cab** to die *US, 2000*

caballo *noun* **1** heroin. Spanish for 'horse' *US, 1970*. **2** a person who smuggles drugs into a prison. Spanish for 'horse', which is almost a MULE *US, 1992*

cabaret *verb* **1** to lie in bed masturbating *US, 1950*. **2** to use an addictive drug in a semi-controlled pattern *US, 1958*

cabbage *noun* **1** money *US, 1903*. **2** the vagina. Perhaps from the image of leaves peeling back *US, 1967*. **3** low grade marijuana. From the quality of the leaves *NEW ZEALAND, 2002*. **4** a coronary artery bypass graft. A loose pronunciation of the acronym CABG *US, 1994*

cabbage *verb* **1** to become vegetable-like *UK, 2001*. **2** to smoke marijuana, especially low grade marijuana *NEW ZEALAND, 1998*

cabbage *adjective* poor-quality *NEW ZEALAND, 1990*

cabbage cutter *noun* on the railways, a freight engine *US, 1977*

cabbaged *adjective* **1** mentally and physically exhausted. Punning on 'a vegetative state' *UK, 1992*. **2** under the influence of MDMA, the recreational drug best known as ecstasy *UK, 1991*. **3** drunk *UK, 2002*

cabbage-eater *noun* a German or Russian immigrant. Offensive *US, 1942*

cabbage hat *noun* a Royal Marine. After the uniform green beret *UK, 1979*

cabbage out *verb* to relax *NEW ZEALAND, 2003*

cabbage patch *noun* a remote, insignificant place *US, 1862*

cabbage patch *nickname* **1** the state of Victoria, Australia. Also referred to as 'cabbage garden' and 'the cabbage state'. Hence, a native may be a 'cabbage patcher', 'cabbage gardener' or 'cabbage stater' *AUSTRALIA, 1882*. **2** Kingston prison in Portsmouth *UK, 1996*

Cabbagetown *nickname* a mixed residential and business area near downtown in Toronto. This term was likely derived from the days when poor people lived downtown and presumably could only afford to eat cabbage *CANADA, 1958*

cabby; cabbie *verb* to drive a motor vehicle; to be driven. Army use *UK, 1974*

cabello *noun* cocaine, *2003*

cabez *noun* intelligence. From the Spanish *cabeza* (head) *TRINIDAD AND TOBAGO, 1956*

cab freight *noun* an attractive woman passenger in a truck *US, 1961*

cabin car *noun* a brakevan (caboose) *US, 1977*

cabin stabbing *noun* (from a male perspective) an act of conventional sexual intercourse. As in the title of the 1990 song 'Cabin Stabbing' by Super Cat (William Maraugh) *JAMAICA, 2001*

cab joint *noun* a brothel whose customers are spotted and transported by taxi drivers *US, 1930*

cabled *adjective* (of a vehicle) equipped with a winch *US, 2004*

cábóg *noun* an ignorant male; a rustic clodhopper *IRELAND, 2004*

caboodle *noun* all of something *US, 1848*

caboose *noun* **1** the buttocks *US, 1919*. **2** the final participant in serial sex. From the phrase PULL A TRAIN used to describe the practice *US,* *1970*. **3** the youngest child in a family *US, 1969*. **4** a jail *US, 1865*. **5** a small house or shack *TRINIDAD AND TOBAGO, 1956*. **6** a cooking shed *CAYMAN ISLANDS, 1985*

caboose bounce *noun* a train consisting of nothing more than an engine and a brakevan (caboose) *US, 1929*

cabouche *noun* ▷ *see:* BAROUCHE

cabron *noun* a guy, especially a brutish or dim-witted one. Border Spanish used in English conversation by Mexican-Americans *US, 1974*

cab sav *noun* cabernet sauvignon wine *AUSTRALIA, 1990*

ca-ca *noun* **1** excrement. Probably from Spanish children's speech; used by non-Spanish speakers. Sometimes seen spelt as 'kaka' or other such variations *US, 1952*. **2** nonsense *US, 1980*. **3** marijuana, especially if poor quality, adulterated or fake *US, 1969*. **4** heroin, especially low quality heroin *US, 1986*. **5** drugs, not necessarily heroin *US, 1995*

caca-hole *noun* the anus *TRINIDAD AND TOBAGO, 2003*

cack; cak; kack *noun* **1** excrement *AUSTRALIA, 1972*. **2** rubbish, nonsense *UK, 1997*. **3** someone or something extremely funny *AUSTRALIA, 1989*

cack; cak; kack *verb* **1** to fall asleep *US, 1959*. **2** to defecate. Like many other words for bodily functions, 'cack' was part of everyday conventional speech for many years before slipping into impolite usage in the late C19 *UK, 1436*. ► **cack it** to be very nervous or worried; to feel thoroughly frightened. A variation of SHIT IT *UK, 2002*. ► **cack your dacks 1** to lose control of your bowels *AUSTRALIA, 1992*. **2** to become scared *AUSTRALIA, 1992*. ► **cack yourself 1** to be terrified. Literally 'to shit yourself'; used figuratively (most of the time), often as an exaggeration *UK, 2000*. **2** to laugh uncontrollably. A variant is 'cack yourself laughing' *AUSTRALIA, 1987*

cack; kack *adjective* contemptible, unpleasant, inferior. Variant spellings abound – 'cak', 'kak', etc *UK, 1996*

cackersarnie *noun* the condition that exists when someone pulls your trousers or underpants forcefully upward, forming a wedge between buttock cheeks; the act of putting someone in that position. Mainly used by schoolboys. From CACK (excrement, faeces) and SARNIE (sandwich) *UK, 2003*

cack-handed *adjective* left-handed; clumsy *UK, 1854*

cackies *noun* trousers, especially khakis *US, 1990*

cackle *verb* **1** to chatter; to talk inconsequentially *UK, 1530*. **2** to confess and/or to inform on others *US, 1949*. **3** as part of a controlled roll of dice, to give them the appearance and sound of being shaken while actually preventing their turning *US, 1963*

cackle crate *noun* in trucking, a truck hauling chickens *US, 1946*

cackle factory *noun* a mental hospital *US, 1950*

cacky *noun* **1** a yellowish-brown colour. From the adjective sense (shitty), giving a joke at the expense of 'khaki' *UK, 1984*. **2** human excrement. Childish *UK, 1961*

cacky *adjective* **1** covered with excrement; hence filthy, malodorous *UK, 1937*. **2** in the language of striptease, overtly if not excessively sexual *US, 1981*

cacto *noun* the moth *Cactoblastis cactorum*, a successful biological control of introduced prickly pear *AUSTRALIA, 1941*

cactus *noun* in hospital usage, a severely burnt patient *US, 1994*. ► **in the cactus** in trouble, especially with one person *NEW ZEALAND, 1953*. ► **out in the cactus** in a very remote area *NEW ZEALAND, 1963*

cactus *adjective* ruined, wrecked *AUSTRALIA, 1945*

cactus juice *noun* tequila; mescal *US, 1971*

cad *noun* **1** an ill-bred, ill-mannered lout *UK, 1827*. **2** a Cadillac car *US, 1929*. **3** *cad*mium *UK, 1978*. **4** one ounce of marijuana. A confusion with CAN expanded to CADILLAC US, 2001. **5** a railway conductor US, 1977

cadaver cadet noun a necrophile US, 1987

cadbury noun a person who gets drunk on very little alcohol. Referring to the advertising slogan of Cadbury Dairy Milk chocolate, which has 'a glass and a half of full cream milk' AUSTRALIA, 1996

caddie shack noun any small building where gold caddies congregate and wait for work US, 1953

caddy adjective sharp, stylish, fashionable US, 1984

Caddy; Caddie noun a Cadillac car US, 1929

caddy blackjack noun a private game of blackjack US, 1981

caddy-old-punch noun an improvised, brown-paper kite GUYANA, 1996

cadet noun **1** a pimp US, 1904. **2** a new drug user US, 1949

cadge verb to beg; to wheedle something from someone US, 1812

cadger noun a beggar; a scrounger UK, 1851

cadie; caddy; caddie noun a hat; originally a bush name for a slouch hat. English gypsy use AUSTRALIA, 1898

cadillac noun **1** cocaine US, 1953. **2** one ounce of a powdered drug US, 1950. **3** phencyclidine, the recreational drug known as PCP or angel dust US, 1994. **4** a cup of coffee with cream and sugar US, 1989. **5** a note-and-string based method of communication in prison US, 2000. **6** the maximum amount which may be spent at a prison canteen US, 1989. **7** in the language of the homeless, a shopping cart US, 1997. **8** the US Army M-1 tank US, 1991. **9** a large surfboard used for big-wave conditions US, 1965

Cadillac bunk noun a single prison bed in a setting where most beds are two-tiered bunk beds US, 1989

cadillac express noun the drug methcathinone US, 1998

Cadillac pusher noun a person whose job it is to push carts with garments through the streets US, 2002

café au lait noun a person of mixed race with skin the shade of milky coffee UK, 1961

caff noun a café UK, 1931

caffuffle noun chaos, confusion BARBADOS, 1975

caffuffle verb to confuse someone or something BARBADOS, 1965

cage noun **1** an elevator US, 1938. **2** a brakevan (caboose) US, 1931. **3** an abandoned house US, 2000. **4** a car. Bikes (motorcycle) usage US, 1981. **5** the body US, 1973

caged lion noun in horse racing, a racehorse battling back from apparent defeat to win a race AUSTRALIA, 1989

cage girl noun a ticket seller in a theatre US, 1952

cagey adjective wary, non-commital, cautious US, 1893

caggie; kaggie noun a cagoule or kagool (a weatherproof outer-garment) UK, 1984

cahoo-hole noun a pothole in the road CANADA, 1992

cahoots noun ▶ **in cahoots with** conspiring or planning with someone US, 1829

Cain and Abel; Cain noun a table. Rhyming slang, based on the sons of Adam and Eve who are remembered as the first murderer and his victim; recorded by Ducange Anglicus in 1857 UK, 1857

caine; cane noun cocaine, crack cocaine US, 1983

Caisse Pop noun in Quebec, a kind of cooperative bank. The term is shortened from Caisse Populaire or 'popular bank', a French term universally used by anglophones CANADA, 2001

cak noun ▷ see: CACK

cake noun **1** a beautiful girl or young woman US, 1941. **2** the female breast US, 1957. **3** the vagina US, 1967. **4** bread TRISTAN DA CUNHA, 2000. **5** a meal provided as compensation in addition to wages US, 1973. **6** money; a good deal of money. Extends, perhaps, from BREAD (money) but 'cake' has traditionally been associated with wealth. 'Qu'il mangent de la brioche' – 'Let them eat cake', attributed to Queen Marie-Antoinette (1755–93) on being told that her people had no bread US, 1965. **7** marijuana resin UK, 2001. **8** a round disc of crack cocaine US, 1994. **9** a rural person. Derogatory IRELAND, 1991.

▶ **get your cake** to date your girlfriend US, 2001. ▶ **off your cake** confused, drug-intoxicated. The latter meaning gained dates from the late C20 and the distinction between the two senses may be blurred UK, 2000

cake adjective **1** easy US, 1968. **2** homosexual. Clipped from FRUITCAKE (a homosexual man) UK, 2001

cake boy noun an attractive, usually younger homosexual male US, 1995

cake-cutting noun short-changing US, 1993

caked adjective **1** to be wealthy, monied. From CAKE (money). Variants include 'caked out', 'caked up' and 'cakeholed' UK, 1940s. **2** drug-intoxicated US, 1994

cake-eater noun **1** an effeminate young man, who may or may not be homosexual. An important word of the flapper era, but seldom heard thereafter US, 1916. **2** a person who enjoys performing oral sex on women US, 1967

cakehead noun an idiot, a fool UK, 1998

cake hole noun **1** the vagina UK, 2001. **2** the mouth. Also heard as 'cake 'ole' UK, 1943

cake-o adjective all right, correct, safe, suitable, what is required, comfortable. Back slang for OK UK, 2001

cakes noun **1** the buttocks, especially female buttocks US, 1993. **2** crack cocaine UK, 2003

cake tin nickname the Wellington, New Zealand, sports stadium NEW ZEALAND, 2001

cakewalk noun an easy or overwhelming success. Originally a boxing term for an easy victory, then expanded to general use US, 1897

cakey adjective foolish, daft UK: SCOTLAND, 1985

calabash cut noun a haircut in which the hair is cut on a line equidistant from the top of the head. A 'calabash' is a squash, and the suggestion is that a hollowed out squash shell was used to guide the scissors TRINIDAD AND TOBAGO, 1990

calaboose noun a jail, especially a local one. From the Spanish calabozo (dungeon) US, 1792

calamity howler noun a person who predicts disaster US, 1892

Calamity Jane noun in a deck of playing cards, the queen of spades. Martha Jane 'Calamity Jane' Canary (1852–1903) was a legendary figure in the settling of the western US US, 1988

calbo noun heroin. Probably from a confusion of CABALLO (heroin) UK, 2003

calc out verb to calculate something US, 1999

calculator noun **1** in horse racing, a parimutuel clerk who calculates odds US, 1976. **2** in poker, a player skilled at assessing the hands of other players US, 1988

Calcutta noun **1** butter. Rhyming slang UK, 1998. **2** a Calcutta sweep AUSTRALIA, 1950

Calcutta sweeps; Calcutta sweep noun a type of sweepstake in which contestants' names are auctioned off AUSTRALIA, 1914

caleche noun in Quebec, a one-horse, two-wheeled carriage CANADA, 1963

calendar noun a prison sentence of one year US, 1926

calendar days; calendar time noun the bleed period of a woman's menstrual cycle US, 1954

calf noun **1** a young teenage girl US, 1959. **2** a Cadillac car US, 1980 ▷ see: COW'S CALF. ▶ **have a calf** to become emotionally overwrought; to lose control. A variation born of HAVE A COW US, 1999

calf-lick noun a limp quiff, or a tuft of hair on someone's forehead which will not lie smoothly. Northern dialect in wider use UK, 1954

calf slobber noun meringue US, 1960

calf's tail noun the cord attached to a railway whistle US, 1946

Calgary Redeye noun a drink made of tomato juice and beer CANADA, 1987

Cali noun **1** California US, 1930. **2** MDMA, the recreational drug best known as ecstasy, originating in California. A shortening of CALIFORNIA ECSTASY, 1999

calibrate *verb* to correct someone's information or opinion. Derives from making minor adjustments to high-tech weaponry *US, 2003*

calico cluck *noun* a female railway worker *US, 1975*

Cali dreamers *noun* a variety of MDMA, the recreational drug best known as ecstasy. The whole plays on the song 'California Dreamin' by The Mamas and Papas, 1966 *UK, 1999*

Califas *nickname* California. Border Spanish used in English conversation by Mexican-Americans *US, 1974*

California bankroll *noun* a single large-denomination note wrapped around small-denomination note, giving the impression of a great deal of money *US, 1980*

California bible *noun* a deck of playing cards *US, 1960*

California blackjack *noun* in blackjack, an ace and a nine, which produce a score of 20, not 21 *US, 1982*

California blankets *noun* newspaper used as bedding *US, 1926*

California C-note *noun* a ten-dollar note *US, 1983*

California coffee *noun* inexpensive wine *US, 1976*

California cornflakes *noun* cocaine *US, 1976*

California Crybaby Division *nickname* in the Korean war, the 40th California National Guard Division *US, 1989*

California ecstasy *noun* MDMA, the recreational drug best known as ecstasy, originating in California, *1999*

California girl *noun* a variety of marijuana *US, 2002*

Californian *noun* a variety of MDMA, the recreational drug best known as ecstasy *UK, 1996*

Californian northern lights *noun* a hybrid marijuana grown in California. The northern lights (*aurora borealis*), a luminous atmospheric display, is a metaphor for potent effects and a romantic simile for the plant's appearance *US, 1999*

California pimping *noun* working as a pimp in a relaxed, low-pressure style *US, 1972*

California quail *noun* a tablet of the recreational drug methaqualone, the recreational drug best known as Quaaludes™ *US, 1997*

California sunrise *noun* **1** a variety of MDMA, the recreational drug best known as ecstasy; a blend of amphetamine and caffeine marketed as MDMA *UK, 1996*. **2** LSD. A variation of CALIFORNIA SUNSHINE *UK, 1998*

California sunshine *noun* LSD *US, 1977*

California tilt *noun* a car with the bonnet (hood) sloping downward to a front end that is lower than the rear end *US, 1976*

California tires *noun* tyres with little remaining tread *US, 1971*

California turnaround *noun* any powerful central nervous system stimulant. So potent that a trucker who takes one can drive to California and back *US, 1976*

Californicator *noun* a Californian, especially one who has moved to Oregon or Washington state *US, 1978*

calipers *noun* dice that are true to an extremely minute tolerance, approximately 1/1000th of an inch *US, 1950*

Cali red beard *noun* a distinctive marijuana grown in California *US, 1999*

call *noun* **1** an opinion; a prediction *US, 1999*. **2** the initial flooding of sensations after injecting heroin *US, 1973*

call *verb* ▶ **call Earl** to vomit *US, 1968*. ▶ **call for a cab** (of a jockey) to make jerky arm movements as he battles to remain in the saddle *UK, 1961*. ▶ **call for Herb** to vomit. An echoic play on the sounds produced by a sudden expulsion of vomit *AUSTRALIA, 1984*. ▶ **call for Hughie** to vomit. Onomatopoeic play on Hughie as the involuntary sounds of vomiting. A joke current in the 1970s described getting drunk on green *crème de menthe* and calling for television personality Hughie Green (1920–97) *UK, 1974*. ▶ **call for the butter** to have completed a task or arrived at your destination. Fishing skippers who claimed the ability to locate fish by the taste of the bottom mud would smear butter on a lead weight, lower it to the bottom, and then taste the mud brought to the surface on the buttered lead *US, 1975*. ▶ **call hogs**

to snore *US, 1973*. ▶ **call it on** to challenge another gang to a gang fight *US, 1955*. ▶ **call Ralph** to vomit *US, 1983*. ▶ **call someone full-mouth** to address your elder without using an honorific Mr or Mrs *GUYANA, 1995*. ▶ **call someone raw** to address your elder without using an honorific Mr or Mrs *ANGUILLA, 1995*. ▶ **call the shots** to be in a position of power; to direct the actions of others *US, 1967*

callabo *noun* a collaboration *US, 2002*

callalloo *noun* a confused set of circumstances; a mix-up. From the name of a popular stew *TRINIDAD AND TOBAGO, 2003*

call book *noun* a list, formal or highly informal, kept by a pool hustler, of locations where money can be made playing pool *US, 1990*

call boy *noun* **1** a male prostitute whose clients book his services by telephone *US, 1942*. **2** a boy or young man who called railway workers to work *US, 1898*

calley *noun* marijuana. From KALI and COLLIE *JAMAICA, 1975*

call girl *noun* a prostitute who makes bookings with customers by telephone *US, 1922*

call house *noun* a brothel from which prostitutes are procured by telephone *US, 1913*

callibogus *noun* an alcoholic drink of spruce beer, rum or whisky, and molasses *CANADA, 1995*

calling card *noun* **1** a fingerprint *US, 1949*. **2** needle marks on a drug user's arm *US, 1971*. **3** during the Vietnam war, a printed card identifying the unit, left on the bodies of dead enemy soldiers *US, 1990*

calling station *noun* in poker, an unskilled player who calls bets prematurely *US, 1979*

call it *verb* while working as a prostitute, to state the price expected for the service requested *UK, 1987*

Call Me God *noun* a CMG (Commander of the Order of St Michael and St George). A pun elaborated on the initials; used by civil servants demonstrating a jocular familiarity with the honour *UK, 1961*

call money *noun* a demand for payment of a debt *US, 1989*

call of the great outdoors *noun* a need to defecate or urinate. An elaboration of 'a call of nature' which is the conventional euphemism *UK, 1965*

call out *verb* to challenge someone to a fight *US, 1980*

call that George! used for expressing finality or completion *TRINIDAD AND TOBAGO, 1983*

call-up *noun* in prison, a summons to a governor's office *UK, 2001*

Cally *nickname* ▷*see:* CARLY

cally dosh *noun* money *UK, 1988*

calmer *noun* a barbiturate or other central nervous system depressant *UK, 1999*

Calumet fever *noun* (among Ottawa valley lumbermen) fear of riding logs down the slide at Calumet, Quebec *CANADA, 1964*

Calvin Klein *noun* **1** wine. Rhyming slang, formed on the name of American fashion designer Calvin Klein (b.1942). Sometimes shortened to 'Calvin' *UK, 1998*. **2** a fine. Rhyming slang, formed on the name of fashion designer Calvin Klein (b.1942) *UK, 1998*

Calvin Klein special *noun* a mixture of cocaine and the recreational drug ketamine. A back formation from the initials *US, 1995*

Calvins *noun* blue jeans or underwear designed by Calvin Klein *US, 1982*

cam *noun* **1** camouflage. Military *UK, 1995*. **2** a camera *2003*

Camberwell carrot *noun* an exceptionally long and fat marijuana cigarette *UK, 1987*

Cambo *adjective* Cambodian *US, 1976*

Cambodian red *noun* marijuana from Cambodia. Named after its reddish hue *US, 1973*

Cambodia trip *noun* a highly potent strain of marijuana from Cambodia *US, 1960s?*

Cambodie *adjective* Cambodian. Vietnam war usage *US, 1964*

Camden Lock *noun* a shock. Rhyming slang, based on a vibrant area of north London *UK, 1998*

Camden rules *noun* poor table manners. A tribute to Camden, New Jersey *US, 1986*

came *noun* cocaine. Probably by misspelling or mishearing of 'cane' (cocaine) *UK, 1953*

camel *noun* **1** in twelve-step recovery programmes such as Alcoholics Anonymous, a person who maintains sobriety. From the sense of 'dry as a camel' *US, 1998*. **2** a poor performing racehorse *AUSTRALIA, 1989*. **3** a marijuana cigarette *US, 1976*

camel driver *noun* an Arab *US, 1985*

camelfucker *noun* an Arab. Offensive *US, 1998*

camel jockey; camel jock *noun* a Arab; anyone mistaken for an Arab. Used with contempt *US, 1961*

camel's hump *noun* an act of defecation. Rhyming slang for DUMP *UK, 2003*

camel stop *noun* a taxi stand. New York police slang; an allusion to the preponderance of immigrants in New York's taxi-driving workforce *US, 2003*

camel toe *noun* the condition that exists when a tight-fitting pair of trousers, shorts, bathing suit or other garment forms a wedge or cleft between a woman's labia, accentuating their shape *US, 1994*

camera *noun* a police radar unit *US, 1976*

Camilla Parker-Bowles *noun* a Rolls Royce car, usually called a 'rolls'. Rhyming slang, formed on the name of the mistress (later wife) of Prince Charles, Prince of Wales. Variants are 'Camilla Parker', 'Parker-Bowles' and 'Parker' *UK, 1998*

Camille *noun* **1** a homosexual man who moves from one unfortunate, failed love affair to another *US, 1972*. **2** a melodramatic hospital patient who always feels on the verge of dying. From the novel by Alexandre Dumas *US, 1994*

camisole *noun* a strait jacket used to restrain the violent or insane *US, 1949*

cammies; camies *noun* a camouflage uniform *US, 1971*

camo *noun* camouflage *US, 1984*

camouflage *noun* the disguise and staged personality assumed by an expert card counter playing blackjack in a casino in the hope of avoiding detection and ejection *US, 1991*

camp *noun* **1** ostentation, flamboyant behaviour; extravagance of gesture, style etc; also, deliberately overt effeminacy used to signal homosexuality. May be further refined (or otherwise) as HIGH CAMP or LOW CAMP *US, 1999*. **2** a dramatically effeminate homosexual man. In Australia not necessarily a flagrantly effeminate homosexual *US, 1923*. **3** a habitual resting place for wild animals *AUSTRALIA, 1947*. **4** a temporary location to stay at *AUSTRALIA, 1994*. **5** a resting or holding place for stock animals *AUSTRALIA, 1845*. **6** a rest *AUSTRALIA, 1899*. **7** jail *US, 1968*. ▶ **in camp** of a government or military officer, being based away from the regular place of duty *INDIA, 2003*

camp *verb* **1** to exhibit humorously exaggerated, dramatic, effeminate mannerisms (usually but not exclusively of a homosexual male). Variants are 'camp around', 'camp about' and 'camp it up' *US, 1925*. **2** to stay at a place temporarily; to have a short rest. Originally (1840s) meaning 'to stop travelling or working and set up a quick camp for making refreshments' *AUSTRALIA, 1848*. **3** to sit on a man's face during heterosexual love-making. A rare non-gay usage, from the conventional sense 'to take up temporary residence' *UK, 2001*. **4** (of wild animals) to rest or sleep *AUSTRALIA, 1861*

camp *adjective* **1** ostentatious, effeminate, affected; usually applied to behaviour or style. Possibly French in origin; however it may well be an ironic reversal of 'unkempt' (ungroomed) or, less likely, derive from the acronym KAMP: 'known *as male prostitute' UK, 1909*. **2** homosexual. In Australia not necessarily flagrantly effeminate *AUSTRALIA, 1941*

campaign *noun* ▶ **on a campaign** drunk *UK, 2002*

campaign *verb* in horse racing, to run a racing stable as a business *US, 1951*

camp as a row of tents *adjective* **1** flagrantly homosexual *AUSTRALIA, 1965*. **2** (often, but not exclusively, of homosexual men) ostentatious, effeminate, extravagantly styled. Elaboration of CAMP (ostentatious, etc.), punning on conventional 'camping'. The phase is often ornamented with adjectives that describe the tents as 'frilly', 'pink', etc *UK, 1967*

camp as Christmas *adjective* (often, but not exclusively, of homosexual men) ostentatious, effeminate, extravagantly styled *UK, 1999*

camp bitch *noun* an overtly, extravagently effeminate male homosexual *US, 1964*

camper *noun* **1** any person. Usually described as a 'happy camper' or 'unhappy camper', but sometimes simply as a 'camper' *US, 1987*. **2** a restaurant customer who lingers too long at their table *US, 1995*

campery *noun* a showing-off of qualities that are considered camp *UK, 1976*

campness *noun* a tendency towards or, simply, a quality of effeminacy or flamboyance, hence of homosexual behaviour *UK, 1971*

camp thief; camp robber *nickname* the grey jay or Canada jay. Also known by these names in the US since 1893, this bird is nicknamed for its habit of scrounging food at outdoor work and play sites *CANADA, 1893*

campus *noun* a prison's grounds *US, 1982*

campy *adjective* melodramatically and blatantly homosexual *US, 1965*

Cam red *noun* Cambodian red marijuana *US, 2003*

cam-stick *noun* a *stick* of face makeup used for *cam*ouflage. Military *UK, 2001*

Cam trip *noun* a highly potent strain of marijuana from Cambodia. An abbreviated form of CAMBODIA TRIP *UK, 2001*

can *noun* **1** a jail or prison *US, 1912*. **2** a toilet; a bathroom or water closet *US, 1914*. **3** the buttocks *US, 1914*. **4** an imprecise amount of marijuana, usually one or two ounces. Derived from the practice in the 1940s of selling marijuana in Prince Albert tobacco cans *US, 1967*. **5** one ounce of marijuana. Probably from a pipe tobacco container, possibly a shortening of 'cannabis' *US, 1959*. **6** marijuana. Probably a shortening of 'cannabis' but possibly from 'can' (a measured amount of cannabis) *UK, 1986*. **7** a Saracen armoured-car *UK, 1995*. **8** a railway tank carriage *US, 1946*. **9** a car *US, 1970*. **10** a safe *US, 1949*. **11** in electric line work, an overhead transformer *US, 1980*. **12** in drag racing, nitromethane fuel *US, 1968*. ▶ **in the can** not trying to win *US, 1951*

can *verb* **1** to discharge someone from employment *US, 1908*. **2** to stop something, to cease something *US, 1906*

canab *noun* marijuana. Also variant 'canaib'. From the *cannabi*s plant *2001*

Canada flash *noun* in the Canadian military, a visible identification badge *CANADA, 1995*

Canada honker *noun* a Canada goose *US, 1927*

Canada potato *noun* a Jerusalem artichoke *CANADA, 1998*

Canadian *noun* **1** a Jewish person *US, 1950*. **2** a multiple bet *UK, 1991*

Canadian bacon *noun* in homosexual usage, an uncircumcised penis *US, 1987*

Canadian black *noun* dark marijuana from Canada *US, 1969*

Canadian bouncer *noun* the central nervous system depressant Seconal™, manufactured in Canada *US, 1971*

Canadian passport *noun* a hair style in which the hair is worn short at the front and long at the back. Most commonly known as a MULLET *US, 2000*

Can Air *noun* a putative merged Air Canada/Canadian Airlines conglomeration *CANADA, 1991*

canal boat *noun* the Horserace Totaliser Board, the Tote. Rhyming slang. The Tote was created by an Act of Parliament in 1928. This term (unlike synonymous NANNY GOAT) does not appear until after 1972 when the legislation was amended to allow the Tote to operate as an on-course bookmaker *UK, 1984*

canal boats *noun* big shoes *US, 1926*

canal conch noun a promiscuous woman. The 'conch' at issue is of the vaginal type TRINIDAD AND TOBAGO, 1985

canal wrench noun in oil drilling, a shovel US, 1954

canamo noun marijuana. From the Spanish cañamo (hemp) and cañamo indio (cannabis) US, 1971

can-a-piss noun a can of beer NEW ZEALAND, 1998

canappa noun marijuana. The Italian name given to the cannabis plant US, 1938

canary noun **1** a female singer UK, 1886. **2** a police informer. Canaries sing, as do informers US, 1929. **3** a person who is perceived to bring bad luck US, 1974. **4** a capsule of pentobarbital sodium (trade name Nembutal™), a central nervous system depressant US, 1973

canary verb to inform to the police US, 1958

can-can noun gossip TRINIDAD AND TOBAGO, 1956

cancel verb ▶ **cancel someone's ticket** to kill someone US, 1970

Cancel Canada's Freedom nickname For the Co-Operative Commonwealth Federation, a leftist political party that evolved into Canada's New Democratic Party. The parody of the acronym CCF arose from critics feeling that the party was too global in its outlook and not nationalistic enough CANADA, 1985

cancelled stick noun a tobacco cigarette that has been emptied of tobacco and refilled with marijuana US, 1966

cancer noun **1** any artificial sweetener. Because of the belief that the sweeteners are carcinogens US, 1986. **2** rust or corrosion on a car body US, 1975

Cancer Alley noun any area with high levels of environmental carcinogens US, 1981

cancer center noun a tobacco shop US, 1955

cancer stick noun a cigarette US, 1958

Cancon noun Canadian Content, a percentage of which is required in broadcasting CANADA, 2002

CanCult noun Canadian Culture. Subsidised by the government, and enjoying a measure of world recognition, this industry is the site of much infighting and jealousy CANADA, 2002

c and b there used as an invitation to an event TRINIDAD AND TOBAGO, 1987

c and d noun cocaine and marijuana UK, 1997

C and E noun **1** a member of the church who only goes to services at Christmas and Easter UK, 1966. **2** in craps, a bet on any craps and eleven US, 1985

C and H noun cocaine and heroin. A borrowing of a branded name for sugar; sometimes used with the sugar company's advertising slogan: 'pure cane sugar from Hawaii' US, 1980

can die! used for expressing despondency SINGAPORE, 2002

candle noun **1** a semi-solid stalactite of nasal mucus UK, 2000. **2** an emergency flare US, 1971

candle money noun a pay-out on fire insurance. Police and underworld use; derives from a candle left burning in an insured property, perhaps deliberately UK, 1958

candlestick noun in electric line work, a fiberglass download bracket US, 1980

C and M noun a mixture of cocaine and morphine US, 1950

can-do adjective confident, optimismtic US, 1921

candy noun **1** any barbiturate capsule US, 1969. **2** cocaine US, 1931. **3** a sugar cube treated with LSD US, 1972. **4** crack cocaine UK, 2003. **5** inexpensive plastic or acrylic jewellery US, 1949. **6** cash US, 2003. **7** anything good or enjoyable US, 1984. **8** a girl with extremely conservative sexual mores US, 1961

candy verb to enhance a marijuana cigarette with another drug US, 1982

candy adjective excellent US, 1991

candy apple red noun bright red; in hot rodding, a clear coated metallic red paint US, 1963

candy-armed adjective injured. Used for describing pitchers in the game of baseball US, 1953

candy-ass noun a weak person US, 1970

candy-ass; candy-assed adjective weak, ineffective, timid US, 1952

candy-bar punk; candy-bar fag noun a male prisoner whose sexual favours are bought with purchases from the prison shop US, 1972

candy butcher noun a walking vendor who sells sweets US, 1966

candy C; candy cee noun cocaine. An elaboration of CANDY (cocaine) by combination with C (cocaine) US, 1953

candycaine; candycane noun cocaine. Punning on the Christmas hard peppermint 'candy cane' and 'cocaine' US, 1989

candy flip noun **1** a combination of LSD and MDMA, the recreational drug best known as ecstasy, taken at the same time US, 1992. **2** an LSD-based drug-experience enhanced with a multiplicity of other intoxicants. From CANDY (cocaine) US, 1996

candy floss noun the recovered entrails of someone who has been hit by a train. From the technique employed UK, 2002

candy grabbers noun in electric line work, channel lock pliers US, 1980

candy kid noun a girl who wears a lot of inexpensive plastic or acrylic jewellery CANADA, 2002

candy maker noun a male homosexual who masturbates a partner to ejaculation and then licks and swallows the semen US, 1964

candyman noun **1** a drug dealer, especially a cocaine dealer; a heavy cocaine user US, 1969. **2** a field enforcement official of the Federal Communication Commission US, 1976

candy pail noun a chamber pot CANADA, 1987

candy stick noun a cigarette with a menthol filter US, 1984

candy store noun a casino with rules that favour gamblers US, 1991

candystore dice noun mass-produced dice that are imperfect even when unaltered by a cheat US, 1974

candy striper noun a teenaged volunteer nursing assistant in a hospital. From their pink and white uniforms US, 1963

candy wagon noun in trucking, a truck with a light load US, 1942

candy wrapper noun a hundred-dollar note. Probably because of its association with the snorting of cocaine, or 'nose candy' US, 1983

cane noun **1** a short crowbar used by criminals for breaking and entering. An ironic allusion to a gentleman's cane UK, 1937. **2** sugar US, 1990 ▷see: CAINE

cane verb **1** to defeat someone in a humiliating fashion UK, 1937. **2** to have sex US, 1966. **3** to do something to excess or, at least, to the limit UK, 2001. ▶ **cane the loop** to play the 9th, 10th and 11th holes at St Andrews golf course, Scotland, in two under par UK, 1986

caned adjective drug-intoxicated, drunk UK, 1997

cane it verb **1** to drive at speed. To 'cane' (to punish) a motor UK, 1997. **2** to react, especially beyond sensible physical limitations, to chemical stimulants taken recreationally UK, 2002

can house noun a brothel US, 1906

Caniac noun an ice hockey fan of the Montreal Canadiens who travels to other cities to see playoff games. The term comes from the combining into one word of shortened forms of 'Canadiens' and 'maniacs' CANADA, 2002

can I do you now, sir? a catchphrase that is usually appropriate to context. Adopted from the radio comedy It's That Man Again, otherwise known as ITMA, that was broadcast on the BBC from 1939–49; the catchphrase was spoken by Mrs Mopp, the office char, played by Dorothy Summers. Still heard occasionally UK, 1939

can I speak to you? used as the commonest euphemism for 'Are you willing to listen to a corrupt proposal I am about to put to you?' UK, 1977

canister noun **1** a safe US, 1950. **2** the head UK, 2000

can it! be quiet!; stop talking! US, 1919

cankle noun a thick ankle. Possibly, as a compound of 'calf' and 'ankle' US, 2000

CanLit noun Canadian literature CANADA, 2002

cannatt noun a mean, insignificant, unpleasant person IRELAND, 1992

canned *adjective* **1** tipsy, drunk *US, 1918*. **2** of music, recorded, especially to serve as background music. Derogatory *UK, 1904*. **3** recorded, repetitive *US, 1903*

canned goods *noun* **1** a virgin *US, 1967*. **2** a male who has never experienced passive anal sex *US, 1972*

canned heat *noun* a gel formed with liquid ethanol and saturated calcium acetate solution; when ignited, the alcohol in the gel burns. Used as a source of fuel in portable cooking stoves and as a source of alcohol by truly desperate derelicts *US, 1950*

canned up *adjective* drunk on *canned* beer or lager *UK, 1999*

cannibal *noun* a person who performs oral sex *US, 1916*

cannon *noun* **1** a large handgun *US, 1846*. **2** a large surfboard designed for big-wave conditions *US, 1965*. **3** an extra large marijuana cigarette *UK, 1999*. **4** a muscular arm *US, 1989*. **5** a pickpocket *US, 1909*

cannonball *noun* **1** an express train *US, 1894*. **2** a dive in which the diver grips and tucks their knees against their chest to maximise the splash *US, 1949*

cannonball *adjective* (used of a road race) unofficial, illegal *US, 1992*

cannon-cocker *noun* a member of an artillery unit. Vietnam war usage *US, 1952*

cannon fodder *noun* infantry soldiers. Used with sympathy or derision by journalists, agitators and, occasionally, the troops *UK, 1948*

canny *noun* a bird; a pheasant. English gypsy use *UK, 2000*

canoe *noun* a marijuana cigarette which burns unevenly or is holed. The resemblance to a simple canoe: 'a log with a hole in one side', *2001*

canoe *verb* **1** to have sex *US, 1954*. **2** (used of a marijuana cigarette) to burn only on the top *US, 1989*

canoe inspection *noun* a medical inspection of a woman's genitals for signs of a sexually transmitted disease *US, 1964*

canoe licking *noun* the act of oral sex on a woman *US, 2001*

canoe-maker *noun* a forensic pathologist. From the image of the body on the autopsy table, opened up to resemble a canoe *US, 1970*

Canoe U *nickname* the US Naval Academy at Annapolis. The 1998 Naval Academy yearbook included a CD-ROM supplement entitled *Canoe U*, providing a virtual tour of the Naval Academy *US, 1963*

can of coke *noun* a joke. Rhyming slang *UK, 1998*

can off *verb* to fall off *NEW ZEALAND, 1984*

can of gas *noun* a small butane torch used in the preparation of crack cocaine *US, 1992*

can of oil; canov *noun* a boil. Usually reduced *UK, 1961*

can of striped paint *noun* a mythical task assigned to a newly hired helper *US, 1963*

can of whip-ass; can of whup-ass *noun* a notional repository for a physical beating *US, 1984*

can of worms *noun* **1** a complex issue or situation, consideration of which may cause further problems, scandal or unpleasantness *US, 1927*. **2** a can of c-ration spaghetti *US, 1991*

canonical *adjective* in computing, in the usual and accepted form. Literally, 'according to religious law' *US, 1981*

can opener *noun* a curved bar used by criminals to prize open a safe *US, 1949*

can or no can used for expressing the decision-making process used by a big-wave surfers *US, 1991*

cans *noun* **1** the female breasts *US, 1959*. **2** headphones *CANADA, 1977*. **3** money. English gypsy use *UK, 2000*

can shooter *noun* a criminal who specialises in breaking into safes *US, 1949*

can spanner *noun* a tin opener. Royal Navy use *UK, 1979*

cantaloupe *noun* a misfit; an outcast *US, 1985*

cantaloups *noun* dice weighted by a cheat to show a four, five or six *US, 1983*

can't be bad! used as an expression of, sometimes envious, approval or congratulation *UK, 1964*

canteen *noun* **1** a truck stop *US, 1976*. **2** goods purchased against earnings credited, or cash. Prison use *UK, 1978*

canteen boat *noun* the rear craft in a sea-borne minesweeping formation *UK, 1995*

canteen cowboy *noun* **1** a ladies' man, especially one who loiters in the NAAFI (the armed forces shop or canteen) for the purpose of meeting women. Royal Air Force use, still current in the 1970s. Formed on US **DRUGSTORE COWBOY** (a young man who loiters in or around a drugstore for the purpose of meeting women) *UK, 1943*. **2** a railway employee on an unexpected or extended tea break *UK, 1970*. **3** an orderly corporal on duty in a Royal Air Force Station Institute, NAAFI or Junior Ranks' Club. Roughly contemporary with the sense as 'ladies' man'; still current in the early 1970s *UK, 1961*

canteen letters *noun* an extra two letters per week if an inmate pays for stamps. Prison use *UK, 1978*

canteen punk *noun* a prisoner who engages in sexual acts for payment in goods bought at the prison canteen or shop *US, 1974*

canter *noun* the speed with which a prisoner believes that his prison sentence will race by. From conventional 'canter' (a horse's easy speed of movement, not quite a gallop), thus a prisoner's boast of an 'easy ride' *UK: SCOTLAND, 2000*

can't go swimming experiencing the bleed period of a woman's menstrual cycle *US, 1999*

can't hear you – your mouth's full of shit used as a refusal to acknowledge what someone else is saying, implying that what is being spoken is nonsense or offensive. Used by some comedians as a 'heckle put-down' *UK, 1994*

can't-help-it *noun* an imagined disease. From an earlier sense of the term as 'menstruation' *US, 1919*

can't-miss *noun* in horse racing, a racehorse that is a sure thing to win a race to the extent that a sure thing is a sure thing *US, 1951*

can to can't all day, from early morning (when you can just see) to late evening (when you can't see) *US, 1919*

can't-see-um *noun* any small, annoying insect *US, 1985*

can't take you anywhere! used as a jocular reprimand to a companion who has just said or done something contrary to the accepted social code; or (replacing *you* with *him* or *her*) to the company at large, as a humorous acknowledgement of such a *faux pas UK, 1975*

Canuck *noun* a Canadian, especially a French-Canadian. Insulting. Most likely to be heard in portions of the US bordering Canada. During the 1972 campaign for US President, a newspaper in New Hampshire printed an anonymous letter accusing candidate Senator Muskie of having used the term 'Canuck' to describe the state's French-Canadian population. The sound and fury created by the accusation stunned Muskie, and by the time it was learnt that the letter had been a concoction of President Nixon's election campaign the damage had been done *US, 1835*

Canuck *adjective* Canadian. Insulting *US, 1955*

can-up *noun* a particularly bad fall while skiing *US, 1963*

canvas *noun* **1** a strait jacket *US, 1949*. **2** a sports shoe, whether or not made from canvas *FIJI, 1997*

canvasback *noun* a boxer or fighter whose lack of skills leads him to find himself on his back *US, 1955*

canyon *noun* the vagina *US, 1980*

canyon-dive *noun* oral sex performed on a woman *US, 1980*

canyon slicker *noun* a condom. Combines **CANYON** (the vagina) with a waterproof outergarment *UK, 1998*

cap *noun* **1** a bullet; a shot *US, 1925*. **2** a capsule of drugs *US, 1929*. **3** a psychoactive mushroom. Conventionally, the domed upper part of a mushroom; possibly an abbreviation of 'liberty cap', the name given to psilocybin mushrooms *US, 1999*. **4** the amount of marijuana that will fit into the plastic cap of a tube of lip gloss *US, 1989*. **5** crack cocaine. Sometimes in the plural *US, 1998*. **6** used as a term of address for someone whose actions are provoking physical violence. Hawaiian youth usage; an abbreviated form of 'capillary' *US, 1982*. **7** captain *US, 1759*. **8** a capital letter. Originally used by printers, then publishers and authors *UK, 1937*. **9** a recapped tyre *US,*

1971. **10** the penis *FIJI, 1993*. **11** in casino gambling, a chip of one denomination on top of a stack of chips of another denomination *US, 1991*

cap *verb* **1** to package a drug in capsules *US, 1952*. **2** to shoot someone *US, 1970*. **3** to insult someone in a competitive, quasi-friendly spirit; to outdo someone *US, 1944*. **4** to steer business to someone *US, 1973*. **5** in casino gambling, to add to an existing bet, usually illegally *US, 1980*. **6** to assist in a fraudulent scheme by fast talk that helps lure the victim into the swindle *UK, 1811*. **7** to fly on combat air patrol (CAP). Royal Air Force use *UK, 1979*

Cape Breton attache case *noun* a plastic bag *CANADA, 1980*

Cape Cod turkey *noun* salt cod *US, 1865*

Cape Doctor *noun* the strong southeasterly trade wind that blows in Cape Town over summer *SOUTH AFRICA, 1861*

cape horn *noun* a condom. The southernmost tip of the South American continent puns on 'cape' (an outer garment, often waterproof) worn on a HORN (the erect penis). A similar pun was behind the C19 sense, now obsolete, as 'the vagina' – the southernmost tip, often subject to stormy weather, where many men have been lost *UK, 1998*

capella *noun* a hat. An affected elaboration of 'cap'; easily confused with the obsolete sense (a coat) which derives directly from Italian *UK, 1993*

Cape of Good Hope *noun* **1** soap. Rhyming slang, based on the South African headland; sometimes shortened to 'cape' *UK, 1925*. **2** the Pope. Rhyming slang *UK, 1994*

caper *noun* **1** a criminal undertaking, especially a swindle or theft *US, 1925*. **2** that which is going on; business; an undertaking *AUSTRALIA, 1954*. **3** the time devoted to pleasure; a hedonistic lifestyle. Probably from the conventional sense (a dance) *UK, 2001*. **4** cocaine. Etymology uncertain; possibly rhyming slang: 'cape of good hope', for 'dope' *UK, 2001*. **5** a costume worn for erotic effect *UK, 2002*

caper *verb* to commit a criminal undertaking, especially a swindle or theft *US, 1976*

caper car *noun* a car used for a crime and then abandoned *US, 1981*

capey; capie *noun* a person who is part of the non-white, or 'coloured' population in South Africa's Cape province. A term that has survived apartheid *SOUTH AFRICA, 1977*

capisce?; capeesh? do you understand? Thanks to gangster films and television programmes, almost always a blatant affectation with an organised, Sicilian ring to it *US, 1977*

capital *adjective* attractive, good-looking *US, 2001*

capital H *noun* heroin. An embellishment of H (heroin) *US, 1975*

capital prize *noun* a sexually transmitted infection *US, 1948*

cap man *noun* a confederate in a swindle *US, 1971*

Cap'n Crunch *nickname* a captain of a British Columbia provincial ferry who had a spectacular collision *CANADA, 1989*

capo *noun* a leader of a Mafia organisation *US, 1952*

capon *noun* an effeminate or homosexual male *US, 1945*

cap on *verb* to look at someone or something *US, 1971*

capoonkle *adjective* confusing, confused *US, 1982*

capper *noun* **1** a clincher; something that beats all others *UK, 1960*. **2** in a drug-selling enterprise, a person who fills capsules with a drug *US, 1958*. **3** in a confidence swindle, a person who lures the victim into the swindle. From the verb CAP *US, 1753*. **4** in an auction, a dummy bidder *US, 1853*

caps *noun* heroin *UK, 1998*

capsula *noun* crack cocaine *UK, 2003*

capsule con *noun* a prisoner convicted on drug charges *US, 1970*

captain *noun* **1** a railway conductor *US, 1946*. **2** the person buying the drinks *AUSTRALIA, 1953*. ▶ **out with the captain** out drinking. Especially in the Maritime provinces, the Captain is of course Captain Morgan rum *CANADA, 2001*

Captain Bob *nickname* corrupt businessman Robert Maxwell (1923–1991) *UK, 1994*

Captain Cook *adjective* ill. Rhyming slang for CROOK (ill), formed on the name of explorer Captain James Cook (1728–1779) *AUSTRALIA, 2002*

Captain Cook; captain's *noun* a look. Rhyming slang, after Captain James Cook, 1728–79, British sea explorer who 'discovered' the east coast of Australia *AUSTRALIA, 1960*

Captain Grimes *nickname* The Times newspaper. Rhyming slang *UK: ENGLAND, 1982*

Captain Hicks *noun* in craps, the number six *US, 1941*

Captain Kirk *noun* a Turk. Rhyming slang, based on a famous character of the original television and film science fiction adventure series Star Trek, since 1969 *UK, 1998*

captain of the head *noun* an orderly assigned to latrine duty *US, 1947*

captain's log *noun* **1** a lavatory. Rhyming slang for 'bog', based on a famous detail of television and film science fiction adventure series Star Trek, since 1969 *UK, 1998*. **2** the penis. A Star Trek cliché punning on WOOD (the erect penis) *US, 2001*

captain's man *noun* a police officer designated to pick up bribes from criminals for his superior officers *US, 1972*

Captain Trips *nickname* Jerry Garcia (1942–1995), lead guitarist and spiritual bedrock of the Grateful Dead *US, 1994*

capture *noun* an arrest and imprisonment *UK, 1958*

capture *verb* ▶ **capture the bishop** (of a male) to masturbate. Punning 'capture' with 'to lay hands on'; a variation of BASH THE BISHOP (to masturbate) *UK, 2005*

capun *noun* capital punishment *US, 1992*

caput *adjective* ▷*see:* KAPUT

cap work *noun* the alteration of dice for cheating by making them resilient on certain surfaces, which makes them more likely to bounce off the altered sides *US, 1950*

car *noun* **1** a clique of prisoners *US, 1989*. **2** a radio *US, 2002*. **3** in lobstering, a slatted box in the water in which lobsters are kept until they are sold *US, 1978*

caramel *noun* ▶ **drop a caramel** to defecate *UK: SCOTLAND, 1988*

caramel *adjective* mixed race *US, 1994*

caramello *noun* a type of hashish from Morocco. From the Spanish for 'caramel'; the Spanish spell the word with one l *UK, 2003*

caravan *nickname* the section of Mountjoy jail where members of the travelling community are incarcerated *IRELAND, 1996*

carb *noun* a carburettor *US, 1942*

car banger *noun* a criminal who specialises in stealing from cars *US, 1982*

carbie; carby *noun* a carburettor *NEW ZEALAND, 1956*

carbo *noun* carboyhydrates *US, 1977*

carbolic dip *noun* the bath or shower with carbolic dip given to prisoners when they arrive at a prison *US, 1950*

car bra *noun* a cover placed on the front of a car in the hope or belief that it will foil radar speed-detection *US, 1990*

carburettor *noun* a tube with holes used for smoking marijuana; a hole that is designed to let air into a pipe used for smoking marijuana. As its automotive namesake forces a mixture of fuel and oxygen into an engine, the marijuana-related carburettor forces a mixture of marijuana smoke and air into the smoker's lungs *US, 1967*

carcass *noun* one's body; oneself *AUSTRALIA, 1956*

car catcher *noun* a rear brakeman on a freight train *US, 1946*

car clout *noun* a thief who breaks into and steals the contents of cars *US, 1962*

card *noun* **1** a tactic held in reserve and then used to win an advantage. Usually in the expression 'playing the (fill in the blank) card' *US, 1973*. **2** an eccentric; a lively personality *UK, 1836*. ▶ **go through the card** to have everything on offer; to cover something comprehensively. Originally, 'to back every winning horse at a race-meeting.' *UK, 1977*. ▶ **on the card** in railway slang, on time *US, 1977*

card verb **1** to ask someone for proof of age before selling or serving them alcohol US, 1975. **2** to trade credit card numbers illegally UK, 1998

cardboard noun in horse racing, a betting ticket AUSTRALIA, 1989

cardboard box noun any sexually transmitted infection. Rhyming slang for POX UK, 1980

cardboard caver noun in caving and pot-holing, a caver who gives up at the first sign of wetness. Derogatory UK, 2004

cardboard city noun a prison segregation unit. Derives from the fact that the furniture in such prison cells is often made from cardboard UK, 1996

card-carrying adjective devout, dedicated. First used in the late 1940s to describe fervent leftists in the US as 'card-carrying Communists', the term was given new life in 1988 when Democratic presidential candidate Michael Dukakis described himself as a 'card-carrying member of the American Civil Liberties Union' US, 1963

cardenales noun barbiturates. From the Spanish for 'cardinal' (a red bird) US, 1997

carder noun a person employed to place prostitutes' advertising cards in telephone boxes and other public places UK, 1994

cardi; cardie; cardy; Cardi noun **1** a cardigan knitted woollen jacket. Named after James Brudenell, the seventh Earl of Cardigan (1797–1868) whose cavalry troops, during the Crimean War (1853–56), wore a similar garment for warmth UK, 1987. **2** an inhabitant of the country of Ceredigion, formerly Cardiganshire; any person who is reluctant to part with cash. Probably originates with the frugal practices of Cardiganshire hill farmers UK: WALES, 2002

cardies noun electronic gambling machines that display playing cards AUSTRALIA, 1998

cardinal noun ► **the cardinal is home** used for conveying that the speaker is experiencing the bleed period of the menstrual cycle US, 1980

card mob noun two or more card cheats working together US, 1979

cards noun ► **on the cards** likely, probable UK, 1849

cards speak noun in high-low poker, the rule that players need not declare whether they are playing for a low or high hand US, 1996

card surfing noun **1** a moving of custom between credit cards to achieve financial advantage UK, 2000. **2** a criminal act in which a criminal closely observes a person using an automatic cash machine (by looking over his or her shoulder) and notes the personal identity number that is enterered on the keypad; the user's card is subsequently stolen, without making the user aware of the theft, and fraudulent withdrawals of cash are the criminal's reward. Also known as 'shoulder surfing' US, 1992

care verb ► **not care less** to be absolutely unconcerned US, 1966

care bear noun a person working in a prison who is seen to be too sympathetic to the prisoners' needs. Derogatory; based on cute cartoon characters The Care Bears, originally created in 1981 for US greeting cards, and subsequently animated for television and film UK, 1996

career girl noun a ewe that refuses to nurse her young NEW ZEALAND, 2002

career mangler noun in the Canadian military, a Career Manager CANADA, 1995

care factor: zero! noun I don't care about what you just said! US, 1997

CARE package noun **1** a box of treats and/or necessities, sent to someone away from home with the hope of cheering them up. Suggested by CARE packages sent by the United Nations US, 1962. **2** a small amount of a drug disguised for safe carrying and later use UK, 1983

careware noun computer software offered free by its developer, with the request that the user make a contribution to a charity in place of paying a fee for the software US, 1991

carga noun heroin. Border Spanish used in English conversation by Mexican-Americans, from its literal sense as 'a charge (of explosive)' US, 1965

cargo noun ostentatious jewellery worn as a status symbol UK, 1994

carhop noun **1** an employee in a drive-in restaurant who serves customers in their cars US, 1939. **2** a girl who chooses partners on the basis of their car US, 1995

cariole noun a horse-drawn sleigh CANADA, 1965

carjack verb to steal a car from its driver under threat of bodily harm. An elision of 'car' and 'hijack' US, 1991

car jockey noun **1** a race car driver US, 1977. **2** a parking attendant US, 1956

cark; kark verb to die. Origin unknown. Suggestions that it is from 'carcass', or from 'cark' (the harsh cry of a crow) are not very convincing AUSTRALIA, 1977

car key noun a screwdriver used for breaking into cars UK, 1996

cark it; kark it verb to die AUSTRALIA, 1982

Carl Rosa noun a poser, a poseur; hence, as 'the old Carl Rosa', fraud or deceipt. Rhyming slang, formed on the name of German musician Carl Rosa, 1842–89; in 1873 he founded the Carl Rosa Opera which is now Britain's oldest opera company UK, 1977

Carly; Cally nickname lager manufacturers Carlsberg™; lager manufactured by Carlsberg™. 'Carly' may be used for the basic brand lager or Carlsberg Special Brew, or combined with 'extra' for Carlsberg Extra, and 'special' for Carlsberg Special Brew UK: SCOTLAND, 1988

carmabis noun marijuana. A visual pun on the word 'cannabis' and a quasi-spiritual reference to KARMA (fate); possibly an error in spelling or reading US, 1977

carn! come on! A call of encouragement especially common amongst sports spectators. Eye-dialect rendering of typical Australian pronunciation. Commonly preceding the name of a team beginning with 'the', e.g. 'carn the Blues' (come on the Blues) AUSTRALIA, 1965

carna used in exhortations AUSTRALIA, 1967

carnal noun among Mexican-Americans, a very close male friend. Border Spanish used in English conversation by Mexican-Americans US, 1950

carnapper noun a person who habitually steals cars. On the pattern of 'kidnapper' UK, 1984

carne noun heroin. From the Spanish for 'meat' US, 1986

carney; carny noun a carnival US, 1931

carnie noun **1** a young person under the legal age of consent. An abbreviated reference to 'carnal knowledge'; sometimes embellished as 'carnie kid'. NEW ZEALAND, 1984. **2** a carnation AUSTRALIA, 1968. **3** cocaine US, 2003

carnival croquet noun the shell game US, 1966

carnival louse noun a person who follows a carnival from town to town and associates with carnival employees, but is not one himself US, 1981

carny noun **1** any person employed by or associated with a travelling carnival US, 1939. **2** the insider's language used by carnival workers US, 1948

carny Bible noun the Amusement Business magazine US, 1985

carny divorce noun an arrangement in which a man and woman who are living together without benefit of a wedding end their relationship, often consisting of one ride backwards around on a ferris wheel US, 1985

carny's Christmas noun Labor Day (the first Monday in September) US, 1981

carny wedding noun an arrangement in which a man and woman live together without benefit of a wedding, often consisting of one ride around on a ferris wheel US, 1980

Carolina noun **1** in craps, a nine US, 1950. **2** a friend, a mate. A Glasgow rhyming slang extension of 'china plate' (mate), a piece of Cockney rhyming slang UK, 1988

Carolina spread noun significant weight gain below the waist US, 1981

Carolina stocker noun in drag racing, a stock car with illegal equipment or with an illegally large engine US, 1968

carp *noun* **1** anchovies as a pizza topping *US, 1996.* **2** a black prisoner *US, 1989.* **3** a carpenter, especially on a theatre set *US, 1952*

car park *noun* an informer. Rhyming slang for NARK (an informer) *UK, 1992*

carped *adjective* drug-intoxicated *UK, 1996*

carpenter *noun* an orthopaedist *US, 1994*

carpenter's dream *noun* a flat-chested woman. From the pun 'flat as a board, and easy to screw' *US, 1974*

carpet *noun* **1** a three month period of imprisonment. A shortening of 'carpet bag' rhyming slang for 'drag' an obsolete term for 'a three month sentence'; this origin is now mainly forgotten; therefore it has since been reasoned that 'carpet' is so-called because it is easy to do *UK, 1956.* **2** a three year sentence of imprisonment *UK, 1956.* **3** in betting, odds of 3–1 *UK, 1967.* **4** a sum of £3 *UK, 1954.* **5** three hundred pounds, £300. Ticket-touting slang. Also spelled 'carpits' *UK, 2002.* **6** an artificial grass playing surface *US, 1978.* ▶ **clean the carpet** (of a female) to masturbate *US, 2001.* ▶ **matching carpet and drapes; carpet and drapes that match** applied to a person, usually a woman, whose hair is neither bleached nor dyed. A jocular suggestion that the hair on the head is of the same natural shade as the pubic hair *US, 1999*

carpet and a half *noun* in betting, odds of 7–2. In bookmaker slang CARPET is 3–1, here the addition of a half increases the odds to 3½–1 or 7–2 *UK, 1991*

carpetbagger *noun* a person who interferes in local politics without being a true part of the local community *US, 1868*

carpet burger *noun* oral sex performed on a woman *US, 2001*

carpet burn *noun* a rawness of the skin due to frictional contact with a carpet. On the model of 'rope-burn'. Tends to be used mainly of knees and elbows and generally in the context of wounds received in the course of unconventionally located love-making *US, 1986*

carpet control *noun* an obsessive belief, held whilst under the influence of crack cocaine, that there are useable traces of crack cocaine on the floor. A variation on CARPET PATROL. From a discreet correspondent *UK, 2001*

carpet crawler *noun* a young child *US, 1976*

carpet game *noun* a swindle in which the swindler holds and then steals the wallet of a customer going to see a non-existent prostitute *US, 1967*

carpet joint *noun* a fancy, high-class casino *US, 1961*

carpet muncher *noun* a cunnilinguist; hence, and especially, a lesbian *US, 1994*

carpeto; carpito *noun* thirty pounds £30. Ticket-touting slang. From CARPET (£300) *UK, 2002*

carpet patrol *noun* smokers of crack cocaine who search the floor for droppings of crack cocaine *UK, 1998*

carpet slashing *noun* a dance party. From the more common CUT A RUG *US, 1947*

carpet walker *noun* a drug addict *US, 1971*

car-popping *noun* car-theft. From POP (to steal) *UK, 1996*

Carrie; Carrie Nation; Carry; Carry Nation *noun* cocaine *US, 1955*

carrier pigeon *noun* a messenger or courier *US, 1933*

carrot *noun* a marijuana cigarette *US, 2001*

carrot cruncher *noun* (from an urban perspective) a country-dweller *UK, 1977*

carrot eater; carrot snapper *noun* a Mormon. Offensive *US, 1968*

carrot-top *noun* a red-headed person *US, 1889*

carry *noun* **1** any victim of a crime who must be taken from the scene by stretcher *US, 1958.* **2** a consignment or substantial quantity of drugs *UK, 1996*

Carry *noun* ▷ *see:* CARRIE

carry *verb* **1** to carry a firearm *US, 1971.* **2** to be in possession of drugs *US, 1961.* **3** to have surplus money *UK: NORTHERN IRELAND, 1996.* **4** to lead or be in charge of something *US, 1972.* ▶ **carry a big spoon**

to stir up trouble *AUSTRALIA, 1989.* ▶ **carry a case** to be out of prison on bail. A neat play on a basic travel requirement and a 'court case' *UK, 1996.* ▶ **carry a torch** to yearn for an unrequited love or a love affair that is over; to be devoted to someone without having your devotion reciprocated *US, 1927.* ▶ **carry it to the door** to serve all of a prison sentence *US, 2002.* ▶ **carry news** to gossip *TRINIDAD AND TOBAGO, 1970.* ▶ **carry someone's bags** to be romantically involved with someone *US, 1973.* ▶ **carry the banner** to stay up all night *US, 1980.* ▶ **carry the bug** in circus usage, to work as a night watchman. From BUG (a torch) *US, 1981.* ▶ **carry the can back; carry the can** to take the blame or punishment on behalf of another; to be made a scapegoat; to do the dirty work while another gets the credit. Navy origins *UK, 1929.* ▶ **carry the mail 1** to buy drinks *AUSTRALIA, 1966.* **2** to commit a murder for hire *US, 1971.* **3** to move quickly *US, 1946.* ▶ **carry the shit bucket** to perform the lowliest tasks *AUSTRALIA, 1977.* ▶ **carry the silks** in horse racing, to race for a particular owner *US, 1951.* ▶ **carry the stick** to live without a fixed abode *US, 1978.* ▶ **carry the target** in horse racing, to run in the last position for an entire race *US, 1976.* ▶ **carry the wheels** to accelerate so quickly that the vehicle's front wheels lift off the ground *US, 1968.* ▶ **carry your bat out** in cricket, to survive your team's innings undismissed *UK, 1934*

carryall *noun* a vehicle for transport, either wheeled or on rails for snow *CANADA, 1963*

carry-away *noun* a robbery in which a safe is taken and opened at leisure away from the crime scene *US, 1958*

carry day *noun* in television and film-making, a day in which the cast and crew are paid but do not have to work *US, 1990*

carry down *verb* to arrest someone *TRINIDAD AND TOBAGO, 1971*

carrying all before her *adjective* of a woman, having a generous bust or obviously pregnant. Jocular *UK, 1984*

carryings-on *noun* conspicuous behaviour *UK, 1859*

carrying weight *adjective* depressed. Beatniks' use, late 1950s-60s; from the notion of being under a heavy burden *UK, 1984*

Carry Nation *noun* ▷ *see:* CARRIE

carry-on *noun* **1** a fuss; an uproar; an outbreak of excited behaviour *UK, 1890.* **2** any continuing activity or catalogue of details *UK, 2001*

carry on *verb* **1** to behave in a conspicuous way, to make a fuss *UK, 1828.* **2** to be involved in a flirtatious or adulterous relationship. Generally phrased 'carry on with', specifying the other person *UK, 1856.* **3** to act in an ostentatiously effeminate manner in public *US, 1963*

carry tos *noun* (around Shigawake in the Gaspe) social welfare. The word is pronounced 'carry toss' *CANADA, 1998*

carry your ass! go away! *GUYANA, 1998*

carsey; karsey *noun* a brothel. From the Italian *casa* (a house) which is also its original use *UK, 2002*

car-shop *verb* to break into a car to steal its contents *US, 1997*

cart *verb* **1** to carry something somewhere. From the conventional sense (to transport by cart) *UK, 1964.* **2** in cricket, to hit the ball or attack the bowling with unrestrained power *UK, 1903*

Carter's Little Liver Pills *noun* any central nervous system stimulant *US, 1976*

cart-nap *verb* to steal a shopping trolley. A jocular combination of 'cart' and 'kidnap' *UK, 1996*

car toad; car tink; car tonk; car whacker *noun* a railway inspector. Named for the squatting position taken when inspecting the underside of a car *US, 1946*

carton-pusher *noun* a person who sells cigarettes that have been stolen or smuggled from a state with lower taxes *US, 1978*

car trick *noun* an act of sex between a prostitute and customer in a car *US, 1968*

carts; cartz *noun* a man's genitalia *UK, 1992*

cartucho *noun* a package containing marijuana cigarettes, equivalent to a packet of cigarettes. From 'cartouche' (a roll or case of paper, etc., containing a charge for a firearm), or Spanish *cartucho* (a roll or case of paper) *UK, 1986*

cartwheel *noun* **1** a feigned drug withdrawal spasm *US, 1936.* **2** an amphetamine tablet *US, 1966.* **3** a silver dollar piece *US, 1949*

cartzo; catso; cartes *noun* the penis. From Italian *cazzo* (to thust) *UK, 1702*

carve *verb* **1** in skateboarding, to take a turn sharply *US, 1976.* **2** in surfing, to change the course of the surfboard by digging it into the water *US, 1980.* **3** in mountain biking, to travel at great speed around corners *US, 1996.* **4** in foot-propelled scootering, to turn sharply while in mid-jump. Glossed as 'pulling off a big, fast, aerial scoot-turn' *UK, 2000.* **5** to outplay another musician in a competition of solos *US, 1970.* ▶ **carve some beef** to grant sexual favours; to consent to sex *US, 2001.* ▶ **carve someone's knob** to make someone understand *US, 1953.* ▶ **carve up the mob** to surf recklessly through a crowd of surfers or swimmers *AUSTRALIA, 1964.* ▶ **carve yourself a slice** from the male point of view, to have sex *UK, 1984*

carved up *adjective* (used of a bodybuilder) without fat *US, 1984*

carve-up *noun* **1** a fight; a battle; a gang war *UK, 1961.* **2** an act of poor driving in which one vehicle cuts in front of another *UK, 1984.* **3** a division of loot, profits or the legacy of a will *UK, 1935.* **4** a swindle *UK, 1937*

carve up *verb* **1** of a driver, to cut in front of another vehicle and force the driver of that vehicle to brake or take other emergency action *UK, 1984.* **2** to spoil the chances of another's business *UK, 1961.* **3** to swindle an accomplice out of a share *UK, 1937*

carvie *noun* **1** a fellow prisoner who shares in a supply of tobacco, perhaps by subscription to a common supply *UK, 1950.* **2** a prisoner who deals in contraband tobacco; a tobacco baron. From the earlier sense (a prisoner who shares your tobacco). This sense describes the prisoner who *carves up* the supply *UK, 1996*

carving knife *noun* a wife. Rhyming slang *UK, 2003*

car wash *noun* during the Vietnam war, an establishment in Vietnam where a man went for a haircut, bath, massage and sex *US, 1977*

car whacker *noun* ▷ *see:* CAR TOAD

casa *noun* the operator of a gambling establishment or game. Spanish for 'house' *TRINIDAD AND TOBAGO, 1952*

casabas *noun* the female breasts *US, 1970*

Casablanca *noun* a wanker (an all-purpose term of abuse). Rhyming slang *UK, 2003*

Casablanca gold *noun* a variety of hashish produced on the higher slopes of the Rif Mountains *UK, 2003*

Cascadia *noun* an imaginary proposed state or area formed of the states of Washington and Oregon and British Columbia *CANADA, 1995*

case *noun* **1** a promiscuous woman *AUSTRALIA, 1967.* **2** a patient with a sexually transmitted infection *US, 1994.* **3** a love-affair *UK, 1860.* **4** to engage in an adulterous relationship *UK, 1977*

case *verb* **1** to look over a place or person, especially in anticipation of criminal activity *US, 1914.* **2** to work as a prostitute. A cynical variation of 'go case' (to have sex with) *UK, 1996.* **3** to tease someone, to scold someone *US, 1971.* **4** to put a prisoner on report for a breach of regulations *UK, 1950*

case! used for asserting that all has gone as planned *TRINIDAD AND TOBAGO, 1966*

case ace *noun* in card games, the fourth and remaining ace when three have been played *US, 1960*

case game *noun* in pool, a situation in which each player can win with their next shot *US, 1985*

case note *noun* **1** a one-dollar note *US, 1962.* **2** a gambler's last money *US, 1962*

case out *verb* to engage in sexual foreplay *US, 1963*

caser *noun* **1** a skilled card-counter in blackjack *US, 1983.* **2** in poker, the last card in a particular rank or suit in a deal. A term borrowed from the card game of faro *US, 1963.* **3** a strict prison officer; one with a reputation for putting prisoners on report *UK, 1950.* **4** a five shilling piece; five shillings. Recorded earliest in Australia. Became obsolete after the introduction of decimal currency in 1966 *AUSTRALIA, 1825.* **5** a sexually aggressive boy *US, 1963*

Casey Jones *noun* **1** in poker, a player who draws the last card of a rank, the case card. John Luther 'Casey' Jones (1864–1900) was an American locomotive engineer whose death in a train accident made him a legend celebrated in ballad and song *US, 1988.* **2** in pool, a case game (one that either player can win with their next shot) *US, 1993*

cash *verb* to finish consuming something. Usage is in the context of drug or alcohol consumption *US, 2001*

cash and carriage *noun* marriage. Rhyming slang. Derives only from CASH AND CARRY (to marry) as the term 'cash and carriage' has no other existence *UK, 1992*

cash and carried *adjective* married. Rhyming slang, from CASH AND CARRY (to marry); not 'cashed' *UK, 1961*

cash and carry *verb* to marry. Rhyming slang *UK, 1961*

cash ass *noun* sex for money *UK, 1987*

cash cow *noun* any business or business-sector that provides a steady cash flow *US, 1974*

cashed *adjective* completely consumed, empty *US, 1997*

cashed up *adjective* with a ready supply of money *AUSTRALIA, 1930*

casher *noun* a front trouser pocket. Pickpockets' use, because that is where coins are usually carried *UK, 1974*

cashew *noun* a psychiatric patient *US, 1994*

cashie *noun* a cash transaction that is tax-free by virtue of not being reported *NEW ZEALAND, 1995*

cash-in *noun* a profitable product or activity that is tied into – and would not exist without – another product or activity that has a greater presence in the marketplace *UK, 1970*

cash in *verb* **1** to die. A shortened form of 'cash in your chips' *US, 1891.* **2** to take advantage of something and profit thereby *US, 1904*

cashish *noun* money *UK, 2000*

cashmere *noun* a jumper, whether actually cashmere or not *US, 1970*

cash money! used for expressing great joy or pleasure *US, 2002*

cashola *noun* money *US, 1977*

cash sale *noun* a US Marine newly arrived in Vietnam and inexperienced in combat. Cash Sales was the name of an outlet found on marine bases in the US; a marine newly arrived in Vietnam looked like and smelled like a Cash Sales outlet *US, 1990*

cash talk *noun* a Canadian male game in which participants aggressively insult each other *CANADA, 2002*

cash up *verb* **1** to get money *AUSTRALIA, 1958.* **2** to pay someone *UK, 1983*

casino-hop *verb* to move from one casino to another *US, 1993*

casino perfects *noun* high quality dice used in casinos. The dice are almost certain to roll true because they are milled to a very precise tolerance *US, 1997*

casket nail *noun* a cigarette. Far less common than COFFIN NAIL *US, 1969*

casper *noun* a very pale white person, especially a tourist at the beach *US, 1991*

Casper; Casper the ghost *noun* crack cocaine. Based on the cartoon-strip character Casper the Friendly Ghost; from the cloud of smoke produced when smoking the product *US, 1994*

cass-cass *adjective* messy, slovenly *GUYANA, 1998*

cast *verb* ▶ **cast an eyeball** to look. Teen slang *US, 1958.* ▶ **cast the runes** in computing, to operate a program that will not work for anyone else *US, 1991*

casters-up mode *adjective* in computing, broken *US, 1991*

cast-eye *noun* a squint *BELIZE, 1998*

casting couch *noun* the notional or real sofa in a director's office, used for sex with an actor hoping for a part. Based on the commonly held belief that a sexual performance is all the audition required *US, 1931*

cast-iron *adjective* irrefutable *UK, 1943*

cast iron college *noun* a local jail. Carnival usage *US, 1968*

castle *noun* **1** a house or apartment *US, 1953*. **2** in cricket, the wicket that a batsman is defending *UK, 1959*

castled *adjective* in cricket, bowled out. From CASTLE (a wicket that is being defended) *UK, 2003*

castor *noun* ▶ **on the castor** popular, well-regarded. Extended from CASTOR (excellent) *AUSTRALIA, 1953*

castor *adjective* excellent; all right *AUSTRALIA, 1944*

Castor and Pollux; Caster and Pollux *noun* the testicles. The classical twins of the Zodiac provide the source for this rhyming slang for BOLLOCKS *UK, 1992*

Castro *nickname* a neighbourhood in San Francisco, California, dominated by homosexual men since the early 1970s. Castro Street is the main artery of the neighbourhood *US, 1987*

Castro clone *noun* a homosexual who conforms to a clean-cut, fashionable image. The Castro is a predominantly gay neighbourhood in San Francisco *US, 1986*

cast up *verb* to vomit *BARBADOS, 1965*

casual *noun* **1** a member of a violent faction of football supporters (A FIRM), aligned to a football team and identified by a uniform of casual wear. In use since the late 1970s. Examples recorded include Aberdeen Soccer Casuals, Cambridge Casuals, Celtic Casuals, Darlington Casuals, Fine Young Casuals (Oldham FC), Suburban Casuals (Southampton) *UK, 1989*. **2** a youth fashion from the late 1970s, based on designer labels. In the 1980s a working-class trend, in the 1990s a positive symbol of urban chic; also refers to a follower of this fashion style. A variant is 'caj' *UK, 1980*

casual *adjective* excellent, fashionable, trendy. Youth usage *US, 1963*

cat *noun* **1** a man *US, 1920*. **2** a black person *US, 1972*. **3** a spiteful, gossiping woman. A back-formation from CATTY (spiteful, sly) *UK, 1950*. **4** the vagina *UK, 1720*. **5** a passive homosexual male; any male homosexual. In prison 'cats' are 'young prisoners who, though usually heterosexual prior to incarceration, submit to the passive role in homosexual relations in prison'. But also in prison 'cat' is used to refer to known homosexuals who are often segregated from other inmates. Outside of prison the term is used generally of homosexual men: perhaps an extension of the meaning as 'a woman'. The suggestion that it is a shortening of 'catamite' has no supporting evidence *AUSTRALIA, 1950*. **6** a lion; a tiger; a leopard. Circus usage, usually in the plural *UK, 1953*. **7** in circus and carnival usage, a trouble-making southern rustic *US, 1981*. **8** a poorly performing racing greyhound *AUSTRALIA, 1989*. **9** in poker, a nonstandard hand such as the 'little cat', 'big cat', etc *US, 1988*. **10** heroin *US, 1993*. **11** methcathinone *US, 1995*. **12** a category *UK, 1984*. **13** a Caterpillar™ tractor or other type of heavy equipment *US, 1918*. **14** a catalytic converter, an emissions-control device *US, 1993*. **15** a hydraulic catapult on an aircraft carrier *US, 1962*. **16** a catamaran *UK, 1984*. **17** a boat of any description *UK, 1961*. ▶ **let the cat out of the bag** to disclose a secret *UK, 1760*. ▶ **on the cat** staying away from home at night *US, 1965*. ▶ **on the cat hop** in railway slang, on time *US, 1946*. ▶ **put a cat among the pigeons; set the cat among the pigeons** to stir up trouble *UK, 1976*. ▶ **something the cat dragged in; something the cat has brought in** used as the epitome of someone who is bedraggled *UK, 1928*

Cat *noun* a Cadillac car *US, 1945*

cat *verb* **1** to stay away from home overnight, prowling for sin. From the alleycat as a role model for behaviour *US, 1949*. **2** to pursue someone in the hopes of sexual relations *US, 1946*

Cat A *noun* the categorisation of most secure prisons, thus the cat-egory for highly dangerous prisoners or those considered most likely to escape. 'Cat B,' 'Cat C,' and 'Cat D' are also used in decreasing order of required security. These categories have been in force since 1966 *UK, 1996*

Cat A *verb* to categorise a prisoner as Cat A. 'Cat B', 'Cat C' and 'Cat D' are also used in decreasing order of required security. *UK, 1996*

catalog man *noun* a gambling cheat whose superficial knowledge of cheating is acquired from studying catalogues of cheating devices. A derisive term when used by cheats who carefully hone their craft *US, 1945*

cat and class *noun* cataloguing and classification. Librarians' use *UK, 1984*

cat and mouse *noun* a house. Rhyming slang *UK, 1857*

catapult *noun* in the language of windsurfing, a high-speed exit from the board assisted by high winds *US, 1985*

catatonia *noun* in computing, the condition that exists when a computer is in suspended operation, unable to proceed *US, 1981*

catatonic *adjective* (of a computer) caught in an inextricable oper-ation and thus suspended beyond reach or response *US, 1991*

catawampus *adjective* crooked, bent *US, 1851*

catbird seat *noun* an advantageous position. Coined or at the very least popularised by humourist James Thurber in 1942 *US, 1942*

catbox *noun* the Middle East *US, 1998*

catcall *noun* a derisive jeer *US, 1839*

catch *noun* **1** a person who is considered matrimonially or romantically desirable *UK, 1749*. **2** a prostitute who has been recruited to work for a pimp *US, 1973*. **3** in Keno, the number of winning numbers that a player has marked *US, 1972*. **4** a hidden condition or consequence *US, 1855*

catch *verb* **1** (used of a pimp) to recruit a prostitute to work for him; to recruit a woman to work as a prostitute *US, 1972*. **2** (used of a prostitute) to engage a customer *US, 1968*. **3** to play the passive sex-ual role in a homosexual relationship *US, 1966*. **4** to take calls or complaints called in to a police station; to be assigned a case *US, 1958*. **5** in an illegal number gambling lottery, to win *US, 1949*. **6** in gin, to draw a card *US, 1971*. ▶ **catch (some) lead** to be shot *US, 1970*. ▶ **catch a bullet** to be shot *US, 1992*. ▶ **catch a buzz** to smoke marijuana and become intoxicated *US, 1997*. ▶ **catch a crab** in rowing, to err in a stroke, disrupting the timing and momentum of the rowing *US, 1949*. ▶ **catch a dummy** in prison, to refuse to speak *US, 1990*. ▶ **catch a fish** in poker, after making a small bet with a good hand (the bait), to lure another player into increasing the bet *US, 1988*. ▶ **catch a glad** to act with spon-taneous joy *TRINIDAD AND TOBAGO, 1984*. ▶ **catch a hit** to be scolded or harshly criticised. Marine usage in the Vietnam war *US, 1991*. ▶ **catch a horse** to urinate. A euphemism *AUSTRALIA, 1942*. ▶ **catch a pay** to be beaten and robbed *US, 1997*. ▶ **catch a run** to wet one side of a marijuana cigarette to promote even burning *US, 1997*. ▶ **catch a stack** to rob someone with a lot of cash *US, 1987*. ▶ **catch a vaps** to become suddenly inspired *GRENADA, 1998*. ▶ **catch air** to become airborne while skateboarding or surfing *US, 1987*. ▶ **catch ass** to have a hard time *TRINIDAD AND TOBAGO, 1956*. ▶ **catch no ball** to fail to understand *SINGAPORE, 2002*. ▶ **catch on the flipper; catch on the (old) flip-flop** to make contact on your return. Citizens' band radio slang *US, 1976*. ▶ **catch on the rebound** to become emotionally involved with a person who has just been rejected from another relationship. Probably the pun from which the emotional condition ON THE REBOUND derives *UK, 1864*. ▶ **catch on the reverse; catch on the rebound** to make contact on a return journey. Citizens' band radio slang *US, 1976*. ▶ **catch some** to engage in heavy sexual caressing *US, 1968*. ▶ **catch squeals** to take calls or complaints called into a police station *US, 1969*. ▶ **catch the bumps** in a striptease act, to synchronise the dancer's pelvic thrusts with the drum and cymbal beat *US, 1981*. ▶ **catch thrills** to engage in an activity that excites or stimulates. Hawaiian youth usage *US, 1982*. ▶ **catch tricks** (used of a drummer in a performance) to create sound effects on sight *US, 1973*. ▶ **catch wreck** to achieve respect for your actions *US, 1995*. ▶ **catch your death of cold; catch your death** to catch a very bad cold. Dating is obscure; the tra-ditional Yorkshire folk song 'On Ilkley Moor baht'at' contains the line 'Then thee will catch thy death of cold' which, while the intent may be literal, means no more than '[If you go out on] Ilkley Moor without a hat [...] you will catch a bad cold' *UK, 1872*. ▶ **catch yourself on** to recover your common sense. Usually in the imperative *UK, 1984*

catch 22 *noun* a self-cancelling dilemma. Coined by Joseph Heller for his 1955 novel *Catch 22*, which was originally to be titled 'Catch 18' – until *Mila 18* by Leon Uris was published *US, 1977*

catch colt *noun* an illegitimate child *US, 1901*

catch driver *noun* in harness racing, a driver hired on the day of the race *US, 1994*

catcher *noun* **1** the passive partner in homosexual sex *US, 1966*. **2** a peripheral member of an illegal drug enterprise hired to retrieve drugs hurriedly thrown out of a window to avoid confiscation and arrest *US, 1989*

catcher's mitt *noun* a dense jungle area with a heavy Viet Cong and North Vietnamese presence northeast of Phu Loi. Based on a vague resemblance between the area and a catcher's mitt on a map *US, 1990*

catch hand *noun* a casual workman who moves from job to job to get more favourable rates and conditions but has no intention of staying with any job until its completion *UK, 1964*

catch it *verb* **1** to get it into trouble with an authority, especially to incur a beating or a severe telling off *UK, 1835*. **2** to be killed *US, 1982*

catch on *verb* **1** to understand; to grasp the meaning or significance of something *US, 1884*. **2** to become popular or fashionable *UK, 1887*

catch one *verb* to drink or use drugs to the point of mild intoxication *US, 1997*

catchy *adjective* attractive, appealing, especially if vulgarly so *UK, 1831*

catch you later used as a farewell *US, 1947*

Cat City *nickname* Cathedral City, California. A resort town just south of Palm Springs in the Coachella Valley *US, 1981*

cat daddy *noun* a male with charm and charisma *US, 2002*

caterpillar *noun* during the war in Vietnam, a convoy of non-combat vehicles on a passably secure road *US, 1991*

caterpillar *verb* in mountain biking, to pedal with a fluctuating, inefficient cadence *US, 1992*

catever; kerterver *adjective* bad. From Italian *cattivo* (bad) but via earlier senses as 'an odd occurence or person' *UK, 2002*

cat-eye *noun* an irregular work shift *US, 1977*

cat eyes *noun* eyes that are anything other than dark brown *US, 1982*

catface *noun* a pucker left in a garment after ironing *US, 1952*

cat fever *noun* catarrhal gastroenteritis, suffered by troops in the field in Vietnam *US, 1945*

cat fight *noun* a no-holds-barred fight between women *AUSTRALIA, 1967*

catfish *noun* a person who speaks too much and thinks too little *US, 1954*

catfish row *noun* a black neighbourhood in a southern US city. For the setting of his 1935 folk opera *Porgy and Bess*, George Gershwin used Catfish Row, a fictionalisation of an alleyway named Cabbage Row off Church Street in Charleston, South Carolina *US, 1965*

cat got your tongue? 'why aren't you talking?'; used for mocking or asking why a temporary speechlessness has struck. Elliptical for 'has the cat got your tongue?'; generally addressed to a child but equally patronising when asked of an adult *UK, 1911*

cath *verb* to insert a catheter into a patient. Medical use *UK, 1980*

cat-haul *verb* to interrogate someone fiercely. From a form of punishment used with slaves – a cat was forcibly dragged by the tail down the slave's bare back *US, 1951*

cat head *noun* a biscuit *US, 1962*

Catherine Wheel *noun* in the youth trend for 'souped-up' motor-scootering, a lifting of the front wheel off the ground due to sudden acceleration performed in conjunction with a flaming trail. Probably from the Catherine Wheel firework as a fiery elaboration of WHEELIE *UK, 2004*

Catho *noun* a member of the Catholic Church *AUSTRALIA, 1996*

cat hole *noun* a one-time, one-man field latrine dug by the user in Vietnam *US, 1978*

Catholic *noun* a pickpocket *US, 1949*

Catholic aspirin *noun* a tablet of Benzedrine™ (amphetamine sulphate), a central nervous system stimulant. From the cross scores on the white tablet *US, 1973*

cathouse *noun* a brothel *US, 1893*

cat in hell's chance *noun* a very slim chance or possibility. In 1796, Francis Grose recorded 'No more chance than a cat in hell without claws'. Almost always phrased in the negative: 'not a cat in hell's chance' (no chance whatsoever) *UK, 1796*

cat lapper *noun* a lesbian; someone who enjoys performing oral sex on women *US, 1967*

cat-lick; cat-licker *noun* a Roman Catholic *US, 1942*

cat-life *noun* a prison sentence of two or more consecutive life terms *US, 1992*

cat man *noun* a burglar who relies on stealth *US, 1962*

catnip *noun* **1** poor quality, adulterated or entirely fake marijuana. Catmint, the botanical genus *nepeta*, known in the US as 'catnip', may be passed off as marijuana to the unsuspecting, or mixed with genuine marijuana as a make-weight; consequently any impotent marijuana *US, 1962*. **2** a marijuana cigarette. An ironic adoption of the previous sense *UK, 2003*

cat out *verb* to sneak away *UK, 1983*

cat pack *noun* a loosely defined group of wealthy, famous and fashionable people *US, 1971*

cat pan *noun* a bowl used for washing the vagina. From CAT (the vagina) *TRINIDAD AND TOBAGO, 2003*

cat-piss-and-pepper *noun* a noisy, unrestrained argument *BARBADOS, 2003*

cat pisser *noun* windscreen wipers *US, 1992*

cat plant *noun* a facility where crude oil is separated by catalysis *US, 1960*

cat rack *noun* a game concession in a carnival in which a player throws balls at stuffed cats on a platform or fence *US, 1960*

cats *noun* **1** trousers *UK, 2002*. **2** heavy rain. From the older (1738) and more familiar adverb form *UK, 1976*. **3** stocks without proven performance *US, 1997*

cat's arse *noun* anything very good, superlative or exceptional; someone who is considered the best by themselves or others *UK, 1984*

cat's ass *noun* **1** an extraordinarily good or extraordinarily bad example of something *US, 1967*. **2** a knot or kink in a wire or rope *US, 1942*

cat's bar *noun* a female-only or mixed-sex bar *NEW ZEALAND, 1953*

cat's breakfast *noun* an unpleasant mess. A variation of DOG'S BREAKFAST *UK, 1984*

cat's eyes *noun* in craps, a roll of three *US, 1945*

cat shit *noun* used as a basis for comparison when describing someone who is mean *US, 1970*

cat shot *noun* a take-off from an aircraft carrier assisted by a catapult. Vietnam war usage *US, 1959*

cat's meat *noun* an easily accomplished task *NEW ZEALAND, 1962*

cat's meow; cat's miaow *noun* anything very good, superlative or exceptional; someone who is considered the best by themselves or others *US, 1921*

cat's mother *noun* ▶ **'she' is the cat's mother; 'she' is a cat's mother** addressed as a catchphrase reproof to a child who fails to show proper respect by referring to the mother, or any other adult woman, as 'she'. Occasionally 'she is the cat'; at other times 'she' is 'the cat's grandmother.' *UK, 1897*

cat's nut *noun* an extraordinary thing or person *US, 1928*

cat's pajamas; cat's pyjamas *noun* anything very good, superlative or exceptional; someone who is considered the best by themselves or others. Coined by, or inspired by, an illustration by New York Journal sports cartoonist Thomas Aloysius 'TAD' Dorgan (1877–1929); in the UK by 1923 but rare by 1939. Still occasionally recorded *US, 1922*

catspraddle *verb* to beat someone with the fists *TRINIDAD AND TOBAGO, 1998*

cat's prick *noun* an elongated ember at the lit end of a cigarette *UK, 2003*

cat's whiskers *noun* anything very good, superlative or exceptional; someone who is considered the best by themselves or others.

A variation of CAT'S PAJAMAS. From the 1960s on, usage is mainly Australian *UK, 1927*

cattie *noun* a mail-order catalogue *UK, 1988*

cattle *noun* racehorses *AUSTRALIA, 1989*

cattle call *noun* a mass audition *US, 1952*

cattle dog *noun* **1** a Catholic school student *NEW ZEALAND, 1998*. **2** a catalogue. Punning on the similarity of the pronunciation *AUSTRALIA, 1984*

cattle truck *noun* **1** any large truck used to transport troops. Vietnam war usage *US, 1968*. **2** in oil drilling, a bus that transports workers to the oil fields *US, 1954*. **3** a driver-operated omnibus *UK, 1973*

cattle truck; cattle *verb* 'fuck', generally in a figurative or expletive sense. Rhyming slang *UK, 1961*

cattle wagon *noun* a large car, especially a station wagon *US, 1973*

cat tranquillizer *noun* the recreational drug ketamine *CANADA, 2002*

catty *adjective* **1** sly, spiteful, mean-spirited *UK, 1886*. **2** nimble and sure-footed in a cat-like manner. Lumberjacks' use *CANADA, 1984*

catty-cat *noun* the vagina *US, 1980*

catty-catty *adjective* promiscuous *TRINIDAD AND TOBAGO, 2003*

cat wagon *noun* a mobile brothel *US, 372*

cat-walk *verb* on a motorcycle or bicycle, to perform a wheelstand and then ride forward on the rear wheel *US, 1992*

cat walker *noun* a burglar who steals at night *UK, 1990*

cat wash *noun* a quick cleaning of the body using a washcloth but not a full bath or shower *BAHAMAS, 1982*

catweed *noun* marijuana *UK, 1996*

cat work *noun* criminal employment as a cat-burglar *UK, 1956*

caught short *adjective* **1** unprepared, especially with regards to bodily functions *AUSTRALIA, 1964*. **2** embarrassed by an untimely lack of whatever is required *UK, 1984*

caught using purple *adjective* apprehended making non-farm use of tax-free farm petrol. To help ease the strain on farm budgets, the prairie provinces allow farmers to buy petrol for farm equipment exempt from certain taxes. The petrol is dyed purple. Police in rural areas check. It also means being caught at some other technical illegality *CANADA, 1987*

Cauliflower Alley *noun* the boxing world. Journalists' use. Extending the punning TIN-EAR ALLEY *UK, 1961*

cauliflower ear; cauliflower *noun* an ear that has been damaged and deformed by blows. Originally and still used as a boxing term *US, 1896*

caulks *noun* ▶ **put the caulks to someone** to stamp with studded boots on someone's face. Lumberjacks' and loggers' use; 'caulks' are the spiked studs on their specialised waterproof boots *CANADA, 1961*

caulk up *verb* to use spiked working boots to stamp on someone. Lumberjacks' and loggers' use; 'caulks' are the spiked studs on their specialised waterproof boots *CANADA, 1939*

cause *verb* ▶ **cause a vacancy** in poker, to win a hand that drives a player from the game *US, 1988*

'cause; cos; coz; cuz because. An accepted and conventional term in C16 that has slipped into dialect and vulgar use *UK, 1977*

cause it *verb* to cause trouble to, or damage something *UK, 1974*

cav *adjective* cavalier. In the pornography industry, an attitude towards sexually transmitted disease *US, 1995*

cavalier *noun* the uncircumcised penis. Probably of Royal Navy origin, then juvenile; derives as an antonym of ROUNDHEAD (a circumcised penis) *UK, 2002*

cavalry *noun* ▶ **the cavalry are coming; the cavalry are here** help is coming; help is here. From the literal military sense, probably informed in use by film Westerns *UK, 1984*

Cav and Pag *nickname* the short operas *Cavalleria Rusticana*, by Pietro Mascagni, and *Pagliacci*, by Ruggero Leoncavallo, when paired as a double bill. *Cavalleria Rusticana* was first performed in 1890, *Pagliacci* in 1892 *UK, 2002*

cave *noun* **1** a deep sore at the site of repeated drug injections *US, 1973*. **2** the vagina. From the conventional meaning (a large hole or crevice) *UK, 2001*. ▶ **keep cave** to keep a lookout. Extends from CAVE! pronounced 'kay-vee' (beware!); school slang *UK, 1906*

cave *verb* to have sex with someone *US, 1973*

cave! beware! School slang, pronounced 'kay-vee', from Latin *cavere* (to beware). Still familiar, but mainly from its convenience as a crossword clue to a generation who read a certain sort of children's fiction *UK, 1868*

caveman *adjective* **1** obsolete *US, 1974*. **2** used of any skateboarding manoeuvre performed in an old-fashioned style *UK, 2004*

cave tubing *noun* a floating exploration of underground river and cave systems on an inflated rubber tube *BELIZE, 2003*

caviar *noun* **1** human faecal matter in the context of a sexual fetish. A euphemism used in pornography *UK, 2002*. **2** residue in whatever utensils are used for manufacturing crack cocaine *US, 1993*. **3** a mixture of marijuana and crack cocaine prepared for smoking in a cigarette *US, 1989*. **4** cocaine; crack cocaine *UK, 2003*

caviar can *noun* an armoured tank from the former Soviet Union *US, 1952*

Cavite all star *noun* marijuana, probably from the Philippines. Cavite was a US military base and is now an 'Export Processing Zone', ninety miles south of Manila *US, 1977*

cav of the cav *nickname* the First Squadron of the Ninth US Cavalry. Organised in 1866, the Ninth Cavalry saw action in every war through to Vietnam *US, 1991*

cavvy *noun* a substitute horse, or person *CANADA, 1987*

cazh *adjective* ▷ *see:* KAZH

cazooled *adjective* drunk *US, 1968*

CB *noun* used as an abbreviation for COCKBLOCK *US, 1980*

CB *adjective* could be. Used in tentative diagnoses, such as 'could be lupus' *US, 1994*

CBC sunshine *noun* rain after a Canadian Broadcasting Corporation forecast of sun *CANADA, 1987*

CBT *noun* in the subculture of consensual sado-masochism, the infliction of discomfort and pain on a male's genitals. An initialism of *c*ock (the penis) 'b'all' (the testicle) and 'torture' *UK, 2002*

CC *noun* **1** Canadian Club™ whisky *US, 1971*. **2** cocaine offered as a gift by a dealer *US, 1989*. **3** a prison segregation unit. An abbreviation of CARDBOARD CITY *UK, 1996*

CC *verb* to send someone to a prison segregation unit, or to replace cell furniture with cardboard items. From CARDBOARD CITY (the segregation unit) *UK, 1996*

CCW *noun* the criminal charge of carrying a concealed weapon. As the US moved to the right, gun enthusiasts have been successful in enacting legislation in many states that permit – not forbid – carrying concealed weapons, changing the meaning of the acronym to 'concealed-carry weapon' *US, 1973*

CD *noun* a condom. Scamto youth street slang (South African townships) *SOUTH AFRICA, 2005*

C-Day *noun* the day when new car models were available for civilian purchase after the end of World War 2 *US, 1944*

C-duct *noun* cocaine *US, 1986*

C-dust *noun* cocaine *US, 1970*

cecil *noun* cocaine. A disguise like CHARLIE, another man's name *UK, 1996*

Cecil B. DeMille *noun* any large job that evolves into a chaotic mess. New York police slang *US, 1997*

Cecil Gee; cecil *noun* one thousand pounds. The high street designer menswear shop Cecil Gee is used for 'dressing up' the common G (£1,000). Noted in use by television presenter Johnny Vaughan *UK, 2002*

ceech *noun* hashish *US, 1992*

ceefa noun a cat. A play on 'c for cat' NEW ZEALAND, 1998

ceiling bet noun the highest bet permitted in a given game or situation US, 1988

ceiling chicken noun an Air Canada baggage handler with a particular assignment CANADA, 1994

ceitful adjective deceitful GUYANA, 1996

celeb noun a celebrity US, 1916

celebrity-fucker noun a person who seeks out sexual relationships with famous people US, 1969

celestial discharge noun death in a hospital US, 1994

cell noun a wireless telephone that is part of a system in which a geographical area is divided into sections served by a limited-range transmitter. An abbreviation of 'cell phone' a term first heard in the late 1980s as an abbreviation of 'cellular' US, 1997

cell verb to occupy a prison cell US, 1901

cell 99 noun a prison morgue US, 1949

cellar noun in a sports league, the last place in team standings US, 1950

cellar dealer noun a card cheat who deals from the bottom of a deck US, 1988

cellar flap; cellar verb to borrow something. Rhyming slang for TAP (to borrow) UK, 1960

cell block noun 1 a condom. A clever play on words: 'cell' (a basic life-form) representing spermatazoa, combined with 'block' (a barrier); the whole ironically suggesting imprisonment (of the penis) UK, 1998. 2 a school classroom. Teen slang US, 1958

cellie; celly noun 1 in jail or prison, a cellmate US, 1966. 2 a cellular telephone US, 1999

cell-shocked adjective deranged from life in prison. An obvious, although sharp, play on 'shell-shocked' US, 1990

cell spin noun a surprise search of a cell by prison authorities. From SPIN (to search) UK, 1996

cell task noun in prison, a pin-up. A focus on location and inspiration for a prisoner's TASK (masturbation) UK, 1996

cell warrior noun a prisoner whose actions outside his cell do not match his aggressive words uttered in the safety of his cell US, 2001

cement arm noun an intravenous drug user's arm that is toughened with scar tissue over the veins US, 1973

cemented adjective very drunk UK, 1983

cementhead noun a stupid person US, 1949

cement mixer noun 1 a dancer who rotates her pelvis in a simulation of sexual intercourse US, 1951. 2 a dance, a ball. A beatnik term not recorded until 1984 UK, 1984. 3 a loud car or truck US, 1914

cement overcoat noun hardened cement in which a murder victim is concealed US, 1969

cement overshoes noun concrete poured around a person's feet, used to weigh them down when their body is disposed of in a body of water US, 1962

census office noun in prison, the office where incoming and outgoing mail is checked UK, 1996

cent noun a dollar US, 1957. ▶ **like a cent worth of shaved ice** humiliated, belittled TRINIDAD AND TOBAGO, 1987

centerfield noun 1 in craps, a field bet on the nine US, 1985. 2 in blackjack played in casinos, the seat directly across from the dealer US, 1985

centre noun in the gambling game two-up, the bets placed with the person spinning the coins AUSTRALIA, 1911

Centre noun ▶ **the Centre** the central parts of the Australian mainland AUSTRALIA, 1899

centurion noun a cricketer who scores 100 runs BARBADOS, 1886

century noun 1 a $100 note US, 1859. 2 one hundred pounds (£100) UK, 1861. 3 one hundred yards US, 1989. 4 one hundred miles US, 1956. 5 in motor racing, 100 miles per hour US, 1965

century verb to save one hundred dollars US, 1970

century note noun a one-hundred dollar note US, 1908

'cept except UK, 1851

cereal noun marijuana, especially when smoked in a bowl, 1999

cert noun 1 a certainty UK, 1889. 2 a horse that is considered to be a certain winner; a likely winner in any contest UK, 1889

certifiable adjective mentally deranged. Carried over from an earlier legal requirement to certify a person as insane UK, 1939

cess noun marijuana, possibly of inferior quality US, 1995

cess!; ciss! used as an expression of contempt or disgust, also used for registering disappointment. Directly from Afrikaans sies. Variants include 'sis!', 'sies!' and 'siss!' SOUTH AFRICA, 1862

cest noun marijuana UK, 2003

CFA noun someone not originating from a particular place in the Maritime Provinces. An acronym for 'come from away', well known to Newfoundlanders and other coastal people CANADA, 2002

CFB adjective very clear indeed. An abbreviation of 'clear as a fucking bell'. Vietnam war usage US, 1980

CFD noun a chilled 12-ounce can of beer. An abbreviation of 'cold frothy dog' US, 2002

CFM adjective sexually suggestive. An abbreviation of COME-FUCK-ME US, 1989

C-H noun a cheating scheme in poker involving two players; if one player signals that he is holding a good hand, his confederate raises the bet. An abbreviation of 'crooked-honest' US, 1988

cha adjective fashionable, trendy, stylish US, 1992

chabobs noun the female breasts US, 1962

chach noun the vagina; a despised woman US, 2003

cha-cha verb to have sex US, 1980

chaff bandit noun a racehorse that does not win enough to pay its way AUSTRALIA, 1989

chaffy noun a fellow prisoner UK, 1996

chain noun a bus or van used to transport prisoners US, 1984. ▶ **off the chain** excellent US, 2001. ▶ **pull someone's chain** 1 to tease someone; to mislead someone US, 1962. 2 to control someone's actions against their will; to treat someone with contempt. The image of a dog on a leash. Variants are 'jerk someone's chain' and 'yank someone's chain' US, 1962

Chain noun ▶ **The Chain** the Aleutian Islands US, 1886

chain-drink verb to drink one beverage after another, barely pausing between drinks US, 1976

chain gang noun 1 a railway crew assembled from the first available workers US, 1946. 2 the Lord Mayor and Lady Mayoress of London. After the chains of office UK, 1976

chain it verb to chain smoke UK, 2001

chains and canes noun restraint and corporal punishment when advertised as services offered by a prostitute UK, 2003

chain-saw verb to exhange positions with someone; to take over; to cut in UK, 2003

chain-smoke verb to smoke cigarettes continuously and addictively UK, 1934

chainsuck noun in mountain biking, a condition that occurs when the bicycle chain doubles back on itself and gets jammed between the frame and the chain rings US, 1996

chair noun 1 the electric chair; the death penalty US, 1895. 2 a motorcycle sidecar UK, 1984

chairbacker noun an unordained, self-taught preacher US, 1955

chairborne adjective in the miliary, assigned to a rear-echelon support job. A pun on 'airborne', applied to 'chairborne commandos', 'chairborne generals', the 'chairborne infantry', 'chairborne rangers', etc US, 1943

chairman of the board noun the most important person of a set of people. Probably extended from its use as a nickname for Frank Sinatra, 1915–98 US, 2002

Chairman of the Board nickname actor and entertainer, Frank Sinatra, 1915–1998. Coined in tribute to his rôle as founder of Reprise Records in 1961 US, 1963

chairwarmer *noun* an idler, a loafer *US, 1960*

chale! no! never! Border Spanish used in English conversation by Mexican-Americans *US, 1950*

chalewa *noun* a marijuana pipe, usually made from coconut shell and tubing, used ritually by Rastas *JAMAICA, 2001*

Chalfont St Giles; chalfonts *noun* haemorrhoids. Rhyming slang for 'piles', formed from the name of a village in Buckinghamshire *UK, 1980*

chalice *noun* a pipe for smoking marijuana. A word with wider religious significance adopted into ritual by Rastafarians and hence into more general use. Celebrated in the song 'chalice to chalice' by Tappa Zukie, 1996 *JAMAICA, 1990*

chalk *noun* **1** a white person. Not flattering *US, 1945*. **2** methamphetamine or amphetamine *US, 1966*. **3** crack cocaine. From the appearance *UK, 2003*. **4** a potent homemade 'wine' made from yeast, sugar, water, and rice or fruit *US, 2001*. **5** low quality beer *US, 1949*. **6** in sports betting, the contestant or team favoured to win *US, 1991*. **7** chocolate syrup *US, 1946*. ▶ **by a long chalk** by much; by a great degree. In the later C20 the predominant usage becomes 'not by a long chalk' with the meaning as 'grossly inferior' *UK, 1859*

chalk *verb* **1** to prepare cocaine for inhalation. The image of white chalk lines *UK, 1997*. **2** to chemically lighten the colour of cocaine for buyers who believe that the white colour reflects purity *US, 1989*. **3** to observe something or someone *US, 1959*. **4** to ban a gambler from a table, game or casino *US, 1950*. **5** to steal something *US, 2001*

chalk and talk *noun* teaching; those methods of teaching which are currently considered old-fashioned. Slightly contemptuous *AUSTRALIA, 1942*

chalk-eater *noun* in horse racing, a bettor who consistently bets on favourites. From the old custom of a bookmaker chalking odds on a blackboard *US, 1951*

chalked up *adjective* under the influence of cocaine *US, 1955*

chalker *noun* a very fat person *US, 1990*

chalker and talker *noun* a teacher. Later use is slightly contemptuous *AUSTRALIA, 1942*

Chalk Farm; chalk *noun* the arm. Rhyming slang, formed on the name of an area of north London *UK, 1857*

chalk hand *noun* in poker, a hand that is almost certain to win *US, 1988*

chalk horse *noun* in horse racing, the favourite in a race *US, 1951*

chalkie *noun* a school teacher. From the use of chalk on a blackboard *AUSTRALIA, 1945*

chalk it up *verb* to claim or give someone the credit for something *UK, 1923*

chalk it up! used for drawing attention to a triumph or extraordinary happening, often accompanied by a gesture of chalking a figure 1 on a wall *UK, 1923*

chalk man *noun* the police employee who chalks the outline of a corpse where it has fallen before the body is removed *US, 1992*

chalk people *noun* people who live far from the ocean *US, 1991*

chaloupe *noun* a wide, heavy, large American car. French used by the English-speaking in Quebec *CANADA, 1992*

chambermaid *noun* a railway machinist working in a roundhouse *US, 1946*

chamber of commerce *noun* **1** a toilet. A pun on 'chamber pot' *US, 1960*. **2** a brothel *US, 1949*

chamber pipe *noun* a type of pipe used to smoke marijuana *US, 1992*

champ *noun* **1** a drug addict who does not inform on others when questioned by the police *US, 1960*. **2** a *champ*ion *US, 1868*. **3** used between contemporary, unrelated males as a familiar form of address *UK, 2004*

champagne *noun* **1** human urine in the context of a sexual fetish *US, 1987*. **2** a well-paying customer of a prostitute *US, 1992*

champagne blonde *noun* a woman with pale blonde hair *UK, 1904*

champagne Charlie *noun* a man who enjoys a luxurious, if somewhat dissipated, lifestyle. After a music hall song about a noted drinker of champagne *UK, 1868*

champagne chins *noun* folds of flesh creating the image of more than one double chin as a result of the good life *UK, 1997*

champagne drug *noun* cocaine *US, 1998*

champagne house *noun* wealthy clubbers. Champagne, generally prefixed with a sense of derision or criticism (as CHAMPAGNE SOCIALISM), combines with HOUSE (MUSIC) (the umbrella-genre for contemporary club music) *UK, 1999*

champagne socialism *noun* a belief in socialist ideals apparently contradicted by an expensively indulgent lifestyle. Critical and derisive *UK, 1987*

champagne socialist *noun* a person attached to socialist politics who enjoys a luxurious lifestyle *UK, 1987*

champagne tap *noun* a bloodless sample from a lumbar puncture,. traditionally rewarded by a bottle of champagne from the consultant *UK, 2002*

champagne tastes and mauby pockets *noun* something said to be possessed by those who do not have the money to live the lifestyle that they affect *BARBADOS, 1976*

champagne trick *noun* a wealthy, big-spending customer of a prostitute *US, 1973*

champers *noun* *champ*agne. The original word is abridged and the suffix '-ers' is added; this process of amendment, credited to students at Oxford University, is discussed by Partridge and Beale in the appendix to the 8th edition of the *Dictionary of Slang and Unconventional English* and called 'Oxford -er(s)' *UK, 1955*

champion *noun* a completely inept and unlucky person *SINGAPORE, 2002*

champion *adjective* excellent. Mainly, or stereotypically from the north of England *UK, 1937*

champion *adverb* excellently. Mainly, or stereotypically from the north of England *UK, 1937*

chance *verb* ▶ **chance your arm** to take unnecessary risks *UK, 1966*

chance 'em *verb* while surfing, to decide to ride a big wave *US, 1991*

chancer *noun* an opportunist, especially one who takes risks in pursuit of criminal gain; someone who takes or creates *chances* *UK, 1884*

chance would be a fine thing!; chance is a fine thing! 'I wish I had that opportunity!' or 'You wouldn't know what to do if you got the opportunity!' or 'that is very unlikely!'. Each variant has all meanings *UK, 1912*

chancre mechanic *noun* a military medic, especially one assigned to diagnose and treat sexually transmitted infections *US, 1944*

chandelier *noun* **1** where non-existent bids in a fraudulent auction are said to come from *UK, 2003*. **2** a homosexual. Rhyming slang for QUEER. Shortened to 'shandy' *UK, 2003*

chandelier sign *noun* a dramatic reaction to being touched in a painful area. It is said that the patient 'hits the ceiling' or 'hits the chandelier' *US, 1994*

chanel *noun* cocaine. A slightly forced formation, playing on the name of designer Coco Chanel *US, 1976*

chang *noun* cocaine *UK, 2002*

change *noun* **1** money *US, 1972*. **2** an approximation or a fraction *US, 1975*. ▶ **the change** the menopause. Elliptical for CHANGE OF LIFE *UK, 1934*

change *verb* ▶ **change address** to leave *TRINIDAD AND TOBAGO, 2003*. ▶ **change tune** to retreat *US, 1991*. ▶ **change water** to engage in an unproductive activity. From lobstermen, who refer to the hauling and baiting of an empty trap as 'changing water' *US, 1975*. ▶ **change your luck** (used of a white person) to have sex with a black person; to have sex with a person of the sex with whom one would not ordinarily have sex *US, 1916*. ▶ **change your tune** to alter your professed opinion or manner of speech *UK, 1578*

change artist *noun* a swindler who gives customers too little change *US, 1960*

change machine *noun* a prostitute who charges very little for sex *US,* *1963*

change of life *noun* the menopause *UK, 1834*

change of luck *noun* (used of a white person) sex with a black person *US, 1916*

change raiser *noun* a swindler who tricks cashiers into giving him too much change *US, 1960*

changes *noun* difficulties *US, 1973*

changies *noun* changing rooms *UK, 2001*

chank *noun* a chancre; any sexually transmitted infection *US, 1960*

chank *verb* to eat loudly and rudely *US, 1844*

channel *noun* a vein, especially a prominent vein suitable for drug injection *US, 1994*

channel *verb* in car customising, to lower the body of the car *US, 1965*

Channel Bore *nickname* UK television Channel 4 *UK, 1999*

channel fever *noun* a strong desire by someone at sea to be back on land *UK, 1929*

channel fleet *noun* a street. Rhyming slang *IRELAND, 1960*

channel-surf *verb* to browse distractedly through a variety of television programmes, switching from channel to channel *US, 1994*

channel swimmer *noun* a heroin user. Punning on 'channel' as 'a vein' *US, 1959*

chant *verb* to sing *UK, About 1386*

chantoosie *noun* in Montreal, a female nightclub singer. The word is adapted from French *chanteuse* (a woman who sings) *CANADA, 2002*

chap *noun* **1** a man, a fellow *UK, 1704.* **2** a young fellow who wouldn't yet know about the ways of the world *IRELAND, 1992.* **3** a juvenile offender or detention centre inmate who is top of the pecking order *UK, 1978*

chapel *adjective* being part of a chapel's congregation *UK, 1946*

chapel hat pegs *noun* used for comparisons with things that are exaggeratedly conspicuous or obvious when not normally so *UK, 1984*

chapess *noun* a girl; a woman. A jocular extension of CHAP (a man) *UK, 2003*

chapopote *noun* heroin *UK, 2003*

chapped *adjective* **1** depressed *US, 1990.* **2** irritated, angry *US, 1966*

chapped off *adjective* very angry *US, 1963*

chappie; chappy *noun* a man, a fellow. Originally (1820s) a diminutive for CHAP (a man), meaning 'a little fellow'; in the current sense and as a form of address by 1880s. Current usage however is often ironic, probably affected by Chappie™, a branded dog food *UK, 1882*

chaps *noun* ▶ **the chaps** (of men) a grouping of peers; us *UK, 1978*

chapstick lesbian *noun* a lesbian who is athletic or has a notable interest in sports. Formed on the model of LIPSTICK LESBIAN *UK, 2004*

chapter and verse *noun* complete detail; detailed knowledge *US, 1956*

chapter herald *noun* a Hell's Angels motorcycle gang member. A play on 'herald angels' combined with the fact that Hell's Angels are grouped into 'chapters' *UK, 1984*

char; cha; chah *noun* tea. From Chinese – Mandarin *ch'a* (tea) used conventionally from C17 *UK, 1919*

character *noun* **1** a man; a fellow; a person *UK, 1931.* **2** a person with an underworld lifestyle *US, 1958.* **3** a chilled 12-ounce bottle of beer *US, 2002*

charas; churus *noun* hashish from India *INDIA, 1957*

charcoal *adjective* (used of skin colouring) grey-brown *BAHAMAS, 1982*

chardie *noun* chardonnay *AUSTRALIA, 2003*

charge *noun* **1** an intoxicated sensation, emotional or narcotic *UK, 1950.* **2** intense excitement *US, 1960.* **3** marijuana. From an earlier sense meaning 'drugs in general'; it contains a charge – produces a KICK *US, 1941.* **4** an injection of a drug *US, 1925.* **5** an alcoholic drink *AUSTRALIA, 1963.* **6** prison contraband secreted in a prisoner's rectum

NEW ZEALAND, 1997. **7** a person arrested and held in charge *UK, 1970.* **8** a Charge Nurse, the nurse in charge of a ward, especially if male. Often after 'the' *UK, 1961*

charge *verb* to go surfing *US, 1991.* ▶ **charge it to the rain and let the dust settle it** to pay for something on credit without fully expecting to pay the charge *US, 1946*

charge account *noun* a person who can be counted upon to post bail if you are arrested *US, 1976*

charged; charged up *adjective* drug-intoxicated *US, 1942*

charge 'em! used as an exortation to action. Hawaiian youth usage *US, 1982*

charger *noun* a bullet-shaped container for anal concealment and storage of drugs *UK, 1996*

charge up *adjective* excited; drunk *TRINIDAD AND TOBAGO, 2003*

charidee *noun* charity seen as a self-serving, publicity-seeking enterprise. Comedians Harry Enfield and Paul Whitehouse captured this heavily ironic mid-Atlantic pronunciation for the comic caricatures Smashie and Nicey *UK, 2001*

Charing *noun* a horse. Rhyming slang, from Charing Cross (considered by traffic-planners to be the absolute centre of London); the rhyme-word was pronounced 'crorse' in C19 Cockney *UK, 1857*

chariot *noun* **1** a car. Ironic, jocular *US, 1935.* **2** a brakevan (caboose) *US, 1945*

charity dame; charity moll *noun* an amateur prostitute, or one undercutting the going-rate *AUSTRALIA, 1953*

charity fuck *noun* sexual intercourse engaged in by one partner as an act of generosity *US, 1978*

charity girl *noun* an amateur prostitute or promiscuous woman *US, 1916*

charity hop *noun* in baseball, the last long hop taken by a ground ball, making it simple to field *US, 1967*

charity stuff *noun* a woman who, while promiscuous, does not prostitute herself *US, 1950*

Charles *noun* **1** cocaine. More familiarly known as CHARLIE (cocaine) *UK, 1997.* **2** a Viet Cong; the Viet Cong *US, 1966.* **3** a female's underwear *US, 1968*

Charles Dance *noun* a chance. Rhyming slang, formed on the name of the British actor born in 1946 *UK, 1998*

Charley *noun* **1** the penis *US, 1969.* **2** heroin, *2002* ▷ *see:* CHARLIE and variants

charley horse *noun* a muscle cramp *US, 1888*

Charley Paddock *noun* used as a personification of a hacksaw *US, 1949*

charley price *noun* a large rat. An allusison to Sir Charles Price, member of the Houses of Assembly of Jamaica for St Mary, 1756–61, and three times speaker, who introduced a large species of rat to Jamaica to kill cane rats *JAMAICA, 2002*

charleys *noun* the testicles *US, 1964*

Charley's dead between schoolgirls, used as a warning that a slip or petticoat can be seen below the hem of a skirt *UK, 1974*

Charley Wheeler *noun* a girl. Rhyming slang for SHEILA (a girl) *AUSTRALIA, 1945*

Charlie *verb* in the circus or carnival, to dump posters or advertising leaflets that have not been distributed or posted *US, 1980*

charlie *adjective* **1** ostentatious but lacking in quality. Upper-class; possibly even an attempt at rhyming slang, 'charlie horse' (coarse) *UK, 1982.* **2** scared, afraid. Probably a shortening of rhyming slang CHARLIE HOWARD (a coward) *UK, 1958*

Charlie; charlie *noun* **1** cocaine. The phonetic alphabet has 'Charlie' for 'C' in use from around the same time that 'charlie' first appears. Also spelt 'charley' *UK, 2000.* **3** crack cocaine *UK, 2000.* **3** a member of the Viet Cong *US, 1965.* **4** the Viet Cong *US, 1966.* **5** a fool. Often as 'a right charlie' or 'a proper charlie'. Possibly a reduction of CHARLIE HUNT (a CUNT) somewhat softened, or simply a jocular nomination, perhaps referring to a professional fool such as Charlie Chaplin (1889–1977) *UK, 1959.* **6** a white man, or white men in general US, 1928. **7** a woman. Short for CHARLIE WHEELER (a woman) AUSTRALIA, 1942. **8** a female prostitute AUSTRALIA, 1950. **9** the bleed period of the menstrual cycle AUSTRALIA, 2002. **10** a glass or bottle of Carlsberg™ lager. Used by the British Army in Germany in the 1950s and 1960s. Noted by Beale, 1974 UK, 1974. **11** a dollar US, 1924. **12** in poker, the third player to the left of the dealer US, 1988. ▶ **go to see Uncle Charlie** to use cocaine, especially to go to a lavatory for discreet ingestion of the drug UK, 2001

charlie bender noun a prolonged session of cocaine abuse. A new influence, CHARLIE (cocaine), for a traditional BENDER (a drinking session) UK, 1997

Charlie bird noun during the Vietnam war, a helicopter used by a tactical commander US, 1974

Charlie boy noun an effeminate man. Patronising US, 1896

Charlie Brown noun a citizens' band radio set. The name of a much-loved cartoon character, created in 1950 by Charles M. Schulz, disguises a conventional initialism UK, 1981

Charlie Chaplin noun a chaplain, especially a prison chaplain. After the famous comedy actor SOUTH AFRICA, 1974

Charlie Chase verb in horse racing, to finish second. Rhyming slang, from 'Charlie Chase' (to place) AUSTRALIA, 1989

Charlie Chester; charlie noun a paedophile, a child molester; often used as a nickname for a headmaster. Rhyming slang, used by schoolchildren, formed, for no reason other than a convenient rhyme, from the name of the comedian and broadcaster, 1914–96 UK, 2003

Charlie Clore; Charlie noun **1** twenty pounds (£20). Rhyming slang for SCORE. Formed, no doubt with irony, on the name of British financier Charles Clore (1904–79), a 1960s symbol of great wealth UK, 1998. **2** a floor, the floor. Rhyming slang, as above, but without any irony UK, 1998

charlie cocaine noun cocaine UK, 1997

Charlie Cong noun the Viet Cong; a Viet Cong US, 1970

Charlie Cooke noun a look. Rhyming slang, formed on the name of Chelsea and Scotland midfielder Charlie Cooke (b.1942) who was especially well-known from the mid-1960s to the late 70s UK, 1998

charlied; charleyed; charlied up; charleyed-up adjective cocaine-intoxicated UK, 1999

Charlie Drake noun **1** a brake. Rhyming slang, formed on the name of British comedian and recording artist Charlie Drake (1925–2006); in the late 1950s and early 60s he was one the UK's most famous entertainers. The plural, unusually, is Charlie Drakes UK, 1998. **2** a break. Rhyming slang, formed as above UK, 1998

Charlie Howard noun a coward. Rhyming slang UK, 1936

Charlie Hunt; Charlie noun **1** the vagina. Rhyming slang for CUNT. Also variant spelling 'Charley Hunt', shortened to 'Charley' UK, 1961. **2** a fool. Rhyming slang for CUNT UK, 1961

Charlie is my darling used as a catchphrase by cocaine-users. From an old Scottish folk-song celebrating Bonnie Prince Charlie, 1720–88, playing on CHARLIE (cocaine) UK, 2002

Charlie Noble noun an exhaust stack or chimney. Originally nautical, referring to a ship's smokestack US, 1940

Charlie Potatoes noun an important man UK, 2000

Charlie Pride noun a ride in or on something. Rhyming slang, formed on the US country and western musician (b.1938) UK, 2003

Charlie rats noun US Army c-rations. A combination of the phonetic alphabet and an abbreviation of 'rations' US, 1982

Charlie Ridge noun a ridge in the mountainous region west of Da Nang at the base of Ba Na Mountain; during the Vietnam war, also used as a jocular, generic term for any piece of landscape in Vietnam US, 1980

Charlie rockets noun a marine contraption in Korea, a small cart with 144 tubes that fire 42-pound projectiles over a range of approximately 5,200 yards US, 1957

Charlie Ronce; Charley Ronce noun a ponce (a man who lives off a prostitute's earnings); hence a derogatory term for any man.

Variants are 'Joe Ronce' and 'Johnnie Ronce'. Rhyming slang, frequently reduced to 'Charlie' but never 'Joe' or 'Johnnie' UK, 1977

charlies noun the female breasts. Always in plural; of uncertain derivation UK, 1909

Charlie's Angels noun police women. From the cult television series about three female detectives that commenced broadcasting in 1976 and is first recorded in this sense in the same year US, 1976

Charlie Sheard noun a beard. Rhyming slang UK, 1980

Charlie Smirke; Charley Smirke noun a fool. Rhyming slang for BERK, formed from a British champion jockey of the 1930s–50s UK, 2003

Charlie Tom noun a communist terrorist. Military slang, based on early phonetic alphabet UK, 2001

Charlie Wheeler noun a woman. Rhyming slang for SHEILA, after Charles Wheeler, the Australian artist of nudes AUSTRALIA, 1953

charlie willy noun a real or imagined state of sexual arousal as a result of cocaine usage. Combines CHARLIE (cocaine) with WILLY (the penis), 1999

charm verb to talk to someone US, 1989

Charmin' noun a timid prisoner. From the advertising slogan for Charmin'™ toilet paper – 'Please don't squeeze the Charmin'' US, 1976

charming! used for expressing disapproval. An ironic variation of the conventional sense, signalled with heavy emphasis on the first syllable UK, 1956

charms noun the parts of a woman's body that are imagined in a sexual context or revealed for titillating effect UK, 1937

charm school noun any leadership training course. Originally applied to officer training in the military US, 1971

charper verb to search for something, to seek something UK, 2002

charperer; charpering omee; charpering omi noun a police officer. From CHARPER (to seek) and OMEE (a man) UK, 1893

charpering carsey noun a police station. From CHARPERER (a policeman) and CARSEY (originally, a house) UK, 1893

charra noun a person of Indian descent living in Durban. A term that is acceptable in Hindu-to-Hindu conversation, but not for outsiders SOUTH AFRICA, 1970

Chartocracy nickname Canada, in which the Charter of Rights and Freedoms gives courts wide powers CANADA, 2002

charver noun **1** a woman, especially when objectified sexually; an act of heterosexual intercourse with a woman. A consequent usage of the verb CHARVER (to have sex) UK, 1979. **2** any member of a subcultural urban adolescent group that wears hip-hop dress and jewellery (and acts older than their years) UK, 1996. **3** a female member of the sub-cultural urban youth grouping loosely identified as CHAV. A narrowing of the previous non-gender-specific sense UK, 2005

charver; charva verb to have sex. From Romany charvo (to interfere with) UK, 1962

charvering donna noun a prostitute. A combination of CHARVER (to have sex) and 'donna' (a woman) UK, 2002

Chas noun **1** cocaine. A conventional diminutive of CHARLIE (cocaine) UK, 1999. **2** a Viet Cong; the Viet Cong. Also spelt 'chaz'. One of not a few variants of CHARLIE US, 1991

Chas and Dave verb to shave. Rhyming slang, formed (perhaps ironically) on the names of two bearded Cockney musicians, Charles (Chas) Hodges and Dave Peacock, who have been known as a double-act since 1975. Also used as a noun UK, 1992

chase noun in horse racing, a steeplechase race US, 1976

chase verb **1** to vigorously pursue a person responsible for some matter and who can achieve a specific result, such as the completion of a piece of work or the provision of urgently needed documents. A variant is 'chase up' US, 1963. **2** in poker, to play against an opponent's superior hand US, 1963. **3** to smoke any drug. An abbreviation and broadening of the meaning of CHASE THE DRAGON (to smoke heroin) UK, 1998. ▶ **chase the bag** to engage yourself in a near constant search for drugs to buy US, 1970.

► **chase the dog** to loaf on the job *US, 1954*. ► **chase the dragon** to inhale heroin smoke, especially from heroin burnt on a piece of aluminium foil *US, 1961*. ► **chase the kettle** to use drugs *US, 1997*. ► **chase the nurse; chase the white nurse** to become addicted to morphine *US, 1992*. ► **chase the tiger** to smoke heroin *UK, 2002*. ► **chase your losses** when losing at gambling, to bet more and more and with less discretion in an increasingly frustrating attempt to win back what has been lost *US, 1998*

chaser *noun* **1** a drink taken immediately after another *US, 1897*. **2** a womaniser *US, 1894*. **3** a prison guard *US, 1982*. **4** a military police officer assigned to escort prisoners in transport. Short for 'brig chaser' *US, 1927*. **5** a supplementary message that demands to know what action has been taken on a previous message. A military usage *UK, 1969*. **6** a crack cocaine user with obsessive compulsive behaviours *US, 1992*

chase-up *noun* a car chase or informal car race *UK, 1967*

chasping *adjective* excellent *UK, 1983*

chassis *noun* **1** a human body *US, 1930*. **2** the female breasts *US, 1957*. **3** the skull *US, 1994*. **4** a car *US, 1947*

chastity belt *noun* in gambling, the loss limit that some players impose on themselves *US, 1996*

chastity rig *noun* a skin-coloured patch worn over a woman's vulva to give the appearance of nudity *US, 1970*

chat *noun* **1** a vocabulary, style or manner of speech or writing *UK, 1968*. **2** a talent for glibly persuasive speech; the gift of the gab *UK, 1968*. **3** a thing, an article, an object *UK, 1906*. **4** the vagina. French *chat* (cat), thus PUSSY *UK, 1937*. **5** an old man, usually a vagrant, deadbeat and alcoholic, or otherwise degraded. Especially in prison use *AUSTRALIA, 1950*. **6** a louse. Prison usage *AUSTRALIA, 1812*

chat *verb* **1** to talk persuasively to someone as a strategy for seduction; to flirt. Also 'chat up' *UK, 1898*. **2** to reveal a secret *JAMAICA, 2003*. ► **chat stupidness; chat foolishness** to talk nonsense *ANGUILLA, 1996*

chatarra *noun* heroin. Possibly from Spanish *chatarra* (scrap iron) *UK, 2003*

chat down *verb* to engage in flirtatious conversation *BARBADOS, 1965*

châteaued *adjective* drunk on wine. Upper-class society pun on the French *château* (origins of good wine) with conventional 'shattered', *1982*

chateaux cardboard *noun* cheap wine that comes contained in a cardboard box *AUSTRALIA, 1996*

chat room *noun* a network on the Internet that hosts real-time typed conversations *US, 1993*

Chattanooga choo-choo *noun* a marijuana cigarette made with two or three rolling papers laid longways *US, 1997*

chatter *noun* the flexing of a surfboard riding over choppy water or the slapping sound created *US, 1963*

chatter *verb* (used of a car) to vibrate as a result of loose parts in the drive line *US, 1954*

chatterati *noun* a grouping of articulate middle-class people, especially those occupied in academic, artistic or media work. A variation of CHATTERING CLASS, by a combination of 'chatter' and -ERATI (a suffix that creates a fashionable grouping) *UK, 2001*

chatterbox *noun* **1** a very talkative person. Conventionally contemptuous, but often affectionate, especially of children *UK, 1774*. **2** a typewriter *US, 1950*

chattering class; chattering classes *noun* articulate middle-class people, especially those occupied in academic, artistic or media work *UK, 1985*

chatty *adjective* dirty; worn out; in poor repair *AUSTRALIA, 1944*

chatty, catty and scatty *adjective* of a woman, talkative, spiteful and incapable of serious thought. Offensive *UK, 1969*

chatty-chatty *adjective* talkative, gossipy. West Indian and UK black usage *UK, 2000*

chat up *verb* **1** to bluff or to trick someone by the use of convincing speech *UK, 1962*. **2** to flatter someone; to flirt with someone *UK, 1963*

chat-up line *noun* a conversational gambit intended to initiate a seduction. Extended from CHAT UP (to talk flirtatiously) *UK, 1986*

chaud *noun* the penis *UK, 2002*

chav *noun* any member of a subcultural urban adolescent group that dresses and acts older than their years. Variants are 'chava', 'charva', 'chavster' and 'charver'. Usually derogatory, even contemptuous; possibly derived from an abbreviation of Chatham, the town in Kent where the genus is reputed to have originated; possibly from, or influenced by, Romany *chavvy* (a child) *UK, 2003*

chavtastic *adjective* unashamedly in the chav style *UK, 2004*

chavvy; chavy; chavvie *noun* a child; occasionally used, in a derogatory sense, for a man. English gypsy use; ultimately from Romany *chavi* (child, daughter) and *chavo* (child, son) *UK, 1860*

chaw *verb* to cut something up, to disfigure something. A figurative use of an old form of 'chew' *UK, 1959*

chawbacon *noun* an unsophisticated country dweller *US, 1834*

ChCh; cheech *nickname* Christchurch, New Zealand *ANTARCTICA, 2003*

che then. In phrases such as 'cheers che' *ANTARCTICA, 1985*

C head *noun* a cocaine user or addict *US, 1982*

cheap *noun* ► **do the cheap** to take a shortcut *CANADA, 1994*. ► **on the cheap** economically, cheaply, and often, too cheaply *UK, 1859*

cheap *adjective* mean, lacking in generosity *US, 1904*

cheap and cheerful; cheap but cheerful *adjective* inexpensive but acceptable. Deprecatory, but not as harsh as the conventional 'cheap and nasty' *UK, 1978*

cheap and nasty *noun* a pasty (a small pastry turnover that may contain a variety of fillings). Rhyming slang, depending on an Australian accent for intelligent delivery *AUSTRALIA, 1937*

cheap as chips *adjective* very good value; under-priced. The catchphrase of television presenter and antique dealer David Dickinson (b.1941) *UK, 2000*

cheap at the half the price! used for extolling or appreciating a very reasonable price. Often ironic. It seems likely that this is a perversion of the more sensible claim: 'cheap at twice the price' *UK, 1977*

cheap basing *noun* crack cocaine. The drug is cheaper and less pure than FREEBASE cocaine *UK, 1998*

cheap Charlie *noun* a cheapskate *US, 1982*

cheap heart *noun* a Purple Heart award resulting from a minor combat wound *US, 1990*

cheapie *adjective* cheap; of inferior quality. Frequently, but not originally, applied to films *UK, 1898*

cheapie; cheapy *noun* something cheap, or that is made available at a cheaper cost *UK, 1898*

cheapies *noun* cheap thrills *AUSTRALIA, 1992*

cheap-jack *adjective* used of goods sold cheaply, or of cheap quality. An elaboration of 'cheap', but based on a partial misunderstanding of the conventional 'cheapjack' (a travelling hawker with a diminishing scale of 'bargain' prices) *UK, 1999*

Cheap John *adjective* shoddy, inferior *US, 1855*

cheap line *noun* a person who buys inexpensive merchandise *FIJI, 1992*

cheapo *noun* **1** a cheap, or inferior, thing *US, 1975*. **2** in chess, a trick move or a game won because of an opponent's error *US, 1971*

cheapo *adjective* inexpensive *US, 1972*

cheapo-cheapo *adjective* very cheap; of inferior quality *UK, 1977*

cheap physical stuff *noun* sexual activity short of intercourse *US, 1968*

cheap play *noun* in dominoes, a move that scores one point *US, 1959*

cheapshit *adjective* inexpensive and inferior. Combines conventional 'cheap' with SHIT (rubbish, something of no value) *UK, 2000*

cheap shot *noun* **1** a petty, unfair insult *US, 1971*. **2** in sports, an unnecessary, unprovoked act of violence *US, 1970*

cheapskate *noun* a miserly person *US, 1896*

cheapskate *adjective* miserly *US, 1903*

cheapy *noun* ▷see: CHEAPIE

cheat *verb* **1** when bodybuilding, to use muscles other than those designed for use in a particular exercise *US, 1984*. **2** in the entertainment industry, to move slightly to create a better camera angle *US, 1991*

cheater *noun* anything that makes a job easier, such as a short length of pipe or anything else that is handy to slip over the handle of a wrench to increase leverage *US, 1941*

cheaterbug *noun* a person who cheats *SINGAPORE, 2002*

cheater five *noun* while surfing, the toes of one foot extended over the nose of the board only because the surfer has stretched his leg far forward *US, 1965*

cheaters *noun* **1** eye glasses *US, 1908*. **2** dark glasses *US, 1938*. **3** the eyes *UK, 1977*. **4** padding that enhances the apparent size of a female's breasts *US, 1972*. **5** metal skis *US, 1963*. **6** in electric line work, channel lock pliers *US, 1980*

cheater's bar *noun* an anti-cheating mechanism in a slot machine *US, 1968*

cheater slicks *noun* car tyres that are smooth but not quite treadless *US, 1970*

cheat sheet *noun* **1** a written memory aid, usually but not always clandestine *US, 1957*. **2** in casino gambling, a listing of the payoffs for a particular ticket *US, 1982*

cheat spot *noun* an establishment that sells alcohol after closing hours *US, 1963*

cheat throat *noun* oral sex performed on a man in which the person doing the performing simulates taking the penis completely into their mouth without actually doing so. A play on DEEP THROAT, the real thing *US, 1995*

che-che *noun* a light-skinned person; an unlikeable person *SAINT KITTS AND NEVIS, 1996*

check *noun* a gambling token *US, 1974*

check *verb* **1** to murder someone *US, 1997*. **2** to forget or ignore something, often deliberately. A variant is 'check out' *UK, 1996*. **3** to have an intimate relationship with someone. West Indian and UK black youth usage *UK, 1998*. **4** as a prank, to pull down a friend's bathing suit from behind *US, 1997*. ▶ **check hat** to prepare to leave *US, 1966*. ▶ **check the cheese** to watch girls as they walk by *US, 1959*. ▶ **check the dictionary** to confirm vague or confusing orders or directions. Vietnam war usage *US, 1991*. ▶ **check the oil level** to pentrate a vagina with your finger *CANADA, 2003*. ▶ **check the war** to stop arguing *US, 1947*. ▶ **check your nerves** to stay calm *US, 1947*. ▶ **check your six** used as a warning to a pilot to check behind his aircraft for enemy planes. Based on the clock configuration, with twelve o'clock being straight ahead and six o'clock straight behind *US, 1991*

checkbook; chequebook *adjective* characterised by a seemingly unlimited ability and will to pay for something. Applied most commonly to journalism (paying for news), but also to enterprises such as baseball *US, 1975*

check cop *verb* to use an adhesive placed on a cheater's palm to steal chips while sliding a pile of chips in a poker game to the winner *US, 1988*

check crew; check gang; check team *noun* a racially integrated work crew *US, 1960*

checkerboard *adjective* racially integrated *US, 1930*

check in *verb* **1** to place yourself in protective police custody *US, 2001*. **2** to be intitiated into a youth gang *US, 1994*

check out *verb* **1** to leave prison *US, 1950*. **2** to die. A euphemism not without its black humour *US, 1927*. **3** to commit suicide while in prison *US, 1992*

checkout chick *noun* a woman who works at a shop checkout *AUSTRALIA, 1983*

check, please! used as a humorous suggestion that a conversation is at an end. Popularised by Keith Olberman on ESPN, used by Woody Allen in *Annie Hall* and Catherine Keener in *Being John Malkovich* *US, 1971*

check this! listen to this! *US, 1998*

check writer *noun* a criminal who passes bad cheques *US, 1972*

check you later; check ya later used as a farewell *US, 1982*

cheddar *noun* money *US, 1998*

cheeba; cheeb *noun* a potent marijuana, now a generic term *US, 1989*

cheech *noun* a leader of an Italian-American criminal organisation *US, 1977*

chee-chee; chi-chi *noun* a person of mixed European and Indian parentage; the English accent of Eurasians in India. Derives from Hindi *chhi chhi* (dirt, filth) *INDIA, 1816*

chee-chee; chi-chi *adjective* of mixed European and Asian parentage; used for describing the English accent of Eurasians in India. Derives from Hindi *chhi chhi* (dirt, filth) *INDIA, 1781*

cheek *noun* **1** the buttock. Variants are 'arse-cheek', 'ass-cheek' and 'butt-cheek'. Usually in the plural *UK, c.1600*. **2** impudence; audacity; effrontery *UK, 1840*. **3** a sexually loose female *US, 1955*

cheek *verb* to address someone with impudence *UK, 1840*

cheekiness *noun* effrontery; impudence *UK, 1847*

cheek up *verb* to speak to someone with a decided lack of respect *BAHAMAS, 1982*

cheeky *adjective* impudent, insolent *UK, 1859*

cheeky-arsed *adjective* impudent, insolent *UK, 1972*

cheeky monkey *noun* an impudent person, often as a term of address and semi-exclamatory. Popularised as a catchphrase by Comedian Al Read (1909–1987) in the late 1950s *UK, 1959*

cheeky possum *noun* an impudent fellow, a cheeky boy *AUSTRALIA, 1953*

cheekywatter *noun* any alcoholic drink, especially when being dismissive of its intoxicating properties *UK: SCOTLAND, 1996*

cheeo *noun* marijuana seeds for chewing. Possibly from an exaggerated pronunciation of 'chew' *US, 1973*

cheep *verb* to betray someone, to inform upon someone *US, 1903*

cheeper *noun* a police informer *US, 1949*

cheer *noun* LSD. an abbreviation of BLUE CHEER *UK, 1998*

cheerful giver *noun* the liver *UK, 1961*

cheeri goodbye. An abbreviation of CHEERIO *NEW ZEALAND, 1984*

cheeribye goodbye. A blend of CHEERIO and 'goodbye' *UK, 1961*

cheerio *adjective* tipsy *SOUTH AFRICA, 1946*

cheerio; cheeri-ho; cheero goodbye *UK, 1959*

cheers! **1** used as a drinking toast *UK, 1959*. **2** thank you. From the drinking toast *UK, 1976*

cheer-up *noun* an anti-depressant tablet; an amphetamine or other central nervous system stimulant *UK, 1999*

cheerybyes goodbye *UK: SCOTLAND, 1988*

cheese *noun* **1** smegma, matter secreted by the sebaceous gland that collects between the glans penis and the foreskin or around the clitoris and labia minora. From the dull whitish colour of this substance *US, 1927*. **2** in auto repair, a plastic body filler used to fill in dents on a car body, usually referring to Bondo Body Filler™ *US, 1992*. **3** the wife. Short for CHEESE AND KISSES *AUSTRALIA, 1919*. **4** an attractive young woman *US, 1959*. **5** a wedge-shaped piece of coloured plastic used in the board game Trivial Pursuit™ *UK, 2002*. **6** in pool, a situation where a player needs to make only one shot to win *US, 1993*. **7** money; a gambler's bankroll. A locution popularised by Minnesota Fats, as in, 'I never lost when we played for the cheese' *US, 1985*. **8** heroin *UK, 2002*. **9** freebase cocaine *US, 1992*. **10** an amphetamine user *US, 1993*. **11** money *US, 2002*. **12** nonsense *US, 1989*. **13** luck *US, 1990*. ▶ **piece of cheese** in poker, a truly terrible hand *US, 1982*

cheese *verb* **1** to leave *US, 1955*. **2** to smile. From the urging by photographers that those having their picture taken say 'cheese' to form a smile *US, 1986*

cheese! spoken by the subject of a photograph in order to shape the lips into a smile. Often heard in the photographer's injunction: 'say cheese!' *UK, 1930*

cheese and crackers *noun* the testicles. Rhyming slang for KNACKERS *UK, 1998*

cheese and crackers! used as a non-profane oath. A euphemistic 'Jesus Christ!' *US, 1924*

cheese and kisses *noun* a wife. Rhyming slang for MISSUS *AUSTRALIA, 1898*

cheese and rice! used for expressing surprise or irritation *TRINIDAD AND TOBAGO, 1950*

cheeseball *noun* a corny, socially inept person *US, 1990*

cheesebox *noun* a telephone device used to transfer calls received by an illegal operation. So named, according to legend, because the first one was found by police hidden in a cheese box *US, 1952*

Cheesebox *nickname* the Stateville Prison in Joilet, Illinois *US, 1992*

cheese bun *noun* a worker who informs on his fellow workers *US, 1960*

cheesecake *noun* a scantily clad woman as the subject of a photograph or artwork *US, 1934*

cheesecutter *noun* a wedge-shaped hat. From the shape, and the memory of the vaguely similar late C19/early C20 'cheese-cutter caps' *UK, 2000*

cheesed off; cheesed *adjective* disgruntled, bored, miserable. 'Cheese off!' (go away!), a euphemistic exclamation from 1890s Liverpool, may be the origin. On the other hand 'say cheese' is a photographer's formula to create a smile and if you don't feel like smiling you may well be 'cheesed off' *UK, 1941*

cheesedog *noun* a socially inept person who perceives himself in somewhat grandiose terms *US, 1997*

cheese-down *verb* to laugh uncontrollably. Military usage; probably extended from CHEESE (to smile) but note obsolete naval slang 'cheese down' (to coil rope into neat spirals for a harbour stow) *UK, 1987*

cheese eater *noun* an informer. Playing on RAT *US, 1886*

cheese-eating surrender monkeys *noun* the French; anyone who does not support American imperialism. Coined on *The Simpsons* television show as a parody of American arrogance; often used by arrogant Americans unaware of the irony of their use. Such is the pervasive presence of this term that it was the subject of a question on *Mastermind* (11th October 2004) *US, 2000*

cheese grater *noun* a waiter. Rhyming slang *UK, 1998*

cheese grater *nickname* the Chateau Champlain Hotel in Montreal *CANADA, 2002*

cheesehead *noun* **1** a Dutch person. Derogatory, if not intentionally so. Probably from the shape and preponderance of Edam and Gouda *UK, 1978.* **2** a resident of the state of Wisconsin. Playful but not particularly kind *US, 2003*

cheesemo *noun* gossip. A corruption, intentional or not, of the Spanish *chisme* (gossip) *US, 1997*

cheese off *verb* to annoy someone *UK, 1947*

cheese off! go away! *US, 1996*

cheese on! used for expressing enthusiastic approval *BARBADOS, 1965*

cheese-on!; cheese-on and bread! used as a euphemistic cry in place of 'Jesus Christ!' *BARBADOS, 1996*

cheeser *noun* **1** a person with smelly feet. From the malodorous quality of ripe cheese *UK, 1976.* **2** a police informer *US, 1979*

cheese table *noun* a metal hole-lined table used in sheet metal fabrication *US, 1955*

cheesy *adjective* **1** of poor quality, inexpensive, shoddy *US, 1863.* **2** smelly. From the malodorous quality of ripe cheese *UK, 1889*

cheesy-feet *noun* used as a derogatory form of address. From the malodorous quality of ripe cheese *UK, 1972*

cheesy-foot *noun* bad-smelling feet *TRINIDAD AND TOBAGO, 2003*

cheesy quaver *noun* a raver. Contemporary rhyming slang, from a branded cheese-flavoured snack *UK, 2002*

cheesy quaver raver *noun* a member of a social grouping within the hardcore rave culture, characterised by a fashion for boiler suits, white gloves and paint masks. After Quavers™, a cheese

flavoured snack food, punning on 'cheesy' (unfashionable) and using RAVER (a party goer) *UK, 2002*

chellum *noun* a clay pipe for smoking marijuana *SOUTH AFRICA, 2003*

Chelsea bun *noun* a son; the sun. Rhyming slang; a variation of CURRANT BUN *UK, 1998*

Chelsea Pier *adjective* queer, odd. Rhyming slang, formed on a London landmark; similar to BRIGHTON PIER but here 'queer' doesn't lead to 'homosexual' *UK, 2003*

chemical *noun* **1** crack cocaine *US, 1994.* **2** any drug with addictive characteristics *UK, 2003*

chemical generation *noun* a section of society identified as the first to have MDMA, the drug best known as ecstasy, as a recreational option, especially those who were actually a part of the attendant dance culture. The chemical generation began in the late 1980s but was probably not identified by this title until the late 90s; the definitive recreational drug culture was not restricted to MDMA but its wide use signalled a greater-than-ever-before acceptance of man-made and designer drugs *UK, 1998*

chemically challenged *adjective* drunk. 'Challenged' is a key word in the lexicon of political correctness, lending an air of humour to this use *US, 1994*

chemical persuasion *noun* in caving and pot-holing, explosives *UK, 2004*

chemise-lifter *noun* a lesbian; an effeminate homosexual male. Originally, a play on SHIRT-LIFTER (a homosexual man) coined by Barry Humphries who defined it in *A Nice Night's Entertainment*, 1981, as 'a female invert'; subsequently, derived perhaps by a misunderstanding of the original definition, the male variation has gained a little currency *AUSTRALIA, 1981*

chemist *noun* a person who uses a mainframe computer for the academic purposes for which it was designed, depriving the speaker of the chance to use it for more interesting, less academic purposes *US, 1991*

chemmie *noun* a shirt; a blouse. Probably from 'chemise' *UK, 2002*

chemmy; shemmy *noun* the card-game 'chemin-de-fer' *UK, 1923*

chemo *noun* **1** *chemo*therapy, a cancer treatment *US, 1978.* **2** a liquid octane booster that is inhaled for its intoxicating effects *US, 1994*

chep *noun* a kiss, intimate or otherwise; kissing *IRELAND, 2001*

chequed-up *adjective* having ready money after receiving payment for seasonal work *AUSTRALIA, 1905*

cheroot *noun* a large marijuana cigarette *US, 1993*

cherry *noun* **1** the hymen; virginity (male or female); the state of sustained sexual abstinence. Combines with a variety of verbs (bust, crack, pop) to indicate the ending of a virgin condition *US, 1918.* **2** a virgin; someone who because of extenuating circumstances has abstained from sex for a long period *US, 1942.* **3** by extension, any innocence that can be lost *US, 1956.* **4** by extension, someone who is completely inexperienced *US, 1946.* **5** a pretty young woman, a girlfriend. Also spelt 'cherrie', 'cherie', 'tcherrie' and 'tjerrie' *SOUTH AFRICA, 1962.* **6** a young woman regarded as the object or subject of a transitory sexual relationship. Scamto youth street slang (South African townships) *SOUTH AFRICA, 2005.* **7** of a male, the 'virginity' of the anus *US, 1997.* **8** an entry-level youth gang member *US, 1981.* **9** in pool, an extremely easy shot *US, 1993.* **10** in horse racing, a horse that has yet to win a race *US, 1951.* **11** in greyhound racing, the inside starting position *AUSTRALIA, 1989.* **12** the clitoris *AUSTRALIA, 1985.* **13** a female nipple *US, 1964.* **14** in cricket, a new ball *UK, 1953.* **15** the flashing red light on top of a police car *US, 1976.* **16** a blush; a red face. From the colour *UK, 2001.* ▶ **pick a cherry** in bowling, to knock over a pin that had been previously missed *US, 1953*

cherry *adjective* **1** virginal *US, 1933.* **2** without a criminal record *US, 1980.* **3** (used of a car) restored to better than mint condition *US, 1953*

cherryade *noun* an assistant to Cherie Booth, wife of UK Prime Minister Tony Blair. Both the drink and the aide may be described as 'red, sweet and fizzing' *UK, 1998*

cherryberry *noun* a uniform red beret of the Parachute Regiment; hence, a soldier of the Parachute Regiment *UK, 1979*

cherry boy *noun* a male virgin *US, 1974*

Cherry Coke *adjective* bisexual. Suggests 'neither one thing nor the other' *UK, 2001*

cherry farm *noun* a prison, or the section of a prison reserved for first-time offenders *US, 1966*

cherry fine *adjective* excellent *US, 1966*

cherry girl *noun* a virgin. US military usage during the Vietnam war *US, 1982*

Cherry Hill *nickname* during the Vietnam war, the base camp of the 3rd Battalion, 16th Artillery Regiment, just outside Chu Lai. So named because the Viet Cong and North Vietnamese did not attack the camp during the 1968 Tet Offensive, hence the 'cherry' *US, 1990*

cherry hog; cherry *noun* a dog, especially a greyhound. Rhyming slang, formed on the old name for 'a cherry stone' *UK, 1960*

cherry juice *noun* hydraulic fluid in a tank turret traversing system. Vietnam war usage *US, 1991*

cherry kicks *noun* the first drug injection enjoyed by someone just released from prison *US, 1971*

cherry menth; cherry meth *noun* the recreational drug GHB *US, 1995*

cherry orchard *noun* a woman's college *US, 1966*

cherry patch *noun* a poker game being played by a group of poor players, ripe for the taking by a good professional *US, 1982*

cherry picker *noun* **1** a boy or youth in a sexual relationship with an older man. Royal Navy use *UK, 1961*. **2** a person who targets virgins for seduction *US, 1960*. **3** the penis. A play on CHERRY (virginity) *UK, 2003*. **4** one pound (£1). Rhyming slang for NICKER (a pound) *UK, 1974*. **5** a machine, mounted on a rail car or caterpillar tractor, for picking up logs dropped from cars or on roadsides *CANADA, 1962*. **6** a crane *US, 1987*. **7** a large bucket on a boom attached to a truck used to raise a worker to work in an elevated position on power lines, telephone lines, etc *US, 1991*. **8** an engine hoist *US, 1992*. **9** a railway pointsman. Named because of the red railway signal lights *US, 1946*. **10** a prominent, hooked nose *US, 1968*

cherry pie *noun* **1** in the entertainment industry, extra money earned for something other than ordinary work *US, 1955*. **2** in circus and carnival usage, extra work for extra pay *US, 1981*

cherry-popping *noun* the act of taking someone's virginity *US, 1975*

cherry red *noun* the head. Rhyming slang *UK, 1998*

cherry ripe *noun* **1** a pipe. Rhyming slang, propbably influenced by 'cherry-wood pipe' *UK, 1857*. **2** nonsense. Rhyming slang for TRIPE. Can be shortened to 'cherry' *UK, 1960*

cherrytop *noun* a police car; a police car's coloured lights *US, 1970*

Chessex girl *noun* an upper-class young woman dressed with the down-market trappings of vulgar glamour. Coined by the *Tatler* magazine, July 2003, as a compound of 'Chelsea' (a traditonally well-off area of London) and ESSEX GIRL (a social stereotype of a loud, vulgar, sexually available woman) *UK, 2003*

chest *noun* a woman's breasts *US, 1986*. ▶ **get it off your chest** to say something that you may have kept private or secret; to confess *UK, 1902*

chestbonz *noun* the marijuana smoker who takes the greatest inhalation from a shared water-pipe *UK, 1999*

Chester and Esther *noun* in craps, a bet on any craps and eleven. A back formation from the initials 'c and e' *US, 1985*

chesterfield *noun* a sofa or couch. Especially in the western provinces of Canada, this word is the universal term for this common piece of furniture *CANADA, 1950*

Chester the Molestor; Chester *noun* a lecherous man *US, 1989*

chestily *adverb* arrogantly, conceitedly *US, 1908*

chestnut *noun* **1** a chestnut horse *UK, 1670*. **2** a stale story or outworn jest. Also known as 'an old chestnut' *US, 1880*

chestnuts *noun* **1** the testicles *US, 1971*. **2** the female breasts *US, 1971*

chesty *adjective* **1** of a woman, who has generously proportioned breasts *UK, 1955*. **2** used of symptoms (such as a cough) that result from an unhealthiness or weakness in the chest; also used of

someone who is inclined to such a condition *UK, 1930*. **3** arrogant, conceited *US, 1899*

Chev; Chevy; Chevvy *noun* a Chevrolet car *US, 1937*

chevoo *noun* a party. A variant of SHIVOO *AUSTRALIA, 1963*

Chevy Chase *noun* the face. Rhyming slang, originally for the scene of a Scottish and English battle recorded in a famous ballad of 1624. The original slang usage, pronounced 'chivvy', flourished from 1857 but was presumed obsolete by 1960. The revival, recorded by www.LondonSlang.com in June 2002, is more likely inspired by a US bank or the comedy actor Chevy Chase (b.1943) *UK, 2003*

Chevy Chased *adjective* drunk. Possibly rhyming slang for SHITFACED (drunk) from CHEVY CHASE (face), possibly a variant of OFF YOUR FACE (very drunk) *UK, 2002*

Chevy eleven *noun* in the used car business, a Chevrolet II *US, 1992*

chew *noun* **1** chewing tobacco *US, 1990*. **2** an act of oral sex *UK, 1962*. **3** food. South African school usage *SOUTH AFRICA, 1961*

chew *verb* ▶ **chew face** to kiss *US, 1980*. ▶ **chew it** in skateboarding, to fall from the board *US, 1976*. ▶ **chew pillows** to be the passive partner in anal sex *UK, 1979*. ▶ **chew steel** (of a racehorse) to strain against the bit *AUSTRALIA, 1989*. ▶ **chew the cud** to consider something; to be very thoughtful *UK, 1749*. ▶ **chew the fat** to gossip, to chatter idly *US, 1907*. ▶ **chew the rag** to discuss something; to complain, to moan; hence, to argue *UK, 1885*. ▶ **chew the scenery** to over-act in a dramatic performance *US, 1973*. ▶ **chew the sugar cane** to gossip *US, 1978*. ▶ **chew your tobacco more than once** to repeat yourself *US, 1893*

chew and choke *noun* a roadside restaurant; a motorway services *US, 1976*

chew and spew; chew 'n' spew *noun* a fast-food outlet; the food served at such a place, especially if the quality of the food is lower than expectations *AUSTRALIA, 1998*

chewed to loon shit *adjective* ground up; ruined *CANADA, 1974*

chewers *noun* the teeth *US, 1970*

chewies *noun* crack cocaine *US, 1994*

chew out; chewing out *noun* a rebuke *US, 1964*

chew out *verb* **1** to perform oral sex on a woman *AUSTRALIA, 1985*. **2** to rebuke someone harshly *US, 1929*

chew over *verb* to consider something, to discuss something *US, 1939*

chewsday *noun* Tuesday. Humorous *US, 1877*

chewy *noun* **1** crack cocaine mixed with marijuana for smoking *US, 1993*. **2** chewing gum. Also spelt 'chewie'. Usually as a non-count noun, but can also be used to refer to a single piece of chewing gum *AUSTRALIA, 1924*

chewy on your boot! I hope your kick goes astray. Used as a cry of discouragement in Australian Rules football *AUSTRALIA, 1966*

Chi *nickname* Chicago, Illinois *US, 1895*

chiac; shack *noun* the dialect of residents of the Shediac, New Brunswick area *CANADA, 2001*

chiack; chiak *noun* teasing *AUSTRALIA, 1869*

chiack; chiak; chyack *verb* to tease someone. From C19 British costermonger's slang 'chi-hike' (a hurrah or friendly commendation) *AUSTRALIA, 1853*

chiacking; chiaking *noun* teasing *AUSTRALIA, 1853*

Chiantishire *nickname* Tuscany, especially the area around Chianti. Humorously formed in the manner of an English county; from the popularity of the area with British expatriates and tourists *UK, 1986*

chib *noun* a knife or razor used as a weapon. Probably a variation of CHIV (a knife) *UK: SCOTLAND, 1973*

chib *verb* to stab or otherwise cut someone with a knife or razor. From CHIB (a knife) *UK: SCOTLAND, 1990*

chiba *noun* **1** heroin. Probably a misspelling or mishearing of CHIVA (heroin) *UK, 2003*. **2** marijuana. Spanish slang embraced by English-speakers *US, 1981*

chiba-chiba *noun* marijuana, especially potent marijuana from Colombia or Brazil *US, 1979*

chibbing *noun* a deliberate wounding by stabbing or razor-cutting *UK,* 2001

chibs; chips *noun* the buttocks *US,* 1957

chica *noun* a girl. Spanish; used largely as a term of address, and largely by those without a working knowledge of Spanish *US,* 2000

Chicago bankroll *noun* a single large denomination note wrapped around small denomination notes, giving the impression of a great deal of money *US,* 1966

Chicago black *noun* a dark-leaved variety of marijuana. Grown in and around Chicago *US,* 1971

Chicago contract *noun* a binding oral agreement, secured by honour *US,* 1992

Chicago green *noun* a green-leafed variety of marijuana. Grown in and around Chicago *US,* 1967

Chicago G-string *noun* a g-string designed to break open, revealing the dancer's completely naked state *US,* 1981

Chicago heavy mess *noun* boiled salt pork *CANADA,* 1961

Chicago leprosy *noun* infections, scars and abcesses caused by prolonged intravenous drug use *US,* 1992

Chicago piano *noun* an anti-aircraft gun or other automatic weapon *US,* 1941

Chicago pill *noun* a bullet *US,* 1949

Chicago rattlesnake *noun* salt pork *CANADA,* 1947

Chicago typewriter *noun* a fully automatic weapon *US,* 1963

chicamin *noun* money. The word is adapted from Chinook jargon 'chikamnin' (iron, metal) *CANADA,* 1963

Chicano *noun* a Mexican-American. Originally a slur; by the later 1960s a term of self-identification and pride *US,* 1951

Chicano time *noun* used for denoting a lack of punctuality *US,* 1972

chi-chi *noun* first aid *US,* 1992 ▷*see:* **CHEE-CHEE**

chi-chi *adjective* **1** homosexual. From the conventional usage denoting a fussy style *UK,* 2002. **2** fashionable; fussy. Also spelt 'she-she' *UK,* 1932

chi-chi gal *noun* a lesbian *JAMAICA,* 2004

chi-chi man *noun* a male homosexual *JAMAICA,* 2000

chi-chis *noun* a woman's breasts *US,* 1961

chick *noun* **1** a young woman *US,* 1899. **2** a male prostitute *UK,* 1984. **3** a friendly fighter aircraft *US,* 1951. **4** cocaine. One of many variations on the cocaine-as-female theme *US,* 1990

chickabiddy *noun* used as a term of endearment for a child. From a C18 childish variation on 'chicken' *UK,* 1829

chicken *noun* **1** a woman *US,* 1981. **2** a boy, usually under the age of consent, who is the target of homosexual advances *US,* 1914. **3** a child, a youthful or inexperienced person; often as an affectionate form of address *UK,* 1711. **4** a young and inexperienced prostitute, especially male *UK,* 1988. **5** someone under the legal drinking age *US,* 1990. **6** used as a term of endearment *IRELAND,* 2003. **7** a test of wills in which two cars drive directly at each other until one driver – the loser – veers off course *US,* 1952. **8** a coward. From the characteristics ascribed to the best of 'chickens'; in an earlier sense, found in Shakespeare, the meaning is 'someone timorous and defenceless' *US,* 1936. **9** marijuana *US,* 1997. **10** a small halibut. Alaskan usage *US,* 1997 ▷*see:* **CHICKEN PERCH.** ► **no chicken; no spring chicken** no longer young *UK,* 1860

chicken *adjective* scared, cowardly, afraid *US,* 1933

chicken bone *noun* a chocolate-filled hard sweet confection invented by the Ganong family firm of St Stephen, New Brunswick *CANADA,* 2002

chickenbone special *noun* any small, local railway *US,* 1970

chicken burner *noun* a Pontiac 'Firebird' car *UK,* 1981

chicken bus *noun* during the war in Vietnam, a troop transport bus. From the chicken wire that covered the windows in the hope of keeping enemy grenades outside the bus *US,* 1990

chicken catcher *noun* in electric line work, an armsling *US,* 1980

chicken colonel *noun* in the US Army, a full colonel. From the eagle insignia of the rank *US,* 1918

chicken cookies *noun* frozen ground chicken patties *ANTARCTICA,* 1991

chicken coop *noun* **1** a women's jail or prison *US,* 1949. **2** an outdoor toilet *US,* 1970. **3** a weight station. Citizens' band radio and trucking slang *US,* 1975

chicken crank *noun* an amphetamine fed to chickens to accelerate their egg-laying *US,* 1989

chicken curry *verb* to worry. Rhyming slang *UK,* 2001

chicken dinner *noun* a pretty woman *US,* 1946

chickenfeed *noun* **1** a less than generous amount of money *US,* 1836. **2** a task that can be accomplished with ridiculous ease *SINGAPORE,* 2002. **3** methamphetamine *US,* 1964

chicken fillet *noun* a gel-filled pad placed into a brassiere cup to uplift and enhance the appearance of a woman's breast; a gel-filled full breast prosthesis *UK,* 2003

chicken fink *noun* an unlikeable, disloyal person *US,* 1973

chickenguts *noun* braided military decorations *US,* 1943

chickenhawk *noun* **1** during a war, someone who supports the war but avoids military service themselves. Virtually every member of the US government that supported the 2003 invasion of Iraq avoided active military service in Vietnam during their youth *US,* 1988. **2** a mature homosexual man who seeks much younger men as sexual partners *US,* 1965. **3** by extension, a woman who seeks out young male lovers *US,* 1978

chickenhead *noun* **1** a female who pursues a male solely because of the male's success and visibility as a musician, athlete, etc *US,* 1999. **2** a person performing oral sex on a man. Also 'chickhead'. From the bobbing motion *US,* 1996. **3** an aggressive or violent woman *US,* 1980. **4** a foolish, frivolous person *US,* 1906

chicken heart *verb* to fart. Rhyming slang, only recorded in the past tense *UK,* 1992

chicken in a basket *noun* in the Canadian military, an Air Command badge worn on the tunic until 1992 *CANADA,* 1995

chicken jalfrezi *adjective* crazy. Contemporary rhyming slang, inspired by a popular curry dish *UK,* 2002

chickenkiller *noun* a Cuban or Haitian. From the stereotype of Cubans and Haitians as voodoo practioners sacrificing chickens in religious rites; insulting *US,* 1970s

chicken oriental *adjective* insane, crazy. Rhyming slang for MENTAL *UK,* 2003

chicken out *verb* to lose courage and retreat from an endeavour *US,* 1934

chicken perch; chicken *noun* a church; church. Rhyming slang *UK,* 1931

chickenplate *noun* a steel vest that helicopter and other aircrew wore in the Vietnam war, designed as bulletproof *US,* 1971

chicken powder *noun* amphetamine in powdered form, used intravenously *US,* 1971

chicken pox *noun* an obsession of an older homosexual male with young men or boys *US,* 1979

chicken queen *noun* a mature male homosexual who is especially attracted to boys or young men *US,* 1963

chicken ranch *noun* a rural brothel. Originally the name of a brothel in LaGrange, Texas, and then spread to more generic use *US,* 1973

chicken run *noun* the exodus of people from Rhodesia (now Zimbabwe) for fear of the future; hence, the exodus of people from South Africa for fear of the future *ZIMBABWE,* 1977

chicken scratch *noun* cocaine. Probably from the sense, 'a search for crack cocaine' *UK,* 2003

chickenshit *noun* a coward *US,* 1929

chickenshit *adjective* cowardly *US,* 1934

chicken skin *noun* the sensation and physical manifestation of the chills. Hawaiian youth usage, instead of the more common 'goose bumps' *US,* 1981

chicken's neck *noun* a cheque. Rhyming slang. A variation of GOOSE'S NECK *UK, 1998*

chicken switch *noun* a switch that will abort a mission; a notional switch that will end a project *US, 1960*

chicken tracks *noun* in electric line work, a device formally known as an Epoxirod tri-unit *US, 1980*

chicken wing *noun* a bowler whose elbow strays outward from the body during the backswing motion of rolling the ball *US, 1987*

chicken yellow *noun* the recreational drug PMA. Also known as 'chicken fever' or 'chicken powder' *US, 2001*

chickey-babe; chicky-babe *noun* a young woman, especially a good-looking one *AUSTRALIA, 1991*

chick flick *noun* a film that is desiged to appeal to a female audience *US, 1993*

chickie! used as a warning *US, 1934*

chickie; chicky *noun* **1** a lookout or decoy *US, 1934*. **2** a young girl. Teen slang *US, 1919*

chickie poo *noun* a young and beautiful girl. Recorded in the usage of counterculturalists associated with the Rainbow Nation *US, 1981*

chickie run *noun* a test of wills in which two cars drive at high speeds towards a cliff; the driver who jumps from his car first loses *US, 1955*

chicklet *noun* a young woman. Elaboration by conventional diminution of CHICK (a young woman) *US, 1922*

chick lit *noun* literature directed at young women; literature written by women *US, 1993*

chick magnet *noun* a male who is attractive to women *AUSTRALIA, 1995*

chicko; chico *noun* a child. Either by elaboration of 'chick' (a child) or adoption of Spanish *chico* (a boy). Remembered in army service in the 1960s–early 1970s, by Beale, 1984 *UK, 1984*

chick with a dick *noun* a transsexual or, rarely, a hermaphrodite. Almost always plural *US, 1991*

chicky *noun* a female. Used with an ironic nod towards the outmoded 'chick' *US, 1994*

chicle *noun* heroin. Spanish for 'gum', alluding to the gummy nature of heroin that has not been processed to powder form *US, 1994*

chiclet keyboard *noun* a computer keyboard with small plastic keys. A visual allusion to a branded chewing gum *US, 1991*

Chic Murray; chic *noun* a curry. Glasgow rhyming slang, formed from the name of the Scottish comedian, 1919–85 *UK: SCOTLAND, 1988*

Chicom *noun* a soldier from the People's Republic of China; a Chinese communist *US, 1967*

Chicom *adjective* Chinese communist *US, 1964*

chiddles *noun* in Newfoundland, cooked cod roe or cod milt *CANADA, 1971*

chief *noun* **1** a Flight Sergeant. Royal Air Force use; a hangover from Chief Petty Officer, the corresponding rank in the Royal Naval Air Service, a military service that predated Royal Air Force. Sometimes personalised to the diminuitive 'chiefie' *UK, 1942*. **2** a Petty Officer. Royal Navy use *UK, 1929*. **3** a Chief Engineer; a Lieutenant Commander; a First Mate. Nautical usage *UK, 1894*. **4** a Chief Inspector. Police usage *UK, 1961*. **5** LSD *US, 1966*. **6** used as a term of address. Jocular, sometimes suggesting deference *US, 1935*

chief *verb* in a group smoking marijuana, to hog the cigarette or pipe *US, 1997*

chief cook and bottle washer *noun* used as a humorous title for someone with important duties and responsibilities. Often, not always, used with irony *US, 1840*

chiefie *noun* used as a friendly term of address to a man *UK: SCOTLAND, 1996*

chief itch and rub *noun* an organisation's key leader *US, 1960*

Chief Nasty-Ass of the No-Wipe-Um Tribe *noun* anyone completely lacking in personal hygiene *US, 1997*

chief of heat *noun* a non-commissioned officer commanding an artillery battery *US, 1988*

chief of staff *noun* a soldier's girlfriend back home. Vietnam war usage *US, 1965*

chief tin shoe *noun* a person who has no money at the moment. A mock native Indian name *US, 1984*

chieva *noun* heroin. Probably a variation of CHIVA (heroin) *UK, 1998*

chiff *noun* ▷ *see:* CHIV

chiffy *noun* in prison, a razorblade fixed to a toothbrush handle as an improvised weapon. A variation on CHIV *UK, 1996*

chigger *noun* a person with Chinese and black ancestors. Derogatory *US, 1992*

Chihuahua town *noun* a neighbourhood where many Mexican immigrants or Mexican-Americans live *US, 2967*

child, please! used for expressing great surprise or disbelief *BAHAMAS, 1982*

child-proof lid *noun* a condom. A pun on a device designed to 'keep children out' *UK, 1998*

chile pimp *noun* a pimp, especially a Mexican-American pimp, who has no professional pride and only mediocre success in the field *US, 1972*

chili *adjective* Mexican *US, 1936*

chili bean *noun* a Mexican or Mexican-American; any Spanish-speaking person. Derogatory *US, 1980*

chili belly *noun* a Mexican or Mexican-American *US, 1967*

chili bowl; chili-bowl haircut *noun* an untapered haircut that looks as if the barber simply placed a bowl on the person's head and trimmed around the edge of the bowl *US, 1960*

chili chaser *noun* an agent of the US Immigration and Naturalization Service Border Patrol *US, 1956*

chili choker *noun* a Mexican or Mexican-American. Derogatory *US, 1990*

chili chomper *noun* a Mexican or Mexican-American. Derogatory. *US, 1970*

chili eater *noun* a Mexican or Mexican-American. Derogatory *US, 1911*

chill *verb* **1** to kill someone *US, 1947*. **2** to calm down; to be calm *US, 1979*. **3** to idle *US, 1972*. **4** to suddenly slow down while driving after spotting a police car *US, 1962*. ▶ **chill like a megavillain** to relax. Especially effective in the participle form – 'chillin' *US, 1992*. ▶ **chill the beef; chill the rap** to escape prosecution by bribery or intimidation of witnesses *US, 1950*

chill *adjective* **1** calm, unexcited *US, 1987*. **2** excellent *US, 1989*

chillax *verb* to calm down and relax *US, 1993*

chilled *adjective* calm, relaxed *US, 1992*

chilled down *adjective* calm and relaxed *UK, 1990s*

chilled out *adjective* relaxed, especially after chemically enhanced dancing *UK, 1980s*

chillen *noun* children. A phonetic slurring *US, 1971*

chiller *noun* in publishing or films, a thriller that 'chills the blood' *UK, 1961*

chillicracker *noun* an Anglo-Indian. Derogatory. Derives, presumably, from the use of hot spices in Indian cooking contrasted with the bland, essentially white nature of a cracker *UK, 1977*

chill out *verb* to calm down, to relax *US, 1983*

chill pill *noun* a mythical pill that will induce calm *US, 1982*

chillum; chilum *noun* a pipe for smoking marijuana. Originally late C18 Hindi for the bowl (*chilam*) of a 'hookah' (*hugga*) intended for tobacco. More than 150 years later a modified usage rolled up in the West Indies. Widely used in the UK thanks, in part, to HEAD SHOP(S) *JAMAICA, 1970*

chill with you later used as a farewell *US, 1987*

chilly *adjective* **1** excellent, fashionable, desirable *US, 1971*. **2** cold-hearted *US, 1971*

chilly bin *noun* a portable cooler *NEW ZEALAND, 1976*

chilly most *adjective* calm and collected *US, 1992*

chime *noun* **1** an hour *US, 1946*. **2** the even firing of a multi-cylinder motocycle engine *UK, 1979*

chimer *noun* a clock or watch *US, 1973*

chimney *noun* **1** a person who smokes, especially a heavy smoker *UK, 1937*. **2** in trucking, a smokestack on a cab *US, 1971*

chimney sweep run *noun* in trucking, a job that requires the driver to handle the freight and get dirty *US, 1971*

chimo! Let's drink! *CANADA, 2002*

chimping *noun* in digital photography, the activity of reviewing captured images on a camera's screen. Originally used of White House press-photographers who accompanied pointing at such images with a chorus of *oohs* and *aahs* and were, naturally, compared to chimpanzees *US, 2004*

chin *noun* **1** gossip, idle conversation *UK, 1862*. **2** on a bomber, the area immediately below and slightly behind the nose of the plane *US, 1983*. ▶ **keep your chin up** to maintain your courage or fortitude; often said as an encouraging injunction *UK, 1938*

chin *verb* **1** to punch someone on the chin *UK, 1984*. **2** to talk idly *US, 1872*

china *noun* **1** a friend, a mate. Rhyming slang for CHINA PLATE. Also variant 'chiner' *UK, 1880*. **2** teeth; false teeth *US, 1942*

China *noun* **1** the whole world other than Europe and English-speaking lands. A Cockney view of the world: 'The place rich folk go for their holidays. The place any person not wearing European dress comes from' *UK, 1961*. **2** heroin. From CHINA CAT (heroin) or CHINA WHITE (heroin). The lower case variant 'china' is sometimes used *UK, 2003*

China cat *noun* strong heroin *US, 1994*

china chin *noun* (of a boxer or fighter) a vulnerability to blows on the chin *US, 1940*

China circuit *noun* in the language of travelling performances, a circuit of small, unsophisticated towns. Named after the Pennsylvania towns of Pottstown, Pottsville and Chambersburg, all of which were home to chamber pot manufacturing concerns *US, 1973*

China clipper *noun* a dishwasher, human or mechanical. Vietnam war usage *US, 1966*

China girl *noun* Fentanyl™, a synthetic narcotic analgesic that is used as a recreational drug *UK, 2004*

chinaman *noun* a numbing substance put on the penis to forestall ejaculation *TRINIDAD AND TOBAGO, 2003*

Chinaman *noun* **1** an addiction to heroin or another opiate *US, 1948*. **2** in politics, a mentor or protector. A term from Chicago, a major cradle of machine politics in the US *US, 1973*. **3** an Irishman *UK, 1956*. **4** in cricket, a left-handed bowler's leg-break to a right-handed batsman. Homage to Elliss 'Puss' Achong, a 1930s West Indian cricketer of Chinese ancestry *UK, 1937*. **5** an unshorn lock on a sheep's rump. Thought to resemble a pigtail *NEW ZEALAND, 1968*. ▶ **must have killed a Chinaman** there must be a reason for your bad luck. Chinese people have been in Australia from the earliest colonial times and there was formerly great superstition attached to them. Today the word 'Chinaman' is long dead and persists only in this saying *AUSTRALIA, 1982*

Chinaman on your back; Chinaman on your neck *noun* the painful symptoms and craving need for drugs experienced by an addict during withdrawal *US, 1959*

Chinaman's chance; Chinaman's *noun* an absence of luck, no real chance at all. Reflecting the status of the Chinese population of early C20 US *US, 1911*

Chinamat *noun* an inexpensive Chinese restaurant *US, 1979*

china plate *noun* a mate. Now generally used as a stock idiom: 'me old china plate' *AUSTRALIA, 1905*

chin armour *noun* a false beard. Theatrical usage *US, 1952*

China white *noun* **1** heroin; less frequently, cocaine. The presumed location of the drug's origin (although it's just as likely to come from Pakistan, Afghanistan or Thailand) plus the colour *US, 1974*. **2** a

tablet of MDMA, the recreational drug best known as ecstasy *UK, 2002*. **3** Fentanyl™, a synthetic narcotic analgesic that is used as a recreational drug *UK, 2004*

chinch; chintz *noun* a bedbug *US, 1946*

chinche *noun* heroin *UK, 2003*

chin-chin used as a toast. Originally used as a salutation to Chinese people *UK, 1909*

chin-chin man *noun* a male homosexual *US, 1990*

chinch pad *noun* an inexpensive, shoddy boarding house or hotel *US, 1958*

chinchy *adjective* **1** cheap; parsimonious, stingy *UK, 1400*. **2** infested with bedbugs *US, 1961*

chinee *noun* **1** a free ticket to a sporting event *US, 1981*. **2** a Chinese meal, a Chinese take-away; a Chinese restaurant *UK, 1984*. **3** a Chinese person *US, 1871*

Chinee *adjective* of presumed Chinese origin *US, 1984*. ▶ **not in a chinee world** impossible; wholly unacceptable. From the notion that Chinese language and culture are beyond comprehension *BARBADOS, 1992*

chinee brush *noun* a numbing liquid put on the penis to delay ejaculation *TRINIDAD AND TOBAGO, 2003*

chinee bump *noun* a black woman's hair temporarily set in neatly aligned clumps to facilitate drying *JAMAICA, 1996*

chinee shop *noun* a small neighbourhood grocery shop, whether owned by Chinese people or not *TRINIDAD AND TOBAGO, 2003*

Chinese *noun* **1** in circus and carnival usage, hard work, especially hard work without payment *US, 1981*. **2** a Chinese meal; a Chinese restaurant *UK, 1980*. **3** a small grocery store *BAHAMAS, 1995*. **4** adulterated heroin *UK, 1996*

Chinese *verb* in the circus or carnival, to perform heavy labour *US, 1980*

Chinese *adjective* in horse racing, said of blurred numbers on the tote board *US, 1947* ▷*see:* CHINESE LACQUERED

Chinese ace *noun* a pilot who makes a landing with one wing lowered; a pilot who has a reputation for crashing planes on landing. After CHINESE LANDING *US, 1928*

Chinese auction *noun* a charity auction, in which a buyer is selected at random for each item *US, 1997*

Chinese burn *noun* a torment inflicted by grasping a victim's wrist or forearm in both hands and twisting the skin harshly in opposite directions. Children's slang for a juvenile cruelty, known in the UK, Canada and Australia. May also be used as a verb *UK, 1956*

Chinese copy *noun* a reproduction that captures the original's defects as well as its strengths *US, 1979*

Chinese cure *noun* an all-natural treatment for the symptoms associated with withdrawal from heroin addiction *US, 1953*

Chinese cut *noun* in cricket, a batting stroke that unintentionally deflects the ball off the inside edge of the bat *UK, 1982*

Chinese cut *verb* in cricket, to perform a Chinese cut *UK, 1982*

Chinese dolly *noun* in the television and film industries, a dolly on slanted tracks *US, 1987*

Chinese dominoes *noun* in road haulage, a load of bricks *UK, 1951*

Chinese dragons *noun* LSD *UK, 2003*

Chinese eyed *adjective* squinting through tired eyes following the use of marijuana. Described by racial stereotype *US, 1998*

Chinese fashion *adverb* sex with both participants lying on their sides, the active male lying behind his partner *US, 1980*

Chinese fire drill *noun* **1** any situation in which confusion reigns. Frequent use in the Vietnam war *US, 1946*. **2** a prank loved by generations of American youth in which a car full of people stops at a red light and the passengers suddenly leap from the car, run around it, and get back in as the light turns green *US, 1972*

Chinese flush; Chinese straight *noun* in poker, a worthless hand approximating but not equalling a flush or straight *US, 1979*

Chinese gunpowder; gunpowder *noun* cement *UK, 1951*

Chinese lacquered; Chinese *adjective* extremely tired. Rhyming slang for KNACKERED (extremely tired). Prison slang *UK, 2002*

Chinese lady *noun* a multiple-seat toilet *NEW ZEALAND, 1998*

Chinese landing *noun* the typical angling of an aeroplane when it lands in Antarctica, with one wing low. Humour based on the premise that 'one wing low' has a certain Chinese ring to it *US, 1918*

Chinese molasses *noun* opium; heroin. From the appearance of opium in an early stage of manufacture *US, 1953*

Chinese needlework *noun* intravenous use of narcotics *US, 1942*

Chinese red *noun* heroin *US, 1977*

Chinese rocks *noun* **1** relatively pure heroin *US, 1975*. **2** crack cocaine *UK, 1996*

Chinese rong *noun* a non-existent disease suffered by soldiers *US, 1947*

Chinese rot *noun* any unidentified skin disease or sexually transmitted infection *US, 1940*

Chinese screwdriver *noun* a hammer *AUSTRALIA, 1974*

Chinese speed *noun* ginseng *UK, 1983*

Chinese Texan *noun* a daring, dangerous driver. Toronto usage *CANADA, 2002*

Chinese tobacco *noun* opium *US, 1951*

ching *noun* **1** in betting, odds of 5–1 *UK, 1991*. **2** five pounds (£5). London slang *UK, 2000*

ching and a half *noun* in betting, odds of 11–2. In bookmaker slang CHING is 5–1, here the addition of a half increases the odds to 5½–1 or 11–2 *UK, 1991*

chingazos *noun* fisticuffs; blows. Border Spanish used in English conversation by Mexican-Americans *US, 1991*

ching! ching! ching! used as a descriptive expression of the speed of a quick succession of events. Echoic of bells ringing *UK, 1974*

chinger *verb* to grumble; to complain; to scold; hence, to deter a prospective customer. Used by market traders *UK, 1979*

chingon *noun* an important person; a leader. Border Spanish used in English conversation by Mexican-Americans *US, 1974*

chingua *adjective* ▷*see:* CHINKER

chink *noun* ▶ **another push and you'd have been a chink** used insultingly as a slur on the morals of the subject's mother, imputing that she would have sex with anyone of any race *UK, 1961*

Chink *noun* **1** a Chinese person. Derives from 'ching-ching', the phonetic interpretation of a Chinese courtesy, adopted as a racist term, now obsolete; this abbreviated, still derogatory, variation is much used in Britain and the US. Variants are 'Chinkie' and 'Chinky' *US, 1878*. **2** a Vietnamese person *US, 1970*

Chink *adjective* **1** Chinese *US, 1957*. **2** Vietnamese *US, 1970*

chinker; chikwa; chinqua *adjective* five. From Italian *cinque*, via mid-C19 ligua franca *UK, 1996*

chinki-chonks; chinky-chonks *noun* the Chinese, or Asian people in general. A derogatory or patronising term, playing on CHINK and CHINKIE in a fashion which suggests a drunken coinage *UK, 1978*

Chinkie; Chinky; Chink *noun* **1** something of Chinese origin; a general description of anything perceived to originate in the Far East. Sometimes spelt (with contemptuous familiarity) with a lower case 'c' *AUSTRALIA, 1879*. **2** a Chinese meal; a Chinese take-away *US, 1948*

chinkie munchy shop *noun* a Chinese restaurant or take-away *UK, 1981*

chink ink *noun* an indelible ink used by card cheats to mark cards *US, 1988*

chinks *noun* a small bit of anything, given up grudgingly *GRENADA, 1998*

chinky *noun* a small firecracker *US, 1997*. ▷*see:* CHINKIE

chinky *adjective* **1** parsimonious *BARBADOS, 1965*. **2** small *TRINIDAD AND TOBAGO, 1956*

Chinky speed *noun* ginseng *UK, 1983*

chinless wonder *noun* an upper-class man who is naïve or foolish; or is considered to be foolish by virtue of his privileged

circumstances. While 'chinless' may be an accurate physical description of some, figuratively it is seen to suggest a weakness of character *UK, 1969*

chin music *noun* gossip, idle conversation *UK, 1826*

Chinook arch *noun* in western Canada, an archway of cloud forecasting the arrival of Chinook winds *CANADA, 1964*

Chinook fever *noun* among Calgary newcomers, a sort of ill-ease like spring fever, during warm winter days caused by Chinook winds *CANADA, 1963*

chin pubes *noun* sparse facial hair *US, 1995*

chinstrap *noun* ▶ **on your chinstrap** extremely tired. Military. Also occasionally, but not military, 'on your nose' *UK, 1995*

chintz *noun* a cheapskate *US, 1949* ▷*see:* CHINCH

chintzy *adjective* cheap, miserly, stingy *UK, 1902*

chinwag *noun* **1** a friendly conversation *UK, 1879*. **2** a chat, a conversation *UK, 1879*

chinwag *verb* to chat, to converse *UK, 1920*

chin-whiskered *adjective* small-time, lacking professionalism. A logging term *US, 1930*

chip *noun* **1** heroin, particularly when weakened below the market norm *US, 1974*. **2** a shilling. Hence, HALF A CHIP (6d) *UK, 1950*. **3** in games of chance, a counter that represents a monetary value *US, 1840*. **4** a cash register *US, 1950*. **5** a *chip*olata sausage. Usually used in the plural. Noted by Anthony Burgess in a letter to Partridge, 1967 *UK, 1967*. **6** a quarrel *AUSTRALIA, 1947*. **7** a small surfboard made from lightweight balsa wood. Also known as a 'potato chip' *US, 1964*

chip *verb* **1** to use drugs occasionally or irregularly. Applied to all narcotics but especially heroin *US, 1964*. **2** to depart, to go *UK, 1994*. **3** to find fault with someone; to reprimand someone *AUSTRALIA, 1915*. **4** in shuffleboard, to barely touch another disc *US, 1967*. ▶ **chip the ivories** to take part in casual conversation *US, 1945*. ▶ **chip your teeth** **1** to become very angry *US, 1962*. **2** to talk incessantly *US, 1973*

Chip; Chippie; Chippy *noun* a member of the California Highway Patrol. Thanks to the 1977–1983 television series *CHiPS US, 1977*

chip along; chip in *verb* in poker, to make the minimum bet required *US, 1988*

chip back *verb* to rebate an amount, to discount an amount. Second-hand car-dealers' use *UK, 1965*

chip dip *noun* an adhesive placed on a cheater's palm, enabling him to steal chips as he helpfully slides a pile of chips in a poker game to the winner *US, 1988*

chip head *noun* a computer enthusiast *US, 1993*

chip in *verb* **1** to contribute to an undertaking; to make a contribution *US, 1861*. **2** to interpose smartly in a conversation, discussion or speech; occasionally, by so doing, to interfere *US, c.1870*

chip off the old block *noun* someone with the same character as a parent; someone with inherited characteristics. Originally 'a chip of the same (old) block' *UK, 1642*

chip on your shoulder *noun* a grievance or a sense of inferiority which is often manifested in defiance or ill-humoured behaviour. Derives, probably, from juvenile conflict: when two boys were determined to fight, a chip of wood was placed on the shoulder of one, and the other challenged to knock it off *US, 1855*

chipper *noun* **1** a chip shop *IRELAND, 1993*. **2** an occasional non-habitual drug-user *US, 1938*. **3** in prison, an illegal tinder box *UK, 1950*

chipper *adjective* well, fit, lively *US, 1840*

chippy *adjective* **1** impudent *UK, 1888*. **2** quarrelsome, dirty, rough *UK, 1898*. **3** unwell, especially as a result of drinking alcohol; hungover *UK, 1877*

chippy; chippie *noun* **1** a fish-and-chip shop *UK, 1961*. **2** a person who uses addictive drugs occasionally without developing a habit *US, 1924*. **3** a modest drug addiction *US, 1964*. **4** a young woman, usually of loose morals, at times a semi-professional prostitute *US, 1886*. **5** a carpenter. Also in the reduced form 'chips' *UK, 1916*. **6** cocaine *UK, 1998*. **7** marijuana *UK, 2003*. **8** a person in a gambling casino who tries to hustle or steal chips *US, 2003*. **9** an inexperienced gambler *US, 1985* ▷ *see:* CHIP

chippy; chippie *verb* **1** to be unfaithful sexually *US, 1930*. **2** to use drugs occasionally and not habitually. Applied particularly to heroin *US, 1924*

chippy chaser *noun* a man obsessed with the seduction of women *US, 1977*

chippy joint; chippie joint *noun* a brothel *US, 1992*

chips *noun* **1** money *US, 1840*. **2** the action of looking out or serving as a watchman. If a school boy is smoking a cigarette in the toilet, his friend will 'keep chips' for him *SOUTH AFRICA, 2002* ▷ *see:* CHIBS.
▶ **get your chips** to be dismissed from employment *UK, 1969*.
▶ **have had your chips** to have been beaten; to be finished or utterly defeated; to have been moved; to have been ruined to have been killed. Ultimately from gambling symbolism *UK, 1959*.
▶ **in the chips 1** well funded *US, 1842*. **2** in poker, winning *US, 1988*.
▶ **when the chips are down** at the crucial moment *US, 1943*

chips and peas; chips *noun* the knees. Rhyming slang *UK, 1998*

chips and salsa *noun* a computer's hardware *US, 1997*

chips and whetstones *noun* odds and ends *US, 1927*

chira *noun* marijuana, especially shredded marijuana. Originally South American Spanish *, 1998*

chiro *noun* a *chiropractor AUSTRALIA, 1991*

chirp *noun* **1** a female singer *US, 1944*. **2** a type of manipulation of a record to create a musical effect. Derives from the 'chirping' sound that is created *UK, 2002*. **3** a quick use of cocaine *US, 1997*

chirp *verb* to make an exaggerated kissing sound *US, 1950*

chirpiness *noun* liveliness, cheerfulness, a pleasing pertness. The state of being CHIRPY *UK, 1867*

chirps *verb* to talk persuasively to someone as a strategy for attempted seduction, to flirt *UK, 2004*

chirpy *adjective* always happy. From the cheerful chirping of songbirds *UK, 1837*

chirrupy *adjective* cheerfully chatty *UK, 1808*

chisboy *noun* a pampered youth. Derogatory or disdainful teenage slang from the South African townships *SOUTH AFRICA, 2003*

chisel *noun* ▶ **on the chisel** involved in a swindle *US, 1958*

chisel *verb* **1** to cheat *UK, 1808*. **2** to place small, conservative bets *US, 1950*

chisel charter *noun* an illegal bush plane charter *CANADA, 1997*

chiseled *adjective* without fat, well sculpted *US, 1984*

chiseler *noun* **1** a cheat, a petty swindler *US, 1918*. **2** a gambler who places small, conservative bets *US, 1950*

chisler *noun* a hardy child, usually a boy *IRELAND, 1993*

chisme *noun* gossip; rumours. Border Spanish used in English conversation by Mexican-Americans *US, 1974*

chit *noun* a youthful-looking homosexual male *US, 1987*

chit *verb* to sign a chit accepting responsbility for an item or amount of money *US, 1986*

chitari *noun* marijuana *US, 2001*

chit-chat *noun* small talk *UK, 1605*

chit-chat *verb* to engage in small talk *UK, 1821*

Chitlin Circuit *noun* the notional collection of ghetto bars and nightclubs where black musicians perform in the hope of having a hit that will launch them into better venues. A term attributed to black singer Lou Rawls *US, 1967*

Chitlins 101 *noun* any black studies course. A derogatory term, drawing from 'chitterlings', a dish made with pork innards *US, 1998*

Chi-town *nickname* Chicago, Illinois *US, 1922*

chiv; chive; chiff *noun* a knife, a razor or other blade used as a cutting weapon. Of Romany origin *UK, 1673*

chiv; chive *verb* to cut someone with a knife or a razor. Multiple variant spellings, including 'shive', 'shiv' and 'shife'. Probably from 'shive' (to slice bread), 1570; originally seen in this sense as 'chive',

1725; 'chiv' is not recorded until 1812; 'shiv' and 'shive' are C20 variations that hark back to the word's origins *UK, 1812*

chiva *noun* heroin. From the Spanish of Mexican-Americans *US, 1967*

chix *noun* a Pacific halibut under 4.5 kg *CANADA, 1989*

chiz *noun* **1** in circus and carnival usage, a swindler. An abbreviation of CHISELER *US, 1981*. **2** an annoying occurrence or circumstance. From the verb CHISEL (to cheat) *UK, 1953*. **3** the best *US, 1997*

Chizler *noun* a Chrysler car or engine *US, 1968*

chol; cha!; chaa! used for registering impatience, disdain or disappointment *JAMAICA, 1827*

choad *noun* **1** the penis *US, 1968*. **2** a person who is easily despised. Sometimes spelt 'chode' *US, 1998*

choc *noun* **1** chocolate, a chocolate. Variants are 'choccy' and 'chocky' *UK, 1896*. **2** a non-white, especially an African. A shortening of 'chocolate' that is both derogatory and offensive *SOUTH AFRICA, 1978*. **3** a person of Mediterranean or Middle Eastern background. Short for CHOCOLATE FROG. Offensive *AUSTRALIA, 1987*

choc beer *noun* an unfiltered ale, sweeter and fruitier than traditional beer, brewed in Oklahoma. From the Choctaw Indians, who are said to have taught immigrant Italians the recipe for the beer *US, 1954*

choccy *noun* a cough after chocolate has been in the mouth *UK, 2003*

choccy! used for expressing approval *UK, 2003*

chocha *noun* the vagina. From Spanish *US, 2002*

chock *noun* home-fermented, vegetable-based alcohol *US, 1972*

chockablock; chocka *adjective* jammed close together, crammed full. From C19 nautical slang *UK, 1840*

chock-a-block (up) *adjective* (of a man) with the penis entirely inserted into a sexual partner *AUSTRALIA, 1969*

chocker; chocka *adjective* **1** completely full *NEW ZEALAND, 1980*. **2** disgruntled, fed up. From 'chock-full' (crammed full) or, more likely, CHOCKABLOCK (crammed full), the variant spellings lend credence to the latter *UK, 1942*

chockers *noun* feet. Market traders' slang *UK, 1979*

chockers *adjective* **1** completely full *AUSTRALIA, 1981*. **2** (of a man) with the penis entirely inserted into a sexual partner *AUSTRALIA, 1975*

chocko; choco *noun* **1** an person of Mediterranean or Middle Eastern background. An abbreviation of CHOCOLATE FROG with the '-o' suffix. Offensive *AUSTRALIA, 1985*. **2** a conscripted soldier or militiaman who remained in Australia and did not fight overseas. World War 2; from CHOCOLATE SOLDIER. In World War 1 the term was simply 'choc' *AUSTRALIA, 1943*

chocks away! let's go!; let's get on with it! From the wooden blocks that were used to stop an aircraft's wheels from rolling; to take the chocks away allowed the plane to take off *UK, 1943*

choco-fan *noun* heroin *UK, 2003*

chocoholic *noun* a person who is excessively fond of chocolate *AUSTRALIA, 1969*

chocolate *noun* **1** a black person *US, 1906*. **2** amphetamines *UK, 2003*. **3** opium *US, 1992*. **4** a twenty rand banknote. Urban, especially township slang, from the brown colour of the note *SOUTH AFRICA, 1984*. **5** a southern European *AUSTRALIA, 1989* ▷ *see:* CHOCOLATE FUDGE, CHOCOLATE THAI. ▶ **in the chocolate** in considerable trouble. A euphemism for IN THE SHIT *UK, 1998*

chocolate *adjective* of African heritage *US, 1906*

chocolate bobby *noun* a community police officer. Used by lower-ranking police *UK, 1981*

chocolate box *adjective* in art, describing a sentimental or romantic style such as you might expect on a chocolate box. Generally used with reproach if not with a degree of contempt *UK, 1901*

chocolate boxey *adjective* in the decorative arts, sentimentally romantic *UK, 1894*

chocolate bunny *noun* a Vietnamese prostitute who favoured black American soldiers over white American soldiers *US, 1991*

chocolate button *noun* an attractive or petite black person. Patronising and offensive *UK, 2002*

chocolate canal *noun* the rectum. Collected during an extensive survey of New Zealand prison slang, 1996–2000 *NEW ZEALAND, 2000*

chocolate chip cookies *noun* MDMA, the recreational drug best known as ecstasy, mixed with heroin or methadone *UK, 2002*

chocolate chips *noun* **1** desert camouflage uniforms *US, 1991*. **2** a type of LSD marketed in brown capsules *UK, 1998*. **3** a variety of MDMA, the recreational drug best known as ecstasy *UK, 2003*

chocolate drop *noun* **1** a black person. Offensive *US, 1900*. **2** a girl below the age of sexual consent who regularly has sex with seamen *UK, 1971*

chocolate ecstasy *noun* crack cocaine blended with chocolate milk powder during processing *US, 1997*

chocolate frog *noun* **1** a person of Mediterranean or Middle Eastern background. Rhyming slang for WOG. Offensive *AUSTRALIA, 1971*. **2** a police informer. Rhyming slang for DOG. A chocolate frog is a popular confectionary *AUSTRALIA, 1971*

chocolate fudge; chocolate *noun* a judge, especially one who shows leniency. Rhyming slang, gently punning on the judge's sweet nature or a SWEET (excellent) result *UK, 1992*

chocolate hearts *noun* a variety of LSD, *2001*

chocolate highway *noun* the anus and rectum *US, 1977*

chocolate rock *noun* a blend of crack cocaine and heroin that is smoked, *2002*

chocolate rocket *noun* crack cocaine blended with chocolate milk powder during processing *US, 1997*

chocolate soldier *noun* a member of an Australian militia during World War 2 who did not serve in a theatre of war. Derogatory *AUSTRALIA, 1943*

chocolate starfish *noun* the anus. A visual pun *UK, 1997*

chocolate Thai; chocolate thi; chocolate *noun* a variety of marijuana *UK, 1995*

chocolate time *noun* the bleed period of the menstrual cycle *US, 2001*

chod *noun* the penis *UK, 2001*

choggy shop *noun* a shop catering to the needs of servicemen and women. Military *UK, 1995*

chogi *noun* a Korean worker *US, 1951*

chogie! move out of here! Korean war usage *US, 1982*

choice *noun* in horse racing, the favoured horse in a race *US, 1960*

choice *adjective* excellent *US, 1958*

choice! used for expressing strong approval *NEW ZEALAND, 1998*

choiceamundo *adjective* excellent *US, 1991*

choirboy *noun* **1** a novice criminal *US, 1949*. **2** a newly initiated member of a youth gang *US, 1956*. **3** a newly recruited police officer *UK, 1996*. **4** a prisoner who informs on others. From the sense of 'to SING' (to inform). Collected during an extensive survey of New Zealand prison slang, 1996–2000 *NEW ZEALAND, 2000*

choir practice *noun* an after-hours gathering of policemen, involving liberal amounts of alcohol and sex, usually in a remote public place *US, 1975*

choke *noun* **1** a swallow or drink of alcohol *US, 1958*. **2** an artichoke of either Jerusalem or globe variety. The punning 'have hearty chokes for breakfast' (to be hanged) dates from 1785; it is difficult to be more accurate with this greengrocers' usage *UK, 1961*. **3** a Mexican-American. Derogatory. A shortened form of CHILI CHOKER *US, 1990*. **4** a garotting *AUSTRALIA, 1953*. **5** a nervous shock; something grievous *UK, 1965*

choke *verb* **1** to forget. Especially in the imperative *US, 1968*. **2** to fail to perform under pressure *US, 1968*. **3** to prevent a horse from winning a race. Strictly, and originally, by pulling back on the reins so strongly that the horse is almost choked *UK, 1962*. **4** in computing, to reject data input *US, 1991*. **5** to borrow something; to scrounge something; to beg *FIJI, 1993*. **6** to turn off a light *US, 1950*. **7** to drink something quickly *UK: SCOTLAND, 1988*. ▶ **choke a darkie** to defecate. Also 'strangle a darkie', and 'sink a darkie' or 'teach a darkie to swim' when on a flush toilet *AUSTRALIA, 1968*. ▶ **choke the chicken 1** (of a male) to masturbate *US, 1976*. **2** (of a male) to

masturbate with the adrenaline-inducing agency of autoerotic strangulation or suffocation *UK, 2002*. ▶ **choke the Chihuahua** (of a male) to masturbate *UK, 2003*. ▶ **choke your chauncy** (of a male) to masturbate in a race *US, 1989*. ▶ **choke your mule** (of a male) to masturbate *US, 1992*

choke *adjective* many. Hawaiian youth usage *US, 1982*

choke and chew *noun* a roadside restaurant *US, 1976*

choke and puke *noun* a restaurant with bad food at low prices *US, 1988*

chokecherry farmer *noun* an unsuccessful farmer *CANADA, 1987*

choked *adjective* emotionally upset, annoyed. The sense of 'a lump in your throat' *UK, 1964*

choked down *adjective* **1** (of a racehorse) experiencing difficulty breathing during a race *US, 1994*. **2** well-dressed *US, 1980*

choked off *adjective* disgusted, fed-up *UK, 1980*

choke down *verb* to force yourself to swallow an alcoholic drink despite any difficulty with taste or capacity *UK, 1988*

choked up tight *adjective* dressed up, especially with button-down collars *US, 1976*

choke off *verb* to punish or berate a prisoner. Prison officer slang, from military origins *UK, 1962*

choke out *verb* to render someone unconscious through a choke hold that cuts off cerebral blood flow at the carotid artery in the neck, usually applied with a police officer's baton across the throat *US, 1985*

choker *noun* a necktie *US, 1945*

choke rag *noun* a necktie *US, 1944*

choke up *verb* to lose your composure; to totter on the verge of tears *US, 1941*

chokey *adjective* crowded, tight-fitting *TRINIDAD AND TOBAGO, 2003*

chokey; choky *noun* **1** a prison; a detention cell; a segregation unit. From Hindustani *chauki* (a four-sided place or building) *UK, 1837*. **2** the time spent in a prison segregation unit; the punishment itself *UK, 1996*. **3** a prison diet of bread and water, served as punishment *UK, 1958*

Chokie *adjective* Chinese. Used of Hong Kong Chinese crew on a Royal Fleet Auxiliary vessel during the Falklands war. The variation 'chogey' is remembered by Beale as in Army usage in Hong Kong during the 1960s *UK, 1982*

choking *adjective* **1** extremely thirsty *UK: SCOTLAND, 1988*. **2** desperate for a cigarette, a drink, sex or whatever may bring relief or satisfaction *UK, 1997*

chokkas *noun* shoes. From CHOCKERS (feet). English gypsy use *UK, 2000*

cholly *noun* cocaine *US, 1970*

cholo *noun* a young, tough Mexican-American. Border Spanish used in English conversation by Mexican-Americans *US, 1971*

chomeur *noun* in Quebec, a person receiving unemployment insurance benefits *CANADA, 1998*

chomo *noun* a child molester *US, 1992*

chomp *verb* to eat *US, 1968*

chompers *noun* **1** the teeth; false teeth *US, 1950*. **2** a snack or meal *ANTARCTICA, 1963*

chong *adjective* good-looking, handsome. Used by urban black youths *UK, 2004*

chonga *noun* marijuana *UK, 2002*

choo-choo *noun* a train. Formed from the child's imitation of a steam whistle *US, 1898*

choof *verb* **1** (of a person) to go; to depart. As used of a steam train in stories for children *AUSTRALIA, 1947*. **2** to smoke marijuana *AUSTRALIA, 2000*

choof off *verb* to depart, to leave *AUSTRALIA, 1972*

chook! a call made to domestic chickens *AUSTRALIA, 1903*

chook; chookie; chuckie *noun* **1** an adult domestic chicken, male or female. First appearing in Australia in the diminutive form 'chuckey' this word is imitative of the cluck of the hen but also owes something to 'chicken'. In general use in British dialect from C18 as *chuck*, *chuke*, and the diminutive *chookie*, *chucky*, where it was also used as a term of endearment from the C19 *AUSTRALIA, 1900.* **2** a slaughtered chicken dressed for cooking; a cooked chicken *AUSTRALIA, 1948.* **3** cooked chicken meat *AUSTRALIA, 1945.* **4** a woman, especially an elderly woman *AUSTRALIA, 1915.* **5** a fool *AUSTRALIA, 1955.* **6** a coward. A variation of CHICKEN *AUSTRALIA, 1997.* ▶ **choke the chook; milk the chook** (of a male) to masturbate. Variant of CHOKE THE CHICKEN. *AUSTRALIA, 1999.* ▶ **I hope your chooks turn into emus and kick your dunny down** I wish you bad luck *AUSTRALIA, 1972.* ▶ **like a chook with its head chopped off; like a chook without a head** without rhyme or reason. A variant of HEADLESS CHICKEN *AUSTRALIA, 1983*

chookas! used for wishing an actor good luck. Actors are, by tradition, superstitious , and to actually wish an actor 'good luck' in so many words is thought to be tempting fate; this abstract (derivation unknown) or surreal benediction was used by Evan Dunstan, an Australian theatrical agent in London during the 1980s *AUSTRALIA, 1984*

chook chaser *noun* a small motorcycle or its rider. A derogatory term used by riders of larger motorcycles *AUSTRALIA, 1996*

chookhouse *noun* an enclosure for domestic chickens *AUSTRALIA, 1938*

chookie *noun* a fool *AUSTRALIA, 1855.* ▶ **will you chookie!** you will not!; used for emphasising a contradiction of a preceding statement *UK: SCOTLAND, 1985*

chook poop *noun* chicken manure *AUSTRALIA, 1986*

chook raffle *noun* a raffle to raise money for charity offering a dressed chicken as a prize *AUSTRALIA, 1979*

chook wheel *noun* a spinning wheel with numbered pegs used for a chook raffle *AUSTRALIA, 1991*

chookyard *noun* an enclosed yard for domestic chickens *AUSTRALIA, 1941*

choom *noun* an Englishman. Representing a toney English pronunciation of CHUM. Used jocularly and mildly derisively *AUSTRALIA, 1916*

choon *noun* within house and other contemporary dance styles, a piece of recorded music. A mispronounced and misspelt 'tune' *UK, 2002*

choose *verb* (of a prostitute) to agree to work for a pimp *US, 1972*

choosing money *noun* the money a prostitute pays a pimp to join his fold *US, 1972*

chop *noun* **1** dismissal from employment *UK, 1945.* **2** approval *US, 1992.* **3** a share or division of something *AUSTRALIA, 1919.* **4** a scathing, cutting remark or joke *US, 1957.* **5** a short and sudden type of scratch (a manipulation of a record to create a musical effect) *UK, 2002.* **6** a wood-chopping contest. Also known as a 'chops' *AUSTRALIA, 1926.* **7** food. US military usage during the Vietnam war *US, 1982.* **8** a dolt, an idiot, a fool *SOUTH AFRICA, 2004.* ▶ **have had the chop** to be no good; to be ruined *AUSTRALIA, 1975.* ▶ **no chop** no good, inferior. From the conventional sense of 'chop' as 'class, rank or quality' implied in 'first chop', 'second chop', etc *AUSTRALIA, 1864.* ▶ **not much chop** not very good. From the British and Anglo-Indian 'chop' (quality) *AUSTRALIA, 1847*

chop *verb* **1** in car and motorcycle customising, to lower the upper portion of the car body or motorcycle by shortening the structural supports *US, 1953.* **2** to cut a car into pieces *US, 1953.* **3** to go into action as a soldier. Extended from the sense 'to shoot' *UK, 2001.* **4** to kill someone *UK, 2001.* **5** to execute someone by hanging them. Prison use, probably dating from the time when the axe was the preferred method of official execution. Capital punishment was abolished in the UK in 1965 *UK, 1950.* **6** to shoot someone to death *US, 1933.* **7** to approve something *US, 1992.* **8** to adulterate a powdered drug *US, 1970.* **9** in handball, to add spin to the ball when hitting it *US, 1970.* **10** (of dice in a crap game) to pass once and then not pass *US, 1981.* **11** in motor racing, to pull sharply in front of another car *US, 1965.* ▶ **chop it up** to talk with enthusiasm and energy *US, 2004.* ▶ **chop sin** to gossip; to talk idly *BERMUDA, 1985.* ▶ **chop ten** to sit with your legs crossed as others work *JAMAICA, 1998.* ▶ **chop the clock** to reset a vehicle's mileometer (odometer) to a reduced

measure *US, 1981.* ▶ **chop wood** to drive off a road or motorway into a tree *US, 1962.* ▶ **chop your gums** to engage in idle talk *US, 1948*

chop-chop *noun* **1** food *US, 1951.* **2** a meal. Used by UN troops in the Korean war, 1950–53 *US, 1950.* **3** oral sex performed on a man. From the vocabulary of Vietnamese prostitutes, taken and used by US soldiers *US, 1990.* **4** trade union factionalism *US, 1961.* **5** loose-leaf tobacco sold illegally *AUSTRALIA, 2001*

chop-chop *verb* during the Korean war, to eat *US, 1951*

chop-chop *adverb* immediately; in an instant. Pidgin or mock pidgin, sometimes used as an imperative *UK, 1836*

chop-chop square *nickname* a large square in Riyadh, Saudi Arabia, that, on a Friday, is the chosen site for public execution by beheading (with a sword) of those the state has sentenced to death, *2001*

chop house *noun* a restaurant *US, 1956*

chop out *verb* to separate a dose of powdered cocaine *UK, 2002*

chopped *adjective* **1** marijuana-intoxicated *US, 1995.* **2** ugly *US, 1993*

chopped and channeled *adjective* (of a car) modified by cutting larger windows and lowering the body of the chassis frame, producing a sleeker profile that hugs the road *US, 1965*

chopped liver *noun* **1** the vagina *UK, 2001.* **2** something of no consequence *US, 1954*

chopped off *adjective* annoyed, angry *US, 1963*

chopped rag *noun* a parachute which has been altered. Vietnam war usage *US, 1991*

chopped top *noun* a hot rod that has had its roof removed *US, 1960*

chopper *noun* **1** a helicopter *US, 1951.* **2** a modified motorcycle with an emphasis on function, not form, usually featuring high handlebars. From CHOP *US, 1966.* **3** a bicycle modified with an emphasis on function, not form, usually featuring high handlebars *UK, 1977.* **4** the penis *UK, 1973.* **5** a machine gun *US, 1929.* **6** a pistol *US, 1957.* **7** a hacksaw; a hacksaw blade *US, 1950.* **8** a logger or lumberjack *US, 1975.* **9** an elderly sow or boar suitable to be turned into pork sausages *NEW ZEALAND, 1988.* **10** a cow destined for slaughter rather than a dairy life *AUSTRALIA, 1987.* **11** a deer-skin mitten with a wool mitten insert. Michigan Upper Peninsula usage *US, 2003.* **12** a car taken in part-exchange. Second-hand car dealers' slang *UK, 1965.* **13** a ticket taker *US, 1960.* **14** a bad mood. Used by printers and compositors. No longer in use by 1960 *UK, 1948*

chopper *verb* to transport something by helicopter. From CHOPPER (a helicopter) *US, 1968*

chopper coppers *noun* the police in helicopters. Quoted as a term used by residents of Berkeley, California *US, 1970*

chopper jockey *noun* a helicopter pilot or crew member *US, 1960*

choppers *noun* **1** the teeth *US, 1944.* **2** the female legs *US, 1963*

choppy *noun* a choppy wave. Surfers' use, reported by Barry Prentice, 1984 *AUSTRALIA, 1984*

choppy *adjective* **1** (of railway track) uneven, producing a rough ride *US, 1975.* **2** in autombile racing, describing abrupt movements in vertical wheel displacement *US, 1980.* **3** (of a temperature chart) uneven. Hospital nurses' use *UK, 1961*

chop-ride *noun* a test-flight to examine a pilot's suitability to continue flying. To fail the test would result in the CHOP *UK, 1979*

chops *noun* **1** the teeth or mouth *UK, 1589.* **2** musical ability *US, 1968.* **3** an ability; a technique. Extends the skilled sense of jazz 'chops' *US, 2002.* **4** the female legs *US, 1960*

chops *verb* to talk. Adapted from CHOPS (the mouth), hence 'to use the mouth' *UK, 2000*

chop shop *noun* a car body repair shop where stolen cars are altered or parts are stripped for sale separately *US, 1978*

chopsocky *noun* oriental martial arts; low-budget martial arts films. Probably a blend of *chop suey* (a popular Chinese dish) and SOCK (to hit) *US, 1978*

chops on *verb* to talk and talk. A variation of CHOPS *UK, 2000*

chopstick *noun* a South Asian person. Offensive *US, 1980*

chopsticks *noun* **1** the number six. Rhyming slang *UK, 1980*. **2** mutual, simultaneous masturbation. From the crossing of hands in the piano piece 'Chopsticks' *US, 1941*

chop suey *adjective* mixed up. Hawaiian youth usage *US, 1981*

chopsy *adjective* loquacious, too talkative *UK, 2001*

choptop *noun* a crewcut haircut *US, 1959*

chop-up *noun* a division of plunder *AUSTRALIA, 1966*

chor *noun* a thief *FIJI, 1997*

chorals; corals *noun* a central nervous system depressant, especially chloral hydrate *US, 1998*

chorb *noun* a spot, a pimple. School slang *SOUTH AFRICA, 1970*

chord-ially used as a humorous closing in letters between singers *US, 1975*

chordy *adjective* stolen. From Romany *côr* (to steal) *UK, 1979*

chore *verb* **1** to steal something. English gypsy use; from original Romany *côr UK, 1979*. **2** to arrest someone *UK, 2000*

chorer *noun* a thief. Derives from CHORE (to steal) *UK, 1979*

chore whore *noun* an assistant *UK, 1996*

chorine *noun* a member of a theatrical chorus *US, 1922*

choro *verb* to steal something *FIJI, 1989*

chorrie; tjorrie *noun* a near-derelict car *SOUTH AFRICA, 1961*

chorus and verse; chorus *noun* the posterior, the backside. Glasgow rhyming slang (reliant on the local accent) for ARSE *UK, 2002*

chossel *noun* a girlfriend *BARBADOS, 1996*

chota *noun* the police; a police officer. Border Spanish used in English conversation by Mexican-Americans *US, 1974*

chovies *noun* anchovies *US, 1996*

chow *noun* food *US, 1856*

Chow *noun* a Chinese person. Offensive *AUSTRALIA, 1864*

chow *verb* to eat *US, 1900*

Chow *adjective* Chinese. Offensive *AUSTRALIA, 1903*

chow used as a greeting and as a farewell. A variation of CIAO. Recorded in this spelling in a 1961 letter to Partridge from Nicholas Bentley noting its popularity as a form of both salutation and goodbye, and particularly at the Royal College of Art *UK, 1961*

chowderhead *noun* a fool *UK, 1819*

chow down *verb* **1** to set to eating. Originally military, then spread into widespread, if affected, use *US, 1945*. **2** to perform oral sex *US, 1994*

chow for now goodbye. An intentional corruption of the Italian *ciao US, 1991*

chow hall *noun* a school cafeteria *US, 1963*

chowhound *noun* an enthusiastic eater *US, 1917*

chowmeinery *noun* in circus and carnival usage, a Chinese restaurant *US, 1981*

chow miaow *noun* Chinese food. Punning on CHOW as food generally, a Chinese person, and a shortening of *chow mein* (itself a root for the sense of CHOW as 'food') with a convenient rhyme to suggest catmeat is a staple ingredient *AUSTRALIA, 1958*

Chriggy; Chriggie *noun* Christmas. A variation of CHRISSY that was recorded in 1984 but has since disappeared without trace *UK, 1984*

Chrimbo; Chrimble; Crimble *noun* Christmas *UK, 2001*

Chrissake!; chrisake! Christ's sake! *UK, 1964*

chrissie *noun* a chrysanthemum *AUSTRALIA, 1977*

Chrissy; Chrissie *noun* Christmas *AUSTRALIA, 1966*

Christ *adjective* used as an adjectival intensifier *BAHAMAS, 1982*

Christ! used as a register of anger, frustration, wonder, etc. Blasphemous by derivation, probably blasphemous in use *UK, 1748*

Christ almighty! used as a register of anger, frustration, wonder, etc. Blasphemous by derivation, probably blasphemous in use *UK, 1987*

Christ almighty wonder *noun* a person of remarkable talent; such a person who is very aware of how special he or she is; an asounding event. A combination of the exclamation CHRIST ALMIGHTY! with 'wonder' (an outstanding thing) *UK, 1961*

christen *verb* **1** to give a name to something, to call something by a particular name. After the Christian tradition *UK, 1642*. **2** to use something for the first time *UK, 2003*. ▶ **christen the queen** to urinate *AUSTRALIA, 1985*

christer *noun* a Christian who proclaims his beliefs to all, whether they wish to hear or not *US, 1921*

Christian *adjective* (of a person) decent; (of a thing) civilised, decent, respectable. In early use the sense was human as opposed to animal. Contemporary use tends towards irony *UK, 1577*

Christians in Action *nickname* the US Central Intelligence Agency. Reverse engineered from the agency's initials *US, 1992*

christina *noun* ▷ *see:* CRISTINA

Christine *noun* **1** in homosexual usage, used as a personification of methamphetamine powder *US, 1980*. **2** cocaine. Another in a long series of personifications of drugs based on the drug's first letter *US, 1973*

Christ-killer *noun* a Jewish person. Offensive *UK, 1861*

Christless *adjective* cursed, damned *US, 1912*

Christmas! used as a mild expletive. A euphemistic evasion of CHRIST! *UK, 1909*

Christmas card *noun* **1** in trucking, a speeding ticket *US, 1976*. **2** a guard, especially a train guard. Rhyming slang *UK, 1960*. ▶ **off your Christmas card list; not on your Christmas card list** used as an expression of displeasure towards someone. A jocular threat, often in verb form: 'to cross someone off your Christmas card list' *UK, 2003*

Christmas cheer; Christmas *noun* beer *UK, 1992*

Christmas crackers *noun* the testicles. Rhyming slang for KNACKERS *UK, 1974*

Christmas dinner *noun* a winner. Rhyming slang *UK, 1992*

Christmases *noun* ▶ **like all your Christmases have come at once** very happy, delighted *UK, 1993*

Christmas hold *noun* a grabbing of another's testicles. That is, 'a handful of nuts' *AUSTRALIA, 1950*

Christmas kitty *noun* a holiday bonus cheque *US, 1954*

Christmas log *noun* a racing greyhound. Rhyming slang for 'dog' *UK, 1974*

Christmas present *noun* in tiddlywinks, a stroke of good luck *US, 1977*

Christmas roll *noun* a multi-coloured assortment of barbiturate capsules *US, 1973*

Christmas shopping; Christmas shop; Christmas *noun* of a male, masturbation. Rhyming slang for STROP(PING) *UK, 1992*

Christmas tree *noun* **1** a capsule of amobarbital sodium and secobarbital sodium (trade name Tuinal™), a combination of central nervous system depressants *US, 1968*. **2** an assortment of multi-coloured pills *US, 1992*. **3** marijuana. Draws a parallel between two plants that appear at times of celebration *US, 1987*. **4** in drag racing, an electronic starting device consisting of a set of lights *US, 1970*. **5** a bank of red and green-coloured lights that are part of an instrument panel *US, 1945*. **6** in the car sales business, a car loaded with accessories and gadgets *US, 1953*. **7** in trucking, a tractor trailer embellished with many extra running lights *US, 1971*. **8** in oil drilling, the collection of equipment at the top of an oil well *US, 1925*. **9** in the television and film industries, a cart used for storing and carrying lighting equipment *US, 1977*. **10** in the television and film industries, a stand with more than one light mounted on it *US, 1987*. **11** in railway terminology, a coloured light signal *UK, 1970*. **12** a woman who over-dresses or over-uses cosmetics *US, 1960*. **13** the knee. Rhyming slang; the plural is 'Christmas trees' *UK, 1998*. **14** in electric line work, a pole-mounted auxiliary arm used for hoisting a conductor *US, 1980*. **15** in Nova Scotia, a piece of fishing gear with many lines, hooks, and pegs attached *CANADA, 1980*. ▶ **(just) come down off the Christmas tree** foolish, inexperienced, gullible *UK, 1999*. ▶ **lit up like a Christmas tree** dazzling; resplendent *AUSTRALIA, 1962*

Christ on a bike!; Jesus Christ on a bike! used as a register of shock or amazement US, 1986

Christ on a boogie board! used for registering surprise or disbelief US, 2001

Christ on a crutch! used for expressing exasperation US, 1928

Christopher Lee noun urine; urination; an act of urination. Rhyming slang for PEE or WEE; formed on the name of British film actor Christopher Lee (b.1922) UK, 1998

Chris Wren noun a fifty pound note. An illustration of Sir Christopher Wren, architect, 1632–1723, featured on Bank of England £50 notes from 1981 UK, 2002

chrome noun **1** in computing, software features that attract buyers but add little functionally US, 1991. **2** the best, judged in terms of appearance; the shiniest examples UK, 1998. ▶ **sit on chrome** of a car, to have alloy wheels UK, 2005

chrome verb in hot rodding, to add chrome features to a car US, 1954

chrome dome noun **1** a bald man; a bald head US, 1962. **2** a fibre helmet used between April and October in Vietnam to protect soldiers from the sun. Aluminium paint gave rise to the 'chrome' US, 1991

chrome-plated adjective nicely dressed. High school student usage, borrowing from car vocabulary US, 1961

chrome to the dome noun a pistol held to the head US, 1998

chromie noun a chromed wheel, popular with hot rodders US, 1968

chromo noun **1** a female prostitute. From 'chromolithograph', a type of painted lithographic picture, referring to the 'painted' (i.e. made-up) faces of prostitutes AUSTRALIA, 1883. **2** anything that is inexpensive, shoddy or inferior US, 1934

chrondo noun potent marijuana. A blend of CHRONIC and INDO US, 1997

chroned out adjective suffering from a hangover US, 2001

chronic noun **1** potent marijuana. A word popularised in hip-hop usage. 'The Chronic' by Dr Dre (1992) is one of the biggest-selling rap albums of all time US, 1993. **2** marijuana mixed with crack cocaine US, 1998

chronic adjective **1** constant; bad, objectionable, severe, unpleasant. From the conventional medical sense UK, 1860. **2** very good US, 1998

chronic bubonic noun marijuana that is more potent than simple 'chronic' or simple 'bubonic' US, 2001

Chryco nickname the Chrysler Corporation, a car manufacturer US, 1993

chub noun **1** a moderately overweight person UK, 1838. **2** the penis US, 1997

chub verb to smuggle items into a prison by secreting the contraband up the anus UK, 1996

chub-a-dub noun an act of masturbation CANADA, 2002

chubb; chubb up verb to lock a prison cell door. From the well-known branded lock UK, 1950

chubbies noun large female breasts US, 1964

chubby noun **1** an overweight man as a homosexual object of desire US, 1971. **2** an erection US, 1997

chubby adjective (of the penis) erect UK, 2003

chubby-chaser noun a person who is sexually attracted to overweight people US, 1976

chubster noun **1** a overweight person. From conventional 'chubby' (overweight/fat) US, 2002. **2** the penis US, 1997

chuc; chuke noun a Pachuco, or young Mexican-American with a highly stylised sense of fashion and a specialised idiom. The Pachuco was the Mexican zoot-suiter of the 1940s, and his legacy is seen today in Mexican-American culture. The term can be used either as a term of pride or as a term of derision US, 1963

chuck noun **1** food UK, 1850. **2** vomit AUSTRALIA, 1966. **3** a white man. A diminutive of Charles or Charlie US, 1965. **4** the Viet Cong US, 1981. **5** a throw, a toss; in cricket, a thrown ball, an illegal delivery UK, 1862. **6** a shove that leads to a fight BARBADOS, 1965. ▶ **give it a chuck** to stop, to desist. Often as an imperative UK: SCOTLAND, 1984

chuck verb **1** to vomit AUSTRALIA, 1957. **2** to throw something UK, 1593. **3** to throw something away, to discard something US, 1911. **4** to throw a case out of court. Police slang UK, 1970. **5** to dismiss someone, to reject someone; to jilt someone AUSTRALIA, 1932. **6** to eat excessively when being withdrawn from drug dependence UK, 1966. **7** to forget. Also 'chuck it' US, 1947. ▶ **chuck a charley; chuck a charlie** to have a fit of temper AUSTRALIA, 1945. ▶ **chuck a dummy** to feign an illness or injury US, 1992. ▶ **chuck a mental** to lose your temper and composure in a manner that suggests emotional instability NEW ZEALAND, 1998. ▶ **chuck a seven 1** to have a fit of temper. From the langauage of dice-playing AUSTRALIA, 1945. **2** to die. From the game of craps, in which to throw a seven (except on the first roll) is to lose AUSTRALIA, 1961. ▶ **chuck a six; chuck a sixer** to have a fit of temper. From dice-playing AUSTRALIA, 1945. ▶ **chuck a willy** to have a fit of temper AUSTRALIA, 1945. ▶ **chuck a wing-ding** to feign a seizure while in prison in the hope of obtaining drugs in treatment US, 1992. ▶ **chuck your weight about; chuck your weight around** to behave in an unpleasant, domineering way; to bully someone UK, 1909. ▶ **chuck yourself about; chuck yourself into something** to move about energetically UK, 1984

chuck and jam adjective crowded TRINIDAD AND TOBAGO, 2003

chucked adjective acquitted. From CHUCK (to throw a case out of court) UK, 1950

chucker noun in cricket, a bowler who is apt to throw the ball UK, 1882

chucker-out noun a man employed to keep out and get rid of unwanted patrons; a bouncer UK, 1884

chucker-outer noun a bouncer AUSTRALIA, 1998

Chuck Fuck noun a man of no real significance US, 1997

chuck horrors noun the painful symptoms of withdrawal from drug addiction US, 1926

chuckie noun ▷see: CHOOK

chuck-in noun a piece of good fortune; a bonus. From an earlier sense (to add to a collection) AUSTRALIA, 1916

chuck in verb **1** to get rid of something, to discard something, to quit something UK, 1944. **2** to contribute something AUSTRALIA, 1907. **3** to include something as an extra AUSTRALIA, 1965

chucking noun in cricket, an illegal act of throwing, not bowling, a ball UK, 1995

chucking-out noun an ejection, especially from a premises UK, 1881

chucking-out time noun closing time in a public house or other licensed premises. An image of forced ejection UK, 1909

chuck it down verb to rain, hail or snow, very heavily. Sometimes elaborated as, for example, 'chuck it down with rain' UK, 2002

chuckle noun an instance of vomiting AUSTRALIA, 1961

chuckle verb to vomit AUSTRALIA, 1964

chucklehead noun a fool UK, 1731

chuckleheaded adjective simple, dim-witted UK, 1768

chuck off verb **1** to voice abuse; to let fly AUSTRALIA, 1915. **2** to throw someone off something. A colloquial use UK, 1841

chuck one up verb to salute. Military UK, 1984

chuck out verb to eject someone forcibly; to get rid of someone. Usage may be actual, figurative or jocular UK, 1869

chucks noun **1** a powerful craving for food associated with withdrawal from heroin addiction. Also 'chuckers' US, 1953. **2** the craving for food that follows the smoking of marijuana US, 1970. **3** high-top sports shoes, especially Converse's Chuck Taylor™ shoes US, 1984

chuck up verb **1** to yield, to abandon, to give in. From pugilism, specifically from the traditional method of conceding defeat; a shortening of 'chuck up the sponge' UK, 1864. **2** to vomit AUSTRALIA, 1984

chuck wagon noun **1** a truck stop or roadside restaurant. A jocular reference to the cooking wagon on cattle drives in the Old West US, 1976. **2** a brakevan (caboose) US, 1977

chuck you, Farley! used as an expression of derision. An intentional spoonerism of 'Fuck you, Charley!', favoured by school children US, 1976

chud *noun* a disgusting person. From the film *Cannabalistic Humanoid Underground Dwellers* US, 1986

chuddie; chuddy *noun* chewing gum. Used by teenagers UK, 1984

chuddies *noun* underpants. Directly from Punjabi into HINGLISH (Asian English); widely popularised as a catchphrase KISS MY CHUDDIES! coined by *Goodness Gracious Me*, a BBC comedy sketch show scripted and performed by four British Asian comedians, first heard on Radio 4 in 1996 but better known from television, since 1999; often misunderstood to mean ARSE UK, 1996

chuff *noun* **1** the anus or buttocks AUSTRALIA, 1945. **2** the vagina UK, 1997. **3** pubic hair US, 1967. **4** a homosexual male. A sexual objectification from the sense as 'buttocks' UK, 1961. ▶ **the chuff** replaces 'the hell' in phrases such as 'where the hell?', a euphemism for 'the fuck'. From CHUFF (the buttocks) UK, 1996

chuff *verb* to fart UK, 1998

chuff all nothing, nothing at all UK, 1997

chuff box *noun* the vagina; in later use, the anus UK, 1961

chuff chum *noun* a male homosexual. An elaboration of CHUFF (a male homosexual). Derogatory UK, 1961

chuffdruff; muffdruff *noun* dried flakes of sexual secretions (male and/or female) clinging to the female pubic hair. An ellipsis of CHUFF (the vagina) or MUFF (the vagina, etc.) and 'dandruff' UK, 1998

chuffed *adjective* **1** pleased, delighted; flattered; very excited. Originally northern English dialect meaning 'proud', adopted by military, then wider society. The current, more generalised usage was possibly spread by jazz fans. Embellishments include 'chuffed to fuck'; 'chuffed to arseholes'; 'chuffed to buggery'; 'chuffed pink'; 'chuffed to little mint-balls'; 'bo-chuffed'; 'chuffed to little naffy breaks'; 'chuffed to naffy breaks' and 'chuffed to oil-bumps'. Often qualified by intensifiers DEAD, REAL, WELL, etc UK, 1957. **2** displeased, disgruntled. Qualifiers and context may be required to distinguish usage from the previous sense as 'pleased'. Variants include 'dischuffed' and 'dead chuffed' UK, 1961

chuffer *noun* **1** a person, euphemistic for 'fucker' UK, 1997. **2** a cigarette-smoker. A play on 'puffer' and CHUFF (the buttocks/an arse) UK, 2003. **3** a train. From nursery use UK, 1999. **4** the buttocks. An elaboration of CHUFF UK, 2004

chuffing *adjective* used as an intensifier, a euphemism for 'fucking' UK, 1997

chuffing Nora! used for registering surprise, anger, amazement, etc. A variation of FLAMING NORA! UK, 1997

chuff it! a general declaration of rejection or dimissal; may also imply resignation to or acceptance of a situation. FUCK IT! euphemistically UK, 1859

chuff muncher *noun* a lesbian. From CHUFF (the vagina) UK, 1998

chuff nut *noun* a piece of faecal matter clinging to anal hair. Elaborated on CHUFF UK, 1961

chuff piece *noun* the anus, the arse. An elaboration of CHUFF UK, 1962

chuftie *noun* the vagina. A variation of CHUFF (the vagina) UK, 1998

chuftie plug *noun* a tampon UK, 1998

chufty badge *noun* a notional award offered to someone who is overly proud of a small achievement UK, 2005

chug *noun* a long, sustained swallow of a drink US, 1969

chug *verb* **1** to swallow a drink in a single draught. An abbreviation of CHUGALUG US, 1989. **2** in computing, to operate slowly US, 1991

chug-a-lug! used as a drinking toast AUSTRALIA, 1984

chugalug; chuglug *verb* to drink without pausing to breathe US, 1936

chugger *noun* a professional fundraiser who is tasked to confront passers-by in the street with a charity's need for regular income and persuade people to sign agreements to make regular donations. A blend of 'charity' and MUGGER (a street robber) UK, 2002

chugging *noun* a method of professional fundraising by persuading passers-by in the street to sign financial agreements for regular donations. A blend of 'charity' and MUGGING (street robbery) UK, 2003

chuke *noun* a knitted cap US, 1966. ▷ *see:* CHUC

chukka chap *noun* a man associated with the game of polo. A 'chukka' is a period of play in a polo match UK, 2003

chukka chick *noun* a woman associated with the game of polo UK, 2004

chum *noun* **1** an associate, a regular companion or a close friend. Originally in conventional use; slipped into colloquial use in C19 UK, 1684. **2** used (of a male) as a form of address, often patronising UK, 1684

chum *verb* **1** in aerial combat, to fly low over enemy territory in order to draw enemy ground fire, which is then answered by airpower flying higher and out of sight US, 1990. **2** to vomit US, 1990

chuma *verb* to kiss. From the Hindi FIJI, 1996

chum buddy *noun* a close friend US, 1952

chummery *noun* in India, a bungalow (or similar) shared by friends (now, usually young and single). From CHUM (a friend) INDIA, 1888

chummified *adjective* drunk US, 1968

chummy *noun* **1** a civilian; a prisoner; a prime suspect; also used as a patronising form of address. Metropolitan Police slang; a diminutive of CHUM (a friend) that threatens intimacy UK, 1948. **2** loose and broken pieces of anything. A closely related word with a different but perhaps related meaning is used in New England and the Canadian maritime provinces fishing: 'chum bait', 'chumming' CANADA, 1999

chummy *adjective* very friendly, intimate, sociable US, 1884

chump *noun* **1** a fool; a naive person who is easily duped US, 1876. **2** the head UK, 1859. ▶ **off your chump** in any degree, mad UK, 1864

chump *verb* **1** to act foolishly US, 1971. **2** to swindle someone, to cheat someone US, 1930

chump change *noun* a small amount of money US, 1968

chump educator *noun* **1** a trade newspaper or magazine used to educate outsiders on the industry's secrets US, 1981. **2** in the circus or carnival, *Billboard* magazine US, 1980

chump expenses *noun* minor expenses US, 1969

chump heister *noun* a carnival ferris wheel US, 1980

chump job *noun* a legal, legitimate job, especially a low-paying and menial one US, 1972

chump off *verb* to better or out-insult someone in a verbal duel US, 1972

chump twister *noun* a carousel US, 1961

chunck *verb* in pinball, to hit the ball into a scoring bumper with such force that the bumper fails to respond US, 1977

chunder *noun* **1** vomit AUSTRALIA, 1953. **2** an instance of vomiting AUSTRALIA, 1983. **3** in poker, a weak hand that wins US, 1996

chunder *verb* **1** to vomit. Probably rhyming slang for 'Chunder Loo' (spew); from the name of an advertising comic strip character that ran in the early C20. The widely held theory that it derives from a clipping of the phrase 'Watch under!', used by seasick passengers on liners to warn the lower decks of an impending vomit-shower, is nothing but ingenious trifling AUSTRALIA, 1950. **2** to mangle someone AUSTRALIA, 1986. **3** to churn AUSTRALIA, 1962

chunderer *noun* a person who habitually vomits, especially as a result of excessive drinking AUSTRALIA, 1971

chundering *noun* vomiting AUSTRALIA, 1964

chunderish *adjective* bilious AUSTRALIA, 1991

chunderous *adjective* sickening AUSTRALIA, 1967

chunk *noun* a large amount US, 1889

chunk *verb* **1** to throw something US, 1835. **2** to vomit US, 1994. **3** in Americans casinos, to bet a great deal, especially to do so unwisely US, 1985. **4** to engage in a fist fight US, 1990

chunka-chunka *adjective* used for representing a steady musical rhythm. Echoic UK, 2003

chunk down *verb* to eat US, 1968

chunker *noun* an M79 grenade launcher. Vietnam war usage US, 1975

chunk of beef; chunka; chunker *noun* a chief, a boss. Rhyming slang; probably no longer in use *AUSTRALIA, 1942*

chunk of change a lot of money *US, 2002*

chunky; chunks; chunkies *noun* hashish. From the similarity in appearance to a block of chocolate *US, 1971*

chunt *noun* an inept, unlikeable person *US, 2004*

church *noun* LSD *UK, 2003.* ▶ **the church** the Investigations Department of HM Customs & Excise *UK, 2001*

churchie *noun* a religious proponent of virtue *NEW ZEALAND, 1997*

church is out 1 an opportunity has passed *US, 1966.* **2** no hope remains; there is nothing to be done *US, 1966*

church key *noun* a can and bottle opener. With the advent of pull-ring (1962), the pop-top (1963), and the stay-on tab can (1974), the device and term all but disappeared *US, 1951*

Church of England *noun* in craps, a bet that the next roll will be 1, 2, 11 or 12. A back-formation from C AND E, itself the initials of 'crap-eleven', the conventional name of the bet *US, 1983*

church rat *noun* a self-serving, pious person *TRINIDAD AND TOBAGO, 1993*

church tramp *noun* a student who changes his church affiliation as necessary to attend various church social functions *US, 1963*

church warden *noun* a pipe with a long stem. Originally made of clay but the name refers to the shape not the material. In 2003 this type of pipe is enjoying a small revival in fashion as a result of the films in the *Lord of the Rings* trilogy *UK, 1863*

churn *verb* to schedule unnecessary return visits to a doctor to increase fees *US, 1991.* ▶ **churn butter** to have sex. Vietnam war usage; slang based on visual images *US, 1991*

churn out *verb* to produce a large quantity of something, especially without too much concern for the finished article's quality *UK, 1912*

chut *noun* a male homosexual; homosexual practices between men. Possibly from CHUTE (the rectum), CHUTNEY (sodomy) or as a variation of CHUFF (a homosexual male) *UK, 1977*

chut *verb* to chew chewing gum *AUSTRALIA, 1945*

chute *noun* **1** the rectum *US, 1976.* **2** the coin slot on a pinball machine *US, 1977.* **3** especially in Quebec, a waterfall *CANADA, 1947.* **4** in sailing, a spinnaker *US, 1990.* **5** a parachute *UK, 1920.* **6** in the usage of youthful model road racers (slot car racers), a straight portion of track *US, 1997.* ▶ **through the chute** smuggled from Venezuela *TRINIDAD AND TOBAGO, 1987*

chutes *noun* a subway (underground) system *US, 1950*

chutney *noun* sodomy. From a similarity in colour and texture between conventional 'chutney' and faecal matter *UK, 1984*

chutney farmer; chutney ferret *noun* a male homosexual. Derogatory. From CHUTNEY (sodomy) *UK, 1996*

chutty *noun* chewing gum *AUSTRALIA, 1942*

chutzpah; chuzpah *noun* gall, intestinal fortitude, extreme self-confidence. One of the best-known Yiddish words in the US *US, 1892*

CHV *noun* Council House Vermin, i.e. people who, it appears, can only afford to live in council houses *IRELAND, 2003*

ciacito, baby used as a farewell. A catchphrase television sign-off of Daisy Fuentes, the too-hip host on the MTV cable network in the 1990s. Repeated with referential humour *US, 1994*

ciao; ciaou goodbye. From an Italian greeting and farewell, affected by English-speakers as a fashionable or ironic farewell *UK, 1959*

'cid; cid; sid *noun* LSD. An abbreviation of ACID *US, 1986*

-cide; -icide *suffix* the conventional suffix, that creates the meaning 'murder' or 'murderer', when used to make a flippant or nonce-word. In June 2003 a quick search of the Internet reveals 'Bushicide', 'Saddamicide' and 'Iraqicide' *UK, 1866*

Cider City *nickname* Hereford, Herefordshire; Taunton, Somerset. Both are historic centres of cider-making *UK, 1981*

ciderhead *noun* a cider drinker. Combines conventional 'cider' with -HEAD (a habitual user) *UK, 1998*

cig *noun* a cigarette or cigar *US, 1894*

cigar *noun* **1** a reprimand, especially at work *US, 1960.* **2** in circus and carnival usage, any compliment *US, 1981*

cigar! correct! An extrapolation from 'Close, but no cigar' *US, 1991*

cigarette *noun* an untalented or personality-free roller derby skater. The cigarette lagged back in the packet, hence the punning term *US, 1999*

cigarette holder *noun* the shoulder. Rhyming slang *UK, 1998*

cigarette paper *noun* a packet of heroin or another drug *US, 1936*

cigarette pimp *noun* a pimp whose lack of professional pride leads him to solicit customers for his prostitutes *US, 1972*

cigarette roll *noun* a type of parachute malfunction *US, 1962*

cigarette swag; cigarette paper swag *noun* a small pack of possessions and necessary items carried by a tramp. From the size and shape of the pack *AUSTRALIA, 1938*

cigarette with no name *noun* a marijuana cigarette *US, 1980*

cigger *noun* a cigarette *AUSTRALIA, 1922*

ciggy; ciggie *noun* a cigarette *US, 1915*

ciggyboo; ciggieboo *noun* a cigarette *UK, 1958*

ciggybutt *noun* a cigarette *US, 1998*

Cilla Black; Cilla *noun* the back. Rhyming slang, formed on the name of singer and television presenter Cilla Black (b.1943) *UK, 1992*

CIL spinner *noun* an illegal charge of dynamite to 'catch' fish in the water without using hooks or nets *CANADA, 1989*

cinch *noun* **1** a certainty *US, 1890.* **2** in horse racing, a horse that is virtually certain to win *US, 1960*

cinchers *noun* brakes *US, 1942*

Cincy; Cinci *nickname* Cincinatti, Ohio *US, 1899*

cinder dick *noun* a railway detective *US, 1925*

cinderella *noun* the nose. Rhyming slang for 'smeller' *UK, 1992*

cinderella *adjective* **1** the colour yellow; in snooker, the yellow ball. Rhyming slang *UK, 1992.* **2** cowardly. Rhyming slang for YELLOW *UK, 2002*

Cinderella liberty *noun* a short release from military duty and from base restrictions. Cinderella had to be home by midnight, as do navy and marine troops *US, 1961*

Cinderella team *noun* a sports team that wins a tournament or championship that it had little hope of winning *US, 1971*

cinders *noun* ▶ **take to the cinders** on the railways, to quit a job *US, 1977*

cinder trail *noun* a railway track *US, 1962*

cinnamon stick *noun* a penis with faeces stains after anal sex *US, 1979*

cipaille *noun* in Quebec, a deep-dish meat pie *CANADA, 1998*

ciphering *noun* arithmetic *US, 1905*

circle *noun* any group of people playing footbag *US, 1997*

circle *verb* ▶ **circle a game** (of a bookmaker) to limit the amount that may be bet on a given game or race when the bookmaker suspects that the game or race is fixed *US, 1978.* ▶ **circle the drain 1** to be near death *US, 1994.* **2** by extension, said of a project or enterprise that is nearing collapse *US, 1997*

Circle City *nickname* Leeds, West Yorkshire *UK, 1981*

circled *adjective* married *US, 1960*

circle jerk *noun* **1** group male masturbation, sometimes mutual and sometimes simply a shared solitary experience *US, 1958.* **2** any non-productive, time-wasting exercise *US, 1973.* **3** a series of exit consoles on websites that link back on themselves, creating an infinite loop *US, 2004*

circle-jerk *verb* to participate in group male masturbation *US, 1971*

Circle K *noun* the recreational drug ketamine. A punning allusion to a US national chain of convenience stores *US, 1998*

circle work *noun* the driving of a car in tight circles to form circular tracks on the ground *AUSTRALIA, 1996*

circs *noun* circumstances *UK, 1883*

circuit *noun* a series of homosexual parties held each year around the US, with participants flying from city to city for the festivities *US, 1990s*

circuit girl *noun* a travelling prostitute *US, 2002*

circuit queen *noun* a male homosexual who follows the circuit from party to party *US, 1994*

circular file *noun* a wastebasket *US, 1947*

circulation *noun* traffic *CANADA, 2001*

circus *noun* **1** sexual behaviour that is public, fetishistic or both *US, 1878*. **2** a state of affairs; a noisy and confused institution, place, scene or assemblage *US, 1899*. **3** a temporary company of people (often moving from place to place), engaged in the same endeavour, e.g. lawn tennis, motor racing, etc. A specialisation of CIRCUS (an assemblage) *UK, 1958*. **4** a group of aircraft engaged in displays of skilful flying. Military origins *UK, 1916*. **5** feigned spasms by a drug addict to convince a doctor to prescribe a narcotic *US, 1949*

circus bees; circus squirrels *noun* body lice *US, 1981*

circus cowboy *noun* a youthful, attractive homosexual male prostitute. A matching of the US MIDNIGHT COWBOY with London geography *UK, 1987*

circus simple *adjective* obsessed with the circus *US, 1975*

circus tent *noun* an apartment or house where customers pay to view sexual exhibitions *US, 1959*

cissy *adjective* effeminate. From 'sister' *CANADA, 1915*

citizen *noun* **1** an ordinary person outside a gang or club *US, 2000*. **2** a fellow member of a youth gang *US, 1953*. **3** a prisoner who has earned the respect of other prisoners *US, 1989*

cits *noun* ▶ **the cits** Minneapolis and St Paul, Minnesota *US, 1966*

City *noun* ▶ **The City** San Francisco, California. Uniformly used by northern Californians, who shun 'FRISCO *US, 1955*

-city *suffix* a good example of the precedent noun *US, 1930*

city block *noun* in horse racing, a large margin of victory or a large lead *US, 1951*

city college *noun* a jail, especially the New York City jail *UK, 1796*

city flyer *noun* a small truck used for local deliveries *US, 1971*

city Jake *noun* a person sophisticated in urban ways *US, 1966*

city kitty *noun* a local police official *US, 1976*

city light *noun* the low-intensity setting on headlights *US, 1950*

city mouse *noun* in Antarctica, a member of support personnel who never leaves McMurdo Station *ANTARCTICA, 2003*

city of the newly-wed and nearly-dead *nickname* Victoria, British Columbia *CANADA, 1989*

city slicker *noun* a smoothly persuasive rogue of a type stereotypically associated with city life; a sophisticated city-dweller. The second sense is derogatory *US, 1924*

city titties *noun* small bumps delineating lanes on motorways and roads *US, 1992*

city tote *noun* a coat. Rhyming slang, formed on the name of a bookmaking firm *UK, 1998*

civilian *noun* **1** anyone who is not a member of the group with which the speaker identifies, especially a motocyle gang *US, 1946*. **2** a non-regular officer *US, 1947*. **3** in twelve-step recovery programmes such as Alcoholics Anonymous, a person who is not involved in and does not need to be involved in a recovery programme *US, 1998*

civil serpent *noun* used as a humorous synonym for 'civil servant' *US, 1980*

civvies *noun* **1** civilian clothes. Military usage *UK, 1889*. **2** manufactured cigarettes. Prison slang, remembering the pleasures of being a CIVVY (a civilian) and a gentle play on CIGGY, CIGGIES *UK, 1996*

civvy *noun* a member of the general public, not a member of the uniformed services: military, police, prison, fire, etc. Abbreviated from 'civilian' *UK, 1895*

civvy *adjective* civilian. Military use *UK, 1915*

civvy street *noun* civilian life; non-military life *UK, 1943*

CJ *noun* phencyclidine, the recreational drug known as PCP or angel dust *US, 1994*

C-jam *noun* cocaine *US, 1986*

c-jame *noun* cocaine *US, 1968*

C-joint *noun* a place where cocaine is sold *US, 2002*

CJ's *noun* a pair of men's close-fitting and revealing nylon swimming trunks. Standing for COCK JOCKS *AUSTRALIA, 2003*

CK *noun* **1** Calvin Klein™ clothing. Favoured by members of the Bloods youth gang, to whom the initials also stand for 'Crip Killer' *US, 2000*. **2** a mixture of cocaine and the recreational drug ketamine *US, 1995*. **3** cocaine *US, 1971*. **4** a man who feels that he has to disparage other women in front of men. An abbreviation of COCK-KNOCKER *US, 2002*

CK1 *noun* a mixture of nine parts cocaine and one part the recreational drug ketamine. The brand name of a popular fragrance by Calvin Klein *UK, 2001*

clack *verb* to rattle the dice when switching altered dice in or out of a game; always inadvertent and usually disastrous to the cheat *US, 1950*

clacker *noun* **1** the backside; the anus. Probably from 'clacker' a ratcheted noise-making device, alluding to farting. Not a perversion of 'cloaca' *AUSTRALIA, 1960*. **2** a young woman; a group of young women; young women in general. Military *UK, 1984*. **3** a dollar *US, 1918*. **4** a triggering device for claymore mines *US, 1990*

clackers *noun* the teeth; false teeth *US, 1950*

clacker valve *noun* the female genitalia *UK, 2003*

clag *noun* excreta, faeces; rubbish *UK, 2003*

claggy *adjective* unpleasantly bedaubed with excreta. From CLAG *UK, 2003*

clag nut *noun* a small lump of excreta or toilet paper that clings to the anal hair. From CLAG (faeces) *UK, 2003*

claim *verb* **1** to arrest someone *UK, 1970*. **2** to challenge someone to a fight *IRELAND, 1989*

claiming *noun* a method of casino cheating, in which a cheat claims that a slot machine malfunctioned and they received no payment or inadequate payment from a win *US, 1985*

Claire Rayners *noun* trainers (footwear). Based on the name of Claire Rayner, popular agony aunt and novelist *UK, 1997*

clam *noun* **1** the vagina *US, 1916*. **2** the anus *US, 1983*. **3** the mouth *US, 1825*. **4** a dollar *US, 1886*. **5** a betting chip in a poker game *US, 1988*. **6** in a musical performance, a missed cue or an off-key note *US, 1955*

clam; clam up *verb* to stop talking *US, 1916*

clambake *noun* a session in which jazz musicians collectively improvise. From CLAM (a missed note) *US, 1937*

clam dam *noun* a condom. Combines CLAM (the vagina) with 'dam' (a barrier) *US, 1990s*

clam-diggers *noun* calf-length trousers. The suggestion is that the trousers are an appropriate length for digging for clams in mud flats *US, 1947*

clam gun *noun* a shovel or other digging implement *US, 1927*

clamp *verb* ▶ **clamp it to** to have sex *US, 1963*

clam patch *noun* the passenger seat on a motorcycle. Biker (motorcycle) slang, coarsely referencing women as CLAM (the vagina) *US, 2003*

clampers *noun* the teeth *US, 1970*

clamp it! be quiet! *UK: SCOTLAND, 1988*

clamps *noun* handcuffs *US, 1949*

clams *noun* money *AUSTRALIA, 1992*

clam-shelled *adjective* ▶ **get clam-shelled** to be engulfed by a wave while surfing *US, 1991*

clam squirt *noun* vaginal secretions *US, 1974*

Clan *noun* ▶ **the Clan** a group of performers and friends surrounding Frank Sinatra in the 1950s and 60s. Better known as the Rat Pack *US, 1960*

clanger noun **1** an error, a mistake UK, 1957. **2** a coward AUSTRALIA, 1953. **3** in poker, a drawn card that does nothing to improve your hand. Also known as a 'clang' US, 1996

clangeroo noun a memorably bad misjudgement. An intensification of CLANGER (an error) with the suffix -EROO; mainly theatrical in use UK, 1957

clangers noun testicles UK, 1961

clank noun an armoured tank US, 1982

clank verb **1** to be nervous US, 1955. **2** to reject a romantic overture or partner US, 1959

clank clank! used in response to an Australian's claim of ancestry that goes back to the days of the early settlers. Echoic of transported prisoners' chains AUSTRALIA, 1968

clanked up adjective anxious, nervous US, 1953

clanks noun delirium tremens US, 1980

clap noun gonorrhoea. From old French clapoir (a sore caused by venereal disease); the term was normal register for centuries, slipping into colloquial or slang in mid-C19 UK, 1587

clap verb to kill someone US, 2002. ► **clap beef** to have sex with a woman JAMAICA, 1980. ► **clap eyes on** to see someone or something UK, 1838

clap checker noun a member of the Medical Corps. Vietnam war usage, identifying medics by the least glorious of their duties US, 1991

clap clinic noun a medical pratice that treats all sexually transmitted disease US, 1976

clapped-out; clapped adjective **1** unserviceable as a result of use or neglect UK, 1946. **2** (of persons) exhausted, no longer effective UK, 1946

clappers noun the testicles. Derives from the clapper of a bell, and is almost always in the plural UK, 1959. ► **like the clappers; like the clappers of hell; like the clappers of fuck** very fast; very hard. Possibly rhyming slang for 'clappers of a bell', 'hell' UK, 1948

clappy adjective infected with a sexually transmitted infection, especially gonorrhoea US, 1937

claps noun gonorrhoea. Largely black usage US, 1965

clap shack noun a clinic or hospital ward where sexually transmitted infections are treated US, 1952

clap sticks noun in the television and film industries, the clapboard used for synchronising sound and picture US, 1987

claptrap noun **1** nonsense, rubbish. From the conventional sense (language designed to win applause) UK, 1915. **2** a brothel with a high incidence of sexually transmitted infections US, 1987

clarabelle noun tetrahydrocannabinal (THC), the psychoactive ingredient in marijuana US, 1971

Clarence nickname a cross-eyed person. From Clarence, a cross-eyed lion that out-acted the human cast in BBC television's Daktari, 1966–69 UK: SCOTLAND, 1988

claret noun blood. Conventional claret is a fortified Bordeaux red wine; the visual connection is obvious UK, 1604

Clarisse noun used as a term of address among male homosexuals US, 1965

clarity noun MDMA, the recreational drug best known as ecstasy US, 1989

Clark Gable noun a table. Rhyming slang, formed on the name of US film actor Clark Gable, 1901–60 UK, 1992

Clark Kent adjective homosexual. Rhyming slang for BENT, formed from the 'secret identity' of Superman UK, 2003

clart noun **1** used as a term of friendly address. Most likely from UK black BLOODCLAAT or PUSSYCLAAT (a contemptible person) into wider youth usage UK, 2004. **2** excrement; also as a euphemism for all senses of 'shit'. From Scottish and dialect clarty (sticky with dirt; sticky; dirty). Also used in the plural UK, 1977

clary noun a clarinet US, 1942 ▷see: JULIAN CLARY

class noun elegant style or behaviour, refined taste, a state of excellence. Originally sports usage UK, 1874

class verb to attend a class US, 2002

class A's noun **1** cocaine, heroin and other drugs that are legally categorised as Class A narcotics UK, 1999. **2** in the US Army, the dress uniform US, 1968

classic adjective **1** excellent US, 1964. **2** handsome, well-dressed US, 1998

classic six noun a common layout of an apartment in Manhattan – two bedrooms, living room, dining room, kitchen and small maid's room US, 2002

class up the ass noun a superlative style US, 1972

classy adjective of superior quality; stylish; having CLASS UK, 1891

classy chassis noun an attractive female body US, 1955

clat noun a dirty person UK: SCOTLAND, 1985

clatch noun your personal belongings ANTARCTICA, 1989

clatter verb to smack someone, to hit someone, to beat someone up UK, 1979

clatters noun a smacking. From CLATTER (to smack) UK, 1979

'clavaed up adjective used when a balaclava helmet is worn UK, 2000

Claven noun someone who purports to know everything. From the Cliff Claven character on the television comedy Cheers US, 1991

claw noun a pickpocket US, 1914

claw verb to pick a glass up from its top US, 1998. ► **claw off a lee shore** to face serious difficulties in a task or project. Nautical origins US, 1963

clay noun **1** a claymore mine US, 1994. **2** tetrahydrocannabinal (THC), the psychoactive ingredient in marijuana US, 1971. **3** hashish US, 1992

clay eater noun a poor rural dweller US, 1841

clay pigeon noun a person who is easily victimised US, 1972

Clayton's noun any substitute for a desired thing NEW ZEALAND, 2002

Clayton's adjective false, pretend, faux. From the proprietary name of a substitute alcoholic drink which was widely advertised as 'the drink you have when you're not having a drink' AUSTRALIA, 1984

clean verb **1** by gambling, fraud or theft, to take all of someone's money. A variant is 'clean out' UK, 1812. **2** to remove seeds, stems and foreign matter from marijuana leaves US, 1967. **3** to rid yourself of altered dice, altered cards or any evidence of cheating US, 1950. **4** in mountain biking, to succeed in negotiating an obstacle or set of obstacles without accident US, 1996. ► **clean it up** to clarify or explain something US, 1942. ► **clean out the kitchen; clean up the kitchen** to perform oral sex on a woman US, 1941. ► **clean road for monkey to run** to labour for someone else's benefit TRINIDAD AND TOBAGO, 2003. ► **clean someone's bones** to thrash or defeat someone soundly in a fight US, 1963. ► **clean someone's clock 1** to severely defeat someone, physically or in a competition US, 1959. **2** in trucking, to pass another vehicle, especially another truck, at high speed US, 1971. ► **clean the books** to induce a criminal to confess to a series of unsolved crimes US, 1984. ► **clean the cage out** to perform oral sex on a woman UK, 2002. ► **clean the clock** on the railways, to make an emergency stop. An allusion to the air gauge that drops to zero in an emergency stop US, 1977. ► **clean the kitchen** to lick your sex-partner's anus UK, 2002. ► **clean the pipes** to ejaculate; to masturbate US, 1998. ► **clean the table** in pool, to shoot all of the remaining balls in one turn US, 1989. ► **clean the tube** (of a male) to masturbate. Using 'tube' to mean 'the penis' US, 2001. ► **clean up the calendar** (used of the police) to extract from a criminal confessions clearing up a number of crimes, regardless of his actual guilt, in exchange for lenient treatment on another crime US, 1992

clean adjective **1** drug-free US, 1949. **2** unarmed US, 1952. **3** innocent; free of suspicion; without a trace of guilt; without a criminal record US, 1925. **4** not subject to police surveillance US, 2003. **5** (used of an illegal betting operation) unafraid of police intervention because of bribes paid to the police US, 1951. **6** excellent, fashionable, stylish US, 1963. **7** (used of a theatrical performance) completely sold out US, 1973. **8** in circus and carnival usage, without value US, 1981. **9** (of an object ball in pool) directly into the pocket without touching a cushion or another ball US, 1993

clean *adverb* completely as in 'He got clean away' or 'I clean forget' *UK, 1999*

clean and ready *adjective* prepared; dressed nicely *US, 1980*

cleaner *noun* **1** in the used car business, a customer who does not have a car to trade in *US, 1956*. **2** a hired killer *US, 2000*. **3** in circus and carnival usage, the person who retrieves money from paid players who have been allowed to win a concession game to drum up business *US, 1981*

cleaners *noun* ► **take someone to the cleaners 1** to thrash someone *UK, 1976*. **2** to thoroughly swindle or rob someone *US, 1907*. **3** to forcibly strip someone *UK, 1996*

clean freak *noun* a person who is obsessed with cleanliness *US, 1967*

cleaning crew *noun* the members of a criminal enterprise who rid the crime scene of possible evidence and at times any bodies resulting from the crime *US, 1997*

cleaning kit *noun* the equipment needed to rid a crime scene of possible evidence *US, 1997*

clean out *verb* to thrash someone *US, 1862*

clean peeler *noun* to a surfer, a perfect wave *US, 1997*

clean sheets *noun* a bed or cot. Vietnam war usage *US, 1991*

cleanskin *noun* **1** a person without a criminal record. Originally applied to an unbranded sheep *AUSTRALIA, 1943*. **2** a novice. From the conventional sense (an unbranded stock animal) *AUSTRALIA, 1907*. **3** a person of integrity, especially in a political context. From the sense of 'a person without a police record' *AUSTRALIA, 1942*. **4** in horse racing, a jockey who has never been disqualified in a race *AUSTRALIA, 1989*

cleansleeve *noun* a low-ranking military recriut *US, 1909*

clean-the-kitchen *noun* corned beef hash *US, 1946*

clean time *noun* the amount of time that has passed since a prisoner was last in trouble *US, 1989*

clean-up *noun* **1** a good alibi *US, 1990*. **2** a wave that breaks seaward of most surfers, causing them to lose their boards and thus cleaning up the area *US, 1964*

clean up *verb* to make a profit, especially a big one *US, 1831*

cleanup team *noun* the members of a criminal enterprise who rid a crime scene of any possible evidence and at times bodies resulting from the crime *US, 1997*

clean wheels *noun* a motor vehicle to be used in crime that has never been previously stolen or come under prior police suspicion in any way *UK, 1977*

clean works *noun* a new needle and syringe. A concept and term new in the age of AIDS *US, 1993*

clear *noun* ► **in the clear** with no evidence against you; therefore, innocent or apparently so *UK, 1934*

clear *verb* to steal something *UK, 1998*. ► **clear the channel** to stop talking *US, 1962*. ► **clear your tubes** to ejaculate; to masturbate *AUSTRALIA, 1985*

clear as mud *adjective* anything but clear; confused *UK, 1842*

clearinghouse *noun* an illegal lottery. More commonly known as a NUMBERS game *US, 1951*

Clear Lake *noun* methamphetamine purportedly manufactured in the Clear Lake region of northern California *US, 1989*

clear light *noun* a stage in some LSD experiences in which the user feels receptive to enlightenment *US, 1971*

clearly! I agree! *US, 2002*

clear off *verb* to depart. Often used as an imperative *UK, 1816*

clearskin *noun* used as a variation of all senses of 'cleanskin' *AUSTRALIA, 1943*

clear-skinned *adjective* with a light complexion *BARBADOS, 1965*

clef *verb* to compose a tune or song *US, 1948*

Clem *noun* in the circus or carnival, a fight with customers *US, 1891*

Clement Freud *noun* a haemorrhoid. Rhyming slang, formed from the name of British writer, broadcaster and politician, Sir Clement Freud (b.1924), father of EMMA FREUD whose name has a synonymous purpose *UK, 2003*

clemo *noun* executive clemency granted to a convicted prisoner *US, 1960*

clennedak *noun* in Quebec, a child's taffy cone (a sweet confection) *CANADA, 1998*

clerk *noun* in American casinos, an exceptionally skilled dealer *US, 1980*

clerks and jerks *noun* clerical support personnel and officers. Vietnam war usage. The high degree of cynicism about officers found in enlisted men was even more intense in Vietnam *US, 1975*

clever *adjective* ► **damned clever these Chinese; dead clever these Chinese; clever chaps these Chinese** a catchphrase used as a comment upon an explanation given about some device or machine, especially if the explanation has not been understood. A back-handed tribute to Chinese ingenuity *US, 1955*

clever bollocks *noun* a clever person *UK, 2001*

clever clogs *noun* a clever person. A variation of 'clever boots' *UK, 1866*

clever creep *noun* a forensic chemist. Police use *UK, 1971*

clever dick *noun* **1** a clever, rather too clever, person. Derisive or sarcastic in use *UK, 1887*. **2** a brick. Rhyming slang *UK, 1992*

clever Dickie *noun* a bricklayer. Rhyming slang for 'brickie', extended from CLEVER DICK (a brick) *UK, 1992*

clever drawers *noun* a knowledgable person. Disparaging *UK, 1966*

cleverguts *noun* a clever person. Childish and sarcastic *UK, 1959*

cleverkins *noun* a clever person *UK, 1937*

cleverly *adverb* (used of a racehorse winning a race) easily *US, 1960*

clever Mike *noun* a bicycle. Rhyming slang for 'bike' *UK, 1961*

clever sticks *noun* a clever person. A variation on the theme of 'clever boots'; often used as a juvenile taunt *UK, 1946*

clevie *noun* the vagina *UK, 2002*

clew up *verb* to hide, to go into hiding. Of naval origins *UK, 1962*

click *noun* **1** a gang. A corrupted spelling of 'clique' *US, 1879*. **2** a kilometer. Also spelt 'klick' or 'klik'. Vietnam war usage *US, 1962*

click *verb* **1** to have a successful encounter with a hitherto unknown member of the opposite sex *UK, 1937*. **2** to get along instantly and famously *UK, 1915*. **3** to suddenly understand something; to suddenly make sense in context *UK, 1939*. **4** to perform at the right moment as needed by a friend *US, 1989*. **5** to enjoy an amorous relationship *IRELAND, 2003*. **6** of a woman, to become pregnant (or in Australia, of a cow) *UK, 1937*. **7** in the theatre or other forms of entertainment, to be a success *US, 1926*. **8** in horse racing, to win a race *US, 1951*. **9** to be well accepted *US, 1982*. **10** to be selected or accepted for a duty or a fate; to be killed. A military colloquialism *UK, 1917*

clicker *noun* **1** crack cocaine mixed with phencyclidine, the recreational drug known as PCP or angel dust *US, 1994*. **2** a brick *US, 1989*. **3** in circus and carnival usage, a free pass *US, 1981*

clickers *noun* false teeth *US, 1950*

clicks *noun* approval; applause *US, 1997*

clicks and mortar; C&M *noun* a business that combines trading from traditonal business premises with Internet-based commerce. A play on 'bricks and mortar', a traditional business *US, 1999*

clientised *adjective* having come to a point of view that is in sympathy with a client's or subject's outlook or situation *UK, 2003*

Cliffie *noun* a student or alumna of Radcliffe College, Harvard University *US, 1961*

C light *noun* in the pornography industry, a light used to illuminate the genitals of the performers. 'C' is in CUNT *US, 1991*

climax *noun* **1** amyl nitrite. Because of the orgasm-enhancing characteristics of the drug *US, 1992*. **2** heroin *UK, 1998*

climb *noun* **1** cat burglary *UK, 1936*. **2** a marijuana cigarette. A climb is necessary if you wish to get HIGH (intoxicated) *US, 1946*

climb *verb* ► **climb the wooden hill; climb the wooden hill to Bedfordshire** to go upstairs to bed. A combination of WOODEN HILL (the stairs) and BEDFORDSHIRE (a bed) *UK, 1984*

climbing trees to get away from it used as a catchphrase reply to the question 'getting any (sexual satisfaction)?' *AUSTRALIA, 1984*

climb into *verb* to criticise someone, to launch a verbal attack on someone *NEW ZEALAND, 1993*

climey *noun* a British social 'climber' in the US, especially New York. A contraction of 'climber' and LIMEY (a Briton) *UK, 1999*

clinch *noun* a prolonged or passionate embrace *US, 1901*

clinch *verb* in bird-watching circles, to identify a rare bird *UK, 1977*

cling *verb* ▸ **cling to the belt** (used of South Vietnamese troops) to stay close to US troops *US, 1988*

clinic *noun* **1** a poker game characterised by over-analysis of each hand *US, 1988*. **2** a poker game played by doctors *US, 1988*

clink *noun* a jail; a police station. Originally an infamous prison in Southwark, London, and then by the mid-C19 applied to any jail, prison or cell *UK, 1785*

clinker *noun* **1** in the entertainment industry, a failure *US, 1961*. **2** a small piece of faeces clinging to anal hairs *UK, 1904*. **3** a wrong note in a musical performance *US, 1937*. **4** a mistake *US, 1937*. **5** a piece of broken-up ice on the water *CANADA, 2001*

clinkeroo *noun* a jail or prison *US, 1992*

clinkers *noun* **1** handcuffs *US, 1949*. **2** leg irons; foot shackles *UK, 1699*

clip *noun* **1** a rate of speed, as in 'a fair old clip' *UK, 1867*. **2** an occurrence or instance *US, 1979*. **3** a blow *UK, 1830*. **4** a swindle or other act of dishonest trickery *US, 1941*. **5** a string of bottles containing doses of crack cocaine *US, 1992*. **6** a vasectomy *US, 1993*. **7** in the circus or carnival, a patron *US, 1980*

clip *verb* **1** to steal something; to swindle someone; to win something, especially through cheating *US, 1922*. **2** to kill someone, especially by gunshot *US, 1928*. **3** to hit someone *US, 1855*. ▸ **clip a steamer** to defecate *US, 2003*

clip and clean *adverb* completely *US, 1975*

clip-a-nines *noun* a 9 mm ammunition clip *US, 2001*

clip girl *noun* an attractive woman employed in a clip joint to encourage customers to part with their money on the promise of (sexual) services to be delivered *UK, 2001*

clip joint; clip dive *noun* a bar, gambling house or other business where customers are routinely cheated *US, 1932*

clip off *verb* (used of ammunition) to explode because of heat from a surrounding fire *US, 1990*

clipped dick *noun* a Jewish person. Derogatory *US, 1960*

clipper *noun* **1** a thief *US, 1954*. **2** a person who collects film clips, usually of a single subject *US, 1978*. **3** a disposable cigarette lighter. A generic from the Clipper™ brand *UK, 1996*

Clipper Club *noun* the abstract brotherhood of men who have undergone a vasectomy *US, 1995*

clippie; clippy *noun* **1** a female conductor on a bus or train. From clipping tickets *UK, 1941*. **2** an employee who checks and clips tickets at railway stations *AUSTRALIA, 1953*

clipping *noun* a robbery facilitated by posing as a prostitute and knocking out the clients with sleeping pills *UK, 1977*

clique *noun* a youth gang. A nuance of the conventional sense *UK, 2003*

clique up *verb* to form small groups *US, 1972*

clit *noun* **1** the clitoris *US, 1958*. **2** a despicable person. A figurative application, similar to PRICK *UK, 1999*

clithopper *noun* a promiscuous lesbian *US, 1982*

clit lit; cliterature *noun* good quality erotica for women. Formed from CLIT (the clitoris) and 'lit' (literature) *US, 1999*

clitoris *noun* any popular model of car. Motor trade slang. Explained as 'every cunt has one' by a car salesman *UK, 1977*

clit ring *noun* a piece of jewellery for a clitoral piercing. As body piercing became more popular through the 1990s this prosaically-named ornamentation, based on an abbreviation of 'clitoris' became a familiar possibility *US, 1995*

clit stick *noun* a small vibrating sex-aid designed for clitoral stimulation. An abbreviation of 'clitoris' combined with the lipstick-sized vibrator's shape *UK, 2002*

clit tease *noun* a heterosexual woman who socialises with lesbians without revealing that she is heterosexual *US, 2002*

clitter *noun* a slap with the open hand. From the Irish *cliotar IRELAND, 2000*

clitty the clitoris *UK, 1866*

clitty clamp *noun* a device that is attached to a clitoris and is designed to cause discomfort or pain in the cause of sexual stimulation *UK, 1995*

clitwobble *noun* a woman's desire for sex *UK, 1998*

cloak *verb* to send an electronic message in a manner that disguises the true origin of the message *US, 1997*

cloak-and-dagger *adjective* very secret; pertaining to espionage *US, 1944*

clobber *noun* clothes, especially any outfit of good or noticeable quality. Probably Yiddish *klbr*, but 'to clobber' is 'to CLOUT' ('to hit' and may also be 'clothing') *UK, 1879*

clobber *verb* **1** to strike someone forcefully *US, 1944*. **2** to criticise someone or something harshly *UK, 1956*. **3** in computing, to overwrite a program *US, 1991*. **4** to impose an onerous duty or unwelcome burden on someone. Usually before 'with'; for example, 'I got clobbered with finishing the weeding' *UK, 1984*

clobbered *adjective* drunk *US, 1951*

clobbering machine *noun* the notional machine that creates conformity *NEW ZEALAND, 1998*

clock *noun* **1** a milometer (odometer) *UK, 1967*. **2** a speedometer *UK, 1942*. **3** a taxi meter. Often in the enquiry 'How much is on the clock?' *UK, 1930*. **4** an air gauge used with air brakes *US, 1946*. **5** a watch. In conventional use from 1559, in slang use since late C19; noted by the *Oxford English Dictionary* as obsolete 'except in modern slang' *UK, 1961*. **6** the face *UK, 1918*. **7** a punch to the face. From the verb *NEW ZEALAND, 1959*. **8** a look. From the verb *UK, 2000*. **9** a one-year prison sentence *AUSTRALIA, 1941*. **10** a prisoner who is at the beginning of their sentence *US, 1962*. **11** bravery, courage *US, 1950*

clock *verb* **1** to catch sight of or notice someone or something; to watch someone or something *US, 1929*. **2** to watch someone patiently; especially to follow someone with the purpose of discovering the details of a bet *UK, 1958*. **3** to keep track of a slot machine in an effort to make an educated guess as to when it will pay off *US, 1984*. **4** to keep track of the money involved in a game or an enterprise *US, 1977*. **5** to register on the speedometer; to attain a particular speed. From CLOCK (a speedometer) *UK, 1892*. **6** to figure something out; to evaluate something *US, 1961*. **7** to earn something *US, 1989*. **8** to punch, to strike with the fist. Perhaps, originally, 'to hit in the CLOCK' (the face) *UK, 1932*. **9** to sell drugs on the street *US, 1992*. **10** to wind back the mileometer (odometer) of a vehicle to increase its sale value *US, 1980*. **11** to identify. After the senses to see and to watch *UK, 2005*. ▸ **clock in** to visit your boyfriend or girlfriend only out of a sense of duty *US, 2004*. ▸ **clock in the green room** while surfing, to take a long ride inside the hollow of a breaking wave *US, 1991*. ▸ **clock the action** to understand what is happening and what is being said *US, 1962*

clock and house *verb* to see and remember suspects' faces, and then follow them to their home. From CLOCK (to see; to watch and follow) *UK, 1977*

clocker *noun* **1** a street drug dealer, especially of crack cocaine *US, 1992*. **2** a watchman or guard, especially one who punches a time clock while making his rounds *US, 1949*. **3** an onlooker *US, 1976*

clocking *noun* a fraudulent act of turning back a vehicle's mileometer (odometer). From the verb CLOCK *UK, 1974*

clock out *verb* to act in a psychotic manner *US, 1989*

clock puncher *noun* an employee whose working day is measured by a time-clock. A worker must 'punch in' and 'punch out' at a time-clock *US, 1932*

clock watcher *noun* **1** an employee who takes care to work only for as long and as hard as is minimally required *UK, 1911*. **2** a person completely lacking in generosity *US, 1956*

clock watching *noun* the act of working no harder, or for no longer, than is minimally required *UK, 1942*

clockweights *noun* the testicles. From the workings of a longcase clock *UK, 2003*

clockwork along *verb* to go smoothly, 'to go like clockwork' *UK, 1990s*

clockworks *noun* the brain *US, 1947*

clocky *noun* sudden waving arm movements of a surfer trying to get his balance *US, 1991*

clod *noun* a stupid person *UK, 1605*

clodbuster *noun* a farmer *US, 1950*

cloddy *noun* a prison officer *UK, 1996*

clodge *noun* the vagina *UK, 2001*

clodhopper *noun* **1** a person with big feet; big feet or big shoes. Evoking the image of a ploughman with large, coarse boots *UK, 1836*. **2** a clumsy person *UK, 1824*. **3** a police officer. Rhyming slang for COPPER; sometimes shortened to 'clod' *UK, 1998*. **4** a copper coin, a penny. Rhyming slang for 'copper'. Sometimes shortened to 'clod' *UK, 1925*

clog *verb* to take a picture with a mobile phone and upload it to a website. A contraction of 'camera' and 'log' *US, 2003*

clog down *adverb* of driving, very fast or accelerating. Military; from the sense of putting your foot down on an accelerator pedal *UK, 1984*

clogger *noun* a footballer who has a reputation for fouling when tackling an opponent *UK, 1970*

cloggie *noun* **1** a clog dancer. Popularised in the late 1960s by *The Cloggies*, a cartoon strip about a clog dancing team, written and drawn by Bill Tidy *UK, 1969*. **2** a Dutch person. Derogatory. Originally military usage, from the extensive use of clogs as a symbol of Netherlands' folk-culture. Also variant 'clog head' *UK, 1987*

cloggy *noun* the Dutch language. From the extensive use of clogs as a symbol of the Netherlands' folk-culture *UK, 1984*

clomp *verb* to walk in a noisy and demonstrative fashion *UK, 1829*

clone *noun* **1** a highly stylised, fashion-conscious homosexual male *US, 1979*. **2** a personal computer that closely duplicates the functions and operations of a leading brand *US, 1991*. **3** a car with an identity that has been fraudulently duplicated from a legitimately registered vehicle *UK, 2005*

clone *verb* **1** to reconfigure a stolen mobile phone so that an existing subscriber is charged for all calls *US, 1994*. **2** to duplicate the detailed identity of one car onto another *UK, 2005*

clonk *verb* to hit someone *US, 1943*

clonked; clonked out *adjective* of a mechanical device, not working. A teenagers' variation of CONKED; CONKED OUT *UK, 1982*

close *verb* ▶ **close the back door** in bombing missions, to provide rear guard protection for the bombers *US, 1990*. ▶ **close the door** in motor racing, to pass another car and then pull sharply in front of it to minimise its chances of passing you *US, 1965*

close *adjective* skilled *US, 1959*

close but no cigar; no cigar *adverb* incorrect. From carnival games giving cigars as prizes *US, 1986*

close call *noun* a near thing, a narrow escape *US, 1881*

closed *adjective* subject to strict law enforcement; unfriendly to criminal enterprises *US, 1969*

closed door *noun* a surf condition where waves are breaking simultaneously all along a beach, creating no shoulder to ride *US, 1963*

closed for maintenance *adjective* in the bleed period of the menstrual cycle *US, 2000*

closed game *noun* a private gambling game, especially poker, usually for high stakes *US, 1992*

close out *verb* (of waves) to become unsuitable for surfing, either because of their size or their breaking pattern *US, 1991*

closer *noun* in a sales team, the individual responsible for the final stages of negotiations *US, 1987*

closet *noun* a person who is secretly homosexual *UK, 2001*. ▶ **in the closet** hidden, not avowed. Almost always applied to homosexuality *US, 1967*. ▶ **on the closet** (of a prisoner and prison officer) to be handcuffed together but separated by a long chain that is intended to reduce embarrassment when using the water closet *UK, 2000*. ▶ **out of the closet** avowed, open *US, 1971*

closet *adjective* hidden, not admitted. Most often but not always, and not first, used in conjunction with homosexuality *US, 1952*

close-talker *noun* a person who speaks to others without respecting the usual cultural protocols on not standing too close to someone you are talking to. A term popularised on Jerry Seinfeld's television programme in an episode called 'The Raincoat Party' first aired on 28th April 1994 *US, 1994*

closet case *noun* **1** a person who is secretly homosexual *US, 1969*. **2** someone to be ashamed of. Teen slang, without any suggestion of the homosexuality later associated with the term *US, 1954*. **3** a potential romantic interest whom you are keeping away from your friends *US, 1955*

closet dyke *noun* a lesbian who conceals her sexual orientation *US, 1967*

closeted *adjective* living with an unrevealed fact, especially homosexuality *US, 1992*

close to the door *adjective* about to be released from prison *US, 1989*

close to the skin *adjective* lacking subcutaneous fat *US, 1984*

closet queen *noun* a male homosexual who conceals his sexual orientation *US, 1957*

close work *noun* sexual activity *US, 1957*

clot *noun* a dolt *UK, 1632*

cloth *noun* ▶ **down to the cloth** (used of a player in a game of poker) almost out of money *US, 1982*

cloth-eared *adjective* deaf *UK, 1965*

cloth-ears *noun* a person with a poor sense of hearing; a person affecting deafness; a condition of convenient deafness. From the ear-flaps on certain headgear *UK, 1912*

clothes *noun* **1** in horse racing, a horse blanket *US, 1951*. **2** a plainclothes police officer or division *US, 1971*

clotheshorse *noun* a person who pays a great deal of attention to fashions and the clothing they wear *US, 1850*

clothesline *noun* the line used to lead a glider plane into the air *US, 1985*

clothes-peg *noun* **1** the leg. Rhyming slang, usually in plural *UK, 1931*. **2** an egg. Rhyming slang *UK, 1961*

clothes queen *noun* a homosexual man who is drawn to ostentatious, flamboyant clothing *US, 1963*

clotted cream *noun* a student at the Royal Agricultural College in Cirencester. A jocular representation of a thick and rich elite *UK, 2004*

clotty *adjective* slovenly, untidy *IRELAND, 2000*

cloud *noun* **1** crack cocaine. From the thick white smoke produced when smoked *US, 1994*. **2** the intoxication from smoking freebase or crack cocaine *US, 1992*

cloudhopper *noun* an air pilot, especially in the bush *CANADA, 1959*

cloud nine *noun* **1** a condition of perfect happiness, euphoria. Probably derives as a variation of CLOUD SEVEN; possibly from US weather forecasting terminology which divides clouds into nine types, the highest being number nine; or, less likely, a spiritual possibility: of the ten names for Buddha, the ninth is 'enlightened one'. It is probable that the US radio adventure series *Johnny Dollar*, 1949–62, popularised the term's usage *US, 1935*. **2** MDMA, the recreational drug best known as ecstasy. From the blissed-out state *UK, 2003*. **3** crack cocaine *US, 1994*

cloud seven *noun* a condition of perfect happiness, euphoria. Derives, possibly, from 'seventh heaven'. Still current but CLOUD NINE attracts more attention *US, 1956*

clout *noun* **1** a heavy blow. Conventional from about 1400, it has slipped into dialect and colloquial use since the C18 *UK, 2003*. **2** power, influence, especially political *US, 1868*

clout *verb* **1** to hit a person with a heavy blow of your hand. Conventional from early C14, by late C19 had slipped into dialect and colloquial use *UK, 2000*. **2** to rob or steal something *UK, 1708*. **3** to fail to bet a debt *AUSTRALIA, 1989*. **4** to arrest someone *US, 1992*

clouter *noun* a thief who steals from parked cars *US, 1993*

clouting *noun* the palming of cards *AUSTRALIA, 1953*

clover *noun* money *US, 1951*

clown *noun* **1** a fool, an incompetent person *US, 1898*. **2** in carnival usage, a local police officer *US, 1929*. **3** a railway pointsman or yard brakeman *US, 1946*

clown alley *noun* on a circus lot, the area of tents where performers, especially clowns, dress and live *US, 1956*

clown bookie *noun* a bookmaker who operates in carnivals *AUSTRALIA, 1989*

clown wagon *noun* a brakevan (caboose) *US, 1931*

club *noun* **1** in pool, a heavier-than-usual cue stick *US, 1990*. **2** in trucking, a dilapidated trailer *US, 1971*. ▶ **in the club** pregnant. A shortening of IN THE PUDDING CLUB *UK, 1890*. ▶ **put someone in the club** to make someone pregnant *UK, 1943*

club *verb* to spend an evening in a nightclub or several nightclubs *US, 1964*

clubber *noun* a patron of nightclubs *US, 2003*

clubbers' cold *noun* a runny nose, as a side-effect of drug use *UK, 1999*

clubbie *noun* a beach lifeguard. An abbreviation of 'life-saving *club*' *AUSTRALIA, 1977*

club-crawl *verb* to move as a group of friends from one nightclub to another *US, 1994*

Club Fed *noun* a minimum-security, well-equipped federal prison housing white-collar criminals, especially the federal prison camp in Lompoc, California. A punning reference to Club Med, a group of holiday resorts *US, 1985*

club-fight *verb* to engage in youth gang warfare *US, 1949*

club-hop *verb* to move from one nightclub to another, especially with a group of friends *US, 1997*

clubhouse lawyer *noun* an athlete who is quick to criticise his team's management when presented with an audience of fellow players *US, 1937*

club kid *noun* a fashionable, attractive young person paid to attend a nightclub in the hope of attracting others *US, 1995*

clubland *noun* an area of London bounded by and mainly comprising St James's Street and Pall Mall; subsequently, with the coming of nightclubs and club culture, any area where a number of clubs are to be found *UK, 1885*

club sandwich *noun* sex involving three people at once. Surviving in the shortened form of a simple 'sandwich' *US, 1970*

club widow *noun* a woman whose husband's pursuits at a country club or other club often leave her at home alone *US, 1928*

clubzine *noun* a single-interest fan magazine published by a fan club *US, 1982*

cluck *noun* **1** a gullible fool *US, 1906*. **2** a crack cocaine user *US, 1994*. **3** counterfeit money *US, 1949*

cluck *verb* to withraw from any drug. Perhaps this derives from a confused attempt at the sound of a COLD TURKEY (the withdrawal period and its symptoms) *UK, 1996*

cluck and grunt *noun* ham and eggs *US, 1972*

clucker *noun* **1** in the urban drug culture, someone who brings buyers to sellers *US, 2002*. **2** a fool *US, 1945*. **3** the two halves of a scallop shell still closed after the scallop has died of natural causes *CANADA, 1955*

cluckhead *noun* a crack cocaine addict *US, 1995*

cluckiness *noun* the state of wanting to be pregnant *AUSTRALIA, 1985*

clucking *adjective* showing an addict's hunger for drugs, especially crack cocaine *UK, 1996*

clucky *adjective* **1** (of a hen) to be sitting on an egg or eggs. This term was in use in the US in the 1940s, but persists in Canadian country areas *CANADA, 1916*. **2** (of a woman) showing signs of pregnancy or of an intense desire for children. Extended from the conventional use referring to a broody hen. Originally and especially used of women, but now also of men *AUSTRALIA, 1941*

cludgie; cludge *noun* a (public) lavatory. Scottish dialect, now in wider use *UK, 1985*

clue *noun* ▶ **have no clue; not have a clue; haven't a clue** to be ignorant. As in the title of a BBC Radio 4 programme, *I'm Sorry, I Haven't a Clue*, on air since 1981 *UK, 1948*

clue; clue in *verb* to inform someone, to update someone *UK, 1948*

clued up *adjective* well-informed *UK, 1970*

clueless *adjective* unaware, especially of fashion, music and other social trends *UK, 1943*

clue up *verb* to brief someone, to inform someone *UK, 1984*

cluey *noun* a well-informed person *AUSTRALIA, 1968*

cluey *adjective* wise; in the know *AUSTRALIA, 1967*

clump *noun* **1** a person whose main talent is hitting other people *UK, 2000*. **2** a heavy blow with the hand *UK, 1889*

clump *verb* to hit someone heavily, to thump someone *UK, 1999*

clumping *adjective* used as an occasional variant of 'thumping' (large) *UK, 1984*

clumsome; clumbsome *noun* in electric line work, a worker who is not a journeyman lineman but who claims some climbing experience. From the worker's claim that while not a journeyman, he has 'clumb some' *US, 1942*

clumsy as a cub-bear handling his prick *adjective* very clumsy indeed *CANADA, 1984*

clunk *noun* **1** an ill-bred or ill-mannered person; a fool *US, 1929*. **2** a man *AUSTRALIA, 1948*

clunk *nickname* ▶ **the clunk** a CF-100 Canuck jet fighter aircraft. The aircraft first flew in 1950, and is also known as ALUMINIUM CROW and LEAD SLED *CANADA, 1994*

clunk!; ker-lunk! used for approximating the sound of a hard object hitting another. As in Jimmy Saville's catchphrase 'Clunk click every trip', in public information films of the 1970s, in which 'clunk' represents a car door closing and 'click' a seatbelt slotting home *UK, 1823*

clunker *noun* **1** an old, beat-up car. The original military usage in the 1940s applied to any old vehicle or machine. By the 1960s, applied almost exclusively to a car *US, 1942*. **2** an inferior item *US, 1971*

clunkhead *noun* a dolt *US, 1952*

clunky *adjective* awkward, clumsy, inelegant *US, 1968*

clusterfuck *noun* **1** group sex, heterosexual or homosexual *US, 1966*. **2** a disorganised, chaotic situation *US, 1969*

clusterscrew *noun* chaos; monumental lack of organisation *US, 1976*

clutch *noun* **1** a despised person *US, 1961*. **2** in poker, a hand that is certain to win *US, 1967*

clutch *verb* ▶ **clutch the gummy** to be caught and blamed for something. An elaboration of HOLD THE BAG *US, 1960*

clutch *adjective* **1** serving as a replacement. Korean war usage *US, 1957*. **2** unkind *US, 1991*

clutched *adjective* scared, anxious *US, 1952*

Clyde *noun* **1** a misfit; an outcast *US, 1950*. **2** during the Vietnam war, a Viet Cong or North Vietnamese regular *US, 1966*. **3** used to refer to any object the name of which you cannot remember or do not know *US, 1992*. ▶ **as deep and dirty as the Clyde** used of someone who is devious, dishonest, secretive or untrustworthy. Glasgow use, formed on the name of its river *UK: SCOTLAND, 1985*

C-man *noun* a sexually successful male student. An abbreviation of 'cunt-man' or COCKSMAN *US, 1968*

c'mon 1 used to solicit a reasonable or common-sense response. Also used in the long form 'come on' *UK, 2002*. **2** used imperatively in a citizens' band radio transmission to request a reply *US, 1976*

C-note noun **1** a one hundred dollar note *US, 1930.* **2** a prison sentence of 100 years *US, 1990*

C-note charlie noun in a casino, a gambler who insists on betting with hundred-dollar notes, not betting chips *US, 1949*

CNS-QNS (in doctors' shorthand) unintelligent. An initialism of 'central nervous system – quantity not sufficient'; medical slang *UK, 2003*

coachman's knob noun an erection of the penis caused by the vibrations whilst travelling on public transport *UK, 2003*

coal noun a marijuana cigarette *US, 1993.* ► **burn coal; deal in coal** (of a white person) to have sex with a black person *US, 1922*

coal and coke; coals and coke adjective penniless. Rhyming slang for BROKE *UK, 1937*

coal candy noun hard black licorice *US, 1997*

coal cracker noun a resident of the anthracite coal region of northeastern Pennsylvania *US, 1997*

coalface noun ► **at the coalface** used to signify the place where actual work is done (as opposed to management or administration). A figurative use of the mining reality *UK, 1995*

coal hole noun **1** a coal mine, especially a closed mine *US, 1997.* **2** the anus *UK, 2003*

coalie noun a wharf labourer who loads and unloads coal *AUSTRALIA, 1882*

coalman's sack adjective very dirty. Rhyming slang for 'black' *UK, 1992*

coalminer's breakfast noun a shot of whisky served in a glass of beer *US, 1990*

coal oil noun kerosene *US, 1980*

Coaly noun the devil *US, 1950*

Coast noun ► **the Coast 1** the west coast of the US *US, 1930.* **2** the northwest coast of Tasmania *AUSTRALIA, 1987*

coast verb **1** to idle; to relax *US, 1981.* **2** to relax and experience the effects of a drug *US, 1969*

coaster noun someone who lives near the beach; a surfer *US, 1982*

Coastie; Coasty noun a member of the US Coast Guard; a Coast Guard ship *US, 1970*

coasting adjective drug-intoxicated to a pleasant degree *US, 1936*

coast-to-coast noun a powerful amphetamine or other central nervous system stimulant. Purportedly strong enough to keep a truck driver awake long enough to drive the 3000 miles from coast to coast *US, 1969*

coat noun ► **on the coat** ostracised. Tugging on the lapel of the coat was used as a signal to be silent to criminals *AUSTRALIA, 1940*

coat verb **1** to belittle someone, to defeat someone with words. From the sense 'to reprimand someone' *UK, 1997.* **2** to reprimand someone, especially of a warder reprimanding a prisoner *UK, 1996.* **3** to ostracise someone *AUSTRALIA, 1973.* **4** in tournament pool, to obscure the view of the tournament judge when making a shot, thus jeopardising the point *US, 1972*

coat and badge noun ► **on the coat and badge** scrounging; on the cadge. Rhyming slang, from the verb COAT AND BADGE (to cadge) *UK, 1960*

coat and badge verb to cadge something. Rhyming slang, formed on Doggett's Coat and Badge Race, the oldest annual sporting event in Britain, a boat race from London Bridge to Chelsea, first contested by Thames watermen in 1715 and continuing still *UK, 1936*

coathanger noun **1** in rugby, a straight-arm, neck-high tackle *NEW ZEALAND, 1998.* **2** a horizontal branch that needs to be removed from trees destined for timber *NEW ZEALAND, 1988*

coathanger nickname the Sydney Harbour Bridge *AUSTRALIA, 1943*

coat of varnish noun a reprimand; a prison sentence. An elaboration of COAT (to reprimand) *UK, 1956*

coat puller noun someone who tips in return for a favour and in the hope of future favours *AUSTRALIA, 1989*

coaxer noun in horse racing, a battery-powered device used illegally by a jockey to shock a horse during a race *US, 1951*

cob noun **1** a mate, a friend. Shortening of COBBER *AUSTRALIA, 1960.* **2** the penis, literally and in the figurative sense of a disagreeable man *US, 1954.* **3** the testicle *UK: NORTHERN IRELAND, 1968.* **4** prison food, originally and especially bread. From a 'cob loaf' *UK, 1996.* **5** brown skin *BARBADOS, 1998.* ► **have a cob on; get a cob on** to be annoyed, moody or angry; to become annoyed, moody or angry. First recorded as Merchant Navy slang, then Royal Navy before more general usage; possibly northern dialect in origin *UK, 1937.* ► **off the cob** overly sentimental. A play on words to achieve 'corny' *US, 1935*

cobalt bomb noun a nuclear device to enable the use of cobalt in medicine *CANADA, 1953*

Cobar shower noun **1** a dust storm. Cobar is an inland town in New South Wales. Other locations similarly used by nature, weather and irony: Bourke, Bogan, Bedourie, Darling, Wilcannia and Wimmera *AUSTRALIA, 1945.* **2** a flower. Rhyming slang *AUSTRALIA, 1945*

cobb noun lung phlegm *US, 2003*

cobber noun a mate, friend, companion. Perhaps originally the agent noun of the Suffolk dialect *cob* (to take a liking to a person). The Yiddish *chaber* (comrade) seems a less likely source. Formerly extremely common but now more well known than actually used *AUSTRALIA, 1893*

cobber dobber noun a person who informs on a friend, workmate or the like. As appealing as this rhyming couplet seems it never attained great popularity *AUSTRALIA, 1966*

cobber up verb to become friends with someone *AUSTRALIA, 1918*

cobbing noun a beating. Listed as 'obsolete' and 'of nautical origin' by the *Oxford English Dictionary*, this term is still in use in the Canadian Maritime Provinces *UK, 1769*

cobbler noun a forger of official documents *US, 1982*

cobblers noun nonsense. From the earlier sense (testicles) *UK, 1955.* ► **load of cobblers; load of old cobblers** nonsense; lies. An elaboration, but not necessarily an intensification, of COBBLERS (nonsense) *UK, 1968*

cobbler's awls; cobbler's stalls; cobblers noun the testicles. Rhyming slang for BALLS (the testicles) *UK, 1936*

cobblers to you! used for expressing rejection of someone. Originally, a euphemistic application of testicles in a form in which BALLS! and BOLLOCKS! also serve. Now so inoffensive that it has been co-opted by shoe-repairers *UK, 1974*

cobitis noun a dislike of prison food. A combination of COB (prison food) and the suffix -ITIS (used to create imaginary medical conditions) *UK, 1950*

COBOL Charlie noun in computing, a COBOL programmer who can use the language but does not fully understand how it works *US, 1990*

coby noun morphine *US, 1992*

coca; coka noun cocaine *US, 1986*

cocaine-voucher noun a currency note. A contemporary variation on BEER VOUCHERS *UK, 2002*

cochornis noun marijuana *US, 1980*

cock noun **1** the penis. Probably from 'cock' (a male bird) *UK, 1450.* **2** the vagina *US, 1867.* **3** used as a male-to-male term of address. Decidedly casual *UK, 1837.* **4** a man who buys more than his share of drinks in a public house or club so as to have company pleasing to him *UK, 1977.* **5** rubbish, nonsense. From 'poppycock' (nonsense) or 'cock and bull story' (a fictitious narrative) *UK, 1937.* **6** a man who fights without restraint *US, 1964.* ► **cocks on the block** used in various phrases and injunctions to define a display of courage or determination. A macho piece of office jargon that is not gender-specific in use *UK, 2005.* ► **get cock** to have sex *US, 1972.* ► **give six inches of hot cock** from a male perspective, to have sex. The measurement is flexible *UK, 1974*

cock verb **1** to have sex *US, 1973.* **2** to prepare an aircraft for take-off *US, 1986.* **3** to trick someone; to outsmart someone *GUYANA, 1975.* ► **cock a deaf 'un** to pretend not to hear someone; or deliberately not listen to, or ignore someone. A variant, possibly a mishearing, of COP A DEAF 'UN *UK, 1973*. ▶ **cock ten** to sit with your legs crossed as others work *GUYANA, 1996*

cock! used as an expression of displeasure *CANADA, 1993*

cockadau *verb* to kill someone. On loan from Vietnamese *US, 1987*

cock-a-doodle-don't *noun* a condom. Contrived play on COCK (the penis) and the feathered variety's crow; possibly informed by DOODLE (the penis) and, less likely, 'doodle' (to make a fool of) *UK, 1998*

cockaleekie *adjective* impudent, cheeky. Rhyming slang, formed on a type of soup *UK, 1998*

cockalize; kokalize *verb* to thrash someone *US, 1947*

cock-almighty *noun* the best. Obsolete euphemism of 'cock' for 'God', hence 'God almighty', with reference to more modern nuances of COCK (chief, man, etc.) *UK, 1999*

cockamamie; cockamamy *adjective* implausible, not credible. Neither Yiddish nor Hebrew, but born of Jewish immigrants in the US *US, 1941*

cock and bull story *noun* a fanciful, exaggerated or outright untrue story *US, 1795*

cockapoo *noun* a crossbreed of cocker spaniel and poodle *US, 2001*

cockatoo *noun* **1** a person acting as lookout, especially for an illegal activity. Flocks of feeding cockatoos often have one or more birds posted up high as sentries to warn of approaching danger *AUSTRALIA, 1827*. **2** a small-scale farmer *AUSTRALIA, 1845*

cockatoo *verb* to act as a lookout *AUSTRALIA, 1954*

cockatoo farmer *noun* a small-scale farmer *AUSTRALIA, 1849*

cockatooing *noun* the act or job of being a lookout *AUSTRALIA, 1945*

Cockbang *noun* Bangkok, Thailand. Offensive to Thai people. A near-Spoonerism that aptly describes Bangkok's reputation and role as a sex destination *US, 1991*

cock bite *noun* an unpleasant person *US, 1971*

cockblock *verb* to interfere with someone's intentions to have sex *US, 1971*

cock book *noun* a sexually explicit book *US, 1968*

cock cap *noun* a condom. Combines COCK (the penis) with protective wear *UK, 1998*

cock cheese *noun* smegma *UK, 1961*

cock chokers *noun* a pair of men's close-fitting and revealing nylon swimming trunks *AUSTRALIA, 2003*

cock Corpsman *noun* a military doctor or medic who inspects male recruits for signs of sexually transmitted disease *US, 1964*

cock custard *noun* semen *UK, 2001*

cock-diesel *adjective* muscular *US, 1988*

cockeater *noun* a person who enjoys performing oral sex on men *US, 1967*

cocked *adjective* drunk *US, 1737*

cocked hat *noun* an informer; an untrustworthy person. Rhyming slang for RAT *UK, 1992*

cocker *noun* **1** the penis *US, 1967*. **2** a man. From the Yiddish *kakker*; used with a lack of kindness *US, 1946*. **3** used as a male-to-male form of address *UK, 1888*. **4** a cockroach *AUSTRALIA, 1953*

cockernee *noun* a Cockney; a Londoner. A jocular attempt at Cockney pronunciation; a Cockney is anyone born within the sound of Bow Bells, although world usage has moved the boundaries to include all of a vaguely defined London *UK, 1999*

cockers-p *noun* a cocktail party *UK, 1983*

cockerwitter *noun* a person from the Woods Harbor and Shag Harbor areas of Shelburne County, Nova Scotia. The name is derived from Cockerwit Passage, the narrow strip of navigable water between Woods Harbour and Soloman, Vigneau, and St John Islands *CANADA, 1979*

cock eye *noun* a wink *TRINIDAD AND TOBAGO, 2003*

cock-eye Bob; cock-eyed Bob; cocky Bob *noun* a sudden squall or thunderstorm in northwest Australia. Occasionally shortened to 'cock-eye' *AUSTRALIA, 1894*

cock-eyed *adjective* **1** squint-eyed *UK, 1821*. **2** drunk. First recorded by Benjamin Franklin *US, 1737*. **3** absurd, ridiculous, topsy-turvy *UK, 1896*

cock-eyes *noun* in craps, a three *US, 1968*

cockfest *noun* a party with many more males than females in attendance *US, 2001*

cock-happy *adjective* over-confident *UK, 1959*

cock hound *noun* a man obsessed with sex *US, 1947*

cockie *noun* the penis. An elaboration of COCK *UK, 2001* ▷*see:* COCKY

cockiness *noun* a personal quality of smug over-confidence *UK, 1864*

cocking stocking *noun* a condom *UK, 1998*

cock it on; cock on *verb* to exaggerate; to overcharge someone. The supplement to the 5th edition of Partridge's *Dictionary of Slang and Unconventional English* records this term as occurring since about 1910 and in virtual disuse by 1960 *UK, 1961*

cock it up *verb* **1** to make a complete mess of something *UK, 1979*. **2** (of a woman) to offer yourself sexually *AUSTRALIA, 1961*

cock jacket *noun* a reputation for sexual prowess *US, 1984*

cock-jockey *noun* a man who thinks that sex is more important than anything else and that his contribution is paramount *UK, 2002*

cock jocks *noun* a pair of men's close-fitting and revealing nylon swimming trunks *AUSTRALIA, 2003*

cock-knocker *noun* a despised person *US, 1959*

cockle and hen *noun* ten shillings; ten pounds; in betting, odds of 10–1; in prison, a ten year sentence; in Bingo (also House and Tombola), the number ten. Rhyming slang; usually as 'cockle', which is a slovening of 'cockerel'. Other variants include 'cockle', 'cock and hen', 'cocks and 'en' and 'cockun' *UK, 1960*

cockleburr *noun* any central nervous system stimulant *US, 1976*

cockle to a penny *noun* in gambling, odds of 10–1. Rhyming slang, combining COCKLE AND HEN (ten) and PENNY BUN (one); mainly in racecourse use *UK, 1984*

cock linnet *noun* a minute. Rhyming slang, formed on the singing bird that is a familiar symbol of Cockney mythology *UK, 1909*

cock, lock and rock *verb* to prepare for and go into armed conflict. A variation of 'lock and load' *UK, 2001*

cock loft *noun* the observation tower of a brakevan (caboose) *US, 1946*

cockmaster *noun* a male proud of his sexual prowess *US, 1951*

cockmeat *noun* the penis, specifically or as a generality *US, 1995*

cock movie *noun* a pornographic film *US, 1967*

cock off! go away! *UK, 2003*

cock of the walk *noun* an important man in any given circumstance. A fighting cock allows no other into its enclosure or 'walk' *UK, 1855*

cockpit *noun* **1** the vagina *UK, 1891*. **2** the clitoris *US, 1982*

cockpit queen *noun* a flight attendant who is more interested in the men flying the plane than doing her job with the passengers *US, 2002*

cockrag *noun* a loincloth *AUSTRALIA, 1964*

cock ring *noun* a device worn on the penis to enhance sexual performance *US, 1977*

cockroach *noun* **1** a white person *TRINIDAD AND TOBAGO, 2003*. **2** a motor coach. Rhyming slang *UK, 1960*. **3** a racing greyhound that never wins *AUSTRALIA, 1989*

cockroach *verb* to steal something. Hawaiian youth usage *US, 1981*

cockroach bite *noun* any lip sore *TRINIDAD AND TOBAGO, 1996*

cockroach killers *noun* pointed shoes or boots *US, 1970*

cock robin *noun* the penis *UK, 1977*

cock rock *noun* aggressively macho heavy rock music performed with pelvic-thrusting posturing. Combines COCK (the penis) and 'rock' *US, 1992*

cock rocker *noun* a performer of cock rock *UK, 2000*

cock rot *noun* an unspecified sexually transmitted disease *US, 1990*

cocksman *noun* **1** a man who prides himself on his sexual prowess *US, 1896.* **2** a male prostitute *US, 1970*

cocksmith *noun* a sexually expert man *US, 1959*

cock-sparrow *adjective* mad. Rhyming slang for YARRA (mad, stupid) *AUSTRALIA, 1973*

cockstand; stand *noun* an erection *UK, 1866*

cocksuck *noun* an act of oral sex on a man *US, 1940*

cocksuck *verb* to perform oral sex on a man *US, 1977*

cocksucker *noun* **1** used as a generalised term of abuse for a despicable person *US, 1918.* **2** a person who performs oral sex on a man, especially a male homosexual. The most well-known use of the term in the US is in a statement attributed to former President Richard Nixon, who upon learning of the death of FBI Director J. Edgar Hoover on 2nd May 1972, is reported to have said 'Jesus Christ! That old cocksucker!'. Nixon was reflecting the widespread belief that Hoover was homosexual *UK, 1891.* **3** a person who performs oral sex on a woman *US, 1942.* **4** during the Vietnam war, a leech. Especially the huge, reddish-black, slimy leeches of the Mekong Delta *US, 1991.* ▶ **third assistant cocksucker at a Mongolian clusterfuck** a lowly assistant *US, 1977*

cocksucker red *adjective* a bright red shade of lipstick. Not a brand name. Garish and conveying a low-life, whorish image *US, 1982*

cocksucker's teeth *noun* used as the epitome of uselessness *US, 1972*

cocksucking *noun* oral sex performed on a man *UK, 1895*

cocksucking *adjective* despicable, loathsome *US, 1902*

cocktail *noun* **1** a marijuana cigarette, partially smoked and inserted into a regular cigarette *US, 1966.* **2** cocaine *UK, 2003.* **3** any mixture of drugs *CANADA, 2002*

cocktail *verb* to insert a partially smoked marijuana cigarette into a tobacco cigarette *US, 1960*

cocktailery *noun* a cocktail lounge *US, 1981*

cocktail hour *noun* the time when all patients in a hospital ward are given medication *US, 1946*

cocktail party *noun* the use of Molotov cocktails *US, 1979*

cock tax *noun* spousal support; alimony *AUSTRALIA, 1964*

cocktease *noun* a cockteaser *US, 1981*

cocktease *verb* to tempt a man with the suggestion of sex *UK, 1957*

cockteaser *noun* a sexually attractive woman who flaunts her sexuality *UK, 1891*

cock-up *noun* an error, a mistake. A number of etymologies have been suggested, among them: bookkeeping amendments written at a tilt, and the 'cock' (spigot) of ale-barrels; while it is possible that the origins lurk in such innocence it is certain that modern usage is influenced by 'fuck-up', 'balls-up', etc., which presumes 'cock' is a 'penis' *UK, 1948.* ▶ **couldn't organise a cock-up in a brothel** used of an inefficient person. A later variation of COULDN'T ORGANISE A FUCK IN A BROTHEL with a neat pun on COCK-UP (an error) and COCK (the penis) *UK, 2001*

cock up *verb* to make a mess of something; to make a mistake. Military in origin *UK, 1974*

cockwood *noun* firewood stolen from work. Coalminers' use *UK, 1984*

cocky *adjective* over-confident; smug; arrogant. From the strutting nature of the rooster *UK, 1768*

cocky; cockie *noun* **1** a cockroach *AUSTRALIA, 1984.* **2** a cockatoo. Occasionally used loosely of other parrots. Frequently as a name for a pet cockatoo *AUSTRALIA, 1834.* **3** a sheep which has lost some of its wool *AUSTRALIA, 1959.* **4** a small-scale farmer. Often preceded by the crop or livestock farmed, such as COW COCKY and SPUD COCKY *AUSTRALIA, 1871.* **5** used as a term of endearment; hence as a more general form of address *UK, 1687.* ▶ **like cocky on the biscuit tin** left out; on the outside looking in. Referring to Arnott's™ biscuits which have since at least 1910 had a logo of a parrot eating a biscuit adorning their biscuit tins *AUSTRALIA, 1970.* ▶ **like the**

bottom of a cocky's cage (of the mouth or tongue) in a disgusting state from being hungover *AUSTRALIA, 1986*

cocky dickie *noun* an over-confident individual *UK, 2003*

cocky's crow *noun* dawn. Extended from a conventional 'cock's crow', playing on COCKY (a small-scale farmer) *AUSTRALIA, 1945*

cocky's joy *noun* **1** golden syrup or treacle *AUSTRALIA, 1902.* **2** rum *AUSTRALIA, 1953*

cocky's string *noun* fencing wire, especially number eight fencing wire. From COCKY (a small-scale farmer) *NEW ZEALAND, 1998*

co-co *noun* cocaine *US, 1997*

cocoa *noun* semen. In the phrase 'come your cocoa' *UK, 1984.* ▶ **come cocoa** to make a complete confession of guilt *UK, 1977*

cocoa puff *noun* a combination of marijuana and cocaine *UK, 2003*

cocoa puff *verb* to smoke cocaine mixed with marijuana. Punning on a branded breakfast cereal *UK, 1998*

cocobay on top of yaws *noun* more trouble than you can handle *GUYANA, 1996*

cocolo *noun* the penis *TRINIDAD AND TOBAGO, 2003*

coconut *noun* **1** a Mexican-American who rejects his heritage and seeks to blend in with the white majority. Like a coconut, brown on the outside but white on the inside *US, 1974.* **2** a black or Indian person who is considered to have exchanged heritage and community values for acceptance by white society. A coconut is brown on the outside, white on the inside *UK, 1981.* **3** an Australian Aboriginal who has adopted the values of white society *AUSTRALIA, 1980.* **4** a Pacific Islander *NEW ZEALAND, 1964.* **5** a clod, a dolt *US, 1965.* **6** cocaine *US, 1994*

coconuts *noun* **1** cocaine *US, 1952.* **2** money *US, 1981*

coconut tackle *noun* in rugby, a head-high tackle *NEW ZEALAND, 1998*

coconut telegraph *noun* the informal way in which news travels in the Caribbean *US, 1989*

cocoon *verb* to stay at home enjoying sedentary activities *US, 1987*

coco rocks; cocoa rocks *noun* crack cocaine combined in its production with a chocolate-flavoured milk powder *UK, 2003*

Coco the Clown *noun* cocaine. A disguise for CO-CO; formed from the professional name (sometimes 'CoCo') of Latvian-born Nicolai Polakovs, 1900–74, who, for forty years from 1930, worked for Bertram Mills' Circus and became the best-known clown in the UK; subsequently the name has become almost a generic for any clown *UK, 2002*

COD *noun* the product a male prostitute sells – cock on demand *UK, 1987*

cod *verb* to hoax someone, to fool someone *UK, 1864*

cod *adjective* **1** mock, parodic, ersatz. Originally theatrical; usually in combination with the term that is being qualified *UK, 2000.* **2** bad. Variants include 'codalina', 'codette' and 'codettareenaronee' *UK, 1968*

cod and hake; cod *noun* the penis. Rhyming slang for TROUSER SNAKE *UK, 2003*

coddy *noun* ▷see: LUCODDY

coddy; cody *adjective* bad, amateurish. An elaboration of COD *UK, 1993*

code brown *noun* used as a vaguely humorous notification that a hospital patient has defecated. An allusion to the colour code jargon heard in hospitals *US, 1989*

code R *noun* rape. Prison slang *NEW ZEALAND, 1999*

code red *noun* in the military, punishment meted out by a group to soldiers to a non-conforming peer *US, 1992*

code two *noun* an escape from prison *CANADA, 1976*

codfish flats *noun* a poor section of town *US, 1969*

codger *noun* a pleasantly eccentric old man. Often found as 'old codger' *UK, 1756*

codi *noun* a codeine tablet *UK, 1968*

codjocks *noun* a pair of men's close-fitting and revealing nylon swimming trunks *AUSTRALIA, 2003*

cod ogle *noun* a contact lens *UK, 1992*

codology *noun* nonsense *IRELAND, 1997*

cod-riah *noun* a wig *UK, 1992*

cods *noun* **1** the testicles *UK, 1632*. **2** courage, daring. Synonymous with BALLS *US, 1972*. **3** a mess, a state of confusion. Possibly rhyming slang for 'cod and skate', STATE *UK, 1994*

cod's roe *noun* money. Rhyming slang for DOUGH *UK, 1998*

codswallop; cods *noun* nonsense *UK, 1963*

Cod War *noun* **1** the political friction in the early to mid-1970s between Britain and Iceland, especially between the British and Icelandic fishing fleets and fishermen, over the fishing rights off Iceland. A journalists' term that allowed the consequent pun: 'Cod peace'. *UK, 1970s*. **2** a female prisoner *US, 1949*

coeey *noun* a rat. English gypsy use *UK, 2000*

coey *noun* a thing; any object *UK, 1979*

C of E; church boys *noun* HM Customs & Excise. A play on the initial similarity to the Church of England *UK, 2000*

coffee *noun* LSD. A euphemism created in Boston, alluding to the fact that LSD was often sold in Cambridge coffee houses *US, 1967*

coffee-and *noun* a light meal *US, 1901*

coffee-and *adjective* small-time, insignificant *US, 1937*

coffee-and-cakes *noun* a small salary *US, 1925*

coffee and tea; coffee *noun* the sea. Rhyming slang *UK, 1992*

coffee grinder *noun* **1** in oil drilling, a worn-out rig *US, 1954*. **2** a sexual dancer who makes grinding motions with her pelvis *US, 1960*

coffeehouse *verb* in poker, to try to deceive your opponents by idle speech and deliberate mannerisms *US, 1949*

coffeemate *noun* any central nervous system stimulant. Punning on a non-dairy coffee cream-substitute *US, 1976*

coffee pot *noun* a restaurant *US, 1928*

coffee shop *noun* a café-style business open for the smoking, or other consumption, of marijuana in its various forms. Originally in Amsterdam *NETHERLANDS, 2003*

coffee stalls *noun* the testicles. Rhyming slang for BALLS; not as popular as ORCHESTRA STALLS *UK, 1961*

coffin *noun* **1** a surfing manoeuvre in which the surfer lines prone on the board, his arms crossed over his chest *AUSTRALIA, 1963*. **2** in skateboarding, a manoeuvre in which the rider lies completely horizontally on the board, feet first *US, 1964*. **3** the canvas bag used to carry cricket equipment *NEW ZEALAND, 1993*. **4** a case housing weapons *US, 1978*. **5** a safe within a safe *US, 1949*. **6** in poker, the smallest possible raise in a game with a limited number of raises permitted *US, 1967*

coffin box *noun* in trucking, a sleeping compartment added onto a conventional cab *US, 1971*

coffin corner *noun* in battle, a vulnerable position *US, 1995*

coffin-dodger *noun* an old or elderly person, especially if infirm. UK medical slang *UK, 1998*

coffin hoist *noun* in electric line work, any type of chain hoist *US, 1980*

coffin lid *noun* a child. Rhyming slang for KID *UK, 2000*

coffin nail *noun* a cigarette. From the link between smoking cigarettes and death. In the C19, it referred to 'a cigar' *US, 1900*

coffin spike *noun* a cigar *US, 1973*

coffin tank *noun* a motorcyle petrol tank shaped like a coffin *US, 1970s*

cog *verb* to copy from another's work *TRINIDAD AND TOBAGO, 2003*

cogger *noun* a Catholic *UK, 1966*

Coggy *adjective* Catholic, especially Roman Catholic *UK, 2002*

cogs *noun* sunglasses *US, 1945*

cog-stripper *noun* in trucking, a driver who has problems shifting gears *US, 1971*

cohangas *noun* the testicles, literally and figuratively as a measure of courage. An intentional butchering of the Spanish *cojones US, 1992*

coin *noun* money *UK, 1820*

coin *verb* to earn an amount of money *US, 1946*

coin it; coin it in *verb* to make money, especially easily or quickly. From the earlier 'coin money' *UK, 1984*

coinkidink *noun* a coincidence. Multiple creative spellings are to be found *US, 1979*

coin-op *noun* a coin-operated pool table *US, 1990*

COIO *noun* a Canadian whose origins are in India *CANADA, 2002*

cojones *noun* the testicles; courage. From Spanish *US, 1932*

coke *noun* **1** cocaine *US, 1903*. **2** crack cocaine. From the previous sense *UK, 2000*

coke bar; coke joint *noun* a bar, club or pub where cocaine or crack cocaine is used openly, *2002*

coke biscuit *noun* a pill of MDMA, the recreational drug best known as ecstasy. Presumably marketed, illegally, under this name to tempt custom with a partial (in fact, non-existent) content of cocaine or, perhaps, Coca-Cola *UK, 2002*

Coke bomb *noun* a crude hand grenade fashioned by the Viet Cong, packed inside a drinks can *US, 1990*

cokebottle *noun* in computing, any character that is not found on a normal computer keyboard *US, 1983*

Coke bottle glasses *noun* spectacles with very thick lenses *US, 1986*

Coke bottles *noun* a person with poor eyesight and thick glasses *US, 1997*

coke bugs *noun* a cocaine-induced conviction that insects or snakes are crawling beneath the skin, *2002*

coke burger *noun* a tablet of MDMA, the recreational drug best known as ecstasy. The name leads to unrealistic hopes that the tablet may contain a trace of cocaine *UK, 2002*

coked; coked out; coked up *adjective* cocaine-intoxicated *US, 1924*

cokehead *noun* a cocaine addict *US, 1922*

coke house *noun* a building or dwelling where cocaine is sold *US, 1989*

coke jumbie *noun* a cocaine user or addict *TRINIDAD AND TOBAGO, 1989*

coke out *verb* to use cocaine to an excess *US, 1995*

coke, smoke, and a puke *noun* a fighter pilot's breakfast *US, 1986*

coke whore *noun* a person who trades sex for cocaine *US, 1992*

Cokey Stokey *nickname* Stoke Newington in north London. A rhyme based on 'Hokey Cokey' (a dance), combining the first element of Stoke Newington and COKE (cocaine), from the reputation of the area as a centre for drugs and other criminal endeavours *UK, 2002*

cokie *noun* **1** a frequent user of cocaine *US, 1916*. **2** a junior member of a youth gang *US, 1949*

Cokomo Joe; Kokomo Joe; kokomo *noun* a cocaine user *US, 1938*

cola *noun* **1** cocaine. Playing off the popular soft drink *US, 1992*. **2** a marijuana bud or buds, especially the long top bud on a marijuana plant. From Spanish *cola* (a tail) *UK, 2004*

cold *noun* ▶ **too slow to catch a cold** applied to someone or something that moves slowly, or someone whose thought processes are sluggish *UK, 1917*

cold *adjective* **1** heartless, cruel *UK, 1849*. **2** bad *US, 1934*. **3** absolute *US, 1973*. **4** not capable of being traced to an owner. Back-formed from HOT (stolen) *US, 1992*. **5** innocent of charges under which someone was convicted. Prison usage *AUSTRALIA, 1944*. **6** in gambling, unlucky *US, 1997*. **7** without preparation; in ignorance. Generally used quasi-adverbially *US, 1896*. **8** used as a substitute for 'cool' in any of its senses *US, 1968*. **9** (used of a take-off from an aircraft carrier) failed, resulting in a crash *US, 1959*

cold *adverb* suddenly, completely *US, 1889*

cold and hot *noun* cocaine and heroin combined for injection. Based on the initials *US, 1986*

cold and hungry *noun* in trucking, a C & H truck *US, 1976*

cold as a Bay Street banker's heart *adjective* very ungenerous, or in metaphor, very cold. This expression is from the Canadian prairies, and refers both to its peoples' resentment of Toronto bankers (Bay is the main banking street) and to the legendary cold winters of Saskatchewan, Manitoba and Alberta *CANADA, 1987*

cold as a nun's cunt *adjective* extremely cold *AUSTRALIA, 1955*

cold as a nun's nasty *adjective* extremely cold *AUSTRALIA, 1971*

cold biscuit *noun* **1** a female who does not respond to sexual overtures *US, 1972*. **2** a person lacking any apparent sex appeal. High school usage. *US, 1961*

cold-blooded *adjective* **1** competent; admirable. Also shortened to 'cold' *US, 1992*. **2** in horse racing, said of any horse that is not a thoroughbred *US, 1960*

cold blow *noun* air conditioning *US, 1971*

cold bluff *noun* in poker, a large bet on a poor hand designed to mislead other players *US, 1980*

cold-bust *verb* to catch someone in the act; to reveal your own guilt inadvertently *US, 1986*

cold-call *verb* to go into a pub hoping to make a sexual contact. Adopted from sales jargon *UK, 2002*

coldcock *verb* to hit someone without warning, especially with a blow to the head that knocks the person to the ground *US, 1918*

cold coffee *noun* beer *US, 1976*

cold comfort *noun* in necrophile usage, sexual activity with a corpse *US, 1987*

cold crotch *noun* the application of an ice pack on the scrotum of a man who has overdosed on heroin *US, 1993*

cold-cunt *verb* (used of a woman) to treat someone with hostility *US, 1982*

cold deck *noun* **1** in card games, a stacked deck of cards *US, 1857*. **2** logs swept into a stack to be moved after drying. British Columbia logging usage *CANADA, 1952*

cold dope *noun* in horse racing, information based on empirical evidence *US, 1951*

cold draw *noun* in curling, a rock curled into an open house or into the house without rubbing or knocking out another rock *CANADA, 1964*

colder than a witch's tit *adjective* extremely cold; extremely unfriendly *AUSTRALIA, 1978*

cold feet *noun* fear or a reluctance to proceed *US, 1896*

cold finger work *noun* picking the pocket of a man preoccupied with sex *US, 1948*

cold fish *noun* **1** an unfriendly person *US, 1924*. **2** a standoffish, unwelcoming girl *CANADA, 1977*

cold-footer *noun* a cowardly soldier, or someone too cowardly to become a soldier. From having COLD FEET (fear) *AUSTRALIA, 1916*

cold hole *noun* during Vietnam, an enemy tunnel that has been verified as empty *US, 1991*

coldie *noun* a cold beer *AUSTRALIA, 1953*

cold in the dong *noun* gonorrhea *US, 1981*

cold like dog nose *adjective* very cold *TRINIDAD AND TOBAGO, 2003*

cold meat party *noun* a funeral or wake *US, 1908*

cold one *noun* **1** a cold beer *US, 1927*. **2** an empty wallet, purse or safe *US, 1962*

cold pit *noun* in motor racing, a member of the pit crew who works behind the wall separating the pit from the race track *US, 1993*

cold-plate *verb* to attach a legitimate licence plate to a stolen vehicle that matches the description of the vehicle to which the licence plate belongs *US, 1993*

cold potato *noun* a waiter, especially a slow or inefficient one. Cockney and theatrical rhyming slang *UK, 1960*

cold prowl *noun* an assumed easy house to rob *CANADA, 1976*

cold-read *verb* (used of a fortune teller) to tell a fortune without background information on the customer, relying on observations

and the customer's answers for the predictions. A term borrowed from acting, where it means 'to read a script out loud without having studied it' *US, 1989*

cold shake *noun* a method of preparing pills for injection by crushing and then dissolving them in cold water instead of heating with a flame *US, 1989*

cold spot *noun* a glass of iced tea *US, 1967*

cold storage *noun* **1** a morgue *US, 1949*. **2** solitary confinement *US, 1949*

Coldstream Guards; coldstreams *noun* playing cards. Rhyming slang, formed on the name of the oldest serving regular regiment in the British Army *UK, 1992*

cold tea sign *noun* an irreverent indicator of a geriatric's death in hospital. A blackly humorous medical symptom, glossed as 'when positive, refers to the several cups of cold tea on the bedside cabinet besides a dead geriatric' *UK, 2002*

cold turkey *noun* **1** an act of withdrawing from addictive drugs suddenly; the time period of that withdrawal *US, 1925*. **2** in blackjack, a hand comprised of two face cards *US, 1980*. **3** in poker, two kings dealt consecutively *US, 1988*

cold turkey *verb* to withdraw from a habit or addiction suddenly and without any tapering off *US, 1949*

cold turkey *adjective* (used of an attempt to break a drug addiction) sudden and complete without narcotics or medication to ease the withdrawal symptoms *US, 1953*

cold turkey *adverb* (used of an attempt to break a drug addiction) suddenly and completely without narcotics or medication to ease the withdrawal symptoms *US, 1922*

cold weather indicators *noun* a woman's nipples *US, 2001*

colgate *noun* any toothpaste *TRINIDAD AND TOBAGO, 2003*

coli *noun* marijuana. A shortening, perhaps, of BROCCOLI (marijuana) or COLIFLOR TOSTAO (marijuana) *US, 1978*

colifor tostao *noun* marijuana. A 'toasted cauliflower' in unconventional Spanish *US, 1973*

colin *noun* an erection *UK, 2002*

coliseum curtains *noun* the foreskin *UK, 2002*

collabo *noun* an artistic collaboration. A hip-hop term *UK, 2003*

collar *noun* **1** an arrest *US, 1871*. **2** a police officer *US, 1973*. **3** hard, laborious work. English gypsy use; shortened from conventional 'collar-work.' *UK, 2002*. **4** an improvised seal between a dropper and needle used to inject drugs *US, 1960*. **5** the steering column of a car *US, 2000*. ▶ **finger a collar** to make an arrest. Police slang; a variation of 'feel your collar' *UK, 1999*. ▶ **have your collar felt; have your collar touched** to be arrested or stopped by the police. The active verb COLLAR (to seize, to arrest) dates from the early C17. In those and other gentler times officers of the law would, reputedly, touch their suspect on the collar or shoulder to signify capture *UK, 1949*

collar *verb* **1** to grab someone by the collar, literally or figuratively; to arrest someone *UK, 1613*. **2** to appropriate something; to steal something *UK, 1700*. **3** to understand something, to grasp something *US, 1938*. **4** in horse racing, to run neck and neck *US, 1951*. **5** (from a male perspective) to have sex. A shortening of HOP INTO THE HORSECOLLAR *AUSTRALIA, 1971*. ▶ **collar a hot** to eat a meal *US, 1947*. ▶ **collar the jive** to understand what is being said *US, 1947*

collar and cuff *noun* a homosexual male. Rhyming slang for PUFF *UK, 1934*

collars and cuffs *noun* ▶ **matching collars and cuffs; collars and cuffs that match** applied to a person, usually a woman, whose hair is neither bleached nor dyed. A jocular suggestion that the hair on the head is of the same natural shade as the pubic hair *US, 1984*

collars-for-dollars *noun* a situation in which an arresting officer trades the criminal's release for a share of the proceeds of the crime *US, 2001*

collats *noun* money. Abbreviated and adapted into predominantly black usage from 'collateral' (a pledge of equal value) *UK, 2000*

collect *noun* a win at gambling *AUSTRALIA, 1966*

collect *verb* **1** to call for a person and proceed with him or her *UK, 1937*. **2** to win at gambling; to take your winnings *AUSTRALIA, 1982*

collect call *noun* a citizens' band radio message for a specific named person *US, 1976*

collection box *noun* the vagina *BAHAMAS, 1982*

college *noun* jail *UK, 1699*

college classique *noun* in Quebec, a specialised, college-preparatory school. These Catholic schools, absorbed into the state system of junior colleges, are still known by their French name, even among anglophones *CANADA, 1963*

College Eye *noun* a Lockheed EC-121 Warning Star aircraft. Vietnam war usage *US, 1991*

college hill *noun* a well-off section of town *US, 1970*

College Joe *noun* a quintessential college student *US, 1961*

college try *noun* a sincere effort, despite the likelihood of failure. Especially common as 'the old college try' *US, 1918*

college widow *noun* a woman who lives in or near a college town and dates men from the college year after year *US, 1900*

collie *noun* marijuana. From KALI *JAMAICA, 1970*

Collie; Colly *nickname* Colchester; hence the Military Corrective Establishment at Colchester; detention therein. Military use *UK, 1974*

collie dug *noun* a man; implying that to some degree the person is a fool or a victim. Glasgow rhyming slang for MUG, formed from the local pronunciation of 'collie dog' *UK: SCOTLAND, 2002*

Collie Knox *noun* the pox. Rhyming slang, noted by Red Daniells, 1980 *UK, 1980*

collie man *noun* a marijuana dealer *JAMAICA, 1977*

colly *noun* **1** an erection. Derives from earlier rhyming slang, 'colleen bawn' for HORN; formed on the name of the heroine of *The Lily of Killarney*, an 1862 opera by Julius Benedict *UK, 1960*. **2** cauliflower. Also variant 'cauli' *UK, 1961*

collywobbles *noun* an unsettled condition of the stomach. Derives from the conventional senses of 'colic' and 'wobble' *UK, 1823*

Colney Hatch; colney *noun* a match. Rhyming slang, formed on the one time lunatic asylum in north London *UK, 1960*

Colombian *noun* extremely potent marijuana from Colombia *US, 1971*

Colombian gold *noun* marijuana from Colombia, yellow in colour *US, 1976*

Colombian marching powder *noun* cocaine *US, 1992*

Colombian necklace *noun* a form of execution intended to set an example in which the victim's throat is slit. Probably formed after the more elaborate COLOMBIAN NECKTIE *US, 1995*

Colombian necktie *noun* a form of execution intended to set an example in which the victim's throat is slit and the tongue pulled down through the gaping wound. From a well-dressed image in which the tongue replaces a tie. A COLOMBIAN NECKLACE is less elaborate *US, 1997*

Colombian red *noun* marijuana from Colombia, reddish in colour *US, 1976*

Colonel Blimp *noun* **1** a shrimp (seafood). Rhyming slang, inspired by the following sense *UK, 1992*. **2** a very conservative, reactionary man. Often shortened to 'blimp'. From the cartoon character invented by British cartoonist David Low, 1891–1963, and brought to life by Welsh actor Roger Livesey, 1906–76, in the film *The Life and Death of Colonel Blimp*, 1943 *UK, 1934*

Colonel Gadaffi; colonel *noun* a café. Rhyming slang, formed on the name of the Libyan leader Colonel Muammar al-Qaddafi (b.1942) *UK, 2002*

Colonel Klink *noun* any high-ranking prison officer. A reference to *Hogan's Heroes*, a popular television comedy of the late 1960s *US, 2002*

Colonel Prescott; colonel *noun* a waistcoat. Rhyming slang, thought to date from the 1930s *UK, 1992*

Colonel Sanders *noun* a mature male homosexual who is especially attracted to boys or young men. An allusion to the founder of the Kentucky Fried Chicken™ franchise *US, 1979*

color *noun* **1** in roller derby, any type of theatrics that would make the skater stand out to fans *US, 1999*. **2** money *US, 1950*. **3** in a casino, any betting token worth more than one dollar *US, 1977*

color *verb* ▶ **color it dos** make that a double *US, 1997*

colorado *noun* **1** cocaine, *2003*. **2** a red barbiturate capsule, especially if branded Seconal™. From Spanish *colorado* (the colour red). Often abbreviated to 'colie' *US, 1971*

Colorado cocktail *noun* marijuana *UK, 1998*

Colorado Kool Aid *noun* Coors™ beer. Brewed in Colorado, and for several decades not marketed nationally *US, 1972*

colored people's time *noun* used for denoting a lack of punctuality. One of the very few instances in which the former ameliorative 'colored people' is still used in the US *US, 1967*

colored showers *noun* a sexual fetish involving urination on your partner *US, 1993*

colored town *noun* a neighbourhood with a large population of black people *US, 1964*

color for color *adverb* in American casinos, the method of paying bets – one denomination at a time *US, 1980*

color me *verb* used ironically in conjunction with an adjective for describing a personal condition *US, 1962*

colors *noun* **1** insignia that indentify group membership, especially in motorcyle gangs *US, 1966*. **2** the coloured clothing worn as a signal of gang affiliation *US, 1989*

color-struck *adjective* overly conscious of skin colour *US, 1965*

color up *verb* in casino gambling, to trade chips of one denomination for chips of a higher denomination *US, 1991*

colour *noun* an Aboriginal Australian *AUSTRALIA, 1995*

colourful *adjective* (of language) robust and lively, some may say offensive *UK, 1957*

colour of his eyes *noun* the size of the penis. Rhyming slang for 'size' *UK, 2002*

Columbia clutch *noun* an overdrive gear *US, 1960*

Columbian *noun* marijuana. A misspelling of COLOMBIAN, also seen as 'Columbian red', 'Columbian gold', etc *US, 1971*

Columbus black *noun* marijuana claimed to originate in Columbus, Ohio *US, 1982*

Columbus Circles *noun* dark circles beneath an actor's eyes *US, 1952*

com *noun* a safe or vault's combination *US, 1949*

combat fishing *noun* sport fishing at a crowded fishing spot *US, 1993*

combat-happy *adjective* deranged by the horrors of combat *US, 1962*

combat jack *noun* an act of masturbation by a combat soldier to relieve the tension or boredom of combat *US, 2003*

combat professor *noun* in Vietnam, an American military advisor. Faint praise *US, 1991*

combats *noun* fashionable trousers with a military design. An abbreviation of 'combat trousers', *2000*

Combat Zone *nickname* an unsavoury area in downtown Boston, dominated by sex shops, bars and drug dealers *US, 1971*

comber *noun* a large wave that breaks on a reef or a beach *US, 1977*

combine harvester *noun* a class 9 goods locomotive *UK, 1970*

combo *noun* **1** a combination of anything physical or abstract *US, 1921*. **2** a white man who cohabits with an Aboriginal woman. A term of derision. From 'combination', as they combine black and white *AUSTRALIA, 1896*. **3** a small jazz band *US, 1924*. **4** in pool, a combination shot, or one in which the cue ball is shot into a numbered ball that then hits the object ball *US, 1990*. **5** a combination lock *UK, 1996*. ▶ **go combo** of a white man, to live with an Aboriginal woman *AUSTRALIA, 1896*

combol *noun* cocaine *UK, 2003*

comb-over *noun* a male hairstyle in which a few long strands grown on one side of the head are contrived to cover a bald pate *UK, 1980*

combusse *noun* a married man's lover. She '*comes bust* up the marriage' *TRINIDAD AND TOBAGO, 2003*

come *verb* **1** to experience an orgasm *UK, 1600.* **2** to yield to bribery or persuasion *UK, 1970.* **3** to behave in a specified way, as in 'Don't come the innocent with me' *UK, 1837.* ► **come a cropper** to fall heavily; to be the victim of an accident. From hunting jargon, 'a cropper' (a fall) *UK, 1999.* ► **come a tumble** to detect something, to fathom something, to understand something. Rhyming slang for RUMBLE *UK, 1992.* ► **come big** (of a bettor in horse racing) to bet more than usual on a race *AUSTRALIA, 1989.* ► **come down like trained pigs** in horse racing, to finish a race exactly as predicted *US, 1951.* ► **come from** to emanate from; to expose the philosophical basis for a statement or action. Another vague term of the 1960s *US, 1978.* ► **come high or come low 1** no matter what *TRINIDAD AND TOBAGO, 2003.* ► **come home** (of the effects of LSD) to dwindle, diminish and vanish *US, 1997.* ► **come home early** in horse racing, to establish and hold an early lead to win a race *US, 1951.* ► **come hot** in a confidence swindle, to complete the swindle which the victim immediately understands to have been a swindle *US, 1985.* ► **come like salt** to be in great abundance *TRINIDAD AND TOBAGO, 2003.* ► **come over all peculiar** to feel suddenly physically indisposed or emotionally upset. A later variant of COME OVER ALL QUEER, avoiding the ambiguous and politically incorrect QUEER (unwell/homosexual) *UK, 2003.* ► **come over all queer** to feel suddenly physically indisposed or emotionally upset *UK, 1937.* ► **come over all unnecessary; go all unnecessary** to become sexually excited *UK, 1984.* ► **come sick** to experience the bleed period of the menstrual cycle *US, 1948.* ► **come the acid; come the old acid; come the old acid drop** to be heavily sarcastic or especially impudent. From ACID (sarcasm) *UK, 1962.* ► **come the bludge on** to sponge upon someone. From BLUDGE (to cadge) *AUSTRALIA, 1958.* ► **come the cunt; come the old cunt** to be particularly obstreperous or unpleasant. From CUNT (an unpleasant or despicable person) *UK, 1984.* ► **come the old soldier 1** to wheedle, to impose on someone. Of military origin *UK, 1818.* **2** to hector someone, to domineer someone, by virtue of supposed greater knowledge. Deriving from the likely behaviour of the longest-serving soldier in the barracks *UK, 1984.* ► **come the raw prawn 1** to try to deceive someone or impose upon them. A raw prawn is hard to swallow *AUSTRALIA, 1942.* **2** to behave in a recalcitrant manner. Heard among Irish labourers *UK, 1979.* ► **come the tin man** to bluff; to make yourself a nuisance *UK, 1962.* ► **come the tin soldier; come the old tin soldier** to be impertinent or obstructive. An elaboration and slight shift in sense from COME THE OLD SOLDIER *UK, 1977.* ► **come to grief 1** to get into serious trouble; to fail *UK, 1850.* **2** to take a tumble; to have a fall. Usually found in sporting contexts *UK, 1854.* ► **come your lot** to experience an orgasm. An elaboration of COME *UK, 1964.* ► **come your mutton** (of a male) to masturbate *UK, 1961.* ► **come your turkey** (of a male) to masturbate *UK, 1961*

come; cum *noun* **1** semen *US, 1923.* **2** an orgasm. From the verb sense (to experience an orgasm) *US, 1967* ▷*see:* COME AND GO

come across *verb* **1** (generally of a woman) to take part in sexual intercourse *AUSTRALIA, 1967.* **2** to have sex as the result of persuasive insistence *US, 1921.* **3** to agree to become an informer *US, 1973.* **4** to give the appearance of having a specified characteristic *UK, 2002*

come again? please repeat or restate what you just said *US, 1970*

come-along; cum-along *noun* a wire grip used for holding wire or conductor under strain *US, 1944*

come and go; come *noun* snow. Rhyming slang, extending from the verb form 'coming and going' (snowing) *UK, 1992*

comeback *noun* **1** a return to a formerly successful status *US, 1908.* **2** a repercussion; repercussions *UK, 1894.* **3** revenge *US, 1964.* **4** a return call on a citizens' band radio *US, 1976.* **5** a boomerang *AUSTRALIA, 1878.* **6** an adulterant used to dilute crack cocaine. A chemical that when baked looks, smells, and tastes like CRACK *US, 1989*

come back *verb* **1** to reply *US, 1896.* **2** to reply to a citizens' band radio broadcast *US, 1976.* **3** to retract something, to take something back, especially to apologetically cancel a previous remark *AUSTRALIA, 1957*

comeback kid *noun* a thief who breaks into a hotel room where he has previously stayed, using a key he failed to return *US, 1954*

come-back money *noun* in horse racing, money from off-track betting operations that is wired to a race track just before a race *US, 1951*

come chugger *noun* a person who performs oral sex on men *US, 1999*

come clean *verb* to tell the truth, to confess *US, 1919*

come day, go day; come day, go day, God send Sunday *adjective* laid back, unruffled *US, 1918*

comedown *noun* **1** a person, thing or event that dampens your spirits or depresses you *US, 1952.* **2** a period during which the diminishing sensations of a drug are felt *UK, 1984*

come down *verb* **1** to experience the easing of drug intoxication *US, 1959.* **2** to arrive in prison *US, 1972.* **3** (of a river) to flood; to be inundated. Many Australian rivers are mostly dry for a large part of the year and then fill, often quite suddenly, during the wet season *AUSTRALIA, 1868*

come down! in the sport of archery, used as an imperative to instruct a pupil to refrain from completing a shot *UK, 1988*

come dumpster; cum dumpster *noun* a promiscuous female *US, 2001*

come freak; cum freak *noun* a person who is obsessed with sex *US, 1966*

come-fuck-me *adjective* sexually alluring. An embellished FUCK-ME *US, 1986*

come gum; cum gum *noun* chewing gum with a liquid centre *US, 1985*

come-here *noun* a person originally from outside a community *US, 1985*

come-hither look *noun* a flirtatious and inviting glance *UK, 1961*

come-in *noun* in a circus, the hour period before the performance, during which patrons are allowed to enter the big top *US, 1980*

come in, Berlin used as a humorous request that someone joins a conversation. Often said with a melodramatic flourish, mimicking a military communication *US, 1978*

come in if you're pretty used in response to a knock on a dressing room door. Theatrical camp; certainly in use since the mid-1980s *UK, 1985*

come in spinner! 1 in the gambling game two-up, used as a call signalling that all bets are laid and it is time to spin the coins *AUSTRALIA, 1943.* **2** begin!, commence! *AUSTRALIA, 1957*

come it *verb* **1** to behave impudently *UK: SCOTLAND, 1934.* **2** to wheedle, to impose on someone. Of military origins; a variation of COME THE OLD SOLDIER *UK, 1925*

come-off *noun* an event or result *US, 1887*

come off *verb* **1** to happen, especially to happen successfully *UK, 1864.* **2** to orgasm. A variation of COME *UK, 1937.* **3** to give the appearance of whatever characteristic is specified *US, 2003*

come off it! don't exaggerate!; don't keep trying to fool me! Elaborated from the earlier US usage: 'come off!' and phrases like 'come off your perch!' and 'come off the 'grass!' *UK, 1912*

come-on *noun* **1** a challenge to fight, often unspoken *UK, 1971.* **2** an invitation, especially unspoken and especially sexual *US, 1942.* **3** an inducement *UK, 2001*

come on *verb* **1** to demonstrate sexual interest *US, 1959.* **2** to commence the bleed period of the menstrual cycle. Euphemistic *UK, 1984.* **3** (of drugs) to start having an effect *US, 1946.* **4** to give the appearance of whatever characteristic is specified. Originally used in jazz circles but exampled here as a song title and lyric by melodic heavy metal band Pretty Maids *UK, 1942*

come on snake, let's rattle! let's dance! Teen slang *US, 1958*

come on worm, let's wiggle let's dance *US, 1954*

come out *verb* **1** to declare your homosexuality openly or publicly *US, 1941.* **2** to declare or admit to a personal fact *UK, 2000.* **3** to leave college or high school amateur athletics and sign a contract to play professionally *US, 1990.* **4** to leave the bush to return to an urban or settled area *CANADA, 1951.* ► **come out of the closet** to declare your homosexuality openly or publicly *US, 1971*

come outside!; outside! used as a challenge to fight. A shortening of any number of variations on 'Come outside and fight!' *UK, 1984*

comer *noun* a promising prospect *US, 1879*

come scab *noun* a dried-on patch of semen on skin *UK, 2002*

come shot; cum shot *noun* a scene in a pornographic film or a photograph of a man ejaculating *US, 1972*

come the revolution at some unknown point in the future everything will change for the better, used as a catchphrase response to an unanswerable complaint, or as a vague, unmeant threat of revenge *US, 1987*

come the revolution you'll be first against the wall used in complaint against any figure of authority *UK, 1997*

come-through *noun* in a big store confidence swindle, the stage when the victim learns that he has been swindled and goes after the swindlers *US, 1997*

come-to-bed-eyes *noun* male or female eyes that offer a glimpse of sexual promise, allegedly *UK, 1982*

come to that! in point of fact!; since you mention it! *UK, 1923*

come undone *verb* in a literal and figurative sense: to fall to pieces; also, to meet with difficulties or disaster *UK, 1937*

come unstuck *verb* in a literal and figurative sense: to fall pieces; also, to meet with difficulties or disaster. Earlier variations are 'come unput' and COME UNDONE. All have the sense 'to fall apart' *UK, 1928*

come-up *noun* a robbery *US, 2003*

come up *verb* **1** (of drugs) to start having an effect. A variation of the earlier COME ON *UK, 1996*. **2** to grow up; to be raised *US, 1990*. **3** of a racehorse (that has been bet on), to win *UK, 1937*. ▶ **come up trumps** to succeed; to turn out well. An image of card playing *UK, 2001*

come up on *verb* to have a win on a lottery, or football pool, or the like *UK, 1984*

comfort lady *noun* a prostitute *US, 2000*

comfy *adjective* comfortable *UK, 1829*

comfy wing *noun* in prison, the enhanced wing for prisoners who have earned the privilege of greater comfort. From COMFY (comfortable) *UK, 2000*

comical *adjective* used as a humorous synonym for 'chemical' *US, 1968*

comical Chris *noun* an act of urination. Rhyming slang for PISS *UK, 1980*

comic book *noun* a truck driver's daily log book. A reflection of the degree of attention given to the log book by some drivers *US, 1976*

comic cuts *noun* the guts. Rhyming slang *AUSTRALIA, 1945*

comics *noun* **1** the testicles. A shortening of 'comic cuts' rhyming slang for NUTS *UK, 1992*. **2** topographical maps. Cynical Vietnam war usage *US, 1991*. **3** weekly motorcycle newspapers and magazines *UK, 1979*. ▶ **read too many comics** to confuse dreams with reality *UK, 2005*

comic strip *noun* a person with many tattoos *US, 1997*

coming down!; coming through! used as a warning by a surfer to other surfers that he is starting a ride on a wave *US, 1991*

coming out party *noun* discharge from prison *US, 1983*

comings *noun* semen. From COME (to orgasm) *UK, 1961*

comm *noun* a commission *AUSTRALIA, 1989*

commando *noun* a person with rough sexual tastes *US, 1964*

commando *adjective* ▶ **go commando** to wear no underwear. Commandos are always ready for action *US, 2001*

commercial *noun* **1** a male homosexual prostitute *US, 1949*. **2** a sex scene in a pornographic film. An intentionally misleading term which makes a public discussion about the production of pornography possible without offending those nearby *US, 1995*

commercial highway engineer *noun* a truck driver. A humorous glamorisation of the job *US, 1971*

commercial traveller *noun* **1** a ram that escapes its paddock *NEW ZEALAND, 2002*. **2** a person with bags under his eyes. From a music-hall joke current in the 1930s *UK, 1961*

commie *noun* **1** a Communist, literally or approximately *US, 1939*. **2** a computer *UK, 1996*

commish *noun* **1** a commission, a percentage on sales *US, 1862*. **2** a Commissioner *US, 1910*

commo *noun* **1** a Communist *AUSTRALIA, 1946*. **2** a military radio; communications *US, 1964*. **3** purchases from a prison shop *US, 1992*

commo *adjective* Communist *UK, 1942*

commodore *noun* the sum of fifteen pounds (£15). Extended from rhyming slang LADY; LADY GODIVA (a FIVER, £5) – via the song 'Three Times a Lady', by the Commodores, 1978 *UK, 2003*

common *noun* common sense. A familiar form in the 1950s and 60s, especially as 'a bit of common', now rare *UK, 1936*

common *adjective* ▶ **as common as cat shit and twice as nasty** extremely ordinary; very cheap and nasty; morally or socially beneath you *UK, 1968*

common dog *noun* common sense. Military slang *UK, 1987*

commo wire *noun* electrical wire used for a wide variety of tasks *US, 1986*

comms *noun* communications, *2001*

community chest *noun* a sexually available girl *US, 1968*

commute *verb* to take DMT, a short-lasting hallucinogen *US, 1970*

Como *noun* a Fred Perry™ shirt, a fashion item with iconic status among skinheads. Via singer Perry Como (1912–2001) *UK, 2001*

comp *noun* **1** a competition. Also called a 'compo' *UK, 1929*. **2** a complimentary benefit given to valued customers *US, 1977*. **3** compensation *US, 1953*. **4** a compositor; a typesetter *US, 1842*

comp *verb* **1** to issue something on a complimentary basis *US, 1961*. **2** to accompany someone musically *US, 1949*

compa *noun* a very close friend. Border Spanish used in English conversation by Mexican-Americans; from the more formal *compadre* (godfather to one's child) *US, 1974*

compadre *noun* a close and trusted male friend. Ultimately from the Spanish word for 'godfather of your child' *US, 1833*

company *noun* sex. Used as a euphemism by prostitutes soliciting customers *US, 1991*

company girl *noun* a prostitute hired to enliven a corporate event or outing *US, 1960*

company jewellery *noun* a railwayman's company hat, badge and switch keys *US, 1946*

company patsy *noun* the person within an organisation who is blamed for everything that goes wrong *US, 1973*

complain *verb* ▶ **can't complain!; musn't complain!** things are tolerable, nothing to *really* complain about. A catchphrase, often given as a by-rote reply without consideration of the sense *UK, 1847*

comp list *noun* a list kept at the door of a club or concert, identifying those who are to be admitted free of charge *US, 1999*

compo *noun* **1** compensation *UK, 2000*. **2** worker's compensation *AUSTRALIA, 1941*. **3** a composition *TRINIDAD AND TOBAGO, 2003*. **4** mixed mortar, plaster or the like *AUSTRALIA, 1971*

comprehensively *adverb* thoroughly, indisputably; in a very big and a delightfully humorous way. Sporting *UK, 1979*

comprehensive physician *noun* a proctologist, a doctor specialising in diseases of the rectum. Based on any number of pale puns about 'holes' and 'whole patients' *US, 1980*

comprenday *verb* to understand. Cod French, from *comprendre* (to comprehend) *UK, 2001*

comprende? do you understand? Spanish used by English speakers without regard to their fluency in Spanish, and with multiple variations reflecting their lack of fluency *US, 1994*

comps *noun* comprehensive college examinations *US, 1961*

compsci *noun* a computer science student. A shortening and compounding of the discipline, pronounced 'comp-ski' *UK, 2002*

compty *adjective* mentally deficient. Army, possibly of Hindustani derivation *UK, 1984*

compute *verb* to make sense. Almost always heard in the negative – 'does not compute'. Popularised in the 1960s television situation comedy *My Living Doll*, in which the robotic character played by

Julie Newmar would respond to anything that she did not understand by saying 'That does not compute' *US, 1964*

computer geek *noun* a person whose life is centred around computers to the exclusion of all other outlets *US, 1991*

computer nerd *noun* a student whose enthusiasm for computers has interfered with the development of a well-rounded personality *US, 1985*

compy *noun* a competition *AUSTRALIA, 1998*

compy? do you understand? A complete corruption of the French or Spanish *US, 1947*

comrat *noun* a political liberal. A derogatory play on the communist use of the term 'comrade' *US, 1951*

comred *noun* a political liberal. A play on the term 'comrade' *US, 1953*

comsymp *noun* a liberal; a *communist symp*athizer *US, 1964*

con *noun* **1** a *con*vict or ex-*con*vict *US, 1888*. **2** a criminal *con*viction *UK, 1925*. **3** deception; an act intended to trick or deceive; a tale intended to deceive *US, 1896*. **4** a *con*vention. Especially popular among fans of science fiction and comic books *US, 1978*. **5** in horse racing, a *con*cession wager *AUSTRALIA, 1989*. **6** a *con*ference; a *con*sultation. Lawyers' use *UK, 1961*. **7** a lavatory attendant *UK, 1961*

con *verb* to subject someone to a *con*fidence trick; to dupe the victim of a criminal enterprise *US, 1892*

Con-Air *noun* any aeroplane flown by the federal Bureau of Prisons to transport prisoners *US, 1996*

Conan Doyle; conan *noun* a boil. Rhyming slang, formed on the name of Sir Arthur Conan Doyle, author and creator of Sherlock Holmes. As the current use is almost exclusively of the shortened form, to many the source of the rhyme, and hence the rhyme itself, has been lost *UK, 1932*

con artist *noun* a skilled confidence swindler *US, 1937*

concert *noun* a play; a show; any theatrical entertainment *UK, 1992*

concertina *noun* a sheep that is hard to shear because of the wrinkles on its skin *AUSTRALIA, 1959*

conch *noun* **1** a conscientious student. Used contemptuously *AUSTRALIA, 1988*. **2** a white native of the Bahamas, especially a poor one *BAHAMAS, 1840*. ▶ **have the conch** to be your turn to speak. From the symbolic value of a conch-shell in William Golding's *Lord of the Flies*, 1954 *UK, 2005*

conchie; conchy *noun* a conscientious objector *UK, 1917*

Conchie Joe; Conchie Joe *noun* a local white Bahamian *BAHAMAS, 1978*

Conchy Joe *noun* ▷*see:* CONKY JOE

Con Club *noun* any provincial headquarters of the Conservative and Unionist Association. Described in *The Sunday Times*, 20th August 1978, as 'that ambiguous abbreviation' *UK, 1978*

con-con *noun* the residue that remains after smoking freebase cocaine *US, 1992*

concrete overcoat *noun* a covering of a corpse with concrete to facilitate its disposal in a body of water *US, 1971*

concrete overshoes *noun* concrete poured around a person or body's feet to faciliate disposal in a body of water *US, 1976*

concrete wheels *noun* a citizens' band radio transmitter situated in a building. Citizens' band radio slang *UK, 1981*

concuss *adjective* suffering the symptoms of a concussion *SINGAPORE, 2002*

condo *noun* an owner-occupied flat, a *condo*minium *US, 1964*

condom *noun* **1** in computing, the plastic bag that protects a 3.5 inch disk *US, 1991*. **2** in pool, a removable rubber sleeve for a cue stick *US, 1993*

condominiums *noun* in bar dice games, a roll from the cup in which some dice are stacked on top of others, invalidating the roll *US, 1976*

conducer *noun* a railway conductor *US, 1946*

conductor *noun* **1** an experienced LSD user who acts as a guide for another who is experiencing the drug's effects; LSD *US, 1982*. **2** the

second active participant in serial sex with a single passive partner. From PULL A TRAIN (serial sex) *US, 1975*

cone *noun* **1** a detachable conical receptacle of a pipe or bong; the contents of one of these *AUSTRALIA, 1995*. **2** a cone-shaped marijuana cigarette *UK, 2000*. **3** a socially inept person. An abbreviation of CONEHEAD *US, 1990*. ▶ **give cone** to perform oral sex *US, 1982*. ▶ **pull a cone** to smoke the entire contents of a a detachable conical receptacle of a marijuana pipe *AUSTRALIA, 1987*

conehead *noun* **1** a habitual smoker of marijuana *AUSTRALIA, 1987*. **2** a socially inept person. From a recurring skit on *Saturday Night Live*, first appearing in 1983; Dan Aykroyd played alien Beldar Conehead and Jane Curtin his wife Prymaat *US, 1990*. **3** a young person with a shaved head and radical racist views. Another name for the common SKINHEAD *NEW ZEALAND, 2001*

coner *noun* a pickpocket who distracts a targeted victim by dropping an ice-cream cone at the victim's feet *UK, 1969*

Coney Island *noun* **1** any room in a police station where suspected criminals are forcefully interrogated *US, 1949*. **2** a lunch cart; a condiment-rich lunch served from a lunch cart *US, 1960*. **3** any travelling carnival or amusement park *TRINIDAD AND TOBAGO, 1927*

Coney Island butter *noun* mustard *US, 1947*

Coney Island whitefish *noun* a used condom. The most prominent use of the term is probably in the title of the 1979 Aerosmith song 'Bone to Bone (Coney Island White Fish Boy)' *US, 1984*

conference *noun* a poker game. An intentionally misleading euphemism *US, 1988*

confessional *noun* a police interview room *UK, 1971*

confetti *noun* **1** bricks. An abbreviation of IRISH CONFETTI *US, 1950*. **2** snow. Obviously, 'wet confetti' is 'sleet' *UK, 1981*

confidencer *verb* an electronic device that screens out background noise from a telephone mouthpiece *US, 1985*

confo *noun* a conference *AUSTRALIA, 1953*

confound! curse!, especially as 'confound it!', 'confound you!', etc; used for mild oaths or imprecations *UK, 1966*

confounded *adjective* inopportune, unpleasant, odious, excessive *UK, 1760*

Confucius he say used as an introduction to either a genuine or cynical philosophical proposition, or as a set-up to a joke that is archly stylised: its lack of the use of 'a' or 'the', approximates 'oriental' words of wisdom. An example (selected at random from a wealth of Internet sites that celebrate this comedic formula): 'Crowded elevator small different to midget'. Confucius, 551–479 BC, was a great Chinese philosopher not best remembered for his jokes and double entendres *UK, 1975*

confuddle up *adjective* confused *BAHAMAS, 1982*

confuffle *noun* confusion *TRINIDAD AND TOBAGO, 1993*

confusion *noun* a street fight; a quarrel leading to a fight. Noted as of West Indian origin *JAMAICA, 1873*

Cong *noun* a Congregational chapel; a follower of the Congregational faith. The *Book of Congregational Praise* was known as 'Cong Praise'. The term faded from use after the Congregational Church merged with the Presbyterian Church of England in 1972. Members of the newly formed United Reformed Church soon became 'Urks' *UK, 1961*

Congo *noun* a Congregationalist *AUSTRALIA, 1953*

Congo brown; Congo dirt *noun* marijuana purportedly grown in Africa *US, 1992*

Congolese *noun* an extremely potent variety of marijuana cultivated in the Republic of Congo *UK, 1970*

congrats *noun* congratulations *UK, 1894*

conhanger *noun* the co-signer of a purchase contract or loan *US, 1975*

con into; con out of *verb* to subject someone to a criminal trick; to fool a victim into giving up something of value. Derives from CON (confidence trick) *1958*

conjugals *noun* conjugal rights *UK, 1937*

conk *verb* **1** to straighten hair using any number of chemical processes *US, 1944*. **2** to hit someone, especially on the head *UK, 1821*. **3** to kill someone *US, 1918*

conk; konk *noun* **1** the head *US, 1870*. **2** the nose; hence, a nickname for anyone blessed with a big nose. Possibly from 'conch' (a large shell) with Latin and Greek derivations *UK, 1812*. **3** a hairstyle in which naturally curly hair is chemically straightened; hence, the hair straightening process; the chemical preparation required *US, 1942*

conkbuster *verb* inexpensive, potent whisky *US, 1947*

conked; conked out *adjective* (of a machine) not working; (of a person) exhausted *UK, 1984*

conker *noun* a line of traffic that builds up behind a slow driver *UK, 1972*

conk out; konk out; clonk out *verb* to fall asleep; to pass out; to stop operating *UK, 1917*

conky *noun* **1** a nose. Market traders' elaboration of CONK. Variants include 'conkey' and 'conkie' *UK, 1979*. **2** used of any person with a large nose. From CONK (a nose). Arthur Wellesley, Duke of Wellington (1769–1852) is perhaps the best known of people so profiled; he was known first as 'conkey', then 'old conkey'. Another variant spelling is 'konsky' *UK, 1961*. **3** the penis *BAHAMAS, 1982*

Conky Joe; Conchy Joe *noun* a white person, or a person with very light-coloured skin *BAHAMAS, 1942*

con man *noun* a confidence swindler *US, 1889*

con merchant *noun* a confidence swindler *US, 1959*

connect *noun* a connection from which an illicit substance may be obtained; a drug dealer *US, 1960*

connect *verb* to make a sexual conquest *US, 1985*

connected *adjective* associated with, if not a formal part of, organised crime *US, 1977*

connection *noun* **1** a drug dealer; a drug deal *US, 1928*. **2** a sexual partner *US, 1985*. **3** a friend *SOUTH AFRICA, 2004*

connections *noun* in horse racing, a horse's owner, trainer and the trainer's assistants *US, 1960*

connectors *noun* in poker, several sequenced cards that might be improved to a five-card sequenced straight *US, 1990*

conneroo *noun* a confidence swindler *US, 1949*

connie *noun* **1** a convict *AUSTRALIA, 1964*. **2** a type of playing marble. A shortening of CONNIE AGATE *AUSTRALIA, 1966*. **3** a tram or train conductor *AUSTRALIA, 1933*. **4** a small stone or rock, especially one for throwing. Used mainly in eastern mainland Australia. Possibly from an Australian Aboriginal language *AUSTRALIA, 1978*

Connie *noun* **1** a Constellation airliner. An aircraft that in the 1950s and 60s linked countries and continents. In 2004, the Dutch National Aviodrome museum completed the restoration of a Lockheed L-749 Constellation. The project was titled 'Connie Comeback' *US, 1953*. **2** a Royal Enfield 'Constellation' motorcycle, introduced in 1958 *UK, 1979*. **3** a Lincoln Continental car *US, 1971*. **4** the vagina. A proper name as a euphemism (perhaps for CUNT) *US, 1998*

connie agate *noun* a type of playing marble made from agate. Perhaps from 'cornelian', with elision of the 'r' *AUSTRALIA, 1916*

Connie's army *noun* the flotilla of supporters of the racing yacht *Constellation* in the 1962 America Cup races. An obvious allusion to 'Arnie's army' *US, 1964*

conniver about *verb* to wander aimlessly *AUSTRALIA, 1953*

con out of *verb* ▷ *see:* CON INTO

conrod *noun* a connecting rod. Used by engineers and mechanics *UK, 1931*

cons *noun* **1** a prison sentence *UK, 1996*. **2** previous convictions. Metropolitan Police slang *UK, 1970*

cons *verb* in computing, to add an item to a list *US, 1983*

con safos used as a warning not to deface the writer's grafitti *US, 1970*

conscious *adjective* socio-politically aware of black race issues *UK, 1994*

con's con *noun* in prison, an ideal prisoner in the opinion of other inmates. From CON (a convict) *UK, 2001*

consent job *noun* any crime committed with the consent of the victim, who then collects on an insurance policy *US, 1950*

conshie *noun* a conscientious person. In contrast to the sense of 'conscientious objector', which seems to have little or no purchase in Australia *AUSTRALIA, 1970*

consig *noun* in an organised crime enterprise, a trusted advisor. Shortened from the Italian *consigliore* *US, 1985*

constant screecher *noun* a teacher. Rhyming slang *UK, 1992*

consti *noun* constipated. Slightly embarrassed if not entirely euphemistic; recorded as a young woman's use *UK, 1982*

constipated *adjective* in tiddlywinks, said of a position in which your winks are tied down and useless *US, 1977*

constipation *noun* a railway station. Rhyming slang; punning, perhaps, on a lack of movement. *UK, 1992*

constitutional *noun* a drug addict's first injection of the day *US, 1959*

contact *noun* **1** (of any situation of any degree of criminality or legality) an acquaintance, especially in business or trade; someone you can call on for assistance or information; a connection; an agent *US, 1931*. **2** a reliable source for something, especially drugs *US, 1966*. **3** a police informer *US, 1962*. **4** a *contact* lens. Usually used in the plural *US, 1961*

contact high *noun* a vicarious, sympathetic experience caused by witnessing another person's drug-induced experience *US, 1955*

contact lens *noun* LSD; LSD mixed with another drug. Possibly from the small size of a dose and its ability to change your view of the world *US, 1977*

containered *adjective* locked in a cell *UK, 1996*

content-free *adjective* said of a computer message that adds nothing to the substance of a discussion or to the reader's knowledge *US, 1991*

continental cuisine *noun* frozen food served to firefighters in remote but not inaccessible locations *US, 1991*

continental kit *noun* in hot rodding, a spare tyre fastened on the boot (trunk) of the car *US, 1958*

contour *adverb* (used of an aircraft) at treetop level *US, 1988*

contours *noun* the curves of a woman's body. Somewhere between poetry and pornography *UK, 1886*

contract *noun* **1** an order to kill someone or a reward offered to anyone who kills the target *US, 1941*. **2** a promise made by one police officer to do a favour for another *US, 1958*

contract rider *noun* in horse racing, a jockey who is under contract with one stable *US, 1976*

contra-rotating death banana *noun* a Chinook helicopter. In Royal Air Force use, 2002 *UK, 2002*

contrary *adjective* (of someone's personality or disposition) adverse, antagonistic, perverse. The earliest example is the undated nursery rhyme 'Mary, Mary, quite contrary' which is supposed to be about Mary Stuart, 1542–87 *UK, 1850*

Control-Alt-Delete *noun* ▷ *see:* CTRL-ALT-DELETE

control C *verb* to stop what it is that you are doing. A borrowing from the command used on many computer operating systems to interrupt a program *US, 1991*

control freak *noun* a person with an obsessive need to control people and events *US, 1977*

controller *noun* a mid-level operative in an illegal gambling enterprise who is in charge of a number of runners *US, 1964*

control O *verb* to stop talking. From the character used on some computer operating systems to abort output but allow the program to keep on running. Generally means that you are not interested in hearing anythimg more from that person, at least on that topic *US, 1991*

Con U *nickname* Concordia University, Montreal. After the formation of Concordia University out of two existing institutions, this short form expressed student dissatisfaction with procedures and policies *CANADA, 1972*

conversate *verb* to converse in a loud and lively style. From the conventional 'conversation' *US, 2000*

conversion job *noun* a disfigurement caused by a violent beating. From the conventional sense *UK, 1969*

convert *noun* a newly addicted drug addict *US, 1949*

convert *verb* to steal something *NEW ZEALAND, 1984*

convict *noun* in circus usage, a zebra. An allusion to the zebra's striped coat, evocative of a prison uniform *US, 1926*

convincer *noun* the stage in a confidence swindle when the victim is fully committed to the scheme *US, 1940*

convo *noun* a conversation *AUSTRALIA, 1987*

convoy *noun* **1** a group of trucks driving as a group, in communication with each other *US, 1971*. **2** serial sex between a woman and multiple male partners *FIJI, 2004*

con wise *adjective* extremely sophisticated in the ways of the world based on lessons learned in prison *US, 1912*

coo *noun* the vagina *UK, 1879*

cool!; coo-er! used for expressing astonishment, disbelief or wonderment *UK, 1911*

cooch *noun* the vagina; sex with a woman *US, 2001*

cooch dancer *noun* ▷*see:* COOTCH DANCER

coocher *noun* a sexually suggestive dancer *US, 1927*

coochie *noun* the vagina; sex with a woman; a woman as a sex object *US, 1995*

coochie-cutters *noun* very short shorts *US, 2002*

coochi snorcher *noun* the vagina. Elaboration of COOCHIE (the vagina) *US, 1998*

cooder *noun* a hairdresser. Probably contrived from the name of US guitarist Ry Cooder (b.1947) as a play on 'riah' (hair), 'Ry' forming a pun on 'hair cut'. Used in contemporary gay society *UK, 2003*

cooee *noun* the call 'cooee' *AUSTRALIA, 1831*. ▶ **within cooee** within calling distance of a 'cooee'; nearby, close *AUSTRALIA, 1836*

cooee *verb* to make the call 'cooee' *AUSTRALIA, 1824*

cooee! used as a call to communicate whereabouts over distance. A direct borrowing of the call in the extinct Australian Aboriginal language Dharug, from the Sydney region. Adopted by the early white colonists, the call is used in the bush to mean both 'where are you?' and the answer 'I am here'. The 'coo' is drawn out and followed by a sharp, rising 'ee' *AUSTRALIA, 1793*

cook *noun* **1** a musician who plays with great passion and energy *US, 1962*. **2** on the railways, a rear brakesman *US, 1977*. **3** a look, in the phrases 'give a cook', 'have a cook', 'take a cook'. Possibly rhyming slang, or may simply be an accidental rhyme formed by confusion with the Yiddish use of German *guck* (a look) *UK, 1960*. **4** extreme criticism *AUSTRALIA, 1989*

cook *verb* **1** to melt a powdered narcotic, especially heroin, in water, prior to injecting or inhaling. The drug is 'cooked up' and 'cooked down' *US, 1952*. **2** to boil dynamite to extract nitroglycerine *US, 1992*. **3** to prepare crack cocaine, heating a mixture of cocaine, lidocaine, baking soda and other chemicals to remove the hydrochloride *US, 1992*. **4** to excel, to excite people *US, 1942*. **5** to falsify accounting figures; to manipulate them *UK, 1636*. **6** to make something radioactive; to become radioactive *US, 1950*. **7** (used of a car radiator in hot rodding) to boil over *US, 1960*. **8** to execute someone by electrocution *US, 1932*. ▶ **cook on all four** to be very busily employed. Adopted from COOK WITH GAS or COOK ON THE FRONT BURNER *CANADA, 1984*. ▶ **cook on the front burner** to excel; to go fast *US, 1956*. ▶ **cook with gas** to perform successfully, especially after a period of trying and failing; to do very well *US, 1941*. ▶ **cook your goose 1** to ruin someone; to kill someone *UK, 1851*. **2** to drink to the point of being drunk *US, 1964*

cookbook *noun* in computing, a book of code segments that can be used to enhance programs *US, 1991*

cooked *adjective* **1** drunk or drug-intoxicated *US, 1997*. **2** in trouble *US, 1959*. **3** embalmed *US, 1987*. **4** finished, exhausted *UK, 1925*

cookem fry *verb* to die. Rhyming slang, from an earlier naval use as 'hell' *UK, 1969*

cooker *noun* **1** any object used to heat heroin preparatory to injecting it *US, 1958*. **2** a person who prepares crack cocaine *US, 1992*. **3** a person or thing that excels or excites *US, 1943*

cooker *verb* to inject a drug intravenously *UK, 2003*

cookie *noun* **1** a person *US, 1917*. **2** the vagina *US, 1970*. **3** a material reward or inducement; money *US, 1972*. **4** a sweet confection that has marijuana as a major ingredient *US, 2002*. **5** cocaine *US, 1949*. **6** a large chunk of processed crack cocaine *US, 1993*. **7** a cigarette *US, 1976*. **8** a cigarette adulterated with crack cocaine *US, 1997*. **9** a file that an Internet webpage leaves on the hard drive of a user's computer, that is retrieved whenever the user returns to that webpage *US, 1993*. **10** a blood clot travelling through the arteries *US, 1994*. **11** in television and film-making, a light screen designed to cast shadows *US, 1990*. ▶ **that's the way the cookie crumbles** that's how things turn out *US, 1956*

cookie breath *noun* the alcoholic fumes arising from someone who has drunk lemon extract or vanilla flavouring *CANADA, 1999*

cookie cutter *noun* **1** in circus and carnival usage, a police badge *US, 1926*. **2** the cap badge worn by officers of the Canadian Cadet Instructors Cadre. The CIC cap badge is brass and maple leaf-shaped. As such, its irregular edges are reminiscent of the serrated edge of a kitchen biscuit cutter *CANADA, 1995*

cookie duster *noun* a moustache *US, 1930*

cookies *noun* the contents of a person's stomach *US, 1927*. ▶ **blow your cookies** to vomit *US, 1976*. ▶ **get your cookies** to experience pleasure, especially in a perverted way *US, 1956*

cookie toss *noun* vomit *US, 1975*

cooking *adjective* **1** in shuffleboard, used for communicating the fact that a disc is in the kitchen *US, 1967*. **2** (used of surf conditions) excellent *US, 1977*

cooking fuel *noun* low-octane petrol *UK, 1979*

cooking lager *noun* a lager of no more than average strength *UK, 2002*

cook off *verb* (used of ammunition) to explode because of heat from a surrounding fire *US, 1990*

cook shack *noun* **1** a truck stop or roadside restaurant *US, 1976*. **2** a brakevan (caboose) *US, 1977*

cook up *verb* **1** to concoct something; to fabricate something; to falsify something. Often in the form 'cook up a story' *UK, 1817*. **2** to manufacture amphetamine *US, 1985*. **3** to process cocaine hydrochloride into crack cocaine *UK, 2002*

cooky *noun* in sabre fencing, a hit on the guard not on the target. A corruption of 'coquille' (the guard) *UK, 1988*

cool *noun* **1** self-control, composure *US, 1953*. **2** a truce between street gangs *US, 1958*. **3** a look. Back slang *UK, 1977*

cool *verb* **1** to calm down; to become less dangerous *US, 1977*. **2** to idle; to pass time doing nothing *US, 1990*. **3** to kill, or at least immobilise someone *US, 1962*. **4** to die *US, 1994*. ▶ **cool it** to unwind, to calm down; to slow down, to ease off; to stop whatever activity you are engaged in. Often used in the imperative *US, 1953*. ▶ **cool your brains** to calm down *TRINIDAD AND TOBAGO, 1928*. ▶ **cool your heels** to rest *UK, 1633*. ▶ **cool your jets** to calm down; to back off *US, 1973*. ▶ **cool your liver** to drink alcohol *BARBADOS, 1998*

cool *adjective* **1** fashionable, attractive, admired *US, 1947*. **2** acceptable, agreeable *US, 1994*. **3** (of jazz or the style of a jazz performer) relaxed, good, modern *US, 1947*. **4** discreet, under control. Similar to the earlier COOL AS A CUCUMBER *UK, 1952*. **5** retaining complete personal control of the need for drugs or whilst drug-exhilarated, or so the user believes *UK, 1973*. **6** not carrying illegal drugs *UK, 1967*. **7** used for emphasising an amount of money *UK, 1728*. ▶ **cool like Gokool** very successful *TRINIDAD AND TOBAGO, 1938*

coolaboola; coder-boder *adjective* excellent, admirable, acceptable. An elaboration of COOL (acceptable) combining a slangy abridgement of the Irish *ruaille-buaille* (a row, noisy confusion, noise) *IRELAND, 1996*

cool as *adjective* extremely pleasing, very good. An intensification of COOL, shortened from COOL AS FUCK, etc *UK, 2002*

cool as a cucumber *adjective* self-possessed *UK, c.1732*

cool as a fish's fart *adjective* calm, composed *IRELAND, 1996*

cool as fuck *adjective* extremely pleasing, very good. An intensification of COOL. In 1990, the phrase 'cool as fuck' was part of the logo-styling for UK band the Inspiral Carpets *UK, 1990*

cool bananas! great! excellent! *AUSTRALIA, 1987*

cool beans! used as an expression of intense approval *US, 1987*

cool breeze *noun* used as a term of address, generally with admiration *US, 1961*

cool breeze *adjective* calm, collected *US, 1967*

cool breezer *noun* a carefree, casual surfer *US, 1988*

Cool Britannia *noun* a marketing categorisation for fashionable British culture. Puns 'Rule Britannia'; originally coined by the Bonzo Dog Doo Dah Band in 1967: 'Cool Britannia / Britannia you are hip' *UK, 1999*

cool-cool; cool-cool so *adverb* as if normal *TRINIDAD AND TOBAGO, 2003*

coolcrack *verb* to kill someone *US, 1947*

cool dad *noun* a well-dressed, popular male. College student usage *US, 1959*

cool deal! used as an expression of assent or praise *US, 2001*

cool down *verb* to calm down *UK, 1882*

cooler *noun* **1** a jail or prison *US, 1872*. **2** a cell used for solitary confinement; a segregation unit *US, 1899*. **3** an infirmary. Where one's social activities are 'put on ice' *US, 1983*. **4** a morgue *US, 1994*. **5** a silencer attached to a hand gun *US, 1962*. **6** a cigarette laced with cocaine *US, 1994*. **7** a stacked deck of cards used by a cheat *US, 1935*. **8** in horse racing, a horse that is not expected to win the race *US, 1935*. **9** a lightweight cotton blanket put on a horse after a warm-up *US, 1964*

cooler-bagger *noun* a man with a paunch. Teen slang; coined in humorous reference to SIX-PACKER (a well-built man) *SOUTH AFRICA, 2003*

coolgardie safe; Coolgardie *noun* a type of storage locker for keeping foodstuffs cool. From the name of a Western Australian mining town *AUSTRALIA, 1924*

cool head main thing! used for urging others to calm down. Hawaiian youth usage *US, 1972*

cool-hunter *noun* a person engaged in the identification of up-coming trends, especially in the media or fashion industry. Formed on COOL (fashionable) *UK, 2002*

coolie *noun* **1** a loner; a person who refuses to join a gang *US, 1958*. **2** a hip, street-smart person *US, 1967*. **3** a cigarette to which crack cocaine has been added *US, 1992*

Coolie *noun* **1** in South Africa, a person of Indian descent. Offensive, insulting *INDIA, 1873*. **2** a Vietnamese civilian. The C19 term for Chinese or other East Asians was revived by US soldiers in Vietnam *US, 1991*. **3** an Asian servant *AUSTRALIA, 1995*. **4** a locomotive fireman *UK, 1970*

coolie *adjective* of East Indian origin *TRINIDAD AND TOBAGO, 1880*

coolie colours *noun* bright colours, especiallly in combination in dress. From the association of these bright colours with Indians *GRENADA, 1998*

coolie-do *noun* the vagina *US, 1972*

coolie food *noun* Indian food *TRINIDAD AND TOBAGO, 2003*

coolie pink *noun* a garish, bright pink. Associated with the bright colours favoured by East Indians *SOUTH AFRICA, 1978*

coolie tonic *noun* any liquid poison. In Trinidad, poison is associated with Indian suicides *TRINIDAD AND TOBAGO, 2003*

cooling *adjective* unemployed *US, 1949*

cooling glasses; coolers *noun* sunglasses *INDIA, 1979*

coolio *adjective* fashionable; acceptable. An elaboration of COOL; probably also a reference to rapper Coolio who enjoyed a huge international success in the mid-1990s *US, 1997*

cool it back *verb* to become calm and composed under pressure *US, 1984*

cool Muther John *noun* a boy who is fashionable, knowledgeable and trendy *US, 1955*

coolness! used for expressing agreement or approval *US, 1988*

cool off *verb* to calm down *UK, 1887*

cool-off man *noun* in a confidence swindling or cheating scheme, the member of the swindling group who stays with the victim calming him down after he learns that he has been swindled *US, 1977*

cool-out *noun* in police interrogations, the practice of leaving the accused alone in the interrogation room before the interrogation begins *US, 1997*

cool out *verb* **1** to idle *BARBADOS, 1965*. **2** in police interrogations, to perform a cool-out on someone *US, 1997*. **3** (used of a confidence swindler or a tout who has given bad tips) to calm a bettor who has lost *US, 1951*

cool points *noun* an imaginary tally of points awarded for cool behaviour and subtracted for uncool behaviour *US, 1989*

cool the beans! calm down!, be patient! *UK: SCOTLAND, 1988*

cool wash; coul wash *noun* a pelting with stones. Probably a corruption of the French *coup de roche* (blow with a stone) to Creole *koul woche* *DOMINICA, 2003*

cool water *noun* strong, illegally manufactured whisky *US, 1999*

cooly *noun* marijuana. Perhaps a deliberate mispronunciation of KALI *JAMAICA, 1998*

cool your jets! calm down! *US, 1982*

cool yule happy Christmas. A very uncool turn of phrase, generally heavily ironic or knowingly *infra dig* for humorous effect *UK, 1999*

coon *noun* in the UK and US, a black person; in Australia, an Aborigine; in New Zealand, a Pacific Islander; in South Africa, a black-faced minstrel. Offensive *US, 1834*

coon *verb* **1** to steal something; someone to cheat *US, 1964*. **2** to bet *US, 1947*. **3** on the railways, to travel over the tops of goods wagons while a train is moving *US, 1975*

coon-ass *noun* a resident of Louisiana; a Cajun. Often, not always, considered a slur *US, 1943*

coon bottom *noun* a poor part of town, especially one where poor black people live *US, 1968*

coondie *noun* a stone or rock, especially a small stone suitable for throwing. Usage chiefly in Western Australia *AUSTRALIA, 1941*

cooney *noun* **1** a white resident of Louisiana. A diminuitive of COON-ASS *US, 1975*. **2** a woman, especially a wife. Northern Canadian usage. Also spelled 'kuni' *CANADA, 1961*

coon killer *noun* a club *US, 1982*

coon light *noun* a light mounted on a truck tracking on the right edge of the road *US, 1971*

coon's age *noun* a long time *US, 1843*

coon stopper *noun* a powerful gun *US, 1977*

Coon Town *noun* a neighbourhood populated largely by black families. Offensive *US, 1987*

coop *noun* **1** a house or apartment *US, 1947*. **2** a police stationhouse *US, 1962*. **3** a place where police sleep or idle during their shift *US, 1973*. **4** in craps, a roll of 12. An abbreviated nickname of Gary Cooper, star of the Western film *High Noon US, 1983*

coop *verb* to sleep or relax while on duty *US, 1962*

coop delight *noun* the body of a murder victim. From the Latin *corpus delicti US, 1976*

cooper *verb* to silence or humiliate someone *CANADA, 1999*

coop-happy *adjective* deranged from confinement *US, 1960*

coo's arse; cow's arse *noun* **1** a cigarette end over-moistened with a smoker's saliva *UK: SCOTLAND, 1988*. **2** by extension, a botched job *UK: SCOTLAND, 1988*

coosie *noun* a Chinese person or other South Asian *US, 1949*

coot *noun* **1** a harmless simpleton, especially an old one; a fellow. Probably from the behavioural characteristics of the bird. Current in south London *US, 1766*. **2** the vagina; a woman as a sex object; sex with a woman *US, 1975*

coot *verb* to have sex *BAHAMAS, 1982*

cootch dancer; cooch dancer *noun* a woman who performs a sexually suggestive dance. A shortened form of HOOCHY KOOCHY *US, 1910*

cootchy-coo; kootchy-koo; kitchy-koo *noun* used as a lexicalisation of talk used with babies. From Irish dialect *kitchy, kitchy, kaw UK, 1984*

cooter *noun* the vagina *US, 1986*

cootie catcher *noun* a somewhat intricately folded piece of paper, manipulated by the fingers, used by children to tell fortunes or to catch imaginary cooties *US, 1987*

cooties *noun* an imaginary disease or infestation that could be transmitted by close contact, thus creating a stigma for the person who is said to have it. A children's corruption of the older sense of the term (a body louse) *US, 1971*

Coot-sac *noun* a cove or bay without an outlet. From the French *cul de sac* (dead end) *CANADA, 2001*

coover *noun* any article or thing. English gypsy use, from Romany *kova* (this; thing) *UK, 2000*

cooze; coozie *noun* **1** the vulva; the female genitals *US, 1927*. **2** a woman, especially a promiscuous woman *US, 1921*

cooze light *noun* in the pornography industry, a light used to illuminate the genitals of the performers *US, 1995*

coozie stash *noun* contraband, especially drugs, hidden in the vagina *US, 1992*

cop *noun* **1** a police officer. False etymologies abound, with formation suggestions of 'copper badges', 'copper buttons', or an initialism of 'Constable On Patrol' at the head of the unruly pack. The verb sense 'to grab' leads to the verb sense 'to arrest' which leads to COPPER which was shortened to 'cop'. No buttons, no badges, no initialisms *US, 1859*. **2** an arrest. Especially familiar in the phrase IT'S A FAIR COP *UK, 1844*. **3** a job or employment; a position *AUSTRALIA, 1915*. **4** treatment; a deal as in 'it's a rotten cop' *AUSTRALIA, 1968*. **5** in carnival usage, a small prize won at a game concession *US, 1980*. **6** winnings from gambling *US, 1930*. **7** a gratuity *AUSTRALIA, 1989*. ▶ **it's a fair cop** used of a good or legal arrest; in later use, as a jocular admission of anything trivial *UK, 1891*. ▶ **no cop; not much cop** worthless, valueless, useless *UK, 1902*

cop *verb* **1** to obtain, to take or to purchase something, especially drugs *US, 1867*. **2** to seduce someone, to have sex with someone *US, 1965*. **3** to come upon someone; to catch someone out *AUSTRALIA, 1933*. **4** to catch sight of someone or something; look at someone or something *AUSTRALIA, 1925*. **5** to see something; to notice something *UK, 1916*. **6** to catch someone *AUSTRALIA, 1889*. **7** to inform; to betray someone *US, 1895*. **8** to endure something *AUSTRALIA, 1971*. **9** to take or receive a bribe *UK, 1977*. **10** to steal something *AUSTRALIA, 1991*. **11** in trainspotting, to record a train's number *UK, 2003*. **12** (used of a rigged carnival game) to malfunction, allowing a player to win *US, 1985*. ▶ **cop a breeze** to leave, especially without calling attention to yourself *US, 1950*. ▶ **cop a deaf 'un** to pretend not to hear; to deliberately not listen to, or ignore, someone *UK, 1920s*. ▶ **cop a drop** to take a bribe. Combines COP (to obtain) with DROP (a bribe) *UK, 1970*. ▶ **cop a feel** to touch someone sexually without their consent *US, 1935*. ▶ **cop a heel** to leave; to run away; to escape *US, 1977*. ▶ **cop a joint** to perform oral sex on a man *US, 1962*. ▶ **cop a load** to take a look, especially to take a good look; to pay attention to something *UK, 1984*. ▶ **cop a minty wrapper** in horse racing, to receive a very small gratuity, or no gratuity at all, after winning a race *AUSTRALIA, 1989*. ▶ **cop a mope** to escape *US, 1951*. ▶ **cop a nod** to sleep *US, 1947*. ▶ **cop a packet 1** to be severely wounded. Originally military *UK, 1982*. **2** to become infected with a sexually transmitted disease *UK, 1984*. **3** to be sentenced to preventive detention. Prison use *UK, 1950*. ▶ **cop a plea** to enter a guilty plea to a criminal charge *US, late 1920s*. ▶ **cop a pose** to adopt the posture of a fashion or shop-window mannequin *UK, 2003*. ▶ **cop deuces** to assume a submissive or defensive position *US, 1976*. ▶ **cop it sweet 1** to enjoy the situation *AUSTRALIA, 1975*. **2** to receive something graciously *AUSTRALIA, 1989*. **3** in prison, to take punishment without complaint *AUSTRALIA,*

1950. **4** to endure unpleasantness without complaint; to resignedly put up with something bad *AUSTRALIA, 1988*. ▶ **cop on to** catch on to something; become aware of something *AUSTRALIA, 1957*. ▶ **cop the lot** to receive everything *AUSTRALIA, 1911*. ▶ **cop z's** to sleep *US, 1961*

cop *adjective* good, worth having, of value *UK, 2000*

copacetic; copasetic *adjective* good, excellent; safe; attractive. Etymology unknown; Chinook jargon, French, Italian and Yiddish sources have been suggested *US, 1919*

cop and blow *noun* the rule of thumb governing a pimp's *modus operandi*, acquiring and losing prostitutes *US, 1967*

cop and blow *verb* to acquire something and then leave *US, 1972*

cop and hold; cop and lock *verb* (of a pimp) to acquire and retain a prostitute *US, 1972*

cop caller *noun* a truck with squeaky brakes or noisy recapped tyres *US, 1938*

cope *verb* to function in normal situations while under the influence of a hallucinogenic drug *US, 1996*

Copenhagen capon *noun* a transsexual. Homosexual usage; an allusion to the sex-altering operation performed on Christine Jorgensen in Denmark *US, 2003*

Copenhagen snoose *noun* damp, grated chewing snuff *CANADA, 1964*

cop for *verb* to get into an intimate relationship with someone. From COP (to catch) *UK, 1985*

cop house; cop factory *noun* a police station *US, 1928*

copilot *noun* **1** a tablet of dextroamphetamine sulphate (trade name Dexedrine™), or any other central nervous system stimulant *US, 1965*. **2** the co-signer of a purchase contract or loan *US, 1975*

cop it *verb* **1** to get or receive something painful, such as a beating; to receive punishment *AUSTRALIA, 1916*. **2** to take or receive something *AUSTRALIA, 1982*. **3** to be killed *AUSTRALIA, 1960*. **4** to be hit with enemy fire *AUSTRALIA, 1932*

cop man *noun* a low-level drug dealer who must pay cash to the supplier for the drugs to be sold *US, 1989*

cop off *verb* **1** to form a liaison with someone based on mutual sexual attraction. Ultimately from COP (to catch) *UK, 1994*. **2** to fondle someone intimately; to engage in foreplay; to have sex *UK, 2001*. **3** to masturbate *UK, 2000*. **4** to shirk, to skive, to play truant *UK, 2002*

cop on *noun* understanding, common knowledge *IRELAND, 1997*

cop on *verb* to understand something; to start behaving reasonably. Sometimes said in angry response to a person's undesirable behaviour: 'cop (yourself) on' *IRELAND, 1991*

cop-out *noun* a drastic compromise of principle *US, 1956*

cop out *verb* **1** to avoid an issue by making excuses; to go back on your word *US, 1952*. **2** to confess; to enter a guilty plea *US, 1938*

cop-out man *noun* in a crooked version of the coin-tossing game two-up, the person who by arrangement takes the winnings *AUSTRALIA, 1953*

cop out on *verb* to inform on someone *UK, 1996*

copped-out *adjective* conventional. From COP OUT (to make excuses, to cease trying) *UK, 2000*

copper *noun* **1** a police officer. Derives from COP (to catch) *UK, 1846*. **2** a police informer *UK, 1937*. **3** a prison informer *UK, 1961*. **4** a pre-decimal penny or halfpenny coin; a post-decimal two-penny or one-penny coin; such coins mixed. Originally, about 1840, of coins actually made of copper; the term has survived bronze and further debasement *UK, 1712*

copper *verb* **1** in craps, to bet that the shooter will lose *US, 1950*. **2** to inform against someone *UK, 1924*. **3** to be engaged as a working police officer *UK, 1984*

copper chopper *noun* a police helicopter *US, 1979*

copper jitters *noun* an excessive fear of contact with the police *US, 1953*

coppers *noun* money *BARBADOS, 1965*

Coppers in Disguise *nickname* the Criminal Investigation Department. An jocular play on the well-known initials CID;

substituting COPPER (a police officer) for 'criminal' and referring to the non-uniformed status of the officers as 'in disguise' *UK, 1984*

copper's nark *noun* a police informer *AUSTRALIA, 1945*

copper time *noun* the reduction of a prison sentence for good behaviour *US, 1992*

copping neighborhood *noun* a neighbourhood where buyers and sellers know that drugs are sold *US, 1990*

copping zone *noun* an area in a city where buyers and sellers of drugs know to congregate and do business *US, 1989*

coppist *noun* a trainspotter, especially one positioned at a level crossing. From COP (to see something) *UK, 1946*

cop shop *noun* a police station *AUSTRALIA, 1941*

cop spotter *noun* a rearview mirror *US, 1971*

cop's rub *noun* a frisking or pat-down for weapons or contraband *US, 1973*

cop's tang *noun* a Ford Mustang modified and enhanced for police use *US, 1992*

cops' tank *noun* a jail cell reserved for policemen/criminals *US, 1985*

'copter; copter *noun* a helicopter *US, 1947*

cop that lot! just look at them!, or that!: especially to express admiration, astonishment or derision *AUSTRALIA, 1960*

copy *noun* a received radio-communication; a message confirming reception *US, 1976*

copy *verb* to understand what has been said. Shortwave radio slang that spread well outside the world of radio *US, 1984*

copybroke *adjective* descriptive of a computer program in which the copyright scheme has been disabled *US, 1991*

copy, copy I am receiving. Citizens' band radio slang *1981*

cop you later goodbye. With an intentional, if somewhat feeble, pun on 'copulator' or 'copulate her' *AUSTRALIA, 1988*

cor! used for registering shock, surprise or sexual desire. A euphemistic rendering of 'God!' *UK, 1931*

coral *noun* a capsule of chloral hydrate *US, 1970*

corals *noun* ▷*see:* CHORALS

coral stomper *noun* a Pacific Islander. Derogatory *NEW ZEALAND, 1998*

cor blimey!; gorblimey! used for registering shock or surprise. A euphemistic rendering of 'God blind me!'; abbreviates to BLIMEY! *UK, 1896*

cords *noun* corduroy trousers *US, 1926*

corduroy *noun* in surfing, a swell lined up like ribbing *US, 1991*

corduroy road *noun* a road built over a swamp or muddy land by laying logs side by side at right angles to the way *CANADA, 1961*

core *adjective* **1** said of pornography that shows penetration. A shortened HARDCORE *US, 1995.* **2** serious, weighty, important *US, 1986*

-core *suffix* when in combination with a (modern) musical style, used for creating a less compromising genre title *UK, 2000*

corella *noun* a sheep with patches of wool hanging loose *AUSTRALIA, 1953*

co-respondent shoes *noun* black and white or brown and white shoes of a type. Deriving, apparently, from the type of people who wore them: co-respondents in divorce cases; they were originally called 'co-respondent's shoes'. Originally fashionable between the World Wars, they were worn in the 1950s by entertainers as diverse as Max Miller and Elvis Presley. They have long been fashionable with golfers and are still available to buy *UK, 1934*

corey; cory; corie *noun* the penis. English gypsy use; probably from Romany *kori* (a thorn) *UK, 2000*

corflu *noun* correction fluid, especially the fluid used for correcting mimeograph stencils *US, 1982*

Corine *noun* cocaine *US, 1967*

cork *noun* a tampon *US, 1981*

cork *verb* **1** to have sex *US, 1983.* **2** to set your fishing gear to obstruct that of another fisherman *CANADA, 1989.* ▶ **cork the air** to sniff

cocaine *US, 1950.* ▶ **cork the bottle** (used of a relief pitcher in baseball) to enter a game and pitch effectively *US, 1967.* ▶ **cork your cryhole** to stop complaining *US, 2002*

corker *noun* **1** something or someone attractive, desirable or wonderful; a stunner *UK, 1882.* **2** something that closes or settles an argument *US, 1835.* **3** an inconsistent, unpredictable poker player *US, 1988*

cork in *verb* to become wedged after falling into a snow crevasse *ANTARCTICA, 2003*

corking *adjective* unusually large, fine or good *US, 1895*

cork off *verb* to sleep *US, 1959*

corkscrew *noun* a black woman's hair temporarily set in neatly aligned clumps to facilitate drying *BARBADOS, 1996*

corkscrew *verb* to move spirally, or cause something to move spirally *UK, 1837*

cork top *noun* a surfer *US, 1963*

corky *noun* a corked muscle *AUSTRALIA, 1986*

cor lummie!; cor lumme!; cor lummy! used as a general-purpose expletive. A Cockney variation of 'God love me!'; almost stereotypically Cockney but later use tends towards irony *UK, 1961*

corn *noun* **1** something that is excessively sentimental. Originally applied to all music that was not jazz in the 1930s, and then eased into general usage *US, 1936.* **3** whisky *US, 1967.* **4** any alcoholic beverage *TRINIDAD AND TOBAGO, 1986.* **5** money. Both corn and money are seen as staples of life *US, 1837.* **6** a hard scar produced by repeated drug injections *US, 1971*

corn *verb* to make a great deal of money without apparent effort *BARBADOS, 1996*

Corn and Broccoli Channel *nickname* the Canadian Broadcasting Corporation. A jocular formation from the network's initials *CANADA, 2002*

corn and bunion *noun* an onion. Rhyming slang; the plural is 'corns and bunions'. Also applied in idiomatic use *UK, 1931*

cornball *adjective* clichéd; overly sentimental *US, 1948*

cornbeef-and-biscuits politics; cornbeef-and-rum politics *noun* the practice of seeking to capture the votes of poor people by offering them gifts of corned beef, biscuits and rum as a bribe during political campaigns *BARBADOS, 1996*

corn belt *noun* the mid-western United States *US, 1955*

corn binder *noun* any International Harvester™ truck *US, 1971*

cornbread *noun* a simple, rural southern black person. Cornbread is a staple in the diet of poor rural southerners, black and white *US, 1954*

corn cob *noun* in electric line work, a thimble adapter pin *US, 1980*

corned *adjective* drunk *UK, 1785*

corned beef *noun* **1** in prison, a chief officer. Rhyming slang *UK, 1950.* **2** a thief. Rhyming slang. Also known as 'bully beef' *UK, 1984*

corned beef; corny *adjective* deaf. Glasgow rhyming slang, reliant on Glasgow pronunciation *UK: SCOTLAND, 1985*

cornelius *noun* marijuana *US, 1997*

Cornel Wilder *noun* a hair-fashion of the 1950s, popular with youths in Sydney. Named after US film actor Cornel Wilde (b.1915) who actually wore his hair shorter than the fashion he inspired *AUSTRALIA, 1953*

corner *noun* **1** in horse racing, a share of the winnings *AUSTRALIA, 1989.* **2** the block in a prison where the cells for solitary confinement are found *US, 1962.* ▶ **around the corner** in poker, said of a sequence of cards that uses the ace as both a high and low card *US, 1988.* ▶ **cut a corner; cut corners; cut the corners** to perform any task in a manner that minimises time, effort or expense, but for equal profit or even greater gain, and perhaps at the cost of safe practice or legality. From the conventional, literal sense *UK, 1957.* ▶ **in the corner** on a fishing or lobstering boat, fully throttled *US, 1978*

corner *verb* **1** to force someone into an embarrassing or difficult position. Figurative *US, 1824.* **2** to go around a corner of a racecourse; to drive a vehicle around a corner, especially at speed *UK, 1861*

corner boy *noun* **1** an urban youth who idles in the street *US, 1971.* **2** a fellow prisoner from a prisoner's neighbourhood *US, 1991*

corner game; cornering *noun* a confidence trick in which payment is received before the promised delivery of goods or sexual services will take place 'around the corner' – the delivery, of course, is never made *UK, 1956*

corner man *noun* a person who is not part of the criminal underworld but whose sympathies lie with the underworld in its constant strife with law enforcement *US, 1964*

cornet player *noun* a cocaine user *US, 1977*

corn-fed *adjective* unsophisticated, simple, rustic *US, 1924*

cornfield clemency *noun* escape from a rural prison *US, 1992*

cornfield meet *noun* a head-on train collision *US, 1931*

cornflake *noun* **1** a youthful, sexually inexperienced male who is the object of an older homosexual's desire *US, 1979.* **2** the cap badge worn by Canadian Forces recruits. Named because of its resemblance to a cornflake in colour and shape *CANADA, 2001*

cornflake *adjective* fake. Rhyming slang *UK, 1992*

corn game *noun* in a carnival, a Bingo game *US, 1960*

cornhead *noun* a long-haired adherent to the racist, fascist philosophy espoused by shaved-head skinheads *US, 2000*

cornhole *noun* the anus *US, 1922*

cornhole *verb* **1** to take the active role in anal sex *US, 1938.* **2** to victimise someone; to force someone into submission. A figurative use of the previous sense *US, 1974*

corn husk *noun* a condom, especially one manufactured for anal intercourse. Derives from CORNHOLE (anal sex); conventionally, 'husk' is the membranous outer covering of the maize plant *UK, 1998*

Cornish pasty; Cornish *adjective* appetising; sexually alluring. Rhyming slang for 'tasty' *UK, 1992*

corn man *noun* a man who is emotionally and sexually inexperienced *TRINIDAD AND TOBAGO, 2003*

corn mule *noun* homemade alcohol using corn as a base *US, 1949*

corn off the cob *noun* mawkish, sentimental music or entertainment. An elaboration of CORN *AUSTRALIA, 1984*

corn on the cob *adjective* used as an intensifier *UK, 1997*

cornpone *noun* an unsophisciated, crude rural southerner. Poet Lawrence Ferlinghetti regularly referred to US President Lyndon B. Johnson as 'Colonel Cornpone' in his poems; cartoonist Al Capp created General Jubilation T. Cornpone, master of grabbing defeat from the jaws of victory *US, 1919*

cornrip *noun* a prostitute *BARBADOS, 1965*

corn row *noun* hair tied in tight braids separated by rows of bare scalp *US, 1946*

corn-row *verb* to fix hair in tight braids *US, 1971*

corn snake *noun* a dried corn stalk gusting across a road. Biker (motorcycle) usage *US, 2003*

corn stalker *noun* a marijuana cigarette rolled in the outer leaf of a corn cob and sealed with honey *US, 2003*

corny *adjective* mawkish, sentimental, hackneyed *US, 1932* ▷ *see:* CORNED BEEF

corp *noun* a corporal, generally as a term of address. Military *UK, 1959*

corpie *noun* a police officer *SAINT KITTS AND NEVIS, 1996*

Corpo *nickname* Dublin Corporation *IRELAND, 2000*

corporation *noun* a prominent belly *UK, 1753*

corporation cocktail *noun* an intoxicating drink made by bubbling coal gas through milk. Current in the 1970s, until wholesale conversion to natural gas *UK, 1984*

corporation pop *noun* tap water. Formed from 'pop' (a soft drink) and the 'corporation' that supplied water to domestic consumers; used in northern England *UK, ENGLAND, 1997*

corpse *noun* **1** an actor's on-stage blunder or fit of laughter. From the verb *UK, 1978.* **2** a corporal. In Royal Air Force use *UK, 2002*

corpse *verb* of an actor, to blunder and so confuse yourself or another actor; while acting, to fall prey to irresistible laughter *UK, 1873*

corpse cop *noun* a homicide detective *US, 1985*

corpser *noun* an actor who is prone to disruptive laughter. From CORPSE (to blunder) *UK, 2002*

corpsing *noun* involuntary laughter, especially among actors. From the verb *UK, 2002*

corpuscle *noun* used as a humourous synonym for 'corporal' *US, 1968*

corr *noun* a fight. English gypsy use, from Romany *koor* (to fight) *UK, 2000*

corral *noun* a group of prostitutes working for a single pimp *US, 1971*

corroboree *noun* any gathering or party; a celebration. Figurative use of the original sense as 'a traditional dance ceremony held by Australian Aboriginals', from the extinct Australian Aboriginal language Dharug, spoken in the Sydney region. Now considered politically incorrect *AUSTRALIA, 1833*

corroded *adjective* ugly *US, 1980*

corset *noun* a bullet-proof vest *US, 1949*

corvey; corvee *noun* in Quebec, a community work project. Originally the word, from French, meant 'community work repairing the road in the spring'. In French, it carries the sense of 'what a bore!' but in English, it is still used *CANADA, 2002*

corybungus *noun* the buttocks. Homosexual usage; perhaps from COREY (the penis) *UK, 2002*

cosa *noun* marijuana. From the Spanish for 'thing', so functionally the equivalent of 'stuff', an intentionally vague inreference to the drug *US, 1992*

cosh; kosh *noun* a bludgeon, a truncheon *UK, 1869.* ▶ **under the cosh** at a disadvantage; under control *UK, 1958*

cosh *verb* to strike someone with a cosh *UK, 1896*

co-signer *noun* a fellow prisoner who is willing to vouch for you or to defend you with action *US, 1989*

coskel *adjective* dressed in conflicting, clashing colours *TRINIDAD AND TOBAGO, 1996*

cosmic *adjective* **1** wonderful, excellent, fabulous. The teenage appetite for superlatives is OUT OF THIS WORLD *UK, 1977.* **2** esoteric, difficult to grasp *US, 1980*

cosmic rays *noun* the source of an unexplained computing problem *US, 1991*

cosmos *noun* phencyclidine, the recreational drug known as PCP or angel dust *US, 1977*

cossie; cozzie *noun* **1** a theatrical costume *UK, 1967.* **2** a swimming costume *AUSTRALIA, 1926*

cost *verb* to be expensive *UK, 1933.* ▶ **cost a bomb** to be very, or unexpectedly, expensive *UK, 1984.* ▶ **cost a packet** to be very, or unexpectedly, expensive *UK, 1984.* ▶ **cost an arm and a leg** to be very, or unexpectedly, expensive *US, 1956*

Costa del *noun* when combined with a place name, an area that is peopled with criminals. After COSTA DEL CRIME *UK, 2003*

Costa del Crime *noun* Spain's Costa del Sol. In the late 1970s, a diplomatic breakdown between Britain and Spain (over Gibraltar) created a safe haven for British criminals. One of the effects of a major armed robbery in London in 1983 was this journalistic coinage *UK, 1984*

Costa del Sludge *noun* the Spanish Riviera. A bitter reference to pollution *UK, 1980*

Costa Geriatrica *noun* the south coast of England; Spain's Costa Brava; any coastal area popular as a retirement destination; hence, also applied to non-coastal areas such as Henley-on-Thames. A jocular but nevertheless derisive reference to the number of old people that retire to the seaside *UK, 1977*

cosy *noun* an act of sexual intercourse. Used by upper-class society females; from the verb sense (to snuggle) *UK, 1982*

cot *noun* a bed AUSTRALIA, 1954

cot case *noun* an incapacitated person, such as a drunk or insane person. That is, 'a person who should be confined to a bed' AUSTRALIA, 1932

cotch *noun* any improvised place to sleep JAMAICA, 1972

cotch *verb* to vomit. From Afrikaans *kots* SOUTH AFRICA, 1974

cotched *adjective* relaxed, especially in a post-dance or post-drug-use situation. Used by some teenagers for 'chilled out' UK, 2003

cotics *noun* narcotics, especially heroin US, 1942

cottage *noun* a public lavatory used for homosexual encounters UK, 1932

cottage *verb* to seek homosexual contact in a public urinal. After COTTAGE (a public lavatory) UK, 1971

cottage cheese *noun* cellulite. A purely visual coining US, 1997

cottage queen *noun* a homosexual man who seeks sexual contact in public toilets. A combination of COTTAGE (a public lavatory) and QUEEN (a homosexual man) UK, 1992

cottager *noun* a homosexual man who seeks sexual contact in public toilets. After COTTAGE (a public lavatory) UK, 2000

cottaging *noun* **1** the practice of engaging in homosexual encounters in public toilets UK, 1972. **2** the practice of going down to your 'cottage' – a second and often quite a large house – in the country for the weekend UK, 1984

cotton *noun* **1** cotton used for straining a dissolved narcotic (heroin, cocaine or morphine) before injection; the bits of cotton saturated with drugs can be aggregated for an injection US, 1933. **2** female pubic hair US, 1970 ▷ *see*: COTTON WOOL

cotton ball *noun* a burst of flak fire as perceived from the air US, 1990

cotton brothers *noun* cocaine, heroin and morphine. From the cotton strainer used when prepararing these drugs US, 1938

cotton-chopper *noun* used as a term of address, especially to someone with a southern accent US, 1977

cotton fever *noun* an intense illness sometimes suffered after injecting heroin leached from used cottons US, 1989

cottonhead *noun* a heroin addict who habitually uses cotton used by other addicts to leach out heroin for his use US, 1970

cotton mouth *noun* a dryness of the mouth as a result of smoking marijuana or hashish, 2003

cotton on to; cotton on; cotton to *verb* to form, or have, a liking or fancy for something or someone; to understand or come to understand AUSTRALIA, 1907

cottonpicker *noun* a fellow; used as a term of address, especially from trucker to trucker US, 1919

cotton-picking *adjective* used as a folksy intensifier US, 1952

cotton shooter *noun* a drug addict who injects residue aggregated from cotton swatches used to strain drugs US, 1951

cotton slut *noun* a person who will attend an event for the sole purpose of obtaining a tee-shirt being given to those in attendance US, 2001

cottontail *noun* an attractive woman US, 1962

cotton-top *noun* an old person. An allusion to the white hair with which some older people are blessed US, 2000

cotton wool; cotton *noun* a casual quest for a sexual partner. Rhyming slang for PULL, in the phrase ON THE PULL (to quest or be questing for a sexual partner) UK, 1998. ▶ **wrap in cotton-wool; keep in cotton-wool** to cosset; to be extremely protective of someone UK, c.1890

couch *noun* ▶ **on the couch 1** undergoing psychotherapy US, 1961. **2** in gambling, without further funds US, 1996

couch casting *noun* the practice of casting roles in performances based on the actor's willingess to have sex with the casting director US, 1973

couch commander *noun* someone watching television with a remote control US, 1991

couch dance *noun* a sexual dance performed in a sex club, with the dancer grinding on the lap of a man seated on a couch US, 1990

couchie *noun* ▷ *see*: KOUTCHIE

couch lock *noun* a feeling of inertia as a result of smoking marijuana UK, 2004

couch potato *noun* a person who habitually idles, watching television. Possibly a pun on 'boob-tuber' (a television addict) and a 'potato' as a 'tuber'; it may also play on VEGETABLE (a person with an undemanding existence); the 'couch', of course, is where the potato is planted. One of the very few slang words or phrases where it is seemingly possible to trace the coining; in July 1976 a group of friends in California coined the term, which was first used in commerce in 1977 and then hit the big time with the *Official Couch Potato Handbook* (1983) US, 1976

couch surfer *noun* a person who sleeps on a friend's couch overnight NEW ZEALAND, 2003

cough *noun* **1** a confession. After COUGH (to confess) UK, 1978. **2** a piece of information or good evidence. Police use; from COUGH UP (to disclose) UK, 1984. **3** money paid out. From COUGH UP (to pay) US, 2000

cough *verb* **1** to confess US, 1899. **2** in drag racing, to suffer complete engine failure. Used as a transitive verb; 'you cough your engine' US, 1968. ▶ **cough your cud** to vomit NEW ZEALAND, 1989

cough! said humorously while pretending to grab at another man's testicles. From the practice in medical examinations of cupping the testicles and testing the healthy movement that is occasioned by a cough UK, 1984

cough and a spit *noun* **1** a small part in a play or a film UK, 1984. **2** a short distance UK, 2003

cough and choke *verb* to smoke. Also used as a noun to mean 'a cigarette' UK, 1998

cough and die *verb* (used of a computer program) to cease operating by virtue of a design feature US, 1991

cough and drag *noun* a cigarette. Rhyming slang for FAG (a cigarette), pitched somewhere between irony and black humour UK, 1992

cough and sneeze *noun* cheese. Rhyming slang, generally thought to date from late C19 UK, 1961

cough and splutter *noun* butter. Rhyming slang UK, 1978

cough drop *noun* an attractive girl SOUTH AFRICA, 1946

cough it up – it might be a gold watch! used as jocular encouragement to someone with a hacking cough UK, 1978

cough syrup *noun* money paid to police informers US, 1951

cough up *verb* **1** to pay; to hand over something US, 1890. **2** to disclose something US, 1896

couillon *noun* a lacrosse-like two ball game played by eastern Canadian Indian women on ice or in a clearing CANADA, 1951

couldn't-care-less *adjective* indifferent, uncaring UK, 1947

council gritter; council *noun* the anus. Rhyming slang for SHITTER UK, 2002

council houses *noun* trousers. Rhyming slang UK, 1934

count *noun* the ratio by which a drug is diluted US, 1964

count *verb* in pool, to make a shot US, 1967. ▶ **count days** in twelve-step recovery programmes such as Alcoholics Anonymous, to track your recovery from addiction US, 1998. ▶ **count your money** to use the toilet US, 1954

counter *noun* **1** in poker, a player who to the annoyance of other players repeatedly counts his chips or money US, 1963. **2** a prostitute's customer US, 1964. **3** in lobstering, a lobster that meets the legal measurement requirements US, 1978

counter hopper *noun* a dedicated follower of youth fashion UK, 1983

countess *noun* an older homosexual man US, 1979

country *noun* ▶ **in country** during the Vietnam war, in Vietnam US, 1971

country *adjective* unsophisticated, rural, not world-wise US, 1964

country bama *noun* a naive, gullible rustic US, 1990

country booboo *noun* any naive, gullible person *VIRGIN ISLANDS, BRITISH, 1996*

country bookie *noun* a naive rustic *TRINIDAD AND TOBAGO, 1904*

country Cadillac *noun* a pickup truck *US, 1976*

country club *noun* **1** a minimum security, comfortable prison generally reserved for corporate and banking criminals *US, 1960*. **2** anything that appears to be relatively comfortable and undemanding *US, 1973*

country cousin *noun* **1** the bleed period of the menstrual period *US, 1908*. **2** a dozen. Rhyming slang *UK, 1909*

country dunny *noun* ▶ **all alone like a country dunny** completely alone; by yourself; friendless *AUSTRALIA, 1988*. ▶ **like a country dunny** glaringly obvious; standing out *AUSTRALIA, 1954*

country mile *noun* a long distance or margin *US, 1951*

country mouse *noun* in Antarctica, a scientist or scientist's assistant whose work takes them into the field, away from McMurdo Station *ANTARCTICA, 2003*

country send *noun* in a big con, sending the victim away to retrieve money *US, 1997*

country store *noun* in the Vietnam war, a military self-service supply centre *US, 1968*

country straight *noun* in poker, a hand consisting of four sequenced cards which can be converted into a five-card sequence with the correct draw at either end of the sequence *US, 1978*

country wool *noun* homespun wool *CANADA, 1956*

count store *noun* a rigged carnival game *US, 1985*

count the hooks!; count the hoops! in the Canadian military, used for demanding that a subordinate recognises the uniform and rank of the superior rebuking him or her *CANADA, 1995*

county *noun* any county jail, where the accused are held before trial and prisoners convicted of misdemeanours are incarcerated for short sentences *US, 1953*

county *adjective* in the manner of the landed gentry; snobbish, pretentious in the manner of, or with pretentions to, the gentry *UK, 1921*

county blues *noun* a blue uniform issued to prisoners in a county jail *US, 1993*

County Kilburn *nickname* the northwest London district of Kilburn. Formed in the manner of an Irish County in recognition of the high density of Irish in Kilburn's population *UK, 2000*

county mountie *noun* **1** a member of the Ulster Defence Regiment (1970–1992). Adopted from the US meaning (a local police officer); a reference to the six counties of Ulster *UK, 1981*. **2** a local police officer *US, 1975*

count your fingers! used with heavy humour to suggest distrust of a person who is shaking, or has just shaken, someone's hand *UK, 1984*

county shoes *noun* inexpensive shoes issued to prisoners by a county jail *US, 1973*

county time *noun* time served in a local county jail, as opposed to a state or federal prison. Less than 'state time' or 'hard time' *US, 1996*

coup *noun* **1** a crime *UK, 2001*. **2** in horse racing, a secret betting plunge in which a great deal of money is bet at favourable odds *AUSTRALIA, 1895*

Coupe *noun* a Cadillac Coupe de Ville car *US, 1980*

coupla *noun* two. A slovening of 'couple of' *UK, 1959*

couple *noun* several drinks, especially beers, not necessarily two *UK, 1935*

couple of bob *noun* **1** a non-specific amount of money. Pre-1971, when decimalisation changed the face and value of sterling, a **BOB** was 'a shilling' (5p) *UK, 1980*. **2** a job. Rhyming slang *UK, 1992*. **3** a lump of phlegm. Rhyming slang for **GOB** (to spit) *UK, 1992*

coupon *noun* **1** the face. Often in the phrase 'fill in your coupon' (attack your face) *UK, 1980*. **2** an 'I owe you' which has not and will not be paid off *US, 1996*. **3** in trucking, a speeding ticket *US, 1976*

courage *noun* sexual potency *BAHAMAS, 1982*

courage pill *noun* **1** a capsule of heroin *US, 1933*. **2** a central nervous system despressant *UK, 2003*

'course of course *UK, 1886*

course-a-grunt; course-a-pig *noun* an error in bricklaying in which opposite ends of a new wall meet at different heights *UK, 1978*

course note *noun* paper money in denominations of $5 or greater *US, 1950*

court *noun* ▶ **hold court in the street** to mete out what a police officer deems justice through physical beatings *US, 2001*

court *verb* ▶ **court Cecil** to become addicted to morphine *US, 1992*

court card *noun* in a deck of playing cards, any jack, queen or king *US, 1961*

courtesy flush *noun* a mid-defecation flush of the toilet as a courtesy to others in a bathroom or other prisoners in the cell *US, 1996*

court-in *noun* a ceremonial beating to initiate a new member into a gang *US, 1990*

court-out *noun* a ceremonial beating of a person leaving a gang *US, 1990*

Cousin Charlie *nickname* the Federal Communications Commission *US, 1976*

cousin Ella *noun* an umbrella. Rhyming slang *UK, 1992*

Cousin Jack *noun* a Cornish man, especially a miner *AUSTRALIA, 1863*

cousins *noun* curly hair on the back of the neck *BAHAMAS, 1982*

cousin Sis *noun* a piss (an act of urination); piss (alcohol), especially in the phrase 'going on the cousin Sis'. Rhyming slang *UK, 1998*

couta *noun* a barracouta *AUSTRALIA, 1933*

cove *noun* a fellow, bloke. From Romany *kova* (a thing, a person) *UK, 1567*

Covent Garden pardon, especially as a shortened version of 'I beg your pardon'. Rhyming slang, replacing the original (1857) sense as 'a farthing' (a coin that was worth 1/4 of a penny); formed on the name of a fashionable area of central London when it still had a reputation as a market for fruit and vegetables *UK, 1992*

cover *noun* **1** an admission fee paid to enter a bar or club. A shortened 'cover charge' *US, 1986*. **2** a single large-denomination note wrapped around small-denomination notes, giving the impression of a great deal of money *US, 1964*. **3** a recording which has been popularised by someone else. A shortened form of the more formal 'cover version' *US, 1970*. **4** the disguise and staged personality assumed by an expert card counter playing blackjack in a casino in the hope of avoiding detection and ejection *US, 1991*

cover *verb* **1** (used of a male) to have sex with a woman. Conventionally applied to a stallion with a mare *TRINIDAD AND TOBAGO, 1980*. **2** (used of a favourite by sports gamblers) to win by at least the margin established as the pointspread by the bookmakers *US, 1991*

covered wagon *noun* **1** an aircraft carrier, especially the USS Langley *US, 1933*. **2** an ugly or unpleasant woman. Rhyming slang for **DRAGON** *US, 1992*

covered with horseshoes *adjective* extremely lucky *US, 1988*

cover for *verb* **1** to act as a substitute for another worker *UK, 1976*. **2** to conceal someone's crime or mistake *UK, 1968*

covers *noun* ▶ **pull the covers off** to reveal someone's homosexuality *US, 1981*

covey *noun* a group of gullible people, likely victims for a swindle or crime *US, 1964*

cow *noun* **1** a contemptible woman *UK, 1696*. **2** a fellow, bloke *AUSTRALIA, 1941*. **3** a despicable person *AUSTRALIA, 1894*. **4** a prostitute attached to a pimp *US, 1859*. **5** something that causes annoyance *AUSTRALIA, 1904*. **6** any unpleasant situation or experience *NEW ZEALAND, 1964*. **7** a can of evaporated milk. Follows 'the' *US, 1975*. **8** a transport aircraft, usually a C-123 or C-130, outfitted with pumps and large rubberised drums *US, 1991*. ▶ **have a cow** to become emotionally overwrought; to lose control *US, 1966*. ▶ **run cow; work cow** to work for personal gain while in the employ of another *GUYANA, 1952*

Cow & Gate *adjective* late, in the sense that the bleed period of the menstrual cycle is overdue. Rhyming slang, formed, with heavy irony, on the name of a well-known baby food manufacturer *UK, 1998*

cowabunga; cuyabunga! used as an expression of triumph. Originally a signature line uttered by Chief Thunderthud on *The Howdy Doody Show* (NBC, 1947–60). Embraced by surfers, American soldiers in Vietnam, and the writers of *Teenage Mutant Ninja Turtles* and *The Simpsons US, 1955*

cow and calf *noun* **1** half; thus, 50 pence (half £1). Rhyming slang. Variants are 'cow calf' and 'cows' *UK, 1950*. **2** a laugh. Rhyming slang. Also used as a verb *UK, 1992*

cow and horse; cow *noun* sexual intercouse. Rhyming slang *UK, 2003*

cowardy custard; cowardy, cowardy custard *noun* a coward. Custard is YELLOW (the colour applied as an adjective for cowardice) and so reinforces the accusation. This taunting form of address is usually hurled or chanted by children *UK, 1836*

cow belt *noun* the rural areas of the Indo-Gangetic plain. Journalistic, from the perception that more traditional Hindu values hold sway in such communities, and, therefore, a cow is revered more there than elsewhere in modern India *INDIA, 2001*

cowboy *noun* **1** a reckless, impulsive, undisciplined person *US, 1926*. **2** a flash fellow; a know-all *UK, 1978*. **3** a young and inexperienced, or irresponsible, driver *UK, 1984*. **4** a motorist prone to breaking the rules of the road *US, 1928*. **5** any tradesman (such as a builder, electrician, mechanic or plumber) who is unreliable, irresponsible and, perhaps, unqualified; the sort to make quick money by undercutting regular, trained craftsmen. As in the sign for Patel Brothers Builders: 'You've tried the Cowboys, now try the Indians!' *UK, 1984*. **6** a minor criminal given to violence. From such a person's tendency to 'come out shooting' *UK, 1977*. **7** during the Vietnam war, an unprincipled, untrustworty, hustling Vietnamese person *US, 1991*. **8** a beginner. Mining usage *CANADA, 1959*. **9** used as a humorous term of address *US, 1999*. **10** in horse racing, any jockey with an unconventional style of riding *AUSTRALIA, 1989*. **11** a bow-legged man. From the gait of such a horse-rider *UK, 1984*. **12** in computing, a person with intelligence, knowledge and dedication to programming *US, 1991*. **13** in a deck of playing cards, a king *US, 1967*. **14** a perfunctory cleaning of the body with a wash cloth but not a full bath or shower *BAHAMAS, 1982*

Cowboy *nickname* Nguyen Cao Ky, Prime Minister of South Vietnam after the murder of Diem. So named by President Diem. 'Cowboy' is a term the Vietnamese then reserved for only the most flamboyant of gangsters. US Secretary of Defense McNamara condemned Ky as 'the absolute bottom of the barrel' *US, 1991*

cowboy *verb* **1** to murder someone in a reckless manner *US, 1946*. **2** to gang-rape someone *US, 1957*

cowboy Bible *noun* a packet of cigarette rolling papers *US, 1970*

cowboy Cadillac *noun* any pickup truck *US, 1976*

cowboy coffee *noun* coffee boiled in an open pot, served without milk or sugar *US, 1943*

cowboy cool *adjective* (used of beer) at room temperature *US, 1984*

cowboy coupe *noun* a pickup truck decked out with accessories *US, 1962*

cowboy hat *noun* a disposable paper toilet seat cover *US, 1992*

cowboys *noun* the police; police officers *UK, 1960*

Cowboys *nickname* ▶ **the Cowboys** third battalion, Royal Green Jackets *UK, 1995*

cowboys and Indians *noun* a prison sentence of 99 years *US, 1990*

cow cage *noun* a livestock carriage on a freight train *US, 1946*

cow cocky *noun* a dairy farmer *AUSTRALIA, 1902*

cow college *noun* a small rural college, especially one offering degrees in agriculture *US, 1906*

cow confetti; cowyard confetti *noun* nonsense, rubbish. A euphemism for BULLSHIT *AUSTRALIA, 1941*

cow cunt *noun* a despicable person *US, 1988*

cow-cunted *adjective* possessing a slack and distended vagina *US, 1980*

Cowdenbeath *noun* the teeth. Glasgow rhyming slang, formed from a Scottish town (and football team) *UK: SCOTLAND, 1988*

cow dust time *noun* evening. A direct translation from Bengali *go-dhuli*, describing the dust that hangs in the air at that time of day when the cattle are returned from the fields *INDIA, 2004*

cowgirl *noun* a sexual position in which the woman is on top, astride and facing her partner *US, 1995*

cow grease *noun* butter. Originally 'cow's grease', 1857 *UK, 1857*

cowing *adjective* used to intensify. Probably military origins; a euphemism for FUCKING *UK, 1962*

cowing lush *adjective* marvellous, wonderful; used as an all-purpose expression of admiration *UK: WALES, 2001*

cow juice *noun* milk *UK, 1796*

cow-kick *verb* (of a horse) to kick outward and upward like a cow *CANADA, 1954*

cow lick *noun* in publishing, inexpensive varnish used on a book cover *US, 1986*

cowpat *noun* a single dropping of cow dung *UK, 1954*

cowpath *noun* a narrow back road *US, 1971*

cowpat lotto *noun* a lottery in which the winner is decided by which part of a paddock a cow first drops dung *AUSTRALIA, 1995*

cow poke *noun* a wooden device to keep a cow from going through a fence *US, 1968*

cow's breakfast *noun* a straw hat *CANADA, 1959*

cow's calf; cow and calf; cow's; calf *noun* until 1971, ten shillings; thereafter, fifty pence. Rhyming slang for 'half' (of £1). Pre-decimalisation, mainly reduced to 'calf'; in later C20 'cows' predominates *UK, 1941*

cowsh *noun* cattle excrement; nonsense. An abbreviation of 'cow shit' *AUSTRALIA, 1937*

cow's lick *noun* prison; a prison. Rhyming slang for NICK (a prison) *UK, 1962*

cowson *noun* a contemptible man. Literally, 'the son of a cow' *UK, 1936*

cowstroke *noun* in cricket, a hefty stroke to the leg side *UK, 1978*

cow-tongue *noun* a gossip *TRINIDAD AND TOBAGO, 2003*

Cow Town *nickname* **1** Forth Worth, Texas *US, 1976*. **2** Calgary, Alberta *CANADA, 1962*

cow trail *verb* to take a motorcyle cruise in the country for recreation *US, 1973*

cowyard *noun* an inexpensive brothel *US, 1964*

cowyard cake *noun* a cake or bun containing a few sultanas *AUSTRALIA, 1953*

cox box *noun* an electronic device that includes an amplifier/microphone system as well as various measurement functions, used by a coxswain in competitive rowing *US, 1999*

coxed *adjective* (of a boat) under the control of a *cox*swain *UK, 2001*

coxey; cocksy *noun* an inexperienced swindler working on a scam by telephone who makes the initial call to potential victims *US, 1988*

coxy *noun* a *cox*swain *US, 1966*

coyote French *noun* the mixture of Canadian French, Cree and English spoken by the older Metis *CANADA, 1963*

coyote ugly *adjective* very ugly. The conceit of the term is that a man who wakes up with a 'coyote ugly' woman sleeping on his arm will, like a coyote caught in a trap, gnaw off his arm to escape *US, 1985*

cozmo *noun* phencyclidine, the recreational drug known as PCP or angel dust *US, 1994*

cozy *adjective* dull, boring *US, 1993*

cozzer *noun* a police officer; the police. A confusion of Hebrew *chazar* (pig) and COPPER (a police officer) *UK, 1958*

CP *noun* corporal punishment *US, 1987*

c phone *noun* a mobile telephone. 'C' is for 'cellular' *US, 1997*

CP pill *noun* a large, orange anti-malaria pill taken once a week. Chloroquine-Primaquine *US, 1991*

CPR strawberry *noun* a prune *CANADA, 1987*

CPT; CP time *noun* a notional system of time in which punctuality is not important. An abbreviation of COLORED PEOPLE'S TIME *US, 1925*

crab *noun* **1** a contemptible person *UK, 1580.* **2** in the language of members of the Bloods youth gang, a member of the Crips youth gang *US, 1987.* **3** a member of the Royal Air Force *UK, 1983.* **4** a first-year college student *US, 1947.* **5** the vulva. Sometimes expanded to 'crabby'. *BAHAMAS, 1982.* **6** in the television and film industries, a device used to support a tripod on a slippery or uneven surface *UK, 1960*

crab *verb* **1** (of an aircraft) to fly close to the ground or water; to drift or manoeuvre sideways. From the sideways movement of a crab. An aircraft flying close to the ground may appear to fly diagonally *UK, 1943.* **2** in the language of parachuting, to direct the parachute across the wind direction *US, 1978.* **3** in the television and film industries, to move the camera sideways *US, 1987.* **4** to spoil something *UK, 1812.* **5** in horse racing, to belittle a horse's performance *UK, 1948*

crab *adjective* perverse; ill-humoured, perpetually mean, cross. A shortening of CRABBY *UK, 1961*

crab air *nickname* the Royal Air Force (RAF). Military use; extends from CRAB (a member of the Royal Air Force) *UK, 1987*

crab bait *noun* a newly arrived prisoner *US, 1976*

crabbie *noun* the vagina *BAHAMAS, 1995*

crabby *adjective* ill humoured, perpetually mean, cross. The villain of the extremely popular 1957 *Tom Terrific* cartoon series from Terry-Toon Cartoon Studios was the aptly named Crabby Appleton, who was, we remember, 'rotten to the core' *US, 1908*

crab-fat *noun* an airman in the Royal Air Force. In army and navy use. From the colour and consistency of a blue ointment used to treat CRABS (pubic lice); the blue is of a similar shade to the Royal Air Force uniform. However, this derivation may not be direct, nor strictly accurate. From the early C20, Admiralty grey paint was called 'crab-fat' and the anti-lice ointment was claimed as the inspiration for that shade. It seems equally likely, therefore, that this later use should derive from the grey paint *UK, 1961*

crabfats *noun* the Royal Air Force. In army and navy use; from the singular sense CRAB-FAT (an airman) *UK, 1961*

crab-foot *noun* childlike, scratchy handwriting *BELIZE, 1996*

crab hole *noun* a depression in swampy ground *NEW ZEALAND, 1964*

crab in a barrel *noun* used as a representation of the inability of people to work together *TRINIDAD AND TOBAGO, 2003*

crab-mash *verb* to do a poor job ironing clothes *BARBADOS, 1965*

crabs *noun* **1** pubic lice *UK, 1707.* **2** in craps, a three *US, 1938.* **3** by extension, in a deck of playing cards, any three *US, 1981*

crabs on the rocks *noun* an itching of the scrotum. A play on CRABS (pubic lice) *UK, 1961*

crack *noun* **1** crystalline lumps of concentrated cocaine *US, 1985.* **2** entertaining conversation in good company. Irish neologism *craic* (an informal entertainment) combines with earlier Eirrean use of 'the crack' (brisk talk, news); ultimately from Old English *cracian* (crack, a loud noise) *IRELAND, 1966.* **3** a witticism; a quick and funny remark *US, 1884.* **4** a witty person *US, 1976.* **5** a smart person *FIJI, 1993.* **6** a top class racehorse *AUSTRALIA, 1960.* **7** the vagina. The imagery from which this derives should be apparent; it remains in widespread use *UK, 1775.* **8** the cleft between the buttock muscles; loosely, the bottom; or, more narrowly, the anus *UK, 1999.* **9** a passing of wind *US, 1946.* **10** an instance; one item *US, 1937.* **11** an opportunity or chance *US, 1893.* **12** an attempt. In phrases 'have a crack', 'take a crack', 'give a crack', etc *US, 1836.* **13** of dawn or day, the break, the instant it commences *US, 1887.* **14** the latest news. Anglo-Irish. Heard on a building site in Lancashire *UK, 1979.* **15** wood; firewood. English gypsy use *UK, 1851.* ▶ **on crack** out of your mind. Used in situations where there is no crack cocaine

involved, usually humorously in a statement such as 'What are you, on crack?' *US, 1995*

crack *verb* **1** to speak *US, 1897.* **2** to ask for something *US, 1928.* **3** to reveal a secret; to inform on someone *US, 1922.* **4** to tease someone; to taunt someone; to insult someone *US, 1930.* **5** to arrest someone *US, 1952.* **6** to break and enter using force with the intent of committing a crime within *UK, 1725.* **7** to change paper money into coin. Originally used by seamen in Liverpool; phrased in use as, for example: 'Can you crack a fiver?', meaning 'Can you change a five pound note?' *UK, 1961.* **8** to have sex with a girl who is a virgin *FIJI, 1992.* **9** in surfing, to catch a wave *AUSTRALIA, 1957.* **10** to strike something or someone in such a way that a sharp noise is produced; to slap, to smack, etc *UK, 1836.* **11** in cricket, to hit a ball hard *UK, 1882.* **12** to drum with expertise. A shortening of 'crack a hand' *TRINIDAD AND TOBAGO, 2003.* ▶ **crack a bennie** to break a Benzedrine™ (amphetamine sulphate) inhaler open *US, 1970.* ▶ **crack a fat** to achieve an erection *AUSTRALIA, 1968.* ▶ **crack a grain** to suffer aching testicles *TRINIDAD AND TOBAGO, 2003.* ▶ **crack a Judy; crack a Judy's tea-cup** to take a woman's virginity. Formed from conventional 'crack' (to break, to open) and JUDY (a girl or woman) *UK, 1937.* ▶ **crack a laugh** to burst into laughter *TRINIDAD AND TOBAGO, 2003.* ▶ **crack a lay** to divulge something secret *AUSTRALIA, 1941.* ▶ **crack a rat** to fart *US, 1998.* ▶ **crack a short** to break into a car *US, 1970.* ▶ **crack a smile** to smile broadly, especially of someone who is usually serious *UK, 1990.* ▶ **crack an egg 1** in bowls, to play with just sufficient weight to move a bowl or a jack an inch or two *SOUTH AFRICA, 1968.* **2** in curling, to touch a stone lightly with the bowled stone *CANADA, 1960.* ▶ **crack the nut** to meet an operation's daily operating expenses *US, 1980.* ▶ **crack wise** to insult someone with a degree of sarcasm and humour. Imparts a slight air of the old gangster life *US, 1921.* ▶ **crack your cherry** to lose your innocence or virginity *US, 1970.* ▶ **crack your face** to smile broadly, especially of a usually serious person *UK, 1966.* ▶ **get cracking** to start, to begin work *UK, 1937*

crack *adjective* excellent *UK, 1793*

crack about *verb* to act vigorously and aggressively. Field Marshal Montgomery spoke of his army, after it had crossed the Rhine in 1945, as having the chance to 'crack about on the plains of North Germany' *UK, 1945*

crackalacking; crackalackin' *verb* happening; doing; occurring; working. Also, in the greeting 'what's crackalackin?' *US, 2003*

crack along; crack on *verb* to move swiftly. From the use of a whip to encourage speed *UK, 1837*

crack attack *noun* the intense craving for crack cocaine felt by an addict *US, 1992*

crack baby *noun* **1** a child born with an addiction to crack cocaine *US, 1990.* **2** someone who is behaving very foolishly. Comparing the person to a baby born addicted to crack cocaine *US, 1990*

crack back *noun* marijuana mixed with crack cocaine *UK, 1998*

CrackBerry *noun* a person who enjoys an obsessive relationship with a BlackBerry mobile telecommunications device *UK, 2005*

CrackBerry *nickname* the BlackBerry™, a wireless instant-messaging device *CANADA, 2002*

crack cooler *noun* pieces of crack cocaine soaked in a wine cooler drink *US, 1994*

crack-crack *noun* hands that are badly chapped *NORFOLK ISLAND, 1992*

crack down *verb* **1** to repress; to suppress by draconian means, especially used of campaigns against lawless persons or acts. Usually before 'on' or 'upon' *UK, 1940.* **2** in horse racing, to be determined to win a race *US, 1994*

crack down on *verb* to seize or make off with something *AUSTRALIA, 1961*

cracked *adjective* mentally impaired *UK, 1692*

cracked ice *noun* diamonds that have been removed from their settings *US, 1962*

cracked out *adjective* suffering symptoms of heavy crack cocaine usage *US, 1988*

cracked squash *noun* a fractured skull *US, 1985*

crack 'em up noun a vehicular accident US, 1977

cracker noun **1** a poor, uneducated, racist white from the southern US US, 1966. **2** a person of Anglo-culture CANADA, 2001. **3** anything excellent. From CRACK (excellent). Contemporary usage is due in part to comedian Frank Carson who has 'It's a cracker!' as a catchphrase UK, 1914. **4** an excellent performance in a game AUSTRALIA, 1986. **5** an attractive woman UK, 1914. **6** the buttocks US, 1948. **7** a person who breaches a computer system's security scheme. Coined by hackers in defence against journalistic misuse of their word US, 1991. **8** a criminal who specialises in breaking into safes. An abbreviation of 'safe cracker' US, 1982. **9** a safe CANADA, 1976. **10** a pound (£1); a pound-note. Often used in phrases such as 'not have a cracker' AUSTRALIA, 1934. **11** the least amount of money AUSTRALIA, 1934. **12** a firework AUSTRALIA, 1907. **13** a gramophone record US, 1947. **14** a brothel AUSTRALIA, 1955. **15** a tooth. Usually in the plural UK, 1978. ▶ **go off like a cracker** to explode into a rage AUSTRALIA, 1995. ▶ **not worth a cracker** entirely worthless AUSTRALIA, 1941

cracker adjective excellent NEW ZEALAND, 1964

cracker! used for expressing approval UK, 2003

cracker-ass noun a thin person US, 1966

crackerbox noun **1** a plain, box-like house US, 1945. **2** a jail from which escape is simple; a safe which is simple to break into US, 1950. **3** a brakevan (caboose) US, 1977. **4** a military truck used as an ambulance US, 1950

cracker-box adjective plain, simple, unsophisticated US, 1911

Crackerdom noun an area inhabited predominantly by racist white people US, 1987

cracker factory noun a mental hospital US, 1970

crackerjack noun an excellent example of something US, 1895

crackerjack adjective highly skilled, excellent US, 1899

cracker night noun a night which is celebrated with fireworks. Currently this is used to commemorate the birthday of Queen Elizabeth II, though it was previously used to celebrate other occasions AUSTRALIA, 1951

crackers noun LSD. From the practice, at least in Boston, of saturating animal cracker biscuits with LSD and selling it in that form US, 1967

crackers adjective crazy, mad UK, 1925

crack gallery noun a building or room where crack cocaine is sold and smoked US, 1989

crack girl noun a girl or woman addicted to crack cocaine US, 1980s

crack hardy verb to endure something bravely; to put on a brave face AUSTRALIA, 1904

crackhead noun **1** a person addicted to crack cocaine US, 1986. **2** a crazy person. From CRACKED (mentally impaired) UK, 2002

crack house noun a building or room where crack cocaine may be bought and consumed US, 1985

crackie noun **1** a crack cocaine user US, 1997. **2** in the Maritime Provinces, a small yapping dog CANADA, 1959

crack-in noun a burglary US, 1949

cracking adjective **1** very fast, vigorous. Also used as an adverb UK, 1825. **2** excellent. Also used as an adverb UK, 1833

crack in the shack noun a homosexual in a jail cell US, 1984

crack it verb **1** to succeed in some endeavour; to attain a desire AUSTRALIA, 1936. **2** to succeed in gaining sexual intercourse; to have sex AUSTRALIA, 1941. **3** to work as a prostitute AUSTRALIA, 1945

crackle noun banknotes. From the sound of new money UK, 1950

crackling noun a woman or women regarded as sexual pleasure. This probably blends the pleasures to be had from tender, juicy meat and CRACK (the vagina). Conventionally 'crackling' is the crisped skin of roast pork UK, 1947

crack mama noun a homeless woman addicted to crack cocaine US, 1997

crack off verb (of a male) to masturbate UK, 2003

crack on verb **1** to tell someone something; to reveal a secret AUSTRALIA, 1965. **2** to go ahead. A variation of the sense 'to hurry',

hence 'to move forward' UK, 2001. **3** to flirt; to try to seduce someone US, 1982. **4** to succeed in gaining sexual favours from another AUSTRALIA, 1955 ▷see: CRACK ALONG

crack out verb **1** to escape from prison US, 1950. **2** in a swindle, to relieve the victim of his money quickly US, 1977

crackpot noun a person who is somewhere in the continuum between odd and crazy UK, 1883

crackpot adjective (of ideas and schemes) crazy, fantastic, unrealistic US, 1934

crack regiment noun the Women's Royal Army Corps, and its predecessor (from 1938–46), the Auxiliary Territorial Service. A pun on CRACK (excellent) and CRACK (the vagina) UK, 1995

crack salesman noun **1** a youthful, attractive homosexual male prostitute US, 1979. **2** a pimp US, 1949

cracksman noun a burglar; a safe-breaker. Originally 'a house-breaker'. As in the title of the 1963 film starring Charlie Drake US, 1797

crack smile noun a slash from ear to mouth, especially one inflicted for failure to pay for drugs US, 1993

cracksmoker noun a person whose sanity is open to question, whether or not they actually smoke crack US, 1997

crack troops noun female soldiers. A pun on 'crack' – here used in the vaginal sense, not the expected expert sense US, 1947

crack-up noun **1** a nervous breakdown US, 1936. **2** a cause for laughter US, 1961

crack up verb **1** to undergo a nervous breakdown US, 1917. **2** to praise someone highly US, 1829. **3** to amuse someone greatly; to cause laughter; to start laughing, especially uproariously US, 1942

crack weed noun marijuana laced with crack cocaine UK, 2003

crack whore noun a prostitute motivated by a desire to buy crack cocaine US, 1990

cracoid noun a crack cocaine addict US, 1990

cradle noun **1** your domicile, be it a room, apartment or house CANADA, 1993. **2** any open-top railway goods wagon, such as a gondola US, 1977

cradle baby noun a novice citizens' band radio user. Based on the initials CB US, 1976

cradle rape noun sex with a girl under the age of consent US, 1969

cradle-rocker noun in placer mining, a trough on a rocker shaken to separate gold flecks from sand and earth CANADA, 1995

cradle-snatch verb to have a sexual relationship with someone much younger than yourself. The image of the partner as a baby UK, 1938

cradle-snatcher noun a person who has a noticeably younger lover. Also known as a 'cradle-robber' US, 1907

Craft's disease noun senile dementia. From the spurious acronym 'can't remember a fucking thing' AUSTRALIA, 1996

craftsman noun a socially inept dolt US, 1992

crafty Alice noun used as the epitome of a woman's wiles UK, 1969

crafty butcher noun a male homosexual. Punningly derived, with Chrismas-cracker-motto corniness, because 'a crafty butcher takes his meat through the back door' UK, 2003

cram verb to study hastily for an examination UK, 1810

cram-book noun a book used for hasty study UK, 1883

cram it! used for registering an imperative rejection US, 1957

crammer noun **1** a period of intense studying for an examination UK, 2005. **2** a teacher who prepares students for examination; a student in a period of intense study for an examination; hence, an institution where students are given such intense preparation UK, 1813

cramming noun intensive study especially in preparation for an examination UK, 1821

cramp noun an unpleasant person US, 1992

cramp verb ▶ **cramp someone's style** to hamper or prevent someone from doing, or being at, their best. From sporting use US, 1917

cramper *noun* a small cage in which a prisoner of war is confined *US, 1986*

cran *noun* a hiding-place for stolen goods *UK, 2003*

crane *noun* **1** in skateboarding, a manoeuvre in which the rider crouches on one foot, extending the other leg outwards *US, 1976*. **2** a superior with a great deal of influence. New York police slang *US, 1997*

crank *noun* **1** methamphetamine hydrochloride in powdered form; any amphetamine; methcathinone *US, 1969*. **2** a mentally unstable person; an unreliable, unpredictable person; a person who is obsessed by a single topic or hobby *US, 1833*. **3** a prison guard who takes pleasure in making life difficult for prisoners *US, 1981*. **4** a prison bully *US, 1958*. **5** a crankshaft. Hot rodder usage *US, 1948*. **6** the penis *US, 1968*. **7** an act of masturbation *AUSTRALIA, 1985*

crank *verb* **1** to use amphetamines or methamphetamine, central nervous system stimulants *US, 1970*. **2** to inject a drug. Also known as 'crank up' *UK, 1978*. **3** to turn up the volume of music to very loud *US, 1994*. **4** to excel *US, 1988*. **5** in computing, to perform well *US, 1991*. **6** in a card game, to deal the cards *US, 1988*. ▶ **crank tail** to physically assault someone *TRINIDAD AND TOBAGO, 1971*

crank *adjective* insane *FIJI, 1995*

crank bug *noun* an insect that is seen by someone under the influence of methamphetamine but not by others *US, 1977*

crankcase *verb* the head *US, 1960*

crank commando *noun* an amphetamine or methamphetamine addict *UK, 1970*

cranked; cranked out; cranked up *adjective* **1** stimulated by methamphetamine or amphetamines *US, 1971*. **2** excited; intensified. Mechanical imagery *US, 1957*

cranker *noun* a bowler who in delivering the ball lifts it high over his head in the backswing *US, 1987*

cranking; cranking up *noun* the act of injecting a drug *UK, 2000*

cranking *adjective* amusing; pleasing; exciting; good *US, 1982*

crank off *verb* to consume something *US, 2001*

crank out *verb* to create something, to make something. The implication is of mechanical manufacture, but that is not necessarily the intention *US, 2001*

crank time *noun* the time set or needed to start up a helicopter *US, 1991*

cranny *noun* **1** the vagina. An adoption, probably in C19, of the conventional sense; it remains in circulation mainly as an occasional variation of a pornographer's theme; the male-inspired 'cranny-hunter', however, is no longer evident *UK, 1937*. **2** a toilet *US, 1968*

crap *noun* **1** nonsense *UK, 1898*. **2** excrement *UK, 1846*. **3** an act of defecation *US, 1926*. **4** marijuana *US, 1961*. **5** weak or highly diluted heroin *US, 1942*. ▶ **take a crap** to defecate *US, 1952*

crap *verb* to defecate *UK, 1673*

crap *adjective* inferior, shoddy, valueless, unpleasant, disliked for whatever reason. From the earlier sense (excrement) *US, 1916*

crap antenna *noun* the ability to detect when someone is speaking nonsense *AUSTRALIA, 1987*

crap around *verb* to idle; to pass time doing nothing; to waste time *US, 1935*

crap artist *noun* a convincing liar *US, 1934*

crap-ass *noun* a despicable person *US, 1975*

crap-ass *adjective* shoddy, inferior *US, 2000*

crapaud-foot writing; crapaud hand *noun* illegible penmanship *TRINIDAD AND TOBAGO, 2003*

crapaud-going-to-wedding *noun* childlike, scratchy handwriting *GRENADA, 1996*

crap course *noun* an easy college course *US, 1956*

crape-hanger *noun* a doomsayer *US, 1949*

crap hat *noun* in a paratroop regiment, a non-jumper. From the different colour of the uniform beret (a non-jumper is not allowed to wear the red 'cherry berry' beret) *UK, 2000*

crap heap *noun* a dilapidated vehicle *AUSTRALIA, 1974*

craphole *noun* a bad place, a disgusting place *US, 1939*

craphouse *noun* **1** a toilet *US, 1934*. **2** a dirty, unpleasant place *US, 1934*

crapness *noun* a lack of style or worth *UK, 2000*

crap off *verb* to annoy someone *AUSTRALIA, 1974*

crapola *noun* used as an embellished 'crap' in any and all of its senses *UK, 1959*

crap out *verb* **1** to be completely exhausted; to go to sleep *US, 1956*. **2** to die *US, 1929*. **3** to come to an end of a horizontal passage while caving or pot-holing. The horizontal equivalent of the conventional mining-term 'bottom out' *UK, 2004*

crapper *noun* **1** a toilet *US, 1927*. **2** the anus, the rectum; the buttocks *UK, 1998*. ▶ **in the crapper** in horse racing, finishing in fourth place or worse *US, 1976*

crapper dick *noun* a police officer who patrols public toilets in search of illegal homosexual activity *US, 1950*

crappereena *noun* a toilet *UK, 1979*

crappers *noun* ▶ **in crappers ditch** in severe trouble. A strikingly unpleasant image akin to UP SHIT CREEK *NEW ZEALAND, 1998*

crappers *adjective* very drunk *UK, 1987*

crappo *noun* a resident of Jersey (in the Channel Islands) according to those on Guernsey *UK, 1991*

crappy *adjective* **1** of poor quality. From CRAP (excrement), synonymous with SHITTY *US, 1942*. **2** befouled with excrement *UK, 1846*

craps *noun* dice, especially used in craps *US, 1965*

craps! used for expressing disgust *TRINIDAD AND TOBAGO, 2003*

crapshoot *noun* an unpredictable, risky situation *US, 1971*

craptabulous *adjective* of extremely inferior quality. a combination of CRAP and FANTABULOUS sometimes used to celebrate that which is so bad it is good *UK, 2005*

craptacular *adjective* of extremely inferior quality. A combination of CRAP and spectacular sometimes used to celebrate that which is so bad it is good. Coinage is credited to the writers of cartoon character Bart Simpson in The Simpsons *US, 2004*

craptastic *adjective* of extremely inferior quality. A combination of CRAP and fantastic sometimes used to celebrate that which is so bad it is good *US, 2003*

craptitude *noun* a state of existence comprising generally negative qualities such as poor taste and feebleness. A variation of CRAPNESS that seems to carry a suggestion of decrepitude *UK, 2000*

crap up *verb* **1** to fill something with clutter *US, 1946*. **2** to spoil something; to ruin something *US, 1953*. **3** to address someone with a complete lack of sincerity *US, 1950*

crapweasel *noun* a deceitful and/or annoying person *UK, 2005*

crash *verb* **1** to enter a party or social event without an invitation *US, 1921*. **2** to enter a place with force with the intention of committing a crime *US, 1924*. **3** to stay somewhere temporarily; to sleep somewhere *US, 1945*. **4** to go to sleep *UK, 1943*. **5** to return to normal perceptions after a drug intoxication; to experience an associated feeling of post-intoxication depression or dismay *US, 1967*. **6** (used of a computer program) to fail completely without warning *US, 1983*. **7** (used of a police case) to fail or be dropped *UK, 1996*. **8** to hit something, to strike something *US, 1989*. **9** to escape from jail or prison *US, 1970*. **10** in circus and carnival usage, to change money *US, 1981*. **11** to pass something; to give something out. Teen slang, recorded in Leicestershire *UK: ENGLAND, 1977*. **12** to intubate a hospital patient quickly and urgently *US, 1994*. **13** to perform a high-priority job as soon as possible *US, 1986*. ▶ **crash and burn 1** to fail *US, 2003*. **2** in computing, to fail in a dramatic and spectacular fashion *US, 1991*. ▶ **crash the ash** to offer someone a cigarette *UK, 1950s*

crash box *noun* in cars, a manual transmission not equipped with synchromesh, requiring forceful gear shifts *US, 1965*

crash car *noun* an old, inexpensive car used in the distribution of illegal alcohol *US, 1974*

crash cart *noun* a mobile cart used to carry equipment. Originally hospital use, since expanded *US, 1982*

crash-course *noun* a short, intensive course on a particular subject *UK, 1973*

crasher *noun* **1** a person temporarily sleeping in someone else's house or apartment *US, 1975*. **2** a very tedious or tiresome person or thing. A variation of CRASHING BORE *UK, 1960*. **3** a powerful, hard-breaking wave *US, 1964*

crash hat *noun* a safety helmet *US, 2003*

crash helmet *noun* a condom. Figurative use of motorcyclists' safety wear: in both uses worn in case of accident. Possibly also a punning reference to 'helmet' (the head of the penis) *UK, 1998*

crash hot *adjective* excellent *AUSTRALIA, 1962*

crash hot! used for expressing enthusiastic approval *NEW ZEALAND, 1998*

crashing bore *noun* a very tedious or tiresome person or thing *UK, 1934*

crash-out *noun* an escape from prison or jail *US, 1940*

crash out *verb* to escape from prison *US, 1954*

crash pad *noun* **1** a room, apartment, or house where people stay for the night or temporarily, with or without knowing the owner, with or without formal invitation *US, 1967*. **2** a pit of soft dirt or sand used for low-level stunt falls *US, 2003*

-crat; -ocrat *suffix* when linked with a subject, used to designate a person that may be dominant, or aspiring to dominance, or pretending superiority within that subject area. A sarcastic or humorous application of the conventional sense found in such words as 'aristocrat', 'democrat', 'plutocrat', etc. The root in most conventional senses ends with an 'o'; in colloquial or journalistic usage the 'o' is generally incorporated *UK, 1937*

crate *noun* **1** an old and dilapidated car *US, 1927*. **2** a railway boxcar *US, 1977*

crate of sand *noun* a truck hauling sugar *US, 1971*

crater *noun* **1** a deep sore caused by repeated injections *US, 1967*. **2** a facial blemish *US, 1968*

crates *noun* the female breasts *NEW ZEALAND, 1984*

c-rat grenade *noun* a crude hand grenade fashioned by the Viet Cong using a US combat rations can as the grenade shell *US, 1990*

c-rats *noun* US Army combat rations. Vietnam war coinage, in continuing use *US, 1965*

craven *adjective* gluttonous, greedy *GRENADA, 1996*

cravenous *adjective* gluttonous, greedy *VIRGIN ISLANDS, BRITISH, 1996*

cravetious *adjective* greedy *TRINIDAD AND TOBAGO, 1956*

cravicious *adjective* gluttonous, greedy *BARBADOS, 1996*

crawfish *verb* to evade someone or something. In nature, the only defence available to the crawfish is to bury itself in mud or silt, moving backwards *US, 1842*

crawl *noun* **1** in television and film-making, titles that roll from the bottom of the screen to the top *US, 1990*. **2** in pool, backspin applied to the cue ball *US, 1954*

crawl *verb* **1** to behave sycophantically *AUSTRALIA, 1880*. **2** to search somewhere *US, 1986*

crawler *noun* **1** a sycophant *AUSTRALIA, 1827*. **2** a despicable or contemptible person; a low person *AUSTRALIA, 1917*

crawling *adjective* verminous. Shortened from 'crawling with lice' *UK, 1961*

crawling horror *noun* in computing, obsolete hardware or software *US, 1991*

crawl with *verb* to be alive, or filled with, people of a specified type *UK, 1925*

cray *noun* **1** a one-hundred dollar note. From the note's red colour, shared with the crayfish *NEW ZEALAND, 1998*. **2** a crayfish *AUSTRALIA, 1909*

crayon *noun* a programmer who works on a supercomputer designed by Cray Research *US, 1991*

craythur *noun* strong alcohol, usually whiskey. The spelling reflects the Hiberno-English pronunciation of 'creature' *IRELAND, 2002*

crazies *noun* phencyclidine, the recreational drug known as PCP or angel dust *US, 1993*

crazy *noun* a person who engages in erratic or unpredictable behaviour *US, 1867*

crazy *adjective* **1** excellent, exciting, superlative *US, 1948*. **2** enthusiastic *for, about* or *to do* something *UK, 1779*. **3** (used of a particular card in poker and other card games) capable of being played as a card of any value. The same as the more common 'wild' *US, 1967*. **4** many *US, 1989*. ▶ **like crazy** of behaviour, to the utmost *US, 1924*

crazy alley *noun* the area in a prison in which mentally ill patients are confined *US, 1992*

crazy as a bedbug *adjective* extremely eccentric, mad *US, 1918*

crazy-ass *adjective* very crazy *US, 1994*

crazy doctor *noun* a psychiatrist or other psychotherapist *US, 1989*

crazy Eddy *noun* high quality phencyclidine, the recreational drug known as PCP or angel dust *US, 1993*

crazy eight; crazy 8 *noun* a discharge from the US Army for mental unfitness. From US Army Regulation 600–208 *US, 1968*

crazy freak *noun* a pretty girl *US, 1955*

crazy house *noun* a mental hospital *US, 1887*

Crazy Joey *nickname* Joey Gallo, reputed member of the Gambino crime family in New York, shot to death at Umberto's Clam House in 1972 *US, 1990*

crazy large *adjective* doing very well *US, 1993*

crazy like a fox; crazy as a fox *adjective* eccentric; cunning *US, 1935*

crazy oats *noun* wild rice *CANADA, 1963*

crazyweed *noun* marijuana *UK, 1998*

creaker *noun* an old person *US, 1958*

cream *noun* **1** a bribe *US, 1982*. **2** a variety of hashish from the Parvatti Valley in Northern India *UK, 2003*. **3** money. *Cash rules everything around me US, 1994*

cream *verb* **1** to ejaculate; to secrete vaginal lubricants during sexual arousal *US, 1915*. **2** by extension, to gush with excitement *US, 1948*. **3** to defeat someone convincingly *US, 1940*. **4** to kill someone *US, 1940*. **5** to hit someone or something *US, 1942*. **6** to rob someone *UK, 1998*. ▶ **cream the rag** to boast in an offensive manner. The mastubatory image is powerful *US, 1971*. ▶ **cream your jeans** while dressed, to respond to a sexual stimulus by secreting fluids *US, 1942*. ▶ **get creamed** to be knocked from your surfboard and pounded into the ocean, ocean bottom or pilings of a pier *US, 1978*

cream bun *noun* a Protestant. Glasgow rhyming slang for HUN *UK: SCOTLAND, 1996*

cream cookie *noun* a bookmaker; a betting shop. Glasgow rhyming slang for BOOKIE *UK: SCOTLAND, 1988*

cream cracker *noun* an unsavoury lower-class person. Rhyming slang for KNACKER; also abbreviated to 'creamers' *IRELAND, 2003*

cream crackered *adjective* tired out, exhausted. Rhyming slang for KNACKERED (exhausted); a conventional 'cream cracker' is a savoury biscuit *UK, 1992*

creamed *adjective* soiled by vaginal secretions as a result of sexual arousal *UK, 1997*

creamer *noun* **1** an employee who steals from the till *UK, 1996*. **2** someone who is over-excited or scared; by implication, someone who is not in control of his emotions or his affairs *AUSTRALIA, 1973*. **3** in the car sales business, an excellent car *US, 1953*

creamie *noun* **1** a sexually attractive young woman *UK, 1982*. **2** an outstanding student selected after advanced flying training to become a flying instructor. Also variant 'creamy' *UK, 1981*

creamies *noun* the viscous discharge of a sexually transmitted infection *US, 1969*

cream off *verb* to orgasm. Based on CREAM (to ejaculate) *UK, 2000*

creampie *noun* semen seeping from a vagina, anus or mouth. A fetish that oozed from US Internet pornography in the early 2000s; the semen is as often as not an artificially concocted look-alike *US, 2002*

cream puff noun **1** a huff. Glasgow rhyming slang *UK, 1985*. **2** an effeminate male *US, 1945*. **3** an easy target, easy prey *US, 1915*. **4** in the used car business, a well-preserved car *US, 1949*

creamy noun a person of mixed European and Australian Aboriginal heritage *AUSTRALIA, 1912*

creamy adjective **1** quarter-caste Australian Aboriginal *AUSTRALIA, 1912*. **2** sexually attractive. Influenced by 'creamy' (delightful), this use is from CREAM (to secrete fluids when sexually aroused) *US, 1947*. **3** pleasing, excellent. Teen slang *UK, 1889*

crease noun in sports betting, a distortion created when strong fan support for one team or contestant creates an imbalance in the odds which can be exploited by a clever bettor *US, 1991*

crease; crease up verb to laugh immoderately, to collapse with laughter; to cause such a condition. An image of being bent double with laughter *UK, 1984*

cred noun credibility *UK, 1998*

cred adjective acceptable to your peers; hence, fashionable. Abbreviated from STREET-CRED (the quality of being understood by urban youth), in turn shortened from 'street-credible' *UK, 1999*

credentials noun the genitals *US, 1968*

credit noun **1** an achievement or accomplishment. From the acknowledgement of service rendered in the entertainment industry *US, 1992*. **2** a reduction of a jail sentence due to good behaviour *US, 1949*

credit card noun **1** a boyfriend *UK, 1981*. **2** a favour owed *US, 1985*

creek noun ▶ **down the creek** in oil drilling, wasted or lost *US, 1954*. ▶ **up the creek** in trouble. Variant phrases include 'up the creek without a paddle' and 'up the creek with a paddle in a barbed-wire canoe' *US, 1918*

creep noun **1** an objectionable or unpleasant person; a dull or insignificant person *US, 1926*. **2** a prisoner who is neither respected nor liked *US, 1951*. **3** a thief who operates in hotels, entering unlocked rooms as the guests sleep *UK, 1877*. **4** a drug addict who relies on the kindness of other addicts for small amounts of drugs *US, 1971*. **5** a furtive arrival or departure *US, 1946*. ▶ **on the creep** used of a thief who is working *US, 1996*

creep verb **1** to work as a sneak-thief *US, 1928*. **2** to ambush someone with the intent of seriously injuring or killing them. Prison usage *US, 1974*. **3** to attempt to have a secret sexual relationship with someone's boyfriend or girlfriend *US, 2001*. **4** to be sexually unfaithful *US, 1972*. **5** to dance. A late 1950s usage, not necessarily in reference to 'the Creep', a short-lived 1950s dance sensation *UK, 1950s*. **6** to escape *US, 1967*

creep! go away! *UK, 1958*

creep-and-cuss adjective (used of car traffic) extremely congested *US, 1964*

creeped out adjective worried, disturbed. Extends from THE CREEPS (a feeling of dread) *US, 2001*

creeper noun **1** a burglar *US, 1906*. **2** a prostitute or prostitute's accomplice who steals from the clothes of the prostitute's customer *UK, 1984*. **3** a marijuana cigarette *US, 1997*. **4** in trucking, a very low gear *US, 1937*. **5** in car repair, a platform on casters that allows a mechanic to lie on their back and roll under a car to work on it *US, 1992*

creeperbud; creeper noun a subtly potent variety of marijuana. Because it 'creeps up on you' *US, 1981*

creepers noun soft-soled, quiet shoes favoured by burglars *US, 1949*

creepers! used for expressing surprise. An abbreviated version of JEEPERS, CREEPERS! *US, 1944*

creep game noun a scheme in which a prostitute and her confederate rob the prostitute's customer *US, late 1960s*

creep house noun a brothel where customers are routinely robbed *US, 1913*

creepie-peepie noun a small, hand-held television camera. An unsuccessful attempt to recreate the popularity of WALKIE-TALKIE *US, 1952*

creeping crud noun any skin rash suffered in tropical and jungle environments *US, 1946*

creeping Jesus noun a hypocritically pious sneak and coward *UK, 1818*

creeping Jesus! used as an expression of surprise, frustration, anger, etc *AUSTRALIA, 1961*

creeping mocus noun a non-existent disease *US, 1947*

creep joint noun a brothel where customers' clothes are searched and robbed *US, 1921*

creepo noun a contemptible person *US, 1960*

creep out verb to create a very uncomfortable feeling in someone *US, 1983*

creep pad noun a creep joint *US, 1946*

creeps noun ▶ **the creeps** a sensation of dread *UK, 1849*

creeps! used as an all-purpose, non-profane expression of surprise *US, 1971*

creepster noun a revolting person. An embellished CREEP *US, 1993*

creepy adjective annoying; producing anxiety or nervousness in others *US, 1919*

creepy-crawly noun an insect; a spider *UK, 1960*

creepy-peepy noun **1** battlefield radar. Vietnam war usage *US, 1965*. **2** a television mini-camera *US, 1986*

crem noun a crematorium. Cremation has been legal in the UK since 1884; it is a matter of conjecture how soon this familiar shortening took a hold *UK, 1971*

Creme de Menthe French noun oral sex performed with a mouth full of creme de menthe alcohol *US, 1993*

cremmie; cremmy noun a crematorium. An elaboration of CREM *AUSTRALIA, 1982*

crepes noun trainers (sneakers) *JAMAICA, 1996*

crepesoles noun trainers (sneakers) *GUYANA, 1996*

crest verb to smile. From the branded toothpaste *US, 1997*

cretin noun an incompetent and despicable person *US, 1981*

cretinous adjective in computing, incompetent, dysfunctional *US, 1981*

crevice noun the vagina. Widespread in pornographic literature *UK, 1937*

crew noun **1** a criminal gang *US, 1946*. **2** a tightly-knit group of close friends *US, 1957*. **3** a group of graffiti artists who work together *US, 1997*

crew chief noun the leader of a unit of a criminal gang *US, 1992*

crew dog noun a crew chief in the US Air Force *US, 1998*

crew hog noun a miscellaneous member of a film crew *US, 2000*

crew pie noun a pizza made by a pizza parlour's employees *US, 1996*

crew runner noun the leader of a criminal gang *US, 2000*

crew up verb to form a group to commit a crime *US, 2000*

cri! used as an expression or shock, surprise, etc. A shortening of CRIKEY! *UK, 1984*

crib noun **1** a person's dwelling; an apartment or house *US, 1809*. **2** a room or shack where a prostitute plies her trade *US, 1846*. **3** a house or shop chosen for a robbery *CANADA, 1976*. **4** in trucking, the sleeping compartment behind the driver *US, 1976*. **5** a holiday cottage *NEW ZEALAND, 1980*. **6** a prison cell *US, 1990*. **7** a gambling establishment *UK, 1823*. **8** a brakevan (caboose) *US, 1977*. **9** a safe *US, 1962*. **10** a receptacle for carrying a meal to work *AUSTRALIA, 1941*. **11** a meal taken during the major break at work *AUSTRALIA, 1890*. **12** any form of written aid to cheating in examinations. The original (1841) meaning was specifically 'a literal translation illicitly used by students'; the current vaguer sense gained purchase during C20 *UK, 1900*. **13** cribbage (a card game) *UK, 1885*. **14** crack cocaine *UK, 1998*

crib verb **1** to reside somewhere *US, 1969*. **2** to cheat in an examination *UK, 1891*. **3** to plagiarise something; to copy something *UK, 1941*

cribbage peg noun the leg. Rhyming slang *UK, 1923*

cribber noun a horse that chews the wood of its stall *US, 1947*

crib course noun a basic, easy course of study *US, 1970*

crib girl noun a woman working in a supply shack or supply room *US, 1945*

cribhouse *noun* a brothel *US, 1916*

cribman *noun* a professional safecracker *US, 1976*

crib sheet *noun* a piece of paper with information used for studying or cheating in an examination or test *US, 1960*

crib time *noun* a meal time during work hours *AUSTRALIA, 1890*

cricket *adjective* fair, following customs and rules *UK, 1900*

cricket score odds *noun* in horse racing, odds of 100 – 1 or higher *AUSTRALIA, 1989*

cricket team *noun* a very sparse moustache. There are eleven men – or hairs – on each side *AUSTRALIA, 1984*

cricks; crix *noun* theatre critics *US, 1952*

crigs *noun* the testicles. From the Irish *creig* (rock) or *cnag* (knob) *UK: NORTHERN IRELAND, 1992*

crikey! used as an expression of surprise, frustration, etc. A euphemism for CHRIST! *UK, 1838*

crikey Moses! used for registering surprise or anguish *UK, 1993*

crill *noun* a marijuana cigarette laced with cocaine. A lazy pronounciation of CRIPPLE *UK, 2001*

crill *adjective* inferior *US, 1993*

crills *noun* crack cocaine *US, 1995*

crillz *noun* an abode *US, 1997*

crim *noun* a *criminal US, 1909*

crim *adjective* involved in crime; criminal *AUSTRALIA, 1987*

crime *noun* someone who doesn't pay debts. From the adage 'crime doesn't pay' *AUSTRALIA, 1989*

crime *verb* in the military, to discipline someone *AUSTRALIA, 1932*

Crime Dog *nickname* Fred McGriff (b.1943), a first baseman (1986 – 2001) with a large impact on the defence of the team he was playing for. An allusion to the comic strip character McGruff, a crime-fighting dog *US, 1992*

crimey *noun* a criminal *US, 1969*

crimp *noun* **1** an obstacle or impediment *US, 1896*. **2** a discreet bend or crease in a playing card that assists a cheat or a conjuror to prosper *US, 2003*

crimp *verb* to intrude; to impede something *US, 1979*

crimp cut *noun* in a card game, a cheating move in which the cheater cuts the deck of cards to an intended spot *US, 1996*

crimper *noun* **1** a hairdresser *UK, 1968*. **2** in gambling, a person who crimps cards so as to be able to identify them in future hands *US, 1992*

crimps *noun* tight curls of hair *BAHAMAS, 1982*

crimson butterfly *noun* the penis *UK, 2003*

crimson rambler *noun* a bedbug *US, 1906*

crimson tide; crimson wave *noun* the bleed period of the menstrual cycle *US, 2001*

cringe *noun* methamphetamine. Probably from CRANK, but the image of cringing is powerful when discussing a methamphetamine user *US, 1993*

cringe!; oh cringe! used as an expression of abject embarrassment, apology or regret; also, in sympathy with another's embarrassment. A vocalisation of a probable physical reaction to such embarrassment *UK, 1984*

crink *noun* **1** a sharp, searing pain *US, 1970*. **2** methamphetamine sulphate in powdered form *US, 1977*

crinkle *noun* paper money *UK, 1954*

crinkle-top *noun* a black person with natural or afro hair *US, 1980*

crip *noun* **1** an easy course in school or college *US, 1923*. **2** a *cripple US, 1893*

cripes! used as a euphemistic exclamation in place of 'christ!' *AUSTRALIA, 1903*

crippen! used for registering surprise or annoyance. Using the name of notorious murderer Dr H. H. Crippen, 1860 – 1910; ultimately a variation of CHRIST! *UK, 1984*

crippie *noun* high quality marijuana *US, 2002*

cripple *noun* **1** a marijuana cigarette. Evolves from CRUTCH (a device to support the butt) *US, 1955*. **2** a knee-boarder; a surfer who rides kneeling rather than standing. Derogatory, spoken with disdain by experienced surfers *US, 1988*. **3** in pool, a shot that cannot be missed or a game that cannot be lost *US, 1964*. **4** a disabled railway carriage *US, 1946*

cripple-cock *noun* **1** cider. Dorset slang, subsequently adopted as a brand name. Possibly playing on BREWER'S DROOP (an inability to acheive an erect penis symptomatic of drunkenness) *UK: ENGLAND, 1979*. **2** used as a general pejorative. A slur on virility *UK, 1980*

crippleware *noun* computer software that operates up to a point but then is disabled until payment for a full working version is made *US, 1991*

crip up *verb* (of an able-bodied actor) to play the rôle of a disabled character. From CRIP (a cripple) *UK, 2004*

cris *noun* amphetamines. A misspelling and/or a play on CRYSTAL (methamphetamine), or an abbreviation of Spanish *cristal US, 1971*

Crisco Frisco *nickname* San Francisco, California. An allusion to the vegetable shortening often used as a sexual lubricant and San Francisco's reputation as a city with a large homosexual population *US, 1979*

crisp *noun* **1** crack cocaine mixed with marijuana *US, 1995*. **2** any alcohol *US, 2001*

crisp *adjective* **1** excellent, perfect, appealing *US, 1995*. **2** said of a table in pool where there is no need to adjust a shot to compensate for the table surface *US, 1993*

crisper *noun* a commissioned act of arson *UK, 2003*

crispie *noun* a currency note; hence the plural is also generalised as money. Extended from 'crisp', the quality of new notes *UK, 1982*

crispo *adjective* mentally deficient due to drug abuse *US, 1993*

crisp packet *noun* a prison bed *UK, 1996*

crispy *noun* a badly burnt person or corpse. An abbreviation of CRISPY CRITTER *US, 1981*

crispy *adjective* **1** good, stylish, pleasing *US, 1997*. **2** slightly diminished in mental facilities due to prolonged alcohol and/or drug use *US, 1979*

crispy critter *noun* **1** a burnt corpse, especially one burnt by napalm. The term was borrowed from the branded name of a sugar-frosted oat cut out in animal shapes, popular in the US in the 1960s *US, 1967*. **2** a badly burnt hospital patient. *US, 1989*. **3** a burnt pizza *US, 1996*

criss; kris *adjective* stylish, attractive, fashionable; used of the new or desirable. Adapted from an abbreviation of 'crisp' (fresh). UK black usage *JAMAICA, 1991*

crissake; crisake; krissake used for expressing frustration or annoyance *UK, 1964*

criss-cross *noun* an amphetamine tablet, especially Benzedrine™ (amphetamine sulphate). From the cross scoring on the tablet; possibly a play on CRIS, a central nervous system stimulant (amphetamine) *US, 1993*

criss-cross *verb* to simultaneously ingest lines of heroin and cocaine by nasal inhalation *2002*

cristal *noun* MDMA, the recreational drug best known as ecstasy *UK, 2003*

cristina; cris; crist; christina *noun* methamphetamine. A personification of CRYSTAL (powdered methamphetamine) *US, 1971*

crit *noun* **1** a critic *UK, 1743*. **2** a criticism; a critique *UK, 1908*. **3** a state of critical mass; critical size. A colloquialism from nuclear physics *US, 1957*

crit-hit *noun* a critical success. A combination of CRIT (a critic) and 'hit' (a success) *UK, 2003*

critical *adjective* **1** dangerously ill or injured *UK, 2003*. **2** impressive, amazing *US, 1990*. **3** (used of a wave) very steep, threatening to break at any moment *US, 1963*

criticism/self-criticism *noun* a structured group discussion in which members of the group analyse and comment on their own behaviour and that of other members of the group. Popular in leftist groups in the US in the late 1960s and early 70s *US, 2002*

critter *noun* a creature, especially a horse or a cow; a person (usually disparaging) *US, 1815*

crivens! used for registering shock, horror or astonishment. Probably a compound of 'Christ!' and 'heavens!' *UK, 1999*

cro *noun* a prostitute. A variation of CROW *AUSTRALIA, 1953*

croack *noun* a mixture of crack and an amphetamine *US, 1993*

croagies *noun* the testicles *US, 1985*

croak *noun* a combination of crack cocaine and methamphetamine. A variation of CRACK with fatal forebodings: CROAK (to die) *UK, 1998*

croak *verb* **1** to die. From the death-rattle *UK, 1812*. **2** to kill someone *UK, 1823*. **3** to inform on someone, to betray someone *US, 1964*. **4** in pool, to miscue *CANADA, 1988*

croaker *noun* **1** a doctor, especially a company doctor. Sometimes abbreviated to 'croak' *UK, 1879*. **2** a doctor who provides narcotics for an addict. A specialisation of the previous sense *US, 1978*. **3** a habitual complainer. In C19 US use, but now obsolete there *AUSTRALIA, 1882*. **4** a dying person, or one who has just died. From CROAK (to die) *UK, 1873*

croc *noun* a crocodile *AUSTRALIA, 1884*

crock *noun* **1** an unpleasant or worthless person, object or experience; a waste of time. Contemptuously abbreviated from the familiar CROCK OF SHIT *US, 1944*. **2** an old and worn-out person or thing *UK, 1889*. **3** a person with medical problems which are the result of abusive living *US, 1978*. **4** a computer program that normally functions but fails if modified at all *US, 1983*. **5** nonsense. An abbreviation of CROCK OF SHIT *US, 1962*

C rock *noun* crack cocaine. C (cocaine) plus ROCK (crack cocaine) *UK, 2001*

crock *adjective* broken; no good *AUSTRALIA, 1957*

crock cut *noun* a haircut which gives the appearance of having been achieved by placing a bowl over the subject's head *US, 1947*

crocked *adjective* **1** wrong, awry *UK, 2000*. **2** drunk *US, 1917*

crock of shit *noun* **1** an unpleasant or worthless person, object or experience; a waste of time. A conventional 'crock' (a pot) of SHIT (excreta) *US, 1951*. **2** nonsense, lies *US, 1945*

crocky *noun* a crocodile. Mostly juvenile *AUSTRALIA, 1943*

crocodile *noun* **1** a long line of school children walking two abreast *UK, 1870*. **2** a smile. Rhyming slang *UK, 1992*. **3** a horse. Possibly a jocular elaboration of CROCK (a worthless or worn-out thing, hence a broken-down horse) *AUSTRALIA, 1897*

crocus *noun* **1** a doctor. Originally 'croakus' *UK, 1785*. **2** a fair-weather trader who appears for a while when winter is over *UK, 1979*

Croker *nickname* Croke Park, the official head quarters of the Gaelic Athletic Association (GAA) *IRELAND, 2000*

Cromwell *noun* a Vauxhall Cavalier car. Citizens' band radio slang; Cromwell and the Cavaliers were on opposing sides in the English Civil War *UK, 1981*

cronky *adjective* **1** fraudulent, dishonest. From 'cronk' (corrupt) *AUSTRALIA, 1971*. **2** applied generally as a disdainful descriptor. Schoolchildren's slang *UK, 1983*. **3** inferior; 'wonky' *UK, 1961*

crook *adjective* **1** dishonest; illegal; (of an item) illegally gained, stolen, illicit *AUSTRALIA, 1898*. **2** (of a racehorse) not being run to win; (of a jockey) not riding to win *AUSTRALIA, 1895*. **3** bad; no good *AUSTRALIA, 1900*. **4** ill; unwell; injured *AUSTRALIA, 1908*. ► **go crook** to express anger verbally *AUSTRALIA, 1910*

crook *adverb* badly *AUSTRALIA, 1959*

crook as a dog *adjective* very unwell *AUSTRALIA, 1955*

crook as Rookwood *adjective* (especially in Sydney) very unwell. Rhyming phrase referring to Rookwood Cemetery, the main cemetery serving Sydney for many years *AUSTRALIA, 1971*

crook book *noun* a piece of crime fiction *UK, 1959*

crooked *adjective* **1** dishonest; of dishonest manufacture *UK, 1864*. **2** annoyed *AUSTRALIA, 1942*

crooked *adverb* illicitly, in a criminal manner, furtively *UK, 1936*

crooked as a dog's hind leg extremely crooked. Both literally and figuratively 'crooked' *AUSTRALIA, 1965*

crookie *noun* a wrong or weak person or thing *NEW ZEALAND, 1962*

crook on *adjective* annoyed with *AUSTRALIA, 1967*

croop *noun* a croupier *UK, 2000*

crop *noun* **1** a fifth of a gallon of wine *US, 1975*. **2** inferior quality heroin. A variation of CRAP *US, 2002*

crop dusting *noun* farting while walking down the aisle of an airliner *US, 2002*

crop-head *noun* a male with closely cut hair *UK, 1983*

cropper *noun* **1** a man who seeks to have sex with a transsexual. Named after *Coronation Street* character Roy Cropper whose 1999 soap opera story-line had him involved with a transsexual *UK, 2003*. **2** a fail; a setback *AUSTRALIA, 1921*. ► **come a cropper** to take a heavy fall; to go wrong. This is the most familiar phrase based-on 'cropper' (a fall, 1858); others are 'get a cropper' and 'fall a cropper' *UK, 1874*

croppie *noun* a crop circle researcher *UK, 2003*

crop-topped *adjective* with short hair, cropped on top *2001*

cross *noun* an act of betrayal, a doublecross *UK, 2001*. ► **in a cross** in trouble *US, 1976*. ► **on the cross** dishonestly *UK, 1819*

Cross *noun* ► **the Cross** the King's Cross district of Sydney *AUSTRALIA, 1946*

cross *verb* **1** to betray someone *UK, 1821*. **2** to cheat a cheat *US, 1950*

cross bar hotel *noun* a jail or prison *US, 1865*

cross-comical *adjective* foolish *BARBADOS, 1965*

crosscut *noun* a Chinese woman; a Jewish woman. A Liverpudlian term, derived from the notion that Asian women's genitals have a different orientation to those of Western women; hence, its yet more ill-informed application to Jewish women *UK, 1966*

crossed wires *noun* a misunderstanding. From the hazards of telephony *UK, 1932*

cross-eye; cross-eyes *noun* a person with a squint. From the conventional sense describing the condition *UK, 1937*

cross-eyed *adjective* annoyed, angry *UK, 1998*

crossfire *noun* in confidence games, conversation between confederates in the swindle that draws the victim into the swindle. Originally used to describe the quick banter of vaudeville, then adapted to criminal purposes *US, 1940*

crossfire *verb* (used of a racehorse) to clip the rear hooves together while running *US, 1951*

crosshairs *noun* ► **put in the crosshairs** to target something. From military sniper/target competition shooting *US, 2002*

crosshaul *noun* a notional tool that a novice logger is often sent to fetch *US, 1913*

crosslift *noun* in poker, a cheating technique in which two confederates on either side of the victim continue raising the bet until the victim withdraws from the hand *US, 1968*

cross my heart and hope to die used as an oath, often with humour *US, 1926*

cross my heart and hope to spit used as an oath and pledge. Popularised by Theodore 'Beaver' Cleaver on the US television comedy *Leave it to Beaver* (CBS and ABC, 1957–63), in place of the more common 'cross my heart and hope to die'. Used with referential humour by those who had watched the show as children *US, 1963*

Crossmyloof *noun* a male homosexual. Glasgow rhyming slang for POOF, formed from the name of an area of the south side of Glasgow *UK: SCOTLAND, 1988*

cross of the north *noun* a stance assumed by a canoer on a portage when meeting someone on a trail *CANADA, 1947*

crossover *verb* to leave one youth gang and join a rival gang *US, 1995*

cross-patch *noun* a peevish, ill-tempered person. A combination of 'cross' (angry, peevish) and obsolete 'patch' (a fool). Originally applied to a girl or a woman; the general sense is first recorded in 1818 *UK, 1700*

crossroad *noun* an amphetamine tablet identified by its cross-scoring. Less commonly heard than CROSS TOP *US, 1980*

crossroader *noun* an itinerant card cheat *US, 1889*

cross-talk *noun* in a radio or television broadcast, speaking simultaneously and thus possibly obscuring what is said *US, 1984*

cross-thread *adjective* contrary *TRINIDAD AND TOBAGO, 1960*

cross top *noun* a tablet of Benzedrine™ (amphetamine sulphate), a central nervous system stimulant. From the appearance: white tablets with a cross cut into the surface *US, 1971*

crossword spanner *noun* a pencil. A term used by Royal Navy engineers *UK, 1962*

crot *noun* excrement, especially as 'soft crot', a loose stool. A schoolboys' term *UK, 1957*

crotch *noun* a woman *US, 1973*

Crotch *nickname* the US Marines Corps *US, 1953*

crotch ball *noun* in handball, a ball that strikes the intersection of two playing surfaces *US, 1970*

crotch crickets *noun* pubic lice *US, 1971*

crotchety *adjective* ill-tempered, cross *UK, 1825*

crotch light *noun* in the pornography industry, a light used to illuminate the genitals of the performers *US, 1977*

crotch magazine *noun* a pornographic magazine *US, 1986*

crotch rocket *noun* a motorcycle, usually a fast racing motorcycle *US, 1974*

crotch rot *noun* any fungal infection in the crotch *US, 1967*

crotch row *noun* in a striptease performance, seats very near the performers *US, 1973*

crotch shot *noun* a photograph focused on a person's genitals *US, 1973*

crotch strap *noun* in motor racing, a safety device that attaches to the buckle of the lap belt and is attached to the chassis under the seat *US, 1963*

crotch walker *noun* a shoplifter who conceals booty between the thighs *UK, 1996*

crovey! used for expressing approval *UK, 2003*

crow *noun* **1** a black person. Offensive *US, 1823*. **2** a female prostitute. Occasionally also spelt 'cro'. Perhaps influenced by CHROMO *AUSTRALIA, 1944*. **3** a mawkish, old-fashioned person *US, 1945*. **4** a drinking friend *BERMUDA, 1985*. **5** an undertaker; an undertaker's employee. From their black clothing *UK, 1947*. **6** used as an abusive term of address *UK, 2003*. **7** cocaine *UK, 2003*. **8** an electronic warfare specialist. Vietnam war usage *US, 1980*. **9** an eagle insignia in the US Navy *US, 1905*. ▶ **as the crow flies** directly; in a straight line *AUSTRALIA, 1902*

Crow *nickname* the Crow's Nest Pass railway freight rates *CANADA, 1987*

crowbait *noun* a horse, especially an older horse *US, 1851*

crowbar palace *noun* a jail *US, 1941*

crowd *noun* **1** a company of people defined by a common denominator, a set *US, 1840*. **2** a fat person *US, 1970*

crowd *verb* **1** to put pressure on someone, to coerce someone *US, 1828*. **2** to verge on a specified age *US, 1943*

crowded cabin *noun* in poker, a hand consisting of three cards of one rank and a pair. Conventionally known as a 'full house' *US, 1988*

crowded space *noun* a suitcase. Rhyming slang; especially, by thieves stealing luggage in crowded spaces *UK, 1961*

crowd engineer *noun* a police dog *US, 1992*

crowd-surf *verb* to pass over the heads of a crowd, propelled and supported by the hands of that crowd *US, 1993*

crow-eater *noun* a person from the state of South Australia *AUSTRALIA, 1881*

crow foot *noun* **1** in car repair, an open-ended wrench with an extension *US, 1993*. **2** in the television and film industries, a device

used to support the legs of a tripod on a slippery or uneven surface *US, 1960*

crowhop *noun* in rodeos, a mild bucking *CANADA, 1987*

crowie *noun* an old woman. From a resemblance to the crow in colour (of plumage/clothing) and tone of voice *UK, 1979*

Crow Jim *noun* anti-white racial discrimination by black people. A reversal of the common term JIM CROW for anti-black discrimination *US, 1956*

crown *noun* **1** a type of MDMA, the recreational drug best known as ecstasy. From the imprint on the pink pill *UK, 1996*. **2** a hat *US, 1976*. **3** a condom *UK, 1998*

Crown *noun* a Crown Prosecutor *CANADA, 2002*

crown *verb* **1** to hit someone on the head *UK, 1746*. **2** to couple a brakevan (caboose) to a freight train *US, 1946*

crown and anchor *noun* a despicable person. Rhyming slang for WANKER, formed on the name of a dice game *UK, 1992*

crown crap *noun* heroin *US, 1975*

crownie *noun* a tram or bus inspector. After the emblem of that rank *AUSTRALIA, 1953*

crown jewels *noun* **1** the male genitals, especially the testicles *AUSTRALIA, 1970*. **2** tools. Rhyming slang, perhaps taking its inspiration from the value a tradesman places on his tools *UK, 1992*. **3** jewels, usually ostentatious if not tacky, worn by a drag queen. The royalty punning thanks to 'queen' *US, 1965*

Crown Vic *noun* a Ford Crown Victoria car *US, 1999*

crows *noun* ▶ **where the crows fly backwards** an arid, desolate region *AUSTRALIA, 1932*

crow's feet *noun* **1** wrinkles at the corner of the eyes *UK, 1374*. **2** MDMA, the recreational drug best known as ecstasy. Specifically used of any tablet of MDMA stamped with an image similar to the single print of a bird's track *UK, 2004*

crow's foot *noun* in electric line work, a device formally known as an Epoxirod tri-unit *US, 1980*

crow's nest *noun* **1** the uppermost balcony in a cinema. A pun on the nautical term, acknowledging that the upper balconies were reserved for black people (CROWS) *US, 1970*. **2** the observation tower of a brakevan (caboose) *US, 1940*

crow storm *noun* a flocking up of noisy crows as cold weather approaches in the autumn *CANADA, 1992*

Croydon facelift *noun* a female hairstyle in which the hair is scraped back (into a ponytail or similar) so tightly that it appears to stretch the skin on the face. Coinage is credited to suburban London local newspaper the *Croydon Guardian*, reflecting the CHAV sub-cultural phenomenon. Also known as a 'Croydon smile' *UK, 2005*

Croydon pineapple *noun* a female hairstyle, popular among an underclass of urban youth, in which all hair is tightly scraped into a spikey top knot. Croydon is an urban area to the south east of London strongly identified with the CHAV sub-culture *UK, 2005*

CRS disease *noun* a sudden loss of memory. The person in question 'can't remember shit' *US, 1997*

crucial *adjective* very good. Recorded in Bermudan and American youth culture *BERMUDA, 1985*

crud *noun* **1** a contemptible person. Originally Scottish dialect for 'excrement' *US, 1930*. **2** rubbish, filth, shit. Originally Scottish dialect *crud* (curdled matter) *US, 1943*. **3** dried or sticky semen *US, 1967*. **4** any sexually transmitted infection *US, 1951*. **5** a common cold or the flu *ANTARCTICA, 2003*. **6** a notional disease, covering many ailments, real and imaginary *US, 1932*. **7** snow that does not produce good snowboarding *US, 1990*

crudded up *adjective* infected with a sexually transmitted disease *US, 1997*

cruddy *adjective* **1** useless, worthless, unpleasant, disgusting. Created from CRUD (filth) *US, 1947*. **2** encrusted with dirt or filth *US, 1949*

crudie *noun* an unsophisticated rustic *US, 1968*

crud up *verb* to foul something; to spoil something *US, 1963*

crudzine *noun* a poorly written and/or poorly produced fan magazine *US, 1976*

cruel *verb* to spoil something, especially to spoil a person's chances. Also spelt 'crool' in an effort to represent an uneducated pronunciation *AUSTRALIA, 1899*. ▶ **cruel the pitch** to spoil someone's chances; to ruin an opportunity *AUSTRALIA, 1915*

cruel *adjective* very *US, 1985*

cruel; cruelly *adverb* severely; extremely hard. In conventional use until later C19 *UK, 1937*

cruet *noun* the head *AUSTRALIA, 1941*. ▶ **do your cruet** to lose your temper *AUSTRALIA, 1976*

cruft *noun* any unpleasant, unidentified substance *US, 1983*

crufty *adjective* in computing, poorly designed or poorly built *US, 1981*

cruise *noun* a male homosexual who picks up multiple short-term sexual partners *US, 1950*

cruise *verb* **1** to search for a casual sex-partner, usually homosexual; to pursue a person as a casual sex-partner, especially by eye contact *US, 1925*. **2** to join others in driving slowly down chosen downtown streets, usually on a weekend night, seeing others and being seen *US, 1957*. **3** to drive. With a suggestion of carefree elan *US, 1957*. **4** to take someone, to lead someone *US, 1946*. ▶ **cruisin' for a bruisin'** heading for trouble, especially a physical beating *US, 1947*

cruise and kill *verb* (of light scout teams during the Vietnam war) to go around looking for solders to kill *US, 1991*

cruise joint *noun* a bar or other establishment where people gather in search of sexual partners *US, 1966*

cruisemobile *noun* any desirable car *US, 1978*

cruiser *noun* **1** a person who habitually searches regular haunts for casual sex-partners, usually homosexual *UK, 1996*. **2** a prostitute *US, 1868*. **3** a surfer who approaches surfing with a casualness that borders on laziness *US, 1988*

cruising *noun* the recreational activity of searching for a casual sex-partner, usually homosexual *UK, 1927*

cruisy *adjective* **1** relaxing, enjoyable *NEW ZEALAND, 1998*. **2** (of a place) characterised by a high degree of activity by homosexual men looking for sexual partners. Also spelt 'cruisey' *US, 1949*

cruit; croot *noun* a new military recruit *US, 1897*

cruller *noun* the head *US, 1942*

crumb *noun* **1** a despicable person *US, 1919*. **2** a body louse *US, 1863*. **3** a small piece of crack cocaine *US, 1994*. ▶ **put on the crumb act** to impose something on another person *AUSTRALIA, 1959*

crumb box *noun* **1** in circus and carnival usage, a small suitcase or box containing personal belongings *US, 1981*. **2** a brakevan (caboose) *US, 1945*

crumb bum *noun* **1** a lowly, inept person *US, 1934*. **2** a gambler who places very small and very conservative bets *US, 1950*

crumb castle *noun* in circus and carnival usage, a dining tent *US, 1981*

crumb-catcher *noun* a young child *US, 1962*

crumb crunchers *noun* the teeth *US, 1945*

crumb-crusher; crumb-cruncher *noun* a child, especially a very young one *US, 1959*

crumb-hunting *noun* housework. Obsolete teen slang, originally from military use in the early 1940s of 'crumb hunt' as meaning 'a kitchen inspection' *CANADA, 1946*

crumble *noun* in hospital, an elderly patient. Medical slang *UK, 2002*

crumbly; crumblie *noun* an older person, certainly one who is over 50 years old. An upper-class society image of crumbling with decay *UK, 1982*

crumbo *noun* ▶ **el crumbo** a socially inept person. Pseudo Spanish *US, 1956*

crumbs *noun* a small amount of money. An offshoot of BREAD *US, 1970*

crumbs! used as a mild exclamation. A euphemism for CHRIST! *UK, 1922*

crumb-snatcher *noun* a child; a baby *US, 1958*

crummy *noun* **1** a brakevan (caboose) *US, 1916*. **2** a truck, a boxcar or an old brakevan (caboose), converted to passenger carrying by adding wooden benches *CANADA, 1964*

crummy *adjective* **1** inferior *US, 1915*. **2** lice-infested *UK, 1859*

crump *verb* **1** to die *US, 1958*. **2** (used of a hospital patient) to become suddenly sicker, especially without hope of recovering *US, 1980*

crumpet *noun* **1** sexually desirable women considered collectively; hence, desirable men. Originally of women only; men weren't so categorised until the 1980s *UK, 1936*. **2** the head *UK, 1891*. ▶ **a bit of crumpet** sexual intercourse *NEW ZEALAND, 1984*. ▶ **bow the crumpet** to plead guilty. Formed on CRUMPET (the head); from bending the head in unspoken affirmative *AUSTRALIA, 1975*. ▶ **not worth a crumpet** worthless *AUSTRALIA, 1944*

crumpet man *noun* a womaniser *UK, 1977*

crump out *verb* to succumb to exhaustion; to die *US, 1953*

crunch *noun* **1** a most severe test of strength, courage, nerve, skill, etc *UK, 1939*. **2** a number sign (#) on a computer keyboard *US, 1991*. **3** a hospital patient with multiple fractures *US, 1989*. **4** an Afrikaner. Also 'crunchie'. Derogatory and offensive *SOUTH AFRICA, 1970*. ▶ **do your crunch** to become enraged. Army use *UK, 1984*

crunch *verb* to analyse something, especially a large amount of data *US, 1981*

crunch and munch *noun* crack cocaine. From the drug's arguable resemblance to breakfast cereal or a snack food *US, 1993*

crunch cap *noun* a fatigue hat, made of cotton canvas with a brim around, that kept the sun and rain off the heads of American soldiers in Vietnam. It could be folded or 'crunched up' easily *US, 1984*

crunch case *noun* a hospital patient with a severe head injury *US, 1994*

cruncher *noun* **1** a dent in a surfboard that can be repaired without a resin filler *US, 1986*. **2** a foot *US, 1946*

crunch hat *noun* in motor racing, a safety helmet *US, 1993*

crunch time *noun* the critical moment *US, 1961*

crunchy *noun* **1** the pavement or sidewalk *US, 1945*. **2** a foot soldier, or member of the infantry. Korean and then Vietnam war usage *US, 1951*

crunchy *adjective* embodying the values or at least the trappings of the 1960s counterculture; a person who embodies these values. An adjective often associated with GRANOLA, used to describe the throwback person *US, 1990*

crunk *noun* **1** an excited state *US, 2001*. **2** a popular genre of hip-hop music *UK, 2005*

crunk *adjective* excellent; intense. Rap coinage; a variation of CRANKED (intensified) *US, 1995*

crunked *adjective* **1** excited. Rap usage; a variation of CRUNK (excellent) *US, 2001*. **2** very drunk *US, 2003*

Crusaders *nickname* the 523rd Fighter Squadron, which served in Korea and briefly in Vietnam *US, 1991*

crush *noun* **1** a romanticised affection for someone; an infatuation *US, 1884*. **2** the object of an infatuation. In C19 US use, but now obsolete there *AUSTRALIA, 1996*. **3** the vagina *US, 1982*. **4** a hat *US, 1916*. **5** in pool, the opening or break shot *US, 1993*

crush *verb* to do very well *US, 1986*

crushed *adjective* ugly *US, 1993*

crusher *noun* **1** in horse racing, a person who works the odds as they shorten *AUSTRALIA, 1965*. **2** a powerful, hard-breaking wave *US, 1964*. **3** something overpowering or overwhelming *UK, 1840*. **4** a police officer. Now rare *UK, 1835*

crushers *noun* fashionable, stylish sunglasses. Biker (motorcycle) usage *US, 2003*

crushman *noun* a good-looking boy *US, 1982*

crust *noun* **1** a livelihood *AUSTRALIA, 1888*. **2** in the UK, members of an alternative culture underclass. Back-formation from CRUSTY (a member of an alternative culture underclass) *UK, 2004*. **3** nerve, courage, gall *US, 1900*

crust *verb* to insult someone *US, 1945*

crustie *noun* an old person *NEW ZEALAND, 1997*

crust of bread; crust *noun* the head, epecially as a source of intelligence. Rhyming slang *UK, 1961*

crusty *noun* a young person who many years later embraces the counterculture values of the late 1960s *UK, 1990*

crusty *adjective* **1** dirty, shabby *US, 1972*. **2** crude, vulgar *US, 1964*

crusty treats *noun* cocaine *UK, 2003*

crut *noun* **1** filth, nastiness, dirt *US, 1940*. **2** a disease *US, 1947*

crutch *noun* **1** an improvised holder for the short butt of a marijuana cigarette. The term of choice before ROACH CLIP came on the scene *US, 1938*. **2** in pool, a device used to support the cue stick for a hard-to-reach shot. As the terminology suggests, the device is scorned by skilled players *US, 1990*. **3** in skating, an experienced skater supporting a novice *UK, 1961*

crutch *verb* to conceal goods (stolen property or contraband) in the vagina – usually contained in a condom and often further protected from discovery by the insertion of a tampon *UK, 1996*

crutcher *noun* a female thief or smuggler who hides goods in her crutch. From CRUTCH. Recorded by a Jamaican inmate of a UK prison *UK, 2002*

Crutches *nickname* Las Cruces, New Mexico *US, 1970*

cry *noun* ▶ **the cry** the best *US, 1955*

cry *verb* ▶ **cry a river** to regret something deeply *US, 1994*. ▶ **cry all the way to the bank** used ironically by, or of, someone whose artistic work is a commercial success yet attracts adverse criticism. Credited to musician and entertainer (Wladziu Valentino) Liberace who, from the mid-1950s, enjoyed great popular success and, in the face of critical disdain, quipped and then included the following quotation in his stage act: 'When the reviews are bad I tell my staff that they can join me as I cry all the way to the bank'. The phrase survives but has also become the more straightforward 'laugh all the way to the bank' *US, 1984*. ▶ **cry Bert** to vomit *AUSTRALIA, 1971*. ▶ **cry blue ruin** to proclaim a family financial disaster *CANADA, 1959*. ▶ **cry Ruth** to vomit. Self-descriptive of its echoic origins *AUSTRALIA, 1971*. ▶ **cry your eyes out; cry your heart out** to weep long and bitterly *UK, 1704*

cry baby *noun* a child swindler who appeals for money from strangers with pitiful tales of woe, accompanied if need be by tears *US, 1982*

cry baby grenade *noun* a hand grenade loaded with tear gas for use in riots and to clear bunkers and tunnels *US, 1990*

cry down *verb* to disparage someone or something *TRINIDAD AND TOBAGO, 1988*

crying *adjective* used as a negative intensifier *US, 1942*

crying towel *noun* a notional linen given to someone who is a chronic complainer *US, 1928*

crying weed *noun* marijuana. The WEED that invites emotional involvement *US, 1953*

cry me a river! used for expressing a lack of sympathy in the face of an implicit solicitation of same *US, 1995*

cryppie; crippie *noun* in computing, a cryptographer *US, 1991*

crypto *noun* a person who is a secret-sympathiser or -adherent of a political group, especially of a communist. Adapted from the conventional prefix *crypto-* (concealed, hidden, secret) in such uses as 'crypto-facist'; ultimately from Greek *kruptos* (hidden) *UK, 1946*

cryptonie; cryppie *noun* marijuana *UK, 2003*

crystal *noun* **1** a powdered narcotic, especially methamphetamine *US, 1964*. **2** phencyclidine. Recorded as a current PCP alias *US, 1977*. **3** a type of marijuana *2003*

crystal *adjective* perfectly understandable. A reduction of 'crystal-clear' *UK, 1994*

crystal chin *noun* a fighter who is easily injured with blows to the chin *US, 1981*

crystal cylinder *noun* the hollow of a breaking wave *AUSTRALIA, 1992*

crystal meth; crystal meths *noun* powdered methamphetamine *US, 2001*

crystal palace *noun* an apartment or house occupied by amphetamine and/or methamphetamine abusers *US, 1997*

crystal pop *noun* a combination of cocaine and phencyclidine, the recreational drug known as PCP or angel dust. Possibly playing on 'Krystal' champagne *UK, 2003*

crystal ship *noun* a syringe filled with a melted powdered drug *US, 1992*

crystal tea *noun* LSD. From the appearance of the drug in crystalline form *UK, 1998*

crywater *noun* tears *ANTIGUA AND BARBUDA, 1998*

c's *noun* **1** combat rations, the standard meals eaten by US troops in the field, consisting of an individual ration of packaged precooked foods which can be eaten hot or cold *US, 1976*. **2** food. An abbreviation of 'calories'; 'to get your c's' is 'to eat' *US, 1968*

CS *noun* **1** used as a euphemism for 'chickenshit'. Far less common than BS (BULLSHIT) *US, 1944*. **2** marijuana *UK, 2003*

C sponge *noun* a contraceptive sponge *US, 1997*

CT *noun* a woman who signals an interest in sex with another woman but does not have sex with her. An abbreviation of CUNT TEASE *US, 1923*

CTD (in doctors' shorthand) for expected to die soon. An initialism for 'circling the drain' *UK, 2003*

CTN used as shorthand in Internet discussion groups and text message to mean 'can't talk now' *US, 2002*

Ctrl-Alt-Delete; Control-Alt-Delete *noun* a notional device or technique which causes something to be reconsidered or restarted. From the combination of character-keys used as a 'short-cut' to restart a computer; the former is written, the latter spoken *US, 1995*

Cuban pumps *noun* in homosexual usage, heavy work boots *US, 1987*

cubbitch *adjective* greedy *TRINIDAD AND TOBAGO, 1960*

cubby *noun* a room, apartment or house *US, 1948*

cube *noun* **1** a complete conformist. An intensification of SQUARE (a conventional person) *US, 1955*. **2** LSD. From the fact that LSD was often administered in sugar cubes *US, 1966*. **3** a tablet of marijuana, approximately one gram in weight. From the shape *US, 1984*. **4** a tablet of morphine *US, 1950*. **5** a cubic inch *US, 1970*. **6** a work space in an open-area office. An abbreviation of 'cubicle' *UK, 1936*

cubeb *noun* a herbal cigarette, pungent and spicy, made from the cubeb berry *US, 1959*

cube head *noun* a regular LSD user *US, 1966*

cubes *noun* **1** the testicles *US, 1968*. **2** dice *US, 1918*. **3** morphine *US, 1980*. **4** crack cocaine *UK, 2003*

cubicle *noun* a Mini Metro car *UK, 1981*

cub reporter *noun* a young, naive and untrained reporter. The term is a popular culture allusion to the Superman legend. When Clark Kent went to work at the *Daily Star*, Jimmy Olsen was an office boy with aspirations to be a great reporter. With help from Superman, Olsen, who was forever tagged with the label 'cub reporter', became a member of the reporting staff. From the much earlier (1845) sense of a 'cub' as an 'apprentice' *US, 1908*

cuck *verb* to defecate *CANADA, 1993*

cuck *adjective* very bad, awful *IRELAND, 1997*

cuckle bucks *noun* curly or kinky hair that has not been chemically straightened *US, 1973*

cuckoo *noun* a fool; a crazy person *UK, 1889*

cuckoo *adjective* crazy, mad, distraught *US, 1906*

cuckoo farm *noun* a mental hospital. A variation of FUNNY FARM *UK, 1980*

cuckoo house *noun* a mental hospital *US, 1930*

cuckoo's nest *noun* **1** the vagina. Survives in folk songs of the US and UK *UK, 1840*. **2** a mental hospital *US, 1962*

cucumber *noun* **1** a number, usually a telephone number. Rhyming slang *UK, 1992*. **2** in gambling, an ignorant victim of a cheat. A play on 'green', the colour of the cucumber and a slang term for 'inexperienced'. Often shortened to 'cuke' *US, 1962*

cucumbers *noun* ▶ **the cucumbers** in prison, Rule 43, which allows a prisoner to be kept apart from the main prison community for 'safety of self or others'. Rhyming slang ('numbers') *UK, 2003*

cuda *noun* **1** a barracuda *US, 1949*. **2** a Plymouth Barracuda car *US, 1965*

cuddle and kiss *noun* **1** an act of urination. Rhyming slang for PISS. Sometimes shortened to 'cuddie' *UK, 1992*. **2** a girl; a girlfriend. Rhyming slang for 'miss'; formed in a time when a cuddle and kiss were the only realistic objectives for a young man with love on his mind *UK, 1938*. **3** piss, in the phrase 'take the piss' (to make a fool of). Rhyming slang *UK, 1992*

cuddle bunny *noun* an attractive girl *US, 1946*

cuddled and kissed; cuddled *adjective* drunk. Rhyming slang for PISSED *UK, 1998*

cuddle puddle *noun* a group of people lying together, especially after taking the type of recreational drugs that enhance feelings of togetherness; a communal jacuzzi *UK, 2003*

cuddle seat *noun* in a cinema, a double seat provided for a couple's convenience. Probably adopted from the brand name Cuddleseat™ (a baby carrier) introduced in 1947 *AUSTRALIA, 1984*

cuddy *noun* a horse. From British dialect *cuddy* (a donkey) *AUSTRALIA, 1897*

cudja? could you? Apparently coined by television production company Brighter Pictures but rapidly gained wider use *UK, 2002*

cuds *noun* the countryside *UK, 1995*

cue *noun* **1** barbecued meat *US, 1992*. **2** barbecue *US, 1908*. **3** a tip or gratuity *US, 1970*. ▶ **put your cue in the rack** to die; to retire *AUSTRALIA, 1989*

cueball *noun* **1** a bald person *US, 1941*. **2** a crew-cut haircut *US, 1955*. **3** one-eighth of an ounce of cocaine *US, 1993*

cue biter *noun* an actor who proceeds with his lines without letting the audience react appropriately to the cue line *US, 1973*

cue-bow *noun* a charge of 'conduct unbecoming an officer' filed against a police officer *US, 1975*

cues *noun* headphones worn by musicians overdubbing a tape *US, 1979*

cuff *noun* ▶ **off the cuff** unrehearsed, improvised. From the discreet *aide-memoire* some performers or speakers jot on their cuffs *US, 1938*. ▶ **on the cuff 1** on credit *US, 1927*. **2** admitted to a theatre without paying for a ticket *US, 1973*

cuff *verb* **1** to handcuff someone *UK, 1851*. **2** to shine something, to polish something *US, 1973*. **3** to drink to excess *TRINIDAD AND TOBAGO, 1956*. **4** to admit someone to an entertainment without charge *US, 1951*. **5** in an illegal betting operation, to accept bets at odds and in a proportion guaranteed to produce a loss for the bookmaker *US, 1951*

cuff down; cuff up *verb* to assault someone; to beat someone *TRINIDAD AND TOBAGO, 1966*

cuff link faggot; cuff link queen *noun* a wealthy, ostentatious homosexual male *US, 1965*

cuff links *noun* handcuffs *US, 1982*

cuffs *noun* handcuffs. Originally used of C17 iron fetters, now used as a shortening of 'handcuffs' *UK, 1861*

cuke *noun* a cucumber. A domestic colloquialism *US, 1903*

CUL used in computer message shorthand to mean 'see you later' *US, 1991*

culchie *noun* a person from rural Ireland. A derogatory term coined during the 1940s at University College Galway for students of agriculture; probably from Irish *Coillte Mach* (County Mayo), regarded (wrongly) as a remote place. Other possible etymologies: *coillte* (woods) and *cúl and tí* (a rear entrance to an important house, used by social inferiors) *IRELAND, 1958*

cull *noun* **1** a prisoner re-assigned to an undemanding job after failing at a more challenging one *US, 1990*. **2** in horse racing, a horse

that is cast off by a stable because it has failed to perform well *US, 1947*. ▶ **on the cull list** unmarried *US, 1933*

cully; cull; cul *noun* a man, a fellow, a companion *UK, 1661*

cultural jammer; jammer *noun* a cultural activist who creatively subverts advertising material *US, 1990*

culture fruit *noun* watermelon *US, 1973*

culture jam; jam *noun* a message subverted by anticorporate activists *US, 2001*

culture jamming; jamming *noun* the act of inverting and subverting advertising matter by anticorporate activists. Derives from the conventional sense of 'jam' (to disrupt a signal) *US, 1995*

culture vulture *noun* an enthusiast for intellectual and artistic culture and cultural events *US, 1947*

cultus *adjective* worthless, bad, useless, insignificant. From the Chinook trading jargon *US, 1851*

cultus coulee *noun* a stroll or ride for pleasure *CANADA, 1963*

cultus potlatch *noun* a present for which nothing is expected in return, especially one of little value *CANADA, 1940*

cum *noun* amyl nitrite. A drug associated with sex *US, 1992* ▷ *see:* COME *and variants*

cumbucket *noun* a despised person *US, 1975*

cum catcher *noun* a condom. Uses COME; CUM (semen) to describe a condom's purpose *UK, 1998*

cum drum *noun* a condom; especially a condom with a bulbous extension to collect semen. Phonetically similar to 'condom' *US, 1987*

cummy face *noun* in a pornographic film or photograph, a close-up shot of a man's face as he ejaculates *US, 1995*

cum shaw *noun* anything procurred through other than legitimate channels. From the Chinese for a 'present' or 'bonus', originally applied to a payment made by ships entering the port of Canton *UK, 1925*

cung *noun* marijuana *US, 1995*

cunkerer *noun* a blundering, poorly trained technician. From 'cunk', imitative of the metallic sound of a clumsily handled tool *GUYANA, 1998*

cunning as a Maori dog *adjective* very cunning; sly. 'Maori dog' is now usually replaced by less objectionable epithets like 'shithouse rat' *NEW ZEALAND, 1947*

cunning as an outhouse rat *adjective* very cunning indeed *NEW ZEALAND, 1996*

cunning as a shithouse rat *adjective* extremely crafty *NEW ZEALAND, 1917*

cunning kick *noun* a place for secreting money *AUSTRALIA, 1979*

cunny *noun* the vagina. A play on CUNT (the vagina) and 'con(e)y' (a rabbit) *UK, 1615*

cunny fingers; cunny thumbs *noun* an awkward, clumsy person. A term originally applied to a weak shooter *US, 1892*

cunt *noun* **1** the vagina. The most carefully avoided, heavily tabooed word in the English language *UK, 1230*. **2** a woman, especially as an object of sexual desire *UK, 1674*. **3** sex with a woman *UK, 1670*. **4** a despicable person, female or male. When used as a reductive term of abuse, 'cunt' is usually more offensive than the male equivalents *UK, 1860*. **5** among homosexuals, a boy or young man as a sexual object *US, 2004*. **6** among homosexuals, the buttocks, anus and rectum *US, 1972*. **7** among homosexuals, the mouth *US, 1972*. **8** a person you admire or pretend to grudgingly admire; a form of address between friends. Mainly jocular usage *UK, 2001*. **9** an idiot, a fool *UK, 1922*. **10** to a drug addict, a vein used for injecting a drug, especially the vein found on the inside of the elbow *US, 1960*. **11** an unfortunate or difficult situation; an unpleasant task; a problem. A logical extension of earlier, still current senses (an irritating person or object) *UK, 1931*

cunt and a half *noun* an extremely unpleasant person. This intensification of CUNT (an unpleasant person) was originally used exclusively of males *UK, 1984*

cunt book *noun* a pornographic book, especially one with photographs or illustrations *US, 1969*

cunt breath *noun* a despicable person *US, 1992*

cunt cap *noun* a narrow green garrison cap worn by enlisted men. Probably of World War 1 vintage. The Chinese Army refer to the same article as a 'cow's-cunt-cap'. Soldiers learn the term in the first few days of training. They now learn not to use the term in the presence of women *UK, 1923*

cunt collar *noun* a desire for sex *US, 1965*

cunt eater *noun* any person who performs oral sex on a woman *US, 1998*

cunted *adjective* drunk *UK, 2003*

cunt-eyed *adjective* squinting *UK, 1916*

cunt face *noun* a despicable person *US, 1948*

cunt-faced *adjective* despicable *US, 1974*

cunt fart *noun* a despicable person *US, 1996*

cuntfuck *noun* an extremely unpleasant individual. Both CUNT and FUCK are synonymous here, each serving to intensify the other *UK, 2002*

cunt hair *noun* a very small distance *US, 1957*

cunt hair grass *noun* an oatgrass or spike rush *US, 1945*

cunt hat *noun* a felt hat. Probably from the shape of the crease in the crown *UK, 1923*

cunthead *noun* a despised fool *US, 1971*

cunt-holes! used for registering frustration, annoyance or anger *UK, 2000*

cunt hook *noun* the hand. Usually in the plural *US, 1994*

cunt-hooks *noun* **1** a gesture that is used to insult or otherwise cause offense, in which the forefinger and middle-finger are extended to form a V-shape, the palm turned in towards the gesturer. An alternative name for a V-SIGN *UK, 1984*. **2** an unpleasant person *UK, 2001*

cunt hound *noun* a man obsessed with the seduction of women *US, 1960*

cuntie *noun* a contemptible person. A patronising elaboration of CUNT *UK: NORTHERN IRELAND, 2001*

cuntiness *noun* unpleasant or stupid characteristics of a person *UK, 2001*

cunting *adjective* used as an intensifier, generally denoting disapproval *UK, 2000*

-cunting- *infix* used as an intensifier, generally negative *UK, 2000*

cuntish *adjective* **1** unpleasant; stupid *UK, 2000*. **2** weak, cowardly *US, 1975*

cunt juice *noun* vaginal secretions *US, 1990*

cunt-lapper *noun* a person who performs oral sex on a woman *US, 1916*

cunt-lapping *noun* oral sex on a woman *US, 1970*

cunt-lapping *adjective* despised *US, 1923*

cunt-licking *noun* oral sex on a woman *US, 1996*

cunt-licking *adjective* despised *US, 1985*

cunt light *noun* in the pornography industry, a light used to illuminate the genitals of the performers *US, 1995*

cunt like a Grimsby welly *noun* an unusually large and pungent vagina. Grimsby is a fishing port on the north east coast of England; the comparison to a 'welly' (Wellington boot) is obvious *UK, 2002*

cunt man *noun* a heterosexual man; a womaniser. Uses CUNT in the generalised sense as 'women' *UK, 1999*

cunt off *verb* to make someone angry; to annoy someone *UK, 2001*

cunt pie *noun* the vagina, especially as an object of oral sex *US, 1980*

cunt prick *noun* a despicable person. A compound of two terms of abuse that may need strengthening after overuse *UK, 1997*

cunt racket *noun* prostitution *US, 1977*

cunt rag *noun* **1** a sanitary towel *US, 1968*. **2** a despicable person or thing *US, 1971*

cunt's act *noun* a major deception *AUSTRALIA, 1985*

cunt screen *noun* a strip of canvas stretched between the open rungs of the accommodation ladder up which lady guests would ascend above the heads of the boat's crew. Similar in purpose and effect to a VIRGINITY CURTAIN *UK, 1984*

cunt-simple *adjective* obsessed with sex; easily distracted by women *US, 1982*

cunt sniff *noun* a contemptible or loathesome individual. As usage of CUNT (a contemptible person) becomes evermore mainstream, elaborations are necessary to maintain the derogatory effect. 'Cunt sniff' contrives CUNT (vagina) and conventional 'sniff' (to inhale, to smell) to suggest something of no more worth than the odour of a woman's genitals *UK, 2001*

cunt splice *noun* any improvised splice *US, 1956*

cunt starver *noun* a prisoner serving time for not making maintenance payments *AUSTRALIA, 1950*

cunt stretcher *noun* the penis *US, 2001*

cunt-struck *adjective* obsessed with sex with a woman or women *UK, 1866*

cunt-sucker *noun* **1** a person who performs oral sex on women *UK, 1868*. **2** a despised person *US, 1964*

cunt-sucking *noun* oral sex on a woman *US, 1998*

cunt-sucking *adjective* despised *US, 1964*

cunt tease *noun* a woman who signals an interest in sex with another woman but does not have sex with her *US, 1971*

cunt-tickler *noun* a moustache *US, 1967*

Cunt Town *nickname* Norfolk, Virginia. A major naval base, and hence a hotbed of prostitution *US, 1982*

cunt wagon *noun* a car perceived to attract women *US, 1974*

cunty *adjective* unpleasant *US, 1972*

cup *noun* **1** the vagina *US, 1973*. **2** a cup of tea. Both figurative and practical *UK, 1952*

cup and saucer *noun* the fifth wheel on a tractor trailer *US, 1961*

cupcake *noun* **1** a cute girl *US, 1939*. **2** a male homosexual, especially if young *US, 1996*. **3** a haircut shaped like a box *US, 1989*

cupcakes *noun* **1** the female breasts. Possibly informed, if not inspired, by a brassiere's 'cups' *UK, 2002*. **2** well-defined, well-rounded buttocks *US, 1972*. **3** LSD *US, 2003*

Cup Day *noun* the day on which the Melbourne Cup horse race is run *AUSTRALIA, 1876*

cupful of cold sick *noun* the epitome of worthlessness *NEW ZEALAND, 1998*

cupid's itch *noun* any sexually transmitted infection *US, 1930*

cupid's measles *noun* syphilis; any sexually transmitted infection *US, 1970*

cupla focal *noun* a paltry knowledge of Irish, literally a few words, enough for a display of national pride but not nearly enough for a conversation *IRELAND, 1996*

cup of chino; cup of cheeno *noun* a cappuccino *AUSTRALIA, 1987*

cup of tea *noun* **1** something that is to your taste. Variants are 'cup of char' and 'cuppa' *UK, 1932*. **2** an act of urination. Rhyming slang for PEE or WEE *UK, 1992*

cup of tea *verb* to see. Rhyming slang *UK, 1992*

cuppa; cupper *noun* a cup of tea or coffee *UK, 1934*

cuppie *noun* a female hanger-on at a World Cup sailing competition *US, 1996*

cups *noun* sleep *US, 1948*. ▶ **in your cups** drinking; drunk *UK, 1406*

Cup week *noun* the week during which the Melbourne Cup horse race is run *AUSTRALIA, 1882*

cura *noun* heroin; specifically an injection of heroin at a moment of great need. From Spanish for 'cure' *US, 1969*

curate's egg *noun* something that is good in parts. From the phrase 'good in parts – like a curate's egg' *UK, 1961*

curb *noun* ▶ **against the curb** without money *US, 1995*. ▶ **to the curb 1** destitute; suffering from hard times *US, 1989*. **2** rejected in romance *US, 1993*. **3** vomiting *US, 1989*

curb *verb* to stop or slow down *US, 1953*

curb hop *noun* a person who takes orders and serves food to customers seated in their cars *US, 1937*

curb serve *verb* to sell crack cocaine on a street corner *US, 1995*

curbstoner *noun* in the used car business, a dealer who operates with low overheads and a small inventory *US, 1968*

cure *noun* **1** treatment for drug addiction. Generally after 'the' *US, 1953*. **2** suicide *US, 1949*

cured *adjective* ▶ **get cured** to get rich *US, 1957*

Curehead *noun* someone who dresses in black similar to members of the band the Cure or other goth-rock bands, wears makeup and has the specific hairstyle of the lead singer *IRELAND, 1991*

curer *noun* an alcoholic drink taken to alleviate the symptoms of a hangover *UK: SCOTLAND, 1996*

cure-the-plague *noun* the bleed period of the menstrual cycle. From the C14 belief that drinking menstrual blood was a remedy for bubonic plague *US, 2000*

curfuffle; gefuffle; kerfuffle *noun* a disturbance or disorder of any kind *UK: SCOTLAND, 1813*

curl *noun* the concave face of a wave as it breaks *US, 1963*

Curl *noun* used of a bald man, or one with *curly* hair, as a form of address. A barely abbreviated form of CURLY *AUSTRALIA, 1984*

curlies *noun* pubic hair. Used both literally and figuratively to suggest complete control over someone *US, 1973*

curl the mo; curl a mo *adjective* great; terrific; excellent *AUSTRALIA, 1941*

curl the mo!; curl a mo! terrific! *AUSTRALIA, 1954*

curly *noun* a challenging situation *NEW ZEALAND, 1998*

Curly *noun* used of a bald-headed man. Ironic or, perhaps, the man so-dubbed began with curly hair and, like the word itself, evolved into this sense *UK, 1961*

curly *adjective* **1** (mainly of decisions, questions, etc) difficult *AUSTRALIA, 1963*. **2** excellent, attractive. Possibly a shortened variation of CURL THE MO *UK, 1981*. ▶ **to give someone the curly lip** to say something displeasing *US, 1989*

curly do *noun* a curly hair style popular with black men and women in the mid-1970s *US, 1975*

curly wolf *noun* an aggressive, belligerent man. A term from the American west *US, 1910*

curp *noun* the penis. Back slang, 'kcirp' for PRICK (the penis). Only ever in limited use, by 2003 completely redundant *UK, 1981*

currant bread *adjective* dead. Rhyming slang *UK, 1992*

currant bun *noun* **1** a nun. Glasgow rhyming slang *UK, 1996*. **2** the sun. Rhyming slang. Sometimes shortened to 'currant' *UK, 1938*. ▶ **on the currant bun** on the run. Rhyming slang, in underworld and police use *UK, 1959*

Currant Bun *nickname The Sun*, a daily newspaper. Rhyming slang, acquired from the solar original *UK, 1979*

currant cake *adjective* awake. Prison rhyming slang *NEW ZEALAND, 1999*

currant-cakes *noun delirium tremens*. Rhyming slang for SHAKES; a back-formation from CURRANT-CAKEY (shakey) *UK, 1992*

currant-cakey; currant-cakie *adjective* shakey. Rhyming slang *UK, 1932*

currants and plums *noun* the gums. Rhyming slang *UK, 1992*

curry *noun* verbal support on the emphatic end of the scale *NEW ZEALAND, 1998*. ▶ **give someone curry 1** to attack someone. That is, make it 'hot' for them *AUSTRALIA, 1936*. **2** to make someone's life difficult, to reprove someone. Possibly from the hot nature of curry *AUSTRALIA, 1936*. ▶ **the Curry** Cloncurry, generally called 'The

Curry', is the western Queensland base of the Flying Doctor Service *UK, 1962*

curry city *nickname* Bradford, West Yorkshire. Citizens' band radio slang, reflecting the large immigrant population *UK, 1981*

curry-mouth *adjective* fond of Indian food *TRINIDAD AND TOBAGO, 1987*

curry muncher *noun* a person from the Indian subcontinent. Derogatory *NEW ZEALAND, 1991*

curse *noun* **1** the bleed period of the menstrual cycle. Used with 'the' *US, 1930*. **2** a swagman's bundle of personal effects, a swag. Variants are 'curse of Cain' and 'curse of God' *AUSTRALIA, 1921*. ▶ **carry the curse; hump the curse** to go on the tramp. After CURSE (a swag) *AUSTRALIA, 1959*

curse *verb* ▶ **curse stink; cuss stink** to use a great deal of profanity *TRINIDAD AND TOBAGO, 1960*

curse of Eve *noun* the bleed period of the menstrual cycle. Adopted from poetic and literary use *UK, 1929*

curse of Mexico *noun* in a deck of playing cards, the two of spades *US, 1949*

curse of Scotland *noun* in a deck of playing cards, the nine of diamonds *UK, 1715*

curse rag *noun* a sanitary towel. Formed on CURSE (the bleed period of the menstrual cycle) *UK, 1961*

curtain *noun* used in conjunction with a precedent noun, indicating isolation, hostility, aggression and/or danger *US, 1955*

curtain-climber *noun* a small child *US, 1973*

curtain-raiser *noun* the first game of a season *US, 1950*

curtains *noun* **1** the end, implying death or dismissal. Theatrical origin (the final curtain of a play) *US, 1901*. **2** the *labia majora US, 1982*. ▶ **curtains and carpet that match; matching curtains and carpet** said when a person's hair colour matches the colour of their pubic hair *US, 2003*

curtain-twitcher *noun* a person who spies on the comings and goings of the world from behind a curtained window *UK, 2002*

curve *noun* ▶ **ahead of the curve** anticipating events or trends; on the cutting edge *US, 1980*. ▶ **behind the curve** lagging behind trends or developments *US, 1989*

curve-breaker *noun* a diligent, smart student. A student whose performance upsets the grading curve *US, 1955*

curved *adjective* corrupt, crooked, criminal. A variation of BENT *UK, 1999*

curve-killer *noun* a student who excels. A reference to the grading curve *US, 1959*

curvy crawler *noun* a prostitute, a streetwalker. A play on KERB CRAWLING (soliciting prostitutes from a vehicle) *UK, 1984*

cush *noun* **1** the vagina; sex; a woman as a sexual object *US, 1960*. **2** loose tobacco *US, 1950*. **3** money *US, 1900*

cush *adjective* comfortable, unstrained. A shortened form of CUSHY *US, 1931*

cushion *noun* a passenger railway carriage *US, 1913*

cushty *adjective* excellent, great. A roughly contemporaneous variation of CUSHY (easy, comfortable); attributed to market traders since the late 1910s; much more widespread since 1981 through usage in BBC television comedy series *Only Fools and Horses UK, 1985*

cushy *adjective* easy, comfortable, unstrained. From Hindu *khush* (pleasant) or Romany *kushto* (good) *UK, 1915*

cuspy *adjective* (used of a computer program) well-designed, highly functional *US, 1981*

cuss *noun* **1** a person; a creature. Usually, slightly contemptuous, reproachful or humorous; probably derived as a shortening of CUSTOMER, pehaps influenced in later usage by CUSS (a curse) *US, 1775*. **2** a curse. A dated euphemism that survives in the term TINKER'S CUSS (a thing of little value) *US, 1848*

cussbud *noun* a person who uses a great deal of profanity *TRINIDAD AND TOBAGO, 1977*

cuss-cuss *noun* insults, profanity *BAHAMAS, 1982*

cussedness *noun* cantankerousness, contrariness *US, 1866*

cuss fight *noun* a loud, angry argument *US, 1923*

cussie *noun* an HM Customs & Excise official *UK, 2002*

cuss out *verb* to reprimand someone with a heavy reliance on profanity *US, 1863*

cuss word *noun* a profanity. After CUSS (a curse) *US, 1872*

custard and jelly; custard *noun* television; a television. Rhyming slang for TELLY *UK, 1974*

custard cream; custard *verb* to dream. Rhyming slang, formed on a biscuit. *UK, 1992*

custards *noun* acne, pimples, spots. From the colour of the swelling or the pus *AUSTRALIA, 1942*

custard tart *noun* a traffic warden *UK, 1981*

custer *noun* a person who poses as a member of a youth gang but is not accepted as a gang member *US, 1995*

custie *noun* a buyer of illegal drugs. Simply put, an abbreviation of 'customer' *US, 1997*

customer *noun* **1** a person, or any creature, generally qualified as a type, as in 'an ugly customer' or 'an awkward customer' *UK, 1589*. **2** any person who is subject to a social worker's professional or charitable attention. A patronising categorisation, now replaced with the equally dishonest 'client' *UK, 1966*. **3** a motorist being stopped by a police officer for a traffic violation *US, 1962*. **4** a potential shop-lifter. In UK Disney Stores in the mid-1990s staff were instructed to refer to customers as 'guests' – anyone referred to as a 'customer' was instantly the subject of an unwelcome attention *UK, 1995*. **5** a prisoner *US, 1949*

cut *noun* **1** an adulterant used to dilute a drug; a dilution of a drug *US, 1966*. **2** a share, usually of profits, often of ill-gotten gains *AUSTRALIA, 1911*. **3** a reduction of a prison sentence *US, 2002*. **4** any district where goods are bought and sold with a minimum of questions asked *UK, 1950*. **5** any place where young people congregate to socialise *US, 1953*. **6** someone's appearance. Usually derogatory *IRELAND, 1997*. **7** a stage or a degree *UK, 1818*. **8** of music, a recording or a special part of one. From the verb sense *US, 1975*. **9** in hip-hop music, a sample or part of a tune that is played repeatedly *US, 2000*. **10** the vagina *US, 1967*. **11** a press cutting *UK, 2003*. **12** a hitting of the open hand with a cane for corporal punishment. Formally common in the Australian school system, now the practice is obsolete. The term is commonly found in the plural as the punishment was generally so given *AUSTRALIA, 1915*

cut *verb* **1** in the drug trade, to dilute drugs *US, 1937*. **2** to dilute anything by the addition of a secondary ingredient. Extended from the previous sense (to dilute drugs) *US, 1985*. **3** (of a drug) to take effect *UK, 1998*. **4** to fart *US, 1967*. **5** to engage in an informal musical competition in which musicians attempt to better each other in extended jazz solos *US, 1937*. **6** to record a song *US, 1937*. **7** to skip something, to fail to attend something *UK, 1794*. **8** to leave quickly *UK, 1790*. **9** to ignore a person, either as a single act or as continuing behaviour *UK, 1634*. **10** to tease or disparage someone *US, 1975*. **11** to divide or share out legal profits or criminal gains *UK, 1928*. **12** to perform surgery *US, 1970*. ▶ **be cut out for something** to have the appropriate qualities for something *UK, 1645*. ▶ **be cut out to be a gentleman** to be circumcised *UK, 1961*. ▶ **cut a chogie** to leave quickly. Korea and Vietnam war usage *US, 1981*. ▶ **cut a fat one** in drag racing and hot rodding, to drive at top speed *US, 1968*. ▶ **cut a hus** to do someone a favour. Marine slang in Vietnam *US, 1991*. ▶ **cut a melon** to fart *UK, 1998*. ▶ **cut a rat** to fart *US, 1995*. ▶ **cut a rug** to dance expertly *US, 1942*. ▶ **cut a rusty** to show off *US, 1838*. ▶ **cut ass; cut arse 1** to leave, especially in a hurry *US, 1972*. **2** to assault someone *TRINIDAD AND TOBAGO, 1980*. ▶ **cut brush** to drive off the road into brush *US, 1962*. ▶ **cut cake; cut the strawberry cake** to short-change someone *US, 1949*. ▶ **cut card straight** to deal in a direct and honest manner *TRINIDAD AND TOBAGO, 2003*. ▶ **cut fine; cut it fine** to narrow something down to a minimum *UK, 1891*. ▶ **cut it** to perform satisfactorily and so meet a requirement. From CUT THE MUSTARD *US, 1987*. ▶ **cut loose 1** to leave someone alone *US, 1974*. **2** to enjoy yourself unrestrained by any sense of moderation *US, 1808*. ▶ **cut no ice** to make no difference *US, 1896*. ▶ **cut one off** in the police, to salute a superior officer. Usually in the form 'cut

someone one off' *UK, 1948*. ▶ **cut skin; cut tail** to physically assault someone; to beat someone *TRINIDAD AND TOBAGO, 1959*. ▶ **cut some slack** to relax the pressure *US, 1968*. ▶ **cut someone dead** to ignore someone completely. An emphasised use of CUT (to ignore) *UK, 1826*. ▶ **cut someone down to size** to reduce someone to a true understanding of his or her status or worth *US, 1927*. ▶ **cut someone's lunch** to cuckold someone; to steal someone's partner; to move in on another's potential pick-up *AUSTRALIA, 1996*. ▶ **cut ten** to sit with your legs crossed as others work *JAMAICA, 1977*. ▶ **cut the cheese** to fart *US, 1959*. ▶ **cut the coax** to turn off a citizens' band radio *US, 1976*. ▶ **cut the gas** to stop talking. Teen slang *US, 1951*. ▶ **cut the mustard 1** to perform satisfactorily and so meet a requirement *US, 1902*. **2** to fart with especially noxious effect *UK, 1998*. **3** to have sex *UK, 1977*. ▶ **cut throat** to have sex with a female virgin *TRINIDAD AND TOBAGO, 2003*. ▶ **cut to the chase** to get on with it. Cinematic imagery; 'to jump to the next exciting sequence' *US, 1983*. ▶ **cut up jackies** in the circus or carnival, to tell stories about the past *US, 1980*. ▶ **cut up jackpots** (used of carnival workers) to engage in carnival insider conversation *US, 1985*. ▶ **cut up pipes** in circus and carnival usage, to gossip, brag or disparage someone *US, 1981*. ▶ **cut up rough 1** to be, or become, quarrelsome or difficult *UK, 1837*. **2** to resist or show resentment with violence *AUSTRALIA, 1944*. ▶ **cut your eyes** to look at someone or something with disdain *BARBADOS, 1965*. ▶ **cut your own hair** to be extremely frugal *AUSTRALIA, 1989*. ▶ **cut your water off** in shuffleboard, to hold an opponent to a scoreless half round *US, 1967*. ▶ **cut Z's** to sleep *US, 1991*

cut *adjective* **1** circumcised *US, 1998*. **2** physically fit, conditioned, well-toned *US, 1998*

cut!; cut it!; cut it out! *adjective* stop!, cease! *UK, 1859*

cut along *verb* to depart. Often as an imperative *UK, 1902*

cut and carried *adjective* married. Rhyming slang *UK, 1960*

cut and paste *noun* cosmetic surgery *US, 1997*

cut and paste *verb* to open a patient's body in surgery only to discover an inoperable condition, and then to close the patient back up *US, 1994*

cut and run *verb* to depart promptly; to decamp hurriedly. Of nautical origin *UK, 1811*

cut and scratch *noun* a match, safety or non-safety. Rhyming slang *UK, 1960*

cut and shut *adjective* used to describe a secondhand car that has been illegally contrived from the best parts of two damaged cars. Often hyphenated as a noun *UK, 1968*

cut and tuck *noun* a male transsexual who has had his penis removed and an artificial vagina surgically constructed *AUSTRALIA, 1985*

cut-ass *noun* a beating *TRINIDAD AND TOBAGO, 1959*

cutback *noun* in surfing, a turn back into the wave *US, 1979*

cut buddy *noun* a close friend *US, 1954*

cutchie *noun* ▷*see:* KOUTCHIE

cut-down *noun* a half bottle of rum *BARBADOS, 1965*

cute *adjective* acute, sharp-witted, clever, shrewd *UK, 1731*

cute hoor *noun* any person, female or male, who is corrupt. May be used affectionately as well as pejoratively. The present Hiberno-English pronunciation was common in England in C16 and C17, and lasted in common use into C19 *IRELAND, 2001*

cutemup *noun* a prison doctor *US, 1962*

cuter *verb* a twenty-five cent piece. A corruption of 'quarter' *US, 1927*

cuteration *noun* the zenith of cuteness *US, 1963*

cutesy *adjective* cloying, annoyingly cute *US, 1914*

cut-eye *noun* a disapproving look *TRINIDAD AND TOBAGO, 1960*

cut from timber to bramble *adjective* (used of a man) sexually active and indiscriminate *TRINIDAD AND TOBAGO, 1987*

cut-glass sledgehammer *noun* a notional tool that a young, inexperienced novice is sent to fetch *US, 1960*

cut-hip *noun* a physical beating; a thrashing *BAHAMAS, 1998*

cutie *noun* an attractive or clever young woman. Originally (UK, C18) a 'clever but shallow person'; this sense is an early example of US term moved into wider usage by Hollywood films *US, 1911*

cutie-pie *noun* an attractive woman *US, 1970*

cut-in *noun* the initial contact with the intended victim in a confidence swindle *US, 1977*

cut in *verb* **1** to attempt a romantic relationship with someone already romantically involved *US, 1950*. **2** to seize a share of a business or enterprise *US, 1980*

cut into *verb* to approach someone and draw them into a swindle; to introduce someone to something *US, 1940*

cutlass carpenter *noun* an unskilled carpenter *TRINIDAD AND TOBAGO, 2003*

cut lunch *noun* a circumcised penis as an object of oral sex *AUSTRALIA, 1985*

cut-lunch commando *noun* a soldier who does not see active service, especially a reservist. A contemptuous term implying that they get a prepared lunch rather than real army rations *AUSTRALIA, 1952*

cut man *noun* the member of a boxer's entourage responsible for treating cuts between rounds *US, 1975*

cut off *verb* to lay someone off due to lack of work *US, 1990*

cut off the joint *noun* from the male perspective, an act of sexual intercourse *UK, 1961*

cut of your jib *noun* your general appearance, hence, nature, character and temperament *UK, 1825*

cutor *noun* a prosecuting attorney *US, 1962*

cut out *verb* **1** to leave *US, 1827*. **2** to die *US, 1955*. **3** to take goods in payment instead of money *AUSTRALIA, 1984*. **4** to pay for something by having sexual intercourse rather than using money *AUSTRALIA, 1971*. **5** (of a power-source controlled by automatic technology) to switch off; to break (electrical) contact *UK, 1984*. **6** to serve time in prison rather than paying a fine *AUSTRALIA, 1939*

cuts *noun* **1** the definition of body muscle from spaces between the muscle that have no fat *US, 1984*. **2** any remote location *US, 1985*. **3** permission from a friend to step into a queue at their place *US, 1989*. **4** clothing *US, 1978*

cutter *noun* **1** a surgeon *US, 1970*. **2** an illegal abortionist *FIJI, 1994*. **3** a person who is proficient with the use of a knife or of a weapon *US, 1947*. **4** a pistol *US, 1908*. **5** a musician who betters another in a competition of solos *US, 1956*. **6** any substance used to dilute a drug, thereby expanding volume while reducing potency *US, 1995*. **7** in American casinos, twenty-five cents. Playing on the sound of 'quarter' *US, 1985*. **8** money *UK, 2000*

cut the cackle! stop talking! From CACKLE (to chatter inconsequentially). When extended to: 'cut the cackle and come to the 'osses [Horses]', the meaning is 'stop the preliminaries and get down to business' *UK, 1889*

cut the crap! stop talking nonsense! *US, 1956*

cutting *noun* the preparation of cocaine for inhalation by chopping lines of powder with a razor blade or credit card *2002*

cutting *adjective* good, excellent *UK, 2003*

cutting gear *noun* oxyacetylene apparatus used to break into safes *UK, 1977*

cutting house *noun* a place where drugs are diluted for resale *US, 1974*

cutting man *noun* a best friend *US, 1970*

cutting plant *noun* a shop where stolen cars are dismantled or altered *US, 1978*

cuttings merchant *noun* in prison, a prisoner who wields power by collecting newspaper cuttings of reported crimes *UK, 2000*

cutty *noun* **1** a cousin *US, 2002*. **2** a playful girl *IRELAND, 1999*

cut-up *noun* a dishonestly fixed outcome of any event, e.g. a competition, an election, a lottery, a job application, etc *UK, 1985*

cut up *verb* **1** to behave without restraint *US, 1846*. **2** (when driving) to overtake in such a manner that other vehicles are adversely affected *UK, 1964*

cut-up *adjective* upset, emotionally distressed *UK, 1844*

cut war *noun* in lobstering, a rivalry that has escalated to the point where lobstermen are cutting each other's buoys *US, 1978*

cuyabunga! ▷*see:* COWABUNGA!

cuz *noun* a friend *US, 1979*. ▷*see:* 'CAUSE

cuzz *noun* a term of address used by one member of the Crips youth gang to another *US, 1990*

cuzzies *noun* HM Customs & Excise *UK, 2002*

cuzzy-bro *noun* a close and loyal friend *NEW ZEALAND, 1991*

cwazy *adjective* used as a jocular substitute for 'crazy' *US, 1952*

c-word *noun* the word cunt. Usually after 'the' *UK, 1986*

CYA *verb* to protect yourself from future criticism for actions being taken now. An abbreviation of 'cover your ass' *US, 1959*

c-ya used in computer messages as shorthand to mean 'see you' *US, 1995*

cyber *adjective* denoting an on-line, Internet or digital state or existence. A back-formation from 'cybernetics' (scientific and mechanical systems of control and communication), coined in 1948 by Norbert Wiener (1894–1964) from the Greek *kybernan* (to steer, to govern). Mainly used in unhyphenated combinations as a prefix, but can stand alone *US, 1966*

cyberspace *noun* the notional locus where on-line communication takes place and from where a digital existence is supposed. Coined by science fiction author William Gibson (b.1948) to describe 'the hallucinatory world existing between computers' in *Neuromancer*, 1984 *US, 1984*

cycle *noun* anabolic steroids. Steroids are taken for a fixed time period – a 'cycle' – and then not taken for the same time period. Professional wrestling usage *US, 2003*. ▶ **having your cycle** experiencing the bleed period of the menstrual cycle *US, 2001*

cycle-lifter *noun* a bicycle thief *INDIA, 1979*

cyclo *noun* a rickshaw pulled by a bicycle *US, 1972*

cyclone *noun* phencyclidine, the recreational drug known as PCP or angel dust *US, 1994*

Cyclops sausage dog *noun* the penis. Probably jocular imagery of a mythical one-eyed giant crossed with a dachshund *UK, 2003*

cylinder *noun* the vagina. A mechanics' simile *AUSTRALIA, 1984*

Cyp *noun* a Cypriot. Pronounced 'sip' *UK, 1984*

Cyril Lord *adjective* bald. Rhyming slang; an imperfect rhyme formed on the name of a British carpet manufacturer (now Carpets International) probably best remembered for an incredibly annoying advertising jingle that haunted the 1960s and 70s. Cyril Lord made rugs and, appropriately, a RUG is a 'hair piece' *UK, 1992*

Cyril Sneer; cyril *noun* a male homosexual. Rhyming slang for QUEER formed from a character in the Canadian cartoon series *The Raccoons* from the 1980s *UK, 2003*

cyring call *noun* in poker, a bet equal to the last bet made in a hesitating fashion *US, 1982*

Dd

D *noun* **1** LSD *US, 1971*. **2** Dilaudid™, a synthetic opiate *US, 1954*. **3** narcotics *US, 1976*. **4** used as a term of address, young man to young man. An abbreviation of DUDE *US, 1997*. **5** a police detective *AUSTRALIA, 1882*. **6** a (pre-decimalisation, 1971) penny. From Latin *denarius*, a rough equivalent of an old penny and used in the standard abbreviation for pre-decimal Sterling: £sd or lsd *UK, 1387*. **7** in poker, the fourth player to the left of the dealer *US, 1988*. **8** a demilitarised zone. A shortening of DMZ, the official abbreviation *US, 1991*

D&D *noun* dungeons and dragons (a genre of fantasy roleplay games) *UK, 2001*

D-5 *noun* a Sony TCD-5M analogue recording tape deck. Favoured by tapers of Grateful Dead concerts until the advent of digital audio tape in the early 1990s *US, 1994*

da *noun* father, a father. An abbreviation of affectionate, informal or childish 'dad' or 'dada', especially in Scotland *UK, 1851*

DA *noun* **1** a hair-style popular in the early 1950s; the hair was tapered and curled on the nape of the neck like the feathers of a duck's tail. Abbreviated from DUCK'S ARSE/ASS *US, 1951*. **2** a drug addict *US, 1946*. **3** a dumb ass *US, 2003*

da 1 the. Fashionable respelling of phonetic slovening; an essential element in Hawaiian youth usage *US, 1981*. **2** so; very. Hawaiian youth usage *US, 1981*

dab *noun* **1** a fingerprint. Police jargon, in everyday use, usually in the plural *UK, 1926*. **2** a moistened finger-tip covered in powdered amphetamine. Possibly as, and then only partly-inspired by, a nostalgic reference to a children's sweet, the Sherbert Dib Dab™, a lolly dipped into a powdered sugar confection *UK, 2000*. **3** in rugby, a short, darting run with the ball *NEW ZEALAND, 1970*. **4** in cricket, a batsman's stroke that deflects the ball gently behind the wicket *UK, 1969*. **5** a criminal charge; a prison disciplinary charge *UK, 1996*

dab *verb* **1** to ingest a powdered drug by sucking or licking the powder collected on a moistened finger *UK, 2001*. **2** in mountain biking, to touch the ground unintentionally with any part of the body *US, 1992*. **3** of a batsman in cricket, to play a tentative stroke that gently deflects the ball behind the wicket *UK, 1985*

dabble *noun* stolen property *UK, 1981*

dabble *verb* **1** to use addictive drugs without succumbing to the addiction *US, 1949*. **2** to experiment with homsexuality *UK, 1996*. **3** to operate an (occasional) trade in stolen or illegal goods, especially antiques or drugs *UK, 1996*

dab-dab *noun* to participate in homosexual sex. Prison usage *US, 1990*

dacha; daiture; deger *adjective* ten. From Italian *dieci*, via lingua franca into polari *UK, 1996*

Dachau *noun* any military stockade. Vietnam war usage *US, 1968*

dachs *noun* a dachshund *UK, 1886*

dachsie; dachsy *noun* a dachshund. An affectionate elaboration of DACHS *UK, 1961*

dack up *verb* to light or smoke (a marijuana cigarette) *NEW ZEALAND, 1991*

dad *noun* **1** used as a term of address for a man, especially an older man. Often patronizing *US, 1928*. **2** a homosexual prisoner's 'owner' (protector and lover) *US, 1992*. ▶ **be like Dad** to keep quiet; to say nothing. From the World War 2 slogan 'be like Dad: keep Mum', playing on MUM (quiet) *UK, 1996*

-dad *suffix* used as a nonce suffix attached to a friend's name *US, 1995*

da-dah! used as a mock fanfare *UK, 2000*

Dad and Dave *noun* **1** a shave. Rhyming slang, after the characters Dad and Dave, the subject of well-known and well-loved humorous sketches concerning pioneering life by 'Steele Rudd' (Arthur Hoey Davis, 1868–1935) *AUSTRALIA, 1944*. **2** a grave. Rhyming slang *AUSTRALIA, 1971*

dad-blamed *adjective* used as a euphemism for 'damned'. 'Dad' is a euphemism for God *US, 1844*

dad-blasted *adjective* damned, confounded. 'Dad' is a euphemism for God *US, 1840*

daddy *noun* **1** the very best *US, 1865*. **2** the most powerful inmate in a borstal (a juvenile offenders penal institution); in prison, the most powerful or very strong inmate, or the prisoner who runs a racket *UK, 1978*. **3** a leader. Originally prison slang, especially of a forceful personality among borstal inmates; now in wider use *UK, 2001*. **4** the dominant partner in a male homosexual relationship *US, 1932*. **5** an aggressive, predatory male homosexual *US, 1996*. **6** the woman who plays the active, masculine role in a lesbian relationship *US, 1940s*. **7** in the US Army, your supervising officer *US, 1968*. **8** used as a term of address to a man *UK, 1681*. **9** a marijuana cigarette *UK, 2001*

daddy-come-to-church *noun* an unusual event *US, 1953*

daddy mac *noun* an attractive young man *US, 1997*

daddy-o *noun* **1** a term of address for a man. Also variant 'daddio'. *US, 1947*. **2** the US Federal Communications Commission *US, 1977*

daddypoo *noun* used as an embellishment of 'daddy', usually from a woman to a man *US, 1966*

daddy's yacht *noun* used rhetorically as a representation of the privileges of civilian life. Military sarcasm, in several variations, most commonly 'Where do you think you are? On your daddy's yacht'; directed mainly at National Service recruits (1945–62) *UK, 1962*

daddy tank *noun* a jail cell reserved for lesbian prisoners *US, 1971*

dadger *noun* the penis. Variation of TADGER (the penis) *UK, 1997*

dadrock *noun* 1990s rock music that sounds like music from a generation earlier, e.g. Oasis play dadrock that bears obvious similarities to the Beatles *UK, 1999*

dads *noun* a father, or in general address, a man. A variation of 'dad' *UK, 1984*

Dad's Army *nickname* the Home Guard (1940–45); hence, any grouping of older men with a united purpose. Gently derogatory. The term survives essentially as a piece of familiar nostalgia mainly because of the popularity of BBC television comedy series *Dad's Army* (1968–77, and which is still being repeated today). The modern sense is therefore informed by the nature of the characters in the programme; variously bumptious and bumbling, etc *UK, 1968*

dad's army *adjective* barmy, foolish. Rhyming slang, after the 1970s television comedy of the UK's World War 2 Home Guard *UK, 1992*

daff *noun* excrement *IRELAND, 1989*

daffies *noun* strong liquor *UK, 1979*

daffodil *noun* a homosexual man *US, 1935*

daffy *noun* a skiing stunt in which one ski is swung up in front of the skier while the other is brought up behind and parallel to the first, the whole being a form of mid-air splits. 'Daffy' is listed under the heading Freestyle skiing in the official lexicon for the 2002 Winter Olympic Games *UK, 1984*

daffy *adjective* odd, eccentric, silly. The original meaning of 'slightly mad' has softened over the years *UK, 1884*

daffydowndilly; daffadowndilly *adjective* silly. Rhyming slang, formed on an informal name for the 'daffodil', or perhaps it is simply an elaboration of DAFFY (silly, daft) *UK, 1960*

daffy-headed *adjective* feather-brained, daft *UK, 1981*

daft *nickname* Nova Scotia's Department of Fisheries and Oceans *CANADA, 2002*

daft and barmy *noun* an army. Rhyming slang, Note also the reversed rhyme: DAD'S ARMY for 'barmy' *UK, 1979*

daft as a brush; mad as a brush *adjective* crazy; stupid *UK, 1945*

daft Doris *noun* a foolish woman *UK, 2000*

daftie *noun* a daft person *UK, 1872*

dag *noun* **1** a matted lock of wool and excrement on a sheep's behind. From British dialect *AUSTRALIA, 1891*. **2** a person who is eccentric and humorous; a real character; a wag. Formerly common, now obsolete (but see sense 3). Some have suggested that the origin of this term lies in the British dialect term 'a feat set as a dare', but the examples given are less than convincing *AUSTRALIA, 1875*. **3** a person who is dull and conservative; a person who has no sense of fashion; an uncool or unhip person. Now the commonest meaning. It is widely believed that it derives from sense 1, but this is not the case. Probably partially from sense 2 and partially a backformation from DAGGY sense 2. Formerly and still to some extent quite an insult, equivalent to GEEK and NERD, but recently also used in an affectionate manner, and jocularly 'reclaimed' as a term of approval. This reclamation has led to a semantic shift where the meaning can be 'uncool in an amusing or eccentric way', and thus this sense now overlaps with that of sense 2 *AUSTRALIA, 1966*. **4** a daring act *NEW ZEALAND, 1984*

dag *verb* **1** to engage in anal sex *US, 2001*. **2** to participate in serial, reciprocal, homosexual oral sex *US, 1990*

dag! used for expressing surprise *US, 1987*

dagdom *noun* the notional realm of dags *AUSTRALIA, 1990*

dage *noun* a foreigner, an immigrant. From DAGO (a foreigner, an immigrant, etc.) *AUSTRALIA, 1955*

Dagenham dustbin *noun* a Ford car. Citizens' band radio slang. Dagenham in Essex is the best-known as the major manufacturing base for Ford cars *UK, 1981*

dagga *noun* **1** marijuana. Dagga is the common name in South Africa for a relatively non-toxic herb (genus: *Leonotis.* varieties: *Cape, red* and *wilde*) which is smoked like tobacco; however, for a slang user one herb predominates *SOUTH AFRICA, 1955*. **2** a marijuana cigarette *US, 1955*

dagga rooker *noun* a marijuana smoker. Combines DAGGA with Afrikaans *rooker* (a smoker). In respectable circles a 'dagga rooker' is recorded as 'a scoundrel; a wastrel' *SOUTH AFRICA, 1998*

dagger *noun* a lesbian. An abbreviation of the full BULLDAGGER *US, 1980*

dagger of desire *noun* the erect penis. Jocular *UK, 2003*

daggers *noun* ▶ **throw daggers; give the daggers** to look angrily at someone. Variations of the conventional form 'look daggers' *UK, 2002*

daggily *adverb* in a daggy manner *AUSTRALIA, 1972*

dagginess *noun* the state of being daggy *AUSTRALIA, 1990*

daggy *adjective* **1** unfashionable; uncool *AUSTRALIA, 1981*. **2** (of clothes, personal appearance, etc.) dirty, filthy *AUSTRALIA, 1967*. **3** cheap or trashy looking in a sexually promiscuous way *US, 1997*. **4** (of sheep) having dags; (of wool) soiled with excrement *AUSTRALIA, 1895*

dago *noun* **1** an Italian or Italian-American. A slur, originally applied to Spaniards, then to Spaniards, Portuguese and Italians, and now only to Italians *US, 1857*. **2** any foreigner. Liverpool use *US, 1968*. **3** in hot rodding, a dropped front axle, especially on older Fords *US, 1965*

Dago *nickname* San Diego, California *US, 1931*. ▶ **the Dago** Frank Sinatra, American singer (1915–1998) *US, 1963*

dago *adjective* foreign *AUSTRALIA, 1900*

dago bomb *noun* a type of firework *US, 1960*

dago red *noun* inexpensive, inferior red wine *US, 1906*

dagotown *noun* a neighbourhood dominated by Italian-Americans *US, 1960*

Dagwood *noun* a large and elaborate sandwich. Named after the sandwiches made by the Dagwood Bumstead character in the *Blondie* comic strip *US, 1948*

Dagwood dog *noun* a deep-fried battered frankfurter on a stick *AUSTRALIA, 2003*

daikon legs *noun* short, pale and fat legs. Hawaiian youth usage. The 'daikon' is also known as an Asian, Oriental or Chinese radish; it is stubby and white *US, 1981*

dailies *noun* film scenes filmed one day, rush processed and delivered for viewing by the director and others the same or next day *US, 1970s*

daily *noun* a regular (daily) bet with a bookmaker *UK, 1984*

daily-daily *noun* during the Vietnam war, anti-malaria pills taken daily, in addition to a second medication taken once a week *US, 1982*

daily double *noun* in poker, two consecutive winning hands. A borrowing from horse racing *US, 1996*

daily dozen *noun* physical exercises, performed on rising; hence, a limited group (or the measure thereof) of anything (voluntarily) experienced on a daily basis. It is unlikely that the 'dozen' was ever a precise sum *UK, 1919*

Daily Express *noun* a dress. Rhyming slang, formed on the title of a leading national newspaper *UK, 1992*

Daily Express *verb* to dress. Rhyming slang, formed on the title of a leading national newspaper *UK, 1992*

Daily Getsmuchworse *nickname* the *Daily Express*. Coined in the 1970s by satirical magazine *Private Eye UK, 1975*

Daily Liar *nickname* the *Daily Mail*. Jocular *UK, 1984*

Daily Mail; daily *noun* **1** a tail; hence, rectum, arse. Rhyming slang, based on the title of a major newspaper *UK, 1956*. **2** a tale, especially 'glib patter' or the story told by an informer; a confidence-trickster's patter. Rhyming slang, formed on the title of a leading national newspaper *UK, 1960*. **3** a prostitute; a sexually available woman. Rhyming slang for TAIL (a woman objectified sexually) or BRASS NAIL (a prostitute), formed on the title of a leading national newspaper *UK, 1977*. **4** bail. Rhyming slang, formed on the title of a leading national newspaper *UK, 1977*. **5** a nail. Rhyming slang, formed on the title of a leading national newspaper; used by carpenters *UK, 1961*. **6** ale. Rhyming slang *UK, 1960*

Daily-Tell-the-Tale *nickname* the *Daily Mail UK, 1960*

Daily Torygraph *nickname* the *Daily Telegraph*. From the paper's political bias *UK, 2003*

dainties *noun* underwear, especially women's underwear worn by transvestites *US, 1972*

dairy; dairies *noun* the female breast(s). Elaborated as 'dairy arrangements' in 1923; most later use tends towards 'dairy' for 'a breast', with 'dairies' as a natural plural; however, 'dairy' is originally recorded as both singular and plural (in the context of a single female); it is current in the plural sense in Scamto (urban youth slang in South African townships) *UK, 2005*. ▶ **the dairy** the best. A play on conventional 'cream' *UK, 2003*

dairy box *noun* a sexually transmitted infection. Rhyming slang, formed on a branded chocolate assortment manufactured by Nestlé *UK, 1992*

daisy *noun* **1** an excellent thing or person *US, 1757*. **2** an attractive young woman *US, 1876*. **3** a male homosexual. Often used in Peter O'Donnell's *Modesty Blaise* stories, 1962–2001 *US, 1944*

daisy bell! hell! Rhyming slang, formed on the name of a music hall song ('Daisy Bell' also known as 'A Bicycle Made for Two', by Harry Dacre, 1892) *UK, 1992*

daisy chain *noun* **1** a group of people, arranged roughly in a circle, in which each person is both actively and passively engaged in oral, anal, or vaginal sex with the person in front of and behind them in the circle. A term that is much more common than the practice *US, 1927*. **2** an abstract grouping of people who have had sex with the same person at different times *US, 1990*. **3** figuratively and by extension, a series of events that return to the beginning *US, 1954*. **4** in computing, a network architecture in which a single cable connects all nodes *US, 1995*. **5** a confidence swindle where funds from successive victims are used to keep the swindle alive with the earlier victims *US, 1985*. **6** a series of (Claymore) mines attached to each other and rigged for sequential detonation. From the general appearance *UK, 1950*

daisy cutter *noun* **1** a 10,000 to 15,000 pound bomb used to clear jungle and create an instant landing zone in Vietnam *US, 1967*. **2** in cricket, a fast ball bowled in such a way that it barely clears the surface of the pitch *UK, 1863*

Daisy Dormer *adjective* warmer, especially of the weather. Rhyming slang, formed on the name of a music hall entertainer; originally used as a noun in the sense as a 'bed-warmer' *UK, 1960*

Daisy Dukes *noun* very short and very tight shorts. Named after a character on the unforgettable US television programme *Dukes of Hazzard US, 1993*

daisy roots; daisies; daisys *noun* boots. Rhyming slang, always in the plural *UK, 1859*

daiture *adjective* ▷*see:* DACHA

dak *noun* **1** marijuana *NEW ZEALAND, 1998*. **2** a C-47A Skytrain plane, also known as a DC-3, most commonly used to transport people and cargo, but also used as a bomber and fighter *US, 1975*

dak; dack *verb* to pull another's trousers down as a prank *AUSTRALIA, 2000*

dakhi *noun* a black person. Scamto youth street slang (South African townships) *SOUTH AFRICA, 2005*

da kine used at any time to mean anything. Hawaiian youth usage. Can be used as a noun, pronoun, adjective and suffix *US, 1951*

daks; dacks *noun* shorts or trousers. From a proprietary name *AUSTRALIA, 1970*

dallacking *verb* play acting, fooling *IRELAND, 2000*

Dallie; Dally *noun* a Dalmatian, especially an immigrant to New Zealand from that area or the Balkans in general *NEW ZEALAND, 1940*

Dally *noun* a New Zealander whose heritage is Croatian (Dalmatian) *NEW ZEALAND, 1950*

dally *verb* in western Canadian rodeos, to loop the lariat around the saddle horn *CANADA, 1987*

dally *adjective* good, kind, nice, sweet. Possibly a variation of DOLLY (attractive) *UK, 2002*

dam *noun* a menstrual cup (a device worn internally, used instead of tampons) *US, 2001*

Dam *nickname* ▶ **the Dam** Amsterdam *UK, 1996*

dama blanca *noun* cocaine. Spanish for 'white lady' *US, 1976*

damage *noun* **1** expense; cost. Probably from damages awarded at law. Especially familiar in the (jocular) phrase, 'what's the damage?' (how much?) *UK, 1755*. **2** a problem *US, 1988*. ▶ **do damage** to cost a lot *US, 1997*

damaged goods *noun* **1** an ex-virgin *US, 1916*. **2** a person who is mentally unstable *UK, 2002*

dame *noun* **1** a woman. While the term originally reflected on the woman involved (an implication of common status), it now reflects more on the speaker, suggesting a tough or old-fashioned viewpoint *UK, 1720*. **2** in a deck of playing cards, a queen *US, 1996*

Dame Judi Dench; Dame Judi; Judi Dench; Judi *noun* a stench. Rhyming slang, formed from the name of celebrated actress Dame Judi Dench (b.1934) *UK, 1998*

damfino used as a jocular abbreviation of 'damned if I know' *US, 1882*

dammit *noun* used, for the purposes of comparison, as the representation of something insignificant. Adapted from 'damn-it'. Examples include 'soon as dammit' (exceedingly quick, or almost immediate); 'near as dammit' (very close indeed); etc *UK, 1908*

damn *noun* something of little or no worth. Usually in phrases like 'not worth a damn', 'not care a damn' and 'not give a damn'. There is a stongly fought historical argument that this derives from 'dam' (an Indian coin of little value); the *Oxford English Dictionary* prefers 'damn' (a 'profane utterance') as the object of this etymology *UK, 1760*

-damn- *infix* used as an intensifier *US, 1867*

damn'; damn *adjective* damned; used for implying anything from distaste to hate for whoever or whatever is so described. A shortening of DAMNED *UK, 1775*

damn!; damn it! used for registering annoyance or irritation *UK, 1589*

damn all *noun* nothing *UK, 1922*

damn and bastardry! used as a mild oath. Modelled on conventional 'damn and blast' *UK, 2000*

damn and blast *noun* the last position in a race. Rhyming slang *UK, 1992*

damn and blast *verb* to curse, to condemn *UK, 2003*

damn and blast! used for expressing anger or frustration. A common coupling of DAMN! and BLAST! *UK, 1943*

damnation alley *noun* in roulette, the twelve-number column on the left of the layout. So named because a dealer may not see a cheat place a late bet in the column, which is sometimes out of the dealer's line of sight *US, 1979*

damned *adjective* used as an all-purpose intensifier, generally to negative effect *UK, 1596*. ▶ **as be damned** very, extremely *IRELAND, 1939*

damned tooting used for expressing emphatic agreement. Folksy *US, 1963*

damn-fool; damfool *adjective* foolish, silly. From 'damned fool' (an absolute fool) *UK, 1959*

damn skippy absolutely! without a doubt! An intensive affirmative *US, 1994*

damn well *adverb* certainly, assuredly, very much *UK, 1934*

Damon Hill; damon *noun* a pill, especially an amphetamine. Rhyming slang, formed on the name of the UK's Formula 1 World Champion (1996) racing driver Damon Hill (b.1960); a discreetly playful reference to SPEED (an amphetamine) *UK, 1998*

damp *adjective* allowing the importation of alcohol for personal consumption but not for public sale. A play on the extremes of 'wet' and 'dry' *US, 1991*

damp blanket *noun* in the theatre, a bad review *US, 1981*

damper *noun* **1** a solitary confinement cell; a cell *US, 1992*. **2** a safe deposit box in a bank *US, 1872*. **3** a bank *US, 1932*. **4** a simple, unleavened, savoury bread traditionally cooked in the ashes of a campfire. So named because it 'dampens' the appetite. Now also applied to a similar style of bread available at bakershops *AUSTRALIA, 1825*

damper *verb* to mute, to quiet *US, 1979*

damps *noun* central nervous system depressants. A playful allusion to 'amps' as 'amphetamines' *US, 1992*

damp squib *noun* a failure; a dud; a fizzler. A 'damp squib' is, literally, a 'wet firework' *AUSTRALIA, 1946*

Dan *noun* **1** a man in charge of a male public convenience. From the children's rhyme, 'Dan, Dan, dirty old man, / Washed his face in the lavatory pan' *UK, 1954*. **2** a Roman Catholic. Glasgow slang *UK: SCOTLAND, 1988*

dance *noun* a fight. Ice hockey usage *CANADA, 1970*. ▶ **what's the dance?** what's going on?; what's going to happen? Used among prisoners *UK, 2002*

dance *verb* **1** of a batsman in a game of cricket, to swiftly advance beyond the crease to meet the pitch of a ball *UK, 1995*. **2** (used of a wink in tiddlywinks) to wobble around *US, 1977*. **3** to cause a car to bounce up and down by use of hydraulic lifts *US, 1980*. ▶ **dance ass** to ignore the needs of others *TRINIDAD AND TOBAGO, 2003*. ▶ **dance in the rain room** to take a shower in prison *US, 1989*. ▶ **dance on the carpet** to be called into a superior's office for questioning about possible misconduct or poor work performance *US, 1946*

danceable *adjective* of music, suitable for dancing to. The earliest sense (1860) was of a dancing partner being suitable to dance with *UK, 1937*

dance fever *noun* Fentany™, a synthetic narcotic analgesic that is used as a recreational drug *UK, 2004*

dancehall *noun* **1** in a prison in which death sentences are executed, the execution chamber *US, 1928*. **2** in oil drilling, a large flat-bed truck *US, 1954*

dance of death *noun* a relationship or marriage between two addicts. Used in twelve-step recovery programmes such as Alcoholics Anonymous *US, 1998*

dancer *noun* **1** a boxer who evades his opponent rather than engaging him *US, 1949*. **2** a cat burglar; a sneak thief *UK, Since C19*

dancers *noun* ▶ **have it on your dancers** to run away. A variation of (have it) ON YOUR TOES *UK, 1977*

dancing *noun* in railway slang, the condition of locomotive wheels slipping on the rail *UK, 1970*

dancing academy *noun* used as a euphemism and legal dodge for an after-hours homosexual club *US, 1974*

dancing girls *noun* in dominoes, the seven tiles with a five *US, 1959*

Dan Dares *noun* flared trousers. Rhyming slang for, 'flares', formed on Dan Dare, the comic strip 'pilot of the future', first seen in *The Eagle* in 1950 *UK, 1996*

D and D *verb* **1** to leave a restaurant without paying your bill. An abbreviation of DINE AND DASH *US, 1997*. **2** to fail to lead; to escape responsibility. Said to stand for (to) 'delegate and *disappear' CANADA, 1995*

D and D *adjective* **1** drunk *and* disorderly. Abbreviated from an official cause of arrest *UK, 1899*. **2** deaf *and* dumb. Usage is both literal (applied to beggars) and figurative (applied to someone who knows nothing and will say nothing). *US, 1937*

dander *noun* **1** anger. Possible etymologies: 'dander' (dandruff), 'dunder' (ferment), or Romany *dander* (to bite), *dando* (bitten) *UK, 1831*. **2** a leisurely stroll. Also used as a verb. In the north of Ireland it is pronounced 'donder' *IRELAND, 2002*. ▶ **get your dander up** to become annoyed or angry *US, 1831*

Dandies *noun* ▶ **the Dandies** the Dandenong Ranges outside Melbourne *AUSTRALIA, 1981*

D and M *noun* a serious conversation, generally relating to personal relationships. Standing for DEEP AND MEANINGFUL *AUSTRALIA, 1996*

dandruff *noun* **1** snow *US, 1976*. **2** cocaine *UK, 2001*

dandy *noun* **1** anything first-rate or excellent *UK, 1784*. **2** a grade of 'D' *US, 1965*. **3** in South Australia, a small container for ice-cream. Origin unknown. Perhaps originally a brand name *AUSTRALIA, 1954*

D and Z *noun* a demilitarised zone *US, 1991*

dang used as a mild oath or intensifier. A euphemised 'damn' *US, 1821*

dange *adjective* extremely good. Rhymes with 'strange', short for 'dangerous' *CANADA, 2002*

danged *adjective* used as a euphemism for 'damned' *US, 1962*

danger *noun* an aggressive flirt *FIJI, 1993*

danger is my business used as a humorous response to a suggestion that a proposed activity is dangerous. The motto of cartoon secret agent *Cool McCool* (NBC, 1966–69), used with referential humour *US, 1966*

danger wank *noun* an act of masturbation with the threat of being discovered as an added stimulus *UK, 2003*

dangle *noun* the penis *US, 1936*

dangle *verb* ▶ **dangle the cat** to drive a Caterpillar truck *US, 1971*

dangleberries *noun* pieces of dried faecal matter clinging to the hairs surrounding the anus *UK, 1984*

dangle from *verb* from a male perspective, to have sex. Heard in the 1970s: 'Cor! I could dangle from *that!' UK, 1961*

dangler *noun* **1** the penis *US, 1971*. **2** a person who has died by hanging *US, 1987*. **3** a lorry's trailer *UK, 1951*. **4** a freight train *US, 1977*

dangling bits *noun* the external male genitals. Variant of DANGLY BITS *AUSTRALIA, 1979*

dangly bits *noun* the external male genitals *AUSTRALIA, 2000*

daniel *noun* the buttocks *US, 1946*

Daniel Boone squad; Daniel Boone team *noun* US soldiers who engaged in cross-border reconnaissance in Cambodia during the Vietnam war *US, 1991*

Daniels *noun* the buttocks *US, 1973*

Danish pastry *noun* a transsexual. An allusion to Denmark's standing as an early pioneer in sex-change operations *US, 1997*

dank *noun* a very potent marijuana. In conventional English, 'dank' conjures the 'stinky' STINKWEED (marijuana) smell of WEED (marijuana) growing in a damp place; or possibly from the slang adjective 'dank' (excellent). Recorded with the use of 'the' *US, 1998*

dank *adjective* **1** inferior; inefficient; bad; unpleasant. Originally recorded as a military term, the semi-conventional usage arrived on a US campus 40 years later providing the spur for the sense that follows *US, 1984*. **2** excellent; brilliant. BAD is 'good', WICKED is 'excellent' *US, 1989*

Dan Leno *noun* a festive event, a jollification, especially a coach trip to the seaside. Rhyming slang for 'a beano' (a jollification); formed on the professional name of Victorian comedian Dan Leno (George Galvin), 1860–1904 *UK, 1992*

Danny La Rue *adjective* blue, applied to any shade whether actual or figurative. Rhyming slang, formed on the name of popular 'comic in a frock' Danny La Rue (b.1926) *UK, 1992*

Danny La Rue; Danny *noun* a clue. Rhyming slang, based on popular 'comic in a frock' Danny La Rue (b.1926) *UK, 2002*

Danny Marr *noun* a car. Rhyming slang, based on an unrecognised source *UK, 1996*

Dan O'Leary *noun* a tour of police duty in which the police officer works every possible minute *US, 1958*

dan up *verb* to spruce up *TRINIDAD AND TOBAGO, 2003*

dap *noun* a handshake hooking thumbs, used by black US soldiers in Vietnam *US, 1972*

dap *verb* to greet another with a ritualistic handshake; to show respect in greeting *US, 1973*

dap *adjective* well-dressed, fashionable. A shortened 'dapper' *US, 1956*

DAP *adjective* dead-*ass* perfect. Golf usage *US, 2000*

dap down *verb* to dress nicely *US, 1980*

dapper *noun* a person dressed in style *US, 1974*

dapper *adjective* perfect, excellent, admirable. Possibly punning on the conventional sense of 'dapper' (neat and tidy) and TIDY (good, correct). Black usage *UK, 2000*

dapper Dan *noun* any well-dressed man *US, 1970*

daps *noun* **1** gym shoes, plimsolls, tennis shoes, trainers. Originally 'slippers', certainly in this general sense since the 1950s, adapting to succeeding fashions *UK, 1924*. **2** proper respect *US, 1997*

Dapto dog *noun* an person of Mediterranean or Middle Eastern background. Rhyming slang for WOG. Named after the Dapto Dogs, a greyhound racing track at Dapto, south of Sydney *AUSTRALIA, 1983*

DAR *noun* a hard-working student; a damned *average* raiser *US, 1955*

darb *adjective* in circus usage, excellent *US, 1981*

darbies *noun* **1** a set of handcuffs or fetters; shackles. Derives from a C17 moneylender's bond called Father Darby's or Derby's bands *UK, 1665*. **2** fingerprints *UK, 1950*

Darby *noun* ▶ **on your Darby** alone, on your own. Rhyming slang, formed on DARBY AND JOAN (the conventional archetype of an elderly married couple or inseparable companions) *UK, 1942*

Darby and Joan *noun* **1** an inseparable couple, with connotations of possible homosexuality. Extending the conventional sense of 'an archetypal elderly married couple' *UK, 1975*. **2** a telephone. Rhyming slang, formed on the conventional archetype of an elderly married couple or inseparable companions. *UK, 1961*. **3** a loan. Rhyming slang *AUSTRALIA, 2002*

Darby and Joan *verb* to moan. Rhyming slang, formed (perhaps ironically) on the conventional archetype of an elderly married or inseparable couple *UK, 1992*

Darby bands *noun* the hands. Rhyming slang, from the old (possibly C16) expression 'Father Darby's bands' (a binding agreement between a money lender and a borrower) *UK, 1992*

dare *noun* a challenge, an act of defiance. In conventional use from late C16 to late C19, usage thereafter is colloquial *UK, 2002*

darg *noun* a certain fixed amount of work for a given time period *AUSTRALIA, 1927*

dark *noun* ▶ **in the dark** (used of a bet in poker) made without having seen your cards *US, 1990*

dark *verb* to spoil, especially by behaving aggressively *UK, 1990s*

dark *adjective* **1** bad, inferior, unpleasant, nasty; used as an all-purpose negative *UK, 1997*. **2** unreachable by telephone. A condition usually resulting from a failure to pay your bill *US, 2004*. **3** good. On the BAD (good) model, the reverse of sense 1 *UK, 1998*. **4** evil, *2000*. **5** secret *AUSTRALIA, 1877*. **6** untelevised *US, 2000*

dark and dirty *noun* rum and coke (Coca-Cola™ or similar). The drink is made, and the term is formed, of *dark* rum and a fizzy accompaniment the colour (some may think) of dirty water. Royal Marines coinage *UK, 1979*

dark as an abo's arsehole *adjective* extremely dark *AUSTRALIA, 1971*

dark brown *adjective* of a voice, low, well-modulated and sexually attractive. Originally of a female voice, then more general *UK, 1946*

dark cheaters *noun* sunglasses *US, 1949*

dark days *noun* a type of bet in an illegal numbers game lottery *US, 1957*

darkers *noun* sunglasses *TRINIDAD AND TOBAGO, 1987*

dark eyes *noun* dizziness *BARBADOS, 1965*

Dark Gable *noun* a handsome black man. Punning on the name Clark Gable. The nickname has been taken by more than one, but perhaps nobody more prominent than Mohammed Ali who briefly called himself Dark Gable in 1981 *US, 1959*

dark-green *adjective* **1** excellent *US, 1954*. **2** black. Marine humour in Vietnam – a black marine was said to be 'dark-green' *US, 1991*

dark horse *noun* **1** in horse racing, a horse that is deemed a poor performer but one that might surprise all and win *US, 1951*. **2** a racehorse that has been trained in secret *AUSTRALIA, 1877*. **3** a person who keeps things about themselves secret *AUSTRALIA, 1917*. **4** a candidate or competitior of whom little is known. A figurative use of racing slang *UK, 1865*

darkie *noun* **1** used as a flattering and affectionate term of address for an attractive, dark-skinned woman *TRINIDAD AND TOBAGO, 1990*. **2** a piece of excrement *AUSTRALIA, 1972* ▷ *see also:* DARKY

dark meat *noun* a black person as a sexual object *US, 1888*

dark money; dark time *noun* extra wages paid for night work *UK, 1970*

dark o'clock *noun* night *UK, 1995*

darks *noun* dark glasses *BERMUDA, 1985*

dark shadow *noun* a tightly-cropped hair cut that stops short of absolute baldness *UK, 1999*

darkside *noun* a category of rave music *UK, 2002*

dark thirty *noun* late at night *US, 1984*

dark time *noun* night *US, 1976*

darktown *noun* a neighbourhood populated largely by black people *US, 1916*

dark 'un *noun* of dock-workers, a 24-hour shift *AUSTRALIA, 1957*

dark-white paint *noun* used as the object of a prank errand for a novice painter *US, 1966*

darky; darkie *noun* **1** a black person. Originally used in a paternalistic, condescending manner, but now mainly to disparage *US, 1775*. **2** an Australian Aboriginal *AUSTRALIA, 1845*. **3** a Polynesian person *NEW ZEALAND, 1863*

Darky Cox *noun* a *box* in a theatre auditorium. Rhyming slang, of unknown derivation *UK, 1961*

darkytown *noun* a neighbourhood with a large population of black people *US, 1971*

darl; darls *noun* used as an address or endearment, darling *UK, 1930*

darling *noun* **1** used both as a general and a theatrically arch form of address *UK, 1933*. **2** used as a term of address between male homosexuals *US, 1949*

darling *adjective* charming, sweet. An affectedly feminine or effeminate usage *UK, 1805*

Darling Buds of May; Darling Buds *adjective* homosexual. Rhyming slang for GAY formed on the title of a 1958 novel by H.E. Bates and, especially, from a 1991 BBC television adaptation *UK, 1992*

darling daughter *noun* water. Rhyming slang. One of several terms that have 'daughter' as the common (dispensible) element *UK, 1992*

darlings *noun* the prostitutes of Darlinghurst and King's Cross, Sydney *AUSTRALIA, 1984*

Darling shower *noun* a dust storm. Ironic; probably from areas of the outback by the western reaches of the Darling River *AUSTRALIA, 1945*

Darlo *nickname* **1** Darlington, County Durham *UK, 1984*. **2** Darlinghurst, Sydney *AUSTRALIA, 1937*

darls *noun* darling *AUSTRALIA, 1967*

darn!; darn it! used for registering annoyance, frustration, etc. A euphemistic variation of DAMN! *US, 1781*

darnation *noun* damnation. Euphemistic; despite the weakening of 'damnation', there is still evidence of use *US, 1798*

darned *adjective* used as an intensifier. Euphemistic for DAMNED *US, 1807*

darned tooting! used as a mock oath affirming that which has just been said. Usually used in a self-mocking way, conjuring the image of an older, confused, country bumpkin *US, 1963*

darn straight! you are right! Used with irony, playing with the use of the heavily euphemised 'darn' *US, 1994*

Darren Gough *noun* a cough. Rhyming slang, formed on the name of Yorkshire and England cricketer (b.1970) *UK, 1998*

dartboard *noun* ▶ **had more pricks than a second-hand dartboard** used of a sexually promiscuous woman. Such a woman may be described as 'a second-hand dartboard'. Currently popular in Australia *UK, 1982*

daru *noun* rum. From Hindi *BARBADOS, 1965*

Darwin rig *noun* an adaptation of the typical business suit worn by men in far northern Australia. Generally a short-sleeved shirt, and often short trousers. A tie is normally included, but a coat is definitely not. Named after Darwin, a major city in the tropical north *AUSTRALIA, 1964*

Darwin stubbie; Darwin stubby *noun* a 2.25 litre bottle of beer. An ironic term: a STUBBIE is one of the smallest bottle sizes. The city of Darwin is located in the tropical north and is well known for prodigious beer-drinking *AUSTRALIA, 1972*

dash *noun* **1** a dashboard *UK, 1902*. **2** an escape from custody *US, 1952*. ▶ **have a dash at** to make an attempt, to try. The surviving form of 'do your dash' *AUSTRALIA, 1923*

dash *verb* to depart in a hurry *UK, 1932*

dash!; dash it!; dash it all! used as a general purpose expletive. Euphemistic only when deliberately replacing DAMN! but note that SHIT is disguised in the extended variations *UK, 1800*

dashed *adjective* damned. Euphemistic; dated *UK, 1881*

dash on to *verb* to chastise *UK, 1979*

dash-pot *noun* a device that can be installed in a car engine to prevent the car from stalling when the driver suddenly lifts their foot off the accelerator *US, 1960*

dash up the channel *noun* from the male perspective, sexual intercourse. A work-related coinage used by (southern) England coastal fisherman *UK, 1961*

dat *noun* pork *JAMAICA, 2000*

date *noun* **1** a person with whom an appointment or romantic engagement is made. From the conventional sense that defines the appointment *US, 1925*. **2** a prostitute's customer *US, 1961*. **3** a sexual liaison between a prostitute and a customer. An ironic euphemism *US, 1957*. **4** a prisoner's expected date of release from prison *US, 1989*. **5** a foolish or silly person. Especially in the phrase 'soppy date'; later use is generally affectionate *UK, 1914*. **6** the anus; the buttocks. First recorded in Australia in 1919 as 'a word signifying contempt'. Possibly a case of rhyming slang reduced to its first element, DATE AND PLUM, BUM *AUSTRALIA, 1919*

date *verb* **1** (used of a prostitute) to have sex with a customer for pay *US, 1951*. **2** to caress the buttocks. From DATE (the buttocks) *AUSTRALIA, 1984*. **3** to poke in the anus; to goose *AUSTRALIA, 1972*

date and plum; date *noun* the buttocks, the backside, the anus. Rhyming slang for BUM *UK, 1998*

date bait *noun* **1** an attractive person of either sex who is sought-after as a date *US, 1944*. **2** anything that might serve as an incentive for a date *US, 1986*

date driller *noun* the active participant in anal sex *NEW ZEALAND, 1998*

date-packer *noun* a male homosexual *AUSTRALIA, 1985*

date roll *noun* toilet paper *AUSTRALIA, 2003*

date with DiPalma *verb* (of a male) an act of masturbation. DiPalma alias 'the hand' *US, 2001*

daughter *noun* **1** a form of address between homosexual men. This CAMP adoption of the feminine form is also reflected in the cross-gender assignment of pronouns *UK, 1992*. **2** a male homosexual in relation to the man who has introduced him to homosexuality *US, 1949*

dauncey *adjective* pregnant. The 'Lucy is Enceinte' episode of the television comedy *I Love Lucy* (1950–57), which aired on 8th December 1952, was the first US television treatment of pregnancy. Lucy avoided the word 'pregnant', instead saying that she was 'feeling real dauncey', explaining that it was a word that her grandmother 'made up for when you're not really sick but you just feel lousy'. The word enjoyed brief popular usage *US, 1952*

Dave Clark *adjective* dark. Rhyming slang, formed from the name of UK drummer, leader of the Dave Clark Five (b.1942) *UK, 2004*

Dave Dee, Dozy, Beaky, Mick and Tich *adjective* rich. Rhyming slang, jocularly contrived from a 1960s UK pop group *UK, 2004*

David Bowie *adjective* windy. Rhyming slang for, 'blowy', formed on the name of singer and musician David Bowie (David Robert Jones, b.1947) *UK, 1992*

David Gower; David *noun* a shower. Rhyming slang, based on the name of cricketer and television personality David Gower (b.1957) *UK, 2002*

Davina McCalls *noun* nonsense. Rhyming slang for BALLS, formed from the name of UK television presenter Davina McCall (b.1967) *UK, 2004*

davvy *noun* a sofa or couch. A corruption of 'Davenport' *US, 1997*

Davy Crockett *noun* a pocket. Rhyming slang, formed on the name of an American folk-hero who lived from 1786–1836; he was not an inspiration for slang until the actor Fess Parker brought him to life in 1954 and a succession of Disney-made television adventures *UK, 1961*

Davy Jones's locker; Davy Jones's; Davy's locker *noun* **1** the last resting place of those lost at sea; the sea. Davy Jones has been used as a personification for the 'spirit of the sea' since 1751, his locker is mentioned in *The Journal of Richard Cresswell, 1774–7*; the etymology, however, is another mystery of the deep. Jones may arise from Jonah (and his biblical adventures at sea), Davy may have been added by Welsh sailors in honour of St David *UK, 1777*. **2** a door knocker. Rhyming slang *UK, 1992*

Davy Large *noun* a barge. Rhyming slang, formed on the name of a docker who later became a Trade Union official *UK, 1961*

daw *noun* a silly, empty person; an obdurate unreasoning person *IRELAND, 1997*

dawamesk *noun* marijuana *UK, 2003*

daw-daw; daw-yaw *adjective* slow-witted. This seems to derive from a yokelish DOH! Certainly the metropolitan notion of countrysiders at the time this slipped into usage was through BBC radio's 'everyday story of country folk', *The Archers*, first broadcast nationally in 1951; actor Robert Mawdesley certainly introduced such a meaningless syllable into his portrayal of Walter Gabriel, an irascible rogue who gave the appearance of being more slow-witted than he actually was *UK*

dawg *noun* **1** a dog. A rural, southern 'dog' *US, 1979*. **2** a fellow youth gang member *US, 2003*

dawner *noun* an engagement between a prostitute and customer that lasts all night, until dawn *US, 1987*

dawn patrol *noun* any activity that requires staying up all night or getting up very early. Originally a military term, later applied figuratively *US, 1945*

day *noun* ▶ **not your day; it's not your day; it just isn't your day** used for expressing a rueful, philosophical acceptance of a day when everything seems to go wrong *UK, 1984*

day! good day!, hello! An shortening of G'DAY *UK, 1907*

day and night *noun* **1** a *light* ale. Rhyming slang, first recorded in 1960, and still fairly current *UK, 1960*. **2** light (illumination). Rhyming slang *UK, 1992*

day-and-night merchant *noun* a lorry driver who breaks the law by driving more than 11 hours in 24 to undercut other drivers *UK, 1964*

day-for-day *adverb* serving a prison sentence without any reduction in the sentence for good behaviour *US, 1990*

dayglo; day-glo *adjective* used of dazzlingly vivid, rebelliously bright, fluorescent colours. Day-Glo™ paints were introduced in 1951, the name was soon applied to the wider world of tastelessness *UK, 1962*

day job *noun* a conventional job, usually used to finance a person's true interest or passion *US, 1994*

daylight *noun* in horse racing, the non-existent second-place finisher in a race won by a large margin. Used with humour *AUSTRALIA, 1989*. ▶ **he (she) wouldn't give you daylight in a dark corner** said of a person with a reputation for meanness. Glasgow use *UK, 1988*

daylight in the swamp! used for rousing people from bed. A logger term *US, 1936*

daylight robbery *noun* an exorbitant price *UK, 1949*

daylights *noun* ▷*see:* LIVING DAYLIGHTS

day number *noun* in an illegal number gambling lottery, a wager on a number for a single day's drawing *US, 1949*

day player *noun* an actor who is called for a single day's work on a television programme or film set *US, 1988*

days *noun* ▶ **good old days** the past, remembered fondly and better than it ever was. Evolved from the early C19 'good old times' *UK, 1986*

day's dawning; days a dawning *noun* morning. Rhyming slang *UK, 1960*

days of rage *noun* a series of violent confrontations between radical members of the Students for Democratic Society and the police in downtown Chicago in the autumn of 1969 *US, 1970*

day to day *adjective* unencumbered by thoughts of the long term, living one day at a time *US, 1983*

dazzle dust *noun* face powder. Obsolete teen slang *CANADA, 1946*

DB *noun* **1** a *dead body US, 1973*. **2** a socially inept person. An abbreviation of DOUCHE BAG *US, 2003*

DBI a doctors' (unofficial) code for classifiying a despicable, offensive or unhygienic person, in a measure indicated by a suffixed numeral. An initialism for *dirt bag index'. UK, 2003*

DC *noun* a hamburger with every possible trimming and condiment *US, 1966*

DD *noun* a person who is *deaf* and *dumb US, 1926*

DD *adjective* by extension, said of a criminal who gives up no information at all if arrested *US, 1950*

D day *noun* used as a designation for the start of an action. Originally applied to military actions, then expanded to general use. For example, in a US veteran's hospital, it is the routine day that Ducolax™ suppositories are given bed-bound patients *US, 1944*

d-dog *noun* a dog trained to detect hidden drugs *US, 1992*

DDT! used for disparaging, urging the listener to *drop dead twice*. Youth usage; punning on the insecticide now banned but used with great effectiveness to kill mosquitos in the years after World War 2 *US, 1947*

deacon *noun* a prison warden *US, 1949*

deacon *verb* to present a job or product in the best possible light, placing more importance on the first impression than on the actual quality *US, 1855*

deacon seat *noun* **1** the seats nearest a fire *US, 1975*. **2** in a lumber camp, the long bench in the bunkhouse *US, 1851*

deacon's nose *noun* the flat lobe at the nether end of a chicken which is like a mammal's tail, base for the tail-feathers. This part of the chicken or turkey is also known in the US as 'the pope's nose' and in the UK as 'the parson's nose' *CANADA, 1967*

dead *noun* **1** a corpse *BARBADOS, 1971*. **2** in any card game, cards that have been discarded *US, 1973*

dead *adjective* **1** absolute *UK, 1894*. **2** used for expressing a very high degree of trouble *UK, 2002*. **3** (of a place) dull, boring; without interest *AUSTRALIA, 1945*. **4** in a bar, used for describing any drink that has been abandoned *UK, 1985*. **5** (of a racehorse) not run on its merits; ridden to lose deliberately *AUSTRALIA, 1957*. **6** (used of dice) weighted to have one face land up more often than the law of averages would predict *US, 1993*. **7** in bar dice games, no longer wild. If a game is played with 'aces wild' (assuming the point value of any other die), a call of 'aces dead' after the first call of a hand nullifies the 'wild' status *US, 1976*. **8** in pinball, said of a bumper that scores when hit but does not propel the ball back into play *US, 1977*. **9** in pool, said of a shot made such that the cue ball stops completely after striking the object ball *US, 1990*. ▶ **not be found dead with; not be seen dead with** used to deny the possibility that you will have anything whatsoever to do with someone or something *UK, 1915*. ▶ **not be seen dead in; not be found dead in** used in expressions of dislike and dismissal for items of clothing; may also, with slight variation, be applied to a place *UK, 1961*

dead *adverb* very, absolutely, extremely, completely. A general intensifier *UK, 1589*

dead air *noun* silence. Telecommunications usage *US, 1976*

dead alive *noun* in Bingo (also House and Tombola), the number five *UK, 1981*

dead-alive *adverb* extremely slowly *TRINIDAD AND TOBAGO, 1971*

dead as disco *adjective* completely dead. From the meteoric rise and fall of the disco fad in the 1970s *US, 1995*

dead ass *noun* the buttocks in seated repose *US, 1950*

dead-ass *adjective* lacking energy *US, 1958*

dead-ass *adverb* absolutely *US, 1971*

dead babies *noun* semen *US, 1998*

dead-bang *adjective* beyond debate *US, 1934*

dead-bang *adverb* absolutely *US, 1919*

deadbeat *noun* **1** a person who won't pay his debts, especially one who does not pay child support after divorce. In modern use, often construed with 'dad' or 'parent' *US, 1871*. **2** a destitute person; a bum or derelict *AUSTRALIA, 1892*

dead beat *adjective* exhausted *UK, 1821*

dead bird *noun* in horse racing, a certainty *AUSTRALIA, 1889*

Dead board *noun* an Internet bulletin board system designed by, and for, fans of the Grateful Dead *US, 1994*

dead cat *noun* in circus usage, a lion, tiger, or leopard that is on display but does not perform *US, 1981*

dead cat on the line *noun* used as a representation of something that is wrong or immoral *US, 1970*

dead centre *noun* a cemetery. Jocular *UK, 1961*

dead cert *noun* a certainty. Originally sporting and gambling usage *UK, 1889*

dead-cert *adjective* certain *AUSTRALIA, 1993*

dead cinch *noun* a certainty. An intensification of CINCH (a certainty) *UK, 1927*

dead-cinch *adjective* certain. From the noun sense *UK, 2001*

dead drop *noun* in espionage or a sophisticated criminal venture, a location where a message can be left by one party and retrieved by another *US, 1986*

dead duck *noun* an absolute failure, a person or thing with no possibility of success *US, 1829*

dead end *noun* in bowls, an end (a stage of play) that has to be replayed when the jack is driven out of bounds *UK, 1990*

deaders *noun* meat *JAMAICA, 2000*

dead eye dick *noun* a person who is an excellent shot *AUSTRALIA, 1986*

deadfall *noun* a dishonest, disreputable, vice-ridden drinking establishment *US, 1837*

dead finish *noun* the end *AUSTRALIA, 1881*

dead fish *noun* a gambler who places small bets to prolong the inevitable *US, 1963*

deadfoot *noun* a slow vehicle *US, 1976*

dead from the neck up *adjective* brainless, stupid, insensitive *UK, 1930*

dead gaff *noun* a premises with no-one in *UK, 1956*

dead give-away *noun* a notable indication, or betrayal, of guilt, or defect *US, 1882*

dead hand *noun* in poker, any hand held by a player who has bet all of his chips or money on the hand *US, 1947*

deadhead *noun* **1** a person who rides free on a railway, bus or aeroplane, usually because of their employment with the carrier *US, 1841*. **2** a boring person *US, 1907*. **3** a non-playing observer of gambling *US, 1974*. **4** a person given a ticket or tickets for having performed minor services in a theatrical production *US, 1973*

Deadhead *noun* a follower of Grateful Dead, a band strongly associated with psychedelic drugs, seen by many to epitomise the hippie ideal. Grateful Dead's choice of name was the result of browsing a dictionary; usually abbreviated to 'The Dead'; their 30-year career as a live band came to an end in 1995 with the death of guitarist Jerry Garcia *US, 1972*

deadhead *verb* **1** to discourage. A gardening image of deadheading roses to discourage growth *UK, 2001*. **2** to ignore *UK, 2002*. **3** to coast in a car with a depleted petrol supply *US, 1976*. **4** (used of an airline or railway employee) to ride as a passenger in available seating *US, 1854*

deadhead *adverb* without cargo *US, 1987*

dead heart *noun* the arid inland regions of Australia *AUSTRALIA, 1906*

dead horse *noun* tomato sauce. Rhyming slang *AUSTRALIA, 1966*

dead house *noun* a funeral parlour *BARBADOS, 1965*

dead-leg *noun* **1** a useless person *UK, 2003*. **2** a corking of the thigh *AUSTRALIA, 1996*

dead letter perfect *adjective* of an actor, absolutely certain of your lines *UK, 1952*

dead lice ▶ **dead lice are falling off; dead lice are dropping off** used for describing someone who is very slow-moving or lazy *US, 1960*

dead line *noun* in prison, a line the crossing of which will bring gun fire from guards *US, 1962*

deadline *verb* to remove from action for repairs. Vietnam war usage *US, 1991*

dead loss *noun* **1** a person or thing that is utterly inefficient, or a complete failure, or an absolute waste of time or money *UK, 1927*. **2** a boss. Rhyming slang, adopting the non-rhyming sense: 'a person that is utterly inefficient or an absolute waste of money' *UK, 1992*

deadly *adjective* **1** excellent. Especially common in Australian Aboriginal English *US, 1970*. **2** very boring *US, 1955*

deadly *adverb* excessively, extremely, very *UK, 1688*

deadly embrace *noun* in computing, the condition resulting when two processes cannot proceed because each is waiting for another to do something *US, 1981*

deadly treadly *noun* a bicycle. Rhyming elaboration of TREADLY, with the suggestion that it is risky to ride *AUSTRALIA, 2003*

dead man *noun* an earth anchor for a wire or cable *UK, 1840*

dead man's arm *noun* a steamed roll pudding *NEW ZEALAND, 1985*

dead man's ears *noun* stewed dried apricots *NEW ZEALAND, 1992*

dead man's hand *noun* in poker, a hand with a pair of aces and a pair of eights. Although it is the modern belief that this was the hand held by Wild Bill Hickok when shot to death in 1876 in Deadwood, Dakota Territory, early uses of the term (which also sometimes referred to three jacks with two red sevens) make no mention of Hickok. In 1942, Damon Runyon wrote that the hand with jacks was sometimes called the 'Montana dead man's hand' *US, 1888*

dead man's head *noun* a spherical plum pudding *NEW ZEALAND, 1994*

dead man's pull-ups *noun* an exercise in which a person hangs with their arms extended from a bar, lifts their chin over the bar, and then lowers themself to the full arm-extended position *US, 1996*

dead man's rounds *noun* ammunition held pointed toward the bearer *US, 1991*

dead man's zone; dead Marine zone *noun* a demilitarised zone. Back-formation from the initials DMZ *US, 1984*

dead marine *noun* an empty bottle *AUSTRALIA, 1854*

dead meat *noun* **1** used for expressing a very high degree of trouble. Originally applied only in situations where death was certain, but then softened to include lesser consquences *US, 1974*. **2** a prostitute. An allusion to the flesh that is sold in a butcher's shop, as opposed to that which is freshly given *UK, 1961*

dead money *noun* **1** obviously counterfeit paper money *US, 1956*. **2** in poker, money bet by a player who has withdrawn from a hand *US, 1992*

deadner *noun* a blow, a thump *IRELAND, 2003*

dead-nuts *adverb* completely *US, 1887*

deado *noun* a corpse *US, 1919*

deado; dead-oh *adjective* deep asleep; unconscious. Possibly from the earlier sense (very drunk), however DEAD in 'dead drunk' serves as an intensifier, whereas the sense here may be a literal allusion *UK, 1984*

dead-on *adjective* accurate *UK, 1889*

dead on arrival *noun* **1** heroin. From official jargon for those who are delivered to hospital too late *UK, 1998*. **2** phencyclidine, the recreational drug known as PCP or angel dust. In honour of the drug's fatal overdose potential *US, 1993*

dead pan *noun* a complete lack of facial emotion *US, 1927*

deadpan *adjective* without expression; displaying no emotion *US, 1928*

dead pigeon *noun* **1** in a criminal enterprise, a double-crosser *US, 1964*. **2** a person who is destined to lose *US, 1919*

dead pony gaff *noun* of circus and fairgrounds, a bad site. Used by travelling showmen *UK, 1961*

dead presidents *noun* US currency notes of any dollar denomination; hence, generically, US money. From the portraits of Washington, Lincoln, Hamilton etc., printed on the different value notes *US, 1944*

dead rabbit *noun* the penis in a flaccid state *US, 1964*

dead ring *noun* an exact likeness *AUSTRALIA, 1915*

dead ringer *noun* an exact likeness *US, 1891*

dead road *noun* MDMA, the recreational drug best known as ecstasy *UK, 2003*

dead set; dead-set; deadset *adjective* complete, utter *AUSTRALIA, 1965*

dead set; dead-set; deadset *adverb* **1** completely, utterly. From the common collocation of 'dead completely' and 'set against/for/on' (determined (not) to do something or have something happen) *AUSTRALIA, 1947*. **2** really; honestly *AUSTRALIA, 1987*

deadshit *noun* a despicable person *AUSTRALIA, 1961*

dead skin *noun* the white inner peel of an orange *BAHAMAS, 1982*

dead sled *noun* in the used car business, a car in extremely poor condition *US, 1997*

dead soldier *noun* an empty alcohol bottle or beer can *US, 1899*

dead spit *noun* an exact likeness *UK, 1901*

dead-stick *verb* to land an aircraft without engine function *US, 1962*

dead-stick *adjective* (used of landing an aircraft) without engine function *US, 1999*

Dead threads *noun* in the language surrounding the Grateful Dead, the layers of clothes worn by a concert-goer *US, 1994*

dead time *noun* time served in jail which does not count towards fulfillment of the prisoner's sentence *US, 1973*

dead to rights denoting an absolute certainty that fully justifies arrest on a criminal charge, as when caught red-handed. DEAD intensifies 'to rights' (fairly, legally) *UK, 1859*

dead to the world *adjective* unconscious, deeply and soundly asleep; unaware of any outside stimulus. Earlier use may also have connoted 'drunk' *UK, 1899*

dead tree format *noun* paper on which computer output is printed *UK, mid-1990s*

dead trouble *noun* an extremely difficult situation, deep trouble *UK, 1971*

dead 'un *noun* **1** unoccupied premises. Criminal use *UK, 1956*. **2** a racehorse deliberately ridden to lose *AUSTRALIA, 1877*

deadwood *noun* **1** an incompetent or otherwise useless person *US, 1887*. **2** a flaccid penis. Extended from WOOD (the erect penis) *US, 1995*. **3** unsold tickets for a performance *US, 1934*. **4** non-playing observers of gambling *US, 1974*. **5** a person caught outright committing a crime *US, 1992*

dead yard *noun* a ceremony after burial in the deceased's yard *JAMAICA, 2003*

deaf and dumb *noun* the buttocks, the backside, the anus. Rhyming slang for BUM *UK, 1992*

deafie *noun* a deaf person. Prominently applied to Dr Eric Williams, Prime Minister of Trinidad from 1956 until 1981 *TRINIDAD AND TOBAGO, 1972*

deal *noun* **1** a business transaction, a trade or a bargain *US, 1838*. **2** an underhand or secret transaction; a trade of questionable legality; a mutually beneficial commercial or political arrangement. A nuance of the broader sense, (a trade, a bargain) *US, 1881*. **3** a small amount of marijuana or hashish *UK, 1978*. ▶ **bad deal; raw deal; rough deal** ill-treatment, exploitative or unfair usage; a swindle *US, 1912*. ▶ **fair deal; square deal** an honest and equitable usage. The *locus classicus* of 'square deal' is in a speech delivered by US President Theodore Roosevelt in 1903: 'We must treat each man on his worth and merits as a man. We must see that each is given a square deal, because he is entitled to no more and should receive no less' *US, 1876*. ▶ **new deal** a new arrangement *US, 1834*. ▶ **the deal; the real deal** the very best *US, 1986*

deal *verb* **1** to sell drugs *US, 1958*. **2** to supervise the blackjack game in a casino *US, 1980*. ▶ **deal off the top** to treat fairly. From the gambling scheme of cheating by dealing off the bottom of a deck *US, 1969*

deal *adverb* much. Derived from the noun sense (a considerable amount) *UK, 1756*

dealer's band *noun* an elastic band used by a drug dealer to secure or to facilitate the jetisoning of drugs for sale *US, 1966*

dealy; dealie *noun* a thing the correct name of which escapes or is not important to the speaker *US, 1997*

dean *noun* **1** a shark *AUSTRALIA, 1977*. **2** a skilled and experienced poker player *US, 1979*

deaner; deener; dener; diener *noun* a shilling. Until decimalisation in 1971; probably from *denier* (a French coin, the twelfth part of a sou). After the introduction of decimal currency in Australia in 1966, it came to mean a ten cent piece, or its value, a similar coin with about the same comparative value; dying out from the 1980s, now seldom heard *UK, 1857*

dean of men *noun* a prison warden *US, 1949*

dear!; oh dear!; dear oh dear! used as a mild register of anxiety, irritation, regret, etc.. Probably 'dear God!' or 'dear Lord!' *UK, 1694*

dear dear! used as a mild exclamation or oath; often used to add a mild or ironic emphasis to what is being said. By reduplication of DEAR! *UK, 1849*

dear dyin' Moses! used as an elaborate, original curse in coastal Nova Scotia CANADA, 1999

dearg noun a stab or a shot, a sharp punch IRELAND, 2000

dearie noun 1 used by women as a form of address. A less intimate variation of conventional 'dear' (a loved one) UK, 1681. 2 used as an affected form of address among male homosexuals. Camp adoption of the previous sense UK, 1962

dearie me!; deary me! used for registering regret. An elaboration of DEAR ME! that is more sorrowful in tone UK, 1785

Dear Jane noun a letter to a girlfriend or wife breaking off the relationship US, 1963

Dear John; Dear John letter; Johnny letter noun a letter from a woman to her husband or boyfriend ending their relationship US, 1945

dear me! used as a mild exclamation or oath; often used to add a mild or ironic emphasis UK, 1773

dear oh dear! ▷see: DEAR!

dear old thing noun ▷see: OLD THING

death noun 1 paramethoxyamphetamine or 4-methoxyamphetamine (PMA), a synthetic hallucinogen AUSTRALIA, 1997. 2 someone or something that is exquisitely perfect US, 1965. 3 a difficult situation, such as an exam, a hangover, etc US, 1965. 4 in harness racing, the position just behind and outside the leader. Because the horse in that position has to travel farther than horses on the inside and does not have the benefit of a lead horse breaking the wind resistance US, 1997. ▶ **at the death** in the finish. Figurative sense of a conventional 'end' UK, 1962. ▶ **like death; like death warmed up** feeling or appearing extremely unwell UK, 1939. ▶ **to death 1** to the extreme; superlative UK, 1998. 2 frequently and ad nauseam UK, 1937

death adder; death adder man noun an unwelcoming man who lives a solitary life in the Australian outback. From the name given to several species of venomous snake found in Australia. Historically 'an outback gossip' was also known as a 'death adder' AUSTRALIA, 1951

death adders noun ▶ **have death adders in your pockets** to be stingy AUSTRALIA, 1944

death ball noun in cricket, any bowled delivery that takes a wicket UK, 1996

death benefit noun in poker, money given to a player to complete a bet US, 1996

death box; fun box noun in snowboarding and skateboarding, an improvised hollow platform such as a wooden or plasic box or barrel, from which to bounce the board US, 1995

death cookie noun in snowboarding, a rock hidden in snow US, 1995

death drinker noun a vagrant alcoholic UK, 2000

death drop noun butyl chloride when taken recreationally UK, 1984

death metal; deathcore noun a category of heavy metal music that draws on violent, blasphemous and mysogynistic imagery UK, 1992

death mitten noun bags slipped over the hands of murder victims to preserve evidence US, 1992

death on call noun Battery C, 4th Battalion, 77th Infantry of the US Army. A gunship unit with the boast of 'kill by profession' US, 1990

death on truckers noun the US Department of Transportation. From the agency's initials: DOT US, 1971

death pen noun a designated pen with black indelible ink used in hospitals for filling out death certificates US, 1994

death rattle noun in cricket, the noise made when a batsman's wicket is hit by the ball UK, 1958

death rim noun any expensive car wheel rim. The rim is an invitation to crime and violence, hence the name US, 1995

death row noun a type of bet in an illegal numbers game lottery US, 1957

death seat noun 1 the front passenger seat of a car or truck. From the probability, actual or notional, that the passenger is the least

likely to survive an accident US, 1975. 2 in a trotting race, the position on the outside of the leader. Derives from the difficulty of overtaking from such a position AUSTRALIA, 1989

death spiral noun a downward spiral of an aeroplane from which recovery is nearly impossible and as a result of which impact with the ground is inevitable US, 1990

death tourist noun a person who travels to a country where euthanasia is legal for the purpose of achieving a medically assisted suicide US, 2003

death trip noun 1 LSD enhanced with botanical drugs from plants such as Deadly Nightshade or Jimsonweed US, 1970. 2 heroin UK, 2002. 3 a fascination with death US, 1969

death watch noun attendance upon a man condemned to death. Hanging was institutionalised in C5 Britain; the death penalty was abolished in the UK in November 1965 – except for the crimes of treason, piracy with violence and arson in Royal Dockyards UK, 1950

death wish noun phencyclidine, the recreational drug known as PCP or angel dust US, 1986

deathy noun a death adder AUSTRALIA, 1951

deazingus noun a dingus, or eye dropper used in drug injecting US, 1973

deb noun 1 a debutante US, 1920. 2 a girl associated with a youth gang, either directly as a member or through a boyfriend. A lovely if ironic borrowing from 'debutante' US, 1946. 3 a depressant, sedative or tranquillizer tablet. From a slovenly pronunciation of 'deps' (depressants); also recorded in the plural US, 1975. 4 a tablet or capsule of amphetamine. A reversal of the chemical effect in the earlier usage; also noted as a plural UK, 2003. 5 a tablet of MDMA, the recreational drug best known as ecstasy UK, 2003

debag verb to remove someone's trousers, often with humorous intention, always with some degree of force. From BAGS (trousers) UK, 1914

deball verb to castrate US, 1961

debaucherama noun an orgy. Combines conventional 'debauch' with a variation of the suffix- 'orama' (indicates largeness) UK, 2000

Debbie Chon noun an overweight soldier. From the Korean; Korean war usage US, 1982

debone verb to bend a playing card so that it can be identified later in another player's hand US, 1968

debriefing noun an after-flight hotel party attended by a flight crew and flight attendants US, 2002

debris noun marijuana seeds and stems remaining after cleaning US, 1971

debthead noun a prisoner who is continually in debt and, therefore, untrustworthy. A combination of conventional 'debt' with- HEAD (a person considered as a single attribute) UK, 1996

debtor's colic noun any feigned illness whereby a man can get into hospital, or remain sick in his cell, in order to avoid meeting his creditors UK, 1950

debts noun in prison, a placing (of an inmate) on report UK, 1996

debug verb 1 to clear an area of listening devices US, 1964. 2 to rectify faults of electrical, mechanical or operational nature; to remove faulty programming from a computer UK, 1945

debut verb 1 to subject a boy to his first homosexual experience UK, 1978. 2 to acknowledge your homosexuality US, 1964

decadence; deccadence noun MDMA, the recreational drug best known as ecstasy UK, 1998

decaf noun decaffeinated coffee US, 1956

decaf adjective decaffeinated US, 1981

decapitation noun the assassination of a head of state. Media-friendly military jargon US, 2003

decapitation strike noun a military attack intended to kill (or render impotent) an enemy's leader US, 2003

decayed adjective drunk US, 1966

dece adjective exceptionally good, 'wonderful'. A shortening of 'decent', pronounced 'deece' UK, 1977

decent *adjective* **1** sufficiently dressed for standards of propriety, especially in the phrase 'are you decent?'. A specialised sense of 'decent', probably of theatrical origins *UK, 1949.* **2** good, pleasing, excellent *US, 1979*

decider *noun* of a sporting contest, the deciding factor: the final heat, the final set; the winning stroke, the winning run, the winning play. From racing, when a 'decider' is a heat run after a dead-heat. Generally used with 'the' *UK, 1883*

decimated *adjective* drunk *UK, 2002*

decision *verb* to win a boxing match by a decision of the judges as opposed to with a knock-out *US, 1979*

deck *noun* **1** a packet of a powdered drug *US, 1916.* **2** a packet of cigarettes *US, 1923.* **3** a gramophone turntable. A critical component of a DJ in the modern sense of the term *US, 1997.* **4** the ground *UK, 1836.* **5** in cricket, the pitch *UK, 1995.* **6** a pack of playing cards. In conventional use from late C16 until about 1720, then dialect and colloquial. In the early part of C20, usage was confined, more or less, to the underworld; from the end of World War 2 it was in common use in the UK and Australia and, by the 1970s, in general and widespread informal use. 'Deck of cards' was a UK number one hit for Max Bygraves in 1973 *UK, 1948*

deck *verb* to knock to the ground *US, 1945*

deck ape *noun* an enlisted sailor in the US Navy *US, 1944*

decked *adjective* **1** unconscious from abuse of alcohol or drugs *US, 1961.* **2** dressed stylishly *US, 1972*

decker *noun* a look *AUSTRALIA, 1951*

deckie *noun* a deck-hand. Nautical *UK, 1913*

deck monkey *noun* a deckhand *US, 1941*

decknician *noun* a disc jockey who is admired for skilful manipulation and mixing of music on turntables *UK, 2003*

decko *noun* ▷*see:* DEKKO

deck off *verb* to dress up *TRINIDAD AND TOBAGO, 1973*

decks *noun* trousers *UK, 1983*

deck up *verb* to package a powdered drug for sale *US, 1964*

declare *verb* ▶ **declare a gang** (used of warring youth gangs) to agree to discuss a truce *US, 1953*

declare out *verb* (of the Canadian Armed Forces) to opt out of service, to resign a commission *CANADA, 1959*

decomp room *noun* the room in a morgue housing decomposed bodies *US, 1983*

decorate *verb* to pay for something at a restaurant or bar. Most commonly in the phrase 'decorate the mahogany' for buying drinks at a bar *US, 1908*

decorated with red roses *adjective* in the bleed period of the menstrual cycle. Remembered as World War 2 usage *US, 1999*

decoy *noun* an undercover police officer whose appearance leads criminals to assume the officer is a promising victim *US, 1981*

dedo *noun* an informant. From the Spanish for 'finger', used by English speakers in the American southwest *US, 1995*

dedud *verb* to clear unexploded artillery shells from a practice range *US, 1968*

dee *noun* **1** a capsule of Dilaudid™, a pharmaceutical narcotic *US, 1986.* **2** a police detective. Variant spelling of D. *AUSTRALIA, 1882*

deeda *noun* LSD. Possibly New York slang *US, 1967*

dee dee *noun* the vagina *US, 1998*

deedee *noun* a drug (or dope) dealer. A pronounced initialism *UK, 1997*

deefa *noun* a dog. Playing on 'd for dog' *NEW ZEALAND, 1998*

deek *verb* to decoy an opposing player into making a wrong move *CANADA, 1942*

deemer *noun* a ten-cent piece. From the colloquial 'dime' *US, 1926*

deep *adjective* **1** filled with the specified number of referential objects. For example, 'four deep' would mean 'four people in a car' *US, 1973.* **2** serious, intense *US, 1990.* **3** (used of language) standard

BAHAMAS, 1982. **4** habitual. This seems to be used in the Black community only *UK, 2000*

deep! used for expressing approval *UK, 2003*

deep and meaningful *adjective* a serious conversation, generally about emotions and relationships *AUSTRALIA, 1988*

deep-dick *verb* (from the male point of view) to have sex *US, 1997*

deep end *noun* ▶ **go off the deep end; go in off the deep end** to become excited, angry, emotional, passionate, maddened. A figurative application of the deep end of a swimming pool *UK, 1921*

deep freeze *noun* solitary confinement *US, 1958*

deep house *noun* a sub-category of house music but with a mellower feel, often featuring profound, rolling bass lines and samples from jazz records *UK, 1996*

deep kimchi *noun* serious trouble. Based on the unflattering comparison of the Korean pickled delicacy with excrement *US, 1998*

deep magic *noun* in computing, an understanding of a technique in a program or system not known by the average programmer *US, 1991*

Deep North; deep north *noun* the far northern parts of the eastern state of Queensland. Modelled on US 'deep south', with identical connotations *AUSTRALIA, 1972*

deep-pocket *adjective* (used of a defendant in civil litigation) wealthy, possessing considerable financial reserves *US, 1976*

deep-sea diver *noun* a fiver (£5). Rhyming slang *UK, 1980*

deep sea fishing *noun* exploratory surgery *US, 1994*

deep serious *adjective* extremely critical, as bad as it gets. Vietnam war coinage and usage *US, 1985*

deep shaft *noun* strong, illegally manufactured whisky *US, 1999*

deep six *verb* to discard; to reject *US, 1952*

deep throat *noun* oral sex performed on a man in which the person doing the performing takes the penis completely into their mouth and throat. A term from the so-named 1972 classic pornography film *US, 1991*

deep throat *verb* to take a man's penis completely into the mouth and throat *US, 1991*

deep-water Baptist *noun* a member of a Baptist sect that practises full-immersion baptism *US, 1949*

deez-nuts me. The reference to 'these nuts' is an intimate, if crude, reference to yourself *US, 1985*

def *adjective* excellent, superlative *US, 1979*

def *adverb* definitely *US, 1942*

de facto *noun* a partner in a de facto relationship *AUSTRALIA, 1952*

defect *noun* a school prefect. A pun to delight the childish *UK, 1961*

deffo; defo *adverb* definitely *UK, 2001*

defiled *adjective* drunk *US, 1997*

definite *adjective* used as a meaningless embellishment *US, 1985*

deft and dumb *adjective* a catchphrase that defines desirable qualities in a wife or mistress *US, 1961*

degomble *verb* to remove snow stuck to your clothes and equipment before going indoors *ANTARCTICA, 1989*

dehorn *noun* **1** denatured alcohol (ethyl alcohol to which a poisonous substance has been added to make it unfit for consumption) *US, 1926.* **2** a person who is addicted to denatured alcohol (ethyl alcohol to which a poisonous substance has been added to make it unfit for consumption) *US, 1926*

dehorn *verb* **1** to have sex after a long period of celibacy *US, 1972.* **2** to demote or discharge from employment *US, 1946.* **3** to cut someone's hair *US, 1972*

dehose *verb* to return a computer that is suspended in an operation to functioning *US, 1991*

dehydrate *verb* to become thirsty, especially for alcohol. Coined at around the same time as dehydrated foods became fairly common *UK, 1946*

dehydrated water *noun* the object of a prank errand for a new or inexperienced worker *US, 1970*

deja dit *noun* a sensation of having said something before; the consequent boredom. Adopted directly from French (already said), following 'déjà vu'. *UK, 1994*

deja fuck *noun* the unsettling sensation that the person with whom you are now having sex is a former sexual partner *US, 2002*

deja vu all over again *noun* the same thing, once again, repeated. An assault on the language attributed to baseball great Yogi Berra *US, 1995*

deke *noun* a decoy *US, 1950*

dekko; decko *noun* a look. Ultimately from Hindi *dekho* (look!) Originally British military use dating from the Raj era. There is an 1854 example of 'dekh' used in Anglo-Indian English, though no doubt the common Hindi imperative *dekho!* would have been in common use *AUSTRALIA, 1957*

delay *verb* in Quebec, a time limit, an extension *CANADA, 2002*

delayer *noun* a railway dispatcher *US, 1946*

delec *adjective* attractive. An abbreviation of 'delectable' *NEW ZEALAND, 1998*

delete *verb* to leave *US, 1993*

Delhi belly *noun* diarrhoea suffered by tourists *US, 1944*

deli *noun* a *deli*catessen *US, 1954*

Delia *noun* a recipe. From Delia Smith (b.1941), arguably the UK's most celebrated cookery writer and broadcaster *UK, 2004*

delicacies *noun* the testicles *UK, 2002*

delicate *adjective* ▶ **in a delicate state of health; in a delicate condition** pregnant. Now rare, but still understood *UK, 1850*

delicatessen book *noun* a betting operation where the odds are constantly cut *US, 1947*

delish; deelish *adjective* delicious *UK, 1920*

delivery boy *noun* in poker, any young, inexperienced, unskilled player *US, 1996*

delivery order *noun* a request that a certain type of car be stolen and sold to the requesting party *US, 1983*

dell *verb* to hit. English gypsy use *UK, 2000*

delo *noun* a delegate *AUSTRALIA, 1961*

delosis *noun* a pretty girl *US, 1953*

delouse *verb* to clear an area of listening devices. A pun on synonymous DEBUG *UK, 1969*

delph *noun* the teeth. Possibly from a play on Delft china *UK, 2002*

Delta delta *noun* a female Red Cross volunteer in Vietnam *US, 1990*

Delta dust *noun* marijuana grown in Vietnam. A subtle pun on the several scientific names for marijuana and its psychoactive component that include 'Delta 1' or 'Delta 9' *US, 1991*

delta sierra *noun* a stupid person. Using the phonetic alphabet for DS – DUMB SHIT or 'dog shit' *US, 1987*

Delta sox *noun* nylon socks that replaced wool socks for US Army troops in Vietnam in 1970. The army concluded that nylon socks were more suited to tropical wear, especially in areas such as the Mekong Delta, than were wool socks *US, 1990*

delts *noun* the deltoid muscles *US, 1981*

delurk *verb* to post a message on an Internet discussion group after previously observing without posting *US, 1995*

deluxe *noun* in circus usage, a box seat *US, 1981*

dem *noun* **1** a *dem*onstration; also, as a verb, to *dem*onstrate, especially how an article works *UK, 1968*. **2** a capsule of merperidine (trade name Demerol™), a synthetic opiate *US, 1992*

Dem *noun* a *Dem*ocrat *US, 1875*

dem *adjective* their. West Indian and black English rendering of 'them' used ungrammatically or shortened from 'belonging to them' *UK, 1994*

dem *pronoun* them. West Indian and black English phonetic variation *JAMAICA, 1868*

demented *adjective* in computing, not functional and not useful. In computing, the condition resulting when two processes cannot proceed because each is waiting for another to do something *US, 1983*

demento *noun* a deranged person *US, 1977*

demi-god *noun* **1** a good-looking boy *US, 1983*. **2** a person recognised by the computing community as a major genius *US, 1991*

demmy *noun* a capsule of Demerol™ (merperidine), a powerful and habit-forming painkiller *US, 1956*

demo *noun* **1** a *demo*nstration model or recording *US, 1963*. **2** an act of having sex in front of observers. Apparently this had a vogue during the 70s *AUSTRALIA, 1971*. **3** a political *demo*nstration *AUSTRALIA, 1904*. **4** a *demo*nstration of how something works or how an action or activity ought to be done *UK, 1961*. **5** *demo*lition *US, 1943*. **6** a laboratory pipette used to smoke crack cocaine *US, 1992*

demob *noun* a release from conscription or other contract of military service. An abbreviation of officialese 'demobilisation'; hence 'demob suit' (clothes issued on return to civilian life), etc *UK, 1945*

demob *verb* to demobilise *UK, 1918*

demoiselle *noun* an odd-shaped pillar of clay or cemented gravel, caused by erosion. The word comes from the French, meaning 'young woman', and is likely to be suggested by the shape, or the shape as it appears to a plains rider who hasn't seen a woman for a long time *CANADA, 1952*

demolish *noun* crack cocaine *UK, 1998*

demolition party *noun* a party held on the last night of a lease for the purpose of destroying furniture, fixtures, etc *NEW ZEALAND, 1987*

demon *noun* a police detective, or, loosely, a police officer. Originally criminal slang. The suggestion in the *Oxford English Dictionary Supplement* (1972) that it is somehow extracted from Van Diemen's Land, a former name of the penal colony of Tasmania, seems tenuous at best *AUSTRALIA, 1898*

demon *adjective* **1** applied to someone, especially in cricket and other sports, who seems superhuman in action. Originally used of Australian cricketer Fred Spofforth, 1853–1926 *UK, 1883*. **2** excellent *US, 1983*

demon tweak *noun* **1** a motorcycle enthusiast who does his own tuning at home *UK, 1979*. **2** in motor racing, a highly clever modification which may or may not improve the car's performance *US, 1980*

demoto *noun* a person lacking motivation; a self-non-starter *US, 1993*

dems *noun* demolitions. Military *UK, 1995*

denari; denarli; dinarlee; dinali; denali *noun* money. Polari *UK, 1914*

Denis Law *noun* a carpenter's saw. Rhyming slang, formed on the name of a Scottish footballer (b.1940) *UK, 1992*

Denmark *noun* ▶ **go to Denmark** to undergo a sex change operation. Homosexual usage; an allusion to the sex-altering operation performed on Christine Jorgensen in Denmark *US, 1957*

den mother *noun* an older, unofficial leader of a group of homosexual men *US, 1997*

Dennis the Menace *noun* a variety of MDMA, the recreational drug best known as ecstasy. From the similarity between the red and black stripes on the comic book character's jumper and those on the tablet *UK, 1996*

Dennistoun Palais *noun* aluminium. Glasgow rhyming slang, on 'ally', formed from a venue in the Dennistown area of the city; used by local scrap-dealers *UK: SCOTLAND, 1988*

dental floss *noun* LSD *UK, 2003*

dental flosser *noun* someone who is considered to be worthless or despicable. Rhyming slang for TOSSER *UK, 2003*

dent for an E-flat bugle *noun* an imaginary item for which a novice musician may be sent. Military in origin, but remembered as a fool's errand enjoyed in the Boys' Brigade during the early 1960s *UK, 1964*

dentist *noun* in oil drilling, a cement worker *US, 1954*

dentist's friend *noun* in circus and carnival usage, any sweet *US, 1981*

Denver mud *noun* a patent medicine applied as a poultice *US, 1970*

dep *noun* **1** a *deposition* (a copy of a transcript of evidence). Usually in the plural *UK, 1996*. **2** a *deputy UK, 1851*. **3** a *deputy* prison governor *UK, 1950*. **4** in the theatre, a company representative of Equity (the actors' union) *UK, 2001*. **5** in Quebec, a corner store. A short form of the French word *dépanneur*, which is also used by anglophones and allophones as well as Quebec French speakers, and is often used to describe what in Ontario is known as a 'confectionery', and in south and central Texas as an 'icehouse' *CANADA, 2001*

depart *verb* in the language of fighter pilots, to accelerate through the plane's limits *US, 1990*

department of fishy things *nickname* Nova Scotia's Department of Fisheries and Oceans *CANADA, 2002*

Department of Holidays *nickname* the British Columbia Ministry of Transportation and Highways *CANADA, 1989*

department of the obvious *noun* a mythical agency that employs people to state the obvious *US, 1991*

departure lounge *noun* in hospital, a geriatric ward. Medical slang, using humour to cope with imminent death *UK, 2002*

depeditate *verb* in computing, to place text in a fashion that cuts off the feet of the letters *US, 1991*

depending on what school you went to a catchphrase used when two distinct pronunciations of a word are offered *AUSTRALIA, 1977*

depend on it!; depend upon it! be certain; used as an assurance that a statement is, or will be, true *UK, 1738*

depth bomb *noun* an amphetamine tablet *UK, 1968*

depth charge *noun* **1** a shot of whisky served in a glass of beer *US, 1956*. **2** a fig or a prune. Of Royal Navy and Royal Air Force origins; comparing an explosion in the deep, which is in the power of such military hardware, to the laxative effect of the fruits *UK, 1943*. **3** any food that is heavy or stodgy, such as dumplings. From the effects on your lower depths; originally recorded in prison use but soon in wider use *UK, 1950*

depth charging *noun* a system of playing blackjack based not on a count of the value of cards played but on the depth of the deck dealt *US, 1991*

deputy *noun* a married person's lover *TRINIDAD AND TOBAGO, 1975*

deputy do-right *noun* a police officer *US, 1980*

der! you idiot! In origin representing a stalling articulation such as 'um' or 'er', implying that you need to spend time thinking about something that is obvious. Always said with a sarcastic tone *AUSTRALIA, 1979*

derange *verb* to bother, to trouble. From the French *déranger CANADA, 2001*

derby *noun* **1** oral sex *US, 1969*. **2** any sporting contest between traditional rivals *UK, 1999*

derby kelly; darby kelly; derby kel; derby kell; derby; darby *noun* the stomach, the abdomen, the belly. Rhyming slang for 'belly' *UK, 1906*

derel *noun* a person lacking in basic intelligence. An abbreviation of the conventional 'derelict' *US, 1991*

derelict *noun* a socially inept, slightly dim person *US, 1979*

derm; derem *noun* an intestine; usually in plural, guts. The phrases 'my derms are clapping together' and 'my derms are flapping together' are vulgarisms for 'hungry' *SOUTH AFRICA, 1970*

dermo *noun* dermatitis *AUSTRALIA, 1948*

dero *noun* a derelict *AUSTRALIA, 1971*

DEROS; deros *verb* to return to the US from combat duty in Vietnam. From the abbreviation for the 'date of estimated return from overseas' *US, 1968*

derrick apple; derrick fruit *noun* in oil drilling, a nut, bolt or piece of dried mud that falls off a derrick *US, 1954*

derrière *noun* the vagina. From French *derrière* (behind), a familiar euphemism for 'the buttocks', 'the behind', adopted here for a new location *US, 1998*

derro *noun* a derelict *AUSTRALIA, 1972*

derry *noun* a derelict house *UK, 1978*

Derry & Toms *noun* bombs. Rhyming slang, formed during World War 2 on the name of a London department store, which closed in 1973 *UK, 1960*

Derry-Down-Derry; DDD; three Ds *noun* sherry. Theatrical rhyming slang *UK, 1960*

'ders *noun* oral sex. An abbreviation of 'headers', itself an embellishment of HEAD *US, 1982*

desert cherry *noun* a soldier newly arrived in Kuwait or Saudi Arabia during the first Gulf war *US, 1991*

desert lamb *noun* kid goat's meat *AUSTRALIA, 1969*

desert rat *noun* any longtime resident of any desert area, especially, in modern usage, Las Vegas, Nevada *US, 1907*

desert rose *noun* a military urinal used in the desert *UK, 2002*

deserve *verb* ▶ **deserve a medal** said of a hard worker: to deserve some kind of reward for effort; also said in regard of an achievment, especially of some act, however trivial, that you would not like to have done (in either use, it is implicit that no reward or official acknowledgement of the act is likely) *UK, 1961*

desi *noun* someone from India *US, 1996*

designer *adjective* (used of pornography) relatively high-brow, designed for couples and first-time viewers *US, 2000*

designer drug *noun* a recreational drug sythesized to mimic the effects of another more expensive or unlawful drug *US, 1996*

desiness *noun* a recognisably Indian quality *UK, 2006*

desk commando *noun* a military support worker who does not face combat *UK, 1958*

desk cowboy *noun* a military or police support worker who does not face combat or street duty *US, 1942*

deskfast *noun* breakfast taken at your desk *US, 1996*

desk jockey *noun* an office worker *US, 1953*

desk piano *noun* a typewriter *US, 1945*

desk pilot *noun* a military or police support worker who does not face combat or street duty *US, 1955*

desk rage *noun* an outburst of enraged hostility within an office environment *US, 2000*

desk rider *noun* a military support worker who does not face combat; an officious bureaucrat *US, 1966*

desmadre *noun* a disaster. Border Spanish used in English conversation by Mexican-Americans *US, 1974*

Desmond *noun* a lower second-class degree, a 2:2. A clever pun which may be considered rhyming slang, based on Archbishop Desmond Tutu (b.1930) *UK, 1998*. ▶ **do a Desmond** to undress, completely or largely, especially at a rock concert. From Desmond Morris, author of *The Naked Ape US, 1983*

desperado *noun* **1** a person who is down and out; an unemployed person scrounging a living from day to day *AUSTRALIA, 1977*. **2** a person who exhibits desperation in seeking sexual partners *AUSTRALIA, 1987*. **3** a desperate gambler *US, 1961*

desperado *adjective* desperate. A borrowed word used as an elaboration *UK, 2001*

desperate *noun* **1** a gambling addict *AUSTRALIA, 1975*. **2** a person who exhibits desperation in seeking sexual partners *AUSTRALIA, 1979*

desperate *adjective* very good. Largely dependent on a melodramatic delivery to impart the slang sense *US, 1951*

desperate *adverb* very *CANADA, 1988*

Desperate Dan *noun* a tan. Rhyming slang, formed on the name of a comic strip hero who has appeared in the *Beano* since 1938 *UK, 1992*

desperate money *noun* in horse racing, money bet by someone who is in a long losing streak and is very anxious to win *AUSTRALIA, 1989*

despizable *adjective* worse than despicable *US, 1975*

des res *a desirable residence*. A cliché of estate agent jargon *UK, 1986*

dessert crack *noun* nitrous oxide. Small containers of nitrous oxide used in canned dessert topping are a prime source of the gas for young users *US, 2002*

dessie *noun* a desert boot *UK, 1995*

destat *verb* to get rid of a property's statutory tenants *UK, 1963*

destructo *noun* in surfing, a large and powerful wave *US, 1978*

det *noun* a *det*onator, *1962*

detainer *noun* a railroad dispatcher *US, 1946*

detectorist; metal detectorist *noun* a person who, for recreation, operates a metal detector *UK, 2002*

dethrone *verb* to order someone to leave a public toilet to prevent homosexual activity. A royal image from the use of QUEEN. (homosexual) *US, 1941*

detox *noun* a facility where an alcoholic or drug addict can begin treatment with the detoxification process *US, 1973*

detox *verb* to undergo, or subject to, a process of detoxification *US, 1972*

Detroit diesel *noun* any General Motors engine *US, 1971*

Detroit iron *noun* a large, American car *US, 1950*

Detroit vibrator *noun* a Chevrolet big-rig truck *US, 1971*

deuce *noun* **1** two of anything, such as two marijuana cigarettes, two women, etc *US, 1943*. **2** a two-year prison sentence *US, 1925*. **3** two pounds or two dollars *US, 1900*. **4** in the restaurant business, a table for two *US, 1935*. **5** an act of defecation. From children's toilet vocabulary: NUMBER TWO (defecation) *US, 2003*. **6** in dice games, the point two *US, 1950*. **7** in pool, the two-ball *US, 1878*. **8** in card games, a two of any suit *UK, 1680*. **9** two dollars' worth of drugs. Originally a $2 package of heroin; with inflation other drugs became more likely to fit the bill *US, 1992*. **10** heroin. From DEUCE BAG; DEUCE (a two-dollar bag of heroin) *UK, 1986*. **11** two hundred *US, 1998*. **12** two hundred dollars *US, 1973*. **13** twenty dollars *US, 1960*. **14** in television and film-making, a 2000 watt spotlight *US, 1990*. **15** an arrest or conviction for driving under the influence of alcohol. California Penal Code Section 502 prohibits driving under the influence of alcohol, hence the 'two' reference *US, 1971*. **16** a 1932 Ford. A favourite of car enthusiasts, immortalised by the Beach Boys in their 1963 song 'Little Deuce Coupe' *US, 1954*. **17** a Chevrolet II car made between 1962 and 1967 *US, 1993*. **18** a small-time criminal *US, 1992*. **19** used as a substitute for 'the devil' or 'hell' *UK, 1694*. **20** the Delta Dagger fighter aircraft *US, 1970*. ▶ **deuce of benders** the knees *US, 1947*

deuce *verb* **1** to shear 200 sheep in a day. Hence, 'deucer' (someone capable of this feat) *AUSTRALIA, 1950*. **2** to back down from a confrontation *US, 1950*. **3** to supply someone with marijuana *US, 1992*

deuce and ace; deuce *noun* a face. Rhyming slang; dated and rare *UK, 1925*

deuce-and-a-half *noun* a two-and-a-half ton cargo truck. Military usage since World War 2 *US, 1944*

deuce-and-a-quarter *noun* a Buick Electra 225 *US, 1968*

deuce bag; deuce *noun* a two-dollar bag of heroin *US, 1971*

deuceburger *noun* a prison sentence of two years *US, 1990*

deuced *adjective* damned; confounded. Dated, but occasionally used with heavy irony *UK, 1782*

deuce-deal *verb* to deal the second card in a deck *US, 1965*

deuce-deuce *noun* a .22 calibre weapon *US, 1990*

deuce-deuce-five *noun* a Buick Electra 225 *US, 1993*

deuce-five *noun* a .25 calibre gun *US, 2003*

deuce gear *noun* a soldier's rucksack and other items carried in the field *US, 1991*

deuce out *verb* to withdraw from a situation out of fear *US, 1949*

deuce-point *noun* in a field patrol, the second soldier in line *US, 1991*

deuces *noun* **1** dice that have been altered to have two twos, the second two being where one would expect to find a five. Used in combination with FIVES, likely to produce a seven, an important number in craps *US, 1974*. **2** a double line *US, 1990*. ▶ **deuces are in** in firefighter usage, pay cheques are prepared and ready to be distributed. From a gong signal of 2–2-2 *US, 1954*

deuce up *verb* to line up in pairs *US, 1990*

deuceway *noun* an amount of marijuana costing two dollars *US, 1979*

devil *noun* **1** a barbiturate or other central nervous system depressant, especially Seconal™. A truncated form of RED DEVIL *US, 1969*. **2** the hallucinogen STP *US, 1971*. **3** a printer's apprentice or errand boy *UK, 1683*. **4** a white person *US, 1980*. **5** in craps, a seven *US, 1993*. ▶ **devil me arse!** used as an expletive. Of Anglo-Irish origins *UK, 1984*. ▶ **devil of a** an extreme (originally diabolical) example of something. May be used with 'a' or 'the' *UK, 1767*. ▶ **devil take him!; devil take you!; devil take me!; devil take it!** used for expressing anger, impatience, frustration. Often used with 'the' *UK, 1548*. ▶ **go to the devil** to fall into ruin. From about 1460, although it is recorded in Latin more than a hundred years earlier *UK, 1460*. ▶ **go to the devil!** used as an angry expression of dismissal. If not an exclamation, certainly imperative *UK, 1859*. ▶ **how the devil!; what the devil!; where the devil!; who the devil!; why the devil!** used as an impatient intensification of how, what, when, where, who, why. In early uses 'the Devil' was capitalised. 'What the devil' since about 1385. 'When the devil' since 1562. 'Where the devil', 1687. 'Who the devil', 1568. 'Why the devil', 1819 *UK, 1385*. ▶ **little devil; young devil** used as a form of address. Often in tones of exasperation to, for instance, a wilful child; conspiratorial or playful to a (mischievous) adult *UK, 1931*. ▶ **the devil is rolling his oats** it is thundering *CANADA, 1998*. ▶ **the devil made me do it!** used as a humorous excuse for misconduct. A catchphrase made wildly popular by comedian Flip Wilson on *The Flip Wilson Show* (NBC, 1970–74). Repeated with referential humour *US, 1970*. ▶ **the devil to pay; the devil and all to pay; the very devil to pay** very unpleasant consequences to face up to. An echo of Faust *UK, 1733*

devil and demon; devil *noun* semen. Rhyming slang *UK, 2003*

devil bridle *noun* spittle dried around the mouth *TRINIDAD AND TOBAGO, 1951*

devil dancing hour *noun* very late at night *TRINIDAD AND TOBAGO, 1971*

devil devil *adjective* (used of rough country) country broken up into holes and hillocks. From Aboriginal pidgin for an 'evil spirit' *AUSTRALIA, 1844*

devil-dog *noun* a member of the US Marine Corps *US, 1918*

devil drug *noun* crack cocaine *UK, 2003*

devilfish *noun* in poker, a skilled player who plays poorly to mask his skill early in a game *US, 1996*

Devil's Asshole *nickname* an area in the Mekong Delta south of Sa Dec with a strong Viet Cong presence *US, 1990*

devil's bedpost *noun* in a deck of playing cards, the four of clubs *UK, 1837*

devil's dancing rock *noun* a large, smooth, flat stone found in a pasture or meadow *US, 1963*

devil's dandruff *noun* cocaine; crack cocaine. A simile for an 'evil white powder' *US, 1981*

devil's dick *noun* a crack cocaine pipe *US, 1992*

devil's dust *noun* **1** crack cocaine *US, 1994*. **2** phencyclidine, the recreational drug known as PCP or angel dust *US, 1992*

devil's half acre *noun* a neighbourhood catering to vice *US, 1959*

devil's herb *noun* hashish (cannabis resin or pollen) *UK, 1994*

devil's luck; devil's own luck *noun* unusually good luck; occasionally, bad luck *UK, 1891*

devil snatcher *noun* larva of the dragon fly *CANADA, 1955*

devil's own *adjective* devilish; troublesome; difficult *UK, 1729*

devil's smoke *noun* crack cocaine *US, 1994*

devil's tar *noun* oil *US, 1949*

devil weed *noun* **1** stramonium, a narcotic herb. A plant that can be eaten or smoked for drug intoxication and hallucinogenic effect, and is sometimes mistaken for marijuana. It is variously known as known as 'jimson weed' (corrupted from Jamestown weed), 'yerba del diablo' (devil's herb), 'devil's apple' and 'thorn apple' (from the appearance of the fruit), 'angel's trumpet' and 'Gabriel's trumpet' (the flower). Native to south-western US, Mexico, Central America, India and Asia; an occasional weed in Britain *US, 2001*. **2** marijuana. Ironic, mocking those who condemn marijuana *US, 1985*

devo *noun* a deviant *AUSTRALIA, 1990*

dew *noun* **1** marijuana; hashish *US, 1971*. **2** rum that has been manufactured illegally *TRINIDAD AND TOBAGO, 2003*. ▶ **knock the dew off the lily; shake the dew off the lily** (of a male) to urinate *US, 1974*

dewbaby *noun* a dark-skinned black male *US, 1972*

dew drop *noun* a drop of clear nasal fluid or mucus that hangs from the tip of the nose *UK, 1984*

Dewey *noun* a socially inept social outcast *US, 1988*

dewey; dooe; dooey; duey *noun* two. From Italian *due* via parleyaree into polari *UK, 1937*

DEWLINE *noun* the network of radar stations and airstrips for interceptor aircraft across Canada's North. An abbreviation of 'Distant Early Warning Line' *CANADA, 1957*

dex *noun* **1** Dexedrine™, a central nervous system stimulant *US, 1961*. **2** dextromethorphan (DXM), an active ingredient in non-prescription cold and cough medication, often abused for non-medicinal purposes *US, 2003*. **3** MDMA, the recreational drug best known as ecstasy. From DECADENCE (MDMA) *UK, 2003* ▷*see:* **ECSTASY**

dexedrine *noun* MDMA, the recreational drug best known as ecstasy. An elaboration of DEX (MDMA) based on Dexedrine™, a branded amphetamine *UK, 2003* ▷*see gloss at:* **ECSTASY**

dexie; dexi; dexo *noun* Dexedrine™, a central nervous system stimulant *US, 1951*

dexter *noun* a diligent, socially inept student *US, 1985*

DFA *noun* describes an imaginary effect employed in the recording industry. An initialism of 'does fuck all' *UK, 2005*

DFFL *dope forever, forever loaded* – a slogan of the Hell's Angels motorcycle gang that enjoyed somewhat wider popularity *US, 1966*

D for dunce; deefer *noun* money, profits, extras, undeclared income. Rhyming slang for BUNCE *UK, 1992*

DFP *noun* in pornography, a scene in a film or a photography showing two men ejaculating on a woman's face; a *double facial pop US, 1995*

DFs *noun* DF118s, painkillers manufactured from synthetic opium, used recreationally *UK, 1996*

DH used as an exhortation while drinking. An abbreviation of 'down the hatch!' *NEW ZEALAND, 1998*

dhobi; dhobie; dohbie *noun* **1** a native Indian washerman. From Hindi *dhobi* or *dhoby* (a member of the 'Scheduled Castes' born to wash and press clothes) *INDIA, 1816*. **2** laundry, washing. From the verb sense; originally a military usage *UK, 2002*

dhobi; dhobie; dohbie *verb* to wash (your clothes). From Hindustani *dhob* (washing); originally a nautical usage, then general in all military services *UK, 1929*

dhobi dust *noun* any washing powder. Military; extended from DHOBI (laundry) *UK, 1984*

dhobi mark *noun* a small laundry mark. Anglo-Indian *INDIA, 2003*

dhobi's itch *noun* a ring-worm infection of the armpit and groin in areas of high humidity or temperature. This 'itch' appears to derive not from DHOBI (the washerman) but from DHOBI (the laundry) as the condition was thought to spread via underwear which had been washed together *UK, 1890*

dhobi wallah *noun* a native washerman serving the military. Of Anglo-Indian military origin. An extension of DHOBI (a washerman), possibly a combination of DHOBI (laundry) and 'wallah' (a man – in relation to his occupation) *INDIA, 1937*

diablo *noun* LSD. The Spanish for 'devil' *UK, 2003*

diabolical *adjective* disgraceful. 'Possessed by the devil' in a weakened sense *UK, 1958*

dial *noun* the face *US, 1842*

dial *verb* **1** in a prayer group, to pray first. Not much language used by the religious qualifies as slang, but this certainly does *US, 1990*. **2** in foot-propelled scootering, to get a trick right *UK, 2000*. ▶ **dial a traf** to fart. When the spelling of each word is reversed the sense is revealed: 'laid a fart' *US, 1998*

DIAL *adjective* dumb in any language. Said of truly incommunicative hospital patients *US, 1994*

dial-a-winner *noun* a Dodge push-button automatic transmission *US, 1968*

dialed in *adjective* **1** in a state of concentration that excludes any and all distractions. Punning on 'connected'. May be reduced to its first element *US, 1995*. **2** belonging to the inner circle *US, 1997*

dialer *noun* a telephone that when called automatically calls another telephone number *US, 1976*

dial in on *verb* to understand what motivates someone else; to grasp their personality *US, 1997*

dial out *verb* to ignore *US, 1967*

dialtone *noun* a personality-free person *US, 1990*

diamaid *noun* in a deck of playing cards, a diamond *TRINIDAD AND TOBAGO, 2003*

diambista *noun* marijuana *US, 1954*

diamond *noun* **1** anything that is considered as the best, especially as an assement of personal qualities *UK, 1990*. **2** an amphetamine tablet scored with a diamond-shape *UK, 2003*. **3** a tablet of MDMA, the recreational drug best known as ecstasy *UK, 2003*. **4** a custom diamond-shaped car window *US, 1980*

Diamond *noun* the central square of an Irish town *IRELAND, 1992*

diamond *adjective* excellent *UK, 1990*

diamond cutter *noun* the erect penis. A later variation on the penis as a type of tool *US, 1975*

diamond dust *noun* crystallized ice in the air *ANTARCTICA, 1958*

diamonds *noun* **1** a type of bet in an illegal numbers game lottery *US, 1957*. **2** the testicles. An evolution from the common FAMILY JEWELS *US, 1964*

diamond season *noun* warm weather *US, 1987*

Diamond Street *nickname* 47th Street just west of Fifth Avenue, New York. Home to many diamond merchants *US, 1982*

diamond white *noun* a white Cadillac *US, 1998*

Diana Dors *noun* knickers, drawers. Rhyming slang, formed on the professional name of 'Blonde Bombshell' actress Diana Fluck, 1931–84. A humorous reference to women's underwear, perhaps by contrast with the enhanced and marketed sexuality that was Diana Dors *UK, 1992*

diaper *noun* **1** a sanitary towel *US, 1980*. **2** any winter covering on the front of a truck *US, 1971*. **3** a rubber insulating blanket used in overhead electric line work *US, 1980*

diaper dandy *noun* an athlete in his first year of college. Coined or popularised by sports announcer Dick Vitale *US, 1993*

diapers *noun* a flotation coat with between-the-legs button flaps issued by the National Science Foundation in Antarctica *ANTARCTICA, 1991*

diazzy *noun* a diazepam tablet *UK, 2001*

dibbi dibbi *adjective* stupid; worthless; insignificant *UK, 1994*

dibble *noun* an encounter with the police; the police; a police officer. Appeared in this sense during the 1990s; after Officer Dibble, the police character in cult television cartoon series *Top Cat*, Hanna Barbera, 1961 *UK, 1994*

dibbler *noun* the penis *US, 1998*

dibbly-dobbler *noun* an accurate, medium-pace cricket bowler; such a cricketer's delivery *UK, 1997*

dib-dabs *noun* a condition of anxiety, uneasiness, nervousness. A variation of 'abdabs' reported by Commander C. Parsons, 1984 *UK, 1984*

dibs *noun* **1** first right to, first claim on. Among the earliest slang a child in the US learns; derives from 'dib' (a portion or a share) which was first recorded in the UK in 1889 *US, 1932*. **2** money *UK, 1807*. **3** a living *US, 1949*. **4** a room, apartment or house *US, 1993*

dibs and dabs *noun* **1** small amounts *US, 1960*. **2** pubic lice. Rhyming slang for CRABS *UK, 1961*

dic; dick *noun* a dictionary. It has been suggested that this term was coined by, or within the family of, Scottish philologist and first lexicographer of the *Oxford English Dictionary*, Sir James Murray, 1837–1915; it would be nice if it were true. 'Dick', in the sense that someone who uses fine words is said to have 'swallowed the dick', is recorded in 1873 *US, 1831*

dice *noun* **1** in motor racing, a duel between two cars within the field of competitors *US, 1962*. **2** crack cocaine *UK, 2003*. **3** Desoxyn™, a branded methamphetamine hydrochloride *US, 1977*. ▶ **dice on the floor, seven at the door** used in casino gambling to express the superstitious gambler's belief that if the dice leave the table and land on the floor during a game of craps, the next roll will be a seven *US, 1974*

dice *verb* **1** to disparage or insult effectively *US, 1993*. **2** to reject, to throw away. The probable derivation is from conventional 'dice' (to lose or throw away) *AUSTRALIA, 1944*. **3** to throw away; reject; discard *AUSTRALIA, 1943*

dice bite *noun* a wound on the hand of a gambler in casino craps when struck by tossed dice *US, 1983*

dice mob *noun* a group of two or more cheats in a dice game *US, 1961*

dicer *noun* **1** a hat *US, 1887*. **2** a fast freight train *US, 1927*. **3** a 'duel' between two drivers. Car racing drivers and commentators' use *UK, 1984*

dice with death *verb* to risk actual death or figurative demise *UK, 1941*

dicey; dicy *adjective* risky, uncertain *UK, 1944*

dicey on the ubble *adjective* balding. Used by Teddy Boys *UK, 1958*

dick *noun* **1** the penis *US, 1888*. **2** the clitoris *US, 1964*. **3** a man *US, 1914*. **4** sex with a man *US, 1956*. **5** a police officer, especially a detective; a private detective *US, 1886*. **6** a despicable person. Losing its taboo in the US, but still chancy. *US, 1966*. **7** a fool *UK, 1553*. **8** nothing, zero *UK, 1925*. **9** a look, a glance. A variation of DECKO; DEKKO *UK, 1979*. **10** during the Vietnam war, the enemy. From the Vietnamese *dich* (enemy) *US, 1991* ▷*see:* DIC. ▶ **cut dicks; talk dicks** to speak clearly and with an affected English accent *VIRGIN ISLANDS, BRITISH, 1973*. ▶ **get your dick tender** to have an emotional need to be with a woman at all times *US, 1972*. ▶ **had the dick** to be ruined *AUSTRALIA, 1971*. ▶ **it's just a dick thing** used as a humorous excuse for typical male behaviour. A catchphrase from the film *Mo' Better Blues US, 1991*. ▶ **put dick** (from the male point of view) to have sex *US, 1973*

dick *verb* **1** to exploit; to take advantage of; to harm. In the 1968 US presidential election, the bumper sticker 'Dick Nixon Before Nixon Dicks You' raised eyebrows *US, 1964*. **2** (from the male point of view) to have sex with *US, 1942*. **3** to look. A variation of DECKO; DEKKO *UK, 1979*. ▶ **have your dick sucked** to be fawned upon; to be flattered *UK, 1993*

Dick & 'Arry *noun* a dictionary *UK, 1992*

dick all *noun* nothing, nothing at all *UK, 2005*

dick around *verb* **1** to behave in a sexually promiscuous fashion *US, 1969*. **2** to make a mess of, to inconvenience *US, 2002*. **3** to pass time idly *US, 1947*

dickbrain *noun* a fool *US, 1971*

dick-breath *noun* used as a term of abuse *US, 1972*

dick cheese *noun* smegma *CANADA, 2002*

dick daks *noun* a pair of men's close-fitting and revealing nylon swimming trunks. From DICK (the penis) and DAKS (shorts) *AUSTRALIA, 2003*

dick-dip *noun* sex *US, 1967*

dick doc *noun* **1** a urologist *US, 1994*. **2** a military doctor or medic who inspects male recruits for signs of sexually transmitted disease *US, 1964*

Dick Emery *noun* memory. Rhyming slang, formed on the name of a British comedian and comedy actor, 1917–83 *UK, 1992*

dickel!; dickin!; dickon! used to express disgust or disbelief. Perhaps from DICKENS! *AUSTRALIA, 1894*

dickens! used as an interjectional expletive to express surprise, impatience, etc, generally combined with how, what, where, etc. Euphemistic for 'the devil' *UK, 1598*

dicker *noun* **1** a look-out, a scout *UK: NORTHERN IRELAND, 1995*. **2** a dictionary. By application of the Oxford -ER *UK, 1937*

dickeroo *noun* a police officer *US, 1945*

dickey *noun* (of clothing, in the Canadian north) a top covering. The word comes from Eskimo *attike* (a covering) *CANADA, 1952*

dickey *adjective* **1** of plans or things, tricky, risky, 'dicey'. Also spelt 'dischy' *UK, 1984*. **2** foolish *NEW ZEALAND, 1998* ▷*see:* UNCLE DICK

dickey-bird *noun* **1** in oil drilling, a loud squeak caused by poorly lubricated equipment *US, 1954*. **2** the penis. An elaboration of DICKY in schoolboy use *CANADA, 1968*

dickey-dido *noun* the external female genital parts. Originally recorded (1887) as a word for 'a fool'; this sense survives in the bawdy song 'The Mayor of Bayswater' (to the tune of 'The Ash Grove'): 'One black one, one white one / And one with a lump of shite on, / The hairs on her dickey-dido hang down to her knees' *UK, 1984*

dick-eye *noun* used as an offensive term of address between males *UK, 2003*

dickface *noun* a contemptible fool *US, 1975*

dick-fingered *adjective* clumsy *US, 1984*

dick flick *noun* an action-oriented film that appeals to a male audience. An opposite and equal reaction to CHICK FLICK *US, 2001*

dickhead *noun* an inept, unlikeable person; an idiot. A satisfying embellishment of DICK (the penis). As a term of abuse this is often accompanied by, or even replaced with, a mime of the masturbation of a flaccid penis, gesturally sited in the centre of the forehead *US, 1964*

dickheaded *adjective* foolish *AUSTRALIA, 1981*

dickie *noun* the penis. Children's vocabulary *US, 1962*

dickie wacker *noun* a disrespectful teenage boy who shows off *AUSTRALIA, 1985*

dickjoke *noun* any coarse joke *US, 1991*

dickless *noun* a female police officer or detective. A shortened form of DICKLESS TRACY that plays on two meanings of dick – 'penis' and 'detective' *US, 1984*

dickless *adjective* used of men to intensify general abuse. Literally: 'without a DICK' (a penis) *US, 1984*

dickless Tracy *noun* a female police officer. A neat pun on DICK (the penis) and the popular comic book hero-detective Dick Tracy created by Chester Gould in 1931; a contemptuous suggestion that a female cannot be as effective as a male *US, 1963*

dickless wonder *noun* a person of either sex who lacks courage or conviction *US, 1997*

dick-lick *noun* used as a term of abuse *US, 1984*

dicklicker *noun* **1** a cocksucker in all its senses *US, 1968*. **2** a greyhound racing enthusiast. Used by horse racing enthusiasts *AUSTRALIA, 1989*

dicklicking *adjective* despicable *US, 1978*

dick mittens *noun* hands that were not washed after urination *US, 2001*

dicknose *noun* used as a term of abuse *US, 1974*

dick off *verb* to waste time, to idle, to shun work *US, 1947*

dickory dock *noun* **1** the penis. Rhyming slang for COCK (the penis), not an elaboration of DICK *UK, 1961*. **2** a clock. Rhyming slang, based on the nursery rhyme 'Hickory dickory dock / A mouse ran up the clock' *UK, 1961*

dick partition *noun* a condom. Combines DICK (the penis) with a barrier *UK, 1998*

dick pointers *noun* a pair of men's close-fitting and revealing nylon swimming trunks *AUSTRALIA, 2003*

dick pokers *noun* a pair of men's close-fitting and revealing nylon swimming trunks *AUSTRALIA, 2003*

dickrash *noun* an annoying or despicable person; a jerk *AUSTRALIA, 1996*

Dick's hatband *noun* used in comparisons, especially as the epitome of tightness *UK, 1781*

Dick Shot Off *noun* the *Distinguished Service Order*, (a medal for bravery). Punning on DICK (the penis) *UK, 1937*

dick-skinner *noun* the hand *US, 1971*

dick-smacker *noun* a prison guard. Not kind *US, 1984*

dicksmith *noun* a US Navy hospital corpsman *US, 1974*

Dick Smith *noun* a drug user or addict who does not socialise with other users *US, 1876*

dickson! ▷ *see:* DICKEN

dicksplash *noun* an awkward or inept person, a fool *UK, 2003*

dick-stepper *noun* a clumsy oaf *US, 1983*

dick stickers *noun* a pair of men's close-fitting and revealing nylon swimming trunks *AUSTRALIA, 1996*

dick-string *noun* a male's ability to achieve an erection *US, 1965*

dick sucker *noun* a homosexual male *US, 1995*

dicksucking *noun* oral sex performed on man *US, 1977*

dick-sucking *adjective* despicable *US, 1972*

dickswinging *adjective* used of an obviously arrogant person (regardless of gender). Office jargon that reflects the macho nature of the workplace *UK, 2005*

dicktease *noun* a woman who creates the impression of being more sexually available than she is. A variant of the more common PRICK-TEASER *US, 1989*

dick teaser *noun* a girl who suggests that she will engage in sex but will not *US, 1962*

Dick the Shit *nickname* Shakespeare's *Richard III*. A play on 'Richard the turd' in theatrical slang *UK, 1985*

dick togs *noun* a pair of men's close-fitting and revealing nylon swimming trunks. From DICK (the penis) and TOGS (a swimming costume) *AUSTRALIA, 2003*

Dick Turpin *noun* thirteen. Rhyming slang, used by dart players; formed on the name of the infamous highwayman, born in 1706, hanged in 1739 *UK, 1937*

dickwad *noun* an unlikeable or despicable person *US, 1989*

dick-waver; dicky-waver *noun* a male exhibitionist *US, 1973*

dickweed *noun* a despicable, dim-witted person *US, 1980*

dickwhacker *noun* a fool *NEW ZEALAND, 2002*

dick-whipped; dick-whupped *adjective* dominated by a man. Formed as an antonym for PUSSY-WHIPPED (dominated by a woman) *US, 1998*

dickwipe *noun* a despicable person *US, 1992*

dickwit *noun* an idiot, a contemptible fool *UK, 2001*

dicky *noun* **1** the penis. An extension of DICK *UK, 1891*. **2** a windscreen on a motorcycle *UK, 1979*

dicky *adjective* **1** inferior; in poor condition or health; insecure; having an odd quality *UK, 1959*. **2** idiotic or annoying; appearing silly. That is, of, or befitting, a DICK(HEAD) *NEW ZEALAND, 1982* ▷ *see:* DICKEY

dickybird *noun* **1** a little bird. Childish. As in the traditional nursery rhyme, 'Two little dicky-birds sitting on a wall, / One named Peter, one named Paul' *UK, 1781*. **2** a word; hence, a thing of little value, the smallest thing. Rhyming slang; most often given in full and usually in the negative context, 'not say a word', hence the second part of

this sense. In the theatre, 'dickies' are an actor's script, 'the words' *UK, 1932*. ▶ **not a dickybird** nothing *UK, 1975*

dicky diddle; diddle *noun* urination. Rhyming slang for PIDDLE; used by juveniles, perhaps playing on DICKY (the penis) *UK, 1961*

dicky dirt; dicky *noun* a shirt. Rhyming slang; also note conventional 'dicky' (a detachable shirt front, since 1811), in turn influenced by obsolete slang 'dicky' (a dirty shirt, 1781) *AUSTRALIA, 1905*

dicky-dunking *noun* sex from the male perspective *US, 1994*

dicty *noun* a snob *US, 1928*

dicty *adjective* **1** excellent *US, 1947*. **2** arrogant, haughty. Also Spelt 'dichty' *US, 1923*

did *noun* a capsule of Dilaudid™, a pharmaceutical narcotic *US, 1986*

di-da, di-da, di-da used to extend an explanation or complaint, especially when reporting an instance thereof. Usually mocking; but also as an alternative to BLAH BLAH. When used by lyricists of pop songs it tends to have no meaning whatsoever *UK, 1940*

diddish *adjective* used to describe anything associated with traditional travellers, especially with regard to degrading or denigratory treatment. Used by late-1980s – early 90s counterculture travellers *UK, 1999*

diddle *noun* **1** an act of masturbation. From conventional 'diddle' (to jerk from side to side) *US, 2001*. **2** a swindle, a deception *UK, 1803*. **3** gin *UK, 2003*. ▶ **on the diddle** engaged in swindling. From DIDDLE (a deception), on the model of ON THE FIDDLE (engaged in a swindle) *UK, 2001*

diddle *verb* **1** (from the male perspective) to have sex *US, 1870*. **2** to masturbate *US, 1934*. **3** to swindle *UK, 1806*. **4** to cheat *US, 1972*. **5** in computing, to make a minor change *US, 1983*. **6** in computing, to work half-heartedly *US, 1991*. ▶ **diddled by the dirty digit of destiny** adversely affected by fate *US, 1977*

diddler *noun* **1** the penis *US, 1969*. **2** a child molester *US, 1976*

diddling *noun* petty cheating, sharp practice, trivial swindling, chronic borrowing *UK, 1849*

diddling Miss Daisy *noun* an act of female masturbation. After the 1989 film *Driving Miss Daisy UK, 2004*

diddly *noun* anything at all. An abbreviation of DIDDLY-SHIT *US, 1964*

diddlybopper; diddybopper; dittybopper; diddley bop; diddy bop *noun* a street thug *US, 1958*

diddly-dick *noun* nothing at all *US, 1972*

diddly-dum *adjective* fine, good *UK, 1976*

diddly-shit; diddly-squat *noun* anything or nothing at all *US, 1955*

diddums *noun* **1** used by adults for soothing and consoling babies and very young children; hence, a childish endearment *UK, 1893*. **2** used for offering heavily sarcastic mock-sympathy to an adult or older child and deride childish behaviour or for suggesting that such behaviour or attitude is childish. Adapted from the nonsense endearment used to soothe very young children. This nonsense is expandable: 'diddums doodums dumpling den' *UK, 1893*

diddy *noun* **1** a toilet. Perhaps originally a fanciful term used when speaking with small children. Also variant 'didee' *AUSTRALIA, 1958*. **2** the female breast or nipple. Recorded in use in Glasgow and Australia *UK, 1991*. **3** a fool; used as a mild insult. Glasgow slang, from the previous sense, and therefore a TIT *UK, 1985*. **4** a gypsy. A familiar diminutive of DIDICOI in all its variant spellings. Can be further reduced to 'did' *UK, 1953*

diddy *adjective* small. Usage popularised by Liverpool comedian Ken Dodd (b.1927) *UK, 1965*

diddy around; diddy about *verb* to fool around. From DIDDY (a fool) *UK; SCOTLAND, 1985*

diddy bag; ditty bag *noun* a small bag issued to soldiers for carrying their personal effects *US, 1947*

diddy bop *verb* to take part in gang fights *US, 1955*

diddybopper *noun* a racially ambitious black person who rejects black culture and embraces the dominant white culture *US, 1980* ▷ *see:* DIDDLYBOPPER

diddy-dum slinger *noun* a radar operator *US, 1947*

Diddys *noun* in the entertainment industry, *per diems*. A back formation, from *per diem* to the initials PD to the initials of rap singer P Diddy *US, 2004*

didee *noun* a water-closet. Generally used with 'the' *AUSTRALIA, 1967*

didge *noun* price or cost. A corruption of 'digits' *US, 1984*

didgy *noun* a dustbin. Glasgow slang *UK: SCOTLAND, 1985*

didgy *adjective* **1** nervous, unsettled. Possibly from EDGY (nerves on edge) *UK, 1999*. **2** digital *UK: SCOTLAND, 1985*

didi; dee-dee *verb* to leave. From the Vietnamese word *di* (goodbye) adapted by US soldiers during the war and made into a verb *US, 1964*

didicoi; diddicoi *noun* gypsy; Romany; half-breed gypsy *UK, 1853*

didj; didg *noun* a didjeridoo (an Australian Aboriginal instrument) *AUSTRALIA, 1919*

didn't oughter *noun* a daughter. Rhyming slang *UK, 1977*

dido *noun* **1** mischief, a prank *US, 1807*. **2** a petty complaint filed against a police officer by a superior *US, 1958*

did you ever?; did you ever! would you believe it! *UK, 1817*

die *verb* **1** to want something very much *UK, 1709*. **2** in roller derby, to fall after an extended and dramatic fight *US, 1999*. ▶ **die for a tie** used as a humorous sobriquet for General MacArthur's prediction that the war in Korea would end in a stalemate unless he were given approval to attack China *US, 1976*. ▶ **die in the arse; die in the bum** to fail completely *AUSTRALIA, 1976*. ▶ **die on the law** on the railways, to work the maximum allowed by the Hours of Service Act *US, 1990*. ▶ **die on your arse** of a comedian, to fail to entertain *UK, 2004*. ▶ **die the death** of an entertainer, especially a comedian, to meet with a complete lack of response from an audience *UK, 1984*. ▶ **die with your boots on** to die while in action *US, 1874*. ▶ **to die for** spectacular, wonderful *US, 1983*

die; dye *noun* a diazepam (trade name Valium™) tablet, used as an anti-anxiety agent *US, 1986*

die before me! used for acknowledging that someone has said exactly what you said at the same time *TRINIDAD AND TOBAGO, 1987*

Diefenbaker meat *noun* canned meat distributed to the poor during the years John Diefenbaker was prime minister (late 1950s-mid 60s) *CANADA, 1987*

Diefenbunker *noun* the secure fallout shelter for high Canadian government officials to use in case of national disaster *CANADA, 1995*

diener *noun* ▷*see:* DEANER

die on the floor, seven at the door; on the floor, hit the door in casino craps, used as a prediction that the next roll after a dice has bounced onto the floor will be a seven *US, 1983*

dies *noun* tablets of diazepam, an anti-anxiety agent with central nervous system depressant properties *US, 1997*

diesel *noun* **1** an aggressive, 'manly' lesbian. An abbreviation of DIESEL DYKE *US, 1959*. **2** a man with a great physique *US, 1993*. **3** prison tea. Probably suggestive of the taste or appearance *UK, 1996*. **4** heroin *UK, 1996*

diesel *adjective* projecting an aggressive and tough image. Originally applied to a lesbian type, the DIESEL DYKE, then to a broader field *US, 1995*

diesel digits *noun* channel 19 on a citizens' band radio, favoured by truckers *US, 1976*

diesel dork *noun* a large penis *US, 1994*

diesel dyke; diesel dike *noun* a strong, forceful, aggressive lesbian *US, 1959*

diesel fitter; diesel *noun* bitter (beer). Rhyming slang *UK, 1992*

diesel therapy *noun* the repeated transfer of a troublesome prisoner from prison to prison *US, 1996*

dieso *noun* a diesel mechanic. An Australian addition to the slang of the South Pole *ANTARCTICA, 1967*

diet pill *noun* an amphetamine tablet. From the drug's association with weight-loss *US, 1972*

diff *noun* **1** difference *US, 1896*. **2** a differential in a motor vehicle *AUSTRALIA, 1941*

diffabitterance *noun* used as a humorous replacement for 'bit of difference' *US, 1921*

difference *noun* **1** notice. Jocular; usually phrased as 'no-one took a blind bit of difference' *UK, 2001*. **2** any weapon used in a fight or crime *US, 1950*

different *adjective* out of the ordinary, special, unusual, recherché *UK, 1912*. ▶ **different strokes for different folks** different things please different people. Singer Syleena 'Syl' Johnson released the song 'Different Strokes' (J. Cameron and J. Zachary) with this line in it in 1967; Sly and the Family Stone's 1968 mega-hit 'Everyday People' put the phrase on the map *US, 1966*

differs *noun* difference. Anglo-Irish *UK, 1959*

diffy *noun* a car or truck's differential *NEW ZEALAND, 1956*

dig *noun* **1** a punch, a blow. Extends the conventional sense of 'poke' *UK, 2001*. **2** a jibe, an insult, a taunt *UK, 1849*. **3** an Australian or New Zealand soldier of either world war. An abbreviation of DIGGER. Commonly used as form of address to such a soldier. Later also a friendly form of address to any man, and now generally only used to men of an age to have fought in a world war *AUSTRALIA, 1916*. **4** a form of male address. A shortening of DIGGER *AUSTRALIA, 1916*. **5** an archaeological excavation, an archaeological expedition *UK, 1896*. **6** in cricket, an innings *AUSTRALIA, 1966*. **7** an injection of a drug *UK, 2000*. **8** in volleyball, contact with the ball below the waist *US, 1972*. **9** a fisherman's stretch or 'area' of water *AUSTRALIA, 1963*. **10** a drag racing event *US, 1993* ▷*see:* DIG IN THE GRAVE

dig *verb* **1** to like, to appreciate *US, 1950*. **2** to understand *US, 1934*. **3** to bother, to concern *AUSTRALIA, 1958*. **4** to inject a drug intravenously, especially heroin *UK, 1996*. **5** in handball, to hit a low ball before it strikes the floor *US, 1970*. **6** in surfing, to paddle energetically *US, 1963*. ▶ **dig a drape** to buy a new dress. Teen slang, reported by a Toronto newspaper in 1946 *CANADA, 1946*. ▶ **dig for gold** to pick your nose *US, 2003*. ▶ **dig horrors** to be suffering; to live with trouble *GRENADA, 1975*. ▶ **dig out your eye** to swindle; to cheat *TRINIDAD AND TOBAGO, 1935*. ▶ **dig the man a neat ditch** in oil drilling, to perform any job well *US, 1954*. ▶ **dig with the left foot** be a Catholic *IRELAND, 1951*. ▶ **dig with the right foot** to be of the same religious persuasion, in Northern Ireland a Protestant *UK: NORTHERN IRELAND, 1997*. ▶ **dig with the wrong foot** to be a Catholic *CANADA, 1968*

dig-away *noun* a festering sore *TRINIDAD AND TOBAGO, 1989*

Digby chicken *noun* a smoked, salted small herring. Digby is a fishing port on the west (Fundy) shore of Nova Scotia *CANADA, 1995*

dig down *verb* to demolish *BARBADOS, 1965*

digger *noun* **1** a goldminer *AUSTRALIA, 1849*. **2** an Australian or New Zealand soldier of either world war. Also extended to soldiers fighting in other military conflicts such as the Korean and Vietnam wars. Originally applied only to infantry soldiers of World War 1 who spent much time digging and maintaining trenches. A term of high approbation *AUSTRALIA, 1916*. **3** by extension, a term of male address *AUSTRALIA, 1920*. **4** an undertaker *US, 1945*. **5** a person who buys a large number of tickets to a popular entertainment and resells the tickets to a broker *US, 1927*. **6** a member of the Digger hippie counterculture support-network. Named for a mid-C17 English sect that practised agrarian communism *US, 1966*. **7** a pickpocket, especially a clumsy one *US, 1931*. **8** a face-first fall *US, 1993*. **9** a solitary confinement cell *US, 1992*. **10** a drag racing car *US, 1993*. **11** the grade 'D' *US, 1968*

diggety used in various combinations for expressing surprise or pleasure *US, 1928*

diggidy *noun* marijuana *UK, 2001*

digging for worms *noun* varicose vein surgery. Medical slang, obvious imagery *UK, 2002*

diggings *noun* lodgings *US, 1837*

diggity *noun* heroin *UK, 2003*

diggys *noun* digital scales *UK, 1999*

dig in *verb* **1** to eat heartily *UK, 1912*. **2** from a standstill, to accelerate a car suddenly, making the tyres squeal on the road *US, 1951*

dig in the grave; dig *noun* a shave. Rhyming slang *AUSTRALIA, 1931*

digit *noun* a number chosen as a bet in an illegal policy bank lottery *US, 1973*

digital manipulation *noun* (of a female) masturbation. A simple pun using computer technology *US, 2001*

digithead *noun* a person whose enthusiasm for mathematics or computers is never hidden *US, 1994*

digits *noun* a telephone number *US, 1995*

digits dealer *noun* an operator of an illegal numbers policy lottery *US, 1982*

dignity *noun* the vagina. A political coinage *US, 1998*

dig out *noun* help getting out of a difficult situation *IRELAND, 1995*

dig out *verb* **1** to work cheerfully and with a will; to make a real effort. Military usage *UK, 1987*. **2** to taunt, to insult *UK, 1998*. **3** in trucking, to start fast *US, 1971*

digs *noun* **1** lodgings, be it a room, flat, or house. An abbreviation of the earlier (1830s) 'diggings'. In the UK theatrical 'digs' have a long and colourful history with most venues still providing a 'digs-list' for touring players *UK, 1893*. **2** a job *US, 1973*

dig up; dig out *verb* to research and discover, or find and obtain *UK, 1611*

dig you later used as a farewell *US, 1947*

dik *adjective* **1** stupid. Derived from its literal Afrikaans sense as 'thick' *SOUTH AFRICA, 1978*. **2** tired of something or someone. Often in the expression 'to be dik of' *SOUTH AFRICA, 1986*. **3** heavy, beefy, big, fat, powerfully built. From Afrikaans *SOUTH AFRICA, 1970*

dikbek *noun* a sulky or surly person. From Afrikaans for 'thick beak' *SOUTH AFRICA, 1970*

dike *noun* stolen brass or copper sold as scrap *US, 1980* ▷*see:* DYKE

dike *verb* in computing, to remove or disable something. Derived from the sense of 'dikes' as 'diagonal cutters used in electrical work' *US, 1991*

dilberry *noun* a fool *NEW ZEALAND, 1952*

Dilbert *noun* **1** in poker, a player with a strong grasp of the mathematics and probabilities associated with the game but a poor set of playing skills *US, 1996*. **2** a blunder *US, 1944*

dilbert *verb* to disabuse an employee of work-place optimism. From the experiences of Dilbert the eponymous anti-hero of the *Dilbert* comic strip *US, 1996*

dildo *noun* a despicable, offensive or dim-witted person *US, 1960*

DILF *noun* a sexually attractive father. A gender variation of MILF (a sexually appealing mother); an acronym of 'dad I'd like to fuck' *US, 2003*

dill *noun* **1** a fool. Back-formation from DILLY (foolish) *AUSTRALIA, 1941*. **2** the penis *AUSTRALIA, 1988*

dillberries *noun* excreta that cling to anal or pubic hair. The original spelling was 'dilberries' *UK, 1811*

dill-brain *noun* a simpleton *AUSTRALIA, 1975*

dill-brained *adjective* foolish *AUSTRALIA, 1975*

dill-dock *noun* a dildo *US, 1949*

dillhole *noun* an easily disliked person *US, 1997*

dilligaf do I look like I give a fuck? Collected as police slang *US, 1999*

dill piece *noun* the penis *US, 2001*

dillpot; dillypot; dill *noun* a fool. Rhyming slang for TWOT, possibly from DILLY (silly) *AUSTRALIA, 1941*

dilly *noun* **1** an excellent or remarkable thing or person. Usually used in a sarcastic sense *US, 1908*. **2** a capsule of Dilaudid™, a synthetic morphine used by heroin addicts trying to break their habit *US, 1971*

Dilly *nickname* Piccadilly, an area of central London. The area around Piccadilly Circus was a popular location for street-walkers and polari-speaking male prostitutes *UK, 1936*

dilly *adjective* silly, foolish. Possibly from DILLPOT (a fool) or, more likely as the first recording of 'dilly' predates 'dillpot' by 35 years, simple rhyming slang *AUSTRALIA, 1905*

dilly bag *noun* a bag, generally small, for carrying odds and ends. From *dilly* a traditional Australian Aboriginal woven bag, from the Australian Aboriginal language Yagara *AUSTRALIA, 1906*

dilly-bags *adjective* much, plenty, many. An elaboration of BAGS *AUSTRALIA, 1953*

dilly boy *noun* a young male prostitute. The DILLY (Piccadilly Circus) is (perhaps was) renowned as a centre for male prostitution *UK, 1979*

dilly-dally *verb* to dawdle; hence to waste time. A reduplication of conventional 'dally' (to loiter) *UK, 1741*

dillzy *noun* the penis. A variation on 'dilly' (penis) *US, 1999*

dim *noun* the night; twilight *US, 1944*

dim *adjective* unintelligent. An antonym for the intellectually bright *UK, 1924*

dimba *noun* marijuana from west Africa. A variation of DJAMBA *UK, 1998*

dimbo *noun* ▷*see:* DIMMO

dime *noun* **1** ten dollars *US, 1958*. **2** one hundred dollars *US, 1988*. **3** one thousand dollars *US, 1974*. **4** ten years; a ten-year prison sentence *US, 1967*. **5** a pretty girl. A product of a one-to-ten scale for rating beauty, with ten being the best; thus an updated way of saying 'a ten' *US, 2002*. ▶ **on a dime** precisely, suddenly *US, 1996*

dime *verb* to betray, to inform on *US, 1970*

dime-a-dip dinner *noun* a fundraising meal *US, 1967*

dime a dozen *adjective* used of anything in very plentiful supply *US, 1930*

dime bag; dime *noun* a packet of drugs sold for ten dollars *US, 1970*

dime-dropper *noun* a police informant *US, 1966*

dimelow; dinelow; dinelo *noun* a fool, an idiot *UK, 1900*

dime-nickel *noun* a 105mm wheeled cannon capable of shooting shells at a high angle *US, 1991*

dime note *noun* a ten-dollar note *US, 1938*

dime paper *noun* ten dollars worth of a powdered drug, especially heroin *US, 1972*

dime special; dime *noun* crack cocaine *US, 1998*

dime-stacking *noun* a system of keeping track of drinks not rung up on a bar's cash register, enabling the bartender to calculate the amount that can be safely embezzled at the end of the shift *US, 1992*

dime store *noun* **1** a store selling a variety of small items *US, 1938*. **2** a small casino or gambling establishment with low-stakes games *US, 1953*

dime's worth *noun* the (variable) amount of heroin that is sufficient to cause death *UK, 2002*

dimmo; dimbo *noun* a stupid person *CANADA, 1977*

Dimmo; Dimo *noun* a Greek. From the pronunciation of '*Demo*', short for *Demosthenes*, a very common given-name among Greeks *UK, 1961*

dimp *noun* a cigarette-end. Originally military, then vagrants *UK, 1940*

dimple *noun* a dent on a car's body *US, 1997*

dimps *noun* a small amount of money, tobacco or other prison currency *UK, 1996*

dimwit *noun* a slow-witted fool. Extends from DIM (not very bright) *US, 1921*

dimwitted *adjective* stupid, slow. The quality of a DIMWIT *US, 1940*

Dinah *noun* dynamite or nitroglycerin *US, 1949*

dinarly; dinarla; dinaly; dinah; dinarlee *noun* money. Ultimately from Latin *dinarii* into Italian or Spanish, via lingua franca to parleyaree; or, pehaps Larin *dinarius*, into Persian and wider Arabic *dinar* (various coins), via gypsy; thence general Cockney usage and adoption as part of the polari vocabulary *UK, 1851*

din-din *noun* dinner; a meal. Children's vocabulary *UK, 1905*

din-dins *noun* a meal. A variation of DIN-DIN *UK, 1920*

dine *noun* dynamite *US, 1992*

dine *verb* ▶ **dine at the Y; eat at the Y** to perform oral sex on a woman. The Y is an effective pictogram for the groin of a woman *US, 1971*

dine and dash *verb* to leave a restaurant without paying your bill *US, 1997*

dine in *verb* in prison, to eat in your cell rather than communally. Hence the derivatives 'diner-in' and 'dining in' *UK, 1950*

ding *noun* **1** the penis *US, 1965*. **2** the buttocks. A shortening of DINGER *AUSTRALIA, 1957*. **3** a party, especiallly a wild party. A shortening of WINGDING *AUSTRALIA, 1956*. **4** marijuana *US, 1954*. **5** a dent, scratch, scrape or rip *US, 1945*. **6** the expenses incurred in operating a carnival concession *US, 1985*. **7** a mentally unstable person. A shortened form of DINGBAT *US, 1929*. **8** a quasi-coercive request for money *US, 1982*

Ding *noun* an Italian; a Greek *AUSTRALIA, 1940*

ding *verb* **1** to physically beat another person. This meaning is attributed by the *Oxford English Dictionary* to dialectal use in East Anglia *UK, 1688*. **2** to dent, scratch, scrape or rip *US, 1968*. **3** in circus and carnival usage, to borrow *US, 1981*. **4** to reject *US, 1965*. **5** to wound *US, 1968*. **6** to kill. Vietnam war usage *US, 1991*. **7** to name for a duty or responsibility. Military *UK, 1984*

dingage *noun* damage to a surfboard or a surf-related injury *US, 1991*

ding-a-ling *noun* **1** the penis. A pet-name; 'dangle' (penis, also conventionally 'to hang down'), compounds with the nursery word 'ding-dong' (the ringing of a bell), to give an image of testicles as bells and penis as a dangling bell-rope. Originally black usage, the success of Chuck Berry's 1972 recording of a twenty-year-old song made this term widely accessible *US, 1952*. **2** a fool *US, 1935*

ding-a-ling *adjective* foolish, crazy *US, 1959*

dingbat *noun* **1** an odd, foolish or eccentric person *US, 1879*. **2** used as a (euphemistic) replacement for any noun the user cannot or will not name. Perhaps this sense is the inspiration for the selection of symbols that comprise the Dingbats typeface *US, 1923*. **3** a daredevil motorcyclist *UK, 1979*. ▶ **go like a dingbat** go fast *UK, 1967*. ▶ **mad as a dingbat** extremely mad; very angry. A reference to *delirium tremens AUSTRALIA, 1940*

dingbats *noun delirium tremens NEW ZEALAND, 1911*

dingbats *adjective* **1** crazy, mad, delusional *AUSTRALIA, 1925*. **2** stupid, foolish *AUSTRALIA, 1950*

ding-ding *noun* a crazy person *US, 1970*

dingdong *noun* **1** the penis *US, 1944*. **2** a sing-song. Rhyming slang for 'a song' *UK, 1960*. **3** a gas-powered railway coach used on a branch line *US, 1945*. **4** a heated quarrel *UK, 1922*. **5** a party. Extended from the sense as 'a sing-song' *UK, 1936*

ding-dong *verb* to telephone *US, 1973*

ding-dong *adjective* **1** of top quality; great; terrific *AUSTRALIA, 1953*. **2** (of a fight, competition, etc) hard fought *AUSTRALIA, 1924*

ding-dong bell; ding-dong *noun* hell. Rhyming slang, used originally by World War 2 Royal Air Force *UK, 1961*

dinge *noun* **1** a black person. Derogatory, from conventional 'dingy' (dark) *US, 1848*. **2** a member of any dark-skinned race. Adopted from the US meaning 'a black person'. Note, also, that during World War 2 Royal Air Force bombing crews used 'the dinge' 'for the blackout' *UK, 1934*

dinged *adjective* concussed, in a confused mental state. Pronounced with a hard 'g'. From the conventional (if archaic) use (to hit) *UK, 1970*

dinged up *adjective* battered *AUSTRALIA, 1979*

dinge queen *noun* a white homosexual man who finds black men attractive; a black homosexual man *US, 1964*

dinger *noun* **1** the backside or anus *AUSTRALIA, 1943*. **2** an extraordinary thing or person. An abbreviation of HUMDINGER *US, 1809*. **3** a railway yardmaster *US, 1929*. **4** a sniper *US, 1972*. **5** a burglar alarm, especially an intentionally visible one *US, 1931*

dinghy *noun* **1** a motorcycle sidecar *UK, 1979*. **2** the penis *BAHAMAS, 1982*

dingle *adjective* (of weather) good *ANTARCTICA, 1989*

dingleberries *noun* **1** the female breasts *UK, 1980*. **2** the splattered molten particles near a weld *US, 1974*

dingleberry *noun* **1** a glob of dried faeces accumulated on anal hairs. Although this sense is not the earliest recorded sense of the word, it is probably the original sense *US, 1938*. **2** a despicable person *US, 1924*. **3** a military decoration *US, 1953*

dingleberry hone *noun* in car mechanics, a hone (a tool used to enlarge and smooth the inside of a hole) that uses a silicon carbide ball attached to spring-like wires that flex *US, 1993*

dinglebody *noun* a foolish, simple person *US, 1957*

dingle-dangle *noun* the penis *UK, 1937*

dinglefuzzy *noun* used in place of a person's name which has been forgotten *US, 1975*

ding list *noun* in female college students' slang, a notional list of boys whom the keeper of the list does not like *US, 1963*

dingnuts! used for registering annoyance or frustration as a euphemism for 'bollocks!'. An elaboration of NUTS! *UK, 2000*

dingo *noun* **1** a cowardly, treacherous or despicable person. From 'dingo' the Australian native dog, to which the attributes of cowardice and treachery have long been incorrectly applied by white people *AUSTRALIA, 1869*. **2** an Australian *NEW ZEALAND, 2002*. ▶ **turn dingo on** to betray someone *AUSTRALIA, 1945*

dingo *verb* **1** to behave in a treacherous or cowardly manner *AUSTRALIA, 1935*. **2** to cancel, especially to cancel a date or romantic assignation. Teen slang *UK, 2003*

dingo's breakfast *noun* an act of urination and a good look round; no breakfast at all *AUSTRALIA, 1965*

ding string *noun* a cord attached to a surfer and his surfboard. The cord has the effect of reducing damage to the board after the surfer falls off *US, 1991*

ding team *noun* a scout and sniper working together *US, 1991*

dingus *noun* **1** the penis *US, 1888*. **2** an artificial penis *US, 1957*. **3** used for identifying a thing, the correct name of which escapes the speaker or is not important in context; a gadget, a contraption *US, 1876*. **4** an eye-dropper used in makeshift drug-injection equipment *US, 1973*

ding ward *noun* a hospital ward for the mentally infirm *US, 1981*

dingy *noun* a police van *US, 1970*

dingy *adjective* eccentric, odd *US, 1907*

dink *noun* **1** a person from South Asia; especially, in later use, a Vietnamese person. Possibly Australian rhyming slang, formed on CHINK (a Chinese person). It was adopted by the US military in Vietnam in 1967 *AUSTRALIA, 1938*. **2** a partner in a relationship that can be defined as 'double (or dual) income, no kids', that is a couple with two jobs and no children; or as an adjective applied to the couple. An acronym *US, 1987*. **3** a clueless, unaware person *US, 1962*. **4** the penis *US, 1888*. **5** in volleyball, a tap of the ball after a faked hitting of the ball downward with great force *US, 1972*. **6** a lift on a bicycle or, formerly, a horse *AUSTRALIA, 1934*

dink *verb* to give someone a lift on a bicycle or, formerly, a horse. British dialect had *dink* (to dangle a baby) and this may be the origin, but it is hardly conclusive *AUSTRALIA, 1932*

dink *adjective* genuine; true; honest. Anbreviation of DINKUM *AUSTRALIA, 1980*

dink around *verb* to idle or waste time *US, 1978*

dinki-di; dinky-die *adjective* genuine. An intensified variation of DINKUM, often associated with nationalistic values *AUSTRALIA, 1918*

dinkie; dinky *noun* a partner in a relationship that can be defined as 'double (or dual) income no kids (yet)', that is a couple with two jobs and no children; also an adjective applied to the couple *US, 1986*

dinkie dow *noun* marijuana. Originally in the Vietnam war to mean 'off the wall' (crazy) – which was ascribed to marijuana, locally-grown or imported by the soldiers. The US servicemen went home in 1975 and took the word with them *US, 1968*

dinkied up *adjective* smartened up, made lively *UK, 1981*

dink pack *noun* a six-pack of beer. The word 'dink' is so close to 'dinky' that it seems to refer to the six-pack as less than a 'real' box of beer: a twelve or a two-four *CANADA, 1993*

dink tank *noun* a condom. Combines DINK (the penis) with an appropriate container *UK, 1998*

dinkum *adjective* **1** serious *AUSTRALIA, 1962*. **2** real, genuine. Originally meaning 'work', or 'an allotted amount of work', 'dinkum' comes from the Lincolnshire and Derbyshire dialects of Britain. The phrase FAIR DINKUM was recorded from north Lincolnshire in 1881 and first recorded in Australia in 1890. The conjecture that it is from Cantonese *dim kum* (real gold), said to have been introduced by Chinese miners during the gold rush (1860s), cannot be true since it fails to explain how a Chinese mining term could have made its way to the British midlands *AUSTRALIA, 1905*. **3** honest; upstanding *AUSTRALIA, 1962*

dinkum *adverb* really; truly; honestly *AUSTRALIA, 1915*

dinkum Aussie a person who embodies all those things seen as characteristically Australian *AUSTRALIA, 1920*

dinkum oil *noun* reliable information *AUSTRALIA, 1915*

dinky *noun* **1** an expensive car. Wealthy humour, based on Dinky Toys *UK, 1980*. **2** an old, dilapidated car. From the older, more common meaning (a kite) *TRINIDAD AND TOBAGO, 1986*. **3** an electric tram with controls at each end *US, 1923*. **4** a small railway engine used for yard switching *US, 1905*

dinky *adjective* **1** small, unassuming *US, 1895*. **2** neat, spruce, dainty *UK, 1788*. **3** of music, pleasant, easy-listening *UK, 1976*. **4** wildly enthusiastic, crazy *US, 1969*. **5** fair; honest *AUSTRALIA, 1941*

dinky dau *adjective* crazy. From the Vietnamese for 'off the wall'. Vietnam war usage *US, 1965*

dinky-di; dinky-die; dinki-di *adjective* real; genuine; true; honest *AUSTRALIA, 1962*

dinky dows *noun* marijuana. Vietnam war usage *US, 1992*

dinky inky *noun* in television and film-making, a low watt spotlight *US, 1990*

dinners *noun* the female breasts *US, 1953*

dinny *noun* the vagina *BAHAMAS, 1982*

dinnyhayser *noun* an excellent thing or person. From boxer Dinny Hayes *NEW ZEALAND, 1998*

dinnyhayzer *noun* a heavy punch; a knockout blow. Commemorates the pugilist Dinny Hayes *AUSTRALIA, 1907*

dinosaur *noun* **1** any person who is old or considered to be out of date, or both *US, 1970*. **2** an older heroin user *US, 2002*. **3** any computer that requires raised flooring and a dedicated power source *US, 1991*

dinosaur juice *noun* petrol, gasoline *US, 1976*

dinosaurs *noun* a type of LSD *UK, 2003*

dip *noun* **1** a pickpocket *US, 1859*. **2** a short swim *UK, 1843*. **3** a foolish person *US, 1932*. **4** diphtheria; a patient suffering from diphtheria and, therefore, classified by disease. Medical *UK, 1961*. **5** crack cocaine *US, 1994*. **6** a member of the *Dip*lomatic Service *UK, 1968*. **7** a cigarette that has been dipped in embalming fluid *UK, 2003*. **8** from a male perspective, a swift act of sexual intercourse *UK, 1976*. **9** an injection of a narcotic *US, 1959*. **10** a pinch of chewing tobacco; the chewing tobacco itself *US, 1997*. **11** a light. Hence 'dips!' (lights out!) *UK, 1947*. ► **on the dip** engaged in pickpocketing *US, 1949*

dip *verb* **1** to pick pockets *UK, 1857*. **2** to display an inappropriate interest in another prisoner's business *US, 1976*. **3** to eavesdrop *US, 1987*. **4** to fail in the commission of a crime, especially theft or robbery *AUSTRALIA, 1975*. **5** to hurry *US, 1997*. **6** to swerve through traffic on a bicycle *BERMUDA, 1985*. **7** to use chewing tobacco *US, 2001*. **8** to leave *US, 1993*. ► **dip south** to search your pockets for money *NEW ZEALAND, 2002*. ► **dip your left eye in hot cocky shit!** get stuffed! *AUSTRALIA, 1972*. ► **dip your lid** to raise one's hat as a polite gesture. Although no longer in common use since the wearing of hats went out of fashion after World War 2, it is still used occasionally *AUSTRALIA, 1915*. ► **dip your wick** to have sex *UK, 1958*

dip-dunk *noun* an unpleasant person, especially one who is not in the know *US, 1992*

diphead *noun* a social outcast *US, 1975*

diplomacy *noun* deception *TRINIDAD AND TOBAGO, 1938*

diply *noun* a socially inept outcast *US, 1965*

dip out *verb* **1** to come off worse; to miss out on an opportunity; to fail *UK, 1987*. **2** to back out of *AUSTRALIA, 1952*. **3** (used of a member of crack cocaine-selling crew) to remove small amounts of crack from the vials for sale, for later personal use *US, 1994*. **4** on a bird-watching trip, to fail to see the object of the quest *UK, 1977*

dipper *noun* a pickpocket *UK, 1889*

dipping *noun* the act of picking pockets *UK, 1882*

dippy *adjective* foolish, unstable, silly *US, 1899*

dippy dog *noun* a deep-fried battered frankfurter on a stick *AUSTRALIA, 2003*

dipshit *noun* a person of no consequence and no intelligence *US, 1962*

dipshit *adjective* offensive, inconsequential, lacking in intelligence *US, 1968*

dip shop *noun* in the used car business, a small finance company with very high interest rates that will offer loans to customers who might not otherwise qualify for financing *US, 1975*

dipso *noun* a person who suffers from an uncontrollable urge to drink. An abbreviated '*dipso*maniac' *UK, 1880*

dipso *adjective* drunk *UK, 2003*

dip squad *noun* a police unit that targets pickpockets. Formed on DIP (a pickpocket) *UK, 1977*

dipstick *noun* **1** the penis *US, 1973*. **2** an inept fool, an idiot. A euphemistic DIPSHIT; possibly punning on the synonymous sense of PRICK. In the UK, usage was popularised by BBC television situation comedy *Only Fools and Horses*, first broadcast in 1981 *US, 1963*

dipstick *verb* to test the abstract qualities of someone or something. From the device used to measure the depth of oil in a car's engine; thus a play on 'take the measure of' *UK, 2003*

dipsy *noun* a gambling cheat *US, 1950*

dipsy-doodle *noun* **1** a zig-zag motion. From baseball jargon *US, 1989*. **2** a long, end-around-end skid *US, 1962*

dipwad *noun* an inept outcast *US, 1976*

dire *adjective* objectionable, unpleasant. A trivialisation of the conventional sense *UK, 1836*

direct action *noun* a political act, especially a violent one, that may lead to arrest *US, 1968*

dirge *noun* a Dodge truck *US, 1971*

dirk *noun* **1** a knife or improvised cutting weapon *US, 1950*. **2** a socially unacceptable person *US, 1964*

dirt *noun* **1** a man or group of men who will prey upon homosexuals *US, 1927*. **2** gossip, criticism, rumour *US, 1844*. **3** heroin. Slightly less judgmental than 'shit' *US, 1973*. **4** marijuana *US, 1995*. **5** a tobacco cigarette *US, 1971*. **6** a trump card, especially when played unexpectedly *UK, 1945*. ► **down in the dirt** (used of flying) close to the ground *US, 1987*. ► **have the dirt on someone** to know some scandal about someone or something; to have the news about someone or something *UK, 1984*. ► **in the dirt** in trouble. Euphemistic for IN THE SHIT *UK, 1964*

dirt *adverb* very *UK, 1821*

dirtbag *noun* **1** a despicable or offensive person *US, 1941*. **2** a prisoner with poor personal hygiene *US, 1989*

dirtball *noun* a dirty, despicable person *US, 1974*

dirt bike *noun* a motorcycle designed for off-road use *US, 1970s?*

dirtbird *noun* a contemptible individual. From the skua and its habit of forcing other birds to regurgitate their stomach contents *IRELAND, 1996*

dirtbox *noun* the anus; the rectum *UK, 1984*

dirtbud *noun* a despicable person *US, 1998*

dirt chute *noun* the rectum *US, 1971*

dirt-dobber *noun* a farmer; an unsophisticated rustic *US, 1947*

dirt farm *noun* the mythical source of gossip *US, 1980*

dirt grass *noun* marijuana of inferior quality *US, 1971*

dirties *noun* work clothing *US, 1954*

dirt nap *noun* death *US, 1981*

dirt road *noun* the anus and rectum *US, 1922*

dirt surfer *noun* a member of the counterculture who has abandoned any pretence of personal hygiene or grooming *US, 1994*

Dirt Town *nickname* McMurdo Station, Antarctica *ANTARCTICA, 2003*

dirt-tracker *noun* a member of a touring sports team who is not selected for the major events *NEW ZEALAND, 2001*

dirt weed *noun* low quality marijuana *US, 1997*

dirty *noun* ▶ **do the dirty** to have sex *US, 1968*. ▶ **do the dirty on someone** to trick or otherwise treat someone unfairly *UK, 1914* ▷*see:* DIRTY DICK

dirty *verb* ▶ **to dirty your Christmas card** in horse racing, to fail dramatically and suffer a great loss of reputation *AUSTRALIA, 1989*

dirty *adjective* **1** guilty *US, 1927*. **2** in possession of drugs or other contraband *US, 1927*. **3** in urine testing, containing drug metabolites *US, 1990*. **4** infected with a sexually transmitted infection *US, 2003*. **5** angry, upset, annoyed *AUSTRALIA, 1972*. **6** in betting on horse racing, said of a day of races that has produced wins for gamblers and losses for bookmakers *AUSTRALIA, 1989*. **7** descriptive of electricity with unstable voltage that causes problems with computers *US, 1991*. **8** of an aircraft, with undercarriage down and flaps suitably aligned in order to fly as slowly as possible *UK, 1979*

dirty *adverb* very, extremely; a general intensifier, especially of adjectives of size *UK, 1894*

dirty air *noun* in motor racing, air turbulence on the race track *US, 1980*

dirty anal *noun* a scene in a pornographic film or a photograph depicting anal sex where traces of faeces are visible on that which is being inserted anally *US, 1995*

dirty and rude *adjective* nude. Rhyming slang *UK, 1992*

dirty arm *noun* a drug addict's arm showing the scars and infections resulting from intravenous drug use *US, 1992*

dirty barrel *noun* the genitals of a person infected with a sexually transmitted disease *US, 1967*

dirty basing *noun* crack cocaine. The drug is cheaper and less pure than FREEBASE cocaine *UK, 1998*

dirty beast *noun* a priest. Glasgow rhyming slang *UK, 1988*

dirty bird *noun* Old Crow™ whisky *US, 1970*

dirty boogie *noun* a sexually suggestive dance *US, 1969*

dirty case *noun* in hospital usage, an operation in which the surgeons discover an infection *US, 1980*

dirty-dance *verb* to dance in an explicitly and intentionally sexual manner *US, 1994*

dirty daughter *noun* water. Rhyming slang. One of several terms that have 'daughter' as the common (dispensible) element *UK, 1961*

Dirty Den *noun* a pen. Rhyming slang, formed on the popular nickname of a character in BBC television's *EastEnders*; the villainous Dennis Watts, who appeared in the first episode, broadcast 19th February 1985, was nicknamed by the tabloid press *UK, 1992*

dirty Dick; the dirty *noun* a police station, a prison. Rhyming slang for NICK *UK, 1992*

Dirty Dicks *noun* a ward for sexually transmitted diseases in a military or other service hospital. A pun on DICK (the penis) *CANADA, 1984*

dirty-dirty *nickname* the southern United States *US, 1999*

dirty dish *noun* fish. Rhyming slang *AUSTRALIA, 2002*

dirty dishes *noun* evidence planted by police or investigators to incriminate someone *US, 1982*

dirty dog *noun* a despicable or untrustworthy person; a lecher *UK, 1928*

dirty dog *nickname* the Greyhound Bus Lines *US, 1997*

dirty dupe *noun* in television and film-making, a crude, black and white, working print *US, 1990*

dirty end of the stick *noun* an unfair position to be in, or inequitable treatment *UK, 1924*

dirty girl *noun* an operating theatre nurse who is not deemed sterile and who is available for tasks that do not require disinfecting *US, 1980*

Dirty Half Mile *nickname* a section of the Sydney inner-city suburb of Kings Cross noted for prositution and vice *AUSTRALIA, 1934*

dirty laundry *noun* embarrassing information *US, 1982*

dirty leg *noun* a woman with loose sexual mores; a common prostitute *US, 1966*

dirty leper; dirt *noun* pepper. Rhyming slang, probably suggested or informed by the appearance of ground black pepper *UK, 1992*

dirty look *noun* a look of contempt or strong dislike *UK, 1961*

dirty mac; dirty mackintosh *noun* used as a generic description for any man who habitually resorts to sex-shops, strip-clubs and the purchase of 'top-shelf' publications *UK, 1975*

dirty mac brigade *noun* a notional collection of sex-oriented older men *UK, 1987*

dirty mack *verb* to speak insults and slander *US, 1999*

dirty money *noun* **1** money that is the proceeds of crime, especially money that can be traced. *Dirty Money (Un Flic)* is a crime drama in which a policeman targets a drug-smuggling operation, directed by Jean-Pierre Melville, 1972 *UK, 2003*. **2** extra pay for very dirty work. An employment issue *UK, 1897*

dirty movie *noun* a sexual or pornographic film *US, 1969*

dirty old man *noun* **1** a lecher; especially a middle-aged or older man with sexual appetites considered more appropriate in someone younger. Given impetus in the UK in the late 1960s – early 70s by television comedy series *Steptoe and Son UK, 1932*. **2** any homosexual man older than the homosexual male speaker *US, 1964*

dirty on *adjective* angry with *AUSTRALIA, 1965*

dirty pool *noun* unfair tactics. From the game of pool *US, 1940*

dirty Sanchez *noun* an act of daubing your sex-partner's upper lip with a 'moustache' of his or her faeces. This appears to have been contrived with an intention to provoke shock rather than actually as a practice, although, no doubt, some have experimented. The use of a Mexican name merely suggests the shape of a drooping moustache *US, 2003*

dirty side *nickname* the eastern coast of the US *US, 1976*

dirty smoke *noun* marijuana *UK, 2002*

dirty stack *noun* in a casino, a stack of betting tokens of different denominations *US, 1983*

dirty stop-out *noun* a person who spends more time than expected away from home in pursuit of pleasure. A jocular cliché when the stress on 'dirty' is admiring; may have an admonishing tone if used by parents, or if 'stop-out' is alone or combined with a harsher adjective *UK, 1906*

dirty thing *noun* a person who behaves amorously, or flirts saucily or unsubtly, especially with heavy innuendo. Originally used for adolescent girls or amorous boys *UK, 1961*

dirty thirty *noun* **1** in the Vietnam war, a US soldier who had killed 30 enemy soldiers *US, 1991*. **2** the US Air Force pilots who served as co-pilots with Vietnamese Airforce crews in 1963 and 1964 *US, 1990*

dirty tricks *noun* secret tactics that are generally considered to be unfair *US, 1963*

dirty tyke *noun* a bike. Rhyming slang *UK, 1992*

dirty up *verb* **1** to render an entertainment (radio, television, film, book, play, etc) more sexually titillating *UK, 1974*. **2** to modify a recording to make it sound more 'authentic' or 'raw' *US, 1983*

dirty water *noun* ▸ **get the dirty water(s) off your chest** (of a male) to ejaculate, either with a partner or as a sole practitioner *UK, 1961*

dirty weekend *noun* a romantic or sexually adventurous weekend (away from home) spent with your lover; or with your partner or spouse but without your children *UK, 1963*

dirty work *noun* in a strip or sex show, movements made to expose the vagina *US, 1971*

dirty work at the crossroads *noun* illegal activity, especially if concealed *US, 1938*

DIS *noun* death while in the saddle, or engaged in sexual intercourse *US, 1979*

dis; diss *verb* **1** to insult in a competitive, quasi-friendly spirit, especially in a competitive rap battle *US, 2000*. **2** to show disrespect, to disparage *US, 1982*. **3** to release (from prison). An abbreviation of 'discharge' *US, 1990*

disappear *verb* to kill someone and dispose of the corpse in a manner that assures it will never be discovered. As a transitive verb, a favourite term – and practice – of right wing death squads and organised criminal enterprises *US, 1964*

dischuffed *adjective* displeased, offended; insulted. Military usage *UK, 1987*

disco *noun* **1** an event where a DJ plays recorded music for dancing. The ubiquitous post-wedding-breakfast or after-dinner entertainment; probably derives from the mobile discothèques which proliferated in the 1970s to take advantage of the then-fashionable disco scene *UK, 1964*. **2** a venue for dancing to recorded music. Abbreviated from 'discothèque' *US, 1964*. **3** by extension, a genre of dance music *US, 1964*

disco *adjective* **1** out of date, out of fashion, out-moded *US, 1993*. **2** acceptable, good. From the film *Pulp Fiction US, 1995*

disco biscuit *noun* **1** a tablet of MDMA, the recreational drug best known as ecstasy. A heavily ironic identity for a fashionable drug; 'disco' as a nightclub for an earlier generation that didn't have ECSTASY and hence, is considered extremely unfashionable, plus 'biscuit' in the conventional sense of 'a basic supply (ship's biscuit) which can sustain life'. In short 'MDMA brings life to clubs' *UK, 1996*. **2** the recreational drug methaqualone, best known as Quaaludes™, a tablet of methaqualone. From the popularity of the drug in the 1970s disco scene *US, 1993*

disco brick *noun* a kilogram of cocaine *UK, 2001*

disco burger *noun* a tablet of MDMA, the recreational drug best known as ecstasy *UK, 1996*

disco dancer *noun* **1** an opportunist. Glasgow rhyming slang for CHANCER *UK, 1988*. **2** cancer. Rhyming slang *AUSTRALIA, 1983*

disco dose *noun* a mild dose of LSD *US, 1995*

disco dust *noun* cocaine *UK, 1999*

disco gun *noun* a Walther PPK pistol *UK, 1995*

disco move *noun* any manoeuvre executed by a novice surfer *US, 1991*

discon *noun* the criminal charge of 'disorderly conduct' *US, 1963*

disco queen *noun* a male homosexual who frequents discos. The title of a 1978 song by Paul Jabara glorifying the energy of the song's hero *US, 1979*

disgustitude *noun* the state of being disgusted *US, 1990*

dish *noun* **1** an attractive female *UK, 1909*. **2** the buttocks, the anus. Polari *UK, 1965*. **3** gossip, especially when disparaging, salacious or scandalous. From the verb sense *US, 1976*. **4** on Prince Edward Island, an undefined amount of alcohol *CANADA, 1956*. ▸ **put on the dish** to apply lubricant to the anus in preparation for anal sex *UK, 2002*

dish *verb* to gossip, to disparage. Originally 'dish the dirt' or 'dish out the dirt' *US, 1941*. ▸ **dish soup** to sell cocaine *US, 1995*. ▸ **dish the dirt; dish it** to gossip indiscreetly or with slanderous intent *US, 1926*

DI shack *noun* the quarters where drill instructors live and the on-duty instructor works *US, 1991*

dish bitch *noun* a television journalist who, when on location, relies on satellite communication for incoming information which is then included in that journalist's report *UK, 2005*

dis-head; diss-head *noun* a person who will not conform and show respect. Combines DIS (to show disrespect) with -HEAD (an enthusiast) *US, 2000*

dishlicker *noun* a dog, especially a racing greyhound *AUSTRALIA, 1983*

dishonourable discharge *noun* ejaculation achieved through masturbation *US, 1964*

dish out *verb* **1** to distribute. Originally military and therefore used of food or medals *UK, 1931*. **2** to dispense (abuse) *US, 1908*. ▸ **dish it out** when fighting or arguing, to attack with punishing force *US, 1930*. ▸ **dish out the gravy; dish out the porridge** of a judge, to deliver a severe sentence of imprisonment *UK, 1950*

dish queen *noun* a male homosexual who takes special pleasure in gossip *US, 1970*

dishrag *noun* a person or thing of no importance *US, 1906*

dish rags *noun* in poker, poor cards *US, 1996*

dishwasher *noun* a railway worker who cleans engines in a roundhouse *US, 1946*

dishwater *noun* poor quality beer *AUSTRALIA, 1972*

dishwater diarrhoea *noun* a notional disease that plagues those reluctant to wash their dishes *US, 1969*

dishy *adjective* sexually attractive. From DISH (an attractive person) *UK, 1961*

disinfo *noun* disinformation *UK, 1976*

disk drive *noun* the vagina *UK, 2001*

dismant *noun* a bit of previously-used electrical or mechanical equipment. From 'dismantle' *SOUTH AFRICA, 1974*

dismo *noun* a fanatic surfing enthusiast who never actually surfs *US, 1997*

Disneyland *noun* a prison with relaxed rules that ease the difficulty of serving a sentence *US, 1992*

Disneyland *nickname* **1** the Pentagon; military headquarters in Vietnam. A critical assessment of reality and fantasy in the military leadership *US, 1963*. **2** the brothel district near An Khe, Vietnam, near the 1st Cavalry Division base *US, 1966*

Disneyland-on-the-Rideau *nickname* National Defence Headquarters, on the Rideau Canal in Ottawa *CANADA, 1995*

disobey *verb* ▸ **disobey the pope** **1** to masturbate. While this may be another ecumenical variation of BASH THE BISHOP (to masturbate), it is certainly a literal reaction to the Catholic view of onanism. It is also theoretically possible to 'please the pope' *UK, 2001*. **2** to have sex. Here the use of frowned-upon contraception seems to be implied *US, 2001*

dispatchers *noun* in a dice game cheating scheme, improperly marked dice *UK, 1811*

dispersal *noun* in prison, the system of managing Category A prisoners by sending them to one of six high-security prisons rather than concentrating them all in one maximum-security facility *UK, 2000*

distress *verb* to impregnate outside marriage *TRINIDAD AND TOBAGO, 2003*

dis war *noun* an exchange of quasi-friendly insults as part of a rap battle; a war of words. Extended from DIS (to show disrespect) *US, 1995*

dit *noun* a tale, a yarn. Origin unknown *AUSTRALIA, 1942*

ditch *noun* **1** the sea; the ocean; the Atlantic Ocean; the English Channel. Generally used with 'the' *UK, 1841*. **2** the antecubial vein inside the bend of the elbow, often used for injecting drugs *US, 1968*. **3** the Tasman Sea *NEW ZEALAND, 2002*. **4** inferior marijuana, especially from Mexico. From DITCHWEED *US, 2001*

ditch *verb* **1** to reject, discard, abandon; to elude *US, 1899*. **2** to release (from prison). An abbreviation and corruption of 'discharge' *US, 1990*. **3** in an emergency, to bring an aircraft down in the sea *UK, 1941*

ditchweed *noun* marijuana of inferior quality that grows wild in roadside ditches, especially in Mexico *US, 1982*

ditso *noun* an absent-minded, somewhat dim person *US, 1976*

ditso *adjective* absent-minded, somewhat dim *US, 1987*

dit-spinner *noun* a person adept at telling stories, anecdotes or the like *AUSTRALIA, 1967*

ditto I agree; the same goes for me *US, 1981*

ditto-head *noun* a fan of radio entertainer Rush Limbaugh. Limbaugh conditioned his callers to begin conversations on the radio with a simple 'Dittos from [hometown]' instead of gushing admiration for him *US, 1992*

dity *adjective* upset, nervous *US, 1978*

ditz *noun* an absent-minded, empty-headed person *US, 1982*

ditzy; ditsy *adjective* (usually of a woman) scatterbrained, silly *US, 1973*

div *noun* a fool; a disagreeable individual. Abbreviated from DIVVY (a fool) *UK, 1983*

dive *noun* **1** a disreputable establishment *US, 1867*. **2** an intentional loss in a sporting event *US, 1916*. ▶ **take a dive** to deliberately lose a boxing match or other sporting contest *US, 1942*

dive *verb* to lose a contest or competition intentionally, especially in boxing. From the image of a boxer diving towards the mat, feigning a knock-out blow *US, 1921*. ▶ **dive for pearls** to work washing dishes in a restaurant *US, 1951*

dive-bomb *verb* to jump into water in a tucked position in order to make a large splash *AUSTRALIA, 1980*

divebombing *noun* an act of picking up dog ends from the pavement. Vagrants' use *UK, 1980*

divel a bissel! used by Nova Scotians of German descent as a mild oath *CANADA, 1999*

diver *noun* **1** a pickpocket *UK, 1611*. **2** a hang glider *US, 1992*

Diver *nickname* Charles Jaco, CNN reporter in Saudi Arabia during the US war against Iraq in 1991. Because of Jaco's athletic dives off camera when a missile attack alert was announced *US, 1991*

divhead *noun* a fool; a disagreeable individual. Elaboration of DIV *UK, 1997*

dividends *noun* money *US, 1997*

divider *noun* a marijuana cigarette that is shared among several smokers *UK, 2001*

divine *adjective* pleasant, 'nice'. A trivial use of the conventional sense *UK, 1928*

divine blows *noun* energetic sex *TRINIDAD AND TOBAGO, 2003*

Divine Brown *noun* ▶ **go Divine Brown; go Divine** to perform oral sex. Rhyming slang for GO DOWN (ON); aptly formed on the professional name of a Los Angeles prostitute who enjoyed some minor celebrity when, in 1995, she was apprehended performing just such a service for film actor Hugh Grant (b.1960) *UK, 1998*

Divine Miss M *nickname* Bette Midler, American singer born in 1945 *US, 1982*

diving board *noun* in electric line work, a work platform board *US, 1980*

diving gear *noun* a condom *US, 1990*

diving suit *noun* a condom *AUSTRALIA, 1984*

divoon *adjective* lovely, delightful. A humorous elaboration of 'divine' *US, 1944*

divorce *noun* in the usage of organised pickpocket gangs, the loss of a crew member to jail *US, 1949*

divot *noun* a toupee. Borrowed from golf's 'sliced piece of turf' *UK, 1934*

divvie *noun* a person with instinctive knowledge. Probably from 'diviner' *UK, 1978*

divvies *noun* **1** used for claiming a share of something that is being divided *US, 1958*. **2** divination *UK, 1947*

divvo *noun* a fool. A variation of DIVVY *UK, 1997*

divvy *noun* **1** a share or portion; a dividend *US, 1872*. **2** a fool *UK, 1989*

divvy *adjective* daft, foolish, idiotic. From DIVVY (a fool) *UK, 1979*

divvy up *verb* to divide into shares. A phonetic abbreviation of 'divide' *US, 1876*

divvy van; divi-van *noun* a police van. From 'divisional van' *AUSTRALIA, 1982*

dixie *noun* **1** (especially in Victoria and Tasmania) a small cardboard ice-cream container *AUSTRALIA, 1941*. **2** unnecesssary body action *BARBADOS, 1980*

Dixie *nickname* the southeastern United States *US, 1859*

Dixie cup *noun* **1** the traditional navy white hat, symbol of the American sailor since the C19 *US, 1973*. **2** a woman who speaks with a southern accent *US, 1977*. **3** a female Red Cross worker in Vietnam *US, 1990*. **4** a person who is considered to be utterly dispensable, who is used and then discarded *US, 1997*

dixie lid *noun* a child, a kid. Rhyming slang *UK, 1998*

Dixie Trail *noun* anal sex facilitated by Dixie Peach hair dressing as a lubricant *US, 1968*

DIY *adjective* do-it-yourself, especially of household maintenance or repair. A colloquial abbreviation *UK, 1955*

DIYer *noun* a do-it-yourself-er, a person who tends to do his own household repairs and maintenance *UK, 1984*

Diz *nickname* Dizzy Gillespie (1917–1993), a jazz trumpeter instrumental in the creation of bebop *US, 1961*

dizz *noun* **1** an odd, absent-minded person *US, 1963*. **2** marijuana *UK, 2003*

dizz *verb* sleep; to sleep. A Royal Navy variation of ZIZZ, perhaps in combination with 'doze' *UK, 1945*

dizzy *adjective* scatterbrained *US, 1878*

dizzy limit *noun* the utmost *AUSTRALIA, 1916*

dizzy three *noun* a C-47A Skytrain plane, also known as a DC-3, most commonly used to transport people and cargo, but also used as a bomber and fighter *US, 1975*

DJ *noun* **1** men's formal evening wear, a dinner jacket *UK, 1967*. **2** an agent of the Federal Bureau of Investigation. An allusion to the Department of Justice, home to the FBI. Sometimes spelt out as 'deejay' *US, 1935*

dj; deejay *noun* a disc jockey *US, 1950*

dj; deejay *verb* to work as a disc jockey *US, 1985*

djamba *noun* marijuana. A West African word, now in wider usage *US, 1938*

DKDC I don't know, I don't care. Combining a lack of intelligence with apathy *US, 1997*

DL *noun* ▶ **on the DL** down low, discreetly *US, 1996*

DM's *noun* Dr Martens™ heavy-duty boots. An abbreviation of the brand name. The boots were designed for industrial use and subsequently adopted as fashionwear, initially by skinheads and bootboys, then as a general fashion item for either sex *UK, 1998*

DMT *noun* dimethyltryptamine, a hallucinogenic drug *US, 1971*

DMZ *noun* any place between two opposing factions or social forces, controlled by neither yet ceded by neither. Originally a military term – 'demilitarised zone' – for an area dividing North and South Korea *US, 1976*

DNF in motorcycle racing, did not finish a race *US, 1970s*

do *noun* **1** a party or social function *UK, 1824*. **2** an action, deed, performance or event *UK, 1860*. **3** a person considered in terms of their sexual performance or willingness *AUSTRALIA, 1950*. **4** a dose of drugs *US, 1971*. **5** in craps, a bet on the shooter *US, 1974*. **6** a hairdo *US, 1966*. ▶ **do the do** to have sex *US, 1993*. ▶ **do your do** to prepare your hairdo *US, 1995*

DO *noun* in hot rodding, dual overhead camshafts *US, 1948*

do *verb* **1** to kill *UK, 1790*. **2** to charge with, or prosecute for, or convict of a crime *UK, 1784*. **3** to use up your money, especially to squander *AUSTRALIA, 1889*. **4** to assault, to beat up *UK, 1796*. **5** to injure (a part of the body) *AUSTRALIA, 1963*. **6** to rob *UK, 1774*. **7** to swindle, to deceive, to trick *UK, 1641*. **8** to have sex with *UK, 1650*. **9** to perform oral sex upon someone *US, 1963*. **10** to consume, especially an alcoholic drink *UK, 1857*. **11** to use drugs *US, 1967*. **12** when combined with a name (of a very recognisable person or group) that is used as a generic noun, to behave in the manner of that person or group of people, as in, for example, 'do a Lord Lucan' (to disappear mysteriously) *UK, 1934*. **13** to visit as a tourist or pleasure-seeker *UK, 1858*. **14** to suffice, to answer its purpose *US, 1846*. ▶ **be doing of** to be doing something. Often in a question, such as 'What are you doing of?' *UK, 1853*. ▶ **do cards** to steal or forge credit cards *UK, 1996*. ▶ **do it 1** to have sex *IRELAND, 1923*. **2** to defecate; to urinate. Euphemistic *UK, 1922*. ▶ **do someone like a dinner** to overcome someone completely in a fight or competition; to vanquish. Punning on the phrase 'dinner's done' (dinner is ready) *AUSTRALIA, 1847*. ▶ **do the Harold Holt; do the Harold** to decamp. From rhyming slang for 'bolt'. Harold Holt (1908–67) was an Australian prime minister whose term of office was cut short when he went ocean swimming one afternoon and presumably drowned – his body was never recovered *AUSTRALIA, 1987*. ▶ **do the thing** to have sex *US, 1968*. ▶ **do your bit** to do your share and so contribute to the greater good, especially in times of trial or conflict *UK, 1902*. ▶ **you'll do me/us** you are entirely suitable for a task; we are more than happy to be supporting you. Used as a cry of encouragement and support *AUSTRALIA, 1952*

DOA *noun* **1** a more than usually dangerous variety of heroin. From the acronym DOA (dead on arrival); DEAD ON ARRIVAL (heroin) *UK, 1998*. **2** phencyclidine, the recreational drug known as PCP or angel dust. The abbreviation is for DEAD ON ARRIVAL – the results of a PCP overdose *US, 1993*

doable *adjective* sexually attractive enough to warrant the speaker's gift of having sex *US, 1997*

do as you like *noun* a bicycle. Rhyming slang for 'bike' *UK, 1960*

doat *noun* someone or something fit to be doted on *IRELAND, 1975*

dob *noun* a small lump or dollop, usually applied to butter, jam, cream, etc. Originally dialect *UK, 1984*

DOB *noun* a lesbian. An abbreviation of 'daughters of Bilitis' *US, 1982*

dob *verb* to inform on someone *AUSTRALIA, 1955*

dobber *noun* **1** a despicable person *UK, 2002*. **2** an informer; a telltale *AUSTRALIA, 1955*. **3** a fool, an idiot. Glasgow slang *UK: SCOTLAND, 1996*. **4** the penis. Also 'dob' *US, 1974*

dobber-in *noun* an informer; a telltale *AUSTRALIA, 1958*

dobbing-in *noun* informing *AUSTRALIA, 1994*

do bears shit in the woods? yes; a nonsense retort used as an affirmative answer to a silly question, often sarcastic. Often mixed with the synonymous 'Is the Pope Catholic?' to achieve DOES THE POPE SHIT IN WOODS? *US, 1971*

dobie *noun* a Doberman Pinscher dog *US, 1981*

dob in *verb* **1** to inform against someone; to tell on someone *AUSTRALIA, 1954*. **2** to contribute funds *AUSTRALIA, 1956*

do-boy *noun* a male who does whatever his girlfriend tells him to do *US, 2001*

doc *noun* **1** a *doctor US, 1840*. **2** a *document*. Originally a military use, especially in the plural, for 'official documents of identity or record' *US, 1868*. **3** in computing, *documentation US, 1991*

docco *noun* a documentary *UK, 2000*

doc in the box *noun* a walk-in medical clinic *US, 1994*

dock *noun* ▶ **in dock 1** of a motor vehicle, being serviced or repaired *UK, 1984*. **2** in hospital, or otherwise unable to carry on as usual due to injury or medical treatment *UK, 1785*

dock asthma *noun* in a trial, the shocked gasps given by the accused as accusations are made or proved. The gasps are ironically considered as symptoms of a notional disease *UK, 1977*

docker *noun* a partially smoked cigarette that has been thrown away or extinguished for use later *UK, 1966*

docker's ABC *noun* ale, baccy (tobacco), cunt, a worker's shopping-list in the spirit of 'wine, women and song', especially well used in Liverpool *UK, 1961*

docker's hankie *noun* the act of clearing the nostrils by blowing the contents onto the ground *UK, 1979*

dockie *noun* a dockside worker *AUSTRALIA, 1935*

dock monkey *noun* a worker who loads and unloads trucks *US, 1939*

dock walloper *noun* **1** a worker who loads and unloads trucks *US, 1971*. **2** a thief who steals cargo before it has been unloaded or passed through customs *US, 1986*

doco *noun* a documentary *AUSTRALIA, 1996*

Docs *noun* Dr Martens™ footwear *US, 1993*

doctor *noun* **1** (used of children) the exploration of each other's genitals *US, 1966*. **2** a male with a large penis. Homosexual usage *US, 1964*. **3** an expert *US, 1990*. **4** a bookmaker who declines to take a bet, telling the bettor he will 'get better' *AUSTRALIA, 1989*. **5** a person who sells illegally manufactured alcohol *US, 1960*. **6** MDMA, the recreational drug best known as ecstasy. Possibly punning on the degrees MD and MA *UK, 1998*. **7** (especially in Western Australia) a refreshing wind coming after a period of stifling weather. Preceded by a placename to form proper nouns for commonly occurring winds of this type, such as the Albany Doctor, Esperance Doctor, Fremantle Doctor, etc *AUSTRALIA, 1870*. ▶ **go for the doctor** to race a horse at top speed *AUSTRALIA, 1969*

doctor *verb* **1** to falsify, to adulterate, to tamper *UK, 1774*. **2** in cricket, to illegally tamper with the condition of the ball to the bowler's advantage *UK, 1996*

doctor and nurse; doctor *noun* a purse. Rhyming slang *UK, 1998*

Doctor Blue; Dr Blue *noun* used in hospitals as a code announcement that a patient is in cardiac arrest *US, 1973*

Doctor Cotton; Dr Cotton *adjective* rotten. Rhyming slang *UK, 1932*

Doctor Crippen; Dr Crippen *noun* dripping (melted fat used like butter). Rhyming slang, formed on the name of the celebrated murderer Dr Hawley Harvey (1862–1910) *UK, 1961*

Doctor Dre; Dr Dre *adjective* homosexual. Rhyming slang for GAY, formed from the stage name of hip-hop performer and producer Andre Young (b.1965) *UK, 2003*

Doctor Feelgood; Dr Feelgood *noun* **1** heroin *UK, 2002*. **2** any doctor who specialises in energy-giving injections *US, 1973*

Doctor Jekyll and Mister Hyde; Dr Jekyll and Mr Hyde *noun* the recreational drug methaqualone, best known as Quaaludes™ *US, 1985*

Doctor K; Dr K *nickname* Dwight Gooden (b.1964), a right-handed pitcher (1984–2000) with an immortal early career and an acceptable mid-career. In the shorthand of baseball scorekeeping, a 'K' is a 'strikeout', and 'Doc' Gooden had many *US, 1986*

Doctor Legg; Dr Legg *noun* an egg. Rhyming slang, formed on the name of a minor character in the BBC television soap opera *EastEnders UK, 1998*

Doctor Livingstone, I presume a catchphrase greeting used for any fortuitous or unexpected meeting. Adopted from Henry Morton Stanley's greeting, in 1871, to African explorer David Livingstone *UK, 1891*

Doctor Pepper; Dr Pepper *noun* one of the several surface-to-air missile patterns used by the North Vietnamese against American aircraft during the Vietnam war. Missile approaches from the ten o'clock, two o'clock and four o'clock positions; 'ten-two-and-four' was a Dr Pepper slogan *US, 1990*

doctor shopping *noun* the practice of visiting multiple physicians to obtain multiple prescriptions for otherwise illegal drugs. A common practice of drug addicts and suppliers of drug addicts *US, 2003*

Doctor Thomas; Dr Thomas *noun* a black person who rejects black culture and takes on the culture of the dominant white society. An elaboration of the common UNCLE TOM, coined long before Clarence Thomas became the prototype of the concept *US, 1980*

Doctor White; Dr White *noun* **1** a drug addiction *US, 1959*. **2** cocaine *US, 1986*

Doctor Who; Dr Who *noun* a prison warder. Rhyming slang for SCREW (a prison warder), based on a time-travelling television hero first seen in 1963 *UK, 1996*

docu *noun* a *docu*mentary film or television programme. As a prefix, such as in 'docudrama' (a documentary drama), 'docu' has been conventional since 1961 *UK, 2003*

docy *noun* the female breast *BAHAMAS, 1982*

Doc Yak *noun* a doctor whose reputation is less than sterling. From a syndicated comic strip that last appeared in 1935 *US, 1956*

do-dad *noun* in American football, a blocking strategy in which offensive players cross over and block each other's defensive opposite *US, 1966*

doddle *noun* an objective acheived with ease; in sport, an easy win or a simple victory. Probably from 'dawdle' or 'toddle', implying a 'walk-over', which is consistent with its earliest use in racing circles, but possibly from Scottish 'doddle', a lump of homemade toffee (hence something desirable and easily acquired). It is recorded with the meaning 'money very easily obtained' in Scotland in 1934 *UK, 1937*

doddle *verb* to achieve; to win something very easily *UK, 1963*

dodge *noun* a scam, a swindle *UK, 1638*. ▶ **on the dodge** in hiding from the police *US, 1976*

Dodge *noun* ▶ **get out of Dodge; get the hell out of Dodge** to leave, usually with some haste. A loose allusion to the Wild West as epitomised by Dodge City, Kansas, and the seriousness of an order by the authorities to leave town *US, 1965*

dodge *verb* ▶ **dodge the column** to shirk, to avoid your duty, work or responsibility. Originally military *UK, 1919*

dodge *adjective* dubious *UK, 2006*

Dodge City *nickname* an enemy-controlled area south of Da Nang, the scene of heavy fighting in November 1968; anywhere in Vietnam with a strong Viet Cong presence *US, 1969*

dodger *noun* **1** a small advertising leaflet *US, 1879*. **2** a shunting truck *UK, 1970*. **3** bread *AUSTRALIA, 1897*

dodger *adjective* excellent, fine *AUSTRALIA, 1941*

dodgy *noun* an informer. From the adjectival sense as 'unreliable', perhaps shortened from 'dodgy geezer' or similar *UK, 1996*

dodgy *adjective* **1** of doubtful character or legality; dubious. Popularised in the 1960s by the comedian Norman Vaughan as a catchphrase, with an accompanying thumbs-down gesture. The thumbs-up opposite was 'swingin!' *UK, 1961*. **2** risky *UK, 1898*. **3** stolen *UK, 1861*

dodo *noun* **1** a fool *US, 1898*. **2** an aviation cadet who has not completed basic training *US, 1933*

do down *verb* to get the better of someone, financially or otherwise; to harm someone's reputation by spreading gossip or rumour *UK, 1937*

doe *noun* a woman *UK, 1909*

doer *noun* **1** an energetic person who gets on with the job; a person who tackles problems or setbacks with good humour *AUSTRALIA, 1902*. **2** the person responsible for a specific crime, especially a murder *US, 1992*. **3** in horse racing, a horse as a performer – either good or poor *UK, 1948*

doer and gone; doer 'n' gone *adjective* very far away. From Afrikaans for 'far away'; a synonym for HELL AND GONE *SOUTH AFRICA, 1972*

does Rose Kennedy have a black dress? yes; a sarcastic nonsense retort used as an affirmative answer to a silly question *AUSTRALIA, 1987*

does she? used as a euphemism for 'does she (or, is she likely to) have sex?' *UK, 1969*

does the Pope shit in the woods? yes; a nonsense retort used as an affirmative answer to a silly question, often sarcastic. The result of combining synonymous DO BEARS SHIT IN THE WOODS? and 'Is the Pope Catholic?' *UK, 1997*

dof *adjective* stupid, idiotic, muddled *SOUTH AFRICA, 1979*

doffie *noun* a stupid, idiotic or muddled person *SOUTH AFRICA, 1991*

do-flicky *noun* any small tool the name of which escapes the speaker *BARBADOS, 1965*

do for *verb* to beat severely, to kill *UK, 1740*

dog *noun* **1** an unattractive woman or man. Originally used by men of women which, in the UK, has remained the predominant sense *US, 1937*. **2** a sexually transmitted infection *US, 1962*. **3** an informer to the police or, in prison, to the prison authorities *AUSTRALIA, 1848*. **4** a prison warder *AUSTRALIA, 1919*. **5** a traitor *AUSTRALIA, 1896*. **6** used as a general form of friendly address (without any negative connotations). A rare positive use of 'dog', synonymous with 'man', possibly influenced by rap artist Snoop Doggy Dogg (Calvin Broadus, b.1972). Also Spelt 'dogg' and 'dawg' *US, 1995*. **7** a freshman, or first-year college student *US, 1947*. **8** the grade 'D' *US, 1964*. **9** a cigarette-end. A shortened DOG END *UK, 1935*. **10** a marijuana cigarette *US, 1997*. **11** in sports betting, the underdog *US, 1975*. **12** in poker, a worthless hand *US, 1988*. **13** in horse racing, a racehorse with little value *US, 1840*. **14** in pool, a difficult shot *US, 1993*. **15** in horse racing, a sawhorse used to keep horses away from the rail during a workout on a muddy track *US, 1976*. **16** in poker, the fourth player to the left of the dealer *US, 1988*. **17** a sausage; a hot dog. Derives from the belief that dog meat was used as a sausage filler; this led to a hot sausage in a roll being called a 'hot dog'. In a fine example of circular etymology 'hot dog' now abbreviates to 'dog', and 'dog' is once again a sausage; most consumers are no longer concerned about dog meat *UK, 1845*. **18** the foot *US, 1913*. **19** a piece of paper money *TRINIDAD AND TOBAGO, 1986*. **20** an F86-DC aircraft *US, 1956*. **21** a failure of a song or film *US, 1929*. ▶ **dog tied up** an unpaid debt *AUSTRALIA, 1905*. ▶ **it shouldn't happen to a dog** a catchphrase used to complain about the manner in which a human has been treated. Thought to be of Yiddish origin *US, 1968*. ▶ **it's a dog's life** used of a meagre existence. A catchphrase, generally used by someone enduring such a life *UK, 1969*. ▶ **like a dog watching television** in the position of doing something you do not understand *US, 2003*. ▶ **on the dog** on credit *US, 1978*. ▶ **put on the dog** to assume a superior, upper-class attitude *US, 1865*. ▶ **run like a dog** to run or perform slowly *AUSTRALIA, 1996*. ▶ **the dog dead** there is nothing more to say on the subject *BARBADOS, 1965*. ▶ **the dog has caught the car** a person (or group of people) who has achieved a goal and is now at a loss for what to do next *US, 2003*. ▶ **turn dog** to become a police informer *AUSTRALIA, 1863*

Dog *noun* the Greyhound bus line. A fixture in American travel until a crippling strike in the 1990s; variants include 'Grey Dog' and 'ol 'Grey Dog' *US, 1974*

dog *verb* **1** to avoid work; to work slowly *US, 1955*. **2** to studiously ignore *US, 1987*. **3** to abuse or harass *US, 1992*. **4** in motor racing, to follow another car very closely, hoping to distract or weaken the resolve of the driver ahead *US, 1965*. **5** of a male, to have sex with a partner who is kneeling on all-fours and entered from behind *UK, 1937*. **6** to perform sexually for money *US, 1989*. **7** to betray *AUSTRALIA, 1896*. **8** in pool, to miss a shot that should be made *US, 1984*. **9** to play truant. Extended from a variation of 'dodge'. With variant 'dog it' *UK: SCOTLAND, 1985*. **10** to hunt dingoes. Variant: to wild dog *AUSTRALIA, 1910* ▷*see:* DOG IT

dog *adjective* referring to the prison authorities, generally seen as officious and corrupt by prisoners *AUSTRALIA, 1978*

dogan *noun* an Irish Roman Catholic *CANADA, 1965*

dog and bone; dog *noun* a telephone. Rhyming slang *UK, 1961*

dog and boned; doggo *adjective* drug-intoxicated. Rhyming slang for STONED *UK, 1998*

dog and cat *noun* a mat. Rhyming slang *UK, 1992*

dog and duck *noun* a fight. Rhyming slang for RUCK (a fight). Possibly formed on the name of a pub where fist-fighting was prevalent *UK, 1992*

dog and pony show *noun* an elaborate presentation *US, 1957*

dog and pup; dog *noun* a cup (a drinking vessel or a trophy). Rhyming slang *UK, 1992*

dog-ass *noun* a despised person *US, 1959*

dog-ass *adjective* **1** shoddy, inferior *US, 1953*. **2** despicable *US, 1953*

dog bait *noun* during a mass prison escape, a prisoner left by others to attract the attention of the tracking dogs *US, 1972*

dogball *noun* in a deck of playing cards, an eight *US, 1996*

dog-behind *verb* to beg for a favour TRINIDAD AND TOBAGO, 2003

dogbone *noun* **1** the weapon panel in the cockpit of an F-4 Phantom aircraft US, 1984. **2** in electric line work, an EHV yoke plate US, 1980

dogbox *noun* **1** a type of small and basic compartment in a railway carriage AUSTRALIA, 1905. **2** a truck's gear box US, 1971. ▶ **in the dogbox** in trouble, especially with one person NEW ZEALAND, 1953

dog breath *noun* **1** a contemptible person; used as a term of abuse US, 2000. **2** bad-smelling breath US, 1944. **3** cigarette smoke US, 1996

dog catcher *noun* any fast truck. The suggestion is that the truck is fast enough to pass a Greyhound bus US, 1971

dog clutch *noun* an involuntary locking of the vaginal muscles, imprisoning the penis (*penis captivus*). Common in dogs, not so common in humans, but common enough for a term to describe it US, 1967

dog cock *noun* chub sausage NEW ZEALAND, 1998

dog collar *noun* **1** a white clerical collar UK, 1861. **2** a choker necklace UK, 1903

dog-dance *verb* to give the impress that you are following someone very closely BARBADOS, 1965

dog-dancing *noun* useless or exaggerated activity CANADA, 1967

dog days *noun* a woman's menstrual period US, 1960

dog do *noun* dog faeces US, 1979

dog doody *noun* dog excrement. Variation on DOGGY DO; euphemistic US, 2001

dog driver *noun* a police officer. Insulting or contemptuous UK, 1977

dog-eater *noun* a member of the Sioux Indian tribe US, 1963

dog eat your shame! used for expressing complete disgust TRINIDAD AND TOBAGO, 1958

dog end *noun* **1** a contemptible person UK, 2002. **2** a cigarette-end. A corruption of 'docked end' (a partially smoked cigarette that is pinched off – 'docked' – and saved for later use) and still found as 'dock end' UK, 1935

dog-ender *noun* a prisoner who rolls new cigarettes from the unsmoked remains of others UK, 1996

dog-eye *noun* ▶ **keep dog-eye** to keep a look-out. From the verb DOG-EYE (to scrutinise) UK, 2001

dog-eye *verb* to scrutinise carefully US, 1912

dogface *noun* **1** an ugly person; used as a general term of abuse US, 1849. **2** a low ranking soldier US, 1930

dog-faced *adjective* despicable US, 1962

dog fashion; doggie fashion *adverb* sexual intercourse from behind, vaginal or anal, heterosexual or homosexual UK, 1900

dog finger *noun* the index finger US, 1926

dog food *noun* **1** Italian sausage US, 1996. **2** heroin US, 1992

dogfuck *noun* a despicable person US, 1993

dogfuck *verb* to have sex from the rear, homosexual or heterosexual, vaginal or anal US, 1980

dogger *noun* **1** a person who engages in *al fresco* sexual activities such as exhibitionism or voyeurism; especially of sexual activities (with multiple partners) in parked vehicles, generally in the countryside. When police approached 'doggers' (before they were so-named), the usual excuse offered was 'walking the dog' UK, 2003. **2** a truant. From DOG (to play truant) UK: SCOTLAND, 1985. **3** a hunter of dingoes AUSTRALIA, 1890

doggers *noun* multi-coloured swimming trunks AUSTRALIA, 1963

Doggett's *noun* ▶ **on the Doggett's** on the scrounge, cadging. Derives from COAT AND BADGE (to cadge) which has, in the past, been used as 'Doggett's coat and badge'. Doggett's Coat and Badge Race, founded by Thomas Doggett, an Irish actor, in 1715, is the oldest annual sporting event in Britain, a boat race from London Bridge to Chelsea contested by Thames' watermen. The race and the slang are both very much alive UK, 1960

doggie *noun* **1** an infantry soldier. A shortened DOGFACE US, 1937. **2** an enlisted man in the US Army US, 1945. **3** a greyhound racing enthusiast AUSTRALIA, 1989

doggie cop *noun* a police officer working with a trained dog US, 1983

doggie pack *noun* a US Army combat field pack. Used derisively by US Marines during the conflict in Vietnam US, 1982

doggie pouch *noun* a small ammunition pouch used by the infantry US, 1971

doggie straps *noun* rucksack straps. Vietnam war usage US, 1991

dogging *noun* **1** *al fresco* sexual activities such as exhibitionism or voyeurism; especially of sexual activities (with multiple partners) in parked vehicles, generally in the countryside. Originally used of the act of spying on people having sex in parked vehicles UK, 1998. **2** the hunting of dingoes AUSTRALIA, 1947

doggins *noun* in the illegal production of alcohol, liquor sweated out of used barrel staves US, 1974

doggo *noun* a sled dog handler ANTARCTICA, 1995

doggo *adjective* **1** lying prone, playing dead UK, 1893. **2** of a car's interior, of poor quality UK, 1981 ▷*see:* DOG AND BONED

doggone *adjective* used as a mild, folksy euphemism for 'damn'. Multiple variants. Usually used with a conscious folksy effect in mind UK, 1826

doggy *noun* **1** the penis BAHAMAS, 1982. **2** a railways' platelayer UK, 1970

doggy bag; doggie bag *noun* **1** a bag in which uneaten food from a restaurant is packed and taken home US, 1947. **2** a condom UK, 1998

doggy do *noun* dog excrement AUSTRALIA, 1995

doghole; doghole mine *noun* a small mine employing less than 15 miners US, 1943

doghouse *noun* **1** in trucking, the engine covering in the driving compartment US, 1971. **2** a brakevan (caboose), or the observation tower of a brakevan US, 1897. **3** the front fender, bonnet and grille of a car US, 1934. **4** a small tool shed US, 1918. ▶ **in the doghouse** ostracised; in disfavour. Alluding to an outside kennel. Commonly used of a man being ostracised by his wife for some misdemeanour US, 1926

doghouse cut *noun* a manner of cutting a deck of cards in which a section of cards is moved from the centre of the deck to the top, leaving the bottom cards undisturbed US, 1967

dogie *noun* heroin US, 1969

dog in the manger *noun* a person who selfishly refuses to give up something that he does not want UK, 1573

dog it; dog *verb* **1** to refuse to pay a lost bet or a debt US, 1950. **2** to back down from a confrontation or situation for lack of courage US, 1979

dog juice *noun* inexpensive alcohol, especially wine US, 1980

dogleg *noun* in oil drilling, a radical change in direction of drilling US, 1954

dogleg *verb* to make an angled detour, to take an angled route. Originally, perhaps, used in aviation UK, 1984

dog license *noun* a Certificate of Exemption to allow an Aboriginal to buy a drink in a hotel. This term derives from the Blackfellows Act, also known as the Dog Act AUSTRALIA, 1959

dog meat *noun* **1** a person who is certain of defeat or death US, 1977. **2** an inept, worthless person US, 1908

dog mouth *noun* bad breath experienced upon waking up. Hawaiian youth usage US, 1982

do-gooder *noun* a well-intentioned person who believes in and supports charity. The term suggests both a naivite and a slightly cloying sense of self-righteousness US, 1927

dog out *verb* **1** to keep a look out UK, 1966. **2** to criticise harshly US, 1986

Dogpatch *nickname* a neighbourhood of bars and shops near the Da Nang US Air Base during the Vietnam war. Dogpatch was the stereotypical Appalachian town in Al Capp's *Li'il Abner* comic strip, which was very popular in the US during the Vietnam war US, 1975

dog pile *noun* the pile of skiers or snowboarders produced when one falls while dismounting from a lift *US, 1990*

dogpile *verb* **1** to jump onto someone or onto a group of people *US, 1945*. **2** to post many critical comments in response to a posting on an Internet discussion group *US, 1995*

dog-piss *adjective* inferior, shabby *US, 1971*

dog puncher *noun* a driver of sled dogs *CANADA, 1964*

dog race *noun* in horse racing, a race featuring cheap racehorses *US, 1951*

dog-rob *verb* to acquire through scrounging or pilfering *US, 1919*

dog-robber *noun* **1** an officer's assistant *US, 1863*. **2** a person assigned the most menial of tasks, especially the acquisition of difficult-to-acquire goods and services *US, 1974*. **3** in the film and television industries, a person whose job it is to find difficult-to-find goods for props *US, 2002*. **4** during the Vietnam war, someone assigned to the rear area as seen by someone in combat *US, 1991*

dog-rough *adjective* disorderly; prone to rowdiness; unsophisticated *UK, 2002*

dogs *noun* **1** the feet; shoes *US, 1914*. **2** in circus and carnival usage, the legs *US, 1981*. **3** a safe's tumblers *US, 1949*. ▶ **go to the dogs** to be slowly ruined *UK, 1619*. ▶ **the dogs** greyhound racing *UK, 1927*

dog's abuse *noun* very harsh abuse (that you would only give to a dog) *IRELAND, 1998*

dog's age *noun* a very long time *US, 1836*

dog's bait *noun* a huge amount *US, 1933*

dog's ballocks *noun* in typography, a colon dash (:-) *UK, 1961*

dog's balls *noun* no money at all *FIJI, 1993*. ▶ **stick/stand out like dog's balls** to be obvious *AUSTRALIA, 1986*

dogsbody *noun* a worker who is given the tedious menial tasks to perform, a drudge. Originally military or naval *UK, 1922*

dog's bollock *noun* an article of little or no value *UK, 1997*

dog's bollocks; dog's ballocks; the bollocks *noun* anything considered to be the finest, the most excellent, the best. Derived from the phrase 'It sticks out like a dog's ballocks' said of something that the speaker considers obvious, hence the sense of 'someone or something that sticks out from the rest'. Often abbreviated in speech to 'the dog's' *UK, 1989*

dog's breakfast *noun* an unmitigated mess *AUSTRALIA, 1934*

dog's cock; dog's prick *noun* in typography, an exclamation mark (!) *UK, 1961*

dog's dick *noun* a mess, a disgusting mess. A variation of DOG'S DINNER (a mess) *UK, 2003*

dog's dinner *noun* **1** used as a comparison for someone who is smartly dressed, stylishly or formally-attired. Variants of the comparison include 'dolled up like a dog's dinner'; 'done up like a dog's dinner'; 'dressed up like a dogs dinner'; and 'got up like a dog's dinner' *UK, 1936*. **2** a mess, a disgusting mess *UK, 1997*

dog's disease *noun* influenza or gastro-enteritis or malaria or a hangover, etc *AUSTRALIA, 1890*

dog's eye *noun* a meat pie. Rhyming slang *AUSTRALIA, 1988*

dog shift *noun* a work shift in the middle of the night *US, 1977*

dogshit *noun* **1** anything or anyone considered to be worthless or disgusting *US, 1968*. **2** Italian sausage *US, 1996*. **3** the epitome of feeling wretched or ill *UK, 1999*

dogshit *adjective* worthless or disgusting *US, 1967*

dog show *noun* in the military, an inspection of the feet *US, 1949*

dog's lipstick *noun* the uncircumcised penis when erect. From an image of the head of the penis extending beyond the protection of the foreskin in a manner reminiscent of a lipstick protruding beyond its decorative protective casing; the reference to a dog is open to interpretation *UK, 2003*

dog's lunch *noun* a physically repulsive person *US, 1964*

dog soldier *noun* a common soldier *US, 1950*

dog squad *noun* undercover police *AUSTRALIA, 1967*

dogster *noun* a member of the Mongrel Mob, a New Zealand prison gang *NEW ZEALAND, 2000*

dog's tooth *noun* truth. Rhyming slang *UK, 1992*

dog-style; doggy style *noun* a sexual position in which the woman or passive male kneels and the man enters her from behind *US, 1957*

dog's vomit *noun* disgusting food *AUSTRALIA, 1966*

dogtag *noun* **1** an identity disc *US, 1918*. **2** a prescription for a narcotic, possibly legal or possibly forged or illegally obtained *US, 1959*

dog-tucker *noun* a person or animal that consistently fails and is deemed worthless. From an earlier, literal sense of the word as 'a sheep to be slaughtered for dog meat' *NEW ZEALAND, 1999*

dog turd *noun* a cigar *US, 1969*

dog wagon *noun* **1** a bus or van used to transport prisoners from jail to prison *US, 1952*. **2** a lunch counter; a diner *US, 1900*

dog-wank *adjective* worthless *UK, 2000*

dogwash *noun* a task that is not particularly important but is pursued instead of a more demanding, more important task *US, 1991*

dog watch *noun* a work or guard shift in the middle of the night *US, 1901*

dog water *noun* colourless seminal fluid *US, 1965*

dog with two dicks; dog with two choppers; dog with two cocks; dog with two tails used as a simile for being delighted or very pleased. Generally in phrases: '... as a dog with...' or 'like a dog with...'. 'A dog with two choppers' is first recorded in 1950; 'a dog with two tails' is noted by the *Oxford English Dictionary* in 1953 *UK, 1950s*

doh! used for registering frustration when things fail to turn out as planned, or at the relisation that you have said something foolish. Popularly associated with, and a catchphrase of, Homer Simpson in the television cartoon *The Simpsons* (since 1987) *UK, 1945*

doight! used for expressing distress. A wildly popular catchphrase verbalization from *The Simpsons* television cartoon *US, 1994*

doily *noun* a toupee *US, 1952*

do in *verb* **1** to kill *UK, 1905*. **2** to injure *UK, 1905*. **3** to exhaust. Thus DONE IN (exhausted) *UK, 1917*. **4** to defeat, to beat *AUSTRALIA, 1916*. ▶ **do yourself in** to commit suicide. A personalised variation of the first meaning *UK, 1999*

doing a party *noun* a tactic employed when performing a three-card-trick: a confederate of the card sharp pretends to be winning so as to encourage the unsuspecting to stake heavily *UK, 1977*

doings *noun* **1** used as a collective noun for unspecified necessities. Generally as 'the doings' *UK, 1919*. **2** excrement *UK, 1967*

doink *noun* a socially inept, out-of-touch person *US, 1968*

do it! used as an exhortation to experience life rather than analyse it *US, 1968*

do-it fluid *noun* alcoholic drink. Based on the observed effect of alcohol on sexual inhibition *US, 1980*

do it now! a catchphrase in jocular or semi-irrelevant use. Originally a business slogan; first recorded in this use in 1927 but dating from no later than 1910, and still common in 1965 *AUSTRALIA, 1927*

do it the hard way! used in derision to an awkward worker who is struggling with a task. Often preceded by 'that's right!' and occasionally completed with 'standing up in a hammock' *CANADA, 1961*

do-it-yourself *noun* masturbation *UK, 1960*

do-it-yourself kit *noun* a steam locomotive or locomotives. As an ironic contrast to diesel technology. Coinage is credited to Mr Bill Handy, a train driver *UK, 1970*

dojah *noun* marijuana *US, 2004*

dole *noun* ▶ **on the dole** in receipt of unemployment benefits *UK, 1925*. ▶ **the dole** unemployment benefit; the local offices from which unemployment benefit is managed *UK, 1919*

dole bludger *noun* a person habitually living off social security payments. A term of high opprobrium, often applied contemptuously to any recipient of the dole with the implication that employment could be found by anyone if they so desired AUSTRALIA, 1976

dole-on-sea *noun* a seaside resort with few visitors and high unemployment. Formed on THE DOLE (unemployment benefit) UK, 2003

doley *noun* a person in receipt of unemployment benefit AUSTRALIA, 1953

doll *noun* 1 a young woman US, 1840. 2 a very attractive person of any sex that you find attractive US, 1963. 3 used as a term of address US, 1949. 4 a barbiturate capsule; an amphetamine capsule or tablet. Coined by Jacqueline Susann, author of *Valley of the Dolls* US, 1966. 5 a tablet of MDMA, the recreational drug best known as ecstasy UK, 2003

dollar *noun* 1 five shillings. Dating from those happy days when the rate of exchange was US$4 to £1 UK, 1848. 2 a variety of MDMA, the recreational drug best known as ecstasy UK, 1996. 3 money UK, 2000

dollar *nickname* Route 100 in eastern Pennsylvania US, 1977

dollar ride *noun* an orientation flight on a military aircraft US, 1975

dollars *noun* a type of bet in an illegal numbers game lottery US, 1957

dollars to doughnut *adverb* at very high odds, indicating a high degree of certainty US, 1984

dollop *noun* a lump; hence, in a figurative sense, a clumsy individual; a formless mess – 'a dollop of custard'. From an earlier sense (a tuft of grass) UK, 1812

dollop; dollop out *verb* to share out a formless mess. From the noun sense UK, 2000

doll's eyes *noun* eyes rolling upward, suggesting neurological depression US, 1989

doll shop *noun* a brothel US, 1990

doll's house *noun* a prison. Most likely inspired by the toy and not the Ibsen play UK, 1996

doll up *verb* to dress up, to refine US, 1906

dolly *noun* 1 the vagina. In the C19, a 'dolly' was a 'penis', possibly from a 'child's dolly' (a toy a girl might play with); equally, it could derive from 'washing dolly' (a device plunged in and out of wet laundry). The etymology here is likely to be the former: 'Can I play with your dolly?' UK, 2001. 2 an attractive young woman. Very much a word of its time UK, 1906. 3 a homosexual who lives in the suburbs UK, 2003. 4 a lesbian prisoner's lover NEW ZEALAND, 1999. 5 a very feminine fashion style of the 1960s UK, 1968. 6 a capsule of Dolophine™, known generically as methadone US, 1954. 7 in cricket, a simple catch. Possibly of Anglo-Indian origin. Reduced from 'dolly catch' UK, 1904

dolly *verb* to interrogate AUSTRALIA, 1975

dolly *adjective* attractive, pretty; nice. Polari UK, 1964

dolly bag *noun* the cloth bag carried by female prisoners UK, 1996

dolly bird *noun* an attractive young woman UK, 1964

dolly boy *noun* a youthful, attractive homosexual male prostitute. An evolution from DILLY BOY UK, 1979

Dolly Cotton *adjective* rotten. Rhyming slang UK, 1931

dolly dimple; dolly *adjective* simple. Glasgow rhyming slang. Current in English prisons February 2002 UK, 1988

dolly flapper *noun* a railroad pointsman US, 1946

dolly mixtures *noun* the cinema, the movies. Rhyming slang for 'the pictures' UK, 1992

dolly-over-teakettles *adverb* head-over-heels US, 1982

Dolly Parton *noun* in craps, a roll of two ones. Dolly Parton is a talented and popular American country singer and songwriter with big hair and big breasts; the single dots on the two dice suggested to someone her breasts US, 1983

dolly sweetness *noun* a pretty girl US, 1947

dolo *noun* methadone. A shortened form of Dolophine™, a protected trade name for methadone US, 1986

do lo *adverb* secret. An abbreviation of DOWNLOW US, 1999

dolphin *noun* 1 a variety of MDMA, the recreational drug best known as ecstasy UK, 1996. 2 a flaccid penis US, 1995. ► **wax the dolphin** of a male, to masturbate US, 2002

dolphin ball *noun* in pinball, a ball that stays in play for a relatively long period without scoring many points US, 1977

DOM *noun* an older homosexual who is attracted to younger men and boys; a *dirty old man* US, 1966

dom *adjective* 1 sexually *dominant* US, 1989. 2 stupid, dumb. An Afrikaans word in the South African English colloquial vocabulary SOUTH AFRICA, 1942

dom; domme *noun* 1 a dominatrix US, 2002. 2 the dominant performer in a pornographic sex scene US, 2000. 3 a sexual dominant in sadomasochistic sexual relationships US, 1989. 4 a person's room, apartment or house. A shortened variant of the more common DOMMY US, 1959

do me a favour; do me *noun* a neighbour. Rhyming slang. Like many next door neighbours the rhyme is not quite perfect UK, 1998

do me a favour! used for expressing disbelief and refutation of a point or suggestion just raised UK, 1958

dome doily *noun* a hat US, 1947

do me good *noun* a *Woodbine cigarette. Rhyming slang that evolved during World War 1, and survived in mid-C20 as an expression of defiance when cigarettes were scientifically linked with cancer UK, 1960

domes *noun* LSD US, 1980

dome slug *noun* in Antarctica, a support personnel assigned to the geodesic dome at the top of the American Scott-Amundsen base ANTARCTICA, 2003

domie *noun* dory-mate (short form) CANADA, 1999

Dominican Dandy *nickname* Juan Marichal (b.1937), a high-kicking, overpowering pitcher (1960 – 75). From the Dominican Republic, and 'a fastidious dresser' US, 1968

domino *noun* 1 a black and white capsule containing a mixture of central nervous system stimulants and depressants US, 1971. 2 a 12.5 mg tablet of Durophet™, an amphetamine US, 1971

domino *verb* to stop or finish US, 1953

domkop *noun* a fool. From Afrikaans *dom* (stupid) and *kop* (head) SOUTH AFRICA, 1910

dommo *noun* one who performs well. Applied to skateboarding, surfing and snowboarding US, 1997

dommo *verb* to perform well; to dominate US, 1990

dommy; dommie *noun* a home. From 'domicile' US, 1943

Dom P *noun* Dom Perignon champagne UK, 2002

doms *noun* dominoes UK, 1982

don *verb* ► **don the beard** to perform oral sex on a woman AUSTRALIA, 1971

don; don man *noun* a respected leader. Ultimately from Spanish *Don* (an honorific), via gangster use. West Indian, hence UK black UK, 2000

dona; donah; donna; doner *noun* a woman, especially a girlfriend. Polari, from Spanish *doña* or Portuguese *dona* (a woman) UK, 1859

dona juana *noun* marijuana. A Spanish 'Lady Jane' US, 1986

dona juanita *noun* marijuana. A Spanish 'Lady Jane' US, 1938

Donald Duck *verb* to have sexual intercourse. Rhyming slang for FUCK AUSTRALIA, 1983

Donald Duck; donald *noun* 1 an act of sexual intercourse. Rhyming slang for FUCK AUSTRALIA, 1983. 2 by extension, a 'fuck' in all other senses. Rhyming slang, from the Disney cartoon character UK, 1992. 3 luck. Rhyming slang, from the Disney cartoon character UK, 1979

Donald Ducked *adjective* exhausted. Rhyming slang for FUCKED UK, 1988

Donald Duck Navy noun the anti-submarine fleet of the US Navy US, 1947

Donald Duck suit noun the blue uniform of sailors in the US Navy US, 1972

Donald Peers; donalds noun the ears. Rhyming slang, formed on the name of popular singer and recording artist Donald Peers, 1909–73 UK, 1984

Donald Trump noun an act of defecation. Rhyming slang for DUMP, based on celebrated US businessman Donald Trump (b.1946), possibly an extravagant play on New York landmark Trump Tower UK, 2002

donar noun a steady girlfriend US, 1993

don dada noun a very important person. Rasta patois for 'TOP DOG, highest of all dons' JAMAICA, 2003

donder; donner noun used as an abusive term of address or reference, a bastard. From Afrikaans donder (a scoundrel) SOUTH AFRICA, 1969

done and dusted adjective 1 completely finished UK, 2001. 2 beaten up UK, 1950

done deal noun an agreement that has been reached. Folksy, a hint of the American South US, 1990

done-done adjective over-cooked BAHAMAS, 1982

done in adjective tired out, exhausted UK, 2001

done thing noun whatever is considered to be the correct etiquette. Always with 'the' UK, 1961

done up adjective dressed up UK, C20

dong noun 1 the penis US, 1900. 2 a thing of no worth UK, 1991

dong verb to punch or hit AUSTRALIA, 1916

donga noun 1 (especially in South Australia) natural bush wilderness AUSTRALIA, 1967. 2 a temporary dwelling AUSTRALIA, 1900. 3 a watercourse AUSTRALIA, 1902. 4 a sleeping area. An Australian contribution to the language of the South Pole ANTARCTICA, 2003

dongce noun the penis UK, 2001

donger noun the penis AUSTRALIA, 1971

dongle noun 1 a security scheme for a commerical microcomputer progam US, 1991. 2 any small device designed to add functionality to a computer, often plugged into a USB port US, 1997. 3 an electronic key that hangs on a cord around the neck UK, 2001

don jem noun marijuana UK, 1998

donk noun 1 a donkey US, 1868. 2 a racehorse. An abbreviation of 'donkey' NEW ZEALAND, 1952. 3 large, protruding buttocks. A term often associated with celebrity Jennifer Lopez US, 2003. 4 an engine US, 1942

donkey noun 1 a black person US, 1857. 2 a manual labourer US, 1932. 3 a fool UK, 1840. 4 (especially in South Australia) a lift on a bicycle AUSTRALIA, 1981. 5 a resident of Guernsey (in the Channel Islands) according to those on Jersey UK, 1991. ▶ **pull your donkey** (used of a male) to masturbate US, 1990

donkey verb (especially in South Australia) to give someone a lift on a bicycle AUSTRALIA, 1981

donkey days noun a very long time BAHAMAS, 1982

donkey deep adjective enthusiastically engaged NEW ZEALAND, 1998

donkey dick noun 1 a man with a large penis; a large penis US, 1980. 2 sausage; unidentified pressed meat US, 1968. 3 the flexible spout attached to the opening of a container US, 1990. 4 a large electrical cable connector US, 1990. 5 a prolonged, insatiable erection due to extended heroin use US, 1997

donkey doctor noun a mechanic who works on donkey engines US, 2003

donkey jammer noun the operator of a donkey (auxiliary) engine CANADA, 1953

donkey-lick verb to defeat convincingly AUSTRALIA, 1890

donkey punch noun during homosexual anal intercourse, a sharp blow given by the active partner to the passive partner's kidneys. The sudden pain from the blow causes a clenching of the

buttocks and tightening of the rectal passage, thereby enhancing the pleasure of the penetrating participant UK, 2005

donkey-puncher noun the operator of a donkey engine US, 1920

donkey's ages noun a very long time. A variation of DONKEY'S YEARS UK, 1984

donkey shins thank you. Intentionally butchered German US, 1990

donkey sight noun an imprecise but easily manoeuvred manual sight on a tank's main gun US, 1990

donkey style adjective (used of sex) anal US, 2002

donkey's years; donkeys' years; donkeys noun a very long time. A pun on the length and sound of a 'donkey's ears' UK, 1916

donkey vote noun a vote made by simply filling out a ballot paper in the order the candidates are listed in AUSTRALIA, 1964

donkey work noun difficult, menial labour UK, 1920

donko noun a lunchroom or tea room at a workplace NEW ZEALAND, 1976

donks noun a very long time. An abbreviation of DONKEY'S YEARS, but it is worth noting the similarity to synonymous YONKS UK, 1995

donner; donder verb to thrash, to beat up SOUTH AFRICA, 1916

donnie; donny noun a fracas. An abbreviation of DONNYBROOK NEW ZEALAND, 1960

donniker noun 1 a toilet US, 1937. 2 the penis US, 1951. 3 a railway brakeman on a freight train US, 1932

donniker location noun a poor location on a carnival midway US, 1985

Donniker Sam noun a man who begs for money in a public toilet US, 1981

donny noun a fight AUSTRALIA, 1969

donnybrook noun a riot, a tumult UK, 1852

Don Revie noun an alcoholic drink, especially beer. Rhyming slang for BEVVY (an alcoholic drink, especially beer), formed from the name of football manager Don Revie, 1927–89, and probably coined during his tenure in charge of the England team (1974–78) UK, 1998

don't noun in craps, a bet against the shooter US, 1950

don't ask, don't tell used as a humorous, if jaded, reminder that some things are best left unknown. An adage coined to describe the official approach to homosexuals in the US military under the Clinton administration; a soldier would not be asked about his or her sexual preference, but would be expected not to reveal their homosexuality US, 1993

don't be rude noun food. Rhyming slang UK, 1992

don't call us, we'll call you used as a catchphrase that is generally understood to be a polite, or not-so-polite, rejection of an application for employment. Adopted from the world of entertainment where it is traditionally supposed to signal the end of an unsuccessful audition US, 1968

don't-care-damn adjective entirely indifferent GRENADA, 1976

don't-care-ish adjective apathetic, indifferent US, 1927

don't come the raw prawn do not attempt to dupe me. Military slang from World War 2. The literal meaning of this phrase has not been satisfactorily explained. 'Prawn' has been used in Australia since C19 to mean 'fool', so a 'raw prawn' could mean a 'naive fool', and if 'come' is to be understood as 'to act the part of', the phrase would imply trying to dupe someone by feigned ignorance. Some have defined 'raw prawn' as 'something far-fetched, difficult to swallow', if this is so, then 'come' would mean 'perpetrate', which is also possible AUSTRALIA, 1948

don't come the uncooked crustacean do not attempt to dupe me. Rare variant of DON'T COME THE RAW PRAWN AUSTRALIA, 1971

don't do anything I wouldn't; don't do anything I wouldn't do used jocularly, as good advice, often as parting advice, and often in a sexual context. Occasionally the sentiment is changed to 'don't do anyone I wouldn't do' UK, 1984

don't do that, then in computing, used as a stock response to a complaint that a certain action causes a problem *US, 1991*

don't give me that! I don't believe you! *UK, 1984*

don't go there!; don't even go there! used for expressing a lack of interest in pursuing a topic *US, 1993*

don't hold your breath! don't expect anything to happen; anything that is expected is unlikely to happen for a long time, if at all *US, 1971*

don't let today be the day! used as an all-purpose, very serious threat *US, 2002*

don't mean nothin' used as an all-purpose reaction to any bad news among American soldiers in Vietnam *US, 1990*

don't sleep! don't kid yourself! *US, 2002*

don't spend it all at once! used as a jocular injunction given when handing over a very small sum of money *UK, 1977*

don't-talk-about *conjunction* not to mention *TRINIDAD AND TOBAGO, 2003*

don't tense! relax! *US, 1951*

don't work too hard! used as a jocular admonition by, for instance, a worker going on holiday to workmates left behind *UK, 1984*

doo *noun* a skidoo, used for transport over ice and snow *ANTARCTICA, 2003*

doob; doub *noun* an amphetamine pill or other central nervous system stimulant *UK, 1969*

doobage *noun* marijuana *US, 1985*

doober *noun* a marijuana cigarette *US, 2000*

doobie; dooby; doob; dube *noun* **1** a marijuana cigarette. The earliest identification is as 'Negro slang for a marijuana roach'. A belief persists that the term was spawned from the 1950s American children's television show, *Romper Room*, in which children were urged to be 'good do-be's'. Alternative spelling with a 'u' for 'dubee' and 'dubbe' *US, 1967*. **2** a pill *UK, 2002*

doobie-head *noun* a smoker of marijuana in cigarette-fashion, *1999*

doobious *adjective* under the influence of marijuana. A play with the conventional 'dubious' and DOOBIE (a marijuana cigarette) *US, 1986*

doobry *noun* used as a replacement for any noun that the user cannot or does not wish to specify *UK, 1950s*

dooby *noun* marijuana *UK, 2000*

dooce *verb* to be dismissed from employment for the contents of a 'blog' (an on-line diary), website or other shared journal. Named after *www.dooce.com;* established in 2001 by Los Angeles website designer Heather Armstrong, who is credited with coining the word, and who, in 2002, was fired from her job for publishing stories about her workmates on her website *US, 2005*

doocing *noun* dismissal from employment for the contents of a 'blog' (an on-line diary), website or other shared journal. From the verb sense *US, 2005*

doodackie *noun* an object the name of which escapes or is not important to the speaker *NEW ZEALAND, 1999*

doodackied up *adjective* dressed up *NEW ZEALAND, 1947*

doodad; dodad *noun* a trivial or useless object *US, 1877*

doodads *noun* the bleed period of the menstrual cycle *AUSTRALIA, 2001*

doodah *noun* **1** used as a replacement for any noun that the user cannot or does not wish to specify. Employed to comic effect by the Bonzo Dog Doo Dah Band, formed in 1965. The 'doodah' was dropped as success beckoned *UK, 1928*. **2** the vagina *US, 2001*. **3** semen *UK, 2003*

dooder *noun* the female breast *BAHAMAS, 1982*

doodle *noun* the penis. Children's vocabulary *US, 1980*

doodle *verb* **1** to have sex *US, 1957*. **2** to play music in a whimsical, relaxed manner *US, 1955*

doodle-a-squat *noun* in circus and carnival usage, money *US, 1981*

doodlebug *noun* **1** in oil drilling, any mechanical or electrical device claimed as a tool to find oil *US, 1924*. **2** any small vehicle, such as a small tractor that pulls dollies in a warehouse *US, 1935*

doodlebugger *noun* in oil drilling, a person who claims divine powers in locating oil *US, 1936*

doodle-gaze *verb* to stare at a woman in a lingering, lustful fashion *US, 1990*

doodles *noun* the testicles. Combines the genital sense of DOODLE (the penis) with the vague sense (a small nameless article) *US, 2001*

doodly *noun* anything at all *US, 1939*

doodly-squat *noun* **1** nothing at all *US, 1934*. **2** low grade marijuana *US, 1979*

doo-doo *noun* **1** excrement, literal or figurative. Also as 'do-do'. A child's euphemism; by reduplication of 'do' or 'doo' (excrement) *US, 1948*. **2** trouble *US, 1989*

doody; dooty *noun* excrement. Childish *US, 1969*

doof *noun* **1** dance music *AUSTRALIA, 1998*. **2** a dance music aficionado *AUSTRALIA, 1998*. **3** a party open to the public, often announced and cited clanedestinely, featuring drugs, music and sensory overload *AUSTRALIA, 2002*. **4** a slow-witted person, a fool. Originally a Scottish dialect word *US, 1971*

doof *verb* to hit someone *UK: SCOTLAND, 1988*

doofah; doofer *noun* a thing, a gadget, an unnamed article. Probably from the sense that such an article will *'do for* now' *UK, 1945*

doofball *noun* an inept social outcast *US, 1977*

doofer *noun* a dance music aficionado *AUSTRALIA, 1998*

doofing *noun* dance music *AUSTRALIA, 1997*

doofus; dufus *noun* **1** a dolt, a fool *US, 1955*. **2** in caving and pot-holing, an inept cave. A specialist variation *US, 2004*

doohickey *noun* an object the exact name of which escapes the speaker *US, 1914*

doojigger *noun* an object the name of which escapes the speaker *US, 1927*

dook *noun* **1** in the gambling game two-up, a throw of heads three times in a row *AUSTRALIA, 1966*. **2** a hand *AUSTRALIA, 1924*. **3** a fist *AUSTRALIA, 1977*. **4** (especially in Western Australia) a playing marble. Has the short vowel of 'book' and may be spelt 'doog' *AUSTRALIA, 1965*

dook *verb* **1** to pass or hand over something secretly *AUSTRALIA, 1915*. **2** to pay a bribe or gratuity *AUSTRALIA, 1945*. ▶ **dook them** in the gambling game two-up, to throw heads three times in a row *AUSTRALIA, 1966*

dooker *noun* a member of a criminal enterprise whose job is to distract the authorities by creating a diversion *US, 1956*

dookie; dookey; dooky; dukey *noun* **1** excrement. Children's vocabulary *US, 1969*. **2** a paymaster. Carnival usage, without variant spellings *US, 1960*

Dookie *nickname* a student, alumni or supporter of Duke University *US, 1990*

doolacky *noun* a thing; a thingumabob *AUSTRALIA, 1950*

doolally; doolali; doolally tap; doodle-ally; doodally; tapped *adjective* **1** mad. From the obsolete noun 'doolally tap' (a form of madness). Deolali (a military sanitorium in Bombay) corrupted and abbreviated as 'doo-lally' plus Hundustani *tap* (fever) *UK, 1925*. **2** extremely drunk. Extends from the previous sense *UK, 1943*. **3** in a state of sensory confusion. A compound of all senses: 'mad', 'drunk' and 'broken' *UK, 2001*

doolander *noun* a powerful blow *UK: SCOTLAND, 1985*

dooley *noun* **1** a privvy; an outdoor toilet *US, 1968*. **2** heroin *US, 1994*

doolie *noun* a fool *UK: SCOTLAND, 1985*

doolin *noun* a Roman Catholic. From Mickey Doolin, the quintessential Irishman *NEW ZEALAND, 1959*

doo-mommie go fuck your mother. A phonetic approximation of the Vietnamese *du ma* (fuck your mother) *US, 1991*

DOOM pussy mission *noun* a night bombing run flown by US bombers over North Vietnam. The DOOM came from the the the Da Nang Officer's Open Mess, the 'pussy' refered to the relative lack of danger in a night mission *US, 1991*

doom tube *noun* the hollow of a wave that does not offer a surfer the ability to leave the hollow *US, 1991*

doomy *adjective* very depressed and discouraged; dismal *UK, 1968*

door *noun* **1** a supplier of drugs *CANADA, 2002*. **2** a capsule of Doriden™, a trade name for glutethimide, a sedative *US, 1992*. ▶ **from the door** from the outset *US, 1967*

doorbell *noun* the nipple of a woman's breast *US, 1973*

doorcard *noun* in seven-card stud poker, a player's first face-up card *UK, 2003*

door-hugger *noun* a girl who sits as far away from her date when he is driving as possible *US, 1966*

door jockey *noun* a doorman *US, 1956*

doorknob *noun* **1** a socially inept person *US, 1994*. **2** a shilling. Pre-decimal rhyming slang for BOB (a shilling) *UK, 1961*

doormat *noun* **1** a person who is easily manipulated by others *UK, 1883*. **2** a toupee *US, 1952*. **3** in surfing, a bodyboarder, that is a surfer who lies down on the surfboard. Derogatory *SOUTH AFRICA, 2003*

door pops *noun* dice that have been altered so that they will score a 7 or 11 more frequently than normal *US, 1950*

door-pusher *noun* a girl who stays as close as possible to the passenger door while riding in a car on a date *US, 1959*

doorshaker *noun* a night watchman *US, 1942*

doorstep *noun* ▶ **not on your own doorstep** a piece of folk-philosophy (often as an injunction): do not get sexually involved with anyone close to home, or at work *UK, 2003*

doorstep *verb* of a journalist, to wait near a subject's door in order to obtain an interview, a photograph, etc *UK, 1981*

doorstep sandwich *noun* a sandwich that uses two very thick slices of bread *IRELAND, 1989*

doorstop *noun* in computing, broken or obsolete equipment *US, 1991*

door whore *noun* **1** someone employed to welcome clubbers to a club but who actually enforces a strict exclusion policy based on the club's style requirements *UK, 1999*. **2** a restaurant hostess *US, 1995*

doos *noun* a despicable person *SOUTH AFRICA, 2004*

doosey *noun* heroin *UK, 2003*

doosh *noun* the face. Glasgow slang *UK: SCOTLAND, 1988*

do out of *verb* to swindle someone out of something *UK, 1825*

doover *noun* **1** a thing; a thingumabob. Originally in World War 2 services slang. Suggested origins include (1) a variant on DOOFAH, (2) from Yiddish, a variant of Hebrew *davar* (a thing), and (3) extracted from HORSES DOOVERS. The first two are much more likely that the last *AUSTRALIA, 1940*. **2** the penis. From the sense as an 'unnamed thing' *AUSTRALIA, 1971*

do over *verb* **1** to beat someone up *UK, 1866*. **2** to swindle or take advantage of *AUSTRALIA, 1952*. **3** to frisk, to search through someone's clothing or property *UK, 1984*. **4** to have sex with someone *AUSTRALIA, 1948*

dooverlackie; doovilackie *noun* a thing; a thingumabob *AUSTRALIA, 1987*

doowally *noun* an idiot, a person with a less than first-class grip on reality. Glasgow slang, perhaps related to DOOLALLY (mad) *UK: SCOTLAND, 1988*

doo-wop *noun* a musical style popular in the 1950s, featuring nonsense syllables sung in close harmony *US, 1969*

doozer *noun* **1** anything that is large or outstanding *CANADA, 1975*. **2** an exceptional example or specimen *US, 1930*

doozy *adjective* an extraordinary example of something *US, 1916*

dop *noun* **1** the head. From Afrikaans *dop* (an empty vessel) *SOUTH AFRICA, 1978*. **2** any brandy. From Afrikaans *doppe* (husks of grapes) *SOUTH AFRICA, 1896*. **3** a short drink of any spirits, a tot; the act of drinking. Variant 'doppie' *SOUTH AFRICA, 1996*

dop *verb* to drink (alcohol). From Afrikaans *dop* (a drink) *SOUTH AFRICA, 1977*

dope *noun* **1** a drug, drugs, especially if illegal *US, 1900*. **2** marijuana *SOUTH AFRICA, 1946*. **3** heroin *US, 1891*. **4** information, especially confidential information *US, 1902*. **5** a stupid fool *UK, 1851*. **6** money. Teen slang *SOUTH AFRICA, 2003*. **7** in oil drilling, a lubricant *US, 1954*

dope *verb* **1** to use recreational drugs *US, 1889*. **2** in the used car business, to hide a car's mechanical flaws *US, 1968*

dope *adjective* **1** stylish, excellent, best. A word that defines and sneers at society's failures; this common hip-hop usage, credited to rap-pioneer Chief Rocker Busy Bee, rejects the negative and promotes the positive in the 'bad-as-good' way *US, 1981*. **2** dull. Teen slang *SOUTH AFRICA, 2003*

dope! used for expressing approval *UK, 2003*

dope cake *noun* a baked confection which has marijuana or hashish as a major ingredient *UK, 2002*

dope corner *noun* a street corner where drugs are usually sold *US, 1992*

dope daddy *noun* a drug dealer *US, 1936*

dopefied *adjective* amazing *US, 2000*

dope fiend *noun* a drug addict *US, 1895*

dopehead *noun* a regular drug user *US, 1903*

dope house *noun* a house or building where drugs are bought and used *US, 1968*

dope kit *noun* the equipment needed to prepare and inject drugs *US, 1973*

dopeman *noun* a drug dealer *US, 1974*

dope off *verb* to fail to pay attention; to fall asleep *US, 1918*

dope on a rope *noun* in the language of hang gliding, a paraglider pilot *US, 1992*

dope out *verb* **1** to become, or spend time, intoxicated on recreational drugs *US, 1970*. **2** to discover, to ascertain, to comprehend; to work out *US, 1906*

dope pull *noun* an addict's need for drugs *US, 1997*

doper *noun* a drug user *US, 1922*

dope rope *noun* a cord attached to a surfer and his surfboard *US, 1991*

dope sheet *noun* **1** a leaflet or pamphlet offering 'inside' tips on horse betting *US, 1900*. **2** in the television and film industries, a running report on shooting kept by an assistant director *UK, 1960*

dope slope *noun* a beginner's ski slope *US, 1963*

dope smoke *verb* to smoke marijuana *US, 1980*

dopester *noun* a person who analyzes the past performance of racehorses and athletic teams in order to predict future performance *US, 1907*

dope stick *noun* a cigarette *US, 1904*

dope up *verb* to use drugs *US, 1942*

dopey *adjective* **1** dull-witted, foolish *US, 1903*. **2** sleepy, lethargic, dull; half-asleep under the influence of drink, medicinal or recreational drugs *US, 1896*

dopey; dopie *noun* a drug user or addict *US, 1929*

dopium *noun* opium; heroin *US, 1942*

dor; door; dorie *noun* a capsule of glutethimide (trade name Doriden™), a hypnotic sedative and central nervous system depressant *US, 1986*

doradilla *noun* marijuana. The Spanish zoological name for a 'wagtail' *US, 1973*

do-rag *noun* a scarf worn on the head after a hair treatment process *US, 1970*

dorcas *noun* used affectionately as a term of endearment. The Dorcas Society is a charitable society founded in the early C19, taking its name and biblical inspiration from the charitable nature of Dorcas recorded in Acts ix, 36. The original slang use, now obsolete, was as 'a seamstress who worked for charity'; that spirit is invested in this polari usage as 'one who cares' *UK, 2002*

dordy! used for registering surprise. English gypsy use, from Romany *dawdi* UK, 2000

do-re-mi; dough-rey-me noun money. Extends from DOUGH (money), punning on 'do-re-mi/doh-ray-mi' in the 'tonic sol-fa' system of music. Most strongly associated with Woody Guthrie's 1937 song '(If You Ain't Got the) Do Re Mi' US, 1926

dorf noun a social outcast US, 1967

Dorian love noun homosexual love and/or sex. From Oscar Wilde's portrait US, 1987

do-right noun a favour US, 1986

do-right adjective righteous, diligent US, 1936

do-right boy noun a police officer US, 1970

do-righter noun a person who does not use drugs US, 1970

Doris noun 1 a woman. From the slightly old-fashioned female name UK, 2001. 2 a police van BARBADOS, 1965

Doris Day noun 1 homosexuality. Rhyming slang for GAY, formed from the name of American singer and actress Doris Day (b.1924), perhaps as a knowingly ironic reference to Rock Hudson, a famously closeted homosexual, with whom she co-starred on several occasions UK, 1992. 2 a way. Rhyming slang which reduces to 'doris' UK, 1992

dork noun 1 the penis US, 1961. 2 a socially inept, unfashionable, harmless person US, 1964

dork verb to act in a socially inept fashion US, 1990

dorkbrain noun an inept outcast US, 1974

dorkbreath noun used as a term of abuse US, 1974

dorkus noun a fool. An embellished DORK US, 1979

dorky adjective odd; out of step with the rest; without social skills. From DORK US, 1970

dorm noun a *dormitory* UK, 1900

dormie noun a student living in a dormitory; a person with whom you share a dormitory room US, 1966

dorm rat noun a person living in a dormitory US, 1963

dorm rot noun a bruise on the skin caused by a partner's mouth during foreplay; a suction kiss US, 1970

do-room noun a room where drugs are used, especially injected US, 1974

Dorothy noun a tyre. Rhyming slang, formed from the name of Welsh torch-singer Dorothy Squires, 1915–98, always used in a reduced form UK, 1992

Dorothy Dixer noun a pre-arranged question put to a Minister in parliament for which he or she has a prepared answer. Named after Dorothy Dix, a popular US question-and-answer columnist AUSTRALIA, 1963

dory plug nickname a member of the Royal Canadian Navy CANADA, 1995

dose noun 1 a case of a sexually transmitted infection US, 1914. 2 a curse, a spell BAHAMAS, 1982. 3 an amount or quantity of something UK, 1607. 4 a four-month prison sentence. In earlier use (1860) as 'three months' hard labour' UK, 1996. 5 a single experience with LSD US, 1967. 6 a dolt US, 1969. ▶ **like a dose of salts** very quickly, and effectively. From the laxative properties of Epsom Salts; especially as 'go through something like a dose of salts' UK, 1837

dose verb 1 to introduce a drug, espsecially LSD, into a host substance; to give a drug to someone without their knowledge US, 1957. 2 to share drugs US, 1997. 3 to ingest; to take a dose of US, 1971. 4 to infect another with a sexually transmitted disease US, 1918

dosed up adjective infected with a sexually transmitted disease US, 1969

dose of the shits noun 1 a case of diarrhoea AUSTRALIA, 1979. 2 a bad mood AUSTRALIA, 1973

doses noun LSD CANADA, 2002

dose up verb to pass a sexually transmitted infection to someone else US, 1950

dosey-doe verb to dance, literally or figuratively. From a basic call in American square dancing US, 1961

dosh noun money. Possibly a combination of 'dollars' and 'cash'; there are also suggestions that the etymology leads back to DOSS (temporary accommodation), hence, it has been claimed, the money required 'to doss', or Scottish dialect *doss* (tobacco pouch, a purse containing something of value) – note, too, that tobacco is related to money via QUID. US 'dosh' didn't survive but in mid-C20 UK and Australia the word was resurrected, or coincidentally recoined US, 1854

dosh verb to give UK, 1999

doss noun 1 sleep US, 1894. 2 a waste of time UK, 1998. 3 an easy thing to do UK, 1999. 4 an attractive female US, 1968. 5 a brakevan (caboose) US, 1977

doss verb to sleep in temporary accommodation, usually on an improvised bed – floor, sofa, etc. Sometimes embellished to 'doss down' UK, 1744

doss about; doss verb to waste time UK, 1935

dossbag noun 1 a sleeping bag. Gulf war usage UK, 1991. 2 a lazy or idle person UK, 2003

dosser noun a homeless person, a vagrant. Originally, 'one who frequented a DOSS HOUSE', now applied equally to one who sleeps rough UK, 1866

doss house noun a very cheap lodging-house; a shelter for the homeless UK, 1889

dossier noun in Quebec, a project. This word is an example of Frenglish CANADA, 2002

doss joint noun an establishment providing cheap, basic sleeping quarters AUSTRALIA, 1969

dossy adjective daft UK, 1958

dot noun 1 LSD; a dose of LSD US, 1967. 2 the anus US, 1964. 3 the clitoris US, 1964. 4 the bleed period of the menstrual cycle. Remembered as late 1970s usage US, 2000. 5 in hot rodding, a taillight US, 1958. ▶ **off your dot** out of your senses UK, 1926. ▶ **on the dot** exactly punctual UK, 1909

Dot nickname Dorchester, Massachusetts US, 1997

dot verb 1 to drop a small amount of LSD on a piece of paper US, 1970. 2 to have anal intercourse. From DOT (the anus) UK, 2002. 3 to hit someone, to strike UK, 1895

dot-and-dash noun 1 money. Rhyming slang for 'cash' UK, 1962. 2 a moustache. Rhyming slang, for, in all probability, TASH (a moustache) and based on the morse code for 'A' UK, 1992

dot ball noun in cricket, a bowled ball from which no runs are scored. From the dot that is recorded in the scorebook UK, 1984

dot-bomb noun a failed dot-com business US, 2001

dot con artist noun a criminal who operates an Internet-based fraud. A play on the Internet business domain and generic 'dot com' US, 1999

Dot Cotton adjective rotten. Rhyming slang, formed from the name of a character played by actress June Brown in BBC television's *EastEnders* UK, 2003

Dot Cottoned adjective drunk. Possibly (imperfect) rhyming slang, 'Dot Cotton' for 'pissed rotten', from the character Dot Cotton, played by actress June Brown, in BBC television's *EastEnders* – the character is known for tipsiness UK, 2002

dot, dot, dot used to imply what happened next, and then, etc. A verbalisation of the written narrative device ... that is often used in romantic fiction to draw a veil over moments of intimacy UK, 2003

do tell! used for expressing doubt. Ironic, sarcastic or mock-incredulous US, 1891

dot head noun an Indian or Pakistani. Offensive. From the caste mark which Hindu women wear on their foreheads US, 1982

dot man noun a Department of Transportation functionary who inspects trucks at motorway stops. Based on the agencys initials: DOT US, 1976

dot on the card adjective definitely, no doubt UK, 1999

dots *noun* sheet music. From the look of written music *US, 1927*

dotty *adjective* eccentric, senile *UK, 1885*

double *noun* **1** a street *UK, 1937.* **2** a pimp with more than one prostitute working for him *US, 1987.* **3** in gambling, a bet on two different events in which the total return on the first selection is automatically staked on the second *UK, 2001.* **4** a twenty-dollar note. An abbreviation of DOUBLE SAWBUCK *US, 1966.* **5** a lift on a bicycle or, formerly, a horse *AUSTRALIA, 1947.* ▶ **on the double** swiftly. From military use for 'marching at twice the regular speed' *UK, 1865*

double *verb* to give someone a lift on a bicycle or, formerly, a horse *AUSTRALIA, 1950.* ▶ **double in brass** to perform two or more tasks at once. A term from the theatre, where an actor might play a brass instrument in the orchestra while not on stage acting *US, 1963*

double *adverb* very much. Often used as an intensifier *UK, 1958*

double 8 *noun* in the television and film industries, 16mm film *UK, 1960*

double ace *noun* in dominoes, the 1–1 piece *US, 1959*

double adaptor *noun* **1** a male who both gives and receives anal sex *AUSTRALIA, 1987.* **2** a bisexual. Scamto youth street slang (South African townships) *SOUTH AFRICA, 2005*

double-aught buck *noun* double-O (.32 calibre) buckshot used in police shotguns *US, 1982*

double bag *verb* to use two condoms at once *US, 1989*

double-bagger *noun* an ugly woman *US, 1982*

double bank *noun* to ride as a second person on a horse, or later, a bicycle *AUSTRALIA, 1876*

double bank *verb* to double the number of animals pulling a load *AUSTRALIA, 1867*

double-barreled *adjective* extreme *US, 1867*

double-bass *noun* a sexual position in which a man, having entered a woman from behind, simultaneously applies manual stimulation to her nipples and clitoris *AUSTRALIA, 2002*

double belly buster *noun* in poker, a hand that requires two cards to make a five-card sequence *US, 1978*

double-blue *noun* a pill containing both amphetamine and barbiturate *UK, 1978*

double bubble *noun* **1** an amount that is twice as much, especially money. A rhyming play on 'double' *UK, 1999.* **2** overtime at double rate *UK, 2005.* **3** a water pipe with two channels, used for smoking marijuana *US, 1998.* **4** cocaine in a smokable form. Marketed as being twice as potent when inhaled *US, 1993.* **5** in prison, interest demanded on an advance of drugs, tobacco or any other form of prison currency. With variant 'double back' *UK, 1996.* **6** a very attractive girl. Teen slang *US, 1951*

double buffalo *noun* fifty-five miles an hour. The US five-cent piece features an engraved buffalo *US, 1976*

double carpet *noun* **1** in betting, odds of 33–1. Dubious accounting 'doubles' the odds from a CARPET (3–1) *UK, 1967.* **2** in prison, a sentence of six months. Literally, 'twice a CARPET' (three months) *UK, 1996*

double century *noun* in motor racing, 200 miles per hour *US, 1965*

double cheese *noun* in pool, the situation when either player can win with one shot *US, 1993*

double cherry drop *noun* a variety of MDMA, the recreational drug best known as ecstasy *UK, 1996*

double-choked *adjective* extremely disappointed or disgruntled, utterly disgusted *UK, 1965*

double click your mouse; double click *verb* of a female, to masturbate. An allusion to manipulation of the clitoris *AUSTRALIA, 2003*

double-clutch *verb* **1** to partake of more than your share of a marijuana cigarette being passed around a group *US, 1980.* **2** to move quickly; to do anything quickly *US, 1968.* **3** to grab someone in the crotch and the buttocks *BAHAMAS, 1982*

double-clutcher *noun* used as a humorous euphemism for 'motherfucker' *US, 1967*

double-clutching *adjective* used as a jocular euphemism for 'motherfucking' *US, 1964*

double-column *verb* to pass another vehicle and stay in the passing lane *US, 1982*

double cross *noun* a double-scored tablet of amphetamine or other central nervous system stimulant *US, 1971*

double-cunted *adjective* possessing a slack and distended vagina *US, 1980*

double damn defo *adverb* very definitely, certainly. An intensification of DEFFO; DEFO *UK, 2003*

double dare; double dog dare *verb* to challenge someone to do something *US, 1945*

double deuce *noun* a .22 calibre gun *US, 1994*

double-diamond lane *noun* the right or slow lane on a motorway. Named for the logo of the McLean Truck Line, believed to have the slowest trucks in the industry *US, 1976*

double dibs! used as a strong assertion of a claim of rights to something *US, 1947*

double-digit fidget *noun* the anxiety felt by US troops in Vietnam with less than 100 days left before leaving Vietnam *US, 1991*

double-digit midget *noun* a soldier with less than 100 days left in their tour of duty *US, 1969*

double dime *noun* twenty *US, 1969*

double dime note *noun* a twenty-dollar note *US, 1961*

double dink *verb* to give someone a lift on a bicycle or, formerly, a horse *AUSTRALIA, 1941*

double-dip *verb* **1** to date both sexes *US, 2002.* **2** to dip a piece of food into a shared sauce or relish after taking a bite *US, 1993*

double dipper *noun* a bisexual *US, 1997*

double-dipping *noun* payment by two different sources for the same work or reason. Slang from the ice-cream parlour, where the 'double dip' cone had two scoops of ice-cream *US, 1986*

double dome; green double dome; green single dome *noun* LSD *US, 1994*

doubledome *noun* an intellectual *US, 1943*

double-door *verb* in pool, to beat someone quickly. The image is that the defeated player has no sooner walked in the front door than he is walking out the back door *US, 1990*

double dooring *noun* an act of criminal fraud perpetrated on a hotel, in which the fraudster arrives in the manner of a legitimate customer but departs by the back door leaving the account unpaid *UK, 1996*

double duke *verb* to arrange a deck of cards so that two players will be dealt good hands *US, 1977*

double Dutch; Dutch *noun* unintelligible speech. Double Dutch is also a secret language in which words are disguised to prevent understanding by outsiders *UK, 1876*

double eighty-eights; double 88s best wishes; warm wishes *US, 1976*

double fever *noun* fifty-five miles an hour. From FEVER (five) *US, 1976*

double fin *noun* ten dollars or ten years *US, 1949*

double-fisted *adjective* large, imposing *US, 1853*

double fives *noun* a hand slap of both hands used for a greeting or for expressing appreciation of that which has just been said *US, 1977*

double-gaited *adjective* bisexual *US, 1927*

double harness *noun* marriage *AUSTRALIA, 1885*

double-hatted *adjective* serving in two positions simultaneously *US, 1990*

double-header; doubleheader *noun* **1** an event where two acts share the headline *UK, 2002.* **2** an activity engaged in twice in a row on the same day, especially sex *US, 1977*

double infinity *noun* in poker, a pair of eights. Turned on its side, a figure eight is an infinity symbol *US, 1996*

double-jointed *adjective* exceptional *US, 1974*

double L *noun* a telephone. An extrapolation from 'landline' *US, 1976*

double loaded *adjective* carrying a large amount, especially of stolen property *UK, 1956*

double net *noun* in betting, odds of 20–1. Literally, 'twice a NET' (10–1) *UK, 1991*

double nickel *noun* **1** fifty-five; five-fifty *US, 1990*. **2** a ten-year prison sentence *US, 1998*. **3** fifty-five miles an hour, the speed limit imposed throughout the US by the federal government in 1974 *US, 1976*

double nickels *noun* in craps, a roll of ten made with a pair of fives *US, 1999*

double nuts *noun* double zero *US, 1981*

double-o *noun* a close examination *US, 1913*

Double-O *nickname* rock musician Ozzy Osbourne (b.1948) *UK, 2002*

double O's *noun* Kool cigarettes *US, 1981*

double packer *noun* a member of the Hell's Angels who is prone to take a girlfriend with him on excursions *US, 1966*

double rock *noun* crack cocaine diluted with procaine *UK, 1998*

double rough *noun* a prison sentence of 50 years *US, 1990*

double rush *verb* to deliver in an expedited fashion. Bicycle messenger slang, used as the title for a short-lived television comedy (CBS, 1995) *US, 1995*

double saw *noun* a twenty-year jail sentence *US, 1976*

double sawbuck; double saw *noun* a twenty-dollar note *US, 1931*

double sawski *noun* a twenty-dollar note *US, 1953*

double stacked *noun* paramethoxyamphetamine, PMA. A drug that is difficult to distinguish from MDMA (ECSTASY) *UK, 2001*

double stacks *noun* MDMA, the recreational drug best known as ecstasy *US, 2002*

double stack white Mitsubishi *noun* an extra thick tablet of paramethoxyamphetamine, PMA, etched with the Japanese car manufacturer's logo, easily confused with MDMA *US, 2000*

double-stakes-about *noun* in gambling, a type of conditional bet *UK, 2001*

double taps *noun* in betting, odds of 15–8. From the TICK-TACK signal for the odds *UK, 1991*

double time *adverb* very much, greatly, absolutely. Variation of BIG TIME (entirely) with DOUBLE as the intensifier *UK, 1994*

double ton *noun* **1** in cricket, a batsman's score of 200 runs or more in one innings *UK, 1995*. **2** in motor racing, 200 miles per hour *US, 1993*

double tre *noun* six *US, 1998*

double trouble *noun* **1** a capsule of sodium amobarbital and sodium secobarbital (trade name Tuinal™), a combination of central nervous system depressants *US, 1967*. **2** any combination of drugs *US, 1990*. **3** a member of Alcoholics Anonymous who is seeking treatment for a second psychological disorder. Those who succeed are known as 'double winners' *US, 1990*

double ups *noun* vials of crack cocaine *US, 1992*

Double Willie *noun* a stagehand who is paid at the doubletime rate for working through meal and rest breaks *US, 1973*

double yoke *noun* crack cocaine. Perhaps this is a reference to the 'yoke' of addiction, punning on the contents of an egg *UK, 1998*

double-yolker *noun* **1** a fool. Prison usage *NEW ZEALAND, 1999*. **2** a ewe carrying twins *NEW ZEALAND, 2002*

double zero; zero zero; zero-zero *noun* a high grade variety of hashish from Morocco; generally, marijuana *UK, 1996*

double zero rocky *noun* cannabis resin *UK, 1999*

doubting Thomas *noun* a perpetually sceptical person *UK, 1877*

douche *noun* a shower. Vietnam war military usage *US, 1991*

douche *verb* **1** to take an enema before or after anal sex *US, 1972*. **2** to reject someone's application for membership in a fraternity, sorority or club *US, 1968*

douche bag *noun* **1** a despicable person; a socially inept person *US, 1945*. **2** a promiscuous woman prisoner *US, 1992*. **3** in trucking, the windscreen was container *US, 1971*. **4** a shower kit. Vietnam war military usage *US, 1991*

douched *adjective* exhausted *US, 1968*

douche job *noun* a wash or steam cleaning of a truck *US, 1971*

douche kit *noun* a shaving kit *US, 1970*

douche out *verb* as a prank, to flood the floor of a room by pouring buckets of water under the crack of the door *US, 1967*

doucher *noun* an annoying, unlikeable person *US, 2004*

doudou *noun* used as a term of endearment. From French Creole, ultimately from French *doux* (sweet) *UK, 1998*

dough *noun* **1** money *US, 1851*. **2** an American infantryman. Korean war usage; shortened from the earlier DOUGHBOY *US, 1951*

doughball *noun* a fool. Glasgow slang *UK: SCOTLAND, 1988*

doughboy *noun* **1** a soldier in the infantry. Many inventive, but unproved, explanations for the term's coining can be found *US, 1847*. **2** a catering employee on a televison or film set *US, 1997*

dough dolly *noun* on Prince Edward Island, a slice of bread cut off for breakfast after rising overnight *CANADA, 1988*

doughfoot *noun* an infantry soldier. World War 2's answer to the DOUGHBOY of World War 1 *US, 1943*

dough-gods *noun* dumplings on top of a stew *CANADA, 1987*

dough-head *noun* a fool. From the thick consistency of conventional 'dough' *US, 1838*

doughnut *noun* **1** a tightly driven full circle, typically executed by young drivers who leave tyre marks from the sharp turns and acceleration *US, 1960*. **2** a tyre; in motor racing, a fat, treadless tyre *US, 1922*. **3** a traffic roundabout *UK, 1981*. **4** an undersized, often illegal, steering wheel *US, 1980*. **5** any material produced to be played on the radio which leaves a silent space in the middle for information provided by the announcer *US, 1980*. **6** the anus *AUSTRALIA, 1985*. **7** the inside of a round, hollow wave *US, 1988*. **8** a fool, a crazy person. Probably abbreviated from DOUGHNUT HEAD; possibly newly coined, combining conventional 'dough' to suggest a thick consistency and NUT (the head); or, possibly, an elaboration of 'nut' (a crazy person). Also spelt 'donut' *UK, 2001*

doughnut *verb* **1** to cluster around a speaker, voicing support. When television cameras were introduced in the House of Commons in 1989, their focus was exclusively on the speaker. To give the impression of support of, or even interest in, what was being said, other MPs would cluster around – 'doughnut' – the speaker, muttering words of support *UK, 1992*. **2** to win a game without your opponent scoring *US, 1971*

doughnut bumper *noun* **1** a lesbian *US, 1997*. **2** an aggressive, dominant lesbian *US, 1992*

doughnut dolly; donut dolly *noun* a female Red Cross volunteer in Vietnam. Vietnam war usage. From the practice of Red Cross volunteers serving doughnuts and coffee to the troops *US, 1968*

doughnut head *noun* used as a term of abuse suggesting an empty head *US, 1977*

doughnut six; donut six *noun* the leader of a group of female Red Cross workers in Vietnam. 'Six' was radio code for a unit's commander *US, 1990*

dough-pop *verb* to hit hard *US, 1972*

dough-roll *noun* a wife *US, 1972*

dough-roller *noun* **1** a baker *US, 1920*. **2** a wife or female lover *US, 1929*

Douglas Hurd; douglas *noun* **1** a third-class university degree. This rhyming slang, based on Britain's former Foreign and Commonwealth Secretary, succeeded a THORA *UK, 2000*. **2** a turd. Rhyming slang, formed from the name of the English Conservative politician (he was Foreign Secretary 1989–95) and novelist, Lord Douglas Hurd (b.1930) *UK, 1992*

dougla tonic *noun* any liquid poison. In Trinidad, suicide by Indians is associated with poison *TRINIDAD AND TOBAGO, 2003*

Douk *noun* a Doukhobor, a member of a Russian fringe religious sect with settlements in Western Canada. The Doukhobors were known for taking off all their clothes when brought to court *CANADA, 1962*

do up *verb* **1** to inject an illegal drug *US, 1952*. **2** to apply a tourniquet before injecting a drug intravenously *US, 1970*. **3** to beat up. A variation of DO *UK, 1959*

douse *verb* ▶ **douse the glim** to turn off the lights *US, 1945*

dove *noun* **1** a five-dollar note *US, 2002*. **2** a tablet of MDMA, the recreational drug best known as ecstasy, identified by an embossed dove-based motif. Variously known, often depending on their appearance, as 'love dove', 'double dove' or 'white dove' *UK, 1992*

Dover boat *noun* a coat. Rhyming slang *UK, 1998*

Dover harbour *noun* a barber. Rhyming slang *UK, 1992*

doves *noun* crack cocaine *US, 1993*

dowager *noun* an elderly, usually affluent, homosexual man *US, 1941*

do what? what are you saying? *UK, 1998*

down *noun* **1** any barbiturate or central nervous system depressant *US, 1971*. **2** a dislike or antipathy *AUSTRALIA, 1835*. ▶ **have a down on** to hold something or someone in low esteem *AUSTRALIA, 1828*

down *verb* **1** to finish a drink *UK, 1922*. **2** to sell stolen goods *US, 1967*

down *adjective* **1** excellent; loyal; fashionable *US, 1946*. **2** willing, prepared, eager *US, 1944*. **3** aware of the current social fashions and opinions; being or feeling a part of a general or specific social scene. A narrowing of the earlier UK C18 sense (wide-awake, suspicious, aware); modern use is mainly black or trendy *US, 1944*. **4** (of surf conditions) flat *US, 1977*. **5** depressed *UK, 1610*. **6** in custody; imprisoned *US, 1927*. ▶ **down on** opposed to; holding a low opinion of something *US, 1848*. ▶ **down to 1** responsible for *UK, 1970*. **2** because of; attributable to *UK, 1958*

down *adverb* **1** down to or down at *AUSTRALIA, 1911*. **2** to hospital *BARBADOS, 1965*. ▶ **get down** to inject (a drug) into a vein *US, 1969*

downalong *adjective* in Barbados, of or pertaining to the other British West Indies islands *BARBADOS, 1965*

down and dirty *adjective* **1** highly competitive, no holds barred *US, 1988*. **2** descriptive of the final card in a game of seven-card stud poker. It is dealt face-down and it greatly affects the chances of a hand winning *US, 1988*

down and out *adjective* homeless; without money *US, 1901*

down beat *noun* ▶ **on the down beat** declining in popularity *US, 1947*

downblouse *noun* a type of voyeurism devoted specifically to seeing a woman's breasts looking down her blouse *US, 1994*

downer *noun* **1** a circumstance that depresses; a depressing experience. From DOWN (depressed) *US, 1967*. **2** a barbiturate or other central nervous system depressant *US, 1965*. **3** an animal being led to slaughter that is too sick or crippled to walk into the slaughterhouse. This sense of the word began to enjoy great popularity in the US in late 2003 with the publicity surrounding Mad Cow Disease in US cattle *US, 1991*. ▶ **have a downer on** to hold something or someone in low esteem *AUSTRALIA, 1915*

down for mine *adjective* willing to stand up for your group *US, 1989*

down hill *adjective* during the second half of a prison sentence *US, 1950*

down home *noun* **1** jail, especially the Manhattan Detention Pens *US, 1982*. **2** the US federal penitentiary in Atlanta, Georgia *US, 1992*. **3** a relatively specific place in the Maritime Provinces *CANADA, 1988*

down home *adjective* exemplifying the essence of black culture *US, 1982*

downhomer *noun* a person who identifies closely with his maritime roots *CANADA, 1988*

downie *noun* a central nervous system depresssant *US, 1966*

Downing Street *noun* in various games, the number ten. From 10 Downing Street, the official address of the British prime minister *UK, 1943*

download *verb* to defecate. Application of computer terminology to the toilet bowl *US, 2001*

downlow *adjective* secret. Black usage *UK, 1990s*

down on your Mamas and Papas *adjective* in dire financial straits. Rhyming slang for DOWN ON YOUR UPPER; formed on a 1960s' US pop-group *UK, 2004*

down on your uppers *adjective* in dire financial straits. When the upper of a shoe is worn down, a person might as well be walking barefoot *US, 1963*

downpressor *noun* an oppressor. Rasta patois *JAMAICA, 1982*

down south *noun, adverb* **1** below the waist; the genitals *US, 1982*. **2** Antarctica *ANTARCTICA, 1913*. **3** the US federal penitentiary in Atlanta, Georgia *US, 1992*. ▶ **it's raining down south** experiencing the bleed period of the menstruation cycle *US, 1999*. ▶ **it's snowing down south** your slip is showing *US, 1955*

downstairs *noun* the genital area, especially of a female *UK, 2002*

down the banks *noun* a reprimand; a piece of your mind *IRELAND, 1968*

down the block *adjective* in prison, in the punishment cells *UK, 1978*

down the drain; down the drains *noun* the brain; brains. Rhyming slang *UK, 1998*

down the drain *adjective* lost, wasted, failed *UK, 1930*

down the food chain *adjective* to be less important in the hierarchy of a business or social organisation, further down the chain of command. An allusion to the natural organisation of species, each being the food source for the next one up the biological chain *UK, 1999*

down the gurgler *adjective* hopelessly lost *AUSTRALIA, 1982*

down the hatch! used as a drinking toast, as a descriptive precursor to taking a drink and as an encouragement to take medicine *US, 1931*

down the mine *adjective* said of the nose of a surfboard that has knifed below the ocean surface *AUSTRALIA, 1964*

down the pan *adjective* lost, wasted, failed. A variation of DOWN THE DRAIN *UK, 1961*

down there *noun, adverb* the genitals. A precious if unmistakable euphemism *US, 1995*

down the road *adjective* in prison *UK, 1982*

down the steps *adverb* used to denote a sentence to imprisonment *UK, 1956*

down time *noun* in prison, free time. Adopted from industry, where the term means that machines aren't working, hence free time for workers *UK, 1996*

down to the ground *adverb* thoroughly, extremely well *UK, 1867*

down to the rivets *adjective* (used of brake pads or a clutch) extremely worn *US, 1992*

downtown *noun* **1** heroin *US, 1983*. **2** in pool, the foot end of the table *US, 1993*. **3** during the Vietnam war, the airspace above Hanoi, North Vietnam *US, 1967*

downtowner *noun* a member of the US embassy staff in Vientiane, Laos. Used with more than a trace of derision by US troops in the field *US, 1991*

down trip *noun* any unpleasant, uninspiring experience *US, 1967*

down trou *noun* the voluntary lowering of your trousers *NEW ZEALAND, 1984*

Down Under; down under *noun* Australia *AUSTRALIA, 1915*

Down Under; down under *adverb* in Australia *AUSTRALIA, 1886*

downy *noun* a bed. A reference to the 'down' found in bedding *US, 1843*

dowry *noun* a great deal, a lot. Probably from the value of a traditional bride's dowry *UK, 1859*

doxy; doxie *noun* a woman; a girlfriend. Originally, in C16, 'a beggar's trull' (the unmarried mistress of a beggar). Beginning in C19 it took on a softer and broader sense *UK, 1530*

Doyle Brunson *noun* in hold 'em poker, a ten and a two as the first two cards dealt to a player. Poker player Doyle 'Texas Dolly'

Brunson won the World Series of Poker two years in a row with this hand *US, 1982*

D'Oyly Carte; d'oyly *noun* **1** a fart. Rhyming slang, formed from the name of the opera company, founded in 1875, that specialises in presenting the works of Gilbert and Sullivan. One of various backstage names for the opera company is 'The Oily Fart' *UK, 1992*. **2** the heart. Rhyming slang *UK, 1992*

do you kiss your mother with that mouth? used as a rejoinder to profanity *US, 1992*

do you know something? used as a gentle if meaningless introduction to what might otherwise come over as unlikely, unkind or abrupt. As an example: 'Do you know something? I rather like you.' *UK, 1974*

do you like the taste of hospital food? used as a jocular threat of violence *UK, 1995*

do you want some? used as a challenging invitation to violent conflict *UK, 2001*

dozens *noun* a game of ritualistic insult *US, 1915*

dozer *noun* **1** marijuana *UK, 2003*. **2** a bulldozer *US, 1942*

dozey *adjective* slow; stupid *AUSTRALIA, 1972*

dozo *noun* a dolt *NEW ZEALAND, 1998*

dozy *adjective* stupid; lazy. Military coinage *UK, 1999*

DP *noun* **1** double penetration. In the pornography industry, this usually refers to a woman who is being penetrated simultaneously in the vagina and anally; viewers of American pornography have been obsessed with this type of double penetration since the 1990s. Technically, it refers to two objects or body parts inserted into the same rectum or vagina simultaneously *US, 1997*. **2** a displaced person *UK, 1945*. **3** Dr. Pepper™ soda. A drink favoured, and hence a term heard, mostly in the southern US *US, 1966*

DPP *noun* a vagina simultaneously penetrated by two penises. An abbreviation of 'double pussy penetration' *US, 2000*

D.P.Q. *noun* a dumb passenger question *CANADA, 1989*

DPs *noun* a pair of men's close-fitting and revealing nylon swimming trunks. An initialism of DICK POINTERS or DICK POKERS *AUSTRALIA, 2003*

drab *noun* a pretty girl, especially one who is new in town *US, 1947*

drack *noun* an unattractive woman *AUSTRALIA, 1960*

drack *adjective* **1** dreary; dull; awful; unpleasant. Possibly derived from Dracula, but others have suggested it is an alteration of DRECK *AUSTRALIA, 1944*. **2** (of a woman) unattractive *AUSTRALIA, 1949*

dracs *noun* the canine teeth. *Dracula*, according to Hollywood at least, has overlarge pointed canines for puncturing the skin of his victims *UK, 2001*

draft beast *noun* a student who studies hard in preparation for exams *TRINIDAD AND TOBAGO, 2003*

drafty *noun* draught beer *US, 1969*

drag *noun* **1** anything or anyone boring or tedious *US, 1863*. **2** a conventional, narrow-minded person *US, 1947*. **3** an unattractive girl *US, 1955*. **4** a transvestite *UK, 1974*. **5** female clothing worn by men; male clothing worn by women. A term born in the theatre, but the non-theatrical sense has long dominated. He or she who wears 'drag' may or may not be a homosexual *UK, 1870*. **6** any kind of clothing *US, 1959*. **7** clout, influence *US, 1896*. **8** a street or road, especially a major urban street *UK, 1851*. **9** a car. From earlier senses 'as a coach', 'a cart', 'a wagon and a van'. English Gypsy use *UK, 1935*. **10** a freight train, especially a slow one *US, 1925*. **11** an inhalation (of a cigarette, pipe or cigar) *US, 1904*. **12** a marijuana cigarette *UK, 1978*. **13** the soldier at the 'very rear of a group of soldiers on patrol. From the older term 'drag rider' (1888) for the cowhand riding at the rear of a herd *US, 1991*. **14** a sentence of three months' imprisonment *AUSTRALIA, 1877*. **15** a confidence game in which a wallet is dropped as bait for the victim *US, 1958*. ▶ **the drag** a several-block area near Independence Square, Port of Spain, Trinidad *TRINIDAD AND TOBAGO, 1984*

drag *verb* **1** to bore or annoy *US, 1944*. **2** to wear clothing of the opposite sex *US, 1970*. **3** to compete in a drag race, a quarter-mile race from a standing start *US, 1950*. **4** in poker, to take (chips) from the pot as change for a bet *US, 1967*. **5** in poker, to take the house

percentage out of a pot *US, 1988*. **6** to rob vehicles *UK, 1970*. **7** to lead on, to entice *US, 1981*. ▶ **drag the chain** to be slow to perform some task; to lag behind. Metaphorically referring to Australia's convict era when prisoners were chained together, but originally in use amongst shearers and only recorded long after chain gangs were a thing of the past *AUSTRALIA, 1912*. ▶ **drag your anchor** to lose control of yourself and drift towards trouble. Clearly understood nautical origins *US, 1963*

drag-ass *adjective* tired, lazy *US, 1952*

drag back *verb* to re-imprison a convict released on licence *UK, 1996*

drag ball *noun* a dance dominated by men dressed as women *US, 1957*

drage; droge; droje; draje *noun* any kind of clothing. Affected variations of DRAG *UK, 1992*

dragged *adjective* annoyed, depressed *US, 1952*

dragger *noun* a thief who steals vehicles or their contents *UK, 1956*

draggin' wagon *noun* **1** a tow truck, especially a military tow truck. Also known as a 'dragon wagon' *US, 1945*. **2** in drag racing, a fast car *US, 1968*

draggy *adjective* boring, tedious *US, 1868*

drag it! let's hurry up! Teen slang *US, 1951*

drag king *noun* a woman who impersonates a man, especially one who performs in a male persona *US, 1995*

drag mag *noun* a magazine targeted at transvestites *US, 1972*

dragon *noun* **1** the penis. Originally in the phrase 'water the dragon' (of a man, to urinate) *UK, 1891*. **2** heroin *US, 1961*. **3** an ugly or unpleasant woman. A variation of the conventional sense of 'an aggressive woman', often as 'old dragon' *UK, 1992*

dragon drawers *noun* brightly coloured men's underpants *TRINIDAD AND TOBAGO, 1987*

dragonfly *noun* an A-37 aircraft, used in the Vietnam war largely as a close air-support fighter for ground forces *US, 1985*

dragon lady *noun* **1** an aggressive, ruthless, ambitious woman. Her traits make a man a leader; from a comic strip character who along with being ruthless etc. is from the Far East *US, 1952*. **2** an armoured cavalry assault vehicle *US, 1991*

Dragon Lady *nickname* Madame Ngo Dinh Nhu, sister-in-law of South Vietnamese President Diem. Madame Nhu, married to Diem's brother, established herself as Vietnam's unofficial First Lady. She supported the abolition of divorce, birth control and abortion, and closed a number of nightclubs *US, 1991*

dragon rock *noun* a mixture of crack cocaine and heroin. A combination of DRAGON (heroin) and ROCK (crack) *UK, 2002*

dragon ship *noun* any of several US helicopter gunships equipped with Gatling guns during the Vietnam war *US, 1967*

Dragon's Jaw *nickname* the Thanh Hoa railway and road bridge, spanning the Song Ma River three miles north of Thanh Hoa, the capital of Annam Province, North Vietnam *US, 1974*

drag queen *noun* a man, usually but not always homosexual, who frequently or invariably wears women's clothing. From DRAG (women's clothes when worn by men) and QUEEN (an effeminate homosexual man). The social conditions that prevailed when this term was coined allowed for less obvious and glamorous cross-dressing *US, 1941*

drags *noun* drag races, a series of quarter-mile events where the cars start at rest and achieve extremely high speeds *US, 1963*

drag show *noun* a performance by men dressed as women *US, 1959*

drag squad *noun* the unit providing rear-guard security behind a larger body of soldiers *US, 1991*

dragster *noun* a person who regularly asks for a puff on others' cigarettes *US, 1963*

dragula *noun* a transvestite who only appears at night. A compounding of DRAG (female clothing worn by men) and Dracula (a legendary creature of the night) *UK, 2003*

drag up *verb* **1** to dress in women's clothes *UK, 2002*. **2** to quit a job *US, 1930*

drag weed *noun* marijuana *US, 1949*

Drain *noun* ▶ **the Drain** the Waterloo and City underground railway *UK, 1970*

drain *verb* (used of a ball in pinball) to leave play at the bottom of the playing field *US, 1977*. ▶ **drain the dragon** (used of a male) to urinate *AUSTRALIA, 1971*. ▶ **drain the main vein** (used of a male) to urinate *US, 1989*. ▶ **drain the radiator** to urinate *US, 1977*. ▶ **drain the train** (used of a male) to have sex *US, 1984*. ▶ **drain the vein** to urinate *US, 1968*. ▶ **drain the weasel** (used of a male) to urinate *US, 1990*. ▶ **drain your crankcase** (used of a male) to urinate *CANADA, 2002*

draino! used by a golfer to celebrate a long putt falling into the hole *US, 1997*

drain pipe *noun* in poker, a conservative player who slowly but surely accumulates winnings, draining money from other players *US, 1996*

drama mama *noun* an elaborately effeminate male *SINGAPORE, 2002*

drama queen *noun* someone who creates an unnecessary or excessive fuss. Originally gay usage *UK, 1990*

drammer damner *noun* a harsh theatre critic *US, 1952*

drape *noun* **1** clothing; a man's suit *US, 1938*. **2** the sag of a suit favoured by zoot suiters and their fellow travellers *US, 1954*

drape *verb* to dress, to attire *US, 1942*. ▶ **drape the shape** to get dressed *US, 1962*

drape *adjective* said of a stylized, baggy men's suit favoured by zoot suiters *US, 1967*

draped *adjective* adorned with a lot of gold jewellery *US, 1995*

drapes *noun* bell-bottom pants *US, 1970*

drape shape *noun* a baggy, loose-fitting style of clothing popular in the 1940s *US, 1955*

drat! used as a mild expletive. From 'God rot!' *UK, 1815*

dratted *adjective* damned *UK, 1845*

draw *noun* **1** a winning bet with a bookmaker *UK, 2000*. **2** marijuana; a marijuana cigarette *UK, 1987*. **3** a cigarette *AUSTRALIA, 1955*. **4** in pool, backspin applied to the cue ball *US, 1866*

draw *verb* while injecting a drug, to pull blood into the syringe to verify that the needle has hit a blood vein *US, 1971*. ▶ **draw dead** in poker, to draw cards into a hand that cannot win *US, 1990*. ▶ **draw the crabs 1** to attract the enemy's attention; to draw fire *AUSTRALIA, 1918*. **2** to attract unwanted attention *AUSTRALIA, 1988*. ▶ **draw the crow** to get the worst job or the worst share of something *AUSTRALIA, 1942*. ▶ **draw water** (of the sun) to exhibit long vertical lines in the sky. Said in Nova Scotia to be a sign of approaching rain, it occurs also in New England, where it is said to be a sign of clear weather *CANADA, 1942*

draw down on *verb* to draw out and point guns at *US, 1974*

draw drapes *noun* the foreskin of an uncircumcised penis *US, 1979*

drawers *noun* sex *US, 1969*

drawing room *noun* a brakevan (caboose) *US, 1977*

drawings *noun* **1** information; gossip; news *US, 1968*. **2** plans for a course of action *US, 1990*

draw up *verb* to inject a drug intravenously. Derives from the initial act of drawing up blood into the syringe to mix with the narcotic before re-injection *UK, 1998*

dread *noun* **1** a Rastafarian. From the distinctive dreadlocks hairstyle worn by Rastafarians *JAMAICA, 1976*. **2** a black person. From the previous sense; prison usage *UK, 1996*

dread *adjective* **1** difficult, hard, impossible; used to ascribe negative qualities to any situation. West Indian and UK black *UK, 1977*. **2** frightening *UK, 1996*

dreaded *adjective* **1** of hair, in dreadlocks *UK, 2003*. **2** fashionable, popular, in style *US, 1998*

dreaded lurgi; the lurgi; the lergy; lerg *noun* any malaise or minor ailment. The 'dreaded' variation is a direct quotation from *The Goon Show*, which was originally broadcast on BBC radio in 1951. So much in the world of the Goons was 'dreaded'. The 'lurgi' found a currency among school-children where it was

further applied to notional illnesses and any vaguely unpleasant or unclean disease that another could be accused of carrying *UK, 1954*

dreadfully *adverb* exceedingly. Often used to imply or intensify a pejorative sense *UK, 1697*

dreadlocks *noun* the long, bundled strands of hair worn by Rastafarians *JAMAICA, 1960*

dreads *noun* dreadlocks, a Rastafarian hairstyle in which the hair is not combed or brushed, forming matted clumps or 'locks' *US, 1977*

dream *noun* **1** an appealing, attractive member of whatever sex attracts you *US, 1895*. **2** opium *US, 1929*. **3** cocaine *UK, 1998*

dreamboat *noun* **1** a sexually attractive person *US, 1944*. **2** a well-maintained, large luxury car *US, 1945*

dream book *noun* a book that purports to interpret dreams, suggesting numbers to be played in an illegal lottery based on symbols in the dreams *US, 1963*

dream cube *noun* a sugar cube impregnated with LSD *UK, 1983*

dream dust *noun* any powdered drug *US, 1957*

dreamer *noun* **1** a motorist who thinks that he can outrun a police car. Police humour *US, 1962*. **2** morphine or a morphine addict *US, 1992*. **3** a blanket *US, 1973*

dreamers *noun* sheets for a bed *US, 1945*

dream gum *noun* opium; heroin *US, 1934*

dreamland *noun* sleep or an unconscious state *US, 1908*

dream number *noun* in an illegal number gambling lottery, a bet based on the bettor's dream, either directly or as interpreted by a dream book *US, 1949*

dreams *noun* heroin. From earlier, obsolete sense as 'opium' *UK, 2003*

dream sheet *noun* a list created by a soldier of the places where he would like to be shipped. Rarely realised *US, 1971*

dream stuff *noun* marijuana *US, 1949*

dream team *noun* any group made up from the best in the field *US, 1942*

dream ticket *noun* an 'ideal' pairing, especially of politicians for the purposes of election. Originally applied to Richard Nixon and Nelson Rockerfeller as running mates for the 1960 US Presidential election. Adopted in the UK during the 1980s, reflecting a new, more American style of political presentation *US, 1960*

dream tobacco *noun* marijuana *UK, 2003*

dreamy *adjective* very attractive, beautiful, desirable *US, 1941*

dreck *noun* **1** excrement; worthless trash. From the Yiddish and German for 'dung' *IRELAND, 1922*. **2** heroin *UK, 2002*

drecky *adjective* rubbishy, trashy, shitty. From DRECK (excrement, trash) *UK, 1979*

dreece *noun* three units of anything *US, 1950*

drenched *adjective* drunk *US, 1926*

drepsley soup *noun* (among Canadian Mennonites) a broth soup with dumplings *CANADA, 1998*

dress down *verb* to dress up. Often intensified with 'for a motherfucker' *US, 1984*

dressed *adjective* armed *US, 1973*

dressed up like a preacher *adjective* overdressed, flashily dressed *US, 1991*

dresser *noun* a car or motorcyle with every possible accessory *US, 1992*

dress for sale *noun* a prostitute *US, 1979*

dress in *verb* to exchange the clothes worn upon arrival for prison-issued clothes *US, 1976*

dressing room lawyer *noun* an actor who is quick to recognise and address wrongs by theatre management *UK, 1952*

dress out *verb* to exchange prison clothing for street clothes upon release from prison *US, 1976*

dress-tail *noun* a woman as a sexual object *TRINIDAD AND TOBAGO, 2003*

dress-up *noun* an unconvincing drag queen (a man dressed as a woman) *UK, 2002*

dressy casual *adjective* of style or fashion, informal yet smart and/or expensive *US*, *1999*

drib *noun* an unskilled poker player *US*, *1967*

dribble *noun* small, weak waves *US*, *1991*

dribble *verb* **1** to cause a car to bounce up and down by use of hydraulic lifts. To 'dribble' a basketball is to bounce it, hence the transference here *US*, *1980*. **2** to meander, to walk *US*, *1960*

dribs and drabs *noun* pubic lice. Rhyming slang for CRABS *UK*, *1992*

drift *verb* to leave *US*, *1853*

drill *verb* **1** to have sex from a male perspective. From the imagery of a long hard tool opening a hole *UK*, *2000*. **2** to inject (a drug) *US*, *1970*. **3** to shoot (with a bullet); to kill by shooting *UK*, *1720*. **4** to interrogate *US*, *1995*. **5** to kick, throw or bowl a ball, directly and forcefully; to score a goal with a forceful kick *AUSTRALIA*, *1998*. **6** in pool, to make a shot in an emphatic and convincing manner *US*, *1993*. **7** to walk, to move *US*, *1953*. ▶ **drill for vegemite** to have anal sex. From Vegemite™, a popular type of black and salty spread made from yeast extract *AUSTRALIA*, *1985*

drill down *verb* to examine or investigate something in depth; to narrow the focus of an investigation and its results. A figurative sense of the conventional use *UK*, *2001*

driller *noun* a poker player who bets very aggressively *US*, *1988*

drink *noun* **1** a bribe *UK*, *1977*. **2** a profit *UK*, *1997*. **3** a large body of water, especially an ocean *US*, *1832*. ▶ **in the drink** in pool, said of a cue ball that falls into a pocket *US*, *1990*

drink *verb* ▶ **drink eight cents** to drink to excess *TRINIDAD AND TOBAGO*, *2003*. ▶ **drink from the furry cup** to perform oral sex on a woman. Probably coined by comedian Sacha Baron-Cohen (b.1970); his influence on late C20 UK slang is profound *UK*, *2001*. ▶ **drink porridge** to serve a prison sentence. A figurative use of 'drink' combined with PORRIDGE (imprisonment) *UK*, *2000*. ▶ **drink the Kool-Aid** to be persuaded, to follow blindly. From the 'Jonestown massacre', 1978, a mass murder and suicide administered through the agency of cyanide in branded soft drink Kool-Aid™ *US*, *1987*. ▶ **drink with the flies** to drink alone when at a public hotel or bar *AUSTRALIA*, *1911*. ▶ **you would drink it through a shitey cloot** applied to anyone who appears to be so thirsty, or desperate, that no obstacle will hinder the taking of a drink. Glasgow slang formed on 'shitey' (faeces-covered) and Scottish dialect *cloot* (a hoof) or, more likely, *clout* (a rag) *UK: SCOTLAND*, *1996*

drinkee *noun* any alcoholic drink. A jocular mock pidgin *US*, *1969*

drinker *noun* a public house; an after-hours drinking club (generally unlicensed) *UK*, *2001*

drinkerama *noun* a party organised around the consumption of alcohol *US*, *1968*

drinker's hour *noun* 3am *US*, *1984*

drinking voucher; green drinking voucher *noun* a currency note, especially a £1 note. Jocular *UK*, *1982*

drinky; drinkies *noun* a drinking session, a drinks party. From the nursery usage *UK*, *1983*

drinkypoo; drinki-poo *noun* any alcoholic drink. Baby talk, thought to give alcohol an innocent demeanour *US*, *1983*

drip *noun* a person lacking in social skills, fashion sense or both; a simpleton, a fool *US*, *1932*. ▶ **the drip** the payment of money owed in instalment payments *AUSTRALIA*, *1989*

drip *verb* to complain *UK*, *1987*

drip and suck *verb* to intubate a hospital patient with intravenous and nasogastric tubes *US*, *1994*

drip drop *noun* the bleed period of the menstrual cycle *US*, *2000*

drip dry; drip *verb* to cry. Rhyming slang *UK*, *1992*

dripper *noun* **1** an old prostitute. One who is 'no longer controller of her emissions' *UK*, *1970*. **2** an eye dropper, used in an improvised method of drug injection *US*, *1953*

dripping *adjective* cowardly, ineffectual. An upper-class exaggeration of WET (ineffectual) from conventional 'dripping wet' (soaked) *UK*, *1982*

dripping toast *noun* a host. Rhyming slang *UK*, *1998*

drippy *adjective* mawkish, overly sentimental, insipid *US*, *1947*

drippy dick *noun* an unspecified sexually transmitted disease *US*, *1990*

drippy faucet *noun* the penis of a man with a sexually transmitted infection that produces a puss discharge *US*, *1981*

dripsy *noun* gonorrhea *US*, *1981*

drive *verb* **1** to walk *US*, *1956*. **2** to lift weights *US*, *2000*. **3** to borrow (a radio). From CAR (a radio) *US*, *2002*. ▶ **drive a desk** to do office-work; to operate a sound-desk. Usually with a derogatory or a disappointed tone. After FLY A DESK *UK*, *1999*. ▶ **drive the bus** to vomit *US*, *2001*. ▶ **drive the porcelain bus** to kneel down and vomit into a toilet bowl. The image of the bowl's rim being held like a steering wheel *UK*, *1998*. ▶ **drive them home** to snore. From C18 'drive pigs to market', and its later variant 'drive the pigs home' *UK*, *1997*. ▶ **drive wooden stake** to irrevocably and permanently end (a project, a business, an idea) *US*, *1974*

drive-by *noun* **1** a drive-by shooting, where shots are fired from a moving car *US*, *1992*. **2** a silent, smelly fart *US*, *2001*

drive-by *verb* to shoot someone, or into a crowd, from a moving car *US*, *1992*

drive call *noun* in a telephone swindle, a high-pressure, follow-up call to the victim *US*, *1985*

drive dark *verb* to drive without headlights at night *US*, *1992*

driver *noun* **1** an amphetamine or other central nervous system stimulant *US*, *1990*. **2** a tablet of MDMA, the recreational drug best known as ecstasy *UK*, *2003*. **3** a pilot *UK*, *1942*. **4** in poker, a player whose aggressive betting is dominating the game *US*, *1996*. **5** the leader of a prison clique. Back formation from CAR (a clique) *US*, *1989*

drive-time *noun* the hours of the morning and afternoon weekday commute, prime time on radio *US*, *1982*

drive-up *noun* a fresh arrival at prison *US*, *1990*

driveway *noun* a scenic road, often in a city, landscaped and planted *CANADA*, *1958*

drizzles *noun* diarrhoea *US*, *1943*

drizzling shits *noun* dysentery *US*, *1980*

dro *noun* marijuana grown hydroponically *US*, *2002*

droge; droje *noun* ▷ *see:* DRAGE

drogle *noun* a dress. Gay slang *UK*, *2002*

droid *noun* a low-level employee who is blindly loyal to his employer *US*, *1980*

drome *noun* in circus and carnival usage, a motordrome *US*, *1981*

drone *noun* **1** a sluggard, a tedious person *UK*, *1529*. **2** in hospital usage, a medical student *US*, *1994*

drone cage *noun* a private railway carriage *US*, *1946*

droned *adjective* simultaneously intoxicated on alcohol and marijuana. A blend of 'drunk' and 'stoned' *US*, *1997*

droner *noun* a boring, spiritless person; an objectionable person *US*, *1943*

drongo *noun* **1** a fool; a hopeless individual. Originally Royal Australian Air Force slang for 'a recruit'. Said in an early RAAF source to be named after the '(spangled) drongo' (a large clumsy flying bird), but drongos are not particularly large (smaller than a pigeon), and while they are somewhat aerobatic and erractic flyers they are certainly not clumsy. Otherwise it has been suggested that it is an allusion to a racehorse named Drongo which gained notoriety for never winning a race and was used as a character in satirical political cartoons in the *Melbourne Herald* in the 1920s, which may be true despite the gap of 20 years *AUSTRALIA*, *1941*. **2** a new recruit to the Royal Australian Air Force *AUSTRALIA*, *1941*

drongo *adjective* foolish *AUSTRALIA*, *1945*

dronk *adjective* drunk. From Afrikaans *SOUTH AFRICA*, *1983*

dronkie *noun* a drunkard. From Afrikaans *dronk* (drunk) *SOUTH AFRICA*, *1969*

droob *noun* a hopeless individual. A connection with US 'droop' (an obnoxious person) is highly suspect as there is nothing to suggest that this uncommon Americanism was ever known in Australia *AUSTRALIA, 1933*

droog *noun* **1** a ruffian; a henchman. Derives from the sense as 'friend' in the novel and play *A Clockwork Orange* by Anthony Burgess (1917–93) and the subsequent film by Stanley Kubrick (1928–99); combined to some degree with DRONE (a tedious person) *AUSTRALIA, 1967*. **2** a good friend *US, 1971*

droogs *noun* drugs. An affected mispronunciation *UK, 2001*

drool *noun* nonsense; drivel. Punning on conventional 'drivel' and 'dribble' *US, 1900*

drooling the drool of regret into the pillow of remorse used as a humorous comment on a person who has not performed up to their expectation. Coined and popularised by ESPN's Keith Olberman *US, 1997*

droolin' with schoolin' *adjective* said of an overly diligent student. Teen slang, now thought to be obsolete *US, 1944*

drool value *noun* sexual attractiveness *AUSTRALIA, 1996*

droop *noun* a socially inept person *US, 1932*

droop-snoot *nickname* the supersonic airliner Concorde. After the fact that the plane's nose could be lowered. Borrowed from an earlier (1945) description of any aircraft with a downward-pointing nose *UK, 1984*

droopy *adjective* dispirited, dejected, sulky *US, 1955*

droopy-drawers *noun* **1** a person, especially a child, with trousers that are too large on a comic scale *US, 1931*. **2** a slovenly or incompetent person. Jocular *UK, 1939*

drooth; drouth *noun* a great thirst; a thirsty person; a drunk. From a dialect variation of 'drought' *UK: SCOTLAND, 1911*

drop *noun* **1** in espionage or a criminal enterprise, a place where goods, documents or money is left to be picked up later by a confederate *US, 1922*. **2** a place where stolen goods or other criminal material may be temporarily stored *US, 1922*. **3** a bribe *UK, 1931*. **4** in horse racing, a cash-handling error that favours the racetrack *US, 1982*. **5** the place where players who are invited to an illegal dice game are told where the game will be held *US, 1964*. **6** the ingestion of a drug *US, 1975*. **7** LSD. From the verb sense (to consume drugs), especially as 'drop acid' *UK, 1998*. **8** an attractive woman. Mimicking the language of wine connoisseurs *AUSTRALIA, 1957*. **9** the act of execution by hanging. Derives from: 'the new drop; a contrivance for executing felons at Newgate, by means of a platform, which drops from under them'. The condemned prisoner would then 'drop' to the end of a rope. Also recorded as 'the last drop' *UK, 1958*. **10** an orphan *US, 1970*. **11** in a casino, the amount of money taken in from betting customers *US, 1935*. ▶ **get the drop on someone; have the drop on someone** to get, or have, an advantage over someone. Originally, and still, 'to be quicker drawing a gun than your opponent' *US, 1867*

drop *verb* **1** to swallow, to ingest (a drug). A favourite word of the LSD culture, but popular for other drugs of abuse before and since; if used without a direct object, almost certainly referring to LSD *US, 1961*. **2** to kill, especially by shooting. In various uses and combinations 'drop' means 'to die' or 'to finish'. This variant is pro-active *US, 1726*. **3** to bribe *UK, 1956*. **4** to release a music recording *UK, 1991*. **5** to lose (especially money). An example of C19 flash slang that has survived *UK, 1676*. **6** to cash a forged cheque *UK, 1956*. **7** to give money *UK, 1974*. **8** to break off a romantic relationship with someone *AUSTRALIA, 1962*. **9** to perform oral sex on a woman *US, 1997*. **10** to fart *AUSTRALIA, 1987*. **11** to knock down with a punch *AUSTRALIA, 1954*. **12** in pool, to hit (a ball) into a pocket *US, 1993*. **13** to cause a car to suddenly drop almost to the ground by use of hydraulic lifts *US, 1980*. **14** to include a tune in a sequence of recorded dance music *UK, 2002*. ▶ **drop a banger** to blunder; to make a mistake, especially one of some consequence. From BANGERS (the testicles); a variation of DROP A BOLLOCK *UK, 1961*. ▶ **drop a bollock; drop a ballock** to make a mistake, especially one of some consequence. Derives from DROP A BRICK (to make a mistake) combined with BOLLOCKS (the testicles) *UK, 1942*. ▶ **drop a bomb; drop one 1** to fart *UK, 1998*. **2** to defecate *US, 2001*. ▶ **drop a bombshell** to reveal a great and shocking surprise *UK, 2002*. ▶ **drop a brick** to make a

faux pas *UK, 1923*. ▶ **drop a bundle** to give birth *NEW ZEALAND, 1948*. ▶ **drop a clanger** to make a mistake, especially in a social context. A variation of DROP A BOLLOCK, based on CLANGERS (the testicles) *UK, 1942*. ▶ **drop a deuce** to defecate. From the children's toilet vocabulary: NUMBER TWO (defecation) *US, 2003*. ▶ **drop a dime** to make a telephone call, especially to the police to inform on someone. From the days when the price of a call from a pay phone was a dime *US, 1966*. ▶ **drop a goolie** to make a mistake. A figurative use of GOOLIES (the testicles); a direct equivalent to DROP A BOLLOCK *UK, 1961*. ▶ **drop a jewel; drop jewels** to create rap music or lyrics *US, 1991*. ▶ **drop a lug** to confront someone about their conduct; to insult *US, 1973*. ▶ **drop a name** to inform on a criminal or suspect *US, 1990*. ▶ **drop a nickel** to become involved in something *US, 1953*. ▶ **drop a sprog** to give birth. Combines 'drop' (to give birth, usually of an animal) with SPROG (a baby) *UK, 1987*. ▶ **drop an oar in the water** to make a mistake. From rhyming slang, OARS AND ROWLOCKS for BOLLOCKS; this is an elaboration and variation of DROP A BOLLOCK *UK, 1998*. ▶ **drop beads** to unintentionally disclose your homosexuality *US, 1970*. ▶ **drop bottom** to set the bass levels on a car stereo system at a high level *US, 2003*. ▶ **drop foot** to dance without restraint *JAMAICA, 1996*. ▶ **drop off the twig** to die *AUSTRALIA, 1974*. ▶ **drop science** to explain; to educate; to make sense *US, 1992*. ▶ **drop some iron** to spend money *US, 1987*. ▶ **drop someone in it** to get someone blamed and into trouble. Euphemistic DROP IN THE SHIT *UK, 1991*. ▶ **drop the bucket on someone** to expose someone's misdeeds; to get someone into trouble. The 'bucket' is a full sanitary bin, in other words, to 'put someone in the shit' *AUSTRALIA, 1950*. ▶ **drop the hammer 1** at the start of a drag race, to release (engage) the clutch in a sudden and forceful move *US, 1965*. **2** to accelerate *US, 1976*. ▶ **drop the hook** to arrest *US, 1953*. ▶ **drop the kids off** to defecate *US, 2003*. ▶ **drop the kids off at the pool** to defecate *UK, 2002*. ▶ **drop them** of a woman, to readily remove her knickers as a practical necessity for sexual activity, and thus said to be symbolic of a woman's sexual availability *UK, 1984*. ▶ **drop trou** as a prank, to lower your trousers, bend over and expose your buttocks to the world *US, 1966*. ▶ **drop your bundle** to lose one's composure; to go to pieces *AUSTRALIA, 1847*. ▶ **drop your candy** to make a serious mistake *US, 1908*. ▶ **drop your guts** to fart *AUSTRALIA, 1978*. ▶ **drop your handbag** to fart. A variation on DROP YOUR GUTS. Royal Navy slang *UK, 1989*. ▶ **drop your lunch** to fart *AUSTRALIA, 1985*

drop-dead *adverb* extremely *AUSTRALIA, 1997*

drop dead! used as a contemptuous expression of dismissal; go away! *UK, 1934*

drop-down *noun* in horse racing, a horse that has been moved down a class or down in claiming price *US, 1990*

drop edge of yonder *noun* a near-death condition *US, 1939*

drop gun *noun* a gun that is not registered and not capable of being traced, and thus placed by the police in the vicinity of someone whom they have shot to justify the shooting *US, 1987*

drop-in *noun* **1** in computing, characters added as a result of a voltage irregularity or system malfunction *US, 1991*. **2** a temporary visitor *AUSTRALIA, 1982*

drop in *verb* in surfing, to start a ride on a wave already occupied by another surfer or other surfers *AUSTRALIA, 1985*

drop it! stop!, especially as an injunction to stop talking or fooling *UK, 1847*

drop-kick *noun* **1** the vagina. Formed as an extension of rhyming slang, 'punt' for CUNT *AUSTRALIA, 1983*. **2** by extension from the previous sense, a fool, especially an annoying or contemptible fool *AUSTRALIA, 1986*. **3** by extension, something that is frustrating or annoying *AUSTRALIA, 1986*

droplifting *noun* an act of secretly placing your own CDs in the display racks of a music retailer *UK, 2003*

drop off *verb* to go to sleep *UK, 1820*

drop-out *noun* a person who has withdrawn from formal education or mainstream society. Usage is conventional but the company that the word keeps gives it the aura of unconventionality *UK, 1930*

drop out *verb* to withdraw from school, college, university or mainstream society *US, 1952*

dropper *noun* **1** a gambler who can be counted on to lose a lot of money *US, 1963*. **2** a criminal who cashes a forged cheque *UK, 1956*. **3** a paid killer *US, 1962*

dropper *verb* to inject a drug intravenously *UK, 1998*

dropping *noun* the criminal act of passing forged cheques *UK, 1956*

dropping! in foot-propelled scootering, a warning shout used when a jump has gone wrong *UK, 2000*

drop-short *noun* an artillery soldier *AUSTRALIA, 1954*

dropstick *noun* pickpocketing. West Indian slang *UK, 1977*

dropsy *noun* a cash bribe, or other money the taxman doesn't know about. The money is 'dropped' in the pocket or hand *UK, 1930*

drop-the-hanky *noun* a pickpocketing scheme in which the victim is distracted when an attractive woman member of the pickpocketing team drops a handkerchief or other small object which the victim stoops to recover *US, 1954*

drop-top *noun* a car with a convertible roof *US, 1973*

drop your cocks and pull up your socks! used for awakening a sleeping man or men. A variation of HANDS OFF COCKS – FEET IN SOCKS! Originally used by drill instructors to military recruits *US, 1962*

drove *adjective* very angry *US, 1992*

Drover's Guide *noun* an imaginary publication that is cited as a source of rumours *AUSTRALIA, 1959*

drown *verb* **1** in oil drilling, to contaminate a well with flooding salt water *US, 1954*. **2** to lose heavily gambling *US, 1974*

drowning *noun* the criminal act of gaining entry to a property with the intent to commit theft by claiming to work for a water supplier *UK, 1998*

drown-proofing *noun* in navy training, an exercise involving extended periods of treading water, especially while restrained to some degree *US, 1987*

drowsy high *noun* a central nervous system despressant. From the effects of intoxication *UK, 1998*

druck steaming *adjective* drunk. What a druck is or why it should be steamed is a mystery that defeats sober logic *UK, 2002*

'druff *noun* dandruff *UK, 1996*

drug; drugg; drugged *adjective* displeased, annoyed *US, 1946*

drug-fuck *noun* a drug-addict, a junkie *UK, 2002*

drug-fucked *adjective* incapacitated from taking drugs *AUSTRALIA, 1991*

drugged *adjective* patently stupid *US, 1991*

druggie; druggy *noun* a drug user, abuser or addict *US, 1966*

druggo *noun* a drug user or addict *AUSTRALIA, 1989*

drughead *noun* a drug addict; a serious abuser of narcotics *US, 1968*

drug monkey *noun* a heavy user of drugs *UK, 2003*

drugola *noun* **1** a bribe in the form of drugs given to encourage play of a particular record on the radio *US, 1973*. **2** bribes paid to police by drug dealers *US, 1997*

drugstore cowboy *noun* a young man who loiters in or around a drugstore for the purpose of meeting women *US, 1923*

drugstore dice *noun* inexpensive shop-bought dice, not milled to casino-level tolerances *US, 1962*

drugstore handicap *noun* in horse racing, a race in which drugs have been given to enhance performance *US, 1948*

drugstore race *noun* in horse racing, a race in which a number of the horses involved have been drugged for enhanced or diminished performance *US, 1960*

drug up *adjective* dragged up (poorly brought up). Deliberately illiterate to mimic its context *UK, 1984*

druid *noun* **1** the promoter of a drag racing event *US, 1965*. **2** a priest *IRELAND, 1958*

druid dust *noun* a narcotic herb that, when smoked as a marijuana substitute, produces a gentle euphoria. Druidism is an ancient religion associated with Wales and Stonehenge in the county of Wiltshire; the latter especially is particularly popular with people who are probably marijuana smokers *UK, 1999*

druk *verb* to stab *SOUTH AFRICA, 1972*

drum *noun* **1** a place of business or residence, a house, a home, a flat, etc *UK, 1846*. **2** by extension from the previous sense, a brothel *AUSTRALIA, 1879*. **3** by extension, a cell *UK, 1909*. **4** a safe *US, 1912*. **5** reliable information; inside information *AUSTRALIA, 1915*. **6** in horse racing, reliable inside information *AUSTRALIA, 1989*. **7** the face. Rhyming slang, from 'drum 'n' bass' (an electronic music genre) *UK, 2001*. ▶ **run a drum** (of a racehorse) to run a winning race, as tipped or expected. Used in negative contexts *AUSTRALIA, 1933*

drum *verb* **1** to steal from unoccupied premises. Probably from an earlier sense (not recorded until 1933) 'to reconnoitre for the purposes of theft by knocking – *drum*ming – on the door of a targeted premises' *UK, 1925*. **2** to inform someone about something *AUSTRALIA, 1919*. **3** to drive a vehicle at speed *UK, 1981*

drum and fife; drummond *noun* **1** a wife. Rhyming slang *UK, 2003*. **2** a knife. Rhyming slang *UK, 1960*

drummed out of the Gestapo for cruelty *adjective* unduly authoritarian, especially when applied to a senior police officer *UK, 1999*

drummer *noun* **1** a housebreaker, especially one who steals from unoccupied premises; a confidence trickster who poses as a door-to-door salesman or similar *UK, 1856*. **2** a poker player who plays only with good hands or good odds favouring his hand. A play on the operative adjective of TIGHT used to describe such a player *US, 1988*. **3** a railway yard conductor *US, 1946*

drummie *noun* a drum-majorette *SOUTH AFRICA, 1972*

drumming *noun* daylight-theft from empty premises. From DRUM (to steal from empty premises) *UK, 1956*

drumstick *noun* a leg, especially a shapely female leg *UK, 1770*

d-runk *adjective* drunk *US, 2001*

drunkalog *noun* in twelve-step recovery programmes such as Alcoholics Anonymous, a long story recounted at a programme meeting, dwelling on the addiction and its manifestations rather than recovery *US, 1998*

drunkard *noun* a passenger train running late on a Saturday night *US, 1977*

drunk as a cunt *adjective* very drunk. Presumed to date from a late C19 variation of the traditional folk song 'Seven Drunken Nights': 'Oh, you're drunk, you're drunk, you stupid old cunt / You're drunk as a cunt can be' *UK, 1984*

drunk as a lord *adjective* being in a state of drunkenness. One of the more notable similes for 'drunk' *UK, 1796*

drunk as a skunk *adjective* very drunk. Derives not from the characteristics of a skunk but, most likely, simply from the rhyme; or possibly as a slurring of DRUNK AS A CUNT. Widely known *UK, 2002*

drunk as a thousand dollars *adjective* very drunk *CANADA, 1989*

drunk as Chloe *adjective* very drunk. The identity of the apparently besozzled Chloe is a mystery *AUSTRALIA, 1892*

drunk as Cooter Brown *adjective* very drunk *US, 1953*

drunkathon *noun* a session of excessive drinking *UK, 2003*

drunk bumps *noun* small bumps delineating lanes on motorways and roads. So named because of their role in alerting drunk drivers that they are straying out of their lane *US, 1992*

drunken *adjective* (used of a wink in tiddlywinks) behaving unpredictably *US, 1977*

drunken forest *noun* in the permafrost area of northern Canada, trees tilted in many directions by natural forces and not held by their shallow root systems *CANADA, 1957*

drunkie *noun* an alcoholic *UK, 1861*

drunkometer *noun* any device used to measure a motorist's blood alcohol content *US, 1962*

drunk tank *noun* a jail cell where drunk prisoners are detained *US, 1947*

drunk wagon *noun* a police van used for rounding up public drunks *US, 1970*

druthers *noun* a preference *US, 1870*

dry *noun* **1** an instance of an actor forgetting the lines *UK, 1945*. **2** a politician who espouses economic caution, especially a Conservative under the leadership of Margaret Thatcher. Coined as an antonym for WET (a middle-of-the-road politician) *UK, 1983*. ▶ **on the dry** in a state of refraining from drinking any alcohol *US, 1957*. ▶ **the Dry** the dry season in Australia's tropical north *AUSTRALIA, 1908*

dry *verb* of an actor, to forget your lines during a performance *UK, 1934*

dry *adjective* **1** of a heavy drinker or alcoholic, doing without alcohol, not drinking, nor under the influence of alcohol *UK, 2002*. **2** without money *US, 1942*

dry *adverb* in a simulated manner *US, 1975*

dry as a dead dingo's donger *adjective* extremely dry; extremely thirsty; parched. That is, as dry 'as the penis of a dead dingo' (a native dog living in arid regions) *AUSTRALIA, 1971*

dry as a kookburra's kyber *adjective* extremely dry, parched *AUSTRALIA, 1971*

dry as a Pommy's towel *adjective* extremely dry; extremely thirsty; parched. From the notion that English people do not wash, a stereotype long held in Australia *AUSTRALIA, 1987*

dry as a whore's cunt on Sunday morning *adjective* extremely dry, especially of exploratory oil drillings *US, 1985*

dry balls *noun* an ache in the testicles from sexual activity not resulting in ejaculation *BAHAMAS, 1982*

dry bath *noun* in prison, a strip search *UK, 1933*

dry clean *verb* to wash your body with just a face cloth *TRINIDAD AND TOBAGO, 2003*

dry clean Methodist *noun* a Christian belonging to a church that does not practise full-immersion baptism *US, 1970*

dry drunk *noun* a person who behaves like an alcoholic even though they are abstaining from drinking. A term used in twelve-step recovery programmes such as Alcoholics Anonymous *US, 1998*

dry Dutch courage *noun* drugs *US, 1987*

dry-eye *adjective* concealing any emotional reaction *BAHAMAS, 1982*

dry-fire; dry-snap *verb* to practise shooting a pistol without live ammunition *US, 1957*

dryfoot *noun* in a Nova Scotia fishing village, a person who never goes fishing *CANADA, 1985*

dry fuck *noun* sex simulated while clothed *US, 1938*

dry-fuck *verb* **1** to stimulate or pantomime sexual intercourse while clothed *US, 1935*. **2** to penetrate a vagina or rectum without benefit of lubricant *US, 1979*

dry goods *noun* clothing *US, 1851*

drygulch *verb* to ambush *US, 1930*

drygulcher *noun* an outlaw who would hide in small canyons and ambush travellers *US, 1930*

dryhanded *adjective* inordinately proud, snobbish *US, 1947*

dry heaves *noun* non-productive vomiting or retching *US, 1991*

dry high *noun* marijuana *US, 1977*

dry hole *noun* a military operation based on poor intelligence and producing no results *US, 1990*

dry hoot *noun* a marijuana cigarette rolled tight and not lit but sniffed *CANADA, 2002*

dry-hump *verb* to simulate sexual intercourse while clothed *US, 1964*

dry lay *noun* sexual intercourse simulated through clothing *US, 1951*

dry out *verb* **1** to undergo a course of treatment designed to break dependence on alcohol *US, 1908*. **2** to detoxify from heroin addiction *US, 1966*

dry root *noun* **1** an act of simulated sexual intercourse while clothed *AUSTRALIA, 1979*. **2** sex without the benefit of lubrication *NEW ZEALAND, 1998*

dry-root *verb* to simulate sexual intercourse while clothed *AUSTRALIA, 2000*

dry rub *noun* body contact, implicitly sexual *US, 1950*

dry run *noun* **1** a trip to court in which nothing happens *US, 1997*. **2** a false alarm *US, 1959*

dry shite *noun* a boring individual *IRELAND, 1995*

dry snitch *noun* a person who unintentionally or indirectly but intentionally betrays or informs on another *US, 1989*

dry-snitch *verb* to betray or inform on someone either unintentionally or indirectly but intentionally *US, 1967*

dry up *noun* to inject a drug intravenously. Probably a variation of DRAW UP *UK, 2003*

dry up *verb* to stop talking. Often used as an imperative *US, 1853*

dry water *noun* in Nova Scotia, an area formerly covered by water but silted in *CANADA, 1999*

D/s *noun* in Sado-masochistic sex, domination and submission *US, 1995*

D's *noun* Dayton tire rims *US, 1997*

DT *noun* **1** a police officer on a street crime beat *US, 1985*. **2** heroin *UK, 2003*

DTK *adjective* handsome, dressed sharply. An abbreviation of 'down to kill', 'down' meaning 'ready' and 'kill' in the figurative sense *US, 1967*

d to d *adjective* door to door *UK, 1985*

D town *nickname* **1** Dallas, Texas *US, 1998*. **2** Denver, Colorado *US, 1986*

DTR *noun* a conversation in which two people define their relationship *US, 2002*

DTs *noun* **1** *delirium tremens*, the withdrawal symptoms of an alcohol or drug addiction *US, 1857*. **2** a pair of men's close-fitting and revealing nylon swimming trunks. Standing for DICK TOGS *AUSTRALIA, 2003*

du *noun* used as a term of address in male-to-male greetings. An abbreviation of the already short DUDE *US, 2000*

dual *noun* a person who is willing to play either the sadist or masochist role in a sadomasochism encounter *US, 1979*

dual sack time *noun* time spent sleeping with someone *US, 1946*

Duane Eddys *noun* cash money. Rhyming slang for READIES, formed from the name of US guitarist Duane Eddy (b.1938) *UK, 2004*

dub *noun* **1** the last part of a marijuana cigarette that is possible to smoke *US, 1989*. **2** a cigarette, especially when used to extend a marijuana cigarette *US, 1975*. **3** a car wheel rim. Usually in the plural *US, 2002*. **4** the Western Hockey League in Canada *CANADA, 1991*. **5** a twenty-dollar note. An abbreviation of DOUBLE SAWBUCK *US, 1981*. **6** an incompetent and inferior person *US, 1887*

Dub *nickname* someone from Dublin *IRELAND, 1996*

dub *verb* **1** to have sex with *US, 1997*. **2** to close, to lock up. Prison use, from the obsolete sense (a key) *UK, 1753*. **3** to criticise, or otherwise dismiss, in speech. Teen slang *UK, 2003*

dubber *noun* a cigarette *US, 1975*

dubbies *noun* the female breasts *US, 1966*

dubbo *noun* a fool. From the country town Dubbo, seen as a place of country bumpkins *AUSTRALIA, 1973*

dub-dub-dub *noun* the World Wide Web (www). A spoken shortening *UK, 2003*

dub dub dub *verb* to contact or use the internet. By ellipsis of each initial in the conventional abbreviation for World Wide Web *UK, 2005*

dubes *noun* a central nervous system stimulant *UK, 1983*

dubich *noun* a marijuana cigarette *US, 1997*

Dublin *noun* any neighbourhood populated by large numbers of Irish immigrants *US, 1963*

dubs *noun* twenty dollars; something sold for twenty dollars *US, 2001*

Dubya *nickname* George W. Bush, 43rd President of the US. A deliberately Texan pronunciation of 'W', necessarily included in his name during the presidential campaign of 1999 and 2000 to differentiate him from his father George Bush, 41st President of the US *US, 1999*

ducat *noun* in prison, a written order given to a prisoner for an appointment *US, 1926*

ducats *noun* money *US, 1866*

duchess *noun* **1** a wife. An affectionate title, adopted from 'the wife of a duke' (the highest hereditary rank of nobility), originally given to costermongers' wives, perhaps in relation to the coster-royalty of Pearly Kings and Queens. May be a shortened form of DUCHESS OF FIFE, or extended from DUTCH (a spouse) *UK, 1895*. **2** a girlfriend *US, 1945*. **3** a female member of a youth gang *US, 1993*. **4** a comfortably-off or grandly well-appointed homosexual man *UK, 2002*

duchess *verb* to treat as a VIP *AUSTRALIA, 1956*

Duchess of Fife *noun* a wife. Rhyming slang; often suggested as the origin of DUTCH (a wife) and/or DUCHESS *UK, 1961*

Duchess of Teck; duchess *noun* a cheque. Rhyming slang, formed from the title of Her Serene Highness Princess Victoria Mary ('Princess May') of Teck (1867–1953), queen consort of George V, or from her mother, Princess Mary Adelaide, who was entitled Duchess of Teck from 1871. The husband, DUKE OF TECK, serves the same purpose in slang *UK, 1960*

Duchess of York *noun* pork. Rhyming slang, not recorded until after Sarah ('Fergie') Ferguson (b.1959) became Duchess of York in 1986 *UK, 1992*

duck *noun* **1** in cricket, a score of zero/nought. A shortening of the original term 'duck's egg' which derived from the shape of 0 written in the scorebook *UK, 1868*. **2** an unrelentingly gullible and trusting person; an odd person. Prison usage *US, 1848*. **3** in pool, a shot that cannot be missed or a game that cannot be lost *US, 1990*. **4** an attractive target for a robbery *US, 1965*. **5** a stolen car discovered by police through serendipitous checking of number plates. An abbreviation of SITTING DUCK *US, 1970*. **6** a portable urinal for male hospital patients *US, 1980*. **7** a prison sentence of two years. Probably from the shape of 2 *US, 1990*. **8** in a deck of playing cards, a two *US, 1988*. **9** a surfer who lingers in the water, rarely catching a wave *US, 1991*. **10** an admission ticket for a paid event. An abbreviation of DUCAT *US, 1945*. **11** a firefighter. New York police slang *US, 1997*. **12** inexpensive wine. An abbreviation and then generic use of Cold Duck, a sparkling red wine that was extremely popular in the 1960s and 70s *US, 1972*. **13** used as a term of address, usually an endearment. Also used in the plural since 1936 *UK, 1590*

duck *verb* **1** to avoid *US, 1864*. **2** in pool, to miss a shot or lose a game intentionally to mislead an opponent as to your true ability *US, 1993*. ▶ **duck a date** in circus and carnival usage, to fail to perform as scheduled *US, 1981*. ▶ **duck and dive** to avoid or evade, especially with regard to legality or responsibility; to dodge work, to shirk; hence, to avoid regular employment but make a living nevertheless. Rhyming slang for SKIVE (to avoid or evade) *UK, 1960*. ▶ **duck arse** when smoking, to wet the cigarette end with saliva. Probably a back-formation from DUCK'S ARSE, changing 'duck' from 'a bird' to a verb *UK, 1968*

duckbill *noun* an experimental 12-gauge shotgun tested by US Navy SEALS in Vietnam *US, 1991*

duck bucket *noun* in poker, a poor hand that wins a pot, especially a pair of twos *US, 1996*

duck butt *noun* **1** a short person *US, 1939*. **2** a hair-style popular in the early 1950s, in which the hair was tapered and curled on the nape of the neck like the feathers of a duck's tail *US, 1955*

duck butter *noun* smegma or other secretions that collect on and around the genitals *US, 1933*

duck day *noun* the day when a member of the US armed forces is honourably discharged. An allusion to the US armed forces insignia designating honourable discharge known as the RUPTURED DUCK *US, 1946*

duck-dive *verb* in surfing, to push the nose of the surfboard down under a breaking wave *US, 1988*

duck egg *noun* a fool. Possibly from the cricketing term which derives from DUCK (zero) *UK, 2003*

duck factory *noun* an area of marsh where ducks nest *CANADA, 1964*

duck-fucker *noun* a lazy person *US, 1986*

duckhouse *noun* ▶ **one up against your duckhouse** something to your detriment; one against you *AUSTRALIA, 1933*

duck out; duck out of *verb* to avoid responsibility; to fail to attend a meeting. An elaboration of DUCK (to avoid) *UK, 1984*

duck plucker *noun* used as a euphemism for 'motherfucker' *US, 1976*

duck rest *noun* a poor night's sleep *BARBADOS, 1965*

ducks *noun* money. An abbreviation of DUCATS *US, 1997*

ducks and drakes *noun* delirium tremens. Rhyming slang for SHAKES *AUSTRALIA, 1967*

ducks and geese *noun* the police *AUSTRALIA, 1966*

duck's arse; duck's ass *noun* **1** a hairstyle popular in the early 1950s, especially among Teddy Boys; the hair was tapered and curled on the nape of the neck like the feathers of a duck's tail. Also widely known by the initials DA, and occasionally by the euphemistic 'duck's anatomy' *UK, 1955*. **2** a cigarette end that is over-moistened with a smoker's saliva *UK, 1993*. **3** an informant. Rhyming slang for GRASS (an informant), probably formed during the 1950s when the 'duck's arse' hairstyle was in fashion *UK, 1950s*. ▶ **tighter than a duck's arse** very drunk or drug-intoxicated. An oddly mixed metaphor *UK, 2002*

duck's disease; ducks' disease; duck-disease *noun* shortness of stature, especially applied to short legs. A humorous reference to an anatomical characteristic of ducks *UK, 1925*

duck's guts *noun* **1** trouble *BARBADOS, 1965*. **2** something superlative *AUSTRALIA, 1979*

duck shoving *noun* the passing of a problem on to another *NEW ZEALAND, 1984*

duck's nest *noun* in oil drilling, a brick-lined hole under a boiler that enhances combustion *US, 1954*

duck soup *noun* an easy task; a cinch *US, 1902*

duck suit *noun* a brown and tan camouflage suit, not dissimilar to the suit worn by a duck hunter, issued to US special forces in Vietnam. The colours were not particularly suited for Vietnam and the suits were largely rejected by the troops *US, 1991*

duck tail *noun* **1** a hair-style popular in the early 1950s in which a boy's hair was tapered and curled on the nape of the neck like the feathers of a duck's tail *US, 1943*. **2** an unruly South African youth *SOUTH AFRICA, 1959*

Ducky *nickname* Le Duc Tho (1911–1990), North Vietnamese politician, who declined the 1973 Nobel Peace Prize which he won jointly with Dr Henry Kissinger of the US *US, 1991*

ducky *adjective* attractive, good *US, 1901*

ducky; duckie *noun* used as a term of address. Originally in general use, especially by women; from mid-C20, usage by men is often affected, implying homosexuality *UK, 1819*

duct *noun* cocaine. An abbreviation of C-DUCT *US, 1986*

dud *noun* a worthless or unsuccessful person or thing, a failure. Originally, 'an unexploded bomb or shell' *UK, 1915*

dud *verb* to fool or deceive; to swindle *AUSTRALIA, 1970*

dud *adjective* worthless, useless, unsatisfactory *UK, 1903*

dud bash *noun* an unsatisifying sexual partner *AUSTRALIA, 1967*

dudder *noun* a swindler; a con artist *AUSTRALIA, 1988*

dude *noun* **1** a regular fellow. In the US, the term had this vague sense in the hippie culture, and then a much more specific sense in the 1970s and 80s *US, 1883*. **2** used as a term of address, young male to young male *US, 1945*. **3** a railway conductor *US, 1946*

Dude *nickname* Lenny Dykstra (b. 1963), a hard-playing and hard-living center fielder and leadoff hitter in baseball (1985–1996) *US, 1989*

dude *adjective* well-dressed *BAHAMAS, 1982*

dude up *verb* to dress up *US, 1899*

Dudley *noun* a beginner gambler *US, 2003*

Dudley Do-Right; Dudley Dogooder *noun* the epitome of a sincere, moral, upstanding citizen, despised by those who live on the fringes of the law. From a cartoon feature *Dudley Do-Right of* *the Mounties* first aired in 1961 as a segment on the *Rocky and Friends Show* US, 1990

Dudley Moore; dudley *noun* a sore, hence any kind of uncomfortable skin condition. Rhyming slang, formed from the name of a British actor, comedian and jazz-musician, 1935–2002 UK, 1992

dudly; dudley *adjective* (used of a boy) extremely boring. Valley girl slang US, 1982

dud root *noun* an unsatisfying sexual partner AUSTRALIA, 1985

duds *noun* **1** clothing UK, 1307. **2** fake drugs. From DUD (a worthless thing) UK, 1996

due *noun* the residue left in a pipe after smoking crack cocaine US, 1989

due *adjective* of a professional criminal, considered likely to be arrested whether or not actually responsible for the crime in question UK, 1996

due-back *noun* something that is borrowed, such as a cigarette, with an expectation of a ultimate return of the favour US, 1951

Duesie *noun* a Duesenberg car US, 1965

duff *noun* the buttocks, the rump. Although first recorded in the UK, modern usage began in the US in 1939 UK, 1840. ▶ **up the duff** pregnant. Perhaps from 'duff' (pudding) AUSTRALIA, 1941

duff *verb* to escape US, 1963

duff *adjective* no good, inferior, useless UK, 1953

duffel drag *noun* the final morning of a soldier's service in Vietnam US, 1991

duffer *noun* **1** a doltish old man. In recent times, the term has come to take on an emphasis on age UK, 1730. **2** an incompetent, a person of no ability. Possibly from Scots *doofart* (a stupid person) UK, c.1730

Duff's Ditch *noun* the Red River floodway, built 1962–68 when Duff Roblin was Premier CANADA, 1987

duff up *verb* to beat up, to assault someone UK, 1961

duffy *noun* **1** a spasm feigned by a drug addict in the hope of eliciting sympathy from a physician US, 1973. **2** a doltish old man. A variation of DUFFER UK, 2002

duffy; duffie *verb* to leave quickly. A simpler version of TAKE IT ON THE ARTHUR DUFFY US, 1945

duggy *adjective* dressed in style US, 1993

dugongs the female breasts UK, 1985

Dugout Doug *nickname* General Douglas MacArthur (1880–1964) of the US Army US, 1982

duh *noun* an offensive, despicable person; a clumsy person; a socially awkward person. From the expression of disgust at someone's stupidity SOUTH AFRICA, 1976

duh! used for expressing disgust at the stupidity of what has just been said. A single syllable with a great deal of attitude US, 1963

duh-brain *noun* a stupid person. Extended from duh UK, 2006

duji; doogie; doojie *noun* heroin US, 1960

duke *noun* **1** a regular fellow; a tough guy US, 1939. **2** poor quality tobacco issued by the State of California to prisoners. Named after former California Governor Deukmejian (1983–91) US, 1989. **3** in card games, a hand (of cards) US, 1967

Duke *noun* **1** a Ducati motorcycle UK, 1979. **2** a socially inept person US, 1983

Duke *nickname* **1** Edwin Donald Snider (b.1926). Snider played center field for the Brooklyn and Los Angeles Dodgers baseball teams of the 1950s and was the most powerful hitter in the Dodgers' line-up. He was more formally known as the 'Duke of Flatbush' US, 1969. **2** the film actor John Wayne, 1907–79 US, 2001

duke *verb* **1** to fight with fists US, 1935. **2** to give US, 1973. **3** to allow US, 2001. **4** to fool; to deceive US, 1975. **5** to have sex US, 1993. **6** to short-change someone by palming a coin given as part of the change US, 1981

duke breath *noun* bad breath US, 1993

duked out *adjective* dressed up US, 1938

Duke of Argyle *noun* a file (a tool). Rhyming slang UK, 1992

Duke of Argyles; the duke *noun* haemorrhoids. Rhyming slang for 'piles' UK: SCOTLAND, 1988

Duke of Kent *noun* rent. Rhyming slang, no earlier than C20 UK, 1932

Duke of Kent *adjective* bent (in all senses). Rhyming slang UK, 1992

Duke of Montrose *noun* the nose. Glasgow rhyming slang UK: SCOTLAND, 1988

Duke of Teck; duke *noun* a cheque. Rhyming slang UK, 1960

Duke of York *noun* **1** a cork. Rhyming slang UK, 1931. **2** talk. Rhyming slang UK, 1992. **3** a fork. Rhyming slang UK, 1992

duke on *verb* to give US, 1967

duker *noun* a person inclined to fight US, 1979

dukes *noun* **1** the hands; fists. The singular is 'duke', or variant 'dook', which is probably rhyming slang, formed on DUKE OF YORK for 'forks' (the fingers) US, 1859. **2** cut-off blue jean shorts. An abbreviation of DAISY DUKES US, 1996

duke shot *noun* any method by which a carnival game operator allows a customer to win a rigged game US, 1985

duke's mixture *noun* **1** a person of mixed race US, 1961. **2** a random conglomeration US, 1914

dukey *noun* **1** a brown paper lunch bag. Chicago slang US, 1986. **2** in the circus, a lunch prepared for circus workers on long train journeys between towns US, 1980. **3** in circus and carnival usage, a meal ticket or book of meal tickets US, 1981 ▷*see:* DOOKIE

dukey rope *noun* a gold chain necklace US, 1989

dukey run *noun* in the circus, a long train ride between shows US, 1980

duky *noun* an operator of a DUKW barge ANTARCTICA, 1966

dull and dowdy *adjective* cloudy. Rhyming slang, that can refer to poorly conditioned beer as well as the weather UK, 1992

dull as arse *adjective* very boring, extremely dull UK, 2002

dullsville *noun* the epitome of a boring existence US, 1960

Dullsville, Ohio *noun* anywhere other than Las Vegas US, 1985

dumb as a mud fence *adjective* very stupid US, 2004

dumb ass *noun* **1** a stupid person US, 1958. **2** stupidity US, 1972. ▶ **eat up with the dumb ass** very stupid US, 1984

dumb-ass; dumb-assed *adjective* stupid, foolish. From the noun sense US, 1957

dumb as two short planks *adjective* used to describe someone who is very stupid CANADA, 1989

dumbbell *noun* a stupid person US, 1918

dumb blonde *noun* a stereotypical (perhaps mythical) blonde-haired, sexually attractive woman who is not especially intelligent US, 1936

dumb bomb *noun* a bomb that must be dropped accurately. Back formation from 'smart bomb' US, 1991

dumbbutt *noun* a dolt US, 1973

dumb cake *noun* in Newfoundland, a cake baked and eaten by unmarried women in silence CANADA, 1998

dumb cluck *noun* a fool AUSTRALIA, 1948

dumb crooker *noun* a social misfit US, 1963

Dumb Dora *noun* an empty-headed woman US, 1922

dumb down *verb* to simplify the content of something so that it can be understood by the general uneducated public US, 1933

dumb dust *noun* cocaine or heroin US, 1986

dumbfuck; dumb-fuck *noun* a despicable, stupid person US, 1950

dumbjohn *noun* a person of no importance, especially a military cadet US, 1951

dumbo *noun* a dolt, a fool US, 1932

Dumbo *noun* during the war in Vietnam, a C-123 US Air Force provider US, 1989

dumbshit *noun* an imbecile US, 1961

dumbshit *adjective* stupid *US, 1967*

dumb sock *noun* a dolt *US, 1932*

dumbwad *noun* an imbecile *US, 1978*

dum-dum *noun* **1** a soft-core bullet that expands upon impact *UK, 1897*. **2** a simpleton *US, 1937*. **3** Demerol™, a central nervous system depressant *US, 1984*

dummies *noun* **1** in horse racing, spurs approved for racing *AUSTRALIA, 1989*. **2** imitation drugs *US, 1995*

dummkopf *noun* a dolt; a fool. German for 'dumb-head' *US, 1809*

dummy *noun* **1** a fool; a mentally retarded person *UK, 1796*. **2** a mute *US, 1962*. **3** a representative of a corrupt police officer in insurance fraud *UK, 1956*. **4** a feigned injury or illness *US, 1992*. **5** a substance other than narcotics sold as narcotics *US, 1992*. **6** a solitary confinement cell in prison *NEW ZEALAND, 1998*. **7** a train that transports railway workers *US, 1946*. **8** a wallet. From an earlier use as 'a pocket-book' *UK, 1958*. **9** the penis *US, 1950*. ▶ **beat your dummy** (used of a male) to masturbate *US, 1977*. ▶ **on the dummy** quiet *US, 1971*

dummy *verb* to pack marijuana into a rolled cigarette butt *US, 1965*

dummy-chucker *noun* a swindler who pretends to be the victim of accidents *US, 1963*

dummy dust *noun* **1** phencyclidine, the recreational drug known as PCP or angel dust *US, 1977*. **2** cocaine *US, 1992*

dummy flogger *noun* a masturbator *US, 1985*

dummy oil *noun* Demerol™, a branded central nervous system depressant *US, 1988*

dummy stick *noun* a bamboo stick used to carry baskets on each end, carried across the shoulders *US, 1965*

dummy up *verb* to stop talking; to be quiet *US, 1928*

dump *noun* **1** the buttocks *US, 1973*. **2** an act of defecation *US, 1942*. **3** an unpleasant place or location *US, 1899*. **4** in a smuggling operation, the place where the goods to be smuggled are assembled *US, 1956*. **5** a ticket returned unsold to a theatre by a ticket agency *US, 1981*. **6** a large, unprocessed amount of information *US, 1991*. **7** a hospital patient who is transferred from one hospital or nursing home to another *US, 1983*. **8** a mortuary. Gallows humour from the Vietnam war *US, 1991*. **9** a fall from a surfboard, usually caused by a wave's impact *US, 1964*. ▶ **take a dump 1** to defecate *US, 1942*. **2** to lose a game intentionally, especially for the purpose of taking advantage of spectator betting *US, 1955*

dump *verb* **1** to beat; to kill *US, 1960*. **2** to assault *US, 1951*. **3** to break off a romantic relationship with someone *AUSTRALIA, 1967*. **4** to derive sexual pleasure from sadistic acts *US, 1957*. **5** in bowling, to release the ball with the fingers and thumb at the same time *US, 1969*. **6** to fall from a surfboard; to be battered by a wave while bodysurfing *AUSTRALIA, 1967*. **7** in motorcyling, to fall to the ground with the motorcyle *US, 1973*. **8** in hot rodding and drag racing, to damage a component partially or completely *US, 1965*. **9** to lose a game intentionally, especially for the purpose of taking advantage of spectator betting *US, 1951*. **10** in horse racing, to bet a large amount on a horse just before a race *US, 1951*. **11** to lose a large sum of money gambling in a short period *US, 1980*. **12** to vomit after injecting heroin or a synthetic opiate *US, 1968*. **13** to complete an illegal drug sale by delivering the drug *US, 1995*. ▶ **dump it out** to defecate *US, 1990*. ▶ **dump the clutch** in drag racing, to engage the clutch in a quick and forceful manner *US, 1970*. ▶ **dump your load** to ejaculate *NEW ZEALAND, 1998*

dumper *noun* **1** a toilet *UK, 2003*. **2** an athlete who dumps a game, intentionally losing *US, 1951*. **3** a person who takes sexual pleasure from sadistic acts *US, 1957*. **4** an uninspiring, boring experience *UK, 1983*. **5** a large and dangerous wave that breaks suddenly *AUSTRALIA, 1920*

dumpi; dumpy *noun* the smallest size (340ml) bottle of beer. From the squat shape *SOUTH AFRICA, 1966*

dumping *noun* a beating in the context of sadistic sex *US, 1957*

dumping table *noun* a blackjack table in a casino where players have been consistently winning *US, 1991*

dumpling *noun* a fool, a dunce *UK: SCOTLAND, 1988*

dump off *verb* (used of a casino dealer) to overpay a bet made by a confederate *US, 1985*

dump out *verb* (of a casino employee) to lose intentionally as part of a scheme with a gambler or gamblers *US, 1977*

dumps *noun* the female breasts *US, 2001*. ▶ **down in the dumps** depressed, melancholy *UK, 1714*. ▶ **the dumps** melancholy. Often in phrases 'in the dumps' and 'down in the dumps' *UK, 1714*

dump stroke *noun* in pool, the minuscule adjustment to a shot that a player makes when intentionally missing a shot *US, 1990*

dump truck *noun* **1** a court-appointed public defender *US, 1984*. **2** a car filled with lesbians *US, 1970*. **3** a prisoner who does not hold up his end of a shared task or relationship *US, 1989*

dumpty *noun* a latrine *AUSTRALIA, 1945*

dumpy *adjective* (used of waves) weak, erratic *US, 1988*

dun *noun* a male friend *US, 2002*

duncey *adjective* stupid *TRINIDAD AND TOBAGO, 1962*

duncy; duncey *adjective* foolish, stupid *BARBADOS, 1965*

dundus *noun* an albino. West Indian and UK black patois *UK, 1994*

dune coon *noun* an Arab. Very offensive *US, 1984*

duner *noun* a person who enjoys driving dune buggies in the desert *US, 1974*

dungarees *noun* battle fatigues. Marine Corps usage in World War 2 and Korea *US, 1979*

dung beetle *noun* used by bookmakers for describing a person who thrives on blather or bullshit *AUSTRALIA, 1989*

dunge *noun* a dent *IRELAND, 1997*

dungeon *noun* a nightclub catering to sado-masochistic fetishists *US, 1996*

dunger; dunga *noun* the penis *NEW ZEALAND, 1998*

dungout *noun* an utter failure *NEW ZEALAND, 1995*

dungpuncher *noun* the male playing the active role in anal sex *AUSTRALIA, 1985*

dung-scuffer *noun* a cowboy. A euphemism for SHITKICKER *US, 1974*

dunk *verb* to humiliate in any context *US, 1999*

dunka *noun* a large posterior *US, 2002*

Dunkirk *noun* work. Rhyming slang *UK, 1992*

dunky; dunkey *noun* a condom *UK, 1997*

Dunlop tyre; dunlop *noun* a liar. Rhyming slang *UK, 1992*

dunnies *noun* a toilet block *AUSTRALIA, 1933*

dunnit? doesn't it? A phonetic slurring *UK, 1984*

dunno; dunna; dunnaw don't know; I don't know. A phonetic slurring *UK, 1842*

dunny *noun* **1** a toilet. A shortening of *dunniken*, from British dialect and cant. Thought to be a compound of 'danna' (excrement) and 'ken' (house). Before the age of septic tanks and flush toilets the 'dunny' was a wooden outhouse standing far back from a dwelling. The spelling 'dunnee' seems only to have been favoured by Barry Humphries in his *Bazza MacKenzie* comic strip *AUSTRALIA, 1933*. **2** the vagina *BAHAMAS, 1982*. **3** money *JAMAICA, 2000*

dunny budgie *noun* a blowfly *AUSTRALIA, 2003*

dunny can *noun* a sanitary bin *AUSTRALIA, 1962*

dunny cart *noun* a vehicle for collecting sanitary bins *AUSTRALIA, 1963*

dunny diver *noun* a plumber *NEW ZEALAND, 2002*

dunny documents *noun* toilet paper *AUSTRALIA, 1996*

dunny man; dunnyman *noun* a man employed to empty sanitary bins *AUSTRALIA, 1962*

dunny paper *noun* toilet paper *AUSTRALIA, 1987*

duns *noun* money *JAMAICA, 1982*

dupe *noun* a duplicate *US, 1891*

dupe *verb* to duplicate *US, 1912*

duper *noun* a duplicating machine, such as a mimeograph *US, 1982*

duppy *noun* a ghost BARBADOS, 1965

duppy and the dog *noun* a crowd made up of everyone you can think of BARBADOS, 1980

duppy tucks *noun* clothes burnt by an iron BARBADOS, 1965

Durban *noun* marijuana from the Durban area of South Africa SOUTH AFRICA, 1997

Durban brown *noun* brownish marijuana, said to have been grown in Natal Province, South Africa UK, 2002

Durban poison *noun* a variety of marijuana SOUTH AFRICA, 1996

durn *adverb* used as a folksy variation of 'darn' or 'darned', a euphemism for 'damned' US, 1958

durog *noun* marijuana. A variant of DUROS, punning on 'drug' US, 1977

durong *noun* marijuana. A variation of DUROG and DUROS UK, 2003

duros *noun* marijuana. The Spanish masculine noun *duro* is a five-peseta coin; the anglicised plural puts a cheap price on the drug US, 1971

durry *noun* a cigarette. Origin unknown. It has been suggested that it is extracted from Bull *Dur*ham™, a brand of tobacco, but this is drawing a long bow indeed AUSTRALIA, 1941

duss *verb* to kill. West Indian and UK black pronunciation of DUST (to kill) UK, 1994

dust *noun* **1** a powdered narcotic, especially cocaine or heroin US, 1916. **2** phencyclidine, the recreational drug known as PCP or angel dust. An abbreviation of ANGEL DUST. US, 1977. **3** inexpensive cigarette tobacco given free to prisoners US, 1967. **4** the powdered malted milk used in soda fountain malt drinks US, 1946. **5** money UK, 1607. **6** a small amount of money TRINIDAD AND TOBAGO, 1987. **7** the condition of being doomed or finished US, 1994. ▶ **on the dust** working as a refuse collector UK, 1999

dust *verb* **1** to beat UK, 1612. **2** to shoot; to kill US, 1972. **3** to leave US, 1945. **4** to use and become intoxicated with phencyclidine, the recreational drug known as PCP or angel dust US, 1989. **5** to combine marijuana and heroin for smoking US, 1986. **6** in horse racing, to administer a drug to a horse before a race US, 1951

dustbin *noun* a gun turret UK, 1990

dustbin lid; dustbin *noun* **1** a child. Rhyming slang for 'kid'; rarely, if ever, singular. May be reduced further to 'binlid' UK, 1960. **2** a Jewish person. Rhyming slang for YID UK, 1979

dust-biter *noun* during the US war against Iraq, an infantry soldier assigned to front line duty US, 1991

dust bunny *noun* a cluster of dust that accumulates under furniture US, 1966

dust-eater *noun* the last vehicle in a military convoy US, 1986

dusted *adjective* **1** drug-intoxicated. Originally of cocaine, then less and less discriminating US, 1959. **2** drunk US, 1966

dusted out; dusted *adjective* under the influence of phencyclidine, the recreational drug known as PCP or angel dust US, 1983

duster *noun* **1** a metal device worn above the knuckles so that, when punching, it both protects the fist and lends brutal force to the blow. An abbreviation of 'knuckleduster'; from DUST (to beat) UK, 1999. **2** an M-2 anti-aircraft tank armed with twin Bofars 40mm guns. The tank was designed for anti-aircraft combat, but the North Vietnamese did not operate in the air, so the M-2 was used on the ground, where it was quite good at DUSTING [killing] enemy soldiers US, 1969. **3** a user of phencyclidine, the recreational drug known as PCP or angel dust US, 1967. **4** in oil drilling, a hole that produces no oil. It may produce salt water, but it is still dry US, 1898. **5** the inner door of a safe US, 1949. **6** the buttocks US, 1946

duster *verb* to punch someone using a knuckleduster UK, 2000

dusters *noun* the testicles US, 1967

dust hawk *noun* a horse driven in sulky races CANADA, 1971

dusties *noun* old gramophone records of out-of-fashion songs US, 1972

dust it *verb* to leave hurriedly TRINIDAD AND TOBAGO, 1990

dust of angels *noun* phencyclidine, the recreational drug known as PCP or angel dust US, 1994

dust-off *noun* medical evacuation by helicopter. Vietnam war usage US, 1967

dust off *verb* **1** to kill US, 1940. **2** to evacuate (the wounded) US, 1971. **3** in hot rodding and drag racing, to defeat in a race US, 1965

dust puppy *noun* a cluster of soft dust that accumulates on the floor US, 1943

dusts *noun* brass knuckles US, 1993

dust-up *noun* a fight; a disturbance; an engagement with an enemy. Military coinage; the image of dust raised in a physical conflict UK, 1897

dusty *noun* an old person, thought to be aged 70 or more. Upper-class society use UK, 1982

dusty *adjective* under the influence of phencyclidine, the recreational drug known as PCP or angel dust US, 1998

dusty and cleaning *noun* a surgical scraping of the uterus. A back-formation from the technical term D & C (dilation and curettage) US, 2003

Dusty finish *verb* the conclusion of a professional wrestling match in which the original referee returns from having been knocked out to overrule a victory declared by a second referee. Refers to Dusty Rhodes, a wrestler who often finished his matches in this dramatic fashion US, 2000

dutch *noun* ▶ **in dutch** in trouble US, 1851

Dutch *noun* **1** a spouse, especially a wife. Usually as 'old Dutch' and preceded by a possessive pronoun. Albert Chevalier (1861–1923) explained the derivation as 'old Dutch clock', likening a wife's face to a clock-face, or punning on CLOCK (a face). The etymology is uncertain, but often confused with DUCHESS (a wife) and DUTCH PLATE (a friend) UK, 1889. **2** suicide US, 1915 ▷*see:* DOUBLE DUTCH, DUTCH PLATE

dutch *verb* ▶ **dutch a book** in an illegal betting operation, to accept bets with odds and in a proportion that guarantees the bookmaker will lose money regardless of the outcome that is being bet on US, 1911

Dutch *verb* in hot rodding and car customising, to paint elaborate pinstripes or flames on the car body in the style of 1950s customiser Kenneth 'Von Dutch' Howard US, 1993

Dutch *adverb* paying your own way US, 1914

Dutch act; Dutch route *noun* suicide US, 1902

Dutch auction; Dutch sale *noun* a mock-auction or sale where goods are sold at nominal prices; especially an auction where the price is slowly decreased until the first bid is made and the lot is sold; in a multiple lot sale the highest bidder wins the right to purchase at the lowest bid price UK, 1859

Dutch bath *noun* a cursory washing of the body using little water US, 1953

Dutch book *noun* in a bookmaking operation, a horse race in which the odds are such that the astute bettor can bet on any horse and win US, 1912

Dutch cap *noun* a diaphragm or pessary US, 1950

Dutch clock *noun* a speed recording device on a railway engine US, 1943

Dutch courage *noun* courage induced by drink UK, 1826

Dutch door action *noun* bisexual activity US, 1997

Dutch dumplings *noun* in homosexual usage, the buttocks US, 1987

Dutch fuck *noun* the act of lighting your cigarette from one that another person is smoking. Often accompanied by the catchphrase: 'Hold it close to mine and take the draws down slowly' UK, 1948

Dutch girl *noun* in homosexual usage, a lesbian. A painful pun alluding to Holland's flood control US, 1987

Dutchie *noun* a Dutch person UK, 2000

Dutch leave *noun* an absence without permission US, 1898

dutchman *noun* **1** any after-the-fact alteration of a flawed work process US, 1859. **2** in oil drilling, the shaft of a screw that remains in a hole after the head has been sheared or twisted off *US, 1954*. **3** a drug dealer *US, 1992*

Dutchman *nickname* Norm Van Brocklin (1926–83), quarterback for the Los Angeles Rams during their glory days (1949–57) and then for the Philadelphia Eagles (1958–60) *US, 1960*

Dutchman's fart *noun* a sea-urchin *UK, 1980*

Dutch Mill *nickname* the infiltration surveillance centre at Nakhon Phonom, Thailand. Sensors along routes of North Vietnamese infiltration into South Vietnam broadcast to an orbiting aircraft which relayed the signals to the US base at Nakhon Phonom, Thailand. Because of the distinctive shape of one of its antennas, the installation was called Dutch Mill *US, 1986*

Dutch nickel *noun* a hug or quick kiss *US, 1949*

Dutch oven *noun* a prank performed by farting in a shared bed and then holding the unfortunate victim under the sheets *AUSTRALIA, 1983*

Dutch Owl *noun* a Dutch Owl™ cigar re-made to contain marijuana *US, 2003*

Dutch pegs *noun* the legs. Rhyming slang *UK, 1923*

Dutch plate; Dutch *noun* a friend. Rhyming slang for MATE, which had some currency in the 1960s and 1970s, mainly in its shortened form. Sometimes, and easily, confused with DUTCH (a spouse, especially a wife) *UK, 2002*

Dutch rod *noun* a Luger pistol *US, 1949*

Dutch rub *noun* a playground torture consisting of rubbing the head of a boy restrained in a headlock with the restrainer's knuckles *US, 1930*

Dutch sea wife *noun* a simulated vagina, used for masturbation by males *US, 1957*

Dutch straight *noun* in poker, a hand with five cards sequenced by twos, worth nothing but not without its beauty *US, 1963*

Dutch treat *noun* an arrangement in which each person pays their own way *US, 1887*

Dutch uncle *noun* a person given to pedantic lectures *UK, 1838*

dutty *adjective* **1** dirty. West Indian and UK black patois pronunciation *UK, 1994*. **2** used as a personal compliment. Derived from dirty *UK, 2005*

duty *noun* a duty officer *US, 1957*

duty dog *noun* the officer acting as prison governor when the governor is absent *UK, 1996*

duvet day *noun* an unofficial day off work that is taken for no good reason. In August 2004 'duvet days' were discussed as employee incentives *UK, 2003*

duw duw! used for registering frustration, exasperation, or sympathy. Pronounced 'jew jew'; a reduplication of Welsh *duw* (god) used widely, and without especial reference to its religious significance, by non-Welsh-speaking South Walians *UK: WALES, 2002*

dux *adjective* smart *FIJI, 1993*

DV *noun* a Cadillac Coupe de Ville car *US, 1980*

dwaddle *verb* to waste time, to dawdle *US, 1950*

dwang *noun* a short piece of timber inserted between wall studs *NEW ZEALAND, 1988*. ▶ **in the dwang** in trouble. From Afrikaans for 'constraint' *SOUTH AFRICA, 1994*

dwarf *noun* the butt of a marijuana cigarette. *Crush That Dwarf, Hand Me the Pliers* was a Firesign Theatre play about the life of Everyman George Tirebiter, punning, as was the fashion of the time, on marijuana use *US, 1970*

dweeb; dweebie *noun* a socially inept person *US, 1985*

dweeby *adjective* foolish, inept, out of touch with current trends *US, 1987*

dwell *verb* ▶ **dwell the box** to be patient *UK, 1956*

DWI *adjective* poorly dressed. 'Dressed without instructions', a play on the usual meaning of the initials, 'driving while intoxicated' *US, 1997*

dwid *noun* a social outcast *US, 1988*

dwim *noun* in computing, a command meaning 'do what I mean' *US, 1983*

dwindles *noun* the condition of an older hospital patient who is fading away *US, 1981*

dyam *adjective* used as an intensifier. A West Indian and UK Black patois variation of 'damn' *UK, 1994*

dye party *noun* a gathering to tie-dye an assortment of clothes for personal use or sale *US, 1994*

dying on its arse *adjective* failing. The image of sitting down to wait for death and decay *UK, 2001*

dyin' holy dyin' used as a curse or oath, especially in Nova Scotia. Unlike a number of the maritime sacrilegious curses, this one is often used to express surprise *CANADA, 1999*

dyke; dike *noun* **1** a lesbian, especially a 'mannish', aggressive one. Safely used by insiders, with caution by outsiders *US, 1931*. **2** a toilet *UK, 1923*. **3** dipipanone, an analgesic opiate used for recreational narcotic effect *UK, 1996*

dyke daddy *noun* a male who prefers and seeks the friendship of lesbians *US, 1991*

dykey *adjective* overtly lesbian, mannish *US, 1964*

dykon *noun* a person or image seen as inspirational to lesbians. A variation on 'gay icon', combining DYKE (a lesbian) and 'icon' (a devotional image) *UK, 1994*

dynamite *noun* **1** powerful alcohol or drugs *US, 1919*. **2** nitroglycerine tablets prescribed to cardiac patients *US, 1975*. **3** any amphetamine, methamphetamine or other central nervous system stimulant *US, 1980*. **4** cocaine *US, 1959*. **5** a blend of heroin and cocaine *US, 1937*. **6** something that is very good *US, 1902*. **7** in an illegal betting operation, money that one bookmaker bets with another bookmaker to cover bets that he does not want to hold *US, 1951*. **8** a fight. Rhyming slang. May be abbreviated to 'dyna' *UK, 1992*

dynamite *verb* to stop a train suddenly *US, 1977*. ▶ **dynamite the brakes** in trucking, to make a sudden, emergency stop *US, 1951*

dynamite *adjective* excitingly excellent *US, 1922*

dyn-no-mite! used for expressing strong approval. A stock laugh-line catchphrase used by the character J.J. Evans, played by Jimmie Walker, in the 1970s situation comedy *Facts of Life US, 1978*

dyno *noun* **1** heroin, especially if nearly pure. An abbreviation of 'dynamite' *US, 1969*. **2** alcohol *US, 1962*. **3** a dynometer (an instrument used to measure engine power) *US, 1954*

dyno *adjective* excellent. An abbreviation of DYNAMITE *US, 1962*

dyno- *prefix* dynamic *US, 1992*

dyno-pure *noun* especially pure heroin. An elaboration of DYNO *UK, 2002*

Dyson *noun* an act of mutual oral-genital sex. Dyson™ is the brand name of a vacuum cleaner that introduced 'dual-cyclone' technology which, it is claimed, provides improved suction; 'Dyson', as a sex-act, stresses the dual functionality of such suction. This is not the first use of a vacuum cleaner as a sexual simile: Electrolux™, another major brand, at one time used the slogan 'Nothing Sucks Like An Electrolux' which, unsurprisingly, lead to its use as an epithet for 'a fellatrix' *UK, 2001*

Ee

E *noun* **1** MDMA, the recreational drug best known as ecstasy. Generally from the initial letter of ECSTASY, specifically in reference to any MDMA tablet stamped with the symbol *UK, 1995.* **2** dismissal, rejection. An abbreviation of ELBOW *UK, 1994.* **3** in poker, the fifth player to the left of the dealer. *US, 1988*

E *verb* to take MDMA, the recreational drug best known as ecstasy. From the noun use *UK, 1996*

e- *prefix* electronic; in practice, mainly applied to communication by computer. A back-formation from 'e-mail', used in such constructions as 'e-address' and 'e-government' *US, 1996*

each-way all each-way *noun* in multiple and accumulator betting, a method of settling each-way bets by dividing the total return from one stage of a bet into equal parts to be wagered on the next stage *UK, 2001*

eager beaver *noun* an annoyingly diligent and hard-working person *US, 1943*

eagle *noun* ▶ **the eagle flies; the eagle screams; the eagle shits** used for expressing payday. Often used with 'when' *US, 1918*

eaglebird *noun* **1** the winner of any long-odds bet, such as the double zero in roulette *US, 1992.* **2** in horse racing, a long-shot winner that nobody has bet on *US, 1947*

eagle day *noun* pay day. On pay day, it it said that THE EAGLE FLIES/SCREAMS, hence this term *US, 1941*

E and E *noun* evasion and escape. Korean war usage *US, 1982*

E and E *verb* to avoid combat duty. From the accepted 'escape and evasion'. Military use in Vietnam *US, 1979*

E and T; ET *noun* in craps, a one-roll bet on eleven and twelve. The bet was originally known as 'E and T'; with the popularity of the film *E.T.*, the terminology quickly changed *US, 1983*

ear *noun* **1** a citizens' band radio antenna *US, 1976.* **2** a person who is not a part of the criminal underworld but who reports what he hears to those who are *US, 1964.* **3** a police officer *SOUTH AFRICA, 1973.* **4** on a playing card, a bent corner used by a cheat to identify the card *US, 1950.* ▶ **keep your ear to the ground; have your ear to the ground** to be alert to whatever is happening *UK, 1920.* ▶ **on your ear 1** easily *UK, 1956.* **2** extremely drunk *IRELAND, 1991*

ear angel *noun* a very small, nearly invisible speaker in a television announcer's ear by which others can communicate with the announcer while on air *US, 1997*

earballs *noun* listeners to commercial broadcasting *US, 1999*

ear banger *noun* a person who enjoys the sound of his own voice *US, 1942*

earbash *noun* a conversation; an unwanted lecture; a tirade *AUSTRALIA, 1951*

earbash *verb* to talk to someone at length; to bore someone with speech *AUSTRALIA, 1944*

earbasher *noun* an incessant talker; a bore *AUSTRALIA, 1941*

earbashing *noun* **1** an insistent barrage of chatter; constant nagging *AUSTRALIA, 1945.* **2** a harsh reprimand *NEW ZEALAND, 1984*

ear bender *noun* an overly talkative person *US, 1934*

earbobs *noun* large, dangling earrings *US, 1986*

ear candy *noun* **1** music that is pleasant, if not challenging *US, 1984.* **2** a platitude *US, 1991*

earcon *noun* an artificial sound that is representative of an action or content. A contrived piece of jargon awkwardly derived from 'icon', its visual equivalent, and slowly creeping into everyday usage *UK, 1988*

earful *noun* a reprimand, especially when robust or lengthy *US, 1911*

earhole *noun* the ear. By synecdoche *AUSTRALIA, 1934.* ▶ **on the earhole; on the ear'ole** on the scrounge. Extends the sense of 'earhole' (whatever you can hear) to 'whatever you can pick up' *UK, 1998*

earhole *verb* **1** to eavesdrop, to listen in on someone's conversation *UK, 1958.* **2** in motorcycle racing, to bank the motorcycle to an extreme degree in a turn, bringing the driver (and the driver's ear) close to the ground *US, 1965*

earie *noun* ▶ **on the earie** alert, informed *US, 1980*

ear job *noun* sexual talk on the telephone *US, 1978*

earl *verb* to vomit. A rhyme with HURL *US, 1968*

Earls Court *noun* salt. Rhyming slang, formed from the name of an area of west London *UK, 1992*

early bird *noun* a word. Rhyming slang *UK, 1937*

early doors *noun* women's knickers, panties, etc. Rhyming slang for 'drawers'; probably since late C19 when 'early doors' was current for a theatrical performance and it was a time when women actually wore 'drawers' *UK, 1979*

early doors *adverb* early on, especially in relation to a sporting contest. Originally applied to admissions to old time music halls; later used, with almost catchphrase status, by football commentator Ron Atkinson *UK, 1998*

early electic *noun* used as a humorous description of a mix of design or decorating styles *US, 1980*

early foot *noun* in horse racing, speed in the initial stages of a race *US, 1960*

early morn *noun* the erect penis. Rhyming slang for HORN *UK, 1992*

early o'clock *noun* shortly after an activity has started *TRINIDAD AND TOBAGO, 1983*

early opener *noun* a public hotel that opens early in the morning to cater for shift workers *AUSTRALIA, 1981*

early out *noun* **1** a separation from the armed forces that is earlier than anticipated *US, 1991.* **2** in American casinos, an early dismissal from work due to smaller than expected numbers of gamblers *US, 1980*

early riser *noun* a prisoner who is about to be released. Discharge from prison usually occurs early in the day *UK, 1996*

early shopper *noun* in horse racing, a bettor who places a bet as soon as the betting windows open *AUSTRALIA, 1989*

early shower; early bath *noun* an ejection from an athletic contest *NEW ZEALAND, 1978*

ear-moll *verb* to listen in; to eavesdrop *UK, 1984*

earn *noun* an amount of money earned, especially earned illicitly *AUSTRALIA, 1977*

earn *verb* to make a dishonest profit *UK, 1977*

earner *noun* **1** a job that pays; something that generates income *UK, 1970.* **2** any circumstance that criminals can turn to profitable advantage *UK, 1977.* **3** a member of an organised crime enterprise who produces high profits, however unpleasant his character may be *US, 1995.* **4** money earned, especially money from an illicit source or corrupt practice *UK, 1970*

earnings *noun* proceeds from crime *SOUTH AFRICA, 1974*

ear'ole *noun* in betting, odds of 6–4. From the TICK-TACK signal used by bookmakers *UK, 1991*

ears *noun* a citizens' band radio receiver. Citizens' band radio slang; usually phrased 'put your ears on', 'have your ears on', etc *US, 1976.* ▶ **be all ears** to listen with close attention *UK, 1865.* ▶ **get your ears raised** to have your hair cut *US, 1954.* ▶ **have your ears flapping; keep your ears flapping** to listen, especially to make an effort to keep up with what is going on *UK, 1984*. ▶ **pull ears** in the language of paragliding, to intentionally collapse both tips of the wing to increase speed *US, 1992*. ▶ **put the ears on** to attempt a controlled roll of the dice *US, 1963*. ▶ **your ears are burning** applied to a sensation that somebody is talking about you. Known in many variations since C14 *UK, 1984*

ear sex *noun* a sexually-oriented telephone conversation with a person working for a telephone sex service *US, 1984*

earth *noun* a marijuana cigarette *BAHAMAS, 1982*. ▶ **the earth** a great expense *UK, 1924*

Eartha Kitt; eartha *noun* **1** faeces; an act of defecation; (as a plural) diarrhoea. Rhyming slang for SHIT, formed on the name of popular singer Eartha Kitt (b.1928) *UK, 1992*. **2** the female breast. Rhyming slang for TIT *UK, 2001*

earthless *adjective* used as a non-profane negative intensifier *BARBADOS, 1965*

earthly *noun* ▶ **no earthly; not an earthly** no chance whatever *UK, 1899*

earth mother; earth mama *noun* a woman who eschews makeup, synthetic fabric, and meat *US, 1980*

earth pads *noun* shoes. Teen slang *US, 1947*

earthshake *noun* an earthquake *JAMAICA, 2003*

earth to .... used as a humorous suggestion that the person named is not in touch with reality *US, 1977*

earwig *noun* an eavesdropper; a lookout man *UK, 1950*

earwig *verb* **1** to eavesdrop. A poor pun on 'to hear' *UK, 1927*. **2** to understand, to realise. Rhyming slang for TWIG *UK, 1992*

ease *verb* to leave *US, 1947*

easel *noun* a motorcycle's prop stand *UK, 1979*

ease off *verb* to urinate *UK, 1970*

ease on *verb* to leave with a parting gesture *US, 1959*

ease up *verb* to have sex *US, 1993*

easie; easy *noun* a latex girdle *NEW ZEALAND, 1991*

east and west *noun* **1** complementary doses of MDMA, the rec-reational drug best known as ecstasy, and amphetamine, both in powder form, inhaled via different nostrils. 'East' is signified by E (MDMA), 'west' extends from an initialism of WHIZZ (amphetamine) *UK, 1996*. **2** the female breast. Or simply 'east west' *UK, 2001*. **3** the breast or the chest, hence the upper body. Rhyming slang *UK, 1923*. **4** a vest. Rhyming slang; in pickpocket usage *US, 1949*

East Anus *nickname* the town of East Angus, Quebec *CANADA, 1977*

Easter bunny *noun* money. Rhyming slang *UK, 1998*

Easter egg *noun* **1** a message hidden in a computer program's object code *US, 1991*. **2** an icon or hidden process on the menu of a DVD that, when selected or followed, leads to hidden features *US, 2002*. **3** the leg. Rhyming slang *UK, 1998*. ▶ **on the Easter egg** begging, scrounging. Glasgow rhyming slang for ON THE BEG *UK; SCOTLAND, 1988*

East Ham *adjective* nearly mad. On the map of the London Underground East Ham is 'one stop short of Barking'; playing on BARKING (raving mad) *UK, 2001*

Eastie *nickname* East Boston, Massachusetts *US, 1979*

East India Docks *noun* **1** any sexually transmitted infection. Rhyming slang for POX, formed from the name of one of the docks of east London *UK, 1992*. **2** socks. Rhyming slang *UK, 1998*

East Jesus; East Jesus Nowhere *noun* the outback *US, 1961*

East Jesus, Arkansas *noun* a fictitious place, difficult to find and peopled with uneducated and poor people *US, 1994*

East Los *nickname* east Los Angeles, California *US, 1974*

eastman *noun* a pimp *US, 1911*

East Overshoe *noun* the mythical town in Maine which is the home to fools and idiots *US, 1975*

Eastside player *noun* crack cocaine *US, 1994*

easy *noun* **1** in craps, a point made by a combination other than a matched pair. From the fuller 'easy way' *US, 1996*. **2** in poker, the fifth player to the left of the dealer. A name based on the scheme of 1 = A, 2 = B, etc *US, 1988* ▷*see:* EASIE

easy *verb* to silence or kill *US, 1992*

easy *adjective* **1** sexually accessible *UK, 1699*. **2** having no preference when given a choice *AUSTRALIA, 1941*. ▶ **easy on the eye** pleasing to look at; good looking, especially of women *UK, 1936*

easy **1** used as a greeting. Noted in current UK use *US, 2003*. **2** used as a warning *UK, 1996*. **3** used as a farewell. Hawaiian youth usage; often accompanied by a hand gesture, wiggling the hand from the wrist emphasising the thumb and little finger. Noted in current UK use *US, 1972*

easy as ABC *adjective* very easy. A simplicity noted by Shakespeare, 'then comes the answer like an Absey booke', 1595 *UK, 1970*

easy as apple pie *adjective* very easy. Variation of EASY AS PIE *AUSTRALIA, 1984*

easy as damn it *adjective* very easy. Recorded by Partridge in the 1st edition of his *Dictionary of Slang and Unconventional English* and still familiar. Other variations noted at that time include 'easy as pissing the bed' and 'easy as shelling peas' *UK, 1937*

easy as falling off a log; easy as rolling off a log *adjective* very easy. Mark Twain used 'easy as rolling off a log' in 1880 *US, 1880*

easy as kiss my arse *adjective* very easy. Recorded, with the euphemistic variation 'easy as kiss my ear', by Partridge in the 1st edition of his *Dictionary of Slang and Unconventional English* *UK, 1937*

easy as kiss my eye *adjective* very easy. Euphemistic variation of EASY AS KISS MY ARSE *UK, 1984*

easy as pie *adjective* very easy *US, 1964*

easy as shaking drops off your john *adjective* very easy. Masculine use; JOHN THOMAS; JOHN (the penis) *UK, 1984*

easy as winking *adjective* very easy *UK, 1937*

easybeats *noun* a team or opponent which is easily defeated. Punning on The Easybeats, an Australian 1960s rock group *AUSTRALIA, 1990*

easy chair *noun* in a group of three or more trucks travelling on a motorway, the middle truck *US, 1976*

easy go *noun* an unstrenuous prison job *US, 1983*

easy greasy *noun* an icy road *US, 1976*

easy, greasy! take it easy! Teen slang *US, 1955*

Easy Hall *noun* a notional place of great comfort and ease *BARBADOS, 1980*

easy like kissing hand *adjective* very easy *TRINIDAD AND TOBAGO, 2003*

easy mark *noun* a person who is easily persuaded *US, 1915*

easy meat *noun* someone who can be seduced, or made a victim; something that is easy to achieve. The original sense is 'a sexually available woman' *UK, 1961*

easy-peasy *adjective* very easy, very simple. A childish reduplication of 'easy', occasionally taken further as 'easy-peasy, lemon-squeezey' *UK, 1976*

easy rider *noun* **1** a pimp *US, 1914*. **2** a guitar. From an earlier use as 'a compliant sexual partner' *UK, 1949*. **3** a type of LSD identified by a design based on the 1969 film *Easy Rider UK, 2004*. **4** cider. Rhyming slang, reducing to 'easy' *UK, 2002*

easy street *noun* a comfortable, affluent situation for little expenditure of effort *US, 1897*

easy way *noun* (used of an even-numbered point in craps) scored in any fashion other than a pair *US, 1974*

eat *noun* eating *US, 1993*

eat *verb* **1** to perform oral sex *US, 1916*. **2** to swallow. Used especially in the context of ingesting LSD *US, 1970*. **3** (of tobacco) to chew *CANADA, 1961*. **4** to bother *US, 1892*. **5** to accept a monetary loss *US, 1955*. ▶ **be able to eat an apple through a bird cage** to have buck teeth *AUSTRALIA, 1998*. ▶ **could eat the hind leg off a donkey** applied to someone who is very hungry. A variation of 'eat a horse', on

the model of TALK THE HIND LEG OFF A DONKEY *UK, 1961*. ▶ **eat a horse and chase the rider/jockey** to be very hungry *AUSTRALIA, 1972*. ▶ **eat a shit sandwich** to accept humiliations as punishment. A variation on EAT SHIT *UK, 1997*. ▶ **eat a stock** to buy undesirable stock to maintain an order market in the stock *US, 1988*. ▶ **eat asphalt** to crash while riding a motorcycle, bicycling, or taking part in any recreational activity on the street *US, 2002*.
▶ **eat bad food** to get pregnant *TRINIDAD AND TOBAGO, 1974*. ▶ **eat cards** in blackjack, to draw more cards than you normally would in a given hand in order to learn more about what cards are remaining unplayed. The card-eater takes a short-term loss in hope of a long-term big win *US, 1991*. ▶ **eat cheese** to curry favour *US, 1968*. ▶ **eat concrete** to drive on a motorway *US, 1971*.
▶ **eat crow** to be forced to accept humiliation. According to legend, a British Army officer tricked then forced an American to eat a crow that the latter had shot *US, 1877*. ▶ **eat cunt** to perform oral sex on a woman *US, 1972*. ▶ **eat dick** to perform oral sex on a man *US, 1988*. ▶ **eat dim sum** to take the passive role in anal intercourse. Rhyming slang for TAKE IT UP THE BUM *UK, 2003*. ▶ **eat dirt** to fall on your face. A literal consequence *US, 1998*. ▶ **eat face** to kiss in a sustained and passionate manner *US, 1966*. ▶ **eat for breakfast** to vanquish, outdo, overcome *AUSTRALIA, 1970*. ▶ **eat from the bushy plate** to engage in oral sex on a woman. Probably coined by comedian Sacha Baron-Cohen (b.1970); his influence on late C20 UK slang is profound *UK, 2001*. ▶ **eat it 1** to suffer an accident, especially a fall. Hawaiian youth usage *US, 1982*. **2** in surfing, to lose control and fall from your surfboard *US, 1991*.
▶ **eat lead** to be shot *US, 1927*. ▶ **eat like a horse** to have a very large appetite *UK, 1971*. ▶ **eat plastic** (used of a hospital patient) to be intubated *US, 1994*. ▶ **eat pussy** to perform oral sex on a woman *US, 1965*. ▶ **eat raw; eat raw without salt** to defeat or destroy mercilessly *TRINIDAD AND TOBAGO, 2003*. ▶ **eat razor blades** to speak harshly and offensively. Collected in 1972 *BARBADOS, 1972*. ▶ **eat sausage** to perform oral sex on a man *NEW ZEALAND, 1984*. ▶ **eat shit 1** as a condition of subservience, to do something disagreeable or humiliating. May be varied to 'eat crap' *US, 1930*. **2** in surfing, to lose control of a ride and fall off your surfboard *US, 1991*. ▶ **eat someone's lunch** to thrash; to exact revenge *US, 1968*. ▶ **eat the cookie** while surfing, to be pounded fiercely by a breaking wave *US, 1997*. ▶ **eat the crutch off a low-flying emu** to be very hungry *AUSTRALIA, 1985*. ▶ **eat the floormat** to throw yourself to the floor of a car *US, 1981*. ▶ **eat the ginger** to play the leading role in a play *US, 1952*. ▶ **eat the head off, eat the face off** to verbally abuse or attack *IRELAND, 2003*. ▶ **eat your gun** to commit suicide by gun *US, 1997*. ▶ **eat your hat** used for expressing a certainty that such and such will not happen. Very occasionally taken literally as 'a wager against fate' *UK, 1837*. ▶ **eat your own dog food** to make use of whatever product or service you provide *US, 2003*. ▶ **eatin' ain't cheatin'** used as a jocular assertion that oral sex does not rise to the level of adultery or infidelity. A maxim that enjoyed sudden and massive appeal in the US during the President Clinton sex scandals *US, 1994*. ▶ **I could eat a baby's bum through a cane chair** I am extremely hungry *AUSTRALIA, 1985*. ▶ **I could eat a scabby horse between bedrags** I am very hungry *UK, 1981*. ▶ **I could eat that; I could eat that without salt** a catchphrase that is used of an attractive girl or young woman. An unattractive girl may inspire the opposite: 'I couldn't eat that'; on the other hand, girls wishing to express desire may use: 'he could eat me without salt'. The sense is occasionally exaggerated as: 'I could boil up her knickers and drink the gravy' *UK, 1951*

ea-tay *noun* marijuana. Pig Latin for 'tea' *US, 1938*

eat chain! used as an insult along the lines of 'drop dead!'. An abbreviation of 'eat a chain saw!' *US, 1997*

eat dick! used as a dismissive retort *UK, 1982*

eater *noun* a person who eats marijuana *US, 2001*

eat flaming death! used as an overblown expression of hostility *US, 1975*

eat fuck! used as a dismissive retort. A variation of 'eat shit!' *US, 1979*

eating tobacco *noun* chewing tobacco *US, 1901*

eat me! used as a somewhat coarse expression of defiance. The taboo component is fading if not faded *US, 1962*

eat my shorts! used as a humorous declaration of defiance *US, 1979*

eat out *verb* to perform oral sex, usually on a woman *US, 1966*

eats *noun* food, a meal *UK, 1782*

eat shit and die! used as a powerful expression of dislike or disapproval *US, 1986*

eat the apple, fuck the Corps used as a defiant yet proud curse of the marines by the marines *US, 1976*

eatum-up stop *noun* a roadside restaurant or truckstop *US, 1976*

eat up *verb* (used of a wave) to overcome and knock a surfer from the surfboard *US, 1965*

eat what you can and can what you can't used for urging someone to be frugal and conservationist *CANADA, 1989*

eau-de-cologne *noun* **1** a telephone. Rhyming slang. Sometimes corrupted to 'the odour' or 'odie' *UK, 1961*. **2** a woman. Rhyming slang on polari 'palone' (a woman) *UK, 1937*

e-ball *noun* MDMA, the recreational drug best known as ecstasy *US, 1992*

Ebeneezer Goode *noun* the personification of the culture surrounding MDMA, the recreational drug best known as ecstasy *UK, 1992*

e-bomb *noun* MDMA, the recreational drug best known as ecstasy *UK, 2003*

E-brake *noun* a vehicle's emergency brake *US, 2003*

ecaf; eek; eke *noun* the face. Back slang used in polari, especially in the abbreviated forms *UK, 1966*

e-car *noun* an electrically powered *car UK, 2003*

eccer *noun* an abbreviation for (homework) exercise. This term makes use of the suffix -ER which is especially common in Dublin Hiberno-English and is used at the end of abbreviated names *IRELAND, 1991*

eccy; ec *noun* economics *US, 1924*

echo *noun* a variety of MDMA, the recreational drug best known as ecstasy. From the international phonetic alphabet, E (MDMA) is ECHO, also playing on the first syllable of ECSTASY (MDMA) *UK, 1996*

echo *verb* to repeat what was just said *US, 1967*

'eck-as-like in answer to a rhetorical question, certainly not, it is very unlikely. A Yorkshire-ism, often used in bad impressions of a northern accent; not recorded, surprisingly, until 1979 *UK, 1979*

ecker; ecky *noun* MDMA, the recreational drug best known as ecstasy; a tablet of MDMA. Based on the first syllable of ECSTASY (MDMA) *UK, 2002*

eckied *adjective* intoxicated with MDMA, the recreational drug best known as ecstasy. From ECKY; ECKIE (ecstasy) *UK, 1996*

ecky; eckie *noun* MDMA, the recreational drug best known as ecstasy; a tablet of MDMA. Plays with the first syllable *UK, 1995*

ecky-becky *noun* a poor white person *BARBADOS, 1965*

ecnop *noun* a person who lives off prostitutes' earnings, a ponce. Back slang *UK, 1956*

eco- *prefix* used to signify an assocation with environmental issues. An abbreviation of 'ecology/ecological' *US, 1969*

ecofreak *noun* a radical environmentalist *US, 1970*

eco-freako *adjective* overly devoted to ethical ecological principles *UK, 2004*

ecology freak *noun* a devoted environmentalist *US, 1984*

econ *noun* economics *US, 1976*

econut *noun* a zealous environmentalist *US, 1972*

ecoporn; eco-porn *noun* aesthetically pleasing pictures of ecological subjects, especially when of no scientific or environmental value; used derisively of any advertising that praises a company's 'green' record or policies *US, 1985*

ecowarrior *noun* a person who is especially active in any political struggle or violent action against forces that are seen to threaten the environment or balance of nature. Formed on 'eco', a widely used abbreviation of 'ecology/ecological'. The natural enemy of the 'ecowarrior' is the 'ecoterrorist', a term first recorded in 1988 *UK*, *2002*

ecstasy *noun* methylene-dioxymethamphetamine, MDMA, a mildly hallucinogenic empathogen and/or entactogen, a drug of empathy and touch. Easily the most recognisable slang name for this widely popular recreational drug; it derives from the senses of well-being and affection felt by users. The illegal status of the drug has encouraged a great many alternative names; some are generic (E is probably the most widely known), and some serve as brand names. Originally synthesized by German pharmaceutical company Merck some time before 1912. Since the 1980s the drug has been inextricably linked with RAVE culture *US*, *1985*

E'd; E-ed; E'd up; E-ed up *adjective* intoxicated with MDMA, the recreational drug best known as ecstasy. Under the influence of E (ecstasy) *UK*, *2001*

Eddie Grundies *noun* underwear. A variation of GRUNDIES, formed from the name Eddie Grundy, a popular character in the BBC radio soap opera *The Archers* *UK*, *2002*

edelweiss *noun* a type of marijuana developed in Holland *UK*, *2003*

e-deuce *noun* an M-14 automatic rifle *US*, *1977*

Edgar Britt; Edgar *noun* an act of defecation. Rhyming slang for SHIT. In the plural, used for 'diarrhoea' *AUSTRALIA*, *1969*

Edgar Britts; Edgars *noun* a bad mood, anxiety, fear. Rhyming slang for THE SHITS *AUSTRALIA*, *1983*

edge *noun* **1** in gambling, a statistical advantage, usually expressed as a percentage *US*, *1977*. **2** antagonism; a tension arising from mutual dislike *UK*, *1979*. **3** a knife, used or intended for use as a weapon *US*, *1972*. **4** an urban area with bars, nightclubs, and prostitution *US*, *1973*. ▶ **on edge** very tense, nervy, anxious *UK*, *1870*. ▶ **on the edge** in gambling, out of funds; broke *US*, *1963*

Edge City *noun* a notional place where people live on the edge of danger *US*, *1970*

edged *adjective* angry *US*, *1982*

edge note *noun* a fifty pound (£50) note. Prison slang *UK*, *2002*

edge work *noun* the alteration of dice by rounding off the edges to affect the roll *US*, *1950*

edgy *adjective* **1** nervous, irritable, tense *UK*, *1837*. **2** leading a trend. Probably from 'cutting-edge' *US*, *1976*. **3** in the used car business, said of a car that needs body work *US*, *1968*

Edinburgh fringe *noun* the female pubic hair; the vagina. Rhyming slang for MINGE *UK*, *2002*

Edison *noun* in horse racing, a hand battery used illegally by a jockey to impart a shock to his horse *US*, *1947*

Edison medicine *noun* electric shock therapy. Alluding to Thomas Edison, a central figure in the early history of electricity; not a common phrase, although not for lack of cleverness *US*, *1990*

Edmonchuk *nickname* the city of Edmonton, Alberta *CANADA*, *1998*

Edmundo Ros; edmundo *noun* a boss. Rhyming slang, formed from the name of Trinidadian band-leader Edmundo Ros (b.1910) who, from 1940, brought Latin American rhythms to Britain *UK*, *1998*

edna! watch out!; be quiet! Rhyming slang, 'Edna May', based on 'way'; originally used for 'on your way' or 'on my way', now an imperative. Based on the name of actress and singer Edna May (May Edna Pettie), 1878–1948 *UK*, *1960*

Ednabopper *noun* a fan of Dame Edna Everage. Coined by Barry Humphries, the man behind the Dame *AUSTRALIA*, *1991*

Edna Everage; Edna *noun* a drink. Rhyming slang for 'beverage'; based on the 'Housewife Superstar' character created by Australian comedian and satirist Barry Humphries (b.1934) *UK*, *2002*

Edsel; Flying Edsel *nickname* the US Air Force F-111 aircraft. An allusion to the single greatest failure in American car manufacture *US*, *1972*

educated currency *noun* in horse racing, bets placed on the basis of what is believed to be authentic, empirical tips *US*, *1951*

educator *noun* in the circus or carnival, the *Billboard* weekly newspaper *US*, *1980*

Edward *noun* MDMA, the recreational drug best known as ecstasy. Early phonetic alphabet for E (predating 'E easy' and 'E echo') *UK*, *1998*

Edward Heath; Ted Heath; Edwards; Teds *noun* the teeth. Rhyming slang, formed on the name of a former UK prime minister, 1970–74, and Conservative party leader, who was famously caricatured with a toothy grin *UK*, *1972*

eed-way *noun* marijuana. Pig Latin for WEED *US*, *1938*

eejit; eedjit; idjit *noun* an idiot. Phonetic spelling of Irish pronunciation; earlier variations include 'eediot' and 'eegit' *IRELAND*, *1955*

eel *noun* **1** an untrustworthy or otherwise despicable person. Adapting the 'slippery character' sense to more general derogatory usage; possibly, also, a disguised reference to a HEEL (a dishonest, untrustworthy person) *UK*, *2001*. **2** a spy or informer *US*, *1956*. **3** the penis. From a perceived resemblance *US*, *1968*

eels *noun* in electric line work, insulated line hose used for covering up lines during work *US*, *1980*

eels and liquor; eels *noun* one pound (£1). Rhyming slang for NICKER, formed from the name of a classic dish of London cuisine *UK*, *1992*

eensy-weensy *adjective* very small. A rarely heard variant of 'teensy-weensy' *US*, *1978*

eeoo-leven *noun* in craps, an eleven *US*, *1985*

eez *noun* sex *BERMUDA*, *1985*

eff; F used as a euphemism for 'fuck' in all its different senses and parts of speech. Originally purely euphemistic, but soon a jocular replacement for FUCK *UK*, *1929*

eff and blind *verb* to swear; to pepper discourse with obscenities. A combination of two euphemisms: EFF (FUCK) and BLIND (BLOODY) *UK*, *1943*

eff and jeff *verb* to swear; to pepper discourse with obscenities. A variation of EFF AND BLIND *UK*, *2004*

effect *noun* ▶ **in effect; in effect mode** relaxed, in-control, unstressed *US*, *1998*

effed up *adjective* used as a euphemism for 'fucked up' *US*, *1971*

effer *noun* a person, a fucker *UK*, *1966*

efficient *adjective* ▶ **get efficient** to smoke marijuana *US*, *1997*

effing; effin'; f-ing *adjective* used as an intensifier; a euphemism for 'fucking' *UK*, *1929*

eff off *verb* used as a euphemism for 'fuck off' *UK*, *1945*

effort *noun* a specific article that is not accurately named. Originally public school usage *UK*, *1925*

efink *noun* a knife. Back slang *UK*, *1859*

egad! used as a mild oath. Possibly 'ah God'. Generally considered to be obsolete from later C19 but survives in ironic usage *UK*, *1673*

egg *noun* **1** a person. From 'bad egg' (a rascal) *UK*, *1864*. **2** a fool, especially an obnoxious fool. Possibly derived from YEGG (a criminal) *US*, *1918*. **3** a white person who associates with, and takes on, the culture of south Asians. The egg, like the person described, is white on the outside but yellow on the inside *US*, *1997*. **4** a novice surfer *AUSTRALIA*, *1963*. **5** a person who is trying to bet his way out of debt and, predictably, failing *AUSTRALIA*, *1989*. **6** a bookmaker who refuses a bet. From the bookmaker's claim 'I've already laid it' *AUSTRALIA*, *1989*. **7** a railway police officer *US*, *1977*. **8** a billiard ball *US*, *1988*. **9** a bomb *US*, *1950*. **10** a theatrical failure *US*, *1952*. **11** crack cocaine *US*, *1994*. **12** a short surfboard with a round tail and a round nose, extremely common in the late 1960s and early 70s *AUSTRALIA*, *2002*

egg *verb* to perform poorly *US*, *2002*

egg; green egg; wobbly egg *noun* a capsule of branded tranquilliser Temazepam™. From the appearance *UK*, *1996*

egg and spoon; egg *noun* **1** a black person. Derogatory; rhyming slang for COON. Subject to some politically correct confusion with earlier 'good egg' (an expression of approval, hence 'good person',

1903) *UK, 1992*. **2** a procurer of prostitutes, a pimp. Rhyming slang for HOON (a pimp) *AUSTRALIA, 1975*

eggbeater *noun* **1** a single-rotor helicopter. Coined well before the war in Korea, but used extensively by US forces in Korea *US, 1936*. **2** a twin-engine training plane *US, 1946*. **3** an oldish, not very powerful motor car. An affectionate usage *UK, 1981*. **4** a small outboard motor for a boat *US, 1942*. **5** a paddle skier. The skier sits on a small bulbous canoe and paddles into the surf using paddles. His whirring repetitive paddling motion, especially when gaining speed to catch a wave, resembles an eggbeater *SOUTH AFRICA, 2003*. **6** a bad head-over-skis fall while skiing *US, 1963*

egg breaker *noun* in electric line work, a guy strain insulator *US, 1980*

egg crate *noun* in hot rodding and car customising, a grille design with a cross hatch *US, 1993*

egg flip *noun* in horse racing, useful information about a horse or race *AUSTRALIA, 1966*

egghead *noun* **1** an intellectual, often a scientist; a very smart person *US, 1918*. **2** a bald person *US, 1907*

egghead brigade *noun* forensic scientists. Police use, from EGGHEAD (an intellectual, often a scientist) *UK, 1971*

eggheaded *adjective* **1** intellectual yet lacking common sense *US, 1956*. **2** bald *US, 1920*

egg in a hole *noun* a slice of bread fried with an egg in a hole cut out of the middle *CANADA, 1995*

egg on your face *noun* humiliation or embarrassment *CANADA, 1964*

eggplant *noun* a black person *US, 1934*

egg roll *noun* **1** an idiot *AUSTRALIA, 1985*. **2** a beginner surfer *AUSTRALIA, 1991*

eggs *noun* the testicles *US, 1976*

eggshell blonde *noun* a bald person *AUSTRALIA, 1977*

eggsucker *noun* **1** a sycophant *US, 1838*. **2** in electric line work, an insulated line tool formally known as a grip-all stick *US, 1980*

egg-sucking *adjective* despicable *US, 1845*

eggy *adjective* **1** unpleasant, tasteless *UK, 1978*. **2** annoyed, angry. Possibly a phonetic variation of 'aggravated' *UK, 1961*

Eglinton Toll; eglinton *noun* the anus; by extension, the buttocks. Glasgow rhyming slang for ARSEHOLE, formed from an area of that city *UK: SCOTLAND, 1988*

egoboo *noun* favourable words, praise *US, 1982*

Egon Ronay; egon *noun* an act of defecation. Rhyming slang for PONY (PONY AND TRAP), imperfectly formed from the name of a celebrated food critic *UK, 1998*

ego surf *verb* to search for mentions of your name on the Internet *US, 1997*

ego trip *noun* any activity that is motivated by self-importance *US, 1967*

egregious *adjective* very bad. Conventional English rendered slang by attitude and drawn-out pronunciation *US, 1991*

Egypt *noun* a neighbourhood populated largely by black people *US, 1979*

Egyptian *noun* a tablet of MDMA, the recreational drug best known as ecstasy *UK, 2003*

Egyptian queen *noun* in homosexual usage, an attractive black man. An incorrect racial label *US, 1987*

eh used after a positive statement without any suggestion of questioning. Usage after virtually every positive statement a speaker makes is characteristic of many speakers of both New Zealand and northern Australia *AUSTRALIA, 1956*

eh? do you agree? *CANADA, 1945*

E-head *noun* a habitual user of MDMA, the recreational drug best known as ecstasy. Combines E, the familiar shorthand for ECSTASY (MDMA) with -HEAD (a user) *UK, 1999*

Eiffel Tower; eiffel *noun* **1** a shower. Rhyming slang *UK, 1992*. **2** a good look. Rhyming slang and homophone, EYEFUL *UK, 1992*

eight *noun* **1** heroin. 'H' is the 8th letter of the alphabet, and there is the phonetic connection to 'H' *US, 1997*. **2** one-eighth of an ounce of a drug *US, 1974*. **3** an eight fluid ounce beer glass; a serving of beer in such a glass *AUSTRALIA, 1972*

eight and out *noun* in pool, a win achieved by sinking all eight balls in a single turn *US, 1993*

eight ball *noun* **1** one eighth of an ounce *US, 1988*. **2** a discharge from the US Army for mental unfitness. From the regulation AF 600–208 *US, 1968*. **3** Old English 800™ malt liquor *US, 1992*. **4** a dark-skinned black person. The 'eightball' in billiards is black *US, 1919*. **5** a conventional, staid, unsophisticated person *US, 1970*. **6** a mixture of crack cocaine and heroin *US, 2001*. ▶ **behind the eight ball** in a difficult position. From a tactical disadvantage when playing pool *US, 1932*

eight-charge *noun* eighty pounds of gunpowder in a satchel *US, 1991*

eighteen *noun* an eighteen gallon keg of beer *AUSTRALIA, 1918*

eighteen-carat *adjective* first-class, excellent. From the 'carat' which is used to classify the weight of diamonds and other precious stones, generally considered to be a measurement of quality *UK, 1880*

eighteen pence *noun* sense, common-sense. Rhyming slang *UK, 1932*

eighter from Decatur *noun* in craps, a roll of eight *US, 1950*

eight miler *noun* a distracted driver who drives for several miles with a turn signal flashing *US, 1971*

eight-pager *noun* a small pornographic comic book that placed well-known world figures or comic book characters in erotic situations *US, 1961*

eight-track *noun* an eight-lane motorway. A borrowing from the name of the 'eight-track' tape player popular in the 1970s *US, 1977*

eighty *noun* eighty dollars worth of crack cocaine *US, 2003*

eighty-deuce *nickname* the 82nd Airborne Division, US Army *US, 1991*

eighty-eight *noun* a piano. From the 88 keys on a standard piano *US, 1942*

eighty-eighter *noun* a piano player. Drawn from the number of keys on a piano *US, 1949*

eighty-eights best wishes; love and kisses *US, 1934*

eighty-five *noun* a girlfriend *US, 2001*

eighty niggers and two white men *nickname* the 82nd Airborne Division, US Army. During the Vietnam war, it was perceived that the 82nd Division enjoyed an above-average black population *US, 1984*

eighty-one mike mike *noun* an 81mm medium extended-range mortar, found in the mortar platoon of an infantry battalion *US, 1991*

eighty-six; eight-six *noun* an order barring a person from entering a bar or other establishment *US, 1943*

eighty-six; eight-six *verb* to eject; to bar from entry *US, 1955*

eina! used as an exclamation of pain or as a cry of sympathy for someone else's pain. Pronounced 'aynah!' *SOUTH AFRICA, 1913*

Einstein *noun* used as an ironic nickname for someone who has mastered basic logic. Albert Einstein (1878–1955) is the one modern scientist, it seems, that everyone has heard of *UK, 1997*

Einstein's mate *noun* an especially unintelligent person. An ironic comparison *UK, 1977*

Eisenhower *noun* a shower. Rhyming slang, formed from the name of the 34th US President, General Dwight D. Eisenhower, 1890–1969 *UK, 1992*

eke *noun* cosmetics; a room used when applying makeup. Derived from polari backslang ECAF (the face), and used within homosexual society *UK, 1984*

ek sê; ek se; ekse used as an emphatic affirmation of a statement. From Afrikaans *ek* (I) *sê* (say), probably a shortening of *ek sê vir jou* (I'm telling you) *SOUTH AFRICA, 1959*

ekusen o'clock *noun* in the morning *SOUTH AFRICA, 2003*

El *noun* an elevated railway. Chicago, New York and Philadelphia are major cities with an El *US, 1906*. ▶ **the El** the boys' reformatory at Elmire, New York *US, 1950*

Elaine *noun* MDMA, the recreational drug best known as ecstasy. A personification of the drug by elaboration of E (MDMA) *UK, 2003*

elbow *noun* **1** a dismissal or rejection *UK, 1971*. **2** a pound (0.45kg) of marijuana. A phoentic rendition of the abbreviation 'lb' (pound) *US, 1997*. **3** in electric line work, an underground cable terminator *US, 1980*. ▶ **on the elbow** freeloading, on the scrounge. Playing, perhaps, with ON THE EARHOLE *UK, 1977*

elbow-bending *noun* immoderate consumption of alcohol *US, 1934*

elbow-bending *adjective* drinking to excess *US, 2002*

elbow cake *noun* in the Gaspe region of Canada, a hot biscuit *CANADA, 1998*

elbow grease *noun* hard manual labour; effort *UK, 1672*

elbow-lifting *noun* drinking, especially as part of a drinking session *UK, 1961*

elbow list *noun* a list, often notional, of despised things or persons *UK, 1983*

elbow-tit *verb* to graze or strike an unknown female's breast with your elbow *US, 1974*

El Cid *noun* LSD. A punning play on the first letter of LSD and the second syllable of 'acid' (LSD), giving the name of a legendary Spanish hero *UK, 2003*

El D; LD *noun* **1** a Cadillac El Dorado car *US, 1970*. **2** Eldorado™ fortified wine *UK: SCOTLAND, 1985*

elderberry *noun* an older homosexual man *UK, 1979*

elder days *noun* in computing, the years before 1980. A conscious borrowing from Tolkien *US, 1991*

el diablito *noun* a mix of cocaine, heroin, marijuana and phencyclidine, the recreational drug known as PCP or angel dust. The Spanish 'little devil' offers a more elaborate recipe than EL DIABLO *US, 1998*

el diablo *noun* a mix of cocaine, heroin, and marijuana. Spanish 'el diablo' (the devil) *UK, 1998*

El Dog *noun* a Cadillac El Dorado car *US, 1975*

electric *adjective* **1** used as a superlative; marvellous, strange, sudden *UK, 1977*. **2** augmented with LSD *US, 1967*

electric bookmaker *noun* a bookmaker who is regularly shocked by the results of the events bet on *AUSTRALIA, 1989*

electric cure *noun* execution by electrocution *US, 1950*

electrician *noun* a person who provokes or accelerates a confrontation *US, 1998*

electric puha *noun* marijuana, especially New Zealand-grown. *Puha* is the Maori name for 'wild sowthistle' *NEW ZEALAND, 1989*

electrics *noun* a vehicle's electric circuitry *UK, 1946*

electric soup *noun* **1** a mixture of metholated spirits and cheap red wine *UK: SCOTLAND, 1985*. **2** Eldorado™, a fortified wine sold in Scotland *UK: SCOTLAND, 1983*

Electric Strawberry *nickname* the 25th Infantry Division, US Army. The Division's insignia is a green taro leaf in a red circle, suggesting a strawberry *US, 1991*

electro- *prefix* when applied to a musical style, involving synthesizers. As well as the examples listed as headwords, the following styles have been recorded: 'electro-baroque', 'electro-boogie', 'electro-bossa', 'electro-death', 'electro-dup', 'electro-funk', 'electro-goth' and 'electro-noir' *UK, 2003*

Electrolux *noun* a person gifted at performing oral sex on men. From the branded vacuum cleaner and its advertising boast – 'Nothing sucks like an Electrolux' *UK, 2001*

electros *noun* electrical equipment employed for sexual stimulation, especially when advertised by a prostitute *UK, 2003*

elef *noun* eleven; in betting, odds of 11–1. A shortening and slovening of 'eleven' *UK, 1991*

elef a vier *noun* in betting, odds of 11–4. A phonetic slurring of ELEF (11) and 'four' *UK, 1991*

elegant *adjective* **1** (used of a homosexual male) polished, effete *US, 1949*. **2** in computing, simple yet extremely efficient *US, 1990*

elegant sufficiency *noun* used as an indication that enough has been had to eat. A jocular mocking of genteel mannners which has, perhaps, become a cliché *UK, 1984*

elephant *noun* **1** heroin *UK, 1996*. **2** marijuana *UK, 2003*. **3** a high-ranking Naval officer. US naval aviator usage *US, 1986*

Elephant and Castle *noun* **1** arsehole, in anatomic and figurative senses. Rhyming slang, based on an area of south London *UK, 2002*. **2** a parcel. Rhyming slang *UK, 1959*

elephant bag *noun* in the usage of forest fire fighters, a large canvas bag used for dropping cargo from aeroplanes *US, 1959*

elephant bucks *noun* a large amount of money *AUSTRALIA, 1994*

elephant ear *noun* in electric line work, a high-strength strain insulator *US, 1980*

elephant gun *noun* **1** any powerful rifle *US, 1918*. **2** an M79 grenade launcher. Vietnam war usage. It is a single-shot, break-open, breech-loading, shoulder-fired weapon *US, 1964*. **3** a surfboard designed for big-wave conditions *US, 1963*

elephant intestines *noun* the cotton tubes used by the Viet Cong to carry rice in the field *US, 1990*

elephant juice *noun* the drug etorphine, a synthetic morphine 1,000 times more potent than morphine *AUSTRALIA, 1989*

elephant motor *noun* the Chrysler Hemi engine. Huge displacement and power *US, 1993*

elephant pill *noun* the large orange anti-malaria chloroquine-primequine pill taken once a week by US troops in Vietnam *US, 1980*

Elephants' Graveyard *nickname* the Boston Naval District headquarters *US, 1971*

elephant snot *noun* in car repair, gasket sealant, usually referring to Permatex™ sealant, a tradmarked product *US, 1992*

elephant's trunk; elephant trunk *noun* a drunk. Rhyming slang *US, 1977*

elephant's trunk; elephant trunk; elephant's; elephants *adjective* drunk. Rhyming slang, influenced by the pink elephants that only drunks can see *UK, 1859*

elephant tracker *noun* a railway detective *US, 1968*

elephant tranquillizer; elephant *noun* phencyclidine, the recreational drug known as PCP or angel dust *US, 2004*

elevator *noun* **1** in trucking, a hydraulic lift on the back of a trailer *US, 1971*. **2** a false cut of a deck of playing cards *US, 1991*

elevator jockey *noun* an elevator (lift) operator *US, 1951*

eleven *noun* **1** a stunningly gorgeous woman who swallows semen after oral sex. An elaboration of the 'perfect TEN' *AUSTRALIA, 1985*. **2** in a deck of playing cards, a jack or knave *US, 1996*

eleven bang-bang *noun* an infantry soldier. 11-B was the numerical MOS code assigned to an infantry soldier *US, 1980*

eleven bravo *noun* an infantry soldier *US, 1991*

eleven bush *noun* an infantry soldier *US, 1970*

eleven-foot pole *noun* an imagined device for touching someone whom another would not touch with a ten-foot pole *US, 1975*

eleven from heaven *noun* a roll of eleven in a craps game *US, 1957*

elevenses *noun* mid-morning refreshments; a mid-morning break from work, generally for refreshments but also used as an opportunity for cigarette smoking. Originally Kent dialect, extended from 'eleven o'clock'; late C19 workmen also had 'fourses' *UK, 1887*

eleventh commandment *noun* any rule which is seen as a mandatory guideline on a par with the Ten Commandments. A term probably coined by Ronald Reagan and applied to his adage that no Republican (except him) should disparage another Republican. Eventually applied, often jocularly, to many different situations. For example: the mythical commandment but very real criminal code – thou shalt not get caught *US, 1975*

eleventh gear *noun* in trucking, neutral, used for conserving fuel when coasting down a hill *US, 1971*

elf *noun* a technical market analyst *US, 1986*

el fabuloso! used for expressing strong approval *NEW ZEALAND, 1998*

el foldo *noun* an utter, relentless collapse *US, 1943*

Eli *nickname* Yale University; a Yale student; a Yale sports team *US, 1879*

Eli Lilly *noun* morphine. From the drug manufacturer's name *US, 1955*

eliminate *verb* to kill a person. Originally jocular, but no longer *UK, 1937*

elite *adjective* in the world of Internet discussion groups, offering the illegal *US, 1997*

Elizabeth Regina *noun* the vagina. Rhyming slang, formed from Queen Elizabeth *UK, 2003*

Elizabeth's corner *noun* gossip *AUSTRALIA, 1989*

elk river *noun* in poker, a hand with three tens *US, 1968*

Elky *noun* a Chevrolet El Camino pickup truck, manufactured from 1959 until 1987 *US, 1993*

-ella *suffix* used to feminise a noun and thus create a derogative sense *US, 1979*

elle momo *noun* marijuana laced with phencyclidine, the recreational drug known as PCP or angel dust. The etymology is uncertain; it looks French, sounds Spanish and is possibly a play on American 'mom' *UK, 2001*

ellie *noun* an elephant seal *ANTARCTICA, 1990*

Ellis Day *noun* LSD. Almost a homophone *UK, 2003*

Elly and Castle *nickname* the Elephant and Castle district of south London *UK, 1976*

Elmer *noun* in circus and carnival usage, an unsophiscticated, gullible local *US, 1926*

El Producto *noun* oil. Texan *US, 1980s*

El Ropo *noun* any cheap cigar. Mock Spanish *US, 1960*

Elsie Tanner *noun* **1** a spanner. Rhyming slang, formed from the name of a character in the television soap opera *Coronation Street*, played, from 1960 to 84, by actress Pat Phoenix, 1923–86 *UK, 1992*. **2** a single instance or example of something. Glasgow rhyming slang for 'wanner' *UK: SCOTLAND, 1988*

El Smoggo; El Stinko *nickname* El Paso, Texas. A tribute to the city's air quality *US, 1970*

el tee *noun* a lieutenant. From the abbreviation 'Lt' *US, 1978*

elton *noun* a toilet. A play on JOHN (a toilet) and musician Elton John (b.1947) *UK, 1977*

Elton John; elton *noun* deception; an act intended to trick or deceive; a tale intended to deceive. Rhyming slang for 'con', formed from the name of popular musician Sir Elton John (Reginald Kenneth Dwight) (b.1947) *UK, 1998*

elvis *noun* LSD *UK, 2003*

Elvis *noun* a poker player who is nearly broke but manages to stay in a game far longer than one would predict. Like Elvis Presley, the poker player refuses to die *US, 1996*

emag *noun* a game. Back slang *UK, 1873*

E-man *noun* a police officer assigned to the Emergency Service Unit. New York police slang *US, 1997*

embalmed *adjective* very drunk *US, 1934*

embalmed beef *noun* canned beef. A term most strongly associated with profiteers during the Spanish–American war; mostly historical use *US, 1898*

embalming fluid *noun* phencyclidine, the recreational drug known as PCP or angel dust *US, 1992*

embroidery *noun* the punctures and sores visible on an intravenous drug user's body *US, 1973*

embugger *verb* to hinder, to hamper. Military *UK, 1995*

embuggerance *noun* any unforeseen hazard that complicates a proposed course of action. Originally military, *1995*

emby *noun* in carnival usage, a gullible player *US, 1985*

EM club *noun* an enlisted men's club *US, 1977*

Eme *noun* the Mexican Mafia, a Mexican-American prison gang. From the Spanish pronunciation of the letter 'M' *US, 1990*

emeffing *adjective* used as a euphemism for 'motherfucking' *US, 1958*

emergency gun *noun* an improvised method to puncture the skin and inject a drug *US, 1973*

emergency handout *noun* in prison, the consequent act of separating an imprisoned mother from her baby when, for disciplinary reasons, the parent is removed from the mother and baby unit – the baby is therefore handed out into local authority care *UK, 1996*

Emma Chisit? how much is it? The most famous and well-remembered piece of STRINE. The story goes that a visiting English writer, Monica Dickens, was autographing copies of her latest book in Sydney and a woman handed her a copy and asked in her best Australian accent 'How much is it?'. Monica Dickens took the book and wrote: 'To Emma Chisit' and signed her autograph below *AUSTRALIA, 1965*

Emma Freud *noun* a haemorrhoid. Rhyming slang, formed from the name of journalist Emma Freud (b.1961), daughter of Sir CLEMENT FREUD, whose name serves a synonymous purpose *UK, 1997*

Emma G *noun* a machine gun. A formation built on the initials MG *US, 1949*

Emma Jesse *noun* an emergency brake *US, 1971*

Emmerdale Farm; emmerdale *noun* the arm. Rhyming slang, formed from the title of a UK soap opera, broadcast since 1972, later changing its name to *Emmerdale UK, 1998*

emmet *noun* a holiday-maker or tourist in Cornwall. Derisive. *Emmet* is a dialect word for 'ant'; in Cornwall the holiday-makers obviously swarm and get everywhere *UK, 1978*

emptyhead *noun* an idiot *UK, 2001*

empty nest *noun* a home in which the children have all grown and gone away *US, 1973*

empty suit *noun* a person of no substance *US, 1980*

emu; emu bobber *noun* a person who picks up tickets at a racecourse in the hope of finding an unclaimed win. From the emu, a large, flightless Australian bird related to the ostrich, with long legs and a long neck, that bends to pick things off the ground *AUSTRALIA, 1966*

emu-bob *verb* to pick things up off the ground, such as litter or kindling *AUSTRALIA, 1926*

emu bob; emu parade; emu patrol; emu stalk; emu walk *noun* a patrol by a group of people over a certain area of ground for the purpose of searching or cleaning the area *AUSTRALIA, 1941*

enchilada *noun* ▶ **the whole enchilada** all of something. Popularised in the US during the Watergate scandal of 1972–1974 *US, 1966*

end *noun* **1** the area where you are born, or where you live and/or are well-known *UK, 2005*. **2** the best; an extreme *UK, 1938*. **3** a share or portion *US, 1887*. **4** the penis *US, 1957*. **5** money *US, 1960*. ▶ **the end** something or someone that tests you to the end of your endurance *UK, 1938*

endo *noun* **1** in mountain biking, an accident in which the cyclist is thrown over the handlebars; the course the cyclist follows in such an accident; a mountain biking trick in which the front brake is sharply applied thus forcing the back wheel to come up off the ground *US, 1996*. **2** in motor racing, an end-over-end flip *US, 1976*. **3** a backwards fall off a surfboard *US, 1988*. **4** in the television and film industry, any stunt in which a vehicle goes through the air end-over-end *US, 2003*. **5** marijuana *US, 1997*

end of enough said, no more. *End of* story *UK, 2001*

end of discussion used as a humorous, if stock, indication that there is nothing more to be said on the subject at hand *US, 1987*

end of story used as a way to indicate that all that needs to be told has been told, all that needs to be said has been said. Often jocular *US, 1996*

end of the line *noun* the absolute end, the finish of something *US, 1948*

end of the road *noun* the finish of something *UK, 1954*

end of watch *noun* death *US, 1983*

ends *noun* **1** money. An abbreviation of DIVIDENDS (money) *US, 1997*. **2** cash in hand *US, 2001*. **3** a rich customer of a prostitute *US, 1987*. **4** the hair. Possibly by back-formation from 'split-ends'. Recorded in use in contemporary gay society *UK, 2003*

endsville *noun* **1** the end *US, 1962*. **2** the best *US, 1957*. **3** the worst *US, 2003*

Ene *nickname* **1** the Northern Structure prison gang. Spanish for the letter 'N' used by English speakers in the American southwest *US, 1995*. **2** a member of the Nuestra Familia prison gang *US, 1950*

enema queen *noun* a male homosexual with an enema fetish *US, 1969*

Enema Sue; Enema Zoo *nickname* New Mexico State University. A cheerful play on the initials NMSU *US, 1970*

energizer *noun* phencyclidine, the recreational drug known as PCP or angel dust *US, 1986*

energy powder *noun* amphetamine *UK, 1996*

enforcer *noun* a criminal who uses violence or intimidation to enforce the will of a criminal gang *US, 1929*

en fuego! used as a humorous observation that somebody is performing very well. Coined and popularised by ESPN's Dan Patrick; probably the most widely used of the ESPN-spawned catchphrases *US, 1997*

Engelbert Humperdinck; englebert *noun* a drink. Rhyming slang, formed from the name of singer Engelbert Humperdinck (Gerry Dorsey) (b.1936) who came to popular fame in the mid-1960s *UK, 1998*

engine *noun* ▶ **on the engine** (used of a racehorse) well in front in a race *US, 1994*

engineer *noun* the first active participant in serial sex with a single passive partner. From 'to PULL A TRAIN' (to engage in serial sex) *US, 1975*

engine room *noun* **1** the forward pack on a rugby union team *NEW ZEALAND, 1998*. **2** the rhythm section of a band *TRINIDAD AND TOBAGO, 1990*. **3** the mid-boat rowers in an eight-person racing shell *US, 1949*

England *noun* ▶ **go to England** to have a baby in secret *TRINIDAD AND TOBAGO, 1960*

English *noun* in pool, spin imparted on the cue ball to affect the course of the object ball or the cue ball after striking the object ball *US, 1869*

English-Channel eyes *noun* bloodshot eyes from exposure to cigarette and/or marijuana smoke. From photographs of swimmers staggering out of the water having crossed the Channel, their eyes bloodshot *US, 1979*

English method *noun* the rubbing of the penis between the thighs of another boy or man until reaching orgasm. More commonly known in the US as the 'Princeton Rub' *US, 1987*

English muffins *noun* in homosexual usage, a boy's buttocks *US, 1987*

English return *noun* dead silence after what was supposed to be a funny joke *US, 1951*

English vice *noun* flagellation *US, 1956*

enin *noun* nine; in betting, odds of 9–1. Backslang *UK, 1859*

enin to rouf *noun* in betting, odds of 9–4. A combination of ENIN (nine) and ROUF (four) when, if used alone, each word signifies more than the number itself *UK, 1991*

enit? don't you know? One of the very few Native American expressions used in a slangy sense by English-speaking Native Americans *US, 1988*

enjoy! used as a benediction by restaurant waiters, and then mimicked in other contexts *US, 1995*

enjoy the trip?; enjoy your trip? a catchphrase readily delivered to anyone who stumbles or trips over something. Often phrased 'did you enjoy the trip?', sometimes elaborated 'send a postcard next time!' *UK, 1974*

enlisted swine *noun* an enlisted soldier *US, 1986*

Enoch *noun* a coloured immigrant child. By ironic transference from Enoch Powell, 1912–98, a noted opponent of immigration into the UK. Recorded as being used by white primary-school children, but the example was surely set by a parent *UK, 1979*

Enoch Powell; enoch *noun* **1** a towel. Rhyming slang, formed from the name of British scholar and politician, Enoch Powell 1912–98 *UK, 1992*. **2** a trowel. Rhyming slang *UK, 1992*

enough *pronoun* ▶ **can never get enough** to be sexually insatiable *UK, 1974*. ▶ **have had enough** to be tipsy, drunk. A not entirely honest form of words – the implied sense is 'to have had more than enough' *UK, 1937*

enthuse *verb* to be enthusiastic, or create enthusiasm in others *US, 1827*

entjie; endjie *noun* a cigarette, especially the stub of a cigarette that may be saved for later; a marijuana cigarette. Formed on Afrikaans *end* (end), 'entjie' is pronounced 'ayn-chee' *SOUTH AFRICA, 1946*

entreprenerd *noun* a computer- or Internet-business entrepreneur. A play on NERD *UK, 2003*

entry *noun* ▶ **up your entry** appropriate to your taste or requirements *UK, 1980*

envelope *noun* **1** a condom *US, 1964*. **2** an aeroplane's performance limits *US, 1990*

Enzed *noun* New Zealand *AUSTRALIA, 1915*

Enzedder *noun* a New Zealander *AUSTRALIA, 1933*

EOT *adjective* dead *US, 1998*

ep *noun* an episode. A broadcasting abbreviation in wider currency *US, 1915*

EPA *nickname* East Palo Alto, San Mateo County, California. A black ghetto surrounded by Silicon Valley wealth *US, 2000*

epic *adjective* excellent, outstanding *US, 1983*

epidoddle *noun* epidural anaesthesia *US, 1994*

eppie scoppie *noun* a tantrum *UK, 1995*

eppis *noun* nothing *US, 1966*

eppo *noun* an attack, an outburst *IRELAND, 2003*

eppy *noun* a display of temper *UK, 1988*

Eppy *nickname* Brian Epstein (1934–67), manager of the Beatles *UK, 2001*

eppy *adjective* epileptic *UK, 1988*

epsilon *noun* a very small amount *US, 1983*

EPT *nickname* El Paso, Texas *US, 1974*

EQ; EQs *noun* an equalizer, the device which controls the tonal quality of domestic and professional sound-reproduction equipment *UK, 2002*

equalizer; equaliser *noun* a gun or any object that can be used in a fight. Not without irony *US, 1899*

equator *noun* the waist *US, 1948*

equipped *adjective* **1** stylish and fashionable *US, 1972*. **2** armed, equipped with a weapon *UK, 1996*

-er; -ers *suffix* used to create a slangy variation of a conventional, generally abridged, word. By this process, the word 'indigestion' becomes, in its simplest form, 'indigesters'; 'football' becomes FOOTER and 'rugby football' becomes 'rugger'. Now known as the 'Oxford -er(s)', it began at Rugby school in 1875 (*Oxford English Dictionary*), but this origin has been disputed and claimed for Harrow School. Usage migrated via Oxford University into general (upper-)middle-class slang, and Royal Navy Service *UK, 1875*

eradication squad; 'radication squad *noun* a unit of armed police *UK, 1994*

-erati *suffix* when added to a type or cultural interest, creates a fashionable group with a common identity or interest. On the model of 'literati'; better-known uses include 'liggerati' (hangers-on), 'niggerati' (successful members of black society) *UK, 1990*

erdie; erdy *noun* an unimaginative, conventional person. From German *erde* (earth, the Earth, the ground) *UK, 1974*

'ere; here said when passing a marijuana cigarette *US, 2001*

erecstasy *noun* a recreational drug cocktail of MDMA, the recreational drug best known as ecstasy, and Viagra™ (a branded drug that enables a male erection). A conflation of 'cause' and 'effect' *IRELAND, 2003*

erector *noun* a semi-erect penis *UK, 1999*

-ereemo *suffix* used as a meaningless appendage. Jocular, maybe just for fun *UK, 1997*

-er -er *suffix* a doer (of the verb). Jocular repetitious use of the agent suffix '-er'. Normally only one 'er' is used for a compound verb, thus 'wash up' becomes 'washer-up'. Then, added to both parts of the compound, 'washer-upper'. And sometimes, for comic effect, with a third '-er' added to the new compound as a whole, 'washer-upperer'. This last especially used by children *AUSTRALIA, 1964*

erie *noun* ▶ **on the erie** engaged in eavesdropping *US, 1950*

E-ring *adjective* high-ranking. Military usage. Refers to the 'E-ring' of the Pentagon where high-ranking officers work *US, 1986*

-erino *suffix* used as a suffix to create humorous variants understood from their base *US, 1890s*

erk! used for expressing disgust *AUSTRALIA, 1981*

erk; irk *noun* a contemptible person. From a military use as 'a serviceman of low rank' *UK, 1959*

erky *adjective* mildly disgusting; unpleasant. From **ERK!** (an expression of mild disgust). The suggestion that it derives from 'disparate*erk*' (a naval rating) is mere clutching at straws *AUSTRALIA, 1959*

ernie *noun* a fool, especially one who does not concentrate. Snowboarders' slang *US, 1995*

-eroo *suffix* used as a meaningless embellishment; also used to intensify *US, 1931*

-erooni; -eroony *suffix* used as a decorative intensifier *US, 1966*

Eros and Cupid *adjective* stupid. Rhyming slang *UK, 1998*

erp *verb* to vomit *US, 1968*

errie *noun* an aeroplane *UK: SCOTLAND, 1988*

Errol Flynn *noun* the chin, in senses anatomic and figurative. Rhyming slang, formed from the name of the swashbuckling film actor, 1909–59 *UK, 1961*

Erroll Flynns *noun* spectacles. Rhyming slang for **BINS** *UK, 1992*

Ervine *noun* a police officer *US, 1992*

esclop *noun* a police officer. Back slang, however the 'c' is not pronounced, and the 'e' is generally omitted, thus, 'slop' *UK, 1851*

escort service *noun* a prostitution business operating euphemistically under the guise of providing an escort, not a prostitute *US, 1982*

ese *noun* used as a term of address to a young male; an aware, street-wise young man. Border Spanish used in English conversation by Mexican-Americans *US, 1950*

eskimo *noun* **1** in oil drilling, a worker from Alaska or Montana *US, 1954*. **2** a Jewish person *US, 1989*

Eskimo ice cream *noun* a mixture of tallow, berries and fish *CANADA, 1962*

Eskimo Nell; eskimo *noun* a bell (a telephone call). Rhyming slang, formed from the heroine of a famously bawdy ballad *UK, 1998*

Eskimo pie *noun* the vagina of a frigid woman *US, 1977*

Eskimo roll *noun* a manoeuvre used by surfers to pass through a wave coming at them by rolling under their surfboard *US, 1977*

Eskimo salad *noun* moss from a caribou stomach, prized as food by Eskimos *CANADA, 1948*

Eskimo sisters *noun* women who have at some point had sex with the same man. Used as the title of a 2002 play by Laline Paull *US, 1994*

esky *noun* a portable cooler for food and drink in the form of an insulated oblong box with a flat lid. Proprietary name; from '*eskimo*' with a '-y' suffix. A quintessential item of Australian suburban life *AUSTRALIA, 1953*

Esky *noun* an Eskimo *US, 1978*

Esky lid *noun* a small bodyboard used for surfing. Used derisively *AUSTRALIA, 1996*

Esky lidder *noun* a bodyboarder *AUSTRALIA, 1996*

esnortiar *noun* cocaine. Of Spanish origin *UK, 2003*

esong *noun* the nose. Back slang *UK, 2002*

esra; esrar; esar *noun* marijuana. A Turkish word now in wider usage *US, 1982*

esroch *noun* a horse. Back slang *UK, 1859*

essence *noun* MDMA, the recreational drug best known as ecstasy *US, 1998*

essence *adjective* beauty, especially when ascribed to a women *UK, 1987*

essence of magic mushrooms *noun* *psilocybin* or *psilocin*, usually in powder or capsule form *UK, 1999*

Essex girl *noun* used as a stereotype for jokes, an Essex girl is brash, vulgar, trashy, sexually available, deeply unintelligent and, allegedly, from Essex. Derogatory. Essex girl jokes such as: 'Q: What do you call an Essex girl with two brain cells? A: Pregnant' have been in circulation since the 1980s *UK, 2001*

establishment *noun* the dominant power in any society *UK, 1955*

esthole *noun* an enthusiastic supporter of the est human growth movement. An appropriate play on 'asshole' *US, 1997*

estuffa *noun* heroin. From border Spanish for 'stuff' (a drug, especially heroin) *US, 1984*

ET *noun* in drag racing, the elapsed time of a particular quarter mile sprint *US, 1963* ▷*see:* **E AND T**

e-tard *noun* a person whose life has been adversely effected by excessive use of MDMA *US, 2001*

etch-a-sketch *verb* to manually stimulate both of a sex-partner's nipples. A similar action is required to operate an Etch-a-Sketch™, a children's toy drawing machine *NEW ZEALAND, 2002*

etched *adjective* drunk *UK, 2002*

E Team *noun* in the language of hang gliding, expert fliers from Lake Elsinore, California *US, 1992*

eternal care *noun* in hospital, intensive care. Medical slang, darkly humorous *UK, 2002*

ethanolic *noun* a drunkard *US, 1978*

Ethiopian paradise *noun* in a racially segregated cinema, the balcony *US, 1900*

Ethy meat *noun* a black woman as a sex object. An abbreviation of 'Ethiopian', a racial rather than national label *US, 1987*

E-tool *noun* an entrenching tool with an extendable telescopic handle and folding blade *US, 1976*

e-type *noun* a person with a professional or recreational interest in electronics *UK, 2003*

Euan Blair; Euan *noun* Leicester Square. Rhyming slang, recalling an incident in July 2000 when Prime Minister Blair's 16-year-old son Euan was found 'drunk and incapable' in Leicester Square *UK, 2002*

euaned *adjective* very drunk. Pronounced 'you-and'. From 6th July 2000: Prime Minister Blair's 16-year-old son was arrested for being 'drunk and incapable' *UK, 2002*

euchre *verb* to ruin or destroy *US, 1853*

eucy; eucy oil *noun* eucalyptus oil *AUSTRALIA, 1977*

euphoria *noun* a combination of mescaline, crystal methadrine and MDMA, the recreational drug best known as ecstasy *UK, 2003*

Europe *noun* ▶ **go Europe** to vomit *BERMUDA, 1985*

Eurotrash *noun* rich foreigners living in the US. Taki Theodora-copulos popularised the term in society columns written for *Vanity Fair* and the *Spectator US, 1987*

eva *noun* a pill marked with E on one side and A on the obverse, sold as MDMA, the recreational drug best known as ecstasy, actually containing a mixture of MDMA and amphetamine *UK, 2002*

evac *noun* an evacuation *US, 1954*

evac *verb* to evacuate *US, 1944*

Eve *noun* MDMA, the recreational drug best known as ecstasy. A play on ADAM, itself almost an anagram of MDMA *US, 1985*

evening breeze; sweet evening breeze *noun* cheese. Rhyming slang *UK, 1992*

evening glass *noun* calm surf conditions in the evening after the afternoon wind has diminished *US, 1978*

Evening News *noun* a bruise, especially a love-bite. Rhyming slang, formed from the title of a London evening newspaper that ceased publication in 1980 *UK, 1992*

even shake; fair shake; good shake *noun* a fair deal *US, 1830*

even steven; even stephen; even stevens; even stephens *adjective* even, equal. 'Steven' adds nothing but the rhyme *US, 1866*

everafters *noun* consequences *UK, 2002*

everclear *noun* cocaine *UK, 2002*

ever hear more!; ever see more! used as an expression of surprise *TRINIDAD AND TOBAGO, 2003*

everlastin joob-joob *noun* a fool, an idiot; a contemptible person. Glasgow rhyming slang for TUBE, formed on an improbable-sounding sweet *UK: SCOTLAND, 1988*

ever-loving *adjective* used as an intensifier *US, 1919*

ever such *adjective* used to describe a great or fine example *UK, 1803*

Everton toffee; everton *noun* coffee. Rhyming slang *UK, 1857*

every crab from the bush everyone *CAYMAN ISLANDS, 1985*

every home should have one a catchphrase generally applied to common objects, babies and non-material things. Thought to have been an advertising slogan in the 1920s *UK, 1974*

every man and his dog everyone *AUSTRALIA, 1979*

every man jack *noun* absolutely everyone *UK, 1828*

Every Minute Sucks *noun* work with an Emergency Medical Service unit. New York police slang; back-formation from the initials EMS *US, 1997*

everything-but girl *noun* a woman who will engage in any and all sexual activity short of intercourse *US, 2002*

everything in the garden's lovely! a catchphrase used to exclaim: all is well, all goes well *UK, 1910*

everything is everything used for conveying that all is well when asked how things are going *US, 1968*

everything's drawing everything's going well, thank you! Nautical origins, suggesting that all sails are set and there is a following breeze *US, 1963*

everything that opens and shuts *noun* everything possible *AUSTRALIA, 1960*

every which way *adverb* in every manner or direction *US, 1824*

every which way but in every manner or direction except the correct one. A specific refinement of EVERY WHICH WAY *UK, 1984*

eve teasing *noun* an act of a male outraging the modesty of a female in a public place by indecent speech or actual and unwanted physical contact *INDIA, 1979*

evil *noun* **1** a look of contempt or strong dislike *UK, 2005*. **2** a man with a body piercing through his penis. New Zealand prison slang *NEW ZEALAND, 2000*

evil *adjective* **1** mean-spirited, inconsiderate *US, 1939*. **2** excellent *UK, 1999*. **3** in computing, not designed for the speaker's purpose *US, 1991*

evo *noun* the evening *AUSTRALIA, 1977*

Ev'o'lene, the Nevada Queen *noun* in craps, the number eleven *US, 1985*

ex *noun* **1** a former lover or spouse. The prefix 'ex-', like those so-named, stands alone *US, 1929*. **2** exercise, games *UK, 1947*. **3** in target shooting, a bullseye. From the notion, perhaps, that 'X marks the spot' *US, 1957*. **4** a car's accelerator *TRINIDAD AND TOBAGO, 1971*

ex!; exie! used for expressing enthusiastic approval. Contractions of EXCELLENT! used by Glasgow schoolchildren *UK: SCOTLAND, 1996*

exacta *noun* in horse racing, a bet on first and second place *US, 1991*

exacto! exactly. Mock Spanish. *US, 1991*

exacts *noun* mundane, easily obtained facts about a person, gathered by an investigator *US, 1997*

excellent *adjective* impressive, amazing. Conventional English turned slang by the young. Stress is on the first syllable, which follows something close to a glottal stop; the 'l' is lazy *US, 1982*

excellent! used for expressing enthusiastic approval *US, 1989*

excellent behaviour! used for registering approval *UK, 2000*

excess leggage *noun* a more than usual display of a person's legs *UK, 2004*

Exchange & Mart *noun* a prostitute. Rhyming slang for TART; formed from the title of a weekly publication (published every Thursday since 1868) devoted to advertisements from people wishing to buy, sell or barter the widest range of goods or services *UK, 1992*

excitement *noun* sexual intercourse; the penis *IRELAND, 1997*

ex-con *noun* an *ex-con*vict, a former prisoner. Also recorded in the UK *US, 1906*

excruciate *verb* to aggravate, to irritate, to anger *UK, 1997*

excuse me? regarding a statement just made, used as an expression of disbelief, either of the content of the statement or of the fact that the statement has been made at all *UK, 2003*

excuse-me; 'scuse-me; bo-excuse-me; ooscuse-me *noun* an educated, middle-class person. Township slang; contemptuous *SOUTH AFRICA, 1963*

excuuuuuse me! used as a humorous admission of error. Made wildly popular by comedian Steve Martin during frequent appearances on NBC's *Saturday Night Live* in the 1970s and 1980s. Repeated with referential humour *US, 1977*

exec *noun* **1** a corporate executive *UK, 1896*. **2** an executive military officer *US, 1898*

executive services *noun* sexual intercourse, as distinct from masturbation, when advertised as a service offered by a prostitute *UK, 2003*

exercise *verb* ▶ **exercise the ferret** (from a male perspective) to have sex *AUSTRALIA, 1971*. ▶ **exercise the one-eyed trouser snake** (of a male) to urinate. Based on ONE-EYED TROUSER SNAKE (the penis) *UK, 2000*

exes *noun* **1** expenses, out-of-pocket costs. Also known as 'ex's', 'exs' and 'x's' *UK, 1864*. **2** six; in betting, odds of 6–1. Backslang. Also variant 'exis' *UK, 1951*

exes and a half *noun* in betting, odds of 13–2. In bookmaker slang EXES is 6–1, here the addition of 'a half' increases the odds to 6½–1 or 13–2 *UK, 1991*

exes to fere *noun* in betting, odds of 6–4. A combination of EXES (six) with a corruption of 'four' *UK, 1937*

exes to rouf *noun* in betting, odds of 6–4. A combination of EXES (six) and ROUF (four) *UK, 1991*

exfil *noun* *exfil*tration (the act of withdrawing troops or spies from a dangerous position). Military *UK, 1995*

ex-govie *adjective* in the Australian Captial Territory, descriptive of a dwelling, formerly owned by a government department but now privately owned *AUSTRALIA, 1988*

exiticity *noun* MDMA, the recreational drug best known as ecstasy *UK, 2003*

exo *verb* to equip an off-road vehicle with an external safety cage. From 'exoskeleton' *US, 1972*

exo *adjective* excellent AUSTRALIA, 1990

expat *noun* an *expat*riate, a person from the UK living overseas US, 1961

expect *verb* ► **expect a flood** to wear trousers that are too short TRINIDAD AND TOBAGO, 1993

expedite *verb* ► **expedite into eternity** to die US, 1994

expendable *adjective* describes casualties of war whose loss is anticipated and considered acceptable as the price of success. A military and political term borrowed from accounting UK, 1942

expensive care unit *noun* a hospital's intensive care unit US, 1989

expensive scare *noun* in hospital, intensive care. Medical slang UK, 2002

experience *noun* an experience of using LSD or mescaline UK, 1978

explorers' club *noun* a group of LSD users. Another 'LSD-as-travel' metaphor US, 1967

expressions *noun* profanity BARBADOS, 1965

exsqueeze me! excuse me! US, 1953

extra *noun* **1** in the coded language of the massage parlour, sex US, 1996. **2** in the language surrounding the Grateful Dead, an extra ticket for that day's concert US, 1994

extra *adjective* of behaviour, unnecessary or extreme UK, 2005

extra *adverb* very NEW ZEALAND, 2002

extract *verb* ► **extract the michael** to make fun of someone; to pull someone's leg; to jeer, to deride. A 'humorous' variation of TAKE THE MICKY, probably on the model of the synonymous EXTRACT THE URINE UK, 1984. ► **extract the urine** to make fun of someone; to pull someone's leg; to jeer, to deride. A 'humorous' euphemistic variation of TAKE THE PISS UK, 1948

extra-curricular activities *noun* adulterous sexual play, especially sexual intercourse UK, 1984

eye *noun* **1** desire, an appetite US, 1934. **2** a person who is not a part of the criminal underworld but who reports what he sees to those who are US, 1964. **3** a private detective US, 1930. **4** a hand-held mirror used by a prisoner to see what is happening down their cellblock US, 1992. **5** an automatic timing light on a drag racing track US, 1970. **6** a railway track signal US, 1946. **7** the anus US, 1990. ► **I will in my eye** used for registering refusal IRELAND, 1993. ► **my eye!; all my eye!; my eye and Betty Martin!** used for registering disbelief UK, 1842. ► **the Eye 1** a metal detector US, 1967. **2** the US Federal Bureau of Investigation. From 'FBI' to 'eye' US, 1997

eyeball *noun* **1** a meeting between two shortwave radio operators who have only known each other over the radio US, 1976. **2** a visual observation US, 1951. **3** the identification of a criminal by a witness to the crime US, 1992. **4** a favoured child or pet TRINIDAD AND TOBAGO, 1986. **5** a truck or car headlight US, 1977

eyeball *verb* **1** to see, to stare, to identify in a police line-up US, 1901. **2** to stare aggressively. After EYEBALL TO EYEBALL (descriptive of an aggressive confrontation) US, 1996

eyeball palace *noun* a homosexuals' bar where there is a lot of looking and not much touching US, 1964

eyeball queen *noun* a male homosexual who looks but does not touch US, 1964

eyeballs *noun* ► **to the eyeballs** to the maximum of capacity, absolutely full, totally UK, 1933

eyeballs, come back here! used by a clever boy for expressing approval of a passing girl US, 1955

eyeball-to-eyeball *adjective* on the verge of a hostile confrontation. A variation of conventional 'face-to-face' US, 1953

eyeball-to-eyeball *adverb* in direct, face-to-face confrontation US, 1953

eyeball van *noun* a police van equipped for surveillance US, 1988

eye black *noun* mascara UK, 1952

eye bleeder *noun* powerful, green marijuana US, 1997

eye candy *noun* an extremely attractive person, regardless of their character or intellect, regardless of their sex, regardless of their sexual orientation US, 1984

eye doctor *noun* the active participant in anal sex. From EYE (the anus) US, 1949

eye! eye!; eye-eye! look out!; also used as a warning that a prisoner is under surveillance; or as an injunction to be vigilant UK, 1950

eye fiddle *noun* an ugly person. From the Irish *aghaidh fidil* (a face-mask made from coloured paper) IRELAND, 2000

eye-fuck *verb* to look at with unmasked sexual intentions US, 1916

eyeful *noun* a good look at something UK, 1899

eye-game *verb* to exchange flirtatious looks TRINIDAD AND TOBAGO, 2003

eyeglasses *noun* used as a warning by an orchestra conductor to the musicians that a particularly difficult passage is coming up US, 1973

eye in the sky *noun* **1** surveillance stations or cameras in casinos concealed above two-way mirrors on the ceiling US, 1961. **2** a police helicopter US, 1992

eye job *noun* cosmetic surgery around the eyes US, 1996

eyelash *noun* an act of urination. Rhyming slang for SLASH (urination) UK, 2000

eye-opener *noun* **1** a strong drink, especially early in the morning US, 1817. **2** a drug addict's first injection of the day US, 1959. **3** any drug that acts as a central nervous system stimulant BAHAMAS, 1982. **4** the active participant in anal sex US, 1949

eyes *noun* ► **keep your eyes peeled; keep your eyes skinned** to be extra-observant. 'Keep your eyes skinned' predated 'peeled' by 20 years US, 1833. ► **the eyes** in craps, a roll of two. An abbreviation of SNAKE EYES US, 1999

eye's front *noun* a contemptible fool. Rhyming slang for CUNT, formed from the military command 'Eyes front!' UK, 1974

eyes like cod's bollocks *noun* protuberant eyes UK, 1961

eyes like piss-holes in the snow *noun* deeply sunken or squinting eyes (whether naturally, or as a result of illness, or – most commonly – as a symptom of a hangover) UK, 1970

eyes of blue *adjective* true. Rhyming slang UK, 1992

Eyetalian *noun* an Italian or, an Italian-American AUSTRALIA, 1900

Eyetalian *adjective* Italian. A spelling that follows pronunciation UK, 1962

Eyetie *noun* **1** an Italian or Italian-American. Originally army use in World War 1 US, 1919. **2** the Italian language. Derogatory, if not intentionally so US, 1925

Eyetie *adjective* Italian UK, 1925

Eyetoe *noun* **1** an Italian AUSTRALIA, 1941. **2** the Italian language AUSTRALIA, 1957

eye trouble *noun* **1** a tendency to stare. Prison usage NEW ZEALAND, 1999. **2** extreme fatigue US, 1971

eye up *verb* to look something or someone over, especially to appraise someone as sexually desirable US, 1957

eyewash *noun* **1** nonsense UK, 1930. **2** intentionally deceptive words or actions US, 1917. **3** tear gas US, 1992

ey up; ey-up used as a greeting; used as a means of directing attention to something. A northern English dialect phrase in wide use UK, 1977

E-Z *adjective* easy. Phonetic American spelling US, 1996

e-zine *noun* a low-budget, self-published magazine made available over the Internet. A combination of 'e-' (a prefix, denoting electronic) and ZINE (a FANZINE, a magazine for and by fans) US, 1998

Ff

F *noun* **1** oral sex. An abbreviation of FRENCH used in personal advertising *US, 1987*. **2** in poker, the sixth player to the left of the dealer *US, 1988*

F *adjective* in the written shorthand of the Internet and texting, in a homosexual context, feminine. Short for FEMME *UK, 2004*

F ▷*see:* EFF

F2F face-to-face, in Internet or texting shorthand *UK, 1996*

F-40; Lilly F-40; forty *noun* an orange-coloured 100 mg capsule of secobarbital sodium (trade name Seconal™), a central nervous system depressant *US, 1977*

fab *adjective* very good, excellent; used for registering general approval or agreement. A shortening of FABULOUS (very good, etc.); hugely popular usage in the 1960s, in part thanks to The Beatles. Subsequently in and out of vogue, surviving between times as irony. The cult science fiction television programme *Thunderbirds* (1964–66) used 'F. A. B.' as an acknowledgement but otherwise meaningless catchphrase; the 1999 UK re-run coincided with a vogue revival *US, 1957*

fabbo *adjective* fabulous; excellent. From 'fabulous' *AUSTRALIA, 2003*

fabe *adjective* very good, excellent. An affected elaboration of FAB *UK, 1967*

fabel *adjective* very good, excellent, lovely. An elaboration of FAB *UK, 2002*

faboo *adjective* fabulous *US, 1999*

fabric *noun* clothing in general *US, 1972*

fabulicious *adjective* good and good tasting. Usually used to describe a sexually appealing man *US, 1997*

fabulous *adjective* used as a clichéd term of praise *US, 1997*

face *noun* **1** makeup *UK, 1946*. **2** pride, self-esteem, confidence, reputation, standing *UK, 1876*. **3** a known criminal *US, 1944*. **4** in racecourse gambling, a bettor who is believed to have useful information regarding the likely outcome of a race. A bookmakers' usage *UK, 2001*. **5** a leading member of the Mod youth fashion movement *UK, 1964*. **6** in professional wrestling, a wrestler who is designed by the promoters to be seen by the audience as the hero. Short for BABYFACE *US, 1990*. **7** a professional pool player who is well known and recognised, making it impossible for him to make a living betting with unsuspecting amateurs *US, 1990*. **8** a stranger; any person *US, 1946*. **9** used as a term of address *UK, 1891*. **10** oral sex *US, 1968*. **11** in betting, odds of 5–2. From the TICK-TACK signal used by bookmakers *UK, 1991*. **12** a clock or watch *US, 1959*. ▶ **between the face and eyes** where a blow or shocking news hits *US, 1975*. ▶ **feed your face; stuff your face** to eat, especially to eat hungrily or in an ill-mannered way *UK, 1939*. ▶ **in your face** adversarial, confrontational *US, 1976*. ▶ **off your face** drunk or drug-intoxicated. Variation of OFF YOUR HEAD *UK, 2001*. ▶ **your face (and) my arse** a catchphrase response to a smoker's request, 'Have you got a match?' *UK, 1984*

face *verb* to humiliate *US, 1983*. ▶ **face the breeze** in horse racing, to be in the position immediately behind and outside the leader *US, 1997*

face! used as the stinging finale to a deliberate insult. Youth slang *US, 1979*

face-ache *noun* used, generally, as a disparaging form of address. Harsher when used behind someone's back *UK, 1937*

face as long as a wet Sunday *noun* used for describing an expression of depression or sadness *CANADA, 1984*

face bubble *noun* in motorcyling, a plastic shield attached to the helmet to cover the face *US, 1973*

faced *adjective* **1** drunk *US, 1968*. **2** under the influence of MDMA, the recreational drug best known as ecstasy *US, 1998*. **3** embarrassed, humiliated. Youth slang *US, 1993*

face-fart *verb* to burp *NEW ZEALAND, 1982*

face-fucking *noun* oral sex, from an active perspective *US, 1996*

face fungus *noun* whiskers, men's facial hair *UK, 1907*

face job *noun* cosmetic surgery designed to alter your appearance *US, 1982*

face lace *noun* whiskers *US, 1927*

facelift *noun* in the used car business, the procedure of turning back the miles on the mileometer (odometer) *US, 1997*

face like a bag of arses *noun* an ugly face. A variation of FACE LIKE A BAG OF SPANNERS *UK, 2003*

face like a bag of spanners *noun* a hard and rough face, mostly used when describing a woman. Recorded as used by a man describing his mother-in-law *UK, 1975*

face like a bulldog *noun* an ugly face, mostly applied to a girl or woman. Embellishments abound, such as 'face like a bulldog chewing a wasp' or 'face like a bulldog licking piss off a nettle' *UK, 2003*

face like a dyin' calf *noun* a morose, sorrowful look *CANADA, 1988*

face like a leper licking piss off a thistle *noun* an ugly face, mostly applied to a girl or woman *UK, 2003*

face like a slapped arse *noun* a very miserable-looking countenance *UK, 1999*

face-off *noun* an ejaculation of semen onto a lover's face *US, 2003*

face-plant *noun* a face-first fall; in snowboarding, a face-first fall into the snow *US, 1984*

faces and spaces *noun* joint consideration of equipment and personnel for the field and non-field positions. Military usage *US, 1986*

face-shot *noun* an air-to-air guided missile *US, 1991*

face time *noun* time spent in a meeting or conversation with an important or influential person; time spent on television *US, 1991*

face train *noun* serial oral sex, from the point of view of the provider *US, 2001*

facety *adjective* rude, arrogant *JAMAICA, 1943*

face-up massage *noun* an erotic massage *CANADA, 2002*

face-welly *noun* a gas mask. Conventional 'face' combined with 'welly' (a protective rubber boot). Royal Air Force use *UK, 2002*

facey *adjective* indicating criminal qualities. From FACE (a known criminal) *UK, 2000*

fachiva *noun* heroin *UK, 2003*

facial *noun* **1** ejaculation onto a person's face. Depictions of the act in pornographic films and photographs promise great pleasure to the recipient *US, 1993*. **2** in rugby, an aggressive rubbing of the face of a tackled opponent *NEW ZEALAND, 1998*

facking *adjective* used as an intensifier. A variant spelling of 'fucking' based on London Cockney pronunciation *UK, 2001*

factoid *noun* a fact, especially when superfluously or gratuitously given *UK, 2003*

factor *noun* in horse racing, a horse who is contending for the lead in a race *US, 1960*

factory *noun* **1** a police station *UK, 1891*. **2** the equipment needed to inject drugs *US, 1971*. ▶ **the factory** the theatre. Jocular usage by actors *UK, 1952*

factory driver *noun* in motor racing, a driver officially representing a car manufacturer *US, 1980*

fac-U *nickname* during the Vietnam war, the forward air controller training facility in Phan Rhang. The FAC from 'forward *air* controller', the U from 'university', and the combination from a sense of mischief *US, 1942*

fade *noun* **1** a departure *US, 1942*. **2** a black person who tries to lose his identity as a black person and to assume an identity more pleasing to the dominant white society *US, 1970*. **3** a white person *US, 1972*. **4** a haircut style in which the sides of the head are closely cut and the top of the head is not. Also heard as a 'fadie' *US, 1989*

fade *verb* **1** to leave, to disappear *US, 1899*. **2** to idle; to waste time *US, 1968*. **3** to match the bet of another gambler; to bet against another gambler's success *US, 1890*. **4** to buy part of something *US, 2004*. **5** to deal with, to handle *US, 1972*. ► **fade a beef** to cause a complaint or criminal charge to be removed *US, 1976*

fadeaway *noun* in hot rodding, a design feature that blends the front fender back into the car body *US, 1954*

fade away *verb* to become quiet *US, 1947*

faded *adjective* **1** drunk *US, 1998*. **2** drug-intoxicated *US, 1998*

fade-out *noun* a disappearance *US, 1918*

faff about; faff around *verb* to mess about; to waste time on matters of no importance. An apparent euphemism for FUCK but originally British dialect *faffle* with the same sense *UK, 1874*

fag *noun* **1** a male homosexual. Shortened from 'faggot' *US, 1921*. **2** a cigarette, a cigarette butt *UK, 1888*. **3** a despicable, unlikeable person. No allegation of homosexuality is inherent in this usage *US, 1982*
▷ *see:* FAG PACKET

fag around *verb* (of presumptively heterosexual male friends) to joke around or engage in horseplay *US, 1997*

fag-bag *verb* to rob a homosexual man *US, 1977*

fag-bait *noun* an effeminate boy or young man *US, 1974*

fag bangle *noun* a homosexual man who accompanies a heterosexual woman. Derives from the purely decorative effect of the relationship *UK, 2002*

fag factory *noun* **1** a place where homosexuals gather. Formed on FAG (a homosexual) *US, 1949*. **2** a prison, especially one with a large homosexual population *US, 1992*

fagged out; fagged *adjective* exhausted *UK, 1785*

fagging *noun* male homosexual anal-intercourse *US, 1996*

faggish *adjective* effeminate, blatantly homosexual *US, 1958*

faggot *noun* a male homosexual *US, 1914*

Faggot Flats *nickname* a neighbourhood in Los Angeles, south of the Sunset Strip and north of Santa Monica Boulevard *US, 1969*

faggot road *noun* a road topped with sapling bundles *CANADA, 1956*

faggotry *noun* male homosexuality; male homosexual practices *US, 1970*

faggot's lunch box *noun* a jock strap; an athletic support *US, 1964*

faggot's moll *noun* a heterosexual woman who seeks and enjoys the company of homosexual men *US, 1969*

faggoty; faggotty *adjective* obviously homosexual *US, 1927*

faggy *adjective* effeminate, blatantly homosexual *US, 1949*

fag hag *noun* **1** a female cigarette smoker. Teen slang, formed on FAG (a cigarette). Noted by a Toronto newspaper in 1946, and reported as 'obsolescent or obsolete' in 1959. This sense of the term is long forgotten in the US but not the UK *US, 1944*. **2** a woman who seeks and enjoys the company of male homosexuals. Formed on FAG (a homosexual). At times now used with derision, at times with affection *US, 1965*

fag-hater *noun* a person with a pathological dislike for homosexuals *US, 1979*

Fagin *noun* **1** a leader of thieves. After the character created by Charles Dickens in *Oliver Twist*, 1837 *US, 1976*. **2** in pool, a person who backs a player financially in his bets *US, 1990*

fag loop *noun* a loop on the back of a man's shirt *US, 2001*

fag mag *noun* a magazine marketed to homosexuals. A compound of FAG (a homosexual) and MAG (a magazine) *UK, 2003*

fag moll *noun* a woman who keeps company with homosexual men *US, 1973*

fagola *noun* a homosexual *US, 1961*

fag out *verb* to go to bed *US, 1968*

fag packet; fag *noun* a jacket. Rhyming slang *UK, 1992*

fag roller *noun* a criminal who preys on homosexual victims *US, 1962*

fag show *noun* in the circus or carnival, a performance by female impersonators *US, 1980*

fag tag *noun* a loop on the back of a man's shirt *US, 1980*

failure to float *noun* drowning or near drowning *US, 1994*

failure to fly a tag applied to failed suicides. Medical slang *UK, 2002*

faints!; fain I!; fains!; fain it!; faynights!; fainites! used to call a playground truce. Schoolchildren's use, probably from conventional 'feign' (to pretend) hence 'to shirk', 'to evade'; often used in conjunction with a fingers-crossed gesture, the middle finger twisted over and around the forefinger, in the traditional sign of the cross, hence the call for truce may actually be a plea for sanctuary derived from conventional 'fen', corrupted from French *fend* (to forbid); note also 'forfend' (to protect) as in the phrase 'Heaven forfend' *UK, 1870*

fainting fits; faintings *noun* the female breasts. Rhyming slang *UK, 1972*

faints *noun* in the illegal production of alcohol, low-proof distillate *US, 1974*

fair *adjective* **1** (used of a gang fight) without weapons *US, 1965*. **2** absolute; total *AUSTRALIA, 1960*

fairbank *verb* in a gambling cheating scheme, to let a victim win at first, increasing his confidence before cheating him *US, 1961*

fair bollix *noun* a fair deal, a just proportion. Variation of FAIR DO'S *IRELAND, 2000*

fair buck *noun* used as a plea for fair treatment *NEW ZEALAND, 1998*

fair cow *noun* an annoying person or circumstance *AUSTRALIA, 1904*

fair crack of the whip *noun* fair treatment, equal opportunity. To give someone a 'fair crack of the whip' is to deal fairly with that person *AUSTRALIA, 1929*

fair crack of the whip! be fair! *AUSTRALIA, 1924*

fair dinks *adverb* honestly *AUSTRALIA, 1983*

fair dinkum *adjective* **1** displaying typical Australian characteristics, such as honesty, directness, guts, sense of humour and the like *AUSTRALIA, 1937*. **2** real; actual *AUSTRALIA, 1937*. **3** serious; in earnest *AUSTRALIA, 1934*. **4** fair; honest; equitable *AUSTRALIA, 1947*. **5** true; genuine *AUSTRALIA, 1908*

fair dinkum *adverb* **1** honestly; really; seriously; in all truth. First recorded in 1881 from the dialect of north Lincolnshire as an exclamation equivalent to 'fair play!', in which usage it had a brief life in Australia from 1890 to 1924 (*Australian National Dictionary*) *AUSTRALIA, 1894*. **2** totally; properly; well and truly *AUSTRALIA, 1918*. **3** fairly *AUSTRALIA, 1947*

fair do's; fair dues *noun* fair and just treatment. A plural of 'do' as action (deeds), sometimes confused with 'dues' (requirements) without substantially altering the sense *UK, 1859*

fair enough *noun* a homosexual. Rhyming slang for PUFF (a homosexual); probably coined as an elaboration of FAIRY (a homosexual) *UK, 1992*

fair enough! used for expressing agreement *UK, 1926*

fair fight; fair one *noun* a fight between members of rival gangs in which weapons or at least lethal weapons are forbidden *US, 1950*

fair fucks *noun* credit, merit *IRELAND, 1992*

fair go *noun* an act or instance of just treatment; a fair or reasonable opportunity *AUSTRALIA, 1904*

fair go! 1 be fair! *AUSTRALIA, 1938*. **2** this is true! *NEW ZEALAND, 1976*

fair go? indeed? *NEW ZEALAND, 1961*

fair go, spinner! in the gambling game two-up, used as a call signifying that the coins are to be tossed *AUSTRALIA, 1945*

fairies *noun* ► **away with the fairies** day-dreaming, possibly drug-intoxicated; mentally deranged; out of this world *IRELAND, 1996*

fair play! used for expressing appreciation. Probably from the Welsh *chwarae teg*, used as an expression of approval by English-speaking Welsh *UK, 2001*

fair shake *noun* ▷*see:* EVEN SHAKE

fair suck of the pineapple! used for registering surprise or complaint. A humorous variation of FAIR CRACK OF THE WHIP *AUSTRALIA, 1971*

fair suck of the sauce bottle! be fair! *AUSTRALIA, 1972*

fair suck of the sauce stick *noun* fair treatment, equal opportunity *AUSTRALIA, 1971*

fair to middling *adjective* average, especially in reply to an inquiry about your health or situation *UK, 1889*

fairy *noun* **1** a male homosexual *US, 1895.* **2** an avionics tradesman in the Royal Air Force *UK, 2002*

fairy dust *noun* phencyclidine, the recreational drug known as PCP or angel dust *US, 1993*

fairy hawk *noun* a criminal who preys on homosexuals *US, 1988*

fairyland *noun* **1** any roadside park. So named because of the belief that homosexuals congregate at roadside parks in search of sexual partners *US, 1971.* **2** a colour light multiple aspect gantry (a railway signal) *UK, 1970*

fairy loop *noun* a cloth loop on the back of a man's shirt *US, 1970*

fairy powder *noun* any powdered drug *US, 1992*

fairy story; fairy *noun* a Tory (Conservative); a Tory politician. Rhyming slang *UK, 1992*

fairy wand *noun* a cigarette holder *US, 1963*

fake *noun* **1** in a magic act, a piece of equipment that has been altered for use in a trick *US, 1981.* **2** a swindler; a confidence man *UK, 1884.* **3** a medicine dropper used by an intravenous drug user to inject the drug. At times embellished as 'fakus' *US, 1973.* **4** an erection *UK, 2002*

fake *verb* **1** to deceive *UK, 1859.* **2** to falsify for the purposes of deception *UK, 1851.* **3** to make, to do *UK, 2002.* **4** to hit. Polari *UK, 1933.* **5** to play music by ear *US, 1926.* ► **fake it** usually of a woman, to pretend to experience an orgasm during sexual intercourse *US, 1989.* ► **fake it till you make it** in twelve-step recovery programmes such as Alcoholics Anonymous, used as a slogan to encourage recovering addicts to modify their behaviour immediately, with their emotional recovery to follow *US, 1998*

fake *adjective* used in combination with a noun to denote an artificially constructed article, e.g. 'fake hair' for a wig *UK, 2002*

fake bake *noun* a suntan acquired in an indoor tanning booth *US, 1991*

fake book *noun* a book of chords used by musicians who improvise off the basic chords *US, 1970*

fakement *noun* **1** personal adornment such as jewellery or makeup. Extends an earlier theatrical sense as 'face-paint' *UK, 2002.* **2** a thing; used of something the name of which escapes you *UK, 2002*

fake out *verb* to bluff, to dupe *US, 1949*

fake riah; fashioned riah *noun* a wig. A combination of FAKE or 'fashioned' (made/artificial) and RIAH (the hair) *UK, 2002*

fakes *noun* breast implants *US, 1997*

fakie *noun* **1** in foot-propelled scootering, a travelling backwards manoeuvre, usually performed with only the rear wheel in contact with the ground *UK, 2000.* **2** in skateboarding, a travelling-backwards manoeuvre *UK, 1996*

fall *noun* an arrest and/or conviction. In the US often formed as 'take a fall', in the UK 'get a fall' *US, 1893*

fall *verb* **1** to be arrested *US, 1873.* **2** of police and shop detectives, to arrive *AUSTRALIA, 1975.* **3** to come; to go *US, 1943.* **4** to become pregnant *UK, 1722.* ► **fall into the bottle** to become a drunkard *US, 1990.* ► **fall off a mango tree** to be extremely naive *TRINIDAD AND TOBAGO, 1991.* ► **fall off the roof** to start the bleed period of the menstrual cycle *US, 1973.* ► **fall on the grenade** in a social situation, to pay attention to the less attractive of a pair of friends in the hope that your friend will have success with the more attractive member of the pair *US, 2002*

fall about *verb* to laugh immoderately *UK, 1967*

Fallbrook redhair *noun* marijuana purportedly grown near Fallbrook, California *US, 1992*

fall by *verb* to visit *US, 1965*

fall down *verb* to fail at something *US, 1899*

fallenatnite *noun* used as a mock scientific name for a stone *CANADA, 1989*

fallen off the back of a lorry; fell off a lorry; off the back of a lorry *adjective* stolen (not necessarily from a vehicle). A pretence at discretion which advertises a conspiratorial acknowledgment of an article's ill-gotten provenance; well known in the latter half of C20 *UK, 1977*

fall for *verb* **1** to be greatly attracted to someone or something, to fall in love with someone; in a less positive sense, to be taken in by someone or something *US, 1903.* **2** to become pregnant *UK, 1968*

fall guy *noun* a person who is set up to be blamed for a crime. From FALL (an arrest/a conviction) *US, 1904*

fall in *verb* **1** to join; to stay *US, 1952.* **2** in horse racing, to barely hold off challengers and win a race *AUSTRALIA, 1989*

fall into *verb* to acquire by chance or without effort *US, 1946*

fall money *noun* money placed in reserve by a criminal for use if arrested *US, 1893*

fall on *verb* to become pregnant *UK, 1976*

fall out *verb* **1** to be overcome with emotion *US, 1938.* **2** to lose consciousness due to a drug overdose *US, 1959*

fall partner *noun* a confederate with whom you have been arrested *US, 1969*

falls *noun* ► **over the falls** said of a surfer carried over the breaking edge of a wave *US, 1964*

fall scratch *noun* money set aside to cover expenses incurred in the event of an arrest *US, 1969*

fall togs *noun* conservative, traditional clothing worn by a seasoned criminal on trial to improve his chances with the jury or judge *US, 1962*

fall up *verb* to go to *US, 1952*

false! used for expressing doubt about the truth of the matter just asserted *US, 1989*

false alarm *noun* the arm. Rhyming slang, always used in its full form to avoid confusion with 'falses' and FALSIES (breast enhancements) *UK, 1992*

falsie basket *noun* crotch padding worn by males to project the image of a large penis *US, 1957*

falsies *noun* pads that aggrandise the apparent size of a girl or woman's breasts *US, 1943*

falsitude *noun* a lie *US, 2001*

falsy *noun* a chipped marble *TRINIDAD AND TOBAGO, 2003*

fam *noun* **1** the hand. English gypsy use *UK, 1699.* **2** a family. Also recorded in the US *AUSTRALIA, 1996*

family *noun* a group of prostitutes and their pimp *US, 1969.* ► **in the family way** pregnant *UK, 1796*

family *adjective* homosexual *US, 1994*

family jewels *noun* the male genitals *US, 1922*

family pot *noun* in poker, a hand in which most of the players are still betting at the end of the hand *US, 1990*

family reunion *noun* in trucking, a meeting of several drivers for one company at a truck stop *US, 1971*

family-style *adjective* (used of parts in a manufacturing plant) stored together *US, 1955*

famine *noun* a lack of availability of an addictive drug *US, 1992*

famous dimes *noun* crack cocaine *US, 1994*

Famous Fourth *nickname* the Fourth Army Division, US Army *US, 1991*

famous last words a catchphrase used as an expression of doubt regarding the certainty of whatever has just been promised *UK, 1948*

fan *noun* **1** the preliminary touching of a targeted victim by a pickpocket *US, 1958*. **2** crack cocaine *US, 1993*

fan *verb* to beat; to spank *UK, 1785*

fanac *noun* an activity for a serious fan *US, 1978*

fananny whacker *noun* a person who cheats at marbles by encroaching over the shooting line *AUSTRALIA, 1977*

fananny whacking *noun* cheating at marbles by edging your hand over the shooting line *AUSTRALIA, 1985*

fan belt inspector *noun* an agent of the Federal Bureau of Investigations. A back formation from the initials FBI *US, 1971*

fancom *noun* a convention put on by fans *US, 1976*

fancy *noun* a man's dress shirt with a coloured pattern *US, 1986*

fancy *verb* **1** to desire, to wish for, to want *UK, 1598*. **2** to desire sexually; to find sexually attractive. From the more general sense, 'to desire'; the sexual shadings were evident by Shakespeare's time. It slipped into current usage towards the end of C19 *UK, 1635*. ▶ **fancy the muff off; fancy the tits off; fancy the pants off** to find a woman extremely desirable. Intensification of FANCY (to desire) by specifiying MUFF (the vagina), TIT(S) (the female breasts) or 'pants' (underwear) *UK, 2000*. ▶ **fancy your chances; fancy your chance** to presume that your charm or skill will suffice to achieve success *UK, 1962*. ▶ **fancy yourself** to have too high an opinion of yourself (probably). Shortened from the conventional 'fancy yourself as' or 'fancy yourself to be something' *UK, 1866*

fancy!; fancy that! used as an exclamation of surprise. Often as an imperative; however, when spoken disinterestedly, it may be used to quench another's excitement *UK, 1813*

fancy boy *noun* in poker, a draw in the hope of completing a hand that is extremely unlikely *US, 1967*

fancy Dan *noun* an elegant, conceited man *US, 1943*

fancy-Dan *adjective* pretentious *US, 1938*

fancy man *noun* a man who lives off the earnings of a prostitute or several prostitutes; a male lover *UK, 1811*

fancy pants *noun* a dandy; a pretentious, superior, self-important person *US, 1934*

Fancy Pants *nickname* Anthony Joseph 'A.J.' Hoyt (b.1935), a stock car racing driver who dominated the sport in the US during the 1950s and 60s. Derived from Hoyt's fastidious dressing habits, alluding to a Bob Hope film of the era *US, 1999*

fancy woman *noun* a kept mistress; a female lover. Often used of a man's woman friend to disapprove of an implied immorality *UK, 1812*

fandabidozi! wonderful! A catchphrase coined by comedy double-act The Krankies; it has some (mainly ironic) currency. Seen, in 2004, as the slogan on a tee-shirt and the message on a greetings card *UK, 1978*

fan dancer *noun* a sexual dancer or striptease performer who employs a large fan in her dance. Most famously exemplified by Sally Rand (real name Harriet Helen 'Hazel' Gould Beck), who popularised the style at the 1933 Chicago Century of Progress World Fair *US, 1936*

fandangee *adjective* overdressed or otherwise assuming an air of superiority *TRINIDAD AND TOBAGO, 2003*

faned *noun* the editor of a single-interest fan magazine *US, 1982*

fanfic *noun* further stories and adventures for characters in familiar television programmes and films written for pleasure by fans of the original, especially widespread on the Internet. From 'fan fiction' *US, 1998*

fan fuck *noun* a heterosexual pornographic film in which male fans of the female pornography star are selected to have sex with her *US, 2000*

fang *noun* **1** a bite *AUSTRALIA, 1988*. **2** eating *AUSTRALIA, 1957*. **3** a drive taken at high speed. From FANG (to drive fast) *AUSTRALIA, 1970*

fang *verb* **1** to drive fast. Said to be from Juan Fangio, 1911–95, Argentine racing car driver, but since the 'g' in Fangio is pronounced as a 'j' some question is thrown over this origin *AUSTRALIA, 1969*. **2** to yell furiously *US, 1962*

fang down *verb* to eat *AUSTRALIA, 1996*

fang man *noun* a man who is a hearty eater *AUSTRALIA, 1982*

fangs *noun* musical ability. An outgrowth of 'chops' *US, 1958*. ▶ **put the fangs in** to ask for a loan of money *AUSTRALIA, 1919*

fan key *noun* the command key on a Macintosh computer. From the symbol on the key, which can be seen to resemble the blades of a fan *US, 1997*

fanner *noun* **1** a pickpocket. Likely a variant of FINGER *US, 1950*. **2** a fan dancer *US, 1981*

fanners in a child's game, pronounced to ward off another child's claim to half of something. The game, under the name 'halfies' or 'halvers', is listed in the *Oxford English Dictionary* as 'very old' *CANADA, 1987*

fanny *noun* **1** the vagina. A popular female name, possibly combined with the vulvic symbolism of a fan-light (a loosely triangular opening). It is worth noting that John Cleland's *The Memoirs of Fanny Hill* features a sexually active heroine; however its publication in 1749 is about a hundred years before 'fanny' came to be used in this sense *UK, 1879*. **2** a woman objectified sexually. From the previous sense *UK, 1997*. **3** the buttocks *US, 1919*. **4** a story, lies *UK, 1933*

fanny *verb* to talk glibly, especially to talk until a crowd has gathered. Recorded in use among market traders *UK, 1949*

fanny about; fanny around *verb* to waste time, to idle *UK, 1971*

Fanny Adams; sweet Fanny Adams; sweet Miss Adams; sweet FA; FA; fanny *noun* nothing at all. From the brutal and maniacal murder, on 24th August 1867, of 8-year-old Fanny Adams, at Alton in Hampshire. Parts of her body were found over several days in different parts of the rural countryside. Upset with the tinned mutton that they were being served, British sailors in 1869 began to refer to the tins as containing the butchered contents of 'Sweet Fanny Adams'. It evolved into a suggestion of 'fuck', or 'nothing', and has been used in that sense in the C20 *UK, 1914*

fanny batter *noun* vaginal secretions *UK, 2002*

fannyboo *noun* the vagina. Childish elaboration of FANNY (the vagina) *US, 1998*

Fanny Cradock; Fanny Craddock *noun* a haddock. Rhyming slang, formed from the name of Fanny Cradock, 1909–94, still remembered as the intimidating (now iconic) presenter of 1950s and 60s television cookery programmes; the second version, as recorded by Ray Puxley in 1992, is a popular misspelling of her name *UK, 1992*

fanny fart *noun* an eruption of trapped air from the vagina, usually during sexual intercourse *AUSTRALIA, 1987*

fanny farter *noun* a woman who can execute fanny farts *AUSTRALIA, 1987*

fanny-flaps *noun* the vaginal labia *UK, 2003*

Fanny Hill *noun* a pill, especially 'the pill' (a contraceptive). Rhyming slang, formed from the title of John Cleland's erotic novel *The Memoirs of Fanny Hill*, 1749. Presumed to be a 1960s' coinage as Cleland's classic was controversially republished at the same time as the contraceptive pill was being introduced *UK, 1992*

Fanny Hill *nickname* the Los Angeles County women's jail *US, 1981*

fanny lips *noun* the vaginal lips; the *labium majora* or *minora*. A combination of FANNY (the vagina; the vulva) and the conventional translation of 'labium' *UK, 2002*

fanny merchant *noun* a glib talker *UK, 1998*

fanny on; fanny *verb* to talk with the intention to persuade or deceive *UK, 1949*

fanny pelmet *noun* a very short skirt *UK, 1995*

fanny quack *noun* a gynaecologist. A combination of FANNY (the vagina) and QUACK (a doctor) *UK, 1999*

fanny rag *noun* a sanitary towel *AUSTRALIA, 1985*

fan on *verb* to decline an offer *US, 1997*

fanoogie; fenugie *noun* during the Vietnam war, a soldier freshly arrived in Vietnam. A back formation from FNG (FUCKING NEW GUY) *US, 1991*

fantabulosa; fabulosa *adjective* wonderful. Arch elaborations of 'fabulous' *UK, 1967*

fantabulous *adjective* very good. A blend of 'fantastic' and 'fabulous'. Contemporary UK gay usage *US, 1958*

fantasia *noun* **1** a variety of MDMA, the recreational drug best known as ecstasy *UK, 1996*. **2** DMT (dimethyltryptamine), a powerful but short-lasting hallucinogen *UK, 2004*

fantastic *adjective* excellent, almost excellent, very good, merely good *US, 1929*

fantastic buy *noun* in poker, a card drawn to make a strong hand in a heavily bet situation *US, 1988*

fantasy *noun* the recreational drug GHB. Coined, no doubt, as an attractive marketing brand; it also stresses GHB's relation to FANTASIA (ECSTASY) *US, 1999*

fantidilysastic *adjective* great. A teenage invention of the 1960s *NEW ZEALAND, 1998*

fanzine *noun* an inexpensively self-published magazine devoted to such topics as hobbies, music, film and politics. A combination of 'fantasy' and 'magazine'; originally a magazine produced for science fiction fans but adopted by and produced by fans of any topic imaginable *US, 1949*

FAQ *noun* *frequently asked questions*. A real-life acquisition from the Internet, where FAQ files were created as a resource of informative and regularly updated information; gently punning on 'fact'. On-screen the acronym is both singular and plural; in speech the plural is generally indicated by the addition of an 's' *US, 1989*

FAR *noun* a hard and fast rule *US, 1991*

far and near *noun* beer. Rhyming slang; glossed as C19, but remains a familiar term, perhaps because of its neat reversal with NEAR AND FAR (a bar) *UK, 1960*

farang *noun* a foreigner. Vietnamese, borrowed by US soldiers *US, 1949*

farbulous *adjective* used approvingly of up-to-the-moment followers of fashion and the trendy clothes they wear; used disapprovingly of wardrobe items worn by historical re-enactors that post-date the intended period. A blend of FAR OUT and fabulous *UK, 2005*

fare *noun* a prostitute's client. Both heterosexual and homosexual usage *UK, 1959*

fark 'fuck', in all its senses. The word 'fuck' as filtered through the Australian accent *AUSTRALIA, 1971*

farm *noun* ▶ **back to the farm** laid off due to lack of work *US, 1946*

farmer *noun* an unsophisticated person *US, 1864*. ▶ **I could eat a farmer's arse through a hedge** used as a declaration of great hunger *UK: SCOTLAND, 1988*

Farmer Giles; farmers *noun* haemorrhoids. Rhyming slang for 'piles'. Used in Australia and the UK *UK, 1955*

farmer's set *noun* in dominoes, the 6–4 piece *US, 1964*

farmer tan *noun* a suntanned face, neck and lower arms *US, 1996*

farm out *verb* to delegate to another *UK, 1862*

farmyard confetti *noun* nonsense. A probable play on BULLSHIT; a later variation of COW(YARD) CONFETTI and FLEMINGTON CONFETTI *AUSTRALIA, 1973*

far out *adjective* **1** excellent, innovative, creative, daring. Originally a jazz term with an emphasis on 'experimental', and then in general use with a more general meaning *US, 1954*. **2** drug-intoxicated *US, 1961*

farshtinkener; fushtookanah *adjective* stinking. From German to Yiddish to American slang *US, 1968*

farsighted *adjective* said of a restaurant waiter or waitress who is intentionally ignoring a customer signalling for service *US, 1995*

far south *noun* Antarctica *ANTARCTICA, 1881*

fart *noun* **1** an anal emission of gases. From Chaucer in 1386 through to the present day *UK, 1386*. **2** an unlikeable, even contemptible person *UK, 1891*. **3** used as a symbol of contempt *UK, 1685*. ▶ **a fart in a thunderstorm** something of negligible worth or impact *UK, 1989*. ▶ **a fart in a windstorm** a fuss made over something unimportant. Several variations on, including 'fart in a whirlwind' 1963 *CANADA, 1963*. ▶ **like a fart in a trance** listless, distracted, indecisive *UK, 1985*. ▶ **the farts** an attack of flatulence *UK, 1998*

fart *verb* to produce an anal emission of gases, to break wind *UK, 1250*. ▶ **fart the Star-spangled Banner** to do everything that is required and more. An ironic claim to super-capability, usually made in addition to a list of everything ordinarily required *US, 1998*. ▶ **fart through silk** to live a life of luxury and ease *US, 1927*

fart about *verb* to waste time foolishly *UK, 1900*

fart along *verb* to dawdle *UK, 1998*

fart around *verb* to waste time *US, 1931*

fart arse *noun* a fool, a useless person. Contemptuous *UK, 2000*

fart-arse *verb* to spend time unproductively; to idle *AUSTRALIA, 1971*

fart-arse about *verb* to waste time very foolishly. An intensification of FART ABOUT *UK, 1984*

fart blossom *noun* a despicable person *US, 1938*

fartbreath *noun* a despicable person *US, 1974*

fart-catcher *noun* a male homosexual *UK, 1967*

farter *noun* **1** a person who farts *UK, 1580*. **2** the anus *AUSTRALIA, 1992*

fart-face *noun* a despicable person *US, 1938*

farthead *noun* a despicable person *US, 1962*

farthole *noun* a despicable person or thing *US, 1972*

fart hook *noun* a worthless, useless person *US, 1973*

farting *adjective* trifling, contemptible, insubstantial *UK, 2001*

farting spell *noun* **1** a moment, a pause *UK, 1998*. **2** a loss of temper. From the previous sense (a moment) via 'to have a moment' (to experience a short-lived change of equanimity) *UK, 1998*

fart-knocker *noun* **1** a despicable person *US, 1952*. **2** an incompetent blunderer. Used with humour and often affection *US, 1952*

fartleberries *noun* **1** haemorrhoids. From an image of faecal remnants that cling to anal hair. Royal Navy slang *UK, 1989*. **2** small pieces of faeces clinging to anal hairs. Also variant 'fart-o-berries' *UK, 1785*

farts *noun* ▶ **the farts** an attack of flatulence *UK, 1998*

fart sack *noun* **1** a bed *US, 1992*. **2** a sleeping bag *US, 1943*

fartsucker *noun* a despicable person *UK, 1891*

farty *adjective* flatulence-inducing *UK, 1975*

fascinoma *noun* a medical case that is unusual and thus interesting *US, 1994*

fascist; fascistic *adjective* descriptive of a computer program with security walls or usage policies that the speaker finds excessive *US, 1991*

fascists *noun* the police. Used by late 1980s–early 90s counterculture travellers *UK, 1999*

fash *adjective* fashionable *AUSTRALIA, 1988*

fa'sheezy ▷*see:* FO'SHEEZY

fash hag *noun* a follower of *fashion*. Modelled on FAG HAG (a woman who seeks the company of gay men) *UK, 2003*

fashion casualty *noun* someone in the thrall of clothes-designers' more ridiculous excesses. A variation of FASHION VICTIM *UK, 1999*

fashionista *noun* someone who dictates, or is in the vanguard of, trendiness *UK, 2001*

fashion victim *noun* someone in the thrall of fashion designers' more ridiculous excesses; often applied, loosely, to someone who is conspicuously expensively dressed *UK, 1984*

fash mag *noun* a fashion magazine *UK, 2002*

fash pack *noun* a loose categorisation of pre-eminent people in the fashion industry. Modelled on RAT PACK and subsequent gangs, real and imagined *UK, 2002*

fast *adjective* overly concerned with the affairs of others *TRINIDAD AND TOBAGO, 2003*. ▶ **as fast as lightning over Cuba** very fast *CAYMAN ISLANDS, 1985*. ▶ **faster than the mill-tails of hell** moving very, very fast *CANADA, 1999*. ▶ **get fast** in a criminal enterprise, to cheat a partner out of money or goods *US, 1987*. ▶ **so fast he's goin' like greased lightnin' thru a gooseberry bush** used for indicating great speed. Note the alliteration – goin', greased, gooseberry – which is often characteristic of Nova Scotia slang *CANADA, 1988*

fast *adverb* in gambling, betting large amounts without fear of loss *US, 1974*

fast and out of place *adjective* emphatically over-concerned with the affairs of others *TRINIDAD AND TOBAGO, 2003*

fast bird *noun* in Vietnam, a high-speed attack jet aircraft *US, 1991*

fast buck *noun* money that is easily earned, especially if done so illicitly *US, 1949*

fast burner *noun* a person who is advancing quickly through the ranks. US Air Force usage *US, 1986*

fast-count *verb* to shortchange *US, 1949*

fastened up *adjective* imprisoned *UK, 2000*

fast in *noun* **1** MDMA, the recreational drug best known as ecstasy *UK, 2003*. **2** amphetamines *UK, 2003*

fast lane *noun* a lifestyle showing no regard for the future *US, 1976*

fast-mouth *adjective* fond of talking *TRINIDAD AND TOBAGO, 2003*

fast mover *noun* in Vietnam, a jet aircraft *US, 1972*

fast one *noun* a trick intended to deceive or defraud, usually in the phrase 'pull a fast one' *US, 1923*

fast pill *noun* in horse racing, a stimulant given to a horse *US, 1947*

fast sheet setup *noun* an apartment or motel that caters to prostitutes and their customers *US, 1969*

fast shuffle *noun* a swindle; a deceptive act *US, 1930*

fast stuff; fast; go-fast *noun* amphetamines, speed *UK, 1996*

fast-talking Charlie *noun* a Jewish person, or someone who is thought to be Jewish *US, 1980*

fast time *noun* daylight saving time *CANADA, 1953*

fat *noun* **1** an erection *AUSTRALIA, 1941*. **2** a fattened cow or bull ready for market *AUSTRALIA, 1888*. **3** used as a euphemism in place of 'fuck' *BERMUDA, 1985*

fat *adjective* **1** good *US, 1951*. **2** wealthy *UK, 1699*. **3** (used of a fuel mixture) too rich. Biker (motorcyle) usage *US, 2001*. **4** (used of a part in a dramatic production) demanding, challenging, rewarding *US, 1973*. **5** when said of a military unit, over-staffed. Vietnam war usage *US, 1977*. **6** (ironically) slim; little. Especially in the phrases 'fat chance' and 'fat hopes' *AUSTRALIA, 1938*. **7** out of fashion, old-fashioned *UK, 1980*

fat Albert; Bert *nickname* any exceptionally large aircraft, especially a Boeing 737, a Lockheed C-5A Galaxy or a Lockheed C-130 Hercules. The Boeing 737 was first manufactured in 1967: The Lockheed C-130 was delivered into service in 1970. The first Lockheed C-5A was delivered in late 1969 *US, 1994*

fat and wide *noun* a bride. Rhyming slang, from a playground variation of 'Here Comes the Bride' *UK, 1992*

Fat Arse Brigade *noun* collectively, the older women who support the People's National Movement party in Trinidad *TRINIDAD AND TOBAGO, 1977*

fat-arsed *adjective* broad-bottomed; hence, wealthy *UK, 1937*

fat ass *noun* a fat person *US, 1931*

fat-ass *adjective* of impressive dimensions *US, 1993*

fatback *adjective* lacking sophistication, rustic *US, 1934*

fat bags *noun* crack cocaine *UK, 1998*

fat bastard *noun* an overweight person *UK, 1988*

fat boy box *noun* a box with enough packaged food to last several days in the wilderness *US, 2000*

Fatboy Slim; Fatboy *noun* a gym. Popney rhyming slang, based on the stage name of musician and DJ Norman Cook (b.1963). Popney was contrived via *www.music365.co.uk*, an Internet music site *UK, 2001*

fat cat *noun* **1** a wealthy, powerful, prominent individual *US, 1925*. **2** an overpaid company director. A specifically British usage of the more general US term *UK, 1971*

fatcha *noun* the face. Polari, from Italian *faccia UK, 2002*

fatcha *verb* to shave, to apply cosmetics. From the noun sense as 'the face' *UK, 2002*

fat chance *noun* no chance at all *US, 1908*

fat city *noun* success, wealth *US, 1964*

Fat City *nickname* **1** Ottawa, Ontario, Canada's capital city. The name derives from the huge largess of taxpayer funds the city gets for museums, the Tulip Festival, the winter canal skating season, and so forth *CANADA, 2001*. **2** the headquarters of the Military Assistance Command Vietnam, located in Saigon *US, 1991*

fat devil *noun* a good-looking woman *US, 1978*

fat farm *noun* a facility where people go to lose weight through a regime of exercise and proper diet *US, 1969*

fat grrrls *noun* a young, radical faction of the 'fat acceptance movement' *US, 1995*

fat guts *noun* nuts (the fruit). Rhyming slang, possibly deriving from an effect of over-indulgence *UK, 1992*

fathead *noun* **1** a fool *US, 1842*. **2** a black person's hair style in which the hair stands out from the head *TRINIDAD AND TOBAGO, 2003*

father *adjective* excellent *BARBADOS, 1965*

fatherfucking *adjective* used as a variant of 'motherfucking' *US, 1963*

father's day *noun* the day each month when fathers appear in court to make child support payments *US, 1973*

Father-Son-Holy Ghost house *noun* a style of three-storey terraced house consisting of three rooms stacked vertically *US, 1970*

father's t'other end *noun* a room built on the end of the house. The odd word 't'other' is a shortened form of 'the other' much used in southwestern Nova Scotia *CANADA, 1999*

father time *noun* **1** a criminal judge who is inclined to give long sentences *US, 1950*. **2** a prison warden *US, 1949*

fatigue *noun* teasing; good-natured insults *TRINIDAD AND TOBAGO, 1904*

fat jabba *noun* ▷ see: JABBA

fat lip *noun* a fist blow to the mouth *US, 1944*

fat lot *noun* (ironically) little or none *UK, 1892*

fatmouth *verb* to insult, to taunt, to tease, to trade barbs *US, 1962*

fat-mouthed *adjective* loud-mouthed *US, 1952*

fat one *noun* **1** a substantial marijuana cigarette *UK, 1996*. **2** a generous line of powdered cocaine *2002*

fat pants *noun* wide-legged trousers *TRINIDAD AND TOBAGO, 1999*

fat pappy *noun* a large marijuana cigarette *US, 1999*

Fat Pill *noun* (among Canadian forces personnel) a sweet snack *CANADA, 1995*

fat pockets *noun* wealth *US, 1997*

fat rat *noun* the US Army's five-quart collapsible water bladder *US, 1990*

fat-rat *adjective* easy, privileged *US, 1983*

fats *noun* fatigues, the military work uniform *US, 1990*

fatso *noun* an obese person; used as a common nickname or rude term of address for an obese person *US, 1933*

fat stuff *noun* a fat person *US, 1926*

fat talk *noun* excessive boasting *TRINIDAD AND TOBAGO, 2003*

fatten *verb* in poker, to increase a bet *US, 1963*

fatty *noun* **1** a fat person, often as an offensive name-calling, sometimes as a nickname *UK, 1797*. **2** an extra-large marijuana cigarette. Also variant 'fattie' *US, 1969*

fatty *adjective* used of a pornographic categorisation that displays obese performers *UK, 2002*

fat zero; big fat zero *noun* nothing at all, none *UK, 1976*

faubourg; fauxbourg *noun* in Quebec, a suburb or a part of a city keeping the old name; a large indoor shopping complex. From the French for 'false town', this term is in use in Montreal to designate the area known as the Faubourg de Melasse (where ships loaded molasses) and the Faubourg, a complex of shops and boutiques in the centre of town *CANADA, 1967*

faucet nose *noun* the condition experienced by surfers who have water forced up their nose while being pummelled by a wave *US, 1991*

faunch; fawnch *verb* to complain vociferously *US, 1911*

fausty *adjective* unpleasant, distasteful. High school usage *US, 1961*

faux-hawk *noun* a hairstyle in which a central section (running from front to back) is grown longer/higher than the hair on the rest of the head. Pronounced 'fohawk'; this is a play on the 'mohawk' haircut (which this style approximates) and 'faux' (fake, artificial). Footballer and style-icon David Beckham sported the style in the summer of 2002 *US, 1996*

fauxmosexual *noun* a homosexual who behaves in the manner of a conventional heterosexual. A compound of 'faux' (fake) and 'homosexual'; as an aural pun only the first consonant is changed *UK, 2003*

fav *noun* in horse racing, the horse with the shortest odds to win a race. An abbreviation of 'favourite' *US, 1960*

fave; fav *adjective* favourite. A term with a definite teen magazine flavour *US, 1921*

fave rave *noun* a notably favourite person or thing, especially with relation to the creative arts *US, 1967*

favourite; favourites *adjective* excellent *UK, 1943*

fawmy *noun* a ring. English gypsy use, from earlier *fawny UK, 2000*

fawnty *noun* a car in a poor state of repair. In Glasgow this is a humorous 'brand name' *UK: SCOTLAND, 1988*

fax *noun* facts *UK, 1837*

fay *noun* a white Caucasian *US, 1927*

fay *adjective* **1** homosexual *US, 1928*. **2** white, Caucasian *US, 1927*

Fayette-Nam *nickname* Fayetteville, North Carolina, home of Fort Bragg and the US Special Forces *US, 1987*

faygeleh *noun* a male homosexual. Yiddish, literally 'little bird' *US, 1968*

faze *verb* to surprise, to disconcert *US, 1830*

fazool *noun* one dollar *US, 1979*

f beep beep k 'fuck' in any use *INDIA, 2002*

FBI *noun* **1** fat, black and ignorant. Used in ritualistic insults *US, 1971*. **2** used for describing people of East Indian origin. An initialism for 'fat-belly Indian', 'fat-bottom Indian', 'fine-boned Indian', or any number of similar constructions *TRINIDAD AND TOBAGO, 2003*. **3** an informer. UK black prison slang *UK, 2002*. **4** a Filipino. An abbreviation of 'full-blooded Ilocano'. Ilocano is a dialect spoken in the Philippines; among Hawaiian youth, the term applies to any Filipino, no matter what dialect, if any, they speak *US, 1982*

F bomb *noun* the word 'fuck', especially when used in a setting where such profanity is not expected *US, 1988*

FDAM *noun* an occasion for ostentatious dress. For 'First Day at (the) Marina' *CANADA, 1995*

fear *noun* ▶ **put the fear of God into** to terrify *UK, 1905*

fear in twelve-step recovery programmes such as Alcoholics Anonymous, used as an acronym for an addict's choices – *fuck everything and run*, or *face everything and recover US, 1998*

fearful *adjective* used as general intensifier *UK, 1991*

fearfully *adverb* very, greatly. Dated but still familiar, especially in the works of P. G. Wodehouse *UK, 1835*

Feargal Sharkey *noun* a black person. Rhyming slang for DARKY, formed from the name of a (white) Irish singer born in 1958 *UK, 1998*

feasty *adjective* excellent. Teen slang *US, 1958*

feather *verb* **1** in hot rodding, to operate the accelerator in a controlled, light manner *US, 1965*. **2** in horse racing, a light jockey *US, 1951*. **3** in pool, to only barely glance the object ball with the cue ball *US, 1990*

feather and flip *noun* a bed; sleep. Rhyming slang for KIP *UK, 1934*

featherbed *verb* to create work rules that require employment of workers who have no real tasks or not enough real tasks to justify their pay *US, 1921*

featherfoot *noun* a racing car driver who uses a light touch on the throttle during turns to control the engine speed precisely *US, 1993*

feather hauler *noun* a trucker with a light load, especially one of dry freight *US, 1971*

featherhead *noun* a superficial, silly and/or dim-witted person *US, 1868*

feather merchant *noun* **1** a civilian employee of the military; a civilian *US, 1941*. **2** a timid, conservative poker player *US, 1996*

feather plucker *noun* **1** a sharp practitioner. Rhyming slang for 'clever FUCKER' *UK, 1964*. **2** an objectionable person. Rhyming slang for FUCKER, generally used only in a jocular or affectionate way *UK, 1961*

feathers *noun* **1** a bed *US, 1899*. **2** body hair, especially fine hair or pubic hair *US, 1966*. **3** sleep *US, 1977*. **4** in darts and Bingo (also House and Tombola), the number thirty-three. Also variant 'fevvers' *UK, 1977*. ▶ **make the feathers fly** to cause uproar, to disturb the status quo *US, 1825*

featherwood *noun* a white woman. Formed with the more common PECKERWOOD in mind *US, 1989*

feature *noun* **1** an act of sexual intercourse *AUSTRALIA, 1972*. **2** in carnival usage, the rigged game that a particular operator operates best *US, 1985*

feature *verb* **1** to have sex. Popularised by the Barry McKenzie cartoon strip *AUSTRALIA, 1965*. **2** to take note of, to pay attention to *US, 1958*. **3** to approve of *US, 1952*. **4** to give an appearance; to look like *BARBADOS, 1965*

feature creature *noun* a computer programmer who enjoys adding features to programs *US, 1991*

featured dancer *noun* a sex club performer whose appearance at the club is advertised and who travels from club to club *US, 2000*

-features *suffix* used, when combined with an appropriate (generally genital) noun, as an unflattering nickname. In 1909 it was sufficient to call someone 'features'. Contemporary examples, found during a cursory search of the Internet on 8th October 2003, include 'bollock-features', 'cunt-features', 'prick-features', and 'twat-features' *UK, 2003*

fecal freak *noun* a person who derives sexual pleasure from eating the faeces of others *US, 1971*

feck *verb* **1** to steal *IRELAND, 1989*. **2** 'fuck', in all senses and derivatives. Scarcely euphemistic; widely popularised by *Father Ted*, a Channel 4 situation comedy, 1995–98 *IRELAND, 1989*

fecked *adjective* drunk. A variation of FUCKED *IRELAND, 2002*

fed *noun* **1** an agent of the federal government *US, 1916*. **2** a police officer *AUSTRALIA, 1966*. **3** a member of the Royal Air Force police. Adopted from the sense 'a member of the FBI' *UK, 2002*

federal *adjective* excellent *US, 2004*

federal court *noun* a floor manager in a casino or cardroom *US, 1996*

federales *noun* the federal government. From the Spanish *US, 2000*

federation *noun* a noisy, tumultuous gathering. An allusion to the attempt in 1876 by John Pope-Hennessy to create a Confederation of the Windward Islands, which resulted in riots *BARBADOS, 1965*

fed ex *noun* a person who has served time in a federal prison. Punning on the name of an express delivery business *US, 1997*

fedlercarp! used as a non-profane oath. Used by spacecraft pilots, especially Lt Starbuck, on the US television series *Battlestar Galactica* (ABC, 1978–80), and briefly in popular speech *US, 1979*

fed up *adjective* bored, disgusted, tired of something, miserable *UK, 1900*

fee *noun* coffee *US, 1966*

feeb *noun* **1** a person who is feeble, in spirit, mind or body *US, 1911*. **2** an agent of the US Federal Bureau of Investigation (FBI); the FBI *US, 1985*

fee-bee *noun* in craps, a five. Almost certainly a corruption of the more common PHOEBE *US, 1968*

feebie *noun* an agent of the Federal Bureau of Investigation (FBI) *US, 1942*

feed *noun* **1** a meal, especially an excellent and lavish one *UK, 1808*. **2** the chords played by a jazz band during a solo *US, 1970*. **3** a comedian's foil *UK, 1952*

feed *verb* **1** in pinball, to put a coin into the machine *US, 1977*. **2** when gambling on a slot-machine, fruit machine or one-armed bandit, to put a coin or coins into the machine's slot *US, 1996*. **3** in a jazz band, to play a chord background for a soloist *US, 1961*. ▶ **feed rice** to speak plainly *UK, 1989*. ▶ **feed the monkey** to sustain a drug addiction *US, 1970*. ▶ **feed the ponies** to bet on horse racing *US, 1997*. ▶ **feed the pony** to manually stimulate the vagina. Possibly related to *Smack the Pony*, a television comedy-sketch programme mainly written and performed by women, first broadcast in 1999 *UK, 2002*. ▶ **feed the warden** to defecate *US, 1996*. ▶ **feed with a long spoon** to be very careful in dealing with someone *TRINIDAD AND TOBAGO, 2003*. ▶ **feed your face** to eat *US, 1968*. ▶ **feed your head** to use psychoactive drugs. A phrase immortalized by Jefferson Airplane in the 1967 song 'White Rabbit', with Grace Slick's commanding vocal of 'Remember, what the dormouse said/ Feed your head, feed your head' *US, 1970*

feed bag *noun* a container of drugs *US, 1992*

feeder *noun* **1** a comedian's foil *UK, 1952*. **2** a hypodermic needle and syringe *US, 1959*

feeding time at the zoo *noun* a period of great disorder and disruption *AUSTRALIA, 1944*

feel *verb* **1** to understand *US, 2002*. **2** to agree with *US, 2004*. **3** to approve of or enjoy *US, 2003*. **4** to fight with someone. Literally, 'to feel the blows of an opponent' *UK, 2000*. ▶ **feel it** to feel good, to enjoy something *US, 2001*. ▶ **feel no pain** to be drunk *US, 1955*

feeler *noun* **1** a finger *UK, 1831*. **2** in poker, a small bet made for the purpose of assessing how other players are likely to bet on the hand *US, 1967*. **3** a citizens' band radio antenna on a truck *US, 1976*

feel fine; feel *noun* nine, especially nine pounds (£9). Rhyming slang *UK, 1992*

feeling *noun* marijuana *UK, 2003*

feeling fine *noun* mutual, simultaneous oral sex between two people. Rhyming slang for 69 *UK, 2003*

feel up *verb* to fondle someone sexually *US, 1930*

feely; feele; feelier; fellia; feely-omi *noun* a young man, a boy. Polari, originally with the more general sense as 'children'; from Italian *figlie* (children). A distinction is sometimes made whereby 'feele' is defined as a 'child' and 'feely omi' as 'a young man (sometimes specifically an underaged young man)' *UK, 1859*

feen *verb* to look at nude pictures *US, 1976*

feep *noun* the electronic alert sound made by a computer terminal *US, 1981*

feet *noun* ▶ **get your feet muddy** to get into trouble, especially with the criminal law *UK, 1977*. ▶ **have two left feet** to be clumsy when moving, especially when dancing *UK, 1915*

feet and yards; feet *noun* playing cards. Rhyming slang; always plural *UK, 1992*

feh! used as a declaration of disapproval or disgust. Yiddish, although the Yiddish etymology is not at all clear *US, 1990*

feisty *adjective* aggressive, spirited, lively *US, 1896*

felch *verb* to suck semen from another's anus and rectum *US, 1972*

felcher squelcher *noun* a condom intended for anal intercourse *UK, 1998*

Felix the cat *noun* a type of LSD. Presumably identified by an image of the cartoon hero created by Otto Messmer in 1919 *UK, 2003*

fella; page 3 fella *noun* an attractive male model; applied in a wider derogatory context to imply that a handsome exterior masks a deeply unintelligent personality. Derives from the use of topless models on page 3 of UK tabloid newspaper, the *Sun UK, 2003*

fellah; fella; feller *noun* **1** a male animal *UK, 1978*. **2** a man. An affected or lazy pronunciation of 'fellow'. 'Feller' since 1825; 'fellah', originally associated with affected and aristocratic speech, since 1825; 'fella' (and variations) since 1934 *UK, 1931*

fellowship *noun* a group activity involving a shared vice. Word play with the conventional, religious usage *US, 1986*

fellow traveller *noun* **1** a person who sympathises with a cause without being a full-blown member of the cause. Originally applied only to communist sympathisers; translated from the Russian *US, 1936*. **2** a flea *UK, 1966*

felony *noun* a girl under the legal age of consent *US, 2004*

felony shoes *noun* expensive training shoes. Favoured by urban youth, often involved in, and more often associated with, crime *US, 1978*

felony sneakers *noun* expensive trainers favoured by urban youth *US, 1979*

female unit *noun* a girlfriend. A cheap imitation of 'parental unit' *US, 1984*

femalia *noun* those parts of the female body that have a sexual resonance *US, 1996*

femdom *noun* a *fem*ale sexual *dom*inant, a dominatrix; female domination as a sexual subculture *US, 1989*

fem grem *noun* an unskilled female surfer. An abbreviation of 'female GREMMIE' *US, 1995*

feminazi *noun* a feminist. A popular term with, and probably coined by, US radio entertainer Rush Limbaugh who uses the term in order to marginalise any feminist as a hardline, uncompromising man-hater *US, 1989*

femme *adjective* **1** blatantly effeminate *US, 1963*. **2** female *UK, 2003*

femme; fem *noun* **1** a young woman *US, 1871*. **2** in a homosexual relationship, the person who plays the passive, 'feminine' role *US, 1934*

femme looker *noun* in circus and carnival usage, an attractive female *US, 1981*

femme queen *noun* an overtly effeminate male homosexual *US, 1963*

femmi *adjective* feminist *UK, 2000*

femmo *adjective* feminist *AUSTRALIA, 1993*

fence *noun* a person who trades in stolen goods *UK, 1698*. ▶ **go over the fence** to escape from prison *UK, 1996*. ▶ **sit on the fence** to be impartial, neutral or waiting to see who wins *UK, 1887*. ▶ **take the fence** (used of a bookmaker) to fail to pay off a winning bet *US, 1947*

fence *verb* **1** to purchase, receive and/or store stolen goods *UK, 1610*. **2** to cheat in a test *US, 1955*

fenced *adjective* irritated, angry *US, 1982*

fence hanger *noun* in motor racing, a spectator, usually female, who is more interested in the participants in the race than in the race itself *US, 1980*

fence painting *noun* a scene in a pornographic film or a photograph of oral sex performed on a woman in a fashion designed to maximize the camera angle, not the woman's pleasure *US, 1995*

fence parole *noun* a prison escape *US, 1990*

fence rider *noun* in motor racing, a driver who moves through the turns on the outside of the curve, nearest the fence *US, 1980*

fence-to-fence *adjective* in carnival usage, in control of all the activities in an engagement *US, 1985*

fencing *noun* a trade in, or the act of dealing in, stolen property *UK, 1962*

fender *noun* a new employee. Like a fender absorbing the impact of a collision, the new employee absorbs the wrath of the supervisor *US, 1955*

fender bender *noun* a minor car accident *US, 1962*

fenderhead *noun* a dolt *US, 1975*

Fenian *noun* an Irish catholic. From the American-Irish 'brotherhood' for the support of the revolutionary overthrow of the English government in Ireland *UK, 2000*

fen-phen *noun* a combination of fenfluramine and phentermine, used as a diet drug and/or central nervous system stimulant *US, 1996*

feral *noun* a person holding strong environmentalist views and living an alternative lifestyle *AUSTRALIA, 1994*

feral *adjective* **1** aggressive; wild *AUSTRALIA, 1994*. **2** living a low-technology, alternative, environmentally-friendly lifestyle *AUSTRALIA, 1994*

ferdutzt *adjective* (among Nova Scotians of German descent) used to describe someone who is confused *CANADA, 1999*

fe real; for real *adjective + adverb* genuine; honestly, genuinely; credibly *US, 1956*

fern *noun* a female's pubic hair *US, 1981*

ferret *noun* **1** the penis. A celebration of the animal's talent for exploring holes *AUSTRALIA, 1971*. **2** a member of the security services engaged to 'sweep' for and remove electronic bugging devices *UK, 1977*. **3** a beret. Royal Air Force use a deliberately poor rhyme *UK, 2002*. ▶ **give the ferret a run** (of a male) to engage in sexual intercourse. Also variant 'exercise the ferret' *AUSTRALIA, 1968*

ferry dust *noun* heroin. A play on magical 'fairy dust' *UK, 1998*

ferschlugginer *adjective* used as a mildly profane intensifier. A Yiddish term *US, 1955*

fer shur; fur shur *adverb* certainly. A staple of the Valley Girl lexicon, often used as an exclamation *US, 1982*

ferstay *verb* to understand *CANADA, 1987*

fertilize *verb* ▶ **fertilize the vegetables** to feed or medicate neurologically depressed hospital patients *US, 1985*

fess; fess up *verb* to confess *US, 1840*

-fest *suffix* a gathering together of, or a concentration of, or an event celebrating the modifying noun with which it combines. Abbreviated from 'festival' *US, 1865*.

festering *adverb* exceedingly. A euphemism for 'fucking' *AUSTRALIA, 1982*

festivity *noun* a drinking party *US, 1955*

festy *adjective* disgusting; dreadful; awful *AUSTRALIA, 1996*

fet *noun* amphetamine *UK, 1996*

fetch *verb* **1** to deliver (a blow). A conventional usage from C12 that slipped into the colloquial register sometime around late C19 or early C20 *UK, 1958*. **2** in computing, to retrieve and import a file from an Internet site to your computer *US, 1995*

fetch up *verb* to arrive, especially to arrive eventually *US, 1858*

fe true; for true; feh true *adverb* honestly, truly. West Indian and UK black patois, 'for true'. Also used as an exclamation and intensifier *UK, 1994*

fetschpatz *noun* (among Ontario's Mennonites) a dumpling *CANADA, 1998*

fever *noun* **1** five. An intentional corruption of FIVER *US, 1985*. **2** in craps, a roll of five. Sometimes embellished to 'fever in the South' *US, 1950*. **3** in a deck of playing cards, any five *US, 1951*. **4** a $5 note *US, 1961*. **5** an enthusiastic interest or, perhaps, mass hysteria *UK, 1885*

fevver clucker *noun* used as a humorous euphemism for 'clever fucker' *NEW ZEALAND, 1998*

few *noun* **1** a few alcoholic drinks *AUSTRALIA, 1903*. **2** any short jail sentence *US, 1949*

fews and twos *noun* very little money *US, 1948*

fey *adjective* effeminate *US, 1952*

Fezzer *noun* a Ford 'Fiesta' car. Essex use *UK, 2003*

fezzie *noun* a festival *UK, 2002*

FFF *verb* to find, fix, and finish. A military axiom for dealing with the enemy; the 'fix' is to fix in position, while to 'finish' is to kill *US, 1990*

FHB family hold back! A directive to family members to take guests into account when serving themselves *AUSTRALIA, 1983*

fid *noun* a British worker in Antarctica. Originally an acronym of 'Falkland Island Dependencies Survey' *ANTARCTICA, 1952*

fiddle *noun* **1** a swindle, a deception; in later use, used mainly of petty fraud *UK, 1873*. **2** a one-pound note; the sum of one pound; (more generally) money *AUSTRALIA, 1988*. **3** in pickpocket usage, a coat *US, 1943*. **4** a radio *US, 1971*. ▶ **on the fiddle** engaged in swindling or petty-fraud *UK, 1961*

fiddle *verb* **1** to swindle *UK, 1590*. **2** to falsify a personal statement of expenses, or corporate accounts and finances; to fraudulently amend examination or election results. A specialised use of the general sense (to swindle) *UK, 1970*. ▶ **fiddle with yourself** to masturbate *US, 1969*

fiddle and fire *noun* in the car sales business, a radio and heater *US, 1953*

fiddle bitch *verb* to potter aimlessly *CANADA, 1989*

fiddlededee; fiddley *noun* an act of urination. Rhyming slang for PEE or WEE. Presumably coined with some euphemistic intent, yet 'to go for a fiddley' seems, somehow, a more ambiguous option *UK, 1992*

fiddlefart around *verb* to waste time doing little or nothing *US, 1972*

fiddlefuck *verb* to waste time *US, 1949*

fiddler *noun* **1** a bookmaker who will only take small bets *UK, 1991*. **2** a paedophile. Prison usage *NEW ZEALAND, 1999*

fiddler's elbow *noun* the right-angled sharp turns in country roads *CANADA, 1950*. ▶ **in and out like a fiddler's elbow** applied to anything or anyone that enters and exits a given situation with unusual rapidity; especially, of a male's enthusiastic thrusting during sexual intercourse *UK, 1994*

fiddler's fuck *noun* a notional item of no value *US, 1961*

fiddlers three; fiddlers *noun* an act of urination. Rhyming slang for WEE or PEE, formed from the lyrics to the traditional nursery-song, 'Old King Cole. A variant of FIDDLEDEDEE *UK, 1992*

fiddlesticks! used as an all-purpose cry of frustration. Considered inoffensive, although it is possibly a pun on 'penis', via 'sword', the Shakespearean 'fiddlestick', although the bawdy pun itself is not made by Shakespeare *UK, 1600*

fiddley *noun* a one-pound note; the sum of one pound. Short for FIDDLEYDID *AUSTRALIA, 1941*

fiddleydid *noun* a one-pound note; the sum of one pound. Rhyming slang for QUID. This lasted briefly after the introduction of decimal currency (1966), and was used to denote the comparative sum of $2 *AUSTRALIA, 1941*

fiddly bits *noun* chrome embellishments on a motorcycle saddle bag and seat. Biker (motorcycle) usage *US, 2001*

fidlet *noun* a British expeditioner recently arrived in Antarctica *ANTARCTICA, 1967*

fido! used for suggesting that a group overcome an obstacle. An abbreviation of 'fuck it, drive on' *US, 1983*

fido dido *noun* a variety of MDMA, the recreational drug best known as ecstasy. From the borrowed image of Fido Dido, a fashionable cartoon youth of Spanish origin, imprinted into the tablet as a brand logo *UK, 1990s*

fi-do-nie *noun* opium *US, 1954*

field *verb* to work as a bookmaker *AUSTRALIA, 1960*

field circus *noun* in computing, field service *US, 1991*

fielder *noun* a bookmaker *AUSTRALIA, 1936*

fielders *noun* a rum ration carried on a field trip *AUSTRALIA, 1972*

field goal *noun* in pool, a shot in which the cue ball passes between the object ball and another ball, touching neither. An allusion to American football, in which a field goal is scored when the ball is kicked between the goalpost uprights *US, goa*

field nigger *noun* a black person who does not curry favour from white people and thus is afforded no degree of privilege *US, 1970*

field of wheat *noun* a street. Rhyming slang, with a deliberately ironic inversion of its original sense *UK, 1859*

fields *noun* ▷ *see:* STRAWBERRY FIELDS

field scarf *noun* a necktie. Marine Corps usage in World War 2 and Korea *US, 1940*

field-strip *verb* **1** to disassemble; to take apart *US, 1947*. **2** to break tobacco loose from a smoked cigarette and disperse it in the wild without leaving a trace of the cigarette *US, 1963*

fiend *noun* **1** a person who habitually or compulsively indulges in narcotics, especially morphine and cocaine. Modern usage is generally ironic, except when politicians and tabloid newspapers need a headline *US, 1881*. **2** a person who smokes marijuana when alone. Marijuana use is considered to be a communal activity hence a solo-smoker is the subject of criticism. Used ironically in this context *UK, 1998*. **3** an enthusiast. From the sense as 'addict' *US, 1884*

fiend *verb* **1** to cause a car to drop suddenly, almost to the ground, by use of hydraulic lifts *US, 1980*. **2** when arresting an unruly person, to use a choke hold *US, 1987*

fiendish *adjective* excellent *US, 1900*

fiend on *verb* to show off; to better *US, 1980*

fierce *adjective* very, very good *US, 1994*

fife and drum *noun* the buttocks *UK, 1960*

fifi bag *noun* a home-made contraption used by a masturbating male to simulate the sensation of penetration *US, 1969*

FIFO fit in or fuck off. An acronym from the world of office jargon where it may seen as general advice regarding Human Resources policy *UK, 2005*

fifteen and two; fifteen-two *noun* a Jewish person. Rhyming slang; Partridge suggests the term originates in scoring for the card game cribbage *US, 1984*

fifteen fucker *noun* a military disciplinary reprimand *US, 1989*

fifteen minutes of fame *noun* the brief period of celebrity that Andy Warhol saw as an element of pop culture *US, 1997*

fifth *noun* ▶ **take the fifth** to listen to a fellow alcoholic recount their worst misdeeds without comment or judgment *US, 1990*

fifth gear *noun* a state of intoxication *US, 1968*

Fifth Street *noun* in seven-card stud poker, a player's third face-up card (the *fifth* card dealt to the player) *UK, 2003*

fifty *noun* **1** a serving of beer that is half new and half old. A shortening of FIFTY FIFTY *AUSTRALIA, 1965*. **2** a .50 calibre machine gun *US, 1977*

fifty-dollar lane *noun* in trucking, the inside passing lane. A name based on the fine at the time on many motorways for truckers who used the inside lane *US, 1976*

fifty-eleven *noun* a mythical large number *US, 1970*

fifty-fifty *noun* **1** oral sex followed by anal sex. Largely supplanted by HALF AND HALF *US, 1941*. **2** in the television and film industries, a shot of two actors facing each other, each taking up half the screen *US, 1977*. **3** a serving of beer that is half new and half old *AUSTRALIA, 1972*

fifty-fifty! give me half of what you are consuming! *FIJI, 2002*

fifty-five *noun* in craps, a roll of two fives *US, 1974*

fifty-mission cap *noun* a cap similar to that worn by bomber crews during World War 2 *US, 1956*

fifty-one; one fifty-one *noun* small pieces of crack cocaine sprinkled in a tobacco or marijuana cigarette *US, 1994*

fifty PSI finger *noun* (among Canadian armed forces personnel) a finger poked into someone's chest to emphasise a point forcefully *CANADA, 1995*

fifty-two *noun* in craps, a roll of five and two – a seven *US, 1973*

fifty-two/twenty club *noun* US military veterans who were entitled to benefits of $20 a week for a year after World War 2, making a life of bohemian leisure possible *US, 1946*

fig *noun* **1** hardly anything at all *UK, 1400*. **2** an effeminate male. An amelioration of FAG *US, 1963*. **3** (of chewing tobacco) a plug *CANADA, 1862*

figary; fegary *noun* a fanciful mood; stylish clothing; whimsical ideas or notions; an impulsive decision *IRELAND, 1984*

figging *adjective* used as a euphemism for the intensifying 'fucking' *US, 1999*

Fightertown USA *nickname* the Miramar Naval Air Station, Miramar, California *US, 1990*

fighting drunk *adjective* in a state of drunken intoxication that prompts aggressive behaviour. Also used as a noun *UK, 1937*

fighting fifth *noun* any sexually transmitted infection. Rhyming slang for 'syph' (syphilis) *UK, 1992*

Fighting Hannah *nickname* the U.S.S. Hancock. An aircraft carrier that saw service in World War 2 and Vietnam *US, 1945*

Fighting Irish *nickname* the athletes of Notre Dame University *US, 1962*

fighting lager *noun* a lager of more than average strength *UK, 2002*

Fightlink *nickname* a Dublin night bus *IRELAND, 2003*

figjam *noun* a boastful person *AUSTRALIA, 1996*

figjam! stop boasting! *AUSTRALIA, 1996*

figmo; fuigmo *noun* fuck it, got my orders; fuck you, I got my orders. Korean and then Vietnam war usage. Descriptive of a somewhat defiant attitude. The sanitised version is FIGMOH: 'finally got y rders home *US, 1957*

figmo chart *noun* a record which a soldier kept of the number of days remaining until he was rotated home from Korea or, later, Vietnam *US, 1966*

fig-skin family *noun* distant relatives whom you rarely see *TRINIDAD AND TOBAGO, 1999*

figure *noun* a number to be bet upon in an illegal lottery or numbers game *US, 1967*

figure *verb* ▶ **it figures; that figures** it is reasonable or understandable; it works out as expected. A figurative use of the arithmetic sense *US, 1952*

figure of eight it *verb* (a notional action) to tighten the vagina *UK, 2002*

figures *noun* an illegal lottery in which winners are those who have bet on a number chosen by some random method. Best known as 'the numbers' or 'policy racket' *US, 1967*

fiji *noun* a member of the Phi Delta Gamma college fraternity *US, 1963*

Fila cunt's trainer *noun* a Fila™ sport shoe. An aural pun on 'feeler'; UK prison slang *UK, 2002*

file *noun* a pickpocket *UK, 1665*

file *verb* **1** to throw away. Office irony *US, 1982*. **2** to dress up. An abbreviation of 'profile' *US, 1989*

file 13 *noun* an office waste-paper basket *US, 1942*

file 17 *noun* the rubbish (trash) *US, 1989*

filet *noun* an attractive female *US, 1989*

filiome *noun* a young man, especially an underage participant in homosexual sex. A combination of FEELY (a boy) and OMEE (a man) *UK, 2002*

fill *verb* ▶ **fill a blanket** to roll a cigarette *US, 1949*. ▶ **fill the bill** to fulfil requirements, to meet the need *US, 1880*. ▶ **fill your boots 1** to do whatever it is you want very much to do, but are hesitating over. This phrase is used to encourage in Nova Scotia. It has been suggested that it derives from either the pursuit of fish while wearing high-top wading boots or the effect on the bowels of extreme enjoyment after restraint *CANADA, 1999*. **2** to have as much of something as you want or need; to do some activity to its limit *UK, 2003*

filled *adjective* **1** (used of a woman) shapely *US, 1997*. **2** of a car's body, repaired with glass fibre *UK, 1968*

filled-in *adjective* pregnant *AUSTRALIA, 1955*

filler pig *noun* in a carnival, a woman hired to entertain customers outside a side show before the featured talent appears *US, 1960*

fillet *noun* cocaine. A metaphor alluding to the drug's high cost and status *US, 1993*

fillet of cod; fillet *noun* an unpleasant individual. Rhyming slang for SOD (a contemptible man) *UK, 1979*

fillet of plaice; fillet *noun* a face; the face. Rhyming slang *UK, 1992*

fill in *verb* **1** to temporarily replace someone at work *US, 1930*. **2** to beat up *UK, 1948*. **3** to make pregnant *AUSTRALIA, 1955*

fillings *noun* loose tobacco *US, 1950*

Fillmore *noun* a potent mixture of alcoholic beverages *US, 1993*

fills *noun* dice which have been weighted for cheating *US, 1950*

fillum; filum *noun* a motion picture. Representing a widely decried but nonetheless common enough Australian pronunciation of 'film' with two syllables; also commonly used and understood in Ireland, Scotland, the north west (particularly Liverpool) and the north east (Newcastle) of England *AUSTRALIA, 1932*

fill up *verb* in poker, to complete a desired hand by drawing cards *US, 1951*

filly *noun* **1** a young woman *UK, 1614*. **2** in poker, a hand consisting of three of the same suit and a pair. Conventionally known as a 'full house' *US, 1951*

filly *adjective* pretty *UK, 2002*

film *noun* underwear *FIJI, 1992*

filth *noun* **1** the police; the CID *UK, 1967*. **2** a very attractive person *US, 1997*

filth *adjective* great; excellent; brilliant *AUSTRALIA, 1996*

filthiness *noun* the bleed period of the menstrual cycle *BAHAMAS, 1982*

filth merchant *noun* a man driven by his sexual appetites *UK, 2001*

filthy *noun* a look of disdain *IRELAND, 2003*

filthy *adjective* **1** excessive, especially unpleasantly so *UK, 1733*. **2** upset, extremely angry *AUSTRALIA, 1992*. **3** great; excellent; brilliant *AUSTRALIA, 1987*. **4** attractive, fashionable, stylish *US, 1993*

filthy dirty *adjective* very dirty. The usage of FILTHY as an intensifier, also duplicating the conventional senses of 'filthy' and 'dirty' has caused this cliché to verge on hyphenated single-word status *UK, 1843*

filthy great *adjective* very large. The usage of FILTHY as an intensifier; here also the play on synonymous 'dirty' has caused this cliché to verge on hyphenated single-word status *UK, 2003*

Filthy McNasty *noun* a dirty, rude person *US, 1969*

filthy rich *adjective* very wealthy. The usage of FILTHY as an intensifier has caused this cliché to verge on hyphenated single-word status *UK, 1940*

filum *noun* ▷*see:* FILLUM

fimps *noun* in craps, a roll of two fives *US, 1968*

fin *noun* **1** a five-pound or five-dollar note *UK, 1868*. **2** a five-year prison sentence *UK, 1925*. **3** a US Navy diver who is not qualified for SCUBA diving. Vietnam war usage *US, 1991*

finagle *verb* to obtain in a manipulative manner *US, 1922*

final *noun* the moment in a confidence swindle when the victim is left to discover his loss *US, 1969*

final curtain *noun* in carnival usage, death. The obituary section in the *Amusement Business* magazine is named 'Final Curtain' *US, 1985*

finale-hopper *noun* a young man who goes to a dance without a partner, cutting in on another's partner at the end of the evening in the hope of leaving the dance with her *US, 1922*

final gallop *noun* the hastening pace of lovemaking that climaxes at orgasm *UK, 1970*

financial *adjective* having ready cash; solvent *AUSTRALIA, 1899*

finders keepers said to signify that the person who finds an object is entitled to keep it. First recorded as 'findee keepee, lossee seekee' in an 1825 *Gloss of North Country Words*. The full phrase, known by every UK and US child, is 'Finders, keepers / losers, weepers' *UK, 1856*

find them, fool them, fuck them, forget them used as a formula for male relationships with females. The earliest form is 'find, feel, fuck and forget'; also known as the 'four F method'. Mutliple variants exist *US, 1966*

fine *adjective* **1** sexually attractive *US, 1944*. **2** in twelve-step recovery programmes such as Alcoholics Anonymous, fucked-up, insecure, neurotic and emotional *US, 1998*. ▶ **fine as May wine** excellent *US, 1964*

fine *adverb* ▶ **cut it fine; run it fine** to succeed by a very narrow margin *UK, 1871*

fine and dandy *noun* brandy. Rhyming slang *UK, 1971*

fine and dandy *adjective* splendid, excellent *US, 1910*

fine how-d' ya do *noun* a dilemma, a problem *US, 1946*

finest *noun* the police. Used with irony, alluding to the popular phrase identifying a city's policemen as 'the city's finest citizens'. In 1875, New York began to claim it had the 'finest police force in the world', a phrase borrowed from the claim of General Joseph Hooker during the US Civil War that he commanded 'the finest army on the planet'. In the early C20, New York began to refer to its fire department as 'the bravest' and the police simply as 'the finest' *US, 1914*

finest kind *noun* the very best *US, 1981*

fine stuff *noun* marijuana that has been cleaned and trimmed, also marijuana in general *US, 1955*

fine thing *noun* a sexually attractive female *IRELAND, 1991*

fine tuner *noun* in car repair, a sledge hammer. Facetious *US, 1992*

fine up *verb* (of weather) to improve *CANADA, 1990*

fine weather *noun* a pretty girl *US, 1947*

f-ing *adjective* ▷*see:* EFFING

fingee *noun* a new member of personnel, especially one who is not wished for or welcomed. Derived, loosely, from 'fucking new guy' *US, 1990*

finger *noun* **1** a gesture of contempt, the index finger raised from a fist with the palm inwards as the hand jerks upward suggesting an intimate destination. Often accompanied with an invitation to 'spin on it' or the elliptical 'oliver!' (OLIVER TWIST). *US, 1961*. **2** an unpopular individual. Metropolitan Police slang *UK, 1970*. **3** a pickpocket *UK, 1925*. **4** a marijuana cigarette. From the shape *UK, 2001*. **5** an individual banana in a bunch *CAYMAN ISLANDS, 1985*. **6** a citizens' band radio antenna *US, 1976*. ▶ **get your finger out; pull your finger out; take your finger out; pull it out** to stop time-wasting and start doing something useful. Often used as a semi-exclamatory injunction. Probably 'out from up your arse' but there is no need to say so *UK, 1959*. ▶ **have your finger up your arse** to be doing nothing *UK, 1964*. ▶ **lift a finger; move a finger** to make the slightest effort, usually applied in a negative sense to a lack of effort *UK, 1936*. ▶ **on the finger** on credit *US, 1951*. ▶ **put the finger on** to identify; to name; to inform on somebody *US, 1924*. ▶ **put your finger on** to identify or explain exactly *UK, 1973*

finger *verb* **1** to identify; to name; to inform upon somebody *US, 1930*. **2** to digitally stimulate/explore the vagina or anus as a part of sexual foreplay *UK, 1937*

finger and ring *adjective* very close *TRINIDAD AND TOBAGO, 2003*

finger and thumb; finger *noun* **1** a mother *UK, 1992*. **2** a companion, a friend. Rhyming slang for CHUM *UK, 1961*. **3** a drum. Rhyming slang *UK, 1992*. **4** the buttocks. Rhyming slang for BUM *UK, 2002*. **5** rum *UK, 1851*

finger artist *noun* a lesbian *US, 1970*

fingerbang *verb* to insert a finger or fingers into a partner's vagina or rectum for their sexual pleasure *US, 1990*

finger bowl faggot *noun* a wealthy, ostentatious, homosexual male *US, 1965*

finger cot *noun* a latex covering used by a doctor on his finger when examining a rectum or vagina *US, 1973*

finger flip *verb* in skateboarding, to perform a jump during which the board moves laterally through 360 degrees *UK, 2003*

fingerfuck *noun* the manual stimulation of another's vagina or anus *US, 1971*

fingerfuck *verb* to insert a finger or fingers into a partner's vagina or rectum. Plain-speaking former US President Lyndon Johnson (1963–1969) was said to have said 'Richard Milhouse Nixon has done for the United States of America what pantyhose did for finger-fucking' *UK, 1793*

finger-fucker *noun* a person who fingerfucks *US, 1969*

finger horse *noun* in horse racing, the favourite *US, 1951*

finger in the pie *noun* an involvement in an activity, especially a share in the profits of something *UK, 1659*

finger job *noun* **1** digital stimulation of the vagina or anus *US, 1963*. **2** an act of betrayal *US, 1974*

finger lid *noun* marijuana *UK, 2003*

finger line *noun* a line-up in which crime victims or witnesses attempt to identify the criminal(s) *US, 1976*

finger louse *noun* a police informer *US, 1956*

finger man *noun* **1** a person who provides criminals with inside information to aid a robbery or other crime *US, 1930*. **2** a professional killer *US, 1930*

finger poker *noun* a game of poker bet on credit *US, 1951*

fingerprint *noun* in poker, a player's signature move *US, 1996*

fingerprint *verb* in trucking, to manually unload a trailer *US, 1971*

finger-puppet audition *noun* an act of masturbation *UK, 2003*

fingers *noun* a piano player *US, 1973*. ▶ **have your fingers in the till** to steal from your employer or place of work *UK, 1974*. ▶ **the fingers** a gesture (the forefinger and the middle finger are extended to form a V shape, the palm turned in towards the gesturer) that is used to insult or otherwise cause offence, especially when made in conjunction with threatening or abusive language e.g. 'fuck off!' or 'up yours!' with which the sign may be considered synonymous *UK, 2003*

Fingers *nickname* used as a pickpocket's nickname *US, 1949*

fingers crossed! used for expressing hope. Describes the action – the middle finger twisted over and around the forefinger – that doesn't always accompany the words. A basic prayer, representing the sign of the cross, although the Christian God is mostly forgotten in familiar and superstitious usage. The gesture, but not the term, may also accompany the swearing of an oath, or may represent friendship and sexual contact *UK, 1924*

finger sheet *noun* in horse racing, a publication giving the entries and odds for a day's races *US, 1951*

fingersmith *noun* **1** a pickpocket *UK, 1823*. **2** a thief *BARBADOS, 1965*

fingers to fingers used as an oath and pledge. The original pledge was heard on the US television comedy *The Life of Riley* (NBC, 1949–58); the full pledge, used by the Brooklyn Patriots of Los Angeles fraternal group, was 'Fingers to fingers, toes to toes, if I break this pact, break my nose'. On the comedy *The Honeymooners* (CBS, 1955–56), the toast version used by the fraternal order of Raccoons was 'Fingers to fingers, thumbs to thumbs, watch out below, here she comes' *US, 1950*

fingertip *noun* in the car sales business, power steering *US, 1953*

fingertips *noun* someone adept at masturbating others *US, 1990*

finger-walk *verb* with one hand, to roll a coin over and through the knuckles *US, 1981*

finger wave *noun* **1** a digital examination of the rectum, either as part of an prostate examination or a drug search *US, 1962*. **2** a

gesture with the middle finger, usually interpreted to mean 'fuck you!' *US, 1976*

fingy *noun* a new arrival in Antarctica. A pronunciation of FNG or FUCKING NEW GUY *ANTARCTICA, 2003*

finif *noun* **1** a five-dollar note. From the Yiddish *finif* (five) *US, 1859*. **2** a prison sentence of five years *US, 1904*. **3** in dice games, a five on one die *US, 1950*

finish *verb* ▶ **finish on the chinstrap** in horse racing, to win a race easily under restraint *US, 1951*

finishing school *noun* a reformatory for juvenile delinquents *US, 1976*

finito the end, no more. Italian *finito* (finished). The elaboration 'finito, Benito' adds an Italian name – thus stressing the word's Italian origin *UK, 1975*

fink *noun* **1** an informer *US, 1902*. **2** a non-union job or worker *US, 1917*. **3** in circus and carnival usage, a broken piece of merchandise *US, 1981*

fink *verb* to inform on *US, 1925*

fink-and-fort it *adjective* used of a London working-class accent. A phonetic representation of 'think and thought it' *UK, 2001*

fink book *noun* the record of a longshoreman's or seafarer's employment. The books were used by employers to punish labour activists and enforce non-union conditions in the workplace *US, 1934*

fink out *verb* to betray; to inform *US, 1962*

finky *adjective* disloyal, cowardly *US, 1948*

Finlay Quaye *adjective* homosexual. Rhyming slang for 'gay', formed from the name of a singer who enjoyed notable success in the late 1990s *UK, 2003*

finny *adjective* (used of a hand or foot) deformed *BARBADOS, 1965*

Finsbury Park *noun* an arc light. Rhyming slang, formed from the name of an area of North London *UK, 1992*

finski *noun* a five-dollar note *US, 1952*

fin-up *noun* a prison sentence of five years to life *US, 1962*

FIP *noun* a scene in a pornographic film or a photograph of a man pretending to ejaculate inside a vagina or rectum. An initialism for 'fake internal pop-shot'; used in softcore pornography *US, 1995*

fir *noun* marijuana *US, 1984*

fire *noun* **1** matches or a cigarette lighter *US, 1959*. **2** a detonator *UK, 1956*. **3** a sexually transmitted infection *NORFOLK ISLAND, 1992*. **4** a combination of crack cocaine and methamphetamine *UK, 1998*. **5** a running car engine. Usually in the context of a comment such as 'your fire went out' when a motorist shuts off his engine *US, 1962*. **6** a car heater *NEW ZEALAND, 1998*. ▶ **I wouldn't spit on him (her) if he (she) was on fire; I wouldn't piss on him if he was on fire** I detest him (her) *UK, 1979*. ▶ **on fire** (used of a homosexual) patently, obviously. As in FLAMING *US, 1994*

fire *verb* **1** to light up a cigarette or a marijuana cigarette. Literally 'to apply a flame' *US, 1950*. **2** (of a mechanical device) to start up. Also 'fire up' as a variant *US, 2000*. **3** to inject a drug intravenously *US, 1936*. **4** to dismiss from employment. A pun on 'discharge' *US, 1887*. **5** to destroy by arson *US, 1957*. **6** to ejaculate *UK, 1891*. **7** to play a sport exceedingly well; to be 'on fire' *AUSTRALIA, 1977*. ▶ **fire a leak** to urinate *TRINIDAD AND TOBAGO, 2003*. ▶ **fire one** to have a drink *BARBADOS, 1965*. ▶ **fire the acid** to drink rum *JAMAICA, 1998*. ▶ **fire the ack-ack gun** to smoke a cigarette dipped in a heroin solution *US, 1969*

fire alarms *noun* arms (weaponry); the arms. Rhyming slang *UK, 1992*

fire-and-forget *adjective* (used of a missile) guided automatically *US, 1991*

fire away *verb* to commence, to start. Generally as imperative or invitation *UK, 1775*

fireball *noun* **1** an extremely energetic person *US, 1949*. **2** in pinball, a ball that leaves play without scoring any points *US, 1977*. **3** a tracer bullet *US, 1962*. **4** a short but intense use of artillery in the Vietnam war *US, 1991*

fire bomber *noun* an aircraft for fighting fire *CANADA, 1961*

firebug *noun* **1** an arsonist; a person with a pathological love of fire *US, 1872*. **2** in poker, a player who bets and plays in a reckless fashion *US, 1996*

fireburner *noun* a zealot *US, 1972*

firecan *noun* a type of radar system in a military aircraft *US, 1999*

firecracker *noun* a secret fragmentation artillery shell used on an experimental basis in Vietnam. The formal name was Controlled Fragmentation Munition, or CoFraM *US, 1991*

fired *adjective* excited, eager, sexually aroused *US, 1968*

fired up *adjective* enthusiastic *1999*

fire-eater *noun* a ferociously brave person *US, 1808*

fire engine *noun* corned beef served in a tomato sauce over white rice *BAHAMAS, 1982*

firefighter cute *adjective* describes an attractive young man. Teenspeak, post-11th September 2001 — the day firefighters became 'American heroes' *US, 2002*

firefly *noun* a helicopter equipped with a powerful search light, usually teamed with several gunships in the Vietnam war *US, 1991*

fire in the hole! **1** used as a warning that an explosive is about to be detonated *US, 1986*. **2** in the illegal production of alcohol, used as a warning of approaching law enforcement officials *US, 1974*

fire into *verb* to approach with an intent to seduce *UK, 1995*

fireless cooker *noun* a gas chamber *US, 1962*

fireman *noun* in a group smoking marijuana from a pipe, the second person to smoke *SOUTH AFRICA, 2004*

fireman's *noun* horse races. Rhyming slang, from 'fireman's braces' *AUSTRALIA, 1989*

fireman's hose; fireman's *noun* the nose. Rhyming slang *UK, 1992*

fire on *verb* **1** to excite sexually *US, 1969*. **2** to punch someone *US, 1973*

fire pie *noun* a red-headed woman's pubic hair and vulva *US, 2003*

fireplace *noun* in hot rodding, the grille on the front of a car *US, 1958*

fireproof *adjective* invulnerable *UK, 1984*

fire-rage *noun* an argument *BARBADOS, 1965*

fire track *noun* an armoured personnel carrier or tank equipped with a flame-thrower *US, 1991*

fire up *verb* **1** to light a pipe, a cigar or a cigarette *UK, 1890*. **2** to light and smoke a marijuana cigarette *US, 1962*. **3** to inject drugs *UK, 1996*. **4** to enthuse *UK, 1986*

firewater *noun* **1** strong alcohol. A term associated with Native Americans, often pronounced with an ambiguous accent approximating an accent used by Indian actors in old cowboy films *US, 1817*. **2** GBL, a drug that is nearly identical in molecular structure to the recreational drug GHB *US, 1999*. **3** spruce beer, and also, phosphorescence in salt water *CANADA, 1950*

fireworks *noun* **1** a great disturbance; dramatic excitement *UK, 1889*. **2** an exchange of gunfire *US, 1864*. **3** a police car with flashing lights *US, 1976*. **4** roadside flares warning motorists of an accident or other problem ahead *US, 1962*

firey; fire-ie; firee *noun* a firefighter, especially of bushfires *AUSTRALIA, 1996*

firing line *noun* ▶ **in the firing line** in danger of dismissal from employment; applied more widely to any who are identified as those who will be blamed or held to account *UK, 1961*

firm *noun* **1** a gang of football hooligans. A business-like self-description, adopted from professional criminals *UK, 1999*. **2** a criminal gang. From the conventional sense as a 'business' *UK, 1969*. **3** a squad of detectives, especially a close-knit group. A humorous adoption of the 'criminal gang' sense *UK, 1977*. **4** a criminal set-up between a police officer or officers, especially CID, and a criminal gang *UK, 1970*. ▶ **on the firm** as a constant arrangement, steadily *UK, 2001*. ▶ **the firm** the British royal family. Monarchy seen as a business is a notion very much in tune with the ethics of the late 1980s *UK, 2001*

firm up *verb* to form into a gang *UK, 2000*

first aid *noun* **1** a *blade* (as a weapon); a razor *blade*. Rhyming slang; thought to be inspired by the catchphrase threat: 'Can your wife [or mum] do first aid? Well get her to stitch this up' *UK, 1992*. **2** a small shop that sells, amongst other commodities, patent medicines *BARBADOS, 1965*

first aid kit; first aid *noun* the female breast. Rhyming slang for TIT, usually plural *UK, 1992*

first base *noun* **1** in teenage categorisation of sexual activity, a level of foreplay, most commonly referring to kissing. The exact degree varies by region and even by school *US, 1928*. **2** in blackjack played in American casinos, the seat immediately to the dealer's left *US, 1985*

first cab off the rank *noun* the first in a series *AUSTRALIA, 1966*

first call *noun* in Antarctica, the first ship to arrive at the South Pole each season *ANTARCTICA, 2003*

first class *adjective* extremely good *UK, 1879*

first dollar *noun* in television and film-making, the first money generated after release *US, 1990*

first drop *noun* in cricket, the 3rd position in the order of batting *UK, 1960*

First Fleeter *noun* a person, or a descendant of a person, who arrived on the first fleet of ships to bring British colonists to Australia in 1788. A great deal of pride is associated with this lineage in Australia *AUSTRALIA, 1826*

first horse *nickname* the First Cavalry Division, US Army *US, 1968*

first Louie *noun* a first lieutenant *US, 1991*

first off *adverb* as a beginning *US, 1880*

first-of-May *noun* **1** an inexperienced worker. A circus word, based on the start of the circus season *US, 1961*. **2** a newcomer to a circus or carnival *US, 1926*

First of the First *noun* the First Battalion of the First Regiment, US Marine Corps. Korean war usage *US, 1982*

first pig *noun* a first sergeant, the most senior non-commissioned officer in the US Army *US, 1975*

first reader *noun* a railway conductor's trainbook *US, 1946*

first sergeant *noun* your wife *US, 1976*

first shirt *noun* a first sergeant in the US Army *US, 1969*

first sleeve *noun* a first sergeant *US, 1956*

first soldier *noun* a first sergeant in the US Army *US, 1946*

first suck of the sauce bottle *noun* first in a queue *AUSTRALIA, 1971*

first today and last tomorrow in horse racing, said of an inconsistent performer *US, 1951*

fish *noun* **1** the vagina *UK, 1891*. **2** a woman, usually heterosexual *UK, 1891*. **3** a male homosexual. Prison slang *JAMAICA, 2002*. **4** a prisoner who has recently arrived in prison *US, 1864*. **5** a lover *NORFOLK ISLAND, 1992*. **6** a person. Always suffixed to an adjective *UK, 1722*. **7** a fool *UK, 2000*. **8** a heavy drinker *US, 1990*. **9** a drug addict who supports his habit by pimping *US, 1955*. **10** in poker, an unskilled player who is a likely victim of a skilled professional *US, 1996*. **11** in on-line poker, the weakest player in the game *2003*. **12** in cricket, a weak batsman *TRINIDAD AND TOBAGO, 1990*. **13** a poor chess player *US, 1971*. **14** in oil drilling, any object inadvertently dropped down a well *US, 1954*. **15** a Plymouth Barracuda car *US, 1976*. **16** a torpedo *US, 1948*. **17** a dollar *US, 1950*. **18** in electric line work, a glass strain insulator *US, 1980*. ▶ **have other fish to fry; have bigger fish to fry** to have other business, or other things to do or achieve *UK, 1660*

fish *verb* **1** to dance in a slow and sexual manner, moving the body but not the feet *US, 1952*. **2** in gin, to discard in a manner that is designed to lure a desired card from an opponent *US, 1965*. **3** in poker, to stay with a bad hand in the hope of drawing the only card that can possibly make the hand a good one *US, 2003*. **4** to use a prison's plumbing system to pass a note from cell to cell *US, 2000*. ▶ **fish for food** to gossip *US, 1947*. ▶ **fish on the half-line** in the Maritime Provinces, to fish for half of the catch as wages *CANADA, 1983*. ▶ **fish or cut bait; fish, cut bait or go ashore** make up your mind! The shorter, two-option phrase is more popular today than the longer original *US, 1860*

fish used as a euphemism for 'fuck', a cry of despair, surprise, rage, resignation; an abbreviated euphemism for 'fuck off', a cry of disbelief. Often lingering on the 'f' before pronouncing the 'ish' so that a disguised intention is made obvious *UK, 1998*

fish and chip; fish *noun* **1** the *lip, lip* (impudence). Rhyming slang *UK, 1992*. **2** a gratuity. Rhyming slang for 'tip' *UK, 1992*

fish and chips *noun* in poker, a group of unskilled players with a lot of money to lose *US, 1996*

fish and shrimp *noun* a pimp. Rhyming slang *US, 1935*

fish and tank *noun* a bank. Rhyming slang *UK, 1998*

fishbelly *noun* a white person *US, 1985*

fishbite *noun* the condition that exists when someone pulls your trousers or underpants forcefully upward, forming a wedge between buttock cheeks *US, 1990*

fishbowl *noun* **1** a room in HMP Wormwood Scrubs where prisoners meet their visitors *UK, 1996*. **2** the area in a prison where newly arrived prisoners are housed *US, 1992*

fish bull *noun* a new and young prison guard *US, 1984*

fish-burner *noun* a sled dog. An extension of the early C20 'hay-burner' (horse) *US, 1967*

fish cake *noun* five dollars *US, 1985*

fishcunt *noun* used by adolescent boys as a derisory term for any girl of similar maturity. Describes an olfactory and physical difference between the genders *UK, 1997*

fish-eater *noun* a Roman Catholic. From the largely forgotten practice of abstaining from eating meat on Fridays *US, 1980*

fisherman's daughter; fisherman's *noun* water. Rhyming slang. One of several terms that have 'daughter' as the common (dispensable) element *UK, 1888*

fisherman's dinner *noun* a steak *CANADA, 1989*

fish eye *noun* an expressionless stare. From the appearance *US, 1941*

fish eyes *noun* tapioca *US, 1918*

fish fingers *noun* said of fingers that have been used to stimulate a woman's vagina *AUSTRALIA, 1985*

fish frighteners *noun* a pair of men's close-fitting and revealing nylon swimming trunks *AUSTRALIA, 2003*

fish gallery *noun* the area in a prison where newly arrived prisoners are kept *US, 1962*

fishhead *noun* a person from Southeast Asia *US, 1971*

fish-hook *noun* **1** in a deck of playing cards, any seven *US, 1967*. **2** in a deck of playing cards, a jack or knave *US, 1981*

fish-hooks *noun* problems *NEW ZEALAND, 2002*

fishies *noun* MDMA, the recreational drug best known as ecstasy *US, 2002*

fishing expedition *noun* a litigation tactic of requesting a broad range of probably irrelevant information in the hope of discovering something helpful *US, 1874*

fishing pole *noun* any contrivance fashioned to pass or retrieve items from cell to cell *US, 2001*

fish line *noun* in a prison, a string used to pull objects from one cell to another *US, 1989*

fishmonger *noun* a lesbian. Conventionally 'one who deals in fish' (*Oxford English Dictionary*), playing on FISH (the vagina) *UK, 2002*

fish 'n' chip mob *noun* anyone who is considered socially wanting due to lack of breeding or hereditary privilege. Patronising upper-class usage; originally military for any regiment considered socially inferior *UK, 1982*

fisho *noun* an angler *AUSTRALIA, 1971*

fish queen *noun* a homosexual male who spends a great deal of time in the company of heterosexual women *US, 1941*

fish scale *noun* crack cocaine. From the appearance *US, 1989*

fish scales *noun* cocaine *US, 2002*

fishskin *noun* a condom *US, 1936*

fishtail *verb* to cause the rear of an aeroplane or car to swerve from side to side *US, 1927*

fish tank *noun* **1** a holding cell for newly arrived prisoners. A wonderful pun with independently formed terms *US, 1962*. **2** a bus *UK, 1981*

fish wife *noun* a married male homosexual's wife *US, 1971*

fishy *adjective* inducing suspicion *US, 1840*

fist city *noun* a physical fight *US, 1930*

fister *noun* a person who inserts their hand into another's vagina or rectum for sexual gratification *US, 1999*

fist fuck; fist *verb* to insert your lubricated fist into a partner's rectum or vagina, leading to sexual pleasure for both *US, 1972*

fist-fucker *noun* **1** a practitioner of fist fucking *US, 1972*. **2** a frequent, obsessive masturbator *US, 1962*

fist-fucking; fisting *noun* **1** the practice of inserting the hand (and part of the arm) into a partner's anus (or vagina) for the sexual pleasure of all involved. Predominantly gay usage but also found in heterosexual practice *US, 1972*. **2** masturbation *UK, 1891*

fist it! be quiet! *US, 1994*

fist sandwich *noun* a punch in the mouth *US, 1982*

fit *noun* **1** the equipment needed to inject a drug. A shortened form of OUTFIT. Also recorded in England *US, 1959*. **2** an outfit of clothing *US, 1972*. ▶ **have a fit; have forty fits** to lose your temper, to become very angry *UK, 1877*

fit *adjective* sexually attractive. Originally a black term, now in wider usage; coinage is obviously informed by the conventional sense as 'healthy' *UK, 2000*. ▶ **are you fit?** are you ready? *UK, 1984*

fit 'n' furry *adjective* used as a description of a hirsute, sexually attractive man *UK, 2003*

fit; fit up; fix up *verb* to ensure that someone is convicted of a criminal charge, often by nefarious means; to frame *AUSTRALIA, 1882*. ▶ **fit just like a smack on the lips** (of a raincoat) to be the perfect size *CANADA, 1988*. ▶ **fit where they touch; fits where it touches** applied to loose or ill-fitting clothes *UK, 1932*

fit and spasm *noun* an orgasm. Rhyming slang, formed on appropriate imagery *UK, 2003*

fit as a fiddle *adjective* in good health or condition *UK, 1616*

fitbin *noun* the vagina *UK, 2001*

fit fanny *noun* a sexually attractive woman or women *UK, 2003*

FITH *adjective* demented, stupid. From 'fucked in the head' *AUSTRALIA, 1987*

fitness *noun* sexually attractive young women. From FIT (sexually attractive) *UK, 1994*

fitted *adjective* **1** falsely incriminated *UK, 1998*. **2** well-dressed *US, 2003*

fit to *adjective* at the point of doing something; likely to do something *UK, 1585*

fit to be tied *adjective* very angry, furious *US, 1894*

five *noun* **1** a slap of the hand in greeting *US, 1959*. **2** five pounds *UK, 2001*. **3** an amphetamine tablet *US, 1993*. **4** a five-year prison sentence *UK, 1958*. **5** Chanel No. 5™ perfume *US, 1994*. ▶ **come and take five** to make a short visit *GRENADA, 1976*. ▶ **get your five** to attain the highest rank in the Canadian civil service *CANADA, 1995*. ▶ **give five** to shake hands or to slap hands in a greeting *US, 1935*. ▶ **take five** to take a short break *US, 1929*

five and dime *noun* in poker, a hand with a five and a ten and three other unpaired cards in between *US, 1968*

five and two *noun* used as a formula for the services of a prostitute – her fee and the room fee *US, 1970*

five-by-five; five-by *adverb* loud and clear *US, 1954*

five by two *noun* a Jewish person *AUSTRALIA, 1984*

five-card Charlie *noun* in casino blackjack games, a bonus paid to a player who draws three cards and still has a total count of 21 or less *US, 1996*

five-cent paper *noun* five dollars' worth of a drug *US, 1971*

five-digit disco *noun* an act of female masturbation *UK, 2004*

five finger *noun* a thief, especially a pickpocket *US, 1932*

five-finger *verb* to shoplift *US, 1919*

five-finger discount *noun* theft by shoplifting *US, 1966*

five-fingered chequebook *noun* acquisition by shoplifting *NEW ZEALAND, 1994*

five-fingered Mary *noun* a man's hand as the means of masturbation *US, 1971*

five-fingered widow *noun* (of a male) the hand as a masturbatory tool; masturbation *UK, 1977*

five fingers *noun* a five-year prison sentence *US, 1992*

five hundred club *noun* the notional association of all those who have been in Antarctica for more than 500 consecutive days *ANTARCTICA, 2003*

five-knuckle shuffle *noun* masturbation *US, 1972*

five-K rig *noun* a 5000 watt public address system *UK, 1985*

five-o *noun* fifty *US, 1983*

five o'clock follies *noun* during the Vietnam war, the daily military press briefings *US, 1966*

five o'clock shadow *noun* fast-growing, dark facial whiskers, which give the appearance of needing a shave by late in the afternoon. President Richard Nixon was known and ridiculed for his *US, 1937*

five of clubs *noun* the fist. Often used in constructions such as 'I dealt him the five of clubs' *US, 1947*

five-oh *noun* the police; a police officer. From *Hawaii Five-O*, a police television series that aired from September 1968 to April 1980, featuring an elite four-man police unit *US, 1983*

five on the sly; five on the soul side *noun* a mutual slapping of palms as an 'inside' greeting *US, 1980*

five-pinner *noun* a bowler in a five-pin game *CANADA, 1957*

five-pound word *noun* any profanity. From the fine that one might receive for using profanity *BAHAMAS, 1982*

fiver *noun* **1** a five-pound or five-dollar note *US, 1843*. **2** in craps, the number five *US, 1985*

fiver-finger *noun* money. Derived from shoplifting and pickpocketing *UK, 1996*

fiver, fiver, racetrack driver *noun* in craps, the number five *US, 1985*

fives *noun* **1** dice that have been altered to have two fives, the second five being where one would expect to find a two. Used in combination with DEUCES, likely to produce a seven, an important number in the game of craps *US, 1974*. **2** the fifth landing or floor level in a prison *UK, 1996*. **3** the fingers *US, 1973*

fives! used to reserve your seat as you briefly leave the room. The promise inherent is to be right back – in, let's say, *five* minutes *US, 1996*

fives-a-pair *noun* fifty-five miles an hour. The near-universal speed limit on US roads from the mid-1970s until the early 90s *US, 1976*

fives artist *noun* an expert at a shortchanging scheme using a five-dollar note *US, 1953*

five-six-seven *noun* collectively, Chevrolets manufactured in 1955, 1956 or 1957. Five-six-seven clubs exist in several North American cities, dedicated to the restoration and preservation of 1955, 1956 and 1957 Chevrolets, Corvettes, Pontiacs and Chevrolet and GMC trucks *US, 1993*

five-spot *noun* **1** a five-dollar note *US, 1892*. **2** a five pound note. Adopted directly from the prervious sense *UK, 1984*. **3** a prison sentence of five years *US, 1901*

five-square *adverb* loud and clear *US, 1956*

five thousand *US* ▷*see:* **5000**

five to four *adjective* *sure*, certain. Rhyming slang *UK, 1992*

five-to-lifers *noun* a pair of shoes issued to prisoners by the state. Purported to last at least five years *US, 1989*

five to two *noun* a Jewish person. Rhyming slang for 'Jew' *UK, 1932*

five twenty-nine *noun* a jail sentence of one day less than six months. The maximum sentence for a misdemeanour charge in some jursidictions *US, 1953*

five watter *noun* *UK* ▷*see:* **5 WATTER**

five-way *noun* a powdered-drug cocktail of cocaine, heroin, flunitrazepam and methamphetamine ingested nasally whilst also drinking alcohol. Probably applies to any mix of five recreational stimulants *UK, 2002*

five will get you ten used for an expression of confidence in the assertion that follows *US, 1990*

fivezies *noun* in poker, a pair of fives *US, 1988*

fix *noun* **1** an injection of a drug, especially heroin *US, 1936*. **2** by extension, what a person craves or needs *US, 1993*. **3** an illegal arrangement *US, 1948*. **4** a well-thought-out plan with criminal intent *AUSTRALIA, 1975*. **5** trouble, a difficult position *US, 1834*. **6** in the slang of pool players, proper position for the next shot or shots *US, 1970*. ▶ **get a fix on** to make a plan of action *US, 1955*

fix *verb* **1** to inject or otherwise ingest a drug, especially heroin *US, 1936*. **2** to prepare *US, 1725*. **3** (with connotations of coercion or violence) to deal with someone, or settle a situation, or exact revenge *UK, 1961*. **4** to falsely incriminate. Also variant 'fix up' *US, 1790*. **5** to neuter (an animal), to castrate *US, 1970*. **6** to have sex with *FIJI, 1992*. ▶ **be fixing to do something** be preparing to do something; be about to do something *US, 1971*. ▶ **fix someone's pipe** in the usage of counterculturalists associated with the Rainbow Nation gatherings, to give someone marijuana *US, 1997*. ▶ **fix your bones** to use drugs, especially while suffering withdrawal pains *US, 1992*

fixed *adjective* situated *US, 1958*

fixer *noun* **1** a person who can solve problems informally *US, 1972*. **2** a person who takes care of legal problems encountered by a circus or carnival *US, 1900*. **3** an agent working for the police *UK, 1996*

fixit *noun* a criminal enterprise in which cars are given new identities *UK, 1972*

fix or repair daily *noun* a Ford truck; any Ford vehicle. A back formation from the initials FORD. Contemporary UK motor trade slang *US, 1971*

fix up *verb* to arrange a (romantic) introduction and meeting on someone else's behalf *US, 1930*

fix up ▷*see:* **FIT; FIT UP**

fizgig; fizzgig *verb* to work as an informer *AUSTRALIA, 1985*

fizgig; fizzgig *noun* a police informer. Also spelt with 'ph' *AUSTRALIA, 1895*

fizz *noun* any sparkling wine *UK, 1864*

fizzed *adjective* gently drunk *UK, 1999*

fizzer *noun* **1** a failure; a dud. From the sense as 'a dud firework.' *AUSTRALIA, 1957*. **2** in the military, a charge of misconduct *UK, 1935*. **3** a police informer. From FIZGIG *AUSTRALIA, 1943*. **4** the face. A variation of PHIZOG used in Glasgow *UK: SCOTLAND, 1996*

fizzler *noun* a failure *NEW ZEALAND, 1984*

fizzog *noun* ▷*see:* **PHIZOG**

fizzy boat *noun* a small but loud motorboat *NEW ZEALAND, 1998*

flab *noun* fat, flabbiness, obesity *UK, 1923*

flabbergast *verb* to astound, to utterly confuse *UK, 1772*. ▶ **my flabber is gasted; never has my flabber been so gasted** I am astounded or astonished. Jocular phrases formed on the verb FLABBERGAST (to astound). The second form is particularly associated with British comedian Frankie Howerd, 1917–92 *UK, 1984*

flabby labby *noun* unusually pronounced vaginal labia *US, 2003*

flack *noun* a publicist; a spokesperson *US, 1939*

fladanked *adjective* drug-intoxicated *US, 1997*

fladge; flage *noun* flagellation *UK, 1948*

flag *noun* **1** a criminal gang's lookout *US, 1949*. **2** while injecting a drug into a vein, the flow of blood up into the syringe, indicating that the vein has been pierced *US, 1989*. **3** a variable which changes value when a certain condition is reached *US, 1991*. **4** in gambling, a wager of 23 bets consisting of four selections *UK, 2001*. **5** the grade 'F' *US, 1968*. **6** the ground floor of a tiered prison cellblock *US, 1992*. **7** a one-pound note *AUSTRALIA, 1989*. ▶ **have the flags out** to experience the bleed period of the menstrual cycle *AUSTRALIA, 1968*. ▶ **have your flag in port** to experience the bleed period of the menstrual cycle *US, 1966*. ▶ **the flag is up; the red flag is up** experiencing the bleed period of the menstrual cycle *US, 1980*

flag *verb* **1** to label or categorise someone *US, 1992*. **2** in the military, to make an entry on a soldier's record which will prevent further promotion *US, 1970*. **3** to give a student in college a notification of academic deficiency *US, 1968*. **4** to display or wear prominently (a handkerchief or other symbol of sexual taste) *US, 1896*. **5** to wear an article of clothing signifying gang membership *US, 1995*. **6** to arrest *US, 1927*. **7** to fail (a test or course) *US, 1965*. **8** to skip, as in missing a class *US, 1997*

flag country *noun* in the US Navy, the area where an admiral works *US, 1991*

flag day *noun* the bleed period of the menstrual cycle *US, 1968*

flag football *noun* a friendly, non-competitive game of poker. In the US, flag football is played with a tame set of rules which forbid most of the physical contact associated with the game *US, 1996*

flagging *adjective* said of a woman experiencing the bleed period of her menstrual cycle *US, 1954*

flag-off *noun* a commencement *INDIA, 2004*

flag off *verb* to start, to commence. From the use of a flag to signal the start of a race *INDIA, 2004*

flagpole *noun* the erect penis. Especially in the phrase 'properly saluting the flagpole' (oral sex) *US, 1922*

flag's up! in circus and carnival usage, used for conveying that a meal is ready *US, 1981*

flag unfurled *noun* the world. Rhyming slang, replacing the earlier sense (man of the world) *UK, 1992*

flag up *verb* to draw attention to, to advertise *UK, 2002*

flag-waver *noun* **1** a rousing, patriotic song or performance *US, 1937*. **2** in horse racing, a horse that flicks its tail up and down while racing *US, 1951*

flah *verb* to have sexual intercourse. The word appears to be most commonly used in Cork *IRELAND, 2003*

flahulach *adjective* generous *IRELAND, 1967*

flail *verb* to surf awkwardly *US, 1990*

flak *noun* abuse, criticism. From the original sense (anti-aircraft fire) *US, 1963*

flake *noun* **1** cocaine *US, 1961*. **2** the shavings off a solid mass of crack cocaine *US, 1983*. **3** an unreliable, unstable person *US, 1959*. **4** the planting of evidence on a suspected criminal *US, 1973*. **5** in the Maritime Provinces, a wooden rack for drying fish *CANADA, 1963*

flake *verb* **1** to plant evidence on a suspected criminal *US, 1972*. **2** to fall asleep; to pass out. Often used as the variant 'flake out' *US, 1955*

flake artist *noun* a police officer inclined to plant evidence on a suspected criminal *US, 1973*

flaked *adjective* unconscious. A shortening of FLAKED OUT *US, 1959*

flaked out *adjective* exhausted, unconscious *US, 1958*

flake of corn *noun* an erection (of the penis). Rhyming slang for HORN *UK, 1992*

flake off *verb* to go away *US, 1957*

flake off and die, dude! used as an all-purpose insult *US, 1988*

flake out *verb* to collapse *UK, 1942*

flakers *adjective* **1** drunk to the point of passing out *NEW ZEALAND, 1978*. **2** tired, exhausted *UK, 1987*

flakie *noun* ▶ **take a flakie; throw a flakie** to have a fit of temper. Glasgow slang *UK: SCOTLAND, 1988*

flak shack *noun* a military hospital or hospital ward where soldiers suffering from war-related psychological problems are treated *US, 1944*

flak trap *noun* a tactic used by the North Vietnamese in which anti-aircraft fire is withheld from the area of a downed US aircraft until the rescue aircraft get near *US, 1955*

flaky *adjective* inattentive, distracted, unreliable. Partridge suggested a connection between the adjective and cocaine, which was 'flaky' in nature *US, 1959*

flam *noun* a deceptive front *UK, 1632*

flam *verb* to swindle, to fool, to deceive *UK, 1637*

flamage *noun* incendiary rhetoric used in a computer posting or internet discussion group *US, 1991*

flame *noun* **1** a cigarette lighter *US, 1994*. **2** an insulting or aggressive e-mail or Internet discussion group posting. The collective noun is FLAMAGE *US, 1983*

flame *verb* to post insulting personal attacks on others posting messages on an Internet bulletin board or in an Internet discussion group, or to send an insulting personal attack by e-mail. From an earlier sense of simply 'insulting', in the absence of any computer technology *US, 1981*

flamebait *noun* a message posted in an Internet discussion group for the express purpose of soliciting insulting messages *US, 1995*

flame bath *noun* the dropping of 55-gallon drums of combustible liquids from a utility helicopter, followed by flares that ignite the fuel *US, 1970*

flame cooking *noun* the process of smoking freebase cocaine by placing the pipe over a flame *2002*

flamefest *noun* a protracted exchange of insulting and inflammatory messages on an Internet discussion group *US, 1995*

flame-out *noun* **1** in hot rodding and motor racing, a complete failure of the ignition system while the car is operating *US, 1965*. **2** an empty petrol tank *US, 1960*

flamer *noun* **1** a blatant and conspicuous homosexual *US, 1948*. **2** an alcoholic drink which is set on fire in the glass (after the flames have been extinguished the fumes are inhaled before the drink is swallowed); an alcoholic drink which is set alight in the drinker's mouth in the hope that swallowing puts the flame out *UK, 2001*. **3** an Internet user who posts vitriolic, insulting messages in Internet discussion groups *US, 1983*. **4** a pistol *US, 1997*

flamethrower *noun* **1** in hot rodding and drag racing, an ignition system that has been greatly enhanced *US, 1958*. **2** a diesel truck with flames showing on the smokestack from an incorrect fuel-to-air ratio *US, 1971*. **3** a cigarette dressed with cocaine and heroin *UK, 1998*

flame war *noun* a virulent exchange of insulting messages in an Internet discussion group *US, 1995*

flaming *adjective* **1** (used of a homosexual) patently, obviously *US, 1941*. **2** used as an intensifier *UK, 1895*

flaming asshole *noun* a truly despicable person *US, 1968*

flaming coffin *nickname* a DH-4 bomber aircraft *US, 1919*

flaming end *noun* a remarkable and pleasing thing or person *UK, 1983*

flaming fury *noun* a toilet built over a deep pit in the ground, the contents of which are periodically set alight *AUSTRALIA, 1960*

flaming hell! used for registering surprise, anger, amazement, etc. A euphemism for FUCKING HELL! rather than a literal elaboration of 'hell' *UK, 1984*

flaming Nora! used as a euphemistic replacement for 'flaming hell!'. Coined for the racial tension situation comedy *Love Thy Neighbour*, 1972–76. The *Coronation Street* character Jack Duckworth, since 1979, also uses the television-friendly term, hence its wider currency *UK, 1979*

flaming onion *nickname* the Ordnance Corps of the US Army. From the flaming grenade insignia *US, 1944*

flaming piss pot *nickname* the Ordnance Corps of the US Army. From the flaming grenade insignia *US, 1980*

flaming well *adverb* damned well *AUSTRALIA, 1955*

Flanagan & Allen; flanagan *noun* a *gallon* (of motor fuel). Rhyming slang, formed from the names of music hall comedians

Bud Flanagan, 1896–1968, and Chesney Allen, 1894–1982, who worked together as a double act and as part of the Crazy Gang *UK, 1992*

flange *noun* **1** the vagina *AUSTRALIA, 1996*. **2** the outer lips of the vagina *AUSTRALIA, 1985*

flange *verb* to walk along *UK, 2002*

flange-head *noun* a Chinese person *US, 1949*

flanger *noun* in target shooting, a shot that strikes outside a close group of shots on the target *US, 1957*

flanker *noun* a trick, a swindle, a doublecross. Originally military; usually as 'do/play/pull/work *a flanker'* *UK, 1923*

flannel *noun* empty and pretentious talk *UK, 1927*

flannel *verb* to flatter; to deceive *UK, 1941*

flannelmouth *noun* a loudmouth; an insincere, silver-tongued talker *US, 1881*

flannel-mouthed *adjective* thick-tongued, especially as the result of drinking to excess *US, 1973*

flannel panel *noun* in a magazine, a list of who did what in that edition *UK, 2002*

flannie *noun* a flannelette shirt *AUSTRALIA, 1996*

flanno *noun* a flannelette shirt *AUSTRALIA, 1996*

flanno *adjective* made from flannelette *AUSTRALIA, 1987*

flap *noun* **1** a disturbance or crisis *UK, 1916*. **2** the mouth *AUSTRALIA, 1960*. **3** the ear. As a plural it is often the nickname for men with large ears *UK, 1977*. **4** strands of hair that a semi-bald man may cultivate and style to lay over his naked pate *UK, 1992*. **5** a cheque. Underworld and prison use *AUSTRALIA, 1955*

flap *verb* **1** to be agitated; to panic, to dither *UK, 1912*. **2** while surfing, to make awkward flapping arm motions trying to gain your balance *US, 1991*. ▶ **flap skin** to have sex *US, 1990*

flapdoodle *noun* nonsense *UK, 1833*

flapjacked *adjective* drunk *US, 2002*

flapjaw *noun* a person who talks incessantly *US, 1950*

flapper *noun* **1** the penis in a flaccid state *US, 1980*. **2** the ear *US, 1933*. **3** a radio antenna *US, 1976*

flapper steak *noun* a pig's ear sandwich *US, 1947*

flapper track *nickname* an unofficial greyhound race track often used so that dogs could get a 'kill' to sharpen their appetites before an official race *IRELAND, 1977*

flapping track *noun* a small, unlicensed dog racing track *UK, 1977*

flaps *noun* **1** the female breasts *US, 1972*. **2** the vaginal lips; the *labia majora* or *minora*. Although there is some evidence of 'flap' meaning 'the vagina' in C17, it is long obsolete; this sense is a shortening of the synonymous PISS FLAPS *UK, 2002* ▷*see:* FLAP

flare *noun* a type of scratch (a manipulation of a record to create a musical effect) that cuts out the middle of a sample. Named after DJ Flare who invented the move in the late 1980s *US, 2002*

flared *adjective* **1** drunk *CANADA, 1965*. **2** angry *US, 1993*

flare kicker *noun* the crew member who operates an airship's flare dispenser *US, 1997*

flares *noun* flared trousers *US, 1964*

flash *noun* **1** a sudden onset of drug-induced effects *US, 1946*. **2** LSD *US, 1994*. **3** any central nervous system stimulant *UK, 1983*. **4** illicitly distilled alcohol. Used by British expatriates in Saudi Arabia *UK, 1981*. **5** a revelation; an epiphany; a satori *US, 1924*. **6** in a striptease show, the stripper's entrance onto the stage *US, 1945*. **7** a large number of small-denomination banknotes with a large-denomination note showing, giving the impression of a great deal of money *UK, 1996*. **8** inexpensive, showy jewellery *US, 1927*. **9** an inexpensive carnival prize that is so appealing that people will spend great sums trying to win it *US, 1927*. **10** a suit of clothes *US, 1950*. **11** the appearance of wealth or success *US, 1975*. **12** a know-all. Used in borstals and detention centres *UK, 1978*. **13** in horse racing, a last-minute change in odds *US, 1951*. ▶ **bit of flash** ostentation, a superficial show *UK, 1962*

flash *verb* **1** to exhibit as naked a part or parts of the body that are usually clothed *UK, 1893*. **2** to show off *UK, 1754*. **3** to show *UK, 1754*. **4** to display official credentials *UK, 1976*. **5** while dealing blackjack in a casino, to briefly and unintentionally expose the down card *US, 1980*. **6** to display prizes in a carnival game in order to attract customers *US, 1966*. **7** to vomit *US, 1968*. **8** to vomit after injecting heroin or while withdrawing from heroin use *US, 1957*. **9** to inhale glue or industrial solvents for the psychoactive effect *US, 1970*. **10** to remember an event from the past in a sudden and powerful manner. An abbreviation of 'flashback' *US, 1984*. **11** to break light bulbs in their sockets, either as an act of vandalism or preparatory to a crime *US, 1953*. **12** to commit a social gaffe *US, 1963*. ▶ **flash a brown** to drop your trousers and expose your buttocks *NEW ZEALAND, 1998*. ▶ **flash a joint** to display prizes in a carnival game *US, 1968*. ▶ **flash the ash** used as a demand that someone offer a cigarette. A variation of CRASH THE ASH; probably arose in the 1950s but now rare *UK, 1984*. ▶ **flash the cash** to spend some money; to offer payment *US, 1999*. ▶ **flash the gallery; flash the range** in prison, to use a small mirror to watch out for approaching guards while conducting some prohibited activity in your cell *US, 1981*. ▶ **flash the hash** to vomit *US, 1965*. ▶ **flash your ass** to commit a social gaffe *US, 1968*

flash *adjective* **1** ostentatious, showy *UK, 1785*. **2** impudent, cheeky *UK, 1980*

flashback *noun* a relapse into a hallucinatory drug experience long after the effect of the drug has worn off *US, 1971*

flash-bang *noun* an explosive device designed to deafen and blind without otherwise injuring *US, 1999*

flash cash *noun* a large, ostentatious bankroll *US, 1979*

flash cloth *noun* colourful draping used in a carnival concession *US, 1985*

flash dough *noun* counterfeit money *US, 1949*

flasher *noun* **1** a person with a psychopathological need to expose his or her genitals *US, 1962*. **2** a casino dealer who inadvertently reveals his down card *US, 1991*

flash flood *noun* in poker, a sudden sequence of good cards *US, 1996*

flash Harry *noun* an ostentatiously or expensively accoutred man. The character of Flash Harry created by George Cole (b.1925) in the *St Trinians* films (mid-1950s–mid-60s) is, perhaps, the most widely known popular usage – adding a shading of criminality to the meaning; Sir Malcolm Sargent (1895–1967), a conductor noted for his elegance and showmanship, is remembered by the nickname Flash Harry *UK, 1964*

flash house *noun* a room, apartment or house where amphetamine addicts gather to inject the drug *US, 1970*

flash mob *noun* a large crowd that materialises in a public place to perform a scripted action for several minutes before dissolving *US, 2003*

flash-mob *verb* to take part in a flash mob *UK, 2004*

flash mobber *noun* a participant in a flash mob *US, 2003*

flash money *noun* money, especially in a bankroll, intended for impressing, not spending *US, 1970*

flash on *verb* to think about with great intensity and focus *US, 1968*

flash paper *noun* paper that dissolves completely and quickly when exposed to water *US, 1973*

flash roll *noun* a large number of small-denomination banknotes with a large-denomination note showing, giving the impression of a great deal of money *US, 1987*

flash trash *noun* a gaudy, cheap woman *US, 1992*

flash up *verb* in circus and carnival usage, to add embellishments to a piece of clothing *US, 1981*

flat *noun* **1** a flat area for spectators in the centre of a racecourse *AUSTRALIA, 1846*. **2** in an illegal number gambling lottery, a bet that two digits will appear in the winning number *US, 1949*. **3** a police officer. Probably a shortening of FLATFOOT *UK, 1966*. **4** good quality tobacco, as opposed to prison issue tobacco *AUSTRALIA, 1902*. **5** a case of beer containing 24 bottles *CANADA, 2001*. **6** a conventional, law-abiding, boring person *UK, 1753*. **7** a smooth-sided subway (underground) carriage that lends itself to graffiti art *US, 1997*. **8** a credit card *UK, 1977*

Flat *noun* the season of flat horse racing *UK, 1937*

flat *adjective* **1** without money, broke. A shortening of 'flat broke' *US, 1832*. **2** (of a prison sentence) full, unqualified *US, 1972*. **3** (used of a bet) unvarying in amount *US, 1978*. ▶ **that's flat; and that's flat** used for emphasis or for concluding a preceding remark. An early usage (late C16) can be found in act 1, scene 3 of Shakespeare's *Henry IV Part 1 UK, 1598*

flat *adverb* completely *US, 1992*

flat-ass *adverb* absolutely *US, 1964*

flat-ass calm *noun* in lobstering, the condition of the sea when there are no waves and no wind *US, 1978*

flat-back *verb* to engage in prostitution. From the image of a prostitute having sex lying on her back *US, 1967*

flat-back; flat-bottom *adjective* possessing modest buttocks *TRINIDAD AND TOBAGO, 1971*

flatbacker *noun* a prostitute of an undiscerning nature *US, 1969*

flat blue; flat; blue flat *noun* a tablet of LSD *US, 1971*

flatcatcher *noun* in horse racing, a horse that looks the part but evades actual achievement *UK, 1948*

flat-chat *adverb* as fast as one can go *AUSTRALIA, 1981*

flat chunks *noun* a combination of crack cocaine and benzocaine *UK, 1998*

flat dog *noun* bologna *US, 1990*

flatfoot *noun* a police officer, especially one assigned on foot patrol *US, 1912*

flatfoot *verb* to walk *US, 1974*

flatfooted *adjective* unprepared, unready, not 'on your toes' *US, 1908*

flat fuck *noun* sex without loss of semen *US, 1982*

flat-hat *verb* to fly very close to the ground at a high speed *US, 1939*

flat joint; flat store *noun* an illegal gambling operation where players are cheated as a matter of course *US, 1914*

flatkey *noun* a fifty-five mile an hour speed limit. A term borrowed from shortwave radio users (to depress the transmit switch) by citizens' band radio users, and then applied to the nearly universal road speed limit implemented in the US after the oil embargo of the early 1970s *US, 1976*

flatline *verb* to die. An allusion to the flat line on a medical monitoring device that indicates death *US, 1981*

flatliner *noun* **1** a dead person; a dead thing. From FLATLINE (to die). *Flatliners* is a 1990 film by Joel Schumacher in which five medical students experiment with the line between life and death *US, 1998*. **2** a mobile phone user who allows the phone's batteries to run down. A Manchester youth usage, from the sense 'a dead person', possibly, here, specifically 'brain dead' *UK, 2003*. **3** in poker, an unskilled and uninspired player. The moral equivalent of 'brain dead' *US, 1996*. **4** 4-methylthioamphetamine, the recreational drug best known as 4-MTA *UK, 2004*

flat-out *adjective* absolute, complete *US, 1959*

flat out *adverb* as fast as possible *AUSTRALIA, 1941*

flat out like a lizard drinking *adjective* going or working as fast as possible *AUSTRALIA, 1935*

flat passer *noun* shaved dice used in cheating schemes *US, 1997*

flatroofer *noun* in the Maritime Provinces, a fishing boat with a reduced sailing rig for winter *CANADA, 1955*

flats *noun* **1** the lowest tier of cells in a prison *US, 1976*. **2** dice, the surfaces of which have been altered for cheating *US, 1950*

flat-spot *verb* (used of a car for sale) to remain in one spot without being driven or even moved *US, 1992*

flat-stick *adjective* very busy; at top speed *NEW ZEALAND, 1972*

flat-strap *adverb* as fast as possible *AUSTRALIA, 2001*

flatten out *verb* to serve a prison sentence completely *US, 1976*

flattie *noun* **1** a flat tyre *AUSTRALIA, 1971*. **2** a flat-heeled shoe, as distinguished from the high-heeled variety. Also as variant 'flat' *UK, 1959*

flat tire *noun* **1** a shoe that has been forced off a person's heel by someone walking behind them *US, 2003*. **2** a sagging breast *US, 1997*

flattop *noun* an aircraft carrier *US, 1942*

flatty *noun* **1** a member of an audience. Gently derogatory; extended by circus showmen from the (probably) now obsolete sense 'a rustic, an unitiated person', first recorded in 1859 *UK, 1933*. **2** a person who works in a flat joint (an illegal gambling operation where players are cheated as a matter of course) *US, 1981*. **3** a uniformed police officer or a plain-clothes officer who is recognisable as a foot-patrol officer. A variation of FLATFOOT *US, 1866*. **4** a flat-bottomed boat *AUSTRALIA, 1934*. **5** a flathead fish *AUSTRALIA, 1962*

flat wheel *noun* a person with a limp *US, 1977*

flatworker *noun* a burglar who specialises in flats (apartments) *UK, 1996*

flava *noun* style, especially when unique. Also with more conventionally spelt variants, 'flavor' and 'flavour' *US, 1982*

flavour *noun* **1** in computing, a type or variety *US, 1983*. **2** cocaine *US, 1995*

flavourful *adjective* in computing, pleasing *US, 1991*

flavour of the month *noun* the latest, short-lived trend or fashion or relationship. Derisive, even contemptuous; originally conceived as a marketing strategy for ice-cream *US, 1946*

flavour of the week *noun* the latest, short-lived trend or fashion or relationship *US, 2001*

flawless *adjective* **1** flawed *US, 1982*. **2** handsome *US, 1972*

flea *noun* **1** someone who has refused to pay a debt *AUSTRALIA, 1989*. **2** in American casinos, a gambler who places very small bets *US, 1985*. **3** in the car sales business, a customer determined to spend a small amount of money but buy an excellent car *US, 1953*. **4** in a hospital, an internist *US, 1994*

flea and louse *noun* **1** a house, especially one that is run down or unsalubrious. Rhyming slang *UK, 1859*. **2** a brothel, a whore house. Rhyming slang *UK, 2003*

fleabag *noun* **1** a low-cost, run-down motel, room, boarding house or apartment *US, 1924*. **2** a person dressed in old or dirty clothes; a smelly person *UK, 2003*. **3** a drug user *CANADA, 1994*. **4** a dishonest, disreputable carnival *US, 1980*

fleabag *verb* to nag. Rhyming slang *UK, 1992*

fleapit *noun* a shabby cinema *UK, 1937*

flea powder *noun* weak and/or diluted heroin *US, 1956*

fleas and itches *noun* motion pictures. Rhyming slang *AUSTRALIA, 1967*

fleas and lice *noun* ice. Rhyming slang *UK, 1992*

flea track *noun* a parting in the hair *NEW ZEALAND, 1998*

flea trap *noun* an inexpensive, shoddy hotel or boarding house *US, 1942*

fleder deder *noun* a handicap *JAMAICA, 2002*

Flemington confetti *noun* nonsense. A probable play on BULLSHIT, after the Flemington stockyards *AUSTRALIA, 1941*

flesh *noun* an actor who appears on stage *US, 1981*

flesh *adjective* in the music industry, appearing and performing live *US, 1948*

flesh agent *noun* a talent agent *US, 1986*

flesh-coloured highlights *noun* baldness. Jocular *UK, 2001*

flesh market *noun* an area where prostitution and other sex businesses thrive *US, 1987*

fleshmeet *noun* a meeting in the *flesh* of on-line correspondents *US, 1996*

flesh peddler *noun* an entertainer's business manager or agent *US, 1935*

flesh pit *noun* a bar or nightclub where people come in search of sexual partners *US, 1991*

fleshpot *noun* a brothel *US, 1950*

flesh torpedo *noun* the erect penis *UK, 2003*

fleshy flute *noun* the penis. Especially in the phrase 'playing a tune on the fleshy flute' (oral sex) *US, 2001*

flex *noun* cocaine *UK, 2003*

flex *verb* **1** to insult someone, to annoy, to frustrate *UK, 2004*. **2** to display power by a show of strength. From 'to flex your muscles' *US, 1993*. **3** to leave *US, 1993*

flex *adjective* flexible *US, 1992*

flexi-flyer *noun* in drag racing, a racing car with a long wheelbase with built-in flexibility to keep the wheels on the tracks *US, 1968*

flick *noun* **1** a film *UK, 1926*. **2** a photograph *US, 1962*. **3** rejection; dismissal. Short for FLICK PASS *AUSTRALIA, 1982*

flick *verb* **1** to reject *AUSTRALIA, 1988*. **2** to turn back or alter a car's mileometer (odometer) to increase resale value *NEW ZEALAND, 1991*. ▶ **flick someone's switch** to sexually excite someone. A play on TURN ON (to thrill) *UK, 2003*. ▶ **flick your bean** (of a woman) to masturbate. Fairly conventional use of 'flick' (to move with the fingers) applied to BEAN (the clitoris) *UK, 2001*. ▶ **flick your Bic** in trucking, to tap your brakes at night signalling to another driver. A borrowing from advertising for Bic™ cigarette lighters *US, 1976*. ▶ **flick your wick** to speed up, to hurry up *NEW ZEALAND, 2002*. ▶ **flick yourself off** of a woman, to masturbate. From the small movements necessary to manipulate the clitoris *UK, 2005*

flicker *noun* a film *US, 1926*

flick pass *noun* rejection; dismissal. Rhyming slang for arse. A 'flick pass' is a type of open-handed pass made in Australian Rules football *AUSTRALIA, 1983*

flicks *noun* the cinema *UK, 1927*

flid *noun* used as term of playground abuse. Derives from thalidomide, pronounced 'flidomide' *UK, 1980*

flier *noun* **1** in sports, a very fast start; in cricket, a swift rate of scoring at the beginning of a match. A shortening of conventional 'flying start', usually in the phrase 'off to a flier' *UK, 1984*. **2** in target shooting, a shot that strikes outside a close group of shots on the target *US, 1957*. **3** a prisoner who commits suicide by jumping or is murdered by being thrown from the top tier of a prison *US, 1942*. ▶ **take a flier** to leave *US, 1914*

flies *noun* ▶ **and no flies** as an exhortation to believe the statement to which it is appended *UK, 1846*. ▶ **no flies on someone** nothing at all wrong or amiss with someone *AUSTRALIA, 1845*

flight attendant *noun* a security guard at a rock concert, usually large and muscular, stationed at the barricades near the stage *US, 1997*

flight deck *noun* the female breasts *UK, 1981*

flightie *noun* a person who has relocated to the Highlands of Scotland from the urban realities of England in search of a rural dream. Derogatory. Probably from the verb 'to take flight' *UK: SCOTLAND, 2004*

flight lieutenant Biggles *noun* giggles. Rhyming slang, based (although wrongly ranked) on the flying-ace hero created by W.E. Johns in 1932 *UK, 2002*

flight lustre *noun* a mythical substance for which new recruits in the Canadian Air Force are sent to search *CANADA, 1995*

flight skins *noun* military flight pay *US, 1945*

flight time *noun* in motor racing, the elapsed time a car unintentionally spends in the air, usually upside down. Grim humour *US, 1980*

flik *noun* a song from which the lyrics have been changed for humorous consumption by science fiction fans *US, 1991*

flim *noun* a five pound note; the sum of £5. Originally an abbreviation of 'flimsy', adjective and obsolete noun use for the early, large white banknotes *UK, 1870*

flimflam *noun* **1** nonsense, pretentious or deceptive nonsense. In conventional use until late C19 *UK, 1546*. **2** a swindle involving a

supposedly lost wallet supposedly found on the ground near the victim *US, 1960*

flimflam *verb* to shortchange, to swindle *US, 1881*

flimflam man *noun* a confidence swindler *US, 1970*

flimflammer *noun* a swindler who engages in the flimflam swindle (a swindle involving a supposedly lost wallet supposedly found on the ground near the victim) *US, 1960*

flimp *verb* to cheat, to swindle; in betting, to underpay or offer bets at below the odds. From an earlier sense of 'theft by snatching'; ultimately from west Flemish *flimpe* (knock, slap in the face) *UK, 1925*

flimsy *noun* any order written on thin, onion skin paper. The orders were written on 'flimsy' paper, hence the nominalisation of the adjective *UK, 1889*

fling *noun* a limited period devoted to self-indulgent pleasures, especially sexual; a short-lived sexual liaison *UK, 1827*

fling *verb* ▶ **fling a dummy** to die suddenly *UK, 1981*. ▶ **fling baby** to undergo an abortion *TRINIDAD AND TOBAGO, 2003*

flinger *noun* **1** an impulsive poker player who is inclined to raise bets without regard to the quality of his hand *US, 1988*. **2** in target shooting, a shot that strikes outside a close group of shots on the target *US, 1957*

fling-wing *noun* a helicopter *US, 1991*

Flintstones *nickname* **1** the UK armed forces. The cartoon television series *The Flintstones* depicted a stone-age world in which C20 technology is comically replaced by prehistoric ingenuity. As a nickname used by the US military it reflects the outdated 'prehistoric' equipment and shortages of everyday supplies that force the UK forces to improvise and scrounge *US, 2003*. **2** a variety of LSD. Identified by a picture of the cartoon characters the Flintstones, created by William Hanna and Joseph Barbera in 1966; sometimes shortened to 'flints' *UK, 1996*

flip *noun* **1** a condition of mental instability *US, 1953*. **2** a person who has lost touch with reality *US, 1952*. **3** an LSD experience *US, 1992*. **4** in trucking, a return trip *US, 1976*. **5** a male homosexual who plays the passive role in sex *US, 1992*. **6** a police informer *US, 1967*

Flip *noun* a Filipino *US, 1931*

flip *verb* **1** to become very angry or agitated; to go temporarily crazy *US, 1950*. **2** to become enthusiastic and excited *US, 1950*. **3** to induce a betrayal *US, 1980*. **4** to betray; to inform on *US, 1960*. **5** to gesture. As used in FLIP THE BIRD (to raise the middle finger) *UK, 1992*. **6** on the railways, to step aboard a moving train *US, 1977*. ▶ **flip a bitch** to make a u-turn *US, 2000*. ▶ **flip a trick** (of a prostitute) to have sex with a customer. Far less common than to 'turn' a TRICK *US, 1979*. ▶ **flip the bird** to gesture in derision with a raised middle finger *US, 1968*. ▶ **flip the bishop** (of a male) to masturbate. Plays on FLIP as euphemistic FUCK and, conventionally, as a 'manipulation'. A variation of BASH THE BISHOP (to masturbate) *UK, 2005*. ▶ **flip the bone** to extend the middle finger in a rude gesture of defiance *US, 1957*. ▶ **flip the grip** to shake hands *US, 1945*. ▶ **flip the lip** to talk *US, 1947*. ▶ **flip your gut** to evoke sympathy or sadness *US, 1997*. ▶ **flip your lid; flipflop your lid** to lose emotional control *US, 1961*. ▶ **flip your stick** to move your penis during an all-cavity strip search *US, 2002*. ▶ **flip your wig** to lose your mental composure *US, 1959*

flip *adjective* pleasant, fashionable, popular *US, 1955*

flip euphemistic replacement for some noun and most verb senses of 'fuck' *UK, 1956*

flip act *noun* feigned insanity *US, 1967*

flipflap *noun* in circus usage, a back handspring *US, 1981*

flipflop *noun* **1** a sandal that is not bound to the foot, usually worn around a swimming pool. From the sound made when walking on concrete *US, 1970*. **2** a return journey *US, 1976*. **3** a traffic lane designed for turning around. Detroit usage *US, 1997*

flip-flop *verb* **1** to change positions on a political issue or issues in response to changing public opinion *US, 1965*. **2** (used of two homosexuals) to reverse sexual roles after sexual satisfaction is achieved by the active partner *US, 1961*. **3** to have sex with both men and women *US, 1992*. **4** (used of two homosexuals) a reversal of sexual roles *US, 1972*

flip-flopping *noun* changing positions on an issue or issues *US, 1976*

flip off! go away!; used as a euphemistic replacement for 'fuck off!' *UK, 1956*

flipped *adjective* smart, attractive *US, 1955*

flipper *noun* **1** the hand *UK, 1812*. **2** to a lineman in American football, the forearm *US, 1967*. **3** the ear *US, 1905*. **4** a temporary partial denture used to mask the absence of a single tooth or several teeth, especially with child actors. Technically known as a 'stayplate', it flips in and out of the child's mouth *US, 1999*. **5** a friend *UK, 1970*. **6** a criminal who informs on friends and associates to reduce his own sentence or to completely avoid charges *US, 1997*. **7** in the television and film industries, a section of set that can be easily replaced *UK, 1960*. **8** the game of pinball *US, 1974*. **9** in hot rodding, a hubcap *US, 1958*. **10** a turn signal in a truck or car *US, 1976*

flippers *noun* anchovies *US, 1996*

flipping *adjective* used as an intensifier. Since about 1940 the commonest of all euphemisms for FUCKING in the UK, as in the common exclamation of disgust 'Flipping 'eck!' (fucking hell!), often used unwitting of the term it disguises *UK, 1911*

flippy *adjective* eccentric, crazy *US, 1965*

flip-side *noun* **1** the reverse side of a vinyl record. From the action of flipping the disc over *US, 1949*. **2** the opposite of something. A figurative application of the earlier sense as 'the reverse side of a record' *US, 1967*. ▶ **on the flip-side** later on *US, 2002*

flip top *noun* **1** the top of a canned food or beverage that peels open without resort to an opening device *US, 1955*. **2** a truck cab that tilts up to expose the engine *US, 1971*

flip-wreck *noun* a habitual masturbator. Referring to the supposed damaging effects of masturbation *AUSTRALIA, 1950*

flit *noun* **1** an effeminate homosexual male *US, 1935*. **2** a discreet and hurried departure to avoid debts. Probably from MOONLIGHT FLIT *UK, 1952*. **3** any insecticide in a spray can. A generic use, from the trade name of an insecticide *TRINIDAD AND TOBAGO, 1993*

flitters *noun* tatters *IRELAND, 1989*

fliv *verb* in circus and carnival usage, to fail or to perform poorly *US, 1917*

flivver *noun* an old, worn car, especially a Ford car. The term was, by the early 1980s, chiefly associated with the early model Ford cars, and had thus become historical *US, 1910*

flix *noun* photographs. Possibly a variation of FLICKS (the cinema) *US, 2002*

flixy *adjective* easy *FIJI, 1994*

FLK *noun* a strange-looking child; a *funny-looking kid*. British medical slang *US, 1961*

flo *noun* **1** a variety of marijuana, *2001*. **2** a young person *CANADA, 1991*

float *noun* **1** a customer's down payment, treated by the salesman collecting it as a short-term loan *US, 1980*. **2** a tyre *US, 1976*. **3** military duty on board a ship. Vietnam war US Marines usage *US, 1991*

float *verb* **1** in the gambling game two-up, to toss the coins so that they only give the appearance of spinning *AUSTRALIA, 1945*. **2** to eat after extensive drinking *UK, 1983*. ▶ **float a log** to defecate *UK, 1985*. ▶ **float a sausage to the seaside** to defecate into a sewage system. The phrase may have originated in the comic VIZ *UK, 2002*. ▶ **float dice** to drop dice suspected of having been weighted into a glass of water to see if they roll over on one side *US, 1997*. ▶ **float someone's boat** to please someone; to make someone happy *US, 1984*. ▶ **float the gears** to shift gears without using the clutch *US, 1976*

floater *noun* **1** a corpse found floating in a body of water *US, 1890*. **2** a particle of food floating in a bottled drink (having been washed into the bottle as it was being drunk from) *UK: SCOTLAND, 1988*. **3** in circus and carnival usage, a slice of imitation fruit floating on the top of imitation fruit juice *US, 1981*. **4** a meat pie served with pea gravy *AUSTRALIA, 1915*. **5** the recreational drug methaqualone, best known as Quaaludes™ *US, 1997*. **6** a person who is temporarily assigned to one job or another™ *US, 1909*. **7** a migratory worker *US,*

1859. **8** a person who is a poor credit risk because of constantly changing employment *US, 1975*. **9** an early release from jail, usually with an order to leave town immediately *US, 1914*. **10** a river-rafting enthusiast *US, 1997*. **11** in the language of wind surfing, a sailboard that can support the weight of a person in the water *US, 1985*. **12** a big, buoyant surfboard *US, 1964*. **13** a pinball machine which is nearly level, lacking the playfield pitch needed for a good game. The fact that the playfield is nearly level makes it seem as if the ball floats on the playfield *US, 1977*. **14** in the gambling game two-up, a coin which does not spin properly and so is illegal *AUSTRALIA, 1944*. **15** in the television and film industries, a section of set that can be easily replaced *UK, 1960*. **16** a mistake *UK, 1913*

floaties *noun* (used by surfers) faeces floating in the sea *US, 1991*

floating *adjective* **1** moving; not settled in a definite place. Almost always applied to an illegal crap game that moves from location to location *US, 1951*. **2** drunk or marijuana-intoxicated *US, 1938*

floating chrome *noun* a commerical truck embellished with a lot of extra chrome *US, 1971*

floating shotgun *noun* a rocket-armed landing craft. Korean war usage *US, 1982*

float-out *noun* a jail sentence suspended contingent upon the criminal leaving town *US, 1968*

floats *noun* dice that have been hollowed out to affect their balance. Because most dice used in casinos are now transparent, the practice and term are almost obsolete *US, 1950*

flob *verb* to spit. Noted at a time when punks showed appreciation of their musical heroes by expectorating at the stage *UK, 1977*

flock *noun* a group of unskilled poker players *US, 1996*

flockatoon *noun* in Quebec's Gaspe area, an event at which people get happily drunk *CANADA, 1992*

flog *noun* **1** a prostitute *AUSTRALIA, 1967*. **2** an act of male masturbation *AUSTRALIA, 1985*

flog *verb* **1** to endorse, to promote, to sell *UK, 1925*. **2** to sell, especially illicitly *UK, 1925*. **3** to steal *AUSTRALIA, 1962*. **4** to go with much effort *UK, 1925*. **5** to have sex *BAHAMAS, 1982*. **6** in drag racing, hot rodding and motor racing, to push the car to its limit or beyond *US, 1993*. ▶ **flog a dead horse** to work hard to little or no purpose *UK, 1872*. ▶ **flog the bishop** (of a male) to masturbate. A variation on BASH THE BISHOP (to masturbate) using conventional 'flog' (to beat); note the synonymous 'flog your donkey' and 'flog your mutton' were coined at around the same time *US, 1999*. ▶ **flog the infidel** (of a male) to masturbate *US, 2001*. ▶ **flog your chops** to wear yourself out *AUSTRALIA, 1968*. ▶ **flog your dong** (used of a male) to masturbate *US, 1994*. ▶ **flog your dummy** (used of a male) to masturbate *US, 1922*. ▶ **flog your guts out** to wear yourself out *UK, 1959*

flogged *adjective* drug-intoxicated *US, 1949*

flogging *adjective* damned. Used as an intensifier. A euphemism for FUCKING *AUSTRALIA, 1955*

flog off *verb* to leave *NEW ZEALAND, 1998*

flog on *verb* to surf the Internet for masturbatory inspiration. Puns 'flog', the root word of many terms for masturbation, with 'log on', IT jargon for connecting to the Internet *NEW ZEALAND, 2002*

flo is coming to town used as a code phrase for the bleed period of the menstrual cycle *US, 2002*

Flo Jo *nickname* Florence Griffith Joyner (1959–1998), a sprinter whose style and speed dominated the 1988 Olympics *US, 1988*

flood *verb* **1** to experience the bleed period of the menstrual cycle, used especially of a heavy flow *US, 1942*. **2** (used of professional wrestlers) to rush into the ring or arena in large numbers *US, 1992*. **3** to wear trousers that don't reach the shoes *US, 1998*

floodgates *noun* ▶ **floodgates open up** the bleed period of the menstrual cycle commences *US, 2001*

floods *noun* long trousers that are too short or shorts that are too long *US, 1982*

flooey *adverb* awry *US, 1905*

flookum *noun* in circus and carnival usage, an artificially flavoured and coloured 'fruit' drink; the syrup used to make the drink *US, 1966*

floor *noun* used as a figurative or notional description of the place where out-of-work workers wait for a job referral at a union hiring hall *US, 1992.* ▶ **on the floor** poor. Rhyming slang; also serves as a metaphor *UK, 1960.* ▶ **take off the floor** to remove a prostitute from service in a brothel *US, 1978*

floor *verb* **1** to confound, to puzzle *UK, 1830.* **2** to push a vehicle's accelerator to the floorboard *US, 1953*

floor box *noun* in hot rodding, a car with a manual transmission *US, 1960*

floorburners *noun* shoes *US, 1972*

floor lamp *noun* a woman actor with good looks but not blessed with acting ability *US, 1973*

floor liner *noun* the vagina. Rhyming slang *UK, 2003*

floor-pop *noun* in the car sales business, a customer who walks into the showroom *US, 1966*

floor whore *noun* an aggressive retail salesperson *US, 2001*

floor work *noun* in a strip or sex show, movements made on the floor simulating sexual intercourse, offering strategic and gripping views as the dancer moves her legs *US, 1965*

flooze *noun* a woman or girl *US, 1952*

floozie; floozy; floosie; floosy *noun* a woman, especially one with few sexual inhibitions; a prostitute *US, 1902*

flop *noun* **1** a place to spend the night *US, 1910.* **2** a house or garage where criminals escaping from the scene of a crime can safely hide themselves or store weapons, tools and stolen property, thus leaving their own homes uncompromised *UK, 1977.* **3** a drunk sleeping in public *US, 1949.* **4** a complete, dismal failure *US, 1919.* **5** a demotion *US, 1973.* **6** the denial of a release on parole by a prison parole board *US, 1944.* **7** an arrest, conviction and/or imposition of a prison sentence *US, 1904.* **8** in hold 'em poker, the first three cards dealt face-up in the centre of the table *US, 1990.* **9** in a dice game, a roll of the dice *US, 1962.* **10** the ear *US, 1945*

flop *verb* **1** to reside temporarily; to stay overnight *US, 1907.* **2** to go to sleep *UK, 1936.* **3** to fail completely *US, 1900.* **4** in police work, to demote in rank or assignment *US, 1970.* **5** in bar dice games, to shake the dice in the dice cup and then roll them onto a surface *US, 1971*

flop box *noun* a hotel room, a bedroom, lodgings. A variation of FLOP (a place to sleep) *US, 1976*

flophouse *noun* **1** an inexpensive, shoddy, tattered, dirty place to stay, catering to transients *US, 1909.* **2** a brakevan (caboose) *US, 1977*

flop joint *noun* a flophouse *US, 1928*

flop on *noun* the penis that has become flaccid when an erection is to be preferred *UK, 2003*

flopper *noun* **1** the arm *US, 1945.* **2** a person who feigns having been struck by a car in hope of collecting insurance payments from the driver *US, 1982.* **3** a modified stock car in which the entire fibreglass body lifts from the front to gain access to the engine and driver seat *US, 1993*

flopperoo *noun* a failure *US, 1931*

flopper-stopper *noun* a brassiere. Jocular *AUSTRALIA, 1984*

flopping *adjective* damned. Used as an intensifier. A euphemism for FUCKING *AUSTRALIA, 1969*

floppy *noun* a black person. An insulting term that is likely to have been military slang in Rhodesia *SOUTH AFRICA, 1978*

flop sweat *noun* a panic associated with the possibility of failure, whether or not actual perspiration is involved *US, 1966*

floptrips *noun* in a game of on-line poker, a three-of-a-kind after the flop (the initial deal of three cards), *2003*

Florida Hilton *nickname* the federal prison camp at Eglin Air Force Base, Eglin, Florida *US, 1974*

Florida snow *noun* cocaine *US, 1994*

floss *noun* **1** cotton candy. The spun sugar is known as 'candy floss' in the UK but not known as such in the US, making what would be a simple UK abbreviated form to be a piece of slang in the US *US, 1960.* **2** a thong-backed bikini bottom *US, 1991*

floss *verb* **1** to behave with ostentatious style and flair *US, 2002.* **2** to show off *US, 1999.* **3** to wear expensive clothes and jewels. Used by urban black youths *UK, 2004*

flossie *noun* a homosexual male *UK, 1974*

flossing *adjective* excellent *US, 2001*

flossy *adjective* **1** in circus and carnival usage, showy *US, 1895.* **2** excellent *US, 2004*

flotsam *noun* new or unskilled surfers in the water *BARBADOS, 1977*

flotty *noun* a hat that, by the inclusion of a little cork in a zippered pocket, is designed to float *SOUTH AFRICA, 2000*

flounder *noun* a native of Newfoundland *US, 1949*

flounder and dab *noun* a taxi. Rhyming slang for 'taxi-cab'; generally abbreviated to 'flounder' *UK, 1865*

flour mixer *noun* **1** a Gentile woman. Rhyming slang for 'shixa' (SHIKSE); employed by Jewish Cockneys *UK, 1961.* **2** a female shop assistant or domestic worker. A nuance of the rhyming slang for a 'Gentile woman' *UK, 1977.* **3** an inoffensive man, especially one who is a clerk. Extended from the previous senses which are specifically of a woman. *UK, 1977*

flow *noun* **1** the style in which a rap artist creates lyrics and/or performs. 'Flow' is a term used to express a quality of conventional poetry *US, 1995.* **2** money. An abbreviation of the conventional 'cash flow' *US, 1997*

flower *noun* **1** a male homosexual *US, 1949.* **2** marijuana *UK, 1998.* **3** in poker, a hand made up of cards of the same suit. Conventionally known as a 'flush' *US, 1988*

flower-bed *verb* to drive a truck with the right wheels on the hard shoulder of the road, kicking up dust *US, 1969*

flower child *noun* a participant in a 1960s youth movement promoting peace and love. Flower children used marijuana (FLOWER) and other drugs as an expression of their culture, and distributed ordinary flowers as symbols of their beliefs. In its first usage 'flower children' meant 'marijuana users'; the media adopted the more openly cultivated flowers as the image to sell *US, 1967*

flowered up *adjective* intoxicated on drugs, especially marijuana, possibly MDMA, the recreational drug best known as ecstasy *UK, 1999*

flower flipping *noun* MDMA, the recreational drug best known as ecstasy *UK, 2003*

flower key *noun* in computing, the comma key on a Macintosh computer *US, 1991*

flower patch *noun* a woman's vulva and pubic hair *US, 1986*

flower pot *noun* **1** an inexpensive, poorly made helmet. Biker (motorcycle) usage *US, 2001.* **2** a cot. Rhyming slang *UK, 1992.* **3** in electric line work, a pad-mount transformer *US, 1980*

flower pot *adjective* hot, especially in the context of a hot (severe) reprimand. Rhyming slang *UK, 1992*

flower power *noun* the amorphous creed or philosophy of the hippie movement, based on drugs, sex, music, non-violence and a rejection of all things material *US, 1967*

flower-power suit *noun* a camouflaged combat-suit. An army term. 'Make love not war' shot through with irony *UK, 1984*

flowers; monthly flowers *noun* the bleed period of the menstrual cycle. From Latin *fluor* (to flow) via French *fleurs* (flowers); in conventional usage from C15 to mid-C19 *UK, 2002*

flowers and frolics *noun* the testicles. Rhyming slang for BOLLOCKS recorded as Anglo-Irish *UK, 1960*

flower sign *noun* fresh *flowers* by a hospital patient's bed seen by medical staff as a *sign* that the patient has a supportive family *UK, 2002*

flowers of spring *noun* used condoms in a sewage system *US, 1973*

flower tops *noun* marijuana. From the most potent part of the plant *US, 1969*

flowery dell; flowery *noun* **1** a room, lodgings, accommodation. Rhyming slang for 'cell' *UK, 2002.* **2** a prison cell. Rhyming slang *UK, 1925*

flox; floxy *noun* a homosexual man. A variation of 'moxy' *UK, 2003*

floxen *noun* a group of homosexual men. The plural of 'flox', recorded in contemporary gay usage *UK, 2003*

flu; 'flu *noun* influenza. A colloquial shortening *UK, 1839*

flub *verb* to botch *US, 1916.* ▶ **flub the dub** to masturbate *US, 1922*

flubadub *noun* a fool. From the name of a puppet on the *Howdy Doody Show US, 1975*

flube tube *noun* a cardboard tube filled with scented cloth that masks the smell of exhaled marijuana smoke *US, 2003*

flue *noun* **1** a room *US, 1972.* **2** a confidence swindle involving money in an envelope; the envelope used in the swindle *US, 1969.* **3** a prison warder. Rhyming slang for SCREW (a prison warder) *UK, 1996.* **4** the stomach *US, 1946*

fluey *adjective* characteristic of, or characterised by, influenza *UK, 1969*

fluff *noun* **1** a woman, especially an attractive woman of no further consequence than her sexual availability. Usually used with 'a bit of' or 'a piece of'. Combines the sense as 'pubic hair', with an image of 'fluff' as something of no consequence. Not kind *UK, 1903.* **2** the female pubic hair. An otherwise obsolete usage that survives in the term BIT OF FLUFF. *UK, 1937.* **3** an effeminate lesbian *US, 1972.* **4** to a homosexual who practises sado-masochism, a homosexual of simpler tastes *US, 1985.* **5** a mistake in the delivery of theatrical lines, also in broadcasting; a minor mistake when playing music. Originally 'lines imperfectly learned' *UK, 1891.* **6** in the television and film industries, a flubbed line of dialogue *UK, 1960*

fluff *verb* **1** to perform oral sex on a male pornography performer who is about to be filmed so that he will enter the scene with a full erection *US, 1977.* **2** to make a mistake in a theatrical performance, such as by mispronouncing or muddling words; likewise in broadcasting; also in musical performance, by playing the wrong note, etc *UK, 1884.* **3** to fart. Juvenile origins in New Zealand schoolboy 'fluffing contests' and US 'laying a fluffy'. Possibly from UK dialect *fluff* (a slight explosion), or 'fluff' (a mistake). UK usage is nursery and childish *NEW ZEALAND, 1944.* **4** to ignore; to discard *US, 1959.* **5** to fail (an examination) *US, 1955*

fluff and buff *noun* a fluff-dried battle dress utility uniform with buff-polished boots, the standard uniform of the US Airborne *US, 1988*

fluffed *adjective* **1** drunk *US, 1904.* **2** cocaine-intoxicated. A new use for the previous sense *UK, 1999*

fluffer *noun* in the making of a pornographic film, a person employed to bring the on-camera male performers to a state of sexual readiness. Extension of the conventional sense of 'fluff' (to make fuller or plumper) *US, 1977*

fluff girl *noun* a fluffer *US, 1991*

fluffie; fluffy *noun* an anti-globalisation activist with a belief in peaceful protest *UK, 2001*

fluff off *verb* **1** to dismiss, to reject *US, 1944.* **2** to evade work or duty *US, 1962*

fluff stuff; fluffy stuff *noun* snow *US, 1976*

fluffy *adjective* **1** light-hearted, non-serious *UK, 2001.* **2** in the theatre, unsure of your lines *UK, 1952*

fluid *noun* whisky *US, 1843*

fluids and electrolytes conference *noun* used in a hospital as humorous code for a drinking party to be held on hospital grounds *US, 1989*

fluke *noun* a stroke of luck, an accident. In the game of billiards a 'fluke' is a 'lucky shot' *UK, 1857*

fluke *verb* to do a thing well by accident *UK, 1860*

fluked out *adjective* drug-intoxicated *US, 1952*

fluke out *verb* to become drug-intoxicated *US, 1958*

fluking iron *noun* in fencing, an épée. A derisory term, suggesting that FLUKE (luck) rather than skill is required when engaging with such weapons *UK, 1988*

fluky; flukey *adjective* more by luck than design *AUSTRALIA, 1867*

flummox *verb* to perplex, to confuse *US, 1834*

flummy dumm *noun* in Newfoundland, a hunters' and trappers' bread *CANADA, 1988*

flunk *noun* a locked and fortified compartment within a safe *US, 1928*

flunk *verb* to completely and irrevocably fail an examination *US, 1837*

flunkey and lackey *noun* a Pakistani; any Asian or Afro-Asian immigrant; loosely, any native of the Indian subcontinent. Rhyming slang for PAKI *UK, 1992*

flunk out *verb* to leave an educational establishment as a result of failing your examinations *US, 1920*

flunky *noun* a person assigned to assist or perform menial jobs. In the US, originally a work camp waiter or assistant cook, and usually not quite as harsh as Partridge's 'parasite' or 'toady' *UK, 1855*

flunky *verb* to work as a low-level assistant *US, 1968*

flurry *noun* a flourish *BARBADOS, 1965*

flush *verb* **1** to draw blood back into a syringe. Drug users' term *UK, 1978.* **2** to leave work *US, 1991.* **3** to fail (a test or course) *US, 1964.* ▶ **flush the john** in a casino, to play slot machines *US, 1979*

flush *adjective* having plenty of money, especially as an exception to the rule *UK, 1603*

flush bucket *noun* in motor racing, a carburettor that feeds the engine more of the air/fuel mixture than it can use *US, 1993*

flute *noun* **1** the penis. Plays on the shape, informed by oral sex. Variations include 'flesh flute', 'living flute', ONE-HOLED FLUTE, SILENT FLUTE, SKIN FLUTE; also PINK OBOE; the sense compares with Romany *haboia* (a hautboy, an early oboe). There are arguable examples in *A Midsummer Night's Dream*, 1600 (or earlier) and *Anthony and Cleopatra*, 1606 – 7 of Shakespeare punning on 'flute' as 'penis'. In more general usage in the C18 *UK, 1671.* **2** a soda bottle filled with alcoholic drink *US, 1971.* **3** a car radio. From the language of car sales *NEW ZEALAND, 1998*

flute around *verb* to waste time, to be unresolved in action *IRELAND, 1996*

flute player *noun* a person who performs oral sex on a man *US, 1916*

fluter *noun* a male homosexual *US, 1962*

fluthered *adjective* completely drunk *IRELAND, 1992*

flutter *noun* a small bet. Originally meant 'a good try' *UK, 1874*

flutter bum *noun* a good-looking and popular boy. Teen slang *US, 1955*

flutter-finger *noun* in the usage of youthful model road racers (slot car racers), a person who fluctuates speed constantly *US, 1997*

fly *noun* an attempt; a try. Usually in the phrase 'give something a fly' *AUSTRALIA, 1915.* ▶ **on the fly** on the railways, said of a moving train that is boarded *US, 1977*

fly *verb* **1** to act cautiously *US, 1965.* **2** to sneak a look *JAMAICA, 2003.* ▶ **be flying it** to do extremely well, to make great progress. Used in the present participle only *IRELAND, 1997.* ▶ **fly a desk** of an aircraft pilot, to work in air traffic administration. Originally military *UK, 1951.* ▶ **fly a kite 1** to tentatively reveal an idea as a test of public opinion *UK, 1937.* **2** to pass a worthless cheque *UK, 1927.* **3** in prison, to write a letter; to smuggle correspondence in or out of prison *US, 1960.* ▶ **fly aeroplane** to stand up *SINGAPORE, 2002.* ▶ **fly by the seat of your pants** to attempt any unfamiliar task and improve as you continue. From aircraft pilots' original use as 'to fly by instinct' *UK, 1960.* ▶ **fly in ever decreasing circles until he disappears up his own asshole** (among Canadian military personnel) to exhibit much ineffective activity while being anxious *CANADA, 1995.* ▶ **fly light** to work through a meal break *US, 1946.* ▶ **fly low 1** to drive (a truck) at a very high speed *US, 1971.* **2** to act cautiously *US, 1965.* **3** to have one's trouser fly unbuttoned or unzipped *CANADA, 1989.* ▶ **fly Mexican Airlines; fly Mexican Airways** to smoke marijuana and experience euphoric effects. From FLYING (experiencing the effects of drugs) plus Mexico which has long been considered a major source of fine quality cannabis such as Acapulco gold. *US, 1972*. ▶ **fly off the handle** to lose your temper; to lose self-control *US, 1843*. ▶ **fly right** to behave in a manner appropriate to the situation *US, 1984*. ▶ **fly the bean flag** to be experiencing the bleed period of the menstrual cycle *US, 1954*. ▶ **fly the flag** to appeal against a conviction in hope of a reduced sentence *AUSTRALIA, 1975*. ▶ **fly the kite** to defraud, to cheat, especially by passing a fraudulent cheque or by obtaining and dishonouring a credit arrangement *UK, 1968*. ▶ **fly the mail** to drive (a truck) very fast *US, 1961*. ▶ **fly the red flag** to experience the bleed period of the menstrual cycle *US, 1954*. ▶ **fly the rod** to gesture with the middle finger, roughly conveying 'fuck you!' *US, 1968*. ▶ **fly without a licence** of a male, to have an undone trouser fly. Generally juvenile *UK, 1977*

fly *adjective* **1** good, pleasing, fashionable. A term which has enjoyed three bursts of popularity – in the swing jazz era of the late 1930s, the emergence of black exploitation films in the early 1970s, and with the explosion of hip-hop culture in the 1980s *US, 1879*. **2** cunning, devious; artful, knowing. From Scottish dialect *fly* (sly; smart) *UK, 1724*. **3** cunningly discreet. A slight variation of the previous sense *UK, 2000*. **4** in the youth trend for 'souped-up' motor-scootering, daring, dangerous, clever *UK, 2004*. **5** aware of what is going on; wise to criminal ways *AUSTRALIA, 1882*. **6** unreliable; dishonest *TRINIDAD AND TOBAGO, 2003*

flybait *noun* **1** an unattractive girl *US, 1947*. **2** a corpse *US, 1992*

fly baker; fly bravo *verb* to experience the bleed period of the menstrual cycle. In the phonetic alphabet from 1941–56 'baker' was given for 'B', from 1956 to date 'bravo' is used; in naval signalling to fly the flag representing 'B' means 'I am taking on, carrying or discharging dangerous goods'; a large red flag is flown *US, 1999*

fly ball *noun* in handball, a shot played off the front wall before it hits the ground *US, 1970*

fly beer *noun* in the Maritime Provinces, beer of potatoes and hop yeast, and molasses or sugar and water *CANADA, 1959*

fly-blown *adjective* broke; penniless *AUSTRALIA, 1853*

flybog *noun* jam *AUSTRALIA, 1920*

flyboy *noun* **1** a military aviator *US, 1937*. **2** in drag racing, a hobbyist who confines their passion to weekend racing. Punning on the 1940s 'aviator' sense of the term *US, 1965*

fly-by *noun* a missile that misses its target and does no damage *US, 1991*

fly-by-night *noun* a person who is drunk. Rhyming slang for TIGHT (tipsy) *UK, 1992*

fly-by-night *adjective* unreliable; likely to disappear *US, 1914*

fly-by-nights; fly-be's *noun* tights *UK, 1979*

fly cemetery *noun* a currant pudding *UK, 1963*

fly chick *noun* an attractive woman *US, 1945*

flyer *noun* **1** a chance, a gamble, a risk. Originally a financial specu-lation. Also spelt 'flier' *US, 2001*. **2** a conversational line used to start conversation when seeking a sexual encounter *US, 1972*. **3** a person who threatens to or has jumped to his death *US, 1987*

fly-fishing position *noun* in fencing, an unconventional guard pos-ition used by some épéeists. From the image of a fisherman casting *UK, 1988*

fly-fly boy *noun* a military aviator *US, 1949*

fly gee *noun* in circus and carnival usage, a clever, sarcastic, sophisti-cated man with a flexible approach to the truth *US, 1981*

fly girl *noun* an attractive, sexually alluring young woman *US, 1986*

fly-in *noun* an extravagant party for homosexual men in which men fly in to the party from all parts of the country *US, 1982*

flying *adjective* **1** experiencing the euphoric or mind-altering effects of a drug. A shortened form of 'flying high' or 'flying in the clouds' *US, 1942*. **2** making great progress, doing exceedingly well *IRELAND, 1992*. **3** in poker, full, as in a full house *US, 1967*

flying a *noun* an extremely obnoxious person. The 'a' is usually understood as ASSHOLE *US, 1968*

flying arse *noun* nothing at all, the very least amount. A variation of FLYING FUCK *UK, 2002*

flying banana *nickname* **1** a military transport helicopter, especially the Piasecki HRP *US, 1950*. **2** an H-21 helicopter. Vietnam war usage with variant 'banana' *US, 1957*

flying boxcar *nickname* a transport aircraft, especially a C-119 *US, 1918*

flying brick *noun* any heavy aircraft that is difficult to control *US, 1944*

flying brickyard *nickname* the Orbiter Space Shuttle. A derisive reference to the 34,000 heat resistant tiles designed to protect the craft during re-entry to the earth's atmosphere; construction began in 1975, and the first mission was flown in 1983 *US, 1994*

flying carpet *noun* a livery taxi. New York police slang; an allusion to the large number of immigrant drivers *US, 1997*

flying coffin *noun* any dangerous aircraft, such as a glider used by paratroopers. A reference to the gliders' vulnerability to artillery *US, 1918*

flying douche *noun* ▶ **take a flying douche** used as an intense expression of 'go to hell' *US, 1965*

flying duck used for all senses of 'fuck'. Rhyming slang *UK, 1992*

flying Dutchman *noun* a drug dealer *US, 1992*

Flying Edsel *nickname* ▷ *see:* EDSEL

flying firetruck *noun* nothing, the very least amount. A barely euphemistic variation of FLYING FUCK *UK, 2003*

flying flapjack *nickname* the XF5 U-1 experimental military hovering aircraft *US, 1973*

flying fox *noun* a device for crossing or transporting goods across rivers, ravines, or the like *AUSTRALIA, 1901*

flying fuck *noun* nothing at all, the very least amount. Usually couched in the negative *US, 1946*. ▶ **take a flying fuck** get lost! *US, 1926*

flying fuckland *noun* a fantasy world; used for registering disbelief *UK, 2000*

flying gas station; gas station in the sky *nickname* a KC-135 aircraft used for inflight refuelling of jet aircraft *US, 1991*

Flying Horsemen *nickname* during the war in Vietnam, the First Air Cavalry Division. An elite reconnaissance unit *US, 1989*

flying Jenny *noun* a US Army shortwave radar set *US, 1947*

flying lesson *noun* **1** the reported US and South Vietnamese practice of pushing suspected Viet Cong or captured North Vietnamese soldiers from helicopters to their death *US, 1991*. **2** the act of throwing a prisoner or guard off a high tier in a prison cellblock *US, 1992*

flying orders *noun* instructions given to a truck driver by a dispatcher *US, 1971*

flying Oscar *nickname* a Boeing-Vertol CH-47 helicopter, the US Army's prime cargo helicopter in Vietnam. So named because of the likeness to an Oscar Meyer™ hotdog *US, 1991*

flying pasty *noun* excrement, wrapped and thrown from a prison window. The term survives where modern sanitation is not easily available *US, 1996*

flying prostitute *nickname* a B-26 bomber aircraft. Like the lady of the night, the B-26 had no visible means of support *US, 1943*

flying saucer *noun* a morning glory seed, thought to have psychoactive properties *US, 1971*

flying saucer cap *noun* a military service cap *US, 1971*

flying sheep's dick *noun* nothing at all, the very least amount *UK, 1992*

flying sixty-nine *noun* mutual and simultaneous oral sex . A vari-ation of SOIXANTE-NEUF *UK, 1984*

flying squad *noun* a fast-moving, versatile group *US, 1967*

flying telephone pole; telephone pole *nickname* a surface-to-air missile, especially an SA-2. Vietnam war usage *US, 1977*

flying ten *noun* a ten-dollar advance on pay given to a soldier when newly assigned to a base *US, 1956*

Flying Tiger Air Force *noun* a collection of American mercenaries who flew air raids in support of Chiang Kai-shek's losing effort on mainland China *US, 1971*

flying triangle *noun* LSD *UK, 2003*

flying twenty-five *noun* a pay advance in the military *US, 1956*

flying wedge *noun* a group of people in a wedge-shaped formation, advancing rapidly into a crowd. A practice and term used by police, security workers and American football players *US, 1970*

fly in the ointment *noun* anything that spoils the perfection of a finished article. Of biblical inspiration (Ecclesiastes 10:1) *UK, 1833*

fly in the sky *noun* an aircraft, especially a police helicopter *US, 1976*

Flynn ▶ **in like Flynn 1** easily, quickly, without effort *US, 1945*. **2** in poker, said of a player who bets before it is his turn *US, 1951*

fly-over *noun* the inability of a mail plane in rural Alaska to land and deliver mail *US, 1972*

fly's eyes *noun* the testicles semi-exposed through tight pants. It can also refer to the act of a male exposing his testicles by pulling his underwear tightly between them with the object of terrorising people with the spectacle *AUSTRALIA, 2000*

flyspeck *noun* Tasmania. A reference to the size of Tasmania relative to mainland Australia *AUSTRALIA, 1966*

flyspeck 3 *noun* any miniscule, unreadable font *US, 1991*

fly-trap *noun* the mouth *UK, 1795*

fnarr! fnarr! used for expressing amusement at a double entendre. A rote catchphrase response that, for a while, threatened to replace actual laughter with young people *UK, 1997*

FNF *noun* used by prison officers to categorise prisoners who are held as a result of a Friday night altercation. An initialism of 'Friday night fracas' *UK, 1996*

FNG *noun* a newly arrived soldier in Vietnam. A 'fucking new guy' *US, 1966*

fnudger *noun* a person who cheats at marbles by advancing over the shooting line. Perhaps an alteration of 'fudge' *AUSTRALIA, 1974*

FOAD used as shorthand in Internet discussion groups and text messages to mean 'fuck off and die' *US, 2002*

FOAF *noun* a friend of a friend. The most common source for an urban legend or other apocryphal story *US, 1991*

foaklies *noun* inexpensive imitations of Oakley™ sunglasses *US, 2003*

foam *noun* beer *US, 1908*

foamer *noun* **1** a railway fan whose love for railways is obsessive *US, 2004*. **2** a glass of beer *US, 1959*

foamie *noun* a surfboard made from polyurethane *US, 1965*

foaming at the mouth *adjective* very angry. From a symptom of utter madness *UK, 1961*

foamy *noun* a glass of beer *US, 1983*

foamy cleanser *noun* in hold 'em poker, an ace and a jack as the first two cards dealt to a particular player. Building on the synonymous AJAX, a branded cleaner and obvious homophonic leap from 'ace-jack' *US, 1981*

fob *noun* a Samoan *NEW ZEALAND, 1998*

FOB *noun* a foreign exchange student; an international student *US, 1993*

FOB *adjective* **1** lazy, inefficient; flat on his behind *US, 1955*. **2** fresh off the boat. An initialism usually applied to recent immigrants, but in the usage of Hawaiian youth applied to visitors to the islands *US, 1981*

focker *noun* a fucker (in all senses). Filtered through a Northern Ireland accent *UK; NORTHERN IRELAND, 2001*

focus *noun* vision, eyesight *US, 1947*

FOD *noun* foreign object damage to an aircraft *US, 1989*

foeitog!; foei tog! used as an exclamation of pity or sympathy, and as a cry of 'shame!'. An Afrikaans term, *foei* (shame) *tog* (nevertheless), that has some currency among speakers of South African English *SOUTH AFRICA, 1910*

fog *noun* **1** a person who is profoundly out of touch with current trends and his social peers *US, 1983*. **2** steam *US, 1954*

fog *verb* to shoot and kill someone *US, 1913*

fog and mist; foggy *noun* drunk. Rhyming slang for PISSED *UK, 1992*

fogey *noun* an increase in military pay *US, 1878*

foggy *adjective* ▶ **haven't the foggiest** to be unclear in your mind. With ellipsis of idea or notion *UK, 1917*

fogscoffer *noun* a rainbow appearing in a fog about to dissipate *CANADA, 1963*

fogy; fogey *noun* an old person with out-dated ideas and values *UK, 1720*

fogy; fogey *adjective* old-fashioned, or unusual. Recorded in use among Leicestershire teenagers *UK, 1984*

foil *noun* **1** a quantity of illegal drugs wrapped in aluminium foil *AUSTRALIA, 1994*. **2** heroin *UK, 2003*. ▶ **put on the foil** in ice hockey, to apply tinfoil layers (illegally) under the gloves to increase the impact of punches in fights *CANADA, 1977*

foilhead *noun* a person with highlighted hair *US, 2001*

fokkin *adjective* used as an intensifier. A variant spelling of 'fucking' based on Irish pronunciation *UK, 2003*

fold *noun* money *UK, 2000*

fold *verb* **1** to fail, to cease to be operational, used of a business venture or theatrical production *UK, 1928*. **2** in poker, to withdraw from a hand, forfeiting your bet *US, 1963*. ▶ **fold hands** to stop working *TRINIDAD AND TOBAGO, 2003*

folded *noun* drunk *US, 1997*

folding; folding stuff; folding green *noun* paper money, hence money *US, 1930*

folding lettuce *noun* money, paper money. A lesser variant of FOLDING STUFF *US, 1958*

Folex *noun* an inexpensive imitation of a Rolex™ wristwatch *US, 2003*

folkie *noun* a folk singer or musician; a folk music enthusiast *US, 1966*

folknik *noun* a member of the folk music counterculture of the 1950s and 60s *US, 1958*

folks *noun* a group of your friends *US, 1997*

follies *noun* the Quarter Sessions. An ironic comparison between justice and vaudeville. The Courts Act 1971 replaced the Quarter Sessions with the Crown Courts *UK, 1950*

follow-cat *noun* a person who imitates others *TRINIDAD AND TOBAGO, 1982*

follow-pattern *adjective* copied, derivative, imitative *BARBADOS, 1965*

follow through *verb* to accidentally defecate at the conclusion of a fart *UK, 1997*

follow your nose! a catchphrase addressed to a person seeking directions *UK, 1664*

follytricks *noun* politics *JAMAICA, 2003*

FoMoCo *nickname* the Ford Motor Company *US, 1971*

fond of her mother; good to her mother *adjective* homosexual. A euphemism based on a stereotype *UK, 1992*

f-one-j-one *noun* Fiji *AUSTRALIA, 1996*

fong *noun* **1** any alcoholic beverage *NEW ZEALAND, 1985*. **2** a kick. With variant 'fon' *IRELAND, 1962*

fonged *adjective* very drunk *NEW ZEALAND, 1965*

fonk *noun* a male homosexual *BAHAMAS, 1982*

foo *noun* in computing, used as an arbitrary, temporary name for something *US, 1983*

food *noun* bullets *UK, 2001*

foodaholic *noun* a compulsive eater *US, 1965*

food boat *noun* in prison, a financial alliance between several prisoners to pay for food *UK, 1996*

food chain *noun* a pecking order or hierarchy *US, 1998*

food coma *noun* the drowsiness often experienced after eating too much *US, 1987*

foodie *noun* a person who has a passionate interest in the latest trends in gourmet food *UK, 1982*

food stamps *noun* in poker, a player's cash reserved for household expenses pressed into action after he has lost his betting money *US, 1996*

foof *noun* the breast. Usually in the plural *UK, 2002*

foofoo *noun* **1** the vagina *UK, 1998*. **2** a prissy or girlish man *US, 1848*. **3** cologne, perfume *US, 1928*. **4** something that is purely decorative without adding functional value *US, 1986*

foofoo dust; foofoo stuff; foofoo *noun* **1** heroin *US, 1998*. **2** cocaine *UK, 2002*. **3** talcum powder. Also called 'foo stuff' and 'foofoo powder' *UK, 1962*

foo gas; phou gas *noun* an explosive mixture in a buried steel drum serving as a defence around the perimeter of a military base *US, 1978*

fook 'fuck' in all senses and forms. A phonetic rendering of accented English *UK, 1997*

fool *noun* used as a term of address, sometimes suggesting foolishness and sometimes not *US, 1986*

fool *adjective* silly, foolish; often a pejorative intensifier. In conventional use from C13 to late C19. Now especially used in the US, often in the phrase 'that fool thing' *UK, 2003*

fool around *verb* to have a casual sexual relationship *US, 1937*

fool file *noun* the mythical library of the stupidest things ever said *US, 1991*

fool-fool *noun* a simple-minded fool. By reduplication *JAMAICA, 1994*

foolio *noun* a fool; a social outcast *US, 1994*

foolish powder *noun* heroin; cocaine; any powdered drug *US, 1930*

fool killer *noun* a notional creature called upon to dispose of fools *US, 1853*

fools seldom differ used as a derogatory retort to the catchphrase 'great minds think alike' *UK, 1977*

foop *noun* ▶ **one swell foop** used as a humorous reversal of 'one fell swoop' *US, 1972*

foop *verb* to have sex *BARBADOS, 1998*

fooper *noun* a homosexual male. Apparently back-slang of POOF *US, 1975*

foops *noun* a fart *TRINIDAD AND TOBAGO, 2003*

foot *noun* ▶ **on the one foot in front of the other caper** on the run *UK, 1984*. ▶ **put your foot in it** to do or say something tactless, to blunder *UK, 1823*

foot *verb* to run fast *US, 1965*

football *noun* **1** a tablet of Dilaudid™, a central nervous system depressant manufactured by the Knoll Pharmaceutical Company *US, 1972*. **2** a tablet of dextroamphetamine sulphate and amphetamine sulphate (trade name Diphetamine™), a central nervous system stimulant *US, 1966*. **3** a simple musical accompaniment used when a performer is ad libbing *US, 1973*. **4** the briefcase carrying the communication equipment that enables the president of the US to launch a nuclear attack *US, 1968*

football team *noun* a very sparse moustache. There are eleven men – or hairs – on each side. The UK version of Australia's cricket team *UK, 1984*

foot burner *noun* a walking plough *US, 1958*

footer *noun* the game of football (soccer). An early example of the Oxford University -ER, a slangifying process *UK, 1863*

footie; footy *noun* **1** the game of football (soccer) *UK, 1940*. **2** the game of rugby union *NEW ZEALAND, 1998*. **3** a football *AUSTRALIA, 1983*. **4** a pedestrian police surveillance operative *UK, 2002*

foot-in-mouth disease *noun* the tendency to say that which ought not to be said *US, 1968*

foot it *verb* to walk, especially a considerable distance. Originally US black *US, 1972*

foot on the till *noun* in horse racing, used for describing the position of a horse that is racing well *AUSTRALIA, 1989*

footpounder *noun* an infantry soldier *US, 1986*

footprint *noun* the portion of a tyre that contacts the track *US, 1972*

footrest *noun* an accelerator pedal *US, 1976*

foots *noun* theatrical footlights *US, 1919*

footsack! go away! An anglicised pronunciation of Afrikaans *voetsek* (a curt command to a dog, offensive when applied to a person) *SOUTH AFRICA, 1855*

footsie *noun* foot-to-foot contact, usually out of sight such as under a restaurant table *US, 1944*

footwarmer *noun* **1** a linear amplifier for a citizens' band radio *US, 1976*. **2** a walking plough *CANADA, 1954*

foozle *noun* in golf, a mis-hit shot *UK: SCOTLAND, 1869*

for Africa *adverb* hugely, in large amounts, greatly *SOUTH AFRICA, 1970*

for-and-aft cap *noun* a military garrison cap *UK, 1940*

for a start-off *adverb* to begin with *UK, 1959*

forbidden fruit *noun* a youthful, attractive male who is under the age of legal consent. Homosexual usage *US, 1979*

force *noun* in stage magic, any method of ensuring that a particular card (or other object) is chosen *UK, 2003*. ▶ **the force** the police *UK, 1868*

for cheese cake! used for registering anger or surprise. Euphemism and rhyming slang, FOR CHRIST'S SAKE! varied as a pun 'for Jesus' sake!' *UK, 1998*

for Christ's sake! used as an expletive, if not employed as a prayer. Recorded in conventional use since late C14; as an expletive since 1944 *UK, 1386*

for crying out loud! used for registering anger, irritation, surprise, astonishment, etc. Probably a euphemistic replacement of FOR CHRIST'S SAKE! *UK, 1924*

for days *adverb* to a great degree *US, 1981*

for days! **1** that's the truth! *US, 1968*. **2** used for expressing amazement *US, 1970*

fore-and-after hat *noun* a military garrison cap *US, 1931*

foreground *verb* to assign a high priority to a task *US, 1991*

forehand *adjective* (used of surfing) facing the wave *AUSTRALIA, 1985*

foreign *adjective* (used of a betting chip) from another casino *US, 1982*

foreigner *noun* an illicit employment using the time and materials of your legitimate employer; any work done while claiming unemployment benefit *UK, 1943*

for England *adverb* (to perform an everyday action) to an extravagant degree *UK, 1999*

forever and a day *adverb* an indefinite but considerable length of time. An intensification of 'for ever' *UK, 1823*

forever-forever used as a motto by the Black Guerrilla Family prison gang *US, 2000*

for fake used as a sarcastic reply when asked 'for real?' *US, 2003*

for free *adverb* free, gratis. The 'for' is redundant *US, 1942*

forget it! don't worry about it! *US, 1903*

for God's sake! used as an expletive, if not employed as a prayer. In conventional use by 1300; as an expletive it is widely recorded since 1932 *UK, 1932*

for it *adjective* due for punishment; in immediate trouble *UK, 1925*

fork *verb* **1** used as a euphemism for 'to fuck' *US, 1999*. **2** to ride (a horse) *US, 1882*

fork and knife *noun* **1** life. Rhyming slang, generally used in the phrases 'not on your fork and knife' and 'never in your fork and knife' *UK, 1934*. **2** a wife. Rhyming slang *UK, 1937*

forked *adjective* in computing, unacceptably slow or dysfunctional. Probably a euphemism for FUCKED *US, 1991*

forked-tongued *adjective* duplicitous. Ascribing stereotypical snake-like qualities; best remembered (although possibly apocryphal) from cowboy films in the phrase 'white man speak with forked tongue' *US, 1961*

forklift *noun* in poker, a substantial win *US, 1996*

fork out *verb* to pay *UK, 1831*

fork over *verb* to hand over *UK, 1820*

forks *noun* the fingers. Originally a pickpocket's term *UK, 1812*

form *noun* **1** a criminal record *UK, 1956*. **2** a person's character or true nature *AUSTRALIA, 1944*. **3** the situation, organisation or position *UK, 1948*. **4** women viewed as sexual prospects *US, 1953*. **5** high spirits. Generally used with 'in' as, for instance, 'he's in form tonight' *UK, 1877*. **6** luck. From 'form' as 'a record of a racehorse's past performance' *AUSTRALIA, 1962*

formal *adjective* ▶ **go formal** to wear a clean flannel shirt *US, 1997*

formerly known as known as. A wildly popular construction after recording artist Prince announced in 1993 that he had changed his name to The Artist Formerly Known as Prince *US, 1993*

for mossies *adverb* for no special reason, for amusement *SOUTH AFRICA, 1973*

form player *noun* in horse racing, someone who bets based on information found in a racing form *US, 1976*

formula one *noun* a hammerhead shark. Used by surfers *AUSTRALIA, 1991*

for Pete's sake! euphemistic for 'God's sake!' *UK, 1924*

for real *adverb* ▷*see:* FE REAL

for real? used for expressing surprise and perhaps doubt *US, 1995*

Forrest Gump; forrest *noun* **1** an act of defecation. Rhyming slang for DUMP formed from the title of a 1994 Oscar-winning film and its eponymous leading character *UK, 1998*. **2** an unpleasant place or location. Rhyming slang for DUMP *UK, 1998*

for Ron for later on. Punning on a diminutive of the name Ronald *UK, 2000*

for shame! used as a humorous admission that you have been cleverly ridiculed *US, 1963*

for sure! used as an enthusiastic, stylish affirmation *US, 1978*

Forsyte Saga *noun* lager. Rhyming slang, after the 1970s television dramatisation of the series of novels by John Galsworthy (1867–1933) *UK, 1979*

Fort Apache *nickname* the police station in the 41st precinct, New York. An allusion to the American West and the wild, lawless character of the neighbourhood *US, 1976*

Fort Bushy *noun* the vulva and female pubic hair *US, 1961*

Fort Fucker *nickname* Fort Rucker, Alabama. Home of the US Army Aviation Center for both fixed wing and helicopter training *US, 1991*

Fort Fumble *nickname* the Canadian National Defence Headquarters in Ottawa *CANADA, 1995*

Forth Bridge job *noun* anything needing constant amendment, or renewal or updating. An allusion to the job of painting the Forth Bridge – the painters are reputed to start again at the other end as soon as they have finished the job *UK, 1984*

Fort Head *nickname* Fort Hood, a US Army installation. From the preponderance of drug use there during the Vietnam war *US, 1968*

for the love of Mike! used for registering exasperation, disbelief, surprise, exaltation, etc. A euphemism 'for the love of Christ' or, possibly, 'Moses' *UK, 1959*

for the love of Pete! used for registering exasperation, disbelief, surprise, exaltation, etc. A euphemistic 'for the love of God'; probably American Irish Roman Catholic origins; a variation of FOR PETE'S SAKE!, on the model of FOR THE LOVE OF MIKE! *UK, 1949*

forthwith *noun* an order to a police officer to report immediately *US, 1958*

Fort Knox *noun* in shuffleboard, a number that is well hidden or guarded *US, 1967*

Fort Liquordale *nickname* Fort Lauderdale, Flordia. A nickname earned from the invasion of heavy-drinking college students each spring *US, 1982*

Fort Lost in the Woods *nickname* Fort Leonard Wood, Missouri *US, 1974*

Fortnum & Mason; fortnum *noun* a basin. Rhyming slang, formed on the name of a London department store. *UK, 1998*

fortnum cut *noun* a short back and sides haircut, mockingly called a basin cut or a pudding-basin cut. Formed from rhyming slang for FORTNUM & MASON (a basin) *UK, 1998*

Fort Piss *nickname* Fort Bliss, Texas. Home to the US Army Air Defense Artillery Center *US, 1991*

Fort Pricks *nickname* Fort Dix, New Jersey. A major training, mobilisation and deployment centre. The scene of frequent demonstrations against the Vietnam war *US, 1974*

Fort Puke *nickname* Fort Polk, Louisiana. Home to the JRT Operations Group, the 2nd Armored Cavalry Regiment, the 519th Military Police Battalion and the Warrior Brigade *US, 1974*

Fortrash *noun* the FORTRAN computer language *US, 1991*

for true *adverb* ▷*see:* FE TRUE

Fort Screw Us *nickname* Fort Lewis, Washington. Home of the I Corps *US, 1991*

Fort Smell *nickname* Fort Sill, Oklahoma. The primary field artillery training facility during the conflict in Vietnam *US, 1991*

Fort Turd *nickname* Fort Ord, Monterey, California *US, 1991*

fortune cookie *noun* **1** an aphorism or joke that appears on a computer screen when a user logs in *US, 1991*. **2** in poker, a bet made without having seen all of your cards *US, 1996*

fortuni *adjective* gorgeous *UK, 2002*

Fort Useless *nickname* Fort Eustis, Virginia. Home to the US Army Transportation School, with training in rail, marine, amphibious operations and other modes of transportation *US, 1974*

forty-deuce *nickname* 42nd Street, New York *US, 1987*

forty-fin *noun* a millipede *BAHAMAS, 1982*

forty-four *noun* a whore. Rhyming slang *UK, 2003*

forty-going-north *adjective* leaving or moving quickly *US, 1993*

fortyleg *noun* a centipede *BARBADOS, 1965*

forty-miler *noun* a new and inexperienced carnival worker or one who never travels far from home with the carnival *US, 1935*

forty-niner *noun* a cocaine user. An allusion to the gold rush of 1849, with cocaine serving as 'gold dust' *US, 1992*

forty-pounder *noun* a 40-ounce bottle of alcohol *CANADA, 1998*

forty-rod *noun* strong, cheap whisky *US, 1861*

Forty Thieves *noun* the mostly white, all wealthy shop owners on Front Street, Hamilton, Bermuda *BERMUDA, 1985*

forty-three *verb* to keep apart from the main prison community for 'safety of self or others' *UK, 1996*

forty-weight *noun* **1** strong coffee. Inviting a comparison with motor oil *US, 1976*. **2** beer, especially Iron City™ *US, 1976*

forty winks *noun* a nap, a short sleep *UK, 1872*

forward *noun* any amphetamine or other central nervous system stimulant *US, 1966*

FOS *adjective* full of shit, literally or figuratively *US, 1978*

fo' sheezy; fo' sheazy; fa' sheezy; fo' sho sho certainly *US, 1999*

fossick *verb* **1** to search for gold in abandoned mines or mining refuse. From the British dialect of Cornwall *AUSTRALIA, 1852*. **2** to rummage about in searching for something *AUSTRALIA, 1855*. **3** to poke about a place *AUSTRALIA, 1941*

fossicker *noun* a person who fossicks *AUSTRALIA, 1852*

fossil *noun* **1** an old person with outmoded ideas and values *US, 1952*. **2** a parent *US, 1957*. **3** in computing, a feature that is retained after it is no longer needed in order to preserve compatibility *US, 1991*

fother mucker *noun* used euphemistically for 'motherfucker' in all senses. A Spoonerism; in the Brite Bar in New York it is possible to buy a 'Fother Mucker' cocktail *US, 2003*

fougasse *noun* napalm-thickened petrol, used in an improvised flame-thrower. Korean and Vietnam war usage *US, 1989*

foul *adjective* unpleasant, unfriendly. Conventional English rendered slang with attitude *US, 1999*

foulball *noun* a despised person *US, 1925*

fouler *noun* a very bad mood *IRELAND, 2003*

foul-up *noun* an instance of something being botched or ruined *US, 1943*

foul up *verb* to botch, to ruin *US, 1942*

found-in *noun* a person arrested for patronizing an illegal bar or gambling club *CANADA, 1960*

fountains of Rome *noun* in homosexual usage, urinals in a public toilet *US, 1987*

four *noun* **1** a capsule of Empirin™ with codeine, designed for pain relief but abused by users of central nervous system depressants and opiates *US, 1977*. **2** a four-ounce glass of beer *AUSTRALIA, 1972*. **3** yes; an affirmative. Also written as '4'. An abbreviation of the conventional citizens' band radio code 10–4 *US, 1976*

four-banger *noun* a four-cylinder engine *US, 1953*

four-be-two *noun* a prison warder. Rhyming slang for **SCREW** *UK, 1996*

four bits *noun* a fifty-year prison sentence *US, 1990*

four-by *noun* a prison warder *AUSTRALIA, 1983*

four-by-four *noun* **1** a vehicle with four wheels and four-wheel drive *US, 1993*. **2** a whore. Rhyming slang *UK, 2003*

four by too's *noun* in twelve-step recovery programmes such as Alcoholics Anonymous, used for describing why recovering addicts don't attend programme meetings – too busy, too tired, too lazy or too drunk. A play on 'two-by-four', the dimensions of the most common timber used in construction *US, 1998*

four by two *noun* **1** a Jewish person. Rhyming slang, originally military. Variants include 'four by', 'fourby' and 'four-he' – but 'three by two', a civilian variation, is now obsolete *UK, 1936*. **2** a prison warder. Rhyming slang for **SCREW** *AUSTRALIA, 2001*

four-colour glossies *noun* any literature that contains some useful information but which emphasises style over substance *US, 1991*

four-cornered *adjective* caught in the commission of a crime *US, 1992*

four-deuce *noun* an M-30 4.2 inch heavy mortar. Vietnam war usage *US, 1968*

fourex fever *noun* a state of drunkenness caused by XXXX™ lager *AUSTRALIA, 1996*

four-eyed *adjective* wearing glasses *US, 1878*

four-eyes *noun* a person who wears glasses *US, 1865*

four five *noun* a .45 calibre handgun *US, 1994*

fourflusher *noun* a liar, a fraud *US, 1904*

four f's *noun* used as a jocular if cynical approach to male relationships with women – find them, feel them, fuck them, forget them. A pun on 4F draft status, which meant that a man was physically unfit to serve *US, 1942*

four-laner *noun* a truck driver who prefers large interstate motorways *US, 1971*

four-letter man *noun* **1** an unpleasant person. Euphemistic disguise for the letters *s h i t* or *c u n t US, 1923*. **2** a male homosexual *US, 1949*

four-letter word *noun* a profanity, especially although not always one with four letters, and usually the word 'fuck' *US, 1936*

four-lunger *noun* a four-cylinder engine *US, 1971*

four-on-the-floor *noun* **1** a car with a four-speed transmission with the gear shift mounted on the floor *US, 1968*. **2** use of the bass drum on every beat, especially in disco music. Playing on the automotive term *US, 1980*

fourpenny dark *noun* cheap wine *AUSTRALIA, 1955*

four percent *noun* a mild beer that was for a time sold in the west *CANADA, 1962*

four plus *adverb* to the utmost degree *US, 1961*

fours *noun* **1** in poker, four of a kind *US, 1967*. **2** the fourth landing or floor level in a prison *UK, 1996*

fours and dors *noun* a combination of number four codeine tablets and Doriden™ sleeping pills, which produces an opiate-like effect on the user *US, 1989*

four-square *noun* in new car sales, the work sheet used by a sales representative *US, 1989*

four-star *adjective* excellent. From a common rating system used with hotels, restaurants and the like *US, 1935*

four-s time *noun* the time before going out on the town; in the armed services, the pre-liberty period. The s's are 'shit, shave, shower and shine' *US, 2001*

four-striper *noun* a captain in the US Navy *US, 1914*

fourteen *noun* **1** an M-14 rifle *US, 1985*. **2** the Grumman F-14 Tomcat, a long-range strike-fighter aircraft. Vietnam war usage *US, 1978*

fourteen and two *noun* a typical punishment of 14 days restricted to barracks with two hours of extra duty each day. Punishment imposed under Article 15 of the Uniform Code of Military Justice for minor misconduct by military members *US, 1991*

fourteener *noun* any one of the 54 peaks over 14,000 feet in the Colorado Rocky Mountains *US, 1997*

Fourteen Feathers *noun* Thunderbird™ wine. On account of the 14 feathers on the label's bird *US, 2003*

four-tens *noun* a work schedule of four ten-hour days a week. A schedule that became popular in the US in the late 1970s and early 80s, keeping the basic 40-hour working week but creating an additional 52 days a year off work *US, 1979*

fourth of July *noun* a tie. Rhyming slang *UK, 1931*

four to the floor *adjective* **1** in music, a four bar beat; describes most modern dance music *UK, 2002*. **2** falling-down drunk. Suggesting the drunkard is possibly a musician and is probably on 'all fours' *UK, 2002*

four-trey, the country way *noun* a roll of seven in a craps game *US, 1957*

four-twenty *noun* **1** marijuana. Also written as '4:20'. False etymologies abound; the term was coined by teenagers in Marin County, California, and does not refer to any police code *US, 1969*. **2** any time that is considered the appropriate time to smoke marijuana. Also written as '4:20'. Coinage is credited to California students in the 1970s then, via the scene surrounding the Grateful Dead into wider usage *US, 2004*

four-way *noun* a mixture of four drugs, usually psychedelics and stimulants *US, 1992*

four-way *adjective* willing to engage in four types of sexual activity, the exact nature of which depends up on the person described and the context *US, 1971*

four-wheeler *noun* **1** in trucking, a passenger car *US, 1986*. **2** a nominal Christian, originally specifically a Catholic, who only goes to church for his or her baptism, marriage and funeral. Shorter form of 'four-wheel Christian'. The four wheels are, in turn, on a pram, a wedding-car and a hearse *UK, 1969*

four wheel skid *noun* ▷ *see:* FRONT WHEEL SKID

four-year lesbian *noun* a woman who takes lesbian lovers in college, planning to return to the safer waters of heterosexuality after graduation from college *US, 1995*

four zero *adjective* 40 years old. This entry stands as an example of all variations from 20 to 90 *UK, 2000*

fox *noun* **1** a beautiful woman or girl *US, 1961*. **2** in poker, the sixth player to the left of the dealer *US, 1988*

fox *verb* **1** to follow; to spy on *NEW ZEALAND, 1905*. **2** to slaughter a horse for fox food *CANADA, 1980*

fox and badger *noun* the penis. Rhyming slang for TADGER *UK, 2003*

fox and hound *noun* a *round* of drinks. Rhyming slang, formed on the name of a pub *UK, 1992*

Fox Charlie Charlie; Friendly Candy Company *nickname* the Federal Communications Commission *US, 1976*

foxcore *noun* rock music played by women *UK, 2003*

fox hunter *noun* an Englishman *AUSTRALIA, 1989*

foxie *noun* **1** an attractive girl *US, 1979*. **2** a fox terrier *AUSTRALIA, 1906*

foxtress *noun* a beautiful woman or girl *UK, 2005*

foxtrot yankee! fuck you! From the military phonetic alphabet – FY *US, 1991*

foxy *adjective* attractive, beautiful. Usually but not always applied to a woman *US, 1895*

frabjous *adjective* joyous, wonderful. A nonsense word coined by Lewis Carroll (C.L. Dodgson), and used vaguely in various contextual senses *UK, 1872*

fracture *verb* to have a strong, favourable effect upon someone *US, 1946*

fractured *adjective* drunk *US, 1953*

frag *noun* **1** a *frag*mentation hand grenade or bomb *US, 1943*. **2** a *frag*ment from a bullet or artillery shell *US, 1966*. **3** a *frag*mentary order *US, 1962*

frag *verb* **1** to kill a fellow soldier, usually an officer and usually with a fragmentation grenade. A term coined in Vietnam to describe a practice that became common if not widespread in Vietnam *US, 1970*. **2** by extension, to score a 'kill' over another player in video and computer games, especially Quake™ *US, 2002*. **3** to dispatch by a fragmentary order *US, 1967*. **4** in motor racing, to cause an engine to explode, sending pieces of motor through the engine block *US, 1992*

fragged-out *adjective* over-stressed. Military, from US military abbreviation of 'fragmentary/fragmentation.' *UK, 2001*

fraggle *noun* **1** in prison, a mentally ill inmate. A Fraggle is a television puppet character from Jim Henson's *Fraggle Rock*, 1983–87; this excerpt from the theme lyric may well explain the derivation: 'Dance your cares away, / Worry's for another day [...] Let the Fraggles play'. Jim Henson also created *The Muppets* which also serve as models for the slow-witted *UK, 1996*. **2** (among Canadian Forces personnel) an avionics technician *CANADA, 1995*

fraggle juice *noun* in prison, medication given to mentally ill inmates *UK, 1996*

Fraggle Rock *noun* **1** a section of a prison dedicated to psychiatric criminal care *UK, 1996*. **2** (among Canadian Air Force personnel) the Air Command Headquarters in Winnipeg *CANADA, 1995*

frag list *noun* a frag order. Vietnam war usage *US, 1986*

frag order *noun* an order setting the day's specific military objectives. Shortened 'fragmentation order'. Vietnam war usage. *US, 1961*

fraho; frajo *noun* marijuana. Originally a 'cigarette' or 'marijuana cigarette' *US, 1952*

'fraid so I'm afraid so. Often answered with ''fraid not' *US, 1895*

fraidy cat *noun* a cowardly person *UK, 1910*

frail *noun* a woman *US, 1899*

frak! used as a non-profane oath. Used by spacecraft pilots, especially Lt. Starbuck on the US television series *Battlestar Galactica* (ABC, 1978–80), and briefly in popular speech *US, 1979*

frame *noun* **1** the general circumstance, especially of a crime. Conventionally a frame fits the picture; figuratively applied *UK, 1970*. **2** the body *US, 1052*. ▶ **in the frame** under suspicion of involvement in a crime that is being investigated *UK, 1996*

frame *verb* to incriminate a person by contriving false evidence *US, 1899*

frame dame *noun* an attractive and sexually active, if not too bright, girl *US, 1979*

frame job *noun* a conspiracy, especially one where blame for a misdeed is placed on someone *US, 1973*

framer *noun* a bed *US, 1973*

frames *noun* eyeglasses *US, 1972*

frame-up; frame *noun* manufactured evidence that is intended to incriminate *US, 1908*

frammis *noun* a commotion *US, 1954*

France *noun* used as a euphemistic subsitute for 'hell' *BARBADOS, 1965*

France and Spain; frarny *noun* rain. Rhyming slang *UK, 1931*

Francis Drake *noun* a brake. Rhyming slang, formed on the name of celebrated circumnavigator and national hero Sir Francis Drake, 1540–96 *UK, 1992*

franger *noun* a condom. Perhaps an alteration of FRENCH LETTER *AUSTRALIA, 1981*

frangler *noun* a condom *AUSTRALIA, 1988*

Franglish *noun* French and English mixed or blended in the same sentence *CANADA, 1964*

frank *noun* a *frank*furter, a hot dog *US, 1925*

Frank and Pat *noun* talk. Rhyming slang for chat, based on long-running characters Frank Butcher (from 1987) and Pat Evans (from 1986) in BBC television soap opera *EastEnders UK, 2002*

Franken- *prefix* in combination with a noun denotes a freakish, genetically modified or ugly form of that thing. After Mary Shelly's 1818 novel *Frankenstein* but from the images provided by C20 Hollywood *US, 1992*

Frankie Boy *nickname* Frank Sinatra, American singer (1915–1998) *US, 1963*

Frankie Dettori *noun* a *story*, the facts or circumstance. Rhyming slang, formed from the name of the champion jockey (b.1970) *UK, 2002*

Frankie Fraser; frankie *noun* a razor. Rhyming slang, formed from the name of 'Mad' Frankie Fraser (b.1923), an ex-gangster with a reputation for violence and a celebrity profile *UK, 2001*

Frankie Howerd; frankie *noun* a coward. Rhyming slang, formed from the name of a popular comedian, 1917–92 *UK, 1984*

Frankie Laine; frankie *noun* a toilet *chain* (to flush the lavatory); hence a handle that operates a cistern. Rhyming slang, formed from the name of a popular American singer (b.1913) *UK, 1992*

Frankie Vaughan; frankie *noun* **1** pornography. Rhyming slang for PORN; formed from the name of Liverpool-born singer and actor Frankie Vaughan (b.1928). Also used as an adjective *UK, 1979*. **2** a prawn. Rhyming slang formed from the name of a popular British singer, 1928–99 *UK, 1984*

Frankie Vaughno *noun* pornography. An extension of the original rhyming slang for PORN, to match PORNO *UK, 2002*

frantic *adjective* exciting, thrilling *US, 1934*

frap *verb* to whip *US, 1894*

frapping *adjective* used as a euphemism for 'fucking' in its different senses *US, 1968*

Fraser and Nash; Frazer-Nash *noun* an act of urination. Rhyming slang for SLASH (an act of urination); from Frazer-Nash, a sports car manufacturer until 1939 *UK, 1974*

frat *noun* a college fraternity *US, 1895*

frat around *verb* to idle, to gossip instead of studying *US, 1963*

fratastic *adjective* displaying characteristics associated with college fraternities *US, 2003*

frat dick *noun* a boorish member of a college fraternity *US, 1989*

fraternity brother *noun* a fellow prisoner *US, 1949*

frat mattress *noun* a girl who is sexually attracted to and available for college fraternity boys *US, 2001*

frat rat *noun* an obnoxious, aggressive, arrogant example of a college fraternity member *US, 1958*

frat tuck *noun* a shirt worn tucked into the trousers in the front but hanging loose in the back *US, 2001*

fratty *adjective* characteristic of college fraternity behaviour, style, or language *US, 2003*

fratty bagger *noun* a stereotypical fraternity member who dresses, talks, and lives the part to a fault *US, 1973*

frau *noun* a wife. A jocular borrowing from German *UK, 1821*

frazzle-assed *adjective* worn out *US, 1951*

frazzled *adjective* **1** confused *US, 1883*. **2** drunk *US, 1906*

freak *noun* **1** a person with strong sexual desires, often fetishistic *US, 1922*. **2** a devotee, an enthusiast *US, 1895*. **3** a member of the 1960s counterculture. Originally a disparaging negative, turned around and used in a positive, complimentary sense. Widely used from the mid-1960s; hurled as abuse at the original hippies, the term was adopted by them and turned back on the critics by the self-confessed 'freaks' with an ability to FREAK OUT themselves and others *US, 1960*. **4** a habitual drug user. Usually suffixed to a defining drug *US, 1967*. **5** used as a term of endearment. Teen slang *US, 1954*. **6** a dance with strong suggestions of sexual movement, first popular as a 1975 disco dance and then again in the late 1990s and early 2000s. Used with 'the' unless used as a verb *US, 1979*. **7** a nonsensical novelty song *US, 1948*. **8** a wrestler whose huge size is obviously the result of the use of anabolic steroids *US, 1996*. **9** in poker, a wild card, which may be played as a card of any value *US, 1949*. ▶ **get your freak on; get your freak out** to enjoy a sexual perversion *US, 2003*

freak *verb* to panic *US, 1964*

freak *adjective* **1** in jazz, unorthodox *US, 1955*. **2** attractive *US, 1994*

freaked *adjective* disturbed, unsettled, nervous *US, 1967*

freak house *noun* **1** an abandoned building used as a temporary residence for drug addicts who have been evicted from their own dwelling *US, 1995*. **2** a room, apartment, or house where amphetamine addicts gather to inject the drug *US, 1970*

freaking *adjective* used as an intensifier where 'fucking' is to be avoided *US, 1928*

freaking A! used as a euphemism for 'fucking A!' in expressing surprise *US, 2002*

freakish *adjective* sexually perverted *US, 1929*

freak jacket *noun* a reputation for unconventional sexual interests *US, 1967*

freaknasty *noun* a sexually active woman who shares her activity with multiple partners *US, 2001*

freaknik *noun* a mass celebration of black students in the streets of Atlanta, Georgia, during college spring break *US, 1992*

freako *noun* a weirdo; a sexual deviant; a habitual drug-user *US, 1963*

freak off *verb* **1** to have sex, especially with vigour and without restraint. An extremely subjective verb, perhaps referring to homosexual sex, perhaps to oral sex, perhaps to heterosexual anal sex *US, 1967*. **2** to go, to leave *US, 1970*

freak-out *noun* **1** a celebratory event, a gathering together of counterculturists to enjoy music and drugs. A response to the critics who called them 'freaks', via FREAK OUT (to panic) *US, 1967* ▷*see:* RAVE. **2** an uninhibited sexual exhibition *US, 1969*. **3** a temporary loss of sanity and control while under the influence of a psychoactive drug *UK, 1966*. **4** a complete panic and loss of control *US, 1970*. **5** a member of the 1960s counterculture *UK, 1970*

freak out *verb* **1** to lose sanity while under the influence of LSD or another hallucinogen *US, 1967*. **2** to panic *US, 1964*. **3** to make someone feel unsettled, astonished, or bizarre *US, 1964*. **4** to snap under intolerable pressure *UK, 1979*. **5** to behave in a crazed manner as a response to an emotional stimulus *US, 1966*

freak show *noun* a fetishistic sexual performance *US, 2001*

freak trick *noun* a prostitute's customer who pays for unusual sex *US, 1971*

freaky *noun* a habitual drug user *UK, 1969*

freaky *adjective* **1** odd, bizarre *US, 1895*. **2** sexually deviant *UK, 1977*. **3** characteristic of the 1960s counterculture *US, 1971*. ▶ **get freaky** to have sex *US, 1996*

freaky-deaky *adjective* acting without restraint, especially in a sexual way *US, 1981*

freckle *noun* the anus. Popularised by the Barry McKenzie cartoon strip *AUSTRALIA, 1967*

freckle-puncher *noun* a male homosexual *AUSTRALIA, 1968*

Fred Astaire *noun* **1** a chair. Rhyming slang *UK, 2003*. **2** a hair. Rhyming slang, formed on the name of the American entertainer, 1899–1987 *UK, 1992*

freddy *noun* an amphetamine tablet, especially a capsule of ephedrine *US, 1992*

Freddy Fraternity *noun* a stereotypical college fraternity member who looks, dresses, talks, and lives the part *US, 1995*

Fred Nerk; Fred Nerks *noun* used as a name for an unknown person *AUSTRALIA, 1967*

Fred's *nickname* Fortnum & Mason, an upmarket grocers and department store in Piccadilly, London. Upper-class society usage *UK, 1982*

Fred's out used as a warning that you have farted *US, 1973*

free *noun* the world outside prison *US, 1966*

free *verb* ▶ **free the tadpoles** of a male, to masturbate *UK, 1999*

free *adjective* unaffected by any conventional values. A critical if vague word from the 1960s counterculture *US, 1967*

freeball *verb* (used of a male) to dress without underwear *US, 1997*

freebase *noun* nearly pure cocaine alkaloid which can be obtained from powdered cocaine hydrochloride and is then burnt and inhaled *US, 1979*

freebase *verb* to remove the impurities from cocaine to advance and heighten the effect. By ellipsis from 'free the base' *US, 1980*

free baser *noun* a user of freebase cocaine *US, 1979*

freebie; freeby *noun* something that is given away at no cost *US, 1928*

freebie *adjective* free of charge *US, 1946*

freeco *noun* something of value given away for free *TRINIDAD AND TOBAGO, 1985*

freedom bird *noun* an aeroplane bringing troops back to the US from Vietnam *US, 1971*

freeganism *noun* a political/ecological philosophy of consuming food and drink that is past its use-by or sell-by date and would, therefore, otherwise be thrown away. A combination of 'free' and 'veganism' *US, 2003*

free, gratis and for nothing *adjective* costing nothing. Tautological *UK, 1841*

free green peppers *noun* a sneeze by a food preparer. Limited usage, but clever *US, 1996*

free it up *verb* to disclose information *US, 1997*

freelancer *noun* a prostitute unattached to either pimp or brothel *US, 1973*

freeload *verb* to cadge; to subsist at other people's expense *US, 1942*

freeloader *noun* a person who manages to eat, drink and socialise at the expense of others *US, 1936*

free lunch *noun* used as a symbol of something that is provided freely *US, 1949*

freeman *noun* ▶ **on the freeman's** gratis, for free *UK, 1999*

freeness *noun* **1** an open-invitation party *TRINIDAD AND TOBAGO, 1948*. **2** a free event *BARBADOS, 1965*

Freep *nickname* the Los Angeles *Free Press*; the Detroit *Free Press US, 1971*

free pass to bankruptcy *noun* a credit card *US, 1971*

free ride *noun* **1** used as a metaphor for attaining something without effort or cost *US, 1899*. **2** in poker, the right to stay in a hand without further betting, most commonly because the player has bet his entire bankroll on the hand *US, 1963*. **3** an orientation flight on a military aircraft *US, 1983*

free-rider *noun* a motorcyclist who shares a gang's philosophy but does not formally join the gang *US, 1992*

Free Shoes University *noun* Florida State University. A back-formation from the initials FSU, playing on the role of athletics and the sponsorship of athletics by a major shoe company at the university *US, 2000*

freeside *adjective* outside prison *US, 1960*

freestyle *noun* heterosexual intercourse *UK, 2000*

freestyle *verb* to improvise and perform a rap lyric, often a capella *US, 1995*

freeware *noun* computer software provided free of charge *US, 1983*

freeway *noun* in a prison dormitory, the aisle through the centre of the room. Alluding to the constant foot traffic *US, 1996*

freeway surfer *noun* a person who embraces the mannerisms of surfing, owns the equipment needed to surf, but who chooses to watch from the safety of the car *US, 1987*

free, white and 21 *adjective* possessing free will and able to exercise self-determination *US, 1949*

free world *noun* life outside prison *US, 1960*

free-world *adjective* civilian; from outside prison *US, 1967*

free-world gal *noun* a male prisoner who practised homosexuality before entering prison *US, 1972*

free-world punk *noun* a male prisoner who engaged in homosexual sex before prison *US, 1972*

freeze *noun* **1** cocaine. From the numbing, cooling effect *US, 1984*. **2** a small amount of cocaine placed on the tongue *US, 1989*. **3** a rejection of affection. Colder than the proverbial 'cold shoulder' *US, 1942*

freeze *verb* **1** to stop moving completely *UK, 1848*. **2** in draw poker, to decline the opportunity to discard and draw any new cards *US, 1971*. ▶ **freeze your nose** to use cocaine. From the drug's numbing effect on mucuous membranes *US, 1972*. ▶ **freeze your nuts** to be extremely cold *UK, 2001*

freeze-out *noun* a poker game in which all participants must play until they lose all their money or win all the other players' money *US, 1975*

freezer *noun* in poker, an early call made even as other players continue to raise their bets *US, 1967*. ▶ **the freezer** Antarctica *ANTARCTICA, 1993*

freeze up *verb* to become paralyzed with fear. An occupational hazard of those who work high above the ground *US, 1989*

freight *noun* the cost of something, especially a bribe *US, 1950*. ▶ **pull freight** on the railways, to quit a job *US, 1977*

freight train *noun* a wave breaking powerfully in perfect formation *US, 1987*

French *noun* **1** oral sex, especially on a man *US, 1916*. **2** an open-mouthed, French kiss *US, 1978*. **3** profanity *US, 1865*. ▶ **excuse my French!; pardon my French!** employed as an apology for a use of spoken language which may cause offence. Often used in a cursory manner or with insincerity. The original intention, presumably, was to allow the apologee the pretence not to have understood a 'foreign' word; now the apology is a cliché which merely acknowledges an inappropriate use of robust unconventional English *UK, 1936*

French *verb* **1** to perform oral sex. The term derives from the widely held belief that the practice is very common in France *US, 1923*. **2** to French kiss; to kiss with open lips and exploratory tongues *US, 1955*. **3** in drag racing and hot rodding, to fit the bonnet (hood) over the headlights to create the apperance of recessed headlights *US, 1968*

French blue *noun* a manufactured combination of tranquillizer (methaqualone) and stimulant (amphetamine) taken recreationally *UK, 1964*

French bull-hook *noun* a deceptive explanation *BAHAMAS, 1982*

French date *noun* oral sex performed on a man by a prostitute *US, 1972*

French deck *noun* a deck of cards decorated with art ranging from naughty and nude to pornographic *US, 1963*

French dip *noun* precoital vaginal secretions *US, 1987*

French dressing *noun* semen. An allusion to FRENCH (oral sex) *US, 1987*

French Embassy *noun* a premises of the Young Men's Christian Association. An allusion to the association between the YMCA and homosexual men who enjoy FRENCH (oral sex) *US, 1963*

French fits *noun* tremens. Possibly combines a conventional fit of the SHAKES with an allusion to the stereotypical French characteristic of shrugging *US, 1940*

French fries *noun* **1** 3 inch sticks of crack cocaine with ridged edges *US, 1993*. **2** the thighs. Rhyming slang *UK, 2002*

French harp *noun* a harmonica *US, 1983*

Frenchie *noun* a light-skinned person; an unlikeable person *SAINT KITTS AND NEVIS, 1998* ▷ *see also:* FRENCHY

French inhale *verb* to draw cigarette smoke into the mouth and then allow it to drift out and upwards for inhalation through the nose. The French credit is presumably to signal how sophisticated such technique is thought to be *US, 1957*

French joint *noun* an over-sized, conical marijuana cigarette *US, 1997*

French kiss *noun* **1** a kiss with the mouths open and tongues adventuring. With variant 'Frenchie' *US, 1949*. **2** an act of urination; urination. Rhyming slang for PISS *UK, 1992*

French kiss *verb* to kiss with the mouth open and the tongue active *US, 1918*

French lay *noun* oral sex *US, 1972*

French leave *noun* a departure without intimation; flight *UK, 1771*

French lessons *noun* oral sex *US, 1970*

French letter *noun* a condom. In the mid-C20 so common in use as to be almost conventional; however usage inevitably diminished with the advent of the contraceptive pill. In post-AIDS society 'French letter' is now just one among hundreds of newer slang terms for the condom. Unusual variations are 'American', 'Italian' or 'Spanish' letters. The French repaid the compliment with *capote anglaise* (a condom), literally an English hooded cape, which abbreviates as *capote*; interestingly, when 'French letter' is abbreviated the nationality remains and it becomes a FRENCHY or a FRENCHIE *UK, 1856*

French loaf *noun* four. Rhyming slang, on back slang 'rofe' (RUOF) *UK, 1974*

Frenchman's acre *noun* an arpent or since the 1970s, a hectare, French measures of land *CANADA, 1992*

French massage *noun* oral sex *AUSTRALIA, 1985*

French postcard *noun* a photographic postcard depicting anything ranging from simple female nudity to full-blown sexual activity *US, 1926*

French safe *noun* a condom *US, 1870*

French screwdriver *noun* a hammer *US, 1987*

French tickler *noun* a condom with external protrusions marketed as giving pleasure to the wearer's partner *US, 1916*

French trick *noun* oral sex performed by a prostitute *US, 1972*

French wank *noun* an act of sexual gratification in which the penis is rubbed between a female partner's breasts *UK, 1997*

Frenchy; Frenchie *noun* **1** a French or French Canadian person, often as a nickname *UK, 1883*. **2** a fundamentally honest gambler who will cheat occasionally if the right opportunity arises *US, 1961*. **3** a condom. A familiar shortening of FRENCH LETTER *UK, 1998*. **4** an act of oral-genital sex *US, 1957*

Frenchy; Frenchie *adjective* French *UK, 1883*

freq; freak *noun* a radio frequency *US, 1969*

frequency *noun* a level of understanding *US, 1959*

frequently outwitted by inanimate objects *adjective* extremely incompetent. US naval aviator usage *US, 1986*

fresca *noun* an affectionate pat on the head. From the film *Caddy Shack* *US, 1984*

fresh *verb* to flatter *US, 1989*

fresh *adjective* **1** good, sharp, stylish. Possibly shortened from 'We're fresh out the pack / so you gotta stay back, / we got one Puerto Rican / and the rest are black', an early 1980s signature routine by

Grand Wizard Theodore and the Fantastic 5 MCs *US, 1984*.
2 impudent. Possibly from German *frech* (impudent) *US, 1845*. **3** bad
smelling *BARBADOS, 1965*

fresh and sweet *adjective* very recently released from jail *US, 1982*

freshener *noun* any alcoholic drink *US, 1969*

freshen up *verb* to clean, to smarten, to revive. An example of a
conventional term, 'freshen', being made colloquial by the
addition of an unnecessary adverb *UK, 1937*

fresher *noun* a university freshman *UK, 1882*

fresh-fucked *adjective* energised and happy, whether the result of
recent sex or not *US, 1994*

freshie *noun* a freshwater crocodile *AUSTRALIA, 1964*

freshies *noun* **1** in snowboarding, the first tracks in virgin snow *US,
1995*. **2** fresh fruit and vegetables *ANTARCTICA, 1990*

fresh meat *noun* **1** a person, especially a virgin, seen merely as a
object for sexual conquest *UK, 1896*. **2** a newly arrived soldier. Also
referred to as 'new meat' *US, 1908*

fresh money *noun* in horse racing, the cash actually brought to the
track and bet on a given day *US, 1947*

fresh-water American; fresh-water Yankee *noun* a person who
has never been to the US but speaks with an American accent and
embraces other American mannerisms *TRINIDAD AND TOBAGO, 1961*

fress *verb* **1** to eat greedily or to excess. From the German for
'devour' *US, 1968*. **2** to engage as the active partner in oral sex. From
the sense 'to eat greedily' *US, 1998*

fret *adjective* enthusiastic; excellent *IRELAND, 1999*

Freud squad *noun* psychiatrists. UK Doctors' slang, punning on
'fraud squad' *UK, 2003*

Friar Tuck; friar; friar's used for all noun, verb and expletive
senses of 'fuck'. Rhyming slang, often in phrases like 'not give a
friar's', from the name of one of Robin Hood's band of merry
men. Friar Tuck is also the source of a popular Spoonerism *UK, 1956*

Friar Tucked *adjective* thwarted. Rhyming slang for *FUCKED UK, 1996*

frick and frack *noun* the testicles *US, 1980*

fricko *noun* a chicken stew *CANADA, 1951*

friction *noun* a match *TRINIDAD AND TOBAGO, 1953*

Friday car; Friday afternoon car *noun* a car that is constantly
going wrong. Hence anything that is imperfect may be prefixed by
'Friday' or 'Friday afternoon'. From the notion that car-factory
workers may skimp on the last shift of the week *UK, 1979*

fridge *noun* **1** a refrigerator *US, 1926*. **2** (usually of a woman) a person
who is sexually unresponsive. A play on 'frigid' *US, 1996*

fried *adjective* **1** drunk or drug-intoxicated *US, 1923*. **2** mentally
exhausted *US, 1980*. **3** in computing, not working because of a
complete hardware failure *US, 1981*. **4** sunburnt *US, 1989*

fried, dried, and swept aside *adjective* said of bleached hair that
suggests straw *US, 1997*

fried, dyed, combed (swooped) to the side *adjective* used as a
description of a black person's hair that has been chemically
straightened *US, 1980*

fried egg *noun* the insignia of the US Military Academy *US, 1908*

fried eggs *noun* small female breasts *UK, 1997*

friend *noun* in poker, any card that improves a hand *US, 1988*.
▶ **have a friend visiting** to experience the bleed period of the
menstrual cycle *UK, 1889*

friend *verb* **1** to engage in sexual foreplay. Reported in Toronto as a
term used by Trinidadian teens *CANADA, 1993*. **2** to have sex; to take
part in a romantic relationship *TRINIDAD AND TOBAGO, 1971*

friendly *adjective* used as a coded euphemism for 'passive' in
sadomasochistic sex *US, 1987*

Friendly City *nickname* Port Elizabeth, South Africa *SOUTH AFRICA, 1951*

friend of Dorothy *noun* a homosexual. Thought to be from the
Judy Garland character in *The Wizard of Oz*; Garland is a gay icon
AUSTRALIA, 1988

friend of Pedro *noun* someone in possession of cocaine. PEDRO
(cocaine) has lots of friends *UK, 1999*

friends *verb* to court. Used only in the present participle *BARBADOS,
1965*

fries *noun* pieces of crack cocaine. Shortened from FRENCH FRIES *US,
1994*

frig *noun* ▶ **give a frig; care a frig** to care, to be concerned –
usually in a negative context *UK, 1955*

frig *verb* **1** to masturbate *UK, 1598*. **2** to digitally stimulate/explore the
vagina as a part of sexual foreplay. A nuance of the sense to
'masturbate' *UK, 2003*. **3** to dawdle or waste time *US, 1975*

frig used now as a euphemism for 'fuck' in all its senses *UK, 1879*

frig about *verb* to waste time doing little or nothing *UK, 1933*

frigger *noun* used as a euphemism for 'fucker' *IRELAND, 1996*

frigging *adjective* **1** damned *AUSTRALIA, 1948*. **2** used as a euphemism
for 'fucking', usually as an intensifier. With variant 'fricking' *UK, 1893*

frigging *adverb* damned well *AUSTRALIA, 1948*

-frigging- *infix* damned *AUSTRALIA, 1983*

frigging hell! used for registering surprise, anger, amazement.
Euphemism for FUCKING HELL! *UK, 1982*

frigging in the rigging wasting time idling when on duty. From a
bawdy ballad *AUSTRALIA, 1962*

fright *noun* an ugly person *UK, 1832*. ▶ **he (she) wouldn't give you
a fright on a dark night** said of a person with a reputation for
meanness. Glasgow use *UK, 1988*

frightener *noun* a scare *UK, 1965*. ▶ **put the frighteners on** to
scare someone *UK, 1958*

frightful *adjective* used as a general-purpose intensifier *UK, 1752*

frightfully *adverb* very, extremely *UK, 1809*

frigidaire *noun* a sexually frigid woman. An allusion to the refrigerator brand *US, 1949*

frig off *verb* to go away, to leave. Often in the imperative *US, 1961*

frig up *verb* to botch, to ruin *US, 1933*

frillies *noun* women's underclothing, especially insubstantial
'feminine' garments *UK, 1937*

fringe *noun* thin strips of material attached to the G-string worn by a
striptease dancer *US, 1981*

fringe *verb* to get something from somebody else by imposing on
their hospitality or generosity *US, 1947*

fringes *noun* the eyes *US, 1947*

fringie *noun* a person on the fringes of a gang, not a hardcore
member *US, 1966*

frios *noun* marijuana mixed with phencyclidine, the recreational
drug known as PCP or angel dust *UK, 1998*

frip *adjective* lousy. Youth usage *US, 1949*

frisbee *noun* **1** a biscuit from an army c-ration *US, 1991*. **2** an agent of
the Federal Bureau of Investigations *US, 1993*

'Frisco *nickname* San Francisco, California. Never used by San
Franciscans, and a sure sign of a tourist *US, 1849*

Frisco speedball; Frisco special; San Francisco bomb *noun* a
combination of cocaine, heroin and LSD. Up, down and out – all
at once; a combination of a SPEEDBALL (cocaine and heroin) with
the drug that made FRISCO (San Francisco) psychedelic *US, 1969*

frisk *verb* **1** to search the person for illicit goods *UK, 1789*. **2** to laugh
UK, 1996

frisker *noun* a pickpocket *UK, 1802*

frisky *noun* cocaine *US, 1986*

frisky powder *noun* cocaine *US, 1955*

frit *noun* in Quebec, a French fried potato *CANADA, 1986*

Frito *noun* a woman who is sexually expert. A pun on the Frito Lay
company name – a 'good lay' *US, 1967*

fritterware *noun* computer software that is seductive to users,
consumes time, and adds little to functionality *US, 1991*

fritz *noun* ▶ **on the fritz** broken *US, 1902*

Fritz *noun* a German *UK, 1915*

fritz *verb* to break *US, 1918*

friznaughti *adjective* drug-intoxicated *US, 1995*

frizzle *adjective* very cold *NORFOLK ISLAND, 1992*

'fro *noun* a bushy Afro hair style *US, 1970*

frob *noun* any small object *US, 1991*

frob *verb* to manipulate dials or settings *US, 1983*

frobnicate *verb* to manipulate dials or settings *US, 1983*

frobnitz *noun* any device the name of which is unknown, escapes the speaker's mind, or is not relevant *US, 1991*

frock *noun* women's clothing; a theatrical costume *UK, 2002*

frock *verb* to decorate as a military officer. From the C19 sense of 'investing with priestly office' *US, 1986*

frock and frill *noun* a *chill*, a cold. Rhyming slang *UK, 1992*

frock billong lallies *noun* trousers. A combination of Tok Pisin, a Melanesian pidgin, *billong* (belong) and polari **FROCK** (clothing) and **LALLY** (the leg) *UK, 2002*

froffy *adjective* poor and shabby looking *BARBADOS, 1998*

frog *noun* **1** a social outcast *US, 1968*. **2** a promiscuous girl *US, 1995*. **3** a French Canadian *CANADA, 1966* ▷ *see:* **FROGEATER**. **4** a condom. Probably as a play on **FRENCH LETTER** or **FRENCHY** (a condom) *AUSTRALIA, 1952*. **5** the French language *UK, 1955*. **6** one dollar *US, 1962*

Frog *noun* a person from France. Like all the 'frog' terms for the French, it refers to the eating of frogs *UK, 1778*

frog *verb* to fail (a test or exam) *US, 1968*

Frog *adjective* French. Said with unkind intensions *US, 1910*

frog! used for expressing disgust *US, 1991*

frog and toad; frog *noun* the road. Rhyming slang *UK, 1859*

frog-choker *noun* a heavy rain *CANADA, 2002*

frogeater *noun* a French person; a French-Canadian. This term, highly derogatory along with 'Frog', has passed out of use, and in any case could be more aptly applied to the Acadians of Louisiana, who are fond of frog-legs from the bayous *US, 1812*

frogeyed sprite *noun* an Austin-Healy Sprite *UK, 1992*

Froggie; Froggy *noun* **1** France *UK, 1999*. **2** a person from France *US, 1870s*

froggy *adjective* **1** aggressive *US, 1939*. **2** used to describe a dry mouth after smoking marijuana. Probably from the phrase 'frog in the throat' (hoarse) *UK, 2002*

Froggy; Froggie *adjective* French *UK, 1872*

frog hair *noun* a very short distance *US, 1958*

frog-march; frog's march *verb* to push someone forward holding them by their collar and the seat of their trousers *UK, 1884*

frog salad *noun* in carnival usage, any performance that features scantily clad women *US, 1981*

frog show *noun* a dance performance that features scantily clad women *US, 1973*

frogskin *noun* **1** money; paper money; a one-dollar note *US, 1902*. **2** a condom *NEW ZEALAND, 1998*

frogskins *noun* a wetsuit and other cold-water garments *US, 1991*

frog-spawn *noun* tapioca pudding. One of the joys of a public school education *UK, 1949*

frogsticker *noun* a knife *US, 1972*

frog-strangler *noun* a torrential downpour *US, 1942*

frog-walk *verb* to forcefully carry somebody face-down *US, 1960*

frolic *noun* a New Brunswick work bee and party *CANADA, 1964*

from arsehole to breakfast time all the time, all the way *UK, 1984*

from away *adjective* from any place other than the area of the eastern Canadian coast speaker's own local region or town. Exactly opposite of 'from around here', this term is flexible in application

and odd in that the object of the preposition is a word not ordinarily used in the noun position *CANADA, 1985*

from here to there without a pair in poker, used for describing a hand of sequenced cards. Conventionally known as a 'straight' *US, 1951*

frompy *adjective* unattractive *US, 1948*

from way downtown – bang used as a humorous comment on a witty remark, a correct answer, or other verbal victory. Coined by ESPN's Keith Olberman to describe three-point shots in basketball *US, 1997*

frone *noun* an ugly woman *US, 1947*

frone *adjective* terrible *UK, 1945*

front *noun* **1** a person's public appearance; stylish clothing *US, 1899*. **2** the genitals; sex *BAHAMAS, 1982*. **3** the beginning. Especially in the phrase 'from the front' *US, 1959*. ▶ **at the front** used of a drug that is taken before another *UK, 1978*. ▶ **more front than Selfridges/Harrods/Buckingham Palace/Albert Hall/Brighton/Brighton beach/Woolworths/Myers** audaciousness; impudence. Puns 'front' (cheek) with the exceptional frontage of Selfridges, a very large department store in Oxford Street; Harrods is another impressive London shop; Buckingham Palace is the Queen's official London residence; the Albert Hall is a major concert venue; and Brighton is a seaside resort on the south coast – 'front' in this instance abbreviated from 'seafront'. In Australia, Myers is a large department store in Melbourne *UK, 1958*. ▶ **out front** owing someone who has extended goods to you for payment later *US, 1989*. ▶ **the front** the main road or street within the area of a Teddy Boy gang's influence *UK, 1959*. ▶ **up front** in advance *US, 1970*

Front *nickname* ▶ **the Front 1** Piccadilly, as an area of homosexual commerce and prostitution *UK, 1964*. **2** Oxford Street, London *UK, 1977*

front *verb* **1** in jazz or popular music, to be a band leader, or lead singer of a band *US, 1936*. **2** to lie; to project a false image of yourself *US, 1993*. **3** to show up; to make an appearance *AUSTRALIA, 1968*. **4** to confront someone *AUSTRALIA, 1945*. **5** to appear before a court *AUSTRALIA, 1941*. **6** to provide something of value to someone with the expectation of being paid later *US, 1989*. **7** to back down from a physical confrontation *US, 1987*. **8** to pretend, to fake *US, 1993*. ▶ **front an air biscuit** to pretend innocence of generating a guilty fart *UK, 2002*. ▶ **front it** to face up to a difficult problem or situation; hence, to leave a Vulnerable Prisoners' Unit and return to the main prison *UK, 1996*

front and back *noun* a sack, the sack. Rhyming slang *UK, 2003*

front bottom *noun* the vulva and vagina *UK, 2003*

front botty; front bum *noun* the vagina *AUSTRALIA, 1988*

front bumpers *noun* the female breasts. An elaboration of **BUMPER** *UK, 1973*

front door *noun* **1** the vagina. As opposed to the **BACK DOOR** (the rectum) *UK, 1890*. **2** the leading vehicle in a convoy of citizens' band radio users *US, 1975*

front doormat *noun* a woman's pubic hair *UK, 1980*

fronter *noun* **1** an inexperienced swindler working on a scam by telephone who makes the initial call to potential victims *US, 1988*. **2** a person who appears to be something he is not and who does not deliver on promised action *US, 1997*

front line *noun* an urban area where a mainly black community may come into conflict with an adjacent white community or with the laws of white society. West Indian and UK black usage *UK, 1978*

front-liner *noun* a person in a youth gang who is capable of murder *US, 1995*

frontload *verb* to drink at home before going out for a night of drinking on the town *US, 1999*

front-loading *noun* a technique for observing the dealer's down card in casino blackjack as the dealer tips the card up to slide it under his up card *US, 1991*

front man *noun* someone who is employed to cover for a criminal operation by posing as the legitimate owner/leader or by acting as spokesperson *US, 1934*

front money *noun* **1** money paid in advance for the purchase of drugs *US, 1978*. **2** money needed to start a venture *US, 1925*

front off *verb* **1** to place yourself in a highly visible position *US, 1960*. **2** to sell drugs on credit *US, 1995*

front porch *noun* in poker, the earliest position in a hand *US, 1996*

front-running *noun* support given to a person or team only when they are doing well *US, 1970*

fronts *noun* legitimate, square, unaltered dice *US, 1950* ▷*see:* GOLD FRONTS

front street *noun* ▶ **on front street** in the open; in public *US, 1992*. ▶ **put on front street** to inform on, to betray *US, 1995*

front up *verb* to appear in *front* of; to con*front*; *AUSTRALIA, 1945*

front wedgy *noun* the condition that exists when a tight-fitting pair of trousers, shorts, bathing suit, or other garment forms a wedge between a woman's labia, accentuating their shape. The WEDGY brought around to the front of the body *US, 2003*

front wheel skid; four wheel skid; four-wheeler *noun* a Jewish person. Rhyming slang for YID. Intentionally offensive *UK, 1943*

front yard *noun* in trucking, the road ahead of you *US, 1977*

frosh *noun* a freshman (first-year student), either in high school or college *US, 1915*

frost *verb* to anger. Often in combination with a body part *US, 1895*. ▶ **frost someone's balls** to anger someone *US, 1994*

frost boil *noun* the irregular road surface caused by frost heave *CANADA, 1995*

frosted *adjective* **1** angry *US, 1956*. **2** bejewelled, well-ornamented *UK, 2005*

frosted face *noun* the photographic depiction of a woman's face covered with semen. American heterosexual pornography has long shown a fascination for ejaculations on a woman's face. In the late 1990s, this fascination expanded to embrace the depiction of multiple ejaculations on a woman's face. Any Internet search engine will uncover dozens of sites boasting 'frosted faces', a term that puns on the branded cereal 'Frosted Flakes' while inviting a visual comparison with the cereal's sugar glaze *US, 2001*

frost freak *noun* a person who inhales freon, a refrigerant, for its intoxicating effect *US, 1970*

frosty *noun* a cold beer *US, 1961*

frosty *adjective* cool, calm, collected *US, 1970*

frot *verb* to rub against another person for sexual stimulation, usually surreptitiously *UK, 1973*

froth *noun* in horse racing, a double. Rhyming slang from 'froth and bubble' to 'double' *AUSTRALIA, 1989*

froth *verb* to engage in an abusive verbal attack *UK, 2001*

froth and bubble *noun* trouble. Rhyming slang *AUSTRALIA, 1955*

frothing *adjective* (used of a party) populated by many girls *US, 1988*

froudacity *noun* lying about something you know nothing about. A blending of 'audacity' and 'fraudulence' *TRINIDAD AND TOBAGO, 1967*

frou-frou *adjective* fussy, overly fancy *US, 1951*

frown *noun* lemon syrup or fresh lemon added to a coca-cola *US, 1946*

frowney; frowney face *noun* the emoticon depicting a frown − :(*US, 1991*

froyo *noun* frozen yogurt *US, 1998*

froze *adjective* **1** cocaine-intoxicated. Evocative of the C18 meaning of the word as 'drunk' *US, 1974*. **2** frozen *UK, 1590*

frozen *adjective* **1** excellent. Teen slang *US, 1954*. **2** dull, lacking action *NEW ZEALAND, 1998*. **3** in pool, directly touching (a ball or the rail of the table) *US, 1984*

frozen chosen *noun* the people who work in Antarctica *US, 1997*

frozen Chosin *nickname* the Chanjin Reservoir, identified on Japanese maps as the Chosin Reservoir, scene of heroic military action by the US Marine Corps in the winter of 1950−51 *US, 1952*

frozen custard *noun* the vagina of a frigid woman *US, 1977*

frozen fireworks *noun* jewellery *US, 1979*

frozen mitt *noun* **1** a rejection; a brush off. A variant of 'cold shoulder' *UK, 1915*. **2** an intentionally unwelcoming reception. With 'icy mitt' as a variant *UK, 1903*

frug *verb* to dance. Originally a fashionable dance which was contrived and flourished briefly in the mid-1960s. Its re-emergence is as an ironic generic for all non-specific dancing *UK, 1999*

fruit *noun* **1** a homosexual, especially an obviously homosexual male person *US, 1900*. **2** an eccentric or even mentally unstable person. A shortening of FRUITCAKE *US, 1959*. ▶ **do your fruit** to go mad; to lose your temper. Probably suggested by BANANAS (crazy, mad); *UK, 1978*

fruitbait *noun* a man who attracts the attention of other men *US, 1973*

fruit basket *noun* the male genitalia when offered to view from behind. Strong homosexual overtones: BASKET (the male genitals) combined with FRUIT (a homosexual) *US, 2001*

fruitbat *noun* a crazy person *AUSTRALIA, 1992*

fruit boot *noun* **1** a style of shoe popular in the 1950s and 60s, ankle-high suede shoes with crepe rubber soles conventionally known as 'desert boots'. English mods embraced desert boots made by Clarks, and their popularity spread to the US, where they were labelled 'fruit boots' because of their perceived popularity with perceived homosexuals *US, 1964*. **2** an in-line skater. Derogatory *UK, 2000*

fruitcake *noun* **1** an eccentric or even mentally unstable person *US, 1942*. **2** a blatantly homosexual man *US, 1960*

fruit cupper *noun* an amateur racing car driver, especially in sports car races *US, 1993*

fruiter *noun* a homosexual *US, 1918*

fruit fly *noun* a heterosexual woman who befriends homosexual men *US, 1965*

fruit fuzz *noun* a police officer assigned to an anti-homosexual vice operation *US, 1979*

fruit hustler *noun* a homosexual prostitute; a criminal who preys on homosexual victims *US, 1959*

fruiting *noun* promiscuous behaviour *US, 1982*

fruit jacket *noun* a prison record identifying a person as a homosexual *US, 1986*

fruitliner *noun* a White Freightliner truck *US, 1971*

fruit loop *noun* **1** an effeminate homosexual man. An elaboration of FRUIT, from the brand name of a popular breakfast cereal *US, 1989*. **2** a psychiatric patient *US, 1994*. **3** the cloth loop on the back of a man's shirt *US, 1966*

fruit on the sideboard; fruit for the sideboard *noun* something easily obtained; unexpected financial gain. It is claimed this originated with the famous Sydney bookmaker Andy Kerr *AUSTRALIA, 1953*

fruit pinch *noun* an arrest of a homosexual man *US, 1970*

fruit ranch *noun* a mental hospital or a psychiatric ward *US, 1985*

fruit roll *noun* the violent robbing of a homosexual *US, 1973*

fruit salad *noun* **1** a display of military medals *UK, 1943*. **2** a pooled mix of different types of pills contributed by several people and then consumed randomly *US, 1969*. **3** a group of stroke patients who cannot care for themselves *US, 1978*. **4** a person of mixed race *FIJI, 1992*. ▶ **do the fruit salad** to expose your genitals in public *US, 1994*

fruit show *noun* a display in which a prostitute will stimulate and masturbate herself utilising any of a variety of fruits or vegetables, especially when advertised as a service *UK, 2003*

fruit tank *noun* a jail cell reserved for homosexual prisoners *US, 1981*

fruity *adjective* **1** of language or content, very rich or strong; sexually suggestive; amorous *UK, 1900*. **2** obviously homosexual *US, 1940*

frumpy *adjective* poorly dressed, rumpled, messy *US, 1947*

frups *noun* a fart *TRINIDAD AND TOBAGO, 1987*

frupse *noun* nothing at all. Something that is 'not worth a frupse' is 'worthless' *BARBADOS, 1965*

fruta *noun* a homosexual. A literal application of Spanish to English slang *US, 1997*

fry *noun* **1** crack cocaine *US, 1994*. **2** crack cocaine mixed with embalming fluid or LSD. Probably from 'fry your brains' but the presence of embalming fluid in this potentially lethal mixture suggests FRY (to execute by electrocution) *US, 1998*. **3** marijuana mixed with embalming fluid or LSD *UK, 2003*. **4** LSD *US, 1992*. **5** a car accident in which an occupant or occupants of the car are burnt *US, 1962*

fry *verb* **1** to put to death by electrocution *US, 1928*. **2** in computing, to fail completely *US, 1983*. **3** to use and be under the influence of LSD *US, 1993*. **4** of a drug, to destroy or impair the mind by extreme intoxication; of a drug-user, to experience the consequences of LSD *US, 1996*. **5** to alter the mind irreparably *US, 1972*. **6** to straighten your hair, chemically or with heat *US, 1945*. **7** in motor racing, to overheat (an engine or component) *US, 1993*

fry daddy *noun* a marijuana and crack cocaine cigarette *US, 1989*

frying size *noun* said of children of elementary school age *US, 1954*

fry stick *noun* a marijuana cigarette laced with embalming fluid or phencyclidine, the recreational drug known as PCP or angel dust *UK, 2003*

fry-up *noun* a quickly cooked collation of any foodstuffs prepared by frying *UK, 1967*

FTA *fuck the army*. A popular sentiment shared by those both in and not in the army during the Vietnam war. Country Joe McDonald of 'Look's Like I'm Fixin' To Die Rag' fame, took an anti-war show named 'FTA!' on the road to GI coffee houses in 1971 *US, 1968*

FTW used as a defiant stance against everything – *fuck the world US, 1972*

FUBAR *adjective* **1** used as an expression of disgust because a situation is *fucked up beyond all recognition*. Of the many military acronyms with a prominent 'F' coined during World War 2, one of the few to survive *US, 1944*. **2** drunk. A sense created by using 'fucked up' to mean 'drunk', not 'botched.' *US, 1985*

fuck *noun* **1** the act of sex *UK, 1675*. **2** a person objectified as a sex-partner *UK, 1874*. **3** a despicable or hapless person *UK, 1927*. **4** used as an intensifier. Often used with 'the', as in 'Get the fuck out of here!' *US, 1934*. **5** an extreme example or degree *UK, 1928*. **6** something of no value *UK, 1790*. ▶ **and fuck** and so on, etc *UK, 2002*. ▶ **as fuck** an intensifier, used in combination with an adjective. Other examples include: 'heavy as fuck', 'daft as fuck', 'queer as fuck', etc *UK, 1999*. ▶ **couldn't organise a fuck in a brothel** used of an inefficient person *UK, 1961*. ▶ **for fuck's sake!; fuck sake!** used as a register of exasperation or impatience *US, 1961*. ▶ **for the love of fuck** used as an expression of exasperation or entreaty *UK, 2005*. ▶ **like fuck** like hell; very much *UK, 1995*. ▶ **running fuck at a rolling doughnut** an extremely difficult manoeuvre or operation *UK, 1979*

fuck *verb* **1** to have sex *UK, 1500*. **2** to damage beyond repair *UK, 1775*. **3** used as an intense verb of abuse, as in 'fuck the police' *UK, 1915*. **4** to confound *AUSTRALIA, 1998*. ▶ **be fucked in the car** to have had something done to you that you did not deserve *CANADA, 1969*. ▶ **fuck a duck** to shirk, to avoid work. Vietnam war usage. *US, 1933*. ▶ **fuck a duck!** used for registering surprise *UK, 1940s*. ▶ **fuck anything that moves** applied to a person's rampant sexuality. The variations of this catchphrase are manifold, all formed on 'fuck anything' – *with* 'a hole', 'a crack', 'a cock', 'a dick', 'a vagina', 'hair on it', 'breasts', 'tits', 'a heart beat', 'a pulse' etc; *that* moves; *on* 'two legs'. *UK, 1977*. ▶ **fuck in the ass** to victimise; to force into submission. Figurative *US, 1995*. ▶ **fuck the arse off** to have exceptionally vigorous sex. Applied to conventional sexual intercourse; despite the use of 'arse', anal sex is neither included or precluded. Usage is generally something of a boast *UK, 2000*. ▶ **fuck the dog** to idle instead of working *US, 1935*. ▶ **fuck the fucking fuckers** used for expressing contempt and defiance of and towards just about everyone *US, 1980*. ▶ **fuck them if they can't take a joke** during the Vietnam war, used as a cynically humorous retort when things went wrong. Multiple variants *US, 1980*. ▶ **fuck up the arse** to betray. Combines FUCK (to damage) with 'up the arse', which makes it personal *UK, 2001*. ▶ **fuck you very much!** used as a humorous expression of defiance *US, 1980*. ▶ **fuck your fist** to masturbate *US, 1966*. ▶ **who do you have to fuck?** used as an impatient enquiry: who do I have to persuade?, who is responsible for something? how can I do or get something? Probably hyperbolic *US, 1968*

fuck *adjective* ▶ **a fuck sight** a lot *UK, 2001*

fuck! used as a simple exclamation *UK, 1929*. ▶ **do you fuck!; will you fuck!** used as a strong and disapproving denial: no you did not, no you will not *UK, 1961*. ▶ **is it fuck!** used as an emphatic negative *UK, 1984*. ▶ **will I fuck!** used as an expression of strong disagreement. Often applied in the third person: 'will he fuck!', 'will they fuck!' *UK, 1961*

fuck *prefix* used to create a non-specific type within a recognisable series, e.g. 'fuckism', fuckology. Dismissive *UK, 1991*

fuckable *adjective* sexually appealing *UK, 1891*

fuck about; fuck around *verb* to play the fool, to waste time; to make a mess of; to inconvenience *UK, 1922*

fuck-a-doodle-doo! used as an ironic exclamation of delight *UK, 1994*

fuckaholic *noun* a person obsessed with sex *US, 1981*

fuck all; fuckall *noun* nothing, nothing at all *UK, 1918*

fuck almighty! used in despair when others may call upon God. Euphemistic use of FUCK for what might otherwise border on blasphemy *UK, 2001*

fuck and blind *verb* to swear. A frank variation of EFF AND BLIND *UK, 1974*

fuck-around *noun* **1** a promiscuous person *FIJI, 1992*. **2** a young street ruffian *FIJI, 1984*

fuck-arse around *verb* to play the fool, to waste time; to make a mess of; to inconvenience *UK, 2000*

fuckass *noun* a despicable person *UK, 1960*

fuckass *adjective* despicable *US, 1961*

fuckathon *noun* an extended bout of sex *US, 1968*

fuckbag *noun* a despicable person *US, 1989*

fuck book *noun* a sexually explicit book, usually heavily illustrated *US, 1944*

fuckboy *noun* a young man as the object of homosexual desire *US, 1971*

fuckbrain *noun* an idiot. A variation of the equally derisive FUCKWIT *UK, 1997*

fuck buddy *noun* a friend who is also a sex companion *US, 1972*

fucked *adjective* **1** ruined, spoiled, potentially doomed *UK, 1955*. **2** extremely weary, exhausted *UK, 1984*. **3** drunk or drug-intoxicated *US, 1965*. **4** insane, crazy, senseless *US, 1970*

fucked if I can it is very unlikely that I will be able to do something *UK, 2000*

fucked off *adjective* **1** fed up, disgruntled, annoyed, angry *US, 1945*. **2** having been told to fuck off or to have been on the receiving end of a similar injunction or intimation *UK, 1998*

fucked up *adjective* **1** drunk or drug-intoxicated *US, 1944*. **2** mentally unstable; depressed; anguished; *UK, 1939*. **3** despicable *US, 1945*. **4** ruined, spoiled, broken *US, 1965*

fucked-upness *noun* a depressed or ruined condition *UK, 2003*

fucken *adjective* used as a general intensifier. A variant spelling of FUCKING *UK, 2001*

fucker *noun* **1** a man, a spirited person. Often used affectionately or derisively; not generally a term of abuse unless combined with an appropriate adjective e.g. 'dirty', 'miserable', etc *UK, 1893*. **2** a contemptible person *UK, 1890*. **3** a nuisance, an awkward thing *US, 1945*

fuckery *noun* **1** oppression; the inherent corruption of a dominant society *US, 1978*. **2** things, concepts *US, 2002*. ▶ **like fuckery** vigorously *UK, 2000*

fuckface *noun* an offensive or despicable person *US, 1945*

fuckfaced *adjective* despicable, ugly *US, 1940*

fuck-features *noun* a contemptible person *AUSTRALIA, 1972*

fuck film; fuck flick *noun* a pornographic film *US, 1970*

fuckhead *noun* used as an all-purpose insulting term of address or descriptive noun for a despicable, stupid person *US, 1966*

fuckhole *noun* the vagina *UK, 1893*

fucking *noun* sexual intercourse. Well known but, aside from macho bragging and fantasising, kept safely between the sheets in a book or a bedroom; however in 1996, advertising the title of Mark Ravenhill's successful play, *Shopping and Fucking*, challenged and, perhaps, changed some media taboos *UK, 1568*

fucking *adjective + adverb* used as an attention-getting intensifier *US, 1857*

-fucking- *infix* used as an intensifier. One of the very few infix intensifiers used in the US or UK *US, 1921*

fucking A! used as an expression of surprise, approval or dismay *US, 1947*

fucking Ada! used for registering annoyance, frustration, etc *UK, 1962*

fucking arseholes! used as an exclamation of surprise, anger, amazement. A standard intensification of ARSEHOLES!; often lazily or deliberately reduced to 'KIN' ARSE'OLES *UK, 1984*

fucking hell! used as an exclamation of surprise, anger, amazement. An intensification of HELL. Often lazily or deliberately reduced to 'KIN' 'ELL or run together as a single word *UK, 1974*

fucking machine *noun* a lustful lover *AUSTRALIA, 1971*

fucking new guy *noun* a recent arrival to combat. A key term and key concept in Vietnam *US, 1977*

fucking well *adverb* used for emphasis *UK, 1922*

fuck-in-law *noun* someone who has had sex with someone you have had sex with. Leading to a punning exploration of the 'sex degrees of separation' between people *US, 1995*

fuck it! used as a general declaration of rejection or dismissal; may also imply resignation to a situation *UK, 1937*

Fuck KKKanada! *verb* in Quebec, used for denigrating the Canadian confederacy *CANADA, 2002*

fuck knows *noun* an uncertain measure of time. Clipped from 'fuck knows how long' *UK, 1997*

fuck knuckle *noun* an annoying or despicable person; an idiot; a jerk *AUSTRALIA, 1981*

fuck load *noun* a considerable quantity *US, 1988*

fuck machine *noun* a very active sexual partner *US, 1992*

fuck-me *adjective* extremely sexually suggestive *US, 1974*

fuck me! used for registering disbelief, despair, surprise, satisfaction. Often used in a wry or semi-humorous manner; since the 1950s usage is likely to provoke the rejoinders 'not now' or 'later' or 'no thanks', etc. Also used in many combinations and elaborations, all with same sense. Often ironic *UK, 1929*

fuck me blue! used as an elaborate variant of 'fuck me!' *US, 1988*

fuck me harder! used as an elaborate and graphic expression of frustration *US, 1991*

fuck-me's *noun* very tight, form-fitting trousers on a man *US, 1972*

fuck movie *noun* a pornographic film *US, 1967*

fuck no used as an emphatic negative, *1979*

fucknut *noun* a contemptible person *US, 1988*

fucko *noun* used as a jocular if derisive term of address *US, 1973*

fuck of a *noun* a considerable or notable quantity or example of something *US, 1928*

fuck-off *noun* **1** a person who shirks their responsibility and duty *US, 1947*. **2** a truant *UK, 2000*

fuck off *verb* **1** to leave, especially to leave immediately; also used as a threatening injection to inspire an immediate departure; 'fuck off!' *UK, 1929*. **2** used for dismissing a foolish statement *UK, 1974*. **3** to treat someone as unworthy of respect or notice *US, 1962*. **4** to postpone, to cancel *UK, 2002*

fuck-off *adjective* **1** obvious, unmissable *UK, 1999*. **2** describes an attitude of not caring for the opinions of others *UK, 1999*. **3** incompetent *US, 1953*

fuck off and die! go away – and don't come back! An emphatic variation of FUCK OFF. Abbreviated for text messaging as FOAD *UK, 2000*

fuckola used as an embellished 'fuck' in any of its senses *US, 1998*

fuck over *verb* to treat another person with contempt or cruelty in any way; to mistreat, to hurt emotionally or physically, to betray, to victimise, to cheat *US, 1961*

fuck pad *noun* a room, apartment or house maintained for the purpose of sexual liaisons *US, 1975*

fuckpole *noun* the penis *US, 1966*

fuckries *noun* trouble; wrongs. West Indian and UK black patois *UK, 1994*

fucks! used as an expression of anger, frustration or resignation. An elaboration of FUCK! *UK: WALES, 2001*

fucksome *adjective* sexually desirable *UK, 1937*

fuck spider! used for expressing extreme frustration *SINGAPORE, 2002*

fuck stick *noun* **1** the penis. Used by Saigon prostitutes during the Vietnam war, adopted by US soldiers *US, 1976*. **2** a despicable person *US, 1958*

fuck-struck *noun* infatuated or obsessed with someone because of their ability in sex *US, 1966*

fuck that for a lark!; fuck this for a lark! no chance!; used as an emphatic dismissal of any activity or notion that you have no wish to subscribe to *UK, 1984*

fuck the bourgeoisie used as a slogan by the hippie counterculture. The first time many young people heard of the bourgeoisie *UK, 1970*

fuck this for a game of soldiers!; fuck that for a game of soldiers! used as an emphatic dismissal of any activity or notion that you have no wish to subscribe to. A military variation of earlier 'fuck that for a game of skittles'; in turn an elaboration of 'fuck that' *UK, 1979*

fuck truck *noun* any car, truck or van used for sexual encounters *AUSTRALIA, 1974*

fuck-up *noun* a chronic, bungling, dismal failure (person or thing) *US, 1944*

fuck up *verb* **1** to spoil, to destroy *UK, 1916*. **2** to make a mistake *US, 1945*. **3** to fail dismally *US, 1970*. **4** to cause drink or drug intoxication, especially if extreme *UK, 1970*

fuckwad *noun* **1** the semen ejaculated at orgasm *UK, 2000*. **2** a contemptible fool; a despicable person; used as a general purpose pejorative. The negative suffix '-wad' intensified *US, 1974*

fuckwit *noun* an annoying or despicable person; a fool; an idiot. A blend of FUCK and NITWIT of HALF-WIT *AUSTRALIA, 1968*

fuckwit *adjective* stupid *UK, 2003*

fuck with *verb* **1** to meddle with; to interfere with; to play around with *UK, 1999*. **2** to impress *US, 2001*

fuck-wittage *noun* a state of stupidity *UK, mid-1990s*

fuckwitted *adjective* idiotic *AUSTRALIA, 1971*

fucky *adjective* **1** trendy, sexy, stylish *UK, 2003*. **2** lustfully erotic *AUSTRALIA, 1989*. **3** used as an intensifier, replacing 'fucking' *UK, 2000*

fucky-fucky *noun* sex. Vietnam war usage *US, 1961*

fucky-fucky sauce *noun* semen *US, 1972*

fuck you! used contemptuously as an expression of disdain, dismissal or disbelief *UK, 2001*

fuck you and the horse you rode in on! used as an emphatic and insulting rejection *US, 1971*

fuck-you lizard *noun* a Vietnamese Tokay Gecko lizard. US soldiers in Vietnam thought that the gecko's call sounded as if the gecko was saying 'fuck you'. In polite company, the lizard was called an 'insulting lizard' *US, 1970*

fuck-your-buddy week *noun* a notional designation of the present week, explaining rude behaviour by your superiors *US, 1960*

fuck yourself!; go and fuck yourself! used as an expression of dismissal *UK, 1879*

fuck you sideways! used contemptuously as an expression of disdain or dismissal. An intensification of FUCK YOU! *UK, 2001*

fucky-sucky *noun* a combination of oral and vaginal sex *US, 1974*

fucky-sucky *verb* to engage in oral and then vaginal sex *US, 1996*

FUD *noun* uncertainty and doubt *US, 1997*

fuddle-duddle! used as a euphemism for 'fuck off'. Said by Canadian Prime Minister Pierre Trudeau in the House of Commons 16th February 1971 *CANADA, 1979*

fuddy *noun* an old-fashioned person. An abbreviation of FUDDY-DUDDY *US, 1958*

fuddy-dud *noun* an old-fashioned, inhibited, conventional person *US, 1904*

fuddy-duddy *noun* a fussy, old-fashioned, narrow-minded person *US, 1904*

fuddy-duddy *adjective* fussy, old-fashioned, narrow-minded *US, 1907*

fudge *verb* to cheat *US, 1958*

fudge used as a euphemism for 'fuck'. Based on the opening sound (as is 'sugar' for SHIT) *UK, 1766*

fudge factor *noun* an allowance made for possible error in estimating the time, material, or money needed for a job *US, 1962*

fudge nudger *noun* someone who engages in anal sex, especially a male homosexual *UK, 2003*

fudgepacker *noun* a gay man. Someone who packs 'fudge' (excrement), thus a graphic description of a participant in anal intercourse *US, 1985*

fudger *noun* a planespotter who claims greater success than is true *UK, 2003*

fuel *noun* **1** cocaine *US, 1984*. **2** marijuana *US, 1993*. **3** marijuana adulterated with psychoactive chemicals *US, 1992*

fueled *adjective* very drunk *US, 1997*

fueler *noun* a drag racing car that does not use petrol as fuel *US, 1970*

fuel-tank justice *noun* a fistfight to settle a dispute at work. This type of conflict resolution often took place behind a fuel tank, near the work location but out of sight, usually after work *US, 2001*

fuel up *verb* to eat quickly *US, 1991*

fuete *noun* a hypodermic needle. From Cuban Spanish *fuete* (a whip) *US, 1973*

FUFA an army deserter during the Vietnam war – *f*ed *u*p with the *f*ucking *a*rmy *US, 1990*

fufnick *noun* in the car sales business, a car part or mechanism that has been altered in appearance but not in substance *US, 1953*

fufu *noun* **1** an eccentric person; a crazy person *CAYMAN ISLANDS, 1985*. **2** a homosexual *US, 1993*

fug used as a euphemism for 'fuck' in all its variant uses and derivatives *US, 1958*

Fugawi *noun* a mythical tribe or people, so named because after years of wandering they asked, 'Where the fuck are we?'. Military origins *US, 1989*

fugazi *adjective* crazy. Coined during the Vietnam war *US, 1980*

fugazzi *adjective* wrong. A disguising of FUCK and, possibly, ARSE *UK, 2002*

fugging *adverb* used as a euphemism for the intensifier 'fucking' *US, 1983*

fugly *noun* an extremely ugly person *AUSTRALIA, 1970*

fugly *adjective* very ugly. A blending of FUCKING (or 'funky') and 'ugly' *US, 1984*

full *adjective* **1** drunk *US, 1844*. **2** heavily drugged. A shortening of 'full of drugs' *UK, 1978*. **3** pregnant *TRINIDAD AND TOBAGO, 1976*

full as a bull's bum *adjective* extremely full *AUSTRALIA, 1971*

full as a fairy's phone book *adjective* extremely full; very drunk. Alluding to the allegedly inherent fickle nature of homosexual males *AUSTRALIA, 1978*

full as a family jerry *adjective* completely full *AUSTRALIA, 1982*

full as a family po *adjective* extremely full; very drunk *AUSTRALIA, 1982*

full as a goog *adjective* extremely full; very drunk *AUSTRALIA, 1941*

full as a pommie complaint box *adjective* extremely full; very drunk *AUSTRALIA, 1985*

full as a state school *adjective* extremely full; very drunk *AUSTRALIA, 1945*

full as a teddy bear *adjective* very drunk *CANADA, 1998*

full as a tick *adjective* extremely full; very drunk *AUSTRALIA, 1892*

full-auto *adjective* (used of a firearm) fully automatic *US, 1992*

full belt *adverb* at top speed *AUSTRALIA, 1901*

full bottle *noun* full speed or maximum volume. A Londoners' term *UK, 1977*

full bull *noun* a colonel in the US Army *US, 1962*

full chart *noun* a sale with maximised profit realised from financing the sale *US, 1980*

full dress *adjective* of a motorcyle, fully equipped and accessorised *US, 1973*

full dresser *noun* a factory stock Harley Davidson Electra-Glide motorcycle with every possible accessory. Biker (motorcycle) usage *US, 2000*

full eek *noun* a face that is fully made-up *UK, 2002*

full French *noun* oral sex performed on a man until he ejaculates *US, 1973*

full Greek *noun* in pinball, a shot up and then back down a lane with a scoring device, scoring twice *US, 1977*

full guns *adverb* to the maximum *US, 1947*

full hand *noun* the state of being infected with multiple sexually transmitted diseases *US, 1964*

full harva *noun* anal intercourse *UK, 2002*

full hit *noun* everything *UK, 2001*

full house *noun* **1** a combination of several non-existent diseases *US, 1947*. **2** infection with both gonorrhea and syphilis *US, 1981*. **3** a state in which a person is infested with more than one form of parasite, such as head and body lice *US, 1977*. **4** in drag racing and hot rodding, a highly modified engine *US, 1948*

full house and no flush *noun* the situation in which all available latrines are occupied *US, 1947*

full house mouse *noun* in hot rodding, a small car with a fully modified engine *US, 1965*

full monty; full monte; monte *noun* everything required within a given context. Usage widely popularised by the success of the film *The Full Monty*, 1997. Three plausible etymologies are well-rehearsed: from the nickname 'Monty', given to Field Marshal Montgomery, 1st Viscount of Alamein (1887–1976); the card game called Spanish Monte or Monte Bank; an abbreviation of Montague Burton, a high street menswear and tailoring company, retailers of a complete suit of clothing *UK, 1985*

full moon *noun* **1** a woman's menstrual period *US, 1954*. **2** buttocks of the large variety *US, 1997*. **3** a large slice of peyote cactus *US, 1970*

Full Nanaimo *noun* a garish dress outfit simulating official naval attire *CANADA, 1989*

full of beans *adjective* vigorous, energetic, in high spirits, full of life *UK, 1854*

full of gob *adjective* talkative; too talkative *UK, 2002*

full of run *adjective* (used of a racehorse) in good racing form *US, 1951*

full of shit *adjective* (of a person) deliberately or congenitally stupid, misleading or misinformed *US, 1954*

full of yourself *adjective* conceited, self-involved *UK, 1866*

full-on *adjective* maximum, complete, absolute, very *US, 1970*

full out *adverb* completely, intensely *US, 1918*

full personal *noun* sexual intercourse, as distinct from masturbation, when advertised as a service offered by a prostitute *UK, 2003*

full sails *adverb* in trucking, driving at top speed with the wind behind you *US, 1976*

full screw *noun* a corporal in the army *UK, 1995*

full service *noun* in the coded language of massage parlours, sexual intercourse *US, 2002*

full stop; full stop – end of story a catchphrase used as a firm signal that a matter is at an end. Verbalised punctuation, exactly matching US use of 'period' *UK, 1976*

full-timer *noun* a person who lives in a recreational vehicle all year *US, 1997*

full tit *noun* an all-out effort *NEW ZEALAND, 1998*

full tub *noun* in poker, a hand consisting of three cards of the same rank and a pair. Conventionally known as a 'full house' *US, 1988*

full up to dolly's wax replete with food; entirely full *AUSTRALIA, 1945*

full weight *noun* a package of drugs that weighs as much as it is claimed to weigh *US, 1992*

fully *adverb* very *US, 1982*

fuma d'Angola; fumo d'Angola *noun* marijuana. Portuguese, meaning 'smoke of Angola' *US, 1969*

fumble *verb* in college, to do poorly and receive a notification of academic deficiency *US, 1968*

fumble fingers *noun* clumsy hands *US, 1986*

fumed-up *adjective* marijuana-intoxicated *UK, 2002*

fumigate *verb* to take an enema before or after anal sex *US, 1972*

fummydiddle *verb* to waste time or to bungle *US, 1975*

fun *noun* a grain of opium *US, 1964*

fun *verb* to tease, to joke *US, 1967*

fun *adjective* amusing, interesting, light-hearted *US, 1950*

fun and frolics *noun* the testicles. Rhyming slang for BOLLOCKS, recorded as Anglo-Irish *1960*

fun and games *noun* 1 a (very) agreeable time; love-making, petting and/or sexual intercourse. The sexual sense is, of course, a specialisation of the general sense *UK, 1961*. 2 ironically, a disagreeable time; a brush with an enemy. Originally navy usage when the enemy was at sea *UK, 1948*

fun bags *noun* the female breasts *US, 1965*

fun book *noun* a collection of discount coupons given to guests by casinos *US, 1991*

fun box *noun* in skateboarding and foot-propelled scootering, any manufactured obstacle (usually made of wood) that provides varying configurations of ramps and surfaces for the boarder to employ *US, 1992*

funch *noun* sex during lunch *US, 1976*

Fun City *nickname* New York. Coined by Mayor John Lindsay in 1965 *US, 1966*

fundage *noun* money *US, 1993*

fundie; fundi; fundy *noun* 1 of religious faith, fundamentalist; a fundamentalist, especially a Christian fundamentalist but also applied in non-religious uses *UK, 1982*. 2 an expert, a teacher *SOUTH AFRICA, 1937*

funeral *noun* ▶ **it's your funeral; your funeral** it's of no concern to me (regardless of what the business, circumstance or situation that is being referred to is) *US, 1895*

funeral train *noun* a long line of cars whose progress is impeded by one slow driver who refuses to pull over and let them pass *US, 1962*

fun factor *noun* the ratio of a car's power to its weight *US, 1992*

fungee; fungy *noun* a fruit dumpling or a deep-dish blueberry pie *CANADA, 1952*

fungoo! fuck you! Often accompanied by graphic body language *US, 1942*

fun hog *noun* an obsessed enthusiast of thrill sports *US, 1992*

funk *noun* 1 a strong human smell; the smell of human sexual activity *US, 1917*. 2 semen; smegma *US, 1976*. 3 a genre of dance music that combines soul, blues, gospel and jazz with irresistible beats and rhythms. From the sense as 'the smell of sex' *US, 1958*. 4 a depressed state of mind *UK, 1820*

funk! used for expressing anger or disgust *US, 1963*

funk; funk it *verb* to lose your nerve, to have your courage or determination give way *UK, 1857*

funked out *adjective* drug-intoxicated *US, 1971*

funki dred *noun* a young black man who wears his hair in dreadlocks as a part of his fashionable style – not as a profession of Rastafarianism. Deliberate misspellings of FUNKY (fashionable) and 'dread' (a dreadlock wearer) *UK, 1994*

funk out *verb* to become exhausted *BAHAMAS, 1982*

funky *adjective* 1 sexual in a primal sense, earthy *US, 1954*. 2 bad, distasteful, dirty, smelly *US, 1946*. 3 earthy, fundamental, emotional, and when applied to music, characterised by blues tonalities *US, 1954*. 4 fashionable *US, 1969*. 5 in computing, descriptive of a feature that works imperfectly but not poorly enough to justify the time and expense to correct it *US, 1991*

Funky Fourth *nickname* the Fourth Army Division *US, 1991*

funky-fresh *adjective* fashionable, stylish *US, 1982*

funky yellow *noun* a variety of LSD *UK, 1996*

funny *adjective* 1 homosexual *US, 1962*. 2 odd, strange; hence, unwell *UK, 1806*

funny bomb *noun* a fragmenting explosive. Army use *US, 1991*

funny bone *noun* the extremity of the *humerus*, specifically that part of the elbow over which the ulnar nerve passes; a notional part of the body that is stimulated by comedy. A pun on 'humerus' and 'humorous', stressing the funny-peculiar sensation that is felt when the nerve is struck *UK, 1840*

funny book *noun* 1 a pornographic book or magazine *US, 1976*. 2 in trucking, a driver's daily log book *US, 1976*

funny boy *noun* a male homosexual *US, 1977*

funny bunny *noun* an eccentric *US, 1966*

funny business *noun* dishonest enterprises, criminal activities *UK, 1891*

funny car *noun* 1 in the language of car salesmen, a small car, especially a foreign-made car *US, 1975*. 2 in drag racing, a car with a drag racing chassis and engine covered with a fibreglass replica of a conventional car body *US, 1960s*

funny cigarette *noun* a marijuana cigarette *US, 1949*

funny fag *noun* a marijuana cigarette. Formed on FAG (a cigarette) *UK, 1998*

funny farm *noun* a hospital for the mentally ill *US, 1959*

Funny Farm Express *nickname* in trucking, a Frozen Foods Express truck. A back-formation from the company's initials *US, 1976*

funny five minutes *noun* a temporary aberration *UK, 2004*

funny ha-ha; ha-ha funny *adjective* amusing, inviting of laughter, as opposed to 'funny' in the sense of peculiar. From the oft-cited contrast of FUNNY PECULIAR and 'funny ha-ha' by British novelist and dramatist Ian Hay *UK, 1938*

funny kine *adjective* strange, unexpected, abnormal. Hawaiian youth usage *US, 1981*

funny money *noun* 1 counterfeit or play currency *US, 1938*. 2 during the Vietnam war, military payment certificates. The certificates were handed out to the military instead of currency to prevent black market use of the US dollar. Denominations of the certificates ranged from five cents to 20 dollars *US, 1965*. 3 any foreign currency. A resolutely English coinage, disregarding Scottish notes and sneering at the Euro *UK, 1984*. 4 the scrip issued in Alberta by the Canadian Social Credit party, which advocated free credit and monetary reform; the party became known as the 'funny-money party' CANADA, 1958. **5** promotional coupons issued by casinos to match money bets US, 2003

funnyosity noun a funny-peculiar curiosity. By elision UK, 1962

funny papers noun **1** LSD. A reference to the cartoon images printed on, or simply the effect of, LSD impregnated blotting paper UK, 1996. **2** topographical maps. Vietnam war usage; a tad cynical about the accuracy of the military's maps US, 1980. **3** building plans US, 1989

funny peculiar adjective funny in the sense of peculiar, as opposed to 'funny ha-ha' (amusing) UK, 1938

funny puff noun a marijuana cigarette US, 1976

funny valentine noun a tablet of Dexedrine™, a central nervous system stimulant. A reference to the tablet's heart shape US, 1966

funny ward noun a hospital ward reserved for the mentally ill US, 1963

funny water noun any alcoholic beverage US, 1974

funster noun a joker; a person who reminds you how much fun we are having. The name of a model of Chrysler outboard boat and given a nod in 'Tenement Funster', a song composed by Roger Taylor and recorded by Queen in 1974 US, 1974

funsy-wunsy noun sex US, 1956

funsy-wunsy adjective fun, cute US, 1995

funt; foont; pfund noun a pound (£); money. From German *pfund* pronounced 'foont' and Yiddish *funt*, incorporated into parleyaree and thence polari UK, 1857

fun tickets noun money US, 1997

funzine noun a purportedly humorous single-interest fan magazine US, 1982

fur noun **1** the female pubic hair; a woman as a sex object. Contemporary use mainly in FURBURGER, FUR PIE, etc US, 1959. **2** a woman's hairpiece US, 1972. ▶ **make the fur fly** to cause uproar, to disturb the status quo US, 1814

furball noun an aerial dogfight involving several planes US, 1983

fur beef noun a prison sentence for rape US, 1976

furburger noun the vagina, especially as an object of oral pleasure-giving; a woman as a sex object. A term that is especially popular with Internet pornographers US, 1965

fur coat and no knickers applied to someone whose surface rectitude masks a less than respectable morality UK, 1980

fur cup noun the vagina US, 1966. ▶ **drink of the fur cup** to perform oral sex on a woman US, 1966

furious fifties noun the latitutes of 50 to 59 degrees south ANTARCTICA, 1906

furkid noun a pet whose owner makes much of it CANADA, 2002

furlough baby noun a baby born after a serviceman's brief visit home CANADA, 1989

furnace and organ noun a car radio and heater US, 1959

furniture noun a rifle's or a similar weapon's stock UK, 1995

furphy noun **1** a rumour. A similar semantic development can be seen with SCUTTLEBUTT. Rarely 'furfy' AUSTRALIA, 1915. **2** an iron water cart. From the name of a manufacturer of such carts AUSTRALIA, 1938

fur pie noun the vulva and pubic hair US, 1934

furra noun heroin UK, 2002

furry folds noun the vagina US, 2001

furry hoop noun the vagina AUSTRALIA, 1971

furry letterbox noun the vagina UK, 2001

furry monkey noun the vagina UK, 1999

fur shur adverb ▷see: FER SHUR

further noun ▶ **in the further** in the future. Used when saying goodbye US, 1973

further adverb ▶ **have it further back** to know a lot and share that knowledge in talk CANADA, 1972

furthermucker noun used as a humorous euphemism for 'motherfucker' US, 1965

fur tongue noun a sycophant or toady US, 1977

fur-trapper noun a thief who distracts hotel guests in the lobby or at the hotel desk long enough to steal their furs US, 1954

fusebox noun the head US, 1946

fuselighter noun an artillery soldier US, 1988

fuss noun ▶ **don't make a fuss** a bus. Rhyming slang UK, 1960

fuss verb used as a euphemistic replacement for 'fuck' US, 1974

fuss-arse noun a fussy person. In 2003, usage appears to be mainly limited to south and southwest Wales UK, 1961

fuss-box noun a finicky, fussy person UK, 1901

fussbudget noun a chronic worrier US, 1904

fussed adjective ▶ **not fussed** unconcerned UK, 1988

fusspot noun a very fussy person. A combination of 'fuss', as an indicator of the dominant characteristic, and -POT (a person) UK, 1921

fussy adjective finicky UK, 2002. ▶ **not fussy** not especially keen; unconcerned CANADA, 1984. ▶ **not that fussy about** having an aversion to something, not liking it CANADA, 2000

futz around verb to waste time; to tinker with no results US, 1930

futz up verb used as a euphemism for 'fuck up', meaning to bungle US, 1947

fuzz noun **1** a police officer; the police US, 1929. **2** the pubic hair, usually on a female US, 1981

fuzz verb to shuffle (a deck of playing cards) by simultaneously drawing cards from the bottom and top of the deck US, 1967

fuzzball noun a fart. Generally phrased in the manner of 'someone dropped a fuzzball' and 'who's made the fuzzballs?' UK, 1979

fuzz box noun in electric line work, a noise-producing voltage tester US, 1980

fuzzburger noun the vagina as an object of oral pleasure-giving US, 1967

fuzz-buster noun an electronic radar-detection device US, 1976

fuzzed adjective drug-intoxicated US, 1961

fuzzie noun a girl or young woman US, 1974

fuzz one; fuzz two; fuzz three noun used as a rating system by US forces in Vietnam for the films shown on base; the system rated films on the amount of pubic hair shown. The more, the better US, 1990

fuzz-spotter noun a rear view mirror. From FUZZ (the police) UK, 1979

fuzztail noun a horse US, 1958

fuzzy noun **1** in horse racing, a horse that is seen as certain to win a race US, 1956. **2** in a deck of playing cards, the joker US, 1988

fuzzy-wuzzy noun **1** any black or dark-skinned native of a foreign land. A soldier's term, originally for a Sudanese warrior, widened to include all of Africa and islands such as Fiji. Now offensive and disdainful UK, 1892. **2** (during World War 2) a native of Papua New Guinea AUSTRALIA, 1942. **3** a dust ball US, 1947

fuzzy-wuzzy angel noun (during World War 2) a native of Papua New Guinea who gave assistance to Australian service personnel AUSTRALIA, 1942

fwefen noun the vagina TRINIDAD AND TOBAGO, 2003

f-word noun **1** the word 'fuck'. The intent is to specify one word, out of thousands that begin with 'f', that the speaker will not use US, 1970. **2** fusion (of musical genres). In music such fusion is viewed with great trepidation, stressed here by its deliberate confusion with 'fuck' UK, 2002

FYA used as Internet shorthand to mean 'for your amusement' US, 1997

FYI used in computer message shorthand to mean 'for your information' US, 1991

Gg

G *noun* **1** one thousand dollars; one thousand pounds; one thousand. From GRAND *US, 1928*. **2** a gram. Used mainly in a drug context *UK, 1997*. **3** one grain (of a narcotic) *US, 1966*. **4** a generic manufactured cigarette *US, 1992*. **5** a gang member *US, 1990*. **6** a close friend *US, 1989*. **7** a girlfriend *US, 1991*. **8** a G-string *US, 1992*

g' *adjective* good, especially in g'day, g'night, g'morning *UK, 1961*

gaar *noun* the buttocks *TRINIDAD AND TOBAGO, 1987*

gab *noun* unimportant conversation *UK, 1790*

gabacho; gavacho *noun* a white person. Derogatory border Spanish used in English conversation by Mexican-Americans *US, 1950*

gabalash *verb* (of quilting) to lash the quilt into the frame with big stitches, so that the precise, tiny stitches of the quilting design itself may be done. The word may derive from blending the two words 'gab' and 'lash', as the quilting sessions are also occasions for talk *CANADA, 1999*

gabber *noun* any central nervous system stimulant *US, 1987*

gabbleguts *noun* a talkative person *AUSTRALIA, 1966*

gabby bench *noun* a bench favoured by idle talkers *BAHAMAS, 1982*

gabbyguts *noun* a talkative person *AUSTRALIA, 1969*

Gabby Hayes hat *noun* the field hat worn by US soldiers in Vietnam. Likened to the narrow brim and low crown of the hat worn by the US western film star Gabby Hayes *US, 1977*

gabfest *noun* a group talk, usually about gossip or trivial matters *US, 1897*

gabins *noun* money *TRINIDAD AND TOBAGO, 2003*

Gabriel *nickname* a prisoner who plays the chapel organ *UK, 1950*

gabs *noun* trousers made of gabardine (a twill-woven cloth) *UK, 1955*

gack *noun* **1** cocaine *UK, 1997*. **2** a despised person *US, 1997*

gack *verb* in poker, to fold holding a hand that would have won had the player stayed in the game *US, 1996*

gack-blowing *noun* the process of anally ingesting cocaine *UK, 2002*

gacked *adjective* cocaine-intoxicated *UK, 2003*

gack-nag; gak-nag *noun* a cocaine user *UK, 2002*

gack scab *noun* a crusting of damaged mucous membrane that forms around the nostrils as the result of inhaling cocaine. Combines GACK (cocaine) with conventional 'scab' *UK, 1999*

gad *noun* in horse racing, the whip used by jockeys *US, 1976*

gadabout *noun* a Lada car. Citizens' band radio slang *UK, 1981*

Gadaffi *noun* the NAAFI (Navy, Army and Air Force Institutes). In Royal Air Force use; rhyming slang, based on the name of Lybian leader Colonel Moammar el Gadaffi *UK, 2002*

gad daigs! used for expressing surprise *BAHAMAS, 1982*

gadget *noun* **1** used as a general term for any cheating device used in a card game *US, 1988*. **2** in poker, any special rule applied to a game using wild cards *US, 1967*. **3** a G-string or similar female article of clothing *US, 1980*. **4** a US Air Force cadet *US, 1944*

gadgie *noun* **1** a man; an idiot or fool *UK: SCOTLAND, 1985*. **2** an old man. Urban youth slang *UK, 2005*

gaff *noun* **1** a location *UK, 1999*. **2** a place of residence; home; a shop or other place of business *UK, 1932*. **3** a prison cell. A narrower sense of 'a place of residence' *UK, 1996*. **4** a fair or fairground; a place of public amusement. Circus usage *UK, 1753*. **5** a cheating device *US, 1893*. **6** a device used to hide the shape of a male transvestite's penis *US, 1973*

gaff *verb* **1** to fix or rig a device *US, 1934*. **2** to cheat *UK, 1811*. **3** to talk aimlessly and pleasantly *TRINIDAD AND TOBAGO, 1994*

gaffer *noun* **1** used as a form of address. A loose variation of 'gaffer' as 'boss' or 'old man', usually showing respect *UK: ENGLAND, 1748*. **2** an employer, a boss, a foreman *UK, 1659*. **3** a senior electrician in a film unit *US, 1969*. **4** on the railways, a track crew supervisor *US, 1977*. **5** in motorcycle racing, a leader of a racing team *US, 1965*. **6** in circus and carnival usage, a manager *US, 1981*

gaffle *noun* in street gambling, a protocol under which the winner shares his winnings with other players *US, 1997*

gaffle *verb* **1** to steal *US, 1900*. **2** to arrest; to catch *US, 1954*. **3** to cheat, to swindle, to defraud *US, 1998*

gaffs *noun* dice that have been altered for cheating *US, 1950*

gaff shot *noun* in pool, an elaborate shot, especially an illegal one *US, 1985*

gaffus *noun* a hypodermic syringe and needle, especially when improvised *US, 1967*

gafu *noun* a colossal mistake. A 'god almighty fuck-up' *NEW ZEALAND, 1998*

gag *noun* **1** a manner of doing something, a practice *US, 1890*. **2** in the television and film industries, a stunt *US, 1988*. **3** any artifice employed by a beggar to elicit sympathy *US, 1962*. **4** an event or activity contrived to provide amusement or excitement *UK, 1996*. **5** an indefinite prison sentence *US, 1958*. **6** a small group of close friends *US, 1994*. **7** a quick use of cocaine *US, 1997*. **8** in craps, a bet that the shooter will make his even-numbered point in pairs *US, 1950*

gag *verb* to panic in the face of a great challenge *US, 1988*

gaga *adjective* **1** infatuated, silly *UK, 1917*. **2** mad, especially as a result of senility *UK, 1920*

gag-awful *adjective* horrible *US, 1981*

gage *noun* **1** marijuana. Also variants 'gayge' and 'gages' *US, 1934*. **2** alcohol, especially whisky *US, 1932*. ▶ **get a gage up** to smoke a marijuana cigarette *UK, 1998*

gage butt *noun* a marijuana fashioned cigarette *US, 1938*

gaged *adjective* drug-intoxicated *US, 1932*

gage out; gauge out *verb* to become, or be, sleepy as a result of marijuana intoxication *UK, 1996*

gagers; gaggers *noun* methcathinone *US, 1998*

gagged *adjective* disgusted *US, 1968*

gagging *adjective* desperately craving something, such as a cigarette, a drink or sex *UK, 1997*

gagging for a blagging *adjective* used of banks, etc, that exhibit poor security. A combination of GAGGING (desperate for something) and BLAGGING (a robbery with violence) *UK, 2001*

gaggle *noun* a formation of several military aircraft flying the same mission *US, 1942*

gaggler *noun* **1** MDMA, the recreational drug best known as ecstasy *UK, 2003*. **2** amphetamines *UK, 2003*

gag mel; gag me with a spoon! used for expressing disgust. A quintessential Valley Girl expression of disgust *US, 1982*

gagster *noun* a comedian *UK, 1935*

Gainesburger *noun* in the military, canned beef patties. Alluding to a dog food product. Vietnam war usage *US, 1983*

Gainesville green *noun* marijuana grown in or near Gainesville, Florida *US, 1976*

gal *noun* a woman or a girl. This gal is a woman with a chequered history: 'Cockney for girl', 1824, but then the pronunciation worked its way up the social ladder until, by about 1840, it was quite upper-class. From around 1850 a 'gal' was a 'servant girl' or a 'harlot', and from about 1860, a 'sweetheart' as used by Albert Chevalier in *My Old Dutch*, 1893. The current sense is recorded in US jazz and jive circles from the 1930s. By the turn of the millennium, having passed through respectability once again, 'gal' was patronising or kitsch, and rarely found without 'guys' *UK, 1795*

galactic *adjective* great, wonderful, amazing *US, 1998*

galah *noun* a fool. From the name of an endemic Australian cockatoo, commonly kept as a cage bird, and able to be coaxed into antic behaviour. The name of the bird comes from the Australian Aboriginal language Yuwaalaraay *AUSTRALIA, 1938*

galba *noun* the penis *TRINIDAD AND TOBAGO, 2003*

gal block *noun* a section of a prison reserved for blatantly homosexual prisoners *US, 1972*

gal-boy *noun* an effeminate young man *US, 1987*

galf *noun* a girlfriend. A reduction of 'galfriend' *US, 1979*

Galilee stompers *noun* in homosexual usage, sandals *US, 1987*

gall *noun* effrontery, impudence *US, 1882*

gallery 13 *noun* a prison graveyard *US, 1982*

gallery god *noun* a theatre-goer who sits in the uppermost balcony *US, 1947*

gallon *noun* a container for liquid, without regard to the precise volume *FIJI, 1993*

gallop *verb* ▶ **gallop the lizard** (of a male) to masturbate *AUSTRALIA, 1985*

galloper *noun* a racehorse *AUSTRALIA, 1960*

galloping *adjective* worsening *UK, 1785*

galloping bones *noun* dice *US, 1920*

galloping dandruff *noun* body lice *US, 1920*

galloping dominoes *noun* dice *US, 1918*

galloping horse *noun* heroin. An elaboration of HORSE (heroin) *US, 1959*

gallops *noun* horse racing *AUSTRALIA, 1950*

gallup *noun* heroin. Building on the HORSE image *UK, 2002*

gallus; gallows *adjective* attractive, wonderful; self-confident, quick-witted, brave, ostentatious, nonchalant; also used as an intensifier. A phonetic slurring of 'gallows', suggesting 'fit for the gallows' and thus 'wicked' – a very early example of 'bad' means 'good'. In the US from the 1840s to 1940s *UK, 1789*

galoot; galloot *noun* a man, especially if hulking, stupid, boorish, foolish, clumsy or otherwise objectionable. Possibly from Dutch *gelubt* (a eunuch) *UK, 1818*

gal pal *noun* **1** a woman's female friend *US, 2001*. **2** a female friend of a male homosexual *US, 1977*

gal tank *noun* a holding cell in a jail reserved for homosexual prisoners *US, 1972*

galvanise *noun* sheets of corrugated iron *BARBADOS, 1965*

galvo *noun* galvanised iron. Iron corrugated sheets are a common building material in rural Australia *AUSTRALIA, 1945*

gam *noun* **1** the leg. Originally applied to a crippled leg, later to a woman's leg *UK, 1785*. **2** an act of oral sex. Also variant 'gambo' *UK, 1954*

gam *verb* **1** to pretend *IRELAND, 1989*. **2** to boast *US, 1970*. **3** to perform oral sex *UK, 1910*

gamahuche *noun* an act of oral sex. Possibly a combination of Scots dialect words *gam* (gum, mouth) and *roosh* (rush), hence a 'rushing into the mouth'; more likely from French *gamahucher* which shares the same sense *UK, 1865*

gambage *noun* showing off *TRINIDAD AND TOBAGO, 1940*

Gamble and Procter; gamble *noun* a doctor. Rhyming slang, formed on a reversal of the pharmaceutical company Procter and Gamble *UK, 1998*

gambler's bankroll; gambler's roll *noun* a bankroll consisting of a large-denomination note on the outside of a number of small-denomination notes *US, 1986*

game *noun* **1** an athlete's style and ability *US, 1997*. **2** a person's style; visual and oral *US, 1976*. **3** a conventional attitude. A counterculture concept that refuses to accept non-drop-out society as anything more than a game with unnecessary rules *UK, 1967*. **4** a criminal activity; crime as a profession *UK, 1739*. **5** business *AUSTRALIA, 1877*. **6** an attempt to con *US, 1975*. **7** sex appeal *US, 1999*. **8** an interest in the opposite sex *US, 2001*. **9** a romantic or sexual relationship outside your primary relationship. Synonymous with PLAY AROUND; also, 'game' has strong sexual overtones, as in ON THE GAME (engaged in prostitution) *UK, 1958*. ▶ **give the game away** to cease doing something; to abandon; to give up *AUSTRALIA, 1953*. ▶ **on the game** to be working as a prostitute *UK, 1898*. ▶ **out of the game** married, engaged or dating only one person *US, 2001*. ▶ **run a game** to fool, to swindle *US, 1940*. ▶ **the game** the business of prostitution *UK, 1898*. ▶ **the Game** the criminal lifestyle *US, 1976*

game *verb* **1** to deceive, to mislead, to trick *US, 1963*. **2** to flirt; to woo *US, 1988*

game! used for expressing that enough is enough *US, 1997*

game as a pissant *adjective* very courageous *AUSTRALIA, 1944*

game face *noun* in sports, a serious expression and demeanour reflecting complete concentration on the competition at hand. Now used outside of sports, extended to any serious situation *US, 1972*

gameless *adjective* unskilled *US, 1983*

game of nap *noun* **1** a cap. Rhyming slang, from the card game *UK, 1976*. **2** an act of defecation. Rhyming slang for CRAP *UK, 1992*

game over! used for expressing that enough is enough *US, 1997*

gamer *noun* **1** a video game or role-playing game enthusiast *US, 1977*. **2** an athlete who can always be counted on for a gritty, all-out effort *US, 1977*. **3** a person engaged in swindles and hustles as a way of life *US, 1975*

game refuge *noun* any institution where traffic violators who are under pursuit are free from further pursuit once they pass the gates *US, 1962*

games and sports; games *noun* warts. Rhyming slang *UK, 2003*

gamey eye *noun* a tendency to flirt *IRELAND, 1995*

gamma delta iota *noun* a college student who is not a fraternity or sorority member; a notional fraternity or sorority comprised of students who don't belong to fraternities or sororities. A back-formation from GDI (**god damn independent**) *US, 2000*

gammon *noun* one microgram. The unit of measurement for LSD doses, even in the non-metric US *US, 1969*

gammon rasher *noun* a superlative thing. Rhyming slang for SMASHER *UK, 1974*

gammy *adjective* **1** inferior, of low quality. As in 'gammy gear' (inferior goods) *UK, 1979*. **2** lame *UK, 1879*

gammy chant *noun* a bad situation *IRELAND, 1997*

gamoosh *noun* a fellow, usually not referring to a winner in the zero-sum game of life *US, 1988*

gamot *noun* heroin; morphine *UK, 1998*

gander *noun* a look *US, 1914*. ▶ **cop a gander** to look at someone or something, especially with discretion *US, 1950*. ▶ **get your gander up** to become annoyed or angry. A variation, probably by mishearing, of DANDER *UK, 2002*

Gandhi's flipflop *noun* used in similes as an example of extreme dryness. Mahatma Gandhi, 1869–1948, wore sandals *UK, 1999*

gandies *noun* underwear *US, 1970*

G and T *noun* gin and tonic. Initialism *UK, 1966*

gandy *noun* in Newfoundland, a pancake *CANADA, 1966*

gandy dancer *noun* **1** a railway track worker. Thought to be so called from the Gandy Manufacturing Company of Chicago, which made many of the tools used by the section gangs *US, 1918*. **2** a road worker *US, 1976*. **3** in trucking, a tractor trailer that weaves back and forth on the road *US, 1971*

gandy gang *noun* on the railways, a crew of track workers *US, 1977*

gang *noun* **1** a work crew. Still heard on occasion, but largely replaced with the standard English 'crew' *US, 1989*. **2** a person's social group. From earlier conventional senses *UK, 1945*. **3** a great many *US, 1811*. **4** marijuana *BAHAMAS, 1982*

gang *verb* to engage in serial, consecutive sex, homosexual or heterosexual, especially to engage in multiple rape. A shortened form of GANGBANG *UK, 1972*

gangbang *noun* **1** successive, serial copulation between a single person and multiple partners *US, 1945*. **2** an orgy at which several couples have sex. **3** a cluster of reporters descending on a public figure with microphones, cameras, notepads and shouted questions. Sometimes shortened to 'bang' or the variant 'major bang' *US, 2001*. **4** a social gathering. A humorously ironic use of the orgiastic sense *UK, 1977*. **5** a group of friends talking together on citizens' band radio *US, 1977*. **6** a television writing session involving multiple writers *US, 1997*. **7** the utilization of a large number of computer programmers to create a product in a short period of time *US, 1991*. **8** a fight between youth gangs *US, 1967*

gangbang *verb* **1** to engage in successive, serial copulation with multiple partners. Also in figurative use *US, 1949*. **2** to be an active part of a gang; to battle another gang *US, 1968*

gangbanger *noun* a youth gang member *US, 1969*

gangbuster *noun* a zealous, energetic police official or prosecutor who targets organised crime *US, 1936*

gangbusters *noun* ▶ **like gangbusters** aggressively, with force *US, 1940*

gang cheats *noun* two or more people working as confederates in a cheating scheme *US, 1988*

gange *noun* marijuana. A shortening of GANJA (marijuana) *US, 1971*

gang-fuck *noun* an uncoordinated mess *UK, 1995*

gang-fuck *verb* to engage in serial, consecutive sex, homosexual or hetereosexual *US, 1916*

gangie *noun* Serial sex between one person and multiple, partners, consensual or not *NEW ZEALAND, 1971*

gangplank *noun* a bridge *US, 1976*

gangplank fever *noun* in the military, a fear of transfer to an assignment overseas *US, 1945*

gang-shag *noun* successive, serial copulation between a single person and multiple partners *US, 1927*

gang-splash *noun* serial sex between one person and multiple partners, heterosexual or homosexual, consensual or not *AUSTRALIA, 1971*

gangsta *noun* a young black member of a (criminal) gang. A deliberate respelling of 'gangster' *US, 1998*

gangsta *adjective* good, exciting. Hip-hop *US, 2002*

gangsta-lette *noun* a female gang member *US, 2001*

gangstamuthafucka *noun* a gangster, especially one who is considered powerful. An intensification of GANGSTA *UK, 1997*

gangsta rap; g-rap *noun* a rap music genre characterised by explicit sex and violence which, it is claimed, reflects black urban existence. Combines GANGSTA or 'g' (a black urban anti-hero) with RAP (a musical style) *US, 1992*

gangsta rapper *noun* a rap artist who reflects on the black urban experience in an explicitly sexual and violent manner. GANGSTA RAP has been an influential music genre since the late 1980s *US, 1990*

gangster *noun* **1** marijuana. Promotes the outlaw self-image enjoyed by smokers of the illegal substance; possibly playing on GANJA *US, 1960*. **2** a cigarette *US, 1972*

gangster bitch *noun* a female who associates with youth gang members *US, 2001*

gangster doors *noun* any four-door sedan *US, 1980*

gangster lean *noun* **1** a style of driving a car in which the driver leans towards the right side of the car, leaning on an arm rest, steering with the left hand; by extension, a slouching walk or posture *US, 1973*. **2** a car with hydraulic shock aborbers that are set to leave the car higher on one side than the other *US, 1991*

gangster pill *noun* any barbiturate or other central nervous system depressant *US, 1994*

gangster whitewalls *noun* showy, flashy, whitewalled tyres *US, 1972*

gang-up *noun* serial sex between multiple active participants and a single passive one *US, 1951*

gangy *noun* a close friend; a fellow member of a clique. Hawaiian youth usage *US, 1982*

ganja *noun* **1** marijuana, notably from Jamaica. Hindi word for 'cannabis', possibly derived from BHANG and adopted around 1920 by 'Anglo-Indian drug addicts', by 1970 the UK Home Office 'could ascribe it to West Indians'. Celebrated in song by, among many others, Clancy Eccles, 'Ganja Free', 1972 and Leslie Butler, 'Ashanti Ganja Dub', 1975. With many spelling variations including 'ganj', 'ganjah', 'ganjuh' and 'ganga' *JAMAICA, 1972*. **2** the white establishment *US, 2000*

ganja *adjective* white-skinned *US, 2000*

gank *noun* **1** marijuana *US, 1989*. **2** a substance sold as an illegal drug that is actually fake *US, 1994*

gank *verb* **1** to steal *US, 1996*. **2** in Internet game-playing, to 'kill' a player, especially unfairly. Also used as a noun *UK, 2003*

ganky *adjective* ugly, repulsive *IRELAND, 2004*

GAP *noun* the Great American Public *US, 1965*

gap *verb* to watch, to witness a crime *US, 1949*. ▶ **gap it** to make a quick exit *SOUTH AFRICA, 2000*. ▶ **gap your axe** to annoy *NEW ZEALAND, 1998*

gape *noun* a completely relaxed, distended anus. A term used by anal sex fetishists, especially on the Internet *US, 1999*

gape *verb* to idle, to wander *US, 1966*

gaper *noun* **1** a dolt. An abbreviation of GAPING ASSHOLE *US, 1966*. **2** a novice skier, or a non-skier watching others ski *US, 1990*. **3** a mirror *US, 1931*

gaper-block; gapers' block *noun* a traffic problem created by motorists slowing down to gawk at an accident *US, 1961*

gaping and flaming *adjective* (used of a party) wild, rowdy, fun *US, 1968*

gaping asshole *noun* a dolt *US, 1966*

GAPO *noun* used as an abbreviation of gorilla armpit odour *US, 1967*

gaposis *noun* a notional disease involving a gap of any kind *US, 1942*

gap out *verb* to daydream and miss something for lack of attention *CANADA, 1993*

gapper *noun* a mirror. Prisoner usage to describe a mirror used to watch for approaching guards as the prisoners do something which they ought not to do *US, 1934*

gappings *noun* a salary *US, 1955*

gap up *verb* to fill capsules with a powdered narcotic *US, 1971*

gar *noun* **1** a black person. An abbreviviation of NIGGER *US, 1962*. **2** marijuana rolled in cigar leaf *US, 2001*

gar *adjective* excellent, pleasing *US, 1993*

garage *noun* a subset of a criminal organisation *US, 1975*

garage action *noun* a legal action for libel (usually against a newspaper) brought by the police on their own behalf. The damages awarded are often substantial enough to buy a new garage for the police officer's home *UK, 1998*

garage band *noun* an amateur rock group with a basic, three-chord approach to music. From the custom of practising in the garage at the home of the parents of a band member *US, 1977*

garage man's companion *noun* a truck manufactured by General Motors Corporation. A back-formation from the initials GMC *US, 1971*

garans! certainly. Hawaiian youth usage; shortened from 'guaranteed' *US, 1981*

garbage *noun* **1** anything of poor quality or little or no worth; nonsense. From the sense as 'refuse' *UK, 1592*. **2** heroin; low quality heroin *US, 1962*. **3** farm produce *US, 1976*. **4** any and all food, usually low in protein and high in carbohydrate, not in a bodybuilder's diet *US, 1984*. **5** cocktail garnishes *US, 1998*. **6** in hot rodding, a surfeit of accessories unrelated to the car's performance *US, 1960*. **7** in poker, the cards that have been discarded *US, 1967*

garbage barge *noun* a tuna fish sandwich *US, 1985*

garbage down *verb* to eat quickly *US, 1959*

garbage dump *noun* the California State Prison at San Quentin *US, 1992*

garbage guts *noun* a glutton *AUSTRALIA, 1977*

garbage hauler *noun* a truck driver hauling fruit or vegetables *US, 1971*

garbage head *noun* an addict who will use any substance available. A term used in twelve-step recovery programmes such as Alcoholics Anonymous *US, 1970*

garbage in – garbage out a catchphrase employed as an admonition to computer users: if you program mistakes into a computer then an output of rubbish will surely result *US, 1976*

garbage mouth *noun* a person who regularly uses profanity *US, 1970*

garbage rock *noun* crack cocaine, especially of inferior quality *UK, 1998*

garbage shot *noun* in pool, a shot made with luck, not with skill *US, 1979*

garbage stand *noun* in circus and carnival usage, a novelty concession *US, 1981*

garbage time *noun* the minutes at the end of an athletic contest when the outcome is not in doubt and substitute players are used freely by either or both teams; games at the end of a season when a team's record is such that a win or loss will not make a difference and substitute players are freely used *US, 1971*

garbage up *verb* **1** to eat *US, 1955*. **2** in bodybuilding, to eat food that is not in your regular diet *US, 1984*

garbage wagon *noun* a standard Harley-Davidson motorcyle. The term came from those who stripped the Harley of all the 'garbage' they didn't want, keeping only the functional necessities *US, 1966*

garbanzos *noun* the female breasts *US, 1982*

garbo *noun* **1** a rubbish collector *AUSTRALIA, 1953*. **2** a rubbish bin *AUSTRALIA, 1987*

garbologist *noun* a rubbish collector *AUSTRALIA, 1973*

garburator *noun* a garbage disposal unit mounted in the sink *CANADA, 1998*

garden *noun* **1** a woman's pubic hair *US, 1982*. **2** a railway yard *US, 1946*

Gardena miracle *noun* in a game of poker, a good hand drawn after a poor deal hand. Gardena is a city near Los Angeles where poker rooms are legal *US, 1982*

gardener *noun* **1** a bookmaker who extends his prices beyond his competitors *AUSTRALIA, 1989*. **2** in pool, a betting player who wins *US, 1990*

garden gate *noun* **1** eight pounds, £8 *UK, 1992*. **2** a magistrate. Rhyming slang *UK, 1859*

garden gate *verb* to perform oral sex on a woman. Rhyming slang for PLATE (to engage oral sex) *UK, 2002*

garden gnome *noun* a comb. Rhyming slang *UK, 1992*

garden plant; garden *noun* an aunt. Rhyming slang *UK, 1992*

garden punk *noun* a male homosexual *BAHAMAS, 1982*

garden tool *noun* a promiscuous girl or woman. Alluding, of course, to a 'hoe' *US, 1990*

Gareth Gate *verb* to masturbate. Rhyming slang, inspired by the name of pop singer Gareth Gates (b.1984) who came to fame in 2002 *UK, 2003*

Gareth Hunt *noun* an unpleasant or despicable person. Rhyming slang, formed on the name of a well known London-born actor (1943–2007) *UK, 2003*

gargle *noun* alcoholic drink *AUSTRALIA, 1965*

gark *noun* a scratch *NEW ZEALAND, 1998*

garlo *noun* a police officer. English gypsy use *UK, 2000*

garm *noun* clothing; an item of clothing. An abbreviation of 'garment'; current in the black community *UK, 1997*

garmed up *adjective* fashionably or smartly dressed *UK, 1997*

gar-mouth *verb* to issue threats which cannot and will not be implemented. In honour of the 'gar', a fish of the pike family with long jaws – a big mouth *US, 1984*

garms *noun* clothes. From conventional garments *UK, 2006*

garn! go on! *AUSTRALIA, 1911*

garnish *noun* cash *US, 2003*

garnot *noun* heroin *UK, 2002*

Garrison finish *noun* in horse racing, a sprinting finish by a horse that has lagged back until the final moment *US, 1890*

garrity *adjective* madly over-excited. Presumably after someone who exhibited such characteristics; possibly Freddie Garrity (b.1940), prancing and dancing lead singer of Freddie & The Dreamers, a 1960s pop group from Manchester *UK, 1999*

Gary Ablett *noun* a tablet, especially of MDMA, the recreational drug. best known as ecstasy. Rhyming slang, ironically based on Australian Rules Football player Gary Ablett whose career was marred by a controversial involvement with drink and drugs. The etymology is confused by Liverpool FC player Gary Ablett *AUSTRALIA, 1992*

Gary Cooper *noun* in craps, a roll of 12. From Cooper's starring role in the western film *High Noon US, 1983*

Gary Glitter *noun* the anus; a lavatory. Rhyming slang for SHITTER. The original 1980s use for entertainer Gary Glitter (Paul Francis Gadd b.1944), as inspiration for a rhyming slang term was as 'bitter' (beer), however in the mid-90s allegations of under-age sex changed the public's perception and Gary Glitter became an ARSEHOLE or was associated with toilets. In 2006 he was found guilty in Vietnam of charges concerning under-age sex . Unlike much rhyming slang this is generally used in full, if only to avoid confusion with GARY LINEKER (vinegar) *UK, 2001*

Gary Lineker *noun* vinegar. Imprecise rhyming slang, based on the name of Gary Lineker (b.1960), a popular footballer and television personality. Walkers Crisps, whose advertising he is closely associated with, introduced a 'Salt and Lineker' flavour after this slang term was in circulation *UK, 1998*

Gary Player; Gary *noun* an 'all-*dayer*' event. Rhyming slang, based on the name of South African golfer Gary Player (b.1936) *UK, 2002*

gas *noun* **1** a pleasing and/or amusing experience or situation. A jazz term that slipped into mainstream youth slang *US, 1953*. **2** anabolic steroids. The term drew national attention in the US on 14th July 1994, when Terry Bollea (aka Hulk Hogan) testified in criminal proceedings against wrestling promoter Vince McMahon in Uniondale, New York. Asked if he had heard any slang for steroids, Bollea/Hogan answered 'Juice. Gas' *US, 1994*. **3** batteries. From the radio as CAR metaphor *US, 2002*. **4** money *SOUTH AFRICA, 1977*. **5** in pool, momentum or force *US, 1993*. ▶ **cut the gas** to stop talking *US, 1951*. ▶ **take gas** to be knocked from a surfboard by a wave; to fall from a skateboard *US, 1963*. ▶ **take the gas** to lose your composure *US, 1961*

gas *verb* **1** to talk idly; to chatter. The 'gas' is hot air *US, 1847*. **2** to tease, to joke, to kid *US, 1847*. **3** to please, to excite *US, 1941*. **4** to inhale glue or any volatile solvent for the intoxicating effect *US, 1970*. **5** to straighten (hair) with chemicals and heat *US, 1953*

gasbag *noun* a very talkative individual, a boaster, a person of too many words *US, 1862*

gas-cooker *verb* to catch out; to put in a difficult position; to trick or delude. Glasgow rhyming slang for SNOOKER *UK: SCOTLAND, 1988*

gaseech *noun* a face *UK, 1992*

gas 'em stop *noun* a petrol station *US, 1976*

gas factor *noun* (among Canadian forces personnel) a measure of a person's commitment to a project. The initials represent '*give a shit*' *CANADA, 1995*

gas gun *noun* a large-bore shotgun loaded with tear-gas cannisters *US, 1962*

gas-guzzler *noun* a motor vehicle that demands immoderate quantities of fuel, either by design or in consequence of a driver's excessive demands *US, 1973*

gash *noun* **1** the vagina; sex with a woman; a woman as a sex object *US, 1866*. **2** a male homosexual who is sexually passive *US, 1950*. **3** rubbish, refuse. A British contribution to South Pole slang *ANTARCTICA, 1958*. **4** a second helping of food *AUSTRALIA, 1943*. **5** marijuana *US, 1986*

gash *verb* to have sex *US, 1989*

gash *adjective* useless, of poor quality *UK, 1997*

gas-head *noun* **1** an abuser of industrial solvents for their psychoactive effects *UK, 1996*. **2** a person with chemically straightened hair *US, 1968*

gash hound *noun* a man who is obsessed with women *US, 1955*

gasket *noun* **1** any improvised seal between the end of a dropper and the hub of a needle *US, 1970*. **2** a doughnut *US, 1942*

gasket jint; gasket *noun* a pint, especially of beer. Glasgow rhyming slang, formed on the local pronunciation of 'joint' *UK: SCOTLAND, 1988*

gasoline! in oil drilling, used as a shouted warning that a boss is approaching *US, 1954*

gasoline alley *noun* in motor racing, the area at the race track where race teams repair and prepare cars for the race *US, 1965*

gasp and grunt; grunt *noun* the vagina; a woman or women sexually objectified. Rhyming slang for CUNT *UK, 1961*

gas-passer *noun* an anaesthetist *US, 1961*

gasper *noun* **1** a cigarette. Descriptive of the respiratory effect of tobacco-smoking. Originally military slang for an inferior cigarette, popularised in World War 1, in wider usage by 1930 *UK, 1914*. **2** a marijuana cigarette. From the earlier sense (cigarette) *US, 1984*. **3** something that is astonishing *US, 1970*. **4** in typography, an exclamation mark (!) *UK, 2003*

Gaspers *nickname* the Asper family of Winnipeg, Manitoba, socially, culturally and politically prominent *CANADA, 2002*

gasper stick *noun* a marijuana cigarette *UK, 1998*

Gaspe steak *noun* fried bologna *CANADA, 1998*

gas pump jock *noun* in the days before self-service, a petrol station attendant *US, 1986*

gas queen *noun* a male homosexual who patronizes young male prostitutes working on the street *US, 1997*

gassed *adjective* **1** tipsy, drunk. World War 1 military use from the stupefying effects of gas; then, its origins soon forgotten, just another synonym for 'drunk' *US, 1919*. **2** describes a drug that is considered to be terrific or very enjoyable, used especially of marijuana, *US, 1946*

gasser *noun* **1** something wonderful, very exceptional; extraordinarily successful *US, 1944*. **2** a cigarette. Partridge suggests 'perhaps a slovening of the synonym GASPER'; a darker etymology reflecting the cough-inducing and life-shortening properties of tobacco is also possible *AUSTRALIA, 1984*. **3** an anaesthetist. Medical slang. Often teamed with surgeons as 'gassers and SLASHERS' *UK, 2002*. **4** in drag racing, a car that only uses petrol for fuel *US, 1965*. **5** in oil drilling, a well that produces no oil *US, 1954*

gassy *adjective* excellent, pleasant, humorous *US, 1962*

Gastown *noun* now a section of downtown Vancouver, named after a Victorian-era saloonkeeper *CANADA, 1952*

gastro *noun* gastroenteritis *AUSTRALIA, 1975*

gat *noun* **1** a gun, especially a pistol; in the Royal Air Force, a rifle *US, 1897*. **2** the anus. From Afrikaans (a hole) *SOUTH AFRICA, 1968*

gat *verb* to shoot *US, 1990*

gat-creeper *noun* a sycophant. From GAT (the anus), and *kruiper* (creeper) *SOUTH AFRICA, 1985*

gate *noun* **1** a jazz musician; hence a fashionable man. A pun on 'swinging' (swing gate, abbreviated from GATOR *US, 1936*. **2** used as a term of address among jazz lovers of the 1930s and 40s *US, 1936*.

3 a young person *US, 1936*. **4** release from prison *US, 1966*. **5** a vein into which a drug is injected *US, 1986*. **6** the mouth *US, 1936*

gate *verb* in private dice games, to stop the dice while rolling, either as a superstition or to check for cheating *US, 1963*

-gate *suffix* used as an embellishment of a noun or name to suggest a far-reaching political scandal. From the Watergate scandal that consumed and ultimately destroyed the Nixon presidency between 1972 (the burglary) and 1974 (the resignation from office) *US, 1973*

gate-crash *verb* to achieve entrance to a place, or an event such as a party, without proper credentials or an invitation *US, 1922*

gate-crasher *noun* a person who achieves entrance to a place, or an event such as a party, without proper credentials or an invitation *US, 1927*

gate-crashing *noun* the act of achieving entrance to a place, or an event such as a party, without proper credentials or an invitation *US, 1927*

gate fever *noun* the anxiety suffered by prisoners as they approach their release date *UK, 1958*

gate happy *adjective* (of prisoners) exuberant or excited at the approach of a release date *UK, 1996*

gate jaw *noun* in trucking, a driver who monopolises conversation on the citizens' band radio *US, 1976*

gatekeeper *noun* a person who introduces another to a first LSD experience *US, 1967*

gate money *noun* the cash given to a prisoner upon release from prison *US, 1931*

gatemouth *noun* a gossip *US, 1944*

Gatemouth *nickname* jazz trumpeter Louis Armstrong (1901–1971) *US, 1936*

gates *noun* **1** used as a term of address, male-to-male, usually collegial *US, 1936*. **2** marijuana *US, 1966*. **3** a house *BERMUDA, 1985*

Gateshead *noun* ▶ **get out at Gateshead** during sex, to withdraw the penis from the vagina just before ejaculation, to practise *coitus interruptus UK, 1970*

gates of Rome *noun* home. Rhyming slang *UK, 1960*

gate to heaven; jade gate *noun* the vagina. Notable for what seems to be the first slang uses of 'gate' as 'vagina' – not for the sub-'Perfumed Garden'-style of metaphorical imagery *US, 2001*

Gateway to the South *noun* Balham, a district in South London. An ironic title, coined in the early 1960s for a satirical 'travelogue' 'Balham – Gateway to the South' written by Frank Muir and performed by Peter Sellers *UK, 1977*

gatey *adjective* of prisoners, suffering anxiety as the date of release from prison approaches *UK, 1959*

gather *noun* a police officer *UK, 1999*

gather *verb* to arrest. Usually as the passive 'be gathered' *AUSTRALIA, 1975*

Gatnick *noun* London *Gatwick* airport. A pun on NICK (to steal), based on the reputation of the baggage handlers *UK, 1999*

gato *noun* heroin. Spanish *gato* (a cat) *US, 1980*

gator *noun* **1** an alligator *US, 1844*. **2** an all-purpose male form of address. Originally a Negro abbreviation of 'alligator'; in the 1930s it was adopted into JIVE (black/jazz slang) as an equivalent of CAT (a man); *gato* is a 'male cat' in Spanish. Eventually rock 'n' roll spread the word and it died out *US, 1944*. **3** a swing jazz enthusiast. An abbreviation of ALLIGATOR *US, 1944*

Gator *nickname* Ron Guidry (b.1950), one of the best pitchers to ever play for the New York Yankees (1975–88). Guidry came from Louisiana, a state with swamps that are home to alligators *US, 1978*

gator boy; gator girl *noun* a member of the Seminole Indian tribe *US, 1963*

gator grip *noun* in television and film-making, a clamp used to attach lights. An abbreviation of 'alligator grip', from the resemblance to an alligator's jaws *US, 1987*

gatted *adjective* drunk *UK, 2002*

gatter *noun* a drink; alcohol, especially beer. English gypsy use *UK, 1841*

gattered *adjective* drunk. Possibly a variation of GUTTERED *UK, 2003*

gauching *adjective* used to describe the glazed-eyed, open-mouthed state of an intoxicated drug taker *UK, 1996*

gauge *noun* a shotgun *US, 1993*

gavel and wig; gavel *verb* to probe your eye or your anus in order to relieve an irritation. Rhyming slang for TWIG *UK, 1992*

gavvers *noun* the police. English gypsy and underworld use *UK, 2000*

gawd; gaw; gor *noun* god. Phonetic spelling of Cockney pronunciation, subsequently treated as almost euphemistic *UK, 1877*

gawd love-a-duck!; cor love-a-duck! used as a mild expression of shock or surprise. A variation of LORD LOVE-A-DUCK! *UK, 1948*

gawjo *noun* ▷*see:* GORGER

gawk *noun* in circus and carnival usage, a local who loiters as the show is assembled or taken down *US, 1981*

gay *noun* a homosexual *US, 1953*

gay *adjective* **1** homosexual *US, 1933*. **2** catering to or patronised by homosexuals *US, 1954*. **3** bad, stupid, out of style. General pejorative in juvenile use; a reversal of the politically correct norm much as 'good' is BAD and WICKED is 'good' *US, 1978*

gay 90s *noun* US Treasury 3.5% bonds issued in 1958, due to return in 1990 *US, 1960*

gay and frisky *noun* whisky. Rhyming slang *UK, 1919*

gay and hearty *noun* a party. Rhyming slang *AUSTRALIA, 1969*

gay as a French horn *adjective* undoubtedly homosexual *UK, 2001*

gay-ass *adjective* extremely out of fashion *CANADA, 2002*

gay bar *noun* a bar catering to a homosexual clientele *US, 1953*

gay bashing *noun* violent beatings targeted on homosexuals *US, 1997*

gay boy *noun* a homosexual male, especially one who is flamboyant and young *US, 1945*

gaycat *verb* to have a good, carefree time *US, 1924*

gay chicken *noun* a young homosexual male *US, 1959*

gaydar; gadar *noun* the perceived or real ability of one homosexual to sense intuitively that another person is homosexual *US, 1982*

gayer *noun* a homosexual. An elaboration of GAY *UK, 2003*

gay for pay *adjective* said of a heterosexual man who portrays a homosexual man in a film or other theatrical performance *US, 1997*

gay ghetto *noun* a section of a city largely inhabited by openly homosexual men. Probably coined by Martin Levine, who wrote 'Gay Ghetto', published in *Journal of Homosexuality*, Volume 4 (1979). Examples include Greenwich Village and Chelsea in New York, the North Side in Chicago and the Castro in San Francisco. Unlike all other ghettos, they are affluent *US, 1971*

gay gordon *noun* a traffic warden. Rhyming slang, probably formed from the Gay Gordons, a traditional Scottish dance *UK, 1992*

gaylord *noun* a homosexual man. An elaboration of GAY via a somewhat obscure male forename; introduced to the UK, and possibly coined by, comedian Sacha Baron-Cohen (b.1970) *UK, 2001*

gayly *adverb* in a manner that is recognised as obviously homosexual *UK, 2002*

gay-marry *verb* to commit to a lifelong relationship with someone of the same sex *US, 1999*

gaymo *noun* used as an insult by very young children *UK, 2004*

gayola; gay-ola *noun* extortion of homosexuals by the police *US, 1960*

gay plague *noun* AIDS. This term, with overtones of pious hate and biblical retribution, spread the misconception that the AIDS epidemic was exclusively reserved for 'ungodly' homosexuals *US, 1982*

gay radar *noun* the ability to recognise a homosexual *AUSTRALIA, 1994*

gay-tastic *adjective* especially wonderful or fabulous in a way that appeals to homosexuals *US, 2004*

gay 'til graduation *adjective* temporarily or situationally homosexual or bisexual *US, 1996*

Gaza II *noun* Concordia University, Montreal, formed of Sir George and Loyola Universities in 1974 *CANADA, 2002*

gazebbies *noun* the female breasts. Vietnam war usage *US, 1965*

gazelle *noun* ▶ **in a gazelle** feeling good. Obsolete teen slang *CANADA, 1946*

gazillion *noun* a very large, if indefinite, number *US, 1995*

gazongas *noun* the female breasts *US, 1978*

gazook *noun* **1** a loud lout *US, 1901*. **2** a boy *US, 1949*

gazookus *noun* in carnival usage, a genuine article *US, 1924*

gazoony *noun* **1** a fellow, especially a low-life *US, 1914*. **2** a manual labourer in a carnival *US, 1966*. **3** the passive participant in anal sex *US, 1918*

gazoozie *verb* to swindle *US, 1992*

gazump *verb* **1** to raise the selling-price of a property after agreeing the terms of sale; hence to outbid an agreed sale. A specialisation of the sense 'to swindle' *UK, 1971*. **2** to swindle *UK, 1928*

gazumping *noun* the act of raising the selling-price of a property after agreeing the terms of sale; hence, outbidding an agreed sale. From the verb GAZUMP *UK, 1971*

gazunder *noun* a chamberpot *AUSTRALIA, 1981*

gazunder *verb* of a house-owner or a swindler, to reduce the selling price of a property, especially shortly before exchange of contracts, with a threat that the sale must go through on the new terms. A play on GAZUMP *UK, 1988*

GB *noun* **1** sex between one person and multiple, sequential partners. An abbreviation of GANG BANG *US, 1972*. **2** any barbiturate or central nervous system depressant. An abbreviation of GOOFBALL *US, 1966*. **3** goodbye *US, 1945*

GBH *noun* **1** the criminal charges of grievous bodily harm and malicious wounding; the act of causing serious injury. Initialism *UK, 1949*. **2** the recreational drug GHB. A jumbling of the letters in GHB gives an abbreviation for GRIEVOUS BODILY HARM *UK, 1996*

GBH of the brain *noun* the activity of studying. From GBH (physical assault and damage) *UK, 1996*

GBH of the eardrums *noun* loud music. From GBH (physical assault and damage) *UK, 1996*

GBH of the earhole; GBH of the ear *noun* a verbal assault. Extended from the criminal offence of GBH (grievous bodily harm). Usually jocular *UK, 1984*

G bit *noun* a prison sentence to a federal penitentiary *US, 1950*

g'bye goodbye *UK, 1925*

G-car *noun* a federal law enforcement agency car *US, 1981*

GCM! used as an expression of frustration or wonder. An initialism of 'God, Christ, Moses' *SOUTH AFRICA, 1984*

g'day; gooday; gidday hello! An extremely common, and now iconic, Australian greeting *AUSTRALIA, 1928*

GDI *noun* a college student who is not a fraternity or sorority member, a god-damn independent *US, 1966*

G-dog *noun* a good friend *US, 1998*

GE *noun* the electric chair. Homage to General Electric *US, 1990*

gear *noun* **1** marijuana; heroin; drugs in general *US, 1954*. **2** anything, especially anything illicit, intentionally undefined *AUSTRALIA, 1975*. **3** the equipment and paraphernalia associated with drug use, especially syringes, etc *UK, 1996*. **4** stolen goods *UK, 1956*. **5** stuff, things *UK, 1415*. **6** clothes *AUSTRALIA, 1970*. **7** (of a woman) the obvious physical attributes. Extended from the purely genital sense *US, 1953*. **8** a homosexual *US, 1972*. ▶ **get your arse into gear; get your ass into gear** to stop idling, to apply yourself to an activity, to start doing something useful *US, 1914*

gear *adjective* very good, outstanding. Brought to the world by the Beatles, dropped from fashionable use in the mid-1960s; revived in the UK, later C20, and continues in ironic use *UK, 1951*. ▶ **gear for something** obsessed with, fanatical about something *US, 1972*

gear bonger; gear banger *noun* a poor driver, especially one who crashes the gears *US, 1971*

gear-box *noun* the vagina. A survival and technological updating of obsolete 'gear '(the vagina), used in East Anglia, notably Suffolk *UK, 1972*

gear down *verb* to dress up *BARBADOS, 1965*

geared *adjective* available for homosexual relations *US, 1935*

geared up *adjective* dressed up. Also used of motorcyclists in full protective wear *UK, 1979*

gear head *noun* in mountain biking, a bicycle mechanic *US, 1992*

gear jammer *noun* a truck driver who has a difficult time shifting gears, especially one who is constantly clashing the gears as he shifts *US, 1929*

gear-lever *noun* the penis. Historically 'gear' has meant both male and female genitals so the derivation here is ambiguous. Remembered by Beale as the term used by UK National Servicemen (National Service ran from 1946–60) *UK, 1973*

gears *noun* the testicles *US, 1952*

gedanken *adjective* in computing, impractical or poorly designed. From the German for 'thought' *US, 1983*

gedunk *noun* 1 ice-cream, sweets, potato crisps and other junk food; the ship store where junk food can be bought. A US Navy term *US, 1927*. 2 a place where sweets and snacks are sold *US, 1956*

gedunk truck *noun* a catering truck *US, 1992*

gee *noun* 1 a man, a fellow *US, 1907*. 2 opium; heroin. Possibly a respelling of the initial letter of a number of synonyms, or from Hindi *ghee* (butter), or playing on the sense as HORSE (heroin) *US, 1938*. 3 $1,000. From the first letter of GRAND ($1,000) *US, 1936*. 4 a piece of praise. Possibly from the verb sense 'to encourage' *UK, 1998*. 5 a market trader's or circus entertainer's assistant who is discreetly positioned in the crowd to incite responses *UK, 1934*. 6 a strong, respected, manipulative prisoner *US, 1951*. 7 any device used to secure a needle to an eye dropper as part of an improvised mechanism to inject drugs *US, 1960*. 8 the vagina. The term gives rise to the 'gee bag' condom, 'missed by a gee hair' (a near miss or accident) and the expression 'do ya the gee' said by a boy to a girl and meaning 'do you have sex' *IRELAND, 1991*. 9 a horse *UK, 1879*

gee *verb* 1 to encourage, to incite. From the commands to a horse: 'gee up!' *UK, 1932*. 2 to inform. From the initial letter of GRASS (to inform) *UK, 1996*

geel; jee! an exclamation used for expressing surprise, astonishment or shock. Probably a euphemism for 'Jesus!'; later use is often ironic *US, 1895*

geech *noun* money *US, 1968*

geechee *noun* an uneducated, rural black person, especially one who is not easily understood *US, 1905*

gee'd up *adjective* 1 drug-intoxicated. Originally of opium (GEE), gradually less discriminating *US, 1936*. 2 excited. Influenced by the meaning as 'drug-intoxicated' but actually from GEE (to encourage) *UK, 1932*. 3 dressed in clothing associated with youth gangs *US, 1995*

geedus *noun* in circus and carnival usage, money *US, 1981*

gee-eyed *adjective* completely drunk *IRELAND, 2001*

gee-gees *noun* 1 horse races. Singular 'gee gee' is a '(race)horse' and 'the gee gees' means 'horse racing' *UK, 1869*. 2 veterinary drugs *IRELAND, 1996*

gee head *noun* a frequent Paregoric user *US, 1970*

geek *noun* 1 a carnival freak, usually an alcoholic or drug addict, who would sit and crawl in his own excrement and occasionally bite the heads off snakes and chickens. Perhaps from German *gucken* (to peep, to look) or synonymous German slang or dialect *kefken US, 1928*. 2 a student whose devotion to study excludes all other interests or society; someone who is considered too studious; someone obsessed with computers. Pejorative *US, 1980*. 3 an offensive, despicable person; a clumsy person; a socially awkward person *UK, 1876*. 4 a prostitute's customer with fetishistic desires *US, 1993*. 5 an awkward skateboarder or a pedestrian who gets in the way *US, 1976*. 6 crack cocaine mixed with marijuana *UK, 1998*. 7 a look; a peek *AUSTRALIA, 1966*

geek *verb* 1 to display severe anxiety when coming off cocaine intoxication *US, 1993*. 2 to act foolishly *US, 1998*. 3 to look, watch, peer *AUSTRALIA, 1966*

geek-a-mo *noun* a geek *US, 1991*

geeked *adjective* 1 in a psychotic state induced by continuous use of amphetamine or methamphetamine *US, 1989*. 2 sexually aroused while under the influence of a central nervous system stimulant *US, 1989*. 3 marijuana-intoxicated *US, 2002*. 4 jittery, childishly excited *US, 1984*

geeked out *adjective* unordinary; injured *US, 2002*

geeker *noun* 1 a user of crack cocaine *US, 1990*. 2 a starer *AUSTRALIA, 1979*

geekerati *noun* an elite grouping of people involved in information technology *US, 2000*

geeker rental *noun* a car stolen by a crack cocaine addict who then trades use of the car for drugs *US, 2002*

geeking *adjective* inept; unfashionable; awkward *US, 1987*

geekish *adjective* obsessed with computers; socially inept *US, 1986*

geek out *verb* to enter a highly technical mode which is too difficult to explain *US, 1991*

geek-o-zoid *noun* a student whose devotion to study excludes all other interests or society, hence an unpopular student; someone who is considered too studious; someone obsessed with computers. An elaboration of GEEK *UK, 2002*

geeksploitation *noun* an act, or general policy, of taking profitable advantage of the enthusiasm and willingness to work of young computer programmers; also used of entertainment designed to appeal to the technologically-obsessed. A combination of GEEK (a studious-type or IT obsessive) and 'exploitation' *US, 1996*

geekster *noun* a geek *US, 1991*

geeky *adjective* socially inept; overly involved with computers *US, 1981*

gees *noun* horse racing *UK, 1959*

geeser *noun* a small amount of an illegal drug *US, 1952*

geet *noun* a dollar *US, 1947*

geets *noun* money *US, 1949*

geetus *noun* money *US, 1926*

gee-up *noun* 1 an act or instance of stirring *AUSTRALIA, 1995*. 2 a swindler's confederate who leads others to spend their money *AUSTRALIA, 1899*

gee up *verb* 1 to motivate; to encourage *AUSTRALIA, 1955*. 2 to tease *UK, 1983*

gee whiz! used for registering shock, surprise, disappointment, or for emphasis. Elaboration of GEE! *US, 1876*

gee willikers! used as a mock oath. There are countless variants *US, 1851*

geez *noun* 1 a friend *UK, 2003*. 2 a look. A variant of GEEK *AUSTRALIA, 1981*

geeze; geaze *verb* to inject by hypodermic needle *US, 1966*

geeze; geaze; greaze *noun* heroin; an injection of heroin; narcotics *US, 1967*

geezer *noun* 1 a man. Possibly from Basque *giza* (a man), picked up by Wellington's soldiers during the Peninsular War (1808–14); alternatively it may derive from C15 English dialect *guiser* (a mummer). Variant spellings include 'geyser' and the abbreviated 'geez' *UK, 1885*. 2 an old person, somewhat infirm. An objectionable reference to a senior citizen *UK, 1885*. 3 a fellow-prisoner *UK, 1958*. 4 a man who is easily duped *UK, 1959*. 5 a young manual worker who lives with his parents and spends his disposable income on leisure and pleasure. Created by a research company as a sociological label for commercial and marketing purposes; a specialised variation *UK, 2003*. 6 an intravenous drug user. Sometimes spelled 'geazer' from the variant verb spelling geeze; geaze *US, 1967*. 7 a small amount of a drug *US, 1971*

geezerbird; geezerchick *noun* a young woman characterised by her behaviour and positive involvement in activites (drinking, swearing, sport, etc) stereotypically enjoyed by males. Combines GEEZER (a man) with a less-than-politically correct term for a 'young woman' *UK, 2002*

geezo *noun* **1** a hardened prison inmate *US, 1951*. **2** an armed robbery *US, 2001*

geggie; gegg *noun* the mouth. Glaswegian use *UK: SCOTLAND, 1985*

gehuncle *noun* a cripple *US, 1954*

gel *noun* **1** a girl. With a hard 'g' *UK, 1969*. **2** dynamite used for opening a safe *US, 1972*. **3** a socially inept person *US, 1991*

gelly; jelly *noun* gelignite *AUSTRALIA, 1941*

gelt; geld *noun* money. Originally conventional English, then out of favour, then back as slang. German, Dutch and Yiddish claims on its origin *UK, 1529*

gen *noun* information. Originally military, possibly deriving from the phrase 'for the *general* information of all ranks' *UK, 1940*

gen; gen up *verb* to learn; to inform, to brief. After the noun *UK, 1943*

gendarme *noun* a police officer. Adopted directly from the French *gendarme UK, 1906*

gender bender *noun* a person with an ambiguous or androgynous sexual identity, or with asexual identity divergent from their biological sex *UK, 1980*

gender mender *noun* a computer cable with either two male or two female connectors *US, 1991*

general *noun* a railway yardmaster *US, 1946*

General *nickname* ► **The General 1** Frank Sinatra, American singer (1915–1998) *US, 1963*. **2** Ireland's most famous criminal, Martin Cahill *IRELAND, 1995*

General Booth *noun* a tooth. Rhyming slang, formed from the name of William Booth, 1829–1912, the founder of the Salvation Army *UK, 1992*

general election *noun* an erection. Rhyming slang, the source of many jokes about standing members, even if we only get one every four or five years *UK, 1992*

general mess of crap *noun* a truck manufactured by General Motors Corporation. A humorous back-formation from the initials GMC *US, 1971*

General Smuts; generals *noun* the testicles. Rhyming slang for NUTS, formed from the name of a South African statesman, 1870–1950 *UK, 1992*

General Westhisface *nickname* US Army General William Westmoreland. Not particularly kind *US, 1977*

Generation X; Gen X *noun* the marketing category that defines people born between the late 1950s and mid-70s. Originally the title of a sociological book by Charles Hamblett and Jane Deverson, 1965; moved beyond jargon when adopted as the name of a UK punk band in the mid-1970s; in 1991 Douglas Coupland employed it to describe a new generation; usage is now almost conventional. Generation Y does not appear to have caught on *US, 1965*

Generation Xer; Gen-Xer; Xer; X *noun* in marketing terms, someone born between the late 1950s and mid-70s, seen as well educated but without direction *US, late 1970s*

Generation XL *noun* a (notional) sociological group of children, teenagers or young adults who are clinically obese. A play on GENERATION X and XL, the retail abbreviation for 'extra large' *UK, 2003*

generic *adjective* stupid, dull, boring *US, 1988*

geni-ass *noun* a smart and diligent student. A play on 'genius' *US, 1968*

genius *noun* **1** a person skilled at performing oral sex. A pun based on HEAD (oral sex) *US, 2002*. **2** in computing, an obvious or easily guessed password *US, 1990*

genny; jenny *noun* a *gen*erator *UK, 1956*

gent *noun* **1** a good man, an honourable man, a man who is admired. From '*gent*leman' and characteristics generously ascribed to the stereotype *UK, 1987*. **2** a man with pretentions to class or status. Used in a derisory context *UK, 1605*. **3** money. Survives as a variant of GELT (money) but, in fact, derives not from German *gelt* but French *argent* (silver; money); original use was especially of silver coins *UK, 1859*. **4** a maggot used as fishing bait *AUSTRALIA, 1998*

gentleman jockey *noun* in horse racing, an amateur jockey, especially in a steeplechase event *US, 1947*

gentleman of leisure *noun* a pimp *US, 1973*

gentleman's call *noun* in pool, an understanding that a shot need not be called if it is obvious *US, 1992*

gentleman's fever *noun* a sexually transmitted infection *BAHAMAS, 1982*

gentlemen's relish *noun* sperm *UK, 2002*

gents *noun* a gentlemen's public convenience *US, 1960*

Geoff Hurst; geoff *noun* **1** a *first* class honours degree. Rhyming slang, based on the name of Geoff Hurst (b.1941), the only footballer to have scored a hat-trick in a World Cup final *UK, 1998*. **2** a thirst *UK, 1994*. **3** urination. Rhyming slang for 'burst' *UK, 2002*

Geoffrey Chaucer *noun* a saucer. Rhyming slang formed on the name of the great English poet, who lived from about 1343 to 1400, and who, fittingly, used slang in his rhyme *UK, 1992*

geog; geoggers *noun* geography, especially as a subject of study *UK, 1940*

geologist *noun* a physician who considers his patients to be as intelligent as a rock *US, 1978*

George *noun* **1** a gambler who tips the dealer or places bets in the dealer's name *US, 1974*. **2** in American casinos, a skilled and lucky gambler *US, 1985*. **3** used as a term of address for any Pullman porter *US, 1939*. **4** an act of defecation. A euphemism by personification, but why a George should be so honoured is not recorded *UK, 1959*. ► **call it George** to agree that a matter is settled *GUYANA, 1962*

George *adjective* excellent *US, 1930*

George and Ringo *noun* bingo. Rhyming slang, formed from the names of two of the Beatles, George Harrison and Ringo Starr, and probably not heard since the Beatles broke up *UK, 1992*

George and Zippy *adjective* (of weather) cold, chilly. Rhyming slang for NIPPY, based on two of the puppet characters in long-running Thames television children's programme *Rainbow* (from 1972) *UK, 2002*

George Bernard Shaw; George Bernard *noun* a door. Rhyming slang, formed from the name of the Irish playwright, 1856–1950 *UK, 1992*

George Blake *noun* a snake. Rhyming slang, formed from the name of a notorious British security and intelligence operative who spied for the KGB from 1944–61 *UK, 1992*

George Martin *noun* farting. Rhyming slang, formed from the name of orchestral arranger and producer Sir George Martin (b.1926) *UK, 2003*

George Melly *noun* the belly, a paunch. Rhyming slang, formed from the name of the jazz singer and surrealist (1937–2007) whose shape echoes the sense *UK, 1992*

George Michael; George *verb* to cycle. Popney rhyming slang, based on popular singer George Michael (b.1963). Popney was originally contrived for *www.music365.co.uk*, an Internet music site; this is one of several terms that caught on *UK, 2001*

George Raft *noun* **1** a draught. Rhyming slang, formed on the name of US film actor George Raft (1895–1980) *UK, 1979*. **2** hard work. Rhyming slang for GRAFT *UK, 1992*

George Smack; George *noun* heroin *US, 1967*

George Spelvin *noun* used in a theatre programme as a fictitious name for an actor *US, 1908*

George the Third *noun* **1** a bird. Rhyming slang, recorded as an alternative to RICHARD THE THIRD *UK, 1961*. **2** a lump of excrement. Rhyming slang for TURD *UK, 1992*

George W. *noun* a person with an inflated sense of self-worth. An unkind allusion to US President George W. Bush *US, 2001*

Georgia; Georgie *verb* to cheat, to swindle; (of a prostitute) to have sex with a customer without collecting the fee. Especially used in the context of prostitution *US, 1960*

Georgia buggy *noun* a wheelbarrow *US, 1918*

Georgia ham *noun* a watermelon *US, 1971*

Georgia homeboy *noun* the recreational drug GHB. A disguise for the initials GHB *US, 1993*

Georgia night rider *noun* a trucker who drives at night in the hope of avoiding police *US, 1976*

Georgia overdrive *noun* coasting down a hill with the car or truck in neutral *US, 1963*

Georgia scuffle *noun* **1** a swindle which fails because the intended victim is not smart enough to be swindled *US, 1992*. **2** in carnival usage, rough handling of an extremely naive customer in a swindle *US, 1950*

Georgie Best *noun* **1** a pest, especially a drunken pest. Rhyming slang, reflecting footballer George Best's fall from grace to alcoholism *UK, 1992*. **2** the female breast. Rhyming slang *UK, 2003*. ▶ **be my Georgie Best!** do as you wish; you are welcome to have whatever has been asked for. Rhyming slang for 'be my guest', formed on the name of Irish footballer George Best (1946–2005) *UK, 1977*

ger *verb* get. A slovenly pronunciation that occurs when the following word commences with a vowel, in uses such as 'ger along' *UK, 1895*

gerbil around *verb* in car repair, to work at a somewhat frantic pace in an effort to hide the fact that the problem at hand, or car repair in general, is too difficult *US, 1992*

geriatrick *noun* an older homosexual man as a one-time sex-partner *UK, 1979*

germ *noun* **1** a German *UK, 1915*. **2** a despised person *US, 1942*

Germaine Greer *noun* a glass of beer. Rhyming slang, formed from the name of an Australian feminist and academic who has become a media personality (b.1939) *AUSTRALIA, 1987*

German *noun* (used by prisoners) a prison officer. A hangover from World War 2 when the Germans were the enemy *UK, 1996*

German band *noun* the hand. Rhyming slang *UK, 1979*

Germans *noun* drug dealers from the Dominican Republic as perceived by African-American drug dealers competing for the same market – the enemy *US, 1992*

germs *noun* gentlemen, as a form of address. A jocular slurring, especially in the pairing 'Ladeez and Germs' *UK, 2001*

Geronimo *noun* **1** an alcoholic drink mixed with a barbiturate. A dangerous cross reaction *US, 1970*. **2** a barbiturate *US, 1990*

gerook; gerooked *adjective* drug or alcohol-intoxicated. From Afrikaans for 'cured/smoked' *SOUTH AFRICA, 1970*

gerrick *noun* piece of rolled up silver foil used as a filter in marijuana pipes. The 'gerrick' is made by laying out a piece of foil (usually from a cigarette box), or thin cardboard (usually from the same box) into a square, rolling it up, bending it into a circle and wedging it into the bottom of a bottleneck pipe to keep the marijuana from falling out when the smoke is sucked in *SOUTH AFRICA, 2003*

gerry *nickname* an old person. An abbreviation of 'geriatric' *NEW ZEALAND, 1998*

gert *adjective* great. A C14 dialect word that is now widely familiar beyond its regional use as a result of media exposure *UK, 1997*

gertchal; gerchal; gertcher! I don't believe you!; used for registering disbelief. An alteration of 'get away!'; immortalised in song by Chas and Dave, 1979 *UK, 1937*

Gertie Gitana; Gertie *noun* a banana. Rhyming slang, based on the name of music hall entertainer Gertie Gitana, 1888–1957; originating in the first decade of C20 with her name replacing the refrain 'Have a banana' in the song 'Let's All Go Down the Strand'. Still in use *UK, 1961*

gert stonkers *noun* large female breasts *AUSTRALIA, 1988*

Gestapo *noun* **1** the police. Originally used of the military police during World War 2 in a (presumably) jocular allusion to the German Secret Police of the Third Reich. Often used with 'the' *UK, 1941*. **2** uniformed personnel (such as bus inspectors) or others (such as teachers) who enjoy the little power of their authority *UK, 1969*. **3** the motorcycle officers of the Metropolitan police traffic div-

ision. Police use (especially the Metropolitan Police Drugs Squad); probably inspired by the jackboots and black breeches uniform *UK, 1999*

get *verb* **1** to understand, to appreciate *US, 1892*. **2** to worry, to vex, to annoy *US, 1867*. **3** to enthral, to appeal to, to affect emotionally, to obsess *UK, 1913*. **4** to obtain sexual intercourse *AUSTRALIA, 1970*. ▶ **get above yourself** to become conceited, arrogant *UK, 1923*. ▶ **get amongst** to perform some task or take part enthusiastically *AUSTRALIA, 1970*. ▶ **get any; get anything; get enough; get a little bit** to have sex *US, 1947*. ▶ **get it 1** to be punished, especially physically *UK, 1851*. **2** to be killed *US, 1964*. **3** to become infected with a sexually transmitted infection *UK, 1937*. ▶ **get it in one** to understand immediately *UK, 1942*. ▶ **get it on 1** to have sex *US, 1970*. **2** to fight *US, 1959*. **3** to join battle. US Marines usage in Vietnam *US, 1991*. ▶ **get it up** to achieve an erection *US, 1943*. ▶ **get some 1** to have sex *US, 1970*. **2** to kill enemy soldiers *US, 1976*. ▶ **get well 2** to make money *US, 1995*. ▶ **get wet** to kill someone using a knife or bayonet *US, 1991*. ▶ **get with** to have sex with *UK, 1987*. ▶ **get with the program** to start to behave in a responsible manner. A generally figurative application of the recovery programmes promoted by Alcoholics Anonymous, Gamblers Anonymous, etc; usually as an injunction *US, 1983*. ▶ **get your end away** to have sex *UK, 1975*. ▶ **get your leather** to have sex *CANADA, 1985*. ▶ **get your own back** to get revenge *UK, 1910*. ▶ **get your skates on** to hurry up. Often as an imperative. Originally military *UK, 1895*. ▶ **get your skin** to have sex *CANADA, 1999*. ▶ **get yours** to get the punishment you deserve *US, 1905*. ▶ **have got something on someone** to possess evidence against someone *UK, 1928*

get!; git! go!; go away! *US, 1884*

get a black dog up you! go to hell! *AUSTRALIA, 1992*

get across *verb* to make yourself (or your subject) understood *US, 1913*

get a dog up you! go to hell! *AUSTRALIA, 1996*

get a grip! control yourself! *US, 1982*

get a life! used to tease someone who is revealing a lack of grounding in reality or who is too obsessed with something *US, 1989*

get along! used for registering incredulity. Similar to the later 'get away!' *UK, 1984*

get along with you! go away! be quiet! *UK, 1837*

get a roll of stamps and mail it in used as a humorous comment on a lack of effort. Coined by ESPN's Keith Olberman to describe 'a lackluster effort on the part of a player or team' *US, 1997*

get a room! used for discouraging public displays of affection *US, 1999*

get at *verb* **1** to attack verbally, to tease *UK, 1891*. **2** to mean, to imply a meaning *US, 1899*. ▶ **get at it** to tease someone, to make a fool of someone *UK, 1958*

getaway *noun* the last morning of a military tour of duty *US, 1968*

get away!; gerraway! don't talk nonsense!; don't flatter! In 2002 a travel company used the slogan 'Get away' in a television advertising campaign, punning on the conventional sense (to escape, to go on holiday) with an exclamation of disbelief that such holidays could be so cheap *UK, 1848*

getaway day *noun* in horse racing, the last day of a racing meet *US, 1962*

get-back *noun* an act of revenge *US, 1984*

get bent! used as an exclamation of defiance, roughly along the lines of 'go to hell!' *US, 1970*

getcha vine *noun* a thorny vine found in the jungles of Vietnam *US, 1990*

get down *verb* **1** to depress *UK, 1930*. **2** in sports betting, to place a bet *US, 1974*. **3** to be a part of, or to relate to, as in 'get down with the kids' *UK, 1999*. ▶ **get down to it** to begin to work with serious application, sometimes used of sexual activity *US, 1937*

get-down time; git-down time *noun* the time of day or night when a prostitute starts working *US, 1972*

get-'em-off *noun* an exit ramp; a motorway exit *US, 1976*

get 'em off!; geremoff! used as a jocular imperative to strip US, 1995

geters noun money US, 1975

get-go; git-go; gitty up noun the very start US, 1966

get-hard adjective sexually arousing to men UK, 2000

get her! ▷ see: GET YOU!

get-high noun crack cocaine US, 1990

get in; get-in verb of a staged entertainment, to bring in and set up staging and technical equipment. The reverse (to deconstruct and entirely remove staging equipment) is 'get out'. Also used as nouns. UK, 1996

get-in Betty noun a crowbar used by burglars US, 1950

get into verb to come to know and like UK, 1968

get-it-on adjective vigorous, energetic in approach US, 1970

get knotted! used for expressing contempt. Usage was frozen in time and soon considered archaic. Later use is marked with irony UK, 1958

get lost! used as a contemptuous imperative of dismissal US, 1902

get off verb 1 to form an initial liaison with someone sexually attractive, especially with a view to greater intimacy UK, 1925. 2 to achieve sexual climax US, 1952. 3 to use a drug; to feel the effects of a drug US, 1952. 4 by extension, to take pleasure from something US, 1952. 5 to crash while riding a motorcycle. Sarcastic and euphemistic biker (motorcycle) usage US, 2003

get off!; get off it! used as a register of impatience or incredulity UK, 1969

get-off house noun a place where you can both purchase and inject heroin US, 1990

get off on verb to greatly enjoy something. After GET OFF (to achieve sexual climax) UK, 1973

get off the stove, I'm ridin' the range tonight! used for expressing enthusiasm about an upcoming date US, 1951

get on verb 1 of people, to agree, to co-exist. Often with a modifying adverb UK, 1816. 2 to become elderly UK, 1885. 3 to use drugs US, 1952. 4 to have US, 1990

get-out noun 1 an escape, an excuse, an evasion UK, 1899. 2 an extreme degree of something US, 1838

get out verb (used of a bettor) to recoup earlier losses US, 1951

get out of here! used for expressing disbelief at what has just been said US, 1994

get out of here, Mary! used for expressing doubt US, 1987

get out of it! used for expressing a lack of belief in what has just been said UK, 1984

get-over noun success through fraud US, 1997

get over verb to take advantage of someone, making yourself look good at their expense US, 1981. ▶ **cannot get over** to be astounded UK, 1899. ▶ **get over on** to seduce US, 1987

get over it! used as a suggestion that the hearer move on from the issue that is dominating the moment US, 1994

get over you! used in order to deflate a person's excessive sense of importance US, 1997

get real verb to face the facts. Often as an imperative US, 1998

get real! used for expressing scorn at that which has just been said US, 1982

get round verb to circumvent US, 1849

get shagged! used as a general expression of disbelief or contempt UK, 1997

get stuffed! used as a general expression of disbelief or contempt UK, 1952

getting any? used as a male-to-male greeting. Instantly jocular due to the inquiry as to the other's sex life US, 1958

getting on adjective (of time) late; growing late UK, 1882

get to verb to annoy someone US, 1961

get-up noun 1 an outfit or costume UK, 1847. 2 manufactured evidence that is intended to incriminate UK, 1967. 3 a piece of criminal trickery, an elaborate deceit UK, 1970. 4 the last morning of a jail sentence or term of military service US, 1967

get up verb 1 to be released from prison US, 1967. 2 to succeed in painting your graffiti tag in a public place US, 1994. 3 to win; to succeed AUSTRALIA, 1904. 4 to cause a racehorse to win AUSTRALIA, 1969

get-up-and-go noun vigour, energy, drive. Earlier variations from which this derives are 'get-up' and 'get-up-and-get' US, 1907

get up off of verb to concede something of importance or value US, 1985

get with the words! verb explain yourself! US, 1965

get you!; get him!; get her! verb 1 (with an emphatic stress on the pronoun) used to deflate a conceited male ego or to imply an unmasculine oversensitivity or homosexuality UK, 1958. 2 used for expressing disbelief at what has just been said. Homosexual use US, 1949

get your arse to an anchor! verb sit down! Adapted from nautical (likely fisherman) usage, this phrase came ashore for general purposes CANADA, 1978

get your kit off! verb used as ribald encouragement to undress UK, 1985

GFE; girl friend experience noun a dinner date followed by sex as a service offered by a prostitute UK, 2005

G force! used as an expression of enthusiastic assent. From a Japanese comic strip US, 1987

GFY go fuck yourself. Used when discretion suggests avoiding the word 'fuck' US, 1987

GG noun in transsexual usage, a genuine or genetic girl US, 1987

GH noun General Hospital, a popular television daytime drama US, 1981

Ghan noun an Afghan. In outback Australia this referred to the numerous immigrants from Afghanistan and nearby regions who came to work in the desert regions as camel-drivers. Not used to refer to recent migrants from Afghanistan AUSTRALIA, 1911

ghana noun marijuana. Possibly a variant spelling of GANJA (Jamaican marijuana) although current usage doesn't acknowledge this etymology nor specify an alternative, such as marijuana from Ghana UK, 1989

ghar noun the buttocks. From the Hindi for 'donkey' TRINIDAD AND TOBAGO, 1976

GHB noun a pharmaceutical anaesthetic used as a recreational drug. Gamma hydroxybutyrate is a foul-tasting liquid, invented in the 1960s by Dr. Henri Laborit, who swore by its powers as an aphrodisiac. The drug has been marketed as an anaesthetic and a health supplement, but it is a heightened sense of touch, sustained erections and longer orgasms that make it popular with 'up-for-it clubbers' US, 1990

gheid noun a Paregoric user US, 1971

gherao verb in India and Pakistan, to surround someone and not allow him or her to go from an office, desk, etc, as a demonstration against that person. From Hindi gherna (to surround, to beseige) INDIA, 1967

gherkin noun the penis, especially a small penis. A variation of 'pickle' (the penis), especially in the phrase JERK THE GHERKIN (to masturbate) US, 2002

ghetto noun the anus US, 1973

ghetto adjective inferior, shoddy, bad US, 1995

ghetto- prefix used to qualify an adjective as being in the style of black culture. Has positive connotations when used by the black community but can be patronising and derogatory US, 2001

ghetto bird noun a police helicopter, especially one flying at night with a bright spotlight US, 1993

ghetto blaster; ghetto box noun a large, portable radio and tape player; a portable music system. Can be considered offensive because it is culture-specific and stereotypical US, 1981

ghetto bootie noun large buttocks US, 2001

ghetto fabulous *adjective* ostentatious, exemplifying the style of the black hip-hop community *US, 1996*

ghetto lullaby *noun* inner-city nightime noises – sirens, gunfire, helicopters, etc *US, 1993*

ghetto rags *noun* clothing typical of the inner-city ghetto *US, 1970*

ghetto sled *noun* a large, luxury car *US, 1997*

ghetto star *noun* a youth gang leader *US, 1993*

'Ghini *noun* a Lamborghini car. A hip-hop abbreviation and aspiration *US, 1999*

ghost *noun* **1** a faint, secondary duplicate video image in a television signal, caused by the mixing of the primary signal and a delayed version of the same signal *US, 1942*. **2** a blank stop on a casino slot machine *US, 1993*. **3** in poker, a player who frequently absents himself from the table *US, 1996*. **4** LSD. Usually used with 'the' *US, 1967*. ► **do a ghost** to leave quickly *US, 1995*. ► **when the ghost walks** in oil drilling, pay day *US, 1954*

ghost *verb* **1** to transfer a prisoner from one prison to another at night after the prison has been secured *US, 1982*. **2** to vanish *US, 1969*. **3** to relax, especially while evading duty. Military use *US, 1982*

ghost battalion *noun* during the Vietnam war, the First Battalion, Ninth Marines. So named because of the large number of casualties suffered at Con Thien and Khe Sanh *US, 1991*

ghostbust *noun* to search in an obsessive and compulsive way for small particles of crack cocaine *US, 1992*

ghosted *adjective* out of sight *UK, 1994*

ghost hand *noun* in poker, a hand or part of a hand that is dealt to the same player twice in a row *US, 1988*

ghost town *noun* ► **send to ghost town** to transfer a prisoner without warning *UK, 1996*

ghost train *noun* ► **on the ghost train** used of a prisoner who is being moved without warning from one prison to another overnight. From GHOST (to transfer overnight) *UK, 1996*

ghost-walking day *noun* in circus and carnival usage, payday *US, 1981*

ghoulie *noun* the vagina. Something frightening that lurks in the dark *US, 1998*

ghoulie *adjective* ghoulish *US, 1993*

GI *noun* **1** an enlisted soldier in the US Army *US, 1939*. **2** an American Indian who has abandoned his indigenous culture and language in favour of mainstream American culture; a government Indian *US, 1963*

GI *verb* **1** to clean thoroughly *US, 1944*. **2** to strip *US, 1968*

Gianluca Vialli; gianluca *noun* cocaine. Rhyming slang for CHARLIE (cocaine); based on the name of Gianluca Vialli (b.1964), a famous Italian football player and manager *UK, 1998*

gib *noun* a man's buttocks *US, 1986*

GIB *noun* the back seat member of the crew on a fighter aircraft. An initialism for 'guy in back' *US, 1967*

Gib *nickname* Gibraltar *UK, 1822*

GIB *adjective* skilled in sex. An initialism for 'good in bed' *US, 1977*

gibber *noun* a small stone used for throwing. From the extinct Australian Aboriginal language Dharug (Sydney region). Originally, since 1833, referring to 'large boulders', it has undergone a reduction in size over the decades. As a technical term of geologists it refers to smallish stones of dark reddish chaceldony that litter the surface of large areas of the arid inland. Colloquially it is used of any rock, stone or pebble suitable for throwing *AUSTRALIA, 1902*

gibbled *adjective* (of a machine) broken down *CANADA, 1989*

gibbs *noun* the lips *US, 1990*

gib-gib *noun* used for mocking another's laughter. From an advertisement for Gibbons Chicken Ration *TRINIDAD AND TOBAGO, 1994*

giblet *noun* a stupid, foolish or inept person. Playing on a turkey image *US, 1984*

giblets *noun* **1** the female gentalia *UK, 2003*. **2** showy chrome accessories on a motorcycle. Biker (motorcycle) usage *US, 2003*

Gibson girl *noun* an emergency radio used when a military aircraft is shot down over a body of water *US, 1943*

gick *noun* excrement *IRELAND, 1993*

gick *verb* to defecate *IRELAND, 1996*

giddy *noun* a tourist, especially on a package holiday. Used by holiday reps *UK, 1997*

giddyap; giddyup *noun* the beginning; the inception *US, 1974*

giddy as a kipper *adjective* dizzy. A 'giddy kipper', although not in this sense, has been a feature of English slang since the late C19 *UK, 1999*

giddy goat *noun* in horse racing, the totalisator. Rhyming slang from 'tote' *AUSTRALIA, 1989*

gif *noun* an aircraft pilot. From the initials of 'guys in the front seat' *US, 1945*

giffed *adjective* drunk *UK, 2003*

giffer *noun* a pickpocket *US, 1949*

gift *noun* in a sex club, used as a coded euphemism for payment for special services *US, 1997*. ► **the gift** the bleed period of the menstrual cycle *US, 2001*. ► **the gift that keeps giving** a sexually transmitted disease *US, 1986*

gifted *adjective* experiencing the bleed period of the menstrual cycle *US, 2001*

gift of the sun; gift of the sun god *noun* cocaine *UK, 1998*

gig *noun* **1** a musical performance or concert. Originally musicians' slang for an engagement at a single venue *US, 1926*. **2** a job *US, 1908*. **3** a party *US, 1954*. **4** a prison or jail sentence *US, 1977*. **5** a police informer. A clipping of FIZGIG *AUSTRALIA, 1953*. **6** a busybody *AUSTRALIA, 1944*. **7** a person who stands out because they look foolish; a fool *AUSTRALIA, 1943*. **8** the vagina *US, 1967*. **9** a look; a peek *AUSTRALIA, 1924*. **10** a demerit or other indication of failure *US, 1968*. **11** in an illegal number gambling lottery, a bet that a specific three-digit number will be drawn *US, 1846*. **12** in harness racing, a sulky *US, 1997*

gig *verb* **1** to work; to have a job *US, 1939*. **2** of a musician or group of musicians, to play an engagement or a series of engagements *UK, 1939*. **3** to go out to bars, clubs and/or parties *US, 2000*. **4** to look or stare; to take a peek *AUSTRALIA, 1959*. **5** to tease *AUSTRALIA, 1969*. **6** in carnival usage, to win all of a player's money in a single transaction *US, 1985*

gigging *noun* teasing *AUSTRALIA, 1966*

giggle and titter; giggle *noun* bitter (beer) *UK, 1992*

giggle band *noun* the decorative hemmed edge at the top of a stocking. Get beyond that and you're laughing *UK, 2001*

giggle bin *noun* an institution for containment and care of the mentally disturbed *UK, 1964*

giggle factory *noun* an insane asylum *AUSTRALIA, 1968*

giggle house *noun* an insane asylum *AUSTRALIA, 1919*

giggle juice *noun* alcohol *US, 1939*

giggler *noun* a scene in a pornographic film involving sex with two women. From the GIRL-GIRL designation *US, 1987*

giggles; good giggles *noun* marijuana *US, 1986*

giggle smoke *noun* marijuana; a marijuana cigarette *US, 1952*

gigglesoup *noun* any alcoholic beverage *US, 1972*

giggle water *noun* alcohol, especially champagne *US, 1926*

giggle weed *noun* marijuana. From the definite effect WEED has on your sense of humour *US, 1937*

giggling academy *noun* a mental hospital *US, 1949*

giggly *adjective* very good. Probably from the euphoric reaction to marijuana. West Indian and UK black use *UK, 2002*

giggy; gigi *noun* the anus and rectum *US, 1953*

GI gin *noun* cough syrup *US, 1964*

gig-lamps; gigs *noun* spectacles, eye-glasses. From the lights placed to each side of a 'gig' (a light carriage); 'headlights' (glasses), a later coinage, reflects similar inspiration *UK, 1853*

GIGO in computing, used as a reminder that output is only as good as input – (garbage *in*, garbage *out*) *US, 1964*

gig shot *noun* in carnival usage, the method used by an operator to win all of a player's money in a single transaction *US, 1985*

gig wagon *noun* transportation used by a rock band during a concert tour *UK, 1985*

GI Joe *noun* a quintessential American soldier. A term fuelled by a cartoon in the 1940s, a Robert Mitchum movie in 1945 and a line of toys starting in 1964 *US, 1935*

gildy *adjective* fancy, ornate *UK, 2002*

gilf *noun* a sexually appealing mature woman. A variation of MILF (a sexually appealing mother) and DILF (a sexually appealing father); an acronym of 'grandma *I'd like to fuck' US, 2003*

gil-gil *noun* used for mocking another's laughter *TRINIDAD AND TOBAGO, 1993*

gilhooley *noun* in motor racing on an oval track, a spin *US, 1965*

gill; gills *noun* in circus and carnival usage, a customer, especially a gullible one *US, 1981*

Gillie Potters *noun* **1** pig's trotters. Rhyming slang; formed from the name of British comedian, an early star of BBC radio, Gillie Potter, 1887–1975 *UK, 1980*. **2** the feet. Rhyming slang for TROTTERS *UK, 1980*

gillie suit *noun* camouflaged uniforms used by the US Army Special Forces. Gulf war usage *US, 1992*

Gilligan *noun* a hapless, socially inept person. From the *Gilligan's Island* television programme, in which Gilligan was a hapless, socially inept person *US, 1991*

Gilligan hitch *noun* any and every method to bind with a chain or tie with a rope *US, 1919*

gillion *noun* ten to the ninth power; untold millions *US, 1991*

gilly *noun* **1** a member of an audience, especially a woman. Theatrical and circus usage *UK, 1933*. **2** a man, especially a gullible rustic. Market traders and English gypsy use, from the previous sense as 'a member of a circus audience' *US, 1882*

gilly-galloo *noun* in circus and carnival usage, an outsider *US, 1981*

gils! used for expressing pleasant surprise *US, 2002*

gilt *noun* money. Derives from German *gelt* (gold) and conventional 'gilt' (silverplate) *UK, 1708*

GI marbles *noun* dice. Because of the love for dice games displayed by American soldiers, especially during World War 2 *US, 1950*

Gimli glider *noun* a Boeing 737 which ran out of petrol and glided to a safe landing in Gimli, Manitoba; later, any car that has run out of petrol. The incident happened because of a confusion between metric and English ways of measuring petrol during the fill-up. One of the pilots had been a glider pilot *CANADA, 2000*

gimme *noun* **1** a request or demand for money. From 'give me' *UK, 2001*. **2** an easy victory or accomplishment *US, 1986*. **3** a pistol *US, 1994*. **4** in pool, a shot that cannot be missed or a game that cannot be lost *US, 1990*

gimme *verb* used for 'give me'. A lazy phonetic abbreviation *US, 1883*

gimme five *noun* a mutual hand-slapping used as greeting or to signify mutual respect. From the phrase 'give me your hand'; 'gimme' (give me) 'five' (fingers, hence hand) *UK, 1999*

gimmel *noun* in betting, odds of 3–1. Probably coined by a Jewish bookmaker with a sense of humour, from *gimel* (the Hebrew letter which, in Judaic teaching, symbolises a rich man running after a poor man) which, in turn, derives from Hebrew *gemul* (the giving of reward and punishment) *UK, 1991*

gimmes *noun* a selfishly acquisitive characteristic *US, 1918*

gimmick *noun* **1** a gadget, an ingenious device or contrivance such as may be used in crime and magic to deceive or distract, or commercially, especially in the entertainment industry, to attract publicity and attention. 'You Gotta Get a Gimmick', Stephen Sondheim, 1959, is a song performed by striptease artistes demonstrating their ingenious methods of standing out from the crowd *US, 1926*. **2** characteristics such as costume, haircut or entrance music that collectively make a professional wrestler stand out as a unique marketable commodity *US, 1993*. **3** the actual device used to rig a carnival game *US, 1968*. **4** in poker, a special set of rules for a game *US, 1988*

gimmick *verb* to rig for a result *US, 1922*

gimmicks *noun* the equipment needed to inject drugs *US, 1967*

gimmie *noun* marijuana and crack cocaine mixed together for smoking in a cigarette *US, 1994*

gimp *noun* **1** a limp; a cripple *US, 1925*. **2** an incompetent or weak person *US, 1924*. **3** a sexual submissive who seeks satisfaction in dehumanising, full fetish clothing and crippling bondage. A specialisation of the previous senses made very familiar by Quentin Tarantino, *Pulp Fiction*, 1993 – the film featured a masked-creature (taking his pleasure at the hands of a dominatrix) known only as 'the gimp' *US, 1993*

gimper; gimpster *noun* a cripple *US, 1974*

gimp out *verb* to panic in the face of great challenge *US, 1988*

gimpy *noun* a (long-haired) member of the counterculture, a hippy *UK, 1998*

gimpy *adjective* **1** crippled; handicapped *US, 1929*. **2** inferior *US, 1970*

gims *noun* the eyes *US, 1945*

gin *noun* **1** a black prostitute *US, 1962*. **2** an Aboriginal female *AUSTRALIA, 1985*. **3** cocaine *US, 1971*. **4** a street fight between youth gangs *US, 1993*

gin *verb* **1** (used of a woman) to have sex *US, 1976*. **2** to fight *US, 1972*

gin and Jaguar bird *noun* a wealthy, usually married, woman from the upper-class districts surrounding London, especially Surrey, regarded as a worthwhile target for sexual adventuring. A BIRD (a woman) who lives in the 'gin and Jaguar belt' *UK, 1977*

ginch *noun* **1** the vagina *US, 2003*. **2** a woman; a woman as a sex object *US, 1936*

ginchy *adjective* **1** fashionable, attractive, pleasing *US, 1959*. **2** sharp-witted, clever, shrewd. A variation of the sense as 'attractive' *UK, 1988*

giner *noun* the vagina *US, 2004*

gin flat *noun* an apartment where alcohol is served illegally to a paying not-so public *US, 1951*

ging *noun* a handheld catapult; a slingshot *AUSTRALIA, 1903*

ginger *noun* **1** a sandy- or red-haired person; often as a nickname. Originally (1785) used of a cock with reddish plumage *UK, 1885*. **2** the backside. From GINGER ALE *AUSTRALIA, 1967*. **3** a prostitute who steals from her clients. Also 'ginger girl', 'gingerer' *AUSTRALIA, 1953*. ▶ **on the ginger** (of prostitutes) working at gingering their clients *AUSTRALIA, 1979*

ginger ale; ginger *noun* **1** jail. Rhyming slang *UK, 1992*. **2** bail. Rhyming slang *NEW ZEALAND, 1963*. **3** the backside. Rhyming slang for TAIL *AUSTRALIA, 1967*

ginger beer; ginger *noun* **1** a homosexual man. Rhyming slang for QUEER *UK, 1959*. **2** a member of the Royal Australian Engineers. Rhyming slang for 'engineer' *AUSTRALIA, 1941*

ginger beer; ginger *adjective* homosexual. Rhyming slang for QUEER *UK, 1960*

gingering *verb* (of a prostitute or accomplice) stealing from a client's clothing *AUSTRALIA, 1944*

ginger minger; ginger minge; ginge minge *noun* a person who has (it is presumed) naturally ginger pubic hair *UK, 1993*

ginger pop *noun* **1** a police officer. Rhyming slang for COP *UK, 1992*. **2** ginger beer *UK, 1827*

gingersnaps *noun* ▶ **(have had) too many gingersnaps last night** to have had too much alcohol to drink *CANADA, 1998*

ginger-top *noun* a redhead. From GINGER *UK, 1998*

ginhead *noun* a habitual drinker of gin *US, 1927*

gin jockey *noun* a white man who cohabits with an Aboriginal woman *AUSTRALIA, 1955*

gink *noun* **1** a naive rustic; a dolt *US, 1906*. **2** a look; a peek. Perhaps a nasalised variant of GEEK *AUSTRALIA, 1945*. **3** an unpleasant smell *UK: SCOTLAND, 1988*

gink *verb* to give off an unpleasant smell *UK: SCOTLAND, 1988*

ginky *adjective* out of style *US, 1969*

gin mill *noun* a bar. The term has shed most of its unsavoury connotations of the past and is now generally jocular *US, 1866*

ginned *adjective* drunk *US, 1900*

ginny barn *noun* a prison for females or a section of a prison reserved for females *US, 1967*

ginola *adjective* supremely attractive. A tribute to the good-looking French footballer David Ginola (b.1967); recorded in use in contemporary gay society *UK, 2003*

ginormous *adjective* very large. Pronounced 'jye-normous' *UK, 1962*

gin's piss *noun* poor quality or weak beer. From 'gin' meaning 'a female Australian Aboriginal'; from the extinct Australian Aboriginal language Dharug (Sydney region) *AUSTRALIA, 1972*

ginzo *noun* an Italian-American or Italian. Offensive. Probably a derivative of GUINEA *US, 1931*

Giorgio Armani; giorgio *noun* a sandwich. Rhyming slang for 'sarnie', formed from the name of the Italian fashion designer (b.1934) *UK, 1998*

gip-gip *noun* used for mocking another's laughter *TRINIDAD AND TOBAGO, 1997*

gipsy's ginger *noun* human excrement found out of doors. From a characteristic colour of excrement combined with a denigratory stereotype of gipsy life *UK, 1984*

gipsy's kiss; gipsey's *noun* an act of urination. Rhyming slang for PISS *UK, 1979*

gipsy's warning; gipsy's *noun* **1** a sinister warning, a final warning, a warning of immediate reprisal. Negative stereotyping *UK, 1918*. **2** morning. Rhyming slang *UK, 1960*

giraffe *noun* a *half* ounce, especially of drugs. Rhyming slang *UK, 2003*

girdle *noun* **1** a waistband. Recorded in use in contemporary gay society *UK, 2003*. **2** an over-the-shoulder car seat belt *US, 1962*. **3** in motor racing, the main support for the engine *US, 1993*

girl *noun* **1** cocaine *US, 1953*. **2** crack cocaine *UK, 2003*. **3** heroin *US, 1981*. **4** a lesbian. A term used by lesbians *US, 1995*. **5** a homosexual male, especially an effeminate one *US, 1912*. **6** (especially in sporting contexts) an effeminate male *AUSTRALIA, 1986*. **7** in a deck of playing cards, a queen *US, 1967*

girl and boy *noun* a toy. Rhyming slang *UK, 1992*

girl-deb *noun* a girl who spends time with a boy's youth gang, whether or not she is a gang member's girlfriend *US, 1967*

girlf *noun* a girlfriend *UK, 2003*

Girl Friday *noun* a young woman who is very useful to have about the place as an assistant. From Defoe's tale of Robinson Crusoe and his Man Friday *US, 1940*

girlfriend *noun* **1** a male homosexual's lover or friend *US, 1965*. **2** used as an affectionate term of address for a friend or acquaintance *US, 1997*. **3** cocaine. An elaboration of GIRL (cocaine) *US, 1979*

girl-girl *noun* a scene in a pornographic film, or an entire pornographic film, involving two women *US, 2000*

girl-girl *adjective* in pornography, involving two women *US, 1973*

girlie *noun* a young woman. Patronising and derisive *UK, 1860*

girlie *adjective* mildly pornographic, featuring naked women but not sexual activity. Mainly in use from the mid-1950s *US, 1921*

girlie bar *noun* a drinking place at which 'hostesses' are available *US, 1971*

girlie film *noun* a film featuring naked women but no sexual activity *US, 1973*

girlie magazine *noun* a commercial publication that features many pictures of naked women. The sex industry sells 'girlies' not 'women' *CANADA, 1920*

girls *noun* a woman's breasts. From the television situation comedy *Anything but Love* (1989–92), in which the character played by Jamie Lee Curtis proudly nicknamed her breasts 'the girls' *US, 2001*

girls and boys *noun* noise. Rhyming slang *UK, 1992*

girl's blouse *noun* an effeminate male *AUSTRALIA, 1996*

girls in blue *noun* female police officers *AUSTRALIA, 1998*

girls' school *noun* a reformatory for female juvenile offenders *US, 1982*

girl's week *noun* the bleed period of the menstrual cycle *US, 2001*

girl thing *noun* **1** a problem or subject best understood by females *US, 1992*. **2** the various hygiene steps taken by a female pornography performer before a sex scene. Also called 'girl stuff' *US, 1995*

girly-girl *noun* **1** a stereotypically feminine female *US, 1991*. **2** a female friend *US, 1997*. **3** a tampon *US, 1999*

giro *noun* **1** a fraud perpetrated on the social security system whereby a Giro cheque benefits payment is signed and cashed by someone other than, but with the connivance of, the intended payee who then reports the cheque as lost and waits for a duplicate payment *UK, 1996*. **2** a social security/benefits cheque. An abbreviation of 'Giro cheque' *UK, 1981*

GI's; GI shits *noun* diarrhoea *US, 1944*

GI shower *noun* a military hazing or punishment in which a group of soldiers forcibly clean a dirty peer with wire brushes *US, 1956*

gism pot *noun* the vagina *UK, 2001*

git; get *noun* an objectionable individual; an idiot. 'Get' was conventional English from the C14 to C18, meaning 'a child', 'one of his get' (one of his begetting); hence a useful synonym for BASTARD. Usuage is now mainly in northwest England. 'Git' is a mispronunciation *UK, 1940*

gitbox *noun* a guitar *US, 1937*

gite *noun* a bed and breakfast. In Quebec, even anglophones know and use 'gite', but it is often accompanied by 'bed and breakfast' so tourists from the US are not confused: Le Gite Park Ave., Bed and Breakfast. Au Gite Olympique is located on a major street in Montreal *CANADA, 2002*

git-faced *adjective* having an objectionable countenance *UK, 2000*

git-fiddle *noun* a guitar. A decidedly rural term *US, 1935*

Gitmo *nickname* the US naval base at Guantanamo Bay, Cuba *US, 1959*

G-Ivan *noun* a Russian enlisted soldier *US, 1946*

give *noun* inside information *UK, 1980*

give *verb* **1** to tell a secret. Mainly imperative *UK, 1956*. **2** to consent to have sex *US, 1935*. **3** to have sex with a woman *UK, 1970*. ▶ **give a fuck** to care, to be concerned. Often in the negative *US, 2001*. ▶ **give good X; give great X** to be notable for the noun that follows. On the original model of GIVE HEAD (to perform oral sex) *US, 1971*. ▶ **give her tarpaper** to work very hard. Used in Michigan's Upper Peninsula *US, 2003*. ▶ **give it 1** to behave in the manner of whatever noun or adjective follows *UK, 1999*. **2** either by speech or action, to make your attitude to someone or something obvious *UK, 1996*. ▶ **give it all that** to brag, to show off *UK, 1977*. ▶ **give it away** to engage in sex without pay; to engage in sex promiscuously *US, 1945*. ▶ **give it some** to put a great deal of effort into something. Possibly abbreviated from 'give it some wellie' *UK, 2001*. ▶ **give it the nifty fifty** (used of a male) to masturbate *US, 1983*. ▶ **give it the off** to go, to leave *UK, 1997*. ▶ **give it to** to copulate with *US, 1992*. ▶ **give it up** to applaud. Often as an imperative to an audience *US, 1990*. ▶ **give Jack his jacket** to give credit where credit is due *BARBADOS, 1975*. ▶ **give laugh for pea soup** to bring gossip or interesting news when you visit, hoping for a meal in exchange *JAMAICA, 1977*. ▶ **give leather** to thrust forcefully while having sex *TRINIDAD AND TOBAGO, 2003*. ▶ **give me a break; gimme a break** used as an expression of dismay at that which has just been said. Ubiquitous in the 1990s *US, 1993*. ▶ **give skin** to slap hands in greeting *US, 1964*. ▶ **give someone hell** to deal with someone in a harsh or severe manner *UK, 1851*. ▶ **give someone one** to have sex with someone *UK, 1974*. ▶ **give someone the reds** to anger. Teen slang *US, 1951*. ▶ **give someone their hat** to release from prison *US, 1976*. ▶ **give the office** to signal or give information *UK, 1804*. ▶ **give the skins** to have sex with someone *US, 1990*. ▶ **give two fucks** to care, to be concerned. An elaboration of GIVE A FUCK, and usually in the negative *US, 1974*. ▶ **give up as a bad job** to abandon something that has no prospect of success *UK, 1862*. ▶ **give what for** to beat, to thrash, to scold. Derives, apparently, from an exchange in which a person threatened with punishment asked 'What for?' and received the formulaic answer 'I'll give you what for' *UK, 1873*. ▶ **give wings** to inject someone else with heroin or to teach them to inject themselves *US, 1968*. ▶ **give your right ball/testicle for** to give everything for *AUSTRALIA, 1988*

give-and-get *noun* a bet. Rhyming slang *UK, 1998*

give-and-take *noun* a cake. Rhyming slang. *UK, 1960*

give-a-shit lobe *noun* the frontal lobe of the brain. If shot in the frontal lobe, the patient rarely cares about anything *US, 1990*

give-away *noun* a revelation or betrayal, either deliberate or inadvertent *US, 1882*

give away *verb* to cease doing something; to give up *AUSTRALIA, 1944*

give over! stop it! *UK, 1984*

giz *noun* the vagina *US, 1975*

giz! give me; give us. A slurring of 'give us', where 'us' is often used for 'me' *UK, 1999*

gizmo *verb* to outfit with a device *US, 1977*

gizmo; gismo *noun* a gadget, device or contraption, the exact name of which is forgotten by, or unimportant to, the speaker *US, 1942*

gizz *verb* to gaze *UK, 1975*

gizza; gissa used for making a demand. Phonetic compound of 'give us [me] a'. 'Gizza job' became a catchphrase in the mass-unemployment circumstances of the early 1980s *UK, 1982*

gizzard *noun* 250 or 300 dollars. An allusion to a 'monkey' ($500), with the gizzard being the guts of the monkey *AUSTRALIA, 1989*

gizzit *noun* a looted item. Short for 'give us it'; used by the military in the 1982 Falklands war *UK, 1982*

gizzuts *noun* guts, courage *US, 1993*

GJ *noun* grand jury *US, 1997*

G-joint *noun* **1** a federal penitentiary *US, 1992*. **2** a crooked carnival game. 'G' is for 'gaffed' (rigged) *US, 1946*

GLA *noun* a car theft; grand *larceny automobile US, 1973*

glacines *noun* heroin. Possibly a misspelling of 'glassine', a material used to make bags in which the drug may be supplied *UK, 1998*

glacio *noun* a glaciologist *UK, 1985*

glad *noun* a *glad*iolus; a cut gladiolus flower *AUSTRALIA, 1968*

glad bag *noun* **1** a body bag, used to cover corpses. Coined in Vietnam; still in use in the Gulf war and after *US, 1983*. **2** a condom *UK, 1998*

gladdy; gladdie *noun* a *glad*iolus; a cut gladiolus flower *AUSTRALIA, 1947*

glad eye *noun* a come-hither look *US, 1903*

glad hand *noun* **1** a welcome, rousing if not always sincere *US, 1873*. **2** on the railways, the metal air hose coupling between carriages. The interlocking connectors vaguely resemble hands clasped in a handshake *US, 1975*

glad-hand *verb* to greet with profuse, if insincere, enthusiasm. Often found in the context of politicians *US, 1895*

glad-handing *adjective* insincere and false *US, 1992*

gladiator school *noun* a violent prison *US, 1981*

glad lad *noun* an attractive male *US, 1945*

glad-on *noun* an erection. A happy variation of HARD-ON (an erection) *UK, 2001*

glad plaid *noun* a bright plaid pattern. Mexican-American youth (Pachuco) usage in the American southwest *US, 1947*

glad rag *noun* a piece of cloth saturated with glue or an industrial solvent, used for recreational inhaling *US, 1971*

glad rags *noun* your best clothes *US, 1899*

glad stuff *noun* any hard drug; cocaine, heroin, morphine, opium *US, 1953*

glad we could get together used as a humorous farewell. A catchphrase television sign-off by John Cameron Swayze on NBC in the 1950s. Repeated with referential humour *US, 1949*

glaiket *adjective* foolish; having a foolish appearance. From an earlier sense as 'inattentive to duty' *UK, 1985*

glam *noun* glamour *US, 1937*

glam *adjective* **1** glamorous *UK, 1964*. **2** flamboyant, especially in dress and appearance *US, 1993*

glam; glam up *verb* to dress more smartly *UK, 1937*

glamazon *noun* a beautiful, well-muscled woman. A compound of 'glamour' and 'Amazon'. *2001*

glammed-up *adjective* dressed or presented in a glamorous manner *UK, 1924*

glamottle *noun* a 13 ounce bottle of Budweiser™ beer. Budweiser advertised that it was a 'glass that holds more than a bottle', which is corrupted here *US, 1948*

glamour *noun* a sexually attractive female *AUSTRALIA, 1983*

glamour boy *noun* a US Air Force flier *US, 1946*

Glamour-don't *noun* a huge fashion mistake. From a fashion 'do's and don'ts' column in *Glamour Magazine CANADA, 1993*

glamour groovie *noun* a fashion-conscious person *US, 1947*

glamour-puss *noun* a sexually attractive person, especially one who has enhanced a natural beauty with artificial glamour *US, 1941*

G-land *noun* Grajagan, Indonesia. A surfing destination *US, 1991*

glare glasses; glares *noun* sunglasses *INDIA, 1979*

glark *verb* to decipher a meaning from context *US, 1991*

Glasgow grin; Glesga grin *noun* a slash or slash-scar on the face *UK: SCOTLAND, 1988*

Glasgow kiss; Glesga kiss *noun* a head butt to your opponent's face *UK, 1988*

Glasgow nod; Glesga nod *noun* a head butt to your opponent's face *UK: SCOTLAND, 1988*

Glasgow Ranger; glasgow *noun* a stranger. Rhyming slang, formed from Glasgow Rangers football club; recorded as an underworld term *UK, 1992*

glass *noun* **1** amphetamine powder; methamphetamine powder *UK, 1998*. **2** heroin *UK, 2003*. **3** a hypodermic syringe *US, 1942*. **4** a shop window *US, 1973*. **5** a five ounce glass of beer *AUSTRALIA, 1972*. **6** a smooth water surface *US, 1979*. **7** a diamond *US, 1918*. **8** in drag racing and hot rodding, fibreglass, used to reduce weight *US, 1968* ▷*see:* **GLASS OF WATER**

glass *verb* **1** to attack someone's face using a glass or bottle as a weapon *UK, 1936*. **2** in hot rodding, to repair a car body with lead compound, or fibreglass *US, 1960*

glassbottle *noun* pieces of broken glass set into the top of a wall *TRINIDAD AND TOBAGO, 1920*

glass ceiling *noun* a notional barrier to personal advancement, especially in the employment prospects of a woman, a disabled person or anyone from an ethnic minority. 'You can't see it but you know it's there' – or 'the sky's the limit' *US, 1984*

glass chandelier *noun* homosexual; a homosexual. Rhyming slang for QUEER *UK, 2003*

glass cheque *noun* a bottle with a deposit on it *UK: SCOTLAND, 1988*

glass chin *noun* a window built in the area immediately below and slightly behind the nose of a bomber *US, 1988*

glass dick *noun* a pipe used to smoke crack cocaine *US, 1995*

glass diet *noun* an addiction to crack cocaine *US, 1997*

glass gun *noun* a hypodermic syringe and needle *US, 1949*

glass house *noun* **1** a guard room, detention barracks or military prison. From the glass-roofed North Camp military prison in Aldershot *UK, 1931*. **2** in prison, a detention cell or cells *UK, 1996*. **3** in surfing, a smooth ride inside the hollow of a wave *US, 1987*

Glass House *nickname* the Parker Center police headquarters in Los Angeles *US, 1963*

glassie *noun* a clear glass marble *AUSTRALIA, 1934*

glass itch *noun* irritation of the skin by fibreglass dust. Surfing usage *US, 1978*

glass jaw *noun* a weak jaw in the context of boxing or fighting *US*, 1955

glass of beer *noun* the ear. Rhyming slang *UK*, 1961

glass of plonk *noun* the nose. Rhyming slang for CONK *UK*, 1992

glass of water; glass *noun* a quarter of an ounce (seven grams) of cocaine. Rhyming slang for QUARTER *UK*, 2002

glass pack *noun* in hot rodding, a muffler that has been stuffed with fibreglass, increasing the roar of the engine *US*, 1960

glass work *noun* in poker, the use of a small mirror or other refective surface to cheat *US*, 1968

glassy *adjective* (used of an ocean condition) smooth, not choppy *US*, 1963

Glasto *noun* the *Glastonbury* Festival; to a lesser extent, the town of Glastonbury. The festival began in 1970 when it was known as The Glastonbury Fayre. The earliest references to the event as 'Glasto' seem to be late 1990s *UK*, 2003

glaze *verb* to daydream *NEW ZEALAND*, 1998

glazed *adjective* drunk *US*, 1972

glazey doughnut *noun* the residue of vaginal secretions ringing a cunnilinguist's mouth *UK*, 2002

gleam *verb* ▶ **gleam the tube** (of a female) to masturbate *US*, 2001

gleamer *noun* any reflective surface used by the dealer for cheating in a card game *US*, 1969

gleaming *adjective* excellent *US*, 1997

gleek *noun* in poker, three of a kind *US*, 1967

gleesome threesome *noun* group sex with three participants *AUSTRALIA*, 1971

Glen Hoddle; Glen *noun* an objective achieved with ease; in sport, and easy win or simple victory. Rhyming slang for 'doddle', based on the name of footballer and former England coach Glen Hoddle *UK*, 2002

glide time *noun* a flexible work schedule *NEW ZEALAND*, 1977

glim *noun* **1** a light *UK*, 1676. **2** the eye *UK*, 1789. **3** a railway lantern *US*, 1946

glim *verb* to see *US*, 1912

glimmer *noun* **1** a light *UK*, 1566. **2** any reflective surface used by a dealer to cheat in a game of cards *US*, 1962

Glimmer Man *nickname* a man appointed by the Gas Company during World War 2 to inspect homes for any contravention of the rationing of gas *IRELAND*, 1968

glimmers *noun* the eyes or eyeglasses *UK*, 1814

glimmer twins *nickname* Mick Jagger and Keith Richard of The Rolling Stones. A self-given nickname, apparently – according to Keith Richard – in response to the question 'Who ARE you? What's it all about? Come on, give us a clue. Just give us a glimmer' *UK*, 1968

glimp *verb* to peer, to peep. Military; an abbreviation of 'glimpse' (to see briefly) *UK*, 1987

gliss around *verb* to make small talk *US*, 1947

glitch *noun* a malfunction. From the Yiddish for 'slip' *US*, 1962

glitching *noun* a temporary or intermittent loss of control (of a radio-controlled aircraft) when interference from another signal occurs *UK*, 1979

glitter *noun* salt *US*, 1981

glitter fairy *noun* a style-conscious, effeminate homosexual man. Usually derogatory *US*, 1978

glittergal *noun* in circus and carnival usage, a female performer *US*, 1960

glitter gulch *noun* downtown Las Vegas, Nevada *US*, 1953

glitz *noun* superficial glamour, especially as applied in show-business *US*, 1977

glitzy *adjective* ostentatious, gaudy, especially with a sense of tawdry show-business glamour; often applied to something that glitters *US*, 1966

GLM *noun* (in doctors' shorthand) *good looking mum*. Medical slang *UK*, 2003

glo *noun* crack cocaine *US*, 1994

glob *noun* expectorated sputum *US*, 1989

globber *noun* an expectoration *US*, 1988

globes *noun* the female breasts *US*, 1889

globetrotter *noun* a heroin addict who contacts many heroin dealers in search of the best heroin *US*, 1970

globule *noun* a contemptible person *UK*, 1988

glom *verb* **1** to steal, to snatch, to grab. Scots dialect *glam*, *glaum*, (to clutch or grasp) *US*, 1897. **2** to attach to, to seize upon, to grab hold of for oneself *US*, 1972. **3** to eat hastily *US*, 1990

gloom note *noun* in college, a notification of academic deficiency *US*, 1968

glop *verb* **1** to drink noisily; to drink quickly; to slurp. Derives from 'glop' (a viscous liquid), or from a mispronunciation of 'gulp' *UK*, 1987. **2** to pour or apply with gusto *US*, 1992

glophead *noun* a habitual drunk. Combines GLOP (to drink) with -HEAD (a user) *UK*, 1987

glopper *noun* someone who is unfashionably dressed. Used among foot-propelled scooter-riders *UK*, 2000

Gloria Gaynors *noun* trainers. Rhyming slang, formed from the name of soul singer Gloria Gaynor (b.1949). *UK*, 1998

Gloria Soames *noun* glorious homes *AUSTRALIA*, 1965

glory *noun* on the railways, an accidental death *US*, 1946. ▶ **get the glory** while in prison, to become religious – a state of being that may well outlast the prison sentence *UK*, 1950

glory be *noun* tea (the beverage or the meal). Rhyming slang *UK*, 1998

glory be! used as an expression of delight or astonishment. Shortened from 'Glory be to God!' but often having to do without God in spirit as well as word *UK*, 1893

glory card *noun* a licence from the Federal Communications Commission to operate a citizens' band radio *US*, 1976

glory fit *noun* an exhibition of religious emotional frenzy *CANADA*, 1946

glory hole *noun* **1** a hole between private video booths in a pornography arcade or between stalls in a public toilets, designed for anonymous sex between men *US*, 1949. **2** any unpleasant place or situation *NEW ZEALAND*, 1951. **3** any room or cupboard where oddments are stored *UK*, 1984. **4** the officer's sleeping quarters on a navy ship *US*, 1889. **5** a clear spot in an otherwise cloudy sky through which a fighter aircraft can reach its target *US*, 1991

glory hour *noun* the hour between noon and 1 pm on Sundays, the only hour of the day when drinking is permitted in pubs *FALKLAND ISLANDS (MALVINAS)*, 1982

glory seeds *noun* seeds of the morning glory plant, eaten for their psychoactive properties *US*, 1992

glory wagon *noun* a brakevan (caboose) *US*, 1977

gloss *noun* a shine *US*, 1969

glossy *noun* **1** a photograph *US*, 1931. **2** a 'glossy' magazine *US*, 1945

glove *noun* a condom. Leading to the safe-sex slogan 'No glove, no love' *US*, 1958

glove *verb* to examine a prisoner's rectum for contraband *US*, 1972

gloves *noun* ▶ **the gloves are off; take the gloves off** used for expressing a commitment to action without compromise, compassion or hesitation *UK*, 2001

glovework *noun* in cricket, a wicketkeeper's skill or performance *UK*, 1996

glow *noun* a pleasant, warming sense of intoxication *US*, 1942

glub *noun* a slob or lazy person *NEW ZEALAND*, 2002

glub out *verb* to idle; to relax completely *NEW ZEALAND*, 2002

glue *noun* **1** semen *UK*, 1998. **2** the residue produced during heroin manufacture *US*, 1992. **3** in computing, any interface protocol *US*, 1991. **4** a police detective *US*, 1950. ▶ **do glue** to sniff glue for the psychoactive effect *UK*, 1996

glued *adjective* drunk US, 1957

glued up *adjective* intoxicated as a result of solvent abuse, especially glue-sniffing UK, 2001

glue gun *noun* a weapon which fires a hardening resin to paralyse the human target UK, 2001

gluehead *noun* a person who inhales glue or any volatile solvent for the intoxicating effect US, 1970

gluepot *noun* **1** the vagina. Rhyming slang for TWAT, combined, perhaps, with allusive imagery UK, 1992. **2** a racehorse that performs very, very poorly US, 1924. **3** in cricket, a wicket with a 'sticky' surface (caused by the sun drying wet turf) UK, 1985

gluer *noun* a person who sniffs model glue for the psychoactive effect US, 1982

gluey *noun* a person who inhales glue or any volatile solvent for the intoxicating effect US, 1967

glug *noun* a swallow, a mouthful, a swig of a drink. Echoic US, 1971

glutes; gloots *noun* the gluteus maximus muscles (the three large muscles in the buttocks) US, 1984

g-ma *noun* grandmother US, 1997

GMFU; GMBU *noun* a situation of organisational choas. Initialism of 'grand military fuck up' or 'grand military balls up'; probably since World War 2 UK, 1982

GMOF *noun* a grossly obese hospital patient. A 'great mass of flesh' US, 1989

GMT *noun* time to clean out the refrigerator. Back-formation from the Greenwich standard, abbreviating here 'green meat time' CANADA, 2002

gnarlatious *adjective* extremely impressive US, 1991

gnarly *adjective* **1** treacherous, challenging. Originally surfer slang applied to waves and surf conditions, and then broadened to an all-purpose adjective US, 1977. **2** bad, disgusting US, 1978. **3** excellent. An absolute reversal of the original sense, used amongst foot-propelled scooter-riders US, 1982

gnashers *noun* the teeth NEW ZEALAND, 1984

gnat bites *noun* small female breasts UK, 1980

gnat-brain *noun* an idiot UK, 2002

gnat's *noun* something very small. A reduction of, or a suggestion of, many terms including: 'gnat's arse', 'gnat's chuff' and 'gnat's whiskers'; in such uses as 'within a gnat's' and 'tight as a gnat's arse', etc UK, 2001

gnat's blood *noun* tea purchased from a railway canteen or refreshment bar UK, 1970

gnat's eyelash *noun* a very small distance. The variant bodyparts are seemingly infinite, with 'eyelash' as the earliest recorded US, 1937

gnat's piss *noun* a weak beverage such as tea or beer UK, 1984

gnawing *noun* kissing NEW ZEALAND, 1998

gnawing-the-nana *noun* oral sex on a man AUSTRALIA, 1971

gnome *noun* a socially inept outcast US, 1959

G-note *noun* a $1000 note US, 1930

go *noun* **1** a turn at something; an attempt UK, 1825. **2** an opportunity AUSTRALIA, 1965. **3** a fair chance. Commonly used in the phrase 'give someone a go' AUSTRALIA, 1937. **4** an attack AUSTRALIA, 1965. **5** a look AUSTRALIA, 1930. **6** a preference AUSTRALIA, 1977. **7** approval, agreement US, 1878. **8** high-spirits, vigour, energy, as a human characteristic. Originally, and still, applied to horses UK, 1825. **9** used of a busy period or energetic activity UK, 1965. **10** a fight, especially a prize-fight; an argument US, 1890. **11** an event AUSTRALIA, 1979. **12** a drag race event US, 1954. **13** amphetamines. From the 'get up and go' nature of the drug's effects UK, 2003. **14** MDMA, the recreational drug best known as ecstasy US, 2003. **15** a goanna. 'Goanna' is the Guyana Indian name for 'lizard', attached here to the monitor lizard AUSTRALIA, 1904. ▶ **from the word go** from the very start. Derived from the starting of a race US, 1838. ▶ **have a go at** to criticise. From the sense 'to attack' UK, 1977. ▶ **make a go of it** to make a success of something US, 1877

go *verb* **1** when reporting a conversation, to say. A thoroughly annoying quotative device found as early as 1942, favoured by teenagers in the 1970s and 80s US, 1942. **2** to take on the mannerisms and customs of a place or group of people US, 1917. **3** to find acceptable, to wish for, to enjoy. Especially, and usually, when applied to food or drink UK, 1953. **4** to urinate; to defecate. Probably a shortening of 'go to the toilet', now a euphemism UK, 1926. **5** to attack physically; to fight AUSTRALIA, 1924. **6** to race US, 1965. **7** to become (of a political constituency, as in 'to go Tory') US, 1937. **8** in a casino, to earn in tips US, 1980. **9** to weigh US, 1999. **10** of a telephone, to ring UK, 2000. ▶ **go all the way** to have sexual intercourse US, 1924. ▶ **go Alzheimers** to forget. Public awareness of Alzheimer's confuses the disease with the premature senile dementia it causes UK, 2000. ▶ **go bent 1** to become dishonest. From BENT (crooked) UK, 2002. **2** (of a police witness) to retract a statement or renege on an undertaking. The implication is that the witness is behaving in a criminal manner, BENT UK, 1970. ▶ **go big, go fat** to achieve substantial height or distance in snow-boarding US, 1995. ▶ **go both ways** to be willing to play both the active and passive role in homosexual sex US, 1972. ▶ **go down the rabbit hole** to use drugs. An allusion to Lewis Carroll and Alice in Wonderland CANADA, 1993. ▶ **go for a burton 1** to to be killed in an air crash. Military slang of uncertain etymology UK, 1941. **2** to be destroyed or ruined, to be forgotten UK, 1957. ▶ **go great guns** to do very well, to prosper UK, 1913. ▶ **go off like a two-bob rocket** to lose your temper in a very unsubtle way UK: SCOTLAND, 1996. ▶ **go on** to talk at length UK, 1822. ▶ **go over jackass hill** to be a teenager CANADA, 1992. ▶ **go over the wall 1** to secretly depart from anywhere you are duty-bound to be. Applies to escape from prison and the wider world US, 1933. **2** to go to prison UK, 1917. ▶ **go some 1** to fight US, 1968. **2** to go well, to proceed with notable vigour US, 1911. ▶ **go south 1** to deteriorate; to break US, 2000. **2** in a gambling cheating scheme, to take dice or money off the gaming table US, 1997. ▶ **go through the card** to cover everything that is available in a given circumstance. Originally a horse racing term UK, 1978. ▶ **go to bat** to stand trial. A baseball metaphor US, 1965. ▶ **go to ground** to go into hiding US, 1990. ▶ **go to higher game** to launch a legitimate business after a period in an underworld enterprise US, 1972. ▶ **go to New Norfolk** to be crazy. A reference to the asylum located in New Norfolk AUSTRALIA, 1988. ▶ **go to the wall** to exert yourself at all costs without regard to the consequences US, 1976. ▶ **go up fool's hill** to be a teenager CANADA, 1999. ▶ **go upside someone's head** to hit someone on the head US, 1959. ▶ **go west** to be spoiled or ruined; to die UK, 1925. ▶ **go west on someone** to fail, to let someone down CANADA, 1999. ▶ **go with the flow** to acquiesce US, 1977. ▶ **not go much on** to not like much AUSTRALIA, 1932

go! used for expressing approval and encouraging further effort US, 1957

go-ahead *adjective* progressive; anxious to succeed US, 1840

go ahead, make my day used to summon defiance. From the film character Dirty Harry played by Clint Eastwood. US President Ronald Reagan used the line in a speech to the American Business Conference in March 1985: 'I have only one thing to say to the tax increasers. Go ahead – make my day!'. He liked the line so much that he repeated it in a speech at his 83rd birthday in 1994 US, 1983

go-ahead man *noun* in horse racing, a person working with someone selling 'inside' information on the horses and races US, 1962

go-aheads *noun* thong sandals US, 1962

goalie *noun* **1** a goal-keeper. In football and ice hockey; first recorded in the modern spelling in 1957 – as 'goalee', known since 1921 UK, 1957. **2** the clitoris US, 1972

goanna *noun* a piano. Rhyming slang for 'pianna', a variant pronunciation AUSTRALIA, 1918

goat *noun* **1** a person responsible for a failure or loss, especially a player in an athletic contest. A short form of 'scapegoat' US, 1894. **2** in horse racing, a poor-performing racehorse AUSTRALIA, 1941. **3** a fool. Often, and originally, in the phrase 'act the goat' UK, 1879. **4** in motor racing, a Dodge car US, 1965. **5** in hot rodding, an old car US, 1948. **6** an engine used in a railway yard US, 1946. **7** a goatee US, 1956.

▶ **get someone's goat** to succeed in making someone lose their temper *US, 1904*

goat boater *noun* a surfer who uses a surfboard/canoe hybrid craft. Mainly derogatory *UK: WALES, 2002*

goat fuck *noun* a colossal, confused mess *US, 1971*

goat hair *noun* illegally manufactured alcoholic drink *US, 1970*

goat head *noun* in electric line work, an angle-iron punch *US, 1980*

goat heaven *noun* bliss *BARBADOS, 1965*

goat knee *noun* a callus, especially one on the head from carrying heavy loads *BARBADOS, 1965*

goat land *noun* in oil drilling, non-productive land *US, 1954*

goat locker *noun* in the US Navy, the kitchen and dining hall reserved for officers *US, 1990*

goat mouth; goat bite *noun* a curse; bad luck *TRINIDAD AND TOBAGO, 1827*

goat pasture *noun* any worthless land sold as part of a confidence swindle *US, 1985*

goat rope *noun* a rumour. Gulf war usage *US, 1991*

goat screw *noun* a disorganised, confusing situation *US, 1988*

goat track *noun* a rough, winding hill road *NEW ZEALAND, 2002*

go away *verb* to be sent to jail or prison *US, 1990*

go-away gear *noun* a truck's highest gear *US, 1971*

gob *noun* **1** the mouth. Originally Scots and northern English dialect *UK, 1550*. **2** a slimey lump or clot, especially of spittle. In conventional use until early C19 *UK, 1964*

gob *verb* **1** to spit *UK, 1872*. **2** to eat *UK, 1999*

go back on *verb* to break a promise or a trust *UK, 1859*

gobble *noun* an act of oral sex *UK, 1984*

gobble *verb* **1** to perform oral sex on a man *US, 1966*. **2** to talk *US, 1947*. **3** in drag racing, to achieve very high speeds *US, 1965*. ▶ **gobble the goop** to perform oral sex on a man *US, 1918*

gobble alley *noun* the upper balcony in a cinema favoured by homosexuals *US, 1966*

gobble down *verb* in computing, to obtain *US, 1983*

gobbledygook *noun* dense, pompous, and unintelligible jargon *US, 1944*

gobble hole *noun* in pinball, a hole near the centre of the playing field which takes a ball from play while scoring a large number of points *US, 1979*

gobble off *verb* to perform oral sex on a man. A more complete elaboration of GOBBLE *UK, 2003*

gobbler *noun* a hospital patient with petty complaints *US, 1980*

gobbling irons *noun* a knife, fork and spoon. A trawlermen's term *UK, 1969*

gobbling rods *noun* a knife, fork and spoon. Gulf war usage *UK, 1991*

gobbo *adjective* stupid *UK, 2002*

gobby *noun* a small lump of dried nasal mucus *UK, 2000*

gobby; gobbie *adjective* loquacious, too talkative; impudent *UK, 1993*

gobdaw *noun* **1** an ordinary fool *IRELAND, 1989*. **2** a dolt, a gullible person *IRELAND, 2003*

go between *noun* a cow gate *CANADA, 1987*

gobgrabbing *noun* in prison, the practice of trying to *grab* and steal drugs concealed in someone's *gob* (the mouth) *UK, 1996*

goblet of jam *noun* marijuana. From the direct translation from Arabic *m'juni akbar* (a hashish-based confection) *US, 1969*

gob off *verb* to talk loudly or too much *UK, 1995*

gobs *noun* **1** a great deal of. In the C16, a 'gob' or 'gubbe' referred specifically to a 'great deal of money' or a 'large mouthful of fatty meat'. By World War 2, the term had acquired this broader meaning, as evidenced by the title of Johnny Viney's 1943 wartime humorous novel *Sailors are Gobs of Fun, Hattie US, 1839*.

2 in a hospital, gynaecology. Rhymed on the model of OBS (obstetrics) *UK, 2002*

gobshite *noun* a fool; an unpleasant person. Combines GOB (the mouth) and SHITE (rubbish), hence 'someone who talks rubbish': the subsequent, more abusive sense depends on the phonetic ugliness of the word *IRELAND, 1961*

gobsmack *noun* a shock that renders you speechless. A back-formation from the verb *UK, 2001*

gobsmacked *adjective* being speechless or lost for words as the result of amazement or shock. Adopted from northern dialect; silence is the suggested result of a 'smack' (hit) in the GOB (mouth) *UK, 1971*

gobsmacking *adjective* shocking *UK, 1996*

gobsmackingly *adverb* surprisingly *NEW ZEALAND, 2003*

gobstopper *noun* **1** a large ball-shaped sweet that reveals layers of colour as sucking diminishes its size. Combines GOB (the mouth) with the effect of a large sweet *UK, 1928*. **2** the penis. Rhyming slang for CHOPPER rejoicing in puns of size and sweetness *UK, 1992*

gobstoppers *noun* the testicles. From GOBSTOPPER (a ball-shaped sweet) *UK, 2002*

gobstruck *adjective* very surprised. From GOB (the mouth) and 'struck' (hit) *UK, 1988*

go button *noun* a car's accelerator *US, 1993*

go-by *noun* a passing by *US, 1949*

goby *noun* a middleman in a criminal enterprise. From 'go-between' *UK, 1970*

go-by-the-wall *noun* a cornerboy *IRELAND, 1989*

God Almighty *noun* a woman's nightdress, a 'nightie'. Rhyming slang *UK, 1998*

God-awful *adjective* terrible, dreadful. 'God' as the intensifier of all that is bad *US, 1897*

God bless you *noun* used as a mnemonic device in snooker for remembering the correct spotting of ball colours – green, brown, yellow *US, 1993*

God-botherer; God-pesterer *noun* an immoderately religious individual *UK, 1937*

God Calls Me God *noun* a GCMG (Grand Commander of St Michael and St George). A pun elaborated on the initials; used by civil servants demonstrating a jocular familiarity with the honour *UK, 1961*

God damn *noun* jam (the preserve). Rhyming slang *UK, 1992*

-goddamn- *infix* used as an intensifier *US, 1968*

godfather *noun* in horse racing, someone who provides financial assistance to a financially failing operation *AUSTRALIA, 1989*

God forbid; Gawd forbid; Gawd fer bid *noun* **1** a child. Rhyming slang for KID *UK, 1909*. **2** a Jewish person. Rhyming slang for YID *UK, 1960*

Godfrey *noun* used in oaths in place of 'God' *US, 1959*

God hates a coward in poker, used for luring a reluctant bettor to bet *US, 1951*

godhead *adjective* excellent at playing Internet games. Possibly an elaboration of 'good' *UK, 2003*

godiva *noun* ▷*see:* LADY GODIVA

God love her *noun* a mother. Rhyming slang *UK, 1974*

go down *verb* **1** to happen *US, 1946*. **2** to be arrested and/or imprisoned *UK, 1906*. **3** while working as a police officer in a patrol car, to park and sleep *US, 1973*

go-down man *noun* in an illegal betting operation, the employee designated to identify himself as the operator in the event of a police raid, accepting risk in place of the actual operator *US, 1951*

go down on; go down; go down south *verb* to perform oral sex *US, 1914*

go downtown *verb* to have sex. Coined for US television comedy *Seinfeld, 1993–98 US, 2003*

God save the Queens *noun* green vegetables, especially cabbage. Rhyming slang for 'greens' *UK, 1992*

God's flesh *noun* **1** psilocybin, a hallucinogenic mushroom *US, 1970*. **2** LSD *UK, 2003*

God's gift to women; God's gift *noun* of a man, a great lover. A familiar idiom, also used in other contexts as 'God's gift to something or someone'; generally heavily ironic *US, 1927*

God's honest truth *noun* the absolute truth *UK, 1959*

God shop *noun* a church *US, 1965*

God-size *adjective* very, very large *US, 1968*

God slot *noun* a regular position in a television or radio broadcast schedule given over to religious programmes *UK, 1972*

God's medicine; God's own medicine *noun* morphine; opium *US, 1925*

God squad *noun* **1** church authorities; evangelical enthusiasts *US, 1965*. **2** the US military Chaplains Corps *US, 1965*

God's waiting room *noun* a nursing home; a rest home *US, 1989*

goer *noun* **1** a proposition that seems a likely success *AUSTRALIA, 1974*. **2** an enthusiastic participant in sexual activity *UK, 1984*. **3** in hot rodding, a fast car *US, 1954*. **4** a person with get-up-and-go *AUSTRALIA, 1983*. **5** a horse being honestly ridden to win *AUSTRALIA, 1966*

go-fast *noun* any amphetamine or other central nervous system stimulant *US, 1993*

go-faster *noun* any amphetamine or other central nervous system stimulant *US, 1986*

gofer *verb* to act as an assistant and errand-runner. From the noun *UK, 2001*

gofer; gopher; go-for *noun* **1** a low-level assistant who typically runs petty errands. He or she *goes for* this and *goes for* that *US, 1930*. **2** in the military, a special team assigned with the task of bypassing normal channels to acquire needed supplies *US, 1990*

goffer *noun* **1** a cold drink of mineral water or lemonade. Derives from drinks manufacturer Goffe & Sons Ltd *AUSTRALIA, 1945*. **2** a wave washing inboard *UK, 1987*. **3** a punch, a blow *UK, 1886*. **4** a salute *AUSTRALIA, 2003*

go for *verb* **1** to attack with words (spoken or written) or with physical force *UK, 1880*. **2** to pay for *US, 1975*

go for it! used as a general exhortation *US, 1978*

go forth and multiply! go away! Genesis 1:28 provides this archly euphemistic variation of 'fuck off!'. *US, 1985*

go for the gusto! used as an exhortation to take risks and live life fully. From a slogan for Schlitz beer; often used ironically *US, 1988*

gog *noun* a person from North Wales. From Welsh *gogledd* (north) *UK: WALES, 2002*

go-getter *noun* a very active, enterprising person *US, 1910*

gogga *noun* **1** something frightening, monstrous or unwanted, especially in a political or business context. From the sense as 'an insect' *SOUTH AFRICA, 1934*. **2** any insect. A generic term, from Khoikhoi *xo-xon* via Afrikaans *SOUTH AFRICA, 1905*. **3** a germ, a disease *SOUTH AFRICA, 1963*

goggatjie; gogga *noun* used as a term of endearment. From Afrikaans for 'little insect' *SOUTH AFRICA, 1972*

goggle *verb* ▶ **goggle the horizon** used by motorcyclists to mean a number of things, most commonly to keep an eye out *US, 2003*

goggle box *noun* a television. Conventional 'goggle' (to stare) elaborates viewers' response to the box (television) *UK, 1959*

goggler *noun* a male homosexual *US, 1970*

goggles *noun* spectacles. From the conventional sense (spectacles for eye-protection) *UK, 1871*

Gogland *nickname* North Wales. From Welsh *gogledd* (north) *UK: WALES, 2002*

go-go *noun* a discotheque; a venue for erotic-dance performance *US, 1965*

go-go *adjective* associated with a discotheque. A very big word for a very few years *UK, 1964*

go-go bird *noun* a CH-47 transport helicopter fitted with window-mounted machine guns and used as a gunship. Not a successful experiment *US, 1991*

go-go boy *noun* an attractive, usually homosexual, young man who is a paid dancer at a nightclub or bar *US, 1971*

go-go dancer *noun* a paid dancer at a nightclub *US, 1967*

go-go dancing *noun* dancing for pay at a nightclub in a cage or platform above the patrons *US, 1993*

go-go juice; go juice *noun* petrol; diesel *US, 1976* ▷ *see:* GO-JUICE

go home used as a humorous farewell. A catchphrase television sign-off on *The Tracey Ullman Show* (Fox, 1987–90). Repeated with referential humour *US, 1987*

gohong *noun* during the Korean war, food or chow. From the Korean word for 'rice' applied by American soldiers to food in general *US, 1951*

goie *noun* a central nervous system stimulant such as Dexedrine™ or Benzedrine™ *US, 1960*

go-in *noun* a fight *AUSTRALIA, 1900*

going! used for encouraging another's action. Hawaiian youth usage *US, 1982*

going home gear *noun* a truck's highest gear *US, 1971*

going-over *noun* **1** a beating; a verbal assault *US, 1942*. **2** a detailed inspection, a search *US, 1919*

goings-on *noun* behaviour or proceedings. Usually with a pejorative implication *UK, 1775*

goitre *noun* a large quantity of banknotes, usually folded into a trouser pocket. From the unsightly bulge *UK, 1977*

go-juice *noun* alcohol (liquor) *US, 1968*

go jump in the creek go away!, be off with you! *AUSTRALIA, 1947*

GOK God only knows. An informal medical acronym *UK, 2003*

gold *noun* **1** money *US, 1940*. **2** used generically for jewellery, especially goods that are traded illicitly *UK, 2000*. **3** a type of bet in an illegal lottery *US, 1957*. **4** potent marijuana *US*. When combined with a place name for the formation of place plus colour *US, 1968*. **5** in drag racing and hot rodding, a trophy or prize *US, 1968*

golda *noun* a Jewish homosexual. Gay slang, formed on the name Golda and originating among Cape coloureds *SOUTH AFRICA, 2000*

Goldberg *noun* used as a stereotype of a Jewish merchant *US, 1965*

goldbrick *noun* a person who shuns work or duty *US, 1918*

goldbrick *verb* to avoid a work detail *US, 1918*

goldbricker *noun* a swindler *US, 1902*

goldbug *noun* a person who buys and hoards gold *US, 1981*

gold buttons *noun* a conductor on a train *US, 1977*

Gold Coast *nickname* **1** a high-rise, high-rent district on Lakeshore Drive bordering Lake Michigan in northern Chicago, Illinois *US, 1950*. **2** an area in Harlem, New York, where police bribes are common and lucrative *US, 1972*. **3** the Atlantic coast of South Florida *US, 1983*. **4** a stretch along the east coast of Queensland, Australia, noted for extraordinarily good surfing *AUSTRALIA, 1991*

gold-digger *noun* someone who pursues another romantically because of their wealth. Used to characterize women as predators of men *US, 1916*

gold-digging *adjective* engaged in the romantic pursuit of a wealthy lover *US, 1994*

gold dust *noun* **1** cocaine. Extends DUST (playing on the expense) *US, 1962*. **2** heroin *UK, 1996*

Gold Dust Twins *nickname* **1** Timothy Leary and Dick Alpert, LSD pioneers *US, 1971*. **2** Byron Nelson and Jug McSpaden, who dominated professional golf in the US during the 1940s *US, 1998*

golden *noun* marijuana. From the colour of the leaf *UK, 2003*

golden *adjective* successful, excellent, charmed *US, 1958*

golden arm *noun* in craps, a player with a long streak of good luck rolling the dice *US, 1993*

golden BB the bullet or anti-aircraft round that hits you *US, 1969*

golden bollocks *nickname* a lucky man *UK, 1984*

golden boy *noun* **1** a favoured male *AUSTRALIA, 1967*. **2** in homosexual usage, a handsome young man at his sexual prime *US, 1981*

golden brown *noun* heroin. An elaboration of BROWN (heroin) *UK, 1981*

golden bullet *noun* the bullet or anti-aircraft round that hits your combat plane *US, 1991*

golden chair! used to reserve your seat as you briefly leave the room *US, 1996*

golden crescent *noun* an area in Afghanistan, Iran and Pakistan where heroin is produced *US, 1992*

golden doughnut *noun* the vagina *AUSTRALIA, 1972*

golden dragon *noun* LSD *UK, 1998*

golden flow *noun* the urine test given to US soldiers upon their return to the US from Vietnam *US, 1971*

golden ghetto *verb* a large, comfortable US Army divisional base camp in South Vietnam. A term used with derision by the marines *US, 1990*

golden girl *noun* **1** a favoured woman *AUSTRALIA, 1992*. **2** high quality cocaine *US, 1980*. **3** heroin *US, 1994*

Golden Girls *nickname* the women's track team from the Bahamas at the 2000 Olympics *US, 2004*

golden glow *noun* a luminous daub used by card cheats to mark cards *US, 1988*

golden leaf *noun* **1** marijuana of excellent quality. Possibly descriptive of the plant's appearance, as well as the value placed upon it *US, 1925*. **2** a marijuana cigarette *UK, 2003*

golden mile *noun* the area west of McGill in central Montreal, characterized by large stone mansions *CANADA, 2002*

golden ointment *noun* a large win in betting; money *AUSTRALIA, 1989*

golden oldie *noun* **1** a song from the past that is still popular, especially a rock and roll song from the 1950s or 60s *US, 1966*. **2** by extension, anything that can be categorised in a nostalgic context. After the old songs a radio DJ announces *US, 1980*

golden shower *noun* a shared act of urine fetishism; the act of urination by one person on another for sexual gratification *US, 1943*. ▶ **couldn't organise a urine sample in a golden shower** used of an inefficient person or organisation. A later variation of '…PISS-UP IN A BREWERY' and '…COCK-UP IN A BROTHEL' *UK, 2005*

golden shower queen *noun* a male homosexual who derives sexual pleasure from being urinated on *US, 1964*

golden spike *noun* a hypodermic needle *US, 1955*

golden T *nickname* in New York, Fifth Avenue from 47th Street north to 57th Street, and 57th Street between Madison and Sixth Avenues *US, 1989*

golden time; golden hours *noun* in the entertainment industry, time worked at a premium overtime rate *US, 1970*

golden triangle *noun* an area in Burma, Laos and Thailand where heroin is produced *US, 1992*

goldfinger *noun* synthetic heroin *US, 1992*

goldfish *noun* a strain of marijuana, also known as 'orange bud' *UK, 2001*

goldfish *verb* to mouth words, to talk without being heard. Imitative of a goldfish *US, 2002*

goldfish bowl *noun* a jail's interrogation room *US, 1962*

goldfishing *noun* the behaviour of visitors being shown around a prison. From the similarity to a naturally wide-eyed, open-mouthed goldfish *UK, 1996*

gold fronts; fronts *noun* ornamental dental work *US, 1994*

Goldie Hawn *noun* a prawn. Rhyming slang, formed from the name of the US movie actress (b.1945) *UK, 1998*

Goldilocks *noun* a sexually transmitted infection. Rhyming slang for POX, caught from a fairytale heroine – 'Who's been sleeping in my bed?' *UK, 1998*

gold mine *noun* an establishment that sells alcohol illegally, by the drink *US, 1978*

gold nuggets *noun* in dominoes, the 5–5 piece *US, 1959*

gold ring *noun* (of playing cards) a king. Rhyming slang, also used of monarchy *UK, 1992*

gold room *noun* a room in the Pentagon where the Joint Chiefs and Staff meet with the Operations Deputies *US, 1986*

gold rush *noun* **1** the frantic searching for jewellery or coins that follows a shift in the slope of a beach, exposing lost articles *US, 1986*. **2** in hold 'em poker, a hand consisting of a four and a nine. An allusion to the California gold rush of 1849 *US, 1996*

gold seal *noun* good quality marijuana *UK, 1996*

gold star *noun* marijuana *UK, 1998*

gold-star lesbian *noun* a lesbian who has never had sex with a man and intends that she never will *UK, 2004*

Goldstein *noun* a Jewish person *US, 1980*

gold watch *noun* Scotch whisky. Rhyming slang, always given full measure *UK, 1992*

golfball *noun* **1** crack cocaine; a large piece of crack cocaine *US, 1994*. **2** any central nervous system depressant *UK, 1998*. **3** a changeable sphere with 88 different characters used on IBM Selectric typewriters *US, 1991*

golfballs *noun* **1** dice *US, 1962*. **2** LSD *UK, 2003*

golfballs and bullets *noun* a US Army c-rations meal of meatballs and beans *US, 1991*

Golf Course *nickname* Camp Radcliff, base camp for the Fourth Infantry Division near An Khe, South Vietnam. From its large helicopter airfield with low-cut grass *US, 1966*

goliath *noun* a multiple bet, gambling on eight horses, combining 247 bets in a specific pattern *UK, 1991*

gollies *noun* ▶ **the gollies** dog racing. From rhyming slang; for GOLLIWOG (a dog) *UK, 1992*

golliwog *noun* **1** a dog, especially a greyhound. Rhyming slang, may be abbreviated to 'gollie' *UK, 1992*. **2** fog. Rhyming slang, often reduced to 'golly' *UK, 1998*

golliwoggy; golly *adjective* foggy *UK, 1998*

gollop *verb* to eat hurriedly and with great gusto. A variation of conventional 'gulp' *UK, 1937*

golly *noun* **1** a black person. A shortening of 'golliwog' *UK, 1976*. **2** any person of non-white ethnicity; a native of the Indian subcontinent; an Arab;. A play on WOG via 'golliwog' (a negroid doll) *UK, 1967*. **3** a gob of phlegm or mucus *AUSTRALIA, 1938*. **4** a half gallon jar of beer *NEW ZEALAND, 1999*

golly *verb* to expectorate *AUSTRALIA, 1978*

golly! used for registering surprise, shock, etc. Euphemistic variation on 'God', which evokes a childish innocence *UK, 1775*

gollyer *noun* a gob of spittle *IRELAND, 1966*

golly gee, Buffalo Bob used for expressing mock astonishment *US, 1969*

golpe *noun* heroin. From Spanish *golpe* (a blow, a shot) *US, 1980*

gom *noun* a foolish, awkward person; a simpleton; an idiot *IRELAND, 1996*

GOM *noun* morphine; opium. An initialism of GOD'S OWN MEDICINE *UK, 1996*

goma; guma *noun* heroin. Possibly an elaboration of GOM *US, 1967*

gomer *noun* **1** a US Marine, especially a clumsy trainee. Terminology used with affectionate derision by the US Army during the Vietnam war. From the television show *Gomer Pyle*, which is not a completely flattering image of the marines *US, 1984*. **2** a repulsive, non-compliant hospital patient. From the plea – 'get out of *my* emergency room!' *US, 1993*

go-minh money *noun* compensation payment to Vietnamese civilians by the US military for accidental losses resulting from military actions. From the Vietnamese for 'extract yourself from a predicament' *US, 1990*

gommed up *adjective* dirty US, 1982

gommie *noun* a silly person CANADA, 1990

gomtor; gom *noun* an uncouth person, especially when applied to an Afrikaner. From Afrikaans *gomtor* (a lout) SOUTH AFRICA, 1970

gon *noun* a gondola train carriage US, 1934

gonad alert *noun* ▷*see:* NAD ALERT

gondola *noun* heroin UK, 2003

gone *adjective* **1** superlative, profoundly in touch with current trends. Nellie Lutcher's 1947 recording of 'He's a Real Gone Guy' did as much as anything to introduce the term into the language US, 1946. **2** drunk or drug-intoxicated US, 1933. **3** completely destitute and physically ruined because of crack cocaine addiction US, 1994. **4** infatuated US, 1957. **5** pregnant AUSTRALIA, 1945. **6** caught AUSTRALIA, 1954

goneburger *noun* anything that is redundant or finished NEW ZEALAND, 2000

gone case *noun* a hopeless cause SINGAPORE, 2002

goner *noun* **1** someone who has died or is unavoidably doomed to die very soon. From 'gone' as a euphemism for 'dead' UK, 1847. **2** someone who is doomed to failure US, 1970. **3** a person who excels US, 1949

gone to bed *adjective* dead UK, 1992

gone to Gowings *adjective* well and truly gone. From an advertising campaign for Gowing Bros, a Sydney department store. Used as an intensifier of 'gone', especially for slang senses of 'gone' AUSTRALIA, 1977

gone to hell *adjective* utterly ruined UK, 1984

gone up *adjective* drunk or drug-intoxicated US, 1970

gong *noun* **1** a medal or decoration UK, 1921. **2** a medal UK, 1945. **3** opium; heroin US, 1936. **4** marijuana US, 1977. **5** a gun US, 1995

gong down *verb* to ring the alarm bell on a police car as a signal to another motorist to stop. Early police cars were fitted with bell-shaped gongs. During the 1930s and 40s the police patrolling in cars were known as 'gongers' UK, 1958

gonies *noun* the testicles. A diminuitive of 'gonads' US, 1970

gonj *noun* marijuana UK, 2003

gonk *noun* **1** a prostitute's client. A contemptuous term used by prostitutes, deriving, perhaps, from a type of humanoid doll UK, 1977. **2** a fool, an idiot. Teen slang UK, 2003

gonk *verb* **1** to sleep UK, 1987. **2** to lie US, 1991

gonna; gunna; gunner; gonner *verb* going to. Slovenly pronunciation US, 1913

gonnabe *noun* a wannabe (someone with ambition) who has a realistic chance of achieving the goal US, 1988

gonnif; gonif; ganef *noun* a thief; a crook. Yiddish from Hebrew. Depending on the tone, can range from laudatory to disdainful UK, 1839

go-no-go *noun* the point on a runway where a pilot taking off must decide whether to abort a take-off or to take off US, 1963

gonski *adjective* gone UK, 2000

gonzo *noun* cocaine UK, 1996

gonzo *adjective* crazed; having a bizarre style. Although coinage is credited to US journalist and author Bill Cardoso, close friend and partner in adventure with the late Hunter S. Thompson, the dust jacket to Cardoso's collected essays claims only that he is 'the writer who inspired Dr. Hunter S. Thompson to coin the phrase "Gonzo journalism"'. Thompson first used the term in print and the term is irrevocably linked with him in the US US, 1971

gonzoid *adjective* crazed; having a bizarre style US, 1979

Gonzo the great; gonzo *noun* a state of drunkenness. Rhyming slang for, 'a state', formed on a popular puppet character in television's *The Muppet Show*, from 1976, and subsequent Muppet films UK, 1998

goo *noun* **1** any semi-liquid or viscous stuff, especially of an unknown origin US, 1903. **2** a look IRELAND, 1991. ▶ **give with the goo** to explain fully. Obsolete teen slang CANADA, 1946

goob *noun* **1** a large facial blemish US, 1976. **2** methcathinone US, 1998

goober *noun* in the usage of young street racers, anyone who drives a car with an automatic transmission US, 2003

gooby *noun* a gob of spit or phlegm NEW ZEALAND, 1985

gooch *noun* an inept, unaware person US, 1976

gooch-eyed *adjective* blind in one eye US, 1972

good *adverb* ▶ **come good** of people, to rise to or surpass expectations; of things, to work out well or better than expected UK, 1892. ▶ **have it good; have it so good** to be possessed of (many) advantages US, 1946. ▶ **make good** in poker, to match another player's increased bet US, 1967

good and *adverb* absolutely, completely, properly UK, 1885

good and plenty *noun* heroin. Playing with a trademarked sweet confection name US, 1994

good and proper *adverb* to the greatest degree, completely UK, 1928

good buddy *noun* used as a term of address. A term that enjoyed meteor-like ascendancy in popularity with the citizens' band radio craze that swept the US in 1976. Still used with jocular irony US, 1956

good butt *noun* a marijuana cigarette US, 1960

Good-bye Girls *nickname* the 2004 US women's Olympic soccer team. An acknowledgement of the fact that many of the team members were playing in their final competition UK, 2004

good-bye, kids used as a humorous farewell. On the final episode of the children's television classic *Howdy Doody Show* (NBC, 1947–60), these final words were uttered by Clarabell the Clown, who for 14 years had not spoken. Repeated with referential humour US, 1951

good-bye kiss *noun* the repurchase at a premium of stock by a target company from the company attempting a takeover US, 1988

good chute *noun* a successful ejection of pilot and crew from a downed US aircraft US, 1990

good cop *noun* in a pair of police, the partner who plays the sympathetic, understanding role during an interrogation US, 1975

good cop, bad cop *noun* a police interrogation method in which one interrogator plays the role of a hardliner, while the other plays the role of a sympathetic friend US, 1975

goodfella *noun* a gangster. Brought into mainstream use by the 1989 film *Goodfellas* US, 2003

good few *noun* a fair number US, 1828

good for *adjective* having sufficient money or credit to pay the specified requirement UK, 1937

good for you! used as a register of approval of something achieved or said by the person addressed or spoken of UK, 1861

good fuck! used for registering surprise UK, 2002

good fun *noun* a great deal of fun. Hawaiian youth usage US, 1981

good gravy! used as an utterly unprofane exclamation US, 1971

good grief! used as an all-purpose expression of surprise, anger, disappointment, dismay. Given great popularity in the 1960s by Charles Schultz's *Peanuts* comic strip US, 1937

good guts *noun* correct and pertinent information AUSTRALIA, 1957

good H *noun* heroin. An elaboration of H (heroin), possibly playing on the conventional exclamation 'good heavens!' UK, 2002

good hands used in farewell BAHAMAS, 1982

good hitter *noun* in pool, an excellent cue stick US, 1990

good horse *noun* heroin. A playful elaboration of HORSE (heroin) UK, 2002

goodie *noun* **1** a valuable possession UK, 2003. **2** something that is special and good US, 1975. **3** a person on the side of right, especially in works of fiction US, 1873. **4** extra parts or equipment for a car, enhancing its performance and/or embellishing its appearance US,

1954. **5** in poker, a card that improves a hand *US, 1961.* **6** an ambush or mechanical ambush *US, 1991*

goodie and baddie; goodie *noun* an Irish person. Rhyming slang, for PADDY *UK, 1992*

goodied up *adjective* (used of a truck) embellished with lights, chrome and other accessories *US, 1971*

goodies *noun* **1** the vagina *US, 1959.* **2** the female breasts *US, 1969*

good looks *noun* employment documents. Rhyming slang for BOOKS *UK: SCOTLAND, 1988*

good man Friday *noun* a pimp *US, 1953*

goodness!; goodness me! used as a mild expletive, or register of shock, surprise, etc *UK, 1704*

goodness gracious!; goodness gracious me! used as a mild expletive, or register of shock, surprise, etc. In 1960 Peter Sellers, in the character of an Indian doctor, recorded a successful comedy duet entitled 'Goodness Gracious Me' with Sophia Loren (written by Herbert Kretzmer); the old exclamation soon had catchphrase status. In 1996, four British-Indian comedians adopted the term as the ironic title for a radio comedy series, subsequently a television success. Now this term, the earliest recorded usage of which is by Charles Dickens, is considered by many to be a part of the stereotypical Indian vocabulary *UK, 1840*

goodness only knows! used as a mild declaration of ignorance; used of something beyond your knowledge or experience *UK, 1819*

goodness' sake!; for goodness' sake! used as a mild register of exasperation or impatience. The earliest use was in reference to the goodness of God *UK, 1613*

Good night Chet. Good night David. used as a humorous exchange of farewells. The signature sign-off of television news anchors Chet Huntley and David Brinkley in the 1960s. Repeated with referential humour *US, 1956*

goodnight kiss *noun* an act of urination; urination. Rhyming slang for PISS *UK, 1992*

good-night nurse *noun* a smoker's last cigarette of the night before going to sleep *US, 1996*

goodnight, nurse used for indicating the end or the finish of an activity *UK, 2000*

good numbers (used in citizens' band radio transmissions) best wishes, regards *US, 1976*

good-oh; good-o; goodoh; goodo *adjective* very good; all right; well; in good health *AUSTRALIA, 1905*

good-oh; good-o; goodoh; goodo *adverb* well; satisfactorily; all right *AUSTRALIA, 1920*

good-oh!; good-o!; goodoh!; goodo! **1** terrific!, well done! *AUSTRALIA, 1904.* **2** all right!, okay! *AUSTRALIA, 1918*

good oil *noun* correct and pertinent information *AUSTRALIA, 1916*

good old *adjective* **1** used as an affectionate (occasionally derisive) modifier of a term of reference or address *UK, 1821.* **2** familiar; used for expressing commendation or approval *UK, 1898*

good old boy *verb* a white male from the southern US who embraces the values of his region and race *US, 1961*

good on you! **1** well done!, good for you! *AUSTRALIA, 1907.* **2** used as a farewell *US, 1997*

good people *noun* a person who can be trusted and counted on *US, 1891*

good plan! used as a humorous expression of approval *US, 1981*

goods *noun* **1** the genuine article, the real thing; exactly who or what is required *US, 1899.* **2** positive evidence of guilt *US, 1900.* **3** any drug *US, 1971.* **4** yourself, especially areas of intimate contact *UK, 1988.* ▶ **the goods** an attractive person *UK, 1984*

good shake *noun* ▷*see:* EVEN SHAKE

good ship venus; good ship *noun* the penis. Rhyming slang *UK, 1992*

good show!; jolly good show! used as an expression of delight *UK, 1940*

good sort *noun* a sexually attractive woman *AUSTRALIA, 1944*

good stuff *noun* among criminals, a respected criminal *UK, 2001*

good style *adverb* excellently *UK, 2001*

good thing *noun* **1** a lucrative opportunity *AUSTRALIA, 1962.* **2** a sucker; someone who is easily tricked *US, 1909.* **3** a horse that is tipped to win *AUSTRALIA, 1877.* **4** a good thing. Made slang by attitude and tone. A signature line of Martha Stewart on her television show *Martha Stewart Living Television*, first aired in 1993. Repeated with referential humour *US, 1993.* ▶ **like a good thing** in an active, pleasing or exciting way *IRELAND, 1996*

good thinking! used as a register of approval for an excellent idea or good suggestion, or ironically in the case of a bad or obvious suggestion *UK, 1968*

good time *noun* **1** a period of incarceration that does not destroy the prisoner's spirit *US, 1975.* **2** a reduction of a prison sentence for good behaviour in jail *US, 1952.* **3** time that counts towards a soldier's military commitment *US, 1971.* ▶ **the original good time that was had by all** used of a sexually promiscuous woman. A twist of the clichéd catchphrase 'a good time was had by all', coined by US film actress Bette Davis, 1908–89. The original catchphrase is credited to poet Stevie Smith, who acquired it for use as a title from the reportage of parish magazines *US, 1981*

good-time house *noun* an establishment that sells alcohol illegally, especially by the drink *US, 1978*

good to go *adjective* prepared to start a mission. Airborne slang in Vietnam, quickly absorbed into the non-military mainstream *US, 1966*

good to me! used for expressing self-praise *US, 1972*

good wood *noun* a dependable, trustworthy white prisoner. Derived from PECKERWOOD *US, 1989*

goody!; goodee! used as an expression of delight. Childish; often reduplicated in excitement *UK, 1796*

goody drawer *noun* any drawer in a bedroom containing contraceptives, lubricants or sex toys *US, 2002*

goody-goody *noun* **1** an excessively good person. Usually uttered with some degree of derision *UK, 1871.* **2** marijuana. From the exclamation of delight. *UK, 2003*

goody-goody *adjective* (of children) too well-behaved; (of adults) hypocritically or sentimentally pious *UK, 1871*

goody gumdrops; goody goody gumdrops; goody gumdrop used as an expression of delight; often ironic in later use *UK, 1959*

goody two-shoes *noun* a person of excessive virtue *US, 1934*

gooey *noun* in computing, a graphic user interface (GUI) such as one with windows and icons *US, 1995*

gooey *adjective* **1** viscous or semi-viscous *US, 1903.* **2** excessively sentimental *UK, 1935*

gooey ball *noun* any sticky confection made with marijuana or hashish *US, 2001*

gooey louey *noun* a second lieutenant in the US Army *US, 1991*

goof *noun* **1** an alcoholic beverage. Found only in Ontario, this term may have derived from GOOFBALL (a barbiturate drug) *US, 1964.* **2** a barbiturate. An abbreviation of GOOFBALL *US, 1944.* **3** a frequent marijuana smoker *US, 1950.* **4** a silly, soft or stupid person *US, 1916.* **5** a joke, a prank *US, 1958.* **6** a swim *SOUTH AFRICA, 2004*

goof *verb* **1** to botch, to ruin *US, 1952.* **2** to tease, to joke *US, 1931.* **3** to give yourself away to the police *UK, 1978.* **4** to spoil an injection of a narcotic, during either preparation or application *UK, 1978.* **5** to smoke marijuana *US, 1970.* **6** to enter what appears to be a near coma as a result of drug intoxication *US, 1951*

goof around *verb* to pass time enjoyably but unproductively *US, 1931*

goofball *noun* **1** a barbiturate used for non-medicinal purposes *US, 1939.* **2** a mixture of heroin and cocaine *US, 1969.* **3** a habitual smoker of marijuana *SOUTH AFRICA, 2004.* **4** a silly and/or dim-witted person *US, 1944*

goof butt; goof-butt; goofy butt *noun* a marijuana cigarette. A combination of GOOF (a marijuana smoker) and BUTT (a cigarette) *US, 1938*

goofed; goofed up; goofed-up *adjective* **1** wrong *US, 1952*.
2 experiencing the effects of drugs, especially barbiturates or marijuana; drunk *US, 1944*

goofer *noun* **1** a barbiturate capsule, especially glutethimide *US, 1969*.
2 someone who toys with recreational drugs *UK, 1998*. **3** a person who regularly uses drugs in pill form *US, 1952*. **4** a homosexual male prostitute who assumes the active role in sex *US, 1941*

goofer dust *noun* a barbiturate *US, 1954*

go off *verb* **1** to happen, occur *UK, 1804*. **2** of a fight, to happen, to start *UK, 1999*. **3** to vehemently display anger *AUSTRALIA, 1979*. **4** to cease to like something or someone *UK, 1934*. **5** to fall asleep *UK, 1887*. **6** to ejaculate *UK, 1866*. **7** to give birth *AUSTRALIA, 1971*. **8** to turn out or pass off in the way indicated *AUSTRALIA, 1867*. **9** to perform brilliantly *AUSTRALIA, 1987*. **10** to behave extravagantly; to go all out *AUSTRALIA, 1995*. **11** to defecate *TRINIDAD AND TOBAGO, 1973*. **12** to pass peak condition; to deteriorate in freshness *UK, 1978*. **13** to be raided by authorities *AUSTRALIA, 1941*. **14** to make a noise. An extension of 'go off' (to start) *UK, 1998*. **15** (of a party or nightclub venue) to be thoroughly exciting and enjoyable *AUSTRALIA, 1993*. **16** (of a prize) to be awarded *AUSTRALIA, 1970*. **17** (of a woman) to engage in sexual intercourse *AUSTRALIA, 1967*. **18** in motor racing, to suffer a diminution of performance, either because of a handling problem or driver fatigue *US, 1980*. **19** (of a racehorse whose true abilities have been kept secret) to be raced to win *AUSTRALIA, 1936*. ▶ **go off on one** to lose your temper *UK, 1997*

goofies *noun* **1** a swimming bath. Children's slang *SOUTH AFRICA, 1970*.
2 LSD *US, 2001*

goof-off *noun* a lazy person *US, 1945*

goof off *verb* to waste time, to idle *US, 1943*

goof on *verb* to joke about, to make fun of *US, 1956*

goof-up *noun* a blunder, an error of judgement *US, 1956*

goofus *noun* **1** a fool *US, 1917*. **2** in circus and carnival usage, an extremely gullible customer who demonstrates great potential as a victim *US, 1981*

goofy *noun* **1** a fool, especially as a form of address. Goofy is the name of the foolish dog in Walt Disney's Mickey Mouse cartoons *UK, 1967*. **2** a skateboarder who skates with the right foot to the front *UK, 2004*

goofy *adjective* gawky, clumsy, foolish, eccentric *US, 1919*

-goofy *suffix* mentally imbalanced as a result of the preceding activity *US, 1969*

goofy butt *noun* ▷*see:* GOOF BUTT

goofy foot *noun* a surfer who surfs with the right foot forward. Most surfers surf with their left foot forward *AUSTRALIA, 1962*

goofy footed *adjective* in foot-propelled scootering, used of someone who rides with the left foot behind the right. From surfing *UK, 2000*

goofy's *noun* LSD *UK, 2001*

goog *noun* an egg. Shortening of GOOGIE *AUSTRALIA, 1941*

googan *noun* in pool, someone who plays for fun *US, 1990*

googie *noun* an egg. From Gaelic *AUSTRALIA, 1903*

google *verb* to search for something on the Internet by means of a search engine; to check a person's credentials by investigating websites that contain that person's name. A generic use of Google™ (a leading Internet search engine) *US, 2000*

google; google hut *noun* an egg-shaped, fibreglass field hut *ANTARCTICA, 1992*

Google bomb *noun* an effort to create a great number of Internet pages with links to a specific website so that it achieves a position near the top of a Google search directory for seemingly unrelated words. Google™ is an Internet search engine *US, 2002*

Google bombing *noun* the deliberate creation of a great number of Internet pages with links to a specific website with an intent that the website achieves a position near the top of a Google search directory for seemingly unrelated words. Google™ is an Internet search engine *US, 2002*

google box *noun* television *NEW ZEALAND, 1984*

googlewhack *noun* among Internet users, the result of a search for any webpage that, uniquely, contains a combination of two randomly chosen words and is therefore indexed by the search-engine Google as '1 of 1' *US, 2002*

googlewhack *verb* among Internet users, to search for any webpage that, uniquely, contains a combination of two randomly chosen words and is therefore indexed by the search-engine Google as '1 of 1'. A back-formation from GOOGLEWHACKING *US, 2002*

googlewhacking *noun* among Internet users, a popular craze for searching for any webpage that, uniquely, contains a combination of two randomly chosen words and is therefore indexed by the search-engine Google as '1 of 1'. Coinage is credited to Gary Stock 'Chief Innovation Officer and Technical Compass' of a company in Kalamazoo, Michigan, who discovered and named this 'compelling' time-wasting activity *US, 2002*

googly *noun* an awkward question. A figurative use of the cricketing sense *AUSTRALIA, 1942*

goo-goo eyes *noun* romantic glances *US, 1897*

googs *noun* in circus and carnival usage, eyeglasses. A corruption of 'goggles' *US, 1924*

goo guard *noun* on a truck, a mudflap *US, 1971*

gooi *noun* a brief sexual liaison. Punning on the idea of FLING from the verb GOOI (to fling) *SOUTH AFRICA, 1978*

gooi *verb* to give; to put; to throw, to fling; to drop; etc. From Afrikaans for 'to fling' *SOUTH AFRICA, 1946*

gook *noun* **1** a Vietnamese person, especially if an enemy of the US; a person from the Far East, especially a Filipino, Japanese or Korean; any dark-skinned foreigner. A derogatory term, too all-encompassing to be directly racist but deeply xenophobic. Coined by the US military; the Korean and Vietnam wars gave the word a worldwide familiarity (if not currency). Etymology is uncertain, but many believe 'gook' is Korean for 'person' *US, 1919*. **2** the Vietnamese language; any Asian language *US, 1981*. **3** an unspecified, unidentified, unpleasant, viscous substance. Sometimes spelt 'guck' *US, 1942*. **4** the recreational drug GHB *US, 1996* ▷*see gloss at:* GHB

gook *adjective* Vietnamese *US, 1979*

gooker *noun* in hot rodding, a car with many cheap accessories but no performance enhancements that would qualify it as a hot rod *US, 1965*

gook sore *noun* any skin infection suffered by a US soldier in Vietnam *US, 1989*

Gookville *noun* a neighbourhood, hamlet or city occupied by Vietnamese people *US, 1967*

gook wagon *noun* in hot rodding, a car with many cheap accessories but no performance enhancements that would qualify it as a hot rod *US, 1953*

goola *noun* a piano *US, 1944*

goolie *adjective* black *UK, 2002*

goolie ogle fakes *noun* sunglasses. A combination of GOOLIE (black), OGLE (the eye) and FAKE (a manufactured article) *UK, 2002*

goolies *noun* the testicles. Originally military, from Hindi *gooli* (a pellet), in phrases such as 'Beecham Sahib's goolis' for 'Beechams pills', and so punning on PILLS (the testicles). Usually in the plural, except in phrases like DROP A GOOLIE/DROP A BOLLOCK (make a mistake) *UK, 1937*

gooly; gooley *noun* a small stone suitable for throwing. Probably from an Australian Aboriginal language. The usual derivation from Hindi *goli* (ball) and 'bullet' is at best farfetched *AUSTRALIA, 1924*

goom *noun* methylated spirits used as a drink by alcoholics. Probably an alteration of a word from an Australian Aboriginal language *AUSTRALIA, 1967*

goombah *noun* a loyal male friend; an Italian-American. An Italian-American usage, sometimes used in a loosely derogatory tone *US, 1954*

goomie *noun* a derelict alcoholic who drinks methylated spirits *AUSTRALIA, 1973*

goon *noun* **1** a unintelligent or slow-witted person. From Alice the Goon, a character in the comic strip *Thimble Theatre* (1919), via a large and stupid character known as 'the goon' in Elzie Segar's comic strip *Popeye the Sailor* (1935–38), which popularised the word and introduced it to the UK. Originally English dialect *gooney* (a simpleton), possibly from Middle English *gonen* (to gape) and Old English *ganian* (to gape, to yawn). UK usage from the 1950s is influenced by *The Goon Show*, a surreal BBC radio comedy with a cast of fools *US, 1921*. **2** a hired thug. A broadening of the original sense *US, 1938*. **3** a partisan on either side of a labour dispute hired to perpetrate violence *US, 1938*. **4** a North Korean soldier *US, 1960*. **5** cheap wine *AUSTRALIA, 2003*. **6** a flagon of cheap wine. It has been suggested that this comes from 'flagoon', a jocular pronunciation of 'flagon', but this is not supported by any evidence *AUSTRALIA, 1982*. **7** phencyclidine, the recreational drug known as PCP or angel dust *US, 1977*. **8** a gooney-bird (a C-47A Skytrain plane) *US, 1937*

go on! used as an expression of surprise, incredulity or derision *UK, 1916*

goonbag; goonsack *noun* the plastic bladder from inside a cardboard wine box *AUSTRALIA, 2003*

goonboards; goonieboards *noun* short, homemade skis *US, 1963*

goon boy *noun* a socially inept, unpopular person *US, 1955*

goonda *noun* a hooligan; a street-rough. Directly from Hindi *INDIA, 1926*

goondaism *noun* hooliganism. Hindi *goondah* Anglicised with '-ism' *INDIA, 1979*

goon dust *noun* phencyclidine, the recreational drug known as PCP or angel dust *US, 2001*

gooned out *adjective* under the influence of a drug *US, 1968*

gooner *noun* a North Vietnamese soldier *US, 1969*

gooney; goonie *noun* a communist Chinese soldier; a North Korean soldier *US, 1957*

gooney bird *noun* **1** a C-47A Skytrain plane, also known as a DC-3, most commonly used to transport people and cargo, but also used as a bomber and fighter *US, 1942*. **2** a foolish or dim-witted person *US, 1956*

goonie party; goon party *noun* a backyard party at which goonbags of different wines are hung on a rotary clothesline which is then spun so that fate decides what you will drink next *AUSTRALIA, 2003*

goon squad *noun* a group of prison guards who use force to quash individual or group rebellions *US, 1967*

goon stand *noun* in the television and film industries, a large stand for supporting large equipment or devices *US, 1977*

goony *adjective* silly, doltish *US, 1939*

goonyland *noun* territory controlled by the North Korean Army and/or Chinese troops during the Korean war *US, 1957*

goop *noun* **1** any sticky, viscid, unpleasant substance the exact chemical composition of which is unknown *US, 1918*. **2** the chemical jelly used in incendiary bombs *US, 1944*. **3** liquid resin used in surfacing surfboards *US, 1965*. **4** the recreational drug GHB *US, 1999*. **5** a fool *US, 1915*

gooper *noun* lung phlegm *US, 1978*

goop gobbler *noun* a person who enjoys and/or excels at performing oral sex on men *US, 1981*

go or blow used to describe a situation in car repair or motor racing where an engine will either perform very well or self-destruct *US, 1992*

goori *noun* a poorly performing racehorse. From an early sense of the word, a corrupted form of the Maori *kuri* (dog) *NEW ZEALAND, 2002*

goose *noun* **1** a socially inept, out-of-fashion person *US, 1968*. **2** in poker, an unskilled player who is a likely victim of a skilled professional *US, 1996*. **3** a shop assistant. Especially in shoplifters' use *AUSTRALIA, 1975*. **4** an act of copulation. Rhyming slang for 'goose and duck', FUCK *UK, 1893*. **5** in television and film-making, the truck carrying the cameras and sound equipment *US, 1990*. **6** a girlfriend, a woman. From an earlier English use. Also variant 'goosie' *SOUTH AFRICA, 1974*

goose *verb* **1** to jab or poke someone, especially between the buttock cheeks *US, 1906*. **2** by extension, to urge into action *US, 1934*

goose and duck; goose *noun* a trifle, something of no value. Rhyming slang for FUCK *UK, 2003*

goose and duck; goose *verb* to have sex. Rhyming slang for FUCK, also used to create euphemistic expletives *IRELAND, 1944*

gooseberry *noun* a person whose presence interferes with the relationship, especially romance, of two other people *UK, 1837*

gooseberry ranch *noun* a rural brothel *US, 1930*

gooseberry tart *noun* **1** the heart. Rhyming slang *UK, 1937*. **2** a fart. Rhyming slang *UK, 1998*

goosed *adjective* drunk *US, 1979*

goosed moose *noun* in hot rodding and car customizing, a car with a front that is substantially lower than its rear *US, 1993*

goose egg *noun* **1** zero; nothing. Originally baseball slang *US, 1866*. **2** a swollen bump *US, 1953*. **3** an oval cylindrical polystyrene float used in fishing *CANADA, 1999*

goose eye *noun* in the illegal production of alcohol, a perfect formation of bubbles on the meniscus of the product, indicating 100 proof *US, 1974*

goose flare *noun* a type of runway flare used in wartime Canada *CANADA, 1984*

goose grease *noun* KY jelly, a lubricant *US, 1985*

goose juice *noun* powerful sedative medication given to mental patients *US, 1986*

goose's neck; goose's *noun* a cheque *UK, 1961*

Goose Village *nickname* the Victoriatown area of waterfront Montreal *CANADA, 2002*

goosey *adjective* jumpy, wary, nervous *US, 1906*

goosie *noun* in male homosexual relations, the passive or 'female' rôle. Prison slang *SOUTH AFRICA, 1965*

gooter *noun* penis *IRELAND, 1991*

go-out *noun* a surfing session *US, 1988*

go out *verb* **1** to die, especially from a drug overdose *US, 1997*. **2** to suffer a relapse while participating in a twelve-step recovery programme such as Alcoholics Anonymous *US, 1998*

go over *verb* to paint over another's graffiti with your art *US, 1997*

Gopaul luck not Seepaul luck used for expressing that one man's good fortune is not another's *TRINIDAD AND TOBAGO, 1990*

go pedal *noun* an accelerator pedal *UK, 1994*

gopher *noun* **1** a person who is easily swindled, who 'goes for' the pitch *US, 1959*. **2** a poker player who plays with a high degree of optimism. So named because of the player's willingness to 'go for' a draw in almost any situation *US, 1996*. **3** a criminal who tunnels into a business to rob it *US, 1928* ▷ *see:* GOFER

go-pill *noun* any amphetamine or other central nervous system stimulant *US, 1957*

gopping *adjective* dirty. Gulf war usage *UK, 1991*

gor *noun* ▷ *see:* GAWD

gora *noun* a white person *INDIA, 1984*

Gorbachoff! used as a blessing when someone sneezes. Possibly related to 'gesundheit!' *US, 1990*

gorbie *noun* a stupid tourist *CANADA, 1989*

gorblimey *adjective* stereotypically (parodically) Cockney *UK, 2001*

Gorby blots; Gorbacher *noun* a type of blotter LSD popular in the early 1990s. The blotters were illustrated with the face of Mikhail Gorbachev, hence the 'Gorby' *US, 1994*

Gordon and Gotch; gordon *noun* a watch. Rhyming slang, formed from the name of a long-gone book-dealing company based in Plaistow, east London *UK, 1960*

Gordon Bank *noun* an act of masturbation. Rhyming slang, formed from football goalkeeper Gordon Banks (b.1937) *UK, 2003*

Gordon Bennett! used as a mild expletive. Probably an alteration of 'gorblimey!'. *UK, 1984*

gorge *noun* in circus and carnival usage, food *US, 1981*

gorge *adjective* used for expressing approbation. A shortening of 'gorgeous' *UK, 2003*

gorgeous *adjective* used for expressing approbation *US, 1883*

gorger; gorgia; gawjo *noun* a non-gypsy, anyone who is not a part of the travelling community. English gypsy use *UK, 1900*

gorgon *noun* a ruthless leader or bully *JAMAICA, 2000*

goric *noun* **1** a paregoric, an opiate-based medicinal syrup *US, 1982*. **2** opium; heroin. From 'pare*goric*' (a medicine that assuages pain) *US, 1977*

gorilla *noun* **1** a criminal who relies on brute strength and force *US, 1861*. **2** a prisoner who obtains what he wants by force *US, 1958*. **3** in the entertainment industry, a technical member of a film crew *US, 1970*. **4** in the music industry, a very popular bestselling song *US, 1982*. **5** one thousand dollars. Building on 'monkey' ($500) *AUSTRALIA, 1989*

gorilla *verb* to manhandle, to beat *US, 1922*

gorilla dust *noun* intimidating bluffing *US, 1986*

gorilla-grip *verb* in skateboarding, to jump holding the ends of the board with the toes *US, 1976*

gorilla pill *noun* a barbiturate capsule or other central nervous system depressant *US, 1969*

gorilla pimp *noun* a brutish pimp who relies heavily on violence to control the prostitutes who work for him *US, 1972*

gorilla salad *noun* thick pubic hair *US, 1981*

gork *noun* **1** a patient with severe mental deficiences *US, 1964*. **2** a fool; a contemptible person *US, 1970*

gorked *adjective* stupefied from anaesthetic *US, 1973*

gorker; gork *noun* in baseball, a weakly hit ball that falls for a base hit. A term coined by legendary professional baseball manager Earl Weaver *US, 1982*

gorm *verb* to bungle; to act awkwardly *US, 1975*

gorm! used for expressing surprise *TRINIDAD AND TOBAGO, 1997*

gormless *adjective* foolish *NEW ZEALAND, 1952*

gorp *noun* **1** a complete social outcast *US, 1976*. **2** a snack of nuts and dried fruit favoured by hikers. From 'good old raisins and peanuts' *US, 1991*

gorsoon *noun* a young male *IRELAND, 2001*

go-see *noun* in modelling, an visual 'interview' *US, 1969*

Gosford dog *noun* a person of Mediterranean background. Rhyming slang for WOG. From Gosford, a satellite city of Sydney which has a greyhound racing track *AUSTRALIA, 1983*

gosh used in expressions of surprise, frustration. A euphemistic 'God' *UK, 1757*

gosh-darned; gosh-derned; gosh-danged *adjective* used as a mild intensifier. A euphemistic replacement for 'God-damned' *US, 1997*

go-slow *noun* a deliberate slowing of production by workers as a type of industrial action *AUSTRALIA, 1917*

gospel true *adjective* entirely true *AUSTRALIA, 1957*

gospel truth *noun* sincerely the truth *AUSTRALIA, 1902*

goss *noun* gossip *NEW ZEALAND, 1985*

gotcha *noun* in computing, a misfeature that generates mistakes *US, 1991*

gotcha! **1** used as a humorous exclamation of a verbal conquest of some sort. Often used as the gloating afterword when a practical joke is played. On 2nd May 1982, during the Falklands war, the Argentine ship Belgrano was torpedoed by the Royal Navy as she sailed away from the exclusion zone. At least 386 lives were lost. The Sun newspaper printed the notorious, gloating one-word headline: 'GOTCHA'. Also used in triumph when a capture or victory has been achieved *UK, 1932*. **2** used for registering an understanding of what someone has said. A slovening of '[I] got you' *UK, 1966*

gotchie *noun* **1** a security guard or park keeper *IRELAND, 2003*. **2** a schoolboy prank, especially around Niagara Falls, Ontario, in which the victim's underpants are pulled up between his buttock cheeks. In the US, it is called a 'wedgie', but in Canada, a 'gotchie', which both comes from 'gotch' for 'underpants' (with Hungarian and eastern European source words) and is a pun *CANADA, 2002*

goth *noun* a member of a youth fashion cult, characterised by a dark, sepulchral appearance and stark white and black makeup. Inspired by C19 *gothic*-romance images of vampires, this dress sense is allied to a style of rock music also called 'goth' *UK, 1984*

Gotham *noun* New York City. Alluding to a mythical village inhabited by wise fools *US, 1807*

gothoid *adjective* recognisably goth in fashion *UK, 1999*

go through *verb* **1** to leave hurriedly; to decamp *AUSTRALIA, 1944*. **2** (of a man) to have sex with a woman *AUSTRALIA, 1967*

got it! used for urging another surfer not to catch this wave, which you claim as yours *US, 1991*

go-to-godamn *adjective* damned *US, 1961*

Go to Hell *nickname* Go Dau Ha, home to a US Naval Advanced Base from 1969 to 71, close to the Cambodian border on the Vam Co Dong River, South Vietnam *US, 1990*

go-to-hell rag *noun* a neckerchief worn by an infantry soldier *US, 1991*

go-to-whoa *noun* in horse racing, the entire length of a race *AUSTRALIA, 1971*

gotta like that! used for expressing approval, genuine or ironic *US, 1987*

got you covered! I understand! *US, 1955*

gouch *noun* a period of drug-induced exhaustion *UK, 2000*

gouge *verb* to surf expertly and stylishly. Applied to a ride on a wave *US, 1990*

Gouge and Screw Tax *noun* ▷*see:* GRAB AND STEAL TAX

gouger *noun* an aggressive lout *IRELAND, 1997*

goulash *noun* **1** an illegal cardroom that is open 24 hours a day *US, 1974*. **2** in prison, a meat stew of any description *UK, 1996*. **3** in electric line work, any insulating compound *US, 1980*

go up *verb* **1** to be sentenced to prison; to be sent to prison *US, 1872*. **2** while acting, to miss your cue or forget a line *US, 1973*

gourd *noun* the head *UK, 1829*. ▶ **bored out of your gourd** extremely bored. The rhyme on GOURD (the head) intensifies 'bored' *US, 1999*. ▶ **out of your gourd 1** extremely drug-intoxicated. Substitutes GOURD (a head) in synonymous 'out of your head' *US, 1967*. **2** crazy *US, 1963*

gourd guard *noun* in drag racing, a crash helmet *US, 1968*

gourmet ghetto *noun* north Berkeley, California; any neighbourhood featuring speciality food shops and gourmet restaurants. Originally applied to a two-block stretch of Shattuck Avenue between Cedar Street and Rose Street in Berkeley *US, 1983*

gov *noun* a prison governor *UK, 1996*

govern *verb* to play the active role in sex, sadomasochistic or not *US, 1985*

government artist *noun* an unemployed person in receipt of state beneifts. From a joke, heard in the high unemployment of the 1980s. A popular choice of occupation still, if questionnaires are to be believed *UK, 2003*

government-inspected meat *noun* **1** a soldier or sailor. Homosexual usage *US, 1970*. **2** a soldier as the object of a homosexual's sexual desire *US, 1981*

government jewellery *noun* restraints worn on prisoners' bodies to restrict movement *CANADA, 1987*

government job *noun* poor craftmanship *US, 1965*

government juice *noun* water *US, 2003*

Government Racing Car *noun* a car of the Gendarmerie Royale du Canada, the French name for the Mounties. Back-formation from the initials GRC *CANADA, 2002*

governor *noun* **1** an acknowledged expert *UK, 1980.* **2** an employer, a superior *UK, 1802*

governor's *noun* a prison governor's adjudication or ruling *UK, 1996*

gov'nor *noun* ▷*see:* GUV'NOR

gow *noun* **1** a drug, especially opium *US, 1922.* **2** sauce *US, 1967.* **3** herring roe *CANADA, 1998*

gowed up *adjective* drunk *CANADA, 1977*

gowhead *noun* a drug addict *US, 1935*

go-with-the-flow *adjective* easy going, relaxed. After the phrasal verb 'go with the flow', *2001*

gow job *noun* used in the 1940s to describe what in the 50s would to be called a hot rod *US, 1941*

gowster *noun* a drug addict or heavy drug user *US, 1936*

goy *noun* a Gentile. Yiddish *UK, 1841*

goyish; goyische *adjective* Gentile *US, 1965*

gozohomey bird *noun* an aircraft that returns you home. Royal Air Force use *UK, 2002*

gozz *noun* gossip *UK, 1983*

GP *noun* a general principle *US, 1944*

GPO (in doctors' shorthand) good for parts only *UK, 2003*

GR8 *adjective* in text messaging, great. A variant spelling; one of several constructions in which a syllable pronounced 'ate' is replaced by the homophone 'eight' *UK, 2002*

gra *noun* appetite; desire. The Hiberno-English word for 'love, liking, affection' *IRELAND, 1995*

grab *noun* **1** an arrest *UK, 1753.* **2** a person who has been arrested *US, 1992.* ▶ **up for grabs** available, especially if suddenly or recently so *US, 1928*

grab *verb* **1** to capture someone's imagination and attention *UK, 1966.* **2** to impress *US, 1970.* **3** to arrest *UK, 1753.* **4** in horse racing, to win a race with a long shot *US, 1951.* ▶ **grab a dab** to engage in male-on-male rape *US, 1990.* ▶ **grab air** to apply a truck's brakes *US, 1971.* ▶ **grab sack** to muster courage *US, 1999.* ▶ **grab the apple** to seize tightly on the saddle horn while riding a bucking animal *CANADA, 1987*

grab-a-granny *adjective* used to describe an event where you can meet mature women *UK, 1987*

grabalishus *adjective* greedy *BAHAMAS, 1995*

grab all, lose all used for expressing the dangers of greed *TRINIDAD AND TOBAGO, 2003*

grab and snatch *noun* the Goods and Services Tax (GST) *NEW ZEALAND, 1998*

Grab and Steal Tax; Gouge and Screw Tax *noun* the Canadian Goods and Services Tax. A back-formation on the initials GST *CANADA, 2001*

grab-ass *noun* horseplay *US, 1947*

grab-ass *verb* to engage in physical horseplay *US, 1953*

grab bag *noun* **1** a loose assortment of anything. From a lucky dip offered at US fairs *US, 1879.* **2** a pooled mix of different types of pills contributed by several people and then consumed randomly *US, 1970.* **3** the theft of a suitcase or briefcase accomplished by placing a look-alike bag near the bag to be stolen and then picking up and leaving with the bag to be stolen; the suitcase or briefcase stolen in such a theft *US, 1977.* **4** a lunch box or lunch bag *US, 1954.* **5** a bag of equipment prepared for grabbing in the event of an emergency *UK, 2004*

grabber *noun* **1** the hand *UK, 1859.* **2** a surfer who ignores surfing etiquette and catches rides on waves 'owned' by other surfers *US, 1991.* **3** a story that captures the imagination *US, 1966.* **4** a shame; a pity *US, 1977.* **5** a railway conductor *US, 1931*

grabble *verb* to grab violently *UK, 1781*

grabby *adjective* **1** attention-grabbing *UK, 1998.* **2** greedy, grasping, selfish *UK, 1953*

grab-iron *noun* a handle on the side of a goods wagon *US, 1975*

grab joint *noun* an eating concession in a circus or carnival *US, 1904*

grad *noun* **1** an amphetamine tablet or other central nervous stimulant *US, 1977.* **2** an ex-convict *US, 1950.* **3** a *grad*uate *US, 1871*

grade *noun* ▶ **make the grade** to achieve a required standard *US, 1908*

grade-grubber *noun* a student whose only goal is to get good grades *US, 1966*

graduate *noun* an ex-convict *US, 1949*

graduate *verb* **1** to complete a prison sentence. A construction built on the jocular 'college' as 'jail' *US, 1945.* **2** to be cured of a sexually transmitted infection *US, 1949.* **3** to begin using more powerful drugs, or to stop taking drugs completely *US, 1992.* **4** (used of a racehorse) to win a race for the first time *US, 1976*

grad wrecks *noun* the Graduate Records Examinations. The standardised testing given to undergraduate students seeking admission to graduate school in the US *US, 1966*

graf *noun* **1** graffiti *US, 1997.* **2** a paragraph *US, 1991*

graffer *noun* a graffiti artist who produces complete works, not just a stylised signature *US, 1993*

graf-head *noun* a graffiti artist *UK, 1998*

graft *noun* **1** personal and financial advantage as the result of dishonest or unethical business or political practice, especially bribery and patronage; corporate corruption in general *US, 1901.* **2** any kind of work, especially hard work *UK, 1859*

graft *verb* **1** to work hard *UK, 1859.* **2** to labour at criminal enterprises *UK, 1859*

grafter *noun* **1** a hard worker *AUSTRALIA, 1891.* **2** among market traders, a market trader *UK, 1979.* **3** a thief, a crook, a swindler *US, 1866.* **4** a criminal who identifies opportunities for other thieves *UK, 1978*

graf-write *verb* to write or draw in the style of graffiti *US, 2000*

graf-writing *noun* the act of *graffiti*-ing *US, 2001*

grain *noun* a heavy drinker *US, 1963*

grain and drain train *noun* solitary confinement *US, 1982*

grains *noun* semen; sperm *TRINIDAD AND TOBAGO, 2003*

grammie *noun* a tape deck, especially one mounted in the dashboard of a truck or car *US, 1976*

grammy *noun* one gram (of a drug) *US, 1992*

gramp; gramps; grampa *noun* a grandfather; also used as an address for an old man. A slurring of GRANDPA *UK, 1898*

gran *noun* a grandmother, especially as a form of address. Childish or affectionate shortening *UK, 1863*

grand *noun* a unit of 1,000, usually applied to US dollars or the pound sterling *US, 1915*

grand bag *noun* in homosexual usage, a large scrotum *US, 1981*

grand canyon *noun* in homosexual usage, a loose anus and rectum *US, 1981*

grand charge *noun* an empty threat or boast *TRINIDAD AND TOBAGO, 1973*

grand dad *noun* a grandfather *UK, 1819*

grand duchess *noun* a heterosexual woman who enjoys the company of homosexual men *US, 1970*

grandfather clock *noun* the penis. Rhyming slang for COCK, often paired with POLISH AND GLOSS (to masturbate) *UK, 1992*

grand fromage *noun* the most important person in a given organisation or enterprise. A cod-French variation of BIG CHEESE *UK, 2005*

grandma *noun* **1** the bleed period of the menstrual cycle *US, 1929.* **2** an older homosexual man *US, 1964.* **3** the lowest gear in a truck, or car. The lowest gear is the slowest gear, hence the reference to grandmother *US, 1941*

grandma's peepers *noun* in dominoes, the 1–1 piece *US, 1959*

grandpa noun a grandfather; also used as an affectionate form of address to an old man. Abbreviation of 'grandpapa' UK, 1848

grandpappy noun grandfather US, 1952

grandpa's dozen noun a twelve-pack of inexpensive beer US, 1994

grandstand noun a large handicap weight for a racehorse AUSTRALIA, 1966

grandstand verb to perform in a flashy manner, with an eye towards audience perception rather than the level of performance US, 1900

granfer noun a grandfather. A slurring of 'grandfather' UK, 1959

granite boulder noun the shoulder. Rhyming slang UK, 1992

grannie grunt; old grannie noun an annoying person. Rhyming slang for CUNT (an idiot) UK, 1992

grannies noun the bleed period of the menstrual cycle US, 1929

grannie's wrinkles; grannies noun winkles (seafood). Rhyming slang. UK, 1992

granny noun **1** grandmother UK, 1698. **2** an old woman. Extended from the previous sense UK, 1699. **3** the bleed period of the menstrual cycle US, 1929. **4** a bungled knot; anything that has been bungled US, 1975. **5** the quality of pride. Derives from the idiomatic phrase 'teach your grandmother to suck eggs', in which 'granny' (an abbreviation of grandmother) represents anyone wiser than you UK, 1851. **6** an apple of the Granny Smith variety AUSTRALIA, 1944

granny-dumping noun the convenient removal of elderly relatives from family responsibility to permanent hospital or nursing-home care UK, 1987

granny farm noun a care home or estate for elderly residents. From 'granny' (generic old woman). An ironic coinage reflecting UK society's apparent treatment of the elderly as so much livestock to be managed by others UK, 1988

granny gear noun **1** tranquillizers and anti-depressants, such as Valium™, Prozac™ and Rohypnol™. Drugs intended for GRANNY (an old woman), or intended to slow you down which is a stereotypical characteristic of a grandmother UK, 2005. **2** a car, truck, or bicycle's lowest gear; in a four-wheel drive automobile, the lowest gear combined with the lowest range in the transfer case US, 1993

granny jazzer noun used as a euphemism for 'motherfucker' US, 1977

granny panties noun large, cotton underpants US, 1991

granny rag noun a red flag used for indicating an oversized load on a truck US, 1971

granny's here for a visit experiencing the bleed period of the menstrual cycle US, 1968

granola noun a throw-back to the hippie counterculture of the 1960s US, 1982

Grant noun a fifty-dollar note. From the engraving of Ulysses S. Grant, a distinguished general and less-than-distinguished president, on the note US, 1961

grape noun **1** wine. Often used in the plural US, 1898. **2** gossip. A shortening of GRAPEVINE (the source of gossip) US, 1864. **3** in the language of car salesmen, a promising potential customer. Like the grape, the customer is 'ripe for picking' US, 1975. **4** a member of a flight deck refuelling crew US, 1986

grapefruit league noun in baseball, a notional league of the teams that conduct spring training in Florida US, 1929

grapefruits noun large female breasts US, 1964

grape parfait noun LSD. From the purple hue of the drug US, 1977

graper noun in oil drilling, a sycophantic worker US, 1954

grapes noun **1** the testicles US, 1985. **2** the female breasts US, 1980. **3** haemorrhoids NEW ZEALAND, 1998. **4** a percent sign (%) on a computer keyboard US, 1991

grapes of wrath noun wine US, 1947

grapevine noun **1** a network of rumour or gossip; the mysterious source of rumours US, 1862. **2** a line, especially a washing line. Rhyming slang, often shortened to 'grape' UK, 1992

graph noun an autograph US, 1975

grappler noun a wrestler. More of a fan word than an insider's word, but heard US, 1990

grass noun **1** an informer. Rhyming slang based on 'grasshopper', COPPER (a policeman) UK, 1932. **2** marijuana. The term of choice during the 1960s and 70s US, 1943. **3** hair, especially a crew cut AUSTRALIA, 1919. **4** a woman's pubic hair US, 1964. ▶ **have more grass than Kew Gardens** used of a person who is known as a regular police informer UK, 1984. ▶ **out to grass** retired from work; hence no longer in use. An image of old horses put out to grass UK, 1969

grass verb **1** to inform; to betray. From GRASS (an informer). Also variant 'grass up' UK, 1936. **2** to engage in sexual intimacy CANADA, 1999. **3** to defeat; to beat US, 2002

grassback noun a promiscuous girl US, 1969

grass bottle noun pieces of broken bottle glass TRINIDAD AND TOBAGO, 2003

grass castle noun a large dwelling owned by someone believed to have made their fortune dealing in marijuana AUSTRALIA, 2003

grass colt noun an illegitimate child CANADA, 1990

grassed up adjective in lobstering, covered with slime US, 1978

grasser noun an informer UK, 1957

grass fight noun a hard-fought argument or fight AUSTRALIA, 1986

grass-fighter noun a tough and willing brawler AUSTRALIA, 1951

grasshead noun a habitual marijuana smoker US, 1958

grasshopper noun **1** a tourist AUSTRALIA, 1955. **2** a customer who inspects one line of goods after another without buying anything UK, 1979. **3** a type of clutch on a motorcycle US, 1998. **4** a police officer; a police informer. Rhyming slang for COPPER (policeman). Rarely heard, but familiar as GRASS (an informer) UK, 1992. **5** marijuana UK, 2003. **6** in electric line work, an open-link cutout US, 1980

Grasshopper noun used as a humorous form of address to someone being instructed in cod-philosophical truths. From the US television series Kung-Fu, 1972–75 UK, 1994

grass in the park noun an informer. Rhyming slang for NARK, and a development of GRASS (informer) UK, 1961

grass palace noun a house bought with profits from the commercial cultivation of marijuana AUSTRALIA, 2002

grass sandwich noun a child born of a sexual union in the outdoors CANADA, 1999

grass stains noun green discoloration on the fingers of a person who has been handling marijuana US, 2001

grass-widow noun a wife who is temporarily apart from her husband. Originally, mainly Anglo-Indian in use UK, 1846

grass-widower noun a husband who is temporarily apart from his wife US, 1862

grassy ass! thank you. An intentionally butchered gracias US, 1990

grata noun marijuana UK, 1998

Grauniad noun ▶ **the Grauniad** the Guardian newspaper. An anagram, coined in the mid- to late 1970s by satirical magazine Private Eye. Despite the improvement in spell-check technology the nickname remains widely popular UK, 1979

gravalicious adjective greedy, avaricious JAMAICA, 1979

grave noun a work shift at night, usually starting at or after midnight. An abbreviation of GRAVEYARD SHIFT US, 1980

gravedigger noun **1** in the dice game crown and anchor, a spade. Of naval origin UK, 1961. **2** in circus usage, a hyena US, 1981

gravedodger noun an old person UK, 1996

gravel noun **1** an air-delivered mine introduced by the US in Vietnam. Formally known as an XM42 mine dispensing system US, 1980. **2** crack cocaine US, 1994

gravel agitator noun an infantry soldier US, 1898

gravel and grit noun faeces. Rhyming slang for SHIT UK, 2003

gravel cruncher noun a non-flying officer in the US Air Force US, 1929

gravel-crusher *noun* an infantry soldier *US, 1918*

gravel puncher *noun* a solitary miner using antiquated equipment *CANADA, 1951*

gravel rash *noun* scraped skin and cuts resulting from a motorcyle accident *US, 1992*

grave-nudger *noun* from the perspective of youth, an older person *UK: SCOTLAND, 1988*

graveyard *noun* the area of a beach where waves break *US, 1965*

graveyard shift; graveyard tour; graveyard watch *noun* a work schedule that begins very late at night and lasts until the morning shift begins, traditionally from midnight until 8 am *US, 1907*

graveyard spiral *noun* a downward spiral of an aeroplane from which recovery is nearly impossible and as a result of which impact with the ground is inevitable *US, 1988*

gravity check *noun* in footbag, the bag dropping to the ground *US, 1997*

gravy *noun* **1** money, especially money that is easily and/or illegally obtained *US, 1930*. **2** an unexpected benefit *US, 1910*. **3** in poker and other games that are bet on, winnings *US, 1967*. **4** any sexual emission, male or female *UK, 1796*. **5** blood *UK, 1999*. **6** a mixture of blood and drug solution in a syringe. Perhaps from 'gravy' as 'blood' in C19 boxing slang *US, 1966*. **7** sexual innuendo or bawdiness when used to enliven a dull script. A pun on SAUCE (impudence) *UK, 1973*. **8** a prison sentence. Especially in the phrase DISH OUT THE GRAVY (to sentence harshly) *UK, 1950*. **9** pasta sauce. Mid-Atlantic Italian-American usage *US, 1976*. ▶ **clear gravy** an unexpected bonus or profit. An embellishment of the more common GRAVY *US, 1975*

gravy *adjective* **1** all right *US, 2002*. **2** excellent, very good *UK, 2005*

gravy used for expressing approval *UK, 2003*

gravy hauler *noun* a truck driver who will only drive high-paying jobs *US, 1971*

gravy run *noun* on the railways, a short and easy trip *US, 1977*

gravy strokes *noun* during sex, the climactic thrusts prior to male ejaculation. Presumably from GRAVY (any sexual emission: semen) *NEW ZEALAND, 2003*

gravy train *noun* a money-making opportunity, a generous situation *US, 1914*

gray *noun* **1** a white person *US, 1944*. **2** a white betting token usually worth one dollar *US, 1983*. **3** a police officer *US, 1967* ▷ *see also:* GREY

gray *adjective* white, Caucasian. Derogatory *US, 1944* ▷ *see also:* GREY

gray area *noun* in motor racing, the portion of the track immediately above the quickest line around the track *US, 1980*

Graybar hotel; Graybar Motel *noun* a jail or prison *US, 1970*

grayboy *noun* a white male *US, 1951*

gray cat *noun* a white male *US, 1997*

gray eye *noun* a work shift that starts in the middle of the night *US, 1977*

grayspace *noun* the brain *US, 1982*

Graystone College *noun* a jail or prison *US, 1933*

graze *noun* **1** in cricket, time spent fielding in a quiet area of the out field *UK, 1997*. **2** food, a meal *SOUTH AFRICA, 2004*

graze *verb* **1** to pay only superficial attention to any television channel, preferring instead to flick from one programme to another *US, 1998*. **2** (used of an amphetamine user) to search obsessively in a carpet for pieces of amphetamine or meth-amphetamine *US, 1989*

grease *noun* **1** any lubricant used in anal sex *US, 1963*. **2** any hair cream *BAHAMAS, 1982*. **3** nitroglycerin *US, 1949*. **4** in trucking, ice or snow *US, 1976*. **5** food, especially US Army c-rations *US, 1991*. **6** a young, urban tough. An abbreviation of GREASER *US, 1967*. **7** a black person *US, 1971*. **8** in pool, extreme spin imparted on the cue ball to affect the course of the object ball or the cue ball after striking the object ball *US, 1993*. **9** a bribe *UK, 1823*. ▶ **shoot the grease** to make the initial approach in a confidence swindle *US, 1982*

grease *verb* **1** to shoot or kill. Vietnam war usage *US, 1964*. **2** to bribe or otherwise favourably induce others to act as desired *UK, 1528*. **3** to eat *US, 1984*. **4** to use nitroglycerin to break into a safe *US, 1949*. **5** to barely pass a course in school or college *US, 1959*. ▶ **grease heel** to run away quickly *TRINIDAD AND TOBAGO, 1939*. ▶ **grease someone's palm** to persuade by bribery *UK, 1807*. ▶ **grease the skids** to facilitate something, especially by extra legal means *US, 1989*. ▶ **grease the tracks** to be hit by a train *US, 1977*. ▶ **grease the weasel** to have sex (from the male perspective) *US, 2003*. ▶ **grease your chops** to eat *US, 1946*

greaseball *noun* **1** a person of Latin-American or Mediterranean extraction. A derogatory generic derived from a swarthy complexion *US, 1922*. **2** an odious, unappealing, unattractive person. Derives from racist usage *US, 1917*. **3** a railway mechanic *US, 1977*. **4** in circus and carnival usage, a food concession stand *US, 1981*

greaseburger *noun* a despicable person *US, 1991*

greased *adjective* drunk *US, 1928*

grease for peace used as a humorous farewell. A catchphrase television sign-off on the *Sha Na Na* programme (1971–81). Repeated with referential humour *US, 1971*

grease gun *noun* the US Army's M-3 submachine gun. Based on GREASE (to kill) *US, 1944*

grease-hand *noun* a bribe *TRINIDAD AND TOBAGO, 1966*

grease it! in playground basketball, used as a cry to encourage a ball tottering on the rim of the hoop to fall through for a score *US, 1980*

grease man *noun* a criminal with expertise in using explosives to open safes *US, 1970*

grease money *noun* a bribe *TRINIDAD AND TOBAGO, 1987*

grease monkey *noun* **1** a car or aeroplane mechanic *US, 1928*. **2** in oil drilling, a worker who lubricates equipment *US, 1954*

grease orchard *noun* an oil field *US, 1954*

grease out *verb* to enjoy good luck *US, 1990*

grease pit *noun* a low-quality, low-price restaurant *US, 1995*

greaser *noun* **1** a Mexican or any Latin American. Offensive *US, 1836*. **2** a motorcycle gang member. The collective noun is 'grease' *UK, 1971*. **3** a hamburger, especially one from a fast-food restaurant *US, 1982*. **4** a young, poor tough *US, 1964*. **5** a slimey lump or clot of spittle and mucus *UK: SCOTLAND, 1988*. **6** a submachine gun, especially the M-3 or M3A-1 submachine gun *US, 1991*. **7** a Teddy Boy. Greased hair was an important part of 1950s fashion *UK, 1964*

grease up *verb* to lubricate the anus, especially in order to smuggle contraband within the body *US, 1996*

greasies *noun* take-away food, especially fish and chips *NEW ZEALAND, 1979*

greasy *noun* a shearer *AUSTRALIA, 1939*

greasy *adjective* having an insincere and ingratiating manner *UK, 1848*

greasy eyeball *noun* a foul or menacing look *AUSTRALIA, 1996*

greasy luck *adjective* good luck. A whaling expression that persisted after whaling in New England *US, 1963*

greasy spoon *noun* an inexpensive and all-around low-brow restaurant *US, 1912*

great *adjective* very skilled *UK, 1784*

great action! used as an expression of happy approval *US, 1980*

great army *noun* in horse racing, the body of regular bettors *AUSTRALIA, 1989*

Great Australian Adjective *noun* the word 'bloody' used as an intensifier. This had an extremely high frequency amongst many speakers, especially formerly, though now it has lost much ground to FUCKING *AUSTRALIA, 1897*

great balls of fire! used as a mockingly profane expression of surprise. Found in *Gone With The Wind* (1939) but made famous by Jerry Lee Lewis in his 1957 hit song written by Jack Hammer and Otis Blackwell *US, 1951*

great big *adjective* intensifies the merely big *UK, 1857*

great Caesar's ghost! used as a non-profane oath. The non-profane outburst of the *Metropolis Daily Planet* editor, Perry White, in *The Adventures of Superman* (1951–1957). Repeated with referential humour *US, 1954*

great divide *noun* the vulva. From the nickname of the continental divide, where north American rivers flow either east or west. Perhaps best known from its usage in the erotic poem 'The Ballad of Eskimo Nell': 'She dropped her garments one by one / With an air of conscious pride / And as he stood in her womanhood / He saw the Great Divide' *US, 1980*

Greatest *nickname* ▶ **the Greatest** Muhammed Ali (b 1942), heavyweight boxer who defined and dominated the sport from 1960 until the late 1970s *US, 1964*

Great Runes *noun* in computing, text displayed in UPPER CASE ONLY. A legacy of the teletype *US, 1991*

great Scott! used for registering exasperation or surprise; also as an oath *UK, 1885*

great stuff *noun* anything excellent *UK, 1934*

great unwashed *noun* ▶ **the great unwashed 1** the proletariat. Originally derisive and jocular, now somewhat snobbish, but familiarity breeds unthinking colloquialisms *UK, 1937*. **2** hippies. At the time, no doubt, this was seen as a literal description of long-haired counterculturists *UK, 1977*

great white combine *noun* a prairie hailstorm *CANADA, 1987*

great white father *noun* any unpopular authority figure *US, 1963*

great white hope *noun* crack cocaine. Used with 'the' *UK, 2003*

great white light *noun* LSD *US, 1966*

great white way; gay white way *noun* Broadway and the theatre district of New York *US, 1901*

great white whale *noun* cocaine. An exaggeration and romantic allusion based on the colour of cocaine *UK, 2001*

greaze *verb* to eat *US, 1968*

grebo; greebo *noun* a member of a British youth cult that flourished in the mid- to late 1980s; grebos/greeboes are characterised as being intentionally unkempt and categorised as rock and heavy metal music enthusiasts. Adapted from GREASER (a youth subculture), perhaps influenced by 'greb' (an insult) *UK: ENGLAND, 1987*

gred *adjective* unpleasant *UK, 2005*

greedy-guts *noun* a glutton; a person (occasionally, thing) driven by greed or appetite. 'Greedy gut ' is the earlier form *UK, 1550*

greedy pig *noun* used by card sharps of a victim *UK, 1977*

greefa; grifa; griff; griffa; griffo *noun* marijuana. Originally border Spanish used in English conversation by Mexican-Americans *US, 1931*

Greek *noun* **1** unintelligible language *UK, 1600*. **2** anal sex; a practitioner of anal sex *US, 1967*. **3** a male homosexual, especially the active partner in anal sex *US, 1938*. **4** in pinball, a shot up a lane with a scoring device with sufficient force to activiate the scoring device *US, 1977*

Greek *adjective* (of sex) anal *US, 1934*

Greek culture; Greek style; Greek way *noun* anal sex *US, 1967*

Greek lightning *noun* arson financed by the owner of a failing business. In Chicago, Greeks enjoy the reputation of being arsonists. Chicago residents cite a rule of Three Ns – 'never give matches to a Greek, whiskey to an Irishman, or power to a Polack' *US, 1982*

Greek massage *noun* anal sex *AUSTRALIA, 1985*

Greek rodeo *noun* anal sex between men *US, 1968*

Greek's *noun* a small cafe or milkbar. Post-World-War-2 migrants from southern Europe commonly opened such businesses, though they were not, of course, all Greek *AUSTRALIA, 1946*

Greek shift *noun* in card trickery, a method of repositioning a card *US, 2003*

Greek shot *noun* in dice games, a controlled roll with a controlled result *US, 1962*

Greek shuffle *noun* in card trickery, a cut of the deck that leaves the cards in the same order as before the cut *US, 2003*

green *noun* **1** money. From the green colour of paper currency in the US *US, 1898*. **2** in American casinos, a $25 chip *US, 1985*. **3** marijuana, especially with a low resin count *US, 1955*. **4** phencyclidine, the recreational drug known as PCP or angel dust. From the practice of sprinkling the drug on parsley or mint *US, 1981*. **5** the recreational drug ketamine. From the drug's natural green colour *US, 1986*. **6** mucus *UK, 1997*. **7** the felt surface of a pool table *US, 1990*. **8** a stage, especially in the phrase 'see you on the green'. All that remains in current use of theatrical rhyming slang 'green gage' *UK, 1931*. **9** an unbroken wave *US, 1964*. **10** a green capsule containing drugs, especially a central nervous system stimulant. Also variant 'greenie' *US, 1966*. **11** a supporter of environmental politics *UK, 1982*. ▶ **in the green** flying with all instruments recording safe conditions *US, 1963*

green *adjective* ▶ **not as green as you are cabbage-looking** more intelligent than you look. Jocular *UK, 1931*

greena *noun* marijuana *UK, 1998*

green about the gills *adjective* ill, nauseous, sickly-pale *UK, 1949*

green and black *noun* a capsule of Librium, a central nervous system depressant *US, 1992*

green and brussel; greens and brussels *noun* a muscle; muscles. Rhyming slang *UK, 1992*

green and friendly *noun* a prison-issue phone card *UK, 1996*

green-and-white *noun* a green and white police car *US, 1991*

green apple quick-step *noun* diarrhoea *US, 1994*

green around the gills *adjective* giving an appearance of being about to vomit *US, 1985*

greenback *noun* **1** a one-dollar note *US, 1862*. **2** a one-pound note. A green-coloured banknote, first issued in 1917, the colour remained despite diminishing size and value, except for the period 1940–48 when it was blue, until 1988 when it ceased to be legal tender. Sometimes shortened to 'greenie' *UK, 1961*. **3** an Australian one-pound note. Fell out of use after the introduction of decimal currency in 1966 *AUSTRALIA, 1919*. **4** in surfing, a swell that has not broken *US, 1963*. **5** an implement for re-railing a train carriage or engine *US, 1946*

green baggy *noun* the cap worn by Australian test cricketers *AUSTRALIA, 1992*

green bait *noun* a cash bonus paid to US soldiers who re-enlisted during the Vietnam war *US, 1991*

green bean *noun* in South Africa, a township municipal police officer. Derisive; from the colour of the uniform *SOUTH AFRICA, 1987*

green bud; green buds *noun* marijuana. From the colour of the plant *US, 1981*

green burger *noun* a blend of amphetamine and caffeine marketed as MDMA, the recreational drug best known as ecstasy *UK, 1996*

green can *noun* a can of Victoria Bitter™ beer *AUSTRALIA, 2003*

green cart *noun* an imaginary vehicle used to take people to an asylum for the insane *AUSTRALIA, 1935*

green door *noun* the door leading to an execution chamber *US, 1976*

green double dome *noun* ▷ *see:* DOUBLE DOME

green dragon *noun* **1** LSD enhanced with botanical drugs from plants such as Deadly Nightshade or Jimsonweed *US, 1970*. **2** any barbiturate or other central nervous system depressant *US, 1971*. **3** heroin *US, 1990*. **4** the M-113 armoured personnel carrier. The primary armoured tracked personnel carrier used by the US forces in Vietnam *US, 1991*

green drinking voucher *noun* ▷ *see:* DRINKING VOUCHER

green egg *noun* ▷ *see:* EGG

greenery *noun* marijuana. College slang *US, 2001*

green eye *noun* on the railways, a clear signal *US, 1946*

green eyes *noun* jealousy, envy *US, 1950*

green fairy *noun* absinthe, a French gin *UK, 2001*

greenfly *noun* used as a collective noun for Army Intelligence Corps personnel. From the bright green beret they adopted in the mid-1970s *UK, 1984*

green folding; folding green *noun* paper money *UK, 1981*

green frog *noun* a central nervous system despressant *UK, 1998*

greengages; greens *noun* wages. Rhyming slang *UK, 1932*

green game *noun* in a casino, a game with a mininum bet of $25 (the green betting token) *US, 1983*

green goblin *noun* absinthe, a French gin. From private correspondence with a rock group whose management prefer to remain anonymous. Named after the arch-enemy of Spiderman *UK, 2001*

green goddess *noun* **1** marijuana. From the colour of the leaf and the elation it inspires; several ancient religions worshipped a green goddess *US, 1938*. **2** an emergency firefighting vehicle that is made available (for operation by the military) when regular firefighters and their fire engines are out of service. First came into the public vocabulary during the 1977 strike by Fire Brigade officers *UK, 1997*

green gold *noun* cocaine *UK, 1998*

green goods *noun* counterfeit money *US, 1949*

green grolly *noun* a deposit of phlegm. Abbreviates as 'grolly'. Schoolboy and military use *UK, 1989*

greenhorn *noun* a person recently arrived in the city or recently immigrated to a new country *UK, 1753*

green hornet *noun* a capsule combining a central nervous stimulant and a central nervous system depressant *US, 1942*

greenhouse *noun* **1** a small room or enclosed space where marijuana is being smoked *US, 2001*. **2** in surfing, a smooth ride inside the hollow of a wave *US, 1987*. **3** in hot rodding and car customising, the upper part of the car body *US, 1993*

green ice *noun* emeralds *US, 1950*

greenie *noun* **1** any paper money *UK, 1982*. **2** a one-pound note. From the colour of the note *UK, 1980*. **3** an Australian one-pound note. Shortening of GREENBACK *AUSTRALIA, 1968*. **4** a gob of thick nasal mucus and catarrhal matter. From the colour *UK, 2000*. **5** a speeding ticket *US, 1976*. **6** a conservationist. From 'green ban' (a ban imposed for environmental reasons) *AUSTRALIA, 1973*. **7** an ocean wave, especially a large breaking wave suitable for surfing *AUSTRALIA, 1964*

greenie in a bottle *noun* a bottle of beer *AUSTRALIA, 1991*

green ink *noun* time spent in aerial combat *US, 1991*

green-ink brigade *noun* collectively, people who write cranky or abusive (often illegible) letters. Derives from the notion that only a person who disdains conventional standards could possibly be ill mannered enough to write in green ink – or, sometimes, green crayon *UK, 2001*

green light *noun* in prison, permission to kill *US, 2000*

green-light *verb* to give approval. In traffic signalling, the green light means 'go' *UK, 2001*

green-light *adjective* approved. After the verb sense *UK, 2001*

green machine *noun* **1** the US Army. Vietnam war usage *US, 1969*. **2** a computer built to military specifications for field use *US, 1991*

green man *noun* **1** marijuana. To 'see the green man' is to smoke or buy marijuana *US, 1997*. **2** a bottle of Ballantine™ ale *US, 1965*

green meanie *noun* any green amphetamine or barbiturate capsule *US, 1981*

green micro *noun* a type of LSD *UK, 1996*

Green Onion *noun* a Montreal parking violation officer *CANADA, 1999*

greenout *noun* the joy felt on seeing and smelling plants after an extended stay on Antarctica *ANTARCTICA, 2003*

green paint *noun* marijuana *UK, 2003*

green paper *noun* money *US, 1979*

green pastures *noun* high earnings for railwaymen; bonus payments; overtime *UK, 1970*

greenpea *noun* a novice *US, 1912*

green penguin *noun* a variety of LSD *UK, 1996*

green queen *noun* a male homosexual who takes pleasure in outdoor sex in public parks *US, 1981*

green room *noun* **1** in surfing, a smooth ride inside the hollow of a wave *US, 1987*. **2** an execution chamber *US, 1981*

greens *noun* **1** currency notes. The colour of money *US, 1904*. **2** marijuana. From the colour and after GREEN (marijuana), possibly informed by the vegetable sense and the UK expression of maternal care 'eat your greens, they're good for you', *1998*. **3** green vegetables, especially cabbage and salad *UK, 1725*. **4** loose green clothing worn by hospital employees, especially in operating theatres *US, 1988*. **5** the green US Army dress uniform *US, 1968*. **6** sexual activity *UK, 1888* ▷*see:* GREENGAGES

greens and beans *noun* basic groceries *US, 1994*

greenseed *noun* a US soldier freshly arrived in Vietnam *US, 1988*

greens fee *noun* the amount charged by a pool room to play pool. Punning on a conventional term found in golf, alluding to GREEN (the surface of a pool table) *US, 1990*

green shield stamps *noun* money. A variation on GREENSTAMPS; Green Shield Stamps were a sales promotional scheme popular in the 1960s and 70s *UK, 1981*

green single dome *noun* ▷*see:* DOUBLE DOME

green slime *noun* green peppers. Limited usage, but clever *US, 1996*

green snow; green tea *noun* phencyclidine, the recreational drug known as PCP or angel dust. The colour reference is to the parsley or mint on which the drug is often sprinkled *US, 1978*

greenstamp *noun* a traffic ticket for speeding *US, 1975*

greenstamps *noun* in trucking, money *US, 1956*

green stuff *noun* currency notes *US, 1887*

green teen *noun* an environmentally conscious young person *US, 1995*

green thumb *noun* in pool, the ability to make money playing for wagers *US, 1990*

green-to-green *adjective* running smoothly, without problem. Nautical origins – ships following the rules of navigation *US, 1975*

green triangle *noun* a variety of MDMA, the recreational drug best known ecstasy. From the colour of the tablet and the embossed motif *UK, 2002*

green 'un *noun* a one-pound note *UK, 1982*

greenwash *noun* a pretended concern for ecological matters. A play on 'whitewash' (a covering-up of faults), possibly also on EYE-WASH (something that is intended to conceal; nonsense) *UK, 2003*

green wedge *noun* LSD *US, 1975*

green womb *noun* the inside of a hollow breaking wave *US, 1991*

green worms *noun* the undulating green lines on a radar screen *US, 1947*

green yoke *noun* a young inexperienced horse *UK, 1969*

greet *verb* ▶ **greet the judge** in horse racing, to win a race *AUSTRALIA, 1989*

greeter; greta *noun* marijuana *US, 1952*

Gregory Peck; gregory *noun* **1** a cheque. Rhyming slang formed on the name of film actor Gregory Peck, 1916–2003 *AUSTRALIA, 1983*. **2** the neck. Also known in the UK, especially after use in mid-1970s BBC television's *Porridge AUSTRALIA, 1966*

Gregory Pecks; gregories *noun* spectacles. Rhyming slang for SPECS, formed from the name of film actor Gregory Peck, 1916–2003 *UK: SCOTLAND, 1985*

grem *noun* an unskilled skateboarder; generally, anyone who is maladroit at anything. Teen slang; probably a shortening of GREMMIE *UK, 1978*

gremlin *noun* **1** a mysterious spirit that haunts aircraft, deluding pilots; hence, any mechanical fault. Originally Royal Ait Force slang *UK, 1929*. **2** an inexperienced surfer who does not respect surfer etiquette *US, 1961*

gremmie *noun* **1** an unpopular, unfashionable person *US, 1962*. **2** an unskilled surfing or skateboarding novice *AUSTRALIA, 1962*.

3 marijuana and crack cocaine mixed for smoking in a cigarette US, 1989

grette noun a cigarette US, 1966

Greville Starkey noun a black person. Rhyming slang for DARKY, formed from the name of the English jockey and Derby winner (b.1939). Noted as predating synonymous FEARGAL SHARKEY UK, 1998

grey noun in a mixed race couple, the other partner BERMUDA, 1985

grey adjective a middle-aged, conventionally minded, conservatively dressed person in the eyes and vocabulary of the counterculture UK, 1967

grey death noun insipid prison stew AUSTRALIA, 1967

greyer noun someone dull who perpetuates dullness UK, 1999

grey ghost noun a parking inspector in Victoria, New South Wales and Western Australian. From the colour of their uniform AUSTRALIA, 1967

grey goose noun a grey California Department of Corrections bus used for transporting prisoners. An allusion to the Greyhound bus line US, 1974

greyhound noun a very short skirt. A pun on (pubic) hair/hare UK, 2002

Greyhound noun an M-8 armoured car. World War 2 vintage, used at the beginning of the Vietnam war by the Army of the Republic of Vietnam US, 1990

greyhound verb (used of a black person) to pursue a white person in the hopes of a romantic or sexual relationship. From GREY MAN (a white person) US, 1972

greylist verb to hold a person under consideration for blacklisting CANADA, 2002

grey man noun **1** a white man. Black slang UK, 1984. **2** a dull, boring undergraduate. Oxford and Cambridge students' term UK, 1960

grey mare noun a bus or train fare. Rhyming slang UK, 1992

grey matter noun brains, thus intelligence US, 1899

grey shield noun LSD UK, 2003

greys on trays noun adult snowboarders US, 1997

grice verb to practise trainspotting. Trainspotters' slang UK, 1982

grice; gricer noun a locomotive (train) spotter. Trainspotters' slang UK, 1982

grick noun a Greek immigrant or Greek-American US, 1997

grid noun **1** the face UK, 2001. **2** the female breast US, 1993. **3** a bicycle AUSTRALIA, 1927

G-ride noun **1** a stolen car US, 1985. **2** a rebuilt, customised vintage car with a suspension system that allows the body to be lifted and lowered US, 1997

gridley grinder noun on Prince Edward Island, a bad storm CANADA, 1988

grief noun trouble, problems. Originally in the phrase COME TO GRIEF (to get into trouble, to fail) US, 1897. ▶ **give someone grief** to tease or criticise someone US, 1968

grief verb to trouble someone UK, 2003

griefer noun an Internet game player who tries to spoil the fun of other players by harassing them. Someone who creates GRIEF (trouble) UK, 2003

griever noun a union spokesman on a contract grievance committee US, 1946

grievous bodily harm noun the recreational drug GHB. Extended from the punning GBH US, 1993

g-riffick noun the recreational drug GHB. A combination of the 'g' of GHB and 'terrific' US, 1997

grifter noun **1** a person who makes their living by confidence swindles, especially short cons. Widely familiar from Jim Thompson's 1963 novel The Grifters and its 1990 film adaptation US, 1915. **2** in horse racing, a bettor who makes small, conservative bets US, 1951

grig verb to annoy, to tease. From the Irish griog IRELAND, 2000

grill noun **1** a person of Mediterranean background. Post-World-War-2 migrants from southern Europe commonly opened businesses selling fried or grilled food AUSTRALIA, 1957. **2** a motor accident in which an occupant or occupants of the car are burnt US, 1962. **3** the bars or mesh of a prison cell US, 1992

grille noun the teeth US, 2001

griller noun a verbal assault, a roasting, especially when given by the authorities AUSTRALIA, 1975. ▶ **to put on the griller** to assault verbally. Mostly in the passive voice AUSTRALIA, 1975

grime noun a modern music genre focused on lyrical and aural interpretation of an inner-city environment and street-culture, that combines the musical influences of hip-hop and UK garage with the practical low-budget, do-it-yourself spirit of punk rock and reggae sound-systems. So-named, apparently, to acknowledge the music's origins in the grimey urban sprawl UK, 2004

grimey adjective excellent, best UK, 2005

grimmy noun **1** a middle-aged woman UK, 1972. **2** marijuana UK, 2003

Grimsby Docks noun socks. Rhyming slang, formed from a location on the northeast coast of England UK, 1988

grimy adjective **1** rude; uncouth US, 2002. **2** excellent UK, 2004

grin noun **1** a good and amusing situation US, 1966. **2** used as Internet shorthand to mean 'your message amused me' US, 1997

grinch noun a bad-tempered person whose negative attitude depresses others. Adopted from the characteristics of the Grinch, a mean-spirited character created by Dr Seuss (Theodor Seuss Geisel) in the novel How The Grinch Stole Christmas, 1957, and subsequently played by Jim Carrey in the 2000 film version US, 2003

grinchy adjective unpleasant, distasteful, bad. High school usage US, 1961

grind noun **1** sexual intercourse; an act of sexual intercourse UK, 1870. **2** in a striptease or other sexual dance, a rotating movement of the hips, pelvis, and genitals US, 1931. **3** hard, dull, routine, monotous work; work in general. Originally with special emphasis on academic work; now more general and often appearing as 'the grind' or 'the daily grind' UK, 1851. **4** a serious, dedicated, diligent student US, 1889. **5** in the used car business, a concerted assault of negotiation with a potential customer US, 1997. **6** a style of hard rock appealing to the truly disaffected, featuring a fast, grinding tempo, bleak lyrics and relentlessly loud and distorted guitars. Also known as 'grindcore' US, 1994

grind verb **1** to have sex UK, 1647. **2** in a striptease or other sexual dance, to rotate the hips, pelvis, and genitals in a sensual manner US, 1928. **3** to study hard US, 1955. **4** in computing, to format code so that it looks attractive US, 1983. **5** to eat. Hawaiian youth usage US, 1981. **6** to call out and invite patrons to enter a performance US, 1968. ▶ **grind someone's ass** to annoy US, 1996

grindage noun food US, 1990

grinder noun **1** a sexual partner US, 1966. **2** a striptease artist US, 1950. **3** a person who calls out and invites patrons to enter a performance US, 1968. **4** a pornographic film with poor production values and little plot or dialogue, just poorly filmed sex US, 1995. **5** the drill field in an armed forces training camp US, 1963. **6** in competition sailing, a person who in tandem operates a winch-like device to raise a large sail very quickly US, 1996

grinders noun the teeth UK, 1676

grind film noun a pornographic film, usually with crude production values and no plot or character development US, 1977

grind house noun a theatre exhibiting continuous shows or films of a sexual or violent nature US, 1929

grinding adjective (used of surf conditions) powerful, breaking consistently US, 1987

grind joint noun a casino dominated by slot machines and low-limit tables US, 1991

grind man noun a person who calls out and invites patrons to enter a performance US, 1968

grinds noun ▶ **get your grinds** to have sex US, 1966

grinds; grines noun food US, 1981

grind show *noun* a carnival attraction that relies on a relentless patter to attract customers inside *US, 1927*

grind store *noun* an illegal gambling operation where players are cheated as a matter of course *US, 1985*

grine *noun* sexual intercourse; an act of sexual intercourse. A variation of GRIND *JAMAICA, 1970*

grine *verb* to have sex. A variation of GRIND *JAMAICA, 1971*

gringo *noun* among Latinos in the US, a white person. The source of considerable false etymology based on the marching song 'Green grow the rushes, o'. Often used with a lack of affection *US, 1849*

gringo gallop *noun* diarrhoea suffered by tourists in Mexico or Latin America *US, 1960*

grinner *noun* a rock which just shows above the ground *CANADA, 1987*

grins and shakes *noun* a tour of a military facility or a visit to the troops *US, 1991*

grip *noun* **1** a small suitcase. A shortened form of 'gripsack' *US, 1879*. **2** money *US, 1993*. **3** a large amount *US, 1997*. **4** a photograph *ANTARCTICA, 2003*. ▶ **get a grip** to get control of your emotions and actions *US, 1971*

grip *verb* **1** to arrest *UK, 2000*. **2** to flatter and curry favour with those in power *US, 1981*. **3** to masturbate *US, 1971*. ▶ **grip your shit** to satisfy your requirements *UK, 1995*

gripe *noun* a complaint *US, 1918*

gripe *verb* to moan, to complain *US, 1928*

gripester *noun* in prison, a chronic complainer *US, 1962*

griping *noun* complaints; the act of complaining *US, 1945*

grip off *verb* to annoy. Used among bird-watchers, usually as 'gripped off' *UK, 1977*

grippers *noun* men's underpants *US, 1985*

grips *noun* **1** a porter on a passenger train *US, 1977*. **2** running shoes *US, 1991*. ▶ **come to grips** to get control of your emotions and actions *UK, 1988*

gripy *adjective* miserable *US, 1946*

gristle *noun* the penis. A relatively obscure term, but well understood when adopted as a confrontational name by 1980s thrash metal pioneers Throbbing Gristle *UK, 1665*

grit *noun* **1** spirit, stamina, courage, especially if enduring *US, 1825*. **2** a member of the Canadian Liberal Party *CANADA, 1995*. **3** a narrow-minded if not reactionary person *US, 1972*. **4** a stereotypical rural, southern white *US, 1972*. **5** food *US, 1959*. **6** crack cocaine. Another rock metaphor, based on the drug's appearance *US, 1994*. **7** a cigarette *US, 1990*

grit *verb* to eat *US, 1968*

gritch *verb* a complaint *US, 1983*

grizzle *verb* to sleep *US, 1997*

grizzle-guts; grizzly-guts *noun* a tearful, whining person. From the verb 'to grizzle' *UK, 1937*

groan *noun* a standup bass fiddle *US, 1945*

groaner *noun* a foghorn with a prolonged monotone *US, 1997*

groats *noun* the epitome of unpleasant *US, 1979*

groceries *noun* **1** the genitals, breasts and/or buttocks, especially as money-earning features *US, 1965*. **2** crack cocaine. A sad euphemism *US, 1994*. **3** in horse racing, horse feed *US, 1951*

grocer's shop *noun* an Italian. Rhyming slang for WOP *UK, 1979*

grocery boy *noun* a heroin addict who is craving food *US, 1973*

grocery French *noun* a barely passable command of the Quebec French language *CANADA, 1980*

grocery getter *noun* a car for everyday use *US, 1993*

grock *noun* a fool. Probably after Adrien Wettach, 1888–1959, the Swiss clown named Grock, who was inducted in the Clown Hall of Fame in 1992 *UK, 2002*

G-rock *noun* cocaine; a one gram rock of crack cocaine *UK, 1998*

grockle *noun* **1** a tourist. Disparaging; sometimes shortened to 'grock'. Grock was the professional clown-name of Charles Adrien Wettach (1880–1959), hence 'grockle' is probably intended to represent a tourist as a clown; however not abbreviated until the 1990s *UK, 1964*. **2** a social inferior. Disparaging, upper-class usage; acquired from the sense as 'tourist' *UK, 1982*

grockly *adjective* common, inferior. Used by upper-class youths, from GROCKLE (a social inferior) *UK, 1982*

grody *noun* a dirty, homeless hospital patient infested with lice *US, 1985*

grody; groady; groaty *adjective* messy, unkempt, disgusting *US, 1963*

grody to the max *adjective* extremely disgusting *US, 1982*

groendakkies *noun* a mental hospital. From Afrikaans for 'green roofs' *SOUTH AFRICA, 1978*

grog *noun* **1** an alcoholic drink, especially beer *US, 1805*. **2** a clot of spittle. Glasgow slang *UK: SCOTLAND, 1985*. ▶ **on the grog** drinking steadily; taking part in a drinking session; binge drinking *AUSTRALIA, 1946*

grog *verb* **1** to drink alcohol *US, 1824*. **2** to spit. Glasgow slang *UK: SCOTLAND, 1985*

grogan *noun* a piece of excrement; a turd *AUSTRALIA, 1980*

grog artist *noun* a heavy drinker *AUSTRALIA, 1965*

grog boss *noun* a person serving alcohol at a work party *CANADA, 1964*

grog-doped *adjective* intoxicated by kava, a herbal beverage made from the root of the tropical shrub *piper methysticum FIJI, 1992*

groggery *noun* a disreputable bar *US, 1822*

grogging *noun* drinking alcohol; boozing *AUSTRALIA, 1962*

grogging-on *noun* drinking heartily, or to excess *AUSTRALIA, 1979*

groggy *noun* a person who drinks to excess *FIJI, 1994*

groggy *adjective* weak, unsteady, faint. From conventional 'groggy' (drunk) *UK, 1828*

grog-on *noun* a drinking session or party *AUSTRALIA, 1971*

grog on *verb* to take part in a drinking session; to drink steadily and heavily *AUSTRALIA, 1951*

grog session *noun* an extended kava drinking session. Kava is a tranquillity-inducing beverage made from the root of a tropical shrub *FIJI, 1991*

grog shanty *noun* a roughly constructed building selling alcohol *AUSTRALIA, 1895*

grog shop *noun* **1** an off-licence (liquor store) *AUSTRALIA, 1799*. **2** a cheap tavern *UK, 1790*

grog swiper *noun* an intemperate kava drinker. Kava, made from the root of a tropical shurb, induces tranquillity *FIJI, 1996*

grog-up *noun* a drinking session or party *AUSTRALIA, 1959*

grog up *verb* to drink heavily and steadily *AUSTRALIA, 1955*

groid *noun* a black person. A shortened 'negroid' *US, 1972*

groin; groyne; growne *noun* a ring *UK, 1931*

groinage *noun* jewellery. From GROIN (a ring) *UK, 2002*

groinplant *noun* in mountain biking, an unintended and painful contact between the bicycle and your groin *US, 1992*

groin-throb *noun* someone, of either sex, who is the object of sexual lust. A play on the more romantic 'heart-throb' *1996*

grok *verb* to understand, to appreciate. Coined by Robert Heinlein (1907–88) for the science-fiction novel *Stranger in a Strange Land*, 1961; adopted into semi-mystical use by the counterculture *US, 1970*

grolly *noun* an unpleasant thing. Ascribes the attributes of a GREEN GROLLY, often abbreviated as 'grolly' (a lump of phlegm) to any given object *UK, 1987*

grom *noun* a beginner surfer. An abbreviation of GROMMET *US, 1990*

grommet *noun* **1** a novice surfer, especially one with a cheeky attitude *AUSTRALIA, 1981*. **2** by extension, a zealous novice in other sports. Recorded in use by skateboarders and scooter-riders *US, 1995*. **3** a kid *AUSTRALIA, 1995*. **4** the anus *UK, 1889*

gromp *verb* in tiddlywinks, to move a pile of winks as a whole onto another wink or pile of winks *US, 1977*

gronk *noun* an unattractive woman *UK, 1987*

gronk *verb* in computing, to shut down and restart a computer whose operation has been suspended. A term popularised by Johnny Hart in his *B.C.* newspaper comic strip *US, 1981*

groom *verb* to attract children into sexual activity. A euphemism that hides a sinister practice *UK, 1996*

groove *noun* **1** the prevailing mood *UK, 1998*. **2** a routine; the regular way of doing something *UK, 1984*. **3** a profound pleasure, a true joy *US, 1946*. **4** (of music) an aesthetic pleasure in tune with the zeitgeist *US, 1996*. **5** a rhythm *UK, 1947*. **6** the act of dancing *UK, 1998*. ▶ **in the groove** totally involved, at that moment, with making or enjoying music. Originally used in jazz but has been applied to most subequent modern music forms *US, 1932*

groove *verb* **1** to enjoy *US, 1950*. **2** to please, to make happy *US, 1952*. **3** to make good progress, to co-operate *UK, 1967*. **4** to have sex *US, 1960*. **5** to be relaxed and happy *US, 1970*

groover *noun* a drug user who enjoys psychedelic accessories to his drug experience *US, 1971*

groovily *adverb* pleasantly *UK, 2002*

groovy *adjective* **1** very good, pleasing. The word enjoyed two periods of great popularity, first in the early 1940s and then in the mid-to-late 1960s, where it caught on both in the mainstream and in hip circles. Since then, it has become a signature word for mocking the attitudes and fashions of the 1960s *US, 1937*. **2** sexually attractive. A nuance of the sense as 'pleasing' *UK, 1967*. **3** profoundly out-of-style *US, 1983*. **4** used to describe the effects of amphetamine. Drug-users' (no-one else could be so subjective) slang *US, 1978*

grope *noun* an act of sexual fondling, especially when such fondling is the entire compass of the sexual contact *US, 1946*. ▶ **come the grope** to feel up sexually *AUSTRALIA, 1971*. ▶ **go the grope** to feel up sexually *AUSTRALIA, 1962*

grope *verb* to grab or caress someone's genitals, usually in an impersonal manner *UK, 1380*

Groper *nickname* a non-Aboriginal native or resident of Western Australia, especially a descendant of an early settler. A shortening of SANDGROPER *AUSTRALIA, 1899*

Groperland *noun* the state of Western Australia *AUSTRALIA, 1900*

gross *adjective* disgusting *US, 1959*

gross-out *noun* a disgusting thing *US, 1968*

gross out *verb* to disgust, to shock. From GROSS (disgusting) *US, 1965*

Grosvenor Squares *noun* flared trousers, flares. Rhyming slang *UK, 1992*

grot *noun* **1** dirt, filth. By back-formation from GROTTY *UK, 1971*. **2** a filthy person *AUSTRALIA, 1985*. **3** a toilet *NEW ZEALAND, 1981*

grotbag; grot-bag; grot *noun* an unpleasantly dirty person. A combination of GROT (dirt), with the suffix -BAG (personifies an unpleasant quality). Glasgow use *UK: SCOTLAND, 1988*

grot-hole *noun* in caving and pot-holing, a small cave that leads nowhere and is difficult to manoeuvre in *UK, 2004*

grots *noun* in caving and pot-holing, any (well used) clothing *UK, 2004*

grotty; grot; grotbags *adjective* unattractive, inferior *UK, 1964*

grouch *noun* an ill-tempered person *US, 1900*

grouch bag *noun* literally, a small bag hidden on the person with emergency funds in it; figuratively, a wallet or a person's supply of money *US, 1908*

Groucho Marx; groucho *noun* an electrician. Rhyming slang for SPARKS, formed from the name of the American comedian, 1890–1977 *UK, 1992*

ground *noun* an area of operation or influence. In police use *UK, 2002*. ▶ **back on the ground; on the ground** freed from prison *US, 1982*. ▶ **on the ground** in horse racing, said of a jockey serving a suspension *US, 1976*

ground *verb* to punish a child by refusing to let them leave the house for any social events *US, 1950*

ground apple *noun* a brick *US, 1945*

ground clouds *noun* fog *US, 1976*

ground control *noun* a person who guides another through an LSD experience. Another LSD-as-travel metaphor *US, 1967*

grounder *noun* a crime that does not demand much effort by the police to solve *US, 1984*

ground floor *noun* ▶ **in on the ground floor** in at the early stages of a project, trend, technical development, etc. Generally phrased 'get in on', 'let in on' and 'be in on' *US, 1864*

ground gripper *nickname* a Hawker Siddeley 'Trident' aircraft. Introduced into service in 1964 *US, 1994*

groundhog *noun* **1** in the language of parachuting, anyone who has not parachuted *US, 1978*. **2** a railway brakeman *US, 1926*

ground joker *noun* any non-flying personnel in the Air Force *US, 1946*

groundlark *noun* a bookmaker who illegally conducts business at a horse race track *AUSTRALIA, 1989*

groundman *noun* in a group of friends taking LSD or another hallucinogen, a person who does not take the drug and helps those who do navigate their experience *UK, 1983*

ground-pounder *noun* a member of the infantry. Coined in World War 2, and used in every war since *US, 1942*

groundscore *verb* to find something of value, real or perceived, on the ground *US, 1997*

ground-sluice *verb* to shoot at a bird on the ground *CANADA, 1999*

groundsman *noun* an assistant to a bookmaker who collects bets and pays off winners *AUSTRALIA, 1989*

ground-trog *verb* in caving and pot-holing, to search the surface for cave entrances *US, 2004*

ground week *noun* the first week of US Army airborne parachute training *US, 1991*

ground zero *noun* **1** the centre of action. From the lingo of atomic weapons, literally meaning 'the ground where a bomb explodes' *US, 1966*. **2** a back-to-basics condition from which a recommence-ment or restructuring may be developed. Figurative, from sense as a 'centre of targeted destruction' *UK, 2001*. **3** an untidy bedroom. Teen slang *US, 2002*

group grope *noun* **1** group therapy *US, 1977*. **2** sex involving more than two people *US, 1967*

groupie; groupy *noun* **1** a girl who trades her sexual availability to rock groups and musicians in exchange for hanger-on status *US, 1966*. **2** a follower or hobbyist devoted to a pre-eminent person within a given field, or to a genre or subject type. An extension of the previous sense, this usage is not restricted to rock groups or music, nor is there a suggestion that sex is a prerequisite; the tone may be derogatory, jocular or ironic *US, 1967*

Group of One; G1 *noun* the United States *CANADA, 2002*

grouse *noun* **1** a grumble; a cause for complaint *UK, 1917*. **2** a good thing; something of the best quality *AUSTRALIA, 1924*

grouse *verb* to grumble *UK, 1885*

grouse *adjective* great; excellent; top quality. Origin unknown. Commonly intensified as 'extra grouse' *AUSTRALIA, 1924*

grouser *noun* a complainer. From the verb GROUSE *UK, 1885*

grouter *noun* ▶ **come in on the grouter** to gain a fortuitous and unfair advantage, especially by appearing at an opportune time. The origin of this term is unknown, although one might conjecture that since grouting is the last task in a tiling job, to come in on the grouter would be to arrive when there is no work left to be done *AUSTRALIA, 1902*

grovel *verb* **1** in computing, to work with great diligence but without visible success *US, 1981*. **2** to ride a wave even as it runs out of force *US, 1990*

Grover *noun* a one-thousand dollar note; one thousand dollars. From the portrait of US President Grover Cleveland on the notes, first issued in 1928 *US, 1984*

grow *verb* ▶ **grow your own** to promote an enlisted man to a non-commissioned officer vacancy in a unit; to promote from within *US, 1990*

growed-up truck *noun* an eighteen-wheeled over-the-road truck *US, 1976*

growl *verb* ▶ **growl at the badger** to engage in oral sex on a woman, especially noisily *UK, 1998*

growl and grunt; growl *noun* the vulva and vagina. Rhyming slang for CUNT *AUSTRALIA, 1941*

growler *noun* **1** a bowel movement *US, 1993*. **2** a fart *UK, 2003*. **3** in the language of barbershop quartets, a strident bass singer *US, 1975*. **4** the lowest gear in a truck *US, 1971*. **5** a largely submerged iceberg *ANTARCTICA, 1912*. **6** the vagina *AUSTRALIA, 1988*. **7** a prison cell used for solitary confinement *US, 1984*. **8** beer, the dregs of a cask *IRELAND, 1999*. **9** a wrestler *US, 1945*. **10** a hotel's activity log *US, 1953*. **11** a beer can *US, 1949*

grub *noun* **1** food; provisions of food *UK, 1659*. **2** bullets. From the previous sense *UK, 2001*. **3** an inferior, lowly person *UK, 1845*

grub *verb* **1** to kiss with passion *US, 1963*. **2** to engage in sexual foreplay *US, 1976*

grubber *noun* **1** a disgusting person *US, 1941*. **2** in cricket, a ball bowled underarm. Also variant 'grub' *UK, 1837*

grubbies *noun* old, worn, comfortable clothes *US, 1966*

grubby *noun* a young male summer resident of a camp on a Canadian lake *CANADA, 1997*

grubby *adjective* not neat, not clean *US, 1965*

grubs *noun* old, worn and comfortable clothes *US, 1966*

grudge-fuck *verb* to have sex out of spite or anger *US, 1990*

gruesome and gory *noun* the penis. Rhyming slang for COREY *UK, 1992*

gruesome twosome *noun* a couple who date steadily *US, 1941*

Grumann Greyhound *noun* the C-2A aircraft. Manufactured by Grumann, a twin engine, prop-driven plane used by the US Navy to transport troops (hence the 'Greyhound' as an allusion to the bus company) or cargo *US, 1991*

grumble and grunt; grumble *noun* the vagina; hence women objectified sexually. Rhyming slang for CUNT *UK, 1938*

grumble and mutter *noun* a bet. Rhyming slang for FLUTTER *UK, 1992*

grume *noun* a filthy, decrepit patient in a hospital casualty department *US, 1978*

grummet *noun* a woman, or women, objectified sexually. From earlier senses, now lost, as 'the vagina' and 'sexual intercourse' *UK, 1960*

grump *noun* an ill-tempered person *UK, 1900*

grumpus-back *noun* a gruff, churlish person *BARBADOS, 1965*

grundies; grunds *noun* underpants. Short for REG GRUNDIES *AUSTRALIA, 1984*

grundy *adjective* mediocre *US, 1959*

grunge *noun* **1** unpleasant dirt or filth *US, 1965*. **2** a rock music genre. From the previous sense, abstractly applied to the 'dirty' guitar sound; it is occasionally recorded from the mid-1960s but until Nirvana and other Seattle-based US groups came to prominence in the early 90s 'grunge' was not a genre *US, 1972*. **3** a style of loose-fitting, layered clothes favoured by fans of the grunge music scene *US, 1998*. **4** an obnoxious, graceless person *US, 1968*

grungejumper *noun* used as a euphemism for 'motherfucker' *US, 1958*

grungie *noun* **1** a filthy or disgusting person *UK, 2000*. **2** a post-hippie youth in rebellion. Also spelt 'grungy' *US, 1982*

grungy *adjective* filthy, dirty, unpleasant, untidy. Of GRUNGE (an unpleasant substance); however contemporary use also refers to the deliberately messy fashion associated with GRUNGE music *US, 1965*

grunt *noun* **1** a member of the US Marine Corps *US, 1968*. **2** An infantry soldier, especially but not necessarily a marine. An important piece of slang in the Vietnam war *US, 1962*. **3** a menial, unskilled worker *US, 1970*. **4** an electrician or electrical lineman's assistant. Some power companies in the US have tried to prohibit use of the term to describe the helper position; in general, linemen have perceived this attempt as political correctness carried to an absurd extreme and have continued calling their helpers 'grunts' *US, 1926*. **5** a railway engineer *US, 1939*. **6** in mountain biking, a steep and challenging incline *US, 1996*. **7** power *NEW ZEALAND, 1998*. **8** marijuana *US, 1993* ▷*see:* GASP AND GRUNT

grunt *verb* to eat *US, 1968*

grunt-and-squeal jockey *noun* a truck driver who hauls cattle or pigs *US, 1971*

grunter *noun* **1** a bed *NEW ZEALAND, 1984*. **2** a foghorn with two tones *US, 1997*

grunts *noun* food *US, 1968*

grunt-tight *adjective* (used of a bolt) tightened by feel rather than by measured torque *US, 1992*

grush *noun* a mad scramble of boys to get a coin or some similar gift thrown at them; a present given to people outside a church after a wedding *IRELAND, 1976*

gruts *noun* underpants *NEW ZEALAND, 1998*

gry; gryer *noun* a horse. Romany *UK, 1978*

GS *noun* a shared act of urine fetishism; the act of urination by one person on another for sexual gratification. Used in personal advertising; an abbreviation of GOLDEN SHOWER *US, 1979*

GSD *noun* an Alsatian. Initialism of *German Shepherd Dog*, the original breed name, which was changed by the UK Kennel Club after World War 1 for reasons of political sensitivity *UK, 2002*

G shot *noun* an injection of a small amount of a drug while in search of a larger amount *US, 1992*

G-star *noun* a youth gang member *US, 1995*

G-string *noun* **1** a small patch of cloth passed between a woman's legs and supported by a waist cord, providing a snatch of modesty for a dancer. A slight variation on the word 'gee-string' used in the late C19 to describe the loin cloth worn by various indigenous peoples *US, 1936*. **2** a BMW Series 3 car. Scamto youth street slang (South African townships) *SOUTH AFRICA, 2005*

GTA *noun* the criminal charge of grand theft, auto. The punch-line of an oft-repeated joke: 'What do you call four [ethnic minority of choice at the moment] in a brand new Cadillac?' *US, 1993*

GTG used as shorthand in Internet discussion groups and text messages to mean '*got to go*' *US, 2002*

G thing *noun* a subject matter best understood by young urban gangsters *US, 1994*

G-top *noun* a tent or trailer in a carnival reserved exclusively for carnival employees. Employees can drink and gamble out of sight of the public and police *US, 1980*

Guardianista *noun* a liberal, politically-correct person. Intended as derogatory; from the stereotype that such a person is a reader of the *Guardian* newspaper and combined with left-wing Nicaraguan revolutionaries the Sandinistas *UK, 2003*

Guat *noun* a *Guat*emalan *UK, 1995*

Guatemala dirt dobbers *noun* sandals *US, 1970*

guava *noun* **1** an upwardly mobile young adult. An acronym for '*grown up and very ambitious*' or '*growing up and very ambitious*' *SOUTH AFRICA, 1989*. **2** the buttocks, the backside. Especially in the phrase 'on your guava' *SOUTH AFRICA, 1975*

guava *adjective* very good, superlative *US, 1991*

guava days; gauva season; guava times *noun* difficult times *TRINIDAD AND TOBAGO, 1979*

gub *verb* to hit in the mouth; to defeat. From 'gub' (the mouth) *UK: SCOTLAND, 1985*

gubbins *noun* used as a replacement for any singular or plural noun that the user cannot or does not wish to specify *UK, 1944*

gubbish *noun* in computing, nonsense. A blend of 'garbage' and 'rubbish' *US, 1983*

Gucci *adjective* stylish, especially cleverly so. From the high-profile fashion brand *UK, 1995*

gucky *noun* Gucci, a fashion-design label. Upper-class society usage; a deliberate and jocular mispronunciation of a favourite brand *UK, 1982*

gucky *adjective* sickening. Upper-class society use *UK, 1982*

gudentight; goot-n-tight *adjective* tight, especially in a sexual context. A mock German or Dutch construction *US, 1969*

guernsey *noun* ▶ **get a guernsey** to be selected for something, such as a team, job, award or the like. Originally 'to be picked for a football team', from 'guernsey' as 'a top worn by football players' *AUSTRALIA, 1918*. ▶ **give someone a guernsey** to select someone *AUSTRALIA, 1962*

guess *noun* ▶ **by guess and by God** a casual form of nautical navigation *US, 1986*. ▶ **miss your guess** to be mistaken *US, 1921*. ▶ **your guess is as good as mine** a catchphrase used to describe a situation where neither party knows the facts *CANADA, 1939*

guessing stick *noun* a slide rule *US, 1941*

guessing tubes *noun* a stethoscope. Medical slang *UK, 2002*

guesstimate; guestimate *noun* a rough calculation. Part 'guess', part 'estimate' *US, 1934*

guest *noun* a prisoner. Used in combinations such as 'guest of the city', 'guest of the governor or guest of the nation' *US, 1982*

guest star *noun* a last-minute replacement to take the place of someone who has cancelled a date *US, 2002*

guff *noun* **1** foolish nonsense, usually spoken or sung. From 'guff' (empty talk), later usage informed by the sense of 'a fart', punning and adding a noxious element to HOT AIR (nonsense) *US, 1888*. **2** back-talk, verbal resistance *US, 1879*. **3** a fart. Probably from the sense 'nonsense', thus a play on HOT AIR *UK, 1998*

guff *verb* **1** to fart. Probably from GUFF (nonsense), hence a play on HOT AIR *UK, 1997*. **2** to eat and drink greedily *INDIA, 1979*. **3** to anger and prepare to fight *TRINIDAD AND TOBAGO, 2003*

guggle *noun* the throat, the gullet *US, 1991*

guide *noun* a person who monitors the LSD experience of another, helping them through bad moments and caring for their physical needs *US, 1966*

guider; glider *noun* a children's makeshift vehicle, typically constructed of a soapbox and pram-wheels *UK, 1979*

guido *noun* an Italian or Italian-American, especially a macho one. Disparaging *US, 1988*

guillotine *noun* the lip of a wave crashing down on a surfer's head *US, 1991*

guilt trip *noun* an effort to make someone else feel guilty *US, 1972*

guilt-trip *verb* to attempt to make someone feel guilty *US, 1977*

guinea *noun* **1** an Italian or Italian-American *US, 1890*. **2** in horse racing, a horse groom *US, 1962*

Guinea football *noun* a homemade bomb *US, 1918*

guinea people *noun* Jamaicans with a strong sense of African identity *JAMAICA, 2003*

guinea pig *noun* **1** a person used as the subject of an experiment *US, 1920*. **2** a wig. Rhyming slang *UK, 1998*

guinea red *noun* cheap Italian red wine. Offensive because of the national slur *US, 1933*

Guineatown *noun* a neighbourhood dominated by Italian-Americans and/or Italian immigrants *US, 1992*

gulch *noun* on Prince Edward Island, junk food or unappetising food *CANADA, 1988*

gulch *verb* to engage in sexual intimacy in the outdoors *CANADA, 1985*

gullwing *noun* a car body style in which the passenger doors are hinged at the top and open upwards *US, 1993*

gully *adjective* **1** inferior; not up to expectations *US, 2002*. **2** excellent. A reversal of the earlier sense on the BAD is 'good' principle; used by urban black youths *UK, 2004*

gully-gut *noun* a glutton *UK, 1542*

gully monkey *noun* a person lacking intelligence and class *TRINIDAD AND TOBAGO, 2003*

guluptious *adjective* big and awkward *TRINIDAD AND TOBAGO, 2003*

gum *noun* **1** crude, unrefined opium *US, 1956*. **2** MDMA, the recreational drug best known as ecstasy *UK, 2003*. **3** in pool, a cushion. Cushions were once fashioned with rubber gum *US, 1993*

gumball *noun* **1** the flashing coloured lights on a police car *US, 1971*. **2** in stock car racing, a soft tyre used for extra traction in qualifying heats but, because it wears out so quickly, not in races *US, 1965*. **3** heroin *UK, 2003*

gumball *verb* to activate the flashing coloured lights on a police car *US, 1983*

gum-beat *verb* to talk, to chat *US, 1942*

gumbies *noun* black tennis shoes *US, 1969*

gumbo *noun* **1** in horse racing, thick mud *US, 1947*. **2** in oil drilling, any viscous or sticky formation encountered in drilling *US, 1954*

gum boot *noun* a condom *NEW ZEALAND, 2002*

gumbooter *noun* a dairy farmer *NEW ZEALAND, 2002*

gumby *noun* in computing, an inconsequential but highly visible display of stupidity. A borrowing from Monty Python *US, 1991*

gumdrop *noun* a capsule of secobarbital, a central nervous system depressant; any drug in capsule form *US, 1980*

gum it *verb* to perform oral sex on a woman *US, 1971*

gummer *noun* a gumboot, a Wellington boot *UK, 1984*

gummi *noun* rubber as a fetish. From German *gummi* (rubber) *UK, 2003*

gummy *noun* a gumboot or Wellington boot *NEW ZEALAND, 1995*

gummy *adjective* old, in poor condition. From Australian *gummy* (a sheep that has lost its teeth) *AUSTRALIA, 2001*

gump *noun* **1** a passive homosexual man *US, 1981*. **2** a chicken (of the fowl persuasion) *US, 1981*

gump stump *noun* the rectum *US, 1970*

gumption *noun* common sense, shrewdness; initiative, application, determination *UK, 1719*

gums *noun* overshoes *US, 1996*. ▶ **flap your gums; beat your gums; beat up your gums** to talk *US, 1955*. ▶ **give your gums a rest** to stop talking *US, 2003*

gumshoe *noun* a private investigator or detective *US, 1908*

gumsucker *noun* a non-Aboriginal inhabitant of the state of Victoria. Referring to the habit of chewing *gum* 'the sap of various native Australian trees (gumtrees)'. Now mainly historical *AUSTRALIA, 1840*

gum tree *noun* ▶ **up a gum tree** in trouble; in a hopeless situation *AUSTRALIA, 1851*

gum tree mail *noun* a non-official mail service in which a letter to be posted is stuck in a cleft stick and passed to the driver or guard of a train passing through a remote area *AUSTRALIA, 1969*

gum up *verb* ▶ **gum up the works** to interfere and so spoil things *US, 1932*

gun *noun* **1** a hired gunman *US, 1920*. **2** an expert at some occupation, especially shearing *AUSTRALIA, 1897*. **3** a pickpocket *US, 1965*. **4** a hypodermic needle and syringe *US, 1899*. **5** the upper arm; the bicep muscle *US, 1973*. **6** the penis *UK, 1675*. **7** any instrument used for tattooing *US, 1989*. **8** an electric guitar. From the symbolic actions of guitarists like Jimi Hendrix (1942–70) who stressed the metaphor when he recorded the song 'Machine Gun' in 1969 *US, 1988*. **9** a brass horn *US, 1960*. **10** a large surfboard used for big-wave conditions *US, 1965*. **11** in the language of wind surfing, a sailboard that is moderately long and tapered at the rear *US, 1985*. **12** in horse racing, a complete effort by a jockey *US, 1976*. **13** on the railways, a track torpedo used to warn an engineer of danger ahead *US, 1975*. **14** any signal that a quarter of a football game has ended *US, 1971*. ▶ **on the gun** engaged in crime as a profession *US, 1950*. ▶ **under the gun 1** (used of a prison) under armed guard *US, 2002*. **2** in poker, said of the player who must act first in a given situation *US, 1947*

gun *verb* **1** to accelerate a vehicle or rev its engine *US, 1920*. **2** to inject a drug intravenously *UK, 2003*. **3** to look over, to examine *UK, 1812*. **4** to attack verbally *UK, 2003*. **5** in computing, to use a computer's force-quit feature to close a malfunctioning program *US, 1983*.
▶ **gun it** (of a vehicle) to travel at top speed. From earlier, now conventional sense of 'gun' (to run an engine at full power) *US, 1976*

gun *adjective* **1** excellent *NEW ZEALAND, 1998*. **2** expert *AUSTRALIA, 1916*

gun and bomb *noun* a condom. Rhyming slang; the plural is 'guns and bombs' *UK, 2003*

gun and rifle club *noun* an inner-city hospital's casualty department *US, 1978*

gun ape *noun* an artillery soldier *US, 1988*

gun belt *noun* the American defence industry *US, 1991*

gunboats *noun* large, heavy shoes *US, 1862*

gun-bull *noun* an armed prison guard *US, 1928*

gun bunny *noun* an artilleryman *US, 1980*

Gunchester *nickname* Manchester *UK, 1994*

gun down *verb* (used of a male) to masturbate while looking directly at somebody else *US, 2002*

gunfighter seat *noun* in a public place, a seat with the back against the wall, overlooking the room. From the caution exercised by gunfighters in the West *US, 1997*

gun for *verb* to be on the lookout for with the intent of hurting or killing *US, 1878*

gun from the gate *noun* in horse racing, a racehorse that starts races quickly *US, 1951*

gunga din *noun* used to address a man with a perceived Indian or Asian ethnicity. Racist, derogatory; a stereotypical appellation from the poem 'Gunga Din', Rudyard Kipling, 1897: 'Of all them black-faced crew/ The finest man I knew / Was our regimental *bhisti* [a water-carrier], Gunga Din' *UK, 1994*

Gunga Din; gunga *noun* the chin. Rhyming slang, formed from Rudyard Kupling's poem *US, 1992*

gunge *noun* **1** an (unidentifiable or disgusting) viscid substance; general filth *UK, 1965*. **2** rubbish, nonsense *UK, 2003*. **3** any tropical skin disease affecting the crotch area of a US soldier in Vietnam *US, 1977*

gunge; gunge up *verb* in a general sense, to make filthy; more narrowly, to deliberately swamp someone with a viscous mess (humorously known as 'gunge') *UK, 1976*

gunged up; gungey; gungy *adjective* filthy, sticky; clogged with filth, especially with an unidentifiable or disgusting viscid substance. From GUNGE *UK, 1962*

gungeon; gunja; gunjeh; gunga *noun* marijuana, especially from Jamaica. A corruption of GANJA. Used to describe the most potent grade of marijuana in the 1940s *US, 1944*

gung-ho *adjective* dedicated, spirited, enthusiastic. Originally coined as a slogan understood to mean 'Work together!' by the US Marines during World War 2, then embraced as an adjective *US, 1942*

gungun *noun* marijuana variously claimed to be from Africa, Jamaica or Mexico. From GUNGEON (marijuana) *UK, 1998*

gungy; gungi *adjective* enthusiastic, spirited, brave. Formed from GUNG-HO *US, 1961*

gun hand *noun* in racquetball, the hand with which a player holds the racquet *US, 1971*

gunk *noun* **1** an unidentified and unpleasant substance *US, 1938*. **2** a thick liquid. Originally the brand name for a chemical cleaner *UK, 1999*. **3** any industrial solvent inhaled for its psychoactive effect *US, 1982*

gun moll *noun* a female gangster *US, 1908*

gun-mouth pants *noun* men's trousers with straight, tapered legs *TRINIDAD AND TOBAGO, 1937*

gunna *noun* a procrastinator *AUSTRALIA, 1996*

gunna going to *AUSTRALIA, 1944*

gunner *noun* **1** a person with sexual expertise and experience *US, 1965*. **2** in poker, the player with the best hand or who plays his hand as if it were the best hand *US, 1951*. **3** the person shooting the dice in craps *US, 1930*. **4** a student who takes competition to an aggressive level *US, 1994*

gunners *noun* braces (suspenders) *US, 1949*

gunnif *noun* a thief, a crook. A variation of GONNIF *UK, 2000*

gunny *noun* **1** a US Marine Corps gunnery sergeant *US, 1976*. **2** a door gunner on an airship, or a crew member of a gunship *US, 1980*. **3** a gun enthusiast *US, 1957*. **4** potent marijuana *US, 1970*

gun pet *noun* a parapet fortified to protect artillery *US, 1990*

guns *noun* **1** a helicopter gunship. Used by the US Army Aero Weapons Platoon in Vietnam *US, 1990*. **2** to marines in Vietnam, a weapons squad or platoon *US, 1990*. **3** the fists *US, 1981*

gunsack *noun* thick, heavy female thighs *TRINIDAD AND TOBAGO, 2003*

gunsel *noun* **1** a young homosexual man *US, 1918*. **2** a thug *US, 1943*

gunship *noun* **1** in the Metropolitan Police, a Flying Squad car when firearms are being carried *UK, 1999*. **2** in the Metropolitan Police, an Armed Response Vehicle *UK, 1999*. **3** a van used in a drive-by shooting *US, 1988*

gun-shot *noun* a single measure of chilled After Shock™ cinnamon or peppermint liqueur imbibed through a straw in a single action *UK, 2001*

gunslinger *noun* a chronic masturbator *US, 2002*

gunsmith *noun* an experienced pickpocket who trains novice pickpockets *US, 1934*

gun talk *noun* tough, threatening talk *TRINIDAD AND TOBAGO, 2003*

guntz *noun* the whole lot, the whole way. Adopted from Yiddish, ultimately German *das Ganze* (all of it) *UK, 1958*

gun up *verb* to prepare to fight, either with fists or weapons *US, 1981*

guppies *noun* anchovies. Limited usage, but clever *US, 1996*

guppy *noun* **1** an individual who is socially categorised as a gay *u*pwardly *m*obile *p*rofessional. A blend of GAY and YUPPIE *UK, 1984*. **2** a navy diver who is not SCUBA qualified *US, 1991*. **3** a heavy drinker. From FISH *US, 1991*

gur *noun* ▶ **on the gur** of a child, sleeping roughly *IRELAND, 1976*

gurner *noun* a person intoxicated by MDMA, the recreational drug best known as ecstasy. From the similarity between the distorted faces pulled by ECTSASY users and the ugly faces deliberately pulled by gurners in traditional gurning competitions *UK, 2000*

gurning *noun* the effect of tightened facial muscles as a result of taking MDMA, the recreational drug best known as ecstasy. From the conventional sense when the facial distortion is both voluntary and humorous *UK, 1996*

gurrier *noun* a lout, a ruffian *IRELAND, 2004*

guru *noun* an expert *US, 1986*

guru you! used as a humorous euphemism for 'screw you' *US, 1971*

gush *verb* **1** to express yourself in an over-effusive or sentimental manner *UK, 1864*. **2** in professional wrestling, to bleed *US, 1992*

gusset *noun* the vagina. Conventionally, a 'gusset' is a piece of material that reinforces clothing, particularly at the crotch and hence in this sense by association of location *UK, 1999*

gussy up *verb* to dress up *US, 1952*

gusto *noun* money *US, 1984*

gut *noun* **1** a school course that requires little effort *US, 1916*. **2** a main street through town *US, 1968*. **3** the belly, the stomach *UK, 1362*. **4** an air hose on a brake system *US, 1946*. **5** in electric line work, insulated rubber hose used on 5kV line *US, 1980*

gut *verb* in hot rodding, to remove all but the bare essentials from a car's interior *US, 1958*

gut bag *noun* a plastic bag containing frozen food, the exact identity of which is not clear *US, 1991*

gut-barge *verb* to use your beer-belly to bump into another's in an informal trial of strength *UK, 2002*

gut bomb *noun* any greasy, tasty, heavy food, especially a greasy hamburger *US, 1968*

gut bucket *noun* **1** an earthy style of jazz music combining elements of ragtime and blues. A 'gutbucket' was a cheap saloon from the name given to a bucket placed beneath a barrel of gin to catch and recycle leakages. The musicians in these type of places played for tips, and the style of music they played there became known as 'gutbucket' *US, 1929*. **2** a rough and rowdy bar with rough and rowdy patrons *US, 1970*. **3** a fish bait boat; by extension a messy space of any kind *US, 1975*

gut card *noun* in gin, a card that completes a broken sequence *US, 1965*

gut check *noun* a test of courage or determination *US, 1968*

gutful; gutsful *noun* too much of something *UK, 1900*

gut hopper *noun* a student who moves from one easy course to another *US, 1955*

gut issue *noun* the one most important issue in a discussion *US, 1986*

gutless *adjective* **1** cowardly, lacking determination *US, 1900*. **2** used to describe an extreme of quality: either very good or very bad *UK, 2002*

gutless wonder *noun* an outstanding coward *US, 1900*

gutrage *noun* a visceral anger *US, 1966*

gut reamer *noun* the active participant in anal sex *US, 1962*

gut-ripper *noun* an antipersonnel grenade that explodes at waist level *US, 1991*

guts *noun* **1** the stomach; the general area of the stomach and intestines. Standard English from late C14; slipped into unconventional usage early in C19 *UK, 1393*. **2** the essentials, the important part, the inner and real meaning *UK, 1663*. **3** the pulp and membrane inside a fruit *TRINIDAD AND TOBAGO, 1990*. **4** the interior of a car *US, 1975*. **5** information *AUSTRALIA, 1919*. **6** courage *US, 1891*. **7** in the gambling game two-up, the bets placed with the spinner of the coins *AUSTRALIA, 1941*. ▶ **have someone's guts for garters** used for expressing a level of personal threat. An idea that has been in circulation since about 1592. Hyperbolical, but none the less real for all that *UK, 1933*

guts and butts doc *noun* a gastroenterologist *US, 1994*

gut sausage *noun* a poor man's meal: cornmeal suet and in an intestine *CANADA, 1958*

gutser *noun* **1** a person who eats a great deal *NEW ZEALAND, 1998*. **2** a heavy fall. Usually in the phrase 'come a gutser'. Variants include 'gutzer' and 'gusta' *AUSTRALIA, 1918*. ▶ **come a gutser** to come undone; to fail miserably *AUSTRALIA, 1918*

gutsful *noun* ▷ see: GUTFUL

gut shot *noun* **1** a bullet wound in the stomach, painful and often fatal *US, 1992*. **2** in poker, a drawn card that completes an inside straight *US, 1951*

gutsiness *noun* courage *UK, 1959*

gutslider *noun* a bodyboarder. A term of derision when used by surfers *SOUTH AFRICA, 2003*

guts like calabash *noun* extreme courage *TRINIDAD AND TOBAGO, 1991*

gutsy *adjective* **1** courageous *UK, 1893*. **2** of music, heartfelt, spirited *UK, 1984*

gutsy; guts *noun* an overweight or obese person. A nickname and derogatory term of abuse; 'gutsy' is a mid- to late C20 variation of 'guts' *UK, 1596*

gutted *adjective* being bitterly disappointed; used to describe a depressed, empty feeling. Derives, possibly, from the image of a gutted fish or similar; how much emptier could you feel? *UK, 1981*

gutter *noun* a vein, especially a prominent one suitable for drug injection *US, 1994*

gutter ball *noun* in pool, a shot in which the cue ball falls into a pocket. Homage to bowling *US, 1993*

gutter bunny *noun* a commuter who bicycles to work. Mountain bikers' slang *US, 1996*

guttered *adjective* drunk. Used in Inverness *UK: SCOTLAND, 2002*

gutter glitter *noun* cocaine *UK, 2003*

gutter junkie; gutter hype *noun* a drug-addict reduced by the circumstances of addiction to living in the streets or, at best, using inferior drugs. A combination of JUNKIE (an addict) or HYPE (an addict) with 'gutter' representing the lowest point achievable *US, 1936*

gutter slut *noun* a sexually promiscuous woman *UK, 2003*

gutter wear *noun* fashionably shabby clothing *US, 1988*

gutty *noun* an unpleasant person *IRELAND, 1998*

guv *noun* an informal style of address to a male of superior status. Short for 'governor' and GUV'NOR *UK, 1890*

guv'nor; guvnor; gov'nor *noun* **1** a boss. Reduced from 'governor' *UK, 1969*. **2** the landlord of a public house. Originally a lazy reduction of 'governor' *UK, 1999*

guy *noun* a man or a boy; a general form of address; in the plural it can be used of and to men, women or a mixed grouping *US, 1847*

guyed out *adjective* drunk. An allusion to the tightness achieved through guy wires *US, 1973*

guy-magnet *noun* a person who is attractive to men *AUSTRALIA, 1996*

guy thing *noun* a problem or subject best understood by males *US, 1992*

guyver; guiver *noun* insincere talk; pretence *AUSTRALIA, 1864*

guzzle-and-grab *noun* eating and drinking, with an emphasis on fast, low-brow food and alcohol *US, 1951*

guzzled *adjective* drunk *US, 1939*

guzzle guts *noun* a glutton or a heavy drinker *UK, 1959*

gwaai; gwai; gwa *noun* tobacco; a cigarette. From the Zulu *ugwayi* (tobacco) *SOUTH AFRICA, 1978*

gwaffed *adjective* drug-intoxicated *SOUTH AFRICA, 2003*

gwan *verb* happening, going on. A patois slurring of 'going on', *1994*

gwarr; gwarry; gwat *noun* the vagina *SOUTH AFRICA, 2004*

GWB the *George Washington Bridge*. It crosses the Hudson River between upper Manhattan and Fort Lee, New Jersey *US, 1997*

gweep *noun* an overworked computer programmer *US, 1990*

G-wheel *noun* in a carnival, a game wheel that has been rigged for cheating. 'G' is for 'gaffed' (rigged) *US, 1990*

gyac *god you're a cunt; give you a clue*. An initialism. Pronounced as if retching *UK, 1994*

gyal *noun* a girl; girls. A phonetic variation. *1994*

gyke *noun* a gynaecologist. Used among middle-class women, especially in hospital *UK, 1984*

gym bunny *noun* someone who makes regular use of a gymnasium *UK, 2001*

gymhead *noun* someone who exercises obsessively and therefore spends a great deal of time in a gymnasium. A combination of 'gym' (a gymnasium) and -HEAD (a user) *UK, 2002*

gym queen *noun* a man who spends a great deal of time at a gym *US, 1994*

gym rat *noun* an exercise fanatic *US, 1978*

gymslip training *noun* the process of instructing, and conditioning the behaviour of, a transvestite who wishes to be treated as an adolescent girl, especially when used in a dominant prostitute's advertising matter *UK, 2003*

gynae *noun* gynaecology *UK, 1933*

gynae; gyno *noun* gynaecology; a gynaecologist *UK, 1933*

gynie *noun* a gynaecological examination *UK, 1995*

gyno; gynae *noun* a gynaecologist *AUSTRALIA, 1967*

gyno shot *noun* a close-up scene in a pornographic film or a photograph showing a woman's genitals *US, 1995*

gyp; gip *noun* **1** someone or something that is considered a cheat; someone who does not honour debts and obligations. Abbreviated from 'gypsy'; an unconsidered racial slur. Also Spelt 'gip' *US, 1859*. **2** in horse racing, someone who owns only a few horses.

An abbreviation of 'gypsy'; not derogatory *US, 1938*. **3** in oil drilling, gypsum *US, 1954*. **4** pain, actual or figurative. Also 'jyp' *UK, 1910*

gyp; gip *verb* to cheat (someone), to swindle *US, 1880*

gypo; gyppo; jippo; gippo; gyppy; gypper *noun* a gypsy; gypsy. Derogatory, casually racist *UK, 1916*

gypo-bashing *noun* racially motivated physical attacks on gypsies. On the model of PAKI-BASHING (attacks on Pakistanis and other Asians) *UK, 2000*

gyppo *noun* an avoidance or shirking of a duty; a shirker. From gypsy or Egyptian via military slang *SOUTH AFRICA, 1978*

gyppo *verb* to dodge an unpleasant responsibility, to shirk a duty; to avoid something. From gypsy or Egyptian via military slang *SOUTH AFRICA, 1971*

gyppo *adjective* small-time *CANADA, 1959*

gyppo's dog *noun* used as a standard of skinniness. Based on a stereotypical image of a gypsy's dog *UK, 2001*

gyppy *adjective* painful; annoying (causing a figurative pain) *UK, 2000*

gypsy *noun* **1** in circus and carnival usage, an undependable employee, especially a drunk *US, 1981*. **2** in trucking, an owner-operator who works independently *US, 1946*

gypsy *adjective* **1** unlicensed, unregulated, usually owned by the operator. Most often applied to a taxicab or truck, although originally to a racehorse owner/jockey *US, 1951*. **2** meddling, nosy, officious *BARBADOS, 1965*

gypsy bankroll *noun* a roll of money in which the top several notes are real large-denomination notes and the rest are counterfeit, plain paper, or small-denomination notes *US, 1981*

gyrene *noun* a US Marine *US, 1894*

gyro; gyro wanker *noun* a surfer who constantly flaps his arms to gain balance on the surfboard *US, 1991*

gyve *noun* a marijuana cigarette. This archly ironic reference to marijuana addiction uses an almost obsolete standard English word meaning 'shackles and fetters' whilst punning on JIVE *US, 1938*

Hh

H *noun* heroin *US, 1926*. ▶ **the H** Houston, Texas *US, 1998*

H-17 *noun* in casino blackjack gambling, a rule that the dealer must draw a card if he has a 17 made with an ace counting 11 points. The 'h' is for HIT *US, 1996*

H8 *verb* in text messaging, hate. A variant spelling; one of several constructions in which a syllable pronounced 'ate' is replaced by the homophone 'eight' *UK, 2002*

hab *noun* a habitual criminal *US, 1963*

habit *noun* an addiction to any drug *UK, 1881*

habitual *noun* ▶ **the habitual** a criminal charge alleging habitual criminal status *US, 1972*

Habra Dabra and the crew *noun* any random representatives of the populace. The functional equivalent of 'Tom, Dick and Harry' *BARBADOS, 1965*

hache *noun* heroin. The Spanish pronunciation of the letter 'h' *US, 1955*

hachi; hodgy *noun* the penis *US, 1954*

hack *noun* **1** a journalist, a reporter *UK, 1810*. **2** a prison guard *US, 1914*. **3** a solution to a computer problem; an impressive and demanding piece of computer work *US, 1981*. **4** in computing, a quick, often temporary, fix of a problem *US, 1983*. **5** a single act of unlawfully invading and exploring another's computer system by remote means *US, 1983*. **6** an opportunist. Used at Oxford University *UK, 1980*. **7** a taxi *US, 1928*. **8** a hot rod *US, 1958*. **9** a brakevan (caboose) *US, 1916*. **10** a game of Hacky Sack *US, 1997*

hack *verb* **1** to tolerate, endure, survive. Usually used with 'it' *US, 1952*. **2** to bother, to annoy *US, 1893*. **3** to unlawfully invade and explore another's computer system by remote means *US, 1983*. **4** to investigate the possibilities of a computer purely for the pleasures of discovery; to create new possibilities for a computer without commercial consideration *US, 1983*. **5** to work with a computer *US, 1981*. **6** to drive a taxi *US, 1903*. **7** to play with a hacky sack beanbag *US, 1995*. ▶ **hack butts** to smoke cigarettes *CANADA, 1993*. ▶ **hack it** to cope with, to accomplish *US, 1952*

hack around; hack off; hack *verb* to waste time, usually in a context where time should not be wasted *US, 1888*

hack driver *noun* in horse racing, a jockey *US, 1951*

hacked; hacked off *adjective* annoyed *US, 1936*

hacker *noun* **1** a person who uses their computer expertise in any effort to breach security walls and gain entry to secure sites *US, 1963*. **2** a person with a profound appreciation and affection for computers and programming *US, 1981*. **3** an expert in any field *US, 1983*. **4** a taxi driver *BAHAMAS, 1982*

hackette *noun* a female journalist. Patronising *UK, 1984*

hackie *noun* a carriage or taxi driver *US, 1899*

hack mode *noun* while working on or with a computer, a state of complete focus and concentration *US, 1991*

Hackney Wick *noun* a penis. Rhyming slang for PRICK. Hackney Wick is an area of East London, located considerably closer to the source of Cockney rhyming slang than the more popular synonym HAMPTON WICK *UK, 1998*

hacktivist *noun* a cultural activist and skilled computer-user who invades a corporate website to leave subversive messages *UK, 2001*

hacky sack *noun* a beanbag used in a game in which a circle of players try to keep the bag from hitting the ground without using their hands. A trademarked product that has lent its name to a game and to rival products *US, 1989*

haddock and cod; haddock *noun* used as a general pejorative, a sod. Rhyming slang *UK, 1962*

had-it *noun* a person who was formerly successful *UK, 1992*

had-it *adjective* exhausted; completely worn out. Hawaiian youth usage *US, 1981*

haemorrhoid *noun* **1** an irritation, an annoying person. An excruciating pun on 'pain in the ass' *US, 1975*. **2** a despised person *US, 1969*

haffie *noun* ▷*see:* HALF-JACK

ha-fucking-ha!; ha-bloody-ha!; ha-di-fucking-ha!; hardy fuckin' ha, ha! used as a jeering response to unfunny jokes; and to dismiss impossible suggestions *UK, 1976*

hag *verb* to annoy, to bother *BARBADOS, 1965*

hagged out *adjective* **1** exhausted *US, 1968*. **2** (of a woman) ugly. From 'hag' (an unattractive woman), possibly punning on SHAGGED; SHAGGED OUT (tired) *US, 2001*

Haggis McBagpipe *nickname* British Columbia radio and television personality Jack Webster *CANADA, 1989*

ha-ha *noun* a glass of beer; beer *US, 1979*

ha-ha bird; ha-ha pigeon *noun* a kookaburra, a well-known Australian bird. From its call which resembles human laughter *AUSTRALIA, 1938*

ha-ha-funny *adjective* ▷*see:* FUNNY HA-HA

Haight *nickname* ▶ **the Haight** the Haight-Ashbury neighbourhood of San Francisco *US, 1967*

Haight-Ashbury *nickname* a neighbourhood in San Francisco, the epicentre of the hippie movement in the mid- to late 1960s. From the intersection of Haight and Ashbury Streets. More recently referred to simply as THE HAIGHT *US, 1987*

hail *noun* **1** crack cocaine. Based on the drug's resemblance to pieces of hail *US, 1994*. **2** in soda fountain usage, ice *US, 1935*

hailer *noun* in the television and film industries, a bullhorn *US, 1977*

Hail Mary *noun* **1** a last-minute, low-probability manoeuvre *US, 1994*. **2** in poker, a poor hand that a player holds into high betting in the hope that other players are bluffing and have even worse hands *US, 1996*

hail smiling morn *noun* the erect penis, an erection. Rhyming slang for HORN *UK, 1980*

haim *noun* ▷*see:* HAME

haint; hain't a have-not; to have not. Verb and noun. A vulgar contraction *UK, 1971*

hair *noun* **1** courage *US, 1959*. **2** in computing, intricacy *US, 1981*. ▶ **get in someone's hair** to annoy or irritate someone *US, 1949*. ▶ **let your hair down** to behave in a (more than usually) uninhibited manner *US, 1933*. ▶ **put hair on your chest; put hairs on your chest** a quality ascribed to an alcoholic drink or, when encouraging a child to eat, used of food (especially crusts and brussel sprouts); also applied more broadly to robust or challenging questions of aesthetic taste or preference *UK, 1964*. ▶ **tear your hair; tear your hair out** to behave in a highly agitated manner, especially as a result of worry *UK, 1606*. ▶ **wear your hair out against the head of the bed; wear your hair out on the bedhead** to go bald. A jocular explanation *UK, 1961*

hairbag *noun* a veteran police officer *US, 1958*

hairbagger *noun* an experienced police officer *US, 1958*

hairball *noun* **1** an obnoxious, boorish person, especially when drunk *US, 1981*. **2** a large, powerful wave *US, 1981*

hairball! terrifying! *US, 1998*

hairblower *noun* a severe telling-off, a scolding *UK, 2002*

hairburger *noun* the vulva, especially in the context of oral sex *US, 1971*

hair burner; hair bender *noun* a hair stylist *US, 1964*

haircut *noun* **1** a short prison sentence. From the short period of time between haircuts *UK, 1950.* **2** a lowering of the true mileometer (odometer) reading of a motor vehicle to increase its resale value *NEW ZEALAND, 1990.* **3** marijuana *UK, 2003.* **4** a sore on a man's penis as the result of a sexually transmitted infection. From the popular belief that the sore was caused by a woman's pubic hair *TRINIDAD AND TOBAGO, 2003*

haircut *adjective* describes an image of fashionability that is without deeper significance *UK, 2000*

hairdresser *noun* a homosexual. From the presumption that all hairdressers are gay *UK, 2001*

hair-dry *adjective* without getting your hair wet *US, 1991*

haired up *adjective* angry. From a dog's bristling back when angry *US, 1914*

hair fairy *noun* a homosexual male with an extravagant hairdo *US, 1964*

hair in the gate *noun* in television and film-making, any foreign object in the camera gate *US, 1990*

hair pie *noun* **1** the vulva; oral sex performed on a woman. Also spelt 'hare' pie or 'hairy' pie *US, 1938.* **2** a pizza with an errant hair embedded in it. Limited usage, but clever *US, 1996*

hairpins *noun* homosexual code phrases inserted casually into a conversation, trolling for a response *US, 1950*

hairtree *noun* a man who wears his hair long and styled as a fashion statement *US, 1996*

hair-trunk *noun* in horse racing, a bad-looking horse that performs poorly *UK, 1948*

hairy *noun* **1** a long-haired, bearded individual *UK, 1976.* **2** a former non-commissioned officer training to become an officer. Military *UK, 1981.* **3** a young woman with a reputation for sluttishness. Glasgow slang *UK: SCOTLAND, 1985.* **4** heroin. A phonetic distortion of HARRY *US, 1973*

hairy *adjective* **1** dangerous; scary (especially if thrilling) *US, 1945.* **2** bad, difficult, undesirable. A popular term in C19, resurrected in later C20 youth usage *UK, 1848.* **3** in computing, complicated *US, 1983.* **4** good, impressive *US, 1959*

hairy-arse; hairy-arsed *adjective* describes a thuggish, insensitive brute *UK, 2001*

hairyback; hairy *noun* an Afrikaner. Derogatory *SOUTH AFRICA, 1970*

hairy bank *noun* a prostitute's vagina *GUYANA, 1998*

hairy belly *noun* in dominoes, the 6–6 piece *US, 1959*

hairy chequebook *noun* the vagina, as used for payment in kind instead of money *AUSTRALIA, 1996*

hairy clam *noun* the vagina. An almost subtle combination of FISH and visual imagery *UK, 2000*

hairy eyeball *noun* a hostile stare. Deriving, perhaps, from the eyelashes that mask the eye *US, 1995*

hairy fairy *adjective* of a man, effeminate to some degree. A pun on AIRY-FAIRY (delicate, insubstantial) and FAIRY (a homosexual man) *UK, 1978*

hairy goat *noun* a racehorse that is a slow runner or poor performer *AUSTRALIA, 1933*

hairy goblet *noun* the vagina *UK, 2001*

hairy growler *noun* the vagina *UK, 2001*

hairy leg *noun* **1** a man. CItizens' band radio slang *UK, 1981.* **2** a railway fettler *AUSTRALIA, 1969*

hairy maclary *noun* a female who invites sexual foreplay but stops short of intercourse *NEW ZEALAND, 1998*

ha-ja *noun* ▷*see:* HALF-JACK

hale and hearty *adjective* a party. Rhyming slang *UK, 1992*

Hale and Pace; hale *noun* the face. Rhyming slang, from comedy double act Gareth Hale and Norman Pace *UK, 2002*

half *noun* **1** used colloquially as an elliptical noun when the original noun is omitted, especially of a half pint (of beer) *UK, 1937.* **2** a child travelling at half-fare *UK, 1961*

half *adverb* **1** used in exaggerations, as in 'I half killed him' *UK, 2001.* **2** used to reverse what is being said, which is usually formed as a negative, and thus stress the intention, i.e. 'not half bad' is pretty good *UK, 1583*

half a bar *noun* until 1971, ten shillings; post-decimalisation, fifty pence *UK, 1911*

half a C *noun* fifty dollars. A shortened allusion to $100 as a 'C-note' *US, 1967*

half a case *noun* fifty cents *US, 1950*

half a chip *noun* sixpence, a sixpenny bit *UK, 1950*

half a cock *noun* five pounds (£5). Based on rhyming slang COCKLE AND HEN (ten) *UK, 1950*

half a crack *noun* a half-crown coin, half-a-crown, two shillings and sixpence. A coin and coinage that paid the price of decimalisation in 1971 *UK, 1933*

half a dollar *noun* **1** a prison sentence of 50 years *US, 1990.* **2** a half-crown coin; two shillings and sixpence. Pre-decimalisation, that is pre-1971, a half-crown coin was valued at two shillings and sixpence (equivalent to 12½ p), and, presumably, at the point of coinage, a pound was worth approximately four US dollars *UK, 1916*

half a football field *noun* fifty crystals of crack cocaine *UK, 2001*

half-a-man *noun* a short person *US, 1997*

half a mo *noun* a very short but vaguely defined time. A shortening of 'half a moment' *UK, 1896*

half and half *noun* **1** oral sex on a man followed by vaginal intercourse *US, 1937.* **2** a hermophrodite *US, 1935.* **3** a pint drink comprising equal measures of two different beers *UK, 1909*

half and half *adjective* **1** mediocre *TRINIDAD AND TOBAGO, 1958.* **2** bisexual *US, 1975*

half a nicker *noun* **1** pre-decimalisation, ten shillings; after 1971, fifty pence. From NICKER (one pound) *UK, 1895.* **2** a vicar. Rhyming slang. Also variant 'half-nicker man' *UK, 1974*

half-apple *noun* in television and film-making, a standard-sized crate used for raising objects or people, half as high as a standard 'apple' *US, 1990*

half-assed; half-arsed *adjective* **1** inferior, unsatisfactory, incompetent *US, 1865.* **2** incomplete, not serious, half-hearted *US, 1933*

half a stretch *noun* **1** a six-month prison sentence. From 'stretch' (a year's sentence) *UK, 1950.* **2** gambling odds of 6–1 *UK, 1984*

half a yard *noun* fifty dollars *US, 1961*

half-baked *adjective* intellectually deficient. Dialect *UK, 1855*

half-chat *noun* a half-caste. Also used in Australia *UK, 1909*

half-cock *noun* ▶ **go off at half-cock** generally, to start without being ready; in sex, to ejaculate prematurely or without being fully erect. A variation of HALF-COCKED *UK, 1904*

half-cock *adjective* ill-considered; inferior *UK, 2002.* ▶ **at half-cock** not fully prepared or ready *UK, 2000*

half-cocked *adjective* **1** not fully capable; not completely thought out; unfinished; incomplete. Derives from the mechanism of a gun *US, 1833.* **2** drunk *AUSTRALIA, early C19.* ▶ **go off half-cocked** generally, to start without being ready; in sex, to ejaculate prematurely or without being fully erect. Gun imagery *UK, 1809*

half colonel *noun* a lieutenant-colonel *US, 1956*

half-cut *adjective* drunk *UK, 1893*

half-cuts *noun* trainers (sneakers) *BARBADOS, 1998*

halfers *noun* ▶ **go halfers; go haufers** to share equally between two parties *UK: SCOTLAND, 1985*

half-fried *adjective* of eggs, fried on one side only. The Indian-English equivalent to SUNNY SIDE UP *INDIA, 1979*

half G *noun* a half-gallon jar of alcohol *NEW ZEALAND, 1971*

half-gone *adjective* half-drunk *UK, 1925*

half-half *adjective* mediocre *FIJI, 1996*

half-hearty *adjective* of medicore health, recovering from an illness but not completely recovered *BARBADOS, 1965*

half-het *noun* a bisexual *US, 1995*

half hour *noun* a short prison sentence. A little bravado in this prisoner's exaggeration *UK, 2002*

halfie *noun* a half-caste person *AUSTRALIA, 1945*

half-inch *verb* to steal; to arrest. Rhyming slang for PINCH (to steal or to arrest) *UK, 1925*

half-iron *noun* a heterosexual or bisexual man who associates with homosexuals. From 'iron' (a homosexual male) *UK, 1950*

half-jack; ha-ja; haffie *noun* a half-bottle (375 ml) of spirits *SOUTH AFRICA, 1953*

half-load *noun* fifteen packets of heroin *US, 1973*

half-man *noun* a kneeboarder, or a surfer who rides without standing *US, 1991*

half-mast *adjective* **1** (used of a penis) partially but not completey erect *US, 1972*. **2** partially lowered *US, 1871*

half of marge *noun* a police sergeant. Rhyming slang for SARGE, formed from a measure of margarine *UK, 1998*

half-ounce *verb* to cheat *UK, 1960*

half-ounce deal *noun* in prison, a trade that swaps a half ounce of tobacco for a single marijuana cigarette *UK, 1996*

half ounce of baccy *noun* a Pakistani, especially a Pakistani child. An elaboration (perhaps a reduction) of OUNCE OF BACCY (PAKI) *UK, 1992*

half ouncer *noun* a physically intimidating individual employed to control the clients of any establishment, usually of a premises offering entertainment, e.g. pub, club, concert venue, music festival, etc; a 'chucker-out'; door-security. Rhyming slang for BOUNCER, with a degree of irony *UK, 1992*

half past six *adjective* incompetent. A sexual reference, with the hands of the clock indicating impotence *SINGAPORE, 2002*

half past two *noun* a Jewish person. Rhyming slang *UK, 1960*

halfpenny dip; ha'penny dip; ha'penny *noun* **1** a sleep. Rhyming slang for KIP *UK, 1980*. **2** a ship. Rhyming slang *US, 1961*

halfpenny stamp; ha'penny *noun* a tramp. Rhyming slang *UK, 1992*

half-pick duck *noun* an incomplete account *TRINIDAD AND TOBAGO, 1975*

half-pie *adjective* half-hearted *AUSTRALIA, 1941*

half-pie *adverb* not fully *AUSTRALIA, 1992*

half piece *noun* 14g (½ oz) of a powdered drug, especially heroin *US, 1938*

half-pint *noun* a short person. From the non-metric measure of volume *US, 1876*

half-pipe *noun* a trough in a snow slope used for aerial manoeuvres in snowboarding *US, 1993*

half-power *noun* a worker working with a hangover *US, 1980*

half-rack *noun* in the US, half a case of beer (12 bottles or cans); in Canada, a six-pack of beer *US, 1997*

half-scooped; hauf-scooped *adjective* tipsy *UK: SCOTLAND, 1988*

half-seas-over *adjective* half-drunk *UK, 1700*

half-sheet *noun* a punishment, usually a fine, received by a prison warder. This generalised term derives from the half-sheet of blank paper that an officer is given to explain his conduct *UK, 1950*

half smart *adjective* stupid *US, 1927*

half-soaked *adjective* moderately competent *UK, 2001*

half stamp *noun* a tramp. Rhyming slang *UK, 1984*

half-step *verb* to make a half-hearted, insincere effort *US, 1990*

half-stepper *noun* a person who does things only halfway and cannot be counted on *US, 1981*

half tanked *adjective* mildy drunk *AUSTRALIA, 1971*

half track *noun* crack cocaine. Rhyming slang *UK, 1998*

half-wit *noun* a stupid fool *UK, 1755*

half your luck you're so lucky! Elliptical for 'I wish I had half your luck' *AUSTRALIA, 1933*

halibut head *noun* to the indigenous peoples of Alaska, a white person *US, 1965*

halter *noun* a necktie *US, 1960*

halvsies *noun* **1** half a share of something that is to be divided. Variants include 'halfsies' and 'halfies' *US, 1927*. **2** mutual oral sex performed simultaneously *US, 1985*

ham *noun* **1** an amateur shortwave radio operator and enthusiast *US, 1919*. **2** theatrical antics *US, 1930*. **3** in circus and carnival usage, food or a meal *US, 1981*. **4** any type of alcoholic drink *US, 1997*. **5** a member of the armed forces in complete dress uniform *US, 1991*. **6** overtime *UK, 1970*

ham *verb* **1** to over-act, to be an inferior actor *US, 1930*. **2** to walk *US, 1962*. ► **ham it up** to behave theatrically, to exaggerate *US, 1955*

ham actor; ham actress; ham *noun* an unsubtle actor *US, 1881*

ham and beef *noun* a *chief* prison warder. Rhyming slang *UK, 1962*

ham and egg; ham *noun* the leg. Rhyming slang *UK, 1932*

ham-and-egger *noun* **1** in professional wrestling, a wrestler whose regular role is to lose to help the careers of others. A slight variation on the boxing original *US, 1999*. **2** in oil drilling, an operator who has suffered loss after loss and is now burdened with poor credit *US, 1954*. **3** an inconsequential person who has achieved little *US, 1985*

ham and egging *noun* a general system or understanding that allows different members of a sports team to achieve best performances at complementary times *US, 1997*

ham and eggs cap *noun* ▷*see:* SCRAMBLED EGGS CAP

hambone *noun* **1** a male striptease act. A popular male display in the 1960s *AUSTRALIA, 1964*. **2** a trombone *US, 1934*. **3** a telephone. Rhyming slang *UK, 1992*. **4** a black prisoner *US, 1989*

hamburger *noun* a socially inept outcast. High school usage *US, 1949*

hamburger helper *noun* **1** crack cocaine. The drug bears some resemblance to a brand name food product *US, 1994*. **2** a linear amplifier for a citizens' band radio *US, 1976*

Hamburger Hill *nickname* Dong Ap Bia Mountain in South Vietnam, close to the Laos border. Taken at great cost by the US Marines in battle in May 1969, and then quietly abandoned a week later. Of marginal tactical importance and ultimately symbolic of the lack of military vision *US, 1971*

hamburger home *noun* a boarding house used by oil field workers *US, 1954*

hame; haim; haym *noun* a job, especially a menial or unpleasant one *US, 1941*

hamfat *noun* an amateur performer *US, 1911*

hamhock circuit *noun* a tour of black bars and nightclubs *US, 1975*

Hamilton *noun* a ten-dollar bill. From the engraving of Alexander Hamilton on the note *US, 1948*

hammed *adjective* drunk *US, 1997*

hammer *noun* **1** the penis *US, 1967*. **2** a handgun *US, 1994*. **3** heroin *NEW ZEALAND, 1982*. **4** an attractive girl or young woman *US, 1970*. **5** a pizza with ham topping *US, 1996*. **6** an accelerator pedal. Citizens' band radio slang, often as 'back off the hammer' (to slow down) and 'put the hammer down' (to accelerate) *US, 1974*. **7** in shuffleboard, the eighth and final shot *US, 1967*. **8** in bar dice games, the player who wins the chance to play first *US, 1971*. ► **on your hammer 1** following close behind; tailing. From HAMMER AND NAIL *AUSTRALIA, 1942*. **2** badgering. From HAMMER AND TACK *AUSTRALIA, 1955*. ► **put the hammer on** to press someone for something *IRELAND, 1984*

hammer *verb* **1** to drive a vehicle at maximum speed *AUSTRALIA, 1960*. **2** to inflict a resounding defeat *UK, 1948*. **3** to beat up *UK, 1973*. **4** to stretch physical limits *UK, 2002*. ► **get hammered 1** while surfing, to be knocked from your surfboard and violently thrashed by the surf *US, 1988*. **2** in mountain biking, to experience a violent accident *US, 1992*

hammer and discus *noun* facial hair, whiskers. Rhyming slang *UK, 1998*

hammer and nail; hammer *verb* to follow, to tail. Rhyming slang *UK, 1961*

hammer and tack *noun* the back. Rhyming slang *AUSTRALIA, 1977*

hammer and tongs *adverb* energetically, vigorously, strongly; violently. From the vigorous use a blacksmith makes of these tools *UK, 1708*

hammer-blowed *adjective* drunk *UK, 2002*

hammered *adjective* drunk *US, 1960*

hammerhead *noun* one of several kinds of inferior horse *US, 1941*

hammerheading *noun* **1** an act of taking a recreational drug cocktail of MDMA, the recreational drug best known as ecstasy, and Viagra™ (a branded drug that enables a male erection). From the after-effect of a throbbing headache *UK, 2003*

hammering *noun* a defeat, a significant defeat; a beating *UK, 1900*

hammer man *noun* a male of considerable sexual prowess. Related to the expression 'going at it hammer and tongs' to describe highly energetic sexual activity *IRELAND, 1997*

hammers *noun* the female thighs *US, 1980*

hammer-slammer *noun* an airframe technician. US Army usage *US, 1998*

hammer time *noun* a decisive point; the time to launch a military attack. Adapted from a catchphrase attached, in the late 1980s, to California rapper MC Hammer *US, 2003*

hammock *noun* a sanitary towel. Generally used by young males, often in the jocular formula: 'hammock for a bleeding lazy cunt' *UK, 2003*

hammock for two *noun* a brassiere *US, 1963*

hammock season *noun* the bleed period of the menstrual cycle. The image of a sanitary towel as a WEE HAMMOCK or 'mouse's hammock' *SOUTH AFRICA, 2001*

hammy *adjective* melodramatic, theatrical *US, 1899*

hammy; hammie *noun* a hamstring *AUSTRALIA, 1986*

ham patch *noun* a telephone connection enabled by shortwave radio *ANTARCTICA, 1997*

Hampden roar *noun* the state of affairs, the current situation. Rhyming slang for THE SCORE, formed from the name of Scotland's national stadium and the roar of a football crowd *UK: SCOTLAND, 1985*

Hampstead Heath; hampsteads; ampstids; hamps *noun* the teeth. Rhyming slang, from a rural area of north London *UK, 1887*

Hampton Court; hampton *noun* salt. Rhyming slang, formed on a historic Surrey location. Do not confuse it with Hampton Wick (the penis) *UK, 1992*

Hampton Wick; Hampton; Wick *noun* **1** a penis. Rhyming slang for PRICK (the penis), after a suburb of London. A polite euphemism in its reduced forms *UK, 1960*. **2** a fool. Rhyming slang for PRICK (general term of offence) *UK, 1977*

ham sandwich *noun* language. Glasgow rhyming slang; this is a convincing rhyme in the appropriate accent *UK: SCOTLAND, 1988*

ham shank *noun* **1** an American. Rhyming slang for YANK. Originally a World War 2 Merchant Navy coinage to describe American ships or men, subsequently adopted by the Americans *UK, 1960*. **2** a bank. Rhyming slang *UK, 1994*. **3** an act of masturbation. Rhyming slang for WANK *UK, 2002*

ham stealer *noun* a thief who steals to eat, rather than for profit *US, 1976*

hamster *noun* a discrete piece of computer code that does what it is supposed to do well *US, 1991*

hamster crab; crab *noun* a type of scratch (a manipulation of a record to create a musical effect). Derives from the crab-like movements of the DJ's fingers; 'hamster' is a reference to the hamster-switch *UK, 2002*

hamster-style *noun* a method of manipulating record turntables in which the priorities are reversed. DJ jargon; on a sound mixer the

hamster switch is a crossfader reverse switch, so named for the 'BulletProof Scratch Hamsters' who are credited with its invention in the mid-1990s *UK, 2002*

Hancock *verb* to sign. A shortened version of JOHN HANCOCK. From his admirable signature on the Declaration of Independence *US, 1967*

hand *noun* five; in betting, odds of 5–1. From the TICK-TACK signal used by bookmakers *UK, 1991*. ▶ **do it with one hand tied behind your back** to do something very easily *US, 1889*. ▶ **hand has no hair** used for expressing a willingness to accept money in the present situation *TRINIDAD AND TOBAGO, 1982*

hand *verb* ▶ **hand it to** to admit the superiority of someone or something *US, 1914*

HAND in text messaging, *have a nice day UK, 2003*

hand and a half *noun* in betting, odds of 11–2. In bookmaker slang HAND is 5–1, here the addition of a 'half' increases the odds to 5½-1 or 11–2 *UK, 1991*

hand and fist *adjective* drunk. Rhyming slang, always used in full, for PISSED *UK, 1992*

H and B *adjective* sexually aroused; hot and bothered *US, 1968*

handbag *noun* **1** an attractive male escort for a woman at a social engagement *AUSTRALIA, 1967*. **2** a male homosexual *AUSTRALIA, 1992*. **3** money. Also variant 'hambag' *UK, 1984*

handbag-positive *adjective* applied to a confused and disoriented patient, lying in a hospital bed, clutching their handbag or purse. A jocular medical condition *UK, 2002*

handbags *noun* a minor verbal or physical disagreement, especially on a sports pitch *UK, 2003*

Handbags *nickname* second battalion, Royal Green Jackets *UK, 1995*

handbags at dawn a minor verbal or physical disagreement *UK, 2001*

handbags at ten paces a conflict that, despite its potential for violent confrontation, comes to nothing more than posturing. The number of paces may vary *UK, 1991*

handball *verb* to insert your lubricated hand into your partner's rectum or vagina, providing sexual pleasure for both *US, 1979*

handballing *noun* the insertion of a hand and fist into a person's rectum or vagina for sexual gratification *US, 1999*

hand bomb *verb* to throw a just-caught salmon using both hands *CANADA, 1989*

handbook *noun* a bookmaker who operates on the street, without the benefit of a fixed office *US, 1973*

handbrake *noun* a wife or girlfriend, seen as preventing a man from having a good time *AUSTRALIA, 1998*

handbrakie *noun* a handbrake turn *AUSTRALIA, 1996*

H and C *noun* a mixture of heroin and cocaine. A play on 'hot and cold', shown on taps as H and C *US, 1971*

hand cannon *noun* a large pistol. Used for effect, quaintly old-fashioned *US, 1929*

handcuff *noun* an engagement or wedding ring *US, 1926*

handcuffed *adjective* married *US, 1945*

hand-doodle *noun* to masturbate *US, 1968*

H and E *noun* high explosives *US, 1971*

-handed *suffix* denotes the specific or general size of a gang when combined with a unit of measurement, e.g. two-, ten-, mob-handed *UK, 1999*

hand fuck *verb* to insert a lubricated fist into a partner's rectum or vagina, leading to sexual pleasure for both *US, 1979*

handful *noun* **1** a troublesome person who is difficult to control; something difficult to control *UK, 1887*. **2** a prison sentence of five years *US, 1930*. **3** in a restaurant or soda fountain, five *US, 1967*. **4** in racing, five. As high as you can count on one hand. To win by 'a couple of handfuls' is to win by ten lengths *UK, 1937*. **5** five pounds (£5) *UK, 1961*. **6** gambling odds of 5–1, especially among bookmakers *UK, 1984*. ▶ **get a handful; have a handful** to fondle a woman's breasts, buttocks or genitals *UK, 1977*

hand gallop *noun* an act of male masturbation *US, 1971*

hand grenaded *adjective* (used of a racing car engine) exploded and damaged *US, 1980*

handicap *noun* a sexually transmitted infection, especially gonorrhoea. Rhyming slang for CLAP *UK, 1992*

handicap chase; handicap *noun* a face, especially an ugly face. Rhyming slang *UK, 1992*

handie *noun* an act of manual masturbation. From HAND JOB *AUSTRALIA, 1994*

handies *noun* fondling of hands by lovers *AUSTRALIA, 1915*

handing out *noun* in prison, the act of separating an imprisoned mother from her baby (subject to disciplinary exceptions the parent and child may spend up to eighteen months in a mother and baby unit) *UK, 1996*

hand jig; hand gig *noun* masturbation *US, 1962*

hand jive *noun* **1** a rhythmic pattern of hand-movements performed to music as a substitute for more usual forms of dance; hence, obscure hand signals *US, 1958*. **2** an act of masturbating a male *UK, 2003*

hand job *noun* **1** manual stimulation of another's genitals *US, 1937*. **2** in trucking, cargo that must be hand-loaded *US, 1971*

hand-job *verb* to masturbate another person *US, 1969*

handle *noun* **1** a name, a nickname *US, 1837*. **2** a self-attributed identity used on citizens' band radio *US, 1974*. **3** a big nose *US, 1750*. **4** a glass of beer served in a 10-fluid-ounce glass with a handle *AUSTRALIA, 1943*. **5** a half-pint glass of beer *NEW ZEALAND, 1994*. **6** in horse racing, the total amount bet, either on a given race or an entire season *US, 1951*. ▶ **get a handle on** to gain a means of comprehending or controlling someone or something *US, 1972*

handle *verb* to stay in control. Hawaiian youth usage as an intransitive verb *US, 1981*. ▶ **handle swollen goods** (of a male) to masturbate. Punning a criminal activity: 'to handle stolen goods' *UK, 2001*

handler *noun* **1** a drug dealer who deals in large quantities to retail-level sellers *US, 1953*. **2** in drag racing, a driver *US, 1968*

handles *noun* in basketball, ball-handling skill *US, 1997*

handle-slammer *noun* a person who manipulates the handles of a slot machine that is in need of repair, forcing the machine to pay out regardless of the spin *US, 1984*

hand like a foot *noun* in card games, a very bad hand of cards. A pun that was previously used of poor handwriting. Currently in popular use at Internet sites devoted to poker *UK, 1956*

handmade *noun* **1** a large penis. An allusion to the belief that excessive masturbation will produce a larger-than-average penis *US, 1967*. **2** a hand-rolled cigarette *US, 1988*

hand mucker *noun* in gambling, a cheat who switches cards *US, 1979*

handout *noun* in prison, the act of giving a prisoner's property to a visitor for removal *UK, 1996*

hand over fist *adverb* very quickly, especially applied to making or losing money *UK, 1888*

hand queen *noun* a male homosexual who favours masturbating his partner *US, 1964*

hand-reared *adjective* endowed with a large penis. A reference to masturbation, presumably with the suggestion that such manipulation promotes growth *UK, 1961*

hand relief *noun* masturbation in the context of a hand massage – a sexual service offered in some massage parlours *US, 1988*

hand ride *noun* in horse racing, a race run without using a whip *US, 1974*

hand-rolled *noun* a marijuana cigarette. Mildly euphemistic, and thus mildly humorous *US, 1978*

hands *noun* ▶ **put your hands up** to confess, especially to admit to a crime. The universal gesture of surrender. The singular 'put your hand up' seems unlikely; it smacks of a schoolchild seeking attention *UK, 1970*

hands and feet *noun* meat. Rhyming slang *UK, 1992*

hands and heels *adjective* in horse racing, used for describing a ride in which the jockey did not use his whip *AUSTRALIA, 1989*

handshake *noun* **1** the synchronisation mechanism of two computers or two programs *US, 1991*. **2** to engage in mutual masturbation *US, 1961*

hand shandy; handy shandy *noun* an act of male masturbation *UK, 1997*

hand shoe *noun* a glove *US, 1977*

hands off cocks – feet in socks!; hands off your cocks and pull up your socks!; hands off cocks – on with socks!; hands off cocks, on socks! used for awakening sleeping men. Military usage *UK, 1976*

handsome! excellent, first-rate; used for registering approval *UK, 1997*

hand thing *noun* the act of masturbating a man. A variation of HAND-JOB *US, 2001*

hand-to-gland combat *noun* an act of masturbation, especially if conducted with vigour. A pun on 'hand-to-hand combat' *AUSTRALIA, 1998*

hand tools *noun* lockpicks, screwdrivers and other tools used by burglars *US, 1982*

hand to rouf *noun* in betting, odds of 5–4. A combination of HAND (five) and ROUF (four) *UK, 1991*

hand up *verb* to incriminate *UK, 2002*

handwave *verb* to oversimplify or give a cursory explanation of a complicated point *US, 1981*

handy *noun* among antique dealers, an antique small enough to conceal in the palm of the hand *UK, 2003*

handy *adjective* good at fighting *UK, 1997*

hane *adjective* disgusting. An abbreviation of HEINOUS *US, 1993*

hang *noun* **1** a little bit. Used as a euphemism for 'damn'; always in the negative *UK, 1861*. **2** used as a euphemism for 'hell' *SOUTH AFRICA, 1960*. **3** a person who regularly spends time in one place, or around people and places that are in some way associated *US, 1996*. **4** a job *US, 1950*. ▶ **get the hang of something** to learn how to do something *US, 1847*. ▶ **give a hang; care a hang** to care, to be concerned – usually in a negative context *UK, 1861*

hang *verb* **1** to turn, especially but not exclusively applied to driving a vehicle. Usually in the phrase 'hang a left/right' (to make a left/right turn) *US, 1967*. **2** to tolerate, to keep up with *US, 1993*. **3** used for registering annoyance, impatience, etc, as in 'hang the expense'. From the sense 'to execute by hanging' *UK, 1392*. **4** to idle *US, 1941*. **5** (used of a computer program) to wait in suspension for something that will not occur *US, 1983*. ▶ **hang crepe** in a hospital, to manage a patient's expectations by leading them to expect the very worst *US, 1994*. ▶ **hang five** to surf with five toes extended over the front edge of the board *US, 1963*. ▶ **hang hard** to suffer a hangover *US, 1996*. ▶ **hang heels** to surf with your heels extended backwards over the tail of the surfboard *US, 1977*. ▶ **hang her alongside awhile before we heist her aboard** (of an idea or plan) to urge someone to think about it before we do anything *CANADA, 1992*. ▶ **hang it up 1** to insult *US, 1989*. **2** to stop talking, to shut up *US, 1963*. **3** to retire. Or 'hang them up' *US, 1936*. ▶ **hang loose** to do little and to do it without angst *US, 1955*. ▶ **hang on the iron** to put snow chains on a truck's tyres *US, 1961*. ▶ **hang on the leg** (used of a prisoner) to associate and curry favour with prison authorities *US, 1992*. ▶ **hang on the wall** (used of a groupie) to loiter at a rock and roll club in the hopes of making contact with a musician *US, 1969*. ▶ **hang one on** to punch *AUSTRALIA, 1974*. ▶ **hang paper 1** to pass counterfeit money *US, 1976*. **2** to pass cheques with fraudulent intent *UK, 1996*. ▶ **hang ten** to surf with all the toes of both feet extended over the front of the board *US, 1963*. ▶ **hang tight** to stay put, to stay resolved *US, 1947*. ▶ **hang up your jock** to quit or retire *US, 1983*. ▶ **hang your hat** to live, to reside *US, 1969*. ▶ **hang your own** in circus and carnival usage, to brag. A metaphor derived from the image of the braggart hanging posters advertising himself *US, 1981*

hang about *verb* to loiter, to hesitate, to haunt *UK, 1892*

hang about! used for demanding a pause in an activity. Always imperative, sometimes used to indicate that the speaker has suddenly understood something *UK, 1974*

hangar *noun* in trucking, a garage *US, 1976*

hangar-flying *noun* a group conversation among combat pilots, reliving combat missions *US, 1918*

hang around *verb* to idle, to pass time aimlessly, to socialise *US, 1830*

hangar queen *noun* an aircraft that spends an inordinate amount of time being repaired *US, 1943*

hangashore; angishore *noun* a person who does not go out fishing and thus is regarded as lazy. Originally from the Irish word *aindeiseoir* (a wretch), this word was adapted by folk etymology to apply to the fishing culture of Atlantic Canada *CANADA, 1988*

hangcher *noun* a handkerchief *TRISTAN DA CUNHA, 1963*

hang-down *noun* the penis *US, 2001*

hanged up *adjective* drug-intoxicated *US, 1949*

hanger *noun* **1** a piece of paper currency that has not fallen all the way through the slot on a casino table where cash is dropped *US, 1980*. **2** in pool, a ball that is at rest right at the edge of a pocket *US, 1937*. **3** a handgun cartridge that fails to detonate immediately after being struck by the firing pin *US, 1957*. **4** a handbag with a strap *US, 1950*

Hanger Lane *noun* a nuisance, an annoyance, a frustration, an irritation. Rhyming slang for PAIN, formed from the name of a traffic-junction on London's North Circular road, probably coined by a driver in a jam *UK, 1992*

hang-gut *noun* a paunchy stomach *BAHAMAS, 1982*

hanging *adjective* **1** of inferior quality *UK, 2002*. **2** drunk; exhausted *UK, 2002*

hanging bacon *noun* the outer labia of the vagina *UK, 2002*

hanging Johnny *noun* the penis in a flaccid state *US, 1980*

Hanging Sam *noun* General Samuel T. Williams of the US Army. Williams fought Pancho Villa in Mexico, and then in World War 1, World War 2, Korea and Vietnam *US, 1972*

hang it!; hang it all! used for registering annoyance, irritation or despair *UK, 1703*

hangman *noun* a difficult person *NEW ZEALAND, 2002*

hangnail *noun* a slow-moving person, a dawdler, especially a slow driver. Rhyming slang for 'snail', from the characteristics of the creature *UK, 1998*

hang on *verb* **1** to wait; to wait while using a telephone. Often used in the imperative *UK, 1959*. **2** to make a criminal charge against *US, 1957*

hangout *noun* a place where people gather to socialise. At times a negative connotation *US, 1892*

hang out *verb* **1** to spend time with someone, usually a friend or friends *US, 1867*. **2** to monitor a citizen's band radio channel *US, 1976*

hangtime *noun* time spent waiting for something to happen *US, 1991*

hang tough! used for expressing support when departing *US, 1990*

hang up *verb* **1** when combined with an article symbolic of a trade, profession or sport, to retire from that field of endeavour. 'Hang up your fiddle', which carries the generalised sense of retiring, is first recorded in 1833; however the current wide use may well owe its generation to Western films, particularly the cliché of an aged or disabled gun-fighter hanging up his guns. Of modern variations 'Hang up (one's) tits' is recorded of a retiring female impersonator in 1984. In 2003 a brief search of contemporary sources reveals a hairdresser hanging up his scissors, a judge hanging up the wig and robe, a Malayan who has hung up his Kalashnikov, a chef who hangs up his toque and white jacket, and a war correspondent who has hung up her flak jacket; jockeys hang up their silks, boxers hang up their gloves, sumo wrestlers hang up their loincloths, etc *UK, 1833*. **2** in a prayer group, to pray last. If 'to pray first' is to DIAL, then it is only logical that 'to pray last' is 'to hang up' *US, 1990*. ▶ **hang up a shingle** to go into business for yourself *US, 1997*

hangup; hang-up *noun* **1** an emotional problem, neurosis or inhibition *US, 1952*. **2** in foot-propelled scootering, a seizing-up of a wheel during the performance of a trick *UK, 2000*

hanhich *noun* hashish. Probably a misspelling of 'hashish' *UK, 2003*

hank *noun* ▶ **take your hank** to masturbate *US, 1967*

hank book *noun* a pornographic book or magazine *US, 1974*

hank freak *noun* a person obsessed with masturbating *US, 1967*

Hank Marvin *adjective* very hungry. Rhyming slang for 'starving'; based on the name of popular guitarist Hank Marvin (b.1941) *UK, 1998*

hankty *adjective* suspicious *US, 1966*

hanky; hankie *noun* a handkerchief; a tissue (often qualified as a paper hankie). In the US a childish shortening virtually conventional in the UK *UK, 1895*

hanky code; hankie code *noun* a designation of a person's sexual preferences, signalled by the colour of the handkerchief and the pocket in which it is worn *US, 1991*

hanky pank *noun* a carnival game in which the customer is allowed to win small, inexpensive prizes *US, 1985*

hankypank *adjective* (used of a carnival game) inexpensive *US, 1950*

hanky-panky; hankie-pankie *noun* **1** trickery, mischief, especially of a sexual nature *UK, 1841*. **2** a boyfriend. Teen slang *UK, 2003*

Hannibal Lecter *noun* a ticket inspector. Rhyming slang, formed from the name of a fictional serial killer who caught the popular imagination, created in 1981 by author Thomas Harris and portrayed on film in 1986 by Brian Cox, and, most famously, by Anthony Hopkins from 1992 *UK, 1998*

Hanoi Hannah *noun* a composite character on Radio Hanoi who broadcast during the Vietnam war with a target audience of US troops and a goal of lessening troop morale *US, 1967*

Hanoi Hilton *nickname* a North Vietnamese prisoner of war camp, formally known as the Hoa Lo Prison (1964–1973). The title of a 1987 film starring Michael Moriarty and Jeffrey Jones as US prisoners of war trying to survive in the camp *US, 1970*

hanyak *noun* a smokeable methamphetamine *UK, 1998*

hap *noun* **1** an event or activity. An abbreviation of 'happening'; usually found in questions such as 'What's the hap?' *US, 1971*. **2** a bite; a mouthful. Directly from Afrikaans *SOUTH AFRICA, 1978*

hapas capas *noun* a writ of *habeas corpus US, 1950*

ha'penny *noun* the female genitals. From the small value halfpenny coin *UK, 1984* ▷ *see:* HALFPENNY DIP, HALFPENNY STAMP

ha'porth *noun* a small or negligible measure of something (cost, potency, wit, etc). A colloquial contraction of 'halfpennyworth' that orginally, surely, suggested greater value and less contempt *UK, 1976*

ha'p'orth; haporth; apeth *noun* a fool. A contraction of 'halfpennyworth' signifying something of little value; gently contemptuous and usually qualified as 'daft ha'porth', 'silly apeth', etc *UK, 1974*

happen *verb* to be successful *US, 1949*

happening *noun* **1** an unstructured event built around music, drugs and a strong sense of bonding *US, 1959*. **2** a party at which there is much drinking; a booze-up *AUSTRALIA, 1971*

happening *adjective* modern, fashionable, chic. In common with many words that define the times, 'happening' is now deeply unfashionable, surviving in irony and the vocabularies of those who were there when it was 'happening' *US, 1977*. ▶ **it's all happening!** used when more than one thing happens at the same time; used of a general state of excitement *UK, 1976*

happily *adverb* in computing, operating without awareness of an important fact *US, 1991*

happiness *noun* MDMA, the recreational drug best known as ecstasy *UK, 2002*

happy *noun* a variety of MDMA, the recreational drug best known as ecstasy *UK, 1996*

happy *adjective* slightly drunk *UK, 1770*. ▶ **are you happy in your work?** asked, ironically, of someone engaged in dirty or dangerous work. Originally military, in the form 'are you happy in the Service?' *UK, 1943*

-happy *suffix* mentally unbalanced or obsessed in the manner denoted by earlier or current circumstances, or impending fate, as affixed. Originally military, from HAPPY (slightly drunk); thus 'bomb-happy' (nerves shattered by exposure to imminent death or mutilation), 'demob-happy' (obsessed by *demob*ilisation, release from service) *US, 1931*

happy as a pig in shit *adjective* extremely happy *UK, 1944*

happy as Larry *adjective* extremely happy. Just exactly who the proverbially happy Larry was is one of those snippets of information lost in time *AUSTRALIA, 1905*

happy bag *noun* a holdall in which an armed robber carries the equipment of his trade *UK, 2002*

happy bunny *noun* a person who is very contented. Childish imagery, originally business jargon. A contented worker, or team member. Often with a negative sense: 'not a happy bunny' *US, 1998*

happy camper *noun* used as a humorous description of a contented person. Often said with sarcasm or used in the negative *US, 1981*

happy cigarette *noun* a marijuana cigarette *US, 1982*

happy-clappy *adjective* filled with spiritual joy, sometimes applied to Christians but rarely in the conventional Church *UK, 1993*

happy day *noun* a mixture of bottled strong ale and draught beer *UK: SCOTLAND, 1996*

happy days *noun* **1** a type of bet in an illegal numbers game lottery *US, 1957*. **2** breadfruit *BARBADOS, 1965*

happy drug *noun* MDMA, the recreational drug best known as ecstasy *UK, 2003*

happy dust *noun* cocaine, morphine or any powdered mind-altering drug. Imparts a sense of nostalgia, not unlike WACKY BACCY (marijuana). The term of choice for cocaine in George Gershwin's *Porgy and Bess US, 1922*

happy fag *noun* a marijuana cigarette *UK, 2002*

happy gas *noun* nitrous oxide, laughing gas *AUSTRALIA, 1986*

happy hacking used as a farewell *US, 1981*

happy happy joy joy used as a humorous, often sarcastic, celebratory remark. First heard in the *Ren and Stimpy* cartoon (1991–1995), and then popularised with a broader audience by Keith Olberman on ESPN *US, 1997*

happy herb *noun* marijuana *UK, 1998*

happy hour *noun* a period of time in the late afternoon when a bar serves free snacks and drinks at reduced prices *US, 1959*

happy hours *noun* flowers. Rhyming slang *UK, 1960*

happy little Vegemite *noun* a happy person, especially a child. From an advertising jingle for Vegemite™, a yeast-based spread popular in Australia *AUSTRALIA, 1988*

happy meal *noun* a mixture of chemical stimulants and depressants. A Happy Meal is more usually a product of McDonalds™ fast-food restaurants *UK, 2001*

happy pie *noun* the vagina *US, 1974*

happy pill *noun* **1** an amphetamine or other central nervous system stimulant *UK, 1956*. **2** a Prozac™ tablet *UK, 2001*. **3** a tablet of MDMA, the recreational drug best known as ecstasy *UK, 2003*

happy powder *noun* cocaine *UK, 1998*

happy Sally *noun* strong, homemade whisky *US, 1986*

happy shop *noun* an off-licence (a liquor store) *US, 1972*

happy slap *verb* to physically assault a randomly chosen person and film the incident on a mobile phone *UK, 2005*

happy slapper *noun* a person who, as part of popular youth craze, violently attacks a randomly chosen individual while the incident is filmed by an accomplice *UK, 2005*

happy slapping *noun* an apparently motiveless violent attack on a randomly chosen innocent person while the incident is filmed by an accomplice; or such attacks collectively; or the teenage craze for such attacks *UK, 2005*

happy stick *noun* a marijuana cigarette enhanced with phencyclidine, the recreational drug known as PCP or angel dust *US, 1999*

happy trails *noun* cocaine. From the cowboy song known by those who came of age in the US in the 1950s and 60s *US, 1993*

happy trails used as a farewell. A catchphrase television sign-off sung on *The Roy Rogers Show* (NBC, 1951–57). Repeated with referential humour *US, 1951*

happy valley *noun* the cleft between the buttock cheeks *US, 1970s*

Happy Valley *nickname* the Vinh Thanh Valley, during the war a dangerous area northeast of An Khe, South Vietnam *US, 1983*

haps *noun* the latest; something that is popular. Often heard as 'the haps' *US, 1961*

harami *noun* a shrewd or cunning person; used as a term of abuse it may carry the same sense as 'bastard'. From Urdu *haram* (that which is sacred), hence Urdu *harami* (a rogue). There is anecdotal evidence that it has been in UK since the 1960s. Current in Pakistan and Indian street slang, as is the equivalent but more abusive Urdu term *haramzada* (a son of wickedness; a BASTARD) *INDIA, 2003*

harass *verb* to flirt *TRINIDAD AND TOBAGO, 2003*

Harbour City *nickname* Sydney *AUSTRALIA, 1964*

harbour light; harbour *adjective* right. Rhyming slang *UK, 1961*

hard *noun* **1** an erection *US, 1961*. **2** hardcore sexual material *US, 1977*. **3** an addictive drug *NEW ZEALAND, 1982*. **4** coins *US, 1950*

hard *adjective* **1** of drinks, intoxicating, spiritous, 'strong' *US, 1789*. **2** (used of drugs) powerfully addictive *US, 1955*. **3** fine, excellent *US, 1948*. **4** muscular, toned *US, 1990*. **5** of rock music, serious, uncompromising, with a strong rhythmic force *US, 1960s*. **6** of rave music, relentlessly rhythmic *UK, 1998*. **7** of pornographic material, descriptive of anything that is more explicit than society finds generally acceptable. A flexible standard depending on where you are. *US, 1969*. **8** in craps, a point made with a matching pair. A bet on a 'hard' number means that the only combination that will win is a pair. Often used in the phrase 'the hard way' *US, 1930*. **9** (used of straightened hair) heavily greased *US, 1970*. **10** in blackjack, said of a hand without an ace or with an ace and a value of 12 or higher *US, 1978*. **11** (used of a theatre ticket) reserved for a specific seat *US, 1973*

hard *adverb* ▶ **go hard** to engage in gunfire *US, 2003*

hard ankle *noun* a working man, especially a trucker *US, 1976*

hard-arsed; hard-ass; hard-assed *adjective* uncompromising, unyielding, tough, stubborn *UK, 1903*

hard ask *noun* a difficult challenge *NEW ZEALAND, 2000*

hard-ass *noun* a strict, unforgiving, unrelenting person *US, 1966*

hard-ass *verb* **1** to endure a difficult situation *US, 1967*. **2** to treat harshly *US, 1970*

hard at it *adjective* very busy, especially when engaged on a particular task *UK, 1749*

hardback *adjective* old *JAMAICA, 2000*

hardball *noun* **1** competition or conflict with no holds barred *US, 1972*. **2** crack cocaine *UK, 2003*

hardballer *noun* a person who competes or pursues an interest with an intense focus and little thought as to the consequences *US, 1984*

hardbelly *noun* a teenage girl or young woman. Biker (motorcyle) usage *US, 1988*

hard bit *noun* a prison sentence that is especially difficult to serve, *1996*

hard-boiled *adjective* callous, cynical, emotionally uninvolved, tough; describing the characteristics of macho tough guys in 'hard-boiled' pulp fiction. Figurative usage of the solid properties of hard-boiled eggs, or clothing vigorously boiled in starch; applied by Mark Twain (1835–1910) to refer to rigid rules of grammar (1886); in the early 1900s it applied to hard or stiff clothing; by 1918 it was being used to describe a person who stuck rigidly to the rules; from which the current sense evolved *US, 1904*

hardboot *noun* a person from Kentucky *US, 1923*

hard candy *noun* **1** heroin *US, 1970*. **2** a person who has been identified for revenge by a prison gang *US, 1997*

hard-case *noun* a hardened, tough person *US, 1836*

hard-case *adjective* eccentric, unconventional *NEW ZEALAND, 1971*

hard cat *noun* a well-dressed, popular male *US, 1959*

hard-charge *verb* in car racing, to drive aggressively *US, 1965*

hard chaw *noun* a thug *IRELAND, 2003*

hard cheddar *noun* bad luck *UK, 1931*

hard cheese *noun* bad luck. Often said in commiseration *UK, 1876*

hardcore *noun* **1** amyl nitrite. Perhaps from 'hardcore' as a grade of pornography because of the drug's reputation as a sexual relaxant *UK, 1996*. **2** a regular soldier of the North Vietnamese Army or the Viet Cong *US, 1991*

hardcore *adjective* **1** of pornography, graphic, explicit. The gradations between SOFTCORE and 'hardcore' vary over time and place; in general, the erect penis, penetration and ejaculation are the hallmarks of hardcore pornography *US, 1970*. **2** extreme *US, 1997*

hardcore *adverb* extremely *US, 1997*

hard cut *adjective* rough, tough, hard-living *CANADA, 1962*

hard-doer; hard doer *noun* a person who struggles valiantly against difficulties. Literally, a person who 'does it hard'. A term of approbation *AUSTRALIA, 1910*

hard dresser *noun* an aggressive, 'mannish' lesbian *US, 1967*

hard-earned *noun* money, especially that identified as earnings, *1975*

hard-ears *noun* said of a stubborn person *TRINIDAD AND TOBAGO, 2003*

har-de-har-har used as a vocalisation mocking laughter *US, 1957*

hardfist *noun* a violence-prone, tough person *CANADA, 1955*

hard graft *noun* hard work *AUSTRALIA, 1873*

hard-grafting *adjective* hard-working *AUSTRALIA, 1972*

hard guy *noun* a serious, violent criminal *US, 1916*

hard hat *noun* an elite, full-time Viet Cong soldier *US, 1965*

hard head *noun* a criminal who uses explosives to break into safes *US, 1949*

hard hit *noun* an act of defecation. Rhyming slang for SHIT, especially in the phrase 'go for a hard hit' *UK, 1978*

Hard John *noun* **1** an agent of the Federal Bureau of Investigation (FBI) *US, 1945*. **2** a tough, uncompromising person *US, 1961*

hard knock *adjective* toughened by life. Having been through the SCHOOL OF HARD KNOCKS *US, 1977*

hard labour *noun* a neighbour. Rhyming slang *UK, 1992*

hard leg *noun* an experienced, cynical prostitute *US, 1967*

hard line *noun* crack cocaine *UK, 1998*

hard lines *noun* bad luck. Probably of nautical origins. Often said in commiseration *UK, 1824*

hard-look *verb* to stare at aggressively *US, 1994*

hard mack *noun* a brutish pimp who relies on force and the threat of force to control his prostitutes *US, 1972*

hard man *noun* **1** a professional thug; a person not afraid of violent action *US, 1970*. **2** an uncompromising politician or businessman *UK, 1976*

hard money *noun* cash *US, 1972*

hard-mouth *verb* to threaten or disparage *TRINIDAD AND TOBAGO, 1960*

hard nail *noun* a hypodermic needle *US, 1955*

hard-nosed *adjective* stubborn, uncompromising *US, 1927*

hard nut *noun* a dangerous foe; a tough individual; a difficult challenge. Clipped from 'a hard nut to crack' *US, 1884*

hard nut to crack *noun* ▷see: TOUGH NUT

hard of hearing *adjective* undisciplined, disobedient *TRINIDAD AND TOBAGO, 1973*

hard-on *noun* **1** the erect penis; an erection *US, 1888*. **2** a grudge *US, 1931*. **3** a stubborn, belligerent person *US, 1968*. **4** a prized possession; something to be desired. Derives from the sense as 'an erection', via the idea that inanimate objects can be SEXY (desirable) *UK, 1999*. **5** a desire for *US, 1971*

hard on *adjective* addicted to *BAHAMAS, 1982*

hard one *noun* in necrophile usage, a corpse that has stiffened with rigor mortis *US, 1987*

hard pimp *noun* a pimp who relies on violence and the threat of violence to control his prostitutes *US, 1973*

hard-pushed *adjective* in difficulties, especially financial *UK, 1834*

hard rice *noun* during the Vietnam war, weapons and ammunition *US, 1985*

hard rock *noun* crack cocaine. An elaboration of ROCK *UK, 1998*

hardshell Baptist *noun* a member of the Primitive Baptist Church, or any other rigidly orthodox Baptist *US, 1838*

hard shells *noun* powerfully addictive drugs, such as heroin, morphine and cocaine *US, 1960*

hard, soft and wet denotes all that is necessary to operate a computer *UK, 1998*

hard sports *noun* sadomasochistic sex-play involving defecation, especially when it is offered as a service in a prostitute's advertising *UK, 2003*

hard spot *noun* an ambush using tanks or other armour as part of the ambush *US, 1991*

hard stuff *noun* **1** alcoholic drink other than beer or wine *AUSTRALIA, 1832*. **2** addictive drugs such as heroin or cocaine *US, 1950*. **3** coins *US, 1788*

hardtail *noun* a motorcyle with no rear shock absorbers *US, 1992*

hard time *noun* a long prison sentence, whether in absolute terms or relative to the crime or relative to the prisoner's ability to survive *US, 1927*

hard-timer *noun* a prisoner serving a long sentence *US, 1986*

hard up *adjective* **1** in want of money, impoverished *UK, 1818*. **2** in need of something specified *UK, 1840*

hardware *noun* **1** weapons, usually guns *US, 1865*. **2** ostentatious jewellery *US, 1939*. **3** silverware *US, 1962*. **4** any medal or trophy awarded in a competition *US, 1921*

hardware shop *noun* a homosexual male brothel *UK, 1987*

hardware store *noun* a poker game in which players generally bet based on the value of their hands and do not bluff. An allusion to the True Value chain of hardware stores in the US *US, 1996*

hard word *noun* ▶ **put the hard word on someone 1** to ask someone for sexual intercourse *AUSTRALIA, 1936*. **2** to make a fervent request of someone *AUSTRALIA, 1918*

hard yakka; hard yacker *noun* hard work *AUSTRALIA, 1888*

hard yard *noun* a difficult challenge *NEW ZEALAND, 2000*

hard yards *noun* exacting work. Originally a sporting metaphor *AUSTRALIA, 2001*

hare and hound *noun* a round of drinks. Rhyming slang; a variation of FOX AND HOUND *UK, 1992*

hare-and-hound race *noun* a long motorcyle race in the desert *US, 1965*

haricot bean; haricot *noun* a male homosexual. Rhyming slang for QUEEN *AUSTRALIA, 1971*

Harlem credit card *noun* a siphon used for stealing petrol from parked cars *US, 1979*

Harlem handshake *noun* a series of hand-to-hand manoeuvres that combine into an idiosyncratic handshake. Harlem, New York, is a centre of the black community and figuratively used to emphasise stereotypical and negative black characteristics *US, 2000*

Harlem heater *noun* any improvised source of heat, such as leaving an oven door open to heat the room. New York police slang *US, 1997*

Harlem sunset *noun* the blood-red line on freshly razor-slashed skin. Harlem New York, is a centre of the black community and figuratively used to emphasise negative black characteristics; here, combined with an allusion to 'blood red sunsets', the suggestion is that only black people get into razor fights *US, 1940*

Harlem taxi *noun* a large, luxury car painted in an extravagant colour *US, 1962*

Harlem tennis *noun* the game of craps *US, 1983*

Harlem toothpick *noun* a pocket knife; a switchblade *US, 1944*

Harley wrench *noun* a hammer. Humorous biker (motorcyle) usage, suggesting a low degree of sophistication among motorcycle mechanics *US, 2003*

harmonic *noun* Indian *tonic* water. Rhyming slang *UK, 1984*

harm reducer *noun* marijuana. A reference to the claim that smoking tobacco mixed with marijuana will cause less harm than unadulterated tobacco *UK, 2001*

harness *noun* **1** reinforcement on the outside of a safe *US, 1949*. **2** a uniform *US, 1853*. **3** the leather clothing worn by some motorcycle riders and embraced as a fashion statement by others *US, 1993*

harness *adjective* uniformed *US, 1903*

harness rack *noun* an old horse *CANADA, 1987*

Harold Lloyd; harold *noun* celluloid (as a housebreaking tool, used for forcing locks). Rhyming slang, formed from the name of the legendary silent film comedian, 1893–1971 *UK, 1959*

Harold Macmillan; 'arold *noun* a villain. Rhyming slang, formed from the name of a British prime minister (1957–63) and statesman, 1894–1986 *UK, 1992*

Harold Pinter; 'arold *noun* a splinter. Rhyming slang, formed from the name of a playwright (b.1930) *UK, 1992*

harolds *noun* knickers. Probably rhyming slang, from HARRY TAGGS, shortened to Harry, thus Harold *AUSTRALIA, 1971*

harp *noun* **1** a harmonica *US, 1887*. **2** an Irish-American or an Irish person *US, 1898*

harpic *adjective* mad, crazy, eccentric. A play on ROUND THE BEND (mad) and branded toilet cleaner Harpic's advertising slogan 'cleans round the bend'. It is interesting to note that a cocktail of blue curacoa, kahlua, vodka and lemonade is named Harpic – probably not just for the colour. Also used as a nickname *UK, 1961*

harpist *noun* a harmonica player. From HARP (a harmonica) *UK, 1993*

harpoon *noun* a needle used to inject drugs intravenously, especially a hollow needle used in an improvised contraption *US, 1938*

Harris tweed *noun* amphetamine. Rhyming slang for SPEED *UK, 1983*

Harry *noun* heroin. Giving an personal identity and disguise to H (heroin) *US, 1954*

Harry-big-button *noun* any cheap electrical appliance characterised by unfashionable design, especially large control knobs *UK, 2002*

harry-carry *noun* suicide. From Japanese *hara-kiri* (ritual suicide by disembowelment) *UK, 1996*

Harry Freemans *noun* anything that is free. Royal Navy, from obsolete 'drink at freeman's quay' (to drink at another's expense) *UK, 1962*

Harry Hill *noun* a tablet of MDMA, the recreational drug best known as ecstasy. Rhyming slang for 'pill'; based on the name of UK comedian Harry Hill (b.1964) *UK, 2001*

Harry Hoof *noun* a male homosexual. Glasgow rhyming slang for POOF *UK: SCOTLAND, 1985*

Harry Huggins *noun* a fool, an idiot, often with an implication that the fool is a victim (and a fool to be so). Rhyming slang for MUGGINS (an idiot) *UK, 1992*

Harry James *noun* the nose. A pun on 'trumpet', connected to band leader and trumpet player Harry James (1916–83) *UK, 1958*

Harry Lauder *noun* a prison warder. Rhyming slang, formed from the name of the Scottish comedian and singer, Sir Harry Lauder, 1870–1950 *UK, 1961*

Harry Lime *noun* time. Rhyming slang, formed from the name of the character played by Orson Welles in the 1950 film *The Third Man UK, 1972*

Harry Monk; harry *noun* semen. Rhyming slang for SPUNK; generally reduced *UK, 1992*

Harry Selby *noun* used in a theatre programme as a fictitious name for an actor. Less common than GEORGE SPELVIN, but serving the same purpose *US, 1973*

Harry Tagg *noun* bag. Rhyming slang; theatrical. Current in 1960 *UK, 1960*

Harry Taggs; harolds *noun* trousers. Rhyming slang for 'bags' (trousers) *UK, 1992*

Harry Tate *noun* **1** eight pounds (£8). Rhyming slang, formed from the stage name of musical hall performer Ronald Hutchinson, 1872–1940 *UK, 1992*. **2** a plate. Rhyming slang *UK, 1992*. **3** a first officer in the Merchant Navy. Rhyming slang for 'mate' *UK, 1961*. **4** a confusion; an attack of nerves; an emotional state. Rhyming slang for 'state' *UK, 1932*

Harry Tate *adjective* late. Rhyming slang, formed from the stage name of musical hall performer Ronald Hutchinson, 1872–1940 *UK, 1960*

Harry Tates *noun* branded cigarettes, Player's 'Weights'. Rhyming slang *UK, 1974*

Harry Wragg; Harry Rag; harry *noun* a cigarette. Rhyming slang for FAG (a cigarette), formed on the name of jockey Harry Wragg, 1902–85 *UK, 1960*

Harry X-ers with Harry preceding and -ers suffixed, a personified variation of an adjective or adverb. Mainly nautical, in applications such as 'Harry Nuders' (naked) *UK, 1925*

harsh *noun* marijuana, hashish. Probably a play on the pronunciation of HASH (hashish) but may well refer to the quality *UK, 2003*

harsh *verb* to criticise or disparage *US, 1988*. ▶ **harsh a mellow** to ruin a calm situation *US, 1997*

harsh *adjective* **1** disagreeable, forbidding, severe. Conventional English rendered slang by the young *US, 1984*. **2** in motor racing, bumpy and rough *US, 1980*

Hart, Schaffner and Marx *noun* in poker, three jacks. An allusion to a men's clothing manufacturer *US, 1988*

harum-scarum *adjective* reckless, careless *UK, 1751*

harum-scarum *adverb* recklessly, wildly *UK, 1691*

harvest moon; harvest *noun* a black person. Rhyming slang for COON *UK, 1992*

Harvey Nichol *noun* a predicament. Rhyming slang for PICKLE, formed from the name of London department store Harvey Nichols *UK, 1932*

Harvey Nichols *noun* pickles, savoury condiments. Rhyming slang, formed from the name of a London department store *UK, 1960*

Harvey Nicks; Harvey Nic's *nickname* Harvey Nichols, a fashionable department store *UK, 1991*

Harvey Smith *noun* a v-sign as an insulting gesture. Following an incident on 15th August 1971 when show-jumper Harvey Smith used the gesture at the British Jumping Derby and as a result was disqualified (a decision subsequently overturned); his spontaneous action swiftly became part of UK folklore *UK, 1979*

Harvey Wallbanger *noun* any unsafe, reckless and/or drunk driver *US, 1976*

has *noun* hashish. An abbreviated variation of HASH *UK, 1998*

has-been *noun* a person whose best days and greatest achievements are in the past *UK, 1606*

has beens *noun* green vegetables, especially cabbage. Rhyming slang for GREENS *UK, 1984*

hasbian *noun* a former lesbian; a woman who took lesbian lovers in college, but who reverted to heterosexuality after graduation from college *US, 1995*

hash *noun* **1** hashish (cannabis resin or pollen). Variant spellings include 'hashi', 'hashis' and 'haschi'. Derived from the Arabic word for 'herb' or 'grass', as though it were the herb 'par excellence' (Sadie Plant, 'Writing On Drugs', 1999) *US, 1948*. **2** a number sign (#)

on a computer keyboard *US, 1991*. ▶ **make a hash** to spoil, to make a mess of something *UK, 1833*

hash *verb* to serve alcoholic drink that is not the brand claimed *US, 1979*

hash and trash *noun* background noise during a citizens' band radio transmission *US, 1976*

Hashbury *nickname* the Haight-Ashbury neigbourhood of San Francisco. A blending of the two street names and an allusion to the drug-using propensities of the area's residents *US, 1967*

hashcake *noun* a confection that has marijuana or hashish as a major ingredient *UK, 2000*

hash cannon *noun* a device for smoking marijuana or hashish, used to force smoke deep into the lungs *US, 1970*

hasher *noun* a waitress in an inexpensive restaurant *US, 1908*

hash house *noun* a restaurant that serves inexpensive, simply prepared food, catering to working men *US, 1868*

hash joint *noun* a hash house *US, 1895*

hash out *verb* to discuss until an issue is resolved *US, 1995*

hashover *noun* a general feeling of lethargy or malaise following marijuana use. A play on 'hangover' and HASH (marijuana) *UK, 1996*

hash-puppy *noun* a dog trained to sniff-out marijuana. A play on Hush Puppies™, US branded footware, introduced in 1958 *AUSTRALIA, 1970*

hash-slinger *noun* a waitress or cook *US, 1868*

hassle *noun* a problem, trouble, harassment *US, 1946*

hassle *verb* **1** to harass, annoy *US, 1959*. **2** to engage in mock plane-to-plane aerial combat *US, 1979*

hasta la bye-bye goodbye. Intentionally butchered Spanish *US, 1990*

hasta la vista, baby! see you later! Popularised by Tone Loc in his 1989 rap hit 'Wild Thing' *US, 1990*

hasta lumbago used as a humorous farewell. An intentional corruption of the Spanish *hasta luego* (until later) *US, 1977*

hat *noun* **1** in drag racing, a crash helmet *US, 1968*. **2** a condom *US, 1992*. **3** a woman *US, 1963*. **4** on the railways, an incompetent worker *US, 1977*. **5** a US Marines drill instructor *US, 1991*. **6** twenty-five dollars *US, 1973*. **7** anything bought with a bribe, used as code for a bribe *US, 1973*. **8** the up-arrow or caret key (^) on a computer keyboard *US, 1991*. **9** a dose of LSD *US, 1994*. **10** in pinball, a piece of plastic that indicates a value when lit. Conventionally known as a 'playfield insert' *US, 1977*. ▶ **get hat** to leave *US, 1966*. ▶ **in the hat** marked for murder by a prison gang *US, 2003*. ▶ **throw your hat in first** to test out a situation before taking part *AUSTRALIA, 1953*. ▶ **wear more than one hat; wear several hats** to simultaneously hold more than one post, or position of responsibility *US, 1924*

hat and coat *noun* a boat, especially a refrigerated cargo ship. Rhyming slang *UK, 1992*

hat and feather; hatton *noun* weather. Rhyming slang *UK, 1992*

hat and scarf *noun* a bath. Rhyming slang, with Cockney pronunciation. *UK, 1992*

hatch *noun* **1** the vagina *US, 1967*. **2** the mouth *US, 1968*

hatch *verb* ▶ **hatch it** to forget about something *US, 1968*

hatchery *noun* a psychiatric ward or mental institution *US, 1994*

hatchet job *noun* an unwarranted and harshly critical attack on someone's or something's reputation *UK, 1944*

hatchet man *noun* **1** a person who is called upon to perform distasteful tasks. From the literal image of a paid assassin armed with a hatchet; sometimes abbreviated to a simple 'hatchet' *US, 1937*. **2** a physically aggressive athlete, especially one who is tasked with roughing up an opponent *US, 1971*

hatchintan *noun* a gypsy site. English gypsy use, from Romany *hatsh* (stop, rest) *UK, 2000*

hatch, match and dispatch *verb* (of a local preacher) to carry a person through life's big events *CANADA, 1992*

hatch, match and dispatch; hatches, matches, dispatches; hatched, matched, dispatched *noun* newspaper

announcements of births, marriages and deaths. A neat summation of life, originally applied by journalists to such newspaper columns; later recognised by church authorities as the times when most people are prepared to be part of a service or congregation *UK, 1937*

hate *verb* used in the phrase 'hate to say' as a substitute for 'have' *US, 2003*. ▶ **hate someone's guts** to hate someone intensely *UK, 1918*

hated *adjective* **1** bad, unpleasant *US, 1989*. **2** (used of a girl) beautiful beyond imagination. Usually as 'hated BETTY' *US, 1988*

hater *noun* a jealous or envious person *US, 2001*

hater juice *noun* derogatory speech *US, 2003*

hating life *adjective* depressed *US, 1989*

hatless tap dance *noun* (among Canadian Forces personnel) the march into the Commanding Officer's office to face a charge *CANADA, 1995*

hat out; hat up *verb* to leave *US, 1970*

hats *noun* LSD *UK, 1998*

hats off congratulations. An imperative variation of 'take your hat off to'; when hats were everyday wear the action would echo the words or make their use unnecessary *UK, 1929*

hatstand *adjective* mad, crazy. From the cartoon character 'Roger Irrelevant: he's completely hatstand' in the comic *Viz UK, 2003*

hatter *noun* **1** a solitary worker in a rural or remote area, especially one who suffers from social phobia. Originally applied to miners who worked their claims without a partner. Possibly from the phrase 'your hat covers your family' (you are alone in the world), though no doubt the concept of the 'mad hatter' must have had an influence. Now only historical *AUSTRALIA, 1853*. **2** a homosexual man. From BROWN-HATTER (a gay man) *UK, 1984*

Hattie Jacques; Hatties *noun* delirium tremens, the shakes. Rhyming slang, based on the name of actress and comedienne Hattie Jacques (1924–80) *UK, 2002*

hat trick *noun* three consecutive successes, usually in a sporting context; three linked events. Originally and conventionally a cricketing term, recorded to mark the bowling of three wickets with consecutive balls; achieving this phenomenal feat entitled the sportsman to a new hat from his club, hence 'hat-trick'. Subsequently adopted by other sports for lesser feats of three, such as three goals scored in a football match (which may well not be rewarded with a hat) *UK, 1909*

hatty *adjective* used to describe the qualities of an elaborate hat *UK, 1959*

hat up! used for urging departure *US, 1971*

haul *noun* the proceeds of a crime or business operation *US, 1950*

haul *verb* ▶ **haul ass** to go swiftly *US, 1918*. ▶ **haul butt** to move quickly *US, 1968*. ▶ **haul coal** (used of a white person) to have sex with a black person *US, 1972*. ▶ **haul someone over the coals** to give a stern reprimand to someone *UK, 1795*. ▶ **haul the mail 1** in trucking, to drive faster to make up for lost time *US, 1971*. **2** in hot rodding and drag racing, to perform at the highest potential *US, 1993*

hauler *noun* **1** in the usage of youthful model road racers (slot car racers), a fast model road car *US, 1997*. **2** a very fast drag racing car *US, 1960s to 70s*

haurangi *adjective* drunk *NEW ZEALAND, 1960*

have *verb* **1** to have sex with someone *UK, 1594*. **2** to believe something, to accept *UK, 2001*. **3** to outwit, to cheat, to deceive *UK, 1805*. ▶ **have a no** I don't have. Korean war usage from Japanese pidgin; a supply officer's perfect answer to a requisition for supplies not in stock *US, 1951*. ▶ **have a pop at** to attack, especially verbally. A variation of 'have a pop at' (to try) adopting a different sense of 'pop' (to hit) *UK, 2001*. ▶ **have got 'em; have got 'em bad** to have the *delirium tremens*, to have a fit of nerves or depression or 'the blues' *UK, 1893*. ▶ **have got it bad; have got it badly** to have fallen in love or to be infatuated *UK, 1911*. ▶ **have had it 1** to be faced with an unavoidable prospect of defeat or ruin; to be defeated, to be ruined; to be dead or to have been killed *UK, 1941*. **2** to have had more than enough of something; to be sick and tired of something *UK, 1984*. ► **have had it up to here** to have had more than enough of; to be sick and tired of. An elaboration of HAVE HAD IT; here accompanied with a gesture that indicates the neck or the top of the head *UK, 1984*. ► **have it** to fight *UK, 1999*. ► **have it away 1** to escape from imprisonment or arrest; to get away *UK, 1958*. **2** to steal *UK, 1984*. ► **have it in for** to bear a grudge against; to wish to harm *UK, 1840s*. ► **have it made; have got it made** to be on the point of succeeding; to be faced with no (more) obstacles; to have it easy *US, 1955*. ► **have it off 1** to have sex *UK, 1937*. **2** to succeed in a criminal enterprise *UK, 1936*. ► **have it on your dancers** to escape; to run away. An elaboration of HAVE IT ON YOUR TOES. *UK, 1984*. ► **have it on your toes; have it away on your toes** to escape; to run away *UK, 1958*. ► **have legs** of an idea, to have the ability to progress. Media jargon that has seeped into wider usage *UK, 1999*. ► **have one in the departure lounge** to feel the urgent need to defecate *UK, 2002*. ► **have yourself** to indulge yourself or provide yourself with something *US, 1929*

have-a-go *adjective* describes a person who bravely attempts to prevent a crime; intrepid *UK, 1971*

have a good one goodbye. Slightly cooler than urging someone to 'have a good day' *US, 1984*

have an apple! get lost, forget it, calm down *CANADA, 1959*

have been! I'll see you later! Youth usage *US, 1949*

have off *verb* **1** to steal from *UK, 1994*. **2** to use without respect. A variation of the previous sense *UK, 1999*. **3** to defeat, to overthrow, to supplant *UK, 2001*

have on *verb* to take up a challenge; to accept an invitation to fight or compete *AUSTRALIA, 1941*

have you been? have you used the lavatory? Euphemistic *UK, 1969*

have you ever wanted a bindi? used with humour to accompany a threatened knuckle blow to a companion's forehead. A catchphrase that offers a red mark in the centre of the forehead *UK, 2003*

Hawaiian *noun* **1** very potent marijuana cultivated in Hawaii *US, 2001*. **2** a marijuana cigarette *UK, 2003*

Hawaiian black *noun* a dark leafed marijuana from Hawaii, *2003*

Hawaiian disease *noun* sexual abstinence due to an absence of women. An allusion to the mythical illness 'lakanuki' (lack of sex) *US, 1987*

Hawaiian head *noun* a strain of marijuana, known elsewhere as New Zealand green, Thai Buddha or Tasmanian tiger *US, 2002*

Hawaiian homegrown hay *noun* marijuana grown in Hawaii *UK, 2003*

Hawaiian number *noun* any elaborate production number in a show or movie *US, 1973*

Hawaiian sunshine *noun* LSD *US, 1982*

haw-eater *noun* an Ontarian from Manitoulin Island *CANADA, 1998*

hawg *noun* a large motorcyle, especially a Harley-Davidson *US, 1984*

hawk *noun* **1** LSD. May be used with 'the' *US, 1966*. **2** a lookout *US, 1956*. **3** any cold night wind, especially a strong wind that blows off Lake Michigan across Chicago, Illinois. Often with 'the' *US, 1946*

Hawk *nickname* Coleman Hawkins, a leading jazz saxophonist of the 1920s and 1930s *US, 1949*

hawk *verb* **1** to expectorate sputum *US, 1989*. **2** to watch closely, to check out *US, 1886*. **3** to make an aggressive romantic approach *US, 1993*. ► **hawk the fork** (of a woman) to work as a prostitute *AUSTRALIA, 1978*. ► **hawk your mutton** to work as a prostitute *UK, 1937*

hawker *noun* expectorated sputum *US, 1974*

Hawkesbury Rivers *noun* the shivers. From the name of a river in New South Wales *AUSTRALIA, 1941*

hawk-eye *verb* to watch closely *US, 1979*

hawkins *noun* cold weather. An embellishment and personification of HAWK *US, 1934*

hawkshaw *noun* a detective. From the name of a detective in the 1863 play *The Ticket of Leave Man* by Tom Taylor, and later and more relevantly from the comic strip *Hawkshaw the Detective*, drawn by Gus Mager (1913–22, 1931–48). In UK West Indian use *US, 1888*

hawkshaw *verb* to snoop, to inquire *US, 1946*

haw maws *noun* the testicles. Glasgow rhyming slang for BAWS (BALLS), from a cry to attract your mother's attention *UK: SCOTLAND, 1988*

hay *noun* **1** a bed, either in the context of sleep or of sex *US, 1903*. **2** marijuana. A play on GRASS *US, 1934*. **3** money *AUSTRALIA, 1939*

hayburner *noun* a horse, especially a poor-performing racehorse *US, 1904*

hay butt *noun* a marijuana cigarette *US, 1942*

hayed up *adjective* marijuana-intoxicated *US, 1952*

hay head *noun* a marijuana user *US, 1942*

haymaker *noun* **1** a powerful fist blow to the head *US, 1902*. **2** in cricket, a batsman's powerful but reckless shot *UK, 1954*

haymaking *verb* in cricket, powerful but reckless batting *UK, 1986*

hayo *noun* cocaine. From a Caribbean name for the coca plant *US, 1984*

hayron *noun* heroin. Possibly a deliberately perverse pronunciation. *UK, 2003*

hayseed *noun* a rustic or country yokel. Strongly suggests a high degree of unsophistication *US, 1851*

hay shaker *noun* a farmer *US, 1924*

haystack *noun* the back, the rear. Rhyming slang. 'Going round the haystack' is noted as a possible euphemism for paying a visit to a toilet *UK, 1960*

hay wagon *noun* a brakevan (caboose) *US, 1977*

haywire *adjective* out of control; crazy; in wild disorder; chaotic. The image of wire on a bale of hay that flails wildly when cut *US, 1920*

haze *noun* **1** LSD. A shortened form of PURPLE HAZE *US, 1994*. **2** a variety of marijuana, *2002*

haze *verb* to bully, insult and ridicule a homosexual. A specialised nuance of the conventional sense (to punish, to bully) *UK, 1977*

hazed *adjective* drug-intoxicated *US, 2001*

Hazel *noun* heroin. Abbreviated WITCH HAZEL (heroin), and subsequently disguised as 'Aunt Hazel' *US, 1949*

haz-mat *noun* hazardous material *US, 1983*

HBI *noun* house breaking implements. Initialism *UK, 1950*

H bomb *noun* heroin mixed with MDMA, the recreational drug best known as ecstasy. Extended from H (heroin), playing on the devastating power of a nuclear weapon *UK, 2002*

H cap *noun* a capsule of heroin *US, 1990*

he; him *noun* the penis. A derivation immemorial *UK, 1970*

head *noun* **1** a member of the counterculture, usually involving drugs *US, 1966*. **2** a habitual user of drugs. In the Vietnam war, the term differentiated between a person who smoked marijuana and a JUICER who abused alcohol *US, 1953*. **3** a state of drug intoxication *US, 1952*. **4** enough marijuana to fashion a single cigarette *UK, 1996*. **5** a fan of hip-hop music *US, 2003*. **6** a respected graffiti artist *US, 1997*. **7** a familiarising term used to address both sexes, but more generally male. Head can also be used to designate certain groups, for example, a 'D4 [Dublin 4] head' is a post southside person, not necessarily living in the D4 postcode *IRELAND, 1997*. **8** oral sex *US, 1941*. **9** the penis *TRINIDAD AND TOBAGO, 2003*. **10** a talking head. With this shortened form, a good expert guest on a television or radio show becomes 'good head' *US, 2001*. **11** deception *TRINIDAD AND TOBAGO, 1993*. **12** a crime victim *US, 1987*. **13** a toilet *US, 1942*. **14** music played without a musical score *US, 1946*. **15** a railway worker *US, 1990*. ► **bite someone's head off; snap someone's head off** to attack verbally, especially as a disproportionate response *UK, 1984*. ► **do it standing on your head; do on your head** to achieve with ease *UK, 1896*. ► **do your head in** to emotionally overload, confuse and make stressed *UK, 1982*. ► **get your head down; get your head**

down to it to plead guilty. From bending the head in unspoken affirmative *AUSTRALIA, 1975.* ▶ **give head** to perform oral sex *US, 1956.* ▶ **have a head like a sieve** to be very forgetful. *1984.* ▶ **have your head screwed; have your head screwed on right; have your head screwed on the right way** to be shrewd and businesslike, to have a practical intelligence *UK, 1821.* ▶ **have your head up your ass** stupid, unaware, uninformed *US, 1944.* ▶ **need to have your head read** to have ridiculous ideas. That is 'you need to see a psychiatrist' *AUSTRALIA, 1938.* ▶ **off your head** in a state of mental confusion; drug-intoxicated. The latter meaning dates from the 1960s and the distinction between the two senses may be blurred *UK, 1999.* ▶ **on your head** in motor racing, flipped (of a race car) *US, 1980.* ▶ **out of your head** in a state of drug or drink intoxication. When combined with a mental or emotional state, the sense varies: 'with grief', 'with worry', etc *UK, 1996.* ▶ **pull your head in** to mind one's own business *AUSTRALIA, 1944.* ▶ **put the head on; stick the head on** to head-butt an opponent's face *UK: SCOTLAND, 1985.* ▶ **you need your head examined; you want your head examining** a catchphrase addressed to someone who has said or done something stupid. Originally 'you want your head read' but it adapted as fashion and technique moved from phrenology to psychiatry *US, 1942.* ▶ **you'd forget your head if it wasn't screwed on** a catchphrase addressed to (or, in the third person, of) an absent-minded person. Variations are mainly concerned with the method of fixing: 'if it wasn't attached', '...tied on', '...stuck on', '...jammed on', etc *UK, 1979*

head *verb* **1** to leave *US, 2003.* **2** to carry (something) on your head *BARBADOS, 1965*

-head *suffix* a habitual user of the indicated substance; hence an enthusiast, a fan *US, 1953*

headache *noun* **1** your spouse *US, 1933.* **2** a journalist. Gulf war usage *US, 1991*

headache! used as a warning in various industries that an object has been accidentally dropped from a height and that those working below should immediately take care *US, 1944*

headache bar *noun* a steel bar welded onto a bulldozer or other piece of heavy equipment to protect the operator from branches or other sources of potential head injury *US, 1990*

headache Mary *noun* low grade marijuana *US, 1979*

headache rack *noun* the grill at the rear of a truck cab designed to protect the driver and any passengers from injury if the load should shift forward due to a sudden stop *US, 1969*

headache stick *noun* a police nightstick *US, 1919*

head-and-a-half *noun* an intellectual person *AUSTRALIA, 1987*

head artist *noun* a person skilled at giving oral sex *US, 1979*

headbang *noun* a meeting intended to generate creative and innovative solutions. Office jargon *UK, 2005*

head-bang *verb* to jerk your head up and down to add to the enjoyment of fast music. Collected from fans of heavy metal music by Seamus O'Reilly, January 1995 *US, 1995*

headbanger *noun* **1** a violent psychotic *UK, 1983.* **2** a devotee of heavy metal music *US, 1979.* **3** a prisoner who bangs his head against walls, doors, etc *UK, 1996*

headbin *noun* a crazy, unstable person *IRELAND, 2001*

head case *noun* an emotionally troubled or mentally disturbed person *UK, 1966*

head cheese *noun* prepuce smegma in a male *US, 1941*

head chick *noun* the dominant and favoured prostitute among a group of prostitutes working for a pimp *US, 1957*

head cook and bottle-washer *noun* a person who does all the work. Humorous. Originally 'bottle-washer' carried the same meaning with or without the head cook's help. The British adaptation of the earlier US CHIEF COOK AND BOTTLE WASHER *UK, 1876*

head cunt *noun* the mouth (as an object of sexual penetration) *US, 1996*

head dab *noun* in mountain biking, a face-first fall *US, 1992*

head down and arse up working busily *AUSTRALIA, 1945*

head drugs *noun* amphetamines *UK, 1998*

head 'em *verb* **1** to take part in the gambling game two-up *AUSTRALIA, 1902.* **2** in the game two-up, to throw a pair of heads *AUSTRALIA, 1925*

header *noun* **1** a head-first dive *UK, 1849.* **2** oral sex. An embellishment of the more common HEAD *US, 1976.* **3** in hot rodding, a type of exhaust manifold that improves engine performance *US, 1948*

head faggot *noun* a male homosexual with an appetite for performing oral sex *US, 1996*

head-faking *adjective* stimulating, exciting *UK, 1983*

headfit *noun* an uncontrolled outburst of temper *UK, 2000*

head fuck *noun* **1** a state of mental confusion *UK, 1996.* **2** something that deliberately confuses or misleads *UK, 2002*

headfuck *adjective* confusing, misleading, especially when deliberately so *UK, 2001*

head game *noun* a psychological ploy *US, 1979*

head gasket *noun* a condom. Conventionally, 'a mechanical seal', with a further pun on HEAD (an act of oral sex) *US, 1964*

head gee *noun* a prison warden *US, 1976*

head-hunt *verb* in boxing, to try to hit the opponent in the head *US, 1960*

headhunter *noun* **1** a person who recruits others for specific jobs with specific firms, especially professionals and executives *US, 1960.* **2** a psychiatrist *US, 1972.* **3** an oral sex enthusiast *US, 1961.* **4** a homosexual male *US, 1990.* **5** a police officer assigned to investigate complaints of misconduct by other police *US, 1965.* **6** a paid killer *US, 1982.* **7** a female who trades sex for money or drugs *US, 1995*

head job *noun* an act of oral sex *US, 1963*

head-job *verb* to shoot in the head *UK, 1993*

head jockey *noun* a practitioner of oral sex on a woman *US, 1971*

headless chicken *noun* used as the object of comparison for something or someone acting without rhyme or reason *AUSTRALIA, 1957*

headlights *noun* **1** the female breasts *US, 1970.* **2** the female nipples when obviously erect although masked by clothing. A more narrowly focused meaning from the previous sense *CANADA, 2003.* **3** large jewels, especially diamonds *US, 1899.* **4** LSD *US, 1994*

head like an unplayable lie *noun* an ugly person *AUSTRALIA, 1995*

head like a robber's dog *noun* an unattractive person *AUSTRALIA, 1971*

head motherfucker in charge *noun* the leader of an enterprise *US, 2002*

head nigger in charge *noun* the leader of an enterprise *US, 1978*

head on *adverb* in gambling games such as twenty-one, playing directly against the dealer without other players *US, 1963*

head over heels *adjective* deeply, completely (especially in descriptions of love). By ellipsis from the cliché 'fall head over heels in love' *UK, 2003*

head over turkey *adverb* upside down; head over heels *AUSTRALIA, 1915*

head phones *noun* a stethoscope *US, 1982*

head plant *noun* to fall face first while snowboarding *US, 1993*

headquarters puke *noun* a member of the military assigned to the rear echelon staff. Gulf war usage *US, 1992*

head rag *noun* a bandana or piece of cloth worn with straightened or processed hair *US, 1973*

heads and heels *noun* a youthful, sexually inexperienced male who is the object of an older homosexual's desire. The suggestion is that you have to lift the inexperienced boy by his head and heels to get him into position for sex *US, 1979*

heads down *adjective* in computing, so focused on a task as to be ignorant of all else *US, 1991*

head serang; head sherang *noun* the person in charge. From Anglo-Indian *serang* (a captain of a native Indian vessel), from Persian *AUSTRALIA, 1918*

head shed *noun* a military headquarters. Vietnam war usage *US, 1963*

head shop *noun* a shop that retails drug paraphernalia, incense, posters, lights, and other products and services associated with drug use *US, 1967*

headshrinker *noun* a pyschiatrist or other therapist *US, 1950*

head shrinking *noun* the practice of psychiatry *US, 1964*

heads I win, tails you lose however a situation is resolved I cannot lose. Mocking the principle that a toss of a coin normally offers a choice of winner *UK, 1832*

heads-up *adjective* **1** clever, alert. From the earlier sense as 'wide-awake' *US, 1934*. **2** in motor racing, said of a competition with no handicap *US, 1993*

heads-up *adverb* (of a game of pool) with no handicaps in effect *US, 1993*

head-the-ball *noun* a crazy person *UK, 2000*

head time *noun* an opportunity to think *UK, 1998*

head-up *adjective* straightforward, direct *US, 2001*

heal *verb* ▶ **heal with steal** to perform surgery *US, 1994*

healthy *adjective* **1** (used of a girl) well built *US, 1970*. **2** large, excellent *UK, 1937*

heap *noun* **1** a car, especially an old and run-down car *US, 1921*. **2** a slovenly woman, usually preceded by an adjective. Originally dialect *UK, 1806*. **3** a large number, a great deal *UK, 1661*

heap *adjective* very. A crude borrowing of the speech of native American Indians as portrayed by pulp fiction and film screenwriters *US, 1958*

heap of coke; heap *noun* a man. Rhyming slang for BLOKE *UK, 1851*

heap of shit *noun* a mechanical item that is old, unreliable or broken *UK, 2000*

heaps *noun* ▶ **give someone heaps** to chastise, denigrate or attack someone unrestrainedly *AUSTRALIA, 1978*

hear *verb* to understand *US, 1973*

hearse *noun* a brakevan (caboose) *US, 1930*

heart *noun* **1** physical courage, especially as displayed in the commission of a crime *US, 1937*. **2** an amphetamine capsule, especially dextroamphetamine sulphate (trade name Dexedrine™). From the shape of the tablet *US, 1965*. ▶ **my heart bleeds for you; my heart bleeds** faux-sympathy, used ironically for expressing bitterness or jealousy *US, 1968*. ▶ **put the heart crossways** to shock *IRELAND, 1995*

heartbeat *noun* **1** any of several signals produced by a computer or software *US, 1991*. **2** a short measure of time *US, 1985*

Heartbreak Hill *nickname* a challenging hill at approximately mile 20 of the Boston Marathon *US, 1998*

heartburn palace *noun* a roadside restaurant that features greasy food *US, 1971*

heart check *noun* a test of courage *US, 1995*

heart check! I defy you!; I dare you!; I challenge you! *US, 2001*

heartface *noun* a form of address used by some homosexual men *UK, 1968*

heart scald *noun* a troublesome individual *IRELAND, 1998*

hearts of oak; hearts *adjective* penniless. Rhyming slang for BROKE *UK, 1934*

heart starter *noun* an alcoholic drink taken upon waking *AUSTRALIA, 1975*

heartthrob *noun* a very attractive man *US, 1926*

heat *noun* **1** pressure, stress *US, 1929*. **2** the police *US, 1931*. **3** intense police interest or pressure following a crime *US, 1928*. **4** a firearm *US, 1926*. **5** crowd or audience reaction. An entertainment industry term embraced by professional wrestling *US, 1958*. **6** popularity, audience appeal *US, late 1970s*. **7** in roller derby, a fight, be it scripted or spontaneous, staged or real *US, 1999*. **8** in pinball, the part of the pinball machine that rises as a panel in the front of the machine. Conventionally known as the 'lightbox' *US, 1977*. **9** the ultimate, the best *US, 1985*. **10** a dildo *US, 1999*. ▶ **on heat** of a woman, sexually aroused. Correctly used of animals *UK, 1937*. ▶ **take the heat** to

sunbathe *US, 1968*. ▶ **take the heat off; take heat off** to relieve the pressure on someone *UK, 1979*

heated hell *noun* the worst of the worst *US, 1945*

heater *noun* **1** a revolver. The term smacks of gangster films *US, 1926*. **2** a linear amplifier for a citizens' band radio *US, 1976*. **3** a good-looking boy *US, 1993*. **4** an excellent thing *US, 2003*. **5** in poker, a period of good luck for one player *UK, 2003*. **6** a large cigar *US, 1918*. **7** a cigarette *US, 1993*. ▶ **take a heater** to defecate *US, 2001*

heater and cooler *noun* a shot of whisky and a glass of beer *US, 1982*

heating food *noun* any food thought to enhance sexual strength and passion. A euphemism of social and spiritual significance. Those seeking a godly and contemplative life (and, according to custom, all women, especially widows) should stick to 'cooling foods' *INDIA, 2003*

heat magnet *noun* anything that draws the attention of the authorities. Based on HEAT (the police) *CANADA, 2002*

heat station *noun* a police station. From HEAT (the police) *US, 1963*

heaty *adjective* under police surveillance or the subject of police interest *US, 1967*

heave *noun* an ejection, a dismissal. Used in the construction 'give someone (or something) the heave' *UK: SCOTLAND, 1985*

heave *verb* to vomit *US, 1832*

heave-ho *noun* an ejection, a dismissal *US, 1932*

heaven *noun* **1** seven or eleven. Rhyming slang, used by dice gamblers *UK, 1961*. **2** cocaine *UK, 2002*. **3** heroin *UK, 2003*. **4** a billboard in the language of graffiti artists *US, 2002*

heaven and hell; heaven *verb* to give off a bad smell. Rhyming slang *UK, 1992*

heaven dust; heavenly dust; heaven flour *noun* any powdered drug; cocaine; heroin. Perhaps a positive alternative to HELL DUST *US, 1933*

heavenly blue; heavenly sunshine *noun* LSD *US, 1977*

heavenly blues *noun* morning glory seeds as a psychoactive agent *US, 1982*

heaven on a stick *noun* a very good thing *US, 1990*

heavens above *noun* love *UK, 1961*

heaven sent *noun* MDMA, the recreational drug best known as ecstasy *UK, 1996*

heavens to Betsy! used as a register of shock, surprise, etc. Charles Earle Funk researched and failed to discover the etymology of this phrase for *Heavens to Betsy!*, 1955; he believed that the phrase is certainly mid-C19 but was unable to discover its usage before 1940 *US, 1940*

heavens to Murgatroyd! used as a register of shock, surprise, etc. A variation of HEAVENS TO BETSY!; popularised by Hanna Barbera's animated lion Snagglepuss, from 1959; also credited to US comedian Red Skelton, 1913–97. The identity of Murgatroyd is a mystery *US, 1959*

heaves and squirts *noun* symptoms of heroin withdrawal. A rather graphic way of describing vomiting and diarrhoea *US, 1973*

heavies *noun* large waves. Always in the plural *US, 1961*. ▶ **the heavies** serious newspapers, as opposed to the tabloid press *UK, 1950*

heaviosity *noun* a quality of some (drug-inspired) heavy rock music *US, 1981*

heavy *noun* **1** an experienced criminal who relies on violence and force *US, 1930*. **2** armed robbery; an armed robber *US, 1950*. **3** sexually aroused, especially if aggressively so. A sense used by prostitutes *UK, 1980*. **4** a physically intimidating prison officer brought in to deal with rioting prisoners *UK, 1996*. **5** a lesbian prison officer *UK, 1996*. **6** in the television and film industries, an antagonist *US, 1926*. **7** an officer. Vietnam war coinage *US, 1976*. **8** an important person *US, 1925*. **9** heroin *US, 1971*. **10** a potent dose or a potent drug or both *US, 1988*. **11** medium gravity beer. Not to be confused with WEE HEAVY (a barley wine) *UK: SCOTLAND, 1985*. **12** a large aircraft *AUSTRALIA, 1962*. **13** an aircraft carrier *US, 1959*

heavy *verb* **1** to threaten with violence; to menace *UK, 1998.* **2** to harass, threaten or victimise someone; to coerce someone threateningly *AUSTRALIA, 1974*

heavy *adjective* **1** very serious, very intense *US, 1963.* **2** wonderful, excellent *US, 1972.* **3** (of drugs) addictive *US, 1959.* **4** violent, inclined to use violence *US, 1902.* ▶ **get heavy** to study *US, 1955*

heavy! used for expressing approval *UK, 2003*

heavy A *noun* an assistant drill instructor, US Marine Corps *US, 1987*

heavy Chevy *noun* a Chevrolet with a big block engine *US, 1992*

heavy closer *noun* in a swindle, a person who makes the final deal with the victim *US, 1986*

heavy cream *noun* a hefty, large-breasted woman *US, 1960*

heavy-duty *adjective* serious, intense *US, 1935*

heavy-fisted *adjective* said of a gambling house operative who takes more than the appropriate share of the winnings of a poker game for the house share *US, 1951*

heavy-footed *adjective* pregnant *UK: NORTHERN IRELAND, 1996*

heavy hammer *noun* any powerful pain medication *US, 1994*

heavy handbag *noun* a rich (homosexual) boyfriend. From HANDBAG (money); recorded in use in contemporary gay society *UK, 2003*

heavy-handed *adjective* used of a person who pours alcoholic drinks too generously, or mixes alcoholic drinks at too great a strength. From the conventional sense (clumsy) *UK, 1971*

heavy hitter *noun* a person with a deserved reputation for violence. A baseball metaphor *US, 1970*

heavy lifter *noun* a dangerous, tough person *US, 2001*

heavy manners *noun* any form of authoritarian control or discipline experienced by black individuals or communities *UK, 1994*

heavy metal; HM; metal *noun* a music genre, characterised by loud amplification, the primacy of electric guitars and simple, powerful – if occasionally lumbering – rhythmic patterns. The origin may be in military and munitions terminology but the popular and probable etymology is as follows: 'The term heavy metal was originally coined by Beat novelist William Burroughs in his *Naked Lunch*, reintroduced into the pop vocabulary by Steppenwolf in their hit "Born to Be Wild" ("heavy metal thunder") and subsequently redefined by rock critic Lester Bangs in the heavy metal fan magazine *Creem*.' (*Rolling Stone Encyclopaedia of Rock & Roll*, 1983). In fact, William Burroughs wrote of Uranium Willie, the Heavy Metal Kid, in *Nova Express*, 1946, 13 years before *Naked Lunch* was published. Lester Bangs was writing about the Yardbirds. In later use 'metal' takes over as the preferred abbreviation, creating a subtle differentiation understood by fans of heavy music *US, 1999*

heavy metaller *noun* a musician or fan of heavy metal music *US, 1989*

heavy mob *noun* **1** a criminal gang that relies on violence; a gang involved in large scale crimes *UK, 1944.* **2** the Metropolitan Police Flying Squad *UK, 1999.* **3** physically intimidating prison officers brought in to deal with rioting prisoners *UK, 1996*

heavy paint-work passers *noun* in a dice cheating scheme, dice that have been altered by drilling the spots and filling them with heavy metallic paint *US, 1963*

heavy petting *noun* mutual sexual caressing that stops shy of full intercourse *UK, 1960*

heavy roller *noun* a very important person *US, 1974*

heavy strings *noun* useful and powerful connections *BAHAMAS, 1982*

heavy thumb *noun* in the usage of youthful model road racers (slot car racers), a fast, reckless racer *US, 1997*

heavyweight Jones *noun* a drug dealer who sells drugs in a manner calculated to lead his customers to addiction *US, 1971*

heavy wizardry *noun* in computing, designs or code that demand a specialised and deep practical understanding *US, 1991*

heavy worker *noun* a criminal who specialises in breaking into safes *US, 1949*

Hebe; Heeb *noun* a Jewish person. Derogatory *US, 1926*

Hebrew hoppers *noun* sandals. From the images of Jesus Christ wearing sandals *US, 1970*

heck *noun* used as a euphemistic alternative to 'hell'. Originally dialect; often exclamatory *UK, 1887*

hecka *adverb* very. A euphemised HELLA *US, 1989*

heck-city *adverb* very *US, 2004*

heckety-heck *noun* used as a euphemistic alternative to 'hell' *UK, 2003*

hecksa *adverb* very *US, 2004*

heck you! used as a euphemistic replacement for 'fuck you!' *FIJI, 1996*

hectic *adjective* **1** (used of a wave) fairly treacherous *US, 1988.* **2** extreme, outrageous (often applied to gruesome or gory acts); good. Teen and youth slang, noted by *Sunday Times* (South Africa), 1st June 2003 *SOUTH AFRICA, 2003*

hector! used as a euphemism for 'heck', itself a euphemism for 'hell' *US, 1965*

H'ed *adjective* addicted to heroin *US, 1997*

hedgehog *noun* any non-white person; a native of the Indian Subcontinent; an Arab; any (non-English) foreigner. Rhyming slang for WOG *UK, 1992*

hedge hopper *noun* a crop dusting pilot *US, 1954*

hedge monkey *noun* a member of the counterculture travellers' community. Derogatory *UK, 2001*

hedge mumper *noun* a tramp. An elaboration of MUMPER (a tramp). English gypsy use *UK, 2000*

H-E-double toothpicks!; H-E-double hockey sticks! hell. Youth slang, euphemistically spelt out *US, 1997*

heeb *noun* a jittery sensation, a fearful feeling. An abbreviation of HEEBIE JEEBIES *UK, 1996*

heebie-jeebies *noun* **1** the jitters, a sense of anxiety. Thought to have been coined by US cartoonist Billy DeBeck (1890–1942) for the comic strip *Barney Google US, 1923.* **2** delirium tremens *US, 1926.* **3** symptoms of withdrawal from an addictive drug *US, 1987*

heebies *noun* jitters *US, 1926*

Heeeeere's Johnny ... used as a humorous introduction. The drawn-out introduction of US late-night talk show host Johnny Carson by sidekick Ed McMahon from 1962 until 1992. Widely repeated, with variations and referential humour *US, 1980*

hee-haw *noun* **1** loud and braying laughter *UK, 1843.* **2** nothing of any worth, zero. The value of a donkey's bray *UK, 2000*

heel *noun* **1** a dishonourable or untrustworthy individual *US, 1914.* **2** in professional wrestling, a wrestler designed by the promoters to be seen by the audience as a villain *US, 1958.* **3** by extension, any figure in the wrestling business designed by the promoters to be disliked by the fans *US, 1998*

heel *verb* to leave without paying a bill *US, 1966*

heel-and-toe *verb* to run away quickly *CANADA, 1870*

heeled *adjective* **1** armed *US, 1866.* **2** provided with funds *US, 1873.* **3** in possession of drugs *US, 1970*

heeler *noun* **1** a political party worker who does readily what is ordered *US, 1876.* **2** an opportunistic sneak thief *US, 1931.* **3** in poker, an unmatched card retained in a player's hand when drawing *US, 1967*

heelie *noun* in skateboarding, a manoeuvre in which the rider elevates the rear wheels of the board while riding forward on the front wheels *US, 1976*

heelish *adjective* in professional wrestling, villainous *US, 1996*

heel list *noun* a list of persons unwelcome as guests at a hotel *US, 1953*

heesh *noun* hashish *US, 1982*

heeze *noun* hashish *CANADA, 2002*

heezie; heezy *noun* ▶ **off the heezie; off the heezie for skeezie** awesome, wonderful, cool, amazing. A hip-hop variation of 'off the hook', apparently coined by rapper Snoop Doggy Dog *US, 1999*

Hef *nickname* Hugh Hefner (b.1926), founding publisher of *Playboy* magazine, which first appeared in December 1953 *US, 1968*

heffa *noun* a stocky girl or woman. A variation of heifer (a young cow) *US, 2005*

hefty *noun* in circus and carnival usage, a performer in a strong-man act *US, 1981*

hefty *adjective* **1** well-funded at the moment. Teen slang *US, 1958*. **2** intense *AUSTRALIA, 2002*

he-girl *noun* a person with mixed sexual physiology, usually the genitals of a male and surgically augmented breasts *US, 2004*

hehe in a game of on-line poker, used for acknowledging luck in winning a hand, *2003*

Heidi *noun* a young woman with back-to-the-earth, 1960s values and fashion sense, especially one with pigtails *US, 2001*

heifer *noun* a stocky girl or woman. An insult, if not a fighting word *US, 1835*

heifer dust *noun* nonsense. A euphemism for BULLSHIT *US, 1927*

heifer paddock *noun* a girls' school *AUSTRALIA, 1885*

heigh-ho! used as a signal of enthusiasm *US, 1930s to 50s*

height *noun* ▶ **from a great height** used to intensify the infliction of punishment or suffering. Always preceded with the passive sense of a verb combined with 'on', e.g. 'come down on' *UK, 1961*

heing and sheing *noun* sex *US, 1993*

Heinie *noun* a German; German *US, 1904*

heinie; heiny *noun* ▷*see:* HINEY

Heinies *noun* Heineken™ beer *US, 1982*

heinous *adjective* offensive, unpleasant. Conventional English elevated to slang by attitude *US, 1982*

Heinz *noun* a multiple bet, combining 57 bets. Based on the advertising slogan for, and synonymous with, the products of the food company H.J. Heinz. A 'super heinz' combines 120 bets *UK, 1983*

heir and a spare two sons, in the context of a male line of succession; hence, one and a spare of anything. Used as a minimum breeding requirement by powerful and privileged families whose bloodline justifies their inheritance, applied especially to monarchies *UK, 2003*

heist *noun* a theft or robbery *US, 1976*

heist *verb* **1** to accept; when used in the negative, to reject a story or idea as untruthful or fanciful *CANADA, 1999*. **2** to steal, especially to shoplift. There are enough Hollywood heist films to make a genre. Also spelt 'hyste' *UK, 1815*

heister *noun* a thief or robber. From the earlier 'hoister' *UK, 1865*

Helen *noun* heroin. Giving an identity and disguise to H (heroin) *US, 1971*

heli *noun* a *heli*copter *US, 1995*

helicopter *noun* **1** in skateboarding, a manoeuvre in which the rider jumps off the board, turns in the air and then lands on the board *US, 1976*. **2** a Chinese-educated person *SINGAPORE, 2002*

helicopter view *noun* a non-detailed overview *CANADA, 2000*

hell *noun* **1** used widely in oaths, and to reinforce imprecations, and questions (often rhetorical) of impatience and irritation *US, 1596*. **2** crack cocaine *UK, 2003*. ▶ **for the hell of it; for the sheer hell of it; just for the hell of it** simply for the pleasure or experience of doing something; also applied to reckless behaviour *UK, 1934*. ▶ **from hell** used for intensifying. Humorous, hyperbolic *US, 1965*. ▶ **get the hell out; get the hell out of here (or somewhere)** to leave, usually with some haste *US, 1971*. ▶ **hell out of** when combined with a verb of violent action, such as knock, punch, thump, etc, to treat a person extremely roughly *IRELAND, 1922*. ▶ **play hell with; play merry hell with** to cause severe trouble for someone or something *UK, 1803*. ▶ **to hell** intensely, when combined with a wish or hope *UK, 1891*. ▶ **to hell with it!** used for registering or reinforcing dismissal *UK, 1929*. ▶ **will I hell!** used as an expression of strong disagreement.

Often applied in the third person: 'will he hell!' or 'will they hell!' *UK, 1931*

hella *adverb* extremely *US, 1992*

hellacious *adjective* especially nasty or difficult *US, 1929*

hell and gone; hell-and-gone *noun* a far-distant place or point in time *US, 1938*

hell-bent *adjective* recklessly determined *US, 1835*

hellcat *noun* a wild, fierce woman *UK, 1605*

hell dust *noun* any powdered drug; heroin; morphine *US, 1953*

heller *noun* a wild, uninhibited party *US, 1975*

hellery *noun* trouble, mischief, bad behaviour *CANADA, 1965*

hell-fire! used as a register of exasperation, frustration, anger, etc *UK, 1997*

hell-for-stout *adjective* very strong *US, 1954*

hell-hole *noun* **1** a horrible, infernal place *UK, 1882*. **2** in a combat helicopter, an approximately 34-inch-square opening in the floor, used for emergencies and roping down to and up from the ground *US, 1976*

hellifying *adjective* used as an adjectival intensifier *US, 1973*

hellish *adjective* **1** unpleasant, difficult *UK, 1569*. **2** used as a positive intensifier; excellent *UK: ENGLAND, 2001*

hellish *adverb* used as a pejorative intensifier *UK, 1768*

hellishing; hellishun *adverb* used as an intensifier. An elaboration of HELLISH (an intensifier) on the model of FUCKING, SODDING, etc *AUSTRALIA, 1931*

hello! used for signalling disbelief when said as if speaking to someone slow-witted *US, 1985*

hell of *adverb* extremely. A reverse correction of the corrupted HELLA *US, 1995*

hell of a *adjective* an extreme, good or great example of something. May be preceded with 'a', 'the' or 'one' *UK, 1776*

Hell Pass Hole *nickname* El Paso, Texas *US, 1970*

hellride *noun* in mountain biking, any bad trail or bad ride *US, 1992*

hell's bells used as a mild oath *UK, 1832*

hell's half acre *noun* during the Vietnam war, an area just north of Cu Chi, dominated if not controlled by the Viet Cong *US, 1991*

hell to breakfast *noun* here to there, all over *US, 1930*

helluva hell of a *US, 1910*

hell week *noun* a period of extreme harassment, especially of new recruits to a college fraternity by their older fraternity brothers *US, 1930*

helmet *noun* **1** the head of the circumcised penis. From the similarity in shape to a World War 2 German Army helmet *US, 1970*. **2** a uniformed police constable *UK, 2002*

helo *noun* a helicopter *US, 1965*

helo *adjective* none *CANADA, 1963*

helpcat *noun* a tutor; a student assistant. A punning allusion to HEP CAT *US, 1955*

helper *noun* any amphetamine or other central nervous system stimulant *US, 1963*

helter skelter *noun* a shelter. Originally a World War 2 coinage for an 'air raid shelter'. Noted as still in occasional use as a 'bus shelter' *UK, 1992*

helter-skelter *adverb* in defiance of order; pell-mell *UK, 1593*

he-man *noun* an especially virile or overtly masculine man, a masterful man *US, 1832*

hem and haw *verb* to stutter, to hestitate while beginning a sentence *UK, 1786*

hemp *noun* marijuana *US, 1883*

hempen fever *noun* execution by hanging *UK, 1785*

hemp head *noun* a frequent user of marijuana *US, 1980*

hempster *noun* anyone involved in the business of retailing hemp. From HEMP (marijuana) and conventional, perfectly legal 'hemp' *UK, 2002*

hempty *noun* leaves from the hemp plant *CANADA, 2002*

hen *noun* **1** a woman *UK, 1626*. **2** used for informally addressing a woman; also, as an endearment *UK: SCOTLAND, 1626*. **3** a flamboyant feminine male homosexual *TRINIDAD AND TOBAGO, 1985*. **4** in a deck of playing cards, a queen *US, 1988*. **5** the Sea Knight military helicopter. A term used by reconnaissance troops in Vietnam *US, 1991*

hen apple *noun* an egg *US, 1938*

hench *noun* a person in attractive physical shape *UK, 2005*

hen fruit *noun* an egg *US, 1854*

Henley regatta *noun* a conversation. Rhyming slang for NATTER, formed from the famous sporting event *UK, 1998*

hen mill *noun* a women's jail or prison *US, 1960*

Henny; Hen' *noun* Hennessy™ cognac *UK, 1999*

henny penny *noun* a female player in a low-stakes game of poker *US, 1988*

henpecked *adjective* ruled by a domineering woman. The surviving form of the original verb 'hen-peck' *UK, 1680*

hen pen *noun* a women's prison *US, 1992*

henry *noun* an eighth of an ounce (three and a half grams) of a drug, especially marijuana or cocaine. Cutting HENRY THE EIGHTH down to size *UK, 1998*

Henry *noun* **1** any Ford Motor Company car or engine *US, 1917*. **2** heroin. From 'heroin' to H to Henry *US, 1953*

Henry Fonda *noun* a *Honda* 90 motorcycle. Rhyming slang, used by (prospective) London taxi drivers; the Honda 90 is the machine of preference when they DO THE KNOWLEDGE *UK, 1998*

Henry IV *noun* the human immunodeficiency virus *US, 2001*

Henry the Eighth *noun* eight grams of cocaine *US, 1993*

Henry the Fourth *noun* four grams of cocaine *US, 1993*

Henry the Third *noun* a piece of excrement. Rhyming slang for TURD *AUSTRALIA, 1971*

Henry was here *noun* the bleed period of the menstrual cycle *UK: WALES, 2000*

hen's night *noun* a woman-only pre-wedding party held for the bride-to-be. The counterpart of the BUCK'S PARTY *AUSTRALIA, 1994*

hen's teeth *noun* the epitome of that which is exceedingly rare *AUSTRALIA, 1965*

hentai *adjective* overtly pornographic. A Japanese term, usually applied to a style of Japanese animation; one of only a few Japanese terms to have worked its way into unconventional English usage, thanks to pornographic websites on the Internet *JAPAN, 1996*

hep *noun* hepatitis *US, 1967*

hep *adjective* **1** aware *US, 1903*. **2** in step with the latest fashion, latest music and latest slang *US, 1942*

hepatic rounds *noun* used in a hospital as a humorous code for a drinking party to be held on hospital grounds *US, 1989*

hepatitis roll *noun* a meat and salad roll. Used by Australian troops during the Vietnam conflict to refer to such rolls commonly sold by street vendors, and reputed to be the cause of gastrointestinal and other complaints *AUSTRALIA, 1988*

Hepburn's Hussars *noun* a special police force organised by Ontario Premier Mitch Hepburn to deal with an Oshawa car workers' strike *CANADA, 1946*

hep cat; hepped cat *noun* a fan of jazz or swing music; a stylish and fashionable man *US, 1938*

heppo *noun* hepatitis *AUSTRALIA, 1987*

heppo roll *noun* a hepatitis roll *AUSTRALIA, 1988*

hep square *noun* a person who lives a conventional life but has some awareness of unconventional lifestyles *US, 1972*

her *noun* cocaine *US, 1981*

Hera *noun* heroin. Disguising 'heroin' with the name of a Greek goddess *UK, 2002*

herb *noun* marijuana. Celebrated in song by Sly & the Revolutionaries, 'Herb', 1979 *US, 1962*

Herb *noun* ▶ **cry herb; call herb** to vomit. Echoic *AUSTRALIA, 1967* ▷ CRY RUTH

herb *verb* to assault a weak person *US, 1995*

herbal *adjective* pertaining to marijuana *US, 1995*

herbal bliss *noun* MDMA, the recreational drug best known as ecstasy *UK, 2003*

herbal ecstasy *noun* a substance that is not restricted by drug control legislation and is claimed to be a natural substitute for MDMA *UK, 2004*

herbals *noun* marijuana *US, 1995*

herb and a' *noun* marijuana and alcohol. A lazy clipping of HERB AND AL *US, 1980s*

Herb and Al; Herbie and Al *noun* marijuana and alcohol *US, 1981*

herbert *noun* **1** a mischievous child or youth. Quite often heard as 'little herbert' *UK, 1999*. **2** a harmless youth; a ridiculous man. An extension of the previous sense *UK, 1960*. **3** a man in a specified field of endeavour *UK, 1956*

Herbie *noun* in Antarctica, a powerful blizzard *ANTARCTICA, 1987*

Herbie Alley *noun* the passage between Black Island and White Island, through which fast-moving Antarctic blizzards develop *ANTARCTICA, 2003*

Herbie Hides *noun* trousers. Rhyming slang for STRIDES, formed from the name of Nigerian heavyweight boxer Henry Hide (b.1971) *UK, 1998*

herbs *noun* **1** marijuana *UK, 2000*. **2** (of a motor engine) power *AUSTRALIA, 1960*

herbsman *noun* a marijuana smoker. Used as a song title by King Stitt and Andy Capp, 'Herbsman', 1970 *JAMAICA, 1975*

Herc; Herk; Herky Bird *noun* the Hercules C-130 medium cargo transport aircraft manufactured by Lockheed. The primary transport aircraft used for US military forces in Vietnam *US, 1980*

hercules *noun* especially potent phencyclidine, the recreational drug known as PCP or angel dust *US, 1981*

herd *noun* **1** a packet of Camel™ cigarettes *US, 1945*. **2** a quantity of something *IRELAND, 1991*

Herd *noun* ▶ **The Herd** the 173rd Airborne Brigade, US Army. The first major US combat unit sent to Vietnam *US, 1991*

herd *verb* in hot rodding, to drive (a hot rod) *US, 1933*

herder *noun* **1** a prison guard assigned to a prison yard *US, 1992*. **2** in horse racing, a jockey or horse that forces the other horses to bunch up behind it *US, 1951*. **3** on the railways, a yard pointsman *US, 1930*

here and there *noun* a chair. Rhyming slang, always used in full *UK, 1992*

here's how used as a toast *UK, 1896*

here we go; here we go again used for registering resignation at the commencement of an anticipated, predictable or otherwise undesirable event *UK, 1954*

her indoors; 'er indoors; 'er *noun* the wife of the user. Coined for television comedy drama series *Minder*, 1979–94 *UK, 1984*

Herman Fink *noun* ink. Rhyming slang *UK, 1960*

Herman the German *noun* the penis *US, 1991*

hermit *noun* a poker player wearing headphones during play *US, 1996*

hero *noun* **1** heroin *US, 1953*. **2** a surfer whose opinion of his own skills exceeds his actual skills *US, 1985*

hero gear *noun* enemy paraphernalia taken from the battlefield *US, 1961*

heroina *noun* heroin *US, 1994*

herone *noun* heroin *UK, 1998*

hero of the underworld *noun* heroin. An elaboration of HERO (heroin) *US, 1986*

herox *noun* 4-bromo-2,5-dimethoxyphenethylaimine, a mild hallucinogen *US, 1995*

herring and kipper; herring *noun* a striptease dancer. Rhyming slang for STRIPPER *UK, 1992*

herringboner *noun* a dairy farmer *NEW ZEALAND, 2002*

herring choker *noun* 1 a person from New Brunswick or elsewhere in the Canadian Maritime Provinces *US, 1899.* 2 a Scandanavian *US, 1936*

herring snapper *noun* a Scandanavian *US, 1930*

herself *noun* a wife, your wife, a female partner *IRELAND, 1989*

Hershey Highway *noun* the rectum *US, 1973*

Hershey road *noun* the rectum *US, 1974*

Hershey squirts *noun* diarrhoea. A joking if unpleasant allusion to Hershey™ chocolate *US, 1972*

he-she *noun* a man living as a woman, either as a transvestite or transsexual; an effeminate male *US, 1871*

hesher; heshen; hesh *noun* a fan of heavy metal music *US, 1997*

hesh girl; hash girl *noun* a prostitute who works in cheap drinking establishments. Urban and township slang *SOUTH AFRICA, 1973*

he shoots! he scores! used for celebrating a minor accomplishment. From the television programme *Saturday Night Live US, 1991*

hesitation marks *noun* scars on the inner wrist from failed suicide attempts *US, 1972*

hessle *noun* heroin *UK, 1998*

het *adjective* heterosexual *US, 1972*

hetboy *noun* a heterosexual male. Internet shorthand *US, 1995*

heter *noun* a heterosexual *UK, 1980*

hetero *noun* a heterosexual *UK, 1933*

hetgirl *noun* a heterosexual female. Internet shorthand *US, 1995*

het up; all het up *adjective* excited. From a dialect variation of 'heated' or 'heated up' *US, 1909*

hex *noun* a number sign (#) on a computer keyboard *US, 1991*

hexy *noun* hexamine (a solid fuel provided in small blocks). Military *UK, 1995*

hey? 1 pardon? Used alone or as the introduction to a question that is formed using a standard interrogative *SOUTH AFRICA, 1961.* 2 used at the end of a question for emphasis or as a means of demanding a response *SOUTH AFRICA, 1969*

hey used as a discourse break that raises emphasis or focus *US, 1974*

hey-diddle-diddle *noun* a swindle, a deception. Rhyming slang for FIDDLE *UK: SCOTLAND, 1988*

hey-hey *noun* a good time *US, 1985*

hey now 1 used as a greeting *US, 1946.* 2 used for getting attention *US, 1987*

hey-presto! a command used by stage magicians; hence, used for registering a sudden or surprising transformation; cynically used for 'as if by magic' when a predictable change occurs *UK, 1731*

hey rube *noun* a fight between swindlers of any sort and their victims *US, 1900*

hey, rube! used as an insider request for help in a fight. Originally and principally an expression used in the circus and carnivals *US, 1900*

hey-you *noun* an uncouth or insolent person. From the signature conversational gambit employed by such people *UK: SCOTLAND, 1988*

HFH used as a jaded abbreviation of a jaded 'ho-fucking-hum' *US, 1990*

H-head *noun* a habitual user of heroin *UK, 1978*

HHOJ; HHOK used in computer message shorthand to mean 'ha-ha only joking' or 'ha-ha only kidding' *US, 1991*

hi-ball *noun* a central nervous system stimulant, especially dextroamphetamine (trade name Dexamyl™) *US, 1971*

hiccup *noun* a fault in administration, an interruption to any smooth-running procedure *UK, 1974*

hiccup *verb* in computing when transferring data, to inadvertently skip some data or send some data twice *US, 1995*

hick *noun* an unsophisticated, simple person from the far rural reaches. A familiar form of 'Richard'. Now chiefly US use *UK, 1565*

hickey *noun* 1 a bruise on the skin caused by a partner's mouth during foreplay; a suction kiss *US, 1942.* 2 a favourable movie review *US, 1997.* 3 in dominoes, a type of side bet *US, 1981.* 4 in pool, a rule infraction *US, 1992*

Hickey *noun* a notional province where there are no manners or courtesy *BARBADOS, 1965*

hickory dickory dock; hickory dickory *noun* a clock. Rhyming slang; an elaboration of DICKORY DOCK, from the nursery rhyme which continues 'A mouse ran up the clock' *UK, 1998*

hiddy *adjective* 1 drunk *US, 1989.* 2 hideous *US, 1990*

hide *noun* 1 the human skin *UK, 1607.* 2 impudence; effrontery; cheek *AUSTRALIA, 1902.* 3 a wallet *US, 1932.* 4 a horse *US, 1934.* 5 in hot rodding, a tyre *US, 1960*

hide *verb* ▶ **hide the salami** to have sex. 'Sausage' as 'penis' imagery; a variation of the earlier HIDE-THE-WEENIE *US, 1983*

hide and seek *noun* impudence. Rhyming slang for 'cheek' *UK, 1992*

hideaway *noun* a pocket *US, 1945*

hi-de-hi a greeting, answered by 'ho-de-ho'. First recorded during World War 2; adopted by Jimmy Perry and David Croft as the title (and catchphrase) of a television situation comedy set in a 1950s holiday camp (BBC, 1980–88); the call and response greeting is still heard, but often ironic *UK, 1941*

hideola *adjective* ugly. A variation of conventional 'hideous' *UK, 1992*

hides *noun* drums. Jazz slang *UK, 1986*

hide-the-baloney *noun* sexual intercourse *US, 1973*

hide-the-sausage *noun* sexual intercourse *AUSTRALIA, 1971*

hide-the-weenie *noun* sexual intercourse *US, 1968*

hidey *noun* the children's game hide and seek *AUSTRALIA, 1957*

hi diddle diddle *noun* 1 middle, especially the middle of a dart board. Rhyming slang *UK, 1992.* 2 a swindle, a deception *UK, 1992.* 3 a violin, a fiddle. Rhyming slang *UK, 1998*

hiding *noun* a beating; a heavy defeat *UK, 1809*

hiding to nothing *noun* ▶ **on a hiding to nothing** faced with a situation in which any outcome is unfavourable *UK, 1905*

hids *adjective* lacking fashion sense. An abbreviation of the conventional 'hideous' *US, 2002*

hidy-hole; hidey-hole *noun* a hiding place *UK, 1817*

hidy-ho, neighbor used as a humorous greeting. A catchphrase salutation from the US television comedy *Home Improvements* (ABC, 1991–99). Repeated with referential humour *US, 1991*

hifalutin *adjective* ▷*see:* HIGHFALUTIN

higgledy-piggledy *adjective* in a confused jumble. Probably derived as a rhyming elaboration of the disordered huddle in which pigs exist *UK, 1598*

high *noun* 1 the sensation produced by consuming drugs or alcohol *US, 1944.* 2 a sense of exhilaration, unrelated to drugs *US, 1970*

High *noun* Miller High Life™ beer *US, 1967*

high *adjective* 1 drunk or drug-intoxicated *UK, 1627.* 2 under the influence of a drug, especially marijuana *US, 1931.* 3 bad-smelling *TRINIDAD AND TOBAGO, 1935.* ▶ **at high warble** angry, especially without justification. Naval aviator usage *US, 1986*

high and light *adjective* pleasantly drug-intoxicated *US, 1952*

high and mighty; high-and-mighty *adjective* arrogant, imperious *UK, 1825*

high and tight *noun* a man's haircut in which the sides of the head are shaved and a quarter-inch of hair is left on top. A military term for a military haircut *US, 1988*

high as a kite *adjective* very drunk or drug-intoxicated. Rhyming slang for TIGHT (drunk); a clever elaboration of HIGH *US, 1939*

high-ass *adjective* haughty; arrogant *US, 1931*

highball *noun* **1** in the used car business, a knowingly inflated price *US, 1975*. **2** a signal to a train engineer to increase speed *US, 1897*. **3** a glass of milk *US, 1946*

highball *verb* **1** to travel fast *US, 1912*. **2** to see. Probably playing on EYEBALL *US, 1965*

high beams *noun* **1** erect nipples on a woman's breasts seen through a garment *US, 1986*. **2** the wide open eyes of a person under the influence of crack cocaine *US, 1994*

high bountious *adjective* very bad-smelling *TRINIDAD AND TOBAGO, 2003*

highboy *noun* in hot rodding, a coupe, sedan or roadster that sits on top of the frame rails at stock height, that has not been lowered *US, 1968*

highbrow *noun* a person of superior intellectual quality or interests; a person who affects interests that imply an intellectual superiority *US, 1907*

highbrow *adjective* of superior intellectual quality or interest *UK, 1884*

high-brown *adjective* of mixed black and white heritage. Originally white usage, then adopted by African-Americans *US, 1915*

high camp *noun* an ostentatious, highly mannered style. A refined variation of CAMP *US, 1966*

high cap *verb* to brag, to banter, to gossip *US, 1990*

high diver *noun* a person who enjoys or excels at performing oral sex on women. A construction built on the image of going down *US, 1981*

high drag *noun* elaborate female clothing worn by a man *US, 1963*

higher-higher *noun* the upper echelons of military command *US, 1991*

highfalutin; hifalutin *adjective* absurdly pompous, snobbish. Probably an elaboration of 'high-flown' or similar; 'highfaluting' (the 'g' is optional) was originally hyphenated which lends strength to this etymology. Yiddish *hifelufelem* (ostentatious, self-glorifying) is also possible *US, 1839*

high five *noun* **1** a greeting or sign of approval accomplished by slapping open palms with arms extended above head-level. The greeting and term originated in sport but quickly spread *US, 1980*. **2** HIV. A construction based on an abbreviation of 'high' to 'hi' and conversion of 'V' to the Roman numeral five *US, 2003*

high five *verb* to raise your open hand above your head and slap it against the open hand of someone else *US, 1981*

high fur *noun* the refuelling of a hovering helicopter *US, 1991*

high grade *noun* marijuana. Recorded by a Jamaican inmate of a UK prison, August 2002 *UK, 2002*

high hard one *noun* forceful sex *US, 1986*

high hat *noun* opium. From an earlier sense (a large opium pill) *US, 1896*

high-hat; high-hatted *adjective* snobbish, superior, supercilious *US, 1924*

high-heel boy *noun* a paratrooper *US, 1948*

high holy *noun* in the usage of counterculturalists associated with the Rainbow Nation gatherings, an older, experienced member of the counterculture. Often used with a degree of irony and lack of reverence *US, 1997*

high horse *noun* a position of arrogant superiority *US, 1947*

high iron *noun* the main line of a railway *US, 1930*

high-jive *verb* to tease, to taunt, to belittle *US, 1938*

high jump *noun* a court higher than a local magistrate's *AUSTRALIA, 1944*. ▶ **be for the high jump 1** to be faced with a severe official reprimand or punishment. Of military origin. With variations 'be up for the high jump' and 'be in for the high jump' *UK, 1919*. **2** to be engaged to be married *IRELAND, 1992*

highland fling *noun* to sing. Rhyming slang, credited to a 1950s recording by Billy Cotton and Alan Breeze *UK, 1992*

highlighter *noun* a political leader or spokesman among prisoners *US, 1976*

highly *adverb* used as an intensifier with an attitude *US, 1991*

highly illogical *adjective* illogical. A signature line of the Vulcan Mr Spock on the first incarnation of *Star Trek* (NBC, 1966–69). Repeated with referential humour *US, 1968*

high maintenance *adjective* (used of a person) requiring a great deal of attention and/or money; needy *US, 1989*

highness *noun* ▶ **her highness; his highness** your spouse. Affectionately ironic *UK, 1961*

high noon *noun* **1** in craps, a roll of twelve *US, 1982*. **2** a spoon. Rhyming slang, formed from the title of the 1952 film *UK, 1992*

high-nose *verb* to snub; to ignore *US, 1954*

high number *noun* an especially fashionable member of the Mod youth fashion movement *UK, 1986*

high octane *adjective* caffeinated. Borrowing from the language of car fuel for application to the world of coffee drinks and, to a lesser extent, soft drinks *US, 1995*

high off the hog *adverb* prosperously *US, 1970*

high play *noun* showy spending designed to impress *US, 1972*

high pockets *noun* the stature of a tall, thin man *US, 1912*

high puller *noun* a devoted player of casino slot machines, especially those with higher bets and higher payouts. A play on the term HIGH ROLLER *US, 1985*

high-rider *noun* a car or truck that has been structurally altered to ride very high; a person who drives such a car or truck *US, 1982*

high-riders *noun* trousers worn above the waist *US, 1975*

highroll *verb* to spend freely and to live fast *US, 1975*

high roller *noun* **1** a gambler who makes large bets and spends freely *US, 1881*. **2** in television and film-making, a large, tall, three-legged light stand *US, 1990*

high rolling *adjective* materially successful. From HIGH ROLLER (a big spender) *US, 1890*

highs *noun* in pool, the striped balls numbered 9 to 15 *US, 1990*

high-school Harriet *noun* a high-school girl who is dating a college boy *US, 1966*

high-school Harry *noun* an immature college male; a typical high-school student *US, 1959*

high-school horse *noun* in horse racing, a racehorse that seems to win only when the odds are very high. Based on the humorous suggestion that the horse is so smart it can read the posted odds *US, 1951*

high shots *noun* in the illegal production of alcohol, liquor that exceeds 100 proof *US, 1974*

high side *noun* **1** the outside of a curve in a road *US, 1966*. **2** in craps, the numbers over 7 *US, 1950*

high-side *verb* to show off *US, 1965*

high speed, low drag *adjective* competent, reliable, dependable. Vietnam war usage *US, 1991*

high sphincter tone *noun* said of a person with a high degree of inhibition and a conservative nature *US, 1994*

high spot *noun* the outstanding part or feature of something *UK, 1926*

high stepper *noun* pepper. Rhyming slang *UK, 1992*

hightail *verb* to move very quickly. Almost always used with 'it' *US, 1919*

high tea *noun* a social gathering of male homosexuals *US, 1981*

high tide *noun* the bleed period of the menstrual cycle *US, 1970*

high-up *noun* a person of high rank or importance *UK, 1929*

high waist *noun* vigorous sex. The 'high' suggests the woman's ability to lift the man up from below during sex *TRINIDAD AND TOBAGO, 2003*

high-waist *adjective* (used of a woman) skilled at sex *TRINIDAD AND TOBAGO, 2003*

high wall job *noun* a burglary that requires climbing *UK, 1996*

high-waters *noun* long trousers that are too short or short trousers that are too long *US, 1971*

highway princess *noun* a prostitute, especially one who works at truck stops *US, 1976*

highway salute *noun* a gesture with the middle finger meaning 'fuck you' *US, 1977*

highway surfer *noun* a person who adopts the mannerisms of surfers, buys the equipment, but never seems to get out of the car into the water *US, 1963*

high, wide and handsome; high, wide and fancy *adjective* excellent; first-rate. The title of a 1937 musical/romance film starring James Burke *US, 1947*

high wine *noun* a mixture of alcohol and flavoured water *CANADA, 1957*

high yellow; high yaller; high yella *noun* a light-skinned black person, especially female; a Creole; a mulatto. 'Objectionable when referring to lighter-colored black persons' according to *Dictionary of Cautionary Words and Phrases*, 1989 *US, 1923*

high yellow; high yaller; high yella *adjective* light-skinned *US, 1958*

hijinks; hijinx *noun* an act or acts of self-indulgent frivolity. An altered spelling of conventional 'high jinks' *US, 1995*

hijo de la chingada *noun* son of a fucked woman. Border Spanish used in English conversation by Mexican-Americans; highly insulting *US, 1974*

hike *verb* to insult in a competitive, quasi-friendly spirit, especially by reference to your opponent's family *US, 2000*

hiker *noun* a prison officer whose duty is to be anywhere in the prison when required *UK, 1996*

hike up *verb* **1** of clothes, to work out of position or to drag into place *US, 1873*. **2** to raise prices *US, 2003*

Hilda Handcuffs; Hilda *noun* a police officer; the police. An example of CAMP trans-gender assignment, in this case an assonant play on handcuffs as stereotypical police equipment *UK, 1992*

hill *noun* ▶ **go over the hill** to desert military duty; to escape from prison *US, 1912*. ▶ **on the hill** in pool, needing only one more score to win *US, 1993*. ▶ **over the hill** past your prime *US, 1950*

Hill *noun* ▶ **the Hill** Parliament Hill in Ottawa *CANADA, 1965*

hill and dale *noun* a tale, of the type told by a confidence trickster. Rhyming slang *UK, 1953*

hillbilly *adjective* chilly. Glasgow rhyming slang *UK: SCOTLAND, 1985*

hillbilly chrome *noun* aluminium paint *US, 1971*

hillbilly craps *noun* craps played on the sidewalk or otherwise as a private game *US, 1950*

hillbilly hell *noun* used as an embellished, intensified 'hell' *US, 1970*

hillbilly heroin *noun* the synthetic opiate oxycodone used recreationally. When dissolved in water and injected, or crushed and inhaled, it has a similar effect to heroin. The drug's popularity in the rural Appalachian Mountains region led to the 'hillbilly' reference. It came to the forefront of the American national conscious in late 2003 when radio entertainer Rush Limbaugh was reported to be addicted to OxyContin™ *US, 2001*

hillbilly operahouse *noun* a truck with a radio *US, 1971*

hillbilly special *noun* a truck manufactured by General Motors Corporation *US, 1971*

Hill Fights *noun* a series of battles in the vicinity of Khe Sanh, South Vietnam, in April and May 1967 *US, 1988*

hill game *noun* in pool, a situation where either player can win with a single pocket *US, 1993*

hillman hunter; hillman *noun* a client or customer of any service that has little respect for the clients and customers. Rhyming slang, formed from the name of a 1970s car *UK, 1992*

hillybin *noun* a lesbian *NEW ZEALAND, 1973*

Hilton *noun* a camp where firefighters fighting a forest fire sleep *US, 1991*

him *noun* heroin *US, 1969* ▷ *see:* HE

Himalaya gold; Himalaya *noun* a potent marijuana with yellow hairs on a pale green bud. A hybrid plant cultivated in the 1990s, not in the Himalayas but with genetic antecedents in Nepal and South India; the naming is, perhaps, also an ironic reference to the highest physical location on planet earth *UK, 2003*

himbo *noun* a man objectified by his good looks and presumed lack of intellectual qualities; a man who trades on this image; a gigolo. Plays on contemporary use of BIMBO (a beautiful and available young woman − if you are a rich older man) *US, 1988*

Hinckley; Hinkley *noun* phencyclidine, the recreational drug known as PCP or angel dust *US, 1984*

hincty *adjective* conceited, vain, arrogant *US, 1924*

hind claw *noun* a means of support secondary to your job *BARBADOS, 1965*

hind hook *noun* the rear brakeman on a freight train *US, 1946*

hind tit *noun* ▶ **on the hind tit; suck the hind tit** to be last in order or standing *US, 1940*

Hindu shuffle *noun* in card trickery, a technique that will keep a card or several cards on the bottom of the deck *UK, 2003*

hiney; heiny; heinie *noun* the buttocks *US, 1921*

hinge *noun* the elbow *US, 1945*

hinges *noun* ▶ **off your hinges** mentally unhinged, crazy. Word play; as 'off the hinges' from 1611 to mid-C19 *UK, 1986*

Hinglish *noun* a hybrid language formed of Hindi and English; also applied to an informal blending of Punjabi and English *UK, 2001*

hinked up *adjective* suspicious, afraid *US, 2000*

hinky *adjective* **1** nervous, anxious *US, 1956*. **2** suspicious *US, 1975*

hinky-dee *noun* a form of comedic song *US, 1949*

hinky-dinky *adjective* small-time, second class, outmoded. A cousin of the more famous RINKY-DINK *US, 1967*

hip *noun* **1** a member of the 1960s counterculture *US, 1967*. **2** a heroin addict *US, 1953*. **3** the buttocks *BAHAMAS, 1982*

hip *verb* **1** to explain, to bring up to date, to inform *US, 1932*. **2** to figure out, to become aware *US, 1975*. ▶ **hip your ship** to let you know *US, 1953*

hip *adjective* **1** knowing, understanding *US, 1902*. **2** in style, fashionable, admired *US, 1944*. ▶ **hip to all happenings** profoundly aware of the latest trends and happenings *US, 1964*

hip cat *noun* a fan of jazz or swing music; a stylish and fashionable man *US, 1947*

hipe *verb* in a cheating scheme in a game of cards, to restore a deck to its original position after a cheating move *US, 1962*

hip-flinger *noun* a dancer in any type of overtly sexual dance *US, 1981*

hip-hop *noun* used as a loose categorisation of (initially) black urban youth culture, encompassing breakdancing, graffiti art, DJing and rap music; used as an umbrella for any music, especially dance and rap-music, that falls within the general style; any fashion or style that is defined by association with the culture. Combining HIP (fashionable) and HOP (dance); like ROCK 'N' ROLL before it, 'hip-hop' is an American phenomenon that has had a worldwide impact *US, 1982*

hip hop daisy age *noun* an early 1990s fashion in hip-hop culture that approximated the 'peace and love' attitudes of the hippie movement *UK, 2003*

hip kick *noun* the rear pocket on a pair of trousers *US, 1981*

hipky-dripky *noun* mischief *US, 1959*

hi-po *adjective* in motor racing, high performance *US, 1993*

hipped *adjective* **1** aware of, knowledgeable of *US, 1920*. **2** carrying a gun *US, 1920*

hipped to the tip *adjective* aware of everything *US, 1947*

hipper *noun* a large, swollen bruise on the hip. Noted as a sports injury suffered by foot-propelled scooter-riders *UK, 2000*

hippie; hippy *noun* a follower of jazz and the jazz scene who strives to be hip *US, 1952*

hippie crack *noun* nitrous oxide. A substance of abuse favoured by hippies and neo-hippies, seductive if not addictive *US, 1992*

hipping *noun* a nappy (diaper) or sanitary towel *TRINIDAD AND TOBAGO, 2003*

hippo *noun* an armoured personnel carrier used by the South African police *SOUTH AFRICA, 1996*

Hippo *noun* any theatre called the Hippodrome. An affectionate shortening of an actor's place of work, such as, in Britain, the Birmingham Hippo, the Bristol Hippo, and, in the US, the Baltimore Hippo *UK, 1937*

hip pocket *noun* a truck's glove compartment *US, 1976*

hippy *adjective* **1** full-hipped *US, 1963*. **2** mentally dulled by years of imprisonment *US, 1950*

hippy-dippy *noun* a hippy or hippie, in either sense. Derogatory *US, 1969*

hippy-dippy *adjective* used to describe the 'peace and love' philosophy of the hippy movement *US, 1960*

hippy hill *nickname* a hill in Golden Gate Park, San Francisco, between the Stanyan Street entrance and Dinosaur Valley *US, 1967*

hippytitis *noun* hepatitis *UK, 1970*

hippy-trippy *adjective* psychedelic. A rhyming combination of the counterculture and the effects of drugs *UK, 2001*

hippy witch *noun* a girl who 30 years later still dresses in the styles popular with the late 1960s counterculture *US, 1997*

hip-square *noun* a conventional person who at moments adopts the drapings of the jazz lifestyle without fully embracing it *US, 1961*

hipster *noun* **1** a devotee of jazz and the jazz lifestyle *US, 1940*. **2** a person at the stylish edge of fashionable. A contemporary variation *US, 2002*

hipsway *noun* dismissal *UK: SCOTLAND, 1988*

hir used as a gender-neutral third-person singular pronoun *US, 1997*

hirsute *adjective* in computing, complicated. Used as a jocular synonym for 'hairy' *US, 1983*

hi-si *noun* high society *US, 1957*

his lordship *noun* used ironically of a male who is perceived to behave in a manner that is somehow above his status. Derisive *UK, 1961*

hiss *noun* to hike rapidly *NEW ZEALAND, 1958*

hissy-fit; hissy *noun* a tantrum *US, 1997*

history *noun* **1** the condition of being doomed or finished *US, 1978*. **2** in a swindle, the background on a victim, people likely to be encountered, a location or event *US, 1977*

history sheeter *noun* a person with a criminal record *INDIA, 2003*

hit *noun* **1** a single inhalation of marijuana, hashish, crack cocaine, or any drug's smoke *US, 1952*. **2** a dose of a drug *US, 1952*. **3** an intravenous injection of a drug, usually heroin *UK, 1996*. **4** a meeting with a drug dealer and a drug user *US, 1952*. **5** in the eastern US in the early 1990s, prescription medication with codeine *US, 1993*. **6** a marijuana cigarette *UK, 2001*. **7** a tablet of MDMA, the recreational drug best known as ecstasy *UK, 2003*. **8** a deliberate inhalation of solvent fumes, such as glue sniffing *UK, 1982*. **9** a blast of euphoria, joy, excitement. Figurative use of a drug term *US, 1971*. **10** the electronic registration of a visit to a website *US, 1995*. **11** a planned murder *US, 1950*. **12** an arrest *US, 1973*. **13** a winning bet in an illegal lottery *UK, 1818*. **14** in blackjack, a card that a player requests from the dealer to add to his hand *US, 1980*. **15** in snowboarding, a snow jump *CANADA, 1996*. ▶ **on hit** excellent *US, 1997*

hit *verb* **1** to inject drugs into a vein *US, 1949*. **2** to take an inhalation of marijuana smoke *US, 1952*. **3** to smoke (marijuana) *US, 1949*. **4** to guess correctly the day's number in an illegal lottery *US, 1947*. **5** to kill in a planned, professional manner *US, 1949*. **6** to rob *US, 1970*. **7** to cover with graffiti *US, 1997*. **8** to visit, to go to a place *US, 1995*. **9** to serve a drink *US, 1932*. **10** to ask for something, especially money *US, 1894*. **11** to telephone someone with a mobile phone *US, 2002*. **12** to win. From cricket *TRINIDAD AND TOBAGO, 2003*. **13** to have sex *US, 2004*. ▶ **be hit with a bit** to be sentenced to prison. From BIT (a prison sentence) *US, 1962*. ▶ **can't hit the bull in the arse with a scoop shovel** to be physically or mentally useless. 'This expression describes someone who is totally uncoordinated.

As this involves both a broad weapon and a broad target it refers not to poor marksmanship, but rather to a total inability to act in a coordinated manner.' Chris Thain, *Cold as a Bay Street Banker's Heart*, 1987 *CANADA, 1987*. ▶ **hit a hurdle** to die; to suffer a severe setback *AUSTRALIA, 1989*. ▶ **hit a lick** to commit a robbery *US, 2001*. ▶ **hit daylight** to be released from prison *US, 1988*. ▶ **hit for six** to demolish another's argument, proposal or plan. A figurative use of a cricketing term *UK, 1937*. ▶ **hit in the seat** an act of anal intercourse *US, 1976*. ▶ **hit it** to leave *US, 1930*. ▶ **hit it a lick; hit it** in poker, to raise a bet *US, 1988*. ▶ **hit it off** to take a mutual liking to someone *UK, 1780*. ▶ **hit it up** to strike up an acquaintance *US, 1934*. ▶ **hit on the hip** to page electronically *US, 1996*. ▶ **hit the books** to study hard *US, 1968*. ▶ **hit the bottle** to bleach your hair blonde. Teen slang, punning on a term associated with drinking *US, 1955*. ▶ **hit the breeze** to leave *NEW ZEALAND, 1974*. ▶ **hit the bricks** to work on the street *US, 1973*. ▶ **hit the bucket** to drink very heavily. A humorous variation on 'hit the bottle' (to drink heavily) *UK: SCOTLAND, 1988*. ▶ **hit the burner** to draw upon all of your inner resources and stamina. US naval aviator usage *US, 1986*. ▶ **hit the ceiling** to become very angry *US, 1914*. ▶ **hit the cinders** to jump or fall from a moving train *US, 1977*. ▶ **hit the deck 1** to fall or throw yourself to the ground *US, 1925*. **2** to land a plane *UK, 1943*. **3** to get out of bed. Often as an imperative *UK, 1918*. **4** to go to bed *UK, 1935*. ▶ **hit the dex** to work as a DJ. Fashionable spelling for (record) 'decks', combined with a vague play on other senses of HIT THE DECK *UK, 2002*. ▶ **hit the Dixie** to stop idling and start doing something *BAHAMAS, 1982*. ▶ **hit the gravel; hit the grit** to fall from a moving train *US, 1946*. ▶ **hit the hay** to go to bed. Originally used by tramps; anglicised in 1929 by Conan Doyle *US, 1912*. ▶ **hit the hop** to use drugs, especially heroin or opium *US, 1963*. ▶ **hit the jackpot** to have great success or good fortune, especially when unexpected or beyond your expectations. A figurative application of 'jackpot', a poker term applied generally to any gambling prize. Known worldwide in its variant forms: 'crack' (favoured in Australia), 'hit', 'strike' or 'win' *US, 2001*. ▶ **hit the mainline** to inject a drug intravenously. A combination of HIT (to inject) and MAINLINE (a vein) *US, 1950*. ▶ **hit the moon** to reach the highest plateau of a drug experience *US, 1971*. ▶ **hit the needle** to inject a drug intravenously. A combination of HIT (to inject) and the means of delivery *US, 1950*. ▶ **hit the pipe** to smoke crack cocaine *US, 1992*. ▶ **hit the pit 1** to inject a drug into the armpit. A combination of HIT (to inject) and PIT (the armpit) *UK, 1998*. **2** to be incarcerated *US, 1992*. ▶ **hit the post** in the language of radio disc jockeys, to talk during the introduction of a song, completing your thought just before the song's vocal begins *US, 1997*. ▶ **hit the prone** to throw yourself to the ground *US, 1977*. ▶ **hit the road; hit the trail** to go; to commence or recommence a journey *US, 1899*. ▶ **hit the roof** to be, or to become very angry; to exhibit that anger *UK, 1925*. ▶ **hit the sack** to go to bed, to go to sleep *US, 1912*. ▶ **hit the sauce** to drink alcohol *US, 1997*. ▶ **hit the sewer** to inject heroin or another drug intravenously *US, 1973*. ▶ **hit the silk** in card games, to withdraw from or end a game or hand. From the military slang for bailing out of an aircraft by parachute (silk) *US, 1972*. ▶ **hit the skids** to deteriorate *US, 1958*. ▶ **hit the slab** to be killed *US, 1950*. ▶ **hit the toe** to depart; to decamp *AUSTRALIA, 1983*. ▶ **hit the wall** to reach a point of exhaustion beyond which lesser athletes will fail to continue, especially of long-distance and marathon runners *US, 1982*. ▶ **hit with a check** to discharge from employment and pay off owed wages *US, 1954*. ▶ **hit your marks** in television and film-making, to move to the proper place at the proper time in a scene *US, 1990*

hit and get *verb* to rob one place and then hurry to rob somewhere else *UK, 1996*

hit and miss; hit or miss *noun* **1** a kiss. Rhyming slang, 'hit me', which evolves to 'kiss me', to 'kiss'. Sometimes abbreviated to 'hit' *UK, 1933*. **2** urine; alcoholic drink or (when used with 'the'), drinking or a session of drinking. Rhyming slang for PISS (and ON THE PISS) *AUSTRALIA, 1960*

hit and run *noun* **1** a betting technique in which a player places a single bet and withdraws from the game if he wins *US, 1950*. **2** the sun. Rhyming slang *UK, 1998*

hit and run *verb* **1** in casino blackjack, to enter a game when the count is advantageous to the players, to play a few games and then to move to another table *US, 1991*. **2** in poker, to play for a short time, win heavily and quit the game *US, 1982*

hit and run *adjective* **1** (used of entertainment engagements) in one city one night, another city the next *US, 1976*. **2** swindled. Rhyming slang for 'done' (DO) *UK, 1992*

hit-and-split *noun* a quick air attack followed by a quick retreat *US, 1991*

hitch *noun* **1** a period of duty or service *US, 1905*. **2** a jail sentence *US, 1964*

Hitch *nickname* Alfred Hitchcock (1899–1980), television and film director *US, 1976*

hitch *verb* to hitchhike. A colloquial shortening *US, 1929*. ▶ **hitch up the reindeers; hitch up the reindeer** to inhale powdered cocaine. Punning variously on SNOW (cocaine) and SLEIGH RIDE (the use of cocaine) *US, 1986*

hitched *adjective* married *US, 1857*

hitchhiker *noun* a commerical message played at the end of a radio programme *US, 1980*

hitch up *verb* to marry, to partner. Figurative application of a conventional 'hitch' (a knot) *US, 1902*

hit kiss *noun* the exchange of crack cocaine smoke from one user to another through a kiss *US, 1989*

Hitler's drug *noun* paramethoxyamphetamine, PMA. The drug was originally created during World War 2 by Hitler's chemists with the intention of enabling Nazi soldiers to fight around the clock. In 1999 the *Observer* reported fears of the drug's arrival in UK clubs, *1999*

hit list *noun* a list of targets for retaliation, either physical or otherwise *US, 1972*

hit man *noun* a professional killer *US, 1963*

hit on *verb* to flirt; to proposition *US, 1954*

hit or sit *verb* used for describing a player's two choices in blackjack or twenty-one – draw another card or not *US, 1962*

hits *noun* **1** LSD *UK, 1998*. **2** a pair of dice that have been altered so that they will not roll a total of seven *US, 1962*

hitsville *noun* success. Used on the normally staid *BBC Light Programme*, 30th June 1963 *UK, 1963*

hit team *noun* during the Vietnam conflict, a small unit of trained scouts sent on a mission to kill the enemy *US, 1987*

hitter *noun* **1** a hired killer *US, 1959*. **2** a crack cocaine pipe designed for a single inhalation *US, 2001*

hit the hay *verb* to smoke marijuana *US, 1942*

hittin' *adjective* excellent *US, 1991*

hitting; hittin' *adjective* tasty *US, 1993*

hitting fluid *noun* heroin *US, 1973*

hit up *verb* **1** to inject a drug intravenously *US, 1969*. **2** to ask for something *US, 1988*. **3** to go to *US, 2002*

hiya used as a casual greeting *UK, 1940*

hiya-butty-bay; hiya-butt-bay *noun* Trecco Bay, Porthcawl in south Wales. In 1947 mining was nationalised and subsequent working practices meant that entire communities relocated to the seaside resort of Porthcawl for 'miners' fortnight'. The friendly greeting 'hiya, butty' (hello, friend) filled the air. The style of holidays changed in the 1960s but the term is still in limited circulation *UK: WALES, 2001*

hiya kids used as a humorous greeting. The signature greeting used on the children's television programme *Ed's Gang* (later *Andy's Gang*) (1951–58). Repeated with referential humour *US, 1955*

hizzie *nickname* the room, apartment or house where someone lives *US, 2002*

Hizzoner *nickname* used as a jocular reference to a mayor, especially Richard J. Daley, mayor of Chicago from 1955 until his death in 1976. A slurred 'his honor' *US, 1882*

HK *nickname* Hong Kong. Current among the UK Chinese population *UK, 1998*

HMCS *how my companion snores*. A jocular back-formation from HCMS (Her Majesty's Canadian Ship) *CANADA, 2002*

HMFIC *noun* a commanding officer, or *head motherfucker in charge* *US, 1993*

HNIC *noun* the leader of an enterprise, the *head nigger in charge* *US, 1972*

HO *verb* to withhold more than your share of something. An initialism of 'hold out' *US, 1950*

ho; hoe *noun* **1** a sexually available woman; a woman who may be considered sexually available; a prostitute. Originally black usage, from the southern US pronunciation of 'whore'; now widespread through the influence of rap music *US, 1959*. **2** a woman. A weakened variation of the previous sense *US, 1959*. **3** a weak or effeminate man *US, 1996*

ho; hoe *verb* to work as a prostitute *US, 1972*

hoaching; hotchin *adjective* full, teeming, crowded *UK: SCOTLAND, 1911*

hoachy *adjective* exceedingly lucky, fortunate *UK: SCOTLAND, 1985*

hoagons *noun* the female breasts *US, 1968*

ho, babe used as a student-to-student greeting *US, 1959*

hobber de hoy; hibber de hoy *noun* an adolescent boy, especially a hooligan. Recorded as rhyming slang by Ray Puxley, *Cockney Rabbit*, 1992; but probably direct from 'hobbledehoy', first recorded in 1540, which, excepting the nuance of hooliganism, is synonymous; 'hobbledehoy', however, is unlikely to be rhyming slang as the earliest explicit reference to rhyming slang does not appear until about 300 years later in John Camden Hotten's *The Slang Dictionary*, 1859 *UK, 1992*

hobby bobby *noun* a special constable, a part-time uniformed police officer *UK, 2005*

ho-bitch *noun* a female who has earned a complete lack of respect. Used on those special occasions when just BITCH or just HO is just not enough *US, 1997*

hobnail *verb* to walk *NEW ZEALAND, 2000*

hobnail express *noun* travel by walking *US, 1918*

hobo *noun* **1** a vagrant. Uncertainly derived from 'hoeboy' (a migrant agricultural labourer) or the exclamation 'Ho boy!' (used by mail carriers) *US, 1885*. **2** in trucking, a tractor trailer that is moved from one terminal to another *US, 1971*. **3** a homing bomb, one with a targeting capability *US, 1975*

hobo bet *noun* in craps, a bet on the number twelve. From the number's association with boxcars *US, 1985*

hobo cocktail *noun* a glass of water *US, 1947*

hobosexual *noun* a person who is sexually active with several partners in a short period of time *US, 1985*

Hobo Woods *noun* an area in South Vietnam which was a major staging area for the North Vietnamese to launch attacks on Saigon or Cu Chi City *US, 1986*

Hobson's choice; hobsons *noun* **1** the only option that is offered and, therefore, no choice at all. Widely claimed, since 1712, to derive from Tobias Hobson, who hired out horses, and is reputed to have compelled his customers to take whichever horse happened to be next in line, or go without; however, 'Hodgson's choise' is recorded in 1617 *UK, 1649*. **2** the voice. Rhyming slang *UK, 1937*

Ho Chi Minh Motel *noun* a rest house used by the Viet Cong along a trail or route *US, 1967*

Ho Chi Minh sandals *noun* slip-on sandals made from the treads of discarded tyres, designed and worn by the Viet Cong during the Vietnam war *US, 1977*

Ho Chi Minh's curse *noun* diarrhoea. An existing formation of 'somebody's curse' adapted in Vietnam *US, 1991*

Ho Chi Minh Trail *noun* Route 209 in northeast Pennsylvania *US, 1977*

hock *noun* **1** the male who takes the active role in homosexual intercourse. Origin unknown. Ted Hartley in his glossary of prison slang (1944) says that 'hocks' can mean 'feet', and is therefore in some way related to the term HORSE'S HOOF. Simes, in his *Dictionary of Australian Underworld Slang* (1993), suggests that ' hock' is 'feeble' and rhyming slang for 'cock'. Neither of these is overwhelmingly convincing AUSTRALIA, *1944*. **2** the foot UK, *1785*. ▶ **in hock 1** in debt, especially to a pawnbroker US, *1883*. **2** in prison US, *1859*

hock *verb* **1** to pawn US, *1878*. **2** to clear the throat of phlegm. From a confusion with conventional 'hawk' US, *1992*. **3** to nag. From the Yiddish US, *1961*

hockey box; hock *noun* a male homosexual prostitute AUSTRALIA, *1985*

hockey hair a hair style: the hair is worn short at the front and long at the back. Better known, perhaps, as a MULLET CANADA, *2000*

hockeystick *noun* a mutton chop NEW ZEALAND, *1990*

hock shop *noun* a pawnbroker's shop UK, *1871*

hocus *noun* a solution of heroin that has been heated and is ready to inject US, *1967*

hocus *verb* to alter legitimate dice for cheating purposes US, *1950*

hocus pocus; hocus *noun* cocaine, heroine, morphine or opium; also marijuana. Best remembered as a stage magician's incantation, but claimed to be a mocking corruption of *hoc est corpus* (this is the body); originally, 1650–1720, 'a juggler/a conjuror'; it was in circulation during C19 and into C20 in the sense of 'criminal deception/shady trickery'; in 1821 as 'to stupefy with alcohol' (for the purposes of robbery) and hence 'hocus' became 'a drugged liquor' from as early as 1725 and well into C19 served as an adjective meaning 'intoxicated'. All these meanings condensed into a catalogue of hard drugs during C20; 'marijuana' joined the list in the 1980s UK, *1938*

hodad *noun* a non-surfer who associates with surfers and poses as a surfer US, *1961*

hoddie *noun* a labourer working for a bricklayer AUSTRALIA, *1952*

hod of shit *noun* a great deal of trouble US, *1981*

hoe *noun* a fellow black man, usually in context of sexual bragging. From HOMEBOY (close friend), punning on 'hero' US, *1987* ▷*see:* HO

hoedown *noun* a street fight between youth gangs US, *1993*

hoe in *verb* to attack physically and with vigour NEW ZEALAND, *2002*

hoe into *verb* to attack a task with vigour, especially the eating of a meal AUSTRALIA, *1935*

hoffing *noun* a fight, especially between youth gangs US, *1971*

hog *noun* **1** a powerful motorcycle, especially a large Harley-Davidson motorcycle US, *1965*. **2** a utility helicopter equipped with rockets and machine guns US, *1991*. **3** a Cadillac or other large luxury car US, *1960*. **4** the penis US, *1968*. **5** a police officer. A variation on PIG (a police officer) US, *1970*. **6** a US Marine Corps recruit during basic training. Contemptuous US, *1968*. **7** a leader; a strong personality US, *1989*. **8** a drug addict who requires large doses to sustain his habit US, *1952*. **9** heroin US, *2000*. **10** marijuana. A term apparently coined by US soliders during the conflict in Vietnam, drawn from 'hash, o, grass' US, *1968*. **11** phencyclidine, the recreational drug known as PCP or angel dust US, *1971*. **12** a strong sedative, trade name Benaceyzine™ US, *1977*. **13** a computer program that uses a high degree of a computer's resources US, *1991*. ▶ **beat the hog** (used of a male) to masturbate US, *1971*. ▶ **hog is pork** there is no difference between the two alternatives being discussed TRINIDAD AND TOBAGO, *2003*. ▶ **on the hog** homosexual US, *1976*

hog *verb* **1** to speak rudely TRINIDAD AND TOBAGO, *2003*. **2** to rape US, *1972*. **3** in high-low poker, to declare for both high and low US, *1996*

Hog-60 *noun* an M-60 machine gun. Each squad in Vietnam was assigned an M-60, the army's general purpose machine gun which entered the service in the 1950s. It was designed to be lightweight (23 pounds) and easy to carry. It produced a low 'grunting' sound and thus the porcine allusions US, *1987*

Hogan's Alley *nickname* the Riviera Country Club, Pacific Palisades, California. Hogan enjoyed great success there, especially in 1947 and 48 US, *1997*

hog board *noun* a bulletin board where soldiers post pictures of their families and girlfriends. Marine usage in Vietnam US, *1974*

hog eye; hogger; hoghead; hogineer; hog jerk; hog jockey *noun* a railway engineer US, *1977*

hog fuel *noun* sawdust and bark produced by sawmills, burnt to generate steam for electricity CANADA, *1989*

hogging *noun* a romantic interest in heavy people US, *2004*

hog jaws *noun* a special plough blade fitted to a D7E bulldozer, or Rome Plow, for use in land clearing operations in Vietnam US, *1991*

hog-leg; hog leg *noun* **1** an oversized handgun US, *1919*. **2** a large marijuana cigarette US, *1997*

hog liver *noun* in electric line work, a flat porcelain guy strain insulator US, *1980*

hogman *noun* a criminal who silences alarms while a crime is committed UK, *1996*

hogmaster; hogmauler *noun* a railway engineer US, *1977*

hog out *verb* in motor mechanics, to enlarge an engine's openings or passages US, *1993*

hog pen *noun* a prison guards' control room US, *1984*

hog-tie *verb* to bind the hands and feet US, *1894*

Hogtown *nickname* Toronto. Nicknamed for the early C20 growth of farmer's markets and slaughterhouses, Toronto has also continued to be known as TORONTO THE GOOD CANADA, *1985*

hog up *verb* to address with a lack of respect BARBADOS, *1965*

hog wallow *noun* the slot used as a sighting plane on the topstrap of a Colt or Smith and Wesson pistol US, *1957*

hogwash *noun* nonsense US, *1882*

hog whimpering *adjective* very drunk UK, *1983*

hoha *noun* a fuss NEW ZEALAND, *1983*

hoha *adjective* weary NEW ZEALAND, *2003*

ho-ho *noun* a fat teenage girl US, *1982*

hoick *verb* **1** to spit AUSTRALIA, *1941*. **2** to throw or chuck; to loft AUSTRALIA, *1972*. **3** to raise, to hoist. Sometimes spelt 'hoik' UK, *1898*

hoicked-up *adjective* raised, especially artificially lifted UK, *2003*

hoi polloi *noun* the common people; the unwashed masses UK, *1822*

hoist *noun* ▶ **on the hoist** engaged in shoplifting UK, *1958*

hoist *verb* **1** to drink (an alcoholic beverage) UK, *1983*. **2** to rob with guns US, *1928*. **3** to shoplift UK, *2000*

hoister *noun* **1** a shoplifter; a pickpocket UK, *1790*. **2** in circus and carnival usage, a ferris wheel US, *1981*

hoisting *noun* shoplifting UK, *1936*

hoisting bloomers *noun* a capacious undergarment used by shoplifters UK, *1956*

hoity-toity *adjective* snobbish, haughty, assuming, uppish. Directly from the earlier form 'highty-tighty' UK, *1720*

Ho Jo's *nickname* a Howard Johnson restaurant. A fixture along US motorways in the 1950s and 60s US, *1965*

hokey; hoky; hokie *adjective* sentimental; mawkish; in poor taste US, *1927*

hokey cokey *noun* karaoke. Rhyming slang for a modern singalong entertainment enjoyed after a few drinks formed from the name of a song and dance that used to be enjoyed after a few drinks UK, *1998*

hokey-pokey *noun* **1** sexual intercourse. A play both on POKE (to have sex) and the childrens' song and dance, the 'hokey cokey' UK, *1983*. **2** in circus and carnival usage, any shoddy, inexpensive merchandise US, *1981*

hokum *noun* nonsense US, *1921*

hold *noun* in casino gambling, the amount of money bet that is retained by the casino US, *1977*. ▶ **in the hold** hidden in a pocket or elsewhere on the body US, *1961*

hold *verb* **1** to be in possession of drugs US, *1935*. **2** to be in possession of money US, *1967*. ▶ **get hold of** to have sex with someone US, *2003*. ▶ **hold court** to get in a shoot-out with police US, *1974*. ▶ **hold feet to the fire** to apply great pressure and demand results UK, *1995*. ▶ **hold no brief for** not to support or actively sympathise with someone UK, *1918*. ▶ **hold the bag** to take the blame US, *1985*. ▶ **hold the fort; mind the fort** to manage temporarily in an absentee's stead *UK, 1870.* ▶ **hold your dick** to do nothing; to wait idly *UK, 2001.* ▶ **hold your mud** to stand up to pressure and adversity *US, 1966.* ▶ **hold your mug** to keep a secret *US, 1970*

hold down *verb* **1** to maintain (a position of employment) *US, 1896.* **2** to control (a block or neighbourhood). Youth gang usage *US, 1985*

holder *noun* a prisoner, usually not a gang member, entrusted with storing drugs controlled by a prison gang *US, 1992*

holding *adjective* in possession of ready cash *AUSTRALIA, 1922*

holding ground *noun* a position, literally or figuratively, where you can weather adversity. From the nautical term for an area where the sea bottom provides a firm hold for anchors *US, 1963*

holding pen *noun* **1** a cell in a local jail where prisoners are held when they first arrive, pending a decision on whether criminal charges will be filed against them or not *US, 1981.* **2** a boarding school *NEW ZEALAND, 2001*

holding tank *noun* a cell at a local jail where the recently arrested are held before being processed *US, 1994*

hold-it *noun* a gratuitous television view of a pretty girl or woman, usually a spectator at a sporting event *US, 1986*

hold out on *verb* to refuse to give something, often information *US, 1907*

hold paddock *noun* a retirement home *NEW ZEALAND, 1994*

hold the bus!; haud the bus! slow down!; wait a minute! *UK: SCOTLAND, 1988*

hold the phone! wait a minute! *US, 1975*

hold with *verb* to agree with or approve of something or someone *UK, 1895*

hold your horses *verb* used imperatively to urge inaction *US, 1844*

hole *noun* **1** the vagina; sex with a woman; a woman; women *UK, 1592.* **2** the anus *UK, 1607.* **3** the mouth *US, 1865.* **4** a passive, promiscuous, unattached lesbian *US, 1992.* **5** in prison, a cell designed for solitary confinement. Always with 'the' *UK, 1535.* **6** an undesirable place; a place that is dirty or disordered *UK, 1876.* **7** any place where a supply of illegal drugs is hidden *US, 1993.* **8** a monetary or social difficulty, a mess, a scrape *UK, 1760.* **9** the subway (underground) *US, 1933.* **10** a mine *US, 1977.* **11** on the railways, a passing track *US, 1946.* **12** in trucking, a position in the gear box *US, 1971.* **13** a tobacco cigarette *US, 1970.* **14** in drag racing, the starting line *US, 1970.* ▶ **after his hole; after his end** of a man, seeking sex with a woman. From HOLE (the vagina) or END (the penis) *UK, 1961.* ▶ **get your hole** to have sexual intercourse *IRELAND, 1991.* ▶ **go in the hole** to fall from a pole, tower, rig or building under construction *US, 1989.* ▶ **in the hole** in police usage, hiding and avoiding work *US, 1973*

hole bit *noun* while in prison, a sentence to solitary confinement *US, 1967*

hole card *noun* **1** in stud poker, a card dealt face-down *US, 1967.* **2** a resource in reserve *US, 1926.* **3** the key to a person's character. From the game of stud poker, in which a 'hole card' is a card dealt face-down *US, 1968*

hole-in-one *noun* sexual intercourse on a first date. A puerile golf metaphor *US, 1972*

hole in the ground; hole *noun* a pound. Rhyming slang *UK, 1992*

hole in the head *noun* the epitome of something that is not needed at all. From Yiddish *US, 1951*

hole in the wall *noun* **1** an automated cash machine *UK, 1985.* **2** in trucking, a tunnel *US, 1976*

hole olie *noun* in stud poker, a card dealt face-down. A jocular embellishment of HOLE CARD *US, 1967*

holes *noun* ▶ **the holes** a location, such as a public lavatory, where men may have anonymous sex with each other by means of holes bored between private cubicles *UK, 1996*

hole shot *noun* in drag racing, the art of starting at the first possible moment without incurring a foul for starting too soon *US, 1970*

holetime *noun* solitary confinement in prison *US, 1967*

hole to bowl *noun* the path taken during defecation on a toilet *US, 1969*

hole up *verb* to hide *UK, 1875*

holey dollar *noun* a Spanish dollar with a hole punched in the centre *CANADA, 1963*

holiday *noun* in horse racing, the term of a suspension from competing *AUSTRALIA, 1989*

Holiday Inn *noun* any large US base camp in Vietnam where field troops would stand down for several days before returning to combat in the field *US, 1986*

HOLLAND written on an envelope, or at the foot of a lover's letter as lovers' code for 'here our love lies and never dies' or 'hope our love lasts and never dies'. Widely known, and well used by servicemen; now a part of the coded vocabulary of texting *UK, 1984*

holler *verb* to talk *US, 2001*

holler *adjective* stylish *US, 1961*

holler and hoot *verb* to engage in an abusive verbal attack *UK, 2001*

holler and shout *noun* a German. Rhyming slang for KRAUT *UK, 1992*

holler boys holler; holler boys *noun* a collar. Old rhyming slang, originally 'holloa boys', 'holloa', from a chant used on Guy Fawkes night, with a use dating back to the time of the detachable collar. Modern use is reduced to the first two elements and often without the 'h' *UK, 1960*

holli *noun* a marijuana cigarette which is placed in a pipe for smoking *US, 2001*

holliers; hollyers *noun* holidays, vacation *IRELAND, 1991*

hollow leg *noun* a characteristic ascribed to someone who is able to eat or drink in great quantities *US, 1992*

Hollyweird *nickname* Hollywood, California *US, 1953*

Hollywood *noun* **1** used as a teasing term of address for someone whose clothes and mannerisms suggest a high level of showmanship *US, 1973.* **2** a dramatic outburst *NEW ZEALAND, 1983.* **3** a feigned injury *NEW ZEALAND, 1972.* **4** in hot rodding, an extravagant, ostentatious exhaust system *US, 1958*

Hollywood glider *noun* the B-17 Flying Fortress. The B-17 appeared frequently in films *US, 1946*

Hollywood no *noun* an answer of 'no' implicit in the failure to return a phone call *US, 1992*

Hollywoods *noun* dark glasses *US, 1966*

Hollywood shower *noun* in Antarctica, a shower that exceeds the two-minute showers permitted by military authorities *ANTARCTICA, 2003*

Hollywood stop *noun* a rolling stop at a traffic signal or a stop sign *US, 1986*

Holmes *noun* used as a term of address from male-to-male. Playing on the term 'homes' *US, 1975*

hols *noun* holidays (both singular and plural), a vacation *UK, 1905*

Holstein *noun* a police car. An allusion to the black and white markings of the cow and a police car *US, 1961*

holy *adjective* great, extreme, *1978*

holy cats! used for registering surprise, shock or alarm *US, 2001*

holy chain lightning! used as a mild oath in Nova Scotia *CANADA, 1988*

holy city *noun* in poker, a high-value hand *US, 1988*

holy cow! used as a mild oath, expressing surprise. Popularised by baseball radio announcers Harry Caray and Phil Rizzuto *US, 1927*

holy crap! used for registering surprise. A variation of HOLY SHIT *US, 2001*

Holyfield *noun* fine quality marijuana. A neat pun using the name of three-time world heavyweight champion boxer Evander 'Real Deal' Holyfield (b.1962); here 'holy' implies 'the purest' and combines with a 'field (of grass)', and Holyfield's nickname 'Real Deal' guarantees the quality *UK, 2000*

Holyfield's ear; 'olyfields *noun* a year. Rhyming slang, formed in honour of boxer Evander Holyfield, whose ear was bitten by his opponent Mike Tyson during a 1997 world heavyweight title fight *UK, 1998*

holy fuck! used for registering shock or surprise *US, 1982*

holy ghost *noun* **1** the corpse of a person who has died from gunshot wounds *US, 1987*. **2** a coast. Glasgow rhyming slang *UK: SCOTLAND, 1988*. **3** in racing, the starting post or the winning post. Rhyming slang *UK, 1932*. **4** toast. Rhyming slang *UK, 1960*

holy guacamole! used satirically as a register of shock or surprise. 'Guacamole' is pronounced to rhyme with 'holy' *UK, 2003*

Holy Joe *noun* any religious leader. The term suggests a lack of sincerity *US, 1864*

Holy Lands *noun* an area of central Belfast. Named for its principal arteries: Damascus Street, Jerusalam Street and Canterbury Street *UK: NORTHERN IRELAND, 2001*

holy man! used as a powerful exclamation. Michigan Upper Peninsula usage *US, 2003*

holy moo cow! used as an expression of complete surprise. A jocular embellishment of the more common HOLY COW! *US, 1968*

holy nail *noun* bail. Rhyming slang *UK, 1992*

holy of holies *noun* **1** the vagina. A crude pun on HOLE *US, 1994*. **2** any inner sanctum *US, 1995*

holy oil *noun* an oil applied to the skin or clothing in the belief that it will bring the bettor luck in an illegal number gambling lottery *US, 1949*

holy old mackinaw! used as a curse *CANADA, 1988*

holy old snappin' arseholes! used as an oath in Nova Scotia with allusions to both the lobster and fear *CANADA, 1988*

holy olie *noun* in stud poker, the hole card *US, 1951*

holy shit! used for registering astonishment *US, 1986*

holy show *noun* an embarrassment, a ridiculous sight *IRELAND, 1984*

holy smoke *noun* branded soft drink Coca-Cola™, Coke™. Rhyming slang, originally used of the solid fuel *UK, 1992*

holy smoke! used as a exclamation of surprise and wonder *UK, 1892*

holy snappin'! used as a curse or oath *CANADA, 1982*

holy Toledo! used for registering surprise. A little bit of Holy Toledo goes a long way. A trademark of Milo Hamilton, radio broadcaster for the Houston Astros baseball team, and often used by Skipper, the son of Jungle Jim on *Jungle Jim* (1955) *US, 1951*

holy war *noun* a debate among computer enthusiasts about a question which has no objective answer *US, 1991*

holy water *noun* **1** official approval. US naval aviator usage; to give such approval is to 'sprinkle holy water' *US, 1986*. **2** a daughter. Rhyming slang *UK, 1992*

holy weed *noun* marijuana *US, 2001*

holy week *noun* the bleed period of a woman's menstrual cycle *US, 1964*

holy whistlin' frig! used as a curse in Nova Scotia *CANADA, 1988*

hom *verb* ▶ **hom it up** to flaunt your homosexuality. Substitutes an abbreviation of 'homosexual' for CAMP (affected) in 'camp it up' (to flaunt affectation) *UK, 2001*

hombre *noun* **1** a man. Spanish *hombre* (a man), spread worldwide by Hollywood Westerns such as *Hombre*, 1967, starring Paul Newman *US, 1846*. **2** a male friend. Adapted from the previous sense; this usage possibly informed by a phonetic similarity to HOMEBOY (a close friend) *UK, 2001*. **3** heroin. From Spanish *hombre* (a man) *US, 1998*

home *noun* **1** a very close male friend. An abbreviation of HOMEBOY *US, 1944*. **2** the vein into which an intravenous drug user injects a drug *US, 1973*. ▶ **at home in the going** in horse racing, said of a horse that is running a track that complements the horse's skills and preferences *US, 1951*. ▶ **send home** to sentence to prison *US, 1990*

Home *nickname* England or Great Britain. As used by C18–19 colonists this is par for the course, and that their direct descendants would use this also is hardly surprising, however, this locution remained in common use (in speech, if not by self-conscious writers) well into C20 and only began to die out in the 1970s. Now it is very much a thing of the past *AUSTRALIA, 1808*

home and dry *adjective* safe and sound; having accomplished an arduous task *UK, 1930*

home and hosed *adjective* **1** (of a racehorse) expected to win *AUSTRALIA, 1975*. **2** all finished and done with. Said of a task that is easily accomplished *AUSTRALIA, 1945*

homebake *noun* morphine or heroin extracted from codeine compounds *NEW ZEALAND, 2002*

homebaker *noun* a person who illegally manufactures drugs *NEW ZEALAND, 1986*

home base; home run *noun* in the teenage categorisation of sexual activity, sexual intercourse *US, 1963*

home box *noun* a computer enthusiast's own computer *US, 1991*

homeboy *noun* a very close male friend, often but not always from the same neighbourhood *US, 1899*

home cooking *noun* sex with your spouse *US, 1964*

homee *noun* ▷ *see:* OMEE

home ec *noun* home economics, in which the theory and practice of homemaking are studied *US, 1899*

home-ec-y *adjective* (used of a girl) conventional, out of touch with current fashions, styles and trends *US, 1970*

homee-palone *noun* ▷ *see:* OMEE-PALONE

homegirl *noun* a very close female friend, usually from the same neighbourhood, gang or faction of a gang; usually applied to a black girl *US, 1934*

homegrown *noun* marijuana, cultivated locally *US, 1974*

homeguard *noun* a local worker, as contrasted with a travelling or migratory worker; a local resident *US, 1903*

homemade *noun* **1** a cigarette rolled by hand from loose tobacco *US, 1954*. **2** a home-made pistol *US, 1949*

home on the range *noun* change. Rhyming slang *AUSTRALIA, 1989*

home on the range *adjective* strange. Rhyming slang, formed from the title of a well-known cowboy anthem (actually, the official song of the state of Kansas) *UK, 1998*

home plate *noun* an aeroplane's home base or carrier *US, 1991*

home port *noun* a trucker's residence. Jocular use *US, 1976*

homer *noun* **1** a job done privately by a tradesman outside of his regular employment. Glasgow slang *UK: SCOTLAND, 1996*. **2** a wound sufficiently serious to require treatment away from the theatre of war *AUSTRALIA, 1945*. **3** a referee or sports official who favours the home team *US, 1888*

Homer *noun* any Iraqi soldier. Gulf war usage; an allusion to the doltish Homer Simpson of television cartoon fame *US, 1991*

homers *noun* home-brewed beer. A gift to the slang of the South Pole from its Australian visitors *AUSTRALIA, 1970*

home run *noun* the journey of a circus from the final engagement of the season to the winter quarters *US, 1980* ▷ *see:* HOME BASE. ▶ **hit a home run** to have sex *US, 2001*

homerunner *noun* an artillery shell that hits its target directly *US, 1991*

homes *noun* used as a term of address, usually establishing comrade status *US, 1971*

home skillet *noun* a close friend *US, 1993*

homeslice *noun* **1** a close friend *US, 1984*. **2** a prisoner from your home city *US, 1992*

homesteader *noun* **1** an American who had been in Vietnam for more than a few years *US, 1991*. **2** a person who is dating one person steadily. High school usage *US, 1961*

Homesteader's Bible *noun* the Eaton department store catalogue *CANADA, 1987*

homesteader's fiddle *noun* a cross-cut saw *CANADA, 1954*

home sweet home *noun* in circus and carnival usage, the final performance of a season *US, 1981*

hometown honey *noun* a college student's date from their hometown *US, 1968*

home twenty *noun* a person's home town. From citizens' band radio code in which '20' means 'location' *US, 1976*

homework *noun* foreplay *US, 1993*. ▶ **bit of homework; piece of homework** a person objectified sexually *UK, 1945*

homewrecker *noun* a person whose affair with a married person leads to divorce, especially when there are children involved *US, 1968*

homey; homie *noun* a male from your neighbourhood; a close male friend; a fellow youth gang member *US, 1944*

homey, don't play dat! don't say that! A catchphrase from the television programme *In Living Color US, 1990*

homicide *noun* heroin or cocaine mixed with prescription drugs, such as scopolamine or strychnine *UK, 1998*

homie *noun* a homosexual *US, 1990* ▷

homing pigeon *noun* the US armed forces insignia designating honourable discharge *US, 1946*

homintern *noun* an aggressive, loyal homosexual subculture. A term coined by W.H. Auden, punning on the Marxist 'comintern' or Communist International *US, 1968*

homme *noun* a homosexual male. A pun on French *homme* (a man) and the first syllable of homosexual *UK, 2005*

homo *noun* **1** a homosexual, especially a male homosexual *US, 1922*. **2** used as an insulting term of address to someone who is not homosexual *US, 1993*

homogrips *noun* sideburns *NEW ZEALAND, 1998*

homo-hater *noun* a person with a pathological dislike for homosexuals *US, 1979*

homo heaven *noun* **1** a public area where homosexuals congregate in hopes of quick sex *US, 1965*. **2** the upper balcony in a theatre patronised by homosexual men *US, 1966*

homosexual adapter *noun* a computer cable with either two male or two female connectors *US, 1991*

hon *noun* used as a term of endearment. A shortened 'honey'. Fiercely claimed by Baltimore, Maryland, as a Baltimore-coinage *US, 1906*

hon bun *noun* used as a term of endearment. A shortened 'honey bunny' *US, 1940s*

honcho *noun* a boss, a big-shot. From the Japanese term for 'a group or squad leader' *US, 1945*

Honda rice *noun* IR8, a high-yielding variety of rice introduced in Vietnam in the 1960s, doubling rice production yields *US, 1985*

hondo *noun* **1** an attractive, popular male *US, 1986*. **2** a zealous enthusiast *US, 1968*

honest *noun* cherry syrup added to a soda fountain drink. From the American legend of George Washington's honesty when asked as a child if he cut down a cherry tree *US, 1946*

honest *adjective* (used of a drug) relatively pure and undiluted *US, 1970*

honest! I am speaking the truth!; I do mean it! A shortening of 'honestly' *UK, 1937*

Honest Abe *noun* General Creighton Williams Abrams, Jr (1914–1974). Abrams succeeded General Westmoreland as US commander in Vietnam, where he championed the Vietnamisation of the war *US, 1991*

honest brakeman *adjective* a person who engages in petty theft at work but not grand theft. From the faint praise – 'he worked for the railroad for thirty years and never stole a boxcar' *CANADA, 2002*

honest injun' used as a pledge of complete honesty *US, 1851*

honest John *noun* **1** a decent, upstanding, law-abiding citizen *US, 1884*. **2** in a shoplifting operation, an honest-looking confederate who distracts the store personnel *US, 1974*

honest kine? is that right? Hawaiian youth usage *US, 1981*

honestly! used as an expression of disgust, exasperation, unpleasant surprise, etc *UK, 1966*

honest reader *noun* a playing card with an unintentional imperfection that enables an observant player to identify it in another player's hand *US, 1988*

honest squeeze *noun* a cherry squeeze soda fountain drink. An allusion to the George Washington myth involving the cutting down of a cherry tree *US, 1952*

honest-to-God; honest-to-goodness *adjective* true, genuine, thorough, honest; truly, genuinely, thoroughly, honestly *US, 1913*

honey *noun* **1** a sexually attractive young woman. Sometimes spelled 'hunny' *US, 1930*. **2** a female surfer or a male surfer's girlfriend *US, 1986*. **3** a sexually desirable person *UK: SCOTLAND, 1985*. **4** an 'effeminate' lesbian *US, 1978*. **5** used as a term of affectionate address *UK, 1350*. **6** anything considered pleasing, attractive, effective, etc *US, 1888* ▷*see:* POT OF HONEY

honey bear *noun* a policewoman. Extended from BEAR (police) *US, 1976*

honey blunt *noun* marijuana rolled in the outer leaves of a cigar which are then sealed with honey *US, 2003*

honey box *noun* the vagina *US, 1969*

honey bucket *noun* **1** a portable toilet *US, 1976*. **2** a chamberpot *US, 1931*. **3** a truck used to empty septic tanks *US, 1971*

honey cart *noun* a vehicle hauling human excrement; a portable toilet *US, 1929*

honey dip *noun* an attractive woman, especially one with a light brown skin colour *US, 1993*

honey dipper *noun* the driver of a truck that drains septic tanks *US, 1961*

honey dipping *noun* vaginal secretions *US, 1949*

honey-fuck *verb* **1** to have sex in a slow, affectionate manner *US, 1964*. **2** to have sex with a Lolita-aged nymphet *US, 1967*

honey, I'm home! used for humorously announcing an entrance. From the *Dick Van Dyke Show* (1961–66), a centrepiece in the golden age of the situation comedy on US television *US, 1988*

honeyman *noun* a procurer of prostitutes; a man who makes his living off the earnings of prositutes *US, 1982*

honeymoon *noun* **1** sex. Used by prostitutes in Southeast Asia during the Vietnam war *US, 1976*. **2** the early period in a drug addiction *US, 1952*. **3** the first few hands played by a new player in a poker game *US, 1996*

honey oil *noun* the recreational drug ketamine *US, 1994*

honey perrs *noun* stairs. Glasgow rhyming slang, formed on a street-vendors cry for 'sweet pears' *UK: SCOTLAND, 1996*

honeypot *noun* **1** the vagina. Recorded as rhyming slang for TWAT (the vagina) It certainly rhymes, but must surely be influenced – if not inspired – by senses that are conventional, figurative and slang. Found once in the UK in 1719, and then in general slang usage with 'candy' *US, 1958*. **2** in male homosexual usage, the anus and rectum *US, 1981*. **3** a chamber pot *US, 1954*. **4** in Maine, a muddy hole in the road *US, 1975*

honey shot *noun* a gratuitous television view of a pretty girl or woman, usually a spectator at a sporting event *US, 1968*

honeytrap *noun* the seduction by a sexually attractive person of a politican or other prominent figure into dishonest or indiscreet behaviour. Used in conversation since the early 1990s *NEW ZEALAND, 2002*

honey wagon *noun* **1** a vehicle hauling human excrement; a portable toilet *US, 1923*. **2** a truck hauling beer *US, 1976*. **3** a catering truck *US, 1992*

Hongcouver *nickname* the city of Vancouver, British Columbia, Canada *CANADA, 2002*

Hong Kong *verb* to be odoriferous. Rhyming slang for PONG *UK, 1992*

Hong Kong *adjective* wrong. Rhyming slang *UK, 1998*

hong-yen *noun* heroin, originally in pill form *US, 1949*

honk *noun* pleasure; enjoyment *US, 1964*

honk *verb* **1** to moan, to complain. A military usage *UK, 1995*. **2** to vomit *UK, 1967*. **3** to fart. Also used as a noun. From the noise of geese – low-flying geese may be offered as an excuse – or 'honk' (to smell), *1998*. **4** to smell badly *AUSTRALIA, 1977*. **5** to inhale drugs, originally through the nose *US, 1968*. **6** when flying an aeroplane or helicopter, to pull, to jerk, to yank *US, 1946*. **7** in drag racing, to defeat *US, 1993*. ▶ **honk your horn** to grab a man's penis *US, 1970*. ▶ **honk your lot** to vomit. An elaboration of HONK *UK, 1974*

honked *adjective* drunk. Of military origin *UK, 1959*

honked off *adjective* angry *US, 1958*

honker *noun* **1** the penis *US, 1968*. **2** the nose *US, 1942*. **3** expectorated sputum *US, 1981*. **4** a goose *US, 1841*. **5** a large and powerful wave *US, 1991*. **6** in drag racing, a fast stock car *US, 1968*

honkers *noun* drunk. Perhaps deriving from HONK (to vomit) as a side-effect of drunkenness. Used in the military for 'very drunk' *UK, 1958*

Honkers *nickname* Hong Kong. Military, especially used by officers *UK, 1984*

honking *adjective* **1** very smelly; of inferior quality *UK: SCOTLAND, 1985*. **2** very large *US, 1995*

honk on *verb* in the usage of youthful model road racers (slot car racers), to race fast *US, 1997*

Honky *noun* a person from Hong Kong *AUSTRALIA, 2003*

honky; honkie; honkey *noun* a white person. Usually not said with kindness, especially when used to describe a member of the white ruling class *US, 1946*

honky nut *noun* in Western Australia, a large gumnut (the hard, dried, inedible fruit of a eucalyptus tree) *AUSTRALIA, 1996*

honky-tonk *noun* a saloon, dance-hall or gambling-house. Also used as an adjective *US, 1894*

honourable member for Fuckinghamshire *noun* the penis. Jocular *UK, 2003*

hoo-ah! used for expressing enthusiastic approval *US, 1991*

hoobly goobly *noun* nonsense *US, 1956*

hooch; hootch *noun* **1** alcohol *US, 1915*. **2** a peasant hut; a small, improvised shelter. Korean and then Vietnam war usage *US, 1952*. **3** marijuana. Sometimes variant 'hoochie' *US, 1972*

hooch dog *noun* a marijuana cigarette *US, 1986*

hooched-up *adjective* drunk. From HOOCH (an alcoholic drink; also, in the UK, a brand name alcoholic drink popular with young drinkers) *US, 1922*

hooch girl *noun* a young Vietnamese woman who worked as a maid or did laundry for US troops *US, 1981*

hooch-head *noun* a drunkard *US, 1946*

hoochie *noun* in British Columbia fishing, a soft plastic lure with tentacles *CANADA, 1989* ▷ *see:* HOOTCHIE

hoochy koochy *noun* a sexually suggestive dance *US, 1895*

hood *noun* **1** a neighbourhood, especially in an urban ghetto *US, 1967*. **2** a rough street youth; a criminal. A shortened 'hoodlum' *US, 1880*. **3** the penis. West Indian and UK black usage. Collected from a UK prisoner in May 2002 *JAMAICA, 1995*. **4** the chest *US, 1989*. **5** heroin *UK, 2003*. **6** a 12 ounce bottle of beer *US, 1967*. ▶ **under the hood** literally, flying by instrumentation; figuratively, operating without knowing exactly what is going on *US, 1956*

hoodie *noun* a sweatshirt or jacket with a hood *US, 1993*

hoodish *adjective* tough, criminal *US, 1967*

hood lifter *noun* a motor mechanic *US, 1971*

hoodlum *noun* a ruffian, a gangster, especially if dangerous. Probably from a printing error on a reversal of Muldoon (a known gangster's name), thus 'noodlum', hence 'hoodlum'; of other folk-etymologies only a gang-cry of 'huddle 'em!' is moderately convincing *US, 1871*

hoodoo *noun* an outcropping of rock in desolate western Canadian land *US, 1879*

hoodrat *noun* **1** a tough youth who prowls the streets of his inner-city neighbourhood, in search of trouble and fun *US, 1997*. **2** a promiscuous girl *US, 1997*

hooer; hoor *noun* a whore. Representing a spelling pronunciation of 'whore'. This came to be a general term of abuse and was applied not only to women, but also to men *AUSTRALIA, 1952*

hooer lure *noun* aftershave lotion. Given the crudeness of typical hockey player talk, the word 'hooer' may refer to any woman, not just a prostitute *CANADA, 1991*

hooey *noun* **1** nonsense *US, 1912*. **2** a rope wrapped around three feet of an animal, secured with a half hitch *CANADA, 1987*

hoof *noun* **1** a foot or shoe *UK, 1598*. **2** a sea turtle's flipper *CAYMAN ISLANDS, 1985*. ▶ **on the hoof 1** working as a prostitute on the streets *US, 1977*. **2** on the spot, spontaneously. From the literal sense of the term, applied to cattle or swine, meaning 'alive' *US, 1992*. ▶ **the hoof** dismissal from employment; expulsion *UK, 1973*

hoof *verb* **1** to dance *US, 1916*. **2** to walk *UK, 1641*

hoof and toof *noun* foot and mouth disease. Farmers' use *UK, 2001*

hoofer *noun* a professional dancer, especially a tap dancer *US, 1916*

hoofprint *noun* footprints that could be identified as or surmised to be made by Viet Cong or North Vietnamese soldiers *US, 1989*

hoof up *verb* to sniff up, to inhale through the nose, to snort. Possibly from a mispronunciation of HOOVER *UK, 2002*

hoo-ha *noun* a fuss or commotion; nonsense *UK, 1931*

hoo-haw *noun* a fight, a dispute *CANADA, 1959*

hoo-ing and ha-ing *noun* a commotion, the making of a fuss. From the noun HOO-HA *UK, 2000*

hook *noun* **1** in a pickpocket team, the confederate who actually makes the theft *UK, 1863*. **2** a thief. Originally applied specifically to a pickpocket *UK, 1863*. **3** a shoplifter *UK, 1961*. **4** a finger, the hand. Usually used in the plural *UK, 1829*. **5** a key or lockpick *US, 1970*. **6** in the used car business, a person who reverses the mileometer (odometer) to reduce the mileage shown *US, 1992*. **7** a person who strives to be that which he is not *US, 1989*. **8** a prostitute. A shortened HOOKER *US, 1918*. **9** a contact in the police department with influence *US, 1973*. **10** a superior with influence and the ability to protect. New York police slang *US, 1997*. **11** a telephone or telephone call *US, 1975*. **12** a CH-47 Chinook helicopter. Vietnam war usage *US, 1968*. **13** a railway demolition crane *US, 1946*. **14** a razor *US, 1962*. **15** the concave part of a wave *US, 1963*. **16** a chevron insignia *US, 1947*. **17** the grade 'C' *US, 1968*. **18** a feature in a computer or computer program designed to facilitate later changes or enhancements *US, 1991*. **19** in a confidence swindle, the stage in the swindle when the victim is fully committed to the scheme *US, 1969*. **20** in pointspreads established by bookmakers in sports betting, half a point *US, 1991*. **21** in a deck of playing cards, a jack or knave *US, 1961*. ▶ **off the hook 1** out of a difficult or embarrasing situation *UK, 1864*. **2** amazing, excellent *US, 1999*. ▶ **on the hook 1** in debt *US, 1957*. **2** in love. Teen slang *US, 1951*. **3** being towed by a tow truck *UK, 1951*. **4** skipping school *US, 1906*

hook *verb* **1** to addict *US, 1922*. **2** to inject by hypodermic needle *US, 1953*. **3** to snare in a swindle *UK, 1730*. **4** to steal *US, 1951*. **5** to take, but not necessarily steal *UK, 1947*. **6** to engage in prostitution *US, 1959*. **7** to ride a racehorse so that it will lose *AUSTRALIA, 1982*. **8** in trucking, to shift gears. Most often heard as 'hook 'er into high' *US, 1971*. **9** to arrest *US, 1928*. ▶ **hook a barracuda** to locate and show a gratuitous television view of a pretty girl or woman, usually a spectator at a sporting event *US, 1986*

hook and book *verb* to handcuff and arrest a criminal suspect *US, 1994*

hook and bullet crowd *noun* hunters and recreational fishermen, collectively as a lobbying force *US, 1990*

hooked *adjective* **1** addicted to drugs. Originally a transitive verb – the drug hooking the person – but that formation is long forgotten in the US *US, 1922*. **2** 'addicted' to anything non-addictive *UK, 1984*. **3** obsessed by an activity or a person. Figurative application of the sense 'addicted to drugs' *UK, 1984*. **4** taken care of *US, 1989*. **5** put together or arranged well *US, 2002*. **6** (of a shot in pool) obstructed *US, 1979*

hooker *noun* **1** a prostitute. Probably derives from the conventional sense of 'hook' (to lure); possibly reinforced by now obsolete slang: 'hook' (to rob); and with reference to Corlear's Hook, popularly The Hook, an area of New York City known for prostitution *US, 1845*. **2** in a deck of playing cards, a queen. An evolved form of the more common WHORE *US, 1967*. **3** a towing truck *US, 1978*. **4** a shunter (a locomotive used for moving train carriages around a shunting yard). Railwaymen's term *UK, 1970*. **5** on a moped, a modified exhaust pipe *BERMUDA, 1985*. **6** the hand. A variant of the more common HOOK *US, 1959*. **7** a strong alcoholic drink *UK, 1833*. **8** a cigarette. Teen slang *US, 1951*

hooknose *noun* a Jewish person. Offensive, based on a stereotyped racial characteristic *US, 1867*

hook-off-the-nail *noun* clothing bought off the rack, ready to wear *BAHAMAS, 1982*

hooks *noun* in electric and telephone line work, climbing irons *US, 1980*

hook shop *noun* a brothel. From HOOKER (prostitute) *US, 1889*

hook up *verb* **1** to meet someone; to meet someone and have sex *US, 1986*. **2** to work in partnership *US, 1996*. **3** to arm yourself *US, 1973*. **4** in drag racing and motor racing, to achieve maximum traction *US, 1980*. **5** to provide *US, 1993*

hooky; hookey *adjective* criminal, stolen, counterfeit. Plays on BENT *UK, 1984*

hooky bob *verb* in icy winter conditions, to grab the bumper of a passing car and use your feet as skis as you are pulled along *US, 1997*

hooley *noun* an especially lively party *IRELAND, 1877*

hoolie *noun* a *hooli*gan *UK, 1996*

hooligan *noun* in motor racing on a dirt track, a consolation race *US, 1965*

hooly-dooly; hooley-dooley wow! *AUSTRALIA, 1965*

hoon *noun* **1** a man who lives off the earnings of prostitutes; a pimp *AUSTRALIA, 1949*. **2** a loud ignorant lout; a hooligan. Origin unknown *AUSTRALIA, 1938*. **3** a person who drives recklessly *AUSTRALIA, 1985*. **4** a trip in a motor vehicle taken for the pleasure of, especially fast, driving *AUSTRALIA, 1996*

hoon *verb* to drive recklessly *AUSTRALIA, 1992*

hoonah light *noun* in the pornography industry, a light used to illuminate the genitals of the performers *US, 1995*

hoondom *noun* an assemblage of louts *NEW ZEALAND, 1983*

hoonered *adjective* drunk *UK, 2003*

hooning *noun* loutish behaviour *NEW ZEALAND, 1986*

hoonish *adjective* loutish *NEW ZEALAND, 1970*

hoonmobile *noun* a lout-driven car *NEW ZEALAND, 1993*

hoop *noun* **1** in criminal circles, a finger-ring. Conventional English for three centuries, and then ascended to criminal slang *US, 1856*. **2** the rectum as a place to hide prison contraband *US, 1989*. **3** a jockey *AUSTRALIA, 1941*

hoopdee *noun* a new, late-model car *US, 1971*

hooped *adjective* drunk *NEW ZEALAND, 1998*

hoopie *noun* a bicycling enthusiast who spends more time and effort buying equipment and clothing than actually bicycling *US, 1997*

hoopla *noun* a commotion. Originally, the cry associated with the fairground game of tossing hoops over blocks *US, 1877*

hoople *noun* a fool, a dolt *US, 1928*

hoople head *noun* an idiot *US, 1985*

hoop rod *noun* a car. Formed from HOT ROD and HOOPTY *US, 2001*

hoops *noun* handcuffs *US, 1949*

hoop snake *noun* a mythical snake that holds its own tail and rolls. A tale told to impress and frighten gullible visitors. An early example of the story (though not the term itself) can be found in J.S. James, *The Vagabond Papers*, 1877 *AUSTRALIA, 2003*

hoopsy-coopsy *adjective* drunk *NEW ZEALAND, 1962*

hoopty *noun* a run-down, shoddy car *US, 1970*

hoor; hure *noun* a whore. Variant early spellings from C14 and C15, surviving in current Irish slang *UK, 1987*

hoo-raw *noun* a fight, a dispute *CANADA, 1958*

hooray *noun* good news *UK, 1983*

hooray goodbye *AUSTRALIA, 1898*

hooray Henry; hooray *noun* a male of the upper-classes who exhibits a superior or anti-social manner. Coined as 'Hoorah Henry' by Damon Runyon in the story *Tight Shoes*, 1936; mainly UK usage *UK, 1959*

hooride *verb* in a group, to berate and humiliate someone *US, 1997*

hooroo goodbye *AUSTRALIA, 1906*

hooroos *noun* phlegm *NORFOLK ISLAND, 1992*

hoor's melt; whore's melt; whoor's melt *noun* a contemptible person. Combines HOOR (a prostitute, perhaps implying no more than a female) with 'melt' (spawn, offspring); alternatively 'melt' may derive from Old English *milte* (the spleen) or as a dialect word for 'the tongue' *IRELAND, 1961*

hoose *noun* in poker, a hand consisting of three cards of the same rank and a pair. Known conventionally as a 'full house' *US, 1951*

hoose *verb* to bowl with speed and force *BARBADOS, 1965*

hoosegow *noun* a jail or prison. A corruption of the Spanish *juzgado* (court or tribunal) *US, 1908*

hoot *noun* **1** a cause for laughter. A bit old-fashioned, often used in a sarcastic or condescending tone *US, 1942*. **2** an inhalation of marijuana *CANADA, 2002*. **3** a little bit. Generally used in phrases that have a negative intent, such as 'not give a hoot', 'not care two hoots', etc *US, 1878*. **4** money *AUSTRALIA, 1881*

Hoot *noun* a member of the Hutterian Brethren. The Hutterites are an Anabaptist group that believe in communal living; they are found in rural areas of the Canadian prairies and the American states of Montana, Washington, North Dakota and Minnesota *US, 1997*

hootched *adjective* drunk *US, 1993*

hootchie; hoochie; hootchy mama *noun* a young woman, especially when easily available for sex *US, 1990*

hootchie-coo *noun* sex *US, 1990*

hootchy-kootchy; hootchie-coochie *noun* a sexually attractive person *US, 1969*

hootenananny *noun* in oil drilling, any complicated piece of equipment that the speaker cannot identify by name *US, 1928*

hooter *noun* **1** the nose. In senses both actual and figurative; from the trumpeting noise emitted when blown *UK, 1958*. **2** cocaine. The drug is sniffed up the HOOTER (nose) *US, 1979*. **3** a large marijuana cigarette *US, 1986*. **4** a party *US, 1978*. **5** a toilet *NEW ZEALAND, 1968*

hooters *noun* female breasts *US, 1972*

hootie mac *noun* marijuana *US, 1996*

hooting *noun* in surfing, shouts that compliment the quality of a wave or a ride on the wave *US, 1988*

hoover *noun* **1** any vacuum cleaner. A widely used generic, from Hoover, a manufacturer of brand name vacuum cleaners since 1908 *UK, 1999*. **2** the nose *UK, 1983*

hoover *verb* **1** to clean with a vacuum cleaner. A generic, almost *the* generic, from Hoover™ vacuum cleaners *UK, 1939*. **2** to suck out, to remove by suction *AUSTRALIA, 1991*. **3** to extract; to draw out *US, 1985*. **4** to inhale drugs. From the similarity to a 'hoover' (a vacuum cleaner) cleaning up dust *US, 1982*. **5** to eat or drink greedily. From the similarity to a 'hoover' (a vacuum cleaner)'s indiscriminate method of swallowing anything in its path *US, 1986*. **6** to perform oral sex on a man. From the supposed similarity to a 'hoover' (a vacuum cleaner)'s suction *UK, 1992*. **7** to perform an abortion. An allusion to the branded vacuum cleaner *US, 2003*

hoover d'amour *noun* an act of oral sex on a man. From the supposed similarity to a vacuum cleaner's suction, lent romance by the French 'of love' *UK, 1992*

hoozy *adjective* absent-minded *US, 2003*

hop *noun* **1** a narcotic – opium, morphine or heroin *US, 1886*. **2** a dance, a party *UK, 1731*. **3** in handball, a ball which breaks to the left or right after rebounding off the front wall *US, 1972*. **4** in craps, a one-roll bet on the next roll *US, 1987*. ▶ **on the hop** playing truant *UK, 1998*

hop *verb* **1** to work as a car hop at a drive-in restaurant where customers are served in their cars *US, 1972*. **2** to go, to travel *UK, 1923*. **3** to flee or escape *US, 1950*. **4** in horse racing, to administer an illegal drug to a horse, either a stimulant or a depressant *US, 1976*. ▶ **hop 'n' pop** in the language of parachuting, to pull the ripcord within three seconds of clearing the aircraft *US, 1978*. ▶ **hop a hole** (used of a ball in pinball) to fall into and then keep moving out of an ejecting hole because of high velocity *US, 1977*. ▶ **hop bells** to work in a hotel as a bell hop *US, 1942*. ▶ **hop in for your chop** to take your share *AUSTRALIA, 1954*. ▶ **hop into the horsecollar** (from a male perspective) to have sex. From HORSECOLLAR (the vagina) *AUSTRALIA, 1971*. ▶ **hop it; 'oppit** to depart, especially to depart quickly *UK, 1910*. ▶ **hop the train** to ride the subway (underground) without paying the fare *US, 1995*

hop-and-drop *noun* **1** a stylised walk *TRINIDAD AND TOBAGO, 1951*. **2** a limp *BARBADOS, 1965*

hop and pop *verb* to wake up and spring into action *US, 1998*

hopdog *noun* an opium addict *US, 1946*

hope *noun* ▶ **not a hope in hell!** not a chance!, not a hope! *UK, 1923*

hopeless *adjective* incompetent *UK, 1922*

hope-to-die *noun* your spouse or romantic partner *US, 1971*

hop gun *noun* a syringe used by intravenous drug users *US, 1949*

hophead *noun* **1** an opium addict, or, less precisely and more commonly, a user of marijuana or other drug *US, 1901*. **2** a heavy drinker *AUSTRALIA, 1957*. **3** in horse racing, a horse that only performs well when under the influence of a stimulant *US, 1947*

hop in *verb* to begin in earnest, especially the eating of a meal *AUSTRALIA, 1939*

hop into *verb* to attack a person, task, meal, etc, with vigour *AUSTRALIA, 1945*

hop it!; hoppit! go away! Used as an injunction, exclamation or both *UK, 1914*

hop it and scram; hop it *noun* ham. Rhyming slang. *UK, 1992*

hop off *verb* to launch an attack *US, 1918*

hop out *verb* to crash (an aeroplane) *US, 1986*

hop-pad *noun* an opium den *US, 1946*

hopped; hopped up *adjective* under the influence of drugs *US, 1918*

hopped up *adjective* (used of a car) modified to increase the engine performance *US, 1941*

hopper *noun* **1** a kangaroo or wallaby *AUSTRALIA, 1879*. **2** a car shock absorber *US, 1970*

hopper fill heist *noun* an attempt to defraud a casino by sitting at a slot machine with a winning combination showing that has paid off partially but requires additional coins to be added to complete the payoff *US, 1999*

hoppers *noun* trainers (sneakers) *ANTIGUA AND BARBUDA, 1998*

hopping *adjective* extremely busy *IRELAND, 2003*

hopping John *noun* a stew made of boiled pig's feet, black-eye peas and rice *US, 1838*

hopping mad *adjective* very angry *US, 1675*

hopping pot; hopping *noun* the lot. Rhyming slang *UK, 1961*

hoppo-bump *verb* to bump into another for fun. From the name of a child's game in which players hop on one leg and bump into each other *AUSTRALIA, 1998*

hops *noun* beer *US, 1902*. ▶ **on the hops** on a drinking binge *AUSTRALIA, 1930*

hopscotch *noun* a watch. Rhyming slang, formed from the name of a traditional children's game *UK, 1998*

hopscotcher *noun* a carnival worker who moves from one carnival to another *US, 1966*

hop squad *noun* a narcotics squad within a police department *US, 1958*

hop stop *noun* in pinball, a brief release of an extended flipper to prevent a ball from rolling up off the end *US, 1977*

hoptoad *verb* on the railways, to derail *US, 1946*

hoptoads *noun* any dice altered for cheating *US, 1950*

hop up *verb* in hot rodding, to increase the power of an engine *US, 1942*

horizontal *adjective* asleep *US, 1991*. ▶ **get horizontal** to sleep *US, 1976*

horizontal bop *noun* sexual intercourse *US, 2001*

horizontal exercise *noun* sexual intercourse *US, 1918*

horizontal folk-dancing *noun* sexual intercourse; lovemaking *AUSTRALIA, 1992*

horizontal gymnastics *noun* sexual intercourse *UK, 2001*

horizontal lubricant *adjective* any alcoholic drink or drinks, especially in the adjectival phrase 'nicely irrigated with horizontal lubricant' *UK, 2002*

horizontal manoeuvres *noun* sexual intercourse. Military origins *UK, 1995*

horizontal refreshment *noun* sexual intercourse *UK, 1889*

horizontal rumble *noun* sexual intercourse *US, 2000*

hork *verb* to spit; hence to vomit. Variation of conventional 'hawk' (to clear your throat) *US, 2001*

Horlicks *noun* a mess. Originally, upper-class society usage of a brand name; Horlicks™ is a malted food drink. Usage here is probably inspired by the salacious possibilities of the separated syllables 'whore licks' and a vague assonance to 'bollocks' (to mess up) *UK, 1982*

horn *noun* **1** the penis; the erect penis; lust *UK, 1594*. **2** adultery *TRINIDAD AND TOBAGO, 1857*. **3** the nose *UK, 1823*. **4** any implement used for snorting powdered narcotics *US, 1977*. **5** a pipe used to smoke crack cocaine *US, 1994*. **6** the telephone *US, 1941*. **7** a trumpet; hence any brass or wind instrument; occasionally a piano. Jazz slang *US, 1966*. ▶ **around the horn 1** the oral stimulation of all parts of a partner's body. In the UK, *Round the Horne* was an innuendo-driven radio comedy originally broadcast from 1965–69 *US, 1976*. **2** from one location to another, in quick succession *US, 1942*. **3** in craps, a single-roll bet on the 2, 3, 11 and 12 *US, 1962*. **4** in baseball, around the infield positions. After an out made at first base, if there are no runners on base the defensive team typically throws the ball 'around the horn' *US, 1956*. ▶ **put the horns on; put horns on 1** to cuckold. After the traditional sign of a cuckold *UK, 1959*. **2** (used of a superstitious gambler) to engage in a personal ritual designed to break a streak of bad luck *US, 1949*

horn *verb* **1** to inhale (a drug) through the nose *US, 1967*. **2** to commit adultery *TRINIDAD AND TOBAGO, 1973*

hornbag *noun* a sexually attractive or highly sexed person *AUSTRALIA, 1981*

horndog *noun* a person who is obsessed with sex *US, 1984*

horner man; horner woman *noun* an adulterer *TRINIDAD AND TOBAGO, 1990*

horn in *verb* to intrude upon, to interfere *US, 1911*

horning *noun* heroin *UK, 1998*

horn movie *noun* a pornographic film *US, 1967*

horn pill *noun* an (allegedly) aphrodisiac tablet for men. Claimed to give the HORN (an erection) *UK, 1961*

hornrim *noun* an intellectual *US, 1974*

horny *adjective* **1** desiring sex *US, 1826*. **2** of an erotic or pornographic image, sexually stimulating. From the HORN (the erect penis) that results *UK, 1984*. ▶ **sleep horny** to go to bed naked (and be sensually aware of it) *UK, 1968*

horny man *noun* a federal law enforcement official. A euphemistic allusion to the devil by those engaged in the illegal production of alcohol *US, 1974*

horny-mone *noun* the substance that drives a cow to mate, to go into heat. A humorous corruption of 'hormone' *CANADA, 1992*

horny porny *noun* pornography *US, 1981*

horrendous *adjective* terrible. A blend of the conventional 'horrible' and 'stupendous' *US, 1968*

Horrids *nickname* Harrods department store in Knightsbridge, West London. Jocular usage, mainly by those who can't afford to shop there; the word play is enhanced by class sensitivities as 'horrid' is considered part of a socially superior vocabulary *UK, 1996*

horrie *noun* a large and dangerous wave that breaks suddenly *AUSTRALIA, 2003*

horries *noun* **1** *delirium tremens*; the ill-effects of drinking or drug-taking. From 'horror' *SOUTH AFRICA, 1959*. **2** a phobia, a horror of something. From 'horror' *SOUTH AFRICA, 1971*

horror *noun* **1** a mischievous person, especially when addressed to a child *UK, 1819*. **2** an extremely unattractive woman who is seen as a sex object, especially one who is ravaged by age *UK, 2002*

horror *adjective* great, wonderful. A contraction of HORRORSHOW *UK, 2001*

horrors *noun* **1** sickness associated with withdrawal from alcohol or drug addiction. Noted specifically of withdrawal from amphetamines or heroin *US, 1839*. **2** the bleed period of the menstrual cycle. Schoolgirl use *UK, 1980*. **3** acute psychosis caused by amphetamines *UK, 1978*

horrorshow *adjective* great, wonderful. Ultimately from Russian *khorosho* (good); coined by Anthony Burgess (1917–93) for the novel *A Clockwork Orange*, 1962. Adopted in US teen slang in the 1990s *UK, 1961*

hors d'oeuvre *noun* drugs in capsule form *US, 1980*

horse *noun* **1** heroin *US, 1950*. **2** a casual girlfriend. Probably from a play on 'whores' *UK, 1962*. **3** a prostitute. An evolution of the STABLE as a group of prostitutes *US, 1957*. **4** a prostitute's customer. Used by prostitutes *SOUTH AFRICA, 1946*. **5** a large man *US, 1947*. **6** an affectionate male term of address *IRELAND, 2003*. **7** in circus and carnival usage, one thousand dollars *US, 1981*. **8** a person who smuggles contraband into prison *US, 1981*. **9** in bar dice games, a turn of rolling the dice *US, 1976*. **10** a poker player with a reputation for stinginess *US, 1988*. **11** a Ford Mustang car *US, 1976*. **12** in television and film-making, a stand that holds film reels while the film is fed through a viewer *US, 1990*. **13** a knife or improvised sharp instrument *US, 1973*

horse *verb* **1** to thrash, to defeat absolutely *UK: SCOTLAND, 2002*. **2** to ruin, to destroy. Extended from the previous sense *UK: SCOTLAND, 2002*

horse and buggy; horse and wagon *noun* heroin and the equipment needed to prepare and inject it *US, 1984*

horse and carriage *noun* a garage. Rhyming slang (the rhyme is accurate when spoken in a London accent). *UK, 1992*

horse and cart; horse *verb* **1** to start *UK, 1992*. **2** to fart. Rhyming slang; reduced to its first element, usually in the past tense *UK, 1992*

horse and trap *noun* **1** an act of defecation. Rhyming slang for CRAP, a rarer form of PONY AND TRAP *UK, 1961*. **2** gonorrhoea. Rhyming slang for CLAP *UK, 1961*

horse and trough *noun* a cough. Rhyming slang *UK, 1992*

horse around; horse about *verb* to fool around *US, 1900*

horse ass *noun* anything at all; nothing *BAHAMAS, 1982*

horse bite *noun* heroin. An elaboration of HORSE (heroin) *UK, 2002*

horse blanket *noun* a filming technique employed to soften faces *US, 1997*

horse box *noun* a control station in a Townsend Thorenson ferry/ship's engine room that contains the engine controls, alarms, etc. Used by ferry crews *UK, 1979*

horsecock *noun* **1** a sausage *US, 1942*. **2** a wooden club *US, 1970*. **3** in oil drilling, a nipple used to connect hoses *US, 1954*

horsecollar *noun* **1** a rescue sling lowered from a hovering helicopter to the ground or sea below *US, 1969*. **2** the vagina, especially large or distended external female genitals. The shape provides a simile *US, 1994*. **3** in an athletic contest, a failure to score *US, 1907*. **4** in hot rodding, the grille from an Edsel automobile, popular for customising other cars *US, 1965*

horsed *adjective* heroin-intoxicated. From HORSE (heroin) *UK, 1962*

horse doofers; horses doovers *noun* hors d'oevres. Jocular mispronunciations *UK, 1959*

horsefeathers *noun* nonsense. A transparent euphemism for HORSESHIT *US, 1927*

horse feed *noun* in circus and carnival usage, poor business *US, 1981*

horsefuck *verb* to have sex from behind and with great vim *US, 1973*

horsehead *noun* **1** an amphetamine *US, 1971*. **2** a heroin user. A straightforward combination of HORSE (heroin) and -HEAD (a user) *US, 1952*

horse heart *noun* a tablet of Dexedrine™, a trade name for dextroamphetamine sulphate, a central nervous system stimulant *US, 1977*

horse hockey! used for expressing disapproval. A signature line of Colonel Sherman Potter on *M*A*S*H* (CBS, 1972–83). Repeated with referential humour *US, 1964*

horse-holder *noun* an assistant to a high-ranking military officer *US, 1982*

horse off *verb* to allow horses to graze in a field, thus ruining it for cows until the crop grows back *CANADA, 1987*

horse piddle *noun* hospital. Word play masquerading as rhyming slang *UK, 1992*

horse pill *noun* the large, orange anti-malarial pill (chloroquine-primaquine) taken once a week by US troops in Vietnam *US, 1990*

horse piss *noun* cheap alcoholic drink, or a brand you don't drink *US, 1970*

horse radish *noun* heroin *US, 1997*

horse room *noun* an illegal betting operation where bets can be placed and collected on horse races *US, 1950*

horse's *noun* a male homosexual. Shortening of HORSE'S HOOF *AUSTRALIA, 1960*

horses *noun* dice that have been altered for cheating by omitting key losing combinations *US, 1964*

horse's arse; horse's ass *noun* a person who is not liked or trusted; an idiot; someone deserving of a generally abusive epithet *UK, 1865*

horseshit; horseshite *noun* nonsense *US, 1923*

horseshit *verb* to deceive, to tease. In the nature of BULLSHIT *US, 1954*

Horseshit Man *noun* Ho Chi Minh. A phonetic approximation used by troops in Vietnam *US, 1991*

horse's hoof; horses *noun* a male homosexual. Rhyming slang for POOF *AUSTRALIA, 1944*

horsespot *noun* the vagina *US, 1998*

horse-to-horse *adjective* in a direct comparison or competition *US, 1950*

horticulturalist *noun* in pool, a player who wins money betting *US, 1990*

HO's *noun* hangers-on attached to a rock band *UK, 1985*

hose *noun* the penis *US, 1928*

hose *verb* **1** to copulate, vaginally or anally *US, 1935*. **2** to shoot with an automatic weapon. Sometimes heard as the more elaborate 'hosepipe' *UK, 1917*. **3** to swindle; to cheat *US, 1940*. **4** to laugh vigorously *SOUTH AFRICA, 2004*. ► **hose yourself** to get drunk *AUSTRALIA, 1979*

hosebag *noun* a prostitute or promiscuous woman. A conventional 'bag', punning on BAG (a promiscuous woman), is a container for a HOSE (penis) *US, 1978*

hosed *adjective* drunk *US, 1987*

hose down *verb* to rain heavily *NEW ZEALAND, 1995*

hose in *verb* to win handily *NEW ZEALAND, 1998*

hose job *noun* **1** oral sex on a man *US, 1978*. **2** a bad situation; a situation in which you are cheated or swindled *US, 1989*

hose off *verb* to annoy or make angry *NEW ZEALAND, 1959*

hoser *noun* **1** an uncouth, dim person. Popularised by Bob and Doug McKenzie's 'Great White North' television skit *CANADA, 1981*. **2** a male with sexual experience and expertise *US, 1968*

hosing *verb* to beat *US, 1947*

hospital *noun* **1** jail. An unabashed euphemism *US, 1959*. **2** in a smuggling operation, the place where the smuggled goods are picked up *US, 1956*

hospital hold *noun* an unsafe grip on a tool *US, 1983*

hospital pass *noun* **1** the responsibility for a controversial project or task. Such a responsibility will inevitably draw down painful and wounding criticism. Derives from an American football usage *US, 2003*. **2** in team sports, a dangerously made pass which allows the opposition a good chance at defence. So called because of the risk of injury to the receiver *AUSTRALIA, 1984*

hoss *noun* **1** used as a term of address, man to man *US, 1834*. **2** heroin. In colloquial US speech, 'hoss' is a shortened form of HORSE (heroin) *US, 1960*

hossie *noun* a hospital *AUSTRALIA, 1971*

hostess *noun* a prostitute *US, 1954*

hostess with the mostest *noun* a good hostess. An apparently irresistible reduplication in the US, going 'host with the most' one better *US, 1970*

hostie *noun* an air hostess *AUSTRALIA, 1960*

hostile *adverb* ▶ **go hostile** to lose your temper *NEW ZEALAND, 1998*

hostile! used for expressing strong approval *US, 1995*

hostilish *adjective* arrogant, haughty, condescending *TRINIDAD AND TOBAGO, 1960*

hot *noun* a hot meal *US, 1926*

hot *adjective* **1** stolen *US, 1924*. **2** wanted by the police *US, 1928*. **3** suspect *UK, 1996*. **4** dangerous for criminal activity *UK, 1618*. **5** dangerous to other criminals because of co-operation with the police *US, 2003*. **6** under enemy fire. Although a critical term in the Vietnam war, it was coined not there, but in the US Civil War 100 years earlier *US, 1864*. **7** (used of a weapons system) activated, armed *US, 1962*. **8** poisoned *UK, 2002*. **9** good *US, 1970*. **10** excellent; used for describing music or musicians that create excitement *US, 1866*. **11** (used of jazz) traditional and spirited, as opposed to modern *US, 1924*. **12** popular *US, 1961*. **13** sexual, sensuous *US, 1931*. **14** (used of a striptease dance) very sexual *US, 1977*. **15** attractive, good-looking *US, 1982*. **16** angry *US, 1225*. **17** brief, quick *US, 1946*. **18** in sports betting, generating heavy betting; favoured *UK, 1882*. **19** (used of a set in the television and film industries) fully prepared for filming *US, 1977*. **20** drunk *BERMUDA, 1985*. ▶ **hot as Mapp's mill-yard** very hot *BARBADOS, 1965*

hot air *noun* spoken nonsense, inconsequential speech, meaningless words *US, 1873*

hot and bothered *adjective* sexually aroused *UK, 1821*

hot and cold *noun* **1** heroin and cocaine combined for injection. Based on the initials *US, 1970*. **2** gold. Rhyming slang, often reduced to its first element *UK, 1961*

hot and heavy *adjective* passionate *US, 1971*

hot and stuck *adjective* said of a player who is losing badly in a game of poker *US, 1982*

hot-arsed *adjective* feeling an urgent sexual desire, lustful *UK, 1683*

hot ass *noun* a tin kettle with a large bottom *CANADA, 1973*

hot bed *noun* a motel room rented without following proper registration procedures and rented more than once a day; a room in a cheap boarding house *US, 1940*

hot box *noun* **1** a sexually excited vagina; a sexually excited female *US, 1964*. **2** a prison cell used for solitary confinement *US, 1983*. **3** a small room or enclosed space where marijuana is being smoked *US, 2001*

hot boy *noun* a thief known to the authorities *BAHAMAS, 1982*

hot-bunk *verb* to sleep in turns or rotation on a bunk or in a sleeping bag *US, 1945*

hot buns *noun* a male homosexual *US, 1990*

hot cakes *noun* **1** phencyclidine, the recreational drug known as PCP or angel dust *US, 1994*. **2** crack cocaine. An elaboration of CAKES *UK, 1998*

hot chair *noun* the electric chair; death by electrocution in an electric chair *US, 1926*

hot cheque *noun* a forged cheque or one intentionally drawn with insufficient funds to cover payment *US, 1972*

hot chrome *noun* a car that appeals to girls *US, 1954*

hot cross bun *noun* **1** a gun. Rhyming slang *UK, 1992*. **2** the sun. Rhyming slang *UK, 1992*. **3** son. Rhyming slang *UK, 1931*. **4** run, as in 'on the run' from the police. Rhyming slang. Sometimes simply 'hot cross' *UK, 1960*

hot damn!; hot dang!; hot diggity damn!; hot damn and double damn! used for registering pleasure, astonishment; occasionally anger *US, 1933*

hot damn, Vietnam! used for expressing surprise, shock or dismay. 'Vietnam' is lengthened to three syllables *US, 1972*

hot deck *noun* logs piled up for immediate loading. British Columbia logging usage *CANADA, 1952* ▷ *see:* COLD DECK

hot diggety!; hot diggety dog!; hot diggety doggity! used for registering pleasure or astonishment. Compounding, and linking HOT DAMN! and HOT DOG! *US, 1923*

hot dinner *noun* **1** used as a measure when claiming greater experience of an activity than either that of someone else or a notional average *UK, 1959*. **2** a winner. Rhyming slang *UK, 1992*

hot dog *noun* **1** a frankfurter or other spiced sausage served in a bread-roll. The term arose at Yale University in 1894 and was quickly embraced by students at other colleges. Past suggestions that the term arose at New York's Polo Grounds have been disproved by US slang lexicographers Barry Popik and Gerald Cohen *US, 1894*. **2** a skilled and cocky person defined as much by their cockiness as their skill *US, 1894*. **3** a police officer *US, 2001*. **4** a pornographic book or magazine *US, 1974*

hot dog *verb* to perform in a flashy manner that displays your skill. Surfing slang in wider usage *US, 1961*

hot-dog *adjective* given to showing off *US, 1923*

hot dog! used for registering delight, pleasure or approval *US, 1906*

hotdog book *noun* a book used for stimulating sexual interest while masturbating *US, 1967*

hot dogger *noun* an expert surfer *US, 1963*

hot dope *noun* heroin. A combination of HOT (excellent) and DOPE (drugs) *UK, 1998*

hot dose *noun* a fatal injection of a narcotic that has been adulterated with a poison *US, 1995*

hotel *noun* a jail *US, 1845*

hotel barber *noun* a thief who steals from hotel rooms *AUSTRALIA, 1895*

hotel parental *noun* your parents' house. Many parents complain that their house is treated as a hotel; this youth coinage confirms parental suspicions *UK, 1999*

hotels *noun* in bar dice games, a roll from the cup in which some dice are stacked on top of others, invalidating the roll *US, 1976*

hot fish yoghurt *noun* semen *UK, 2001*

hotfoot *noun* a prank in which a matchbook is lit and inserted in to an unsuspecting victim's shoe *US, 1934*

hotfoot *verb* to move quickly *US, 1896*

hot footer *noun* somebody who is in a perpetual hurry *US, 1946*

hot fudgey *noun* a savoury piece of gossip *US, 1994*

hot-fuel *verb* to fuel an aircraft while the engine is running *US, 1990*

hot funky *noun* a sexually attractive, sexually available woman *US, 1993*

hot hay *noun* marijuana *US, 1952*

hot-hot *adjective* very hot, very spicy. Intensification by reduplication *INDIA, 1979*

hothouse *noun* the vagina *US, 2001*

hot karl; hot carl *noun* an act of defecating on a sexual partner; an act of defecating on a person who is asleep; an act of hitting someone with a sock full of human excrement. In Chicago, the comedy troupe Hot Karl have been in existence since 1999; a humorous reference to scatalogical practice is inferred but not confirmed. The earliest unequivocal usage is on the Internet in 2002. In 2004 a white rapper called Hot Karl is noted; also tee-shirts with the image of a pile of steaming faeces and the slogan 'hot carl' *US, 2002*

Hotlanta *nickname* Atlanta, Georgia *US, 1976*

hot-lap *verb* in motor racing, to drive around the track fast before a race or qualifying run starts, testing the car's performance *US, 1973*

hot lead *noun* bullets *US, 1949*

hot-lot *verb* to move quickly; to hurry *US, 1972*

hot mix *noun* in trucking, hot asphalt being transported to a construction site *US, 1971*

hot mouth *noun* a tendency to speak without editing *TRINIDAD AND TOBAGO, 1988*

hotness *noun* something good or desirable *US, 2002*. ▶ **the hotness** an excellent example of something *US, 2003*

hot-nose *verb* in aerial combat, to approach from behind and below, rising up in front of and ahead of the target plane *US, 1990*

hotnot *noun* a black person. Offensive, insulting; from Hottentot (an indigenous people of South Africa) *SOUTH AFRICA, 1846*

hot nuts *noun* intense male sexual desire *US, 1935*

hot pants *noun* **1** sexual desire *US, 1929*. **2** tight, skimpy shorts as a (surprisingly enduring) fashion item. Deriving, no doubt, from the sexual sense *UK, 1970*

hot peas *noun* the knees. Glasgow rhyming slang *UK, 1988*

hot peckers *noun* hot peppers. Limited usage, but clever *US, 1996*

hot pee; hot piss *noun* a pressing desire to urinate *TRINIDAD AND TOBAGO, 1990*

hot-pillow *adjective* said of a hotel or motel that rents rooms for sexual liaisons for cash, without registering the guests using the room *US, 1954*

hot pit *noun* in motor racing, the area where a pit crew works on a car during a race *US, 2001*

hot plate *noun* the electric chair; execution by electrocution *US, 1949*

hot-plate hamster *noun* a prison officer who eats food intended for prisoners *UK, 1996*

hot poop *noun* the latest information. Combines HOT (quick) and POOP (news) *UK, 1996*

hot pot *noun* **1** in poker, a large amount of money bet on a hand *US, 1988*. **2** in horse racing, a favourite *AUSTRALIA, 1904*

hot potato *noun* a waiter, especially an efficient one. Cockney rhyming slang, pronounced 'pertatah' ('waitah') *UK, 1960*

hot potato *verb* to prioritise or juggle priorities *NEW ZEALAND, 2001*

hot ringer *noun* a burglar alarm that advises police that an armed robbery is in progress *US, 2001*

hot rock *noun* a person who through dress or manner strives to be noticed *US, 1945*

hot rod *noun* a car modified for speed and, sometimes, flashy looks *US, 1945*

hot rod *verb* to masturbate *US, 1971*

hot roller *noun* a stolen car that is being driven *US, 1970*

hots *noun* **1** sexual desire, intense interest *US, 1947*. **2** electric hair curlers *US, 1975*

hot seat *noun* **1** the position of responsibility, especially if the situation attracts critical attention *UK, 1942*. **2** the electric chair; death by electrocution in the electric chair *US, 1925*

hot seat game *noun* a swindle in which all the players in a game except the victim are confederates *US, 1989*

hot sheet *noun* a list of cars reported as stolen *US, 1926*

hot-sheet *adjective* said of a motel or hotel that rents rooms for sexual liaisons for cash, without registering the guests using the room *US, 1977*

hot shit *noun* an exceptionally good person or thing *US, 1960*

hot-shit *adjective* exciting; fashionable *US, 1962*

hotshot *noun* **1** an adulterated dose of a drug that is designed to be fatal when injected *US, 1936*. **2** a gun shot fired after an emergency

call to police *US, 1994*. **3** an electric cattle prod *US, 2003*. **4** execution by electrocution in the electric chair *US, 1951*. **5** a flashy, successful person whose self-esteem is perhaps excessive *US, 1927*

hot spike *noun* a dose of a drug that has been adulterated and produces serious injury or death when injected *US, 1974*

hot spot *noun* in oil drilling, an area that has indications of a productive field *US, 1997*

hot squat *noun* the electric chair; execution by electrocution *US, 1928*

hot stepper *noun* a fugitive from justice *JAMAICA, 1982*

hotstick *noun* a marijuana cigarette *US, 1957*

hot stove *adjective* said of a discussion of sports between periods in games *CANADA, 1962*

hot stuff *noun* **1** promotional literature produced as part of a telephone sales swindle *US, 1988*. **2** illegal whisky *US, 1840*. **3** coffee *US, 1977*. **4** napalm *US, 1990*

hotsy-totsy *adjective* fancy *US, 1926*

hotsy-totsy; hotsy *noun* an attractive young woman *US, 1928*

hottentots *noun* the buttocks *US, 1974*

hotter *noun* a thrill-seeking criminal who drives stolen high-performance cars *UK, 1991*

hotter than Dutch love *adjective* very hot *US, 1950*

hot ticket *noun* something that is extremely popular and in demand *US, 1978*

hottie *noun* **1** a celebrity *NEW ZEALAND, 2002*. **2** an attractive, sexually appealing young person *US, 1991*. **3** a great wave or surfer *US, 1991*. **4** a black person, especially of the Khoikhoi race. May be insulting or affectionate; from Hottentot (an indigenous people of South Africa) *SOUTH AFRICA, 1970*

hotting *noun* the thrill-seeking activity of stealing and driving stolen high-performance cars *UK, 1998*

hot toddy *noun* the body. Rhyming slang *UK, 1992*

hot tot *noun* a very attractive young woman. A comination of HOT (sexually attractive) and a variation of TOTTY (a sexually attractive woman) *UK, 1999*

hot to trot *adjective* ready and eager for sexual activity. Extended from HOT (sexually eager, passionate) *US, 1951*

hotty; hottie *noun* a hot water bottle *UK, 1947*

hot up *verb* **1** to become increasingly lively or exciting *UK, 1923*. **2** to identify, or point the finger of suspicion at someone to the police *UK, 1996*. **3** to increase the power, speed and performance (of a car) *UK, 1928*

hot walker *noun* in horse racing, a groom who walks a horse after a race, letting it cool down *US, 1976*

hot water *noun* a state of trouble, a difficult situation *UK, 1537*

hot wire *noun* a linear amplifier for a citizens' band radio *US, 1976*

hot-wire *verb* to bypass a car's ignition system and start the car by cutting and connecting wires under the dashboard *US, 1954*

hot with two t's *adjective* extremely sexy *US, 2000*

hot ziggedy!; hot ziggetty!; hot ziggity!; hot ziggety damn! used for registering pleasure or astonishment; occasionally anger. A variation of HOT DIGGETY! *US, 1995*

hou-bro *noun* a fellow fraternity member. An abbreviation of 'house brother' *US, 1977*

hound *noun* **1** a person who is obsessed with the preceding combining noun. Not, as the definition might suggest, a grammarian *US, 1911*. **2** an unattractive woman. A variation of DOG *UK, 1988*. **3** a Greyhound bus *US, 1959*

hound dog *noun* an air-to-ground missile *US, 1991*

hound-dog *verb* to track down, to follow, to find *US, 1998*

house *noun* **1** a prisoner's cell or the area immediately surrounding the prisoner's bed in a dormitory-style room *US, 1970*. **2** a police station *US, 1909*. **3** in poker, a hand consisting of three cards of the same rank and a pair. An abbreviation of the conventional 'full house' *US, 1990* ▷*see:* HOUSE MUSIC. ▶ **go under the house** to perform oral sex on a woman *US, 1981*. ▸ **in the house 1** here and now, present, currently *US, 1993*. **2** popular, stylish *US, 1994*. ▸ **mind your house** watch your back, be careful. Often used in sports matches: when a player has the ball a team mate will shout 'mind your house' if an opponent is coming up behind him *IRELAND, 1999*. ▸ **on the house** paid for by management of the establishment *US, 1889*. ▸ **the house** the New York House of Detention for female prisoners *US, 1966*

house *verb* **1** to steal *US, 1989*. **2** to carry contraband, such as a weapon or drugs *US, 1997*

house *adjective* casual, verging on sloppy *US, 1993*

house ape *noun* a child *US, 1968*

house ball *noun* in pinball, a ball that leaves play without having scored any points *US, 1977*

housecat *noun* a soldier not assigned to combat duty. Vietnam war usage *US, 1977*

housed *adjective* drunk *US, 1997*

house dancer *noun* a sex club dancer who regularly appears at one club *US, 2000*

house dick *noun* a private detective working for a hotel or other establishment *US, 1951*

house fee *noun* the amount charged for entering a crack house *US, 1992*

house girl *noun* **1** a prostitute working in a brothel *US, 1957*. **2** in a sex club, a local dancer who regularly works at the club, as distinguished from pornography stars who make limited engagements at the club *US, 1997*

housekeeper *noun* in prison, the passive, weaker partner in a relationship who is subservient to his dominant partner's needs and wants *US, 1991*

housemaid's knee *noun* **1** a sea, the sea. Rhyming slang *UK, 1979*. **2** a key. Rhyming slang *UK, 1992*

housemaid's knees *noun* the condition caused by Osgood-Schlatter disease, calcium deposits on the lower outside quadrant of the knee *US, 1973*

houseman *noun* the best regular player in a pool hall *US, 1990*

house mother *noun* a madame in a brothel *US, 1987*

house mouse *noun* **1** a prisoner who takes or accepts responsibility for cleaning a prison cell, dormitory or common room *US, 1989*. **2** in Antarctica, support personnel assigned to the base, especially someone assigned to domestic duties *ANTARCTICA, 1958*. **3** an American soldier who explored Viet Cong tunnels *US, 1989*. **4** during the Vietnam war, a Vietnamese maid or mistress *US, 1991*

house music; house *noun* an umbrella genre for much contemporary dance music with strong repetitive rhythms – in 4/4 time, generally between 115 and 135 beats per minute. The name derives from the Ware*house* club in Chicago where the music originated in the mid-1980s *UK, 1998*

house nigger; house nigga *noun* a black person who curries favour from white people and in return is given some small degree of privilege. An updated 'house slave' *US, 1968*

house nut *noun* in the cinema business, the weekly operating expenses of the cinema *US, 1990*

House of Commons *noun* an outdoor toilet *CANADA, 1987*

House of D *nickname* the New York Women's House of Detention, Greenwich Avenue *US, 1964*

house of dark shadows *noun* any building that is occupied, or thought to be occupied, by Viet Cong *US, 1991*

House of Do Right *nickname* the New York City jail *US, 1967*

House of Fraser; hoosie Fraser; howser *noun* a razor, especially as a weapon. Rhyming slang, formed from the name of a retailing chain *UK, 1992*

house of intake *noun* a restaurant. A term coined by writers of the Coneheads skits on *Saturday Night Live* in the late 1970s, featuring three Remulakian aliens who lived quiet and normal lives in the suburbs of New Jersey. Most of the Remulakian phrases were too

forced for everyday slang, such as 'molten lactate extract of hooved animals' for 'melted cheese', but a few such as this were temporarily in vogue *US, 1977*

house of joy *noun* a brothel *US, 1948*

House of Lords *noun* corduroy trousers. Rhyming slang for CORDS *UK, 1992*

house of wax *noun* a prison *US, 1973*

house piece *noun* a gift of a dose of crack cocaine, given to the owner of a crack house in appreciation for the use of the premises *US, 1992*

houseplant *noun* a person who never leaves the home *US, 1917*

houser *noun* **1** a person who is part of the club music and party set *US, 1994*. **2** a group of close friends *US, 1993*

house-stoy *noun* (among Nova Scotians of German descent) a wedding present *CANADA, 1975*

House that Ruth Built *nickname* Yankee Stadium, Bronx, New York. The stadium opened in 1923 at the height of Ruth's career *US, 1998*

housewife *noun* an elementary sewing kit *UK, 1968*

housewives' choice *noun* voice. Rhyming slang, formed from the title of a record request programme broadcast on the *BBC Light Programme*, 1946–67 *UK, 1992*

house wizard; house guru *noun* the technical expert in a business or organisation *US, 1991*

house-wrecker *noun* in surfing, a large and powerful wave *US, 1978*

housey housey *adjective* itchy. Rhyming slang for 'lousy' (lice-ridden, hence itchy). Formed from the name of one of Bingo's variations *UK, 1992*

Hovis *noun* the head of a brown-skinned person. A refinement of the rhyming slang LOAF OF BREAD (the head); Hovis™ is a well-known brand of *brown* bread *UK, 1998*

how ADJECTIVE can you get? used of someone who has a more than average measure of a specified quality *US, 1951*

Howard Johnsons *noun* an outdoor street food vendor in Vietnam during the war. From the name of a roadside restaurant which at the time of the Vietnam war was immensely popular in the US *US, 1965*

Howard's Way *adjective* homosexual. Rhyming slang for GAY, from the title of a BBC television drama series, 1985–90 *UK, 2003*

how are you going? how are you? Used as a greeting *AUSTRALIA, 1930*

how bad is that? that's great! *US, 1965*

how can I tell? used in prison to question the truth of that which has just been said *US, 1992*

how come? why *US, 1848*

how cool is that! used for expressing delight *US, 1999*

how-de-do; how-d'ye-do *noun* a shoe. Rhyming slang *UK, 1979*

how-do-you-do; how-d'ye-do *noun* a fuss, a noisy difficulty, an embarrassing or awkward problem. Rhyming slang for 'stew' *UK, 1835*

how do you like me now? *noun* crack cocaine *UK, 1998*

howdy-do; howdy used as a friendly greeting. A reduction of 'how d'ye do' (1697) *US, 1970*

Howdy Doody *noun* an unspecified chemical agent used in Vietnam *US, 1991*

how goes it? used as a greeting *US, 1966*

how high is a Chinaman? used as a catchphrase reply to an unanswerable, or stupid, question. From a children's pun that How Hi *is* a Chinaman *UK, 1977*

howie *noun* a howitzer, field artillery *US, 1990*

howk *verb* to dig, to excavate *UK: SCOTLAND, 1911*

howl *noun* a source of great amusement *US, 1930*

howl *verb* ▸ **howl at the moon** to experience the bleed period of the menstrual cycle *US, 2001*

howler *noun* **1** a glaring mistake *UK, 1885*. **2** a child *UK, 1980*

howling *adjective* **1** drunk *UK, 2002*. **2** very smelly *UK, 1988*. **3** superlative *UK, 1865*

howling fifties *noun* the latitutes of 50 to 59 degrees south *ANTARCTICA, 1962*

Howling Mad Smith *nickname* General Holland M. Smith, US Marine Corps, The NBC action series *A-Team* (1983–87) featured a character named Captain H. M. 'Howlin' Mad' Murdock, played by Dwight Schultz, presumably named after General Smith *US, 1988*

how much? what do you mean? *UK, 1852*

how rude! used for expressing disgust. A catchphrase from the television programme *Full House US, 1990* ▷*see:* RUDE!

how's hacking? used as a greeting *US, 1981*

how's it going? used as a greeting *US, 1944*

how's it hanging? used as a greeting, usually male-to-male. Sometimes testicularly inclusive and increased to 'they' *US, 1974*

how-so? how is that so? Found in the C14, but not a complete path to the current usage *US, 1980*

how's tricks? used as a friendly greeting. Probably from the terminology of card games but may also have had nautical origins *UK, 1904*

how sweet it is! used for expressing pleasure. One of comedian Jackie Gleason's several signature lines, often used on *The Jackie Gleason Show* (CBS, 1952–70). Repeated with obviously referential humour *US, 1957*

how's your arse for lovebites? used as a greeting between young men *UK: SCOTLAND, 1996*

how's-your-father *noun* **1** any act of sexual intimacy from petting to intercourse; non-conventional sexual behaviour. Originally from the music halls, 'how's your father' or 'howsyerfather' was an all-purpose catchphrase, a euphemism for anything; subsequent usage, especially in the services during World War 2 mainly narrowed the sense to 'a sexual dalliance' *UK, 1931*. **2** any activity or business that is complicated or annoying, a fuss. Rhyming slang for 'palaver' *UK, 1998*. **3** a fight *NEW ZEALAND, 2002*. **4** cocaine *UK, 2000*

how's your love life?; how's your sex life? used as a greeting, often flirtatious *UK, 1969*

how's your mind? are you mad? Generally asked in exasperation or irritation *SOUTH AFRICA, 2004*

howzat? how's that? Often heard as a cricketer's appeal to the umpire *UK, 1961*

howzit? used as a greeting. In South Africa, the usual reply is: 'No, fine', which actually means 'Yes, I am fine' (the word 'no' is often taken to mean 'yes'); an Afrikaner might reply: 'Ja, well, no fine' *US, 1950*

hoy *verb* to throw *AUSTRALIA, 1971*

hozzo *noun* a large and dangerous wave. From 'horrible', with '-o' suffix *AUSTRALIA, 1987*

hozzo *adjective* (of a wave or surfing conditions) large, powerful and dangerous *AUSTRALIA, 1987*

hozzy; ozzy; ozzie *noun* a hospital *UK, 2001*

HP *noun* a man. Gay slang; an initialism of polari HOMEE-PALONE (a man) *UK, 2002*

HRN *noun* heroin. Whilst this looks like an acronym it is simply 'heroin' devowelled *US, 1959*

HTH *noun* a spouse or lover who is waiting for you back home. An abbreviation of 'hometown honey' *US, 1993*

hubba *noun* crack cocaine *US, 1988*

hubba-hubba! used for expressing enthusiastic appreciation of a good-looking woman *US, 1941*

hubba, I am back *noun* crack cocaine. Rhyming slang *UK, 1998*

hubba pigeon *noun* a crack cocaine addict who searches for bits of crack cocaine on the ground *US, 1995*

hubbly-bubbly *noun* a water pipe used for smoking marijuana, hashish or crack cocaine *US, 1970*

hubboo *adjective* pregnant *NORFOLK ISLAND, 1992*

hubby; hubbie *noun* a husband. Often used in a sardonic sense *UK, 1688*

hubcap *noun* **1** an important person. Playing on WHEEL (a very important person) *US, 1960*. **2** a person whose sense of importance outweighs his actual importance *US, 1951*

huck *verb* in snowboarding, to launch yourself into the air *US, 1995*

huckery *adjective* ugly. Often used to describe a woman or 'moll' *NEW ZEALAND, 1993*

huckle *verb* to be bundled into a place; to be thrown out; to arrest *UK: SCOTLAND, 1985*

hudda *noun* a police officer; the police *US, 1993*

huddle *verb* while working as a police officer in a patrol car, to park and sleep *US, 1973*

huddy keep left (of a horse) *CANADA, 1957*

hudge *verb* in pinball, to apply physical force to a machine to affect the trajectory of the ball without activating the tilt mechanism *US, 1977*

huevon *noun* a very lazy person. Border Spanish used in English conversation by Mexican-Americans; from the image of the man who is so lazy that his testicles (HUEVAS) grow large *US, 1974*

huevos *noun* **1** the testicles; courage. Border Spanish used in English conversation by Mexican-Americans; literally 'eggs' *US, 1974*. **2** waves. Spanish for 'eggs', but a near-homophone for 'waves', hence the play *US, 1991*. **3** a variety of Moroccan hashish. From Spanish for 'eggs', named for its shape and texture *SPAIN, 2003*

Huey *nickname* a Bell utility military helicopter *US, 1962*

Huey shuffle *noun* a common hesitation in the flight pattern by an inexperienced helicopter pilot *US, 1983*

huff *verb* **1** to inhale household or industrial chemicals for recreational purposes *US, 1969*. **2** to steal *TRINIDAD AND TOBAGO, 1990*

huff and puff *noun* a state of high anger *TRINIDAD AND TOBAGO, 1978*

huff and puff *verb* to breathe heavily. From the childhood tale of *The Three Little Pigs UK, 1890*

huffer *noun* **1** an act of oral sex on a man. Probably a mistaken understanding of HUMMER *US, 1973*. **2** a person who inhales household or industrial chemicals for recreational purposes *US, 1969*. **3** in drag racing and hot rodding, a supercharger *US, 1968*

hug *verb* ▶ **hug the bowl** to vomit *US, 1997*

hug and slug *noun* (among Canadian Forces members) any place where girls or fights are to be found *CANADA, 1995*

hug drug *noun* MDMA, the recreational drug best known as ecstasy. From the affectionate feelings roused by the drug *UK, 1996*

hugger-mugger *noun* **1** chaos *US, 1972*. **2** a prostitute who beats and robs customers or who serves as a decoy for someone who beats and robs the customer *US, 1970*

huggie *noun* a styrofoam or plastic cylinder that slips over a beer can, serving as insulation *US, 2000*

hugging *adjective* bad, crazy *US, 1997*

huggy *adjective* given to hugging; hence, sensitive and caring *US, 1999*

huggy-bear *noun* prolonged hugging and kissing *US, 1964*

hughie; huey *noun* an act of vomiting. A joke was told of a person calling out the name of television presenter Hughie Green, 1920–1997; it was, in fact, the cry of someone vomiting after drinking green Chartreuse *UK: SCOTLAND, 1985*

hughie; huey *verb* to vomit. Echoic of the involuntary vocal accompaniment to the action *UK: SCOTLAND, 1985*

Hughie; Hughey; Huey *noun* a supposed rain god. Used in the phrase 'send her/it down Hughie!', said when the rains first appear after a dry spell or the dry season. The earliest instance of this is from the *Bulletin*, 3rd December 1912, where it is stated that it referred to a Mr Huie 'an amateur meteorologist who had luck in prophesying rain'. This story has not been verified and would probably carry more force if it weren't for the fact that Hughie sounds more like a first name than a surname, and also in light of the variants that have from time to time cropped up, such as 'send her down Steve!' and 'send her down David!' *AUSTRALIA, 1912*

hugs and kisses; hugs; ugs *noun* a wife. Rhyming slang for MISSUS *UK, 1992*

huh-huh-huh; huh-huh-huh-huh used as a representation of unspirited laughter. Caricatured as the smirking laugh of teenage heavy metal fans in the animated television series *Beavis and Butthead*, Mtelevision, 1993–97 *US, 1997*

hulk *noun* an unusually large bodybuilder *US, 1980*

hulking *adjective* large, especially of an unwieldy mass *UK, 1698*

hull *noun* an empty pistol cartridge case *US, 1957*

hullabaloo *noun* a loud noise; an uproar; confusion *UK, 1762*

hulloo *noun* a completely inconsequential person *NORFOLK ISLAND, 1992*

hully-gully *adjective* stylish, especially in a Rastafarian sense *BAHAMAS, 1973*

hum *verb* **1** to be busy, to be crowded; to be lively *US, 1887*. **2** to have an unpleasant odour, to stink *UK, 1902*

human sea *noun* an infantry tactic of the North Korean Army, of swarming enemy positions in overwhelming numbers *US, 1964*

humble *noun* a false criminal accusation or charge *US, 1940*

Humbolt green *noun* marijuana. This should, perhaps, be 'Humboldt green', indicating the county in northern California in which this green-leafed marijuana plant originates *UK, 2003*

humbug *noun* **1** false or trumped-up criminal charges *US, 1972*. **2** a fight, especially between youth gangs *US, 1962*

humbug *verb* **1** to fight *US, 1968*. **2** to interfere with, to bother *TRINIDAD AND TOBAGO, 1904*

humdinger *noun* a remarkable thing or person *US, 1905*

hum job *noun* oral sex performed on a male *US, 1964*

hummel *noun* the hair. English gypsy use *UK, 2000*

hummer *noun* **1** an act of oral sex performed on a man *US, 1971*. **2** an exceptionally good thing *US, 1681*. **3** an arrest for something the person did not do; an arrest for a minor violation that leads to more serious charges *US, 1932*. **4** a minor mistake *US, 1959*. **5** a joke, a prank *US, 1990*. **6** the Grumman E-2, an early warning aircraft. Given the official nickname 'Hawkeye', it was instantly renamed by the troops *US, 1989*. **7** an army weapons carrier. The official designation is a High Mobility Multipurpose Wheeled Vehicle. The slang is easier *US, 1983*

hummer days *noun* (from a male perspective) the bleed period of the menstrual cycle *US, 2001*

hummingbird ass *noun* used for suggesting that a person lacks the courage to back up his taunts *US, 1977*

humongous; humungous *adjective* very large *US, 1968*

hump *noun* **1** a fit of sulks, a bad mood, depression *UK, 1873*. **2** an offensive or despicable person *US, 1963*. **3** a dolt, a dull person *US, 1963*. **4** an act of sexual intercourse *US, 1918*. **5** a Camel™ cigarette *US, 1989*. **6** a bridge. Citizens' band radio slang *UK, 1981*. **7** the air route over the Himalaya Mountains during World War 2 *US, 1942*. **8** the middle section of a prison sentence *US, 1962*. **9** a large wave. Surfer usage *US, 1957*. **10** a military combat patrol. Recorded in Australia in the C19, but not again until the US war in Vietnam *US, 1971*. **11** a lookout during a crime *US, 1949*. **12** in circus usage, a camel *US, 1926*. ▶ **over the hump** while gambling, having won enough to be gambling now with the house's money *US, 1950*

hump *verb* **1** to have sex *US, 1784*. **2** to carry, to lug, to march. An essential word to US soldiers in Vietnam *AUSTRALIA, 1851*. **3** to earn money working as a prostitute *US, 1973*. **4** in trucking, to drive fast *US, 1976*. ▶ **hump it** in poker, to raise the maximum bet allowed *US, 1988*. ▶ **hump like a camel** to engage in sexual intercourse with great physical enthusiasm *US, 1970*. ▶ **hump the dog** to waste time completely. Similar construction to the synonymous 'fuck the dog' *US, 1980*. ▶ **hump your bluey/drum/swag** to carry one's belongings in a swag while seeking work on foot *AUSTRALIA, 1851*

hump-and-jump *adjective* (of a job) physically demanding and fast-paced *US, 1977*

hump and thump *noun* cardiovascular resuscitation *US, 1994*

humpback job *noun* a local freight train *US, 1946*

hump date *noun* during the Vietnam war, the date when half of a soldier's tour of duty in Vietnam is completed *US, 1965*

hump day *noun* Wednesday. Visualised as a hill, the peak or hump of the work week or school week is Wednesday *US, 1955*

humper *noun* **1** a member of a rock band's crew who carries heavy items *UK, 1985*. **2** a large and unbroken wave *US, 1977*. **3** in motor racing, a slick drag racing tyre that has been grooved for use on a dirt track *US, 1980*

hump-hump *verb* to have sex. Mock pidgin *US, 1997*

hump night *noun* Wednesday night *US, 1955*

hump rat *noun* a railway yard brakeman *US, 1968*

humpty dumpty *noun* an extreme reaction to MDMA, the recreational drug best known as ecstasy. A probable reference to the fate of the nursery rhyme character *UK, 1996*

Humpty Dumpty language *noun* any word or vocabulary given an unusual or eccentric sense by the user. Derives from *Through the Looking Glass and What Alice Found There* by Lewis Carroll (Charles Dodgson), 1871: '"When I use a word," Humpty Dumpty said, in rather a scornful tone, "it means just what I choose it to mean – neither more nor less."' *UK, 1984*

humpy *noun* a makeshift dwelling. Originally used of a temporary shelter made by Aboriginals; from the Australian Aboriginal language Yagara (Brisbane region) *AUSTRALIA, 1846*

humpy *adjective* handsome, sexy. Homosexual usage *US, 1968*

humpy-bump *verb* to have sex *US, 1974*

hun *noun* one hundred dollars; a one hundred dollar note *US, 1895*

Hun *noun* **1** a German; a person of German descent. As German troops set sail for China on 27th July 1900, Wilhelm II urged them to fight 'just as the Huns a thousand years ago'. The name stuck. It was the main pejorative for the enemy in World War 2 *UK, 1900*. **2** a Protestant *UK: SCOTLAND, 1996*

hunch *noun* an intuition or premonition. Now verging on conventional *US, 1888*

hunch *verb* to bring someone up to date; to inform *US, 1973*

hundoe *noun* one hundred dollars *US, 2001*

hundred-mile coffee *noun* strong coffee. So named because it is strong enough to keep a trucker awake to drive one hundred miles *US, 1971*

hundred to eight *noun* a plate. Rhyming slang, formed from bookmaker's odds *UK, 1998*

hundred to thirty *adjective* dirty *UK, 1974*

hung *adjective* **1** endowed with a large penis. Shakespeare punned with the term 400 years ago *UK, 1600*. **2** fascinated or obsessed with *US, 1950*. **3** (used of a computer program) suspended, waiting for something that will not happen *US, 1983*

hung like a cashew blessed with a small penis *UK, 1998*

hung like a hamster blessed with a small penis *US, 2004*

hung like a jack donkey; hung like a donkey endowed with an impressively large penis *UK, 1984*

hung like a pimple blessed with a small penis *US, 1995*

hung over *adjective* suffering from the after-effects of having drunk too much alcohol. Derives from 'hangover' *US, 1942*

hungries *noun* the craving for food that follows the smoking of marijuana *US, 1970*

hungry *adjective* stingy; mean *AUSTRALIA, 1855*

hung up *adjective* **1** obsessed, infatuated *US, 1950*. **2** addicted *US, 1950*. **3** of a drug-addict who is unable to get drugs, depressed, let down, disappointed. A nuance of the previous sense *US, 1948*. **4** inhibited, neurotic *US, 1952*. **5** while surfing, caught along the steep wall of a wave and unable to pull out *US, 1963*

hungus *adjective* in computing, extremely large *US, 1981*

hunk *noun* a good-looking, muscular boy or man *US, 1945*

hunka chunka *noun* sexual intercourse *US, 2005*

hunkin *adjective* enormous *US, 1997*

hunky *adjective* attractive, muscular *US, 1972*

hunky; hunkie *noun* **1** a white person. Derogatory *US, 1959.* **2** an Eastern European; a Slav; a Hungarian. Disparaging, but usually more illustrative of the speaker's lack of geographic knowledge *US, 1909*

hunky dory *adjective* satisfactory, fine *US, 1861*

hunt *noun* ▶ **in the hunt** in contention *AUSTRALIA, 1957*

hunt *verb* to chase off, away or to somewhere *AUSTRALIA, 1917.* ▶ **hunt owls** to drive at night with your full headlight beams on, blinding oncoming traffic *US, 1962.* ▶ **hunt rabbits** in a game of poker, to go through the cards that were not played after a hand is finished in search of what might have been *US, 1951.* ▶ **hunt the great white whale** to search for a source of cocaine. The GREAT WHITE WHALE is a literary allusion to *Moby Dick*, the classic novel by Herman Melville (1819–91), and a play on the colour and power of cocaine *UK, 2001*

hunter *noun* **1** a pickpocket *US, 1949.* **2** cocaine *UK, 1998*

hunt for Red October *noun* the bleed period of the menstrual cycle. Elaboration of 'red' – the colour of blood – by adoption of the title of a novel by Tom Clancy, and subsequent film *US, 2000*

hunting license *noun* an assignment given by a prison gang to kill someone *US, 1992*

huntsabber *noun* a hunt saboteur *UK, 2001*

hunty-hunty *adjective* (of a woman) used to describe a husband-hunter or a 'manhunter'. Reduplication of the woman's essential quality. West Indian, hence UK Black *UK, 2000*

huppie *noun* an individual socially categorised as an *Hispanic urban professional* or *Hispanic upwardly mobile professional*. On the familiar model of YUPPIE (young upwardly mobile professional) *US, 1986*

hurdy *noun* a dance hall girl *CANADA, 1958*

hurl *noun* an act of vomiting; vomit *AUSTRALIA, 1967*

hurl *verb* to vomit *AUSTRALIA, 1964*

hurler *noun* a person who suffers from bulimia nervosa *US, 1998*

hurly-burly *adjective* confusing, tumultuous *UK, 1596*

hurrah *noun* in a big store confidence swindle, the stage of the swindle when the victim is fully duped *US, 1997*

hurricane deck *noun* the back of a bucking bronco *US, 1862*

hurricane ham *noun* conch *BAHAMAS, 1982*

hurricane lamp; hurricane *noun* a *tramp*, a vagrant. Rhyming slang *UK, 1998*

hurricane lamp job *noun* in horse racing, a horse that finishes last by a great distance. The horse is so far back that it is joked that a hurricane lamp is needed to find it *AUSTRALIA, 1989*

hurricane on a ten-cent piece *noun* a wife furious with her husband *CANADA, 1995*

hurry-come *adjective* done with haste and without care *TRINIDAD AND TOBAGO, 1987*

hurry-on *noun* a quickening of pace *AUSTRALIA, 1983*

hurry-up *noun* **1** a hurry, speed. Since the 1960s *UK, 1962.* **2** a request for a quickening of pace *AUSTRALIA, 1916*

hurryup wagon *noun* a police van *US, 1893*

hurt *noun* ▶ **put the hurt on** to inflict pain *UK, 2001*

hurt *verb* to crave a drug *UK, 1996*

hurt *adjective* undesirable, unattractive, inept *US, 1973*

hurting *adjective* inferior; not up to expectations *US, 2002*

hurt me! used for expressing extreme pleasure or displeasure *US, 1983*

hurve *verb* to move quickly; to hurry *AUSTRALIA, 1983*

husband *noun* in a homosexual relationship (male or female), the more aggressive and domineering partner *US, 1941*

husband and wife; husband *noun* a knife. Rhyming slang *UK, 1992*

hush *noun* silence *UK, 1976*

hush-em *noun* a silencer attached to a handgun *US, 1949*

hush-hush *adjective* secret. Reduplicated 'hush' (to be quiet); military origins *UK, 1916*

hush money *noun* a bribe paid to obtain silence *UK, 1709*

hush puppy *noun* **1** a Smith and Wesson 9 mm pistol; the silencer attached to the pistol. Carried by US Navy SEALS. So named, the legend goes, because of its use in killing guard dogs *US, 1982.* **2** a yuppie (a young upwardly mobile professional). Rhyming slang, formed from a footwear-manufacturer's brand name *UK, 1992*

hush-puppy *adjective* (used of jazz) old-fashioned, conventional *US, 1958*

husk *verb* to undress *US, 1945*

Husky *noun* in trucking, a Brockway truck. From the company logo *US, 1976*

huss; hus; huz *noun* a favour. Vietnam war usage, especially by marines *US, 1971*

hustle *noun* **1** an illegal enterprise, especially one involving swindling *US, 1943.* **2** effort, exertion, desire *US, 1898.* ▶ **on the hustle 1** engaged in a career of swindling *US, 1997*

hustle *verb* **1** to engage in prostitution *US, 1895.* **2** to obtain after a diligent effort, especially one using unorthodox, if not illegal, means *US, 1840.* **3** to beg, to cadge. Used by beggars and tramps *US, 1902.* **4** to flirt; to make a sexual advance *TRINIDAD AND TOBAGO, 2003*

hustler *noun* **1** a prostitute, especially a male homosexual *US, 1924.* **2** a drug pusher *UK, 1996.* **3** a person who makes his living by playing pool for wagers, feigning a skill level below his true level to secure bets *US, 1967.* **4** a person who lives by his charm and wits, dishonest but usually not violent *US, 1896*

hustler's row *noun* any outdoor area where prostitutes loiter in search of customers *UK, 1966*

hustling *noun* **1** the practice of dealing drugs *UK, 2000.* **2** prostitution *UK, 1977*

hustling gal *noun* a prostitute *US, 1954*

hut *noun* **1** a house *US, 1989.* **2** a jail cell *US, 1949.* **3** a brakevan (caboose) *US, 1946*

hutch *noun* **1** a domicile, be it a room, apartment or house *US, 1966.* **2** a prison *US, 1956*

hutzelsup *noun* (among Nova Scotians of German descent) a confused mess *CANADA, 1999*

Hyack *noun* in British Columbia, a volunteer fireman. The term, from a Chinook jargon word, is preserved in the Honorable Hyack Battery of New Westminster, BC *CANADA, 1959*

hyak *verb* in British Columbia, to hasten. The term comes from Chinook jargon *CANADA, 1959*

hyas *adverb* big, large, very *CANADA, 1953*

hyas tyee *noun* a great chief, an important person. A combination of two Chinook jargon words, HYAS and *tyee* (chief, king) *CANADA, 1956*

hybolic *adjective* pompous, wordy, bombastic. Hawaiian youth usage *US, 1972*

hybrid *noun* in the car sales business, used as a euphemism for a car that has at least some parts that do not belong *US, 1953*

Hyde Park *noun* **1** an actor's mark. Rhyming slang, from the film world *UK, 1972.* **2** an informer. Rhyming slang for NARK *UK, 1992*

hydraulic *noun* in drag racing, a massive engine failure resulting from fuel failing to ignite within a cylinder *US, 2003*

hydraulic *adjective* inclined to steal. Like a hydraulic jack, he will 'lift' anything *AUSTRALIA, 1989*

hydraulics *noun* bollocks, in all senses. Euphemistic rhyming slang *UK, 1998*

hydro *noun* **1** marijuana which is grown *hydro*ponically *US, 1996.* **2** MDMA, the recreational drug best known as ecstasy. Probably from the dehydration experienced by users of the drug *UK, 2003.* **3** amphetamines *UK, 2003.* **4** electric power generated by the flow of water *CANADA, 1964*

hydroponic *noun* marijuana that is cultivated hydroponically. The soilless culture of cannabis results in plants that are up to ten time as potent as those grown outdoors *US, 1989*

hyiu *adjective* great, many, much, very. The word is adapted into English from Chinook jargon *CANADA, 1966*

hyke *noun* **1** codeine. From the brand name Hycodan™ *US, 1997*. **2** hydrocodone, a synthetic codeine *US, 1970*

Hymie *noun* a Jewish male. Like Mick (for Mickey) as a label for the Irish, Hymie is a shortened Hyman. Not used kindly *US, 1973*

hype *noun* **1** a syringe *US, 1910*. **2** a needle-using drug addict *US, 1924*. **3** a frequent user of marijuana. Use of the term 'addict' is controversial in the context of marijuana users, but the suggestion here is that the person has let marijuana control his life *US, 1999*. **4** exaggeration, nonsense *US, 1938*. **5** deception; an act of deception; something intended to stimulate sales, etc *US, 1955*. **6** a swindle or cheat *US, 1980*. ▶ **put the hype on** to raise prices because of demand without regard to fairness of the price *US, 1980*

hype *verb* **1** to lie, to swindle *US, 1914*. **2** to stimulate interest or sales *US, 1942*

hype *adjective* excellent *US, 2002*

hyped up *adjective* stimulated or excited, especially if by artificial means *US, 1946*

hype guy *noun* in circus and carnival usage, a short-change swindler *US, 1981*

hype marks *noun* scars and sores on a drug addict's body indicating intravenous drug use *US, 1973*

hyper *noun* **1** in circus and carnival usage, a short-change swindler *US, 1981*. **2** a person employed to stimulate music sales in an attempt to influence the pop charts, *1998*

hyper *adjective* emotionally stressed. Abbreviated and adapted from 'hyperactive' *US, 1942*

hyper- *prefix* extremely *UK, 1984*

hype stick *noun* a hypodermic syringe *US, 1933*

hype tank *noun* a jail holding cell reserved for drug addicts *US, 1964*

hypo *noun* **1** a hypodermic syringe *US, 1905*. **2** a needle-using drug addict *US, 1904*. **3** a swindle *US, 1949*

Hy-town *nickname* Hyannis, Massachusetts *US, 1998*

Ii

I *noun* ▶ **the I** an interstate highway *US, 2003*

I ain't even tryin' to hear you! I am not listening *US, 1993*

I ain't here to brag used for demonstrating that the speaker understands that he is bragging. A paralipsis of the first order. Many grammatical variants exist, as well as the simpler, 'Not to brag' *US, 2004*

I am a Ranger. We live for the One, we die for the One. used with humour as an affirmation of support. The motto of the interplanetary police on the US science fiction television programme *Babylon* (1994–98) *US, 1994*

I am Canadian *noun* a drink made with fruit juice, Quebec maple syrup and whisky or Molson Canadian beer *CANADA, 2002*

I am so sure! used for expressing strong doubt about what has just been said *US, 1982*

I and I *noun* used in the military as a jocular substitute for the official 'R and R' (rest and recreation). An abbreviation of 'intercourse *and* intoxication', the main activities during rest and recreation *US, 1960*

I believe you but thousands wouldn't a catchphrase retort that is used to express doubt or, at best, reserve judgement about the veracity of the person being addressed. This phrase exists in a number of minor variations, and is so well known that 'I believe you but!' carries the full sense *UK, 1927*

I bet!; I'll bet! I am certain. Elliptical for 'I bet you did' or 'do' or 'did'; often derisive or ironic *UK, 1939*

Ibiza Hilton *noun* the police station of the Guardia Civil Ibiza. An ironic reference to the international Hilton hotel chain *SPAIN, 1999*

IBM *noun* **1** a smart, diligent student *US, 1960*. **2** a member of an organized crime family; an Italian businessman *US, 1997*

IBM discount *noun* a price increase *US, 1991*

iboga *noun* **1** amphetamines. A reference to the African shrub *tabernathe iboga* and *ibogaine*, a natural stimulant that is compounded therefrom *UK, 2003*. **2** MDMA, the recreational drug best known as ecstasy *UK, 2003*

IC *noun* during the Vietnam war, an innocent civilian *US, 1985*

I can catch *noun* the US Interstate Commerce Commission. A back formation from the agency initials: ICC *US, 1971*

I can read his lips, and he's not praying used as a humorous comment on a profanity. Popularised by ESPN's Keith Olberman *US, 1997*

I can't fight that! used by a clever boy for expressing approval of a girl who has just passed by *US, 1955*

I can't HEAR you! used as a humorous solititication of more enthusiastic support. A signature line of marine drill instructor Vince Carter on the television situation comedy *Gomer Pyle, USMC* (CBS, 1964–69). Repeated with referential humour *US, 1966*

I can't take you anywhere used as a humorous, if stock, tease of someone who has commited a faux pas *US, 1994*

ice *noun* **1** diamonds *UK, 1905*. **2** cocaine, especially in blocks *US, 1971*. **3** smokeable amphetamine or methamphetamine *US, 1989*. **4** heroin *US, 1987*. **5** protection money paid by a business to criminals or by criminals to the police *US, 1887*. **6** a pay-off, a bribe; an added charge *US, 1968*. **7** the difference between the listed price and the price actually paid for theatre tickets for a very popular show *US, 1973*. **8** in poker, a stacked deck *US, 1967*. **9** solitary confinement in prison *US, 1990*. **10** any computer program designed as a system security scheme *US, 1995*. ▶ **on ice** incarcerated *US, 1931*. ▶ **on the ice** (of a racehorse) being secretly, and illicitly, kept from running to win *AUSTRALIA, 1966*

Ice *noun* in-car entertainment, especially audio equipment *UK, 2003*. ▶ **the Ice** Antarctica *ANTARCTICA, 1834*

ice *verb* **1** to kill *US, 1941*. **2** to place in solitary confinement *US, 1933*. **3** to ignore with a vengeance *US, 1932*. **4** to give up; to stop *US, 1962*. **5** to reject; to stand up *US, 1997*. ▶ **ice it 1** to stop doing something *US, 1974*. **2** to forget something *US, 1960*

iceberg *noun* **1** an emotionally cold person, especially a woman *UK, 1840*. **2** a sexually frigid woman *US, 1949*

iceberg act *noun* unfriendly treatment *US, 1953*

ice blink *noun* a whitish glow on the horizon or on clouds caused by light reflecting off ice *CANADA, 1995*

ice-block *noun* an ice confection on a stick *AUSTRALIA, 1948*

icebox *noun* **1** a morgue *US, 1928*. **2** a jail or prison. An extension of the more common COOLER (jail) *US, 1938*

ice cold *noun* a chilled beer *AUSTRALIA, 1968*

ice cold *adjective* rude *US, 1990*

ice cream *noun* a white child; white children. Used defensively by children of different hues *UK, 1979*

ice-cream freezer; ice-cream *noun* a man. Rhyming slang for GEEZER *UK, 1962*

ice-cream habit *noun* the irregular consumption of drugs by an occasional user. 'Ice-cream eater' and 'ice-creamer' are obsolete slang terms for an irregular user of opium, an earlier application (late C19 to the 1930s) based on the notion that ice-cream is an occasional pleasure and not an every day diet *US, 1970*

ice-cream man *noun* a drug dealer, especially one selling opiates *US, 1952*

ice-cream truck *noun* ▶ **and the ice-cream truck you rode in on!** used to extend and emphasise an absolute rejection *US, 2001*

ice cube *noun* crack cocaine *US, 1994*

iced *adjective* drunk, drug-intoxicated *US, 1953*

iced down *adjective* wearing many diamonds *US, 1998*

iced out *noun* wearing a great deal of diamond-bearing jewellery *US, 2000*

ice down *verb* to completely cover with graffiti *US, 1997*

icehouse *noun* a jewellery store. From ICE (a diamond) *US, 1949*

Icelandic Air Force *noun* (around Gimli, Manitoba) flocks of pelicans *CANADA, 1987*

ice luge *noun* a block of ice used in a drinking game in which a shot of vodka, tequila or other alcoholic drink is poured down the ice into the drinker's mouth *US, 2001*

iceman *noun* **1** a person who bribes a government official or otherwise 'fixes' difficult situations. From ICE (a bribe) *US, 1981*. **2** in horse racing, a jockey who rides without using the whip or vigorous kicks *AUSTRALIA, 1989*. **3** a mechanic who works on truck refrigeration units *US, 1971*

ice money *noun* money used to bribe *US, 1993*

ice pack *noun* high quality marijuana *US, 1971*

ice palace *noun* **1** a jewellery store *US, 1956*. **2** a hockey rink *CANADA, 1955*

ice widow *noun* a woman whose husband is in Antarctica *NEW ZEALAND, 1971*

icing *noun* cocaine *US, 1984*

ick *noun* **1** any unpleasant sticky substance *UK, 2002*. **2** in the language surrounding the Grateful Dead, a bacterial or viral infection that quickly spreads among those following the band on tour. Always with 'the' *US, 1994*. **3** a social outcast *US, 1942*

ick *adjective* mawkishly sentimental, hence unpalatable. An abbreviation of ICKY *US, 2001*

ickies *noun* foreign money of any type. Royal Navy usage, possibly a variation of ACKER (money). One 'ickie' equals one hundred KLEBBIES *UK, 1989*

ickle *adjective* little. A small child's pronunciation employed archly by those old enough to know better *UK, 1864*

icky *noun* a rich person *US, 1953*

icky *adjective* **1** unattractive, distasteful. First found in jazz to describe oversweet music other than jazz, then migrated into general use with the more general meaning *US, 1929*. **2** unwell. Probably from baby-talk variations of 'sick' or 'sickly' *UK, 1939*. **3** overly sentimental, especially of music or of a taste in music. Originally from jazz *US, 1929*

icky-poo *adjective* unwell. Baby-talk variation of 'sick' or 'sickly' *UK, 1920*

ICL used as shorthand in Internet discussion groups and text messaging to mean 'in Christian love' *US, 2002*

I could cure the plague used by a woman to describe her condition when experiencing the bleed period of the menstrual cycle *US, 2000*

I could just scream! used as an expression of frustration. A signature line of Captain Wallace B. Binghamton on the television comedy *McCahle's Navy* (ABC, 1962–66). Repeated with referential humour *US, 1962*

icy-pole *noun* an ice confection on a stick. Generic use of a trademark term *AUSTRALIA, 1932*

ID *noun* an identity card or other means of identification *US, 1941*

ID *verb* to identify someone. Derives from the noun uses as 'identification/identity' *US, 1944*

idea hamster; ideas hamster *noun* a person who is employed to generate new ideas *UK, 2001*

identity *noun* a noted person; an odd or interesting person *AUSTRALIA, 1874*

idi *adjective* cruel. Probably after Ugandan dictator Idi Amin, 1925(?)-2003; recorded in use in contemporary gay society *UK, 2003*

idiot blocks *noun* options placed at the end of a staffing paper designed to allow the reader simply to tick the option which describes his decision *US, 1986*

idiot board *noun* in television, an out-of-camera board on which a performer's lines are displayed *UK, 1952*

idiot box *noun* **1** the television *US, 1955*. **2** an automatic car transmission *US, 1993*

idiot card *noun* in the television and film industries, a poster board with the dialogue written in large letters for actors to read *US, 1957*

idiot-head *noun* a stupid person. Used by young children *AUSTRALIA, 1988*

idiot juice *noun* any alcoholic beverage brewed in prison, especially a nutmeg/water mixture *US, 1974*

idiot light *noun* in a car, a warning light on the dashboard in place of a gauge *US, 1968*

idiot pill *noun* a barbiturate or central nervous system depressant *US, 1953*

idiot's delight *noun* in dominoes, the 5-0 piece *US, 1959*

idiot spoon *noun* a shovel *US, 1947*

idiot stick *noun* **1** a small carved copy of a totem pole *CANADA, 1989*. **2** a shovel *US, 1930*. **3** a digging bar *US, 1980*

idjit *noun* ▷*see:* EEJIT

I don't think so used as a humorous rejection of the sentiment that has been expressed *US, 1969*

I don't want to know used as refusal to accept unwelcome news or facts *UK, 1946*

idren *noun* friend; friends. West Indian, Rastafarian and UK black patois for 'brethren' (brothers), with religious and political overtones *UK, 1994*

idyat bwai *noun* a fool. West Indian patois (idiot boy) *UK, 1997*

if bet *noun* in horse racing, a bet that is made contingent upon winning a bet in an earlier race *US, 1947*

if cash *noun* in gambling, a type of conditional bet: an instruction to re-invest all or part of a winning return on another bet *UK, 2001*

iffiness *noun* a quality of unreliability, subject to doubt. From IFFY *UK, 2001*

iffy *adjective* **1** tenuous, uncertain *US, 1937*. **2** dangerous, risky. Extends from the previous sense *UK, 2001*

if I'm lying, I'm dying I am telling the truth. There are multiple reduplicative variations *US, 1981*

If it ain't broke, don't fix it used as a humorous suggestion to leave well enough alone *US, 1961*

if it isn't... (used as an acknowledgement of someone) it is that person *US, 1951*

if it's too loud, you're too old used for dismissing complaints of loudness at rock concerts. A saying attributed to Kiss. *US, 1995*

if-lose; if-win *noun* in gambling, a type of conditional bet: a bet is required only if the prior selection loses/wins or is a non-runner *UK, 2001*

ifs, ands or buts *noun* conditions, contingencies, exceptions *US, 1982*

if they back up the truck used in the entertainment industry for expressing a recognition that if the offer is lucrative enough, the actor speaking will accept the role despite its dramatic limitations. The phrase conjures up the image of a truck full of bags of money backing up the driveway to be emptied. *US, 2001*

if ya wonders, then ya is used in twelve-step recovery programmes such as Alcoholics Anonymous as a judgment on those who stop to wonder if they might be an addict *US, 1998*

if you say so used for indicating (grudgingly, or to placate) acceptance of what has been said *UK, 1956*

ig *verb* to ignore *US, 1946*

iggie *noun* a feigned ignorance. Circus and carnival usage. Often used in the phrase 'give them the iggie' *US, 1961*

igloo *noun* a one-hundred-dollar note. From the resemblance between '100' and 'loo' *AUSTRALIA, 1989*

ign'ant *adjective* ignorant *US, 2002*

ignorant *adjective* ▶ **make ignorant** to make angry. A south London term *UK, 1977*

ignorant end *noun* in poker, the low card in a five-card sequence *US, 1990*

ignorant oil *noun* alcohol, especially cheap and potent alcohol *US, 1954*

ignorant spoon *noun* in oil drilling, a shovel *US, 1954*

ignuts *noun* an ignorant fool *US, 1934*

I-guy *noun* a member of a team who thinks of himself – the individual – more than the team. Related to the sports adage: 'There is no "I" in "team"' *US, 1997*

I hate it! used for expressing solidarity with the misfortune just described by another *US, 1984*

I hate it when that happens used for introducing humour, usually after someone else has described an extremely unlikely situation *US, 1987*

I have nothing more to say about this that is either relevant or true used as a humorous comment when there is nothing worthwhile to say. Popularised by ESPN's Keith Olberman, paraphrasing Winston Churchill's claimed reaction when confronting an entrance essay at Eton *US, 1997*

I heard it on the marl road used for expressing rumour as the source of information *CAYMAN ISLANDS, 1985*

I heard that! I agree with you! *US, 1992*

I heard ya used for expressing assent *US, 1992*

ike *noun* a feeling of displeasure, a bad mood *UK, 1998*

Ikey *noun* **1** a Jewish person. Derogatory; an abbreviation of the name Isaac *UK, 1835.* **2** a student of the University of Cape Town, especially a member of one of the University's sports teams *SOUTH AFRICA, 1921*

Ikey Mo *noun* a Jewish person *UK, 1922*

I kid you not used for humorously assuring the truth of the matter asserted. The signature line of Jack Parr, host of the late-night *Jack Parr Show* (NBC, 1957–62). Repeated with referential humour *US, 1967*

Ilie Nastase *noun* a lavatory. Rhyming slang for KARZY, formed from the name of the Romanian tennis player (b.1946) *UK, 1998*

I liiiiike it! used for expressing approval. A catchphrase from the film *The Rocketeer*, 1991 *US, 1991*

ill *verb* **1** to perform excellently; to do anything superbly. Originally black usage, generally 'to be illin' rather than 'to ill'; became widespread with hip-hop culture *US, 1992.* **2** to undergo severe mental stress *US, 1989*

ill *adjective* **1** good, pleasing, desirable, admirable *US, 1991.* **2** wild or crazy. Originally black usage, from the verb sense; spread through hip-hop culture *US, 1979.* **3** wrong. Originally black usage, probably a variation on 'sick'; widespread with hip-hop culture *US, 1994*

ill-ass *adjective* excellent, superb *US, 2001*

I'll be buggered!; I'm buggered! used for registering surprise *UK, 1966*

I'll be damned!; well, I'm damned! used as a general-purpose exclamation; also as an intensification of a personal opinion *UK, 1925*

ill-behaved *adjective* said of a computer program that becomes dysfunctional because of repeated error *US, 1991*

I'll bet! ▷*see:* I BET!

I'll be there *noun* a chair. Rhyming slang *UK, 1961*

I'll bet you a fat man used for expressing supreme confidence *US, 1963*

illegal tegel *noun* any native or game bird taken illegally for food. Tegel™ is a brand of dressed poultry *NEW ZEALAND, 1989*

illegit *noun* a person or thing of questionable legality *US, 1954*

illegits *noun* dice that have been altered for cheating *US, 1977*

iller *adjective* worse *US, 1979*

illest *adjective* best *US, 2002*

I'll holla used as a farewell *US, 1998*

illies *noun* marijuana *UK, 2003*

illin'; ill *verb* to behave in a wild or crazy manner. Originally black usage, generally 'to be illin' rather than 'to ill'; became widespread with hip-hop culture *US, 1986*

illing *noun* marijuana *UK, 2003*

illing *adjective* bad, troubling *US, 1980*

illo *noun* an illustration *US, 1982*

ill piece *noun* a male homosexual despised by his peers *US, 1970*

I'll tell you what I'm gonna do used as a humorous, self-explanatory if nonce announcement of intent. Popularised by Sid Stone, announcer on the *Texaco Star Theater*, hosted by Milton Berle (1948–1951). One of the very first television-spawned catchphrases to become part of the national vocabulary *US, 1948*

illy *noun* **1** a cigarette infused with embalming fluid *US, 2001.* **2** marijuana, especially sensimillia (a very potent marijuana from a plant with seedless buds) *US, 1995*

illywhacker *noun* a confidence trickster. Agent noun from the obsolete phrase 'whack the illy' (to swindle; to perform confidence tricks). 'Illy' may possibly be a variant of obsolete 'eelie' (a confidence trick) which in turn is possibly from 'eeler-spee', a Pig Latin variant of SPIELER. This word was all but dead prior to gaining new life due to Peter Carey's 1985 novel *Illywhacker AUSTRALIA, 1941*

I'ma used to preface an intention. A slurred elision of 'I am going to', or 'I'm LIKE' *US, 2001*

I'm about it! I agree with your plan of action! *US, 1999*

imaginitis *noun* an overactive imagination *AUSTRALIA, 1944*

I'm all right, Jack! a smug declaration of self-satisfaction. Used as the title of a 1959 film *UK, 2002*

I-man *noun* an investigator from the Interstate Commerce Commission *US, 1938*

I'm Audi; I'm Audi 5000 I'm leaving now *US, 1995*

imbo *noun* a fool; an imbecile *AUSTRALIA, 1953*

I'm deep enough I quit, pay me *US, 1954*

I mean used for emphasis on that which follows *US, 1967*

I mean that! I agree with what you just said! *US, 1977*

I mean to say! used as an emphasis of the speaker's sincerity *UK, 1843*

I'm gone used as a farewell *US, 1993*

I'm history used as a farewell *US, 1984*

IMHO in my humble opinion. A ubiquitous piece of computer shorthand *US, 1991*

immo *adjective* imitation *US, 1994*

immortal *noun* in stud poker, any hand that is certain to win; the best possible hand *US, 1947*

IMNSHO used as Internet shorthand to mean 'in my not so humble opinion' *US, 1995*

IMO used as Internet shorthand to mean 'in my opinion' *US, 1995*

Imp *noun* a Chrysler Imperial car *US, 1961*

impact zone *noun* an area where the waves are breaking. Surfer usage *SOUTH AFRICA, 2003*

import *noun* a date who comes from out of town *US, 1926*

impressionist *noun* a person who is more interested in the impression they are making than they are in their substance *TRINIDAD AND TOBAGO, 1989*

improve *noun* ▶ **on the improve** improving *AUSTRALIA, 1959*

Improved Scot *noun* in Hudson Bay, a person of mixed Scottish and Indian blood *CANADA, 1987*

imps file *noun* a journalists' dossier on an important person or persons *UK, 1976*

I'm serious! used for expressing strong agreement with what has just been said *US, 1981*

I'm sideways used as a farewell *US, 1993*

I'm sure!; I'm so sure! used for expressing great doubt *US, 1982*

I'm there! I agree! I approve! *US, 1977*

in *noun* **1** an inside connection *US, 1929.* **2** an introduction *US, 1945.* **3** in a casino, the amount of cash collected at a table in exchange for chips. An abbreviation of 'buy-in' *US, 1980.* ▶ **the in** exclusive and positive access to something *UK, 2003*

in *adjective* **1** fashionable *UK, 1960.* **2** socially accepted; popular *US, 1929.* **3** assured of having amatory success *AUSTRALIA, 1960.* **4** experiencing good luck or the like *AUSTRALIA, 1960.* **5** incarcerated *US, 1903*

in *preposition* ▶ **be in it** to be actively and ethusiastically involved *AUSTRALIA, 1928*

-in *suffix* used in combination with a simple verb to create a communal activity as a means of protest, as in 'love-in' or 'teach-in' *US, 1937*

in a minute used as a farewell *US, 1992*

in-and-out *noun* **1** sex at its most basic *US, 1996.* **2** the nose. Rhyming slang for 'snout' *UK, 1960.* **3** a tout; a ticket tout. Rhyming slang *UK, 1998.* **4** a cigarette; tobacco. Rhyming slang for SNOUT *UK, 1998*

in-and-out-man *noun* an opportunist thief or burglar *UK, 1957*

in a pig's valise! used for expressing how very unlikely something is. The title of a late-1990s play by Eric Overmyer *US, 1957*

in betweens *noun* amphetamine tablets; depressant tablets; a mixture of amphetamines and barbiturates *US, 1975*

inbred *noun* a doctor with doctor parents. Medical slang *UK, 2002*

Inca message *noun* cocaine. A specific allusion to Peru, but generally a reference to South America as a source of cocaine *US, 1984*

incandescent *adjective* furiously angry *UK, 2004*

incantation *noun* in computing, an esoteric command *US, 1991*

incense *noun* **1** amyl nitrite or butyl nitrite. The pungent vapours are inhaled, hence the term *US, 1980*. **2** heroin *UK, 2003*

incest *noun* sex between two similar homosexual types, such as two effeminate men *US, 1972*

inch-and-a-half *noun* overtime pay at the standard overtime rate of one and a half the regular rate *US, 1984*

inch boy *noun* a male who has or is thought to have a small penis *US, 1997*

include me out! leave me out! A catchphrase coined by film mogul Samuel Goldwyn, 1882–1974 *US, 1938*

include war *noun* a prolonged inflammatory debate in an Internet discussion group in which the mass of former postings and counterpostings included make it impossible to follow who is saying what and when *US, 1995*

income tax *noun* fines paid by prostitutes *UK, 1947*

incoming *noun* enemy fire, especially artillery or mortar fire that is about to land *US, 1977*

incoming! used as a warning of impending enemy mortar or rocket fire *US, 1976*

increase the peace! used as a call for an end to violence *US, 1990*

indeedy *adverb* indeed. An intentionally folksy and intensifying addition of a syllable *US, 1856*

In Deep Shit *nickname* Iain Duncan Smith, Conservative Party leader (2001–2003). Back-formation from Smith's initials: IDS *UK, 2001*

index *noun* the face *US, 1945*

India *noun* marijuana. Variations of INDIAN HAY or INDIAN HEMP. Also known as 'Indian' *UK, 1978*

Indian *noun* **1** an Indian meal, especially in, or prepared by, a restaurant *UK, 1998*. **2** an active firefighter, as distinguished from a Chief and other officers *US, 1954*

Indiana green *noun* green marijuana claimed to have been grown in the state of Indiana *US, 1965*

Indiana pants *noun* boots *US, 1964*

Indian boy marijuana *UK, 2001*

Indian charm *noun* the arm. Rhyming slang *UK, 1998*

Indian cocktail; Indian tea; Indian tonic *noun* liquid poison as a means of suicide *TRINIDAD AND TOBAGO, 1985*

Indian Country; Injun Country *noun* during war, any area with a strong enemy presence *US, 1945*

Indian hand-rubbed *noun* a powerful hashish from Himachel Pradesh in Northern India *2003*

Indian hay *noun* marijuana *US, 1936*

Indian Heads *noun* the Second Infantry Division, US Army. So named because of the Division's insignia *US, 1991*

Indian hemp *noun* marijuana. From 'East Indian hemp', the familiar name for *Cannabis indica US, 1986*

Indian ice cream *noun* a bitter confection made from soopolallie berries, water, and white sugar *CANADA, 1989*

Indian Indian *noun* an American Indian who has retained his indigenous culture and language *US, 1963*

Indian list *noun* the Interdict list, a law forbidding a person from buying, selling or consuming alcohol; by extension any list of those who may not buy alcohol *CANADA, 1958*

Indian nigga *noun* a member of a British Indian (Hindi) urban youth gang or subculture *UK, 2006*

Indian rope *noun* marijuana. A play on 'hemp' as a material used in the making of ropes, HEMP (marijuana) and, perhaps, the Indian rope trick as a magical method of getting high *US, 1986*

Indian steak *noun* bologna *US, 1963*

Indian talk *noun* in trucking, smoke rising from a diesel smoke stack. An allusion to smoke signals used by American Indians to communicate over long distances *US, 1971*

Indian time *noun* used for denoting a lack of punctuality *US, 1963*

Indian weed *noun* marijuana. A variation of INDIAN HAY or INDIAN HEMP *US, 1986*

indie *noun* a vague categorisation within rock music, familiar since the 1980s and identified as 'serious' music that is marketed as independent and non-commercial, in its bid for commercial success. Also used as an adjective *UK, 1993*. ▶ **the Indie** the *Independent* (the youngest of the UK's national daily newspapers) first published in October 1986. The Sunday edition is less well-known as 'the Sindie' *UK, 2003*

indie; indy *adjective* independent *US, 1928*

Indo *noun* **1** Indonesia *AUSTRALIA, 1991*. **2** an Indonesian *AUSTRALIA, 1966*. **3** marijuana cultivated in Indonesia *US, 1993*

Indon *noun* an Indonesian. This has for the most part died out in favour of INDO *AUSTRALIA, 1966*

Indonesian bud *noun* **1** marijuana cultivated in Indonesia *UK, 1998*. **2** heroin *UK, 2003*

industrial language *noun* swearing, profanity *US, 1984*

Indy *nickname* the Indianapolis Speedway, home to a 500-mile race every May *US, 1965*

inexplicable mob *noun* a large crowd that materialises in a public place to perform a scripted action for several minutes before dissolving *US, 2003*

infant killer *noun* a paedophile. Prison use *UK, 2002*

infant mortality *noun* the tendency of computer components to fail within the first few weeks of operation *US, 1991*

infernal *adjective* execrable, detestable, annoying *UK, 1764*

infernally *adverb* detestably, execrably, annoyingly *UK, 1638*

infil *verb* (of military troops or spies) to *infil*trate. Military *UK, 1995*

infinitely fine *adjective* in computing, used as the ultimate praise *US, 1990*

in flaggers *noun* in *flagrante delicto* (in the commission of a crime; red-handed). The first syllable elaborated by application of the Oxford -ER *AUSTRALIA, 1973*

influence *noun* ▶ **under the influence** drunk or drug-intoxicated *UK, 1937*

info *noun information US, 1907*

Ingerland *noun* England, especially the England football team. A phonetic representation of the word England as chanted by a sports crowd *UK: ENGLAND, 2005*

Ingersol Willie *noun* in horse racing, the track's official timer of morning workouts *US, 1951*

In Hock Constantly *noun* the owner of an International Harvester Company truck. A back-formation from the company's initials: IHC *US, 1971*

ink *noun* **1** space or coverage in a newspaper *US, 1953*. **2** oil *US, 1976*. **3** inexpensive wine *US, 1917*. **4** alcoholic drink. Probably a back-formation from INKED which appears from C19 *AUSTRALIA, 1977*. ▶ **ink in the pen** the ability to achieve erection and to ejaculate *US, 1967*

ink *verb* in the production of comics books, to draw over pencil art with a pen *US, 1997*

ink-and-paper man *noun* a counterfeiter who uses a printing press *US, 1985*

inked; inked up *adjective* drunk *AUSTRALIA, 1898*

inked in *adjective* planned *UK, 1994*

inkie *noun* in the television and film industries, an incandescent light bulb *UK, 1960*

inkie-dinkie *noun* in the television and film industries, a 250-watt light source *UK, 1960*

ink-slinger *noun* a clerical employee *US, 1889*

ink stick *noun* a fountain pen *US, 1942*

inky *noun* **1** a newspaper, especially one dedicated to music journalism *UK, 2003*. **2** a felt-tipped pen. Used in Glasgow schools *UK: SCOTLAND, 1988*

inland squid *noun* a surfer who does not live at or near the beach *US, 1987*

inmate *noun* used as a term of derision, applied to a prisoner who follows prison rules and curries favour with the prison administration *US, 1984*

innards *noun* **1** the entrails, the stomach, the guts. A dialect and vulgar alteration of 'inwards' *UK, 1825*. **2** the inner workings of a car's engine or transmission *US, 1993*

inner space *noun* a person's deepest psychological being *US, 1967*

innie *noun* an inward-turned navel *US, 1966*

innit isn't it?; also used as a general purpose tag regardless of grammatical context. Originally, and still, a lazily pronounced interrogative referring back to the verb 'is' in the preceding sentence, e.g. 'It's raining, innit?' *UK, 1959*

in on *preposition* being a part of something; participating in or sharing in something *UK, 1923*

ins-and-outs *noun* ▶ **want to know the ins-and-outs of a cat's arse; want to know the ins-and-outs of a duck's arse** to be very inquisitive. Generally in catchphrase form as 'you want to know', 'he'd want to know', etc. Variations include 'the ins-and-outs of a nag's arse', also 'of a duck's backside' and 'of a duck's bum' *UK, 1984*

insane *adjective* **1** excellent *US, 1955*. **2** fearless; willing to try anything for fun *US, 1997*. **3** ridiculous, in either a good or bad way *US, 1997*

insanely great *adjective* in computing, magnificent to a degree that can be fully grasped by only the most proficient practitioners *US, 1991*

insaniac *noun* a lunatic. A compound of 'insane' and 'maniac' *UK, 1999*

insanity stripe *noun* in the US armed forces, the insignia designating a three-year enlistment *US, 1946*

insects and ants *noun* men's underpants. Rhyming slang *UK, 1960*

insensitive care unit *noun* a hospital's intensive care unit *US, 1989*

inside *adverb* imprisoned *UK, 1888*

inside job *noun* a crime committed by, or with the assistance of, someone who lives or works in the place where it occurs *UK, 1908*

inside man *noun* in a big con swindle, a confederate to whom the victim is turned over once he has been lured into the enterprise *US, 1940*

inside oil *noun* inside information *AUSTRALIA, 1966*

insider *noun* a pocket *US, 1945*

inside the Beltway *noun* literally, the area of Washington D.C. surrounded by a motorway known as the Capital Beltway; figuratively, the Washington political and journalistic establishment *US, 1977*

inside track *noun* a position of advantage; information which provides such an advantage. A figurative use of racing wisdom *US, 1857*

inside work *noun* any internal alteration of dice for cheating *US, 1963*

instaga; instagu *noun* marijuana *UK, 2003*

Instamatic *noun* a police radar unit used for measuring vehicle speed. A brand name extrapolation from CAMERA (a generic term for radar) *US, 1976*

Instant Dictator Kit *noun* in the Canadian military, items of brass and braid that transform an ordinary uniform into a ceremonial one *CANADA, 1995*

instant LZ *noun* a 10,000- to 15,000-pound bomb used to clear jungle and create an instant landing zone in Vietnam. The bomb was designed to create a wide but shallow crater in the jungle, literally creating an instant landing zone *US, 1981*

instant zen *noun* LSD *US, 1972*

insurance cheater *noun* in oil drilling, a safety belt *US, 1954*

intel *noun* military intelligence *AUSTRALIA, 1961*

intellectual *noun* in the army, a member of the intelligence section *UK, 1993*

intellectual hour *noun* all time spent watching cartoons on television *US, 1980*

intelligence centre *noun* a field latrine. Gulf war usage *US, 1991*

intense *adjective* extreme, wild. A conventional adjective rendered slang by attitude and pronunciation, emphasis on the second syllable *US, 1982*

Inter *nickname* the intermediate examination taken after completing the first three years of secondary school in Ireland *IRELAND, 1998*

Intercourse 80 *nickname* Interstate 80, a major east–west motorway in the US *US, 1977*

intercoursed *adjective* exhausted. Archly euphemistic for FUCKED *UK, 1979*

interesting *adjective* in computing, annoying or difficult *US, 1991*

interesting, yes – provocative used for expressing possible interest in what has just been said. A catchphrase from the film *Tommy Boy US, 1997*

interior decorating *noun* the act of having sex during the day. Upper-class society usage *UK, 1982*

Interlake potato *noun* a rock *CANADA, 1987*

internal *noun* a person who smuggles drugs inside their bodies *US, 1997*

internals *noun* intrusive medical examinations as part of sexual role-play, especially when advertised as a service offered by a prostitute *UK, 2003*

International House of Pancakes *noun* a hospital ward for severe stroke victims, who lie in bed muttering in their own language *US, 1978*

international milk thief *noun* a petty thief. An example of police humour; heavily ironic *UK, 1977*

interrogation by altitude *noun* the reported practice by US troops of interrogating a group of suspected Viet Cong in a helicopter, throwing those who refused to answer to their death below and thus encouraging cooperation from those left *US, 1990*

in the nude *noun* food. Rhyming slang *UK, 1979*

in there; in thar *adjective* excellent. An allusion to surfing inside the hollow of a breaking wave *US, 1991*

into *preposition* **1** in debt to *US, 1893*. **2** in organised crime, in control of *US, 1985*. **3** interested in; participating in *US, 1965*

intro *noun* an introduction *UK, 1923*

intro *verb* to introduce *US, 1986*

invertebrated *adjective* very drunk *US, 1982*

investment *noun* a bet, especially on a horse race *NEW ZEALAND, 1944*

invitation *noun* a speeding ticket. A humorous euphemism *US, 1976*

invite *noun* an invitation. A verb-as-noun that began as standard English and then evolved into slang *UK, 1659*

in with *preposition* in a friendly or social relationship with someone *UK, 1677*

in you go, says Bob Munro used as a toast. If a real Bob Munro gave his name to this toast, he is lost in the alcohol fog of history *NEW ZEALAND, 1999*

in-your-chops *adjective* direct, provocative *UK, 2004*

in-your-face; in-yo-face *adjective* aggressive, provocative *US, 1988*

in your oils *adjective* delighted; in your element. From Welsh *hwyl* (mood) *UK: WALES, 1985*

IOW used as Internet shorthand to mean 'in other words' *US, 1997*

I owe you money or what? why are you looking at me that way? Hawaiian youth usage *US, 1981*

IQ anniversary *noun* the anniversary of a person's quitting smoking. The 'IQ' stems from '*I Quit*', punning on the more commonly understood sense of the abbreviation *US, 1998*

IQ Charley *noun* a half-wit. Teen slang; unkind *US, 1955*

irie; irey *adjective* good, great, wonderful *JAMAICA, 1994*

iris *noun* an Indian homosexual male. Gay slang, formed on the name Iris, probably elaborating the initial 'I' for 'Indian', and originating among Cape coloureds *SOUTH AFRICA, 2000*

Irish *noun* Irish imports, such as snuff, whisky, linen, tea, etc. Linen from 1784, snuff from 1834 and whisky from 1889 *UK, 1982*

Irish *nickname* any athletic team from Notre Dame University. An abbreviation of the fuller FIGHTING IRISH *US, 1975*

Irish apple *noun* a potato *UK, 1896*

Irish baby buggy *noun* a wheelbarrow *US, 1919*

Irish banjo *noun* a shovel *US, 1941*

Irish clubhouse *noun* a police stationhouse *US, 1904*

Irish confetti *noun* **1** semen spilled on a woman's body *US, 1987*. **2** stones, bricks, etc, when used as offensive missiles *US, 1913*. **3** small stones kept in a pocket for disciplining sheepdogs *NEW ZEALAND, 1961*

Irish curtain *noun* on Prince Edward Island, a cobweb inside the house *CANADA, 1988*

Irisher *noun* a person of Irish descent *US, 1807*

Irish horse *noun* **1** salted beef *UK, 1748*. **2** a flaccid or impotent penis *US, 1987*

Irish hurricane *noun* a flat calm sea *US, 1803*

Irish jig; Irish *noun* a wig. Rhyming slang *UK, 1972*

Irish lace; Irish lace curtains *noun* a spider's cobweb *US, 1950*

Irish linen *noun* in pool, the cloth used as a grip on the end of a cue stick *US, 1993*

Irishman's gate *noun* any makeshift gate *NEW ZEALAND, 1977*

Irish pennant *noun* a dangling thread on a recruit's uniform. Marine humour, marine usage *US, 1941*

Irish picnic wagon *noun* a police van *US, 1996*

Irish pop *noun* a shot of whisky and glass of beer *US, 1982*

Irish rose *noun* the nose. Rhyming slang *UK, 1961*

Irish shave *noun* an act of defecation *US, 1979*

Irish steak *noun* cheese. An allusion to Irish poverty *UK: SCOTLAND, 1988*

Irish sulk *noun* a fit of depression after being spirited and happy *CANADA, 1982*

Irish toothache *noun* **1** an erection *UK, 1882*. **2** pregnancy *US, 1972*

Irish turkey *noun* corned beef *US, 1915*

Irish waterfall *noun* a manner of cigarette smoking in which smoke is drawn into the mouth and then allowed to drift out and upwards for inhalation through the nose *UK, 2003*

Irish wedding *noun* masturbation *US, 1987*

Irish whip *noun* in handball, a stroke hitting the ball close to the body *US, 1972*

iron *noun* **1** a gun, especially a handgun *US, 1838*. **2** the penis *UK, 1706*. **3** money *UK, 1705*. **4** in the used car business, collectively the worst cars on the sales lot *US, 1975*. **5** an old, dilapidated truck *US, 1971*. **6** in hot rodding, a custom-built chrome bumper *US, 1956*. **7** an older mainframe computer *US, 1991*. **8** a railway track *US, 1977*. ▶ **push iron; bump iron; drive iron; pump iron** to lift weights. Prison use *US, 1965*

Iron Age *noun* in computing, the period approximately between 1961 (the first PDP-1) and 1971 (the first commercial microprocessor) *US, 1991*

iron ass *noun* a stern, demanding, unrelenting person *US, 1942*

iron ben *noun* a bullet-proof vest *US, 1949*

ironbender *noun* a severe foreman, a strict disciplinarian *CANADA, 1956*

iron bomb *noun* a conventional aerial bomb that is simply dropped from the sky without any targeting capability in the bomb *US, 1962*

iron box *noun* a domestic iron *INDIA, 1979*

iron cure *noun* the sudden and complete deprivation of a drug to an addict in jail who suffers intensely *US, 1973*

iron curtain *noun* a girdle *US, 1968*

iron dog *noun* a snowmobile *US, 1961*

iron door *noun* ▶ **behind the iron door** in prison *US, 1992*

iron duke *noun* in poker, a hand that is either certain to win or at least played as if it is certain to win *US, 1967*

iron girder *noun* a murder. Rhyming slang *UK, 1998*

iron God *noun* the Burroughs B-550 computer *US, 1968*

iron hat *noun* a safety helmet. Most commonly known as a 'hard hat' *US, 1954*

iron hoof; iron *noun* a male homosexual. Rhyming slang for POOF *UK, 1936*

iron horse *noun* a tank or other armoured vehicle *US, 1918*

iron idiot *noun* an imprecise but easily manoeuvred manual sight on a tank's main gun *US, 1986*

Iron Lady *nickname* British Prime Mininster (1979–90) Margaret Hilda Thatcher (b.1925). Coined by the Soviet media for Thatcher's unyielding anti-communist sentiments; always used with 'the' *UK, 1976*

iron lot *noun* a used car business specialising in old, inexpensive cars *US, 1975*

iron lung *noun* a tip, a gratuity. Glasgow rhyming slang for BUNG *UK, 1985*

iron man *noun* one US silver dollar ($1). From the metal coin *US, 1908*

Iron Mike *noun* **1** a bicycle. Rhyming slang for 'bike', formed from the nickname of US boxer Mike Tyson (b.1966) *UK, 1998*. **2** a pair of brass knuckles *US, 1949*

iron mouth *noun* any person with orthodontia *US, 1979*

iron nose *noun* in British Columbia, a steelhead trout *CANADA, 1963*

iron out *verb* **1** to correct a misunderstanding, to negotiate differences and achieve agreement, to put right *UK, 1930*. **2** to knock a person down; to flatten *AUSTRALIA, 1953*

iron pile *noun* the area in a prison recreation yard where the weightlifting equipment is kept *US, 1962*

iron pony *noun* a motorcyle *US, 1945*

irons *noun* **1** handcuffs. Also used in the singular *US, 1929*. **2** in horse racing, stirrups *US, 1951*. **3** tyre chains used for winter driving *US, 1971*

iron skull *noun* on the railways, a boilermaker *US, 1946*

iron tank *noun* a bank. Rhyming slang *UK, 1960*

Iron Triangle *noun* **1** a major North Korean industrial complex between Pyongyang to the north, Chorwon to the west and Kumhwa to the east *US, 1968*. **2** a dense jungle area near the Cu Chi District of South Vietnam, about 20 miles northwest of Saigon, dominated by the Viet Cong and the scene of heavy fighting *US, 1966*

iron undies *noun* the notional underwear worn by a woman who is not willing to have sex *NEW ZEALAND, 2002*

iron worker *noun* a criminal who specialises in breaking into safes *US, 1949*

iron yard *noun* the area where weight lifting equipment is left and used, especially in prison *US, 1995*

I say! used for attracting attention or for registering surprise or pleasure *UK, 1909*

I say, I say, I say! used as a catchphrase introduction to a corny joke. From music hall comedy routines *UK, 1927*

isda *noun* heroin *US, 1977*

I see nothing used as a humorous expression of complicity. A catchphrase from the unlikely wacky-Nazi-POW-camp-comedy television programme *Hogan's Heroes* (CBS, 1965–71). Uttered frequently by Sergeant Hans Schultz, the full phrase was 'I see nothing, I hear nothing, I know nothing!'. Repeated with referential humour *US, 1965*

I see, said the blind man (and he saw) used for expressing sudden comprehension in a teasing and humorous way *US, 1991*

ish *noun* an *issue* (of a magazine, especially a single-interest fan magazine) *US, 1967*. ▶ **the ish** a Royal Marine *issued* with all possible kit; or a full complement of equipment. Derives from '*issue*' *UK, 1987*

-ish *suffix* **1** added to an adjective or phrase to form a less precise adjective, or to suggest a vaguer, often wider, interpretation of the proceeding adjective or phrase *UK, 1815*. **2** added to a proper name to form an adjective *UK, 1845*

I shit them I am superior *UK, 1979*

I shit you not I am very serious *US, 1986*

I should cocoa!; I should coco! I should say so. Rhyming slang, 'coffee and cocoa', unusually reduced to its second element. Derisive and sarcastic *UK, 1936*

I shouldn't wonder! I should not be surprised *UK, 1836*

ishy *adjective* disgusting, unappealing *US, 1968*

is it? **1** used for registering a mild disbelief *UK, 1994*. **2** used for indicating polite interest, astonishment, incredulity, etc. Used rhetorically without regard to gender, subject or number. Sometimes spelt '*izzit*' *SOUTH AFRICA, 1970*

Island *noun* ▶ **the Island** the Isle of Wight, off the south coast of England; in particular the prisons: HMP Camp Hill, HMP Albany or HMP Parkhurst *UK, 1956*

Isle of Man *noun* a pan. Rhyming slang, formed on the name of the island off the north west of England *UK, 1992*

Isle of Wight *noun* a light. Rhyming slang *UK, 1998*

Isle of Wight *adjective* **1** right; both as an expression of approval and indicative of direction. Rhyming slang, formed from the name of the island off the south coast of England *UK, 1960*. **2** tight (in a state of drunkenness or mean with money). Rhyming slang *UK, 1992*

I smell bacon! there are police nearby! A catchphrase from *Wayne's World*, heard before but popularised by it *US, 1993*

isn't it? used rhetorically, without regard to gender, subject or number: is that not so? *SOUTH AFRICA, 1956*

isn't that special? used for expressing sarcastic disdain. From Dana Carvey's 'Church Lady' skit on *Saturday Night Live US, 1987*

Israelite *noun* someone who is temporarily without money *JAMAICA, 1969*

issue *noun* a problem. Often used in a mocking way, borrowing from the lexicon of self-improvement and popular psychotherapy. Most often heard in the plural *US, 1999*

issues *noun* crack cocaine *UK, 2003*

-ista *suffix* when combined with a subject-noun, a follower or aficionado of something or someone. From Spanish. An example is FASHIONISTA *UK, 2003*

is the Pope (a) Catholic? yes; a nonsense retort used as an affirmative answer to a silly question, often sarcastic. Often mixed with the synonymous DO BEARS SHIT IN THE WOODS? to achieve DOES THE POPE SHIT IN THE WOODS? Used in the UK since the 1970s *US, 1977*

I suppose *noun* a nose. Rhyming slang *UK, 1859*

I swallow! used as a cry of submission *UK, 2000*

iswas *noun* a contemptible, very much disliked person. This appears to be a compound of 'is' and 'was' and is therefore perhaps implying that the person so described is (soon to be) in the past tense. Noted in connection with a legal dispute over rap lyrics by *BBC News*, 6th June 2003 *UK, 2003*

is your father a glass maker? used to suggest that somebody in front of you at a public event sit down and stop blocking your view *TRINIDAD AND TOBAGO, 2003*

it *noun* **1** sex *UK, 1599*. **2** the penis *US, 1846*. **3** a short-term sexual partner, a casual pick-up *UK, 2002*. **4** in male homosexual usage, a heterosexual male or a homosexual male who is not part of the speaker's inner circle *US, 1981*

It *noun* sweet vermouth. Originally *I*talian vermouth as used in 'gin and it' *UK, 1937*

it ain't over 'til the fat lady sings used as a humorous aphorism meaning that something is not over until it is over. The battle cry of those who are about to lose *US, 1992*

ital *adjective* natural, unadulterated; (of food) organic, salt-free; (of sex) without a condom *JAMAICA, 1994*

Italian airlines *noun* walking *US, 1987*

Italian mausoleum *noun* a car boot (trunk). From the stereotype of the corpses of Mafia murder victims being stuffed in car boots *US, 1982*

Italian shower *noun* a liberal application of aftershave or scent *UK, 1997*

ITALY written on an envelope, or at the foot of a lover's letter, as lovers' code for 'I trust and love you'. Widely-known, and well-used by servicemen but, apparently, has not transferred to the coded vocabulary of texting *UK, 1960*

itch *noun* ▶ **he (she) wouldn't give you the itch** said of a person with a reputation for meanness. In Glasgow use *UK, 1988*

itch *verb* to have a desire to do something *UK, 1225*

itch and scratch; itch *noun* a match (a vesta) *UK, 1931*

itchy backside *noun* said of a restless person *SINGAPORE, 2002*

itchy feet *noun* **1** attributed to a person who is restless *UK, 1984*. **2** attributed to a prison inmate who is considered to be a potential absconder. A specialisation of 'have itchy feet' (to be restless) *UK, 1978*

itchy pussy *noun* a Mitsubishi car *US, 1992*

ite all right (as an adjective, or a greeting). A shortening of 'all right'. Teen slang *UK, 2003*

item *noun* a romantically-linked couple. Expressing a commitment that the two individuals be considered as a single item *US, 1981*

Itie *noun* an Italian. Variation of EYETIE *UK, 1941*

Itie *adjective* Italian *AUSTRALIA, 1988*

-itis *suffix* used to create imaginary medical conditions, such as lazyitis (congenital laziness) and cobitis (an aversion to prison food) *US, 1912*

it's all good used for expressing optimism or a sense that all is well in the world *US, 1995*

it's been great used as a farewell *US, 1969*

it's been real used as a farewell, suggesting that the time spent together has been enjoyable *US, 1982*

it's better to give than receive used as a declaration that it is better to be the active rather than passive partner in homosexual anal intercourse. A charitable philosophy *UK, 2000*

it's breakfast! used by firefighters in the woods to mean that the fire is out and their work is finished *US, 1991*

it's dead the issue being discussed need not be discussed any further *US, 2002*

it's hard to feel good about that used as an intentionally laconic expression of sympathy or commiseration *US, 1987*

it's not my job used for expressing a lack of interest in helping to do something. A signature line of comedian Freddie Prinze on the television comedy *Chico and the Man* (NBC, 1974–78). Repeated with referential humour *US, 1974*

it's not the end of the world! offered as consolation to someone who has suffered a mishap *UK, 1984*

it's on! used for announcing the start of hostilities between youth gangs *US, 1953*

it's the oil that counts in oil drilling, used for expressing doubt about any new process, equipment or idea *US, 1954*

it's there used as a stock answer about something that is acceptable but not great *CANADA, 1993*

itsy bitsy *noun* the vagina. Childish euphemism *US, 1998*

itsy-bitsy *adjective* tiny *US, 1938*

it's you used as a greeting *US, 1973*

it takes all sorts an elliptical variation of the homespun philosophy: it takes all sorts to make a world (or a universe) *UK, 1951*

it takes one to know one you are as bad as the person you are criticising *UK, 1984*

itty *adjective* tiny. A childish form of 'little' *UK, 1798*

itty-bitty *adjective* tiny. A reduplicated variation of ITTY, perhaps by combination with BITTY *UK, 1938*

Ivan *noun* a Russian, especially a soldier; the nation of Russia; sometimes used in the plural to represent Russians in general. Originally military; the popular male forename is the Russian equivalent to John *US, 1944*

ivories *noun* **1** the teeth *UK, 1782*. **2** the keys of a piano or a similar instrument *UK, 1818*. **3** dice *US, 1962*. **4** billiard or pool balls *UK, 1875*.
▶ **spank the ivories** play the piano in a jazz-style *US, 1944*.
▶ **tickle the ivories** to play the piano *UK, 1930*

ivory flake *noun* cocaine *US, 1983*

ivory soap *noun* in dominoes, the double blank piece *US, 1959*

ivory tower *noun* used as a metaphor for an attitude that is elitist, intellectual and removed from the real world *US, 1911*

I wonder! I doubt it!, I can't believe it!; I think it may be so *UK, 1922*

I wouldn't fuck her with your dick used as a jocular disparagement of a woman's sexual attractiveness *US, 1974*

I wouldn't kick her out of bed; I wouldn't kick that out of bed used as an expression of general sexual interest. Sometimes elaborated as 'I wouldn't kick her out of bed for farting' or '... for eating crackers' *UK, 1984*

ixnay no. Pig Latin for 'nix' *US, 1929*

-iz- *infix* used as an infix to hide the meaning of a word. Used in prison and other fields with a tentative relationship to the law. 'Dope' becomes 'dizope' *US, 1976*

-iz-i *infix* an embellishment that adds no meaning to a word. Popularised by Frankie Smith in the 1999 song 'Double Dutch Bus' *US, 1999*

IZM; ism; izm *noun* marijuana *US, 1992*

Izzy *noun* any Jewish male *US, 1949*

Jj

J *noun* **1** a marijuana cigarette. 'J' is for JOINT *US, 1967.* **2** in a deck of playing cards, a jack *US, 1988.* **3** money. An abbreviation of JACK *US, 1982*

JA *noun* **1** Jamaica *JAMAICA, 1994.* **2** a Jamaican *JAMAICA, 2000*

jab *noun* an intravenous drug injection *US, 1914*

jab *verb* to inject a drug intravenously *US, 1908*

jabba; fat jabba *noun* an overweight or unattractive person, especially a school fellow; especially used as a playground insult. After the character Jabba the Hutt, introduced to cinema goers in *Return of the Jedi*, 1983 *UK, 2003*

jabber *noun* **1** a syringe *US, 1982.* **2** a drug user who injects drugs *US, 1973.* **3** a boxer *US, 1904*

jabbing jabba *noun* the act of anal sex. A nicely alliterative turn of phrase. Jabba the Hutt, created by George Lucas, is an excrementally ugly character from the *Star Wars* films; hence 'jabbing' (thrusting) into SHIT *UK, 2001*

jab-off *noun* the flooding sensations of exhilaration and euphoria following a heroin injection *US, 1973*

jack *noun* **1** anything at all; nothing at all *US, 1973.* **2** the anus. Notably in 'up your jack!' *UK, 1984.* **3** an act of masturbation *US, 2003.* **4** semen. Possibly by back-formation from JACK OFF (to masturbate) *US, 1997.* **5** a sexually transmitted infection. Short for 'jack in the box', rhyming slang for POX *AUSTRALIA, 1944.* **6** methylated spirits as an alcoholic drink. Probably a variation of JAKE *UK, 1961.* **7** a homemade alcoholic beverage, usually applejack or raisinjack *US, 1894.* **8** tobacco *US, 1949.* **9** a small heroin pill *UK, 1967.* **10** in bowls, the small white ball that serves as a target for the bowls *UK, 1611.* **11** money *US, 1890.* **12** a counterfeit double-headed coin. Origin unknown *AUSTRALIA, 1936.* **13** a robbery *US, 1988.* **14** a police officer or detective *UK, 1889.* **15** a friend *BAHAMAS, 1995.* **16** a kookaburra. Shortening of 'laughing jackass' *AUSTRALIA, 1898.* **17** a peek or a look *NEW ZEALAND, 1984*

Jack *noun* an all-purpose male name; any man; used as a male-to-male form of address. Predominantly black use *UK, 1706* ▷*see:* JACK JONES

jack *verb* **1** to steal, to take by force – especially of street crime. Adopted from 'JACK' (to hijack) *US, 1930.* **2** to lift or raise or move something, as with a carjack *AUSTRALIA, 1961.* **3** (of a male) to masturbate *US, 1995.* **4** to convey a cartridge into the chamber of a firearm *AUSTRALIA, 1995.* **5** to abandon, to dismiss *UK, 1961.* **6** to serve (a prison sentence) *US, 1966.* **7** to move the plunger of a hypodermic syringe back and forth *AUSTRALIA, 1970.* **8** to flush blood in and out of a hypodermic syringe *AUSTRALIA, 1970.* **9** to cease; to shirk *UK, 1947.* ▶ **jack someone's root** to frustrate someone *US, 1980.* ▶ **jack your jaw** to talk incessantly *US, 1983.* ▶ **jack your joint** to manoeuvre your penis during sex *US, 1997*

jack *adjective* **1** used for describing any medium used for inspiration while masturbating. Followed by the medium – 'jack pictures', 'jack flick', 'jack book', etc *US, 1990.* **2** had enough of; fed up with *AUSTRALIA, 1889*

Jack; Jack's *nickname* Jack Daniels™ whisky *US, 1972*

jackabaun *noun* in Newfoundland, a mischievous person not to be trusted. This word may have descended from the British 'jacobin' (a political reformer) *CANADA, 1982*

jackal's wedding *noun* a time when the sun shines and it rains; a sunshower. Glossed as a 'village expression' by Nigel Hankin, *Hanklyn-Janklyn,* 2003 *INDIA, 2003*

Jack and Danny *noun* **1** the buttocks, the anus. Rhyming slang for FANNY, formed from characters played by Jack Nicholson and Danny Lloyd in the Stanley Kubrick film, *The Shining,* 1980 *UK, 1992.* **2** the vagina. Rhyming slang for FANNY (the vagina) *UK, 2000.* **3** a story, lies. Rhyming slang for FANNY *UK, 2000*

Jack and Jill; Jack-and-Jill; jack *noun* **1** a bill. Rhyming slang *UK, 1960.* **2** a till, a cash register. Rhyming slang *UK, 1932.* **3** a hill. Rhyming slang, formed on the nursery rhyme couple who went up the hill *UK, 1934.* **4** a fool. Rhyming slang for DILL (a fool) *AUSTRALIA, 1973.* **5** the (contraceptive) pill. Rhyming slang *UK, 1988.* **6** a pill. Rhyming slang *UK, 1992*

Jackanory *noun* a story. Either deriving from, or the inspiration for, BBC television storytelling programme *Jackanory,* 1965–96 *UK, 1972*

jack around *verb* **1** to engage in horseplay *US, 1963.* **2** to fool around *US, 1962*

jackass *noun* a fool. A male ass and thus an elaboration of ASS (a fool) *UK, 1823*

jackatar *noun* a Newfoundlander of mixed French and Micmac ancestry *CANADA, 1966*

jack benny *noun* in hold 'em poker, a three and a nine as the first two cards dealt to a player. Comedian Benny perpetually claimed that he was 39 years old *US, 1981*

jack boat; jack schooner *noun* a two-spar gaff-rigged fishing boat in Cape Breton and Newfoundland *CANADA, 1982*

jack boy *noun* a street criminal who relies almost exclusively upon force and terror *US, 1989*

Jack Canuck *noun* a Canadian *CANADA, 1963*

Jack Dash *noun* an act of urination. Glasgow rhyming slang for SLASH *UK: SCOTLAND, 1988*

jackdaw and rook *noun* a book; specifically, in the theatre, the text of a play ('the book'). Originally theatrical *UK, 1960*

Jack Dee *noun* urine; an act of urination. Rhyming slang for WEE or PEE, formed from the name of a UK comedian-actor (b.1962). Also used as a verb *UK, 1998*

Jack Doyle *noun* a boil. Rhyming slang, formed from the name of an Irish boxer, 1913–78 *UK, 1992*

jacked *adjective* **1** stolen, especially if taken in a mugging (a violent street-crime). Alas, in ever wider-use since the early 1980s *US, 2002.* **2** caffeinated. Borrowing from the language of car fuel for application to the world of coffee drinks and, to a lesser extent, soft drinks *US, 1996.* **3** very muscular *US, 2003*

jacked up; jacked *adjective* **1** drunk, drug-intoxicated, exhilarated *US, 1935.* **2** infected with a sexually transmitted infection *AUSTRALIA, 1950*

jackeen *noun* a Dubliner. A derivative of Jack, an abbreviation of John (Bull), the national nickname for an English man originating from the character named John Bull who features as a stereotypical Englishman in 'The History of John Bull', a collection of pamphlets written by John Arbuthnot (1667–1735), issued in 1712 *IRELAND, 1998*

jacker *noun* **1** a robber, a hijacker *US, 1985.* **2** a camouflage expert *US, 1956*

jackeroo; jackaroo *noun* an apprentice station hand working on, and learning how to manage, a cattle or sheep station. Origin unknown. Suggestions have been legion, such as: the male name Jack blended with 'kangaroo'; a corruption of Johnny Raw; and borrowings from various Australian Aboriginal languages. Originally it was a Queensland word referring to a man living away from settled areas, and so may be referable to a native Queensland language *AUSTRALIA, 1845*

jackeroo; jackaroo *verb* to work as a jackeroo *AUSTRALIA, 1875*

jacket *noun* **1** a personnel file, especially in prison or the military *US, 1944.* **2** an executive not involved with actual production *US, 1997.* **3** a capsule of Nembutal™, a central nervous system depressant *US, 1952.* ▶ **get a jacket; wear a jacket** (used of a man) to accept, unknowingly, another man's child as your own *JAMAICA, 1997.* ▶ **give (someone) a jacket** (used of a woman) to name someone as the father of her child who is not actually the father *JAMAICA, 2003*. ▶ **put the jacket on someone** to frame someone, setting them up to take the blame *US, 1982*

jacket *verb* (used of a school boy) to give a girl your school jacket, signifying a steady dating relationship *US, 1954*

jack flaps *noun* fancy clothes worn by a man in pursuit of female companionship *US, 1976*

Jack Flash *noun* a crash, a smash. Rhyming slang, probably formed from the title of the Rolling Stones' song, 'Jumping Jack Flash',1968 *UK, 1992*

jack hat *noun* a condom. Combines JACK (semen) with a cover; possibly a reference to Jack 'The Hat' McVitie, a murder victim of the Kray twins *UK, 1998*

Jack Herer *noun* an extremely potent strain of marijuana, a hybrid of three of the strongest varieties. Named in honour of Jack Herer, also known as 'The Emperor of Hemp', a high-profile campaigner for the legalisation of cannabis *UK, 2003*

Jack Horner; little Jack Horner *noun* a corner. Rhyming slang; its various uses glossed as 'may be stood in, turned around or cut' *UK, 1931*

jackie *noun* in the circus or carnival, a story of past deeds or escapades *US, 1980*

Jackie Dash; jackie *noun* an act of urination. Rhyming slang, formed, apparently, from the name of a union official in London's dockland, JACK DASH, however, is recorded in Glasgow in 1988 *UK, 1998*

Jackie Howe; Jacky Howe; jacky-howe *noun* a dark blue or black sleeveless singlet worn by rural labourers. Named after Jackie (John Robert) Howe (d.1920), a champion shearer *AUSTRALIA, 1930*

Jackie Trent *adjective* dishonest, corrupt. Rhyming slang for BENT, formed from the name of a popular singer (b.1940) *UK, 2002*

jack in; jack it in *verb* 1 to abandon, to quit *UK, 1961*. 2 to log onto the Internet *US, 1995*

jackin' the beanstalk *verb* (of a male) masturbating. Cleverly punning JACK OFF (to masturbate) and STALK (the erect penis) with the famous fairytale *US, 1999*

Jack-in-the-black *noun* black-labelled Jack Daniels™ whisky *US, 1990*

jack in the box *noun* 1 the penis. Like the toy, it pops up at the least touch *UK, 1999*. 2 syphilis. Rhyming slang for POX. The shortened form 'jack' is first recorded in Australia, 1944 *UK, 1954*

jack it up to have sexual intercourse with (someone) *AUSTRALIA, 1974*

jack-jawed *adjective* dim-witted *US, 1985*

Jack Johnson *noun* an axe with the blade sticking up. Jack Johnson was a heavyweight champion boxer, the first black to win the title; his victory spurred the search for a 'Great White Hope' *CANADA, 1992*

Jack Jones; Jack; Jack Malone *noun* a state of isolation, alone. Imperfect rhyming slang for 'alone', yet in practice the rhyme often seems to be with 'own': 'on your jack' (on your own); a feeling of abandonment is often implied *UK, 1925*

Jack Ketch *noun* a term of imprisonment. Rhyming slang for STRETCH *UK, 1998*

jack-knife *verb* to double up at the waist *US, 1951*. ▶ **jack-knife your legs** (used of a man) to straighten your legs so that the crease of the trousers stands out and the turn-ups fall over the shoes *US, 1994*

Jack Lang *noun* slang; rhyming slang; Australian slang. Rhyming slang, formed from the name of Australian state politician Jack (John Thomas) Lang 1876–1975 *AUSTRALIA, 1977*

jackleg *noun* a gambler who cheats *US, 1949*

jackleg *adjective* unschooled, untrained *US, 1837*

jacko *noun* an oppossum *NEW ZEALAND, 1984*

jack-off *noun* 1 an act of masturbation *US, 1952*. 2 a despised person *US, 1938*

jack off *verb* 1 (used of a male) to masturbate. Derives from 'jack' (an erection) now obsolete, combined with JERK OFF (to

masturbate) *US, 1916*. 2 to manipulate the injection of a drug such that the drug enters the blood stream slowly *US, 1967*

jack-off artist *noun* a masturbator *US, 1991*

jack-off bar *noun* a truck's emergency brake *US, 1971*

jack-off flare *noun* a small, hand-launched aerial flare. The term is based on comparing images *US, 1987*

jack-off party *noun* a male gathering for mutual masturbation *UK, 2003*

jack of spades *noun* sunglasses. Rhyming slang for SHADES *UK, 1992*

jack of the dust *noun* aboard ship, a storekeeper of cleaning supplies *US, 1986*

jack-pack *noun* a contraption used by a masturbating male to simulate the sensation of penetration *US, 1979*

jack picture *noun* a photograph used while masturbating *US, 1972*

jackpot *noun* 1 serious trouble *US, 1887*. 2 a lot of logs crossed in every direction *US, 1905*. 3 in the circus or carnival, a story of past deeds *US, 1980*

jackrabbit *noun* a driver who starts through an intersection at the first hint of a green light *US, 1962*

jackrabbit parole *noun* escape from prison *US, 1992*

jack ready *adjective* sexually aroused *US, 1990*

Jack Rice *noun* used as a notional figure in descriptions of large objects. From the name of a famous racehorse *AUSTRALIA, 1945*

Jack Robinson *noun* ▶ **before you can say Jack Robinson; quicker than you can say Jack Robinson** instantly; almost instantly; very quickly *UK, 1700*

jack-roll *verb* 1 to rob or pick a pocket, especially to rob a drunk *US, 1916*. 2 to abduct a woman. As a crime, this was especially commonplace in the late 1980s; after 'the Jackrollers', a gang of kidnappers from the Diepkloof area of Soweto *SOUTH AFRICA, 2003*

jack-roller *noun* a person who robs drunks *US, 1922*

jacks *noun* a toilet *IRELAND, 1991*

jack's alive *noun* five, especially as five pounds sterling. Rhyming slang for 'five', sometimes abbreviated to 'jack's' *UK, 1931*

jack shit *noun* nothing, a pittance *US, 1969*

jack-slap *verb* to slap (someone) forcefully *US, 1981*

Jackson *noun* 1 a twenty-dollar note. From the portrait of US President Andrew Jackson on the note *US, 1969*. 2 used as a male-to-male term of address *US, 1941*

Jackson five *noun* one hundred dollars in twenty-dollar notes. A portrait of US President Andrew Jackson is found on the face of a $20 note, enabling this pun on the 1970s Motown recording group *US, 1983*

Jackson Pollocks; jacksons *noun* the testicles; hence, nonsense, rubbish. Rhyming slang for BOLLOCKS, based on artist Jackson Pollock (1912–56) *UK, 2002*

Jack Sprat *noun* 1 the fat (of meat). Rhyming slang *UK, 1960*. 2 an annoying or troublesome child. Rhyming slang for BRAT *UK, 1992*

Jack Straw *noun* marijuana. Jack Straw MP, UK Home Secretary 1997–2001, responsible for strengthening anti-drug legislation, was embarrassed when his son was arrested for possession of marijuana. Within days the rhyming slang 'Jack Straw' for DRAW (marijuana) had been added to the lexicon *UK, 1998*

jacksy; jacksie; jaxie *noun* the buttocks; the anus *UK, 1943*

Jack Tar; jolly Jack Tar *noun* 1 a sailor. An elaboration of TAR *UK, 1781*. 2 a bar. Rhyming slang *UK, 1960*

Jack the Bear *noun* in motor racing, a driver who performs very well *US, 1993*

Jack the biscuit *noun* a show-off; someone who is important or self-important enough to be ostentatious. JACK (a man) 'takes the biscuit' (defeats all rivals) *UK, 2002*

Jack the Dripper *noun* the penis. A pun on the name of legendary serial killer Jack the Ripper *UK, 2003*

Jack the Lad *noun* **1** someone noticeably sharper, smarter or smugger than the rest; a rogue. In *Prison Patter*, 1996, Angela Devlin notes that this term is used to excuse dubious – possibly criminal – behaviour by young males *UK, 1977*. **2** in criminal circles, an exemplary criminal *UK, 1974*

Jack the Lad *adjective* bad. Rhyming slang *UK, 1992*

Jack the Ripper *noun* **1** a kipper (a smoked fish) *UK, 1992*. **2** a striptease artist. Rhyming slang for STRIPPER *UK, 2003*. **3** a slipper. Rhyming slang, based on the name of legendary late C19 Whitechapel murderer *UK, 2002*

jack-up *noun* **1** a tablet of sodium amobarbital (trade name Amytal™), a central nervous system depressant *US, 1973*. **2** an injection of drugs. From the verb *UK, 1996*

jack up *verb* **1** to inject drugs *US, 1975*. **2** to raise *US, 1904*. **3** (of the surf) to increase in swell *AUSTRALIA, 1987*. **4** to rob with force *US, 1965*. **5** to arrest or detain for questioning by police *US, 1967*. **6** to be uncooperative; to object, to refuse to comply *AUSTRALIA, 1898*

jack-up fence *noun* a large wire fence with barbed wire across the top. Criminals lift victims and hang them on the top of the fence as they rob them *US, 2000*

Jacky *noun* a kookaburra *AUSTRALIA, 1898*. ▶ **sit up like Jacky** to sit up straight in a perky or self-important manner. It has been suggested that this refers to sitting up straight 'as an aboriginal is supposed to do in company with whites', though it should be noted that the kookaburra habitually sits up on an exposed branch or fencetop surveying an area of ground for insect and reptile food, and impertinently ignores the frequent attacks of other birds *AUSTRALIA, 1941*

Jacky Jacky; Jacky *noun* an Australian Aboriginal man *AUSTRALIA, 1845*

Jacob's crackers *noun* the testicles. Also shortened form 'jacobs'. Rhyming slang for KNACKERS; from the branded savoury biscuits. Usage popularised by comedian Joe Pasquale in the television programme *I'm A Celebrity, Get Me Out of Here*, December 2004 *UK, 2004*

Jacob's crackers *adjective* tired, exhausted. Rhyming slang leading to KNACKERED; a variant of CREAM CRACKERED formed on a premier brand of cream crackers *UK, 2003*

Jacob's ladder *noun* a sturdy rope ladder dropped from a hovering helicopter for descent to and ascent from the ground *US, 1985*

jader *noun* in Newfoundland, a person not liked, a nuisance *CANADA, 1944*

jafa *noun* **1** a resident of Auckland. From 'just another fucking Auklander' *NEW ZEALAND, 1998*. **2** a scientist. An abbreviation of 'just another fucking academic'. 'Jafo' is a variant where the scientist is an 'observer' *ANTARCTICA, 1987*

jaffa *noun* an infertile man. Probably an allusion to a seedless Jaffa orange *UK, 2001*

jag *noun* **1** a period of time spent entirely focused on a single activity, often with the defining term prefixed *US, 1913*. **2** a drinking or drug binge *US, 1892*. **3** a state of alcohol or drug intoxication *UK, 1678*. **4** an act of solvent abuse *UK, 1963*. **5** a social engagement; a date *IRELAND, 1983*. **6** a loner lacking social skills *US, 1993*. **7** a small load on a truck *US, 1971*

Jag *noun* a Jaguar car *US, 1953*

jag *verb* to work as a male prostitute *US, 1972*

jagabat *noun* a promiscuous woman; a prostitute *TRINIDAD AND TOBAGO, 1992*

jagged *adjective* drunk or drug-intoxicated. First recorded by Benjamin Franklin *US, 1737*

jagger *noun* a tattoo artist *US, 1947*

Jagger's lip; jagger's *noun* a chip. Rhyming slang, formed from a prominent characteristic of Rolling Stones' singer Mick Jagger (b.1943) *UK, 1998*

jaggy nettle; jaggy *noun* a kettle. Glasgow rhyming slang; 'jaggy' means 'prickly' *UK: SCOTLAND, 1988*

jag house *noun* a brothel that caters to male homosexuals *US, 1972*

jag-off *noun* a despicable, offensive or dim-witted person *US, 1938*

jag off *verb* to manipulate the injection of a drug such that the drug enters the blood stream slowly *US, 1958*

jags *adjective* sexually aroused *SOUTH AFRICA, 2004*

jag up *verb* to inject drugs. In Glasgow slang, presumably a variation of JACK UP *UK: SCOTLAND, 1996*

jahalered *adjective* drunk *UK, 2002*

jail *noun* in horse racing, the first month after a claimed horse is in a new stable. Racing rules limit the conditions under which the horse may be raced during the first month *US, 1976*. ▶ **in jail** in pool, said of a cue ball that is touching another ball or the rail, leaving the player with no good opportunity to make a shot *US, 1990*

jail *verb* to serve a prison sentence, especially without losing hope or sanity *US, 1967*. ▶ **be jailing** to wear your trousers or shorts very low, below the buttocks, with your boxer shorts visible above the trouser line. From the image of prisoners who are not allowed to have belts and whose trousers thus sag *US, 1993*

jail arithmetic *noun* in prison, any method used to keep track of your time served and the time remaining on your sentence *US, 1949*

jailbait; gaol-bait *noun* a sexually alluring girl under the legal age of consent *US, 1930*

jailbird; gaol-bird *noun* a prisoner or ex-convict *UK, 1661*

jail bollocks *noun* difficulties presented by fellow-prisoners and officers *UK, 1996*

jailcraft *noun* a prison-officer's knowledge of the day-to-day running of a prison *UK, 1996*

jailee *noun* a prison officer. A deliberate role-reversal for the jailer *UK, 1996*

jail gay *noun* a prisoner who, while generally heterosexual, adopts homosexuality as a temporary practice while in prison *UK, 2000*

jailhouse *noun* a type of bet in an illegal numbers game lottery *US, 1957*

jailhouse flowers *noun* the solicitation of sexual relations by non-lexical verbalisation *US, 1974*

jailhouse lawyer *noun* a prisoner with some expertise, real and/or perceived, in the criminal justice system *US, 1926*

jailhouse punk *noun* a man who becomes a passive homosexual while in prison *US, 1982*

jailhouse turnout *noun* a previously heterosexual man who becomes homosexual in prison *US, 1965*

jail politician *noun* a prisoner who stirs up disaffection and unrest, or one who manipulates prison officers *UK, 1996*

jail-wise *adjective* sophisticated with respect to survival in prison *US, 1967*

jake *noun* **1** Jamaica ginger, a potent and dangerous illegally manufactured alcohol *US, 1923*. **2** methylated spirits as an alcoholic drink *UK, 1932*. **3** a vagrant alcoholic addicted to methylated spirits *UK, 1966*. **4** a social outcast *US, 1989*. **5** a person identified as a potential crime victim *US, 1997*. **6** a uniformed police officer *US, 1987*

jake *adjective* honest, upright, equitable, correct *US, 1914*

jaked *adjective* drunk *UK: SCOTLAND, 1988*

jaked out *adjective* in a drunken stupor *UK: SCOTLAND, 1988*

jaked up *adjective* drunk. Derives from JAKE (methylated spirits as an alcoholic drink) *UK: SCOTLAND, 1988*

jake (it) *verb* to give something less than a full effort; to feign an injury *US, 1967*

Jake man *noun* a vagrant alcoholic addicted to methylated spirits. From JAKE (methylated spirits) *UK, 1966*

jaker *noun* in sports, a player who chronically claims injuries. From basketball *US, 1967*

jakerloo; jakealoo; jakeaboo *adjective* all right; fine. An elaboration of JAKE. The obsolete faux Latin term 'jakalorum' was recorded as early as 1905 *AUSTRALIA, 1919*

jakes *noun* the police *US, 1993*

jakey noun **1** Jamaica ginger, a fruit flavoured alcoholic drink *CANADA, 1999*. **2** a meths drinker, thus an alcoholic in desperate straits. From JAKE (methylated spirits as an alcoholic drink) *UK, 2001*

jakey adjective **1** alcoholic *UK, 2002*. **2** socially inept, unaware of current fashions and trends *US, 1989*. **3** odd looking *US, 1964*. **4** said of a light jail sentence. From JAKE (methylated spirits as an alcoholic drink) *UK, 2000*

jallopy; jalopy; jaloppie; jollopy; gillopy noun a cheap, dilapidated or old motor vehicle, especially a car *US, 1926*

jam noun **1** a difficult position, an awkward situation; a difficulty; trouble *US, 1914*. **2** a recorded song *US, 1937*. **3** a record album. Usually in the plural *US, 1981*. **4** blues, jazz or rock music simultaneously improvised by an informal gathering of musicians; a period spent making such music *UK, 1929*. **5** a party with loud music *US, 1993*. **6** cocaine *US, 1972*. **7** amphetamines *US, 1953*. **8** sex *US, 1949*. **9** the vagina *US, 1980*. **10** in homosexual usage, any heterosexual man. An abbreviation of 'just a man' *US, 1981*. **11** the corpse of a person who has died with massive injuries *US, 1987*. **12** a fight, especially a gang fight *US, 1992*. **13** a gathering of skateboarders *US, 1976*. **14** petty smuggling *US, 1956* ▷*see:* CULTURE JAM

jam verb **1** to play music with others, improvising *US, 1935*. **2** to dance *TRINIDAD AND TOBAGO, 1986*. **3** to excel *US, 1984*. **4** to have sex *US, 1972*. **5** to coerce, to threaten, to pressure *US, 1971*. **6** to leave quickly; to travel at high speeds *US, 1965*. **7** in gambling, to cheat (another player) *US, 1997*. **8** to subvert advertising matter *US, 2001*. **9** in surfing, to obstruct or block another surfer's ride *US, 1967*. **10** to surf with speed and intensity *US, 1988*

jam adjective heterosexual. Eventually supplanted by STRAIGHT *US, 1935*

JAM used as Internet shorthand to mean 'just a minute' *US, 1997*

Jamaican noun marijuana cultivated in Jamaica *US, 1974*

Jamaican assault vehicle noun any sports utility vehicle. New York police slang; SUV's are favoured by Jamaican criminals *US, 1997*

Jamaican blue mountain noun a type of marijuana cultivated in Jamaica *US, 1994*

Jamaican bomber noun a large marijuana cigarette, made with what is claimed to be Jamaican marijuana *US, 1997*

Jamaican gold noun a variety of marijuana cultivated in Jamaica *US, 1986*

Jamaican switch noun a type of confidence swindle. There are many variations of the swindle, but the common element is the swindler pretending to be a foreigner with a lot of money in need of help *US, 1973*

jam and bread noun the bleed period of the menstrual cycle. Red on white imagery *US, 1999*

jam and butter! used as a mild oath *NEW ZEALAND, 1998*

jam band noun a musical band known for long improvisations *US, 1981*

jam box noun a portable radio and cassette player with large speakers *US, 1982*

jam-buster noun **1** an assistant yardmaster in a railroad yard *US, 1938*. **2** in Winnipeg, a jam doughnut *CANADA, 1998*

jam butty noun a police car. A combination of JAM-JAR (a car) and BUTTY (a sandwich), describing a white car with a red stripe *UK, 1990*

jam Cecil noun **1** cocaine *US, 1975*. **2** amphetamines *UK, 1977*

Jam Down adjective Jamaican *JAMAICA, 1994*

James Earl dog noun a marijuana cigarette *US, 1986*

James Hunt noun a cunt (in all senses, but especially as a term of abuse). Rhyming slang, formed from the name of the UK racing driver, 1947–93 *UK, 2003*

Jamie noun any General Motors truck *US, 1971*

jam-jar noun a motor car. Rhyming slang, originally (late C19) applied to a tram, and probably almost as old as the car *UK, 1960*

jammed adjective **1** describes the altered state of a public image, usually a billboard, once it has been subverted by cultural activists *US, 2001*. **2** experiencing a drug overdose *US, 1949*. **3** (used of the collective bets in a hand of a poker game) formed by many bets and raised bets *US, 1996*. **4** (used of prison sentences) concurrent *US, 1982*

jammed up adjective **1** under great pressure *US, 1973*. **2** experiencing a drug overdose *US, 1971*

jammer noun **1** in American casinos, a skilled and adaptable dealer *US, 1985*. **2** a popular, trend-setting, respected person. Hawaiian youth usage *US, 1982* ▷*see:* CULTURAL JAMMER

jammered verb of a place, packed with people *IRELAND, 1991*

jammers adjective very-crowded, jam-packed *IRELAND, 2004*

jammie noun a party with loud music. A variation of 'jam' *US, 1995*

jammies noun pyjamas *US, 1967*

jamming; jammin' adjective excellent *US, 1982*

jammy noun the penis *US, 1997* ▷*see:* JEMMY

jammy adjective exceedingly lucky, fortunate; profitable. Jam has long been seen as a luxury, hence phrases like JAM ON IT (something pleasant) and a general sense that possession of jam is a definition of luck or prosperity *UK, 1915*

jammy dodger verb from the male perspective, to have sex. Rhyming slang for ROGER (to have sex), formed from the brand name of a popular biscuit. The noun is 'a jammy dodgering' *UK, 1998*

jammy-jams; jam-jams noun pyjamas *US, 1976*

jamoke noun **1** a despicable or ignorant person *US, 1946*. **2** coffee *US, 1895*

jam on it noun an agreeable surplus or an enhancement; a cause of extra satisfaction *UK, 1919*

jam pail curling noun in the Canadian prairies, curling with cement poured into old jam pails as curling stones *CANADA, 1987*

jampot noun in homosexual usage, the anus and rectum *US, 1941*

jam rag noun a sanitary towel. Plays on conventional 'jam' (to block) and the conventional colour of jam, red, for the menstrual blood, with 'rag' for the materials involved *UK, 1966*

jam roll noun **1** unemployment benefit; any government office from which it is administrated. Rhyming slang for THE DOLE *UK, 1992*. **2** a fool; a despised person. Rhyming slang for ARSEHOLE *UK, 2003*. **3** parole. Rhyming slang. Shortened to 'jam' *UK, 1995*

jams noun **1** pyjamas *US, 1973*. **2** trousers *US, 1968*. **3** bright, long, multi-coloured swimming trunks *AUSTRALIA, 1966*

jam sandwich noun a police car. JAM-JAR (a car), plus visual metaphor *UK, 1981*

jam session noun **1** a gathering of musicians who play in a collective, improvised fashion *US, 1933*. **2** an informal, unstructured group discussion *US, 1963*

jam tart noun **1** heart. Rhyming slang *UK, 1979*. **2** a girlfriend; hence (patronisingly) a young woman. Often simplified to 'jam'. Simple rhyming slang for 'sweetheart'; however when used more generally it may also be an elaboration of TART (a young woman, especially of easy morals) *UK, 1960*

jam up verb **1** to cause trouble; to place in a troubling situation *US, 1836*. **2** to confront *US, 1992*

jam-up adjective **1** excellent, pleasing *US, 1823*. **2** in pool, playing well and luckily *US, 1990*

jam week noun the bleed period of the menstrual cycle *UK, 2003*

jandals noun rubber sandals *NEW ZEALAND, 1984*

Jane; jane noun **1** a public toilet for women. Playing on JOHN (a toilet) *US, 1997*. **2** marijuana *UK, 1966*. **3** a woman, a girlfriend. Generic use of popular name. Also 'Janie' *US, 1865*

Jane, please, not in front of the men! used for expressing disapproval of a public display of affection. A signature line of Captain Wilton Parmenter to Jane Angelic Thrift on the television comedy *F Troop* (ABC, 1965–67). Repeated with referential humour *US, 1965*

Janet Street-Porter; Janet noun a quarter (1/4 oz measure of marijuana). Rhyming slang, formed from the name of a well-known broadcaster and journalist *UK, 1998*

Jane Wayne Day *noun* a day on which wives of US Marines go through a series of exercises designed to give them a sense of what their husbands go through *US, 1989*

jang *noun* the penis *US, 1972*

janglers *noun* ▶ **take the janglers** to become upset *IRELAND, 1999*

janglies *noun* in caving and pot-holing, assorted pieces of single-rope-technique (SRT) metallic equipment. Echoic *UK, 2004*

Jan Hammered; Jan'd *adjective* drunk. An elaboration of HAMMERED (drunk), playing on the name of Czech born jazz keyboardist Jan Hammer (b.1948) *UK, 2002*

janitor *noun* an ordinary infantry soldier. Gulf war usage *US, 1991*

jank *verb* to steal *US, 2001*

jankers *noun* confinement to barracks (as a military punishment) *UK, 1916*

jankity *adjective* old, broken down *US, 2004*

janky *adjective* broken, dysfunctional, inoperative *US, 1999*

janner *noun* 1 a West Countryman. Originally restricted to someone with a Devon burr *UK, 1984*. 2 a member of a southwest England subcultural urban adolescent grouping defined by a hip-hop dress and jewellery sense (and an urge to act older than their years). By extension of the previous sense *UK, 2004*

janny talk *noun* the speech of a mummer, distorted to conceal identity. 'Janny' is a variant of 'John,' as in 'John Jacks', listed by the *English Dialect Dictionary* as a common name in England for mummers *CANADA, 1969*

JAP *noun* a spoiled Jewish girl or woman; a Jewish-American princess. The term was wildly popular in the early 1980s, with the expected onslaught of joke books, J.A.P. handbooks, etc *US, 1972*

Jap *noun* 1 a Japanese person. Derogatory *US, 1854*. 2 someone who attacks from behind and/or without warning *US, 1949*. 3 an unannounced test *US, 1967*

jap *verb* to attack without warning. An allusion to the Japanese attack at Pearl Harbor *US, 1942*

Jap *adjective* Japanese. Unkind *US, 1869*

Japanese beetle *noun* any small, Japanese-made car. Punning on the insect and the Volkswagen *US, 1976*

Japanese safety boots *noun* rubber flip-flops (footwear) *AUSTRALIA, 2003*

Japanglish *noun* a blend of Japanese and English spoken in Japan. A variation of conventional 'Japlish' *UK, 2001*

Jap crap *noun* imports from Japan, especially motorcycles *US, 1986*

Jap cunt *adjective* Japanese; a Japanese. Deliberately offensive combination of JAP (Japanese) and CUNT (someone or something unpleasant) *UK, 2000*

Jap hash *noun* chop suey or chow mein *US, 1979*

japie; jaapie; jarpie; yarpie *noun* 1 an Afrikaner. Contemptuous; derived from Jaap a diminutive of the Afrikaans name Jakob *SOUTH AFRICA, 1949*. 2 a South African. May be jocular, contemptuous or affectionate *SOUTH AFRICA, 1956*. 3 an unsophisticated person, especially one from a rural area. Patronising if not offensive *SOUTH AFRICA, 1964*

Jap on Anzac Day *noun* a person to whom you would wish ill luck. Australians fought against the Japanese in World War 2, and Anzac Day is a national holiday commemorating Australian service men and women *AUSTRALIA, 1982*

Japper *noun* a motorcycle manufactured in Japan *AUSTRALIA, 1996*

jap scrap *noun* a motorcyle manufactured in Japan *US, 1988*

Jap's eye; japer *noun* the opening in the glans of the penis. From the resemblance in shape to the racial stereotype *UK, 2001*

Jap-slapper *noun* a martial artist. A reference to the Japanese who invented or developed so many of the recognised disciplines *UK, 1995*

Jap-slapping *noun* the martial arts of unarmed combat *UK, 1995*

Jap-slaps *noun* a sandal that is not bound to the foot, usually worn around swimming pools or at the beach. Hawaiian youth usage *US, 1982*

jar *noun* 1 a glass of beer. Originally Lincolnshire dialect *UK, 1925*. 2 any dark-skinned person. Prison usage *NEW ZEALAND, 1997*

jar *verb* ▶ **jar the deck** to wake up and get up *US, 1962*

jar *adjective* (of jewellery) fake. Abbreviated from JARGOON *UK, 1956*

jar dealer *noun* a drug dealer who sells pills in large quantities *US, 1971*

jarg *adjective* fake. From JARGOON (fake jewellery) *UK, 2001*

jargon *noun* confusion *US, 2001*

jargoon; jar *noun* an item of replica jewellery with less value than the original; counterfeit or paste-jewellery used in confidence tricks. From conventional 'jargoon' (a type of zircon) *UK, 1956*

jarhead *noun* 1 a US Marine. Originally an army mule, then a member of the US Army, especially a member of the football team (1931) *US, 1943*. 2 a habitual user of crack cocaine *US, 1993*

jark *verb* to 'neutralise' a weapon by planting a transmitter. Military; probably from the obsolete sense as 'a pass guaranteeing safe conduct' *UK, 2001*

jarking *noun* the act of 'neutralising' a weapon by planting transmitters. Military *UK, 1995*

jarmies *noun* pyjamas *NEW ZEALAND, 2001*

jarms *noun* pyjamas *AUSTRALIA, 1971*

jar of jam *noun* a pram. Rhyming slang. The earlier sense as 'tram' is now obsolete *UK, 1992*

jar pot *noun* marijuana that is so potent that it must be stored in a pot or airtight jar to contain the smell *US, 1992*

jarrah-jerker *noun* in Western Australia, a bush worker, especially a logger. Jarrah is a type of Australian native tree *AUSTRALIA, 1965*

jarred up *adjective* drunk. After JAR (a glass of beer) *UK: SCOTLAND, 1988*

J. Arthur Rank; J. Arthur *noun* 1 an act of masturbation; a masturbator. Rhyming slang for WANK, based on the name of UK cinema tycoon Lord Rank (1888–1972) *UK, 1980*. 2 a bank. Rhyming slang, based on the name of film millionaire Joseph Arthur Rank (1888–1972). Sometimes shortened to the simple 'Arthur' *UK, 1977*

jasper *noun* 1 a lesbian or a bisexual woman. Robert Wilson hypothesises that the Reverend John Jasper, a pious man of God, lent his name in this good-is-bad etymology *US, 1954*. 2 a person of no consequence. From a stereotypical rural name *UK, 1896*

jasper broad *noun* a lesbian or bisexual woman *US, 1972*

Jasper Carrot *noun* a parrot. Rhyming slang, formed from the name of a popular Birmingham-born comedian *UK, 1998*

Jatz crackers *noun* the testicles. Rhyming slang for KNACKERS. From the name of a brand of savoury cracker *AUSTRALIA, 1992*

jaunt *noun* in horse racing, a race, especially an unimportant one *US, 1951*

java *noun* coffee *US, 1850*

java patrol *noun* in trucking, a stop for coffee *US, 1946*

jaw *verb* 1 to talk, especially in an argumentative or scolding fashion *UK, 1748*. 2 in pool, to hit a ball that bounces off the sides of a pocket without dropping *US, 1990*

jaw artist *noun* a person skilled at the giving of oral sex *US, 1972*

jawblock *verb* to chat, to talk *US, 1946*

jawbone *noun* credit obtained by arguing for it *US, 1862*

jawbone shack *noun* on the railways, a small office in a switching yard *US, 1977*

jaw dropper *noun* a great surprise *CANADA, 1993*

jawfest *noun* 1 a long, aimless conversation *US, 1915*. 2 a prolonged session of oral sex *US, 1967*

jawflap *noun* a gossip *US, 1952*

jaw-jack *verb* to chatter loudly and with no purpose; hence, to talk on citizens' band radio *US, 1962*

jaws *noun* **1** the buttocks *US, 2002.* **2** in dominoes, the 6–6 piece *US, 1959.* ▶ **case of the jaws** a harsh reprimand *US, 1968*

jaws of Jewry *noun* in Newfoundland, great risk or danger *CANADA, 1982*

Jax *nickname* Jacksonville, Florida. Also known as 'The Cesspool of the South' *US, 1936*

jaxied *adjective* drunk. Probably from JACKSY (the anus), thus a form of ARSEHOLED (drunk) *UK, 2002*

jay *noun* **1** a bank. An abbreviation of JUG (a bank) *US, 1950.* **2** a jungle. Vietnam war usage *NEW ZEALAND, 1999.* **3** coffee. Probably an abbreviation of JAVA *US, 1962*

Jay Kay *noun* a take-away meal. Popney rhyming slang, based on singer Jay Kay (b.1969) of popular group Jamiroquai. Popney was contrived for *www.music365.co.uk*, an Internet music site *UK, 2001*

jay-naked *adjective* completely naked *US, 1975*

jay neg *noun* an older black person *TRINIDAD AND TOBAGO, 2003*

Jayzus!; Jaysus! a Hiberno-English pronunciation of 'Jesus', used as a blasphemous expletive *IRELAND, 1989*

jazz *noun* **1** nonsense *US, 1951.* **2** stuff *US, 1951.* **3** semen *US, 1932.* **4** heroin *CANADA, 1986.* ▶ **the jazz** the general details (of something) *UK, 1999*

jazz *verb* **1** to have sex with someone *US, 1918.* **2** of a male, to orgasm. After JAZZ (semen) *UK, 2004*

jazz about; jazz around *verb* to cause trouble, to annoy *US, 1917*

jazzbo *noun* a fervent jazz enthusiast *US, 1921*

jazz cigarette *noun* a marijuana cigarette *UK, 2001*

jazzed *adjective* excited, enthusiastic *US, 1918*

jazzed-up *adjective* revised and augmented, improved *US, C20*

jazz joint *noun* a brothel *US, 1927*

jazz nazi *noun* a purist jazz fan *CANADA, 2002*

jazz up *verb* to modernise; to enliven; in a specialised sense, to convert classical music into pop *UK, 1984*

jazz Woodbine *noun* a marijuana cigarette. A variation of JAZZ CIGARETTE; WOODBINE is a slang generic for 'a cheap cigarette' *UK, 1983*

jazzy *adjective* showy; ostentatious *US, 1923*

JB *noun* a person with 'jet black' skin *US, 1946*

J Bay *nickname* Jeffrey's Bay, west of Port Elizabeth, South Africa *SOUTH AFRICA, 1991*

J-bird *noun* **1** a person in or recently released from jail. An abbreviation of JAILBIRD *US, 1971.* **2** in a deck of playing cards, a jack or knave. An elaboration of J *US, 1951*

JBM *adjective* in horse racing, said of a horse that has only won one race. An abbreviation of 'just beaten maiden' *US, 1976*

JB's *noun* sandals, flip-flops. An abbreviation of 'Jesus boots' *US, 2003*

J Carroll Naish *noun* an act of urination. Rhyming slang for SLASH, formed from the name of the US film actor, 1897–1973 *UK, 1979*

J-cat *noun* a person who is more crazy than eccentric *US, 1997*

J City *nickname* Juarez, Mexico *US, 1970*

J C water-walkers *noun* sandals. An allusion to Jesus Christ (JC) walking on water, presumably in sandals *US, 1970*

JD *noun* **1** a juvenile delinquent *US, 1956.* **2** Jack Daniels™, a brand name Tennessee sourmash whisky. Initialism *US, 1981*

JD card *noun* a police citation issued to a transgressing juvenile, requiring participation in a Police Athletic League team to avoid incarceration *US, 1972*

Jean *noun* a female customer of a prostitute. An extrapolation of JOHN *US, 1976*

Jean and Dinah *noun* prostitutes *TRINIDAD AND TOBAGO, 1993*

Jean-Claude Van Damme; Jean-Claude *noun* ham. Rhyming slang, formed with cruel wit – HAM (to be a poor actor) – from the name of the Belgian film actor, also known as 'the muscles from Brussels' (b.1960) *UK, 1998*

jeans at half mast *noun* engaged in the passive role in anal sex *US, 1950*

Jedi *noun* a member of an exclusive and influential group. Based on a cast of characters created by George Lucas and introduced in the film *Star Wars*, 1977 *UK, 2000*

Jedi master *noun* in the language of hang gliding, an experienced, expert flier *US, 1992*

jeegee; jee gee *noun* heroin. Possibly plays on 'gee gee' (a horse) and HORSE (heroin) *US, 1971*

jeely jar *noun* a car. Glasgow rhyming slang *UK: SCOTLAND, 1988*

jeep *noun* an inexperienced enlisted man. Air Force usage during the Vietnam war *US, 1970*

jeepers creepers!; jeepers!; creepers! used as a mild oath. A euphemism for 'Jesus Christ!' *US, 1928*

Jeep girl *noun* a Chinese prostitute attached to US armed forces *US, 1946*

jeeter *noun* a lieutenant *US, 1941*

jeez!; jeese!; geez! used as a mild oath. A euphemised 'Jesus' *US, 1830*

jeezan ages!; jeezan peas!; jeezan rice! used for expressing shock and surprise. Euphemisms for 'Jesus Christ!' *TRINIDAD AND TOBAGO, 1992*

jeezer *noun* a fellow *US, 1972*

Jeez Louise! used as a mild oath *US, 1957*

jeezly *adverb* used as an all-purpose intensifier. This variation on 'Jesus' is a staple of language in maritime Canada *US, 1885*

Jeezo-groveler *noun* a Christian. Based on an unconventional diminutive of Jesus this is literally, if offensively, someone who kneels before Jesus *US, 1989*

Jeezuz! used for expressing exasperation. An exaggeratedly stressed 'Jesus!' *UK, 1999*

Jeff *noun* **1** an all-purpose name for a man *US, 1953.* **2** a white person, especially one who is hostile towards black people *US, 1959.* **3** a dull individual, a pest. Originally a shortened form of Jefferson Davis, the president of the Confederate States of America throughout its existence during the US Civil War, 1861–65. Afro-American slang remembered him as a southern white racist, and reduced him to the status of pest *US, 1938*

jeff *verb* to behave obsequiously in the hope of winning approval *US, 1960*

Jeff *verb* to lie or at least to exaggerate *US, 1992*

Jefferson airplane *noun* a used match split to hold the butt of a partially smoked marijuana joint. Many musicians take names from drugs slang, but the reverse happened here. Jefferson Airplane was a successful San Franciscan rock band associated with 1960s drugs culture and psychedelic culture. The name, a humorous coinage for an imaginary blues musician, Blind Thomas Jefferson Airplane, was first given to a dog; only later to an improvised DOG END holder *US, 1967*

Jekyll and Hyde; jekyll *noun* a forgery, a fake. Rhyming slang, extended from the adjective sense of SNIDE (false, counterfeit, sham, bogus, etc.) *UK, 1992*

Jekyll and Hyde; jekyll *adjective* false, counterfeit, sham, bogus, two-faced. Rhyming slang for SNIDE; a neat pun formed from, and referring to the dual personality of the eponymous character in *The Strange Case of Dr Jekyll and Mr Hyde*, by Robert Louis Stevenson, 1886 *UK, 1959*

Jekyll and Hydes; jekylls *noun* trousers. Rhyming slang for STRIDES *UK, 1992*

jell *noun* a person with few thoughts and no sense of fashion *US, 1982*

jell *verb* to leave hastily, to escape. English gypsy use *UK, 2000*

jellied eel *noun* a wheel. Rhyming slang *UK, 1992*

jellied eel *verb* to transport. Rhyming slang for 'wheel' *UK, 1992*

jellied eels *noun* a private vehicle. Rhyming slang for 'wheels' *UK, 1992*

jellies *noun* soft, plastic, apparently edible sandals *US, 1995*

jello arms *noun* in surfing, exhausted, rubbery arms from paddling *US, 1987*

jelly *noun* **1** the vagina *US, 1926*. **2** sexual intercourse *US, 1926*. **3** a sexually permissive female *UK, 1989*. **4** a capsule of Temazepam™, a branded tranquillizer; any central nervous system depressant; in the plural it refers to the drug in general. A term embraced by US youth after seeing the film *Trainspotting UK, 1996*. **5** cocaine *UK, 1998* ▷*see:* GELLY

jelly *verb* to explode, especially with gelignite *UK, 2002*

jelly *adjective* excellent. From a song performed by Destiny's Child *UK, 2003*

jelly baby *noun* **1** an expert in the use of gelignite. From the name of a popular sweet manufactured in the shape of a 'baby', extending 'jelly' (gelignite) *UK, 1974*. **2** a tablet of Temazepam™, a branded tranquillizer *UK, 1998*. **3** an amphetamine tablet *US, 1971*

jellybag *noun* **1** a condescending Englishman in the Canadian West *CANADA, 1987*. **2** a large fuel cell made of rubber or plastic. Vietnam war usage *US, 1965*. **3** a 1936 Chevrolet lowered in the rear *US, 1955*

jellybeans *noun* crack cocaine *UK, 1998*

jelly belly *noun* a fat person *UK, 1896*

jelly blubber *noun* a jellyfish *AUSTRALIA, 1943*

jellybone *noun* a telephone. Rhyming slang, used by courier controllers *UK, 1992*

jelly box *noun* the vagina *AUSTRALIA, 1988*

jelly doughnut; jelly donut *noun* an overweight female Red Cross volunteer in Vietnam *US, 1991*

jellyhash *noun* an extremely potent variety of hashish produced in Holland *UK, 2003*

jellyhead *noun* a habitual user of crack cocaine. Combines 'jelly', as in JELLYBEANS (crack cocaine) with HEAD (a user) *UK, 1999*

jelly on the belly *noun* semen ejaculated on a woman's stomach *AUSTRALIA, 1985*

jelly roll *noun* **1** the vagina *US, 1914*. **2** a used tampon or sanitary towel *US, 1972*

jelly sandwich *noun* a sanitary towel *US, 1980*

jelly tight *adjective* excellent *US, 1972*

jelly tot *noun* a young boy who tries to act older than he is. Teen slang *US, 1951*

jemmy *verb* to force open with a short crowbar *UK, 1893*

jemmy; jammy *noun* a short crowbar used by burglars. Known in the US as a 'jimmy' *UK, 1811*

Jennifer Justice; Jennifer *noun* a police officer; the police. An example of CAMP trans-gender assignment *UK, 2002*

jenny *noun* **1** a fence-wire spinner *NEW ZEALAND, 1978*. **2** a merry-go-round *US, 1985*. **3** in the television and film industries, a mobile source of direct current *UK, 1960* ▷*see:* GENNY

Jenny barn *noun* the ward for women in a narcotic treatment hospital *US, 1955*

Jenny Hill; jenny *noun* a pill. Rhyming slang, formed from the name of a music hall performer, 1851–96 *UK, 1937*

Jenny Lea; Jenny Lee *noun* **1** a key. Rhyming slang *UK, 1961*. **2** tea. Rhyming slang *UK, 1960*

Jenny Lind *noun* wind. Rhyming slang, used in reference both to the weather and bodily functions; formed from the name of a mid-C19 singer and cultural icon, popularly known as 'The Swedish Nightingale', 1820–87 *UK, 1992*

Jenny Riddle *noun* an act of urination. Rhyming slang for PIDDLE; a variation/feminisation of the better known JIMMY RIDDLE *UK, 1998*

Jenny Wren; jenny *noun* Ben Truman™ beer. Rhyming slang *UK, 1992*

jere; jeer *noun* **1** the buttocks, the backside. Rhyming slang for 'rear'; informed by the earlier sense as 'turd' *UK, 1936*. **2** a turd *UK, 1979*. **3** a male homosexual. Rhyming slang for QUEER, playing on the word's sense as 'buttocks' *UK, 1961*

jerecase; jeercase *noun* the buttocks. An elaboration of JERE; JEER *UK, 1979*

Jeremiah *noun* a fire. Rhyming slang, especially among urban labourers; occasionally 'Obadiah' *UK, 1934*

Jeremied *adjective* drunk. Probably in celebration of a man called Jeremy who may not even remember the reason why *UK, 2002*

Jeremy Beadle *verb* to irritate, to annoy, to provoke. Rhyming slang for NEEDLE, formed from the name of a television prankster (b.1949) *UK, 1998*

jerk *noun* **1** an idiot, a fool *US, 1919*. **2** in a gambling establishment, a hanger-on who runs errands for gamblers *US, 1979*

jerk *verb* to tow a disabled car home with the help of a neighbour *CANADA, 1987*. ▶ **jerk the chicken** of a male, to masturbate *UK, 2003*. ▶ **jerk the gherkin** of a male, to masturbate *UK, 1962*. ▶ **jerk the turk; jerk your turkey** of a male, to masturbate. It is said of a man's genitalia that when shaved it resembles 'a plucked turkey hanging in a shop' yet this appears to be a lone instance of a 'turkey' used as a 'penis'; 'turk', an abbreviation of 'turkey', is a convenient rhyme for 'jerk' which describes the physical action *UK, 1999*. ▶ **jerk your mutton** to masturbate. 'Mutton' (penis) dates from the C16 and is now obsolete except in uses such as this and 'mutton bayonet', 'mutton dagger'; 'mutton' (vagina) dates from the same period: subsequent usages are as 'a woman or women', 'a promiscuous woman', 'a prostitute' and the surviving 'mutton dressed as lamb' *UK, 1984*

jerk around; jerk about *verb* to tease someone, sometimes maliciously *US, 1972*

jerker *noun* in the car sales business, a car manufactured before World War 2 *US, 1953*

jerk fitting *noun* (on a car, truck or tractor) a grease nipple *CANADA, 1987*

jerk-off *noun* **1** a single act of masturbation, especially by a male *US, 1928*. **2** a contemptible fool *US, 1932*

jerk off *verb* **1** to masturbate. A reasonably accurate description of the physical activity involved *UK, 1896*. **2** to tease; to mislead *US, 1968*. **3** to cause the withdrawal (of a criminal charge, a witness scheduled to testifiy, etc) *US, 1950*

jerk-silly *adjective* obsessed with masturbation *US, 1962*

jerkwater *noun* a dull-minded person *US, 1958*

Jerkwater *noun* a contemptuous name for a location *US, 1982*

jerkwater *adjective* provincial *US, 1897*

jerky *noun* used as a male-to-male, peer-to-peer term of address. Jocular, from 'The Jerky Boys' (two young men who elevated prank telephone calls to comedic art) *US, 1996*

jerky *adjective* foolish, stupid. From JERK (an idiot) *US, 1932*

jerry *noun* something that is not as well made as it appears *TRINIDAD AND TOBAGO, 1987*

Jerry *verb* to realise; to comprehend; to 'tumble' to an idea *AUSTRALIA, 1894*

Jerry; Gerry *nickname* **1** a German; the Germans. Derogatory, often as an abstract reference to Germans as the enemy whether at war or football. Possibly derived from 'Jerry' (a chamber pot) in reference to the shape of German military helmets; more likely, as 'Gerry', an elaborated abbreviation of 'German' *US, 1915*. **2** a foreman on a railway track crew *US, 1867*

Jerry Lee *noun* urination; an act of urination. Rhyming slang for WEE or PEE, formed from the name of rock 'n' roll singer and piano player, Jerry Lee Lewis (b.1935) *UK, 1992*

Jerry Springer *noun* **1** an ugly person. Rhyming slang for MINGER, formed from the name of the UK-born US television personality (b.1944) *UK, 2003*. **2** heroin. Named after a US chat-show host *UK, 2002*

Jersey *noun* the state of New Jersey *US, 1949*

Jersey bean *noun* a resident of Jersey (in the Channel Islands) *UK, 1991*

jersey chaser *noun* a female college student who is attracted to athletes *US, 2002*

Jersey girls *nickname* a small group of women living in New Jersey whose husbands were killed in the World Trade Center on 11th September 2001, and who pressured a reluctant Bush administration into appointing a commission to investigate the attack. Evocative of an unrelated song by Bruce Springsteen *US, 2002*

Jersey highball *noun* a glass of milk *US, 1947*

Jersey lightning *noun* inexpensive, inferior whisky *US, 1848*

Jersey side of the snatch play *noun* middle age. Borrowed from the slang of bowlers, where the 'Jersey side' is to the left of the head pin *US, 1961*

Jesse James *noun* **1** in craps, a nine rolled with a four and a five. Jesse James was shot with a 45 calibre handgun *US, 1985*. **2** in hold 'em poker, a four and a five as the first two cards dealt to a player *US, 1981*

Jesse Owens *noun* ▶ **on the Jesse Owens** fast *US, 1948*

jessie *noun* **1** an effeminate man; a male homosexual. A female name used as a generic *UK, 1958*. **2** a pretty red-headed girl *US, 1947*

jesum crow! used for expressing surprise, dismay or disgust *US, 1971*

Jesus *adjective* used as an adjectival intensifier *BAHAMAS, 1982*

Jesus and his brothers *noun* J & B™ whisky. Scamto youth street slang (South African townships) *SOUTH AFRICA, 2005*

Jesus boots; Jesus shoes; Jesus slippers *noun* sandals *US, 1942*

Jesus Christ almighty!; Jesus Christ!; Jesus! used as a register of anger, frustration, wonder, etc. Blasphemous by derivation, probably blasphemous in use *US, 1994*

Jesus Christing *adjective* used as an intensifier *UK, 2000*

Jesus clip *noun* any small clip that is destined to be dropped, leading to an outburst of 'Oh Jesus!' because it will not be found. Biker (motorcycle) and bicyclist usage *US, 2001*

Jesus freak *noun* a fervent Christian, especially a recent convert *US, 1966*

Jesus freakery *noun* fervent Christianity *UK, 1996*

Jesus fuck! used for registering an intense reaction. This combination of two individually powerful words serves when neither 'Jesus!' nor FUCK! has strength enough *UK, 2001*

Jesus fucking Christ! used as an all-purpose oath of surprise, approval, disapproval, anger, etc. The most common use of the intensifying infix in the US *US, 1969*

Jesus gliders *noun* sandals *US, 1990*

Jesus H. Christ! used in oaths. Occasional substitutions of the middle initial, which is nothing more than a humorous, intensifying embellishment *US, 1892*

Jesus juice *noun* white wine. Allegedly coined by singer Michael Jackson. It was also claimed, in a *Vanity Fair* article, that Jackson called red wine 'Jesus blood'. Within months the term was widespread *US, 2004*

Jesus nut *noun* the main nut and bolt holding a helicopter's rotor blade to the body of the aircraft. Presumably one prayed to Jesus that the nut and bolt did not fail *US, 1977*

Jesus stiff *noun* a person who feigns religion to obtain food, lodging, or better privileges in prison *US, 1950*

Jesus to Jesus and eight hands around! used as a cry of disbelief *US, 1975*

Jesus weejuns *noun* sandals *US, 1969*

Jesus wept! used as an expression of annoyance, despair, disgust, impatience, etc. The shortest verse in the Bible (John 11: 35) used as a catchphrase *UK, 1937*

jet *noun* the recreational drug ketamine *US, 1994*

jet *verb* to leave in a hurry *US, 1968*

jet bumper *noun* in pinball, a bumper that upon impact with the ball scores and then propels the ball back into play *US, 1977*

jet fuel *noun* phencyclidine, the recreational drug known as PCP or angel dust *US, 1994*

jethro *noun* a coat. English gypsy use *UK, 2000*

jet jockey *noun* a jet pilot *US, 1950*

jew *noun* a jewfish or jewfish collectively *AUSTRALIA, 1902*

Jew; Jew down *verb* to bargain aggressively about a price. 'An offensive and stereotypical phrase.' (Multicultural Management Program Fellows, *Dictionary of Cautionary Words and Phrases*, 1989) *US, 1818*

Jewboy *noun* a Jewish man. Not said kindly *UK, 1796*

Jew canoe *noun* **1** a Cadillac *US, 1973*. **2** a Jaguar car. Upper-class society usage *UK, 1982*

jeweller's shop *noun* in mining, a rich deposit of opal or gold *AUSTRALIA, 1853*

jewellery *noun* **1** handcuffs *US, 1845*. **2** highly polished brass fittings on any firefighting equipment *US, 1954*. **3** ornamental lights on a long-haul truck *US, 1977*

Jew flag *noun* paper money *US, 1915*

Jew gear *noun* neutral gear, used while coasting downhill *US, 1963*

jewie *noun* a jewfish or jewfish collectively *AUSTRALIA, 1917*

jewish *noun* clothes; fabrics and materials. Scamto youth street slang (South African townships) *SOUTH AFRICA, 2005*

Jewish by hospitalization *noun* in homosexual usage, circumcized but not Jewish *US, 1987*

Jewish corned beef *noun* in homosexual usage, a circumcised penis *US, 1987*

Jewish foreplay *noun* pleading without results *US, 1987*

Jewish joanna *noun* a cash register. A variation of JEWISH PIANO; formed from a racial stereotype and rhyming slang JOANNA (a piano) *UK, 1977*

Jewish lightning *noun* an act of arson as a part of a fraudulent insurance claim *US, 1987*

Jewish overdrive *noun* coasting down a hill with the car or truck in neutral *US, 1969*

Jewish penicillin *noun* chicken soup *US, 1968*

Jewish people's time *noun* used for denoting a lack of punctuality *US, 1967*

Jewish piano *noun* a cash register. A racial stereotype is at the root of this allusion to another instrument with keys that makes 'music'. 'Jewish pianola' is an Australian variant *US, 1935*

Jewish sidewall *noun* white rubber sidewalls affixed to blackwall tyres *US, 1979*

Jewish typewriter *noun* a cash register. Racial stereotyping *UK, 1977*

Jew sheet *noun* an accounting, literal or figurative, of money owed by friends *US, 1987*

Jewtown *noun* a neighbourhood inhabited predominantly by Jewish people *US, 1955*

Jewy Louis *noun* vulgar ostentation masquerading as tasteful interior decor. Upper-class society usage, damning the fake-furniture of the *nouveau riche* by comparing it with the genuine exuberance and style of Louis XV or Louis XVI period furniture and design *UK, 1982*

jhaat *noun* pubic hair. Hindi used by English speakers *TRINIDAD AND TOBAGO, 2003*

jhatoor *noun* the penis. Hindi, used in English conversation *TRINIDAD AND TOBAGO, 2003*

jheri curl *noun* a relaxed, wet-look styling for naturally kinky black hair. Created by and named after Jheri (Robert) Redding (1907–98) *UK, 1994*

J-hole *noun* someone who makes despising easy. From a Will Farell skit on *Saturday Night Live US, 2001*

jib *noun* **1** the mouth *UK, 1860*. **2** on the coast of Nova Scotia, a small piece of land, especially triangular in shape *CANADA, 1980*

jib *verb* to tease. From 'jibe' (to taunt or insult) *UK, 1999*

jibberjabber; jibber-jabber *noun* meaningless chatter *UK, 1922*

jiboney; jabroni; jabroney *noun* **1** a low-level gangster, a tough *US, 1921*. **2** a newly immigrated foreigner; hence someone inexperienced or unsophisticated *US, 1960*

jibs *noun* the teeth *US, 1970*

jiffy *noun* **1** a moment, a short space of time. Also shortened to 'jiff' *UK, 1785*. **2** in computing, a tick of the computer clock, usually one millisecond *US, 1983*

jiffy *adjective* instant *US, 1949*

jig *noun* **1** a black person. Offensive *US, 1922*. **2** sexual intercourse *AUSTRALIA, 1988*. **3** a deception; trickery; mischief *US, 1777*. **4** in Newfoundland, a thread from a garment used to predict a date with a person of the opposite sex *CANADA, 1982*

jig *verb* **1** to stab (someone) *US, 1997*. **2** to play truant from school *AUSTRALIA, 1977*

jigaboo *noun* a black person. Offensive *US, 1926*

jigaboo joy shop *noun* a car supply shop specialising in chrome and other tawdry car accessories *US, 1950*

jig act *verb* to act foolishly or disruptively *IRELAND, 1997*

jig-a-jig; jig-jig *noun* sexual intercourse *US, 1896*

jigger *noun* **1** a bank robber *US, 1950*. **2** a lookout during a crime *US, 1925*. **3** an illegally constructed radio receiver. Prison usage *AUSTRALIA, 1944*. **4** a concealed device for giving an electric shock to a horse in a race *AUSTRALIA, 1953*. **5** a woman who will dance with a man for a fee *US, 1951*. **6** a door. An early cant word that survives in English gypsy use *UK, 1567*. **7** a slow freight train *US, 1927*. **8** a small railway line hand-car or trolley used in line maintenance *NEW ZEALAND, 1953*

jigger *verb* **1** to adjust, especially of numbers or statistics *US, 1997*. **2** to serve as a lookout during a crime *US, 1995*. ▶ **I'll be jiggered!; I'm jiggered!** used for registering surprise *UK, 1886*

jiggered *adjective* **1** damned, in great trouble. Euphemistic replacement for BUGGERED *UK, 1837*. **2** useless, broken *NEW ZEALAND, 2002*

jiggered up; jiggered *adjective* exhausted. As 'jiggered up', a nautical coinage first recorded in 1867; possibly a fusing of 'Jesus' and 'buggered', intended as a euphemism for BUGGERED UP (exhausted) *UK, 1999*

jigger man *noun* a lookout during a crime *US, 1924*

jigger moll *noun* a female lookout for a criminal operation who can also serve as a diversion or distraction *US, 1956*

jiggers! used as a warning to confederates that a prison guard is approaching *US, 1911*

jiggin; jigging *noun* an organised dance. Glasgow slang *UK: SCOTLAND, 1985*

jigging veil *noun* in Newfoundland, a widow's veil. As with JIG, these uses of the word seem to be akin to 'jigging' as a type of fishing *CANADA, 1982*

jiggle *verb* (of a woman) to walk so as to accentuate the movement of the breasts *US, 1965*

jiggle and jog *noun* a French person. Rhyming slang for FROG *UK, 1979*

jiggle bars *noun* the raised bars dividing motorway lanes *US, 1962*

jiggler *noun* **1** a skeleton key for a pin tumbler lock *UK, 1977*. **2** a wire used to manipulate a pay phone to make a call without charge *US, 1997*. **3** in electric line work, a secondary voltage tester with a glow light indicator *US, 1980*

jiggles and wires *noun* excitement *US, 1984*

jiggy *adjective* rich; hence fashionable, stylish; attractive *US, 1995*. ▶ **get jiggy; get jiggy with it 1** to dance, or feel the need to dance to the music *US, 1997*. **2** to have sex; to become sexually intimate *US, 2003*

jiggy swiggy *noun* the current drink of popular choice. JIGGY (fashionable), plus a play on SWIG (to drink) *UK, 2000*

jig lover *noun* a white person who, in the eyes of the racist using the term, treats black people as equals *US, 1950*

jig rig *noun* a car that has been given cheap, showy, useless modifications with no effect on its performance. From a racist stereotype of black values *US, 1986*

jigs *noun* a key *US, 1949*

jigtown *noun* a neighbourhood populated largely by black people *US, 1987*

jig up *verb* to dance in an animated fashion *BAHAMAS, 1982*

jihad *noun* enforcement of school discipline. The Islamic term for 'holy war' adopted as teenspeak, post 11th September 2001 *US, 2002*

jildi! quick!, hurry! Military slang, from Hindustani *jaldi INDIA, 1948*

jill *noun* the female form of the jock strap, worn to protect the genitals. The term derives from the 'Jack and Jill' nursery rhyme, as the male version, the 'jockstrap', is also known as the 'jackstrap' *CANADA, 1988*

jilleroo *noun* a female hand working on a cattle or sheep station. Modelled on JACKEROO *AUSTRALIA, 1943*

jilleroo *verb* to work as a jilleroo *AUSTRALIA, 1970*

jillick *verb* to throw a stone across water, underhand, to see how many times it skips *CANADA, 1937*

jillion *noun* a large, imagined number *US, 1939*

jillo! quick!, hurry! Military slang, from Hindustani *chalo*. Influenced by JILDI! *INDIA, 1984*

jill off *verb* (of a woman) to masturbate. Derivative of the male JACK OFF, and used far less frequently *US, 1989*

jillpots *noun* ▶ **his jillpots; her jillpots** that person, him, her. Circus, itinerant entertainers; probably an elaboration of JILLS *UK, 1937*

jills *noun* self, when combined with an appropriate pronoun – thus 'I jills' for me or myself, 'her jills' for her or herself, 'his jills' for him or himself, etc. Part of the Shelta vocabulary that is often used by sections of gypsy and Romany society as a means of discreet communication *UK, 1906*

Jim *noun* **1** the name given to a friend or offered as a gesture of friendliness. Black/jazz slang subverting the racism of JIM CROW *US, 1899*. **2** in film-making, an all-purpose forename that is prefixed to a worker's informal job title *UK, 1980*. **3** an interested loiterer and observer in an area where sexual trade is conducted *UK, 1977*

Jim and Jack *noun* the back. Rhyming slang *UK, 1967*

Jimbroni *noun* in American casinos, a dealer with neither great skills nor great reactions to situations *US, 1985*

jim cap; jim hat *noun* a condom *US, 1990*

Jim Crow *noun* **1** racial segregation; a racially segregated facility *US, 1921*. **2** in British Columbia logging, a single log load; in Vancouver Island coal mining, a bar for bending track or changing an underground rail switch *CANADA, 1989*. **3** on the railways, a tool used to straighten rails *US, 1952*

Jim-Crow *verb* to segregate racially *US, 1918*

Jim Crow *adjective* **1** racially segregated, reserved for black people *US, 1842*. **2** worthless *CANADA, 1962*

Jim Fish *noun* a black person. Offensive and derogatory *SOUTH AFRICA, 1930*

Jiminy Cricket! used as a mild expletive. Extended from obsolete 'jiminy!'; 'geminil', etc., which may derive from *Jesu domine*; modern use is probably intended to be a euphemism for JESUS CHRIST! *US, 1848*

jim-jams *noun* pyjamas *AUSTRALIA, 1961*

jimjams *noun* a heightened sense of anxiety *US, 1896*

Jim Johnson *noun* the equipment needed to inject heroin or another narcotic *US, 1977*

Jim Jones *noun* marijuana adulterated with cocaine and phencyclidine, the recreational drug known as PCP or angel dust. An eponym from the self-proclaimed messiah of the People's Temple, James (Jim) Warren Jones, 1931–78, who promised followers utopia. In 1977 the sect established Jonestown, an agricultural commune in Guyana, South America. On the 18th November 1978, Jones commanded cultists to drink a punch adulterated with cyanide. The majority obeyed: the mass suicide ('the Jonestown Massacre') took 913 lives, including 276 children. This marijuana cocktail is a metaphor for a dream, represented here as marijuana, that is poisoned *UK, 1998*

jimmies *noun* **1** gym shoes NEW ZEALAND, 1995. **2** tiny pieces of candy sprinkled on ice-cream, biscuits or cake US, 1947

jimmy *noun* **1** the penis US, 1988. **2** a condom US, 1990. **3** an injection of an illegal drug into the skin, not a vein US, 1952. **4** a short crowbar used by burglars UK, 1811. **5** a glass of beer. Homage to James Boag, a brewer AUSTRALIA, 1995. **6** a railway coal truck US, 1946

Jimmy *noun* **1** in Glasgow, used as a term of address to any male stranger UK: SCOTLAND, 1985. **2** anything produced by the truck division of General Motors US, 1953

jimmy *verb* **1** to pry open US, 1854. **2** to obtain free entry into a cinema, or a theatre, or an enclosure at a race meeting, by underhand means UK, 1977

jimmy bottle *noun* a gallon bottle TRINIDAD AND TOBAGO, 2003

Jimmy Boyle; jimmy *noun* foil (used in the preparation of heroin). Rhyming slang, based on the name of Jimmy Boyle (b.1944), a convicted murderer turned sculptor and novelist UK, 1996

Jimmy Britt *noun* shit. Rhyming slang based on the name of a boxing champion who toured Australia during World War I AUSTRALIA, 1977

Jimmy Britts *noun* **1** diarrhoea. Always used with 'the'; rhyming slang for THE SHITS, possibly based on the name of a US baseball player in the first decade of C20. Sometimes shortened to 'jimmys' AUSTRALIA, 1950. **2** a state of extreme annoyance. Rhyming slang for SHIT! AUSTRALIA, 1959

jimmy cap; jimmy hat *noun* a condom. Worn on a JIMMY (penis) US, 1988

Jimmy dog *noun* a marijuana cigarette US, 1986

Jimmy Hicks; Jimmy Hix *noun* **1** an injection of drugs. Rhyming slang for FIX, based on either an unknown Mr Hicks/Hix or guitarist Jimi Hendrix (1942–70), another variation, along with 'jimmy' and 'jimi' UK, 1950. **2** in craps, a roll of six. From the rhyme US, 1919. **3** in a deck of playing cards, a six US, 1951

Jimmy Hill; jimmy *noun* **1** a bill. Rhyming slang, based on the name of former footballer now television sports presenter Jimmy Hill (b.1928) UK, 2002. **2** a pill. Rhyming slang, formed from the name of former footballer now television sports presenter Jimmy Hill (b.1928) UK, 1992

jimmy jacket *noun* a condom US, 1997

jimmy jar *noun* a demijohn, or container of alcohol CANADA, 1977

Jimmy joint *noun* the penis US, 1976

Jimmy Logie *noun* a small lump of dried nasal mucus. Rhyming slang for 'bogie'; formed from the name of an Arsenal footballer of the mid-1950s UK, 1992

Jimmy Mason *noun* a basin, generally in the sense 'to have had a basinful' (as much as you can tolerate)'. Rhyming slang UK, 1992

Jimmy Nail *adjective* stale. Rhyming slang, formed from the name of the actor and singer (b.1954) UK, 1998

Jimmy Riddle; jimmy *noun* an act of urination; urine. Rhyming slang for PIDDLE UK, 1931

Jimmy Riddle; jimmy *verb* to urinate. Rhyming slang for PIDDLE UK, 1937

Jimmy Rollocks *noun* the testicles. Rhyming slang for BOLLOCKS UK, 1961

Jimmy Savile *verb* to travel UK, 1983

Jimmy the sleek *noun* a condom. A play on the nickname Jimmy the Greek (Demetrios Synodinos, later James George Snyder) (1919–96), a well-known gambler. The sleek finish is provided by latex which also takes the gamble out of the situation US, 1990s

Jimmy Valentine *noun* a criminal who specialises in breaking into safes US, 1949

Jimmy White *noun* shite (in all senses). Rhyming slang, formed from UK snooker player Jimmy 'Whirlwind' White. (b.1962) UK, 2003

Jimmy Woodser *noun* a person drinking alone at a public bar; a drink taken alone. From Jimmy Wood, the name of the protagonist in the eponymous song by Australian poet Barcroft Boake (1892). The song originally appeared with a footnote

explaining the term, perhaps indicating that it was otherwise unknown and therefore a coinage of Boake's. Some believe that the name refers to a real person, but this has not been substantiated AUSTRALIA, 1973

Jimmy Young; jimmy *noun* **1** a tongue. Rhyming slang UK, 1992. **2** a bribe. Rhyming slang for BUNG; formed from the name of a singer-turned-radio disc jockey (b.1923) UK, 1992

Jim Pike *noun* someone who is financing an illegal betting operation. Rhyming slang for MIKE AUSTRALIA, 1989

Jimson *noun* used as a male-to-male term of address US, 1953

jing *noun* money. A shortened 'jingle' US, 1973

jing-bang *noun* an uneducated, dirty, noisy person JAMAICA, 1952

jing-jang *noun* the penis US, 1960

jingle *noun* a telephone call US, 1949

jingle *verb* to make a telephone call US, 1959

jingle bell crew *noun* a team of pickpockets US, 1982

jingles *noun* pocket change US, 1989

jingly-jangly *adjective* of music, characterised by the use of acoustic guitars, bright tonal quality and (generally) happy songs UK, 2004

jink *verb* **1** in aerial combat, to make sudden, evasive movements UK, 1917. **2** to swindle. Originally a term from a card game that evolved into wider usage NEW ZEALAND, 1998

jinker *noun* in Newfoundland, on a boat, a bringer of bad luck CANADA, 1964

jinkers *noun* harness racing AUSTRALIA, 1989

jinkies *noun* ▶ **the jinkies; the wee jinkies** applied to anything that is considered excellent UK: SCOTLAND, 1988

jinky *adjective* unlucky. From 'jinx' US, 1969

jinx note *noun* a two-dollar note US, 1970

jipsy *adjective* anxious, energetic, flighty TRINIDAD AND TOBAGO, 1984

jislaaik!; jisl; jiss! used as an exclamation of such negative feelings as anger, frustration, distress, regret, etc; and of positive feelings such as admiration, approval, wonder, etc. Possibly a euphemism for 'Jesus!' (by intention, not etymology) SOUTH AFRICA, 1960

jism trail *noun* semen on a partner's body after ejaculation. A pun on the Chisholm Trail, the major route for cattle drives from Texas to Abilene US, 2003

jiss *noun* excitement, character IRELAND, 1992

jit *noun* **1** a nickel; five cents US, 1913. **2** semen US, 1974

jitney *noun* **1** a sexually available girl. Like the bus, anyone can get on if they have the fare BAHAMAS, 1982. **2** in poker, a $5 chip US, 1988

jits *adjective* excellent, nice SOUTH AFRICA, 2003

jitterbug *noun* a swing jazz enthusiast US, 1938

jitterbug *verb* **1** to fool around US, 1942. **2** to cause a car to bounce up and down suddenly through the use of hydraulic lifts operated by the driver US, 1980. **3** to fight, especially between gangs US, 1958

jitters *noun* uncontrolled shaking; extreme nervousness US, 1929

jittery *adjective* nervous, jumpy, on-edge UK, 1931

jive *noun* **1** swing jazz US, 1937. **2** a highly stylised vernacular that originated with black jazz musicians. Spoken by HEP CAT(S), incorporating a mix of new coinages or meanings with older adoptions; few original words remain in circulation US, 1928. **3** insincere talk; nonsense US, 1928. **4** marijuana or a marijuana cigarette US, 1963. **5** heroin or, less often, opium US, 1946

jive *verb* **1** to speak with a lack of sincerity US, 1928. **2** to dance US, 1938

jive *adjective* insincere, phony, pretentious US, 1946

jive-ass *noun* an insincere, unreliable person US, 1967

jive-ass; jive-arse *adjective* worthless, unreliable US, 1959

jive bomber *noun* a skilled dancer US, 1945

jive doo jee *noun* heroin UK, 1998

jiver *noun* an inveterate flatterer US, 1947

jive stick *noun* a marijuana cigarette US, 1945

jizz *verb* to ejaculate *US, 1983*

jizz; jizzum; jism; jiz; jizm; gism; gizzum *noun* semen. Links to an earlier use as 'life-force, energy, spirit'; a meaning that, occasionally, may still be intended *US, 1941*

jizzbag *noun* an offensive and disgusting person. Literally, 'a condom' *US, 1993*

jizzer *noun* a scene in a pornographic film or photograph showing a man ejaculating *US, 1995*

jizz joint *noun* a sex club *US, 2000*

jizz-mopper *noun* an employee in a pornographic video arcade or sex show who cleans up after customers who have come have left *US, 1994*

jizz rag *noun* a rag used for wiping semen *US, 1983*

JJ Cale *noun* a jail. Rhyming slang, formed from the name of the US musician (b.1938) *UK, 2004*

JK! just kidding! Used after saying something that sounds improbable *US, 2002*

JLD (in doctors' shorthand) *just like dad*. Medical slang *UK, 2002*

J-load *nickname* a generously proportioned backside. After the widely appreciated hindquarters of film actress and singer Jennifer Lopez (b.1970), popularly known and marketed by the nickname 'J Lo'. Recorded in use in contemporary gay society *UK, 2003*

JO *noun* **1** an act of male masturbation. An abbreviation of JERK-OFF *US, 1972*. **2** a job *US, 1993*

JO *verb* (used of a male) to masturbate. An abbreviation of the oh-so-common JERK OFF *US, 1959*

joan; jone *verb* to insult in a competitive, quasi-friendly spirit *US, 1939*

Joanie *adjective* profoundly out of touch with current fashions and trends *US, 1982*

joanna; joana; joanner; johanna *noun* a piano. Rhyming slang *UK, 1846*

Joan of Arc *noun* **1** a lark, in phrases such as 'fuck this for a lark'. Rhyming slang *UK, 1998*. **2** a park. Rhyming slang *UK, 1998*. **3** a shark. Rhyming slang *AUSTRALIA, 1998*

job *noun* **1** used as a substitute for a noun which is apparent from context, especially of cars. Sometimes embellished to 'jobby' *US, 1896*. **2** an inanimate or mechanical article, a thing *UK, 1943*. **3** a person. Usually prefixed with a noun or adjective characteristic *US, 1927*. **4** a criminal venture, usually a robbery *UK, 1690*. **5** a medical procedure. A variant of 'job' (a variety), usually combined with a body part: 'nose', 'boob', etc *US, 1943*. **6** an act of defecation *US, 1975*. **7** in professional wrestling, a planned, voluntary loss *US, 1999*. **8** the injection of a drug for non-medicinal purposes *US, 1970*. ► **do a job** to defecate. Sometimes embellished to 'jobbie' *AUSTRALIA, 1942*. ► **just the job; the job** exactly what is required *UK, 1943*. ► **on the job** having sex, engaged in sexual intercourse *UK, 1966*. ► **the job** the police (as a profession). Police slang *UK, 1999*

job *verb* **1** to rob, to steal, to cheat *US, 1889*. **2** to suffer a planned, voluntary loss in a professional wrestling match *US, 1990*. **3** to hit or strike; to punch *AUSTRALIA, 1915*. **4** to inject a drug *US, 1967*

jo bag *noun* a condom *UK, 1961*

job and finish *noun* a period of employment that is limited by the time it takes to do a specific task. Originally in Merchant Navy use *UK, 1984*

jobbed *adjective* incriminated by false evidence *UK, 1996*

jobber *noun* a professional wrestler who is regularly assigned to lose to advance the careers of others *US, 1990*

jobber to the stars *noun* a moderately talented professional wrestler who is assigned to lose to the most popular wrestlers *US, 1996*

jobbie *noun* **1** used as a substitute noun which is apparent from its context; an item. Extension of JOB *US, 1960*. **2** a transaction; a situation; a piece of work; an event; a procedure; an occurrence. A variation of conventional and unconventional JOB *US, 2001*. **3** a turd. From Scottish dialect *jobbie* (a little job); compare with BIG JOBS (defecation). Widely popularised in the 1970s by comedian Billy Connolly *UK, 2000*. **4** a racehorse *US, 1974*

Jobbie *noun* a Job Centre *UK, 2001*

jobbie-jabber *noun* a male homosexual. A reference to anal sex formed on JOBBIE (a turd) *UK, 2003*

jobo; joro *noun* a woman, mistress or prostitute. From the Japanese, used by US military in Korea *US, 1947*

job out *verb* to assign a wrestler to lose intentionally to advance the career of another *US, 1990*

jobroni; jobrone; gibroni *noun* a professional wrestler who is regularly assigned to lose. Embellishments of the standard JOBBER *US, 1999*

jobsworth *noun* anyone in a position of authority (no matter how petty) who reinforces the personal power of office by insistence on the finer details of whichever bureaucracy or rulebook is represented, generally to veto or reject a course of action. From the expression, 'It's more than my job's worth' *UK, 1970*

jock *noun* **1** an athlete, especially a student athlete. Originally referred to a man's genitals, leading to 'jock strap' as an athletic support, leading to a clipped 'jock' for the support, leading to application to the man wearing the support. Usually, but not always, suggestive of a certain mindlessness *US, 1958*. **2** a jockey *UK, 1826*. **3** a disc jockey *US, 1947*. **4** a navy fighter pilot *US, 1959*. **5** the penis; the male genitals *US, 1790*. **6** an athletic support. An abbreviation of 'jock strap' *US, 1985*. **7** a computer programmer who enumerates all possible combinations to find the one that solves the problem *US, 1983*

Jock *noun* a Scot. Originally armed services' use, then widespread; from the Scottish variant of proper name John *UK, 1788*

jock *verb* **1** to have sex *UK, 1699*. **2** to like; to find attractive *US, 1986*

Jock *adjective* Scottish. Of military origin *UK, 1984*

jock collar *noun* a rubber ring fitted around the base of the penis. Later and better known as a COCK RING *US, 1969*

jocked off *verb* of a professional jockey, to have been deprived of an agreed mount *UK, 1964*

jocker *noun* **1** an aggressive, predatory male homosexual *US, 1893*. **2** an older homosexual male living with and by virtue of the earnings of a younger companion. Originally tramp slang *US, 1890s to 1970s*

jockette *noun* a female student athlete. Spoken for effect, rarely spontaneously *US, 1980*

jockey *noun* **1** a prostitute's client *UK, 1977*. **2** a rapist *IRELAND, 1996*. **3** a driver of any heavy-load vehicle *UK, 1951*

jockey *verb* to drive, to operate *US, 1948*

jockey slut *noun* a girl who trades her sexual availability to disc jockeys in exchange for hanger-on status. The dance music magazine *Jockey Slut* was first published in 1997 *UK, 1997*

jockey's whip *noun* a bed; a sleep. Rhyming slang from KIP *UK, 1960*

jockey's whips *noun* **1** chips. Rhyming slang *UK, 1969*. **2** LSD. Rhyming slang for TRIPS (LSD) *UK, 2002*

jock itch *noun* a sweat-induced rash in the crotch *US, 1950*

jock jacket *noun* a condom *UK, 1998*

Jock Mackay *noun* a pie, especially a 'Scotch pie'. Glasgow rhyming slang, formed from an imagined or generic Scotsman, also heard of in the wistful expression 'Och aye, Jock Mackay' *UK: SCOTLAND, 1988*

jocko *noun* an athlete, a jock *US, 1970*

Jocko land *noun* Scotland. Extended from JOCK (a Scot) *UK: ENGLAND, 1994*

jocks *noun* male underwear *IRELAND, 1996*

jock-sniffer *noun* an obsequious sports fan who tries to associate with athletes *US, 1971*

jockstrap *noun* an athlete *US, 1944*

jock strapper *noun* an athlete *US, 1970*

Jodrell Bank; jodrell *noun* an act of masturbation. Rhyming slang for WANK formed on the observatory located in Cheshire *UK, 1992*

Jody *noun* **1** the anonymous seducer of a soldier's girlfriend back home *US, 1944*. **2** a male civilian during wartime *US, 1944*. **3** a black seducer of white women *US, 1967*

joe *noun* **1** coffee. Originally tramp slang *US, 1930*. **2** a condom *NEW ZEALAND, 1976*

Joe *noun* **1** a fool. Especially in constructions such as 'make a joe of yourself' *NEW ZEALAND, 1965*. **2** a new worker who cannot perform up to expected standards *US, 1989*. **3** a regular fellow *US, 1911*. **4** used to create an imaginary person, first name Joe, last name the quality or characteristic that is personified *US, 1912*. **5** a member of the Navajo Indian tribe. An abbreviation of Nava-Joe *US, 1963*. **6** a prison inmate who is easily imposed upon *UK, 1978*. **7** a police officer *US, 1987*. **8** Schlitz™ beer. From the full name, the Joseph Schlitz Brewing Company *US, 1979*. ▶ **out the Joe** completely drunk *NEW ZEALAND, 1964*

Joe Baksi; Joe Baxi *noun* a taxi. Rhyming slang, based on a US heavyweight boxer well known in the UK. In Glasgow use and also noted in UK prison use *UK, 1988*

Joe Balls *noun* used as a derogatory personification of the typical US soldier *US, 1946*

Joe Blake *noun* **1** a snake. Rhyming slang *AUSTRALIA, 1905*. **2** a gambling stake; a wooden stake. Rhyming slang *UK, 1992*

Joe Blakes *noun* the shaking symptoms of extreme alcoholism. Rhyming slang for the SHAKES *AUSTRALIA, 1944*

Joe Bloggs *noun* everyman; a notional average man *UK, 1969*

Joe Blow *noun* **1** an average, typical citizen *US, 1924*. **2** an excellent musician *US, 1945*

Joe Blow biography *noun* a glowing biographical story about a soldier in his hometown newspaper *US, 1946*

Joe Bucks *noun* any wealthy man *BAHAMAS, 1982*

Joe Chink *noun* a heroin addiction. A further personification of the older CHINAMAN (a heroin addiction) *US, 1973*

Joe College *noun* a stereotypical male college student *US, 1932*

Joe Cool *noun* used for expressing the ultimate in fashion and modernity *US, 1971*

Joe Daki *noun* a Pakistani. Rhyming slang for PAKI *UK, 1998*

Joe Doe; Joe Roe *noun* used as a name for a male blind date. Teen slang *US, 1951*

Joe Erk *noun* a fool. Rhyming slang for BERK – in turn, rhyming slang for CUNT (a fool) *UK, 1998*

Joe Gurr *noun* prison. Rhyming slang for STIR *UK, 1938*

Joe Hero *noun* a typical hero *US, 1977*

Joe Hook *noun* **1** a crook. Rhyming slang, probably influenced by HOOK (to steal) or HOOKY (stolen, counterfeit) *UK, 1932*. **2** a book. Rhyming slang *UK, 1960*

Joe Hunt; joey *noun* a foolish or unlikeable person. Rhyming slang for CUNT. The shortened form is probably influenced by JOEY (a clown) *UK, 1960*

Joe Loss *noun* something of little or no value. Rhyming slang for TOSS, formed from the name of the London-born bandleader, 1909–90 *UK, 1992*

Joe Loss *verb* to toss. Rhyming slang *UK, 1992*

Joe PakiPaki from Opunaki *noun* the notional, typical New Zealander *NEW ZEALAND, 1984*

Joe Patriot *noun* a prototypical patriot *US, 1994*

Joe-pot *noun* a coffee pot. Korean war usage *US, 1979*

Joe Public *noun* an average citizen; the regular man on the street. Originally theatrical of an audience member; gently derogatory *US, 1942*

Joe Punter *noun* an (imagined) average customer. A variation of JOE PUBLIC (the public). Combines JOE (a regular fellow) with PUNTER (a generic customer) *UK, 2000*

Joe Rook *noun* **1** a crook. Perhaps a variant of JOE HOOK, possibly influenced by 'rook' (to defraud); may also be an adaptation of JOE ROURKE (a pickpocket) *UK, 1960*. **2** a book, in particular the book made by an on-course bookmaker; hence, a bookmaker *UK, 1961*

Joe Rookie *noun* a bookmaker. Rhyming slang for 'bookie', from JOE ROOK (a bookmaker's book) *UK, 1998*

Joe Rourke *noun* a pickpocket. Rhyming slang, formed on synonymous but obsolete 'fork' *UK, 1938*

joes *noun* a fit of irritation or depression *AUSTRALIA, 1910*

Joe Schmo; Joe Shmo *noun* an average, if dull and dim, person *US, 1947*

Joe Sixpack *noun* a stereotypical working-class male *US, 1972*

Joe Skinner; Jim Skinner; Jimmy Skinner *noun* a dinner. Rhyming slang *UK, 1938*

Joe Soap *noun* an easily put-upon employee, a fool. Rhyming slang for DOPE; originally military *UK, 1943*

Joe Strummer *noun* a disappointing or depressing event. Rhyming slang, formed from the name of the celebrated rock musician, 1952–2002 *UK, 1998*

Joe the grinder *noun* used as a generic term for the man that a prisoner's wife or girlfriend takes up with while the man is in prison *US, 1964*

Joe the toff *adverb* off, away. Glasgow rhyming slang *UK: SCOTLAND, 1988*

joey *noun* **1** a clown. An abbreviation of the name of legendary clown Joseph Grimaldi (1779–1837) *UK, 1889*. **2** an errand-runner in a drug-dealing operation. Probably from the previous sense as 'clown' *UK, 1999*. **3** a baby *AUSTRALIA, 1968*. **4** a youthful, attractive homosexual male prostitute *AUSTRALIA, 1979*. **5** a young kangaroo or wallaby still living in the pouch; the young of any marsupial. Origin unknown; the earliest example (1828) refers to a young possum. Later 'joey' was also applied to the young of various animals, such as parrots, horses and cattle, but is now restricted as defined *AUSTRALIA, 1839*. **6** an Anglo-Australian person. Used as a, somewhat mild, derogatory term by Australians of Mediterranean and Middle Eastern background *AUSTRALIA, 1987*. **7** in prison, illicit goods, an illegal parcel *UK, 1950*. **8** a condom *NEW ZEALAND, 1984*. **9** the bleed period of the menstrual cycle *UK, 1984*

Joey *noun* someone of little importance. Rhyming slang for JOE HUNT (CUNT) informed by JOEY (a clown) *UK, 1990*

Joey Grey *noun* a rabbit stew. English gypsy use *UK, 2000*

Joeys; Johies *nickname* Johannesburg *SOUTH AFRICA, 1974*

jog *verb* **1** to push with one foot while skateboarding *US, 1984*. **2** in Newfoundland, of a boat, to stop (heave to) into the wind, or sail slowly *CANADA, 1960*

jogger; jogar *verb* to entertain, to sing, to play. Polari, from Italian *giocare* (to play) *UK, 2002*

joggering omee *noun* an entertainer. A combination of JOGGER (to entertain) and OMEE (a man) *UK, 2002*

joggy *noun* a hacksaw *US, 1949*

joharito *noun* heroin *UK, 2003*

john *noun* **1** a prostitute's client. From the sense as 'generic man', probably via the criminal use as 'dupe' or 'victim' *US, 1906*. **2** a police officer. An abbreviation of John Darm, an obsolete pun on French *gendarme* (a police officer) which appears in several variations in the US from 1858, or an abbreviated form of the older John Hop, rhyming with COP. First recorded standing alone in Australia, 1898 *AUSTRALIA, 1898*. **3** in a deck of playing cards, a jack or knave *US, 1967*. **4** a toilet *US, 1942*. **5** a condom. A shortened form of JOHNNY used with over-familiar contempt by prostitutes *UK, 1977* ▷ *see:* JOHN THOMAS

John *noun* a lieutenant *US, 1937*

John Audley; John Orderly abridge the performance!; quickly. Theatrical, from actor-manager John Richardson (d.1837) who would ask 'Is John Audley here?' to cue a speedy conclusion in readiness for his next audience; by legend this was a technique learnt from a John Audley or Orderly *UK, 1864*

John book *noun* a prostitute's list of customers *US, 1973*

John Brown! used as a non-profane oath *BAHAMAS, 1982*

John Bull *adjective* full; drunk *AUSTRALIA, 1971*

John Bull; john *noun* **1** a tug, a pull. Rhyming slang *UK, 1956*. **2** an arrest. Rhyming slang for PULL *UK, 1984*. ▶ **on the John Bull; go**

on the John Bull engaged in a casual or recreational quest for a sexual partner. Rhyming slang for 'on the pull' *UK, 1992*

John Cleese *noun* cheese. Rhyming slang, formed from the name of the comedy actor and writer (b.1939) who, as a member of *Monty Python's Flying Circus* was, in 1972, partly responsible for the 'Cheese Shop' sketch *UK, 1998*

John D *noun* kerosene. An allusion to John D. Rockefeller and hence petroleum-based products *US, 1975*

John Dory *noun* the story *AUSTRALIA, 1987*

John Grieg *noun* the leg. Glasgow rhyming slang, formed from the name of the Glasgow Rangers footballer *UK: SCOTLAND, 1996*

John Hancock *noun* a person's signature. From the attention-getting manner in which Hancock signed the Declaration of Independence *US, 1887*

John Henry *noun* **1** a person's signature. A variant of the more common JOHN HANCOCK *US, 1972.* **2** the penis *US, 1888*

John Hop *noun* a police officer. Rhyming slang for COP *AUSTRALIA, 1907*

John Law *noun* the police *US, 1906*

Johnnie; Johnny *noun* a man *UK, 1673*

johnny *noun* **1** a condom *UK, 1965.* **2** a police officer *US, 1997.* **3** a toilet *UK, 1850.* **4** a prison guard *US, 1950.* **5** a loose-fitting, abbreviated hospital nightshirt with a slit down the back *US, 1958.* **6** an inexperienced firefighter *US, 1954*

johnnybait *noun* a sexually alluring young woman or young man *UK, 1963*

johnny ball *noun* in electric line work, a guy strain insulator *US, 1980*

johnny-be-good *noun* a police officer; the police. Plays on Chuck Berry's 1958 rock 'n' roll classic 'Johnny B. Goode', punning the inherent quality of goodness displayed by the police; possibly ironic. Black usage *US, 2005*

Johnny Black *nickname* Johnny Walker™ Black Label whisky *US, 1990*

Johnny Bliss *noun* an act of urination. Rhyming slang for PISS *AUSTRALIA, 1969*

Johnny Canuck *noun* a Canadian, especially a soldier *CANADA, 1957*

Johnny Cash *noun* an act of urination. Rhyming slang for SLASH, formed from the name of the US singer, 1932–2003 *UK, 1992*

Johnny-come-lately *noun* a new recruit; a newcomer; hence, someone inexperienced or unsophisticated *US, 1839*

Johnny Darky *noun* a black man. Offensive *UK, 2000*

Johnny Foreigner *noun* anyone who is not British *UK, 1990*

Johnny Giles *noun* haemorrhoids. Rhyming slang for 'piles'; formed from the name of an Irish footballer (b.1940) *UK, 1998*

Johnny-go-fast *noun* amphetamines *UK, 2003*

Johnny Gyppo *noun* an Egyptian; Egypt personified *UK, 1985*

Johnny Ham *noun* a private investigator *US, 1986*

Johnny Horner *noun* a corner. Rhyming slang *UK, 1909*

Johnny Long Shoes *noun* the man who steals a prisoner's girlfriend or wife after incarceration *US, 1991*

Johnny-no-stars *noun* a person of limited intelligence and/or ambition. From a system employed by fast-food giant McDonald's™ that is designed to recognise a worker's achievements and acquisition of skills; to have no stars is seen to be a badge of no intelligence *UK, 2002*

Johnny O'Brien *noun* in railroading, a boxcar *US, 1977*

Johnny-on-the-spot *noun* a person who is available whenever needed *US, 1896*

Johnny Pissoff *noun* a very annoying person *US, 1971*

Johnny pump *noun* a fire hydrant *US, 1955*

Johnny Raper *noun* a newspaper. Rhyming slang based on the name of an Australian Rugby League football player *AUSTRALIA, 1983*

Johnny Reb *noun* any rural white male from the southern US *US, 1884*

Johnny Rollocks *noun* the testicles. Rhyming slang for BOLLOCKS; a member of the JIMMY ROLLOCKS and TOMMY ROLLOCKS family *UK, 1984*

Johnny Rotten *nickname* Sir William Wratten, commander of all Royal Air Force assets in the Gulf war *UK, 1991*

Johnny Skinner *noun* a dinner. Rhyming slang; a part of the JOE SKINNER family *UK, 1960*

Johnny Thunder *noun* the combination of an M-16 antipersonnel mine and a M-79 grenade launcher *US, 1991*

johnny-too-bad *noun* a hoodlum, a criminal. A reversal of JOHNNY-BE-GOOD (a police officer). Immortalised by the thus-titled song by the Slickers in the 1973 Jamaican film *The Harder They Come*. UK black usage *JAMAICA, 1994*

Johnny Tourist *noun* a holiday-maker. A personification of the average tourist *UK, 1999*

Johnny Vaughan *noun* pornography. Rhyming slang for PORN, based on television presenter Johnny Vaughan *UK, 2002*

Johnny Walker *noun* an overly talkative person; an informer. Rhyming slang, 'talker'; possibly derived from the brand name whisky (from its tongue-loosening properties) or, perhaps, formed from the name of a BBC radio disc jockey, in tribute to his fluency *UK, 1992*

Johnny Walker *nickname* **1** Pope John XXIII. A pun on a whisky brand name; Pope John XXIII (born 1881, ascended 1958, died 1963) earned this nickname from his habit of sneaking out of the Vatican and walking the streets of Rome *ITALY, 1972.* **2** Lt General Walton H. Walker (1889–1950). Walker served with great distinction in World War I, World War 2, and Korea; he was killed in a car accident in Korea *US, 1973*

Johnny Woodser *noun* a person drinking alone in a pub *NEW ZEALAND, 1941*

John O'Groats *noun* sexual satisfaction. Rhyming slang for OATS, as in 'get your oats' *UK, 1992*

John Peel *noun* a jellied eel. Rhyming slang, formed from the name of a legendary huntsman (1776–1854) or BBC radio disc jockey (1993–2004) *UK, 1992*

John Prescott *noun* a waistcoat. Rhyming slang, formed from the name of the Labour politician (b.1938), UK's Deputy Prime Minister (1997–2007). The latest of many men, real or imagined, named Prescott who have lent a name to this rhyme *UK, 1998*

John Q. Law *noun* the personification of law enforcement *US, 1994*

John Selwyn Gummer *noun* a disappointing or depressing event. Rhyming slang for BUMMER, formed from the name of a Conservative politician and sometime government minister *UK, 1998*

johnsie *noun* the room, apartment or house where you live *US, 2002*

johnson *noun* **1** the penis. Despite an 1862 citation, the word was not widely used in this sense until the 1970s *UK, 1862.* **2** a pound of marijuana, especially a pound of marijuana cigarettes. A pound of marijuana cigarettes would be an 'lb. of J's', hence the initials and the leap to President Lyndon 'LBJ' Baines Johnson *US, 1976.* **3** a marijuana cigarette *UK, 2002.* **4** crack cocaine *UK, 1998.* **5** coffee *US, 1962*

Johnson bar *noun* the emergency brake on a truck *US, 1971*

Johnson family *noun* **1** collectively, the underworld *US, 1926.* **2** a mythical family, all of whose members believe that everything is legitimate and righteous *US, 1982*

Johnson grass *noun* marijuana. Johnson grass is a ubiquitous weed in the US, hence the pun *US, 1971*

John Thomas; john *noun* the penis *UK, 1879*

John Wayne *noun* **1** in the television and film industries, an exaggerated punch *US, 2003.* **2** a bulldozer tank *US, 1991.* **3** a small, collapsible can opener for use in the field. Officially known as a P-38 *US, 1973.* **4** a train. Rhyming slang, formed from the name of the US film actor, 1907–79 *UK, 1998*

John Wayne *verb* to act with reckless disregard for life and safety. One of several military slang terms based on John Wayne (1907–79), the US actor who portrayed a series of tough Western and army heroes *US, 1973*

John Wayne cookie *noun* a US Army c-ration biscuit or candy bar *US, 1986*

John Wayne High School *nickname* the US Army's Special Warfare Training School, Fort Bragg, North Carolina *US, 1991*

John Wayne's hairy saddle bags *noun* the testicles hanging in the scrotum *UK, 1997*

John Woo *noun* excrement, faeces. Rhyming slang, formed from the name of the Chinese film director (b.1946) *UK, 2003*

join *verb* ► **join the Air Force** to die *US, 1994*. ► **join the birds** to jump from a moving train before an unavoidable collision *US, 1975*

joined-up thinking *noun* coherent, considered and well-organised logic *UK, 1989*

join out *verb* to go to work for a circus *US, 1895*

joint *noun* **1** a marijuana cigarette.. For 50 years, the top of the slang pile, easily deposing its predecessors and fending off challengers *US, 1942*. **2** the equipment used to smoke opium *US, 1946*. **3** a syringe *US, 1953*. **4** a pistol *US, 1949*. **5** the penis *US, 1931*. **6** a place, anything from a country to a house *AUSTRALIA, 1945*. **7** a prison *US, 1933*. **8** an establishment that sells alcohol illegally; any disreputable establishment *US, 1877*. **9** an artistic creation (recording, film, etc), also a trainer as a fashion item, especially in black or hip-hop culture *US, 1988*. **10** a hip-hop recording that features more than one leading rapper. Clipped from 'joint recording' *US, 2001*. **11** in horse racing, a battery-powered device used illegally by a jockey to shock a horse during a race *US, 1951*

joint girl *noun* a prostitute working in one specific disreputable establishment *US, 1972*

joint of beef *noun* a boss. Rhyming slang for 'chief' *UK, 1992*

joints *noun* a pair of any popular brand of athletic shoes *US, 1993*

joint-wise *adjective* sophisticated and skilled at the ways and means of serving a prison sentence gracefully *US, 1950*

JOJ *adjective* just off the jet. Applied to a recent immigrant or, in the usage of Hawaiian youth, to a tourist recently arrived in Hawaii *US, 1981*

jojee *noun* heroin *US, 1971*

joke *noun* **1** a person who is not taken seriously *AUSTRALIA, 1992*. **2** an operation that offers the possibility of improper gain *AUSTRALIA, 1989*

joke and farce *noun* the posterior, the buttocks, the anus. Rhyming slang for ARSE *UK, 2003*

joke box *noun* a good teller of jokes *BAHAMAS, 1982*

joker *noun* a person; a bloke or fellow *AUSTRALIA, 1810*

joker poker *noun* any game of poker played with 53 cards, including the joker *US, 1988*

jokers' jailhouse *noun* a lunatic asylum *US, 1971*

jol; joll; jall; jawl; joil; jola; jorl *verb* **1** to go somewhere (especially in search of entertainment); to depart *SOUTH AFRICA, 1946*. **2** to flirt; to have a love-affair *SOUTH AFRICA, 1969*. **3** to make merry, to party. From Afrikaans *SOUTH AFRICA, 1970*

jol; joll; jorl; jaul *noun* a good time; a party, a dance, or similar social occasion. The variations 'jorl' and 'jaul' are representative of the word's pronunciation *SOUTH AFRICA, 1957*

Joliet Josie *noun* a sexually attractive girl under the legal age of consent. Joliet is the site of the major prison in Illinois *US, 1950*

joller; jawler *noun* a person who frequents (unsavoury) places of entertainment; a hedonist, a party-goer, etc. 'Jawler' is spelt as 'joller' is pronounced *SOUTH AFRICA, 1963*

jollier *noun* a good time, a party. An elaboration of 'jolly' *UK, 2002*

jollies *noun* **1** pleasure *US, 1956*. **2** thrills *AUSTRALIA, 1982*. **3** the female breasts *UK, 2002*

jollo *noun* a party or celebration. From 'jolly', or perhaps, 'jollification' *AUSTRALIA, 1907*

jollop *noun* **1** a strong liquor, especially whisky. From an earlier medical sense *AUSTRALIA, 1942*. **2** liquid drugs, usually methadone or morphine. An extension of the original sense as 'a medicine' *UK, 2001*. **3** a large meal of leftovers *CANADA, 1988*

jollup *noun* semen *UK, 2002*

jolly *noun* **1** a good time; an pleasant excursion; a party. An abbreviation of 'jollification' *UK, 1905*. **2** a Royal Marine. The Royal Marines are known as 'the Jollies' *UK, 1825*. **3** in horse race betting, the favourite *UK, 1991*

jolly *verb* to treat a person with such positive cheeriness that a state of a good humour is encouraged or maintained *UK, 1865*

jolly *adjective* drunk. Originally euphemistic, then colloquial *UK, 1652*

jolly *adverb* very, exceedingly *UK, 1838*

jolly bean *noun* an amphetamine tablet *US, 1969*

jolly for polly *adjective* eager for money *UK, 1987*

jolly green *noun* marijuana. A suggestion that GREEN (marijuana/GRASS) might make you JOLLY (drunk), especially if taken in giant portions implied by the brand name character the Jolly Green Giant *UK, 1998*

Jolly Green Giant *noun* any of several large military helicopters, especially the CH-3C helicopter, used during the Vietnam war for counterinsurgency airlifts *US, 1965*

jolly hockey sticks *adjective* redolent of the atmosphere or culture of a girls' public school; also used of a feminine 'country' accent. Used parodically. Coined for the BBC radio comedy of the early 1950s *Educating Archie*, by comedy actress Beryl Reid, 1918–96 *UK, 1999*

jolly joker *noun* a poker. Rhyming slang *UK, 1992*

jolly juice *noun* alcoholic drink *UK, 2001*

jolly pop; jolly popper *noun* an occasional, non-addicted user of heroin *US, 2002*

jolly well *adverb* used as an intensifier *UK, 1898*

jolt *noun* **1** a shock *US, 1966*. **2** a strong and bracing alcoholic drink *US, 1904*. **3** an injection or dose of a drug *US, 1907*. **4** a prison sentence *US, 1912*

jolt *verb* **1** to shock *US, 1961*. **2** to inject a drug *US, 1953*

Jolting Joe *noun* Joe DiMaggio. An extraordinarily gifted player for the New York Yankees baseball team from 1936 to 1951 *US, 1965*

Jo Maxi *noun* a taxi. Also abbreviated to 'Jo' *IRELAND, 2003*

Jonah *noun* a superstitious gambler; a gambler perceived by other gamblers to bring bad luck *US, 1849*

Jonah *verb* in craps, to try to influence the roll of the dice with body movements, hand gestures or incantations *US, 1974*

Jonathan Ross; jonathan *noun* something of little or no value. Rhyming slang for TOSS used in the sense 'not give a toss' formed from the name of a television and radio presenter, chat-show host and film critic (b.1960) *UK, 1998*

jone *verb* to put a spell on someone *CANADA, 1982* ▷ *see:* JOAN

jones *noun* **1** an addiction *US, 1962*. **2** an intense craving or yearning *US, 1970*. **3** heroin *US, 1970*. **4** the penis *US, 1966*

jones *verb* to crave *US, 1974*

Joneses *noun* the notional family next door who are the basis for your aspirations for social equality *UK, 1932*

jones man *noun* a heroin dealer *US, 1972*

jong *noun* **1** a black person, especially a black man. An offensive term, from older senses as 'a black male servant or slave' derived from Afrikaans *jongen* (a boy) *SOUTH AFRICA, 1908*. **2** used as a friendly, informal term of address, regardless of gender; a boyfriend *SOUTH AFRICA, 1911*

jong! used as an expression of anger, frustration, surprise, pleasure, etc *SOUTH AFRICA, 1956*

jonnic; jonnick; jonic; jonick *adjective* **1** true. From British dialect *AUSTRALIA, 1874*. **2** genuine *AUSTRALIA, 1960*

joog *noun* **1** in Newfoundland, especially of alcohol, a small amount, a drop *CANADA, 1968*. **2** the jugular vein. Also spelt 'jug' *US, 1994*

joog *verb* **1** to have sex. Sometimes spelt 'jewg' *JAMAICA, 1942*. **2** in Newfoundland, to drain or drink completely *CANADA, 1968*. **3** to tease *US, 2002*

jook *noun* sexual intercourse *TRINIDAD AND TOBAGO, 1993*

jook verb **1** to poke with a sharp object BARBADOS, 1965. **2** to stab TRINIDAD AND TOBAGO, 1827

jooks noun trousers UK: SCOTLAND, 1988

josh verb to mock, to tease; to banter US, 1852

joshed up adjective stylishly dressed and well-presented. From 'zhoosh' (clothes) UK, 2002

josh it verb to die UK, 1999

joskin noun a country bumpkin UK, 1811

josser noun an outsider. Polari UK, 1933

jostle verb to engage in petty swindles US, 1953

jostler noun the member of a pickpocket crew whose clumsy bumping into the victim distracts him while a confederate picks the pocket US, 1929

jotters noun ▶ **get your jotters; be given your jotters** to be dismissed from employment. Glasgow slang UK, 1985

joual noun the working-class dialect of Frenglish, a mixture of languages, used in Quebec. This term, used by English Quebec speakers rather than 'Frenglish', may derive from a corruption of cheval French for 'horse', i.e. 'French spoken on horseback'. Famed and favourite playwright Michel Tremblay wrote all his early plays in 'joual' and refused to allow them to be translated until the separatist party won power in 1976 CANADA, 2001

jouk verb to play truant; to dodge, duck, avoid, hide CANADA, 1988

jounts noun clothing US, 1987

journo noun a journalist AUSTRALIA, 1965

journo adjective being of journalists or journalism AUSTRALIA, 1999

joust noun a physical encounter with sexual overtones. From the conventional sense as 'combat on horseback' with, perhaps, the phallic suggestion of thrusting lances UK, 2001

jowlster noun a useless troublesome male individual IRELAND, 1984

joxy noun the vagina US, 1967

joy noun **1** luck, satisfaction; especially in the question 'any joy?' and the negative response or interrogative 'no joy'. Originally Royal Air Force usage UK, 1945. **2** marijuana US, 1980. **3** heroin UK, 2002

Joy noun ▶ **the Joy** Mountjoy Prison in Dublin IRELAND, 1959

joy!; rapture! used for expressing pleasure in what has just been said. Somewhat sarcastic or, at least, melodramatic US, 1986

joy bang; joy noun an injection of a narcotic, especially heroin, without succumbing to the drug's addictive nature US, 1953

joy booter noun an infrequent smoker US, 1996

joybox noun a piano US, 1942

joyboy noun a young male homosexual, especially a young male homosexual prostitute UK, 1961

joy flakes noun a powdered drug, especially cocaine or heroin US, 1942

joy girl noun **1** a prostitute US, 1931. **2** in a deck of playing cards, any queen US, 1973

joy jelly noun in electric line work, a silicone compound used on underground cable terminators US, 1980

joy juice noun **1** semen US, 1969. **2** any alcoholic beverage, especially whisky US, 1907. **3** a powerful hallucinogenic drink made from seeds of the datura plant TRINIDAD AND TOBAGO, 1991. **4** a central nervous system despressant US, 1954. **5** chloral hydrate, used to render someone unconscious US, 1971

joy knob noun an attachment to a car steering wheel that facilitates steering with one hand, leaving the other hand free US, 1974

Joynson-hicks noun six. Rhyming slang, formed from the name of Sir William Joynson-Hicks, 1865–1932, who is best remembered as the Conservative Home Secretary at the time of the general strike of 1926 UK, 1960

joy of my life noun a wife. Rhyming slang, often ironic UK, 1936

joy plant noun opium; heroin UK, 1998

joy pop noun an injection of a drug into the skin, not a vein US, 1922

joy-pop verb **1** to inject a drug under the skin, not into a vein US, 1936. **2** to fly a helicopter at a low elevation and high speed US, 1991

joy popper noun an intravenous drug user US, 1936

joy powder noun any powdered drug, especially cocaine, heroin or morphine US, 1922

joy-ride noun an impulsive excursion in a car that is, from the point of view of the riders, borrowed, but from the point of view of the law, stolen US, 1915

joyride verb to steal a car for a joy-ride US, 1949

joy-rider noun **1** a person who takes pleasure in driving another's vehicle without permission. Extended from JOY-RIDE US, 2000. **2** an infrequent user of an addictive drug US, 1950

joyriding noun the criminal act of taking another's car for the thrilling pleasure of driving it US, 1910

joy smoke noun marijuana. 'Joy hemp', 'joy root' and 'joy weed' are also recorded in the 1940s; only 'joy' and 'joy smoke' seem to have survived US, 1938

joystick noun **1** the penis. Probably derived from mechanical imagery, but there is a suggestion that this may be rhyming slang for PRICK US, 1916. **2** a marijuana cigarette US, 1962. **3** the pole used to carry a pair of balanced objects on your shoulders US, 1968

joy water noun vaginal lubricant produced as a result of sexual arousal US, 1973

JP nickname Jamaica Plain, Massachusetts US, 1997

JPT noun used for denoting a lack of punctuality. An abbreviation of JEWISH PEOPLE'S TIME US, 1967

J. Random noun used as a humorous first initial and middle name of a mythical person US, 1983

J-smoke noun a marijuana cigarette; marijuana US, 1969

JT noun the penis. An abbreviation of JOHN THOMAS (the penis) UK, 1923

J-town noun a neighboorhood populated by a large number of Japanese-Americans. An abbreviation of 'Japan Town' US, 1973

Juana noun marijuana. A personified abbreviation US, 1989

Juan Doe noun an unidentified Hispanic male US, 1993

Juanita noun marijuana. Another of the seemingly endless 'MARY JANE' offspring US, 1969

Juan Valdez noun marijuana. Juan is probably taken from 'marijuana', but other than its obvious Spanish roots the etymology of Juan Valdez is uncertain US, 1984

jubilee noun the buttocks US, 1967

juck; juk; juckie noun a dog; hence, used disparagingly of a man. Directly from Romany jook (a dog). In English gypsy use UK, 1979

Judas goat noun an animal trained to lead other animals into slaughter US, 1941

Judas hole; Judas eye; Judas window; Judas noun a small peep-hole in a door through which one can see who is outside the door without been seen from outside US, 1865

Judas priest! used as an expression of surprise or outrage. Multiple embellishments US, 1914

judder noun in motor racing, a shuddering effect felt during braking because of tyre imbalance US, 1980

judder bars noun haemorrhoids NEW ZEALAND, 1998

Judge noun a 1968–73 Pontiac GTO US, 1992

Judge Dread; Judge Dredd noun the head. Rhyming slang, formed from the title of a series of graphic comic-strip adventures and a 1995 film, or, less likely, a reggae entertainer UK, 1998

Judge Duffy; Judge Dean noun in poker, three tens. The suggestion is that the mythical Judge Duffy, Judge Dean, or whoever, commonly handed out sentences of thirty days US, 1963

Judy noun **1** a woman, a girl. Possibly adopted from traditional Punch and Judy puppet shows, or simply from the proper name. Earlier variations of the definition specified that she looked ridiculous (giving credence to Punch's wife) or that she was promiscuous UK, 1812. **2** the meal fed to a prisoner in solitary confinement US, 1992

Judy *adjective* locked in on a target *US, 1990*

jug *noun* **1** a jail or prison *US, 1816*. **2** a bank *US, 1848*. **3** a glass of beer. No longer common. Only used colloquially and not when ordering beer at a hotel where a 'jug' is precisely that, a jug of beer that you take back to a table and fill glasses from *AUSTRALIA, 1960*. **4** a large table jug for beer *AUSTRALIA, 1990*. **5** a glass ampoule holding liquid drugs *US, 1971*. **6** a small container of amphetamine or methamphetamine in liquid form *US, 1980*. **7** a cylinder in an aeroplane engine *US, 1963*. **8** a carburettor *US, 1942*. **9** in electric line work, a horizontal post insulator *US, 1980*

jug *verb* **1** to arrest or imprison *US, 1841*. **2** to attack someone with a jug of boiling water, especially sugared water *UK, 1996*. **3** to have sex with *US, 1965*. **4** to stab *US, 1970* ▷ *see:* JUKE

jug and pail *noun* a prison or jail. A rhyming slang elaboration of JUG (a prison) *UK, 1992*

juge *verb* **1** to have sex *US, 1967*. **2** to stab *US, 2000*

jugged *adjective* **1** drunk. Noted as being used by office- and shop-girls *US, 1923*. **2** imprisoned *UK, 1996*

jugging *noun* in prison, an attack with a jug of boiling sugared water *UK, 2000*

juggins *noun* a dolt *UK, 1882*

juggle *verb* **1** to sell (drugs) *US, 1969*. **2** to engage in criminal business activities *UK, 1994*

juggler *noun* **1** a retail-level drug dealer *US, 1969*. **2** a member of a train crew who loads and unloads freight at stops on a run *US, 1946*

jughandle *noun* in caving and pot-holing, a handle-shaped outcrop of rock used as an anchor-point *UK, 2004*

jughandles; juglugs *noun* prominent ears *UK, 1969*

jug heavy *noun* a criminal who specialises in robbing bank vaults and safes *US, 1949*

jughustler *noun* **1** in oil drilling, a cable-car crew member with a geophone *CANADA, 1958*. **2** in oil drilling, the most inexperienced member of a seismic crew. The recording devices carried by the crew resembled and were called 'jugs' *US, 1954*

jug it! save your prattle for someone who cares! *US, 1951*

jugs; milk jugs *noun* the female breasts. A reference to the source of mother's milk; widely known and used *US, 1957*

jug up *verb* to eat *US, 1992*

juice *noun* **1** alcohol *US, 1932*. **2** methadone, used to break an opiate addiction. In many US clinics, the methadone given to recovering heroin addicts is mixed in orange juice so that it cannot be injected *US, 1981*. **3** a powdered narcotic dissolved for injection *US, 1962*. **4** crack cocaine mixed with marijuana *US, 1993*. **5** anabolic steroids *US, 1992*. **6** blood. Among others, professional wrestling usage *US, 1938*. **7** in drag racing and hot rodding, any special blend of racing fuel *US, 1968*. **8** petrol, diesel *UK, 1909*. **9** nitroglycerin, used by thieves to blow open vaults or safes *US, 1924*. **10** energy *US, 2004*. **11** sex *BAHAMAS, 1982*. **12** pleasure, satisfaction *UK, 1999*. **13** power, influence, sway *US, 1957*. **14** a bribe *UK, 1698*. **15** interest paid to an loan shark *US, 1935*. **16** in sports betting, the bookmaker's commission *US, 1975*. **17** in pool, spin imparted to the cue ball to affect the course of the object ball or the course of the cue ball after it strikes the object ball *US, 1993*. **18** surging surf with big waves *US, 1981*. **19** in a deck of playing cards, a two. An intentional corruption of DEUCE *US, 1951*. ▶ **get some juice on** to achieve a drug intoxication *US, 1980*

juice *verb* **1** to drink, especially to the point of intoxication *US, 1893*. **2** to energise *US, 1977*. **3** to bleed. Professional wrestling usage *US, 1992*. **4** to bribe; to pay for influence *US, 1953*. **5** to obtain something through the influence of another *US, 1980*. **6** to have sex *BAHAMAS, 1982* ▷ *see:* JUICE UP. ▶ **juice the G-spot** to engage in oral sex on a woman *US, 2001*

juice bar *noun* a clinic where recovering heroin addicts are administered methadone. Playful, alluding to JUICE (methadone) *US, 1989*

juice box *noun* the vagina *CANADA, 2002*

juice brakes *noun* in hot rodding and drag racing, hydraulic brakes *US, 1968*

juiced; juiced up *adjective* **1** drunk *US, 1941*. **2** energised *US, 1978*. **3** caffeinated. Borrowing from the language of car fuel for application to the world of coffee drinks and, to a lesser extent, soft drinks *US, 1996*

juiced in *adjective* enjoying powerful political connections *US, 1995*

juice freak *noun* an alcoholic *US, 1971*

juice hand *noun* an electrician, especially in the theatre *US, 1952*

juicehead *noun* an alcoholic *US, 1954*

juice jockey *noun* the driver of a petrol-fuelled truck *US, 1971*

juice joint *noun* **1** an establishment where alcohol is served illegally *US, 1932*. **2** a cigarette made with a mixture of marijuana and crack cocaine *UK, 1998*. **3** a crooked gambling operation *US, 1950*

juice man *noun* **1** a usurer, loan-shark, illegal lender *US, 1961*. **2** an AM radio disc jockey who broadcasts on a powerful, all-night station heard by truckers *US, 1976*. **3** an electrician *US, 1923*

juice money *noun* a bribe *US, 1981*

juicepot *noun* a carburettor *US, 1971*

juicer *noun* **1** a person who abuses alcohol *US, 1960*. **2** an electrician, especially in the television and film industries *US, 1928*. **3** in television and film-making, a lamp operator *US, 1990*. **4** a persuasive and resourceful woman sent out to acquire crack cocaine for others *US, 1992*. **5** a collector of repayments for a loan shark *UK, 1996*. **6** in hot rodding, hydraulic brakes *US, 1954*

juice racket *noun* usury, loan-sharking, illegal lending *US, 1988*

juices *noun* in poker, a pair of twos. Probably a corruption of DEUCE(S) *US, 1951*

juice up; juice *verb* **1** to make exciting or powerful *US, 1964*. **2** to drink to intoxication *US, 1971*

juicy *adjective* **1** scandalous, sensational, especially in a sexual way *UK, 1883*. **2** (used of a woman) sexually aroused *US, 1970*. **3** said of a traffic accident involving serious injuries *US, 1962*. **4** a low-skill poker game or poker play *US, 1982*. **5** (of a wave) powerful, with a large fringing crest *US, 1977*

juicy fruit *noun* an act of sexual intercourse. Rhyming slang for ROOT. From the name of a flavour of chewing gum *AUSTRALIA, 1950*

juicy G *noun* salacious gossip *US, 1989*

juicy Lucy *noun* the vagina. is an adjective with suggestive and sexual uses; Lucy is a convenient rhyming name. It may also be worth noting that Juicy Lucy was a moderately successful UK blues band in the late 1960s and early 70s. A controversial, and hence memorable illustration on their 1969 eponymous debut album depicted a plump, naked lady disported in 'juicy fruit' – grapes, etc. Also a slang term for 'sexual intercourse' *UK, 2001*

juju; ju-ju *noun* a marijuana cigarette. Clipped and reduplicated from 'marijuana' *US, 1940*

jujubes; joobs; jubes *noun* the female breasts; the male pectorals *UK, 1980*

juke *noun* a jukebox *US, 1941*. ▶ **up your juke** under the front of your clothing (as a place of concealment or protection) *UK: SCOTLAND, 1985*

juke; jug *verb* **1** to dance in a boisterous fashion. It is theorised that the word, today only recognised in the formation JUKE BOX, was derived from the African Wolof, Banut or Bambara languages. The term spread through southern blacks from the Gullah, and then into wider slang usage, although with a distincly southern flavour *US, 1933*. **2** to fool, to trick *US, 1873*. **3** to hit *US, 1872*. **4** to avoid a blow. Circus and carnival usage *UK, 1513*

jukebox *noun* an coin-operated recorded-music player *US, 1939*

juke house *noun* a brothel *US, 1987*

juke joint *noun* a bar or club with a jukebox; usually rowdy and teeming with sin *US, 1937*

jukey *noun* a jukebox *UK: SCOTLAND, 1996*

Julian Clary *adjective* vulgar, flashy, ostentatious; impudent; conceited. Rhyming slang for LAIRY *UK, 1998*

Julian Clary; clary *noun* a male homosexual. Rhyming slang for FAIRY, formed from the name of an ostentatiously gay comedian (b.1959) *UK, 1998*

Julius Caesar *noun* **1** a wedge-shaped cheesecutter flat cap. Rhyming slang for 'cheeser' *UK, 1992*. **2** a freezer. Rhyming slang *UK, 1992*

jumble *noun* a white person. Derived from the pronunciation of 'John Bull' (a symbol of Britain) by Nigerian immigrants in London *UK, 1957*

jumblie; jumbly *noun* a jumble sale *UK, 1977*

jumbo *noun* **1** an elephant. From the name of a famous elephant sold to circus impressario P. T. Barnum by London Zoo in 1882. The elephant died in collision with a train in Ontario in 1885 *UK, 1882*. **2** a jumbo-jet *UK, 1984*. **3** a large vial of crack cocaine *US, 1986*. **4** a quart bottle of beer. Heard in Michigan's Upper Peninsula *US, 2003*. **5** a uniformed police constable, especially a clumsy or stupid police constable. A derogatory term employed by detectives *UK, 1970*. **6** the buttocks *NEW ZEALAND, 1998*

jumbo-size *adjective* very large; or, in the language of advertising, slightly larger than normal *UK, 1967*

Jumbo's trunk *adjective* drunk. Rhyming slang. Jumbo was a famous elephant in 1880s London. His name became an eponym for elephants and an adjective for great size. He inspired this variation on 'elephant's trunk' (drunk) *UK, 1923*

jumbuck *noun* a sheep. The origin of this word has long been conjectured. 'Jumbuck' arose in Australian Aboriginal pidgin, which also had 'jump up' (to appear, to come, to be reincarnated), which may be related, though it is difficult to see how exactly. In 1896 a Mr Meston surmised the hardly credible theory that it was from an Aboriginal word meaning 'the white mist preceding a shower, to which a flock of sheep bore a strong resemblance'. 'Jumbuck' is now all but forgotten except that it occurs in the lyrics of the national song 'Waltzing Matilda' *AUSTRALIA, 1824*

jump *noun* **1** an act of sexual intercourse *US, 1931*. **2** a thrill *UK, 2001*. **3** a party, especially a party with music *US, 1954*. **4** the start *US, 1848*. **5** the beginning of a horse race *AUSTRALIA, 1988*. **6** in prison, an unexpected attack *UK, 1978*. **7** in the entertainment industry, a move in between engagements, especially by rail *US, 1916*. **8** the bar in a public house or other licensed premises. Following the notion that you have to jump to get attention; alternatively, it's what you have to jump over to get a free beer *AUSTRALIA, 1978*. ▶ **get the jump on; have the jump on** to get, or have, an advantage over someone *US, 1912*

jump *verb* **1** to have sex *US, 1999*. **2** to be lively, wild, full of activity *US, 1938*. **3** to attack physically, especially by surprise or all of a sudden *UK, 1789*. **4** (of a horse) to begin a race *AUSTRALIA, 1984*. **5** to board a moving train in order to catch a free ride *US, 1885*. **6** to escape, to abscond. Originally, 'to jump ship' *UK, 1865*. **7** to travel from an engagement in one town to the next town where an engagement is scheduled *US, 1975*. **8** to steal a car by creating a short circuit with the ignition system wires to start the engine *US, 1969*. **9** to use specially designed equipment to cause a car to bounce up and down *US, 1992*. **10** in drag racing, to cross the starting line too soon *US, 1970*. ▶ **jump a rattler** to board a train illegally *AUSTRALIA, 1905*. ▶ **jump bail** to deliberately fail to appear in court after bail has been posted, especially by moving away in order to avoid recognition or the court's jurisdiction. From JUMP (to escape) *US, 1865*. ▶ **jump out of your skin** to be greatly startled *UK, 1937*. ▶ **jump salty** to become angry *US, 1969*. ▶ **jump someone's bones** to have sex *US, 1965*. ▶ **jump sore** to anger *US, 1960*. ▶ **jump stink** to become angry *US, 1946*. ▶ **jump the broomstick** to enter into a common-law marriage. Probably a figurative use of a traditional custom, hence, also, the many variations: 'to jump (over) the besom', 'broom', 'bucket', 'ditch', 'doorstep', etc. Brewer in his *Phrase and Fable* suggests that 'broomstick' is an eleboration of 'brom' (the bit of a bridle) and is thus symbolic of skipping over the restraint of marriage *UK, 1898*. ▶ **jump the green** to start quickly just after, or before, a traffic light turns green *CANADA, 1992*. ▶ **jump the gun** to act prematurely. From athletics *US, 1942*. ▶ **jump the shark** of a television programme, to pass a peak of popularity; may also be applied to other entertainments, entertainers or fashions. Coined after a 1977 episode of long-running US television comedy *Happy Days* in which a central character in need of fresh impetus took to water-skis and attempted to leap over a shark *US, 1998*. ▶ **jump through hoops** to be seen to do everything that is required and more *UK, 1917*. ▶ **jump to it** to make an energetic start or respond energetically to the bidding to do so. Often used as an imperative *UK, 1929*. ▶ **jump wires** to steal a car and start the engine by creating a short circuit with the ignition system wires *US, 1969*. ▶ **jump yellow** to act in a cowardly manner *US, 1974*

jump-a-dick *noun* a cricket *CAYMAN ISLANDS, 1985*

jump back *verb* **1** to initiate a fight *US, 1975*. **2** to relent, to ease off *US, 1986*

jump ball *noun* in pool, a ball that leaves the surface of the table *US, 1850*

jump collar *noun* an arrest made for show, which will not produce a conviction *US, 1953*

jump CP *noun* a hastily created, very temporary command post *US, 1991*

jump down *verb* to attack physically *US, 2001*. ▶ **jump down your throat** to flare up in anger and snap in criticism of, and at, you *UK, 1806*

jumped-up *adjective* conceited, arrogant. Similar imagery to GET ABOVE YOURSELF *UK, 1870*

jumper *noun* **1** a person who threatens to or has jumped to his death, either from heights or in front of a train *US, 1964*. **2** a small amount of stimulating liquor *CANADA, 1988*

jumper church *noun* any fundamental Christian church *BAHAMAS, 1982*

jumper lead; jumper wire *noun* a wire designed for starting a car engine while bypassing the key and ignition system *UK, 1977*

jumpers *noun* **1** a hat. Rhyming slang from 'jumpers flat' (a type of horse race) *AUSTRALIA, 1989*. **2** sports shoes *US, 1972*

jumper steak *noun* venison or rabbit meat *CANADA, 1987*

jumpies *noun* sexual intercourse. An elaboration of JUMP *UK, 1984*

jump-in *noun* a timed beating used as an initiation into a youth gang *US, 1987*

jump in *verb* to initiate (someone) into a youth gang through a timed group beating *US, 1990*

jumping *adjective* used as an intensifier in mild oaths *US, 1815*

jumping jack *noun* a *black* person; a *black* snooker ball. Rhyming slang *UK, 1992*

jumping junky *noun* a paratrooper *US, 1991*

jump joint *noun* a brothel *US, 1939*

jump juice *noun* anabolic steroids *US, 1997*

jump off *verb* **1** to happen; to begin *US, 1946*. **2** to assault *US, 1975*

jump-out squad *noun* a unit of police officers in a cruising, unmarked police-vehicle, detailed to jump out of their car and apprehend drug-dealers *US, 1980*

jumpover *noun* a shop robbery *IRELAND, 1996*

jump-start *verb* to light a fresh cigarette with the ember of one being finished *US, 1984*

jump-steady *noun* **1** strong, illegally manufactured whisky *US, 1923*. **2** a drink of gin *US, 1950*

jump street *noun* the inception; the very beginning *US, 1972*

jump-up *noun* **1** theft from lorries. The criminal *jumps up* onto the back of the vehicle; usually used with 'the' *UK, 1956*. **2** a steep section of road, as when going up an escarpment *AUSTRALIA, 1847*

jump-up artist; jump-up merchant; jump-up man *noun* a criminal who steals from the back of goods-vehicles *UK, 1951*

jump upon; jump on *verb* to severely criticise or punish *UK, 1868*

jump wire *noun* a wire designed for starting a car engine while bypassing the key and ignition system *US, 1970s*

junco *noun* heroin. A variation of JUNK (heroin) *UK, 2002*

Juneau sneakers *noun* slip-on rubber boots *US, 1982*

Junebug *noun* used as a nickname for a male named after his father *US, 1970*

jungle *noun* **1** a dangerous, rough part of town, especially one where black people live *US, 1926*. **2** an outdoor area favoured by homosexuals for sexual encounters *US, 1963*. **3** the female pubic hair; hence the vagina *US, 2001*. **4** a tramp encampment *US, 1908*. **5** a prison's recreation yard *US, 1983*. **6** an extremely fast (130–160 beats per minute) form of popular dance music genre that developed in London in 1990–91 *UK, 1990*

jungle bunny *noun* **1** a black person. Highly offensive *US, 1959*. **2** an Asian person *UK, 1984*

jungle-bunny outfit *noun* Royal Air Force-issue camouflaged battledress. A casually and institutionally racist term used by Royal Air Force officer cadets *UK, 1981*

junglee *noun* a wild, unsophisticated, uncivilised person *FIJI, 1995*

jungle eater *noun* a Caterpillar D&E bulldozer modified for military land-clearing work *US, 1991*

jungle fever *noun* used of white people, a strong attraction towards black people. The prominent title of a Spike Lee film (1991) *US, 1990*

jungle fuck *noun* energetic, even athletic sex *US, 1994*

jungle-happy *adjective* deranged from prolonged combat in the jungle *US, 1944*

Jungle Jim *noun* a Roman Catholic. Rhyming slang for TIM (a Roman Catholic) *UK: SCOTLAND, 1985*

Jungle Jim *verb* to swim. Rhyming slang, in contemporaneous use with the television series *Jungle Jim*, 1955–56 *UK, 1956*

jungle job *noun* sex outdoors *US, 1966*

jungle juice *noun* **1** alcoholic drink *AUSTRALIA, 1942*. **2** any improvised alcoholic beverage *US, 1947*. **3** illicit alcoholic liquor brewed by soldiers in the tropics. Used by World War 2 military *AUSTRALIA, 1942*. **4** in prison, serious talk about serious situations *US, 1990*

jungle light *noun* in the pornography industry, a light used to illuminate the genitals of the performers *US, 1995*

jungle meat *noun* in homosexual usage, a black man *US, 1981*

jungle mouth *noun* very bad breath *US, 1975*

jungle pussy *noun* a black woman's vagina; hence black women objectified sexually *US, 1974*

jungle rot *noun* any skin rash suffered in tropical and jungle environments *US, 1945*

jungle rules *noun* a code of competition or combat in which all is fair *US, 1986*

jungle telegraph *noun* the informal and haphazard but effective communication by which rumour spreads *UK, 1966*

jungle up *verb* in oil drilling, to sleep outside *US, 1954*

junglist *noun* a purveyor or follower of jungle music, a music genre of the 1990s favoured at raves *UK, 1996*

junior *noun* in television and film-making, a 1000-watt or 2000-watt light *US, 1990*

junior jumper *noun* a juvenile male who commits a rape *US, 1992*

junior wolf *noun* a younger brother. Teen slang *CANADA, 1946*

junk *noun* **1** heroin; morphine; cocaine *US, 1918*. **2** any illegal drug *US, 1967*. **3** a drug addict *AUSTRALIA, 1975*. **4** the genitals *US, 1997*. **5** graffiti *US, 1997*. **6** in theatre usage, a monologue *US, 1981*

junk *verb* to throw away, to discard, to treat as rubbish *UK, 1916*

junk bonds *noun* in poker, a hand that appears attractive but is in fact a poor hand *US, 1996*

junked; junked up *adjective* under the influence of heroin *US, 1930*

junker *noun* **1** an old and broken-down vehicle *US, 1948*. **2** a heroin addict *US, 1922*. **3** in competitive surfing, an extremely low score *US, 1991*

junk food *noun* food with a high calorific and low nutritional content *US, 1971*

junk hawk *noun* a heroin addict whose life is completely controlled by the addiction *US, 1972*

junkhead *noun* a heroin addict *US, 1963*

junk hog *noun* an opium addict *US, 1950*

junkie *noun* **1** a drug addict, specifically one addicted to heroin. A user of JUNK (drugs, opiates, heroin) *US, 1922*. **2** by extension, a person fiercely devoted to an activity *US, 1962*

junkmobile *noun* a dilapidated car *US, 1991*

junk mooch *noun* a heroin addict who trades information for heroin *US, 1972*

junk-on-the-bunk *noun* a military inspection of a soldier's gear displayed on his bed *US, 1978*

junks *noun* expensive, brand name basketball trainers *US, 1987*

junk tank *noun* a jail cell reserved for drug addicts. A play on the earlier and more common DRUNK TANK *US, 1966*

junkyard dog *noun* **1** a ferocious, territorial person *US, 1983*. **2** a junkyard operator with connections to organised crime *US, 2003*

junt *noun* a large marijuana cigarette *US, 1997*

jurassic *adjective* very old *US, 1997*

jury-nobbling *noun* an act of corrupting, or otherwise tampering with, a jury or jury member. From 'nobble' (to corrupt a jury) *UK, 2000*

jury tax *noun* the perceived penalty of an increased sentence for an accused criminal who refuses a plea bargain, takes his case to jury trial, and loses *US, 1997*

jussus!; jussis!; jissus!; jisses! used for expressing anger, frustration, shock, surprise, etc. From the Afrikaans pronunciation of 'Jesus', as an oath or exclamation *SOUTH AFRICA, 1942*

just as I feared; just as *noun* a beard. Rhyming slang *UK, 1960*

just for today *adverb* used in twelve-step recovery programmes such as Alcoholics Anonymous to describe an addict's commitment to refraining from his addiction *US, 1998*

justin *noun* a half-gallon container. Filled with beer, *just in* case you run out *NEW ZEALAND, 1998*

just-in-caser *noun* a getaway driver *UK, 1996*

just kidding! used for humorously acknowledging an error *US, 2002*

just now *adverb* any time soon, in a little while (at the appropriate time, eventually, or never, may be implied). Influenced by Afrikaans *netnou*. Universally used in South Africa *SOUTH AFRICA, 1900*

just off the banana boat *adjective* gullible, used of an innocent abroad. An allusion to the cultural innocence of a newly arrived immigrant *UK, 1966*

just one of those things a catchphrase philosophy to explain the inexplicable, the impossible or the inevitable. It was used by Cole Porter as the title for a popular song in 1935 *US, 1947*

just quietly *adverb* just between you and me *AUSTRALIA, 1938*

just the facts, m'am used for expressing a wish that the speaker confine their remarks to factual matters. A catchphrase from the 1960s US television series *Dragnet US, 1985*

jute *noun* a teasing *NEW ZEALAND, 1998*

juve *noun* a juvenile part or act. Theatrical *UK, 1967*

juvie; juvey *noun* a juvenile detention hall where young offenders are housed or juvenile court where they are tried *US, 1965*

Kk

K *noun* **1** one thousand dollars; one thousand pounds. Also spelt 'kay' *US, 1965.* **2** a kilometre *UK, 1996.* **3** a kilogram, especially of an illegal drug *US, 1974.* **4** the recreational drug ketamine. Ketamine hycrochloride is an anaesthetic used recreationally for its hallucinogenic properties *US, 1996.* **5** leaves of *catha edulis*, a stimulant also called 'qat', originating in the Horn of Africa and the Arabian peninsula, legally available in the UK and similar to amphetamine in effect when chewed. Also known as 'khat' and 'kat' *UK, 1996.* **6** in a deck of cards, a king *US, 1991.* **7** a knighthood. Used by civil servants; suggestive of a casual familiarity with the honour *UK, 1961.* **8** oral sex on a woman performed according to the strictures of the 'Kivin Method' *US, 2001.*

K2 *noun* **1** phencyclidine, the recreational drug known as PCP or angel dust *US, 1970.* **2** a hybrid marijuana. Named after the second highest place on earth *UK, 2003.*

KA *noun* a known associate of a criminal *US, 1986.*

kaalgat *adjective* in the nude, naked. From Afrikaans *kaal* (bare) and *gat* (hole; anus) *SOUTH AFRICA, 1978.*

kabak *noun* marijuana *UK, 2003.*

kabayo *noun* heroin. A phonetic approximation of Spanish *caballo* (horse); HORSE (heroin) *US, 1977.*

ka-ching used as a representation of the sound of a sale entered on a cash register *US, 1995.*

kack *noun* faeces *NEW ZEALAND, 1984.* ▷*see:* CACK

kacks *noun* **1** trousers. A variation of KECKS; sometimes spelt 'cacks'. Noted in teenage use and still current in 2003 *UK, 1983.* **2** underpants, knickers. Sometimes spelt 'kaks' *IRELAND, 1991.*
▶ **relax the kacks** take it easy *IRELAND, 2003.*

kaff *noun* a marijuana cigarette *UK, 2003.*

kaffall *noun* the face. Polari; probably an elaboration of ECAF *US, 1993.*

kaffies *noun* trousers *UK, 2002.*

kaffir *noun* **1** a black person, especially a black African. Offensive, contemptuous, often abusive; its use is actionable under South African law as a *crimen injuria* (a wilful injury to a person's dignity caused by, for instance, the use of obscene language or racial insults). Also applied in an adjectival sense *SOUTH AFRICA, 1607.* **2** any person who does not accept Islam. From the Hindi for 'infidel' *TRINIDAD AND TOBAGO, 2003.*

Kafflik *noun* a Catholic *UK: SCOTLAND, 1998.*

kag; kaggage *noun* useless or unwanted equipment. Royal Marine slang; combining 'baggage' and KACK *UK, 1989.*

kahuna *noun* **1** a great or important person or thing. From a Hawaiian term for 'priest, wise man'; in this sense often used with 'big' *US, 1987.* **2** in computing, an intelligent and wise practitioner *US, 1991.* **3** a type of marijuana *UK, 2003.*

kai *noun* food; also, drink. 'Kai' is the term for 'food' in many Polynesian languages, but in Australia borrowed either from New Zealand English, where it is taken from Maori, or from various Melanesian pidgins *AUSTRALIA, 1872.*

kaka hole *noun* **1** the anus *TRINIDAD AND TOBAGO, 2001.* **2** by extension, a despicable person *TRINIDAD AND TOBAGO, 2001.*

kakalaylay *noun* dancing with clear sexual overtones *TRINIDAD AND TOBAGO, 1998.*

kaka pipe *noun* a sewage discharge pipe *ANTARCTICA, 2003.*

kaks *noun* Khaki trousers *US, 1968.*

kalakit *noun* marijuana *UK, 2003.*

kale *noun* money *US, 1902.*

Kalgoorlie cooler *noun* a hessian-walled cabinet for keeping foodstuffs cool by evaporation. After the West Australian mining town Kalgoorlie *AUSTRALIA, 1962.*

kali; kali weed *noun* marijuana from Jamaica. Rastafarians consider the smoking of 'kali' to be a religious act. This spirituality is apparent in a number of Hindi words adopted into their lexicon. Conventionally, Kali is the Hindu goddess of time, mother and creator of all things, the personification of cosmic force *JAMAICA, 1982.*

kali mist *noun* a variety of marijuana *UK, 2002.*

kali water *noun* champagne. From KAYLIED; KALIED (drunk) *UK, 1981.*

kalsominer *noun* a person who claims mining experience and skills he does not have. The word is derived from 'calcimine', a kind of whitewash *CANADA, 1964.*

kamikaze *noun* a fall from a surfboard while standing near the nose of the board *AUSTRALIA, 1963.*

kamp *adjective* a homosexual male. Rare spelling variant of CAMP, based on the incorrect folk etymology that it is a C19 acronym for 'known as male prostitute' *AUSTRALIA, 1974.*

kanga *noun* **1** a kangaroo. By shortening *AUSTRALIA, 1917.* **2** money. From rhyming slang 'kanga(roo)' for SCREW *AUSTRALIA, 1953.*

kangaroo *noun* **1** a Jewish person. Rhyming slang, sometimes corrupted to 'kanker' or 'canker' *UK, 1943.* **2** crack cocaine *US, 1994.* **3** a tractor adapted for apple-picking *CANADA, 1989.* **4** a prison warder. Prisoners' rhyming slang for SCREW (a prison warder), often reduced to 'kanga' *UK, 1996.*

kangaroo *verb* to use a toilet, especially a public toilet, by squatting on the seat *AUSTRALIA, 1942.*

kangaroo court *noun* a body that passes judgment without attention to due process *US, 1853.*

kangarooer *noun* a hunter of kangaroos *AUSTRALIA, 1836.*

kangaroo-hop *verb* (of a motor vehicle) to jerk about because the clutch is not released smoothly, an engine problem or the like *AUSTRALIA, 1943.*

kangaroos *noun* ▶ **have kangaroos loose in the top paddock** to be slightly crazy *AUSTRALIA, 1908.*

Kangaroo's Arse *noun* a notional brand name applied to poor quality or cheap Australian wine *UK, 2002.*

Kangaroo Valley *nickname* Earls Court, London. A favourite haunt of Australian tourists *AUSTRALIA, 1965.*

kangkalang; kangkatang *noun* chaos; arguing *TRINIDAD AND TOBAGO, 1993.*

Kansas City roll *noun* a single large-denomination note wrapped around small-denomination notes, giving the impression of a great deal of money *US, 1964.*

Kansas grass *noun* marijuana originating in Kansas *US, 2003.*

Kansas yummy *noun* an attractive woman who is not easily seduced. A term that need not, and usually does not, apply to a woman actually from Kansas *US, 1985.*

Kantwork *noun* a Kenworth truck. Said with irony of an extremely reliable and respected truck *US, 1976.*

kanya *noun* marijuana *US, 1995.*

kappa slapper *noun* a girl member of a sub-cultural urban adolescent grouping that dresses in Kappa™ clothing. Certainly in Cheshire, possibly more widespread. Formed from the Kappa brand name and SLAPPER (a sexually promiscuous woman) *UK, 2003.*

kaput; caput *adjective* used up, useless, destroyed. From the German *US, 1919.*

karachi *noun* a mixture of heroin, phenobarbital and the recreational drug methaqualone, best known as Quaaludes™; heroin. Named after Karachi in Pakistan, the source of much heroin *UK, 1998*

kareem *noun* a car. While appearing to be an elaboration of 'car' this is rhyming slang, based on the name of legendary basketball player Kareem Abdul-Jabbar (b.1947) *UK, 2002*

Karen Carpenter Airlines *nickname* Quebecair, a charter airline with service from Canada to Europe which, allegedly, rarely had food on board. Karen Carpenter, of the music family, died at age 32 in 1983 of acute anorexia nervosa *CANADA, 2002*

karma *noun* fate, luck, destiny. A Buddhist concept adopted by hippies, vaguely understood, simplified and debased in all-purpose usage. 'Good karma' is recognition or portent of good luck, while 'bad karma' generally ascribes blame *US, 1967*

karzy *noun* a lavatory; also used in a figurative sense. From the Italian *casa* (a house) which is also its original use. Many slang words have alternate spellings but users of the karzy have more choices than most: 'khazi'; 'kharzi'; 'kharzie'; 'kazi'; 'karsi'; 'carsey'; 'carsie'; 'carzie'; 'cawsey'; 'cawsy'. The variations spelt with a 'k' date from the mid-C20. Brendan Behan, *Borstal Boy*, 1958, uses 'cawsy' *UK, 1961*

kashittery *noun* (among Nova Scotians of German descent) a verbal fuss *CANADA, 1999*

Kashmir *noun* pungent and very powerful hashish originating in Kashmir, northern India *UK, 1999*

kate *verb* to act as a pimp *US, 1976*

kate; Kate *noun* **1** an attractive prostitute *US, 1949*. **2** used as a term of address among male homosexuals *US, 1965*. ▶ **the kate** the army. Shortened form of obsolete rhyming slang 'Kate Carney' (or Karney), for 'army'; Kate Carney was a popular music hall entertainer in the late C19 *UK, 1964*

Kate and Sidney *noun* steak and kidney, especially in a steak and kidney pudding or pie. Rhyming slang that appears to be a Spoonerism until you look again *UK, 1998*

Kate Bush *noun* marijuana. Named after British singer Kate Bush (b.1958), disguising KB (KIND BUD) and gently punning on BUSH *UK, 1996*

Kate Moss *verb* to masturbate. Rhyming slang for TOSS, formed from the name of the British model (b.1974) *UK, 2003*

Kathleen Mavourneen *noun* **1** a habitual criminal *AUSTRALIA, 1917*. **2** an indefinite jail sentence *AUSTRALIA, 1910*

Kathleen Mavourneen *adjective* lasting for an indefinite time. From the refrain of a popular song 'It may be for years, it may be forever' *AUSTRALIA, 1903*

katydid *noun* any Kenworth truck *US, 1971*

kaya *noun* marijuana; a marijuana cigarette *JAMAICA, 1978*

Kaybecker *noun* a French-speaking Canadian. An intentional 'Quebec' corruption *US, 1975*

kayfabe *noun* the protection of the inside secrets of professional wrestling *US, 1993*

kaylied; kalied *adjective* drunk *UK, 1978*

kayrop *noun* pork. Back slang *UK, 1992*

kazh; kasj; cazh *adjective* pleasant in a casual sort of way. A word deeply rooted in the Valley Girl ethic *US, 1981*

KB *noun* **1** a rejection, a setback. From KNOCKBACK *UK, 1996*. **2** high quality marijuana *US, 1997*

KB *verb* to refuse; to reject. Abbreviated and adapted from KNOCK BACK (to reject) *UK, 1998*

k-bar *noun* a US Marine Corps survival knife *US, 1979*

K-boy *noun* in a deck of playing cards, a king *US, 1943*

KC; Kay Cee *nickname* Kansas City, Missouri *US, 1895*

K capsule *noun* a capsule containing a mixture of the recreational drug ketamine and MDMA, the recreational drug best known as ecstasy. From K (ketamine) *UK, 2002*

keb *noun* a French-speaking Canadian *CANADA, 2002*

kebab *noun* the vagina *UK, 2001*

kecks; kegs *noun* trousers. A northern variation of obsolete 'kicks' (trousers), now well known. Also spelt as 'keks' and 'kex'. In Glasgow, the meaning is specialised to 'men's underpants' *UK, 1900*

ked *noun* in India, used generically for a gym shoe or a canvas shoe. From a branded range of shoes *INDIA, 1979*

kee *noun* a kilogram (especially of drugs). Alternative spelling for KEY *UK, 1997*

keebler *noun* a white person *US, 1992*

keech *noun* **1** excrement, shit. Also applied figuratively. Variants include 'keegh' and 'keek' *UK: SCOTLAND, 1988*. **2** a contemptible person. Extends from the previous sense *UK: SCOTLAND, 1985*

keech *verb* to defecate *UK: SCOTLAND, 1988*

keechy *adjective* soiled with excrement. From KEECH (excrement, faeces) *UK: SCOTLAND, 1985*

keek *verb* to peek. Dialect *UK: SCOTLAND, 1911*

keel over *verb* to collapse. From the conventional sense (to capsize) *UK, 1897*

keen *adjective* good, fashionable. Still heard, but by the late 1960s used almost exclusively with irony, especially when intensified with 'peachy' *US, 1915*

keener *noun* **1** a sycophant *US, 2003*. **2** a school pupil who is enthusiastic about school work. From conventional 'keen' (eager). Shortened to 'keeno' *UK, 1984*

keen on *adjective* enthusiastic about *UK, 1889*

keep *verb* to be in possession of drugs *US, 1966*. ▶ **keep Bachelor's Hall** (of a man) to live alone, even temporarily. In use in the US as well as Canada *CANADA, 1999*. ▶ **keep dog** to act as lookout *UK, 1995*. ▶ **keep him honest** in poker, to call a player who is suspected of bluffing *US, 1963*. ▶ **keep it dark** to say nothing about something; to keep a secret. Used mainly as an imperative *UK, 1857*. ▶ **keep nix** to keep lookout *IRELAND, 1989*. ▶ **keep on keeping on** to persevere in the face of all discouragement or misfortune *US, 1977*. ▶ **keep something under your hat** to maintain secrecy about something; especially used as an imperative for discretion *UK, 1953*. ▶ **keep tabs on someone; keep a tab on someone** to keep an account of; to note someone's movements or activity, to follow and record. The original use was of simple accounting: 'to keep a (financial) table on' *US, 1889*. ▶ **keep the peek** to serve as a lookout during a criminal act *US, 1976*. ▶ **keep your cool** to retain your self-possession *US, 1975*. ▶ **keep your head down** to stay out of trouble. Military origins *UK, 1996*. ▶ **keep your mouth off something** to stop talking about *TRINIDAD AND TOBAGO, 1971*. ▶ **keep your nose clean** to stay out of trouble, to behave yourself *US, 1887*. ▶ **keep yow** to act as lookout while an illegal activity takes place *AUSTRALIA, 1942*

keeper *noun* **1** something or someone worth keeping *US, 1984*. **2** any weapon or instrument that can be used as a weapon *US, 1992*. **3** an arrest that results in criminal charges being filed *US, 1987*. **4** in common-law, a spouse *TRINIDAD AND TOBAGO, 1884*. **5** the person running a two-up gambling game. Shortening of RING-KEEPER *AUSTRALIA, 1941*

keep in *verb* used in a range of expressions to suggest that someone has a satisfactory supply of income, for example 'enough cash to keep him in petrol' *AUSTRALIA, 1936*

keep it real! stay honest!, tell the difficult truth! *US, 1997*

keep-miss *noun* a kept mistress *BARBADOS, 1965*

keep on trucking! persevere!; continue *US, 1972*

keeps *noun* ▶ **for keeps** permanently *US, 1861*

keep the greasy side down and the shiny side up used as an admonition to drive safely. Popularised during the citizens' band radio craze of the later 1970s *US, 1976*

keep up your front to make your game! don't give up! *US, 1968*

keep your hair on! don't get upset! *NEW ZEALAND, 1984*

keep your shirt on! calm down!, relax!, compose yourself! *UK, 1854*

keg *noun* **1** a barrel of beer *AUSTRALIA, 1895*. **2** beer *NEW ZEALAND, 1998*. **3** 25,000 capsules of an illegal drug such as amphetamine, or more generally, a drum containing a very large amount of this or similar drugs *US, 1970*. **4** in television and film-making, a 750-watt spotlight that resembles a beer keg *US, 1990*

kegger *noun* a party with a generous supply of beer. From KEG (a beer barrel) *US, 1966*

kegging *adjective* good, fun *US, 1991*

keg-legs *noun* generously oversized thighs or calves. Anecdotal evidence of 1960s UK usage, often as an unkind name shouted at girls with 'fat' thighs *US, 1999*

kegler *noun* a bowler. From the German *US, 1962*

keg-on-legs *noun* a prodigious drinker of beer *AUSTRALIA, 1996*

keg party *noun* a party at which a keg of beer is supplied for the guests *AUSTRALIA, 1950*

keister; keester; keyster *noun* **1** the buttocks. From the German *US, 1931*. **2** a travelling bag or satchel *US, 1881*. **3** a safe *US, 1913*. **4** a jail or prison *US, 1949*

keister bandit *noun* an aggressive male homosexual who takes the active role in anal sex *US, 1950*

keister stash *noun* a container of contraband hidden in the rectum *US, 1967*

keister stash *verb* to hide (contraband) in your rectum *US, 1967*

Keith Moon *noun* a crazy person. Rhyming slang for LOON formed from the name and nickname of rock musician 'Moon the Loon', 1946–78 *UK, 1992*

keki *noun* the vagina. From the Hindi *TRINIDAD AND TOBAGO, 2003*

kelly *noun* **1** the stomach, the abdomen, the belly. Rhyming slang, abbreviated from DERBY KELLY *UK, 1970*. **2** a hat *US, 1908*

kelly bow *noun* money. Glasgow rhyming slang, perhaps from the name of a gang in the Govan area of Glasgow *UK: SCOTLAND, 1985*

kelper *nickname* a native of the Falkland Islands *FALKLAND ISLANDS (MALVINAS), 1900*

kelsey hair *noun* straight hair *US, 1976*

kelt; keltch *noun* a white person *US, 1912*

Kembla Grange; Kembla *noun* small change. Rhyming slang, after a racecourse just south of Sydney *AUSTRALIA, 1955*

kemp *noun* a customised car *US, 1953*

Ken Dodd *noun* a roll of banknotes. Rhyming slang for 'wad' formed from the name of the British comedian (b.1929) who fell foul of the taxman in 1989 *UK, 1992*

Ken Dodds; kenny's *noun* the testicles. Rhyming slang for CODS formed from the name of British comedian Ken Dodd (b.1929) *UK, 1992*

kenna; kenner *noun* a house. A variation of 'ken' (a house). English gypsy use *UK, 1923*

kennec *noun* a non-gypsy or traveller. English gypsy use *UK, 2000*

kennel *noun* **1** a house *US, 1947*. **2** a prison cell *UK, 1996*

kenner *noun* a school pupil who is enthusiastic about school work. From conventional 'keen' (eager). Shortened to 'keeno' *UK, 1984*

Kennie *noun* any Kenworth truck *US, 1971*

Kennington Lane *noun* pain, a pain. Rhyming slang, formed from a street name in South London *UK, 1961*

Kenny Whopper *noun* in trucking, a Kenworth truck *US, 1976*

Kenosha Cadillac *noun* any car manufactured by American Motors. American Motors had its main factory in Kenosha, Wisconsin *US, 1976*

Kentish Town *noun* a halfpenny or penny. Rhyming slang for 'brown', from the copper colour of the coin *UK, 1961*

Kentucky blue *noun* marijuana grown in Kentucky, 'the Bluegrass State'. A play on GRASS (marijuana) *US, 1969*

Kentucky chrome *noun* trim on a truck painted with aluminium *US, 1971*

Kentucky right turn *noun* a move to the left before making a righthand turn while driving *US, 1999*

Kentucky waterfall *noun* a hairstyle in which the hair is worn short at the front and long at the back. Best known as a MULLET *US, 2001*

Kentucky windage *noun* the adjustment of the aim of a rifle based on intuition *US, 1945*

Kepler Wessels *noun* the testicles *AUSTRALIA, 1984*

keptie *noun* a kept woman supported by a rich benefactor *US, 1950*

keptive *noun* a youthful, sexually inexperienced male who is supported by an older homosexual *US, 1987*

kept man *noun* a procurer of prostitutes; a man who makes his living off the earnings of prositutes *US, 1987*

kerb crawling *noun* soliciting for prostitution from a vehicle *AUSTRALIA, 1989*

kerb-crawling *adjective* working as a prostitute from a vehicle *AUSTRALIA, 1972*

kerchief code *noun* a designation of a homosexual man's sexual preferences, signalled by the colour of the handkerchief and the pocket in which it is worn. For example, a black handkerchief worn on the left signifies that the wearer is into 'Heavy S&M, Top', while on the right it means 'Heavy S&M, Bottom' *US, 1978*

kerching! used in response to a profitable triumph. Echoic of a cash till. Popularised by BBC television children's programme *Kerching!*, the story of a 14-year-old entrepreneur *UK, 2002*

kerdoing!; kerdoink!; gerdoying! used as a representation of a moment of violent impact; crash!; wallop! Echoic. Originally recorded in Royal Air Force use *UK, 1945*

kerist *noun* used for 'Christ' *AUSTRALIA, 1971*

Kermit the Frog *noun* a lavatory. Rhyming slang for BOG formed from the name of a television puppet character in *The Muppet Show*, from 1976 *UK, 1992*

kernel *noun* a swollen groin gland *BARBADOS, 1965*

kero *noun* kerosene *AUSTRALIA, 1930*

kerosene cowboy *noun* an air force jet pilot *NEW ZEALAND, 1996*

kerplop *noun* used for imitating the sound of something being dropped *US, 1969*

kerry-fisted *adjective* said of a left-handed person *CANADA, 1992*

Kerry Packered *adjective* tired, exhausted. Rhyming slang for KNACKERED formed on the name of Australian media tycoon Kerry Packer (b. 1937) *UK, 2003*

Kerry Packers; kerry's *noun* the testicles. Rhyming slang for KNACKERS, formed on the name of Australian media tycoon Kerry Packer (b.1937) *UK, 1992*

ket *noun* **1** the recreational drug ketamine *AUSTRALIA, 1996*. **2** a kettle *NEW ZEALAND, 1998*

ketaine *adjective* used to describe someone or something in bad taste. This term, from Quebec French, is used by both anglophones and francophones *CANADA, 1997*

Ketama; Ketama crumble *noun* varieties of hashish from the Ketama region of Morocco *UK, 2003*

kettle *noun* **1** a fob watch; a wristwatch. Possibly rhyming slang, 'kettle on the hob' for 'fob'; a red kettle is a gold watch, a white or tin kettle is silver *UK, 1889*. **2** a steam locomotive. From the image of steam rising *US, 1934*. **3** a boiler of a steam engine *US, 1828*. **4** in electric line work, an overhead transformer *US, 1980*

kettled *adjective* drug-intoxicated *UK, 1992*

kettle on the hob; kettle *noun* Bob (the diminutive form of Robert). Rhyming slang, originally for 'bob' (a shilling); recorded in use between 1946–52 *UK, 1961*

Kevin; Kev *noun* a working-class youth considered to be a vulgar or threatening presence. This derogatory usage by Kevin's upper- and middle-class contemporaries derives from the commonness of the name. Originally restricted to Cornwall and London *UK, 1998*

Kevin Costner; kevin *noun* a male who pretends to date his female friend(s). Teen slang, after the 1992 film *The Bodyguard* which starred US actor Kevin Costner (b.1955) *SOUTH AFRICA, 2003*

kewl *adjective* good, sophisticated, self-possessed. Variation of COOL. *US, 1998*

key *noun* **1** a kilogram. From the first syllable of 'kilogram'; the one unit of the metric system that at least some Americans have grasped *US, 1966*. **2** the declaration, under the Habitual Criminals Act, that one is a habitual criminal; an indefinite sentence under this act. The joke being that one is given the key to let oneself in and out *AUSTRALIA, 1944*. **3** a prison officer. Often 'keys', even in the singular *US, 1934*

key *adjective* excellent, great *US, 1980*

keyed *adjective* **1** excited *US, 1968*. **2** drug-intoxicated. From an earlier sense as 'drunk' *US, 1972*

key happy *adjective* used of a prison officer who is keen to keep inmates locked in their cells *UK, 1996*

keyhole *verb* (used of a bullet) to enter a target sideways *US, 1957*

keyholing *noun* eavesdropping. From the notion of spying at a keyhole *UK, 2001*

key man *noun* a person declared a habitual criminal *AUSTRALIA, 1944*

key picker *noun* a thief who operates in hotels, stealing keys left at the front desk for safekeeping by guests before they are retrieved by a hotel clerk *US, 1954*

keystone *noun* in circus and carnival usage, a local prosecutor *US, 1981*

keys to St E's *noun* phencyclidine, the recreational drug known as PCP or angel dust. A phencyclidine user in Washington might well find himself at St Elizabeth's hospital for treatment *US, 1984*

key up *verb* **1** to unlock a door *US, 1991*. **2** to become drug-intoxicated *US, 1964*

K-factor *noun* (when on a skiing holiday) the presence and number of Germans. Upper-class society slang; euphemistic for KRAUT (a German) *UK, 1982*

KFC *noun* a male homosexual who is under the age of consent. An elaboration of CHICKEN, from the branding of Kentucky Fried Chicken™ fast-food outlets; recorded in use in contemporary gay society *UK, 2003*

KGB *noun* **1** a potent variety of marijuana. An abbreviation of KILLER GREEN BUD, playing on the familiar initialism of *Komitet Gosudarstvennoi Bezopasnosti*, the Soviet Union's Committee of State Security, 1954–91 *US, 1997*. **2** the police *UK, 1982*. **3** the security office of a prison *US, 1991*

K grave *noun* a state of extreme intoxication with the recreational drug ketamine *US, 2002*

khaki *noun* a uniformed police officer *US, 1986*

khaki down *verb* to dress like other members of a youth gang, including khaki trousers *US, 1985*

khaki wacky *adjective* attracted to men in military uniform *US, 1944*

khat *noun* amphetamine; methcathinone; MDMA, the recreational drug best known as ecstasy. From the common name for the African plant that contains the stimulant cathinone as its main active ingredient *US, 2003*

khayf *noun* a marijuana cigarette *UK, 2003*

khazi *noun* a toilet *UK, 1983*

khazi *verb* to be very nervous, scared or afraid. From KHAZI (a toilet) hence 'to shit yourself' – based on the bowel-churning properties of fear *UK, 2001*

Khe Sanh shuffle *noun* a method of walking honed by combat, always on the lookout for enemy fire. Referring to the US air base in Vietnam during the war *US, 1989*

khola *noun* a potent variety of marijuana *NETHERLANDS, 1990s*

K-hole *noun* a state of intense confusion induced by use of the recreational drug ketamine *US, 1993*

Khyber-diver *noun* a homosexual male *AUSTRALIA, 1992*

Khyber Pass; Khyber *noun* the buttocks, the posterior, the anus. Rhyming slang for ARSE based on the geographical feature that links Afghanistan and Pakistan *UK, 1943*

ki *noun* **1** a kilogram *US, 1966*. **2** in prison, cocoa or chocolate *UK, 1950*

kibbles and bits *noun* small pieces of crack cocaine. A reference to a popular dog food product, suggesting that the pieces of crack cocaine bear some resemblance to the product *US, 1993*

kibitz *verb* to comment while others play a game. From Yiddish (ultimately German) *kiebitzen* (to look on at cards) *US, 1927*

kibitzer *noun* a watcher rather than a participant, especially one who offers unsolicited advice. From Yiddish *kibitser*. The Kibitzer, a play by Jo Swerling (1929), made both the title and Edward G. Robinson, its star, famous in the US *US, 1922*

kibosh; kybosh *noun* **1** an end, a finish. Almost always heard in the context of 'put the kibosh on' or 'to' *UK, 1836*. **2** (of pre-decimalisation currency) one shilling and sixpence *UK, 1845*

kibosh; kybosh *verb* to put an end to *UK, 1884*

kick *noun* **1** pleasure, fun *US, 1928*. **2** a fad, a temporary preference or interest *US, 1946*. **3** the sudden onset of the effects of a drug *US, 1912*. **4** a trouser pocket *US, 1846*. **5** (of pre-decimalisation currency) sixpence, 6d. Rhyming slang that would be more convincing if the 'kick' was plural; usually as 'and a kick' in denominations such as 'two and a kick' (two shillings and sixpence) *UK, 1700*. **6** money *US, 1947*. **7** a bribe *US, 1953*. **8** anything that is shared with another *US, 1995*. **9** the start of a horse race *AUSTRALIA, 1988*. ▶ **hit the kick** to pay *AUSTRALIA, 1972*

kick *verb* **1** to stop using; to break an addiction *US, 1927*. **2** to defer the gratification of a drug injection by slowly injecting the drug while drawing blood from the vein to mix with the drug in the syringe *US, 1952*. **3** to complain *US, 1857*. **4** to release from police custody *US, 1994*. **5** (of a jockey) to urge a horse on in a race *AUSTRALIA, 1982*. **6** (of a horse) to speed up in a race *AUSTRALIA, 1980*. **7** in surfing, to force the nose of the surfboard up out of the water *US, 1973*. **8** in trucking, to shift gears *US, 1971*. **9** in gambling, to raise a bet *US, 1963*. ▶ **kick ass** to be especially energetic and exciting; to succeed by your vigorous efforts. 'Kick arse' and 'Kick butt' are common variations *US, 1979*. **2** to use force, to beat up *US, 1962*. ▶ **kick ass and take names** to overwhelm someone or something in a methodical and determined fashion *US, 1962*. ▶ **kick brass** to complain strongly *TRINIDAD AND TOBAGO, 1986*. ▶ **kick for the other team** to be homosexual *AUSTRALIA, 1987*. ▶ **kick it; kick** to idle, to relax *US, 1983*. ▶ **kick mud** to work as a prostitute *US, 1963*. ▶ **kick out the jams** to remove all obstacles, to fight for freedom *US, 1968*. ▶ **kick sawdust** in circus and carnival usage, to follow or join a show *US, 1981*. ▶ **kick someone's teeth so far down their throat** to beat someone up *AUSTRALIA, 1972*. ▶ **kick something into the long grass** to postpone something *UK, 2003*. ▶ **kick something into touch** to finish an activity, to stop doing something or stop something happening. A sporting allusion *UK, 2000*. ▶ **kick ten bells out of; kick ten bells of shit out of** to physically beat someone very severely. A variation of KNOCK SEVEN BELLS OUT OF *UK, 1996*. ▶ **kick the bucket** to die *UK, 1785*. ▶ **kick the gong** to fool around *US, 1945*. ▶ **kick the tin** to contribute money *AUSTRALIA, 1965*. ▶ **kick to the curb** to break off a relationship *US, 1991*. ▶ **kick up bobsy-die** to make a fuss *NEW ZEALAND, 1960*. ▶ **kick upstairs** to promote to a higher-sounding but less-important position *UK, 1887*. ▶ **kick with the left foot** to be a Catholic *UK, 1984*. ▶ **kick your own arse** to berate yourself. A Glasgow variation of the more familiar 'kick yourself' *UK: SCOTLAND, 1988*. ▶ **kick yourself** to blame yourself, especially to berate yourself *UK, 2003*

kick *adjective* **1** excellent *US, 1972*. **2** out of style *US, 1999*

kick about *verb* to be around *AUSTRALIA, 1933*

kick along *verb* to serve out a prison sentence without letting it get you down *AUSTRALIA, 1950*

kick around *verb* **1** to discuss something *US, 1939*. **2** to idle; to pass time doing nothing *US, 1993*

kick-ass *adjective* **1** fantastic, excellent, thrilling *US, 1980*. **2** vigorous, powerful, aggressive, assertive *US, 1970*

kickback *noun* **1** a commission on a more or less shady deal *US, 1930*. **2** the resumption of drug use after a prolonged period of non-use *US, 1971*

kick back *verb* to relax *US, 1972*

kickdown *noun* **1** an object or commodity that has been donated *US, 1997*. **2** the automatic shift into the next lower gear that occurs with an automatic transmission when applying full throttle *US, 1993*

kick down *verb* to give, to provide *US, 1992*

kickdown gear *noun* in a car, a gear designed for sudden bursts of acceleration *US, 1965*

kicker *noun* **1** an unforeseen complication *US, 1941*. **2** in poker, an unmatched card held in the hand while drawing *US, 1963*. **3** in the illegal production of alcohol, any nitrate added to the mash *US, 1974*. **4** a small, yeast-rich amount of an alcoholic beverage used to start the fermentation process in a homemade alcohol-making venture *US, 1992*. **5** in television and film-making, a small light used to outline objects in the foreground *US, 1990*. **6** in dominoes, the 6–1 piece or any piece with a 5 *US, 1959*. **7** a member of a civilian air crew dropping supplies by parachute to troops in remote areas. The handlers literally kicked the supply crates with parachutes out of the plane doors *US, 1990*. **8** a member of the Mountjoy prison riot squad *IRELAND, 1996*. **9** on the railways, a jammed air brake valve *US, 1975*. **10** a linear amplifier for a citizens' band radio *US, 1976*

kick in *verb* to contribute, to share an expense *US, 1906*

kicking; kickin' *adjective* excellent, wonderful, etc *US, 1988*

kick in the ass; kick in the pants *noun* in horse racing, a horse heavily favoured to win a race *US, 1951*

kick in the balls; kick in the arse; kick in the ass; kick in the pants; kick in the head *noun* a grave disappointment; a serious setback *UK, 1989*

kick-off *noun* **1** a start; a beginning; the time something begins. A figurative use of a sporting actuality *UK, 1875*. **2** a rough-house fight *UK, 2001*

kick off *verb* **1** to begin; to get going *AUSTRALIA, 1924*. **2** to sleep off the effects of an illegal drug *US, 1951*. **3** to die *US, 1908*. **4** to make a fuss, to raise an objection *UK, 2000*

kick on *verb* **1** to commence *AUSTRALIA, 1949*. **2** to keep on; to persevere, to continue, especially against adversity *AUSTRALIA, 1949*

kick out *verb* **1** while surfing, to step on the rear of the surfboard while raising the lead foot and then to pivot the board to end a ride *US, 1962*. **2** to leave a gang *UK, 1996*

kickout hole *noun* in pinball, a hole in the playfield that registers a score and then ejects the ball back into play *US, 1977*

kick pad *noun* a drug rehabilitation facility *US, 1973*

kick pots *verb* to work mess hall duty *US, 1991*

kick rocks! go away! *US, 2001*

kicks *noun* shoes *US, 1897*

kicks race *noun* a drag race with no prize, entered for the fun of competing and winning *US, 2003*

kick-start *verb* to give a good start to something; to get something working well *AUSTRALIA, 1992*

kick stick *noun* a marijuana cigarette. A combination of KICK (an intoxicating effect) and STICK (a cigarette) *US, 1967*

kick up *verb* **1** to complain vigorously, to respond unfavourably and therefore cause problems or trouble. Usually in phrases such as 'kick up a row', 'kick up a fuss', 'kick up trouble', etc *UK, 1789*. **2** (of a jockey) to urge a horse on to a burst of speed *AUSTRALIA, 1960*

kicky *adjective* amusing, entertaining *US, 1942*

kid *noun* **1** a child *UK, 1618*. **2** used as a form of address, usually affectionate *UK, 1959*. **3** the passive member of a male homosexual relationship, especially in prison *US, 1893*. **4** a (young) follower of a stated music style. A UK rock band called the Heavy Metal Kids was formed in 1973 *UK, 2003*. ▶ **our kid** the eldest boy in the family. A colloquial term from the north of England *UK, 1984*

kid *verb* to fool, to pretend *UK, 1811*

Kid Creole *noun* unemployment benefit; the local offices from which unemployment benefit is managed. Rhyming slang for THE DOLE *UK, 2000*

kidder *noun* **1** a teaser, a mocker *UK, 1888*. **2** used as an affectionate form of address to a friend or child. An elaboration of KID *UK, 1982*

kiddie *noun* the boss. A variation of THE MAN; 'kiddy' (late C18) is a mainly obsolete term for 'man', surviving here and as 'Kid' when applied to a boxer *UK, 2000*

kiddie can; kiddie car *noun* a school bus *US, 1976*

kiddie fiddler *noun* a paedophile *UK, 2003*

kiddie stroll *noun* a street in Vancouver where under-age prostitutes work *CANADA, 2002*

kiddiwink; kiddywink; kiddiewinkie *noun* a child. An elaboration of KID; also recorded as 'kiddywinkle', 'kiddywinky' and 'kiddlywink' *UK, 1957*

kiddles *noun* a young woman *US, 1947*

kiddo *noun* **1** used as a term of address, often affectionately *US, 1905*. **2** a youngster, a teenager. An elaboration of KID *US, 1942*

kiddy; kiddie *noun* a small child *UK, 1858*

kiddyana *noun* antique toys. The conventional suffix '-ana' combined with KIDDY (a child) *UK, 2003*

kiddy cop *noun* a police officer assigned to juvenile crime *US, 1975*

kiddy kingdom *noun* bliss *BARBADOS, 1965*

kiddy porn *noun* child pornography *US, 1977*

kid fruit *noun* a male homosexual who achieves gratification from performing oral sex on young men or boys *US, 1961*

kid gloves *noun* ▶ **with kid gloves** delicately, gently, circumspectly, in such a manner so as to avoid upset *US, 1888*

kid in the khaki shirt *noun* in horse racing, an imaginary jockey who wins races on horses not favoured to win *AUSTRALIA, 1989*

kidney *noun* the brain; by extension, intelligence *TRINIDAD AND TOBAGO, 2003*

kidney-buster *noun* a truck, especially a military truck, that rides roughly *US, 1938*

kidney punch; kidney *noun* a lunch. Rhyming slang *UK, 1960*

kidney-wiper; kidney-scraper *noun* the penis. A ribald celebration of a penis of heroic dimensions *US, 1888*

kidology; kiddology *noun* a notional science of teasing or deceiving; a notional science of dealing with children *UK, 1964*

kids *noun* a group of homosexual men friends *US, 1972*

Kids *noun* ▶ **The Kids** *All My Children*, a popular television daytime drama *US, 1987*

kid show *noun* a circus or carnival side show *US, 1980*

kid-simple *noun* a male homosexual who is obsessively attracted to young men and boys *US, 1962*

kidstake *noun* a fake. Rhyming slang, from KIDSTAKES (a pretence) *UK, 1992*

kidstakes *noun* childish behaviour, especially childish pretence or kidding around; joking. From 'kid' (to trick) and 'stakes' (games, competitive undertaking). This unusual sense for the word 'stakes' is also found in the obsolete Australian World War 1 slang term 'bluff-stakes' (a deceitful attempt to coerce someone by bluffing) *AUSTRALIA, 1912*

kid-stuff; kid's stuff; kids' stuff *noun* any activity characteristic of, or suitable for, children; hence, something easy to do *US, 1929*

kielbasa *noun* the penis. From *kielbasa* (a red-skinned Polish sausage) *US, 1978*

kife *verb* in circus and carnival usage, to swindle *US, 1931*

kiff *noun* a marijuana cigaratte *UK, 2003*

kiff-kiff *noun* a modest, suppressed laugh *TRINIDAD AND TOBAGO, 2003*

kike *noun* a Jewish person. Not much room for anything but hate with this word. It is believed that the term originated at the Ellis Island immigration facility in New York harbour, where Jewish immigrants who could not write were instructed to make a circle, or *kikel* in Yiddish *US, 1904*

kike; kike it *verb* to walk *US, 1979*

kike killer *noun* a club or bludgeon *US, 1982*

kiki *noun* a homosexual male. A derisive, short-lived insider term; sometimes spelt 'kai-kai' *US, 1935*

kiki *adjective* **1** in a homosexual relationship, comfortable with playing both roles in sex *US, 1941.* **2** bisexual *US, 1970*

Kilburn priory; Kilburn *noun* a diary, especially a police diary. Rhyming slang *UK, 1992*

kill *noun* **1** in roller derby, an extended attack on the other team's jammer (a skater who is eligible to score) *US, 1999.* **2** semen *US, 1998.* ▶ **the kill** the moment when a sale is confirmed. A hunting image with the salesperson as the hunter and the customer as prey; a variation of the sense 'to win' *UK, 1999*

kill *verb* **1** to cause someone to laugh uproariously *UK, 1856.* **2** to cause pain to someone *UK, 1800.* **3** to excite, to please, to thrill *US, 1844.* **4** to excel *US, 1900.* **5** to cover with graffiti *US, 1997.* **6** in the sport of clayshooting, to hit the target accurately *UK, 1983.* **7** in handball, racquetball and squash, to hit the ball so low on the front wall that it cannot be returned *US, 1970.* **8** in pool, to strike the cue ball such that it stops immediately upon hitting the object ball *US, 1984.* **9** in volleyball, to hit the ball downward with great force from the top of a jump *US, 1972.* **10** in bar dice games, to declare that a formerly wild point is no longer wild *US, 1976.* **11** to finish consuming something *US, 1995.* ▶ **kill big six** to play dominoes *US, 1990.* ▶ **kill brain cells** to get drunk *US, 1983.* ▶ **kill the change** keep the change *UK, 2000.* ▶ **kill the clock** in a game governed by time, to delay the game near the end when winning *US, 1970.* ▶ **kill the sin** to relieve all the blame of something *BAHAMAS, 1982.* ▶ **would kill a brown dog** to be lethal; (of food) dreadful, disgusting, inedible *AUSTRALIA, 1966*

kill *adjective* excellent *US, 1985*

Killarney carrot *noun* a large marijuana cigarette. A regional variation of the CAMBERWELL CARROT *IRELAND, 2000*

kill button *noun* the switch button under a motorcyle hand grip that turns the engine off *US, 1962*

Kill City *noun* a 'branded' variety of heroin *UK, 2002*

killed end *noun* in bowls, an end (a stage of play) that has to be replayed when the jack is driven out of bounds *UK, 1900*

kill 'em and count 'em used as a creed by US troops in Vietnam, referring to the importance attached to body counts of enemy dead *US, 1984*

killer *noun* **1** an extraordinary example of something *UK, 1835.* **2** a marijuana cigarette *US, 1943.* **3** parramethoxyamphetamine, PMA *UK, 2004.* **4** an animal ready to be killed for meat *AUSTRALIA, 1897.* **5** hair pomade *US, 1945*

Killer *nickname* Jerry Lee Lewis, an early US rocker (b.1935) *US, 1982*

killer *adjective* **1** very good *US, 1951.* **2** extremely difficult *US, 1982*

killer B's *nickname* on a sports team, a group of skilled, spirited second stringers *US, 1991*

killer-diller *noun* a remarkably attractive or successful thing; a wildly good time or thrill *US, 1938*

killer green bud *noun* a potent strain of marijuana *US, 1980s*

killer Kane *noun* used as a generic name for a scouting and assassination specialist in the US armed forces *US, 1991*

killer rim *noun* a gold-plated or chrome-plated spoked car wheel *US, 1994*

killer stick *noun* a marijuana cigarette *US, 1982*

killer weed *noun* **1** marijuana *US, 1967.* **2** phencyclidine mixed with marijuana or another substance in a cigarette *US, 1978*

killer whiffer! used for acknowledging an especially bad-smelling fart. Hawaiian youth usage *US, 1982*

kill fee *noun* a fee paid when a creative project is cancelled *US, 1982*

kill-fire *noun* an aggregation of Claymore land mines *US, 1986*

kill game! used as warning to end a conversation *US, 2000*

killick *noun* a leading hand *AUSTRALIA, 1960*

killing *noun* a great financial success *US, 1888*

killing *adjective* extremely funny. From the notion encompassed in the phrase 'to die laughing' *UK, 1874*

killing box *noun* a strategic situation in which it is relatively easy to kill a group of enemy soldiers *US, 1988*

kill rag *noun* a cloth used by a male to clean up after masturbating *US, 1998*

kills *noun* in the language surrounding the Grateful Dead, the very best concert tapes. Always with 'the' *US, 1994*

kill switch *noun* in a racing car, a switch that deactivates the car's electric system, used in an emergency *US, 1993*

kill team; killer team *noun* a small unit of highly trained scouts sent on a mission to kill enemy *US, 1984*

kill-time joint *noun* in circus and carnival usage, a cocktail lounge or bar *US, 1981*

kilo man *noun* a drug dealer who deals at the wholesale level, buying and selling kilograms *US, 1992*

kilos *noun* unwanted body weight *AUSTRALIA, 1989*

kilter *noun* marijuana; a marijuana cigarette *US, 1969*

kiltie kiltie cauld bum a childish chant directed at any male wearing a kilt. An elaboration of 'kilt', repeated, then 'cold' (spelt phonetically in a Glasgow accent) and BUM (the buttocks) *UK: SCOTLAND, 1996*

Kimberley *adjective* used derogatorily or jocularly to denigrate by association something as better than it is. From Kimberley, Western Australia; in such uses as 'Kimberley mutton' (goat meat) and 'Kimberley oyster' (a meat fritter) *AUSTRALIA, 1945*

kimchi *noun* trouble. 'Kimchi' is used as a euphemism for SHIT, with the comparison between excrement and the Korean dish made with salted and fermented cabbage not particularly favourable to the dish *US, 1979*

'kin; 'king *adjective* used as an intensifier. A shortening of FUCKING *UK, 2000*

'kin' arse'oles used as an exclamation of surprise, anger, amazement. Lazily or deliberately abbreviated from FUCKING ARSEHOLES! *UK, 1984*

kind *noun* marijuana, especially high quality marijuana. As is the case with many drug slang terms, 'kind' is a bit amorphous, at times referring to a marijuana cigarette, at times to the smoker, at times to the drug itself *US, 1997*

kinda *adjective* approximately, sort of. A ubiquitously contracted 'kind of' *US, 1963*

kinda sorta *adjective* almost *US, 1995*

kind bud *noun* potent marijuana. A combination of KIND (marijuana) and BUD (marijuana) that suggests twice the normal potency *UK, 1997*

kinder *noun* **1** high quality marijuana *US, 2002.* **2** (especially in New South Wales) kindergarten; a kindergarten *AUSTRALIA, 1955.* **3** a child in kindergarten *AUSTRALIA, 1985*

kindergarten *noun* a reformatory for juvenile offenders *US, 1949*

kinderwhore *noun* a young woman whose dress suggests both youthful innocence and sexual abandon *US, 1994*

Kindest Cut *noun* a vasectomy *CANADA, 2002*

Kindly Call Me God *noun* a KCMG (Knight Commander of the Order of St Michael and St George). A pun elaborated on the initials; used by civil servants demonstrating a jocular familiarity with the honour *UK, 1961*

kindy; kindie *noun* kindergarten; a kindergarten *AUSTRALIA, 1969*

kineahora! God forbid! From the German (not one) and Hebrew (evil eye) *US, 1968*

kinell!; 'kin' 'ell!; kinnell! used as a register of shock or amazement. A contraction of FUCKING HELL! *UK, 1982*

king *noun* **1** an aggressive, 'mannish' lesbian *US, 1964.* **2** a male leader of a group of Australian Aboriginals *AUSTRALIA, 1830.* **3** a skilled person (at a specified thing); an adept *AUSTRALIA, 1919.* **4** in Keno, any single number that a player circles to bet on *US, 1972.* **5** an outstanding piece of graffiti art *US, 1997.* **6** cocaine *UK, 2002*

king *adjective* great; excellent *AUSTRALIA, 1964*

king and queen; king *noun* a bean, a baked bean. Rhyming slang, usually in the plural *UK, 1992*

king brown *noun* (especially in Western Australia) a 750 ml bottle of beer. Named after a large venomous Australian snake; such beer bottles are typically of brown glass *AUSTRALIA, 2003*

king bud *noun* marijuana *UK, 2003*

king crab *noun* in hold 'em poker, a king and a three as the first two cards dealt to a particular player. In the game of craps, a three is sometimes referred to as a 'crab' *US, 1981*

King Dick *noun* a brick. Rhyming slang *UK, 1961*

King Dickie; King Dicky *noun* a bricklayer. Rhyming slang for 'brickie' *UK, 1961*

kingdom-come *noun* **1** the after-life; a notional point in the far-distant future *UK, 1785.* **2** the buttocks. Rhyming slang for BUM *UK, 1979*

King Farouk *noun* a book. Rhyming slang, formed from the name of the Egyptian king, 1920–65 *UK, 1998*

kingfish *noun* a powerful or political figure. Predates but influenced by the adoption as a nickname for the governor of Louisiana, Huey P. Long (1893–1935) *US, 1926*

king george *noun* a gambler who tips generously *US, 1979*

King Hassan *noun* a variety of hashish from Morocco. Named to honour the Moroccan King who gave official permission for the cultivation of a marijuana crop *UK, 1998*

king-hit *noun* a powerful punch; a punch or blow that drops a person; the winning blow in a fight; now, a cowardly and unfair punch given to someone unawares or from behind *AUSTRALIA, 1917*

king-hit *verb* to deliver a powerful punch to someone, especially from behind or when they are unawares *AUSTRALIA, 1949*

king-hit merchant *noun* a person who king-hits others; a cowardly thug *AUSTRALIA, 1944*

kingie *noun* a kingfish *AUSTRALIA, 1936*

king james version *noun* the most authoritative and best in its class *SINGAPORE, 2002*

King Kong *noun* **1** cheap and potent alcohol, usually illegally manufactured *US, 1940.* **2** the penis. A pet name from the legendary (fictional) beast *UK, 2001.* **3** in motor racing, a Dodge or Plymouth with a cylinder head with hemispherical combustion chambers, built for stock car racing *US, 1965.* **4** a powerful drug addiction *US, 1970*

King Kong pill *noun* any barbiturate or central nervous system depressant *US, 1977*

King Lear *noun* the ear. Rhyming slang, formed from the name of a Shakespeare character *UK, 1932.* ▶ **on the King Lear** on the scrounge. Rhyming slang KING LEAR, for 'the ear', extended into a variation of ON THE EARHOLE *UK, 1992*

King Lear *adjective* homosexual. Rhyming slang for QUEER. *UK, 1960*

King Muhammed *noun* a variety of hashish from Morocco *UK, 2003*

king of the hill *noun* an important man in a limited circumstance. From the adult cartoon series *King of the Hill*, 1997 *US, 1977*

king of the ring *noun* a leading bookmaker *AUSTRALIA, 1966*

king of the trough *noun* in the Maritime Provinces, used as a nonsense reply to 'how are you?' *CANADA, 1998*

kingpin *noun* an indispensable leader *US, 1867*

king's elevator *noun* monumental mistreatment. A back-formation from 'the royal shaft' *US, 1969*

king's habit *noun* cocaine. Surely not a reference to the British royal family. *UK, 1986*

king's head *noun* a shed. Rhyming slang, formed ironically from the name of a pub *UK, 1992*

kingshit nigger *noun* a black person who is in charge of an enterprise or event *US, 1978*

king snipe *noun* a foreman of a railway track crew *US, 1916*

King Spliff *nickname* Bob Marley (Robert Nesta Marley, 1947–81), rastafarian, reggae singer *UK, 1999*

king's ransom *noun* an enormous amount of money; an exorbitant price *AUSTRALIA, 1936*

King Tut *noun* a book that translates dreams into 'lucky' lottery numbers *BAHAMAS, 1982*

'kin hell! used for registering anger, amazement, despair, surprise, etc *UK, 1993*

kink *noun* **1** a criminal *US, 1962.* **2** a thief *US, 1950.* **3** non-conventional sexuality, especially when fetishistic or sado-masochistic *UK, 1959.* **4** in a deck of playing cards, a king *US, 1951*

kinker *noun* a circus performer, especially an acrobat or contortionist. Not praise *US, 1909*

kink pie *noun* a pizza with sausage and mushroom toppings. From the initials for the toppings: S & M. Limited usage, but clever *US, 1996*

kinky *adjective* **1** used for describing any sexual activity that deviates from the speaker's sense of sexually 'normal'; also of any article, enhancement or manner of dress that may be used in such activity *US, 1942.* **2** eccentric, bizarre *US, 1847.* **3** illegal; dishonest. In prison, used without a sense of perversion *US, 1903.* **4** stolen *US, 1950*

kinky blaggard *noun* a persuasive talker who gets the desired result. There seems to be an element of envy in 'a blagger who gets away with it'. Probably a variation on 'lucky bastard' *UK, 2001*

kinnikinik *noun* tobacco of mixed leaves and bark and some real tobacco *CANADA, 1987*

kip *noun* **1** sleep; a period of sleep. Following the sense as 'bed' *UK, 1893.* **2** a bed *US, 1859.* **3** an undesirable place; a place that is dirty or disordered *IRELAND, 1991.* **4** a small, narrow bat of wood used to toss the coins in a game of two-up. Origin unknown. May be connected to the dialect word *kep* (to throw up into the air, to throw up a ball and catch it) *AUSTRALIA, 1887.* ▶ **on the kip** asleep *US, 1950*

kip *verb* to sleep *UK, 1889*

kip bag *noun* a bedroll or sleeping bag *US, 1949*

kip dough *noun* money to be spent on lodging *US, 1950*

kip down *verb* to go to bed, to prepare for bed, to sleep. Mainly services usage, a variation of kip *UK, 1959*

kipe; kype *verb* to steal *US, 1934*

kipper *noun* **1** someone with red hair *IRELAND, 2001.* **2** the vagina *UK, 1984.* **3** a Royal Navy sailor; hence, a English person. Derogatory *AUSTRALIA, 1943.* **4** a doss-house; a bed; anywhere to sleep. Used by down-and-outs *UK, 1984.* ▶ **do someone up like a kipper** to ruin a person's chances. A variation of KIPPER *UK, 1984*

kipper *verb* to ruin a person's chances *UK, 1961*

kipper and bloater *noun* **1** a *motor* vehicle, a motor. Rhyming slang *UK, 1979.* **2** a photograph. Rhyming slang on a London pronunciation of 'photo'. Can be shortened to 'kipper' *UK, 1992*

kipper and plaice; kipper *noun* a face, especially one that is not particularly attractive. Rhyming slang *UK, 1992*

kipper feast *noun* oral sex performed on a woman. From the tired comparison between the smell of fish and the smell of the vagina *UK, 1983*

kipper's knickers *noun* the acme of perfection, the best. Always used 'with' the; this is a Glasgow variation on such constructions as BEE'S KNEES and CAT'S PAJAMAS *UK: SCOTLAND, 1988*

kipps *noun* a brakevan (caboose) *US, 1977*

kippy *adjective* (of a woman) attractive, well-dressed *CANADA, 1988*

kipsy *noun* a house or dwelling. From 'kip' (a doss house) and the diminutive suffix '-sy' *AUSTRALIA, 1905*

kishkes *noun* the intestines. Yiddish, from the Russian *US, 1902*

kismet *noun* fate, luck, predestination. From Turkish, Farsi and/or Arabic *US, 1849*

kiss *noun* **1** in games such as pool and marbles, a shot that barely touches another *US, 1973.* **2** a student who curries favour with the teacher. An amelioration of KISS ASS *US, 1963*

kiss *verb* **1** in games such as pool and marbles, to cause one object to barely touch another *US, 1978.* **2** in pool, to try to make a shot by bouncing the object ball off another ball *US, 1990.* **3** to perform oral sex *US, 1941.* ▶ **kiss and tell** to reveal personal and confidential information, usually of a sexual nature *US, 1970.* ▶ **kiss arse; kiss ass**

to behave subserviently. A figurative use of perhaps the most demeaning act that one human can demand another to perform. Mediaeval engravings show devil-worshippers pledging their utter subservience to Satan by lifting his goat-tail and kissing his backside; at that time both 'kiss' and 'arse' were conventionally available to describe such an activity *UK, 1968*. ▶ **kiss butt** to behave subserviently. A variation of KISS ARSE *US, 2001*. ▶ **kiss goodbye** to concede defeat; to accept an involuntary loss *US, 1906*. ▶ **kiss Mary** to smoke marijuana *US, 1968*. ▶ **kiss the couch** to die *AUSTRALIA, 1989*. ▶ **kiss the eighth pole** in horse racing, to finish far behind the leader *US, 1976*. ▶ **kiss the fish** to smoke hashish *US, 1971*. ▶ **kiss the porcelain** to vomit *US, 1984*. ▶ **kiss the toe** to drink a shot of Yukon Jack™ whisky in a single gulp, in a glass containing a pickled human toe *CANADA, 2002*. ▶ **kiss your ass goodbye** to concede defeat, to lose all hope of success or survival *US, 1995*. ▶ **kiss your sister** in poker, to come out even in a game *US, 1996*. ▶ **kiss your teeth** to make a scornful sound *JAMAICA, 2003*

KISS simple enough to be easily understood, even by the slowest person. Acronym for 'keep it simple, stupid!' *US, 1960*

kiss and cry *noun* the part of Canadian figure skating championship rinks where contestants wait for their results *CANADA, 2002*

kiss and cuddle *noun* a muddle. Rhyming slang that is never reduced to its first element *UK, 1992*

kiss-and-ride *adjective* pertaining to areas at transport interchanges designated for dropping off and picking up motor vehicle passengers without parking *AUSTRALIA, 1974*

kiss-ass; kiss-arse *noun* a sycophant; one who curries favour in a self-demeaning fashion *US, 1973*

kisser *noun* **1** the mouth. Originally boxing slang *UK, 1860*. **2** the face *US, 1904*. **3** a sycophant. Shortened 'ass-kisser' *US, 1951*

kissing Mrs *noun* the act of rubbing the clitoris with the penis. Elaborated on THE MRS (vagina) *UK, 2001*

kiss it! used as contemptuous expression of dismissal. A shortening of KISS MY ARSE! *UK, 1999*

kiss kiss goodbye *US, 1991*

kiss-me-arse *noun* in British Columbia ocean waters, the marbled murrelet *CANADA, 1989*

kiss-me-ass; kiss-me-tail *adjective* inconsequential; petty *TRINIDAD AND TOBAGO, 1972*

kiss me Hardy; kiss me *noun* Bacardi™ (a branded white rum). Rhyming slang, formed from Lord Nelson's legendary last words *UK, 1992*

kiss me quick; kiss me *noun* the penis; a fool. Rhyming slang for PRICK, reflecting, to some degree, the type of person who will wear a 'comical' novelty hat bearing the legend 'kiss me quick' when the opportunity arises *UK, 1992*

kiss-me-quick; kiss-me-kwik *adjective* describes a seaside resort given to cheap, dated commercialism. A kiss-me-quick hat is, in many ways, a cultural touchstone *UK, 2003*

kiss-me-quick hat *noun* any novelty hat sold at a funfair or seaside resort, especially one bearing a slogan. The predominant legend writ large on such hats was 'kiss me quick' *UK, 1963*

kiss my arse!; kiss my ass! used as a contemptuous expression of dismissal *UK, 1996*

kiss my chuddies! used as an expression of disdain or rejection. Formed on CHUDDIES (underpants), possibly coined and certainly popularised as a catchphrase by *Goodness Gracious Me*, a BBC comedy sketch programme scripted and performed by four British Asian comedians, first heard on Radio 4 in 1996 but better known from television, since 1999 *UK, 2003*

kiss my grits! used for humorously expressing defiance. A signature line of Polly Holiday's character Florence Jean 'Flo' Casteleberry on the television comedies *Alice* (CBS, 1976–85) and *Flo* (CBS, 1980–81). Repeated with referential humour *US, 1980*

kiss my tits! used for showing disdain or rejection *US, 1995*

kiss of death *noun* a generally innocent or well-meant action or contact that results (often predictably) in disastrous consequences. By association with the kiss by which Judas betrayed Jesus *UK, 1948*

kiss-off *noun* **1** a complete rejection *US, 1926*. **2** any form of compensation paid to someone who has been dismissed or rejected *UK, 2002*

kiss off *verb* to dismiss, to reject *US, 1904*

kiss up *verb* to curry favour *US, 1965*

kissy *noun* an effeminate male *US, 1964*

kissy *adjective* in homosexual usage, exciting, worthy of enthusiasm (usually of an inanimate object) *US, 1949*

kissy-face *noun* prolonged kissing. Introduces a childish tone *US, 1958*

kit *noun* **1** clothes. Conventionally used for sports clothing *UK, 2001*. **2** in prison, contraband goods *UK, 1996*. **3** the equipment needed to prepare and inject heroin or another drug *US, 1959*. **4** in prison, a letter *UK, 1996*

kit and caboodle *noun* all of something *US, 1888*

Kit Carson *noun* a former Viet Cong who has become a scout or translator for the US Army. The allusion is to the scouting abilities of Kit Carson (1809–68), a legend of the US West *US, 1970*

kitchema *noun* a pub, a club or a bar. English gypsy use, from Romany *kitshima* (a tavern) *UK, 1979*

kitchen *noun* **1** an illicit methamphetamine laboratory *US, 1989*. **2** in pool, the end of the table where the cue ball is placed at the start of the game. Technically, it is the area between the head string and the head rail of the table *US, 1990*. **3** the hairs on the back of the neck *US, 1987*. **4** in shuffleboard, the scoring area of the court *US, 1967*. **5** a brakevan (caboose) *US, 1977*. **6** the cab of a railway engine *US, 1946*. ▶ **down in the kitchen** in trucking, in the truck's lowest gear *US, 1971*

kitchen bait *noun* in shuffleboard, a shot made to entice the opponent to try to go after the disc *US, 1967*

kitchen door *noun* the fly on a pair of trousers *TRINIDAD AND TOBAGO, 2003*

kitchen lab *noun* a laboratory where illegal drugs are manufactured, whether or not it is located in a kitchen *US, 1970*

kitchen rackets *noun* in Cape Breton, a *ceilidh* or house dance *CANADA, 2000*

kitchen range *noun* **1** a change (of scene or costume). Theatrical rhyming slang *UK, 1960*. **2** change (small coins). Sometimes abbreviated to 'kitchen' *UK, 1992*

kitchen sink *noun* a stink. Rhyming slang, also used as a verb *UK, 1992*

kitchen sink *adjective* of a piece of dramatic fiction, grittily realistic in a domestic setting *UK, 1960*

kite *noun* **1** a letter, note or message. Largely prison usage *US, 1859*. **2** a cheque, especially a blank or worthless cheque; a stolen credit card or cards *UK, 1805*. **3** a criminal who deals in cheque and credit card fraud. Variation of KITER *US, 2001*. **4** a hand-rolled tobacco cigarette *US, 1992*. **5** a fool *AUSTRALIA, 1961*. **6** a Christian. Prison usage *NEW ZEALAND, 1997*. **7** the face *US, 2001*. **8** an ounce of drugs *US, 1958*. **9** a bus *UK, 1954*. **10** any type of aircraft. Modern use has a mainly ironic tone *UK, 1917*. **11** a glider used in hang-gliding; a hang-glider *AUSTRALIA, 1996*. **12** a newspaper *AUSTRALIA, 1919*. ▶ **fly a kite; lay a kite** to fraudulently issue or pass a worthless cheque. Based on KITE (a cheque); probably criminal in intent but possibly issued in hope *IRELAND, 1805*

kite *verb* **1** to obtain money or credit from a cheque that is drawn against uncollected funds in a bank account *US, 1839*. **2** to send a note or letter *US, 1924*

kite blue *noun* a worthless cheque. An elaboration of KITE *AUSTRALIA, 1975*

kite-flying *verb* passing worthless cheques *UK, 1956*

kite-man *noun* a criminal specialising in cheques and bills of exchange; an issuer of worthless cheques *UK, 1950*

kiter *noun* a criminal who issues worthless and fraudulent cheques *UK, 1970*

kiting-book *noun* a cheque book *UK, 1962*

kit kat *noun* **1** a fool. Rhyming slang for PRATT formed from a popular branded chocolate confectionery bar *UK, 1998*. **2** the recreational drug ketamine *AUSTRALIA, 1996*

kitsch *noun* in any of the arts, a work considered to be inferior or pretentious or in dubious taste. From German *kitschen* (to throw together, especially if hastily) *UK, 1926*

kitschy *adjective* vulgarly sentimental *US, 1967*

kitten *noun* a young girl *US, 1923*

kittens *noun* ▶ **have kittens** to become overly excited *US, 1900*

kittle *noun* the collection of empty beer containers that accumulate on a table during a drinking session *AUSTRALIA, 2003*

kitty *noun* **1** a pool of money. Originally a poker term *US, 1887*. **2** the vagina. A diminutive of PUSSY *US, 2000*. **3** a woman *US, 1936*. **4** a guy, a young man. An extension of CAT *US, 1952*. **5** a jail or prison *US, 1950*. **6** a Cadillac car *US, 1970*

kitty litter *noun* any mixture of sand and salt or other compounds sprinkled on a snowy road or an oil spill on a road *US, 1976*

kiwi *noun* a person who shirks work *US, 1991*

Kiwi *noun* a New Zealander. Named after the national bird of New Zealand. The kiwi is a flightless bird native to New Zealand *NEW ZEALAND, 1918*

Kiwi *adjective* of or relating to New Zealand or New Zealanders *AUSTRALIA, 1935*

Kiwi Ferns *nickname* the New Zealand women's international Rugby League team. From the logo of New Zealand Rugby League: a pictogram of a kiwi and a fern *NEW ZEALAND, 1998*

Kiwi green *noun* a variety of marijuana grown in New Zealand *NEW ZEALAND, 1976*

KJ *noun* **1** high quality marijuana. From 'kind joint' *US, 1997*. **2** a marijuana cigarette enhanced by phencylidine *US, 2001*. **3** phencyclidine, the recreational drug known as PCP or angel dust *US, 1972*

klahowya(h) used as a greeting. A word from the Chinook jargon *CANADA, 1964*

K land *noun* the catatonic intoxication experienced when taking the recreational drug ketamine *US, 1995*

klap *verb* to slap, to smack. From Afrikaans *klop SOUTH AFRICA, 1960*

klatawa *noun* a journey *CANADA, 1963*

klebbies *noun* small denominations in any foreign currency. Royal Navy slang has ICKIE as the generic unit of foreign money, which then subdivides into one hundred 'klebbies' *UK, 2003*

kleenex *noun* **1** a youthful, sexually inexperienced male who is temporarily the object of an older homosexual's desire *US, 1987*. **2** MDMA, the recreational drug best known as ecstasy *US, 1994*

klep; klepper *noun* a kleptomaniac; a thief *UK, 1889*

klepto *noun* a kleptomaniac *US, 1953*

klim *noun* any powdered milk. From the branded product manufactured by Borden *TRINIDAD AND TOBAGO, 2003*

klingon *noun* a crack cocaine addict. A play on 'cling on', describing an addict's behaviour; based on the Klingons, creatures from outer space in television science fiction series *Star Trek US, 2003*

Klondike *noun* **1** a prison cell used for solitary confinement. An allusion to Klondike, Alaska, the epitome of remoteness *US, 1982*. **2** brass or copper, often stolen, sold for scrap *US, 1980*

klooch; klootch *noun* a wife, an Indian woman. The term comes from Chinook jargon for 'female/wife' *CANADA, 1963*

klotsick *adjective* (among Nova Scotians of German descent) said of a cake that has fallen, failed to rise, or rose and then fell *CANADA, 1975*

kluge; kludge *noun* in computing, a makeshift solution to a hardware or software problem *US, 1962*

klutz; clutz *noun* a clumsy, awkward person. Yiddish, from German *US, 1956*

klutzy; clutzy *adjective* clumsy, awkward *US, 1965*

KMAG *noun* during the Korean war, the US advisors assigned to Republic of Korea troops – the Korean Military Advisory Group. The Korean troops performed so poorly early in the war that the initials took on a new meaning – Kiss My Ass Goodbye *US, 1952*

knacked *adjective* exhausted. Used by teenagers too exhausted to manage every syllable of KNACKERED (exhausted) *UK, 1982*

knacker *noun* an unfit or useless individual, especially if overweight. Royal Navy slang: any food with a high calorie count may be called 'fat knacker pie' *UK, 1987*

knacker *verb* **1** to ruin; to kill. From the conventional sense (to slaughter a horse) *UK, 1887*. **2** to steal *IRELAND, 1998*

knacker drinking *noun* drinking alcohol outside *IRELAND, 1991*

knackered *adjective* tired, worn-out, exhausted. Derives from the obsolete 'knacker' (a worn-out horse) *UK, 1949*

knacker out; knacker *verb* to tire out *UK, 1946*

knackers *noun* **1** the testicles. From an earlier sense (castanets) *UK, 1866*. **2** nonsense. Identical in use to all senses of BALLS or BOLLOCKS *UK, 1984*. ▶ **off your knackers** drunk or drug-intoxicated *UK, 2001*

knackers! used for registering anger, frustration, dismissal, etc. Identical in use to BALLS! or BOLLOCKS! *UK, 1984*

knead *verb* ▶ **knead the noodle** (of a male) to masturbate *US, 2001*

knee-bangers *noun* long shorts *US, 1991*

kneecap *verb* to break someone's kneecap or shoot them in the kneecap, almost always as a planned act of retribution *US, 1974*

kneehigh to a grasshopper *adjective* very young. Many variations on this theme have been recorded since 'knee-high to a toad', 1814, and continue to be coined *US, 1914*

kneel *verb* ▶ **kneel at the altar 1** to engage in anal sex *US, 1962*. **2** to kneel while performing oral sex on a man *US, 1965*

kneelo *noun* a surfer who rides kneeling *AUSTRALIA, 1985*

knee machine *noun* a short surfboard, a kneeboard or bellyboard *US, 1977*

kneesies *noun* knee-to-knee contact, usually out of sight such as under a restaurant table *US, 1947*

knee-slapper *noun* a small, white-water wave *US, 1991*

knees-up *noun* an energetic dance party, a lively gathering. From the song 'Knees up Mother Brown!' by Weston and Lee, 1939 *UK, 1963*

knee-tremble *verb* performing sexual intercourse while standing *AUSTRALIA, 1985*

knee-trembler *noun* **1** sex while standing *AUSTRALIA, 1896*. **2** a sexually attractive woman *UK, 1999*

knicker-nicker *noun* a stealer of clothes (especially underwear) from a clothesline *UK, 1984*

knickers *noun* ▶ **keep your knickers on!** stay calm!, don't get excited!; don't lose your temper! *UK, 1973*

knickers! used as an expression of dismissal, contempt or annoyance. A children's 'naughty' word, now in adult hands *UK, 1971*

knickers in a twist; knickers in a knot *noun* an agitated or flustered condition; a state of panic. A figurative sense of an uncomfortable condition *AUSTRALIA, 1978*

knick-knack *noun* **1** a trinket; a small trivial article pleasing for ornament *UK, 1682*. **2** a small penis *US, 1981*

knife and fork *noun* **1** a meal, especially in a restaurant *UK, 2001*. **2** pork. Rhyming slang *UK, 1992*. **3** the money that a betting pool player leaves in reserve for living expenses *US, 1990*. ▶ **do you need a knife and fork?; do you want a knife and fork?** a catchphrase jibe directed at a driver struggling to find the right gear *UK, 1975*

knife and gun club *noun* a hospital casualty department *US, 1994*

knife-happy *adjective* (used of a surgeon) over-eager to treat with surgery *US, 1961*

Knifepoint *nickname* HM Prison Highpoint in Suffolk *UK, 2000*

knight *noun* in homosexual usage, a person with syphilis *US, 1981*

knight of the asphalt *noun* an long-distance trucker *US, 1977*

knit *noun* a shirt or sweater *US, 1972*

knit *verb* ▶ **like knitting fog** impossible *UK, 2003*

knitting circle *noun* in homosexual usage, a group of men who are too engaged in conversation to seek sex *US, 1981*

knitting needle *noun* in oil drilling, a tool used to splice wire cable *US, 1954*

knitting needles *noun* a rapid movement of blades and series of clicks produced when two fencers are practising. From the similarity in sound and action to that of knitting needles, not the earlier, obsolete 'knitting needle' (a sword) *UK, 1988*

knives *noun* ▶ **at it like knives** very sexually active *UK, 1985*

knob *noun* **1** the head *UK, 1673*. **2** the penis *UK, 1660*. **3** a fool; an obnoxious, despised person *UK, 1997*. **4** the knee *US, 1970*. **5** a sexually transmitted infection *UK, 1966*. ▶ **polish a knob** to perform oral sex on a man *US, 1947*

knob *verb* to have sex with someone. Derives from KNOB (the penis) but usage is not gender-specific *UK, 1988*

knobber *noun* **1** oral sex performed on a male *US, 1989*. **2** a fool, used as a general term of contempt. An elaboration of KNOB *US, 1990*

knobbing *adjective* used as an intensifier. Substitutes for FUCKING *UK, 2000*

knobbly knee *noun* a key. Rhyming slang *UK, 1992*

knobby *noun* a motorcycle tyre with large treads, used for riding on dirt and trails *US, 1973*

knob-cheese *noun* smegma collected under the foreskin. A variation of COCK CHEESE *UK, 1997*

knob-end *noun* a despised person *UK, 1998*

knob gag *noun* a joke about a penis *UK, 2003*

knob-gobbling *noun* oral sex on a man *US, 1980*

knobhead; nobhead *noun* a despised person; a fool. From KNOB (the penis) *US, 1926*

knob job *noun* oral sex performed on a man *US, 1968*

knob-jockey *noun* a homosexual male; a promiscuous heterosexual female. A rider of the KNOB (the penis) *UK, 1998*

knob off *verb* go away *UK, 2001*

knobs *noun* the female breasts, especially the nipples *US, 1968*. ▶ **with knobs on** with interest, intensified, with embellishments *UK, 1930*

knob throb *noun* (of a male) an intense desire for sex *UK, 1998*

knock *noun* **1** a setback, especially a monetary loss *UK, 1889*. **2** a bite (that moment when a fish takes the bait). Used by anglers *UK, 1969*. **3** a promiscuous woman *AUSTRALIA, 1965*. ▶ **do a knock 1** to partake in an amorous outing; to go on a date *AUSTRALIA, 1934*. **2** to have sex. From 'knock' (an act of sexual intercourse) *AUSTRALIA, 1933*. ▶ **on the knock 1** on credit; engaged in hire purchase *UK, 1968*. **2** to be working as a prostitute *UK, 1969*. ▶ **take a knock** to suffer a setback or a financial loss *UK, 1649*. ▶ **take the knock** to fail to meet your debts *AUSTRALIA, 1966*

knock *verb* **1** to criticise, to disparage *US, 1865*. **2** to defraud, to cheat, especially by passing a fraudulent cheque or by obtaining and dishonouring a credit arrangement *UK, 1962*. **3** to steal; to rob *UK, 1919*. **4** to arrest *US, 1987*. **5** to kill *AUSTRALIA, 1911*. **6** to wound *AUSTRALIA, 1917*. **7** to exhaust; to debilitate *AUSTRALIA, 1957*. **8** to have sexual intercourse with someone *UK, 1598*. **9** to make an amorous approach to (a person) *AUSTRALIA, 1934*. **10** to be unable to make a move in a game, such as dominoes. Almost certainly derived from the player's action of knocking on the table to signal an inability to move *UK, 1984*. **11** to disclose that a pool player is a professional *US, 1990*. **12** to post (a letter) *US, 1947*. ▶ **couldn't knock the skin off a rice pudding** weak, impotent; used contemptuously of an inferior fighter *UK, 1946*. ▶ **knock 'em cold; knock 'em dead** to amaze an audience, to have a sensational success. From boxing *UK, 1961*. ▶ **knock a chunk off** to have sex from the male perspective *US, 1973*. ▶ **knock a fade** to leave *US, 1973*. ▶ **knock a scarf** to eat a meal *US, 1947*. ▶ **knock at the door** in horse racing, to have nearly won several recent races *US, 1960*. ▶ **knock boots** to have sex, especially anal sex *US, 1994*. ▶ **knock dog** to be

for sale at a low price *TRINIDAD AND TOBAGO, 2003*. ▶ **knock for six 1** to utterly overcome, to inconvenience gravely. Cricketing imagery, where a 'six' or 'sixer' is a shot that clears the boundary *UK, 1902*. **2** to astound *UK, 1949*. ▶ **knock into a cocked hat** to damage someone or something very considerably. By late C20 other violent verbs often replace 'knock' *US, 1833*. ▶ **knock into the middle of next week; knock into next week** to hit violently, even fatally; especially, to deliver a blow that causes insensibility. Originally used of boxers *UK, 1821*. ▶ **knock it off** to have sexual intercourse *AUSTRALIA, 1983*. ▶ **knock it on the head** to stop talking; to stop doing something. Often as an imperative *AUSTRALIA, 1965*. ▶ **knock it out** to have sex *US, 1980*. ▶ **knock one off** to have sex, especially in a perfunctory manner *US, 1924*. ▶ **knock one out** to masturbate to orgasm. Possibly related to KNOCK OUT (to manufacture or supply cheaply) *UK, 1990*. ▶ **knock out tongue** to kiss with open mouths *US, 1993*. ▶ **knock seven bells out of someone** to physically beat someone very severely *UK, 1929*. ▶ **knock someone rotten** to punch or strike fiercely; to daze (a person) by hitting them; to stun *AUSTRALIA, 1965*. ▶ **knock someone's eyes out** to astound someone *AUSTRALIA, 1940*. ▶ **knock something on the head** to finish an activity, to stop doing something or stop something happening. Often as the exclamatory injunction (knock it on the head!) Obviously derives from a final blow that renders someone unconscious, or kills a snake, or drives a nail home *UK, 1871*. ▶ **knock spots off** to surpass *US, 1856*. ▶ **knock the drawing room out of someone** to condition or toughen someone physically *NEW ZEALAND, 1952*. ▶ **knock the slack out** to accelerate (a truck or car) *US, 1976*. ▶ **knock your wig** to comb your hair *US, 1947*

knockabout *noun* an itinerant *AUSTRALIA, 1889*

knock about *verb* **1** to be around *AUSTRALIA, 1889*. **2** to wander without purpose and without a home *TRINIDAD AND TOBAGO, 1904*. **3** to beat someone *UK, 1926*

knockabout *adjective* **1** experienced, well-travelled *AUSTRALIA, 1965*. **2** of theatrical entertainment, noisy and violent, slapstick *UK, 1892*

knock around *verb* **1** to spend time with no fixed abode; to travel about as an itinerant *AUSTRALIA, 1901*. **2** to spend time (with someone); to idle *US, 1846*

knockaround *adjective* experienced in the ways of the world, especially the underworld *US, 1949*

knockback *noun* **1** a refusal; a rejection *AUSTRALIA, 1918*. **2** an 'offer by a bookmaker to accept a wager at lower odds or for a lesser stake, in part at full odds with the balance at reduced odds, or at SP (starting price) terms only' *UK, 2001*

knock back *verb* **1** to reject, especially sexual advances *AUSTRALIA, 1918*. **2** to drink *UK, 1931*. **3** to cost a person a specified amount. For example the phrase 'that knocked him back a fiver' *UK, 1961*. ▶ **knock back with a stick** to get more than enough casual sex. A jocular boast of sexual prowess *AUSTRALIA, 1950*

knockdown *noun* an introduction (to someone) *US, 1959*

knock down *verb* **1** to earn *US, 1929*. **2** to make a sale at auction. From the significant action of an auctioneer's gavel in marking the conclusion of a sale *UK, 1760*. **3** to steal *CANADA, 1976*. **4** to rob *US, 1976*. **5** to spend the entire sum of money earned for seasonal work in a drinking spree. Once a veritable institution this practice was especially common amongst shearers and sailors *AUSTRALIA, 1845*. **6** to drink. A variation of KNOCK BACK (to drink) *UK, 1960*. **7** to introduce *US, 1953*

knock-down drag-out *adjective* (of a fight) vicious *US, 1827*

knocked *adjective* drunk *US, 1974*

knock 'em down rains *noun* in tropical Australia, seasonal torrential rain *AUSTRALIA, 1946*

knocker *noun* **1** an inveterate critic; a person addicted to finding faults and making criticisms *US, 1898*. **2** a person who defaults (deliberately) on a hire-purchase agreement. A narrowing of an earlier use applied to a person who contracts a debt with no intention of repaying it *UK, 1968*. **3** a thief or confidence trickster posing as a door-to-door salesman *UK, 1996*. **4** in circus and carnival usage, a member of the audience who warns others that something is a fraud *US, 1981*. **5** someone who discloses that a pool player is in fact a professional *US, 1990*. **6** in pinball, a sound effect

when an additional ball is won *US, 1977*. ▶ **on the knocker**
1 exactly, precisely *AUSTRALIA, 1960*. **2** right away; promptly *AUSTRALIA, 1962*. **3** used of a door-to-door canvasser or salesman *UK, 1934*. ▶ **up to the knocker** thoroughly, perfectly, entirely *AUSTRALIA, 1911*

knocker and knob *noun* a job. Rhyming slang, probably formed of door furniture (rather than body parts) *UK, 1992*

knockers *noun* **1** the female breasts, especially large ones *US, 1934*. **2** dice that have been loaded with mercury that shifts when the dice are tapped *US, 1950*

knocker shop *noun* a brothel *AUSTRALIA, 1985*

knockin' *adjective* great *US, 2004*

knocking *noun* criticism; fault-finding *AUSTRALIA, 1978*

knockings *noun* the facts or details, an explanation *UK, 1999*

knocking shop *noun* a brothel *UK, 1860*

knock it off!; knock off! stop it!, shut up! *UK, 1883*

knock, knock! 1 used as the verbal equivalent of an actual knock on the door when entering another's room, office, etc *UK, 1984*. **2** in a game of dominoes or such, used as a signal (often accompanied by the action of knocking on the games' table) that the game-player is unable to make a move *UK, 1984*

knocko *noun* a narcotics police officer *US, 1992*

knock-off *noun* **1** a product that is designed to be mistaken for an expensive, brand name product *US, 1963*. **2** the end of a work shift; quitting time *AUSTRALIA, 1916*. **3** a murder *US, 1928*. **4** in hot rodding and drag racing, a wheel lug that is easily removed *US, 1960*

knock off *verb* **1** to cease; to stop *UK, 1649*. **2** to finish a work shift, job, etc. *UK, 1649*. **3** to kill *US, 1879*. **4** to defeat; to despatch *US, 1927*. **5** (of police) to arrest; to raid *US, 1925*. **6** to rob, to steal *US, 1917*. **7** to reproduce a branded item, less expensively and usually illegally *US, 1963*. **8** to sell or dispose of *NEW ZEALAND, 1985*. **9** of a male, to have sex *AUSTRALIA, 1965*. **10** to have sexual intercourse with someone *US, 1943*. **11** to seduce *AUSTRALIA, 1950*. ▶ **knock off a piece** to have sex *US, 1921*

knock-off gear *noun* an item or items of stolen property *UK, 2000*

knock-off time *noun* the end of a work shift; quitting time *AUSTRALIA, 1867*

knock out *verb* **1** to have a very powerful effect on, to impress profoundly *US, 1890*. **2** to manufacture or supply cheaply. The currency of market-traders and sweat-shops, 'knock it out cheap', 'knock them out', adopted into wider use *UK, 1876*. **3** to produce *AUSTRALIA, 1946*. **4** to go to sleep *US, 2003*. **5** to burgle in such a thorough manner that nothing of any value remains *UK, 1950*

knockout *adjective* excellent, impressive *US, 1920*

knockout; knock-out *noun* **1** an outstanding, beautiful or outrageous person *UK, 1892*. **2** an excellent thing. Literally, 'a thing so excellent that it will render you insensible' *UK, 1892*

knock out drops *noun* a sedative added to a drink to cause unconsciousness, especially with criminal intent *US, 1876*

knock over *verb* **1** to rob *US, 1925*. **2** to raid an establishment *US, 1929*. **3** to kill; to slaughter *US, 1823*. **4** to arrest *US, 1924*. **5** to drink *AUSTRALIA, 1924*

knockround *noun* a period spent wandering about idling *AUSTRALIA, 1934*

knock round *verb* to spend time (with someone); to accompany *AUSTRALIA, 1955*

knock shop *noun* a brothel *AUSTRALIA, 1968*

knock sideways *verb* to astound *UK, 1925*

knock together *verb* to prepare a marijuana cigarette. A specialisation of the conventional sense *UK, 2000*

knock-up *noun* a fraudulent system operated to rig the bidding at an auction *UK, 1966*

knock up *verb* **1** to impregnate *US, 1813*. **2** to hammer on the door of a cell to attract the attention of a warder *AUSTRALIA, 1944*

knolly bike *noun* any low-powered motorcycle used by probationary taxi-drivers in the process of learning the geography of London's

streets (DO THE KNOWLEDGE). Formed on a shortening of 'the knowledge' *UK, 1998*

knot *noun* **1** the head *US, 1954*. **2** a large sum of money *US, 1993*

knot-flashing *noun* public self-exposure by a male for sexual thrills. Police slang, formed on an otherwise obsolete use of 'knot' (the [head of the] penis) *UK, 1968*

knotty *adjective* (of hair) in tight curls *BAHAMAS, 1982*

Knotty Ash *noun* cash. Rhyming slang, from the name of a Liverpool suburb; probably inspired by comedian Ken Dodd, a famous resident of the area, and in particular by his clash with the taxman *UK, 1992*

know *noun* ▶ **in the know** trendy, fashionable *US, 1958*

know *verb* ▶ **know b from bull foot** to know anything at all. Usually used in the negative *TRINIDAD AND TOBAGO, 2003*. ▶ **know backwards** to have a thorough knowledge of something *UK, 1904*. ▶ **know how many beans make five** to be not easily fooled *UK, 1830*. ▶ **know inside out** to have a thorough knowledge of something *UK, 1921*. ▶ **know like the back of your hand** to have a thorough knowledge of something. A simile that is easier said than done *UK, 1943*. ▶ **know someone who knows someone** to be able to obtain an article for less than its retail price, referring to either wholesale rates or the acquisition of stolen property *UK, 1984*. ▶ **know the score** to understand what is going on. Referring to a musical score, not the score of a sports contest *US, 1946*. ▶ **know your onions** having knowledge that comes from experience. Also in the variations: 'know your apples' (since 1945); 'oats' (since 1926); 'oil' (since 1925). The formula is also used to describe a specified field of knowledge, e.g. 'know your hockey' (about 1929) *US, 1922*. ▶ **know your shit** to have knowledge that comes from experience *US, 1984*. ▶ **not know from a bar of soap** to not know at all *AUSTRALIA, 1918*. ▶ **not know from the hole in your arse** to be ignorant of *UK, 1999*. ▶ **not know whether you are Arthur or Martha** to be in a state of confusion *AUSTRALIA, 1966*. ▶ **not know whether you are coming or going** to be in a state of confusion, befuddlement or perplexity *UK, 1924*

know-all *noun* a person who displays their knowledge in a conceited manner *AUSTRALIA, 1934*

know-all *adjective* conceitedly knowledgeable *AUSTRALIA, 1965*

knowed-up *adjective* lucky, and believing that skill not luck produced success *US, 1954*

know-it-all *noun* a person who knows less than he thinks *US, 1895*

know-it-all *adjective* conceitedly knowledgeable *UK, 1935*

knowledge *noun* skill at performing oral sex; a person who is skilled at performing oral sex. An elaboration and play on HEAD (oral sex) *US, 2002*. ▶ **do the knowledge** of probationary taxi drivers, to learn the geography of London's streets (especially by driving around on a low-powered motorcycle); to take a written examination that tests the newly acquired knowledge *UK, 1978*

knowledge box *noun* **1** the head; the brain *UK, 1785*. **2** in railway terminology, the yardmaster's office *US, 1926*

knowmean?; na mean? do you know what I mean? Used either as a question or as a stress at the end of a statement *UK, 1997*

knuckle *noun* physical violence; the act of punching. From the verb sense *UK, 2001*. ▶ **go the knuckle** to attack with the fists; to take part in a fist fight *AUSTRALIA, 1944*

knuckle *verb* to punch with a bare fist *AUSTRALIA, 1983*

knuckle-buster *noun* **1** in car repair, a nut that is tightly fastened, guaranteeing a difficult and painful removal process *US, 1992*. **2** a crescent wrench *US, 1941*

knuckle down *verb* to make an effort and apply yourself to a task *UK, 1864*

knuckleduster *noun* a large, heavy or over-gaudy ring which may, or may not, be worn for violent purposes. An extension of the sense as 'a weapon' *UK, 1896*

knuckledusters *noun* a pair of brass knuckles. The derivation is as blunt as the practical usage: where it's worn, on the knuckles; what it does, DUST (to thrash). Abbreviates as 'duster' *US, 1858*

knucklehead *noun* a fool, an idiot US, 1942

knuckle junction *noun* fisticuffs US, 1994

knuckle merchant *noun* a fist-fighter, a rough and ready brawler UK, 2000

knuckle sandwich *noun* a punch in the mouth US, 1955

knuckle shuffle *noun* an act of male masturbation US, 2000

knuckle-shuffle *verb* to masturbate UK, 2002

knuckles on the ground *noun* an illustrative quality ascribed to a person of low intellect and primitive appearance UK, 1975

knuckle up *verb* to fight US, 1968

knucks *noun* knuckles; brass knuckles US, 1858

knucks-in *adjective* doing well. From marbles, where the term is used of a player whose aim is true TRINIDAD AND TOBAGO, 1987

KO; kayo *noun* in boxing, a knock-out US, 1911

KO *verb* to knock-out; to destroy US, 1921

KO *adjective* exhausted. An initialism of 'knocked-out'; used by black urban youths UK, 2004

Kodak *noun* police radar used for measuring vehicle speed US, 1976

Kodak courage *noun* a brief burst of fearlessness encountered when being photographed US, 1997

Kodak moment *noun* a clichéd moment or event. From a series of Kodak advertisements, urging consumers to take pictures at 'Kodak moments' US, 1991

Kodak poisoning; Kodak-Fuji poisoning *noun* an imaginary ailment contracted by the subjects of (over-?)enthusiastic photographers. Jocular; based on the names of major film manufacturers Kodak and Fuji ANTARCTICA, 1983

'koff! (jocular) don't be stupid!; (serious) go away! Phonetic abbreviation of 'fuck off!' UK, 1999

koffiemoffie *noun* a non-white, non-black homosexual male; an air steward on South African Airways. Elaborations of **MOFFIE** (a homosexual male), rhymed with 'coffee', in the first instance for a colour tone, in the second as a humorous reference to the steward's duties. Gay slang originating among Cape coloureds SOUTH AFRICA, 2000

Kojak *noun* **1** a blue flashing lamp that is temporarily attached (by magnets) to the roof of an unmarked police car. Named after the US television police drama *Kojak*, first shown in the UK on BBC television in 1974, and by which the UK police and public were first made aware of this new crime-fighting tool UK, 1999. **2** in hold 'em poker, a king and a jack as the first two cards dealt to a player. The sound of 'king-jack' suggests the name of this popular police television programme (1973–78) starring Telly Savalas US, 1981.
▶ **the Kojak** a totally depilated pubic mound. After the eponymous bald-headed detective UK, 2002

Kojak's moneybox *noun* the penis. Kojak, a television detective of the 1970s, was played by bald-headed actor Telly Savalas, 1924–94; thus this unsettling image of a bald head with a slot for coins UK, 2003

Kojak with a Kodak *noun* a police officer operating a radar camera; police radar. Combines television detective series *Kojak* (1973–78) with the corporate identity of a leading camera and film manufacturer US, 1976

kokomo *noun* crack cocaine. Plays phonetically on 'coke' in the same way as the earlier sense as 'cocaine user' UK, 1998 ▷ *see:* **COKOMO JOE**

kong *noun* cheap and potent alcoholic drink. An abbreviation of KING KONG US, 1945

kooch *noun* a sexually suggestive dance move by a female dancer US, 1946

koochie *noun* the vagina, 2001

kook *noun* **1** a mentally disturbed person US, 1922. **2** an unskilled novice surfer or snowboarder US, 1961. **3** in television and film-making, a light screen designed to cast shadows US, 1990

kook box *noun* a paddle board, used by beginner surfers US, 1964

kook cord *noun* a line that attaches a surfer's ankle to his surfboard US, 1991

kooky *noun* in drag racing and hot rodding, a bobtail roadster (with a short rear overhang) US, 1965

kooky *adjective* eccentric, if not crazy US, 1959

Kool and the Gang *adjective* unemotional and relaxed, calm, imperturbable; excellent, admirable, wonderful IRELAND, 2003

Kools *noun* cigarettes made with tobacco mixed with marijuana US, 1990

kooratz *noun* a socially inept person CANADA, 1994

korea *noun* anal sex FIJI, 1984

Korean forklift *noun* an A-frame backpack used by Koreans to carry large and heavy objects. Korean war usage US, 1982

kosh *adjective* acceptable, agreeable. An abbreviation of KOSHER US, 1994

kosher *verb* to give the appearance or effect of being fair, honest or legal UK, 1962

kosher *adjective* **1** Jewish. Offensive, a figurative application of the Jewish diet US, 1972. **2** fair, square, proper, satisfactory. Yiddish, technically meaning 'fit to eat' (ritually clean in keeping with religious dietary laws). Brought into English slang originally in the East End of London UK, 1896. **3** in homosexual usage, circumcised US, 1987

Kosher Canyon *nickname* a neighbourhood dominated by Jewish people. The most famous is the Fairfax neighbourhood in Los Angeles US, 1975

koutchie; cutchie; kouchie; couchie *noun* a pipe for the smoking of marijuana. Celebrated in song by the Mighty Diamonds 'Pass the Koutchie'. This in turn inspired Musical Youth's UK hit 'Pass the Dutchie': the name was presumably changed so that the BBC censors would miss any reference to drugs JAMAICA, 1975

K-pot *noun* the standard US Army helmet US, 1990

krab *noun* in caving, pot-holing and mountaineering, a karabiner (a coupling device). A colloquial abbreviation, noted in current use UK, 1963

kraut *noun* **1** a German. From the German dish *sauerkraut*; not necessarily disparaging US, 1841. **2** the German language US, 1948

krauthead *noun* a German-American or German immigrant US, 1928

krautland *noun* Germany US, 1955

krautrock *noun* German rock music UK, 1975

kreeble *verb* to ruin, partially or completely US, 1970

Kremlin *noun* **1** Scotland Yard UK, 1966. **2** the headquarters of British Railways UK, 1970

kress *adjective* cheap, inexpensive. From the name of a chain of dime stores US, 1947

krills *noun* crack cocaine US, 2000

kronenburg *noun* a women who looks a lot younger from the front than she does from behind. Formed from the '1664' branding used by Kronenburg™ lager, punning 16 in front and 64 behind UK, 2005

kru *noun* a tightly knit group of close friends. A deliberate respelling of CREW UK, 2003

krunk used in place of profanity. Coined by the writers of *Late Nite with Conan O'Brien* in 1994 as 'America's newest swear word'. It enjoyed brief popularity US, 1994

kryptonite *noun* crack cocaine. From the fictional mineral that weakens comic book superhero Superman (a native of Planet Krypton) UK, 1998

kudos *noun* glory, fame, prestige. From Greek κῦδος (praise); originally university slang, in widespread use by 1890 UK, 1831

kuduffle soup *noun* (among Nova Scotians of German descent) a soup of homemade noodles, potatoes, gravy and browned flour CANADA, 1999

kuf *noun* cocaine UK, 1997

ku klux klan *noun* in poker, three kings. From the klan's initials: KKK US, 1967

kumba *noun* marijuana *UK, 1998*

kung-fu fighter *noun* a lighter. Rhyming slang, based on the popular song by Jamaican-born Carl Douglas *UK, 2002*

kunka *noun* the vagina *BAHAMAS, 1982*

kunkun *noun* the vagina *TRINIDAD AND TOBAGO, 2003*

kush *noun* in circus and carnival usage, money *US, 1981*

kushempeng *noun* marijuana *UK, 2001*

kustom *adjective* custom *US, 1965*

kutchie; kutchi *noun* marijuana. Derived from KOUTCHIE (a marijuana pipe) *JAMAICA, 1972*

Kuwaiti tanker *noun* used as an all-purpose form of abuse. Rhyming slang for WANKER *UK, 1998*

kvell *verb* to overflow with joyful pride. Yiddish *US, 1967*

kvetch *verb* to complain, gripe, whine. Yiddish, used by those who know only five words of the language *US, 1950*

kwaai *adjective* **1** bad, bad-tempered, aggressive. From Afrikaans *kwaad* (bad, evil) *SOUTH AFRICA, 1955*. **2** used as an expression of approval; great, excellent, cool. A reversal of the existing sense on the good-equals-bad formula *SOUTH AFRICA, 1974*

K-wobbler *noun* a Kenworth truck *US, 1986*

K-word *noun* kaffir (a black person, especially a black African); also applied in an adjectival sense. Euphemistic for all South African senses, and offensive in all senses, whether abbreviated or used conventionally *SOUTH AFRICA, 1982*

KY *noun* any sexual lubricant. From the branded name of KY Jelly™ *US, 1971*

KY *nickname* the federal narcotic treatment hospital in Lexington, Kentucky *US, 1962*

kyaw-kyaw *noun* sarcastic laughter. Also used as a verb *US, 1946*

kybo *noun* an outdoor toilet. From a children's acronym – 'keep your bowels in order' *US, 1972*

LI

L *noun* **1** LSD *UK, 1969*. **2** marijuana. Rap and hip-hop slang *US, 1993*. **3** elevation. A surfer 'gets L' when his surfboard soars high into the air on an aerial move *US, 1991*. ▶ **take an L** to lose a game. From the designation in newspapers of 'wins and losses' as 'W's and L's' *US, 1999*

L-12 *noun* an extremely social outcast. The 'L' is for 'loser', twelve times *US, 1993*

L7; l-seven *noun* a staid person who is uninterested in or unsympathetic to the fashionable interests of teenagers. The shapes of L and 7 can combine to form a SQUARE (a conventional person). This slang may be entirely gestural in expression: the forefinger and thumb on each hand extended at right angles, left (L) and right (7) combining to make the shape of a square *US, 1956*

L8R *adverb* used in text messaging, to mean 'later'. One of several constructions in which a syllable pronounced 'ate' is replaced by the homophone 'eight' *UK, 2003*

LA *noun* any amphetamine or other central nervous system stimulant. A shortened form of 'long-acting' or LA TURNABOUT *US, 1986*

LA *nickname* Los Angeles, California *US, 1901*

la; la-la *noun* a toilet. An abbreviated 'lavatory' *NEW ZEALAND, 1998*
▷*see:* LAR

lab *noun* **1** a *lab*oratory *UK, 1895*. **2** a *Lab*rador dog. Also variants 'labbie' and 'labby' *UK, 1984*

labbe *noun* the vagina. Possibly derived from 'labia' *US, 1998*

label *noun* the name by which a person is known *US, 1928*

labial contact *noun* a kiss; kissing *US, 1947*

labor skate *noun* a trade union official *US, 1930*

Labour *noun* ▶ **the Labour** the Labour Exchange, later the Job Centre (government offices where unemployed persons must register to search for work as a condition for the receipt of state benefits) *UK, 1964*

labour day junkie *noun* someone who uses heroin only occasionally *IRELAND, 1996*

labradoodle *noun* a crossbreed of labrador and poodle *US, 2001*

la buena *noun* heroin. From Spanish *buena* (good) *UK, 2003*

lac *noun* a Cadillac *US, 1990*

lace *noun* **1** a combination of marijuana and cocaine *UK, 1998*. **2** money *US, 1971*

lace *verb* to have sexual intercourse. The female is seen here as a drink to be 'laced' by the male's semen *US, 1996*. ▶ **lace up your boots** to prepare for a fight *US, 1998*

lace card *noun* **1** a computer punch card with all the holes punched out *US, 1991*. **2** the foreskin of an uncircumcised penis *US, 1941*

lace curtain *noun* beer. Rhyming slang, formed on the name of Burton, and originally applied only to beers from that brewery *UK, 1961*

lace-curtain Irish *noun* middle-class Irish-American or Irish immigrants *US, 1934*

lace-curtain lesbian *noun* a lesbian whose mannerisms and affectations do not suggest her sexual preference *US, 1969*

laced *adjective* drug-intoxicated, especially marijuana-intoxicated *US, 1988*

lace queen *noun* a homosexual who prefers men with uncircumcised penises *US, 1988*

lace-up *noun* a shoe or boot that is laced up (as opposed to sandals, slip-ons, etc) *UK, 1887*

lack *adjective* lacking money, style or both. Hawaiian youth usage *US, 1982*

lackery *noun* ▶ **give them lackery** a beating *IRELAND, 1989*

lad *noun* ▶ **bit of a lad** a young man who is full of self-confidence with which he pursues sensual ambitions. An elaboration of 'lad' *UK, 1960*. ▶ **one of the lads** a woman, especially a young woman, who is seen to be on equal terms with, or part of a society of, men *UK, 2003*. ▶ **the lad 1** the penis *UK, 2001*. **2** cancer or tuberculosis *IRELAND, 1997*. ▶ **the lads** male friends, the men of a regular social group, team, etc *UK, 1896*

ladder *noun* the main track in a railway yard *US, 1946*

laddie *noun* in a deck of playing cards, a jack *US, 1988*

laddish *adjective* used, often disapprovingly, of the lively behaviour of young men responding to those things (alcohol, sport, sex) that appeal to them *UK, 1841*

laddishness *noun* the lively behaviour of young men responding to those things (alcohol, sport, sex) that appeal to them *UK, 1886*

laddo *noun* a spirited youth, a bit of a lad. Slightly patronising *IRELAND, 1870*

ladeez *noun* ladies, often as a form of address. Most often in the phrase 'ladeez and germs' (ladies and gentlemen) *UK, 1995*

ladette *noun* a young woman characterised by her behaviour and positive involvement in activites (drinking, swearing, sport, etc) stereotypically enjoyed by males *UK, 1995*

la di da *noun* the *Daily Star* newspaper. Rhyming slang *UK, 1998*

la-di-da; la-di-dah *verb* to behave in an affectedly cultured manner, when noted from a lower social station *UK, 1964*

la-di-da; la-di-dah *adjective* pertaining to the affectedly cultured speech and manners of the upper-classes, especially when noted from a lower social station; hence, pretentious. Jocular or pejorative usage *US, 1890*

la-di-dah; lardy; la-di-da *noun* a cigar. Rhyming slang, cleverly echoing the LA-DI-DAH status of a cigar smoker *UK, 1991*

ladies' aid *noun* in pool, a device used to support the cue stick for a hard-to-reach shot. As the terminology suggests, the device is scorned by skilled players *US, 1990*

ladies a plate, gents a crate used in party invitations to request female guests to bring a dish of food and male guests to bring something to drink *NEW ZEALAND, 1984*

ladies' delight *noun* the penis *UK, 2003*

ladies' man *noun* a man who pays great attention to women; a womaniser *AUSTRALIA, 1901*

lads-mag *noun* a commercial publication that targets young men with aspirational features on hedonistic lifestyles and, in particular, pictures of semi-naked young women *UK, 2000*

lady *noun* **1** a prostitute *US, 1972*. **2** a homosexual man. An example of CAMP trans-gender assignment *UK, 1932*. **3** in a deck of playing cards, a queen *US, 1900*. **4** cocaine *US, 1974*

lady *adjective* effeminate. Recorded in contemporary gay use *UK, 2003*

ladybits *noun* the female genitals *UK, 2003*

Lady Blamey *noun* a drinking glass made by cutting the top off a bottle using a kerosene-soaked string. Taught to the troops by Lady Blamey, the wife of Sir Thomas Blamey, commander of Allied Land Forces in the south-west Pacific *AUSTRALIA, 1945*

ladyboy *noun* a person with mixed sexual physiology, usually the genitals of a male and surgically augmented breasts; a pre-surgery transsexual or a transvestite. A term used most often in association with the sex industry in Bangkok, Thailand. The first widespread use of the term was in association with a television documentary aired in November 1992 *UK, 1992*

lady caine *noun* cocaine. A compound of LADY (cocaine) and CAINE (cocaine) *UK, 1998*

lady come back *noun* a type of bet in an illegal numbers game lottery *US, 1957*

lady five fingers *noun* a boy's or man's hand in the context of masturbation; masturbation *US, 1969*

lady from Bristol *noun* a pistol. Rhyming slang *UK, 1968*

Lady Godiva; godiva; lady *noun* a five-pound note or the sum of £5. Rhyming slang for a FIVER; an appropriately financial allusion to the C11 English noblewoman who rode naked through Coventry to protest against taxes – according to the legend which arose in the C13 *UK, 1960*

lady in the red dress *noun* the bleed period of the menstrual cycle. An elaboration on red imagery stressing the feminine nature of the term *US, 1999*

lady in waiting *noun* in male homosexual usage, a man who loiters in or near public toilets in the hope of sexual encounters *US, 1981*

Lady Jane *noun* a common-law wife or girlfriend *CANADA, 1987*

ladykiller *noun* a man who is sexually fascinating to women *UK, 1811*

lady luck *noun* good fortune personified *UK, 1205*

Lady Muck *noun* a woman who is, in the speaker's opinion, unjustifiably self-important or esteemed. The counterpart to LORD MUCK *UK, 1957*

lady of the night *noun* a prostitute *UK, 1925*

Lady Snow *noun* cocaine *US, 1967*

lady's waist *noun* a small, waisted glass for serving alcoholic drinks *AUSTRALIA, 1934*

Lafayette *noun* a bet. Rhyming slang *AUSTRALIA, 1989*

laff *noun* a laugh *UK, 1962*

laff *verb* to laugh *UK, 1997*

laffmeister *noun* a comedian. A combination of LAFF (a laugh) and German *meister* (a master, a champion) *UK, 2002*

lag *noun* **1** a convict who has been imprisoned for many years *UK, 1812*. **2** an act of urination. A survival from the obsolete verb form *UK, 1979*

lag *verb* **1** to inform against a person *AUSTRALIA, 1832*. **2** to arrest *UK, 1835*. **3** to be serving a prison sentence. Originally, 'to be transported for a crime' *UK, 1927*. **4** to urinate. From an earlier sense as 'water'. A variant spelling is 'lage' *UK, 2002*

lage *noun* a convict. A variation of LAG *UK, 2002*

lager lout *noun* a hooligan fuelled by alcohol, especially lager *UK, 1987*

lagged *adjective* **1** exhausted, especially from travelling. An abbreviation of conventional 'jet lagged' (suffering disrupted body rhythms as a result of flying across time zones), from 'lag' (to fail to keep pace) *UK, 1999*. **2** drunk. Also 'lagged up' *UK, 2000*

lagger *noun* **1** a contact man in a smuggling enterprise *US, 1956*. **2** an informer to the police or authorities *AUSTRALIA, 1967*

lagging *noun* a prison sentence *UK, 1812*

lagging boat *noun* a drunk *UK, 2000*

LA glass *noun* a smokeable methamphetamine that does not dissolve rapidly *US, 1989*

Lah *noun* Los Angeles, California. Rarely heard, and then in northern California and derisively *US, 1978*

lahdee; lahdie *adjective* smart or fashionable. From LA-DI-DA (pretentious) *UK, 1973*

lah-di-dah; lah-di *noun* a famous entertainer, a star. Rhyming slang *UK, 1979*

laid-back *adjective* relaxed, passive, easy-going *US, 1969*

laid in the aisle *adjective* very well dressed *US, 1971*

laid out *adjective* drunk to the point of passing out *US, 1928*

laid, relayed and parlayed *adjective* thoroughly taken advantage of. There are multiple variants of the third element – 'waylaid', 'marmalade', etc *US, 1957*

lair *noun* a person who dresses and behaves in a showy manner. Back-formation from LAIRY. A term of great contempt *AUSTRALIA, 1923*

lair *verb* to behave in a showy, ostentatious way; to be a lair *AUSTRALIA, 1928*

lairise *verb* to behave in a showy, ostentatious way; to be a lair *AUSTRALIA, 1945*

lairy; lary; larey *adjective* showy, ostentatious, attention-seeking *AUSTRALIA, 1898*

lakanuki *noun* a prolonged period of sexual abstinence. An imitation pidgin 'lack of NOOKIE' *US, 1944*

lakbay diva *noun* a dark leafed marijuana. *Diva* is 'goddess' in Latin; 'lacbay' is Pig Latin for BLACK; this marijuana is a 'black goddess' *UK, 1998*

Lake Acid *nickname* Lake Placid, New York. Coined during a concert stop by the Grateful Dead in 1983 *US, 1983*

Lake Atlantic *nickname* the Atlantic Ocean on the Florida coast. A tribute to the flat surf conditions found in summer *US, 1991*

lake pipes *noun* in hot rodding, straight exhaust pipes, originally designed for speed runs on dry lake beds *US, 1963*

lakes of Killarney; lakes; lakie; lakey *adjective* **1** mad, crazy; stupid. Imperfect rhyming slang for BARMY, formed on a feature of Irish geography *US, 1934*. **2** sly, two-faced. Rhyming slang, on obsolete slang word 'carney' (sly, two-faced) *UK, 1992*

lakester *noun* in hot rodding, a car with a streamlined body and exposed wheels, designed for racing on dry lake beds *US, 1993*

la-la *noun* a toilet *AUSTRALIA, 1963*

lala *noun* the vagina *BAHAMAS, 1982*

La-La Land *noun* Los Angeles, California *US, 1972*

lalapalooze *noun* in poker, a hand that entitles the player to special payment from all other players *US, 1988*

laldy *noun* ▶ **give it laldy** to do something enthusiastically, or with great vigour. Glasgow slang *UK: SCOTLAND, 1985*. ▶ **give someone laldy** to beat or thrash someone. Glasgow slang *UK: SCOTLAND, 1985*

lally; lallie; lall; lallette; lyle; lally-peg *noun* the leg. Polari; usually in the plural *UK, 1967*

lally-covers *noun* trousers. Polari, from LALLY (the leg) *UK, 2002*

lally-drags *noun* trousers. Polari; a combination of LALLY (the leg) and DRAG (clothing) *UK, 2002*

lam *noun* **1** in cheating schemes, a victim. The victims are like 'lambs to slaughter' (easily duped) *UK, 1668*. **2** a young, innocent-looking male prisoner recently arrived at prison, identified as an easy sexual conquest by the population of sexual predators *US, 1922*. ▶ **on the lam** running away; trying to escape *US, 1928*. ▶ **take it on the lam** to escape, to run away *US, 1990*

lam *verb* to escape, especially from prison *US, 1886*

lamb-brained *adjective* foolish *NEW ZEALAND, 1998*

lamb down *verb* to defraud a worker out of their entire end-of-season pay packet by keeping them drunk until it is all spent. Now historical *AUSTRALIA, 1850*

Lambeth Walk *noun* chalk. Rhyming slang, used by snooker and pool players *UK, 1992*

lambsbread *noun* marijuana from Jamaica, with especially large buds *JAMAICA, 2002*

lamb's tongue *noun* a five-dollar note *US, 1950*

lame *noun* a naive, conventional, law-abiding person *US, 1960*

lame *adjective* **1** unfashionable, weak, unspirited *US, 1935*. **2** short of money *US, 1988*

lamebrain *noun* a fool, an idiot *US, 1919*

lame-brained *adjective* stupid *US, 1929*

lame duck *noun* **1** a person or organisation that is handicapped or disadvantaged *UK, 1761*. **2** an act of sexual intercourse. Rhyming slang for FUCK *UK, 2003*

lamed-vovnik *noun* in Jewish legend, a hidden saint *CANADA, 2001*

lame-o *noun* a fool, an idiot. The suffix '-o' is used here to create a noun from an adjective *US, 1977*

lamer *noun* an uninformed Internet user who passes himself off as an expert *US, 1997*

lame rap *noun* an unfounded arrest *US, 1971*

lame stain *noun* a completely inept, despised person *US, 1997*

lamington *noun* a type of small, oblong sponge cake covered with chocolate and desiccated coconut. Probably named after Lord Lamington, governor of Queensland 1895–1901 *AUSTRALIA, 1909*

lamister *noun* a fugitive from justice *US, 1955*

lammie *noun* a lamington *AUSTRALIA, 1998*

lammo *noun* a lamington *AUSTRALIA, 1987*

lamo *noun* a person lacking fashion sense and social skills *US, 1993*

lam off *verb* to escape, to run away. An elaboration of LAM *UK, 2003*

lamor *noun* a kiss. Possibly from French *l'amour* (love) *UK, 2002*

lamp *noun* **1** the eye. Usually used in the plural *UK, 1811*. **2** a look *US, 1926*

lamp *verb* **1** to look *US, 1907*. **2** to hit, to beat *UK, 1954*. **3** to pass time idly, without purpose *US, 1988*

lamped *adjective* drunk *UK, 2002*

lampers *noun* the eyes *US, 1973*

lamp habit *noun* an opium addiction *US, 1949*

lamp man *noun* an electrician, especially in the theatre *US, 1952*

lamps *noun* female breasts *IRELAND, 1993*

lamster *noun* a fugitive from justice or retribution *US, 1904*

lance-comical *noun* a lance corporal *UK, 1995*

lance jack *noun* a lance corporal. Army slang *UK, 1912*

Lancy; Lanky *noun* a Lancashire – hence, loosely, also a Yorkshire – employee on the railways *UK, 1970*

land *noun* **1** a fright *IRELAND, 1992*. **2** a neighbourhood *US, 1989*. ▶ **on the land** making a living by farming or other rural occupation *AUSTRALIA, 1902*

land *verb* to succeed in getting *UK, 1854*

land icing *noun* manure. Variant 'land dressing' is a term for the same thing *CANADA, 1992*

Landie *noun* a Land Rover vehicle *AUSTRALIA, 1992*

landing deck *noun* the top of the head *US, 1947*

landing gear *noun* **1** the legs *US, 1941*. **2** on an articulated lorry, the supports that prop up the trailer when it is unhitched *US, 1971*

landing strip *noun* a woman's pubic hair trimmed into the shape of a narrow vertical bar. A visual comparison *US, 2000*

landlady *noun* a brothel madame *US, 1879*

land line *noun* a conventional telephone line, as distinguished from a mobile phone or radio *US, 1987*

land of cakes *noun* (from the perspective of people on Nova Scotia islands) the mainland *CANADA, 1984*

land of hope *noun* soap. Rhyming slang *UK, 1961*

land of the big PX *noun* the United States. The US seen in its commercial glory as one big PX (supermarket/department store). From Vietnam *US, 1968*

land shark *noun* a person made wealthy by speculating in land *AUSTRALIA, 1836*

land with *verb* to impose an onerous duty or unwelcome burden on someone *UK, 1984*

lane; lain; laine *noun* a sucker, a gullible victim *US, 1933*

lane louse *noun* a driver who appears oblivious to traffic lanes *US, 1962*

lang ▶ **on the lang** playing truant *IRELAND, 1998*

langar *noun* the penis, also used figuratively as a fool *IRELAND, 2002*

langerated *adjective* drunk. A variation of LANGERED *IRELAND, 2002*

langered; langers *adjective* drunk. From Scottish *langer* (weariness); ultimately conventional English 'langour' *IRELAND, 1982*

language *noun* bad language, swearing, obscene speech *UK, 1886*

Language of the Garden *noun* in Cape Breton, Gaelic *CANADA, 2000*

languid *adjective* utterly relaxed *US, 1987*

Lanky *noun* a native of Lancashire *UK, 1972* ▷ *see:* LANCY

Lanky *adjective* of Lancashire *UK: ENGLAND, 1972*

Lao green *noun* a greenish marijuana grown in Southeast Asia, smoked by US troops in Vietnam *US, 1991*

Laotian red *noun* a reddish marijuana, purported to have been grown in Laos *US, 1990*

lap dance *noun* an intimate sexual performance, involving some degree of physical contact between a female performer and a sitting male *US, 1988*

lap dance *verb* to engage in a sexual performance in which a woman dancer, scantily clad if at all, grinds her buttocks into a sitting male customer's lap *US, 1993*

lap dancer *noun* a woman who performs lap dances in a sex club *US, 1985*

La Perouse *noun* alcoholic drink. Rhyming slang for BOOZE; from the name of a Sydney suburb *AUSTRALIA, 1981*

lap job *noun* an act of oral sex on a woman *US, 1969*

lapper *noun* the hand *UK, 2002*

lappy *noun* in Queensland, a circuit of a street block in a vehicle done, especially repeatedly, for entertainment *AUSTRALIA, 2003*

lap up; lap it up *verb* **1** to enjoy receiving flattery; to enthusiastically enjoy any distraction or entertainment *UK, 1890*. **2** to approve of and enjoy *UK, 1890*

lar; lah; la *noun* used to address a companion or friend. Mainly Liverpool use *UK, 1982*

larceny *verb* to manipulate through insincere flattery *US, 1960*

lard *noun* money *UK, 1954*

lard-ass; lard-arse *noun* an overweight person *US, 1918*

lard-assed; lard-arsed *adjective* fat; in the manner of a fat person *US, 1967*

lard-butt *noun* a fat person. A variation of LARD-ASS/ARSE (a fat person); literally FAT ASS *US, 1968*

lard head *noun* a fool. Conventional 'lard' is a soft white fat, hence the usage here as FATHEAD *US, 1936*

lardy-arsed *adjective* blessed with a fat bottom. A variation of LARD-ASSED; combines conventional 'lard' (a cooking fat) with 'arse' (the bottom) *UK, 1999*

larf *noun* nonsense, rubbish *US, 1966*

Largactil shuffle *noun* the stumbling walk of a heavily sedated prisoner. Largactil™ is a brand name for *chlorpromazine*, an anti-psychotic drug *UK, 1996*

large *noun* in betting, the largest wagering unit *AUSTRALIA, 1989*. ▶ **give it the large** to boast, to brag *UK, 2001*

large *verb* to live an extreme and hedonistic lifestyle to its fullest extent *UK, 2001*

large *adjective* **1** famous, successful *US, 2001*. **2** enthusiastic *US, 1967*. **3** very enjoyable, wonderful *US, 1874*. ▶ **have it large; give it large; have it** to enjoy in a very enthusiastic or excessive fashion *UK, 1999*

large *adverb* impressively, (of a lifestyle) in an excessive, successful, comfortable or self-indulgent manner *US, 1883*

large charge *noun* a big thrill *US, 1951*

large chest for sale; large chest for sale – no drawers used by prostitutes as an advertising slogan. A punning euphemism, certainly familiar from shopwindow postcards in the 1970s *UK, 2001*

large one; large *noun* one thousand US dollars; one thousand pounds sterling *US, 1972*

large-type *adjective* extreme *US, 1997*

lark *noun* **1** a light-hearted adventure, a spree *UK, 1802*. **2** a line of work *UK, 1934*

lark *verb* to be criminally active. Puns on the senses 'a line of work' and 'behaving mischievously' *UK, 1958*

lark about; lark around *verb* to have fun by behaving foolishly or mischievously *UK, 1813*

Larkin *noun* ▶ **down to Larkin; for Larkin** free, gratis. Possibly from LARKING (theft) *UK, 1977*

larking *noun* theft *UK, 1958*

larmer *noun* an alarmist *BARBADOS, 1965*

larney; lanie *noun* a white man; a boss (it is possible to be both at once). Derogatory *SOUTH AFRICA, 1956*

laroped; larrupt *adjective* drunk. Derives from LARRUP (to thrash) *UK, 2002*

larp; larping *noun* the adult activity of recreating fantasy, generally quasi-mediaeval, adventures, such as those depicted in Tolkein's *Lord of the Rings* trilogy, usually performed with more enthusiasm than skill or accuracy. An acronym of 'live-action role-play' or 'role-playing' that first appeared in the early 1990s *UK, 2003*

larper *noun* a *live-action role-player*. From LARP *UK, 2003*

larrikin *noun* **1** a trouble-making youth, usually a male; a thug or tough. From British dialect, recorded in Warwickshire and Worcestershire; originally a term of the greatest contempt and the youths so labelled were the subject of much C19 media hype. Journalist Nat Gould described them (1898) as 'hideous-looking fellows, whose features bear traces of unmistakable indulgence in every loathsome vice'. The amelioration of the term relies on the difference between a 'healthy' disregard for authority and social convention and an 'unhealthy' one *AUSTRALIA, 1868*. **2** a fun-loving, good-natured mischief-maker; a scallywag. Seen as typically Australian and much romanticised in literature, as C.J. Dennis' character, the Sentimental Bloke. Now the prevailing sense *AUSTRALIA, 1891*

larrikin *adjective* of or befitting a larrikin *AUSTRALIA, 1979*

larrikinism *noun* **1** delinquent behaviour *AUSTRALIA, 1870*. **2** good-hearted playfulness *AUSTRALIA, 1987*

larrup *verb* to beat, to thrash, to hit vigorously *UK, 1823*

larruping *noun* a thrashing. From LARRUP (to beat) *UK, 1889*

larry *noun* **1** in a card game, the player who has the last chance to act in a given situation *US, 1950*. **2** in carnival usage, an unprofitable day or engagement *US, 1966*. ▶ **doing a Larry** working as a *locum tenens*, a (temporary) substitute in a professional medical position *UK, 2002*

Larry *adjective* in circus and carnival usage, worthless *US, 1939*

Larry Cadota *noun* a worthless novelty sold in the circus or carnival *US, 1980*

larry-dooley *noun* a beating; a hiding. Origin unknown. There is possibly a connection with a boxer named Larry Foley (1890s), but this seems hardly creditable *AUSTRALIA, 1946*

larval stage *noun* the initial burst of enthusiastic and single-minded focus experienced by computer enthusiasts *US, 1991*

lase *verb* to print a document on a laser printer *US, 1991*

lash *noun* **1** an attempt; a try-out; a go. From the earlier sense (a fight; fighting). Often in such phrases as 'have a lash at', 'give it a lash', etc *AUSTRALIA, 1840*. **2** an act of urination *UK, 2001*. ▶ **on the lash** engaged in a hedonistic, alcohol-inspired quest for pleasure *UK, 2002*

lash *verb* to dispose of. Extends the sense of LASH (an act of urination) *UK, 2001*. ▶ **lash into** to do something in a vigorous manner. From Irish dialect *IRELAND, 2003*

lashed; lashed up *adjective* drunk. Possibly from LASH-UP (a party) or directly from LASH (an act of urination), hence a variation of PISSED *UK, 1999*

lasher *noun* a female whose only appeal is sexual *IRELAND, 2003*

lashings *noun* plenty *IRELAND, 1829*

lash-up *noun* **1** a heavy drinking session *UK, 2000*. **2** an informal social occasion, especially a party *UK, 1968*

lason sa daga *noun* LSD. From the initials, but of unknown origin *US, 1977*

last call *noun* death *US, 1977*

last card in the pack *noun* **1** a snack. Theatrical rhyming slang *UK, 1960*. **2** dismissal from employment. Rhyming slang for 'sack'; sometimes abbreviated to 'last card' *UK, 1992*

last-card Louie *noun* in stud poker, a player who stays in a hand until his last card, improbably hoping for the one card that can produce a winning hand *US, 1951*

last chance *noun* the upper balcony in a cinema favoured by homosexuals *US, 1966*

lastish *noun* the most recently published issue of a single-interest fan magazine *US, 1982*

last mile *noun* in prison, the walk from the death cell to the execution chamber *US, 1950*

last of the big spenders; last of the big-time spenders *noun* used ironically of a mean person, or ruefully of yourself *AUSTRALIA, 1975*

LA stop *noun* a rolling stop at a traffic signal or stop sign *US, 1999*

last-out *noun* a work shift that starts at approximately midnight and ends eight hours later *US, 1989*

last rose of summer *noun* a hospital patient with an ever-melodramatic belief that death is near *US, 1994*

last waltz *noun* the walk taken by a prisoner condemned to death from the death cell to the execution chamber *US, 1945*

last week's pay *noun* used in horse racing as the epitome of speed *AUSTRALIA, 1989*

last year's fun on wheels *noun* a baby in a pram *US, 1976*

lat; lats; lat-house *noun* a latrine. Mainly military use *UK, 1984*

latch *noun* a railway engine throttle *US, 1977*

latch *verb* to understand *US, 1938*

latchico *noun* a ruffian *IRELAND, 2003*

latchkey *adjective* (of a child) unsupervised at the end of the school day because of working parents *US, 1944*

latch low *noun* in trucking, a very low gear *US, 1946*

late *adjective* ▶ **late as Ellick** proverbially late *BARBADOS, 1965*

Late Late *nickname* The Late Late Show, a very popular and long-running television chat-show hosted by Gay Byrne *IRELAND, 1995*

late-late show *noun* any television show that airs very late at night *US, 1956*

late-night *noun* **1** a bus ticket found on the street that is still valid. Prized by drug addicts desperate to raise funds to buy their next dose *US, 1989*. **2** a party after a party *US, 2001*

late-nighter credit card *noun* a length of rubber hose for siphoning petrol out of other people's cars *CANADA, 1989*

late night line; late night *noun* cocaine *UK, 2002*

later; laters; lates; later on; late goodbye *US, 1954*

later for that! I don't like that idea at all! *US, 1987*

later for you goodbye *US, 1983*

later, 'tater goodbye. An embellished LATER, with the 'tater' (potato) used only for the sake of reduplication *US, 1978*

latex *noun* a condom *US, 1992*

lather *noun* a condition of excitement; agitation, anxiety *UK, 1839*

lathered *adjective* drunk *UK, 2002*

Latin *noun* a Mexican, Latin American or Spanish-speaking person *US, 1964*

latrine Gene *noun* a soldier with a pathological need to be clean *US, 1946*

latrine lips *noun* a citizens' band radio user who employs a vocabulary that is considered foul or obscene *US, 1976*

latronic used as a farewell. A corruption of LATER ON *US, 1991*

lats *noun* **1** the *latissimus dorsi* muscles on the lower back *US, 1939.* **2** skis. Used in Michigan's Upper Peninsula *US, 2003* ▷*see:* LAT

latte *adjective* pale. Italian *latte* (milk), widely used for a style of milky coffee, from which this derives – although *latteo* (milky) would be more correct. Recorded in contemporary gay use *UK, 2003*

lattie; latty *noun* a house or a flat. Polari *UK, 1859*

LA turnabout; LA turnaround *noun* a long-lasting amphetamine *US, 1970*

lau *verb* to place. Polari *UK, 1967*

laugh *noun* ▶ **a laugh** something funny, something merely amusing, often used ironically *UK, 1930*

laugh *verb* to be in a favourable position *AUSTRALIA, 1969.* ▶ **be away laughing** to make a good start *NEW ZEALAND, 1964.* ▶ **laugh all the way to the bank** to be financially successful, especially in the face of long odds or disapproval *UK, 1984.* ▶ **laugh like a drain** to laugh noisily; to guffaw. Referring to the noisy rushing of water down a drain or plughole *UK, 1948.* ▶ **laugh your bollocks off** to laugh uproariously *UK, 2001.* ▶ **laugh your nuts off** to laugh uproariously. NUTS (the testicles) punning on NUT (the head), hence a dubious pun on the more conventional idiom 'laugh your head off' *UK, 2000.* ▶ **laugh your tits off** to laugh a great deal *UK, 1996*

laugh and a joke; laugh *noun* a smoke: a cigarette, a cigar, a pipe or marijuana prepared for smoking. Rhyming slang *UK, 1880*

laugh and scratch *verb* to inject a drug, especially heroin. Derives from physical reactions *UK, 1998*

laugher *noun* in sports, an easy and overwhelming victory *US, 1961*

laughing academy *noun* a mental institution *US, 1947*

laughing boy; laughing girl *noun* used ironically as the title of a gloomy-looking person *US, 1940*

laughing Buddha *noun* a variety of LSD *UK, 1996*

laughing farm *noun* a mental institution *US, 1965*

laughing gear *noun* the mouth *NEW ZEALAND, 1964.* ▶ **wrap your laughing gear around** to eat *AUSTRALIA, 1962*

laughing grass *noun* marijuana. Derives from the tendency to laughter experienced by marijuana smokers *US, 1954*

laughing jackass *noun* a kookaburra, *Dalceo novaeguineae*; a well-known Australian bird with a loud laugh-like call. Now but a little used term *AUSTRALIA, 1798*

laughing potato *noun* a new, dry potato *CANADA, 1998*

laughing-sides *noun* elastic-sided boots *AUSTRALIA, 1937*

laughing tobacco *noun* marijuana *UK, 2003*

laughing weed *noun* marijuana. Derives from the tendency to laughter experienced by marijuana smokers *US, 1925* ▷*see also:* GIGGLEWEED

launch *noun* in drag racing, a quick and powerful start *US, 1993*

launching pad *noun* **1** a place where LSD is taken. Punning both on PAD (a place) and LSD as 'travel' *US, 1971.* **2** a lavatory seat in a (moving) train. Inspired by the image of an evacuation into space *UK, 1970*

launder *verb* to pass ill-gotten gains through a system of changes designed to legitimise their status *UK, 1973*

laundromat *noun* a business used to legitimise money gained in criminal enterprises. A play on LAUNDER (to decriminalise money) *UK, 1998*

laundry *noun* **1** a business used by organised crime to give illegally gained money the appearance of legitimacy *US, 1997.* **2** in homosexual usage, a bulge in a man's crotch. Humourous, suggesting that the bulge is produced by something other than the man's genitals *US, 1964*

laundry queen *noun* in circus and carnival usage, a female dancer *US, 1981*

Laura Norda *noun* law and order *AUSTRALIA, 1971*

Laurel and Hardy *noun* **1** Bacardi™ (a branded white rum). Rhyming slang, formed from the names of film comedians Stan

Laurel (1890–1965) and Oliver Hardy (1892–1957) *UK, 1992.* **2** a yardie (a Jamaican gangster). Rhyming slang, based on film comedians Stan Laurel (1890–1965) and Oliver Hardy (1892–1957) *UK, 2001*

lav *noun* **1** a word *UK, 2002.* **2** a *lav*atory. Variant 'lavvy' *UK, 1913*

lavaliers *noun* the female breasts *US, 1969*

lavender *adjective* effeminate, homosexual *US, 1929*

lavender fascist *noun* an uncompromising, politically motivated homosexual *US, 1999*

lavvy-diver *noun* a plumber. From 'lavvy' (a lavatory) *UK: SCOTLAND, 1985*

law *noun* ▶ **have the law on someone** to inform the police about someone *UK, 1800.* ▶ **the law 1** the police, the law enforcement authorities *US, 1893.* **2** your parents. Teen slang *US, 1955*

law *verb* **1** to arrest *US, 1935.* **2** to impersonate the police for the purposes of extortion *UK, 1956*

lawing *noun* the act of impersonating a police officer for criminal purposes *UK, 1956*

lawn *noun* a woman's pubic hair *US, 1964*

lax up *verb* to have a laxative effect *UK, 1990s*

lay *noun* **1** an act of sexual intercourse *US, 1928.* **2** a girl or a woman regarded as a sex-partner, usually with a modifying adjective such as easy, good, great, etc *UK, 1635*

lay *verb* to have sex. Most often heard in the passive *UK, 1800.* ▶ **lay a batch** to accelerate a car quickly and in so doing to leave rubber marks on the road *US, 1969.* ▶ **lay a cable** to defecate *AUSTRALIA, 1979.* ▶ **lay a fart** to fart *US, 1951.* ▶ **lay a log** to defecate. Extended from LOG (a turd) *UK, 2003.* ▶ **lay chilly** to relax *US, 1981.* ▶ **lay dead 1** to remain silent *US, 1976.* **2** to stay in one place; to stay still *US, 1949.* **3** to idle, to waste time fooling around. Vietnam war usage *US, 1991.* ▶ **lay dog** to lie motionless in the jungle. Vietnam war reconnaissance patrol usage *US, 1991.* ▶ **lay down some sparks** to accelerate a car suddenly from rest, bringing the car frame or body into contact with the road and producing a shower of sparks *US, 1980.* ▶ **lay down the law** to dogmatise, especially in an argument; to insist on a mode of behaviour *UK, 1762.* ▶ **lay eggs** to drop bombs *US, 1998.* ▶ **lay heat** to fart *US, 1998.* ▶ **lay in the cut** to wait in hiding *US, 1976.* ▶ **lay it down 1** in motorcycle racing, to spin out or fall, causing the motorcyle and the earth to meet; to intentionally throw a motorcycle on its side in the face of an impending accident *US, 1962.* **2** to explain the rules of a carnival midway game to a potential customer *US, 1985.* ▶ **lay it on** to inform, to report or explain fully *US, 1975.* ▶ **lay it on thick; lay it on with a trowel; lay it on** to do something in an excessive manner *UK, 1600.* ▶ **lay on the iron** in motor racing, to move inside another car on a turn, forcing it up and out of the fastest part of the track *US, 1993.* ▶ **lay paper** to pass counterfeit money or bad cheques *US, 1972.* ▶ **lay pipe** (used of a male) to have sex *US, 1939.* ▶ **lay the leg** to seduce or attempt to seduce *US, 1981.* ▶ **lay the note** to shortchange someone *US, 1977.* ▶ **lay the smack down** to engage in a physical fight *US, 1999.* ▶ **lay track** to lie *US, 1992*

layabout *noun* an unemployed idler *UK, 1932*

lay and pay in casino blackjack games, the practice of laying hands down, turning them over, and paying or collecting all bets at once *US, 1980*

layback *noun* a barbiturate, a central nervous system depressant *US, 1970*

lay bear *noun* in the carnival, a stuffed bear given to a girl by a game operator in return for sex *US, 1985*

lay-by *noun* on the railways, a passing track *US, 1946*

lay dead! wait just a minute! Teen slang *US, 1958*

laydeez *noun* ladies. Jocular; a phonetic spelling of an overly sincere or quasi-American pronunciation *UK, 2001*

laydown *noun* a gullible customer or buyer; an easy victim *US, 1935*

lay down *verb* **1** to play in a musical performance *US, 1943.* **2** to remand in custody *UK, 1996*

laydown merchant *noun* a criminal who passes or distributes forged money *UK, 1996*

lay down misère *noun* a certainty. A card-game usage brought into wider circulation *AUSTRALIA, 1966*

layer *noun* a bookmaker *UK, 1937*

layette *noun* the equipment necessary to prepare and inject a narcotic drug *US, 1882*

lay-for-pay *noun* sex with a prostitute *US, 1956*

lay-in *noun* permission from prison authorities to remain in bed in your cell instead of working *US, 1972*

lay into *verb* to attack verbally or physically *UK, 1838*

lay off *verb* **1** in betting, for one bookmaker to place a bet with another bookmaker to reduce the risk of loss *AUSTRALIA, 1877*. **2** to stop aggravating or interfering, to cease. Often as an imperative *US, 1908*

lay-off bet *noun* a hedging bet *AUSTRALIA, 1966*

lay of the day *noun* in horse racing, the best wager of the day *AUSTRALIA, 1989*

lay of the land *noun* in circus and carnival usage, a lead dancer in a sexually oriented dance show *US, 1981*

lay-on *noun* a gift of drugs *UK, 1997*

lay on *verb* to give *US, 1936*

layout *noun* **1** an apartment or house *US, 1883*. **2** the equipment used to prepare and inject, or smoke, narcotic drugs *US, 1881*. **3** a soldier who lies hidden in a hole observing enemy movements. Korean war usage *US, 1957*

lay out *verb* to engage in sexual two-timing *IRELAND, 2003*

lay up *verb* **1** to relax *US, 1962*. **2** to paint graffiti on train carriages while standing in a siding *US, 1997*

Lazarus ball *noun* in pinball, a ball that passes between the flippers but then miraculously bounces back into play *US, 1979*

laziosis *noun* laziness, presented with humour as a disease *BELIZE, 1975*

lazy arm *noun* in the television and film industries, a hand-held microphone boom *UK, 1960*

lazy-bones *noun* a loafer, a lazy person *UK, 1592*

lazyitis *noun* laziness, as a 'medical' condition. A combination of 'lazy' and the suffix -ITIS (used to create an imaginary disease) *UK, 1967*

Lazy K *nickname* HM prison Long Kesh. Military *UK: NORTHERN IRELAND, 1979*

lazy lob *noun* a partial erection of the penis *UK, 1998*

lazy money *noun* money kept in reserve, especially secretly *AUSTRALIA, 1989*

lazy wind *noun* a cold, biting wind *AUSTRALIA, 2003*

LBJ *noun* **1** LSD, especially when combined with some other drug. Probably a jocular transference of initials with those of former US President Lyndon Baines Johnson, 1908–73 *US, 1982*. **2** piperidyl benzilate, a hallucinogen *US, 1970*. **3** heroin *UK, 1998*. **4** phencyclidine, the recreational drug known as PCP or angel dust *UK, 2002*

LBJ *nickname* during the Vietnam war, the Long Binh military stockade, South Vietnam *US, 1977*

LBJ Ranch *nickname* the Long Binh military stockade, South Vietnam. Playing on US President Lyndon B. Johnson's ranch in Johnson City, Texas, outside Austin *US, 1973*

L-bomb *noun* an explicit declaration of love *US, 2002*

LB's *noun* pounds, extra weight *US, 1986*

lead *noun* a pencil *BARBADOS, 1965*. ▶ **get the lead out** to stop dawdling, to hurry up *US, 1919*

lead *verb* ▶ **lead up the garden path** to lead on, to entice *UK, 1925*

lead balloon *noun* ▶ **go down like a lead balloon; go over like a lead balloon** of an action, to be poorly received, to be unsuccessful, to fail *US, 1960*

lead cocktail *noun* bullets *US, 1949*

leaded *adjective* caffeinated. Borrowing from the language of car fuel for application to the world of coffee drinks and, to a lesser extent, soft drinks *US, 1996*

Leader *noun* ▶ **The Leader** Frank Sinatra, US singer (1915–98) *US, 1963*

leadfoot *noun* a driver who consistently drives faster than necessary *US, 1938*

lead-foot *verb* to drive fast *US, 1986*

lead in the pencil *noun* the ability of a man to achieve an erection and ejaculate *UK, 1925*

lead joint *noun* in circus and carnival usage, a shooting gallery concession on the midway *US, 1981*

lead on, McDuff! let's go!; let's get started! A mis-quotation from Shakespeare's *Macbeth* ('Lay on, McDuff') that became a catchphrase *UK, 1912*

lead pants *noun* a slow-moving, work-averse person *US, 1947*

lead-pipe cinch *noun* an absolute certainty *US, 1894*

lead poisoning *noun* wounds inflicted by a gun. From the lead in bullets *US, 1883*

lead singer *noun* a leader of a criminal gang *US, 1997*

lead sled *noun* **1** any aircraft that is considered underpowered or unresponsive *US, 1961*. **2** a CF-100 Canuck jet fighter aircraft. The aircraft first flew in 1950, and is also known as ALUMINIUM CROW and THE CLUNK *CANADA, 1994*. **3** a Boeing 727 aircraft. Allegedly from its heaviness during take off; the plane was produced from the early 1960s to 1984 *US, 2002*. **4** the US Air Force F-105 fighter-bomber. So named because it was the heaviest single-seat fighter plane in the world *US, 1968*. **5** in hot rodding and drag racing, a slow car *US, 1968*

leaf *noun* **1** marijuana *US, 1961*. **2** cocaine *US, 1942*. **3** a banknote. An extension of the imagery of LETTUCE (money) *US, 1929*

leaf colonel *noun* a lieutenant colonel *US, 1946*

leafer *noun* a cheque, especially when forged or issued fraudulently *UK, 1996*

leaf pipe *noun* a credit-card sized pipe for smoking marijuana *UK, 1999*

league *noun* ▶ **out of your league** used of anything or anyone of a superior quality; to be out of your league is to be of a lesser condition, out-classed *UK, 1966*

leaguey *noun* a Rugby League player or follower *AUSTRALIA, 2003*

leak *noun* **1** an act of urination. The verb 'leak', found in Shakespeare as a vulgar synonym for 'urinate', has been supplanted by the noun use of the term *US, 1918*. **2** an unauthorised disclosure of confidential or secret information; the person making such a disclosure *US, 1939*. **3** in casino gambling, any dealer error or weakness *US, 1991*

leak *verb* **1** to urinate *UK, 1596*. **2** to sweat *UK, 1995*. **3** to ejaculate. Also embellished as 'leak out' or 'leak off' *FIJI, 1984*. **4** to weep *US, 1883*. **5** to reveal secret or confidential information in an underhanded, secret manner *US, 1859*

leakage *noun* in a casino or gambling operation, the money lost to cheats and thieves *US, 1963*

leaker *noun* **1** in gambling, a bettor who loses large amounts of money quickly *US, 1997*. **2** in motor racing, an engine that is not well maintained, whether or not it actually leaks lubricants or other fluids *US, 1993*

leak light *noun* in television and film-making, unwanted light *US, 1990*

leaky bladder *noun* a ladder. Rhyming slang *UK, 1992*

leaky faucet *noun* a urinary tract or reproductive system disorder causing a urinary or vaginal discharge *US, 1988*

leaky leak *noun* phencyclidine, the recreational drug known as PCP or angel dust *US, 2001*

lean *noun* a combination of codeine-infused cough syrup and alcohol or soda *US, 1998*

lean and linger *noun* a finger. Rhyming slang *US, 1929*

lean and lurch *noun* a church. Rhyming slang *UK, 1992*

leaner *noun* a shelf or high table in a bar provided for standing drinkers *NEW ZEALAND, 1995*

lean on *verb* **1** to threaten with force as a means of persuasion; to bring pressure to bear *US, 1931*. **2** to physically assault *US, 1911*

leaper *noun* **1** any central nervous system stimulant, especially amphetamine *US, 1961*. **2** a cocaine user after sustained cocaine use. From the nervousness produced by cocaine use *US, 1973*. **3** a person who threatens to or actually does jump to their death *US, 1954*

leapers *noun* wads of cotton soaked in Benzedrine™ (amphetamine sulphate, a central nervous system stimulant) extracted from an inhaler *US, 1967*

leaping *adjective* drug-intoxicated *US, 1925*

leaping heap *noun* a Harrier aircraft. Royal Air Force use *UK, 2002*

Leaping Lena *noun* **1** a light truck *US, 1971*. **2** a train that ran from Darwin to Birdum. Also known as the 'abortion express' *AUSTRALIA, 1940*

leaps *noun* anxiety, nervousness *US, 1922*

learn *verb* to teach. In conventional use from about 1300; in C19 it came to be considered colloquial and, now, vulgar *UK, 1937*

Leary's *noun* LSD. Named after 'LSD guru' Timothy Leary, 1920–1996 *UK, 2003*

lease louse *noun* a dealer in oil field leases *US, 1953*

leash *noun* a line attached at one end to a surfer and at the other to the surfboard *US, 1977*

leather *noun* **1** a wallet or purse *US, 1949*. **2** in circus and carnival usage, a pickpocket *US, 1936*. **3** in homosexual usage, the anus *US, 1941*. **4** in horse racing, the small whip carried by jockeys *US, 1951*

leather *verb* to thrash. Originally, from early C17, 'to beat with a leather strap'; during mid- to late C19 usage became more generalised *UK, 1998*

leather *adjective* used for denoting leather fetishistic and sado-masochistic symbolism in sexual relationships *US, 1964*

leather ass *noun* in poker, the bodily manifestation of great patience *US, 1981*

leather bar *noun* a bar with a homosexual clientele whose fashion sense is leather-oriented and whose sexual tastes are sado-masochistic *US, 1963*

leather cesspool *noun* a bar or club that caters to low-lifes *US, 1971*

leathered *adjective* drunk. Derives from LEATHER (to thrash) *UK, 2002*

leathering *noun* a physical thrashing; a verbal thrashing *UK, 1791*

leatherneck *noun* a US Marine. Possibly from an earlier usage as 'Royal Marine' (a BOOTNECK); ultimately from a leather collar, part of the historical uniform of both services *US, 1890*

Leatherneck Square *nickname* four US Marine bases in South Vietnam that formed a quadrilateral *US, 1976*

leather up *verb* to prepare the cracks of a safe for the placement of nitroglycerin which will blast it open *US, 1949*

leave *noun* in pool, the position of the balls after a shot *US, 1990*

leave *verb* ▶ **leave it 1** to stop talking about something, to change the subject. Often as an imperative *UK, 1997*. **2** used imperatively, to resist a temptation to get into a fight. A widely used call for peace that appears to be generally ignored and serves, therefore, as little more than a rhetorical spur in the arsenal of aggression *UK, 2001*. ▶ **leave seeds** to impregnate *US, 1998*. ▶ **leave someone cold** to fail to arouse any interest or excitement in someone *UK, 1857*. ▶ **leave someone holding the baby** to abandon a responsibility and, instead, leave someone else to deal with any difficulties *UK, 1928*

leave it out! stop that!, shut up! *UK, 1982*

leave off *verb* to cease doing something; often as an imperative *UK, 1400*

leaver *noun* in drag racing, a driver who starts before the start signal, thereby forfeiting the race *US, 1993*

leaverite *noun* a worthless mineral *CANADA, 1989*

leaves *noun* cigarette papers *UK, 1996*

Leb; Lebanese *noun* **1** hashish from cannabis plants cultivated in the Lebanon *UK, 1975*. **2** a Lebanese person, or any person from an Arabic background. 'Leb', 'Lebo' and 'Lebbo' are commonly used derogatorily by Anglo-Australians, but amongst the Arabic-based ethnic community used positively, much the same as wog *AUSTRALIA, 1994*

lebanese *noun* a lesbian. A deliberate malapropism, recorded in contemporary gay use *UK, 2003*

Lebanese gold; gold Lebanese; gold leb *noun* golden-hued cannabis resin from the Middle East *UK, 2002*

Lebo; Lebbo *noun* a Lebanese person, or any person from an Arabic background *AUSTRALIA, 2000*

Lebo; Lebbo *adjective* Lebanese; from an Arabic background *AUSTRALIA, 1995*

leccy; lecki *noun* electricity *UK, 1999*

leccy; lecky *adjective* electric, as in 'lecky kettle', 'leccy blanket', etc *UK, 1984*

ledge *noun* an impressive person. Shortening of LEGEND *AUSTRALIA, 1988*

lee-gate *verb* to peep *US, 1975*

leem *noun* a completely inept person *CANADA, 1994*

Lee Marvin *adjective* very hungry. Rhyming slang for 'starving'; based on the name of film actor Lee Marvin, 1924–87 *UK, 1998*

leery *adjective* **1** bad-tempered, disagreeable; insolent *UK, 1977*. **2** distrustful, cautious. Originally underworld usage. Also spelt 'leary' *UK, 1718*

leet *noun* an Internet user who is categorised, often self-categorised, as 'elite'. A reduction of 'elite'; used (especially on bulletin-boards) as an antonym for LAMER *US, 1998*

leet talk; leet; l33t; leet speak; l33t 5p34k *noun* a written slang used for Internet and text communications in which numerals and non-alphabet characters replace letters. After LEET (an 'elite' Internet user) *US, 2001*

Lee Van Cleef; lee van *noun* beef (meat). Rhyming slang, formed from the name of a US film actor, 1925–89 *UK, 1998*

left and right *noun* a fight. Rhyming slang *UK, 1961*

left field *noun* ▶ **out of left field** unexpected, unforeseen, from nowhere *US, 1946*

left field *adjective* different, out of the ordinary. Figurative use of baseball jargon *US, 1967*

left-footer *noun* **1** a Roman Catholic. Used by Northern Ireland Protestants. Probably derives from a turf-cutting spade that is pushed into the ground with the left foot, but there is also a suggestion that a left-footer is simply 'out of step' with the 'right-minded' user *UK, 1961*. **2** a homosexual *NEW ZEALAND, 1998*

left-handed *adjective* homosexual *US, 1929*

left-handed bricklayer *noun* a Freemason. An army coinage *UK, 1975*

left-handed cigarette *noun* a marijuana cigarette *US, 1991*

left-hander *noun* a criminal. Superstition holds the dextrous (right-handed) to be righteous and the sinister (left-handed) to be evil *UK, 2000*

left-sided *adjective* homosexual. A variation of LEFT-HANDED current in UK prisons, August 2002, explained by one inmate as 'they are not on the right side of sexuality' *UK, 2002*

lefty; leftie *noun* a political left-winger *US, 1935*

lefty; leftie *adjective* politically left-wing, liberal *UK, 1939*

leg *noun* **1** sex; women as sex objects. The functional equivalent of 'ass' *US, 1966*. **2** a straight-leg or infantry soldier *US, 1964* ▷ *see:* LEG OF MUTTON. ▶ **around the leg** currying favour with prison administration *US, 1989*. ▶ **find another leg; grow another leg** (used of a racehorse) to perform well in muddy track conditions *AUSTRALIA, 1989*. ▶ **get the leg over; get your leg over; get a leg over** to have sex, generally from a male perspective *UK, 1975*. ▶ **give someone leg** to tease someone *US, 1971*. ▶ **not have a leg to**

stand on in an argument or dispute, to be in a defenceless position *UK, 1594*

leg *verb* to shoplift by hiding merchandise between your legs under a skirt *US, 1972*. ▶ **leg a hand** in poker, to reserve the right to make a bet even though the player has a good hand *US, 1979*. ▶ **leg it** to walk, to walk fast, to run; to hurry; to run away *UK, 1601*

legal *noun* a lawyer *UK, 1996*

legal aid *noun* lemonade. Glasgow rhyming slang *UK: SCOTLAND, 1988*

legal beagle *noun* a lawyer, especially one who is sharply intelligent or keen *US, 1949*

legal eagle *noun* a lawyer *US, 1939*

legalese *noun* in computing, inpenetrable language *US, 1991*

legal high *noun* any substance that is not restricted by drug control legislation that mimics (or is claimed to mimic) the effect of an illegal drug *UK, 2004*

legalize it *verb* in trucking, to slow down to the speed limit *US, 1976*

legal needle *noun* the legal speed limit *US, 1976*

leg bail *noun* escape from jail or prison *UK, 1759*

leg before wicket; LBW *noun* a ticket, especially in the sense of something pleasing or satisfying. Rhyming slang, from the cricketing term (and its abbreviation) *UK, 1962*

leg bus *noun* the adult leg when walking and carrying/dragging a child along *UK, 2002*

legend *noun* **1** an impressive person *AUSTRALIA, 1989*. **2** a surfer with an old-fashioned, long surfboard *AUSTRALIA, 1991*

legend *adjective* excellent, admirable *IRELAND, 2003*

leger *noun* a stand at a racecourse some distance from the finishing post. After St Leger, a famous English horse race *AUSTRALIA, 1907*

legger *noun* ▶ **do a legger** to run away, to escape on foot *IRELAND, 1991*

leggins *noun* the rubbing of the penis between the thighs of another man until reaching orgasm *US, 1934*

leggner *noun* a year's prison sentence *UK, 1950*

leggo! let go! An urgent slovening *US, 1884*

leggo beas' *adverb* wild, disorderly. From 'let go beast' (an uncontrolled animal) *JAMAICA, 1991*

leggo beast *noun* a promiscuous young woman *GRENADA, 1976*

leggy *noun* a cord attached to a surfer and their surfboard *US, 1987*

leg irons *noun* climbing irons used in electric and telephone line work *US, 1980*

legit *noun* ▶ **on the legit** legitimate; legitimately *US, 1930*

legit *adjective* **1** legitimate *UK, 1909*. **2** used to describe serious theatre (drama, as opposed to variety, revue, etc), the acting or an actor employed therein *UK, 1908*

legit *adverb* honestly, *legit*imately *UK, 1908*

legits *noun* dice that have not been altered *US, 1977*

legless *adjective* **1** drunk *UK, 1976*. **2** in horse racing, lacking ability *AUSTRALIA, 1989*

legman *noun* an assistant who does the leg work *US, 1923*

lego *noun* an infantry soldier, not attached to an airborne division *US, 1971*

leg of beef *noun* a thief. Rhyming slang *UK, 1992*

leg of lamb *noun* an impressive person. Jocular alteration of LEGEND *AUSTRALIA, 1996*

leg of mutton; leg *noun* a button. Rhyming slang *UK, 1992*

leg of pork *noun* chalk. Rhyming slang *UK, 1998*

leg opener *noun* something, usually an alcoholic drink, which assists in persuading a woman into having sexual intercourse *AUSTRALIA, 1945*

legover; leg over *noun* (from a male perspective) conventional sexual intercourse. Often in phrases 'a bit of leg over', 'get your leg over', etc *UK, 1969*

leg piece *noun* a dance performance in which the female dancers are scantily dressed or naked *US, 1973*

leg-pull *noun* an act of teasing or mockery. From PULL SOMEONE'S LEG *US, 1895*

leg-rope *verb* to marry or tie down in a relationship *NEW ZEALAND, 1956*

legs *noun* **1** in the entertainment industry, staying power and continuing popularity *US, 1978*. **2** stamina in sport; staying power *AUSTRALIA, 1986*. **3** the duration of the intoxication from a central nervous system stimulant *US, 1989*. **4** (of a shot in pool) momentum, force *US, 1835*. **5** an ability to continue or last *AUSTRALIA, 1995*. **6** a bicycle messenger *CANADA, 1993*. ▶ **do your legs** in police slang, to severely damage your career prospects *UK, 1999*. ▶ **have legs all the way up to your armpits/bum** to have long, beautiful legs *AUSTRALIA, 1944*

leg show *noun* a stage performance featuring bare-legged female dancers *UK, 1882*

Leicester square; leicester *noun* a chair. Rhyming slang *UK, 1998*

lekker; lecker *adjective* pleasant, excellent, delicious, etc. From Afrikaans *SOUTH AFRICA, 1847*

lel; lell *verb* to take. Polari; the original Romany sense implied seizure or arrest *UK, 1889*

lem *noun* a person who is on his or her own. A shortening of 'lemon'. Teen slang *UK, 2003*

lemac *noun* a Camel™ cigarette *US, 1989*

lemon *noun* **1** in used-car sales, a mechanically unsound vehicle, or one with a dubious history *UK, 2005*. **2** a simple-minded fool *US, 1906*. **3** anything or anyone that is undesirable. Probably from the least valuable symbol on a fruit-machine *US, 1906*. **4** in marketing, a woman who lives alone and is unlikely to be interested in financial sector products. Fruit-machine imagery, informed by the previous sense; the complete opposite is a PLUM *AUSTRALIA, 1983*. **5** a lesbian. Perhaps playing on FRUIT *AUSTRALIA, 1983*. **6** a heavily diluted narcotic *US, 1952*. **7** a woman's pubic hair, hence the vagina *UK, 1976*. **8** in pool, a person who loses intentionally *US, 1990*. **9** a light-skinned black person *US, 1970*. ▶ **up the lemon; up the lemon puff** pregnant. Rhyming slang for UP THE DUFF (pregnant); a lemon puff is a popular biscuit *UK, 2001*

lemon *adjective* ostentatious *UK, 2000*

lemon 714 *noun* a tablet of the recreational drug methaqualone, best known as Quaaludes™. Quaaludes™ were originally manufactured by Rorer, and were stamped 'Rorer 714'. Lemon eventually bought the patent from Rorer, continuing the '714' stamp. Virtually all pills stamped with '714' today are counterfeit *US, 1993*

lemonade *noun* **1** a spade, either as a suit of cards or in the offensive slang sense of a black person *UK, 1992*. **2** poor quality heroin. Often shortened to 'lemon' *US, 1957*

lemonade *verb* in poolroom betting, to miss a shot or lose a game intentionally *US, 1967*

lemonade stand *noun* the small house-like cabin on a lobster boat *US, 1978*

lemon and dash *noun* a *wash*-place. Rhyming slang *UK, 1961*

lemon and lime *noun* time. Rhyming slang *UK, 1992*

lemon and limes *noun* a variety of MDMA, the recreational drug best known as ecstasy *UK, 1996*

lemon barley *noun* cocaine. Rhyming slang for CHARLIE *UK, 1996*

lemon curd *noun* **1** a young woman. Rhyming slang for BIRD. Sometimes abbreviated to 'lemon' *UK, 1988*. **2** a piece of excrement. Rhyming slang for TURD *UK, 1998*

lemon drop *noun* **1** a police officer. Rhyming slang for COP. Sometimes abbreviated to 'lemon' *UK, 1998*. **2** a birth control pill. Alluding to a popular hard sweet *US, 1970*

lemon flavour; lemon *noun* a favour. Rhyming slang *UK, 1998*

lemon player *noun* a person who plays lemon pool *US, 1969*

lemon pool *noun* a pool swindle in which a skilled player lets an opponent win until high stakes are bet and then wins, making it look like he was extremely lucky *US, 1969*

lemon pop *noun* a piece of plastic or thin metal used to slip between the moulding and the top of the window on push-button locking cars, from which a loop of dental floss is dropped over the post on the door and yanked to open the door *US, 1996*

lemon squash *noun* a wash. Rhyming slang *UK, 1992*

lemon-squeezer; lemon *noun* a fellow, a man. Rhyming slang for GEEZER *UK, 1979*

lemon squeezy *adjective* easy. Rhyming slang, taken from an elaboration of EASY-PEASY *UK, 1998*

lemon tart *noun* a fart. Rhyming slang *UK, 2003*

lemon tea *noun* urination; an act of urination. Rhyming slang for WEE or PEE, perhaps inspired by the appearance of the drink *UK, 1998*

lend *noun* a loan. A colloquial or dialect term, also recorded in Australia and New Zealand *UK, 1575*

length *noun* the penis, especially when erect *NEW ZEALAND, 2002*.
▶ **you would not walk the length of yourself** used of a very lazy person *UK: SCOTLAND, 1988*

Len Hutton *noun* a button. Rhyming slang, formed from the name of a famous cricketer, 1916–90; probably no longer in use *UK, 1992*

lenllo *noun* a marijuana cigarette *US, 2001*

Len Lott *adjective* hot. Rhyming slang alluding to an Australian jockey *AUSTRALIA, 1989*

Lenny the Lion *noun* a male homosexual. Rhyming slang for IRON (IRON HOOF), which is itself rhyming slang for POOF (a male homosexual); formed from the name of a ventriloquist's dummy, a slightly effeminate lion, created by Terry Hall, popular on UK television during the 1950s and 60s *UK, 1992*

leño *noun* marijuana; a marijuana cigarette. Spanish for a LOG *US, 1955*

leños *noun* phencyclidine, the recreational drug known as PCP or angel dust. Probably related to LEÑO (marijuana) *US, 1984*

lens *noun* a dose of LSD; LSD *US, 1994*

Leo Fender; Leo *adjective* homosexual. Rhyming slang for BENDER (a homosexual). Leo Fender (1909–91) was an inventer and designer of electric guitars *UK, 2002*

Leo Sayer *noun* an event that lasts all day, especially a drinking spree or a rave. Rhyming slang for 'all-dayer', based on the name of singer/songwriter Leo Sayer (b.1948) *UK, 2002*

Leo's loot *noun* the major portion of criminal profits. A play on 'lion's share' *UK, 1956*

lepping *noun* in a highly emotional state *IRELAND, 1951*

lepta *adjective* eleven *UK, 2002*

lergy lerg *noun* a completely non-existent disease *US, 1947* ▷ *see:* DREADED LURGI

Leroy *noun* used as a term of address by US soldiers for black soldiers from the rural south *US, 1991*

les *noun* a lesbian *UK, 1929*

lesb *adjective* lesbian *US, 1968*

lesbian bed death *noun* a marked drop in libido experienced in some long-term lesbian relationships *US, 1994*

lesbie *noun* a lesbian *AUSTRALIA, 1966*

lesbie friends *noun* a pair of lesbians. Punning on LESBIE and the phrase 'let's be friends'. Generally used by teenagers as an innuendo *AUSTRALIA, 1987*

lesbo; lezbo *noun* a lesbian *US, 1927*

lesbro *noun* a male who prefers the company of lesbians. A compund of *lesbian* and *brother* *UK, 2005*

les girls *noun* lesbians *US, 1982*

lesionaire *noun* an AIDS patient. Gallows humour to an extreme *US, 1989*

leslie *noun* a lesbian *US, 1967*

Leslie Ash *verb* to urinate. Rhyming slang for SLASH, formed from the name of the British actress (b.1960) *UK, 2003*

leso *noun* a lesbian *AUSTRALIA, 1941*

leso; lezo; lezzo *adjective* lesbian *AUSTRALIA, 1987*

lessie *noun* a lesbian *US, 1938*

lessie *adjective* lesbian *AUSTRALIA, 1987*

let *verb* ▶ **let fly** to hit out, to attack physically or verbally *UK, 1859*. ▶ **let it all hang out** to behave in an uninhibited manner; to be free of convention; to hide nothing. Originally black musicians' usage; adopted into the counterculture of the 1960s and 70s, then absorbed into the psychobabble of 'alternative' and 'new age' therapies, where it remains current *US, 1970*. ▶ **let off; let one off; let go; let one go; let one loose** to fart *UK, 1970*. ▶ **let on** to reveal a secret *UK, 1725*. ▶ **let rip** to let go with considerable, or maximum, force; to shout; to accelerate *UK, 1843*. ▶ **let someone down easily; let someone down gently** to disappoint someone in as non-hurtful a manner as possible *UK, 1834*. ▶ **let someone have it** to attack someone, to give someone a beating or a severe reprimand. The ambiguous nature of the phrase 'Let him have it, Chris' is key to understanding the 1952 murder of a policeman by teenager Chris Craig: did the instruction given by 19-year-old Derek Bentley mean hand over the gun to the police officer, or shoot him? Bentley was executed and posthumously pardoned. The 1991 film of the crime is entitled *Let Him Have It UK, 1848*. ▶ **let the eel swim upstream** to have sex *US, 2001*

letch; lech *noun* **1** a sudden, powerful sexual urge *UK, 1796*. **2** a lecher *US, 1943*

letch; lech *verb* to behave lecherously; to ogle *US, 1943*

letch water *noun* pre-orgasm penile secretions; semen. Ultimately comes from 'lechery' *UK, 2002*

letchy; lechy *adjective* lecherous *UK, 1968*

letdown *noun* a disappointment *UK, 1861*

let George do it! on the railways, used as a humorous attempt to delegate an unpleasant task. Pullman porters, low men on the food chain of railway workers, were known as George *US, 1975*

let in on *verb* to admit into a secret *US, 1929*

let it lay! forget about it! *US, 1947*

let's be having you! used as a summons to work. This phrase also serves as the foundation for a well-known slang-pun on the location of lesbians: 'Lesbie Avenue' *UK, 1984*

let's face it! used for expressing a requirement for an honest appraisal of the facts when confronting or discussing something; often used as meaningless verbal padding *UK, 1937*

let's get ready to rumble! used for evoking the onset of a competition of some sort. Made famous by Michael Buffer, who introduced boxing, sporting and entertainment events with the signature 'Let's get ready to rumble'. Wildly popular in many contexts *US, early 1990s*

let's have some! let's fight A call to arms *UK, 2000*

let's squirm, worm used as an invitation to dance *US, 1945*

let's talk trash used as a formulaic greeting *US, 1951*

letterbomb *noun* a piece of e-mail with features that will disrupt the computers of some or all recipients *US, 1991*

letter from home *noun* a black African *US, 1972*

letterhack *noun* a fan who corresponds with many other fans *US, 1978*

letters *noun* those abbreviations of degree, or degrees, or other educational qualifications, honours or awards for gallantry that are displayed after a person's name *UK, 1961*

letterzine *noun* a fan magazine that only publishes letters *US, 1976*

let the dog see the bone!; let the dog see the rabbit! a catchphrase used by, or of, someone who wishes to do or see something. *UK, 1961*

lettie *noun* a lesbian. Gay slang, originating among those known in the racial categorisation of South Africa as Cape coloureds *SOUTH AFRICA, 2000*

letties *noun* lodgings. Polari, from parleyaree; the plural of 'letty' (a bed) *UK, 1859*

lettuce *noun* money, especially paper money *US, 1903*

lettuce leaves *noun* money, especially one-pound notes. Used by beatniks of the late 1950s and early 60s; extending the imagery of LETTUCE (money) *UK, 1966*

letty *verb* to sleep. Polari; from 'letty' (a bed) *UK, 2002*

level *noun* ▶ **on the level** honest, truthful, trustworthy. Also used as an adverb *US, 1872*

level *adjective* good, excellent *CANADA, 1993*

level; level with *verb* to speak or act honestly, to be frank about something previously concealed, to tell the truth *US, 1921*

level best *noun* your absolute best or utmost *US, 1851*

levels *noun* legitimate, square, unaltered dice *US, 1950*

levels on the splonk *noun* in betting odds, evens. Used in racing circles, especially amongst bookmakers *UK, 1967*

levels you devils; levels *noun* in betting odds, evens *UK, 1967*

leviathan *noun* a heavy backer of horses *AUSTRALIA, 1874*

leviathan *adjective* (of a bookmaker or gambler) wealthy, heavy betting *AUSTRALIA, 1950*

Levy and Frank; levy *noun* an act of masturbation; also used as a verb. Rhyming slang for WANK, formed from the name of a well-known firm of public house and restaurant proprietors *UK, 1958*

Lewinsky *noun* an act of oral sex. Usually in the passive phrase 'get a Lewinsky' but the active 'give good Lewinsky' has been used. In 1995 Monica Lewinsky was a White House intern; she was a central figure in US President Bill Clinton's later attempt to exclude oral sex from a general definition of sexual relations *US, 1999*

Lex *nickname* **1** the Federal Narcotics Hopsital in Lexington, Kentucky *US, 1960*. **2** a Lexus car *US, 1997*

lez *noun* a lesbian *US, 1929*

lez *verb* ▶ **lez it up** to behave (sexually) as lesbians *UK, 2003*

lez *adjective* lesbian *US, 1969*

lezo; lezzo *noun* a lesbian *AUSTRALIA, 1945*

lezza *noun* a lesbian *UK, 2002*

lezzer *noun* a lesbian *AUSTRALIA, 1968*

lezzie; lezzy *noun* a lesbian. Usually offensive *US, 1938*

LF gear *noun* the proceeds of a long firm fraud *UK, 1977*

liamba; lianda *noun* cannabis. African slang *US, 2001*

liar *verb* to tell lies *UK, 1999*

liard *noun* a pathological liar *TRINIDAD AND TOBAGO, 2003*

liar's bench *noun* a settee in front of a country store *US, 1963*

lib *noun* **1** *lib*eration. Usually allied to a specific political cause, most famously 'women's lib' *UK, 1970*. **2** *lib*erty *UK, 1996*. **3** Librium™, a branded depressant *US, 1996*

lib *verb* to release from prison. Abbreviated from 'liberate' *UK, 2000*

libber *noun* a feminist. From 'Woman's Liberation' as the name for the feminist movement of the late 1960s *US, 1972*

libbo *noun* a liberty *UK, 2000*

libe; libes *noun* a library *US, 1915*

liberate *verb* **1** to steal. Coined in irony by US soldiers during World War 2, and then recycled by the political and cultural left of the 1960s *US, 1944*. **2** to take control of *US, 1968*

liberated *adjective* free from narrow, conventional thinking *US, 1970*

liberati *noun* a notional grouping of people who promote liberal principles. Formed with the suffix -ERATI. Used, in a derogatory sense, by British politician David Blunkett *UK, 2004*

liberation *noun* **1** theft in the name of a cause. Said either with irony or a complete lack of humour, depending on the self-righteousness of the speaker *US, 1970*. **2** left-wing politics *US, 1968*

liberty *noun* a twenty-five-cent piece. From the inscription on the coin *US, 1947*

liberty act *noun* in the circus, an act in which horses perform without riders *US, 1973*

library *noun* a brakevan (caboose) *US, 1946*

lice bin *noun* a dirty, unsanitary place *US, 1971*

license *noun* freedom to break the law in an area by virtue of having bribed the police *US, 1950*

-licious *suffix* used in combination with a general or generic characteristic to describe the object as especially attractive within or with regard to the genre *UK, 2002*

lick *noun* **1** a musical phrase *UK, 1932*. **2** a small amount *US, 1814*. **3** in betting, a huge win *AUSTRALIA, 1989*. **4** a robbery *US, 2002*. **5** a fast speed *UK, 1847*. **6** an intoxicating experience with crack cocaine *UK, 2000*. **7** any mistake, from a slight error to a complete disaster. Vietnam war usage *US, 1991*. **8** oral sex *US, 1973*. **9** a serving of ice-cream *NEW ZEALAND, 1998*. ▶ **the lick** anything that is currently considered as stylish, fashionable or best *UK, 2003*

lick *verb* **1** to beat, to thrash *UK, 1535*. **2** to shoot and kill *US, 1994*. **3** to move or act quickly *BERMUDA, 1985*. **4** to smoke (marijuana) *JAMAICA, 2000*. ▶ **lick arse; lick ass** to behave in a subservient manner. A variation of KISS ARSE *UK, 1959*. ▶ **lick butt** to behave subserviently. A variation of KISS BUTT *US, 1990* ▷*see:* KISS ARSE. ▶ **lick like lizard** to use a technique of short, quick laps while performing oral sex on a woman *JAMAICA, 2002*. ▶ **lick shit** to lick crack cocaine for a short-lived sensation of intoxication *UK, 1996*. ▶ **lick the cat** to perform oral sex on a woman *US, 2001*. ▶ **lick the dew off her lily** to engage in oral sex on a woman *US, 2001*. ▶ **lick the rock** to use crack cocaine *UK, 1996*

lick about *verb* to live a carefree, hedonistic life *BARBADOS, 1965*

lick-box *noun* a person who performs oral sex on women *US, 1949*

lick down *verb* to physically assault, to force submission. Elaboration of LICK (to beat) *UK, 1994*

licked *adjective* defeated *UK, 1976*

lickety-split *adverb* speedily, headlong. In recognisable variations from 1831 and uncertain spelling from 1848 *US, 1831*

lickle; likkle *adjective* little. Originally childish and twee as 'lickle me' and 'ickle me', and continues to be so. Contemporary use in UK black patois, however, is not cute *UK, 1994*

lick length *phrase* used to refuse or reject. 'To lick LENGTH' (the penis) is 'to perform oral sex', used here to suggest an extremely unlikely alternative *UK, 2001*

lick-mouth *noun* a gossip *BARBADOS, 1965*

lick-mouth *adjective* salacious, gossip-bearing, inappropriately concerned with the business of others *BARBADOS, 1980*

lick my helmet! used emphatically to dismiss or reject. Based on HELMET (the head of the penis) *UK, 2001*

lick papers *noun* the thin paper used to roll a marijuana cigarette. A term first applied to paper used to hand-roll tobacco cigarettes, and then later, and briefly, to paper used to roll marijuana cigarettes *US, 1986*

licks *noun* a beating. From conventional 'lick' (a blow). Probably since late C18, contemporary usage mainly black *UK, 1994*

licorice stick; liquorice stick *noun* a clarinet *US, 1935*

lid *noun* **1** a hat *US, 1896*. **2** a motorcycle helmet with face protection *US, 1994*. **3** a submarine hatch cover *UK, 1979*. **4** in a card game, the top card of the deck *US, 1988*. **5** an approximate measure (variously twenty-two grams, or one to two ounces) of loose, uncleaned marijuana. Derived from the lid of a tobacco tin, a convenient measure of sufficient marijuana to roll about forty cigarettes *US, 1966* ▷*see:* SAUCEPAN LID. ▶ **on its lid** (of a vehicle) overturned *US, 2004*. ▶ **out of your lid** drug-intoxicated *UK, 2003*. ▶ **put the lid on; put the tin lid on** to conceal something; to bring some activity or enterprise to an (unwelcome) end *UK, 1909*

lid-poppers *noun* an amphetamine or other central nervous system stimulant. The 'lid' in question is a head *US, 1971*

lid-propper *noun* an amphetamine or other central nervous system stimulant *US, 1967*

lids *noun* units of currency *IRELAND, 2003*

lie *verb* to talk *US, 1973*. ▶ **lie through your teeth** to lie deliberately *UK, 1952*

lie box *noun* a polygraph *US, 1955*

lie-down *noun* in prison, time spent in the segregation unit *UK, 1996*

lie down *verb* in pool, to play below your skill level to lure strangers into playing against you for money *US, 1993*

lie low *verb* to be in hiding; to behave in a manner that ought not to attract attention *UK, 1880*

lie sheet *noun* a truck driver's log book *US, 1971*

lieut; loot *noun* a lieutenant *US, 1759*

lieuty *noun* a lieutenant *US, 1998*

life *noun* life imprisonment *AUSTRALIA, 1833*. ▶ **go for your life** to partake enthusiastically; to go all out *AUSTRALIA, 1920*. ▶ **have a life; get a life** to enjoy a well-rounded life including work, family, friends and interests *US, 1985*. ▶ **in the life** homosexual *US, 1963*. ▶ **not for the life of you** expresses the impossibilty of your doing, understanding 'something', etc. Hyperbole *UK, 1809*. ▶ **the life 1** the criminal lifestyle; the lifestyle of prostitution *US, 1916*. **2** the business and lifestyle of professional wrestling *US, 1999*. ▶ **there's life in the old dog yet; there's life in the old girl yet** he, or she, is still very much alive, and, especially, capable of sexual activity *UK, 1857*

life and death; life *noun* breath, especially bad breath. Rhyming slang *UK, 1992*

lifeboat *noun* release from prison as a result of parole board action or a commutation of sentence *US, 1908*

lifed-up *adjective* sentenced to life imprisonment *UK, 2002*

life in London *noun* used for describing an easy, carefree lifestyle *TRINIDAD AND TOBAGO, 1991*

life jacket *noun* a condom. Safe sex saves lives *US, 1989*

life off *verb* to sentence someone to life imprisonment *UK, 2000*

life of Riley *noun* a pleasurable, carefree existence. Occasionally spelt 'Reilly' *UK, 1919*

life on the installment plan *noun* a series of prison sentences with brief periods of freedom between, which have the cumulative effect of a life sentence *US, 1949*

lifer *noun* **1** a career member of the armed forces *US, 1962*. **2** a prisoner sentenced to penal servitude for life *AUSTRALIA, 1827*. **3** a person who has been given a traffic ticket. Ironic usage *US, 1984*. **4** a drug addict *US, 1971*

lifer's dream *noun* a Soviet-made SKS Type 54 carbine rifle, used by the North Vietnamese and Viet Cong during the Vietnam war. Treasured as the ultimate war trophy by US Marines in Vietnam *US, 1990*

life saver *noun* heroin *UK, 2003*

Liffey water *noun* porter (ale); any dark beer or stout, especially Guinness™. Rhyming slang. Later use is heavily influenced by the association of Guinness with water drawn in Dublin from the River Liffey *UK, 1961*

lift *noun* **1** the act of shoplifting *US, 1971*. **2** the early euphoric sensation after using a drug *US, 1973*

lift *verb* **1** to steal *UK, 1526*. **2** to arrest *UK, 1979*. **3** to work out with weights *US, 1990*. **4** to transfer matter from one periodical to another. Used by journalists and printers *UK, 1891*

liftbird *noun* any troop transport plane. Vietnam war usage *US, 1982*

lift doesn't go to the top floor descriptive of a fool *UK, 1999*

lifted *adjective* drug-intoxicated *US, 1942*

lifter *noun* an explosive charge. Mining slang *NEW ZEALAND, 1965*

liftie *noun* a ski-lift operator *CANADA, 1996*

lift-one-drag-one *noun* a person with a pronounced limp *US, 1997*

lift-op *noun* a ski-lift operator *US, 1995*

lifts *noun* hydraulic lifts installed in a car, operated from within the car body to make the car rise or fall suddenly. A key component of a LOWRIDER's car *US, 1980*

lig *noun* a music industry social event *UK, 1983*

ligger *noun* a shameless name-dropping hanger-on attached to a rock band *US, 1985*

light *noun* a tracer bullet *US, 1965*

light *verb* ▶ **light a shuck** to depart suddenly, to move fast. This phrase is derived from the use of flaming cornhusks for light *CANADA, 1903*. ▶ **light the rugs** in drag racing, to accelerate in a fashion that makes the tyres smoke *US, 1965*. ▶ **light the wienies** in drag racing, to smoke the tyres when the race begins *US, 1965*

light *adjective* **1** short of funds, especially in the context of a payment owed *US, 1955*. **2** in poker, owing chips to the collective bet on a hand *US, 1967*. **3** (used of an arrest warrant) susceptible to attack by a skilled defence attorney *US, 1973*. **4** unarmed; without a weapon *US, 1974*

light across the carpet *adjective* homosexual *UK, 2000*

light and bitter *noun* a shitter (in all senses). Rhyming slang, formed from a mix of beers *UK, 2003*

light artillery *noun* **1** the equipment needed to inject a drug *US, 1950*. **2** beans *US, 1946*

light, bright, damn near white; bright, white and dead white *adjective* (used of a black person) very light-skinned *US, 1945*

light colonel *noun* a lieutenant colonel *US, 1954*

lightem *noun* crack cocaine. Evocative of the urging 'light 'em up' *US, 1993*

lighten *verb* ▶ **lighten the tongue** to avoid Creole and make a point of using conventional English *BELIZE, 1996*

lighten up *verb* to become less serious, to calm down; to cease aggravating. Often an imperative; from the conventional sense 'to relieve (the heart or mind)' *US, 1946*

lighter *noun* a crewcut haircut. Teen slang *US, 1951*

light-fingered *adjective* inclined to thievery *UK, 1547*

lightfoot *noun* a sneak thief *UK, 1996*

light green *noun* **1** a white person; a Caucasian. Marine usage in Vietnam *US, 1991*. **2** marijuana, especially inexpensive, low grade marijuana *US, 1973*

lighthouse *noun* in dominoes, a double played by a player who has no matching pieces *US, 1964*

light housekeeping *noun* cohabitation as an unmarried couple *US, 1971*

lightie *noun* a child *UK, 2000*

light infantry *noun* bedbugs, body lice and/or fleas *US, 1949*

light in the loafers *adjective* homosexual. A wonderful, old-fashioned euphemism *US, 1967*

lightning *noun* any amphetamine, methamphetamine or other central nervous system stimulant *US, 1977*

lightning and thunder *noun* whisky and soda *US, 1945*

lightning bug *noun* a helicopter equipped with a powerful search light or flares, usually teamed with several gunships *US, 1990*

lightning flash *noun* LSD. A variation on FLASH *UK, 1998*

lightning hashish *noun* high quality hashish retained by dealers for their own use *US, 1982*

light off *verb* to experience an orgasm *US, 1971*

light of love; love *noun* a prison *governor*. Rhyming slang *UK, 1996*

light of my life *noun* a wife. Rhyming slang, often with ironic or parodic intent *UK, 1998*

light on *adjective* in sparse supply of *AUSTRALIA, 1944*

light on her feet *adjective* (of a man) homosexual *US, 1967*

light out *verb* to leave, especially in a hurry *US, 1865*

light pipe *noun* fibre optic cable *US, 1991*

light rations *noun* in horse racing, a drastic diet undertaken by a jockey to lose weight *AUSTRALIA, 1989*

lights *noun* **1** the eyes *UK, 1820*. **2** in poker, the chips owed by a player who bet without sufficient funds to back his bet *US, 1996*

lights on but there's nobody home; lights on but nobody home said of someone who appears to be normal but is empty-headed *US, 1990*

lights out! used to warn of the presence of police *US, 1997*

light stuff *noun* marijuana or any non-addictive illegal drug *US, 1969*

light up *verb* **1** to light a cigarette or a pipe, etc *UK, 1861*. **2** to share drugs with others *US, 1922*. **3** to shoot someone *US, 1967*. **4** to train a police car's red light on a car *US, 1962*

lightweight *noun* **1** a person who is not taken as a serious threat *US, 1878*. **2** a marijuana smoker who cannot consume as much of the drug as others *US, 2001*

light years *noun* an immeasurably great time, distance or style between one thing and another. From the conventional measure of the distance light travels in a year *UK, 1971*

like *verb* ▶ **like a price** in horse racing, to hold a horse back from winning unless the odds on the horse are high *US, 1951*

like *adverb* **1** (preceding an adjective) in the manner described, eg 'like crazy' *US, 1959*. **2** in a manner of speaking; as it were *UK, 1778*. **3** (after an adjective) in the manner described. Performing the function of the suffix '- ly' *AUSTRALIA, 1867*

like *conjunction* as. A conventional C16 usage that is now considered poor or unconventional English *UK, 1886*

like **1** used for reducing the specificity, precision or certainty of what is being said, eg 'could you like help me?'. In the wake of disaster, use of 'like' all but disappears. Linguist Geoffrey Nunberg first observed this after shootings at a San Diego high school in March 2001, and language columnist Jan Freeman of the *Boston Globe* made the same observation after the terrorist attacks in New York and Washington on 11th September 2001. There is no need for distance in certain situations *US, 1950*. **2** habitually used in informal speech as inconsequential ornamentation *US, 1982*. **3** used as an introduction to a gesture or expression *US, 2003*. ▶ **be like** used for indicating a quotation, or a paraphrase of what was said, or an interpretation of what was said, or a projection of what was thought but not said *US, 1982*

like anything *adverb* with vigour or speed; used, as an intensifier *UK, 1681*

like a plasterer's radio *adjective* semen-spattered *UK, 2002*

like as not; as like as not *adverb* probably, possibly, likely *UK, 1897*

like beef? do you want to fight? Hawaiian youth usage *US, 1981*

like butter! nice, smooth, lovely. A catchphrase from a Mike Myers *Saturday Night Live* skit *US, 1992*

like hell! used as an expression of disbelief or contradiction *UK, 1922*

like it's my job used as an intensifier *US, 2003*

likely *adjective* ▶ **a likely story** used ironically as an expression of profound disbelief *UK, 1984*

like no other *adverb* extremely *US, 2002*

like real used for expressing doubt *SINGAPORE, 2002*

like that *adjective* very closely associated (often described with an accompanying gesture). May be figurative or metaphorical *UK, 1998*

likewise I agree, especially when reciprocating a compliment. Often in the (parodic) elaboration 'likewise, I'm sure' *CANADA, 1984*

l'il *noun* not much *US, 1987*

l'il *adjective* little. A colloquial contraction *UK, 1881*

lil *noun* the female breast. Usually in the plural *UK, 2003*

lilac *adjective* effeminately homosexual *UK, 1978*

lill *noun* the hand *UK, 2002*

Lilley and Skinner *noun* **1** dinner. Rhyming slang; after the shoe shop, established in 1835 *UK, 1976*. **2** a beginner *UK, 1961*

Lillian Gish *noun* **1** fish. Rhyming slang, based on the name of film actress Lillian Gish (1893–1993) *UK, 1960*. **2** an act of urination; urine. Rhyming slang for PISH *UK, 1988*

Lillian Gished *adjective* drunk. Glasgow rhyming slang for PISHED, formed from the name of film actress Lillian Gish (1893–1993) *UK: SCOTLAND, 1988*

lillies *noun* the hands *US, 1973*

Lilly; Lily; Lilly F-40 *noun* a capsule of secobarbital sodium, brand name Seconal™, a barbiturate. From the manufacturer *US, 1986*

lily *noun* **1** the penis. Most commonly heard when describing urination as KNOCK THE DEW OFF THE LILY *US, 1974*. **2** an ear-trumpet. Also used figuratively, as in 'get your lily at the key-hole' (to eavesdrop) *UK, 1979*

Lily; Lily Law; Lilly Law; Lillian; Lucy Law *noun* used as a personification of a police officer, especially a policeman; the police. An example of CAMP trans-gender assignment. Sometimes accompanied by Inspector Beastly. *US, 1949*

lily on a dustbin *noun* something out of place; an incongruous thing *AUSTRALIA, 1943*

lily pad *noun* a flat disc of wood. British Columbian logging usage *CANADA, 1989*

Lily the Pink; Lily *noun* a drink. Rhyming slang, based on 'Lily the Pink' a popular song which begins: 'We'll drink-a-drink-a-drink' *UK, 2001*

lily-white *noun* **1** the hand *US, 1935*. **2** an unidentified terrorist with no history or past suspicion of criminal activity. Used during a report on a bomb explosion in Ealing, West London, *BBC Television News*, 3rd March 2001 *UK, 2001*

lily-white *adjective* populated entirely by white people; discriminating against black people *US, 1903*

lily whites *noun* bed sheets *US, 1946*

lima *noun* marijuana. Possibly implying Peruvian cultivation *UK, 1998*

limb *noun* ▶ **on the limb** in horse racing, said of a horse forced to the outside *US, 1964*. ▶ **out on a limb** in a difficult or exposed position *US, 1897*

limberneck *noun* in electric line work, a lineman's helper or groundman. So named because of the need to look upwards all day *US, 1980*

limbo *noun* **1** a prison *UK, 1590*. **2** marijuana cultivated in Colombia. Possibly derived from the effect of intoxication *US, 1981*

limbo log *noun* in mountain biking, a tree limb overhanging the trail at approximately face height *US, 1992*

limburger *noun* a girl who cannot get a date. From the song 'Dance this Mess Around' by the B-52's *US, 1984*

limby; limbie *noun* an amputee, especially a member of the armed forces who has lost a limb *NEW ZEALAND, 1978*

lime *verb* **1** to relax; to loiter *UK, 2005*. **2** to take part in an informal gathering *TRINIDAD AND TOBAGO, 1941*. **3** in the illegal production of alcohol, to whitewash the interior of a fermenter *US, 1974*

lime acid *noun* LSD *US, 1970*

limer *noun* an idler *BARBADOS, 1964*

limeskin *noun* a worn-out felt hat *BARBADOS, 1965*

limey *noun* a Briton. Derives, as an abbreviation of 'lime-juicer', from the compulsory ration of lime juice that was issued in the British Navy; originally used of British immigrants in Australia, New Zealand and South Africa; in this more general sense since 1918 *US, 1917*

limey *adjective* British *AUSTRALIA, 1888*

limit *noun* the maximum prison sentence for a given offence *US, 1949*. ▶ **go the limit** to have sexual intercourse *US, 1922*. ▶ **the limit** the degree of anything that is the extreme (or beyond) of what you are prepared to tolerate. It may be 'the dizzy limit', 'the giddy limit' or 'just about the fucking limit' *US, 1904*. ▶ **the sky's the limit** the possibilities of something are boundless *UK, 1933*

limo *noun* a *limo*usine *US, 1929*

limo *adjective* luxurious. From the luxury afforded by a LIMO (a limousine) *UK, 1982*

limp *verb* in poker, to reserve the right to make a bet even though holding a good hand *US, 1979*

limp *adjective* drunk *US, 1982*

limp dick; limp prick *noun* someone who is weak or cowardly. The flaccid DICK (penis) as a symbol of impotency *US, 1970*

limper *noun* a defective used car *US, 1978*

limp out; limp *verb* to relax *US, 1997*

limp wrist *noun* an effeminate man, almost always homosexual; used as a symbol of homosexuality *US, 1950*

limpy-go-fetch *noun* a disabled person *US, 1997*

limpy up *adjective* disabled *BAHAMAS, 1966*

Lincoln *noun* **1** a five-dollar note *US, 1945*. **2** a five-dollar prostitute *US, 1965*

Lincoln drop *noun* the small tray near a shop's cash till with pennies which customers may use for making exact payments *US, 1997*

Lincoln Tunnel *noun* in homosexual usage, a loose anus and rectum. Homage to the tunnel connecting New Jersey and Manhattan *US, 1981*

line *noun* **1** a dose of powdered cocaine arranged in a line for snorting *US, 1973*. **2** a vein, especially in the context of injecting drugs *US, 1938*. **3** political philosophy. An important term of the New Left in the US, often modified by 'correct', a precursor of political correctness *US, 1968*. **4** an assembly line in a factory *US, 1996*. **5** collectively, the prostitutes in a brothel who are available for sex at a given moment *US, 1987*. **6** an attractive female *AUSTRALIA, 1941*. **7** a special verbal approach, especially as an introduction to seduction. A chat-up line *UK, 1903*. **8** in the business of dealing with stolen goods, twice the actual price *US, 1969*. **9** the area housing a prison's general population *US, 1989*. **10** in sports betting, the points or odds established by a bookmaker that govern the bet *US, 1977*. **11** money *US, 1972*. ▶ **do a line 1** to inhale a measured dose of a powdered drug, especially cocaine *US, 1979*. **2** to make an amorous approach; to date *AUSTRALIA, 1934*. ▶ **down the line** a psychiatric hospital *NEW ZEALAND, 1963*. ▶ **go on line** to become part of a (criminal or street) gang *UK, 2005*. ▶ **on the line** at risk, at stake, in jeopardy *US, 1940*

line crosser *noun* in the Korean war, a soldier who crossed the main line of resistance to find and retrieve prisoners of war *US, 1967*

line doggy *noun* an infantry soldier *US, 1967*

line duty *noun* in the language surrounding the Grateful Dead, the hours spent waiting in queue to buy tickets or to enter a concert venue *US, 1994*

line forty used for expressing the price of twenty dollars *US, 1946*

line jumper *noun* an enemy spy who sneaks across allied lines. Korean war usage *US, 1957*

linemaker *noun* in a sports betting operation, the oddsmaker *US, 1976*

linen *noun* a letter *US, 1947*

linen draper; linen *noun* a newspaper. Rhyming slang *UK, 1857*

liner *noun* a short promotional statement recorded for a radio station by a famous artist or personality, professing that they listen to that station *US, 2001*

liners *noun* cash *US, 2003*

lines *noun* **1** cocaine. A multiple of LINE (a single dose of cocaine); used in contemporary gay society *UK, 2003*. **2** money *US, 1973*. ▶ **do lines** to use cocaine *US, 2001*. ▶ **get lines** in bodybuilding, to achieve definition, or well-developed and sculpted muscles *US, 1984*

line screw *noun* a prison guard assigned to a cell block *US, 1976*

line storm *noun* an equinoctial gale, at the time of the solstice *CANADA, 1960*

line swine *noun* a driver who appears oblivious to traffic lanes *US, 1962*

line-up *noun* **1** serial sex between one person and multiple partners *US, 1913*. **2** the place where waves line up to break *AUSTRALIA, 1963*. **3** a display of the prostitutes available for sex in a brothel at a given moment *US, 1978*

line up *verb* to arrange *US, 1906*

line work *noun* the addition of fine lines or other markings on the design of a card to aid a cheat *US, 1979*

lingo *noun* slang or another unconventional English language dialect, jargon or vocabulary. Conventional 'lingo' (since 1660) is 'a contemptuous designation for a foreign tongue' *UK, 1859*

linguist *noun* a person who enjoys performing oral sex. Leading, inevitably, to cunning puns *US, 1967*

linguistic exercise *noun* oral sex *US, 1964*

lingy *noun* the penis *BAHAMAS, 1982*

link *noun* a police officer, prosecutor or judge who has been bribed *US, 1964*. ▶ **the link** a person who provides what is needed at a particular moment. From the conventional 'missing link' *US, 1986*

linked *adjective* **1** dating (someone) steadily and exclusively *US, 1966*. **2** bribed *US, 1964*

Link the Chink *noun* any Vietnamese person. War usage *US, 1971*

lion *noun* **1** a greatly respected or revered Rastafarian; a great soul *JAMAICA, 1994*. **2** in pool, a skilled and competitive player *US, 1990*

Lionel Bart; Lionel *noun* a fart. Rhyming slang from the name of the English composer (1930–99) *UK, 1985*

Lionel Blair *noun* a chair. Rhyming slang, based on the name of UK dancer and entertainer Lionel Blair (b.1931) *UK, 1979*

Lionel Blairs; lionels *noun* flares (trousers with flared legs). Rhyming slang, formed from the name of the UK dancer and entertainer (b.1931) *UK, 1992*

lion food *noun* middle management. From a joke, the punch-line of which features a lion boasting of eating one IBM manager a day and nobody noticing *US, 1991*

lion's lair *noun* a chair *UK, 1992*

lion's roar *noun* snoring. Rhyming slang *UK, 1992*

lion's roar *verb* to snore. Rhyming slang *UK, 1992*

lion's share *noun* a chair. Rhyming slang *UK, 1992*

lip *noun* **1** impudence; talking back *UK, 1803*. **2** a lawyer, especially a criminal defence lawyer. From the image of a lawyer as a mouthpiece *US, 1929*. **3** in the car sales business, a potential buyer *US, 1997*

lip *verb* **1** in horse racing, to win by the slightest of margins *AUSTRALIA, 1989*. **2** to kiss *US, 1947*

lip in *verb* to interrupt *US, 1899*

lip it *verb* to stop talking *UK, 1999*

lipkisser *noun* a regular practitioner of oral sex on women *US, 1985*

lip-lock *noun* oral sex performed on a man *US, 1976*

lip music *noun* bragging, boasting, teasing *US, 1992*

lipo *noun* liposuction, a surgical procedure for the cosmetic removal of fat. By ellipsis *UK, 1992*

lipper *noun* a pinch of chewing tobacco *US, 1997*

lippie; lippy *noun* lipstick *AUSTRALIA, 1955*

lippy *adjective* impudent, impertinent; talkative. From LIP (impudence). With an 1803 UK usage of 'lip' as 'back-chat', the likelihood of an earlier adjective sense is high *US, 1865*

lip read *verb* to kiss. An inspired use of a conventional sense *UK, 1974*

lips *noun* ▶ **your lips are bleeding!** used sarcastically to someone using big words. Juvenile *AUSTRALIA, 1953*

lips! used as a cry to summon a makeup artist to apply more lipstick to a performer *US, 1995*

lip service *noun* oral sex *US, 1975*

lipsin' *noun* the act of kissing, snogging. Teenage slang *UK, 2002*

lip-sloppy *adjective* talkative to a fault *US, 1962*

lip spinach *noun* a moustache *US, 1972*

lipstick *noun* **1** in the new and used car business, purely cosmetic touches *US, 1959*. **2** a grease pencil. Used by first aid workers to note tourniquet time on an injured person *US, 1962*. ▶ **lipstick on your dipstick** oral sex performed on a man *US, 1970*

lipstick lesbian; lipstick *noun* a feminine, stylish, upwardly mobile lesbian *US, 1984*

Lipton's *noun* poor quality marijuana. An allusion to a popular, if weak, tea *US, 1964*

lip up! stop talking!; say nothing! A variation of BUTTON YOUR LIP! *UK, 1980*

lip work *noun* oral sex on a woman *US, 1967*

LIQ *noun* an off-licence (liquor store) *US, 1970*

liquid *noun* money, cash. Abbreviated from 'liquid assets' *UK, 1997*

liquid cosh *noun* any tranquillizer or sedative used by prison authorities to subdue an inmate *UK, 1996*

liquid courage *noun* the bravado produced by alcohol *US, 1942*

liquid diet *noun* used humorously for describing a period when someone is drinking a lot of alcohol *US, 1991*

liquid ecstasy; liquid e *noun* the recreational drug GHB *US, 1993*

liquid gold; LG *noun* amyl or butyl nitrate. From the appearance and brand name *UK, 1996*

liquid grass *noun* tetrahydrocannabinol, the purified pyschoactive extract of marijuana *US, 1971*

liquid laugh *noun* vomiting *AUSTRALIA, 1964*

liquid lunch *noun* alcohol but no food for lunch *US, 1963*

liquid sky *noun* heroin *US, 1987*

liquid sunshine *noun* rain *UK, 1970*

liquid wrench *noun* alcohol. Like a wrench, alcohol will loosen things *US, 1996*

liquid X *noun* the recreational drug GHB *UK, 1993*

liquored up *adjective* drunk. Current use in South Carolina *US, 1924*

liquorhead *noun* a drunkard *US, 1923*

Lisa *noun* a perfect, idealised girlfriend *US, 1993*

listener *noun* a person whose only role in conversation is to listen and verify what was said *US, 1982*

listen up! used for commanding attention. Almost always heard in the imperative *US, 1962*

Listerine *adjective* anti-American. The name of a branded antiseptic applied as a punning extension of rhyming slang for SEPTIC TANK (an American) *UK, 2003*

lit *adjective* drunk *US, 1899*

-lit *suffix* literature, when in combination with a defining style *UK, 2001*

lit crit *noun* literary criticism *UK, 2003*

lite; -lite *adjective* denotes a less substantial version of an original. In widespread use; a re-spelling of 'light', devised as a commercial strategy to sustain a brand name while advertising that the product's less marketable ingredients (sugar, nicotine, etc.) have been reduced *US, 1962*

literally *adverb* used as an intensifier. In colloquial use this is generally employed inaccurately or hyperbolically *UK, 1937*

litterbug *noun* a person who drops litter *US, 1947*

litter lout *noun* a person who drops litter *UK, 1927*

Little and Large *noun* margarine. Rhyming slang for MARGE, formed from the name of a comedy double act *UK, 1998*

little bird; little birdie *noun* an unnamed source *UK, 1940*

little bit *noun* a prostitute *US, 1976*

little black book *noun* **1** an address book containing clients' names and telephone numbers, especially in an illegal enterprise *US, 1980*. **2** a (notional) notebook in which bachelors are reputed to keep girls' telephone numbers *AUSTRALIA, 1984*

little black gun *noun* the M-16 rifle. Vietnam war usage *US, 1968*

little blister *noun* a younger sister. Rhyming slang *AUSTRALIA, 1996*

little blues *noun* capsules of the synthetic opiate oxycodone used recreationally *US, 2003*

little bomb *noun* **1** an amphetamine capsule or tablet. Possibly a direct translation of Spanish BOMBITA (an amphetamine capsule) *UK, 1998*. **2** heroin *UK, 1998*

little boy *noun* a small, cocktail frankfurter sausage *NEW ZEALAND, 1984*

little boy blue *noun* a prison officer. Rhyming slang for SCREW *UK, 1992*

little boys' room *noun* a toilet, especially one for men. Juvenile and jocular *US, 1935*

little brown jug *noun* a sink or bath *plug*, an electric *plug*; a tampon. Rhyming slang *UK, 1992*

little Bush *noun* US President George W. Bush *US, 2003*

little casino *noun* in a deck of playing cards, the two of spades *US, 1988*

little cat *noun* in poker, a hand comprised of five cards between three and eight and no pairs among them *US, 1963*

little D *noun* a tablet of hydromorphone (trade name Dialudid™), a narcotic analgesic *US, 1986*

little death *noun* an orgasm. Often in the verb phrase 'have a little death'. From the French petite mort *UK, 1959*

Little Detroit *nickname* Van Dien, North Vietnam. Like Detroit, Van Dien was highly industrialised *US, 1991*

little Dick; little Dick Fisher *noun* in craps, a four *US, 1957*

little dog *noun* in poker, a hand comprised of five cards between two and seven and no pairs among them *US, 1963*

little fella *noun* **1** a child (of either gender) *UK, 1959*. **2** a tablet of MDMA, the recreational drug best known as ecstasy *UK, 2001*

little friend *noun* a fighter plane *US, 1944*

little girls' room *noun* a toilet, especially one for women *US, 1949*

little green friends *noun* marijuana buds *UK, 2003*

little guy; little man; little people *noun* a Japanese soldier; a Viet Cong or soldier in the North Vietnamese Army *US, 1950*

little guy with the helmet *noun* the penis *US, 2001*

little Harlem *noun* a black ghetto *US, 1951*

little help *noun* a linear amplifier for a citizens' band radio *US, 1977*

little Hitler *noun* a self-important person who wields a small amount of official authority with despotic zeal *UK, 1957*

little house *noun* an outside toilet *AUSTRALIA, 1886*

Little Italy *noun* a neighbourhood populated by a large number of Italian immigrants and Italian-Americans *US, 1970*

little jobs *noun* urination by a child *AUSTRALIA, 1886*

little Joe *noun* a roll of four in craps. Often elaborated with a rhyming place name, in the pattern 'little Joe from Kokomo' (or Chicago, Idaho, Lake Tahoe, Mexico, Ohio, Tokyo) *US, 1890*

little Joe in the snow *noun* cocaine *US, 1992*

little Judas *noun* the sliding door in a confession box *IRELAND, 1995*

Little Korea *nickname* Fort Leonard Wood, Missouri. Based on a comparison of the climates *US, 1968*

little lady *noun* the wife *AUSTRALIA, 1917*

little lunch *noun* a mid-morning break at school *AUSTRALIA, 1982*

little madam; proper little madam *noun* a spoilt, conceited or bad-tempered female child *UK, 1787*

little man *noun* **1** the penis *UK, 1998*. **2** a tradesman. An upper- or middle-class female's patronising term *UK, 1984* ▷*see:* LITTLE GUY

little man in a boat; little man; man in the boat; boy in the boat *noun* the clitoris. The 'little man' or 'boy' represent the clitoris as a small penis, and the vulva is imagined to be boat-shaped *UK, 1896*

little Miss Muffet *verb* used as an emphatic rejection. Rhyming slang for 'stuff it', formed from the name of a nursery rhyme character *UK, 1992*

Little Mo *nickname* Maureen Connolly (1934–1969), who dominated women's tennis for several years in the early 1950s until a career-ending accident in 1953. Connolly's aggressive style was compared to the *Missouri*, a battleship with the nickname that she was given *US, 1953*

little muggins *noun* your child. From MUGGINS (yourself, as a fool) *UK, 2000*

little Nell *noun* a door *bell*. Rhyming slang, formed from the name of a Charles Dickens' heroine *UK, 1992*

little office *noun* the toilet *AUSTRALIA, 1981*

little old lady in tennis shoes *noun* used as a stereotype of an energetic, quirky old woman. In 1972, *Sports Illustrated* titled an article about tennis great Hazel Wightman (1886–1974) 'The Little Old Lady in Tennis Shoes' *US, 1984*

little peter *noun* a gas or electric meter. Rhyming slang *UK, 1992*

little pigs *noun* small sausages *US, 1946*

little ploughman *noun* the clitoris *US, 1980*

little R *noun* during the Korean and Vietnam wars, rest and rehabilitation. Distinguished from the BIG R (rotation home) *US, 1960*

littles *noun* in pool, the solid-coloured balls numbered 1 to 7 *US, 1990*

little Saigon *nickname* a neigbourhood with a large number of Vietnamese immigrants and businesses *US, 1979*

Little Sir Echo *noun* a person who always agrees with his superiors *AUSTRALIA, 1989*

little sisters *noun* a group of US magazines aimed at women *US, 1986*

little smoke *noun* marijuana *UK, 1998*

little thing *noun* a bullet *UK, 2001*

little Tokyo *noun* an urban neighbourhood with a high concentration of Japanese people *US, 1945*

little white mouse *noun* a tampon. Used euphemistically in mixed company *AUSTRALIA, 1996*

little woman *noun* the wife. Intentionally archaic, revoltingly coy, and condescending *UK, 1795*

littlie; littley *noun* a child *AUSTRALIA, 1953*

littl'un *noun* a child *AUSTRALIA, 1962*

lit up *adjective* drunk or drug-intoxicated *US, 1899*

live *verb* ► **live caseo** to cohabit for sexual purposes. From 'caseo' (a brothel, or overnight hire of a prostitute) *UK, 1956*. ► **live it up** to have a good time, to enjoy an extravagent lifestyle *US, 1951*. ► **live large** to enjoy a life full of material pleasures *US, 1975*. ► **live on the smell of an oil rag** to live on very meagre means *AUSTRALIA, 1903*

live *adjective* **1** (used of the potential customer of a prostitute) eager to spend money *US, 1969*. **2** in horse racing, said of a horse that has attracted heavy betting *US, 1975*. **3** extreme, intense, exciting, good *US, 1987*. **4** impressive *US, 1991*

live bait *noun* one young drug user selling drugs to other young users *US, 1951*

lived-in look *noun* a complete mess *US, 1968*

live gaff *noun* a premises that is occupied whilst being burgled. Based on GAFF (a place of residence or business) *UK, 1956*

live gig *verb* to masturbate; to have sex. Rhyming slang for FRIG *UK, 2003*

live long and prosper used as a humorous parting. From the original *Star Trek* television series *US, 1991*

livener *noun* **1** a dose of cocaine. Abbreviated from conventional 'enlivener', ascribing to cocaine the bracing attributes of a pick-me-up; an earlier (late C19) use was as 'the first drink of the day' *UK, 1999*. **2** any alcoholic drink that serves as a pick-me-up *UK, 1887*

live one *noun* a person worth noticing *US, 1896*

liverish *adjective* having symptoms loosely diagnosed as the result of a disordered liver. Coined for an advertisment *UK, 1896*

Liverpool kiss *noun* **1** a head butt to your opponent's face. A regional variation of the GLASGOW KISS *UK, 1986*. **2** a blow struck on the mouth *UK, 1968*

liver rounds *noun* used in a hospital as humorous code for a drinking party to be held on hospital grounds *US, 1989*

live, spit and die *noun* LSD. An elaboration of the initials. *UK, 2003*

liveware *noun* **1** a human being. A playful evolution of 'software' and 'hardware' *UK, 1966*. **2** a living organism *US, 1991*

live wire *noun* a male homosexual. Prison slang *UK, 2002*

living daylights; daylights *verb* life; spirit. Ultimately from 'daylights' (the eyes) but here in the consequent sense, 'vitality' or 'vital organs' *UK, 1960*

living shit; living crap used in combination with various transitive verbs to intensify the action to a severe level *US, 1983*

livity *noun* a vocation or calling in life. A Rastafarian term *JAMAICA, 1992*

livvener *noun* an alcoholic drink. Probably from LIVENER (a drink that serves as a pick-me-up) *UK, 1979*

lizard *noun* **1** an uncooperative, dirty hospital patient with scaly skin *US, 1978*. **2** the penis *US, 1962*. **3** a mechanical device used by card cheats to hold cards in the player's sleeve *US, 1988*. ► **flog the lizard; drain the lizard** (of a male) to urinate *AUSTRALIA, 1968*

lizard hit *noun* the last draw on a water pipe *US, 1997*

lizards *noun* lizard-skin shoes *US, 1980*

lizard scorcher *noun* a railway cook *US, 1977*

lizzie *noun* a lesbian *UK, 1949*

Lizzie *noun* a car, especially a Ford. A shortened form of 'Tin Lizzie' (the US stock market nickname for the Ford Motor Company) *US, 1913*

LK; LK Clark; Elkie Clark *noun* a mark; a place and time of starting. Rhyming slang *UK, 1962*

LL *noun* marijuana. A play on the name of rap artist and film actor LL Cool J: COOL (agreeble) and J (a JOINT) *UK, 1998*

LLDB *noun* the special forces of the Army of the Republic of Vietnam *US, 1985*

llesca *noun* marijuana. From Portugese *lhesca* (tinder). Similar to YESCA which derives in the same way from Spanish *US, 1970*

Lloyd's List *adjective* drunk. Rhyming slang for PISSED, formed from the title of the newspaper that reports maritime news *UK, 1998*

loach *noun* during the Vietnam war, a light observation helicopter. From the initials LOH *US, 1973*

load *noun* **1** an ejaculation's worth of semen *US, 1927*. **3** a stock of illegal drugs *UK, 1978*. **4** 25 bags of heroin. It is interesting to note that a 'half load' adds up to 15 bags (of heroin) *US, 1969*. **5** a dose of a drug *US, 1952*. **6** a codeine pill combined with a Doriden™ sleeping pill, producing an opiate-like effect *US, 1989*. **7** a state of intoxication *US, 1947*. **8** any sexually transmitted infection *AUSTRALIA, 1936*. **9** an inept, ludicrous, stupid or unpleasant person *US, 1950*. **10** a car *US, 1937*. **11** fabricated evidence *AUSTRALIA, 1975*. **12** a car in poor condition *US, 1937*. ► **get a load of** to look at; to observe *US, 1922*. ► **take a load off** to sit down *US, 1922*

load *verb* **1** to fabricate evidence *AUSTRALIA, 1975*. **2** to alter (dice); to weight (dice) to score a certain point *US, 1962*

load call *noun* in a telephone swindle, a repeat call to a recent victim *US, 1985*

loaded *adjective* **1** drunk or drug-intoxicated. The abbreviated variation of a mainly obsolete range of similes beginning 'loaded to' *US, 1879*. **2** wealthy *US, 1948*. **3** pregnant *US, 1973*. **4** full of the symptoms of a cold *UK: SCOTLAND, 1988*. **5** armed with a gun *US, 1952*. **6** (used of a car) equipped with every possible accessory *US, 1996*

loaded down *adjective* pregnant *BAHAMAS, 1982*

loaded for bear **1** prepared for an emergency, heavily armed. The term arose in the late C19 as a literal description of a weapon loaded with ammunition suitable for killing a bear, and then in the 1950s came to assume a figurative meaning that dominates today *US, 1927*. **2** in trucking, equipped with a citizens' band radio. With BEAR meaning 'police', the trucker with a citizens' band radio is better prepared to evade speeding tickets *US, 1976*

loader *noun* **1** in American casinos, a blackjack dealer who carelessly exposes his down card while dealing *US, 1985*. **2** an experienced and skilled confidence swindler who makes a second sale to a prior victim *US, 1988*

load exchange *noun* the passing of semen to its maker, mouth to mouth *US, 1970s*

loadie *noun* a drug user *US, 1979*

loadies *noun* dice loaded with weights that affect the roll *US, 1997*

load-in *noun* the carting in and setting up of equipment before a concert or show *US, 1999*

load of cock *noun* nonsense *UK, 1978*

load of postholes *noun* in trucking, an empty trailer *US, 1946*

load of toffee *noun* nonsense. From TOFFEE (flattery), but less sweet *UK, 2001*

load plane *noun* an aircraft loaded with illegal drugs being smuggled *US, 1992*

loads *noun* dice that have been altered with weights so as to produce a certain score *US, 1963*

loadsa a large amount of something; a great number of something. A slovening of 'loads of' *UK, 1988*

load-up *noun* a false allegation *AUSTRALIA, 1996*

load up *verb* (of the police) to plant incriminating evidence in order to secure a conviction, arrest or the like *AUSTRALIA, 1983*

loaf *noun* 1 marijuana *UK, 2003*. 2 a one kilogram unit of hashish *CANADA, 2002*

loaf *verb* to strike with the head *IRELAND, 1991*

loafer *noun* in horse racing, a horse that does not perform well without constant urging by the jockey *US, 1976*

loaf of bread; loaf *noun* the head, especially as a source of intelligence. Rhyming slang *UK, 1925*

loan *noun* ▶ **have a loan of** to play a joke on someone; to pull someone's leg *AUSTRALIA, 1902*

loaner *noun* a piece of equipment that is loaned out while the owner's piece of equipment is being repaired *US, 1926*

loan shark *noun* a person who loans money privately with usurious interest rates and criminal collection procedures *UK, 1905*

loan-sharking *noun* usury with severe repayment terms *US, 1914*

lob *noun* 1 in prison, wages, the weekly pay received by prisoners *UK, 1950*. 2 a prisoner who displays excessive zeal on his job *US, 1951*. 3 a penis. Original use as 'a partially erect penis' has been replaced to mean 'an erect penis', as used in the phrase 'to have a lob on' *UK, 1890*. 4 in a gambling establishment, a hanger-on who runs errands for gamblers *US, 1979*. 5 in horse racing, a horse pulled back by its jockey to prevent it from finishing first, second or third in a race *US, 1935*

lob *verb* 1 to throw or chuck; to place roughly; to plonk *AUSTRALIA, 1934*. 2 (of something airborne) to land *AUSTRALIA, 1943*. 3 to arrive at a place; to turn up, especially unexpectedly *AUSTRALIA, 1911*. 4 (of a racehorse) to win a race *AUSTRALIA, 1988*

lobby *noun* a lobster or freshwater crayfish *AUSTRALIA, 1952*

lobby louse *noun* a non-guest who idles in a hotel lobby *US, 1939*

lobe in *verb* to listen *US, 1973*

LOBNH unintelligent. Doctor's shorthand: an initialism of LIGHTS ON BUT NOBODY HOME *UK, 2003*

lobo *noun* marijuana *US, 1984*

lob-on *noun* an erection. From LOB (a penis, especially if erect), hence 'to have a lob on' is 'to have an erection', from which 'lob-on' now stands alone. Acceptable for broadcast in a comedy context by BBC television *UK, 2001*

lobster *noun* 1 a twenty-dollar note *AUSTRALIA, 1992*. 2 in poker, an unskilled and/or inexperienced player *US, 1988*. 3 dried nasal mucus *BAHAMAS, 1982*. 4 an unexpected and unwelcome erection *UK, 2004*

lobster claw *noun* in electric line work, a device formally known as an adjustable insulator fork *US, 1980*

lobster cop *noun* a fisheries officer *CANADA, 1959*

Lobster Lad *noun* a young male from Prince Edward Island *CANADA, 1955*

lobster shift *noun* a work shift starting at midnight *US, 1942*

lobster skin *noun* badly sunburnt skin. Hawaiian youth usage *US, 1982*

lob up *verb* to arrive *AUSTRALIA, 1990*

local *noun* 1 a resident of a location, contrasted to the visitor *UK, 1835*. 2 a nearby public house; a public house that has your regular custom *UK, 1969*. 3 a person who surfs in an area and asserts territorial privileges there *US, 1991*. 4 during a massage, hand stimulation of the penis until ejaculation *US, 1972*

local *adjective* pertaining to or representing the essence of Creole culture *TRINIDAD AND TOBAGO, 1983*

localism *noun* an attitude, defiant if not hostile, of local surfers towards visiting surfers at 'their' beach *US, 1991*

local smokal; local smokel *noun* local police; a police panda car. Blends SMOKEY BEAR (the police) with the model of LOCAL YOKEL (a foolish country-dweller) *US, 1976*

local talent *noun* a pretty female *US, 1955*

local white *noun* a light-skinned person, born in Trinidad *TRINIDAD AND TOBAGO, 1956*

local yokel *noun* an indigenous inhabitant of a rural area. A slightly contemptuous term, originally used by military personnel *UK, 1950*

loc'd out *adjective* psychotic from drug use *US, 1993*

loced out; loqued out *adjective* exciting, crazy *US, 1995*

locho *adjective* despicable. From the Hindi *lchcha* (lewd loafer), to the corrupted Anglo-Indian 'loocher' *TRINIDAD AND TOBAGO, 1989*

loci; lokey *noun* a small locomotive used for hauling logs or coal *CANADA, 1964*

lock *noun* 1 control; complete control *US, 1966*. 2 a sure thing, a certainty *US, 1942*. 3 in poker, a hand that cannot lose *US, 1990*. 4 in bar dice games, a perfect hand that at best can be tied *US, 1971*

lock *verb* in prison, to reside in a cell *US, 1931*. ▶ **lock neck** to choke a robbery victim with one arm while rifling through their pockets with the other hand *TRINIDAD AND TOBAGO, 1959*

lock and load *verb* to prepare for an imminent confrontation. Originally military, and originally 'load and lock', then reversed for the sound (perhaps to conform with 'rock and roll') and generalised *US, 1949*

lock-down *noun* 1 in prison, a state of security in which all inmates are locked in their cells *UK, 1996*. 2 any situation in which your complete freedom is restricted. Like 'warden' (girlfriend or wife), jail slang brought home *US, 1997*

locked *adjective* 1 drunk *IRELAND, 2002*. 2 drug-intoxicated *US, 1997*. 3 tense, stressed *US, 1955*

locker *noun* 1 a safe or a locked compartment within a safe *US, 1949*. 2 a jail *US, 1997*

locker room *noun* 1 amyl or butyl or isobutyl nitrate as a recreational drug. Popular as a sex-aid in the gay community, the name (possibly deriving from a brand name) reflects the locality of use *US, 1998*. 2 the group of professional wrestlers under contract with a promoter at any given moment *US, 1999*

lock-in *noun* an after-hours and behind locked doors drinking session in a public house *UK, 2003*

lock-in-a-sock *noun* an improvised prison weapon – a combination lock inside in a sock *US, 1996*

lock-mortal cinch *noun* in betting, the surest possible certainty *US, 1975*

lockpicker *noun* an illegal abortionist *US, 1976*

locks *noun* knotted hair in the Rastafarian fashion *JAMAICA, 1976*

locksmith *noun* 1 in pool, a betting professional who only plays games that he is sure of winning *US, 1990*. 2 a poker player who only plays excellent hands *US, 1966*

lockstep *noun* an undeviating order; absolute conformity. A figurative application of a military style of close-marching *UK, 1955*

lockup *noun* 1 a jail or prison *US, 1839*. 2 in pool, a shot that cannot be missed or a game that cannot be lost *US, 1990*

lock-up lattie *noun* a cell; a jail. Polari, formed on LATTIE (a house, a place) *UK, 2003*

lock-worker *noun* a thief who steals from hotel rooms *US, 1954*

loco *noun* marijuana. An abbreviation of LOCOWEED *US, 1982*

loco *adjective* crazy. From the Spanish *US, 1887*. ▶ **go loco** to smoke (and experience the effects of) marijuana *US, 1942*

loco-mote *verb* to drive fast *US, 1976*

locoweed *noun* marijuana. Directly from the name given to several species of poisonous plants of the genera *Astragalus* and *Oxytropis* which may cause frenzied behaviour in grazing stock; ultimately from Spanish *loco* (mad) *US, 1930*

locs; lokes *noun* sunglasses *US, 1997*

log *noun* **1** a turd. From a similarity in appearance to a log of wood; possibly also from the shared characteristic of an ability to float. Especially in the phrasal verb LAY A LOG (to defecate) *US, 1973*. **2** a marijuana cigarette *US, 1977*. **3** phencyclidine, the recreational drug known as PCP or angel dust *UK, 1998*. **4** a carton of cigarettes *US, 1991*. **5** the counter surface in a bar *US, 1967*. **6** a bar or tavern *US, 1950*. **7** a heavy, cumbersome surfboard *US, 1963*. **8** a dullard *US, 1895*.
▶ **behind the log** (used of a betting style in poker) conservative, even when winning *US, 1971*

LOG *adjective* without money, low on green *US, 1997*

log bird *noun* a logistical supply helicopter, used to bring fresh supplies and provisions to troops in the field *US, 1982*

log-flogger *noun* a male masturbator *UK, 2003*

logger *noun* an old, wooden surfboard *AUSTRALIA, 1985*

logger's smallpox *noun* facial scars caused by spiked boots. Lumberjacks' and loggers' use *US, 1938*

logic bomb *noun* code secretly included in a program that causes a computer to fail when certain conditions are met *US, 1991*

logjam *noun* constipation *US, 1991*

logor *noun* LSD *UK, 2003*

logy *adjective* lethargic, without energy *US, 1997*

loid *noun* a strip of celluloid, used to force locks *UK, 1958*

loiner *noun* an inhabitant of Leeds in West Yorkshire *UK, 1950*

loin landlord *noun* a male homosexual *UK, 1983*

Loisaida *nickname* the Lower East Side of New York. A Spanish adaptation of English, borrowed back into English *US, 1981*

loked out *adjective* improved, modified, enhanced *US, 1997*

LOL *noun* (in doctors' shorthand) a *l*ittle *o*ld *l*ady. Medical slang *UK, 2002*

LOL used as Internet shorthand to mean '*l*aughing *o*ut *l*oud' *US, 1991*

lola *noun* cocaine *US, 1993*

Lolita *noun* a young teenage girl objectified sexually; a girl of any age up to the legal age of consent who dresses in a manner that is considered sexually provocative or predatory. Generic use of a proper name, after the sexually aware 12-year-old girl in Vladimir Nabokov's controversial 1955 novel *Lolita* and subsequent films in 1962 and 1998 *UK, 1959*

lollapalooza *noun* an outstanding example of its type. 'Lollapalooza' was adopted as the title for an annual series of peripatetic music festivals that commenced in Phoenix, Arizona in July 1991 *US, 1896*

lollapoloosa *noun* in bar dice games, a roll that produces no points for the player *US, 1971*

lollipop *noun* **1** a police officer. Rhyming slang for COP. A shorter variant is 'lolly' *UK, 1965*. **3** in cricket, a delivery that is easy to play *AUSTRALIA, 1985*. **4** in trucking, a mile marker at the side of the road *US, 1976*. **5** in sport, a clever or ostentatious trick. Rhyming slang on 'lollipop stick' *UK, 2003*. **6** a sugar daddy (an older man who supports or helps support a young woman). Recorded as being used by 'shopgirls and typists' *UK, 1961*. **7** marijuana *FIJI, 2003*

lollipop; lollypop; lolly up; lolly *verb* to betray to the police. Rhyming slang for SHOP (to inform on) *UK, 1933*

lollipop artist *noun* a male homosexual *US, 1977*

lollipop stop *noun* a rest stop on a motorway known as a place where male homosexuals may be found for sexual encounters *US, 1985*

lolly *noun* **1** money. From rhyming slang on 'lollipop' for DROP (a bribe) *UK, 1943*. **2** a sweet *AUSTRALIA, 1854*. **3** the vagina *BAHAMAS, 1982*. **4** the head *AUSTRALIA, 1971*. ▶ **do your lolly** to lose self-restraint in anger *AUSTRALIA, 1951*

lollybags *noun* a pair of men's close-fitting and revealing nylon swimming trunks. From the resemblance to a paper bag full of sweets *AUSTRALIA, 2003*

lollygag; lallygag *verb* **1** to kiss; to have sex *US, 1868*. **2** to dawdle, to dally *US, 1869*

lollypop *noun* **1** an attractive young woman seen only in terms of her sexuality *US, 1984*. **2** a shop. Rhyming slang *UK, 2000*

lolly scramble *noun* a distasteful scramble for a portion of something. Lollies are sweets, and a 'lolly scramble' was originally a children's party activity where guests frantically gathered sweets thrown in the air. *NEW ZEALAND, 1984*

lolly water *noun* a soft drink *AUSTRALIA, 1905*

lolo *noun* the penis. Children's vocabulary *TRINIDAD AND TOBAGO, 1966*

lo-lo; low-low *noun* a custom-designed low rider car *US, 1997*

London taxi *noun* the buttocks, the anus. Rhyming slang for JACKSY *UK, 1992*

London to a brick used of something that is an almost certainty. Coined by race-caller Ken Howard (1913–76), literally meaning that one can safely make an odds-on bet of the city of London against a BRICK (the sum of ten pounds) *AUSTRALIA, 1965*

lonely as a bastard on father's day *adjective* very lonely *AUSTRALIA, 1971*

Lone Ranger *noun* danger. Never in the sense of 'peril' but rather of 'a chance' *UK, 1992*

lonesome *noun* ▶ **on your lonesome** alone *AUSTRALIA, 1902*

lone wolf *noun* a criminal who works alone *US, 1909*

long *noun* a rifle *UK, 1995*

long *adjective* (used of money) a lot of *US, 1947*. ▶ **as long as your arm** very long *UK, 1846*

long acre *noun* a baker. Rhyming slang *UK, 1857*

long and flexy *adjective* sexy. Rhyming slang *UK, 2003*

long and short *noun* wine. Rhyming slang *UK, 1992*

long bread *noun* a lot of money *US, 1963*

long con *noun* an elaborate confidence swindle in which the victim is initially allowed to profit, and then returns with a large sum of money which he loses *US, 1969*

long cut *noun* the pervasive desire for sweets experienced by a drug addict withdrawing from drug use *US, 1971*

long-day/short-day *noun* in lobstering, a schedule in which more traps are hauled every other day than on the intervening days *US, 1978*

long dedger *adjective* eleven. From Italian *undici* (eleven) *UK, 2002*

long-dick *verb* to win a woman away from another; to cuckold *US, 1994*

long drink *noun* a sustained, lingering, sexually inquisitive look *US, 1982*

long drink of water *noun* a very tall thin person *US, 1936*

long end *noun* a confidence game in which the victim is sent for his money, as opposed to a confidence game in which the spoils are limited to the amount on the victim's person *US, 1963*

longer and linger; long and linger *noun* a finger. Rhyming slang, in which, unusually, both nouns are inflected in the plural form: 'longers and lingers'; 'longs and lingers' *UK, 1961*

long eye *noun* the vulva *AUSTRALIA, 1988*

long-eye *adjective* covetous *TRINIDAD AND TOBAGO, 1956*

long firm; LF; LF scam *noun* a commercial fraud in which a good credit rating is first established and then abused *UK, 1869*

long green *noun* a large amount of money *US, 1887*

long green line *noun* an infantry unit marching through the jungle in single file *US, 1991*

long-guts *noun* a tendency to eat too much *GUYANA, 1973*

longhair *noun* **1** an intellectual *US, 1919*. **2** a participant in the 1960s counterculture *US, 1969*. **3** classical music *US, 1951*

long-handled underwear *noun* warm underwear with long sleeves and legs *US, 1882*

longies *noun* long underwear *US, 1941*

long john *noun* a sleeveless wet suit *US, 1985*

Long John *noun* a 175 mm gun *US, 1991*

long johns *noun* long-legged underpants *US, 1943*

long john silver *noun* a car with one headlight burned out *US, 1976*

long jump *noun* an act of sexual intercourse *UK, 1999*

long-mouth *adjective* perpetually hungry *GUYANA, 1996*

longneck *noun* a bottle of beer with a long neck *US, 1980*

long-nose *noun* an American or European. From the Vietnamese, adopted by US soldiers *US, 1967*

long-nosed Henry *noun* a Ford Capri car. Citizens' band radio slang, ascribing the length of the bonnet to Henry Ford's physiognomy *UK, 1981*

long on *adjective* having a substantial amount of something *US, 1913*

long one *noun* one hundred pounds (£100) *UK, 1998*

long paddock *noun* grassed areas along the sides of a public road used for grazing *AUSTRALIA, 1929*

long rats *noun* special pre-cooked rations used by long-range reconnaissance patrols in the field during the Vietnam war *US, 1973*

longs *noun* trousers with long legs *TRINIDAD AND TOBAGO, 1967*

long shoe *noun* a stylish shoe with a tapered toe *US, 1968*

long-shoe game *noun* a swindle *US, 1955*

longshot *noun* a venture involving great risk; in horse racing, a bet on a horse with very long odds. Originally race track slang *UK, 1869*. ▶ **by a long shot** by a long way, by a great degree. Generally as an emphatic negative *US, 1848*

long side *noun* in sports betting, a bet on the underdog *US, 1975*

long sight *noun* ▶ **by a long sight** by a long way. Generally as an emphatic negative *US, 1844*

long skirt *noun* a Maxi car. Citizens' band radio slang; punning the length of a maxi-skirt *UK, 1981*

long sleeve *noun* the foreskin *FIJI, 1993*

long streak of cocky's shit *noun* a tall, thin person *AUSTRALIA, 1986*

long streak of misery *noun* a very tall thin person (who is not necessarily miserable) *UK, 1961*

long streak of piss *noun* a very tall thin person *UK, 2000*

longtail *noun* a single female tourist *BERMUDA, 1985*

long time no see used as a greeting after an extended separation *US, 1900*

long time, no smell used as an affectionate greeting. Hawaiian youth usage *US, 1982*

Long Tom *noun* a long-range artillery gun *US, 1991*

long 'un *noun* a hundred pounds, or a thousand pounds sterling *UK, 1999*

long way *noun* ▶ **by a long way; by a long chalk** by a great degree or measure. Often in a (implied) negative context *UK, 1859*

long white roll *noun* a factory-made cigarette *US, 1945*

long-winded *adjective* **1** slow in doing something. In conventional use when applied to talking *UK, 1961*. **2** in homosexual usage, said of a man who takes a long time to reach orgasm *US, 1981*

loo *noun* a lavatory. Many possible etymologies, mostly from French sources. Contracted from C18 *bordalou* (a portable ladies' privy, shaped like a sauce-boat and carried in a muff); *l'eau* (water) or the C18 warning-cry 'gardy-loo', from pseudo-French *gare de l'eau* (beware of the water), given when emptying the contents of a chamber pot out of a window into the street beneath; an anglicised *lieu* (the place), as in the frequently mispronounced 'time off in *lieu*/loo'. The only entirely English suggestion is a corruption of 'leeward', the sheltered side of a ship over which excretory functions were sensibly performed. The most convincing possibilites are an abbreviated pun on Waterloo, the London railway station named to commemorate the famous battle of Waterloo in Belgium (1815); and the darkly witty reduction of *l'oubliette* (a secret dungeon, often with a pit below) *UK, 1940*

looder *noun* a blow *IRELAND, 2002*

loogie *noun* phlegm that has been expelled from the respiratory passages *US, 1985*

loogin *noun* an awkward, unaccomplished person *US, 1919*

looie; louie; looey *noun* **1** a gob of phlegm or nasal mucus *US, 1970*. **2** a lieutenant *US, 1916*

look *noun* **1** appearance; style *US, 1959*. **2** in the entertainment industry, the right to review and consider a script or project *US, 1999*

look *verb* ▶ **look alive** to be alert, to bestir yourself, to make haste. Often as an imperative *UK, 1858*. ▶ **look a million; look like a million bucks** to look exquisitely stunning *AUSTRALIA, 1956*. ▶ **look at the gate** to near the end of a prison sentence *US, 1984*. ▶ **look at the procter and gamble** to cheat during an examination or test. A pun alluding to the well-known corporation *US, 1968*. ▶ **look at you** to judge someone by their appearance *UK, 1846*. ▶ **look down your nose at** to regard someone or something with contempt, to despise *UK, 1921*. ▶ **look for a hole in the fence** (used of a racehorse) to perform very poorly, as if the horse would rather find a hole in the fence and return to the stable *US, 1976*. ▶ **look like nothing on earth** to have an appearance that is wretched, or indicative of illness, or that is somehow eccentric or ludicrous *UK, 1927*. ▶ **look out the window** in horse racing, to fail to bet on a horse in a race it wins after betting on the horse in a number of previous losing efforts *US, 1951*. ▶ **not look back** to enjoy a continuing success since a defining moment *UK, 1893*

lookalikie; lookylikey *noun* a lookalike, a person who looks like another (generally the similarity is to a celebrity and often used to professional advantage) *UK, 2001*

looker *noun* an attractive woman *US, 1892*

look here! used as a demand for attention to what is being said *UK, 1861*

lookie *verb* to look. A diminutive that introduces a folksy tone; almost always used in the imperative *US, 1972*

lookie-loo *noun* **1** a customer who enjoys looking at merchandise but has no intention of buying *US, 1978*. **2** an inquisitive observer. A Los Angeles term, personified in the character Look-Loo Woman in Quentin Tarantino's 1994 film *Pulp Fiction US, 1989*

looking glass *noun* a car's rear view mirror *US, 1962*

looking good! used for expressing approval. A signature line of comedian Freddie Prinze on the television comedy *Chico and the Man* (NBC, 1974–78). Repeated with referential humour *US, 1974*

look of eagles *noun* in horse racing, the proud look perceived in the eyes of a great racehorse *US, 1976*

look-see *noun* a viewing, an observation *US, 1854*

look-see *verb* to look around *US, 1868*

looks like rain used by a criminal to indicate an imminent arrest. The future isn't sunny *UK, 1996*

look that up in your Funk and Wagnalls! used for a humorous observation about a word or fact. One of the most popular catchphrases from the US television series *Laugh-In* (1967–73) and repeated referentially *US, 1967*

look up *verb* **1** to visit, usually informally *UK, 1788*. **2** to get better *UK, 1806*

look who it isn't used as a facetious greeting on a surprise meeting *UK, 1959*

looky here! used as a demand for attention to what is being said. A variation of LOOK HERE! *US, 1876*

look you! used as a demand for attention to what is being said; especially (when spoken by a non-Welsh) as catchphrase of stereotypical Welshness *UK: WALES, 1937*

loo la *adjective* drunk *UK, 2002*

loomer *noun* a large wave that suddenly appears seaward *US, 1964*

loon *noun* a madman. An abbreviation of 'lunatic' *US, 1823*

loon *verb* to fool about; to move to music in an uncontrolled manner Often followed by 'about' *UK, 1966*

loon about; loon *verb* to play the fool; to enjoy leisure time in a non-conformist manner: dancing, idling, wandering *UK, 1966*

looney tune; loony tune *noun* a crazy person. From the television cartoons created by Warner Brothers beginning in 1960. The variant 'looney tunes' is also used as a singular *US, 1967*

looney tunes *adjective* insane *US, 1971*

loon pants; loons *noun* casual trousers fashioned with a very wide flare below the knee *UK, 1971*

loon shit *noun* boggy land *CANADA, 1987*

loony *noun* **1** a madman. An abbreviation of 'lunatic'; may also be spelt 'looney' *US, 1883*. **2** a one-dollar coin *CANADA, 2002*

loony *adjective* extremely erratic; mildly crazy *US, 1841*

loony bin *noun* a hospital (or other institution) for the treatment of psychiatric problems and mental illness *UK, 1919*

loony bird *noun* a person who is at least eccentric, at most mentally unstable *US, 1964*

loony left *noun* used by 'moderate' politicians to demonise committed socialists as fanatical extremists. Combines LOONY (mad) with 'left' (the sinister positioning of socialist politics) *UK, 1977*

loony toons *noun* LSD *UK, 2003*

loop *noun* **1** a short pornographic video shown on a recurring cycle *US, 1973*. **2** in television and film-making, voice recordings that are used with previously recorded video *US, 1980*. **3** an intrauterine contraceptive device *US, 1972*. **4** in table tennis, a shot with topspin *US, 1971*. **5** a crazy individual. Sometimes expanded to 'loop-de-loop' *UK, SCOTLAND, 1996*. ▶ **in the loop** to be part of an inner-circle that receives restricted information *UK, 1970*. ▶ **out of the loop** not part of a process or inner circle *US, 1976*

Loop *noun* ▶ **the Loop** the core central area of Chicago. From the elevated railway constructed in 1897 that loops around two square miles of central Chicago *US, 1946*

loop-de-loop *noun* simultaneous, reciprocal oral sex between two people *US, 1971*

looped; looping *adjective* drunk. Descriptive of the inability when drunk to maintain a straight line *US, 1934*

looper *noun* **1** a person who is capable of crazy actions *IRELAND, 2003*. **2** a wave that breaks over itself, creating a hollow through which a surfer can ride *US, 1964*

loopie *noun* a tourist *NEW ZEALAND, 1984*

loop joint *noun* an arcade showing recurring pornographic videos in private booths *US, 1986*

loop-scoop *verb* to steal something quickly *US, 1972*

loop-the-loop; loop-de-loop; loopers; loop *noun* soup *UK, 1961*

loopy *adjective* slightly mad; drunk. A conventional 'loop' is an obvious aberration from a straight line *UK, 1925*

loopy juice *noun* **1** an alcoholic drink. A drink with the 'juice' (power) to make you LOOPY (drunk) *UK, 2001*. **2** a strong medication *UK, 1996*

loopy looney juice *noun* alcohol. Royal Navy slang; LOOPY (eccentric) plus LOONY (crazy) and JUICE *UK, 1987*

loose *noun* ▶ **on the loose** (used of a wager) made on credit *AUSTRALIA, 1989*

loose *adjective* **1** (of a slot machine) advantageous to the gambler, both in terms of the frequency of payouts and a small house advantage *US, 1984*. **2** romantically unattached *US, 1968*

loose belly *noun* diarrhoea *TRINIDAD AND TOBAGO, 1991*

loose bump *noun* in the military, an unsolicited and unwanted promotion *US, 1947*

loose cannon *noun* a person whose actions or words cannot be controlled or predicted. From the image of a cannon rolling loose on the deck of a fighting ship *US, 1977*

loose goose *adjective* applied to something or someone that can be described as loose in whatever sense *US, 1958*

loose horse *noun* a tractor truck without a trailer *US, 1971*

loose wig *noun* a wild demeanour *US, 1959*

loosey-goosey *adjective* very loose in any sense *US, 1967*

loosie *noun* **1** an individual cigarette sold over the counter *US, 1981*. **2** in rugby, a loose forward *NEW ZEALAND, 1977*

loosie goosie *noun* a sexually promiscuous young woman *US, 1979*

loot *noun* **1** money *US, 1929*. **2** a lieutenant *US, 1967*

loot-in *noun* politically motivated group shoplifting *US, 1970*

loot money *noun* after World War 2, Chinese national currency obtained by looting *US, 1949*

lope *verb* to stroke *US, 1974*. ▶ **lope your donkey** (of a male) to masturbate *US, 1985*. ▶ **lope your mule** (of a male) to masturbate *US, 1967*

lop-ear *noun* an easily duped person *US, 1950*

lop-ear; lop-eared *adjective* naive, gullible *US, 1863*

loper *noun* **1** a resident of Michigan's Lower Peninsula. Upper Peninsula usage *US, 2003*. **2** in hot rodding, a big and powerful engine that is noisy when it idles *US, 1993*

lopp *noun* a perpetually naive and ignorant person *US, 1989*

lord and master *noun* **1** the backside, the buttocks. Rhyming slang, extending the sequence 'plaster' – PLASTER OF PARIS – ARIS – ARISTOTLE – BOTTLE; BOTTLE AND GLASS – ARSE. Sometimes seen in the abbreviated form of 'lord' *UK, 1998*. **2** a plaster (a first aid dressing). Rhyming slang *UK, 1998*

lord and mastered *adjective* drunk. Rhyming slang *UK, 1998*

lord boards *noun* sandals. From paintings of Jesus Christ wearing sandals *US, 1994*

Lord Jesus *noun* a curly hairstyle popular with black men and women in the mid-1970s *US, 1975*

Lord Lovat! used as an emphatic rejection of something. Rhyming slang, pronounced 'Lord love it', formed from the name of a long aristocratic line *UK, 1992*

Lord love-a-duck! used as a mild expression of shock or surprise. Sometimes varied as 'cor love a duck!' or reduced to 'love a duck!'; it is often regarded as a quintessentially Cockney turn of phrase *UK, 1917*

Lord Mayor *verb* to swear. Rhyming slang *UK, 1992*

Lord Muck *noun* a man who is, in the speaker's opinion, unjustifiably self-important or esteemed. The earlier counterpart to LADY MUCK, although they are often seen as a couple *UK, 1937*

Lord Sutch *noun* in a car, the clutch. Rhyming slang, formed from the name of rock musician and politician Screaming Lord Sutch, 3rd Earl of Harrow, 1940–99 *UK, 1992*

Lord tunderin' Jesus used as one of many elaborate Nova Scotian curses *CANADA, 1985*

Lord Wigg *noun* a glutton, an ill-mannered person. Rhyming slang for 'pig', formed from the name of politician George Cecil Wigg, 1900–83 *UK, 1992*

Lordy!; lawdy! Lord!, mildly calling upon God *US, 1853*

Loretta Young; loretta *noun* the tongue. Rhyming slang, formed from the name of the US television and film actress, 1914–2000 *UK, 1998*

Lorna Doone *noun* a spoon. Rhyming slang, formed from the eponymous heroine of R.D. Blackmore's romantic novel, 1869, widely-known from many film and television versions *UK, 1992*

lorry *noun* ▶ **up the lorry** in a great deal of trouble *SINGAPORE, 2002*

Los *noun* Los Angeles, California. Border Spanish used in English conversation by Mexican-Americans *US, 1913*

lose *verb* **1** to get rid of *US, 1931*. **2** to fail to understand *UK, 1962*. **3** (used of a computer program) to fail to work as expected *US, 1983*. ▶ **lose a load** to ejaculate *US, 1964*. ▶ **lose fire** (used of a car engine) to stop operating *US, 1970*. ▶ **lose it 1** to lose your mental focus to drugs, rhythmic sound and movement, and temporarily lose touch with the reality beyond the rave. A refined sense of 'lose it' (to temporarily lose control) *UK, 1998*. **2** to come off your motorcycle accidentally *UK, 1979*. ▶ **lose the plot** to lose your grasp of a situation *UK, 2001*. ▶ **lose water** in bodybuilding, to perspire. Done intentionally before competition in bodybuilding in order to improve muscle definition *US, 1984*. ▶ **lose your cool** to become angry, excited, nervous, etc; to lose your self-possession *US, 1984*. ▶ **lose your lunch** to vomit *US, 1918*

lose or win *noun* the foreskin. Rhyming slang *UK, 2003*

loser *noun* **1** a socially inept person; a person with consistently bad luck; anyone deemed unacceptable or an outcast *US, 1955*. **2** a convicted felon *US, 1912*. **3** a hospital patient who dies *US, 1970*

losersville *noun* a notional place where all socially inept people live *INDIA, 2002*

lossage *noun* the ongoing effect of a computer malfunction *US, 1991*

loss-leader *noun* something displayed prominently, and at a cut-price rate, to encourage further buying of other stock *US, 1922*

lossy *adjective* (used of a data-compression computer program) apt to lose some data *US, 1997*

lost *adjective* murdered, especially as a victim of 'criminal justice' *US, 1962*

lost-and-found badge *noun* a US Army name tag. Gulf war usage *US, 1991*

lost fart in a haunted milk bottle *noun* the epitome of distraction or indecision. Royal Navy slang. *UK, 1989*

lost in the sauce *adjective* daydreaming, completely inattentive *US, 1988*

lost-it *noun* a person under the sway of drug intoxication *UK, 1997*

lost sailor *noun* in the language surrounding the Grateful Dead, a follower of the band who has lost all touch with reality. From the title of a Grateful Dead song *US, 1994*

lost time *noun* the reduction of time from a prison sentence for good behaviour *US, 1950*

Lost Wages *nickname* Las Vegas, Nevada *US, 1951*

losum game *noun* in the language of carnival workers, a game that for whatever reason should be terminated immediately *US, 1985*

lot *noun* ▶ **do the lot** to lose all your money *UK, 1961*. ▶ **the lot** a life sentence in prison *NEW ZEALAND, 1997*

lotion *noun* alcohol *UK, 1876*

lot lady *noun* in circus and carnival usage, a local woman who is attracted to and makes herself sexually available to circus or carnival employees. In short, a circus or carnival GROUPIE *US, 1981*

lot lizard *noun* **1** an aggressive car salesman *US, 2001*. **2** a prostitute who works at transport cafes *US, 1987*

lot loafer *noun* in circus and carnival usage, a local resident who loiters as a show is assembled or taken down *US, 1981*

lot louce *noun* a patron of a circus or carnival who spends little or no money *US, 1930*

lot of it about a catchphrase applied to the prevalence of anything *UK, 2002*

lotsa *noun* a large amount. A slovenly contraction of 'lots of' *US, 1927*

lotta; lorra a large amount. A slovening of 'lot of' *UK, 1906*

lottery *noun* in horse racing, a race with no clear favourite *AUSTRALIA, 1989*

lottery ticket *noun* a currency note. In use at least fifteen years before the lottery was introduced to the UK *UK, 1982*

lotto *noun* money. Teen slang *SOUTH AFRICA, 2003*

Lotusland *noun* the city of Vancouver, British Columbia and sometimes the whole province of BC *CANADA, 2002*

lou *noun* a lieutenant *US, 1973*

loud *verb* to arrest; to be arrested. English gypsy use *UK, 2000*

loud *adjective* subject to detection by smell *UK, 1641*

loud and clear *adjective* expensive, overpriced, *dear*. Rhyming slang *UK, 1998*

loud and proud *adjective* (used of a citizens' band radio signal) clear *US, 1976*

loud pedal *noun* the accelerator on a drag racing car or hot rod *US, 1952*

louie *noun* a left turn *US, 1967* ▷*see:* LOOIE

Louisiana lottery *noun* an illegal numbers game *US, 1949*

Louisville Lip *nickname* the boxer Mohammed Ali, born Cassius Clay in 1942 in Louisville, Kentucky *US, 1968*

lounder *noun* a generous portion of anything *CANADA, 1999*

loungecore *noun* a particular style of easy-listening music. An ironic combination of 'lounge' music (easy-to-listen but hard to define) and -CORE, which is usually suffixed to forms of rock music *US, 1996*

lounge lizard *noun* a male sexual predator who seeks prey to seduce in fashionable bars and parties *US, 1918*

Lou Reed *noun* amphetamine. Rhyming slang for SPEED. Based, perhaps with more than a hint of irony, on rock singer and songwriter Lou Reed (b.1943) *UK, 1996*

louse *noun* a despicable person *US, 1864*

louse book *noun* an illegal betting operation that accepts only very small bets *US, 1951*

louse cage *noun* a brakevan (caboose) *US, 1960*

loused up *adjective* covered with scars and abscesses from repeated drug injections *US, 1970*

louse house *noun* a run-down, shoddy boarding house *UK, 1785*

louse up *verb* to ruin, to spoil *US, 1934*

lousy *adjective* contemptible, shoddy, bad. Because of the association with body lice, the term was deemed vulgar if not taboo in the US well into the C20 *UK, 1386*

lousy with *adjective* full of something, rich with something. From the prevalence of lice in an infestation *UK, 1594*

lova *noun* an unemployed person. Scamto youth street slang (South African townships) *SOUTH AFRICA, 2005*

love *noun* **1** used as an endearment, or a form of address (generally to the opposite sex, sometimes considered patronising); also for anything that is charming and admired *UK, 1814*. **2** crack cocaine *UK, 1998* ▷*see:* LIGHT OF LOVE

love-a-dove *adjective* extremely affectionate as a result of intoxication with MDMA, the recreational drug best known as ecstasy. A play on LOVEY-DOVEY and DOVE (a type of ecstasy) *UK, 1999*

love a duck!; luvvaduck! used as a mild expletive. Often preceded by 'Cor!,' 'Lord!' or 'Gawd!;' probably a gentling of fuck a duck! *UK, 1934*

love affair *noun* cocaine; a mixture of heroin and cocaine *UK, 2002*

love and kisses *noun* a wife. Rhyming slang for MISSUS *UK, 1992*

love and marriage *noun* a carriage. Rhyming slang, possibly acquired from the 1955 song 'Love and Marriage', lyrics by Sammy Cahn: 'Love and marriage, love and marriage / Go together like a horse and carriage' *UK, 1992*

love an romancin *noun* dancing. Glasgow rhyming slang *UK: SCOTLAND, 1988*

love bladder *noun* a condom *US, 1968*

love blow *noun* marijuana *US, 1986*

love boat *noun* **1** phencyclidine, the recreational drug known as PCP or angel dust *US, 1983*. **2** marijuana dipped in formaldehyde *US, 1998*

love child *noun* a member of the 1960s counterculture *US, 1990*

love conkers *noun* the testicles. Drawing an image of the fruit of the horse chestnut tree while playing on the familiar quotation 'love conquers all' *UK, 2003*

love cushion *noun* your boyfriend or girlfriend *US, 1986*

love doctor *noun* MDMA, the recreational drug best known as ecstasy. Descriptive of the way that ECSTASY treats your emotions *UK, 2003*

love drug *noun* **1** MDMA, the recreational drug best known as ecstasy. Descriptive of the effect that ECSTASY has on your emotions; widely used *UK, 1998*. **2** the recreational drug methaqualone, best known as Quaaludes™ *US, 1985*

loved up; luvdup; luvved up *adjective* under the influence of MDMA, the recreational drug best known as ecstasy, and experiencing the emotional need to share the boundless affection that is associated with the drug *UK, 1996*

love-'em-and-leave-'em; love 'em and leave 'em *adjective* used as a description of philandering or a philanderer *UK, 1961*

love factory *noun* a brothel *US, 1983*

lovefest *noun* a close, happy relationship. Combines 'love' with -FEST (a concentration of) *US, 1995*

love glove *noun* a condom *US, 1987*

love handles *noun* a roll of fat on either side of the body, just above the waist *US, 1970*

love heart *noun* a tablet of MDMA, the recreational drug best known as ecstasy, possibly mixed with the recreational drug methaqualone, best known as Quaaludes™, identified by an embossed heart. These variously coloured tablets are named after a sherberty children's sweet *UK, 1996*

love-in *noun* a communal gathering for a hands-on celebration of interpersonal love *US, 1967*

love in a punt *noun* very weak beer. A play on 'fucking near water' *UK, 1973*

love it! used for registering definite approval *UK, 2001*

love juice *noun* semen *UK, 1882*

love lips *noun* the vaginal labia *UK, 2003*

lovely *noun* 1 an attractive woman *UK, 1938*. 2 phencyclidine, the recreational drug known as PCP or angel dust. A longer variant is 'lovely high' *US, 1978*

lovelyboy *noun* used as a form of address. Sterotypically Welsh, perhaps as a result of its use by actor Windsor Davies in BBC television comedy series 'It Ain't Half Hot Mum', 1974–81 *UK: WALES, 2000*

lovely jubbly; luvly jubbly *adjective* wonderful, fantastic. Coined by John Sullivan (b.1946) as a catchphrase for the popular character Del Boy in the BBC television comedy Only Fools and Horses (1981–96), possibly inspired by a remembered response to a 'Jubbly', a pyramid-shaped frozen ice popular with children during the 1950s and 60s *UK, 1994*

love muffin *noun* the vagina *UK, 2001*

love muscle *noun* the penis *US, 1958*

love mussel *noun* the vagina. A neat pun on LOVE MUSCLE (the penis) and FISH (the vagina) *US, 2001*

love nest *noun* 1 a secluded room, apartment or house where lovers rendezvous *US, 1919*. 2 the vagina *US, 1994*

love nuggets *noun* marijuana *UK, 2003*

love nuts *noun* testicles that ache because of sexual stimulation that has not led to ejaculation; sexual frustration *US, 1971*

love off *verb* to love greatly *UK, 2000*

love pill *noun* a capsule of MDA, a synthetic amphetamine *US, 1970*

love plank *noun* the penis. Popularised in the film Kevin & Perry Go Large, (2000) *UK, 2000*

love pole *noun* the penis, *1999*

love potion #9 *noun* MDMA, the recreational drug best known as ecstasy. Descriptive of the effect that ECSTASY has on your emotions, from a 1959 song by Lieber and Stoller *UK, 2003*

love pump *noun* the penis. Popularised if not coined for the film This Is Spinal Tap *US, 1984*

lover *noun* 1 used as a form of address to someone who is not the speaker's lover. Possibly West Country dialect, certainly used as a characteristic of stereotypical West Country MUMMERSET speech *UK, 1973*. 2 any sex offender *US, 1950*

loverboy; lover boy; lover man *noun* a sexually promiscuous man, or one who tries hard to be so *US, 1952*

lover cover *noun* in drag racing, a protective shield between a driver's legs to prevent injury in the event of an engine explosion *US, 1993*

love rocket *noun* the penis *UK, 2003*

lover's leap *noun* in backgammon, the customary play with a first roll of 6–5: moving a back man 11 points *US, 1970*

lover's nuts *noun* testicles that ache because of sexual stimulation that has not led to ejaculation; sexual frustration *US, 1961*

lover's speed; speed for lovers *noun* MDMA, the recreational drug best known as ecstasy. MDMA is an amphetamine derivative that encourages empathy that is often confused with feelings of love *UK, 2003*

lover's tiff; lovers' tiff *noun* a sexually transmitted infection. Rhyming slang for 'syph' (syphilis), but applied more widely *UK, 1992*

love sacks *noun* the testicles *UK, 2002*

love sausage *noun* the penis *US, 2001*

love, security and devotion *noun* LSD. A sobriquet formed from the drug's initials *US, 1970*

love spuds; spuds *noun* the testicles *UK, 1998*

lovesteak *noun* the penis *US, 1989*

love tap *noun* 1 in motor racing, minor yet intentional contact between cars *US, 1993*. 2 in motor, gentle contact between one pin and another *US, 1987*

love trumpet *noun* the penis. Especially in the phrase 'blowing the love trumpet' (performing oral sex) *US, 2001*

love truncheon *noun* the penis. From the shape and purpose; humorous yet aggressive *UK, 1999*

love up *verb* to engage in sexual activity short of intercourse *TRINIDAD AND TOBAGO, 1964*

love weed; loveweed *noun* marijuana *US, 1938*

lovey *noun* used as an endearment, or an over-familiar or patronising form of address. In conventional use until late C19, thereafter colloquial *UK, 1731*

lovey-dovey *adjective* extremely affectionate, sentimenal, romantic. Heard at the turn of the century, then obsolete; heard again in the late 1940s. When not a genuine endearment, it tends to be used contemptuously *US, 1886*

low *noun* a depression, a state of depression (mental, physical or commercial). The opposite of HIGH *UK, 1961*

low and slow *adjective* describing the manner in which lowriders drive their cars, low to the ground and at a crawl *US, 1985*

lowball *noun* in the used car business, a knowingly deflated price *US, 1961*

low bandwidth *adjective* lacking useful information *US, 1995*

lowbrow *noun* a person who is not, or has no pretensions to be, of above-average intellectual capability or aesthetic refinement *US, 1903*

lowbrow *adjective* of little or no intellectual interest or aesthetic refinement *US, 1903*

lowbush moose *noun* in Alaska, a snowshoe rabbit *US, 1997*

low camp *noun* a coarsely ostentatious style, often unintentional. An elaboration of CAMP (flamboyance) *US, 1963*

lowdown *noun* detailed information *US, 1907*

lower 48 *noun* in Alaska, all states except Alaska *US, 1984*

lower 49 *noun* in Alaska, all states except Alaska *US, 1984*

lower deck *noun* the genitals, male or female *US, 1967*

lower states *noun* in Alaska, all states except Alaska *US, 1984*

lowest form of life; lowest form of animal life *noun* used to categorise or insult the despised, the overlooked and the most junior *UK, 1961*

low-flyer *nickname* Famous Grouse™ whisky. After the characteristic behaviour of the feathered grouse *UK: SCOTLAND, 1996*

lowgrade *verb* to disparage with great effect *US, 1973*

low-hangers *noun* testicles that dangle well below the body. Used in Sex and the City, a late 1990s television comedy to indicate testicles that may get in the way of sexual penetration *US, 2000*

lowheel *noun* a street-walking prostitute; any prostitute; a promiscuous woman. Inferring that the heels are worn down from persistent street-walking *AUSTRALIA, 1939*

low-hung *adjective* possessing a large penis *US, 1964*

lowie *noun* **1** a period of clinical depression. Liverpool usage. Also spelt 'lowey' UK, 2001. **2** a prostitute; a promiscuous woman. From LOWHEEL AUSTRALIA, 1944

Lowies *noun* Lowenbrau™ beer US, 1982

low maintenance *adjective* (used of a person) not requiring a great deal of attention or emotional support. A term that did not achieve anywhere near the fame of its cousin HIGH MAINTENANCE US, 1989

low-man feed *noun* in pinball, an understanding among friends playing a game that the person with the lowest score on one game will pay for the next game US, 1977

low man on the totem pole *noun* in poker, the player with the worst hand US, 1988

low marble count *noun* low intelligence US, 1994

low neck; low neck and short sleeves *noun* an uncircumcised penis US, 1941

low on the totem pole; low on the totem *adjective* occupying an unimportant position in a hierarchy UK, 1974

low pass *noun* a preliminary review of a situation. US naval aviator usage US, 1986

low-rate *verb* to denigrate; to insult US, 1906

low rent *adjective* cheap, inferior; despicable US, 1957

lowrider *noun* **1** a young person who restores and drives a car with a hydraulic system that lowers the car's chassis to just above the ground. A lifestyle and art form in the American southwest, especially among Mexican-American youth US, 1963. **2** a person wearing trousers without a belt and very low on the waist US, 1997

low road *noun* the railway from Glasgow to Dalry. Surely formed from the famous Scottish song 'Loch Lomond': 'O ye'll tak the high road and I'll tak the low road, / And I'll be in Scotland afore ye' UK, 1970

lows *noun* in pool, the solid-coloured balls numbered 1 to 7 US, 1990

low side *noun* in craps, all the points below seven US, 1950

low-tech *adjective* using basic technology. Combines 'low' (basic) with an abbreviation US, 1981

low wines *noun* in the illegal production of alcohol, the low-proof distillate produced by the first run of a still US, 1974

lox *verb* to refill an aircraft's stock of liquid oxygen, used for breathing at high altitudes CANADA, 1995

loxed; loxed out *adjective* in a diminished state of consciousness after a heart attack or respiratory arrest. An abbreviation of 'lack of oxygen' US, 1978

loxion *noun* a neighbourhood. Township slang, from 'location' SOUTH AFRICA, 2003

loyal to the dollar *adjective* bribed and compliant with the intent of the bribe US, 1989

L-plate; L-plater *noun* a prisoner serving a life sentence. A play on L for 'life' and the L-plates that signify learner-drivers UK, 1996

L's *noun* a driver's license US, 2001

LSD *noun* ▶ **new LSD** Vicodin™, a prescription painkiller taken recreationally US, 2001

LSD *nickname* Lake Shore Drive, Chicago US, 1985

LT; el tee *noun* a lieutenant. From the common abbreviation US, 1977

L-town; Lousetown *nickname* Klondike City, Yukon Territory CANADA, 1963

L train *noun* ▶ **take the L train** to lose, to fail miserably US, 1993

L train! used for a warning that police are nearby US, 1993

lubage *noun* marijuana. A variation of LUBANGE (marijuana) US, 1998

lubange *noun* marijuana. Originally East African usage US, 1982

lube *noun* a lubricant US, 1970

lube *verb* to lubricate US, 1956

lubed *adjective* drunk. An abbreviated form of LUBRICATED US, 1979

lube job *noun* the process of lubricating a car or other piece of machinery US, 1950

lubra *noun* an Aboriginal woman. Probably from an Australian Aboriginal language. Now only used derogatorily AUSTRALIA, 1830

lubra lips *noun* large lips AUSTRALIA, 1975

lubricated *adjective* drunk US, 1911

Luby Lou; Luby *nickname* a Jewish person. Rhyming slang; probably formed on Looby Loo, a rag doll character in children's television programme *Andy Pandy*, BBC since 1950 UK, 2000

Lucas *noun* marijuana US, 1998

lucifee; lucivee *noun* a Canada lynx CANADA, 1949

luck *noun* ▶ **you never know your luck** something unexpected may well happen. Probably an elaboration of YOU NEVER KNOW UK, 1961

luck into *verb* to be the beneficiary of good fortune US, 1920

luck money *noun* a tip or gratuity US, 1948

luck out *verb* to experience some good luck US, 1945

lucky 15 *noun* a multiple bet, based on a yankee, combining 15 separate bets UK, 1991

lucky 31 *noun* a multiple bet covering five selections to '31 win stakes or 62 each-way stakes' UK, 2001

lucky 63 *noun* a multiple bet covering six selections to '63 win stakes or 126 each-way stakes' UK, 2001

lucky boy; luck boy *noun* a swindler; a pickpocket US, 1922

lucky buck *noun* a casino gambling coupon US, 1974

lucky charm *noun* the arm. Rhyming slang UK, 1998

Lucky Country; lucky country *noun* Australia. From *The Lucky Country*, 1964, by Donald Horne, Australian author. Often used ironically AUSTRALIA, 1968

lucky dip *noun* **1** a chip. Rhyming slang, possibly derived from the action of eating a bag of chips UK, 1992. **2** a whip. Rhyming slang UK, 1998

lucky lady *noun* a type of bet in an illegal numbers game lottery US, 1957

lucky last *noun* in horse racing, the final race of the day AUSTRALIA, 1989

lucky Pierre *noun* the man (or the woman) sandwiched between the outer layers of a sexually active threesome. Glorified in the following lyric: 'Pierre gave it to Sheila, / Who must have brought it there. / He got it from François and Jacques, / A-ha, Lucky Pierre!' (Tom Lehrer, 'I Got It From Agnes', 1953). Predominately gay male usage US, 1942

lucky shop *noun* in Victoria; an establishment for betting with the TAB (a legal gambling agency) AUSTRALIA, 1979

lucky stiff *noun* in blackjack, a poor hand that is transformed by a lucky draw into a winning hand US, 2003

lucoddy; leucoddy; coddy *noun* the body UK, 1967

Lucozade *noun* a black person. Rhyming slang for SPADE (a black person); formed on the name of a branded drink UK, 1984

lu-cu-pu good night. A short-lived, but intensely used, piece of bebop slang US, 1948

Lucy *noun* an individual cigarette sold over the counter US, 1996

Lucy in the Sky with Diamonds; Lucy *noun* LSD. One of the Beatles' most psychedelic songs, 'Lucy in the Sky with Diamonds', 1967, has always been seen as a (not very discreet) LSD reference UK, 1975

Lucy Locket *noun* a pocket. Rhyming slang, from a nursery rhyme UK, 1971

lude; lud *noun* a tablet of the recreational drug methaqualone, best known as Quaaludes™ or, in a manner not inconsistent with the imprecision of the drug culture, any central nervous system depressant. Quaalude™ was a brand name for methaqualone, a muscle relaxant and barbiturate substitute introduced in 1965 and made illegal in the US in 1984 US, 1973

lúdramán; ludramaun *noun* an idiot, a stupid person. From the Irish for 'an idle person' IRELAND, 1997

luego used as a farewell. Spanish for 'later' US, 1981

luer *noun* a glass syringe with a slip-on needle and a solid plunger *US, 1973*

lug *noun* **1** a large, clumsy, dim man *US, 1927.* **2** a woman who takes lesbian lovers in college and then reverts to heterosexuality after graduation from college. An abbreviation of 'lesbian until graduation' *US, 1993.* **3** the ear *UK, 1507.* **4** an inhalation of marijuana smoke, especially from a water pipe *UK, 1996.* **5** a demand *US, 1929.* **6** luggage *US, 1977*

lug *verb* to bring, to accompany *UK, 1884*

lugan *noun* a Lithuanian. Coined in Chicago *US, 1947*

luger lout *noun* a German. Rhyming slang for KRAUT formed from the well-known brand of German side-arm and a pun on LAGER LOUT *UK, 1992*

lugger *noun* **1** in a big store confidence swindle, somebody who is assigned to provide background ambience, an extra *US, 1931.* **2** a person who physically transports players to an illegal poker game *US, 1979*

lughole; lug'ole *noun* the ear. A variation of LUG (the ear) *UK, 1895*

lug in *verb* (used of a racehorse) to tend to run toward the rail *US, 1964*

luke *noun* pre-coital vaginal secretions *US, 1960s*

luken *noun* in circus and carnival usage, a naive, gullible person *US, 1981*

Luke the Gook *noun* during the Korean war, a north Korean; during the Vietnam war, any Vietnamese person. War usage *US, 1953*

Luke the Gook's castle *noun* a fortified North Korean position *US, 1964*

lullaby *verb* to knock unconscious; to kill *US, 1990*

lulu *noun* something that is amazing *US, 1886*

Lulu's parlor *noun* a brothel *US, 1946*

lumber *noun* **1** the stems of a marijuana plant *US, 1982.* **2** stolen goods *UK, 1956.* **3** an action or piece of information intended to cause trouble *UK, 1956.* **4** a member of the opposite sex that you form an initial liaison with, especially with a view to greater intimacy *UK: SCOTLAND, 1966.* **5** a non-playing, non-betting observer of a game of chance *US, 1961.* ▶ **in lumber; in dead lumber** in trouble *UK, 1967*

lumber *verb* **1** to steal *UK, 1956.* **2** to fight *US, 1982.* **3** to form an initial liaison with someone sexually attractive, especially with a view to greater intimacy *AUSTRALIA, 1933.* **4** to encumber with problems or trouble *UK, 1956.* **5** to arrest. First recorded in 1812 meaning 'to jail', from 'lumber' (to pawn) *UK, 1812*

lumbered *adjective* **1** arrested, in custody. Still in current use. *AUSTRALIA, 1812.* **2** in (any sort of) trouble; having been given unwelcome responsibility *UK, 1984*

lumbering *noun* sexual intercourse *AUSTRALIA, 1992*

lumberjack *noun* the back. Rhyming slang, playing on 'lumbar'. *UK, 1998*

lumberman's strawberries *noun* prunes *CANADA, 1947*

lumber wagon *noun* an old, dilapidated car *US, 1962*

lumber yard *noun* **1** the trees around and in a golf course *US, 2000.* **2** a prison exercise yard *AUSTRALIA, 1956*

lumins *noun* rays of the sun. Often found as 'soaking up a few lumins' *US, 1968*

lummed up *adjective* drunk *UK: SCOTLAND, 1988*

lump *noun* **1** a stupid, inept person *UK, 1909.* **2** a tracking device *UK, 2002.* **3** in hot rodding and drag racing, an engine *US, 1963.* **4** a small lunch carried in your pocket *US, 1980*

lump *verb* **1** to dislike something that must be endured *UK, 1833.* **2** to reluctantly accept. Usually in the phrase 'lump it' *UK, 1791.* **3** to strike; to hit *UK, 1780.* ▶ **lump lips** to talk on the telephone. Teen slang *US, 1951*

lumper *noun* **1** any unskilled worker. Originally applied to an unskilled worker who helped load and off-load vessels, and then more generally *UK, 1785.* **2** in carnival usage, a confederate who is hired to play and win a game in order to generate business *US, 1981*

lump of coke; lump *noun* a man. Rhyming slang for BLOKE *UK, 1859*

lump of ice *noun* advice. Rhyming slang *UK, 1909*

lump of lead *noun* the head. Rhyming slang, often used in connection with a hangover *UK, 1857*

lumps *noun* the consequences of your actions, punishment or other unpleasantness, either physical or by reprimand *US, 1930*

lumpy gravy *noun* the Royal Navy. Rhyming slang *UK, 1984*

lumpy jumper *noun* a female member of the Royal Air Force. A less than flattering allusion to female breasts *UK, 2002*

lun *noun* in Newfoundland, a spot in the lee of the wind *CANADA, 1958*

Luna Park bookmaker *noun* a bookmaker who appears to be operating his business just for fun. Luna Park was an amusement park on Coney Island, New York, and later in Sydney. The Sydney park has long used the sobriquet 'just for fun' in advertisements *AUSTRALIA, 1989*

lunar *noun* the bleed period of the menstrual cycle. Emphasises the monthly rhythm of the cycle *US, 2000*

lunar occurence *noun* the bleed period of the menstrual cycle *US, 1968*

lunatic patrol *noun* a police operation to bring a mentally ill person to a hospital *CANADA, 1945*

lunatics *noun* ▶ **the lunatics are running the asylum; the lunatics have taken over the asylum** used of any situation that is managed by those who are incapable *UK, 1981*

lunatic soup *noun* alcoholic drink *AUSTRALIA, 1933*

lunch *noun* **1** the male genitals, especially as may be hinted at or imagined when the man is dressed *AUSTRALIA, 1944.* **2** oral sex performed on a woman *US, 1995.* ▶ **do lunch** to have lunch, usually a working lunch. Hollywood lingo, embraced elsewhere with a sense of mocking *US, 1987.* ▶ **drop your lunch** to fart *AUSTRALIA, 1988.* ▶ **out to lunch 1** distracted, insensible, foolish, stupid, vacant; being there with the mind elsewhere. A figurative use of a favourite excuse for someone not being there, in this case extended to 'not all there' *US, 1955.* **2** knocked from your surfboard by a wave *US, 1977*

lunch *verb* **1** to fail, to do poorly *US, 1966.* **2** to cause a car engine to explode, scattering parts on the track or road. An especially common event and term in drag racing *US, 1997.* **3** to perform oral sex *UK, 1996.* ▶ **get lunched** to be knocked from your surfboard and thrashed by the ocean *US, 1988*

lunch *adjective* without a care, absent-minded *US, 1975*

lunchbox *noun* **1** the male genitalia, especially when generously presented in tight clothing. An indiscreet euphemism that makes people smile; perhaps its most famous usage occurred during track athlete Linford Christie's impressive performance at the 1992 Olympic Games, when he took gold in the 100 metres *US, 1992.* **2** someone who is completely out of touch *US, 1964*

lunch bucket *noun* a socially inept outcast *US, 1956*

lunch hooks *noun* the hands *US, 1896*

lunchie *noun* a lunchtime drink consumed in place of a meal *UK, 2001*

lunchin' *adjective* foolish. A formation based on OUT TO LUNCH *US, 1987*

lunching *noun* the act of oral sex *UK, 1996*

lunching *adjective* completely out of touch and unaware of what is happening. An evolved OUT TO LUNCH *US, 1999*

lunchmeat *noun* **1** in the pornography industry, an extremely appealing and sexual woman *US, 1995.* **2** in poker, bad cards or a player who proceeds with a bad hand *US, 1996*

lunch out *verb* **1** to perform oral sex *US, 1986.* **2** to experience a psychotic break during drug intoxication *US, 1988*

lunchpail *noun* an ugly, stupid and/or despised person *US, 1968*

lunch tray *noun* a short snowboard *US, 1995*

lund *noun* a despicable person *TRINIDAD AND TOBAGO, 1980*

Lunenburg champagne *noun* rum. Lunenburg, on the Nova Scotia South Shore coast, is long known for its fishing and trading, and the nickname comes from the old three-cornered trade with England and the West Indies – salt fish, rum and lumber *CANADA, 1999*

Lunenburg pudding *noun* pork sausage *CANADA, 1998*

lung butter *noun* phlegm *US, 1993*

lunger *noun* **1** phlegm expelled from the lungs *US, 1946*. **2** a person suffering from tuberculosis *US, 1893*

lungs *noun* the female breasts *US, 1951*

lunk *noun* a dolt *US, 1867*

lunkhead *noun* a dolt *US, 1868*

lupper *noun* the finger. Polari *UK, 1967*

lurk *noun* a cunning scheme or stratagem. A positive term. When referring to a fraudulent or otherwise illegal activity a 'lurk' is only ever a misdemeanour or a bending of the rules. Commonly refers also to a job that is easy yet sounds like hard work, or has some clever trick to being profitable *AUSTRALIA, 1891*

lurk *verb* to read postings on an Internet discussion group without posting your own comments *US, 1984*

lurker *noun* **1** a person who reads postings on an Internet discussion group without posting their own comments *US, 1991*. **2** a market-stallholder who is new to the trade, and who operates in non-traditional markets. Used by veterans who were 'born to the job' *UK, 1983*. **3** a Canadian pilot waiting in Thompson, Manitoba, for a flying job *CANADA, 2002*

lurk man *noun* a man who is adept at obtaining lurks *AUSTRALIA, 1945*

lurk merchant *noun* a person adept at obtaining lurks *AUSTRALIA, 1964*

lurp *noun* **1** a misfit *US, 1955*. **2** a long-range reconnaissance patrol; a member of such a patrol. From the initials LRRP *US, 1968*

lus *noun* enthusiasm, appetite. From 'lust' or synonymous Afrikaans *lus*. Used, for example, in the expression a 'lus for politics' *SOUTH AFRICA, 1994*

lus *adjective* longing for something; lusting after something. From Afrikaans *lus* (desirous) *SOUTH AFRICA, 1970*

luser *noun* a computer neophyte *US, 1995*

lush *noun* **1** alcohol. At one time deemed obsolete slang, but revived *UK, 1790*. **2** an alcoholic *US, 1851*

lush *verb* to drink alcohol excessively *UK, 1811*

lush *adjective* **1** sexually attractive *UK, 1890*. **2** drunk *UK, 1812*. **3** very good, great, especially nice; attractive. Reported in mid-1970s as being used in Wigan, south Lancashire, and in 2002, by south Wales schoolchildren to describe an impressive room in an historic house *UK, 1953*

lush! used for expressing approval *UK, 2003*

lushed *adjective* drunk *US, 1927*

lusher *noun* a drunkard *US, 1848*

lush green *noun* money *US, 1951*

lushhead *noun* a habitual drinker. Combines LUSH (an alcoholic) with -HEAD (a user) *UK, 1938*

lushhound *noun* a drunkard *US, 1935*

lush puppy *noun* a young person who drinks to excess. A play on the branded shoes Hush Puppies™ *UK, 1983*

lush-roll *verb* to rob drunkards *US, 1957*

lushwell *noun* a drunkard *US, 1960*

lush-worker *noun* a thief who preys on drunks who have passed out *US, 1908*

lushy *noun* a drunkard *US, 1944*

lust *noun* ▶ **in lust** sexually attracted to someone. A play on the conventional 'in love' *US, 1963*

lust dog *noun* a passionate, promiscuous female *US, 1975*

lusty wench *noun* an attractive teenage girl. The term assumes a degree of respectability in the girl *NEW ZEALAND, 1984*

luv *noun* love, especially as a form of address. A variant spelling; also used for reasons of alphabetic economy in text messaging *UK, 1898*

luvvie; luvvy; luvvie-darling *noun* **1** an actor of either sex, especially one given to public extravagance or theatrical gesture; an actor who is considered intensely serious about theatre work. Satirical, gently derogatory, often self-descriptive; from the stereotypical thespianic greeting and form of address 'Luvvie, darling' *UK, 1990*. **2** used as a form of address, generally affectionate (usually of the opposite sex, sometimes considered patronising). An extension of LOVE *UK, 1968*

lux *adjective* *lux*urious *US, 2002*

L'ville *nickname* Louisville, Kentucky *US, 1981*

lye *noun* marijuana *US, 1990s*

lying squad *noun* the *Flying* Squad of the Metropolitan Police *UK, 1996*

lyrics *noun* **1** talk, especially when stretching truth or reality. A play on 'words' *UK, 1994*. **2** profanity; disparagement *TRINIDAD AND TOBAGO, 1987*

LZ *noun* a combat aircraft landing zone, especially an improvised one *US, 1971*

Mm

M *noun* **1** morphine *US, 1914*. **2** marijuana. Extended from the previous sense *US, 1955*. **3** an *MBE* (Member of the Order of the British Empire). Used by civil servants, suggestive of a casual familiarity with the honour *UK, 1961*

M & M *noun* a 9 mm pistol *US, 1999*

M20 *noun* a meeting place. Citizens' band radio jargon, originally US; UK use is interesting as the M20 is a motorway route to Folkestone *US, 1981*

M25 *noun* a tablet of MDMA, the recreational drug best known as ecstasy. The initial letter of MDMA leads to the designation of the London orbital motorway (M25) thus memorialising the road's pivotal role in reaching the (often) illegal locations of early raves *UK, 1996*

M8 *noun* used in text messaging to mean 'a mate'. A variant spelling; one of several constructions in which a syllable pronounced 'ate' is replaced by the homophone 'eight' *UK, 2002*

ma *noun* a mother; used for addressing your mother. An abbreviation of 'mama' *UK, 1823*

ma'a *noun* crack cocaine, *2003*

maaga; maga *adjective* thin. From West Indian and UK black patois pronunciation of 'meagre' *UK, 1994*

ma and pa *adjective* (used of a business) small-scale, family-owned *US, 1972*

ma bubby and Choon *noun* any two things that are very close to each other *TRINIDAD AND TOBAGO, 1990*

mac *noun* **1** an automated cash machine. Originally from the trademarked acronym Money Access Centre, then applied to any such device *US, 1996*. **2** a mackintosh, hence any waterproof outercoat. Sometimes spelt 'mack' *UK, 1901*

Mac; mac; mack *noun* **1** used as a term of address for a man whose name is not known by the speaker *US, 1918*. **2** a red McIntosh apple, usually from British Columbia *CANADA, 1958*

mac; mack *verb* to eat voraciously. From the Big Mac, a hamburger speciality from the McDonald's™ hamburger chain *US, 1990*

macaroni *noun* **1** an Italian-American or Italian. From the pasta product *UK, 1845*. **2** excrement. Rhyming slang for 'pony' (the reduced form of PONY AND TRAP), CRAP (excrement). Sometimes reduced to 'maca' *UK, 1974*. **3** a pony; hence £25. Rhyming slang for PONY *UK, 1857*. **4** in betting, odds of 25–1. From rhyming slang for PONY (£25) *UK, 1991*. **5** in oil drilling, small-diameter pipe *US, 1954*

macaroni *verb* to defecate. Rhyming slang for PONY AND TRAP (CRAP) *UK, 1974*

macaroni and cheese *noun* marijuana worth $5 and cocaine worth $10 *US, 2002*

macaroon *noun* a black person. Rhyming slang for COON *UK, 1992*

MacArthur sweep *noun* a combing of the hair from the side of the head over a bald spot on top of the head *US, 1953*

macca; macker *noun* a recruit in the armed forces. Origin unknown *AUSTRALIA, 1944*

macca *adjective* enormous. School slang *UK: ENGLAND, 2003*

Maccas *noun* **1** food from a McDonald's™ restaurant *AUSTRALIA, 1996*. **2** a McDonald's™ restaurant *AUSTRALIA, 1995*

macdaddy *noun* the very best of something *US, 1995*

mace *verb* **1** to swindle, to defraud *UK, 1790*. **2** to owe money. From the previous sense *UK, 1979*. **3** to steal or cheat, especially by means of the three card trick. A variation of the sense 'to swindle' *UK, 1977*

MacGuffin *noun* a device or a gimmick within a film that while often peripheral to the storyline is iconic in and of the overall storytelling. Coined by film director Alfred Hitchcock (1899–1980) *US, 1939*

macher *noun* an important and powerful man. Yiddish *US, 1930*

machine *noun* **1** a fast and attractive car. Often pronounced 'machine' *US, 1908*. **2** a machine gun *US, 1995*. **3** a trumpet *UK, 1983*. **4** in horse racing, a pari-mutuel betting machine *US, 1976*. **5** in horse racing, a battery-powered device used to impart a shock to a horse during a race *US, 1976*

Machine *noun* ▶ **the Machine** in big city politics, the over-arching political organisation that runs all facets of life *US, 1992*

machine gun; machine *noun* a syringe used for injecting an illegal drug *UK, 1978*

Machine Gun Murphy *noun* a stereotypical fearless soldier *US, 1971*

machinery *noun* **1** the equipment used to prepare and inject narcotics *US, 1970*. **2** marijuana. Also simply 'mach' *US, 1977*

macho *noun* excessively masculine, virile and brave. A direct loan from Spanish *US, 1959*

Macintoy; Macintrash *noun* an Apple Macintosh™ computer *US, 1991*

Macintyre *noun* fire. Rhyming slang *UK, 1996*

mack *noun* **1** a pimp *US, 1903*. **2** a person who is a smooth and convincing talker *US, 1962*. **3** the speech a pimp makes to recruit a woman as a prostitute *US, 1972*. **4** a male who attracts females *US, 1997* ▷*see:* MAC

mack *verb* **1** to speak with a stylish flair and flattery *US, 1968*. **2** to work as a pimp *UK, 1887*. **3** to behave with ostentatious style and flair *US, 2002*. **4** to kiss *US, 1993* ▷*see:* MAC

Mack Daddy *noun* a skilled ladies' man; a pimp *US, 1959*

macker *noun* a very large wave *US, 1991* ▷*see:* MACCA

mackerel and sprat; mackerel *noun* a fool. Rhyming slang for PRAT (a fool); however, as this generally appears in the shortened form, an alternative rhyming derivation has appeared: mackerel – fish in the pool – fool *UK, 1998*

mackerel-snapper *noun* a Roman Catholic. From the practice of eating fish on Fridays *US, 1850s*

mack man *noun* a pimp *US, 1960*

Mack the Knife *noun* any surgeon *US, 1980*

Macnamara *noun* a barrow. Glasgow rhyming slang *UK: SCOTLAND, 1988*

macocious *adjective* inclined to gossip *TRINIDAD AND TOBAGO, 1977*

macon; maconha; machona; mach *noun* marijuana. From Brazilian *maconha* (marijuana) *US, 1938*

mac out *verb* to eat ravenously *US, 1982*

Mactown *nickname* McMurdo Station, Antarctica *ANTARCTICA, 2003*

mad *adjective* **1** exciting, good *US, 1941*. **2** in homosexual usage, unrestrained and ostentatious *US, 1949*. **3** used as an all-purpose, dramatic intensifier *US, 1972*

mad *adverb* ▶ **like mad** to an extraordinary extent, very much *UK, 1653*

mad about *adjective* enthusiastic about, having a strong liking for, sexually infatuated *UK, 1744*

madam *noun* in a deck of playing cards, a queen *US, 1988*

Madam de Luce; madam *verb* to deceive. Rhyming slang for 'spruce' *UK, 1938*

madame *noun* **1** an older homosexual man *US, 1979*. **2** the victim of an extortion scheme *US, 1982*

Madame *nickname* Madame Ngo Dinh Nhu, sister-in-law of South Vietnamese President Diem *US, 1965*

Madame Tussaud *noun* bald. Rhyming slang, formed on the name of the famous waxworks' founder *UK, 1998*

mad as a beetle *adjective* extremely mad; very angry *AUSTRALIA, 1942*

mad as a boiled... *mentally* deranged. A seemingly endless source of nonsense similes; 'mad as a boiled dictionary compiler' makes as much sense, which is probably the point *UK, 2000*

mad as a Chinaman *adjective* extremely mad; very angry *AUSTRALIA, 1942*

mad as a cut snake *adjective* extremely mad. Either meaning 'out of one's mind with anger' or 'insane' *AUSTRALIA, 1932*

mad as a goanna *adjective* extremely mad; very angry. A goanna is a large lizard *AUSTRALIA, 1942*

mad as a gum tree full of galahs *adjective* totally mad; crazy. The galah is a striking native bush parrot noted for loud calls and antic behaviour *AUSTRALIA, 1942*

mad as a meat-axe *adjective* extremely mad. Generally meaning 'insane' rather than 'out of one's mind with anger' *AUSTRALIA, 1946*

mad as a satchel of knees *adjective* insane, crazy *UK, 2003*

mad as a snake *adjective* extremely mad. Either meaning 'out of one's mind with anger' or 'insane' *AUSTRALIA, 1917*

mad as sand *adjective* mentally deranged. Liverpool usage *UK, 1999*

mad ball *noun* in circus and carnival usage, a fortune teller's glass globe *US, 1948*

mad bastard *noun* a variety of MDMA, the recreational drug best known as ecstasy *UK, 1997*

mad bomber *noun* a mortar air delivery system. From the initials MADS *US, 1991*

Madchester *nickname* Manchester, the UK city that was, between 1989–92, more in touch with youth, music and drug fashions than any other. 'Mad' puns on craziness and MDMA (ecstasy) *UK, 1996*

mad dog *noun* **1** a fearless, aggressive, uninhibited criminal *US, 1956*. **2** any cheap red wine. Originally applied to Mogen-David wine, later to any cheap wine *US, 1974*

mad-dog *verb* **1** to behave in an intensely aggressive fashion, giving the appearance of near insanity *US, 1992*. **2** to annoy *NEW ZEALAND, 1998*

maddy *noun* ▶ **throw a maddy** to have a fit of ill-temper *UK: SCOTLAND, 1985*

made *adjective* **1** officially admitted into a crime family *US, 1966*. **2** (used of a woman) formerly virginal *US, 1949*

made in heaven *noun* in Bingo, the number sixty-seven. Rhyming slang *UK, 2003*

made in the shade *adjective* successful, accomplished *US, 1951*

made of money *adjective* wealthy *UK, 1786*

Ma Deuce *noun* a Browning .50 calibre machine gun *US, 1982*

made up *adjective* happy, satisfied, pleased *UK, 1999*

mad for it *adjective* very eager. The phrase, originating in Manchester in the north of England, gained its wider currency as a catchphrase to justify the excesses of Liam and Noel Gallagher and their band Oasis *UK, 1997*

madhead *noun* a crazy person *UK, 2002*

madhouse *noun* a brakevan (caboose) *US, 1977*

Madison Avenue crash helmet *noun* a kind of businessman's hat *US, 1965*

mad keen on *adjective* very enthusiastic about something or someone *UK, 1949*

madly *adverb* passionately, fervently, extremely *UK, 1756*

madman *noun* a pill of pure MDMA, the recreational drug best known as ecstasy; MDMA in powdered form. A playful disguise of MaDMAn *UK, 2002*

Mad Max *noun* tax. Rhyming slang, formed on the eponymous hero of three films, 1979–85, set in a post-apocalyptic wasteland; suggesting, perhaps, that taxes will both pay for and survive the apocalypse *UK, 1994*

mad mick *noun* a pick (the tool). Rhyming slang *AUSTRALIA, 1919*

mad mike *noun* a mad minute. From the military phonetic alphabet in which 'm' is 'mike' *US, 1991*

mad minute *noun* an intense, short-lived burst of weapon fire *US, 1917*

mad money *noun* money set aside to use in an emergency or to splurge *US, 1922*

mad monkey *noun* a staff worker at the US Military Army Command, Vietnam. Another of many terms expressing the combat soldier's disdain for those who were in the service but did not see combat *US, 1991*

madon! used as a moderately profane exclamation. Originally Italian-American usage *US, 1977*

Madonna *noun* someone who has died or is unavoidably doomed to die very soon. Rhyming slang for GONER, formed on the popular US singer Madonna Louise Ciccone (b.1958) rather than the religious icon *UK, 2004*

madonna claws *noun* an ugly hand. Contemporary gay use *UK, 2003*

mad out of it *adjective* drunk or drug-intoxicated *IRELAND, 2001*

mad props *noun* effusive compliments *US, 1994*

mad railer *noun* a racing greyhound that will veer towards the inside rail no matter what its starting position *AUSTRALIA, 1989*

Madras in the evening, mad arse in the morning given as a proverbial warning against eating a curry that is spicier than your body can comfortably handle. In Glasgow use *UK: SCOTLAND, 1988*

mad skull *noun* a crazy or mentally unstable person *UK: SCOTLAND, 1985*

mad spun *adjective* deeply under the influence of LSD *US, 1997*

madukes *noun* a mother *US, 2002*

mad weed *noun* green, weak marijuana *JAMAICA, 1979*

mad wey it; mad wi' it *adjective* drunk; mad with drink *UK: SCOTLAND, 2002*

madwoman *noun* a pill of pure MDEA, an analogue of MDMA, the recreational drug best known as ecstasy. Probably as a variation of MADMAN (MDMA) *UK, 2002*

madza; madzer; medza; medzer; midzer *adjective* half. From Italian *mezzo* (a half). Used, for example, in 'madza beagered' (half-drunk) and 'medzer caroon' (a half-crown) *UK, 2002*

Mae *noun* among male homosexuals, a term of endearment. Probably adopted from the name of glamorous film actress Mae West; used in such conversational gambits as: 'Hello, Mae, how are you today?' *UK, 2003*

Mae West *noun* **1** the chest or the breast. Rhyming slang, formed from the name of buxom US actress and writer, 1892–1980 *UK, 1992*. **2** a life-jacket worn by aircrews. Military. Remains familiar thanks to its popularity with crossword compilers *UK, 1940*. **3** in the language of parachuting, a partial inversion of the canopy resulting from a deployment malfunction *US, 1958*. **4** a French-Canadian sugar roll *CANADA, 1979*

mafia *noun* used as part of a jocular formation referring to a large number or influential group of people *US, 1989*

mafioski *noun* Russian criminals. Conventional 'mafia' with the suffix '-ski' to indicate a Russian heritage *UK, 1998*

mafu *noun* marijuana *UK, 2003*

mag *noun* **1** a magazine, in any sense of the term *UK, 1801*. **2** a magnesium steel wheel on a race car *US, 1970*. **3** a magneto, used on drag racing engines with no battery or generator *US, 1968*. **4** a brief conversation; a chat; a gossip *AUSTRALIA, 1895*

Mag *noun* a Magnum™ pistol *US, 1970*

mag *verb* to chat; to prattle *UK, 1820*

maga dog *noun* a mongrel. West Indian and Rastafarian patois, from *maaga* or *mawga* meaning meagre, hence skinny *2004*

magazine *noun* a six-month sentence to jail *US, 1949*

maggie *noun* **1** the Australian magpie, *Gymnorhina tibicen* *AUSTRALIA, 1901*. **2** marijuana. Variants on the name Maggie, all diminutives of Margaret, play very loosely on marijuana: 'Maggie', 'meg', 'megg', 'meggie', 'meggs' *US, 1959*

Maggie *noun* any revolver that fires a cartridge that is more powerful than standard ammunition *US, 1957*

Maggie *nickname* British Prime Minister (1979–90) Margaret Hilda Thatcher (b.1925). The UK wasn't really on first name terms with Mrs Thatcher until she became PM; earlier in her political career, however, she was vilified as 'Maggie Thatcher, milk snatcher'. Also known as 'Attila the hen' *UK, 1994*

Maggie's drawers *noun* a red flag indicating a 'miss' on a rifle range *US, 1936*

Maggie's millions *noun* the unemployed during the premiership of Margaret Thatcher (1979–90) *UK, 1984*

maggot *noun* **1** a loathsome person *AUSTRALIA, 1961*. **2** a white person. Urban black usage *US, 1985*. **3** a repulsive female *AUSTRALIA, 1987*. **4** in the US Air Force, someone who is very dedicated to service *US, 1998*. ▶ **act the maggot** to play the fool *IRELAND, 1937*

maggot; maggotted *adjective* drunk *AUSTRALIA, 2003*

maggot bag *noun* a meat pie *AUSTRALIA, 2003*

maggotbox *noun* an Apple Macintosh™ computer *US, 1991*

maggot wagon *noun* a catering truck *US, 1992*

maggoty; maggotty *noun* angry; in a bad mood *AUSTRALIA, 1919*

magic *adjective* **1** excellent, first class; used for showing approval and enthusiasm *UK, 2001*. **2** in computing, complicated or not yet understood *US, 1981*

magic bean *noun* a tablet of MDMA, the recreational drug best known as ecstasy. From the fairystory *Jack and the Beanstalk UK, 1996*

magic flagon *noun* marijuana *NEW ZEALAND, 1990*

magic fudge; fudge *noun* an intoxicating confection that has marijuana as a central ingredient *UK, 1970*

magic hour *noun* the time between sundown and dark. A filming term; according to Singleton, 'The light is very warm, the sky is a magical deep blue, and shadows are long' (*Filmmaker's Dictionary*, 1990) *US, 1960*

magic money machine *noun* an automated cash machine. Used widely in conversation since the 1990s *NEW ZEALAND, 2002*

magic mushie *noun* a hallucinogenic mushroom *AUSTRALIA, 1982*

magic mushroom *noun* any mushroom with an hallucinogenic effect – the most commonly grown and used in the UK is *Psilocybe Semilanceata* or Liberty Cap mushroom *US, 1968*

magic numbers used as a farewell. Referring to 73 and 88, citizens' band radio code for 'good wishes' *US, 1976*

magic roundabout *noun* used as an informal name for the system whereby a difficult prisoner is contantly moved from prison to prison. Named after *The Magic Roundabout*, a stop-motion animation children's and cult television programme first broadcast in the UK in 1965 *UK, 1996*

magic smoke *noun* marijuana *UK, 1998*

magic sponge *noun* a towel or sponge applied to injured players during a game who then have a miraculous recovery *AUSTRALIA, 2003*

magic up *verb* to improve, to enhance, to encourage *UK, 2003*

magic wand *noun* the penis *UK, 1969*

magistrate's court; magistrate's *noun* a drink of spirits; an alcoholic drink. Rhyming slang for SHORT *UK, 1992*

magnacious *adjective* excellent, great. An elaboration of 'magnificent' *US, 1997*

magnet *noun* a person who attracts the precedent thing or personality type *US, 1993*

Magnificent Mile *noun* a stretch of Michigan Avenue running from the river to Oak Street in Chicago, Illionois. A Chamber of Commerce phrase that took root in the vernacular *US, 1982*

Magnus Pike; magnus *noun* a lesbian. Rhyming slang for DYKE, formed from the name of a British scientist and television presenter *UK, 2003*

magoo *noun* in circus usage, a cream or custard pie thrown by clowns at each other *US, 1926*

magsman; maggs-man *noun* **1** a confidence trickster whose prime device is conversation *AUSTRALIA, 1877*. **2** a talkative person; a raconteur *AUSTRALIA, 1924*

mag wheel *noun* a racing car wheel made of magnesium alloy *AUSTRALIA, 1981*

maha *adjective* very large. From Sanskrit *INDIA, 1995*

maharishee *noun* marijuana *US, 1980s*

Mahatma Gandhi *noun* a shandy. Rhyming slang, formed from the name of the Indian leader, 1869–1948 *UK, 1992*

Mahatma Gandhi; mahatma *adjective* sexually aroused. Rhyming slang for RANDY, formed from the name of the great Indian leader and pacifist, 1889–1948 *UK, 2003*

mahogany bomber *noun* the desk which an office-bound pilot 'flies' *UK, 1981*

mahogany gaspipe *noun* used as a mock representation of intonations of Irish *IRELAND, 1992*

mahooha *noun* ridiculous political manoeuvres and pointless talk *US, 1930*

mahoot *noun* in bar dice games, a roll that produces no points for the player *US, 1971*

mahoska; hoska *noun* an addictive drug, especially heroin *US, 1949*

maid *noun* **1** a black woman (regardless of age or occupation). Offensive, demeaning *SOUTH AFRICA, 1961*. **2** female virginity. Also called 'maiden' *TRINIDAD AND TOBAGO, 1972*

maiden *noun* **1** in horse racing, a horse that has never won a race *US, 1951*. **2** by extension, a jockey who has never won a race *US, 1971*

maidenhead *noun* a woman's toilet. Punning on the hymen and HEAD as 'a toilet' *US, 1968*

maid training *noun* the process of instructing, and conditioning the behaviour of, a sexual submissive. The submissive's menial service becomes part of a sexual relationship (in which an element of transvestism is usually implied); used in a dominant prostitute's advertising matter *UK, 2003*

mail *noun* **1** an overheard conversation on citizens' band radio *US, 1976*. **2** in horse racing, information about a horse or race useful for wagering *AUSTRALIA, 1989*

mail-call; mail *noun* enemy mortar, rockets or artillery being received. Coined in World War I, still used by World War 2 veterans in Vietnam *US, 1919*

main *noun* any large blood vein *US, 1952*. ▶ **the main** to island dwellers off the coast of Maine, the mainland *US, 1975*

Main *noun* ▶ **the Main** St Laurent Street in Montreal. Even though St Catherine Street, running east and west through the centre, has become the main street of the city, St Laurent (or St Lawrence) was originally the centre of shopping, immigrant settlement and the garment district, and so it has held the name *CANADA, 2001*

main *verb* to inject a drug into a main vein *US, 1952*

main line *noun* **1** any large blood vein, especially the median cephalic vein *US, 1930s*. **2** a major vein used for the injection of narcotics, usually heroin *US, 1931*. **3** at a horse racing track, the area with the greatest concentration of mutual betting machines *US, 1951*. **4** the general population of a prison *US, 1967*

Main Line *nickname* the wealthy suburbs just to the west of Philadelphia, Pennsylvania, extending from Merion to Bryn Mawr to Paoli. From the Paoli Local commuter train that ran out of the main line of the now-defunct Pennsylvania Railroad, carrying businessmen to work and future lexicographers in blue wool jerseys with five white stripes on each arm to school *US, 1987*

mainline *verb* to inject drugs, especially heroin, into a main vein *US, 1938*

mainliner *noun* a drug user who injects the drug into a vein *US, 1934*

main man *noun* **1** an important man. From circus jargon *US, 1977*. **2** a pimp, in relation to a prostitute *US, 1985*

main pin *noun* a railway official *US, 1930*

main punch *noun* a man's favoured girlfriend *US, 1994*

main queen *noun* a man's primary girlfriend *US, 1948*

main squeeze *noun* a person's primary partner in romance *US, 1926*

mainstreeting *noun* the use of the main street of a town, especially by a politician, for campaigning *CANADA, 1959*

maintain *verb* ▶ **maintain your low tones** do not raise your voice at me. A phrase coined by writers of the 'Coneheads' skits on *Saturday Night Live* in the late 1970s, featuring three Remulakian aliens who lived quiet and normal lives in the suburbs of New Jersey. Most of the Remulakian phrases were too forced for everyday slang, such as 'molten lactate extract of hooved animals' for 'melted cheese', but a few such as this were temporarily in vogue *US, 1977*

main vein *noun* **1** the penis *US, 2001*. **2** the vagina. Usage is recorded as 'especially among drug addicts' *UK, 1984*. ▶ **stab in the main vein** from a male perspective, to have sex. Formed on MAIN VEIN (the vagina) *UK, 1984*

mainy *adjective* fearless, crazy *US, 2004*

mais oui *adverb* of course, certainly. An affected usage, adopted directly from French *mais oui* (but yes) *UK, 2002*

Maizie *noun* used as a term of address among male homosexuals *US, 1965*

maj *noun* majesty. An informal, generally affectionate, reduction *UK, 1994*

major *noun* a dependable, reliable person *US, 1956*

major *verb* ▶ **major in plumbing** in college, to take nothing but easy courses. An allusion to 'pipes' (easy courses) *US, 1955*

major *adjective* **1** very good *US, 1984*. **2** absolute. Used as an intensifier *AUSTRALIA, 1995*. **3** handsome, dressed well *TRINIDAD AND TOBAGO, 1967*

Major Dee *noun* a maître d'. Possibly influenced by 'major domo' *UK, 2000*

major-league *adjective* prominent, accomplished, prestigious. On 4th September 2000, US presidential candidate George W. Bush leaned to his running mate Dick Cheney at a campaign stop in Naperville, Illinois, and, pointing to a reporter, said 'There's Adam Clymner – major-league asshole from the *New York Times*'. 'Major-league' had major-league arrived *US, 1941*

major leagues *noun* the highest level of achievement in a field *US, 1951*

Major Loder *noun* soda, especially soda water. Rhyming slang, formed from the name of a famous racehorse owner in the early part of C20 *UK, 1961*

majorly *adverb* very much *US, 1983*

Major Stevens *noun* in betting odds, evens. Rhyming slang *UK, 1961*

mak *noun* a machete. Critically important during the Vietnam war for hacking through jungles *US, 1990*

makable *adjective* (used of a wave) in surfing, possible to catch for a ride *US, 1973*

make *noun* an identification *US, 1950*. ▶ **on the make 1** in search of sexual company *US, 1929*. **2** seeking any opportunity or profit *UK, 1992*. ▶ **put the make on** to try to seduce *US, 1963*

make *verb* **1** to identify (a person) *UK, 1906*. **2** in planespotting, to record ('collect') an aircraft *UK, 2003*. **3** to seduce or have sex with someone *US, 1923*. **4** to admit someone into membership in an organised crime organisation *US, 1964*. **5** to manage to catch and travel on a scheduled vehicle *UK, 1955*. **6** to fix a price. In stock market use *UK, 1895*. **7** to steal, to appropriate *UK, 1700*. ▶ **as pretty/clever/happy as they make them** used for indicating an extreme. Current examples (found in a quick search of the Internet, December 2003): 'as bad as they make them', 'as American as they make them' and 'as happy as they make them' *UK, 1896*. ▶ **make (a period of time)** to be sentenced to or to serve a jail sentence *TRINIDAD AND TOBAGO, 1904*. ▶ **make a break** to escape or make an attempted escape from prison *US, 1930*. ▶ **make a bubble; make a jail; make jail; make prison; make years** to be sentenced to or to serve a jail sentence *TRINIDAD AND TOBAGO, 1937*. ▶ **make a thing of; make a thing about** to make a fuss about something *UK, 1934*. ▶ **make a zeef** to show off *TRINIDAD AND TOBAGO, 2003*. ▶ **make ass** to blunder; to make a spectacle of yourself. Hawaiian youth usage *US, 1981*.

▶ **make fares** to work as a prostitute *TRINIDAD AND TOBAGO, 1987*. ▶ **make fart** to make life difficult for someone *TRINIDAD AND TOBAGO, 1990*. ▶ **make friends** (among women) to take a lesbian lover *TRINIDAD AND TOBAGO, 1960*. ▶ **make good** to succeed; to meet expectations *US, 1901*. ▶ **make hole** to drill for oil *US, 1984*. ▶ **make it 1** to have sex *US, 1952*. **2** to leave *US, 1913*. **3** to be accepted by *US, 1955*. **4** to be acceptable *US, 1955*. **5** to succeed, to become prosperous, to reach an objective *UK, 1885*. ▶ **make it up to** to compensate someone for a loss or a wrong that has been suffered *US, 1860*. ▶ **make like 1** to behave in a suggested manner. Used in conjunction with 'and' to join a noun and a verb in a pun *US, 1954*. **2** to behave in the manner of something, to act like *US, 1881*. ▶ **make like a boid** to leave. Teen slang *CANADA, 1946*. ▶ **make love** to steal *CANADA, 1988*. ▶ **make love to the lav** to vomit into a toilet bowl *AUSTRALIA, 1971*. ▶ **make nice** to be act politely *US, 1957*. ▶ **make no bones** without hesitation, to deal with or react to an awkward or unpleasant situation, no matter how difficult *UK, 1459*. ▶ **make one** to plan and carry out an escape attempt from prison *UK, 1974*. ▶ **make one out** to successfully escape from prison *UK, 1996*. ▶ **make smiles** to have sex *UK, 2003*. ▶ **make the hole** to rob drunks sleeping on underground platforms and in carriages *US, 1980*. ▶ **make the show** in motor racing with qualifying heats, to qualify for the race *US, 1993*. ▶ **make time** to flirt, to attempt to seduce *US, 1953*. ▶ **make tracks** to depart hurriedly *US, 1978*. ▶ **make with** to use, to bring into action *US, 1940*. ▶ **make your day** to make a highlight or moment of happiness in an ordinary day; to be the highlight *UK, 1907*

Make and Break engine *noun* a massive, one-cylinder boat motor with a flywheel. It is also known as a 'one-lunger' in Nova Scotia and Maine *CANADA, 1977*

make-believe *noun* pretence *UK, 1811*

make for *verb* to steal, to obtain *US, 1936*

make mine; make it *verb* used for denoting a requirement (a drink, details of an appointment, an amount, a quantity, a price), generally in response to a question or a proposal *US, 1883*

make my day used as a jocular challenge. The phrase entered the popular lexicon in 1983 as a line uttered by the Clint Eastwood character 'Dirty Harry' Callahan in the film *Sudden Impact US, 1985*

make out *verb* **1** to kiss with passion and in a sustained fashion *US, 1949*. **2** to pretend *UK, 1659*

makeover *noun* a complete transformation of fashion and hairstyle *US, 1999*

make the scene with 18 used as a jingle to remind US troops in Vietnam to limit their M-16 rifles to 18 rounds because the rifle sometimes jammed when loaded to its 20-round capacity *US, 1991*

make-up *noun* the final result of any event that is the subject of spread-betting *UK, 2001*

makeup! used as a nonce interjection. Popularised by Milton Berle in the early days of US television; the running gag was that Berle would be knocked off his feet with sacks of flour or a makeup man with an oversized makeup powder puff after mentioning the word 'makeup'. A meaningless catchphrase that swept the nation *US, 1951*

-making *suffix* used to create a word that describes something as having the ability to cause the condition of a prefixed adjective. A linguistic formula credited to the author Evelyn Waugh, 1903–66 *UK, 1930*

makings *noun* the tobacco and rolling paper needed to make a cigarette *US, 1905*

mal *noun* in parachuting, a *mal*function *UK, 2002*

Malabar Hilton *nickname* the Long Bay Correctional Complex, Sydney *AUSTRALIA, 1988*

malad *noun* a *malad*justed child. Used by social workers *UK, 1980*

malarkey; malarky; mullarkey *noun* nonsense *US, 1929*

Malcolm Scott *adjective* hot. Rhyming slang, of theatrical origins, formed from the name of a female impersonator, 1872–1929 *UK, 1960*

Malcolm X *noun* a tablet of MDMA, the recreational drug best known as ecstasy. Uses the adopted name of Malcolm Little, 1925–1965, a leading figure in the US black civil rights movement, to disguise X (ECSTASY) *UK, 1995*

male beaver *noun* featuring shots of the naked male genitals *US, 1969*

malehouse *noun* a homosexual brothel *US, 1963*

male twigs *noun* low quality marijuana *US, 1979*

malky *noun* **1** a safety razor used as a weapon; hence an improvised weapon (a broken bottle, etc). Possibly rhyming slang, based on Malcolm (Malky) Fraser, for 'razor' *UK: SCOTLAND, 1973*. **2** a cut given from a razor as an act of violence; a blow; a beating. From the previous sense *UK: SCOTLAND, 1973*

malky *verb* to attack and cut someone with a razor; to stab. From the noun sense *UK: SCOTLAND, 1985*

mallard *noun* a hundred-dollar note *US, 1985*

mall crawl *noun* an outing to a shopping centre, slowly moving from shop to shop. A play on PUB-CRAWL or BAR-HOP with a rhyme to boot *US, 1996*

mall crawler *noun* a person who spends their spare time at shopping centres *US, 1993*

mallee *adjective* ▶ **fit as a mallee bull** extremely fit and healthy *AUSTRALIA, 1960*

mallet *verb* to smash, to defeat. Used by the SAS in the Falkland Islands, 1982 *UK, 1982*

mallethead *noun* a fool, a stupid person, a numbskull. A variation of MULLETHEAD *US, 1960*

mallie *noun* a young person who spends their free time at shopping centres *US, 1985*

malling *noun* the practice of spending hours at a shopping centre, socialising with other young people *US, 1989*

Mall Madonna *noun* a girl who spends a lot of time in shopping centres *CANADA, 2002*

mallowpuff Maori *noun* a Maori student who excels in school. From a branded chocolate-covered marshmallow biscuit – brown on the outside, white on the inside *NEW ZEALAND, 1998*

mall rat *noun* a young person who spends a great deal of time at a shopping centre *US, 1982*

malpalant *adjective* inclined to gossip. From the French *mal parlant* (speaking poorly) *TRINIDAD AND TOBAGO, 2003*

malt *noun* a Maltese; Maltese *UK, 1959*

malt sandwich *noun* a beer *AUSTRALIA, 1968*

mam *noun* **1** a mother, your mother. Probably early C16; mainly childish now, but earlier usage was also familiar or vulgar *UK, 1573*. **2** a lesbian *UK, 1962*

mama *noun* **1** used as a term of address towards a woman *US, 1959*. **2** a young woman, a woman. Originally Black usage. Also spelt 'mamma' *US, 1917*. **3** in motorcycle clubs and gangs, a female who is available to all the gang members and attached to none *US, 1965*. **4** a sexually promiscuous female *UK, 1977*. **5** in a lesbian couple, the more traditionally feminine partner *US, 1941*. **6** used as a disparaging term of address for an Indian female *SINGAPORE, 2002*. **7** in a deck of playing cards, a queen *US, 1988*. **8** the lead aeroplane in a combat flight formation *US, 1986*

mama! used for expressing surprise, especially by women *TRINIDAD AND TOBAGO, 2003*

mama bear *noun* a policewoman. A feminisation of BEAR (the police) *US, 1976*

mama coca *noun* cocaine *US, 1984*

mama-jammer *noun* used as a euphemism for 'motherfucker' *US, 1969*

mamaloos; mamaloosh *adjective* dead, dying. The word comes from Chinook jargon *memaloost* (dead) *CANADA, 1956*

mama man *noun* an effeminate man, heterosexual or homosexual *TRINIDAD AND TOBAGO, 1973*

mamapoule *noun* an effeminate, demanding man. From the French for 'mother hen' *TRINIDAD AND TOBAGO, 1928*

mamary *noun* a boy who will not leave his mother's protection *TRINIDAD AND TOBAGO, 1978*

mama-san *noun* in Southeast Asia usage, a woman whose age demands respect, especially a brothel madam. The Japanese honorific *san* added to English 'mama' *US, 1946*

mama shop *noun* a small neighbourhood grocery shop, especially one owned by Indians *SINGAPORE, 2002*

mama's lane *noun* the passing lane of a motorway. So named because the trucker, anxious to see his wife, is driving fast and passing cars *US, 1976*

mama's little helper *noun* in shuffleboard, a score that is accidentally provided to you by an opponent *US, 1967*

mama's mellow *noun* the calming effect of secobarbital (brand name Seconal ™), a barbiturate *US, 1971*

mamby pamby *noun* a stupid man *TRINIDAD AND TOBAGO, 1956*

mammaries *noun* the female breasts. After the conventional sense of 'mammary' (relating to the female breast) *UK, 1967*

mammoth *adjective* huge. The stuff of advertising: 'MAMMOTH RUG SALE!' (but who'd want a mammoth rug?) *UK, 1937*

mamms; mams *noun* the female breasts. A reduction of MAMMARIES *UK, 2003*

mammy *noun* **1** a mother *UK, 1523*. **2** in a striptease act, a woman, usually older, who waits backstage, catching a stripper's clothing as she flings it offstage *US, 1981*. **3** the most; the ultimate example. An English language version of the famous Arabic MOTHER OF ALL *US, 1971*. ▶ **the mammy** my mother. There is no indefinite article in Irish. The definite article in Hiberno-English, following and sometimes extending the usage of the indefinite article 'an' in Irish, has some distinctive functions which mark it out from standard English, for example, 'Better give her the both o' them', (Roddy Doyle, *The Van*, 1991) *IRELAND, 1996*

mammy *adjective* a lot of. Placed after the noun *US, 1992*

mammy-fugger *noun* used as a euphemism for 'motherfucker' *US, 1998*

mammy-jammer *noun* used as a euphemism for 'motherfucker' *US, 1973*

mammyjamming *adjective* used as a euphemism for the intensifier 'motherfucking' *US, 1946*

mammy mine *noun* wine. Glasgow rhyming slang *UK: SCOTLAND, 1985*

mammy-screwing *adjective* used as a euphemism for 'motherfucking' *US, 1963*

mammy-sucker *noun* used as a euphemism for 'motherfucker' *US, 1972*

mampy *noun* a buxom, generously voluptuous woman *JAMAICA, 1994*

mampy *adjective* (of a woman) buxom, generously proportioned, Rubenesque *JAMAICA, 1994*

man *verb* in team sports, to defend an opponent man-to-man *US, 1972*

man; mandy *noun* **1** me, myself, I. English gypsy use, from Romany *mandi* *UK, 2000*. **2** a drug dealer *US, 1942*. **3** in a deck of playing cards, a king *US, 1988*. ▶ **a man's got to do what a man's got to do; a man's gotta do what a man's gotta do** homespun philosophy in use as a catchphrase. Jocular *US, 1977*. ▶ **a man's not a camel** I am thirsty and require a drink *AUSTRALIA, 1998*. ▶ **the man** a police officer; an authority figure *US, 1928*. ▶ **yer only man** something that possesses a unique quality *IRELAND, 1997*

man and man *noun* people in general *JAMAICA, 1989*

man and wife *noun* a knife. Rhyming slang *UK, 1925*

man boobs *noun* flabby chest protrusions of an overweight man *AUSTRALIA, 2002*

Manc *noun* **1** Manchester in northwest England *UK, 2002*. **2** a Mancunian; a native of Manchester *UK, 1999*

Manc *adjective* Mancunian, of Manchester *UK, 2001*

Manch *noun* Manchester *UK, 2000*

Manchester City; manchester *noun* the female breast. Rhyming slang for 'titty' (TIT) noted as 'rare' *UK, 1961*

Manchester United *noun* a red and black capsule of MDMA, the recreational drug best known as ecstasy. Designed and branded in tribute to the football team, but someone got the team colours wrong *UK, 2002*

Mancy *adjective* Mancunian, of Manchester. Perhaps, given Manchester's reputation for wet weather, punning deliberately on MANKY (bad) *UK, 2002*

man dem *noun* male friends. Used by black urban youths *UK, 2004*

M and G track *noun* in a pornographic film, additions to the sound track amplifying moans and groans *US, 1991*

mandie *noun* a tablet of the recreational drug methaqualone, best known as Quaaludes™. From the trade name Mandrax™ *US, 1985*

M and M *noun* any tablet drugs used for recreational purposes: amphetamine, barbiturate, MDMA, the recreational drug best known as ecstasy. Named for M&Ms (branded in the US since 1940s) the candy-coated chocolate sweets which, in appearance, are similar to multi-coloured pills *US, 1977*

mandoo-ed *adjective* drunk *UK, 2002*

man down! used in prison for alerting the guards that a prisoner has been injured or fallen ill *US, 1990*

mandrake *noun* **1** a tablet of the recreational drug methaqualone, best known as Quaaludes™. From Mandrax™, the trade name for a synthetic non-barbiturate sedative consisting of methaqualone and a small amount of the antihistamine diphenhydramine *US, 1985*. **2** a sexually aggressive male homosexual *US, 1978*

mandy *noun* a tablet of Mandrax™ a branded tranquillizer *UK, 1970* ▷ *see:* MAN

mane *noun* a streak of unmown hay left in the field after it has been cut *CANADA, 1992*

man-eater *noun* **1** a woman with a strong sexual appetite. A figurative application of the term for dangerous big cats *UK, 1906*. **2** a homosexual man *US, 1979*

man fat *noun* semen *UK, 1974*

Manfred Mann *noun* a tan, a suntan. Glasgow rhyming slang, formed from the successful 1960s pop group and the South African musician who gave his group his name *UK: SCOTLAND, 1996*

man Friday *noun* a black soldier who curried favour from white superiors and thereby avoided combat *US, 1991*

man from Cairo *noun* a social security/benefits cheque. Glasgow rhyming slang for GIRO *UK: SCOTLAND, 1996*

man from the Pru *noun* a cocaine dealer. A play on the UK investment firm Prudential Building Society's advertising campaign and Peru as a source country for much of the world's cocaine *UK, 1983*

manga *noun* a comic book or graphic novel. One of the few Japanese words to be transplanted into English-speaking slang, thanks in large part to the proliferation of pornographic websites on the Internet *JAPAN, 1993*

manged *adjective* damaged without hope of repair *US, 1991*

mangia-cake *noun* a white person, especially British, but very North American (said by an Italian) *CANADA, 1998*

mangle *noun* a bicycle *AUSTRALIA, 1941*

mangle and wringer *noun* a (not especially talented) singer. Rhyming slang *UK, 1992*

mangled *adjective* drunk or drug-intoxicated *UK, 2001*

mango *noun* a fifty-dollar note. From the orange colour *NEW ZEALAND, 1998*

mango head *noun* an oval-shaped head *TRINIDAD AND TOBAGO, 1994*

mango madness *noun* in tropical Australia, a feeling of agitation and oppression experienced leading up to the monsoon season *AUSTRALIA, 1984*

Manhattan silver; Manhattan white; New York City silver; Subway silver *noun* marijuana. Originally, 'a flight of fancy', a genetic variation cultivated from seeds which, having been flushed

into the New York City sewage system, were white or silver. A highly potent and purely fictional urban myth; now, also, just another synonym for 'marijuana' *US, 1975*

manhaul *noun* in Antarctica, an overland trip where a sledge is hauled by people, not vehicles *ANTARCTICA, 1986*

manhole *noun* the vagina *US, 1916*

manhole cover *noun* a brother. Rhyming slang for 'bruvver', perhaps also playing on MANHOLE (the vagina) hence, a playfully insulting CUNT *UK, 1992*

manhood *noun* the penis. Euphemism *UK, 1997*

man hunt *noun* a search for a male as a sexual companion. Humorous use of a term originally meaning 'a search for a criminal or escaped convict' *US, 1996*

man-hunter *noun* a woman, especially a spinster or a widow, particularly one who has, or is reputed to have, a strong sexual appetite *UK, 1961*

maniac *noun* a railway mechanic *US, 1930*

Maniblowba *nickname* the Canadian province of Manitoba. So named because of the cold, windy winters *CANADA, 2002*

manicou-man *noun* an effeminate man, especially a homosexual *TRINIDAD AND TOBAGO, 1996*

manicure *verb* to prepare marijuana for smoking, trimming the leaves and stems and removing foreign objects *US, 1938*

manifestation *noun* in Quebec, a demonstration. In a province marked by a tradition of public service strikes, this unconventional use of a French word has had much use for a long time *CANADA, 2002*

Manila General *noun* used as a humorous if xenophobic nickname for any hospital with a largely Filipino staff *US, 1989*

man in blue *noun* a police officer, *1976*

man in Kokomo *noun* in horse racing, any mysterious source of inside information on a horse or race *US, 1951*

man in the boat *noun* ▷ *see:* LITTLE MAN IN A BOAT

man in the moon *noun* a madman, a fool. Rhyming slang for LOON *UK, 1992*

man in the white coat *noun* a supposed employee of an insane asylum. Now generally in the plural: 'men in white coats' *AUSTRALIA, 1961*

Manisnowba *nickname* the Canadian province of Manitoba. Home to long, cold winters *CANADA, 2002*

Mank *noun* a person from Manchester, a *Mancunian UK, 2000*

manked in *adjective* confined indoors by extreme bad weather *ANTARCTICA, 1986*

manky *adjective* **1** poor quality, inferior; dirty. Possibly from French *manque* (a deficiency) *UK, 1958*. **2** (of weather) bad. A narrowing of the general sense *ANTARCTICA, 1989*. **3** drunk. Possibly deriving from the previous sense, thus 'under the weather' (tipsy) *UK, 2002*

man-love *noun* male homosexuality. A very arch euphemism *UK, 2003*

manly Alice *noun* a masculine homosexual man *UK, 2002*

man-man *noun* a male who exhibits a high degree of virility *US, 1999*

manna *noun* easy-pickings; a heaven-sent opportunity. A biblical allusion *UK, 2001*

manny *noun* a tablet of Mandrax™, a branded tranquillizer. A variation of MANDY *UK, 1968*

mano *noun* used as an embellished 'man' as a term of address *US, 1967*

mano a mano *noun* a one-on-one confrontation. Made quite famous in the US by Colonel Oliver North during the moral collapse of the Reagan presidency, the Iran-Contra debacle of 1986–87. Adapted from bull-fighting, where the term refers to a competition between two matadors and two or more bulls each *US, 1968*

man of the cloth *noun* in pool, a skilled player who makes a living betting on his ability *US, 1990*

man oil *noun* semen *US, 1949*

man o Manishewitz! used as a jocular, mild oath. From a commercial for Manishewitz kosher wine *US, 1992*

man on the land *noun* a farmer or other rural worker *AUSTRALIA, 1911*

man on the moon *noun* a spoon. Rhyming slang *UK, 1998*

manor *noun* **1** a district designated to a specified police authority *UK, 1924*. **2** the area where you are born, or where you live and/or are well known *UK, 1962*

man overboard! **1** in dominoes, used for announcing the fact that a player is forced to draw a piece *US, 1959*. **2** in craps in American casinos, used for announcing that the dice or a die are off the table *US, 1985*

man o'war *noun* a bore. Rhyming slang *UK, 1992*

manscaping *noun* the clipping, shaving and shaping of male body hair for aesthetic effect. Popularised in the US, and then the UK, by the varying national productions of television programme *Queer Eye for the Straight Guy US, 2004*

man-size *adjective* difficult *US, 1945*

man's man *noun* a police informer. From THE MAN (the police) *US, 1972*

Manson lamps *noun* a look full of hate, a murderous look. Formed from a reference to US serial killer Charles Manson and LAMP (the eye) *US, 1999*

manteca *noun* heroin *UK, 2003*

man teef *noun* a woman who 'steals' another's man. Combines 'man' and TEEF (to steal); current in south London according to *Johnny Vaughan Tonight*, 13th February 2002 *UK, 2002*

manthrax *noun* unfaithful men. A combination of 'man' and 'anthrax' coined for *Sex and the City*, a late 1990s television comedy *US, 2002*

mantlepiece *noun* ▶ **you don't look at the mantelpiece when you're poking the fire** a semi-proverbial catchphrase that means a woman's looks are irrelevant during sexual intercourse *UK, 1961*

manto *noun* a condom. Teen slang, after South African Health Minister Manto Tshabalala-Msimang *SOUTH AFRICA, 2003*

man-trap *noun* an attractive, seductive woman *US, 1963*

manual exercises *noun* masturbation *US, 1964*

manual release *noun* manual stimulation of a man's genitals *US, 1996*

Man United are playing at home the bleed period of the menstrual cycle. The Manchester United football team play in a red strip *UK, 2000*

man upstairs *noun* God. Always used with 'the' *US, 1948*

man with the minties *noun* in horse racing, a mythical, anonymous person responsible for a series of bad tips about horses and races *AUSTRALIA, 1989*

Maoriland *nickname* New Zealand *AUSTRALIA, 1859*

Maori overdrive *noun* coasting downhill in neutral *NEW ZEALAND, 1998*

Maori screwdriver *noun* a hammer, especially when used on screws *NEW ZEALAND, 1998*

Maori sidestep *noun* in rugby, a direct confrontation with a potential tackler, relying on brute force rather than guile or finesse *NEW ZEALAND, 1998*

Maori splice *noun* any time-saving solution to a problem *NEW ZEALAND, 1998*

Maori time *noun* a sensibility that is not consumed with worry about punctuality *NEW ZEALAND, 2002*

map *noun* **1** the face *US, 1899*. **2** a musical score; a piece of sheet music *US, 1970*. **3** a cheque *US, 1979*

map *verb* to hit, to strike *US, 1989*

Mapes *nickname* the Maples Inn, a popular bar and music venue in Pointe Claire, Quebec. *CANADA, 2002*

maple key *noun* the maple tree seed, which has wings so as to make it twirl in the wind *CANADA, 1989*

map of Tasmania *noun* the female pubic hair or pubic region *AUSTRALIA, 1978*

map of Tassie *noun* the female pubic hair or pubic region *AUSTRALIA, 1978*

maquillage; maquiage *noun* makeup, cosmetics. From French *maquiller* (to make up the face) *UK, 1992*

maracas *noun* the testicles. Rhyming slang for KNACKERS *UK, 1998*

marathon *noun* **1** in horse racing, any race that is longer than a mile and a quarter *US, 1976*. **2** any amphetamine, methamphetamine or other central nervous system stimulant *US, 1980*

marauder *noun* a surfer who is indifferent to safety, if not reckless *US, 1985*

marble *noun* **1** a slow-witted person. Teen slang *US, 1958*. **2** a tablet of ethchlorvynol (trade name Placidyl™), a central nervous system depressant *US, 1986*. ▶ **make your marble good** to improve one's prospects *AUSTRALIA, 1928*

Marble Arch *noun* starch. Rhyming slang, formed from a famous London landmark *UK, 1998*

marble halls; marbles *noun* the testicles. Rhyming slang for BALLS, perhaps formed after an earlier use of 'marbles' in the same sense (but inspired by a similarity of shape and size) *UK, 1992*

Marblehead turkey *noun* salt cod *US, 1955*

marble orchard *noun* a graveyard *US, 1925*

marbles *noun* **1** the testicles *US, 1916*. **2** dice *US, 1962*. **3** money, cash, salary. Theatrical *UK, 1864*. ▶ **all the marbles** used as a symbol of complete success *US, 1924*. ▶ **hand in your marbles** to give up; to die. Variant forms are built on the verb: 'toss in your marbles', 'throw in your marbles, etc' *AUSTRALIA, 1908*. ▶ **in the marbles** in motor racing, in the outside portion of a curve where there is less traction *US, 1992*. ▶ **lose your marbles** to become insane, to lose your mind *US, 1902*

marbles and conkers; marbles *adjective* mad, crazy. Rhyming slang for BONKERS, formed from two games played by children, but probably inspired by phrases like 'lose your marbles' (to become mad) *UK, 1992*

marblish *adjective* displaying a lack of sportsmanship when losing *TRINIDAD AND TOBAGO, 2003*

marcel *noun* a hairstyle characterised by deep, regular waves made by a heated curling iron. After Marcel Grateau (1852–1936), a French hairdresser *UK, 1963*

marching dust *noun* cocaine *UK, 1998*

marching orders *noun* a dismissal from employment or romantic involvement. From the military use *US, 1856*

marching powder *noun* cocaine. A shortening of BOLIVIAN, COLUMBIAN or PERUVIAN MARCHING POWDER *US, 1984*

Marcia *noun* in horse racing, odds of 9–1. Rhyming slang based on Marcia Hines, an extremely popular singer in Australia in the mid-1970s *AUSTRALIA, 1989*

marconi *noun* an eavesdropper *UK, 2001*

mardy *adjective* sulky, moody. English dialect creeping into the mainstream via television programmes like *Coronation Street UK, 1903*

mardy-arse *noun* a sulker. From the dialect word MARDY (sulky) *UK, 1999*

mardy-arsed *adjective* sulky, whining, 'spoilt'. A combination of dialect word MARDY (sulky) with '-arsed' (having the characteristics of) *UK, 2002*

mare *noun* **1** something good that is hard to believe, a dream. Amends conventional 'nightmare' (a bad dream) and slang 'nightmare' (something bad) *UK, 1997*. **2** something undesirable *IRELAND, 2001*. **3** an unpleasant, bad-tempered woman, especially as an insulting term of address *UK, 1303*

mare and foal *noun* a bankroll. Rhyming slang *NEW ZEALAND, 1998*

mares' nest *noun* a bar for women and their escorts *NEW ZEALAND, 1953*

marga *adjective* skinny *UK, 2005*

Margaret Rose; margaret *noun* the nose. Rhyming slang *UK, 1998*

margarine legs *noun* used as a symbol of a woman's sexual availability *AUSTRALIA, 1987*

Margarita *noun* marijuana *US, 1979*

Margate sand *noun* the hand. Rhyming slang, formed from a seaside resort on the East Coast of England *UK, 1992*

marge *noun* margarine *UK, 1970s*

Marge *noun* the passive, 'feminine' partner in a lesbian relationship *US, 1956*

mari *noun* a marijuana cigarette. A clipping of 'marijuana' *US, 1933*

Maria *noun* in a deck of playing cards, the queen of spades *US, 1950*

Mariah Carey *adjective* scary. Rhyming slang, formed on the name of the popular US singer (b.1970) *UK, 2004*

Maria Monk; maria *noun* semen. Rhyming slang for SPUNK, based on the name of the author of *Awful Disclosures*, 1836, a popular erotic book of its time *UK, 2002*

maricon *noun* a homosexual man. Spanish slang on loan to American slang *TRINIDAD AND TOBAGO, 1950*

Marie Corelli; marie *noun* television; a television. Rhyming slang for TELLY, formed from the pen name of romantic novelist Mary Mackay, 1855–1924 *UK, 1971*

marihooch; marihoochie; marihootee; marihootie *noun* marijuana *US, 1971*

marijuana martini *noun* marijuana smoke blown into, and then inhaled from, a chilled glass *US, 2001*

marimba *noun* marijuana *UK, 2001*

marinate *verb* **1** to relax, to idle *US, 2000*. **2** to ponder, to debate internally *US, 2002*

Marine Tiger *noun* a recent arrival in New York City from Puerto Rico. From the name of a converted C4 troopship that brought many early Puerto Rican immigrants to the US *US, 1952*

marish and parish *noun* everyone *TRINIDAD AND TOBAGO, 1987*

mariweegee *noun* marijuana. A jocular mispronunciation *US, 1994*

marji *noun* marijuana *AUSTRALIA, 1953*

marjoon *noun* a sweet confection with marijuana as a major ingredient *ALGERIA, 1970*

Marjorie *noun* marijuana *US, 1979*

mark *noun* **1** a victim, a potential victim of a swindle *UK, 1749*. **2** a number bet on in the lottery game whe-whe *TRINIDAD AND TOBAGO, 1909*

mark *verb* **1** in casino gambling, to place in a stack chips equal to the amount of marker (a loan) extended to a gambler *US, 1980*. **2** to realise, to see, to understand *UK, 1970*. ▶ **mark your card** to inform; to warn. From the marking of race cards *UK, 1956*

marked wheel *noun* a rigged roulette wheel *US, 1975*

marker *noun* **1** in a casino or gambling enterprise, an advance with an IOU; by extension, any debt or obligation *US, 1887*. **2** a person who bets on a number in the lottery game whe-whe *TRINIDAD AND TOBAGO, 1930*. **3** a vehicle's licence plate *CANADA, 1949*

market price *noun* the going rate for sex with a prostitute *US, 1982*

Mark Ramprakash *noun* a urination. Rhyming slang for SLASH, formed from the name of the English cricketer (b.1969) *UK, 2003*

marks *noun* signs of intravenous drug use, such as scars or abcesses *US, 1983*

Marks and Sparks *nickname* the retailer Marks and Spencer *UK, 1964*

Marlboro country *noun* a remote place; the wilderness *US, 1968*

Marlboro man *noun* a rugged, masculine, handsome cowboy type. Derived from the decades-long advertising campaign for Marlboro cigarettes, featuring ultra-masculine cowboys smoking *US, 1969*

Marley *noun* a marijuana cigarette. From Bob Marley, Rastafarian and marijuana-lover *US, 1997*

Marley's collie *noun* a potent variety of marijuana, a hybrid of Jamaican sensimillia. Named in memory of reggae musician Bob Marley (1945–81), a Rastafarian; COLLIE (marijuana) *JAMAICA, 1990s*

Marlie-Butt *noun* a cigarette *AUSTRALIA, 1996*

marmalade dropper *noun* something shocking, surprising or upsetting, especially a newspaper article. From the idea that someone, especially a newspaper reader, will be so stunned that breakfast may fall from the fingers *UK, 2003*

Marmite *noun* excrement; hence, rubbish. Rhyming slang for SHITE, formed on the name of a branded yeast extract – a brown paste which is apparently an acquired taste *UK, 1998*

Marmite driller; Marmite miner *noun* a male homosexual. Pejorative; a reference to anal sex, based on MARMITE (excrement) *UK, 2003*

Marmite motorway *noun* the rectum. From MARMITE (excrement) *UK, 2003*

Marmon *noun* morphine *US, 1945*

maroc *adjective* extremely drunk. A shortening of the Glasgow pronunciation of MIRACULOUS *UK: SCOTLAND, 1985*

maroon *noun* a moron. A malapropism that emphasises the point being made *US, 1941*

marquee player *noun* a leading or pre-eminent professional athlete with the ability to attract a large audience *US, 1984*

Marrakesh *noun* a variety of Moroccan hashish *UK, 2003*

marriage *noun* in car manufacturing, the installation of the powertrain (the engine, transmission, pinion, ring and differential gears) *US, 1993*

Marrickville Mercedes *noun* in Sydney, any of various cars popular with New Australians. From Marrickville, a suburb with a high population of New Australians *AUSTRALIA, 1987*

married *adjective* **1** handcuffed together *US, 1962*. **2** in trucking, part of a two-driver team *US, 1971*. **3** (used of opium) adulterated with foreign substances *US, 1956*

married quarters *noun* in prison, the section where men who prefer to adopt a gay lifestyle tend to congregate *UK, 2000*

married to Mary Fist *adjective* obsessed with masturbating *US, 1950*

marry *noun* ▶ **marry under bamboo** to be married in Hindu rites *GUYANA, 1996*

marry *verb* in police work, to serve as partners *US, 1992*

marry and bury *verb* (of a minister of the local church) to carry a parishioner through life's big events *CANADA, 1978*

marryjuwanna *noun* marijuana. A less common example of the many personifications of marijuana intended as humorous *US, 1970*

marry money *verb* to wed a wealthy man or woman *UK, 1858*

Mars and Venus; mars *noun* the penis. Rhyming slang *UK, 1992*

Mars Bar; mars *noun* **1** the penis. Extended from the shortened form of rhyming slang MARS AND VENUS (the penis), playing on the name of a famous branded item of confectionery that helps you 'work, rest and play', apparently *UK, 1992*. **2** a scar. Rhyming slang, after a popular chocolate confection introduced to the UK in 1932 *UK, 1985*

marsh *noun* in soda fountain usage, a marshmallow *US, 1946*

marshmallow *noun* a pillow *US, 1976*

marshmallow red; marshmallow *noun* a barbiturate, a central nervous system depressant *US, 1977*

marshmallows *noun* **1** the female breasts *US, 1971*. **2** the testicles *US, 1971*

mart *noun* the finger. All that remains of old rhyming slang 'Martin-Le-Grand; martin' (the hand); recorded in gay use about 1970 *UK, 1984*

mart cover *noun* a glove. From MARTINI (the hand) *UK, 2002*

Martens *noun* heavy-duty boots designed for industrial use and subsequently adopted as fashionwear, initially by skinheads and bootboys, then as a general fashion item for either sex. An abbreviation of the brand name Doctor Martens™ *UK, 2000*

martin-eye *noun* a martini. A jocular embellishment *US, 1969*

Martin Harvey *noun* an act of pretence intended to mislead. Circus, etymology unknown *UK, 1953*

martini noun **1** a ring UK, 2002. **2** the hand; the arm. May be abbreviated to 'mart' UK, 1992. ▶ **dry martini** the left hand. Based on the popular branded drink UK, 2002. ▶ **sweet martini** the right hand. Based on the popular branded drink UK, 2002

Marty Wilde noun mild ale. Rhyming slang, from the stage-name of a singer (b.1939) who had a number of hit records in the late 1950s and early 60s, when mild ale was also a popular choice UK, 1992

marvel noun an impressive person. Also commonly used ironically AUSTRALIA, 1956

marvellous Melbourne nickname the city of Melbourne, Australia's second biggest city AUSTRALIA, 1885

marvy adjective marvellous US, 1931

marvy-groovy adjective bad. A combination of two clichéd adjectives for 'good', meaning 'bad' US, 1967

Mary noun **1** an Australian Aboriginal, Papuan or Islander woman AUSTRALIA, 1830. **2** any woman of Indian descent. Offensive, though not originally intended to be so SOUTH AFRICA, 1927. **3** any black woman, especially a domestic worker; any non-white woman. Offensive, demeaning; from the previous sense SOUTH AFRICA, 1952. **4** used as a term of address from one male homosexual to another US, 1925. **5** a homosexual man who is a Catholic UK, 2002. **6** marijuana. Simply being on first name terms with MARY JANE, MARY WARNER and many other similar personifications of marijuana. Also written as lower case US, 1952. **7** morphine US, 1945

Mary and Johnny noun marijuana. A playful personification of marijuana US, 1935

Mary Ann noun **1** a fan (for cooling the air). Rhyming slang UK, 1992. **2** marijuana. A personification based on varying the vowel-sounds in 'marijuana', So may also appear as Maryanne' or Mary Anner' US, 1936

Mary Decker noun a fast-moving police vehicle, especially an armoured vehicle; a minibus, especially one made by Mitsubishi. Township slang; after the US athlete (b.1958) who failed to win a 1984 Olympic medal in the 3,000 meters, as a result of an incident involving South African athlete, Zola Budd (who was actually running for the UK) SOUTH AFRICA, 1985

Mary-do-you-wanna-dance noun marijuana UK, 2000

Mary Ellen man noun a pickpocket who distracts the victim by telling a sexually charged story US, 1976

Mary Ellens noun large female breasts. Rhyming slang for MELONS; described as 'fairly modern' by Ray Puxley, Cockney Rabbit, 1992, but surely an ironic reference to the music hall song of some 80 years earlier: 'I'm Shy, Mary Ellen, I'm Shy' UK, 1992

Mary Fist noun used as a personification of male masturbation US, 1950

Mary Green; the Mary noun in any suit of cards, the Queen. Rhyming slang UK, 1992

Mary Jane noun **1** marijuana. From the disputed presumption that marijuana is formed of two Mexican Spanish names: Maria and Juan or Juanita, hence Mary Jane, and many variants, such as Mary J, Mary Jonas, Mary Juana and so on US, 1928. **2** cocaine. Rhyming slang UK, 1996

Marylou noun glue. Rhyming slang UK, 1992

Mary Rose noun a nose, especially a notably large specimen. Rhyming slang, apparently formed from the name of a sunken ship which was raised with much hoop-la in 1982 UK, 1998

Mary unit noun a motorcyle police officer US, 2001

Mary Warner; Mary Warmer; Mary Weaver; Mary Werner; Mary Worner noun marijuana. Giving a feminine identity by mispronunciation US, 1933

Mary Worthless noun an older homosexual man US, 1979

masacree noun a massacre UK, 1823

masala relationship noun a romantic relationship between a black man and an Indian woman. From the film Mississippi Masala, alluding to the spice mixture used in Indian cooking TRINIDAD AND TOBAGO, 1994

Masarati noun an improvised pipe for smoking crack cocaine, made from a plastic bottle US, 1992

mash noun **1** mashed potato. Also variant 'mashed' UK, 1923. **2** a romantic infatuation; a sweetheart US, 1877. **3** any homemade liquor US, 2002

mash verb **1** to beat up, to 'beat to a pulp'. Derives from conventional 'mash' (to crush, smash utterly) US, 1872. **2** to flirt aggressively US, 1877. **3** to go away. Usually used as a command to dogs TRINIDAD AND TOBAGO, 1956. **4** to pass, to hand to someone, to give US, 1944

mash and dash verb to kiss and run US, 1996

mashed adjective **1** drunk US, 1942. **2** marijuana-intoxicated. Extending the previous sense, 1997. **3** astonished US, 1968

mashed potato transmission noun in the used car business, a worn, loose, mushy automatic transmission US, 1997

mashed up adjective damaged, 1997

masheer adjective on Prince Edward Island, used for describing a garment CANADA, 1988

masher noun **1** an attractive man IRELAND, 1999. **2** an unsophisticated flirt US, 1973. **3** a person who takes sexual pleasure from physical contact with strangers in crowded places US, 1875

mash list noun a tally of all those with whom you have had sex US, 1996

mash mouth adjective toothless TRINIDAD AND TOBAGO, 1987

mash out verb to complete US, 1973

mashup noun a creative remixing of separate pieces of recorded dance music UK, 2002

mash up verb **1** to beat up, to thrash UK, 1999. **2** (of a disc jockey) to mix dance records together UK, 1996

mask noun **1** a tight, stretched face resulting from extensive cosmetic surgery US, 1997. **2** oversized sunglasses US, 1962

mason noun **1** an extremely frugal person. A reference to stone walls, a methaphor for frugality US, 1950. **2** a male homosexual who takes the active role in sex US, 1949

mass noun a lot of, a great many US, 1994

mass adjective a lot of US, 1981

Massa Charlie noun used as a stereotype of the dominant white male in relation to blacks US, 1965

Massachusetts driver noun in the northeastern US, an inconsiderate and dangerous driver US, 1975

massa day done! used for reminding someone that the colonial era and slavery are a thing of the past TRINIDAD AND TOBAGO, 1961

massage noun sexual services. A euphemism so well known that a legitimate masseuse may hesitate to announce his or her profession US, 2001

massage verb to kill. Vietnam war usage US, 1926

masses noun a large amount UK, 1892

mass gas noun a group of tanker aircraft refuelling a group of receiver planes US, 1963

massive noun **1** a group of friends or peers JAMAICA, 1989. **2** a gang. Predominantly West Indian and UK Black usage, 1994. **3** a social grouping with a shared leisure interest, often identified by location. West Indian and UK Black usage JAMAICA, 1995

massive adjective excellent US, 1982. ▶ **give it massive** to enjoy in a very enthusiastic or excessive fashion. Punning on GIVE IT LARGE UK, 2000

massive! used for expressing enthusiastic approval NEW ZEALAND, 1998

massive humanity noun a large crowd US, 1983

Ma State; Ma nickname New South Wales, Australia. A tribute to NSW's status as Australia's earliest colony, thus the 'mother state' AUSTRALIA, 1906

master adjective excellent TRINIDAD AND TOBAGO, 1956

master blaster noun a large piece of crack cocaine US, 1992

master key noun in law enforcement, a sledge hammer US, 1995

master maniac noun the railways, a master mechanic US, 1975

mastermind *noun* a railway official *US, 1946*

master of your domain *noun* a person who can refrain from masturbation for a prolonged period. Coined and popularised by Jerry Seinfeld in an episode of his television comedy *The Contest* that first aired on 18th November 1992 *US, 1992*

masturbation *noun* self-indulgent nonsense. Used in a euphemistic attempt to avoid WANK *UK, 2001*

masturbation mansion *noun* a cinema theatre showing pornographic films *US, 1972*

mat *noun* ▶ **go to the mat** to engage in a full-scale struggle. From wrestling *US, 1908*

mataby *noun* marijuana grown in Zaire, *1980*

matador *adjective* a stylish, fashionable, independent woman *TRINIDAD AND TOBAGO, 1956*

Matapedia screwdriver *noun* a hammer. Matapedia is a small town in Quebec, poised on the border with New Brunswick *CANADA, 2002*

match *noun* approximately half an ounce of marijuana. An abbreviation of 'matchbox', which contains approximately the same amount *US, 1980*

match *verb* ▶ **match dials** the railways, to synchronise watches *US, 1977*

match bash *noun* a drag racing event built around a series of races between two types of vehicles *US, 1965*

matchbox *noun* **1** an approximate measure, ½ ounce, 5–10 grams, of marijuana. Derives from the capacity of a matchbox, a convenient measure *US, 1996*. **2** a small house *IRELAND, 1920*

matchbox Jimmy *noun* a cab over truck built by General Motors Corporation *US, 1971*

match head; match-head *noun* **1** a small single dose of heroin sold individually *US, 1993*. **2** a football fan, especially one who goes to the game. Those interested in a specific football fixture refer to 'the match'; this combines with -HEAD (an aficionado). A derisory term punning on the small size of a matchhead *UK, 2001*

mate *noun* **1** a good friend; a buddy or chum. This word is used to the near exclusion of its various synonyms in Australia. Originally used only by men, but since the 1980s increasingly by women *UK, 1380*. **2** used as a form of address to a stranger. Generally used in a friendly manner, but also used when being confrontational *UK, 1450*. **3** in poker, a card that forms a pair *US, 1988*

maternity blouse *noun* a large, loose shirt worn untucked by a heavy man *US, 1981*

mateship *noun* masculine friendship. In 1999 Prime Minister John Howard tried to introduce this word into a 'preamble' to the Australian Constitution and came under much criticism and ridicule since it was seen to exclude women – the referendum on the matter was not passed *AUSTRALIA, 1864*

mate's rates; mate rates *noun* especially cheap prices applied to one's friends *AUSTRALIA, 1996*

matey *noun* a man; a companion; a comrade. Used as an affectionate form of address; in a friendly way for someone whose name is not known; in a pseudo-friendly manner for patronising effect *US, 1841*

matey *adjective* friendly. Whereas 'matey' as a form of address is generally used of a man, this usage ignores gender *UK, 1915*

matey boy *noun* used dismissively, a man *UK, 2002*

math out *verb* to render a presentation beyond comprehension by virtue of dense mathematical content *US, 1991*

'matic *noun* an automatic pistol *UK, 1994*

matinee *noun* **1** a sexual encounter in the mid-afternoon *US, 1944*. **2** a repeat robbery of a victim *US, 1950*

matlock *noun* a tooth. Hence 'matlock mender' (a dentist) *UK, 2002*

matrimonial peacemaker *noun* the penis *US, 1967*

matsakaw; matsakow *noun* heroin *US, 1977*

mattie *noun* a woman's very close female friend *BARBADOS, 1965*

mattress *noun* a sexually active, promiscuous girl from a nearby village *CANADA, 1992*

mattresses *noun* ▶ **go to the mattresses; hit the mattresses** during gang warfare, to retreat in an armed group to a fortified room, apartment or house *US, 1964*

mattress fall *noun* uterine prolapse *TRINIDAD AND TOBAGO, 2003*

mattress joint *noun* a hotel catering to prostitutes *US, 1956*

Mattress Mary *noun* used as a personification of the stereotypical sexually loose female *US, 1955*

Matty Mattel; Matty Mattel mouse gun *noun* the M-16 rifle. Named after the toy manufacturer because many soldiers in Vietnam found the M-16 to be a seriously flawed rifle *US, 1978*

matzoh ball; matzo ball *noun* a Jewish dance or party held at Christmas. From a pun on a staple of Jewish cuisine, adopted commercially for a series of events, and from there into wider usage *US, 2002*

Maud; Maude *noun* a male prostitute. From the female name. Also used amongst male homosexuals as an adopted name. Probably since the 1940s *UK, 1984*

Maud and Ruth *noun* the truth. Rhyming slang *UK, 1977*

Maugerville slippers *noun* hip waders. Maugerville is a town on the St John River near Fredericton, New Brunswick *CANADA, 1991*

Maui wowie; Maui wauie; Maui wowee; Maui *noun* a potent marijuana cultivated in Hawaii. The island of Maui plus WOW (a thing of wonder) *US, 1977*

Maui-zowie *noun* a strain of marijuana. A variation of MAUI WOWIE *UK, 2000*

mauler *noun* a set of brass knuckles *US, 1953*

maulsprigging *noun* a beating *BARBADOS, 1965*

Mau-Mau *noun* a black person who uses the fact that he is black to get his way with guilty white people *US, 1965*

mau-mau *verb* to bully, especially using confrontational political arguments that play on racial guilt. Coined as a verb by Tom Wolfe based on the name of a secret society organised to expel European settlers from Kenya *US, 1970*

mauve *noun* a person who appears to be homosexual *UK, 2002*

mauzy *adjective* in Newfoundland, a foggy, misty day with a gentle ocean breeze *CANADA, 1969*

maverick *noun* a stolen, or 'reappropriated', military vehicle. From the western US sense of the word as 'stolen cattle' *US, 1990*

mavis *noun* a male homosexual. Gay slang, formed on the name Mavis and originating among Cape coloureds *SOUTH AFRICA, 2000*

Mavis Fritter *noun* the anus. Rhyming slang *UK, 2003*

maw *noun* a mother *US, 1826*

MAW *noun* an attractive woman who is highly visible at fashionable events. An acronym of 'model, actress, whatever' *UK, 1998*

max *noun* **1** maximum; a maximum *US, 1851*. **2** a maximum security prison *US, 1961*. ▶ **to the max** as far as possible, to the limit *US, 1971*

max *verb* to wear *UK, 2003*

max *adjective* maximum security *US, 1976*

max and relax *verb* to take things easy, to take leisure with pleasure *US, 1994*

max BBs *noun* a tactic in aerial combat of using the highest rate of fire and filling the air with rounds *US, 1991*

maxed to the onions *adjective* extremely large. US military usage during the Vietnam war *US, 1982*

Max Factor *noun* an actor. Rhyming slang, formed from the name of a cosmetics company *UK, 1992*

maximum brilliant *adjective* extremely good *US, 1982*

maxi taxi; maxi *noun* a van used as a taxi *TRINIDAD AND TOBAGO, 1979*

Max Miller *noun* a pillow. Rhyming slang, formed from the name of one of the greats of British stand-up comedy, 1895–1963 *UK, 1992*

max out; max *verb* **1** to reach a limit *US, 1977*. **2** to complete a maximum prison sentence *US, 1972*. **3** to relax *US, 1984*

Max Walls; maxies *noun* the testicles. Rhyming slang for BALLS from the name of Max Wall (1908–90), a great British comedian *UK, 1992*

Maxwell House *noun* a mouse. Rhyming slang, formed on an instant-coffee brand *UK, 1992*

may all your consequences by happy ones used as a humorous farewell. A catchphrase television sign-off on *Truth or Consequences* (1950–1987), a game show. Repeated with referential humour *US, 1962*

Mayflower *noun* a Plymouth car *US, 1965*

Mayne Nickless job *noun* in horse racing, an extremely large bet. The amount bet is so staggering that it must have been stolen from a payroll van of Mayne Nickless, Australia's largest corporate provider of health care *AUSTRALIA, 1989*

mayo *noun* **1** cocaine, heroin, morphine *US, 1949*. **2** mayonnaise *US, 1960*

Mayor Hunna; Mayor John *noun* marijuana *US, 1968*

maypop *noun* in the used car business, a tyre that is not guaranteed. Because it may pop at any moment *US, 1980*

May snow *noun* on Prince Edward Island, a late spring snow, supposed to help cure blindness and sore feet *CANADA, 1988*

maytag *noun* a weak prisoner, especially one who does laundry for others as a sign of submission *US, 1987*

may you live in interesting times used as a curse. Generally jocular. In a speech given in South Africa in 1966, US President John F. Kennedy introduced this allegedly ancient Chinese curse to the world *US, 1998*

Mazatlans *noun* beach sandals made with tyre treads for soles *US, 1965*

mazawatee *adjective* crazy, foolish. Rhyming slang for POTTY, formed from Mazawatee Tea, an old brand name for tea, perhaps also punning on '(tea)pot' *UK, 1992*

Mazola party *noun* group sex, enhanced by the application of vegetable oil to the participants' bodies. An allusion and tribute to Mazola Corn Oil™ *US, 1968*

mazoola *noun* money *US, 1951*

mazuma *noun* **1** money. From Hebrew to Yiddish to English *US, 1901*. **2** a female professor *US, 1947*

MB *verb* to return a carnival customer's money. From 'money back' *US, 1985*

MBNWA *noun* ▶ **Management By Not Walking Around** the extensive use of e-mail to keep in touch with subordinates in business *CANADA, 2002*

Mc- *prefix* used in combination with the noun that follows for expressing a cheap, mass-produced product. From the McDonald's™ hamburger chain *US, 1984*

MC; emcee *noun* **1** a master of ceremonies *US, 1790*. **2** a rap artist. From 'microphone controller' *US, 1996*

MC; emcee *verb* **1** to serve as a master of ceremonies *US, 1937*. **2** to perform *US, 2000*

McFired *adjective* fired from a low-skill, low-wage menial job *US, 2003*

McFly *noun* used as a term of address to someone who does not think often or well. From a character in the *Back to the Future* films *US, 1989*

McGimper *noun* a pimp *US, 1949*

McJob *noun* a temporary job; a job with little or no future prospects. Characterised as the sort of work available at McDonald's™, the multinational fast food brand. A term coined and trademark-registered by McDonald's itself in 1983 as a positive expression of an affirmative hiring program aimed at those with disabilities; by the late 1980s a derisive term for the low-skill, low-wage jobs that were proliferating in the US during the presidency of Ronald Reagan *US, 1991*

McJobber *noun* a person in temporary employment or employment with little or no prospects. After MCJOB *UK, 2003*

McLean lane *noun* in trucking, the right hand or slow lane on a motorway *US, 1976*

McMudhole *nickname* McMurdo Station, Antarctica *ANTARCTICA, 2003*

McNamara Special *noun* a transport plane specially equipped for flying dignitaries to Vietnam during the war *US, 1988*

McNamara's War *noun* the Vietnam war. Robert Strange McNamara was US Secretary of Defense from 1961 until 1967, much of the Vietnam war *US, 1990* ▷*see:* MISTER TRUMAN'S WAR

MCP *noun* a male chauvinist pig. In common usage by those involved in the cause of women's liberation *UK, 1971*

McPaper *noun* a poorly researched, poorly thought out, and poorly written term paper or essay. From McDonald's™, the ubiquitous purveyor of fast-food *US, 1991*

McPhillips Street Station *nickname* the intersection of McPhillips Street (Winnipeg) and the Canadian Pacific Railway main line *CANADA, 1987*

McShit *noun* ▶ **go for a McShit** to use a fast-food outlet's toilet facilities without purchasing from the restaurant's menu. Based on McDonalds™ but available at Burger King™, etc. *UK, 2002*

McTheatre *noun* a derisory categorisation of heavily marketed, big-budget, low-brow musical theatre *US, 1996*

MD *noun* **1** Dr. Pepper™ soda *US, 1967*. **2** a managing director. Only when spoken as 'em dee' *UK, 1963*

MDA *noun* a synthetic hallucinogen (methylenedioxy-amphetamine) that also contains a central nervous system stimulant. Used as a technical term in the late 1950s, in a slang sense later when the drug became popular, largely with gays *US, 1978*

MDB *noun* a hospital patient with an appalling lack of hygiene. A 'mega dirtball' *US, 1989*

MDO *noun* a day missed at work due to a feigned illness. An abbreviation of 'Maori day off' *NEW ZEALAND, 1998*

me *adjective* my *UK, 1947*

meal *noun* a socially inept person. Youth usage *US, 1949*

meal-a-mat *noun* a vending machine dispensing food *US, 1977*

meals rejected by Ethiopians; meals refused by Ethiopians *noun* military MREs (meals ready to eat) *US, 1988*

meal ticket *noun* a source of support, especially a person *US, 1899*

mealymouth *noun* a person who speaks insincerely or with a complete lack of conviction *UK, 1600*

mean *adjective* excellent *US, 1919*. ▶ **so mean he wouldn't pay a dime to see the Statue of Liberty piss** very stingy *CANADA, 1988*. ▶ **so mean he wouldn't shit away from home** used for expressing a high degree of stinginess and bad temper *CANADA, 1988*

mean *adverb* very *US, 1998*

mean as black cat shit *adjective* used for expressing a high degree of stinginess *CANADA, 1988*

me and the devil, pretty soon just the devil in poker, said when all players but two have withdrawn from a hand *US, 1951*

me and you *noun* **1** a menu. Rhyming slang, or merely a play on words *UK, 1932*. **2** in Bingo, the number two. Rhyming slang *UK, 1998*

meanest *adjective* best, fastest *US, 1965*

mean green *noun* phencyclidine, the recreational drug known as PCP or angel dust. The 'green' is from the parsley or mint on which the drug is at times sprinkled; the 'mean' is reduplicative yet accurately describes the behaviour of most users *US, 1981*

meanie *noun* *copelandia cyancens* or *panaeolus cyanescens*: a mushroom with potent psychactive properties. A shortening of 'blue meanie' *UK, 1999*

meanies *noun* the police or other authorities of enforcement; specifically those opposed to citizens' band radio. Abbreviated from 'blue meanies' *US, 1981*

mean mugging *noun* hateful glances *US, 2004*

mean out *adjective* good; bad. Hawaiian youth usage *US, 1982*

mean reds *noun* the bleed period of the menstrual cycle *US, 1961*

meanwhile, back at the ranch used as a humorous indication that a story is about to change to another thread. From a clichéd device used in cowboy films *US, 1956*

meany *noun* an exceedingly mean person. The Beatles, in the cartoon film *The Yellow Submarine*, 1968, popularised the term 'the blue meanies' as an intensification for those that cast a blight on joyfulness *UK, 1927*

me an' you *noun* in Bingo (also House and Tombola), the number two *UK, 1981*

measle sheet *noun* a military map with a large number of small circled numbers indicating checkpoints *US, 1966*

measly *adjective* contemptible, of little value, petty *UK, 1864*

meat *noun* **1** the penis *UK, 1595*. **2** the vagina *US, 1973*. **3** the human body *US, 1834*. **4** a corpse *US, 1949*. **5** in a hospital, tissue taken for a biopsy *US, 1994*. **6** in motor racing, a large racing tyre *US, 1993*. **7** in hot rodding, structural metal in the engine block *US, 1965*. **8** a musical instrument's sound before any electronic alteration *UK, 1983*. ▶ **the meat** athletes; in the entertainment industry, the actors, the performers *US, 1967*

meat *verb* ▶ **be on a meat-free diet** to be a lesbian. A euphemism formed on MEAT (the penis) *UK, 1995*

meat and two veg; meat *noun* used for Reg, a diminutive of the name Reginald. Rhyming slang; an apparently teasing application of the non-rhyming sense as 'the male genitals' *UK, 1992*

meat and two veg; meat with two vegetables *noun* the penis and testicles *US, 1964*

meat axe *noun* in television and film-making, a rod used on scaffolding to hold light screens *US, 1990*. ▶ **as a meat axe** as hell *AUSTRALIA, 1949*

meatball *noun* **1** a dim-witted, gullible person *US, 1939*. **2** a false or petty criminal charge *US, 1944*. **3** a coloured light that serves as a visual aid in an optical landing system for an aeroplane landing on an aircraft carrier *US, 1957*. **4** in horse racing, a combination of cathartics administered to a horse *US, 1951*

meat book *noun* at a college or university, a book with the names and photographs of all incoming students *US, 1996*

meat box *noun* a prison service van for transporting prisoners *UK, 1996*

meat curtains *noun* the vagina *UK, 2001*

meat cutter *noun* a surgeon *US, 1980*

meat district *noun* an area where sex is available *US, 1984*

meat drapes *noun* the condition that exists when a tight-fitting pair of trousers, shorts, bathing suit or other garment forms a wedge between a woman's labia, accentuating their shape *US, 2004*

meat eater *noun* a corrupt police officer who aggressively seeks out bribes and other personal advantages *US, 1972*

meat factory *noun* a college or university that recruits athletes solely for their athletic ability and without any real expectation that they will graduate *US, 1978*

meat fleet *noun* a military hospital ship. Gulf war usage *US, 1991*

meat hangers *noun* a pair of men's close-fitting and revealing nylon swimming trunks *AUSTRALIA, 2003*

meathead *noun* a stupid person; hence a general derogative implying stupidity. No brains between the ears, just meat *US, 1928*

meat hook *noun* in electric line work, a handline hook *US, 1980*

meat injection *noun* the sexual insertion of the erect penis *AUSTRALIA, 1942*

meat mag *noun* a homoerotic, often pornographic, magazine *US, 1979*

meat market *noun* **1** a bar or other public place where people congregate in search of sexual companionship *UK, 1957*. **2** a modelling agency *US, 1972*

meat parlour *noun* an establishment where sex is the most important commodity *US, 1969*

meat-pie *adjective* of average quality *AUSTRALIA, 1988*

meat puppet *noun* **1** the penis *UK, 2003*. **2** a prostitute *US, 1997*

meat rack *noun* **1** a restaurant, bar or other public place where people gather in search of sexual partners *US, 1962*. **2** Piccadilly in London's West End, an area where homosexuals and homosexual prostitutes offer their services. Like so much meat displayed in a butchers *UK, 1972*. **3** a gymnasium *US, 1976*

meat seat *noun* the vagina *UK, 2001*

meat shot *noun* **1** a photograph or scene in a pornographic film focusing on a penis *US, 1974*. **2** a bullet wound in a muscle, not involving a bone or organ damage *US, 1992*

meat show *noun* a striptease act or other performance featuring naked or near-naked women *US, 1943*

Meat Street *nickname* West 14th Street, New York. An allusion both to the meatpacking industry in the area and the transvestite prostitutes who work there at night *US, 1997*

meat wagon *noun* **1** an ambulance *US, 1925*. **2** a coroner's ambulance *US, 1942*. **3** medical evacuation equipment, especially a helicopter *US, 1991*. **4** a prison-service or police vehicle used for confining and transporting prisoners *UK, 1954*

meat whistle *noun* the penis *US, 1965*

meaty *adjective* (used of a wave) powerful *US, 1991*

mebbe *adverb* maybe. From North Country dialect *UK, 1825*

mech *noun* a mechanic *UK, 1918*

mechanic *noun* **1** in the underworld, a specialist for hire *US, 1949*. **2** a hired killer *US, 1989*. **3** in gambling, a cheat who manipulates the cards or dice *US, 1909*. **4** any safety device worn by a circus performer *US, 1980*. **5** an accomplished, skilled lover *US, 1985*

mechanical digger; mechanical *noun* a black person. Rhyming slang for 'nigger' *UK, 1992*

mechanic's grip *noun* in card trickery, a method of holding the deck that favours cheating *US, 2003*

Med *noun* ▶ **the Med** the Mediterranean sea; the lands generally known as the Mediterranean *UK, 1943*

med *adjective* medical *US, 1933*

med head *noun* a member of the military police *NEW ZEALAND, 1998*

media flu *noun* a runny nose and consequent sniffing as symptoms of cocaine use. Some symptoms of influenza translated to a profession noted for cocaine use, on the model of 'Asian flu', etc *UK, 2002*

media whore; meeja whore *noun* someone prepared to do anything for publicity *UK, 1999* ▷see: MEEJA

medic; medico *noun* a *medic*al doctor, whether physician or surgeon; someone who uses medical skills in a professional capacity *UK, 1659*

medical shot *noun* in a pornographic film, an extreme close-up of genitals *US, 1977*

medicate *verb* to use an illegal drug *US, 2003*

medicine *noun* **1** alcohol; liquor *US, 1847*. **2** illegal drugs or narcotics *US, 1976*

medicine line *noun* the border between Canada and the US, especially in the west *CANADA, 1987*

meditation *noun* solitary confinement in prison *US, 1990*

meditation manor *noun* a prison cell used for solitary confinement *US, 1962*

Mediterranean back *noun* a phoney injured back used as an excuse for taking leave from work. A racial slur referring to New Australians, many of whom were from a Greek, Italian or Lebanese background *AUSTRALIA, 1972*

medzers *noun* money. Parleyaree, theatrical and polari. Variants include 'medzies', 'metzers', 'metzes', 'metties', 'metzies', 'measures' and 'mezsh' *UK, 1933*

meeces *noun* mice. From the *Huckleberry Hound* television cartoon series of the late 1950s, in which Mr Jinx the beatnik cat regularly described his feelings towards Pixie and Dixie, two mice, as 'I hate those meeces to pieces' *US, 1991*

meeja; meejah; meejer *noun* media. A phonetic slurring in fashionable currency; slightly derogatory and generally used with 'the' *UK, 1983*

mee-maws *noun* the police. Echoic of a two-tone siren *UK: SCOTLAND, 1988*

meemies *noun* a feeling of anxiety and fear. A shortened form of the SCREAMING MEEMIES *US, 1946*

meese *adjective* plain. Recorded in contemporary gay use *UK, 2003*

meet *noun* **1** a meeting, especially one convened to discuss illegal matters *UK, 1865*. **2** a session in which musicians collectively improvise; a jam session *US, 1957*

meet *verb* in poker, to make a bet equal to the previous bet *US, 1990*

meeting *noun* ▶ **take a meeting** to attend a business meeting. Entertainment industry terminology, used outside the industry in a mocking, pretentious tone *US, 1977*

meff'd *adjective* drunk *UK, 2002*

mega *adjective* great, successful, excellent, special. A multi-purpose superlative, from Greek prefix *mega-* (great) *UK, 1969*

mega- *prefix* used for intensifying *US, 1966*

megablast *noun* a dose of crack cocaine *US, 1993*

megabuck *adjective* very expensive *US, 1992*

mega dirtball *noun* a hospital patient with an appalling lack of hygiene *US, 1989*

megapenny *noun* ten thousand dollars (one cent times ten to the sixth power) *US, 1991*

megg *noun* a marijuana cigarette *US, 1942*

megger *noun* in the television and film industries, a director. From the long-gone practice of directors' using megaphones *US, 1977*

megillah *noun* all of something. For observant Jews on Purim, the reading of the entire Megillas Esther is deemed an obligation *US, 1954*

MEGO my eyes glaze over *US, 1977*

Meg Ryan *noun* a homosexual male. Rhyming slang for 'iron' (IRON HOOF), POOF formed from the name of the US film actress (b.1961) *UK, 1998*

meig *noun* a penny; a five-cent piece *US, 1962*

Mekong Delta *nickname* a neigbourhood with a large number of Vietnamese immigrants and businesses *US, 1979*

mel *noun* in the language surrounding the Grateful Dead, a conventional, law-abiding citizen *US, 1994*

melana cream *noun* a powerful variety of hashish from the Kulu Valley in Himachel Pradesh *UK, 2003*

Melba *noun* ▶ **do a Melba** (especially of an entertainer) to retire and then come out of retirement over and over again. Referring to Dame Nellie Melba, 1861–1931, Australian opera singer *AUSTRALIA, 1971*

Meldrew *noun* a middle-aged or elderly man who is a complainer or a moaner, or is characteristically intolerant, pessimistic or curmudgeonly. Named after Victor Meldrew, the central character in BBC situation comedy, *One Foot in the Grave* (from 1990), written by David Renwick and played by Scottish character actor Richard Wilson *UK, 1990*

mellow *noun* a good friend *US, 1976*

mellow *verb* to calm *US, 1974*

mellow *adjective* **1** pleasing, relaxed, good *US, 1938*. **2** mildly and pleasantly drunk or drug-intoxicated *UK, 1699*. **3** (used of a friend) close *US, 1941*

mellow d *adjective* relaxed, enjoyable. A glorious pun on 'melody' *US, 1973*

mellow man *noun* an attractive male *US, 1945*

mellow yellow *noun* **1** fried banana skin scrapings, sold for their nonexistent psychoactive effect *US, 1966*. **2** LSD *US, 1971*

melon *noun* **1** the head *AUSTRALIA, 1907*. **2** a fool. Probably a shortening of melonhead *AUSTRALIA, 1937*. ▶ **bust your melon** to confuse.

Combines 'bust' (to break) with MELON (the head) *US, 2002*. ▶ **twist your melon** to confuse, to scramble your thoughts. Combines 'twist' (to derange) with MELON (the head). Survives as a catchphrase with the meaning barely understood *UK, 1990*

melon gear *noun* a crash helmet *US, 2003*

melon hut; melon *noun* a prefabricated red field hut *ANTARCTICA, 2000*

melons *noun* large female breasts *US, 1957*

meltdown *noun* the complete and total malfunctioning of a casino slot machine *US, 1999*

melted butter *noun* semen *US, 1980*

melted out *adjective* broke; without funds *US, 1948*

melton *adjective* hot. A pun on 'melting' originally recorded in 1885, however current use is probably freshly coined. Recorded in contemporary gay use *UK, 2003*

Melvin *noun* the condition that exists when someone pulls your trousers or underpants forcefully upwards, forming a wedge between buttock cheeks *US, 1989*

Melvin *verb* **1** to seize someone's testicles and twist them, especially as a girl's revenge for sexual harassment. Obviously extends from the senses that convey a painful and forceful adjustment to someone's underwear *UK, 2003*. **2** to dupe *US, 1991*

Melvyn Bragg; melvyn *noun* **1** a cigarette. Rhyming slang for FAG, based on the name of author and television presenter Lord Bragg of Wigton (b.1939) *UK, 1998*. **2** an act of sexual intercourse. Rhyming slang for SHAG, based on the name of author and television presenter Lord Bragg of Wigton (b.1939); this term came into use shortly after the explicitly sexual television adaptation of his 1990 novel *A Time to Dance* was first broadcast in 1992 *UK, 1992*. **3** a contemptible person. Rhyming slang for SLAG, based on the name of author and television presenter Lord Bragg of Wigton (b.1939) *UK, 1998*. **4** a sexually promiscuous woman, a slut. Rhyming slang for SLAG *UK, 1998*

member *noun* a fellow homosexual *US, 1970s*

Memphis dominoes *noun* dice *US, 1942*

ménage à moi *noun* an act of female masturbation *UK, 2004*

menali *noun* potent hashish originating in the Himalayas *, 1999*

mender *noun* in circus and carnival usage, a claims adjuster *US, 1981*

men in white coats *noun* **1** medical or laboratory personnel *UK, 1967*. **2** psychiatric staff. Usually humorous, and in a context that questions a person's sanity *UK, 1968*

menopause manor *noun* in the Canadian Forces, the Sergeants and Warrant Officers' Mess *CANADA, 1995*

mensch; mensh; mench *noun* an honourable person. German *mensch* (a person) into Yiddish *US, 1953*

mensh *noun* a mention; also, as a verb, to mention *UK, 1984*

mental *noun* an outburst of anger or madness *AUSTRALIA, 1979*

mental *adjective* **1** insane, crazy *UK, 1927*. **2** wonderful, amazing, mind-blowing *UK, 1998*. ▶ **go mental** to become very enraged, to have a fit of ill-temper *UK: SCOTLAND, 1985*

mental blooter *noun* a spree of any kind of excessive behaviour *UK, 1988*

mentalist *noun* a crazy person; a lunatic; an eccentric *UK, 1997*

mentaller *noun* a mad or crazy person *UK, 2001*

mentalness *noun* a state of madness *UK: SCOTLAND, 1996*

mental pygmy *noun* a dolt *US, 1968*

menu *noun* **1** the list of services available in a brothel *US, 1993*. **2** grafitti describing sex preferences and telephone numbers *US, 1972*

merc *noun* a mercenary. With the official US use of the term 'private civilian contractor' instead of 'mercenary' in the invasion and occupation of Iraq, use of the term 'merc' in the future is doubtful *ZIMBABWE, 1967*

Merc *noun* **1** a Mercedes car *US, 1970*. **2** a *Merc*ury car *US, 1951*

Mercedes *noun* **1** in horse racing, odds of 10–1. Rhyming slang, formed from Mercedes Benz *AUSTRALIA, 1989*. **2** a variety of MDMA, the recreational drug best known as ecstasy. After the luxury car; describing the logo stamped on the pill *UK, 1999*

merch *noun* merchandise *US, 1995*

merchant *noun* a prisoner who sells goods to other prisoners *US, 1958*

merchant banker; merchant; banker *noun* a contemptible person. Rhyming slang for WANKER (a contemptible person), coined in response to YUPPIE (a young upwardly mobile professional), many of whom were merchant bankers, moving into the East End of London during the 1980s *UK, 1992*

merck; merk *noun* cocaine. From the name of a pharmaceutical company *US, 1969*

mercy! used for expressing mild surprise *US, 1992*

mercy buckets! thank you. An intentional butchering of the French *UK, 1960*

mercy Mary! used for expressing surprise in a melodramatic fashion *US, 1970*

mercy Miss Percy! used for embellishing any exclamation *US, 1953*

mercy sakes!; mercy's sakes alive! used euphemistically in citizens' band transmissions to register anger, shock, surprise, etc *US, 1976*

mere gook rule *noun* a belief during the Vietnam war that a crime committed against a Vietnamese person was not a crime *US, 1976*

Merlin the magician; merlin *noun* a pigeon. Rhyming slang *UK, 1992*

merry *noun* marijuana. A play on the name Mary, featured in many slang terms for 'marijuana' *US, 1938*

merry and bright *noun* light, a light. Rhyming slang *UK, 1992*

merry dancers *noun* the northern lights *CANADA, 1946*

merry-go-round *noun* **1** the visits to many different prison offices the day before a prisoner is released *US, 1996*. **2** a railway turntable *US, 1946*. **3** a pound (£1). Rhyming slang; often reduced to 'merry' *UK, 1961*

merry hell *noun* ▶ **play merry hell; raise merry hell** to make a disturbance, to complain or quarrel noisily and angrily, to make a din *US, 1911*

merry laird *noun* a beard. Glasgow rhyming slang (a good rhyme in the local accent) *UK: SCOTLAND, 1988*

merry old soul *noun* **1** a hole. Rhyming slang *UK, 1992*. **2** the anus. Rhyming slang for ARSEHOLE; a specialism of the previous sense. Logically, this will be applied with irony to any ARSEHOLE (a contemptible person) *UK, 2003*

merry syphilis and a happy gonorrhoea used as a humorous replacement for 'Merry Christmas and Happy New Year' *AUSTRALIA, 1985*

merry widow *noun* **1** a bust-emphasising corset *US, 1957*. **2** in pool, a cue stick with a butt made with a single, unspliced piece of wood *US, 1983*

mersh *noun* marijuana that is commercially produced for a mass-market *US, 2004*

Meryl Streep; meryl *noun* sleep. Rhyming slang, formed from the name of the US film actress (b.1949) *UK, 1998*

mesc; mezc *noun* mescaline *US, 1970*

meself *pronoun* myself. Representing a common Australian pronunciation *AUSTRALIA, 1898*

mesh *noun* on a computer keyboard, the # character *US, 1983*

meshugge; meshuga; meshuggener; meshigener *adjective* crazy. Yiddish *US, 1888*

mesmeric *adjective* used for expressing approval *UK, 2003*

mess *noun* **1** a person who is dirty or untidy; a person who is disorganised or incapable of being organised *UK, 1891*. **2** excrement *UK, 1903*. **3** a large amount *US, 1826*. **4** drugs *US, 1978*. **5** in poker, a draw of replacement cards that fails to improve the hand *US, 1979*

mess; mess with *verb* to confront; to mess with; to interfere; to bother; to fight *US, 1935*

messages *noun* shopping; hence, message bag, shopping bag. Dialect *UK: SCOTLAND, 1911*. ▶ **do the messages** to go on a small local shopping trip *AUSTRALIA, 1902*

mess around *verb* to engage in sexual foreplay; to have sex *UK, 1896*

messed up *adjective* drunk or drug-intoxicated *US, 1963*

messenger *noun* a bullet *US, 1962*

messer *noun* a joker *IRELAND, 1998*

mess up *verb* to beat someone up *US, 1914*

messy *adjective* good. Another example of BAD meaning 'good' *UK, 2002*

met *noun* methamphetamine *US, 1993*

Met *noun* ▶ **the Met** London's Metropolitan Police, established in 1829 *UK, 1962*

meta- *prefix* used for indicating a higher level than super- or hyper- *UK, 2003*

metabolic clinic *noun* a hospital tea-room. Medical humour *UK, 2002*

metalhead *noun* a lover of heavy metal music and the attendant lifestyle *US, 1982*

metal jacket *noun* a condom *US, 1993*

metal mouth *noun* any person with orthodontia *US, 1978*

meter *noun* twenty-five cents *US, 1945*

-meter; -ometer *suffix* the conventional suffix that creates a means of measuring, when used to make a flippant or nonce-word, especially as a measurer of sexual arousal. In 2003 a brief search of the Internet revealed 'shagometer', from SHAG (to have sex), 'hornometer', from HORN (an erection) and 'pain-in-the-assometer' *UK, 1837*

meter maid *noun* a policewoman who checks cars on city streets for parking infractions *CANADA, 1965*

meter reader *noun* in the US Air Force, a co-pilot *US, 1946*

meth *noun* **1** methamphetamine hydrochloride, a powerful central nervous system stimulant, brand name Methedrine™ *US, 1966*. **2** methadone (a drug prescribed as a substitute for heroin) *US, 1980*. **3** marijuana. An abbreviation of METHOD (marijuana) *US, 1994*

mether *noun* a methylated spirits addict *UK, 1995*

meth head *noun* a habitual user of methamphetamine *US, 1966*

methical *noun* marijuana. A combination of METHOD and TICAL, slang terms for 'marijuana' adopted as aliases by rap artist *Methical*/Method Man *US, 1994*

meth monster *noun* **1** an amphetamine addict *US, 1967*. **2** any paranoid delusion suffered after sustained methamphetamine use *US, 1989*

metho *noun* **1** methylated spirits *AUSTRALIA, 1933*. **2** a habitual drinker of methylated spirits *AUSTRALIA, 1933*

Metho *noun* a Methodist *AUSTRALIA, 1940*

method; method murder *noun* marijuana *US, 1995*

Methodist hell *noun* the epitome of heat *US, 1975*

meths *noun* methylated spirits *AUSTRALIA, 1981*

meth speedball *noun* methamphetamine mixed with heroin. A combination of METH (methamphetamine) and SPEEDBALL (cocaine and heroin mixed, or an UPPER and DOWNER mixed) *2002*

metric miles *noun* haemorrhoids. Rhyming slang for 'piles' *UK, 2003*

metrosexual *noun* an urban, heterosexual male who, in matters of style or recreation, has similar tastes to those stereotypically associated with women or homosexual men *UK, 1994*

Metro Tux *noun* in Los Angeles, the police officer's uniform except for his shirt, which is replaced by a white t-shirt. With this slight modification, policemen may drink at a bar without violating the department rule against drinking in uniform *US, 1994*

Mex *noun* **1** a Mexican or Mexican-American. Offensive *US, 1847*. **2** the Spanish language *US, 1858*

Mex *adjective* Mexican. Offensive *US, 1854*

Mexi *noun* low quality marijuana, claimed to be from Mexico *US, 2001*

Mexican *noun* in eastern Australia, a person from a state south of one's own. In Queensland it refers to either New South Welshmen or Victorians, whereas in New South Wales it refers to Victorians *AUSTRALIA, 1991*

Mexican breakfast *noun* any combination of a glass of water, a cigarette and the chance to urinate *US, 1960*

Mexican brown *noun* inferior heroin that originates in Mexico. The adjective 'Mexican' has a negative value *US, 1975*

Mexican Buick *noun* a Chevrolet *US, 1979*

Mexican Cadillac *noun* a Chevrolet *US, 1962*

Mexican carwash *noun* a rainstorm *US, 1950*

Mexican cashmere *noun* a cotton sweatshirt *US, 1957*

Mexican chrome *noun* aluminium paint *US, 1955*

Mexican cigarette *noun* a poorly made marijuana cigarette *US, 1987*

Mexican compromise *noun* a decision in which you lose property but save your life *US, 1954*

Mexican credit card; Mexican filling station *noun* a siphon used for stealing petrol from a parked car *US, 1979*

Mexican diamond *noun* a stone cut and polished to look like a diamond *US, 1950*

Mexican fox-trot *noun* diarrhoea *US, 1979*

Mexican green *noun* an inferior marijuana cultivated in Mexico *US, 1961*

Mexican hayride *noun* a car overloaded with passengers *US, 1962*

Mexican horse *noun* brown heroin originating in Mexico. The source plus HORSE (heroin) *US, 1979*

Mexican jumping bean; Mexican red *noun* a capsule of barbiturate, especially Seconal™, manufactured in Mexico. Named for the capsule's appearance, not its effect, which is sedative *US, 1971*

Mexican locoweed; Mexican tumbleweed *noun* marijuana *US, 1969*

Mexican mud *noun* brown heroin that originates in the Sierra Madre mountains of Mexico; heroin *US, 1977*

Mexican muffler *noun* a tin can stuffed with steel wool functioning as a car silencer *US, 1953*

Mexican mushroom *noun* psylocybin or psylocin, powerful psychedelic drugs extracted from *Psilocybe mexicana* and *Stropharia cubensis* mushrooms which are native to Mexico *US, 1969*

Mexican nose guard *noun* a jock strap (an athletic support). An unkind linkage of the penis and nose *US, 1979*

Mexican overdrive *noun* while driving, coasting down a hill in neutral gear *US, 1955*

Mexican paint *noun* silver paint *US, 1954*

Mexican red *noun* **1** a potent variety of marijuana with a red-brown colour cultivated in Mexico *US, 1971*. **2** a capsule of secobarbitral sodium (trade name Seconal™), a central nervous system depressant *US, 1977*

Mexican retread *noun* a tyre that has been hastily and superficially repaired *US, 1962*

Mexican shower *noun* a hurried washing of the face and armpits *US, 2004*

Mexican sidewalls *noun* blackwall tyres that have been painted white *US, 1979*

Mexican standoff *noun* **1** a situation in which nobody clearly has the advantage or emerges a clear winner *US, 1891*. **2** the quitting of a poker game when a player is slightly ahead, slightly behind, or even *US, 1958*

Mexican straight *noun* in poker, any hand, a knife and a threat to use the knife. Reminiscent of the simple announcement, 'My Smith and Wesson beats your full house' *US, 1979*

Mexican strawberries *noun* dried beans *CANADA, 2002*

Mexican time *noun* used for denoting a lack of punctuality *US, 1967*

Mexican toothache *noun* dysentery *US, 1960*

Mexican traffic light *noun* a speed bump *US, 1992*

Mexican Valium *noun* Rohypnol™ (flunitrazepam), popularly known as the 'date-rape drug' *US, 1995*

Mextown *noun* a neighbourhood with a large population of Mexicans and Mexican-Americans *US, 1957*

mezz *noun* marijuana, a marijuana cigarette. An eponym honouring Milton 'Mezz' Mezzrow, a jazz musician who was better known for his missionary work on behalf of marijuana than his jazz, and who is better remembered for his writing than his jazz *US, 1937*

mezzony; mizzony *noun* the money required for a purchase of marijuana. A combination of MEZZ (marijuana) and 'money' *US, 1936s*

mezzroll; mezz roll; Mezz's roll; meserole; messorole; mezzrow *noun* an extra-large marijuana cigarette *US, 1944*

MF; em ef *noun* a motherfucker *US, 1959*

MFI *noun* **1** MI5, the UK's security intelligence agency. From the name of the retail chain that pioneered self-assembly furniture in the UK, and became the butt of many jokes *UK, 2002*. **2** a very large myocardial infarction; a major heart attack. Medical slang, elaborating the conventional abbreviation for the condition, MI, with F for, presumably, -FUCKING-. MFI is also a well-known flat-pack furniture retailer *UK, 2002*

MFIC; MFWIC *noun* the person in charge of a situation. An abbreviation of *motherfucker (who's) in* charge *US, 1968*

mf-word *noun* the word motherfuck, motherfucker or motherfucking *US, 1992*

MIA *adjective* difficult to locate. From the military label for 'missing in action' *US, 2002*

miaow!; mee-ow! used of a malicious gossiper, or as a commentary on the gossip itself. Intended as an impression of a cat's mew, from CATTY (spiteful) *UK, 1984*

mic *noun* a microphone. Pronounced 'mike' *US, 1927* ▷*see:* MICRODOT

michael *noun* the vagina *NEW ZEALAND, 1998*

Michael *noun* an alcoholic beverage that has been adulterated with a strong tranquilliser; the narcotic that is so used. An abbreviation of MICKEY FINN *US, 1942*

Michael Caine; michael *noun* a pain. Rhyming slang, formed from the name of the London-born film actor (b.1933) *UK, 1992*

Michael Miles; michaels *noun* haemorrhoids. Rhyming slang, 'piles', formed from the name of a popular television 'quiz inquisitor', host of *Take Your Pick*, 1955–68; or, less likely, from a US banjo player *UK, 2003*

michael-muncher *noun* a person who enjoys performing oral sex on a woman *NEW ZEALAND, 1998*

Michael Schumacher *noun* tobacco. Rhyming slang, formed from the name of the German-born world champion Formula 1 racing driver (b.1969); the rhyme, while not perfect, is informed with irony – Michael Schumacher has long been associated with Marlboro cigarettes *UK, 1998*

Michael Winner *noun* dinner. Rhyming slang, formed from the name of the British film director (b.1935) perhaps better known, in this context, as *The Sunday Times* restaurant critic (with his column: 'Winner's Dinners') *UK, 1998*

Michelle *noun* in cricket, a score of five wickets taken in an innings. Rhyming slang, on the imperfect rhyme of the name of film actress Michelle Pfeiffer (b.1958), with 'five for...' *UK, 2001*

Michigan bankroll *noun* a single large-denomination note wrapped around small-denomination notes, giving the impression of a great deal of money *US, 1914*

Michigan handshake *noun* a firm handshake that imparts a farewell. Newspaper advice columnist Ann Landers used the term in a column on 27th June 1996, in which she urged 'Embarrassed in Pittsburgh' to give her friend Fred 'a Michigan handshake' 'and tell him to hit the bricks' because he had taken a picture of her sleeping in the nude. Landers' use of the term generated a number of inquiries as to its meaning, and placed the term into the public lexicon. Landers herself pointed to Traverse City, Michigan, in the 1960s as the source of the term *US, 1996*

Michoacan; Michoacan green *noun* a powerful grade of marijuana, claimed to have been grown in the Mexican state of Michoacan *US, 1973*

mick *noun* **1** an Irish person or Irish-American *US, 1850*. **2** a car that is used in Ireland before being imported into, and reregistered in, England – the documentation on such a vehicle gives the impression of a much newer car. Car dealers' term *UK, 1968*. **3** a prisoner *US, 1950*. **4** the vagina *NEW ZEALAND, 1998*. **5** a young bull, especially if unbranded. A shortening of MICKEY *AUSTRALIA, 1894*

Mick *noun* a Catholic. From Mick, hypocoristic form of Michael, a common name amongst Catholics in Australia *AUSTRALIA, 1902*

mick *adjective* (used of a school or college course) easy *UK, 1972*

Mick *adjective* **1** Irish *US, 1849*. **2** Catholic *AUSTRALIA, 1985*

mickey *noun* **1** the vagina. Earlier also 'michael' (1950) and 'mick' (1930s) *AUSTRALIA, 1969*. **2** the penis *IRELAND, 1909*. **3** a young bull, especially if unbranded *AUSTRALIA, 1876*. **4** an ordinary fellow *US, 1949*. **5** a potato *US, 1936*. **6** an alcoholic drink adulterated with knock-out drops. A shortened form of MICKEY FINN *US, 1936*. ► **throw a mickey** to throw a tantrum. Perhaps related to MICKEY (a young bull) *AUSTRALIA, 1952*

mickey; mickey out *verb* to drug someone's drink *US, 1946*

mickey-dick *verb* to cheat, to engage in petty thievery *UK, 2005*

Mickey D's *noun* a McDonald's™ fast-food restaurant *US, 1977*

Mickey-Finn *verb* to incapacitate someone with a drink that has been adulterated with a tranquillizer. From the noun *US, 2002*

Mickey Finn; Mickey Flynn; Mickey's *noun* an alcoholic beverage that has been adulterated with a strong tranquillizer; the narcotic that is so used *US, 1928*

Mickey House *noun* in poker, an unplayable hand *US, 1988*

mickey juice *noun* sexual vaginal secretions *AUSTRALIA, 1996*

Mickey man *noun* a radar operator *US, 1946*

Mickey Mouse *noun* **1** a house. Rhyming slang *UK, 1960*. **2** a Liverpudlian. Rhyming slang for SCOUSE, no doubt informed by the use of 'Mickey Mouse' to mean 'inferior'. Noted in mocking use among London football supporters *UK, 1992*. **3** Famous Grouse™ whisky. Glasgow rhyming slang *UK: SCOTLAND, 1988*. **4** a wrist watch. From the watches with the face of Mickey Mouse first popular in the 1930s *US, 1959*. **5** a variety of MDMA, the recreational drug best known as ecstasy, identified by the embossed motif *UK, 2002*. **6** in American casinos, a $2.50 chip *US, 1985*. **7** an ultra-shortwave radar used for aircraft spotting. From a distance, the apparatus may be said to resemble a mouse *US, 1947*

Mickey Mouse *adjective* **1** inferior, trivial, cheap. Originally coined to describe inferior dance music, then given a broader sense *US, 1947*. **2** outmoded, old-fashioned or unnecessarily conventional *US, 1971*. **3** excellent. Rhyming slang for GROUSE *AUSTRALIA, 1973*

Mickey Mouse around *verb* to fool around. School usage *US, 1961*

Mickey Mouse boots *noun* heavy rubber boots issued to soldiers during the Korean war *US, 1952*

Mickey Mouse mission *noun* a simple, undemanding, relatively safe military task *US, 1990*

Mickey Mouse money *noun* **1** any unfamiliar or foreign currency; an unfeasible amount of any money. Originally used by the US military for Japanese currency; contemporary usage may be applied to, for instance, the Euro or Scottish banknotes *US, 1945*. **2** military scrip issued to soldiers in the Korean war *US, 1957*

Mickey Mouse movie *noun* a pornographic film that shows little or no detailed activity *UK, 1976*

Mickey Mouser; mickey *noun* a person from Liverpool, a Liverpudlian. Rhyming slang for SCOUSER *UK, 2000*

Mickey Rooney *noun* a madman, a crazy person. Rhyming slang for LOONY formed from the name of US film actor and entertainer (b.1920) *UK, 1988*

mickey's *noun* LSD *UK, 2003*

mickey-take; micky-take *verb* to make fun of someone; to pull someone's leg; to jeer at, to deride. From TAKE THE MICKY (to mock). Also used as a noun *UK, 1959*

mickey-taking; micky-taking *noun* an act of derisive taunting *UK, 1959*

mickie *noun* a bottled alcoholic drink *US, 1914*

Mick Jagger *noun* lager. Glasgow rhyming slang (a good rhyme in the local accent), formed from the singer with The Rolling Stones (b.1943) *UK: SCOTLAND, 1985*

micks *noun* Michelin™ tyres *US, 1971*

Mick's blood *noun* Guinness™ stout. The quintessential Irish beer *UK: SCOTLAND, 1996*

Mick-takers *nickname* Scotland Yard's anti-IRA Intelligence Unit. A play on MICKEY-TAKE (to make fun) *UK, 1974*

Micky Duff; Mickey Duff *noun* unwell, rough. Rhyming slang, formed from the name of a boxing manager and matchmaker (b.1929) *UK, 1998*

micky muncher *noun* a cunnilinguist *AUSTRALIA, 1988*

microbod *noun* in caving and pot-holing, a small adult or child with the ability to fit into narrow passages and around difficult corners *UK, 2004*

microchip *noun* a Japanese person. Rhyming slang for NIP *UK, 1992*

microdot; mic; micro; mike *noun* a small tablet of LSD *UK, 1996*

Microsloth Windows *nickname* Microsoft Windows™ *US, 1991*

mid-air *noun* in the language of hang gliding, a collision involving two fliers *US, 1992*

middle *noun* **1** in sports betting, a combination of bets that produce a win no matter what the outcome of the game *US, 1975*. **2** the waist. From Old English *middel* and *middil* *UK, 2002*

middle comb *noun* hair parted in the centre. Hawaiian youth usage *US, 1982*

middle leg *noun* the penis. Still in popular use *UK, 1896*

middle name *noun* anything which is your passion or speciality or outstanding characteristic may be claimed as your middle name *US, 1905*

Middlesex *adjective* homosexual. A pun on the place *US, 1948*

middle-sexed *adjective* homosexual *US, 1950*

middle stump *noun* the penis. From cricket *UK, 1937*

middlings *noun* in the illegal production of alcohol, livestock feed used instead of grain *US, 1974*

middy; middie *noun* a ten ounce glass of beer; a serving of beer in such a glass *AUSTRALIA, 1945*

midget *noun* **1** a very young member of a youth gang *US, 1981*. **2** in motor racing, a small, single-seat, open race car *US, 1980*

midgy *adjective* small. Probably derived from 'midget' *UK, 1999*

Midland Bank *noun* an act of masturbation. Rhyming slang for WANK, formed from the name of a high street bank *UK, 1998*

midnight *noun* in dice games, a roll of 12 *US, 1919*

midnight auto parts; midnight auto service; midnight auto supply *noun* stolen car parts; their notional source *US, 1966*

midnight cowboy *noun* a homosexual prostitute, originally one who wears cowboy clothes; hence a homosexual man. Brought from gay subculture into wider use by the film *Midnight Cowboy*, 1969. The less subtle, general sense resulted from the film's success *US, 1972*

midnight lab *noun* a laboratory where illegal drugs are manufactured *US, 1970*

midnight mass *noun* an informer. Rhyming slang (probably from the north of England by the accent required for the rhyme) for GRASS (an informer) *UK, 1996*

midnight oil *noun* opium *US, 1949*

midnight overdrive *noun* coasting down a hill with the car or truck in neutral gear *US, 1971*

midnight revue *noun* serial consecutive sex between one person and multiple partners, usually consensual *US, 1949*

midnights *noun* the midnight shift, a work schedule beginning at midnight and ending at 8am *US, 1994*

midnight shopper *noun* a burglar US, 1976

midnight supply man *noun* a person who traffics in stolen equipment US, 1954

midnight toker *noun* a person who smokes marijuana before retiring to bed US, 1973

midrats *noun* a meal served between midnight and 1am. An abbreviation of 'midnight rations' US, 1973

midway bonus *noun* in circus and carnival usage, an extravagant, empty promise US, 1981

MIG alley *noun* during the Korean war, airspace controlled by North Korea and its allies US, 1951

mighty *adjective* excellent NEW ZEALAND, 1984

mighty *adverb* very, greatly. Often ironic UK, 1715

Mighty Joe Young *noun* a central nervous system depressant UK, 1998

mighty mezz *noun* a generous marijuana cigarette, or simply marijuana US, 1946

mighty mite *noun* **1** a marijuana variety with large buds CANADA, 2002. **2** an airblower used by the military in Vietnam to blow smoke or tear gas into enemy tunnels. Also spelt 'mity-mite' US, 1967

mighty Quinn *noun* LSD US, 1975

mike *noun* **1** a microgram (1/1,000,000th of a gram). The unit of measure for LSD doses, even in the non-metric US US, 1967. **2** a microdot (of LSD), 1998. **3** a microphone US, 1927. **4** a minute. From the military phonetic alphabet – 'mike' for 'm', and 'm' for 'minute' US, 1986. **5** a person who secretly finances a licensed bookmaker AUSTRALIA, 1989

mike; mike up *verb* to equip with a microphone UK, 1984

Mike Bliss; Micky Bliss *noun* the act of urination; urine. Rhyming slang for PISS, which leads to TAKE THE MICKY, TAKE THE MICHAEL and variants such as TAKE THE PISS (to jeer) UK, 1961

mike boat *noun* a military landing craft US, 1977

mike check *noun* oral sex on a male US, 1992

mike fright *noun* an overwhelming fear that confronts an actor when facing a microphone US, 1952

Mike Hunt *noun* a fictitious name, used as a prank for waiting lists. The announcement 'table for Mike Hunt' sounds very much like 'table for my cunt', thus a source of amusement US, 1994

mike juliet *noun* marijuana. Vietnam war usage. The military phonetic alphabet for MJ (marijuana) US, 1977

Mike Malone *noun* a telephone. Rhyming slang UK, 1992

mike-mike *noun* a millimeter, or a weapon with a calibre measured in millimeters. From the military phonetic alphabet for 'mm' US, 1967

mik-e-nik *noun* a car or truck mechanic US, 1976

mileage *noun* **1** any extra use or advantage that may be derived from a situation US, 1955. **2** a record of previous convictions UK, 1996

Mile End *noun* a friend. Rhyming slang, formed from an area of east London UK, 1992

Mile High Club *noun* a collective noun for people who claim to have had sex on an airborne plane. Interestingly, the equivalent 'club' on a train is not measured in height but distance travelled: 'the nine mile club' US, 1972

miles *noun* ▶ **make some miles** to drive (a truck) US, 1971

miles *adverb* much UK, 1885

milf; MILF *noun* a sexually appealing mother US, 1999

milk *verb* **1** to exploit, to cheat UK, 1536. **2** to masturbate UK, 1616. **3** in card games, to draw the top and bottom cards (off a new pack) before the first shuffle US, 1845. ▶ **get off and milk it!** used for heckling a bicyclist. Mainly schoolchildren use UK, 1975. ▶ **milk a rush** while injecting a drug, to draw blood into the syringe and slowly release the drug into the vein, controlling the immediate effect of the drug US, 1986. ▶ **milk it** to squeeze the shaft of the penis towards the head of the penis US, 1978. ▶ **milk the anaconda** (of a male) to masturbate US, 1985. ▶ **milk the bushes** to move a boat by pulling on shore bushes CANADA, 1940. ▶ **milk**

the lizard (of a male) to masturbate; to cause sexual ejaculation UK, 1997. ▶ **milk the one-eyed aphid** of a male, to masturbate UK, 2003

milk? used as a tease of someone whose demeanour is just a bit catty US, 1994

milk-ball *noun* any alcoholic beverage served with milk US, 1983

milk bar *noun* the female breasts. Probably dating from the 1950s when conventional milk bars had their peak of popularity UK, 1984

milkbar cowboy *noun* a motorcyclist given to frequenting milk bars. A term from the 1950s and 60s NEW ZEALAND, 1988

milk-drop *noun* an auction fraud in which the auctioneer inflates the price of an item by accepting non-existent bids before selling the item to the victim of the fraud US, 2003

milker *noun* in poker, a player who bets only on a very good hand or with very good odds US, 1988

milkie; milky *noun* a milkman UK, 1886

milking stool *noun* in electric line work, a yoke used for supporting hot line tension tools US, 1980

milkman's horse *adjective* CROSS, angry. Rhyming slang (the Cockney accent should be obvious) UK, 1961

milko *noun* a milk vendor AUSTRALIA, 1907

milk rope *noun* a pearl necklace US, 1956

milk route *noun* an easy, lucrative sales route US, 1930. ▶ **do the milk route** as a prostitute, to visit late-night venues in search of customers US, 1987

milk run *noun* **1** a routine trip, especially one that calls at several places. Originally military. Also called a 'milk round' UK, 1942. **2** a simple, undemanding, undangerous military task US, 1943. **3** the first run of a ski-lift on a given morning, or the first run down the mountain of the day US, 1963

milkshake *noun* **1** a solution of baking powder administered to a racehorse to improve its performance NEW ZEALAND, 1990. **2** semen that is sucked and swallowed from a rectum US, 1987. **3** oral sex performed on a male NEW ZEALAND, 1998

milkshake *verb* to administer a milkshake to a horse NEW ZEALAND, 1992

milksop *noun* a cowardly or effeminate man UK, 1382

milksucker *noun* a young child US, 1975

milk-train *noun* a train with an early morning schedule US, 1853

Milky Way *noun* a homosexual. Rhyming slang for GAY, created from a galaxy far far away, or, more likely, from a popular chocolate confection with the well-remembered slogan: 'the sweet you can eat between meals without spoiling your appetite' UK, 1998

mill *noun* **1** millimetre, especially as a measure of a gun's calibre, or a width of still- and cine-camera film US, 1960. **2** one thousand dollars US, 1961. **3** a million, especially and usually a million dollars or pounds. Sometimes simply 'mile' US, 1942. **4** in hot rodding and drag racing, an engine US, 1918

Millennium Dome *noun* **1** a comb. Rhyming slang, formed from the famous folly while it was no more than a building site UK, 1998. **2** a telephone. Rhyming slang (that barely rhymes) UK, 2002

millennium domes *noun* female breasts that are enhanced to misleading dimensions. After the UK's much-criticised celebration of 2000 years: the Millennium Dome UK, 2002

Miller time *noun* hours spent drinking beer after work or play. An advertising slogan by the Miller Brewing Company, expanded to non-product-specific ironic usage US, 1981

milling *noun* the action of fighting a companion, no holds barred, as a test of your ability. Military UK, 1810

million *noun* a certainty, a safe bet. Probably from gambling odds of 1,000,000 – 1. Examples: (of a plan) 'It's a million'; (for promotion) 'You're a million' UK, 1970. ▶ **gone a million** utterly undone; defeated; unable to recover AUSTRALIA, 1913

million dollar wound *noun* during war, a wound that was serious enough to get a soldier sent home but not so serious as to affect the rest of their life US, 1947

millioni *noun* millions. An unnecessary elaboration phonetically similar to Italian *milione* (million) *UK, 2001*

Milli Vanilli *noun* the penis. Rhyming slang for WILLY, formed from a controversial US music duo of the late 1980s and early 90s *UK, 2003*

Millwall brick *noun* a weapon made from a tightly rolled newspaper. Named after, or by association with, Millwall Football Club and the awesome reputation of its 'fans' *UK, 1999*

Millwall Reserves; millwalls *noun* nerves. Rhyming slang, formed from a London football team *UK, 1998*

Milton Keynes; miltons *noun* **1** beans, especially baked beans when served on toast. Rhyming slang, based on the Buckinghamshire town *UK, 1998*. **2** homosexuals. Rhyming slang for QUEEN(S), based on the Buckinghamshire town *UK, 1998*. **3** jeans, denims. Rhyming slang, based on the Buckinghamshire town *UK, 2002*

mimeo *noun* a mimeograph machine; a document produced by mimeograph *US, 1970*

Mimeo Minnie *noun* the stereotypical female office worker *US, 1953*

mimi *noun* an act of urination. From the Maori *NEW ZEALAND, 1983*

Mimi *noun* the vagina. A given name punning the centrality of the vagina to the user's perception of herself – 'me me' *US, 1998*

mimic-man *noun* a Trinidadian who has adopted European or American mannerisms and style *TRINIDAD AND TOBAGO, 1971*

mimi hill *noun* a stop during a road trip to use the toilet. From the Maori for 'urinating' *NEW ZEALAND, 1998*

mince *noun* **1** rubbish, nonsense *UK: SCOTLAND, 1911*. **2** anything unpleasant *UK: SCOTLAND, 1985*. **3** used in similes for listlessness or unintelligence *UK: SCOTLAND, 1985*. **4** Guinness™ stout *UK: SCOTLAND, 1988*

mince *adjective* used of an unpleasant thing, especially when in the wrong place *UK: SCOTLAND, 1985*

minced *adjective* drunk *UK, 2002*

mincemeat *noun* ▶ **make mincemeat of** to defeat absolutely *UK, 1876*

mince pies; minces *noun* the eyes. Rhyming slang *UK, 1857*

minch *noun* in circus and carnival usage, an unengaged, low-spending customer *US, 1928*

mincy *adjective* stupid, silly *UK: SCOTLAND, 1988*

mind *noun* ▶ **give someone a piece of your mind** to reprimand, to censure *UK, 1861*. ▶ **the mind boggles!** a catchphrase used as an ironic comment on any marked absurdity. Widely popularised in the *Daily Mirror* cartoon strip *The Perishers*, by Maurice Dodd, from the 1950s in print and the late 70s as an animation *UK, 1984*

mind *verb* **1** to work as a bodyguard, especially for a criminal; to look after a criminal activity *UK, 1924*. **2** to bribe regularly *UK, 1970*. ▶ **don't mind me!; don't mind me, I only live here!; don't mind me, I only work here!** used by someone who feels disregarded as an ironic suggestion that whatever is happening, and that has caused such feelings of alienation, should continue (and continue to disregard the speaker) *UK, 1937*. ▶ **never mind!; never you mind!** mind your own business!, don't let it trouble you! *UK, 1814*

mind! pay attention!, note what I say!, used to add emphatic force to a statement *UK, 1779*

mindbender *noun* **1** anything that challenges your knowledge or assumptions *UK, 1963*. **2** a hallucinogenic drug *US, 1971*

mindblower *noun* **1** an event, experience or situation that completley surprises or shocks *US, 1968*. **2** a hallucinogenic drug *US, 1973*

mind-blowing *adjective* **1** of drugs, especially hallucinogenic *UK, 1967*. **2** amazing, almost unbelievable. Hyperbole *UK, 1967*

mind-boggling *adjective* astounding *UK, 1964*

mind detergent *noun* LSD; any psycho-active drug, legal or otherwise. Coined during the Cold War, this term is suggestive of brainwashing *UK, 2003*

minder *noun* a criminal's bodyguard or enforcer. Made very familiar to the UK public with the television series *Minder*, 1979–94 *UK, 1924*

mindfuck *noun* **1** anything that causes an internal paradigm shift *US, 1971*. **2** the mental aspects of sex *US, 1970*

mindfuck *verb* to baffle; to manipulate psychologically *US, 1967*

mind-fucking *adjective* having the quality to confuse, puzzle or astound. Conventional use of 'mind' plus FUCK (to confound) *US, 1971*

mindle *noun* a stupid girl. Possibly derived as a shortening of 'mindless'. Recorded in contemporary gay use *UK, 2003*

mindless *adjective* (used of waves) immense and powerful *US, 1987*

mind your back!; mind your backs! get out of the way!; also used to 'warn' of the presence of a male homosexual *UK, 1983*

mine *noun* your job *US, 1954*. ▶ **down the mine** lost *AUSTRALIA, 1969*

mine *adjective* a 'minus' attached to a grade *US, 1968*

mine! used for acknowledging in shorthand form responsibility for a problem *US, 1989*

minehost; mine host; mine-host *noun* a tavern keeper, a pub landlord *UK, 1904*

miner *noun* ▶ **the miner's** silicosis *US, 1951*

miner's con *noun* silicosis. An abbreviation of 'consumption' *US, 1951*

ming *noun* an unpleasant smell *UK: SCOTLAND, 1985*

ming *verb* to stink *UK: SCOTLAND, 1986*

minge *noun* **1** the vagina. From the Latin *mingere* (to urinate) and the mistaken belief that urine passes through the vagina *UK, 1903*. **2** the pubic hair. Extends from the previous sense to include the general pubic area. A natural redhead is known as a 'ginger minge' *UK, 1903*. **3** a contemptible person. Extending the sense as 'vagina', synonymous with CUNT *UK, 2001*

minge bag *noun* a contemptible woman. Combines MINGE with BAG (an unattractive woman) *UK, 1982*

minge-muncher *noun* a person who enjoys performing oral sex on women *NEW ZEALAND, 1998*

minger *noun* a person who smells bad; hence, an unattractive person of either sex. From Scottish MING (to stink). Pronounced with a hard 'g' *UK, 2003*

Minge Whinge *nickname* *The Vagina Monologues* by Eve Ensler. Actors' slang for the widely popular theatre piece *UK, 2003*

ming-ho *adjective* drunk. Deriving, perhaps, from MING (to stink), thus playing on STINKING (very drunk) *UK, 2002*

minging *adjective* **1** unattractive, unpleasant; descriptive of anthing bad. Also shortened to 'mingin'. From the verb MING (to stink), hence to look STINKING (disgusting) *UK: SCOTLAND, 1985*. **2** drunk. Royal Navy slang; from MING (to stink) hence STINKING (drunk) *UK, 1987*

minglewood *noun* a hollowed cigar refilled with hashish and potent marijuana *US, 2004*

mingo *noun* an unpleasant person. Perhaps a combination of MING (to stink) and MINGE (the vagina), or perhaps an evolution of the older sense (1775) of the word as a 'chamberpot' *UK, 2001*

mingra *noun* a police officer *UK, 1979*

ming-ray *noun* a mischievous 'game' of spreading a school-fellow's possessions over as wide an area as possible without being noticed by the victim *UK, 2003*

mingy *adjective* **1** mean, miserly. Probably a blend of 'mangy' (shabby) or 'mean', and 'stingy' (mean) *UK, 1911*. **3** in pool, a shot that cannot be missed or a game that cannot be lost *US, 1990*

mini *noun* a mini-skirt, a very short skirt *UK, 1966*

mini-bean *noun* an amphetamine capsule; a tablet of MDMA, the recreational drug best known as ecstasy *UK, 2003*

mini-bennie *noun* an amphetamine or Benzedrine™ (amphetamine sulphate, a central nervous system stimulant) tablet or capsule *US, 1977*

mini L *noun* a Pontiac Grand Prix car. A car with a strong resemblance to the El Dorado *US, 1970*

mini-me *noun* a smaller version of somebody. From a character introduced in 1997 in the *Austin Powers* films *UK, 2003*

Mini Moke *noun* a cigar, cigarette or pipe. Rhyming slang for SMOKE, formed on a type of small car *UK, 1998*

mini-moo *noun* the vagina. MOO (an unpleasant woman) playing on Mini-Me, the miniature alter-ego of the villainous Dr. Evil in the film *Austin Powers, The Spy Who Shagged Me*, 1999 *UK, 2001*

mini skirt *noun* a woman *US, 1977*

mini-tanker *noun* a small mobile beer tank hired for social gatherings *NEW ZEALAND, 1977*

MiniWac *nickname* Bill Bennett, premier of British Columbia from 1975 to 86 *CANADA, 1989*

mink *noun* 1 a female friend or lover *US, 1899*. 2 a female whose romantic interest in a man is overshadowed by her interest in his financial worth *US, 1960*

minky *noun* the vagina *UK, 2001*

Min Min light; Min Min; min min *noun* a will-o'-the-wisp. Probably from an Australian Aboriginal language *AUSTRALIA, 1956*

Minnesota mule *noun* a prostitute recently arrived in New York City from a small town or city *US, 1987*

Minnesota strip *nickname* an area in New York City frequented by prostitutes *US, 1986*

minnie *noun* a homosexual man. An example of CAMP trans-gender identification *UK, 2002*

Minnie *noun* in lowball or low poker, the lowest possible hand. A personification of 'minimum' *US, 1967*

minnie *verb* to mince *UK, 2002*

Minnie Mouse *noun* of a woman, the pubic hair. Named after a cartoon character *UK, 2003*

minnow *noun* a poker player who joins a no-stakes game without sufficient funds *US, 1978*

minny *noun* a minimum security jail or prison; the minimum security wing of a jail or prison *US, 1976*

minoo *adjective* a 'minus' attached to a grade *US, 1968*

minor-league *adjective* mediocre, less than impressive. From the minor leagues in US professional baseball *US, 1949*

minors *noun* ► **the minors** in horse racing, the second and third place finishes *AUSTRALIA, 1989*

minors! that's not a problem! Hawaiian youth usage *US, 1981*

mint *noun* 1 a great deal of money. From the coinage of coins *UK, 1655*. 2 money *US, 1997*. 3 a tablet of MDMA, the recreational drug best known as ecstasy *UK, 1996*

mintage *noun* a mint-flavoured breath freshener or hard sweet *US, 1993*

minted *adjective* 1 very rich. A play on conventional 'mint' (the place where money is made) and being 'made of money' *UK, 1999*. 2 excellent *UK: SCOTLAND, 1988*

mintie *noun* a lesbian who plays the aggressive or dominant role *US, 1972*

mintox; mont *adjective* excellent. Noted as being in use since the 1970s *UK, 2001*

mint rocks; mints; rocks *noun* socks. Rhyming slang; a latter day variation of ALMOND ROCKS reflecting the predominant flavour of modern seaside rock *UK, 1996*

mintweed; mint *noun* phencyclidine, the recreational drug known as PCP or angel dust *US, 1981*

minty *adjective* 1 less than good, filthy, bad *UK, 2002*. 2 fashionable, stylish *CANADA, 2002*. 3 homosexual, effeminate *US, 1965*. 4 excellent *US, 1987*

miracle *noun* in the language surrounding the Grateful Dead, an extra ticket for that night's show *US, 1994*

miracle meat *noun* a penis that is almost as large flaccid as erect *US, 1970*

Miracle Mile *nickname* a stretch of Wilshire Boulevard, a main artery in Los Angeles, California. A nickname coined by an estate agent but then accepted in the vernacular *US, 1987*

Miracle of the Doughnuts *noun* an apparition of the image of Christ which occurred in September 1998 at a doughnut shop in Cape Breton *CANADA, 2001*

miracle rice *noun* IR8, a high-yielding variety of rice introduced in Vietnam in the 1960s, doubling rice production yields *US, 1985*

miraculous *adjective* extremely drunk *UK: SCOTLAND, 1873*

Miranda *noun* a warning read or recited to criminal suspects before an interrogation, informing them of their consitutional rights in the situation. From a 1966 decision of the US Supreme Court *US, 1966*

mirror *noun* a military sentry's enemy counterpart *US, 1992*

mirror man; mirror *noun* a person with decision-making authority who avoids making decisions. From the stock answer of 'I'll look into it' *AUSTRALIA, 1987*

misbehave *verb* to shave. Rhyming slang *UK, 1992*

mischief *noun* ► **do you a mischief** to cause you trouble or harm *UK, 1385*

mischievious *adjective* mischievous. A frequent solecism in both speech and writing *UK, 1937*

misdee *noun* a misdemeanour or minor crime *US, 1992*

miserable *adjective* miserly; stingy *AUSTRALIA, 1903*

misery *noun* low quality coffee *US, 1949*. ► **the misery** the bleed period of the menstrual cycle. Euphemism *US, 1999*

misery fiddle *noun* (among Canadian loggers) a cross-cut saw *CANADA, 1995*

misery guts *noun* a habitually miserable or complaining person *AUSTRALIA, 1981*

misery lights *noun* the coloured lights on the top of a police car *US, 1992*

misery machine *noun* a motorcycle *US, 1962*

misery parade *noun* alcoholics pacing on the pavement waiting for an off-licence or bar to open in the morning *US, 1998*

misfeature *noun* in computing, a feature of a program that was carefully planned but that produces undesirable consequences in a given situation *US, 1983*

misfire *noun* an instance of sexual impotence or premature ejaculation *US, 1981*

mish *noun* the missionary position for sexual intercourse – man on top of prone woman *US, 1995*

mishegoss *noun* nonsense; craziness *US, 1969*

miss *noun* ► **give something a miss; give it a miss** to avoid doing something *UK, 1919*

miss *verb* to inject a drug intravenously. Humorous use of an antonym, 1998. ► **miss a trick** to fail to take advantage of a situation *UK, 1943*. ► **miss out on** to lose an opportunity, to fail to achieve something *US, 1929*. ► **miss the boat** to lose an opportunity, to be late for something. Originally nautical *UK, 1929*. ► **miss the bus** to lose an opportunity *UK, 1915*. ► **miss the pink and pot the brown** to engage in heterosexual anal intercourse. A snooker metaphor playing on 'pink' (the open vagina) and 'brown' (the anus) *UK, 1997*

Miss Ann; Missy Ann *noun* the prototype of the white southern woman *US, 1925*

Miss Carrie *noun* a small supply of drugs carried on the person of a drug addict. Carried to get the addict through a short incarceration in the event of an arrest *US, 1973*

misses *noun* dice that have been weighted, either to throw a seven less (for the opening roll in craps) or more (for subsequent rolls) than normal *US, 1962*

Miss Green *noun* marijuana *US, 1952*

missing *noun* a report of a missing person *US, 1985*

missing link *noun* zinc. Rhyming slang, used by scrap-dealers in Glasgow *UK: SCOTLAND, 1988*

missing you already used as a farewell. A popular catchphrase; alas the sincerity of the sentiment is often undermined by sarcasm *US, 2000*

mission *noun* **1** a search to buy crack cocaine. Another *Star Trek* metaphor *US, 1992*. **2** an assignment given to a youth gang member *US, 1995*

mission bum; mission stiff *noun* a tramp who frequents the dining rooms and sleeping quarters offered to the desitute by religious missions *US, 1924*

Mississippi flush *noun* in poker, any hand and a revolver *US, 1999*

Mississippi marbles *noun* dice *US, 1920*

Mississippi mudflap *noun* a hairstyle: the hair is worn short at the front and long at the back. Best known as a MULLET *US, 2001*

Mississippi saxophone *noun* a harmonica, a mouth organ *US, 1996*

Miss It *noun* used as a term of address to a person with excessive self esteem *US, 1968*

Miss Muggins *noun* a notional seller of out-of-fashion clothing *BARBADOS, 1965*

Missouri marbles *noun* dice *US, 1962*

Missouri pass *noun* in the US, pulling off a road onto the hard shoulder to pass a vehicle on the right *US, 1999*

Missouri stop *noun* a rolling stop at a traffic signal or stop sign *US, 1999*

Miss Palmer and her five daughters *noun* masturbation *BAHAMAS, 1971*

Miss Piggy *noun* **1** a fat, aggressive, loud homosexual man. An allusion to a main character on the *Muppets* children's television programme *US, 1980*. **2** a cigarette. Rhyming slang for CIGGY *UK, 1998*

Miss Priss *noun* used as a friendly female-to-female term of address *US, 1996*

Miss Thing *noun* used as a term of address for someone (female or homosexual male) with excessive self-esteem *US, 1957*

missus *noun* **1** a wife. A phonetic rendering of 'Mrs'; ultimately from 'mistress'. Always modified as either 'the missus', or 'my', 'your', 'his missus' *UK, 1833*. **2** the 'woman of the house' on a country property. Counterpart of the masculine BOSS *UK, 1836*. **3** lady; madam. Used as a term of address to an unknown woman *UK, 1861*

mist *noun* **1** phencyclidine, the recreational drug known as PCP or angel dust *US, 1977*. **2** the smoke produced when crack cocaine is smoked *US, 1994*

mista *noun* mister. A deliberate misspelling *UK, 1997*

mister *noun* **1** the male manager of a homosexual brothel *US, 1966*. **2** a steady boyfriend or common-law husband *TRINIDAD AND TOBAGO, 1945*

Mister; Mr *noun* a stereotype of the adjective that follows *US, 1940*

Mister B; Mr B *nickname* Billy Eckstine (1914–93), jazz vocalist *US, 1948*

Mister B-52; Mr B-52 *nickname* Lt Colonel John Paul Vann (1934–72), killed in a helicopter crash in Vietnam *US, 1988*

Mister Big; Mr Big *noun* the head of an organisation, especially a criminal enterprise *US, 1940*

Mister Bitchy; Mr Bitchy *noun* a Mitsubishi car *US, 1992*

Mister Brown; Mr Brown *noun* the passive male in homosexual anal sex *US, 1950*

Mister Busy; Mr Busy *noun* in prison, any officer with an antagonistic attitude toward the prisoners *UK, 1996*

Mister C; Mr C *nickname* Perry Como (b.1912), US singer *US, 1982*

Mister Charles; Mr Charles *noun* a white man *US, 1970*

Mister Charlie; Mr Charlie *noun* used as a stereotypical representation of white authority over black people. A piece of slang used as a gesture of resistance by US black people *US, 1928*

Mister Chatsby; Mr Chatsby *noun* a non-existent member of a circus administration used to fob off unwelcome visitors. Possibly an elaboration of CHAT (a thing) *UK, 1953*

Mister Clean; Mr Clean; Miss Clean *noun* a person in the public-eye who maintains an image that is beyond reproach *US, 1974*

Mister Dictionary has deserted us yet again used as a humorous comment on profanity *US, 1994*

Mister Fixit; Mr Fixit *noun* used as an informal title for someone who is able to 'fix' things, whether from a technical knowledge or political influence. 'Mr' may be replaced with another title as appropriate *UK, 1984*

Mister Floppy; Mr Floppy *noun* the penis that has become flaccid when an erection is to be preferred *UK, 2003*

Mister Foot; Mr Foot *noun* the penis. An imperial measure of bragging *UK, 2001*

Mister Geezer; Mr Geezer *noun* the penis. Both parts of this combination indicate 'a man' *US, 2001*

Mister Green; Mr Green *noun* money *US, 1973*

Mister Happy; Mr Happy *noun* **1** the penis. Adopted from the character created by UK cartoonist Roger Hargreaves (1935–88) for his *Mr Men* children's books *US, 1984*. **2** a nappy. Glasgow rhyming slang *UK: SCOTLAND, 1988*

Mister Hawkins; Mr Hawkins *noun* a cold winter wind. An embellishment and personification of HAWK *US, 1970*

Mister Hyde; Mr Hyde *noun* an untrustworthy person. Rhyming slang for SNIDE, informed by rhyming slang JEKYLL AND HYDE (two-faced) and the character of Mr Hyde in Robert Louis Stevenson's *The Strange Case of Dr Jekyll and Mr Hyde UK, 1992*

Mister Jones; Mr Jones *noun* used as a personification of the dominant white culture *US, 1971*

Mister Lovely; Mr Lovely *noun* marijuana *UK, 2003*

Mister Man; Mr Man *noun* used as a disparaging term of address *TRINIDAD AND TOBAGO, 1904*

Mister Matey; Mr Matey *noun* the penis. A pet name; possibly a reference to Matey™, a brand name bubble bath for children, marketed in a phallic-shaped character-bottle that is suited to playing games in the bath *UK, 2001*

Mister Miggles; Mr Miggles *noun* heroin *NEW ZEALAND, 1997*

Mister Money; Mr Money *noun* a Jewish person *US, 1980*

Mister Nasty; Mr Nasty *noun* the penis *US, 2001*

Mister Nice; Mr Nice *noun* one of the most powerful hybrid-strains of marijuana. Named in honour of Howard Marks, a campaigner for the legalisation of cannabis. 'Mr Nice' was one of forty-three aliases Marks used in his former career as marijuana smuggler and the one by which he is publicly recognised *UK, 2002*

Mister Period; Mr Period *noun* used of a personification of the fact that a woman has missed her normal menstrual period *US, 1980*

Mister Sin; Mr Sin *noun* a police officer assigned to the vice squad *US, 1980*

Mister Softy; Mr Softy *noun* a flaccid penis *US, 1995*

Mister Speaker; Mr Speaker *noun* a handgun *US, 1945*

Mister Television; Mr Television *nickname* Milton Berle, US comedian of vaudeville, radio and television fame (1908–2002). Berle was the first superstar of US television, hosting the very popular Tuesday night *Texaco Star Theater*. Berle personified the early days of television; when he died in March 2002, newspaper headlines across the US proclaimed that 'Mr Television' had died *US, 1949*

Mister TFX; Mr TFX *nickname* Albert W. Blackburn, a special assistant to Secretary of the Defense Robert McNamara in the early 1960s and an advocate of the controversial TFX (Tactical Fighter, Experimental) *US, 1967*

Mister Thirty; Mr Thirty *noun* a tiger. During the Vietnam war, tigers were occasionally seen near the end of the lunar month when there was less light at night *US, 1991*

Mister Truman's War *noun* the Korean war. A Republican party coining *US, 1964*

Mister Twenty-six; Mr Twenty-six *noun* a hypodermic needle *US, 1973*

Mister Winky; Mr Winky *noun* the penis. Especially in the phrase 'giving Mr Winky an oral report' (oral sex) *US, 2001*

Mister Wood; Mr Wood *noun* a police truncheon. From the crime-fighting technology employed at the time *UK, 1998*

Mister Wood in the house; Mr Wood in the house used to describe a poorly attended circus performance. It is easier to see the wooden benches than the audience that should be sitting on them *UK, 1953*

Mister Zippo; Mr Zippo *noun* the operator of a flame thrower. Vietnam war slang based on the Zippo™ manufacturing company's many cigarette lighters *US, 1991*

mistie; misty *noun* a tablet of morphine sulphate. Probably because the sensation described by users is 'misty' *NEW ZEALAND, 2002*

Mitcham Gypsy *noun* a person who wishes, or pretends, to be a gypsy. Mitcham in Surrey is a town where a number of travelling families have taken residence in houses *UK, 2000*

mites and lice *noun* in poker, a hand with a pair of threes and a pair of twos *US, 1967*

mitsubishi; mitsi *noun* a variety of MDMA, the recreational drug best known as ecstasy. From the Mitsubishi car manufacturer's logo embossed on the tablet *UK, 2001*

Mitsubishi Turbo *noun* a tablet of PMA, a synthetic hallucinogen, etched with the Japanese car manufacturer's logo *UK, 2001*

mitt *noun* **1** the hand *US, 1893*. **2** in poker or other card games, a hand of cards *US, 1896*

mitt *verb* to grab, to seize *US, 1915*

mitt camp *noun* a fortune-telling booth in a carnival *US, 1980*

mitten money *noun* extra money, either in the form of a tip or a bribe. From the practice of sea-going pilots charging an extra fee for winter work *US, 1975*

mitt man *noun* in gambling, a cheat who switches cards *US, 1997*

mitt reader *noun* in circus and carnival usage, a fortune teller who reads palms *US, 1981*

Mitzi *noun* a Mitsubishi car *UK, 2002*

mix *noun* kava, a tranquillity-inducing herbal beverage *FIJI, 1995*. ▶ **in the mix** involved with youth gang activity *US, 1995*

mix *verb* to fight *US, 1895*. ▶ **mix it 1** to stir up trouble *US, 1899*. **2** to fight *UK, 1900*. ▶ **mix your peanut butter** to play the active role in anal sex *US, 1971*

mix and muddle *noun* a cuddle. Rhyming slang *UK, 1992*

mixed jive *noun* crack cocaine *UK, 2003*

mixed up *adjective* confused *US, 1884*

mixer *noun* **1** a troublemaker, a mischief-maker *UK, 1938*. **2** a woman who works in a bar, encouraging customers through flirtation to buy drinks, both for themselves and for her *US, 1950*

mix in *verb* to join a fight *UK, 1912*

mixing stick *noun* the gear shift of a truck *US, 1961*

mixmaster *noun* **1** a Cessna O-1 Super Skymaster aircraft, used in forward air control missions in Vietnam *US, 1951*. **2** a complex motorway interchange *US, 1976*. **3** a dance music disc jockey. With variant form 'mixmeister' *US, 1995*

mixo *noun* a bartender *US, 1950*

mixologist *noun* a bartender *US, 1950*

miz! that's too bad! An abbreviation of 'miserable' *US, 1997*

mizzi *noun* a type of MDMA, the recreational drug best known as ecstasy *UK, 2000*

mizzle *verb* to depart hurriedly *UK, 1781*

MJ; mj *noun* marijuana. From MARY JANE (marijuana) *US, 1966*

MLR *noun* in the Korean war, the main line of resistance or the front *US, 1957*

MMM *noun* an automated cash machine. An abbreviation of MAGIC MONEY MACHINE; used widely in conversation in the 1990s *NEW ZEALAND, 2002*

'mo *noun* a homosexual *US, 1968*

mo *noun* **1** a moment *UK, 1896*. **2** in a prison, a prisoner subject to mental observation *US, 2000*. **3** a moustache *AUSTRALIA, 1894*. **4** a month *US, 1928*. **5** a homosexual *US, 1968*

MO *noun* **1** a criminal's method of operating. From the Latin *modus operandi US, 1954*. **2** marijuana. Also without the capitals *US, 1977*

mo' *adjective* more *US, 2002*

moan *noun* a complaint or grievance, an instance of spoken complaining. Originally military, probably from the verb 'moan' (to grumble) *UK, 1911*

moaning Minnie *noun* a persistent grumbler. Formed on a girl's name but applied to moaners of either gender *UK, 1962*

moan-o-drama *noun* a romance story in a girls' magazine *CANADA, 1997*

mob *noun* **1** a group of friends *US, 1939*. **2** a group of people sharing some connection *AUSTRALIA, 1848*. **3** a gang of criminals *UK, 1791*. **4** a military unit *UK, 1894*. **5** a group of surfers *AUSTRALIA, 1964*. **6** a group of Aboriginal Australians; in Aboriginal English, a tribe, language group or Aboriginal community *AUSTRALIA, 1828*. **7** in circus and carnival usage, the men employed by the show as a group *US, 1981*. **8** a group of animals; a flock or herd *AUSTRALIA, 1828*

Mob *noun* ▶ **the Mob** organized crime; the Mafia *US, 1969*

mob *verb* **1** to idle, to relax with friends *US, 1995*. **2** to surround, yell at and assault *US, 1998*

MOB money over bitches *US, 1998*

mobbed up *adjective* associated with organized crime *US, 1973*

mobbie *noun* **1** a female willing to take any and all sexual partners *AUSTRALIA, 1985*. **2** a member of an organized crime organisation *US, 1994*

Mobe *noun* the Student Mobilization Committee Against the War in Vietnam (SMC), the most powerful and visible anti-war group in the US in the late 1960s and early 70s *US, 1970*

mob-handed *adjective* used to denote that the person specified is within a group or accompanied by a gang of people *UK, 1934*

mobie; moby *noun* a mobile phone *UK, 1998*

mobile *noun* a mobile phone *UK, 2005*

mobile *adjective* sexually attractive *US, 1993*

mobile parking lot *noun* a car transporter *US, 1976*

moblog; moblogging *noun* a diary or a miscellany of random observations, text-messages and pictures collected on a mobile phone and posted on the Internet; the act of creating, keeping or updating such a record. From 'mobile weblog' (see BLOG) *UK, 2002*

moboton *noun* a splendid example of something *BARBADOS, 1965*

mobs *noun* a great number *AUSTRALIA, 1927*

Moby *noun* a completely depillated female pubis. Named for the totally bald-headed musician Moby (Richard Melville Hall, b.1965) *US, 2003*

moby *adjective* enormous. A term brought into the world of computer programming from the model railway club at MIT *US, 1965*

Moby Dick *noun* cocaine. Refers to the GREAT WHITE WHALE in *Moby Dick*, the classic novel by Herman Melville (1819–91). Cocaine, thereby, is claimed to be great and white (and you can have 'a whale of a time'?) *UK, 2001*. ▶ **on the Moby Dick; on the moby** on sick leave. Rhyming slang *UK, 1992*

Moby Dick; moby *adjective* sick. Rhyming slang *UK, 1992*

moby grape *noun* an improvised mechanism for injecting drugs, consisting of a syringe with a rubber bulb from a child's dummy attached to the end. The connection between this term and the late 1960s pyschedelic rock band by the same name seems obvious, yet eludes proof or explanation *US, 1971*

moccasin telegraph *noun* passing information through rumour, gossip or the Internet. The original meaning referred to the use of Indian people as runners to carry messages; it has been adapted to the Internet world *US, 1908*

mocker *noun* clothing; attire. Origin unknown. 'Thirty-five' (author of a glossary of Australian prison slang) writing in 1950 gave the definition 'a coat' *AUSTRALIA, 1953*

mockered up *adjective* dressed up *AUSTRALIA, 1938*

mockers *noun* ▶ **put the mockers on 1** to jinx *AUSTRALIA, 1911.* **2** to thwart, to frustrate someone's plans. A variation of earlier 'put the mock(s) on', which had a sense akin to 'put a jinx on someone' *AUSTRALIA, 1949*

mock fighting *noun* simulated fighting *US, 1978*

mockit; mawkit *adjective* very dirty. Originally meant 'maggoty', now applied equally to actual dirt and notional obscenity *UK: SCOTLAND, 1911*

mockitness *noun* dirtiness. From MOCKIT (very dirty) *UK: SCOTLAND, 1988*

mockney *noun* an ersatz London accent and vocabulary; someone who affects such artificial speech and background in search of cool. A compound of 'mock' (false) and 'Cockney' (the accent and identity of anyone born 'within the sound of Bow bells' or, loosely, an East Ender) *UK, 1989*

mock out *verb* to imitate *US, 1960*

mockstick *noun* a person who is the subject of mockery *BARBADOS, 1965*

mocky; mockie *noun* a Jewish person *US, 1893*

mocumentary *noun* a film or television entertainment in the style of a documentary *US, 1990*

mod *noun* **1** a member of the 1960s youth cult that is characterised by its detailed dress sense and use of motor-scooters. Abbreviated from 'modernist'. Wittily defined in the 6th edition of *The Dictionary of Slang and Unconventional English*, 1967, as 'a teenager unable to afford a motorcycle, and doing his damnedest with a scooter' and pedantically riposted by David Holloway, who writes in his review of the dictionary: '"Mods" ride scooters because the machines protect their clothes[.]' 'Mod' survives in C21 as a convenient music genre, and as small living-history groups who dressup in period costumes, ride scooters and dance to music marketed as 'Mod' *UK, 1960.* **2** in computing, a modification *US, 1991.* **3** a percent sign (%) on a computer keyboard *US, 1991*

modams *noun* marijuana *US, 1977*

mod con *noun* a modern convenience. From estate agent jargon *UK, 1934*

modder *noun* a modifier *UK, 2003*

moddy boy *noun* a young male who embraces the fashion and style of the mods *UK, 1983*

mode *verb* to show disrespect; to exploit *US, 2001*

model *noun* a prostitute *UK, 1995*

model C *adjective* applied to teenagers in South Africa who attend private schools or mixed-race public schools *SOUTH AFRICA, 2003*

model D *noun* a black student who attends, or attended, a government school in a township. Scamto youth street slang (South African townships) *SOUTH AFRICA, 2005*

modified *adjective* used of a car that has been in an accident *UK, 1981*

modplod *noun* a member of the military police. Combines the acronym MOD (the Ministry of Defence) with 'plod' (the police) *UK, 1987*

mods and rockers; mods *noun* the female breasts. Rhyming slang for KNOCKERS, formed from two youth gangs who battled their way into 1960s folklore *UK, 1992*

mod squad *noun* any group of black and white people. An allusion to a US television series (1968–73) that featured three hipper-than-hip juvenile delinquents turned police – Julie, Linc and Pete, one black, one white and one blonde *US, 1971*

modulate; modjitate *verb* to talk on a citizens' band radio. Adopted from technical jargon *US, 1975*

moer as an expletive, used as an expression of rage or disgust; used as an obscene and abusive form of address; in intensifying phrases, 'the moer', 'moer of a', 'moer and gone', etc, a synonym of hell. From Afrikaans for 'mother' (of animals) or 'womb' *SOUTH AFRICA, 1946*

moer; moera *verb* to thrash, to beat-up. Not in polite use *SOUTH AFRICA, 1960*

mofa *noun* marijuana *US, 2001*

moff *noun* a hermaphroditic animal *AUSTRALIA, 1953*

moffie; mophy *noun* a homosexual male; a male transvestite. Deriving, possibly, from 'hermaphrodite', but other etymological theories are interesting: *mofrodite* (a castrated Italian opera singer); Dutch *mof* (an article of clothing); English 'mauve' (as a variant of lavender, a colour associated with homosexuality). The word 'moffie' or 'mophy' first appears in South African sea slang in 1929 as 'a delicate, well-groomed young man' *SOUTH AFRICA, 1929*

moffiedom *noun* homosexual society. From MOFFIE (a homosexual) *SOUTH AFRICA, 1977*

mofo *noun* motherfucker *US, 1965*

mog *noun* a cat. A docking of MOGGY *UK, 1927*

mo-gas *noun* gasoline fuel used for ground vehicles. Vietnam war usage *US, 1977*

moggie *noun* Mogodon™, a brand name tranquillizer *UK, 1998*

moggy; moggie *noun* a cat *UK, 1911*

mogue *verb* to deceive, to fool *UK, 1854.* ▶ **and no mogue?** used to imply a slight incredulity, 'That's true?'. From 'mogue' (to deceive); since late C19 a tailors' catchphrase that slipped into polari *UK, 2002*

mohasky *noun* marijuana. Variants include 'mohaska', 'mohasty' and 'mohansky' *US, 1938*

moired *adjective* drunk. Probably from conventional 'moiréd' (of materials such as silk, 'watered'), thus 'well watered' *UK, 2002*

mojo *noun* **1** a spell, magic *US, 1926.* **2** sexuality, libido, sexual attraction. The song 'Got My Mojo Working' was sung on stage by Ann Cole in 1956 – the lyric continues: 'but it just won't work on you'. In 1971, The Doors released a song entitled 'Mr Mojo Risin'; the title serves as an anagram for the singer Jim Morrison and as an advertisement for his dangerous sexuality. This meaning, however, was not widely appreciated before the second *Austin Powers* film opened in 1999, but it caught on quickly thereafter *US, 1999.* **3** hard drugs, especially powdered drugs: cocaine, heroin, morphine. From the sense 'a kind of magic'; first recorded in this sense as is 'morphine' *US, 1935.* **4** an early version of the fax machine. Very slow, very cumbersome, but for its day a great advance, almost 'magical', hence the term. Popularised by Hunter S. Thompson's writings *US, 1990*

mojo juice *noun* liquid dolophine, a drug commonly known as methadone, used for the rehabilitation of heroin addicts *US, 1987*

moke *noun* **1** a fool. From the conventional sense (a donkey) *UK, 1855.* **2** a horse *AUSTRALIA, 1863*

moko longer than plantain used for signalling to a woman that her slip is showing *TRINIDAD AND TOBAGO, 2003*

molasses *noun* used as a euphemism for 'shit' *UK, 1994*

mole *noun* **1** a promiscuous woman. Commonly used as a term of disparagement implying promiscuity. Merely a respelling of MOLL in the same sense, representing the usual Australian pronunciation *AUSTRALIA, 1965.* **2** in electric line work, a lineman or cable-splicer who works underground *US, 1980*

mole hole *noun* the underground barracks where air attack alert crews live *US, 1963*

moll *noun* **1** an unmarried female companion of a criminal *UK, 1823.* **2** a promiscuous woman. Commonly used as a term of contempt, especially amongst teenagers, implying promiscuity. Commonly pronounced to rhyme with 'pole' *AUSTRALIA, 1972.* **3** a prostitute. Now obsolete in Britain but survives in Australia *UK, 1604.* ▶ **like a moll at a christening** uncomfortably out of place *AUSTRALIA, 1945*

moll buzz *noun* a female pickpocket *US, 1949*

moll-buzzer *noun* a thief who specialises in snatching handbags from women with children in prams or pushchairs *US, 1859*

molly *noun* **1** an effeminate male homosexual *UK, 1709*. **2** any central nervous system stimulant *US, 1979*. **3** MDMA, the recreational drug best known as ecstasy *UK, 2003*

molly-booby *noun* a foolish person *BARBADOS, 1965*

mollycoddle *noun* an effeminate man, especially an effeminate homosexual man *UK, 1833*

molly-dooker *noun* a left-handed person *AUSTRALIA, 1934*

Molly Hogan *noun* in logging, a wire strand, cut from cable, used as a cotter pin *CANADA, 1989*

Molly Hogan deal *noun* a deal with a catch, something wrong *CANADA, 1966*

Molly Maguired *adjective* tired. Rhyming slang, formed, probably, from the title of the 1970 film *The Molly Maguires* rather than the C19 originals *UK, 1998*

Molly Malone; molly *noun* a telephone. Rhyming slang, formed from the name of the tragic heroine of the traditional ballad, 'Cockles and Mussels' *UK, 1971*

Molly O'Morgan *noun* an organ (in any sense). Rhyming slang, originally for 'a barrel organ' *UK, 1961*

molly the monk *adjective* drunk. Rhyming slang *AUSTRALIA, 1966*

molo *adjective* drunk. Origin unknown *AUSTRALIA, 1906*

Molsonland *nickname* Canada *CANADA, 2002*

Molson muscle *noun* the rounded belly of the habitual beer drinker. Molson is one of the two largest breweries in Canada *CANADA, 2001*

mom *noun* the 'feminine' or 'passive' member of a lesbian relationship *US, 1957*

mom-and-pop *adjective* small-time, small-scale. From the image of a small grocery store owned and operated by a husband and wife *US, 1943*

momgram *noun* the postcard that many US Marine recruits sent home upon arriving at basic training in Parris Island, South Carolina *US, 1991*

momma-hopper *noun* used as a euphemism for 'motherfucker' *US, 1977*

mommy-o *noun* used as a term of address for a woman. Far rarer than DADDY-O *US, 1955*

momo *noun* **1** a motor; a car. Childish, reduplication of first syllable *UK, 1982*. **2** an idiot *US, 1960*

momo boy *noun* a member of the Mongrel Mob gang *NEW ZEALAND, 1977*

moms *noun* a mother *US, 1965*

momzer; momser *noun* a bastard; a brute; a detestable man. From the Hebrew for 'bastard' *US, 1947*

Mon *nickname* the Monongahela River *US, 1982*

Mona Lisa *noun* **1** a pizza. Rhyming slang, formed from the English name of the famous portrait by Leonardo da Vinci *UK, 1998*. **2** a freezer. Rhyming slang *UK, 1992*

monarch *noun* in a deck of playing cards, a king *US, 1988*

Monday morning quarterback *noun* **1** in American football, a fan who from the distance of the day after a game knows exactly what should have been done *US, 1967*. **2** a self-styled expert who from the safety of distance knows exactly what should have been done in a given situation in which he was not a participant *US, 1950*

Monday pill *noun* the large, orange anti-malarial pill (chloroquine-primaquine) taken once a week by US troops in Vietnam *US, 1990*

mondo *adjective* large *US, 1982*

mondo *adverb* very *US, 1968*

money *noun* **1** someone who is attractive, nice and generally a good catch. Popularised as a catchphrase by the film *Swingers US, 1997*. **2** a close friend or trusted colleague *US, 1992*. **3** in prison, anything of value in trade *US, 1976*. ▶ **have money to burn** to be rich, to have plenty to spend *US, 1896*. ▶ **in the money 1** wealthy, especially if exceptionally so; comfortably off *UK, 1902*. **2** in horse

racing, finishing first, second or third in a race *US, 1964*. ▶ **it's only money** said to yourself or another, as encouragement to spend or consolation, when faced with an unwanted or unexpected expense *UK, 1984*. ▶ **money talks and bullshit walks** used as a humorous suggestion that talk is cheap *US, 1984*. ▶ **money to stone dogs** a lot of money. Pelting anything handy at foraging stray dogs is a common habit among the poor. *JAMAICA, 2001*. ▶ **put your money where your mouth is** to back up your words with a wager or a payment *US, 1942*. ▶ **you pays your money and you takes your choice!; you pays your money!** only if you contribute to something in some manner are you entitled to hold an opinion or take advantage of that something. A catchphrase. Originally, and in its literal sense, a stallholder's cry to customers, recorded in *Punch* in 1846. Familiarity has shortened the phrase without amending its sense *UK, 2000*

moneybags *noun* a wealthy individual *IRELAND, 1818*

money ball *noun* in pool, a shot that if made will win a wager *US, 1990*

money box *noun* **1** a Royal Mail train *UK, 1970*. **2** any money that remains after the necessities of life are paid for *NEW ZEALAND, 1984*

money for jam *noun* easily obtained or earned money *AUSTRALIA, 1960*

money for old rope *noun* money easily earned, hence anything gained by little or no effort *UK, 1936*

money from home *noun* any money won easily, betting *US, 1951*

money-getter *noun* the vagina *US, 1973*

money-grabber *noun* in motor racing, a driver who enters an event and competes only long enough to claim the fee for appearing and then quits the race *US, 1993*

money in the bank and cattle in the hills *noun* independently wealthy *US, 1954*

money machine *noun* a generous person *US, 1997*

moneymaker *noun* **1** the genitals; the buttocks *UK, 1896*. **2** a success *US, 1899*. **3** a low-priced, reliable truck *US, 1971*

money player *noun* an athlete who performs well in critical situations *US, 1922*

moneypuker *noun* an automatic cash machine *CANADA, 1993*

money rider *noun* in horse racing, a winning jockey *US, 1951*

money row *noun* a type of bet in an illegal numbers game lottery *US, 1957*

money shot *noun* a scene in a pornographic film or photograph of a man ejaculating outside his partner. Perhaps because it is the one shot that justifies the cost of the scene *US, 1977*

money-spinner *noun* anything that makes easy profits *UK, 1952*

money talks those who have money have power *US, 1905*

Monfort lane *noun* the passing lane on a motorway *US, 1977*

mong *noun* **1** a fool; used as an all-purpose insult. Abbreviated from the offensive usage of 'mongoloid' (affected with Down's syndrome) *UK, 1996*. **2** a dog of mixed breed. Shortening of 'mongrel' *AUSTRALIA, 1903*

mong; mong out *verb* (of drugs) to intoxicate; to become intoxicated. Derives from the conventional sense of 'mongol' (a person affected by Down's syndrome, also meaning 'a stupid person') *UK, 1996*

monged *adjective* **1** drunk *UK, 2002*. **2** being fatigued after drug use *UK, 2002*

monged-out; monged *adjective* intoxicated with MDMA, the recreational drug best known as ecstasy, or, occasionally, another drug. Derives from the conventional sense of 'mongol' (a person affected by Down's syndrome, also meaning 'a stupid person') *UK, 2000*

mongee *noun* a good student who is socially inept. School usage *US, 1961*

mongie *noun* a member of the Mongrel Mob gang *NEW ZEALAND, 1982*

mongie *adjective* **1** dirty, fusty, evil smelling; nasty. Reported in use amongst Leicestershire children during the 1970s. Presumably expanding the insulting use derived from 'mongoloid' *UK, 1984*. **2** dull, stupid. From 'mongoloid'. Teen slang *UK, 1984*

mongish *adjective* dull, stupid. From 'mongoloid' *UK, 1980*

mongo *noun* **1** an idiot. Abbreviated from the offensive usage of 'mongoloid' (affected with Down's syndrome); probably used without thinking *US, 1975*. **2** the vagina *US, 1998*. **3** a member of the Mongrel Mob gang *NEW ZEALAND, 1977*

mongo *adjective* very large *US, 1985*

mongo *adverb* in foot-propelled scootering, with the wrong foot. From MONGO (an idiot) *UK, 2000*

mongo-footed *adjective* in foot-propelled scootering, used of someone who pushes with the wrong foot. From MONGO (an idiot) *UK, 2000*

Mongolian clusterfuck *noun* an orgy *US, 1986*

mongrel *noun* a contemptible person. Without any suggestion of mixed breeding *AUSTRALIA, 1902*

mongrel *adjective* displeasurable; unsatisfying; annoying. Used as a negative intensifier *AUSTRALIA, 1967*

mongy *adjective* stupid. From MONG, ultimately 'mongoloid' *UK, 1998*

moniker; monicker *noun* **1** a nickname or sobriquet *UK, 1851*. **2** a signature. Extended from the sense as 'a person's name' *UK, 1851*. **3** the mark that identifies dice as being from a given casino or gambling house *US, 1950*

moniker file *noun* a list of street names or aliases maintained by the police *US, 1981*

monjaree *verb* ▷*see:* MUNGAREE

monk *noun* a monkey *US, 1841*. ▶ **have a monk on** to be angry *UK, 1995*. ▶ **out the monk** completely drunk *NEW ZEALAND, 1964*

monkey *noun* **1** an addiction, especially to heroin or another drug *US, 1949*. **2** five hundred pounds sterling; five hundred US dollars; five hundred Australian dollars *UK, 1832*. **3** fifty pounds sterling. A prison variation; the reduction in value from the outside world's 500-unit is an economic reality *UK, 1950*. **4** 500 shares at £100 each, £50,000 (fifty thousand pounds worth of stock) *UK, 1984*. **5** a naughty rascal; generally said of someone younger *UK, 1604*. **6** in circus and carnival usage, a gullible customer who has been swindled *US, 1922*. **7** a carnival worker who climbs to assemble rides *US, 1966*. **8** a press photographer. Journalists' slang, allegedly from the ungainly gait a press photographer adopts to manage all his equipment; a less disingenuous possibility derives the term from the organ grinder and his monkey *UK, 2004*. **9** a gambler who complains to the police about an illegal gambling operation after losing *US, 1950*. **10** a band leader. A reference to the tuxedo, or MONKEY SUIT, worn by many band leaders *US, 1942*. **11** a poor poker player *US, 1988*. **12** in motorcycle racing, the passenger in a sidecar who works in tandem with the driver *US, 1973*. **13** your boyfriend's or girlfriend's 'other' person *US, 1989*. **14** a white person *US, 1992*. **15** the vagina *US, 1888*. **16** the penis. As in phrases SPANK THE MONKEY (to masturbate) and MARINATE THE MONKEY (to perform oral sex) *US, 1989*. **17** a two-wheeled trailer designed to carry extra long loads *UK, 1951*. **18** in horse racing, a $100 bet *US, 1991*. **19** nonsense *US, 1997*. **20** in card games, a face card *US, 1985* ▷*see:* MONKEY ON YOUR BACK. ▶ **marinate the monkey** to perform oral sex *US, 2001*. ▶ **monkey has a nosebleed** experiencing the bleed period of the menstrual cycle. From MONKEY (the vagina) *US, 2001*. ▶ **put it where the monkey put the nuts!; shove them where the monkey shoved his nuts!; stick it where the monkey stuck his nuts!** used as an angry expression of dismissal or refusal. Anatomically: 'in the anus'; figuratively: UP YOUR ASS/ARSE! *UK, 1879*

monkey *verb* to fiddle, to tamper, to fool around with *US, 1876*

monkey around; monkey about *verb* to behave foolishly, to waste time *US, 1884*

monkey bath *noun* a very hot bath. So hot that when lowering yourself into the water an involuntary (monkey-like?) cry of 'Ooh! Ooh! Aah! Aah!' is emitted *NEW ZEALAND, 2002*

monkey bite *noun* **1** a bruise on the skin produced by extended sucking *US, 1942*. **2** a painful pinch *US, 1997*

monkey boots *noun* a heavy work shoe embraced as a fashion statement by punks and post-punks *US, 1997*

monkey box *noun* the vagina. Either a combination of MONKEY (the vagina) and BOX (the vagina) or MONKEY (the penis) and BOX (the vagina) *US, 1998*

monkey business *noun* mischief; foolishness. The term is powerfully etched in American culture because of revelations in 1987 that Gary Hart, then a married US Senator campaigning for the presidential nomination, had taken an overnight cruise to Bimini with a stunningly attractive woman, Donna Rice, on the aptly named yacht 'Monkey Business'. Hart withdrew from the race under attack as an adulterer *US, 1883*

monkey cage; monkey house; monkey hut; monkey wagon *noun* a brakevan (caboose) *US, 1977*

monkey dick *noun* a link sausage *US, 1965*

monkey drill; monkey pump *noun* a hypodermic needle and syringe *US, 1986*

monkey dust *noun* phencyclidine, the recreational drug known as PCP or angel dust *US, 1981*

monkey flush *noun* in poker, three cards of the same suit, unpaired and without value *US, 1963*

monkey-full *adjective* drunk *UK, 2002*

monkey house *noun* a brothel *US, 1949*

monkey maze *noun* a confusing, complicated traffic interchange *US, 1962*

monkey meat *noun* in Nova Scotia, the small white edible pods or nuts at the base of the fiddlehead fern *CANADA, 1999*

monkey money *noun* **1** an excessive price to pay; silly money. Acquired an earlier US usage, now obsolete, as 'foreign money' *UK, 1999*. **2** the salary paid to film extras in US films shot in Canada *CANADA, 2002*. **3** on the railways, a pass to ride for free *US, 1977*

monkey motion *noun* in hot rodding and drag racing, unwanted movement in any mechanical device *US, 1965*

monkey-on-a-stick *adjective* a style of horse racing using short stirrups. Popularised by jockey Ted Sloan (1874–1933), whose abnormally short legs made the style – widely used today – a necessary innovation. Also applied in the UK to the riding position adopted on early motorcycles *US, 1949*

monkey on your back; monkey *noun* **1** an addiction to drugs, especially heroin. A tenacious monkey is hard to shake off *US, 1959*. **2** in sports, the inability to beat a certain opponent. Used in many sports, but probably most commonly in tennis *US, 1988*

monkey pants *noun* a difficult situation *TRINIDAD AND TOBAGO, 1950*

monkey-parade *noun* an informal but regular event, in some public place, in which (generally) young people, intent on meeting and flirting with the opposite sex, stroll in couples and groups of friends to advertise themselves to others similarly engaged. Recorded in London around the beginning of C20 *UK, 1914*

monkey rum *noun* illegally manufactured alcohol coloured by molasses *US, 1985*

monkey's; monkey's fuck *noun* a notional article of no value. Used in the phrase '(not) give a monkey's fuck', an elaboration of (not) GIVE A FUCK; generally reduced to '(not) give a monkey's' *UK, 1960*

monkey see monkey do! a catchphrase warning against imitating an action, or of doing something that may be imitated; used teasingly of someone who copies an action; applied to an action that is performed by imitation but without understanding *US, 1977*

monkey's fist *noun* a knot tied on the end of a heaving line *US, 1975*

monkeyshines *noun* foolish antics, embarrassing behaviour *US, 1828*

monkey's nuts *noun* cigarette butts. Rhyming slang in current use by prison inmates; a possible play on DOG END (a cigarette butt) via DOG'S BOLLOCKS (the best) *UK, 2001*

monkeyspunk *noun* nonsense *UK, 2004*

monkey's tail *noun* a nail (for hammering). Rhyming slang *UK, 1934*

monkey strap *noun* a lifeline that secures a helicopter gunner to the helicopter *AUSTRALIA, 1945*

monkey suit *noun* **1** a formal evening dress suit; a tuxedo *US, 1895*. **2** any uniform worn by a railway employee on a passenger train *US, 1901*

monkey's uncle *noun* used in non-profane oaths to register surprise *US, 1926*

monkey wagon *noun* ▷ *see:* MONKEY CAGE

Monkey Ward *nickname* Montgomery Ward, a department store chain. A play on the sound *US, 1912*

monkey wrench *verb* to repair (a car or truck engine) *US, 1961*

monk-on *noun* a gloomy, introspective mood *ANTARCTICA, 2003*

mono *noun* **1** mononeucleosis glandular fever *US, 1964*. **2** a black and white television set; a monophonic sound reproduction system. An abbreviation of 'monochrome', 'monaural' or 'monophonic'; a term only needed, outside of its jargon application, until colour television and stereo sound were widely available *UK, 1970*

monobrow *noun* two eyebrows joined by hair growth above the nose *AUSTRALIA, 1990*

monolithic *adjective* extremely drug-intoxicated *US, 1971*

mono-rump *noun* the buttocks formed into a single mass by a garment *US, 1974*

monsoon bucket *noun* a helicopter-borne water container used for aerial bombardment of forest fires *CANADA, 1997*

monsta *adjective* formidable; excellent. A deliberate misspelling of MONSTER (excellent) *US, 1999*

monster *noun* **1** something that is extremely and unusually large *UK, 1759*. **2** a formidable piece of equipment *US, 1955*. **3** an immense wave, surfed by a special and small class of surfers *US, 1987*. **4** a string of multiple Claymore mines arranged to detonate sequentially *US, 1991*. **5** in poker, a great hand or large amount of money bet *US, 1982*. **6** any powerful drug; cocaine *US, 1975*. **7** used as a term of endearment. Teen slang *US, 1954*. **8** an extremely unattractive woman who is seen as a sex object, especially one who is ravaged by age *UK, 2002*. **9** a sex offender, a convicted paedophile. Prison usage *UK, 1996*

monster *verb* **1** to make a verbal attack on someone or something; to put pressure on *AUSTRALIA, 1967*. **2** to harass, threaten or victimise someone *AUSTRALIA, 1967*

monster *adjective* **1** large, formidable, impressive *US, 1975*. **2** excellent. Originally black usage *US, 1953*

monstered *adjective* drunk *UK, 2003*

monstering *noun* **1** a severe telling-off. From MONSTER (to attack verbally) *1998*. **2** a sudden swoop by paparazzi photographers on their subject *UK, 2004*

monster lane *noun* in the US, the lane used for overtaking; in the UK, the slow lane *US, 1976*

monster munch *noun* the vagina. Derives, probably, from Monster Munch™, a branded savoury snack food *UK, 2001*

monster net *noun* during the Vietnam war, the secure radio network connecting radios in the field and headquarters *US, 1990*

monster shot *noun* in pornography, a close-up shot of genitals *US, 1970*

monster truck *noun* a pickup truck with oversized wheels and tyres (large enough to drive over and crush a standard passenger car) and an enhanced engine and transmission. Only in America *US, 1984*

Montana maiden *noun* a ewe. Sheep will be sheep and men will be men. Collected from a former resident of Iowa, March 2001 *US, 2001*

monte *noun* **1** a potent marijuana from Mexico; marijuana from South America; marijuana. From the Spanish for 'bush'- BUSH (marijuana) – or clipping of MONTEZUMA GOLD *US, 1980*. **2** the three card trick, also known as three card monte *UK, 1977* ▷ *see:* FULL MONTY

Monte *nickname* Monte Carlo *UK, 1959*

Monte Cairo *noun* a social security/benefits cheque. Rhyming slang for GIRO *UK, 2000*

Montezuma gold *noun* potent marijuana cultivated in Mexico. From Montezuma II (1466–1520), the ninth Aztec emperor of Mexico *US, 1978*

montezumas *noun* bloomers (capacious underpants for women). Rhyming slang *UK, 1992*

Montezuma's revenge *noun* diarrhoea suffered by tourists in Mexico. Montezuma II (1466–1520), the ninth Aztec emperor of Mexico, famously died as a result of his confrontation with Spanish invaders. Former US President Ronald Reagan in 1981 exhibited what commentator David Brinkley referred to as 'excruciatingly bad taste' by telling a joke about Montezuma's revenge at a state dinner in Mexico City *US, 1960*

month in Congress *noun* a period served in solitary confinement *US, 1976*

monthlies *noun* the bleed period of the menstrual cycle *UK, 1872*

monthly bill *noun* the bleed period of the menstrual cycle *US, 1989*

monthly blues *noun* the bleed period of the menstrual cycle *US, 1954*

monthly evacuations *noun* the bleed period of the menstrual cycle *US, 1999*

monthly monster *noun* the bleed period of the menstrual cycle *US, 2000*

monthly return *noun* the bleed period of the menstrual cycle *US, 1999*

monthly turns *noun* the bleed period of the menstrual cycle *US, 1999*

monthly visitor *noun* the bleed period of the menstrual cycle *US, 2001*

month of Sundays *noun* a long time, with time passing slowly *US, 1986*

montrel *noun* a watch. From obsolete 'montra' (a watch) *UK, 2002*

monty *noun* **1** everything required within a given context. An abbreviation of the FULL MONTY *UK, 2000*. **2** a certainty *AUSTRALIA, 1894*

moo *noun* **1** an unpleasant or contemptible woman. A variation of COW. With the descriptor 'silly' the sense is often softened (foolish woman), or even made affectionate. Widely associated with mid-1960s BBC television bigot, the comic creation Alf Garnett, played by Warren Mitchell *UK, 1967*. **2** a silly person *AUSTRALIA, 1970*. **3** money *US, 1941*

mooch *noun* **1** a person who gives his money to swindlers, a dupe *US, 1927*. **2** in the car sales business, a customer who thinks that with arithmetic skills, a calculator and his sharp mind he can outsmart the salesman *US, 1975*. ▶ **on the mooch** alert for any chance to beg or borrow *UK, 1864*. ▶ **the mooch** idling, scrounging, skulking *UK, 1859*

mooch *verb* **1** to wander without purpose; to loiter *UK, 1851*. **2** to beg from friends, to sponge *UK, 1857*

moocher *noun* a beggar; one who sponges off others, a freeloader *US, 1851*

mooching *noun* in British Columbia, very simple, inexpensive fishing *CANADA, 1960*

moo-cow *noun* a cow. Childish *UK, 1812*

mood *noun* ▶ **in the mood** desiring sex. A euphemistic colloquialism *UK, 1984*

moodies *noun* faked tablets of MDMA, the recreational drug best known as ecstasy. By ellipsis from MOODY (fake) and E (ecstasy tablets) *UK, 1996*

moody *verb* **1** to sulk or be bad-tempered *UK, 1962*. **2** to put into good humour by means of ingratiating talk, to wheedle, flatter or humour *UK, 1934*

moody *adjective* simulated, faked *UK, 1958*

moody; old moody *noun* **1** a fit of sulking. May be preceded by either 'the' or 'a', often in forms such as: 'pull a/the moody' and 'throw a/the moody' *UK, 1969*. **2** lies, deceit, especially deceit by flattery, a confidence trick (see, especially, the 1977 citation) *UK, 1934*. **3** a period of (extreme) moodiness *UK, 1968*. **4** in prison, a psychiatrist's man-to-man, or even genial, approach to a prisoner.

Usually with 'the' *UK, 1945.* ▶ **do a moody** to behave suspiciously. Prison use *UK, 1978*

Moody and Sankey; moody *noun* deception, trickery. Rhyming slang for HANKY PANKY, formed on US evangelists Dwight Lyman Moody and Ira D. Sankey, jointly known (and vilified) as Moody and Sankey, who brought their message to the UK in the mid-1870s. This term may well have evolved separately or be bound up with MOODY; OLD MOODY (lies, deception) *UK, 1961*

mooey; moey; mooe *noun* the mouth. From Romany *mooi* (mouth, face) *UK, 1859*

mooi *adjective* pretty, pleasant, fine, nice. From Afrikaans *mooi* (pretty) *SOUTH AFRICA, 1850*

moo juice *noun* milk *US, 1942*

mook *noun* an incompetent person who is to be more pitied than despised *US, 1930*

mooksey *adjective* dim-witted, stupid-looking *TRINIDAD AND TOBAGO, 1993*

moola; moolah; mullah *noun* money *US, 1939*

moo-moo maker *noun* in Nova Scotia, a livestock caller *CANADA, 1962*

moon *noun* **1** used as a quaint, indefinite measure of time *US, 1988.* **2** a month's imprisonment *UK, 1830.* **3** a smooth, convex wheel cover *US, 1980.* **4** a flat, circular piece of hashish *US, 1972.* **5** illegally manufactured alcoholic drink. An abbreviation of MOONSHINE *US, 1928.* ▶ **over the moon** extremely pleased, delighted *UK, 1974.* ▶ **the moon** the bleed period of the menstrual cycle. Euphemism *US, 1999*

moon *verb* **1** to flash your exposed buttocks at someone. From the venerable sense as 'the buttocks' *US, 1963.* **2** to experience the bleed period of the menstrual cycle. Emphasises the monthly rhythm of the menstrual cycle *US, 2000.* **3** to idle, especially to move listlessly. Generally combined with 'about', 'along', or 'around' *UK, 1848.* **4** in a split-pot game of poker, to declare or win both high and low. An abbreviation of 'shoot the moon' *US, 1988*

moonbeam *noun* a flashlight *US, 1991*

mooneas *noun* in the Canadian West, a newcomer, a greenhorn. The word comes from Cree, where it originally meant 'a white man' *CANADA, 1966*

moonie *noun* **1** a deliberately provocative display of a person's naked buttocks. From the verb MOON, *2000.* **2** any blind, unthinking, unquestioning follower of a philosophy or person. An extension of the early 1970s labelling of followers of the Reverend Sun Myung Moon *US, 1991.* ▶ **pull a moonie** to deliberately display naked buttocks. From MOONIE (a provocative display of naked buttocks); logically you would 'make a moonie', however, among older children and young teenagers in South Wales in 2003, 'pull a moonie' appears to be the predominant form *UK, 2003*

moonlight *noun* a discreet and hurried departure to avoid debts, especially of such an absconding made at night. A shortening of MOONLIGHT FLIT *UK, 1958*

moonlight *verb* to work a second job, especially at night *US, 1957*

moonlight express *noun* trucking by an independent, illegal and inexpensive operation *US, 1971*

moonlight flit *noun* a discreet and hurried departure to avoid debts, especially of such an absconding made at night *UK, 1824*

moonlight flits; moonlights *noun* the female breasts. Rhyming slang for TIT(S) *UK, 1998*

moonlight freight *noun* freight hauled illegally *US, 1963*

moonlight requisition *noun* the notional procedure attached to stolen materials *US, 1946*

moon rock *noun* the combination of heroin and crack cocaine *US, 1989*

moon rocks *noun* crack cocaine. An elaboration of ROCK *UK, 2003*

moonshine *noun* **1** privately and illegally distilled alcohol *UK, 1782.* **2** an aircraft used for dropping magnesium-based flares to illuminate the ground at night *US, 1990*

moonshine 1; moonshine 2 *noun* hybrid varieties of hashish produced in Holland *UK, 2003*

moonshot *noun* **1** anal sex *US, 1972.* **2** outdoor sex at night *US, 1986*

moonstomp *verb* an ungainly dance associated with the skinhead youth cult. Popular with authors looking back to the 1960s and 70s *UK, 1999*

moon-time *noun* the bleed period of the menstrual cycle. Emphasises the monthly rhythm of the cycle *US, 2000*

moonwalk *verb* to perform a dance-step which, when it is done well, gives the impression of walking forward whilst gliding in reverse. Popularised by pop singer Michael Jackson (b.1958); it derives from a supposed similarity to walking on the moon *US, 1984*

moony *noun* any slow or romantic dance, or the music for it, played at an organised dance or disco, especially at the end of an evening *UK: SCOTLAND, 1988*

moop *noun* a person suffering from chronic disorientation in Arctic regions or Antarctica produced by long days and then long nights *ANTARCTICA, 1959*

moo poo *noun* cow manure *AUSTRALIA, 1994*

Moor *noun* ▶ **the Moor** Dartmoor prison *UK, 1869*

moose *noun* **1** in the Korean war, a girlfriend, mistress or prostitute. From the Japanese *musume US, 1951.* **2** an unattractive female *IRELAND, 1995.* **3** in poker, a large pot *US, 1996*

moose call *noun* a howling sound emitted by the Lockheed Starfighter *CANADA, 1995*

moose-eyed *adjective* infatuated; in love *US, 2000*

moose farm *noun* a college sorority whose members are perceived as not particularly attractive *US, 1968*

moose-gooser *noun* an Alaska Railroad train *US, 1948*

moose knuckle *noun* the condition that exists when a tight-fitting pair of trousers, shorts, bathing suit or other garment forms a wedge between a woman's labia, accentuating their shape *US, 1988*

moose milk *noun* an improvised alcoholic mixed drink, especially a homebrew Yukon cocktail made of milk and rum *US, 1957*

moose pasture *noun* **1** in the Canadian West, worthless or unproven mining claims *CANADA, 1962.* **2** any worthless (or nonexistent) land sold as part of a confidence swindle *US, 1985*

moose pasture con *noun* a big con in which the victim is induced to invest in a company that appears on the verge of a great secret success *US, 1997*

moosh *noun* **1** the mouth. After MUSH *AUSTRALIA, 1916.* **2** jail porridge *AUSTRALIA, 1944*

moosh *verb* to shove in the face *US, 1998*

moosh; mush; mushie; mooshy *adjective* fine, excellent, pleasant, nice, super, etc *ZIMBABWE, 1973*

mooshay *noun* a light-skinned person; an unlikeable person *SAINT KITTS AND NEVIS, 1998*

moot *noun* the vagina. Origin unknown *AUSTRALIA, 1978*

moota *noun* marijuana. The Mexican Spanish slang *mota* (marijuana) was smuggled north with the drug. Variant spellings include 'moocah', 'mootah', 'mooter', 'mootie', 'mooster', 'mootos', 'motta', 'muta' and 'mutah' *US, 1926*

mooters *noun* a marijuana cigarette. From MOOTA *UK, 2003*

mop *noun* **1** a head of hair *UK, 1821.* **2** your date for an evening. Teen slang *US, 1954*

MOP *adjective* in the military, missing on purpose *US, 1985*

mop and bucket! a general declaration of rejection or dimissal; may also imply resignation to, or acceptance of, a situation. Rhyming slang for FUCK IT! *UK, 1992*

Mop and Pail *nickname* the *Toronto Globe and Mail* newspaper. This derogatory nickname is surely jocular, as the newspaper is the foremost national newspaper of Canada *CANADA, 2001*

mop booth *noun* a private booth where pornographic films are shown for a fee *US, 2001*

mope *noun* **1** a person who is not particularly bright. From C16 to C19 a part of colloquial speech, 'mope' reappeared 200 years later as slang *US, 1919.* **2** in hospital usage, a nonsurgeon physician. A derogatory evolution of the term 'medical outpatient' US, 1994. **3** a thug US, 1997

mope verb a stealthy escape US, 1926

mope away; mope verb to quit your job in the circus US, 1980

moped noun a fat female; a promiscuous female. From a joke, because both are fun but you don't want anybody to see you on one US, 2001

mopery noun incompetence, stupidity US, 1907

mop jockey noun a janitor or custodian US, 1958

mopp verb to don protective clothing and breathing apparatus against chemical warfare. From the official designation 'mission oriented protective posture.' US, 1993

mopper noun a person who tends to wheedle drinks from friends TRINIDAD AND TOBAGO, 1950

moppet noun a child UK, 1601

mop-squeezer noun in a deck of playing cards, a queen US, 1949

mopsy noun a girlfriend TRINIDAD AND TOBAGO, 1938

moptop noun a youth or a young man who wears his hair in a fringed style popularised by the Beatles in the early 1960s UK, 1964

mop-up noun the end-game of a conflict, in which the stragglers of the losing side are rounded up UK, 1917

mop up verb **1** to win UK, 1861. **2** to consume drinks bought by others TRINIDAD AND TOBAGO, 1971

mop-up boy noun a worker performing janitorial work at an arcade where men masturbate while watching videos US, 1997

moragrifa noun marijuana US, 1966

moral noun a certainty. From the phrase 'a moral certainty' UK, 1861

morale-booster noun any stupid act by the authorities that has the immediate effect of lowering morale US, 1968

morale-raising flour noun cocaine. A play on the name and appearance of self-raising flour UK, 2002

more noun phencyclidine, the recreational drug known as PCP or angel dust US, 1994

more fool used to describe the subject as foolish for acting in a given manner. Often as an exclamation UK, 1959

more hide than Jessie adjective extremely cheeky AUSTRALIA, 1951

more like; more like it adjective would be nearer, better, more acceptable, more accurate UK, 1888

more or less noun a dress. Rhyming slang UK, 1992

more power to your elbow! a catchphrase of encouragement or good wishes. Used as a headline UK, 1860

more pricks than a pincushion an alleged achievement of a promiscuous woman AUSTRALIA, 1971

more tea, vicar(?) used humorously to acknowledge a fart or a belch UK, 1985

more than somewhat adverb very, extremely, to a great degree, very much. Coinage credited to US writer Damon Runyan US, 1930

Moreton Bay fig; Moreton Bay; Moreton noun **1** a busybody. Rhyming slang GIG. From the name of a type of large native figtree AUSTRALIA, 1944. **2** a police informer. Rhyming slang for GIG. May be spelt 'Morton' AUSTRALIA, 1975

MORF used as Internet shorthand to mean 'male or female' US, 1997

morgue noun in circus and carnival usage, a performance or series of performances in a town that fail to attract more than a few customers US, 1904

Moriarty; mori noun a party, a celebration. Rhyming slang; informed, if not inspired, by one of two fictional characters: either the arch-enemy of Sherlock Holmes or the comic creation of Spike Milligan in The Goons UK, 1981

Mork and Mindy adjective windy. Rhyming slang, based on cult US television comedy Mork and Mindy (first broadcast 1978–82) UK, 2002

Mormons noun in hold 'em poker, a king and two queens. An allusion to the practice of plural marriage US, 1996

morning noun ▶ **the top of the morning!; top of the morning to you!** used as a cheery greeting. A stereotypical Irish-ism IRELAND, 1815

morning after the night before noun a morning hangover; applied generally (as a diagnosis) to someone suffering the effects of drinking to excess UK, 1922

morning glory noun **1** an erection upon waking up in the morning. Rhyming slang for COREY (the penis), formed from the name of a popular garden flower (Ipomoea violacea) UK, 1992. **2** an act of sexual intercourse in the morning AUSTRALIA, 1960. **3** a drug addict's first injection of the morning US, 1959. **4** in horse racing, a horse that runs well in early morning workouts but not during races US, 1904

morning line noun in horse racing, the odds established by the racetrack handicapper the morning before a race US, 1967

morning prayers noun a daily briefing on the work to be done. First recorded as 'prayers, family prayers and morning prayers' a World War 2 military term for daily staff conference at HQ UK, 1995

morning shot noun a drug user's first injection that day US, 1986

morning wood noun an erection experienced upon waking US, 1997

Moroccan black noun a variety of marijuana. Named for its source and colour UK, 1996

moron noun a stupid person, a fool. Adopted from the Greek in 1910 to classify a person with an IQ of between 50 and 70; this correct technical sense is now largely avoided US, 1921

moron corps noun the US Army during the Vietnam war. The US Armed Forces qualification test passing score was lowered substantially in the late 1960s to help swell the ranks of the army with poor urban black men, poor rural white men and Mexican-Americans US, 1990

morotgara noun heroin US, 1977

morph verb **1** to change body shape or image. From cinematographic jargon for blending one image into another by means of computer manipulation UK, 2002. **2** to create an electronic message in a manner that gives the appearance of having been sent by someone else US, 1997

morphing noun the act of taking morphine. A shape-changing pun UK, 1996

morphy noun an hermaphrodite BARBADOS, 1965

Morris Minor noun a black eye. Rhyming slang for 'shiner', formed from a type of car manufactured from 1948–71 UK, 1992

mort noun a dolt. Prison usage NEW ZEALAND, 1997

mortal adjective drunk UK, 1994

mortal combat noun very potent heroin US, 1997

mortalled adjective drunk UK: SCOTLAND, 1996

mortaller noun literally a mortal sin, figuratively a terrible thing IRELAND, 2002

mortal lock noun in horse racing, a bet that is sure to win US, 1951

mortal nuts noun in poker, a hand that is sure to win US, 1979

morto adjective mortified IRELAND, 2001

MOS noun the typical man on the street US, 1997

MOS adjective in television and film-making, said of a scene shot without sound US, 1977

Moscow noun a pawnshop AUSTRALIA, 1941

Moscow mule noun a cocktail of vodka, lager (or ginger ale) and lime. 'Moscow' in honour of the vodka, 'mule' for the kick UK, 1967

mosey verb to move slowly and seemingly aimlessly; to amble. Introduces a folksy tone US, 1829

mosey at verb to casually investigate or explore. Possibly from MOSEY (to amble) combined with the sense of 'nosey' (inquisitive) UK, 2001

mosh verb (at a rock music concert, especially hardcore, punk or metal) to jump/dance in a violent and ungainly manner, deliberately crashing into other moshers US, 1983

mosher noun a dancer at a rock concert (especially hardcore, punk or metal) who responds to the music with violent and ungainly bouncing – mainly off other moshers; by extension a dedicated fan of a rock genre *UK, 2002*

moshie *noun* a mosher *AUSTRALIA, 1996*

moshky *noun* a marijuana user *US, 1971*

mosh pit *noun* an area in a dance hall where dancers mosh *US, 1992*

mosquitos; mosquitoes *noun* cocaine *US, 1994*

moss *noun* **1** hair *US, 1926*. **2** seaweed *BARBADOS, 1965*

mossback *noun* **1** an old person with outmoded ideas and values *US, 1878*. **2** a promiscuous girl *US, 1982*

mossie; mozzie; mozzy *noun* **1** a mosquito *AUSTRALIA, 1936*. **2** a sparrow *SOUTH AFRICA, 1884*

most *noun* ▶ **the most** the best *US, 1953*

most *adverb* very *US, 1989*

most def!; mos' def! used for expressing emphatic agreement *US, 1998*

mostie *noun* a sexually attractive woman *NEW ZEALAND, 1998*

most ricky tick *adverb* promptly, immediately. Mock pidgin, used by US soldiers during the Vietnam war *US, 1987*

MOT *noun* a Jewish person identified as such by another Jewish person *US, 1989*

MOT *verb* to conduct an MOT test of a vehicle's roadworthiness. From the official abbreviation of the Ministry of Transport test, introduced in 1960 and grown more stringent since *UK, 2002*

mot; mott *noun* a woman, a girlfriend, a wife. Liverpool Irish usage *UK, 1785*

mota; moto *noun* marijuana. The Mexican Spanish slang *mota* (marijuana) was smuggled north with the drug, *US, 1933*

motate *verb* to move *US, 1967*

MOT'd *adjective* of a vehicle, having passed the MOT test, having an MOT certificate *UK, 1984*

motel time used to signal that a bar is closing and that customers must leave *US, 1965*

moth *noun* in horse racing, a groom or racehorse attendant who is attracted to the bright lights of nightlife *AUSTRALIA, 1989*

mothball *noun* an ether ball used to start a cold diesel truck engine *US, 1971*

mothball *verb* to take out of service; to set against possible future use *US, 1949*

mother *noun* **1** a man; a thing. A slightly euphemistic MOTHERFUCKER; sometimes a low form of abuse, sometimes merely jocular; *US, 1951*. **2** used of, or to, a wife if she is also a mother *UK, 1961*. **3** a male homosexual in relation to a man whom he has introduced to homosexuality *US, 1946*. **4** a (very) senior secretary. Civil service use *UK, 1977*. **5** a drug dealer *US, 1970*. **6** marijuana. Probably an anglicised 'mutha' *US, 1968*. **7** heroin; a heroin dealer; a homosexual heroin dealer. Perhaps a euphemistic reduction of MOTHERFUCKER *US, 1992*. ▶ **be mother** to assume reponsibility for dispensing hot drinks or refreshments. Of either sex but reflecting a general perception of a mother's traditional role *UK, 1934*. ▶ **you love your mother better than your father; you love your father better than your mother** between schoolgirls, used as a warning that a slip or petticoat can be seen below the hem of a skirt *UK, 1977*. ▶ **your mother** used as a self-reference by older homosexual men *US, 1974*

mother and father of all *noun* an epic, if not the epic, example. An elaboration of MOTHER OF ALL *UK, 2002*

mother-ass; mother-arse; mudder ass *noun* used as an abusive term of address or term of reference *TRINIDAD AND TOBAGO, 1958*

mother blood! used for expressing surprise. Almost certainly a euphemism for 'motherfucker!' *BAHAMAS, 1982*

Mother Brown *nickname* the West End of London. Rhyming slang for 'town' *UK, 1992*

Mother Corp *nickname* the Canadian Broadcasting Corporation *CANADA, 2000*

mother crusher *noun* used euphemistically for 'motherfucker' *UK, 2002*

mother-cunt *noun* used as an abusive term of address or term of reference *TRINIDAD AND TOBAGO, 1972*

mother dear *noun* methedrine, a central nervous system stimulant. A phonic pun *US, 1969*

motheren; motherin *noun* used as a euphemism for 'motherfucker' or 'motherfucking' *US, 1959*

motherfather *noun* used as a euphemism for 'motherfucker'. Used by comedian Redd Foxx on *The Royal Family* (CBS, 1991–92) *US, 1992*

motherferyer *noun* used as a euphemism for 'motherfucker' *US, 1946*

motherflipping *adjective* used as a euphemism for the intensifier 'motherfucking' *US, 1961*

mother-for-you *noun* used as a euphemism for 'motherfucker' *US, 1957*

motherfouler *noun* a motherfucker *US, 1947*

motherfuck *verb* used to damn or curse *US, 1942*

motherfucker *noun* **1** a despised person. In 1972, the US Supreme Court reversed the conviction of a man who had used the word 'motherfucker' four times during remarks at a school board meeting attended by some 40 children and 25 women, accepting 'motherfucker' as constitutionally protected speech (Rosenfeld v. New Jersey, 1972) *US, 1928*. **2** a fellow, a person *US, 1958*. **3** a difficult thing or situation *US, 1958*. **4** used as a basis for extreme comparisons *US, 1962*. **5** methamphetamine hydrochloride, a powerful central nervous system stimulant *US, 1993*

motherfuckers and beans *noun* canned beans and frankfurters served as field rations by the US Army *US, 1980*

mother-fucking *noun* sexual intercourse between a son and his mother. The literal sense which precedes the rest *UK, 2000*

motherfucking *adjective* used as an emphatic intensifier. In 1972, the US Supreme Court found the statements 'mother fucking fascist pig cops' and 'god damned mother fucking police' to be constitutionally protected speech. The following year, the California Supreme embraced 'white motherfucking pig' as constitutionally protected *US, 1897*

motherfucking A! used for expressing dismay, surprise or strong assent. An embellished FUCKING A! *US, 1977*

motherfugger *noun* used as a euphemism for 'motherfucker' *US, 1948*

motherfugging *adjective* used as a euphemism for 'motherfucking'. Found throughout Norman Mailer, *The Naked and the Dead*, 1948 *US, 1948*

motherfukka *noun* a fellow, a person. A variant spelling of MOTHERFUCKER *UK, 2002*

mothergrabbing *adjective* used as a euphemism for 'motherfucking' *US, 1958*

Mother Green *nickname* the US Marine Corps. Coined in Vietnam; sometimes embellished to 'Mother Green and her Killing Machine' *US, 1978*

motherhopper *noun* used as a euphemism for 'motherfucker' *US, 1977*

Mother Hubbard *noun* a cupboard. Rhyming slang, formed from a nursery rhyme character *UK, 1992*

motherhugger *noun* used as a euphemism for 'motherfucker' *US, 1956*

motherhumper *noun* used as a clumsy euphemism for 'motherfucker' *US, 1963*

mothering *adjective* used as an intensifier. From MOTHERFUCKING *US, 1951*

mother-in-law *noun* **1** an enemy aeroplane *US, 1991*. **2** a carpenter's saw. Rhyming slang *UK, 1992*. **3** a torn cuticle *BARBADOS, 1965*

mother-in-law job *noun* a racehorse that performs well in long-distance races. The long-distance horse has staying power, and like a mother-in-law seems to stay forever *AUSTRALIA, 1989*

motherjumper *noun* used as an affected euphemism for 'motherfucker' *US, 1949*

motherjumping *adjective* used as a euphemism for 'motherfucking' *US, 1950*

Mother Kelly *noun* **1** jelly; a jelly. Rhyming slang, probably formed from the music hall song 'On Mother Kelly's Doorstep' *UK, 1992*. **2** television; a television. Rhyming slang for TELLY, noted as 'more recent' than the previous sense *UK, 1992*

motherless *adverb* absolutely, completely; especially in the phrase 'motherless broke' (penniless) *AUSTRALIA, 1898*

motherless broke *adjective* completely broke; bankrupt; destitute *AUSTRALIA, 1898*

mother lover *noun* used as a euphemism for 'motherfucker' *US, 1950*

mother loving *adjective* used as a euphemism for 'motherfucking'. Also used as an infix: 'abso-mother-lovin'-lutely!' *US, 1951*

motherlumping *adjective* used as a euphemism for the intensifier 'motherfucking' *US, 1961*

mother McCree! used for expressing disapproval. A signature line of Colonel Sherman Potter on *M*A*S*H* (CBS, 1972–83). Repeated with referential humour *US, 1976*

mother nature *noun* marijuana *US, 1969*

mother nature's gift *noun* the bleed period of the menstrual cycle *US, 1999*

Mother Nature's maracas *noun* the testicles *UK, 2003*

mother of all *adjective* an epic, if not the epic, example. From Saddam Hussein's somewhat hyperbolic prediction that the western invasion of the Persian Gulf in 1991 would be the 'mother of all battles'. Hussein's use of a common Arabic vernacular expression immediately appealed to the American and British ear, with hundreds of variations appearing over several years – 'the mother of all retreats', 'the mother of all confirmation hearings', 'the mother of all eclipses', 'the mother of all government mistakes', etc *US, 1991*

mother of God *noun* LSD *UK, 2003*

mother of pearl *noun* cocaine *US, 1983*. ▶ **the old mother of pearl; my old mother of pearl** a wife; my wife. Rhyming slang for 'old girl' *UK, 1960*

mother of shit! used for registering surprise, rage, etc. Variation on the prayer 'Mother of Christ' *US, 1988*

mother-raper *noun* used as a euphemism for 'motherfucker'. Intended as a euphemism, but one which does not leave much room for the affectionate side of MOTHERFUCKER *US, 1959*

mother-raping *adjective* used as a euphemism for 'motherfucking' *US, 1932*

mother-robbing *adjective* used as a euphemism for 'motherfucking' *US, 1948*

mothers and lovers *noun* a very small crowd at a competition *AUSTRALIA, 1989*

motherscratcher *noun* used as a euphemism for 'motherfucker' *US, 2001*

mother's day *noun* **1** payday. Because on payday you pay the money you owe to one mother(fucker) after another *US, 1965*. **2** the day when welfare cheques arrive *US, 1973*

motherseller *noun* used as a euphemism for 'motherfucker' *US, 1953*

mother's little helper *noun* **1** any tranquilliser; meprobamate (trade names Equanjill™, Meprospan™ and Miltown™), a habit-forming antianxiety agent *US, 1977*. **2** amphetamines *UK, 2003*

mother's pride *noun* a bride. Rhyming slang, possibly influenced by Mother's Pride™, a popular brand of sliced bread *UK, 1992*

mother's ruin; mothers *noun* gin. Some claims have been made that this should be noted as a piece of rhyming slang; the rhyme is certainly slurred enough for gin to be an influence *UK, 1937*

Mother Superior *noun* an older, experienced homosexual man *US, 1941*

mother wit *noun* common sense *US, 1972*

motion lotion *noun* motor fuel *US, 1976*

motions *noun* ▶ **go through the motions** to give the appearance of doing something, without actually doing it, or without doing it wholeheartedly; to conform to social expectations for the sake of appearances *UK, 1816*

motivate *verb* to leave *US, 1955*

moto *noun* a motivated self-starter *US, 1993* ▷ *see:* MOTA

motor *noun* a *motor* car *UK, 1984*

motor *verb* **1** to perform a task very well *UK, 1983*. **2** to leave *US, 1980*

Motor City *nickname* Detroit, Michigan. Because of the car manufacturing concerns in Detroit *US, 1961*

motor crap *noun* car parts made by Motorcraft, a Ford subsidiary *US, 1992*

motored out *adjective* said of a scoring device in pinball which fails to register a score because the scoring register is already in use *US, 1977*

motorhead *noun* **1** a person with more than a passing interest in the internal combustion engine *US, 1974*. **2** a fool *US, 1973*

motormouth *noun* someone who talks without end, or when it would be better not to talk *US, 1963*

motor mouth *verb* to talk incessantly *US, 1985*

motor scooter *noun* used as a euphemism for 'motherfucker' *US, 1960*

motorway *noun* (when skiing) a broad, easy piste *UK, 1982*

motorway draw *noun* marijuana. Extends DRAW (marijuana) *UK, 2001*

Motown *noun* Detroit, Michigan. After MOTOR CITY, thus 'motor *town*' from Detroit's motor industry *US, 1971*

motser; motzer; motza *noun* a large sum of money. Presumed to be from Yiddish *matse* (bread): BREAD (money). Especially used of gambling winnings *AUSTRALIA, 1936*

mott *noun* the female genitalia. From MOT (a woman) *UK, 1984*

mottled *adjective* drunk *UK, 2002*

Mott the Hoople *noun* a scruple. Rhyming slang, formed from the British rock band of the late 1960s and early 70s *UK, 2004*

mouldy *adjective* drunk *IRELAND, 1996*

mouldy fig *noun* a very dull person; specifically, used by young supporters of modern jazz of any jazz aficionado who remains loyal to a traditional form *US, 1945*

Moulin Rouge *noun* a stooge (a comedian's assistant). Theatrical rhyming slang *UK, 1980*

mouly *noun* a black person *US, 1990*

mount *noun* in hot rodding, a driver's car. A deliberate and jocular borrowing from horse racing *US, 1948*

mount *verb* ▶ **mount the red flag** to have sex with a woman experiencing the bleed period of the menstrual cycle *US, 1972*

mountain canary *noun* a mule *US, 1997*

mountain dew *noun* **1** whisky, distilled illegally *UK, 1816*. **2** rum, distilled illegally *TRINIDAD AND TOBAGO, 1926*

mountain goat *noun* **1** a comic who made his name in the Borscht Belt and then came to New York clubs to perform *US, 1973*. **2** a coat. Glasgow rhyming slang *UK, 1988*

mountain oysters *noun* lamb or calf testicles as food *US, 1857*

mountain passes *noun* spectacles, *glasses*. Rhyming slang *UK, 1960*

mountain pay *noun* working on the railways, overtime *US, 1977*

Mountie *nickname* **1** a member of the Royal Canadian Mounted Police (the Mounties). A colloquial term in such widespread use, especially via films (and the slogan: 'The Mounties always get their man'), that it is often accepted as conventional *CANADA, 1914*. **2** a student of the prestigious all-girl Dublin secondary school, Mount Anville *IRELAND, 2003*

mouse *noun* **1** a bruise *US, 1842*. **2** in the used car business, a customer or potential customer *US, 1968*. **3** the soldier on point in the front of a patrol *US, 1991*

mouse *verb* to blackmail someone *UK, 1987*

mouse droppings *noun* in computing, single pixels on a computer screen that do not reappear when the cursor of the mouse is moved away from the spot *US, 1991*

mouse house *noun* **1** a finance company *US, 1975*. **2** in the used car business, an enterprise that compartmentalises the different functions in the sales process *US, 1968*

mouse motor *noun* a small-block Chevrolet V-8 engine. Introduced in 1955, it was relatively small for its power *US, 1993*

mousetrap *noun* **1** any strong or inferior hard cheese. From the use of such cheeses to bait mousetraps *UK, 1947*. **2** a series of exit consoles on websites that link back on themselves, creating an infinite loop *US, 2003*. **3** in oil drilling, a type of tool used to retrieve objects inadvertently dropped down a hole *US, 1954*

mousetrap *verb* to ambush an enemy by drawing them into position with some sort of bait *US, 1989*

moustache *noun* a Moustache Pete *US, 1973*

moustache mob *noun* first generation immigrants from Sicily or southern Italy *US, 1955*

Moustache Pete *noun* an older Italian-American criminal, associated with outdated ways of doing things *US, 1938*

moustache ride *noun* an act of oral sex *US, 1981*

moustache rider *noun* a woman as the object of oral sex with a man *AUSTRALIA, 1985*

mouth *noun* **1** back-talk, insults *UK, 1896*. **2** a dry or furry mouth caused by too much eating or drinking. Often elaborated on the formula a 'mouth like...' – recorded examples vary from 'the bottom of a bird cage' to 'the inside of a Turkish wrestler's jockstrap' *UK, 1937*. **3** a play's reputation *US, 1973*. ▶ **give off a lot of mouth** to shout abuse *UK, 1999*. ▶ **have a mouth like a cow's cunt** to be excessively or indiscreetly talkative. An exaggerated variation of BIG MOUTH *UK, 1967*. ▶ **in the mouth** in poker, said of the first player to act in a given situation *US, 1979*. ▶ **with his mouth wide open** said of a racehorse that easily wins a race *US, 1951*

mouth *verb* to inform on someone to the police *US, 1965*

mouth and trousers *noun* a braggart *UK, 1998*

mouth bet *noun* in poker, a bet made without putting up the funds, binding among friends *US, 1889*

mouth breather *noun* a fool *UK, 1986*

mouthful *noun* **1** a word or phrase that is difficult to speak (for reasons of complexity or length, not content) *UK, 1883*. **2** something spoken which has importance or other significance. From earlier use as 'a long word' *US, 1916*. ▶ **give a mouthful** to swear or be otherwise verbally abusive to someone *US, 1941*

mouth music *noun* oral sex on a woman *UK, 1977*

mouth off *verb* to brag; to insult. Derives from the synonymous verb *US, 1958*

mouth open, story jump out used for explaining why something that was perhaps better unsaid was said *TRINIDAD AND TOBAGO, 1988*

mouthpiece *noun* **1** a lawyer *UK, 1857*. **2** a spokesperson *UK, 1805*

mouth pig *noun* a male homosexual who offers his mouth anonymously to any penis that is presented through a glory hole *US, 1996*

mouthwashing; mouthwash *noun* a non-conventional method of drinking Cointreau™ (a branded liqueur): swill a measure of the liquor around the mouth, swallow and immediately draw in a large breath. Also used as a verb *UK, 2001*

mouthy *adjective* loquacious, too talkative *UK, 1589*

move *noun* ▶ **get a move on** to hurry. Often as an imperative *US, 1888*. ▶ **on the move** about to commit a crime, especially a burglary *UK, 1996*. ▶ **put the move on** to make sexual advances *US, 1987*

move *verb* to sell, especially in bulk *US, 1938*. ▶ **get moving** to urgently begin to do or go *UK, 1963*. ▶ **move the line** in sports betting, to change the point spread that is the basis for betting on one team or the other *US, 1975*. ▶ **move under an ashen sail** to row a boat. As paddles are often made out of ash wood, to say 'he's moving under an ashen sail' is a jocular way of saying that he is not sailing, but rowing *CANADA, 1975*

move in *verb* in poker, to bet your entire bankroll *US, 1979*

movement *noun* collectively the various organisations fighting for social justice and peace in the US in the 1960s *US, 1966*

mover *noun* **1** someone who imports drugs *US, 1995*. **2** a police ticket for a moving violation *US, 1970*. **3** in casino gambling, a dice cheat who places his bet after a roll has started *US, 1962*

mover and shaker *noun* a powerful person with powerful connections *US, 1972*

moves *noun* sexual advances. Always used with 'the' *US, 1968*

movie job *noun* sex, especially sex for pay, in cinema *US, 1966*

movies *noun* police radar recordings of vehicle speed *US, 1977*

movie star drug *noun* cocaine. A reference to Hollywood's reputation for excess in the 1980s and 90s *UK, 2001*

movin' *adjective* good, pleasurable, fashionable, popular *US, 1997*

moving doctor *noun* a medical doctor. A jocular back-formation from the initials MD *CANADA, 2002*

mow *verb* **1** to shave. Usually used in describing a woman shaving her legs or her pubic area *US, 1991*. **2** to eat with gusto and stamina *US, 1991*. ▶ **mow the grass; mow the lawn** to smoke marijuana. Punning on GRASS (marijuana) *UK, 1998*

mowed lawn *noun* a shaved vulva *US, 1964*

mox; moxy *noun* a homosexual man. Recorded in contemporary gay use *UK, 2003*

moxen *noun* a group of homosexual men. The plural of MOX, recorded in contemporary gay use *UK, 2003*

moxie *noun* nerve, courage, gall. Moxie was the first mass-marketed soft drink in the US. Founded in Lowell, Massachusetts in 1884 by Dr Augustin Thompson, Moxie was touted as a patent medicine guaranteed to cure almost any ill including loss of manhood, 'paralysis, and softening of the brain'. These claims were revised with the passage of the Pure Food and Drug Act in 1906. Its sphere of influence was largely in New England *US, 1930*

moxy *adjective* lousy, very bad *IRELAND, 1999*

Mozart and Liszt; Mozart *adjective* drunk. Rhyming slang for PISSED (drunk) *UK, 1966*

mozz *noun* bad luck; a jinx. A shortening of obsolete 'mozzle', from Hebrew *mazzal* (luck). Generally in the phrase 'to put the mozz on' *AUSTRALIA, 1924*

mozz *verb* to jinx someone; to bring bad luck to someone *AUSTRALIA, 1941*

mozzle *noun* ▶ **on the mozzle** cadging, especially when seeking to borrow something small from a friend or neighbour. This derives from an obsolete piece of rhyming slang, 'mozzle and brocha' for ON THE KNOCKER (used of a door-to-door salesman); ultimately from Yiddish *mazel* (good luck) and *brocha* (a blessing) *UK, 1992*

Mrs *noun* ▶ **the Mrs** the vagina. The conventional abbreviation for 'mistress' meaning 'wife'; pronounced 'missis' *UK, 2001* ▷ *see:* MRS MORE

Mrs Doyle *noun* a boil. Rhyming slang, formed from the name of a character in UK Channel 4 television situation comedy *Father Ted*, 1995–98 *UK, 1998*

Mrs Duckett! used as a general declaration of rejection or dismissal; may also imply resignation to, or acceptance of, a situation. Rhyming slang for FUCK IT! *UK, 1960*

Mrs Mop; Mrs Mopp *noun* **1** a woman who works as a cleaner, a charwoman. After a character introduced in the fourth series of the 1940s BBC radio comedy *ITMA*; Mrs Mopp, with the catchphrase 'Can I do you now, sir?', was played by Dorothy Summers *UK, 1948*. **2** a shop. Rhyming slang. Also employed as a verb *UK, 1992*

Mrs Mopping *noun* shopping. Rhyming slang, extended from MRS MOPP (a shop) *UK, 1992*

Mrs More; the Mrs *noun* a floor, the floor. Rhyming slang, from the music hall song 'Don't Have Any More, Mrs More' *UK, 1992*

Mrs Palm and her five lovely daughters; Mrs Palmer and her five daughters *noun* the hand (seen in the context of male masturbation) *AUSTRALIA, 1955*

Mrs Ples *nickname* the skull of an Australopithecine man-ape found at Sterkfontein in 1947. Indicating the (possibly wrong) gender and his/her generic name *Plesianthropus SOUTH AFRICA, 1959*

MSM *noun* homosexual males. Initialism formed from 'men who have sex with men' *UK, 1998*

MTF *noun* a very tactile admirer of young ladies. Initialism, 'must touch flesh'. Upper-class society usage *UK, 1982*

M to F *adverb* Monday to Friday *UK, 1996*

mu *noun* **1** marijuana *US, 1936*. **2** used for expressing the sentiment that 'your question cannot be answered because it depends on incorrect assumptions'. A Japanese word borrowed by computer enthusiasts *US, 1991*

much *adverb* used for ironic emphasis *US, 1988*. ▶ **not much of a** of limited quality, quantity or degree *UK, 1889*. ▶ **not up to much** inferior *UK, 1864*

much more *adjective* very good *US, 1994*

mucho *adjective* much, a lot of. A direct borrowing from Spanish *US, 1942*

mucho *adverb* very. Directly from Spanish *US, 1973*

much of a muchness *noun* very similar, of much the same degree, size, value, etc *UK, 1728*

muck *noun* **1** semen *UK, 1997*. **2** any unpleasant, vile or disgusting thing to eat or drink *UK, 1882*. **3** bad weather *UK, 1855*. **4** stage makeup *US, 1926*. **5** in poker, the pile of discarded cards *US, 1990*. ▶ **as muck** very, exceedingly. Especially used in the phrase 'common as muck' *UK, 1782*. ▶ **make a muck of** to ruin *UK, 1906*

muck *verb* **1** in poker, to fold, to discard your hand *UK, 2003*. **2** in a casino, to spread playing cards on the table and move them randomly as part of the shuffling process *US, 2003*

muck about *verb* **1** to fool around; to trifle with *AUSTRALIA, 1946*. **2** to mess someone about *AUSTRALIA, 1965*. **3** to behave amorously towards *AUSTRALIA, 1959*

muck-a-muck; muckety-muck *noun* an important and prominent person *US, 1856*

muck around; muck about *verb* to fool around *UK, 1856*

mucked up *adjective* in disarray; confused; spoiled. A euphemism for FUCKED UP *US, 1951*

mucker *noun* **1** a friend. From MUCK IN (to share the circumstances of basic living) *UK, 1947*. **2** a person who uses sleight-of-hand to cheat at cards *US, 1996*

mucker-upper *noun* a bungler *UK, 1942*

muck in *verb* to share, on an informal basis, food, accommodation and other facilities, or work. Of military origin *UK, 1919*

mucking *noun* used as a euphemism for 'fucking'. A literary euphemism from the days when it was not permissable to reproduce the word 'fuck' in print. Not used in real language *AUSTRALIA, 1962*

mucking; muckin' *adverb* used as an intensifier. A euphemistic disguise for FUCKING *UK, 1887*

muck out *verb* to kill *US, 1984*

muck sack *noun* a lazy person *US, 1959*

mucksavage *noun* a country person *IRELAND, 1998*

muck stick *noun* a shovel *US, 1908*

muck truck *noun* in prison, a food trolley *UK, 1996*

muck-up *noun* a confusion, a muddle, a botch *UK, 1939*

muck up *verb* to botch, to ruin, to interfere *UK, 1886*

muck-up day *noun* the last day of high school where leaving students play pranks, etc *AUSTRALIA, 1994*

mucky *adjective* **1** contemptible, sordid. An old English regional term that survives in the colloquial vocabulary *UK, 1683*. **2** pornographic, especially when mildly so; lewd. From the previous sense as 'sordid' *UK, 1972*

mucky pup *noun* a dirty or untidy child. A term of disapproval *UK, 1984*

mud *noun* **1** excrement *AUSTRALIA, 1993*. **2** unprocessed opium; opium; heroin *US, 1915*. **3** coffee *US, 1875*. **4** chemical fire retardant dropped from the air *US, 2000*. **5** in circus and carnival usage, any cheap merchandise used as a prize *US, 1981*. **6** on the Internet, a multi-user dungeon, a text-based, networked, mutliparticipant virtual reality system *US, 1995*. **7** a billiard ball *US, 1993*. ▶ **up to mud** no good *AUSTRALIA, 1931*

mud *verb* (used of a racehorse) to run well on muddy track conditions *US, 1978*

mud baby *noun* faeces *US, 2003*

mud ball *noun* a doughnut or other pastry eaten with coffee. Harkened to MUD (coffee) *US, 1976*

mud butt *noun* diarrhoea *US, 2004*

muddafukka *noun* a motherfucker (in all senses) *US, 1995*

mudder *noun* any athlete who performs well in rainy conditions; a racehorse that performs well on wet or muddy track conditions *US, 1942*

muddie *noun* the mud crab *Scylla serrata AUSTRALIA, 1953*

muddlefugging *adverb* used as a euphemism for the intensifier 'motherfucking' *US, 1961*

muddy feet *noun* said of someone who needs to urinate *US, 1963*

muddy fuck *noun* anal sex that brings forth faeces or faecal stains on the penis *US, 1979*

muddy trench *noun* the French. Rhyming slang, possibly based on 'bloody French' *UK, 1992*

muddy water *noun* coffee. Elaboration of MUD (coffee) playing on Muddy Waters, the stage-name of bluesman McKinley Morganfield (1915–83) *UK, 1981*

Muddy York *nickname* York, a suburb of Toronto *CANADA, 2002*

mud flaps *noun* the condition that exists when a tight-fitting pair of trousers, shorts, bathing suit or other garment forms a wedge between a woman's labia, accentuating their shape *US, 2003*

mudge *noun* a hat. From a particular type of hat worn by C19 women *UK, 2002*

mudguard *noun* a person whose outward geniality masks a vicious nature. Both are shiny on the outside and filthy underneath *AUSTRALIA, 1989*

mudhead *noun* a fanatic enthusiast for multi-user dungeon computer play *US, 1991*

mud hog *noun* football played in rainy, muddy conditions *TRINIDAD AND TOBAGO, 1992*

mud hook *noun* **1** an anchor. Nautical use *US, 1827*. **2** in the dice game crown and anchor, an anchor. From the non-symbolic previous sense *UK, 1961*. **3** a finger. Usually in the plural *CANADA, 1968*

mud hop *noun* a clerk in a railway yard *US, 1929*

mudkicker *noun* a prostitute, especially of the street-walking variety *US, 1932*

mudlark *noun* a racehorse that performs well on muddy track conditions *US, 1909*

mud mark *noun* in horse racing, an indiciation in a past performance report that a horse runs well in muddy track conditions *US, 1965*

mud-moving *noun* close-in air support for a ground operation in the Canadian Air Force *CANADA, 1995*

mud puppy *noun* a very ugly girl *US, 1983*

mud-stick artist *noun* a member of a railway track crew *US, 1977*

mud turtle *noun* a black prisoner *US, 1976*

mud wallow *noun* a coffee house. Citizens' band slang, elaborating on MUD (coffee) *UK, 1959*

muff *noun* the vulva; a woman as a sex object *UK, 1699.* ▶ **buff the muff** to manually stimulate a woman's genitals *US, 1999*

muff *verb* to bungle *UK, 1827*

muff-dive *verb* to perform oral sex on a woman *US, 1948*

muff-diver *noun* a person who performs oral sex on a woman *US, 1930*

muff-diving *noun* oral sex performed on a woman *US, 1974*

muffin *noun* a woman objectified sexually. Probably a disguised MUFF (the vagina) *US, 1870*

Muffin the Mule; muffin *noun* a fool. Rhyming slang, formed from the name of a television puppet who was famous in the 1950s *UK, 1998*

muff job *noun* oral sex on a woman *US, 1990*

muffler burn *noun* a bruise on the skin caused by sucking. Hawaiian youth usage *US, 1982*

muff mag *noun* a magazine featuring photographs of naked women, focusing on their pubic hair and vulvas *US, 1972*

muff merchant *noun* a procurer of prostitutes; a man who makes his living off the earnings of prositutes *US, 1987*

muff muncher *noun* a person who performs oral sex on women; a lesbian *AUSTRALIA, 1972*

muff-noshing *noun* oral sex on a woman *US, 1980*

muffydile; muffydite *noun* a person or animal with female and male characteristics. A corruption of 'hermaphrodite' *TRINIDAD AND TOBAGO, 1986*

mufti squad *noun* individually anonymous, uniformed enforcers for the police or prison authorities. Prison usage *UK, 2000*

mu-fucka; muhfucka *noun* a motherfucker. Alternative spelling *UK, 2002*

mug *noun* **1** a man, a bloke *US, 1859.* **2** a gullible fool, an easy dupe. A 'mug' is a vessel into which you can pour anything *UK, 1857.* **3** the face, especially an ugly one *UK, 1821.* **4** the mouth *AUSTRALIA, 1902.* **5** a member of a criminal gang by virtue of brawn not brains *US, 1890.* **6** a client of a prostitute *AUSTRALIA, c. 1906*

mug *verb* **1** to rob with violence or the threat of violence *UK, 1864.* **2** to stare at *US, 2001.* **3** to grimace theatrically, especially while posing for a photograph *UK, 1762.* **4** to kiss *US, 1947.* **5** to photograph a prisoner during the after-arrest process *US, 1899.* ▶ **mug someone off** to show someone as a fool; to play someone for a fool; to consider someone foolish. From MUG (a fool) *UK, 1997*

mug *adjective* foolish. Especially in the terms MUG COPPER and MUG PUNTER *AUSTRALIA, 1954*

mug about *verb* to kiss and fondle someone *AUSTRALIA, 1945*

mug book *noun* a collection of photographs of criminals consulted by the police *US, 1902*

mug chop *noun* a sale of a faulty second-hand car made by a dealer posing as a customer *UK, 1968*

mug cop *noun* a police officer, viewed as inherently stupid *AUSTRALIA, 1971*

mug copper *noun* a police officer, viewed as inherently stupid *AUSTRALIA, 1945*

mug down *verb* to kiss. From MUG (the face) on the model of CHOW DOWN (to set to eating) *US, 1995*

mug gallery *noun* in a carnival, a concession where people pay to have their picture taken *US, 1960*

mugger *noun* a criminal who commits street robbery with violence (or the threat of violence) *US, 1863*

muggie *noun* marijuana. A variation of MUGGLES (marijuana) *2003*

mugging *noun* a street robbery from a person, especially robbery with violence or the threat of violence *US, 1943*

muggins *noun* a fool, an idiot, often with an implication that the fool is a victim (and a fool to be so), a gullible fool *US, 1855*

muggle *noun* **1** a marijuana cigarette *US, 1933.* **2** a person with little or no understanding of computers. The opposite of a WIZARD; derived from the *Harry Potter* novels of JK Rowling *UK, 1999*

mugglehead *noun* a marijuana user *US, 1926*

muggles *noun* marijuana *US, 1928*

muggy *adjective* foolish, in the manner of a mug (a fool, a dupe) *UK, 1997*

muggy-cunt *noun* a fool *UK, 2000*

mug joint *noun* in circus and carnival usage, a concession where customers are photographed *US, 1931*

mug lair *noun* a showy but foolish person *AUSTRALIA, 1944*

mug money *noun* in horse racing, money bet by uninformed bettors *AUSTRALIA, 1989*

mug punter *noun* a gambler, viewed as inherently stupid *AUSTRALIA, 1943*

mug's game *noun* a thankless activity *UK, 1910*

mug shot *noun* **1** a police photograph of a (convicted) criminal. Combines MUG (the face) and 'shot' (a photograph) *US, 1950.* **2** a photographic portrait *UK, 1978*

mugsnapper *noun* in circus and carnival usage, a travelling photographer *US, 1981*

mugsnatcher *noun* a photographer who operates in the street, at a fairground or at the seaside *UK, 1979*

mug's ticker *noun* a counterfeit Swiss watch *UK, 1977*

mug-up *noun* a coffee break or snack, at work or home *US, 1958*

mug up *verb* **1** to flirt, to kiss *US, 1947.* **2** to study hard. Also 'mug up on' *UK, 1848*

muhfuh; muhfuhkuh *noun* motherfuck; motherfucker *US, 1969*

mujer *noun* cocaine. Spanish for 'woman' *US, 1994*

mukluk telegraph *noun* a radio show that makes announcements delivering messages to people in rural Alaska who have no telephone or mail service. The 'mukluk' is 'an insulated boot designed for arctic wear' *US, 1945*

mukums *noun* the female pubic mound *TRINIDAD AND TOBAGO, 2003*

mula *noun* marijuana *US, 1946*

mulady *noun* a ghost, a devil. English gypsy use from Romany *mûlo* (dead, ghost) *UK, 2000*

mulberry bush *noun* ▶ **go round the mulberry bush** to waste time in a misdirected effort. From a children's singing game – a perfect example of using up energy in pointless activity *UK, 1962*

mule *noun* **1** a person who physically smuggles drugs or other contraband *US, 1922.* **2** a Vietnamese who carried supplies for the Viet Cong or the North Vietnamese Army *US, 1990.* **3** in motor racing, a car used for tests and practice *US, 1993.* **4** a small, motorised platform used for transporting supplies or personnel *US, 1903.* **5** a railway brakeman *US, 1929.* **6** an infertile woman *TRINIDAD AND TOBAGO, 1986.* **7** marijuana that has been soaked in whisky *US, 1955*

mule nose *noun* the condition that exists when a tight-fitting pair of trousers, shorts, bathing suit or other garment forms a wedge between a woman's labia, accentuating their shape *US, 2004*

mulenyam; moulonjohn *noun* a black person. From the Italian, referring to an eggplant *US, 1967*

mule's ear *noun* a hidden mechanism used to control the spin of a roulette wheel *US, 1982*

mule teeth *noun* in craps, a roll of twelve *US, 1999*

mule train *noun* in humorous smuggler usage, a car *US, 1956*

mulga *noun* uninhabited or sparsely populated remote regions of Australia. From *mulga* (a type of native acacia), from the Australian Aboriginal language Yuwaalaraay *AUSTRALIA, 1898*

mulga wire *noun* an information network utilising word of mouth *AUSTRALIA, 1899*

mull *noun* marijuana prepared for smoking *AUSTRALIA, 1988*

mull *verb* to break up marijuana buds in preparation for smoking *AUSTRALIA, 2004*

mullah *noun* an Irish person who is not from Dublin *IRELAND, 1996* ▷*see:* MOOLA

mull bowl *noun* a bowl used to mull marijuana AUSTRALIA, 1995

muller *noun* **1** a murderer UK, 1979. **2** an ugly or unattractive person. Teen slang UK, 2003

muller *verb* to roundly beat the opposition in a physical fight. German tailor Franz Müller (executed 1864) was the first person to commit a murder on a British train; his name survives here as a synonym for 'murder' but is used only as an exaggeration UK, 1997

mullered *adjective* **1** drunk or drug-intoxicated UK, 2000. **2** dead UK, 2000

mullering *noun* a beating UK, 1997

mullet *noun* **1** a hairstyle: the hair is worn short at the front and long at the back. Fashionable in the 1980s and much derided by the fashion-conscious generations that followed US, 1997. **2** a gullible person US, 1955. **3** a socially inept outcast US, 1959

mullethead *noun* a fool, a stupid person US, 1857

mull head *noun* a habitual smoker of marijuana AUSTRALIA, 1996

mulligan *noun* a prison guard. Used with derision by prisoners US, 1939

mulligan stew; mulligan *noun* a stew made without a recipe, relying on ingredients that are left over from previous meals US, 1904

mulligatawny *noun* desiring sex. Rhyming slang for HORNY UK, 1998

mullion *noun* an ugly person US, 1959

mullock *noun* mining refuse. From British dialect AUSTRALIA, 1855

mullock heap *noun* a mound of mullock AUSTRALIA, 1859

mull up *verb* to prepare marijuana for smoking. Refers to cutting it up and, usually, mixing it in tobacco AUSTRALIA, 1987

mullygrub *verb* to sulk. A venerable noun (meaning 'depressed spirits'), now surviving in verb form US, 1984

multi *noun* a multiple bet covering seven selections to '120 win stakes or 240 each-way stakes'. Also known as a 'Super Heinz' UK, 2001

multi; multie; multi; multy *adverb* very. Polari UK, 1887

multi; multie; multy; multa *adjective* poor, bad. Polari; a weakening of MULTI KATIVA (very bad). Also used as an expletive and intensifying adjective UK, 1887

multi-coloured yawn *noun* an act of vomiting; vomit AUSTRALIA, 1977

multi kativa; multee kertever; multicattivo *adjective* very bad. Polari; from Italian *molto cattivo* (very bad) UK, 1859

multiples *noun* sex involving multiple people; an orgy US, 1968

multo *adjective* many UK, 2003

mum *noun* **1** a wife or a woman in a long-term relationship UK, 1977. **2** a woman objectified as unattractive. A logical extension of the belief that you would not fancy your mother. Current in the City of London during the 1990s UK, 1998

mum *adjective* quiet, silent UK, 1950

mum and dad *noun* a cricket pad. Rhyming slang, usually in the plural, with both elements pluralised UK, 2003

mum and dad *adjective* mad. Rhyming slang UK, 1976

mumblage *noun* stuff US, 1981

mumble used as a verbal placeholder when an answer is either too difficult or unknown US, 1983

mumbler *noun* a woman wearing a tight-fitting pair of trousers, shorts, bathing suit or other garment that forms a wedge between her labia, accentuating their shape; the trousers in question. Derives from the humorous logic that you can see the lips moving but can't make out what is being said UK, 2002

mumbo jumbo *noun* **1** meaningless jargon UK, 1896. **2** any religion or religious practice, especially one that has or appears to have its roots in Africa UK, 1956

mummerset *noun* actor's all-purpose West Country dialect accent and speech. A punning blend of 'mummer' (an actor) and 'Somerset' UK, 1984

mummy; mum *noun* a mother, your mother. Affectionate diminutives of 'mother' UK, 1964

mummy bag *noun* a sleeping bag which can enclose the sleeper's head US, 1956

mummy dust; whiffle dust *noun* an imaginary magic powder used by conjurors, manufacturers, marketing professionals and others to enhance their product or presentation AUSTRALIA, 2000

mump *verb* **1** to obtain cheap or free goods from tradesmen by virtue of being a police officer. Metropolitan Police slang; a variation in sense of obsolete 'mump' (to get by begging) UK, 1970. **2** to take a bribe. A variation of the previous sense UK, 1996

mumper *noun* a tramp, a vagrant; a beggar. Current use as 'a beggar or scrounger' noted by David Powis, *The Signs of Crime*, 1977 UK, 1665

mums *noun* a mother UK, 1939

mumsie; mumsy *noun* a mother UK, 1876

mum's the word used as an injunction to keep quiet. 'Mum' originates in C16, from the onomatapoeic qualities of speech contained by compressed lips UK, 1704

mumsy *adjective* motherly UK, 1970

mun *noun* used as a general form of individual address to either gender; also used as a means of stressing what has been said. Originally used of a man. Later use is less discerning UK: WALES, 1985

munch *noun* food US, 1998. ▶ **put the munch to** to kiss with passion if not aggression US, 1985

munch *verb* **1** to eat UK, 1923. **2** to kiss US, 1985. **3** to fall or be knocked from a surfboard US, 1977. **4** in computing, to explore flaws in a system's security scheme US, 1991. ▶ **munch the trunch** to perform oral sex on a man. Formed on an abbreviation of 'truncheon', as in LOVE TRUNCHEON UK, 2003

munched *adjective* angry US, 1993

munchie *noun* **1** food, especially a snack or light meal. Earliest reference is in 1917 as a brand name for a chocolate confection UK, 1959. **2** an injury sustained in a fall from a skateboard or bicycle US, 1987

munchies *noun* a sensation of hunger experienced when smoking marijuana US, 1959

munchkin *noun* **1** a child. In general usage. The Munchkins were diminutive characters created by Frank L. Baum for his book *The Wizard of Oz*, 1900. The film of the book, made in 1939, has proved to be an iconographic touchstone for gay culture (FRIEND OF DOROTHY, etc.) US, 1971. **2** an acutely short person. From the race of small people in Frank Baum's *Wizard of Oz* US, 1975. **3** a young computer enthusiast. From diminutive characters in the *Wizard of Oz* US, 1991

munchy *noun* a shark AUSTRALIA, 1991

munchy *adjective* excellent, trendy, fashionable. School usage US, 1961

Muncie *noun* in hot rodding, a Chevrolet four-speed gearbox. Built at a Chevrolet plant in Muncie, Indiana US, 1965

mundane *adjective* unrelated to science fiction US, 1982

mundowie; mundowee *noun* the foot. From the extinct Australian Aboriginal language Dharug (Sydney region) AUSTRALIA, 1822

mung *noun* dirt of any kind US, 1948

mung *verb* **1** to beg. Used by tramps; from Romany *mang* (to beg) UK, 1811. **2** to sell lucky heather. English gypsy use; a variation of the previous sense UK, 2000

munga *noun* food. A shortening of MUNGAREE. Originally in military speech AUSTRALIA, 1918

mungaree *noun* food. From Italian *mangiare* (to eat). Variants include 'mungare', 'munjari', 'munjary' and 'menjarie' UK, 1861

mungaree *verb* to eat; hence food. From Italian *mangiare*, via parleyaree and tramps' slang, into polari. Variants include 'mungarly', 'munja', 'munjarry', 'mangiare', 'manjaree', 'monjaree', 'giare' and 'jarry' UK, 1992

munge *noun* darkness UK, 2002

munge; mung *verb* in computing, to destroy data, accidentally or maliciously US, 1983

mungers *noun* the female breasts, especially when of above average dimensions. Possibly derived from 'humungous' *UK, 2003*

mung-pusher *noun* a poker player who habitually plays hands that have no chance of winning *US, 1966*

mung rag *noun* a cloth used to wipe up spilled alcohol at a bar; a cloth used to wipe off the penis after masturbating *US, 2003*

mung up; mung *verb* to botch, to blunder, to ruin *US, 1969*

munjacake *noun* a bland, uninteresting person. Italian-Canadian coinage and usage *CANADA, 1993*

munjon *noun* an Aboriginal who has little or no contact with white people. From the Western Australian Aboriginal language Yindjibarndi *AUSTRALIA, 1947*

munt *verb* to be ugly *UK, 2003*

munt; muntu *noun* a black African. From Bantu *muntu* (a human being), made abusive and offensive during apartheid *SOUTH AFRICA, 1948*

munted *adjective* **1** drunk or drug-intoxicated *UK, 2001*. **2** having become sexually intimate with an unattractive, promiscuous drunk. Student use; explained as 'to have pulled a MUNTER' *UK, 2002*

munter; munta; munt *noun* **1** an unattractive person who adds to the personal allure with drunkenness and/or promiscuity, especially but not exclusively of young women. Student usage *UK, 1998*. **2** a useless person or object *NEW ZEALAND, 1997*

muppet *noun* **1** a person who is mentally or physically incapacitated or disabled, or considered ugly; someone who represents any permutation of such characteristics; hence, any fool. Created by Jim Henson (b.1936), *The Muppet Show*, a successful television programme of the 1970s and subsequently in films, introduced the gallery of grotesque puppets on which this allusion is founded *UK, 1983*. **2** a magistrate. Police slang *UK, 2002*

muppet house *noun* a prison psychiatric unit; a mental hospital. Extended from MUPPET (a person who is mentally incapacitated) *UK, 1996*

muppetshop *noun* a prison workshop. Extended from MUPPET (a person who is mentally incapacitated; a fool) for the mindless nature of the work *UK, 1996*

mural *noun* a person with many tattoos *US, 1997*

murder *noun* **1** something that is extremely good *US, 1927*. **2** an absolute nuisance; dreadful trouble *UK, 1857*

murder *verb* to consume voraciously *IRELAND, 1991*. ▶ **could murder** to want, to be desirous of something *UK, 1935*

murdered *adjective* very drunk *UK, 1983*

murder house *noun* a school dental clinic *NEW ZEALAND, 1984*

murder one *noun* a mixture of heroin and cocaine *US, 1994*

murder weed; murder *noun* marijuana. Anti-marijuana propaganda adopted into regular slang usage *US, 1935*

murder-your-wife brick *noun* in television and film making, an imitation brick. The imitation brick was first used in the 1965 comedy *How to Murder Your Wife*, starring Jack Lemmon and Virna Lisi *US, 1990*

murk *noun* coffee *US, 1949*

murk *verb* to shoot with a gun *US, 2003*

murky *adjective* low-spirited, depressed *US, 1997*

murotogura *noun* heroin *US, 2002*

murphy *noun* **1** a potato. A belief that potatoes formed the basic diet in Ireland is reflected in this adoption of a common Irish surname *UK, 1811*. **2** the condition that exists when someone pulls your trousers or underpants forcefully upwards, forming a wedge between the buttock cheeks. Most commonly known as a 'wedgie' *US, 1990*

Murphy; Murphy game *noun* a swindle involving a prostitute and her accomplice, usually entailing robbing the prostitute's customer *US, 1954*

Murphy man *noun* the prostitute's male accomplice in a Murphy swindle *US, 1966*

Murphy's law *noun* a cynical 'law' of existence that decrees that 'if something can go wrong it will – and even if it can't, it still might'. Said to derive from a remark (or philosophy) of Captain E. Murphy at Edwards Air Force Base. The underlying maxim or 'law' is found as early as 1941, as 'an old legend' from Peru in 1952, and in 1957 it is offered as 'an old theatrical saying'. At best, it seems to be the attribution of an old saying to a new, glamourous aviation context *US, 1955*

Murray *noun* in horse racing, to bet on credit. Rhyming slang from 'Murray Cod' (a delicious inland fish) to ON THE NOD (on credit) *AUSTRALIA, 1989*. ▶ **on the Murray cod** (of a wager) agreed upon without money changing hands. Rhyming slang for ON THE NOD. Also in the short form 'on the murray' *AUSTRALIA, 1967*

Murray Walker; murray *noun* a talker. Rhyming slang, based on broadcaster (and, therefore, professional talker) Murray Walker (b.1923) *UK, 2002*

muscle *noun* **1** a person or persons using violence and intimidation, usually in the service of another *US, 1942*. **2** physical violence *US, 1879*. ▶ **on the muscle** threatening, coercive *US, 1859*

muscle *verb* to inject a drug intramuscularly, as opposed to intravenously *US, 1970*

muscle boy *noun* a hired intimidator *US, 1963*

muscle car *noun* a passenger car with a powerful engine, a light chassis and two-door body *US, 1969*

muscle-dancing *noun* a sexually suggestive dance *US, 1950*

muscle-happy *adjective* said of a prisoner who concentrates on physical fitness in jail *US, 1958*

muscle in *verb* to intrude, by force or threat of force, on another's activity or business; to intrude, by subterfuge, on another's activity or business *UK, 1929*

muscleman *noun* an enforcer for a criminal enterprise *US, 1929*

muscle Mary *noun* a homosexual man who is a bodybuilder *UK, 2002*

muscles *nickname* used as a form of address for a strong or well-muscled man; also used, with heavy irony, of a weakling *UK, 1984*

muscle uncle *noun* a stereotypically masculine homosexual male. Readily available in specialist Internet sites *US, 2005*

musgro *noun* a police officer. English gypsy use from Romany *mûskro* (a policeman) *UK, 2000*

mush *noun* **1** the mouth or face. Sometimes seen as 'moosh' *US, 1859*. **2** a man; used as a greeting or as a dismissive term of address *US, 1906*. **3** money *UK, 1962*. **4** in circus and carnival usage, an umbrella *UK, 1821*. **5** a weak, slow wave *US, 1977*. **6** in the television and film industries, low-level sound used as background *UK, 1960*

mush *verb* **1** to kiss *US, 1926*. **2** (used of an aeroplane) to run out of airspeed *US, 1935*

mushburger *noun* in surfing, a weak, poorly formed wave *US, 1988*

musher *noun* **1** a man. An elaborataion of MUSH *UK, 2002*. **2** a villain; someone who moves in criminal circles. Liverpool usage; possibly puns MUSH (the face) into FACE (a known criminal) *UK, 2001*

mushfake *noun* to manufacture in defiance of prison rules and prohibitions. A term originally applied to the makeshift repair of umbrellas *US, 1952*

mushie *noun* **1** a mushroom *AUSTRALIA, 1981*. **2** an hallucinogenic mushroom, a magic mushroom *UK, 1996*

mushied-up *adjective* intoxicated by hallucinogenic mushrooms. From MUSHIE (a mushroom) *UK, 1999*

mushmellow *noun* the vagina. A clever play on 'marshmallow' (a pink flower and a sweet confection), combining 'mush' (anything soft and moist) and 'mellow' (relaxed, comfortable) *US, 1998*

mushmouthed *adjective* unable to speak clearly *US, 1977*

mushrat *noun* a muskrat *CANADA, 1954*

mushroom *noun* **1** a person who is given no information. From the US witticism/poster and T-shirt slogan: 'I feel like a mushroom: everyone keeps me in the dark and is always feeding me bullshit' *UK, 1979*. **2** in firefighter usage, a fire that spreads out and downward when reaching a ceiling *US, 1954*. **3** an innocent bystander killed in crossfire *US, 1988*

mushroom *verb* (of the felt tip on a pool cue stick) to compress and spread outward *US, 1988*

mushroom pills *noun* psilocybin or psilocin, in powder or capsule form. A strong psychedelic drug extracted from *Psilocybe mexicana* and *Stropharia cubensis* mushrooms. One capsule has an equivalent effect to forty or more MAGIC MUSHROOM(s) *UK, 1999*

mushy *noun* a weak, slow wave *US, 1964*

mushy *adjective* sentimental, insipidly or gushingly romantic. A figurative application of the conventional sense *US, 1848*

musical vegetables *noun* baked beans *UK, 1988*

music stand *noun* in electric line work, a rack for holding insulated line tools *US, 1980*

Muskoka chair *noun* an outdoor wooden chair with wide flat armrests and a backrest in a fan shape. This is the Canadian name for what is known in the US as the 'Adirondack chair'. The Muskoka Lakes region is north of Toronto *CANADA, 2001*

muskra *noun* a police officer. A corruption of Romany *moskero*; *mooshkero* (a constable) *UK, 1979*

muskrat *noun* a child *US, 1976*

muso *noun* a musician *AUSTRALIA, 1967*

mussie *noun* a tough woman *UK, 1953*

mustang *noun* an officer appointed from the enlisted ranks *US, 1878*

mustard *noun* AIDS [Acquired Immune Deficiency Syndrome], a disease that is transmitted by sexual contact. There are very few synonyms for AIDS despite the huge impact of the disease; the etymology here is uncertain *US, 1996*

mustard *adjective* excellent, best, skilled, keen. From the phrases 'keen as mustard' and 'hot as mustard' *UK, 1925*

mustard and cress; mustard *noun* a dress. Rhyming slang *UK, 1998*

mustard case *noun* a supreme show-off. The suggestion is of a HOT DOG, dosed with mustard *US, 2001*

mustard chucker *noun* a pickpocket who spills mustard on the victim as a diversion and excuse to approach *US, 1989*

mustard keen; mustard *adjective* very keen. From the proverbial phrase 'keen as mustard' *UK, 1979*

mustard pickle; mustard *noun* a cripple. Rhyming slang, imperfectly rhymed *UK, 1998*

mustard pot *noun* the vagina. Rhyming slang for TWOT (TWAT) *UK, 1896*

mustard pot; mustard *adjective* hot *UK, 1998*

mustard shine *noun* the application of mustard to the shoes in the hope of throwing tracking dogs off the scent *US, 1949*

must be nice! used for expressing envy or congratulations *US, 2002*

mutant *noun* a social outcast *US, 1984*

mute *noun* **1** the vagina. Gay slang *UK, 1972*. **2** in horse racing, a pari-mutuel betting machine *US, 1942*

mutha *noun* anything or anyone. An abbreviation of MOTHERFUCKER *US, 2000*

muthafucka *noun* a motherfucker. Alternative spelling *US, 1979*

muthafucking *adjective* used as an all-purpose intensifier. Variant spelling of MOTHERFUCKING *US, 2001*

mutt *noun* **1** a dog, especially a mongrel. Affectionately disparaging *US, 1900*. **2** a despicable low-life *US, 1899*. **3** a thug, a criminal *US, 1997*. **4** the American shethbill, a small Antarctic bird *ANTARCTICA, 2003*

Mutt and Jeff *noun* a pair of men who are physically mismatched, especially in height. From the popular comic strip *US, 1914*

Mutt and Jeff; mutton *adjective* deaf. Rhyming slang from the US cartoon strip characters created by Bud Fisher (1855–1954). Mutt first appeared in the *San Francisco Chronicle* in 1907, Jeff was drawn in shortly after and by 1915 the pair were a national phenomenon. Adopted into UK theatrical slang and consequently reduced in pronunciation to 'mutton' *UK, 1960*

mutter and stutter *noun* butter. Rhyming slang *UK, 1960*

mutton *noun* the penis *AUSTRALIA, 1071*

mutton flaps *noun* the *labia majora* *NEW ZEALAND, 1998*

muttonhead *noun* a railway dispatcher *US, 1977*

mutton-headed *adjective* stupid *UK, 1768*

mutton merchant *noun* a male sexual exhibitionist *AUSTRALIA, 1971*

mutton of the sea *noun* the hawksbill sea turtle *BAHAMAS, 1982*

mutt's nuts *noun* anything considered to be the finest, the most excellent, the best. Variation of DOG'S BOLLOCKS; MUTT (a dog) and NUTS (the testicles) combine literally and figuratively to mean 'outstanding' *UK, 2001*

muvva *noun* used as an abbreviation of 'motherfucker'. A slovening of 'mother' *UK, 2001*

muzzie *adjective* stupid. Probably from 'muscle-headed' *UK, 2001*

muzzle *noun* heroin *US, 1959*

muzzle guzzle *noun* a party organised around alcholic drink *US, 1968*

muzzler *noun* in circus and carnival usage, a person lacking morals *US, 1981*

muzzy *noun* a moustache *UK, 2001*

mwah! the vocal accompaniment to a kiss, especially an air-kiss *UK, 1994*

MX *noun* Mandrax™, a sedative drug *UK, 1978*

Myakka gold *noun* marijuana grown in Florida *US, 2001*

myall *adjective* (of an Australian Aboriginal) traditional; unaffected by white society *AUSTRALIA, 1971*

myall; Myall *noun* an Aboriginal who has little or no contact with white people. From the extinct Australian Aboriginal language Dharug, Sydney region, *mayal* (stranger) *AUSTRALIA, 1962*

my arse!; my ass! used to register disbelief or contempt *UK, 1933*

my arsehole! used for registering disbelief or contempt. A variation of MY ARSE! *UK, 1982*

my Aunt Fanny! used as a register for disbelief, sometimes exclamatory. A euphemism for the bolder MY ASS! *UK, 1945*

my bad! used for acknowledging responsibility for and apologising for a mistake *US, 1989*

my bloody oath! yes indeed! Intensified form of MY OATH! *AUSTRALIA, 1952*

my bust! used for accepting responsibility for a mistake or error *US, 1985*

my colonial oath *noun* my word. Formerly a common exclamation *AUSTRALIA, 1962*

my dog ate it used as a humorous explanation of why a person does not have something that they are supposed to have. From the clichéd student excuse for not having a homework assignment *US, 1999*

my face! used for expressing embarrassment *US, 2003*

my foot! used for registering an emphatic rejection; used as a direct denial of a point just made. A polite variation of MY ARSE!, often used as a suffix to the repeated point of contention *UK, 1999*

my hen laid a haddock *nickname* the Welsh national anthem. A phonetic transliteration of the title and first-line of *Mae Hen Wlad Fy Nhadau* (The Land of my Fathers), first published in 1860. There are a number of humorous variations of the continuing lyric but the first line is a constant; dating from the 1990s. Credited to the poet Nigel Jenkins, it may have been inspired by English politicians inability to learn the Welsh words *UK: WALES, 1994*

my hole! used for registering disbelief or contempt *UK, 2002*

my oath! certainly!, yes indeed! *AUSTRALIA, 1869*

MYOB used in colloquial speech as well as shorthand in Internet discussion groups and text message to mean 'mind your own business' *US, 2002*

Myrna Loy *noun* a saveloy. Rhyming slang, formed from the name of the US film actress, 1905–93 *UK, 1992*

my sainted aunt! used as an exclamation of trivial delight or shock *UK, 1921*

mystery *noun* a young woman, especially when she is a new arrival in a town or city *UK, 1937*

mystery bag *noun* **1** a sausage. So called because the contents are unknown *AUSTRALIA, 1982*. **2** a meat pie *AUSTRALIA, 2003*

mystery meat *noun* cold cuts of suspicious heritage *US, 1918*

mystery punter *noun* a man who spends his time obsessively on the lookout for young women who are newly arrived in a town or city with an intention to live with, and take advantage of, them; such a man is said to be 'mystery mad' *UK, 1977*

Mystic Meg *noun* **1** a leg. Rhyming slang, formed from a television fortune teller who came to fame in the mid-1990s by association with the National Lottery *UK, 1998*. **2** the penis. Rhyming slang for THIRD LEG; a specialisation of the previous sense *UK, 2003*

mysto *adjective* mystical *US, 1980*

my wave! used by surfers to express 'ownership' of a wave and to warn other surfers to get out and stay out of the way *US, 1991*

my word *noun* a piece of excrement. Rhyming slang for TURD *UK, 1992*

my word! **1** used as an expression of surprise or despair *UK, 1841*. **2** yes indeed! Shortening of 'upon my word!' *AUSTRALIA, 1857*

myxo *noun* the viral disease myxomatosis introduced to control feral rabbits *AUSTRALIA, 1953*

Nn

'n' *conjunction* and. An abbreviation; notably (since 1955) in ROCK 'N' ROLL *US, 1858*

NAAFI; Naafi *noun* a military organisation that operates shops and canteens for military personnel; any shop or canteen within that organisation. Acronym of *Navy, Army and Air Force Institutes UK, 1921*

naavo *noun* a secret hiding place *IRELAND, 1999*

nab *noun* the police; a police officer *UK, 1813*

nab *verb* **1** to catch, to arrest *UK, 1686*. **2** to snatch or steal something *UK, 1665*

nabber *noun* a police officer *US, 1837*

nabe *noun* **1** a neighbourhood cinema *US, 1935*. **2** a tavern *US, 1950*

naches; nakhes *noun* proud pleasure. Yiddish from the Hebrew for 'contentment' *US, 1968*

nack *noun* ▶ **in the nack** naked *UK, 2002*

nada *noun* nothing; none. From the Spanish, used by English speakers who do not understand Spanish, often heard in the 1980s advertising phrase 'Nothing – nada – zilch'. Recorded in UK gay currency *US, 1914*

nad alert; gonad alert *noun* used as a warning in a hospital that an x-ray is about to be taken *US, 1994*

nada to vada in the larder referring to a man's genitals, less than averagely endowed. Polari; a clever combination of NADA (nothing) and VADA (to see) with a conventional location where meat is stored *UK, 2002*

nadger *noun* in horse racing, a horse's nose or head *AUSTRALIA, 1989*

nadgers *noun* the testicles. Possibly deriving from 'gonads', and with a similarity to KNACKERS, 'nadgers' was an all-purpose nonsense word used by the radio comedy series *The Goon Show* during the 1950s *UK, 1998*

nads *noun* the testicles. From 'gonads' *US, 1964*

naff *adjective* vulgar, bad, unlovely, despicable; generally contemptible; when used in gay society it may mean heterosexual. Theatrical and CAMP origins but the actual derivation is disputed; possibly an acronym for 'not available for fucking', 'not a fuck' or 'normal as fuck'; or a play on the military acronym NAAFI (Navy, Army and Air Force Institutes) as 'no ambition and fuck-all interest'; otherwise it may originate as back slang for FANNY (the vagina or the buttocks), a shortening of 'nawfuckingood' or in the French phrase *rien à faire* (nothing to do) *UK, 1965*

naff used as a euphemism for 'fuck' (in all senses except sexual intercourse/to have sex) *UK, 1977*

naffette; naffeen *adjective* vulgar, bad, despicable, unlovely. Polari; CAMP variations of NAFF *UK, 1992*

naffing *adjective* used as a euphemism for 'fucking'. Extended from NAFF *UK, 1959*

naff it up *verb* to spoil something *UK, 1981*

naff off *verb* to go away. From NAFF; made very familiar in the UK during the 1970s by the prison-set television situation comedy, *Porridge*, written by Clement and La Frenais. Perhaps the social highpoint of this word's history was during the 1982 Badminton Horse Trials when Princess Anne (now Princess Royal) asked the press, 'Why don't you just naff off?' *UK, 1982*

nagware *noun* free computer software that frequently asks the user to send a voluntary payment for further use *US, 1995*

nah emphatically no. A variation of pronunciation *US, 1971*

nail *noun* **1** a hypodermic needle *US, 1936*. **2** a marijuana cigarette. Possibly another 'nail in your coffin' *US, 1978*. ▶ **on the nail** (of a payment) promptly *UK, 1600*

nail *verb* **1** to apprehend; to arrest *UK, 1732*. **2** to kill *UK, 1824*. **3** to have sex *US, 1957*. **4** to get right, to master *US, 1989*. **5** (of a wave) to knock a surfer from the surfboard. Always in the passive voice *US, 1977*. ▶ **nail someone's bollocks to the door** to physically beat up, to figuratively neuter and mentally defeat *UK, 1998*. ▶ **nail the core** in the language of hang gliding, to find the centre of a thermal and ride it up *US, 1992*

nailed *adjective* deranged *US, 1836*

nail-em-and-jail-em *noun* a police officer *US, 1980*

nailer *noun* a police officer *US, 1973*

nail nicker *noun* in gambling, a cheat who marks cards by nicking them with his fingernails *US, 1997*

nails *noun* a disappointment; a failure. Hawaiian youth usage *US, 1981*

naked *adjective* (used of a truck) driving without a trailer *US, 1976*

Naked Fanny *nickname* Nakhon Phanon, Thailand. Vietnam war humour *US, 1967*

Nam *nickname* Vietnam. Often used with 'the'. Originally military, then widespread, and now slightly arch *US, 1962*

namby-pamby *noun* an effeminate male *US, 1968*

name *noun* **1** an important or famous person *US, 1975*. **2** a known criminal *UK, 1984*. **3** a popular, high-profile professional wrestler *US, 1995*. ▶ **have your name on it** to be meant for you. Originally military, applied to a bullet (or similar) that was destined to hit a particular person; later use is far more general, being used, for instance, when a house-hunter finds the perfect property or, more trivially, of a drink *UK, 1917*. ▶ **no names – no pack drill** the guilty party (or parties) will not be named and, therefore, cannot be punished. Originally used of, or by, army lower-ranks; now general use *UK, 1923*

nan; nana; nannie; nanny *noun* a grandmother, especially as a form of address *UK, 1940*

nana *noun* **1** a banana *US, 1929*. **2** the head *NEW ZEALAND, 1998*. ▶ **do your nana** to lose control; to get angry *AUSTRALIA, 1968*. ▶ **off your nana** crazy, insane *AUSTRALIA, 1966*

nance *noun* an effeminate male or homosexual. Disparaging *US, 1910*

nance *verb* to behave in an exaggeratedly feminine fashion *US, 1968*

nancy *adjective* effeminate; homosexual *UK, 1937*

nancy boy *noun* an effeminate or homosexual man; the former may be construed to be the latter *UK, 1904*

Nancy Lee *noun* tea. Rhyming slang *UK, 1960*

nancy story *noun* an elaborate fabrication. From a traditional Caribbean folktale about Anancy *TRINIDAD AND TOBAGO, 1858*

nan flap *noun* a pendulous spread of flabby upper arm that is characteristic of some older women *UK, 2004*

nang *adjective* excellent. Used by urban black youths *UK, 2004*

nanna *adjective* awful *UK, 2002*

nannie; nanny *noun* a black woman, also as a term of address. Offensive and demeaning *SOUTH AFRICA, 1956* ▷ *see:* NAN

nanny *noun* a prostitute who will, by arrangement, dress and treat a client as an infant *UK, 2003*

nanny goat; nanny *noun* **1** the Horserace Totaliser Board. Rhyming slang. The Tote was created by Act of Parliament in 1928 as 'an independent body with a monopoly of horse-race pool betting'; the legislation to allow the Tote to operate as an on-course bookmaker was not in force until 1972 *UK, 1960*. **2** a coat. Rhyming slang *UK, 1971*. **3** the throat. Rhyming slang *UK, 1992*. **4** a boat. Rhyming slang *UK, 1989*. ▶ **get your nanny goat; get your nanny** to annoy you. A variation of GET YOUR GOAT *US, 1909*

nanny whamming *noun* in rodeo, the joke event of goat tying CANADA, 1987

nano *noun* a very short period of time. An abbreviation of 'nanosecond', used figuratively US, 1991

nanoo *noun* heroin UK, 1998

Nanook *noun* a polar bear. The word comes from Eskimo CANADA, 1963

nante; nantee; nanti; nanty no; nothing, none; stop, shut up!; not. Polari, from Italian *niente* (nothing, anything). Recorded in contemporary gay use UK, 1851

nante pile on the carpet *adjective* bald UK, 1992

nante pots in the cupboard *adjective* toothless UK, 1992

nanti polari!; nanti panarly!; nantee palaver!; nanti parlaree! be quiet!, don't talk! Imperative; literally, 'no talk' UK, 2002

nanti that! stop it!, don't do that! Imperative UK, 2002

nantoise; nantois; nantoisale no; nothing; none. A variation of NANTE UK, 1997

nants no; nothing; none. A variation of NANTE UK, 1950

nanty worster *adjective* being no worse UK, 2002

nap *noun* 1 the short, curly hair of a black person US, 1969. 2 the hair; your hairstyle US, 1996. 3 in horse racing, a tipster's best bet UK, 1991. 4 a good bet, a sure thing. From the racing use UK, 2001

nape *noun* napalm, a mixture of petrol and a thickening agent for use in flame throwers or incendiary bombs, used extensively by the US during World War 2 and later wars US, 1968

napper *noun* the head UK, 1724

napper-wrapper *noun* a turban. Based on NAPPER (the head) UK, 1998

napps *noun* morphine sulphate tablets used to treat cancer patients IRELAND, 1996

nappy *adjective* of hair, usually of the hair of a black person, naturally tightly curled, frizzy. Often derogatory US, 1885

nappy dugout *noun* (of a black woman) the vagina. The imagery of 'dugout' is twofold: literally 'a trench', and, in baseball, the enclosure in which a batsman prepares to play; combined with NAPPY which typically describes black hair US, 1998

nap trap *noun* a roadside rest area US, 1976

nar *adjective* treacherous. An abbreviation of GNARLY US, 1988

narc; nark *noun* 1 an undercover narcotics officer US, 1967. 2 a social outcast US, 2001

narc ark; nark ark *noun* an undercover narcotic officer's car US, 1973

narco *noun* 1 narcotics US, 1954. 2 a narcotics detective US, 1955. 3 any person involved in the manufacture or distribution of drugs. An abbreviation of 'narcotics' US, 1958. 4 the Lexington (Kentucky) Federal Narcotics Hospital US, 1955

narcotic *adjective* wild, intense US, 1980

nards *noun* the male genitals US, 1970

narg *noun* an Indian NEW ZEALAND, 1998

narghile *noun* a water pipe used for smoking marijuana or hashish US, 1970

nark *noun* 1 a police informer. Also spelt 'narc' UK, 1839. 2 an aggravating person AUSTRALIA, 1846. 3 a spoilsport AUSTRALIA, 1927. 4 an awkward customer, one with no intention of buying UK, 1979. 5 a spiteful argument UK, 1979. 6 temper; a fit of annoyance AUSTRALIA, 1946. 7 umbrage UK, 1979. ▶ **put the nark on** to discourage UK, 1979

nark *verb* 1 to annoy UK, 1888. 2 to thwart AUSTRALIA, 1891. 3 to complain, to grumble UK, 1916. 4 to nag NEW ZEALAND, 1984. 5 to act as an informer UK, 1859

nark it! be quiet!, stop it!, shut up! UK, 1925

narks *noun* ▶ **the narks** decompression sickness (a medical condition that may be suffered by deep-sea divers). From the medical term 'nitrogen narcosis' UK, 1964

narky *adjective* bad-tempered, aggravated, annoyed; sarcastic UK, 1895

narrow *adjective* serious. Recorded in use in urban black society UK, 1999

narrowback *noun* 1 an unskilled, unfit labourer US, 1987. 2 a construction electrician. A term used with derision by power linemen to describe their intra-union rivals US, 1980

narrow yellow *noun* a military form (OCSA Form 159) used to pass routine actions to staff agencies US, 1986

narsty *adjective* disgusting. An embellishment of 'nasty' US, 2002

nary *adverb* neither; no US, 1746

nash *verb* to leave, especially in a hurry. From Romany *nash*, *nasher* (to run) UK, 1819

nash *adjective* weak, sickly, coddled CAYMAN ISLANDS, 1985

Nasho; nasho *noun* 1 a person serving in the National Service, a form of compulsory military service 1951–72 AUSTRALIA, 1962. 2 the National Service. Often used in the plural Nashos or Nashoes AUSTRALIA, 1962

nasodrain *noun* while surfing, the sudden and violent expulsion of sea water through the nose US, 1991

nastiness *noun* poor quality drugs UK, 2000

nasturtiums *noun* aspersions. A deliberate malapropism, usually as 'cast nasturtiums' UK, 1984

nasty *noun* 1 the vagina. A usage that calls to mind Grose's definition of C**T – 'a nasty name for a nasty thing' NEW ZEALAND, 1998. 2 the penis AUSTRALIA, 1971. 3 a violently pornographic or horrific film. Often combined as VIDEO-NASTY but the content appears to be outlasting the technology UK, 1982. 4 an authority or agency that enforces citizens' band radio regulations UK, 1981. ▶ **do the nasty** to have sex. A squeamish euphemism applied in a jocular manner US, 1977. ▶ **the nasty** heroin UK, 1996

nasty *adjective* 1 excellent US, 1940. 2 sexy, attractive, appealing; sluttish. A reversal of the conventional sense US, 1995

nasty-assed *adjective* cruel US, 1995

nasty boat *noun* a patrol boat developed for the coastal anti-invasion mission of the Royal Norwegian Navy. The 'nasty' is a technical term adopted to the vernacular US, 1991

nasty days *noun* a woman's menstrual period BAHAMAS, 1982

nastygram *noun* any unpleasant or unwanted e-mail US, 1991

nasty-nasty *noun* sex US, 1993

nasty neat *adjective* cleaner than clean US, 1975

nasty piece of work *noun* an objectionable person UK, 1961

nasty up *verb* to ruin or spoil BARBADOS, 1965

Nat; nat *noun* in politics, a nationalist SOUTH AFRICA, 1926 ▷ *see:* NAT KING COLE

natalie *noun* a black homosexual. Gay slang, formed on the name Natalie, possibly as a play on Natal, and originating among Cape coloureds SOUTH AFRICA, 2000

natch *noun* ▶ **on the natch** withdrawing from drug addiction without medication to ease the pain US, 1969

natch; nach *adverb* naturally US, 1945

nate *noun* 1 nothing US, 1993. 2 an Alaskan native US, 1983

nates *noun* the buttocks US, 1993

national *noun* ▶ **on tour with the national** being moved from prison to prison via the national inter-prison transport system. A pun appreciated by actors of the National Theatre UK, 1996. ▶ **the national** the national inter-prison transport system UK, 1996

national debt *noun* a bet. Rhyming slang UK, 1960

National Front *noun* an unpleasant or despicable person. Rhyming slang for CUNT, formed on a political organisation of the extreme right; a neat pun UK, 1992

national game *noun* the gambling game two-up AUSTRALIA, 1930

national handbag *noun* unemployment benefit; the local offices from which unemployment benefit is managed. From HANDBAG (money). Recorded as a contemporary gay usage UK, 2003

National Hunt *noun* audaciousness; impudence. Rhyming slang for 'front' (SEE MORE FRONT THAN SELFRIDGES), formed from the official name given to horse racing over jumps UK, 1992

native *noun* **1** a native American Indian *US, 2000*. **2** to the employee of a circus or carnival, a local patron *US, 1980*

native sport *noun* during the Vietnam war, looking for and killing Viet Cong *US, 1991*

Nat King Cole; nat *noun* **1** unemployment benefit; a government office from which unemployment benefit is managed. Rhyming slang for THE DOLE; formed on the name of US singer and musician Nat 'King' Cole, 1919–65. Often in the phrase 'on the Nat' *UK, 1961*. **2** a mole (on the skin). Rhyming slang *UK, 1992*. **3** a bread roll. Rhyming slang *UK, 1992*

nato *adjective* used for describing someone who is not sexually aggressive *US, 1968*

natter *noun* aimless conversation; incessantly complaining talk. From northern English dialect *gnatter* (to grumble in conversation) *UK, 1943*

natter *verb* to engage in aimless conversation, to chat *UK, 1943*

natty *noun* **1** any natural light beer *US, 2002*. **2** a wearer of dreadlocks, especially a Rastafarian *JAMAICA, 1976*

natty *adjective* **1** stylish, smartly neat *UK, 1785*. **2** of hair, matted, uncombed, in a condition to be formed into dreadlocks *JAMAICA, 1974*

Natty Bo *noun* National Bohemian™ beer *US, 1990*

natural *noun* **1** a hairstyle embraced largely by black people, featuring longer, unprocessed, unparted hair *US, 1969*. **2** in craps, a winning roll of seven on the first toss *US, 1962*. **3** Seven-Up™ soda. An allusion to the game of craps, where a seven is a 'natural' *US, 1967*. **4** in pool, a shot that cannot be missed or a game that cannot be lost *US, 1990*. **5** a conventional (as opposed to countercultural) person. Used by beatniks, and then hippies; generally in the plural *UK, 1967*

natural punk *noun* in prison, a man who had been homosexual outside prison *US, 1972*

nature *noun* the penis; sexual arousal *US, 2002*

nature boy *noun* a boy in need of a haircut *US, 1955*

nature calls used for announcing, and for excusing yourself for, a needed visit to the toilet; the condition of needing to relieve yourself *UK, 1984*

nature's scythe *noun* the penis *UK, 2003*

Naughton and Gold *noun* a cold. Rhyming slang, formed from a comedy double act that was part of the Crazy Gang, Charlie Naughton, 1887–1976, and Jimmy Gold, 1886–1967 *UK, 1961*

naughty *noun* **1** an act of sexual intercourse *AUSTRALIA, 1959*. **2** a physical injury; hence, a disservice *UK, 1984*

naughty *verb* to have sex *AUSTRALIA, 1961*

naughty *adjective* **1** corrupt or violent. An archaic sense, used by Shakespeare to describe the criminally wicked, re-emerged in the C20 *UK, 2000*. **2** of antique furniture, being passed off as something better or other than it is *UK, 1971*

naughty Nazi salute *noun* the fully erect penis. A parallel with the arm raised stiffly from the body at a similar angle *UK, 2003*

nause; nauze *noun* an inconvenience, a difficulty, an unpleasant person or thing. 'Nausea' abbreviated and adapted *UK, 1977*

nause; nause up *verb* to spoil. From NAUSE (an inconvenience, an unpleasant thing) *UK, 1978*

nausea *noun* trouble, a fuss. In military use *UK, 1959*

Naussie *noun* a New Australian, especially a recent migrant from Europe. A blend of 'new' and AUSSIE *AUSTRALIA, 1959*

nautch *noun* a brothel; a striptease; a sex show of any kind. American Dialect Society member Douglas G. Wilson has suggested that the term is a mildly anglicised version of the Hindi word for 'a dance' *US, 1872*

Nautics *noun* ▶ **the Nautics** the Royal Navy. Used, originally, by the Royal Air Force; shortened from 'nautical' *UK, 1951*

nav *noun* a navigator. In Royal Navy and Royal Air Force use *US, 1956*

Nava-Joe *noun* a member of the Navajo Indian tribe *US, 1963*

naval engagement *noun* sexual intercourse. Used, originally, by naval officers; in speech it's a perfect pun *CANADA, 1984*

navy brat *noun* the child of a career member of the navy *US, 1992*

Navy cake *noun* homosexual anal sex *US, 1964*

naw no *US, 1990*

nay-nays *noun* a woman's breasts *US, 1967*

nay-no no, said with kindness. From the film *Pootie Tang US, 2003*

Nazi *noun* a fanatic about the preceding noun. Not coined but rendered wildly popular on the 'Soup Nazi' episode of Jerry Seinfeld's television comedy that first aired on 2nd November 1995 *US, 1984*

Nazi *adjective* unreasonably authoritarian *UK, 2001*

Nazi crank *noun* methamphetamine *UK, 2004*

Nazi go-cart; Nazi go-kart *noun* a Volkswagen car. Citizens' band radio slang remembering that Volkswagen were German manufacturers before and during World War 2 *US, 1976*

NBG *adjective* of no use. An abbreviation of 'no bloody good' *UK, 1903*

NDG *adjective* no damned good *CANADA, 1997*

near and far *noun* **1** a bar in a public house. Dated rhyming slang that remains a familiar term because of its neat reversal with FAR AND NEAR (beer) *UK, 1909*. **2** a car. Rhyming slang *UK, 1971*

near-beer *noun* a beer-like product with a very low alcohol content, legal during Prohibition. There is some dispute about who said the cleverest thing ever said about 'near bear' – 'The guy who called that near beer is a bad judge of distance' *US, 1909*

near the bone *adjective* barely within contemporary moral standards of taste *UK, 1941*

near the knuckle *adjective* barely within contemporary standards of decency *UK, 1909*

neat *adjective* **1** pleasing, very good. Found as early as 1808, rejected late in the C19, and then returned to favour in the 1930s. Still heard; inescapably HOKEY. Considered as an Americanism in the UK but used by teenagers without irony *US, 1936*. **2** (used of an alcoholic drink) served without ice or water *UK, 1579*

neat as a pin *adjective* very neat *UK, 1787*

neato *adjective* good *US, 1901*

neatojet *adjective* excellent *US, 1972*

neb *noun* **1** the nose *UK: SCOTLAND, 1985*. **2** an act of prying *UK: SCOTLAND, 1985*. **3** an inquisitive person *UK: SCOTLAND, 1985*

neb *verb* to pry. From NEB (a nosey person or an instance of prying) *UK: SCOTLAND, 1985*

nebbie; neb *noun* Nembutal™, a branded central nervous system depressant *US, 1963*

nebbish; nebish; nebbech *noun* a hapless individual; an insignificant nobody. From Yiddish *ne'bech* (too bad!, alas!) thus Yiddish *nebech* (the poor thing); the many variant spellings – not all of which are listed here – result from the difficulty of pronunciation *UK, 1892*

nebby *adjective* inquisitive, prying *US, 1982*

Nebraska sign *noun* a completely flat reading on an electrocardiogram. An allusion to the endless flat prairies of Nebraska *US, 1994*

Nebruary morning *adverb* never *BARBADOS, 1965*

nebular *adjective* excellent *US, 1995*

necessaries *noun* ▶ **the necessaries** the male genitals *UK, 1962*

necessary *noun* **1** money, funds *UK, 1897*. **2** a latrine *US, 1991*

neck *noun* **1** the throat *UK, 1818*. **2** a drink. From the verb sense *UK, 2002*. **3** a white prisoner. A shortened 'redneck' *US, 1976*. **4** in horse racing, a distance of less than half a horse-length *US, 1951*. **5** impudence, effrontery, self-confidence. From Northumberland dialect *UK, 1894*. ▶ **get it down your neck; get that down your neck** to swallow it. Often, when in reference to an alcoholic drink, a light-hearted imperative *UK, 1909*. ▶ **get it in the neck; catch it in the neck; take it in the neck** to be severely punished or reprimanded *US, 1887*. ▶ **get under your neck** to usurp someone else's prerogative *AUSTRALIA, 1989*. ▶ **neck like a jockey's bollocks** used descriptively of a scrawny neck and analogously for personal qualities of toughness and insensitivity; said of someone who is not afraid to take advantage of a situation for their own gain *IRELAND, 1992*. ▶ **up to the neck; up to your neck** deeply *US, 1998*

neck *verb* **1** to kiss in a lingering fashion *UK, 1825*. **2** to swallow *UK, 1514*. **3** to drink *AUSTRALIA, 1998*. **4** in prison, to swallow a package of drugs with the intention of retrieval after excretion *UK, 1996*. **5** to commit suicide *AUSTRALIA, 1995*

necking *noun* the act of kissing, caressing and cuddling *UK, 1825*

necklace *verb* to set fire to a car tyre that has been doused in petrol and placed around a victim's neck. An innocent sounding term for a horrid practice, usually practised black-on-black in the waning days of the white supremacist government in South Africa *SOUTH AFRICA, 1986*

necklace; necklace of fire *noun* a tyre doused or filled with petrol, placed around a victim's neck or shoulders, and set alight *SOUTH AFRICA, 1985*

necklacer *noun* an executioner who, in the name of some informal justice, kills by means of the necklace *SOUTH AFRICA, 1987*

necklacing *noun* an act, or the action, of killing by means of the necklace *SOUTH AFRICA, 1986*

neck oil *noun* alcohol, especially beer *UK, 1860*

necktie party *noun* a hanging, especially an extra-judicial lynching *US, 1882*

necro *noun* a necrophile *US, 1987*

nectar *noun* alcohol. Formerly standard English, now slumming in slang with an archaic tone *US, 1966*

nectar *adjective* excellent *US, 1989*

ned *noun* **1** a young hooligan; a petty criminal *UK: SCOTLAND, 1977*. **2** a member of a Scottish subcultural urban adolescent grouping defined by loutish behaviour and a fondness for sportswear and jewellery *UK, 2004*

Ned *noun* the personification of malnutrition *BARBADOS, 1965*

neddy *noun* a horse *AUSTRALIA, 1887*

nederhash *noun* any or all varieties of hashish produced in the Netherlands. A compound of Dutch *Nederland* (Netherlands) and HASH *NETHERLANDS, 2003*

Ned Kelly *noun* **1** a television; television. Rhyming slang for TELLY; based on Australian bushranger Ned Kelly (1854–80). Current in UK prisons in 2002 *UK, 1979*. **2** the belly. Rhyming slang *AUSTRALIA, 1945*. **3** a thief. From Edward 'Ned' Kelly, Australian bushranger and folk hero (1855–80), famed for wearing self-made armour during his final showdown with police *AUSTRALIA, 1962*. ▶ **game as Ned Kelly** extremely game; courageous *AUSTRALIA, 1938*

needies *noun* gypsies. English gypsy use *UK, 2000*

needle *noun* **1** a feeling of resentment or irritation. Originally tailors' slang *UK, 1873*. **2** a vehicle's speedometer *US, 1976*. ▶ **do the needle** to inject drugs, especially heroin *UK, 1996*. ▶ **get the needle (at, with or to)** to become angry or ill-tempered (towards a stated someone or something) *UK, 1874*. ▶ **on the needle** using or addicted to drugs injected intravenously *US, 1942*

needle *verb* **1** to irritate, to annoy, to provoke *UK, 1873*. **2** in the illegal production of alcohol, to simulate ageing by inserting an electric needle into the keg *US, 1974*

needle and pin *noun* a twin. Rhyming slang. The plural is 'needles and pins' *UK, 1998*

needle and thread *noun* bread. Rhyming slang *UK, 1859*

needle beer *noun* beer which has been fortified with another form of alcohol *US, 1962*

needle candy *noun* any drug that can be injected *US, 1971*

needledick *noun* **1** a small, thin penis; a man so equipped *US, 1970*. **2** a despicable man *US, 1998*

needle-dicked *adjective* endowed with a small penis *UK, 1995*

needle freak *noun* an intravenous drug user *US, 1967*

needle jockey *noun* a nurse or doctor who administers shots *US, 1960*

needleman *noun* in a confidence swindle, an agent who inspires the victim with confidence in the scheme *US, 1988*

needle park *noun* a public park or public area where drug addicts gather and inject drugs. Brought into the idiom by the *Panic in Needle Park* (1966), referring to a traffic island at 74th and Broadway on Manhattan's Upper West Side, where heroin addicts congregated *US, 1966*

Needle Park *nickname* Sherman Square (71st Street and Amsterdam Avenue and Broadway), New York. So named because it was a spot favoured by drug users *US, 1982*

need-one-take-one *noun* the small tray near a shop's cash till with pennies which customers may use for making exact payments *US, 1997*

neek *noun* a socially awkward or unfashionable person *UK, 2005*

neff *adjective* bad, generally contemptible. A variation of NAFF *UK, 2003*

negatory no. Coined in the military, popularised in the US by truck drivers in the 1970s *US, 1955*

neg driving *noun* the crime of negligent driving *AUSTRALIA, 1969*

negotiable grass *noun* money *US, 1951*

negrogram *noun* gossip. An effort to euphemise the more popular NIGGERGRAM *TRINIDAD AND TOBAGO, 2003*

negs *noun* in prison, child neglect *UK, 1996*

neighbor *noun* the number on either side of the winning number on a roulette wheel *US, 1961*

neil *noun* an LSD capsule. An allusion to Neil Young, whose music is suitable for enjoyment by young LSD users *CANADA, 1993*

neither use nor ornament *adjective* applied to a useless person or thing. Contemptuous. Not noted until 1978, however '[D]idn't appear to me to be either useful or ornamental[.]', recorded in 1942, implies an earlier use *UK, 1978*

nekkid *adjective* naked. Jocular spelling *US, 1973*

nellie *noun* an obviously homosexual man; an effeminate homosexual man. Recorded at least as early as 1916, but not fully emerged until the outing of gay culture *UK, 1916*

nelly *noun* **1** cheap wine. Shortening of earlier 'Nelly's death' (1935, *Australian National Dictionary*) *AUSTRALIA, 1941*. **2** the pelvic muscles *TRINIDAD AND TOBAGO, 2003*

nelly! used, by effeminate homosexual men, as an exclamation of disgust or contempt. Remembered, or otherwise dated, as 'mid-1950s', by Beale *UK, 1984*

nellyarda *verb* to listen *UK, 2002*

nelly-assed *adjective* effeminate *US, 1963*

Nelly Bligh; Nelly Bly *noun* **1** a meat pie. Rhyming slang, formed on the protagonist of a folk song *AUSTRALIA, 1950*. **2** a fly. Rhyming slang *AUSTRALIA, 1955*

nelly, nellie *adjective* extremely, even outrageously, effeminate *US, 1963*

Nelly's room *noun* ▶ **up in Nelly's room behind the wallpaper** the presumed location of something missing *IRELAND, 2003*

Nelson Eddy; nelson *adjective* ready. Rhyming slang, based on US entertainer Nelson Eddy (1901–67) *UK, 1992*

Nelson Mandela; nelson *noun* lager, especially the Belgian lager Stella Artois™. Rhyming slang, 'Mandela' for 'Stella'. Based on African statesman, Nelson Rolihlahla Mandela (b.1918), emphasising lager drinkers' grasp of world affairs *UK, 2002*

nelsons *noun* cash. Formed from NELSON EDDY (ready), thus READIES (cash) *UK, 1991*

Nelson's blood *noun* rum *AUSTRALIA, 1924*

nembie; nemby *noun* a barbiturate, especially Nembutal™ *US, 1950*

nemish *noun* a capsule of pentobarbital sodium (trade name Nembutal™), a central nervous system depressant *US, 1969*

nemmie *noun* a capsule of pentobritral sodium (trade name Nembutal™), a central nervous system depressant *US, 1950*

Nep; Nepalese *noun* potent hashish from Nepal *UK, 1999*

Nepalese blue; Nepalese; Royal Nepalese *noun* marijuana cultivated in Nepal *UK, 1970*

Nepalese temple balls; Nepalese temple hash *noun* hashish from Nepal, originally prepared for religious use *US, 1989*

nephew *noun* a young, passive male homosexual in relation to his older lover *US, 1950*

neppy *noun* a person from northeast Philadelphia. A combination of 'North East Philly' *US, 1996*

Nepsha and Kiah *noun* a random selection of people from the populace *BARBADOS, 1965*

'ner *noun* dinner *US, 1969*

nerd; nurd *noun* a person lacking in social skills, fashion sense or both *US, 1951*

nerdbomber *noun* a pest. A catchy term from the television programme *Full House US, 1990*

nerd box *noun* a study cubicle *US, 1997*

nerdistan *noun* a dormitory community for information-and-communication-technology workers. A play on NERD (a dull social stereotype) *US, 1997*

nerdly *noun* a socially inept outcast *US, 1965*

nerdvana *noun* the world of computer enthusiasts who surf the Internet every night *CANADA, 1995*

nerf *verb* in motor racing, to bump a competitor during a race *US, 1952*

nerf bar *noun* in hot rodding, a car bumper *US, 1953*

nerk; nurk *noun* a contemptible person. Possibly compounds NERD and JERK (a fool) or BERK (a fool). A floral tribute in the shape of the word 'nurk' featured in the comedy-documentary *Life Beyond The Box*, BBC 2, 3rd May 2004 *UK, 1966*

nerve *noun* effrontery, audacity *UK, 1893*

nerves *noun* ▶ **get on your nerves** to affect morbidly *UK, 1937*

Nervo and Knox *noun* **1** television; a television. Rhyming slang for BOX, formed from the names of a comedy double act, members of the Crazy Gang, Jimmy Nervo, 1890–1975, and Teddy Knox, 1896–1974 *UK, 1971*. **2** syphillis, a sexually transmitted infection. Rhyming slang for POX, sometimes abbreviated to 'nervo' *UK, 1977*. **3** socks. Rhyming slang *UK, 1961*

nervous *adjective* excellent, well done *US, 1926*

Nervous Air *nickname* Service Air, the Canadian military administrative term for the rough and ready travel using military transport *CANADA, 1995*

nervous Nellie *noun* an excessively nervous person *US, 1926*

nervous wreck *noun* a cheque. Rhyming slang *UK, 1998*

nervy *adjective* nervous *US, 1891*

Nessie *nickname* the Loch Ness monster. This familiar name for a shadow on which part of the Scottish economy exists developed not long after the newspapers announced, on 2nd May 1933, that a giant marine creature had been seen in Loch Ness. It is interesting to note that Nessie reappears in the papers about the same time each year *UK, 2001*

nest *noun* **1** a bed *US, 1990*. **2** a hairdo. High school student usage *US, 1961*

nest egg *noun* money saved for the future *UK, 1700*

nester *noun* a member of the Mexican-American prison gang Nuestra Familia. A corrupted pronunciation of 'Nuestra' *US, 1990*

Nestle's Quick *noun* a non-commissioned officer recently arrived in Vietnam after graduation from training school. The short time it took to earn their rank bothered enlisted men, who struck back with this allusion to Nestlé Quik™ (later Nesquik™), a powdered milk flavouring *US, 1991*

net *noun* **1** ten; in betting, odds of 10–1. Back slang *UK, 1851*. **2** the Internet *US, 1995*

net and bice *noun* in betting, odds of 12–1. A combination of NET (ten) and BICE (two) adds up to twelve *UK, 1991*

net and ex *noun* in betting, odds of 16–1. A combination of NET (ten) and a slurring of 'six', adding up to sixteen *UK, 1991*

net and rouf *noun* in betting, odds of 14–1. A combination of NET (ten) and ROUF (four), adding up to fourteen *UK, 1991*

nethead *noun* in the language surrounding the Grateful Dead, a follower of the band who is part of the Grateful Dead cyber community *US, 1994*

netiquette *noun* the protocol, implicit or explicit, observed by members of an Internet discussion group *US, 1995*

netlag *noun* an inordinate delay in an Internet relay chat. A pun on the standard 'jet lag' *US, 1995*

net police *noun* a participant in an Internet discussion group who on a self-appointed basis polices the discussion for protocol and etiquette violations *US, 1991*

neuron *noun* a neurologist *US, 1994*

neutral *noun* ▶ **to put someone into neutral** to castrate someone *NEW ZEALAND, 2002*

Nevada lettuce *noun* a one-thousand-dollar note. Nevada, formerly the only state in the US with legal gambling, is still the most popular gambling destination in the US and the only state with legal brothels *US, 1962*

Nevada nickel *noun* a five-dollar gambling token *US, 1979*

never *adverb* not *UK, 1999*

never again *noun* Ben Truman™, a branded beer. Rhyming slang, from the promise made the morning after the night before *UK, 1992*

neverendum *noun* either of the two referenda on Quebec sovereignty or independence. The term is a sarcastic allusion to the independentist government's having called two votes on the subject and vowing to keep calling them till it won *CANADA, 1999*

never fear – NAME is here a catchphrase announcement – using the speaker's name, of course – of the speaker's reassuring presence; also used, by the speaker, as a general greeting; or, ironically (and, occasionally, disdainfully) of a third party *UK, 1975*

never happen! used for expressing supreme doubt *TRINIDAD AND TOBAGO, 1956*

never in a pig's ear never. Rhyming slang for 'never in a year' *UK, 1977*

nevermind *noun* ▶ **makes no nevermind** makes no difference *US, 1924*

never mind! **1** don't worry; mind your own business. Semi-exclamatory imperative *UK, 1959*. **2** used as a humorous admission of misunderstanding. A key signature line of the early years of NBC's *Saturday Night Live*, uttered by the Emily Litella character played by Gilda Radner who would end rants about 'Soviet Jewelry' or 'the deaf penalty' with the humble 'never mind'. Repeated with referential humour *US, 1977*

never-never *noun* **1** hire purchase. A suggestion that you will never, never pay off your debts, with an ironic reference to J.M. Barrie (1860–1937)'s idealised home for Peter Pan, 'Never Never Land', first realised in 1904 *UK, 1964*. **2** the remote regions of interior Australia. Origin unknown. Sometimes upper case *AUSTRALIA, 1833*

never-never country *noun* the remote regions of interior Australia *AUSTRALIA, 1889*

never-never land *noun* **1** an imaginary, ideal world. From J. M. Barrie's *Peter Pan* novels *UK, 1900*. **2** the hire purchase method of payment by instalments *UK, 2005*

never pitch a bitch used in confidence swindles as a humorous rule of thumb meaning 'never try to do a sales job on a woman' *US, 1985*

never smarten a sucker up used by gambling cheats and confidence swindlers as a prime rule of the trade *US, 1950*

never this year not a chance *UK, 2000*

never-was *noun* a person to whom actual achievement has eluded *US, 1891*

neves; nevis *noun* **1** in betting, odds of 7–1 *UK, 1991*. **2** the number seven. Back slang *UK, 1851*. **3** a prison sentence of seven years.

A specific application of the number seven. Sometimes extended to 'nevis stretch' *UK, 1958*

neves and a half *noun* In bookmaker slang NEVES is 7–1, here the addition of 'a half' increases the odds to 7½–1or 15–2. In bookmaker slang NEVES is 7–1, here the addition of 'a half' increases the odds to 71/2–1or 15–2 *UK, 1991*

neves to rouf *noun* in betting, odds of 7–4. A combination of NEVES (seven) and ROUF (four) when, if used alone, each word signifies more than the number itself. Pronounced 'nevis to roaf' *UK, 1991*

Neville *noun* a stupid or annoying person; a person lacking in social skills, fashion sense or both *AUSTRALIA, 1995*

new *noun* a lager-style beer brewed by the bottom-fermentation method. As opposed to OLD *AUSTRALIA, 1935*

new! used for commenting humorously on a new purchase *US, 1963*

new addition *noun* crack cocaine *UK, 2003*

newb *noun* a new user of the Internet; a newcomer to an Internet discussion group or multi-player game. A shortening of 'newbie' *UK, 2003*

newbie *noun* **1** a new user of the Internet; a new arrival to an Internet discussion group. The general sense 'newcomer' used condescendingly *US, 1995.* **2** a newcomer. Originally military *US, 1970*

new boy *noun* used of a man or a corporate entity, a new arrival to an existing community. From school usage, applied less accurately in military, business and other closed-circles *UK, 1948*

New Brunswick credit card *noun* a rubber siphoning hose for stealing petrol. An analogous term is the Texas OKLAHOMA CREDIT CARD. People from better-off adjacent states or provinces seem convinced that their poorer neighbours are thieves *CANADA, 1992*

newbug *noun* a new boy or new girl. Originally from Marlborough School and only of a boy, now widespread *UK, 1900*

newby *verb* to fail to perform at a critical moment *US, 2002*

Newcastled *adjective* filled with Newcastle Brown Ale™; drunk (probably as a result of drinking Newcastle Brown Ale). Newcastle Brown Ale was first brewed (in Newcastle) in 1927 *UK, 2002*

new chum *noun* **1** a newly arrived immigrant from Britain who has little knowledge of local life and customs. Originally applied to newly incarcerated prisoners (1812 Vaux), it was applied to migrants as early as 1828 (*Australian National Dictionary*); the opposing term was 'old chum' but this did not survive into the C20 *AUSTRALIA, 1969.* **2** a novice *AUSTRALIA, 1851*

New Delhi *noun* the belly. Rhyming slang, formed, possibly, on a sly reference to Indian food *UK, 1992*

Newf *noun* a Newfoundlander *CANADA, 1958*

Newfie *noun* any person from Newfoundland *US, 1942*

Newfie banana *noun* the root of the cinnamon fern *CANADA, 1988*

Newfie Bullet *noun* a train that traversed the interior of Newfoundland. Ironic *CANADA, 1965*

Newfiejohn *noun* the city of St John's, Newfoundland *CANADA, 1945*

new girl *noun* a new arrival to an existing community. From school use, applied to a female adult joining military, business or other closed group *UK, 2003*

New Guinea crud *noun* any skin rash suffered in tropical and jungle environments *US, 1946*

new guy *noun* a freshly arrived soldier to combat. Often embellished to FUCKING NEW GUY *US, 1970*

New Hampshire screwdriver *noun* a hammer. Maine usage, looking down on the workmanship of carpenters from the south *US, 1975*

newie *noun* something new *AUSTRALIA, 1924*

Newington Butts; newingtons *noun* the stomach, abdomen, guts; in a figurative sense the essential qualities of a person. Rhyming slang for GUTS. Newington Butts is an area of south London *UK, 1960*

new jack *noun* a newcomer (especially one likely to be a success) *US, 1988*

new jack swing *noun* heroin and morphine in concert *UK, 1998*

new kid *noun* in roller derby, a skater who has not yet been accepted by other skaters *US, 1999*

new kid on the block *adjective* in bar dice games, a player just joining an ongoing game *US, 1971*

Newky brown; Newky *noun* Newcastle Brown Ale™. As widely used as the beer is appreciated *UK, 1984*

new-man-rule *noun* an unwritten rule among some units of the US Army in Vietnam that a newly arrived soldier would be placed at the front of the unit as pointman *US, 1990*

new meat *noun* **1** a new student at a school *US, 1962.* **2** an inexperienced prison inmate *US, 1938.* **3** an inexperienced soldier freshly arrived at the front *US, 1971*

new nip *noun* a small boy, or a new boy at a school *UK, 1947*

new one applied to a previously unheard joke or anecdote, or to something seen, or heard of, for the first time. Generally phrased 'that' or 'it's a new one on' followed by a pronoun or person's name *US, 1887*

new pussy *noun* a woman unknown to gang members *US, 1966*

news bunny *noun* a female television reporter or anchor hired for her cute looks *US, 1990*

new school *adjective* (used of rap music) current, modern. The functional reciprocal of OLD SKOOL *US, 2001*

news hawk *noun* a newspaper reporter *US, 1931*

new-sick *noun* a new influenza virus *BARBADOS, 1965*

newspaper *noun* a thirty-day jail sentence *US, 1926*

newspapers *noun* LSD *UK, 2003*

newsstand *noun* a dealer in pornographic literature and magazines *US, 1986*

newsy *adjective* **1** full of information, especially of trivial or personal matters *UK, 1832.* **2** nosy; too interested in gossip *US, 1970*

newszine *noun* a fan magazine that does not contain any fiction, just news *US, 1976*

newted *adjective* drunk. From PISSED AS A NEWT *UK, 1984*

Newton and Ridley *adjective* mildly drunk. Rhyming slang for TIDDLY, formed from the name of the fictitious brewery that supplies the drinking requirements of the characters in the long-running television soap opera *Coronation Street UK, 1998*

Newton Heath *noun* teeth. Rhyming slang from Manchester, formed on the name of an industrial suburb of the city *UK, 1959*

new toy *noun* in the Metropolitan Police, a newly introduced piece of equipment; a new recruit *UK, 1999*

New Year *noun* ▶ **not know if it's New Year or New York** applied to anyone who is failing to think clearly (for whatever reason) *UK: SCOTLAND, 1988*

New Yorker *noun* a variety of MDMA, the recreational drug best known as ecstasy. A play on APPLE (a variety of MDMA) and THE APPLE (New York) *UK, 1996*

New York kiss *noun* a punch to the face *US, 1999*

New York minute *noun* a very short period of time. A nod to the impatience associated with New Yorkers *US, 1948*

New York reload *noun* a second (concealed) pistol; an act of drawing a second gun. Derives from a legal loophole: New York police used not to be allowed the use of a speed loader but a second, concealed gun was apparently permissible *US, 2002*

New York Slime *nickname* the *New York Times* newspaper *US, 1981*

newzak *noun* trivial news, or broadcast news that exists in the background but is ignored. A play on 'muzak' *UK, 2003*

New Zealand green *noun* a strain of marijuana, known elsewhere as Tasmanian tiger, Thai Buddha and Hawaiian head *NEW ZEALAND, 2002*

New Zealand mafia *noun* a notional organisation of New Zealand professionals in London *NEW ZEALAND, 1986*

next *noun* during the Vietnam war, a soldier whose rotation home was due in only a few days *US, 1991*

next *adjective* within a few days of returning to the US after a tour of duty in Vietnam *US, 1990*

nextish *noun* the next issue of a single-interest fan magazine *US, 1982*

nexus *noun* 4-bromo-2,5-dimethoxyphenethylamine, a mild hallucinogen *US, 1995*

NF *nickname* the Nuestra Familia prison gang *US, 2000*

NF *verb* as an act of racial hatred, to set fire to a property that houses members of an ethnic minority. Derives from the initials of the National Front, a politically right-wing organisation founded on muddled philosophies of racial intolerance and violent intervention *UK, 2005*

NFG *adjective* used as shorthand to mean *'no fucking good'* *US, 1977*

NFN doctors' shorthand for the facetious diagnosis: *normal for Norfolk*. Recorded in an article about medical slang in British (3 London and 1 Cambridge) hospitals *UK, 2003*

NG *adjective* no good *US, 1879*

NHI *adjective* used for describing a crime against a criminal, especially one involving only black people. An abbreviation of *'no humans involved'* *US, 1973*

Niagara Falls; niagaras *noun* the testicles. Rhyming slang *UK, 1943*

nibble *noun* a non-commital expression of interest. From the image of a fish trying a bait *UK, 1959*

nibby *noun* a walking stick, especially one used in rounding up sheep *NEW ZEALAND, 1964*

nibs *noun* ▶ **his nibs; her nibs** himself; herself; a self-important person. Usually styled as a mock-title *UK, 1821*

nice and easy *noun* heroin *US, 1994*

nice as pie *adjective* very polite, very agreeable *US, 1922*

nice bit *noun* a prison sentence of three years or more *UK, 1996*

nice enough *noun* a homosexual male. Rhyming slang for PUFF *UK, 1992*

nice kitty *noun* a Christmas bonus *US, 1954*

nice little earner *noun* a well-paid job or profitable scheme, almost always criminal to some degree. An elaboration of EARNER, made popular by actor George Cole as small-time crook and wheeler-dealer Arthur Daley in *Minder*, 1979–94 *UK, 1996*

nicely irrigated with horizontal lubricant *adjective* drunk. Some people, when drinking, use too many words *UK, 2002*

nice-nice *adjective* very attractive *UK, 1994*

nice one used in a congratulatory sense to express praise for an action *UK, 1997*

nice one Cyril; nice one *noun* a squirrel. Rhyming slang *UK, 1992*

nice one, Cyril used for expressing praise. A very popular catchphrase of the mid-1970s. It originated in a television commercial and was taken up in the early 70s as a football chant by Tottenham Hotspur FC's supporters in celebration of Cyril Knowles, one of the club's leading players *UK, 1984*

nice talk *noun* a line of conversation intended to seduce. Urban black youth usage *UK, 2003*

nice up *verb* to make something more acceptable or presentable, to improve, to refine *UK, 2004*

nice weather for ducks wet weather. Known in variant forms since 1840 *UK, 1973*

nicey nice *adjective* Extremely nice, even excessively nice. A diminutive, childish formation usually used with some degree of mocking or irony *UK, 1859*

nick *noun* **1** a prison; a police station. In either case it is where one is taken after getting 'nicked' (arrested); the former dates from 1882, the latter 1957 *UK, 1950*. **2** condition or quality, especially in phrases 'in good nick', 'in poor nick', etc. Originally dialect *UK, 1905*. **3** in horse racing, a mating that results in the sought-after qualities *AUSTRALIA, 1989*. **4** five dollars' worth of marijuana. A shortened form of 'nickel' as in NICKEL BAG *US, 2002*. **5** in craps, a winning roll of seven on the first toss *US, 1962*. **6** a nickname *US, 1995*. ▶ **in the**

nick naked *NEW ZEALAND, 1998*. ▶ **on the nick** engaged in thieving *UK, 1977*

nick *verb* **1** to arrest, to apprehend *UK, 1622*. **2** in prison, to place on report *UK, 2001*. **3** to steal *UK, 1869*. **4** to win a gamble, possibly by taking an unfair advantage or cheating. A variation of earlier obsolete senses: 'to cheat at cards', 'to defraud' *UK, 1676*. **5** (of a person) to move quickly. Followed by an adverb. Perhaps a specialised use of the sense 'to cheat' *AUSTRALIA, 1894*. **6** to throw dice *BARBADOS, 1965*. ▶ **get nicked** get lost. Euphemistic for 'get fucked' *AUSTRALIA, 1968*. ▶ **nick a living** to make enough money to survive *UK, 1998*. ▶ **nick the title** to win a sporting contest and thereby to take the title *UK, 1998*

nick about with *verb* to go around in the company of, or associate with, someone or some group of people *UK: SCOTLAND, 1985*

nick away *verb* to leave, to steal away *NEW ZEALAND, 1998*

nicked *adjective* stolen. From the verb NICK (to steal) *UK, 2001*

nickel *noun* **1** a five-year prison sentence *US, 1953*. **2** five dollars *US, 1946*. **3** in American casinos, a five-dollar betting chip *US, 1980*. **4** five hundred dollars *US, 1974*. **5** a mediocre object or situation *US, 1977*

nickel *adjective* inferior *US, 1932*

nickel and dime *verb* to wear down in small increments *US, 1961*

nickel-and-dime *adjective* small-time, operating on a small scale *US, 1941*

nickel and dime; nickel *noun* **1** time. Rhyming slang *US, 1998*. **2** in pool, a table that is five feet by ten feet *US, 1993*

nickel-and-dime pimp *noun* a small-time pimp *US, 1972*

nickel bag *noun* five dollars' worth of a drug *US, 1966*

nickel-dime-quarter *noun* poker played with very small bets *US, 1968*

nickel game *noun* a game of craps in which the true and correct odds are paid *US, 1950*

nickel gouger *noun* the operator of a dishonest carnival game *US, 1950*

nickel note *noun* a five-dollar *US, 1926*

nickelonian *noun* a crack cocaine addict. A play on 'nickelodian', after the NICKEL BAG that the addict hungers for *US, 1998*

nickel-pincher *noun* a cheapskate. A variation on the much more common 'penny-pincher' *US, 1949*

nickels *noun* in craps, a roll of two fives *US, 1983*

nickels and dimes *noun* in hold 'em poker, a five and ten as the first two cards dealt to a player *US, 1981*

nickel seats *noun* inexpensive seats at an event, usually far from the action *US, 1990*

nickel's worth *noun* a five-minute conversation on a citizens' band radio. Five minutes was once the longest conversation allowed at one time *US, 1976*

nick 'em and stick 'em used of the professional approach of a prison officer who is interested only in the discipline and confinement of prisoners *UK, 1996*

nicker *noun* **1** one pound sterling (£1); pounds *UK, 1910*. **2** pounds *AUSTRALIA, 1965*

nicker bit *noun* a one-pound coin. From NICKER (£1) *UK, 1992*

nicker bits *noun* diarrhoea. Rhyming slang for THE SHITS, formed from NICKER BIT (a £1 coin) *UK, 1992*

nick joint *noun* a dishonest gambling operation *US, 1978*

nick-nacker *noun* an infrequent drug user *US, 1984*

nick nick used of catching or arresting, or the act of being caught. Reduplication of NICK (to arrest); directly from the catchphrase popularised in the later 1970s by comedian Jim Davidson (b.1953) *UK, 1981*

nick off *verb* **1** to depart, to leave *AUSTRALIA, 1901*. **2** to play truant. Teen slang *UK, 1982*. **3** to take or steal something *AUSTRALIA, 1968*

Nicky Butt *noun* a testicle. Rhyming slang for NUT(S), formed from a Manchester United footballer (b.1975) *UK, 1998*

nic-nac party *noun* a party for a bride-to-be. At the party, the gifts for the bride focus on her future home *AUSTRALIA, 1988*

niddy-noddy *noun* a stick about a foot long, with end-pieces, used for wrapping yarn *CANADA, 1986*

niebla *noun* phencyclidine, the recreational drug known as PCP or angel dust. Spanish for 'cloud' *US, 1994*

nieve *noun* cocaine. Spanish for 'snow' *US, 1993*

niff *noun* an unpleasant smell. Possibly derives from 'sniff' *UK, 1903*

niff *verb* to smell unpleasantly. From the noun sense *UK, 1927*

niffy *adjective* smelly. From Sussex dialect *UK, 1937*

nifty *noun* the sum of fifty pounds sterling (£50). Not really rhyming slang, merely a convenient rhyme *UK, 1999*

nifty *adjective* smart, fashionable, fine, splendid. Old-fashioned and affected; probably a corrupted 'magnificent' *US, 1805*

nifty fifty *noun* an act of masturbation. A rhymed approximation of the number of movements required. Often in the phrase 'give it the nifty fifty' *UK, 1984*

nifty-keen *adjective* excellent *US, 1972*

nig *noun* **1** a black person. A shortened form of NIGGER, no less offensive *US, 1828*. **2** an Australian Aboriginal. Racially offensive; now not very common *AUSTRALIA, 1880*. **3** a new soldier, either a recruit or one just out of recruit training *UK, 1980*

Nigel Benn *noun* a pen. Rhyming slang, formed from the name of a champion boxer (b.1964) *UK, 1998*

Nigerian *noun* in homosexual usage, any black man *US, 1987*

Nigerian lager *noun* Guinness™, the branded stout. From the deep black colour of the beer *UK, 1977*

Nigerian scam spam *noun* a swindle that uses e-mail to solicit potential victims to help an African correspondent transfer millions of dollars into an American bank account *US, 2002*

nigga *noun* a black person. A deliberate misspelling, reinventing NIGGER for exclusive black use; widely used in gangsta rap *US, 1980s*

nigger *noun* **1** a black person. When used by white speakers, highly offensive; used by black speakers, especially the young, with increasing frequency *UK, 1574*. **2** an Australian Aboriginal. Racially offensive *AUSTRALIA, 1845*. **3** a Maori *NEW ZEALAND, 1858*. **4** a friend. The word having been reclaimed by the black population, usage in the racially-mixed community of St Pauls, Bristol, resulted, in 2003, in white youths emulating black peers and calling their friends, of any skin-colour, 'nigger' *UK, 2003*. **5** in the television and film industries, a screen on a stand used to achieve lighting effects *UK, 1960*. ▶ **another push and you'd have been a nigger** used insultingly as a slur on the morals of the subject's mother, implying that she would have sex with anyone of any race *UK, 1961*

niggerati *noun* a high profile grouping of successful members of black society. A black coinage, combining NIGGER (a black person) and -ERATI (a suffix which suggests the fashionable) *UK, 2000*

nigger babies *noun* dirt specks, especially in the creases of the neck *US, 1970*

nigger bait *noun* a great deal of chrome on a car *US, 1960*

nigger bankroll *noun* a single large-denomination bill wrapped around small-denomination notes, giving the impression of a great deal of money *US, 1980*

nigger bet *noun* an uncommon amount wagered *US, 1968*

nigger flicker *noun* a small knife; a razor blade used as a weapon *US, 1980*

niggergram *noun* gossip *TRINIDAD AND TOBAGO, 1950*

nigger-hater *noun* an overt racist *US, 1951*

niggerhead *noun* **1** tobacco, twisted into a plug *US, 1843*. **2** an eight-gallon milk can *CANADA, 1992*. **3** a tuft of grass *US, 1859*. **4** in lobstering, a winch head *US, 1978*

niggerhead keister *noun* a steel safe shaped like a ball *US, 1976*

nigger heaven *noun* **1** a simple, perfect happiness *US, 1906*. **2** the highest, least expensive seats in a theatre *US, 1866*

nigger in the woodpile *noun* anything that spoils the perfection of a finished article. Originally used without any sense that offence may be caused; now taboo *US, 1852*

niggeritis *noun* laziness; sloth after eating *TRINIDAD AND TOBAGO, 2001*

nigger-knockers *noun* heavy work boots *US, 1964*

niggerlip *verb* to moisten the end of a cigarette with saliva *US, 1940*

nigger local *noun* on the railways, a freight train that makes frequent local stops that involve heavy work for the crew *US, 1916*

nigger-lover *noun* a white person who mixes with or admires black people; a white person who believes that all men are created equal. Originally white usage, it was intended to be offensive and disparaging *US, 1856*

nigger-loving *adjective* used for describing a white person who does not share the speaker's pathological hatred of black people *US, 1879*

nigger navel *noun* a type of daisy *US, 2002*

nigger pennies *noun* an illegal lottery game *US, 1977*

nigger pool *noun* an illegal numbers gambling lottery *US, 1949*

nigger rich *adjective* maintaining outward signs of wealth *US, 1930*

nigger-rig *verb* to improvise in a shoddy way *US, 1965*

nigger's lip *noun* a (potato) chip. Rhyming slang *UK, 1980*

niggers' man *noun* a white person who is less prejudiced than most *BAHAMAS, 1905*

Niggerstan *noun* any country with a black population. Racist *UK, 1994*

nigger stick *noun* a reinforced baton used by police on suspected criminals, criminals and prisoners *US, 1971*

nigger sticker *noun* a long, sharp knife *US, 1969*

nigger ten *noun* a cross near where a person has died *BARBADOS, 1965*

nigger toe *noun* a Brazil nut *US, 1896*

nigger toes *noun* black olives *US, 1996*

niggertown *noun* a neighbourhood with a large population of black people *US, 1904*

nigger up *verb* to make many purely decorative, inexpensive, flashy modifications to a car *US, 1992*

niggerville *noun* a section of a city or town populated by black people. Offensive *US, 1857*

niggle *noun* a complaint *UK, 1886*

niggle *verb* **1** to do something in a finicky, fussy or time-wasting manner. Originally, certainly from about 1640 in conventional use; now, according to the *Oxford English Dictionary*, chiefly colloquial *UK, 1893*. **2** to irritate, to cause a slight but persistent annoyance. Generally considered to be a conventional use; included here for its derivatives which are certainly in this dictionary's domain *UK, 1796*. **3** to have sex *US, 1962*. **4** in horse racing, to urge a horse with hands and rein *UK, 1948*

niggled *adjective* annoyed, irritated, especially when made so by disappointment or the pettiness of others. From Cumberland dialect *UK, 1878*

niggliness *noun* irritability; a state of being short-tempered *UK, 1982*

niggling *adjective* petty, persistently irritating *UK, 1854*

niggly *adjective* **1** bad-tempered, especially about trifling concerns; irritable *UK, 1840*. **2** annoying, irritating *UK, 1840*

night *noun* ▶ **it'll be all right on the night; it will all come right on the night** used as an optimistic reassurance that everything will be fine. Originally theatrical, expressing the belief that all will be well for the first night. *It'll Be Alright on the Night*, a television programme celebrating the things that go wrong (despite its reassuring title) has been broadcast since 1977 *UK, 1899*. ▶ **make a night of** to spend the night in pursuit of (dissolute) pleasures *UK, 1693*

night; 'night good night. Elliptical reduction of the customary good wishes at parting or sleep *UK, 1912*

night and day *noun* a play. Rhyming slang *UK, 1960*

night and day *adjective* grey. Rhyming slang *UK, 1992*

night bull *noun* a prison guard assigned to a night shift *US, 1967*

nightcap *noun* **1** the final alcoholic drink of the night *UK, 1818*. **2** a marijuana cigarette, especially the last one of the day. No doubt for the relaxant properties of the drug *UK, 1996*. **3** in horse racing, the last race of the day *US, 1951*

nightclub tan *noun* a pale complexion *UK, 1973*

night cocky *noun* in prison, a night patrolman *UK, 2000*

night compass *noun* a chamber pot *CAYMAN ISLANDS, 1985*

nightery; niterie *noun* a nightclub *US, 1934*

night eye *noun* an irregular growth on the inside of a horse's legs, useful as a means of identification *US, 1938*

night for night *noun* in television and film-making, a scene set at night that is also shot at night *US, 1988*

nighthawk *noun* **1** a person who is active late at night *UK, 1818*. **2** a taxi driver who works late at night *US, 1868*

night house *noun* an illegal lottery operating at night *US, 1957*

nightie; nighty *noun* a nightgown *UK, 1871*

nightingale *noun* a police informer. From the SING metaphor *US, 1968*

night manoeuvres *noun* a social date *US, 1962*

nightmare *noun* an unpleasant experience; an unpleasant person *UK, 1927*

night nurse *noun* a cigarette smoked in the middle of the night by an addict whose body is awakened by the craving for nicotine in the night *US, 1996*

night rider *noun* **1** a person who enjoys the wild side of life at night *US, 1951*. **2** in horse racing, someone who takes a horse out for a night workout in the hope of lessening its performance in a race the next day *US, 1951*

nights belong to Charlie used as a rule of thumb by US soldiers in Vietnam, acknowledging the ascendancy of the Viet Cong during the dark *US, 1990*

night train *noun* suicide *US, 1984*

night work *noun* at night, urination or defecation other than in a toilet *TRINIDAD AND TOBAGO, 1959*

nighty-night; night-night; nigh'-nigh' good night. Originally children's vocabulary but now widely used and not always ironically *UK, 1896*

nig in *verb* to sneak in without paying *UK, 2003*

nig-nog *noun* **1** any non-white person. Rhyming slang, by virtue of the rhyme with WOG, this racist and derogatory term is a compound of NIGGER (a black person) and WOG (any foreigner); it is not always considered abusive by the speaker. In *Love Thy Neighbour*, a UK television comedy which ran to seven series, 1972–76, the white-skinned characters routinely called their black neighbours SAMBO(s) and 'nig-nogs' *UK, 1959*. **2** a fool; a novice. Military use, possibly from obsolete slang 'nigmenog' (a fool), probably informed by racist sentiments *UK, 1959*

nigra *noun* marijuana *UK, 2003*

-nik *suffix* a supporter or follower of the precedent activity or principle *US, 1963*

Nike air jerusalem *noun* Nike Air Jordans™, a branded sport shoe. A weak pun replacing Jordan with Jerusalem, current in UK prisons August 2002 *UK, 2002*

Nike down *verb* to dress in nothing but Nike™ clothing and shoes *US, 1998*

Niki Lauda; Niki *noun* cocaine. Rhyming slang, Lauda (pronounced 'louder') for POWDER, based on the name of racing driver Nikolaus Andreas Lauda (b.1949) *UK, 1985*

niks *noun* nothing. From Afrikaans into South African English *UK, 1860*

nimby *noun* **1** used as an acronym for 'not in my back yard', a description of the philosophy of those who support an idea in principle but do not want to be personally inconvenienced by it. The acronym followed the phrase by only a year *US, 1980*. **2** a capsule of pentobarbital sodium (trade name Nembutal™), a central nervous system depressant *US, 1962*

nimrod *noun* a fool, a stupid person, a bungler. Jonathan Lighter writes that 'currency of the term owes much to its appearance in a 1940s Warner Bros. cartoon in which Bugs Bunny refers to the hunter Elmer Fudd as "poor little Nimrod"'. It is not clear that watchers of the cartoon understood the C18 sense of the word as 'a great hunter', but the term has stuck *US, 1932*

NINA no Irish need apply *US, 1987*

Nina; Nina from Carolina; Nina from Pasadena *noun* in craps, a roll of nine or the nine point *US, 1939*

nincompoop *noun* a foolish person, a simpleton. In *A Classical Dictionary of the Vulgar Tongue*, 3rd edition, 1796, Francis Grose defines 'nincompoop' as 'a foolish fellow' and 'one who never saw his wife's ****', which adds a little bite to its use *UK, 1673*

nineball *noun* a socially inept person *US, 1997*

ninebar *noun* nine ounces of cannabis *UK, 1996*

nine-day blues *noun* the incubation period for gonorrhea *US, 1981*

nine-nickel *noun* ninety-five *US, 1998*

nine of hearts *noun* a racehorse that is not likely to win *US, 1951*

ninepennyworth *noun* a prison term of nine months *UK, 1957*

niner *noun* **1** an erect penis that is nine inches long *UK, 1997*. **2** a nine gallon keg of beer *AUSTRALIA, 1957*

nines *noun* ▶ **to the nines** to an impressive degree *UK, 1793*

nine-strand splicer *noun* in oil drilling, a big and strong man *US, 1954*

nineteen *noun* **1** amphetamines. This may well derive from a shortening of the conventional phrase 'nineteen to the dozen' (very fast) as a play on SPEED (amphetamine) *UK, 2003*. **2** MDMA, the recreational drug best known as ecstasy *UK, 2003*. **3** nothing at all. From the game of cribbage (a hand with no points) *US, 1975*

nineteen canteen *noun* a long time ago *SOUTH AFRICA, 1974*

nineteen-eighty cell *noun* a secure prison cell used for prisoners at risk to themselves or others. From the official paperwork, a '1980 form', which must be completed each time before such a cell may be occupied *UK, 1996*

nineteenth hole *noun* a golf course bar where golfers retire after a round of golf *US, 1901*

nine-to-five *noun* the usual working day; the rut of daily existence. Based on an average working day, nine in the morning to five in the afternoon, but applied to regular employment whatever the hours worked, and especially to routine drudgery *US, 1936*

nine-trey *noun* ninety-three *US, 1993*

ninety *noun* **1** the 90-mm cannon mounted on an M-48 Patton battle tank *US, 1991*. **2** the M-67 90-mm recoilless rifle *US, 1991*

ninety days *noun* in dice games, a roll of nine *US, 1909*

ninety-day-wonder *noun* a recent graduate of the US Army's Officer Candidate School *US, 1917*

ninety-in-ninety *noun* in twelve-step recovery programmes such as Alcoholics Anonymous, used as a prescription for starting recovery – ninety meetings in ninety days *US, 1998*

ninety-niner *noun* a driver from Canada's prairies driving into mountain (Alberta and British Columbia) roads for the first time *CANADA, 1989*

ninety-six *noun* reciprocal anal sex *US, 1949*

ninety-weight *noun* **1** any strong alcohol *US, 1976*. **2** strong, 90-proof whisky *US, 1976*

ning nong *noun* a fool, an idiot. Probably a variant of British dialect ning-nang, recorded since the 1830s (*English Dialect Dictionary*) *AUSTRALIA, 1957*

ninny *noun* **1** a fool, a dolt *UK, 1593*. **2** the vagina or vulva *BAHAMAS, 1982*

nip *noun* **1** a nipple, especially a woman's. The nickname given to the character Elaine Benes (played by Julia Louis-Dreyfus) on *Seinfeld* (NBC, 1990–98) after a snapshot that she took for a Christmas card showed a breast nipple *US, 1965*. **2** a small drink *US, 1736*. **3** in Winnipeg, a hamburger *CANADA, 1987*. **4** a manoeuvre, especially while driving *BERMUDA, 1985*

Nip *noun* **1** a Japanese or Japanese-American person. Shortened from 'Niponese'. Deemed offensive by Multicultural Management Program Fellows, *Dictionary of Cautionary Words and Phrases*, 1989 *US, 1942*. **2** a Honda car. Citizens' band radio slang for the product of a Japanese manufacturer; a specific use of a generally racist term *UK, 1981*

nip *verb* **1** (of a person) to move quickly *UK, 1825*. **2** to grab *UK, 1566*. **3** to open a locked door using a special pair of pliers that can grasp the key from the other side of the door *US, 1962*. ▶ **nip it** to stop doing something *US, 1983*

Nip *adjective* Japanese *AUSTRALIA, 1946*

nip and tuck *noun* cosmetic surgery *US, 1981*

nip and tuck *adjective* in a contest, neck and neck, or alternately holding the lead *US, 1845*

nip factor *noun* the degree of coldness *US, 1997*

nip it in the bud! used for humorously suggesting the emerging presence of a problem. A signature line of deputy Barney Fife, played by Don Knotts, on the situation comedy *Andy Griffith Show* (CBS, 1960–68). Repeated with referential humour *US, 1965*

nipper *noun* **1** a baby or young child *UK, 1859*. **2** a young lad employed to do menial tasks for a group of labourers *AUSTRALIA, 1915*. **3** a sandfly *BAHAMAS, 1982*. **4** in target shooting, a shot that just nicks a ring, scoring as if it had fallen within the ring *US, 1957*. **5** a railway brakeman *US, 1977*

nippers *noun* **1** the female breasts *US, 1968*. **2** the teeth *US, 1965*. **3** thickly knit gloves with no fingers *CANADA, 1955*. **4** any cutting tool *US, 1950*. **5** a special pair of pliers that can grasp the key from the other side of the door *US, 1962*

nippie *noun* the nipple *UK, 1997*

nipple gripple; nipple cripple *noun* a violent gripping and twisting assault on someone's (usually a male's) nipples *UK, 2003*

nipple palm *noun* a Nipa palm, found in swampy and marshy land in South Vietnam *US, 1984*

nipplitis *noun* (used of a woman) erect nipples *US, 1997*

Nippon Clipon *noun* the Auckland Harbor Bridge. Through Japanese technology, the bridge was expanded from two to four lanes *NEW ZEALAND, 1976*

nippy *adjective* **1** speedy *UK, 1853*. **2** chilly. Almost always applied to the weather *US, 1898*

nips *adjective* afraid, anxious. Probably from NIP STRAWS *SOUTH AFRICA, 1977*

nip slip *noun* a photograph revealing at least a part of a woman's nipple. The premise is that the reveal is accidental; major usage of the term on Internet photograph sites *US, 2004*

nip straws *verb* to be nervous, anxious or afraid. From the clenching of the jaw; generally as 'nipping straws' *SOUTH AFRICA, 1970*

Nirvana Scotia *noun* Nova Scotia *CANADA, 2002*

nishi *noun* the vagina *US, 1998*

nishte; nish; nishta *noun* nothing. From German *nichts* (nothing), via Yiddish usage. 'Nishta' is recorded as a contemporary gay usage *UK, 1958*

nishtoise; nishtoisale *noun* nothing. A variation of NISHTE *UK, 2002*

nit *noun* a simpleton, a moron, a fool. Widespread UK term of abuse since about 1950 *AUSTRALIA, 1941*. ▶ **keep nit** to act as lookout while an illegal activity takes place *AUSTRALIA, 1903*

nit! run for it! Used to notify wrongdoers of the approach of authority. Probably a variant of NIX *AUSTRALIA, 1882*

nite *noun* night. Generally in a commercial or advertising context *US, 1928*

nit-keeper *noun* a lookout for an illegal activity *AUSTRALIA, 1935*

nit nit! be quiet!; used as a warning that someone is listening. In prison use *UK, 1950*

nitro *noun* a streetlight bulb *US, 1980*

nitro *adjective* volatile. Derived from the unstable nature of nitroglycerin *US, 1977*

nitrous *noun* the gas nitrous oxide used as a recreational drug *AUSTRALIA, 1994*

nits and buggers *noun* in poker, a hand with a pair of threes and a pair of twos *US, 1967*

nits and lice *noun* in poker, a hand with two low-valued pairs *US, 1967*

nitto! stop!; be quiet!; used as a general cry of warning. A variation of NIT NIT! *UK, 1959*

nitty *adjective* idiotic. From NIT (a fool), possibly influenced by NUTTY (crazy) *UK, 1967*

nitty-clitty *noun* oral sex on a woman. A play on CLIT (the clitoris) and NITTY-GRITTY (the essence of the matter) *US, 1975*

nitty-gritty *noun* the essence of the matter. Coined by black people, then spread into wide use. In the early 2000s, the belief that the term originally applied to the debris left at the bottom of slave ships when the slaves were removed from the ship circulated with speed, certainty and outrage. Whether the initial report was an intentional hoax or merely basis-free speculation, it is a false etymology. All authorities agree that the etymology is unknown yet some ill-informed politically correct types consider the word to have racist overtones *US, 1956*

nitwit *noun* a simpleton, a moron, a fool *US, 1914*

nix; nicks *noun* nothing; no. Probably from colloquial German *nichts* via Dutch (colloquial Afrikaans has *niks*) *UK, 1789*

nix *verb* to reject, to deny *US, 1903*

nixer *noun* work undertaken outside normal work, usually without an employer's knowledge *IRELAND, 1994*

nixie *noun* an incorrectly addressed letter. A term used by railway mail clerks *US, 1890*

nixies *noun* a female undergarment with a cut-out crotch permitting vaginal sex while otherwise clothed *US, 1978*

Nixon's revenge *noun* an American Ford car. Citizens' band radio slang; a reference to US President Richard Nixon *US, 1976*

nizzel; nizzle *noun* a close friend. A hip-hop, urban black coinage, formed as a rhyming reduplication of SHIZZLE (sure, yes) *US, 2001*

nkalafaker *noun* a person who is not so much to be admired as was originally thought; a confidence trickster. Teen slang *SOUTH AFRICA, 2003*

nkalakatha *noun* a trustworthy person. Current teen slang *SOUTH AFRICA, 2003*

N.O. no. Spelt for emphasis, usually humorous *US, 1973*

no-access tool *noun* a light cleaning brush carried by telephone installers and repair technicians. If for any reason the installer or repair technician would rather not make a particular service call, they sneak up to the door and leave a 'sorry-we-missed-you' tag. In jest, a fellow worker might accuse him of using a light cleaning brush to faintly tap on the door *US, 2003*

noah *noun* a shark. Rhyming slang from 'Noah's ark' *US, 1963*

Noah's ark *noun* **1** an informer. Rhyming slang for NARK (an informer); used in England since the first decade of the C20. 'Noah's ark' is spoonerised into 'oah's nark', which infers the deeply contemptuous 'whore's nark' *UK, 1996*. **2** a person who accompanies a customer but deters him or her from making a purchase. Rhyming slang for NARK (an awkward customer) *UK, 1979*. **3** a spoilsport. Rhyming slang for NARK *AUSTRALIA, 1898*. **4** a park. Rhyming slang *UK, 1971*

Noah's ark *adjective* dark. Rhyming slang *UK, 1934*

Noah's nobles *noun* female volunteers from the American Red Cross. Korean war usage; Noah is suggested by the Red Cross initials (ARC) *US, 1968*

no ass *adverb* extremely. Placed after the verb *GUYANA, 1996*

no ass! used for expressing the serious nature of what is being said *TRINIDAD AND TOBAGO, 1974*

nob *noun* **1** a person of rank, position or wealth *UK, 1703*. **2** a completely reliable and dependable person *AUSTRALIA, 1989*. **3** the penis. A variation of KNOB *UK, 1961*. **4** the head. Probably from KNOB; since about 1690 but now feels dated and tired *UK, 1690*

nob *verb* to collect money from an audience after a performance or other attraction. Possibly from passing the hat round, a NOB (a head) more usually being put in a hat *UK, 1851*

nobber *noun* a person who collects money for a street entertainer *UK, 1890*

nobber; nobba *adjective* nine. Polari; from Spanish *nueve* or Italian *nove*, via parleyaree and lingua franca *UK, 1996*

nobbins *noun* money collected from an audience, especially money thrown into a boxing ring. From NOB (to collect money from an audience) *UK, 1998*

nobble *verb* **1** to sabotage, especially to hinder or defeat a rival. From horse-tampering *UK, 1856*. **2** to corrupt, or otherwise tamper with, a jury or jury member *UK, 1856*. **3** in horse racing, to drug a horse to impair its performance *UK, 1847*. **4** to appropriate dishonestly, to steal *UK, 1854*

nobbler *noun* **1** a person who drugs racehorses or racing dogs to affect their racing performance *US, 1982*. **2** a small glass of spirits *AUSTRALIA, 1842*

Nobby Hall *noun* a testicle. Rhyming slang for BALL(S), formed from the name of the eponymous hero of an old and bawdy song: 'They call him Nobby Hall, Nobby Hall / They call him Nobby Hall, 'coz he's only got one....finger / They call him Nobby Hall, Nobby Hall' *UK, 1992*

Nobby Stiles; nobbys *noun* haemorrhoids. Rhyming slang for 'piles', formed from footballer Norbert 'Nobby' Stiles (b.1942) who was a member of the England team that won the World Cup in 1966 *UK, 1992*

nob end *noun* the part of town where the money lives *UK, 1964*

no biggie don't worry about it *US, 1982*

no bitch! I don't have to sit in the middle of the back seat of the car! Quickly shouted after someone else reserves the front passenger seat by shouting 'shotgun!' *US, 1989*

noble *noun* an influential, respected prisoner *US, 1976*

noble weed *noun* marijuana *US, 1970*

nobody *noun* ▶ **like nobody's business** to an extraordinary extent, very much *UK, 1938*

nobody's home said of a person who is empty-headed. An abbreviation of LIGHTS ON BUT THERE'S NOBODY HOME *US, 2001*

no brag, just fact used for humorously calling attention to having bragged. Cavalry scout Will Sonnett, played by Walter Brennan, used this line to instill fear on the television Western *The Guns of Will Sonnett* (ABC, 1967–69). Repeated with referential humour *US, 1969*

no-brainer *noun* **1** an opinion so easily formed or decision so easily made that no thinking is required *US, 1980*. **2** in croquet, a lucky shot *US, 1977*

nobs *noun* shoes *US, 1968*

No Cal *noun* northern California *US, 1991*

no can do, Madame Nhu used as a humorous if emphatic suggestion that something cannot be done. Madame Nhu was the sister-in-law of South Vietnamese President Diem *US, 1991*

no chance! used as an emphatic negative, often scornful *UK, 1984*

no chance outside *noun* a non-commissioned officer of the US Army. From the initials NCO and a healthy distrust of military authority *US, 1968*

nochy *noun* night. Polari, from Italian *notte* or Spanish *noche* *UK, 1998*

no comment! used as a jocular catchphrase. In imitation of politicians everywhere *UK, 1977*

no comprende I do not understand. Partial Spanish used by English speakers without regard to their fluency in Spanish, and with multiple variations reflecting their lack of fluency *US, 1971*

nod *noun* **1** a drug-induced state of semi- or unconsciousness. From 'nod' (a sleep) *US, 1936*. **2** a new recruit to the Royal Marines. A variant of 'Noddy', which supposedly derives from a standard issue woollen hat that when worn by recruits looks like Noddy (a children's character)'s hat *UK, 1987*. **3** the head. An abbreviation of

NODDLE (the head) *UK, 2000*. **4** in horse racing, a very small margin of victory or lead *US, 1971*. ▶ **nod is as good as a wink; nod is as good as a wink to a blind horse; nod's as good as a wink to a blind bat** applied to a covert yet comprehensible hint. The 'blind bat' variation was created in 1969 for the ground-breaking television comedy series *Monty Python's Flying Circus* and, like many of that programme's catchphrases, remains in circulation *UK, 1802*. ▶ **on the nod 1** lost in mental stupefaction brought on by heroin or other narcotics *US, 1951*. **2** within a committee, to be agreed without argument; to be *nodded* through. Conventionally, a nod is a sign of assent *UK, 1999*. **3** (of a wager) agreed upon without money changing hands *AUSTRALIA, 1902*. ▶ **the nod** official approval, *UK, 2001*

nod *verb* to enter a near-coma state after drug use *US, 1958*

nod betting *noun* betting on credit *AUSTRALIA, 1981*

nodder *noun* the head *UK, 1956*

noddle *noun* the head *UK, 1509*

noddle *verb* to idle, to waste time *UK, 2003*

noddy *noun* **1** in a film or television interview, a brief shot of the interviewer listening or nodding. In full, a 'noddy-shot' *UK, 1982*. **2** a police motorcyclist. A back-formation from NODDY-BIKE *UK, 1980*

Noddy *noun* a tracked snow vehicle manufactured by the Robin Nodwell Manufacturing Company *ANTARCTICA, 1978*

noddy *adjective* **1** (used of a computer program) trivial, useless but illustrative of a point *US, 1991*. **2** foolish. From Essex dialect *UK, 1971*

noddy-bike; noddy *noun* a police motorcycle. Originally of a light motorcycle used by police before the introduction of the PANDA CAR. Generally presumed to come from Noddy, the character created by Enid Blyton (1897–1968), in turn named after 'a simpleton', but that would better describe the driver than the vehicle and Noddy drove a car; more likely to be derived from obsolete Irish *noddy* (a one-horse conveyance) with just a hint of Enid Blyton *UK, 1964*

noddy boat *noun* a canal-using pleasure boat (not a conventional narrow boat). Derisory *UK, 1972*

noddy shop *noun* a prison workshop. From the nature of the work carried on therein: so basic that it can be understood by children so young that they are still reading *Noddy*, the character created by Enid Blyton (1897–1968) *UK, 1996*

noddy suit *noun* a suit of protective clothing worn against nuclear, biological or chemical threat *UK, 1972*

no dice! 1 originally and literally, in a dice game a roll of the dice that does not count because of a rule violation *US, 1950*. **2** positively no *US, 1931*

nod off *verb* to fall asleep *UK, 1845*

no doubt! used as a formulaic expression of agreement *US, 1988*

nod out *verb* to fall asleep, especially as a result of recreational drug use *US, 1953*

no duh! used for expressing sentiment that what was just said is patently obvious to even the casual observer *US, 1982*

no end *adverb* immensely *UK, 1859*

no end of *adjective* a great number or quantity of. Colloquial *UK, 1623*

no fear! used as an expression of refusal *UK, 1887*

no flies on nothing at all wrong or amiss with someone *AUSTRALIA, 1845*

NoFuck, Virginia *nickname* Norfolk, Virginia *US, 1998*

nog *noun* **1** a Vietnamese or Korean person or soldier; any Southeast Asian person. From NIG-NOG *AUSTRALIA, 1969*. **2** a short piece of wood inserted between wall studs. A variant is 'noggings' *NEW ZEALAND, 1963*

no gain without pain used to urge sacrifice. A catchphrase beloved by athletic coaches as inspiration for bulletin board reading *US, 1968*

noggin *noun* the head *US, 1859*

noggy *noun* a Vietnamese or Korean person or soldier; hence, any Southeast Asian person *AUSTRALIA, 1954*

no go; no-go *noun* a failure, something that is not good; a hopeless attempt. Although the term has an undeniable US 1960s space programme ring to it, it was 140 years old and had crossed the Atlantic before we heard it from NASA's lips *UK, 1824*

no-go-showboat *noun* a car that has been restored and modified with an emphasis on its appearance, not its speed *US, 1963*

no-go zone *noun* an area to which access is prohibited or ill-advised. The term came to the attention of Americans in 2004 in the context of the US occupation of Iraq *US, 1979*

no great shakes *adjective* nothing remarkable, important or special *UK, 1819*

no harm in looking! used as a motto, excuse or philosophy for a husband or boyfriend who finds the sight of the opposite sex irresistible *UK, 1984*

NoHo *nickname* the neighbourhood in New York City just north of Houston Street *US, 1999*

no holds barred *adjective* without constraint, 'anything goes'. Taken from the sport of wrestling *US, 1942*

no-hoper *noun* **1** a worthless person; a person with no prospects *AUSTRALIA, 1944*. **2** a horse considered unable to win a race; a rank outsider *AUSTRALIA, 1943*

nointer *noun* in Tasmania, a brat or mischievous child. Survival of a British dialect word, clipping of 'anointer' in the same sense. Formerly (C16, *Oxford English Dictionary*) the word 'anoint' meant 'to beat soundly', thus 'anointer' would mean 'one who requires anointing/beating' *AUSTRALIA, 1994*

noise *noun* **1** foolish talk; nonsense *US, 1871*. **2** heroin *US, 1928*

noisemaker *noun* in trucking, a radio *US, 1971*

noisemaker *adjective* producing the impression of force through loud sounds. Professional wrestling usage *US, 1998*

noisenik *noun* a contemporary musician whose compositions appear (to most auditors) to be formless noise. The suffix '-nik' forms the person out of the noise *UK, 1999*

noise pollution *noun* in poker, excessive chatter at the table *US, 1996*

noises *noun* ▶ **make the right noises** to use unexceptional platitudes, to pay lip-service *UK, 1976*

noise up *verb* to cause trouble *UK, 2000*

noisy *adjective* of a television programme, talked-about *US*

no joke *noun* a serious matter; hence, a difficulty *UK, 1809*

no kid seriously. Shortening of 'no kidding' *AUSTRALIA, 1946*

no kidding! honestly!, it's the truth! *UK, 1914*

no lie! as unbelievable as what I just said may seem, it is true! *US, 1992*

noly *noun* a simpleton. Pronounced to rhyme with 'holy' *UK, 1979*

nomad *noun* a member of a motorcycle gang who is not a member of any specific chapter of the gang *US, 1992*

no make! stop what you are doing! Hawaiian youth usage, shortened from 'no make like that' *US, 1982*

no man's Nam *nickname* Vietnam. A blend of the historic 'no man's land' and 'Vietnam' *US, 1991*

no-mark *noun* a nobody; someone who has failed to make a mark *UK, 2001*

no mention you're welcome. Hawaiian youth usage *US, 1981*

no more forever *adverb* never again. Echoing the 1877 surrender speech of Chief Joseph of the Nez Perce nation – 'I will fight no more forever' *US, 1998*

non *noun* an socially inept person. An abbreviation of the much longer 'non-factor in the game of life' *US, 1983*

nonce *noun* **1** a sex offender; a child-molester; a pervert. The etymology is uncertain: possibly from dialect *nonce* (good for nothing), or with origins in NANCY BOY (homosexual, hence pervert); however, given the prison context of the coinage and the violent disdain in which sex-offenders are held by their fellow inmates, the very existence of one may be considered as little more than 'for the nonce', literally 'for the time-being'. It is also worth noting in

this context the rhyme on PONCE (someone who lives off immoral earnings), another type held in low-esteem in the pecking order of prison life. It is regrettable that modern society feels the need for this term in wider circulation *UK, 1975*. **2** a police informer, someone who betrays a criminal enterprise *UK, 2000*. **3** a fool *UK, 2002*

nonch *adjective* utterly relaxed, completely at ease. From 'nonchalant'. A Teddy Boy usage *UK, 1958*

nondy *noun* a nondescript vehicle used by the police for maintaining a surveillance. A shortening of 'nondescript' *UK, 1999*

non-event *noun* any unexciting or unsatisfactory event, especially one that fails to fulfill expectations *UK, 1962*

nong *noun* a fool. Shortening of NING NONG *AUSTRALIA, 1944*

non-goer *noun* a racehorse that is not being run to win *AUSTRALIA, 1982*

nonhacker *noun* a soldier who cannot keep up with his fellow soldiers; an ineffective, incompetent soldier. Coined in Vietnam and used heavily there. Back-formation from HACK IT (to cope with) *US, 1976*

non-heinous *adjective* good *US, 1991*

no-no *noun* **1** something that ought not to be done *US, 1942*. **2** an impossibility; a failure; any negative outcome. Reduplication for stress *UK, 1975*

no nothing *noun* nothing whatever *UK, 1884*

no-no war in never-never land *noun* the US secret war against Pathet Lao communist forces in Laos *US, 1990*

nonproducer *noun* a professional gambler who cannot be counted on to lose a great deal of money while gambling in a casino *US, 1963*

nonseller *noun* a plan that almost certainly will be rejected *US, 1986*

non speaks *noun* a state of having been excluded from society. An example of Eton College illiteracy *UK, 1977*

non starter *noun* something or someone that has no chance of success *UK, 1934*

non trier *noun* a racehorse that is not being run to win *AUSTRALIA, 1966*

nontrivial *adjective* extremely complex *US, 1997*

noob *noun* in snowboarding, a beginner. Derives from *newbie* *UK, 2005*

no object no obstacle, or, not an objection. In such phrases as 'distance no object' and 'money no object' *UK, 1984*

noodenaddy *noun* a dithering person; someone who is unable to make up their mind *IRELAND, 1999*

noodle *noun* **1** the head; the brain; intelligence *UK, 1803*. **2** the penis *US, 1975*

noodle *verb* **1** to think, to ponder *US, 1942*. **2** to play music in a tentative, exploratory fashion *US, 1937*

noodles *noun* brains, intelligence. An extension of NOODLE *UK, 2002*

noogie *noun* a blow, usually repeated, to the head with a protuberant knuckle. A hazing of youth. A recurring skit on *Saturday Night Live* in the 1970s vaulted the phrase 'Noogie Patrol' into great popularity, with a nerdish Todd DiLaMuca (played by Bill Murray) grabbing Lisa Lupner (played by Gilda Radner) for a rash of noogies *US, 1972*

nook and cranny *noun* the buttocks, the backside; the vagina. Rhyming slang for FANNY *UK, 1979*

nookie; nooky *noun* the vagina; hence a woman as a sex object; sexual intercourse *US, 1928*

nookie wood *noun* in logging, a core of wood soaked with sap and emerging from a rotted stump *CANADA, 1989*

nooky-nooky *noun* sex *US, 1974*

nooner *noun* a bout of sex at about noon *US, 1973*

no-pay *noun* a person who refuses to repay a debt or loan *US, 1982*

nope no, emphatically no *US, 1888*

no prob; no probs no problem; no problems *AUSTRALIA, 1971*

no problem 1 that is easy; do not worry about that; okay. A catchphrase of affable non-concern *AUSTRALIA, 1965*. **2** you're welcome. At some point in the 1980s, the term 'you're welcome' suddenly vanished from the vocabulary of America's young, replaced suddenly and completely with 'no problem' *US, 1982*

no problemo no problem. A popular elaboration *US, 1991*

noras *noun* breasts *AUSTRALIA, 1992*

nordle *noun* marijuana *UK, 1997*

Norfolk 'n' Chance *nickname* used as a team name in light-hearted contests. A barely euphemistic rendering of 'no fucking chance'; especially popular among quiz teams. Recorded in 1983 as the winners of the University of Essex Rugby 7's Plate *UK, 1983*

no risk! for sure; with certainty *AUSTRALIA, 1969*

nork *noun* the female breast. The suggestion (originally in Baker, *The Australian Language*, 1966) that this derives from Norco, a popular brand of butter which at one time had a picture of a cow with an udder on the packaging, is as far fetched as it sounds, and yet it is the standard folk etymology for this term. Baker also records that 'the form *norg* is reported from Melbourne' and this variant is still in occasional use *AUSTRALIA, 1962*

norm *verb* to behave in an unremarkable or conventional manner. From NORM (an ordinary person) *UK, 2001*

norm; normal *noun* a *norm*al person; a dully conventional person *US, 1983*

Normandy Beach; normandy *noun* a speech. Rhyming slang *UK, 1998*

Norma Stockers *noun* large female breasts. An intentional, humorous corruption of 'enormous KNOCKERS' *AUSTRALIA, 1988*

normie *noun* someone who is not addicted to anything. Used in twelve-step recovery programmes such as Alcoholics Anonymous *US, 1998*

Norris McWhirter *noun* diarrhoea. Rhyming slang for 'squirter', based on author Norris McWhirter (b.1925) *UK, 2002*

north and south *noun* the mouth. Rhyming slang *UK, 1857*

North Circ *nickname* London's North Circular road *UK, 1997*

North End Round *noun* bologna *CANADA, 1987*

norther *noun* a strong, cold wind from the north. A Texas phrase to describe a Texas winter weather condition *US, 1827*

northern lights *noun* **1** in British Columbia, a local variety of marijuana *CANADA, 2002*. **2** a superior variety of hashish produced in Holland from northern lights marijuana pollen *NETHERLANDS, 2003*

Norwegian steam *noun* brute physical exertion *US, 1944*

NORWICH written on an envelope, or at the foot of a lover's letter as lovers' code for '(k)nickers off ready when I come home'. Widely known, and well used by servicemen but, apparently, has not transferred to the coded vocabulary of texting. Used by John Winton in *We Saw the Sea*, 1960 *UK, 1960*

nose *noun* **1** cocaine *US, 1980*. **2** in horse racing, any very short distance that separates winner from loser *US, 1908*. **3** an informer *UK, 1789*. **4** an innate ability to find things *UK, 1875* ▷*see:* NOSEY. ▶ **get up your nose 1** to annoy *UK, 1951*. **2** to irritate, to anger *US, 1968*. ▶ **get your nose bent** to be convicted of a traffic violation *US, 1962*. ▶ **get your nose cold** to use and become intoxicated on cocaine *US, 1980*. ▶ **have a nose for someone** to be sexually attracted to someone *US, 1958*. ▶ **have your nose open** to be strongly attracted to *US, 1957*. ▶ **keep your nose to the grindstone; put your nose to the grindstone** to be (or start) studying hard, working hard. From earlier senses denoting harsh treatment *UK, 1828*. ▶ **on the nose 1** exactly *US, 1883*. **2** in horse racing, a bet on a horse to finish first *US, 1980*. **3** (used of a person's bet in an illegal numbers gambling lottery) invariably the same *US, 1949*. **4** at the start of a song *US, 1982*. **5** smelly *AUSTRALIA, 1946*. **6** (used of ocean water) polluted *AUSTRALIA, 1991*. **7** recreational time spent under the influence of inhaled drugs. Compares with ON THE TILES (having a good time under the influence of alcohol) *UK, 1996*. ▶ **put someone's nose out of joint** to annoy, to upset the plans of, to inconvenience, to disconcert *UK, 1576*. ▶ **shove your nose in; stick your nose in** to interfere, to interpose rudely *UK, 1887*

nose *verb* to curry favour through obsequious conduct. A shortening of BROWN-NOSE *US, 1968*

nose and chin *noun* a win, a winning bet *UK, 1960*

nosebag *noun* **1** a lunch box or paper bag with lunch inside *UK, 1873*. **2** a take-away restaurant, a chip shop *UK, 1981*. **3** a plastic bag used for solvent abuse *UK, 1996*. **4** cocaine *UK, 1999*. **5** in electric line work, a canvas tool pouch *US, 1980*. ▶ **put on the nosebag** to have a meal *AUSTRALIA, 1992*

nosebleed *noun* a stupid, inept person. Teen slang *US, 1951*

nosebleeder *noun* a heavy user of cocaine by nasal inhalation. From a physical side-effect experienced by users *UK, 2002*

nosebleeds *noun* the highest seats in an auditorium or a stadium. Because high altitudes can cause nosebleeds *US, 1978*

nose-burner; nose-warmer *noun* the still-lit butt of a marijuana cigarette *US, 1973*

nose candy *noun* cocaine or, rarely, another powdered drug that can be snorted *US, 1925*

nose drops *noun* liquefied heroin; liquefied methadone *UK, 1998*

no-see-um *noun* any small, nearly invisible insect that bites *US, 1842*

nosefull *noun* a strong dose of a powdered drug that is snorted *US, 1980*

nose garbage *noun* poor quality cocaine *US, 1993*

nose hose *noun* the tubing used for nastrogastic intubation *US, 1994*

nose job *noun* cosmetic surgery to enhance the nose. Combines a conventional 'nose' with JOB (a medical procedure) *US, 1960*

nose kiss *noun* a head butt *UK, 1999*

nose out *verb* to discover by searching *UK, 1630*

nose packer *noun* a cocaine user *US, 1988*

nose paint *noun* any alcoholic drink. From its effect (as mentioned by the Porter in Shakespeare's *Macbeth*) on the colour of a serious drinker's nose *UK, 1880*

nose-picking speed *noun* an extremely slow pace. US naval aviator usage *US, 1986*

nose powder; nose stuff *noun* cocaine, or any other drug that has been powdered for inhalation *US, 1936*

noser *noun* an informer *US, 1992*

nose-ride *verb* in surfing, to ride on the front of the board *US, 1979*

nose-up *noun* cocaine-taking as a cultural activity *UK, 2000*

nosey; nose; nose around *noun* an act of casual surveillance or inquisition *UK, 1984*

Nosey O'Grady *noun* an inquisitive person, usually female *CANADA, 1981*

Nosey Parker; Nosy Parker *noun* a personification of inquisitiveness. From NOSEY (inquisitive), first recorded in a captioned illustration in 1907. Various etymologies suggest links with peeping Toms and eavesdroppers at the Great Exhibition in Hyde *Park*, a link with Archbishop of Canterbury Matthew *Parker* (1504–75) or the characteristics of rabbits in *parks*. Whatever its true origins 'Nosey Parker' is the source of 'nosey-parkering' (being inquisitive); 'nosey-park' (to be inquisitive); 'nosey-parkerdom', 'nosey-parkery', 'Nosey-Parkerism' (the condition of an inquisitve nature or a demonstration of invasive inquisitiveness); 'nosey-parkerishness' (a tendency towards inquisitive behaviour) *UK, 1966*

nosh *noun* **1** food. From Yiddish, ultimately German *nachen* (to eat slyly), since early 1960s *US, 1951*. **2** an act of oral sex on a man or, perhaps, a woman. A punning adoption of the previous sense *UK, 2001*

nosh *verb* **1** to eat; to nibble. From Yiddish *US, 1947*. **2** to perform oral sex. From the more familiar sense 'to eat' *UK, 1998*. **3** to kiss in a sustained fashion *US, 1994*

no shame! you act as if nothing embarrasses you! Hawaiian youth usage *US, 1981*

nosher *noun* an eater. From NOSH (to eat) *UK, 1957*

no shit! used as emphasis that what has just been said is true *US, 1960*

no shit, Dick Tracy! used for pointing out that another person has just made an obvious statement. A variant of the more common allusion to Sherlock Holmes, this based on the US cartoon detective *US, 1981*

no shit, Sherlock! used for pointing out that another person has just made an obvious statement. Sherlock Holmes extends NO SHIT! *US, 1989*

no-show *noun* a non-appearance at an appointed time or place *US, 1957*

nosh up; nosh *noun* a meal, a period of eating, meal time. After NOSH (to eat) *UK, 1964*

no sir; nossir used for registering a strong refusal or denial *US, 1856*

no siree; no siree, Bob absolutely no *US, 1848*

no soap used for signifying that the deal is off, not a hope, you're wasting your time *US, 1926*

no sound, no picture *noun* a person who does not appear for an appointment *SINGAPORE, 2002*

no squash *noun* irreparable brain damage *US, 1978*

nostril *noun* in horse racing, any very short distance between winner and loser that is shorter even than a nose *US, 1951*

no surrenders *noun* suspenders. Rhyming slang *UK, 2003*

no sweat no problem; no need to worry. Therefore no sweat will be produced by fear or exertion *US, 1955*

no-sweat pill *noun* a potent anti-bacterial pill *US, 1986*

not! used as a humorous cancellation of what has just been said in jest. Coined a hundred years before it was broadly popularised by Mike Myers in the 'Wayne's World' sketches on *Saturday Night Live* *US, 1893*

not a dry seat in the house used of a theatre audience that is helpless with laughter or a male audience that is sexually aroused. A blend of the drama critic's cliché: 'not a dry eye in the house', and PISS YOURSELF (to laugh uproariously) *UK, 1974*

not a hundred miles from *adjective* very close to *UK, 1821*

no-talent assclown *noun* a socially inept person. From the film *Office Space* *US, 2002*

not all there *adjective* slightly mad, mentally or intellectually disadvantaged *UK, 1864*

not backward in coming forward not shy *UK, 1830*

not bad *adjective* rather good, or (either patronisingly or with reservations) quite good *UK, 1909*

not bloody likely used as an emphatic negative. First used in print (and, presumably, polite society) in George Bernard Shaw's play, *Pygmalion*, 1914 *UK, 1914*

notch *verb* to wound. Vietnam war usage *US, 1991*

notchback *noun* a car with a dent in its boot. A play on the conventional 'hatchback' *US, 1992*

notch up *verb* to achieve *UK, 1837*

not cricket *adjective* unfair. From the rigid rules of the game, but now always in phrases 'it's not cricket', 'that's not ...', etc *UK, 1978*

note *noun* a one-pound note; the sum of £1. Became obsolete in Australia after the introduction of decimal currency in 1966 but it still used in the UK *AUSTRALIA, 1863*

note from mother *noun* official permission. US naval aviator usage *US, 1986*

no-tell motel *noun* a motel with discreet management favoured by prostitutes and couples seeking privacy *US, 1974*

notes *noun* ▶ **get good notes** in Quebec, to get good marks or grades *CANADA, 2002*

not even no, not at all *US, 1984*

not fucking likely used as an emphatic negative *UK, 1937*

not half *adverb* used as a very positive intensifier of the verb to which it is attached. Usually as 'can't half', 'doesn't half', 'don't half', etc *UK, 1851*

not half! used for registering assent, approval, agreement, etc *UK, 1920*

not half bad *adjective* quite good *UK, 1867*

not having any; not having any of *adjective* refusing to agree *UK, 1902*

nothing *noun* **1** something. Also shortened to 'nothin'. A reversal of sense on the model BAD (good); used in hip-hop culture *US, 2000*. **2** no more than (the height specified). Used to emphasise shortness *AUSTRALIA, 1971*. ▶ **have nothing on** to be greatly inferior to something or someone *US, 1906*. ▶ **nothing shaking** nothing happening *US, 1975*. ▶ **nothing to write home about; nothing worth writing home about** unremarkable. Probably military in origin *UK, 1914*. ▶ **thank you for nothing!; thanks for nothing!** used in refusal or dismissal of help or advice: I owe you no thanks for that and scorn the offer *UK, 1969*. ▶ **you aint seen nothing yet!; you ain't heard nothing yet!** no matter how impressive or extreme something may be there is better or worse yet to come. A catchphrase made famous by the singer Al Jolson in the first 'talkie' film, *The Jazz Singer*, 1927. Especially popular with advertising copywriters *US, 1919*

nothing *adjective* inconsequential *US, 1960*

nothing! when combined with a (partial) repetition of a statement just made, used in denial of that statement *US, 1883*

nothing-ass bitch *noun* used as a stern term of contempt for a woman *US, 1972*

nothing but a thing *noun* something that is not important *US, 1993*

nothing but the bacon! used as a stock answer when greeted with 'what's shakin'?' *US, 1951*

nothing but the bottom of the cup; nothing but the bottom of the net used as a humorous comment on a job well done or a remark well made. Coined by ESPN's Dan Patrick to describe a great shot in golf and basketball *US, 1997*

nothing doing! used as an expression of rejection or denial *UK, 1910*

nothing flat *adverb* very quickly *US, 1947*

notice *noun* a contract to do a job, especially an illegal commission *UK, 1970*

no tilt! used as a euphemism for 'no shit!' in expressing surprise or affirmation *US, 1983*

no time flat *adverb* very quickly *US, 1957*

not in my name; not in our name used worldwide by various humanitarian and anti-war protesters as a slogan of disavowal of prevailing attitudes. 'Not In My Name' (NITM) was adopted, in November 2000, as the name of a Chicago-based Jewish peace group opposed to Israel's occupation of Palestinian Territories *US, 1994*

not likely! used for registering refusal *UK, 1893*

not many yes, a term of emphatic agreement *UK, 1998*

not many benny a great deal, a lot; an intensifying agreement *UK, 1999*

not much to look at *adjective* unattractive, ugly *UK, 1861*

not off *adjective* of a horse – or, more precisely, of a jockey – that is considered not to be trying to win a race *UK, 1991*

not on *adjective* unacceptable; impossible; not permissible *UK, 1984*

not on your life! used for registering emphatic refusal or denial *US, 1896*

not on your nelly used as an absolute denial, refusal or rejection. Rhyming slang, 'not on your Nellie Duff' for PUFF (breath, hence life), thus NOT ON YOUR LIFE! *UK, 1941*

no-top *noun* a convertible with its top down *US, 1976*

not Pygmalion likely! not very likely! Formed on the shocking-in-its-day 'Not bloody likely!' in George Bernard Shaw's play *Pygmalion*, first seen in London in 1914 *UK, 1948*

no-trump *noun* a life prison sentence without chance of parole *US, 1976*

not the full quid *adjective* lacking *NEW ZEALAND, 1984*

nottie *noun* an unattractive person. A back-formation from HOTTIE (an attractive person) *US, 2002*

not tonight, Josephine! a catchphrase used by a man to defer his sexual duties to a wife or lover; hence, applied to any postponement. Originally a quotation, apocryphally attributed to Napoleon dashing his mistress's hopes. In its current sexual context there is obviously a reliance on jocularity of delivery to deflect any serious subtext. Familiar from a music hall poem: 'I'll tell you in a phrase, my sweet, exactly what I mean: / . . . Not tonight, Josephine' (Colin Curzon, 'Not Tonight, Josephine') *UK, 1960*

noughties *noun* the years 2000 through to 2009 *UK, 2001*

no VERB about it!; there is no VERB about it! by enclosing the active verb from a preceding statement, an absolute negation of that verb *UK, 1924*

novhere *adjective* unattractive; unpleasing. A mock German or Dutch accent *US, 1955*

Novie boat *noun* a large, low cost lobster boat built in Nova Scotia *US, 1888*

now *adjective* fashionable, in style, current *US, 1955*

now *adverb* soon; in time; in a vaguely specified time. A stereotypical example of 'Wenglish' (a blending of English and Welsh typical of the valleys of southeast Wales) *UK: WALES, 1985*

Now American Friends Take All *noun* the North American Free Trade Agreement. Back-formation from the agreement's initials *CANADA, 2002*

now and thener *noun* in horse racing, a horse that is an uneven or inconsistent performer *US, 1951*

no way! used for expressing disbelief at that which has just been said *US, 1968*

no way, Jose used as a humorous, if emphatic, denial. The catchy reduplication makes this a favourite early in a young person's process of slang acquisition *US, 1981*

now cut that out used as a humorous attempt to end a tease. A signature line of comedian Jack Benny, heard often on *The Jack Benny Show*, 1950–65. Repeated with referential humour *US, 1954*

no what *adverb* certainly not. Adapted from Afrikaans *nee wat SOUTH AFRICA, 1900*

nowhere *adjective* **1** unaware of what is happening, extremely naive, utterly at a loss *US, 1843*. **2** badly defeated in a race; utterly unsuccessful, to be out of the running *US, 1853*. **3** without money. Usually in the phrase 'ain't nowhere' *GUYANA, 1998*. ► **get nowhere fast** to try hard to do something and yet be frustrated in your endeavour *UK, 1984*. ► **the middle of nowhere** any place that is remote, any place that is an inconvenient distance away from urban 'civilisation' or your personal lifestyle requirements *UK, 1960*

nowhereness *noun* the state of complete unawareness of current trends or complete lack of grounding in reality *US, 1958*

now it's time to say good-bye used as a humorous farewell. A catchphrase television sign-off on *The Mickey Mouse Club* (ABC, 1955–59). Repeated with referential and reverential humour *US, 1956*

now-now *adverb* in the immediate past; immediately; very soon. Adopted from synonymous Afrikaans *nou-nou SOUTH AFRICA, 1948*

now now used as a gentle admonition to cease *UK, 1959*

no worries 1 do not worry about that; everything is all right *AUSTRALIA, 1969*. **2** you're welcome *US, 2001*. **3** yes indeed; certainly *AUSTRALIA, 1986*

nowt *noun* nothing; a worthless person. Dialect word from northern England for conventional 'naught'; made popular by the televison programme *Coronation Street*, and in clichéd phrases such as 'nowt so queer as folk' *UK, 1998*

now then! used as a mild rebuke, or a call for attention *UK, 1791*

nowty *adjective* moody, grumpy. Manchester dialect into wider use *UK, 1999*

no wucking furries do not worry about that! An intentional Spoonerism of 'no fucking worries', both euphemistic and jocular. Also, in the shortened forms 'no wuckers' and 'no wucks' *AUSTRALIA, 1996*

now what? can you top what I just said? *US, 2001*

now you're asking! used in response to a difficult question *UK, 1959*

now you're railroading! used on the railways as an all-purpose expression of praise *US, 1977*

now you tell me!; now he tells me! used when information that has just been supplied is given too late to be of use. A Hebraism *US, 1969*

nozzle *noun* the penis *US, 1994*

NRC *adjective* (by police) nobody really cares *US, 1992*

'n stuff used either as a substitute for 'et cetera' or to complete a sentence that has run out of steam *US, 2001*

NT *noun* in pornography, a scene showing nipple teasing (or torture) *US, 2000*

NTBH *adjective* unavailable for sexual encounters; ugly. Gay usage. The definition varies with the point of view; either way it derives from '*not to be had*' *UK, 2002*

nu *adjective* in rock music, new *UK, 2002*

nub *noun* the clitoris *UK, 2002*

nubbies *noun* short, matted hair on its way to growing into dreadlocks *JAMAICA, 1980*

nubbin *noun* **1** the clitoris. Making 'rubbin' the nubbin' female masturbation *UK, 2004*. **2** the penis *US, 1968*

nub bush *noun* a black female. A shortened 'nubian' and a coarse BUSH. Vietnam war usage *US, 1991*

nubian *noun* in homosexual usage, a black man *US, 1987*

nuddy *adjective* nude, naked *AUSTRALIA, 1953*

nude *adjective* (used of a car) stripped of chrome *US, 1977*

nudge *noun* in pinball, subtle physical force applied to the machine to affect the trajectory of the ball without activating the tilt mechanism *US, 1979*

nudge *verb* **1** to nag; to annoy. Yiddish. Various transliterations including 'nudzh', 'nudj' and 'noudge' *US, 1968*. **2** to drink (alcohol) heavily *AUSTRALIA, 1979*. **3** in pool, to touch the cue ball with the cue stick accidentally while preparing to shoot *US, 1993*

nudge-nudge *adjective* gossipy, especially of gossip with a sexual inference. From NUDGE NUDGE – WINK WINK! *UK, 2003*

nudge nudge – wink wink! used as an indicator of lust or an inference a lewd sexual behaviour. A catchphrase, originally 'nudge nudge – wink wink – say no more!', written by Eric Idle for BBC television comedy *Monty Python's Flying Circus* ('Is your wife a...goer...eh? Know what I mean? Know what I mean? Nudge nudge. Nudge nudge. Know what I mean? Say no more...know what I mean?'), 1969 *UK, 1979*

nudger *noun* **1** the penis *UK, 2001*. **2** a pickpocket *UK, 1996*

nudge show *noun* a safe family comedy *US, 1973*

nudie *noun* a performance or film featuring naked women but no sexual activity *US, 1935*

nudie *adjective* featuring naked or near-naked women *US, 1966*

nudie book *noun* a men's magazine featuring pictures of naked women *UK, 1977*

nudie booth *noun* a private enclosure affording privacy while a paying customer views a nude woman or nude women, usually through a glass partition *US, 1994*

nudie-cutie *noun* a genre of sex film popular in the 1960s, featuring frolicking, cute, nude women *US, 1967*

nudnik; noodnik *noun* a pest, a fool *US, 1925*

nuff *adjective* enough. Once abbreviated, 'enough' could not be spelt 'nough' and understood, hence this phonetic variation. UK school dinner ladies in the 1960s accompanied their service with the question, slovened by repetition, 'nuff?'. Since the 1980s it has been widely used in the black community *US, 1840*

nuff respect used as a greeting and to register admiration, assent or approbation. Misspelling of 'enough respect'. West Indian and UK black usage *UK, 1994*

nuff said used as an assertion that nothing more needs to be said *US, 1840*

nug *noun* **1** a female *US, 1993*. **2** marijuana. Variant 'nugs' *US, 1997*

nugget *noun* **1** a fool, an idiot, especially if prone to violent behaviour or mentally handicapped. Figurative use of 'nugget' (a lump) for 'the head' *US, 1990*. **2** a new, inexperienced soldier or pilot *US, 1966*. **3** an attractive girl *US, 1998*. **4** a young enthusiast of heavy metal music *US, 1983*. **5** an amphetamine tablet *US, 1994*. **6** a piece of crack cocaine *US, 1994*. **7** a one-pound coin. Prison slang, current February 2002 *UK, 2002*

nuggets *noun* the testicles *US, 1963*

nuggety; nuggetty *adjective* **1** (of a person) compact, strong and tough; stocky *AUSTRALIA, 1856*. **2** (of an animal) small, sturdy and strong *AUSTRALIA, 1893*

nugs *noun* **1** female breasts *US, 1994*. **2** great waves for surfing *US, 1991*

nuisance *noun* ▶ **the nuisance** the bleed period of the menstrual cycle. Euphemism *US, 1999*

nuisance grounds *noun* a rubbish dump *CANADA, 2002*

nuke *verb* **1** to attack with a nuclear bomb *US, 1962*. **2** to lay waste, to ravage, to devastate. A metaphorical, if less dramatic, sense *US, 1969*. **3** to heat in a microwave oven *US, 1984*. **4** in computing, to delete *US, 1991*

nuke; nook *noun* a nuclear weapon *US, 1958*

nuke and pave *verb* to reformat the hard drive of a computer *US, 2001*

nuke-and-puke *noun* a microwave frozen dinner *US, 1990*

nuke-knob *noun* a bald or shaved head *US, 1997*

number *noun* **1** a person, particularly someone attractive, originally of a woman *US, 1896*. **2** a prostitute's client (especially in a male homosexual context) *US, 1967*. **3** a casual sex-partner *US, 1970*. **4** sex involving more than two people *US, 1973*. **5** a situation *US, 1908*. **6** a job, a position *UK, 1948*. **7** used as a vague catch-all susceptible of several meanings, usually related to sex or drugs *US, 1978*. **8** in prison, a sex offender; a convicted paedophile. Such prisoners are kept apart from the main body of the prison on rule *number* 43 *UK, 1996*. **9** in craps, any roll except the shooter's point or a seven *US, 1950*. **10** a marijuana cigarette *US, 1963*. **11** a song *US, 1878*. ▶ **do a number on 1** to use emotional pressure, to humiliate *US, 1971*. **2** to kill *US, 1982*. ▶ **have your number; get your number** to understand you, to know your weaknesses, to be in a position to criticise you *UK, 1853*

number 3 *noun* **1** cocaine. C (cocaine) is the third letter of the alphabet *US, 1953*. **2** heroin *UK, 2003*

number 9 *noun* MDMA, the recreational drug best known as ecstasy *UK, 2003*

number cruncher *noun* a computer designed especially for arithmetic operations *UK, 1966*

number dummy; number grabber *noun* a clerk in a railway yard *US, 1946*

numbered off; on the numbers *adjective* in prison, used of sex offenders, convicted paedophiles, etc. Such prisoners are kept apart from the main body of the prison on rule *number* 43 *UK, 1996*

number four; number 4 *noun* heroin *UK, 1998*

number one *noun* **1** yourself, your own interests *UK, 1705*. **2** urination. The plural variant 'number ones' is also used *UK, 1902*. **3** a closely cropped haircut. Originally military, from the most extreme setting on the clippers; it is also possible to have a 'number two', etc *UK, 1925*

number one; numba one *adjective* the very best. Although coined in the 1830s in a pure English sense, it took on a pidgin or mock pidgin tone in the C20; very popular in the Vietnam war *US, 1838*

numbers *noun* **1** an illegal lottery based on guessing a number determined by chance each day *US, 1897*. **2** a telephone number *US, 2002*. ▶ **by the numbers** precisely, correctly *US, 1918*. ▶ **do numbers** to urinate or defecate *TRINIDAD AND TOBAGO, 1990*. ▶ **take the numbers down** in horse racing, to disqualify a horse from a race and announce a new winner *US, 1947*. ▶ **the numbers** in prison, Rule 43, which allows a prisoner to be kept apart from the main prison community for 'safety of self or others'. Explained by former Cabinet Minister Jonathan Aitken, describing his prison

experience 1999–2000, *Have I Got News for You*, 28th November, 2003 *UK, 2003*

numbers banker *noun* the operator of an illegal numbers racket or lottery *US, 1959*

numbers drop *noun* a place where bets on an illegal lottery are turned in or made *US, 1957*

numbers game *noun* sex expressed in numeric terms. The most common is, of course, 69, with other lesser known variants *US, 1964*

number ten; numba ten *adjective* the very worst. Southeast Asian pidgin, commonly used during the Vietnam war *UK, 1953*

number ten thousand *adjective* worse than the very worst. Vietnam war usage *US, 1968*

number three *noun* sexual relief, by any means (conventional, non-conventional or unaccompanied). The next in a logical sequence: NUMBER ONE (urination); NUMBER TWO (defecation) *UK, 1984*

number two *adjective* applied to illegal or irregular activity. 'Number one' is all things legal and above-board *INDIA, 2003*

number two; number twos *noun* defecation. Adult usage of children's bathroom vocabulary *US, 1936*

number two man *noun* a skilled card cheat adept at dealing the second card instead of the top card in a deck *US, 1979*

Numbies *noun* Players' Number 6™ cigarettes *UK: SCOTLAND, 1988*

numbnuts *noun* an idiot *US, 1960*

Numbo *noun* Number 6, a branded cigarette *UK, 2001*

numb out *verb* to feel or show the effects of crack cocaine *UK, 1996*

numbskull; numskull *noun* a dolt; a fool *UK, 1742*

numerologist *noun* a person who claims to have devised a winning system for an illegal numbers gambling lottery *US, 1949*

numero uno *noun* **1** the very best. Spanish for 'number one' *US, 1960*. **2** yourself *US, 1973*

nummy *noun* a fool, a dim-witted person. A shortened 'numbskull' *US, 1902*

nummy *adjective* delicious. Probably after YUMMY (delicious) *US, 1989*

num-nums *noun* the female breasts *US, 1993*

numpty; numptie *noun* a fool *UK: SCOTLAND, 1911*

nunce; nince *noun* a fool. Student use; derogatory *UK, 2002*

nunga *noun* the penis *AUSTRALIA, 1971*

nunga-muncher *noun* a person who performs oral sex on men *AUSTRALIA, 1971*

nun's cunt *noun* used as a comparison for something that is cold, dry or tight *CANADA, 1985*

nun's fart *noun* a treat made with leftover piecrust dough, cinnamon and sugar *CANADA, 1992*

nunu; nuzni *noun* the vagina *TRINIDAD AND TOBAGO, 1994*

nunya *noun* used for conveying that something is 'none of your business' *US, 2000*

nurds *noun* the testicles *US, 1981*

Nuremburg trials; nuremburgs *noun* haemorrhoids. Rhyming slang for 'piles' *UK, 1998*

nurse *verb* in a card game, to nervously fondle and adjust your cards *US, 1988*

nursery *noun* **1** a reformatory for juvenile offenders *US, 1950*. **2** a gentle slope where beginning skiers practice *US, 1963*

nursery race *noun* in horse racing, a relatively short distance race for two-year-olds *US, 1976*

nursery rhyme *noun* time served in prison. Rhyming slang *UK, 2000*

nursery rhymes *noun* the *Times*. Rhyming slang; ironically, perhaps, suggesting that some content of the esteemed newspaper is of a similar character to the more newsworthy nursery rhymes *UK, 1998*

nu-skool *adjective* applied to a new variation on an old theme *UK, 2003*

nut *noun* **1** a regular and recurring expense *US, 1909*. **2** an act of sexual intercourse; sex as an activity. Extending back from NUT (an orgasm) *US, 1991*. **3** an orgasm, especially of a male *US, 1968*. **4** semen

US, 1991. **5** the female breast. Usually in the plural *UK, 2002*. **6** the head; hence, brains, intelligence *UK, 1846*. **7** a crazy person, an eccentric, a crank. Probably by back-formation from NUTTY (crazy) *US, 1908*. **8** an enthusiast *US, 1934*. **9** a person *UK, 1856*. **10** in horse racing, a horse picked by a racing newspaper to win a race *US, 1951*. **11** in horse racing, the tax levied on bets by the track and the state *US, 1990*. **12** a bankroll *US, 1951*. **13** a rugby ball *NEW ZEALAND, 1998*. ► **crack the nut** in gambling, to make enough money to meet the day's expenses *US, 1961*. ► **do your nut 1** to explode with anger *UK, 1919*. **2** to go mad, to feign madness *UK, 1959*. ► **make the nut** to suffice *US, 1966*. ► **nod the nut** to plead guilty. Formed on NUT (the head); from bending the head in unspoken affirmative *AUSTRALIA, 1975*. ► **off your nut 1** in a state of drunkenness or drug intoxication. Parallel to the sense as 'mad'; possibly the original sense, a variation of OFF YOUR HEAD *UK, 1860*. **2** in a state of madness. A variation of OFF YOUR HEAD *UK, 1873*. ► **on the nut** in horse racing, to have lost a large amount of money betting *US, 1951*. ► **out of your nut** drunk or drug-intoxicated. A variation of OUT OF YOUR HEAD *UK, 1999*

nut *verb* **1** to head-butt an opponent's face. Derives from NUT (the head) *UK, 1937*. **2** to execute *IRELAND, 2001*. **3** to have sex *US, 1971*. **4** to orgasm, especially of a male *US, 1999*

nut and gut *adjective* mental and physical *UK, 2002*

nutbag *noun* a mesh restraint used by police to restrain violent people *US, 1997*

nutbox *noun* a mental hospital *US, 1965*

nutcake *noun* an eccentric or crazy person *US, 1967*

nut case *noun* an eccentric; a madman. Combines NUT (a lunatic) with conventional medical use of 'case' *AUSTRALIA, 1944*

nut-chokers *noun* men's underpants. Formed on NUTS (the testicles) *AUSTRALIA, 1971*

nutcracker *noun* **1** a stern person; a strict disciplinarian, especially a woman who crushes a man's spirit *US, 1977*. **2** a railway roundhouse mechanic *US, 1977*

nutcrackers *noun* the testicles. Rhyming slang for KNACKERS; extending, and, possibly deliberately, disguising, NUTS (the testicles) *UK, 1998*

nutcrusher *noun* a hard man (or woman); a strict disciplinarian. Crushed nuts are a standard ingredient in many sweet recipes, hence this readymade pun and variation of BALLBREAKER *UK, 1999*

nutcut *noun* the critical point in an enterprise or operation *US, 1972*

nut-cutting *noun* the most critical and distasteful stage in a project or operation. An image from the West and cattle raising *US, 1968*

nut farm *noun* a hospital for the mentally ill *US, 1940*

nut flush *noun* in poker, a hand with all cards of the same suit and an ace as the high card *US, 1979*

nut graf *noun* in journalism, the key paragraph in an article *UK, 2005*

nut hatch *noun* a mental institution *US, 1942*

nuthouse *noun* a mental hospital *US, 1906*

nut hustle *noun* a swindle involving a prostitute and a confederate *US, 1978*

nut job *noun* someone who is mentally unstable *US, 1972*

nut man *noun* a male homosexual *AUSTRALIA, 1985*

nut mob *noun* a group operating three-shell games in carnivals *US, 1950*

nut nectar *noun* semen *US, 1996*

nut-nut *noun* **1** a crazy person. By reduplication of NUT (a crazy person) *UK, 2000*. **2** in high-low poker, a hand that is the best possible hand either high or low *US, 1996*

nut off *verb* to send a prisoner to a secure psychiatric hospital. From NUT (a crazy person) *UK, 1996*

nut out *verb* **1** to think out; to work out *AUSTRALIA, 1919*. **2** to act mentally ill *US, 1966*

nut player *noun* in poker, a player who only plays a hand that is excellent as dealt. From NUTS (the best possible hand in a given situation) *US, 1979*

nutrients *noun* food *US, 1993*

nut role *noun* the act of feigning eccentricity or mild insanity *US, 1969*

nut-role; nut-roll *verb* to feign mental instability *US, 1967*

nut-runner *noun* in car repair, a pneumatic wrench *US, 1993*

nuts *noun* **1** the testicles; the scrotum *US, 1863*. **2** in poker, the best possible winning hand at a given moment *US, 1977*. **3** the advantage in a bet *US, 1990*. ► **do your nuts over** to become infatuated with someone *AUSTRALIA, 1987*. ► **get your nuts off** to ejaculate *US, 1932*. ► **have your nuts in the wringer** to be trapped in a very weak position *UK, 1998*. ► **the nuts** excellent, outstanding, very impressive. Possibly a shortening of MUTT'S NUTS *UK, 2000*. ► **the nuts are running the fruitcake** used of any situation that is managed by those who are incapable. A neat variation, formed on NUT (a mad person) and FRUITCAKE (a mad person) of THE LUNATICS ARE RUNNING THE ASYLUM *UK, 2001*

nuts *adjective* enthusiastic about; having a strong liking for; sexually infatuated *UK, 1785*

nuts! used as an expression of defiance. From the sense as 'testicles', thus BALLS! *US, 1910*

nut sack *noun* the scrotum *US, 1971*

nutso *noun* a crazy person, an eccentric. From 'nuts' (crazy) *US, 1975*

nutso *adjective* crazy *US, 1979*

nut splitter; nut buster *noun* a railway machinist *US, 1903*

nuts to...! when combined with a name, a noun or a pronoun, used for expressing defiance of that person or thing. Used as a euphemism for 'balls to...!' *UK, 1984*

nutsy *adjective* eccentric, odd, crazy *US, 1923*

nutted *adjective* drug-intoxicated *UK, 1997*

nutter *noun* a crazy person; a lunatic; an eccentric. Extended from NUT (a lunatic) *UK, 1958*

nutters *adjective* crazy, wildly mad *UK, 1982*

nutty *noun* any confectionery; used generically for all chocolate and sweets. Royal Navy slang *UK, 1987*

nutty *adjective* **1** crazy, eccentric *US, 1892*. **2** excellent. A variation on 'crazy' *US, 1953*

nutty as a fruitcake *adjective* insane, crazy. An elaboration of NUTTY *UK, 1935*

nutty putty *noun* in electric line work, a compound formally known as Seal-A-Conn, used for covering connectors *US, 1980*

nut up *verb* **1** to lose your composure completely *US, 1972*. **2** in poker, to shift into a more conservative mode of betting *US, 1982*

nut ward *noun* the psychiatric ward of a prison *US, 1984*

NWAB *adjective* (of a girl) promiscuous, because she will neck with any boy. Youth usage *US, 1949*

n-word *noun* the word 'nigger'. This clumsy euphemism was popularised during the 1995 O.J. Simpson murder trial by F. Lee Baily's cross examination of Mark Fuhrman about a taped interview that Fuhrman had given in 1985 *US, 1987*

nyaff *noun* an irritating or contemptible person, especially if that person is short. Probably derived from Scots *nyaff* (of a dog, to bark) *UK: SCOTLAND, 1985*

nyam *noun* food; something to eat. From the verb. West Indian, hence UK black *UK, 1828*

nyam *verb* to eat. African origins, from 'yam' (a sweet potato) *JAMAICA, 1790*

nylon disgusters *noun* a pair of men's close-fitting and revealing nylon swimming trunks *AUSTRALIA, 2003*

nymph *noun* a nymphomaniac *US, 1916*

nymphet *noun* a sexually attractive, or sexually adventurous, young girl. First applied to a real, as opposed to mythic, creature by Vladimir Nabokov, *Lolita*, 1955 *UK, 1999*

nympho *noun* a nymphomaniac. A creature of men's dreams; used to disparage a woman whose sexual appetites may threaten to make the dream come true *US, 1910*

Oo

O *noun* **1** an *OBE* (Officer of the Order of the British Empire). Used by civil servants; suggestive of a casual familiarity with the honour *UK, 1961*. **2** opium *US, 1933*. **3** an ovation. Most commonly heard in the term 'standing O' *US, 1984*

O *nickname* the Nuestra Familia prison gang *US, 2000*

-o *suffix* used for making colloquial or slang nouns and nicknames. In Australia, where there was no influence from Spanish, this suffix originated from early nominal uses of the cries of various street vendors. Thus the milkman used to sing out 'milk-oh!' and so became the MILKO, the rabbit seller cried 'rabbit-oh!' and so became the RABBIT-O. It is appended to monosyllablic words or to the first syllable of polysyllablic words *AUSTRALIA, 1865*

OAE *noun* anybody who has spent at least one winter in Antarctica. An abbreviation of 'old Antarctic explorer' *ANTARCTICA, 1960*

oafo *noun* an oaf, a socially inferior fool, a lout. A conventional 'oaf' embellished *UK, 1959*

Oak; the Austrian Oak *nickname* Arnold Schwarzenegger (b.1947), the dominant bodybuilder in the steroid-enhanced 1970s *US, 1984*

oak and ash *noun* cash. Rhyming slang *UK, 1960*

oaktoe *noun* the numbing of toes by cold water, creating the sensation that your toes are wooden. Surfing usage *US, 2004*

OAP *noun* an over-anxious patient. Doctors' shorthand, playing on the conventional abbreviation for 'old age pensioner' *UK, 2002*

oar *noun* ▶ **put your oar in; put in your oar; shove in your oar** to interfere in someone else's business *UK, 1730*

oars and rowlocks *noun* nonsense. Rhyming slang for BOLLOCKS *UK, 1998*

oasis *noun* **1** a bar *US, 1956*. **2** in motor racing, a refreshment stand *US, 1965*

oatburner; oatmuncher *noun* in horse racing, a racehorse that does not perform well *US, 1916*

oater *noun* a cowboy film, story or song *US, 1946*

oatie *noun* ▶ **go for an oatie** to go to the toilet. A darkly humorous Antarctic euphemism recalling Captain Oates's heroic last words to his tent-mates in 1912: 'I am going outside, and may be some time' *NEW ZEALAND, 1996*

oatmeal *noun* a small, mushy wave *US, 1991*

oatmeal Chinaman *noun* in mining in the Cariboo, a Canadian *CANADA, 1963*

oatmeal savage *noun* a Scotsman *CANADA, 1954*

oats *noun* **1** sexual gratification. Usually in phrases such as: 'have your oats', 'get your oats', 'need', 'want', etc. Perhaps from 'sow your wild oats' (to commit youthful indiscretion) *UK, 1923*. **2** money which a carnival worker steals from his boss *US, 1985*. **3** enthusiasm *US, 1831*. ▶ **off your oats** off your food *UK, 1890*. ▶ **on his oats** (used of a racehorse) racing without the benefit of a stimulant *US, 1994*

oats and barley; Oats *noun* Charley or Charlie. Rhyming slang. Ostensibly and rarely a man's given name but usually in its older slang senses (a nightwatchman; to make a Charlie of; a ponce; etc) *UK, 1859*

oat soda *noun* beer. An evolution of BARLEY POP *US, 1994*

obbo; obo; obbs; obs *noun* surveillance, observation; a lookout. Varying abbreviations for 'observation' *UK, 1933*

OBE *adjective* overcome by events; overtaken by events *US, 1986*

OBE (used of a bettor in debt) owes bookies everywhere *AUSTRALIA, 1989*

OBH *noun* someone who smokes marijuana constantly. An abbreviation of 'original buddha head' *US, 1995*

obies; OB's *noun* old brown sherry, a drink especially popular among students. Formed on the initials OB *SOUTH AFRICA, 1979*

obit *noun* an obituary *UK, 1874*

obliterated *adjective* very drunk *US, 1987*

oblivion *noun* the state of complete intoxication *US, 1984*

oboy *noun* marijuana. Presumably this drug is, on occasion, greeted with an exclamation of delight: 'Oh boy!' *UK, 2001*

obs *noun* **1** *obs*ervation. Probably military origin *UK, 1999*. **2** in a hospital, *obs*tetrics *UK, 1985*

obscure *adjective* in computing, completely beyond all understanding *US, 1991*

obscuro *adjective* weird, strange (or simply obscure) *US, 1997*

obzocky *adjective* lacking grace and coordination *TRINIDAD AND TOBAGO, 1956*

OC *noun* **1** organised crime *US, 1975*. **2** the synthetic opiate oxycodone used recreationally *US, 2001*

OC *nickname* Orange County, California. Immediately south of Los Angeles *US, 2001*

ocal; opal *noun* the eye. Punning variations on OGLE (the eye) *UK, 2002*

occy; occi *noun* an octopus *AUSTRALIA, 1968*

occy strap; ockie strap *noun* an elastic strap. An abbreviation of 'octopus strap' *AUSTRALIA, 1981*

ocean *noun* **1** in pool, the expansive centre of a table *US, 1993*. **2** in oil drilling, salt water encountered while drilling *US, 1954*

ocean liner *noun* a black eye. Rhyming slang for SHINER *UK, 1992*

ocean rambler *noun* a herring; a sardine *UK, 1961*

oceans *noun* a large amount of something *UK, 1840*

-ocentric *suffix* used with humour as a suffix attached to a person's name, suggesting that they believe that the world revolves around them *US, 1996*

ocker; Ocker *noun* **1** an Australian male who is especially boorish and uncouth; the stereotypical Australian male yob. Originally a colloquial nickname for someone named Oscar. It became associated with typical male boorishness in the 1970s partly under the influence of a character named Ocker in the television comedy *The Mavis Bramston Show* (1965–68) *AUSTRALIA, 1971*. **2** Australian English *AUSTRALIA, 1979*

ocker; Ocker *adjective* characteristic of an ocker *AUSTRALIA, 1972*

ockerdom *noun* the state of being an ocker *AUSTRALIA, 1974*

O club *noun* in the US armed forces, an officer's club *US, 1986*

-ocracy *suffix* when linked with a subject, used to designate (and mock) a grouping that may be dominant, or aspiring to dominance, or pretending superiority within that subject-area. A sarcastic or humorous application of '-cracy' (power, rule), found in such words as 'democracy', 'plutocracy', etc. The root in all conventional senses ends with an 'o'; in colloquial or journalistic usage the 'o' is incorporated *UK, 1860*

ocs *noun* the synthetic opiate oxycodone used recreationally *US, 2000*

octopus *noun* a sexually aggressive boy *US, 1932*

OD *noun* a drug overdose *US, 1959*

OD *verb* to overdose, to take an excessive dose of a drug, usually heroin *US, 1966*

o-dark-hundred *noun* very early in the morning. Mock military time *US, 1982*

oday *noun* money. A Pig Latin construction of DOUGH *US, 1928*

odd *noun* **1** a small number over and above a round number *UK, 1845*. **2** the police; a police-officer *UK, 1958*

oddball *noun* an eccentric *US, 1948*

oddball *adjective* eccentric, peculiar *US, 1957*

oddball trick *noun* a prostitute's customer who pays for fetishistic sex *US, 1973*

odd bod *noun* **1** an eccentric *UK, 1955*. **2** an extra person in a given situation *NEW ZEALAND, 1984*

odd-lot *noun* a police car *UK, 1958*

odds *noun* **1** a vague number, as a part of a greater number. A variation on ODD *UK, 1958*. **2** (of money) small change. A shortening of 'odd coins' *UK, 2002*. ► **make no odds** to make no difference, not better or worse. Originally (from 1776) conventional, now colloquial *UK, 1826*. ► **over the odds** more than is expected; more than is tolerable *UK, 1922*. ► **what's the odds?** what's the difference? *UK, 1840*

odds *verb* to risk, to chance; to avoid. Perhaps deriving from 'to bet against the odds' *UK, 1958*

odds and sods *noun* bits and pieces. Now used as a variant of conventional 'odds and ends'; originally military slang for 'miscellaneous men or duties' *UK, 1935*

odds-on *adjective* **1** very probable, most likely. Adopted from gambling use to denote any form of actuarial or notional likelihood *UK, 1888*. **2** in horse racing, said of odds that pay less than even money *US, 1974*

o-dom *noun* an odometer (a milometer) *US, 2000*

OD's *noun* a drab olive military uniform *US, 1955*

OE *noun* Old English™ malt liquor *US, 1997*

Oedipus Rex; Oedipus *noun* sex. Rhyming slang, based on a king of ancient Thebes used by psychiatrists as a model for the sexual relationship between a boy and his mother *UK, 1979*

ofaginzy *noun* a white person *US, 1946*

ofay *noun* a white person. Origin unknown. Suggestions of a Pig Latin etymology (foe) are implausible. More plausible are suggestions of a basis in an African language or the French *au fait* (socially proper) *US, 1925*

ofer; o-for *adjective* used to describe a male pornography performer who either cannot achieve an erection or cannot ejaculate when needed. Borrowing from sports lingo, identifying the performer as 'oh' (zero) for however many tries *US, 1995*

off *noun* **1** the start of a race; the beginning of something, the start of a journey. From racing *UK, 1959*. **2** time off, a day off, etc. By ellipsis *SOUTH AFRICA, 1966*. **3** a warning given to an illegal betting operation by corrupt police of a pending raid *US, 1952*. **4** in dominoes, a piece that does not contribute to the value of your hand *US, 1959*

off *verb* **1** to kill *US, 1967*. **2** to sell, especially contraband *US, 1960*

off *adjective* **1** distant, aloof, negative *UK, about 1555*. **2** having lost interest in; averse to *UK, 1908*. **3** disgusting, revolting *AUSTRALIA, 1987*. **4** of a street-prostitute, being with a client (and, therefore, *off* the street where the service is offered for sale) *UK, 1959*. **5** not using drugs *US, 1952*. ► **be off!; be off with you!** go away! Old-fashioned, but still in use *UK, 1842*

offbeat *adjective* unconventional, but not unique *US, 1938*

off-brand cigarette *noun* a marijuana cigarette *US, 1980*

off-brand stud *noun* a male homosexual *US, 1962*

off-by-one error *noun* in computing, any simple and basic error, such as starting at 1 instead of 0 *US, 1991*

off colour *adjective* **1** applied to jokes that may be considered impolite or indecent *UK, 1875*. **2** unwell *UK, 1876*

offensive potatoes *noun* canned potatoes *ANTARCTICA, 2003*

offer *verb* ► **offer someone out** to challenge someone to a fight *AUSTRALIA, 1943*

office *noun* **1** a warning; a private signal *UK, 1818*. **2** any secret signal used by gambling cheats to communicate among themselves *US, 1950*. **3** a hint or tip *AUSTRALIA, 1874*. ► **give the office** in prison, to explain the way things are, especially to a new inmate *UK, 1996*

office bike *noun* a woman who readily has sexual intercourse with fellow staff in an office *AUSTRALIA, 1945*

office hours *noun* **1** minor discipline issued by a US Marine Corps company commander *US, 1898*. **2** in poker, pairs of 9s and 5s, or a straight from 9 to 5 *US, 1963*

office piano *noun* a typewriter *US, 1945*

officer material *noun* a mentally deficient enlisted soldier *US, 1945*

office worker *noun* a shirker. Rhyming slang, used by manual labourers, with a subtext of bitter irony *UK, 1992*

offie; offy *noun* an off-licence (a shop licensed to sell alcoholic drinks for consumption *off* the premises) *UK, 1977*

off it *adjective* drug-intoxicated. A variation of OFF YOUR HEAD *UK, 1998*

offshore *adjective* foreign *US, 1997*

offsider *noun* an assistant. Originally (late C19) an assistant/apprentice to a bullock-driver who worked on the 'off side' *AUSTRALIA, 1903*

offski *verb* to go away, to leave *UK, 2001*

off to another NASA convention used for humour when someone who has been displaying their ignorance leaves a room *US, 1991*

off-trail *adjective* unconventional, eccentric *US, 1954*

Offy *noun* a racing engine or any other piece of equipment manufactured by Meyer-Drake *US, 1993*

OG *noun* **1** your mother. An abbreviation of OLD GIRL *US, 1878*. **2** a founding member of a youth gang. An abbreviation of ORIGINAL GANGSTER *US, 1993*

oggin *noun* the ocean *ANTARCTICA, 2003*

ogle *noun* the eye. Survives mainly as a part of the polari vocabulary; usually in the plural *UK, 1676*

ogle; ogale *verb* in homosexual use, to look longingly or amorously at a man. From the wider conventional sense first recorded in the 1680s *UK, 1682*

ogle and leer *noun* gonorrhoea. Rhyming slang *UK, 2003*

ogle fake; ogle riah fake; ogle fake riah *noun* a false eyelash. Polari; literally 'articles (of hair) made for the eye' *UK, 1992*

ogle fakes *noun* spectacles. Polari; literally 'articles made for the eye' *UK, 2002*

ogle filters *noun* sunglasses. Polari; based on OGLE (the eye) *UK, 2002*

ogle riahs *noun* eyelashes. Polari; a combination of OGLE (the eye) and RIAH (the hair) *UK, 2002*

ogle riders *noun* the eyebrows or eyelashes *UK, 2002*

ogle shades *noun* glasses; sunglasses. Polari; based on OGLE (the eye) *UK, 2002*

Ogopogo *noun* a legendary monster in Okanagan Lake, British Columbia *CANADA, 1964*

ogoy *noun* heroin *US, 1977*

oh, behave used as a catch-all catchphrase, usually in the context of a sexual innuendo. Wildly popular for several years after the release of the first *Austin Powers* film in 1997 *US, 1997*

oh, fiddle-faddle! used as a non-profane expression of frustration. Used with regularity by the Aunt Bee character on *The Andy Griffith Show* (CBS, 1960–68). Repeated with referential humour *US, 1963*

Ohio bag *noun* one hundred grams of marijuana. Under Ohio's decriminalisation laws, this is the maximum amount for a fine for simple possession *US, 1982*

ohmigod!; omigod! used for expressing surprise or horror *US, 1982*

oh my Gawd; oh my good Gawd *adjective* bald. Rhyming slang; the second variation is reserved for extreme baldness *UK, 1992*

oh my stars! used for expressing frustration. Popularised by the sexy blonde witch Samantha on *Bewitched* (ABC, 1964–72). Repeated with referential humour *US, 1966*

oh nelly! used for humorously expressing surprise or upset *US, 1997*

ohnosecond *noun* an instant of realisation when you have made a mistake, especially in computing. A punning combination of 'nanosecond' and the exclamation 'oh no!' *UK, 2002*

oh-shit *noun* a criticism *US, 1997*

oh snap! used as a mild oath *US, 2002*

oh the pain, the shame! used as a humorous comment on humiliation. Coined on the television programme *Lost in Space* (1965–68), and then revived and popularised by Keith Olberman on ESPN *US, 1997*

oh yeah? used in questioning veracity or likelihood, or confirming that a person being addressed has understood or is in agreement *US, 1930*

oil; oy! a meaningless noise used to draw attention or cry in protest. Derives from the obsolete 'hoy!', which was a combination of 'ho!' and 'hullo!' *UK, 1936*

oicery *noun* the sleeping quarters of the officer in charge (OIC) *ANTARCTICA, 1959*

-oid *suffix* used as a suffix that embellishes without changing the base word's meaning *US, 1978*

oik *noun* someone considered to be a social inferior; a disagreeable youth. Originally a public school coinage used to categorise status: 'a townee'; then generalised as 'working-class'; also used within that circle as general abuse for an unpopular fellow pupil or someone from a rival school. Generated from HOICK (to hawk and spit) *UK, 1925*

oil *noun* **1** alcohol *US, 1912*. **2** a potent distillate of marijuana or hashish *US, 1996*. **3** heroin *UK, 1998*. **4** news; information about something. Metaphorically because oil is essential for the smooth running of a machine *AUSTRALIA, 1915*. **5** in horse racing, confidential and reliable information about a horse *AUSTRALIA, 1989*. **6** in pool, extreme spin imparted to the cue ball to affect the course of the object ball or the cue ball after striking the object ball *US, 1912*.
▶ **the oil** the complete truth, the lowdown *NEW ZEALAND, 1998*

oil *verb* **1** to inject yourself with a drug, especially heroin *US, 1981*. **2** to bribe *US, 1982*. ▶ **oil it** to study late into the night *US, 1975*

oil and water king *noun* aboard ship, the engineer controlling fresh water distillation *US, 1986*

oil burner *noun* **1** a serious drug addiction *US, 1938*. **2** in trucking, a diesel engine *US, 1971*. **3** in horse racing, a fast horse *US, 1951*

oil-burning *adjective* (used of a drug addiction) severe *US, 1972*

oil can *noun* a railway tank wagon *US, 1946*

oil-can *verb* (of a boat) to make a hollow booming sound striking the water *US, 1990*

oiled; oiled up *adjective* **1** drunk *US, 1737*. **2** readied; well-prepared *UK, 1999*

oilies *noun* work clothes *US, 1954*

oil in the can *noun* in horse racing, a horse believed by its backers to be a sure winner *US, 1951*

oil leak *noun* a Sikh. Rhyming slang *UK, 1998*

oil merchant *noun* a smooth-talking swindler *US, 1935*

oil patch *noun* the oil industry *US, 1980*

oil slick *noun* a Spaniard. Rhyming slang for SPIC *UK, 1992*

oil tanker *noun* used as an all-purpose form of abuse. Rhyming slang for WANKER *UK, 1992*

oil well *noun* in a deck of playing cards, an ace. From the visual comparison of an 'A' with an oil well *US, 1988*

oily *adjective* mean-spirited, tough *US, 1958*

oily rag *noun* **1** a worker's assistant *UK, 1994*. **2** a cigarette. Rhyming slang for FAG (a cigarette). Also shortened to 'oil-rag' and 'oily' *UK, 1932*

oink *noun* a police officer. A far less common usage than the related PIG (police) *US, 1970*

oink *verb* to lure by greed *US, 1954*

oinseach *noun* a female fool *IRELAND, 2001*

Oirish *adjective* Irish. From the stereotypically Irish pronunciation of 'Irish' *UK, 1962*

OJ *noun* **1** marijuana. Possibly, an initialism of 'oint-jay' (JOINT) *US, 1970*. **2** a marijuana cigarette dipped in liquid opium or heroin. In other words, an 'opium joint'. Popular with US troops in Vietnam *US, 1970*. **3** an online jockey who hosts Internet discussions. Initialism, on the model of DJ (disc jockey) *UK, 1998*

OK when appended to a slogan, used as a strengthening affirmative, especially when phrased 'X rule (or rules) OK'. Nigel Rees, *Graffiti Lives, OK*, 1979, writes: 'The addition of "OK" to slogans first became noticeable in Northern Ireland during the early 1970s, as in "Provos Rule, OK" referring to the Provisional IRA' *UK, 2002*

OK; okay *noun* **1** consent, approval *US, 1841*. **2** a bribe paid by an illegal gambling establishment to the authorities to stay in business *US, 1979*

OK; okay *verb* to approve *US, 1988*

OK; okay *adjective* **1** comfortable, at ease. Especially common as 'OK about' or 'OK with' *US, 1978*. **2** safe, unhurt *US, 1839*. **3** decent, mediocre, satisfactory. In 1963, the late Allen Walker Read published his extensive and definitive research on the term, tracing its coinage to 1839 as an abbreviation of 'oil korrect', itself a then-popular slang term *US, 1839*

OK; okay used for expressing assent, approval, understanding, or agreement *US, 1839*

OK Corral *noun* a group of men masturbating while watching a female. An extrapolation of the GUN DOWN image, alluding to the site of a famous American gun battle in 1881 *US, 2002*

oke *noun* used as an affectionate or patronising term of address or reference to a man or boy. A shortened form of OKIE *SOUTH AFRICA, 1970*

okey-doke *noun* **1** a swindle or deception *US, 1969*. **2** a wallet, especially its contents. Rhyming slang for POKE used by pickpockets. Sometimes shortened to 'okey' *UK, 1961*

okey-doke used for communicating agreement. A shortening of OKEY-DOKEY *US, 1936*

okey-dokey *adjective* acceptable *US, 1942*

okey-dokey used for communicating agreement. An old-fashioned, affected, still popular perversion of OK *US, 1932*

Oki; Okie *noun* Okinawa. Coined in World War 2, still used in Vietnam *US, 1945*

Okie *noun* a poor, white resident or native of rural Oklahoma; a poor, white resident or native of the south-central US. Used with derision or pride but not neutrally *US, 1938*

okie; oakie *noun* used as an affectionate or patronising term of address or reference to a man or boy. Anglicised form of Afrikaans *outjie* *SOUTH AFRICA, 1943*

Okie blower *noun* in trucking, an air scoop attached to the air-intake system *US, 1971*

Okie chrome *noun* aluminium paint *US, 1961*

Okie trap *noun* a confusing, complicated traffic interchange *US, 1962*

Oklahoma credit card *noun* a hose used to steal petrol by siphoning it from a parked car. Presenting the myth of Oklahoma as a state filled with poor, crafty and dishonest people *US, 1962*

Oklahoma toothbrush *noun* the penis. In Oklahoma, known as a 'Texas toothbrush' *US, 1994*

OK Yardie *noun* a stereotypical Briton of the upper- or middle-class who lives in west London's gangland. A conflation of 'OK, yah' (a catchphrase cliché of the social grouping) and YARDIE (a Jamaican gangster) *UK, 1998*

-ola *suffix* a meaningless embellishment of a suffix *US, 1919*

olalliechuk *noun* (on the Pacific coast) a homebrew made from berries. The name comes from Chinook jargon *CANADA, 1966*

old *noun* a dark lager-style beer brewed by the top-fermentation method. As opposed to NEW *AUSTRALIA, 1935*

old; ol'; ole *adjective* **1** used to intensify some intensifiers. A slight narrowing of use since first recorded in the 1440s as 'grand, great, plentiful' now mainly seen in such constructions as: 'high old time' (1858) and 'gay old boys' (1887) *UK, 1844*. **2** old. The first headword is, of course, standard English; the second and third variants are variously colloquial, informal and slang as circumstances dictate *UK, 1844*. **3** used as a signal of familiarity with the person so described. As spoken in the southern US, not necessarily indicative of affection, cordiality, or good humour *US, 1984*. **4** tiresome *US, 1864*

old bag *noun* **1** an unattractive or unloveable old woman. Disparaging; possibly a variant of OLD BAT, cognisant of the following sense as 'an elderly prostitute' which itself may derive from OLD BAT *UK, 1949*. **2** an elderly, slatternly prostitute; hence pejorative for a younger prostitute *UK, 1961*

old bastard *noun* a man; fellow. Used as an ironic form of friendly personal address, generally amongst males. Such is the love for this expression amongst working-class Australians, a charity organisation was formed in the 1970s under the name the Australasian Order of Old Bastards. Part of the rules of the order is that 'On encountering other O.B.'s in a bar one must administer a hearty slap on the back, accompanied with the cheerful salutation, "Hello you Old Bastard!". Membership card must be carried at all times. Failure to produce same when challenged by fellow O.B. incurs a penalty of one round of drinks' *AUSTRALIA, 1944*

old bat *noun* a disagreeable, middle-aged or elderly woman. An elaboration of BAT (an ugly woman), originally 'a prostitute' *UK, 1886*

old bill *noun* **1** the penis *UK, 1998*. **2** a signal, by hand or word, asking 'Are there any other cheaters in this game?' *US, 1979*

Old Bill *noun* a police officer; the police. Original usage was singular, now mainly collective. Feasible etymologies, in no particular order of likelihood: i) 'Old Bill', a cartoon strip character created by Bruce Bairnsfather (1888–1959), was a veteran of World War 1 with a distinctive 'authoritarian-looking' moustache – a status and description shared by many pre-World War 2 policemen. This derivation may be reinforced by the 1917 UK government's advertising campaign, featuring Old Bill dressed as a special constable, using the heading 'Old Bill says...' to disseminate important wartime information. ii) Derived from a blend of popular song 'Won't You Come Home, Bill Bailey' punning with 'The Old Bailey' (London's Central Criminal Court). iii) 'Old Bill' was King William IV (1765–1837), during whose reign (1830–37) the police force is wrongly thought to have been established. iv) 'Kaiser Bill', Kaiser Wilhelm I of Prussia (1797–1888), visited England in 1864 when the police uniform changed to helmet and tunic. v) Constables of the watch were nicknamed for the bills or billhooks that they carried as weapons. vi) In Victorian times the 'old bill' was the bill, or account, presented by police accepting bribes, or for services rendered. vii) New laws are introduced as parliamentary *bills*. viii) The London County Council registered all public service vehicles (police, fire and ambulance) with number plates BYL, leading villains to spot unmarked police cars as 'old Bill'. ix) Similarly, Scotland Yard's 'Flying Squad' (established 1921) was reportedly issued with BYL registrations so that the Squad became known as 'old Bill', and hence the police in general. x) In the 1860s, Limehouse police sergeant Bill Smith, of apocryphal memory, was nicknamed 'Old Bill' *UK, 1958*

old bird *noun* a mature, older or old woman *UK, 2003*

old bird *adjective* of a prisoner, having traditional values *UK, 2001*

old blind Bob *noun* the penis *UK, 1974*

old bloke *noun* the penis *AUSTRALIA, 1992*

Old Blue Eyes *nickname* Frank Sinatra, US singer (1915–98) *US, 1984*

old bollocks *noun* an older man *UK, 2000*

old boot; boot *noun* an unattractive woman, a woman with qualities that are considered unattractive *UK, 1958*

old boy *noun* **1** the penis *US, 1943*. **2** used as a friendly form of address to another man. A colloquial vocative since the C17 *UK, 2000*. **3** an old man *UK, 1500*. **4** a father *UK, 1892*

old boy network; Old Boy network *noun* a social and, especially, business connection between former public school pupils which is presumed, by those without such a connection, to give unfair advantages in matters of employment and social advancement;

also applied to connections made at university, and at other institutions which may be considered as for the privileged *UK, 1959*

old breed *noun* the First Marine Division, US Marine Corps, which saw service in World War 2, North China, Korea and Vietnam *US, 1991*

old cat *noun* A Morris Minor car. Citizens' band radio slang *UK, 1981*

old chap *noun* **1** used as a friendly form of address to another man *UK, 1822*. **2** the penis *UK, 1992*

old comic *noun* a Vauxhall Victor car. Citizens' band radio slang; it sounds like a name a music hall comedian would use *UK, 1981*

Old Corncob *nickname* General Douglas MacArthur (1880–1964) of the US Army. From his love for a corncob pipe *US, 1982*

old country *noun* **1** to the US armed forces at the end of World War 2, the United States *US, 1949*. **2** Beverly Hills, California. Used with irony by transplants, especially Jewish transplants, to the San Fernando Valley *US, 2004*

Old Country *nickname* England or the United Kingdom *AUSTRALIA, 1834*

old cow *noun* a despicable old woman *AUSTRALIA, 1864*

old D *noun* a mother. Initially 'dear' or 'darling' *UK, 1996*

Old Dart *nickname* England or the United Kingdom; specifically, London. First recorded in use in England in 1832 (Wilkes). 'Dart' represents the pronunciation of the word 'dirt' in the Essex dialect, and so 'Old Dart' would correlate with 'old sod' (one's native district or country) *AUSTRALIA, 1892*

old dear *noun* an old woman *UK, 1958* ▷*see:* OUL ONE

old dog *noun* a Rover car *UK, 1981*

old face *noun* a chorus dancer whose long tenure makes her unmarketable *US, 1948*

old faithful *noun* the bleed period of the menstrual cycle *US, 1954*

old fart *noun* an old or older person, especially one who is unpleasant or disliked. Often elaborated as 'boring old fart.' *US, 1971*

old-fashioned look *noun* a glance of quizzical disapproval *UK, 1961*

old fellow *noun* **1** the penis *AUSTRALIA, 1968*. **2** a father (regardless of age) *AUSTRALIA, 1954*. **3** used as a friendly form of address to another man; a man *UK, 1825*

old fogey *noun* a small lump of dried nasal mucus. Rhyming slang for BOGEY *UK, 1998*

old folks *noun* **1** parents (regardless of age) *AUSTRALIA, 1957*. **2** in circus and carnival usage, monkeys *US, 1981*

old fruit; my old fruit *noun* used as a friendly form of address to another man *UK, 2003*

old gent *noun* the penis *UK, 2000*

old girl *noun* **1** a mother; a wife *UK, 1887*. **2** an old woman *UK, 1791*

old git *noun* any man who is considered past his prime *UK, 2000*

old grinder *noun* a promiscuous woman *UK, 2000*

old hand *noun* an experienced person, an expert *UK, 1785*

old hat *adjective* old-fashioned, out-of-date *UK, 1911*

old head *noun* **1** an older prisoner *US, 2002*. **2** a returning student to a school *US, 1963*

old horsey *noun* strong, illegally manufactured whisky *US, 1999*

old house *noun* on the railways, a warehouse of salvaged parts *US, 1977*

oldie *noun* **1** an older or elderly person *UK, 1874*. **2** a song from the past that is still popular. A shortened form of GOLDEN OLDIE or 'oldie but goody' *US, 1939*

oldies *noun* parents (regardless of age) *AUSTRALIA, 1964*

old iron and brass; old iron *noun* **2** a pass. Rhyming slang, in military use *UK, 1992*

old iron and grass; old iron *noun* **1** grass. Rhyming slang *UK, 1992*

old Joe *noun* any sexually transmitted infection *US, 1967*

old King Cole *noun* unemployment benefit; a government office from which unemployment benefit is managed. Rhyming slang for THE DOLE; formed on the name of a nursery rhyme character – he was 'a merry old soul' so this rhyme may be intentionally ironic UK, 1960

old kit bag noun a cigarette. Rhyming slang for FAG; possibly from the song by George Asaf and Felix Powell: 'Pack up your troubles in your old kit bag and smile, smile, smile', 1915 – but still familiar UK, 1998

old lad noun used as a friendly form of address to another man UK, 1588

old lady noun **1** a mother US, 1877. **2** a wife, common-law or legal; a girlfriend US, 1836. **3** the more passive member of a same-sex couple US, 1937. **4** any old woman UK, 1824

Old Lady of Threadneedle Street nickname the Bank of England. From a cartoon by James Gillray UK, 1797

old lady white; old white lady noun a powdered drug: cocaine, heroin or morphine US, 1942

old lag noun **1** a regular prisoner or one who has become institutionalised, a recidivist. From LAG (a prisoner) UK, 1950. **2** a prisoner who has been in jail for a long time AUSTRALIA, 1950. **3** a former prisoner AUSTRALIA, 1812. **4** a person who has been contracted to a single employer for a very long time, especially of the armed services. Humorous use of the sense as 'a convict who has been imprisoned for many years' UK, 2001

old man noun **1** a father UK, 1811. **2** a boyfriend or husband UK, 1768. **3** a commanding officer, military or police US, 1830. **4** a pimp in relation to a prostitute US, 1891. **5** an elder amongst the Australian Aboriginals AUSTRALIA, 1848. **6** used as a form of address to another man UK, 1885. **7** the penis UK, 1984. **8** a shark US, 1965

old man comforts noun high-top shoes with ankle support and extra laces US, 1973

old man kangaroo; old man 'roo noun an adult male kangaroo AUSTRALIA, 1834

old man's aid noun in pool, a device used to support the cue stick for a hard-to-reach shot. As the terminology suggests, the device is scorned by skilled players US, 1977

old man's milk noun coconut water mixed with gin TRINIDAD AND TOBAGO, 2003

old Mick adjective nauseated, sick. Rhyming slang UK, 1967

Old Miss nickname the University of Mississippi US, 1989

old money noun an earlier system of measuring, when applied to anything except money UK, 2000

old navy noun heroin US, 2002

Old Nick noun mischief. Nearly obsolete US, 1817

old oak noun London. Probably rhyming slang for THE SMOKE; used by trainspotters; however, Garth Andrews, a retired deputy head of Records and Archives at the British Railways Board, wrote to this dictionary in May 2003, to suggest that 'this has nothing to do with rhyming slang for "smoke". Old Oak Common was the premier engine shed on the Great Western Railway, providing the motive power for crack expresses out of Paddington. It is, of course, possible that Old Oak Common provided the inspiration for the rhyme – if rhyme it is UK, 1970

old pair noun parents IRELAND, 2001

old people noun parents (regardless of age) AUSTRALIA, 1941

old person's friend noun pneumonia CANADA, 1987

old rag noun a flag. Rhyming slang UK, 1992

olds noun parents AUSTRALIA, 1979

old sailor noun a Morris Marina car. Citizens' band radio slang; pun on 'mariner' UK, 1981

old school noun a past generation with an old-fashioned but reliable way of doing things US, 1970

old shaky noun a C-124 long-range transport aircraft US, 1986

old skool; old school noun the original style of hip-hop music viewed retrospectively; subsequently, any hip-hop music that could

not be categorised as house music; finally, any style of music under the hip-hop umbrella that is not absolutely current US, 1989

Oldsmobile noun in hold 'em poker, a nine and an eight as the first two cards dealt to a player. An allusion to the Oldsmobile 98, a popular model US, 1981

Old Smokey noun the electric chair US, 1929

old soak; soak noun a drunkard. From the verb sense (to drink immoderately) UK, 1820

Old Sod noun Ireland UK, 1891

old sort noun a wife, a husband or any partner in a living-together relationship UK, 2000

Old Sparky noun an electric chair, especially Florida's electric chair US, 1971

old stager noun a person of considerable age or experience UK, 1570

oldster noun an older person UK, 1848

old Steve noun heroin US, 1936

old style noun fashion sense that is excessive to the point of ridicule TRINIDAD AND TOBAGO, 1956

old sweat noun an old soldier; a veteran police officer UK, 1919

old thing; dear old thing noun used as a term of address, usually as an endearment UK, 1864

oldtimer's disease noun Alzheimer's disease US, 1988

old Tom noun an aggressive, 'mannish' lesbian US, 1978

old woman noun **1** a wife; a woman you cohabit with UK, 1775. **2** a mother UK, 1829. **3** a male who behaves like an old woman AUSTRALIA, 1963

ole gal noun a male roommate US, 1947

o-levels noun oral sex, especially when advertised as a service offered by a prostitute. A play on the name given to 'ordinary-level' examinations in the British education system UK, 1978

olive oil; olive noun silver foil (used in the preparation of heroin). Rhyming slang UK, 1996

Oliver noun in circus and carnival usage, a police officer US, 1981

Oliver Reed; Ollie; Olly noun **1** tobacco; marijuana. Rhyming slang for WEED (tobacco/marijuana), based on the name of actor Oliver Reed, 1938–99 UK, 1992. **2** amphetamine. Rhyming slang for SPEED (amphetamine), based on the name of actor Oliver Reed, 1938–99 UK, 1992

Oliver Twist adjective drunk. Rhyming slang for PISSED, formed from Charles Dickens' eponymous hero UK, 1998

Oliver Twist!; oliver! a derisive suggestion that accompanies the offensive gesture of a raised middle finger. An elaboration and extension of TWIST!, formed from Charles Dickens' famous hero UK, 2001

Ollie Beak noun a Sikh. Rhyming slang, formed from a puppet – a Liverpudlian owl – that used to introduce children's television programmes in the 1960s UK, 1998

Ollie, Molly and Dolly noun in poker, three queens US, 1948

olly; ollie noun in skateboarding, a jumping manoeuvre, the basis of most skating tricks US, 1989

Oly nickname Olympia, Washington US, 1997

om noun MDMA, the recreational drug best known as ecstasy. Possibly from the Buddhist mantra 'Om', playing on the drug's association with 'trance' (a contemporary dance music genre formed on repetitive rhythms), or, perhaps, an abbreviation of OMEGA UK, 1996

OM noun a male; a partner; a husband. An abbreviation of 'old man'. Frequent usage by shortwave radio operators, carried over into citizens' band radio slang US, 1976

-omatic suffix used as an embellishment that adds nothing to the meaning of the word embellished US, 1982

omee; omey; omer; ome; homee; homi; homie; homey noun a man; a master; a landlord. Polari, from Italian uomo (a man) UK, 1845

omee-palone; omee-paloney; ome-palone; homee-palone; omi-palome; omie-palome *noun* a homosexual man. Polari; a combination of OMEE (a man) and POLONE; PALONE (a woman) *UK, 1966*

omega *noun* MDMA, the recreational drug best known as ecstasy. Possibly a play on 'the end' or, perhaps, an elaboration of OM *UK, 1996*

omen *noun* low grade phencyclidine, the recreational drug known as PCP or angel dust *US, 1993*

omo; OMO *adjective* used for signalling that a woman's husband is not at home: *old man out*. OMO™ is an established branded soap powder *UK, 1995*

omygod *noun* a Plymouth Omega *US, 1992*

on *adjective* **1** in the bleed period of the menstrual cycle. Euphemistic abbreviation of, or an alternative to, ON THE RAG or 'on (your) period' *UK, 1971*. **2** ready and willing *UK, 1888*. **3** willing to take part *AUSTRALIA, 1880*. **4** willing to take part in an amorous liaison *AUSTRALIA, 1907*. **5** dating *AUSTRALIA, 1945*. **6** (of a fight or dispute) begun in earnest *AUSTRALIA, 1945*. **7** persistently asking *AUSTRALIA, 1969*. **8** of a criminal enterprise, under way *UK, 1969*. **9** possible, feasible, worthy of an attempt. Originally recorded in use among billiard and snooker players *UK, 1935*. **10** having secured a bet *AUSTRALIA, 1903*. **11** protected from policy action by bribes *US, 1973*. **12** of a food dish, on the menu *UK, 1949*. **13** drug-intoxicated *US, 1946*. ▶ **not on** not going to happen; forbidden *AUSTRALIA, 1972*

on *preposition* **1** (used of a drug) under the influence of *US, 1925*. **2** so as to affect or disadvantage *US, 1925*. **3** to the detriment of, or the disadvantage of, or the ruin of, etc *UK, 2000*. **4** at or in (a place) *AUSTRALIA, 1853*. **5** to be paid for by *US, 1871*. ▶ **be on about** to talk in such a manner that the speaker is not entirely understood or listened to by the auditor. As in, 'What's he on about now?' *UK, 1984*. ▶ **be on at** to nag, to constantly reprove *UK, 1974*. ▶ **go on about; be on about** to grumble; to complain, especially loudly; to talk on a subject for far too long *UK, 1863*

on and off *noun* a cough. Rhyming slang *UK, 1998*

on bob *adjective* happy. Variation of BOB (pleasant) *UK, 2001*

once a week *noun* **1** a magistrate. Rhyming slang for BEAK *UK, 1960*. **2** impudence. Rhyming slang for CHEEK *UK, 1925*

once in a blue moon very rarely *UK, 1959*

once-over *noun* a brief look that assesses something or someone *US, 1913*

oncer *noun* **1** something or someone unique *AUSTRALIA, 1966*. **2** a person who has sex only once with any given partner *US, 1959*. **3** a one-pound note *UK, 1931*. **4** an impudent person. Derives from rhyming slang ONCE A WEEK for CHEEK *UK, 1992*

one *noun* **1** an eccentric, amusing or outrageous person *UK, 1880*. **2** a devotee, or an adherent, or a champion, of something *UK, 1888*. **3** a grudge; a score; a blow; a kiss; a drink; an act of sexual intercourse; any non-specified noun. By ellipsis of the specific noun *UK, 1830*. **4** a lie; a joke or an anecdote *UK, 1813*. **5** an act of urination. An abbreviation of NUMBER ONE *TRINIDAD AND TOBAGO, 1987*. ▶ **do one for me; have one for me** a jocular catchphrase addressed to someone on the way to the lavatory *UK, 1984*. ▶ **in one** in bar dice games, to make a hand in one roll of the dice *US, 1971*. ▶ **on one** in a state of intoxication as a result of use of MDMA, the recreational drug best known as ecstasy *UK, 1999*

one *adjective* used as an emphatic indefinite article *UK, 1828*

one goodbye. An abbreviation of ONE LOVE. *US, 2002*

one and a half *noun* a prison sentence of eighteen months *UK, 1961*

one and eight *noun* a plate (in all uses, conventional or slang). Rhyming slang *UK, 1992*

one and half *noun* a scarf. Rhyming slang *UK, 1992*

one and one *noun* **1** an inhalation of cocaine using both nostrils *UK, 2003*. **2** a dose of heroin accompanied by a dose of cocaine *US, 1997*. **3** a bag of deep-fried cod and chips *IRELAND, 1963*

one and t'other *noun* **1** a brother. Rhyming slang *UK, 1981*. **2** a mother. Rhyming slang *UK, 1932*

one-armed bandit *noun* **1** a slot machine gambling device *US, 1938*. **2** a petrol pump. From a vague similarity in appearance to a fruit machine *UK, 1981*. **3** that part of an automatic warning system mounted in a diesel locomotive's cab *UK, 1970*

one away! used by prison officers to raise the alarm when a prisoner escapes *UK, 1950*

one day for thief, one day for police used for expressing the conviction that wrongdoers will eventually be caught *TRINIDAD AND TOBAGO, 1990*

one day job *noun* a car that can be disassembled and sold in one day after being stolen *US, 1992*

One Day of the Year *noun* Anzac Day *AUSTRALIA, 1962*

one day, one day, congotay one day there will be justice *TRINIDAD AND TOBAGO, 2003*

one-digit midget *noun* during the Vietnam war, a soldier with less than 10 days to serve before his date of expected return from overseas *US, 1984*

one 'em *verb* in the gambling game two-up, to throw a head and a tail *AUSTRALIA, 1966*

one-eye *noun* **1** the penis. A variation of the 'one-eyed bestiary' *US, 1961*. **2** in a deck of playing cards, a face card drawn in profile, the jack of hearts, the jack of spades or the king of diamonds *US, 1967*. **3** a car with only one headlight working *US, 1962*

one-eyed *adjective* used in combination with a variety of suitably shaped or characterised nouns to depict the penis *UK, 1775*

one-eyed jack *noun* a car with only one headlight working *US, 1998*

one-eyed monster *noun* the penis. Neither Cyclops nor the character from the film *Monsters Inc US, 1972*

one-eyed snake *noun* the penis. A short 'one-eyed trouser snake' *US, 2001*

one-eyed trouser snake *noun* the penis *AUSTRALIA, 1971*

one foot in the grave *adjective* old, perhaps very old. Used as the title of a popular BBC situation comedy about an ageing (but not elderly) couple, written by David Renwick and broadcast from 1990–2000 *UK, 1632*

one for his nob *noun* a shilling. Rhyming slang for BOB that fell into disuse following decimalisation in 1971 *UK, 1961*

one for Ron *noun* an extra cigarette taken when one is offered. Typically the person cadging cigarettes says they'll take one 'and one for Ron', when the person giving the cigarettes asks 'Who is Ron?' the answer given is 'one for later on' *AUSTRALIA, 1966*

one for the boy *noun* in horse racing, a bet placed on a horse by the owner and given to the jockey before the race *US, 1951*

one for the road *noun* a final drink before leaving a bar *US, 1943*

one goer *noun* a race in which only one horse is being run to win *AUSTRALIA, 1966*

one-hand magazine; one-handed magazine; one-handed literature *noun* a pornographic magazine. The image of one hand free *UK, 1978*

one hitter *noun* a device designed for holding a single inhalation worth of marijuana *US, 2003*

one hitter quitter; one hitta quitta *noun* a powerful variety of marijuana. It takes just one HIT (an inhalation) to get an intoxicating effect *UK, 1995*

one-hit wonder *noun* a recording artist or group with a single hit song *US, 1994*

one-holed flute *noun* the penis. Variation of FLUTE (the penis) *UK, 1984*

one-horse *adjective* of little consequence, unimportant, inferior, small *US, 1853*

one hundred *noun* a marijuana cigarette dipped in an opium solution *US, 1991*

One Hung Low *nickname* used as a name for a Chinaman. Intended to be humorous, as in the imagined book title 'The Ruptured Chinaman' by One Hung Low *UK, 1984*

one love used as a farewell *US, 2002*

one lunger *noun* a single cylinder motorcycle. Motorcyclists' slang, noted by Partridge, 1979 *US, 1908*

one man *noun* first degree manslaughter *US, 1982*

one-nighter *noun* a sexual relationship lasting a single night *US, 1969*

one-night stand *noun* a sexual relationship lasting a single night *UK, 1937*

one-off *noun* a unique person, object or event. From manufacturing jargon *UK, 2000*

one off the wrist; quick one off the wrist *noun* (of a male) an act of masturbation. The adjective 'quick' (or occasional variations) does not denote an especially speedy endeavour, its purpose is to elaborate the basic term *UK, 1973*

one of the original twelve *noun* an extremely high-ranking officer. US naval aviator usage *US, 1986*

one of these fine days at a vague point in the future. Minor variations abound: 'some fine day', 'one of these fine mornings', etc *UK, 1846*

one of those; one of them *noun* a homosexual *UK, 1933*

one of those days *noun* a day when everything seems to go wrong, or is more hectic than usual *UK, 1936*

one of us *noun* a male homosexual. Especially in the phrase, 'he's one of us' *UK, 1961*

one on! used as a shouted warning that a train is approaching *UK, 1970*

one-one *noun* in horse racing or harness racing, the position one off the rail and one behind the challenger. A favoured position, close enough to challenge the lead and benefiting from the wind broken by the challenger *US, 1997*

one-on-one house *noun* a place where cocaine and heroin can be bought *UK, 1998*

one-o-one *adjective* basic. Alluding to basic college courses such as 'English 101' *US, 1993*

one out by oneself; on one's own; alone *AUSTRALIA, 1950*

one over the eight *adjective* drunk; the final drink that makes you drunk *UK, 1925*

one over the pocket *noun* a woman who is easily available for sex. Adopted from snooker terminology *UK, 2002*

one pen used by small children to ask foreign tourists for money. A request, sometimes a demand. Derives, perhaps, from a 1961 visit to India by US Vice President Lyndon B. Johnson who handed out ballpoint pens marked with his name *INDIA, 2003*

one-percenter; two-percenter *noun* used as a self-identification by members of outlaw motorcycle clubs. When the president of the American Motorcycle Association proclaimed that 99% (or later 98%) of motorcyclists are 'decent, hardworking, law-abiding citizens', outlaw bikers did the maths and proclaimed themselves the remainder *US, 1966*

one-piece overcoat *noun* a condom *UK, 1984*

one-pipper; one pip *noun* a second lieutenant. Army, from the sleeve or shoulder insignia *UK, 1915*

one-plus-one sale *noun* heroin and cocaine sold together *UK, 2002*

one-pub *adjective* (of a town) small enough to have only one public hotel; inconsequential *AUSTRALIA, 1901*

oner *noun* a one-pound note *UK, 1889*

ones *noun* **1** the first landing or floor level in a prison *UK, 1996*. **2** in the gambling game two-up, a throw of a head and a tail *AUSTRALIA, 1911*. ▶ **all the ones** eleven. In Bingo, House or Housey-Housey calling, the formula 'all the' announces a double number *UK, 1943*. ▶ **on the ones and twos** in prison, used of a sex offender, convicted paedophile, etc. A variation of NUMBERED OFF; ON THE NUMBERS *UK, 1996*

ones and twos *noun* shoes *US, 1928*

one-shot wonder *noun* a man who is unable to achieve a second erection within a short time after orgasm *UK, 1997*

one-side *verb* to hit without warning *FIJI, 1995*

one singer, one song; wan singer, wan song used as a call for order when many people are contributing to a debate at the same time. Originally shouted at people who, uninvited, join in a singer's song, and, inevitably, fail to add a pleasing harmony. Popularised by Glaswegian actor, comedian and folk-singer, Billy Connolly (b.1942) *UK: SCOTLAND, 1996*

one-skin joint *noun* a marijuana cigarette made with just one cigarette paper *UK, 2003*

one-skinner *noun* a marijuana cigarette made with just one cigarette paper *UK, 1999*

one-spot *noun* a prison sentence of one year *US, 1949*

one star artist *noun* a second lieutenant. Military, from the sleeve or shoulder insignia. In World War 1 one star – 'one stunt' was an army catchphrase that reflected the frequency with which second lieutenants got killed in their first battle *NEW ZEALAND, 1984*

onesy *noun* an act of urination *AUSTRALIA, 1995*

one-time *noun* the police *US, 1990*

one toke no joke powerful marijuana. Rhyming elaboration on TOKE (to smoke marijuana) *UK, 2000*

one-toke weed *noun* marijuana of such potency that only a few inhalations induce intoxication *US, 1982*

one to one *noun* in betting odds, evens *UK, 1991*

one-track mind *noun* an overwhelming interest in a single topic, especially sex. Especially familiar, to some, in the catchphrase 'you've got a one-track mind', and various elaborations along the lines of 'and it's a dirt-track' *UK, 1984*

one way *noun* LSD. Possibly plays on the type of ticket you would purchase for a conventional 'trip'; TRIP (a hallucinatory drug experience) *US, 1970*

one-way *adjective* heterosexual *US, 1964*

one-way taxi *noun* a hearse *UK, 1981*

one-wire *noun* an electrician. US Navy usage *US, 1998*

one-woman show *noun* (of a female) an act of masturbation. Figurative sense of a theatrical presentation that itself is often critically described as 'intellectual masturbation' *US, 2001*

one word from you and he does as he likes he ignores your commands. With various pronominal variations. Especially popular amongst parents and pet-owners *UK, 1977*

oney *noun* one *UK, 2002*

on for young and old *adjective* having begun in earnest *AUSTRALIA, 1951*

onion *noun* **1** one hundred dollars *US, 1988*. **2** crack cocaine *UK, 2003*. **3** a native Bermudian *BERMUDA, 1985*. **4** a Ford Orion car. Motor trade slang *UK, 2004*. **5** an absolutely unskilled skateboarder. Teen slang; because 'it makes you cry to watch' *UK, 1978*

onion ballad *noun* a painfully sad song. An allusion to the relationship between onions and tears *US, 1981*

onion church *noun* the Greek Orthodox church. From the dome on many Greek Orthodox churches *US, 1997*

onion hotel *noun* a boarding house used by oil field workers *US, 1954*

onion peeler *noun* a switchblade knife *US, 1973*

onions *noun* ▶ **get up your onions** to irritate, to anger. A variation of GET UP YOUR NOSE *UK, 1988*. ▶ **pain in the onions** an irritation; an annoying person *UK, 1988*

on it *adjective* prepared and ready *US, 2000*

onk *noun* the nose *UK, 2002*

onkaparinga; onka *noun* a finger. Rhyming slang, from Onkaparinga, a steeplechase track in Australia *AUSTRALIA, 1967*

onkus *adjective* no good. Origin unknown *AUSTRALIA, 1918*

onliest *adjective* only *US, 1907*

only *adverb* very. Hawaiian youth usage *US, 1982*

only suckers beef used as a catchphrase in Chicago to affirm a guiding principle of that city, that losers should not complain *US, 1982*

on my honour as a Rocket Ranger used as a humorous oath or pledge. On the US children's television programme *Rod Brown of the Rocket Rangers* (CBS, 1953–54), the children in the television audience were asked to pledge on their honour, among other things, 'to chart my course according to the Constitution of the United States of America'. Used in following years with irony by those who had been children during the dark years of the early 1950s *US, 1954*

on my skin used as a profound oath of honour by white prisoners *US, 1989*

OnO used as an Internet shorthand farewell to mean 'over and out' *US, 1997*

on offer *adjective* available *UK, 2000*

on point *adjective* alert, ready for anything. Military; the man 'on point' leads a patrol *UK, 2001*

on the floor, hit the door ▷*see:* DIE ON THE FLOOR, SEVEN AT THE DOOR

on the hob *noun* the penis. Rhyming slang for KNOB *UK, 2003*

on the in in prison *UK, 2000*

on the strength! seriously! *US, 1989*

on time *adjective* excellent *US, 1992*

on top *adjective* **1** about to happen *UK, 1978*. **2** wrong; destroyed or defeated *UK, 1999*

on top! used as a warning that a prison officer is close. From the sense 'something is about to happen' *UK, 1996*

onya used as praise for a job well done *AUSTRALIA, 1948*

on your bike! go away! *UK, 1967*

o-o *noun* a quick inspection, a once-over *US, 1913*

oo-ah *verb* (used of a woman) to sit or lie with legs spread immodestly *NORFOLK ISLAND, 1992*

oodles *noun* a large number; a large amount *US, 1867*

oo-er!; ooo-er! used for expressing surprise, disgust or embarrassment *UK, 1912*

oo-er missus! used for stressing a sexual innuendo, or as a catchphrase-response to such a double-entendre. A narrowing of the senses used for OO-ER! *UK, 2001*

ooga-booga-land *noun* a non-specific African location. A racist notion based on the presumed phonetics of African tribal chants, probably filtered through a Hollywood reality *UK, 1998*

oogley *adjective* good, excellent. Teen slang *US, 1955*

ooh and aah *verb* to express admiration *US, 1957*

ooh la la *noun* a brassiere. Rhyming slang for 'bra' *UK, 1998*

ooh-la-la used as an expression of admiration *US, 1957*

oojah; oojar; oojamaflip; oojah-ma-flip *noun* a gadget; a non-specific thing. Etymology is unknown, however it has been theorised that it may come from Hindustani, or derive as a corruption of the nautical term 'hook-me-dinghy'; earlier variations include 'ooja-ka-piv' and 'ooja-cum-pivvy' *UK, 1917*

Ookpik *noun* a doll that looks like an owl *CANADA, 1964*

oolies *noun* marijuana *UK, 2003*

ooloo *noun* a knife used by Eskimo women *CANADA, 1966*

oomph *noun* the quality of sexual attraction; hence enthusiasm, vigour, energy. Echoic, from the mating bellow (perhaps of a bull) *US, 1937*

oonock *noun* an Eskimo implement for harpooning seals *CANADA, 1941*

oop north *adjective* in the North of England. A parodic use of a non-specific northern accent *UK, 2002*

oop-pa-a-da used as a greeting by bebop musicians and followers. A highly stylised greeting, widely publicised in the early years of bop jazz, used sparingly *US, 1949*

oops! used in response to an accident or mistake, suggesting an acknowledgement of fault *US, 1989*

ooroo goodbye. Variant of HOOROO *AUSTRALIA, 1967*

ooze *verb* to move, especially slowly, carefully, without enthusiasm *US, 1929*

op *noun* **1** a surgical operation *UK, 1925*. **2** an operator *US, 1930*. **3** a private detective; a private operator *US, 1947*. **4** a military operation *UK, 1996*

op *verb* to operate; to do; to set up *US, 1953*

OP *adjective* other people's *US, 1972*

OPB *noun* used as an initialism for other people's brand, a mythical and humorous brand of cigarettes *US, 1970*

ope *noun* opium; heroin. An abbreviation of 'opium' *UK, 1929*

open *noun* in computing, a left parenthesis – the (*US, 1991*

open *verb* **1** used of a film actor who is a big enough box office attraction that success of a film project is almost guaranteed, to start and carry such a film production *US, 2003*. **2** to turn on *CANADA, 2002*. ▶ **open the kimono** of a business, to reveal company accounts, to publish business information. Business slang *UK, 1998*. ▶ **open the lunchbox** to fart *US, 1997*

open *adjective* **1** excited; drunk or drug-intoxicated; infatuated. From HAVE YOUR NOSE OPEN *US, 1995*. **2** in organised crime, safe for anyone without fear of violence *US, 1963*

open at both ends *adjective* in poker, four cards in sequence that could form a five-card straight with a draw at either end of the sequence *US, 1988*

open door *noun* in surfing, a wave that breaks such that the surfer can ride away from the peak onto the shoulder *US, 1963*

openers *noun* ▶ **for openers** to begin with; for starters *AUSTRALIA, 1969*

open go *noun* a total lack of restriction *AUSTRALIA, 1940*

open heifer *noun* a woman looking for a mate *CANADA, 1987*

open-kimono *adjective* characterised by complete honesty and full disclosure. Sometimes formulated as OPEN THE KIMONO or a variation thereon. Ronin International, a computer consulting firm, promises 'open-kimono' in its published mission statement, explaining that the term 'stems from feudal Japanese times where the term signified that the party will hide nothing within his clothing (the kimono was the dominant clothing of that era) that could conceivably be used as a weapon' *US, 1974*

open-mike *adjective* said of a club where anybody may perform briefly and without payment *US, 1999*

open room *noun* an establishment where it is possible to bet on sporting events and listen to or watch the event as it takes place *US, 1978*

open season *noun* said when there are a lot of police monitoring vehicle speeds on a stretch of road *US, 1976*

open shadow *noun* in a surveillance operation, a follower who lets himself be spotted *US, 1958*

open slather *noun* unrestrained freedom. From British dialect *slather* (to spill, to squander) *AUSTRALIA, 1919*

open work *noun* safecracking *US, 1949*

opera *noun* a travelling show *US, 1980*

Operation Big Switch *noun* the final exchange of prisoners of war in Korea in 1953 *US, 1964*

Operation Killer *noun* a main US offensive in the Korean war, 20th February–6th March 1951 *US, 1968*

Operation Little Switch *noun* a preliminary exchange of prisoners of war in Korea in 1953 *US, 1964*

Operation Yo-Yo *noun* the battle for Wosan, North Korea, in October 1950. So named by the US Marines who arrived at Wosan too late to take part in the capture because they had sailed back and forth around Wosan as the harbour was cleared of mines *US, 1964*

operator *noun* **1** someone who is popular, crafty and perhaps manipulative *US, 1944*. **2** a drug dealer *US, 1952*

opie switch *noun* in car repair, an oil pressure switch *US, 1992*

OPM *noun* other people's money *US, 1901*

oppo *noun* a friend, a pal. Short for 'opposite number' *UK, 1939*

opposite *adjective* obscene, especially of language *SOUTH AFRICA, 1946*

op shop *noun* a charity store. From 'opportunity shop' *AUSTRALIA, 1976*

optic *noun* **1** an eye *UK, 1600*. **2** a look. Short for OPTIC NERVE *AUSTRALIA, 1974*

optical illusions *noun* LSD. From the effect of the drug *UK, 1998*

optic nerve *noun* a look. Rhyming slang for PERV *AUSTRALIA, 1977*

orace *noun* an offensive, despicable person; a clumsy person; a socially awkward person. Recorded in contemporary gay use *UK, 2003*

oral *noun* oral sex. A 2002 Incident Report from the Sausalito (California) Police Department describes the activities at a local massage parlour as follows: 'Only a few girls will do full service (sexual intercourse) and oral (oral copulation) massages' *US, 2002*

orale hello. Border Spanish used in English conversation by Mexican-Americans *US, 1950*

orange *noun* a tablet of dextroamphetamine sulphate (trade name Dexedrine™), a central nervous system stimulant *US, 1967*

orange barrel *noun* a type of LSD *UK, 2003*

orange bud *noun* marijuana. From the colour *UK, 2001*

Orange Crush *noun* in Canadian prisons, a special squad used to restore calm after a disturbance *CANADA, 2002*

orange cube *noun* a dose of LSD given on a sugar cube *US, 1975*

orange haze *noun* a type of LSD *UK, 2003*

orange line *noun* heroin *UK, 2002*

orange magic *noun* a type of LSD *UK, 1996*

orange micro *noun* a type of LSD *UK, 2003*

orange peel *noun* a highly visible orange jacket worn by railway workers *UK, 1970*

orange-peel *verb* (used of freshly applied paint) to wrinkle or form small ridges *US, 1998*

orange pip; orange *noun* a Japanese person. Rhyming slang for NIP *UK, 1979*

orange squash; orange *noun* money. Rhyming slang for DOSH *UK, 1998*

orange sunshine *noun* a type of LSD *US, 1988*

orange wedge *noun* a type of LSD *UK, 2003*

orbit *verb* to engage in oral sex *US, 1985*

orbital *noun* **1** a person who lives permanently in the vicinity of one travellers' settlement. Used by late 1980s – early 90s counterculture travellers *UK, 1999*. **2** a breast. Recorded in contemporary gay usage *UK, 2003*

orchestra stalls; orchestras; orchestrals; orks *noun* the testicles. Rhyming slang for BALLS, based on the front seating in a theatre auditorium. Probably late C19 or early C20 but not recorded until 1960 *UK, 1979*

orchid *noun* a beautiful woman *US, 1948*

order; orderly *verb* **1** to go, to leave *UK, 1997*. **2** to orgasm. From an earlier sense as 'leave', thus 'to come' (to orgasm) *UK, 2002*

orderly daughters *noun* the police *UK, 2002*

order of the boot *noun* dismissal from work; the sack *UK, 1917*

ordinary *adjective* **1** not very good; below standard *AUSTRALIA, 1992*. **2** used by bookmakers for describing a losing day *AUSTRALIA, 1989*

Oregon boots *noun* leg irons *US, 1949*

or else used for indicating consequences that will be unwelcome *UK, 1833*

Oreo *noun* a black person whose values are seen as white values. Borrowed from a trade name of a chocolate biscuit with a white filling. Never used kindly *US, 1968*

orft *adverb* off. A deliberately illiterate pronunciation for jocular effect; especially familiar in 'orft we jolly well go', a catchphrase of broadcaster Jimmy Young (b.1923) *UK, 1980*

organ *noun* **1** a car radio. From the language of used car sales *US, 1978*. **2** the penis. Euphemistic *UK, 1903*

organ-arse *noun* a person who deliberately farts in company *AUSTRALIA, 1998*

organ donor *noun* a motorcyclist who is not wearing a crash helmet *US, 1994*

organ grinder *noun* a criminal's bodyguard or enforcer. Rhyming slang for MINDER *UK, 1992*

organized chicken shit *noun* Officer Candidate School. From the initials *US, 1992*

orgasm! used for registering any transitory pleasure *UK, 2001*

orgasmic *adjective* great, excellent. Hyperbole, probably *US, 1999*

orge *verb* to indulge in an excess of 'sinful' pleasures, especially of food, drugs, shopping or sex. Based on 'orgy', informed by 'gorge' *UK, 1999*

orgy room *noun* a room designated for group sex *US, 1969*

Oriental dancer *noun* in circus and carnival usage, a sexually explicit female dancer *US, 1981*

Orient Express *noun* **1** any route used to smuggle opiates from Southeast Asia to Europe, especially via Amsterdam. An allusion to the famed Paris-to-Istanbul train *US, 1982*. **2** the #7 subway line to Flushing, Queens, New York. An allusion to the large number of Asian-Americans who commute on this line *US, 1997*

orifice *noun* **1** an office. Jocular *UK, 1984*. **2** a (police) officer. Jocular; certainly since the late 1990s *UK, 1996*

original *noun* **1** an unconventional or eccentric person *UK, 1824*. **2** a male prisoner who selects and maintains a primary sexual partner in jail *US, 1972*

original gangster *noun* a member of the founding generation of a youth gang; somebody who is so committed to a gang that he remains a gang member at all costs *US, 1995*

originals *noun* the clothes worn by a member of Hell's Angels when he is initiated into the gang, and worn thereafter in perpetuity *US, 1966*

or, in English used as a humorous bridge between a butchered attempt at verbalisation and an attempt to correct. Coined as a self-parody by ESPN's Keith Olberman *US, 1997*

O-ring *noun* a novice surfer; a dolt *US, 1992*

orinoco; orinoko *noun* **1** cocoa. Rhyming slang. Also shortened to 'ori' *UK, 1992*. **2** a poker. Rhyming slang. Also variant 'orinoker' *UK, 1992*

or is he?; or am I?; or are you? a catchphrase added to a statement for rhetorical effect *UK, 1984*

o'river goodbye. An intentional mispronunciation of the French *US, 1991*

ornament *noun* on the railways, a stationmaster *US, 1977*

ornery *adjective* ill-humoured and uncooperative *US, 1816*

orphan *noun* **1** in craps, a bet on the table that a gambler has forgotten belongs to him *US, 1981*. **2** a computer that has been phased out due to technological advances *US, 1986*

orphan Annie; orphan *noun* the vagina. Rhyming slang for FANNY, formed from the character Little Orphan Annie, introduced to the US in comic strip form in 1924, but best known to British audiences from *Annie* the stage-musical, 1977, and film, 1982 *UK, 1998*

or something used as a final tag, a vague et cetera *UK, 1961*

ort *noun* the anus. Origin unknown *AUSTRALIA, 1952*

orthopod *noun* an orthopaedist *UK, 1960*

or what!? used as an all-purpose, sentence-ending intensifier *TRINIDAD AND TOBAGO, 1983*

or whatever used as a non-specific alternative to a previously stated noun *UK, 1967*

or what-have-you used as a non-specific continuation of a list or suggestion of further details *UK, 1948*

Osama yo mama used as a general-purpose insult. Teen slang; combines 'yo mama!' (a general-purpose insult) with the name of Osama bin Laden, presumed to be ultimately responsible for the atrocities of 11th September 2001 *US, 2002*

Oscar *noun* **1** a male homosexual. Surely a reference to Oscar Wilde *US, 1967*. **2** an offensive, unlikeable person *US, 1905*. **3** a prejudiced, narrow-minded person *US, 1973*. **4** a handgun *US, 1949*

Oscar Asche; Oscar Ash; oscar *noun* cash; money. Rhyming slang, formed on the name of Australian actor, producer and director, Oscar Asche (1871–1936) *AUSTRALIA, 1905*

Oscar Slater *adverb* later. Glasgow rhyming slang, formed from a man who, in 1909, was wrongly convicted of murder in a famous and scandalous travesty of justice; Arthur Conan Doyle, author of the *Sherlock Holmes* stories, took an interest and caused uproar by publishing *The Case of Oscar Slater* in defence of the man *UK: SCOTLAND, 1985*

O-sign *noun* the open mouth of a very sick hospital patient. Medical wit; an especially humorous image when the 'O-sign' becomes the Q-SIGN (as above but with the tongue hanging out) *US, 1980*

Ossie Potter *noun* water. Rhyming slang, from the name of a prominent Australian racehorse owner of the 1950s *AUSTRALIA, 1989*

ossifer; occifer *noun* a police officer. An intentional metathesis, spoken in imitation of the slurred speech of intoxication *US, 1819*

ossified *adjective* very drunk *US, 1901*

OT and E *adjective* over-tired and emotional. Upper-class society usage to describe children who are behaving unsociably. To be TIRED AND EMOTIONAL (drunk) is usually a condition for older family members *UK, 1982*

other *noun* sexual intercourse, especially heterosexual but also homosexual. Mainly used as a BIT OF THE OTHER. Partridge, in the 1st edition of his *Dictionary of Slang and Unconventional English*, 1937, suggests that the unqualified term indicates 'homosexuality as a criminal offence' and that the other alternative is 'prostitution' *UK, 1937*

other half *noun* a significant other, husband or wife *UK, 1976*

other lot *noun* the police *UK, 2001*

Other People *noun* among criminals, the police *UK, 2000*

others *noun* homosexuals *FIJI, 1996*

other side *noun* homosexuality. Usually in a phrase such as 'gone over to the other side'. Collected in 1960 *BARBADOS, 1960*

other thing *noun* ▶ **do the other thing!** used as an expression of contemptuous dismissal: do as you please! *UK, 1848*. ▶ **the other thing 1** the penis. Euphemistic *UK, 1923*. **2** sexual intercourse. Euphemistic *UK, 1846*

OTL *adjective* distracted, foolish, stupid. An abbreviation of OUT TO LUNCH *US, 1968*

OTOH used as Internet shorthand to mean 'on the other hand' *US, 1995*

OTR *adjective* literally, experiencing the bleed period of the menstrual cycle; figuratively, complaining. An initialism of ON THE RAG *US, 1968*

OTT *adjective* to excess; beyond the boundaries of conventional expectations; exaggerated. Ultimately from World War 1 troops leaving the trenches to attack the enemy; 'going over the top' *UK, 1999*

otto; otter; otta *adjective* eight; eight (pre-decimal) pence. Polari, from Italian *octo* via parleyaree *UK, 1893*

ouch *noun* an injury *US, 1962*

ouch! how unfortunate! *US, 1997*

ouchy *adjective* (used of a racehorse) sore *US, 1976*

oudish *adjective* used for expressing approval *UK, 2003*

ought hole *noun* in trucking, the shifting position for the lowest gear *US, 1971*

oughties *noun* the first decade of the 21st century *UK, 2003*

ouija board *noun* in horse racing, the official odds board at the racetrack *US, 1951*

oul fella *noun* a father *IRELAND, 1989*

oul one; auld wan; old dear *noun* a mother *IRELAND, 1989*

ounce man *noun* a drug dealer at the wholesale level, buying and selling in ounces *US, 1966*

ounce of baccy; ouncer *noun* a Pakistani. Rhyming slang for PAKI, formed from a measurement of tobacco *UK, 1992*

our concrete brethren *noun* members of the US Air Force. US Army usage *US, 1998*

our friend with the talking brooch *noun* a uniformed police officer. A reference to the police radio worn on the uniform's breast *UK, 1992*

out *noun* an excuse, an alibi, a means of avoiding responsibility or difficulty *US, 1910*. ▶ **on the out** used of a prisoner when not imprisoned *UK, 1984*

out *verb* **1** to disclose another person's homosexuality. Usually done to a public figure, and most commonly to one who is publicly anti-homosexual, such as J. Edgar Hoover or the cadre of gay men who surrounded Lt Col. Oliver North in the Reagan White House *US, 1990*. **2** to suspend or ban a player or competitor *AUSTRALIA, 1962*. ▶ **out someone's light** to kill someone *TRINIDAD AND TOBAGO, 1987*

out *adjective* **1** publicly and openly homosexual. An abbreviation of the full 'out of the CLOSET' *UK, 1979*. **2** unfashionable; no longer fashionable *UK, 1966*. **3** no longer imprisoned *UK, 1974*. **4** experiencing the bleed period of the menstrual cycle *US, 2000*

out used in farewell *US, 1993*

outa here; outta here *adjective* about to leave *US, 1980*

out-and-out *adjective* complete, absolute, thorough-going *UK, 1813*

out-and-outer *noun* a thorough-going person or thing; an absolute lie *UK, 1812*

outback *noun* the remote regions of Australia *AUSTRALIA, 1893*. ▶ **go outback** to go to the toilet for the purpose of defecation *AUSTRALIA, 1979*

outback *adjective* situated in a remote country area *AUSTRALIA, 1893*

out-country *noun* during the Vietnam war, used for reference to any other country in Southeast Asia *US, 1991*

outdoors *adverb* ▶ **all outdoors** a great amount *US, 1830*

outer *noun* ▶ **on the outer** excluded from the mainstream; out of favour; ostracised *AUSTRALIA, 1902*

outerlimits *noun* a combination of crack cocaine and LSD *UK, 1998*

outers *noun* an excuse, an alibi; a means of escape, or of avoiding responsibility *UK, 1977*

outers *adjective* drug-intoxicated. From a number of phrases that commence 'out of' *UK, 2000*

outfit *noun* **1** a criminal organisation *US, 1933*. **2** a still used in the illegal production of alcohol *US, 1974*. **3** heroin *UK, 2003*. **4** the needle and syringe used to inject a drug *US, 1951*. **5** a vehicle. Idaho usage *US, 1997*

out for the count *adjective* fast asleep. From boxing *UK, 1984*

out front *adjective* direct, honest *US, 1968*

outgribing *noun* a written contribution to a single-interest fan magazine *US, 1982*

outhole *noun* in pinball, the hole beneath the flippers through which a ball leaves play *US, 1977*

outhouse *noun* in poker, a full house (three of a kind and a pair) that is inferior to another full house hand *US, 1996*

outie *noun* an outward-turned navel *US, 1966*

outie *adverb* ▶ **be outie** to leave *US, 1995*

outlaw *noun* **1** a prostitute working without the services of a pimp *US, 1935*. **2** a worker who has been identified as an activist troublemaker and thus blacklisted *US, 1977*. **3** a horse that cannot be tamed or is very difficult to handle *AUSTRALIA, 1900*

outlaw *verb* on the railways, to exceed the 16-hour maximum legal work limit *US, 1968*

outlaw *adjective* in roller derby, outside the official Roller Derby League *US, 1999*

outlet *noun* a bootlegger's house *CANADA, 1999*

out like a light *adjective* suddenly and deeply unconscious *UK, 1944*

out of here used as a farewell *US, 1991*

out of it *adjective* **1** crazy, mentally ill *US, 1979*. **2** in an advanced a state of drug- or drink-intoxication *US, 1963*

out of order; bang out of order *adjective* used to describe behaviour that is unacceptable *UK, 1979*

out of sight; outasight *adjective* excellent, amazing. Nearly a hundred years old before being swept up as a core adjective of the 1960s hippie lexicon *US, 1876*

out of the money *adjective* in horse and dog racing, finished below third place *US, 1988*

out of this world *adjective* extraordinary *US, 1928*

out of town *adjective* used to describe behaviour that is unacceptable *US, 1942*

out of whack *adjective* out of tune, malfunctioning *US, 1885*

out-out *verb* to put out *BARBADOS, 1965*

outro *noun* the concluding section, especially of music or broadcast-programmes. The opposite of INTRO (introduction) *UK, 1967*

outrun *verb* ▶ **outrun the note** (of a car) to last longer than it takes to pay off the loan incurred to buy it *US, 1992*

outs *noun* in poker, the playing of a weak hand in the hope of a drastic improvement in drawing *US, 1979*

outside *noun* **1** in Alaska, anywhere in the US other than Alaska *US, 1900*. **2** the world outside the armed forces *US, 1898*

outside *adjective* **1** out of the ordinary *US, 1969*. **2** (of a child) illegitimate *TRINIDAD AND TOBAGO, 1952*. **3** (of a lover) adulterous *TRINIDAD AND TOBAGO, 1971*. **4** in surfing, seaward of the swell *US, 1963*

outside *adverb* not in prison *US, 1871*. ▶ **get outside of** to eat *US, 1869*

outside! used for calling to the attention of other surfers the presence of an approaching series of waves seaward *US, 1964* ▷*see:* **COME OUTSIDE!**

outside child *noun* an illegitimate child *CAYMAN ISLANDS, 1985*

outside work *noun* any external alteration of dice for cheating *US, 1963*

outstanding *adjective* excellent. Conventional English converted to slang by attitude and a drawn-out pronunciation *US, 1964*

out there *adjective* **1** in a state of extreme marijuana-intoxication *US, 1977*. **2** in the alternative society; out of the mainstream *US, 1975*. **3** crazy, mentally ill *UK, 1996*

out ticket *noun* in horse racing, a winning bet not presented for payment on the day of the race *US, 1982*

out to lunch weird, being in a state that does not conform to peer-group expectations; distracted;crazy *US, 1955*

oven *noun* ▶ **in the oven** pregnant. Especially in the phrase 'bun in the oven' *UK, 1937*

over *adjective* **1** popular with the audience. Professional wrestling usage *US, 1999*. **2** disgusted by; done with *US, 1983*

overamp *verb* to overdose on narcotics *US, 1967*

over-and-under *noun* **1** a capsule containing both a barbiturate and an amphetamine *US, 1973*. **2** an M-16 rifle with an M-79 grenade launcher tube under the rifle barrel *US, 1972*

overboard *adjective* drunk *US, 1948*. ▶ **go overboard 1** to be over-enthusiastic about something, to exaggerate *US, 1931*. **2** to refuse or fail to pay a gambling debt *US, 1947*

over-boogie *verb* to over-indulge in the pleasures of vice *US, 1982*

overbroke *adjective* used of betting with no profit margin for the bookmaker *UK, 1991*

overcoat *noun* **1** a coffin *US, 1949*. **2** in pool, a player who has mastered the foibles of a particular table *US, 1990*

overcoat maker *noun* an undertaker. Rhyming slang, with more than a passing reference to (wooden) OVERCOAT (a coffin) *UK, 1992*

overdue *adjective* used of a criminal who, not having been convicted of a crime, is statistically likely to, or should, be found guilty of something (if there is any justice). Police use *UK, 1984*

overfix *verb* to overdose using a drug *US, 1972*

overground *noun* a commercialised milieu for a previously underground culture *UK, 2001*

overjolt *noun* a drug overdose *US, 1959*

overjolt *verb* to suffer a drug overdose *UK, 1983*

overland route *noun* ▶ **to take the overland route** in horse racing, to race on the outside portion of the track because a horse prefers passing around a pack to accelerating through it *US, 1947*

overlay *noun* in horse racing, a situation where a horse that should win a race is given higher odds than it should *US, 1965*

over-much *adjective* astonishing, difficult to believe *US, 1968*

over my dead body used as an expression of the strongest will to resist. Hyperbole *UK, 1936*

overparted *adjective* having been cast in a *part* that demands more of an actor than he or she is capable of *UK, 2003*

overripe fruit *noun* an older homosexual man *UK, 1979*

over-round *adjective* used of betting when the probable or actual profit margin is entirely in a bookmaker's favour *UK, 1991*

overs *noun* **1** more money than you need *UK, 2000*. **2** surplus or undivided profits from a crime *UK, 1991*. **3** money a bookmaker has overpaid *UK, 1991*. **4** a wager at odds better than those prevailing elsewhere; any extravagence *AUSTRALIA, 1989*. **5** in a game of poker, the small amount of money left in the centre of the table after a pot is divided among two or more players, held over for the next hand *US, 1988*

over there *noun* in Europe. Originally used of the military during World War 1 *AUSTRALIA, 1967*

over the shoulder boulder holder *noun* a brassiere *UK, 1998*

ovies *noun* overtime pay *UK, 2002*

ow *noun* ▶ **on the ow** not in prison. A shortening of 'on the outside' *UK, 2002*

OW *noun* a wife, a girlfriend. Citizens' band radio slang, abbreviated from OLD WOMAN *UK, 1981*

owf; owff *verb* to steal *UK, 2003*

owie *noun* any minor injury. Children's vocabulary *US, 1988*

o-without *noun* an act of oral sex performed without the protection of a condom, especially when advertised as a service offered by a prostitute. From O-LEVELS (oral sex) *UK, 2003*

owl *noun* **1** on the railways, anything related to the night, such as a late-night train *US, 1946*. **2** marijuana. A possible play on HOOTER (a large marijuana cigarette) *UK, 2003*

owlhead *noun* a revolver. Originally referred to a revolver manufactured by Iver Johnson Arms, featuring an owlhead logo; later applied to any revolver *US, 1927*

Owl Shit Junction *noun* any extremely remote town *US, 1977*

own *verb* to dominate; to command complete deference *US, 1997*

ownio *adjective* ▶ **on your ownio** alone *IRELAND, 1922*

ownsome *adjective* ▶ **on your ownsome** alone *UK, 1939*

own up *verb* to admit, to confess *US, 1853*

own-way *adjective* obstinate, mulish *BARBADOS, 1965*

Owsley; Owsley acid; owsley *noun* high quality LSD. From the name of legendary LSD manufacturer Augustus Owsley Stanley III. Other variations include: 'Owsley blue dot'; 'Owsley blues'; 'Owsley power'; 'Owsley purple'; PURPLE OWSLEY 'pink Owsley'; 'white Owsley'; 'Owsley's stuff'; 'Owsleys' *US, 1967*

owt *noun* something, anything. A dialect word from northern England for conventional 'aught'; made popular by the televison programme *Coronation Street*, and in clichéd phrases such as 'you don't get owt for nowt' *UK, 1847*

owzat?; zat? as an appeal to a cricket umpire, how's that? *UK, 1934*

Oxford *noun* a dollar *AUSTRALIA, 1990*

Oxford bag *noun* a cigarette. Rhyming slang for FAG *UK, 1998*

Oxford scholar; Oxford; scholar *noun* **1** (of pre-decimalisation currency) five shillings; (post-1971) 25p. Rhyming slang for DOLLAR (five shillings). The Oxford English Dictionary notes reported usage in southwest England in the 1870s *UK, 1938*. **2** a dollar. Rhyming slang *AUSTRALIA, 1937*

Oxo cube *noun* the London Underground. Rhyming slang for THE TUBE based on the branded beef extract, manufactured in cube form since 1909 *UK, 1960*

oxy *noun* the synthetic opiate oxycodone used recreationally; a capsule of OxyContin™ *US, 2000*

oxy *adjective* having a second-hand or dated appearance. Derives from the appearance of goods sold in the charity shops of Oxfam *UK, 2003*

oxygen section *noun* seats in a stadium or coliseum that are high up and far from the action *US, 1993*

oy gevalt! used for expressing a lament, protest, dismay or delight. Yiddish from German *US, 1968*

oyster *noun* **1** the vagina. From an image of the labia, but note also the following sense as 'the mouth' *UK, 1707*. **2** the mouth, especially as an instrument of homosexual oral sex. Following from the previous sense *UK, 2002*. **3** a gob of thick phlegm. From the appearance. First recorded in *A Classical Dictionary of the Vulgar Tongue*, Francis Grose, 1785, with the further observation 'spit by a consumptive man' *UK, 1785*

oyster stew *noun* cocaine *UK, 2002*

oy vey! used for expressing surprise. Yiddish *US, 1992*

Oz *nickname* Australia. Although the pronunciation would always have had a final 'z' (the 's' becomes voiced) it was first recorded as 'Oss' in 1908 (*Australian National Dictionary*), and not as 'Oz' until 1944, which spelling is partially influenced by the immensely popular 1939 film *The Wizard of Oz*. Became common in the 1970s *AUSTRALIA, 1908*

Oz *adjective* Australian *AUSTRALIA, 1974*

OZ; oh-zee *noun* an ounce of marijuana or other drugs. Spelling out the standard abbreviation for 'ounce' *US, 1933*

ozone *noun* **1** the highest seats in a stadium or auditorium, farthest from the action *US, 1980*. **2** a state of drug or alcohol intoxication *US, 1971*. **3** phencyclidine, the recreational drug known as PCP or angel dust *US, 1994*. **4** marijuana *UK, 2003*

ozoner *noun* an outdoor cinema *US, 1948*

ozone ranger *noun* a person who appears to live in an inner-world, not necessarily as a result of drug or alcohol consumption *US, 1978*

ozone theatre *noun* an outdoor cinema *US, 1957*

Ozzie *adjective* Australian. Variant spelling, representing pronunciation, of AUSSIE *AUSTRALIA, 1918*

ozzy; ozzie *noun* ▷*see:* HOZZY

Pp

P *noun* **1** pure or nearly pure heroin *US, 1971.* **2** a Vietnamese piastre *US, 1965*

P *adjective* **1** pretty. Hawaiian youth usage *US, 1982.* **2** a price *UK, 1997*

-p *suffix* used for turning a word into a question *US, 1981*

P-38 *noun* **1** a police-issue .38 calibre revolver *US, 1976.* **2** in Vietnam war usage, the small can-opener included with individual field rations. A humorous application of bureaucratic nomenclature *US, 1968*

P45 *noun* ▶ **give someone their P45** to break off a romantic relationship with someone. A P45 is the form given by an employer to a dismissed employee *UK: SCOTLAND, 1996*

pa *noun* a father; used to address your father. An abbreviation of 'papa' *UK, 1811*

PA a prosecuting attorney *US, 1992*

Pablo *noun* cocaine. In memory of Colombian Pablo Escobar (1949–93) of the medellín Cartel *UK, 1996*

Pachuco *noun* a young Mexican-American, especially a tough or gang member. A highly stylised fashion sense, a private language and a rage against white oppression of the 1940s *US, 1943*

Pacific steroid *noun* the Southeast Asian plant, taro. Common in conversation in New Zealand since the 1990s *NEW ZEALAND, 2002*

pack *noun* **1** a *pack*age of illegal drugs, especially heroin. Also variant 'packet' *US, 1952.* **2** marijuana *UK, 2003.* **3** in the used car business, a fixed amount that is added to the price the dealer has paid for the car *US, 1975.* ▶ **go to the pack** to deteriorate *AUSTRALIA, 1919*

pack *verb* **1** to carry a weapon, usually a concealed one *US, 1949.* **2** to tuck the male genitals into the left or right trouser leg *US, 1972.* **3** to be fearful. A shortening of PACK SHIT *AUSTRALIA, 1988.* **4** while snowboarding, to hit the snow hard *US, 1990.* **5** to take someone along on a motorcycle cruise *US, 1966.* ▶ **pack a punch** of a thing, to be powerful. A figurative use of the pugilistic sense *US, 1938.* ▶ **pack a rod** to carry a gun. In literature by 1940 *US, 1940.* ▶ **pack a sad** to break off a relationship *NEW ZEALAND, 1994.* ▶ **pack a shitty 1** to sulk *AUSTRALIA, 1985.* **2** to become angry *NEW ZEALAND, 1998.* ▶ **pack death** to be fearful *AUSTRALIA, 1975.* ▶ **pack double** to carry a passenger on a motorcycle *US, 2000.* ▶ **pack fudge** to play the active role in anal sex *US, 1987.* ▶ **pack heat** to carry a gun *US, 1930.* ▶ **pack it** to be fearful. Euphemistic for PACK SHIT *AUSTRALIA, 1945.* ▶ **pack shit; pack the shits** to be fearful. The metaphor is of one so scared that they are straining not to shit themselves *AUSTRALIA, 1971.* ▶ **pack the cracks** to endure injections of collagen *US, 1997.* ▶ **pack the payment** in new car sales, to make a sale for a price slightly below what the customer has said they are willing to spend *US, 1989.* ▶ **pack'em; pack them** to be fearful. Euphemistic for PACK THE SHITS *AUSTRALIA, 1944*

package *noun* **1** a man's genitals as seen through trousers *US, 1997.* **2** a good-looking woman *US, 1945.* **3** the female posterior *US, 2001.* **4** a sexually transmitted infection, especially gonorrhoea *US, 1950.* **5** AIDS or HIV *US, 2002*

package of trouble *noun* the bleed period of the menstrual cycle *US, 1999*

pack away *verb* to consume food or drink with gusto *AUSTRALIA, 1972*

Packer-backer-maki *noun* a beer-drinking, snow-suit wearing, Skoal-chewing, snowmobile-riding fan of the Green Bay Packer professional football team. Michigan Upper Peninsula usage *US, 2004*

packet *noun* **1** the genitals, especially as may be hinted at or imagined when dressed, usually male. Gay slang *UK, 2002.* **2** a large sum of money *UK, 1922*

packet of three; pack of three *noun* a packet of three condoms. A dated semi-euphemism that was widespread before the onset of AIDS and the subsequent positive marketing for condoms *UK, 1996*

pack horse *noun* a person, usually a guard, who brings contraband into prison *US, 1984*

packie *noun* an off-licence. From US states where off-licences are known as 'package stores' *US, 1991*

pack in; pack up *verb* to stop; to cease an activity; to retire *US, 1942*

pack of rocks *noun* a packet of ready-to-smoke marijuana fashioned in the manner of cigarettes. An abbreviation of 'pack of rockets' *UK, 2003*

pack out *verb* to unpack *SOUTH AFRICA, 1969*

pack-rape *noun* rape by a gang of men in succession *AUSTRALIA, 1969*

pack-rape *verb* (of a gang of men) to serially rape a woman *AUSTRALIA, 1965*

pack-rapist *noun* a person who commits pack-rape *AUSTRALIA, 1972*

pack-sack citizen *noun* a short-term resident of any place, living, as it were, out of a packsack (backpack or rucksack) *CANADA, 1966*

pack up *verb* to cease doing something; to retire from work (of a machine, etc) to stop working because of a fault *UK, 1925.* ▶ **pack up shop** to cease trading *UK, 2003*

pacotee *noun* a sexually available woman. From the French and Spanish for 'inferior goods', at times corrupted back into English as 'pack o' tea' *TRINIDAD AND TOBAGO, 1950*

pacy; pacey *adjective* fast, speedy *UK, 1906*

pad *noun* **1** an apartment or house; a room, especially a bedroom. In the C18 'pad' referred to a bed. By the 1930s, it took on the new meaning and was spread by jazz musicians. Still heard, with a retro feel *US, 1938.* **2** a bed *UK, 1718.* **3** a prison cell *US, 1943.* **4** a padded cell *UK, 1996.* **5** the bribery paid by a criminal enterprise to police *US, 1970.* **6** an animal track *AUSTRALIA, 1893.* ▶ **on the pad** bribed *US, 1971*

pad *verb* **1** to reside *US, 1963.* **2** (used of police) to add to the narcotics confiscated from a suspect in order to render the charge against them more serious *US, 1972.* ▶ **pad the ring** in horse racing, to place many small bets on several horses in a race while placing a large bet on one horse away from the track, hoping that the small bets on other horses will drive the odds on your horse up *US, 1951*

paddle *noun* on the railways, a semaphore signal *US, 1977*

paddle *verb* in horse racing, to try hard without success *AUSTRALIA, 1989.* ▶ **paddle the pickle** (of a male) to masturbate *US, 1967.* ▶ **paddle the pink canoe** (of a female) to masturbate *UK, 2004*

paddle bull *noun* a young male moose, whose unbranched antlers look like table tennis bats *CANADA, 1989*

paddle pop *noun* a block of ice. Rhyming slang *NEW ZEALAND, 1998*

paddock-basher *noun* a worn-out old vehicle used to drive around a country property *AUSTRALIA, 1983*

pad down *verb* to go to sleep *US, 1993*

paddy *noun* **1** a white person *US, 1945.* **2** a police officer *US, 1946.* **3** a temper, a rage *UK, 1894*

Paddy *noun* an Irish person *UK, 1780*

Paddy *nickname* used as a nickname for any Irishman. Diminutive of the name Patrick *UK, 1959*

Paddy and Mick *noun* a pick-axe. Rhyming slang, drawing on the stereotype of Irish labourers *UK, 1998*

Paddy and Mick *adjective* stupid. Rhyming slang for THICK, drawing on an Irish stereotype *UK, 1992*

paddy hustler *noun* a criminal who targets white people as victims *US, 1970*

Paddy McGuigan *noun* dancing, jigging. Glasgow rhyming slang for 'jiggin', formed on no Irishman in particular *UK: SCOTLAND, 1996*

Paddy McGuire *noun* a fire. Glasgow rhyming slang, formed on no Irishman in particular *UK: SCOTLAND, 1988*

Paddy O'Rourke *verb* to talk. Rhyming slang; derivation unknown *UK, 1998*

Paddy's Day *nickname* St Patrick Day. A national holiday in Ireland to celebrate St Patrick, Ireland's patron saint *IRELAND, 2003*

Paddy's pig *noun* the epitome of ignorance *NEW ZEALAND, 1974*

Paddy's taxi *noun* a police 'Panda' car *UK, 1969*

paddy strength *noun* in the Vietnam war, the combat strength of a unit, measured by the actual number of troops in the field *US, 1974*

Paddy's Wigwam *nickname* the Roman Catholic Metropolitan Cathedral in Liverpool. 'Wigwam' is an obvious simile for the shape of the 1960s building, PADDY (an Irishman) reflects a cultural perception of Roman Catholics *UK, 2003*

paddy wagon *noun* a police transport van *US, 1909*

Paddy water *noun* Guinness™ Irish stout. From PADDY (an Irish person) *UK, 2000*

paddywood *noun* a white person. Not used kindly *US, 1980*

padiddle *noun* a car with only one headlight functioning. A childish word for the childish activity of spotting cars with one broken headlight *US, 1976*

padlock *noun* the penis. Rhyming slang for COCK *UK, 1972*

pad mate *noun* in prison, the inmate with whom a cell is shared. From PAD (a cell) *UK, 1996*

pad roll *noun* a controlled roll of the dice by a skilled cheat, best made on a blanket spread on the ground *US, 1950*

pad-roll *verb* to roll dice in a controlled fashion. So called because it can best be made on a blanket, rug or other soft pad *US, 1950*

padrone; padroni *noun* a boss (especially in a gangster-related context). From Italian *padrone* (an owner, master), via films about the mafia. The plural is 'padroni' *ITALY, 2000*

pads *noun* tyres. Biker (motorcycle) usage *US, 2003*

pad shark *noun* a prisoner who steals from others' cells. From PAD (a cell) *UK, 1996*

paedie-pump *noun* a prison-issue training shoe worn by sex offenders. Based on an abbreviation of 'paedophile'. In use August 2002 *UK, 2002*

paedo *noun* used as a short form of paedophilia, paedophile and related terms. The Greek for 'child', used as the root for many conventional terms, has lately been been associated in the public imagination with the worst of its uses *UK, 2002*

Pag *noun* the short opera *Pagliacci* by Ruggero Leoncavallo *UK, 1987*

page *noun* one thousand doses of LSD soaked into paper *US, 1999*

page biz *noun* the publishing business. Combines BIZ (a business) with a small example *US, 2002*

page oner *noun* a screenplay in need of a complete rewrite *US, 1997*

page three girl *noun* a girl whose scantily clad, or nude, picture appears as a newspaper pin-up. From a 'Page Three' feature in *The Sun* but applied far more widely *UK, 1975*

pagger *verb* to break or smash; to wreck. Market traders' use; influenced by BUGGER (to ruin) *UK, 1979*

paggered *adjective* drunk. From PAGGER, hence 'smashed' (drunk) *UK, 2002*

pagne *noun* a hangover caused by drinking cham*pagne*. A pun *UK, 1999*

pagoda *noun* in horse racing, the stand where race officials are seated *US, 1951*

paid *adjective* financially stable if not wealthy *US, 1998*

pail *noun* the stomach. An abbreviation of 'lunch pail' (a container) *US, 1945*

pain *noun* an irritation; an annoying person *UK, 1933*

Pain *noun* Main Street in Winnipeg, which at its crossing of Portage is the exact centre. 'Pain' for 'Main' at the intersection of Portage Street is evocative of windy, very cold winter weather *CANADA, 2001*

pain in the ass; pain in the arse; pain in the backside *noun* a great nuisance *US, 1934*

pain in the neck *noun* **1** an irritating nuisance *UK, 1941*. **2** a cheque. Rhyming slang *UK, 1992*

pain in the net *noun* a person who posts inflammatory attacks on Internet discussion groups *US, 1991*

pain slut *noun* a person who derives sexual satisfaction from physical and verbal abuse *UK, 1996*

paint *noun* **1** make up *UK, 1660*. **2** the inside rails of a horse racing track *AUSTRALIA, 1965*. **3** in card games, a face card or a ten *US, 1985*. ▶ **come round on the paint** of a racehorse, to take a bend on the inside *AUSTRALIA, 1953*

paint *verb* **1** to apply make up *UK, 1382*. **2** in lowball poker, to draw a face card to a hand of four low cards *US, 1967*. **3** in hearts, to play a heart on a non-heart trick *US, 1987*. **4** to mark a target with laser beams. Gulf war usage *US, 1991*. ▶ **paint the barn** to apply makeup *CANADA, 2002*. ▶ **paint the bus** to change something's appearance without changing its basic foundations *US, 1974*. ▶ **paint the town red** to have a raucous time on the town *US, 1884*

painted pony *noun* in circus and carnival usage, a zebra *US, 1981*

painter *noun* **1** a card cheat who marks cards for identification in another player's hand *US, 1993*. **2** a firefighter assigned to a hook-and-ladder truck. Owing to the ladder *US, 1954*

painters *noun* ▶ **have the painters in; painters are in** to be in the bleed period of the menstrual cycle. A euphemistic fact of life *UK, 1961*

paint-stripper *noun* cheap and nasty alcohol *UK, 1999*

paipsey *adjective* ugly *BARBADOS, 1965*

pair *noun* **1** a pair of female breasts *US, 1957*. **2** a pair of testicles, hence manliness or courage *US, 1985*

pair of ducks; pair *noun* in cricket, the score of a batsman who is out for no score in each leg of a match. From DUCK (zero) *UK, 2003*

pair of fives; pair of nickels *noun* fifty-five miles an hour, the nearly uniform road speed limit in the US in the mid-1970s *US, 1976*

pair of nostrils *noun* a sawn-off shotgun. From the appearance of the gun *UK, 2002*

pair of panties *noun* paragliding. From the French term *parapente* (paragliding) *US, 1992*

paisan; paisano *noun* an Italian-American; used as a term of address that evokes a common heritage, especially Italian *US, 1947*

pajama *noun* the vagina. Something you slip into at bedtime *US, 1998*

pajama wagon *noun* in trucking, a truck cab with a factory-manufactured sleeping compartment *US, 1971*

Pak *noun* Pakistan *UK, 2004*

pakalolo *noun* a variety of marijuana from Hawaii *US, 1981*

pakapoo ticket *noun* something indecipherable or overly complicated. Pakapoo is a Chinese gambling game that appears to outsiders to be quite complicated *AUSTRALIA, 1951*

Paki *adjective* Pakistani *UK, 1984*

Paki; paki; pakki; Pak *noun* a Pakistani; any Asian or Afro-Asian immigrant; loosely, any native of the Indian subcontinent; Pakistan. Derogatory or patronising *UK, 1964*

Paki-basher; Pakki-basher *noun* a violent racist who, usually as part of a group, attacks members of the Asian community *UK, 1970*

Paki-bashing; Pakki-bashing *noun* an organised or opportunistic assaulting of Asian immigrants by gangs of white youths. Political and racist agenda are claimed in an attempt to dignify these attacks by thrill-seeking youths; however, it is worth noting that an average PAKI-BASHER is unable to draw a distinction between targeted races. This social phenomenon seems to have originated in London and continues, sporadically, nationwide *UK, 1970*

Paki pox *noun* smallpox. From ill-informed racist opinion *UK, 1984*

Pakistaner *noun* a big-breasted girl. Teen slang *SOUTH AFRICA, 2003*

Pakistani black; paki black *noun* a potent, black-brown marijuana cultivated in Pakistan. In other contexts the use of 'Paki' may be seen as derogatory, in this case it is attached to a high quality product *UK, 1998*

Paklish *adjective* of Anglo-Pakistani birth *AUSTRALIA, 2003*

pal *noun* **1** a close friend; used as a term of address, usually sarcastically. From the English, Turkish and Transylvanian Romany tongues *UK, 1681*. **2** a studio musician *US, 1982*

palace *noun* a brakevan (caboose) *US, 1946*

Palace of Varieties *nickname* the House of Commons. A derisive allusion to a place of entertainment *UK, 1999*

pal around *verb* to associate with; to socialise with *US, 1879*

palatic *adjective* drunk. A drunken slurring of **PARALYTIC** (drunk) *UK, 1885*

palaver *noun* business; any activity or business that is complicated or annoying, an unnecessary fuss *UK, 1899*

palaver *verb* to talk; to chat; to argue *UK, 1733*

paleets *noun* used as a male-to-male term of address. An embellished 'pal' *TRINIDAD AND TOBAGO, 1976*

pale-face *noun* when spoken by a black person, a white person. From C18 American Indian usage *US, 1945*

palf *noun* Palfium, a heroin substitute *IRELAND, 1996*

palintoshed *adjective* drunk *UK, 2002*

palled-in *adjective* cohabiting with a woman *UK, 1981*

palliness *noun* comradeship, the condition of being pals *UK, 1937*

pallish *adjective* friendly *UK, 1892*

Pall Mall *noun* a girl. Rhyming slang, formed on the London street; recorded as 'now obsolete' by Julian Franklyn, *A Dictionary of Rhyming Slang*, 1960, who explained the rhyme as 'Cockney dialect makes Paow Maow – Gaow'. Despite Franklyn's assertion, it is apparently still in circulation *UK, 1998*

pally *noun* a friend; a comrade *US, 1979*

pally *adjective* friendly *UK, 1895*

pally up *verb* to make friendly overtures; to make friends *UK, 2002*

palm *noun* napalm. Vietnam war usage *US, 1991*

palming *noun* masturbation *BAHAMAS, 1982*

palm oil *noun* **1** a bribe *UK, 1627*. **2** a gratuity *US, 1949*

palm shiner *noun* in gambling, an object that reflects the image of cards, small enough to be held in the user's hand *US, 1997*

palm-warmer *noun* a person who tips *US, 1951*

palone-omee *noun* a lesbian. Polari; a combination of 'palone' (a woman) and 'omee' (a man), the reverse order 'omee-palone' means a male homosexual *UK, 2002*

palonie *noun* a circus pony used in comedy routines *UK, 1953*

palooka *noun* a person who is mediocre at their craft. Originally a boxing term *US, 1925*

palsy-walsy *adjective* friendly, often with an undertone of insincerity *US, 1937*

pal up *verb* to make friends *US, 1953*

pamp *verb* to place or put something somewhere *UK: SCOTLAND, 1990*

pamphlet *noun* one ounce of a drug *US, 1976*

pan *noun* the face *US, 1923*. ▶ **on the pan** (used of a truck driver) summoned to appear before a public utility commission for violations of driving laws *US, 1961*

pan *verb* **1** to criticise something as unsuccessful *US, 1911*. **2** to utterly defeat someone in a fight; to thrash someone *UK, 2002*. **3** to beg. An abbreviation of 'panhandle' *US, 1997*

Panama cut *noun* a variety of marijuana cultivated in Panama *UK, 1998*

Panama gold; Panamanian gold *noun* a potent, gold-leafed marijuana cultivated in Panama *US, 1968*

Panama red; Panamanian red *noun* a potent variety of marijuana cultivated in Panama *US, 1967*

panatella *noun* **1** a marijuana cigarette *US, 1944*. **2** potent marijuana, especially that originating in South or Central America *US, 1956*

panatic *noun* a devoted, die-hard fan of steelband music *TRINIDAD AND TOBAGO, 1988*

pan breid *adjective* dead. Glasgow rhyming slang for 'pan bread' (a type of crusty loaf) *UK: SCOTLAND, 1988*

pancake *verb* using hydraulic lifts operated from inside the car, to drop suddenly first the back and then the front of a car *US, 1980*

pancake saddle *noun* in western Canada, an English saddle *CANADA, 1987*

panda car; panda *noun* a black and white police patrol car, hence a police patrol car. The logic is black and white: the car was introduced at a time when the pandas at London Zoo were making headlines *UK, 1966*

Pandemonium World Scareways *nickname* US airline company Pan Am. Most airlines attract jocular variations of their names: Pan Am's include: 'Painful, Nauseating and Miserable' and 'Passengers Always Neglected at Mealtimes' *US, 2002*

P and Q *noun* solitary confinement in prison. Abbreviated 'peace and quiet' *US, 1982*

pane *noun* a dose of LSD on a tiny, clear gelatin chip. A shortened form of **WINDOWPANE** *US, 1994*

panel-beater *noun* an employee in a car body shop *AUSTRALIA, 1984*

panel house *noun* a brothel with sliding walls through which thieves steal from the clothes of customers *US, 1848*

panels of fences *noun* in horse racing, a long lead *AUSTRALIA, 1989*

pangonadalot *noun* heroin *US, 1977*

panhandle *verb* to beg *US, 1884*

panhandler *noun* **1** a beggar *US, 1897*. **2** a nurse. Jocular reference to bedpans *US, 1976*

panic *noun* **1** a widespread unavailability of an illegal drug *US, 1937*. **2** a very good time *US, 1958*

panic button *noun* any switch or button which activates an emergency alarm, or summons urgent assistance, or stops a mechanical operation *UK, 1971*

panic flip *noun* in pinball, the premature activation of a flipper *US, 1977*

panic merchant *noun* a person who habitually panics *AUSTRALIA, 1962*

panic stations *noun* a frenzied state of alarmed or confused thinking. A jocular adaptation of the military term 'action stations' *UK, 1961*

pan-loaf *adjective* of a superior social status or well-to-do. Glasgow rhyming slang for **TOFF** – a good rhyme in the local accent – formed from a type of bread with a soft crust *UK: SCOTLAND, 1985*

pannikin boss *noun* a person with a modest amount of authority; a minor boss; a foreman *AUSTRALIA, 1898*

panno *noun* **1** a panel van *AUSTRALIA, 1998*. **2** a foreman. An abbreviation of **PANNIKIN BOSS** *AUSTRALIA, 1957*

panoramas *noun* pyjamas. Rhyming slang *UK, 1992*

pan out *verb* (of an event) to turn out; to result. A figurative application of panning for gold *US, 1871*

pansy *noun* a male homosexual; an effeminate man *UK, 1929*

pansy-ass *adjective* effeminate, weak *US, 2002*

pansy-boy *noun* an effeminate male homosexual *AUSTRALIA, 1976*

pansy-man *noun* a male homosexual *ANTIGUA AND BARBUDA, 1999*

pansy patch *nickname* an area in west Hollywood, California, largely populated by homosexual men since the 1960s *US, 1971*

Pansy Potters *noun* the documents given to someone who is dismissed from employment. Glasgow rhyming slang for **JOTTERS**, formed on a comic strip character *UK: SCOTLAND, 1996*

pansy prattle *noun* the snide remarks and witty insults characteristic of male homosexual banter *US, 1980*

pant *noun* trousers *INDIA, 1979*

panther *noun* a condom. The image of a large black beast. Collected from UK prisoners in May, 2002 *JAMAICA, 2002*

panther breath *noun* strong, illegally manufactured whisky *US, 1999*

panther juice *noun* strong, homemade alcohol *US, 1960*

panther piss *noun* illegally manufactured, low quality alcohol *US, 1971*

panther sweat *noun* **1** surgical spirit and Italian vermouth mixed as a potent drink. After the US slang for inferior whisky. Reported by a correspondent of Partridge as in Beatnik use around 1959, but not recorded until 1984 *UK, 1984*. **2** low quality whisky *US, 1977*

pantload *noun* a great deal of something *US, 1968*

pant moustache *noun* a fringe of pubic hair that escapes the confines of a female's underwear or swimwear *UK, 2003*

pantomime cow *noun* a row; an argument. Rhyming slang *UK, 1998*

pants *noun* **1** rubbish, nonsense, often applied adjectivally *UK, 1998*. **2** sex. In the spirit of 'cunt', 'ass' or 'leg', but a bit more restrained *US, 1965*. ▶ **frighten the pants off; scare the pants off** to frighten or scare someone, especially severely or (when horror is presented as entertainment) thrillingly *UK, 1967*. ▶ **get into someone's pants** to seduce someone; to have sex with someone *US, 1952*

pants *verb* to pull someone's trousers down as part of a prank or practical joke *US, 1989*

pants *adjective* applied to something that is very easily done *UK: SCOTLAND, 1996*

pants and vest; pants *noun* best bitter beer. Rhyming slang *UK, 1992*

pantsful *noun* a great deal, especially of something bad. A suggestion of a lot of excrement *US, 1993*

pantsman *noun* a womaniser *AUSTRALIA, 1968*

pants rabbits *noun* pubic lice; body lice; fleas *US, 1949*

panty hamster *noun* the vagina *UK, 2002*

pantyman *noun* an effeminate heterosexual man; a homosexual man *TRINIDAD AND TOBAGO, 1993*

pantypop *verb* to fart *US, 2003*

panty raid *noun* a college fad in which male students invade the dormitories of female students, seizing underwear as trophies. The practice and term faded quickly with the onset of 1960s culture *US, 1952*

panty-stretcher *noun* a heavy woman. Also recorded in UK usage *US, 1976*

pantywaist *noun* a weakling or coward; a homosexual man *US, 1936*

pantzilla *noun* Sildenafil citrate marketed as Viagra, an anti-impotence drug taken recreationally for performance enhancement, in combination with other chemicals that stimulate the sexual appetites. A jocular reference to the monster in your underpants. The monster, of course, is Godzilla *UK, 2001*

pan up *verb* to prepare a powdered drug for heating prior to injection *US, 1971*

Panzer *noun* a Mercedes-Benz car *US, 1997*

pap *verb* to work as a press photographer who specialises in the sensational and the celebrated. A back-formation from PAPARAZZI *UK, 2004*

paparazzi *noun* press photographers who specialise in the sensational and the celebrated, or a single photographer similarly engaged. From the Italian *paparazzo* which is the correct, though rarely used, singular form. Named after a character in *La Dolce Vita*, a 1960 film by Frederico Fellini *UK, 1968*

pape *noun* a Roman Catholic. A shortening of 'papist' *UK: SCOTLAND, 1985*

paper *noun* **1** money *US, 1974*. **2** a cigarette paper *UK, 1950*. **3** personal identification papers *US, 1982*. **4** promotional literature produced as part of a telephone sales swindle *US, 1988*. **5** a free pass to a performance *UK, 1785*. **6** a cheque *US, 1972*. **7** a speeding ticket *US, 1976*. **8** a deck of cards that have been marked for cheating *US, 1977*. **9** heroin sold in a paper packet; a folded paper containing any powdered drug *US, 1953*. **10** probation in lieu of a jail sentence;

parole from prison *US, 1973*. **11** an underworld contract to have someone killed *US, 1983*

paper *verb* ▶ **paper the house** to give away free tickets to an event in order to secure a large audience *UK, 1859*

paper acid *noun* LSD, especially on blotting paper *US, 1977*

paper and plastic *noun* in gambling, a combination of cash and betting chips. A play on the grocery clerk's query to a customer – 'Paper or plastic bag?' *US, 1996*

paper asshole *noun* an adhesive reinforcement attached to holes punched on a piece of paper to prevent the page from ripping out of a binder. The object is shaped like a small life buoy, visually evocative to some of an anus. Collected from union negotiating committee members in northern California, September 2002 *US, 2002*

paper bag *noun* ▶ **go pop like a paper bag** (of a woman) to copulate vigorously *AUSTRALIA, 1984*. ▶ **you couldn't fight your way out of a paper bag; you couldn't punch your way out of a paper bag** addressed to (or, in the third person, used of) a person boasting of strength or fighting ability *AUSTRALIA, 1961*

paper bag; paper *verb* to nag someone. Rhyming slang *UK, 1992*

paperbag case *noun* an ugly woman. A suggestion that the paper bag be worn over her head *US, 1976*

paper blunt *noun* a marijuana cigarette *UK, 2003*

paper boy *noun* a drug dealer, especially a heroin dealer. Because heroin is often sold in paper envelopes; punning on a newspaper delivery boy *US, 1970*

papered *adjective* used of a stadium or an auditorium filled by people given free tickets *US, 1978*

paper grower *noun* a recycling bin for paper *CANADA, 1989*

paper-hang *noun* the passing of counterfeit money or forged securities *US, 1976*

paper-hanger *noun* **1** a criminal whose expertise is the use of fraudulent securities *US, 1954*. **2** in trucking, a police officer writing a ticket *US, 1976*

paper hat *noun* a fool. Rhyming slang for TWAT *UK, 1998*

paper mushrooms *noun* LSD. LSD on blotting paper having the hallucinogenic properties of MAGIC MUSHROOM(S) *UK, 1998*

paper-puncher *noun* used as a jocular description of a handgun target shooter *US, 1957*

paper-pusher *noun* **1** a bureaucrat; in the military, anyone with a desk job and not in combat *US, 1980*. **2** a person who places counterfeit money into circulation *US, 1985*

papers *noun* in prison, a person's background *US, 2000*

paper soldier *noun* a rear-area military personnel who supported those in combat *US, 1990*

paper time *noun* the additional years added to a prison sentence because of publicity surrounding the crime, criminal and/or trial *US, 1962*

paper top *noun* a convertible car top *US, 1973*

paperweight *noun* **1** in horse racing, a very small weight allowance in a weight-handicapped event *AUSTRALIA, 1989*. **2** a railway office clerk *US, 1946*

paperwork *noun* **1** any alteration of playing cards as part of a cheating scheme *US, 1962*. **2** a speeding ticket *US, 1976*. **3** money; currency notes *UK, 1997*

papes *noun* **1** cigarette rolling papers *US, 1997*. **2** money *US, 2000*

pappy *noun* a father. A childish, rural ring *UK, 1763*

pappy-mammy *noun* a homosexual man *TRINIDAD AND TOBAGO, 1956*

pappyshow *noun* a fool, or someone who presents the appearance of a fool. A corruption of 'puppet show' *TRINIDAD AND TOBAGO, 1940*

paps *noun* press photographers who specialise in the sensational and the celebrated. An abbreviation of PAPARAZZI *UK, 2002*

par *noun* ▶ **below par; under par** less than average or less than projected. A term that migrated from conventional English into golf and then back into broader slang usage *UK, 1767*

para *noun* **1** a *para*trooper *US, 1990*. **2** paranoia, especially as a result of drug abuse *UK, 1996*

para; parro *adjective* **1** paranoid *UK, 1996*. **2** drunk. A shortening of PARALYTIC *AUSTRALIA, 1988*

parachute *noun* **1** a combination of crack cocaine and phencyclidine, the recreational drug known as PCP or angel dust *UK, 1998*. **2** heroin. From its effect of slowing down other drug highs *UK, 2002*

parade *noun* in a striptease show, the dancer's fully clothed walk across the stage before beginning to strip *US, 1945*

paradise *noun* the highest gallery in a theatre *UK, 1952*

paradise stroke *noun* (generally plural) the final thrust before male orgasm *UK, 1984*

paradise white; paradise *noun* cocaine *UK, 1998*

paraffin lamp; paraffin *noun* a tramp, a homeless person; used as an insult for someone in need of a wash. Rhyming slang *UK, 1997*

paraffin oil; paraffin *noun* style. Glasgow rhyming slang (a good rhyme in a local accent) *UK: SCOTLAND, 1988*

parakeet *noun* a Puerto Rican *US, 1962*

parallel *adjective* lying down. Hawaiian youth usage *US, 1982*

paralysis by analysis *noun* inaction produced by over-thinking a situation *US, 1971*

paralytic; paraletic *adjective* very drunk; drunk and incapable. 'Paraletic' is a phonetic misspelling *AUSTRALIA, 1891*

parboiled *adjective* drunk *US, 1960*

parcel *noun* a quantity of stolen goods being delivered to the receiver. A specialisation of the conventional sense *UK, 1981*

pard *noun* partner. A definite Western flavour; a highly affected shortening of 'partner' *US, 1850*

pardner *noun* used as a term of address, male-to-male. Used with an intentional folksiness that harkens to cowboy films *US, 1795*

pardon me for living!; pardon me for breathing! used as an elaborate mock apology offered in answer for a minor error or trivial criticism *UK, 1961*

Paree; Gay Paree *noun* Paris, France. From the French pronunciation *UK, 1848*

parental units *noun* your parents *US, 1982*

parish bull *noun* a man with illegitimate children *BERMUDA, 1985*

park *verb* **1** to (temporarily) place something or someone in a position of some safety or convenience. Often extended – in worldwide variations – as an invitation or imperative: 'park your arse!' 'park your carcass!' 'park your fanny!' 'park your frame!' and, the nautically inspired, 'park your stern!' *UK, 1908*. **2** to stay at a place for a short time *AUSTRALIA, 1961*. **3** to engage in sexual foreplay in a parked car *US, 1972*. **4** to give. A shortening of obsolete PARKER *UK, 1972*. ▶ **park a custard** to vomit. Upper-class society usage *UK, 1982*. ▶ **park a tiger; park the tiger** to vomit *AUSTRALIA, 1985*. ▶ **park it** (of a person) to sit down *AUSTRALIA, 1962*. ▶ **park the ball** in pool, to leave the cue ball roughly in the centre of the table after an opening break shot *US, 1992*. ▶ **park your carcass** (of a person) to sit down *AUSTRALIA, 1977*. ▶ **where I'd like to park my bike** said by a man of a woman considered as a sexual object. The wheel of a bicycle is held in a slot, which puns on vagina *UK, 2003*

parked out *adjective* in horse racing, said of horses forced to the outside on turns *US, 1994*

Parker *noun* a chauffeur. The name of Lady Penelope's chauffeur in *Thunderbirds* (a cult television series of the early 1960s, relaunched in the 90s) adopted as a generic nickname *UK, 1999*

parker *verb* to pay; to give. From 'parleyaree', an early form of POLARI *UK, 1914*

Parkheid smiddy *noun* the female breast. Glasgow rhyming slang for, DIDDY, from the local pronunciation of Parkhead Smithy, a famous forge in Glasgow's East End *UK: SCOTLAND, 1988*

parkie; parky *noun* a park keeper *UK, 2001*

parking lot *noun* **1** a traffic jam *US, 1976*. **2** the vagina. An obvious pun until you start to seek an appropriate vehicle for the penis *US,* *1974*. ▶ **in the parking lot** in gambling, without further funds *US, 1996*

parking space *noun* a grave *UK, 1998*

Park Lane No. 2's *noun* marijuana from Cambodia, often pre-rolled into cigarettes. The term was coined and popularised by US soldiers in Vietnam *US, 1970*

parky *adjective* of the weather, chilly, cold, very cold *UK, 1895*

parlay *noun* crack cocaine *US, 1994*

parlay *verb* to socialise at clubs, bars or parties *US, 2000*

parloo *verb* to masturbate *NORFOLK ISLAND, 1992*

parlour *noun* a brakevan (caboose) *US, 1946*

parlour maid *noun* a rear railway brakeman *US, 1946*

parlour pink *noun* a wealthy person who espouses socialist views from the safety of luxury *US, 1920*

parma violet *noun* a variety of MDMA, the recreational drug best known as ecstasy. From the purple colour of the tablet and overall similarity to a sweet of the same name *UK, 2002*

parnee *verb* to rain. From the noun sense *UK, 1859*

parnee; parnie; parny *noun* **1** rain; tears. Polari, originally Anglo-Indian, from 'parnee' (water) *UK, 1859*. **2** water. Current in English gypsy use, from Romany *pâni* (water) *UK, 1859*

parole dust *noun* fog. A term coined at the San Quentin state penitentiary just north of San Francisco, where fog invites escape attempts *US, 1976*

Parra *noun* in the Sydney region, a visting non-resident of a beachside area. Derogatory. Perhaps from *Parra*matta, a western suburb of Sydney *AUSTRALIA, 1985*

Parry *nickname* the Paremoremo maximum security prison *NEW ZEALAND, 1982*

parsley *noun* **1** marijuana. From the similarity of appearance between one HERB and another *UK, 1996*. **2** phencyclidine, the recreational drug known as PCP or angel dust. Because one method of administration of the drug is to sprinkle it on parsley *US, 1981*

parsley bud *noun* in British Columbia, a local variety of marijuana *CANADA, 2002*

part *adjective* of mixed race *FIJI, 1995*

partial *noun* a partial fingerprint *US, 1996*. ▶ **partial to** having a fondness or liking for something *UK, 1696*

Partick Thistle *noun* **1** a whistle. Rhyming slang, formed on the name of a Scottish football club; also serves as a verb *UK, 1992*. **2** a variety of MDMA, the recreational drug best known as ecstasy, identified by PT embossed on the tablet. Disguising PT with the name of a Scottish football team *UK, 2002*

partied out *adjective* exhausted from excessive party-going *US, 1992*

partner *noun* **1** a very close associate who can be counted on in almost any situation *US, 1994*. **2** any Audi car. Motor trade slang. A pun on 'Howdy, partner' *UK, 2004*

partridge *noun* a good-looking girl or woman *US, 1947*

parts *noun* ▶ **get parts** to engage in sexual activity short of intercourse *US, 1979*

parts changer *noun* in car repair, a mechanic who replaces parts until a problem is solved instead of diagnosing the problem at the outset *US, 1993*

part timer *noun* a variety of MDMA, the recreational drug best known as ecstasy, identified by PT embossed on the tablet *UK, 2002*

party *noun* **1** a person. In conventional use from 1650 but considered to be slang since later C19. Not to be confused with a party to a legal action *UK, 1956*. **2** a woman; a girlfriend. Royal Navy slang *UK, 1987*. **3** sex, especially with a prostitute. A prostitute euphemism *US, 1956*

party *verb* **1** to enjoy a good time. From the conventional noun sense *US, 1922*. **2** to have sex, especially with a prostitute *US, 1963*. **3** to use drugs *US, 1999*

par-ty! used as an exhortation to relax and enjoy yourself. The break between syllables is key *US, 1988*

party animal *noun* a person dedicated to making merry and having a good time. A creature born of the 1990s *US, 1997*

party central *noun* an apartment or house where parties are frequently in progress *US, 2000*

party favours *noun* drugs *US, 1989*

party foul *noun* a faux pas; a substantial breach of etiquette *US, 2004*

party girl *noun* a prostitute *US, 1960*

party hat *noun* **1** the signal light(s) on the roof of a police car. When the light is flashing the police are said to have a 'party hat on' *US, 1976*. **2** a condom *US, 1989*

party hearty *verb* to party in a diligent fashion *US, 1979*

party lights *noun* the coloured, flashing lights on top of a police car *US, 1992*

party line *noun* the 'official version' that must be adhered to whether truthful or not. Originally (1834) a political party's policy; thence into much wider usage *UK, 1937*

party nap *noun* a nap taken in anticipation of a night of drinking and partying *US, 2004*

party on! used as an encouragement for revelry *US, 1989*

party pack *noun* a packet of ten rolled marijuana cigarettes for sale in Vietnam during the war *US, 1991*

party piece *noun* a woman who makes herself sexually available at Hell's Angels gatherings'. A pun formed on PIECE (a woman as a sexual object) *UK, 1982*

party pooper; party poop *noun* a killjoy; a spoilsport *US, 1954*

party powder *noun* cocaine *UK, 2003*

party reptile *noun* an enthusiastic party-goer *US, 1986*

pash *noun* **1** a romanticised affection for someone; an infatuation *UK, 1914*. **2** a fiancée; the woman you enjoy more than a casual relationship with; the primary girlfriend. Royal Navy slang; an abbreviated form of 'passion' *US, 1960*. **3** a passionate kiss or kissing session, especially French kissing *AUSTRALIA, 1962*

pash; pash off *verb* to kiss someone passionately *AUSTRALIA, 1979*

pashing *noun* kissing and petting *AUSTRALIA, 1964*

pash on *verb* to spend time kissing and petting *AUSTRALIA, 1983*

pashpie *noun* an attractive boy or girl. Teen slang *US, 1951*

pash rash *noun* sore lips or irritation of the area surrounding the mouth as a result of kissing *AUSTRALIA, 2002*

pashy *noun* a passionate kiss. An elaboration of PASH *UK, 2000*

pashy *adjective* passionate *US, 1949*

pasray *verb* (used of a woman) to sit in an immodest position *TRINIDAD AND TOBAGO, 2003*

pass *noun* an amorous approach to someone; an introductory attempt at seduction *UK, 1928*

pass *verb* to seek acceptance as white because of fair skin colouring *US, 1933*. ▶ **pass change** to bribe *TRINIDAD AND TOBAGO, 1989*. ▶ **pass the time of day** to exchange greetings; to chat and gossip *UK, 1851*

pass-by *noun* a stranger *JAMAICA, 1958*

passenger *noun* **1** a member of any group who does not fully contribute and is 'carried' by the rest. Originally sporting *UK, 1852*. **2** a member of a prison clique. Formed from CAR (a clique) *US, 1989*

passenger stiff *noun* a railway passenger *US, 1977*

passer *noun* **1** a person who places counterfeit money into circulation *US, 1981*. **2** a drug dealer *US, 1952*

passers *noun* dice that have been altered so as to roll a seven less often than normal *US, 1950*

passion-killers *noun* sensible knickers. Originally of military-issue knickers *UK, 1943*

passion mark *noun* a bruise caused by extended sucking *US, 1966*

passion pit *noun* a drive-in cinema. Teen slang *US, 1951*

passion wagon *noun* a panel van or the like used for sexual encounters *AUSTRALIA, 1966*

pass out *verb* to lose consciousness. From an earlier sense 'to die' *UK, 1915*

passover *noun* a seizure *BARBADOS, 1965*

passover party *noun* a party where those who have been passed over for promotion drown their sorrows *US, 1996*

passport *noun* standing permission from a youth gang to enter the territory which they consider their 'turf' *US, 1972*

past *adjective* ▶ **past it** because of your age or infirmity, to be no longer able to do that which you used to. Applied generally or to a specific inability *UK, 1928*. ▶ **past its sell-by date** no longer of interest; out of fashion. Adopted from product information on packaged goods *UK, 2001*

pasta *noun* cocaine. From 'paste', a step in the production process *US, 1984*

pasta rocket *noun* any Italian sports car *US, 2004*

paste *noun* **1** finely crafted fake gems *US, 1950*. **2** the peanut butter in combat rations *US, 1991*. **3** crack cocaine. From an intermediary step in the production of crack *US, 1994*

paste *verb* to thrash someone *UK, 1846*

pasteboard *noun* in horse racing, a dry track in good condition *US, 1971*

pastie *noun* a fool; used as a friendly term of abuse. Possibly from the thick crust of a Cornish pastie *UK, 2004*

pasties *noun* decorative coverings for a female dancer's nipples *US, 1961*

pasting *noun* a beating. Either physical or figurative *UK, 1851*

pasto *noun* marijuana. From Spanish *pasto* (pasture, grass), thus GRASS (marijuana) *US, 1980*

pastry cutter *noun* a person who applies pressure with the teeth while performing oral sex on a man *UK, 2002*

pastry wagon *noun* a truck owned by the Pacific Intermountain Express. Back-formation from PIE, the company's initials *US, 1976*

pasture *noun* a place where teenagers engage in various levels of sexual activity in parked cars at night *US, 1960*. ▶ **out to pasture** incarcerated *US, 1992*

Pat *noun* ▶ **on your Pat** on your own. A shortening of PAT MALONE *AUSTRALIA, 1908*

Pat *nickname* used as a nickname for an Irish man; also used in jokes which need a stereotypical Irishman as the butt. Pat, a diminutive of Patrick, is a stereotypically Irish name *UK, 1806*

pat *verb* ▶ **pat the pad** to go to bed *US, 1955*

patacca *adjective* used for describing inferior or fake jewellery, especially of a counterfeit Swiss watch. An Italian slang term, pronounced 'pataka', meaning 'worthless; rubbish'; used at the less-honest end of the jewellery trade, and amongst air stewards *UK, 1977*

Pat and Mick *noun* the penis. Rhyming slang for PRICK, formed from two stereotypical Irish names, often featured in jokes. As the butts of these jokes Pat and Mick are inevitably thick, a characteristic which may well pun here as an implied quality of girth *UK, 1961*

Pat and Mick *adjective* sick. Rhyming slang *UK, 2003*

Pat and Mike *noun* a bicycle. Rhyming slang for 'bike' *UK, 1931*

Pat Cash *noun* to urinate. Rhyming slang for SLASH, based on the name of Australian tennis player Pat Cash (b.1965) *UK, 1998*

patch *noun* **1** a district which is the responsibility of a specified police authority; a geographical area designated as the responsibility of public servants, e.g. probation officers, social workers; an area of specialist reponsibility. Originally northern and Midland police, by the mid-1960s it had become common to all public services *UK, 1963*. **2** the territory claimed by a prostitute, a drug dealer or a gang *UK, 1996*. **3** a small community *US, 1997*. **4** the zone assigned to a military reconnaissance team *US, 1991*. **5** a small piece of material covering a striptease dancer's vulva *US, 1973*. **6** a gang emblem sewn to the back of a member's jacket, signifying full membership in the gang *NEW ZEALAND, 1975*. **7** in computing, a temporary modification of code to repair an immediate problem

US, 1991. **8** in the circus or carnival, the person who adjusted legal problems *US, 1960.* **9** an ad hoc payment to a police officer to allow a crime to take place *US, 2001.* **10** the proceeds of a crime, confiscated and kept by corrupt police in lieu of arrest *US, 1987.*
▶ **not a patch on** not in any way to be compared with *UK, 1860*

patched *adjective* thirsty *US, 1968*

patches *noun* **1** a prison uniform issued to inmates who have been assessed as potential escapees *UK, 2000.* **2** a prisoner considered likely to attempt an escape. From the yellow patches worn on the prisoner's jacket and trousers *UK, 1996*

patch money *noun* in a carnival, the money paid by concession operators to the 'patch' or 'fixer' for adjusting legal problems *US, 1985*

pate *noun* a father. Abbreviated from Latin *pater US, 1988*

patent *noun* a multiple bet, gambling on three different horses in separate races in a total of seven bets *UK, 1991*

pater *noun* a father. A familiar use of Latin *pater* (a father), mainly as schoolboy slang, and often considered pretentious *UK, 1728*

path *adjective* pathology; pathological. Originally medical use now widely known, mainly in 'path lab' (a pathology laboratory) *UK, 1937*

pat hand *noun* in blackjack, a hand with points totalling between 17 and 21. A 'pat hand' is a potentially winning hand *US, 1991*

pathetic *adjective* ineffectual, contemptible. From the conventional sense (worthy of pity) *UK, 1937*

pathy *noun* a pathologist *UK, 1956*

patico *noun* crack cocaine. Spanish slang used by English-speakers who would not know what the word means in Spanish *US, 1994*

patient zero *noun* the first person to transmit a disease. Usually used in the context of AIDS *US, 1987*

Pat Malone *noun* alone. Rhyming slang for 'on your own' *AUSTRALIA, 1908*

patoot *noun* the vagina *US, 1974*

patootie *noun* the arse *US, 1948*

pat poke *noun* the hip pocket. Pickpocket usage *US, 1949*

Pats *nickname* the New England Patriots professional football team *US, 1971*

patsy *noun* **1** a dupe; someone blamed for a crime or accident. Perhaps the most famous maybe-patsy of the C20 was Lee Harvey Oswald, who told reporters shortly before being killed: 'They're taking me in because of the fact that I lived in the Soviet Union. I'm only a patsy' *US, 1903.* **2** in poker, a hand that requires no draw. Conventionally known as a 'pat hand' *US, 1988.* **3** a half-gallon jar filled with beer. A fairly complicated rhyme: Patsy Riggir is a country music singer, and her last name evokes RIGGER, which is another term for a half-gallon jar of beer *NEW ZEALAND, 1998*

Patsy Cline; Patsy *noun* a dose of cocaine prepared for inhaling. Rhyming slang for LINE, based on country and western singer Patsy Cline, 1932–63 *UK, 1996*

patsy mouth *noun* a dryness of the mouth as a result of smoking marijuana or hashish *CANADA, 2004*

Patsy Palmer and her five daughters *noun* the hand (seen in the context of male masturbation). A variation of MRS PALM AND HER FIVE LOVELY DAUGHTERS, formed on the name of an actress who came to prominence playing Bianca in the BBC television soap opera *EastEnders* from 1994–99 *UK, 2003*

patter *noun* talk, speechifying *UK, 1778*

Patty Hearst *noun* a *first* class degree. Rhyming slang for 'first', formed from the name of the heiress, who was kidnapped by left-wing extremists, and involved in bank-robbery, before becoming a professional actress (b.1954) *UK, 1998*

Paul Anka *noun* used as an all-purpose form of abuse. Rhyming slang for WANKER; formed from the name of the US singer (b.1941) *UK, 2004*

Paul Weller *noun* branded Belgian lager Stella Artois™. Rhyming slang for 'Stella', based on the name of musician Paul Weller (b.1958) *UK, 2002*

pause *verb* ▶ **pause for a cause** to pull off the motorway to use a toilet *US, 1977*

pav *noun* a pavlova. A type of meringue desert topped with fruit, named after Russian ballerina Anna Pavlova *AUSTRALIA, 1966*

Pavarotti *noun* ten pounds, £10. Punning TENNER on 'tenor'; formed on the great Italian tenor Luciano Pavarotti (b.1935) *UK, 1998*

pavement *noun* ▶ **the pavement** the streets, especially as an area of criminal operation *UK, 1998*

pavement artist *noun* a criminal specialising in street fraud *UK, 2001*

pavement oyster *noun* an expectoration of phlegm that has been deposited in the street *UK, 1981*

pavement pizza *noun* a splash of vomit *AUSTRALIA, 1996*

pavement-pounder *noun* a prostitute who solicits customers on the street *US, 1960*

pavement princess *noun* a prostitute, especially one who works at truck stops *US, 1977*

pavement surfing *noun* being thrown from a motorcycle. Biker (motorcyle) usage *US, 2003*

pavilion *noun* a brakevan (caboose) *US, 1977*

paw *noun* the hand *UK, 1605*

pawn *noun* ▶ **got out of pawn; got out** born *UK, 1992*

paws up *adjective* dead. New York police slang *US, 1997*

pay *noun* a debtor *US, 1989*

pay *verb* ▶ **get paid** to commit a successful robbery *US, 1987.*
▶ **pay black** to pay a blackmailer's extortion. Combines conventional 'pay' with 'black' (blackmail) *UK, 1984.* ▶ **pay crow tax** to lose a farm animal by accidental death or disease *CANADA, 1992.*
▶ **pay the grandstand** in horse racing, to place a bet that will generate a huge earning *AUSTRALIA, 1989.* ▶ **pay through the nose** to pay a high (financial) price for something *UK, 1672.* ▶ **pay your dues** to persevere through hardship *US, 1956*

pay and lay *noun* used for describing the exchange of payment and services involved in prostitution *US, 1969*

pay ball *noun* in pool, a shot that, if made, wins a wager *US, 1993*

pay dirt *noun* money; success *UK, 1857*

pay-for-play *noun* sex that is paid for *US, 1969*

pay hole *noun* in trucking, a truck's highest gear *US, 1971*

pay lawyer *noun* a privately retained lawyer, as contrasted with one provided for indigents by the state *US, 1992*

payola *noun* **1** an illegal payment to a radio station or individual to encourage the playing of a particular song. The word leapt into the American vocabulary in late 1959 as pay-off scandal after pay-off scandal toppled the first generation of rock 'n' roll disc jockeys. Later broadened to include other forms of bribery *US, 1938.* **2** reward money for anonymous police informants *UK, 2002.* **3** oil *US, 1984*

pay out on *verb* to upbraid someone for a wrongdoing. Originally 'to get revenge; to mete out corporal punishment', from British dialect *pay* (to beat/thrash). Now only referring to verbal dressing down *AUSTRALIA, 1977*

pay school *noun* a school charging a tuition fee *US, 1992*

payware *noun* commercially available computer software *US, 1991*

PB *nickname* Pacific Beach, San Diego, California *US, 1993*

PB and J *noun* a peanut butter and jelly (jam) sandwich. A culinary staple of American youth for decades *US, 1981*

PC *noun* **1** a latex finger glove used during digital examinations. A 'pinkie cheater' *US, 1958.* **2** probable cause to arrest someone *US, 1995.* **3** a percentage. Applied to drug sales *US, 1956*

PC *adjective* politically correct. Originally used of left-on-left criticism, appropriated and exploited by the right to marginalise any and all dissent from the left *US, 1986*

PCH *nickname* the Pacific Coast Highway, US route 1 in Los Angeles *US, 1981*

PCOD *noun* pussy cut-off date. When soldiers were returned to the US from the war in Vietnam, they were tested for sexually transmitted diseases. To be sure that any problems were identified and cured before that test, most stopped having sexual relations before the end of their rotation to avoid any delay in returning home *US, 1991*

P'cola *noun* Pensacola, Florida, home to a naval air station known as the 'cradle of Navy aviation' *US, 1991*

PCP *noun* phencyclidine, the recreational drug known as PCP or angel dust *US, 1969*

PD *adjective* pretty disgusting *UK, 1996*

PDA *noun* a public display of affection *US, 1968*

P-dogs *noun* cocaine *UK, 2003*

P-dope *noun* relatively (20%–30%) pure heroin *US, 1997*

PDQ pretty damn quick *UK, 1875*

p'd up *adjective* paranoid *UK, 2001*

pea *noun* **1** in Keno, a small ball with a number between one and 80 painted on it, drawn to establish winning numbers *US, 1987*. **2** in pool, a small tally ball used as a scoring device *US, 1993*. **3** a bullet *US, 1988*. **4** a person expected to win; in racing, a favourite *AUSTRALIA, 1911*

pea-brain *noun* a person lacking common sense, intelligence or both *US, 1950*

pea-brained *adjective* **1** very stupid *UK, 1950*. **2** under the influence of LSD *US, 1982*

peace goodbye. Dave Garroway, host of the morning television news programme *The Today Show* from 1952 to 61, closed each programme raising one hand and saying the single word 'Peace'. In 1988, comedy host Arsenio Hall, whose programme ran until 1993, began to use the same sign-off, at times embellishing it with 'Peace, and think number one' *US, 1991*

peace and quiet *noun* **1** solitary confinement in prison *US, 1982*. **2** a diet. Rhyming slang *UK, 1992*

peacemaker *nickname* the MX missile. Originally applied to the Colt .45 revolver, which made peace by death. Applied by US President Reagan and his administration in 1982 to the missile that carries thermonuclear warheads, apparently unaware of the irony of the term *US, 1982*

peacenik *noun* a person who is opposed to war or a war *US, 1963*

peace 'n' love *adjective* in the style of 1960s counterculture. The twin aims of the counterculture packaged as a marketing slogan; often derogatory *UK, 2001*

peace out used as a farewell *US, 1992*

peace pill *noun* a combination of the hallucinogen LSD and the stimulant methedrine *US, 1971*

PeaCe Pill; peace *noun* phencyclidine, the recreational drug known as PCP or angel dust. A rather clumsy back-formation from the initials *US, 1977*

peace tab *noun* a tablete of psilocybin, a mushroom-based hallucinogen *US, 1971*

peace tablet *noun* a tablet (of any description) with a drop of LSD on it *US, 1982*

peaceweed *noun* phencyclidine, the recreational drug known as PCP or angel dust *US, 1981*

peach *noun* **1** an excellent person or thing *UK, 1863*. **2** a sexually attractive person, usually a woman *UK, 1754*. **3** the vagina *US, 1997*. **4** a tablet of amphetamine sulphate (trade name Benzedrine™), a central nervous system stimulant *US, 1967*

peach *verb* to inform against or on someone. In conventional use from C16 to mid-C19, thereafter considered slang or colloquial *UK, 1991*

peach picker *noun* a cabover truck that is built high off the ground *US, 1971*

peachy *adjective* good, pleasing, attractive. If used at all, used with irony *UK, 1926*

peachy-keen *adjective* excellent *US, 1960*

peacocky *adjective* used of a racehorse, high-headed *US, 1976*

pea-eye *noun* an English-speaking person from Canada's Maritime Provinces. From, if awkwardly, 'Prince Edward Island' *US, 1975*

peak *verb* **1** to become highly excited; to thrill *AUSTRALIA, 1985*. **2** (of a wave) to reach its highest point before breaking *AUSTRALIA, 1987*

peaker plant *noun* a power-generating facility that is brought online only during periods of peak demand *US, 2000s*

peaky *adjective* feeling unwell, or appearing sickly *UK, 1821*

peanut *noun* **1** the penis. An unusually modest pet name; similar to the derogatory joke-description 'hung like a cashew' *UK, 2001*. **2** a transvestite. From northern England, likely to derive from the sense as 'a small penis' *UK, 1966*. **3** a capsule of a barbiturate or other sedative *US, 1967*

peanut butter *noun* low quality, impure amphetamine *US, 1989*

peanut gallery *noun* the least expensive seats in a theatre; more abstractly, an audience *US, 1888*

peanut grifter *noun* a small-time swindler *US, 1953*

peanut heaven *noun* the uppermost gallery in a theatre or arena *US, 1946*

peanut poker *noun* poker played for very small stakes *US, 1988*

peanuts *noun* a very small sum of money *US, 1934*

peanuts and donkey farts *noun* in poker, three two's *US, 1948*

peanut smuggler *noun* a woman whose nipples, especially when erect, are apparent through her clothing *AUSTRALIA, 2003*

peanut wagon *noun* in trucking, a small tractor pulling a large trailer *US, 1946*

pea-picker *noun* a gambler who only bets very small sums. A pun on 'p' (pence) *UK, 1984*

pea, pie, and pud *noun* a meal consisting of a meat pie, peas and mashed potatoes *NEW ZEALAND, 1984*

pea pod *noun* ▶ **on your pea pod** alone. Glasgow rhyming slang on Cockney rhyming slang 'on your tod' (**TOD SLOAN**) *UK: SCOTLAND, 1985*

pearl *noun* **1** an ampoule of amyl nitrite *US, 1971*. **2** cocaine *US, 1984*

pearl dive *noun* when surfing, an occasion when you are forced deep under the water by a wave *US, 1957*

pearl dive *verb* to perform oral sex on a woman. From the metaphor of the clitoris as a pearl *US, 1994*

pearl-diver *noun* **1** a dishwasher in a restaurant *US, 1913*. **2** a five-pound note; the sum of £5 *UK: SCOTLAND, 1985*

pearl diving *noun* oral sex *US, 1949*

pearler *noun* something exceptional. Variant of **PURLER** *AUSTRALIA, 1941*

Pearl Harbour *adjective* of weather, cold. From the Japanese air attack on Pearl Harbour, 7th December 1941; punning **NIP** (Japanese) and the conventional phrase 'a nasty nip in the air' (cold weather). This term seems to have emerged following the 2001 release of the film *Pearl Harbor UK, 2002*

pearlies *noun* **1** the teeth. A shortened form of **PEARLY WHITES**. Also variant 'pearls' *UK, 1914*. **2** a chronic shaking of the bowing arm suffered by violinists *UK, 1974*

pearl necklace *noun* semen ejaculated on a woman's throat and breasts, especially after penis-breast contact *US, 1984*

pearl of a great price *noun* in horse racing, a pure-bred Arabian racehorse *AUSTRALIA, 1989*

pearly gate *noun* a plate. Rhyming slang *UK, 1992*

pearly gates *noun* **1** LSD *US, 1971*. **2** morning glory seeds, rumoured to have hallucinogenic powers *US, 1971*

Pearly Girl *noun* in British Columbia, a local variety of marijuana *CANADA, 2002*

pearly king; pearly *noun* the anus. Rhyming slang for **RING**, formed on a traditional, well-decorated Cockney character *UK, 1992*

pearly whites *noun* the teeth *US, 1935*

pear-shaped *adjective* no longer perfect; describing anything that is now wrong *UK, 2001*

peas and rice boongy *noun* large buttocks *BAHAMAS, 1995*

peasant *noun* **1** a person below your station. Originally British military slang *UK, 1943*. **2** in circus and carnival usage, a customer who does not show proper appreciation for a performance *US, 1981*

peasants *noun* ▶ **the peasants are revolting** a catchphrase that is applied to a general swell of grumbling, used by more senior officers of junior ranks in the military, of a workforce as distinct from management, of students in relation to their educators, etc. A tireless pun on 'revolting' *UK, 1984*

pease pudding hot; pease pudding *noun* nasal mucus. Rhyming slang for SNOT, formed on a traditional rhyme: 'Pease pudding hot / Pease pudding cold / Pease pudding in the pot / Nine days old'. This is *not* a pun on the colour of peas – pease pudding is a golden-hued dish, made from yellow split-peas *UK, 1992*

peashooter *noun* **1** a small-calibre handgun *US, 1950*. **2** the nose. Rhyming slang for HOOTER *UK, 1992*

peas-in-a-pot; peas in the pot; peas; peasy *adjective* hot. Rhyming slang *UK, 1960*

peas on a drum *noun* small female breasts *UK, 1980*

pea-soup *noun* a French-Canadian. In the citation, Richler is referring indirectly to the Montreal hockey team, the Canadiens *CANADA, 2002*

pea-souper *noun* **1** a dense yellowish fog. From the adjective PEA-SOUPY *UK, 1890*. **2** a French-Canadian. This term derives from the ubiquitous Quebec pea-soup, made with ham, still a favourite despite the negative connotations *CANADA, 1978*

pea-soupy; soupy *adjective* descriptive of dense, yellowish fog *UK, 1860*

peasy; peasie *adjective* used of hair, short and curled tightly *BAHAMAS, 1982*

peata; pata *noun* a spoiled child; a favourite child *IRELAND, 1999*

pebble *noun* a piece of crack cocaine. The ROCK metaphor used again; the plural means crack generally *US, 1989*

pebble-dash *verb* to splatter a lavatory bowl with faeces as the result of a dramatic expulsion of diarrhoea *UK, 2003*

Pebble Mill *noun* **1** a pill, especially one that is taken recreationally. Rhyming slang, formed from an area of Birmingham that is best known as the address of BBC television studios, and the title of a programme broadcast from there, 1973–86 *UK, 1998*. **2** a slight or perfunctory kiss *UK, 1893*. **3** on the railways, the lunch period *US, 1977*

peck *verb* **1** to eat *UK, 1665*. **2** to kiss someone in a slight or perfunctory manner *UK, 1969*

pecker *noun* **1** the penis *UK, 1902*. **2** by extension, a despicable person *US, 1988*. **3** courage, especially in the phrase 'keep your pecker up' *UK, 1853*

pecker checker *noun* **1** a military doctor or medic who inspects male recruits for signs of sexually transmitted disease *US, 1967*. **2** a member of a police vice squad targeting homosexual activity *US, 1970*

pecker-foolish *noun* used of a woman, overly obsessed with men and sex *US, 1977*

peckerhead *noun* a despicable or offensive person. Formed from PECKER 'penis', not PECKERWOOD 'racist' *US, 1802*

peckerman *noun* a rapist *US, 1990*

peckerneck *noun* on the railways, a newly hired apprentice *US, 1975*

pecker pole *noun* an undersize tree, not worth logging *CANADA, 1989*

pecker tracks *noun* stains from seminal fluid *US, 1964*

peckerwood *noun* **1** a non-Italian *US, 1980*. **2** a white rural southerner, especially an uncouth and racist one. Not praise. Also shortened variants 'peck', 'pecker' and 'wood' *US, 1904*

Peckham Rye; Peckham *noun* a tie (an article of menswear). Rhyming slang, after an area of south London *UK, 1925*

pecks *noun* food *US, 1958*

pecky *adjective* characterised by well developed chest muscles *US, 1997*

pecs *noun* the pectoralis major muscles *US, 1966*

ped *noun* a pedestrian *UK, 1999*

pedalling with both feet; pedalling *verb* (used of a vehicle, or driver of that vehicle) to achieve top speed. Conjures a misleading image of pedalling a bicycle; the pedal in question is an accelerator *US, 1976*

pedal pusher *noun* a bicyclist *US, 1934*

pedal-pushers *noun* calf-length trousers for women or girls. Originally designed to be suitable for a PEDAL PUSHER (a bicyclist), and variously in and out of fashion since *US, 1944*

pedal to the metal *adjective* used of a motor vehicle, throttled to the maximum *US, 1993*

'ped boy *noun* a young, male, moped rider; a younger, male, BMX cyclist *UK, 2003*

peddle and crank *verb* to masturbate. Rhyming slang for WANK *UK, 2003*

peddler *noun* **1** a prisoner who sells goods to other prisoners *US, 1980*. **2** on the railways, a local freight train *US, 1960*

peddle run *noun* in trucking, a job with frequent stops for deliveries *US, 1971*

pedestrian spear *noun* a large, sharp car radiator ornament *US, 1962*

'ped-head *noun* a motor-scooter enthusiast. Apparently derived from 'moped' and -HEAD (an enthusiast) *UK, 2004*

pedigree *noun* a person's background *US, 1976*

pedigree chum *noun* semen; an orgasm. Rhyming slang for COME, formed on branded dog food Pedigree Chum™ *UK, 1992*

pedlar's pack *noun* dismissal from employment. Rhyming slang for 'sack' *UK, 1992*

pedo *noun* trouble; nonsense. Border Spanish used in English conversation by Mexican-Americans *US, 1974*

Pedro *noun* **1** cocaine. Given a Spanish name (Peter) to suggest a South American nationality for the supplier *UK, 1999*. **2** a survival winch mounted on a military helicopter *US, 1991*

pee *noun* an act of urination; urine *UK, 1902*

pee *verb* to urinate *UK, 1879*. ▶ **pee yourself laughing** to laugh uproariously *UK, 1946*

pee halt *noun* a brief stop during a combat patrol so soldiers could urinate *US, 1991*

peek *noun* ▶ **the peek** in prison, the observation cell *UK, 1950*

peekaboo *adjective* **1** said of a garment with decorative holes or slashes *US, 1895*. **2** used of a mirror, see-through from outside the room *US, 1992*

peeker *noun* a thief who operates by observing the numbers given at a clockroom and then using a counterfeit check to retrieve valuable items that have been checked in *US, 1954*

peek freak *noun* **1** a voyeur *US, 1967*. **2** a casino blackjack gambler who consistently tries to see the dealer's down card *US, 1981*

peek man *noun* a lookout during an illegal or forbidden activity in prison *US, 1976*

peel *noun* a caustic chemical treatment of the skin (dermabrasion) *US, 1997*

peel *verb* **1** to undress *UK, 1785*. **2** to perform a striptease. Originally a term used by and with athletes, later by and with stripteasers *US, 1948*. **3** to pry something open *US, 1968*. **4** (used of a pimp) to entice a prostitute away from her current pimp *US, 1993*. **5** to fire a gun *US, 2001*. ▶ **get peeled** when filming a film or television programme, to extend the shooting into overtime for the crew *US, 1997*. ▶ **peel caps** to shoot someone *US, 1993*. ▶ **peel one off** to fart. Perhaps this should be 'peal' for the ringing tones *UK, 1978*. ▶ **peel wheels** to accelerate a car quickly, squealing the tyres and leaving rubber marks on the road. 1989 *US, 1989*. ▶ **peel your banana** to pull back the foreskin of your penis for inspection or as part of masturbating *US, 2002*

peeled *adjective* of the eyes, open, thus alert and observant. 'Keep 'em peeled' is a catchphrase associated with Shaw Taylor, presenter of a television police assistance programme *Police 5* since the early 1970s *US, 1853*

peeler *noun* **1** a police officer. After Robert Peel, as founder of the Irish constabulary *IRELAND, 1817*. **2** a striptease dancer *US, 1948*. **3** a fast, well-developed wave *US, 1964*

peel-off *noun* a theft of part of a common booty. Criminal and police slang *UK, 1959*

peel out *verb* to accelerate a car suddenly from a stopped position, squealing the tyres on the road *US, 1973*

peelywally *adjective* drunk. From Scottish *peelie-wallie* (sickly) *UK: SCOTLAND, 2002*

peeny *adjective* very small *BARBADOS, 1965*

peeny-weeny *adjective* tiny *TRINIDAD AND TOBAGO, 1993*

peep *noun* **1** a quick glance *UK, 1730*. **2** a two-way mirror *US, 1975*. **3** a clandestine photographer *US, 1982*. **4** a sexually desirable woman. An abbreviation of the somewhat coarse 'perfectly elegant eatin' pussy' *US, 1977*. **5** something spoken, especially in a negative context *UK, 1903*

peep *verb* **1** to look at something, to discover something. Variation of conventional 'peep' (to look) *US, 1992*. **2** to listen to someone or something *US, 2000*. **3** to read music *US, 1964*. ▶ **peep the holecard** to gain deep insight into someone's character *US, 1981*

pee pad *noun* a motorcycle passenger seat *US, 2003*

peepe *noun* the vagina *US, 1998*

pee-pee *noun* **1** urine; urination. Childish *UK, 1923*. **2** the penis. Children's toilet vocabulary. Also variant 'pi-pi' *US, 1967*

peeper *noun* **1** an eye. A definite old-fashioned feel to the term. Popularised in 1938 with the film *Going Places* and the song by Harry Warren: 'Jeepers, creepers/ Where'd you get them peepers?' *UK, 1700*. **2** a voyeur *UK, 1652*. **3** a private investigator or private detective *US, 1943*. **4** a police detective. From an earlier sense as 'policeman' *UK, 1996*. **5** a card player who tries to see another player's cards *US, 1988*. **6** a one-way eye-hole in a door allowing the person on the inside to see who is outside; a peephole *US, 1996*

peepers *noun* **1** a vehicle's headlights *US, 1976*. **2** night-vision enhancing equipment *US, 1991*

peep freak *noun* a voyeur *US, 1975*

peep-hole special *noun* sex in a public toilet *US, 1966*

pee pill *noun* a pill containing an agent that increases the excretion of urine *US, 1968*

peeping Tom *noun* **1** a voyeur; a person who spies on others *UK, 1795*. **2** in poker or other card games, a player or spectator who tries to see another's hand *US, 1996*. **3** a variety of MDMA, the recreational drug best known as ecstasy, identified by PT embossed on the tablet *UK, 2002*

pee-poor *adjective* very poor. A variation on the much more common PISS-POOR *US, 1964*

peep out *verb* to look at something carefully; to examine something *US, 1990*

peeps *noun* people; friends. A probably coincidental usage, based on accidental English, was popularised in the UK by 'Stavros the Greek kebab seller', a character created by comedian Harry Enfield for Channel 4 television's *Friday Night Live* in 1988 *US, 1995*

peep show *noun* an arcade where it is possible to view pornographic videos or a nude woman in private booths; formerly an arcade where it was possible to view photographs of scantily clad women *US, 1947*

peep this look at this *US, 1997*

peer queer *noun* a male homosexual who takes pleasure in watching others have sex *US, 1970*

pee-spout *noun* the penis *UK, 1998*

peeties *noun* dice that have been altered with small weights to produce a desired number when rolled *US, 1962*

peeve *noun* alcohol; drink. Market traders and English gypsy use *UK, 1979*

peevied *adjective* drunk *UK, 2002*

peewat *noun* a person of neither importance nor signficance *TRINIDAD AND TOBAGO, 1982*

pee wee *verb* in dice games with no bank, to roll the dice to see who will play first *US, 1950*

peewee *adjective* composed of children *US, 1877*

peewee; pee wee *noun* **1** the penis *US, 1998*. **2** a very young member of a youth gang *US, 1981*. **3** a small, tightly rolled marijuana cigarette *US, 1970*. **4** crack cocaine *US, 1994*. **5** in craps, a roll of three *US, 1999*

peg *noun* **1** a look *AUSTRALIA, 1973*. **2** a person's leg *UK, 1878*. **3** heroin *US, 1994*. **4** a golf tee *US, 1946*. ▶ **give a peg** to reconnoitre, especially with criminal intent *AUSTRALIA, 1975*. ▶ **on the peg** of driving, at the speed limit. Citizens' band radio slang *UK, 1981*

peg *verb* **1** to watch or look at someone *AUSTRALIA, 1970*. **2** to identify someone or something *US, 1940*. **3** to push a disabled motorcycle with a second motorcycle by reaching out and putting your leg on the foot-rest (peg) of the disabled motorcycle *US, 2000*. **4** to throw something *AUSTRALIA, 1941*. **5** to put someone on report. Originally military, then recorded in use in borstals and detention centres *UK, 1948*. **6** in a card cheating scheme, to prepare a deck for a manoeuvre *US, 1962*. **7** to fix the market price of something. Originally Stock Exchange slang, then more general *UK, 1882*. ▶ **peg it 1** to walk; to walk fast; to run; to hurry. A variation of LEG IT formed on PEG (the leg) *UK, 2004*. **2** to die. A variation of PEG OUT *UK, 1994*

peg away *verb* to labour persistently; to continue to toil *UK, 1818*

peg boy *noun* in male homosexual intercourse, a passive partner *US, 1960*

pegged *adjective* under surveillance *UK, 1996*

pegged out *adjective* dead. From PEG OUT (to die) *US, 2000*

pegger *noun* a tooth *BARBADOS, 1965*

peggy *noun* a person employed to make tea and lunch for labourers *AUSTRALIA, 1971*

Peggy Lee fastball *noun* in baseball, a fast ball that is not particularly fast. From Peggy Lee's hit recording of 'Is That All There Is?' *US, 1980*

Peggy's Leg *nickname* a sweet in the form of a longish stalk; a stick of rock *IRELAND, 1983*

peg leg *noun* a wooden or artificial leg *UK, 1833*. ▶ **peg out** to die. Possibly from the game of cribbage, less likely from croquet *UK, 1855*

pegs *noun* **1** tapered trousers very fashionable in the US in the late 1950s and 60s *US, 1969*. **2** the external vaginal lips *TRINIDAD AND TOBAGO, 2003*

peke-a-poo *noun* a crossbreed of a pekinese and a poodle *US, 2001*

Pekinese *adjective* ▶ **do the Pekinese pop-out** to become wide-eyed with shock or wonder. An allusion to the appearance of a pedigree Pekinese dog *US, 1999*

pekkie; perkie *noun* a black person. Offensive *SOUTH AFRICA, 1963*

pelican *noun* a water bomber, for firefighting *CANADA, 1997*

pellet *noun* a tablet or capsule of LSD *US, 1990*

pelt *noun* a woman's pubic hair; sex; a woman as a sex object. Building on the vulva-as-BEAVER image *US, 1980*. ▶ **stroke the pelt** (of a female) to masturbate *US, 2001*

pelt *verb* ▶ **pelt wood** to thrust with vigour during sex *TRINIDAD AND TOBAGO, 2003*

pelter *noun* in poker, a non-standard hand consisting of a 9, a 5, a 2, one card between 5 and 9 and one card between 2 and 5 *US, 1963*

pen *noun* **1** a jail or prison. Shortened from 'penitentiary.' *US, 1884*. **2** a detention or holding room at a jail or courthouse *US, 1979*

penalty box *noun* the area behind the back seat of an SUV or station wagon *US, 2004*

pen and ink; pen *noun* **1** a noisome smell; a stink. Rhyming slang *UK, 1859*. **2** a mink as an item of wardrobe. Rhyming slang *UK, 1956*. **3** a drink. Rhyming slang *NEW ZEALAND, 1963*

pen and ink; pen *verb* **1** to smell rank; to stink. Rhyming slang *UK, 1977*. **2** to drink *AUSTRALIA, 1983*

pen and pencil set *noun* in electric line work, a digging bar and spoon shovel *US, 1980*

pen bait *noun* a girl under the age of sexual consent. A variation on the more common JAILBAIT *US, 1964*

pencil *noun* **1** the penis. Perhaps borrowing a Mark Twain pun: 'the penis mightier than the sword' *UK, 1937*. **2** in a casino, the authority to give a gambler complimentary drinks or meals. Often phrased as 'power of the pencil' *US, 1977*

pencil *verb* to work as a penciller *AUSTRALIA, 1919*

pencil dick *noun* a thin penis; used, generally, to insult a man by attacking a perception of his masculinity *US, 1998*

penciller *noun* a bookmaker's clerk who writes out betting tickets *AUSTRALIA, 1891*

pencil-neck geek *noun* a bookish, timid, weak man. The term was popularised, if not coined, by US professional wrestler 'Classy' Freddie Blassie to describe his opponents. Blassie recorded a novelty song so titled, written by Johnny Legend and Pete Cicero, in 1979 *US, 1985*

pencil-pusher *noun* **1** a person who works with words; a clerk or secretary. Usually derisive *US, 1881*. **2** in the US Air Force, the navigator on a bomber aircraft *US, 1946*

pencil-sharpener *noun* the vagina. Corresponds, quite logically, with PENCIL (the penis) *UK, 2003*

pencil stiff *noun* a clerical worker. Derisive *US, 1957*

pencil talk *noun* bargaining over a price in a bazaar carried on by writing down the offer. Vietnam war usage *US, 1968*

pencil-whip *verb* **1** to file constant lawsuits and complaints against prison authorities *US, 1992*. **2** to write someone a traffic ticket or notice of a criminal infraction *US, 2001*

pend *verb* to listen; to pay attention *US, 1968*

pendejo *noun* a fool. From the Spanish of Mexican-Americans, literally translated as 'a pubic hair' *US, 1974*

Penelope *noun* a well-built, attractive, somewhat dim woman. The personification of a BIMBO, probably named after an identified celebrity, recorded in contemporary gay usage *UK, 2003*

penetrate *verb* to understand something after analysis *JAMAICA, 2003*

penguin *noun* **1** LSD. Presumably from the picture printed on the blotting paper dose *UK, 1998*. **2** a prison officer. From the black and white uniform *UK, 1996*. **3** a nun *US, 1980*. ▶ **go penguin** in pool, to enter a formal tournament. A reference to the tuxedo that is mandated by the dress code of some tournaments *US, 1990*

penguin *adjective* pregnant *AUSTRALIA, 1985*

penguin food *noun* anchovies. Limited usage, but clever *US, 1996*

penguin suit; penguin outfit *noun* a tuxedo or formal evening dress *UK, 1967*

penis breath *noun* used as a general-purpose insult *US, 1986*

penitentiary pull *noun* influence within a prison *US, 1985*

penitentiary punk *noun* a male who starts taking part in homosexual sex in prison *US, 1972*

penitentiary turn-out *noun* a man who begins engaging in homosexual sex in prison *US, 1972*

penman *noun* a forger *UK, 1865*

pennies *noun* a substantial amount of money *UK, 1999*

penn'orth of chalk; penn'orth *noun* a walk. Rhyming slang *UK, 1938*

Pennsy *nickname* the Pennsylvania Railroad *US, 1953*

Pennsylvania caps *noun* in trucking, tyres that have been recapped with a seamless tread line *US, 1971*

penny *noun* one dollar *US, 1972*. ▶ **the penny drops; the penny's dropped; the penny will drop in minute; did I hear a penny drop?** used in marking the belated understanding of something, often of a delayed appreciation of humour. There are more variations on this theme than are shown here *UK, 1951*

penny *verb* to force pennies into the space between a door and the jam near the hinges, making it difficult or, if done correctly, impossible to open the door from the inside *US, 1989*

penny a mile *noun* a smile. Rhyming slang *UK, 1960*

penny-ante *adjective* petty, insignificant. From a poker game with a one-cent 'ante' or buy-in, an insignificant stake *US, 1935*

penny a pound; penny *noun* the ground. Rhyming slang *UK, 1932*

penny banger *noun* a mistake. Rhyming slang for CLANGER *UK, 1992*

penny black; penny *noun* **1** the back. Rhyming slang, based on a famously rare stamp *UK, 1992*. **2** the floor. By extension from 'penny black' (the back) via the sense to be knocked on your back, thus onto the floor *UK, 2002*

penny bun *noun* **1** one, especially in connection with racing odds. Rhyming slang *UK, 1984*. **2** the sun. Rhyming slang *UK, 1992*

penny for the guy *noun* a pie. Rhyming slang, formed from the catchphrase of children collecting funds to celebrate Guy Fawkes' night *UK, 1998*

penny game *noun* the gambling game two-up *AUSTRALIA, 1966*

penny locket *noun* a pocket. Rhyming slang *UK, 1998*

penny-nickle-nickle *noun* an M-114 155-mm howitzer. The standard infantry heavy artillery weapon during the Vietnam war *US, 1990*

penny-pinching *adjective* frugal *US, 1920*

penny stamp *noun* a tramp. Rhyming slang *UK, 1984*

pension *noun* ▶ **on a pension** of a policeman, having been bribed *UK, 1996*

pension run *noun* in trucking, an easy, undemanding, regular route *US, 1971*

Pentagon East *noun* the US military command in Tan Son Nhut air base, South Vietnam *US, 1975*

penthouse *noun* a brakevan (caboose) cupola *US, 1977*

pen yan *noun* opium; heroin. Originally used of opium only and thought to be from a Chinese term for opium. Many variants, including 'pen yang', 'pan yen', 'pen yen', 'pen yuen', 'pin yen', 'pinyon' and 'pin gon' *US, 1922*

peon *noun* an ordinary computer user with no special privileges *US, 1995*

people *noun* **1** narcotics police *US, 1957*. **2** a prisoner's closest friends and associates *US, 1992*

People *noun* ▶ **the People** the masses, at least to the extent that the masses support the agenda advocated by the speaker. Egalitarian or communist undertones *US, 1961*

people zapper *noun* a Vehicle Mounted Active Denial System or VMADS, a tank or jeep-mounted crowd control weapon *US, 2001*

pep *noun* **1** energy *UK, 1912*. **2** pepperoni *US, 1996*. **3** phencyclidine, the recreational drug known as PCP or angel dust *US, 1982*

pep-em-up *noun* an amphetamine or other central nervous system stimulant *US, 1980*

pepper *noun* **1** an inexperienced, gullible victim of a gambling cheat. Playing on 'green' as a colour and as a slang badge of inexperience *US, 1974*. **2** cinders spread on a snowy road *US, 1976*

pepper and salt punter *noun* a bettor who places bets by telephone from home *AUSTRALIA, 1989*

pepperbelly *noun* a Mexican or Mexican-American *US, 1970*

pep pill *noun* a central nervous system stimulant in a tablet form. A deceptive yet accurate euphemism that persisted for several decades, especially with students *US, 1937*

Pepsi *adjective* sexually frigid. Presumably because Pepsi™ is 'best served chilled' *UK, 2001*

Pepsi; pepper *noun* a French-Canadian. Originally directed as an insult, because it was said by anglophones that French-Canadians chose Pepsi™ over Coca-Cola™ because they thought the cans were larger, it has been adopted as a badge of pride, especially in the derived form 'pepper' *CANADA, 1978*

Pepsi habit; Pepsi Cola habit *noun* the occasional use of a drug, short of an all-out addiction *US, 1970*

pep talk *noun* a brief, emotional speech made to encourage or increase morale *US, 1925*

pep up *verb* to invigorate someone; to strengthen or enhance something *UK, 1925*

per *noun* percentage *US, 1974*

perambulator *noun* a brakevan (caboose) *US, 1977*

percentage *noun* a profit; an advantage. Originally military *UK, 1948*

percentage dice *noun* dice that have been altered to favour a certain roll *US, 1975*

percentage joint *noun* a carnival concession that relies on volume for profit *US, 1985*

percentage player *noun* a gambler who appreciates odds and percentages, absorbing losses in the belief that the odds will ultimately favour him *US, 1961*

percenter *noun* an ex-girlfriend *BAHAMAS, 1982*

perch *noun* ▶ **drop off the perch; fall off the perch** to die *UK, 1937*

percher *noun* among the police, an easy arrest or an easy victim; in cricket, a very easy catch *UK, 1977*

percia *noun* cocaine *UK, 2003*

percolate *verb* to meander; to be doing fine *US, 1945*

percolator *noun* a carburettor *US, 1971*

percussion adjustment *noun* a blow to mechanical equipment with a large hammer. A jocular term for a popular technique, in Royal Air Force use *UK, 2002*

Percy *noun* **1** the penis. Used as the title of a 1971 British film comedy about a penis-transplant *UK, 1977*. **2** an effeminate male *US, 1955*. **3** a rock band's road manager *UK, 1985*. **4** cocaine *UK, 1999*

percy *adverb* per se (intrinsically) *UK, 1994*

Percy Thrower *noun* a telephone. Rhyming slang for BLOWER, formed on the name of television's first 'gardening superstar', 1913–88 *UK, 1992*

perdue *noun* in poker, an unplayable hand abandoned by a player. From the French for 'lost' *US, 1988*

perf *noun* a performance *UK, 2004*

perf *verb* to retire someone on medical grounds. From the acronym of the *Police Employment Rehabilitation Fund* *NEW ZEALAND, 1991*

perf *adjective* perfect *AUSTRALIA, 1979*

perfect high *noun* heroin *UK, 1998*

perfection *noun* perfect surfing conditions *AUSTRALIA, 1992*

perfecto *adjective* first-class, perfect, wonderful. A simple embellishment in the Spanish style *US, 1988*

perfects *noun* dice that are true to an extremely minute tolerance, approximately 1/1000th of a inch *US, 1950*

perform *verb* to behave histrionically *AUSTRALIA, 1891*

performer *noun* a person who behaves histrionically *AUSTRALIA, 1960*

perf surf *noun* excellent surfing conditions *AUSTRALIA, 1987*

perico *noun* cocaine. Spanish slang, adopted by some English speakers; in Spanish *Perico* is a pet name for *Pedro*, and the name PEDRO also serves in English slang as another alias for cocaine *US, 1994*

perish *noun* ▶ **do a perish** to suffer great deprivation, especially of water or sustenance *AUSTRALIA, 1897*

perisher *noun* a person. Usually contemptuous or pitying. *The Perishers* cartoon strip by Maurice Dodd and Dennis Collins/Bill Melvin has appeared in Mirror Group newspapers since 1957 *UK, 1896*

perishing *adjective* very cold. Shortened from 'perishing cold' *UK, 2003*

perishing *infix* used as an intensifier *UK, 1999*

perjohnny *noun* a poor white person *BARBADOS, 1965*

perk *noun* **1** an advantage, in addition to salary, that is offered by a particular employment. An abbreviation of 'perquisite' *UK, 1869*. **2** a tablet of Percodan™, a painkiller. Also variant 'perc' *US, 1971*

perk *verb* to vomit *AUSTRALIA, 1941*

perk up *verb* to recover good spirits or vigour *UK, 1656*

perky *adjective* said of a woman with large buttocks but otherwise a slender body *US, 2004*

perlix *verb* to flaunt your technical skills *BARBADOS, 1965*

perm *noun* in hairdressing, a permanent wave *UK, 1927*

perm *verb* to give hair a permanent wave hair treatment *UK, 1928*

perma- *prefix* permanent; permanently. Acts as adjective or adverb as required *UK, 2004*

permafried *adjective* drug-intoxicated *UK, 2003*

perma-tan *noun* a permanent suntan *UK, 2003*

perp *noun* **1** a criminal suspect. From 'perpetrator' *US, 1987*. **2** wax and baking soda made to look like crack cocaine *US, 1994*

perpetrate *verb* to start a fight *US, 2001*

perp walk *noun* a purposeful display of a charged criminal, especially when being transported from jail to court *US, 1994*

Perry *noun* a member of a 1970s youth movement identified by a uniform of casual wear. From the branded Fred *Perry* casual shirts they wore *UK, 1996*

Perry Como *noun* a homosexual. Rhyming slang for HOMO formed, for no apparent reason other than rhyme, on the popular singer, 1912–2001 *UK, 1992*

pers *adjective* personal *UK, 1997*

Persian *noun* heroin purportedly grown in or near Iran *US, 1981*

Persian brown *noun* heroin *US, 1993*

Persian mafia *noun* a group of influential Iranians *US, 1997*

Persian rugs *noun* drugs. Rhyming slang *UK, 2003*

persnickety *adjective* fussy, snobbish. An alteration of 'pernickety' *US, 1905*

personality girl *noun* a popular woman who works in a bar, encouraging customers through flirtation to buy drinks, both for themselves and for her *US, 1950*

persuader *noun* **1** any weapon, the more deadly the more persuasive *UK, 1796*. **2** a whip, as used by a bullock driver or a jockey *AUSTRALIA, 1890*. **3** a linear amplifier for a citizens' band radio *US, 1977*

persuasion *noun* nationality; sex; kind. From the conventional sense (religious belief or opinion) *UK, 1864*

Peruvian *noun* cocaine, probably from Peru *UK, 1998*

Peruvian flake *noun* a powerful type of cocaine. From its country of origin *US, 1984*

Peruvian lady *noun* cocaine *US, 1994*

Peruvian marching powder *noun* cocaine. A variation of BOLIVIAN/COLOMBIAN MARCHING POWDER *US, 1995*

Peruvian pink *noun* a type of cocaine originating in Peru *UK, 2002*

perv; perve *noun* **1** a sexual pervert. Sometimes 'perv' carries the same force as its origin 'pervert', thus 'someone with a kinky sexual bent', 'a person obsessed with sex', 'a lecher' or 'a homosexual' (by those who regard this as unnatural). Can also be used in a weaker sense to refer to anyone whose sexual behaviour is unwanted *AUSTRALIA, 1942*. **2** in prison, a sex offender; a convicted paedophile. An abbreviation of 'pervert' *AUSTRALIA, 1949*. **3** a person watching or staring sexually; a voyeur *AUSTRALIA, 1944*. **4** a voyeuristic look *AUSTRALIA, 1963*. **5** a look *AUSTRALIA, 1993*

perv; perve *verb* **1** to lust after another person; to behave as a voyeur *AUSTRALIA, 1941*. **2** to look at or watch sexually *AUSTRALIA, 1944*. **3** to look at; to observe *AUSTRALIA, 1984*

pervert squad *noun* a police sex crime investigative squad *US, 1996*

perving *noun* sexual ogling; voyeurism *AUSTRALIA, 1967*

pervy *adjective* sexually perverted; pornographic *UK, 1944*

pesky *adjective* annoying, disagreeable *US, 1775*

pessimal *adjective* as bad as bad can be. Computer slang *US, 1983*

pest control *noun* a psychiatrist; psychiatrists. Medical slang *UK, 2002*

pet *verb* ▶ **pet the cat** to stroke the air or water while getting through a difficult moment surfing *US, 1991*

petal *noun* used as an informal or affectionate term of address *UK, 1980*

Pete *noun* **1** a truck manufactured by Peterbilt *US, 1971*. **2** nitroglycerin *US, 1949*. ▶ **for Pete's sake** used as a mild, non-profane oath used in times of exasperation or annoyance *US, 1924*

pete man *noun* a criminal specialising in breaking into safes *US, 1931*

Pete Murray *noun* a curry. Rhyming slang, formed on the name of a radio DJ (b.1928) *UK, 1998*

peter *noun* **1** the penis *UK, 1902*. **2** a cell in a prison or a police station. The likely derivation is in the the proper name Peter, which comes from Greek *petros* perhaps influenced by *petra* – with the implication 'firm as a rock' *AUSTRALIA, 1890*. **3** a safe *US, 1859*

Peter and his fuzzy pals *noun* the male genitals. An elaboration of PETER (the penis) *US, 2001*

peter-crazy *adjective* obsessed with having sex with men *US, 1972*

peter drops; peter; petes *noun* specifically, knock-out drops; generally, any central nervous system depressant *US, 1933*

peter-eater *noun* a person who enjoys performing oral sex on men *US, 1978*

peter-gazer *noun* a prisoner who cannot hide his interest in other men's penises while in the showers *US, 2001*

peter heater *noun* **1** an act of urination while wearing a wetsuit *US, 1991*. **2** in Canadian military aviation, the pitot heater. The 'pitot tube' is a small tube pointed forward into the airstream, to compare inside and outside pressure and measure airspeed. In cold weather, it can freeze up and must be heated electrically *CANADA, 1995*

peterman *noun* a safe-breaker *UK, 1900*

Peter O'Toole *noun* a stool, especially a bar stool. Rhyming slang, formed from the name of the celebrated Irish actor (b.1932) *UK, 1998*

peter out *verb* to gradually cease; to come to an end *US, 1854*

peter pan *noun* **1** a van. Rhyming slang, formed from J.M. Barrie's immortal hero Peter Pan *UK, 1992*. **2** a pan used by prostitutes while washing a customer's penis. A crude if smart allusion to J.M. Barrie *US, 1974*

peter parade *noun* a mass inspection of soldiers for signs of sexually transmitted infections *US, 1947*

peter pilot *noun* a co-pilot, especially one in training *US, 1987*

peter pocket *noun* the vagina. Seen as a container for a PETER (PENIS) *US, 2001*

peter-puffer *noun* a person who performs oral sex on a man *US, 1987*

Peters and Lee; peters *noun* an act of urination. Rhyming slang for PEE or WEE, formed from a 1970s recording act *UK, 1998*

peter thief *noun* a prisoner who steals from others' cells. From PETER (a cell) *AUSTRALIA, 1950*

peter thin *noun* a prisoner who steals from others' cells. From PETER (a cell) *UK, 1996*

peter tracks *noun* stains from seminal fluid *US, 1993*

Pete Tong *noun* a variety of MDMA, the recreational drug best known as ecstasy, identified by PT embossed on the tablet. Disguising PT with the name of a UK DJ associated with the RAVE scene *UK, 2002*

Pete Tong *adjective* wrong. Rhyming slang, based on the name of popular club and BBC Radio 1 DJ, Pete Tong (b.1960) *UK, 1996*

peth *noun* Pethidine™ a branded central nervous system depressant *UK, 1998*

petro *adjective* anxious, nervous, afraid *US, 2003*

petrol bowsers; petrols *noun* trousers. Rhyming slang. Petrol bowser is a proprietary name for a pump *AUSTRALIA, 1971*

petrol head *noun* **1** a motor vehicle enthusiast *AUSTRALIA, 1985*. **2** a fast and reckless driver *NEW ZEALAND, 1998*

petrol tank *noun* an act of masturbation. Rhyming slang for WANK *UK, 1998*

Petticoat Lane *noun* a physical pain; a pain (a nuisance). Rhyming slang, formed on London's famous Sunday market *UK, 1992*

Petula *noun* central London. Almost certainly a reference to singer Petula Clark (b.1932) who enjoyed lasting success with the songs 'Downtown' and 'Don't Sleep in the Subway' *UK, 2003*

Peyton Place *noun* the face. Rhyming slang, formed from the title of 1956 novel by Grace Metalious, probably remembered here for the television drama series, 1964–69 *UK, 1998*

pezzy; pez *adjective* inferior, of poor quality. Derives from 'peasant' *UK, 2003*

PFC *noun* a private fucking citizen. What a private first class became upon his discharge from duty in Vietnam *US, 1985*

Pfizer riser *noun* sildenafil citrate marketed as Viagra™, an anti-impotence drug. Viagra™ is manufactured by Pfizer, and 'riser' is a convenient rhyme that suggests the drug's power to stimulate an erection *US, 1998*

PFO *adjective* a hospital patient who was injured while drunk. From 'pissed, fell over' *AUSTRALIA, 1987*

PFQ pretty fucking quick. A variation of PDQ (pretty damn quick) *UK, 1998*

pfund *noun* ▷*see:* FUNT

p-funk *noun* **1** heroin. After the drug-driven music of George Clinton's *Parliament-Funk*adelic *UK, 1998*. **2** crack cocaine and phencyclidine mixed for smoking *US, 1994*

PG *noun* **1** paregoric elixir, a flavoured tincture of opium designed to assuage pain *US, 1953*. **2** a paying guest. An initialism *UK, 1963*

PG *adjective* excellent. An abbreviation of 'past gone' *US, 2004*

PG&E *noun* electric shock treatment. From the electric utility Pacific Gas and Electric Company *US, 1962*

PG bag *noun* a small bag for carrying your personal effects, your personal gear *US, 2000*

PGT *adjective* doctors' shorthand for the facetious diagnosis (applied to a casualty patient): pissed (drunk), got thumped. Recorded in an article about medical slang in British (3 London and 1 Cambridge) hospitals *UK, 2003*

PG Tips *noun* the lips. Rhyming slang, formed from a well-known brand of tea; a product which is famously, perhaps not coincidentally, advertised by chimpanzees *UK, 1992*

phantasmagoria *noun* an astonishing visual display. The term was coined for an 1802 exhibition of optical illusions in London. It was used throughout the C19, forgotten, and then briefly revived in the hippie era of the 1960s and 70s *UK, 1802*

phantom gobbler *noun* an anonymous giver of oral sex *UK, 2002*

phantom off *verb* in surfing, to end a ride voluntarily *AUSTRALIA, 1977*

phantom punch *nickname* the punch thrown by Muhammed Ali (then Cassius Clay) that was not seen but which knocked out his opponent Sonny Liston on 25th May 1965 *US, 1998*

Phar Lap odds *noun* in horse racing, very high odds. Phar Lap (1926–32), one of the greatest racehorses of all time, often ran with very high odds *AUSTRALIA, 1989*

pharmies *noun* prescription medication *US, 2003*

pharming *noun* the mixing and then consumption of the mixed prescription drugs *US, 2001*

phase 4 *noun* a pill of MDMA, the recreational drug best known as ecstasy, mixed with sufficient amphetamine for a 4-hour effect. Similarly, a 'phase 8' has an 8-hour effect *UK, 2002*

phat *adjective* excellent, admirable. A deliberate misspelling of FAT (good); originally black usage, now widespread via hip-hop culture *US, 1999*

phat 2 death *adjective* extremely good *US, 1999*

phat-phat; put-put *noun* a motorcycle; a three-wheeled motor-scooter taxi. Echoic *INDIA, 2003*

phatty! great! *US, 1997*

P-head *noun* a frequent user of phenobarbital, a central nervous system depressant *US, 1982*

pheasant *noun* in a gambling cheating scheme, a victim *US, 1974*

pheasant plucker *noun* a 'pleasant fucker'. A popular Spoonerism that is also part of the well-known tongue-twisters: 'I'm not a pheasant plucker / I'm a pheasant plucker's son / And I'm only plucking pheasants / 'Til the pheasant plucker comes' and 'I'm not the pheasant plucker / I'm the pheasant plucker's daughter / And I'm not plucking pheasants / When some pheasant plucker oughta'. Often used ironically with the sense 'unpleasant fucker' *UK, 1973*

phenie *noun* a capsule of phenobarbital, a central nervous system depressant *US, 1971*

phennie *noun* a capsule of phenobarbital, a central nervous system depressant *US, 1974*

pheno *noun* a capsule of phenobarbital, a central nervous system depressant *UK, 1966*

phenomenon *noun* a prodigy; a remarkable person, animal or thing *UK, 1803*

phet freak *noun* an amphetamine addict *US, 1975*

phew! used for expressing relief or suffering, as in the legendary, clichéd tabloid weather headline 'Phew! What a scorcher!' *UK, 1604*

Philadelphia bankroll *noun* a single large-denomination note wrapped around small-denomination notes, giving the impression of a great deal of money *US, 1968*

Philadelphia lawyer *noun* a shrewd and skilled lawyer who is not guided by scruples or ethics. One of many unwarranted slurs on a fine city *US, 1788*

Philadelphia mafia *noun* recording artists, record producers and radio personalities based in Philadelphia in the late 1950s *US, 1982*

Philadelphia roll *noun* a Philadelphia bankroll *US, 1972*

phile *noun* a computer file intended to assist computer hacking *US, 1996*

philharmonic *noun* *tonic* water. Rhyming slang *UK, 1992*

Philistine *noun* a usurer *US, 1974*

Phillies Blunt; Phillies; Philly; Phillie *noun* a cigar re-made to contain marijuana. Generic usage but originally made with a brand name Phillies Blunt™ cigar *US, 1992*

Philly *noun* Philadelphia, Pennsylvania *US, 1891*

philosopher *noun* a card cheat *US, 1967*

Phil the fluter; phil *noun* a gun. Rhyming slang for SHOOTER, from the eponymous hero of an Irish comic ballad, 'Phil the Fluter's Ball', 1915 *UK, 1992*

Phil the Greek *nickname* His Royal Highness Prince Philip (b.1921), Duke of Edinburgh, Earl of Merioneth and Baron Greenwich, born Prince of Greece and Denmark. Probably coined by satirical magazine *Private Eye*; it overlooks the fact that Prince Philip is actually Danish *UK, 1994*

phish *noun* an instance of stealing credit card data on the Internet *US, 2004*

phish *verb* to steal credit card data on the Internet *US, 2003*

phishing *noun* the act of stealing credit card data on the Internet *US, 1997*

phiz *noun* **1** physics, especially as a subject of study *HONG KONG, 1984*. **2** the face; the expression on the face. An abbreviation of 'physiognomy'. Also variants 'phizz' and 'phyz' *UK, 1688*

phizgig *noun* a police informer. Variant of FIZGIG *AUSTRALIA, 1956*

phizog; physog; fizzog *noun* the face; the expression on the face. An abbreviation of 'physiognomy' *UK, 1811*

Phoebe *noun* in dice games, a roll of five *US, 1945*

phoenix *noun* LSD *UK, 2003*

phone *noun* in prison, the toilet bowl in a cell. When the bowl empties of water, it is possible to talk to prisoners in other nearby cells using the pipes to carry the soundwaves *AUSTRALIA, 1978*

phone *verb* ► **phone it in** of an entertainer, to go through the motions; to produce a half-hearted performance *UK, 2003*

phone box *noun* a temporary latrine *US, 2002*

phone call *noun* in prison, a remark that someone wants to talk to you *US, 1990*

phonecard deal *noun* in prison, a trade that values a marijuana cigarette at one phonecard *UK, 1996*

phone phreak; phone freak; phreaker *noun* a person who electronically and fraudulently manipulates international telephone calls. UK use. The original phone phreaks thought of themselves as telecommunications hobbyists (John Markoff, *Wired Style*, 1996) *US, 1972*

phone phreak; phreak *verb* to hack into a telecommunications system. A play on 'freak' *US, 1998*

phone spot *noun* a telephone location used in a bookmaking operation *US, 1973*

phone wench *noun* a female customer service representative *US, 1996*

phoney; phony *adjective* fraudulent; fake; without substance *US, 1894*

phoney; phony *noun* a person who lacks sincerity and substance *US, 1900*

phoney-baloney *adjective* utterly false *US, 1989*

phonus balonus *noun* nonsense. An elaboration of PHONEY-BALONEY *US, 1932*

phony *noun* a deck of playing cards that is either stacked or marked for cheating *US, 1979*

phooey used for registering disbelief or disgust *US, 1929*

photies *noun* photographs *UK, 2002*

photo finish; photo; photer *noun* Guinness™, the branded Irish stout. Rhyming slang *UK, 1960*

photog; fotog *noun* a photographer *US, 1913*

photogenic *verb* to remember something or someone in photographic detail *UK, 1996*

phucked *adjective* drug-intoxicated. Deliberate misspelling of FUCKED (intoxicated) inspired by widespread use of PHAT (excellent) *UK, 1999*

phull on *adjective* enthusiastic. Deliberate misspelling of FULL ON (absolute) probably inspired by the widespread use of PHAT (excellent) *UK, 1999*

phunky; phungky *adjective* funky in all its senses, but especially fashionable or as a descriptor of music. Deliberate misspellings inspired by the widespread use of PHAT (excellent) *UK, 1994*

phus-phus *noun* whispering, murmuring *TRINIDAD AND TOBAGO, 1984*

phwoar *noun* a sexually attractive person. From the lecherous exclamation 'phwoar!' *UK, 2002*

phwoar!; phoor!; fwoarrrgh! used for registering an enthusiastic, possibly lecherous, reaction to a sexy someone or something *UK, 1980*

phy *noun* methadone. An shortening of Physeptone™, a branded methadone hydrochloride *UK, 1971*

physical *adjective* ► **get physical** to become violent *US, 1996*

physical jerks *noun* physical exercises. Originally jocular, now commonplace *UK, 1919*

physio *noun* **1** a physiotherapist *AUSTRALIA, 1960*. **2** physiotherapy *AUSTRALIA, 1988*

physsie *noun* a physical fitness enthusiast *BARBADOS, 1965*

PI *noun* a pimp *US, 1955*

pi *adjective* *pi*ous *UK, 1891*

piano *noun* ► **on the piano** lost *US, 1968*. ► **play the piano** to search for particles of crack cocaine with your fingers in an obsessive and compulsive manner *US, 1992*

PIB *noun* someone who dresses completely in black. A 'person in black' *US, 1990*

pic *noun* **1** a picture *UK, 1884*. **2** a phonograph record *US, 1960*

Picasso *noun* a card cheat who marks cards for identification in another player's hand *US, 1993*

Picasso arse *noun* a woman whose knickers are too tight. The works of celebrated artist Pablo Picasso (1881–1973) inspire this abstract image of a multi-buttocked female *UK, 2002*

Piccadilly; picca *adjective* silly. Rhyming slang, based on the famous central London location *UK, 1992*

Piccadilly Percy *noun* mercy. Rhyming slang *UK, 1979*

piccalilli *noun* the penis. Rhyming slang for **WILLY**, formed on a popular pickle *UK, 1998*

piccaninny *noun* **1** an Australian Aboriginal child. Considered offensive *AUSTRALIA, 1817*. **2** a small black child; children; occasionally any black person. From Spanish *pequeño* (small) or Portuguese *pequeno* (small). Originally applied in the West Indies and US without being considered racist; now highly offensive and derogatory or, in a black-on-black context, judgemental and negative. Also variants 'piccanin', 'picaninny', 'pickaninny' and 'pickney' *UK, 1785*

piccaninny daylight; piccaninny dawn *noun* the beginning of dawn; first light *AUSTRALIA, 1866*

piccie; piccy *noun* a picture *AUSTRALIA, 1967*

piccolo *noun* **1** the penis, especially as the object of oral sex *US, 1967*. **2** a record player *US, 1953*

piccolo and flute; piccolo *noun* a suit (of clothes). Rhyming slang; a variation of **WHISTLE AND FLUTE** *UK, 1960*

Piccy *noun* Piccadilly, London *UK, 1962*

piche *noun* the vagina *US, 1998*

pick *noun* **1** a pickpocket *US, 1949*. **2** an oversized comb, used for bushy hair *US, 2000*. **3** a needle and syringe *NEW ZEALAND, 1995*. ▶ **on the pick** drinking (alcohol). Based on **PICK AND CHOOSE**, this is the rhyming slang equivalent of **ON THE BOOZE** *UK, 1992*

pick *verb* **1** to challenge someone to a fight *AUSTRALIA, 1953*. **2** to tease or kid someone *US, 2003*. ▶ **pick fruit** to find and select a homosexual partner *US, 1950*. ▶ **pick lint** to focus on petty imperfections in a play or performance *US, 1973*. ▶ **pick the cherry** to drive through a red traffic light *US, 1997*. ▶ **pick up your marbles and go home** to quit an effort, especially to do so with a lack of good sportsmanship *US, 1991*. ▶ **pick your arse** to waste your time *UK, 1995*. ▶ **pick your brains** to seek and obtain information from someone with specialist knowledge *UK, 1838*

pick and choose; pick *noun* alcohol, drink. Rhyming slang for **BOOZE** *UK, 1960*

pick and pay *noun* in a casino, a method of paying off bets in blackjack, in which the dealer evaluates each player's hand and pays or collects that player's bet, and then moves to the next player *US, 1980*

pick-ed wiss *noun* urination after a period of discomfort. An intentional spoonerism of 'a wicked piss' *US, 1968*

pick 'em *noun* in sports betting, a game in which neither team is favoured and the bettor must pick the winner *US, 1991*

pickem up truck *noun* a pickup truck. Jocular *US, 1976*

picker *noun* **1** a finger *US, 1945*. **2** a pickpocket *US, 1950*

Pickettywitch *noun* a ditch. Rhyming slang, jocularly contrived from the name of a UK pop group of the late 1960s and early 70s *UK, 2004*

pickle *noun* **1** a predicament; a sorry plight; an unpleasant difficulty *UK, 1562*. **2** a torpedo *US, 1948*. **3** a handgun *US, 1950*. **4** in horse racing, a regular but uninformed bettor *AUSTRALIA, 1989*. **5** in lobstering, the brine that accumulates in a bait box produced by decomposing bait fish and the salt used to preserve the bait fish *US, 1978*. ▶ **off your pickle** drunk *UK, 2002*

pickle *verb* to embalm a corpse *US, 1949*

pickled *adjective* drunk *UK, 1633*

pickled onion *noun* a bunion. Rhyming slang *UK, 1998*

pickled pork *noun* chalk. Rhyming slang *UK, 1998*

pickled punks *noun* in a carnival, a side-show display of jars, each with a foetus preserved in formaldehyde *US, 1960*

pickle fork *noun* in electric line work, an insulated line tool formally known as a prong tie stick *US, 1980*

pickle me tit! used for expressing surprise *NEW ZEALAND, 1964*

pickle party *noun* male masturbation *US, 2001*

pickle, pull and climb *verb* to drop a load of bombs and then climb to evade groundfire *US, 1991*

picklepuss *noun* an overtly and infectiously unhappy person. In the same vein as **SOURPUSS**, with 'pickle' conveying the sour quality *US, 1963*

pickle-stabbers *noun* shoes or boots with sharply pointed toes *CANADA, 2001*

pickle tickle *noun* an act of sexual intercourse *US, 2001*

pick-me-up *noun* **1** an alcoholic drink *US, 1982*. **2** a dose of a central nervous system stimulant *US, 1984*

pick mooch *noun* in sports betting, a bettor who will not pay for handicapping information, but instead bets as those who have paid for the information bet *US, 1997*

pick off *verb* in poker, to catch a player bluffing *US, 1979*

pick on *verb* to tease or victimise someone *UK, 1937*

pick the bones out of that! **1** used as a challenge to unravel, or retort to, or refute, an argument *UK, 1961*. **2** a catchphrase that accompanies expectoration *UK, 1984*

pickup *noun* **1** a short-term sexual partner *US, 1871*. **2** a police order to detain and bring a person to the station for questioning *US, 1977*. **3** in the entertainment industry, a commitment to finance production of a set number of episodes of a television programme *US, 1993*

pick up *verb* **1** to meet someone and form a casual liaison in which at least one of the pair has sexual ambitions involving the other *UK, 1698*. **2** to pay a bill, especially when the accounting is for more than one person; to meet the expense of financing or sponsoring something *US, 1945*. **3** to smoke marijuana *US, 1952*. ▶ **pick up on** to comprehend something *US, 1959*

pickup girl *noun* a street prostitute *AUSTRALIA, 1956*

pickup man *noun* in an illegal lottery, a person who takes bets from players to a central location and pays off winning bets *US, 1963*

picky *adjective* used of hair, tightly curled and short *BAHAMAS, 1982*

picky-head *noun* a black person with short hair *BARBADOS, 1965*

picky-puck *noun* a one-cylinder, two-stroke engine; a boat powered by such an engine *CANADA, 1986*

picnic *noun* **1** oral sex, especially on a man *US, 1964*. **2** extended foreplay and/or sexual intercourse *US, 1993*. **3** sex involving many people and many acts; an orgy *US, 1964*. **4** a difficult situation *NEW ZEALAND, 1998*. **5** something difficult, unpleasant, messy, confusing, etc. An ironic use *AUSTRALIA, 1896*. ▶ **no picnic** a difficult situation or circumstance *UK, 1888*

picnic *verb* (used of fishing boats) to congregate in one area where fish are plentiful *BARBADOS, 1965*

pic pac *noun* in the film industry, a contract to make a set number of films. An abbreviation of 'picture package' *US, 1990*

picture *noun* a beautiful person or thing. Often in the phrase 'pretty as a picture' *UK, 1815*. ▶ **get the picture** to understand a situation *UK, 1938*. ▶ **in the picture** aware of what is going on *UK, 1900*

picture card; picture *noun* in a deck of playing cards, any jack, queen or king *US, 1961*

picture gallery *noun* in circus and carnival usage, a heavily tattooed person *US, 1960*

picture of the queen *noun* a sterling currency note. Basically a copy of US 'picture of Abe' (a $5 note), except that the queen's face appears on all denominations issued in England and Wales *UK, 2002*

pictures *noun* money *US, 1972*. ▶ **take pictures** to use radar to measure a vehicle's speed *US, 1976*

picture-taker *noun* a police officer using radar *US, 1976*

picturize *verb* **1** to explain something; to put someone in the picture. Royal Navy slang *UK, 1987*. **2** to film something *INDIA, 1979*

piddle *noun* urine; an act of urination *UK, 1901*

piddle *verb* **1** to urinate *UK, 1796*. **2** to rain *UK, 1887*. **3** to steal something *US, 1952*. **4** in bar dice games, to roll the dice to determine who will go first in the game *US, 1971*. **5** in tiddlywinks, to make a minute change in a pile *US, 1977*. **6** to build something with matchsticks *US, 1989*

piddle about *verb* to busy yourself doing nothing *NEW ZEALAND, 1984*

piddle around *verb* to loaf or fool around *UK, 1545*

piddler *noun* in prison, a prisoner assigned to work in a craft shop *US, 1990*

piddling *adjective* small; trivial, insignificant *UK: SCOTLAND, 1559*

pie *noun* **1** the vulva *US, 1981*. **2** a woman as a sexual object *US, 1975*. **3** a person who is overweight. Probably from the chant 'who ate all the pies?' *UK, 2003*. **4** a pizza. An abbreviation of the rarely used, full 'pizza pie' *US, 1997*

pie and chips used by women as a generic instance of the difference between the sexes, especially with an ironic regard to equal opportunities *UK, 1996*

pie and liquor; pie and licker *noun* a vicar. Rhyming slang *UK, 1992*

pie and mash *noun* **1** an act of urination. Rhyming slang for SLASH *UK, 1974*. **2** radio interference. Rhyming slang for citizens' band radio jargon 'hash' (channel interference) *UK, 1981*. **3** cash. Rhyming slang *UK, 1992*

pie and mash *adjective* showy. Rhyming slang for FLASH *UK, 2002*

pie and one *noun* a son; the sun. Rhyming slang *UK, 1961*

pie book *noun* a railwayman's meal ticket *US, 1977*

pie car *noun* in the circus, a dining car on the circus train *US, 1980*

pie card *noun* a meal ticket; a means of surviving; a union card *US, 1909*

pie cart *noun* a catering truck *NEW ZEALAND, 1959*

piece *noun* **1** a woman as a sexual object; sex *US, 1942*. **2** an ounce of drugs *US, 1936*. **3** cocaine *US, 2003*. **4** crack cocaine *UK, 2003*. **5** a handgun. Conventional English from C16 until the late C19, then dormant, then slang, chiefly used in the US *US, 1930*. **6** a snack *US, 1970*. **7** a slice of bread, especially bread and spread; a sandwich. Originally just 'a slice of bread'. Also seen in English dialect use from Northumbria to Cornwall *UK: SCOTLAND, 1787*. **8** (especially with children) a sandwich. Used in the south and west of mainland Australia *AUSTRALIA, 2003*. **9** a well executed work of graffiti art. An abbreviation of 'masterpiece' *US, 2001*. **10** a domicile, be it a room, apartment or house *US, 2001*

piece book *noun* a graffiti artist's notebook containing ideas, outlines, sketches and plans for future graffiti pieces *US, 1990*

piece man *noun* an armed bodyguard; a hired killer *US, 1974*

piece of ass *noun* a woman as a sexual object; sexual intercourse *US, 1930*

piece of brass *noun* a prostitute. Elaboration of BRASS NAIL; BRASS (a prostitute), playing on 'piece of arse' (an attractive woman) *UK, 2001*

piece of cake *noun* anything that is considered to be easily achieved or acquired. Originally Royal Air Force usage *US, 1936*

piece of change *noun* a sum of money *US, 1946*

piece of cunt *noun* sex with a woman; a woman as a sexual object *US, 1947*

piece of duff *noun* a young male homosexual prostitute, a rent boy. On the model of PIECE OF ASS (a woman as a sex object); from DUFF (the buttocks), probably informed by DUFF (inferior), and possibly by a rhyme of PUFF (a homosexual male) *UK, 1996*

piece off *verb* to divide an ounce of drugs. From PIECE (an ounce) *US, 1984*

piece of leg *noun* sex *US, 1977*

piece of meat *noun* a woman as a sexual object; sex *US, 1965*

piece of piss *noun* anything that can be achieved easily. This alliterative variation on PIECE OF CAKE was originally Royal Air Force slang *UK, 1949*

piece of pistachio *noun* anything that can be achieved easily. Euphemistic elaboration of PIECE OF PISS *UK, 2002*

piece of shit *noun* something disgusting or of very poor quality; a person who is greatly disliked *US, 1986*

piece of skin; piece of flesh *noun* an attractive woman *UK, 1956*

piece of steel *noun* in prison, a homemade knife *UK, 1996*

piece of trade *noun* a male who self-identifies as a heterosexual but will let homosexual men perform oral sex on him *US, 1965*

piece of wet shit *noun* something disgusting or of very poor quality; a person who is greatly disliked. A slight intensification of PIECE OF SHIT *US, 1979*

piece of work *noun* **1** a contemptible person *UK, 1928*. **2** a killing *US, 2001*

piece-o-idiot *noun* a complete fool *BARBADOS, 1998*

pieces of eight; pieces *noun* weight. Rhyming slang *UK, 1992*

piecey *noun* a slice of bread with a topping. Used especially in Victoria *AUSTRALIA, 2003*

pie-chopper *noun* the mouth *US, 1953*

piecrust *noun* a thin layer of hard snow over soft snow *ANTARCTICA, 1911*

piedras *noun* crack cocaine. From the Spanish for 'hailstones', thus the image of small white rocks *UK, 1998*

pie-eater *noun* a person of no consequence. Calling to mind an image of someone whose principal fare is the meat pie, in other words, a person with a mundane and narrow view of the world judging by their culinary habits. It is claimed that the word was coined during World War 2, and referred then specifically to conscripted criminals who deserted and thence scrounged free pies from the army buffet in Hyde Park, Sydney. There may be some truth in this, but there is an example of 'pie-biter' dating to 1911, and so perhaps 'pie-eater' may also predate the war *AUSTRALIA, 1944*

pie-eating *adjective* inconsequential *AUSTRALIA, 1944*

pie-eyed *adjective* extremely drunk *US, 1904*

pie factory *noun* a mental institution *US, 1967*

pie hole *noun* the mouth *US, 1994*

pie horse *noun* a racehorse that has performed very poorly. So named because of the horse's figurative future as the makings of a meat pie *AUSTRALIA, 1989*

pie in the sky *noun* unattainable dreams. Often, 'there'll be pie in the sky when you die' denoting an illusory happy ever after; taken from a parody of the hymn 'In the Sweet Bye and Bye': 'You will eat, bye and bye, / In that glorious land in the sky; / Work and pray, live on hay, / You'll get pie in the sky when you die' by radical labour activist Joe Hill (aka Joel Haggstrom and Joseph Hillstrom), 'The Preacher and the Slave', ?1911. Joe Hill was executed in Utah in 1915 *US, 2000*

pierced up *adjective* used of someone who is ornamented with body piercings *UK, 1996*

piercing *noun* graffiti *US, 1997*

piercing *adjective* overbearing *US, 1960*

pier rat *noun* a surfer with no regard for surf etiquette *US, 1977*

pier six brawl *noun* an all-out brawl *US, 1929*

pies *noun* the eyes *US, 1945*

pie taster *noun* a person who enjoys performing oral sex on women *US, 1981*

pie wagon *noun* a police transport truck or van *US, 1904*

piff *verb* to throw something. Chiefly used in Victoria; onomatopoeic of something whizzing through the air *AUSTRALIA, 1999*

piffle *noun* nonsense. From the verb (to talk or act in a feeble manner) *UK, 1890*

pig *noun* **1** a police officer; in the plural it may mean a number of police personnel or the police in general *UK, 1811*. **2** a male chauvinist *US, 1992*. **3** a person who has a large or indiscriminate appetite. A shortened form of 'greedy pig' *UK, 1546*. **4** a chorus dancer *US, 1948*. **5** a promiscuous woman *US, 1955*. **6** an unattractive female *UK: SCOTLAND, 1988*. **7** a prostitute *CANADA, 1960*. **8** an inferior or bad example of anything. From an earlier sense as 'an unpleasant person' *UK, 1925*. **9** a 'Humber' one-ton 4x4 armoured personnel carrier. Nicknamed by troops serving in Northern Ireland during the 1970s; taken out of service in the early 1990s *UK, 1974*. **10** an M-60 machine gun. Each squad in Vietnam was assigned an M-60, the army's general-purpose machine gun which entered the service in the 1950s. It was designed to be lightweight (23 pounds) and easy to carry. It produced a low 'grunting' sound and thus the porcine allusions *US, 1974*. **11** in circus usage, an elephant, male or female *UK, 1934*. **12** in a split-pot game of poker, a player who declares both high and low *US, 1988* ▷ *see:* PIG IN THE MIDDLE. ▶ **in pig** pregnant *UK, 1945*. ▶ **kill your pig** to spoil your chances of doing something *UK: NORTHERN IRELAND, 1996*

pig board *noun* a surfboard with a narrow, tapered point and a broad tail *US, 1963*

pig book *noun* a student directory with photographs of each student *US, 1969*

pig-dog *noun* a bull terrier *AUSTRALIA, 1982*

pig down *verb* to alter a car's body or frame *US, 1947*

pigeon *noun* **1** a gullible victim of a swindle *UK, 1593*. **2** a young woman, especially an attractive one *UK, 1586*. **3** a new participant in a twelve-step recovery programme such as Alcoholics Anonymous *US, 1998*. **4** an informer. A shortened form of STOOL PIGEON *US, 1849*. **5** in horse racing, a losing ticket that someone tries to cash in for winnings *US, 1947*. **6** in shuffleboard, a disc straddling the 7/10 off line *US, 1967*. **7** a urinary bottle used in hospital *IRELAND, 1999*

pigeon *verb* to betray someone; to inform on someone *US, 1959*

pigeon drop *noun* a swindle in which two confederates pretend to find a wallet and convince a third person to share in the proceeds of the find *US, 1940*

pigfoot *noun* marijuana *US, 1960*

pigfucker *noun* a despicable person *US, 1994*

piggie bank *noun* the stockings worn by an overweight woman *US, 1981*

piggies *noun* ▶ **make piggies** to have sex *US, 1969*

pigging *adjective* used as an all-purpose intensifier, generally to negative effect; euphemistic for 'fucking', 'sodding', etc *UK, 1974*

piggle *noun* the penis. Children's vocabulary *TRINIDAD AND TOBAGO, 1980*

piggy *noun* the toe. Childish, from the nursery rhyme 'This little piggy went to market, / This little piggy stayed at home' *UK, 1984*

piggyback *verb* **1** in casino blackjack, to place a bet in another player's square *US, 1996*. **2** to transport loaded tractor trailers on railway flat wagons *US, 1971*

piggyback *adjective* used of a vehicle, stacked on top of another vehicle for transport *US, 1936*

piggybacking *noun* the reclamation of an abandoned building, floor by floor *US, 1989*

piggy bank *noun* **1** savings. After the traditional money box *UK, 1984*. **2** a toll booth on a turnpike road *US, 1976*. **3** an act of masturbation. Rhyming slang for WANK. Also shortened form 'piggy' *UK, 1992*

piggy in the middle; pig in the middle *noun* a person caught in the middle of a dispute. From the traditional children's game *UK, 1962*

piggy parts *noun* ham *US, 1996*

pig-ignorant *adjective* very ignorant *UK, 1972*

pig in knickers *noun* a very unattractive female. An elaboration of PIG *UK: SCOTLAND, 1988*

pig in shit *noun* ▶ **happy as a pig in shit; like a pig in shit** very happy *UK, 1944*

pig in the middle; pig *noun* urine; an act of urination. Rhyming slang for PIDDLE or WIDDLE *UK, 1992*

pig in the wall *noun* an error in bricklaying in which opposite ends of a new wall meet at different heights *UK, 1978*

pig iron *noun* **1** in horse racing, any illegal drug given to a racehorse *AUSTRALIA, 1989*. **2** a carnival ride; the metal assembly of a carnival ride *US, 1960*

Pig Iron Express *noun* the steel-hauling division of Pacific Intermountain Express company *US, 1971*

pig iron monkey *noun* in oil drilling, a derrick construction worker *US, 1954*

pig killer *noun* phencyclidine, the recreational drug known as PCP or angel dust *US, 1981*

pig-out *noun* a session of gorging on food *US, 1978*

pig out *verb* to eat a lot quickly and messily *US, 1978*

pig party *noun* serial consensual sex between one person and multiple partners *UK, 1988*

pigpen *noun* **1** a police headquarters *US, 1993*. **2** an illegal gambling operation *US, 1982*. **3** in nine wicket croquet, the crossed centre wickets *US, 1977*

pig pile *noun* an orgy with homosexual men *US, 1972*

pig-root *verb* (of a horse) to prop with the front legs and kick up the back legs *AUSTRALIA, 1900*

pigs *noun* ▶ **pigs to** to hell with *AUSTRALIA, 1906*

pigs! used for registering derision or contempt. An abbreviation of PIG'S ARSE! *AUSTRALIA, 1933*

pig's arse! nonsense! Although the earliest record of this exclamation is from 1951, the existence of euphemistic forms such as 'pig's ear' (dating to 1919) show that it was clearly in use much earlier *AUSTRALIA, 1951*

pigs' ballroom *noun* a bar or club where unattractive females congregate *UK: SCOTLAND, 1988*

pig's bum nonsense *AUSTRALIA, 1998*

pig scabs *noun* pork scratchings, a packaged snack sold in bars *UK, 2003*

pig's ear *noun* beer. Rhyming slang. Sometimes shortened to 'pigs' in UK usage *AUSTRALIA, 1924*. ▶ **make a pig's ear; make a pig's** to bungle; to blunder; to make a mess of something *UK, 1954*

pig shit run *noun* a supply transport flight in the early years of US involvement in the Vietnam war, including transport of live farm animals that left reminders of their presence in the planes *US, 1990*

pig-sick *adjective* irritated; annoyed and disgusted *UK, 1961*

pigskin *noun* a saddle *AUSTRALIA, 1989*

pig's Latin *noun* any coded language used by prison guards *US, 1984*

pig's lattie *noun* a sty. Polari; a play on LATTIE (a house) giving 'pig's house' *UK, 2002*

pig slices *noun* ham *US, 1996*

pig station *noun* in prison, a guard control room *US, 1984*

pig-sticker *noun* **1** a knife, especially a large knife *UK, 1890*. **2** a stick with a nail or sharp metal point on one end used for picking up paper litter *US, 1996*

pig's trotter *noun* a squatter (an unauthorised occupant). Rhyming slang *UK, 1998*

pigsty *noun* **1** a untidy or ill-kept place *UK, 1820*. **2** a police station *US, 1976*

pigtail *noun* **1** in trucking, an electrical cable that connects the electrical systems of the trailer and the tractor cab *US, 1971*. **2** in electric line work, an insulated line tool formally known as a spiral link stick *US, 1980*

pig water *noun* weak, low quality alcohol *US, 1958*

pike *noun* **1** a toll road, a toll motorway *US, 1971*. **2** a railway *US, 1946*. **3** a glance *US, 1950*

pike *verb* **1** in a card game, to peek at an opponent's cards *US, 1962*. **2** (of a man) to tape the penis and testicles to the body as part of an effort to pass as a woman *US, 1987*

pike out *verb* to back out of a commitment *NEW ZEALAND, 1984*

piker *noun* **1** a rank amateur or beginner; a gambler who makes small, cautious bets *US, 1872*. **2** a person who opts out of an agreement or abandons someone; a weak, cowardly person. A term of high contempt in Australia *AUSTRALIA, 1950*

pikey *noun* a tramp; a gypsy; a traveller. Generally used of travellers by non-travellers. Ultimately from early C16 'pike' (to depart). The actor Brad Pitt played a 'pikey' in the film *Snatch*, written and directed by Guy Ritchie, 2000 *UK, 1847*

pikkie *noun* **1** a photograph or film *NEW ZEALAND, 1998*. **2** a small person, a child, a small child; a small thing. Directly from Afrikaans *pikkie*. Between children, usage may be contemptuous. Also shortened form 'pik' *SOUTH AFRICA, 1948*

pilchard *noun* a fool *UK, 2001*

pile *noun* **1** a great deal of money *UK, 1741*. **2** in poker, the amount of money (cash and/or chips) a player has in front of him available for betting *US, 1979*. ▶ **on the pile** in prison *US, 1970*

pile *verb* (from the male point of view) to have sex *US, 1968*. ▶ **pile it on** to exaggerate; to show-off. A variation of PILE ON THE AGONY [see: AGONY] *US, 1876*

pile driver *noun* **1** a sexual position in which the woman stands on her head and the man enters her directly and powerfully from above. A term (and practice) found more commonly in pornography than real life *US, 1995*. **2** the active participant in anal sex *US, 1979*. **3** a hole in a road, jarring to the driver when encountered *US, 1962*

pile in *verb* to enter en masse, especially a vehicle or a bar *US, 1841*

pile of rocks *noun* a type of bet in an illegal numbers game lottery *US, 1957*

pile-on *noun* an offensive, despicable person; a clumsy person; a socially awkward person. An image, perhaps, of this person as victim *INDIA, 2002*

piles *noun* crack cocaine *UK, 1998*

pileup; pile-up *noun* a crash involving multiple vehicles. Originally World War 1 Royal Air Force for 'a plane crash', from an earlier verb sense used by the navy. Widely used by mid-C20, this sense was virtually conventional by the mid-1970s *UK, 2000*

pilgrim *noun* **1** in northwestern Canada, a tourist or newcomer; also, a cow newly imported to the region *CANADA, 1962*. **2** a newcomer to a game of poker *US, 1988*

pill *noun* **1** any central nervous system stimulant *US, 1966*. **2** a tablet of MDMA, the recreational drug best known as ecstasy. A generic usage *UK, 1996*. **3** a pellet of opium *US, 1946*. **4** a cigarette *UK, 1914*. **5** a rugby ball *NEW ZEALAND, 2002*. **6** in pool, a small tally ball used as a scoring device *US, 1993*. **7** an unpleasant person *UK, 1871*. ▶ **the pill 1** the contraceptive pill. Not in practical currency until the early 1960s *UK, 1957*. **2** the weekly anti-malaria pill taken by US troops in Vietnam. Playing on the birth control pill, then very much in vogue back home *US, 1991*

pillar and post *noun* a ghost. Rhyming slang *UK, 1960*

pilled; pilled up *adjective* under the influence of central nervous system stimulants or depressants *US, 1966*

pillhead *noun* a habitual user of amphetamines, barbiturates, or MDMA, the recreational drug best known as ecstasy *US, 1966*

pillion pussy *noun* a woman attracted to motorcyclists. A 'pillion' (probably from the Scottish Gaelic or Irish Gaelic for 'rug') is a motorcycle saddle *NEW ZEALAND, 1956*

pillock *noun* a fool. From a variation of dialect *pillicock* or *pillcock* (the penis) *UK, 1967*

pillow *noun* **1** a weak, effeminate, gutless male *AUSTRALIA, 1992*. **2** a sealed polyethylene bag of drugs *US, 1970*. ▶ **an extra pillow** used as a coded references for a prostitute arranged by a hotel concierge *UK, 2005*

pillow-biter *noun* a homosexual male; specifically the passive partner in anal intercourse *AUSTRALIA, 1981*

pillow-biting *adjective* homosexual *AUSTRALIA, 1985*

pillowcase *noun* an empty-headed fool *US, 1988*

pillow pigeons *noun* bedbugs *US, 1947*

pillow talk *noun* intimate discussions in bed. Suggests secrets shared, not sexually oriented talk *US, 1977*

pill party *noun* execution in the gas chamber. Pills of cyanide dropped into a bucket of water produce the lethal gas, hence the blackly humorous term *US, 1971*

pill popper *noun* a habitual user of drugs in pill form *US, 1979*

pill-pusher *noun* **1** a doctor, especially a specialist in internal medicine *UK, 1909*. **2** a pharmacist *US, 1980*

pill-roller *noun* a doctor *US, 1951*

pills *noun* the testicles *UK, 1937*. ▶ **on pills** dieting. Teen slang *US, 1958*

pilly *noun* an abuser of drugs in pill form *US, 1970*

pilot *noun* **1** a person who remains drug-free to guide another through an experience on a hallucinogenic drug *US, 1966*. **2** a driver of any heavy-load vehicle; a bus driver *UK, 1936*. **3** in horse racing, a jockey *US, 1983*. **4** a pimp *BARBADOS, 1965*

pilot error *noun* in computing, a user's misconfiguration that produces errors that at first appear to be the fault of the program *US, 1991*

pim *noun* the clitoris *TRINIDAD AND TOBAGO, 2003*

pimp *noun* **1** a man who, for a percentage of the income derived, arranges clients for a prostitute; a man who lives off the earnings of a prostitute *UK, 1600*. **2** a charming man who attracts women *US, 1997*. **3** in a deck of playing cards, a jack or knave *US, 1988*. **4** an informer to the police or other authorities *AUSTRALIA, 1899*. **5** cocaine *US, 1994*

pimp *verb* **1** to work as a pimp; to exert control over a prostitute *US, 1972*. **2** to take advantage of *US, 1942*. **3** to act in a stylised, fashionable way *US, 1970*. **4** to inform; to betray *AUSTRALIA, 1938*. **5** to win away the affection of another person's date *US, 1966*. ▶ **pimp your pipe** to loan or rent a pipe used for smoking crack cocaine *US, 1994*

pimp *adjective* excellent, fashionable, stylish *US, 1970*

pimp-ass *adjective* in the manner of a pimp *US, 1995*

pimp-crazy *adjective* psychologically controlled by a pimp *US, 1972*

pimp dust *noun* cocaine. Before the era of crack cocaine, cocaine was an expensive drug enjoyed only by the wealthy, notably by pimps *US, 1980*

pimped-up *adjective* flashy; of a car, laden with flashy accessories, usually not related to the car's performance *US, 1993*

pimping *adjective* expensive, fashionable *US, 2003*

pimple *noun* a steep hill. Hauliers' slang *UK, 1951*

pimple and blotch; pimple *noun* Scotch whisky. Rhyming Slang for 'Scotch' *UK, 1960*

pimple and wart *noun* port (wine). Rhyming slang, always used in full *UK, 1961*

pimplie; pimply *noun* a youth, especially a spotty-faced youth *UK, 1980*

pimpmobile; pimp-car *noun* a large, expensive and ostentatious car, whether or not it is actually owned by a pimp *US, 1973*

pimp playa *noun* a man who presents himself in the style and manner of a pimp but without, necessarily, trading as an agent for prostitution. Urban black slang *UK, 2005*

pimp post; pimp rest *noun* an armrest or console between the driver's seat and the passenger seat of a car. Used for the GANGSTER LEAN *US, 1980*

pimp roll *noun* a highly stylised manner of walking, projecting an image of control and dispassion *US, 1990*

pimp's arrest *noun* used to describe a pimp causing the arrest of a prostitute who has left his control *US, 1972*

pimp shoes; pimping shoes *noun* flashy, expensive shoes *US, 1972*

pimp slap *verb* to strike someone forcefully, usually with the back of the hand across the face *US, 1997*

pimp steak *noun* a frankfurter *US, 1970*

pimp stick *noun* a cigarette holder *US, 1967*

pimp sticks *noun* wire coathangers used by pimps to beat prostitutes *US, 1972*

pimp suit *noun* a showy, extravagant, tasteless suit *US, 1980*

pimpsy; pimps *adjective* too easy. Upper-class society use; possibly the result of silly word play (simple, simps, pimps, pimpsy) *UK, 1982*

pimp title *noun* a pimp's claim on the loyalty, services and earnings of a prostitute *US, 1979*

pimp up *verb* to add flashy touches to something; to dress something up *US, 1993*

pin *noun* **1** the leg or foot. Usually in the plural *UK, 1530*. **2** a hypodermic syringe and needle used for the injection of narcotics *US, 1973*. **3** a very thin marijuana cigarette *US, 1967*. **4** a person who serves as a lookout *US, 1992* ▷*see:* PIN POSITION

pin *verb* **1** to scrutinise someone or something to look at someone or something intently *US, 1965*. **2** to inject a drug *UK, 2003*. **3** to tattoo something with improvised equipment *US, 1972*. **4** (from the male perspective) to have sex *UK, 1961*. ▶ **pin for home** on the railways, to leave work and go home *US, 1977*. ▶ **pin on** to fix the blame on someone *UK, 1979*. ▶ **pin one on** to consume a drink *AUSTRALIA, 1957*

pin and needle *noun* a beetle. Rhyming slang. The plural is 'pins and needles' *UK, 1992*

pin artist *noun* an illegal abortionist *US, 1962*

pin-brain *noun* an idiot *UK, 1998*

pinch *noun* **1** an arrest *US, 1900*. **2** a technique used by a man to maintain an erection, compressing the base of his penis *US, 1995*. **3** very potent heroin, bought and used in small amounts *US, 1993*. **4** a small amount of marijuana *UK, 1996*. **5** a five-dollar note or five-dollar betting chip *US, 1988*. **6** a steep incline *AUSTRALIA, 1846*

pinch *verb* **1** to arrest someone *UK, 1837*. **2** to steal something *UK, 1656*. **3** in horse racing, to win. A jockey may; 'pinch' a race. A bookmaker might manage to 'pinch a little.' *AUSTRALIA, 1989*. ▶ **pinch a loaf** to defecate *US, 1994*

pinch *adjective* substitute. Back-formation from 'pinch-hit' (in baseball, to bat as substitute) *US, 2002*

pinch and press *verb* to cheat at gambling, secretly taking back chips from your bet when dealt a bad hand and adding chips when dealt a good hand *US, 1985*

pinche *adjective* used as an intensifier, roughly the same as 'fucking'. Border Spanish used in English conversation by Mexican-Americans *US, 1974*

pinchers *noun* shoes, especially tight shoes *US, 1945*

pinch hit *noun* a single inhalation of marijuana *US, 1993*

pinch pipe *noun* a small pipe designed to hold enough marijuana for a single inhalation. Small, easily hidden from parents and teachers, and economical *US, 1993*

pin dick *noun* a male with a small penis *US, 2003*

pin-drop silence *noun* absolute silence. Indian English, from the familiar phrase 'so quiet you could hear a pin drop' *INDIA, 2001*

pine *noun* marijuana *UK, 2001*

pineapple *noun* **1** a hand grenade, especially a MK-2 hand grenade or Type 59 grenade *US, 1918*. **2** a combination of cocaine and heroin *US, 1973*. **3** a male homosexual. Perhaps as a specialisation of FRUIT, possibly punning on anal sex as 'taking the ROUGH END OF THE PINEAPPLE' *UK, 1972*. **4** a fifty dollar note. From its yellowish colour *AUSTRALIA, 1992*. **5** a chapel. Glasgow rhyming slang, with a stress on the second and third syllables *UK: SCOTLAND, 1982*. **6** in electric line work, a spool insulator *US, 1980*. **7** unemployment benefit *UK, 1937*

pineapple chunk; pineapple *noun* **1** a *bunk* bed; a bunk (an act of running away) *UK, 1961*. **2** semen. Rhyming slang for SPUNK *UK, 2003*

Pineapple Express *noun* a wind from the south, onshore in British Columbia, which is said to have the scent of Hawaiian pineapples and is warm, occasionally blowing in the winter. An explanation for the warmer climate on Canada's west coast than inland *CANADA, 2001*

pineapple juice *noun* a rain storm in Hawaii *US, 1991*

pine box release; pine box parole *noun* death while in prison *US, 1978*

pine top *noun* strong, illegally manufactured whisky *US, 1999*

ping *noun* **1** an attempt; an effort; a shot *AUSTRALIA, 1988*. **2** an injection of a drug *NEW ZEALAND, 1982*. **3** the sound caused in a car engine by low quality fuel or bad timing *US, 1992*

ping *verb* **1** to recognise or identify someone or something. Royal Navy slang; probably echoic of a radar's noise *UK, 1987*. **2** to hit something with a projectile *AUSTRALIA, 1934*. **3** of a racehorse, to jump well *UK, 2003*. **4** to penalise or fine someone or for breaking a rule or law *AUSTRALIA, 1934*. ▶ **ping the pill** to remove a small amount of a drug from a capsule or packet for your later use *US, 1970*

pinger *noun* a chunk of gold that makes a noise as it hits the pan *CANADA, 1958*

pingers *noun* money, especially coins. Commonly used in New Zealand since the 1950s *NEW ZEALAND, 2002*

ping-in-wing; ping in the wing; ping-wing; ping shot *verb* to inject a drug into the arm. An elaboration of PIN (a syringe) combined with WING (the arm) *US, 1949*

ping-pong *noun* a small photographic portrait *BARBADOS, 1965*

pingpong *verb* (used of a doctor engaged in insurance fraud) to needlessly refer a patient to a number of specialists *US, 1982*

pinhead *noun* **1** a fool; an imbecile *US, 1896*. **2** a person whose interest in playing pinball approaches the level of obsession *US, 1977*. **3** an amphetamine user *US, 1971*. **4** in the language of snowboarding, a skier *US, 1990*. **5** a railway brakeman *US, 1946*

pink *noun* **1** a white person *US, 1945*. **2** a liberal; a socialist; a communist sympathiser *US, 1927*. **3** the open vagina. Widely used in pornography, and beyond *US, 1991*. **4** proof of car ownership. A shortened form of PINK SLIP *US, 1965*. **5** a capsule of secobarbital sodium (trade name Seconal™), a central nervous system depressant *US, 1967*. **6** a casino gambling token worth $2.50 *US, 1991*. **7** in poker, a flush consisting of either hearts or diamonds *US, 1963*. **8** in horse racing, a track police officer. Derived from the *Pink*erton Agency *US, 1947*

Pink *noun* a 'detective' from the Pinkerton Agency. Strikebreaking was among the several roles played by the Pinkerton Agency *US, 1904*

pink *adjective* **1** homosexual. Traditionally 'pink for a girl, blue for a boy'. As an absolutely negative association the colour pink was used in Nazi Germany to label homosexuals for segregation, internment and extermination; in post-World-War-2 Britain, pink had connotations of effeminacy; in the 1970s politically active homosexuals adopted the colour-coded symbolism and pink slowly took on a generally positive tone both in the gay and wider community, especially as a marketing designation *UK, 2003*. **2** white; Caucasian *US, 1945*. ▶ **all pink** in poker, a flush consisting of all hearts or all diamonds *US, 1967*

pink 125 *noun* a tablet of MDMA, the recreational drug best known as ecstasy. From the colour and the 125 mg dosage *UK, 2002*

pink-assed *adjective* somewhat angry *US, 1962*

pink blotters *noun* a type of LSD *UK, 1998*

Pink Cadillac *noun* a variety of MDMA, the recreational drug best known as ecstasy. The colour of the tablet inspires the ultimate in rock 'n' roll luxury transport *UK, 1996*

pink champagne *noun* **1** methamphetamine with a pinkish colour produced by the presence of the stimulant pemoline *US, 1989*. **2** a mix of cocaine and heroin *UK, 1996*

pinker *noun* in poker, a timid bettor *US, 1967*

pinkers *noun* a pink gin. Naval in origin *UK, 1961*

pink eye *noun* **1** cheap, low grade whisky *CANADA, 1953*. **2** special contact lenses worn by card cheats to see luminous markings on the back of cards *US, 1988*

Pink Floyd *noun* a potent type of LSD. Honouring the rock group Pink Floyd, from their early days in the late 1960s when they were considered avant garde and psychedelic *UK, 1999*

pink heart *noun* an amphetamine tablet *US, 1997*

pinkie *noun* **1** the little finger. Originally Scottish, mostly among children, but now widespread. Also variant 'pinky' *UK, 1808*. **2** a white person, especially a male. Recorded in use by black teenagers *UK, 1967*. **3** a pink-eyed albino. Also variant 'pinky' *UK, 1962*. **4** the vagina *TRINIDAD AND TOBAGO, 1986*. **5** a bruised eye *US, 1970*. **6** in Vancouver, a warning ticket *CANADA, 1962*. **7** a racing greyhound that

races best from the outside position AUSTRALIA, 1989. **8** in Newfoundland, cheap wine CANADA, 1958. **9** an early model long-wheel base '110' Land Rover. Used by the British military UK, 1995
▷*see:* PINK SPEEDBALL

pinkie cheater noun a latex finger glove used during digital examinations US, 1973

pinkie-load noun in caving and pot-holing, a piece of equipment so light that it can be picked up by a little finger; hence, a person in a group who is not carrying his or her fair share. From PINKIE (the little finger) UK, 2004

pinkie ring; pinky ring noun a ring worn on the little finger, especially an ostentatious ring worn by a criminal US, 1975

pinkies noun underwear US, 1954

pink lady noun a capsule of secobarbital sodium (trade name Seconal™), a central nervous system depressant US, 1968

pink lemonade noun cleaning fluid injected intravenously. An often lethal substitute for methedrine US, 1971

pink lint adjective having little or no money, penniless. Rhyming slang for SKINT UK, 1961

pink mafia noun any group of women banded together, especially lesbians US, 1997

pinko noun a liberal; a socialist; a communist. Originally applied to Communist party members, subsequently (in the late 1950s) to anyone who disagreed with the dominant culture and politics. Also used attributively US, 1936

pink oboe noun the penis. Coined by satirist Peter Cook (1937–95) for a sketch performed in Amnesty International's *The Secret Policeman's Ball* UK, 1979

pink palace noun **1** a homosexual venue. Combines PINK (homosexual) with an alliterative location UK, 2000. **2** the prison at Hobart AUSTRALIA, 1995

Pink Panther noun a variety of MDMA, the recreational drug best known as ecstasy, identified by the colour and embossed Pink Panther motif UK, 2002

pink pants noun rubbish. An elaboration of 'pants' (rubbish) UK, 2004

pink piccolo noun the penis UK, 2001

pink puffer noun a patient suffering from emphysema US, 1973

pink-ribbon case noun a criminal case that has been thoroughly and professionally investigated by the police. It is said that the police hand the prosecutor a case like this with a pink ribbon tied around it US, 1962

pink robots noun a type of LSD US, 1998

pink slip noun the proof of car ownership US, 1963

pink snapper noun the vagina. Combines PINK (the open vagina) with 'snapper' (various fish are so-called), thus FISH (the vagina); 'snapper' also suggests the image of a mouth that closes US, 2001

pink speedball; pinkie noun a mixture of pharmaceutical cocaine and Dipipanone, an opiate marketed under the brand name Diconal™ UK, 2001

pink tea noun an effeminate male homosexual US, 1957

pink-top noun a small vial of heroin sealed with a pink plastic cap. The pink plastic cap denotes a variation in purity and price US, 2002

pink torpedo noun the penis, especially when erect. Aggressive imagery US, 1984

Pinkville noun an area in the province of Quang Ngai, South Vietnam. Either named because of the area's appearance on maps or because of the strong presence of communist forces in the area US, 1970

pink wedge noun a type of LSD US, 1970

pink witch noun a type of LSD US, 1970

pinky verb in dice games with no bank, to roll the dice to see who will play first US, 1950

Pinky and Perky; pinky noun turkey (meat). Rhyming slang, formed on the puppets of twin pigs who, from 1957, became children's television stars and recording artists UK, 1992

pinky's out of jail! your slip is showing! US, 1955

pin-money noun spending money. Originally a C16 practice of a husband allotting to his wife a certain amount each year for personal expenses UK, 1697

pinned adjective **1** (used of eyes) constricted after opiate use US, 1966. **2** addicted to drugs. From PIN (a hypodermic syringe) US, 1997

pinned up adjective drug-intoxicated. From PINNED (the condition of the pupils when intoxicated) UK, 1996

pinny noun a pinafore US, 1851

pinny adjective very small BARBADOS, 1965

pin position; pin noun the front position in an authorised taxi rank UK, 1977

pin shot noun an improvised injection of a drug in which the skin is pricked and an injection made directly into the wound US, 1949

pinster noun a bowler US, 1953

pint noun a short person US, 1997

pinta noun **1** a pint of milk. From the advertising slogan, 'Drinka pinta milka day' UK, 1958. **2** a prison. Spanish slang used by English-speaking Mexican-Americans US, 2000

pint pot noun a pint glass, usually for draught beer UK, 1999

pint-size; pint-sized adjective used of a person's stature, small UK, 1938

pin-up noun a photograph or printed reproduction of a sexually attractive person; the person who is the subject of, or has the characteristics required for, such a picture. Originally, from the fact that such images were pinned up on walls US, 1941

PIO's noun in the language of hang gliding, over-control by the flier. An abbreviation of 'pilot-induced oscillations' US, 2004

pip noun **1** the best, the finest. From 'pippin' (the best) US, 1897. **2** a star worn by military officers as an indication of rank UK, 1917. **3** an unidentified spot on a radar screen US, 1947. **4** a woman's menstrual period US, 2001. **5** in the whe-whe lottery game, a bet that is close to the winning number TRINIDAD AND TOBAGO, 2003. ▶ **give someone the pip** to annoy someone UK, 1896

pip verb to defeat someone by a narrow margin. Sometimes elaborated to 'pip at the post' UK, 1939

pipe noun **1** the penis US, 1962. **2** any large vein, well suited for drug injection US, 1952. **3** any wind or reed instrument US, 1964. **4** an exhaust pipe US, 1952. **5** a telephone UK, 1951. **6** the firing chamber of a handgun US, 1987. **7** an electric outlet BARBADOS, 1965. **8** a sufficient measure of marijuana for smoking in a pipe. Recorded as Afrikaans *pyp* in 1967 SOUTH AFRICA, 1970. **9** a measurement of time: the distance that could be travelled between rest periods at which a pipe could be smoked CANADA, 1957. **10** the vertical bar (|) on a computer keyboard US, 1991. **11** an academically unchallenging course US, 1968. ▶ **do the pipe** to smoke crack cocaine US, 1996. ▶ **on the pipe 1** addicted to crack cocaine US, 1991. **2** used of a conversation between two jail cells conducted through plumbing emptied of water US, 1992. ▶ **put that in your pipe and smoke it!; stick that in your pipe and smoke it!** accept the situation, or what you have been told, whether you wish to or not UK, 1824. ▶ **take the pipe** to commit suicide US, 1982. ▶ **The Pipe** General Douglas MacArthur (1880–1964) of the US Army. From his love of a corncob pipe US, 1982. ▶ **the pipe** the Greenwich tunnel (under the River Thames) UK, 2001

pipe verb **1** to smoke crack cocaine in a pipe UK, 2000. **2** to look at someone or something UK, 1874. **3** to fabricate a story US, 1976

pipe and drum; pipe noun the anus. Rhyming slang for BUM, especially in the retort 'up your pipe!' UK, 1961

pipe course noun an easy course in college. From the older, largely forgotten sense of 'pipe' as 'easy to accomplish' US, 1927

piped adjective drunk or drug-intoxicated US, 1949

pipe down verb to be quieter; to shut up. Often exclamatory. From the nautical sense (to dismiss by sounding the pipe) UK, 1965

pipehead noun a crack cocaine addict US, 1992

pipe job noun **1** oral sex performed on man US, 1973. **2** an elaborate, fanciful fabricated story US, 1968

pipeline *noun* **1** a citizens' band radio channel which is popular *US, 1976*. **2** in the era of analogue phone exchanges, a telephone number with a recorded message which several people could call at the same time, circumvent the recorded message, and speak to each other *US, 1997*. **3** the rapidly spreading curl of a breaking wave *US, 1965*

pipeliner *noun* in the era of analogue phone exchanges, a person who called a number with a recording, where it was possible to communicate with others calling at the same time *US, 1997*

pipe-opener *noun* in horse racing, a short, intense workout several days before a race *US, 1976*

piper *noun* a crack cocaine addict *TRINIDAD AND TOBAGO, 1993*

pipes *noun* **1** the vocal chords *US, 1969*. **2** the upper arm muscles *US, 1997*

pipesmoker *noun* a homosexual male. An allusion to oral sex *US, 1997*

pipe up *verb* **1** to commence speaking, especially in a situation which may require a degree of boldness on the speaker's part *UK, 1889*. **2** to smoke crack cocaine *US, 1992*

pipickhead *noun* a stupid person. The word is a combination of the Yiddish *pipick* (navel/bellybutton) and the English word *CANADA, 2002*

pip jockey *noun* a radar operator *US, 1947*

pipped *adjective* drunk *US, 1982*

pipper *noun* in Canadian military aviation, an aiming device on a fighter's gunsight *CANADA, 1995*

pippie *noun* the penis *BAHAMAS, 1982*

pips *noun* the female breasts *US, 1981*

pipsqueak; pip-squeak *noun* an insignificant person *UK, 1910*

piranha *noun* a poker player who bets aggressively on any hand with any chance of winning *US, 1988*

pirate *noun* an unlicensed taxi driver *UK, 1977*

pirate's dream *noun* a flat-chested woman. From the association of pirates enjoying sex with captive teenage boys, or perhaps from the punning association of a girl with 'a sunken chest and a box full of treasure' *US, 1972*

pish *noun* rubbish, nonsense *UK, 1988*

pish *verb* used as an alternative spelling for 'piss' (to urinate); hence, to rain heavily *UK, 1997*

pished *adjective* drunk. A variation of PISSED (drunk) *UK: SCOTLAND, 1988*

pisher *noun* a person of no consequence. Yiddish from German, literally 'a bed-wetter' *US, 1968*

piso *adjective* someone who is miserly with money. Military usage; derives from Indian currency: a pais or pice is one quarter of an anna which, in turn, is one sixteenth of a rupee *UK, 1987*

piss *noun* **1** alcohol, especially beer *AUSTRALIA, 1945*. **2** the act of urination; urine. The verb produced the noun. Late Middle English then standard English, until it was deemed vulgar during C19. The sound of the word echoes the sound of urination *UK, 1958*. ▶ **on the piss** on a drinking binge *AUSTRALIA, 1965*. ▶ **take the piss out of** to satirise someone or something; to make a joke of someone or something; to send up someone or something *AUSTRALIA, 1976*. ▶ **the piss** the hell *AUSTRALIA, 1976*

piss *verb* **1** to urinate. Derives from Old French *pisser* and has been perfectly good English since C13, but from mid-C18 it has been considered a vulgarism *UK, 1290*. **2** to rain heavily *IRELAND, 1991*. **3** to accomplish a task easily *UK, 1983*. **4** to whinge *UK, 1995*. ▶ **I wouldn't piss in your ear if your brain was on fire** I could not care less about you *AUSTRALIA, 1985*. ▶ **I wouldn't piss on you if you were on fire** used for expressing the utmost personal contempt *UK, 1994*. ▶ **piss in someone's pocket** to ingratiate yourself with someone; to flatter someone *AUSTRALIA, 1944*. ▶ **piss in the wind** to engage in a hapless, futile activity *US, 1974*. ▶ **piss into someone's tent** to impinge upon another's interests *UK, 2002*. ▶ **piss it in** to win easily *AUSTRALIA, 1996*. ▶ **piss money against the wall; piss it up the wall** to squander or waste money, especially on drinking *UK, 1785*. ▶ **piss on 1** to despise or feel contempt for someone or something *UK, 2000*. **2** to drink heavily; to continue a drinking binge *AUSTRALIA, 1998*. ▶ **piss your**

trousers; piss your pants to soil your clothing by accidental urination *UK, 1966*. ▶ **piss yourself** to laugh uproariously. Abbreviated from 'piss yourself laughing', from the notion that loss of physical control is a consequence of overwhelming laughter *UK, 1951*

piss- *prefix* extremely *AUSTRALIA, 1963*

piss about *verb* to play the fool, to waste time; to make a mess of something; to inconvenience someone *UK, 1961*

piss and moan *verb* to complain loud and long *US, 1971*

piss and punk *noun* bread and water *US, 1970*

piss and vinegar *noun* energy, enthusiam, vigour *US, 1942*

pissant *noun* a small person *US, 1946*

pissant *adjective* insignificant, small-time *US, 1981*

pissaphone *noun* a funnel-shaped urinal used by the military *AUSTRALIA, 1943*

piss around *verb* to play the fool, to waste time; to make a mess of something; to inconvenience someone *UK, 1998*

piss-arse about *verb* to play the fool, to waste time; to make a mess of something; to inconvenience someone *UK, 1948*

piss artist *noun* a heavy drinker *AUSTRALIA, 1968*

piss-ass *adjective* despicable, unworthy, inconsequential *US, 1974*

piss away *verb* **1** to waste or to squander something *US, 1948*. **2** to move away, especially at speed *UK, 1978*

piss-can *noun* a local police station or jail *US, 1950*

piss-cutter *noun* **1** a clever, resourceful and tough person *US, 1941*. **2** a person who disparages a friend *BAHAMAS, 1982*. **3** in oil drilling, the third man on a cable tool rig *US, 1954*

piss down *verb* to rain heavily *UK, 1950*

piss easy *adjective* very easy *NEW ZEALAND, 1988*

pissed *adjective* **1** drunk *UK, 1929*. **2** angry, annoyed. An abbreviation of PISSED OFF *US, 1971*

pissed as a bastard *adjective* very drunk *UK, 2003*

pissed as a cunt *adjective* extremely drunk *UK, 1961*

pissed as a fart; pissed as a brewer's fart *adjective* very drunk *UK, 1998*

pissed as a newt *adjective* very drunk *AUSTRALIA, 1977*

pissed as an owl *adjective* very drunk *AUSTRALIA, 1986*

pissed as a parrot *adjective* extremely drunk *AUSTRALIA, 1977*

pissed as a rat *adjective* very drunk *UK, 1980*

pissed as arseholes *adjective* extremely drunk *UK, 1984*

pissed as a twat *adjective* very drunk *UK, 2003*

pissed off *adjective* fed up; disgruntled; annoyed; angry *US, 1946*

pissed out of your mind; pissed out of your skull *adjective* very drunk *AUSTRALIA, 1969*

pissed up *adjective* in a drunken condition. A variation of PISSED *UK, 1999*

piss-elegant *adjective* conceited, haughty *US, 1957*

pisser *noun* **1** a urinal *UK, 1961*. **2** the penis; the vagina *UK, 1901*. **3** a criminal who urinates in their clothing when caught by authorities *AUSTRALIA, 2001*. **4** an extraordinary person or thing *US, 1943*. **5** an annoyance. Literally something that will PISS OFF (annoy) *US, 1943*. **6** during the Vietnam war, an observer of enemy supply trails *US, 1991*. **7** solitary confinement in prison *US, 1990*. **8** a pub *NEW ZEALAND, 1998*. **9** an electric pylon. Perhaps from as sense as 'the penis' after its phallic shape *UK, 1977*. **10** a type of cicada which releases a liquid when held *AUSTRALIA, 1980*. ▶ **pull your pisser** to befool, or mislead, or tease someone. A variation of PULL YOUR LEG *UK, 1969*

piss-fart around *verb* to waste time *AUSTRALIA, 1988*

piss fat *noun* an erection caused by a full bladder *AUSTRALIA, 1984*

piss flaps *noun* the vaginal lips. *Roger's Profanisaurus*, 1997, also offers its use as an exclamation of disappointment: 'Oh *piss-flaps*! I never win the Lottery!' *AUSTRALIA, 1985*

piss-head *noun* a drunk; a habitual drinker. A combination of PISS (alcohol) with -HEAD (a user) *UK, 1961*

piss-hole *noun* **1** the entrance to the urethra *US, 1996*. **2** a urinal *UK, 1959*. **3** an unpleasant location *UK, 1973*

piss-hole bandit *noun* a homosexual man who seeks sexual contact in a public urinal *UK, 1977*

piss house *noun* a public toilet *US, 1947*

piss in *verb* to win or achieve something easily *NEW ZEALAND, 1998*

pissing *adjective* used as an intensifier, generally denoting disapproval *UK, 1984*

pissing contest *noun* a duel of unpleasantries *US, 1983*

pissing match *noun* a dispute based on mutual negative attacks. From the graphic if vulgar image of two men urinating on each other *US, 1992*

pissing rain *noun* heavy or persistent rainfall *UK, 2000*

piss in the hand *noun* something that is very simple *NEW ZEALAND, 1984*

piss it *verb* to succeed or achieve very easily *UK, 1982*

piss-off *noun* an annoyance, an irritation *UK, 2000*

piss off *verb* **1** to depart. Also used in an exclamatory or imperative sense *UK, 1958*. **2** to irritate or annoy someone. First recorded in the normally slang-free poetry of Ezra Pound *US, 1937*. **3** to get rid of someone *AUSTRALIA, 1972*

piss play *noun* sexual behaviour involving urination and urine *US, 1999*

piss-poor *adjective* extremely poor or feeble. Brought into general usage from British service usage during World War 2 *UK, 1946*

pisspot; piss-pot *noun* **1** a vessel for urine. Originally conventional; it slipped into vulgar use during the C18 whilst still being very much a household necessity *UK, 1440*. **2** a terrible thing or place *US, 1964*. **3** a drunkard; a despicable person. Figurative use of the sense as 'a chamber pot' *AUSTRALIA, 1969*. **4** a US military M-1 helmet *US, 1990*

piss-proud *adjective* having an erect penis as a result of urinal pressure *UK, 1788*

piss-take *noun* an act of mockery or teasing *UK, 1977*

piss-take *verb* to mock; to tease; to deride; to ridicule *UK, 2002*

piss-taker *noun* a mocker; a person who ridicules something *UK, 1976*

piss-taking *noun* mockery *UK, 1967*

piss-to-windward *noun* an entirely inept person *BARBADOS, 1965*

piss tube; pee pipe *noun* a metal tube partially buried in the ground, into which soldiers urinate. Vietnam war usage *US, 1977*

piss-up *noun* a drinking session *UK, 1952*. ▶ **couldn't organise a piss-up in a brewery** used of an inefficient person or organisation. Formed on PISS-UP (a drinking session) *UK, 1984*

piss up; piss up large *verb* to drink beer or other alcoholic beverages *NEW ZEALAND, 1998*

piss-weak *adjective* puny and cowardly *AUSTRALIA, 1971*

pisswhacker *noun* a type of cicada which releases a liquid when held *AUSTRALIA, 1981*

piss-willie *noun* a despicable coward *US, 1977*

pissy *noun* a heavy drinker *AUSTRALIA, 1979*

pissy *adjective* **1** unpleasant, distasteful *UK, 1997*. **2** puny; insignificant; weak *AUSTRALIA, 1985*. **3** angered, crotchety, fussy *US, 1973*. **4** given to drinking *AUSTRALIA, 1979*. **5** drunken *AUSTRALIA, 1971*

pissy *adverb* extremely *BAHAMAS, 1982*

pissy-ass *adjective* dirty, inconsequential *US, 1975*

pissy-eyed *adjective* drunk *NEW ZEALAND, 1998*

pistol *noun* **1** the penis *US, 2002*. **2** a hired gunman *US, 1964*. **3** a reliable person *US, 1984*. **4** a lobster that has lost one or both claws *US, 1975*. **5** in electric line work, an underground cable terminator *US, 1980*

pistola *noun* a cigarette enhanced with freebase cocaine *US, 1979*

Pistol Pete *noun* a chronic male masturbator *US, 2002*

pistorically; pistoratically *adverb* very (drunk) *BARBADOS, 1965*

pit *noun* **1** the armpit *US, 1965*. **2** the vein at the antecubital site, opposite the elbow, commonly used for drug injections *US, 1964*. **3** Pitocin™, a drug used for inducing labour *US, 1994*. **4** phencyclidine, the recreational drug known as PCP or angel dust *US, 1994*. **5** the area in a club or concert hall where dancers can slam dance. An abbreviation of MOSH PIT *US, 1995*. **6** a bed *UK, 1948*. **7** an inside jacket pocket *US, 1958*. ▶ **no pit** no trouble. From 'armpit' to 'pit' to 'sweat' to 'trouble' *US, 1968*

pit *verb* to sweat under the arms *US, 1966*

PITA used as Internet shorthand to mean *'pain in the ass/arse' US, 1995*

pit bull *noun* a variety of MDMA, the recreational drug best known as ecstasy *UK, 1996*

pitch *noun* a persuasive or exaggerated sales act or talk *UK, 1876*

pitch *verb* to play the active sexual role in a homosexual relationship *US, 1966*. ▶ **pitch a stink** to complain loudly *BAHAMAS, 1982*. ▶ **pitch a tent** to have an erection *US, 2001*. ▶ **pitch it strong; pitch it high** to make a forceful case for something *UK, 1837*. ▶ **pitch woo; pitch the woo** to commence a courtship *US, 1867*

pitch and toss *noun* a boss. Rhyming slang *AUSTRALIA, 1945*

pitcher *noun* **1** the active partner in homosexual sex *US, 1966*. **2** a dealer in a casino card game *US, 1973*

pitchhole *noun* a deep pothole in a road *CANADA, 1962*

pitch in *verb* **1** to commence work in a vigorous manner; to join in with another, or others, doing such work *US, 1847*. **2** to start eating; to eat heartily *US, 1937*

pitch up; pitch *verb* to arrive *UK, 2003*

pit cupcake *noun* in motor racing, a female hanger-on in search of romance with drivers or members of the pit crew *US, 1992*

pit girl *noun* a female casino employee whose job is to provide company and encouragement for heavy-betting gamblers *US, 1963*

pit guard *noun* an underarm deodorant *US, 1968*

pit lamp *verb* to engage in illegal jacklighting in hunting; also, to dismiss someone from employment. The first meaning of this slang term comes from the use of a lamp like a miner's lamp *CANADA, 1966*

pit room *noun* a bedroom *ANTARCTICA, 2000*

pits *noun* in a hospital, the medical screening area *US, 1978*. ▶ **the pits** the very bottom; the depths; the nadir; the worst. Perhaps from 'arm*pits*' *US, 1953*

pit stop *noun* **1** while driving, a stop at a restaurant, petrol station or rest area to use the lavatory and/or buy food and drink; a visit to the toilet *US, 1968*. **2** a short stay in prison, especially one occasioned by a parole violation *US, 1984*. **3** an underarm deodorant *US, 1969*

Pitstop *nickname* used as a humorous nickname for Pittsburgh, Pennsylvania *US, 1981*

pitter-patter *verb* **1** to walk in small, quiet steps *US, 1864*. **2** to talk persuasively or glibly *UK, 1979*

Pittsburgh feathers *noun* coal *US, 1949*

Pitt Street farmer *noun* (especially in New South Wales) a city person with a small country property, often run at a loss for tax purposes. From Pitt Street, a principle street in Sydney *AUSTRALIA, 1945*

pitty *noun* a pit bull dog. Formerly known as a Staffordshire Terrier or an American Pit Bull Terrier *US, 1990*

pitty *adjective* messy, dirty *US, 1975*

pity pot *noun* used in twelve-step recovery programmes such as Alcoholics Anonymous as a name for the imaginary place where the addict sits feeling sorry for himself *US, 1995*

pivvy *noun* a very small amount *BARBADOS, 1965*

pix *noun* photographs or films. An abbreviation of the pronunciation of 'pictures' *US, 1932*

pixie *noun* **1** a male homosexual. The term was enshrined in US popular/political culture during the McCarthy hearings in April, 1954. Joseph Welch, the lawyer for the US Army, demanded to know the origins of a doctored photograph, asking if it had come from a 'pixie', alluding to a suspected homosexual relationship involving Roy Cohn, a member of McCarthy's staff. Senator McCarthy asked Mr Welch to define the term, which he happily did: "I should say, Mr Senator, that a pixie is a close relative of a fairy" *US, 1941*. **2** a frequent user of marijuana *UK, 1983*. **3** an amphetamine tablet *US, 1994*. **4** hair that has been chemically straightened *US, 1972*

pixies *noun* ▶ **away with the pixies** daydreaming *NEW ZEALAND, 1998*

pixilated *adjective* whimsical, slightly crazy; befuddled; drunk *US, 1848*

pizlum *noun* a pig's penis *US, 1952*

pizza *noun* **1** marijuana *US, 1965*. **2** a large area of grazed skin. Skateboarders' slang; from the appearance of the wound *UK, 1998*

pizza cutter *noun* in drag racing, an extremely narrow front wheel *US, 1993*

pizza dude *noun* the pizza delivery person *US, 1988*

pizzaface *noun* a person with a bad case of acne *US, 1971*

pizza plate *noun* in electric line work, an insulated tool attachment formally known as a fork suspension attachment *US, 1980*

pizzazz; pizazz; p'zazz *noun* energy, vim, vigour, excitement *US, 1937*

PJ *noun* an unofficial, unlicensed if not illegal, job. An abbreviation of 'private job' *TRINIDAD AND TOBAGO, 1990*

PJ's *noun* pyjamas *US, 1964*

PK *noun* preacher's kid. Used without regard to denomination or even religion, applied even to children of rabbis; denotating a certain bond among those who have grown up in the shadow of organised religion *US, 2004*

placa *noun* a nickname, especially the artistic representation of the nickname on a public wall. Spanish slang used by English-speaking Mexican-Americans *US, 1974*

placcy; placky; plakky; plaggy; plazzy *adjective* plastic *UK, 1999*

place *noun* ▶ **you make the place untidy; you are making the place untidy** used as an ungracious or jocular invitation to be seated *UK, 1978*

placenta poker *noun* the penis. Jocular *UK, 2003*

plague *noun* ▶ **the plague 1** the bleed period of the menstrual cycle *UK, 1961*. **2** HIV *US, 1990*

plague *verb* to trouble, torment, tease, bother or annoy someone. A weakening of the conventional sense *UK, 1594*

plagued *adjective* infected with HIV *US, 1990*

plaguer *noun* a person infected with HIV *US, 1990*

plain Jane *noun* **1** an unremarkably ordinary or unattractive woman *UK, 1912*. **2** an innocent looking, performance-enhanced unmarked motorway patrol car *US, 1992*

plait your shit! used for registering dismissal, either of a notion or a person *AUSTRALIA, 1971*

plamas *noun* flattery, exaggeration *IRELAND, 1999*

plane *verb* in the language of wind surfing, to hydroplane *US, 1985*

planet *noun* when combined with a personal characteristic or interest, applied to a person's narrow or exclusive focus on that characteristic or interest. A remote place that it is hard to contact *UK, 2001*. ▶ **on another planet** very drug-intoxicated *UK, 1999*

Planet Zog *noun* a supremely unrealistic place; the home of unrealistic ideas; where daydreamers go. To be said to have arrived from Planet Zog is 'to have no idea what's going on' *UK, 2003*

plank *noun* **1** a stupid person. The phrase THICK AS TWO SHORT PLANKS (stupid) gave rise to the adjective PLANKY (stupid), hence 'plank' *UK, 1999*. **2** an electric guitar. From the instrument's original construction in the late 1940s, and an insult hurled at later Fender guitars *UK, 2000*. **3** a heavy surfboard, especially an older wooden one *US, 1957*. ▶ **make the plank** in homosexual usage, to take the passive position in anal sex *US, 1981*. ▶ **put the plank to someone** (from a male perspective) to have sex with someone. A variation of PLANK (to have sex) in which 'plank' is understood to be a 'penis' *UK, 2001*

plank *verb* **1** to have sex with. A 'plank' may be a 'floorboard' or, possibly, a 'table'; hence this probably originates from an occurrence on a wooden surface in much the same way as BED (to have sex); it may also be a reference to the erect penis which is, no doubt, 'stiff as a board' *US, 1972*. **2** to conceal something *UK: SCOTLAND, 1823*

plank-spanker *noun* a guitarist. From PLANK (a guitar) *UK, 1998*

plank-whacker *noun* a guitarist. From PLANK (a guitar) *UK, 2001*

planky *adjective* stupid. From THICK AS TWO SHORT PLANKS *UK, 1984*

plant *noun* **1** a person, such as a magician's assistant, who has been secretly placed in an audience, in order to assist whoever is addressing or manipulating that crowd *US, 1984*. **2** a police surveillance action *US, 1984*. **3** a cell used for solitary confinement *US, 1976*. **4** an electrical generator *US, 1985*. **5** the equipment and work animals of a drover or other rural worker travelling through the countryside *AUSTRALIA, 1867*

plant *verb* **1** to bury a body *US, 1855*. **2** to deliver a blow; to drive a ball *UK, 1808*. **3** to station a person for use in an underhand manner *UK, 1693*. **4** to incriminate someone suspected of a crime by hiding evidence where it is certain to be found by the appropriate authorities *UK, 1865*. ▶ **plant it** in motor racing, to accelerate to the fullest extent possible *US, 1965*

plantation *noun* any small garden *CAYMAN ISLANDS, 1985*

planting *noun* a burial *US, 1977*

plant you now, dig you later used as a farewell *US, 1947*

plaque whacker *noun* a dental hygienist *US, 2001*

plaster-caster *noun* a groupie who makes plaster casts of celebrities' penises *US, 1968*

plastered *adjective* drunk *US, 1912*

plaster of Paris; plaster *noun* the backside, the buttocks. Rhyming slang, extending the sequence ARIS – ARISTOTLE – BOTTLE; BOTTLE AND GLASS – ARSE *UK, 1998*

plastic *noun* **1** a credit card; consumer credit in general *US, 1979*. **2** a person who is liable to act in an unpredictable manner *UK, 2003*. **3** a condom *US, 1993*. ▶ **on the plastic** using stolen credit cards, etc *UK, 1977*. ▶ **pull plastic** (used of a prisoner) to place your belongings in a plastic rubbish bag when you are transferred *US, 1997*

plastic *adjective* conventional; superficial; shallow *US, 1967*

plastic badge *noun* a private security guard *US, 2001*

plastic fantastic *noun* **1** a credit card or credit card transation *NEW ZEALAND, 1995*. **2** a yacht with a fibreglass hull *NEW ZEALAND, 1986*

plastic fantastic *adjective* wonderful. If not coined, widely popularised by Jefferson Airplane's 1967 song, 'Plastic Fantastic Lover' *US, 1970*

plastic gangster; plastic *noun* a tough guy who is not anywhere near as tough as he pretends *UK, 1996*

plastic hippie *noun* a person who assumes the outer trappings of the counterculture without fully immersing himself in it *US, 1967*

plastic job *noun* cosmetic surgery *US, 1953*

plastic money *noun* a credit card or cards; consumer credit in general *US, 1974*

plastics *noun* prison-issue plastic cutlery *UK, 1996*

plate *noun* **1** a plate of food brought by a guest to a party. The notion of 'bringing a plate' to supplement the food laid on by the host is an Australian social tradition *AUSTRALIA, 1961*. **2** a badge *US, 1949*. **3** a phonograph record *US, 1935*. ▶ **on a plate; on a platter** easily acquired; with little or no effort required *UK, 1935*

plate *verb* **1** to engage in oral sex. Rhyming slang for 'plate of ham', GAM (to perform oral sex) *UK, 1968*. **2** to engage in oral stimulation of the anus *UK, 2003*

plate and dish *noun* a wish. Rhyming slang *UK, 1998*

plater *noun* **1** in horse racing, a horse that competes in minor, low-paying races. From the practice of awarding a silver plate instead of a cash prize *US, 1923*. **2** in horse racing, a farrier *US, 1976*

plates and dishes; plates *noun* a wife. Rhyming slang for MISSIS *UK, 1960*

plates of meat; plates *noun* the feet. Rhyming slang, since 1857; abbreviated to 'plates' since 1896 *UK, 1857*

plats *noun* platform shoes *US, 1997*

platter *noun* a phonograph record *US, 1931*

platter pusher *noun* a radio disc jockey *US, 1973*

platters of meat; platters *noun* the feet. Rhyming slang; an elaboration of PLATES OF MEAT since 1923; the abbreviation 'platters' since 1945 *UK, 1923*

play *noun* **1** sexual activity *US, 1995*. **2** a manoeuvre; a tactical move *US, 1982*. **3** a legitimate scheme or a criminal venture. From the previous sense *US, 2000*. **4** the deception surrounding a confidence swindle *US, 1940*. **5** in horse racing, a bet *US, 1994*. ▶ **in play** falling into a confidence swindle *US, 1997*

play *verb* to work as a pimp; to hustle *US, 1977*. ▶ **play ball 1** to have sex. Punning on BALL (to have sex) and 'play ball' (to cooperate with) *US, 2001*. **2** to stop idling and start working *US, 1977*. **3** to cooperate with someone else; occasionally applied to inanimate objects such as computers *US, 1957*. ▶ **play bingo** to try to determine the reason for a cash shortage by comparing orders with receipts *US, 1996*. ▶ **play catch-up** in an athletic contest, to try to catch up and surpass an opponent that at the moment is leading *US, 1971*. ▶ **play checkers** to move from empty seat to empty seat in a cinema, looking for a sexual partner. Homosexual usage *US, 1972*. ▶ **play dead** to act dumb *US, 1953*. ▶ **play for the other team** to be homosexual *US, 1997*. ▶ **play handball** to smoke crack cocaine. A highly euphemistic code *US, 1993*. ▶ **play hard to get** to resist amorous advances (especially while intending to acquiesce); hence, more generally, to be reluctant to comply with what is expected *UK, 1945*. ▶ **play hookey; play hooky** to absent yourself from school or work *US, 1848*. ▶ **play inside right** to be mean with money. Rhyming slang for TIGHT, elaborated into football terminology *UK, 1998*. ▶ **play it by ear** to improvise as circumstances dictate. As a musician picking up a tune without sheet music to guide *UK, 1984*. ▶ **play it cool** to remain calm and composed *UK, 1942*. ▶ **play mums and dads; play dads and mums** to have sex. An adult version of a children's game. 'Play fathers and mothers' is also recorded but in the strongest current usages it seems that the female comes first *UK, 1967*. ▶ **play past something** to overcome an obstacle or impediment to progress *US, 1972*. ▶ **play silly buggers** to be a nuisance; to cause trouble or disruption; to 'mess about' *UK, 2001*. ▶ **play someone cheap** to assume that someone is stupid *US, 1947*. ▶ **play the blocks** to idle on a street corner *BAHAMAS, 1982*. ▶ **play the chill 1** to act calm *US, 1920*. **2** to snub someone *US, 1985*. ▶ **play the kerbs** to sell drugs on the street *US, 1989*. ▶ **play the queens** to have sex with a passive, effeminate male prisoner *US, 1984*. ▶ **play the whale** to vomit *AUSTRALIA, 1971*. ▶ **play them as they lay** used as a wisely humorous acceptance of the need to work with what has been given to you *US, 1992*. ▶ **play too close** to take advantage of another's good nature by excessive teasing or abuse *US, 1992*. ▶ **play took and banjo** to sing or whistle a secular tune on a Sunday or religious holiday *BARBADOS, 1965*. ▶ **play up to someone** to humour someone; to flatter someone, to take your cue from another; to behave according to expectations. Originally in theatrical use *UK, 1809*. ▶ **play with yourself** to masturbate. The earliest usage recorded of this sweet little euphemism is by James Joyce *IRELAND, 1922*

play around *verb* to have an extra-marital amorous liaison *US, 1943*

play-away *noun* a weekend at someone else's place in the country. Upper-class society usage; predates BBC television childrens' programme *Playaway*, 1984 *UK, 1982*

playback *noun* a scheme by which the odds on a particular horse race are engineered lower by heavy betting on that horse *US, 1963*

Playboy *noun* a tablet of MDMA, the recreational drug best known as ecstasy *UK, 2004*. ▶ **the Playboy** a pubic hairstyle *UK, 2002*

play dough *noun* bread found in a US Army combat ration. Word play on the inedible mix of flour, water and salt called 'play dough' and played with by children *US, 1991*

played *adjective* out of money *US, 1984*

player *noun* **1** a person who takes pride in the number of sexual partners they have, not in the depth of any relationship; a selfish pleasure-seeker *US, 1968*. **2** a pimp *US, 1972*. **3** a schemer; an important figure in a field *US, 1995*. **4** a drug user or drug seller *US, 1971*. **5** an active member of a terrorist organisation. Used by police, military and other security services *UK, 1995*. **6** in casino gambling, a craps player *US, 1974*. **7** a hip-hop artist. Also variant 'playa' *US, 1995*

player hater *noun* someone who is envious or jealous of another's social success *US, 1999*

player of the pink oboe *noun* a person who performs oral sex on a man. Coined by satirist Peter Cook (1937–95) for a sketch performed in Amnesty International's *The Secret Policeman's Ball. UK, 1979*

play-for-pay *adjective* **1** available for paid sex *US, 1956*. **2** receiving compensation while competing as an amateur athlete *US, 2003*

playground's muddy *noun* experiencing the bleed period of the menstrual cycle *US, 2001*

playing *noun* amongst women prisoners, homosexual flirtation and involvement *UK, 1980*

playing bingo *adjective* in prison, said of a sex offender. From the call of the numbers in RULE FORTY-THREE *UK, 1996*

playing with confederate money *adjective* having silicone breast implants. Very impressive to look at but ultimately valueless. Coined for US television comedy *Seinfeld*, 1993–98 *US, 2003*

play-lunch *noun* a mid-morning break at primary school; also, the food eaten during this break *AUSTRALIA, 1962*

playmates *noun* the testicles *UK, 2002*

play out *verb* **1** (of a DJ) to perform in public; (of a dance record) to be included in a DJ's repertoire *UK, 2003*. **2** to escape from confinement *US, 1972*

play-play *adjective* make-believe *BARBADOS, 1965*

playtime *noun* a time in a prison's schedule when the inmates are out of their cells mixing with each other. From school usage *UK, 1996*

please; per-lease; puh-lease used for humorously asking please or expressing scepticism. An affectation popularised in any number of television situation comedies in the mid- to late 1980s and thereafter a staple of US popspeak *US, 1990*

pleasure and pain *noun* rain. Rhyming slang *UK, 1960*

pleb *noun* **1** an unsophisticated or uneducated person. An abbreviation of conventional 'plebeian' (a lower-class person) *UK, 1865*. **2** an annoying person; a nuisance. A generally derogative application of the sense as 'a plebeian' *UK, 1981*

pleb; plebbie; plebby *adjective* of a plebeian character; coarse; uneducated *UK, 1962*

pleckie *noun* a *plectrum UK: SCOTLAND, 1988*

pledges *noun* cash *US, 2003*

plenty *adverb* very *UK, 1934*

plenty-plenty *adverb* to a great extent *BAHAMAS, 1982*

plier *noun* in a confidence swindle or sales scheme, an agent who for a commission locates potential victims *US, 1988*

pliers *noun* a railway ticket inspector's punch *US, 1946*

plimmie *noun* a plimsoll (a rubber-soled canvas shoe) *UK, 1994*

pling *noun* an exclamation mark (!) on a computer keyboard *US, 1991*

pling *verb* in circus and carnival usage, to beg *US, 1981*

plink *noun* cheap wine. Variant of PLONK with a change of vowel influenced by other couplets such as 'ding dong, 'sing song *AUSTRALIA, 1943*

plinker *noun* an inexpensive, simply designed gun marketed for casual use *US, 1982*

plod; plodder; PC Plod; Mr Plod; the plod *noun* a uniformed police officer; the police. Derives from Mr Plod the Policeman, a character in the Noddy stories of Enid Blyton (1897–1968), possibly a pun on 'plodding the beat' or, simply, 'to plod' (to proceed tediously) *UK, 1977*

ploddite *noun* a police officer *UK, 2003*

plod shop *noun* a police station *UK, 1996*

plokta *verb* in computing, to press keys randomly in an effort to obtain a response from the computer. An acronym of 'press lots of keys to abort' *US, 1991*

plonk *noun* **1** cheap wine. Alteration of French *blanc*, from *vin blanc* (white wine); occasionally used of other alcoholic drinks *AUSTRALIA, 1930*. **2** alcohol, especially beer *NEW ZEALAND, 1984*. **3** a woman police constable *UK, 1996*. **4** the surreptitious wagering of a large amount of money *AUSTRALIA, 1981*

plonk *verb* **1** to place something, especially with a lack of finesse *AUSTRALIA, 1942*. **2** (of a male), to have sex. In use among National Servicemen in the 1950s *UK, 1984*. **3** to wager money *AUSTRALIA, 1981*

plonker; plonk *noun* **1** the penis *UK, 1947*. **2** a fool; used (often humorously) as an everyday form of abuse. Euphemistic extension of the previous sense for name-calling as PRICK. Popularised from the early 1980s by BBC television situation comedy *Only Fools and Horses UK, 1966*

plonkie *adjective* foolish; displaying the qualities of a plonker *UK, 2001*

plonko *noun* an alcoholic *AUSTRALIA, 1963*

ploo *adjective* a 'plus' attached to a grade *US, 1968*

plooky *adjective* pimply, spotty. Extended from PLUKE; PLOOK (a spot) *UK: SCOTLAND, 1985*

plootered *adjective* drunk. Probably from Scottish *plouter* (to splash in water) *UK, 1984*

plop *noun* excrement *US, 1984*

plop *verb* to fall or to drop heavily *UK, 1839*

plop down *verb* to lay down forcefully; to lie down with abandon *US, 1986*

ploppy *noun* an unskilled gambler who describes his systems to all around him *UK, 1996*

plot up *verb* **1** to establish a singular, group or gang presence in an area and represent it as the territory of that individual, group or gang *UK, 1999*. **2** to conceal something *UK, 2001*

plotzed *adjective* drunk. From German *plotzen* (to burst) via Yiddish *plotz* (to burst) *US, 1962*

plow *noun* marijuana. The means by which you become PLOWED (drug-intoxicated) *UK, 2003*. ▶ **get your plow cleaned** to be killed in combat *US, 1968*

plow *verb* (used of a male) to have sex *US, 1970*. ▶ **plow the field** to drive off the road at a high rate of speed into a field *US, 1962*

plowboy *noun* a rustic; an unsophisticated person from the far reaches of the countryside. Disparaging *UK, 1569*

plowed *adjective* **1** drunk *US, 1974*. **2** drug-intoxicated. From the previous sense *US, 1981*

plow jockey *noun* **1** a farmer *US, 1951*. **2** a soldier who cannot keep cadence when marching, who appears to be walking as if behind a plough with one foot in the furrow *US, 1946*

plu *noun* tea *AUSTRALIA, 1960*

pluck *noun* **1** wine *US, 1964*. **2** the recruiting of a prostitute to work for a pimp; a prostitute recruited to work for a pimp *US, 1973*

pluck *verb* **1** to recruit a prostitute into the services of a pimp *US, 1973*. **2** (used of a male) to have sex with a virgin *BAHAMAS, 1982*. ▶ **pluck the chicken** to swindle a victim in a phony investment or sales scheme *US, 1988*

plucky *adjective* brave, daring *UK, 1842*

plug *noun* **1** a piece of publicity, a promotional pitch *US, 1902*. **2** a tampon. Understood to be a variation on conventional 'plug', possibly from abbreviation of technical jargon 'catamenial plug' (a tampon) *US, 2001*. **3** a bullet hole *UK, 2001*. **4** a poker player with a

steady, competent and predictable style of play *US, 1988*. **5** a horse that has seen its best days *US, 1860*. **6** a temporary worker *US, 1997*

plug *verb* **1** to support, to endorse, to promote *US, 1927*. **2** to shoot someone *US, 1870*. **3** (of a male) to have sex with someone *US, 1888*. **4** to insert contraband items into the anus during a prison visit *UK, 1996*. **5** to engage in a fist fight without any weapons *US, 1992*. **6** on the railways, to use the reverse gear to help stop a train *US, 1977*. **7** to tease or taunt someone *US, 2002*. ▶ **plug in** to help. In the usage of counterculturalists associated with the Rainbow Nation gatherings *US, 1997*. ▶ **plug in both ways** (of a male) to be bisexual. A play on AC/DC *UK, 1980*. ▶ **plug your mug** to stop talking *US, 1947*

plug away; plug *verb* to continue doing something or making an effort, to persist doggedly *UK, 1865*

plugged in *adjective* connected to something fashionable *US, 1989*

plugged nickel *noun* literally, a five-cent piece that has been altered by the insertion of a plug of base metal; figuratively, something of no value *US, 1988*

plugger *noun* a person whose job it is to promote a record or recording artist *US, 1945*

plughole *noun* ▶ **go down the plughole** to become lost; to go to waste; to fail. A variation of DOWN THE DRAIN *UK, 1973*

plug-ugly *noun* a violent, rough person *US, 1856*

pluke; plook *noun* a spot, boil or other pus-filled skin blemish. Directly from Scottish dialect *plook UK, 1997*

plum *noun* **1** the testicle. From its shape and fruitfulness. One notable precursor to its unambiguous sense as a testicle is in the innuendo-laden song 'Please Don't Touch My Plums' by Sammy Cahn, 1913–93, written for the film *The Duchess and the Dirtwater Fox*, 1976, in which it was sung in a Golden Globe-winning performance by Goldie Hawn *UK, 2003*. **2** a fool; used as a general term of abuse. From the previous sense *UK, 1982*. **3** an exceptional person or thing *AUSTRALIA, 1956*. **4** in marketing, a married man with above-average income who is keen to improve his pension. A specific sense of the general use of 'plum' as 'something desirable'. The opposite is a LEMON *UK, 1998*. **5** in pool, the plum-coloured four-ball *US, 1990*. **6** in pool, an easy shot *US, 1970*

plumb; plum *adverb* absolutely; completely; utterly. From the earlier, conventional sense (exactly) *UK, 1587*

plumbay *noun* the vulva; a woman's pubic mound *TRINIDAD AND TOBAGO, 2003*

plumber *noun* **1** a urologist *US, 1961*. **2** a male pornography performer *US, 1995*. **3** in the Royal Air Force, an armament tradesman. Still in Royal Air Force use, 2002 *UK, 1942*. **4** a golfer who is a good putter. Built on 'drain' in the sense of putting into the hole *US, 2000*

plumbing *noun* **1** the reproductive system *US, 1960*. **2** any wind instrument *US, 1935*

plumbing problem *noun* the inability of a male pornography performer either to maintain an erection or to ejaculate on demand *US, 1995*

plum-in-the-mouth *adjective* upper-class, privileged *UK, 1926*

plummer *noun* a pickpocket. Misspelling of 'plumber' recorded in prison use August 2002 *UK, 2002*

plummy *adjective* used for describing an affectedly upper-class manner of speech. The original meaning was 'rich, desirable' *UK, 1926*

plum pud; plum pudd *noun* good. Rhyming slang *AUSTRALIA, 1927*

plums *noun* no sexual contact (when the expectation of intimacy is high). Royal Navy slang; derives, possibly, from a 'plum' representing the figure 0 (hence 00 = nothing, nowhere). Alternatively PLUM (the testicle) hence BOLLOCKS (used as a general negative). A 'plums rating' is a sailor who has little luck with the opposite sex *UK, 1989*

plunderphonics *noun* in music, a style of sampling that alters the original, usually without seeking permission from the copyright holder. A compound of 'plunder' (to rob) and 'phonic' (of sound). Coinage is credited to electronic music artist John Oswald (b.1953) *CANADA, 1985*

plunge *noun* **1** a surreptitious wagering of a great amount on a high-odds horse; a large bet. If bookmakers become aware that a great deal of money is being bet on a horse, they shorten the odds *AUSTRALIA, 1895*. **2** a large cumulative amount of money wagered on a competitor *AUSTRALIA, 1960*

plunge *verb* **1** to stab someone; to kill someone by stabbing *UK, 1996*. **2** to wager a great deal of money *AUSTRALIA, 1877*

plunger *noun* a heavy bettor *AUSTRALIA, 1895*

plungeroo *noun* a pinball enthusiast *US, 1945*

plunked *adjective* pregnant *NEW ZEALAND, 2002*

plurry *adjective* bloody. The Australian Aboriginal English pronunciation of the word **BLOODY**, occasionally used in a jocular or euphemistic way by non-Aboriginals *AUSTRALIA, 1950*

plurry *adverb* bloody *AUSTRALIA, 1988*

PL-US *noun* like-minded individuals. Initialism contrived from '*people like us* *US, 1990s*

plus-15s *noun* (pedestrian) overpasses connecting buildings in Calgary, Alberta *CANADA, 2002*

plush *noun* stuffed animals *US, 1985*

Plush family *noun* used as a humorous personification of empty seats in a theatre *UK, 1052*

plush out *verb* to completely refurbish a car's upholstery and interior *US, 1993*

plus-minus *adverb* approximately, about. As the mathematical formula represented by the symbol ± *SOUTH AFRICA, 1970*

Pluto pup *noun* a deep-fried battered saveloy on a stick *AUSTRALIA, 1986*

Pluto water *noun* a natural mineral water that acts as a strong laxative *US, 1972*

pluty *adjective* wealthy; upscale. An abbreviation of 'plutocratic' *NEW ZEALAND, 1984*

Plymouth Argyll *noun* a file (a tool). Rhyming slang, formed on the name of a football club *UK, 1992*

PM *noun* **1** a *post mortem* examination of a corpse *US, 1989*. **2** in horse racing, the odds listed before a race. Also known as the 'PM line' *US, 1955*

PMJI used as Internet discussion group shorthand to mean '*pardon my jumping in*' *US, 1997*

PMS *noun* something or someone irritating or unpleasant. Ascribing the stereotypical symptoms of *pre-menstrual syndrome US, 2001*

PMS *verb* (of a woman) to feel the emotions associated with *pre-menstrual syndrome*; thus to feel angry, irritable, irrational, anxious, etc. PMS is the recognised abbreviation for 'pre-menstrual syndrome' *US, 1990*

pneumonia hole *noun* a car window *US, 1973*

pneumonia sedan *noun* a truck with no window glass or being driven with the windows down in cold weather *US, 1971*

po *noun* **1** a chamber pot. From the pronunciation of 'pot' in French *pot de chambre*. Survives, mainly, through the efforts of the antique trade *UK, 1880*. **2** in pool, position. A horrid contraction, but one that is in actual use *US, 1993*. **3** a promiscuous girl, one who will 'put out' *US, 1963*

PO *noun* a probation officer or parole officer *US, 1966*

po' boy *noun* a public assistance cheque *US, 1971*

pocaution *noun* contraception *BAHAMAS, 1982*

poc doc *noun* a short television documentary. An abbreviation of '*pocket documentary*' *CANADA, 1995*

pocket *noun* ▶ **in pocket** in possession of drugs to be sold *US, 1989*. ▶ **in the pocket** in poker, dealt face-down *US, 1990*. ▶ **in your pocket** of someone else, under your control or direction *UK, 1851*. ▶ **out of pocket** out of line; inappropriate *US, 1972*

pocket *verb* ▶ **pocket the red** to put the penis in the vagina. A pun from the game of billiards. Snooker offers a wider choice of puns with **PINK** and **BROWN** *UK, 1937*

pocket billiards *noun* the manipulation of your testicles for masturbation or comfort, performed by your hand hidden in your trouser pocket. Often in the phrase 'play pocket billiards' *UK, 1940*

pocket change *noun* a small amount of drugs when that is all that is left. From private correspondence with rock musicians *UK, 2001*

pocket club *noun* a police truncheon *US, 1962*

pocket engine *noun* a large pocket watch *TRINIDAD AND TOBAGO, 1939*

pocket man *noun* in a functionally compartmentalised criminal enterprise, the person who holds the cash *US, 1987*

pocket pistol *noun* a roasted cob of corn *BARBADOS, 1965*

pocket pole *noun* the penis. Plays on branded Pocket Pals™, a range of collectible 'whimsies' *US, 2001*

pocket pool *noun* used of a man, self-stimulation or masturbation while clothed. Word play based on ball play; the title of a song by Killer Pussy on the 'Valley Girl' soundtrack *US, 1960*

pocket rocket *noun* **1** the 1973–74 Oldsmobile Cutlass, the first small car from Oldsmobile *US, 1992*. **2** any small, fast, imported car *US, 1994*. **3** an improvised syringe filled with a drug and ready for injection *US, 1989*. **4** marijuana *UK, 1998*

poco loco *adjective* crazy; eccentric. Directly from Spanish *poco* (little) and *loco* (mad) *UK, 2003*

pod *noun* **1** marijuana *US, 1952*. **2** a marijuana cigarette *CANADA, 1958*. **3** the head *US, 1960*. **4** an orthopaedist *US, 1994*. **5** the tail of a surfboard *CANADA, 1977*

PO'd *adjective* angry; pissed off *US, 1957*

poddle *verb* in bowling, to roll the ball into the gutter *US, 1962*

poddy *noun* **1** a user of an iPod™ branded digital music player; often used as a nickname for an iPod *UK, 2004*. **2** a young, unbranded calf. From British dialect *poddy* (obese) *AUSTRALIA, 1872*

poddy *verb* to handfeed a young calf, lamb or foal *AUSTRALIA, 1960*

poddy-dodge *verb* to steal unbranded cattle *AUSTRALIA, 1919*

poddy-dodger *noun* a person who steals unbranded cattle *AUSTRALIA, 1919*

poddy-dodging *adjective* the theft of unbranded cattle *AUSTRALIA, 1919*

podge *noun* a short and fat person; fatness. From conventional **PODGY** *UK, 1876*

podger *verb* to have sex. A possible conflation of **POKE** and **ROGER** *UK: SCOTLAND, 1996*

podgy *noun* a girlfriend, mistress or prostitute. Korean war usage; from the Korean word for 'vulva' *US, 1968*

podgy *adjective* fat *UK, 1846*

podner *noun* used as a jocular term of address. Approximating a Western drawl of 'partner' *US, 1986*

pods *noun* the female breasts *US, 1968*

Podunk *noun* any remote, small town *US, 1977*

podunk *adjective* worthless, remote *US, 1968*

poegaai *adjective* exhausted; drunk *SOUTH AFRICA, 1942*

poep *noun* a fart; faeces; hence, contemptuously, of a person *SOUTH AFRICA, 1969*

poep *verb* to fart. From Afrikaans into impolite South African English *SOUTH AFRICA, 1983*

poep *adjective* bad, unpleasant. From the noun sense as 'faeces' *SOUTH AFRICA, 1970*

poetical *adjective* drunk *UK, 2001*

poets' day *noun* Friday, especially when used as an excuse to finish work early on a Friday. An acronym for '*piss off early – tomorrow's Saturday*' or '*push off early – tomorrow's Saturday*' *UK, 1984*

po-faced *adjective* having an impassive expression. Influenced by **POKER FACE**, but most likely to derive from **PO** (a chamber pot) or 'pohl' (an old exclamation of rejection) *UK, 1934*

pogey *noun* **1** a male homosexual who prefers the passive role in anal sex *US, 1950*. **2** unemployment insurance or welfare *CANADA, 1976*

pogey bait *noun* any food with high calorific, low nutritional content. In prison, sweets, cigarettes or other inducements given to men willing to play the passive role in anal sex *US, 1950*

poggled *adjective* of a car, having had crash damage repaired. A car dealers' term *UK, 1968*

poggler *noun* **1** a purse; a wallet *UK, 1977*. **2** a motor vehicle that has had crash-damage repaired. A car dealers' term *UK, 1977*

pogo *noun* **1** a form of dancing (essentially wildly jumping up and down on the spot) associated with punk rock music *UK, 1978*. **2** a contemptible person. In army use, a member of the administrative personnel, anyone not in the arms corps. From POGO STICK, rhyming slang for PRICK but influenced by imagery of aimlessly bouncing around as one does on a pogo-stick *AUSTRALIA, 1972*

pogo-pogo *noun* cocaine *US, 1970*

pogo stick *noun* **1** the penis. Rhyming slang for DICK or PRICK, influenced by apt imagery *UK, 2003*. **2** a Chinese rocket launcher, used in Vietnam by the Viet Cong *US, 1966*. **3** in electric line work, any telescoping insulated line tool *US, 1980*. **4** in poker, a player with wildly fluctuating play and success *US, 1996*

pogue *noun* **1** a homosexual male who plays the passive role during anal sex, especially if young. Deriving perhaps from Irish Gaelic *pogue* (to kiss) *US, 1941*. **2** a member of the armed forces assigned to the rear echelon, safely away from combat; a soldier newly arrived in combat. Seemingly unconnected to the C19 sense as 'purse' with 'pogue-hunter' as 'pickpocket' *US, 1975*

pogy *noun* a jail or prison *US, 1970*

poindexter *noun* a serious student *US, 1981*

point *noun* **1** a hypodermic needle and syringe *US, 1961*. **2** a pen; a pencil. Gay slang *UK, 1971*. **3** a percentage point *US, 1981*. **4** a man who ensures that order reigns at a brothel *US, 1987*

point *verb* ► **point Dennis at the Doulton** (of a male) to urinate. Doulton is a manufacturer of china *AUSTRALIA, 1971*. ► **point Percy** (of a male) to urinate. A familiar shortening of POINT PERCY AT THE PORCELAIN *AUSTRALIA, 1971*. ► **point Percy at the porcelain** (of a male) to urinate. Conventionally 'point PERCY (the penis) at *porcelain* (the china of a lavatory). Popularised in the UK in the late 1960s and early 70s via a *Private Eye* magazine cartoon strip and two films featuring Barry Mackenzie, an OCKER (a loutish Australian) created by Barry Humphries (b.1934). Coincidentally, the famously Australian Mr Humphries appeared in a 1974 film called *Percy's Progress*, about a man who had a penis transplant. All of which lends credence to the unproven assertion that this phrase is an Australian coinage *AUSTRALIA, 1968*. ► **point the bone** to point blame at someone; to accuse someone. Figuratively recalling the Australian Aboriginal ritual practice of pointing a bone at a person in order to wish death upon them *AUSTRALIA, 1943*. ► **point the finger** to testify on behalf of the prosecution *NEW ZEALAND, 1982*. ► **point the finger at** to identify someone or something as having a specific responsibility *UK, 1833*

pointer *noun* **1** a criminally inclined youth, especially a youth gang member *US, 1963*. **2** a large facial blemish *US, 1976*

pointers *noun* female breasts with prominent pointed nipples *US, 1983*

point-five *noun* a homosexual *FIJI, 1995*

point-out *noun* a member of a confidence swindle who introduces the intended victim to someone whom he identifies as a former acquaintance with good connections, who then lures the victim further into the swindle *US, 1997*

pointy-head *noun* an intellectual. Derogatory *US, 2000*

pointy-head; pointy-headed *adjective* intellectual, if at the expense of common sense. Derogatory *US, 1972*

Poirot *noun* a Belgian police officer. After Hercule Poirot, Agatha Christie's famous fictional detective *UK, 2002*

poison *noun* **1** a narcotic or an alcoholic drink, especially a person's favourite. Used in a jocular tone *US, 1805*. **2** narcotics, especially heroin *US, 1984*

poisoner *noun* a cook to a group of rural workers, especially shearers *AUSTRALIA, 1905*

poison shop *noun* a pharmacy *US, 1988*

poke *noun* **1** a wallet or purse *US, 1859*. **2** money; a roll of money *US, 1926*. **3** the stomach *US, 1975*. **4** power, especially horsepower *UK, 1965*. **5** a punch; a hard hitting verbal thrust. Both uses derive from the conventional sense (a thrust, a push) *UK, 1788*. **6** an inhalation of marijuana or opium smoke *US, 1955*. **7** marijuana. From 'pokeweed', *Phytolacca americana*, a strong smelling shrub native to North America *UK, 2001*. **8** a woman sexually objectified *UK, 1937*. **9** a poor person who attempts through demeaning behaviour to be accepted by upper-class people *BAHAMAS, 1982*

poke *verb* **1** (from a man's point of view) to have sex with a woman *UK, 1868*. **2** used as an emphatic rejection. Synonymous with STUFF or FUCK IT! *UK, 2003*. **3** to smoke marijuana *US, 1998*. **4** to inject a drug *UK, 2003*. ► **poke borak** to make fun of someone or something; to deride someone or something; to ridicule someone or something. Contextually in this phrase 'borak' means 'rubbish; nonsense'. It has its origins in the Australian Aboriginal language Wathawurung where it expressed negation *AUSTRALIA, 1873*. ► **poke mullock at** to deride someone; to make fun of someone *AUSTRALIA, 1916*. ► **poke squid** (of a male) to have sex *US, 1982*

poked *adjective* exhausted *NEW ZEALAND, 1978*

pokee *noun* the vagina. Children's vocabulary *TRINIDAD AND TOBAGO, 1974*

poker *noun* **1** the erect penis *US, 1969*. **2** in fencing, any weapon with a stiff, heavy blade. A derisory term, from the similarity to a conventional poker *UK, 1988*

pokerarse *noun* someone who is not relaxed or easy going *IRELAND, 1992*

poker face *noun* a blank expression that gives nothing away *US, 1885*

poker voice *noun* an even speaking tone that does not reveal any underlying emotion *US, 1986*

pokey *noun* a jail *US, 1919*

pokey *adjective* **1** of an enclosed space, small and dark; inadequate *UK, 1849*. **2** dawdling, slow. From SLOWPOKE *US, 1991*

pokie *noun* an electronic poker machine *NEW ZEALAND, 2002*

pol *noun* a politician *US, 1942*

Polack; Polak *noun* a Polish immigrant or a Polish-American. Disparaging *US, 1898*

Polack; Polak *adjective* Polish *US, 1964*

Polack fiddle *noun* a bucksaw, a one-man tool. Because of the skill attributed to Polish loggers in handling a bucksaw *US, 1975*

Poland-and-China *noun* a black and white police car *US, 1962*

polari; palare; parlare *noun* a slang vocabulary used by theatricals and homosexuals. Variants include: 'polare' and 'parlaree'. Probably from Italian *parlare* (to talk). This 'language' itself derives in great part from Italian and Romany roots, incorporating back slang, Cockney rhyming slang and Yiddish among its influences. The earliest form, known as 'parleyaree', was used by C17 actors who, as a despised section of society, needed a discreet means of communication; as theatricals achieved a degree of respectability so the use of the language changed and polari emerged. By the late 1930s the tolerance of theatre-life had attracted many homosexuals who, as a despised section of society, needed a discreet means of communication *UK, 1966*

polari; palare; parlare *verb* to talk, especially to talk in polari *UK, 1997*

polari lobe *noun* the ear *UK, 2002*

polari pipe *noun* a telephone *UK, 2002*

Polaroid *noun* a police radar unit used for measuring vehicles' speed *US, 1976*

pole *noun* **1** the penis *UK, 1972*. **2** an aircraft's control column *UK, 1981*. **3** in planespotting, a telescope *UK, 2003*. ► **up the pole 1** pregnant *IRELAND, 1922*. **2** in a bad way; at a disadvantage *AUSTRALIA, 1906*. **3** insane *UK, 1896*

pole *verb* **1** from a male perspective, to have sex *UK, 1984*. **2** to steal something *NEW ZEALAND, 1964*. ► **pole on** to impose on someone; to not do one's fair share of work *AUSTRALIA, 1906*

poleaxe *verb* to shock someone into helplessness; to stupify someone. From the antique weapon that combines an axe and a hammer *UK, 2003*

poleaxed *adjective* drunk. From the sense 'to render helpless; to stupify' *UK, 2002*

pole buddy *noun* in electric line work, a transformer gin *US, 1980*

polecat *noun* 1 a police car. From the animal's black and white fur *US, 1976*. 2 in the television and film industries, a lamp support *US, 1990*

poleclimbers *noun* heavy work boots with steel-reinforced toes and arches *US, 1995*

poledad *noun* an annoying, new-to-the-sport skateboarder *US, 1964*

pole dance *noun* a sexual dance performed with a vertical pole as a main prop *US, 2000*

pole day *noun* in motor racing, the first day of qualifying heats when the pole position is decided *US, 1973*

pole hog *noun* in Canadian military aviation, a pilot who tries to keep his hand on the control column *CANADA, 1995*

pole in the hole *nickname* the Spire monument in O'Connell Street, Dublin *IRELAND, 2003*

pole jockey *noun* a telephone or power lineman *US, 1960*

pole orchard *noun* the half-acre of utility poles at the Fort Gordon, Georgia Signal Corps School where linemen are given climbing instruction *US, 1968*

poles *noun* trousers. Vietnam war slang *US, 1991*

pole work *noun* utilisation of a pole by a dancer in a sex club *US, 2001*

poley; poly *noun* a hornless cow or bull *AUSTRALIA, 1843*

poley *adjective* 1 of a beast, hornless. From British dialect *poly, polly, poll,* variant of *polled* (de-horned) *AUSTRALIA, 1843*. 2 of a container, missing a handle *AUSTRALIA, 1901*

polgarize *verb* during the Vietnam war, to give unrealistic and optimistic reports of the US progress in the war. Named after Thomas Polgar, CIA station chief in Saigon in the early 1970s *US, 1990*

po-lice *noun* the police. By stressing the first syllable, the conventional term becomes unconventional *US, 1970*

police discount *noun* a great, if not complete, reduction in the price of goods or services provided to police in their area of duty *US, 1975*

policeman *noun* in horse racing, a horse entered in a claiming race solely for the purpose of permitting the owner to claim another horse in the race *US, 1951*

policeman lesion *noun* in an x-ray, a lesion that is unmissable. Medical wit; the lesion must be so obvious that a policeman would spot it *UK, 2002*

policeman's helmet *noun* the glans of the erect penis. From a similarity in shape to the traditional headwear of the British constable *UK, 1961*

police pimp *noun* an informer to the police *AUSTRALIA, 1956*

police psychology *noun* brute physical force *US, 1973*

policy *noun* an illegal lottery. Better known as the NUMBERS racket *US, 1843*

policy banker *noun* the operator of an illegal numbers racket or lottery *US, 1975*

polio weed *noun* extremely potent marijuana. Marijuana so strong as to reduce the user to a 'polio-like' condition *US, 1982*

polis *noun* the police; a police officer. Mainly Scottish and Irish use *UK, 1878*

poli sci *noun* political science. College shorthand *US, 1971*

polish *noun* oral sex performed on a man *NEW ZEALAND, 1998*

polish *verb* ▶ **polish the mug** to wash your face *US, 1962*

polish and gloss; polish *verb* (of a male) to masturbate. Rhyming slang for TOSS *UK, 1992*

polisher *noun* an alcoholic who drinks metal polish *UK, 1966*

Polish jew *noun* a firecracker *US, 1991*

Polish martini *noun* a shot of whisky and a glass of beer *US, 1982*

Polish matched luggage *noun* two shopping bags from Goldblatt's, a low-end Chicago department store chain *US, 1982*

polish off *verb* to defeat someone; to finish or get rid of something; to eat something without leaving anything (especially with gusto) *UK, 1873*

Polish smoking jacket *noun* a sleeveless tee-shirt or undershirt vest *US, 2002*

Polish victory lap *noun* circling a track in the opposite direction to which a race has been run in celebration of victory. A calculated creation in 1988 of driver Alan Kulwicki, who died in an aeroplane crash in 1993 *US, 1990*

political holy water *noun* alcohol *CANADA, 1999*

politician *noun* in prison, a trusted prisoner given responsibilities and liberties exceeding those of normal prisoners *US, 1946*

politico; politicko *noun* a politican either ambitious or unscrupulous, or both. From the Italian or Spanish *UK, 1893*

pollakaun *noun* a hoard of money; savings *IRELAND, 2000*

Pollard's cellar *noun* a notional representation of homelessness *BARBADOS, 1965*

pollatic *adjective* drunk *UK, 2002*

pollie *noun* a politician *AUSTRALIA, 1967*

pollutant *noun* amphetamine; MDMA, the recreational drug best known as ecstasy. It makes you POLLUTED (intoxicated) *UK, 2003*

polluted *adjective* 1 drunk *US, 1976*. 2 warped, perverse *US, 1988*

polly *noun* a politician *US, 1974*

Polly Flinder *noun* 1 a window. Rhyming slang, noted as a 'shiner's (window cleaner's) term' *UK, 1961*. 2 a cinder, especially when used to describe over-cooked food. Rhyming slang, formed from the nursery rhyme character Polly Flinders *UK, 1992*

polly parrot *noun* a carrot. Rhyming slang *UK, 1992*

polo *noun* a mixture of heroin and a motion-sickness drug. From the middle syllables in 'sco*polo*mine' *UK, 2002*

polo mint *noun* 1 without money. Rhyming slang for SKINT, based on the famous 'mint with the hole' *UK, 2002*. 2 a girlfriend; a young woman. Rhyming slang for BINT. Also based on the branded mint sweet *UK, 2003*. 3 a traffic roundabout. Citizens' band radio slang, from the similarity of shape with Polo™ branded peppermints *UK, 1981*

polone; pollone; polony; polonee; *noun* a woman; a girl; an effeminate man. Polari. Also variants with an 'a' to include 'palone', 'paloney' and 'palogne' *UK, 1934*

Polski *noun* a Polish immigrant or Polish-American *US, 1997*

polvo *noun* 1 phencyclidine, the recreational drug known as PCP or angel dust *US, 2001*. 2 powdered drugs; heroin; cocaine. Directly from Spanish *polvo* (powder): POWDER (heroin). Also variant 'polvito' *UK, 1980*

polvo blanco *noun* cocaine. From Spanish for 'white powder' *UK, 1998*

poly *noun* 1 a person who loves and has sex with multiple partners. An abbreviation of 'polyamorous' *US, 2000*. 2 a polytechnic *UK, 2002*. 3 marijuana of a supposedly Polynesian origin *UK, 1997*. 4 a surfboard manufactured with *poly*urethane *US, 1963* ▷see: POLEY

polyster queen *noun* a girl or woman with no fashion sense *US, 1985*

Pom; pom *noun* an English person, or more loosely, a person from Britain. Shortening of POMMY *AUSTRALIA, 1912*

Pom; pom *adjective* English, or more loosely, British *AUSTRALIA, 1960*

Pomland *nickname* England *AUSTRALIA, 1984*

Pommified *adjective* having taken on an English character *AUSTRALIA, 1936*

Pommy; Pommie *noun* an English person, or more loosely, a person from Britain. Originally used of English immigrants to Australia, it is a shortening of the now obsolete 'Pomegranate', rhyming slang for 'immigrant'. The rhyming slang term and the shortened variants 'Pom' and 'Pommy' all appear in the lexical record at the same time. The occasional spelling 'pommygrant' shows the rhyming pronunciation. Although this word carries a definite negative connotation, it also can be used as a term of affectionate abuse (see POMMY BASTARD and WHINGEING POM). The suggestion that Pommy is actually a respelling of P. O.M.E., standing for the reputed term Prisoner Of Mother England, or P. O.H.M.I.E, standing for Prisoner Of Her Majesty In Exile, and other variations on this theme, are implausible on phonetic grounds and are in themselves anachronistic as acronyms were not a common feature of English in the early part of C20 *AUSTRALIA, 1912*

Pommy; Pommie *adjective* English, or more loosely, British *AUSTRALIA, 1915*

Pommy bastard *noun* an English person (stereotypically viewed as noisome to the Australian) *AUSTRALIA, 1951*

pommy cock *noun* an uncircumcised penis *AUSTRALIA, 1985*

Pommyland *nickname* England or the British Isles *AUSTRALIA, 1915*

po-mo; postie *noun* a postmodernist philosopher *UK, 2003*

pomosexual *noun* a person who will not be defined by his or her sexuality. A contrived play on 'post-modern' and 'homosexual'. 'Pomosexuality' is first recorded in 1995 *US, 1997*

pom-pom *noun* sex. Used by US soldiers in Japan and the Phillipines *US, 1947*

ponce *noun* **1** a pimp *UK, 1872*. **2** a despised or unpleasant person *UK, 1953*. **3** an effeminate male *AUSTRALIA, 1971*

ponce *verb* **1** to obtain something by poncing, usually money *UK, 1938*. **2** to live on the earnings of another's prostitution; to act as a pimp (a prostitute's manager) *UK, 1932*. **3** to scrounge; to sponge. A general sense of acquiring something for nothing extended from the previous sense *UK, 1915*. ▶ **go out poncing** (of the police) to search for pimps *UK, 1996*. ▶ **ponce off; ponce on** to live on the earnings of another's prostitution, but not taking any active part in the trade *UK, 1936*

ponce about; ponce around *verb* **1** to behave in an exaggeratedly camp manner *AUSTRALIA, 1978*. **2** to act the fool; to show off *UK, 1996*

ponce up *verb* to dress up smartly; to decorate something. Originally military *UK, 1965*

poncey *adjective* **1** affectedly stylish *UK, 1964*. **2** blatantly, affectedly homosexual *NEW ZEALAND, 1984*

Poncho *nickname* a Pontiac car *US, 1965*

poncified *adjective* affectedly stylish; effeminate. From PONCE *UK, 2001*

pond *noun* ▶ **the pond** a sea, especially the Atlantic Ocean. An ironic understatement of the distance between the UK and the US, shortened from earlier 'great pond' which it replaces *UK, 1780*

pond life *noun* an unintelligent person or people *UK, 1998*

pond scum *noun* a person with no redeeming features *US, 1997*

pone *noun* in a card game, the player immediately to the right of the dealer *UK, 1901*

pong *noun* an unpleasant smell *AUSTRALIA, 1919*

pong *verb* **1** to stink *UK, 1927*. **2** in the theatre, to substitute lines when the correct lines are forgotten *UK, 1952*

ponga *noun* the vagina *BAHAMAS, 1982*

Pongo; Percy Pongo; Perce *noun* a member of the British Army. The Royal Navy perpetuate the wicked myth that this derives from PONG (a smell) suggesting that soldiers smell and sailors don't. 'Percy' appears to be merely alliterative *UK, 1987*

Pongo Pete *nickname* General Sir Peter de la Billiere (b.1934), commander of British armoured forces during the Gulf war *UK, 1991*

pongy *adjective* smelly *UK, 1936*

ponies *noun* **1** horse races held for ponies *AUSTRALIA, 1950*. **2** horsepower *US, 1993*. ▶ **push ponies** to work as a pimp *US, 1987*. ▶ **the ponies** horse racing *UK, 1961*

Ponsford odds *noun* in horse racing, odds of 100–1 or greater. An allusion to Bill Ponsford, a high scoring cricket legend *AUSTRALIA, 1989*

pont *verb* in the harsh climate of Antarctica, to pose for a photograph, especially in an uncomfortable position. Eponym from Herbert George *Ponting*, photographer on Scott's 1910–13 expedition *ANTARCTICA, 1911*

PONTI; ponti *noun* in military terms, a person of no tactical importance. An acronym *UK, 2002*

pontoon *noun* a period of twenty-one months' imprisonment; also twenty-one years in prison or in military service. From the card game 'pontoon' in which the winning hand scores twenty-one *UK, 1950*

Ponty *nickname* Pontypridd, Pontypool, Pontefract in West Yorkshire, or any town so constructed. From Welsh *pont y* (bridge of) *UK: WALES, 1937*

pony *noun* **1** twenty-five pounds *UK, 1797*. **2** in betting, odds of 25–1. Adapted from the previous sense *UK, 1991*. **3** a racehorse. Used especially in the phrase 'play the ponies' *US, 1907*. **4** a chorus girl or dancer, especially a small one *UK, 1908*. **5** a female who moves quickly from sexual relationship to sexual relationship, manipulating and using her partners *US, 1999*. **6** crack cocaine *US, 1994*. **7** a Pontiac car *US, 1967*. **8** in Western Australia, a small glass of beer. Now generally 5 fluid ounces, though formerly 4 , or even 2 fluid ounces. Obsolescent *AUSTRALIA, 1895*. **9** dried nose mucus *BAHAMAS, 1982*. **10** a literal, line-by-line translation of a work in a foreign (usually classical) language *US, 1827*

pony *verb* in horse racing, to send a stable pony out with a racehorse to limber up *US, 1947*

pony and trap; pony *noun* an act of defecation; hence excreta; rubbish, nonsense. Rhyming slang for CRAP (excrement); it can substitute for any sense of 'crap' *UK, 1960*

pony and trap; pony *verb* to defecate. Rhyming slang for CRAP, usually reduced to 'pony' *UK, 1984*

pony and trap; pony *adjective* rubbishy, trashy, valueless. Rhyming slang for CRAP *UK, 1979*

pony pecker *noun* sausage; unidentified pressed meat *US, 1968*

ponyplay *noun* an animal transformation sexual fetish, in which the dominants train, ride and groom people who dress and act like ponies *US, 2000*

pony up *verb* to contribute your share of a bet or collection *US, 1979*

poo *noun* **1** faeces, excrement; the act of defecation. Childish or jocular. Many variant forms, including 'pooh', 'poo poo' and 'pooh pooh' *UK, 1960*. **2** the buttocks; the anus *BAHAMAS, 1982*. ▶ **in the poo** in trouble. Euphemistic for IN THE SHIT *AUSTRALIA, 1961*

poo; pooh *verb* to defecate *UK, 1963*

-poo; -poos *suffix* used for creating an informal elaboration of a person's name *UK, 2000*

poo and spew syndrome *noun* amoebic dysentery or similar complaint *AUSTRALIA, 1988*

poo butt *noun* a coward. Black street gang terminology *US, 1995*

pooch *noun* **1** a dog. Also used as a term of address for an unknown dog *US, 1924*. **2** the buttocks *BARBADOS, 1965*

Pooch *noun* a Porsche car *US, 1965*

poochi *noun* the vagina. Sounds more like a dog – (a POOCH) – than the traditional PUSSY (the vagina); probably a play on Poochi™, an electronic toy dog promoted with such phrases as: 'The more you play with me the happier I will be!' and 'Feed me my special dog bone whenever I get hungry' *US, 1998*

pooch out *verb* to purse your lips *US, 1989*

poodle; pootle *verb* to travel or move forward without urgency *UK, 1999*

poof *adjective* of a male homosexual *AUSTRALIA, 1992*

poof; pouf; pouff *noun* a male homosexual. In origin probably connected with French slang *poufiasser*, which Barrère (*Argot and Slang* ,1889) defines as a person 'of either sex whose fondness for the opposite sex leads them into a life of questionable description', that is, presumably, a life of prostitution including homosexual prostitution, and *pouffiace* or *pouffiasse* 'a low prostitute' *AUSTRALIA, 1833*

poof-juice *noun* after-shave lotion, eau-de-cologne for men *UK, 1997*

poofster *noun* a homosexual man; an effeminate man. Variation of POOFTER *US, 1995*

poofteenth *noun* a very small amount; an umpteenth AUSTRALIA, *1996*

poofter *noun* **1** a homosexual male. Variants include 'pooftah' and 'poofdah' AUSTRALIA, *1903*. **2** an effeminate looking man, not necessarily homosexual. Also variant 'poofta' AUSTRALIA, *1903*. **3** a contemptible person. Used as a general term of abuse AUSTRALIA, *1986*. **4** a braggart NEW ZEALAND, *1990*

poofter *adjective* **1** (of a male) homosexual AUSTRALIA, *1964*. **2** befitting or suitable for an effeminate homosexual man AUSTRALIA, *1984*

poofter bash *verb* to beat up a male homosexual AUSTRALIA, *1983*

poofter basher *noun* a man, usually as part of a group, who beats up homosexual men AUSTRALIA, *1974*

poofter bashing; poofter-bashing *noun* the practice of physically assaulting male homosexuals AUSTRALIA, *1978*

poofterism *noun* male homosexuality AUSTRALIA, *1971*

poofter rorter *noun* **1** in a men's prison, a prisoner who induces another inmate into homosexual relations AUSTRALIA, *1945*. **2** a person who entices a male homosexual, especially a prostitute, to a secluded place and then robs them AUSTRALIA, *1938*

poofy *adjective* overtly homosexual. Also variant 'poufy' AUSTRALIA, *1962*

pooh *noun* an act of defecation. Children's vocabulary NEW ZEALAND, *1984*

pooh bah *noun* an important person. The name of a character in the Gilbert and Sullivan light opera *The Mikado* UK, *1888*

pooh-bum *noun* a female fan of a rock band who is willing to have sex with band members UK, *1985*

pooh-butt *noun* a despicable person US, *1994*

pooh-pooh *verb* to belittle someone or something; to dismiss someone or something as inconsequential UK, *1827*

poo-jabber *noun* **1** a male homosexual AUSTRALIA, *1994*. **2** a contemptible person. Used as a mild insult, especially amongst children AUSTRALIA, *1996*

pooker *noun* a signpost. English gypsy use from Romany *pûkinger* (to tell) UK, *2000*

pookey; pookie *noun* used as a term of contempt IRELAND, *1989*

pooki *noun* the vagina US, *1998*

pooky *noun* marijuana US, *2001*

pool *noun* in horse racing, the total amount bet in the win, place and show bets for a race US, *1947*

Pool *noun* ▶ **the Pool** Liverpool UK, *1962*

pooley *noun* urine IRELAND, *1995*

poolhall cowboy *noun* a pool player who has perfected a reckless manner US, *1976*

pool harpy *noun* a pool player who plays for money, relying on a combination of skill and deceptive behaviour US, *1966*

pool shark *noun* an expert pool player who makes a living by feigning a lack of expertise and convincing strangers to play against him US, *1908*

poom *verb* to fart TRINIDAD AND TOBAGO, *1992*

pooma *noun* a delapidated car BARBADOS, *1965*

poom bag *noun* large buttocks TRINIDAD AND TOBAGO, *1987*

poomp *noun* to fart BAHAMAS, *1982*

poon *noun* **1** the vagina; a woman; a woman as a sex object; sex with a woman. A shortened form of POONTANG US, *1957*. **2** a fool; a contemptible person. Used as a mild insult AUSTRALIA, *1940*

poonce *noun* an effeminate male AUSTRALIA, *1941*

pooner a male with sexual experience and apparent expertise US, *1968*

poon light *noun* in the pornography industry, a light used to illuminate the genitals of the performers US, *1995*

poontang *noun* the vagina; sex; a woman regarded as a sexual object. Suggestions that the term comes from an American Indian language, Chinese, Bantu, Peruvian or a Filipinio dialect notwithstanding, it almost certainly comes from the French *putain* (prostitute) US, *1929*

poon up *verb* to dress in a flashy manner in order to impress AUSTRALIA, *1972*

poony *noun* the vagina; women as sex objects. A variation of PUNANI UK, *1994*

poop *noun* **1** information, news. Probably from the sense as 'nonsense' (SHIT) US, *1942*. **2** the buttocks BAHAMAS, *1982*. **3** faeces; an act of defecation. Children's toilet vocabulary US, *1948*. **4** rubbish, nonsense UK, *2003*. **5** a pledge to a college fraternity US, *1955*. ▶ **in the poop** in trouble AUSTRALIA, *1971*

poop *verb* **1** to defecate UK, *1927*. **2** in poker, to raise a bet US, *1951*

poopadoop *noun* the rectum US, *1977*

poop-butt *noun* a lazy person US, *1972*

poop chute; poop shute; poop shooter *noun* the rectum and anus US, *1970*

pooped *adjective* exhausted US, *1932*

poopelu *noun* the vagina US, *1998*

pooper *noun* the rectum and anus. From POOP (excrement) US, *1997*

pooper-scooper *noun* an implement for gathering canine excrement, designed to meet the social responsibilities or legal requirements placed upon dog owners. Combines POOP (faeces) with a conventional tool. Also shortened forms 'pooper-scoop' and 'poop-scoop' US, *1972*

poop file *noun* a collection of (school, college, university) examinations given in the past US, *1976*

poophead *noun* a boring, conventional person US, *1955*

poopi *noun* the vagina US, *1998*

poo-poo head *noun* an objectionable person. A variation of SHITHEAD, perhaps more insulting by the use of childish, 'poo-poo', (excrement) US, *1995*

poop-poop *noun* a slow motorboat BAHAMAS, *1982*

poop pusher *noun* a male homosexual UK, *1983*

poops *verb* to fart TRINIDAD AND TOBAGO, *1987*

poop sheet *noun* a bulletin or other document containing news and information US, *1964*

poopy *adjective* **1** filthy with excrement. From POOP (faeces) US, *2003*. **2** bad, awful; of poor quality. A euphemistic synonym for SHITTY US, *2002*. **3** in a bad mood. A euphemistic form of SHITTY US, *1990*. **4** afraid SOUTH AFRICA, *1963*

poopy suit *noun* in the Canadian military, any bulky official garment CANADA, *1995*

poor *adjective* cruel, heartless; lacking good taste US, *2003*

poor-ass *adjective* wretched, unimportant US, *1998*

poorboy *noun* a small bottle of alcohol US, *1952*

poor-donkey *noun* a sandal of plaited rope or one cut from a piece of tyre or wood BARBADOS, *1996*

poor-great *adjective* foolishly pompous GUYANA, *1996*

poor-man blanket *noun* the sun BAHAMAS, *1982*

poor man's *adjective* describes the lesser status or inferior quality of someone by comparison and reference to the greater name with which it is combined. Only colloquial when applied to people UK, *1984*

poor man's roulette *noun* the game of craps US, *1953*

poor man's velvet *noun* a drink of mixed stout and cider. An economic variation of BLACK VELVET (stout and champagne); remembered from the 1970s, notwithstanding the drink's amnesiac effects UK, *2001*

poor man's weather glass *noun* seaweed, especially kelp CANADA, *1974*

poor pearl *noun* an unpopular girl US, *1960*

poor-rakey *noun* thin, gaunt BARBADOS, *1965*

poot *noun* **1** faeces. Children's vocabulary; a variation of poop US, *1981*. **2** anything which is considered to be contemptible US, *1989*. **3** a very small thing; anything at all. Usually heard in the negative, as 'that ain't poot' US, *1978*

poot *verb* **1** to defecate *US, 1945*. **2** to fart *US, 1972*. **3** (used of a hospital patient) to become suddenly more ill, especially without hope of reversing the course *US, 1989*

poot-butt *noun* a lazy fool *US, 1972*

pootenanny; pooties *noun* the female buttocks. Probably derived from Jamaican PUNANI (the vagina) *US, 1997*

pootie *noun* the vagina *US, 1999*

pootle *verb* ▷*see:* POODLE

poov; poove *noun* food, especially grass for grazing. Circus and English gypsy use *UK, 1933*

poov; poove *verb* ▶ **poov the gry; poov the grey** to graze a horse, especially without permission from the land's owner. English gypsy use; a combination of POOV (grass) – thus 'pooving' (grazing) – and GRY (a horse) *UK, 1968*

poove; pouve *noun* a homosexual. Variations of POOF *UK, 1967*

pooze *noun* the vagina *US, 1975*

poozle *noun* a scavenged object *NEW ZEALAND, 1971*

poozle *verb* to strip fixtures from buildings scheduled for demolition *NEW ZEALAND, 1984*

pop *noun* **1** an instance or occurrence *US, 1868*. **2** an attempt, a try *UK, 1929*. **3** an arrest *US, 1972*. **4** an attack. Combination and variation of the senses 'attempt' and 'go' *UK, 2001*. **5** an ejaculation *US, 1986*. **6** one event of sexual intercourse *US, 1982*. **7** in prison, an escape attempt *UK, 1996*. **8** a father, especially as a term of address *US, 1838*. **9** the 'masculine' or 'active' member of a lesbian relationship *US, 1957*. **10** a musical genre, characterised as trivial and without serious artistic intent. Originally widely used to cover the opposite of 'classical music', now denotes just a particular type of popular music: carefully crafted, packaged or manufactured for mass-market appeal *US, 1935*. **11** any non-alcoholic sparkling drink. From the sound of a bottle being opened *UK, 1812*. **12** champagne *UK, 2000*. **13** a drink, usually at a bar *US, 1977*. **14** cough syrup containing codeine *US, 1970*. **15** an injection of a drug *US, 1952*. **16** a strong crowd reaction. Professional wrestling usage *US, 2000* ▷*see:* POP GOES THE WEASEL. ▶ **go off pop** to lose your temper *NEW ZEALAND, 1946*. ▶ **have a pop at** to attack verbally *UK, 1999*. ▶ **on the pop** drinking alcohol *UK, 2000*

pop *nickname* used as a nickname for any male stagedoor manager *US, 1952*

pop *verb* **1** to ejaculate; to experience orgasm *US, 1961*. **2** to have sex with someone *US, 1965*. **3** (used of a male) to have sex with a virgin *BAHAMAS, 1982*. **4** to give birth *US, 1990*. **5** to fart. Childish; used in the US, UK and Australia. Also phrased as 'pop off' and 'pop a whiff' *UK, 1998*. **6** to administer medication *UK, 1991*. **7** to inject a drug *US, 1952*. **8** to take a pill *US, 1968*. **9** when using amyl nitrate, to break the glass ampoules containing the gas *US, 1995*. **10** to inhale a powdered drug *UK, 1998*. **11** to steal something. Originally in black use *US, 1994*. **12** to obtain confidential or classified information about someone as part of an investigation *US, 1997*. **13** to arrest someone *US, 1975*. **14** to fire a gun *UK, 1725*. **15** to hit someone *US, 1980*. **16** to kill someone *US, 1952*. **17** to pay for something *US, 1958*. **18** to praise or promote someone or something *US, 1984*. **19** to applaud and cheer enthusiastically. Professional wrestling usage *US, 2000*. **20** to send an e-mail to someone *US, 2004*. **21** to go to or from somewhere, especially swiftly or suddenly. Usually used with 'up', 'down', 'in', 'out', 'over', 'about', 'off', 'between', etc *UK, 1530*. **22** in pinball, to win a replay or additional ball, activating the sound effect known as a knocker *US, 1977*. **23** (of a car boot or bonnet) to open remotely *US, 2000*. ▶ **pop a cap** to shoot a gun *US, 1965*. ▶ **pop a top** to open a can of beer. An inevitable reduplication with the advent of aluminium cans with pull-tabs in the early 1970s *US, 1967*. ▶ **pop corn** to engage in a swindle or dishonest scheme *US, 1995*. ▶ **pop junk** to gossip *US, 1990*. ▶ **pop smoke** to detonate a smoke grenade *US, 1982*. ▶ **pop the chute** in sailing, to release the spinnaker *US, 1990*. ▶ **pop ya collar** to respect yourself *UK, 2003*. ▶ **pop your clogs** to die. Literally, 'to put your shoes in the pawnbroker's' (because you have no further use for them) *UK, 2000*. ▶ **pop your nuts** to ejaculate *US, 1970*. ▶ **pop your pumpkin** to lose your temper *US, 1954*. ▶ **pop your rocks** to ejaculate *US, 1977*. ▶ **pop your water** to ejaculate *BAHAMAS, 1971*

pop bumper *noun* in pinball, a bumper that scores and kicks the ball on contact *US, 1977*

popcorn; poppy *noun* an erect penis. Rhyming slang for HORN *UK, 1992*

popcorn pimp *noun* a small-time pimp; a pimp who fails to live up to pimp standards *US, 1972*

pope *noun* ▶ **for the pope** used of work without pay *US, 1963*

Pope *noun* ▶ **The Pope** Frank Sinatra, US singer (1915–98) *US, 1963*

Pope's phone number *noun* VAT 69™ Scotch whisky. Dating from a time when telephone exchanges were given as the first three letters of the area name *UK, 1961*

popeye *noun* a car or truck with only one headlight working *US, 1977*

Popeye the sailor *noun* a tailor. Rhyming slang, formed on the cartoon character *UK, 1992*

pop goes the weasel; pop *noun* diesel. Rhyming slang, formed, possibly with an ironic regard to the high costs of motoring, on the traditional rhyme: 'That's the way the money goes, / Pop goes the weasel' *UK, 1992*

popla *noun* beer *SOUTH AFRICA, 1977*

po-po *noun* the police; a police officer *US, 1995*

pop-off *noun* someone who talks too much *US, 1951*

pop off *verb* **1** to die *UK, 1764*. **2** to brag, to boast; to speak out when discretion would suggest silence *US, 1940*. **3** to kill someone *UK, 1824*. **4** to ejaculate *US, 1969*

pop-out *noun* a mass-produced surfboard with little or no handwork involved in the making *US, 1964*

poppa *noun* in prison, a lesbian *US, 1953*

poppa-lopper *noun* used as a euphemism for 'motherfucker' *US, 1977*

pop party *noun* a party where drug users inject drugs *US, 1971*

popped out *adjective* drug-intoxicated *US, 1954*

popper *noun* **1** a finger *US, 1947*. **2** a pistol *US, 1976*. **3** a popcorn wagon *US, 1985*. **4** a pneumatic drill. Mining slang *NEW ZEALAND, 1986*. **5** a fart *UK*. Childish, descriptive. Also called 'multipopper', *1998*. **6** a capsule containing vapours of amyl nitrate or (iso)butyl nitrate inhaled as a stimulant. Often used in the plural form *US, 1967*. **7** any drug addict. A very loosely defined, or understood, usage *UK, 1967*

poppet *noun* **1** used as an endearment. A 'puppet', hence a 'doll' *UK, 1729*. **2** the object of ridicule *BARBADOS, 1965*

popplin *noun* kindling wood, used to start a fire *CANADA, 1984*

poppy *noun* **1** opium. Earlier pharmaceutical usage into slang *UK, 1935*. **2** heroin *UK, 1998*. **3** money *UK, 1977* ▷*see:* POPCORN

poppy *verb* to pay *UK, 1979*

poppycock *noun* nonsense *US, 1857*

poppy love *noun* an older Jewish man *US, 1987*

poppy pad *noun* a room or apartment where heroin users congregate *US, 1959*

pops *noun* **1** used as a term of address for a man, especially an older man *US, 1844*. **2** father *US, 1989*

pop shop *noun* a place where criminals sell stolen goods *US, 1949*

pop shot *noun* a scene in a pornographic film or photograph depicting a man ejaculating *US, 1991*

popsicle *noun* used as a term of abuse *US, 1984*

popsie *noun* an ampoule of amyl nitrite *US, 1971*

popskull *noun* strong, homemade whisky *US, 1999*

popsy; popsie *noun* a young woman who is the object of a romantic or sexual attraction *UK, 1862*

poptastic *adjective* fantastic. Created for the BBC television programme *Harry Enfield's Television Programme*, 1990, written by Harry Enfield and Paul Whitehouse for the comedy characters Smashie and Nicey *UK, 2003*

pop top *noun* a truck carrying bottled soft drinks. Citizens' band radio slang, elaborated on POP (a carbonated drink) *UK, 1981*

population *noun* the general population in a prison *US, 1975*

pop-up *noun* **1** an electronic advertisement delivered to a computer via the Internet that is superimposed over the original browser window *US, 1996*. **2** any mushroom with an hallucinogenic effect *UK, 2000*

pop-up hell *noun* an unfriendly web-surfing environment characterised by multiple console advertisements in pop-up windows. A term used frequently on the web but not in conventional print sources *US, 2004*

porcelain god *noun* a toilet *US, 1986*

porcelain king; porcelain queen *noun* someone who habitually drinks alcohol to the point of vomiting *US, 1993*

porch climber *noun* homemade alcohol or cheap British Columbia wines *CANADA, 1989*

porch monkey *noun* a black person. Offensive, slurring the stereotype of laziness (porch) and the African jungle (monkey) *US, 1981*

porcupine head *noun* in hot rodding and motor racing, the cylinder head on the big-block engines manufactured by Chevrolet. John Edwards, *Auto Dictionary*, 1993, gives a neat etymology: 'When the valve covers are removed, the valve stems appear to stick out at odd angles, like the needles on a porcupine' *US, 1993*

Po' Rican *noun* Puerto Rican *US, 1975*

pork *noun* **1** flesh, especially in a sexual context *UK, 1996*. **2** the genitals, male or female *BAHAMAS, 1982*

pork *verb* to have sex with someone *US, 1968*

pork and bean *noun* a male homosexual. Rhyming slang for QUEEN *AUSTRALIA, 1944*

pork chop *noun* in electric line work, a wire grip used for holding a conductor under tension *US, 1980*

Pork Chop Hill *noun* a hill which was the site of extensive fighting in the final months of the Korean war, from 16th April to 18th April and again from 6th July to 10th July, 1953 *US, 1964*

pork chop in a synagogue used as a simile for anything that is badly, especially embarrassingly, out of place or unwelcome *UK, 1984*

pork-dodger *noun* a Jewish person. From the dietary restrictions of observant Jews *US, 1997*

porker *noun* **1** a fat person *US, 1959*. **2** a police officer. An extension of PIG *US, 1998*

pork-man *noun* a white man *UK, 2000*

pork patrol *noun* a police car *US, 1993*

pork pie *noun* **1** a lie. Rhyming slang. Now stands alone in the reduced form PORKY *UK, 1984*. **2** a serious bruise *NEW ZEALAND, 1998*

pork pies; porkie pies; porkies *noun* the eyes. Rhyming slang *UK, 1999*

pork scratch *noun* a match. Rhyming slang, contrived from the savoury snack pork scratchings *UK, 1996*

pork sword *noun* the penis *US, 1966*

porky *noun* **1** a lie. Abbreviated from rhyming slang PORK PIE *UK, 1992*. **2** the vagina *BAHAMAS, 1982*. **3** a police officer *US, 1973*

porky *adjective* obese *UK, 1852*

Porky Pig *adjective* big; generous. Rhyming slang, from the name of a Warner Bros' cartoon character. The sense of 'big' is often heavily ironic *UK, 1992*

porn; porno *noun* pornography *UK, 1962*

porn and prawn *adjective* of a party, arranged for the purpose of showing pornographic films and catered for with epicurean food including prawns *AUSTRALIA, 1996*

pornbroker *noun* a seller of pornographic literature. A pun on 'pawnbroker' *UK, 1967*

pornflakes *noun* crusty, dried semen. A pun on the branded name of a popular breakfast cereal, Corn Flakes™ *AUSTRALIA, 2003*

porn flick *noun* a pornographic film *UK, 1970*

porn mag; porno mag *noun* a pornographic magazine *UK, 1972*

porno *noun* a pornographic film or video *UK, 1997*

porno *adjective* pornographic *US, 1952*

pornographically *adverb* used in a sexual context for more than averagely *UK, 2002*

pornshop *noun* a shop where pornography is sold. A pun on 'pawnshop' *UK, 1984*

porn weed; horny weed *noun* marijuana with, allegedly, aphrodisiac properties. Combines WEED (marijuana) with sexual possibilities, HORNY (sexually stimulating), PORN (pornography) and 'love' *UK, 1999*

porny *adjective* pornographic *US, 1969*

porpoise *noun* a landing by an aeroplane in which the plane bounces from the main gear to the nose gear *US, 1963*

porpoise *verb* in mountain biking, to ride responding to, instead of controlling, the bike *US, 1992*

Porra; porra *noun* a person of Portuguese descent *SOUTH AFRICA, 1975*

porridge *noun* **1** a sentence of imprisonment; the time served in prison. Possibly puns on STIR (prison) and the staple prison diet of porridge. The term settled in the wider public conciousness during the 1970s with BBC television prison situation comedy *Porridge UK, 1955*. **2** the brain. A visual link between varying consistencies of grey matter *UK, 1997*. **3** sludge removed from drains *UK, 1970*

porridge gun *noun* the penis *UK, 2003*

porridge pot *noun* in motor racing, a crash helmet that covers only the top of the head *US, 1965*

porridge wog *noun* a Scot. Combines WOG (a foreigner) with a stereotypical Scottish dish *UK, 2002*

port *noun* **1** in New South Wales and Queensland, a suitcase or schoolbag. From 'portmanteau' *AUSTRALIA, 1898*. **2** a railway porter *US, 1977*

portable *noun* a foot-patrol police officer *US, 1987*

Portagee *noun* a person from Portugal, or of Portuguese heritage *US, 1978*. ▶ **go Portagee on me** to back out of an agreement. Portuguese immigrants, mostly fishermen, fishbuyers and sailors, settled near where this phrase is current *CANADA, 1999*

Portagee beer *noun* any beer in a quart bottle *BERMUDA, 1985*

Portagee chrome *noun* aluminium paint *US, 1961*

Portagee lawnmower *noun* a goat *US, 1989*

Portagee lift *noun* in manual labour, said when one worker does not carry his fair share *US, 1960*

Portagee overdrive *noun* to coast down a hill while driving *US, 1961*

port and brandy *adjective* sexually aroused; feeling lecherous. Rhyming slang for RANDY *UK, 1992*

portapotty *noun* a portable toilet, transported to construction sites, campgrounds, outdoor concerts, etc. *US, 1993*

porthole duff *noun* homosexual anal sex. A naval use – another dish on the NAVY CAKE menu; the 'porthole' may refer to the anus or, in specialised use, mean that the passive partner has his 'head out of a porthole' *UK, 1961*

portion *noun* an act of sexual intercourse as something given to a woman *UK, 2000*

portnoy *noun* a male masturbator. A reference to *Portnoy's Complaint*, a novel by Philip Roth, 1969 *UK, 1970*

Port of Spaniard *noun* a resident of Port of Spain, Trinidad *TRINIDAD AND TOBAGO, 1990*

portrait painter *noun* speed radar; a police officer operating a speed camera *US, 1976*

port-sider *noun* a left-handed person *US, 1971*

Portuguese parliament *noun* a meeting where everybody talks and nobody listens *US, 1951*

Portuguese shop *noun* a small grocery shop attached to a rum shop, whether or not it is owned by Portuguese people *TRINIDAD AND TOBAGO, 1989*

Portuguese straight *noun* in poker, a straight formed with different suits, thus without value. Hawaiian youth usage *US, 1982*

porty *noun* a portable telephone *US, 1996*

pos *noun* position *US, 1986* ▷ *see:* POSS

POS *noun* a patient regarded by hospital personnel as a *piece of shit US, 1978*

pose *verb* to pretend a station in life that has yet to be achieved *US, 1946*

poser *noun* a person who imitates that which he is not *US, 1990*

posh *adjective* **1** being stylish, smart; of the best class; elegant and sophisticated. In popular folk etymology, reinforced by the song 'Posh' in the 1968 film *Chitty Chitty Bang Bang*, 'posh' is an acronym of *port out starboard home*, supposedly the location of the 'best' cabins on an England to India P&O line cruise; unfortunately P&O has no record of such a phrase ever being used. Other suggested derivations: a contraction of 'polished', an earlier sense as 'money', and a corruption of Scottish *tosh* (smart). However, this is slang and 'port out starboard home' is the more entertaining etymolology and therefore likely to continue as the popular favourite *UK, 1918*. **2** being in possession of drugs *UK, 2002*

Posh and Becks; Posh 'n' Becks *noun* sex *UK, 2003*

Posh and Becks; Posh 'n' Becks *nickname* singer Victoria Beckham and her husband, footballer David Beckham, considered as a single celebrity icon *UK, 2000*

poshie *noun* a posh person *IRELAND, 1997*

posho *noun* a member of the middle- or upper-classes *UK, 2001*

posh totty *noun* a sexually attractive upper-class woman *UK, 2001*

posh wank *noun* **1** an act of male masturbation while the penis is sheathed in a condom. Combines POSH (upper-class) with WANK (to masturbate) *UK, 1999*. **2** used as abuse of a contemptible person, especially one you consider to be of a superior status. A combination of POSH (upper-class) with WANK (an act of masturbation); informed by contemporaneous 'posh wank' (the act of masturbation in a condom) *UK, 1999*

poshy *adjective* elegant and sophisticated. Later variation of POSH *UK, 2000*

poshy-poshy *adjective* extremely elegant and stylish. Reduplication of POSHY for emphasis *UK, 2002*

pository yes, affirmative. Citizens' band radio slang *US, 1976*

poss; pos *adjective* possible *UK, 1886*

poss; pos *noun* a possibility *UK, 1964*

posse *noun* **1** a group of close friends *US, 1985*. **2** a gang *US, 1994*

possible *noun* **1** the vagina. A probably Freudian etymology *US, 1998*. **2** in target shooting, a perfect score *US, 1957*. **3** in poker, any hand that can be completed with the draw of one card. Variant 'possibulletee' *US, 1951*

possie; possy; pozzie; pozzy *noun* a position. Originally in World War 1 a soldier's chosen position from which to snipe, observe, etc *AUSTRALIA, 1915*

possum *noun* darling. A term of affectionate address *AUSTRALIA, 1894*

Possum; Ole Possum *nickname* George Jones, a country singer and songwriter (b.1931) *US, 1995*

possum belly *noun* the tool box located on the underside of a brakevan (caboose). *US, 1946*

post *noun* an autopsy. From the more formal 'post mortem' *US, 1942*. ▶ **left at the post** (of a horse in a race) to lose badly *AUSTRALIA, 1895*

post *verb* to leave someone in the lurch, especially during the commission of a crime *AUSTRALIA, 1975*. ▶ **post a flyer** to use coded language in a conversation to advertise your homosexuality and sexual availability *UK, 1987*. ▶ **post a letter** to go to the toilet *TRINIDAD AND TOBAGO, 2003*

postage stamp *noun* **1** a woman. Citizens' band radio slang, etymology unknown, although licking is almost certainly a component *US, 1976*. **2** a public house bar counter. Rhyming slang for RAMP. Shortened to 'postage' *UK, 1992*. **3** in horse racing, a very small weight allowance in a weight-handicapped event *AUSTRALIA, 1989*

postal *adjective* extremely angry; furious to the point of violence. From a series of highly publicised workplace shootings by frustrated and furious employees of the US Postal Service *US, 1994*

postcode *adjective* used for describing any matter in which domestic, economic or political status may be defined by geographic location; where your postal address affects the provision of medical care, education and publicly funded services, or insurance, or credit rating; especially as 'postcode lottery', 'postcode prescribing' and 'postcode discrimination' *UK, 1999*

poster boy *noun* a very good example of an attitude or condition. Used facetiously *US, 1993*

posteriors *noun* the penis and testicles *BAHAMAS, 1982*

postie *noun* **1** a postman or postwoman *UK, 1887*. **2** The Royal Mail, the Post Office *UK, 2001* ▷ *see:* PO-MO

postman *noun* in horse racing, someone who can be counted on for inside tips on horses and races. A term built on MAIL as 'inside information' *AUSTRALIA, 1989*

postman's knock *noun* **1** a lock. Rhyming slang, ascribed to burglars when used by lockmakers Chubb's in an advertisement *UK, 1962*. **2** a clock. Rhyming slang, sometimes seen in an abbreviated form as 'postman's' *UK, 1992*. **3** in pool, a shot in which the cue ball hits the object ball twice in rapid succession, producing a knock-like sound *US, 1993*

post-mortem *noun* in poker, an analysis of a hand after it has been played *US, 1988*

postop *noun* a transsexual who has undergone all surgery necessary to complete a sex change *US, 1995*

post up *verb* to idle *US, 1998*

pot *noun* **1** marijuana. The most popular slang term for marijuana in the 1950s. No agreement on the etymology, with competing conjectures and little supporting evidence *US, 1938*. **2** heroin *US, 1999*. **3** in Queensland, Victoria and Tasmania, a 10 fluid ounce glass of beer *AUSTRALIA, 1915*. **4** a tooth. Polari; usually in the plural *UK, 1992*. **5** in poker, all of the chips or money bet on a single hand *US, 1947*. **6** the jack in a game of bowls. In Midlands' use. The southern equivalent is 'kitty' *US, 1979*. **7** in electric line work, a transformer. An abbreviation of 'potential transformer' *US, 1980*. **8** a carburettor *US, 1941*. **9** a hospital patient with many trivial complaints *US, 1980*. ▶ **not have a pot to piss in; not have a pot to pee in** to be extremely poor *CANADA, 1961*

pot *verb* **1** to shoot or kill someone *US, 1860*. **2** to put a baby on a potty (a chamber pot) *UK, 1961*. ▶ **pot the white** to have sex. An allusion to billiards *UK, 1955*

-pot *suffix* a person of a type defined or suggested by the word to which it is joined. The best known current forms are FUSSPOT and SEXPOT *UK, 1880*

pot *A noun* a prisoner who has received a minimum of ten years is regarded as a *potential* Category A prisoner *UK, 1996*

potable *noun* drinking water *US, 1968*

pot and pan; old pot and pan; old pot *noun* a man; a husband; a father. Rhyming slang *AUSTRALIA, 1905*

potater juice; potato juice; potata juice *noun* vodka *US, 1976*

potato *noun* **1** marijuana. An elaboration of POT *UK, 1999*. **2** LSD *UK, 1998*. **3** a woman. Short for POTATO PEELER *AUSTRALIA, 1959*

potato digger *noun* an amphibious tracked personnel carrier fitted with a dozer blade used for clearing mines during the Vietnam war *US, 1991*

potatoed *adjective* sluggish; in a non-responsive state (possibly as a result of drug use) *UK, 1999*

potatoes *noun* money. One of life's basics *US, 2001*

potato hook *noun* in electric line work, an insulated line tool formally known as a fixed prong tie stick *US, 1980*

potato-masher *noun* a German fragmentation hand grenade. Korean war usage *US, 1982*

potato patch *noun* a group of neurologically depressed patients *US, 1978*

potato peeler *noun* a woman. Rhyming slang for SHEILA *AUSTRALIA, 1971*

potato soup *noun* vodka *US, 1970*

potato wagon *noun* a police van *US, 1970*

pot belly *noun* in trucking, a trailer with a dropped frame middle used for hauling cattle or hogs *US, 1971*

potch *verb* to spank or smack someone *US, 1969*

potchkeh *verb* to dawdle; to spend time inefficiently. Yiddish from German. Also variants 'potchee' and 'potchky' *US, 1954*

pot head *noun* a user of marijuana *US, 1959*

pot hook *noun* in a deck of playing cards, a nine *US, 1967*

pot hound *noun* a despised, inferior person *TRINIDAD AND TOBAGO, 1956*

pot house *noun* a mad or psychotic person *UK, 2000*

Pot. Kettle. Black. used as Internet shorthand to criticise someone for engaging in precisely the same conduct or reasoning that they are attacking in another *US, 1995*

potless *adjective* without money *UK, 1984*

pot-licker *noun* an older dog *NEW ZEALAND, 1981*

pot likker; pot liquor *noun* 1 tea brewed with marijuana leaves. The intentional spelling error gives a rustic, moonshining feel to the term *US, 1967*. 2 strong, homemade whisky *US, 1972*

pot lot *noun* a used car business specialising in old, inexpensive cars *US, 1975*

pot of glue *noun* 1 a Jew. Rhyming slang. Also shortened form 'potter' *UK, 1992*. 2 a clue. Glasgow rhyming slang. Shortened forms include 'pot' and 'potter' *UK: SCOTLAND, 1988*

pot of honey; honey *noun* money. Rhyming slang *UK, 1961*

pot pig *noun* a marijuana user who takes more than a fair share *UK, 2001*

pots *noun* a large amount of money *UK, 1871*

POTS *noun* plain old telephone service *US, 1997*

pots and dishes *noun* wishes. Rhyming slang *UK, 1979*

pot shot *noun* in poker, an early and aggressive bet designed to drive other players from the field of play. Borrowed from hunting and punning on 'pot' as the collective bets *US, 1951*

potsy *noun* a firefighter's or police officer's badge *US, 1954*

potted *adjective* 1 tipsy, drunk *US, 1924*. 2 in a state of marijuana intoxication *US, 1955*

potten bush *noun* hashish *US, 1977*

pottit heid *adjective* dead. Glasgow rhyming slang, 'deid' in the local accent, formed from local dialect for 'potted meat' *UK: SCOTLAND, 1996*

pottsville *noun* a notional location or state of consciousness imagined by marijuana smokers. Compared to Utopia, Nirvana and Xanadu *US, 2001*

potty *noun* ► **go potty** to use a toilet. Children's toilet vocabulary *US, 1942*

potty *adjective* crazy; silly; eccentric. From 'pot' (a tankard), hence to be inebriated and to have the characteristics of drunken logic *UK, 1920*

potty about in love, infatuated or obsessed (to some degree) with something or someone *UK, 1923*

potty mouth *noun* a person prone to use profanity; profanity *US, 1968*

potty talk *noun* speech that is considered obscenely offensive. From childish 'potty' (a chamber pot or toilet); an almost euphemistic variation of TOILET TALK *US, 2002*

pot-walloper *noun* a person employed to wash dishes *US, 1975*

pot-wrestler *noun* a restaurant cook or dishwasher *US, 1860*

poultice *noun* a large sum of money, especially a large wager *AUSTRALIA, 1904*

pound *noun* 1 a five-dollar note *US, 1935*. 2 a five-year jail sentence *US, 1967*. 3 an 's' unit (five decibels) in measuring the level of a citizens' band radio signal *US, 1976*. 4 an amount of heroin worth

five dollars *US, 1982*. 5 a prison cell used for solitary confinement *AUSTRALIA, 1950*. 6 a jail or prison *US, 1977*. 7 in poker, a heavy bet *US, 1988*. ► **have a pound on yourself** to be conceited; to think very well of yourself. From betting terminology *UK, 1959*

pound *verb* to drink (alcohol) *US, 1995*. ► **pound cotton** to strain the residue of a narcotic from a bit of cotton used to strain the drug for a previous injection *US, 1990*. ► **pound ground** to march *US, 1977*. ► **pound her pee-hole** from the male perspective, to have energetic sex *US, 1994*. ► **pound sand** to engage in futile behaviour. Usually used as a command, where the term takes on a meaning not unlike 'go fuck yourself' *US, 1981*. ► **pound the bishop** (used of a male) to masturbate *US, 1977*. ► **to get pounded** while surfing, to be knocked from your surfboard and thrashed by the wave *US, 1988*

poundage *noun* weight that should be lost *US, 1972*

pound and crown *noun* a lot of money *TRINIDAD AND TOBAGO, 1993*

pounder *noun* 1 a police officer assigned to foot patrol *US, 1945*. 2 a powerful, hard-breaking wave *US, 1964*. 3 a 16-ounce can of beer *US, 1997*

pound note *noun* a coat. Rhyming slang, now fallen into disuse, a victim of the pound coin introduced in 1983 *UK, 1992*

pound of butter *noun* a crazy person; a lunatic; an eccentric. Rhyming slang for NUTTER *UK, 1998*

pound off *verb* (used of a male) to masturbate *US, 1969*

pounds *noun* money *US, 1971*

pounds and pence *noun* sense. Rhyming slang, an updated form of SHILLINGS AND PENCE *UK, 1992*

pound to a penny a certainty, a sure thing. A ludicrously confident wager *UK, 2001*

pour *verb* to move or place a drunk *UK, 1948*. ► **pour on the coal** to throttle up an engine. A borrowing from steam-powered train engines *US, 1956*. ► **pour on the coals** in trucking, to drive fast *US, 1971*. ► **pour the pork** (from the male point of view) to have sex *US, 1973*

poured into *adjective* said of someone wearing very tight clothing, usually of a woman, and generally complimentary *UK, 1960*

pour (it) out *verb* to urinate *US, 1990*

pouve *noun* ▷ see: POOVE

pov *noun* a person who is judged to be less well off than the speaker. Shortened from poverty or impoverished *UK, 2006*

poverty pimp *noun* a person who makes their living from the poverty of others, especially by working for government-funded programmes for the poor. The Coalition on Homelessness in San Francisco presents a Poverty Pimp Award each year *US, 1979*

poverty poker *noun* a style of poker in which a player who loses their bankroll may play for free until they win a hand *US, 1988*

povo *adjective* cheaply produced for a poor marketplace. Derives from 'poverty' *UK, 2001*

pow! used as a register of instant excitement *UK, 1881*

powder *noun* a powdered narcotic, usually heroin or cocaine *US, 1975*. ► **take a powder** 1 to leave *US, 1934*. 2 to inhale or ingest powdered drugs *US, 1982*

powder *verb* ► **powder your nose** 1 to sniff cocaine *US, 1983*. 2 to use the lavatory. A euphemism *UK, 1984*. ► **powder your schnoz** to inhale cocaine. Variation of POWDER YOUR NOSE with SHNOZ; SCHNOZ (the nose) *UK, 2000*

powderbox *noun* the vagina *US, 1998*

powder diamonds; powdered diamonds *noun* cocaine. From the crystalline appearance, and the cost *US, 1977*

powdered *adjective* under the influence of cocaine *US, 1986*

powdered chalk *noun* a walk. Rhyming slang *UK, 1992*

powder monkey *noun* 1 an explosives expert on a work crew *US, 1949*. 2 a cocaine user. Plays on POWDER (cocaine) *UK, 2002*

powder puff *noun* 1 an effeminate homosexual male *US, 1997*. 2 in trucking, a small convex mirror mounted on the outside of the cab *US, 1971*

powder puff *adjective* in various sports, describing an event limited to female competitors *US, 1973*

powder train *noun* a US Navy SEALS diver with expertise in underwater explosives *US, 1991*

power *noun* a charge of explosives *US, 1949*

power *adjective* in a concentrated, intense manner. Almost always used mockingly *US, 1989*

powerdyke *noun* a militant feminist, whether she is a lesbian or not *US, 2003*

power hit *noun* the act of inhaling marijuana smoke and then exhaling it into another's mouth as they inhale *US, 1970*

power lunch *noun* a lunch meeting where business or deals, not eating, is the central focus *US, 1986*

power pill *noun* a tablet of any variety of MDMA, the recreational drug best known as ecstasy *UK, 1996*

powerplant *noun* a variety of marijuana *SOUTH AFRICA, 2003*

power rangers *noun* a variety of LSD. Named after the fantasy television programme *UK, 1996*

power table *noun* a prominent table at a restaurant, seating at which is a recognition of fame or power. Used in the entertainment industry *US, 1984*

power trip *noun* any activity that is motivated by a desire for power *US, 1967*

pow-pow *noun* powder snow. Snowboarders, usage *US, 1995*

pow-wow *noun* a meeting. Originally an Algonquin word for an 'Indian priest' or 'ceremony' *US, 1812*

pox *noun* **1** syphilis; hence any sexually transmitted infection. Altered spelling of 'pocks', originally applied to the pustules of any eruptive disease *UK, 1503*. **2** marijuana; hashish *UK, 1996*. **3** opium; heroin *US, 1942*

pox *verb* to spoil something. From an earlier sense, 'to infect with syphilis' *UK, 1802*

poxbottle *noun* a despicable person *IRELAND, 1991*

pox docs *noun* doctors at a clinic for sexually transmitted diseases. A happy rhyme enjoyed in the medical profession *UK, 2002*

pox doctor's clerk *noun* used as the epitome of someone dressed in a flashy manner *AUSTRALIA, 1950*

poxy *adjective* loathsome, objectionable, disgusting. From POX (syphilis), equating the target of the adjective with venereal diseases *UK, 1922*

pozzie *noun* a location *NEW ZEALAND, 1984*

pozzle *noun* the vagina *US, 1962*

pozzy *noun* ▷ see: POSSIE

PP *noun* **1** a person whose regular apperance in a hospital casualty department has earned him the label *professional patient US, 1978*. **2** influence within a prison. A shortened form of 'penitentiary pull' *US, 1985*

PP nine *verb* to attack someone with a weapon improvised with a PP9 battery, often by concealing the battery in a sock *UK, 1996*

PPP *noun* a severely debilitated hospital patient, with piss-poor protoplasm *US, 1978*

PQ *noun* a half-pint of rum. An abbreviation of 'petit quart' *TRINIDAD AND TOBAGO, 1987*

PR *noun* **1** Puerto Rico *US, 1909*. **2** a Puerto Rican. Also attributed as an adjective *US, 1957*. **3** panama red, a variety of marijuana cultivated in Panama *US, 1969*

practice bleeding *noun* engaging in night-training flights off an aircraft carrier *US, 1986*

prad *noun* a horse. From Dutch *paard* (a horse). Not recorded separately before 1799 but implied in 'prad-lay' (to steal property from horses), now obsolete, noted in Grose's *Dictionary of the Vulgar Tongue*, 2nd edition, 1788 *UK, 1953*

prairie chicken *noun* a grouse, or a newcomer to the prairies *CANADA, 1961*

prairie nigger *noun* a native American Indian *US, 1989*

prairie oyster *noun* an anti-hangover tonic: an unbroken raw egg in a glass of dry red wine, or an unbroken raw egg in Worcestershire Sauce and sherry *US, 1883*

praise *verb* ▶ **praise the porcelain god** to vomit *US, 1986*

pram *noun* ▶ **get out of your pram** to become very angry or over-excited *UK, 1970*. ▶ **throw your toys out of the pram** to become angry; to lose your temper; to become over-excited *UK, 2002*

prang *noun* car accident or collision *US, 1959*

prang *verb* **1** in aviation, to crash-land an aircraft *UK, 1941*. **2** to crash a car *UK, 1952*. **3** to make a short call to a mobile telephone with the sole purpose of registering yourself on the receiving phone's 'caller ID' (thus delivering a private signal but avoiding the cost of a connection) *UK, 2003*

prang *adjective* scared. Urban youth slang *UK, 2005*

prannet; prannie; pranny *noun* a fool; a general term of contempt. After an obsolete sense of 'prannie' (female genitals, hence CUNT) *UK, 1977*

prat *noun* **1** used as a general insult with no particular meaning beyond the derogatory tone; a fool. Variant 'pratt'. From the earlier use as 'buttocks' *UK, 1968*. **2** the buttocks *UK, 1567*. **3** the vagina. From the earlier sense as 'buttocks' *UK, 1937*. **4** in horse racing, interference during a race *AUSTRALIA, 1989*

prat *verb* to engage in coy or fawning behaviour *US, 1969*

prat about *verb* to mess about; to play the fool. From PRAT (a fool) *UK, 1961*

pratfall *noun* in the theatre, a comedy fall, especially one that lands buttocks-first. Often applied figuratively *UK, 1939*

prat in *verb* in pickpocket usage, to back into the potential victim, getting him into position for a confederate *US, 1981*

prat powder *noun* powdered amphetamine. From the power of the powder to make you behave like a PRAT (a fool) *UK, 2002*

pratt *noun* a woman objectified sexually. Extended from the sense as 'vagina' *UK, 1977*

pratt boy *noun* a weak or effeminate person; an outcast *US, 1952*

pratty *adjective* stupid, foolish. From PRAT (a fool) *UK, 1998*

prawn *noun* **1** a fool; a worthless individual *AUSTRALIA, 1893*. **2** an ugly person with an attractive body *UK, 2004*

prawnhead *noun* a fool; a worthless individual *AUSTRALIA, 1961*

prawn-headed *adjective* stupid *AUSTRALIA, 1962*

pray *verb* ▶ **pray to the porcelain god; pray to the enamel god** to vomit into a toilet *US, 1980*

prayer bones *noun* the knees *US, 1946*

prayer meeting *noun* **1** a private dice game *US, 1949*. **2** a propaganda session conducted by Viet Cong with South Vietnamese villagers *US, 1990*

praying John *noun* a gambler who believes that he can influence the fall of the dice by uttering the right, magical words *US, 1950*

pre; pre-game; pre-party *verb* to drink before going to an event where there will be drinking *US, 2001*

preach *verb* ▶ **preach to the choir** to talk to those who are already convinced *US, 1986*

preacher *noun* **1** a traffic police officer who is too kind-hearted to issue citations *US, 1962*. **2** a log that is partially submerged in a river *US, 1974*

preacher's car *noun* in the used car business, a car with no accessories at all *US, 1968*

preacher's pasttime *noun* the shell game *US, 1966*

precious *adjective* egregious, arrant; very, exceedingly; especially as an intensifier of something bad or worthless *UK, 1430*

pre-cum *noun* penile secretions prior to orgasm. A refinement of COME (orgasm/semen) *UK, 1995*

predator *noun* heroin *UK, 1998*

preemie *noun* a premature baby *US, 1927*

preesh! I appreciate that! *US, 1987*

prefab *noun* a prefabricated house, specifically a temporary dwelling (usually a bungalow) that served as a stop-gap measure in the years immediately following World War 2. Some are still in use nearly 60 years later *UK, 1942*

prefab *adjective* prefabricated *US, 1937*

preggers *adjective* pregnant *UK, 1942*

preggo *adjective* pregnant *AUSTRALIA, 1951*

preggy; preggie *adjective* pregnant *UK, 1938*

pregnant duck *noun* the B-24 Liberator bomber. A nod to the plane's clumsy appearance *US, 1946*

pregnant rollerskate; pregnant skateboard *noun* a Volkswagen 'Beetle' car. Citizens' band radio slang *US, 1976*

prelim *noun* a preliminary sporting match *UK, 1923*

prellies *noun* Phenmetrazine, a chemical stimulant marketed as Preludin™, used in the US as a diet drug *UK, 2002*

premie *noun* a premature sexual ejaculation; a man who is subject to such a thing *US, 1975*

premium *noun* a brand name manufactured cigarette *US, 1992*

prenup *noun* an agreement entered into before marriage concerning the division of property in the event of divorce. Shortened from 'prenuptial' *US, 1983*

pre-op *noun* a transsexual who has yet to undergo all surgery necessary to complete a sex change *US, 1986*

pre-op *adjective* in a hospital, pre-operative *US, 1997*

prep *verb* to prepare someone or something *US, 1927*

pre-papier *noun* in Quebec, advance publicity about cultural events (production teams, casts and plays) prior to reviews. This word is a French term adapted fully into English *CANADA, 2002*

pre-party *verb* ▷ *see:* PRE

prepone *verb* to rearrange something for a future date. A definite variation of 'postpone' *INDIA, 2003*

preppy; preppie *noun* a well-groomed, well-heeled, conventional young person with upper-class prep-school values *US, 1968*

Presbo *noun* a presbyterian *AUSTRALIA, 1965*

Presbyterian poker *noun* low-key, low-limit, friendly poker *US, 1996*

prescription *noun* a marijuana cigarette. An assertion that marijuana is just what the doctor ordered *UK, 1998*

prescriptions *noun* commercially manufactured drugs used for non-medicinal purposes *US, 1980*

presence *noun* MDMA, the recreational drug best known as ecstasy *US, 1989*

presento *noun* during the Korean war, a piece of merchandise used by US servicemen to trade with Koreans for services *US, 1960*

presh *adjective* good, pleasing. An abbreviation of the conventional 'precious' *US, 1986*

president *noun* an established, respected graffiti artist, often the leader of a group *US, 1997*

President *nickname* Lester Young (1909–59), jazz saxophonist *US, 1949*

press *noun* **1** in betting, a doubling of the bet in effect *US, 1962*. **2** cocaine; crack cocaine *UK, 1998*

press *verb* **1** to pursue criminal charges *US, 1993*. **2** to dress up *US, 1974*. ▶ **press the blocks** to idle on a street corner *BAHAMAS, 1982*. ▶ **press the bricks** to walk *US, 1949*. ▶ **press the flesh** to shake hands, especially in a political context *US, 1926*. ▶ **press the meat; press the sausage** while gambling, to continue betting your winnings after several consecutive wins *US, 2003*. ▶ **press the sheets** to sleep in a bed *US, 1976*

pressed *adjective* **1** worried, stressed *US, 1989*. **2** dressed stylishly *US, 1980*

pressed duck *noun* a human corpse that has been flattened by traffic. A truly grim comparison *US, 1962*

pressed ham *noun* the bare buttocks pressed against a car window as a rude prank *US, 1966*

pressie; prezzie *noun* a gift, a *present UK, 1937*

pressure cooker *noun* a sports car. Citizens' band radio slang *UK, 1981*

pressure out *verb* to lose your composure completely under pressure. Hawaiian youth usage *US, 1981*

pressurize *verb* to intimidate; to threaten; to coerce *US, 2001*

pre-stiff *noun* a patient close to death *US, 1994*

pretender to the throne *noun* a heterosexual who is attempting to pass as a homosexual *US, 1980*

pretendica *noun* poor quality or counterfeit marijuana. A play on 'pretend' mixed with cannabis indica (a major genus of marijuana) *UK, 1998*

pretendo *noun* a poor quality or counterfeit marijuana. An elaboration of 'pretend' *UK, 2003*

Pretentious? Moi? used self-satirically as an admission of pretentious qualities. A somewhat tired catchphrase *UK, 1975*

pretties *noun* **1** the female breasts *UK, 1973*. **2** on a film or television crew, the makeup, hair and wardrobe departments *US, 1997*. **3** in trucking, state permit stickess affixed on a cab window *US, 1971*

pretty *noun* a youthful, sexually inexperienced male who is the object of an older homosexual's desire *US, 1979*

pretty boy *noun* **1** an effeminate young man *AUSTRALIA, 1942*. **2** a sexually active young man *US, 2003*

pretty face *noun* ▶ **not just a pretty face** used, often ironically, when claiming to be intelligent *UK, 1968*

pretty pictures *noun* in computing, graphical representations of statistics *US, 1991*

pretty please an emphatic or wheedling intensification of please *UK, 1959*

pretty-print *verb* in computing, to format code so that it looks attractive *US, 1983*

pretzels *noun* a small amount of money. An evolution from the more common PEANUTS *US, 1988*

previous *noun* a criminal record. An abbreviation of 'previous convictions' *UK, 1999*

previous *adjective* premature; early; hasty *US, 1885*

Prez *nickname* Lester Young (1909–59), jazz saxophonist. Singer Billie Holiday nicknamed Young 'Prez' as a shortened form of 'President of the Tenor Saxophone' *US, 1957*

prez; pres *noun* president *IRELAND, 1922*

prezzies *noun* paper money. An abbreviation of the common DEAD PRESIDENTS *US, 1997*

prezzo *noun* a gift or present *AUSTRALIA, 1968*

price *noun* **1** a chance. Sporting slang, from bookmakers quoting a 'price' (betting odds) *UK, 1977*. **2** in betting on horse racing, the approximate equivalent odds to $1 *US, 1951*. **3** a discount. A euphemism that saves face for both the seller and buyer *US, 1991*

pricey *adjective* expensive *UK, 1932*

prick *noun* **1** the penis. From the basic sense, 'anything that pricks or pierces'; in conventional English until around 1700. William Shakespeare (1564–1616) played word games with it, Robert Burns (1759–96) toyed with it with vulgar good humour and the Victorians finally hid it away *UK, 1592*. **2** a despicable man; a fool; used as a general term of offence or contempt, often as an abusive form of address, always of a male or an inanimate object. Since the 1940s, when qualified by the adjective 'silly', the sense need not be derogatory or contemptuous, as 'you silly prick', 'the silly prick' etc. An unembellished prick, however, is considered very offensive *US, 1929*. **3** a marijuana cigarette. Presumably based on phallic imagery *UK, 1984*

pricked off *adjective* annoyed, angry *US, 1968*

prickface *noun* a contemptible person *AUSTRALIA, 1971*

pricklick *noun* a homosexual male *US, 1972*

prick parade *noun* a group inspection by a military doctor or medic of male recruits for signs of sexually transmitted disease *US, 1964*

pricksmith *noun* a military doctor or medic who inspects male recruits for signs of sexually transmitted disease *US, 1967*

prick-teaser *noun* a woman who invites sexual advances but does not fulfil that which she seems to promise *US, 1970*

pride and joy *noun* a boy, especially a new-born son. Rhyming slang *UK, 1992*

pride of Deadwood *noun* in poker, a hand consisting of aces and eights. From the belief, true or legendary, that when Wild Bill Hickock was shot and killed in Deadwood, Dakota Territory, he was holding a hand consisting of aces and eights, all black *US, 1988*

pride of the morning *noun* the erection experienced by a man upon awakening in the morning *US, 1972*

priest's dick *noun* something of little or no worth *UK, 2000*

prim *verb* (used of a female) to walk in a sexually inviting fashion *BAHAMAS, 1982*

prime *verb* ▶ **prime the spunk gun** (used of a male) to masturbate *UK, 2003*

primed *adjective* drunk or under the influence of drugs *US, 1950*

prime time *noun* **1** time spent with a spouse or lover. Trucker slang, punning on television terminology *US, 1976*. **2** cocaine; crack cocaine *UK, 2003*

primo *noun* **1** a very high grade of marijuana, consisting of a high degree of potent flowering tops of the plants *US, 1971*. **2** marijuana mixed with crack cocaine *US, 1995*. **3** a conventional tobacco cigarette laced with cocaine and heroin *UK, 1998*. **4** heroin *UK, 2002*

primo *adjective* excellent *US, 1977*

Prince Albert; PA; Albert *noun* a piece of jewellery for a penile piercing; also applied to the piercing itself. This etymology is the stuff of romantic myth: the procedure and bejewelling is named after Queen Victoria's consort who, it is claimed, endured the embellishment of his member to enhance his Queen's pleasure *UK, 2001*

Prince Alberts; Alberts *noun* rags worn by tramps in the place of socks. Folk etymology suggests the alleged poverty of Prince Albert before marriage to Queen Victoria *AUSTRALIA, 1888*

Prince Charming *nickname* used ironically of someone who is anything but *UK, 1998*

Prince of Darkness *nickname* Joseph Lucas, British electrical equipment manufacturer of unreliable headlight systems *US, 1997*

Princess Di *noun* a pie. Rhyming slang, formed on a familiar name for Diana, Princess of Wales, 1961–97; recorded in use before and, following a respectful pause, after her death *UK, 1998*

Princeton rub; Princeton style *noun* the rubbing of the penis between the thighs of another boy or man until reaching orgasm. Princeton is a prestigious and cultured East Coast university *US, 1971*

pringle *noun* multiple orgasms. From the advertising slogan for Pringles™, a savoury snack: 'once you pop you can't stop' *UK, 2001*

print *verb* to take the fingerprints of a prisoner during the after-arrest process *US, 1939*

prior *noun* a prior arrest or prior conviction *US, 1985*

Priscilla *noun* a police officer. Gay slang, using a female name, probably elaborating the initial 'p' for 'police' *SOUTH AFRICA, 2000*

prison air conditioning *noun* a wet towel *CANADA, 2002*

prison bent; prison gay *adjective* used of a heterosexual prisoner who adopts a homosexual or lesbian lifestyle for the duration of his or her sentence *UK, 1996*

prissy *adjective* **1** prudish. *2001*. **2** effeminate. Perhaps a blend of 'prim' and SISSY *US, 1946*

prissy lad *noun* a homosexual man *US, 1954*

priv *noun* a privilege *UK, 1996*

private dance *noun* a one-on-one sexual performance by a woman for a man *US, 1991*

private dick *noun* a private detective. Conventional use of 'private' combined with DICK (detective) *US, 1912*

private eye *noun* a private detective *US, 1938*

privates *noun* the genitals of either sex *UK, 1602*

private slick *noun* a physician in private practice *US, 1994*

private star *noun* a private detective *US, 1958*

privy queen *noun* a homosexual male who searches for sexual partners in public toilets *US, 1941*

prize *adjective* describes a prime example (of whatever it is appended to); complete, utter *UK, 1976*

prize jewels carrier *noun* the scrotum *UK, 2002*

pro *noun* **1** a professional, especially in a field of endeavour that is also enjoyed by amateurs (such as sport or theatre); also used as an Internet domain name for a professional practitioner *UK, 1866*. **2** a professional prostitute *UK, 1937*

prob *noun* a problem *US, 1992*

probate *noun* in a criminal case, a sentence of probation. A person who is arrested for the illegal production of alcohol and is sentenced to probation is said to 'get probate' *US, 1974*

probie *noun* a probationary employee *US, 1973*

procesh *noun* a procession or graduation parade *NEW ZEALAND, 1977*

process *noun* a chemical straightening of curly hair *US, 1967*

procon *noun* a professionally run fan convention *US, 1978*

procure *verb* ▶ **procure for a cause** to steal something *US, 1970*

prod *noun* **1** the penis *US, 1975*. **2** in horse racing, an illegal, battery-powered device used to impart a shock to a horse during a race *US, 1976*. ▶ **on the prod** looking for something; on the offensive; provoked *US, 1904*

Prod; Prot *noun* a Protestant. Mainly Catholic use across the UK *UK, 1942*

Proddie; Proddy *adjective* Protestant; a Protestant. Mainly Catholic use across the UK *UK, 1954*

Proddy dog *noun* a Protestant *AUSTRALIA, 1979*

proddywhack *adjective* Protestant *UK, 1998*

prodigal boy *noun* a person who excels at the game of footbagging *US, 1997*

produce *noun* food *US, 1957*

producer *noun* **1** an official requirement that you produce your driving licence, motor insurance and any other necessary documentation for police scrutiny. In police use, form HO/RT/1 (Home Office/Road Traffic/1) *UK, 1994*. **2** a serious gambler who, like most gamblers, usually loses *US, 1963*

product *noun* illegal drugs *US, 1982*

prof *noun* a professor; also as a form of address *US, 1838*

professional scene *noun* a sado-masochistic encounter for pay *US, 1979*

professor *noun* **1** a diligent student *US, 1955*. **2** a piano player in a brothel *US, 1939*. **3** a skilled and experienced poker player *US, 1979*

proffing *noun* stealing *UK, 2002*

profile *verb* **1** (used of the police) to stop, question and search someone based on their race and age *US, 1992*. **2** to act in an arrogant and conceited fashion *US, 1997*

profiles *noun* in a deck of playing cards, the king of diamonds, jack of spades and jack of hearts, all one-eyed and drawn in profile *US, 1963*

pro from Dover *noun* an expert *US, 1970*

prog *noun* a radio or television programme. Particularly associated with the *JY Prog* presented by Jimmy Young, a BBC radio DJ and presenter from 1959, especially on Radio 2, which he joined in 1973 until his retirement in 2001 *UK, 1975*

prog *adjective* progressive, as used of a school or method *UK, 1969*

proggy *adjective* having the characteristics of progressive house music *UK, 2002*

programme *noun* the twelve-step Alcoholics Anonymous programme for recovery from alcoholism *US, 1991*

programme *verb* in prison, to follow the rules and avoid trouble in hope of an early release *US, 1981*

prohi *noun* a federal law enforcement official. Used by those in the illegal production of alcohol *US, 1974*

prole *noun* a member of the proletariat *US, 1887*

prole *adjective* proletariat; of the working-class *US, 1965*

prom *noun* a dance at a school or college *US, 1894*

promise *noun* ▶ **on a promise** having been promised sexual intercourse *AUSTRALIA, 1960*

prommer *noun* a member of the audience, especially a promenader, at a Henry Wood Promenade Concert (now branded the *BBC Proms*). So named by James Loughran, in the conductor's traditional last-night-of-the-Proms speech, 11th September 1982 *UK, 1982*

promo *noun* public relations; promotional item(s); in the music business, an advance copy of an unreleased tune sent to an influential DJ *US, 1966*

promo *adjective* promotional *US, 1963*

promote *verb* in the circus or carnival, to obtain illegally something that is badly needed *US, 1980*

prong *noun* the penis *US, 1968*

pronger *noun* the penis *US, 1977*

prong me! used for registering disbelief, despair, surprise, or satisfaction. From PRONG (the penis), in the manner and sense of FUCK ME!, suggesting that 'prong' is also used for FUCK (to have sex, etc) *US, 1962*

pronto *adverb* immediately. From the Spanish *US, 1911*

proof *noun* an identification card establishing you as old enough to buy alcohol *US, 1983*

proof *verb* to show identification proving that you are old enough to be where you are, buying what you are buying *US, 1987*

proof shot *noun* a photograph, or a scene in a pornographic film, of a man ejaculating. *US, 1995*

prop *noun* **1** a proposition *UK, 1871*. **2** any portable article used in acting. An abbreviation of 'property': theatrical, film-making, television, etc. also used by those seeking to create an impression *UK, 1864*. **3** in casino gambling, a casino employee who poses as a player to draw interest to a game. An abbreviation of 'proposition player' *US, 1996*. **4** the leg *US, 1969*. **5** a prisoners' strike *NEW ZEALAND, 1985*

prop *verb* **1** to organise a criminal enterprise *UK, 1956*. **2** to take part in a prison strike *NEW ZEALAND, 1982*

propellerhead *noun* an expert computer enthusiast *US, 1997*

propeller key *noun* the command key on an Apple Macintosh™ computer keyboard *US, 1991*

proper *noun* proper respect *US, 1974*

proper *adjective* **1** excellent, complete, perfect. In conventional use until during the C19 *UK, 1375*. **2** of a criminal, respected *UK, 2001*

proper *adverb* excellently, superbly; without subterfuge; handsomely. An intensifier *UK, 2000*

proper little madam *noun* ▷*see:* LITTLE MADAM

proper lush *adjective* great, excellent, wonderful. An intensified variation of LUSH *UK, 1999*

propper; prop *noun* in youth-oriented holiday resorts, a person who encourages custom into clubs and bars. Probably adapted from a reduction of 'proposition' *UK, 1997*

props *noun* **1** proper respect; due credit. Variant 'propers' *US, 1993*. **2** false breasts *US, 1967*

prop up *verb* to suggest or arrange a story or an explanation, especially through a third person. *UK, 1977*

pros *noun* in circus and carnival usage, a prosecutor *US, 1981*

Prosecute Coppers Association *noun* the Police Complaints Authority. A cynical alternative meaning for the PCA; in police use *UK, 2001*

prospect *noun* a prospective member of a club or gang *US, 2000*

prospect *verb* over a period of time, to prove yourself to be a worthy recruit before initiation as a full member of a motorcycle club *US, 1971*

pross; pros *noun* a prostitute *UK, 1905*

pross collar *noun* an arrest of a prostitute for a direct solicitation *US, 1973*

prossie; prossy; prozzy *noun* a prostitute *AUSTRALIA, 1941*

prosso *noun* a prostitute *AUSTRALIA, 1965*

pross van *noun* a police van used in mass arrests of prostitutes *US, 1973*

prosty; prostie *noun* a prostitute *US, 1930*

protection *noun* **1** contraception, especially a condom *US, 1967*. **2** an extortion scheme in which the victim pays the extorting party to protect him from crime, especially crime committed by the extorting party *US, 1999*

protein shake *noun* in the pornography industry, semen that is swallowed *US, 1995*

proto *noun* protection from prosecution by law enforcement *US, 1945*

proverbial; proverbials *noun* used as a general-purpose euphemism. Always reliant on context for sense *UK, 1984*

provo *noun* **1** a 1960s Dutch counterculture revolutionary *NETHERLANDS, 1970*. **2** a military police officer. From *provost* marshall. Can be used with a capital: 'Provo' *AUSTRALIA, 1943*

Provo; Provie; Provvie *noun* a member of the *Provisional* wing of the IRA, subsequently *Provisional* IRA. More than a simple abbreviation, Provo is probably influenced by 'Provo' (a member of a group of 1960s Dutch political activists) derived from French *provocateur* (an aggressor) *UK: NORTHERN IRELAND, 1971*

provvy *noun* an approved school (for juvenile offenders) *UK, 1974*

prozie *noun* a branded antidepressant Prozac™ tablet *UK, 2001*

prozine *noun* a professionally published fan magazine *US, 1978*

prozzy *noun* a girl who is (allegedly) sexually available. Derogatory; shortened from 'prostitute' *UK, 2002*

Pru *noun* ▶ **the Pru** the Prudential Insurance Company *UK, 1927*

prune *noun* the anus. An allusion to the wrinkles found on each *US, 1967*

prune *verb* to out-race someone in a car race from a stationary position *US, 1962*

prune and plum; prune *noun* the buttocks; occasionally and specifically, the anus, the rectum. Rhyming slang for BUM *UK, 1998*

prune pusher *noun* the active participant in anal sex *US, 1979*

prunes *noun* testicles; courage *US, 1984*

pruno *noun* a potent, homemade alcohol, often made with fermented prune juice *US, 1990*

Prussian *noun* a male homosexual who prefers the active role in anal sex *US, 1950*

P's *noun* parents *US, 1989*

PS *noun* penal servitude. An abbreviation. This type of prison sentence was ordered from the C19 until 1948 *UK, 1923*

p's and q's *noun* shoes. Rhyming slang *UK, 1992*. ▶ **mind your p's and q's** to be careful, exact, prudent. Perhaps from the old custom of alehouse tally, marking 'p' for pint and 'q' for quart, care being necessary to avoid over- or under-charging. Whether the source is in printing, or 'pints and quarts', or learning to read, is unknown *UK, 1779*

pseud *noun* a pretentious, image-conscious person. Usage popularised by 'Pseud's Corner' in *Private Eye* magazine *UK, 1954*

pseudo *adjective* pretentious. From the conventional prefix *UK, 1945*

pseudy *adjective* pretentious. A variation of PSEUDO *UK, 1989*

psst; psst! used for attracting someone's attention discretely *IRELAND, 1922*

psych *noun* **1** psychology; psychiatry *US, 1895*. **2** a psychiatrist or psychologist *US, 1971*

psych *adjective* psychedelic, when used in combination with a type of music or musicans, e.g. 'psych rock' or 'psych band' *UK, 2003*

psych; psych up *verb* to use *psych*ological techniques to stimulate, to enthuse, to excite *US, 1957*

psyche! I fooled you! *US, 1990*

psyched *adjective* excited, enthusiastic *US, 1970*

psychedelic martini *noun* DMT, a short-lasting hallucinogen *US, 1970*

psycher; neo-psycher *noun* a musician or fan of psychedelic rock or neo-psychodelia. From PSYCH *UK, 2003*

psychic energizer *noun* an amphetamine or other central nervous system stimulant *US, 1967*

psycho *noun* a psychopath, or someone who is otherwise psychologically disturbed *US, 1942*

psycho *adjective* **1** psychiatric or psychological *US, 1927*. **2** crazy. An abbreviation of 'psychopathic' *US, 1936*

psychobabble *noun* psychological and pseudo-psychological jargon. Derogatory. Popularised, but not coined, by R.D. Rosen in *Psychobabble*, 1977 *US, 1976*

psycho block *noun* an area in a prison where the most violent prisoners are held *US, 1985*

psychopathic *noun* traffic. Rhyming slang, inspired, perhaps, by the state of mind that you (or the driver behind you) get into when stuck in traffic *UK, 1998*

psych out *verb* **1** to intimidate someone completely on a psychological level *US, 1994*. **2** to lose your mental composure or stability *UK, 1971*. **3** to figure out or discover something *US, 1978*

PT *noun* **1** a woman who promises more sex than she delivers. An abbreviation of PRICK-TEASER *US, 1958*. **2** in sports, playing time *US, 2001*

PTA *noun* a hasty washing by a female. The most common association with PTA is the school-support Parent-Teacher Assocation. The PTA in question here refers to the woman's *p*ussy, *t*its and *a*ss *US, 1971*

ptomaine palace *noun* a restaurant serving inexpensive, low quality food *UK, 1952*

ptomaine wagon *noun* a catering truck *US, 1937*

P-town *nickname* Provincetown, Massachusetts *US, 1980*

PU! used for registering disgust of anything that smells. A jocular spelling (pronounce each letter) of the two syllable stretching of 'phew' *US, 1960*

pub *noun* a *pub*lic house, an inn, a tavern *UK, 1859*

pub band *noun* a band of musicians who play principally in public hotels. Pub rock, an umbrella genre for such bands and their music, was popular in the UK in the mid-1970s and is seen as the precursor to PUNK ROCK *AUSTRALIA, 1988*

pubber *noun* a publisher, especially of a single-interest fan magazine *US, 1982*

pub-crawl *noun* a drinking session that moves from one licensed premises to the next, and so on. Combines PUB (a public house, licensed for the sale of alcohol) with a less-and-less figurative sense of 'crawl' *UK, 1915*

pub-crawl *verb* to move in a group from one drinking establishment to the next, drinking at each *UK, 1937*

pub dog sex *noun* an act of sex performed under a pub table *UK, 2001*

pube *noun* a high school girl *US, 1969*. ▶ **get pube** in the categorisation of sexual activity by teenage boys, to touch a girl's vulva *US, 1986*

pube *adjective pube*scent *US, 1995*

pubes *noun* pubic hair *US, 1970*

pubies *noun* pubic hairs *US, 1968*

public relations *noun* a member of a swindling enterprise who promotes the swindle *US, 1977*

pub pet *noun* a two-litre plastic container for draught beer *NEW ZEALAND, 1988*

puck *noun* **1** in a number of casino games, a disc used to mark a point or position *US, 2003*. **2** car brake pad *US, 1993*

pucker *noun* the anus *US, 1995*

pucker factor *noun* the degree of fear or anxiety. From the image of the sphincter tightening in a frightening situation *US, 1982*

puckeroo *adjective* useless, broken *NEW ZEALAND, 2002*

pucker paint *noun* lipstick. Teen slang *CANADA, 1946*

pucker palace *noun* a drive-in cinema. High school student usage *US, 1961*

pucker up *verb* **1** to tighten your rectal and anal muscles *US, 1972*. **2** to behave sycophantically *UK, 2000*

pud *noun* a pudding *UK, 1943*. ▶ **pound your pud; pull your pud; pull your pudding** (of a male) to masturbate *UK, 1944*

pudding *noun* **1** money *US, 1993*. **2** the penis. The abbreviation 'pud' does not appear until the 1930s *UK, 1719*

pudding and gravy; the pudding *noun* the Royal Navy. Rhyming slang *UK, 1961*

pudding-basin *noun* a hairstyle that looks as though a basin has been inverted over the head and the hair cut up to the rim of the basin *UK, 1951*

pudding club *noun* ▶ **in the pudding club** pregnant *UK, 1890*

pudding wagon *noun* in circus and carnival usage, a frozen custard truck *US, 1981*

puddle *noun* a generous dose of liquid LSD *US, 1994*

puddle about *verb* to busy yourself doing nothing *NEW ZEALAND, 1984*

puddle-jumper *noun* **1** a small plane making a relatively short journey *US, 1961*. **2** in trucking, a lightweight truck *US, 1971*

puddy tat *noun* a cat. From the Looney Tunes cartoons with Sylvester the cat and Tweety Bird, with Tweety Bird's constant mantra of 'I taut I taw a puddy-tat' (I thought I saw a pussy cat) *US, 1986*

pudge *noun* a short squat person; anything short and thick; someone who is overweight. A probable variant of PODGE (a short and fat person) *UK, 1999*

pudgy *adjective* short and fat *UK, 1836*

pud puller *noun* a male masturbator *US, 1990*

pudwapper *noun* a male masturbator; hence, a despicable person. Combines 'pud '(the penis) with 'W(h)ap' (to hit) *US, 1988*

puff *noun* **1** a homosexual man; a weak, effeminate man. Pejorative; probably a variation of POOF *UK, 1902*. **2** marijuana. From PUFF (to smoke marijuana). Also variant 'puffy' *UK, 1987*. **3** breath. A puff of wind *UK, 2001*. **4** existence; life-span *UK, 1921*. **5** a charge of explosives *US, 1949*. ▶ **on your puff** on your own, alone *UK, 1995*

puff *verb* to smoke marijuana *UK, 1996*. ▶ **puff the dragon; puff the magic dragon 1** to smoke marijuana. 'Puff, The Magic Dragon', 1963, a song by Peter, Paul and Mary, is, according to a popular myth, about smoking marijuana or a weapon of war – nothing in the lyric sustains this but nevertheless the song inspired this term, 1998. **2** to perform oral sex on a man. Plays on DRAGON (the penis) and the song 'Puff, The Magic Dragon' *US, 2001*

puffa; puffa jacket *noun* an extravagantly bulky jacket generally made of lightweight synthetic materials. Surely coined by marketing experts to account for the fashion-garment's puffed-up appearance *UK, 1991*

puff and dart *noun* in the dice game crown and anchor, a heart. Rhyming slang, probably dating from about 1860 but first recorded in 1936 *UK, 1936*

puff and drag *noun* a cigarette. Rhyming slang for FAG *UK, 1992*

puffed *adjective* exhausted *NEW ZEALAND, 1984*

puffer *noun* **1** a marijuana smoker *UK, 2002*. **2** a crack cocaine user *US, 1994*. **3** in drag racing and hot rodding, a supercharger *US, 1968*

puff-juice *noun* men's toiletries. Based on PUFF (a male homosexual) *UK, 2001*

Puff the Magic Dragon; Puff *nickname* a C-47 aircraft modified as a gunship and redesignated an AC47, heavily used by the US Air

Force in Vietnam. From the gentle 1963 folk song recorded by Peter, Paul and Mary *US, 1983*

pug *noun* 1 a boxer; a fighter. A shortened form of the conventional 'pugilist.' *UK, 1858*. 2 a male homosexual *US, 1992*. 3 in trucking, a cabover tractor *US, 1971*

pug *verb* to fight *US, 1994*

puggie *noun* a hardened criminal *US, 1965*

puggled *adjective* given to foolish behaviour; tipsy *UK: SCOTLAND, 1985*

puggy *noun* a kitty in a card game; a one-armed bandit; an ATM cash dispenser. From a Scots word for 'monkey' *UK: SCOTLAND, 1985*. ▶ **full as a puggy** very drunk; having eaten too much *UK: SCOTLAND, 1985*. ▶ **take a puggy** to become very angry *UK: SCOTLAND, 1985*

puggy work *noun* hard physical labour. From a Scots word for 'monkey' *UK: SCOTLAND, 1988*

pug-ugly *adjective* very ugly. Probably a confusion with PLUG-UGLY (a thug); based on the appearance of a PUG (a boxer) or the broad wrinkled face of a 'pug' (a breed of dog) *UK, 2000*

pug up *verb* to hide something *UK, 2001*

puke *noun* 1 vomit *US, 1961*. 2 a despised person. In the mid-C19, the term was applied with some degree of scorn to residents of the state of Missouri; it later gained a broader sense. In *Rogue Warrior*, Richard Marcinko gives a virtual litany of pukes – Academy puke, admin puke, fleet puke, jet puke, puke ensign, staff puke and Team-puke *US, 1966*

puke *verb* 1 to vomit *UK, 1600*. 2 in the illegal production of alcohol, to allow the still to boil over *US, 1974*. 3 while on a combat air mission, to separate out from formation while under attack *US, 1986*. ▶ **puke your ring up** to vomit violently *UK, 2001*

Puke hole *noun* a shabby, shoddy, dirty place *US, 1973*

pukepot *noun* a despicable person *US, 1973*

puker *noun* a tourist. In Alaska, an allusion to the tendency of tourists on fishing charters to get seasick *US, 1997*

puking buzzards *nickname* the 101st Airborne Division, US Army. From the official nickname of 'Screaming Eagles' *US, 1991*

pukka *adjective* certain; reliable; genuine; hence excellent; fashionable. Derives from Hindu *pakka* which has the meaning of 'substantial' *UK, 1776*

pulborn; pulboron; polboron *noun* heroin. Possibly from Spanish *polvo grande* (big powder) or *polvorón* (a sweet made with almonds) *US, 1977*

pull *noun* 1 in policing, an act of temporarily detaining a suspicious person or vehicle for investigation. Derived from PULL (to arrest) *UK, 1977*. 2 a woman as a sex object *UK, 1985*. ▶ **on the pull** engaged in a casual or recreational quest for a sexual partner *UK, 2002*

pull *verb* 1 (of police) to stop a vehicle; to stop someone for questioning. A broader usage of the earlier sense 'to arrest' *UK, 1970*. 2 to arrest someone *UK, 1811*. 3 to engage in a casual or recreational quest for a sexual partner *UK, 1965*. 4 to recruit someone into prostitution *US, 1967*. 5 to serve time in prison or in the armed forces *US, 1961*. 6 to leave *US, 1960*. 7 (of an adult) to buy beer or cigarettes illegally for a minor. This term is especially, almost exclusively, used in Saskatchewan *CANADA, 2001*. 8 (of a jockey) to deliberately ride a racehorse to lose *AUSTRALIA, 1895*. ▶ **pull a fast one** to do something daring (often a criminal act) and hope to get away with it by being smarter, faster and more deceitful than those set to prevent you; to play a dirty trick. Originally military *UK, 1943*. ▶ **pull a stroke** to do something daring (often a criminal act) and get away with it by being smarter, faster and more deceitful than those set to prevent you; to play a dirty trick *UK, 1970*. ▶ **pull my mouth** to try to get me to say something in particular *CANADA, 1999*. ▶ **pull on** to tackle someone; to contend with someone to test someone; *AUSTRALIA, 1953*. ▶ **pull on the rope** to masturbate a man *US, 1972*. ▶ **pull out (all) the stops** to apply maximum effort to the task in hand. From the stops that limit the full sound of a pipe-organ *UK, 1974*. ▶ **pull pud** (used of a male) to masturbate *UK, 1994*. ▶ **pull someone's coat** to warn someone; to alert someone *US, 1954*. ▶ **pull someone's covers**

to reveal a person's true character *US, 1970*. ▶ **pull someone's leg** 1 to tease someone; to make fun of someone *UK, 1888*. 2 to good naturedly hoax or deceive someone *UK, 1888*. ▶ **pull someone's pisser** to good-naturedly hoax or deceive someone. A variation of PULL SOMEONE'S LEG *UK, 1984*. ▶ **pull someone's plonker** 1 to fool someone; to tease someone; to take a liberty with someone. Variation of PULL SOMEONE'S LEG, similar to PULL SOMEONE'S PISSER, with PLONKER (the penis) supplying the image *UK, 2000*. 2 to waste time. From the sense 'to masturbate' *UK, 1982*. ▶ **pull someone's tit** to good-naturedly hoax or deceive someone; to make a fool of someone *AUSTRALIA, 1959*. ▶ **pull the head off it** (of a male) to masturbate *UK, 2002*. ▶ **pull the monkey** to pull a rubber disc through a cess drain in order to clean the drain *UK, 1970*. ▶ **pull the pin** to resign or retire from a job. Based on the US railroad imagery of uncoupling train wagons by pulling a pin on the couplers *US, 1927*. ▶ **pull the plug** 1 to stop; to finish. An electrical image *UK, 1988*. 2 in submarining, to dive *US, 1948*. ▶ **pull the rein** to advise. The 'right rein' is good advice, the 'bad rein', bad advice *AUSTRALIA, 1989*. ▶ **pull the rug out** to disturb the status quo *UK, 1974*. ▶ **pull the wool over someone's eyes** to deceive someone, especially as regards the deceiver's intentions *US, 1842*. ▶ **pull time** to be sentenced to imprisonment *US, 1950*. ▶ **pull up stakes** to depart; to move house *AUSTRALIA, 1961*. ▶ **pull wires** to use personal influence to achieve a desired outcome. A variation of 'pull strings' *UK, 1984*. ▶ **pull your head in** mind your own business *AUSTRALIA, 1942*. ▶ **pull your pud; pull your pudden; pull your pudding** (of a male), to masturbate *UK, 1944*. ▶ **pull your punches** to exercise moderation, especially in punishment or blame. From boxing *UK, 1934*. ▶ **pull your wire** (of a male), to masturbate *UK, 1937*

pull away *verb* to divert attention from the scene of of a crime *AUSTRALIA, 1975*

pull down *verb* 1 to earn money *US, 1917*. 2 to rob a place *US, 1992*

pulled up *adjective* former *US, 1972*

puller *noun* 1 a sneak thief *US, 1984*. 2 a dealer in stolen or smuggled goods *US, 1956*. 3 a racehorse that strains to run at full speed *US, 1994*. 4 a crack cocaine user who obsessively/compulsively tugs at different body parts *US, 1992*

pulleys *noun* suspenders *US, 1945*

pullie; pully *noun* a pullover, a jumper *UK, 1984*

pull in *verb* to earn (money) *UK, 1529*

pulling *noun* 1 casual or recreational questing for a sexual partner *UK, 2004*. 2 a challenge from a gang, or from one of its members. Teddy Boys' slang *UK, 1959*

pulling gear *noun* in trucking, the gear best suited for climbing a hill *US, 1971*

pulling time *noun* in an illegal numbers gambling lottery, the time of day when the winning number is drawn or selected *US, 1949*

pull off *verb* 1 (used of a male) to masturbate *IRELAND, 1922*. 2 to succeed in doing, or effecting, something *UK, 1887*

pull out of *verb* to be released *US, 1973*

pull the other one!; pull the other one – it's got bells on! used as a sarcastic response from 'leg-pulling' (a humorous act of bluff or deception). The invitation is to pull the other leg *UK, 1964*

pull through *noun* a Jew. Rhyming slang *UK, 1974*

pull up *verb* 1 (of a jockey) to deliberately ride a racehorse to lose *AUSTRALIA, 1936*. 2 to stop (doing something) *US, 1972*

pummel *verb* to skateboard fearlessly, without regard to the effect on the board or body *US, 1984*

pummelled *adjective* very drunk *US, 1990*

pump *noun* 1 the heart *US, 1946*. 2 a fart *UK: SCOTLAND, 1985*. 3 a fire hydrant *US, 1979*. 4 an illegal linear amplifier for a citizens' band radio *US, 1976*

pump *verb* 1 to have sex, usually from the male perspective *UK, 1730*. 2 to exert yourself in a labour *US, 1992*. 3 to obtain a free ride *BARBADOS, 1965*. 4 to interrogate someone *UK, 1656*. 5 to fart *UK: NORTHERN IRELAND, 1937*. 6 to sell drugs, especially crack cocaine *US, 1989*. 7 in poker, to increase a bet made by another player *US, 1983*. ▶ **pump the stump** to shake hands *US, 1947*

pumped *adjective* pregnant *US, 1969*

pumped up *adjective* **1** with muscles inflated and defined *US, 1997*. **2** excited, energised. Current usage is informed by bodybuilding jargon with muscles 'pumped up' for display *UK, 1791*

pump gas *noun* petrol as it is available to the general public, which must be used in some drag racing events *US, 1970*

pumpie *noun* a pump-action shotgun *AUSTRALIA, 1995*

pumping *adjective* **1** (used of contemporary dance music, and of the atmosphere it generates) exciting, energetic *UK, 1999*. **2** (used of surf conditions) powerful, excellent *US, 1977*

pump iron; pump *verb* to exercise by lifting weights. Sports jargon; possibly from PUMP UP (to inflate muscles) *US, 1972*

pump jockey *noun* a petrol station attendant *US, 1966*

pumpkin *noun* **1** used as a sentimental term of address. The affectionate tone of the term of address runs counter to the earlier sense of an 'ineffective, incompetent person' *US, 1998*. **2** in car repair, a pumpkin-shaped differential cover *US, 1992*. **3** in trucking, a flat tyre *US, 1971*

pumpkin belly *noun* the abdomen of a pregnant woman *TRINIDAD AND TOBAGO, 1973*

pumpkin positive *adjective* unintelligent. A doctors' joke: if you shine a light in the mouth, the head will light up. Recorded in an article about medical slang in British (3 London and 1 Cambridge) hospitals by *UK, 2003*

pumpkin seed *noun* a yellow, oblong mescaline tablet *US, 1971*

pumpkin time *noun* a curfew. An allusion to the Cinderella tale *US, 1970*

pump monkey *noun* a petrol station attendant *US, 1961*

pump off *verb* (of a male) to masturbate *UK, 1937*

pumps *noun* **1** the female breasts *US, 1949*. **2** trainers, sneakers *BARBADOS, 1996*

pum-pum *noun* the vagina *JAMAICA, 1972*

pump up *verb* **1** to increase something, to inflate something, to turn something higher *US, 1987*. **2** when lifting weights, to engorge the muscles with blood in order to inflate and define them *US, 1984*. **3** to conduct an exhaustive and detailed briefing *US, 1986*. **4** while gambling, to lose at a steady rate *US, 1980*

punani *noun* the vagina; hence a woman regarded as a sexual object; hence sex with a woman. Probably West Indian. The etymology is uncertain, possibly rooted in POONTANG (the vagina, hence sex). Variant spellings include 'punany'; 'punyani'; 'punaany'; 'punanny'; 'pudenany'; 'punnanny'; 'punaani'; 'poonani'. Black slang, popularised in the wider community by comedian Ali G (Sacha Baron-Cohen, b.1970) and rap music *UK, 1972*. ▶ **ride the punani** to have sex. West Indian slang popularised in the UK in the late 1990s by comedy character Ali G (Sacha Baron-Cohen) *UK, 2003*

punch *noun* **1** an act of sexual intercourse; a person viewed only in terms of sex *US, 1983*. **2** in volleyball, a one-fist overhead pass or volley *US, 1985*

punch *verb* **1** to open something by force. Most commonly, but not exclusively, applied to breaking into a safe *US, 1931*. **2** to have sex *US, 1971*. **3** in a card cheating scheme, to prepare a deck for a manoeuvre *US, 1962*. ▶ **punch it 1** to accelerate to high speed *US, 1987*. **2** to escape (from prison) *US, 1990*. ▶ **punch someone's ticket 1** to kill someone *US, 1983*. **2** to have sex with someone *US, 1992*. ▶ **punch the sun** while driving, to accelerate to make it through an intersection on a yellow light *US, 1997*

Punch and Judy *noun* deception; an unbelievable story. Formed on traditional puppet characters whose tale of domestic disharmony and dishonesty, perhaps, informs the sense *UK, 1992*

punchboard *noun* a sexually available and promiscuous woman. A 'punchboard' is a game which used to be found in shops, where for a price the customer punched one of many holes on the board in the hope of winning a prize *US, 1977*

Punch Bowl *noun* a valley on the east-central coast of Korea formed by the Taebaek-San Maek Mountains, home to some of the bitterest battles of the war *US, 1989*

punch buggie *noun* a Volkswagen 'Beetle' car. Shouted by the first child in a car to see it, which entitles him or her to slug all other children playing the game *US, 1997*

punch-drunk *adjective* of a boxer, deranged or debilitated to some degree as a result of punches received. Hence the condition of being punch-drunk: 'punch-drunkenness' *US, 1918*

puncher *noun* a safe cracker *US, 1949*

punching bag *noun* a promiscuous woman. From PUNCH in its sexual sense *US, 1974*

punch-in-the-mouth *noun* oral sex on a woman *US, 1967*

punch job *noun* a safe robbery in which the combination lock is punched out to gain access to the safe *US, 1958*

punch-out *noun* in Keno, a template with 20 holes punched out for the numbers called in a game, used to compare a player's ticket with the winning numbers *US, 1972*

punch out *verb* **1** to beat someone up *US, 1969*. **2** to leave *US, 1998*. **3** to eject someone from a fighter plane *US, 1986*

punch-up *noun* a fist fight *UK, 1958*

punch up *verb* to enhance something, especially to enhance a script with humour, more lively dialogue, or the like. In the 1950s, the entertainment industry used the term to mean to increase the volume of the sound track or brightness of the picture. Towards the end of the century, the meaning changed to a writing term *US, 1984*

punchy *adjective* discomposed, deranged. Abbreviated from punch-drunk *UK, 1985*

punga *noun* the penis *NEW ZEALAND, 1998*

punishing *adjective* exhausting, gruelling *UK, 1882*

punishment *noun* severe handling; pain, misery *UK, 1811*. ▶ **put to the punishment** in horse racing, to use any physicality such as whipping or kicking to an extreme degree *US, 1951*

punk *noun* **1** a fan of punk rock music and the associated fashions *UK, 1976*. **2** a young and/or weak man used as a passive homosexual partner, especially in prison *US, 1904*. **3** a child *US, 1985*. **4** a lesbian *BAHAMAS, 1982*. **5** in horse racing, a mildly talented jockey *US, 1951*. **6** marijuana *UK, 2003*. **7** the middle position in the back seat of a car *US, 1980*

punk *verb* **1** to have anal sex with someone *US, 1949*. **2** to assault someone *US, 1991*

punk *adjective* poor, lousy, inferior *US, 1896*

punkasals *noun* trainers, sneakers *GRENADA, 1996*

punker *noun* **1** a fan of punk music *US, 1989*. **2** a punk rock song *UK, 2003*

punkette *noun* a female follower of punk music and fashion *US, 1982*

punkfucker *noun* a male prisoner who has sex with homosexual prisoners, especially taking the active role *US, 1972*

punk-hunt *verb* to search for homosexuals and assault them for the sole reason of their homosexuality *US, 1968*

punki; punkin *noun* the vagina. Children's vocabulary *TRINIDAD AND TOBAGO, 1973*

punk in the bunk *noun* used for expressing the fact that the speaker has an effeminate homosexual prisoner under his control *US, 1984*

punk out *verb* **1** to withdraw from a task out of fear *US, 1920*. **2** to inform on or betray a compatriot *US, 1976*

punk pill *noun* any central nervous system depressant *US, 1968*

punk ride *noun* an amusement ride for children *US, 1985*

punk rock; punk *noun* a genre of basic, high-energy rock music that came to prominence in the mid-1970s *US, 1972*

punks *noun* an unsophisticated, rural audience *US, 1952*

punksy *adjective* spunky *BARBADOS, 1965*

punk tank *noun* a holding cell in a jail or prison reserved for homosexuals *US, 1972*

punny eccy; punny *noun* in school, a piece of written work given as a punishment. From a shortening of *'punishment exercise'*; used by Glasgow teachers and pupils *UK: SCOTLAND, 1988*

punt *noun* **1** a gamble; a chance *AUSTRALIA, 1958*. **2** gambling *AUSTRALIA, 1988*

punt *verb* **1** to gamble *UK, 1873*. **2** to do poorly; to give up in some fashion because you are doing poorly. A metaphor from American football, where a team that has not advanced the ball ten yards after three plays will often choose to punt the ball to its opposition rather than risk giving up field position *US, 1968*. **3** to vomit *IRELAND, 1996*. ▶ **punt the pail** to die. A jocular variation of KICK THE BUCKET *UK: SCOTLAND, 1988*

punta-rosa *noun* a hybrid marijuana from Mexico *MEXICO, 2003*

punter *noun* **1** a customer, a consumer; in the plural, an audience *UK, 1965*. **2** a prostitute's customer *UK, 1970*. **3** a gambler *UK, 1873*. **4** a drug dealer's customer *UK, 2000*. **5** a confidence trickster's victim *UK, 1934*

pup *noun* **1** a young person *US, 1964*. **2** the early part (of some specified period). Most commonly in the phrase 'the night's a pup' (the night is still young) *AUSTRALIA, 1915*. **3** in the television and film industries, a 500-watt light source mounted on a stand *UK, 1960*

puppies *noun* the female breasts *US, 2000*. ▶ **like two puppies under a blanket; like two puppies fighting under a blanket** used by men as an appreciation or critical commentary of a female posterior, especially one in undulating motion *UK: SCOTLAND, 2003*. ▶ **the puppies** greyhound racing or coursing. A play on THE DOGS *AUSTRALIA, 1984*

puppies in a box *noun* in the pornography business, a group of bare-breasted women cavorting *US, 1991*

puppy *noun* **1** a person of a specified type *US, 2004*. **2** a fierce one. New York police slang *US, 1997*. **3** a small penis *US, 1980*. **4** in pool, a shot that cannot be missed or a game that cannot be lost *US, 1990*. **5** a small bottle of wine *US, 1980*. **6** a gun. Jamaican gang terminology *US, 1995*

puppyfoot *noun* in a deck of playing cards, a club, especially the ace *US, 1967*

puppy love *noun* a youthful infatuation *US, 1834*

puppy lover *noun* a person who is completely infatuated with someone *US, 1970*

puppy paws; puppy feet *noun* in craps, a ten rolled with a pair of fives *US, 1981*

puppy show *noun* an act that makes you look foolish *BAHAMAS, 1995*

pup tents *noun* in circus and carnival usage, overshoes *US, 1981*

Purdey *noun* a Hillman Avenger (a popular car manufactured in the UK from 1969–82). Citizens' band radio slang; from the tongue-in-cheek spy adventure television series *The New Avengers* (1976–77) which featured actress Joanna Lumley as Purdey, a character named by the actress after a world-renowned shotgun *UK, 1981*

pure *noun* pure, unadulterated heroin *US, 1967*

pure *adverb* absolutely, entirely, utterly; used as a general intensifier *UK, 2001*

pure! surely! *US, 1993*

pure-food law *noun* on the railways, a crew sent to relieve a crew that has reached the maximum work hours allowed by law *US, 1977*

pure laine *noun* in Quebec, a French person who claims direct ancestry among the original French settlers. The phrase means 'pure wool', but even anglophones say 'pure laine' *CANADA, 2001*

pure love *noun* LSD *US, 1977*

pure merino *noun* a person who can trace their ancestry back to free settlers (as opposed to convict transportees) *AUSTRALIA, 1826*

purge *noun* an alcoholic drink *NEW ZEALAND, 1994*

purl; pearl *verb* (used of the nose of a surfboard) to plunge under the surface of the ocean *US, 1963*

purler; pearler *noun* a thing of outstanding excellence or beauty *AUSTRALIA, 1941*

purple *noun* the recreational drug ketamine *US, 1994*

purple *adjective* sexually suggestive but not explicit. Not quite BLUE *US, 1986*

purple death *noun* inexpensive red wine *NEW ZEALAND, 1987*

purple gnome *noun* a variety of LSD *UK, 1996*

purple haze *noun* **1** LSD. Whether the drug inspired the song – 'Purple Haze all in my brain' (Jimi Hendrix, 'Purple Haze', 1967) – or the song inspired the branding is uncertain *US, 1967*. **2** a potent variety of marijuana. Named after the 1967 song by Jimi Hendrix *UK, 1996*

purple-headed love missile *noun* the erect penis. Jocular *UK, 2003*

purple-headed warrior; purple warrior *noun* the erect penis. This could almost be the superhero identity into which an ordinary comic book penis transforms *US, 1998*

purple-headed womb ferret *noun* the penis *UK, 2003*

purple heart *noun* **1** a capsule of phenobarbital (trade name Luminal™), a central nervous system depressant *US, 1966*. **2** a tablet of amphetamine Drinamyl™ used as a recreational drug. From the lilac colour of the pill; playing on the US military decoration awarded to any member of the armed forces wounded by the enemy. Also shortened to 'heart' or 'purple' *US, 1962*

purple-helmeted warrior *noun* ▶ **send in the purple-helmeted warrior** to have sex *US, 2001*

purple hempstar *noun* in British Columbia, a local variety of marijuana *CANADA, 2002*

purple Jesus *noun* an alcoholic drink based on grape juice *CANADA, 1991*

Purple Nike Swirl E *noun* a tablet MDMA, the recreational drug best known as ecstasy, with a Nike logo *UK, 2001*

purple nurple; purple herbie *noun* a violent gripping and twisting assault on someone's (usually a male's) nipples *UK, 2003*

purple ohm; purple om *noun* a type of LSD *UK: NORTHERN IRELAND, 2001*

purple Owsley *noun* a powerful type of LSD. From its colour and the name of legendary LSD manufacturer Augustus Owsley Stanley III. Other variations include 'purple dot'; 'purple dragon'; 'purple microdot'; 'purple owsky'; PURPLE OZOLIN and 'purple wedge' *US, 1970*

purple ozolin; purple ozoline; purple ozzy *noun* a powerful variety of LSD *US, 1986*

purple passion *noun* red wine *US, 1966*

purple patch *noun* a string of good luck *AUSTRALIA, 1989*

purple piccolo *noun* the erect penis *UK, 2003*

purple pickle *noun* the bar awarded to US Air Force flight officers *US, 1946*

purple-suiter *noun* a military officer assigned to the US Department of Defense *US, 1986*

purple Thai *noun* a variety of marijuana *CANADA, 2002*

purple warrior *noun* ▷*see:* PURPLE-HEADED WARRIOR

purr *noun* the belly. English gypsy use *UK, 2000*

purse play *noun* croquet played for money *US, 1997*

pus-ball *noun* ▷*see:* PUSS-BALL

push *noun* **1** a group of friends or associates; a clique. Originally 'push' referred to 'an organised gang of street hoodlums' *AUSTRALIA, 1884*. **2** in betting, a doubling of the bet in effect *US, 1986*. **3** in British Columbia logging, the boss, the foreman *CANADA, 1953*. **4** in blackjack, a tie between the dealer and a player *US, 1978*. **5** a radio frequency. As in 'the battalion push'. Vietnam war usage *US, 1968*. ▶ **the push** a dismissal from employment or romantic involvement *UK, 1875*

push *verb* **1** to sell something, especially drugs *US, 1938*. **2** to make a special effort to promote a professional wrestler's image and status *US, 2000*. ▶ **push poo-poo** to take the active role in anal sex *FIJI, 1997*. ▶ **push some leg** to have sex *US, 1983*. ▶ **push the boat out** to be more generous or extravagant than usual, to act generously; especially with money. Originally naval slang, used of someone buying a round of drinks *UK, 1937*. ▶ **push the bush** (used of a male) to have sex with a woman *US, 1984*. ▶ **push the**

envelope to challenge current parameters. From aviation where ENVELOPE is the limit of a plane's range and powers, via 1990s' marketing speak US, 1998. ▶ **push up the daisies; pushing up the daisies** to be dead, especially dead and buried; use is occasionally extended to the dying. An image first sketched as dated 'turn up your toes to the daisies' in 1842 – from which we derive turn up your toes, (to die). Other variations that have slipped from use: 'under the daisies', 'kick up daisies' and, less certainly, 'grin at the daisy-roots', which may also relate to 'roots' (boots) UK, 1918. ▶ **push your luck** to take a risk UK, 1911

push-bike noun a bicycle. The 'push' providing a motive distinction from a motorbike UK, 1913

pushed adjective short of something, usually time or money UK, 1942

pusher noun **1** a drug dealer US, 1935. **2** in the circus or carnival, a foreman US, 1980

push-in noun a robbery accomplished by knocking on a door and pushing your way into a house or apartment US, 1982

pushing adverb of years of age, approaching, nearly UK, 1974

push in the bush noun vaginal sex US, 1980

push in the truck noun an instance of sexual intercourse. Rhyming slang for FUCK in the transport industry UK, 1992

pushke noun a drive soliciting funds. The term comes from Yiddish, and derives from a charitable collection box in Jewish homes passed around on Sabbath eve to collect for philanthropic purposes CANADA, 2002

push-me-toe noun any thong sandal TRINIDAD AND TOBAGO, 2003

push-oline noun gasoline, petrol US, 1977

push out in the language of hang gliding, used as an all-purpose greeting or farewell US, 1992

pushover noun **1** someone who is gullible or easily manipulated; a person who is easily persuaded into sexual activity US, 1944. **2** something that is easy to do US, 1906

pushunder noun a chamber pot BARBADOS, 1965

push water noun petrol or diesel fuel US, 1977

pushy adjective **1** self-assertive, especially when unpleasantly so US, 1936. **2** used of a woman, in the second stage of labour US, 1994

pusillanimous polecat noun used as a general term of disapproval. A term used by George 'Gramps' Miller, played by George Cleveland, on the television drama Lassie (CBS, 1954–57). Repeated with referential humour US, 1957

puss noun **1** the vagina; sex UK, 1958. **2** a girl or woman; an effeminate man UK, 1991. **3** a 'feminine' lesbian UK, 1977. **4** the mouth; the face. A term hatched simultaneously in Ireland and the US US, 1891. **5** a disgruntled facial expression. From Irish pus IRELAND, 2004

puss-ball; pus-ball noun a contemptible person UK, 2003

puss boots noun trainers, sneakers JAMAICA, 1996

pusser; pusser's adjective official. Royal Navy slang, adapted from the old navy rank of Purser; used in many combinations UK, 1987

pusser's noun rum. Royal Navy slang; derives from 'pusser's ' (official issue), not to be confused with branded Pusser's Rum UK, 1989

pusser's brown noun toilet paper. Royal Navy slang UK, 1984

pusser's cow noun tinned milk. Naval slang AUSTRALIA, 1943

pusser's dip noun a candle. Royal Navy slang; originally 'purser's dip' UK, 1948

pusser's dirk noun a service clasp-knife. Royal Navy slang; a variant of 'pusser's dagger' UK, 1960

pusser's dust noun instant coffee powder. Royal Navy slang UK, 1988

pusser's fix-all noun WD40™, a multi-purpose lubricant. Royal Navy slang UK, 1988

pusser's hard noun navy-issue soap. Royal Navy slang UK, 1962

pusser's leaf noun navy-issue rolling tobacco. Royal Navy slang UK, 1988

pusser's medal noun a food stain on clothing. Royal Navy slang UK, 1988

pussified adjective effeminate US, 1994

pussin noun the vagina; a woman as a sexual object TRINIDAD AND TOBAGO, 1993

pussy noun **1** the vagina; a woman as a sexual object; sex UK, 1880. **2** the mouth (as an object of sexual penetration) US, 1988. **3** a weak or effeminate boy or man; a coward US, 1942. **4** a fur skin or fur garment. Criminals' slang UK, 1937. **5** anchovies. Based on the puerile comparison of the smell of fish and the vagina US, 1996. **6** the middle position in the back seat of a car US, 1980. ▶ **pet the pussy** (of a female) to masturbate US, 2001. ▶ **sling pussy** to work as a prostitute US, 1990

pussy adjective weak; effeminate; not manly US, 1986

pussy; pussy in verb to move quietly; to enter unobtrusively. To a degree synonymous with conventional 'pussyfoot' AUSTRALIA, 1975

pussy-ass noun a weak or effeminate man; a coward US, 1995

pussy beard noun female pubic hair US, 1967

pussy bumping noun genital-to-genital lesbian sex US, 1949

pussycat; pussy cat noun **1** the vagina US, 1980. **2** a sexually attractive woman US, 1965. **3** a pleasant, surprisingly gentle or amenable person US, 1978

pussy cat has a nosebleed a woman who is in the bleed period of the menstrual cycle. A euphemistic elaboration on PUSSYCAT (the vagina) US, 2001

pussyclot; pussyclaat noun someone despicable. Combines PUSSY (vagina) and 'clot' (West Indian pronunciation of 'cloth') to mean 'sanitary towel'; however 'clot' may be understood conventionally as coagulated blood which intensifies the insult JAMAICA, 1978

pussy cloth noun any improvised sanitary towel JAMAICA, 1985

pussy collar noun a desire for sex US, 1963

pussycratic adjective obsessed with sex JAMAICA, 1976

pussy drunk noun a sex offender; a rapist UK, 1996

pussy eater noun a practitioner of oral sex on women US, 2002

pussy fart noun an eruption of trapped air from the vagina during sexual intercourse US, 1995

pussyfence noun a receiver of stolen furs UK, 1956

pussy finger noun the index finger US, 1977

pussyfoot verb to act with such caution that your behaviour appears evasive or cowardly. From the cautious progress of cats US, 1903

pussyfooter noun a railway police officer US, 1977

pussy game noun prostitution US, 1978

pussy hair noun female pubic hair US, 1969

pussy holder noun the passenger seat on a motorcyle US, 1967

pussy hole noun a despicable person or object; used abusively. A synonym for CUNT; seemingly euphemistic but possibly more derogatory than the original PUSSY (the vagina), with extra detail UK, 1994

pussyhole noun a despised person UK, 2006

pussy hook noun a thief who specialises in stealing furs. A combination of PUSSY (a fur) and HOOK (a thief) UK, 1956

pussy hound noun a man obsessed with sex and women US, 1984

pussy lips noun the labia US, 1969

pussy man noun a pimp US, 1967

pussy Nellie; pussy Nelly noun a male homosexual. Mainly naval usage, apparently from early in the C20 UK, 1984

pussy out verb to back out of a task because of fear US, 1992

pussy patrol; pussy posse; pussy squad noun a police vice squad focusing on prostitution US, 1973

pussy posse noun **1** a police vice squad UK, 1963. **2** a group of female friends US, 2001

pussy queer noun a lesbian US, 1982

pussy-seller noun a prostitute BAHAMAS, 1982

pussysucker; pussysugger noun the mouth US, 1964

pussywhip *verb* (used of a woman) to dominate a man *US, 1974*

pussy-whipped *adjective* dominated by a woman *US, 1956*

pussy whisker *noun* a pubic hair *US, 1986*

pussy willow *noun* a pillow. Rhyming slang *UK, 1968*

pussy-wood *noun* stolen firewood. Coalminers' use *UK, 1984*

put *verb* to dilute a drug *US, 1992*. ▶ **put a (number) on** to dilute a drug by the identified numerical factor *US, 1971*. ▶ **put it about** to be sexually promiscuous *UK, 1975*. ▶ **put it on** to declare hostilities with another youth gang *US, 1953*. ▶ **put it to someone** to have sex with someone *UK, 2001*. ▶ **put me in** give me some drugs *UK, 1985*. ▶ **put next to** to introduce one person to another or to acquaint one person with another *US, 1906*. ▶ **put on** to fool someone, to tease someone, to deceive someone *US, 1958*. ▶ **put one on 1** to plan a crime *UK, 1996*. **2** to hit or punch someone *UK, 1974*. ▶ **put paid to** to put a stop to something *UK, 1919*. ▶ **put yourself about 1** to get around and be seen. Originally police usage, now widespread probably as a result of television and film crime dramas *UK, 1970*. **2** to work as a prostitute. A variation of the previous sense *UK, 1980*

puta *noun* a sexually promiscuous woman; a prostitute. From Spanish *puta* (a whore) *US, 1964*

put away *verb* **1** to eat or drink something especially in large quantities *UK, 1878*. **2** to put someone in jail *UK, 1883*. **3** to bribe a jockey to lose a race *UK, 1978*

put-down *noun* a verbal belittling or criticism *UK, 1984*

put down *verb* **1** to belittle someone; to treat someone with humiliating contempt *US, 1958*. **2** to euthanise an animal *UK, 1899*. **3** to implicate someone as guilty *US, 1965*

put it there used as a greeting, soliciting a handshake *US, 1978*

puto *noun* a male homosexual. Border Spanish used by English-speakers in the American southwest *US, 1965*

puto mark *verb* to cross something out. *Puto* is Spanish slang for 'a male prostitute' *US, 2000*

put-on *adjective* affected, insincere *UK, 1621*

put out *verb* **1** to consent to sex *US, 1947*. **2** to be deserving of some punishment *IRELAND, 1997*

put-put *noun* ▷ *see:* **PHAT-PHAT**

putrid *adjective* excellent; brilliant *AUSTRALIA, 1993*

put some water on it! used as a demand that a person using a communal toilet flush to rid the room of the smell of faeces *US, 2001*

putt *verb* to fart. Also used as noun; a childish variation of POOT, probably coined in the mid-1990s by Sylvia Branzei for *Grossology US, 1996*

putter *noun* in hot rodding, a car that has been customised for show rather than performance and is used for 'putting around' *US, 1993*

put the name in the hat *verb* to inform *UK, 1996*

putting green *noun* in pool, the largest regulation-size table *US, 1990*

putt-putt *noun* a boat or vehicle with a puny motor *US, 1959*

putty *noun* ▶ **up to putty** no good *AUSTRALIA, 1916*

put up *verb* to serve time in prison *US, 1976*

put-up job *noun* a pre-arranged deception *UK, 1838*

put up or shut up! used as a challenge to take action to defend what you say, or be quiet *US, 1878*

put you up to *verb* to incite, induce or persuade you to do something *UK, 1824*

putz *noun* **1** the penis *US, 1934*. **2** by extension, an inept, contemptible person *US, 1964*

putz *verb* ▶ **putz around** to idle; to do nothing; to waste time *US, 1972*

PW *adjective* dominated by a female. An abbreviation of PUSSY-WHIPPED *US, 1966*

p-whipped *adjective* dominated by a female. An abbreviated and euphemised PUSSY-WHIPPED *US, 1999*

pyjama cricket; pyjama game *noun* one-day cricket. So-called from the colourful uniforms worn by players instead of the usual cricket whites *AUSTRALIA, 1982*

pyjama-python *noun* the penis *AUSTRALIA, 1971*

pylons *noun* the legs *US, 1947*

PYO Pick-Your-Own, applied to soft fruits and farm vegetables. Usually seen in roadside advertising *UK, 1982*

pyro *noun* a pyromaniac; pyrotechnics *UK, 1977*

python *noun* the penis *AUSTRALIA, 1971*

Pythonesque *adjective* of an event, or series of events, more than bizarre but less than surreal. From the television comedy series *Monty Python's Flying Circus*, BBC, 1969–74 *UK, 1979*

Qq

Q *noun* **1** a homosexual. An abbreviation of QUEER *US, 1968*. **2** of drugs, generally marijuana, a quarter of an ounce *UK, 1997*. **3** the recreational drug methaqualone, best known as Quaaludes™ *US, 1977*. **4** in a deck of playing cards, a queen *US, 1991*. **5** barbecue *US, 2001*. **6** in American casinos, a $25 chip. An abbreviation of QUARTER *US, 1983*

Q *nickname* the San Quentin state prison in San Rafael, California *US, 1951*

Q and A a question and answer session *US, 1997*

qat *noun* **1** methcathinone *US, 2003*. **2** leaves of *catha edulis*, a stimulant also called K, khat or kat, originating in the Horn of Africa and the Arabian peninsula, legally available in the UK and similar to amphetamine in effect when chewed. Also known as 'qaadka' *UK, 1996*

Q boat *noun* an unmarked police car with plain clothes officers. From the name given to disguised naval vessels in World War 1 *UK, 1977*

QE *verb* to turn Queen's Evidence (to give evidence for the prosecution against your alleged accomplices) *UK, 1996*

Q-ship *noun* among hot rodders, a high-performing car that appears to be a conventional car. Taken from the early C20 meaning of an armed and camouflaged merchant ship used as a decoy *US, 1965*

Q-sign *noun* of a very sick hospital patient, the open mouth with the tongue hanging out. Medical wit; the 'Q' is an image of the mouth and tongue as described. The O-SIGN is not quite as serious *UK, 2002*

QT *noun* ▶ **on the QT** quietly, in strict confidence *UK, 1884*

Q tip *noun* in poker, a queen and a ten *US, 1996*

quack *noun* **1** a doctor of medicine. Following an earlier (mid-C17) sense as 'a pretended doctor', abbreviated from 'quacksalver' (one who sells his salves by noisy patter or 'quacking'). The current sense, spread through military use, does not imply any lack of qualification or a degree of salesmanship *AUSTRALIA, 1919*. **2** a hospital patient who feigns symptoms in order to receive attention, prescription medication or both *US, 1978*. **3** in poker, a player who complains loudly when losing *US, 1979*. **4** the recreational drug methaqualone, best known as Quaaludes™ *US, 1985*. **5** a firefighter. New York police slang *US, 1997*. **6** a novice surfer *US, 1977*

quacker *noun* a Kawasaki motorcycle *UK, 1979*

quackery *noun* forensic scientists; a forensic science department. Police use; always used with 'the'. Probably a pun on QUACK (a doctor) *UK, 1971*

quackie *noun* a white person *TRINIDAD AND TOBAGO, 1971*

quack-quack *noun* **1** a duck. An echoic term, used by, or to, infants *UK, 1865*. **2** a commotion *TRINIDAD AND TOBAGO, 1982*

quad *noun* **1** a quadriplegic *US, 1980*. **2** in trucking, a quadriplex transmission that provides twenty forward gears and four reverse *US, 1971*. **3** the recreational drug methaqualone, best known as Quaaludes™ *US, 1980*. **4** a carburettor with four barrels *US, 1965*. **5** a clumsy, inept fool. An evolved SQUARE *CANADA, 1993*

quad-fifty *noun* a quadruple mount .50 calibre machine gun, a devastating truck-drawn trailer-mounted weapon. Originated in World War 2 *US, 1953*

quadruplets *noun* in poker, four cards of the same rank *US, 1979*

quads *noun* **1** the quadriceps muscles *US, 1984*. **2** in poker, a hand with all four cards of the same rank *US, 1996*

quaff *verb* to drink alcohol *UK, 1955*

quail *noun* **1** a woman *US, 1859*. **2** a girl under the legal age of consent. A shortened form of SAN QUENTIN QUAIL *US, 1976*. **3** a twenty-five cent betting token used in of craps *US, 1983*

Quaker oat *noun* a coat. Rhyming slang, formed from Quaker Oats™, a brand of porridge *UK, 1932*

quality *noun* ▶ **the quality** anyone who is not a member of the travelling community *IRELAND, 1993*

quango *noun* a government-financed, notionally independent body with a powerful interest in a given field of interest. An acronym for *Quasi* Non-Government(al) Organisation or *Quasi*-Autonomous National Government Organisation *UK, 1973*

quanker *noun* in Nova Scotia, a duck-calling device *CANADA, 1945*

quare *adjective* mediocre *UK, 1983*

quare hawk *noun* someone who is unconventional in some way *IRELAND, 1989*

quare one *noun* wife *IRELAND, 1997*

quar ice *noun* water that has oozed through the ground through snow and frozen on the surface *CANADA, 1955*

quarked out *adjective* under the influence of drugs *US, 1999*

quarm *verb* (used of a man) to behave in an exaggerated, effeminate manner *BAHAMAS, 1982*

quart *noun* **1** a twenty-five cent piece *BARBADOS, 1965*. **2** in poker, four cards of the same suit in sequence *US, 1979*

quarter *noun* **1** a quarter of an ounce of drugs, especially cocaine *US, 1968*. **2** a quarter of a kilo of drugs *UK, 1996*. **3** twenty-five dollars' worth of drugs. Also called a 'quarter bag' *US, 2001*. **4** a prison sentence of 25 years *US, 1964*. **5** a jail sentence of three months. Also referred to as 'quarter bit' and 'quarter stretch' *UK, 1977*. **6** in American casinos, a $25 chip *US, 1980*. **7** twenty-five pounds of weights used in lifting *US, 1989*. **8** a cigarette *US, 1958*

quarter bird *noun* one quarter pound of cocaine *US, 1999*

quarter-deck *verb* during US Marine Corps basic training, to administer physical discipline or Incentive Physical Training *US, 2004*

quarter house *noun* a place where mid-level heroin dealers do business *US, 1978*

quarter rock *noun* crack cocaine *US, 1993*

quart store *noun* a store that sells beer on the retail level *US, 1997*

quartz *noun* methamphetamine that is smoked *UK, 1998*

Quasar *noun* a woman. A strained allusion to a Quasar television advertising slogan – 'works in a drawer', and then punning on 'drawers' as an item of female underwear *UK, 1976*

quashie *noun* a country-dweller; an unsophisticated peasant. Possibly from C18 *Quashee*, an African name, adopted by white people as a general name for any black person *UK, 1997*

Quasimodo *noun* soda water. Rhyming slang, formed from 'The Hunchback of Notre Dame' *UK, 1992*

quat *noun* in betting, odds of 4–1 *UK, 1991*

quater *noun* twenty-five cents. A corruption of 'quarter' *US, 1980*

quater; quarter; quaterer *adjective* four. Polari, from Italian *quattro* *UK, 1996*

quaver *verb* **1** to dither, especially over whether or not to make a purchase *UK, 1979*. **2** to potter about; to tinker *UK, 1979*

quaverer *noun* a vacillating, or uncertain, customer. From QUAVER *UK, 1979*

quawk *noun* uncooked frozen meat or fish *CANADA, 1947*

quay; quas *noun* the recreational drug methaqualone, best known as Quaaludes™ *US, 1997*

quean *noun* **1** an effeminate male homosexual; an ageing passive homosexual *UK, 1935*. **2** a lesbian. A term used by male homosexuals *UK, 1984*

quean up *verb* in male homosexual society, to adopt girlish mannerisms and affectations; to use cosmetics and to primp. British gay slang *UK, 1972*

queased out *adjective* nauseated, sick *US, 1993*

Quebec wrench *noun* a beer bottle opener. The high consumption rate of beer in Quebec is the source of this oral slang item *CANADA, 2001*

queber *noun* a social outcast *US, 1987*

queeb *noun* a bisexual *US, 1988*

queef *noun* the passing of air from the vagina *US, 2002*

queef *verb* to expel air from the vagina, intentionally or not *US, 2000*

queen *noun* **1** an obviously homosexual male *AUSTRALIA, 1924*. **2** a mother. As the ruler of the house *UK, 2002*. **3** a popular girl *US, 1959*. **4** a girlfriend, mistress or prostitute *US, 1968*. **5** an enthusiast of the preceding thing or activity *US, 1999*

Queen *noun* ▶ **for the Queen** used to describe extra days added as punishment to a sentence of imprisonment *UK, 1996*. ▶ **go Queen's; turn Queen's** to turn Queen's evidence, that is, to give evidence against co-defendants, usually to your own advantage *UK, 1996*. ▶ **the Queen** the National Anthem. Before this we stood for 'the King' *UK, 1952*

Queen Anne is dead a catchphrase retort on old news. Later variations – 'Queen Elizabeth and my Lord Baldwin' – have not survived *UK, 1722*

queen bee *noun* **1** the alpha male in a group of homosexuals. Punning on QUEAN. *The Guild Dictionary of Homosexual Terms*, 1965, offers this definition: 'usually, but not always, an auntie with money, an entourage, and numbers (sex-partners). Frequently he is elderly and, most always, an agreeable person.' *US, 1965*. **2** a heterosexual woman who seeks out the company of homosexual men *US, 1957*

Queen Charlotte tuxedo *noun* a heavy grey Stanfield's undershirt *CANADA, 1989*

queenie *noun* a prostitute *US, 1964*

Queenie *nickname* Queensland, Australia *AUSTRALIA, 1994*

Queen Mary *noun* **1** a surfboard that is too big for the surfer using it. Named after the ocean liner, not a royal female *US, 1964*. **2** a large tank truck. An ocean liner reference *US, 1954*

Queen of Mean *nickname* Leona Helmsley (b.1920), American hotelier and prototype of greed during the Reagan era *US, 1997*

Queen of the Jukebox *nickname* Dinah Washington (1924–1963), a brilliant vocalist in the jazz, pop and R&B genres *US, 1975*

Queen of the South *noun* the mouth. Rhyming slang, formed from the name of a Scottish football club *UK, 1992*

Queen's Cowboys *nickname* the Royal Canadian Mounted Police *CANADA, 1989*

queen's gaff *noun* the anus. An allusion to WINDSOR CASTLE, a royal GAFF (residence) in Berkshire which also serves as rhyming slang for 'arsehole' *UK, 1992*

Queenslander *noun* a type of weatherboard house raised on stilts *AUSTRALIA, 1994*

Queen's Necklace *nickname* in Mumbai, the view after dark of the sparkling lights on Marine Drive (now Netaji Subhash Road) *INDIA, 2002*

Queens Park Ranger *noun* a stranger. Rhyming slang, formed from the full name of QPR, the London football club, Queens Park Rangers *UK, 1961*

queen's row *noun* an area in a prison reserved for blatantly homosexual prisoners *US, 1967*

Queen Street bushie; Queen Street cowboy; Queen Street ringer *noun* in Queensland, a city person with pretences to country living, such as dressing like a cowboy or driving a 4WD *AUSTRALIA, 2003*

queen tank *noun* a jail holding cell reserved for flamboyantly effeminate homosexual men *US, 1988*

queeny *adjective* **1** blatantly homosexual *US, 1979*. **2** showy, melodramatic, affected *US, 1997*

queer *noun* **1** a homosexual man or a lesbian. Usually pejorative, but also a male homosexual term of self-reference within the gay underground and subculture *US, 1914*. **2** counterfeit money *UK, 1812*

queer *verb* to spoil something; to ruin something; to interfere with something *UK, 1812*. ▶ **queer a pitch** to spoil a situation or a circumstance; to undermine someone's efforts *UK, 1875*

queer *adjective* **1** homosexual. Derogatory from the outside, not from within *US, 1914*. **2** catering to or patronised by homosexuals *US, 1957*. **3** driven by deep and perverse sexual desires *US, 1967*. **4** not good; out of fashion. Like 'gay', 'queer' has been hijacked from its homosexual context *US, 1997*. **5** counterfeit *US, 1951*. ▶ **to be queer for** to be fond of someone or something *US, 1953*

queer and nasty, try another service *nickname* the Australian airline QANTAS. Most airlines seem to be the subject of jocular puns. 'Queers and Nancies Trading as Stewards' had some circulation in the 1980s *AUSTRALIA, 2002*

queer as a clockwork orange *adjective* **1** obviously homosexual. Plays on QUEER (unusual/homosexual) *UK, 1973*. **2** unusual or suspicious. Predates the novel *Clockwork Orange* (1962) by Anthony Burgess *UK, 1980*

queer as a four-speed walking stick *adjective* unusual; ostentatiously homosexual. Popularised by raconteur 'Blaster' Bates (b.1922) *UK, 1984*

queer as a left-handed corkscrew *adjective* unusual; ostentatiously homosexual *UK, 1970s*

queer as a nine-bob note *adjective* **1** ostentatiously homosexual. Plays on QUEER (unusual/homosexual) *UK, 1984*. **2** unusual or suspicious. The most 'queer' (unusual) thing about a nine BOB (shilling) note is that it has never existed; the phrase survived decimalisation in 1971, which 'bob' failed to do *UK, 1984*

queer as a nine-bob watch *adjective* suspicious. So cheap it must be suspect *UK, 1984*

queer as a three-dollar bill *adjective* ostentatiously homosexual *US, 1966*

queer as fuck *adjective* definitely homosexual; ostentatiously gay. QUEER (homosexual) plus 'as fuck' (an intensifier); punned in the popular television drama series about gay culture, *Queer As Folk AUSTRALIA, 1997*

queerbait; queer-bait *noun* a man who commands the attention of homosexual men, whether he is homosexual or not *US, 1957*

queer-bashing *verb* an attack (usually physical) of a homosexual because of his sexuality *UK, 1970*

queer beer *noun* weak, watery beer. More commonly reduplicated as 'near beer' *US, 1976*

queerie *noun* a homosexual *NEW ZEALAND, 1998*

queer jack *noun* counterfeit money *US, 1949*

queer-rolling *noun* the practice of attacking and robbing homosexuals *UK, 1977*

queer's lunch box *noun* the male crotch *US, 1964*

Queer Street *noun* ▶ **in Queer Street; on Queer Street** experiencing difficulties, especially financial difficulties; in a vulnerable position *UK, 1952*

queeve *verb* to experience a loss of energy *US, 1984*

quegg *noun* a homosexual. Possibly a compound of QUEER (homosexual or odd) and EGG (a person) *UK, 2001*

Quel Chagrin *noun* Queen's Counsel. From the initials QC *CANADA, 2002*

query *noun* a test or examination *US, 1976*

ques *noun* the question mark (?) character on a computer keyboard *US, 1991*

queue *noun* ▶ **put on a queue** (of a woman) to have sex with a line of partners, one after the other *AUSTRALIA, 1970*

quezzie *noun* a question *UK, 2002*

quiche-eater *noun* a sensitive male; an effeminate male *US, 1984*

quiche out *verb* to concede defeat in a cowardly manner; to behave in a weak or effeminate manner. Probably from the notion that 'real men don't eat quiche' *UK, 2006*

quick and dirty *adjective* constructed as quickly as possible *US, 1991*

Quickdraw McGraw *noun* the US Secret Service agent who is closest to the president. *Quickdraw McGraw* was a Hanna Barbera cartoon that first aired in 1959; ironically, the character Quickdraw McGraw was not a quick draw, but his name has survived, implying that which the character was not *US, 1981*

quick-go *noun* in a sport, a player who does not last very long on a team *US, 1972*

quickie *noun* **1** a sexual encounter that is carried out quickly *US, 1950*. **2** an alcoholic drink taken hastily *AUSTRALIA, 1969*. **3** something that is accomplished quickly *US, 1940*. **4** an unexpected, quickly executed manoeuvre or piece of trickery *US, 1950*

quickie *adjective* carried out quickly *US, 1940*

quick-lunch *noun* a fast-food small restaurant *CANADA, 1959*

quickness *noun* ▶ **with a quickness** as soon as possible *US, 1997*

quick one *noun* an unexpected act of betrayal *US, 1950*

quick one off the wrist *noun* ▷ *see:* ONE OFF THE WRIST

quick pussy *noun* a secure NATO communications system *CANADA, 1995*

quick-smart *adverb* quickly *AUSTRALIA, 1952*

quick-starts *noun* running shoes *US, 1990*

quick thinking, Batman! used for a humorous, if sarcastic, response to another's observation or conclusion. From the *Batman* comic and television series (1966–1968). The television series launched several catchphrases into the vocabulary to a far greater extent than the comic books had *US, 1968*

quick-turn burn *noun* the refuelling and reloading of an F-18 fighter jet in less than five minutes *US, 1991*

quid *noun* **1** a pound sterling; pounds sterling. Deriving perhaps from Latin *quid* (what?), later suggesting 'the wherewithal'. Note too UK dialect *quid* (a wad of tobacco). The quid has survived decimalisation (1971) and several centuries of inflation; originally coined as 'a guinea' (1 pound, 1 shilling), in C 19 it became 'a sovereign' *UK, 1688*. **2** some money. Still in use despite the fact that pounds went out in 1966 when Australia changed over to decimal currency (dollars and cents) *AUSTRALIA, 1976*. **3** five dollars. If a pound is five dollars, so must be a quid *US, 1988*. ▶ **not the full quid** without a full complement of intelligence *AUSTRALIA, 1944*

quid deal *noun* a drug sale involving one pound's worth of drugs, usually marijuana *UK, 1983*

quids *noun* a large amount of money *AUSTRALIA, 1930*. ▶ **not for quids** not for anything *AUSTRALIA, 1941*. ▶ **wouldn't be dead for quids** I am generally happy with my life and circumstances *AUSTRALIA, 1986*

quids in *adjective* prospering; at an advantage. Figurative use of actual profit measured by the QUID (£1) *UK, 1919*

quietie *noun* a quiet drink *AUSTRALIA, 1995*

quiet-side *adjective* secret *US, 1976*

quiff *noun* **1** the vagina; a woman as sex object; a prostitute. Archaic in the US, but understood in context *UK, 1923*. **2** by extension, a male homosexual *US, 1977*

quill *noun* **1** anything used to snort powdered drugs; the drugs themselves *US, 1935*. **2** cocaine *UK, 1998*. **3** heroin *UK, 1996*

quill pig *noun* a porcupine. Michigan Upper Peninsula usage *US, 2003*

quilty *adjective* luxurious *US, 1976*

quim *noun* the vagina; used objectively as a collective noun for women, especially sexually available women *UK, 1735*

quimby *noun* a person completely lacking in social graces *US, 1997*

quimmo *noun* a fool; an unpleasant individual. Extending QUIM (the vagina) as a synonym for CUNT *UK, 1999*

quince *noun* an effeminate male; a homosexual *AUSTRALIA, 1941*. ▶ **get on your quince** to annoy you *AUSTRALIA, 1941*

quinella *noun* in horse racing, a bet on the first two to finish in either order *US, 1991*

quinine *noun* in the game of craps, the number nine *US, 1950*

quint *noun* in poker, five cards of the same suit in sequence *US, 1979*

quint major *noun* in poker, a sequence of five cards, same suit, ending with the face cards *US, 1988*

quitter *noun* a suicide *US, 1982*

quiver *noun* **1** a selection of surfboards used for different surf conditions *US, 1977*. **2** cocaine *UK, 1999*

quivver-giver *noun* an attractive person *US, 1947*

quiz *noun* a roadside sobriety test *US, 1976*

quiz room *noun* a room where the North Vietnamese interrogated US prisoners of war *US, 1990*

quizzy *adjective* nosey *NEW ZEALAND, 1988*

quoit *noun* the anus; the backside *AUSTRALIA, 1919*

quokka soccer *noun* on Rottnest Island, running around kicking quokkas as a type of entertainment. The 'quokka' is a small rare native marsupial, *Setonix brachyurus*, of southwestern West Australia *AUSTRALIA, 1999*

quong *noun* the testicle. Usually in the plural *UK, 2002*

quorum *noun* in poker, the agreed-upon minimum number of players to continue a game *US, 1979*

quote *verb* in criminal circles, to vouch for someone *UK, 2000*

quo vadis *noun* unfashionable or unpopular music. Probably refers to the 1951 film *Quo Vadis* and the rock group *Status Quo*, formed in 1967 and, in 2003, still working, with the implication that both entertainments are dated *UK, 2003*

quozzie; quoz *noun* a disabled or deformed person. Derived from Quasimodo, 'The Hunchback of Notre Dame' *UK, 2000*

Rr

RA *noun* ► **the RA** the Irish Republican Army *IRELAND, 2003*

raas *noun* **1** an arse; hence your being *JAMAICA, 1994*. **2** a contemptible person. Probable origin in the phrase 'your arse', although some suggest Dutch *raas* (rage). The early, especially West Indian, sense was considered extremely offensive, however modern UK black usage is roughly equivalent to ARSE or ARSEHOLE. There is a, possibly disingenuous, belief amongst some Jamaicans that Raas was a king of Africa *JAMAICA, 2000*. **3** nonsense. From West Indian. Black usage *UK, 2000*. ► **the raas** used in order to intensify. Synonymous with 'the hell', 'the fuck', etc *UK, 1994*

raasclat *noun* used as an extreme derogative. Combines RAAS (arse) and 'clat' (West Indian pronunciation of 'cloth') to mean 'a sanitary towel' *JAMAICA, 1978*

raashole *noun* a contemptible person; used as a general term of abuse. A cross-cultural variation on ARSEHOLE, using West Indian and UK black RAAS (an arse) *UK, 2000*

rabbi *noun* a mentor or protector *US, 1970*

rabbit *noun* **1** a woman who has a large number of children. Collected at a UK prison, August 2002 *JAMAICA, 2002*. **2** a man who ejaculates with little stimulation *US, 1987*. **3** a white person *US, 1991*. **4** a nervous, timid, cautious person *US, 1951*. **5** a new member of a Rastafarian gang *NEW ZEALAND, 1988*. **6** a prisoner who is known for attempting to escape prison *US, 1972*. **7** a person who regularly borrows money from an illegal money lender and pays back promptly *US, 1950*. **8** on the railways, a side track on a downhill incline used to divert runaway trains and prevent crashes *US, 1946*. **9** a poor poker player *US, 1967*. ► **go like a rabbit** to demonstrate eagerness during sex *UK, 1972*. ► **the rabbit died** used for indicating a state of pregnancy. From the (former) methodology used to test pregnancy that was introduced in 1949 *UK, 1998*. ► **the rabbit's hopping** experiencing the bleed period of the menstrual cycle. A reversal of the phrase THE RABBIT DIED (pregnant) *US, 2001*

rabbit *verb* to run away *UK, 1887*

rabbit and pork; rabbit *noun* the act of talking; a conversation. Rhyming slang for 'talk' *UK, 1980*

rabbit and pork; rabbit *verb* to talk. Rhyming slang. 'To rabbit on' is 'to talk at length' *UK, 1941*

rabbit blood *noun* a seemingly unstoppable urge to try to escape from prison *US, 1950*

rabbit ears *noun* **1** a v-shaped aerial placed on top of a television set *US, 1967*. **2** in a casino Keno game, the two clear plastic tubes through which the number balls are blown *US, 1993*. **3** an athlete or official who is quick to take offence at teasing *US, 1967*

rabbiter's breakfast *noun* a visit to the toilet and a cigarette *NEW ZEALAND, 1975*

rabbit fever *noun* the urge to try to escape from prison *US, 1962*

rabbit food; rabbit's food *noun* any salad vegetable, especially lettuce. A generally dismissive term from the carnivorous lobby *UK, 1936*

rabbit hunt *verb* in poker, to look through undealt cards after a hand is completed to see what might have been *US, 1967*

rabbit hutch *noun* the crutch or crotch. Rhyming slang *UK, 1980*

rabbit-killer *noun* a short and vicious punch to the neck, generally with the open hand *AUSTRALIA, 1941*

rabbit-oh; rabbit-o *noun* a door-to-door seller of slaughtered rabbits. From the cry 'rabbit oh!', used by the vendor to attract attention *AUSTRALIA, 1902*

rabbit season *noun* spring, when prisoners are inclined to try to escape *US, 1967*

rabbit's paw; rabbit *verb* to talk. Rhyming slang for JAW. The shortened form is identical in sense to the shortened form of RABBIT AND PORK *UK, 1961*

rabbit tracks *noun* in craps, a six rolled with a pair of threes *US, 1985*

rabbit turds *noun* Italian sausage. Limited usage, but graphic *US, 1996*

race *noun* **1** a single game in an illegal numbers lottery *US, 1963*. **2** a single game of Keno *US, 1973*. ► **not in the race** not having any chance of success *AUSTRALIA, 1904*. ► **the race** the game of roller derby *US, 1960s and 70s*

race *verb* ► **race for pink slips (pinks)** in drag racing, to compete for the prize of ownership of the opponent's car *US, 2003*. ► **race off** to conduct a person away to some other place for the purpose of seduction *AUSTRALIA, 1965*

race bird *noun* an enthusiastic fan of horse racing *US, 1971*

race face *noun* in motor racing, the look of total concentration and focus seen on drivers just before a race begins *US, 1993*

racehorse *noun* **1** an accomplished, sought-after prostitute *US, 1972*. **2** a thinly rolled cigarette *AUSTRALIA, 1944*

racehorse Charlie; racehorse Charley *noun* heroin; cocaine. Perhaps from the long-ago brand name White Horse *US, 1936*

race record *noun* a recording by a black artist; rock 'n' roll before whites discovered rock 'n' roll *US, 1927*

racerhead *noun* in mountain biking, someone who competes in races. A mild put-down to describe riders so into competition that they have lost their perspective on the cosmic absurdity of mountain biking *US, 1992*

racers *noun* close-fitting nylon swimwear used for competitive swimming. So-called because they are used in competitive swimming *AUSTRALIA, 2003*

races *noun* ► **at the races** unsuccessful, uncompetitive *IRELAND, 2003*

racetracker *noun* in horse racing, a person who makes their living in some capacity at racetracks *US, 1951*

racing stripe *noun* a faecal stain in the underpants *US, 1991*

racing tackle *noun* amphetamines or other central nervous system stimulants *UK, 1983*

rack *noun* **1** a woman's breasts *US, 1982*. **2** a set of antlers *US, 1945*. **3** bed *US, 1955*. **4** a room or apartment *US, 1993*. **5** a maximum security prison cell *US, 1982*. **6** a hotel's front desk *US, 1954*. **7** a foil-wrapped package of amphetamines *US, 1997*. **8** a packet of five barbiturate capsules or other drugs, give or take several *US, 1972*. **9** a one-month supply of birth control pills *US, 1980*. **10** a six-pack (of beer) *US, 1991*. **11** a case (24 cans) of beer *US, 2000*. ► **hit the rack** to go to bed; to go to sleep *US, 1973*. ► **on the rack** available for prostitution *US, 1977*

rack *verb* **1** to go to sleep *US, 1993*. **2** to steal *US, 1997*. **3** to shoplift *US, 2001*. **4** to perform well *US, 1955*. **5** to load (a gun) *US, 1997*. **6** in the television and film industries, to adjust the camera lens in the middle of a shot to keep the subject in focus *US, 1990*. ► **rack the bars** to open or close a prison cell door *US, 1992*

rack attack *noun* a nap; sleep *US, 1975*

racked *adjective* asleep *US, 1075*

racked up *adjective* upset *US, 1970*

racket *noun* **1** a criminal enterprise; a swindle or a means of deception. Any illicit or dubious enterprise may be termed a 'racket' by prefixing the area of criminal operation, hence 'narcotics racket', 'loan-shark racket', etc *UK, 1894*. **2** a job, trade or profession. A jocular reference: 'What racket are you in?' or 'What's your racket?' *UK, 1891*. **3** a private, police-only party *US, 1987*. **4** any rigged carnival game or attraction *US, 1960*

racket boy *noun* a member of an organised criminal enterprise US, 1953

racket jacket *noun* the jacket of a zoot suit US, 1945

racketty coo *noun* a Jewish person. Rhyming slang for 'Jew' AUSTRALIA, 1971

rackety *adjective* noisy US, 1975

rackey *noun* a boy who affects a style of dressing reminiscent of a gangster. Teen slang US, 1955

rack face *noun* lines on your face left from a blanket, sheet or pillow US, 1996

rack monster *noun* a person who spends a great deal of time in bed US, 1976

rack off *verb* to go away. Commonly but not exclusively used in the imperative. A euphemistic alternative to PISS OFF and FUCK OFF. Origin unknown. The *Oxford English Dictionary* (supplement) suggests a connection with 'rack' meaning 'of a horse, to move by alternately raising two legs on one side', but this seems hardly creditable due to the rarity of that term in Australia AUSTRALIA, 1975

rack off hairy legs! go away! An intensive form of the usual RACK OFF with the rather feeble insult 'hairy legs' tacked on AUSTRALIA, 1988

rack out *verb* to go to sleep US, 1991

rack up *verb* **1** to accumulate things; to score points US, 1961. **2** in a casino or gambling establishment, to have your chips placed in a chip rack to be cashed in US, 1982. **3** to prepare lines of cocaine UK, 1997. **4** in prison, to return prisoners to their cells US, 1990

racy bopper *noun* a female fan of motor racing whose attraction to the sport is a function of her attraction to the race participants US, 1993

rad *noun* **1** a political radical UK, 1973. **2** a radiator UK, 1935. **3** a radio UK, 1996

rad *adjective* extreme; intense; exciting; good. An abbreviated 'radical' US, 1982

radar *noun* a petty thief. Someone who will 'pick up anything' AUSTRALIA, 1989

radar alley *noun* any stretch of a motorway heavily patrolled by radar; especially, Interstate 90 between Cleveland and the New York state line US, 1971

radar Charlie *noun* a poker player with a strong intuitive sense of other players' hands US, 1988

RadCan *noun* Radio Canada, the francophone side of the Canadian Broadcasting Corporation. The 'Rad' in RadCan suggests 'radical', a view held by Canadian federalists of Radio Canada (pronounced, even by anglophone speakers, in the French way, as 'Raaahdio Canada') CANADA, 2002

raddie *noun* **1** an Italian or Anglo-Italian living in London. From the raddled-seeming complexion of some Italians compared to that of a pale Londoner, possibly influenced by REDDY (an Italian). Originally used of Italian families in Clerkenwell UK, 1938. **2** a political radical UK, 1964

radge *noun* a psychotic; a madman UK, 1995

radge *adjective* **1** used in order to express approval UK, 2003. **2** mad; psychotic UK, 2003. **3** silly. Northen dialect radgy (mad) UK, 1961

radgepot *noun* a fool. Probably direct from Northern dialect radge (mad). Natural derivations are 'radgy' and 'radgified' UK, 1979

radiate *verb* ▶ **radiate a mortgage** in Quebec, to cancel a mortgage CANADA, 2001

radiator whiskey *noun* strong, homemade whisky US, 1999

radic *noun* a police officer, especially armed police. Shortened from 'eradicator' UK, 1994

radical *adjective* extreme; outrageous; good. Originally surfer slang, then migrated into the argot of the San Fernando Valley and then into mainstream US youth slang US, 1967

radio *noun* a prisoner who talks loudly and without paying attention to who might be listening US, 1976

Radio Ones *noun* diarrhoea. Rhyming slang for THE RUNS, formed on (the verbal out-pourings of the DJs on) BBC Radio One UK, 1992

radio rental; radio rentals; rentals *adjective* wonderful, amazing; insane, crazy. Rhyming slang for MENTAL; based on Radio Rentals, a high street shop UK, 1973

radio that!; radio that shit! used in prison as a demand for quiet US, 1981

'rado *noun* a Cadillac El Dorado car US, 1980

rad pad *noun* in skateboarding, a rubber wedge used as a shock pad that changes the angles at which the axle assembly is mounted US, 1976

rads *noun* the police UK, 2000

Rafferty's rules; Rafferty rules *noun* an entire lack of rules altogether. From the Irish surname Rafferty, with the implication that the Irish were unruly. Connection with the Northumberland dialect word raffety 'irregular; applied by sinkers to stratified deposits', and the Lincolnshire term raffatory 'refractory' (see *English Dialect Dictionary*), amount to nothing more than hopeful guesswork AUSTRALIA, 1918

raffle ticket; raffle *noun* a mistake. Rhyming slang for RICKET UK, 1992

raft *noun* a large amount US, 1830

rag *noun* **1** a sanitary towel US, 1966. **2** the bleed period of the menstrual cycle US, 1971. **3** a despicable person US, 1997. **4** a newspaper, especially a disreputable one UK, 1889. **5** a used car that is in very poor condition US, 1980. **6** a well-worn tyre US, 1961. **7** a banknote; paper money UK, 1817. **8** in pool, a cushion US, 1985. **9** in horse racing, an outsider (a horse considered unlikely to win a race) UK, 1991. **10** in poker, a useless card in the dealt hand or a drawn card that does not improve the hand US, 1978. **11** in a carnival midway game, a small prize in a plastic bag US, 1985. **12** a railway pointsman US, 1946. ▶ **get your rag out** to lose your temper. A combination of LOSE YOUR RAG and the earlier 'get your shirt out' UK, 1956. ▶ **lose your rag** to lose your temper UK, 1959. ▶ **on the rag; have the rag on 1** experiencing the bleed period of the menstrual cycle US, 1974. **2** figuratively, to be distracted and irritable US, 1963

rag *verb* to mock, bully, tease or ridicule someone UK, 1808

rag *adjective* unpleasant, bad NEW ZEALAND, 1998

ragamuffin *noun* the bleed period of the menstrual cycle. A play on RAG (a sanitary towel) AUSTRALIA, 2001

rag and bone *noun* **1** a telephone. Rhyming slang UK, 1984. **2** a lavatory pedestal and receptacle, especially the lavatory seat. Rhyming slang for THRONE UK, 1992

rag and boner *noun* a telephone. Extended from rhyming slang RAG AND BONE (telephone) UK, 1984

raga-raga *adjective* of clothes, worn-out, ragged. A variation on conventional 'ragged' JAMAICA, 1943

ragbag *noun* **1** an odd assortment UK, 1999. **2** an untidily or shabbily dressed person UK, 1888. **3** in circus and carnival usage, a show that has fallen on hard times or is fundamentally dishonest US, 1981

rage *noun* a large wave US, 1991

rage *verb* **1** to enjoy a party with great enthusiasm US, 1992. **2** to dominate someone or something US, 1984

-rage *suffix* when combined with a subject noun, an outburst of enraged hostility within or occasioned by that subject area UK, 1998

rager *noun* **1** a skilled, aggressive surfer or skateboarder US, 1997. **2** a large party US, 1990

ragga; ragamuffin; raggamuffin *noun* a ruffian, usually of West Indian racial origin. Originally a West Indian and UK black term with an approving tone; probably derived from the conventional sense of a 'raggedy' (a disreputable person); ultimately from Ragamoffyn, a demon in the Middle English poem 'Piers Plowman' by William Langland (perhaps 1330–86). The derivation is likely to be influenced by Jamaican 'raga-raga' (ragged) and 'ragamofi' (ragged clothes) UK, 1996

raggagansta; raggagangsta *noun* a West Indian/UK black gangster. Compounds RAGGAMUFFIN (a ruffian) with GANGSTA (a gangster) UK, 1997

raggastani *noun* a member of a British Indian (Hindi) urban youth gang or subculture *UK, 2006*

ragged *adjective* **1** without money *US, 1990.* **2** tired; unwell *AUSTRALIA, 1958*

ragged edge *noun* in hot rodding, drag racing, and motor racing, the absolute limit of the car's ability *US, 1965*

raggedy *adjective* ragged; rough; dishevelled *US, 1890*

raggedy jack *noun* in Newfoundland, a homemade pile rug *CANADA, 1979*

raggedy jacket *noun* in Newfoundland, a harp seal moulting from the white coat to the bedlamer stage *CANADA, 1976*

raggin' *adjective* dressed in fashionable and expensive clothing *US, 1987*

raggy-arse *adjective* of poor quality *UK, 2002*

rag head *noun* **1** an Arab person, or a native of any race that wears a cloth-covering on the head; by extension a native of Muslim countries. Offensive *US, 1921.* **2** in circus and carnival usage, a gypsy *US, 1981*

raging *adjective* very good; very exciting *US, 1995*

Raging Bull *nickname* Jake LaMotta (b.1921), a middleweight boxer who fiercely made his presence felt in the ring in the 1940s and 50s *US, 1980*

raging queer *noun* a particularly ostentatious or importunate male homosexual. An intensification of QUEER (a male homosexual) *UK, 1984*

rag joint *noun* a carnival concession in a canvas booth *US, 1985*

ragman's coat *noun* on a woman, an untrimmed and naturally abundant mass of pubic hair *UK, 2002*

rag order *noun* chaotic disorder, a mess. Military *UK, 1983*

rag store *noun* a big con swindle in which the lure is the promise of wealth from stocks traded based on allegedly inside information *US, 1969*

rag stuffer *noun* a parachute rigger *US, 1991*

ragtime *noun* the bleed period of a woman's menstrual cycle. A play on ON THE RAG (menstruating), after the musical style *US, 2001*

ragtop *noun* a convertible car *US, 1955*

rag town *noun* a town built in prosperous times, bound to fall into poverty with the end of prosperous times *US, 1954*

ragweed *noun* **1** poor quality marijuana. After botanical genus *Ambrosia* the which grows wild across North America *US, 1969.* **2** poor quality heroin *US, 1998*

rag week *noun* the week of the month when a woman has a menstrual bleed. Combines RAG (a sanitary towel), as in 'on the rag', with conventional 'week' to form a play on university rag week *UK, 2001*

rah!; rah rah! used as a cheer, a shouted expression of support or encouragement. A shortening of 'hurrah!' in college sports use. As 'rah! rah! rah!' it is the climax of a Maori war cry that has been adopted by New Zealand rugby teams *US, 1870*

rah-rah *adjective* characterised by excessive spirit and enthusiasm, usually associated with college or high school *US, 1914*

rahtid; raatid; rhaatid *adjective* used as an intensifier that implies anger or strong disapproval. Urban black usage *UK, 1994*

rail *noun* **1** a line of cocaine or other powdered drug, laid out for snorting *US, 1984.* **2** any railway employee *US, 1946.* ▶ **on the rail** in American casinos, observing the gambling but not playing *US, 1985*

rail *verb* to arrest or detain someone *US, 1995*

railbird *noun* **1** in horse racing, an enthusiast who watches morning workouts, carefully clocking performances *US, 1931.* **2** in American casinos, a thief who steals chips from inattentive gamblers *US, 1985.* **3** in pool, a spectator *US, 1993*

raildog *noun* a backstage technician who works with set rigging on a catwalk *US, 1991*

railfield *verb* a thief who simply grabs shop merchandise and runs from the shop *US, 1960*

rail job; rail *noun* a drag racing car with a chassis made of rail-like metal bars; a drag racing car regardless of the chassis construction *US, 1963*

rail lugger *noun* in horse racing, a horse that prefers to run near or next to the inside rail *US, 1947*

rail on; rail *verb* to criticize or reprimand someone *US, 1987*

railrat *noun* in the language surrounding the Grateful Dead, a member of the audience who prefers to see the show from as close as possible to the band, right on the rail *US, 1994*

railroad *verb* to move your jaw from side to side obsessively and involuntarily after sustained amphetamine use *US, 1989*

railroad bible *noun* a deck of playing cards *US, 1976*

railroad dick *noun* a private guard employed by a railway company *US, 1958*

railroad flat *noun* an apartment consisting of connected long, narrow rooms *US, 1956*

railroad tracks *noun* the bars on a captain's uniform signifying his office *US, 1947*

railroad weed *noun* marijuana, especially of inferior quality. From the weeds that flourish alongside railway lines, not necessarily WEED (marijuana) *US, 1974*

rails *noun* that part of a racecourse where the rails bookmakers are situated; hence, big-time bookmaking *AUSTRALIA, 1981*

rail sandwich *noun* a surfboard between your legs *US, 1978*

rails bookmaker; rails bookie *noun* one of the more prestigious bookmakers *AUSTRALIA, 1950*

railway station *noun* an 'allocation' prison from which prisoners are forwarded *UK, 1999*

ráiméis *noun* foolish, nonsensical, ill-founded talk *IRELAND, 2001*

rain *verb* ▶ **if it was raining …** I am extremely unlucky *AUSTRALIA, 1965.* ▶ **rain pups and pussies** to rain very hard *US, 1990*

rain and pour; rain *verb* to snore. Rhyming slang *UK, 1992*

rainbow *noun* **1** a capsule of amobarbital sodium and secobarbital sodium (trade name Tuinal™), a combination of central nervous system depressants *US, 1966.* **2** in casinos, a bet comprised of different colour and different value betting chips *US, 1991.* **3** in oil drilling, a very small showing of oil in a hole *US, 1954.* **4** a soldier who joins a fighting unit after conflict has ceased. Used in both World Wars; a rainbow comes after a storm *AUSTRALIA, 1919.* ▶ **go up the rainbow** to experience sexual ecstasy *UK, 1972*

rainbow hand *noun* a poker hand with cards of all four suits *US, 1950*

rainbow jumper *noun* in basketball, a high, arcing jump shot *US, 1974*

rainbow party *noun* oral sex on one male by several females, all wearing different colours of lipstick *US, 2003*

rainbow roll *noun* a multi-coloured assortment of barbiturate capsules *US, 1973*

rainbows *noun* **1** LSD. Presumably from the pictures printed on the blotting paper dose *UK, 1998.* **2** the recreational drug methaqualone, best known as Quaaludes™ *UK, 1983*

rain check *noun* **1** a request or promise to take up an invitation at a convenient time; a postponement of any arrangement. From the ticket given to a spectator at an outdoor event providing for a refund/admission at a later date, should the event be interrupted by rain *US, 1930.* **2** the reduction of a criminal penalty; parole, probation *US, 1949*

raincoat *noun* a condom. Figurative use of waterproof wear *US, 1970*

Raincoat Charlie *noun* a striptease audience member who masturbates beneath the safety of his raincoat *US, 1981*

raincoater *noun* a stereotypical perverted pornography fan *US, 2000*

raincoat job *noun* a sexual fetish involving urination on your partner *US, 1993*

rain dance *noun* in computing, an action that is expected to be taken but will likely produce no results *US, 1974*

rained out *adjective* postponed. A term from sports, especially baseball, but applied more broadly to refer to, for example, a class on a given day that has been postponed *US, 1995*

raining and pouring; raining *noun* snoring. Rhyming slang *UK, 1992*

rainmaker *noun* a member of an enterprise whose job includes procuring clients or business by the use of charm *US, 1985*

rain room *noun* a shower room *US, 1968*

Rainy City *nickname* Manchester, UK *UK, 1981*

rainy day woman *noun* marijuana. This seems to have been inspired by the following lyric: 'Everybody must get stoned' by Bob Dylan, 'Rainy Day Women #12 & 35', 1966 *US, 1982*

raise *noun* **1** stake money; a monetary profit *UK, 2000*. **2** parents *US, 1972*. **3** the arm *US, 1973*

raise *verb* **1** (used of a male) to achieve an erection *BAHAMAS, 1971*. **2** to identify yourself to a fellow traveller *US, 1957*. **3** to bail someone out of jail *US, 1973*. ▶ **raise Cain** to make a disturbance; to complain or quarrel noisily and angrily *US, 1930*. ▶ **raise hell** to make a disturbance; to make a din; to cause trouble *US, 1896*. ▶ **raise sand** to argue loudly, creating a problem *US, 1965*

raiser *noun* **1** a lookout who warns confederates of approaching police *US, 1992*. **2** a criminal who specialises in forging increases in the amount payable to an otherwise legitimate cheque or security *US, 1950*

raise up *verb* **1** to make someone angry *US, 2001*. **2** to warn someone *US, 1992*. **3** to be released from prison *US, 1990*

raisinhead *noun* a black person. Offensive *US, 1978*

raisin jack *noun* a potent and vile alcoholic beverage brewed by letting raisins ferment, usually in prison *US, 1986*

raisin picker *noun* on the railways, a worker from Fresno, California. Fresno is regarded as the raisin capital of the US *US, 1975*

raisin snap *noun* alcohol made from fermented raisins *US, 1988*

raize *verb* to annoy or harass someone *US, 1991*

rajah *noun* an erection *NEW ZEALAND, 1998*

rajamuffin *noun* a member of a British Indian (Hindi) urban youth gang or subculture. A play on raggamuffin *UK, 2006*

Rajputana *noun* a banana. Rhyming slang, formed from a ship that berthed in London's Royal Docks *UK, 1998*

rake *noun* **1** an amount of something; a large quantity *IRELAND, 1995*. **2** a comb *US, 1960*. **3** in pool, a device used to support the cue stick for a hard-to-reach shot *US, 1990*

rake *verb* to lower the front end of a car *US, 1970*. ▶ **rake a game** to charge card players for the privilege of playing *US, 1977*. ▶ **rake the leaves** to drive at the back of a group of trucks travelling on a motorway together, watching for police from the rear *US, 1976*

raked *adjective* drunk *US, 1990*

rakehell *noun* an utter scoundrel *UK, 1554*

rake-in *noun* the financial results of an enterprise *US, 1947*

rake in; rake *verb* to make money, especially in generous quantities or at an enviable speed *UK, 1583*

rake-off *noun* money obtained from a crime or as a bribe *US, 1899*

Rakkasans *nickname* the 3rd Battalion, 187th Infantry Regiment. Distinguished airborne and air assault soldiers in World War 2, Korea, Vietnam and the Persian Gulf. From the Japanese for 'parachute', named during the first four years of occupation duty in Japan *US, 1989*

rakli *noun* a girl; a woman. Romany in current English gypsy use *UK, 2000*

Raleigh bike *noun* a lesbian. Rhyming slang for DYKE, formed on a product of a well-known bicycle manufacturer *UK, 1992*

rally *verb* to go out drinking *US, 1974*

ralph *noun* **1** a right turn *US, 1968*. **2** vomit *US, 1975*

ralph *verb* to vomit *US, 1966*

Ralphed up *adjective* dressed in a smart casual style. From Ralph Lauren (b.1939), designer of the Polo™ range of casual clothing *UK, 1997*

ram *noun* amyl or butyl nitrite. Reflecting popular male gay use, possibly deriving from a brand name *US, 1998*

ram *verb* (from a male perspective) to have sex, perhaps violently. Mainly derived from 'ram' (a male sheep), but the thrusting action echoes 'ram' (to batter with a long pole) *UK, 2001*

-rama; -erama; -orama *suffix* used for conveying a superlative quality or quantity. From Greek *orama* (a view) *US, 1954*

rama-lama *noun* rock 'n' roll music. From the doo-wop song 'Rama Lama Ding Dong' recorded by the Edsels in 1959, and somehow thought to capture the *joie de vivre* of the music *UK, 2001*

Rambette *noun* a female Rambo – reckless, fearless, the warrior woman *US, 1992*

rambler *noun* a (portable) radio *UK, 1996*

rambling ROK's *noun* ground troops of the Army of South Korea (the Republic of Korea) *US, 1964*

Rambo *noun* **1** a soldier with too much of a sense of drama and too little intelligence. After the 1982 film starring Sylvester Stallone as an invincible if mentally unstable Vietnam veteran *US, 1989*. **2** an intolerant prison officer who would rather punish inmates. From the 1982 film starring Sylvester Stallone as a military man who uses the most extreme measures to quell his opponents. In use in UK prisons in 2002 *UK, 2002*. **3** heroin *UK, 1998*

Rambo rag *noun* a handkerchief worn on the head. Worn by Stallone in the film *US, 1991*

ramjam *adverb* absolutely crammed *UK, 1879*

rammed *adjective* crammed, stuffed full *UK, 1996*

rammies *noun* trousers; pants. Rhyming slang. Shortening of 'rammy rousers', rhyming slang for 'trousers' *AUSTRALIA, 1906*

rammy *noun* a brawl; a noisy argument, a row; a bustling crowd *UK: SCOTLAND, 1935*

rammy *verb* to take part in crowd violence *UK: SCOTLAND, 1996*

ramp *noun* **1** a search of a prisoner or prison cell. Conducted to search for contraband, though often carried out with much destruction in order to harass the prisoner *AUSTRALIA, 1919*. **2** a public house bar counter; hence, a public house. From an earlier, more general, sense as a shop counter *UK, 1935*

ramp *verb* **1** to swindle, to con; to rob, to mug; to make trouble. Contemporary use is mainly West Indian and UK black *UK, 1812*. **2** to pretend. A variation of the sense 'to swindle, to con' *UK, 2000*. **3** to search a prisoner or a prison cell *AUSTRALIA, 1919*

ramped *adjective* drunk *US, 1992*

ram-raid *verb* to rob a premises using a vehicle as a battering ram and driving it through a window or a wall *UK, 1987*

ram-raid; ram-raiding *noun* a method of robbery that utilises a motor vehicle as a battering ram to gain entry, often using the vehicle to make off with stolen goods *UK, 1991*

ramraider *noun* **1** a criminal involved in ram-raiding *UK, 1991*. **2** a powerful amphetamine sulphate *UK, 1990s*

ramrod *noun* the penis; the erect penis *UK, 1902*

Ramsgate Sand; Ramsgate *noun* the hand. Rhyming slang, formed on the Kent seaside resort *UK, 1992*

ram's pasture *noun* in oil drilling, non-productive land *US, 1954*

ram tube *noun* in a drag racing car, an injector that forces air into a carburettor *US, 1970*

ranch *noun* **1** a house *US, 1960*. **2** any place where marijuana is sold *US, 1945*. **3** to a trucker, anywhere you spend the night *US, 1976*

ranch *verb* to idle; to spend time doing little *US, 1991*

Ranch Hand *noun* a C-123 aircraft equipped with tanks filled with defoliants used on the Vietnam jungle *US, 1969*

rancid *adjective* **1** in poor taste *US, 1989*. **2** excellent; brilliant *AUSTRALIA, 1993*

randan *noun* a spree of wild, debauched, hedonistic behaviour, especially if heavy drinking is involved. Usually in the phrase 'on the randan' *UK: SCOTLAND, 1985*

Randolph Scott; Randolph *noun* a spot. Rhyming slang, based on the name of film actor Randolph Scott, 1903–87 *UK, 1992*

random *adjective* ordinary if unexpected. A major word of the 1990s US youth, just a tad to the slang side of conventional English *US, 1968*

R and R *noun* **1** rest and rehabilitation; rest and recovery; rest and recreation; rest and recuperation; rape and restitution; rape and ruin; rape and run. Despite disagreement on the 'R's', the meaning is the same – a brief stint away from combat or regular duty *US, 1953*. **2** rock 'n' roll *UK, 1977*. **3** rape and robbery. A cynical play on the US military 'r and r' (rest and recreation) *UK, 1996*

randy *adjective* **1** sexually aroused; feeling lecherous. From Scottish dialect *randy* *UK, 1847*. **2** homosexual, perhaps seen as a threatening or predatory characteristic. Public schools use, probably deriving from the more general sense as 'lecherous or sexually aroused' when applied in a single-sex environment *UK, 1968*

randy Andy *nickname* Prince Andrew; any man named Andrew *UK, 1984*

randy comedown *noun* a desire for sex as the effects of drug use wear off *UK, 2002*

rane *noun* cocaine; heroin *UK, 2003*

rang *noun* a person who is acting very oddly. An abbreviation of 'orangutan' *US, 1966*

rangdoodles *noun* in poker, a temporary increase in the betting limit after a player has won a hand with an agreed-upon, rare and excellent hand *US, 1967*

Ranger's Bible *noun* the US Army Ranger handbook, a supplemental training document for long-range reconnaissance patrols *US, 1990*

rangood *noun* wild marijuana. Probably a playful misspelling of RANGOON *UK, 2003*

rangoon *noun* wild marijuana *US, 1968*

Rangoon *noun* a prune. Rhyming slang, formed from the Burmese capital *UK, 1992*

rank *verb* **1** to disparage; to insult, especially in a formulaic or ritual manner *US, 1945*. **2** to bungle or ruin something *US, 1950*

rank *adjective* unpleasant; stupid; bad-smelling. In the world of bad-is-good alienated youth, 'rank' can be good or bad *US, 1955*

ranking *adjective* **1** excellent; admirable. Also shortened to 'ranks' *UK, 1985*. **2** average, mediocre *JAMAICA, 2000*

rank out *verb* to offend or disgust someone by doing something rank *US, 1997*

ran-tan *noun* ▶ **on the ran-tan** on a drinking spree *IRELAND, 1977*

rap *noun* **1** a criminal charge *US, 1903*. **2** blame or responsibility *US, 1927*. **3** a prison sentence *US, 1927*. **4** a clever line of improvised chat, speech or conversation. Black coinage, adopted and popularised by hippies *US, 1967*. **5** a popular music genre in which a rhythmic lyric is spoken over a musical background *US, 2002*. **6** a meandering, unstructured group discussion *US, 1967*. **7** the way in which a person expresses himself or herself *US, 1975*. **8** a very small amount *US, 1973*. ▶ **ride the rap** to serve a prison sentence without losing control, hope or sanity *US, 1991*

rap *verb* **1** to talk without an agenda, aimlessly but honestly. Found before the 1960s, but truly a word of the 60s *US, 1929*. **2** to criticise someone *US, 1957*. **3** to accuse someone falsely or to seek a more serious sentence for someone than their crime deserves *US, 1965*. **4** to perform semi-spoken lyrics over a musical background *US, 1979*

raparazzi *noun* an elite grouping within hip-hop culture. Extends RAP (the pre-eminent hip-hop music style) on the model of PAPARAZZI (photographers who prey on celebrities); the suggestion of preying remains *UK, 2002*

rape *verb* in computing, to destroy a program or data without hope of recovering it *US, 1991*

rape tools *noun* the penis and testicles *US, 1962*

rapid *adjective* excellent *IRELAND, 2003*

rapo; rape-o *noun* a rapist *US, 1972*

rap parlor *noun* a brothel in disguise as a massage parlour in disguise as a business where you pay to talk to women. For those entrepreneurs who do not have what it takes to obtain a massage licence *US, 1982*

rap partner *noun* in a criminal enterprise, a person who will accept responsibility for a venture gone poorly and serve a jail sentence *US, 1977*

rapper *noun* **1** a performer of rap lyrics *US, 1979*. **2** the mouth; the voice *US, 1969*. **3** the chief witness for the prosecution in a criminal trial *US, 1962*

rappie *noun* a partner in crime *US, 1981*

rap session *noun* a group discussion, unstructured and uninhibited *US, 1969*

rap sheet *noun* a record of a person's past arrests and convictions *US, 1960*

rapt *adjective* delighted. Variant of WRAPPED *AUSTRALIA, 1963*

raptor *noun* a rap performer who is also an actor *US, 1998*

Raquel Welch *noun* a belch. Rhyming slang formed from the name of the film actress (b.1940) *UK, 1992*

Raquel Welch *verb* to belch. Rhyming slang, formed from the name of the US actress (b.1940) *UK, 1971*

rare *adjective* **1** excellent; very enjoyable *UK: SCOTLAND, 1985*. **2** of someone, unusual, eccentric. Sometimes 'wild rare' is also used *IRELAND, 1992*

rare as rocking horse shit *adjective* extremely rare or scarce *AUSTRALIA, 1944*

rare groove *noun* a fashionable style of dance music and its presentation. Coined by pirate radio presenter Norman Jay *UK, 1999*

raring to go *adjective* eagerly impatient to get started *US, 1935*

rark-up *noun* an argument or rebuke *NEW ZEALAND, 1995*

rark up *verb* to rebuke or annoy someone *NEW ZEALAND, 1997*

ras! used for expressing surprise *US, 2004*

rash *noun* ▶ **be all over someone like a rash 1** to smother someone with affection, kisses, etc *AUSTRALIA, 1965*. **2** to be easily outdoing an opponent *AUSTRALIA, 1961*

rashie *noun* an upper garment worn by surfers. Originally worn under a wetsuit in order to prevent WETTIE RASH *AUSTRALIA, 1996*

raspberry *noun* **1** a disapproving fart-like noise. From out-of-date rhyming slang, 'raspberry tart' for FART *UK, 1890*. **2** a light grazing of the skin. Skateboarders' slang; from the appearance *UK, 1998*. **3** a sore or abcess on an intravenous drug user from repeated injections in the same spot *US, 1973*. **4** a male who trades sex for drugs *US, 1995*

raspberryland *nickname* Tasmania. From the crop. Hence, a Tasmanian is called a 'raspberrylander' *AUSTRALIA, 1966*

raspberry ripple; raspberry *noun* a disabled individual. Rhyming slang for 'cripple' *UK, 1977*

raspy *adjective* **1** excellent *US, 1982*. **2** bad, unpleasant *US, 1977*

rass *noun* the buttocks; hence, used as a term of abuse. From ARSE *JAMAICA, 1790*

rasta box *noun* a large portable stereo system associated, stereotypically, with black youth culture *US, 1988*

Rastafarian *noun* MDMA, the recreational drug best known as ecstasy. Specifically used of any tablet of MDMA stamped with a stylised image of a dreadlocked head *UK, 2004*

rasta weed *noun* marijuana. Marijuana is famously central to *Rasta*farian ritual *US, 2001*

Rastus *noun* used as a derogatory personification of a black male *US, 1949*

rat *noun* **1** a person who informs on or otherwise betrays compatriots *UK, 1902*. **2** a despicable person *UK, 1594*. **3** an enthusiast of the preceding activity or thing *US, 1864*. **4** a railway detective *US, 1977*. **5** a prostitute *BARBADOS, 1965*. ▶ **like a rat up a drainpipe; like a rat up a drain** very swiftly. Often used with 'up that/her', in which case it is usually of a woman objectified in a sexual context *AUSTRALIA, 1971*. ▶ **like a rat up a rhododendron** very swiftly. A jocular variation of LIKE A RAT UP A DRAIN *AUSTRALIA, 1971*. ▶ **like a rat up a rope/shoreline** with great speed *AUSTRALIA, 1945*. ▶ **not give a rat's ass; not give a rat's arse** to not care at all *US, 1971*. ▶ **rat's died up your arse** used of an especially noxious fart *UK, 2001*

rat *verb* **1** to inform. Perhaps from an earlier political sense of changing political parties *US, 1934*. **2** to rob or loot a person or place *AUSTRALIA, 1898*

rat *adjective* disloyal, untrustworthy; *US, 1955*

rat and mouse *noun* **1** a house. Rhyming slang; first recorded in *Songs and Slang of the British Soldier: 1914–1918*, John Brophy and Eric Partridge, 3rd edition, 1931. Recorded in the US in 1943 *UK, 1931*. **2** an informer. Rhyming slang for LOUSE (a despicable person) *UK, 1961*

rat-arsed; ratarsed *adjective* drunk *UK, 1982*

ratatouille *noun* a nightclub that caters to a mix of gay and straight customers. A culinary allusion *UK, 2003*

ratbag *noun* a contemptible person. A 'ratbag' can be merely a person with odd notions, an eccentric, or someone whose ideas or behaviour verge on the insane *AUSTRALIA, 1890*

ratbaggery *noun* behaviour which is eccentric, despicable or otherwise contemptible *AUSTRALIA, 1943*

rat belt *noun* in computing, a self-locking cable tie *US, 1991*

rat bite *noun* a skin bruise caused by sucking. Hawaiian youth usage *US, 1982*

ratboy *noun* **1** among a group of drug users, a person who will sample any drug before the group uses it. An allusion to the rat as the subject of laboratory experiments *US, 1987*. **2** a member of a subcultural urban adolescent grouping defined by a hip-hop dress and jewellery sense *UK, 2000*

rat caper *noun* a minor crime *CANADA, 1976*

ratchet *noun* any weapon *US, 2003*

ratchet jaw *noun* a person who talks too much and says too little *US, 1965*

ratchet-mouth *verb* to talk incessantly *US, 1981*

rat-cunning *noun* craftiness *AUSTRALIA, 1979*

rat cunning *adjective* crafty *AUSTRALIA, 1970*

rat-drawn *adjective* used of shoes, pointed *US, 1976*

rat-eyed *adjective* drunk *UK, 1998*

ratfink; rat fink *noun* **1** a despised person. Combines RAT (someone unpleasant) and FINK (someone despised, an informer) *US, 1964*. **2** an informer. Combines RAT (an informer) and FINK (an informer) *US, 1965*

rat fuck *noun* **1** a chaotic military disaster *US, 1930*. **2** a despicable person *US, 1922*. **3** a damn *US, 1971*. **4** a prank *US, 1965*

Rat Fuck *noun* the Reaction Forces of the South Vietnamese Army *US, 1990*

ratfuck *verb* to pull a prank *US, 1965*

ratfuck operation *noun* any operation characterised by poor planning, confusion or chaos. Frequently used in the Vietnam war *US, 1990*

rat head *noun* a person, especially a woman, who conveys a complete lack of taste and finesse *US, 2004*

rat hole *noun* **1** a small, messy, cluttered place *UK, 1812*. **2** a railway tunnel *US, 1975*

rat-hole *verb* to stash something away, usually secretively *US, 1948*

rat house *noun* an insane asylum *AUSTRALIA, 1900*

rat jacket *noun* a reputation for being an informer *US, 1973*

rat-legged *adjective* drunk. A variation of RAT-ARSED *UK, 2002*

rat motor *noun* in hot rodding, a Chevrolet engine, usually 396 cubic inches or larger *US, 2001*

rat-on *noun* an erection *NEW ZEALAND, 1995*

rat out *verb* to inform on someone *US, 1990*

rat pack *noun* **1** in competition surfing, competitors vying for the lead *US, 1988*. **2** a group of young gang members *US, 1951*. **3** a ration of food issued to South African soldiers; a package of food *SOUTH AFRICA, 1984*

rat-pack *verb* to surround and attack someone *US, 1971*

rat race *noun* **1** any hectic and non-productive situation, activity or lifestyle *US, 1947*. **2** the face. Rhyming slang *UK, 2003*

rat row *noun* an area in a jail or prison reserved for police informers who would not be safe in the general population of the facility *US, 1982*

rat run *noun* a narrow way between buildings; a back alley; a side road, especially if used in a short-cut; a route through back streets that is used by motorists avoiding heavy traffic *UK, 1977*

rats *noun* combat rations *US, 1976*

rats! used as an expression of annoyance or dismissal *US, 1886*

rats and mice; rats *noun* **1** dice. Rhyming slang *UK, 1932*. **2** rice. Rhyming slang *UK, 1992*

rat's coffin *noun* a meat pie *AUSTRALIA, 2003*

ratshit *noun* a despicable person or thing *US, 1994*. ▶ **go to ratshit** to go very wrong *UK, 1995*

ratshit *adjective* no good; dreadful *AUSTRALIA, 1970*

ratted *adjective* drunk *UK, 2002*

ratter *noun* **1** a police informer; a traitor to a cause or enterprise *US, 1975*. **2** a thief, especially one who steals opal from another's mine *AUSTRALIA, 1932*

rattle *noun* dice *US, 1983*. ▶ **give a rattle** to have sexual intercourse with a female *IRELAND, 2001*

rattle *verb* to agitate or to unnerve someone *US, 1887*. ▶ **rattle beads** to complain *US, 1970*. ▶ **rattle your cage** to annoy or to aggravate you; to arouse your indignation *UK, 1990*. ▶ **rattle your dags** to hurry *NEW ZEALAND, 1968*

rattle and clank; rattle *noun* a bank. Rhyming slang *UK, 1962*

rattle and hiss; rattle *noun* an act of urination; urine. Rhyming slang for PISS *UK, 1998*

rattler *noun* **1** a train *UK, 1871*. **2** Boston's underground system, the Massachusetts Transit Authority *US, 1997*

rattler-jumping *adjective* travelling by illegally catching trains *AUSTRALIA, 1969*

rattlesnake *noun* ▶ **like a rattlesnake** of a woman, describes vigorous participation in sexual intercourse *UK, 2000*

rattlesnakes; rattles *noun* delirium tremens. Rhyming slang for SHAKES *UK, 1992*

rattling *adjective* in an energetic state, possibly as a result of drug abuse *UK, 2000*

rattling *adverb* used as an intensifier, especially when describing adventure fiction *UK, 1829*

rattling-cove *noun* a taxi. Derived from late C17-C18 usage (a coachman) *UK, 2002*

rat trap *noun* **1** a dilapidated, shoddy building *UK, 1838*. **2** a fox hole that accommodated two or three Viet Cong who hid and slept there during the day *US, 1990*. **3** a Japanese person. Rhyming slang for JAP, a pejorative term dating from World War 2 and lingering among veterans of that conflict (especially prisoners of war). Also shortened to 'rat' *UK, 1992*

rat turds *noun* an Oak Leaf Cluster, a military decoration indicating that the soldier has received another decoration more than once *US, 1990*

ratty *adjective* **1** wretched, miserable, mean; stained, tattered *US, 1867*. **2** angry, irritated *UK, 1909*. **3** foolish, odd, eccentric *NEW ZEALAND, 1998*. **4** crazy *AUSTRALIA, 1895*

raunch *noun* in the usage of youthful model road racers (slot car racers), a slow car *US, 1997*

raunchy *adjective* **1** sexually provocative, risqué; used as a euphemism for pornographic *US, 1967*. **2** inept, poorly done;

unpleasant, contemptible; dirty *US, 1939*. **3** used of music, abrasive, aggressive *US, 1982*

ravaged *adjective* drunk *UK, 2002*

rave *noun* **1** a party; a bottle party; a party open to the public, often announced and sited clandestinely, featuring drugs, music and sensory overload. Variant of 'rave up'. First used of wild parties in the late 1950s, then by MOD(s) in the 60s; revived in the 80s for parties on such a scale that both UK culture and law were significantly changed *UK, 1992*. **2** an enthusiastic review *US, 1926*. **3** the object of a passionate liking or craze *UK, 1959*

rave *verb* **1** to express an enthusiasm for something *UK, 1704*. **2** to enjoy the music and other sensations of a rave *US, 1995*. **3** to persist in discussing something that does not interest anyone else involved in the discussion *US, 1981*

rave drug *noun* any chemical or 'designer' drug associated with dance and club culture *UK, 2003*

rave energy *noun* MDMA, the recreational drug best known as ecstasy. The rave culture was fuelled by MDMA *UK, 2003*

raven *adjective* gluttonous; greedy *GRENADA, 1996*

raver *noun* **1** a dedicated hedonist, party-goer, sexual adventurer or drug taker. Extended from the sense as a 'passionate enthusiast'. Defined as 'a young woman who is enthusiastically promiscuous or merely of a passionate (but not promiscuous) nature *UK, 1968*. **2** someone who goes to a rave *UK, 2000*. **3** a homosexual male *UK, 1996*

rave-up *noun* a social gathering. Used ironically of a mild, as opposed to wild, party, by people old enough to remember the rave-ups of the 1960s *UK, 1984*

ravey *adjective* characteristic of raving *UK, 2000*

raving *adjective* used as an intensifier; complete, excellent, utmost, etc *UK, 1959*

Ravi Shankar *noun* a wanker. Rhyming slang, formed from the name of the celebrated Indian musician (b.1920) *UK, 2003*

raw *noun* crack cocaine *US, 1994*. ► **in the raw** naked *US, 1934*

raw *adjective* **1** exciting; excellent *US, 1987*. **2** naked *US, 1931*. **3** undiluted *US, 1974*. **4** unembalmed *US, 1987*

raw fusion *noun* heroin *UK, 2002*

rawhide *noun* heroin *UK, 2002*

rawhide *verb* to drive those under your supervision to work very hard *US, 1962*

raw-jaw *verb* to ignore someone; to bless someone with silence *US, 1992*

raw meat *noun* a new recruit in the US Army *US, 1948*

raw prawn *noun* a raw deal *AUSTRALIA, 1957*

raymond yes, affirmative. Citizens' band radio French *vraiment* (truly, indeed) *UK, 1981*

rays *noun* radiology *US, 1994*. ► **bag some rays; catch some rays; cop some rays** to sunbathe *US, 1963*

razed *adjective* drug-intoxicated *UK, 1998*

razoo *noun* **1** the smallest amount of money. Only ever used in negative contexts, generally 'to not have a razoo,' but also 'not worth a razoo,' 'not get a razoo', etc. Contextually referring to a low value brass coin, the origin of this term remains a mystery despite many guesses over the years. Needless to say no such coin ever existed. Also commonly a 'brass razoo', and formerly spelt 'rahzoo' or 'razzoo' though only rarely *AUSTRALIA, 1919*. **2** harassment *US, 1949*

razor *verb* to slash something with a razor *UK: SCOTLAND, 1999*

razorback *noun* a worker on a circus train; any circus worker other than a performer. Circus historian and linguist Joe McKennon suggested that the term may have derived from the common work command of 'Raise 'er back, let 'er go' when placing circus equipment on train wagons *US, 1904*

razor blade; razor *noun* a black person. Rhyming slang *UK, 1970*

razored *adjective* muscular and sculpted *US, 1984*

razor edges *noun* dice that are true to an extremely minute tolerance, approximately 1/1000th of a inch *US, 1950*

razoring *noun* an attack on someone with a razor. From RAZOR (to slash with a razor) *UK, 1996*

razz *noun* a telling-off; a harangue. An Eton school term *UK, 1967*. ► **on the razz; on the razzle** a period of drinking, partying and other self-indulgent pleasures. Derives from a shortening of 'razzle-dazzle' (excitement). 'Razzle' (a good time) is first recorded in 1908 *UK, 1915*. ► **the razz** a beating *IRELAND, 1962*

razz *verb* to heckle; to show contempt; to jeer. Short for RASPBERRY, a derisive sound *US, 1919*

razzberry *noun* a jeering, derisory, farting noise. Extends RAZZ (to jeer) back to a variation of its source: RASPBERRY *US, 1922*

razzled *noun* drunk. Derives from ON THE RAZZLE, (having a good time, partying) *UK, 2002*

razzle-dazzle *noun* **1** confusion; chaos; bewilderment *US, 1889*. **2** sexual intercourse *UK, 1973*. **3** in circus and carnival usage, a prostitute *US, 1981*

razzmatazz *noun* **1** old-fashioned, sentimental jazz. The term was originally used, before use of the word 'jazz', to describe an early jazz-like music *US, 1936*. **2** a showy outward appearance *UK, 1958*. **3** extreme pleasure *US, 1953*

razzy *adjective* tattered; unkempt *BARBADOS, 1965*

RB *noun* an enthusiastic sportsman whose character is formed by the aggressive pursuit of masculinity and frequently demonstrated by his boorish behaviour and drunken socialising. An abbreviation of RUGGER BUGGER *SOUTH AFRICA, 1991*

RC *adjective* Roman Catholic *UK, 1762*

RCH *noun* a tiny notional unit of measure. An abbreviation of RED CUNT HAIR, perceived as a smaller unit even than a simple CUNT HAIR *US, 1968*

RCMP *noun* in Canada, a Roman Catholic Member of Parliament *CANADA, 1985*

RD *noun* a red-coloured capsule of secobarbital sodium (trade name Seconal™), a central nervous system depressant. An initialised RED DEVIL *US, 1977*

reach *verb* to be prepared to fight *US, 2004*. ► **reach out and touch someone** to telephone. From a 1982 American Telephone and Telegraph advertising slogan *US, 1989*

reach-around *noun* manual stimulation of the passive partner's genitals by the male penetrating from behind *US, 1987*

read *verb* **1** in poker, to try to discern an opponent's hand *US, 1979*. **2** in sports, to anticipate an opponent's movement *US, 1984*. **3** in transsexual usage, to detect a person's genetic sex *US, 1987*. ► **read (someone) the riot act** to give someone a very stern lecture or reprimand. From a law enacted by George I limiting the activities of groups of 12 or more *UK, 1906*. ► **read a shirt** to look for signs of body lice *US, 1981*. ► **read between the lines** said when three fingers are raised in an insolent gesture. The index finger is the one 'between the lines'; this is, therefore, a catchphrased elaboration of a familiar insulting gesture. Reported by a variety of mothers in Cardiff and Bristol during April 2005 and generally credited to 8-year-old children *UK, 2005*. ► **read the riot act** to instruct a prisoner who is about to be released on the legal restrictions concerning firearms. From the sense 'to give someone a very stern lecture or reprimand' *UK, 1996*. ► **you wouldn't read about it** you wouldn't believe such bad luck! *AUSTRALIA, 1950*

readable *adjective* used of a casino blackjack gambler, sloppy in dealing or generous with body language, in either event revealing to players the strength of his hand *US, 1991*

read and write *noun* a fight. Rhyming slang, never used in a shortened form *UK, 1857*

reader *noun* **1** a book; a magazine; a newspaper. From the early C18 usage as a 'pocket-book' which moved into the current sense during the mid-C19 *UK, 1996*. **2** a 'Wanted' poster or handbill *US, 1926*. **3** a counterfeit driving licence *US, 1985*. **4** a prescription for a narcotic *US, 1950*. **5** a marked card *US, 1894*

readers *noun* **1** reading spectacles *UK, 1961.* **2** special tinted eye glasses used for reading marked cards *US, 1985*

readies; reddies *noun* cash money. A variation, not a plural, of READY, in turn an abbreviation of 'ready money' *UK, 1937*

read my lips pay attention to what I am saying, for it is the bedrock truth. A pop phrase embraced in a show of bravado by George Bush when he was running for president of the US in 1988: 'Read my lips – no new taxes' and then the gist of endless ridicule when, two years later, he advocated a new tax. Actor Tim Curry named an album that he recorded in 1978 *Read My Lips*, later explaining to William Safire that he took the phrase to mean 'Listen and listen very hard, because I want you to hear what I've got to say' *US, 1988*

ready *adjective* competent *US, 1946*

ready; reddy *noun* cash money. An abbreviation of 'ready money' *UK, 1639*

ready eye *noun* a police trap. From READY-EYED (well informed or betrayed to the police) *UK, 1996*

ready-eye *verb* (of police) to operate an official surveillance *UK, 2000*

ready-eyed *adjective* **1** used by criminals of a planned crime that has been betrayed and is therefore a police trap *UK, 1975.* **2** in police use, well informed, knowing the detailed truth of a situation *UK, 1977*

ready for Doctor Jesus *adjective* about to die *US, 1966*

ready, Freddie used for signalling readiness *US, 1952*

ready-made *noun* a commercially manufactured cigarette *US, 1952*

ready rocks; redi rocks *noun* a form of cocaine prepared for smoking *US, 1989*

ready-rolls *noun* commercially manufactured cigarettes *US, 1951*

ready-to-run *noun* in the usage of youthful model road racers (slot car racers), a shop-bought car that has not been modified or enhanced *US, 1997*

ready whip *noun* a non-commissioned officer fresh out of training. From the pressurised sweet topping advertised as instant whipped cream *US, 1991*

real *noun* the truth *US, 1972.* ▶ **on the real 1** genuine. Black usage *UK, 2000.* **2** seriously *US, 1993*

real *adjective* homosexual *US, 1997*

real *adverb* really, truly; hence, used as an intensifier, greatly. The *Oxford English Dictionary* offers both Scottish and US origins, but the earliest slang sense is from English writer R.H. Froude *UK, 1827*

real bikini *noun* something that is excellent. Teen slang *US, 1955*

real bush *noun* a white woman. Used by US troops in Vietnam jaded by their experiences with Vietnamese prostitutes *US, 1991*

real case *noun* a serious medical emergency *US, 1994*

real deal *noun* **1** an authentic item or person; the plain truth *US, 1991.* **2** a youth gang member who is fully committed to the gang *US, 1995*

Real Deal *nickname* Evander Holyfield (b.1962), three times world heavyweight champion boxer *US, 1992*

real estate *noun* in war, territory to be taken, held, abandoned or lost *US, 1982*

reality check *noun* in computing, a simple test of a computer's or program's operating ability *US, 1991*

real live *adjective* genuine, actual. Jocular; often used of an inanimate article *UK, 1887*

really! used for expressing emphatic agreement *US, 1973*

Really Canadian Modest Police *noun* the Royal Canadian Mounted Police. A back-formation from the initials RCMP *CANADA, 2002*

Real McCoy *noun* a variety of marijuana *CANADA, 2002*

real McCoy; McCoy *noun* the genuine article *US, 1883*

real thing *noun* ▶ **the real thing** the genuine article. Figurative slang from the conventional sense *UK, 1939*

real world *noun* the non-pornographic entertainment industry; the world outside the pornography industry *US, 1995*

ream *verb* **1** to have anal intercourse *US, 1942.* **2** to cheat someone. Figurative from the more literal sense of poking something up one's rectum. Also variant 'rim' *US, 1933.* **3** to scold or punish someone. From the sense of 'ream' as widening a hole. 'Ream out' is also used *US, 1950*

ream *adjective* excellent. An intensification of the C19 sense as 'good, genuine, honest' *UK, 2002*

ream job *noun* **1** anal sex *US, 1995.* **2** a difficult situation *US, 1968*

rear *noun* the buttocks. Euphemistic *UK, 1796.* ▶ **get your rear in gear** to get going *US, 1972*

rear admiral *noun* a proctologist *US, 1973*

rear-area hawk *noun* an officer stationed away from the field of battle who has strong, bellicose opinions about what should be done in battle. Vietnam war usage *US, 1989*

rear-area pussy *noun* a support personnel safely away from combat. Occasionally abbreviated to RAP *US, 1991*

rear-echelon commando *noun* a soldier assigned to duty safely away from combat *US, 1947*

rear-echelon motherfucker *noun* a member of the armed forces serving behind lines well away from combat. Often abbreviated to REMF *US, 1976*

rear-end loader *noun* a prisoner who hides items in their rectum *AUSTRALIA, 2001*

rear exit *noun* a retreat or flight from danger *US, 1957*

rear-gunner; rear seat gunner *noun* a male homosexual. A masculine image that employs weaponry in a metaphor for anal intercourse *UK, 2000*

rearrange *verb* ▶ **rearrange the deck chairs on the Titanic; rearrange the deck chairs** to focus on petty matters while ignoring major problems. From the image of the folly of worrying about the arrangement of deck chairs on the Titanic as the ship sank *US, 1972*

reat pleat *noun* fashionable trousers. Usage by Mexican-American youth (Pachucos) in the southwestern US *US, 1947*

reb *noun* any poor, rural, white southerner *US, 1978*

rebbish *adjective* poor, white and racist. From the shortened REB or JOHNNY REB, harkening to Confederate soldiers *US, 1945*

rebellious henchman *noun* the penis *UK, 2003*

rebel trap *noun* in pool, the largest regulation-size table. In the US, the large tables were unknown in the south, giving rise to this term in the north *US, 1990*

rebound *noun* **1** a person with whom you have a romantic relationship in close proximity to the unhappy ending of a prior relationship *US, 1997.* **2** in trucking, a return trip *US, 1976.* ▶ **on the rebound** emotionally vulnerable following rejection by a loved-one *UK, 1864*

rec *noun* **1** a recreation ground (a municipal park) *UK, 1931.* **2** in prison, a recommendation given by the judge on sentencing *UK, 1998*

recap *noun* a recapitulation *US, 1926*

recap *verb* to recapitulate *UK, 1950*

recce; reccy *noun* a reconnaissance. Originally military; wider usage tends toward vaguer and more figurative shadings of the sense *UK, 1941*

recce *verb* to go on a reconnaissance; to look around. Originally military *UK, 1943*

receipt *noun* in professional wrestling, an arguably unacceptable manoeuvre that is acceptable in the context of justifiable revenge *US, 2002*

reck *verb* to consider; to think. A shortening of RECKON *UK, 1997*

reckon *verb* to esteem someone or something as worthwhile *UK, 1964*

recognize *verb* to pay attention *US, 2001*

recon *noun* reconnaisance. Often used in an adjectival sense *US, 1918*

recon *verb* to reconnoitre. Shortened for military purposes *US, 1966*

recon by fire *noun* in a military situation, random gunfire designed to ascertain the presence of the enemy by return fire *US, 1971*

record *noun* ▶ **change the record!; put another record on!** used to demand a change of style, subject or substance in what is being said *UK, 1966*

recovery room *noun* a golf course's bar *US, 2000*

rec room *noun* a recreational room. A mandatory feature of suburban 1960s life in the US, where the family gathered to watch television, play table tennis, set up model trains, etc *US, 1962*

rectum rocket *noun* a fast-moving vehicle *UK, 1981*

recycle *noun* LSD *UK, 1998*

recycle *verb* ▶ **recyle the dice** in bar dice games, to roll again after a roll that produces no points for the player *US, 1971*

red *noun* **1** any central nervous system depressant, especially a capsule of Seconal™ or another barbiturate *US, 1979*. **2** marijuana. A generic term for golden-red marijuana, clipping PANAMA RED etc *US, 1982*. **3** morphine *US, 1945*. **4** blood. Professional wrestling usage *US, 2002*. **5** in a deck of playing cards, any heart or diamond. A flush of hearts or diamonds is referred to as 'all red' *US, 1988*. **6** in American casinos, a five-dollar betting chip *US, 1982*. **7** a penny *US, 1950*. **8** a liberal; a socialist; a Marxist; a Marxist-Leninist; a Maoist; a Trotskyite; a communist; an anarchist *UK, 1848*. ▶ **in the red** in debt. From the use of red ink to show debt in account ledgers *UK, 1926*

red *adjective* **1** made of gold, golden. In conventional use from C14, slipped into slang during C17. Also in occasional use as a noun *UK, 1981*. **2** of a mixed (black and white) racial heritage *US, 1969*. **3** drug-intoxicated. From the *red*dening of the smoker's eyes *JAMAICA, 1998*

red and blue *noun* a capsule of amobarbital sodium and secobarbital sodium (trade name Tuinal™), a combination of central nervous system depressants *US, 1969*

red ass *noun* anger *US, 1975*

red-ass *verb* to annoy or tease someone *US, 1994*

red-assed *adjective* very angry *US, 1962*

redback *noun* in western Canada, a Hereford cow or steer *CANADA, 1962*

red badge of courage *noun* a notional badge awarded to someone who performs oral sex on a woman who is experiencing the bleed period of the menstrual cycle *US, 1994*

red ball *noun* **1** a fast freight train *US, 1946*. **2** a trail, path or road used by the Viet Cong or North Vietnamese during the Vietnam war *US, 1991*

red band; red-band *noun* a prisoner with privileges; a trusty *UK, 1950*

red biddy *noun* cheap red wine; also a drink of cheap red wine and methylated spirits *UK, 1928*

red bike *noun* the bleed period of the menstrual cycle *AUSTRALIA, 2002*

red bird *noun* **1** a capsule of secobarbital sodium (trade name Seconal™), a central nervous system depressant *US, 1953*. **2** the AH-1G Cobra helicopter. Used purely as a gunship in the Vietnam war from 1971 until the end of the conflict *US, 1991*

red blanket *noun* the corpse of a person who died with massive injuries *US, 1987*

red board *noun* in horse racing, the official sign announcing that a race's results stand *US, 1947*

red box *noun* an ambulance *US, 1976*

red bread *noun* payment for donating blood *US, 1971*

red bud *noun* marijuana *UK, 2003*

Red Bull *nickname* Black Label™ beer. Scamto youth street slang (South African townships) *SOUTH AFRICA, 2005*

red bullet *nickname* a capsule of secobarbital sodium (trade name Seconal™), a central nervous system depressant *US, 1977*

red button *noun* a foreman *US, 1955*

red can *noun* a can of Melbourne Bitter™ beer *AUSTRALIA, 2003*

red cap *noun* a member of the military police. From the red-topped cap that forms part of the uniform. Generally familiar from

television drama series such as: *Red Cap* (ABC, 1964–66) and *Red Cap* (BBC, 2001–03) *UK, 1931*

red caps *noun* crack cocaine *UK, 1998*

red cent *noun* the lowest value denomination, hence the least amount possible. A *copper* cent, thus 'red' *US, 1839*

Red Centre *noun* the central desert regions of the Australian mainland *AUSTRALIA, 1935*

red chamber club *noun* the Senate in the Canadian Parliament. The source of the term is that the senate (the 'Red Chamber') has red carpets, leather chairbottoms and desk blotters *CANADA, 1963*

red chenke *noun* a light-skinned person; an unlikeable person *ANTIGUA AND BARBUDA, 1996*

red chicken *noun* heroin, especially Chinese heroin *US, 1969*

red cross *noun* marijuana *UK, 2003*

red cunt hair *noun* a very small unit of measure. Sterling Johnson, in *English as a Second F*cking Language*, 1995, notes: 'The term originated with the master carpenters of Cape Cod and is now universally used' *US, 1968*

redders *noun* harness racers. Rhyming slang, from 'red hots' to 'trots' *AUSTRALIA, 1989*

red devil *noun* **1** a capsule of secobarbital sodium (trade name Seconal™), a central nervous system depressant *US, 1969*. **2** a type of amphetamine tablet *UK, 1997*. **3** heroin *UK, 2003*. **4** a woman's menstrual period *US, 1954*

red diaper baby *noun* a person who was raised by Communist parents who instilled Communist beliefs and values *US, 1970*

red dirt marijuana; red dirt *noun* uncultivated marijuana *US, 1960*

red doll *noun* a capsule of secobarbital sodium (trade name Seconal™), a central nervous system depressant *US, 1977*

red dollars *noun* US military scrip in Vietnam *US, 1965*

red dope *noun* wild cannabis that has been sprayed with a bright red herbicide. The colour plus DOPE (marijuana) *US, 2001*

red dot *noun* ▶ **the red dot** the bleed period of the menstrual cycle *US, 2001*

red dot special *noun* the bleed period of the menstrual cycle *US, 2001*

red dragon *noun* a variety of LSD *UK, 1996*

reddy *noun* an Italian. May derive from RADDIE (an Italian living in London), or take root in Italian red wine *UK, 1961* ▷*see:* **READY**

red-eye *noun* **1** a long, aggressive stare *US, 1985*. **2** an overnight aeroplane flight, arriving at its destination early in the morning *US, 1968*. **3** potent, impure homemade alcohol, especially whisky *US, 1819*. **4** fermented catsup. A prison concoction *US, 1976*. **5** on the railways, a stop signal *US, 1946*. **6** in pinball, an activated special scoring device, usually lit in red *US, 1977*. **7** a flashing red light on top of a police car *US, 1976*. **8** the anus *US, 1966*

Redfern *noun* ▶ **get off at Redfern** to practise coitus interruptus. Redfern is the railway station immediately prior to Central Station, the principal station in Sydney *AUSTRALIA, 1956*

red flag *noun* **1** an obvious indication that all is not well *US, 1968*. **2** when injecting a drug into a vein, the practice of drawing blood up into the syringe to verify the finding of a vein and to control the pace of the injection *US, 1987*. **3** a show of menstrual blood on outer clothing; hence, the bleed period of the menstrual cycle *US, 2001*. ▶ **be flying the red flag** to be in the bleed period of the menstrual cycle *UK, 2000*

red flag day *noun* any day during the bleed period of a woman's menstrual cycle *US, 2000*

red flag week *noun* the bleed period of the menstrual cycle. Also used in Scotland *CANADA, 2000*

red goddess *noun* a firefighting vehicle that is generally used for training but made available (for operation by the military) when regular firefighters and their fire-engines are out of service *UK, 2002*

red gunyon *noun* smashed marijuana seeds or gum hashish smoked in a pipe *US, 1973*

red head *noun* a match *US, 1981*

redheaded aunt from Red Bank *noun* the bleed period of the menstrual cycle *US, 1999*

redheaded friend *noun* the bleed period of the menstrual cycle *US, 1999*

Red Heart *nickname* the central desert regions of the Australian mainland *AUSTRALIA, 1931*

red hot *noun* **1** a variety of MDMA, the recreational drug best known as ecstasy *UK, 1996*. **2** a frankfurter *US, 1950*

red hot *adjective* extremely unfair *AUSTRALIA, 1896*

red hots *noun* **1** diarrhoea. Rhyming slang for TROTS *UK, 1992*. **2** trotting races. Rhyming slang for TROTS *AUSTRALIA, 1966*

red Ibo *noun* a light-skinned person of mixed black and white heritage *JAMAICA, 1996*

red Leb *noun* hashish with a reddish colour produced in the Lebanon *UK, 2002*

red-leg *noun* a poor white person *BARBADOS, 1892*

red-legs *noun* the artillery. From the red stripes on the trousers of Union artillerymen during the US Civil War *US, 1971*

red letter *noun* a letter that is smuggled out of prison *UK, 1996*

red letter day *noun* the day each cycle that the menstrual bleed commences. A neat pun on the colour of blood and the date in a calendar *US, 2001*

red light *noun* the bleed period of the menstrual cycle. As in 'red light – stop – there will be no sex' *US, 1954*

red-light *verb* (used of a police car) to activate flashing lights and pull a vehicle off the road *US, 1976*

red-light *adjective* pertaining to prostitution *US, 1900*

red lilly *noun* a capsule of secobarbital sodium (trade name Seconal™); any central nervous system depressant. From the colour of the capsule and the name of the manufacturer *US, 1977*

red line *noun* in the used car business, the minimum which a dealer will accept for a car *US, 1975*

red lips *noun* a type of LSD. Possibly from an image printed on the drug *UK, 2003*

Red Mary *noun* the bleed period of the menstrual cycle *US, 1980*

Red Mike *noun* a woman-hater *CANADA, 1946*

red Mitsubishi *noun* PMA (paramethoxyamphetamine) or PMMA (paramethoxymethylamphetamine) when taken as a recreational drug *UK, 2000*

redneck *noun* a country-dweller, especially one whose views are considered bigoted by 'sophisticated' citizens. Generally derogatory *US, 1830*

redneck radio *noun* citizens' band radio *US, 1977*

Red Ned *noun* cheap red wine *AUSTRALIA, 1941*

redner *noun* ▶ **take a redner** to be embarrassed *IRELAND, 1996*

red nigger *noun* a native American Indian *US, 1998*

red one *noun* **1** in carnival usage, a profitable engagement *US, 1973*. **2** a very short distance. A euphemized abbreviation of RED CUNT HAIR *US, 1980*

red onion *noun* on the railways, an eating establishment *US, 1977*

red-out *noun* a flood of the colour red in your vision just before you pass out from lack of oxygen *US, 1990*

red-penny man *noun* a procurer of prostitutes, a pimp *AUSTRALIA, 1975*

red phosphorus *noun* smokeable metamphetamine. From a process in the synthesis of the drug *UK, 2003*

red pill *noun* ▶ **take the red pill** to go all-out for the active option. From a choice between reality and euphoria offered in the film *The Matrix* (1999) *UK, 2005*

red pussy hair *noun* a very short distance. Slightly less offensive than RED CUNT HAIR *US, 1987*

red-ragger *noun* a Communist *AUSTRALIA, 1916*

red-ragging *adjective* Communist *AUSTRALIA, 1938*

red rattler *noun* a type of passenger train with dark red carriages that became noisy when travelling at speed *AUSTRALIA, 1981*

red river *noun* the bleed period of a woman's menstrual cycle *US, 1954*

red rock *noun* granulated heroin originating in China; heroin generally *US, 1969*

red rock opium *noun* a mixture of heroin, barbital, strychnine and caffeine *UK, 2002*

red rum *noun* **1** a variety of heroin. An allusion to the qualities of the legendary racehorse (steeplechaser Red Rum won the UK Grand National a record three times). Also rhyming slang for 'dumb' and 'murder' spelt backwards *UK, 2001*. **2** a mixture of heroin, barbital, strychnine and caffeine. Also known as RED ROCK OPIUM from which this may be formed by elision; it is interesting to note with regard to the dangerous nature of this cocktail that 'red rum' is 'murder' backwards *UK, 2002*

red rush *noun* amyl nitrite *UK, 1996*

reds *noun* **1** the bleed period of the menstrual cycle *US, 1999*. **2** a sense of anger *US, 1951*

red sails in the sunset the bleed period of the menstrual cycle *AUSTRALIA, 1968*

red seal *noun* a variety of cannabis resin. Branded with a red seal *UK, 1996*

Red Sea pedestrian *noun* a Jewish person. Offensive, intended as jocular; from the crossing of the Red Sea (Exodus 14: 21–22) *UK, 1979*

red shirt *noun* **1** a troublemaker *US, 1967*. **2** a volunteer firefighter *US, 1954*. **3** a college athlete who, because he did not play in his freshman year, may matriculate and play at the varsity level for a fifth year *US, 1950*. **4** in roller derby, a skater who engages in rough, 'bad guy' tactics *US, 1999*. **5** a professional wrestler who is regularly scripted to lose matches to advance the careers of other wrestlers *US, 2002*

redskin *noun* in a deck of playing cards, any face card *US, 1967*

red snapper *noun* in blackjack, a dealt hand of two red cards that add up to 21 *US, 1996*

Red Sox are in town experiencing the bleed period of the menstrual cycle. The colour of blood signals this euphemistic adoption of the Boston baseball team *US, 2001*

red squad *noun* a police unit that engages in systematic investigation and record-keeping about leftist political and social action organisations unrelated to criminal conduct *US, 1970*

red steer *noun* a bushfire *AUSTRALIA, 1936*

red stuff *noun* gold *UK, 1956*

reds under the bed *noun* the communist presence lurking in Western society *UK, 1972*

red tape *noun* excessive formality; bureaucratic obstacles. Originally a literal term, referring to the red-coloured tape used in securing legal documents; later used figuratively *UK, 1837*

red tide *noun* **1** hordes of communists seen as ready to overwhelm western civilisation *US, 1991*. **2** the bleed period of the menstrual cycle *US, 1999*

red-top *noun* a tabloid newspaper at the more populist end of the readership. From the red masthead characteristic of such papers *UK, 1997*

reducer *noun* in gin, any card drawn or held for the sole purpose of reducing the number of points in unmatched cards in a hand *US, 1965*

red up; rid up *verb* to clear and clean a table after eating *CANADA, 1998*

red wedge *noun* the bleed period of the menstrual cycle. Combines 'red', for the colour of blood, with a pun on conventional 'wedge' (something that fills a gap) and 'wedgie' (a trick with underpants) suggesting underwear; the whole being a play on Red Wedge (a 1980s alliance of musicians and actors with the UK Labour party) *UK, 2001*

red week *noun* the bleed period of the menstrual cycle *US, 2001*

red, white and blue *noun* a shoe. Rhyming slang *UK, 1972*

red wings *noun* sexual intercourse or oral sex with a woman who is experiencing the bleed period of the menstrual cycle. From motorcycle gang culture *US, 1971*

reeb *noun* beer. Back slang, noted as current in the UK due to its use in the US, possibly reinvigorated by *The Simpsons* television cartoon *UK, 1859*

reebs *noun* marijuana *US, 1988*

reeds *noun* long shorts, favoured by surfers *US, 1985*

reef *noun* a marijuana cigarette *US, 1958*

reef *verb* **1** to fondle another person's genitals. Probably from the earlier sense 'to pick a pocket' *UK, 1962*. **2** to remove something from someone's pocket *US, 1949*

reefdogger *noun* a marijuana cigarette *US, 1982*

reefer *noun* **1** a marijuana cigarette. Almost certainly from the Spanish word meaning 'to twist'. Still used, with a nostalgic air to it *US, 1931*. **2** marijuana *US, 1931*. **3** a refrigerator; a refrigerated railway wagon *US, 1914*. **4** a pickpocket *US, 1949*

reefer madness *noun* a unusually great appetite or determined devotion to the use of marijuana. An ironic adoption of the title of a 1936 film that famously exposed the immoral excesses of marijuana addicts *AUSTRALIA, 1996*

reefer room *noun* in a morgue, a refrigerated room where bodies are stored *US, 1997*

reegie *noun* a police officer in the Regional Crime Squad *UK, 2002*

reeker *noun* a bad-smelling hospital casualty department patient *US, 1978*

reek-ho *adjective* drunk *UK, 2002*

reekstick *noun* a conventional tobacco cigarette laced with cocaine *UK, 2003*

reel *verb* ▶ **reel someone in** to triumph over gullibility, especially regarding a piece of trivial teasing. Often accompanied by the action of reeling in a fish; sometimes the action may replace the words *UK, 1999*

reeling and rocking *noun* a stocking. Rhyming slang, inspired by the fashions of the rock 'n' roll era; usually seen in pairs *UK, 1992*

reels *adjective* without money. Rhyming slang, from 'reels of cotton' to 'rotten' (without money) *AUSTRALIA, 1989*

reels of cotton *adjective* rotten. Rhyming slang *UK, 1979*

reet; reat *adjective* good, pleasing *US, 1934*

reeve *verb* to cheat *CANADA, 1999*

ref *noun* in a sporting contest, a *referee UK, 1899?*

ref *verb* in a sporting context, to *referee UK, 1929?*

reffo *noun* a migrant to Australia who is a refugee from their home country *AUSTRALIA, 1941*

refusenik *noun* a non-conformist. Adopted without a full understanding from the name given in 1970s to Jews in the Soviet Union who were refused permission to emigrate to Israel *UK, 2002*

reg *noun* **1** a regular customer or guest *UK, 2001*. **2** marijuana of average quality. An abbreviation of 'regular'. The variant 'regs' also exists *US, 1973*

regale *noun* a festive occasion. The term is adopted from French, where it has a similar meaning *CANADA, 1947*

reggaematic *adjective* in or of a reggae style *UK, 1992*

reggin *noun* a black person. The offensive NIGGER spelt backwards *US, 1981*

Reg Grundies; grundies; grunds; reginalds; reggies *noun* underwear. Rhyming slang, playing on UNDIES, formed from the name Reg Grundy, an Australian televison producer *AUSTRALIA, 1984*

Regiment *noun* ▶ **the Regiment** the SAS (22 Special Air Service regiment) *UK, 1995*

regmaker; reggie *noun* a drink, pick-me-up or medication taken to relieve (or 'cure') a hangover. A compound of Afrikaans *reg* (right) and English '-maker' *SOUTH AFRICA, 1954*

rego; reggo *noun* vehicle registration *AUSTRALIA, 1967*

regreen *verb* while working in the office of the US Department of Defense, to receive an update briefing on affairs in the army *US, 1986*

regroup *verb* to recover from a surprise or a setback *US, 1966*

regs *noun* regulations. Military in origin *UK, 1996*

regular *noun* **1** a prisoner who serves his sentence with dignity and strength *US, 1974*. **2** a skateboarder who skates with the left foot to the front *UK, 2004*

regular *adjective* **1** complete; absolute; thorough *UK, 1821*. **2** kind; decent; honest *US, 1946*

regular P *noun* crack cocaine *UK, 1998*

regulars *noun* common black ants *BARBADOS, 1965*

rehab *noun* rehabilitation (a medical regime for the cure of alcohol and drug addiction); also, the clinic or hospital environment where *rehabilitation* takes place. Both senses may serve concurrently *UK, 1961*

rehash *verb* in the circus or carnival, to resell ticket stubs to patrons and pocket the funds *US, 1980*

rehitch *verb* to re-enlist; to re-marry *US, 1953*

reindeer dust *noun* any powdered drug; cocaine; heroin. A play on SNOW *US, 1942*

reject *noun* a socially inept person; a pathetic individual; a person who does not fit in with the fashionable, trendy majority *US, 1968*

relate *verb* to understand; to like or appreciate someone or something. A quintessential, over-used vague verb of the 1960s *US, 1959*

relay spot *noun* a room with a telephone used to relay calls placing bets in a bookmaking operation *US, 1973*

release *noun* in the coded language of massage parlours, ejaculation. A 2002 Incident Report from the Sausalito (California) Police Department describes the activities at a local massage parlour as follows: 'Every massage ends with some type of "release" (orgasm). The release is accomplished by the employee masturbating the client to an orgasm' *US, 2002*

release *verb* ▶ **release a chocolate hostage** to defecate *UK, 2002*. ▶ **release the hounds** to defecate *US, 2003*

relievers *noun* shoes *US, 1962*

re-light *noun* a cigarette butt retrieved and smoked *US, 1996*

religious issue *noun* in computing, a topic that is bound to launch an endless debate which cannot be resolved *US, 1991*

rellie *noun* a *relation*, a *relative AUSTRALIA, 1981*

rello; relo *noun* a *relative AUSTRALIA, 1987*

reload *verb* to give the victim of a confidence trick or fraudulent gambling game a false sense of confidence, then cheat the by-now willing victim of all he or she possesses *UK, 1977*

rels *noun* *relatives AUSTRALIA, 1991*

Rembrandt *noun* in poker, a hand of face cards *US, 1988*

remf *noun* a soldier assigned to a combat support role. Acronym of a 'rear-echelon motherfucker' *US, 1982*

Remington warrior *noun* a rear support troop. Named after the Remington typewriter, the 'warrior's weapon' *US, 1990*

remish *noun* remission (of a prison sentence) *UK, 1958*

remodel *verb* in car repair, to damage a vehicle or part severely *US, 1992*

remould *noun* a sex-change operation *UK, 2002*

Ren and Stimpy *noun* the female breasts. Ren and Stimpy are shamelessly gross cartoon characters created by John Kricfalusi, first seen in 1991 *UK, 2001*

Ren Cen *nickname* the Renaissance Center in Detroit, Michigan. An expensive, bold and risky attempt to revive the dying Detroit central district in the 1970s *US, 2003*

rendered *adjective* drunk *UK, 2002*

renk *adjective* impudent; offhand; rude; yobbish. Variation of 'rank' (offensive) *JAMAICA, 1994*

Reno *noun* in bar dice games, two dice that add up to seven *US, 1976*

renob *noun* a person who acts foolishly *US, 2001*

rent *noun* **1** a youthful, attractive homosexual male prostitute *UK, 1967*. **2** road tax. Motor trade slang *UK, 2004*. ▶ **up me for the rent!** used to register pleasurable astonishment *AUSTRALIA, 1971*

renta- *prefix* hired, rented. In commercial usage often used to create a company name, for instance: 'Rentacar' (examples found in Australia, Ireland, Spain, UK, US) and 'Rentavan' (examples found in Australia, Ireland, Mexico, UK). Both 'rentacar' and 'rentavan' are also used informally of a hired vehicle. Other use is often derogatory: 'rentacrowd' (a hired clique), 'rentamob' (a crowd assembled at political demonstration) and 'rentamouth' (a speaker for hire) *US, 1921*

rent-a-cop *noun* a private security guard. A tad disparaging *US, 1968*

rent-a-gob *noun* a citizens' band radio user who chats on a channel reserved for making contact; a person who talks too much and to little effect *UK, 1981*

rental units *noun* parents. From PARENTAL UNITS, a neat pun describing parental worth from a youth perspective *US, 1996*

Rent-a-Svend *nickname* Canadian politician Svend Robinson, the first openly gay, New Democratic member of Parliament. The controversial Svend Robinson has drawn criticism for his espousal of unpopular causes, such as the Palestinian side in the Arab–Israeli war and gay rights *CANADA, 2002*

rent-a-tile *noun* dancing very closely, barely moving your feet *TRINIDAD AND TOBAGO, 1993*

rent boy *noun* a young male prostitute *UK, 1969*

renter *noun* a homosexual male prostitute *UK, 1893*

rent party *noun* a party thrown for the purpose of collecting donations from friends to pay your rent *US, 1925*

rents *noun* parents. Teen slang that cuts parents down to size *US, 1968*

renzos *noun* Lorenzo™ decorative wheel rims *US, 1993*

reo *noun* **1** a reinforcement *AUSTRALIA, 1931*. **2** a difficult surfing manoeuvre on the breaking lip of a wave. An abbreviation of 're-entry' *US, 1988*

rep *noun* **1** reputation *US, 1705*. **2** a repetition, or complete cycle of an exercise *US, 1984*. **3** a repertory theatre or theatre company; a repertoire *US, 1925*. **4** in prison, a written representation *UK, 2002*. **5** a representative, often a travelling salesman *UK, 1896*. **6** a repellent *UK, 1995*

rep *verb* **1** to represent someone; to give someone a reputation *UK, 2002*. **2** to work as a representative of a company *UK, 1938*

Repat *noun* **1** the Repatriation Commission which gave assistance to ex-service personnel returning to civilian life *AUSTRALIA, 1920*. **2** a hospital for repatriated service personnel *AUSTRALIA, 1968*

repeater *noun* in horse racing, a horse that won the last race it entered *US, 1974*

repo *noun* repossession *US, 1971*

repo depot *noun* the Replacement Detachment of any large military force or installation *US, 1968*

repo man *noun* an agent of a finance company who repossesses, by an assortment of techniques, cars which have not been paid for. From 'repossess' *US, 1984*

repple-depple *noun* a replacement depot where soldiers arriving in Vietnam were assigned to units and soldiers leaving Vietnam were processed for homecoming *US, 1945*

reppoc; reppock *noun* a police officer. Back slang for COPPER *UK, 1996*

represent *verb* **1** to serve as a pimp for a prostitute *US, 1991*. **2** to project a positive image and attitude *US, 1997*

reptile *noun* a railway pointsman *US, 1977*

Republic of Mali *noun* cocaine. Rhyming slang for CHARLIE (cocaine) *UK, 2003*

re-rub *noun* a re-mixed dance music recording *UK, 2002*

res *noun* **1** a resident physician in a hospital *US, 1994*. **2** a dormitory or residence at a university or college *CANADA, 2001*. **3** the oily residue in a pipe after crack cocaine has been smoked *US, 1992*

resemble *verb* to resent. Usually in the jocular 'I resemble that remark' *UK, 1984*

resin *noun* cannabis resin *UK, 1996*

respec; respect; respeck; rispeck used for registering approval of someone's action or attitude. An abbreviation in all variant spellings of 'respect due'; occasionally ironic. Originally West Indian and UK black *UK, 1994*

respect due used for registering approval of someone's action or attitude. Originally West Indian and UK black *UK, 1998*

ressie *noun* a resident DJ *UK, 2001*

rest *noun* ▶ **give it a rest** to stop talking, especially to stop talking about a specific topic. Often as an imperative *UK, 1984*

rest *verb* ▶ **rest your mouth** to stop talking *BAHAMAS, 1982*. ▶ **rest your neck** to stop talking *US, 1989*

rest cure *noun* in the car sales business, sending a car into the shop while the customer waits and then returning it, claiming that work which has not been done has been done *US, 1953*

resting *adjective* of an actor, unemployed. Originally positive thinking, now arch *UK, 1999*

rest in peace *noun* crack cocaine. Imagery of death. *UK, 2003*

restroom *noun* a brakevan (caboose) *US, 1977*

result *noun* **1** the winning score in a sporting contest; a victory in any sport. Conventionally 'result' means 'outcome', hence a 'good result'; this usage clips and implies the positive adjective, exclusively acquiring the result for victors and so denying losers any achievement *UK, 1981*. **2** a satisfying or appropriate outcome; an achievement *UK, 1973*. **3** a successful or profitable robbery *UK, 1998*. **4** an arrest or a criminal conviction *UK, 2004*

ret *noun* a cigarette *US, 1971*

retail action *noun* recreational shopping *US, 1997*

retail therapy *noun* shopping when considered as an empowering leisure activity *US, 1986*

retard *noun* a slow, dim-witted person. From 'mentally retarded', but not necessarily indicative of actual mental retardation *US, 1970*

retarded *adjective* **1** stupid, foolish *US, 2003*. **2** drunk *US, 2003*. **3** in Quebec, delayed, late *CANADA, 2001*

retardo *noun* a mentally challenged person *US, 1981*

retread *noun* **1** in the military: a short-service officer on a second commission; a retired officer recalled to service; a retired officer re-employed as a civilian in an administrative post; an officer who has been promoted from the ranks; an aviator returned to flying duties after a period of ground service. The origin is in the new life given to a tyre by the application of a new tread; there is also a pun on 'retired/re-tyred'. The earliest use is for a World War 1 veteran recalled to serve in World War 2 *AUSTRALIA, 1943*. **2** a recently divorced person *US, 1985*

retread *verb* in the language surrounding the Grateful Dead, to tape over a tape that has been recorded once *US, 1994*

retriever *noun* a prisoner who intimidates other prison inmates for the purpose of 'retrieving' drugs that those inmates are suspected of carrying *UK, 1996*

retro *verb* to return something or someone from Antarctica to the country of origin. An abbreviation of 'retrograde' *ANTARCTICA, 2003*

retrosexual *noun* a heterosexual man who enjoys traditional male pastimes and spends as little time and money as possible on his appearance. A play on METROSEXUAL (a man with aesthetic tastes), suggesting a throwback to an earlier type *US, 2004*

rette *noun* a cigarette *US, 1997*

reunion in my bureau *noun* in Quebec, a meeting in my office. Both 'reunion' and 'bureau' are used in their French sense in English in Montreal *CANADA, 2001*

re-up *verb* to replenish a stack of something; to re-supply something; to re-sign or re-enlist. Originally a military slang term for re-enlisting *US, 1906*

rev *verb* to leave, to go *US, 1952*

RevCan *noun* Revenue Canada, the federal tax collection agency *CANADA, 2002*

revenge of the cradle; revenge of the nursery *noun* Quebec's high birthrate, perceived as being in retaliation for the loss of the province to England by France *CANADA, 1964*

revenoo; revenuer; revenooer *noun* a federal law enforcement official. Used by those in the illegal production of alcohol *US, 1974*

Reverend Ronald Knox; the Reverend; the Right Reverend *noun* syphilis; hence any sexually transmitted infection. Rhyming slang for POX, formed from the Catholic priest and detective storywriter, 1888–1957 *UK, 1980*

reverse *adjective* ▶ **reverse gears** to vomit *US, 1989*

reverse cowgirl *noun* a sexual position in which the woman straddles the prone man, facing his feet *US, 1991*

reverse o *noun* a position for mutual, simultaneous oral sex between two people, or the act itself, especially when advertised as a service offered by a prostitute *UK, 2003*

rev-head *noun* a motor vehicle enthusiast *AUSTRALIA, 1987*

revolt of the admirals *noun* a highly public clash between the US Navy and the US Air Force in 1949 over basing of the country's strategic airpower *US, 1949*

rev up and fuck off go away and don't annoy me; don't annoy me *IRELAND, 1991*

rewind *noun* in trucking, a return trip *US, 1977*

rex *noun* a (small) quantity of money *IRELAND, 1989*

Rexall ranger *noun* someone who wears cowboy clothes but has never worked on a ranch. Rexall is a chain drugstore, giving a touch of specificity to the more common DRUGSTORE COWBOY *US, 1970*

rez *noun* a Native American Indian reservation *US, 1998*

RF *verb* to play a prank. An abbreviation of RATFUCK *US, 1965*

RFB *noun* room, food and beverage – the basic components of a complimentary pass at a casino or hotel *US, 1996*

RG *noun* in homosexual usage, a biological female. A fellow homosexual is a GIRL, while a woman is a 'real girl', or RG *US, 1971*

rhine *noun* heroin. Probably by abbrevation of a particular pronunciation *UK, 1998*

rhino *noun* **1** money *UK, 1688*. **2** a large and powerful wave *US, 1991*

rhino chaser *noun* a large surfboard made for big-wave conditions *US, 1987*

RHIP rank has its privileges *US, 1968*

Rhodey *noun* a white Zimbabwean. Derogatory. A reference to Rhodesia, the country which became Zimbabwe in 1980 *SOUTH AFRICA, 2000*

rhody; rhodie *noun* a rhododendron *UK, 1851*

rhubarb *noun* **1** nonsense. From its use by actors as an 'unintelligible murmur' *UK, 1963*. **2** said repeatedly by muttering actors to give the impression of background conversations; hence, spoken nonsense. Theatre slang *UK, 1934*. **3** a fight; an uproar; a riot *US, 1943*. **4** an advance of wages, a loan; as 'rhubarbs': a membership subscription. Rhyming slang, pronounced 'roobub', for SUB (a subscription) *UK, 1929*

rhubarb and custard *noun* a variety of MDMA, the recreational drug best known as ecstasy. From the red and yellow colour of the pill; the syllable 'barb' is possibly an indication that the tablet contains barbiturate *UK, 1996*

rhubarb pill; rhubarb *noun* a bill (for payment). Rhyming slang, based on a homeopathic remedy for constipation; noted by Julian Franklyn, *A Dictionary of Rhyming Slang*, 1960, who suspected (or perpetrated) the pun 'that both necessitate an outpouring' *UK, 1998*

rhubarbs *noun* **1** suburbs. Rhyming slang, pronounced 'roobubs', formed on an elision of 'suburbs' *UK, 1960*. **2** a variety of LSD *UK, 1996*

rhyme off *verb* to recite; to talk. From Scottish dialect *rame* (to talk nonsense; to reiterate) *UK: SCOTLAND, 2000*

rhythm *noun* an amphetamine tablet *US, 1993*

rhythm and blues; rhythms *noun* shoes. Rhyming slang *UK, 1998*

rhythm method *noun* a method of cheating while playing a slot machine by controlling the spins of the inner-wheels. Playing on the name of the least successful method of birth control *US, 1977*

riah *noun* the hair. Polari back slang *UK, 1967*

riah zhoosher; riah shusher *noun* a hairdresser. A combination of ZHOOSH (to tidy) with RIAH (the hair) *UK, 2002*

riah-zshumpah *noun* a hairdresser *UK, 1992*

rib *noun* **1** a wife or girlfriend. From the Biblical creation tale, with Eve springing from Adam's rib *UK, 1589*. **2** Rohypnol™ (flunitrazepam), popularly known as the 'date-rape drug' *US, 1995*. **3** MDMA, the recreational drug best known as ecstasy *UK, 2003*

rib *verb* **1** to make fun of someone *US, 1930*. **2** to insult someone in a semi-formal quasi-friendly competition. A variation of 'rib' (to tease) *US, 2000*

ribbon and curl *noun* a girl. Rhyming slang *UK, 1992*

ribbon clerk *noun* a poker player who withdraws from a hand at any sign of serious betting *US, 1988*

ribena on toast *adjective* awful; tasteless; in bad taste. Possibly a literal translation of a bad taste; coinage is credited to ballet master David Kerr *UK, 1992*

ribtapper *noun* a heavy-duty boot *UK: SCOTLAND, 1988*

Rican *noun* a Puerto Rican *US, 1975*

rice *noun* effort. Royal Marine slang *UK, 1989*

rice-and-peas boongy *noun* large buttocks, especially those of a woman *BAHAMAS, 1998*

rice-and-ring *verb* to get married *US, 1947*

rice-a-roni *noun* in necrophile usage, a badly decomposed corpse. A comparison to the branded soft-boiled rice product *US, 1987*

rice bandit *noun* a Japanese person. Offensive *AUSTRALIA, 1995*

rice belly *noun* the protruding stomach of a child *GUYANA, 1996*

rice-burner *noun* a Japanese car or motorcycle *US, 1979*

rice eye *noun* a Japanese person. Hawaiian youth usage, especially in the taunt 'No lie, rice eye' *US, 1982*

rice machine *noun* a car manufactured in Japan or by a Japanese manufacturer *US, 1993*

riceman *noun* a Chinese person. Offensive *US, 1945*

rice paddy Hattie *noun* any rural Chinese prostitute *US, 1949*

rice queen *noun* a gay man attracted to men of South Asian origin *US, 1972*

ricer *noun* a person from South Asia. Offensive *US, 1980*

rice rocket *noun* a motorcyle made by a Japanese manufacturer. Offensive *US, 1993*

Richard *noun* **1** any police official, especially a detective. An embellished DICK *US, 1950*. **2** the penis. An extension of DICK (the penis), which is the short form of the first name Richard *UK, 2001*. ▶ **had the Richard** to be ruined or irreparably broken; to be finished. In the *Australian National Dictionary* it is claimed that this is from British rhyming slang 'Richard the Third' (the bird), from theatrical slang 'to get the bird' (to get a bad reception on stage), but there is little semantic overlap to warrant this explanation. Rather if something has 'had the dick' then it is 'fucked', and therein lies the metaphor. Richard here is merely euphemistic for DICK (the penis). Supporting this explanation are the other variants HAD THE STICK, HAD THE ROD and of course HAD THE DICK *AUSTRALIA, 1967*

Richard and Judy *adjective* moody. Rhyming slang, formed from husband and wife television presenters Richard Madeley and Judy Finnegan *UK, 2004*

Richard Burton *noun* a curtain. Theatrical rhyming slang, formed from the name of the Welsh actor, 1925–84 *UK, 1992*

Richard the Third; Richard *noun* **1** a young woman; a sweetheart. Rhyming slang for BIRD *UK, 1950*. **2** a bird. Rhyming slang; originally recorded in *Songs and Slang of the British Soldier*, John Brophy and Eric Partridge, 1930. In theatrical use as THE BIRD (a farting noise masquerading as criticism) *UK, 1979*. **3** a piece of excrement. Rhyming slang for TURD *UK, 1961*

Richard Todd *noun* a portion of fried cod. Rhyming slang formed on the name of the British actor (b.1919) *UK, 1992*

Richibucto goose *noun* a salted shad. Named after a town in Nova Scotia *CANADA, 1939*

rich man's drug *noun* cocaine. Because of its high cost. Although the phrase sounds a bit literary, it was used by those without any particular literary background *US, 1972*

rick *noun* **1** a mistake. Probably a shortening of RICKET (a mistake) *UK, 1991*. **2** an accomplice who pretends to be a client in order to encourage trade, originally used of a cheapjack or showman, later of a less than scrupulous bookmaker *UK, 1898*

rick *adjective* fake; spurious. From the noun *UK, 1967*

rick; ric *verb* to make a mistake. From RICK (a mistake) *UK, 1996*

ricket *noun* a mistake *UK, 1958*. ▶ **drop a ricket** to make a mistake *UK, 1998*

rickety-raw *adjective* attractive, fashionable *US, 1987*

Rick Stein *noun* a fine. Rhyming slang, formed from the name of the UK television chef (b.1947) *UK, 2004*

Rick Witter *noun* a shitter (in all senses). Rhyming slang, formed from the lead singer of Shed Seven *UK, 2003*

Ricky Martin; Ricky *noun* a side-parting. Popney rhyming slang, from popular singer Ricky Martin (b.1971). Popney was contrived for *www.music365.co.uk*, an Internet music site *UK, 2001*

Ricky Racer *noun* a fanatic mountain bike enthusiast who rarely if ever rides *US, 1997*

ricky-ticky; ricky-tick *adjective* used of a jazz rhythm, old-fashioned, even, boring *US, 1952*

rid *verb* ▶ **rid a fit** to get rid of an outfit of clothes *US, 1994*

riddle *verb* in Newfoundland, to weave up-and-down rods between rails to make a fence *CANADA, 1966*

riddle-me-ree *noun* urine; an act of urination. Rhyming slang for PEE or WEE; always used in full to avoid confusion with other slang, such as JIMMY RIDDLE or PIDDLE *UK, 1992*

riddle me this, Batman answer this question. From the *Batman* television series (1966–68) and one of its arch-villains, The Riddler *US, 1993*

riddy *noun* (as a result of embarrassment) a red face. Glasgow slang *UK: SCOTLAND, 1985*

ride *noun* **1** a car *US, 1930*. **2** a person who you are counting on to drive you somewhere *US, 2001*. **3** a sexually desirable person. From RIDE (to have sex) *UK, 2002*. **4** an act of sexual intercourse *UK, 1937*. **5** a companion, especially a companion who is a fellow gang member *US, 1981*. **6** a criminal enterprise *US, 1995*. **7** a style of jazz music with an easy-going rhythm *US, 1930*. ▶ **get a ride** in circus and carnival usage, to receive unfavourable publicity *US, 1981*

ride *verb* **1** to have sex. Usually from the female perspective *US, 1994*. **2** (used of a lesbian) to straddle your prone partner, rubbing your genitals together *US, 1967*. **3** to engage in sycophantic flattery *US, 1988*. **4** to irritate or worry someone *US, 1918*. **5** to play jazz with an easy-moving rhythm *US, 1929*. ▶ **let it ride 1** in gambling, to continue a bet from one play to another, increasing the bet with winnings *US, 1980*. **2** to tolerate something; to take no action about something *US, 1921*. ▶ **ride a beef** to accept a charge for a crime that you did not commit *US, 1967*. ▶ **ride a g-string; ride in a g-string** to drive a BMW car. Scamto youth street slang (South African townships) *SOUTH AFRICA, 2005*. ▶ **ride a pony** to cheat on a test in college or school *US, 1959*. ▶ **ride bitch** to sit in the middle of the front seat in a pickup truck, between the driver and another passenger *US, 1992*. ▶ **ride dirty** to drive under the influence of alcohol *US, 2001*. ▶ **ride ghost** to drive at night without headlights

US, 1995. ▶ **ride it** to endure or cope with imprisonment *UK, 1996*. ▶ **ride it a treat** in horse racing, to ride a skilled and intelligent race *AUSTRALIA, 1989*. ▶ **ride old smokey** to be executed by electrocution *US, 1950*. ▶ **ride rubber** to ride in a car *US, 1981*. ▶ **ride Santa's sleigh** to use cocaine. A phrase that combines SNOW as 'cocaine' with 'flying' as 'intoxication' *UK, 2001*. ▶ **ride shotgun 1** to act as a security or military escort. From the time when stage coaches carrying valuables were protected by a man carrying a shotgun who sat on top of the coach alongside the driver *UK, 1979*. **2** to be prepared for any eventuality in business *US, 1974*. **3** to travel in the passenger seat *US, 1921*. **4** to oversee and control someone with a firm hand *US, 1972*. ▶ **ride the broom** to threaten someone; to predict harm *US, 1990*. ▶ **ride the bubbles** in hot rodding and drag racing, to rise slightly off the ground as a result of aerodynamics *US, 1965*. ▶ **ride the bus** to defecate *US, 1990*. ▶ **ride the card** to ride a winner on every race at a race meeting *AUSTRALIA, 1984*. ▶ **ride the circuit** to move someone who has been arrested from stationhouse to stationhouse, making his timely release difficult *US, 1949*. ▶ **ride the cotton pony; ride the cotton horse** to experience the bleed period of the menstrual cycle. This 'cotton pony' is a 'sanitary towel' *US, 1954*. ▶ **ride the grub line** to travel and survive by scrounging food wherever it can be found *CANADA, 1987*. ▶ **ride the Hershey Highway** to engage in anal sex *US, 1935*. ▶ **ride the lightning** to be put to death by electrocution *US, 1935*. ▶ **ride the pine** to sit on the sidelines of an athletic contest as a substitute player *US, 1938*. ▶ **ride the pipe** to pilot a jet after engine failure. Korean war usage *US, 1991*. ▶ **ride the red tide** to experience the bleed period of the menstrual cycle *US, 1999*. ▶ **ride the short bus** to be mentally deficient. From the literally short bus that special education students use in the US *US, 1995*. ▶ **ride the showing** to tour an area evaluating billboards for potential advertising use *US, 1980*. ▶ **ride the sick book** to feign illness; to malinger *US, 1968*. ▶ **ride the silver steed** to participate in bismuth subcarbonate and neoarsphenamine therapy for syphilis *US, 1981*. ▶ **ride the splinters** to sit on the sidelines of an athletic contest as a substitute player. The 'splinters' are an allusion to the bench which the substitute 'warms' or 'rides' *US, 1949*. ▶ **ride the turtles** to drive on the raised reflective road markers that delineate motorway lanes *US, 1997*. ▶ **ride the white horse** to experience euphoria after using heroin *US, 1955*. ▶ **ride the wire** to travel by tram *US, 1970*

ride along *verb* in poker, to remain in a game without betting because you have bet your entire bankroll on the hand *US, 1967*

ride and a rasher *noun* sexual intercourse followed by breakfast *IRELAND, 1999*

ride man; ride jock; ride monkey *noun* the operator of a carnival amusement ride *US, 1985*

ride out *noun* a group motor-scooter excursion *UK, 2001*

ride out *verb* to depart. Used by London teenagers in the late 1950s. *UK, 1958*

rider *noun* **1** a visible, aggressive member of a gang *US, 2001*. **2** a police officer *US, 2003*. **3** 5 kg of heroin supplied free with a 100 kg shipment of cocaine *UK, 2002*. **4** a cheater. From the phrase RIDE A PONY (to cheat on a test) *US, 1959*. **5** in trucking, a flat tyre on a set of dual tyres *US, 1971*

ridge *adjective* all right; okay. Probably a figurative use of now obsolete 'ridge' (gold). Now superseded by RIDGY DIDGE *AUSTRALIA, 1938*

ridge cottage *noun* a bunker in the Korean demilitarised zone. Korean war usage *US, 1982*

ridge-runner *noun* any white male from the Appalachian Mountain region in the southern US *US, 1980*

ridgy didge; ridgy-didge *adjective* all right; okay *AUSTRALIA, 1953*

ridiculous *adjective* excellent *US, 1959*

riding Saint George; the dragon on Saint George *noun* heterosexual sex with the woman straddling the man, her head upright *US, 1980*

riding the waves; riding a wave *adjective* experiencing drug intoxication *US, 1930*

R-ie *noun* a Returned Servicemen's League club. From the initials *RSL AUSTRALIA, 1992*

rif *verb* to separate someone from military service or employment. From the initialism for 'reduction in force' *US, 1983*

riff *noun* **1** a rhythmic musical phrase played repeatedly, used in jazz and rock. Probably an abbreviation of 'refrain' *US, 1935*. **2** an oft-repeated argument or point of view. A figurative usage of the previous sense *UK, 2000*. **3** the theme or gist of a conversation *UK, 2000*. **4** a verbal embellishment that adds no meaning to what is being said *US, 1967*. **5** an activity or experience *US, 1975*. **6** a refrigerated railway wagon *US, 1946*

riff *verb* **1** to repeatedly play a rhythmic musical figure, usually on a piano or guitar *US, 1955*. **2** to brag; to lie *US, 1990*. **3** to complain *US, 1989*

riffage *noun* rhythmic style(s) of rock music *UK, 2002*

riffle *noun* in a restaurant or soda fountain, to refill (an order) *US, 1967*

riffology *noun* in rock music, simple musical learning or skill *UK, 1999*

riff on *verb* to tease someone; to disparage someone or something *US, 1995*

riff-raff *noun* **1** the lowest class *UK, 1470*. **2** a Welsh person. Rhyming slang for TAFF *UK: ENGLAND, 1992*. **3** a café. Rhyming slang for CAFF *UK, 1998*

riffs *noun* music. Teen slang *CANADA, 1946*

rifle range *noun* **1** the ward in a hospital reserved for patients withdrawing from heroin addiction. A pun on SHOOTING GALLERY *US, 1973*. **2** change (money). Rhyming slang. Shortened form 'rifle' *UK, 1980*

rifle spot *noun* in the television and film industries, a spotlight that produces a long, thin beam of light *US, 1990*

rift *noun* a refrigerated freight railway wagon *US, 1977*

rig *noun* **1** a car, truck or bus *US, 1938*. **2** the collective equipment used by a musical group in concert *UK, 1983*. **3** a hypodermic needle and syringe *US, 1969*. **4** a still used in the illegal production of alcohol *US, 1974*. **5** a holster *US, 2001*. **6** the penis *US, 1971*. **7** surgically augmented breasts *US, 1997*. **8** a bad situation *US, 1997*

rigger *noun* **1** in the Royal Air Force, an airframe tradesman. An official Royal Air Force job title that was dropped as the job description changed in the 1930s yet has continued in colloquial use; still in Royal Air Force use, 2002 *UK, 1943*. **2** a half-gallon jar of beer *NEW ZEALAND, 1998*

rigger mortis *noun* an ineffectual member of the Royal Canadian Air Force. A 'rigger mortis' is a useless airman, based on RIGGER (an airframe tradesman) *CANADA, 1995*

rig gig *noun* a job driving a truck *US, 1976*

right *noun* in craps, a bet for the shooter *US, 1974*

right *adjective* **1** intensifies the good or bad character or condition of someone or something; complete, utter *UK, 1956*. **2** understanding and accepting the mores of the underworld *US, 1950*. ▶ **not right in the head** unsound of mind *UK, 1934*

right *adverb* very *CANADA, 1988*

right 1 used as a greeting or farewell *TRINIDAD AND TOBAGO, 1966*. 2 I do not believe you. Heavily sarcastic, emphasising the negative interpretation. Variants include 'yeah right' and 'aye right' *UK, 1998*

right as rain *adjective* in good health; satisfactory *UK, 1909*

right enough *adverb* certainly, indeed *UK, 1885*

righteous *adjective* **1** very good, excellent, fine; honest; satisfactory. Conventional English with a religious overtone propelled into hip slang by context and emphasis in pronunciation *US, 1942*. **2** used of a drug, relatively pure and undiluted *US, 1967*

righteous bush *noun* any potent variety of marijuana. A combination of RIGHTEOUS (good) and BUSH (marijuana) *US, 1946*

righteous name *noun* a person's true name *US, 1975*

righteous nod *noun* a refreshing sleep *US, 1947*

right guy *noun* a dependable, trustworthy and reliable criminal *US, 1964*

right here used as a set answer to an inquiry as to how you are *BAHAMAS, 1982*

rightie *noun* in craps, a gambler who bets that the shooter will make his point before rolling a seven *US, 1974*

rightiol; righty-o!; righteho!; righty-ho! all right!; certainly!; gladly! *UK, 1927*

right numbers; right price *noun* in horse racing, higher than normal odds that merit a wager *US, 1968*

righto; right-oh okay!; all right! *AUSTRALIA, 1911*

right on! yes; excellent; correct; also used to signal enthusiastic agreement. Originally black usage, perhaps from 'right on the button', 'right on time' or RIGHTO. Subsequently adopted by the hippie generation *US, 1930*

right one *noun* a person whose behaviour does not conform to expectations *UK, 1981*

rights *noun* ▶ **do the rights** to seek or gain revenge *UK, 2002*

right-said-Fred *noun* the head. Rhyming slang, formed on the name of a pop group who enjoyed success in the early 1990s; the group took its name from the title of a humorous song by Bernard Cribbins which was a top ten hit in 1962 *UK, 2000*

righty *noun* someone who looks very much like someone else; a double or near double *US, 1962*

right you are! certainly!; agreed! *UK, 1864*

rigid *adjective* drunk *US, 1972*

rigid *adverb* greatly; used to intensify, especially 'bore', 'scare' and 'shake'. Modelled on synonymous STIFF, always used after the verb it modifies *UK, 1943*

rigmarole *noun* a string of incoherent statements; a disjointed or rambling speech; a trival or almost senseless harangue *UK, 1736*

rigor mortis *noun* in croquet, the condition of not being able to hit any opponent's ball on a turn *US, 1977*

RIH rest in hell. A bitter version of RIP (rest in peace) *US, 1999*

rile *verb* to annoy or anger someone *UK, 1836*

rim *noun* ▶ **above the rim** of the highest quality *US, 2002*

rim *verb* **1** to lick, suck and tongue another's anus *US, 1941*. **2** to swindle someone *US, 1949*

rim-jag *verb* to make an indentation on a playing card with your fingernail or thumbnail to identify the card later in another player's hand *US, 1988*

rim job *noun* the licking of a partner's anus for the purposes of sexual pleasure *US, 1969*

rimmer *noun* a person who provides mouth in mouth-to-anus sex *US, 1979*

rim queen *noun* a male homosexual who is proficient at mouth-to-anus stimulation *US, 1970*

rimrock *verb* to drive livestock into an enclosure; to entrap someone *CANADA, 1951*

rims *noun* sunglasses *US, 1997*

rinctum *noun* an especially violent fit of temper *CANADA, 1953*

Rinehart!; Oh Rinehart! used as a shout to announce the onset of a student disturbance, started in fun but not always ending as such. Specific to Harvard University, honouring John Rinehart, Harvard Law School class of 1903 *US, 1933*

ring *noun* **1** a telephone call *UK, 1900*. **2** the anus. From the shape *UK, 1949*. **3** a circular area where the game of two-up takes place *AUSTRALIA, 1896*. **4** collectively, the bookmakers at a racecourse *AUSTRALIA, 1877*. ▶ **get a ring in your nose** in horse racing, to lose all your money betting *US, 1951*. ▶ **put the ring around it** to confirm something as definite *NEW ZEALAND, 1978*

ring *verb* **1** to provide one thing disguised as another *UK, 1812*. **2** to open and pilfer a cash register *US, 1965*. **3** to shout *BARBADOS, 1965*. ▶ **ring it on** to outwit someone *US, 1977*. ▶ **ring the bell 1** to make a successful attempt at something. Probably from a fairground challenge *UK, 1966*. **2** to achieve success beyond expectations *US, 1950*. ▶ **ring the berries** in ice hockey, to hit the goalie with a hard shot between the legs *CANADA, 1985*. ▶ **ring your chimes** to strike someone on the head with great force *US, 1981*

ring-a-ding *noun* an excellent example of something *US, 1965*

ring-a-ling on the ting-a-ling *noun* a telephone call *US, 1968*

ring angel *noun* a 'blip' on a radar screen, often a flock of birds *US, 1947*

ringas *noun* conversation; a conversation. Scamto youth street slang (South African townships) *SOUTH AFRICA, 2005*

ringburner *noun* an act of defecation that is attended by burning, stinging or other painful sensations in the anus; often applied to the spicy food that causes such effects. Combines RING (the anus) with a conventional sense of 'burn'; upper-class society origins. The following definition is offered by Ann Barr and Peter York in their 1982 *Official Sloane Ranger Handbook*: 'The results of a heavy curry the morning after' *UK, 1982*

ringer *noun* **1** a perfect resemblance. Often intensified with DEAD *US, 1891*. **2** an athlete or horse fraudulently entered in a game or race *US, 1890*. **3** a false vehicle registration number plate *US, 1956*. **4** a criminal who builds new cars from the parts of stolen cars *UK, 1970*. **5** a single inhalation of crack cocaine with a strong effect *US, 1994*. **6** a stockman *AUSTRALIA, 1979*. **7** the fastest shearer in a shearing shed *AUSTRALIA, 1871*

ring game *noun* a game of poker with all seats at the table occupied *US, 1982*

ringie *noun* the person running a game of two-up *AUSTRALIA, 1941*

ring-in *noun* **1** an illegal competitor substituted for another in a race *AUSTRALIA, 1918*. **2** any surreptitious substitute *AUSTRALIA, 1956*. **3** one who doesn't belong; an outsider *AUSTRALIA, 1987*

ring in *verb* **1** to illegally substitute a racehorse or greyhound for another in a race; to substitute a phoney in a competition *AUSTRALIA, 1895*. **2** to secretly introduce altered dice into a dice game *US, 1950*

ringing-in *noun* the illegal substitution of a racehorse or greyhound in a race *AUSTRALIA, 1975*

ring-keeper *noun* the person running a game of two-up *AUSTRALIA, 1896*

ring-knocker *noun* a graduate of one of the US military academies. From the school rings worn by graduates *US, 1991*

ringmaster *noun* a railway yardmaster *US, 1946*

ringpiece *noun* the anus. An ARSEHOLE in both the anatomical and figurative senses *UK, 1949*

ring raider *noun* a male homosexual. An allusion to anal intercourse, based on RING (the anus) *UK, 2003*

ring-sting *noun* a burning sensation in and of the anus caused, generally, by spicy food. Formed on RING (the anus). Occasionally, and originally, known as 'ring-burn' *UK, 1984*

ring-stinger *noun* a curry that produces, as an after-effect, a burning, stinging or other painful sensation in the anus *UK, 2002*

ringy *adjective* irritable *US, 1932*

rink rat *noun* a young boy who hangs around ice rinks, totally involved in hockey *US, 1945*

rinky-dink *noun* **1** something that is second rate, cheap or trivial *US, 1912*. **2** in trucking, the 4000 model White tractor *US, 1971*. **3** in snooker, the *pink* ball *UK, 1992*

rinky-dink *adjective* inexpensive; poorly made; worthless *US, 1912*

rinse *noun* a selection of dance tunes mixed into a seamless whole; an event which features such a musical blend *UK, 1997*

rinse *verb* to mix dance tunes into a seamless whole. Perhaps because of the wash of sound *UK, 1999*. ▶ **rinse arse; rinse skin; rinse tail** to administer a severe beating *TRINIDAD AND TOBAGO, 1992*

rinsebag *noun* a plastic bag that once contained amphetamine *US, 1989*

rinsed *adjective* exhausted. A play on 'washed out' *UK, 2005*

rinsing!; rinsin'! excellent; a general-purpose superlative. The cry of approval offered up to a DJ who is rinsing tunes together (see RINSE), adopted by clubbers into wider usage *UK, 2000*

Rin-Tin-Tin; rinty *noun* the leg. Rhyming slang for PIN, formed from the name given to several generations of a German Shepherd dog television and film star of the 1930s–50s and beyond *UK, 1998*

Rio *noun* Rio de Janeiro *US, 1935*

riot *noun* something or someone that is very amusing or greatly funny *UK, 1933*

riot bell *noun* in prison, any bell *UK, 1996*

riot grrrl; riot girl *noun* a cultural movement of aggressive young feminists; a member of the riot grrrl movement; the sub-genre of punk rock music associated with the movement. Lazy journalism seems to be responsible for 'girl/grrl' variations *US, 1991*

Riot Hyatt; Riot House *nickname* The Continental Hyatt House, Sunset Boulevard, Los Angeles, famous for its association with rock musicians *US, 1989*

riot panic *noun* in circus and carnival usage, enthusiastic applause *US, 1981*

rip *noun* **1** a current travelling seawards from shore, usually moving swiftly. An abbreviation of 'rip tide' or 'rip current' *US, 1990*. **2** a method of breaking into a safe that employs mechanical force and no explosives *US, 1950*. **3** in a cheating scheme in a dice game, the switching of tampered dice into a game *US, 1962*. **4** an injustice; an action that is fundamentally unfair *US, 1982*. **5** a complaint lodged against a police officer *US, 1970*. **6** a fine or punishment imposed for breaking a police department conduct rule *US, 1958*. **7** one pound sterling *UK, 1999*. **8** marijuana *UK, 2003*. **9** a coarse, unattractive woman *IRELAND, 1910*

rip *verb* **1** to cheat or swindle someone *US, 1904*. **2** to steal something *US, 1984*. **3** to kill someone *US, 1974*. **4** to travel quickly *UK, 1971*. **5** to surf in a bold, skilled manner *US, 1988*. **6** to excel *US, 1994*. ▶ **rip a new asshole** to berate someone severely *US, 1995*. ▶ **rip into** to attack someone or something with vigour or gusto. Either physically or verbally *AUSTRALIA, 1970*. ▶ **rip it up** to enjoy energetically; to dance *US, 1956*. ▶ **rip off a piece (of ass)** to have sex *US, 1971*

rip and tear; rip *verb* to swear. Rhyming slang. Possibly an influence on LET RIP (to shout) *UK, 1937*

ripe *adjective* **1** bad-smelling *US, 1995*. **2** too strong for general acceptability *UK, 1999*. **3** used of a girl, over the legal age of consent *US, 1988*. **4** in the language surrounding the Grateful Dead, poised for enlightenment in the mysteries of the band *US, 1994*

rip job *noun* a safe robbery in which the front of the safe is peeled off *US, 1973*

rip-off *noun* **1** a copy; an imitation *US, 1970*. **2** a robbery; a theft; a swindle; exploitation *US, 1975*

rip off *verb* **1** to steal something. If the speaker is doing the stealing, the term suggests an act of political heroism; if not, it suggests corporate greed. The subject of this verb can be either the goods stolen, the location or the owner; the subject can split the verb without changing the sense *US, 1967*. **2** to overcharge someone *UK, 1977*. **3** to rape someone *US, 1984*

rip-off *adjective* **1** in an imitative style, especially with the intention to exploit a commercial advantage *AUSTRALIA, 1973*. **2** exploitative; cheating *US, 1975*

rip-off artist *noun* a swindler; a thief *UK, 1975*

ripped *adjective* **1** drunk or drug-intoxicated *US, 1969*. **2** muscular; lacking body fat; well-sculpted *US, 1984*

ripped out of your tits *adjective* very drunk *UK, 2002*

ripped to the tits *adjective* very drunk *US, 1983*

ripper *noun* **1** a very unattractive (young) woman. Variant 'old ripper' *UK, 2003*. **2** an amphetamine or other central nervous system stimulant *US, 1986*. **3** a skilled skateboarder *US, 1984*. **4** a skilled scooter-rider *UK, 2000*. **5** in pinball, a ball that is forcefully hit into play *US, 1977*

ripper *adjective* intense; extreme; excellent *AUSTRALIA, 1974*

ripper! used for expressing strong approval *AUSTRALIA, 1987*

ripping *adjective* **1** excellent *UK, 1846*. **2** very angry *US, 1968*

ripping iron *noun* a jacket slit up the back *BARBADOS, 1965*

rip-rap noun loose, crushed stone used to form embankments US, 1822

riproodling adjective excellent. A rare variant of 'rip-roaring' US, 1954

rips noun ▶ **do rips** to smoke marijuana US, 1997

rip, shit or bust verb to throw yourself wholeheartedly into a task without fear of the consequences NEW ZEALAND, 1999

rip-snorter noun a remarkable person; an exceptional thing US, 1842

rip track noun on the railways, a hospital US, 1977

Rip Van Winkle verb to urinate. Rhyming slang for TINKLE or SPRINKLE, formed from the eponymous character in an 1820 story by Washington Irving UK, 1992

rise noun an erection US, 1998

rise verb ▶ **rise to the occasion** to achieve an erection when the moment requires it. A punning application of a conventional phrase UK, 1984

rise and shine noun wine. Rhyming slang UK, 1992

rising damp noun cramp. Rhyming slang UK, 1992

rissole noun 1 the anus. Euphemistic for ARSEHOLE AUSTRALIA, 1971. 2 a Returned Servicemen's League club. From a jocular pronunciation of RSL as a vowelless word, punning on 'rissole' (a meat patty) AUSTRALIA, 1983. ▶ **like a rissole** used as a jocular catchphrase tacked onto the farewell expressions 'catch you round' and 'see you round'. Punning on 'round' (circular), the shape of a rissole AUSTRALIA, 1996

ritual spirit noun MDMA, the recreational drug best known as ecstasy UK, 2003

ritzy adjective classy, stylish, fashionable. After the Ritz luxury hotels in New York, London and Paris US, 1920

Riv; Rivie; Rivie hog noun a Buick Riviera car US, 1980

river noun in a hand of poker, the final card received by a player UK, 2003. ▶ **across the river** dead US, 1949. ▶ **up the river; upriver** to a prison US, 1947

riverina noun a shilling, hence, 5p. Rhyming slang for DEANER AUSTRALIA, 1943

river job noun as a result of betting, an enormous loss. So great is the loss that the bettor thinks of jumping in a river AUSTRALIA, 1989

River Lea noun tea, especially a poor quality cup of tea. Rhyming slang, formed on one of London's rivers UK, 1859

River Nile noun a smile. Rhyming slang UK, 1992

River Ouse; river ooze; the river noun strong drink. Rhyming slang for BOOZE UK, 1930

river rat noun a river-rafting enthusiast US, 1997

River Tyne noun wine, especially inferior wine. Rhyming slang, formed on a major river in the northeast of England UK, 1992

Riviera; Riviera of the south nickname any place in Antarctica perceived to be slightly warmer than the rest of the continent, especially the Antarctic Peninsula or Davis station ANTARCTICA, 1963

rivvel noun among Nova Scotians of German origin, a noodle soup. Like another Lunenburg County word, 'roovled' this word is probably a derivative of the German word *runzeln* (wrinkled) CANADA, 1999

Rizla noun a cigarette rolling paper. A brand name that acquired a generic meaning UK, 1996

RJR noun inexpensive cigarette tobacco given free to prisoners. An abbreviation of R.J. Reynolds, a major tobacco company US, 1990

R 'n' R noun rock 'n' roll. An initialism UK, 1999

roach noun 1 a cockroach AUSTRALIA, 1985. 2 the butt of a marijuana cigarette. The variant 'roche' also exists US, 1938. 3 a still-lit and smokeable cigarette end. From the previous sense UK, 1996. 4 Rohypnol™ (flunitrazepam), popularly known as the 'date-rape drug'. From the manufacturer, Hoffman-La Roche. The variant 'roachie' also exists US, 1995. 5 a police officer. A disliked insect found nearly everywhere US, 1963. 6 an unpopular girl US, 1959. 7 in new car sales, a bad credit risk US, 1989

roach verb 1 to smoke a marijuana cigarette UK, 2004. 2 to have sex with someone's spouse or lover; to cuckold someone BAHAMAS, 1982. 3 in computing, to destroy a program US, 1991

roacha noun marijuana UK, 2003

roach and dace noun the face. Rhyming slang. A less common variation of KIPPER AND PLAICE UK, 1874

roach bender noun someone who smokes marijuana. An elaboration of the noun and verb senses of ROACH US, 1942

roach clip noun a device, improvised or manufactured, designed to hold the butt of a (marijuana) cigarette and make smoking the final portion possible US, 1997

roach coach noun 1 a dustcart UK, 1981. 2 a catering truck. The reduplicative suggestion is of a lack of hygiene that attracts cockroaches US, 1985

Roachdale College nickname an 'alternative' institution within the University of Toronto, officially named Rochdale College. Founded in the 1960s, this irreverent nickname captured the flavour of the spirit of the place. Its history is memorialised in an exhibit which includes memoirs of drug use, a Can-Cannabis flag and other 'Counter-Cultural Ephemera' CANADA, 1969

roached adjective under the influence of Rohypnol™ (flunitrazepam), popularly known as the 'date-rape drug'. From the name of the manufacturer, Hoffman-La Roche US, 1996

roach haven noun a hotel/motel lacking in hygiene US, 1995

roach killers noun pointed shoes US, 1974

roach motel noun a used car dealership that targets customers with poor credit US, 1997

roach wagon noun a catering truck US, 1984

roachy noun the penis BAHAMAS, 1982

road noun the realities of contemporary urban existence. A refinement of STREET UK, 2005. ▶ **the road** in Roller Derby, anywhere outside the nine San Francisco Bay Area counties, the home of the game US, 1999. ▶ **up the road** committed for trial before a judge and jury UK, 1977

road verb to ride a bicycle on the road in a large Canadian city CANADA, 2002

road agent noun a highway patrolman or state police officer. Biker (motorcycle) usage US, 2003

road apple noun 1 a piece of horse manure US, 1996. 2 a touring performer US, 1981

roadblock dance noun an unofficial street party UK, 1994

road burn noun in the language surrounding the Grateful Dead, the deteriorated grooming and personal hygiene that serve as physical manifestations of a long tour following the band US, 1994

road dog noun 1 an extremely close friend US, 1989. 2 in sports betting, a team picked as the underdog playing away from home US, 1989

road dope noun amphetamines. Derives from the drug's use by long-distance drivers UK, 2003

road engineer noun a long-haul truck driver US, 1963

road face noun a stoic expression giving no sign of emotion TRINIDAD AND TOBAGO, 2003

road game noun a criminal's field of expertise US, 1984

road head noun oral sex received while driving US, 2001

road helper noun an amphetamine or other central nervous system stimulant US, 1969

roadie noun 1 a member of a rock band's entourage who is responsible for setting up and dismantling the band's equipment while on tour UK, 1968. 2 among mountain-bikers, a derogatory term for a cyclist who only rides on paved surfaces US, 1996. 3 a final drink before starting a road journey. From 'one for the *road*' AUSTRALIA, 1996. 4 a can or bottle of beer drunk while driving. Also used as a measure of distance, as in 'It's a three roadie trip' AUSTRALIA, 1996

roadie's screwdriver noun a hammer or any blunt instrument used to strike something that is not working UK, 1985

road kill *noun* literally, an animal or bird carcass on the side of the road; figuratively, an unattractive mess *US, 1979*

road louse *noun* a chorus dancer who can no longer get work in the major metropolitan dance halls *US, 1948*

road map *noun* **1** multiple facial lacerations *US, 1989*. **2** in craps, the dice placed before the shooter with the point needed to win face up *US, 1983*. **3** a peace plan. Originally, and especially, applied to the Israel–Palestine conflict *US, 2002*

road pizza *noun* an animal carcass on the road *CANADA, 1987*

road rage *noun* a driver's violent reaction to the frustrations of traffic hindrances and the discourtesies of other road users *US, 1988*

road rash *noun* **1** scraped, bruised and/or cut skin earned in falls while skateboarding or engaging in activity on the road *US, 1976*. **2** scraped, bruised and/or cut skin earned by moped riders in road accidents *UK, 2003*

road rocket; rocket *noun* an extremely fast motorcycle *UK, 1978*

road soda *noun* alcohol drunk in a car on the way to a party or concert *US, 2004*

road stake *noun* enough money to get someone to their next job *US, 1965*

roadster *noun* a tramp *US, 1890*

road talk *noun* gossip; a rumour *BAHAMAS, 1982*

road tar *noun* coffee, especially strong and bitter coffee *US, 1976*

road trouble *noun* problems encountered on the street, usually between a pimp and prostitute *US, 1973*

roam *noun* ▶ **on the roam** away from home *US, 1976*

roarer *noun* in horse racing, a horse that coughes loudly while galloping *US, 1947*

roaring forties *nickname* the latitudes between 40 and 49 degrees south. Strong winds from the west produce choppy ocean conditions *ANTARCTICA, 1897*

roaring game *noun* the sport of curling *CANADA, 2002*

roaring twenty *noun* a type of amphetamine tablet *UK, 1998*

roar up *verb* (of a male) to have sex *UK, 1995*

roast *noun* a person killed by a fire *US, 1976*

roast *verb* **1** (from an active perspective) to have sex with someone *UK, 2002*. **2** to criticise someone or something severely; to be mercilessly disparaging of someone or something; to denounce someone *UK, 1782*. **3** to earn money after hours, especially when doing so with some degree of dishonesty *JAMAICA, 1990*

roast beef *noun* the teeth. Rhyming slang *UK, 1992*

roast beef *verb* in the used car business, to suggest a higher trade-in value to the dealer management than will be approved, giving the salesman who does so a cushion to fall to the value he expects will be approved *US, 1975*

roasted *adjective* drunk or drug-intoxicated *US, 1989*

roastie *noun* **1** a roast potato *UK, 2001*. **2** a traditional English roast dinner *UK, 2002*

roasting *adjective* **1** of an ambient temperature, very hot *UK, 1768*. **2** anxious; unhappy *UK, 1996*

roast pork; roast *noun* a fork. Rhyming slang *UK, 1992*

roast pork; roast *verb* to talk. Rhyming slang *UK, 1961*

roast potato; roastie *noun* a waiter. Rhyming slang *UK, 1992*

rob *noun* ▶ **on the rob** engaged in thievery *UK, 1999*

rob *verb* to steal. Unconventional passive usage *UK, 1999*. ▶ **rob the cradle** to be romantically involved with a young person *US, 1978*. ▶ **we wuz robbed; we woz robbed** used as an excuse for losing. As a jocular exclamation this is a fine example of 'many a true word spoken in jest'; widely used (with serious intent) as an indignant cliché. Apparently coined in 1932 by boxing manager Joe Jacobs when his client, Max Schmeling, lost the world heavyweight title as the result of a controversial split-decision *US, 1988*

robber talk *noun* threatening talk *TRINIDAD AND TOBAGO, 1985*

robe *noun* in circus and carnival usage, a judge in criminal court *US, 1981*

Roberta Flack *noun* dismissal from employment. Rhyming slang for SACK, formed from the name of the US singer (b.1939) *UK, 1998*

Robert E. Lee *noun* **1** a quay. Dockers' rhyming slang, formed on the name of the Confederate army general (1807–70) *UK, 1961*. **2** the knee. Sometimes abbreviated to 'Robert E.' or the simple 'Robert' *UK, 1992*. **3** urine; an act of urination. Rhyming slang for PEE or WEE *UK, 1998*

Robert's your father's brother everything's all right. A humorous variation of BOB'S YOUR UNCLE *UK, 1994*

Robert's your mother's brother everything's all right. A humorous variation of BOB'S YOUR UNCLE *UK, 1999*

Robin Hood *noun* wood; a wood; a Woodbine™ cigarette. Rhyming slang, formed on the name of the legendary hero of Sherwood Forest *UK, 1992*

Robin Hood *adjective* good. Rhyming slang, formed on the name of the legendary hero of Sherwood Forest *UK, 1932*

Robin Hoods *noun* merchandise, goods. Rhyming slang *UK, 1992*

robin run *noun* in Canadian maple sugaring, the first flow of the maple tree sap, which is especially sweet *CANADA, 1995*

Robinson Crusoe *verb* to do so. Rhyming slang, formed from the eponymous hero of Daniel Defoe's 1719 book *UK, 1960*

rob my pal *noun* a girl. Rhyming slang for GAL *UK, 1960*

robo *noun* dextromethorphan (DXM), an active ingredient in non-prescription cold and cough medication, often abused for non-medicinal purposes *US, 2003*

robo *verb* to drink Robitussin™ (a branded cough medicine with codeine) *US, 1993*

robodose *verb* to abuse cough syrups for recreational purposes. From the name of the most popular syrup of abuse, Robitussen™ *US, 1995*

robotard *noun* a person who abuses for non-medicinal purposes non-prescription medication containing dextromethorphan (DXM). From the branded cough syrup, Robitussen™ *US, 2003*

robotrip *verb* to abuse for non-medicinal purposes non-prescription medication containing dextromethorphan (DXM). From the branded cough syrup, Robitussin™ *US, 2003*

ROC *noun* the rest of Canada, i.e. all of Canada except Quebec *CANADA, 2002*

roca *noun* **1** MDMA, the recreational drug best known as ecstasy *UK, 2003*. **2** crack cocaine. Corrupted Spanish-English for 'rock' *US, 1994*

Roche; La Roche; rochie *noun* Rohypnol™ (flunitrazepam), popularly known as the 'date-rape drug'. Because Roche Pharmaceuticals markets the Rohypnol™ sleeping pill *US, 2004*

rock *noun* **1** a rhythmic style of (usually) amplified music that provides the umbrella for any number of music genres. Originally abbreviated from ROCK 'N' ROLL; in the US it has continued in use for all forms of driving, rhythmic music. Meanwhile, in the UK early variant forms were called 'beat' or POP; not until the mid-1960s was 'rock' used as a title for some contemporary music and then only applied to the more serious music that derived from rock 'n' roll *US, 1957*. **2** a diamond *US, 1908*. **3** cocaine *US, 1973*. **4** crack cocaine. Describes the crystalline lumps of purified cocaine *US, 1983*. **5** a pool ball *US, 1990*. **6** in the usage of youthful model road racers (slot car racers), a slow car *US, 1997*. **7** a solid, reliable, dependable fellow prisoner *US, 1976*. **8** in prison, a predatory homosexual *US, 1967*. **9** a frugal and stingy person *US, 1950*. **10** a dollar *US, 1950*. **11** a packet of brand name manufactured cigarettes, used as a basic medium of exchange in prison *US, 1992*. **12** a crystal tuning device used in a citizens' band transceiver *US, 1976*

Rock *nickname* ▶ **the Rock 1** Gibraltar. From Gibraltar's main feature *UK, 1829*. **2** the Alcatraz federal penitentiary, located in San Francisco bay *US, 1970*. **3** Rocky Marciano (1923–69), the only undefeated heavyweight champion in boxing history *US, 1975*. **4** Guam. A nickname used by US military pilots during the Vietnamese war *US, 1990*. **5** Riker's Island jail, New York *US, 1975*. **6** the island of Newfoundland. This term, almost universal in use in both Newfoundland and the rest of Canada, derives from the stony soil of the island CANADA, 2001

rock verb **1** to have sex US, 1922. **2** to excel US, 1996. **3** to excite someone US, 1955. **4** to work UK, 2001. **5** to prepare crack cocaine from powdered cocaine US, 1995. **6** to distress someone; to disturb someone; to startle someone US, 1940. ► **rock ass** to produce rock music that inspires a vigorous audience response. On the model of KICK ASS (to behave energetically) US, 1979. ► **rock the boat** to upset the status quo; to make difficulties; to cause trouble UK, 1931. ► **rock the clock** in the used car business, to spin the odometer (mileometer) backwards US, 1997. ► **rock the groove** (of hip-hop music or musicians) to give pleasure UK, 1998

rock adjective hard UK, 2001

rockabilly noun a mid-1950s US fashion; a late 1970s British youth fashion and music genre identified as an exaggeration of hillbilly country and western style. An ellision of ROCK 'N' ROLL and 'hillbilly' US, 1993

rock and boulder noun the shoulder. Rhyming slang UK, 1931

rock and roll noun used of an automatic or semi-automatic weapon, full automatic fire US, 1979

rock and roll; rock 'n' roll verb to begin and perform the task at hand US, 1990

rock ape noun **1** a black person. Offensive AUSTRALIA, 1972. **2** a lout or hooligan AUSTRALIA, 1994

rock attack noun crack cocaine. An elaboration of ROCK. UK, 2003

rock bud noun a powerful variety of marijuana UK, 2003

rock cake noun a small bet. Possibly rhyming slang for 'stake'; or possibly a dismissive comparison to an article of little value UK, 1991

rock candy noun diamonds US, 1970

rockchopper noun a Roman Catholic. A derogatory term originating amongst Protestants. In earlier use (1908, Australian National Dictionary) used of a 'navvy' (i.e. one who breaks up rock), and thus in origin probably a slur labelling all Australian Catholics descendants of Irish Catholic convicts AUSTRALIA, 1981

rock college noun prison NEW ZEALAND, 1998

rock crusher noun in poker, a hand that is certain to win US, 1988

rockdance noun walking barefoot over a rocky surface to retrieve a surfboard US, 1963

rocked out adjective under the influence of crack cocaine US, 1991

rocker noun **1** any of the several curved stripes below the three chevrons on the insignia of a sergeant in the US Army or Marine Corps US, 1944. **2** a curved patch designating a motorcyle gang or the gang-member's home city or country, worn as part of the colours. A borrowing from the military US, 1971. **3** a member of the 1960s youth cult that is characterised by the use of motorcycles and leathers, and chiefly remembered as the opposite to Mod UK, 1971. **4** a non-surfer who associates with surfers and poses as a surfer AUSTRALIA, 1964. **5** a rock musician/singer UK, 2003. **6** a song, or instrumental, exhibiting the rhythmic characteristics of rock 'n' roll UK, 1975. **7** the convex curvature of the bottom of a surfboard US, 1965. ► **off your rocker** crazy UK, 1897

rocker; rokker verb to speak Romany; to talk. English gypsy use from Romany roker (to speak) UK, 2000

rocket noun **1** a marijuana cigarette US, 1942. **2** a hypodermic needle and syringe US, 1989. **3** a bullet US, 1965. **4** an Oldsmobile V-8 engine US, 1965. **5** a tampon. From the shape US, 2001 ▷ see: ROAD ROCKET

rocket alley nickname Phuoc Binh, South Vietnam. The nickname came from the frequent Viet Cong rocket attacks US, 1990

rocket burns noun faecal stains in the underwear or on a toilet bowl CANADA, 2002

rocket cap noun a dome-shaped cap on a vial in which crack cocaine is sold US, 1994

Rocket City nickname Tay Ninh, South Vietnam; Lai Khe, South Vietnam US, 1983

rocket fuel noun **1** phencyclidine, the recreational drug known as PCP or angel dust US, 1976. **2** a combination of assorted alcoholic beverages NEW ZEALAND, 1997

rocket man noun a person who sells syringes to drug addicts. Illegal in the US, but profitable US, 1989

rocket ripple noun a barrage of 144 rockets fired from a small cart. Korean war usage US, 1957

rocket science noun any difficult, demanding task US, 1997

rocket stains noun faecal stains in the underwear or on a toilet bowl CANADA, 2002

rock fiend noun a crack cocaine addict. From ROCK (crack cocaine) UK, 2003

Rockford Files noun haemorrhoids. Rhyming slang for 'piles', formed from the title of a US television series, 1975–82 UK, 2003

rock hard noun amyl or butyl nitrite. Reflects male use as a sex-aid; possibly derives from a brand name UK, 1998

rockhead noun **1** a crack cocaine addict US, 1991. **2** a dim-witted person US, 1957

rock-hog noun in mining, a tunneller or driller CANADA, 1954

rockhopper noun an angler who fishes from coastal rocks AUSTRALIA, 1966

rock hound noun in oil drilling, a geologist, especially one who focuses on the earth's surface US, 1954

rock house noun a premises used for the sale and consumption of crack cocaine US, 1985

rocking chair noun **1** retirement with a pension US, 1946. **2** in a group of trucks travelling together, the truck in the middle US, 1976

rocking chair money noun unemployment insurance or Old Age Security CANADA, 1959

rocking horse noun sauce, whether the condiment, garnish or impudence. Rhyming slang UK, 1979

Rock Jaw nickname Rach Gia, South Vietnam US, 1990

rock jockey noun in the language of paragliding, the pilot of a hang glider US, 1992

rockman noun a dealer in crack cocaine US, 1989

rock med noun medical treatment targeted for rock 'n' roll concert goers US, 1994

rock 'n' roll noun **1** a genre of music with a driving rhythm; an umbrella for most simply rhythmic music produced since the 1950s. The etymology is laden with sexual overtones, thus 'My Man Rocks Me With One Steady Roll', sung by blues singer Trixie Smith in 1924, and a song entitled 'Rock and Roll' is recorded in 1934. It is not until 1954 that the music now recognised as 'rock 'n' roll' is given its identity; coinage is generally credited to US disc jockey Alan Freed US, 1924. **2** a hole. Rhyming slang, used practically or figuratively UK, 1992. **3** unemployment benefit; any government office from which it is administrated. Rhyming slang for THE DOLE UK, 1994

rock 'n' roll! used as an good-humoured exclamation of dismissal UK, 2000

rock of ages; rocks noun wages. Rhyming slang UK, 1937

rock of Gibraltar noun in shuffleboard, a disc that is well hidden and guarded US, 1967

rock-on noun an erection. A variation of HARD-ON (an erection) UK, 1999

rock on the chest; rock on the box noun silicosis US, 1951

rockpile noun any prison job US, 1984

rocks noun **1** salt US, 1981. **2** money US, 1950. **3** dominoes US, 1959. **4** jewels; pearls. From the US sense (diamonds) UK, 1937. **5** the testicles US, 1948. **6** courage US, 1977 ▷ see: ALMOND ROCKS, MINT ROCKS. ► **get your rocks off 1** to ejaculate US, 1969. **2** to be satisfied with or excited about something. Figurative application of the sense 'to ejaculate' US, 1995. ► **on the rocks 1** used of a drink, served over ice US, 1946. **2** in severe trouble UK, 1889. ► **shoot your rocks** to ejaculate US, 1975. ► **the rocks** a confidence swindle involving fake diamonds US, 1969

rock slinger noun a seller of crack cocaine US, 1993

rocks of hell noun crack cocaine. An elaboration of ROCK. UK, 1998

rock solvent *noun* in caving and pot-holing, any explosive. This is slang with a euphemistic purpose: when communicating by telephone, e-mail, etc., it is thought ill advised to use words like 'explosive' *UK, 2004*

rockspider *noun* **1** an Afrikaner. Derogatory. Sometimes shortened to 'spider' *SOUTH AFRICA, 1970*. **2** a child molester. Originally in prison use, but now part of general slang *AUSTRALIA, 1984*

rock star *noun* **1** a crack cocaine dealer *US, 1988*. **2** a woman who engages in sex for payment in crack cocaine or money to buy crack cocaine; a prostitute addicted to crack cocaine *US, 1993*

rock starring *noun* an act of having sex with a partner in exchange for a payment of crack cocaine *UK, 2002*

rock whore *noun* a woman who will trade sex for crack cocaine *US, 1991*

rock wing *noun* in the language of paragliding, the pilot of a hang glider *US, 1992*

rocky *noun* **1** hashish. Probably from a specific use into generic *UK, 1999*. **2** crack cocaine *UK, 1998*

Rocky *noun* Coors™ beer. Coors boasts of being brewed with 'pure Rocky Mountain spring water' *US, 1967*

rocky black; rocky *noun* a type of marijuana *UK, 1996*

rocky hash *noun* a type of marijuana *UK, 1997*

Rocky III *noun* crack cocaine. An elaboration of ROCK, using the title of a 1982 film *UK, 1998*

Rocky Mountain deadshot *noun* pancakes; hotcakes; griddle cakes; flapjacks *CANADA, 1989*

Rocky Mountain Kool Aid *noun* Coors™ beer. Once available only in Colorado, where it is brewed *US, 1977*

Rocky Mountain oyster *noun* an animal testicle, usually that of a steer formerly known as a bull, prepared for eating as a regional delicacy *US, 1986*

rocy *noun* any variety of hashish from Morocco *UK, 2003*

rod *noun* **1** the penis; the erect penis *UK, 1902*. **2** a gun, usually a pistol. A perfect example for those who like to ascribe phallic symbolism to the tools of man's aggression *US, 1903*. **3** a hired gunman *US, 1964*. **4** a car modified for speed or looks; a hot rod *US, 1945*. **5** the draw-rod underneath a railway goods wagon *US, 1904*. ▶ **had the rod** wrecked; ruined. Variant of HAVE HAD THE DICK *AUSTRALIA, 1975*

rodadio *noun* a radio. Trucker embellishment *US, 1976*

rodda *noun* a Cadillac El Dorado car *US, 1972*

rodded up *adjective* armed with a handgun or handguns *US, 1950*

rodder *noun* a hot rod enthusiast *US, 1949*

rodeo fuck *noun* used for describing sex between a man and woman; the man enters the woman from behind, insults her ('you're almost as good as your sister' for example) and then holds on. A term heard mostly in jokes *US, 2002*

Rodino *noun* a Mexican citizen permitted to stay in the US during an immigration amnesty period in the late 1980s. After Congressman Peter Rodino, sponsor of the legislation that made the amnesty possible *US, 1993*

Rodney boater *noun* a boat-dweller who does not care for the upkeep of the boat-home *UK, 1987*

rod out *verb* to install high performance equipment in a car's engine *US, 1994*

Rods; Rod's *nickname* Harrod's, a department store in Knightsbridge, London. An abbreviation that seems to be a diminutive. Upper-class society use *UK, 1982*

Rod the Bod; Rod the Mod *nickname* rock singer Rod Stewart *US, 1993*

rod walloper *noun* a male masturbator. Formed on ROD (the penis) with a variation of 'beater' *AUSTRALIA, 1971*

rod-walloping *noun* male masturbation *AUSTRALIA, 1971*

roger *verb* **1** from a male perspective, to have sex. From its, now obsolete, use as a slang term for 'the penis' *UK, 1711*. **2** to acknowledge receipt of a message *US, 2001*

roger! used for expressing agreement or affirmation. 'R' or 'roger' signified that a message or command had been received *US, 1941*

roger dodger; roger dodge; roger D; roger splodge yes; affirmative. Variations of ROGER! (yes) *US, 1976*

Roger Hunt *noun* a cunt in all senses. Rhyming slang, formed, for no apparent reason other than the rhyme, from the name of a Liverpool and England footballer *UK, 1998*

rogering *noun* from a male perspective, sexual intercourse. From the verb ROGER (to have sex) *UK, 1998*

Roger ramjet *noun* any speeding and reckless driver *US, 1976*

rogue *noun* **1** a horse that is difficult to handle *AUSTRALIA, 1947*. **2** in surfing, a wave that appears without warning *US, 1977*

rogue *verb* to take something without permission *US, 1984*

rogue *adjective* strange; threatening *US, 2003*

rogue's badge *noun* in horse racing, blinkers. Usually worn by horses that do not behave well, hence the label of 'rogue' *US, 1947*

rogue's gallery *noun* a collection of photographs of criminals *US, 1859*

roidhead *noun* a habitual user of steroids. An abbreviation of 'ster*oid*' combined with -HEAD (a user) *UK, 2001*

roid rage; 'roid rage *noun* violently ill-tempered behaviour resulting from excessive steroid use. An abbreviation of 'ster*oid*', playing on ROAD RAGE *US, 1987*

roids *noun* anabolic steroids *US, 1980*

rojas *noun* Malboro™ cigarettes. Spanish for 'red', which is the colour of the packaging *US, 1990*

rojito *noun* a red central nervous system depressant, especially Seconal™. From the Spanish for 'little red one' *US, 1971*

rojo *noun* dextromethorphan (DXM), an active ingredient in non-prescription cold and cough medication, often abused for non-medicinal purposes. Spanish for 'red', which is the colour of the cough syrup *US, 2003*

rojo flow *noun* the bleed period of the menstrual cycle. A use of the Spanish word *rojo* (red) *US, 2001*

roko *noun* a riot, protest or demonstration *INDIA, 2003*

rolf *verb* to vomit *US, 1982*

roll *noun* **1** an act of sexual intercourse. An abbreviation of ROLL IN THE HAY *US, 1962*. **2** a roll of money *US, 1965*. **3** a single cigarette or marijuana cigarette *FIJI, 1993*. **4** MDMA, the recreational drug best known as ecstasy *UK, 2003*. **5** ten barbiturate capsules sold as a unit *US, 1973*. **6** a double-breasted suit *US, 1970*. ▶ **on a roll** enjoying continuing success *US, 1976*

roll *verb* **1** to rob someone, especially with force and especially someone bemused with drink *US, 1873*. **2** to avoid paying a bill for services provided by an establishment such as a hotel or restaurant *US, 1977*. **3** to betray friends by changing sides; to inform on someone. A variation of ROLL OVER *US, 1997*. **4** to leave *US, 1982*. **5** to arrive on the scene *AUSTRALIA, 1861*. **6** to ride in a car *US, 1990*. **7** (used of a woman) to walk with a rolling motion of the pelvis *TRINIDAD AND TOBAGO, 1973*. **8** in prison, to open a cell *US, 1976*. **9** to take MDMA, the recreational drug best known as ecstasy *US, 2001*. ▶ **roll bones** to play dice *US, 1950*. ▶ **roll in on someone** to attack someone *US, 2000*. ▶ **roll it back** to decelerate a motorcycle; to close the throttle-twist grip *UK, 1979*. ▶ **roll on** let it proceed or happen swiftly. Often used in an imperative or exclamatory manner *UK, 1901*. ▶ **roll the dice** to take a chance on something *US, 1992*. ▶ **roll the drums** in betting, to double the bet in effect *US, 1986*. ▶ **roll your own** to reload your own ammunition *US, 1957*

roll deep *verb* to go somewhere with a large group of friends; to have a large group of friends *US, 2001*

roller *noun* **1** a police officer *US, 1964*. **2** a robber who relies on brute force *US, 1975*. **3** a prostitute who takes a client's money without delivering a service. From ROLL (to rob someone) *UK, 1996*. **4** a Rolls Royce car *UK, 1975*. **5** in the car sales business, a car that can be driven home the same day it is bought *US, 1966*. **6** a car that is being driven *US, 1970*. **7** a machine used to start the engine of a drag racer by spinning the rear wheels while the driver turns on the ignition *US, 1970*. **8** a wave *US, 1988*. **9** a vein that tends to roll away from a needle *US, 1970*. **10** a bowler *US, 1953*. **11** a tablet of MDMA, the recreational drug best known as ecstasy *US, 2002*. **12** a hot dog *US, 1991*

roller-rings *noun* the police *US, 1987*

rollers *noun* dice with rounded edges. A roller may be intentionally crafted or not; a naturally occurring roller makes a controlled shot by a cheat difficult *US, 1950*

rollerskate; skate *noun* a small car *UK, 1951*

roll for the bowl *noun* toilet paper *US, 1991*

rollicking *noun* a telling-off. Probably a euphemistic replacement for synonymous BOLLOCKING *UK, 1938*

rollie *noun* **1** a hand-rolled cigarette *AUSTRALIA, 1981*. **2** a marijuana cigarette. A variation of the previous sense *UK, 1999*. **3** a tablet of Rolypnol™, a brand name for flunitrazepan, a sedative *NEW ZEALAND, 1989*

rollies *noun* loose tobacco, used for hand-rolling cigarettes. Prison usage *US, 1967*

rolling *adjective* **1** very rich. Variants include 'rolling in it' and 'rolling in money' *UK, 1782*. **2** under the influence of MDMA, the recreational drug best known as ecstasy *US, 1996*

rolling bones *noun* dice *US, 1950*

rolling hot! used by helicopter gunship pilots in Vietnam to announce that a strafing attack was about to begin *US, 1990*

rolling lighthouse *noun* in trucking, a tractor and trailer embellished with many extra running lights *US, 1971*

rollings *noun* loose cigarette tobacco *US, 1945*

roll in the hay *noun* an act of sexual intercourse *US, 1945*

roll me in the gutter; roll me *noun* butter. Rhyming slang *UK, 1925*

rollocks *noun* the testicles. Rhyming slang for BOLLOCKS. The reduced form of JIMMY ROLLOCKS, JOHNNY ROLLOCKS and TOMMY ROLLOCKS *UK, 1984*

roll-on *noun* a secret lover in addition to your regular partner. Teen slang *SOUTH AFRICA, 2003*

roll on *verb* to travel; to go. Wheeled transport is probably implied *US, 2001*

roll-on, roll-off *noun* a used, sometimes stolen, car imported for sale *TRINIDAD AND TOBAGO, 2002*

rollout *noun* in handball, a ball hit off the front wall so low that the ball does not bounce off the floor *US, 1977*

roll out *verb* to leave *US, 1997*

rollover *noun* an informant *US, 2000*

roll over *verb* to turn against or inform against someone *AUSTRALIA, 1995*

Rolls *noun* a Rolls-Royce car *US, 1928*

Rolls Royce *noun* the voice, especially a good singing voice. Rhyming slang *UK, 1960*

roll-up *noun* **1** a hand-*roll*ed cigarette. A prison coinage *UK, 1950*. **2** a type of bet where the amount won on one event becomes the stake for the next event. Better known as an 'accumulator' *UK, 2001*

roll up *verb* **1** to arrive *AUSTRALIA, 1920*. **2** to roll a marijuana cigarette *US, 1971*

rolly *noun* a match. Rhyming slang, from Rolly Hatch, a prominent and popular horse racing figure in New Zealand and later Australia *AUSTRALIA, 1989*

roll-your-own *noun* a hand-rolled cigarette *NEW ZEALAND, 2002*

roly *noun* a hand-rolled cigarette. From ROLL-UP *UK, 2002*

roly-poly *adjective* overweight *UK, 1820*

Roman candle *noun* **1** in homosexual usage, the penis of an Italian or Italian-American *US, 1987*. **2** in target shooting, a poorly loaded cartridge that produces a spray of red sparks when detonated *US,*

1957. **3** a burst of tracer bullets *US, 1962*. **4** a sandal. Rhyming slang, formed from a firework *UK, 1992*

Roman culture *noun* group sex *US, 1967*

Roman engagement *noun* in homosexual usage, anal sex with a woman *US, 1987*

Roman fingers *noun* the hands of a boy wandering over a girl's body *NEW ZEALAND, 1984*

Roman roulette *noun* birth control by the rhythm method. A variation of VATICAN ROULETTE *UK, 1969*

romantic ballad *noun* a salad. Rhyming slang *UK, 1998*

rom-com *noun* *rom*antic *com*edy. Media jargon that has insinuated itself into mainstream consciousness *UK, 2002*

romo *noun* a follower of the New Romantic youth fashion of the early 1980s *UK, 2003*

romp *noun* in horse racing, an easy victory *US, 1976*

romp *verb* **1** to excite; to excel; to be lively *US, 1946*. **2** to win easily. Also as 'romp home' *UK, 1881*

rompered *noun* severely beaten. Derives from 'romper room'; used by the British military in Northern Ireland to describe a brand of justice dispensed by illegal kangaroo courts *UK: NORTHERN IRELAND, 1974*

rompums *noun* marijuana *UK, 2003*

Romulan *noun* in British Columbia, a local variety of marijuana. A *Star Trek* inspired term *CANADA, 2002*

ron *noun* a homosexual Mafia don *US, 2002*

Ronan Keating *noun* a beating. Rhyming slang, formed from the name of the popular Irish singer (b.1977) *UK, 2004*

ronies *noun* pepperoni *US, 1996*

Ronnie Biggs *noun* lodgings. Rhyming slang for DIGS, formed from the name of the 'Great Train Robber' (1929–2005) *UK, 1992*

Ronnie RayGun *nickname* Ronald Reagan (1911–2004), US President 1981–89. A neat pun that refers particularly to Reagan's 'Star Wars' initiative *UK, 2000*

ronson *noun* **1** a ponce, a man who lives on the earnings of a prostitute. Very imperfect rhyming slang, apparently adopted under the influence of high-powered advertising for the branded cigarette lighters *UK, 1984*. **2** a despised or unpleasant person. Rhyming slang, formed on a very weak rhyme for PONCE *UK, 1960*

roo *noun* **1** a kangaroo. By front clipping *AUSTRALIA, 1898*. **2** an apprentice station hand working on, and learning how to manage, a cattle or sheep station. An abbreviation of 'jackaroo' *AUSTRALIA, 1891*

-roo *suffix* used as an meaningless, affected embellishment of a noun *US, 1984*

roo bar *noun* a metal grille attached to the front of a vehicle as protection from kangaroos when driving in the country *AUSTRALIA, 1973*

roodle *adjective* in poker, said of a hand in which the stakes have been temporarily raised *US, 1947*

roody-poo *noun* someone who is ignorant or unsophisticated *US, 1999*

roody-poo *adjective* second-rate; shallow *US, 1998*

roof *noun* the flight deck of an aircraft carrier *UK, 1998*. ▶ **on the roof** paid for by the management of the establishment. A variation of ON THE HOUSE *UK, 2002*

roof *verb* to break into a building through the roof *US, 1972*

roofer *noun* Rohypnol™ (flunitrazepam), popularly known as the 'date-rape drug' *US, 1997*

roofies; ruffles; ropies *noun* the recreational drug Rohypnol™ (flunitrazepam) *US, 1997*

roof monkey *noun* a television journalist who, when on location, relies on satellite communication for incoming information which is then included in that journalist's report *UK, 2005*

roof-sniffing *noun* in caving and pot-holing, the act of moving on your back along a small, water-filled passage with only sufficient air-space for the eyes and nose *UK, 2004*

rook *noun* a beginner. An abbreviation of ROOKIE *US, 1905*

rook *verb* to cheat someone; to swindle someone; to defraud someone *UK, 1590*

rookety *adjective* rocky; bumpy *BARBADOS, 1965*

rookie *noun* **1** a raw recruit, especially a new recruit in the army or police. Probably a perversion of 'recruit' *UK, 1892*. **2** a novice at a sport; a player in his or her first year with a particular team. From the wider sense as a 'recruit' *US, 1913*. **3** a college freshman *US, 1979*

rooly; roolly *adverb* really. Representing a pronunciation of young children, though also used to represent supposed uneducated speech *AUSTRALIA, 1979*

room *noun* **1** in prison, a cell *UK, 1996*. **2** a bar or cocktail lounge *US, 1970*

roomdawg *noun* a person who shares your room, apartment or house *US, 2002*

roomdog *noun* a roommate *US, 1996*

roomie *noun* **1** a roommate *US, 1918*. **2** a prison cellmate *US, 1982*

room-rifler *noun* a thief who steals from hotel rooms *US, 1954*

'rooms *noun* mushrooms *US, 1969*

rooms *noun* a roommate *US, 1970*

room temperature IQ *noun* a very low intelligence *US, 1981*

room time *noun* time spent surfing in the breaking hollow of a wave *US, 1991*

rooney *noun* the penis *US, 1968*

roost *noun* **1** the highest rows in the highest gallery in a theatre *UK, 1952*. **2** a residence, be it room, apartment or house *US, 1945*

roost *verb* to sit *US, 1983*

rooster *noun* **1** the buttocks *US, 1946*. **2** crack cocaine *US, 1994*. **3** a member of the Piru youth gang *US, 1994*

rooster comb *noun* a swath of unmown hay left in the field after cutting *CANADA, 1992*

rooster tail *noun* a spray of water directly behind an object or person moving fast through the water *US, 1965*

root *noun* **1** the penis *US, 1968*. **2** an act of sexual intercourse *AUSTRALIA, 1959*. **3** a sexual partner. Especially used in contexts where a person's sexual abilities are rated; see DUD ROOT *AUSTRALIA, 1969*. **4** marijuana; a marijuana cigarette *US, 1959*. **5** an amphetamine or other central nervous system stimulant *US, 1971*. **6** a kick. The variant 'rooter' also exists *IRELAND, 1962*

root *verb* **1** to copulate with someone *AUSTRALIA, 1958*. **2** to confound someone; to defeat someone *AUSTRALIA, 1944*. **3** to give a hefty blow to someone or something *AUSTRALIA, 1975*. ▶ **get rooted** go away; piss off. An analogue to 'get fucked' *AUSTRALIA, 1961*. ▶ **root like a rattlesnake** (usually of a woman) to have sex with vigour and uninhibited enthusiasm *AUSTRALIA, 1969*

rootable *adjective* sexually desirable *AUSTRALIA, 1973*

root around *verb* to be sexually promiscuous *AUSTRALIA, 2001*

rooted *adjective* wrecked; ruined *AUSTRALIA, 1944*

rooter *noun* a person who copulates promiscuously *AUSTRALIA, 1975*

root for *verb* to support someone ardently *US, 2000*

rootin' tootin' oil *noun* semen *US, 1962*

root up *verb* to mess something up *AUSTRALIA, 1992*

root ute *noun* a panel van or the like used for sexual encounters *AUSTRALIA, 2000*

rooty-ma-toot *noun* a suit. Glasgow rhyming slang *UK: SCOTLAND, 1988*

roovle *noun* among Nova Scotians of German descent, a wrinkle. In Lunenburg County, the descendants of German soldiers of fortune who were awarded land by King George in the late C18 use unconventional, slightly altered German words in their English conversation. This term is close in sound to 'rivvel' and thus may also come from German *runzeln* (to wrinkle) *CANADA, 1999*

rope *noun* **1** marijuana; hashish; a marijuana cigarette. Conventional 'rope' is often made from Indian hemp. *Cannabis sativa*, a plant genus that gives us marijuana, is true HEMP but sometimes called INDIAN HEMP which may well explain the origins of this usage; it is likely that the sense as 'a marijuana cigarette' is influenced by appearance *US, 1944*. **2** Rohypnol™ (flunitrazepam), popularly known as the 'date-rape drug' *US, 1995*. **3** a vein used for drug injections *UK, 1996*. **4** a thick gold chain necklace *US, 1989*. **5** an Afrikaner. Contemptuous, insulting; a reference to a rope that is, according to a 1975 informant, 'thick, coarse, twisted, hairy' *SOUTH AFRICA, 1970*. **6** tough talk *TRINIDAD AND TOBAGO, 1983*

rope *verb* **1** to lure someone into a swindle *US, 1848*. **2** in a card game, to cheat or mislead someone *US, 1985*

ropeable *adjective* livid; splenetic; furious *AUSTRALIA, 1874*

rope-a-dope *noun* **1** a defensive tactic employed by Muhammed Ali, resting against the ropes and letting his opponent exhaust himself with punches that Ali evaded or absorbed *US, 1975*. **2** a tactic of feigning weakness in order to lure an opponent into an ill-advised offensive. From the boxing sense *US, 1979*

rope dope *noun* low grade marijuana *US, 1995*

ropehead *noun* **1** a Rastafarian with long matted braids *JAMAICA, 1987*. **2** a dark-skinned person. Prison usage *NEW ZEALAND, 1997*

roper *noun* in a confidence swindle, a confederate who identifies and lures the victim into the swindle. Originally used in the context of gambling houses, and then in confidence swindles *US, 1840*

rophie *noun* Rohypnol™ (flunitrazepam), popularly known as the 'date-rape drug' *US, 1993*

ropy; ropey *adjective* bad; rough; unattractive; unsatisfactory; unwell. Originally Royal Air Force use *UK, 1942*

ro-ro *noun* **1** in prison, a type of educational course that makes it possible for short-term prisoners to complete individual modules. A figurative application of RO-RO (roll on, roll off) *UK, 1996*. **2** a Rolls Royce car *UK, 1984*

ro-ro *adjective* roll on, roll off. Said of a containerisation system used to ship military cargo during the Vietnam war *US, 1990*

rort *noun* **1** a confidence trick; an illicit scheme or dodge; a swindle. Also used of legitimate practices imputing that they are unfair or a rip-off *AUSTRALIA, 1926*. **2** a wild party; an unrestrained good time; a drunken orgy *AUSTRALIA, 1950*. **3** in horse or greyhound racing, a large and unexpected bet *AUSTRALIA, 1989*

rort *verb* **1** to fraudulently manipulate an organisation, system or the like; to rip someone off; to rig an election *AUSTRALIA, 1919*. **2** to party boisterously *AUSTRALIA, 1960*. **3** to engage in petty crime *AUSTRALIA, 1919*

rorter *noun* a swindler; a cheat *AUSTRALIA, 1926*

rorty *adjective* wild, boisterous *AUSTRALIA, 1929*

Rory O'More; rory *noun* **1** a floor. Rhyming slang, on the name of a legendary Irish rebel. The earliest of three uses for the rhyme; however, the second sense, 'a whore' is obsolete *UK, 1857*. **2** a door. Rhyming slang, on the name of a legendary Irish rebel. This is the only sense of the word also recorded in the US, where it is sometimes misspelt Rory O'Moore *UK, 1892*

rosa *noun* an amphetamine tablet *US, 1994*

Rosa Maria; rosa maria *noun* marijuana *US, 1938*

roscoe *noun* a handgun *US, 1914*

roscoe *verb* to point a handgun at someone and order them not to move *US, 1974*

rose *noun* a tablet of Benzedrine™ (amphetamine sulphate), a central nervous system stimulant *US, 1967*

Roseanne Barr *noun* a bra. Rhyming slang, formed from the name of the US actress, comedienne and producer (b.1952) *UK, 1998*

rosebud *noun* **1** the anus *US, 1965*. **2** a textbook example of a primary lesion *US, 1981*. **3** following a colostomy, the pink tissue that marks the opening of the intestine on the abdomen *US, 1980*. **4** a potato. Rhyming slang for SPUD. Sometimes shortened to 'rose' *UK, 1943*

rosebud *verb* (of the anus) to become puffy and pronounced *UK, 1996*

rose garden *noun* **1** in prison, a solitary confinement cell *UK, 1978*. **2** a group of neurologically depressed hospital patients *US, 1978*

Rose Marie *noun* marijuana. An anglicisation of ROSA MARIA *UK, 2003*

rose tree trimmer *noun* a person hired to clean latrines *BARBADOS*, *1965*

rosewood *noun* a police nightstick *US, 1970*

rosey lee; rosie lee; rosie *noun* tea. Rhyming slang; originally military, probably from the 1914–18 war *UK, 1925*

rosie *noun* a rubbish bin *UK, 2002*

Rosie O'Grady's *noun* a *ladies'* toilet. Rhyming slang, originally 'Rosie O'Grady' (a lady) but now used only of a public convenience, formed from the film musical *Sweet Rosie O'Grady*, 1943 *UK, 1998*

Rosie Palm and her five sisters; Rosie Palm; Rosie *noun* the male hand as the instrument of masturbation *US, 1977*

rosiner; roziner; rozener *noun* a large serving of an alcoholic drink *AUSTRALIA, 1933*

rosser *noun* a police officer *AUSTRALIA, 1944*

Rossy Docks *noun* socks. Glasgow rhyming slang, based on local pronunciation of Rothesay *UK: SCOTLAND, 1985*

rot *noun* 1 nonsense, rubbish. In *Eats, Shoots & Leaves*, 2003, Lynne Truss records the following marginal note, made by a long-ago reader, in the 1st edition of Partridge's *You Have a Point There*: 'Rot! You lazy swine Partridge' *UK, 1848*. 2 an unidentifed disease or malady *US, 1947*

rot *verb* to be terrible *US, 1997*

rotary *adjective* in circus and carnival usage, emotionally unbalanced *US, 1981*

rot corps *noun* the ROTC, or Reserve Officer Training Corps, found at many colleges *US, 1972*

rote; rout *noun* in Nova Scotia, the sound of the surf on the shore, a fisherman's locating device. This word, not long in print, descended orally from an Old Norse word *rauta* meaning 'roar'. The different sounds of the surf tell fishermen whose GPS has broken down whether they are near sand, cliff, shingle or gravel beach, and their knowledge of the coastline does the rest *CANADA, 1975*

ROTF used in computer message shorthand to mean 'rolling on the floor (laughing)' *US, 1991*

rotgut *noun* any unwholesome alcohol *UK, 1633*

rothe *noun* two hundred pounds. Ticket-touting slang, recorded August 2002; possibly an ironic abbreviation of Rothschild (a rich man) *UK, 2002*

rotheo *noun* twenty pounds. Ticket-touting slang, recorded August 2002. From **ROTHE** *UK, 2002*

Rothman's-sign *noun* nicotine-stained fingers as a diagnostic indicator. An informal medical term, formed on the name of a cigarette manufacturer *UK, 2002*

roti and rum; rum and roti *noun* a tactic in a political campaign in which voters are given food and drink to encourage their vote. 'Roti' is an Indian bread *TRINIDAD AND TOBAGO, 1960*

rotorhead *noun* a helicopter pilot or crew member *US, 1991*

roto-rooter *noun* a person who kisses with an active and probing tongue *US, 1963*

rotted *adjective* drunk or drug-intoxicated *US, 1993*

rotten *adjective* 1 unpleasant *UK, 1964*. 2 ill; depressed; worthless *UK, 1881*. 3 drunk *AUSTRALIA, 1864*. 4 used to intensify a negative quality *UK, 1964*

rotten row *noun* a blow. Rhyming slang, from the name given to the ride in London's Hyde Park *UK, 1992*

rotten squash *noun* brain damage *US, 1985*

rotter *noun* a despised person *UK, 1894*

rottie *noun* 1 a *Rott*weiler dog *US, 1987*. 2 a foul mood *NEW ZEALAND, 1998*

rouf *noun* four; in betting, odds of 4–1. Back slang; pronounced as 'loaf' *UK, 1851*

rouf and a half *noun* in betting, odds of 9–2. In bookmaker slang 'rouf' is 4–1; here the addition of 'a half' increases the odds to 4½–1 or 9–2 *UK, 1991*

rough *noun* turbulent seas following a storm *CANADA, 1979*

rough *verb* 1 to rob someone with force or threat of force *US, 1973*. 2 to jostle or shove a member of a rival gang *US, 1955*. ▶ **rough it** to have sex al fresco. To voluntarily go without such creature comforts as a bed *UK, 2001*. ▶ **rough it up** in poker, to bet heavily *US, 1979*. ▶ **rough up the suspect** (of a male) to masturbate *US, 2001*

rough *adjective* 1 unwell. Dialect *US, 1883*. 2 good. On the **BAD** (good) model *UK, 2003*. 3 excellent; fashionable, trendy *US, 1963*. 4 in lowball poker, unfavourable *US, 1967*

rough as a badger's arse *adjective* ugly; unsophisticated; unwell, especially as a result of too much drinking *UK, 1998*

rough as bags *adjective* extremely rough; unrefined, uncouth; also, of shabby appearance *AUSTRALIA, 1927*

rough as diamonds *adjective* unsophisticated; unpolished. A play on ROUGH DIAMOND *AUSTRALIA, 1971*

rough as guts *adjective* extremely rough; unrefined; uncouth *AUSTRALIA, 1970*

rough diamond *noun* a genuinely good person who is nevertheless unrefined in manners *AUSTRALIA, 1907*

rough end of the pineapple *noun* the raw end of the deal *AUSTRALIA, 1978*

rough-house *verb* to brawl in a playful if rowdy and boisterous manner *US, 1900*

rough hustle *noun* an amateurish, unpolished swindle. The term does not connote any physical roughness, simply a lack of polish *US, 1977*

roughie *noun* 1 an unrefined person or thing. Arthur Chipper notes, in *The Aussie Swearer's Guide*, 1972, that the term is 'Perhaps most commonly assigned to young ladies who aren't good-looking or too well-mannered' *AUSTRALIA, 1907*. 2 a racehorse or greyhound not expected to win; an outsider *AUSTRALIA, 1922*. 3 a sheep with two seasons of wool growth *FALKLAND ISLANDS (MALVINAS), 1993*

roughneck *noun* 1 a thug, a lout, a rowdy person *US, 1836*. 2 in oil drilling, a skilled oil field worker *US, 1954*. 3 on the railways, a brakeman on a goods train *US, 1946*

rough off *verb* to steal something using brute force *US, 1985*

rough rider *noun* 1 a condom of any style or brand thought to bring extra satisfaction to the female partner. West Indian and UK black usage *JAMAICA, 2002*. 2 an armed guard on a vehicle *US, 1991*

rough riding *noun* sexual intercourse without the protection of a condom *UK, 1961*

rough stuff *noun* 1 violent or sadistic sexual behaviour *US, 1925*. 2 marijuana that contains unusable detritus *US, 1972*

rough trade *noun* a tough, often sadistic male homosexual, especially as a casual sex-partner *US, 1927*

rough trip *noun* an unpleasant experience with LSD or another hallucinogen *UK, 1983*

rough trot *noun* a difficult period *AUSTRALIA, 1944*

rough up *verb* to beat or intimidate someone; to facilitate a street robbery with violence *US, 1996*

roughy *noun* a manual labourer in a carnival *US, 1966*

round *noun* an ejaculation *TRINIDAD AND TOBAGO, 2003*

round *verb* to make the rounds *US, 1961*

roundabout; rounder *noun* a conditional bet on three selections *UK, 2001*

round-brown *noun* the anus *US, 1972*

rounder *noun* 1 a migratory, transient worker, especially one living on the edges of legality. Originally applied to railway workers *US, 1908*. 2 a street criminal *CANADA, 1987*. 3 a prisoner associated with traditional Italian-American organised crime *US, 1992*. 4 a highly skilled professional poker player who travels and plays less skilled players *US, 1979*

rounders *noun* confusing talk *TRINIDAD AND TOBAGO, 1977* ▷*see:* ROUND THE HOUSES

round eye *noun* **1** the anus; by extension, a male homosexual who plays the passive role in anal sex *US, 1950*. **2** an American or European. From the Southeast Asian perspective, adopted by US soldiers in Vietnam to describe themselves *US, 1960*

round-eyed *adjective* American or European, Caucasian *US, 1966*

round file *noun* a wastebasket *US, 1975*

roundhead *noun* the circumcised penis. A visual joke, probably of Royal Navy origin, then polari, or juvenile *UK, 2002*

roundheel *noun* a woman who is easily talked into sexual relations. Boxing slang from the 1920s for a poor fighter – a 'push-over' – applied later to women of easy virtue *US, 1943*

round-heeled *adjective* easily seduced *US, 1957*

round heels *noun* a promiscuous or sexually compliant woman. Derogatory; from the anatomical notion that a woman with round heels is more easily put on her back *US, 1926*

roundhouse *noun* a punch that swings round to hit your opponent side-on *US, 1920*

roundie; roundy *noun* a factory-made cigarette. Prison usage *NEW ZEALAND, 1948*

round of drinks *noun* a small bet relative to the bettor's wealth *AUSTRALIA, 1989*

round robin *noun* **1** a story begun by one writer and completed by another or multiple writers *US, 1982*. **2** a wager of ten conditional bets on three selections *UK, 2001*

round robin shift *noun* a work schedule in which the worker rotates between several different shifts *US, 1984*

rounds *noun* an ejaculation *BAHAMAS, 1982*

round sound *noun* a fashionable, current song. 'Round' means nothing, but contrasts with SQUARE *US, 1955*

roundtable *noun* in organised crime, a meeting of leaders convened to discuss and decide with finality pressing business issues *US, 1975*

round the bend; around the bend *adjective* mad, crazy; eccentric. Probably a naval coinage, widespread by the mid-C20 *UK, 1929*

round-the-clock *noun* an elaborate conditional wager on a minimum of three selections *UK, 2001*

round the houses; round me's; rounders *noun* trousers. Rhyming slang on the Cockney pronunciation of 'trousers'. The abbreviation 'round me's' suggests a variation as 'round me houses' – this is not so. In the US the abbreviation 'rounds' was not recorded until 1944 *UK, 1857*

round the twist *adjective* crazy. A variation of ROUND THE BEND *UK, 1960*

round-up *noun* in college, a notification of academic deficiency *US, 1968*

roundy-round *adjective* used of a motor race track or course oval *US, 1993*

rouse *verb* ▶ **rouse on** to castigate someone verbally *AUSTRALIA, 1896*

rouseabout *verb* a general assistant on a rural property. Hence, also, any general assistant *AUSTRALIA, 1881*

roust *verb* **1** to harass someone, especially when done deliberately by the police or other authorities *UK, 1995*. **2** to upbraid someone *AUSTRALIA, 1916*

roustabout *noun* **1** in oil drilling, an unskilled oil field worker *US, 1948*. **2** a general assistant on a rural property. Variant of ROUSEABOUT *AUSTRALIA, 1940*

rouster *noun* a rough and ready western Canadian man. This expression is likely derived from ROUSTABOUT (an oil field worker), but adapted to describe any rough-hewn male *CANADA, 1987*

rousting *noun* **1** a vigorous act of sexual intercourse *UK, 1999*. **2** an act of deliberate (police) harassment *UK, 1980*

rout *noun* a wild, rowdy party *US, 1968* ▷ *see:* ROTE

router *noun* in horse racing, a horse that performs well in longer races *US, 1965*

rover *noun* in a casino, a gambler who moves from game to game, never staying at any one game very long *US, 1987*

row *noun* ▶ **go for a row** to get into trouble *AUSTRALIA, 1965*

row *verb* to fight; to battle. An exaggeration of the sense as 'to argue' *UK, 1999*. ▶ **row down the red river** to experience the bleed period of the menstrual cycle *US, 2001*

rowbottom *noun* a student disturbance, started in fun but not always ending as such. Specific to the University of Pennsylvania in Philadelphia, claimed to have been named for J.T. Rowbottom, a rowdy member of Penn's Class of 1913 *US, 1940*

row dog *noun* in prison, another prisoner whose cell is on the same tier *US, 1995*

rowdy *noun* a person who inhales glue for the psychoactive effect *US, 1971*

rowdy dowdy *noun* in pickpocketing, the seemingly accidental jostling of victims or potential victims by members of the gang *US, 1962*

rowed out *adjective* excluded *UK, 2000*

rower *noun* an argument *UK, 1996*

rowers' revenge *noun* the ritual of throwing the coxswain into the water after a rowing team wins an event *US, 2001*

row in *verb* to implicate someone in a crime *UK, 1970*

row out *verb* **1** to contrive the innocence of someone in relation to a particular crime *UK, 1970*. **2** to distance yourself from something or someone *UK, 1974*

rox *noun* crack cocaine. A phonetic play on ROCK(S) *US, 1994*

Roxanne *noun* cocaine; crack cocaine. A ROCK personification *US, 1994*

Roy *noun* a refined and cultured Australian male. Counterpart to the ALF *AUSTRALIA, 1960*

royal *adjective* effeminately homosexual. 'Queenly' *UK, 2002*

royal blue *noun* a blue tablet variety of LSD *US, 1971*

royal crown *noun* a British Leyland 'Princess' car *UK, 1981*

Royal Docks *noun* syphilis; hence any sexually transmitted infection; hence an irritated condition. Rhyming slang for POX *UK, 1992*

royally *adverb* greatly, extremely *US, 2002*

royal mail; royal *noun* bail. Rhyming slang *UK, 1961*

Royal Navy *noun* gravy. Rhyming slang. Presumably served in a 'Royal Navy boat' *UK, 1992*

Royal Navy situation *noun* a need for money. A pun on SUB (a loan) *UK, 1994*

royal shaft *noun* monumental mistreatment *US, 1983*

royal temple ball *noun* hashish and LSD formed into a ball *US, 1978*

royal wedding *noun* in hold 'em poker, a king and queen, especially of diamonds *US, 1996*

Roy Castle *noun* the anus. Rhyming slang for ARSEHOLE, used here in its anatomical, non-figurative sense; formed from the name of the multi-talented entertainer, 1932–94 *UK, 2003*

Roy Rogers *noun* building tradesmen who are not as skilled as may reasonably be expected. Rhyming slang on the plural form of BODGER. Formed on the name of a famous film cowboy, 1911–98, and thus a play on COWBOY (any tradesman who is unreliable, irresponsible and, perhaps, unqualified) *UK, 1992*

roz *noun* crack cocaine. Possibly a misspelling of ROX *UK, 1998*

rozzer; roz *noun* a police officer. Possibly from Yiddish *khazer* (a pig). 'Roz' is first recorded in 1971 *UK, 1893*

RPG *noun* a role-playing game *US, 1986*

RSN used as Internet shorthand to mean 'real soon now' *US, 1995*

RTA *verb* to return to Australia; to be returned to Australia *AUSTRALIA, 1963*

RTAer *noun* a person returning to Australia after expeditioning in Antarctica. From RTA *AUSTRALIA, 1996*

RTFM read the fucking manual *US, 1997*

ru *noun* a member of the Piru youth gang *US, 1994*

rub *verb* ▶ **rub in; rub it in** to emphasise something annoyingly; to continue to insist, especially in an unkindly or vexing manner

UK, 1870. ▶ **rub off on someone** (of abstract qualitities, such as luck or enthusiasm) to transfer from one person to another *US, 1959.* ▶ **rub someone up the wrong way** to annoy someone *UK, 1862.* ▶ **rub someone's nose in it** to humiliate someone by reminding them of a mistake *UK, 1963.* ▶ **rub the magic lamp** (of a male) to masturbate *US, 2001*

rub-a-dub; rub-a-dub-dub; rubberdy; rubbidy; rubba *noun* a public house. Rhyming slang for PUB; from the nursery rhyme 'Rub-a-dub-dub, / Three men in a tub' *UK, 1932*

rub-a-dub-dubs *nickname* HMP Wormwood Scrubs (a prison in north London). Rhyming slang, in current prison use February 2002 *UK, 2002*

rubber *noun* **1** a condom. The most common, and almost only, slang term for a condom in the US *US, 1947.* **2** balloons *US, 1966.* **3** collectively, a car's tyres. A car might be said to have 'good rubber' *US, 1882.* **4** a car *US, 1964.* **5** a rubber bullet *US, 1982.* ▶ **burn rubber** to spin a car's wheels in a fast start, leaving rubber tracks on the road *US, 1957.* ▶ **chirp rubber** to shift gears in a car in a manner that produces a chirping sound of tyre meeting road *US, 1965.* ▶ **on rubber** driving a car *US, 1945.* ▶ **peel rubber** to spin a car's wheels in a fast start, leaving rubber tracks on the road *US, 1971*

rubber *adjective* used of a cheque, unfunded. A back-formation from the metaphor of an unfunded cheque bouncing *US, 1991*

rubber and rocks *noun* bacon and eggs. Collected during an extensive survey of New Zealand prison slang, 1996–2000 *NEW ZEALAND, 2000*

rubber arms *noun* the sensation experienced by a surfer paddling into a large wave that might be a little larger than the surfer cares to tackle *US, 1964*

rubberband *noun* a vehicle manufactured by DAF. Citizens' band radio slang; a slur on DAF technology *UK, 1981*

rubber bitch *noun* the inflatable rubber air mattress given to US troops in the field in Vietnam *US, 1991*

rubber bum *noun* a derelict hitchhiker *CANADA, 1961*

rubber cheque; rubber kite *noun* a worthless cheque. An unfunded cheque bounces back from the bank *US, 1931*

rubber chicken circuit *noun* the tour made by an after-dinner speaker, with reference to tough chicken as the usual main course *CANADA, 1959*

rubber cow *noun* in circus usage, an elephant, male or female *US, 1981*

rubber duck *noun* **1** a trifle; something of no value. Rhyming slang for FUCK *UK, 1992.* **2** an inflatable rubber dinghy *SOUTH AFRICA, 1986*

rubber ducker *noun* a rubber duck (an inflatable rubber dinghy) enthusiast *SOUTH AFRICA, 1994*

rubber duckie *noun* a short, flexible, rubber-coated vehicle-mounted radio aerial. A jokey reference to 'Rubber Duck' as referring to the HANDLE (a citizens' band radio identity) of the hero of the film *Convoy*, 1975 *UK, 1981*

rubbered *adjective* drunk *UK, 2002*

rubber heels; rubber heelers *noun* the Metropolitan Police internal affairs division at New Scotland Yard. From the silence and secrecy of its methods *UK, 1964*

rubber johnny; rubber johnnie; rubber johney *noun* a condom. An elaboration of JOHNNY *UK, 1980*

rubber lip *noun* a citizens' band radio user who monopolises conversation *US, 1976*

rubber man *noun* in circus and carnival usage, a balloon seller *US, 1981*

rubberneck *verb* to stare with undue interest *US, 1896*

rubberneck bus *noun* a tour bus *US, 1958*

rubberneck car *noun* on the railways, an observation carriage *US, 1946*

rubbernecker; rubberneck *noun* a person who stares with curiousity, especially a motorist who slows to view an accident *US, 1934*

rubber numbers *noun* very approximate statistics *US, 2003*

rubbers *noun* **1** a wet suit; a garment made of rubber or synthetic neoprene worn next to the skin while in cold water *CANADA, 1977.* **2** sneakers, trainers *VIRGIN ISLANDS, BRITISH, 1996*

rubber vag *noun* in circus and carnival usage, someone who lives in a mobile trailer *US, 1981*

rubber walls *adjective* crazy. In gay use, especially in the phrase 'I'll go rubber walls' *US, 1972*

rubbins; rubbings *noun* rubbing alcohol. A drink of desperation *US, 1980*

rubbish *noun* **1** anything of poor quality or little or no worth; nonsense. From the sense as 'refuse' *UK, 1601.* **2** a contemptible person or persons *SOUTH AFRICA, 1941*

rubbish *verb* to criticise someone or something unfavourably; to disparage someone or something; to discard someone or something *AUSTRALIA, 1953*

rubbish *adjective* bad; inferior *UK, 2001*

rubbisher *noun* a person given to detraction *AUSTRALIA, 1972*

rubbishing *noun* an act of denigration. From RUBBISH (little or no worth) *AUSTRALIA, 1971*

rubbishy *adjective* of inferior quality *UK, 1824*

rubbity-dub; rubbity; rubbitty; rubbidy *noun* a public hotel. Rhyming slang for PUB *AUSTRALIA, 1898*

rubby *noun* a derelict who drinks rubbing alcohol. The word is not to be confused with 'rummy' *US, 1962*

rubby-dub *noun* an ignorant soldier from a rural mountain area, a poor candidate to be a good soldier *US, 1946*

rub down *noun* a cursory search of a prisoner by running hands over clothes and body *UK, 1887*

rub down *verb* to search a prisoner *UK, 1887*

rube; reub *noun* an unsophisticated, naive, inexperienced person. From the older, UK 'reuben' (a country bumpkin) *US, 1896*

rubia de la costa; rubia *noun* a light-coloured marijuana originating in Columbia. Directly from Spanish, *rubia* (fair-haired) is used by the Spanish to describe Virginian tobacco, plus *de la costa* (of the coast) *US, 1976*

rubies *noun* the lips *US, 1947*

Rubik's cubes; rubik's *noun* pubic hair. Rhyming slang for PUBES, formed from a puzzling toy *UK, 2003*

rub joint *noun* a dance hall where men can, for a small price, dance intimately with women *US, 1981*

rub 'n' tug *noun* a massage that includes masturbation *US, 2000*

rub of the brush *noun* a beverage made from the remnants of drinks in a bar *US, 1950*

rub-out *noun* a killing *US, 1927*

rub out *verb* **1** to kill someone *US, 1848.* **2** to disqualify a competitor *AUSTRALIA, 1902*

rub up *verb* to assault someone *US, 1952*

rubyfruit *noun* the vagina *US, 1982*

Ruby Murray; ruby *noun* a curry. Rhyming slang, based on popular singer Ruby Murray, 1935–96. In Cardiff, a local variant is Don Murray, named after the Cardiff City footballer *UK, 1992*

ruby rose; ruby *noun* the nose. Rhyming slang *UK, 1992*

ruck *noun* **1** a heated argument; a fight. Possibly derives from obsolete 'rux' (bad temper, anger, passion, noise) or conventional 'ruckus' *UK, 1958.* **2** a rucksack or backpack *US, 1982*

ruck *verb* **1** to fight, especially as part of a gang *UK, 1999.* **2** to masturbate. Prison slang *UK, 1974*

ruck and row; ruck *noun* a cow, especially in the sense a contemptible woman. Rhyming slang, formed from a combination of RUCK (a fight) and 'row' (a disturbance, a violent quarrel) *UK, 1992*

rucker *noun* **1** a fighter *UK, 1968.* **2** a customer given to complaining and making a fuss. A barely euphemistic variation of FUCKER, possibly influenced by 'ruckus'. Used by second-hand car dealers *UK, 1968*

rucking *noun* a severe reprimand. Mostly in prison use *UK, 1958*

ruck up *verb* to pick up your rucksack and other combat gear and proceed with a march. Used as a modernised SADDLE UP, which has definite overtones of cavalry days *US, 1990*

ruckus juice *noun* strong, homemade whisky *US, 1999*

ruco *noun* a boyfriend or husband. Border Spanish used in English conversation by Mexican-Americans; also used in the feminine 'ruca' (a girlfriend or wife) *US, 1950*

ruction *noun* a disturbance; agitation; disorderly behaviour *UK, 1890*

ruddy *adjective* used as an intensifier. A rhyming euphemism for BLOODY that also puns on the colour red *UK, 1914*

ruddy well *adverb* certainly, definitely *UK, 1933*

rude *noun* a youth who steals by mugging. Adapted from RUDE BOY (a Jamaican youth/gangster) *UK, 2002*. ▶ **in the rude** naked. Light-hearted rhyming euphemism for 'in the nude' *UK, 1974*

rude *adjective* **1** sexual; sexy. Upper-class society use. Not to be confused with IN THE RUDE (naked); one condition does not necessarily lead to the next *UK, 1982*. **2** attractive *US, 2003*. **3** intense; superior. Collected from fans of heavy metal music *US, 1995*. **4** used of a computer program, poorly designed *US, 1983*

rude!; rudeness!; how rude!; how rudeness! used for suggesting that the speaker has crossed an etiquette line that is better not breached *US, 1989*

rude bits *noun* genitals *AUSTRALIA, 1994*

rude boy; rude bwoy; rudebwai; rudie *noun* a Jamaican youth associated with gang activities. West Indian and UK black patois *JAMAICA, 1967*

rudeness *noun* sex *TRINIDAD AND TOBAGO, 1973*

rude parts *noun* the most obvious erogenous zones: male and female genitals and posteriors, and female breasts. Upper-class society use; combines RUDE (sexual) with 'private *parts*' *UK, 1982*

ruderalis skunk *noun* an extremely potent hydroponic marijuana which is a hybrid of ruderalis (a variety of marijuana from Russia) and skunk *UK, 1999*

rudery *noun* rudeness, impolite or risqué speech or conversation; sexually implicit or explicit gestures or behaviour *UK, 1932*

Rudolph Hess; rudolph *noun* a *mess* (a failure). Rhyming slang, formed from the name of the high-ranking Nazi officer, 1894–1987 *UK, 1998*

ruff *noun* a twenty-five cent piece *US, 1945*

ruff *adjective* acceptable, good, cool *US, 1985*

ruffie *noun* Rohypnol™ (flunitrazepam), popularly known as the 'date-rape drug' *US, 1995*

ruffle *noun* the passive participant in lesbian sex or a lesbian relationship *US, 1970*

ruffneck *noun* a male or female gangster; a non-conformist or rebellious youth;. A misspelling of 'roughneck' (a thug). West Indian and UK black use into the US via hip-hop culture *UK, 1994*

ruff-puff *noun* a South Vietnamese local defence force. RFs were regional forces, PFs were platoon-size village forces. Quick American minds took RF with PF to form 'ruff-puff' *US, 1977*

rug *noun* **1** a hairpiece, especially a poorly executed one *US, 1940*. **2** pubic hair, especially on a female *US, 1964*. **3** in horse racing, a heavy horse blanket *US, 1976*

rugby ball *noun* a capsule of Temazepam™, a branded tranquillizer. From the shape *UK, 1990s*

rug-cutter *noun* a great time *US, 1951*

rug-eater *noun* a lesbian *US, 1997*

rugger bugger *noun* an enthusiastic sportsman whose character is formed by the aggressive pursuit of masculinity and frequently demonstrated by his boorish behaviour and drunken socialising. From 'rugger' (rugby football) but encompassing a wider field of endeavours *SOUTH AFRICA, 1970*

rug joint *noun* a well-appointed, even luxurious gambling operation *US, 1964*

rug munch *noun* an instance of oral sex on a woman *US, 1995*

rug-muncher *noun* a lesbian. From the image of oral sex as 'munching a hairpiece' *US, 1997*

rug out *verb* to endure a difficult situation. An awkward attempt to render 'rugged' as a verb *US, 2002*

rug rat *noun* a young child. A bit derisive *US, 1970*

rug up *verb* in horse racing, to cover the horse with a blanket after a workout or race *UK, 1948*

ruined *adjective* drunk *UK, 2002*

rule *noun* ▶ **on the rule** of a prisoner, segregated from the general prison population for that prisoner's protection. A reference to rule 43 which is, according to HM Prison Service in 2003: 'A now defunct rule that allowed the segregation of prisoners' *UK, 2000*

rule *verb* used as an expression of supremacy for the preceding collective or plural noun(s) *US, 1968*

rule forty-three; rule 43; the rule *noun* in prison, a sex offender, or other prisoner, kept apart from the main prison community for 'safety of self or others' *UK, 1996*

rule of five *noun* a piece of (unofficial) medical lore: if more than five orifices are obscured by plastic tubing then a patient's condition is critical *UK, 2002*

rum *noun* **1** an unsophisticated, unaware person *US, 1972*. **2** a prisoner deemed inferior or too odd by other prisoners *US, 1972*. **3** a drunkard *US, 1960*

rum *adjective* strange; eccentric; disreputable; questionable *UK, 1774*

rumble *noun* **1** a fight, especially between teenage gangs *US, 1948*. **2** a wild party *US, 1968*. **3** a difficult encounter with law enforcement *US, 1972*. **4** a concerted police search for narcotics *US, 1958*

rumble *verb* **1** to fight *US, 1946*. **2** in circus and carnival usage, to spoil something *US, 1981*. **3** to come to an understanding or realisation of something that has been concealed *UK, 1886*

Rumble in the Jungle *nickname* the October 1974 heavyweight championship fight between Muhammed Ali and George Foreman in Kinshasa, Zaire, in which Ali knocked Foreman out in the 8th round *US, 1974*

rumbleseat *noun* a truck that is not equipped with a citizens' band radio following a truck that is *US, 1976*

rumble-tumble *noun* scrambled eggs. Originally military *UK, 2003*

rum blossom *noun* a red welt produced from excessive consumption of alcohol *US, 1976*

rum boy *noun* a drunk *BAHAMAS, 1982*

rum, bum and bacca; rum, bum and baccy *noun* the mythic three graces of a sailor's life. A (presumed) later variation of 'beer, bum and bacca'. *Rum, Bum and Concertina*, a pun on 'wine, women and song', is the title of the second part of George Melly's autobiography published in 1977. In 1992, the Pogues, reflecting an earlier view of naval life, released an album entitled *Rum, Sodomy and the Lash UK, 1973*

rumdum; rum-dumb *noun* a drunk *US, 1891*

rumdummed *adjective* extremely drunk *US, 1891*

rum goblet; rum goggles *noun* a large Adam's apple *TRINIDAD AND TOBAGO, 2003*

rummy *noun* an alcoholic *US, 1851*

rummy *adjective* **1** prone to drink too much, if not alcoholic *US, 1834*. **2** poor; inferior; bad *US, 1947*

rumoured *adjective* married. English gypsy use, from Romany *romer* (to marry) *UK, 2000*

rump *verb* to cheat someone *UK, 1998*

rump bump *noun* in a sexual dance, a pelvic thrust that emphasises the buttocks moving backwards *US, 1956*

rumper *noun* in hot rodding, a powerful engine *US, 1965*

rumpo *noun* sexual intercourse. Possibly influenced by (or vice versa) Rambling Syd Rumpo, an innuendo-laden character played by Kenneth Williams in *Round the Horne*, BBC radio, 1965–69 *UK, 1986*

rump-ordained *adjective* used for describing a preacher who has no formal theological training or denominational affiliation *US, 1974*

rumpty *adjective* in poor repair; below standard *NEW ZEALAND, 1995*

rumpty pumpty; rumpty *noun* intimate sexual activity. A variation of RUMPY-PUMPY with a nursery rhyme feel thanks to Humpty Dumpty *UK, 1998*

rumpus *noun* a brawl; a riot *UK, 1764*

rumpy-pumpy *noun* sexual intercourse *UK, 1983*

rum-runner *noun* an importer, transporter and/or purveyor of illegal alcohol, especially rum *US, 1920*

rum-sucker *noun* a heavy drinker *TRINIDAD AND TOBAGO, 1845*

rumty *noun* an admirable or excellent person or thing *NEW ZEALAND, 1998*

rum'un; rumun; rumin *noun* especially in Tasmania, an eccentric person; a character; a scallywag *AUSTRALIA, 1967*

run *noun* **1** a group motorcyle excursion *US, 1966*. **2** a period of extended amphetamine use *US, 1967*. ▶ **on the run** escaping from justice; being a fugitive *UK, 1887*

run *verb* **1** to associate; to socialise *US, 1946*. **2** to smuggle something *UK, 1706*. ▶ **run a pot** in poker, to make a sustained, pre-planned bluff on a hand *US, 1967*. ▶ **run blues** to use blue lights in a car's tail lights *US, 1985*. ▶ **run hot** to drive with sirens and flashing lights activated *US, 2002*. ▶ **run like a hairy goat** (of a racehorse) to run poorly in a race *AUSTRALIA, 1941*. ▶ **run rings round someone** to defeat someone with absolute ease *UK, 1891*. ▶ **run speed limit** to do something with great speed. Hawaiian youth usage *US, 1982*. ▶ **run to seed** with age or lack of care, to become ill-kempt, shabby or undesirable. The imagery of the garden *UK, 1837*. ▶ **run your mouth** to talk too much *US, 1977*. ▶ **run your neck** to make threats or boasts which you are not prepared to back up with actions *US, 2001*

runabout *noun* a small car *UK, 1900*

run along *verb* to depart; often used as a gentle imperative *UK, 1902*

run-around *noun* ▶ **give someone the run-around; get the run-around** to treat someone, or be treated, with contempt, or so as to serve a mere whim; to cause someone trouble, or be caused trouble *US, 1924*

run, chicken, run *noun* the Royal Canadian Regiment. Formed from the initials RCR. Note that 'chicken' does not insinuate cowardice. Rather this insult alludes to a story which alleges that a member of the regiment was found, in flagrante delicto, with a chicken. Members of the RCR counter that he was a cook *CANADA, 1995*

rundown *noun* a complete explanation *US, 1969*

runes *noun* in computing, any esoteric display character or computer language *US, 1991*

run-fast *noun* on the railways, oil *US, 1946*

rung-in *adjective* substituted; phoney *AUSTRALIA, 1969*

run-in *noun* **1** an argumentative or violent encounter *UK, 1999*. **2** a concealed location used by criminals for the division or transfer of recently stolen goods *UK, 1959*

run in *verb* to arrest someone *US, 1973*

run, Johnny, run *noun* inexpensive loose cigarette tobacco. Formed from the initials of the R.J. Reynolds tobacco company *US, 1962*

run letter *noun* a final deportation letter from the US Immigration and Naturalisation Service *US, 2002*

runner *noun* **1** in an illegal betting operation, a person who physically collects and pays off bets placed with sheet writers *US, 1947*. **2** a prison inmate who collects dues for a baron (a powerful criminal whose influence is built on illegal trading) *UK, 1978*. **3** someone who carries illegal drugs between dealer and purchaser *US, 1972*. **4** a clerk or collector for a street bookmaker *UK, 1934*. **5** somebody sent to buy alcohol for others *US, 1963*. **6** in the television and film industries, an errand-running production assistant *US, 1990*. **7** a deserter from the armed services; an escapee from prison or borstal *UK, 1959*. **8** in the language surrounding the Grateful Dead, a fan who queues before a show and then quickly claims space for friends who will follow *US, 1994*. ▶ **do a runner** to escape by running away; to abscond; to leave hastily *UK, 1981*

runner and rider *noun* cider. Rhyming slang, from the vocabulary of horse racing *UK, 1992*

runners *noun* **1** sneakers, trainers *AUSTRALIA, 1988*. **2** any shoes *US, 1995*. ▶ **the runners** diarrhoea *US, 1948*

running *noun* **1** diarrhoea *BAHAMAS, 1982*. **2** MDMA, the recreational drug best known as ecstasy *UK, 1998*

running buddy *noun* a close friend and confederate in crime *US, 1970*

running dog *noun* a servant of the ruling class, subservient to counter-revolutionary powers. From Chinese communist terminology originally applied to the Kuomintang *US, 1937*

running partner *noun* a close friend joined for criminal and social activities *US, 1965*

runnings *noun* **1** diarrhoea *ANTIGUA AND BARBUDA, 1996*. **2** a sexually transmitted infection with discharge *TRINIDAD AND TOBAGO, 2003*. **3** whatever is happening or is planned to happen *UK, 1994*

run-off *noun* a prostitute who has attempted to break off from her pimp *US, 1993*

run of outs *noun* a succession of losses or failures *AUSTRALIA, 1953*

run-out *noun* a well-worn tyre *US, 1961*

run out *verb* ▶ **run out of road** to fail to keep control of a motor vehicle, especially on a bend, and consequently be involved in an accident *UK, 1981*. ▶ **run out of steam** to lose vigour *UK, 1961*

run-out powder *noun* the departure of a gambler who has not paid off his gambling debts *US, 1979*

run-over days *noun* the first three days of the bleed period of the menstrual cycle *BAHAMAS, 1982*

runs *noun* a sexually transmitted infection with discharge *TRINIDAD AND TOBAGO, 1951*. ▶ **the runs** a case of diarrhoea *US, 1962*

Runs Empty Only *noun* a truck manufactured by REO. A back-formation *US, 1971*

runt *noun* **1** in circus and carnival usage, a dwarf or midget *US, 1980*. **2** in poker, a pairless hand *US, 1963*

runts and cunts *noun* used for expressing disapproval of the composition of the US armed forces in the decades after Vietnam *US, 1993*

runty *adjective* delicate; sickly *IRELAND, 1989*

runway *noun* a generous dose of powdered cocaine arranged in a line for snorting. A clever play on a conventional 'runway', (a long straight path used to achieve lift-off) *UK, 1999*

run-what-you-brung *noun* a drag race between amateur drivers driving their own cars *US, 1970*

ruof; rofe; roaf; rouf *noun* four. Back slang *UK, 1863*

rupert *noun* **1** an army officer; any young upper-class type. A generic based on the perception that Rupert is a popular name in 'quality' families, but note another military use of 'rupert' as 'the penis'. Current usage seems to date from the 1970s *UK, 1996*. **2** the penis. Military; possibly related to the sense as officer *UK, 1961*

ruptured duck *noun* the US armed forces insignia designating honourable discharge *US, 1946*

rush *noun* **1** a sudden and powerful sense of euphoria or energy. Figurative use of the drug term *US, 1971*. **2** the sudden onset of drug intoxication *US, 1966*. **3** amyl, butyl or isobutyl nitrite. From the sudden effects of the drug *UK, 1996*. **4** cocaine *US, 2003*. **5** in poker, an unusual streak of good cards *US, 1982*

rush *verb* **1** to charge an amount of money *UK, 1887*. **2** to charge for goods or services, especially to overcharge or cheat *UK, 1887*. **3** to be infatuated with someone *BARBADOS, 1965*. **4** to make sexual advances *TRINIDAD AND TOBAGO, 1934*. ▶ **rush the knocks** in drug sales, to ignore the order of customers and make a sale *US, 2002*

rush-and-snatch job *noun* a search and rescue mission without the complications of enemy fire *US, 1991*

Rushina *noun* in homosexual usage, a personification of amyl nitrite or butyl nitrite. From RUSH, a popular name for amyl nitrite *US, 1980*

rushy *adjective* descriptive of an energetic and euphoric reaction to MDMA, the recreational drug best known as ecstasy *UK, 1997*

Russell Crowe *noun* an attack. Rhyming slang for GO, formed from the name of the notoriously pugnacious New Zealand-born film actor (b.1964) *UK, 2003*

Russell Harty *noun* a party. Rhyming slang, formed from the name of the television presenter (1934–88) *UK, 1992*

Russian boots *noun* leg irons *US, 1949*

Russian duck *noun* an act of sexual intercourse. Rhyming slang for FUCK *UK, 1992*

Russian jack *noun* a homemade alcoholic beverage made from sugar, yeast, water and flavouring *FIJI, 1984*

Russian roast *noun* a sexual act in which a woman performs oral sex on a man who is, at the same time, being sodomised by another man *UK, 2004*

Russian roulette *noun* LSD *UK, 1996*

Russki *adjective* Russian *UK, 1859*

Russki; Russky; Rusky *noun* a Russian *UK, 1858*

rust *noun* faecal stains in the underwear or on a toilet bowl *CANADA, 2002*

rust belt *noun* the northern central US, highly industrialised prior to the economic decline in the US in the 1980s *US, 1987*

rust bucket *noun* an old, dilapidated vehicle *AUSTRALIA, 1965*

rustle up *verb* to obtain something; to organise the supply of something *US, 1891*

rusty *adjective* of a skill, having deteriorated as a result of lack of practice *UK, 1796*

rusty bullet wound; rusty bullet hole; rusty sheriff's badge; rusty washer *noun* the anus. 'Rusty' (brown, the colour associated with the anus) plus a visual metaphor *UK, 1997*

rusty dusty *noun* the buttocks *US, 1942*

rusty fuck *noun* a notional object of no value whatsoever *US, 1969*

rusty trombone *noun* a sexual technique in which a man receives oral stimulation of his anus and manual stimulation of his penis at the same time and from the same person. Imagery which becomes apparent if you picture the penis as a trombone's slide and the anus as its mouthpiece *US, 2002*

Ruud Gullit *noun* dismissal from employment. Rhyming slang for BULLET, formed from the name of the Dutch footballer (b.1962) when he was given 'the bullet' as player-manager of Chelsea football club in 1998 *UK, 1998*

RV; r.v. *noun* a recreational vehicle or large motor home *US, 1967*

Ryan Giggs *noun* lodgings. Rhyming slang for DIGS, formed from the name of the Welsh footballer (b.1973) *UK, 1998*

Ss

s- *prefix* it's, especially preceding a word spelt with an 'n', such as *not snot* and *nice snice*. A slovening that allows the childish to say SNOT *UK, 1917*

Sa *noun* a Samoan *NEW ZEALAND, 1992*

sab *verb* to act as a hunt saboteur *UK, 1996*

saccharine lips *noun* a glib talker. Not quite as glib as 'sugar' *AUSTRALIA, 1989*

sachie *noun* Versace™ clothing *US, 1998*

sack *noun* **1** a bed. Probably related to the C19 sailor's use of 'sack' as a 'hammock' *US, 1942*. **2** a bag of heroin; hence, heroin *UK, 1998*. **3** the scrotum. Originally dialect *UK, 1928*. **4** courage. A testicular reference *US, 1984*. **5** a coat or jacket *US, 1972*. ▶ **in the sack** used for suggesting sexual activity. Literally 'in bed' *US, 1995*. ▶ **the sack** dismissal from employment *UK, 1841*

sack *verb* **1** to dismiss someone from employment; to jilt someone *UK, 1841*. **2** to abruptly stop any activity *UK, 2001*. **3** to dispose of something *UK, 2001*. **4** to sleep; to spend the night *US, 1966*. ▶ **sack it** to receive an accidental blow to the scrotum *UK, 2000*

sack, back and crack *noun* a treatment for removing a man's body hair by waxing it and stripping it off *UK, 2003*

sack drill *noun* sleep *US, 1963*

sack duty *noun* sleep *US, 1963*

sack hound *noun* a lazy person, overly fond of sleep *US, 1959*

sack off *verb* to reject something *UK, 2002*

sack of garbage *noun* in bar dice games, a roll that produces no points for the player *US, 1971*

sack of sauce *noun* a used condom *US, 1997*

sack of shit *noun* used abusively of an unpleasant person. A conventional 'sack' full of SHIT (excrement); probably a revision of SAD SACK OF SHIT *US, 2001*

sack out *verb* to go to bed *US, 1946*

sack rat *noun* a lazy person, overly fond of sleep *US, 1947*

sack ship *noun* a big ship used to carry supplies from Europe to the East Coast fisheries *CANADA, 1965*

sack weather *noun* inclement weather during which air missions cannot be flown *US, 1949*

sacky dacky *noun* a depressed misfit *US, 1946*

sacrament *noun* LSD. An arguably pretentious euphemism *US, 1990*

sacré bleu! used for registering shock, frustration, anger, anguish, etc; especially in a context of Frenchness. Directly from the French euphemism *sacré Dieu!* (sacred God!) *UK, 1869*

sacred *adjective* excellent *US, 1991*

sacred cow; sacred ox *noun* on the railways, an extra engine used on a mountain *US, 1977*

sacred site *noun* a place one holds in reverence. From the meaning as 'a place sacred to Australian Aboriginals' *AUSTRALIA, 1987*

sad *adjective* terrible *US, 1945*

sad and sorry *noun* a lorry. Rhyming slang *UK, 1992*

sad-ass; sad-assed *adjective* contemptible *US, 1971*

sad bastard *noun* a contemptible person; an ineffectual person *UK, 2003*

Saddam Hussein *noun* a pain; an irritation; an annoying person. Rhyming slang for conventional 'pain', also on a shortened PAIN IN THE ASS/ARSE; formed, with all due respect, from the name of the former Iraqi leader *UK, 1998*

sad day! used for expressing commiseration with another person's troubles *US, 1989*

saddle *noun* **1** in trucking, the driver's seat *US, 1971*. **2** in a group of trucks travelling down the motorway together, the truck in the middle *US, 1976*. **3** a two-part bet in an illegal numbers gambling lottery *US, 1949*. ▶ **in the saddle 1** engaged in sexual intercourse. The term enjoyed widespread popularity in the US during discussions of the 1979 death of former Vice President and New York Governor Nelson Rockefeller *US, 1979*. **2** in control *US, 1950*

saddle-fuck *verb* to have sex, the woman astride the prone man *US, 1972*

saddler *noun* a ride on a bicycle's saddle while another person pedals *UK, 1979*

saddles *noun* the testicles hanging in the scrotum. Probably from JOHN WAYNE'S HAIRY SADDLE BAGS *UK, 2004*

saddle tramp *noun* **1** a person who rides horseback through the countryside *US, 1942*. **2** a motorcyle gang member *US, 1989*

saddle up *verb* **1** to pick up your gear and resume a combat patrol *US, 1976*. **2** to engage in mutual oral sex simultaneously *US, 1985*

saddo *noun* a pathetic or contemptible individual. Jocular if not derogatory *UK, 2000*

sadfuck *noun* a contemptible person *UK, 1997*

Sadie Masie *noun* sado-masochism. A jocular personification *US, 1965*

Sadie the Office Secretary *noun* used as a personification of the stereotypical female office worker *US, 1953*

Sadie Thompson *verb* to rape (a man) *US, 1985*

sad kecks *noun* a killjoy. Pejorative; conventional 'sad' combined with KECKS (trousers) *UK, 1999*

sadlands *noun* the suburbs of a city *UK, 2002*

sad-on *noun* a bad mood. Royal Navy slang *UK, 1989*

sad sack *noun* a miserable and depressing individual; an inept misfit. Originally US military *US, 1942*

sad sack of shit *noun* a miserable and depressing individual. Abbreviates as SAD SACK *US, 1978*

safe *noun* **1** the rectum. Referring to the rectum as a depository for drugs to be smuggled into prison *US, 1992*. **2** a condom *UK, 1965*. **3** in a pickpocketing team, the thief who takes the wallet or object stolen by the wire and leaves the scene with it *US, 1954*. ▶ **in the safe** concealed in the anus *UK, 1996*

safe *adjective* **1** worthy of approval *SOUTH AFRICA, 1970*. **2** hopelessly out of style. Hawaiian youth usage *US, 1982*. **3** all right; used as an expression of approval or agreement *SOUTH AFRICA, 1981*

safe and sound; safe *noun* the ground *UK, 1992*

safe house *noun* a room, apartment or house where it is safe to stay, work and hide from the authorities, rival criminals or rival spies *US, 1963*

safe screw *noun* a corrupt prison officer *UK, 1996*

safety *noun* **1** a condom *US, 1973*. **2** a safety pin used for an improvised injection of an illegal drug *US, 1952*

safe word *noun* a code word, agreed between a sexual dominant and submissive masochistic partner, for use by the masochist as a signal that the current activity should stop *US, 1987*

safey *noun* in horse racing, a riding assignment for a jockey on a horse that stands little chance of winning *AUSTRALIA, 1989*

sag *verb* to wear trousers that are too big and which consequently ride very low on or below the hips *US, 1991*

saga lout *noun* an elderly person who behaves badly. Saga is a UK company that supplies a wide range of services to the over-50s; a pun on LAGER LOUT (a hooligan fuelled by lager) *UK, 2004*

sage *noun* a hybrid marijuana. An initialism of 'Sativa Afghani genetic equilibrium', contrived, perhaps, as a reference to the herb *UK, 2003*

saggie *noun* a central nervous system depressant such as Seconal™ *US, 1960*

sag off; sag *verb* to truant from school or work *UK, 1959*

Saigon cowboy *noun* a rear-echelon troop or civilian who dressed the part of a combat soldier but did not experience combat *US, 1977*

Saigon quickstep *noun* diarrhoea *US, 1991*

Saigon Suzie *noun* used for describing a stereotypical Vietnamese sex worker during the Vietnam war *US, 1990*

Saigon tea *noun* a whisky-coloured drink served to bar girls in Vietnam, passing for expensive whisky bought by US servicemen *US, 1966*

Saigon Tech *noun* the war in Vietnam; military service in Vietnam *US, 1969*

sailing *adjective* **1** drunk *US, 1968*. **2** marijuana-intoxicated *US, 1993*

sailor's elbow *noun* an act of ending a relationship with a lover. An elaboration, perhaps a specialisation, of ELBOW (an act of dismissal) *UK, 2003*

sailors on the sea; sailors *noun* tea *UK, 1961*

saint *noun* an incorruptible prison officer or police officer *UK, 1996*

saint and sinner *noun* dinner. Rhyming slang *UK, 1992*

Saint Loo *nickname* St. Louis, Missouri *US, 1961*

Saint Moritz *noun* diarrhoea. Rhyming slang for THE SHITS, based on the Swiss resort *UK, 1998*

Saint Peter *noun* the penis. Perhaps because he 'opens the gate to heaven' *UK, 2003*

saints preserve us! used for expressing fear. A signature line of the chief of police on *Batman* (ABC, 1966–68), Chief O'Hara. Repeated with referential humour *US, 1966*

Saint Vitus dance *verb* to move in a fidgety, jerking manner *UK, -1621*

sais a ching *noun* in betting, odds of 6–5. A slurring of 'six' combined with CHING (five pounds) *UK, 1991*

sal *noun* a friend or pal *BARBADOS, 1965* ▷*see:* SAL'TING

sala *noun* an idiot. Adopted into hip-hop, urban usage from subtly insulting Hindi *sala* – the literal sense of which is 'a man's wife's brother'; the abusive sense is 'to someone who is not the speaker's wife's brother: the insult lies in the implication that the sister of the person abused is available to the speaker as a wife' (Nigel Hankin, *Hanklyn Janklyn*, 2003) *US, 2003*

salad *noun* **1** marijuana *US, 1997*. **2** a mixture of two or more drugs *US, 1970*

salad bowl *noun* a serendipitous mixture of inferior (and, hence, uncommercial) bud and leaf remains of varying marijuana varieties *UK, 2003*

salad days *noun* a period of youthful inexperience and innocence *UK, 1606*

salad dodger *noun* a person who is overweight *UK, 1999*

salad parade *noun* a group of ballet dancers *UK, 1952*

salad toss *noun* any of several sexual practices involving oral-anal stimulation *CANADA, 2002*

salad wagon *noun* a dustcart *US, 1962*

salami *noun* the penis. The image of a large, dark sausage *US, 2000*

salaud *noun* a contemptible person, mainly applied to a French person. From French *salaud*, ultimately from French *sale* (dirty) *UK, 1962*

saleslady *noun* a prostitute *US, 1962*

salesman *noun* **1** a professional wrestler who does a good job of feigning pain, anger or fear *US, 1999*. **2** in gin, a card discarded to lure a desired card from an opponent *US, 1965*

Sally *noun* a chilled, twelve ounce can of beer *US, 2002*

Sally Army; Sally Ann; Sally *noun* the Salvation Army; a Salvation Army hostel *US, 1915*

Sally Gunnell; sally *noun* a tunnel, especially the Blackwall Tunnel. Rhyming slang, formed on the name of the British Olympic athlete (b.1966) *UK, 1998*

salmon *noun* a twenty-dollar note. From the orange-red colour *AUSTRALIA, 1983*

salmon and trout; salmon *noun* **1** tobacco; a cigarette. Rhyming slang for SNOUT *UK, 1974*. **2** gout. Rhyming slang. Sometimes varied as 'salmon trout' *UK, 1932*. **3** the nose. Rhyming slang for 'snout' *UK, 1974*. **4** an informer. Rhyming slang for SNOUT *UK, 1992*. **5** a ticket tout. Rhyming slang, originally applied to a racecourse tout *UK, 1932*. **6** stout (beer). Rhyming slang *UK, 1960*

salon *noun* a semi-private area created by shrubs and trees where homosexual liaisons take place. For example, Coco Chanel's salon was found in a large grove of trees at Land's End in San Francisco *US, 1972*

saloon *noun* **1** in poker, a hand consisting of three cards of the same rank and a pair. Known conventionally as a 'full house' *US, 1988*. **2** a brakevan (caboose) *US, 1977*

salt *noun* **1** a sailor, especially an experienced sailor. Often in the phrase 'old salt' *UK, 1840*. **2** an experienced veteran in any calling *UK, 1970*. **3** a woman. Possibly by extension from obsolete (mid-C17 to mid-C18) 'salt' (the sex act); possibly by abbreviation from obsolete (C19) 'salt-cellar' (the vagina); most likely of unknown etymology *UK, 1969*. **4** a drunkard *BARBADOS, 1965*. **5** heroin. From the appearance of the powdered drug *US, 1971*. **6** plain tobacco mixed with marijuana *SOUTH AFRICA, 1946*

salt *verb* **1** to make something appear to be worth more than it is. Originally mining slang *US, 1852*. **2** to swindle someone by baiting them *US, 1950*. **3** to plant or place something to be found *US, 1981*

salt and pepper *noun* **1** marijuana, especially if of poor quality; marijuana adulterated with oregano *US, 1946*. **2** a police car. From the black and white colour scheme of many police cars *US, 1976*

salt and pepper *adjective* white and black *US, 1915*

salt and rob *noun* assault and robbery *SOUTH AFRICA, 1946*

salt away *verb* to save money; to hide money and valuables *UK, 1902*

salt-banker *noun* a fishing boat on the Grand Banks carrying enough salt to preserve fish caught, allowing a longer stay on the water *CANADA, 1961*

salt beef *noun* an attractive woman married to someone else *BAHAMAS, 1982*

saltee; salter; salty; saulty *noun* a penny. From Italian *soldi* (money) *UK, 1859*

saltie *noun* a saltwater crocodile *AUSTRALIA, 1951*

sal'ting; saltfish; sal *noun* the vagina *JAMAICA, 1991*

salt junk; salted *adjective* drunk. Rhyming slang, from a military and nautical name for 'salted beef' *UK, 1909*

saltmine *noun* a workplace *US, 1976*

salt-rising *adjective* sourdough retained as leavening for future baking *CANADA, 1951*

Salt River *noun* ▶ **go up Salt River** to die *US, 1945*

salt shaker *noun* a road-gritting or -salting vehicle *US, 1976*

salt struck *adjective* of cod, dressed with enough salt to be pickled *CANADA, 1957*

salt water *noun* a US police officer born in Ireland *US, 1982*

saltwater taffy *noun* an attractive woman on the beach. An allusion to a brightly coloured sweet sold at US beaches *US, 1990*

salty *adjective* **1** angry, hostile *US, 1938*. **2** uncouth; unpleasant *US, 1985*

salty dog *noun* during the Vietnam war, a piece of equipment lost in combat *US, 1991*

salty water *noun* the recreational drug GHB. Caustic soda mixed with industrial cleaner *gamma butyrolactone* produces a *salt* which is dissolved in *water* to produce the clear solution GHB *US, 1997*

salute *verb* ▶ **salute the judge** to win a horse race *AUSTRALIA, 1977*

Salvador Dali; salvador *noun* **1** cocaine. Rhyming slang for CHARLIE (cocaine) *UK, 2000*. **2** a drink. Glasgow rhyming slang for SWALLY *UK: SCOTLAND, 2002*

salvation army *adjective* mad; eccentric. Rhyming slang for BARMY
UK, 1992

Salvo *noun* a Salvation Army officer *AUSTRALIA, 1891*

Salvosh *noun* the Salvation Army *UK, 2003*

sam *noun* **1** a federal narcotics agent. An abbreviation of Uncle Sam,
the personification of the US federal government *US, 1971*. **2** a
southern Appalachian migrant *US, 1981*

Sam and Dave *noun* a grave. Rhyming slang, formed from US soul
singers Sam Moore and Dave Prater who first came to prominence
in the mid-1960s *UK, 2004*

Samantha Janus *noun* the anus. Rhyming slang based on the name
of model and actress Samantha Janus (b.1975) *UK, 2002*

sambie *noun* a sandwich *AUSTRALIA, 1976*

sambo *noun* **1** a black person. Originally neutral, gradually accepted
as taboo and derogatory; popular etymology holds that 'sambo'
derives from 'sandboy' as in 'happy as a sandboy'; however
Spanish or African origins account for the use from about 1704 as
a proper name, slipping into a generic sense later in the C18 *US,
1957*. **2** a sandwich *AUSTRALIA, 1984*

Sam, Cow and the Duppy *noun* a random selection of the
populace. The functional equivalent of 'Tom, Dick and Harry'
BARBADOS, 1965

same bat time, same bat channel used as a humorous farewell.
A catchphrase television sign-off on *Batman* (ABC, 1966–68).
Repeated with referential humour *US, 1966*

same-day service *noun* in computing, a lengthy response time *US,
1991*

same difference; same diff *noun* the same thing, no difference *UK,
1999*

same mud, same blood used for explaining the absence of racism
in combat troops *US, 1981*

same odds *noun* an equal effect; no difference worth consideration.
From horse racing betting jargon *UK, 2001*

same-old *noun* an unchanged condition. An abbreviation of SAME
OLD SAME OLD *UK, 2000*

same old same old; same-o same-o *noun* more of the same *US,
1972*

same old six and seven used for expressing a certain lack of
progress in life. A borrowing from the game of craps – having
established six as the point (the easiest point to make), the
shooter rolls a seven, thus losing *US, 1959*

same shit, different day used as a stock answer when asked how
things are going *US, 1992*

samey *adjective* monotonous; no different *UK, 1929*

samey-same; same same *adjective* the same. Korean and Vietnam
war usage *US, 1956*

Sam Hill *noun* used as a very quaint euphemism for 'hell' *US, 1839*

Sami *adjective* Samoan *NEW ZEALAND, 1998*

sammo *noun* a sandwich *AUSTRALIA, 1972*

sammy *noun* an Indian man. An offensive word used as a term of
address and reference *SOUTH AFRICA, 1906*

Sammy *nickname* Saddam Hussein. Used by US soldiers during the
1991 war against Iraq *US, 1991*

Sammy Hall *noun* a testicle. Rhyming slang for BALL(S), apparently
formed on a character in a bawdy song *UK, 1992*

Sammy Lee *noun* urine; an act of urination. Rhyming slang for PEE
or WEE, formed on Liverpool and England footballer (b.1959) *UK,
1998*

Samoan family car *noun* a used police car bought at auction.
Hawaiian youth usage *US, 1982*

Sam Sled *noun* in drag racing, a driver who consistently
underperforms *US, 1965*

Samuel Pepys; samuels *noun* a sensation of dread or unease.
Rhyming slang for THE CREEPS, formed from the name of the
diarist, 1633–1703 *UK, 1998*

Samurai *noun* a Japanese man who is abundantly masculine, virile,
brave and demeaning towards women. Hawaiian youth usage *US,
1982*

San Antone! used as a mild oath *US, 1951*

sana wanga; sana banga *verb* to have sex. Probably an
embellishment of WANG (the penis) *TRINIDAD AND TOBAGO, 1935*

San Bernaghetto *nickname* San Bernadino, California. Collected in
San Bernadino, August 2004. Numerous Internet usages, but none
in print *US, 2004*

sanction *noun* in organised crime, punishment by death *US, 1997*

sand *noun* **1** courage *US, 1962*. **2** cocaine *US, 2002*

sand *verb* to mark the edges of playing cards with sandpaper or
another abrasive for the purpose of cheating *US, 1979*

sandbag *noun* a sanitary towel or tampon *US, 2001*

sandbag *verb* **1** to lull someone into a false sense of security, and
then suddenly attack them. Originally a term from poker, used to
describe a betting strategy, and then expanded to broader use *US,
1940*. **2** in poker, to decline to raise a bet while holding a good hand
in the hope of driving up the bet later in the play *US, 1947*

sandbagger *noun* **1** a person who lulls an opponent into security,
and then suddenly attacks *US, 1940*. **2** in the sport of clayshooting, a
competitor 'who by devious methods shoots in a lower class than
his true form warrants' *UK, 1983*

sandbox *noun* **1** a toilet; a lavatory. A reference to a cat's toilet
habits, intended as cute *US, 1968*. **2** in computing, the research and
development department. A recognition of the playing nature of
research *US, 1991*

Sand Box Express *noun* military transport to Saudi Arabia or Kuwait
during the first Gulf war *US, 1991*

sandburner *noun* a Jeep *UK, 1981*

sand flea *noun* someone who associates with surfers at the beach
but rarely if ever enters the water *US, 1985*

sandgroper *noun* a person from the state of Western Australia.
Western Australia has vast tracts of desert *AUSTRALIA, 1896*

sandhog *noun* a tunnel construction worker; any underground
worker *US, 1903*

S and J *noun* a beating by a police officer. An abbreviation of
'sentence and judgment' *US, 2001*

S and M *nickname* Santa Monica Boulevard in Los Angeles, California
US, 1987

S and M; s-m; S & M *noun* **1** sado-masochism *US, 1964*. **2** in a sado-
masochistic relationship, slave and master (or mistress). A confusion of meaning with 'sado-masochism' though not of context
US, 1977. **3** sausage and mushrooms *US, 1996*

sand nigger *noun* an Arab; an Indian or Pakistani person. Highly
offensive *US, 1984*

Sandoz; Sandoz's *noun* LSD. Named after Sandoz Pharmaceuticals,
the original Swiss manufacturer of the drug *US, 1967*

sandpaper *noun* playing cards that have been altered for cheating
by a minute sanding of the edges *US, 1962*

sandpaper *verb* ▶ **sandpaper the anchor** to perform a job that
need not and, in fact, cannot be performed *US, 1975*

sandwich *noun* **1** sex involving more than two people, the specific
nature of which varies with use, usually sex between one woman
and two men, one penetrating her vagina and one penetrating her
anus. A term given a lot of attention in 2000 when actress Cybill
Shepherd dedicated a chapter of her autobiography to a
description of her having taken the part of the filling in a 'Cybill
Sandwich' with two stuntmen *US, 1971*. **2** heroin *sandwiched*
between layers of cocaine *UK, 1998*. ▶ **a sandwich short of a
picnic (basket)** not completely sane. May be 'a sandwich', 'one
sandwich', 'two sandwiches' or 'a few sandwiches' *short of a
picnic*; all variations of the NOT ALL THERE theme. You may also be
'a pork pie' or 'two apples' *short of a picnic UK, 1992*

sandwich *verb* **1** to rob someone *TRINIDAD AND TOBAGO, 1990*. **2** in
poker, to surround a player with two confederates whose collusive

betting tactics relieve the middle player of his bankroll and drive him from the game *US, 1973*

sandwich job *noun* condemnation surrounded on either side by faint praise *US, 1981*

Sandy *nickname* a Douglas A-1E Skyraider, especially effective in providing cover for combat rescue missions in Vietnam *US, 1980*

Sandy McNab; Sandy MacNab *noun* a taxi. Rhyming slang for 'cab' *UK, 1960*

Sandy McNabs; sandies *noun* pubic lice. Rhyming slang for CRABS *UK, 1977*

Sandy Powell *noun* a towel. Rhyming slang, formed from the name of the popular northern comedian, 1900–82 *UK, 1974*

san fairy ann it doesn't matter, it makes no difference; don't worry. From French *ça ne fait rien UK, 1927*

San Fran *nickname* San Francisco, California *US, 1957*

San Francisco bomb *noun* ▷*see:* FRISCO SPEEDBALL

sanga-wanga *noun* sex *TRINIDAD AND TOBAGO, 1980*

sanger *noun* a sandwich *AUSTRALIA, 1943*

sanitary *noun* a well-built, efficient car *US, 1956*

sanitary *adjective* used of a car, built well and without cosmetic frills. A wonderful example of standard English promoted into slang *US, 1960*

sanitary ride *noun* in a horse race, the tactic of riding away from the rail to avoid the mud flung by the pack of racehorses near the rail *US, 1978*

sannie *noun* a shoe sandal. From 'sandshoe' *UK: SCOTLAND, 1985* ▷*see:* SARNIE

sanny *noun* a sanitary towel; hence, a tampon *UK, 1971*

sano *adjective* used of surf conditions, excellent *US, 1988*

sano; sanno *noun* a person employed to empty toilet cans from unsewered households. From 'sanitary' *AUSTRALIA, 1971*

San Q *nickname* the San Quentin state prison, San Rafael, California *US, 1993*

San Quentin breakfast *noun* a male under the age of legal consent as an object of sexual desire *US, 1976*

San Quentin briefcase *noun* a large portable stereo system associated, stereotypically, with black youth culture. San Quentin is the most famous of California's state prisons *US, 1990*

San Quentin quail *noun* a girl under the age of legal consent. San Quentin is California's largest state prison. In the 1940 film *Go West*, Groucho Marx played a character named S. Quentin Quale, an inside joke *US, 1940*

Santa Barbara *noun* in hold 'em poker, an ace and a king as the first two cards dealt a player *US, 1981*

Santa Claus rally *noun* an increase in stock prices between Christmas and the end of the year *US, 1976*

Santa Marta; Santa Maria *noun* potent marijuana with a reddish-gold colour, originally cultivated in northern Colombia *US, 1979*

san toy *noun* a gang member. Rhyming slang for 'boy', as in 'the boys' *UK, 1932*

sap *noun* **1** a gullible fool *UK, 1815*. **2** in borstal, a weak trainee who is 'not very bright'. From the previous sense *UK, 1978*. **3** a short club; a police officer's nightstick *US, 1899*

sapazzola *noun* semen *US, 1985*

saperoo *noun* a complete fool *US, 1950*

sap gloves *noun* gloves weighted for maximised damage when used to strike someone *US, 1975*

sapper *noun* **1** a Viet Cong or North Vietnamese commando. Members of the North Vietnamese Army's combat engineers, and thus the name, derived from the longstanding UK sense of the word as 'a soldier in the Engineer Corps, the Royal Sappers and Miners'. 'Sappers inside the wire!' was a warning call that US soldiers did not want to hear *US, 1987*. **2** during the Vietnam war, an Australian combat engineer, especially one who searched and destroyed enemy tunnels *AUSTRALIA, 1990*

sap weather *noun* the period in the spring when maple sap is running. This period is also known as 'sugar weather' *CANADA, 1963*

Saracen Pig, Spartan Dog! used as a humorous description of an argument. From Woody Allen's 1996 film *What's Up, Tiger Lily?* (followed by *Take this! And this!*), revived and popularised by ESPN's Keith Olberman while broadcasting footage of ice hockey fights *US, 1997*

Sarah *noun* a single, rich and happy woman *UK, 2002*

sardine *noun* **1** a shark. Surfer humour *US, 1965*. **2** a despised person *NEW ZEALAND, 1989*

sarf London *noun* south London. A jocular attempt to say it correctly *UK: WALES, 1999*

sarge; sar'nt *noun* a sergeant, often as a form of addresss *US, 1867*

sarky *adjective* sarcastic *UK, 1912*

sarnie; sannie *noun* a sandwich. Reduced from an upper-crust pronunciation of 'sandwich'. In Glasgow a 'sannie' is preferred *UK, 1961*

sars-fras *noun* a low grade marijuana cigarette *US, 1948*

sarvey; sarvie *noun* this afternoon. Only in the phrase 'the sarvey', by metanalysis from 'this arvie' *AUSTRALIA, 2003*

sarvo *noun* this afternoon. Only in the phrase 'the sarvo', by metanalysis of 'this arvo' *AUSTRALIA, 1942*

sash *noun* anything used to tie around your arm while injecting a drug *US, 1972*

sashay *verb* to walk in a casual, often provocative, manner. A corruption of the French *chasse*, (a gliding dance step) *US, 1928*

Saskatchewan grunt *noun* a dessert of berries and dough on top, as in Nova Scotia, but with saskatoon berries *CANADA, 1987*

sass *noun* disrespectful, flippant back talk. A corrupted pronunciation of the British SAUCE *US, 1835*

sass *verb* to talk back to someone; to speak to someone with disrespect *US, 1856*

sassafras *noun* marijuana. Adopting the innocent identity and coincidental uses of the sassafras tree (*Sassafras albidum*); a native of North America which is used as a source of natural medicine and tea *US, 1944*

sassy *noun* rude speech. Used in the phrase 'give sassies' *BAHAMAS, 1982*

sassy *adjective* spirited; impudent; used to describe someone who answers back *US, 1833*

satchel *noun* ▶ **in the satchel** corrupted; bribed; beholden to someone else. A variation of the more common IN THE BAG *US, 1955*

satchel-swinger *noun* a bookmaker *AUSTRALIA, 1965*

sat-com *noun* satellite communications *UK, 2001*

satellite *noun* **1** a prisoner who remains on the fringes of a prison gang without actually joining it *US, 1992*. **2** a small-stakes poker tournament, the winning of which entitles the player to entry in a higher stakes tournament *US, 1990*

satin *noun* Italian Swiss Colony Silver Satin wine. An inexpensive wine *US, 1980*

satin and lace *noun* the face. Rhyming slang *UK, 1998*

satin and silk *noun* milk. Rhyming slang *UK, 1985*

Saturday night *noun* in dominoes, the double blank piece *US, 1959*

Saturday night special *noun* **1** an inexpensive handgun, usually small calibre *US, 1968*. **2** in computing, a program designed under intense time restraints *US, 1991*. **3** a hospital patient who regularly appears in the casualty department at weekends in search of food and a bed *US, 1978*

Saturday night syndrome *noun* **1** tachycardiac fibrillation *US, 1992*. **2** prolonged local pressure on a limb with resulting prolonged ischemia (inadequate blood supply). So named because of the tendency to drink to the point of extreme intoxication and then pass out with a limb dangling across the arm of a chair or the edge of a bed *US, 2004*. **3** the stress and fear suffered by preachers who wait until Saturday night to write their Sunday sermon *US, 2000*. **4** the tendency of a restaurant kitchen to fail to live up to its highest potential on the busiest night of the week, Saturday night *US, 2001*

sauce *noun* **1** any and all alcohol *US, 1940*. **2** in drag racing, a fuel mixed from nitromethane and alcohol *US, 1968*. **3** impudence; impertinence *UK, 1835*. **4** spirit; courage. From the song 'Baby's Got Sauce' by G. Love & Special Sauce *US, 1997*. ▶ **the sauce** the best *BAHAMAS, 1982*

sauce *verb* to speak impudently or impertinently to someone *UK, 1862*

saucebox *noun* an impudent person *UK, 1588*

sauced *adjective* drunk *US, 1985*

saucepan lid; saucepan; lid *noun* **1** a pound. Rhyming slang for QUID *UK, 1951*. **2** a Jewish person. Rhyming slang for YID *UK, 1960*. **3** a child. Rhyming slang for KID *UK, 1960*

saucepot *noun* an impudent person. A variation of SAUCEBOX *UK, 1998*

saucer *noun* **1** a tablet of MDMA, the recreational drug best known as ecstasy. Perhaps there is an implied pun on flying saucers *UK, 1996*. **2** a silver dollar coin *US, 1959*. **3** in pinball, a scoring hole with a bevelled lip *US, 1977*

saucer cap *noun* a US Army wool serge AG-44 service cap *US, 1990*

saucered and blowed *adjective* all ready to go; prepared for use in any way *CANADA, 1987*

saucy *adjective* **1** attractive; desired *US, 2004*. **2** very drunk *US, 1997*

Saudi cool *adjective* warm to hot. Gulf war usage *US, 1991*

sausage *noun* **1** the penis *AUSTRALIA, 1944*. **2** someone foolish or gullible; used as a gently reproving term of address. Affectionate, childish and jocular *UK, 1982*. **3** used, often while reproving or gently chiding a child or lover, as an affectionate form of address, usually qualified with an adjective *UK, 1982*. **4** marijuana *US, 1968*. **5** a marijuana cigarette *UK, 1978*. ▶ **hide the sausage; sink the sausage** (of a male) to copulate *AUSTRALIA, 1971*. ▶ **not a sausage** no money; hence nothing at all. From rhyming slang, on SAUSAGE AND MASH (cash) *UK, 1938*

sausage and mash *noun* **1** cash; money. Rhyming slang *UK, 1976*. **2** a collision. Rhyming slang for 'crash' or 'smash' *UK, 1961*

sausage board *noun* a surfboard that is rounded at both ends *AUSTRALIA, 1963*

sausage dog *noun* a dachshund *UK, 1938*

sausage fest; sausage party *noun* a party with far more boys than girls *US, 2001*

sausage grappler *noun* a male masturbator *AUSTRALIA, 1971*

sausage roll *noun* **1** unemployment benefit. Rhyming slang for THE DOLE *UK, 1972*. **2** a pole. Rhyming slang *UK, 1992*. **3** a Pole. Rhyming slang *UK, 1959*. **4** the poll (the head), especially in reference to 'Poll Tax'. Rhyming slang *UK, 1992*

sausage roll; sausage *verb* to have sex. Rhyming slang for POLE *UK, 1992*

sauskee *noun* in circus and carnival usage, fifteen dollars *US, 1981*

savage *adjective* good; excellent *US, 1965*

Savannah *noun* in craps, a seven *US, 1983*

save *verb* ▶ **save me** please save for me *US, 1968*. ▶ **save right to the blossom** in British Columbia logging, to fell a tall tree without breaking it *CANADA, 1989*

saveloy *noun* a boy, also in the sense 'one of the boys' (a gang member). Often heard in the catchphrase greeting, challenge or terrace-chant: 'oi oi saveloy!' *UK, 1961*

saver *noun* **1** in a pool tournament, an agreement between two or more players to share their winnings *US, 1993*. **2** a hedging bet *AUSTRALIA, 1891*

savoury rissole *noun* a lavatory; an unpleasant or dirty place, or location. Rhyming slang for PISS-HOLE, formed on an English dish also known as a 'faggot' *UK, 1992*

savvy *noun* knowledge; intelligence; experience. From the Spanish *saber* (to know) *US, 1825*

savvy *verb* to understand. Horribly butchered Spanish *saber* (to know), used by a monoglot English speaker trying to make himself understood by a foreigner *UK, 1785*

-savvy *suffix* aware, intelligent, informed. From French *savoir* (to know). Used for forming adjectives, it follows the noun *UK, 1905*

saw *verb* ▶ **saw logs** to snore. From cartoon illustrations comparing the sounds *US, 1980*. ▶ **saw wood** in pool, to play with an awkward stroke *US, 1990*

sawbones *noun* a doctor, especially a surgeon *UK, 1837*

sawbuck *noun* **1** a ten-dollar note *US, 1850*. **2** a ten-year prison sentence *US, 1950*

sawdust *noun* **1** dynamite *US, 1949*. **2** dehydrated cabbage *ANTARCTICA, 2003*

sawdust joint *noun* an unassuming, barebones gambling operation *US, 1963*

sawdust machine; sawdust pump *noun* a hand drill *US, 1980*

sawdust nobility *noun* an owner of a lumber mill or large timber stand *CANADA, 1956*

sawed-off *noun* a shotgun with a barrel less than 18 inches breech-to-muzzle or 26 inches overall *US, 1982*

sawn-off *noun* a shotgun with the barrels *sawn off* to a much shorter length to aid concealment of the weapon and enhance the lethal spread of the shot *UK, 1959*

saw-off *noun* an agreement to compromise with mutual benefits, especially political *CANADA, 2002*

sawski; sawsky *noun* a ten-dollar note. From SAWBUCK *US, 1957*

say *noun* a story. English gypsy use *UK, 2000*

say *verb* ▶ **say goodbye** to die. Apposite imagery for this piece of unusually sentimental rhyming slang *UK, 1992*. ▶ **say Greg** used for inviting a challenge *TRINIDAD AND TOBAGO, 2003*. ▶ **say your morning prayers** to vomit in the morning, especially as a result of morning sickness *TRINIDAD AND TOBAGO, 1979*

sayanora goodbye *US, 1968*

say dooey *adjective* eight. Polari; SAY (six) plus DOOEY (two) *UK, 2002*

saying hello to Mr Armitage *adjective* drunk, perhaps so drunk as to be sick. Derives either as a tribute to an unknown man or, perhaps, as a reference to lavatory manufacturer Armitage Shanks *UK, 2002*

say kids, what time is it? used as a humourous call to action. The signature opening of *Howdy Doody Show* (NBC, 1947–60). Repeated often with referential humour *US, 1947*

say now used as a greeting *US, 1973*

say oney *noun* seven. Polari; SAY (six) plus ONEY (one) *UK, 2002*

say-so *noun* **1** authority *UK, 1637*. **2** a person's word of honour *UK, 1637*

say tray *adjective* nine. Polari; SAY (six) plus TRAY (three) *UK, 2002*

say what? **1** used as a request to repeat what has just been said. An Americanism *UK, 1999*. **2** used for expressing disbelief at what has just been said *US, 1987*

say what and so what? intended as a clever dismissal of what has just been said *US, 1992*

say when! used to ask *when* enough food has been served or drink been poured. By ellipsis *UK, 1889*

SBD *adjective* used of a fart, inaudible but smelly. An abbreviation of 'silent but deadly' *CANADA, 2002*

sca *noun* information; news; gossip *IRELAND, 1997*

scab *noun* **1** a strike-breaker. From earlier usage as 'a generally contemptible person' *US, 1777*. **2** a thief *UK, 2003*. **3** a stingy person; a miser *AUSTRALIA, 1987*. **4** a citizens' band radio operator. A derisive term used by purist shortwave radio operators *US, 1976*. **5** in western Canada, a saddle *CANADA, 1951*

scab *verb* **1** to act as a strike-breaker *US, 1806*. **2** to search for a possible sex-partner. Hawaiian youth usage *US, 1982*. **3** to cadge something *AUSTRALIA, 1986*. **4** in pinball, to obtain a result through luck, not skill *US, 1977*

scabby *adjective* non-union *AUSTRALIA, 1892*. ▶ **I could eat a scabby dog** used as a declaration of great hunger. In Glasgow use *UK: SCOTLAND, 1996*

scabby eye *noun* a pie. Rhyming slang *UK, 1992*

scabby-headed *adjective* ▶ **I could eat a scabby-headed wean** used as a declaration of great hunger. In Glasgow use. 'I could eat a scabby-headed cat' is the familiar variant in the English midlands *UK: SCOTLAND, 1988*

scab duty *noun* especially in Western Australia and New South Wales, the picking up of litter as a school punishment *AUSTRALIA, 2001*

scablifter *noun* a doctor *UK, 1996*

scad! used in expressing anger *US, 2001*

scadge *noun* a tramp *UK: SCOTLAND, 1996*

scads *noun* a large quantity of anything. From an earlier sense specific to money *US, 1869*

scaffle *noun* phencyclidine, the recreational drug known as PCP or angel dust *US, 1994*

scag; skag *noun* **1** heroin; cocaine *US, 1967*. **2** a cigarette *US, 1945*. **3** inferior alcohol *US, 1947*. **4** an unattractive girl or woman *US, 1962*

scaggy *adjective* addicted to heroin. Extended from SCAG (heroin) *UK, 2002*

scag-hag; skag-hag *noun* **1** a female heroin addict. Combines SCAG (heroin) with conventional 'hag' (a woman), on the model of FAG-HAG (a woman smoker) *UK, 1999*. **2** someone who enjoys the company of heroin-users. A gay coinage; combines SCAG (heroin) with conventional 'hag' (a woman), on the model of FAG-HAG (someone who enjoys the company of gays) *UK, 1998*. **3** a heterosexual woman who takes pleasure in the company of homosexual men *US, 1970*

scag-head; skag-head *noun* a heroin addict. A combination of SCAG (heroin or cocaine) and HEAD (a user) *UK, 1999*

scag jones; skag jones *noun* a heroin addiction *US, 1982*

scag nasty; skag nasty *adjective* repulsive in the extreme *US, 1994*

scald *noun* tea *IRELAND, 1996*

scale *verb* to ride a bus, train or tram without paying. Earlier, since 1904 (*Australian National Dictionary*) used intransitively to mean 'to avoid paying' *AUSTRALIA, 1941*

scaley *noun* a signaller in the British military *UK, 1995*

scalie *noun* a person employed on a vehicle weighbridge *AUSTRALIA, 1976*

Scallicon Valley *nickname* the Information Technology sector in Liverpool. A pun on SCALLY (a Liverpool rogue, hence a Liverpudlian) and California's mythical Silicon Valley, in the world's eyes the home of computer science *UK, 2001*

scally *noun* a rogue; a hooligan; a rough youth. A shortening of SCALLYWAG used in Liverpool slang *UK, 1986*

scally *verb* to behave in a lawless manner. From the noun sense *UK, 2001*

scallybip *verb* to burgle a house while the housewife is outside hanging washing on the line to dry *US, 1972*

scallywag; scallawag; skallywag *noun* a disreputable fellow *US, 1849*

scalp *noun* **1** the appearance of a pornography performer's photograph on the video box. From the sense of a 'scalp' as a 'trophy' *UK, 1995*. **2** a toupee *US, 1952*

scalp *verb* **1** to buy tickets for an event and resell them, usually outside the event itself. Originally stock exchange slang, then passed into broader general usage *US, 1886*. **2** to beat up a rival gang member and steal his gang patch *NEW ZEALAND, 1999*

scalper; scalp *noun* a person who buys tickets for a sporting or entertainment event and resells them at a profit *US, 1869*

scaly *noun* an acting detective constable in a Metropolitan Police Crime Squad *UK, 2002*

scaly leg *noun* a common prostitute *US, 1972*

scam *noun* **1** a scheme by which a legitimate business is forced into bankruptcy and taken over by organised crime *US, 1982*. **2** a scheme to defraud people *US, 1963*. **3** a report; the latest information *US, 1977*

scam *verb* to cheat or defraud someone *US, 1963*

scammer *noun* a petty confidence trickster; a fraudster *US, 1972*

scammered *adjective* drunk *UK, 2003*

scamp *noun* a rascal *UK, 1808*

scampi *noun* a very attractive man. Noted in connection with a legal dispute over rap lyrics by *BBC News*, 6th June 2003 *UK, 1997*

scan *verb* to examine someone or something *US, 1988*

scandal bag *noun* a plastic shopping bag *JAMAICA, 2003*

scandalous *adjective* **1** extremely competent *US, 1992*. **2** mean-spirited. The variant 'scan'lous' also exists *US, 2001*

scandalous! used for expressing disbelief or shock *US, 1997*

Scandi *adjective* Scandinavian *UK, 1996*

Scando-pop *noun* popular music originating in any Scandinavian country *UK, 2003*

scanger; skanger *noun* a rough, uncouth youth *IRELAND, 2003*

scanties *noun* skimpy knickers, hence, skimpy underwear (usually women's) *UK, 1937*

scants *noun* skimpy underpants (usually women's). A shortening of SCANTIES *UK, 1968*

Scarborough Fair; scarborough *noun* hair. Ephemeral rhyming slang, formed from the title of a 1966 recording by Simon and Garfunkel *UK, 1998*

scare *verb* ▶ **scare the shit out of someone** to terrify someone *UK, 1961*

Scare Air *noun* any of the many small airlines operating, on land, bush or water, in British Columbia *CANADA, 1989*

scare cards *noun* in poker, the strongest cards in a player's hand, exposed to other players accidentally on purpose *US, 1996*

scarecrow *noun* an empty police car parked at the side of a road to deter speeding *US, 1976*

scare-do *noun* an unflattering or unfashionable hairdo *US, 1990*

scaredy-cat *noun* a cowardly person. Childish *UK, 1933*

Scare Ontario *noun* Air Ontario *CANADA, 1997*

scarers *noun* ▶ **put the scarers on someone** to frighten someone *AUSTRALIA, 1985*

scare up *verb* to find something by hunting it out; to discover something. From the hunting of game *US, 1852*

scarf *noun* food *US, 1967*

scarf *verb* **1** to eat, especially to eat greedily and hurriedly *US, 1951*. **2** to lick, suck, and tongue a woman's vagina *US, 1966*. ▶ **scarf pussy** to perform oral sex on a woman *US, 1972*

scarfer *noun* **1** the supporter of a football club. The supporter's loyalty is advertised by the colours, pattern or insignia of a scarf *UK, 1999*. **2** in the usage of youthful model road racers (slot car racers), a fast car. From SCARF (to eat), suggesting that the car 'is eating up' the track *US, 1997*

scarfing *noun* self-asphyxiation as a masturbatory aid *UK, 1994*

scarf up *verb* to acquire. Extends from SCARF (to eat hungrily), possibly playing on SCARE UP (to discover) *US, 1973*

scarlet collar *adjective* working in the sex industry. Using 'scarlet woman' with the model of 'white collar' and 'blue collar' workers *US, 1985*

scarlet sister *noun* a prostitute *US, 1951*

scarper *verb* **1** to depart, especially in a hurry. Ultimately Italian *scappare* (to run away) or, less likely, rhyming slang for Scapa Flow for (to go); via polari into more general usage. Variants include 'scarpa', 'scaper', 'scarpy' and 'scapli' *UK, 1844*. **2** to remove something; to dismiss someone. Circus; a variation of the previous sense *UK, 1953*

scary *adjective* good *US, 1969*

scat *noun* **1** excrement, especially as a sexual fetish. From Greek *skat* (dung) *US, 1927*. **2** sado-masochistic sex play involving defecation *US, 1979*. **3** heroin *US, 1949*. **4** low quality, low cost whisky *US, 1950*

scat *verb* to travel fast; to leave. Often used as an imperative *US, 1954*

scattered *adjective* drunk *UK, 2002*

scatty *adjective* crazy; slightly mad; feather-brained. From 'scatter-brained' *UK, 1911*

scatty-yatty *noun* an attractive girl. Teen slang, probably acquired from West Indian slang *UK, 2003*

scav *verb* to scavenge; to scrounge *UK, 2001*

scavenger *noun* in drag racing and hot rodding, a car that wins often, that 'eats up' its competition *US, 1968*

sceg *noun* a surfer. Variant of SKEG. *AUSTRALIA, 1988*

scene *noun* **1** a situation. A superfluous word to describe further a person, place, thing, or happening *US, 1966*. **2** a personal choice or taste; a favoured setting or milieu. Originally black usage, then via jazz into hippy circles *US, 1966*. **3** a sexual interlude *US, 1971*.
▶ **make the scene 1** to arrive and participate in a social gathering *US, 1958*. **2** to go where something of interest is happening *US, 1950*. **3** to have sex *US, 1966*

scenester *noun* a person who is part of contemporary fashionable society *US, 2003*

sceney *adjective* fashionable; part of the scene *UK, 1968*

scenic route *noun* in horse racing, running outside the pack on turns *US, 1978*

schainer yid; shayner Yid *noun* an honest and absolutely trustworthy Jewish man. Yiddish for 'beautiful Jew', especially in the second spelling *UK, 1968*

scheitl; shietel; shyckle; shyker *noun* a wig. Polari; from Yiddish *sheytl* (a wig worn by Jewish women who have married in the Orthodox tradition) *UK, 1992*

scheme *noun* a housing estate *UK: SCOTLAND, 1985*

scheme-on *noun* a person's regular opening line in a singles bar *US, 1985*

schemie *noun* someone who lives on a council estate. The element of Scotland's social housing system that is popularly known as 'the schemies' *UK: SCOTLAND, 2000*

schimmel *noun* among Nova Scotians of German descent, a blond, colourless person *CANADA, 1975*

Schindler's List; Schindler's *adjective* drunk. Rhyming slang for PISSED, formed on the title of a 1993 Oscar-winning film by Steven Spielberg *AUSTRALIA, 1994*

schinwhars; chinois *noun* a Chinese person *UK, 2002*

schitz *verb* to behave in an abnormal fashion because of sustained methamphetamine use. From 'schizophrenia' *US, 1993*

schitz; schiz; schizo; skitz; skiz *noun* anyone who is considered to be mentally ill; generically a mad person; specifically, a *schizo*-phrenic *US, 1945*

schizo; schitzi; schizy; schizzy *adjective* schizoid or *schizo*phrenic; used derogatively of anyone whose behaviour is considered eccentric, illogical or mad. Schizophrenia is a severe mental disorder mistakenly understood by readers of modern thrillers to be little more than a split-personality *US, 1951*

schizz *noun* a person suffering from *schizo*phrenia *US, 1973*

schlanting *noun* cheating *AUSTRALIA, 1982*

schlump *verb* to move heavily *US, 1978*

schlumph *verb* to drink alcohol *UK, 1996*

schmende *noun* the vagina. Possibly (a woman's) 'end' elaborated in cod-Yiddish *US, 1998*

schmick; smick *adjective* exquisite; immaculate *AUSTRALIA, 1996*

schmock; shmock *noun* heroin *UK, 1978*

schmoogie *noun* a friend *US, 1993*

Schneider *verb* **1** in gin, to win a game leaving an opponent scoreless. Also in the shortened form 'Schneid' *US, 1965*. **2** in gambling, to defeat someone completely *US, 1997*

schnoink *noun* a Jewish person. A deliberately offensive and insulting term used by non-Jews; it appears to be 'oink' (the cry of a pig) dressed up in mock-Yiddish *UK, 1977*

schonk *verb* to hit someone *UK, 2002*

school *noun* **1** in poker, a group of players who customarily play together *UK, 1967*. **2** a group of people engaged in a gambling game, especially two-up *AUSTRALIA, 1812*

schoolboy *noun* **1** cocaine; codeine; codeine cough syrup. An inference that these are beginners' drugs *US, 1969*. **2** heroin *UK, 2003*

schoolboy draw *noun* in poker, a draw in a highly unlikely attempt to improve a hand *US, 1988*

schoolcraft *noun* crack cocaine *UK, 1998*

schoolie *noun* **1** a school student *AUSTRALIA, 1994*. **2** one of a group of a young persons holidaying having just finished high school *AUSTRALIA, 1993*. **3** a school teacher *AUSTRALIA, 1889*

Schoolies Week *noun* chiefly in New South Wales and Queensland, a week following final high school exams during which vast numbers of students descend upon certain tourist areas to celebrate *AUSTRALIA, 1984*

schoolmarm tree *noun* a piece of firewood where two trunks have grown together and crossed; also, the tree itself *CANADA, 1942*

schoolmate *noun* a fellow prisoner *US, 1949*

school of crime *noun* a prison *US, 1982*

school of hard knocks *noun* the difficult emotional and physical experiences of growing up, seen as enriching. The UNIVERSITY OF LIFE for the working-classes *US, 1912*

school solution *noun* a military tactic as taught in the classroom *US, 1988*

schooner *noun* a 15-fluid-ounce glass of beer. In South Australia the same name is used for a 10-ounce glass of beer *AUSTRALIA, 1892*

schtonker *noun* anything impressive in its field. Misspelling of STONKER falsely suggesting a Yiddish etymology *UK, 2002*

schuss *noun* a dim-witted person *CANADA, 1999*

schussley; schusslish *adjective* giddy, silly *CANADA, 1999*

schwag; shwag *noun* marijuana, especially low quality marijuana *US, 1995*

schwallied *adjective* drunk *UK, 2003*

schweenie *noun* the penis. A variation of WEENIE (the penis) using a Yiddish model of reduplication amended with 'sch' or 'schm' *US, 1995*

schweinhund *noun* a despicable person. From German *schwein* (pig) and *hund* (dog), as used in British propaganda and fiction as one of the few words employed by any Nazi guard to refer to a British prisoner, and hence into the British vocabulary of abuse *UK, 1941*

schwindely *adjective* among Nova Scotians of German descent, dizzy, unfocused *CANADA, 1999*

schwing! used as a vocalisation of the sound a penis makes getting suddenly erect at the passing of a beautiful woman. A gift to teen slang from Mike Myers and his 'Wayne's World' sketches *US, 1992*

science fiction *noun* the US Army Special Forces. From the initials *US, 1991*

scissorbill *noun* **1** in any group setting, an outsider *US, 1962*. **2** a incompetent, stupid, or dull logger *CANADA, 1989*. **3** on the railways, a new and incompetent worker. Not praise *US, 1977*

scissor-fingers *verb* to shorten a performance. Often accompanied by finger gestures mimicking the use of scissors *US, 1981*

scissors *noun* marijuana *US, 1977*

scissor-sister *noun* a lesbian who engages in vagina-on-vagina sexual contact by spreading her legs as scissor-blades and so conjoining with another woman in a similar position. Adopted as a name by New York band *Scissor Sisters* who found international success in 2004 *US, 2004*

scluttery *adjective* overweight *CANADA, 1999*

scobie *noun* a young uncouth male *IRELAND, 1997*

scobo *noun* a black person *US, 1947*

scody *adjective* **1** excellent *NEW ZEALAND, 1998*. **2** disagreeable *US, 1966*

scoff *noun* **1** food; a meal *SOUTH AFRICA, 1846*. **2** in the Maritime Provinces, a feast *CANADA, 2002*

scoff *verb* to eat *US, 1846*

scoffins *noun* in circus and carnival usage, food. If SCOFF is 'to eat', it is only logical that 'scoffins' are 'that which is eaten' *US, 1981*

sconce *noun* the head *UK, 1567*

scone *noun* the head *AUSTRALIA, 1945*. ▶ **duck the scone** to plead guilty. Formed on SCONE (the head); from bending the head in unspoken affirmative. A variation of BOW THE CRUMPET and NOD THE NUT AUSTRALIA, 1984. ▶ **off your scone** mad. A variation of OFF YOUR HEAD AUSTRALIA, 1958. ▶ **suck your scone in!** mind you own business!; stop talking nonsense! A variation of PULL YOUR HEAD IN! AUSTRALIA, 1984

scone verb to hit someone on the head AUSTRALIA, 1948

scone hot adverb vigorously AUSTRALIA, 1927

Sconnie nickname a resident of the state of Wisconsin US, 1997

scoob noun a beverage. Gulf war usage UK, 1991

scoobied adjective drunk UK, 2003

scooby adjective to treat a prisoner unfairly. From SCOOBY-DOO (a prison officer) UK, 1996

scooby-doo; scooby; scoob noun 1 a clue. Rhyming slang, based on a popular animated cartoon character produced by Hannah Barbera since 1969 UK: SCOTLAND, 1985. **2** a prison officer. Rhyming slang for SCREW (a prison officer); from the cartoon character UK, 1996. **3** a look. Rhyming slang for 'view' UK, 2001. **4** a marijuana cigarette. Scooby Doo, a popular animated cartoon character produced by Hannah Barbera since 1969, disguises DOOBY US, 2000

scooby snack noun 1 marijuana US, 1997. **2** a drug that acts as a depressant or relaxant, usually Valium™ US, 1995

scooby snacks noun 1 any food that is hungered for while under the influence of marijuana. From the insatiable appetite of cartoon character Scooby Doo US, 1996. **2** MDMA, the recreational drug best known as ecstasy UK, 2003

scooch verb while sitting or lying down, to move your body by sliding US, 1985

scoof verb to steal something UK: SCOTLAND, 1996

scoop noun 1 the latest information or news US, 1874. **2** a drink IRELAND, 1991. **3** the convex curvature of the bottom of a surfboard US, 1965. **4** the recreational drug GHB US, 1993

scoop verb 1 to be the first to report a news story US, 1946. **2** (of a beer enthusiast) to drink any type of beer as a means of collecting and recording that particular brew UK, 2003. **3** to kiss someone US, 1997. **4** to arrest someone US, 1977. **5** in high-low poker, to declare for both high and low US, 1979

scooping noun the practice of collecting and recording different types of beer by the simple expedient of drinking each one UK, 2003

scoot noun 1 a foot-propelled scooter UK, 2000. **2** a motorcycle. A shortened 'scooter' US, 1943. **3** a dollar US, 1981. **4** an obnoxious drunk NEW ZEALAND, 1998. ▶ **on the scoot** on a drinking binge AUSTRALIA, 1916

scoot verb 1 to leave in a hurry US, 1882. **2** to slide UK, 1838

scooter noun marijuana US, 1997

scooter tracks noun faecal stains in underwear US, 1989

scooter trash noun a motorcyle gang member US, 1989

scoots noun 1 money US, 1997. **2** diarrhoea US, 1975

scope verb to see or to look at someone or something US, 1974. ▶ **scope on** to look at or examine someone or something US, 1990

scope; scoper; scopey noun an inept, clumsy or stupid individual. A rebranding of 'spastic' in line with the Spastic Society's 1994 name-change; the change to Scope was intended to avoid the 'most common use of the word "spastic" [which] has insidiously assumed misrepresentation that intends the word as an insult' UK, 2002

scope out verb to investigate something; to examine something; to check something out US, 1973

scoper; scope jockey noun a pathologist US, 1994

scope, scam and scheme used as a formula for seduction US, 1990

scope worker noun in circus and carnival usage, an astrologer. An abbreviation of 'horoscope worker' US, 1981

scorch noun a car's performance potential US, 1959

scorch verb to stare at someone or something US, 1991. ▶ **scorch the iron** to operate a train at a high rate of speed US, 1977

scorcher noun 1 a very hot day UK, 1874. **2** in ball games, an extremely hard shot UK, 1977

scorching adjective extremely hot UK, 1940

score noun 1 a robbery; the proceeds of a robbery US, 1949. **2** a one-time payment from a criminal to the police to avoid prosecution US, 1972. **3** a sale, especially of drugs or something else illegal US, 1914. **4** a prostitute's customer US, 1963. **5** a sexual conquest US, 1970. **6** twenty pounds, twenty dollars UK, 1929. **7** in betting, odds of 20–1 UK, 1991. ▶ **keep score** to perform the paperwork required of a police team US, 1970. ▶ **the score** the state of affairs, the current situation. Often in the verb phrase 'know the score' US, 1938

score verb 1 to obtain something, especially drugs and especially dishonestly US, 1914. **2** to make a sexual conquest AUSTRALIA, 1907. **3** (of a police officer) to extract a one-time bribe from a criminal to avoid prosecution US, 1972. **4** (of a horse or rider) to win a race AUSTRALIA, 1969. ▶ **score on** to get the best of someone verbally US, 1963

score! 1 used as a humorous acknowledgement of a correct answer US, 1994. **2** used for expressing joy US, 2002

scorebag noun twenty pounds' worth of a drug UK, 1996

scorpion noun 1 a variety of MDMA, the recreational drug best known as ecstasy UK, 1996. **2** cocaine UK, 1998. **3** in dominoes, the 4–4 piece US, 1959

scotch noun an improvised place to sleep BARBADOS, 1996

Scotch noun in betting odds, even UK, 1991

scotch call; scotch ring; scotchie noun a telephone call that is unanswered by pre-arrangement and which acts as a signal or message without entailing the cost of a telephone call SOUTH AFRICA, 2002

scotch egg; scotch noun the leg. Rhyming slang; usually plural UK, 1962

Scotchman noun a Scotsman. In conventional use until during C19 and, whilst not strictly incorrect, had been superseded by 'Scotsman' on both sides of the border UK, 1998

Scotchman's shout noun a date where each person pays their own way NEW ZEALAND, 1942

scotch mist noun ▶ **turn scotch mist** to vanish; to fade away UK, 1994

Scotch mist adjective drunk. Rhyming slang for PISSED (drunk), playing on the nebulous sense of Scotch mist and a taste of Scotch (whisky) UK, 1984

Scotch screw noun a nocturnal emission of semen US, 1987

Scotch twist noun in handball, a serve that strikes the front wall very near to a corner US, 1972

Scotland the brave; scotland verb to shave. Rhyming slang UK, 1998

Scotland the brave; scotland noun a wave. Glasgow rhyming slang UK: SCOTLAND, 1988

Scotsman's grandstand noun a vantage point overlooking a sportsground, permitting viewing with little or no payment. NEW ZEALAND, 1993

scott; scot noun heroin. Probably a variation of SCAT (heroin) US, 1971

Scottish adjective sexually uninhibited. The etymology is a mystery CANADA, 2000

Scotto- prefix Scottish UK, 2000

Scotty noun crack cocaine; the intoxication produced by crack cocaine. Taken from the catchphrase 'Beam me up, Scotty', first heard in cult science-fiction television series 'Star Trek' (1966–69) US, 1989

scouse noun a meat and vegetable stew. An abbreviation of 'lobscouse' (a favourite dish of sailors since the C17) UK, 1840

Scouser; Scouse; scouse noun a person from Liverpool UK, 1959

scout noun familiar term of address for a male IRELAND, 1996

scout around; scout about verb to search and explore a place or area UK, 1886

scout's honour noun used as a mocking pledge or oath to tell the truth. A reference to the Boy Scouts of America and their pledge to be truthful US, 1984

scow *noun* in trucking, an especially large truck US, 1946

scrabble *noun* crack cocaine. Probably derives from scrabbling on the floor for fragments of the drug. UK, 2003

scradge *noun* food. A British contribution to the slang of the South Pole ANTARCTICA, 2003

scrag *verb* **1** to manhandle someone roughly UK, 1835. **2** to murder someone US, 1930

scraggy *adjective* shabby US, 1946

scraggy Lou *noun* influenza. Rhyming slang for FLU UK, 1992

scram *noun* a black person US, 1940

scram *verb* to leave quickly. Probably a reduction of 'scramble', possibly from German *schrammen* (to run away) US, 1928

scram bag *noun* in circus and carnival usage, a suitcase that is always packed in the event that a hasty departure has become the prudent course of action US, 1981

scramble *noun* **1** adulterated heroin US, 1984. **2** crack cocaine. From the effect on the user US, 1994. **3** in motorcycle racing, a race in difficult terrain US, 1965. ► **the scramble** the chaotic movement of pedestrians as soon as traffic lights permit AUSTRALIA, 1984

scramble *verb* **1** to live hand-to-mouth by a variety of hustles US, 1989. **2** to sell drugs US, 1990

scrambled egg; scrambled eggs *noun* the gold braid insignia on an officer's cap or uniform UK, 1943

scrambled eggs *noun* mental confusion or mental illness US, 1984. ► **have scrambled eggs** to be drunk. Rhyming slang for, 'scrambled' (out of control) legs UK, 1992

scrambled eggs cap; ham and eggs cap *noun* a Captain or First Officer's cap, with gold 'scrambled eggs' applique US, 1982

scrambler *noun* a street-level drug seller US, 1990

scram heat *noun* the urge to attempt escape from prison US, 1962

scram switch *noun* in computing, an off switch for use in an emergency US, 1991

scran *noun* **1** food; a meal. Originally naval slang UK, 1916. **2** an informer. Back slang from NARC (an undercover narcotic officer) UK, 1996

scranker *noun* in the language surrounding the Grateful Dead, a follower of the band who has lost all touch with reality US, 1994

scrap *noun* **1** a fight UK, 1887. **2** a problem; a complaint. Hawaiian youth usage US, 1982. **3** change from a one-pound note or coin UK, 1983

scrap *verb* to fight US, 1997

scrape *noun* **1** a risky situation UK, 1709. **2** a shave. Semi-conventional usage UK, 1859. **3** a gynaecological dilation and curettage (D&C) of the uterus UK, 1994. **4** an abortion US, 1968

scrape *verb* ► **scrape the bottom of the barrel; scrape the barrel** to employ, but not through choice, someone or something of inferior standard US, 1942. ► **scrape the mug** to shave US, 1962. ► **scrape the paint** in horse racing, to race very close to the inside rail AUSTRALIA, 1989

scrape job *noun* an abortion, especially an illegal one US, 1972

scrap iron *noun* **1** a potent and dangerous alcoholic concoction made from wood alcohol, mothballs and chlorine US, 1992. **2** in prison, weights for body building US, 1981

scrap metal; scrap *noun* a kettle. Rhyming slang UK, 1992

scrapper *noun* a fighter US, 1978

scrap track *noun* on the railways, a hospital US, 1977

scratch *noun* **1** money US, 1914. **2** unemployment benefit IRELAND, 2000. **3** a masturbatory manipulation of the clitoris UK, 1979. **4** a sound or rhythmic effect created by the manipulation of a vinyl recording US, 1995. **5** a drug addict US, 2001. **6** rubber marks left on a surface when a car speeds away US, 1966. **7** an attestation by a superior that a police officer was on his beat at a given time US, 1973

scratch *verb* **1** to manipulate a vinyl record to create sounds and rhythms. Scratching, as a technique, was invented in the late 1970s by 13-year-old Theodore Livingstone (later Grand Wizard Theodore) and widely recognised by the mainstream in 1983 with the release of 'Rockit' by Herbie Hancock which featured Grandmixer DST scratching US, 1995. **2** to sign-on for unemployment benefit UK, 2000. **3** to forge US, 1962. **4** to erase something; to withdraw something from a competition UK, 1685. **5** to whip someone; to mark someone with a whip UK, 1956. **6** to paddle a surfboard energetically US, 1963. ► **scratch gravel** to leave quickly, especially in a car US, 1968. ► **scratch head** to have sex. From the sense of HEAD as 'penis' TRINIDAD AND TOBAGO, 2003. ► **scratch your monkey** (used of a drug addict) to satisfy your drug habit with an injection or other ingestion of the drug US, 1992

scratcher *noun* **1** a person who scratches their stylised signature into a window on the underground US, 1997. **2** a tattoo artist, especially an unlicensed amateur US, 1997. **3** a forger US, 1962. **4** a prison warder who is expert in searching a cell UK, 1980. **5** a rough bed or sleeping bag NEW ZEALAND, 1964

scratch house *noun* an inexpensive boarding house or brothel US, 1962

scratching *noun* the searching of prison premises UK, 1978

scratch man *noun* a forger US, 1962

scratch off *verb* to leave, especially in a hurry US, 1956

scratch pad *noun* very inexpensive lodging US, 1946

scratch sheet *noun* a leaflet or pamphlet offering 'inside' tips on horse betting US, 1912

scraven *adjective* gluttonous; greedy GUYANA, 2003

scrawbee-looby *noun* a badly scored goal, a fluke, or one that barely got past the goalkeeper IRELAND, 2000

scream *noun* **1** an extremely ridiculous or funny person or thing. Originally used in theatre slang, now simply melodramatic US, 1888. **2** an appeal against criminal conviction. Prison slang UK, 1990s. **3** a police search UK, 1956

scream *verb* **1** to complain US, 1984. **2** to inform the police or prison authorities UK, 1903. ► **scream like Tarzan; scream like ten Tarzans** to shout loudly TRINIDAD AND TOBAGO, 1989

screamer *noun* **1** a blatant and conspicuous homosexual US, 1997. **2** a hysterical hospital patient US, 1978. **3** an arrest warrant US, 1990. **4** a police siren US, 1992. **5** in drag racing and hot rodding, a very fast car US, 1958. **6** a hamburger with hot sauce and onions US, 1997. **7** in typography, an exclamation mark (!) UK, 1933

screamer and creamer *noun* a woman who is vocal during sex US, 1977

screamers *noun* pieces of metal scrap packed with an artillery shell, which makes a screaming sound as the shell moves through the air US, 1990

screaming *adjective* **1** striking; conspicuous; obvious. Used as an intensifier since the mid-C19, but in a slangy homosexual sense much more recently US, 1848. **2** excellent; the best US, 1989

screaming area *noun* in a hospital, the medical screening area US, 1978

screaming chickens *noun* the 101st Airborne Division, US Army. Like the PUKING BUZZARDS, a play on the official 'screaming eagles' US, 1991

screaming Jimmy *noun* a large General Motors Corporation diesel truck. A reference to the high-pitched noise of the GMC engine US, 1962

Screaming Lord Sutch *noun* the crutch or crotch. Rhyming slang, formed from the name of rock musician and politician, founder of the Monster Raving Loony Party, David Edward Sutch, 3rd Earl of Harrow, 1940–99. In the 1960s he changed his name by deed poll to Screaming Lord Sutch UK, 1992

screaming meemies *noun* hysteria; excessive fear noisily expressed US, 1927

screaming shits *noun* **1** a non-existent disease. It is commonly found in expressions such as, 'I'd rather die with the screaming shits' US, 1947. **2** diarrhoea. used with 'the' US, 1971

screaming sixties *noun* the latitudes of 60 to 69 degrees south ANTARCTICA, 1976

screamy *adjective* melodramatic; exhibitionist; extremely extroverted. Homosexual usage US, 1979

screech *noun* **1** the mouth, the throat, the face *UK, 1984*. **2** dark, strong Jamaican rum imported into Newfoundland *CANADA, 2001*. **3** powdered lime juice. Military *UK, 1995*

screechie *noun* in circus and carnival usage, an audio technician *US, 1981*

screech-in *noun* in Newfoundland, an event in which a newcomer is given screech to drink and then asked to sample the ocean temperature with a foot or kiss a cod *CANADA, 2002*

screel *verb* to complain loudly *TRINIDAD AND TOBAGO, 1971*

screeve *noun* a car *UK, 1979*

screw *noun* **1** a prison officer. Possibly from an obsolete sense of 'screw' (a skeleton key), hence a 'turnkey' or 'warder', or perhaps from 'thumbscrew' (an instrument of torture used in C17 prisons) *UK, 1812*. **2** an act of sexual intercourse *US, 1929*. **3** a sexual partner, potential or actual, of either gender, objectified *UK, 1937*. **4** a wage *UK, 1858*. **5** a salary *NEW ZEALAND, 1984*. **6** a mischievous scheme *TRINIDAD AND TOBAGO, 1935*. **7** a look *AUSTRALIA, 1907*. ▶ **have a screw loose** to be or become eccentric, crazy or insane *UK, 1833*

screw *verb* **1** to have sex *UK, 1725*. **2** used dismissively as a synonym for 'fuck' in exclamations and curses *UK, 1949*. **3** to burgle. A C20 usage from the earlier senses (a skeleton key; and to break into a building using a skeleton key) *UK, 1812*. **4** to swindle or cheat someone *UK, 1900*. **5** to ruin something. Probably a shortening of SCREW UP *UK, 1976*. **6** to stare at someone; to look at someone accusingly *AUSTRALIA, 1917*. **7** to leave *US, 1985*. **8** in pool, to apply spin to the cue ball to affect the course of the object ball or the cue ball after striking the object ball *US, 1990*. ▶ **don't screw the crew** a catchphrase injunction: do not have sex with your workmates. A corporate updating of NOT ON YOUR OWN DOORSTEP *UK, 2003*. ▶ **screw daft** to have sex to the point of insensibility. Generally something of a boast *UK, 2000*. ▶ **screw the arse off someone** to have vigorous sex with someone *UK, 1967*. ▶ **screw the pooch** to bungle or to ruin something. ▶ **screw your brains out** to have sex with great regularity and force *US, 1971*

screwage *noun* a computer malfunction due to design error *US, 1991*

screw around *noun* to fool around; to waste time *US, 1939*

screwball *noun* an odd, eccentric, or crazy person *US, 1933*

screwball *adjective* odd, eccentric *US, 1936*

screwdriver *noun* **1** a principal prison officer. An elaboration of SCREW (a prison officer) *UK, 1950*. **2** a person who evades work or duty. Rhyming slang for SKIVER *UK, 1992*

screwed *adjective* drunk *UK, 2002*

screwed, blued and tattooed *adjective* in such misfortune or trouble that there is no likely escape *CANADA, 1969*

screwed up *adjective* **1** troubled, disturbed *UK, 1907*. **2** spoilt; wrecked; fouled up. A euphemism for FUCKED UP *US, 1943*. **3** being locked in a prison cell. A pun on BANGED UP, via BANG (to have sex) and SCREW (to have sex) *UK, 1977*

screwface *noun* the look presented by a person who is staring *UK, 2006*

screwhead *noun* a crazy person. What you are when you HAVE A SCREW LOOSE *UK, 1997*

screw-hole *noun* an unpleasant location *UK, 2001*

screwing *adjective* anxious, unhappy. Probably from the Jamaican patois verb 'screw' (to frown) *UK, 1996*

screw job *noun* an exploitation or other maltreatment *US, 1987*

screw over *verb* to treat another person with contempt or cruelty in any way; to betray someone, to victimise someone, to cheat someone. A variation of SCREW *UK, 2000*

screws *noun* ▶ **put the screws on; put the screws to** to put pressure on someone, especially in relation to economic operations or debt recovery *US, 1834*

screwsman *noun* a housebreaker, a burglar, a thief. Originally 'a thief using a skeleton key' *UK, 1812*

screw-up *noun* **1** an action or circumstance that has been handled badly *US, 1960*. **2** an awkward person an incompetent, a blunderer; an inadequate person *US, 1960*

screw up *verb* to bungle; to fail in a task; to perform something poorly *US, 1942*

screwy *adjective* crazy; (very) eccentric *US, 1887*

screw you! used as contemptuous dismissal. Substituting SCREW for FUCK in FUCK YOU! with the same senses *US, 2000*

screw your buddy *noun* in pool, a three-player game in which all players play against all other players *US, 1993*

scribble *verb* in computing, to inadvertently and detrimentally modify a data structure *US, 1991*

scribe *noun* a letter *US, 1970*

scriber *noun* in the television and film industries, a writer *US, 1977*

scrid *noun* a very small amount *BARBADOS, 1965*

scrilla; skrilla *noun* money *US, 1998*

scrimy *adjective* despicable; lowdown *US, 1952*

script *noun* **1** a prescription for a narcotic, especially a forged prescription *US, 1936*. **2** in prison, a letter. Possibly from a (medical) prescription seen as a piece of writing with the intention of making you feel better *UK, 1996*. **3** a forged cheque *US, 1950*

script jockey *noun* a screenwriter *US, 1964*

scroat; scrote *noun* a despicable man. Probably from an abbreviation of 'scrotum' *US, 1975*

scrod *noun* **1** an ageing motorcyclist who still looks the part but for whom the motorcycle is a stage prop, not a way of life *US, 2003*. **2** any small fish, usually haddock or cod. This word is part of an old joke: 'Did you get scrod in Boston?'-'It's the first time I've been asked in the pluperfect subjunctive!' Boston is a usual destination for Nova Scotia fish *CANADA, 1841*

scrog *verb* to have sex *US, 1983*

scroggin *noun* a mixture of dried fruits, chocolate, nuts, and grains *NEW ZEALAND, 1991*

scromp *verb* to have sex *US, 1993*

scronies *noun* pepperoni *US, 1996*

scroogie *noun* a screwdriver *US, 1991*

scrot rot *noun* general discomfort, itchiness or sweatiness of the scrotum and surrounding areas *UK, 2003*

scrotty *adjective* dirty; unattractive. A variation of GROTTY, probably by elision of 'it's grotty'; in teenage use *UK, 1982*

scrotum *noun* ▶ **on the scrotum** alert, prepared. A play on the more common 'on the ball' *US, 1949*

scrounge *noun* a habitual borrower; a freeloader *UK, 1937*

scrounge *verb* to rummage; to search *UK, 1909*. ▶ **scrounge off someone** to freeload; to sponge off someone *UK, 1959*

scrounger *noun* a person known for their ability to beg, borrow, buy or steal what is needed. Respected and valued *US, 1918*

scroungy *adjective* cheap, always in search of help *US, 1959*

scrub *noun* **1** a contemptible or insignificant person, especially one who does not share your high standards of morality, style or personal hygiene *UK, 1900*. **2** a person attending a dance who is not asked to dance for long periods of time *TRINIDAD AND TOBAGO, 1971*. **3** a first-year college student *US, 1989*. **4** a substitute player on a sports team *US, 1892*. **5** in hip-hop culture, a performer of little or no talent *US, 1992*

scrub *verb* to cancel something; to forget something; to reject something. A figurative application of the conventional sense 'to erase'; originally recorded in 1828, current use dates from military use in World War 2 *UK, 1943*. ▶ **scrub round** to cancel something; to forget something, especially by agreement *UK, 1943*

scrub-bash *noun* a journey through thick bushland *AUSTRALIA, 1972*

scrub bash *verb* to make a path through thick bushland; to drive a vehicle through bushland *AUSTRALIA, 1964*

scrub-bashing *noun* the clearing of bushland *AUSTRALIA, 1959*

scrubber *noun* **1** a sexually promiscuous woman *UK, 1959*. **2** an unattractive woman *AUSTRALIA, 1977*. **3** an inferior horse bred in the country *AUSTRALIA, 1874*

scrubout *noun* a weekly mass cleaning *ANTARCTICA, 2003*

scrubs *noun* loose-fitting, sterilised clothing worn in hospital operating rooms *US, 1991*

Scrubs *noun* ► **the Scrubs** Her Majesty's Prison Wormwood Scrubs in west London *UK, 1999*

scrub up *verb* to appear after grooming. Always followed by a positive adjective or adverb *AUSTRALIA, 1985*

scruffbag *noun* a scruffy person. Originally, 'a down-and-out' *UK, 1973*

scruff puppy *noun* a girl as the object of social and sexual desire *US, 1988*

scruffy and dirty *noun* in betting, odds of 100–30. Rhyming slang *UK, 1991*

scrum *noun* something of little or no value. Obsolete rhyming slang for a 'threepenny bit', rhymes on synonymous 'thrums'; back in circulation as the perceived worth of the old coin *AUSTRALIA, 1998*

scrumdiddliumptious *adjective* extremely delicious or delightful. An elaboration of SCRUMPTIOUS *UK, 2000*

scrummy; scrummie *adjective* excellent; delicious. An abbreviation of SCRUMPTIOUS; often used as an exclamation of delight *UK, 1915*

scrump *verb* to steal apples from orchards. From an old dialect word for a 'withered apple' *UK, 1866*

scrumper *noun* a stealer of apples from orchards *UK, 1946*

scrumping *noun* an act of stealing apples from an orchard. From the verb SCRUMP *UK, 1999*

scrumptious *adjective* delicious. Often used as an exclamation of delight *UK, 1881*

scrumpy *noun* an alcoholic drink of fermented apples; an (often illicitly made or homemade) rough cider. West country dialect, now widely known *UK, 1904*

scruncheons *noun* in Newfoundland, cut-up pork fat, fried and used to garnish fish and brewis *CANADA, 1966*

scrunch up *verb* to squeeze in; to huddle *US, 1902*

scrungies *noun* swimming trunks worn for surfing *AUSTRALIA, 1991*

scrunt *verb* to live at an absolute minimum standard of living *TRINIDAD AND TOBAGO, 1976*

scruples *noun* crack cocaine *US, 1994*

scuba diver; scuba *noun* a five-pound note. Rhyming slang for FIVER *UK, 1998*

scud *noun* **1** wine *UK: SCOTLAND, 1996*. **2** crack cocaine *UK, 1996*. **3** a state of nudity. Variant elaborations include 'scuddy' and 'scuderoony' *UK: SCOTLAND, 1911*

scud *verb* to slap someone or deliver someone a glancing blow *UK: SCOTLAND, 1985*

scudded *adjective* drunk. Used by US troops during the 1991 war against Iraq, playing on the missile *US, 1991*

scudder *noun* a disagreeable, unlikeable person *US, 1972*

scuddy *adjective* naked *UK: SCOTLAND, 1996*

scuddy-book *noun* a pornographic magazine *UK: SCOTLAND, 1996*

scuds *noun* the female breasts. A comparison with Scud missiles *US, 2001*

scuff *noun* in motor racing, a new racing tyre that has not been broken in *US, 1993*

scuff *verb* **1** in circus and carnival usage, to barely make a living *US, 1981*. **2** to prepare new racing tyres for a race *US, 1993*

scuffer *noun* **1** a police officer *UK, 1860*. **2** a prostitute *US, 1971*

scuffle *noun* life, perceived as a struggle *US, 1946*

scuffle *verb* **1** to survive by your ingenuity, not by working *US, 1961*. **2** to weed a patch of potatoes without disturbing the plants *CANADA, 1990*

scuffler *noun* a person who scrounges to earn a living on the fringes of legality *US, 1965*

scuffs *noun* **1** bedroom slippers. So named because of the scuffing sound they make when you walk *US, 1985*. **2** shoes *US, 1987*

scuff up *verb* to engage in a fist fight *US, 1992*

scugly *adjective* very ugly *US, 1975*

scull *verb* to quaff or down a drink in one draught. Variant spelling of SKOAL; SKOL *AUSTRALIA, 1984*

scum *noun* **1** a despicable, unlikeable person *US, 1971*. **2** in prison, a sex offender; a convicted paedophile *UK, 1996*. **3** semen *US, 1965*

scumbag *noun* **1** a low, despicable person. The highest profile use of the term in recent years was in late April 1998, when US Congressman Dan Burton publicly called then-President Clinton 'a scumbag'. This was shortly before the revelation that Burton was the father of a child born out of wedlock, a revelation that silenced his public judgments on President Clinton's morality. In May 2004, the word got another 15 minutes of fame when it was used in the family-friendly *Blondie* comic strip, provoking serious outrage among some readers *US, 1957*. **2** a condom. Combines SCUM (semen) with a conventional container; however it is not until the 1960s that 'scum' stands apart from this usage *US, 1960*. **3** a prostitute *US, 1973*

scumball *noun* a despicable person *US, 1991*

scumbucket *noun* a despised person *US, 1983*

scumff *verb* to massage the genitals through clothing. Etymology uncertain *UK, 2001*

scumhead *noun* a contemptible person *US, 1995*

scummer *noun* a despicable lowlife whose services are for hire. Perhaps from the C14 sense of the word as 'a pirate' *US, 1985*

scummy *adjective* unpleasant; despicable. Figurative use of the conventional sense (polluted) *US, 1932*

scum of the earth *noun* an extremely unappealing, unattractive or despicable person *US, 1986*

scum out *verb* to live in filth *US, 1993*

scumpig *noun* a low, despicable person *UK, 1997*

scumteen *noun* a vague, large number *US, 1946*

scum-scrubber *noun* an employee of a pornography arcade whose job is to clean up the semen left by customers *US, 1986*

scumsucker *noun* a low, despicable person *US, 1971*

scum-sucking *adjective* despicable *US, 1982*

scunds *noun* a second helping *US, 1966*

scunge *noun* **1** filth *AUSTRALIA, 1966*. **2** a stingy person; a miser *AUSTRALIA, 1988*. **3** a habitual cadger *AUSTRALIA, 2003*

scunge *verb* to cadge something *NEW ZEALAND, 1995*

scungeel *noun* a low-life, a disreputable person. From the Italian *scungili*, (squid) *US, 1977*

scungies *noun* a pair of men's close-fitting and revealing nylon swimming trunks *AUSTRALIA, 2003*

scungy *adjective* sordid; dirty *AUSTRALIA, 1983*

scunner *noun* a nuisance. First recorded of persons in 1796, and of things in 1865 *UK: SCOTLAND, 1988*

scup *verb* to swing. Rarely heard *US, 1951*

scupper *noun* a promiscuous woman. From an earlier sense as 'a prostitute', in turn deriving from 'a hole in a ship's side' *UK, 1970*

scupper *verb* to put an end to something; to thwart someone; to destroy something *UK, 1918*

scurb *noun* a suburban skateboarder who confines his skateboarding to streets and sidewalks *US, 1984*

scurve *noun* a graceless person; someone who is disliked *US, 1951*

scurvy *adjective* **1** unkempt; sloppy; ugly *US, 1965*. **2** very thin *US, 2001*

scuse; 'scuse *verb* to excuse someone; especially in, or as an abbreviation of, the phrases: excuse me, please excuse me. In conventional use from C15, and considered a colloquial slovening since C19 *UK, 1967*

scut *noun* **1** the end of a cigarette *IRELAND, 1984*. **2** a contemptible person; someone of bad character *IRELAND, 1975*. **3** any menial medical procedure *US, 1978*

scut *verb* to ride on the back of a truck or van *IRELAND, 1991*

scut duty; scut work *noun* tedious, menial work *US, 1960*

scuttered *adjective* drunk *IRELAND, 2002*

scuttlebutt *noun* gossip, rumours. From the name of the drinking-water cask found on board a ship, around which sailors gathered to gossip *US, 1901*

scutty *adjective* filthy; decrepit *IRELAND, 1992*

scuz *noun* a dirty, disreputable person *US, 1973*

scuzbag; scuzzbag *noun* a despicable, undesirable person. A variation on SCUMBAG *US, 1980*

scuz rag *noun* during the Vietnam war, a rag used to wipe floors *US, 1991*

scuzz *verb* to be involved in sleazy activities; to keep unpleasant company; to move in low circles *UK, 1997*

scuzzball *noun* a despicable person *US, 1986*

scuzzhead *noun* a despicable person *UK, 1997*

scuzzy *adjective* disgusting *US, 1968*

scwhag *adjective* inferior; shoddy *US, 1998*

seaboard *adjective* used of an order for take-away food at a restaurant *US, 1952*

sea daddy *noun* in the US Navy, a mentor *US, 1992*

seafood *noun* a sailor as an object of homosexual desire *US, 1963*

seafood breakfast *noun* oral sex performed on a woman in the morning *AUSTRALIA, 1985*

seafood plate please. An intentionally butchered French *s'il vous plaît US, 1984*

sea-going bellhop *noun* a member of the US Marine Corps. Derisive, used by other branches of the armed services to mock the USMC dress uniform *US, 1960*

seagull *noun* **1** a person who constantly complains *US, 1968*. **2** a casual wharfside worker *AUSTRALIA, 1965*. **3** a person who watches what bets are being made by big spenders and then makes a small bet on the horses favoured by the big spenders *US, 1966*. **4** a combat pilot who has become reluctant to fly *US, 1990*. **5** a rugby union player who remains outside tight play in the chance that the ball will break loose *NEW ZEALAND, 1975*. **6** chicken *US, 1945*

seam shooter *noun* a criminal who specialises in blowing up safes by placing small amounts of explosives in the safe's seams *US, 1949*

seam squirrels *noun* in circus and carnival usage, body lice *US, 1981*

Seamus Heaney *noun* a bikini. Rhyming slang, formed from the name of the Irish poet (b.1939) *UK, 2003*

Sea of Green *noun* a marijuana growing technique from British Columbia *CANADA, 2002*

sea pie *noun* in the Ottawa valley, a Sunday meat dish *CANADA, 1998*

sea pig *noun* a fat surfer *US, 1988*

sea pussy *noun* the sea anemone. Based on a visual comparison with the vagina *BAHAMAS, 1982*

sea queen *noun* a homosexual sailor or ship's steward; a homosexual man with a taste for seamen *UK, 2002*

sea rat *noun* a seagull *US, 1991*

search *verb* to try to buy illegal drugs *US, 1997*

search and avoid; search and evade *verb* used by US forces to describe the activities of the South Vietnamese Army. Not praise *US, 1972*

searcher *noun* a prisoner who intimidates other prison inmates who are suspected of carrying drugs *UK, 1996*

search me I don't know *US, 1947*

sea stack *noun* a tall column of granite, created by erosion, just off the shore in the ocean near Newfoundland *CANADA, 2002*

sea story *noun* a tale about the teller's exploits, real and imagined *US, 1961*

seat *noun* a police officer assigned to ride as a passenger with another officer *US, 1970*

seat *verb* to perform anal sex on someone *AUSTRALIA, 1950*

seat back! used to reserve your seat as you briefly leave the room *US, 1996*

seat cover *noun* an attractive woman. Citizens' band radio slang *US, 1976*

Sea Thing *noun* the Sea King helicopter, acquired for the Canadian Navy from Sikorsky in 1963 *CANADA, 1995*

seatman *noun* **1** in prison, a male homosexual who takes the active role in anal sex *AUSTRALIA, 1983*. **2** in circus and carnival usage, a paid customer, employed to show enthusiasm *US, 1981*

seat-surf *verb* to move from empty seat to empty seat in a stadium or auditorium, gradually improving your position *US, 1994*

Seattle tuxedo *noun* a clean flannel shirt *US, 1997*

seaweed muncher *noun* a surfer *AUSTRALIA, 1987*

Sebastian Coe; sebastian; seb *noun* the toe. Rhyming slang, formed on the name of a celebrated British athlete (b.1956) who went into politics *UK, 1992*

sec *noun* **1** a second *UK, 1909*. **2** a capsule of secobarbital sodium (trade name *Seconal*™), a central nervous system depressant *UK, 1996*

seccy *noun* **1** a second. An elaboration of SEC rather than an abbreviation of 'second' *AUSTRALIA, 1971*. **2** a capsule of secobarbital sodium (trade name *Seconal*™), a central nervous system depressant *US, 1969*

secko; secoo; sekko *noun* a sexual deviant; a sex offender *AUSTRALIA, 1949*

seco *noun* Seconal™, a barbiturate *US, 1972*

second *noun* a close friend *BARBADOS, 1965*

second balloon *noun* a second lieutenant *US, 1956*

second banana *noun* a person in a supporting role. Originally applied to a supporting comedian *US, 1953*

second base *noun* **1** in a teenage categorisation of sexual activity, a level of foreplay, most usually referring to touching a girl's breasts. The exact degree varies by region or even school *US, 1977*. **2** in casino games of blackjack, the seat or player in the centre of the table directly across from the dealer *US, 1980*. **3** in a deck of playing cards, the card second from the bottom of the deck *US, 1988*

Second Chance University *noun* Sir George Williams University *CANADA, 2002*

second-generation joint *noun* a marijuana cigarette made with the remains of other marijuana cigarettes *US, 1977*

second hat *noun* an assisant drill instructor, US Marine Corps. Usually the most verbally abusive of the three drill instructors who work together as a team *US, 1991*

second John *noun* a second lieutenant *US, 1956*

second nuts *noun* in poker, a good hand that is beaten by a better hand *US, 1976*

seconds *noun* **1** sex with someone who has just had sex with someone else. Often preceded by the adjective 'sloppy' *US, 1966*. **2** a second helping of food *US, 1792*. **3** playing cards that have been altered for cheating *US, 1950*. ▶ **the seconds; touch of the seconds** *second* thoughts; a fear of consequences. Metropolitan Police slang *UK, 1954*

second second *noun* in the television and film industries, an additional second assistant director *US, 1990*

second-story man *noun* **1** a burglar *US, 1886*. **2** a skilled card cheat who deals the second card in a deck *US, 1988*

second to none *noun* heroin *UK, 2003*

secret squirrel *noun* an intelligence operative. In military use in Northern Ireland during the 1970s; from the animated cartoon hero created by Hanna Barbera and first seen in his own television show in 1965 *UK, 1979*

seducing vampires *adjective* experiencing the bleed period of the menstrual cycle *CANADA, 2001*

see *noun* a visual inspection *US, 1973*

see *verb* **1** to understand something; to believe something. Elaborated in the wordplay: '"I see," said the blind man, as he put down his hammer and saw.' *US, 1850*. **2** to have the ability to read music *UK, 1955*. ▶ **see a brown friend out to the coast** to defecate *UK, 2002*. ▶ **see a man about a dog** to go to the toilet. Jocular and euphemistic *UK, 1885*. ▶ **see it coming a mile off** to predict an obvious event, often only with the benefit of hindsight. An elaboration and intensification of 'see it coming' *UK, 1966*. ▶ **see red** to be angry *UK, 1901*. ▶ **see Steve** to use cocaine *US, 1952*. ▶ **see the colour of your money** to see your money; to be paid *UK, 1718*. ▶ **see you coming** to take advantage of your gullibility *UK, 1937*

seed *noun* **1** a child *US, 1998*. **2** a person who is hopelessly out of touch with current fashions and trends. A shortened form of HAYSEED *US, 1968*. **3** in a deck of playing cards, an ace *US, 1988*. **4** in private poker games, a one-dollar betting chip *US, 1971*. **5** a dollar *US, 1961*. **6** the butt of a marijuana cigarette *US, 1982*

seed money *noun* money needed to start a business *US, 1943*

seeds *noun* marijuana; a marijuana cigarette. Usage is generally as a singular noun *US, 1969*

seeds and stems *noun* the detritus of marijuana, unsmokeable but a reminder of what was *US, 1971*

seed spitter *noun* the penis *US, 2001*

seedy *adjective* **1** ill, unwell *UK, 1858*. **2** in car repair, rusty *US, 1992*

seedy rom *noun* a compact disc (CD-ROM) which is sexually explicit *CANADA, 1995*

seeing red *adjective* experiencing the bleed period of the menstrual cycle *US, 1999*

seeing-to *noun* **1** the act of sexual intercourse, generally considered as the man *doing it* to the woman. A sense of aggression is implied; consider the contemporaneous 'seeing-to' (a beating) *UK, 1985*. **2** a beating. Often as 'a proper seeing-to' *UK, 1968*

seek *verb* ▶ **seek the sheets** to crawl into bed *US, 1967*

seek and search *noun* a church. Rhyming slang *UK, 1998*

seen! used for registering agreement or approval. Originally West Indian *JAMAICA, 1967*

seen? understood? Originally West Indian *UK, 1994*

see off *verb* to attend to something; to defeat someone *UK, 1915*

see seven stars *noun* strong, illegally manufactured whisky *US, 1999*

see the Chaplain! used for silencing a soldier who complains excessively *US, 1941*

see ya round like a Polo goodbye. A variation on SEE YOU ROUND LIKE A RECORD, playing on the shape of a Polo™ mint *UK, 1996*

see ya, wouldn't want to be ya goodbye *US, 1993*

see you around campus goodbye. Jocular *US, 1972*

see you, Jimmy used as an aggressive or threatening address to a male stranger. A cliché in the stereotypical drunken Scotsman's vocabulary. Tartan hats with a wild fringe of ginger hair, intended as a comic representation of the generic JOCK, are marketed as 'See You Jimmy hats' *UK, 2001*

see you later, alligator goodbye. From the use of GATOR as an all-purpose form of male address. A catchphrase to which the automatic response was 'in a while, crocodile'; in vogue around 1956, when Bill Haley and His Comets had great success with the song 'See You Later Alligator' (although the actual call and response in the lyric was a slight variation: 'See you later alligator, after a while crocodile') *US, 1956*

see you next Tuesday used as an insider's code for 'cunt'. The 'see you' make the 'cu' and the initials 'nt' follow. *See You Next Tuesday* is the title of Ronald Harwood's 2002 adaptation and translation of Francis Veber's 1993 play *Le Diner De Cons* *UK, 1978*

see you round like a record *noun* goodbye *UK, 1978*

seg; seggie *noun* in prison, segregation; a segregation unit *US, 1967*

seggy *noun* a capsule of secobarbital sodium (trade name Seconal™), a central nervous system depressant *US, 1967*

sei-cordi box *noun* a six-string guitar. Polari; a combination of Italian *sei*; SEY; SEI (six) and *corda* with BOX (a guitar) *UK, 1984*

seized *verb* ▶ **seized of** in Quebec, gripped by, seized by (an idea or project, for example) *CANADA, 2002*

seizure! used as a cry of triumph, no matter how petty the success. Reported as a children's usage, Hay-on-Wye, May 2003 *UK, 2003*

seldom seen *noun* a queen; the Queen. Rhyming slang *UK, 1992*

selecta! used as an expression of approval or pleasure. Deriving from a dance music term for a DJ, via BO SELECTA! (expressing approval of a DJ's performance). Partly popularised in the UK in the late 1990s by Ali G (comedian Sacha Baron-Cohen) *UK, 2003*

selector; selecta *noun* a DJ. A shortening of 'music selector', used in modern dance culture, especially in the term BO SELECTA! *UK, 1999*

self-love *noun* masturbation *UK, 2003*

self-propelled sandbag *noun* a US Marine. US Army Gulf war usage *US, 1991*

self-toast *verb* to incriminate yourself. Office jargon *UK, 2005*

Selina Scott; selina *noun* a spot (a skin blemish). Rhyming slang, formed from the name of a UK television presenter and newspaper columnist *UK, 1992*

sell *verb* **1** to convince someone of something; to trick someone *US, 1996*. **2** to gamble on a result lower than the bookmaker's favoured spread *UK, 2001*. ▶ **sell a hog** to scare someone by bluffing *US, 1990*. ▶ **sell a pup** to swindle someone *UK, 1901*. ▶ **sell backside** to prostitute yourself, literally or figuratively *SINGAPORE, 2002*. ▶ **sell Buicks** to vomit *US, 1978*. ▶ **sell someone down the river** to betray someone *US, 1927*. ▶ **sell tickets** to engage in ritualistic, competitive insulting *US, 2001*

seller *noun* a gambler who bets on a result lower than the bookmaker's favoured spread *UK, 2001*

sell-out *noun* **1** an act of betraying principle or loyalty *US, 2001*. **2** in pool, a missed shot that leaves your opponent with a good shot *US, 1978*

sell out *verb* **1** to betray a cause of conviction, especially for financial reward. Around long before the 1960s, but promoted and glorified in the idealistic haze of the 60s *US, 1888*. **2** to vomit after drinking to excess *NEW ZEALAND, 2002*

selohssa *noun* used as a nonce name for a person or company. 'Assholes' spelled backwards. Peter Tamony collected examples from the San Francisco telephone directory in 1965, 1966 and 1967. In 1953, Welsh playwright Dylan Thomas introduced the village of 'Llareggub' ('bugger all' backwards) in the play *Under Milkwood* *US, 1965*

semi *noun* **1** a *semi*-detached house *UK, 1912*. **2** a *semi*-final *US, 1942*. **3** a *semi*-trailer *AUSTRALIA, 1956*. **4** the penis in a state between flaccid and erect *US, 1994*

semi-retired *adjective* unable to find work *US, 1995*

semolina *noun* a professional cleaner. Rhyming slang *UK, 1992*

semolina pilchard *nickname* Detective Sergeant Norman Pilcher of the Metropolitan Police. Probably coined by the Beatles. Pilcher secured a small celebrity and lasting notoriety in the late 1960s, by arresting, or attempting to arrest, pop stars such as Brian Jones of the Rolling Stones, and John Lennon and George Harrison of the Beatles, for drug offences, and was himself later imprisoned for corruption *UK, 2001*

semper fi used as a shortened version of the US Marine Corps creed – *semper fidelis* (always faithful). Used as a greeting, an affirmation, and in practically any situation to mean practically anything *US, 1986*

semper Gumby *adjective* flexible *US, 1991*

sen; sens *noun* marijuana. A clipping of SENSIMILLIA *UK, 1998*

senator *noun* in a game of poker, a dealer who does not play *US, 1988*

send *noun* the phase of a confidence swindle when the victim is sent to retrieve money *US, 1940*. ▶ **put on the send** in a confidence swindle, to send the victim off to retrieve the money that will pass to the swindlers *US, 1972*

send *verb* **1** to excite someone; to please someone *US, 1935*. **2** to produce a drug intoxication *US, 1950*. ▶ **send a boy to do a man's work** in poker, to make a small bet with a good hand in the hope of luring players with inferior hands to continue betting *US, 1951*. ▶ **send out a salesman** in gin, to discard in a manner that is designed to lure a desired card from an opponent *US, 1965*

▶ **send someone packing** to dismiss someone; to reject someone with immediate effect *UK, 1594.* ▶ **send the little sailor to sea** to have sex *US, 2001.* ▶ **send to Long Beach** to flush a toilet. Long Beach is a community to the south of Los Angeles *US, 1968*

send down *verb* to commit someone to prison *US, 1840*

sender *noun* something or someone that arouses or excites. Originally (mid 1930s) a jazz term referring to a musician who excites and inspires a jazz band; in the early 1940s extended to general usage. Often emphasised as SOLID SENDER *US, 1935*

send-off *noun* **1** a funeral. A specialised use of the sense relating more generally to any journey *US, 1876.* **2** an occasion at which friendly good wishes are offered to someone leaving a current situation (for a journey or different employment, etc) *US, 1841*

send off *verb* **1** to apprehend or arrest someone *AUSTRALIA, 1956.* **2** to steal something *AUSTRALIA, 1950*

send-up *noun* a satirical act; a parody. From the phrasal verb SEND UP *UK, 1958*

send up *verb* **1** to mock someone or something satirically or parodically *UK, 1931.* **2** to sentence someone to prison *US, 1852*

senile street *noun* an area in a hospital or nursing home frequented by senile patients *AUSTRALIA, 1987*

senior moment *noun* a short interval in which an older person succumbs to a mental or physical lack of energy or consistency *US, 1996*

sense; sens *noun* marijuana. An abbreviation of SENSIMILLIA *US, 1984*

sensi; sensee *noun* marijuana. Clipped from SENSIMILLIA *JAMAICA, 1983*

sensimillia; sinsemilla; sinse *noun* a very potent marijuana harvested from a hybrid cannabis plant with seedless buds. From the Spanish *sin se milla* (seedless). Celebrated in song by 'Cocaine will blow your brain, but sinsemilla is IR-IE!' by Yellowman, quoted in *Waiting For The Man*, Harry Shapiro, 1999 *JAMAICA, 1982*

seppo *noun* an American. From SEPTIC *AUSTRALIA, 1985*

Sept. 10 *adjective* petty; inconsequential. Teen slang, post 11th September 2001 *US, 2002*

September morn *noun* the erect penis. Rhyming slang for HORN *UK, 1998*

septic *noun* an American. Short for SEPTIC TANK *AUSTRALIA, 1970*

septic tank *noun* an American. Rhyming slang for YANK. Certainly derogatory in origin, and demonstrating a general low-level anti-American sentiment prevalent in Australia. In the same way that POM demonstrates an anti-English sentiment it is always more joking than serious *AUSTRALIA, 1967*

serenity, tranquility and peace *noun* STP, a synthetic hallucinogen that appeared on the drug scene in 1967. Because of its claimed psychedlic powers, the drug was named STP after the engine oil additive (scientifically treated petroleum), with this trinity of virtues produced through back-formation *US, 1972*

sergeant from K company *noun* in a deck of playing cards, a king *US, 1988*

sergeant-major *noun* in the dice game crown and anchor, a crown. From 'crown', an army colloquialism for 'sergeant-major' *UK, 1961*

serial speedball *verb* to use cocaine, cough syrup and heroin in a continual cycle over a 1–2 day period *UK, 1998*

serio *adverb* in a serious manner. This corruption of 'seriously', making use of the familiarising suffix, especially common in Dublin colloquial speech *IRELAND, 1996*

serious *adjective* **1** used to enhance or intensify *UK, 1982.* **2** seriously ill. Indian English *INDIA, 1979*

serious chep *noun* intimate sexual contact; sexual intercourse. An intensified CHEP (a kiss) *IRELAND, 2001*

serious headache *noun* a gunshot wound to the head *US, 1982*

seriously *adverb* used to intensify or enhance *US, 1981*

serpent *noun* a railway pointsman. From the snake-like 'S' on the pointsman's union pin *US, 1977*

Serpico; Serpico 21 *noun* cocaine; crack cocaine. From the film *Serpico*, 1973 *UK, 1998*

serve *verb* **1** to insult someone in a semi-formal quasi-friendly competition. After 'serve' (a criticism) *AUSTRALIA, 2000.* **2** to humiliate someone; to hit someone *US, 1989.* **3** to sell drugs to someone *US, 1990.* **4** in card games, to deal *US, 1988.* ▶ **serve you right; serves you right** used as an expression of satisfaction that you have got your just deserts *UK, 1837*

server *noun* a person who hands crack cocaine to a buyer as part of a multi-layered selling operation *US, 1994*

service stripes *noun* bruises, punctures and sores visible on the skin of an intravenous drug user *US, 1973*

serving *noun* a beating *AUSTRALIA, 2002*

servo *noun* a service station *AUSTRALIA, 1994*

sesh *noun* **1** a period of sustained drinking. A shortening of SESSION *UK, 1985.* **2** a session *US, 1982*

sess; sces; sezz *noun* potent marijuana. Variations on SENSIMILLIA *US, 1982*

session *noun* **1** a prolonged period of steady drinking *AUSTRALIA, 1949.* **2** an instance of sexual intercourse *US, 1997.* **3** any period of time spent scooter-riding with friends *UK, 2000.* **4** a series of waves *US, 1963*

session; sesh *verb* to concentrate effort on a single objective *US, 1995*

set *noun* **1** a neighbourhood; a specific place in a neighbourhood where friends congregate *US, 1965.* **2** a neighbourhood faction of a gang *US, 2001.* **3** a party, especially a party with music *US, 1966.* **4** a group of breaking waves *AUSTRALIA, 1963.* **5** a woman's breasts *AUSTRALIA, 1967.* **6** in horse or dog racing, a wager or the cumulative amount of wagers taken against a particular contestant *AUSTRALIA, 1988.* **7** a still used in the illegal production of alcohol *US, 1974.* **8** in prison usage, a continuance of a parole hearing *US, 1981.* ▶ **have a set on** to be hostile towards someone *AUSTRALIA, 1866*

set *verb* to make a bet with someone *AUSTRALIA, 1915.* ▶ **set (her) down** in trucking, to make a sudden stop *US, 1971.* ▶ **set in the woods** in lobstering, to set traps close to the shore *US, 1978.* ▶ **set the centre** in the gambling game two-up, to ensure that the spinner's wager is covered by the other players *AUSTRALIA, 1930.* ▶ **set them up** to organise a round of drinks *UK, 1959*

set *adjective* having a wager settled upon *AUSTRALIA, 1915*

set about *verb* to attack or assault someone *UK, 1879*

set back *verb* to cost, especially to cost a great deal *UK, 1856*

set in concrete *adjective* immutable; unalterable. A variation of SET IN STONE *UK, 2002*

set in stone *adjective* immutable; unalterable. A figurative application of the conventional sense *UK, 2003*

set joint *noun* a carnival game which is rigged to prevent players from winning *US, 1968*

setter; setta *adjective* seven; seven (pre-decimal) pence *UK, 1859*

settle *verb* ▶ **settle your hash** to subdue you; to silence you; to defeat you; to kill you *UK, 1803*

settler *noun* in an illegal betting operation, the person who determines the final odds on an event after all bets are taken *US, 1964*

settlers *noun* dice that have been weighted and are thrown with an altered cup with great effect by a skilled cheat *US, 1963*

set-up *noun* **1** an organisation or establishment *UK, 1959.* **2** an arrangement, organisation or situation *US, 1890.* **3** a scheme for the entrapment of a criminal or the incrimination of an innocent *US, 1968.* **4** the equipment used to inject a drug *US, 1952.* **5** a place setting at a dining table *US, 1934*

set up *verb* especially of criminals, to arrange circumstances in such a way that the target of this arrangement is rendered vulnerable; to create a victim; to incriminate someone *US, 1928*

set-up man *noun* a criminal who identifies, plans and organises crimes *US, 1953*

seven *noun* **1** a telephone number. From the seven digits used in US telephone numbers *US, 1998.* **2** in eastern Australia, a seven-fluid-ounce glass of beer *AUSTRALIA, 1972*

seven and seven *noun* **1** a drink made by mixing equal parts of Seven-Up™ soda and Seagrams Seven Whiskey™ *US, 1976*. **2** after 1971 in the Vietnam war, seven days of rest and recuperation, followed by seven days of leave *US, 1991*

seven and six *noun* **1** a fix (a difficult position). Rhyming slang *UK, 1992*. **2** a young Mod. Apparently the MOD favoured tee-shirts from Woolworths costing seven shillings and sixpence *UK, 1983*

seven and six *verb* to fix something. Rhyming slang *UK, 1992*

seven and sixer *noun* a married person. From the cost of a 1960s' wedding licence, seven shillings and sixpence *UK, 1998*

Seven Dials *noun* haemorrhoids. Rhyming slang for PILES, formed on a once notorious area of central London *UK, 1998*

seven-eleven *noun* a small amount of money given to a gambler who has lost all their money, either by a casino or his fellow gamblers *US, 1950*

seven-o *noun* seventy; 70th Street *US, 1972*

seven out *verb* in craps, to roll a seven before making your point, thus losing *US, 1974*

seven-ply gasser *noun* the very best thing *US, 1968*

sevens *noun* ▶ **all the sevens** seventy-seven. In Bingo, House or Housey-Housey calling, the formula 'all the' announces a double number *UK, 1943*

seventeen-wheeler *noun* an eighteen-wheel truck with a flat tyre *US, 1976*

seventh cavalry *noun* any agency that promises or effects an eleventh-hour rescue or last-minute relief from an awkward situation *UK, 2000*

seventh wave *noun* the difficulty that follows many others and proves to be climactic disaster. From the belief that every seventh wave is larger than the six before or after *US, 1975*

seven-up *noun* crack cocaine. A pun on 'coke' as a soft drink and drug *US, 1993*

seven-year itch *noun* a (notional) need to be unfaithful to your spouse after seven years of marriage *UK, 1936*

severe clear *adjective* of the weather, perfect for flying *CANADA, 1989*

severe like *noun* a strong desire for something *US, 1984*

severely *adverb* very much *UK, 1854*

sew *verb* ▶ **sew the button on** in oil drilling, to finish a job *US, 1954*

sewer *noun* **1** a vein, especially a prominent vein suitable for drug injection *US, 1994*. **2** in pool, a pocket that is receptive to shots dropping *US, 1990*. **3** a person who cannot keep a secret *US, 1955*

sewer hog *noun* a ditch digger *US, 1962*

sewer trout *noun* white fish of unknown origin *US, 1945*

sewing machine *noun* a small, foreign-made car. Drag racing usage, heard before the great influx of foreign cars into the US *US, 1970*

sewn-up *adjective* finished *UK, 1966*

sew up *verb* to organise or achieve a satisfactory conclusion; to ensure a favourable outcome *UK, 1904*

sex *noun* the genitals. A literary nicety *UK, 1938*

sex *verb* to have sex with someone *US, 1966*

sex appeal *noun* false breasts *US, 1981*

sexational; sexsational *adjective* very sexy; very sexually attractive *US, 1928*

sex-bomb *noun* a sexually alluring person, especially a woman, particularly one with exaggerated but stereotypical sexuality *UK, 1963*

sexcapade *noun* a sexual adventure. A combination of 'sex' and 'escapade' *US, 1955*

sex case *noun* a sex offender *UK, 1996*

sex changer *noun* a computer cable with either two male or two female connectors *US, 1991*

sex down *verb* to make a thing less appealing. Derived as an antonym for SEX UP *UK, 2003*

sexed up *adjective* sexually aroused *UK, 1942*

sexile *verb* to force your roommate from your shared housing while you have sex *US, 2000*

sex kitten *noun* an especially attractive young woman who exploits her appeal. Coinage apparently inspired by film actress Brigitte Bardot (b.1933) *UK, 1958*

sexo; sex-oh *noun* **1** a sex offender *NEW ZEALAND, 1963*. **2** a person who is preoccupied with sex *NEW ZEALAND, 1959*

sexpert *noun* an expert on sexual behaviour. Mix 'sex' with an 'expert' *US, 1924*

sexploitation *noun* the exploitation of sexual imagery for commercial gain. A combination of 'sex' and 'exploitation' *US, 1998*

sexpot *noun* a sexually exciting woman *US, 1957*

sexstasy; sextasy *noun* MDMA, the recreational drug best known as ecstasy, taken with the erection enhancing drug Viagra™ *US, 1999*

sex tank *noun* a holding cell reserved for homosexual prisoners *US, 1963*

Sexton Blake; sexton *noun* **1** a fake; a forgery. Rhyming slang, formed on the name of a fictional detective who first appeared in 1893 and continued in print well into the 1960s. British artist Tom Keating, 1917–84, famously forged works attributed to Gainsborough, Degas, Boucher, Fragonard, Renoir and Modigliani; in 1976 he confessed to having painted 2,000 Sexton Blakes *UK, 1984*. **2** a cake. Rhyming slang, formed on the fictional detective. Considered obsolete by Julian Franklyn, *A Dictionary of Rhyming Slang*, 1960; however, Ray Puxley, *Cockney Rabbit*, 1992, records it as 'long established' *UK, 1960*. **3** a 'take' in television and films. Rhyming slang, formed on the fictional detective *UK, 1972*

sex up *verb* to present a thing in a manner designed to make it more attractive and appealing. Recorded in 1984 as 'to render a manuscript (more) sexually exciting' *UK, 1984*

sex wagon *noun* a car that appeals to girls *US, 1954*

sexy *adjective* used to describe anything considered to be desirable, very interesting or influential. A figurative application of the sense as 'sexually attractive' *UK, 1980*

sey; sei; sa; say *adjective* six. Polari, from Italian *sei UK, 1996*

sez *verb* says *UK, 1844*

shack *noun* **1** a house that exudes wealth and invites burglary *US, 1950*. **2** especially in Tasmania, and south and west Australia, a holiday house of any size or quality *AUSTRALIA, 1998*. **3** a room, apartment or house *US, 1955*. **4** any room where a citizens' band radio set is housed *US, 1976*. **5** a direct hit on the target by a bomb *US, 1991*. **6** a sexual episode *US, 1995*. **7** a rear brakeman on a train *US, 1977* ▷ *see:* CHIAC

shack *verb* **1** to live together as an unmarried couple. Very often used in the variant 'shack up' *US, 1935*. **2** to spend the night with someone, sex almost always included. Not the ongoing relationship suggested by the older term SHACK UP *US, 1996*

shacker *noun* a sexual partner who spends the night but does not live with you *US, 2002*

shack house *noun* a brakevan (caboose) *US, 1977*

shacking *noun* a party or social gathering *US, 1972*

shack job *noun* a person with whom you are living and enjoying sex without the burdens or blessings of marriage; the arrangement *US, 1960*

shack rat *noun* a soldier who has moved in together with a woman *US, 1947*

shack-up *noun* a person with whom you are living and enjoying sex without the burdens or blessings of marriage *US, 1960*

shack up *verb* **1** to take up residence, usually of a temporary nature *US, 1942*. **2** to provide living quarters for a lover *US, 1960*

shaddup! be quiet! A slurring of SHUT UP! *UK, 1959*

shade *noun* **1** a black person. Offensive *US, 1865*. **2** a suntan *US, 1997*. **3** a legitimate business that acts as a cover for an illegal enterprise *US, 1978*. **4** detached superiority *US, 1994*

shade *verb* **1** to reduce something slightly and gradually *US, 1997*. **2** to mark the backs of cards with a subtle shading of the existing colour *US, 1979*

shades *noun* **1** sunglasses *US, 1958*. **2** police *IRELAND, 1997*

shade spade *noun* an Arab. Offensive *US, 2000*

shade-tree mechanic *noun* an amateur car mechanic of dubious skill, questionable honour and the best of intentions *US, 1992*

shadie *noun* a man, especially a young man, who spends his life on the edges of crime *US, 1976*

shadow *noun* **1** a collector for an illegal money lender *US, 1950*. **2** a truck that is not equipped with a citizens' band radio following one that is *US, 1976*

shadows *noun* dark glasses *US, 1955*

shady *adjective* **1** giving an impression of dishonesty; disreputable; not quite honourable *UK, 1862*. **2** detached, aloof *US, 1994*

shady lady *noun* a prostitute *US, 1976*

shaft *noun* **1** the penis *UK, 1772*. **2** an act of sexual intercourse; hence, a woman objectified sexually. From the verb *UK, 1984*. **3** poor treatment *US, 1959*. **4** a crankshaft. Hot rodder usage *US, 1948*. **5** the leg *US, 1970*

shaft *verb* **1** from a male perspective, to have sex. After SHAFT (the penis) *UK, 1962*. **2** to mistreat or abuse *US, 1959*

shaft artist *noun* a person who is prone to cheat or behave unfairly *US, 1977*

shafted *adjective* in deep trouble; in such deep trouble that your previous position is unrecoverable. Synonymous with FUCKED *UK, 1994*

shafter *noun* a single ox in an ox-pull contest or for work *CANADA, 1985*

shafting *noun* trouble; unfair treatment *UK, 2000*

shaftsman *noun* a person who is prone to cheat or behave unfairly *US, 1977*

shafty *adjective* (used of a thing) fashionable, popular *US, 1951*

shag *noun* **1** an act of sexual intercourse *UK, 1999*. **2** a sexual partner *UK, 1788*. **3** a friend *NEW ZEALAND, 1984*. **4** in trucking, a small trailer used for city driving *US, 1971*. ▶ **like a shag on a rock** all alone *AUSTRALIA, 1845*

shag *verb* **1** to have sex. Possibly from obsolete 'shag' (to shake); usage is not gender-specific *UK, 1788*. **2** to leave *US, 1851*. **3** to run someone down; to arrest someone *US, 1911*. ▶ **shag ass** to leave *US, 1964*. ▶ **shag senseless** to have sex to the point of exhaustion. Generally used as a boast *UK, 2000*

shagadelic *adjective* exciting; great. Combining two clichés of 'swinging sixties London' (from a Hollywood perspective): SHAG (to have sex) and 'psychedelic' (of mind-expanding drugs). Usage has added sexual overtones to this comic coinage which appears just once in the film *Austin Powers, The Spy Who Shagged Me*: 'New case? Very shagadelic, Basil!' (Mike Myers, 1998) *US, 1998*

shaganappi *adjective* worthless *CANADA, 1961*

shagbox *noun* the vagina *UK, 2001*

shagbucket *noun* a worthless or despicable person. Related to obsolete synonym 'shag-bag' *UK, 1997*

shagged; shagged out *adjective* exhausted. From SHAG (to have sex); compares with FUCKED (exhausted) *UK, 1932*

shagger *noun* a person, especially a male, who has sex *UK, 2002*

shagger's back *noun* any backache, whether or not produced by over-exertion in sex *AUSTRALIA, 1988*

shagging *adjective* used as an intensifier. A direct replacement of FUCKING *UK, 2000*

-shagging- *infix* used as an intensifier *UK, 2002*

shagging Nora! used as a register of surprise, anger, amazement, etc *UK, 1982*

shagging pad *noun* a room kept for sexual encounters *AUSTRALIA, 1995*

shagging room *noun* in a brothel, a room or cubicle set aside for the business of sex *UK, 2002*

shag-happy *adjective* obsessed with sex *AUSTRALIA, 1994*

shag me! used for expressing surprise *NEW ZEALAND, 1998*

shag-merchant *noun* a man who is only interested in having sex (and not a relationship) *UK, 2002*

shag-nasty *noun* an unpopular person *UK, 1961*

shag pad *noun* a premises used for sexual liaisons *UK, 2003*

shag-rag *noun* a tabloid newspaper that relies on sexual content for a healthy circulation. Combines SHAG (the sex act) with RAG (a newspaper) *UK, 2000*

shagspot *noun* a pimple (to which adolescents are prey); hence, also used as a nickname (not necessarily for the afflicted) *UK, 1968*

shagtastic *adjective* wonderful, especially in a sexual context *UK, 2002*

shag wagon; shaggin wagon; shaggin'-wagon *noun* a panel van, station wagon or the like used for sexual encounters *AUSTRALIA, 1966*

shag-worthy *adjective* sexually attractive; sexy *AUSTRALIA, 1985*

shaka *adjective* excellent. Hawaiian youth usage *US, 1981*

shaka used as a greeting or to signify fraternity. Spoken in conjunction with a hand signal that emphasizes the little finger and thumb. Hawaiian youth usage *US, 1981*

shake *noun* **1** a moment, an instant of time. Most often used in all manner of elaborations: 'in a shake' (C19), 'in the shake of a hand' (C19, probably obsolete), 'in a brace of shakes' (mid-C19), 'in a couple of shakes' (mid-C19), 'in two shakes' (late C19); later C20 variations are more whimsical: 'in the shake of a lamb's tail', 'in the shake of a dead lamb's tail', 'in two shakes of a lamb's whiff-whoff' (mid-C20), 'two shakes of a donkey's tail' and 'two shakes of a monkey's tail' *UK, 1962*. **2** marijuana, especially the resinous matter that is shaken to the bottom during transit or what remains after the buds have been removed *US, 1978*. **3** any adulterant added to cocaine powder *US, 1989*. **4** a party; a rent party *US, 1946*. **5** a blunt demand for money supported by the threat of physical force. A shortened form of SHAKEDOWN *US, 1953* ▷ *see:* SHAKE AND SHIVER

shake *verb* **1** to search a person's clothing and body *US, 1972*. **2** to get rid of someone or something *US, 1872*. ▶ **shake a leg** to hurry, to get a move on. Extends from the sense 'to dance'; generally used in the imperative *US, 1904*. ▶ **shake hands** (of a male) to urinate. The indirect object has been euphemistically omitted *AUSTRALIA, 1962*. ▶ **shake hands with an old friend 1** used by a male as a jocular euphemism when excusing himself to go and urinate *US, 1994*. **2** (of a male) to masturbate. After the previous sense *UK, 1984*. ▶ **shake hands with him 1** (of a male) to urinate. An allusion to the penis *UK, 1984*. **2** (of a male) to masturbate *UK, 1984*. ▶ **shake hands with Mr Right** (of a male) to urinate. Mr Right is what every woman is searching for, hence this humorous reference to the penis *UK, 1960*. ▶ **shake hands with my friend** (of a male) to urinate. A humorous allusion to the penis; a variation of SHAKE HANDS WITH AN OLD FRIEND *UK, 2000*. ▶ **shake hands with the Devil** (of either sex) to masturbate *US, 1975*. ▶ **shake hands with the unemployed** (of a male) to urinate. The notion behind 'unemployed' is a wry admission that the man in question has not been getting any sex of late *AUSTRALIA, 1972*. ▶ **shake hands with the wife's best friend** (of a male) to urinate; to masturbate *AUSTRALIA, 1968*. ▶ **shake leg** to idle *SINGAPORE, 2002*. ▶ **shake the bushes; shake the leaves; shake the trees** to look for the police, especially so as to warn other drivers. Citizens' band radio slang *US, 1976*. ▶ **shake the leaves** in a group of trucks travelling down the motorway together, to drive in the lead position, risking first contact with police watching for speeders *US, 1976*. ▶ **shake the trees** to drive in the lead position in a group of trucks travelling on a motorway together in a group effort to avoid speeding tickets while driving fast *US, 1976*. ▶ **shake them up** on the railways, to switch wagons or trains *US, 1946*. ▶ **shake white coconuts from the veiny love tree** (of a male) to masturbate. Coinage credited to surreal BBC comedy *The League of Gentlemen UK, 2001*. ▶ **shake your booty** to dance in a lively manner. Literally, 'to shake your buttocks' *US, 1978*. ▶ **shake your skirt** (of a woman) to go dancing *US, 1989*

shake 'n' vac *noun* an act of male masturbation, especially when performed by one sexual partner upon another. Shake 'n' Vac™ is a household cleaning product that achieved cult status as the result of a 1970s television commercial. During the all-singing and dancing demonstration, 'Do the Shake 'n' Vac / and put the freshness back' an attractive actress shook the tube-shaped packaging and white powder was scattered – the perfect metaphor *UK, 2001*

shake and bake noun **1** a non-commissioned officer fresh out of training US, 1985. **2** a portable fire shelter used by workers fighting forest fires US, 1991

shake and shiver; shake noun a river UK, 1960

shakedown noun **1** a search of a person or place US, 1914. **2** an act of extortion US, 1902

shake down verb **1** to search a person or a place US, 1915. **2** to extort US, 1872

shakers noun a bar featuring topless dancers US, 1994

shaker wire noun a motion-detector system used for perimeter security in prisons US, 1996

shakes noun any disease or condition characterised by trembling, especially *delirium tremens* UK, 1782

shake-up noun a mixture of wine and corn whisky US, 1973

Shakey Isles nickname New Zealand. Noted for its earthquakes AUSTRALIA, 1933

shake your shirt! hurry up! NEW ZEALAND, 2002

shakey side noun the west coast of the US, especially California. A term popularised during the citizens' band radio craze of 1976, recognised by many but used by few. A reference to the seismic instability of the west coast US, 1976

Shakies noun New Zealand. From the sobriquet 'the shakey isles' AUSTRALIA, 1989

Shaky noun a Chevrolet car US, 1965

shaky jake nickname the Jacobs radial engine, powering Canadian-built variants of the Anson, a training and liaison aircraft CANADA, 1995

sham noun a streetwise young male; a friend; an untrustworthy individual IRELAND, 1989

sham verb during the Vietnam war, to fabricate an injury or aggravate a real injury in the hope of being sent home US, 1991

sham-battle verb to engage in youth gang warfare US, 1949

shambolic adjective disordered, chaotic. From 'shambles' UK, 1958

sham dunk noun in poker, a poor hand that wins a pot as a result of successful bluffing US, 1996

shame-face adjective shy CAYMAN ISLANDS, 1985

shameful! used as a humorous admission that you have been cleverly ridiculed US, 1963

shame out verb to ridicule vociferously US, 1963

shameration noun the epitome of shame US, 1963

shammer noun a soldier who prolongs a legitimate absence from the frontline to avoid combat US, 1970

shampoo noun **1** champagne. A soundalike pun UK, 1957. **2** a scene in a pornographic film or photograph depicting a man ejaculating onto a person's hair US, 1995

shamrock noun MDMA, the recreational drug best known as ecstasy UK, 1998

shamshes noun good-looking men. Possibly back slang from 'smashers' UK, 1947

shamus noun a police detective; a private detective US, 1925

shanghai noun **1** a sudden and unexpected transfer of a prisoner to another facility as a form of punishment AUSTRALIA, 1977. **2** a handheld catapult. Probably from northern British dialect *shangie*, a variant of *shangan*, from Scottish Gaelic *seangan*: 'a cleft stick for putting on a dog's tail' AUSTRALIA, 1863

shanghai verb **1** to abduct someone; to compel someone to do something. From military usage, 'to transfer forcibly' US, 1934. **2** to transfer a prisoner without warning AUSTRALIA, 1980. **3** to detail someone to a task; to enlist someone to do something that they are not entirely willing to do. From US nautical slang describing a method of recruiting sailors consisting of drugs and force US, 1915

Shania Twain; shania noun a pain. Rhyming slang, formed from the name of the popular Canadian singer (b.1965) UK, 2003

shank noun a homemade knife or stabbing and slashing weapon US, 1967

shank verb to stab someone, especially with a homemade weapon US, 1955

shanks's pony noun walking, as a mode of transport. Ultimately from 'shank' (the leg) UK, 1898

shant noun a drink; a drinking session UK, 1999

shant verb to drink heavily UK: SCOTLAND, 2002

shantoozy noun a female singer. A corruption of *chanteuse* UK, 2002

shanty noun **1** a brakevan (caboose) US, 1977. **2** in poker, a hand consisting of three cards of the same rank and a pair. Conventionally known as a 'full house' US, 1988

shanty Irish noun poor Irish immigrants US, 1970

shantyman's smallpox noun marks from hard physical fighting CANADA, 1965

shape noun **1** a person of unconventional physical appearance. Disparaging UK: SCOTLAND, 1985. **2** a surfboard AUSTRALIA, 1963

shape verb **1** to improve your behaviour or attitude UK, 1960. **2** to adopt a fighting stance; to prepare to fight UK, 1855

shapes noun dice altered by cheats so as to be not true cubes US, 1950

shape up or ship out! used as a last warning to someone whose ways need mending US, 1956

shareware noun computer software that is freely available but for which the developer asks a payment US, 1988

shark noun **1** an unscrupulous businessman or lawyer given to unethical practice and exploitation. Derives from the voracious appetites and predatory behaviour of the fish UK, 1713. **2** a loan shark US, 1990. **3** a swindler. The variant 'sharkie' also exists UK, 1599

shark verb in a dice game such as craps, to make a controlled (cheating) throw of the dice US, 1950

shark and tatties noun fish and chips NEW ZEALAND, 1984

shark bait noun **1** a person who swims out past the surf at a beach; a person in shark-infested waters AUSTRALIA, 1920. **2** a person with very pale skin. Hawaiian youth usage US, 1982

shark city noun Looe, Cornwall UK, 1981

shark-fucker noun a surfer AUSTRALIA, 1987

sharking noun **1** among women, the practice of man-hunting; subsequently also used by men hunting women. Also used in the verb form 'shark'. In 1999, in answer to the question 'What are you doing tonight?' a professional Soho media-type in her mid-20s offered a non-verbal shorthand: she placed both hands palm to palm above her head in imitation of a shark's fin UK, 1999. **2** the illegal loaning of money at extremely high interest rates US, 1974

shark meat noun an easy victim of a cheat, swindler or hustler US, 1990

sharky adjective used of a surfboard nose, pointed US, 1991

Sharon; Shaz noun a stereotypical working-class young woman. Pejorative, in the sense that such a woman is socially unacceptable; from a name widely associated in the 1980s and 90s with that generation and class. Shaz is a diminutive of Sharon UK, 1994

Sharon Stone; sharon noun a telephone, especially a mobile phone. Rhyming slang, formed from the name of the US film actress (b.1958) UK, 1998

sharp noun **1** in gambling, a cheat. A shortened from of SHARPER UK, 1797. **2** a number sign (#) on a computer keyboard US, 1991

sharp adjective stylish, fashionable, attractive US, 1944. ▶ **you are so sharp you'll cut yourself** used to note someone's (over-) cleverness, also to reprove someone for that over-cleverness; especially implying a sharp-tongued cleverness UK, 1910

sharp and blunt noun the vagina. Rhyming slang for CUNT UK, 1937

sharpen verb ▶ **sharpen the pencil** to have sex. Possibly derisive, the use of 'pencil' indicates a small penis US, 2001. ▶ **sharpen your pencil** to reduce the price UK, 1997

sharp end noun in any given endeavour, the position which is exposed to the greatest difficulty or criticism; the vanguard. From the nautical use as 'the bow of a ship' UK, 1976

sharper *noun* in gambling, a cheater *UK, 1681*

sharpering omee; sharper *noun* a police officer. Polari; a variation of CHARPERER; CHARPERING OMEE *UK, 2002*

sharper's tool *noun* a fool. Rhyming slang *UK, 1937*

sharpest *adjective* ▶ **not the sharpest tool in the box** applied to someone of below average intelligence *UK, 2002*

sharpie *noun* **1** a gambling cheat *US, 1942*. **2** in pinball, a player who can play for long periods of time without paying because of his ability to win free games *US, 1977*. **3** a stylishly dressed teenage delinquent. From SHARP (stylish). During the 1960s and 70s only, coming after the BODGIE and WIDGIE and preceding PUNK ROCK *AUSTRALIA, 1965*. **4** an uncircumcised penis *US, 2002*

sharpish *adverb* quickly *UK, 1984*

sharps *noun* a hypodermic needle and syringe. Drug addict usage, borrowed from the medical terminology for any skin-piercing device *US, 1994*

sharpshoot *verb* to question a speaker after a lecture *US, 1968*

sharpshooter *noun* **1** a man whose wife is always pregnant; a man whose children are of the desired sex *FIJI, 1994*. **2** an intravenous drug user who usually hits a vein on the first attempt to inject a drug *US, 1986*. **3** in electric line work, a narrow blade shovel used in hard dirt *US, 1980*. **4** in oil drilling, a long, narrow shovel *US, 1954*

sharp top *noun* in a deck of playing cards, an ace *US, 1988*

shasta *noun* a sexual partner who is not particularly attractive, but who was available at the time. An allusion to Shasta™ soda, not especially liked but available and inexpensive *US, 2001*

shat *verb* ▶ **shat along on my uppers** to have fallen on hard times *CANADA, 1999*. ▶ **shat it** to have been frightened into giving up. A variation in the past tense of SHIT IT (to be afraid) *UK, 2000*

shat on *adjective* having been insulted and humilated. The past tense of SHIT ON *UK, 2000*

shattered *adjective* **1** very tired, exhausted *UK, 1930*. **2** emotionally battered; depressed. Prison usage *NEW ZEALAND, 1997*. **3** very drunk *UK, 1962*

shave *noun* a man with a shaved head; a shaved head. Unlike the SKINHEAD, a 'shave' has no racist or Nazi ideology *NEW ZEALAND, 1997*

shave *verb* **1** to alter the edges or surfaces of dice for use by a cheat *US, 1974*. **2** in hot rodding, to remove body trim from a car prepatory to customising the car *US, 1950s to 70s*. ▶ **shave points** to reduce scoring during a sports contest in furtherance of a gambling conspiracy *US, 1982*

shave and a haircut – two bits describes a particular repeated musical phrase that is characterised by the rhythm of the words in the spoken phrase. This musical RIFF is often credited to guitarist Bo Diddley (b.1928) but the rhythm was already familiar as a pattern of raps used for door-knocking *CANADA, 1940*

shave off *verb* to deliver a severe reprimand; to rant disapprovingly on any topic. Royal Navy slang *UK, 1989*

shave off! used to denote surprise, disgust, frustration or amazement. The Royal Navy is the only arm of the UK military that may allow a beard to be worn, hence the adoption, as expletive, of the order 'Shave off!' *UK, 1989*

shaver *noun* **1** a discounter of notes, at high interest rates *CANADA, 1946*. **2** in the Korean war, a booby trap used by South Korean troops to sabotage North Korean transportation carts *US, 1982*

shave-tail *noun* **1** a cigarette stub *US, 1949*. **2** a newly promoted second lieutenant *US, 1970*

shazam!; shazzam! used for registering triumph. An incantatory ritual from the comic book character created by Bill Parker and C.C. Beck in 1940 – a metaphorically God-like character whose name is called on by the superhero Captain Marvel in moments of crisis; Shazam is an acronym of *Solomon* (wisdom), *Hercules* (strength), *Atlas* (stamina), *Zeus* (power), *Achilles* (courage) and *Mercury* (speed) *US, 1940*

she *noun* **1** cocaine *US, 1958*. **2** used of an effeminate homosexual man, he *UK, 1950*. **3** the penis. An owner's usage, in much the same way a boat or a car is often identified *UK, 1922*

shears *noun* playing cards that have been trimmed for cheating *US, 1961*

shebang *noun* any thing, matter or business at issue at the moment. Usually as 'the whole shebang'. The former senses of 'a hut', 'vehicle' or 'tavern' are all but forgotten *US, 1869*

shebang *verb* to ingest cocaine by spraying a solution of cocaine and water up the nose *UK, 2002*

shebeen *noun* an unlicensed drinking place. Irish *síbín* (illicit whisky) led to original use in Ireland. Adopted in the C20 for use in South African townships and UK West Indian communities *IRELAND, 1847*

she-bill; she-note *noun* a two-dollar note *US, 1996*

shed *noun* in poker, a hand consisting of three cards of the same rank and a pair. Known conventionally as a 'full house' *US, 1988*. ▶ **off your shed** in a state of mental confusion, insane. A variation of OFF YOUR HEAD *UK, 1991*

shed *verb* in poker, to discard a card or cards *US, 1967*

shedded *adjective* drunk. Recorded by 'e-cyclopaedia', BBC News, 20th March 2002, with the somewhat oblique explanation 'as in "My shed has collapsed taking most of the fence with it"' *UK, 2003*

shedder *noun* a moulting lobster *US, 1978*

shedful *noun* a great quantity. A variation of SHED LOAD *UK, 2002*

shed load; shedloads *noun* a great quantity. Probably euphemistic for SHITLOAD rather than a genuinely approximate measure *UK, 1997*

shed row *noun* in horse racing, the row of barns where horses are stabled *US, 1951*

sheeba *noun* a sensimilla variety of marijuana; a type of hashish produced from the pollen of the plant. Derived, perhaps, from CHIBA (a marijuana variety) *US, 2003*

Sheela *noun* an effeminate man or boy. Defined by Bernard Share in *Slanguage*, 2003, as a man or boy who takes an interest in 'affairs properly belonging to women' *IRELAND, 2003*

sheen *noun* a car. An abbreviation of 'machine' *US, 1968*

Sheena *noun* a melodramatic black homosexual male. From the comic book, *Sheena, Queen of the Jungle* *US, 1980*

sheeny *noun* a Jewish person *UK, 1816*

sheep *noun* a woman who volunteers to take part in serial sex with members of a motorcyle club or gang *US, 1972*

sheep-dipping *noun* the use of military equipment or personnel in an intelligence operation under civilian cover *US, 1989*

sheep-fucker *noun* a New Zealander *AUSTRALIA, 1991*

sheep-herder *noun* an inferior driver *US, 1976*

sheepie *noun* hair permed into a fleece of curls *UK, 2001*

sheep's back *noun* the wool industry *AUSTRALIA, 1962*

sheep's eyes *noun* a look that indicates attraction or sexual interest *UK, 1811*

sheepshagger; sheep shagger *noun* **1** a native of Wales. Literally, 'someone who has sex with sheep'; derogatory *UK, 1997*. **2** a New Zealander. Reflecting the high density population of sheep in New Zealand *UK, 2000*. **3** an Australian *NEW ZEALAND, 1999*

sheepshagging *adjective* contemptible *UK, 2002*

sheepskin *noun* **1** a university diploma *US, 1843*. **2** an executive criminal pardon *US, 1962*. **3** a condom *US, 1991*

sheero *noun* the head. English gypsy use *UK, 2000*

sheesh *adjective* very stylish; unnecessarily ornamented; elaborate; fussy. Probably from French slang *chichi* (used of affected looks and manners) *UK, 1967*

sheesh! used as a mild expletive. Euphemistic for, and possibly a slovening of, 'Jesus!' *US, 1997*

sheet *noun* **1** a police record of arrests and convictions. Probably a shortened RAP SHEET, but earlier sources for 'sheet' than this raise questions *US, 1958*. **2** a one-pound note; £1 in value. This survived, perhaps surprisingly, the introduction of the coin in 1983 *UK, 1968*. **3** a newspaper *US, 1981*. **4** one hundred doses of LSD soaked into paper *US, 1999*

sheet *verb* to charge someone with a criminal offence. Police use *UK, 2002*

sheet! used for registering surprise, rage, etc. May be a euphemism or an emphasised pronunciation of SHIT! depending on your needs *US, 1995*

sheet rocking *noun* a combination of crack cocaine and LSD *UK, 2003*

sheets *noun* a daily report of recent criminal activity, circulated among police going on shift *US, 1975.* ▶ **between the sheets** in bed, especially in a reference to sex *UK, 1865*

sheet writer; writer *noun* in an illegal sports betting operation or lottery; a functionary who takes and records bets *US, 1949*

sheezy *noun* ▶ **for sheezy** a very attractive teenager or young woman. Adopted from FO' SHEEZY (certainly) *SOUTH AFRICA, 2003*

she-he *noun* a transvestite or transgender person *US, 1970*

sheila *noun* a woman; a girl. From the given name Sheila. In the C19 spelt 'shelah' and 'shaler', settling down to its current form in the early part of the C20. Although not highly derogatory it certainly is not complimentary, and many women take exception to it. Women as a rule do not refer to other women as 'sheilas' *AUSTRALIA, 1832*

shekels *noun* money. From the ancient Babylonian unit of weight and coin *US, 1883*

shelf *noun* **1** an informer *AUSTRALIA, 1916.* **2** solitary confinement *US, 1967.* **3** in circus and carnival usage, an upper sleeping berth *US, 1981.* ▶ **on the shelf** unlikely to marry *UK, 1839*

shelf *verb* to inform on someone *AUSTRALIA, 1936*

shelf life *noun* the period of time during which something or someone remains popular or in demand. From the literal sense meaning the period of time during which a product may be stored and remain suitable for use *US, 1996*

shelfware *noun* a computer program bought but not used *US, 1991*

shell *noun* **1** a bullet. From the conventional senses as 'an explosive projectile' or 'cartridge case' *UK, 2001.* **2** a person who is somewhat lacking in mental faculties *US, 2002.* **3** a safe with a thin door and walls *US, 1950*

shell *verb* to move quickly, most likely derived from Shell Motor Spirit *BARBADOS, 1965*

shellacking *noun* a beating; a defeat *US, 1931*

shell back *noun* a reactionary. Originally nautical, meaning 'an experienced sailor' *UK, 1943*

she'll be right everything will be okay *AUSTRALIA, 1947*

she'll be sweet everything will be all right *AUSTRALIA, 1957*

shell-like *noun* the ear. Extracted from the phrase WORD IN YOUR SHELL-LIKE *UK, 1994*

Shell Mex *noun* sex. Rhyming slang, formed from the oil company *UK, 1992*

shell out *verb* to pay *UK, 1801*

shells *noun* money. Probably adapted from 'clamshell' ($1) *UK, 1997*

shemale *noun* a transvestite, transsexual or other transgender person; a person with mixed sexual physiology, usually the genitals of a male and surgically augmented breasts *US, 1954*

shemozzle; schemozzle; schlemozzle *noun* a fuss; an altercation; a difficulty; an unfortunate incident. An East End corruption of German *schlimm* (bad) and Hebrew *mazel* (luck), thus Yiddish *schlimazel* (an unlucky person) *UK, 1889*

shenanigans *noun* trickery; mischief *US, 1855*

shepherd *noun* a firefighter assigned to a hook-and-ladder truck. Probably named for the hook which he carries, evocative of a shepherd's staff *US, 1954*

shepherd *verb* in croquet, to guide your ball illegally through the hoop by pushing with your mallet *US, 1977*

Shepherd's Bush *noun* **1** dismissal from employment. Rhyming slang for THE PUSH, from an area of west London *UK, 1992.* **2** the face. Rhyming slang for MUSH (the face), from an area of west London *UK, 1998*

shepherd's pie; shepherd's *noun* the sky. Rhyming slang *UK, 1992*

shepherd's plaid; shepherds *adjective* bad. Rhyming slang *UK, 1932*

sherbert; sherbet *noun* alcoholic drink, especially beer; a drink of beer. Originally (late C19) any warm alcoholic drink; ultimately Turkish *sherbet* (a cooling non-alcoholic drink) *AUSTRALIA, 1904*

sherbet dab; sherbet *noun* a taxi, a *cab.* Rhyming slang *UK, 1998*

sherbet dip *noun* a gratuity, a *tip.* Rhyming slang *UK, 1992*

Sheridan Morley *adverb* unwell. Rhyming slang for 'poorly'; based on the name of noted author, radio presenter and theatre critic Sheridan Morley (b.1941) *UK, 2001*

sherm *noun* **1** a marijuana cigarette that has been supplemented with phencyclidine, the recreational drug known as PCP or angel dust. From Shermans™, a cigarette brand *US, 1982.* **2** crack cocaine *US, 1993.* **3** a social outcast *US, 1998*

sherman tank; sherman *noun* **1** an American. Rhyming slang for YANK, based on the main US battle tank of World War 2 *UK, 1979.* **2** an act of masturbation. Rhyming slang for WANK *UK, 1992*

shermed *adjective* intoxicated with phencyclide, an animal tranquilizer *US, 1990*

sherms *noun* **1** phencyclidine, the recreational drug known as PCP or angel dust *US, 1981.* **2** crack cocaine *US, 1994*

Sherwin-Williams overhaul *noun* in the used car business, a paint job and no further effort to repair or restore a car for sale. Sherwin-Williams is a paint manufacturer *US, 1992*

she-she *adjective* effeminate *BARBADOS, 1965*

she's right that's okay; everything is all right *AUSTRALIA, 1938*

sheuch *noun* the cleft between the buttocks. Glasgow slang from broader Scots *sheuch* (a trench, a ditch) *UK: SCOTLAND, 1996.* ▶ **up the sheuch** mistaken *UK: SCOTLAND, 1996*

shibby *noun* a man who does housework *UK: SCOTLAND, 1996*

shibby *adjective* positive; pleasing. Probably coined by Phil Ashton for the 2001 film *Dude Where's My Car?* in which it is used as a replacement for nouns, verbs, adjectives, proper names, etc.; the original intention in the film was to use the word to mean 'marijuana'; when all drugs references were removed the word remained. This multi-purpose word is also used as a replacement for any verb, and as a lover's nickname *US, 2004*

shicer; sheister *noun* a despicable man; a cheat; a welsher. From German *scheisser* (a shitter) *UK, 1846*

shick *noun* a slice, a share, a rake-off. Perhaps from Schick, a US manufacturer of safety and electric razors since 1926 *UK, 1968*

shicker; shickered; schicker *adjective* drunk. From Yiddish *shiker* (drunk); like many words for 'intoxicated' (or the causes thereof), there are a number of understandably inconsistent spellings, including: 'shiker', 'shikker', 'shikkered', 'shikkured' and 'shikkared' *AUSTRALIA, 1898*

shield *noun* a police officer *US, 1965*

shift *verb* **1** to move or be moved from prison to prison *UK, 1996.* **2** to engage in sexual activity. The exact type of sexual activity is not specified, unlike, for example, RIDE which implies penetrative sex *IRELAND, 1998.* ▶ **shift your arse; shift your ass** to start moving; to move with speed *UK, 1996.* ▶ **shift your cock** (of a man) to start moving; to move with speed *UK, 1997*

shiftless *noun* in the car sales business, equipped with an automatic transmission *US, 1953*

shifty *noun* sex with a prostitute *US, 1954*

shikse; shiksa; shixa *noun* a Gentile woman *UK, 1892*

shikse from Dixie *noun* the ultimate in Gentile femininity. The reference to Dixie is soley for the rhyme; it does not connote that the woman in question is from the south *US, 1945*

shill *noun* **1** in a confidence swindle, a confederate who appears to be prospering as a result of the scheme which is designed to fleece the victim *US, 1940.* **2** a person posing as an enthusiastic and satisfied customer in order to boost sales by a confederate *US, 1916*

shill *verb* to pose falsely as a satisfied customer or successful gambler in order to encourage genuine customers, gamblers, etc *US, 1914*

shillelagh *noun* **1** in hot rodding, a Chevrolet engine, especially a V-8. Only related to the Irish *blackthorn cudgel* in sound *US, 1965*. **2** in horse racing, a jockey's whip *AUSTRALIA, 1989*

shillings *noun* money *UK, 2000*

shillings and pence; shillings *noun* sense. Rhyming slang, updated to POUNDS AND PENCE in the wake of 1971's decimalisation *UK, 1992*

shilly-shally *verb* to be undecided; to hesitate. Rarely heard in the US, but understood in context *UK, 1782*

shilly-shallying *noun* indecision, hesitation *UK, 1842*

shim *noun* **1** a plastic strip used for forcing locks *US, 1968*. **2** a person whose sex is not easily guessed on the basis of their hair and clothing *US, 1970*

shim *verb* to force a lock with a plastic strip *US, 1972*

shimmy *noun* **1** the game *chemin de fer US, 1961*. **2** an undershirt. Perhaps an abbreviation of 'chemise' *NORFOLK ISLAND, 1992*

shimmy act *noun* a feigned seizure *US, 1988*

shimmy dancer *noun* a woman who performs sexual dances *US, 1962*

shindig *noun* a party. A rural term that moved to the city; it gained wide usage as a result of the musical television programme *Shindig* which aired on ABC from September 1964 until January 1966 *US, 1871*

shine *noun* **1** a black person. Abusive in any context *US, 1908*. **2** a government bureaucrat. From the shine on the seat of the bureaucrat's trousers *US, 1987*. **3** alcohol *US, 1933*. **4** a still used in the illegal production of alcohol *US, 1974*. **5** an act of oral sex. A possible play on spit and polish as a means of getting a shine; it seems only to have been noted in the plural *UK, 2002*. ▶ **take a shine to someone** to take a liking to someone or something *US, 1839*

shine *verb* **1** to speak evasively and avoid a subject, often through flattery *US, 1993*. **2** to mock someone *US, 1993*. **3** on the railways, to start a work shift *US, 1977*. ▶ **shine for someone** to appeal to someone *US, 1949*. ▶ **shine on** to ignore something completely *US, 1981*

shine box *noun* a nightclub for an exclusively black clientele; a nightclub providing entertainment by black jazz musicians. Combines SHINE (a black person) and otherwise obsolete 'box' (a tavern, from French *boîte*) *US, 1940*

shine parlour *noun* an establishment that sells alcohol illegally, by the drink. The 'shine' is an abbreviated MOONSHINE *US, 1978*

shiner *noun* **1** a black eye *US, 1904*. **2** a torch *US, 1950*. **3** a railway lantern *US, 1946*. **4** in carnival usage, a diamond *US, 1981*. **5** in gambling, an object that reflects, enabling the user to cheat by seeing cards as they are dealt *US, 1997*

shiner player *noun* in gambling, a cheat who uses a shiny object to reflect the cards as they are dealt *US, 1997*

shiney *noun* a clerk. A reference to the shiny seat of a clerk's trousers – caused by an excess of sitting down. In Royal Air Force use, 2002 *UK, 2002*

shin fight *noun* a sham gang fight *US, 1958*

shingle *noun* **1** a name plate above a prison cell door *US, 1961*. **2** a car number plate *US, 1976*. **3** a lawyer *US, 1958*. ▶ **a shingle short** lacking a full complement of intelligence. From 'shingle' (a wooden roofing tile), thus 'a shingle short of a roof' *AUSTRALIA, 1844*

shining time *noun* starting time for work *US, 1946*

Shinner *noun* a member of Sinn Fein *IRELAND, 1921*

shinola *noun* used as a contrast in describing ignorance as not knowing shit from shinola. Shinola was a patented name (1903) for a boot polish *US, 1940*

shinplaster *noun* a dollar *CANADA, 1963*

shiny and bright; shiny *adjective* right. Rhyming slang *UK, 1992*

shiny-arse *noun* a desk worker. Disparaging. During World War 2 used of base personnel who saw no combat *AUSTRALIA, 1945*

shiny buttons *noun* money *US, 1947*

shiny wing pilot *noun* a pilot who has just completed his flight instruction training *US, 1963*

ship *noun* ▶ **on the ship** in prison, an unofficially worded instruction for immediate transfer to another prison *UK, 1996*

ship; ship out; ship off *verb* to move or be moved from prison to prison *US, 1950*

ship driver *noun* a US Navy officer. Gulf war usage *US, 1992*

shipfucker *noun* a rabble rouser; a troublemaker *US, 1970*

ship in full sail; ship *noun* ale. Rhyming slang *UK, 1857*

shipoopi *noun* a woman *US, 1954*

shippie *noun* a prostitute focused on visiting sailors as customers *NEW ZEALAND, 1999*

ship's anchor *noun* a contemptible person. Rhyming slang for WANKER *UK, 2003*

ship-tick *noun* in college, a notification of academic deficiency *US, 1968*

shiralee *noun* a swag. Now only historical *AUSTRALIA, 1892*

shirt-lifter *noun* a male homosexual *AUSTRALIA, 1966*

shirty *adjective* angry, especially if only temporarily; characteristically ill-tempered. From 'shirt' as a symbol of anger in such obsolete phrases as: 'lose your shirt' or 'have your shirt out' (to become angry) *UK, 1897*

Shishkaberry *noun* in British Columbia, a local hybrid strain of marijuana *CANADA, 2002*

shishkebob *noun* the penis. Rhyming slang for KNOB (the penis); based on the appropriately shaped Turkish dish shish kebab (roast meat on a skewer) *US, 1999*

shisty *adjective* cold-hearted, mean *US, 2004*

shit *noun* **1** heroin *US, 1950*. **2** marijuana *US, 1946*. **3** crack cocaine *UK, 1996*. **4** narcotics; drugs in general *US, 1967*. **5** things; possessions *US, 1969*. **6** anything at all *US, 1995*. **7** nothing; something of no value *IRELAND, 1922*. **8** et cetera *US, 1999*. **9** used as a basis for extreme comparisons *US, 1957*. **10** a foul mood *AUSTRALIA, 1973*. **11** trouble *US, 1937*. **12** a contemptible person. Figurative use of excrement, since C16; often in combination as 'regular shit', 'arrogant shit', etc *UK, 1508*. **13** criticism *UK, 2003*. **14** abuse; unfair treatment *UK, 1980*. **15** nonsense *UK, 1930*. **16** used as a term of endearment. Especially common in the phrase 'little shit' *US, 1970*. **17** business *US, 1994*. **18** in the recording industry, a hit single *US, 1982*. **19** excrement; an act of defecation. Conventional from the C16, since the C19 has been considered vulgar *UK, 1585*. **20** used as a meaningless discourse marker *UK, 1997*. **21** a bombardment, especially with shrapnel. A military usage recorded in use in the Falkland Islands during 1982 *UK, 1931*. ▶ **all about like shit in a field** everywhere *UK, 1999*. ▶ **drop someone in the shit** to get someone blamed and into trouble. A variation of LAND IN THE SHIT; a conventional sense of 'drop' combined with IN THE SHIT (in trouble) *UK, 2001*. ▶ **fall in the shit** to get into trouble. A conventional sense of 'fall' combined with IN THE SHIT; leading to the clichéd envy of 'he could fall in the shit and come out smelling of roses' *UK, 1984*. ▶ **get your shit together** to take control of your personal condition; to get your mind and emotions under control; to become organised. A variation of 'pull yourself together' *US, 1969*. ▶ **give a shit** to care, to be concerned – usually in a negative context *UK, 1970s*. ▶ **have shit for brains** to be stupid; to lack intelligence *AUSTRALIA, 1986*. ▶ **have shit on the liver** to be irritable *AUSTRALIA, 1935*. ▶ **have your shit together; get your shit together** to be focused, organised, self-confident *US, 1970*. ▶ **in deep shit** in serious trouble *US, 1999*. ▶ **in the shit 1** in considerable trouble. You can be IN DEEP SHIT, FALL IN THE SHIT or LAND (someone else) IN THE SHIT *UK, 1937*. **2** in combat *US, 1987*. ▶ **land in the shit** to get someone blamed and into trouble. A conventional sense of 'land' (to set down) combined with IN THE SHIT, generally heard as 'landed (someone) in the shit' *UK, 1984*. ▶ **like shit off a shovel** extremely fast, swift, prompt *UK, 1998*. ▶ **not for shit** of a person's ability to do something, not at all, by no means, not in any circumstances *UK, 2001*. ▶ **run shit down** to discuss something; to inform someone; to explain something *US, 1970*. ▶ **talk shit** to say disparaging things *UK, 1993*. ▶ **the shit** the best *US, 1990*. ▶ **the shit will fly** there will be trouble *UK, 1974*. ▶ **three kinds of shit** a lot of trouble *AUSTRALIA, 1995*. ▶ **treat someone like shit** to treat someone in a disdainful or humiliating manner *UK, 1999*.

▶ **up to shit** no good; hopeless AUSTRALIA, 1978. ▶ **when the shit hits the fan; when the shit flies** the moment when a crisis starts, especially if such trouble has been expected UK, 1966.
▶ **you're shit and you know you are** used by football fans as a chant to disparage (and enrage) the opposing team and fans UK, 2001

shit verb **1** to defecate. Conventional English for about 500 years from the C14, then, sometime in the C19, slipped into vulgarity UK, 1308. **2** to deceive someone; to lie to someone or stretch the truth. An abbreviated form of BULLSHIT US, 1934. ▶ **shit a brick** to have a difficult time accepting something; to react with anger US, 1971. ▶ **shit all over** to surpass someone or something by a great degree UK, 2003. ▶ **shit in** to win easily or by a large margin AUSTRALIA, 1979. ▶ **shit it** to be very nervous or worried; to be thoroughly frightened. An allusion to the bowel-loosening effect of terror UK, 2000. ▶ **shit it in** to do something with ease AUSTRALIA, 1992. ▶ **shit nickels** to be very frightened US, 1968. ▶ **shit on someone** to disparage or abuse someone UK, 1984. ▶ **shit or get off the pot** to get out of the way and let someone else try to do it; make your mind up. Originally directed at dice players CANADA, 1966. ▶ **shit the life out of someone** to frighten someone. Variation of conventional 'scare the life out of' combined with SCARE THE SHIT OUT OF UK, 1999. ▶ **shit your pants 1** to soil your underpants by accidental defecation UK, 2001. **2** to be terrified. To lose control over your excretory functions is noted as a symptom of extreme terror; however, this is used figuratively (most of the time), often as an exaggeration UK, 1994. ▶ **shit your shorts** to behave in a nervous or frightened manner US, 2002. ▶ **shit yourself** to be terrified. Losing control over your excretory functions is noted as a symptom of extreme terror; it is used here (and most of the time) in a figurative sense, certainly as an exaggeration UK, 1914.

shit adjective **1** inferior; shoddy; valueless; unpleasant; disliked for whatever reason UK, 1930. **2** unfashionable; in poor taste UK, 2001. **3** bad US, 1950. **4** despicable US, 1977. **5** good UK, 1996

shit! used for registering annoyance, frustration, despair, etc UK, 1920

shit a brick!; shit-a-brick!; shit on a brick! used for expressing annoyance, disgust or shock AUSTRALIA, 1968

shit-all noun nothing, nothing at all. A variation of FUCK ALL US, 1981

shit and a shave noun a short sentence of imprisonment. An inference that the sentence is for no more time than it takes to get ready to go out UK, 1996

shit and derision!; shit and corruption!; shit and molasses! used for registering annoyance and frustration. Originally air force, describing weather conditions UK, 1982

shit and git verb to leave quickly US, 1994

shit and shinola noun in poker, three two's US, 1948

shitaree noun a toilet UK, 1994

shit-ass adjective despicable, of poor quality US, 1967

shit-ass; shirt-arse noun a despicable person US, 1942

shitbag noun a despicable person or object UK, 1964

shitbag verb to denigrate or criticise someone or something AUSTRALIA, 1986

shitball noun a despicable person US, 1998

shitbird noun a despicable person US, 1952

shit-blitz noun an intensive media campaign of attack designed to present a negative image of someone or something UK, 2004

shit bowl noun a toilet US, 1967

shit box noun **1** the anus UK, 1997. **2** a despicable person AUSTRALIA, 1979. **3** a small and shoddy dwelling AUSTRALIA, 1995. **4** the Chevrolet Chevette US, 1992

shit-box adjective no good AUSTRALIA, 1995

shitbrains; shit-brain noun a stupid person US, 1970

shit-burner noun a person assigned to the task of cleaning out latrines, dousing the spoils with fuel and burning the mixture. Coined during the Vietnam war US, 1991

shitcan noun **1** any rubbish bin US, 1948. **2** a cheap car US, 1971

shitcan verb **1** to throw something away; to discharge someone from employment US, 1975. **2** to denigrate or criticise someone AUSTRALIA, 1950

shitcan adjective rubbishy UK, 1998

shit-chute noun the rectum US, 1977

shit creek noun ▶ **up shit creek; up shit creek without a paddle; up the creek** stranded, in trouble. Embellishments abound US, 1941

shitcunt noun a contemptible person; used as a harsh term of contempt. When neither SHIT nor CUNT is abusive enough this combination may serve UK, 1979

shit disturber noun a troublemaker US, 1977

shite noun excrement; hence rubbish. A variation on SHIT phonetically similar to German Scheiße UK, 1976. ▶ **give a shite** to care, to be concerned – usually in a negative context. A variation of GIVE A SHIT UK, 1971

shite adjective **1** poor quality, inferior UK, 1997. **2** awful; unhappy; emotionally upset UK, 2002

shite! used as an expression of frustration, anger, etc UK, 1937

shit-eater noun a coprophiliac US, 1996

shit-eating adjective sycophantic UK, 1974

shit-eating grin noun a broad smile, ingratiating and unctuous US, 1957

shite-awful adjective being of very inferior quality UK: SCOTLAND, 1996

shit eh! wow! AUSTRALIA, 1972

shitehawk noun a despicable, worthless person UK, 2000

shitehead noun a contemptible person; used as a general term of abuse. A variation of SHITHEAD UK, 1997

shitepoke noun a despicable person US, 1926

shiters noun ▶ **put the shiters up someone** to frighten someone UK: SCOTLAND, 1996

shiters adjective scared. From SHIT-SCARED (terrified) and other variations on the theme UK, 2002

shitey adjective faeces-covered; of poor quality UK: SCOTLAND, 1994

shit-face noun **1** a despised person UK, 1937. **2** used as an intensifier of the degree of intoxication US, 1977

shitfaced adjective drunk US, 1968

shitfire! used as an oath US, 1970

shit fit noun **1** a bad case of diarrhoea US, 1975. **2** a tantrum US, 1968

shit-for-brains adjective stupid US, 2003

shit-for-brains; shite-for-brains noun an idiot US, 1994

shit-fuck noun a despicable person AUSTRALIA, 1997

shit happens used for conveying the inevitability of misfortune. A tremendously popular catchphrase in the mid-to late 1980s in the US, spawning dozens of jokes with the predictable punch-line, tee-shirts with lists of various religions' interpretations of the phrase, etc US, 1983

shit-hawk noun a seagull CANADA, 1993

shithead noun an objectionable, obnoxious, despised person UK, 1961

shitheap noun a motor vehicle that is in poor repair or that lacks power AUSTRALIA, 1984

shitheel noun a despicable person US, 1935

shit heroin noun heroin, especially if of poor quality UK, 1950

shithole; shitehole noun **1** a bad place; a dirty, run-down or disreputable place US, 1965. **2** the anus UK, 1937

shithook noun **1** the hand US, 1970. **2** a thoroughly unpleasant person US, 1968. **3** a CH-47 Chinook helicopter. Vietnam war usage US, 1991

shit-hot noun a highly skilled fighter pilot US, 1983

shit hot adjective excellent, wonderful. A positive sense of SHIT intensifies HOT (popular, fashionable) UK, 1961

shithouse noun **1** a toilet bowl; a toilet; a lavatory UK, 1795. **2** a shoddy, dirty, unpleasant place US, 1973. **3** jail or prison US, 1969. **4** an extremely unpleasant individual *UK, 1999*. **5** a coward *UK, 2002*. ▶ **to the shithouse** to hell *AUSTRALIA, 1987*

shithouse *adjective* **1** disgusting, nasty, unpleasant *AUSTRALIA, 1971*. **2** no good; hopeless; abysmal *AUSTRALIA, 1973*

shithouse rumour *noun* gossip. A blunt version of the kinder and gentler 'latrine rumour' *US, 1968*

shitkicker *noun* **1** a tough, belligerent person *US, 1954*. **2** a country-dweller, a peasant *US, 1966*. **3** a person employed to do menial jobs *AUSTRALIA, 1950*. **4** a prostitute. Far less common than the term MUDKICKER *US, 1967*. **5** a fraudster, especially one who adopts a pose of extreme modesty *US, 1981*

shitkickers *noun* heavy work shoes or work boots *US, 1974*

shitless *adverb* completely, entirely, to a great degree *UK, 1936*

shitlips *noun* a person who talks nonsense. Extended from SHIT (rubbish, nonsense) with 'lips' representing the mouth that emits it *US, 1991*

shit list *noun* an imagined list of those in disfavour *US, 1942*

shitload *noun* a great deal of *US, 1991*

shitman used as an intensifier of what follows *US, 1967*

shitmobile *noun* a poor quality motor vehicle *AUSTRALIA, 1995*

shit-nasty *adjective* very unpleasant *UK, 2001*

shit off! go away! *UK, 1966*

shitogram *noun* an especially virulent e-mail message *US, 1991*

shit on a shingle *noun* minced or creamed beef on toast. A visual simile in UK military use, possibly of US origin *US, 1994*

shit on a string *noun* an elusive or difficult task *US, 1981*

shit or bust *verb* to make a determined final effort. A less extreme variation of RIP, SHIT OR BUST *UK, 2005*

shit order *noun* a dirty or untidy condition, especially when applied to military accommodation or equipment *UK, 1971*

shit-out *noun* a coward *UK, 2000*

shit out *verb* to run away; to yield *UK, 1999*

shit out of luck *adjective* very unlucky *US, 1983*

shitpacker *noun* an anal-sex enthusiast *US, 1964*

shit paper *noun* toilet paper *US, 1969*

shitparcel *noun* a prison officer *UK, 1996*

shitpicker *noun* a notional menial, demeaning job *US, 1971*

shit pie *noun* a comparative example for anything of no value *UK, 1999*

shit pit *noun* a field-latrine. Military *UK, 1995*

Shitport *nickname* Norfolk, Virginia *US, 1982*

shitpot *noun* **1** a contemptible, worthless individual *UK, 1937*. **2** a great deal of *US, 1968*. **3** marijuana of inferior quality. A combination of synonyms SHIT and POT *US, 2001*

shitpuncher *noun* a male homosexual *NEW ZEALAND, 1998*

shits *noun* ▶ **for shits and giggles** for no good reason. Something is done, for example, for shits and giggles *US, 2001*. ▶ **put the shits up someone** to frighten someone *UK, 2002*. ▶ **the shits** **1** diarrhoea *UK, 1947*. **2** the worst *US, 1971*. **3** fear. Following logically from the earlier sense as 'diarrhoea' *UK, 1967*

shit sandwich *noun* a troubling, odious situation *US, 1968*

shit-scared *adjective* terrified *UK, 1958*

shit-shaped *adjective* used of a prison cell that has been daubed with excrement. A pun on 'ship-shape'. From private correspondence with a serving prisoner in 2001 *UK, 2001*

shit, shave, shower, shine used as a jocular reminder of a man's tasks before going out on the town. Multiple variants, probably coined in the US Marine Corps as a pre-liberty litany *US, 1968*

shitshover *noun* a male homosexual. An obvious allusion to anal intercourse *UK, 1996*

shitstabber *noun* a male homosexual *UK, 2002*

shit stain *noun* a stupid, despicable person *US, 1997*

shitstain *adjective* despicable, unpleasant, foolish *US, 1995*

shit-stick *noun* a despised person *US, 1964*

shit sticks! used as a mildly profane expression of disappointment *US, 1964*

shit-stir *verb* to tell tales, or spread rumours, with the specific intention of causing trouble. A limited variation of 'stir the shit' *UK, 1999*

shit-stirrer *noun* a troublemaker; a person who heckles or harasses, especially for the fun of it *AUSTRALIA, 1971*

shit-stirring *noun* harassing; heckling; troublemaking *AUSTRALIA, 1971*

shit stompers *noun* heavy work boots *US, 1975*

shit stopper *noun* a prank *US, 1981*

shit stoppers *noun* drain-pipe trousers (a tight-cut, narrow-legged part of a Teddy Boy's 'uniform') *UK, 2003*

shitstorm; shit storm *noun* an extremely serious situation *US, 1962*

shit street *noun* an unpleasant place to be; serious trouble. You can be 'in' or 'up' shit street; a similar location to SHIT CREEK *UK, 1961*

shitsure *adverb* certainly, definitely *US, 1981*

shittalay *noun* a Chevrolet car *US, 1992*

shit-talk *verb* to engage in bragging, insulting conversation *US, 2004*

shitted *adjective* afraid. A variation of SHIT-SCARED *UK, 1997*

shitter *noun* **1** an example of something *UK, 2005*. **2** a toilet or bathroom *US, 1969*. **3** a criminal, usually a burglar, who fetishistically defecates at the scene of the crime *US, 1970*. **4** a liar; a braggart; a bluffer. A shortened form of BULLSHITTER *US, 1982*. **5** a coward *UK, 2000*. **6** a horse *US, 1958*. **7** a prison cell used for solitary confinement *US, 1972*. **8** the hell. Used as an intensifier *AUSTRALIA, 1971*

shit the bed! used for registering wonder or satisfaction. An elaboration of SHIT! *UK, 2002*

shit ticket *noun* a piece of toilet paper *AUSTRALIA, 1996*

shitting *adjective* used as a negative intensifier *UK, 1966*

shitting in high cotton (and wiping with the leaves) enjoying prosperous times *US, 1984*

shitting-it *adjective* scared; very nervous *UK, 1996*

shittings *noun* diarrhoea *BAHAMAS, 1982*

shitting up *noun* in prison, a deliberate act of protest by decorating a cell with excrement *UK, 1996*

shit train *noun* a great number; a lot of *US, 1989*

shitty *noun* a bad mood *AUSTRALIA, 1979*

shitty *adjective* **1** awful; of poor quality *US, 1924*. **2** in a bad mood *AUSTRALIA, 1971*. **3** drunk *US, 2003*

shitty end of the stick *noun* an unfair position to be in; inequitable treatment *UK, 1974*

Shitty Mcshit! used for registering frustration, annoyance, anger, etc. SHIT! intensified by an elaborated reduplication *UK, 2000*

shit up *verb* to scare someone *UK, 2000*

shitville *noun* any remote, forsaken town *US, 1977*

shitwork *noun* any unglamorous occupation, often dirty work *UK, 1968*

shitwrap *noun* a despicable person *US, 2001*

shiv *verb* to stab someone *US, 1951*

shiv; chiv; shivvie *noun* a homemade knife-like weapon, especially one fashioned in prison. Almost certainly evolved from C17 'chive' (knife) *US, 1915*

shivaree *noun* a group mocking *US, 1805*

Shiva Skunk *noun* in British Columbia, a local variety of marijuana *CANADA, 2002*

shiver and shake; shiver *noun* a cake. Rhyming slang *UK, 1998*

shivoo *noun* a party; a celebration. From French *chez vous* (at your place) *AUSTRALIA, 1844*

shivver *noun* a criminal who attacks victims with a knife *US, 1957*

shiznit *noun* the very best; something of great quality. Used with 'the'. A euphemistic embellishment of THE SHIT *US, 1996*

shizzle; fo' shizzle certainly; emphatically yes. A hip-hop, urban black coinage; the opening sound of 'sure' elaborated to a pattern; especially in rhyming reduplications, 'fo' shizzle my nizzle' (for sure my nigger), 'fo' shizzle my sizzle' (for sure my sister) and 'fo' shizzle my bizzle' (for sure my brother) *US, 2003*

shizzle my mizzle fizzle dizzle! used as a contemptuous expression of dismissal. Popular hip-hop cryptography disguising 'suck my mother fucking dick!' *US, 2003*

shizzy *adjective* great *UK, 1993*

shlemiel; schlemiel; schlemihl *noun* a bungler with chronic bad luck. Yiddish. During the opening montage of the US situation comedy *Laverne and Shirley* (ABC, 1976–83), the lead characters, played by Penny Marshall and Cindy Williams, skip down a Milwaukee sidewalk singing '1–2–3–4–5–6–7–8, Shlemiel, shlamazzel, Hassenpepper Incorporated', giving 'shlemiel' its highest profile to date *US, 1948*

shlep *noun* **1** stealing from parked cars *US, 1950*. **2** influence *US, 2002*

shlep; schlep *verb* to move or travel laboriously. From Yiddish *schlep* or *schlepen* (to drag) *IRELAND, 1922*

shlepper; schlepper *noun* an inconsequential person; a nobody *US, 1934*

shlepper bag; schlepper bag *noun* a tote bag *US, 2000*

shlimazel; schlimazel *noun* a person with chronic bad luck. A blend of German and Hebrew, literally translated as 'bad luck' *US, 1948*

shlock; schlack; schlock *noun* shoddy, defective or cheaply made merchandise. From German to Yiddish to American slang *US, 1915*

shlocker; schlocker *noun* a cheaply produced horror or thriller film. A compound of SHLOCK; SHLOCK (something cheap or inferior) and SHOCKER *UK, 2002*

shlocky; schlocky *adjective* shoddy *US, 1968*

shlong *noun* **1** the penis. From the Yiddish. Also spelt 'schlong' *US, 1969*. **2** a hairstyle in which the hair is worn short at the front and long at the back. An ellision of 'short-long'. Better known, perhaps, as a MULLET *US, 2005*

shlubby *adjective* ill-mannered; poorly dressed. Yiddish from the Slavic *zhlob* (a coarse person) *US, 1968*

shm-; schm- *prefix* used for creating a Yiddish-sounding reduplication of an English word, usually with the intention of diminishing the importance of the original word *US, 1929*

shmagma *noun* marijuana *UK, 2003*

shmaltz; schmaltz *noun* excessive sentimentality, especially in music, writing, etc. From German *schmaltz* (fat, lard) via Yiddish, with a suggestion of something too greasy to be easily digested *US, 1935*

shmams *noun* the female breasts. Derives, apparently, from MAMMARIES on the Yiddish model of reduplication ('mams, shmams') *UK, 2003*

'shman *noun* a first-year college student, a freshman *US, 1987*

shmatte; schmatte *noun* **1** the clothing trade *CANADA, 2002*. **2** a less than elegant house dress. Yiddish *US, 1970*

shmear; schmear *noun* a bribe *US, 1950*

shmear; schmear *verb* to bribe someone *US, 1985*

shmeck; schmeck; shmee *noun* heroin; cocaine. From German *schmecken* (to taste), but note an assonant similarity to SMACK (heroin) *US, 1932*

shmecker; schmecker *noun* a heroin user. Yiddish, formed from SHMECK *US, 1952*

shmeckler *noun* a heroin user or addict *US, 1988*

shmeer; schmear *noun* a package or deal. From the Yiddish *US, 1969*

shmegegge; schmageggy *noun* an incompetent person. An American-born 'Yiddish' word *US, 1975*

shmendrick *noun* a naive, cowardly person. From the name of a character in an operetta by Abraham Golfaden *US, 1980*

shmo; schmo; schmol *noun* a gullible, hapless fool. An American addition to Yiddish. In August 1948, just as 'shmo' was coming into the American lexicon, US cartoonist Al Capp introduced the 'shmoo' in the *L'il Abner* comic strip. The loveable and selfless 'shmoo' loved to be eaten and tasted like any food desired *US, 1948*

shmooze; schmooze *noun* an agreeable conversation; persuasive talk *US, 1939*

shmooze; schmooze *verb* to gossip; to chat, to engage in idle talk; to network; to persuade someone indirectly. Yiddish from the Hebrew *US, 1897*

shmoozy *adjective* chatty; friendly *US, 1954*

shmuck; schmuck *noun* **1** a fool; an objectionable person. Taken into general usage from Yiddish; the literal meaning is 'penis', hence the original Yiddish usage in this sense had a particularly derogatory tone. The variant 'schmuck' seems to have been adopted in error due to a similarity in sound to Yiddish *schmuck* (jewel) *UK, 1892*. **2** the penis *UK, 2003*

shmuck; schmuck *verb* to make a fool of someone *US, 2001*

shmucko; schmucko *noun* a reprehensible person *AUSTRALIA, 1987*

shmutter; schmutter *noun* clothing, especially a suit. From Yiddish *shmatte* (a rag), ultimately from Polish *szmatte* (a rag) *UK, 1977*

shmutz; schmutz *noun* filth; dirt. Yiddish from German *US, 1959*

shnitzel; schnitzel *noun* the penis *US, 1967*

shnook *noun* an inoffensive, unassertive person; a 'nobody'. American Yiddish coinage *US, 1948*

shnookered *adjective* drunk *US, 1985*

shnorrer; schnorrer *noun* a freeloader. Yiddish from the German for 'begging' *US, 1948*

shnoz; schnoz; shnozz; scnozz *noun* the nose. A shortening of SHNOZZLE *US, 1942*

shnozzle; shnozzola; schnozzle; schnozzola *noun* the nose *US, 1930*

shoat boat *noun* in trucking, a trailer used for hauling livestock *US, 1971*

shock a brew! have a beer! An intentional corruption of the Hawaiian SHAKA *US, 1989*

shocked-as *adjective* very shocked *UK, 2001*

shocker *noun* a person or thing that is shockingly bad *AUSTRALIA, 1962*

shock jock *noun* a radio personality who tests the limits and tries to win listeners by outrageous language, thoughts or stunts *US, 1986*

shock shop *noun* a room where electric shock therapy is administered *US, 1962*

shock treatment *noun* in the used car business, a very low assessment of the value of a customer's trade-in car *US, 1980*

shoddy-doo *noun* palms slapped in greeting *US, 1976*

shoddy-dropper *noun* a vendor of low quality clothing passed off as high quality *AUSTRALIA, 1950*

shoe *noun* **1** a detective. An abbreviation of GUMSHOE *US, 1988*. **2** a black person. A play on BOOT *US, 1960*. **3** in drag and motor racing, a driver *US, 1980*. **4** among Quebec anglophones, the Centre Hospitalier Universitaire de Sherbrooke. The word 'shoe' indicates how the acronym CHUS is pronounced, leaving off the last consonant in the French way *CANADA, 2001*. **5** a linear amplifier for a citizens' band radio *US, 1976*

Shoe *nickname* Willie Shoemaker (b.1931), the most successful jockey in the history of horse racing in the US *US, 1977*

shoebite; shoe-bite *noun* a blister on the foot caused by a shoe's rubbing *INDIA, 1979*

shoe boot *noun* a prostitute. Rhyming slang *UK, 2003*

shoe clerk *noun* a poker player who withdraws from a hand at any sign of serious betting *US, 1996*

shoe dog *noun* a shoe salesman *US, 1997*

shoegazer *noun* an aficionado of 'serious' introspective rock music; hence the music itself *UK, 1999*

shoegazing *noun* 'serious', introspective rock music *UK, 2003*

shoe laces and collar buttons *noun* in poker, a hand consisting of a pair of aces and a pair of twos *US, 1988*

shoe-leather express *noun* walking *US, 1949*

shoemaker *noun* a boy who is not particularly intelligent. Teen slang *US, 1955*

shoes *noun* **1** tyres *US, 1917*. **2** car wheel rims *US, 2003*

shoes and socks; the shoes *noun* syphilis; hence any sexually transmitted infection. Rhyming slang for POX *UK, 1992*

shoestring *noun* a very small amount of money; a low budget *US, 1904*

s-h-one-t *noun* used as a euphemism for 'shit' *UK, 2002*

shonk *noun* a person who engages in dishonest business dealings. Back-formation from SHONKY *AUSTRALIA, 1982*

shonker *noun* the nose *UK, 1998*

shonky *noun* a dishonest person *AUSTRALIA, 1979*

shonky *adjective* of an item, phoney; of business dealings, dishonest *AUSTRALIA, 1969*

shoo *adjective* well-dressed. Teen slang *US, 1958*

shoo-fly *noun* **1** a police officer assigned to investigate the integrity of other policemen *US, 1958*. **2** on the railways, a temporary track bypassing an unusable section of track *US, 1946*

shoofti; shufti *noun* a look *AUSTRALIA, 1944*

shoo-in *noun* a person, idea or thing with no serious competition. Originally (1935) applied to a fixed horse race and four years later in a more general sense *US, 1939*

shook *adjective* excited; enthusiastic *US, 1973*

shookon infatuated with *AUSTRALIA, 1868*

shook-up *adjective* alienated; confused; dehumanised *US, 1914*

shoop *verb* to have sex. From the song by Salt-N-Pepa *US, 1994*

shoosh *noun* silence *AUSTRALIA, 1949*

shoosh *verb* ▶ **shoosh your noise** to become quiet. Especially when used as an injunction *UK, 2003*

shoot *noun* **1** anything legitimate, unscripted or unstaged *US, 1996*. **2** heroin *UK, 2002*

shoot *verb* **1** to ejaculate. Most likely a shortened form of the C19 'shooting one's roe' *IRELAND, 1922*. **2** to inject a drug intravenously *US, 1914*. **3** to depart. Variants include 'shoot off' and 'shoot out' *UK, 1897*. **4** to flirt; to make sexual advances *US, 1967*. **5** to throw or toss something *AUSTRALIA, 1929*. **6** to play. Usually as 'shoot pool', 'shoot crap', etc *US, 1926*. **7** to drink alcohol in shot glass units *US, 1991*. **8** to pick a pocket *US, 1969*. **9** used as an imperative; to start; to continue *US, 1915*. **10** (used of a plant) to show signs of producing fruit *CAYMAN ISLANDS, 1985*. ▶ **he shoots, he scores; he shoots, he scores, he wins** used for registering admiration of a small but telling personal victory. A cliché of football commentary applied to the ordinary moments of life; always in the third person, even if used of the first person *UK, 2002*. ▶ **shoot a beaver** to look for and see a girl's crotch *US, 1966*. ▶ **shoot a blag** to gossip *TRINIDAD AND TOBAGO, 1992*. ▶ **shoot a good stick** to play pool well *US, 1961*. ▶ **shoot a jug; shoot a peter** to break into a safe using explosives *US, 1950*. ▶ **shoot a wave** to surf a wave, especially if difficult *US, 1963*. ▶ **shoot an air rifle; shoot an air gun** in pool, to bet without money to back your bet *US, 1990*. ▶ **shoot an azimuth** to take a compass bearing *US, 1991*. ▶ **shoot blanks** (said of a male) to engage in sex with a low or non-existent sperm count *US, 1960*. ▶ **shoot down in flames** to absolutely defeat in an argument *UK, 1942*. ▶ **shoot for two** to defecate. A combination of basketball terminology and children's bathroom vocabulary *US, 2003*. ▶ **shoot gravy** to inject a mixture of blood and drug solution that has been reheated after failing to make a direct hit on the vein *US, 1973*. ▶ **shoot it** to lie. Euphemistic variation of SHOOT THE SHIT (to tell tall tales) *UK, 1959*. ▶ **shoot off your mouth; shoot your mouth off** to speak with a complete lack of discretion; to speak boastfully *US, 1864*. ▶ **shoot the breeze** to chat idly *US, 1919*. ▶ **shoot the bull** to engage in small talk *US, 1902*. ▶ **shoot the con** to engage in goal-oriented, truth-deficient conversation *US, 1965*. ▶ **shoot the crow; shoot the craw** to abscond; to depart hurriedly, especially without paying money that is owed *UK, 1887*. ▶ **shoot the curl; shoot the tube** to surf through the hollow part of a wave *US, 1957*. ▶ **shoot the doughnut** to aim

artillery strikes at enemy forces encircling a US defensive position *US, 1990*. ▶ **shoot the duck** to skateboard crouched on one leg with the other leg extended outward *US, 1976*. ▶ **shoot the pier** to surf, or attempt to surf, through the pilings of a pier *US, 1962*. ▶ **shoot the scales** (used of a truck driver) to bypass a weigh station *US, 1963*. ▶ **shoot the shit; shoot shit** to engage in idle conversation; to tell lies *UK, 1984*. ▶ **shoot the V** to make a V-sign (the first and index fingers raised from a clenched fist, knuckles forward). 'Shoot' as 'to fire a gun' accentuates the aggressive or dismissive nature of this action *UK, 2000*. ▶ **shoot the works** on the railways, to make a sudden, emergency stop *US, 1977*. ▶ **shoot your bolt** to ejaculate *NEW ZEALAND, 1998*. ▶ **shoot your cuffs** (used of a man wearing a suit or sports jacket) to straighten your arms so that the cuffs of the shirt extend beyond the jacket sleeves. The modern version of the older (1878) 'shoot your linen' *UK, 1909*. ▶ **shoot your load** figuratively, to exhaust your resources early in a contest *US, 1954*. ▶ **shoot your trap** to talk too much *US, 1947*. ▶ **shoot your wad** to ejaculate *US, 1972*

shoot! **1** yes! Hawaiian youth usage *US, 1982*. **2** used as a euphemism for 'shit' in an exclamation *US, 1934*

shoot and scoot *verb* to engage in warfare involving brief contact with the enemy and then a quick withdrawal *US, 1987*

shoot-em-up *noun* used as a loose category for any film or computer game with violent gunplay as a main element in advancing the storyline *UK, 2002*

shooter *noun* **1** a gun; a pistol, especially a revolver *UK, 1840*. **2** a professional killer *US, 1972*. **3** a criminal who specialises in breaking into safes *US, 1949*. **4** an intravenous drug user *US, 1991*. **5** in a functionally compartmentalised illegal drug enterprise, the person who holds and turns over the drugs to buyers *US, 1987*. **6** a pinball player *US, 1977*. **7** in pinball, the device that propels a ball into the playfield. Known conventionally as a 'plunger' *US, 1977*. **8** a television camera operator *US, 1986*

shooting gallery *noun* a place where addicts congregate to buy and inject drugs *US, 1951*

shooting match *noun* all of something; the entire matter *US, 1968*

shoot it! in surfing, used to encourage a surfer to catch a wave breaking behind them *US, 1957*

shoot (someone) out *verb* to train or prepare someone *US, 1972*

shoot through *noun* a person who fails to honour an undertaking. Royal Navy slang, from the verb sense 'to go absent without leave' *UK, 1989*

shoot through *verb* to depart hastily; to go absent without leave *AUSTRALIA, 1947*. ▶ **shoot through like a Bondi tram** to depart hastily. Referring to trams formerly running from the centre of Sydney to Bondi beach, noted for their speed. Appearing slightly earlier (1945, *Australian National Dictionary*) was the variant 'go through like a Bondi tram' *AUSTRALIA, 1951*

shoot up *verb* to inject heroin or another drug intravenously *US, 1914*

shoot-up; shoot-up man *noun* a person who promotes a card game or other activity involved in a swindle *US, 1977*

shooty *noun* a shotgun. Jamaican gang terminology *US, 1995*

shop *noun* **1** any place of business, where you work *UK, 1779*. **2** any home or apartment where drugs are sold *US, 1997*. **3** a theatrical engagement; a job *UK, 1888*

shop; shop up *verb* to inform the police authorities against, or reveal the whereabouts of, someone with the expected result of arrest and imprisonment for the subject. The original (1583) sense 'to imprison' began, during C19, to also mean 'to cause to be imprisoned', which sense survives *UK, 1976*

shop around *verb* **1** to search for and compare different possibilities. Extended from the practice of making actual comparisons between shops *UK, 1922*. **2** to search for a conversation on a citizens' band radio *US, 1976*

shop door *noun* the fly on a man's trousers *US, 1965*

shopping accident *noun* an impulse purchase later regretted *CANADA, 1993*

shoppy *noun* **1** a shop assistant; a shop-keeper *UK, 2002*. **2** a shoplifter *AUSTRALIA, 1975*

shoppying *noun* shoplifting AUSTRALIA, 1975

shoppying job *noun* an act of shoplifting AUSTRALIA, 1975

shore dinner *noun* a sailor, as seen by a homosexual US, 1965

short *noun* **1** a car, especially a restored older car or hot rod US, 1914. **2** a drink of spirits (as opposed to wine, beer, etc), or a spirit and a mixer. Used of drinks taken in *short* measures, although the original use is also of undiluted alcohol UK, 1837. **3** the unsmoked butt of a cigarette UK, 1990. **4** a brief nap US, 1976. **5** in lobstering, a lobster that is not legal size US, 1978. **6** a railway carriage left between stations US, 1977

short *adjective* **1** lacking money; lacking enough money to meet an obligation US, 1960. **2** near the end of a prison sentence or military tour of duty US, 1967. **3** used of an amount of a drug, underweight US, 1989. ▶ **a NOUN (part) short of a NOUN (whole)** used as the central part of a generally humorous formula – a something short of a greater – that infers a lack of mental capacity, not completely sane, 'not all there'. Inspiration for these phrases seems to be universal: 'one planet short of a full galaxy'. Religions account for, among others: 'one candle short of a menorah'; 'two candles short of a mass'; 'a few wafers short of a communion'; 'several fishes short of a miracle'. UK politics and current affairs: 'quite a few red boxes short of a successful Prime Minister'; 'various wheezes short of a Scottish parliament'; 'a few pence short of a euro'; 'a few pence short of a first-class stamp'; 'a few digits short of a dialling code'; 'a couple of programmes short of a series'. Sports and games: 'one player short of a cricket team'; 'a couple of cubs short of a full Lion's pack'; 'one helmet short of a huddle'; 'two cards short of a full-house'; 'several pawns short of a full set'; 'several pieces short of a full set'. Animals are also popular: 'two sheep short of a flock'; 'a couple of kangaroos short of a full paddock'. Food and drink: 'several currants short of a bun'; 'one liquorice stick short of a Pontefract cake'; 'two bottles short of a crate'; 'a nosebag short of a sack of oats'; 'two luncheon vouchers short of a ploughman's'; 'several prawns short of a cocktail'; 'a few stock-cubes short of a full polar ration'; 'several gondolas short of a Cornetto [a branded ice-cream associated with Venice]'. Fashion: 'three diamond clusters short of a tiara'; 'several gemstones short of a full tiara'; 'more than a Dolce short of a Gabbana [Dolce & Gabbana is a well-known fashion-house]'. And so on. Two final examples, both with obviously limited circulation but they demonstrate the possibilities: 'a few billion neurons short of a full load'; 'a few shards of pottery short of a full anthropological theory' UK, 1941. ▶ **a sheep short of a paddock** lacking a full complement of intelligence AUSTRALIA, 1994. ▶ **get short** to near the end of a prison sentence or military enlistment US, 1951. ▶ **have short arms and long pockets** to be stingy AUSTRALIA, 1966

short-and-curlies *noun* pubic hair US, 1967. ▶ **have by the short and curlies** to hold someone at a disadvantage; to exercise complete control over someone. Fanciful but convincing imagery in which 'short and curlies' represent pubic hairs; a variation of HAVE BY THE SHORT HAIRS UK, 1948

short-arm *verb* to perform a rectal examination US, 1994

short-arm bandit; short-arm heister *noun* a rapist US, 1950

short-arm inspection; small-arm inspection *noun* an inspection for a sexually transmitted infection. Soldiers or prisoners are lined up, each holding his penis. At the command 'Skin it back and milk it down', each man 'milks' down his penis from the base to the tip so that the inspecting doctor can check for pus at the tip of the urethra UK, 1919

short-arm parade *noun* an inspection of the genitals of a group of men for sexually transmitted infection AUSTRALIA, 1977

short-arse; short-ass *noun* a short person UK, 1706

short-arsed *adjective* small, not tall. Extended from SHORT-ARSE (a short person) UK, 1997

short bus *noun* used as a reference to the mentally retarded. Referring to the smaller school buses used to transport special education students in the US US, 1998

short buy *noun* a purchase of a small amount of drugs US, 1955

shortcake *noun* the act of shortchanging someone deliberately. Used with 'the' US, 1974

shortcake *verb* to shortchange someone US, 1961

shortcake artist *noun* an expert at shortchanging US, 1980

shortchange artist *noun* a swindler who gives customers too little change US, 1960

short con *noun* a confidence game in which the victim is swindled once, without being sent home for a bigger prize US, 1940

short con *verb* to engage in a short con swindle US, 1964

short dog *noun* a half pint bottle of alcohol; cheap wine US, 1968

short end *noun* in the television and film industries, unexposed film remaining after cutting off the exposed film US, 1990

short eyes *noun* a child molester US, 1976

short fuse *noun* an impending deadline US, 1986

short go; short order *noun* a drug dose that is smaller than the addict is accustomed to US, 1959

short hairs *noun* ▶ **have someone by the short hairs** to hold someone at a disadvantage; to exercise complete control over someone. A figurative use of the literal meaning 'to hold by the pubic hair' UK, 1888

short heist *noun* an act of masturbation US, 1974

short house *noun* a short person. A euphemistic variation of SHORT ARSE UK, 1964

shortie pyjamas *noun* summer pyjamas with short sleeves and trousers legs AUSTRALIA, 1987

shortitis *noun* the mental state of knowing that you have almost finished a prison sentence or military tour of duty US, 1950

short-long *noun* a hairstyle in which the hair is worn short at the front and long at the back. Most commonly known as a MULLET US, 2001

short of cars *adjective* on the railways, without a job US, 1977

short on *adjective* less than is adequate, expected or required UK, 1922

short ones *noun* ▶ **have someone by the short ones** to have absolute control of someone; to force submission. A figurative use of the literal meaning 'to hold by the pubic hair'; a variation on HAVE BY THE SHORT HAIRS US, 1971

short pair *noun* in poker, a pair of tens or lower US, 1963

short round *noun* gunfire or artillery fired by friendly forces US, 1985

shorts *noun* **1** a condition of low or no funds US, 1932. **2** the last portion of a cigarette US, 1992. **3** in poker, a pair that is beaten by a larger pair US, 1988

short short *adverb* soon US, 1976

short-shorts *noun* very brief shorts US, 1958

short skirt *noun* a Mini car. Citizens' band radio slang, punning on the length of a mini-skirt UK, 1981

short-sleeves *noun* in homosexual usage, an uncircumcised penis US, 1981

short stick *noun* a stick notched by a US soldier in Vietnam counting the days until the end of his tour of duty US, 1983

shortstop *noun* **1** a temporary arrangement or relationship US, 1972. **2** a gambler who makes small and conservative bets US, 1950. **3** in pool, a very skilled player who is just below the highest tier US, 1990. **4** in a group eating setting, to take a second helping despite an earlier request from another for seconds US, 1947

short time *noun* a brief session with a prostitute, long enough for sex and nothing more US, 1965

short-time *verb* **1** to serve the final days of a jail sentence or term of enlistment US, 1975. **2** to engage in a quick sexual encounter with a prostitute US, 1960

short-timer *noun* **1** a soldier near the end of his tour of duty in Vietnam. All but the US Marines served exactly 12 months in Vietnam; the Marines served 13 months US, 1964. **2** a prisoner whose release date is approaching US, 1966. **3** someone whose retirement date is rapidly approaching US, 1993. **4** a prostitute engaged for a short period of time US, 1960

short-timer's calendar *noun* a calendar showing the days remaining in a soldier's tour of duty in Vietnam US, 1965

shorty *noun* **1** a female, especially an attractive one *US, 1997*. **2** a close friend *US, 1997*. **3** in a casino, a shorter-than-expected shift at a table *US, 1980*

shot *noun* **1** an opportunity *US, 1972*. **2** an attempt *UK, 1756*. **3** the right way to do something *AUSTRALIA, 1953*. **4** an occurrence or instance; a thing *US, 1960*. **5** an instance of sexual intercourse. An abbreviation of SHOT OF COCK *US, 1968*. **6** an ejaculation *US, 2001*. **7** an injection of drugs *UK, 1929*. **8** cocaine *UK, 2003*. **9** Coca-Cola™ *US, 1946*. **10** a single measure of spirits *US, 2000*. **11** a blow, especially a severe one *US, 1996*. **12** an illegal move by a gambler *US, 1980*. **13** a competent pickpocket *US, 1976*. **14** a person or thing *UK: SCOTLAND, 1988*. **15** an incident report describing a prisoner's misconduct *US, 1976*. ▶ **have a shot at** to heckle or harass someone *AUSTRALIA, 1947*. ▶ **like a shot** exceedingly quickly *UK, 1809*. ▶ **make a shot** to secret something on your body while shoplifting *US, 1971*

Shot *noun* ▶ **the Shot** Aldershot (the home of the British Army) *UK, 1925*

shot *adjective* especially of a mechanical contrivance, broken; wrecked; ruined *AUSTRALIA, 1983*. ▶ **shot of** rid of *UK: SCOTLAND, 1823*

shot! well done! *BERMUDA, 1985*

shotcaller *noun* the nominal leader of a youth gang *US, 1995*

shot down *adjective* drug-intoxicated *US, 1982*

shot-for-shot *noun* an arrangement between two homosexuals in which they switch sex roles to satisfy each other *US, 1950*

shotgun *noun* **1** a pipe with air-holes used for smoking marijuana. The shotgun gives a BLAST *US, 1977*. **2** a ritual of drinking beer, forcing the beer out of the can into the drinker's mouth by opening the down-facing top after puncturing the up-facing bottom *US, 1988*. **3** a potent mix of heroin, cocaine, nitroglycerine, phenol and kola nut administered to racehorses as a stimulant *US, 1961*. **4** the front passenger seat in a car. Also called the 'shotgun seat'. The earliest use of the term, not yet applied to a car, seems to be in the 1939 film *Stagecoach*. To date, the earliest discovered use in the sense of a car is in 1963 *US, 1963*. **5** a male passenger in a vehicle equipped with citizens' band radio *UK, 1981*. **6** a police radar unit *US, 1976*. **7** in blackjack, the player to the immediate left of the dealer *US, 1979*. **8** in electric line work, an insulated line tool formally known as a grip-all stick *US, 1980*. **9** an unannounced test *US, 1968*

shotgun *verb* **1** to share marijuana smoke with someone else in the following manner: you blow through a lighted joint or blunt which is held with the burning end in your mouth, while your fellow-smoker inhales the stream of smoke that is produced *US, 1974*. **2** to smoke an entire marijuana cigarette in one go *AUSTRALIA, 1995*. **3** while treating a hospital patient, to order every possible treatment to avoid being wrong *US, 1994*

shotgun *adjective* **1** used of a house or apartment, having rooms set on both sides of a central hall *US, 1903*. **2** wide-ranging *US, 1994*

shotgun! used as a claim on riding in the front passenger seat of a car *US, 1973*

Shotgun Alley *nickname* the A Shau Valley, dense jungle terrain near the border of South Vietnam and Laos, southeast of Khe Sanh. A phonetic approximation *US, 1990*

shotgun bunk *noun* a sleeping space into which one must crawl *CANADA, 1963*

shotgun mike *noun* in the television and film industries, a directional microphone *US, 1990*

shotgunner *noun* a door gunner on an air gunship *US, 1990*

shot house *noun* an establishment that sells alcohol illegally, by the drink *US, 1978*

shot of cock *noun* sexual intercourse *US, 1968*

shot on the swings *noun* an instance of sexual intercourse *UK: SCOTLAND, 1988*

shot out *adjective* in very bad physical shape *US, 1989*

shot rod *noun* a fast car. Teen slang *US, 1955*

shottie *noun* a shotgun *US, 1997*

shot to shit *adjective* ruined, utterly spoiled *UK, 2001*

shotty; shotti *noun* the front passenger seat in a car. A shortened SHOTGUN *US, 2004*

shotty-gotty! used as a claim on riding in the front passenger seat of a car. A variation on SHOTGUN! *US, 1997*

shoulder *noun* in betting, odds of 7−4. From the TICK-TACK signal used by bookmakers *UK, 1991*

shoulder boulder *noun* an abandoned vehicle on the side of the road. The hard shoulder of the road, rhymed and contrived to make an obstacle *US, 1976*

shoulder hopper *noun* a surfer who surfs in another surfer's right of way *US, 1987*

shoulders *noun* ▶ **on the shoulders** in betting, odds of 9−2. From the TICK-TACK signal used by bookmakers *UK, 1991*

shouse *noun* a toilet. Euphemistic for SHITHOUSE *AUSTRALIA, 1941*

shouse *adjective* no good. Euphemistic for SHITHOUSE *AUSTRALIA, 2003*

shout *noun* **1** a drink or round of drinks bought for others; the purchase of a round *AUSTRALIA, 1854*. **2** your turn to buy drinks for someone else *AUSTRALIA, 1882*. **3** your turn to buy anything *AUSTRALIA, 1911*. **4** a call on the police radio. Derived from conventional 'shout' (used to hail) *UK, 1970*. **5** a greeting *US, 1999*

shout *verb* **1** to buy a round of drink for others *AUSTRALIA, 1854*. **2** to buy something as a present for another *AUSTRALIA, 1949*. **3** to write exclusively in upper case *US, 1995*. ▶ **shout at your shoes** to vomit *US, 1987*. ▶ **wouldn't shout if a shark bit you** to be stingy *AUSTRALIA, 1986*

shout-out *noun* a greeting; a recognition *US, 1999*

shove *noun* the member of a pickpocketing team who jostles the victim, diverting his attention so that a confederate can actually pick the victim's pocket *US, 1981*. ▶ **give someone the shove** to dismiss someone from employment or reject the partner in a romantic relationship *UK, 1899*

shove *verb* to have sex *UK, 1969*. ▶ **shove it** used as a harsh rejection of a suggestion. A shortened form of 'shove it up your ass' *AUSTRALIA, 1941*. ▶ **shove it up the ass** to reject something completely *US, 1957*. ▶ **shove paper** to pass counterfeit money or stolen or forged cheques *US, 1962*. ▶ **shove shit uphill** to take the active role in anal intercourse *UK, 1996*

shovel *verb* ▶ **shovel coal** (of a motor vehicle) to accelerate. An allusion to steam-driven, coal-fired transports *US, 1976*

shovel and broom; shovel *noun* a room. Rhyming slang *UK, 1960*

shovel and pick; shovel *noun* a prison. Rhyming slang for NICK *UK, 2000*

shovel and tank *noun* a bank. Rhyming slang *UK, 1961*

shovelhead *noun* the V-twin Harley Davidson engine, manufactured 1966−83. Biker (motorcycle) usage *US, 1995*

shovel pilot *noun* a manual worker *UK, 2003*

shovels and spades *noun* AIDS. Rhyming slang *UK, 1998*

shove off *verb* to go away. Naval coinage, from shoving a boat away; often used as an injunction *UK, 1909*

shover *noun* a person who passes counterfeit money *US, 1945*

show *noun* an opportunity; a chance; an opening *AUSTRALIA, 1876* ▷*see:* SHOW PRICE

show *verb* to arrive; to make an appearance *US, 1958*. ▶ **show hard** to reveal to other men that you have an erection *US, 1975*

show and shine *verb* in car customising, to prepare a car and then exhibit it in a car show *US, 1993*

show-and-tell *noun* a public display and explanation. From the name of a school activity for young children *US, 1948*

showbiz *noun* the entertainment industry. A reduction of 'showbusiness'; originally theatrical *US, 1945*

showbizzy *adjective* used of the stereotypical excesses of showbusiness *UK, 1969*

showboat *verb* to show off; to pay attention to the performance aspects of a task. From the C19 river steamers with theatrical performances and melodramatic, showy gamblers *US, 1951*

show buddy *noun* in the language surrounding the Grateful Dead, a friend with whom you team up for Grateful Dead tours *US, 1994*

showcase *verb* to show off *US, 1945*

showdown *noun* **1** in prison, private time for sex *US, 1972*. **2** in poker, the moment when betting is completed and the players show their hands *US, 1982*

shower *noun* a worthless collection of people *UK, 1941*. ▶ **not come down in the last shower** to be aware *AUSTRALIA, 1902*

shower bath; showers *noun* ten shillings; hence 50p. Rhyming slang for '*half* a pound' *UK, 1960*

shower cap *noun* a condom. Figurative application of a conventional item *US, 1969*

shower of shit; shower of shite *noun* an unpleasant and worthless collection of people. Derogatory. An elaboration of 'shower' *UK, 1999*

showers *noun* urination by one person on another, or other acts of urine fetishism, especially when offered or sought in advertisements *UK, 2003*

shower-spank *verb* (of a male) to masturbate in the shower *US, 1989*

show house *noun* a homosexual brothel *US, 1981*

showie *noun* a person who runs or works in a stall or ride at agricultural shows *AUSTRALIA, 1980*

show me the money used as a humorous urging that a statement be backed up. A key catchphrase in the US in the late 1990s *US, 1996*

show-off lane *noun* in trucking, the passing lane of a motorway *US, 1976*

show-out *noun* a discreet signal from an informer to a police officer *UK, 1959*

show out *verb* to behave ostentatiously *US, 1993*

show pony *noun* a prissy, prancing fop more concerned with image than performance *AUSTRALIA, 1964*

show price; show *noun* in gambling racing, the betting odds displayed by a bookmaker at a point in time *UK, 1976*

show shop *noun* a theatre *US, 1981*

showstopper *noun* a proposal that would lead to a breakdown in negotiations; a deal-killer *US, 1997*

showtime *noun* time for something to begin *US, 1992*

show-up *noun* a process used by police to have witnesses to a crime identify the criminals *US, 1969*

show-up box *noun* a room in a jail where suspects are shown for identification by witnesses *US, 1953*

show us your tits used as a crass male heckling catchcry *AUSTRALIA, 2000*

shpilkes *noun* an inability to sit still *US, 1992*

SHPOS *noun* a critically ill hospital patient who fails to follow medical instructions, worsening their own condition; a sub-*human* piece of shit *US, 1978*

shpritz; schpritz *verb* to squirt or spray. Yiddish *US, 1967*

shrapnel *noun* **1** low denomination coins *UK, 2005*. **2** the ripple effect in poker of a player completely losing his composure and infecting other players with his poor play *US, 1996*

shred *verb* to perform very well; to excel *US, 1977*

shredache *noun* the headache resulting from extreme exertion while surfing. A punned version of the standard 'headache', built on SHRED (performing well) *US, 2004*

shredded *adjective* **1** muscular as the result of intense workouts *US, 2001*. **2** weary; weak *US, 1986*

shredded wheat *adjective* excellent. Rhyming slang for SWEET, based on the branded breakfast cereal; current in UK prisons February 2002 *UK, 2002*

shredder *noun* a snowboarder *US, 1995*

shreddies *noun* male underpants; army-issue underpants; panties; female underwear. Originally a reference to the stereotypically disgusting state of bachelor's underwear; Shreddies™, a branded breakfast cereal, are brown and have a woven appearance *UK, 1991*

shredding *adjective* extreme; exciting; good *US, 1987*

shrewd *adjective* attractive; popular; savvy *US, 1962*

shrewd head *noun* a cunning or shrewd person *AUSTRALIA, 1915*

shrewdie *noun* **1** a cunning or shrewd person *AUSTRALIA, 1904*. **2** a clever action *NEW ZEALAND, 1998*

shriek *noun* **1** distilled, concentrated heroin *US, 1987*. **2** an exclamation mark (!) *US, 1983*

shrieking sixties *noun* the latitudes of 60 to 69 degrees south *ANTARCTICA, 1921*

shrimp *noun* **1** a short person *UK, 1386*. **2** a small penis *US, 1972*. **3** marijuana *UK, 2003*

shrimp job; shrimp *noun* the act of toe-sucking for sexual pleasure. A foot-fetishist's view of an appetising similarity between toes and shrimps *UK, 1999*

shrimp queen; shrimper *noun* a person with a fetish for the toes *US, 1971*

shrink *noun* a psychiatrist or therapist. From the longer and older HEADSHRINKER *US, 1966*

shrinkage *noun* the condition of a man's genitals after swimming in cold water. Coined and popularised on an episode of Jerry Seinfeld's television programme (*The Hamptons*) that first aired on 24th May 1994 *US, 1994*

shroomer *noun* a recreational drug user who takes hallucinogenic mushrooms; also, more innocently, a person who gathers wild mushrooms *US, 2003*

shroomers *noun* mushrooms as a pizza topping *US, 1996*

shrooms *noun* psychoactive mushrooms *US, 1987*

shroud *noun* from the perspective of a man not accustomed to dressing up, a suit *US, 1962*

shtarker *noun* a strong and brave person. Yiddish, from German *US, 1959*

shtetl *noun* a predominantly Jewish neighbourhood. From the German for 'village', originally applied to small Jewish villages in eastern Europe *UK, 1949*

shtick; schtick; shtik; schtik *noun* **1** a theatrical routine, an act; hence a style, routine or behaviour. From German *stück* (a bit, a piece) into Yiddish, and thence more widespread *US, 1961*. **2** an area of interest. From the Yiddish for 'piece' or 'play' *US, 1968*

shtuck; schtuck; schtook; stuk *noun* trouble. Not Yiddish despite appearances, but probably formed on the Yiddish model of a reduplicated word commencing with a 'sh' sound, in which case 'shtuck' is a variant of 'stuck' (in a difficult situation) *UK, 1936*

shtum; shtoom; stumm *adjective* quiet; saying nothing. Anglicised phonetic spelling of synonymous German *stumm* which, it is presumed, reached England through Yiddish *UK, 1958*

shtunk; shtonk *noun* a nasty person; a jerk. Yiddish, from German *US, 1977*

shtup *noun* an act of sexual intercourse *US, 1986*

shtup; shtoop; schtup *verb* to have sex. Yiddish from the German for 'to push' *US, 1965*

shubs *noun* a party. Urban youth slang *UK, 2005*

shuck *noun* **1** nonsense; something of little worth *US, 1851*. **2** a deception; a tease *US, 1959*. **3** in poker, a card that may be discarded and replaced *US, 1981*

shuck *verb* to deceive someone in a blustery, teasing manner. Often used with 'jive' *US, 1959*. ▶ **shuck the ice** to remove stolen diamonds from their settings *US, 1949*

shucker *noun* a striptease dancer *US, 1981*

shuckman *noun* a swindler *US, 1965*

shucks used as a register of dismay or contempt. Used where SHIT! might do *US, 1847*

shucky darn used as a mock, mild oath *US, 1976*

shuffle *noun* **1** the movement by a surfer forward on the board while surfing, executed without crossing the feet *US, 1965*. **2** counterfeit money *US, 1950*

shuffle *verb* ▶ **shuffle off to Buffalo** to leave. The reference to Buffalo, New York, is for the sake of rhyme and adds nothing to the meaning *US, 1986*. ▶ **shuffle the deck** on the railways, to switch wagons onto side tracks at stations along a line *US, 1946*

shufti; shuftie; shufty; shoofti *noun* a quick look. Military adoption of Arabic *sufti* (did you see?) *UK, 1943*

'shun! Attention! A military command, abbreviated from the extended delivery 'Atten... shun!' *UK, 1888*

shunk; shunkie *noun* a toilet *UK: SCOTLAND, 1988*

shunt *noun* a car accident *UK, 1959*

shunt *verb* in motor racing, to bump a competitor *US, 1965*

shunter *noun* a drug dealer who becomes addicted and continues to deal in order to fund the habit. Formed on PUNTER (a customer) *UK, 2000*

shurrit! be quiet! A phonetic slurring of SHUT IT! *UK, 1982*

shurrup! be quiet! A slurring of SHUT UP! *UK, 1964*

shush *verb* to steal something. Polari; a possible variant sense and spelling of ZHOOSH (to swallow) *UK, 2002*

shush bag *noun* a bag for carrying away stolen property. Polari; from SHUSH (to steal) *UK, 2002*

shusher *noun* a person who is employed to keep people quiet on the street outside a nightclub. From 'shush!' (be quiet!) *UK, 2004*

shushing *noun* the work of keeping people quiet on the street outside a nightclub *UK, 2004*

shush the mush! be quiet!, shut up! A combination of conventional 'shush!' and MUSH (the mouth or face) *UK, 2004*

shush up *verb* to become quiet. Often in the imperative. Combines conventional 'shush!' (be quiet!) with SHUT UP *UK, 1999*

shut *verb* ▶ **shut the gate** in motor racing, to pass another car and immediately pull in front of the other car, minimising its ability to pass in return *US, 1965*

shut-door *noun* a rejection; a refusal. The image of a door being slammed in your face *UK, 2001*

shuteye; shut-eye *noun* sleep *UK, 1896*

shuteyes *noun* a sex offender *US, 1982*

shut-in *noun* a person who stays at home and never goes out *US, 1904*

shut it! be quiet! *UK, 1886*

shutout *noun* any situation in which a person fails to score, literally or figuratively *US, 1957*

shutter *noun* **1** the eyelid *US, 1945*. **2** a gunman. Recorded by a Jamaican inmate in a UK prison, August 2002 *UK, 2002*

shutterbug *noun* **1** a photography enthusiast; a photographer *US, 1940*. **2** a photographer who selects subjects for personal sexual gratification, often without the subject's knowledge or consent *US, 1999*

shut the fuck up! be quiet! An intensified, very imperative SHUT UP! (be quiet!) *US, 1991*

shuttup! be quiet!; stop talking! A variation of SHUT UP! *UK, 1955*

shut up *verb* to cease talking; to stop making a noise. Used as a two word exclamation the sense is imperative or (since the 1960s) disbelieving *US, 1840*

shut up! *verb* used as a humorous, kind, even flirtatious way to change the subject *US, 1978*

shut UP! shut up. The difference between the slang 'shut up' and the colloquial is the emphasis on a drawn out 'up' with register rising slightly for the 'up' *US, 1989*

shut-up sandwich *noun* a punch in the mouth *CANADA, 2002*

shut your crunch! be quiet! *UK, 1978*

shut your face! be quiet!; shut up! *UK, 1809*

shut your head! be quiet!; shut up! *US, 1876*

shut your teeth! be quiet!; stop talking! *UK, 2003*

shut your trap! be quiet! From TRAP (the mouth) *UK, 1959*

shuzzit *noun* marijuana. A discreet variation of SHIT *US, 1971*

shvartz; schvartz *noun* a black person; an Indian or Pakistani person. Also seen as 'schwartz', 'schvartze' and ' schvartza'. The Yiddish term *schvartz* (from the German for 'black') is an adjective, with *schvartzer* as the noun for 'a black person'. 'Schvartz' the adjective became an inside, 'code' word among Jews for 'a black person' *US, 1961*

shvartz; schvartz; schwartz; schvartze *adjective* black, especially as a skin colour. Derogatory *UK, 2002*

shvitz; schvitz *verb* to perspire. Yiddish, from German *US, 1992*

shvontz; shwantz *noun* the penis *US, 1965*

shy *verb* to cook opium pellets for smoking *US, 1946*

shy *adjective* **1** having less of something than is desired, required or necessary *US, 1895*. **2** in debt; owing money *US, 1950*

shylock *noun* **1** a person who illegally loans money at very high interest rates and often has violent collection procedures. The allusion to Shakespeare's usurious money-lender in *The Merchant of Venice* cannot be missed *US, 1930*. **2** in circus and carnival usage, the show's office secretary *US, 1981*

shylock *verb* to engage in usurious loan practices *UK, 1930*

shypoo *adjective* inferior; shoddy *NEW ZEALAND, 1952*

shyster *noun* **1** a lawyer, especially an unprofessional, dishonest or rapacious lawyer; any dishonest professional. In his Origin of the Term Shyster, slang lexicographer Gerald Cohen demonstrates the craft of slang etymology at its highest: 'coined by New York journalist Mike Walsh' *US, 1843*. **2** a very poorly attended circus performance *UK, 1953*

siamesed *adjective* in motor racing and repair, closely connected or joined together *US, 1993*

sib *noun* a sibling *UK, 2000*

Siberia *noun* solitary confinement *US, 1984*

sice *noun* in craps, the point and number six *US, 1950*

Sicilian price *noun* death, usually slow and painful, as punishment *US, 1997*

sick *noun* withdrawal symptoms suffered by a drug addict *US, 1972*. ▶ **on the sick** in receipt of sickness benefit *UK, 1996*

sick *adjective* **1** suffering the symptoms of withdrawal from a drug addiction *US, 1938*. **2** experiencing the bleed period of the menstrual cycle *BAHAMAS, 1982*. **3** infected with HIV or suffering from AIDS *US, 1990*. **4** scary. Perhaps from the sensations aroused *US, 1995*. **5** tedious; boring; disaffecting *US, 1973*. **6** excellent; wonderful. On the principle that BAD means 'good' *US, 1987*. **7** in poker, without further funds *US, 1988*

sick and tired of *adjective* bored or fed-up with someone or something *UK, 1783*

sick and wrong! used for conveying a strong disagreement or disapproval *US, 1989*

sick as an ANIMAL *adjective* physically sick, but not necessarily vomiting. The earliest recorded is 'dog' (1705); followed by 'horse' (1765); 'cat' shows up in 1915, and 'sonofabitch' in 1953. 'Sick as a parrot' is a jocular variation from 1979. On 20th November 2000, Judith Keppel was the first contestant to win a million pounds on the television quiz *Who Wants To Be A Millionaire*; the first question she answered (for £100) was: 'Complete this phrase. As sick as a – Puffin – Penguin – Parrot – Partridge' *UK, 1999*

sick-bay commando *noun* a soldier who feigns illness to avoid combat duty *US, 1991*

sickener *noun* anything that is depressing or disappointing *UK, 2001*

sickest *adjective* best *TRINIDAD AND TOBAGO, 1987*

sickie; sicky *noun* a feigned illness cited as grounds for missing work *AUSTRALIA, 1953*

sickle; motorsickle *noun* a motor*cycle*. Re-pronounced abbreviation punning on CHOPPER (a motorcycle) *US, 1967*

sickler *noun* a person suffering from sickle-cell anaemia US, 1994

sickness *noun* the range of symptoms experienced when a drug addict is deprived of the drug US, 1987

sicko *noun* an emotionally or psycho-sexually disturbed person US, 1963

sicko *adjective* depraved AUSTRALIA, 1993

sick pad *noun* a sanitary towel US, 1966

sick puppy *noun* a perverted person US, 1984

sick squid *noun* six pounds. A play on on 'six QUID' UK, 2002

sick to death of *adjective* bored or fed-up with someone or something UK, 1890

siddi *noun* marijuana UK, 1998

side *noun* **1** a recorded tune or song. Early gramophone records held one recording on each side US, 1936. **2** a girl US, 1972. **3** a group of friends TRINIDAD AND TOBAGO, 1973. ▶ **on the ... side** somewhat; to a noticeable degree UK, 1713. ▶ **on the side 1** describes an extra-marital sexual liaison US, 1893. **2** of work or commerce, extra to regular or legitimate practice, often discreetly so UK, 1961. **3** used as an announcement that you are monitoring a citizens' band radio channel; describes someone monitoring a citizens' band radio channel US, 1976. ▶ **over the side** engaged in private business or sexual liaisons during duty hours. Originally navy, 'over the side (of a ship)', meaning 'absent without leave'; adopted into police use UK, 1970. ▶ **put on side** to assume airs and graces. Possibly derived from the game of billiards UK, 1878

side ▶ **on the ... side** somewhat; to a noticeable degree UK, 1713

side arms *noun* **1** in poker, the lower value pair in a hand consisting of two pairs US, 1988. **2** sugar and cream US, 1945

sideboards *noun* side whiskers UK, 1857

sidebox *verb* to surround someone in a menacing manner UK, 1982

side-buster *noun* a person whose deeds do not match his description of his deeds US, 1989

side comb *noun* hair parted on the side. Hawaiian youth usage US, 1982

side dish *noun* a mistress US, 1949

sidehill winder; sidehill gouger *noun* a mythical animal whose legs are shorter on one side than the other from years of grazing on a hillside US, 1975

sidekick *noun* a close friend and accomplice US, 1906

sideman *noun* in a whe-whe lottery game, an assistant to the banker TRINIDAD AND TOBAGO, 1966

side-roader *noun* a rural marijuana thief; a person who grows marijuana in a remote outdoor garden NEW ZEALAND, 1990

'sides *adverb* in addition; used to introduce a further matter. An abbreviation of 'besides' UK, 1579

side squeeze *noun* a partner in romance other than your primary partner; a romantic affair US, 1991

sidewalk pizza *noun* a puddle of vomit US, 1997

sidewalk Susie *noun* a prostitute US, 1949

sideways *adjective* **1** of a sum of money being gambled, split each way (to win or place). Racing slang UK, 1960. **2** in motor racing, out of control, whether or not the car is actually sideways to the track traffic US, 1973

sideways trip *noun* a suicide in prison US, 1984

sidewinder *noun* **1** a South Asian prostitute; a promiscuous South Asian female. The allusion is to a poisonous snake found in North America US, 1997. **2** an unknown but very fast horse CANADA, 1974. **3** in trucking, a U-model Mack truck with a slightly off-centre driver's compartment US, 1971

side work *noun* prostitution US, 1996

sideys; sidies *noun* side whiskers. An abbreviation of 'sideburns' or 'sideboards' UK, 1967

sidity; sididy; seditty *adjective* arrogant, boastful, showing off US, 1968

sieg heils *noun* haemorrhoids. Rhyming slang for PILES UK, 2003

sieve *noun* a hospital or admitting physician that freely admits patients US, 1994

sieve *verb* to drill holes in a safe for the placement of explosives to be used in opening it US, 1970

siff *noun* syphilis US, 1972

sift *verb* to move swiftly through a crowd. Adopting conventional 'sift' (to pass through a sieve), perhaps incorporating a gentle pun on 'shift' (to move) UK, 1997

SIG (in doctors' shorthand) a bad-tempered, thoroughly objectionable individual. An (unofficial) medical initialism: STROPPY (bad-tempered) *i*gnorant GIT (objectionable individual) UK, 2002

sight *noun* a large quantity UK, 1390

sight *verb* to understand BAHAMAS, 1980

sight *adverb* very much. Often used with 'damn', 'damned' or another intensifier UK, 1928

sight-hit *verb* to stare at someone or something; to ogle someone INDIA, 1979

signal-to-noise ratio; s/n ratio *noun* the amount of useful content found on an Internet site. A figurative use of a technical term US, 1997

signature *noun* the backblast of flame or smoke from a weapon US, 1990

signify *verb* to engage in ritualistic insults, goading and teasing. Unlike DOZENS, signifying does not make a person's mother the subject of the tease US, 1932

sign on *verb* to register unemployed; hence to be unemployed US, 1885

signs *noun* hand signals showing youth gang affiliation US, 1993

Sigourney Weaver *noun* the vagina. Rhyming slang for BEAVER, formed from the name of the US actress (b.1949) UK, 2003

sig quote *noun* in computing, an aphorism automatically included with the user's formatted signature US, 1991

silencer *noun* a motorcycle muffler. The UK conventional English 'silencer' is US slang US, 1973

silent *adjective* of an entry in a criminal's file, unofficial; showing crimes for which the criminal was not charged but probably committed US, 1990

silent but deadly *adjective* applied to the unpleasant smell that hangs in the air as a result of a silent fart. Unpleasant but hardly deadly. Anecdotal evidence and experience place this term in the 1970s UK, 1999

silent captain *noun* in shuffleboard, the scoreboard US, 1967

silent death *noun* an electric train. By comparison with steam engines, at the date (around 1950) of the introduction of electric trains UK, 1970

silent flute *noun* the penis. Variation of FLUTE (the penis) UK, 1788

silent flute of love *noun* the erect penis UK, 2003

silent night *noun* a *light* ale. Rhyming slang UK, 1992

silent violent *noun* an unpleasantly aromatic fart that pollutes without warning, a silent fart. A variation of SILENT BUT DEADLY UK, 2003

silk *noun* **1** a white person US, 1960. **2** a homosexual US, 1972. **3** in the categorisation of sexual activity by teenage boys, a touch of a girl's crotch outside her underwear US, 1986. **4** money US, 1950. **5** heroin UK, 2002. ▶ **hit the silk; take to silk** to open a parachute after jumping from a plane US, 1933

silk *adjective* **1** white-skinned US, 1960. **2** homosexual US, 1962

silk and satin *noun* any combination of central nervous system stimulants and central nervous system depressants US, 1980

silk department *noun* the very best AUSTRALIA, 1989

silk glove *noun* a guard on a passenger train. Not praise US, 1977

silk hat *noun* in circus and carnival usage, an egocentrist US, 1981

silkies *noun* a woman's underpants US, 1986

silks *noun* silk or nylon socks *US, 1972*

silk-stocking *adjective* wealthy *US, 1970*

silky *adjective* excellent; pleasing; smooth *US, 1973*

silky-straight *noun* any hairstyle with artificially straightened hair *US, 1981*

Silky Sullivan *noun* in horse racing, any horse that comes from far behind to win a race. Ridden by Willie Shoemaker, the original Silky Sullivan came from 30 lengths behind to win the 1958 Santa Anita Derby by three lengths *US, 1997*

silly affairs *noun* used as a humorous synonym for 'Civil Affairs' *US, 1968*

silly as a two-bob watch *adjective* very silly *NEW ZEALAND, 1984*

silly billy *noun* a fool. Formed on Billy, a familiar diminutive of William; originally used as a nickname for William Frederick, Duke of Gloucester (1776–1834) and William IV (1765–1837), then as a popular name for a clown, especially a clown's juvenile stooge *UK, 1834*

silly bollock; silly bollocks *noun* a contemptible fool *UK, 1999*

silly cunt *noun* a fool *UK, 2000*

silly dust *noun* a powdered drug *UK, 2003*

silly season *noun* from a police perspective, the summer as a period of counterculture, pop, rock and dance festivals. From the familiar journalistic sense. Used by late 1980s–early 90s counterculture travellers *UK, 1999*

silly side bin *noun* psilocybin or psilocin, in powder or capsule form. Nonsense pun on the chemical name *UK, 1999*

sillyvillian *noun* a civilian, seen from the cynical eyes of the military *US, 1963*

silly walk *noun* in computing, an absurd procedure that must be followed. A borrowing from Monthy Python *US, 1991*

sillywatter *noun* any alcoholic drink, especially in reference to a drinker's foolish behaviour *UK: SCOTLAND, 1996*

silver *noun* **1** marijuana. Based on the colour of the leaves *UK, 2000*. **2** in American casinos, a silver coin or $1 chip *US, 1980*. **3** money *US, 1966*. **4** a type of bet in an illegal numbers game lottery *US, 1957*

silver and gold *adjective* old. Rhyming slang *UK, 1998*

silver bike *noun* a metal syringe. Drug addict usage *US, 1970*

silver bullet *noun* **1** an ideal, usually notional, solution to a problem. From the mythology that a silver bullet is fatal to a werewolf; this symbol was also adopted by the eponymous hero of television western *The Lone Ranger*, 1956–62 *UK, 2002*. **2** a martini *US, 1988*

silver goose *noun* a proctoscope *US, 1989*

silver haze *noun* a hybrid strain of marijuana. From the frosty colour of the leaf *UK, 1999*

silver lady *noun* a hypodermic needle and syringe *US, 1993*

silvermine *verb* to patrol a casino in search of coins left in the tray of a slot machine or dropped on the floor *US, 1985*

silver plate please. Intentionally butchered *s'il vous plaît US, 1990*

silvers *noun* any coins *TRINIDAD AND TOBAGO, 2003*

silver spoon *noun* **1** used as a metaphor of wealth at birth, especially in the expression 'born with a silver spoon in your mouth' *US, 1972*. **2** the moon. Rhyming slang *UK, 1992*

silver surfer *noun* an elderly or retired person who uses the Internet. Adopting the identity of cartoon superhero the Silver Surfer, created in 1966 by Stan Lee and Jack Kirby for Marvel Comics; this puns 'silver' (the hair colour) and 'surfer' (someone who browses the Internet) *UK, 2001*

silvertail *noun* **1** a member of the privileged class. Derogatory *AUSTRALIA, 1891*. **2** a prisoner who enjoys privileges *AUSTRALIA, 1950*

silvertail *adjective* pretentious *AUSTRALIA, 1962*

silvery moon *noun* a black person. Rhyming slang for COON *UK, 1979*

silvery spoon *noun* a black person. Rhyming slang for COON *UK, 1977*

sim *noun* a simulator; a simulation *UK, 1979*

simmer down *verb* to calm down *US, 1871*

simoleon *noun* a dollar *US, 1896*

simp *noun* a fool; a simpleton *US, 1903*

simp *adjective* **1** foolish. From SIMP (a simpleton) *US, 2000*. **2** fashionable *US, 1965*

simple as very easy. The familiarity of the phrase 'it is as *simple as* that' has allowed a gradual clipping; first the verb was generally considered unnecessary to express the intention, then 'as' was slurred aside, finally 'that' is understood; it is as simple as that *UK, 2001*

simple pimp *noun* a pimp who fails to live up to the high standards of his fellow pimps *US, 1972*

simple Simon *noun* **1** a diamond (the precious stone; the suit of cards); Double Diamond™ (a branded beer). Rhyming slang, formed from a nursery rhyme character *UK, 1992*. **2** psilocybin, a hallucinogenic mushroom *US, 1970*

simp twister *noun* in circus and carnival usage, a carousel *US, 1981*

sin *noun* ▶ **as sin** extremely, especially in phrases 'ugly as sin' and 'miserable as sin' *UK, 1821*

sin! used for registering shock or surprise. Ironic euphemism for FUCK! *UK, 2001*

sin bin *noun* **1** in team sports, an off-field area a player can be sent to for a period as a punishment for breaking the rules *CANADA, 1970*. **2** in prison, a punishment cell or the punishment block *UK, 1996*. **3** a panel van or the like used for sexual encounters *AUSTRALIA, 1984*. ▶ **in the sin bin** ostracised *AUSTRALIA, 1995*

sin-bin *verb* **1** to temporarily remove a person from duty or office while they are under investigation for some misdeed *AUSTRALIA, 1983*. **2** in team sports, to send a player to the sin bin *AUSTRALIA, 1983*

since Adam was a pup for a very long time *AUSTRALIA, 1956*

since Hector was a pup for a very long time *US, 1904*

since time for a very long time *UK, 2003*

sin city *noun* the neighbourhood in An Khe, Vietnam, housing brothels, bars and other vice dens *US, 1968*

Sinead O'Connor; Sinead *noun* a *doner* kebab. Popney rhyming slang, based on the name of Irish singer Sinead O'Connor (b.1966). Popney was contrived for *www.music365.co.uk*, an Internet music site *UK, 2001*

sine-died *adjective* permanently barred (from a bar or sporting endeavour). From Latin *sine die* (without a day) used in legal language for 'an indefinite adjournment' *UK: SCOTLAND, 1996*

sing *verb* **1** to give information or evidence, usually to the police *US, 1929*. **2** in carnival usage, to make a sales pitch *US, 1981*. **3** in a big store confidence swindle, to provide false information to the intended victim *1997*. ▶ **sing in the choir** to be homosexual. Cute code *US, 1994*. ▶ **sing like a canary** to give information or evidence, usually to the police. An elaboration of SING *US, 1950*

Singapore grey *noun* hashish purportedly manufactured in Singapore *US, 1971*

singbird *noun* a police informer *US, 1982*

sing-cerely used as a humorous closing in letters between singers *US, 1975*

singer *noun* **1** in a confidence swindle, a participant who passes information about the false enterprise to the victim *US, 1985*. **2** in trucking, a recapped tyre. Named after the road noise *US, 1971*

Singin' Johnny *noun* homebrew *CANADA, 1998*

single eye *noun* a Japanese person. Hawaiian youth usage *US, 1982*

single-fish *noun* a urination. Glasgow rhyming slang for PISH (a PISS) *UK: SCOTLAND, 1988*

single-O *noun* a criminal, gambling cheat or a prisoner who acts alone *US, 1962*

single-O *verb* to operate as a criminal without confederates; to operate selfishly within a criminal enterprise *US, 1950*

single-O *adjective* selfish *US, 1950*

singles bar *noun* a bar that caters to a young, unattached clientele *US, 1969*

single-skinner *noun* a single fence *UK, 2002*

single-stakes-about *noun* in gambling, a type of conditional bet *UK, 2001*

singlie *noun* a single man *UK, 1995*

Singlish *noun* a Singaporean adaptation of the English language; a variety of English used in Sri Lanka *SINGAPORE, 2001*

sing on *verb* in the context of a calypso song, to disparage or tease someone *TRINIDAD AND TOBAGO, 1958*

singular! great! *US, 1992*

sinistered area *noun* in Quebec, a disaster area. The French phrase *zone sinestress* is the source of this phrase when used in English in this way *CANADA, 2001*

sink *noun* in the language of hang gliding, falling air that increases the speed of descent *US, 1977*. ▶ **behind the sink** depleted of funds *US, 1974*

sink *verb* to down a drink *AUSTRALIA, 1911*. ▶ **sink the pink** to have sex. Snooker imagery *US, 2001*

sinker *noun* **1** a doughnut *US, 1962*. **2** a dent on a surfboard that requires a resin filler *US, 1986*

sin loi, motherfucker sorry about that. *Xin loi* or *sin loi* is Vietnamese meaning something in the nature of 'sorry about that'. It was widely heard and widely used by US troops in Vietnam *US, 1990*

sinner *noun* a person *IRELAND, 1991*

Sip *nickname* the state of Mississippi *US, 1970*

sip *verb* ▶ **sip at the fuzzy cup** to perform oral sex on a woman *US, 1980*. ▶ **sip suds; sip on suds** to drink beer *US, 1986*

siphon *verb* ▶ **siphon the python; syphon the python 1** (of a male) to urinate. A jocular construction rhyming a reasonably conventional use of 'syphon' with PYTHON (the penis) *AUSTRALIA, 1968*. **2** (of a male) to have sex *US, 1984*

Sippie *noun* a member of the Student Information Processing Board at the Massachusetts Institute of Technology. Acronym *US, 1990s*

sipple *adjective* slippery *TRINIDAD AND TOBAGO, 1973*

sip-sip *verb* to whisper, especially when gossiping *BAHAMAS, 1982*

sir and miss *noun* syphilis. Rhyming slang *UK, 2003*

Sir Anthony Blunt; Sir Anthony *noun* a fool; a despicable fool. Rhyming slang for CUNT, probably coined by comedian and satirist Peter Cook (1937–95). Sir Anthony Blunt (1907–83) was an art historian and traitor who spied for the Soviet Union ('the fourth man') and, eventually, had his knighthood removed *UK, 1979*

Sir Charles *noun* the Viet Cong *US, 1982*

Sir Walter Scott *noun* a pint glass, a pint *pot*. Rhyming slang, formed from the name of the Scottish novelist and poet, 1777–1832 *UK, 1992*

sis *noun* **1** used as a term of address for a sister *UK, 1656*. **2** used as a form of address for a girl or young woman; also (when used by a man of a younger woman) may imply no sexual interest *US, 1859*

sissified; sissy; cissy *adjective* effeminate. From SISTER via SIS *US, 1846*

sissy *noun* an effeminate boy or man, especially a homosexual; a coward *US, 1879*

sissy bar *noun* **1** on a motorcyle or bicycle, a back rest for the passenger seated behind the driver. The suggestion is that a manly man or tough woman has no need for the back rest *US, 1969*. **2** a bar patronised by homosexuals *US, 1982*

sissy stick *noun* in pool, a mechanical device used to support the cue on hard-to-reach shots *US, 1970*

sissy tank *noun* a jail holding cell reserved for homosexual prisoners *US, 1981*

sister *noun* **1** used as a form of address for a woman whose name is unknown *US, 1906*. **2** a black woman *US, 1968*. **3** a form of address between homosexual men. This CAMP adoption of the feminine form is also reflected in the cross-gender assignment of pronouns *UK, 1992*. **4** a fellow homosexual *US, 1949*. **5** a female fellow member of a countercultural or underground political movement *US, 1968*

sister act *noun* a relationship, usually sexual, between two homosexuals with the same orientation *US, 1965*

sister girl *noun* used as a female-to-female term of address, often sternly *US, 1989*

sister hix *noun* in craps, a six *US, 1983*

sisterhood *noun* the bond that unites male homosexuals *US, 1979*

sistren *noun* (of women) friends. Conventional 'sisters' with religious and political overtones adopted for everyday use by the West Indian and UK black communities *UK, 2000*

sit *noun* **1** in harness racing, the position immediately behind another horse, thus using the other horse as a wind-break *US, 1997*. **2** in horse racing, a contract for a jockey to ride a race *AUSTRALIA, 1989*

sit *verb* ▶ **sit like Miss Queenie** to sit with your legs crossed as others work *DOMINICA, 1977*. ▶ **sit on your hands** to refrain from applause at a moment when applause would be appropriate *US, 1981*. ▶ **sit tight** to stay where you are; especially to remain in place when it would be easier to go *UK, 1999*. ▶ **sit up and beg** describes elderly cars and old-fashioned bicycles and motorcycles; also the position adopted by old-drivers of such vehicles *UK, 1979*

sit-and-grab *noun* in a carnival, a food concession with seating *US, 1960*

sit-arse *verb* to wait; to do nothing. A contraction of 'sit on your arse' *UK, 2001*

sit beside her *noun* a spider. Rhyming slang that seems to have its origins in the nursery rhyme 'Little Miss Muffet' *UK, 1992*

sitch *noun* a situation *US, 1967*

sitcom *noun* a situation comedy. A protocol for television comedies since the early 1950s in which the humour is drawn from the confluence of characters and situations *US, 1964*

sit-down *noun* **1** a meeting or conversation over a meal or while sitting *UK, 1861*. **2** in organised crime, a discussion of a dispute between members of the crime enterprise with a final and binding decision rendered by a leader or group of leaders *US, 1975*. **3** a base camp or town in the rear, away from combat. Vietnam war use *US, 1990*

sit down *verb* to join a poker game *US, 1963*

sit-down money *noun* amongst Australian Aboriginals, government welfare or unemployment benefits *AUSTRALIA, 1978*

sit hard *verb* (of ducks) to stay on an egg-nest as long as possible in the approach of danger *CANADA, 1958*

sit in *verb* **1** to play by invitation with a band to which the musician does not belong *US, 1936*. **2** to join a poker game *US, 1967*

sit on it! used as an expression of disapproval. Popularised in the 1970s by frequent use on the television series *Happy Days US, 1979*

sitrep *noun* a situation report. Military *UK, 1995*

sit-still *noun* in horse racing, a style of riding based on patience *US, 1976*

sitter *noun* **1** a woman who works in a bar, encouraging male customers to drink and to buy them drinks *US, 1987*. **2** a hostess in a brothel, neither prostitute nor madam *AUSTRALIA, 1985*. **3** a person who monitors and comforts an alcohol or drug addict who is going through the initial stages of detoxification. A term used in twelve-step recovery programmes such as Alcoholics Anonymous *US, 1998*. **4** a person who guides another or others through an LSD experience. An allusion to the practice of babysitting *US, 1966*. **5** in pool, a ball perched on the lip of a pocket *US, 1924*

sitting breeches *noun* the trousers worn (figuratively) by visitors who have over-stayed their welcome *BARBADOS, 1965*

sitting britches *noun* the trousers worn (figuratively) by an idler or laggard *US, 1963*

sitting down *noun* in fencing, the 'on guard/en garde' position. From the bending of the legs *UK, 1988*

sitting duck *noun* **1** an easy target. Originally military; figurative use of hunting imagery *UK, 1944*. **2** a stolen car discovered by police through serendipitous checking of number plates *US, 1970*

sitting on a goldmine used admiringly of a sexually attractive person, especially one who does not take financial advantage of his or her attraction *US, 1972*

sit upon *noun* the posterior. Euphemistic *UK, 1961*

sitzmark *noun* among British Columbia skiers, the imprint left in the snow from a skier's fall *CANADA, 1989*

Siwash *noun* a stupid person. Originally from Chinook jargon, this term was used by explorers for Native American Indians, but over time it has become an insult both to the native peoples and to the person so designated *CANADA, 1976*

Siwash *verb* to place a non-Native American Indian person on the list of people not allowed to buy alcohol *CANADA, 1989*

Siwash blanket *noun* low cloud cover *CANADA, 1998*

Siwash logger *noun* a beachcomber. This term carries on the early derogatory use of siwash for any Indians or their customs *CANADA, 1962*

Siwash wind *noun* a storm that comes on quickly *CANADA, 1998*

six *noun* **1** a lookout during a crime *US, 1987*. **2** a six-pack of a beverage *US, 1992*. **3** a six-fluid-ounce glass of beer *AUSTRALIA, 1972*. **4** a unit commander *US, 1976*. ▶ **behind the six** without funds *US, 1967*. ▶ **take six** to re-enlist in the military for six years *US, 1968*

six-and-eight *noun* a poor condition. Rhyming slang for STATE *UK, 1980*

six-and-eight *adjective* honest, legitimate. Rhyming slang for STRAIGHT (honest) *UK, 1959*

six and four *noun* heroin mixed with other substances. Probably from the ratio of ingredients *UK, 1996*

sixer *noun* **1** anything that counts or scores as six, especially a six in cricket *UK, 1870*. **2** a six-pack of beer *US, 1993*. **3** a jail sentence of six months *US, 1949*. **4** a corporal punishment of six strokes with a cane. A variation of SIX OF THE BEST *UK, 1927*

sixes *noun* a small drink of rum. Originally costing six cents *TRINIDAD AND TOBAGO, 1968*. ▶ **all the sixes** sixty-six. In Bingo, House or Tombola the formula 'all the' announces a double number *UK, 1943*

six feet under *adjective* dead and buried *UK, 1942*

six-for-fiver *noun* a money lender who operates informally to advance workers money on their wages *US, 1953*

sixie; sixie from Dixie *noun* in craps, the number six *US, 1985*

six moon *noun* a six-months prison sentence *UK, 2000*

six o'clock girl *noun* a thin girl *US, 1947*

six o'clock jump *noun* an enema given to a patient the night before surgery *US, 1946*

six o'clock swill *noun* a last minute rush for drinks in a hotel bar prior to six o'clock closing time. Now obsolete as opening hours for hotels have been expanded *AUSTRALIA, 1955*

six of the best *noun* a corporal punishment of six strokes with a cane *UK, 1912*

six-pack *noun* **1** a well developed and defined abdominal musculature. From the superficial resemblance between the muscles and a six-pack of beer cans *US, 1997*. **2** a car carburettor system with six barrels *US, 1993*

six-packer *noun* a man with well-developed and defined abdominal musculature; a well-built man. Teen slang *SOUTH AFRICA, 2003*

six-packs *noun* in craps, a roll of twelve *US, 1999*

sixpennyworth *noun* a prison term of six months *UK, 1957*

six, six, and a kick *noun* military discipline consisting of six months imprisonment, six months forfeiture of pay and a bad-conduct discharge from the service *US, 1991*

sixteen *noun* an M-16 rifle *US, 1985*

sixteenth *noun* a sixteenth of an ounce (of drugs) *US, 1988*

six tits *noun* in poker, three queens *US, 1948*

six-to-five!; sixty-five!; sixty fifth street! used as a warning among criminals or swindlers that a police officer is nearby *US, 1950*

six to four *noun* a whore. Rhyming slang, from racing odds *UK, 1939*

six-to-six *noun* **1** a prostitute. From their working hours – evening to dawn *FIJI, 1996*. **2** a conversation between two unit commanders *US, 1991*

six-trey *noun* sixty-three; 63rd Street *US, 1972*

sixty days *noun* in dice games, a roll of six *US, 1962*

sixty-eight *noun* used as a humorous variation on sixty-nine – you give me oral sex and I'll owe you one *US, 1982*

sixty-four dollar question; sixty-four thousand dollar question; sixty-four million dollar question *noun* a question that gets to the heart of the matter. The US radio quiz show *Take It or Leave It* offered a highest prize of $64, giving rise to the catch-phrase 'sixty-four dollar question'. The phrase gained currency and three decimal places in televised quiz shows on both sides of the Atlantic *US, 1942*

six up! used as a warning in the usage of counterculturalists associated with the Rainbow Nation gatherings and the Grateful Dead that law enforcement officials are approaching *US, 1994*

size queen *noun* a homosexual male or a woman who is attracted to men with large penises *US, 1963*

sizzle *noun* **1** a sister, in the sense as a female companion, especially in the phrase 'fa' shizzle my sizzle'. A hip-hop, urban black coinage, formed as a rhyming reduplication of SHIZZLE (sure, yes). After 'fa' shizzle my nizzle' (yes my nigger) *US, 2003*. **2** an illegal drug *US, 1969*

sizzle *verb* to be executed by electrocution in the electric chair *US, 1982*

sizzler *noun* **1** in cricket, an exceedingly fast ball; an extremely fast horse, etc *UK, 1961*. **2** an unskilled cook *US, 1975*

sizzle seat *noun* the electric chair; capital punishment by electrocution *US, 1982*

SK8 *noun* in text messaging, a skate or to skate. A variant spelling; one of several constructions in which a syllable pronounced 'ate' is replaced by the homophone 'eight' *US, 2002*

ska *noun* a rhythmic musical style that evolved into reggae. Coinage, in the late 1950s or very early 60s, is generally credited to Jamaican bassist Cluet Johnson when trying to explain the sound and rhythm of ya-ya music; Cluet Johnson is also recorded as using 'skavoovee' and 'love skavoovie' as a nonsensical but American-sounding greeting *JAMAICA, 1993*

skagged up *adjective* intoxicated by or addicted to heroin *UK, 1993*

skanger *noun* a member of a Dublin/Kilkenny subcultural urban adolescent, teenage and young-adult-male grouping that is given to hanging around and causing trouble *IRELAND, 2001*

skank *noun* **1** a girl whose sole attraction is her immorality and sexual availability. An abusive description possibly derived from 'skunk' *US, 1966*. **2** a prostitute *US, 2002*. **3** a confidence trick; a fraud. After SKANK (to steal). West Indian, hence UK black *UK, 1994*. **4** nastiness, filth *US, 1995*

skank *verb* **1** to work a confidence trick; to operate a fraud; to work behind someone's back. West Indian and UK black slang which spread into wider criminal circles. An earlier, surviving usage is a dance style, which imagery suggests the possible etymology is of a figurative dance around the victim of the trick *UK, 2000*. **2** to move to reggae rhythms in a particular loose-limbed style *JAMAICA, 1992*. **3** to steal something *UK, 1997*

skank off *verb* to play truant *UK, 1997*

skank-pit *noun* an unpleasant, distasteful place *US, 1999*

skanky *adjective* ugly; cheap; nasty *US, 1975*

skat; skattie *noun* used as a term of endearment. From Afrikaans *schat* (treasure) *SOUTH AFRICA, 1964*

skate *noun* **1** an easy task *US, 1976*. **2** an extremely unattractive woman who is seen as a sex object, especially one who is ravaged by age. Possibly from obsolete 'skate' (an inferior horse) and influenced by the sense 'an unpleasant man' *UK, 1896*. **3** an unpleasant man *US, 1896*. **4** a lazy and/or incompetent worker. US Army usage *US, 1998*. **5** an act of letting someone escape wrongdoing without punishment *US, 1992*. **6** a tyre *US, 1976*. **7** a motorcycle *US, 1970* ▷ *see:* ROLLERSKATE. ▶ **do a skate** to vanish *NEW ZEALAND, 1998*

skate *verb* **1** to get away with something; to escape punishment *US, 1945*. **2** to win easily *UK: SCOTLAND, 1996*. **3** in the used car business, to steal another salesman's sale *US, 1975*. **4** to dance *IRELAND, 1991*. **5** to be without money *TRINIDAD AND TOBAGO, 1996*

skate Betty *noun* a girl who associates with skateboarders, perhaps skateboarding herself *US, 1989*

skate jockey *noun* a driver of a small car, especially a sports car. Citizens' band radio slang, combines 'skate' (small car) with another form of 'driver' *US, 1976*

skate rat *noun* a devoted, perhaps skilled skateboarder *US, 1989*

skating *adjective* drunk *UK, 1984*

sked *noun* in remote country regions, a schedule for a radio call *AUSTRALIA, 1946*

sked *verb* to schedule. A shortening of the US pronunciation *US, 2004*

skedaddle; skiddadle *verb* to leave in a hurry. Originally US Civil War slang, with claims of Swedish and Danish origins probably disproved *US, 1861*

Skedaddle Ridge *noun* a hill in southern New Brunswick *CANADA, 1995*

skee *noun* **1** whisky, especially low quality, low cost whisky *US, 1950*. **2** opium; heroin *US, 1960*

skeef *noun* an attractive female *JAMAICA, 2000*

skeef *adverb* disapprovingly. From Afrikaans *skeef* (askew) *SOUTH AFRICA, 1969*

skeenteen *noun* used as an imaginary high number *US, 1968*

skeet *noun* **1** a girl *UK, 2003*. **2** in poker, a nonstandard hand consisting of a 9, a 5, a 2, one card between 5 and 9 and one card between 2 and 5 *US, 1963*

skeet *verb* **1** to ejaculate *US, 2002*. **2** to eject liquid from a syringe *US, 1971*

skeeve *noun* a disgusting individual *US, 1976*

skeeve; skeeve out *verb* to disgust *US, 1976*

skeevie *noun* a disgusting person. Teen slang *US, 1955*

skeevie; skeevy *adjective* disgusting *US, 1976*

skeevosa *noun* a disgusting individual. An extension of SKEEVE (a disgusting individual) *US, 1995*

skeeze *verb* to have sex *US, 1990*

skeezer *noun* a woman who will perform sex for crack cocaine *US, 1990*

skeezix *noun* a fool. After a character (a foundling, adopted by Walt and Phyllis Rumpus Blossom, who grew up to be the father of Chipper and Clovia) in Frank O. King's newspaper comic strip *Gasoline Alley US, 1975*

skeff *noun* a confidence swindle *TRINIDAD AND TOBAGO, 1975*

skeg *noun* **1** a surfer. The variant 'sceg' also exists *AUSTRALIA, 1985*. **2** a member of a subcultural social grouping of pubescent or adolescent girls *IRELAND, 2001*. **3** a fin on a surfboard *US, 1962*

skeg-first *adverb* while surfing, said of the beginning of a ride with the tail of the surfboard pointing towards shore *US, 1988*

skeg-head *noun* a surfer *AUSTRALIA, 1988*

skein of thread; skein *noun* a bed. Rhyming slang *UK, 1979*

skeletons fucking on a tin roof used as a perfect simile for a rattling noise *US, 1961*

skell; skel *noun* a vagrant, especially of the thuggish sort. Seemingly related to the C17 'skelder', an honorable cant term for 'a professional beggar' which was long obsolete when 'skell' started to show up in New York in the early 1970s. A favourite word of police television dramas in the 1990s; the screenplay by Gardner Stern for episode 2 of season 2 of *NYPD Blue* that aired in September 1994 was titled *For Whom the Skell Rolls US, 1957*

skerrick *noun* a small amount of something. From British dialect *AUSTRALIA, 1854*

sketch *noun* **1** a situation, an arrangement *UK, 2000*. **2** a term of endearment for someone *IRELAND, 1997*. ▶ **keep sketch** to keep watch *IRELAND, 1996*

sketch *adjective* suspicious; threatening *US, 2003*

sketchy *noun* an odd or weird person. Used amongst foot-powered scooter-riders *UK, 2000*

sketchy *adjective* dangerous; possibly dangerous *US, 2002*

skew-whiff; skiwift *adjective* awry; askew; at the wrong angle *UK, 1754*

ski *verb* in soccer, to kick the ball unnecessarily high in the air *US, 1945*

-ski *suffix* used in combination to intensify an adjective or adverb *UK: SCOTLAND, 1988*

ski bum *noun* a ski enthusiast who spends as much time as possible skiing and as little time as possible working *US, 1963*

ski bunny *noun* a female who is learning to ski; a female who visits ski resorts for the company but does not ski *US, 1963*

skid *noun* heroin, especially when heavily adulterated *US, 1977*

skid *verb* while snowboarding, to slide down a slope sideways *US, 1993*

skid artist *noun* a getaway driver *UK, 1996*

Skid Blvd. *noun* a jocular honorific for a living area for poor people *CANADA, 1963*

skiddies *noun* **1** underpants *UK, 1995*. **2** faecal marks in underwear *UK, 1999*

skidge *verb* attack! A command inciting a dog to attack. A variant of SKITCH! *AUSTRALIA, 1983*

skid lid *noun* **1** a safety helmet or crash helmet *US, 1968*. **2** a paratrooper's helmet *US, 1991*

skid mark *noun* a faecal stain on a toilet bowl or underwear *AUSTRALIA, 1971*

skidoo *noun* a snowmobile *CANADA, 1961*

skidoo *verb* **1** to depart hastily *US, 1905*. **2** to travel by skidoo (a snowmobile) *CANADA, 1986*

skid row *noun* **1** in any town, the run-down area where the socially disadvantaged and marginalised tend to congregate *US, 1931*. **2** in prison, cells for troublesome prisoners *UK, 1996*

skids *noun* underpants. Derives from SKID MARK(s) (faecal stains in underwear) *UK, 1996*. ▶ **put the skids under** (of a person or circumstances) to ensure the imminent dismissal of someone; to dismiss someone from employment *UK, 1948*

skid shot *noun* in pool, a shot made with backspin on the cue ball *US, 1993*

skied *adjective* drug-intoxicated. A play on 'sky' not 'ski', as 'HIGH in the sky' *US, 1989*

skiff *noun* an attractive girl *BAHAMAS, 1982* ▷*see:* SKIT

skiffle *noun* **1** a music genre, a sort of poor-man's rock 'n' roll, played on homemade or low budget instruments, popular in the late 1950s. Originates in 1930s and 40s US black society, meaning a house-party at which a subscription was charged to cover costs and raise money to meet the rent. Music was played by groups of amateur musicians. From conventional 'scuffle' (an impromptu struggle) *UK, 1957*. **2** a very short hairstyle *JAMAICA, 1999*

skill! used as a register or exclamation of approval *UK, 2003*

skim *noun* money stolen from a business or enterprise, skimmed from the business funds like cream from milk *US, 1988*

skim *verb* to divert a portion of your earnings or winnings to avoid paying taxes or to avoid paying your superiors in the enterprise their share *US, 1966*

skimaged *adjective* drunk. English gypsy use *UK, 2000*

skimmer *noun* a hat *US, 1972*

skimming *verb* criminal acquisition of credit or debit card details by use of an electronic reader *UK, 2003*

skim money *noun* money taken from an enterprise's net proceeds before any accounting of the proceeds *US, 1981*

skimpy *noun* in Western Australia and the Northern Territory, a topless barmaid *AUSTRALIA, 2003*

skin *noun* **1** a person *UK, 1958*. **2** an immature or inexperienced young person. Royal Navy slang *UK, 1989*. **3** contact between hands in greeting, acknowledgement or congratulations *US, 1942*. **4** sex *US, 1976*.

5 a woman as a sex object *TRINIDAD AND TOBAGO, 1936*. **6** the foreskin *UK, 1961*. **7** a condom. Literally, 'an extra layer of (latex) skin' *US, 1965*. **8** a thin paper used to roll marijuana or tobacco cigarettes *US, 1996*. **9** one dollar *US, 1930*. **10** in carnival and amusement park usage, a shirt *US, 1982*. **11** a wallet *US, 1950*. **12** a tyre, especially a well-worn one *US, 1954*. **13** fist fighting *US, 1957*. **14** an American Indian. An abbreviated form of 'redskin' *US, 1989* ▷*see:* SKINHEAD. ► **get under your skin** to irritate; to become constantly irritating *UK, 1896*. ► **no skin off your nose** it makes no difference to you. Variations have included: 'no skin off your ear', 'off your ass', 'off your bugle', 'off you' and 'off Jeff' (thus, any person's name) *UK, 1926*

skin *verb* **1** to inject (a narcotic) into the skin as opposed to a vein *US, 1953*. **2** to swindle someone *US, 1819*. **3** to defeat someone *US, 2002*. **4** in hot rodding, to remove a car's upholstery *US, 1958*. **5** to surf without a wetsuit *US, 1991*. ► **skin (it) back** to withdraw the foreskin from your penis, either as part of a medical inspection or masturbation *US, 2002*. ► **skin teeth** to smile; to grin. The image of showing your teeth. West Indian and UK black *JAMAICA, 1994*. ► **skin the cat** to perform oral sex on a woman *US, 2000*

skin *adjective* **1** young, youthful; fresh, new. Royal Navy slang *UK, 1989*. **2** used of a film or a publication featuring nudity *UK, 1977*

skin and blister *noun* a sister. Rhyming slang *UK, 1925*

skin beater *noun* a drummer *US, 1947*

skin beef *noun* a prison sentence for an unspecified sexual crime *US, 1976*

skin book *noun* a sex-themed book *US, 1970*

skin boy *noun* an uncircumcised male *NEW ZEALAND, 1999*

skin chimney *noun* the vagina *UK, 2002*

skin complaint *noun* a bullet wound *US, 1982*

skinder; skinner *noun* gossip; slanderous rumour. From the verb *SOUTH AFRICA, 1979*

skinder; skinner *verb* to gossip. From Afrikaans *SOUTH AFRICA, 1942*

skinderer *noun* a gossip. From SKINDER (to gossip) *SOUTH AFRICA, 1993*

skindering *noun* an act of gossiping. From SKINDER (to gossip) *SOUTH AFRICA, 1981*

skin diver *noun* **1** a five-pound note; the sum of £5. Glasgow rhyming slang for FIVER *UK: SCOTLAND, 1988*. **2** a person who performs oral sex on a male. The reverse of a 'muff diver' *US, 1969*

skin fighting *noun* a fight between members of rival gangs in which weapons or at least lethal weapons are forbidden *US, 1967*

skin flick *noun* **1** a pornographic film *US, 1968*. **2** a slide used by a dermatologist to illustrate diseases during teaching rounds *US, 1980*

skin-flick house *noun* a cinema showing pornographic films *US, 1972*

skinflint *noun* a mean person *UK, 1700*

skin flute *noun* the penis. Often arises in the phrase 'play the skin flute' (to perform oral sex) *US, 1941*

skinful *noun* more than enough alcohol to achieve a drunken state *UK, 1788*

skin full of *noun* drunk *US, 1985*

skin game *noun* **1** in gambling, a rigged game that honest players always lose *US, 1962*. **2** the science of dermatology *US, 1980*

skingraft *noun* an intramuscular injection of a drug *US, 1968*

skin habit *noun* a drug addiction based on intramuscular, not intravenous, injections *US, 1972*

skinhead; skin *noun* **1** a member of a youth fashion and gang movement, characterised by close-cropped or shaven scalp and smart utilitarian wear, associated with football hooliganism, racist violence and neo-Nazism. Early in the 1970s Richard Allen, a pseudonym of James Moffat (1922–93), published a series of 'youthsploitation' novels under the general title *Skinhead UK, 1969*. **2** a British Leyland 'Allegro' car. Citizens' band radio slang, playing on AGGRO *UK, 1981*

skinhound a sexually aggressive person *CANADA, 2002*

skin house *noun* a brothel or place where the entertainment is of a sexual nature *US, 1970*

skin magazine; skin mag *noun* a magazine featuring photographs of nudes, usually women *US, 1968*

skin man; skinner *noun* a sex offender *US, 1976*

skinner *noun* **1** a big win on an unbacked horse or other race competitor; a betting coup *UK, 1874*. **2** a gambling cheat *US, 1974*. **3** a police officer *US, 1965*

skinny *noun* **1** inside information, rumour or fact *US, 1959*. **2** in circus and carnival usage, a ten-cent piece *US, 1981*

skinny *adjective* **1** miserly; niggardly *UK, 1998*. **2** prepared with low-fat or non-fat milk *US, 1997*

skinny as a broom; skinny *noun* a bridegroom. Rhyming slang *UK, 1992*

skinny-dip *verb* to swim in the nude *US, 1966*

skinny dipping in the love pond *noun* from a male perspective, the act of sex without a condom *US, 2001*

skinny Dugan *noun* in craps, any combination of seven *US, 1985*

skinny end *noun* in horse racing, a third place finish *AUSTRALIA, 1989*

skinnymalink *noun* a thin person *UK: SCOTLAND, 1911*

skinny-minny *adjective* very thin; small and thin *US, 1997*

skin one; skin two; skin three *noun* used as a rating system by US forces in Vietnam for the films shown on base; the system evaluated films on the amount of nudity. Higher ratings reflected higher amounts of nudity *US, 1990*

skin out *verb* to clean something out; to finish something *CANADA, 1999*

skinpix *noun* pornographic films *US, 1964*

skin pop *noun* an injection of a drug into the skin or muscle, not into a vein *US, 1952*

skin-pop *verb* to inject a drug into the skin or muscle, not into a vein. Usually practised in the early stages of drug use *US, 1952*

skin popper *noun* a drug user who does not inject the drug into a vein *US, 1967*

skin-popping *noun* an act of injecting a drug subcutaneously, not into a vein *UK, 1973*

skin-pump *verb* to inject a drug under the skin, not into a vein *US, 1952*

skins *noun* drums *UK, 1926*

skin shake *noun* a thorough search of a person's body, including orifices *US, 1967*

skin show *noun* a show featuring women approaching or reaching nudity *US, 1973*

skinsman *noun* **1** a drummer *UK, 1983*. **2** a prolific lover *BARBADOS, 1965*

skint *adjective* having little or no money, penniless. Figurative application of conventional 'skinned' *UK, 1925*

skint as a kipper's backbone *adjective* having no money. An elaboration and intensification of SKINT punning on 'skinned', the original derivation *US, 1956*

skinto *adjective* having little or no money, penniless. A variation of SKINT used in Glasgow *UK: SCOTLAND, 1988*

skin trade *noun* the sex industry in all its facets *US, 1986*

skin up *verb* **1** to roll a marijuana cigarette. From SKIN (cigarette paper) *UK, 1990*. **2** to expose a woman's genitals and breasts *TRINIDAD AND TOBAGO, 1986*

skinz *noun* a sexually attractive woman *US, 1993*

skip *noun* **1** a skipper (a captain, a leader, etc) *UK, 1830*. **2** a coach; used as a term of address for a coach. A shortened form of SKIPPER *US, 1970*. **3** a uniformed police sergeant. An abbreviation of SKIPPER (a US police captain or sergeant) *UK, 2002*. **4** an Anglo-Australian. From Skip, shortening of Skippy, the name of the kangaroo star of the children's television programme *Skippy, The Bush Kangaroo AUSTRALIA, 1987*

skip *verb* ► **skip it** to forget it; to drop the subject; to dispense with something. Often used as an imperative *US, 1934*. ► **skip on** to leave *US, 1989*. ► **skip the cinders; skip the ties** to walk along a railway track *US, 1977*

skip *adjective* Anglo-Australian AUSTRALIA, 1995

skip and jump *noun* the heart. Rhyming slang for PUMP UK, 1992

skip-out *noun* a hotel guest who leaves without paying the bill US, 1958

skip out *verb* to leave in a hurry in order to avoid obligations UK, 1865

skipper *noun* **1** a police chief, captain or sergeant. Jocular, from the C14 nautical sense US, 1929. **2** a sport's team captain. From the use as 'a ship's captain', originally (in this sense) used of the captain of a curling team UK, 1830. **3** a mid-level boss in an organised crime enterprise US, 2003. **4** a prison warden US, 1950. **5** a railway guard US, 1946. **6** a derelict property used as shelter by the homeless. From the C16 when the original sense was 'a barn' (from Welsh ysgubor or Cornish sciber), hence 'a bed out of doors' and, finally, the current use UK, 1925. **7** in poker, a hand with five cards sequenced by twos US, 1963

skipper *verb* **1** to live rough. From SKIPPER (a place of rest for the homeless) UK, 1845. **2** to move from house to house, staying a few nights at each, with all your worldly possessions in tow US, 1971

skippies *noun* inexpensive shoes US, 1990

skippy *noun* a homosexual male US, 1970

skip rat *noun* a litter collector UK, 1996

skirt *noun* a woman or women objectified sexually. In conventional English usage until the late C19 when Victorians deemed it slang; not necessarily pejorative or contemptuous, however various compounds, some now obsolete, objectify women: 'a light skirt' (a loose woman), a BIT OF SKIRT or 'piece of skirt' (a woman as sex object), 'flutter a skirt' (to be a harlot) 'run a skirt' (to keep a mistress) and 'the skirt' (women, collectively) UK, 1899

skit; skiff *noun* a small amount of snow CANADA, 1990

skitch *verb* in icy winter conditions, to grab the bumper of a passing car and use your feet as skis as you are pulled along US, 1997

skitch! attack! A command inciting a dog to attack AUSTRALIA, 1955

skite *noun* **1** a boaster AUSTRALIA, 1897. **2** boastful talk AUSTRALIA, 1860. **3** a glancing blow UK: SCOTLAND, 1985. ▶ **on the skite** engaged in a drinking binge IRELAND, 1992

skite *verb* **1** to boast. From British dialect AUSTRALIA, 1857. **2** to hit someone or something with a glancing blow UK: SCOTLAND, 1911

skitters *noun* diarrhoea. Recorded as 'skitter' in the Scots Dialect Dictionary, 1911 UK: SCOTLAND, 1988

skittery *adjective* worthless IRELAND, 1992

skittle *verb* **1** to knock someone or something down AUSTRALIA, 1938. **2** to kill someone AUSTRALIA, 1971

skittle meon *noun* a sexually available woman JAMAICA, 2002

skittles *noun* dextromethorphan (DXM), an active ingredient in non-prescription cold and cough medication, often abused for non-medicinal purposes US, 2003

skitz *adjective* used for expressing approval UK, 2003

skive *noun* an evasion of duty, work or occupation; an instance of such evasion UK, 1958

skive *verb* to evade a duty, work or occupation; to play truant from school. Possibly from dialect skive (to skim or dart about), more probable is French esquiver (to avoid, to slip away). Adopted into military slang during World War 1, and in widespread use by the middle of the century UK, 1919

skiver *noun* a person who evades work or duty, a shirker UK, 1941

skiving *adjective* work-shy. From SKIVE (to evade work, to shirk) UK, 1959

skivvies *noun* underwear. Originally applied to an undershirt or vest, now to underwear in general US, 1918

skivvy *noun* **1** a domestic servant, especially a maid-of-all-work UK, 1902. **2** during the Vietnam war, a prostitute US, 1991

skivvy *verb* to perform heavy, boring, menial household chores. From the noun UK, 1984

skizziest *adjective* the best US, 1960

skoal; skol *verb* to drink; to down a drink US, 1957

skolly; skollie; scolly *noun* especially in Cape Town, a non-white street hoodlum or petty criminal. From Dutch schullen (to lie low) via Afrikaans SOUTH AFRICA, 1934

skoofer *noun* a marijuana cigarette US, 1980

skookum *adjective* big; powerful; terrific; smart CANADA, 1965

skoon *noun* one dollar US, 1988

skoosh *noun* **1** something that is easily achieved or accomplished UK: SCOTLAND, 1985. **2** any carbonated soft drink UK: SCOTLAND, 1985

skooshed *adjective* drunk UK: SCOTLAND, 1996

skop, skiet and donner *noun* physically violent and threatening behaviour or activity. From Afrikaans skop, skiet en donder (to stop, shoot and beat up). In South African colloquial use: skop (to kick, to enjoy yourself); skiet (to shoot, to gamble with dice, to lie); DONDER (beaten up, also an abusive term of address); skiet and donder (used of action entertainment, 'blood and thunder') SOUTH AFRICA, 1970

skosh; skoshi *noun* a small amount. Korean pidgin, used by US soldiers in Korea and brought back to the US as 'skosh'. The word was given a second wind in the 1970s with a radio advertisement for jeans that promised 'just a skosh more room' in the crotch area for men US, 1970

SKP *noun* an escaped prisoner. A play on 'escapee' US, 1962

skrep *noun* a worn-out, decrepit prostitute TRINIDAD AND TOBAGO, 1973

skronk *noun* in contemporary music, dissonant sounds UK, 1996

skronky *adjective* of an electric guitar's sound or style of playing, excitingly raw and basic; hence, applied to fans of such music US, 2003

skua *noun* frozen chicken. The 'skua' is a large predatory gull; the comparison with chicken is not in the nature of praise ANTARCTICA, 1991

skuif; skuifie; skyf; skyfie *noun* a cigarette, especially a hand-rolled tobacco cigarette, or one containing marijuana. From Afrikaans skuif (a puff of smoke) SOUTH AFRICA, 1946

skull *noun* **1** oral sex US, 1973. **2** a confidence swindle TRINIDAD AND TOBAGO, 1979. **3** a passenger in a lorry. Road hauliers' slang UK, 1951. **4** in circus and carnival usage, a free ticket US, 1981. ▶ **out of your skull** very drunk or drug-intoxicated. Variation on OFF YOUR HEAD UK, 1968. ▶ **take a skull** in a dramatic performance, to react slowly to a line US, 1973

skull *verb* **1** to strike someone; to attack someone IRELAND, 1997. **2** to shun someone JAMAICA, 2003

skull and brains *noun* oral sex US, 2002

skull cracker *noun* strong, homemade whisky US, 1999

skulldrag *verb* in prison, to awake a prisoner in the early hours for immediate transfer to another prison UK, 1996

skulled *adjective* drunk US, 1955

skull-fry *noun* chemically straightened hair US, 1970

skull fuck *noun* an intense assault on all the senses CANADA, 2002

skullfuck *verb* **1** to perform oral sex on a man; (from the male perspective) to receive oral sex CANADA, 2002. **2** (notional) to have sex with a head in symbolic victory. A less realistic variation of the previous sense US, 2000

skullie *noun* a skullcap US, 1993

skull job *noun* an act of oral sex US, 1971

skull money *noun* money earned in illegal ways UK, 2000

skull session *noun* a group analysis and discussion; a conference US, 1959

skunk *noun* **1** a woman, especially a promiscuous woman with deficiencies in the area of hygiene US, 1965. **2** an unpleasant man; a contemptible person. After the North American animal UK, 1841

skunk *verb* in various games, to defeat an opponent by an overwhelming margin US, 1843

skunk beer *noun* inexpensive, bitter, poor quality beer US, 1997

skunked *adjective* drunk US, 2001

skunk juice; skunk juicer; skunk junker *noun* an illegal linear amplifier for a citizens' band radio *US, 1976*

skunk oil *noun* any odorising agent injected into natural gas *US, 1954*

skunk weed; skunk *noun* an extremely potent variety of marijuana which will produce an hallucinogenic effect; also, good quality marijuana *US, 1982*

sky *noun* **1** in a casino, the ubiquitous overhead surveillance system. An abbreviated form of EYE IN THE SKY *US, 1991*. **2** a hat *US, 1976*

sky *verb* **1** to jump high and with great elan *US, 1980*. **2** to leave quickly. Vietnam war slang *US, 1982*

sky-blue-pink *noun* an unknown, indeterminate or fantasy colour. Jocular *UK, 1942*

sky diver *noun* a five-pound note; the sum of £5. Glasgow rhyming slang for FIVER *UK: SCOTLAND, 1988*

sky hook *noun* **1** in oil drilling, a non-existent tool that is often the subject of hazing of new workers *US, 1954*. **2** a citizens' band radio antenna *US, 1976*

sky jockey *noun* a fighter pilot. Gulf war usage *UK, 1991*

sky juice *noun* a cheap refreshment of flavoured ice *JAMAICA, 1972*

skylark *verb* to *park* a vehicle. Rhyming slang *UK, 1964*

sky man *noun* a preacher. A variant of the more common SKY PILOT *US, 1959*

sky-nest *noun* an apartment on an upper floor of an apartment building *US, 1950*

sky palace *noun* a church. The home of a SKY PILOT (a preacher) *UK, 1981*

sky-piece *noun* a hat *US, 1948*

sky pilot *noun* a clergyman, especially in the forces or the prison service. Originally nautical slang *UK, 1887*

skyrocket *verb* (of prices or statistics) to increase steeply *US, 1895*

sky rocket; sky *noun* pocket. Rhyming slang *UK, 1879*

sky scout *noun* an air force chaplain *US, 1945*

skyscraper *noun* paper; writing paper; toilet paper; a newspaper. Rhyming slang *UK, 1992*

sky-shooters *noun* sunglasses *US, 1997*

sky six *noun* God. From 'sky' (a unit commander) *US, 1876*

sky's the limit *noun* in poker, any game played with no limit on the amount of bets *US, 1967*

slab *noun* **1** a road; a highway. A specific application of the generally conventional use as 'a broad, solid mass' *US, 1976*. **2** a thick, dark, cold wave *US, 1991*. **3** a sandwich. Teen slang *CANADA, 1946*. **4** a cardboard carton of 24 cans or bottles of beer *AUSTRALIA, 1997*. **5** a phonograph record; any audio recording *US, 1974*. **6** a package of crack cocaine *US, 1998*. **7** crack cocaine that is heavily adulterated *US, 1992*

slab *verb* in necrophile usage, to engage in sexual activity with a corpse *US, 1987*

slabbed and slid *adjective* 'dead and gone'; also used in prison of an ex-prisoner who has been forgotten *UK, 1950*

slab boy *noun* a necrophile *US, 1987*

slab house *noun* a modest restaurant serving barbecued meat *US, 1975*

slabs *noun* the testicles. Back slang *UK, 1960*

slack *noun* **1** less than harsh treatment *US, 1968*. **2** money *US, 1972*. **3** in a military patrol, the soldier immediately behind the lead soldier in formation *US, 1971*

slack *verb* to wear trousers, especially jeans, oversized, baggy and sagging *US, 1992*

slack *adjective* **1** of a woman, objectionable; of loose morals *AUSTRALIA, 1977*. **2** of poor quality, below standard, unacceptable; lewd, vulgar *UK, 1994*. **3** unproductive; inefficient; lazy *US, 1978*. **4** dreadful; awful; pathetic *NEW ZEALAND, 1981*. **5** contemptibly unfair; unkind *AUSTRALIA, 2000*

slack Alice *noun* a slovenly woman. A fictitious friend called Slack Alice featured in the television comedy monologues of Larry Grayson during the early and mid-1970s *UK: ENGLAND, 2002*

slackarse *noun* a lazy person *AUSTRALIA, 1971*

slack-arse *adjective* tired out, lazy or both *NEW ZEALAND, 1998*

slacker *noun* a person who avoids work, study and responsibility. The most recent burst of popularity for the term is not its first *US, 1898*

Slackers *nickname* Halifax, Nova Scotia. The following etymology is offered by William Pugsley in his 1945, *Slackers, Sinners and other Seamen*: so called because of the relatively slack discipline ashore following duty at sea *CANADA, 1945*

slack jaw *noun* a dolt; a stupid person *US, 1994*

slack man *noun* in a combat march, the second man in line *US, 1989*

slackmeister *noun* someone who has perfected the art of doing nothing *US, 1987*

slackness *noun* **1** lewd and vulgar language. West Indian and UK black patois *UK, 1994*. **2** sexual aggression, promiscuity or perversion *TRINIDAD AND TOBAGO, 1940*

slag *noun* **1** a contemptible person *UK, 1943*. **2** a prostitute; a sexually promiscuous woman *UK, 1958*. **3** an unattractive woman *AUSTRALIA, 1988*. **4** a petty criminal; petty criminals *UK, 1955*. **5** a coward. The earliest of many meanings, all of which are pejorative *UK, 1788*. **6** a negative criticism *AUSTRALIA, 2003*. **7** an insult *UK: SCOTLAND, 1985*

slag *verb* **1** to verbally attack, to slander. Variants include 'slag off' and 'slag down' *UK, 1971*. **2** to spit *AUSTRALIA, 1965*

slag about *verb* to move around; to come and go *UK, 1979*

slag-bag *noun* a contemptible woman. A rhyming combination of SLAG (a contemptible person; a sexually promiscuous woman) and BAG (an unattractive woman) *UK, 1997*

slagging rag *noun* a parachute that is slow to open or does not open at all *US, 1991*

slaggy *noun* a groupie who is promiscuous and sluttish, even by groupie standards *US, 1969*

slaggy *adjective* sluttish *UK, 1943*

slake *verb* ▶ **slake the snake** (of a male) to have sex *US, 1984*

slam *noun* **1** a jail or prison. A shortened form of SLAMMER sometimes; used as a plural *US, 1960*. **2** sexual intercourse *US, 1982*. **3** in foot-powered scootering, a very hard fall *UK, 2000*

slam *verb* **1** to inject an illegal drug intravenously *US, 1996*. **2** to violently jar a mix of alcoholic spirit (usually a shot of tequila) and carbonated soft drink. To prepare a SLAMMER from the action of slamming a covered glass containing the mixture down on a hard surface, e.g. a bar counter *UK, 2001*. **3** to hide prison contraband in your rectum *US, 2000*. **4** to defecate *US, 2001*. **5** to criticise someone or something harshly *US, 1916*. **6** to refuse to work. Prison usage *US, 1950*. **7** in hot rodding and car customising, to modify a car's suspension so as to lower the body *US, 1993*. **8** while riding a surfboard or skateboard, to lose your balance and fall *US, 1984*. **9** to slam dance *US, 1995*

slam bam *noun* **1** homemade whisky *US, 1980s*. **2** a hastily prepared sandwich consisting only of bread and bologna *BAHAMAS, 1995*

slambang *verb* to successfully cheat other gamblers *US, 1950*

slam-bang *adverb* with force or noise *UK, 1840*

slam book *noun* a book with a series of questions to which friends write answers *US, 1969*

slam dance *verb* to dance in a violent manner popular in punk and post-punk settings. Slam dancing was good fodder for popular television in the US, with the *Chips* episode that aired on 31st January 1982 and the *Quincy* episode of 2nd December 1982, both of which centred around the relatively new phenomenon *US, 1981*

slam down *verb* to confine someone to a jail cell *US, 1989*

slam dunk *noun* **1** in the language of wind surfing, an unintended, sudden end of a ride when the board steers too hard to windward *US, 1985*. **2** anything accomplished with ease *US, 2001*

slam-dunk *verb* to defeat someone convincingly, if not overwhelmingly. From the basketball sense of jamming the ball through the hoop *US, 1992*

slam-dunk *adjective* certain *US, 1992*

slam hammer; slam puller *noun* a tool used by car thieves to pull out the cyclinder of the ignition lock *UK, 1977*

slammed *adjective* incarcerated *US, 1982*

slammed back *adjective* under the influence of heroin *US, 1997*

slammer *noun* **1** a door *US, 1946*. **2** a jail or prison. Also in UK use *US, 1952*. **3** solitary confinement *US, 1984*. **4** a mix of alcoholic spirit (usually a shot of tequila) and carbonated soft drink, violently jarred together and gulped down whilst fizzing *UK, 2001*. **5** a person who slam dances *US, 1995*. **6** an illegal linear amplifier for a citizens' band radio *US, 1976*

slammin'; slamming *noun* MDMA, the recreational drug best known as ecstasy *UK, 2003*

slamming *adjective* excellent; beautiful; fabulous. Originally late C19; current usage started in 1980s black society and spread with hip-hop music *US, 1994*

slammin', jammin', throw down happy feet! used for expressing great pleasure *US, 1986*

slam partner *noun* a partner for sex, pure and simple *US, 1993*

slam up *verb* to imprison someone *US, 1990*

slang *noun* in carnival and amusement park usage, a watch chain *US, 1981*

slang *verb* **1** to sell drugs, especially crack cocaine *US, 1991*. **2** to berate someone with abusive language *UK, 1844*. **3** to exhibit or perform in a circus, fair or market; to perform on a stage *UK, 1789*

slanged *adjective* in fetters; in chains *UK, 1812*

slanger *noun* **1** a drug dealer *US, 1997*. **2** a showman. Circus use; from obsolete slang (a travelling show; a single performance of a travelling show) *UK, 1933*

slanging match *noun* an exchange of harsh abuse *UK, 1896*

slangs *noun* slang words or terms. Hawaiian youth usage *US, 1972*

slanguage *noun* a slang vocabulary. A jargon-like attempt to dignify slang as a language *US, 1879*

slanguist *noun* a linguist with a special interest in slang; an expert user of a slang vocabulary. An inevitable construction that lends some dignity to a misunderstood academic; it is first recorded in William Safire's *New York Times* column, 26th October 1980, although 'slangist' was recorded in 1885 as 'a user of slang' *US, 1980*

slant *noun* a South Asian person. Offensive *US, 1942*

slanter *noun* **1** a dishonest trick *AUSTRALIA, 1864*. **2** the eye *US, 1970*

slant-eye *noun* a person from southern Asia. Offensive *US, 1962*

slant six *noun* a six-cylinder engine configured with all six cylinders in line slanted over 30 degrees. Introduced in 1959 for the Plymouth Valiant, it is considered by many to be the most durable engine ever manufactured commercially *US, 1960*

slantville *noun* a neighbourhood dominated by South Asian people *US, 1959*

slanty-eyed; slant-eye *noun* a car of Japanese manufacture. Citizens' band radio slang; a specific application for generally racist terms *US, 1976*

slap *noun* **1** a beating. From the conventional use (to hit with an open hand); as with SPANK it is applied with heavy irony *UK, 2001*. **2** a prison sentence. From a conventional 'slap' given as a punishment *UK, 2000*. **3** theatrical makeup cosmetics. You *slap* it on; theatrical; survives in the face of lighting technology that has made much makeup unnecessary. Also variant 'schlep' *UK, 1860*

slap *verb* **1** to increase the charge for something; to implement a punitive condition *UK, 1922*. **2** especially in jazz or funk music, to play the double bass or bass guitar by pulling at the strings and letting them 'slap' back. 'Slap-style' is also known as 'thumb-style' *US, 1933*. ▶ **slap skins 1** to have sex *US, 1995*. **2** to slap palms in greeting, farewell or approval *US, 1967*. ▶ **slap the bacon in the pan** to have sex *US, 1977*. ▶ **slap the iron to her** to put snow

chains on a truck's tyres *US, 1961*. ▶ **slap the monkey** (of a male) to masturbate. A variation of SPANK THE MONKEY *UK, 2002*

slap *adverb* exactly; perfectly *UK, 1829*

slap and tickle *noun* **1** sex. A little slap and tickle never hurt anyone *UK, 1984*. **2** a pickle. Rhyming slang *UK, 1992*

slap-back *adjective* self-congratulatory *UK, 2001*

slap circuit *noun* the underworld *US, 1963*

slap-down *noun* a humiliating situation *US, 1986*

slap down *verb* to contradict and prevent someone's action, especially when it is done with humiliating effect *UK, 1938*

slap hammer *noun* a hammer designed for pulling dents but used to break open the top of a car's steering column to obtain access to the ignition *US, 1996*

slap-happy *adjective* **1** dazed; confused *US, 1936*. **2** obsessed with masturbation *US, 1962*

slaphead *noun* a bald person, whether naturally so or shaven *UK, 1990*

slaphead *adjective* bald-headed *UK, 1997*

slap-in-the-chops *noun* a shot of pure alcohol *BERMUDA, 1985*

slap on the wrist *noun* any minor punishment *UK, 2002*

slapper *noun* **1** a sexually promiscuous woman. Possibly from SLAP (makeup) or, simply, the sound of flesh on flesh *UK, 1999*. **2** a small, heavy club *US, 1976*. **3** a windscreen wiper *US, 1976*

slapping *noun* a beating *UK, 1997*

slaps *noun* plastic flip-flops (sandals). Skateboarding usage *US, 1976*

slapsie-maxi *noun* a taxi. Rhyming slang *NEW ZEALAND, 1963*

slap-slap *noun* a small police club that fits into a police officer's hand *US, 1962*

slap-up *adjective* (of a meal) excellent, generously provisioned, superior. Originally (1823) used to describe anything or anyone that was considered excellent *UK, 1889*

slash *noun* **1** a urination *UK, 1950*. **2** the vagina *US, 1972*. **3** an attractive, white woman *US, 1987*

slash *verb* **1** to urinate *UK, 1950*. **2** to cut a military-style peaked cap in such a way that the downward angle of the peak is exaggerated *UK, 2001*. **3** to surf aggressively back and forth across the face of a wave *US, 1991*

slash-and-burn *adjective* ruthless; unconcerned with the consequences of a tactic. From a term describing a jungle agricultural practice first recorded in the early 1940s *US, 1989*

slasher *noun* **1** a person who takes a perverse pleasure from vandalism by slashing *US, 1954*. **2** in prison, a self-mutilator *UK, 1996*. **3** a surgeon. Often teamed with anaesthetists as 'GASSERS and slashers' *UK, 2002*. **4** in greyhound racing, a dog that cuts to the inside rail after the first turn *US, 1997*

slash-house *noun* a toilet *AUSTRALIA, 1971*

slat *noun* **1** used to denote five shillings, or the post-decimalisation equivalent of 25p. Originally (1788) 'a half-crown coin'; subsequently, perhaps as a result of inflation, used of a crown (a five-shilling coin) and its value. Thus, pre-1971, 'half-a-slat' was 'a half-crown coin; half-a-crown in value', and so it remained, despite metrication, to represent equivalent values *UK, 1979*. **2** a dollar *US, 1969*. **3** a jail or prison sentence *US, 1973*

slate *noun* marijuana *UK, 1996*

slate *verb* to criticise someone or something harshly *UK, 1848*

slating *noun* an instance of harsh criticism *UK, 1870*

slats *noun* **1** ribs *US, 1898*. **2** prison bars *US, 1950*. **3** skis *US, 1963*

slaughter *noun* a concealed location used by criminals for the division or transfer of recently stolen goods *UK, 1970*

slaughter *verb* **1** to utterly defeat someone *UK, 2001*. **2** to severely criticise someone or something *UK, 1991*. **3** to use a concealed location for temporary storage, distribution or transfer of recently stolen goods *UK, 2001*

slaughtered *adjective* very drunk or drug-intoxicated *US, 1989*

slaughterhouse *noun* **1** a premises where a drug dealer stores drugs *UK, 2003*. **2** a school. Teen slang *US, 1958*

Slaughter on the Water *noun* the 1995 America's Cup sailing race, a lopsided victory by New Zealand *US, 1996*

slave *noun* **1** in a sado-masochistic relationship, a person who endures many forms of humiliation, including extreme pain and public displays of submission *US, 1963*. **2** a submissive prisoner who performs all types of menial tasks for others *US, 1988*. **3** a job *US, 1946*

slave *verb* to work, especially at a menial job *US, 1974*

slave bracelet *noun* a bracelet showing romantic devotion to another *US, 1947*

slave-driver *noun* a stern taskmaster *US, 1854*

slave market *noun* **1** any place where day labourers congregate *US, 1978*. **2** a National Employment Service office *CANADA, 1960*

slave training *noun* the process of instructing, and conditioning the behaviour of, a sexual submissive in order that the submissive's menial service and status become part of a sexual relationship, especially when used in a dominant prostitute's advertising matter *UK, 2003*

slay *verb* to cause someone to laugh uproariously *UK, 1927*

slayer *noun* an assertive young woman. An allusion to the eponymous lead in the television series *Buffy the Vampire Slayer*. Teen slang *UK, 2003*

sleaze *noun* **1** sordidness, sleaziness; immorality *UK, 1967*. **2** political corruption *US, 1983*. **3** a person with low moral standards *US, 1976*

sleazebag *noun* an undesirable, unlikeable person. A useful term when you cannot decide whether to call someone a SCUMBAG or a SLEAZEBALL *US, 1992*

sleazeball *noun* an utterly despicable person *US, 1983*

sleazemeister *noun* an acknowledged expert on, or practitioner of, sordidness, sleaziness, immorality or political corruption. By a combination of SLEAZE and German *meister* (master) *US, 1993*

sleazo *noun* a despicable, sleazy person *US, 1972*

sleazoid *noun* a person of low character *US, 1986*

sleazy *adjective* **1** cheap; inferior; low *US, 1941*. **2** disreputable, especially in a sexually enticing way *UK, 1960*

sleb *noun* a celebrity. A phonetic slurring and reduction *UK, 1997*

sled *noun* **1** a motorcycle. Biker (motorcycle) usage *US, 2003*. **2** a car *US, 1985*

sledge *noun* a verbal criticism designed to put a player off their game *AUSTRALIA, 2000*

sledge *verb* to needle an opponent in order to put them off their game *AUSTRALIA, 1995*

sledgehammer *noun* in pool, a stroke lacking in finesse but full of force *US, 1990*

sledger *noun* in cricket, a fielder who baits, taunts and abuses an opponent as tactical gamesmanship *UK, 2002*

sledgied *adjective* under the influence of MDMA, the recreational drug best known as ecstasy *UK, 1991*

sledging *noun* the practice of needling an opponent in order to put them off their game. Originally, and still principally, in cricket, but now also used in reference to other sports *AUSTRALIA, 1975*

sleekit *adjective* cunning, sly. Dialect *UK: SCOTLAND, 1911*

sleep *noun* **1** a prison sentence of one year *US, 1949*. **2** cocaine. Rich irony; if you do, you won't *US, 1987*

sleep *verb* ▶ **sleep with someone** to have sex with someone *UK, 1819*. ▶ **sleep with the fishes** to be dead as a result of a murder *US, 1972*

sleep around *verb* to be sexually promiscuous *US, 1928*

sleeper *noun* **1** a barbiturate capsule; a sleeping tablet *US, 1961*. **2** heroin *UK, 1998*. **3** a book, film, song, etc, that, having failed to sell successfully on its initial release, eventually becomes a 'hit' *UK, 1984*. **4** in sports, a player who performs exceptionally well in spite of very low initial expectations *US, 1878*. **5** in betting, uncollected winnings; a stake that is illegally retained by the bookmaker when a bet is won *UK, 1956*. **6** in circus and carnival usage, money that a customer overlooks *US, 1981*. **7** in craps, a bet on the table that a

gambler has forgotten is his *US, 1981*. **8** in dominoes, an unused piece that rests numbers-down *US, 1997*. **9** in hot rodding, a conventional-looking, deceptively high-performing car *US, 1965*. **10** a train with sleeping carriages *US, 1958*. **11** a rock just below the land surface *CANADA, 1987*

sleeper jump *noun* any long distance move between performances *US, 1973*

sleeping Bill *noun* a police truncheon *US, 1949*

sleeping policeman *noun* a speed bump *UK, 1973*

sleeping time *noun* a very short jail or prison sentence *US, 1992*

sleep off *verb* to serve a short prison sentence without difficulty *US, 1950*

sleep on *verb* to give overnight consideration to something; to put off making a decision until the following day *UK, 1519*

sleep-out *noun* **1** an enclosed verandah, or part thereof, fitted with a bed for sleeping *AUSTRALIA, 1927*. **2** chiefly in Victoria, a separate outbuilding used as sleeping quarters *AUSTRALIA, 2003*

Sleepy-R *noun* the Canadian Pacific Railway *CANADA, 1987*

sleepy seeds *noun* the deposits of mucus formed about the eyes during sleep *US, 1975*

sleet *noun* crack cocaine. From the drug's resemblance to sleet *US, 1994*

sleeve *noun* a condom *UK, 1998*. ▶ **on the sleeve** used of someone who injects drugs. From the need to roll up a sleeve before injecting *UK, 1996*. ▶ **put the sleeve on someone** to arrest someone *UK, 1996*

sleeve *verb* to tattoo the lower half of the arm *US, 1989*

sleeveen *adjective* sly, devious *IRELAND, 2004*

sleeves *noun* a wetsuit of any style *US, 1977*

sleezer *noun* a person, usually female, who is substandard in some important way *US, 1992*

sleigh ride *noun* the use of cocaine or heroin; cocaine or heroin. Building on the SNOW metaphor *US, 1973*

sleveen *noun* in Newfoundland, a person not to be trusted, a rascal *CANADA, 1968*

slevered *adjective* drunk. Hip-hop, urban slang noted in connection with a legal dispute over rap lyrics by *BBC News*, 6th June 2003 *UK, 2003*

slew *noun* a large amount *US, 1839*

slew; slew a head *verb* to distract someone, especially in the commission of a crime *AUSTRALIA, 1975*

slice *noun* **1** a woman or women, objectified sexually. From the phrase 'take a slice' recorded in 1796 as 'to intrigue, particularly with a married woman, because a slice of a cut loaf is not missed'; the etymology is further thought to trace back to the proverbial phrase 'it is safe taking a shive [a slice] of a cut loaf', and 'shive' is easily exchanged with 'swive' (to have sex). Perhaps from an image of the vagina as a slice in the flesh, but also taking a slice of bread as something necessary and in plentiful supply *UK, 1796*. **2** an act of sexual intercourse (with a woman). After the previous sense, possibly influenced by synonymous PORTION *UK, 1955*. ▶ **cut off a slice** to have sex (with a woman). A punningly contrived verb form of 'slice' (an act of sexual intercourse) *UK, 1980*

slice *verb* ▶ **slice bread** to make a payoff *UK, 1970*

sliced *adjective* **1** muscular, lacking body fat, well-sculpted *US, 1984*. **2** circumcised *US, 1988*

slice of knuckle pie *noun* a punch in the mouth *UK, 1962*

slice of toast *noun* a ghost. Rhyming slang *UK, 1992*

slick *noun* **1** a car tyre without a tread, used in drag racing. Usually heard in the plural *US, 1960*. **2** a glossy magazine *US, 1953*. **3** in pool, a skilled player who bets on his own ability *US, 1990*. **4** a field of criminal expertise *US, 1992*. **5** an unarmed aircraft *US, 1990*. **6** a helicopter used for troop transport *US, 1971*

slick *adjective* **1** attractive; charming *US, 2001*. **2** in lowball poker, favourable *US, 1967*

slick chick *noun* an attractive girl *US, 1947*

slickdick *adjective* smooth; plausible. Elaboration of conventional 'slick' *UK, 1997*

slicker *noun* **1** a world-wise, sophisticated, urban person *US, 1900*. **2** a police officer *US, 1998*. **3** a stolen car with all identification markings erased or removed *US, 1950*. **4** an oversized, wide, smooth tyre used in racing *US, 1958*

slick leggings *noun* the rubbing of the penis between the thighs of another man until reaching orgasm *US, 1961*

slicklicker *noun* an oil-spill cleaning machine *CANADA, 1995*

slick-sleeve *noun* a US Army private E-1; a US Air Force airman basic; a police recruit. 'Slick' because he has no stripes on his sleeve *US, 1970*

slick superspeed *noun* methcathinone. From the superior quality of the drug when compared to average SPEED (amphetamine) *US, 2003*

slick top *noun* an unmarked police car with no light on its roof *US, 1976*

slick-wing *adjective* used of a pilot in the air force, junior. The wing insignias of the junior pilot did not have a star above them like those of senior and command pilots *US, 1986*

slicky; slickey *verb* to obtain something through ingenious and unorthodox diligence, up to and including theft. An adaptation of pidgin English by United Nations troops in Korea in the early 1950s, from 'slick' (not-quite-honestly smart) *US, 1968*

slicky boy *noun* a thief or swindler. Coined by Koreans, borrowed by US and UN troops in Korea *US, 1967*

slide *noun* a trouser pocket *US, 1932*

slide *verb* **1** to depart, to go *US, 1859*. **2** to ride a wave *US, 1965*. ▶ **slide your jive** to talk freely. Teen slang *CANADA, 1946*

slide *adjective* used of a college course, easy *US, 1974*

slide and sluther *noun* a brother. Rhyming slang *UK, 1998*

slider *noun* **1** an electronic device that allows operation between authorised channels on a citizens' band radio *US, 1976*. **2** a gambler who slides rather than rolls dice in an effort to control the result *US, 2003*. **3** a hamburger or cheeseburger. Originally the small hamburgers sold by the White Tower™ chain, later any hamburger *US, 1987*

sliders *noun* men's shorts with an elastic waistband *TRINIDAD AND TOBAGO, 1939*

slide-rule jockey *noun* a navigator in an aeroplane crew *US, 1959*

slides *noun* shoes *US, 1962*

slim *noun* a handgun *US, 1950*

slime *noun* **1** heroin *US, 1994*. **2** British Army Intelligence Corps personnel *UK, 1995*

slimeball *noun* a despicable person *US, 1973*

slimedog *noun* a dirty, offensive person *US, 1994*

slimemouth *noun* a foul-talking person *US, 1985*

slim-fast diet *noun* HIV or AIDS *US, 2002*

slim jim *noun* a device that is slipped into a car door and used to open the door's locking mechanism *US, 1988*

slim off *verb* to strip to your underwear *US, 1958*

slimy *adjective* having an insincere and ingratiating manner *UK, 1602*

sling *noun* **1** a monetary gift or tip. Wilkes records a slightly earlier (1948) variant 'sling back' *AUSTRALIA, 1950*. **2** in horse racing, a gratuity given the jockey and attendants by the owner after a win *AUSTRIA, 1989*. **3** a bribe or illegal payment *AUSTRALIA, 1948*. ▶ **beat it for the sling** to fail to appear in court *AUSTRALIA, 1975*. ▶ **in the sling** said of a woman experiencing her menstrual period *US, 1954*

sling *verb* **1** to throw something (or someone) in a specific direction; hence to pass something from one person to another. Common in C14 and C15, now dialect or colloquial *UK, 2002*. **2** (to discard or abandon) someone or something; to quit something *UK, 1902*. **3** to pay a tip to someone *AUSTRALIA, 1875*. **4** to pay a bribe to someone *AUSTRALIA, 1939*. **5** to sell illegal drugs *US, 2001*. **6** to engage in pro-

miscuous sexual behaviour *BAHAMAS, 1982*. ▶ **sling hash** to work as a waitress or short-order cook *US, 1906*. ▶ **sling ink** to tattoo *US, 1989*. ▶ **sling your hook** to go, to leave. A naval derivation, perhaps inspired by slinging grappling hooks preparatory to swinging across to another ship. Later use seems to be mainly imperative *UK, 1874*

sling-backs *noun* used generically for high-heeled shoes *UK, 2002*

sling-ding *noun* in fishing, a weight attached to a line of trawl to be set, to moor the end *CANADA, 1955*

slinger *noun* **1** a criminal who passes counterfeit money *UK, 1950*. **2** a striptease artist *US, 1981*

sling off *verb* to speaking disparagingly to someone *AUSTRALIA, 1900*

sling out *verb* to reject something; to eject someone *UK, 1959*

slingshot *noun* **1** a drag racing car design in which the driver is seated behind the rear wheels *US, 1962*. **2** any vehicle that passes others on the motorway at great speed *US, 1976*. **3** in motor racing, a passing method in which the car follows another's draught and then quickly passes *US, 1973*. **4** an extremely skimpy man's bathing suit *US, 1991*

slingshotting *noun* in bungee jumping, a reverse jump, beginning with the cord stretched out, yanking the participant up in the air *US, 1992*

slip *noun* **1** in cricket, a fielder or fielding position close to the wicket keeper *UK, 1816*. **2** the price of the fare home given to a punter who has lost all their money *AUSTRALIA, 1977*

slip *verb* **1** to give birth to a child *AUSTRALIA, 1968*. **2** to act inappropriately *US, 1993*. **3** to insult someone in a semi-formal quasi-friendly competition *US, 2000*. ▶ **slip a fatty** to have sex *UK, 1983*. ▶ **slip a lock** to open a locked door by sliding a plastic credit card between the door and jamb and then sliding the lock open *US, 1981*. ▶ **slip her a length** (from the male perspective) to have sex with a woman *UK, 1949*. ▶ **slip it to someone** (of a male) to have sex with someone. Euphemistic and naughty, both at once *US, 1952*. ▶ **slip one to someone** (of a male) to have sex with someone *UK, 2001*

slip-and-fall *noun* a run-of-the-mill, often fraudulent law suit or insurance claim resulting from an injury suffered slipping and falling in a business establishment *US, 1996*

slip-in *noun* any lubricant used for faciliating sex, especially anal sex *US, 1962*

slipper-training *noun* spanking with an old-fashioned gym shoe, especially when advertised as a service offered by a prostitute *UK, 2003*

slippery *adjective* in hot rodding and drag racing, streamlined *US, 1968*

slippery Anne *noun* in a deck of playing cards, the queen of spades *US, 1950*

slippery Sid; slippery *noun* a Jewish person. Offensive. Rhyming slang for YID *UK, 1998*

slippings *noun* any lubricant used in anal sex *US, 1979*

slipping stick *noun* a slide rule *US, 1954*

slippy *adjective* **1** quick; spry; nimble. From dialect. Perhaps the best known contemporary usage is the song that became the theme of the film *Trainspotting* *UK, 1885*. **2** slippery *US, 1982*

slip-slap *noun* an old shoe, especially a slipper *TRINIDAD AND TOBAGO, 1973*

slip-slop *noun* a strap sandal with a wooden sole *BARBADOS, 1965*

slip-sloppy *adjective* very drunk *CANADA, 1988*

slipstick *noun* a trombone *US, 1970*

slip-stick jockey *noun* a radar technician *US, 1947*

slip up *verb* to make a mistake *US, 1855*

S list *noun* used as a euphemism for 'shit list', a list of enemies *US, 1974*

slit *noun* **1** the vagina *UK, 1648*. **2** A person from South Asia. Offensive. From the European perception of South Asian eyes as slanted slits *US, 1980*. **3** a tablet of MDMA, the recreational drug best known as ecstasy.

Possibly from the sense as 'a vagina', punning on CUNT (a vein for injecting) *UK, 2003*

slitch *noun* a despicable and/or promiscuous girl. A blend of SLUT and BITCH *US, 1963*

slither *noun* counterfeit coins *US, 1982*

Sloane ranger; Sloane *noun* a conventional person, part of a fashionable set, born to the privileges of the upper-/middle-class, especially one who dwells in London. A playful blend of *Sloane* Square (in Chelsea, London) and The *Lone* Ranger (since the 1930s, a fictional hero of the American west) *UK, 1975*

slob *noun* **1** a slovenly person; a fat, lazy person; hence, when the characteristics are applied to the intellect: a simple-minded person, or, when applied to the morals, a delinquent *UK, 1861*. **2** anyone of Slavic heritage. Offensive *US, 1978*. **3** used as a derogatory nickname for a member of the Bloods youth gang *US, 1994*

slob; slob out *verb* to behave in a lazy, slovenly manner *UK, 2002*

slobber *noun* food; a meal *UK: SCOTLAND, 1988*

slog *noun* an act or period of hard work *UK, 1888*

slog *verb* **1** to work hard at something *UK, 1888*. **2** to punch someone *UK, 1824*. **3** to walk heavily. From obsolete 'foot-slogger' (an infantryman, a pedestrian) *UK, 1872*. ▶ **slog it out** to work hard at some activity. An elaboration of SLOG (to work hard) *AUSTRALIA, 1971*. ▶ **slog your guts out** to work hard at something. An intensification of SLOG *UK, 1984*

sloo *noun* a look; a visual examination *AUSTRALIA, 1989*

sloosh *verb* to wash in a hurry and in a perfunctory fashion *NORFOLK ISLAND, 1992*

slooze *noun* a promiscuous female *US, 1976*

slop *noun* **1** prison food, *1996*. **2** poorly formed waves for surfing purposes *US, 1965*. **3** in pool, a shot made unintentionally *US, 1990*. **4** in computing, a built-in margin of error in one direction only *US, 1983*. **5** a second-year college student *US, 1947*

slop *verb* ▶ **slop the hogs** in trucking, to fill a truck radiator with water *US, 1971*

slop and flop *noun* meals and lodging *US, 1953*

slope *noun* a person from South Asia *US, 1948*

slopehead *noun* a Vietnamese; any South Asian. Derogatory, perjorative, offensive, demeaning *US, 1966*

slope off *verb* to depart, especially surreptitiously or in embarrassment *UK, 1861*

slope-out *noun* an easy task *US, 1957*

slopey *adjective* used of a wave steep *US, 1991*

slopie *noun* a Chinese person or other South Asian. Offensive *US, 1949*

slop out *verb* **1** in prison, to dispose of bodily waste collected in unplumbed toilet facilities. The first order of the day according to *Lag's Lexicon*, Paul Tempest, 1950; however, according to HM Prison Service in 2003: 'Slopping out was officially ended on 12th April 1996' *UK, 1950*. **2** to remove and clean plates, bowls, etc, that have been used in a prison cell. A play on SLOP (prison food), and the previous sense *UK, 1996*

slopping out *noun* in prison, the regular emptying of unplumbed toilet facilities *UK, 2000*

sloppy *adjective* **1** very sentimental *US, 1883*. **2** drunk *US, 2002*

Sloppy Joe *noun* a multi-layered sandwich from which the fillings ooze. The name comes from the inevitable mess on fingers and face, the sign of a sloppy eater *US, 1961*

sloppy seconds *noun* sex with someone who has just had sex with someone else *US, 1969*

slops *noun* beer *AUSTRALIA, 1944*. ▶ **go slops** to have sex with a woman who has very recently had sex with another man or other men *AUSTRALIA, 1985*

slopshoot *noun* food with little nutritional value but which appeals to popular taste. US Marine Corps slang *US, 1991*

slops merchant *noun* a habitual drinker of beer *AUSTRALIA, 1962*

slopsucker *noun* a low priority project *US, 1991*

slop time *noun* in prison, meal time. From SLOP (prison food) *UK, 1996*

slop up *verb* to drink to the point of intoxication *US, 1962*

slosh *noun* **1** a small indeterminate measure of some liquid *UK, 1888*. **2** a blow. From SLOSH (to hit) *UK, 1936*. **3** a drink, especially if watery or weak; tea; coffee; beer; drink in general; hence, sodden or mushy food *UK, 1819*. **4** the back-slash (\) on a computer keyboard *US, 1991*

slosh *verb* **1** to pour a liquid or a sodden mass carelessly; to swallow a drink, an oyster, etc carelessly. Usually combined with an adverb: 'slosh down', 'slosh out', 'slosh over', etc *US, 1875*. **2** to hit someone *UK, 1890*

slosh and mud; slosh *noun* a stud. Rhyming slang *UK, 1998*

sloshed *adjective* drunk *UK, 1946*

sloshing *noun* a beating; a thrashing *UK, 1931*

sloshy *adjective* drunk *US, 1993*

slot *noun* **1** a prison cell *AUSTRALIA, 1947*. **2** prison *AUSTRALIA, 1976*. **3** used as a term of address among jazz lovers of the 1930s and 40s *US, 1946*. **4** the perfect spot to ride a wave *US, 1964*. **5** a crevasse in the snow *ANTARCTICA, 2000*

slot *verb* **1** to imprison someone *AUSTRALIA, 1950*. **2** to shoot someone dead. Military *UK, 1998*. **3** to give something *UK, 1999*

slotties *noun* **1** a handbag. Polari *UK, 1992*. **2** money *UK, 1992*

slouch *noun* a lazy non-performer *US, 1796*

slough *noun* a jail or prison *US, 1950*

slough *verb* **1** to arrest someone *US, 1962*. **2** to close down a poker game. Also used in the variant 'slough up' *US, 1979*

slow *verb* ▶ **slow your roll** to calm down *US, 1993*

slow boat *noun* ▶ **get someone on a slow boat** to win all of a person's money by luring them into making ill-advised bets *US, 1951*

slowcoach *noun* a slow-moving (or slow-thinking) person *UK, 1837*

slow-em-up *noun* any central nervous system depressant *US, 1980*

slow-me-down *noun* a sedative tablet *UK, 2000*

slow-mo *adjective* slow-motion *US, 1993*

slow-pay *noun* a person in debt who has been remiss in making repayment *US, 1973*

slow pill *noun* in horse racing, a depressant given to a horse to decrease its performance *US, 1947*

slow-play *verb* **1** to stall; to delay *US, 1992*. **2** in poker, to underbet a hand to lure other players with inferior hands into betting *UK, 1990*

slowpoke *noun* a person who moves slowly or dawdles *US, 1848*

slow set *noun* in a disco, a set of songs (usually three) played at slow tempo with the purpose of bringing the dancers closer together *IRELAND, 1997*

slow smoulder *noun* a person whose career is going nowhere fast. US Air Force usage; the opposite of a 'fast burner' *US, 1998*

slow the row, papa! take it easy! *US, 1947*

slud *verb* to fall victim to a chemical warfare attack. From the official military warning that the victim will *s*alivate, *l*achrymate, *u*rinate, and *d*efecate' *US, 1991*

sludge *noun* beer *UK, 1958*

SLUF *nickname* an A-7 Corsair attack bomber. An acronym for 'short /little (or low) ugly fucker (or fellow)' *US, 1994*

sluff *verb* to play truant *US, 1951*

slug *noun* **1** a drink *UK, 1756*. **2** a dollar *US, 1981*. **3** the penis. Figurative application of the slimy invertebrate found in damp places; the pun on conventional 'slug' (a bullet) into BULLET (an ejaculation of semen) is later *AUSTRALIA, 1945*. **4** an idler. Either an abbreviation of 'sluggard' or a comparison to the slow-moving slimy gastropod or land-snail *UK, 1425*. **5** a seal. A visual similarity *ANTARCTICA, 1940*. **6** a group of cards that have been arranged and then inserted into a deck *US, 1996*. **7** a hospital patient who refuses to participate in therapy or self-help *US, 1989*. **8** in drag racing and hot rodding, a piston *US, 1958*. **9** in the television and film industries, a piece of unusable film that is temporarily used to fill in for footage that will be added *US, 1990*. ▶ **put the slug on someone** to hit someone with your fist *US, 1980*

slug *verb* **1** to strike someone hard *UK, 1862*. **2** to drink directly from a bottle. From the noun sense *UK: SCOTLAND, 1996*. **3** to cheat playing slot machines by inserting something other than the proper coin in the machine *US, 1985*. **4** to lie in bed. Verb formation from the more common usage as a noun *US, 1986*

slug and snail; slug *noun* a fingernail, a toenail. Rhyming slang *UK, 1992*

slugfest *noun* a bruising, drawn-out fight; hence, a military engagement at close-quarters. A combination of SLUG (to strike) and -FEST (a concentration of the preceding noun) *US, 2003*

slugger *noun* **1** a brutish fist-fighter *US, 1942*. **2** a casino cheat who tries to play slot machines with objects other than the proper coin *US, 1985*

sluggo *noun* an extremely skimpy bikini *AUSTRALIA, 1991*

sluggos *noun* tight-fitting men's nylon swimming briefs. So called since they display the SLUG (the penis) *AUSTRALIA, 1987*

slug huggers *noun* a pair of men's close-fitting and revealing nylon swimming trunks *AUSTRALIA, 2003*

slugout *noun* a fight, especially between youth gangs *US, 1962*

sluice *noun* an act of sexual intercourse; sex. From an earlier sense (the vagina) *UK, 1970*

slum *noun* **1** an apartment or house. *The Oxford English Dictionary* offers several early C19 cites in this sense but deems the term obsolete. Robert Beck (Iceberg Slim) wrote the language of the streets, not C19 England, suggesting a slang life for the word in the C20 US *US, 1969*. **2** inexpensive costume jewellery; any low-value merchandise *US, 1914*. **3** prison food *US, 1950*

slum *verb* **1** to visit a poor neighbourhood out of curiosity; to live beneath your station *UK, 1884*. **2** to voluntarily mix with social inferiors *UK, 1928*

slum *adjective* cheap; shabby; in poor taste *US, 1973*

slumber slot *noun* in trucking, a sleeping compartment behind the seat *US, 1971*

slumgullion *noun* a make-shift stew made with whatever ingredients are at hand *US, 1963*

slum hustler *noun* a person who sells fake jewellery *US, 1973*

slumlord *noun* a landlord who rents poorly kept-up properties in the ghetto, often with a large profit margin *US, 1953*

slummadelic fire *noun* excellent and exciting rap music *US, 2002*

slummy *noun* small change; coins. Liverpool use *UK, 2001*

slung up *adjective* relaxed; at ease *US, 1990*

slurp *verb* ▶ **slurp at the sideways smile** to perform oral sex on a woman *US, 2001*

slurpage *noun* any beverage *US, 1997*

slush *noun* **1** counterfeit paper money *UK, 1924*. **2** tea *UK: SCOTLAND, 1988*. ▶ **in the slush** very drunk *US, 1991*

slush box *noun* an automatic transmission; a car with automatic transmission *AUSTRALIA, 1981*

slush car *noun* a car with an automatic transmission *US, 1958*

slush fund *noun* **1** a discretionary fund, where the source of the money and the exact way in which it is spent is not subject to any accounting or accountability *US, 1874*. **2** money collected by a prisoner's associates for a prisoner's family *UK, 1996*

slushing fuck pit *noun* the vagina *UK, 2001*

slush pump *noun* **1** a trombone. Musicians' slang *US, 1937*. **2** an automatic transmission; a vehicle with an automatic transmission. 'Not used so much these days,' noted Clive Graham-Ranger, *Sunday Times*, 9th August 1981 *US, 1968*

slush up *verb* to drink to the point of intoxication *US, 1949*

slushy *noun* a kitchen hand *AUSTRALIA, 1880*

slushy *adjective* extremely sentimental *US, 1889*

slut *noun* **1** a promiscuous girl or woman *UK, 1450*. **2** a promiscuous boy or man *US, 2002*. **3** a prostitute *US, 1961*. **4** used as an affectionate female-to-female term of address. Use of the term does not suggest promiscuity *US, 1983*

-slut *suffix* in combination with a sexual fetish or activity, a sexual fetishist or (in pornography) specialist; in such forms as pain-slut, nipple-slut, come-slut, etc. Intended to, or, at best, tends to, diminish the status of a person so described. Widespread in Internet pornography *UK, 2003*

slut-mouth *noun* a person whose language is often coarse and vulgar *US, 2001*

slut puppy *noun* a promiscuous girl *US, 1990*

slutted out *adjective* broken down; in disrepair *US, 1984*

sluttish *adjective* sexual in a cheap way *US, 2004*

slutty *adjective* promiscuous; having a sexual appearance *US, 1991*

slutwear *noun* extremely sexually provoking clothing *US, 2000*

sly *adjective* unfair. Liverpool usage *UK, 2001*

sly-boots *noun* a cunning person. Jocular *UK, 1700*

sly-grog *noun* illegally made or supplied alcohol *AUSTRALIA, 1825*

sly-grogger *noun* a person selling sly-grog *AUSTRALIA, 1897*

sly-groggery *noun* an establishment selling alcohol without a licence to do so *AUSTRALIA, 1907*

sly-grogging *noun* the practice of selling alcohol illicitly *AUSTRALIA, 1952*

sly-grog joint *noun* an establishment selling alcohol without a license to do so *AUSTRALIA, 1956*

sly-grog shop *noun* an establishment selling alcohol without a licence to do so *AUSTRALIA, 1826*

sly mongoose *noun* an extremely clever and devious person. Hawaiian youth usage *US, 1981*

smack *noun* **1** heroin. Derives, possibly, from Yiddish *shmeker* (a sniffer of drugs) *US, 1942*. **2** alcohol *US, 1973*. **3** disparaging talk *US, 1999*. **4** slang *US, 1997*. **5** a swindle based on matching pennies *US, 1940*

smack *verb* to murder someone *UK, 1999*. ▶ **smack the pony** (of a female) to masturbate. *Smack the Pony* is an all-women television sketch show, first broadcast on Channel 4 in 1999 *UK, 2002*

smack *adverb* precisely. A shortened SMACK-DAB *US, 1951*

smack-bang *adverb* of a location, exactly, in the middle *UK, 1984*

smack-dab *adverb* exactly. At times reversed for comic effect *US, 1892*

smacked back *adjective* heroin-intoxicated *US, 1981*

smacked out *adjective* in an extreme state of heroin- or cocaine-intoxication *UK, 1983*

smacker *noun* **1** a loud kiss *UK, 1775*. **2** a one-dollar note *US, 1945*. **3** a pound sterling. From the earlier sense *UK, 1924*

smackeroonie *noun* **1** a kiss. A teenage elaboration of SMACKER, noted by Joanna Williamson, 1982 *UK, 1982*. **2** a pound sterling. An extension of SMACKER (a pound), popularised by UK television personality Christ Tarrant (b.1946) on *Who Wants To Be a Millionaire?* on Itelevision from 1998 *UK, 2002*

smackers *noun* the lips *UK, 2002*

smackhead *noun* a heroin addict. A combination of SMACK (heroin) and HEAD (user) *US, 1972*

smack in the eye *noun* a pie. Rhyming slang *UK, 1992*

smack up *verb* **1** to attack someone; to beat someone up *AUSTRALIA, 1945*. **2** to inject oneself with heroin *US, 1995*

smacky lips *noun* prolonged kissing *US, 1965*

smage *verb* to masturbate *NORFOLK ISLAND, 1992*

small *noun* one hundred dollars *US, 1988*

small *adjective* **1** afraid *US, 1986*. **2** drug-intoxicated. Comedian Steve Martin's refrain of 'Let's get small' inspired a wider usage of the term *US, 1978*

small beer *noun* something or someone of little consequence or importance *UK, 1777*

small fortune *noun* an extravagantly large sum of money *UK, 1874*

small fry *noun* an insignificant thing or things, person or people *UK*, *1797*

small house *noun* a latrine *TRINIDAD AND TOBAGO, 1986*

smallie *noun* **1** in Jamaica, a person from any other Caribbean island *JAMAICA, 1994*. **2** on Trinidad and Tobago, a person from any of the smaller English Caribbean islands northwest of Trinidad and Tobago *TRINIDAD AND TOBAGO, 1945*

small nickel *noun* fifty dollars or, in a casino, fifty dollars' worth of betting tokens *US, 1961*

small one *noun* one hundred dollars *US, 1988*

small potatoes *adjective* something of little consequence *US, 1838*

smalls *noun* **1** underwear *UK, 1943*. **2** a small amount of money as a bribe *JAMAICA, 2003*

small suppository in anticipation of the broom handle *noun* the opening volley in a battle. US Naval aviator usage *US, 1986*

small thing *noun* ▶ **do that small thing** used in a request for a favour, or to signal compliance with a request *UK, 1984*

small-time *adjective* insignificant, unimportant; minor. Of vaudeville origins *US, 1938*

small-timer *noun* an insignificant person; someone of trivial importance in any given field *UK, 1935*

smanker *noun* an unmarried, middle-aged person who has no children, objectified as a lifestyle category. Formed on the acronym of 'single *middle-a*ged *n*o *k*ids', and probably contrived for marketing purposes *UK, 2003*

smarm *verb* to behave in an ingratiating manner; to flatter someone insincerely *UK, 1911*

smarmy *adjective* smug, self-satisfied; overly sentimental *UK, 1909*

smart *adjective* fine; well; alright *UK, 2001*

smart alec; smart aleck; smart alick *noun* an offensively smart person; a know-it-all *US, 1865*

smart armpit *noun* a know-all. Euphemistic for SMART-ARSE *UK, 2000*

smart-arse; smart-ass *noun* a person with a conceited view of their own intelligence *AUSTRALIA, 1937*

smartarsed; smart-arsed *adjective* conceited about one's intelligence *US, 1960*

smart as a new pin *adjective* very smartly dressed *UK, 1893*

smarter than the average bear used for a humourous, if at times ironic, observation about another's intelligence. Yogi Bear's boast about himself in the television cartoon series that first aired in 1958 *US, 1958*

smart-eye *verb* to give someone a look that may be aggressive, challenging or disapproving *US, 2000*

smartie *noun* **1** a shrewd operator; a person who is wise to the various devices used by criminals *AUSTRALIA, 1950*. **2** an impudent, cheeky person; an offensively smart person *AUSTRALIA, 1969*. **3** an intelligent person *AUSTRALIA, 1982*

smarties *noun* tablets of MDMA, the recreational drug best known as ecstasy. From a branded multi-coloured confection *UK, 2001*

smartman *noun* a man who engages in confidence swindles *TRINIDAD AND TOBAGO, 2003*

smart mob *noun* a group of protesters (or some other demonstration of social unrest) organised and mobilised by text messaging. A play on conventional 'mob' and an abbreviation of 'mobile' *US, 2003*

smart money *noun* in horse racing, money bet on the basis of solid, empirical data *US, 1951*

smart-mouth *verb* to talk insolently to someone *US, 1968*

smart pill *noun* rabbit droppings. In the US, Michigan Upper Peninsula usage *AUSTRALIA, 2001*

smarts *noun* intelligence *US, 1970*

smarty *noun* in horse racing, a person purporting to have inside information but who is not to be trusted *AUSTRALIA, 1989*

smarty-pants *noun* a person who is smart, but not quite as smart as they think they are *US, 1941*

smash *noun* **1** a great success. A shortening of 'smash hit' *UK, 1930*. **2** momentum. Air combat slang *US, 1986*. **3** money; pocket change *US, 1953*. **4** wine *US, 1962*

smash *verb* ▶ **smash case** in computing, to disregard any differentiation between upper and lower case *US, 1991*

smash and grab *noun* **1** a black taxi or a minicab. Rhyming slang *UK, 1992*. **2** a simplistic burglary involving very little planning or thought *US, 1969*

smashed *adjective* **1** drunk *US, 1960*. **2** drug-intoxicated *US, 1967*

smash 'em-up *noun* a vehicle accident *US, 1976*

smasher *noun* **1** a very attractive female *US, 1959*. **2** a superlative thing *UK, 1894*. **3** a baggage handler on a train *US, 1977*

smasheroo *noun* **1** a great success. An elaboration of SMASH *US, 1948*. **2** a good-looking female *US, 1959*

smash-face *adjective* physical; aggressive *US, 1990*

smashing *adjective* fine; excellent; possessed of great charm; large. It is often claimed, improbably, that this derives from the Irish phrase *is maith sin* (that's good) *UK, 1911*

smash-mouth *noun* prolonged kissing *US, 1965*

smash-mouth *verb* to kiss passionately *US, 1968*

smash-mouth *adjective* physical, aggressive *US, 1989*

smazzmo *verb* to move in an uncoordinated, jerky manner *US, 1977*

smear *noun* theatrical cosmetics *US, 1952*

smear *verb* to drop napalm on a target *US, 1991*. ▶ **smear a queer** to assault a homosexual *US, 1993*

smears *noun* LSD *US, 1982*

smeg *noun* **1** used as an all-purpose, non-profane insult. Used in many different forms – 'smegl', 'smegging', 'smeghead' – by space castaway Dave Lister in the science fiction comedy television show *Red Dwarf*, BBC since 1988 *UK, 1988*. **2** any viscous matter of unknown origin. The variant 'shmeg' also exists *US, 1995*

smell *noun* digital-vaginal contact *US, 1974*

smell *verb* ▶ **smell Apple pie** to be near your date of expected return from military service in Vietnam in the US *US, 1991*. ▶ **smell for water** to find a spring using a divining rod *CANADA, 1960*. ▶ **smell some gas** to be transported by motor vehicle *US, 2002*

smeller *noun* the nose *UK, 1700*

smell-fart *noun* an inquisitive know-it-all *NEW ZEALAND, 1994*

smellies *noun* **1** perfume; perfumed deodorants *UK, 2002*. **2** anchovies *US, 1996*

smell of broken glass *noun* a strong body odour, especially male. Probably from the 'sharp' nature of the offending smell *UK, 1973*

smell of clay *noun* a condition ascribed to a person likely to die soon *UK: SCOTLAND, 1988*

smellybridge *noun* the perineum (the area of skin between the anus and the scrotum or vagina) *UK, 2002*

smelly hole *noun* the vagina *UK, 2001*

smell you! used for replying to an obvious brag *US, 1995*

smesh *noun* in circus and carnival usage, money *US, 1981*

smidge *noun* the smallest amount. A shortened SMIDGEN. First recorded in 1905, but popularised by ESPN's Dan Patrick telling viewers that *Sports Center* will resume 'in a smidge.' *US, 1905*

smidgen; smidgin *noun* a very small amount *US, 1845*

smile *noun* something that is amusing *US, 1982*

smile and smirk; smile *noun* work; also, as a verb: to work. Rhyming slang *UK, 1992*

smiley *noun* **1** a simplistic image of a smiling face, used for indicating laughter or happiness. First seen as an icon and later in electronic communications formed with punctuation marks, generally as :) but with multiple variations *US, 1995*. **2** a tablet of LSD with the smiley icon printed or etched thereon *UK, 1998*. **3** a variety of

MDMA, the recreational drug best known as ecstasy, identified by the smiley motif embossed on the tablet *UK, 2002*. **4** a large chain with a padlock worn around the arm or neck *US, 1997*

smithereens *noun* small pieces or fragments; shreds *UK, 1829*

Smitty *noun* in hot rodding, a silencer packed with fiberglass, increasing the roar of the engine *US, 1960*

smock *noun* heroin. A corruption of SMACK or the Yiddish SHMECK *US, 1960*

smog *verb* **1** to smoke marijuana *US, 2001*. **2** to execute someone with lethal gas *US, 1992*

smoke *noun* **1** a cigarette; a cigar *UK, 1882*. **2** marijuana; heroin; opium; any drug that may be smoked *US, 1946*. **3** a marijuana cigarette *US, 1967*. **4** crack cocaine when smoked; heroin mixed with crack cocaine when smoked *US, 1991*. **5** denatured alcohol (ethyl alcohol to which a poisonous substance has been added to make it unfit for consumption) mixed with water for drinking *US, 1950*. **6** toxic, potentially fatal solvents used as substitutes for alcohol for the truly desperate *US, 1955*. **7** a black person. Offensive *US, 1913*. **8** a non-commissioned officer commanding an artillery battery *US, 1988*. **9** a forest fire *US, 1991*. **10** one dollar *US, 1975*. ► **bring smoke** to fire a gun *US, 1997*. ► **in smoke** in hiding *AUSTRALIA, 1908*. ► **put smoke** to fire a single round of artillery to help others mark a target *US, 1990*. ► **the Smoke; Big Smoke; Great Smoke; the Smokes** London; any large city. All variations are used with 'the' *UK, 1848*. ► **up the Smoke** to London; to central London (from the suburbs). Originally tramps' usage; you go '*up* THE SMOKE' (London) even when heading *down* from the north *UK*

smoke *verb* **1** to shoot someone *US, 1926*. **2** to drive fast *US, 1976*. **3** to defeat someone soundly, especially in a contest of speed *US, 1996*. **4** to perform oral sex on a man. Simple imagery, perhaps influenced by the Freudian notion that smoking is an 'oral' habit *UK, 1984*. ► **smoke a bowl** to smoke a pipe filled with marijuana *US, 1982*. ► **smoke a pipe; smoke the pipe** to surf through the hollow tube of a wave *US, 1987*. ► **smoke butt** to curry favour through obsequious behaviour *US, 1992*. ► **smoke it** to commit suicide by a gunshot wound in the mouth *US, 1984*. ► **smoke like a chimney** to smoke cigarettes heavily *UK, 1840*. ► **smoke with the devil** to drive too fast for road conditions *US, 1976*

smokeasy *noun* a clandestine venue for the illegal sale and consumption of marijuana. Modelled on SPEAKEASY (a bar that sells alcohol illegally) *UK, 2004*

smoke Canada *noun* marijuana, presumed to originate in Canada *UK, 2001*

smoked cheaters *noun* dark glasses *US, 1959*

smoked haddock *noun* at a racecourse, the paddock. Rhyming slang *UK, 1961*

smoked Irishman *noun* any person with black, brown or coffee-coloured skin *UK, 1966*

smoked out *adjective* **1** extremely intoxicated on marijuana or crack cocaine *US, 1993*. **2** without any crack cocaine to smoke *US, 2003*

Smoked Scotchman *noun* a person whose parentage is Scottish and Indian *CANADA, 1960*

smoked Welshman *noun* any dark-skinned man speaking little English. Maybe simple racial stereotyping, but is probably influenced by the fact that an English person attempting a Welsh accent sounds generically Indian *UK, 1984*

smoke house *noun* **1** a room where meetings of twelve-step recovery programmes such as Alcoholics Anonymous are held. A term based on the heavy cigarette smoking that is often characteristic of the meetings *US, 1998*. **2** crack cocaine *UK, 2003*

smoke pole *noun* a shotgun *CANADA, 1970*

smoker *noun* **1** a social gathering, limited to men, especially one with sexual entertainment; a film shown during such a gathering *UK, 1887*. **2** a marijuana smoker *US, 1961*. **3** a passenger train car in which smoking is permitted *US, 1977*. **4** any diesel-powered truck *US, 1962*. **5** a car for sale that a car trader is using for personal transport *UK, 1965*. **6** a stolen car *US, 1997*. **7** a high-mileage car. A car-dealers' term *UK, 1981*

smokestack *noun* a pile of gambling tokens in the hands of an unskilled gambler *US, 1996*

smoke train *noun* a cigarette *US, 2001*

smoke-up *noun* in college, a notification of academic deficiency *US, 1961*

smoke wrench *noun* in car repair, an oxy-acetylene torch *US, 1992*

smokey *noun* **1** in prison, a segregation unit *UK, 1996*. **2** a Maori. Offensive *NEW ZEALAND, 1984*

smokey bear; smokey; bear *noun* a police officer; the police. Citizens' band radio slang; from Smokey Bear (aka Smokey the Bear), a caricatured black bear, from Capitan, New Mexico, used since 1950 to promote forest fire prevention. The symbolic bear wears a hat similar to that worn by US highway patrol officers and state troopers. Also used to designate police in various forms: 'smokey beaver' (a policewoman), 'smokey convention' (two or more police cars), 'smokey on four legs' (mounted police), 'smokey with a camera' (police using speed detection equipment), 'smokey with ears' (police with radio), etc *US, 1975*

Smokey the bear *noun* **1** a drill sergeant in the US Army *US, 1965*. **2** a military aircraft used for dropping magnesium-based flares to illuminate the ground at night *US, 1989*

smoking *adjective* **1** excellent; thriving; exciting *US, 1975*. **2** fashionably dressed *US, 1989*

smoking gun *noun* **1** unarguable evidence, or an unmissable clue. A term that came into popular use during the President Nixon Watergate scandal in the US in the early 1970s *US, 1974*. **2** a mixture of heroin and cocaine; heroin *UK, 1998*

smoko *noun* **1** a break from work. Originally a break for a cigarette and normally long enough for a hot beverage *AUSTRALIA, 1865*. **2** marijuana *AUSTRALIA, 1987*

smoky *noun* an Indian. Offensive *CANADA, 1953*

Smoky Joe *noun* a military aircraft that marks targets for bomber aircraft with smoke bombs *US, 1946*

smoo *noun* the vagina *AUSTRALIA, 1992*

smooch *verb* to kiss in a lingering manner *US, 1932*

smoochy *adjective* of music, suitable for slow, romantic dancing *UK, 1966*

smoochywoochypoochy *noun* marijuana. A pet name *UK, 2001*

smoodge; smooge *verb* **1** to play the sycophant *AUSTRALIA, 1898*. **2** to kiss and cuddle *AUSTRALIA, 1915*. **3** to win someone around; to charm someone *AUSTRALIA, 1940*

smoodger; smooger *noun* a flatterer *AUSTRALIA, 1897*

smoodgingly *adverb* ingratiatingly *AUSTRALIA, 1962*

smooth *noun* **1** a member of the aggressive youth fashion and gang movement that was the final and least notable stage in the evolution of the skinhead. A SKINHEAD with fractionally longer hair became SUEDEHEAD which, in turn, grew smooth − and not distinctive enough to survive *UK, 1972*. **2** on the railways, a tip of ten cents *US, 1977*

smooth *verb* in hot rodding and drag racing, to remove ornaments and hardware from the car body *US, 1968*

smooth *adjective* **1** used of a man's body, hairless *US, 1997*. **2** calm *US, 1967*. **3** in lowball poker, favourable *US, 1967*. **4** sophisticated, urbane *US, 1991*

smooth used to intensify a phrasal verb *US, 1984*

smooth and glassy *adjective* easy-going *US, 1984*

smoothie *noun* **1** the complete removal of a woman's pubic hair; the result thereof *US, 2001*. **2** a person who stays calm and avoids trouble *US, 1967*. **3** a man who is attractive, persuasive, crafty, and a bit manipulative. Often, but not always, pejorative *US, 1929*. **4** a skilled gambling cheat *US, 1964*

smooth leg *noun* a woman. Citizens' band radio slang *UK, 1981*

smooth operator *noun* someone who is attractive, crafty, and a bit manipulative *US, 1951*

smooth trade *noun* an urbane, fashion-conscious homosexual man *US, 1965*

smother *noun* an overcoat. Allied to the practical sense of the coat worn over a pickpocket's arm to mask criminal activity *UK, 1934*

smother *verb* to conceal a person, a thing or a movement *AUSTRALIA, 1932*

smouch *verb* to kiss *AUSTRALIA, 1968*

smoush *noun* a kiss. With the long vowel of 'smooch' *AUSTRALIA, 1963*

smudge *noun* **1** a photograph. Originally photographers' jargon, from blurred pictures *UK, 1931*. **2** a pornographic magazine or magazines. Extended from the previous sense *UK, 1996*. **3** a photographer, especially a press photographer. Shortened from SMUDGER *UK, 1968*

smudger *noun* a photographer, especially a press photographer. From SMUDGE (a photograph) *UK, 1961*

smurf *noun* **1** an ordinary citizen whose personal bank accounts are used to launder drug money. The Smurfs are well-known children's cartoon characters, adopted here to suggest the innocent appearance of a money launderer *US, 1998*. **2** in an Internet discussion group, a frequent poster who adds little in the way of content *US, 1997*

Smurf Juice *noun* the recreational drug GHB. As a marketing strategy the clear liquid is dyed blue, which is the colour of Smurfs™ (internationally known children's characters) *SOUTH AFRICA, 2003*

smush *verb* to crush. A blending of 'crush' and 'smash' *US, 1991*

smut *noun* pornography *UK, 1698*

smut-hound *noun* a man with a marked predilection for bawdiness or indecent publications; a censor who seeks out such works *US, 1927*

smuts *noun* sexually explicit photographs or postcards *US, 1962*

snack *noun* **1** a youthful, sexually inexperienced male who is the object of an older homosexual's desire *US, 1987*. **2** something easily accomplished *AUSTRALIA, 1941*

snacker *noun* aboard a trawler, a deck-boy or odd-job man *UK, 1974*

snackpack *noun* the male genitals as seen in a jock strap or tight, skimpy underwear *US, 1988*

snaffle *verb* to acquire something for your own *UK, 1902*

snafu *noun* a chaotic mess. An acronym of 'situation normal, all fucked up', or the more polite 'situation normal, all fouled up' *US, 1941*

snafu *verb* to bungle something; to reduce something to chaos. From the noun sense *US, 2001*

snag *noun* **1** a girl, especially an ugly one *US, 1962*. **2** a tooth *US, 1967*. **3** a sausage *AUSTRALIA, 1941*

snag *verb* **1** to grab something; to acquire something *US, 1895*. **2** to outdo someone *US, 1946*

snag bag *noun* a small bag for carrying personal effects. Prison usage *US, 1967*

snagged stag *noun* a boy who is steadily and exclusively dating one girl *US, 1961*

snaggle tooth *noun* a young woman or girl with irregular (or missing) teeth. Among US boys in 2004 'summer teeths' is a nickname for British girls – some are teeth that point here, some are pointing there *UK, 1909*

snail mail *noun* mail sent by normal postal service. A term that was coined after the advent of electronic mail *US, 1983*

snail track *noun* **1** a verticle line of hair on the stomach *AUSTRALIA, 2002*. **2** the residue of vaginal secretions, semen and/or saliva on a woman's thighs after sex *US, 1986*

snail trail *noun* the vagina *UK, 2001*

snake *noun* **1** the penis *US, 1997*. **2** among anglers, a very long rag-worm used as bait *UK, 1968*. **3** in electric line work, insulated rubber line hose *US, 1980*. **4** a long, serpentine putt *US, 1962*. **5** a subway, an underground system *US, 1960*. **6** a surfer who surfs in another surfer's right of way *US, 1987*. **7** an informer *US, 1958*. **8** in foot-powered scootering, another rider who cuts in, especially one who take's another's line into a trick *UK, 2000*. **9** an AH-1G Cobra attack helicopter. The US Army's primary gunship in Vietnam *US, 1986*. **10** a railway pointsman. From the serpentine 'S' on the pointsman's union pin *US, 1946*. ▶ **able to crawl under a snake; lower than a snake's belly** morally reprehensible; despicable. Variations include 'a snake's hips', since World War 2, and 'able to crawl under a snake's belly with a top hat on', 1959 *AUSTRALIA, 1932*. ▶ **the snake** in firefighting, the hose. Used by the London Fire Brigade *UK, 1984*

snake *verb* **1** to have sex from the male perspective *US, 2001*. **2** in snowboarding or skateboarding, to cut in front of someone *US, 1984*. **3** to go quietly, to move silently. The variant 'snake off' also exists *IRELAND, 1958*

snakebite; snakie *noun* a mixture of cider and lager *UK, 1988*

snake-charmer *noun* in Western Australia, a railway maintenance worker. From the prevalence of snakes along railway tracks *AUSTRALIA, 1937*

snake-eaters *noun* the US Army Special Forces. From their jungle survival skills *US, 1991*

snake-eye; snake-eye bomb *noun* during the Vietnam war, one of several aircraft bombs with descent-slowing devices to permit low-level attacks *US, 1966*

snake eyes *noun* **1** in dice games, a roll of two one's. A visual metaphor *US, 1929*. **2** in dominoes, the 1–1 piece *US, 1959*. **3** in poker, a pair of aces *US, 1988*

snake fence *noun* a rail fence, split cedar, in six or eight interlocking zigzag patterns *US, 1805*

Snake Gully *noun* an imaginary remote and backward place *AUSTRALIA, 1945*

snakehead *noun* a smuggler of Chinese people. Direct translation from a Chinese term *US, 2002*

snake juice *noun* strong liquor, especially of rough quality *AUSTRALIA, 1890*

Snakenavel, Idaho *noun* a fictitious rural place *US, 1994*

snake pit *noun* **1** used in the US military during the conflict in Vietnam for describing any operational headquarters *US, 1966*. **2** a sergeant's mess *AUSTRALIA, 1941*

snake ranch *noun* a bachelor's house *US, 1990*

snake room *noun* a bar *CANADA, 1912*

snake's *noun* an act of urination. Shortening of SNAKE'S HISS *AUSTRALIA, 1966*

snake's hiss *noun* an act of urination. Rhyming slang for PISS *AUSTRALIA, 1966*

snakey-snakey *noun* sexual intercourse. From SNAKE (the penis) *UK, 2001*

snaky *adjective* in a foul mood *AUSTRALIA, 1894*

snap *noun* **1** amyl nitrite; an ampoule of amyl nitrite. From the sound/action of breaking open the ampoule *UK, 1962*. **2** an amphetamine tablet *US, 1994*. **3** a mouthful of alcohol or a drink taken in one gulp *CANADA, 1988*. **4** a negative statement or taunt, often as part of a rap performance *US, 1994*. **5** a humourous statement or person *US, 1970*. **6** something that is simple or easy *US, 1877*. **7** in pool, the first shot of the game *US, 1990*. **8** a photograph *US, 1894*. **9** a snack; a packed meal. In dialect from 1642; usage appears to have spread via the railways *UK, 1980*

snap *verb* **1** to insult someone in a semi-formal quasi-friendly competition *US, 1979*. **2** to realise something suddenly; to experience an epiphany *US, 1967*. **3** to flex, and thus contract, the sphincter during anal sex *US, 1972*. ▶ **snap in** to engage in rifle target practice. Korean war usage *US, 1953*. ▶ **snap out of it** to stop dreaming; to face reality; to change your mind-set. Often used as an imperative *UK, 1918*. ▶ **snap to it** to urgently begin to do something *UK, 1918*. ▶ **snap your cap** to lose your sanity *US, 1973*

snap! used for registering a (usually minor) concidence. From the children's card game during which players cry 'snap!' whenever matching cards are exposed *UK, 1959*

snap cap *noun* a dummy shotgun cartridge *UK, 1983*

snapped up *adjective* **1** under the influence of snap (amyl nitrate) *UK, 1962*. **2** very drunk *CANADA, 1999*

snapper *noun* **1** the vagina, especially one with exceptional muscular control *US, 1975*. **2** a girl or young woman *US, 1971*. **3** an infant *IRELAND, 2003*. **4** the foreskin *US, 1941*. **5** a photographer *UK, 1910*. **6** in blackjack, an ace and ten-point card dealt as the first two cards to a player *US, 1980*. **7** amyl nitrite; an ampoule of amyl nitrite *US, 1967*. **8** a small, fast-breaking wave *AUSTRALIA, 1977*. **9** in lobstering, a lobster that is not legal size *US, 1978*. **10** a wooden match *US, 1970*. **11** the mythical ingredient in baked beans that can be removed to prevent flatulence *US, 1975*

snapper-rigged *adjective* improvised; repaired in a makeshift fashion. Nautical terminology brought ashore in Nova Scotia *CANADA, 2002*

snappers *noun* the teeth, especially false teeth *UK, 1924*

snappy *adjective* **1** fashionably smart. Especially as 'snappy dresser' *UK, 1881*. **2** short-tempered; irritable *US, 1834*. ▶ **make it snappy; look snappy** to be quick. Often used as an imperative *UK, 1926*

snaps *noun* **1** praise; recognition *US, 1995*. **2** money *US, 1997*. **3** handcuffs *US, 1949*. **4** snack food *US, 1986*

snard lumps *noun* snow and ice clumps that build up under the fender of the car. In eastern Canada, they have been called 'snowbirds' *CANADA, 1987*

snarf *verb* **1** to drink or to eat something, especially greedily. Possibly abbreviated and adapted from an affected UK pronunciation of SNAFFLE (to acquire) *UK, 2002*. **2** to take something; to grab something *US, 1968*

snark *noun* a caustic witticism *US, 2003*

snark *verb* to act grumpily or nastily *US, 1997*

snarky *adjective* snide, sarcastic; irritable. From the Scottish snark (to find fault, to nag) *UK, 1906*

snarler *noun* a sausage *NEW ZEALAND, 1963*

snarl-up *noun* a chaotic mess; often applied to a near-gridlock in a traffic system *UK, 1960*

snatch *noun* **1** the vagina; sex; a woman (or women) as a sexual object *UK, 1904*. **2** a kidnapping *US, 1931*. **3** something stolen *UK, 2000*. **4** an air rescue of ground troops or the crew of a downed aircraft *US, 1988*

snatch *verb* to kidnap someone *US, 1932*. ▶ **snatch it** to quit work taking the wages due *AUSTRALIA, 1911*. ▶ **snatch your time** to quit work taking the wages due *AUSTRALIA, 1916*

snatch 22 *noun* a woman who is considered so sexually unattractive that a man would have to be drunk to attempt sex with her, but too drunk to perform. A logical knot, formed on SNATCH (the vagina); after *Catch 22*, the novel by Joseph Heller, 1961, and the conventional usage it inspired *UK, 2002*

snatch box *noun* the vagina. An elaboration of SNATCH *UK, 1961*

snatch box decorated with red roses *noun* the bleed period of the menstrual cycle. Formed on SNATCH BOX (the vagina) with blood imagery *US, 1999*

snatcher *noun* **1** a thief *US, 1965*. **2** a police detective *US, 1948*

snatch fur *noun* female pubic hair *US, 1972*

snatch hair *noun* the pubic hair (of either gender) *US, 1995*

snatch hound *noun* a person who is obsessed with sex and women *US, 1992*

snatch man *noun* a press photographer *UK, 2001*

snatch patrol *noun* a combat mission in which the object is to capture enemy troops for interrogation *US, 1977*

snatch-plug *noun* a tampon *US, 1972*

snavel *verb* to steal something *AUSTRALIA, 1892*

snazzy *adjective* stylish; fashionable; smart *US, 1932*

sneak *noun* **1** a schoolchild who tells tales or informs on his or her fellows. School slang, from an earlier, more general sense as 'a despicable person, or one who behaves in an underhand manner' *UK, 1840*. **2** a soft-soled shoe; a running shoe, a trainer *UK, 1862*

sneak *verb* **1** to tell tales; to inform upon someone. School slang *UK, 1897*. **2** to break into a building *US, 1949*. ▶ **sneak a peak** to take a look at something or someone *US, 1999*

sneak *adjective* ▶ **on the sneak tip** in secret *US, 1995*

sneak-and-peak *adjective* **1** designed to be quiet *US, 1973*. **2** undertaken for the purpose of reconnaissance *US, 1974*

sneaker *noun* **1** a person engaged in an illegal enterprise who does not pay a regular bribe to the police but does when confronted *US, 1973*. **2** a smuggler *US, 1956*. **3** a linear amplifier for a citizens' band radio *US, 1977*. **4** in hot rodding or motor racing, an unusually large tyre *US, 1992*

sneaker bitch *noun* a person who is too focused on conspicuous consumption, such as high priced trainers *US, 1989*

sneakernet *noun* in computing, to carry a disk from one computer to another *US, 1991*

sneakers *noun* car wheel rims *US, 2003*

sneak go *noun* any secretive action *AUSTRALIA, 1989*

sneak-in *noun* a bar that surreptitiously remains open after the legal closing time *US, 1951*

sneak job *noun* housebreaking *UK, 1996*

sneaky *adjective* used of a recording device, easily hidden *US, 1982*

sneaky beaky *noun* a spy. Often used attributively as an adjective *UK, 1995*

sneaky man *noun* a married woman's adulterous sexual partner *BAHAMAS, 1982*

sneaky Pete *noun* **1** any potent, potentially fatal, alcoholic concoction, favoured by those whose need outweighs their ability to pay *US, 1947*. **2** marijuana mixed in wine *US, 1955*. **3** a member of a US Army long-range reconnaissance patrol unit *US, 1990*. **4** an unannounced in-flight examination by a crew that boards the plane just before take-off *US, 1963*. **5** in pool, an expert player's custom cue, designed to look like an ordinary cue *US, 1993*

sneeze *noun* pepper *US, 1981*

sneeze *verb* to arrest someone *US, 1950*

sneeze and squeeze *noun* cocaine and sex *US, 1984*

sneezed *adjective* arrested; kidnapped *UK, 1996*

sneeze out *verb* to confess *UK, 1996*

sneezer *noun* **1** the nose *US, 1945*. **2** in marketing, a person whose opinion the market listens to and trusts. A logical by-product of VIRAL MARKETING (word-of-mouth) *US, 2000*. **3** a jail or prison *US, 1953*

sneezing powder *noun* heroin *US, 1958*

snide *noun* **1** a cunning person; an untrustworthy person; a contemptible person; an informer. German *aufschneiden* (to boast, brag), reaching English via Yiddish. Also used in the variant 'shnide' *UK, 1950*. **2** a stolen pearl *AUSTRALIA, 1933*

snide *adverb* secretly; deceitfully *UK, 2002*

snide; shnide; snidey *adjective* false, counterfeit, sham, bogus; hence mean, contemptible; underhand *UK, 1859*

snidey *adjective* sneering; contemptuous; disdainful *UK, 1964*

snidey up *verb* to adulterate drugs, to prepare fake drugs for sale. Extended from SNIDE; SNIDEY (fake) *UK, 1996*

sniff *noun* **1** cocaine *US, 1990*. **2** any solvent that can be inhaled for its psychoactive effect *US, 1974*. **3** a sycophant. From an image of the sycophant's brown nose being in the near proximity of an anus *US, 1968*. **4** a girlfriend *UK, 2002*. ▶ **the sniff** a recreational hunt for sexually attractive company *UK, 1998*

sniff *verb* to ingest drugs by nasal inhalation *UK, 1925*

sniffed-up *adjective* under the influence of cocaine *UK, 1999*

sniffer *noun* **1** the nose *UK, 1858*. **2** an ampoule of amyl nitrite *US, 1970*. **3** a cocaine user *US, 1988*. **4** a device placed on a vehicle's exhaust pipe to measure the pollutants in the emission *US, 1993*. **5** a claims investigator of unemployment and other benefit fraud *UK, 1982*. **6** a computer program that surreptitiously records user passwords and other log-in data *US, 1994*. **7** an outsider who tries to be part of the pornography industry *US, 1995*. **8** a handkerchief *US, 1945*

sniffer and snorter *noun* a reporter. Rhyming slang *UK, 1998*

sniffer bag *noun* a small bag of heroin intended for inhaling *US, 2002*

sniffings *noun* any industrial solvent that is inhaled for its psychoactive effect *US, 1984*

sniffing snow *noun* cocaine. An instructive elaboration of SNOW (cocaine) *UK, 2000*

sniff queen *noun* a homosexual who is a heavy user of amyl nitrite or butyl nitrite during sex *US, 1972*

sniffy *adjective* scornful, disdainful *UK, 1871*

snifter *noun* **1** a small drink of alcoholic liquor; hence, specifically, a brandy glass; more generally, a glass for spirits. The difference between the senses is not always apparent *US, 1844*. **2** a single inhaled dose of cocaine *US, 1930*

snig *verb* to drag something heavy by means of ropes or chains *AUSTRALIA, 1897*

snip *noun* **1** a bargain *UK, 1926*. **2** something that is easily achieved or done; a certainty *UK, 1890*. **3** a thing that is more fortunate, excellent or pleasing than might normally be expected. In the phrase 'snip of a *thing*' *UK, 1952*. **4** a ticket collector *UK, 1970*. ▶ **the snip** any invasive medical procedure that sterilises a patient; a vasectomy, an orchidectomy, etc *UK, 2001*

snip *verb* to borrow money on short notice *AUSTRALIA, 1989*

snipe *noun* **1** the butt of a marijuana cigarette. In the late C19, a 'snipe' referred to the discarded stub of a cigar or cigarette. It briefly enjoyed standing in the vocabulary of marijuana users before falling victim to ROACH *US, 1969*. **2** the butt of a cigarette that can still be relit and smoked *US, 1891*. **3** the nose. From the long straight bill of the bird *UK, 2002*. **4** a sniper's hide *UK: NORTHERN IRELAND, 1979*. **5** on board a ship, a crew member, especially an engineering officer *UK, 1918*. **6** a railway track worker *UK, 1946*

snipe *verb* **1** to disparage someone *US, 1980*. **2** to snoop; to spy on someone *US, 2002*

sniper *noun* **1** a person who posts inflammatory attacks on the Internet *US, 2001*. **2** a sexually promiscuous girl of limited intellect *BAHAMAS, 1982*

snippy *adjective* impatient; argumentative. Originally used in the UK to mean 'parsimonious' (C18), and then in the US (C19) in the current sense. The term enjoyed a brief moment of fame in the early morning hours of 9th November 2000, when US Vice President Al Gore told future President George Bush, 'You don't have to get snippy with me' as he retracted a concession made several minutes earlier *US, 1848*

snips *noun* any cutting tool, for example scissors or wire cutters *US, 1962*

snirt *noun* a stormy mixture of snow and dirt *CANADA, 1987*

snit *noun* **1** a mild temper tantrum *US, 1939*. **2** among Nova Scotians of German descent, an apple slice *CANADA, 1999*

snitch *noun* **1** an informer, especially a police informer. A high profile use of the term was in the motto of the television police drama *Richard Diamond, Private Detective* (1957–60) – 'A detective is only as good as his snitch' *UK, 1785*. **2** a piece of information supplied by a police informer *UK, 2002*

snitch *verb* **1** to inform upon someone *UK, 1801*. **2** to steal something *US, 1904*. **3** to shoot a marble *NORFOLK ISLAND, 1992*

snitchball *noun* any game played by prisoners in the protective unit reserved for informers *US, 1992*

snitch box *noun* an in-house prison post box *US, 1992*

snitcher *noun* **1** a metal detector *US, 1950*. **2** a dislike or grudge *NEW ZEALAND, 1953*

snitch jacket *noun* a reputation for being an informer *US, 1973*

snitch kite *noun* a note sent by a prisoner to prison authorities, informing on other prisoners *US, 2000*

snitty *adjective* bad-tempered *US, 1978*

snob mob *noun* a group of friends with a very high opinion of themselves *US, 1955*

snockered; schnockered; shnockered *adjective* drunk *US, 1955*

snodger *adjective* great; excellent *AUSTRALIA, 1917*

snog *noun* a passionate kiss; a short but intense period of kissing and cuddling *UK, 1959*

snog *verb* to kiss and cuddle *UK, 1945*

snog and fuck *noun* a public house called the 'Dog and Duck'. Rhyming slang *UK, 1992*

snogger *noun* someone who kisses with passion. From SNOG *UK, 2000*

sno-go *noun* a snowmobile *US, 1961*

snogtastic *adjective* sexually attractive; kissable. Elision of SNOG (to kiss) and 'fan*tastic*' *UK, 1998*

snooge *noun* in Newfoundland, a way of attaching sled dogs *CANADA, 1957*

snooker *verb* **1** to trick someone; to place someone in an impossible position. From the game played with balls on a billiard table *UK, 1915*. **2** to conceal something or someone *AUSTRALIA, 1950*

snookered *adjective* placed in a deliberately difficult position. From the game of snooker *UK, 1915*

snookums *noun* used as an affectionate term of address. As the *Oxford English Dictionary* so gracefully puts it, 'usually applied to children or lap-dogs' *US, 1919*

snoop *noun* a detective. From SNOOP (to pry) *US, 1942*

snoop *verb* to pry *US, 2001*

snoop and pry; snoop *verb* to cry. Rhyming slang *UK, 1992*

snooper *noun* an investigator *US, 1889*

snoopers *noun* the flashing lights on top of a police car *US, 1976*

snoopy *noun* the vagina. A pet name; probably from the character Snoopy, a pet beagle, in *Peanuts* cartoon strip by Charles M. Schulz (1922–2000) *US, 2001*

snoose *noun* damp, grated, chewing snuff *CANADA, 1951*

snoot *noun* **1** the nose *UK, 1861*. **2** cocaine *US, 1993*. **3** a conceited, snobbish person *AUSTRALIA, 1938*. **4** in the television and film industries, a cone attachment that directs light to a specific area *US, 1990*. ▶ **give someone the snoot** to treat someone in a condescending manner *US, 1989*

snootch *noun* the vagina *CANADA, 2002*

snootchie bootchie nootchies!; snootchie bootchies! used as an all-purpose, meaning-free catchphrase. The term was apparently coined by actor Jason Mewes in Kevin Smith's films of the 1990s *US, 1995*

snooter *noun* a habitual drug user who ingests drugs by nasal inhalation *UK, 1996*

snoot full *noun* enough alcohol to make you drunk *US, 1918*

snooty *adjective* arrogant, unpleasant, supercilious, snobbish *UK, 1919*

snooze *noun* **1** a short sleep; a doze *UK, 1793*. **2** a bore *US, 1997*

snooze *verb* to sleep; to doze *UK, 1789*. ▶ **snooze hard** to sleep deeply *US, 1995*

snoozer *noun* **1** a Pullman sleeping carriage on a passenger train *US, 1975*. **2** in a poker game using the joker, the joker. Perhaps related to the earlier sense of the word as 'a thief' *US, 1950*

snoozing and snoring; snooze and snoring *adjective* boring. Rhyming slang. Sometimes shortened to 'snoozing' *UK, 1992*

snop *noun* marijuana *US, 1969*

snorbs *noun* the female breasts *US, 1969*

snore-off *noun* **1** a sleep; a nap *AUSTRALIA, 1949*. **2** a place to sleep *AUSTRALIA, 1967*

snore off *verb* to sleep or fall asleep *AUSTRALIA, 1925*

snore sack *noun* a sleeping bag *US, 1945*

snore shelf *noun* a bed; a sleeping compartment in an over-the-road truck *US, 1976*

snorker *noun* **1** a sausage *AUSTRALIA, 1941*. **2** the penis. From the previous sense *AUSTRALIA, 1971*. **3** a contemptible fool. From the sense as 'penis', thus synonymous with PRICK *US, 1977*. **4** in poker, a player who berates the other players when he wins a hand *US, 1988*

snorrer; snorer *noun* a difficult customer, a scrounger. Derived from Yiddish *shnorrer* (a beggar) *UK, 1977*

snort *noun* **1** a drink of an alcoholic beverage *US, 1889*. **2** cocaine *US, 1975*

snort *verb* **1** to ingest drugs by nasal inhalation *US, 1951*. **2** to take a measure of alcohol nasally *UK, 1999*

snorter *noun* a tablespoonful of alcoholic spirit (tequila and vodka are popular) taken nasally *UK, 2001*

snortin' Norton *noun* a Norton motorcyle. Biker (motorcycle) slang *US, 2003*

snort rag *noun* a piece of cloth holding a powdered drug *US, 1969*

snot *noun* **1** nasal mucus. Originally conventional English and in common usage; considered to be dialect or vulgar since the C19 *UK, 1425*. **2** the residue produced by smoking amphetamine *US, 1993*. **3** an arrogant, conceited and flippant person *US, 1941*. **4** a slut *US, 2001*. ▶ **in a snot** annoyed *IRELAND, 2003*

snot *verb* to blow nasal mucus from the nostrils *UK, 2002*

snot and tears *noun* maudlin misery. Also in Afrikaans *snot en trane SOUTH AFRICA, 1969*

snot nose *noun* **1** an arrogant person; a snob *UK, 1964*. **2** conceit *US, 1984*

snot rag *noun* **1** a handkerchief *UK, 1886*. **2** an insignificant or contemptible person *UK, 1973*

snotsicle *noun* frozen mucus hanging from the nose *ANTARCTICA, 1997*

snotter *noun* a gob of thick nasal mucus and phlegm *UK: SCOTLAND, 1869*

snotterybeak *noun* a person with a runny nose *UK, 1988*

snottie *noun* the hagfish. From its production of slime *NEW ZEALAND, 1991*

snottily *adverb* conceitedly, arrogantly, aloofly *UK, 1864*

snotty *adjective* **1** conceited, arrogant, aloof *UK, 1870*. **2** dirty with nasal mucus. While accepted in conventional usage, the root-word SNOT (nasal mucus) is considered vulgar *UK, 1570*. **3** used of a drag racing track surface, slippery *US, 1965*

snotty-nosed *adjective* contemptible, dirty *UK, 1964*

snout *noun* **1** tobacco; a cigarette. From 'snout' (the nose), mainly prison use. 'The word originates from the days when smoking was prohibited in prison. When smoking, the lag cupped his hand and pretended to rub his nose[.]' (Paul Tempest, *Lag's Lexicon*, 1950) *UK, 1885*. **2** an informer, especially one who seeks a reward for giving information. Derives from a conventional 'snout' (the nose) which is poked into other people's business *UK, 1910*. **3** a grudge against someone *AUSTRALIA, 1919*

snout-baron *noun* in prison, a trafficker in tobacco. SNOUT (tobacco) plus BARON (a powerful convict whose influence is built on illegal trading) *UK, 1962*

snoutery *noun* a tobacco warehouse *UK, 1956*

snow *noun* **1** a powdered drug, especially cocaine but at times heroin *US, 1914*. **2** silver; silver money *UK, 1925*. **3** passes for free admission to a performance; audience members who attend a performance using a free pass *US, 1981*. ▶ **no snow on your shoes** in the context of a betting operation, trustworthy. From the belief that someone who has been inside the operation long enough for the snow to have melted off his shoes does not have advance information on a bet *US, 1951*

snow *verb* **1** to deceive someone; to flirt insincerely *US, 1943*. **2** in poker, to bluff or fake *US, 1963*

snow and ice *noun* a price; in gambling, a starting price. Rhyming slang *UK, 1992*

snowball *noun* **1** a variety of MDMA, the recreational drug best known as ecstasy *UK, 1996*. **2** a mixture of cocaine and heroin *UK, 2000*. **3** a white person. Offensive *US, 1980*. **4** in hot rodding, a whitewall tyre *US, 1958*. ▶ **not a snowball's chance in hell; not a snowball's** not a chance *UK, 1962*

snowball *verb* to pass semen to the donor through a kiss *US, 1972*

snowballing; snowdropping *noun* after oral sex, passing semen to the donor by kissing. Originally an exclusively homosexual use *US, 1972*

snowballs *noun* **1** crack cocaine *US, 1995*. **2** dice altered for cheating with only the numbers four, five and six on the faces *US, 1993*

snowbanker *noun* a big American car *CANADA, 1999*

snowbird *noun* **1** a person from the northern US or Canada who migrates to Florida or elsewhere in the southern US during winter. Originally applied to men who enlisted in the army just before winter, and then to workers who flocked south in the winter, and then to tourists *US, 1914*. **2** a cocaine user or addict. Building on SNOW (cocaine) and reaching to pun with the more conventional sense of the term 'snowbird' *US, 1914*. **3** cocaine *UK, 2002*. **4** a glob of snow that sticks under a fender *CANADA, 1978*

snowblind *adjective* impaired from excessive cocaine use *UK, 1983*

snow-bug *noun* a motor toboggan, predecessor to the snowmobile *CANADA, 1964*

snow bunny *noun* **1** a young woman who hangs around ski resorts in conspicuous dress *CANADA, 1964*. **2** a Royal Marine trained in arctic warfare. After the white camouflage suiting *UK, 1978*

snowcaine *noun* cocaine, or a related drug such as benzocaine or lidocaine *US, 1993*

snow cap *noun* cocaine combined and smoked with marijuana *US, 1995*

snow coke *noun* crack cocaine. A combination of two terms meaning 'cocaine' *UK, 2003*

snowcone; snowcones *noun* cocaine *US, 1994*

snowdrop *noun* a US military police officer. An allusion to the white helmets, gloves, belts and socks *US, 1946*

snow-eater *noun* in Colorado, warm, dry winds that can quickly melt snow *US, 1997*

snowed *adjective* cocaine-intoxicated *US, 1949*

snowed under *adjective* over-burdened with work *US, 1984*

snowflake *noun* **1** a white person. From racial tension situation comedy *Love Thy Neighbour*, 1972–76 *UK, 2000*. **2** cocaine. Also used in the plural *US, 1997*. **3** a military mail control record *US, 1986*

snowheart *noun* a variety of MDMA, the recreational drug best known as ecstasy *UK, 1996*

snow hole *noun* among Nova Scotians living on the coast, the part of the sea from which wind and later snow comes *CANADA, 1968*

snow job *noun* deception by flattery *US, 1943*

snowman *noun* **1** a cocaine dealer *US, 1988*. **2** a handsome, popular boy. High school usage *US, 1961*

snowmen *noun* LSD *UK, 2003*

snow queen *noun* a black homosexual who is attracted to white men *US, 1985*

snow seal *noun* a combination of cocaine and amphetamines. From SNOW (cocaine) *UK, 1998*

snow storm *noun* ▶ **caught in a snow storm** under the influence of cocaine *US, 1949*

snow tank *noun* an older, large car that is reliable in snow driving. The older and more worn out, the more likely that the car will get you to your destination when road conditions make driving difficult. Michigan Upper Peninsula usage *US, 2003*

snow time *noun* the infatuation stage of a relationship *US, 1959*

snowtubing *noun* a sporting recreation, racing across snow on an inflated inner-tube *US, 1986*

Snowturkey *noun* a member of the Canadian Forces Flying Demonstration Team, the 'Snowbirds' *CANADA, 1995*

snow white *noun* cocaine *US, 1993*

Snow Whites *noun* tights. Rhyming slang, formed on the fairytale character Snow White *UK, 1992*

snozzled *adjective* drunk *US, 1947*

snubby; snubbie *adjective* a short-barrelled pistol. From 'snub-nosed' *UK, 1981*

snuff *noun* a murder *US, 1994*. ▶ **up to snuff** enough, sufficient, good enough *US, 1994*

snuff; snuff out *verb* to kill someone. In C19 slang, 'to die', and then later the transitive 'to kill' *UK, 1932*

snuff-dipper *noun* a prostitute who works at truckstops *US, 1976*

snuffer *noun* **1** a film purporting to depict the actual killing of someone, usually a woman *US, 1990*. **2** the nose *US, 1945*

snuff film; snuff flick; snuff movie *noun* a film purporting to depict the actual killing of someone, usually a woman *US, 1976*

snuff it *verb* to die. An image of a candle being extinguished *UK, 1885*

snuff muff *noun* a dead woman used for sex. From SNUFF (to kill), in the adjectival sense found in SNUFF FILM, etc., and MUFF (the vulva; a woman as a sex object) *UK, 2002*

snuff-out *noun* a fast and violent loss of position on a surfboard, usually followed by a sudden trip below the ocean surface *US, 1977*

snuff powder *noun* adulterated heroin or a white powdered poison used to injure or kill someone using it in the belief it is heroin. Much better known as a HOTSHOT *US, 1960*

snuff stick *noun* a cigarette *NEW ZEALAND, 1978*

snuffy *noun* any low-ranking soldier in the US Army or Marines, performing a servile or degrading task *US, 1991*

Snuffy Smith *noun* in trucking, any driver for the Smith Transfer Company *US, 1976*

snug *verb* in horse racing, to rein the horse in to preserve energy for a sprint later in the race *US, 1951*

snuggle-bunny *noun* a girlfriend *UK, 1963*

snurgle *verb* to advance with caution; to crawl forward *UK, 1983*

snye *noun* in the Ottawa valley, a side channel bypassing falls or rapids *CANADA, 1995*

SO *noun* used as Internet discussion group shorthand to mean 'significant other' *US, 1997*

so *adjective* homosexual. Dating from the late C19, during the 1930s the pronunciation was affected with a lisp *UK, 2002*

so *adverb* very, extremely. Attitude and pronunciation separate the slang sense from the standard sense *US, 1988*. ▶ **so many women/books/etc, so little time** used as a humorous expression of regret for lost opportunity. So many variations, so little dictionary space *US, 1953*

so used within a sentence as introduction to an intensifying repetition. Tautological. Originally recorded as a 'proletarian colloquialism', there appears to be a widespread usage in Northern Ireland *UK, 1935*

soak *noun* a drunk *UK, 1820*

soak *verb* to use something as collateral for a loan *US, 1972*

soaked *adjective* drunk. First recorded by Benjamin Franklin in 1737 *US, 1737*

soaker *noun* **1** a surfer who lingers in the water, rarely catching a wave *US, 1991*. **2** a pawnshop *CANADA, 1976*. **3** an extremely large halibut *US, 1997*

so-and-so *noun* **1** used as a substitute for a person's name that is either forgotten or that is not important to the point being made *UK, 1596*. **2** used as a euphemism for any derogatory form of address *UK, 1943*

soap *noun* **1** a soap opera, either in the literal sense of a radio or television melodramatic series or in the figurative sense *US, 1943*. **2** the recreational drug GHB *US, 1995*. **3** ordinary soap used to fill cracks when using explosives to open a safe *US, 1970*. **4** a bribe *US, 1972*

soap and flannel *noun* the National Health Service. Rhyming slang for 'panel', a term that relates to healthcare under the system that preceded the advent of the NHS in 1946 *UK, 1992*

soap and lather *noun* a father. Rhyming slang. Ray Puxley, *Cockney Rabbit*, 1992, notes that this 'makes the pope the "holy soap"' *UK, 1961*

soap and water *noun* a daughter. Rhyming slang *UK, 1925*

soap bar; soap *noun* a small block of cannabis resin, often heavily adulterated, especially with animal tranquillizers; thus hashish, especially if adulterated. From the similarity to a conventional bar of soap *UK, 1996*

soap box *noun* a Mini car. Citizens' band radio slang, from the shape and size *UK, 1981*

soap-box artist *noun* a skilled public speaker *NEW ZEALAND, 1938*

soapbox derby syndrome *noun* any rapidly progressing disease or medical condition. The Soap Box Derby is a downhill coasting race sponsored by the Cub Scouts *US, 1983*

soapdogger *noun* a person who always seems unwashed. From DOG (to dodge, to avoid) *UK: SCOTLAND, 1996*

soap opera *noun* a never-ending radio or televison drama series, designed to attract long-term audience loyalty and emotional involvement. The original of the genre, broadcast on US radio from 1932, was *The Puddle Family* sponsored by Procter & Gamble, a soap manufacturer; the product giving the entertainment its identity *US, 1939*

soapy *noun* the balance after a day of betting. Rhyming slang based on Soapy Vallance, a legendary Australian athlete of the 1930s *AUSTRALIA, 1989*

soapy *adjective* dirty; in a mess; in need of a wash *UK, 1996*

soapy bubble; soapy *noun* trouble. Rhyming slang, first recorded in Glasgow. Later used as Cockney rhyming slang *UK, 1985*

sob *noun* one pound sterling. Probably a mishearing of SOV(£1) *UK, 1970*

SOB *noun* **1** used as a term of abuse: *son of a bitch US, 1918*. **2** a sober old bastard. A term used with affection in twelve-step recovery programmes such as Alcoholics Anonymous *US, 1998*

SOB *adjective* short of breath; dyspeptic *US, 1989*

sobriety coach *noun* someone who aids or mentors an alcoholic or a drug addict in the maintenance of a drink- or drug-free life *US, 2002*

sob sister *noun* a soft-hearted, naive person *US, 1912*

sob story *noun* a sentimental narrative that is told to arouse sympathy *UK, 1913*

sob-story artist *noun* a swindler whose method of operating includes a sentimental narrative of misfortune and an appeal to the emotions of the victim *US, 1954*

sociable *adverb* in poolroom betting, for a small wager *US, 1967*

social *noun* a government social worker *US, 1995*. ▶ **go social** to stop fighting *US, 1968*

Social *noun* ▶ **on the Social** receiving Social Security or other state benefits *UK, 1996*. ▶ **the Social** the Department of Health and Social Security (DHSS), reformed as the Department of Social Security (DSS). In 2001 the Department for Work and Pensions (DWP) replaced the DHSS *UK, 1997*

social lubricant *noun* alcohol *US, 1986*

socials *noun* alcoholic beverages *UK, 1991*

societ *verb* to associate with someone *BARBADOS, 1965*

society high *noun* cocaine. A neat reversal on 'high society' suggesting the social circles that can afford cocaine *UK, 1998*

sock *noun* **1** a blow, physical or figurative *UK, 1700*. **2** a condom *US, 1992*. ▶ **put a sock in it** to stop talking. Usually as an imperative *UK, 1919*

sock *verb* **1** to hit or thrash someone *UK, 1700*. **2** to place something somewhere; to hide something *US, 1942*. **3** used for conveying encouragement and support *US, 1960s*. **4** (of a male) to have sex *US, 1969*. ▶ **sock it to someone 1** to attack someone, literally or figuratively *US, 1946*. **2** to have sex with a woman *US, 1969*

socket *noun* the vagina *UK, 2001*

sock hop *noun* a dance for teenagers. The term was coined on account of the practice of removing your shoes and dancing in your socks. The practice changed but the term did not *US, 1975*

socking great *adjective* very large *UK, 1985*

sock it to me! surprise me!; liven things up! Borrowed from the vocabulary of black jazz musicians. Between 1968 and 1970 it was Judy Carne's catchphrase in television variety show *Rowan & Martin's Laugh-In US, 1967*

socko *adjective* excellent; outstanding *US, 1938*

socko-boffo *adjective* absolutely excellent; in a showbusiness or film context, in a 'knock-'em-dead' style. A combination of SOCKO and BOFFO, intensifying either element *US, 1981*

socks *noun* a linear amplifier for a citizens' band radio. From the term FOOTWARMER (a linear amplifier in a truck) *US, 1976*. ▶ **give socks** to copulate *IRELAND, 1984*. ▶ **your socks off** with great effect; with great commitment *UK, 2001*

So Co *noun* Southern Comfort™ whisky *US, 1997*

Socrates' pleasure *noun* anal sex *US, 1993*

Socred *noun* a member of the Social Credit party *CANADA, 1966*

sod *noun* **1** a sodomite; generally used of a male homosexual *UK, c. 1855*. **2** a contemptible man. An abbreviation of 'sodomite' *UK, 1818*. **3** a difficult circumstance; an awkward thing. From the previous sense *UK, 1936*. **4** used as a general form of address *UK, 1942*. **5** a person of the stated characteristic, thus: lucky sod, jammy sod, miserable sod, etc *UK, 1931*

sod! used for dismissing, or registering exasperation with, whatever or whoever is the subject of this injunction *UK, 1904*

soda *noun* **1** cocaine. Playing on Coke™ as the most popular soda in the US *US, 1993*. **2** something easy to do *AUSTRALIA, 1917*

sod about *verb* to play the fool; to potter about; to waste time *UK, 1961*

soda jerk *noun* a person, usually a teenaged boy, who works at a counter at a soda fountain, mixing drinks for customers. An abbreviation of the earlier (1889) 'soda jerker' *US, 1910*

sod-all *noun* nothing, not a thing *UK, 1958*

sod buster *noun* a business that appears to be legitimate but is in fact a front for criminal activity *US, 1982*

sodding *adjective* used as an all-purpose intensifier, generally to negative effect; interchangeable with bloody, fucking, etc *UK, 1912*

sodding Nora! used as a register of surprise, anger, amazement, etc *UK, 1982*

sodding well *adverb* used as an intensifier *UK, 1962*

sod it! used for registering resignation, exasperation, aggravation, etc *UK, 1953*

sod-off *adjective* very obvious *UK, 2000*

sod off! go away! *UK, 1960*

Sodom and Gomorrah; sodom *verb* to borrow; hence, an act of borrowing. Cockney rhyming slang, which gives rise to the phrase: 'on the sodom' *UK, 1998*

sod's law *noun* a cynical 'law' of existence that decrees that 'if something can go wrong it will' and is therefore named or cited as explanation or justification whenever such circumstances conspire *UK, 1970*

sod this for a game of soldiers!; sod that for a game of soldiers! used as an emphatic dismissal of any activity or notion that you have no wish to subscribe to *UK, 1979*

sod this for a lark!; sod that for a lark! used as an emphatic dismissal of any activity or notion that you have no wish to subscribe to *UK, 2004*

sod you! used for registering antipathy or hostility towards or dismissal of the person(s) addressed *UK, 1904*

soft *noun* **1** cocaine *US, 2002*. **2** paper money *US, 1950*. **3** in the usage of telephone swindlers, a cash sale *US, 1959*

soft *adjective* **1** denotes all recreational drugs that are loosely categorised as less harmful or addictive *UK, 2001*. **2** stupid, dull, half-witted; 'soft in the head' *UK, 1775*. **3** in blackjack, said of a hand with an ace where the bettor has the option of treating the ace as 1 point or 11 points *US, 1978*

softarse *noun* a person who is easily imposed upon *UK, 2002*

soft-arsed *adjective* stupid, dull, half-witted *UK, 2002*

softball *noun* any barbiturate or central nervous system depressant *US, 1977*

soft cock *noun* a weak-willed or timid person; a wimp *AUSTRALIA, 1999*

soft-cock *adjective* weak; insipid *AUSTRALIA, 1981*

soft-cock rock *noun* rock music that lacks power and aggression. Blend of SOFT COCK and COCK ROCK *AUSTRALIA, 1996*

soft con *noun* a confidence swindle accomplished through charm and warmth *US, 1977*

softcore *noun* sexual material that does not show insertion, penetration, an erect penis, spread labia or ejaculation *US, 1977*

soft cover *noun* the official government-issued armed forces baseball cap. Marine usage in the Vietnam war *US, 1990*

softly-softly *adjective* describing a circumspect approach to achieve an objective. An abbreviation of 'softly softly catchee monkey'. Later use is probably influenced by *Softly Softly,* a BBC television police drama series, 1966–76 *UK, 1959*

soft-nose *adjective* easily learned. A term of derision applied to the 'soft' sciences, for example sociology *US, 1974*

soft-on *noun* a penis flaccid from being sexually turned off *AUSTRALIA, 1995*

soft one *noun* in necrophile usage, a corpse that has yet to stiffen with rigor mortis *US, 1987*

soft option *noun* an easier or the easiest choice in any given circumstances. Often in a disapproving or derogatory tone *UK, 1923*

soft parts *noun* in car repair, parts or equipment that can be expected to wear out and can normally be replaced at a car parts shop *US, 1992*

soft-pedal *verb* to proceed in a circumspect, less forceful or subdued manner. A figurative application of a piano or organ's volume control *UK, 1915*

softplay *verb* in poker, to play less than ruthlessly against a friend *UK, 1990*

soft shoes *noun* sneakers, trainers *BARBADOS, 1998*

soft slugger *noun* a casino cheat who inserts counterfeit currency into a slot machine *US, 1999*

soft-soap *noun* flattery, especially as an act of deception or manipulation *US, 1830*

soft-soap *verb* to flatter or deceive someone *UK, 1840*

soft time *noun* a relatively short jail sentence, especially one served in an easy-going prison *US, 1983*

soft touch; easy touch *noun* a person who is easily manipulated or parted from a thing of value; a task that is easily done *US, 1940*

soft walkers *noun* sneakers, trainers *ANGUILLA, 1992*

software rot *noun* in computing, an imaginary condition in which unused software or software features stop working if not used *US, 1981*

softy *noun* **1** a flaccid penis *US, 1995*. **2** an inexperienced and/or unskilled poker player *US, 1988*. **3** in computing, a programming expert who lacks any substantial understanding of computer hardware *US, 1991*

soggy *adjective* drunk *AUSTRALIA, 1945*

soggy Sao *noun* a game in which a group of men simultaneously masturbate onto a biscuit which is then eaten. From Sao™, the brand of dry cracker *AUSTRALIA, 1992*

so help me cripes good lord! *AUSTRALIA, 1947*

so help us Fort Knox used with humour as a pledge or oath. From the US television situation comedy *How to Marry a Millionaire* (1958–60), in which three young women seeking rich husbands pledge to help each other, sealing the pledge with 'So help us Fort Knox', referring to the depository of gold held by the US government. Used with referential humour *US, 1960*

SOHF *noun* a sense of humour failure on the part of outsiders who fail to appreciate the graceless antics of the user's social set. Upper-class society use *UK, 1982*

so I says used for effect in introducing a humorous statement. Made famous by Sophie Tucker in her onstage banter about her love life with a fictional Ernie *US, 1998*

soixante-neuf *noun* mutual and simultaneous oral sex. A direct translation into French of synonymous **69**; perhaps with euphemistic intention, or to lend sophistication to the act *UK, 1888*

sol *noun* solitary confinement *US, 1992*

SOL *noun* ill temper. Initialism of 'shit on liver' *AUSTRALIA, 1951*

solarist *noun* a single-minded sunbather *UK, 1979*

solar-panel on a sex-machine *noun* a man's bald-spot. Jocular *UK, 1995*

soldi *noun* a penny. From Italian *soldi* (money) *UK, 2002*

soldier *noun* **1** a regular, low-level member of a criminal organisation who can be counted on to follow orders *US, 1963*. **2** a male lookout for a criminal operation *US, 1956*. **3** a bottle of alcohol; a can of beer *US, 1945*. **4** a finger of bread or toast *UK, 1977*

soldier ants; soldiers *noun* underpants. Rhyming slang *UK, 1992*

soldier on *verb* to persevere against peril; to continue doggedly in the face of difficulty or hardship *UK, 1954*

soldier's farewell *noun* any abusive term of dismissal *UK, 2004*

soldier's wash *noun* a method or act of washing in which cupped hands are used instead of a flannel *UK, 1980*

sold on *adjective* convinced by, or enthusiastic about, something *US, 1928*

soles *noun* shoes *US, 1995*

solicit *verb* (of a homosexual man) to walk in public dressed in female clothes – not necessarily for the purposes of prostitution. An ironic adoption of the stricter legal sense *UK, 2002*

solid *noun* **1** a trustworthy, dependable person *US, 1997*. **2** a favour *US, 1973*

solid *adjective* **1** very good. A jazz term that arrived on the scene with 'swing' in 1935 *US, 1935*. **2** especially amongst criminals, loyal; staunch *AUSTRALIA, 1950*. **3** harsh; severe; unreasonable; unfair *AUSTRALIA, 1915*. **4** usually of time, continuously, uninterrupted; complete *UK, 1718*

solids *noun* in pool, the solid-coloured balls numbered 1 to 7 *US, 1984*

solid sender *noun* a person, particularly a musician, who is especially inspired or inspiring. From the jive vocabulary into the rock 'n' roll lexicon *US, 1946*

solid six *noun* in Keno, a bet on a block of three numbers, two rows deep *US, 1973*

solid sweet! used as strong approval *US, 1980*

solo box *noun* a pornographic video cover showing photographs of only one performer *US, 1977*

Solomon Gundy *noun* salt herring in marinade *CANADA, 1998*

so long goodbye *US, 1865*

so long for now, and spaceman's luck to all of you used as a humorous farewell. A catchphrase television sign-off on *Tom Corbett, Space Cadet* (1950–55), a children's adventure programme. Repeated with referential humour *US, 1955*

solo sack time *noun* time spent sleeping alone *US, 1946*

solve *noun* a crime that has been solved *US, 1992*

Somali tea *noun* **1** leaves of *catha edulis*, a stimulant also called qat or qaadka. Originating in the Horn of Africa and the Arabian peninsula, legally available in the UK and similar to amphetamine in effect when chewed *US, 2003*. **2** methcathinone *US, 2003*

somatomax *noun* the recreational drug GHB. In Aldous Huxley's *Brave New World*, 1932, 'soma' is the drug of social conditioning *US, 1990*

some *adjective* exceptional, remarkable. Used in ironic understatement *US, 1808*

some *adverb* very *US, 1981*

somebody up there *noun* God; a higher power. Used in a jocular and secular vein in expressions such as 'somebody up there likes me' *US, 1957*

some cunt from Preston *noun* country and western music. Rhyming slang *UK, 1988*

some hope!; some hopes! used as an expression of hopelessness or extreme scepticism *UK, 1940*

some mothers do 'ave 'em used of someone who is clumsy, foolish or laughable. A slight variation on a saying from Lancashire: 'don't some mothers 'ave 'em?'. Widely popularised as the title of a BBC television comedy series, 1974, and still repeating *UK, 1960*

Somerset Maugham; somerset *adjective* warm. Rhyming slang, formed from the name of the British author, 1874–1965 *UK, 1998*

something *noun* a remarkable thing *UK, 1958*. ▶ **do you want to make something out of it?; do you want to make something of it?** do you want to fight about it?; do you want to argue about it? *US, 1948*. ▶ **have something on** to have information about someone or something *US, 1919*

something *adverb* used for intensifying. Amends an adjective into an adverb: 'something cruel', 'something horrible', etc *UK, 1964*

something chronic *adverb* constantly; badly, objectionably, severely, unpleasantly *UK, 1916*

something else *adjective* beyond description; unbelievable *US, 1968*

something-something *noun* sex *US, 2003*

something strange *noun* sex with someone other than your regular partner *BERMUDA, 1985*

sometime *noun* a person who cannot be relied upon *US, 1981*

sometimesy; sometimey *adjective* moody; unstable; emotionally inconsistent *US, 1972*

sometimish *adjective* insincere; unreliable *BARBADOS, 1965*

sommat *noun* something. A phonetic distortion *UK, 1978*

son; my son *noun* used between contemporary, unrelated males as a familiar form of address. Occasionally patronising, used in order to establish social ascendancy *UK, 1914*

son-bitch *noun* used as a slightly jocular form of son of a bitch *US, 1981*

song *noun* ▶ **on song** in good form, especially in a sporting context *UK, 1974*

song *verb* to advertise a delinquent debtor by putting his name and offence in a song *CANADA, 1975*

song and dance *noun* **1** an elaborate performance or presentation of a story, especially in an effort to persuade *US, 1895*. **2** a fuss, an outcry. Something trivial or of little account is 'nothing to make a song and dance about' *US, 1895*. **3** a strip search *US, 1976*. **4** a chance. Rhyming slang *UK, 1992*

song and dancer *noun* an opportunist. Glasgow rhyming slang for CHANCER *UK: SCOTLAND, 1988*

songbird *noun* **1** a female singer *UK, 1886*. **2** a police informer *US, 1970*

songplugger *noun* a person employed to promote a recorded song by any of a variety of means *US, 1923*

sonic *noun* a type of LSD identified by a picture of computer game hero 'Sonic the Hedgehog' *US, 1996*

sonk *noun* a foolish, feeble or otherwise objectionable person. Back-formation from SONKY *AUSTRALIA, 1922*

sonky *adjective* foolish, silly; feeble *AUSTRALIA, 1917*

sonno *noun* used generally for addressing a *son*, a boy or a man *AUSTRALIA, 1910s*

sonny *noun* used for addressing a boy or younger man. Often patronising *UK, 1870*

sonny boy; sonny Jim; sunny Jim *noun* used to address a boy or younger man. An elaboration of SONNY; often patronising *UK, 1959*

son of a successor of something. A jocular derivation from the imaginative formula used to title some Hollywood film sequels (a fine example: *Son of Paleface*, 1952, in which Bob Hope played the son of the character he portrayed in *The Paleface*, 1948) *UK, 1971*

sonofabitch; sonuvabitch *noun* a fellow *US, 1951*

son of a bitch *noun* **1** a despicable person *UK, 1605*. **2** used in extreme comparisons *US, 1953*

son of a bitch! used as a mild expletive *US, 1953*

son-of-a-bitching *adjective* used as a somewhat profane intensifier *US, 1930*

son-of-a-bitch with slides *noun* an expert guest speaker at a medical meeting *US, 1985*

son of a gun *noun* a fellow. Originally, 'a soldier's bastard', now mildly disparaging or pejorative. Occasionally used as an exclamation of surprise *UK, 1708*

sook; sooky; sookie *noun* a person easily brought to tears; a crybaby *AUSTRALIA, 1941*

sooky *adjective* apt to burst into tears; weak; timid or cowardly. From British dialect (Clydesdale) *sooky* meaning 'effeminate', recorded in the *English Dialect Dictionary* under the word 'soaky' *AUSTRALIA, 1901*

sool *verb* **1** to incite someone to attack or go after someone; to spur someone on *AUSTRALIA, 1924*. **2** to set a dog onto someone *AUSTRALIA, 1889*. **3** (especially of a dog) to attack someone *AUSTRALIA, 1849*

sooner *noun* **1** a person or thing which fails to perform. Because 'they would *sooner* do nothing than something' *AUSTRALIA, 1892*. **2** a mixed-breed dog *BARBADOS, 1965*

sooty; soot *noun* a black person. A derogatory term *US, 1838*

sooty *noun* **1** a Maori. Offensive *NEW ZEALAND, 1989*. **2** an engine tradesman in the Royal Air Force. In Royal Air Force use, 2002 *UK, 2002*

sooty tunes *noun* reggae music *UK, 1983*

SOP *noun* in motor racing, seat of the pants *US, 1993*

sope *noun* a tablet of the recreational drug methaqualone, best known as Quaaludes™ *US, 1985*

soph *noun* a second-year student in high school or college. An abbreviation of 'sophomore' *US, 1778*

Sophie *noun* a girlfriend. Teen slang *US, 1951*

sophisticated lady *noun* cocaine *US, 1980*

sop joint *noun* a Turkish bath *US, 1968*

sopor; soper; soaper *noun* a tablet of the recreational drug methaqualone, best known as Quaaludes™. From a brand name, ultimately from 'soporific' *US, 1973*

soppings *noun* gravy or sauce. From the act of sopping up with a piece of bread. Southern US *US, 1984*

soppy *adjective* foolishly sentimental; naive. A play on 'sopping wet' (excessively sentimental) *UK, 1918*

soppy date *noun* a fool; someone who is foolishly sentimental *UK, 1959*

soppy ha'p'orth; soppy 'a'p'orth; soppy apeth *noun* a fool; someone who is foolishly sentimental. An elaboration of HA'P'ORTH, and a variation of SOPPY DATE; certainly in parental use during the 1950s *UK, 1984*

sore *adjective* angry; bitter; disappointed; disgruntled *UK, 1694*

sore as a boil *adjective* extremely upset *AUSTRALIA, 1955*

sore bitch *noun* a member of a college sorority *US, 1968*

sore-neck *noun* the sense of resentment arising from not being invited to a social event *NORFOLK ISLAND, 1992*

sore thumb *verb* the epitome of something that is patently obvious or conspicuous *US, 1936*

sorority *noun* **1** male homosexuals collectively as a group *US, 1979*. **2** a woman's prison *US, 1949*. **3** a poker game or tournament limited to female players *US, 1996*

Sorority Sal *noun* a stereotypical sorority member who looks, dresses, talks and lives the part *US, 1959*

sorority sauce *noun* ketchup *US, 1985*

sorostitute *noun* a member of a college sorority. Derisive, suggesting sexual promiscuity *US, 1998*

sorrowful tale *noun* a sentence of three months' imprisonment. Rhyming slang for '(three months in) jail' *UK, 1859*

sorry about that used as a jaded response to something bad that has just happened, especially when caused by the speaker. A keystone of military vernacular during the conflict in Vietnam *US, 1965*

sorry and sad; sorry *noun* a father. Rhyming slang for 'dad' *UK, 1998*

sorry and sad; sorry *adjective* bad. Rhyming slang *UK, 1960*

sorry-ass *adjective* pathetic; despicable *US, 1998*

sort *noun* **1** in combination with an adjective (usually *good* or *bad*), a person of whatever character is indicated *UK, 1869*. **2** a woman; a companion of the opposite sex *AUSTRALIA, 1933*. **3** an attractive woman. Without a distinguishing epithet this word equates with GOOD SORT *AUSTRALIA, 1933*. **4** a woman considered in terms of sexual attraction. Concentrating on the physical aspect of a person, as opposed to their character. An attractive woman is described as a 'beaut sort', 'great sort', 'grouse sort', 'not a bad sort', 'terrific sort,' etc. An ugly woman can be described as a 'rough sort', 'drack sort', 'awful sort', etc *AUSTRALIA, 1948*

sort *verb* **1** to have sex with someone; to satisfy someone's sexual requirements *UK, 2001*. **2** to provide someone with drugs *UK, 2000*. **3** to beat up a fellow prisoner *UK, 1996*

sorta *adjective* in a way; to some extent; somehow; one might say. 'Sort of' lazily pronounced *US, 1980*

sorted *adjective* provisioned with sufficient drugs *UK, 1996*

sort out *verb* to use violence to resolve a difference with someone *UK, 1937*

SOS *noun* **1** the same old stuff *US, 1963*. **2** a somewhat older student. Used by college students to describe, usually unkindly, students in their late twenties or older *US, 2002*

SOS *adjective* unable to learn; stuck on stupid *US, 1994*

SOS between schoolchildren, used as advice that a slip or petticoat can be seen below the hem of a skirt. An initialism of 'slip on show', playing on the emergency code 'save our souls' *UK, 1979*

sosh *noun* **1** a member of upper-class society *US, 1993*. **2** a student whose emphasis is on social activities *US, 1968*

soshe; the soshe *noun* the Social Security, a UK government agency responsible for welfare payments; the welfare (sickness, old-age, unemployment, etc) payments given by the UK government *UK, 1999*

soshing *noun* manipulating someone with criminal intent. Derived from social engineering *US, 2000*

so-so *adjective* mediocre *UK, 1570*

soss; sossy *noun* the penis. From an abbreviation of 'sausage' *NEW ZEALAND, 1998*

sosso *noun* a sausage *AUSTRALIA, 1992*

sosso roll *noun* a sausage roll *AUSTRALIA, 1985*

sot *noun* an alcoholic dulled by drinking *UK, 1592*

so there! used at the end of an argumentative or threatening proposition as the final stress. Abbreviates 'so there you have it', 'so there you are'; often childish *UK, 1982*

so? throw party! used for dismissing the importance of what has just been said. Hawaiian youth usage *US, 1982*

soul *noun* the essence of black culture *US, 1965*

soul *adjective* pertaining to the essence of black culture *US, 1946*

Soul Alley; Soul City; Soulsville *noun* an area in Saigon with bars and brothels patronised largely by black US soldiers *US, 1970*

soulboy *noun* a member of a mid-1970s youth fashion and music sub-culture *UK, 2000*

soul brother *noun* a black man *US, 1970*

soul-case *noun* heart and soul *AUSTRALIA, 1901*

soul food *noun* food associated with southern black culture *US, 1964*

soulie *noun* a member of a mid-1970s youth subculture identified by its dedication to soul music; a soulboy or a soulgirl *UK, 1996*

soul kiss *noun* a sustained, open-mouthed kiss *US, 1948*

soul kiss *verb* to give someone a deep and intimate kiss, usually involving tongue or tongues *US, 1951*

soul patch *noun* facial whiskers that are grown and worn beneath the lower lip and above the chin *UK, 2006*

soul sister *noun* a black woman *US, 1967*

soulville *noun* a part of a city inhabited largely by black people *US, 1975*

sound *noun* **1** a style of speech, including vocabulary, syntax and attitude *US, 1958*. **2** a taunt or tease; an insult *US, 1967*

sound *verb* **1** to speak or inform; to tease someone; to flirt; to insult someone in a semi-formal quasi-friendly competition *US, 1959*. **2** to glare at or intimidate someone with a look *US, 1955*

sound that's good; used in a congratulatory sense to express praise for an action *UK, 2002*

sound as a pound *adjective* reliable; perfectly sound, good or healthy *UK, 2001*

sound as a trout *adjective* perfectly sound, good or healthy *UK, 1635*

soundbox *noun* the throat *US, 1946*

sound down *verb* to speak to someone in a probing or inquiring way *US, 1990*

sound off *verb* to complain angrily about a particular something; to speak your mind *US, 1918*

sounds *noun* **1** recorded music *US, 1955*. **2** a radio. From its use as a provider of 'sounds' (music) *UK, 1996*

sounds like a personal problem used for silencing a complaint without sympathy *US, 1968*

soundtrack *verb* to supply the musical accompaniment to an activity *UK, 2002*

soup *noun* **1** nitroglycerin, or any explosive used for opening a safe *US, 1902*. **2** in the television and film industries, the chemicals used to develop film *US, 1990*. **3** in hot rodding and drag racing, race fuel *US, 1954*. **4** cocaine *US, 1995*. **5** foaming water left after a wave breaks *US, 1963*. **6** rain *US, 1945*. **7** in shuffleboard, the scoring area of the court *US, 1967*. ▶ **in the soup** in grave trouble *US, 2001*

soup and gravy; soup *noun* a navy *UK, 1960*

soup can *noun* a gas grenade *US, 1978*

souped *adjective* of a car, power-enhanced *UK, 1951*

souped-up *adjective* usually of a standard model car, supercharged, performance-enhanced *US, 1931*

soup job *noun* a car with many performance-enhancing features *US, 1993*

soup jockey *noun* a cook for a railway work crew *US, 1975*

soup out *verb* to ride a wave into the foaming water produced by the breaking wave *US, 1963*

soup-plate feet *noun* large hooves on a horse *UK, 1948*

soup-strainer *noun* a moustache *US, 1946*

soup suit *noun* a dinner-jacket *US, 1954*

soup up *verb* to make modifications which increase a car's performance *US, 1933*

sourball *noun* a person with a sour disposition *US, 1900*

sourdough *noun* **1** a person with considerable experience in Alaska *US, 1898*. **2** in Alaska, homebrew alcohol *US, 1915*

sour grape *noun* rape. Prison slang. *NEW ZEALAND, 1999*

sourpuss *noun* a grumbler; a misery; a killjoy. From the 'sour' look on his or her PUSS (face) *US, 1937*

soused *adjective* drunk *US, 1932*

south *noun* ▶ **go south** to palm and hide something, usually dice or cards *US, 1962*

South *noun* ▶ **the South** Antarctica *ANTARCTICA, 1901*

south 48; south 49 *noun* in Alaska, all states except Alaska *US, 1984*

South American snowflakes *noun* cocaine *UK, 1999*

South Austin suitcase *noun* a brown paper bag used to conceal a beer you want to drink on the street *US, 2001*

South County Indian *noun* a Portuguese immigrant or Portuguese-American. Rhode Island usage, alluding to the large Portuguese population *US, 1989*

Southend-on-Sea *noun* urine; an act of urination. Rhyming slang for PEE OR WEE, formed from the stereotypical Cockney's traditional seaside resort *UK, 1992*

Southend Pier *noun* the ear. Rhyming slang *UK, 1992*

southerly buster *noun* on the east coast, a sudden strong and cooling wind from the south arriving towards evening after a hot day and often bringing rain *AUSTRALIA, 1850*

Southern and Seven *noun* an alcoholic drink consisting of Southern Comfort™ whisky mixed with Seven-Up™ soda *US, 1989*

Southern engineering *noun* a sloppy job of design or manufacture *US, 1984*

Southern love *noun* mouth-to-penis contact immediately after the penis is withdrawn from a rectum *US, 1995*

Southie *nickname* an Irish-American enclave in south Boston. An area famous for its support of the Irish Republican Army, its opposition to school busing to achieve racial integration and its anti-homosexual stance *US, 1984*

South of France *noun* a dance. Rhyming slang *UK, 1992*

south of the border *adjective* unacceptable. Glasgow rhyming slang for OUT OF ORDER. Not a reference to England but (thanks to Hollywood) Mexico *UK: SCOTLAND, 1988*

south of the border *adverb* in or to the area of the genitals, especially a woman's *US, 1945*

south of the border; south *noun* order; an orderly condition. Glasgow rhyming slang *UK: SCOTLAND, 1988*

southpaw *noun* a left-handed person, especially a left-handed athlete *US, 1891*

South Pole *noun* the anus. Rhyming slang for HOLE *UK, 1992*

souvenir *verb* to take an object as a souvenir. Originally World War 1 military slang *AUSTRALIA, 1918*

sov *noun* one pound sterling (£1). An abbreviation of 'sovereign', which, at one time, was a coin valued at £1; since the departure of the coin as currency it has denoted first a one-pound note, and then a one-pound coin *UK, 1850*

sovvy *noun* a gold sovereign; a sovereign ring *UK, 2005*

sow belly *noun* on the railways, a coal tender with a drop bottom *US, 1946*

so what? used for registering dismissal of, or disinterest in, what has gone before *US, 1934*

sox *noun* socks *UK, 1905*

so you feel that is your opinion, that is what you think. Recorded in use among young urban blacks *UK, 1999*

sozzled *adjective* drunk. From dialect word *sozzle* (to mix messily) *UK, 1886*

SP *noun* **1** the latest information. Bookmakers abbreviation of jargon 'starting price' *UK, 1974*. **2** starting price bookmaking *AUSTRALIA, 1941*. **3** a starting price bookmaker *AUSTRALIA, 1949*. **4** an establishment operating starting price bookmaking *AUSTRALIA, 1965*. **5** the US Navy's Shore Patrol, or internal police *US, 1951*

SP *adjective* relating to horse race betting at starting price odds *AUSTRALIA, 1932*

SP *adverb* at starting price odds *AUSTRALIA, 1949*

spa *noun* a small, privately owned convenience/grocery shop *US, 1997*

Spa *noun* the Saratoga race track, Saratoga Springs, New York *US, 1960*

spac *adjective* stupid; awful *AUSTRALIA, 1988*. ▶ **go spac** to lose control in anger *AUSTRALIA, 1988*

spac *adverb* dreadfully AUSTRALIA, 1988

spac; spack; spak *noun* **1** a stupid or unfashionable person. Alteration of SPASTIC. Used by schoolchildren AUSTRALIA, 1988. **2** a person with spastic paralysis; a person who has any disability UK, 1996

spac attack; spack attack *noun* an instance of idiotic behaviour. From SPAC UK, 2003

spacbrain *noun* a stupid or unfashionable person AUSTRALIA, 1988

spacco *adjective* ▶ **go spacco** to behave in an idiotic, erratic or hyperactive manner. From SPAC UK, 2003

space *noun* **1** a mental attitude or position UK, 1971. **2** a year, especially a year in prison US, 1950

space *verb* to daydream; to wander off mentally US, 1995

spacebase *noun* a cigar wrapper filled with phencyclidine and crack cocaine US, 1992

space cadet *noun* **1** a drug user UK, 2002. **2** a heavily drugged hospital patient US, 1989

space case; space cadet; space head *noun* a person who is completely out of touch with their surroundings US, 1974

space cookie; space cake *noun* a sweet confection with marijuana in the recipe UK, 1998

space cowboy *noun* a disoriented, distracted person US, 1977

spaced *adjective* **1** in a state of drug intoxication, especially as a result of hallucinogen use but loosely of any drug US, 1967. **2** unaware; unfocused; highly distracted US, 1967

spacedancing *noun* in the language surrounding the Grateful Dead, the freeform dancing practised by band followers US, 1994

spaced out *adjective* **1** drug-intoxicated; disoriented. Conventionally 'space' is beyond the frontiers of normality US, 1970. **2** stupefied from anaesthetic US, 1973

space pill *noun* MDMA, the recreational drug best known as ecstasy UK, 2000

spacer *noun* **1** a hallucinogenic recreational drug UK, 1971. **2** a mace cigarette US, 1967. **3** someone who is capable of crazy actions IRELAND, 2003

space shake *noun* a milk-based drink which has marijuana as an important ingredient UK, 2003

space suit *noun* untearable prison-issue pyjamas UK, 1996

spacies *noun* computerised arcade games. From *Space Invaders* , one of the earliest popular games of this type. Modelled on POKIE AUSTRALIA, 1986

spacker; spacka; spack *noun* a stupid person. A later variation of SPASTIC as a general derogative, in juvenile use in the UK UK, 2001

spacy; spacey *adjective* in a state of confusion; denoting an unbalanced normality or a dazed condition; similar to or of a hallucinogenic experience. Compares a perception of reality to that of being SPACED (drug-intoxicated) but does not always describe a drugged state US, 1970

spad *nickname* a Douglas aircraft A-1 Skyraider, used for close air support of ground troops US, 1989

spade *noun* a black person US, 1928. ▶ **in spades** to a great degree US, 1929

spades *noun* shoes with pointed toes. Teen slang US, 1955

spaff *verb* to ejaculate semen UK, 2003. ▶ **spaff your load** to ejaculate semen. An elaboration of SPAFF UK, 2003

spag *noun* spaghetti UK, 1948

Spag *noun* an Italian. From 'spaghetti' AUSTRALIA, 1967

spag bol; spag bog *noun* spaghetti bolognese UK, 1970

spag fag *noun* a gay man attracted to Italians. Combines SPAG (an Italian) and FAG (a gay man) UK, 1998

spaghetti *noun* **1** in hot rodding, a surfeit of chrome US, 1958. **2** in oil drilling, small-diameter piping US, 1954

spaghetti *adjective* Italian US, 1969

spaghetti and macaroni *noun* sado-masochism. Disguising the initialism S AND M US, 1989

spaghetti-bender *noun* an Italian or Italian-American US, 1967

spaghetti-eater *noun* an Italian or Italian-American US, 1958

Spaghetti Junction *nickname* **1** junction 6 of the M6 motorway, the interchange at Gravelly Hill, near Birmingham. So-called for the complicated pattern of roads; it opened for use in 1972, but was already known by this name in late 1971 UK, 1972. **2** a motorway overpass 10 kilometres from Durban SOUTH AFRICA, 1999

spaghetti strap *noun* very thin shoulder straps on a woman's garment; the garment itself US, 1972

spaghetti western *noun* a cowboy film about the American 'wild west' produced by the Italian film industry US, 1973

spaginzy *noun* a black person US, 1973

Spahn and Sain and then, dear Lord, two days of rain used as a humorous entreaty for a bit of luck to accompany a bit of skill or hard work. Coined by sports writer Gerald Hern in 1948 to describe the strategy of the Boston Braves baseball team – win games pitched by the skilled pitchers Warren Spahn and Johnny Sain and then hope for the best US, 1948

spak *noun* ▷ *see:* SPAC

spam *noun* unsolicited, unwanted, often fraudulent advertising messages sent by e-mail US, 1994

spam *verb* **1** to post e-mail in unwanted quantities, especially advertising matter to people who don't want it. Ultimately from branded tinned meat Spam™ (a compound of spiced ham); popular etymology insists that this usage is inspired by the Monty Python sketch, 1970, set in a café in which nothing but unwanted Spam is served US, 1994. **2** to assign an unpleasant task to someone. Gulf war usage UK, 1991

spam can *noun* **1** a Southern Region 4–6–2 passenger locomotive of the 'West Country' class; a class Q freight locomotive also known as a 'biscuit box'. Railway slang with a derogatory edge; an allusion to the shape UK, 1979. **2** any metal-skinned light aeroplane. A derogatory term used by flying club pilots of veteran, fabric-covered aircraft UK, 1979

spam fritter *noun* the anus. Rhyming slang for SHITTER UK, 2003

spam fritters *noun* the vaginal labia. A pink highlight of UK cuisine UK, 2002

spam javelin *noun* the erect penis. A meat weapon UK, 1997

spam lance *noun* the penis, especially when erect UK, 2001

spam medal *noun* the Canadian Volunteer Service Medal, given to all Canadian servicemen during World War 2 who volunteered rather than being conscripted CANADA, 1995

spamouflage *noun* software designed to mask the fact that an e-mail is an unsolicited mass advertisement US, 2002

Spandau Ballet *noun* an alley. Rhyming slang, formed from the name of a 1980s UK pop group UK, 2004

spang *verb* to beg on the streets. Etymology is uncertain, possibly a compound of 'Spare any change?' or, less likely, an abbreviation of 'spangle' (something that glitters, hence a coin) UK, 1998

spangled *adjective* drunk UK, 2002

Spanic *noun* in Toronto, a person of South American descent CANADA, 2001

Spanish archer *noun* dismissal; a rejection. An excruciating pun: ELBOW (dismissal, a rejection) and 'El Bow' UK, 2000

Spanish curse *noun* in dominoes, the 3–3 piece US, 1959

Spanish football *noun* a sexually transmitted infection. Navy 'lower decks' usage; possibly a pun on 'dribbling' UK, 1961

Spanish guitar; spanish *noun* a cigar. Rhyming slang UK, 1952

Spanish Main; spanish *noun* a drain. Rhyming slang UK, 1992

Spanish onion *noun* a bunion. Rhyming slang UK, 1992

Spanish radio station *noun* used as the epitome of something that is always in the way TRINIDAD AND TOBAGO, 1984

Spanish surrealist *noun* cocaine. A discreet reference to SALVADOR DALI *UK, 2002*

Spanish waiter *noun* a potato. Rhyming slang *UK, 1992*

spank *noun* a beating *UK, 1984*

spank *verb* **1** to beat someone with violent intent. Extends from 'spank' (to beat with an open hand) *UK, 1999*. **2** to rob someone *US, 1976*. **3** to fraudulently amend financial accounts *US, 1999*. **4** (used of a male) to masturbate *US, 1994*. **5** to slap the inside of the arm to draw out veins for a drug injection *US, 1997*. ▶ **spank the monkey** (used of a male) to masturbate *US, 1999*. ▶ **spank the plank 1** (of a male) to masturbate *UK, 1998*. **2** to play an electric guitar *UK, 2004*

spankadocious *adjective* ▷*see:* SPOKADOCIOUS

spanked *adjective* worn out; over-used *US, 1992*

spanking *noun* a serious beating. From 'spank' (to hit with the open hand); a blackly humorous understatement of violent intent *UK, 1999*

spank off *verb* (of a male) to masturbate *UK, 2002*

spanner *noun* **1** a promiscuous female; a sexually provocative woman. From the name of the tool used to tighten nuts *UK, 1983*. **2** in prison, a key *UK, 1996*. **3** a fool; an idiot *IRELAND, 2003*

spannered *adjective* drunk or drug-intoxicated *UK, 2000*

spansula *noun* a combination of central nervous system depressants and stimulants *US, 1971*

Span-yard *noun* a Spaniard *UK, 2000*

spar *noun* **1** a friend; a companion. Shortening of SPARRING PARTNER *BARBADOS, 1965*. **2** a close male friend *JAMAICA, 2003*. **3** a man. From the meaning as 'a friend'. Mainly black usage. The variant 'spa' is also used *UK, 1998*

spare *noun* **1** in a social context, any or all unattached members of the opposite sex *UK: SCOTLAND, 1985*. **2** a friend *US, 1947*

spare *adjective* distraught, distracted or distressed; angry; crazy *UK, 1964*. ▶ **go spare** to become very angry *UK, 1958*

spare me days! heavens above! With ME for 'my' *AUSTRALIA, 1915*

spare prick *noun* a useless fellow; someone who is surplus to requirements. A shortening of 'spare prick at a wedding', from the phrase 'standing about like a spare prick at a wedding' *UK, 1982*

spare rib *noun* a trivial lie. Rhyming slang for 'fib' *UK, 1998*

spare time *noun* the possession of marijuana. The implication is that you must have spare time if you are to use the marijuana *US, 1999*

spare tire; spare tyre *noun* a roll of fat around the waist *US, 1961*

spark *verb* **1** to light a cigarette or a marijuana cigarette. Also variant 'spark up' *US, 1995*. **2** to hit someone hard; to knock someone out *UK, 2002*. **3** to see something or someone. Hawaiian youth usage *US, 1972*. **4** in horse racing, to use an electrical device to shock a horse during a race *US, 1951*. ▶ **spark it up** to smoke marijuana *UK, 1998*

sparked *adjective* knocked out, unconscious *UK, 1996*

sparkers *adjective* unconscious or deeply asleep. A variation of SPARK OUT *UK, 1977*

sparkle *noun* strong and pure methamphetamine with a crystalline appearance *US, 1989*

sparkle plenty *noun* an amphetamine tablet. Named after a character in the *Dick Tracy* comic strip *US, 1969*

sparkler *noun* **1** a diamond *UK, 1822*. **2** a tablet of amphetamine *US, 1994*

sparklers *adjective* clean white socks. Michigan Upper Peninsula usage *US, 2003*

sparkly *adjective* dishonest; criminal. An opposite to dull, STRAIGHT (honest) *UK, 1999*

sparko *adjective* **1** in a state of unconsciousness. Abbreviated from SPARK OUT *UK, 1999*. **2** psychotic; deranged *UK, 1983*

spark out *verb* to become unconscious; to faint; to die. The spark of life goes out, to some degree *UK, 1936*

spark-out *adjective* unconscious. The *spark* of life has (temporarily) gone *out UK, 1958*

sparkplug *noun* a tampon *US, 1999*

sparks; sparky; sparkie *noun* an electrician *UK, 1914*

spark scene *noun* a sexual fantasy; the imagined or remembered *scene* that *sparks* or enhances a sexual reaction *UK, 2001*

sparky *noun* a fool; a mentally handicapped person. Probably derived as a variation of SPAC; SPACK *UK, 2003*

sparky *adjective* lively. Electric, giving off sparks *UK, 2000*

sparring partner *noun* a friend; a companion; a husband or wife. From boxing jargon *UK, 1961*

sparrow *noun* an attractive, single female *BERMUDA, 1985*

Sparrow *noun* in Canada, an Englishman, particularly a Cockney *CANADA, 1966*

sparrow-fart; sparrow's fart *noun* dawn *UK, 1886*

sparrow grass *noun* asparagus *CANADA, 2001*

sparrow's kneecaps *noun* undeveloped or non-existent arm muscles. Parodic, jocular, derisive *UK, 1984*

spastic *noun* a stupid or uncoordinated person. A general term of abuse commonly used by schoolchildren *AUSTRALIA, 1981*

spastic *adjective* incompetent; uncoordinated; unfashionable. A cruel allusion to spastic paralysis *US, 1973*

spat *noun* a short, sharp quarrel; a tiff *US, 1804*

spatmobile *noun* the Toronto airport's Special Assistant Team vehicle *CANADA, 1994*

spawgee *noun* a poor white person *BARBADOS, 1965*

spaz *noun* **1** a person with spastic paralysis; a person who has any disability *UK, 2003*. **2** an uncoordinated or incompetent individual; a fool. Contemptuous and derogatory use of '*spastic*' (a person with spastic paralysis). Also used in the variants 'spazz' and 'spas' *US, 1964*

spaz; spazzo *adjective* crazy; foolish *AUSTRALIA, 1966*

spaz chariot *noun* a wheelchair. From SPAZ (a person who has any disability) *UK, 2003*

spaz cut *noun* any hairstyle that is alleged to make the wearer look mentally or physically handicapped. From SPAZ (a person with a disability) *UK, 2003*

spazmo *noun* an uncoordinated or incompetent individual; a fool. A variation of SPASTIC *UK, 1984*

spaz out; spazz out *verb* to act in a very awkward or uncoordinated manner; to lose emotional control *US, 1984*

spazzed *adjective* drunk *UK, 2002*

spazzer *noun* a spastic (a person with spastic paralysis) *UK, 2003*

SP betting *noun* illegal betting at starting price odds *AUSTRALIA, 1936*

SP book *noun* a starting price bookmaker's ledger *AUSTRALIA, 1948*

SP bookie; SP bookmaker *noun* an illegal off-course bookmaker who offers starting price odds *AUSTRALIA, 1938*

SP'd up *adjective* informed *UK, 1999*

speak *noun* a bar where alcohol is served illegally. A shortened form of SPEAKEASY *US, 1930*

speak *verb* ▶ **speak the real** to speak the truth, unpleasant as it might be *US, 1998*. ▶ **speak the same language** to share a way of thinking about something *UK, 1948*. ▶ **speak white** to speak English. Anglophone Canadian usage *US, 1978*

-speak *suffix* vocabulary or jargon. 'Newspeak' is the language of Oceania in George Orwell's 1948 novel *1984*. This coinage seeped into the language and, post-1984, provides a neat formula for book titles and media headlines concerned with jargon and slang. 'Jackspeak' 1989, 'Low Speak' 1989, 'Artspeak' 1990, 'Eurospeak' 1992, 'Rockspeak' 1996, 'Freshspeak' 1997, 'Double Speak' 1999, 'Teen Speak' 2001 among others *UK, 1949*

speak! tell me what's on your mind! *US, 1975*

speakeasy *noun* a bar that sells alcohol illegally *US, 1889*

speaker *noun* a gun *US, 1970*

speak to the hand ▷*see:* TALK TO THE HAND

speak up *verb* ▶ **speak up Brown – you're through!; speak up Ginger – you're almost through!** said, as if on a telephone, as a comment on an audible fart. Occasionally heard as 'come on Brown', etc *UK, 1961*

spear *noun* **1** a hypodermic needle *US, 1961*. **2** a firefighter's hook *US, 1954*. ▶ **take the spear** to accept responsibility. Colonel Oliver North popularised the phrase during the moral collapse of the Reagan presidency in 1986 and 87, explaining that while he had said that he would 'take the spear' for the administration's misdeeds in Iran and Nicaragua, he did not mean that he would accept responsibility if criminal prosecution became a possibility *US, 1989*. ▶ **the spear** dismissal from work *AUSTRALIA, 1941*

spear *verb* **1** to dismiss someone from employment *AUSTRALIA, 1911*. **2** to eject someone from a shop, pub, etc *AUSTRALIA, 1975*. ▶ **spear the bearded clam** (from a male perspective) to have sex. Formed on BEARDED CLAM (the vagina) *AUSTRALIA, 1971*. ▶ **spear the keg** to broach a keg of beer *AUSTRALIA, 1994*

spear-carrier *noun* a non-speaking role in a play; an actor who appears in the background or only plays minor roles *UK, 1984*

spear-chucker *noun* **1** a black person. Offensive. An allusion to the jungles of Africa *US, 1969*. **2** a vocal, aggressive advocate *US, 1997*

spec *noun* **1** an operational *specification*; a detailed description of something *UK, 1956*. **2** a position, a view-point. Probably abbreviated from 'spectate' *UK, 1999*. **3** a pair of eye-glasses *BAHAMAS, 1982*. ▶ **on spec** on the off chance; speculatively *UK, 1832*

speccy; speckie *noun* in Australian Rules football, a spectacular catching of the ball *AUSTRALIA, 1989*

special *noun* a potent marijuana cigarette *US, 1938*

special *adjective* applied to a disabled person. More patronising than euphemistic *UK, 2003*

special a la coke *noun* the recreational drug ketamine in powder, capsule or tablet form *US, 1998*

special friend *noun* a woman's menstrual period *US, 2001*

Special K *noun* ketamine hydrochloride, an anaesthetic used as a recreational drug, in powder, capsule or tablet form. Kellogg's Special K™, a well-known breakfast cereal, is the inspiration for this variation on K (ketamine) *US, 1993*

specimen *noun* a person of a stated character. Generally derogatory *UK, 1854*

speck *noun* a black person. Offensive *US, 1980*

Speck *noun* ▶ **the Speck** Tasmania. A reference to the shape and size of Tasmania on a map; shortened from obsolete the 'Fly-speck Isle' *AUSTRALIA, 1916*

speck *verb* **1** to search for gold or opal on the surface of the ground *AUSTRALIA, 1888*. **2** to place a highly speculative bet on a horse *AUSTRALIA, 1960*

specker *noun* **1** a speculative bettor. Agent noun of SPECK *AUSTRALIA, 1960*. **2** one year of a prison sentence. Used in numeric constructions such as 'three-specker' or 'five-specker' *US, 1950*

specking *noun* an act of randomly searching for houses to burgle. From ON SPEC (speculatively) *UK, 1996*

specky *adjective* bespectacled *UK, 1956*

specs *noun* **1** eye-glasses. A shortened form of 'spectacles' *UK, 1807*. **2** a person with poor eyesight and thick glasses *US, 1997*. **3** in horse racing, blinkers on a horse *US, 1951*

spectacles, testicles, wallet and watch the positions of the hand when making the sign of the cross. Part Catholic mnemonic, part joke *UK, 1999*

sped *noun* a social outcast *US, 1997*

speed *noun* **1** an amphetamine, especially Dexedrine™, which is a central nervous system stimulant *US, 1966*. **2** crack cocaine *UK, 2003*. **3** ability in pool *US, 1967*

speed *verb* **1** to be under the influence of a central nervous system stimulant *US, 1995*. **2** in poker, to bet heavily and to bluff often *US, 1983*

speedball *noun* **1** a mixture of a central nervous system stimulant (especially cocaine) and a narcotic (especially heroin) *US, 1936*.

2 an alcoholic beverage fortified with a drug *US, 1962*. **3** a rissole *AUSTRALIA, 1965*

speedball *verb* to inject or smoke a mixture of cocaine and heroin. After the noun sense *UK, 2002*

speedboat *noun* marijuana *UK, 1998*

speedbomb *noun* amphetamine powder rolled in a cigarette paper (for the purpose of swallowing) *UK, 2000*

speed bump *noun* **1** a red bump on the skin sometimes suffered after injecting impure amphetamines *US, 1989*. **2** a non-military obstacle that is likely to hinder an army's progress, especially civilians but also used of geographic features. Military jargon *US, 2003*

speed bumps *noun* **1** small female breasts *US, 2003*. **2** Saudi Arabian troops. Gulf war usage *US, 1991*

speed-dating *noun* an intensive method of meeting a number of prospective partners, organised so that each meets each for a short period before moving on to 'date' the next *US, 2003*

speed for lovers *noun* ▷ *see:* LOVER'S SPEED

speedfreak *noun* a person who is addicted to or compulsively uses amphetamines or methamphetamine *US, 1967*

Speed Gordon *noun* used as the epitome of trouble or strife *AUSTRALIA, 1961*

speed hump *noun* a skindiver *AUSTRALIA, 1996*

speed jaw *noun* an aching jaw which is a symptomatic after-effect of amphetamine use *UK, 2002*

speed merchant *noun* in American football, a fast runner *US, 1962*

speed money *noun* a bribe that purchases official cooperation of bureaucratic machinery *INDIA, 2002*

speedo *noun* a speedometer *UK, 1934*

speed of heat *noun* a high speed. US naval aviator usage *US, 1986*

speedometer *noun* in computing, a graphic depiction of a computer's current operating speed *US, 1991*

speedy *adjective* of drugs, displaying stimulant qualities; of a person, under the influence of a central nervous system stimulant. From SPEED (amphetamines) *UK, 1995*

speedy dog *nickname* a Greyhound bus; the Greyhound corporation *US, 1988*

speedy squib *noun* in horse racing, a horse that runs well for most of the race but does not finish well *AUSTRALIA, 1989*

Speewah; Speewa *noun* an imaginary remote country property or locale used as a setting for tall tales. Named after an actual place in northwest Victoria *AUSTRALIA, 1890*

speiler *noun* a swindler *AUSTRALIA, 1879*

spell *noun* a sentence of three months' imprisonment *UK, 1996*

spell *verb* ▶ **spell it out** to explain something that should be apparent and make it absolutely clear *UK, 1968*

spelling flame *noun* an inflammatory Internet posting attacking another's spelling *US, 1995*

spell-o *noun* a rest period, a break *ANTARCTICA, 1916*

spelunk *verb* ▶ **spelunk without a partner** (of a female) to masturbate. Figurative sense of 'spelunking' (caving as a sport), hence this solo exploration of a 'grotto' (the vagina) *US, 2001*

spelunker *noun* a caver. Ultimately from Latin *spelunca* (a cave) *US, 1942*

Spenard divorce *noun* a shooting of one spouse by the other *US, 1965*

spend *verb* ▶ **spend a penny** to urinate. This derives from the charge made for use of a public convenience. The first to charge a penny was opened outside the Royal Exchange, London, in 1855; however, a euphemistic use is not recorded until 1945. Since then prices have risen to beyond a point where the term has any practical meaning *UK, 2003*

spends *noun* *spend*ing money *UK, 2002*

spendy *adjective* expensive *US, 1993*

speng *noun* a fool *UK, 1996*

spent up *adjective* having no more money *UK, 1996*

sperm wail *noun* an involuntary cry from a male experiencing an orgasm *UK, 2002*

spesh *noun* Carlsberg Special Brew™ lager. Phonetic abbreviation of 'special' *UK, 1997*

spesh *adjective* special *AUSTRALIA, 1996*

spew *noun* **1** vomit *US, 1997*. **2** semen *US, 1989*. **3** a temper tantrum *NEW ZEALAND, 1998*

spew *verb* **1** to vomit *US, 1988*. **2** to ejaculate. Adopted from the more common sense 'to vomit', suggesting a more than generous ejaculation *US, 1989*. **3** to reject an agreement or responsibility. Possibly a play on synonymous BLOW OUT *UK, 2002*. **4** to be extremely angry *AUSTRALIA, 1987*. **5** to post an excessive number of messages to an Internet discussion group *US, 1995*. ▶ **spew your guts** to inform on your friends to the police *UK, 1961*. ▶ **spew your guts up** to vomit violently *UK, 1984*. ▶ **spew your ring; spew your ring up** to vomit violently *UK, 1963*

spewing! used for expressing anger *AUSTRALIA, 1988*

spewsome *adjective* dreadful; awful. That is, 'enough to make you vomit' *AUSTRALIA, 1996*

sphynx *noun* the removal by wax of all of a woman's pubic hair; the results thereof *US, 2001*

spic *noun* **1** a Spanish-speaking person. Derogatory and offensive *US, 1913*. **2** a Spaniard. This usage reflects the fact that Spain is the closest Spanish-speaking community to the UK *UK, 2000*. **3** the Spanish language *US, 1946*. **4** a West Indian *US, 1945*. **5** a railway track worker. Many track workers in the American southwest were Mexican; the racial epithet was applied to Mexican and non-Mexican alike *US, 1977*

spico *noun* a Spanish-speaking person. A modestly embellished SPIC *US, 1967*

Spictown *noun* a Spanish-speaking neighbourhood *US, 1969*

spide *noun* a member of a Belfast subcultural urban adolescent grouping that seems to be defined by a hip-hop dress and jewellery sense *UK: NORTHERN IRELAND, 2003*

spider *noun* **1** in the television and film industries, a device used to support the legs of a tripod on a slippery or uneven surface *UK, 1960*. **2** in harness racing, a sulky *AUSTRALIA, 1989*. **3** a tall glass of carbonated soft drink with a dollop of ice-cream in the top *AUSTRALIA, 1941*

spider blue *noun* heroin. Referring probably to the web of blue veins into which heroin users inject the drug *US, 1994*

spider box *noun* in the television and film industries, an electrical junction box *US, 1990*

spider hole *noun* a sniper's lair in a cave. Korean war usage *US, 1957*

spider's legs *noun* the pubic hair that can be seen outside the confines of a girl's bikini or underwear *UK, 2003*

spiel *noun* **1** a long-winded explanation *US, 1896*. **2** a speech intended to attract customers *US, 1966*. **3** an illegal gambling operation *UK, 1996*. **4** a drinking club. Probably a shortening of SPIELER *UK, 1981*

spiel *verb* to talk, especially at length; to patter *US, 1894*

spieler *noun* **1** a facile and smooth speaker *US, 1894*. **2** a person who stands at the door of a business calling out to people passing by, trying to lure them into the business *US, 1894*. **3** an (illegal) gambling or drinking club *UK, 1931*

spiff *noun* **1** a loner. An articulation of the initials SBF (surrounded by friends), used with irony *US, 1987*. **2** a tip, gratuity or commission *US, 1997*. **3** a bonus paid by a record company to a promoter who has succeeded in getting a record played *US, 1980*

spiff *verb* to dress up. Coined in the UK in the 1870s, obsolete by the 1930s, and then resurfaced in the US in the 1970s, used with 'up' *US, 1979*

spiffed *adjective* drunk *US, 1987*

spiffing; spiffin' *adjective* excellent, first-rate; fashionable or smart. Often seen to be dated, redolent of the C19 to mid-C20 upper-

and middle-class society, hence current usage tends towards irony. However, it is also current in its original unambiguous sense *UK, 1872*

spifflicated; spiflicated *adjective* drunk *US, 1906*

spiffy *adjective* well-dressed, elegant, sharp *UK, 1853*

spiflicate *verb* to deal with someone in a way that confounds, silences, dumbfounds or defeats. A humorous colloquialism that by mid-C20 survived mainly as a vague threat to children. Recorded as a form of intimidation used among Yorkshire schoolchildren by Iona and Peter Opie, *The Lore and Language of Schoolchildren*, 1959 *UK, 1785*

spig *noun* a Spanish-speaking person. A corruption of the prevalent SPIC *US, 1969*

spike *noun* **1** a syringe and needle; a hypodermic needle *US, 1936*. **2** a mixture of heroin and scopolamine or strychnine *UK, 2002*. **3** in a deck of playing cards, an ace *US, 1988*. **4** in volleyball, hitting the ball downward with great force from the top of a jump *US, 1972*. **5** a casual ward (a temporary accommodation facility for vagrants) *UK, 1866*. ▶ **the spike** the hypodermic syringe as a symbol of drug addiction *UK, 1973*

spike *verb* **1** to adulterate a drink or ply a person with alcohol or drugs *US, 1909*. **2** to inject a drug *US, 1935*. **3** in American football, to slam the football to the ground in a ritualistic celebration after scoring a touchdown *US, 1975*. **4** to attach electrical tape on a stage floor to mark positions for props and sets *US, 1991*

spiked *adjective* in a state of intoxication as the unwitting victim of an adulterated drink or drug *UK, 1996*

spiker *noun* a (branded antidepressant) Prozac™ tablet *UK, 2001*

spikes *noun* **1** sports shoes with cleats *US, 1997*. **2** woman's shoes with narrow high heels that taper into a point, formally known as spike-heel shoes *US, 1996*

spikey; spikie *noun* an anti-globalisation activist with a philosophy of violent protest *UK, 2001*

spiky *adjective* uncompromising in Anglican faith or practice *UK, 1881*

spill *verb* **1** to fall off a surfboard *US, 1957*. **2** to talk with energy and no clear agenda *US, 1970*. ▶ **spill the beans** to tell that which one is not supposed to tell *US, 1993*. ▶ **spill your guts (out)** to confess your secrets; to tell all you know *US, 1927*

spin *noun* **1** a tactical, revisionist interpretation of an event for public consumption. Although the term came to the forefront during the Reagan presidency, it is an ancient practice that was simply taken to new heights by Reagan's handlers *US, 1986*. **2** an excursion in a car. Originally applied to horse training, meaning 'a run of some duration', then to a bicycle ride, and now the present sense *UK, 1907*. **3** a period of time considered in terms of how you fared during it; an experience; a time of it *AUSTRALIA, 1917*. **4** five years' imprisonment *AUSTRALIA, 1950*. **5** a five-pound note; the sum of £5. An abbreviation of SPINNAKER. After decimalisation in 1966 also briefly used for $5 *AUSTRALIA, 1941*. **6** a single playing of a song by a radio station *US, 1999*. **7** a turn at spinning the coins in the gambling game two-up *AUSTRALIA, 1919*. **8** a Separation Program Number. The numbers corresponded to several hundred reasons for discharge from the service. Also known as 'spin number' *US, 1984*

spin *verb* **1** to manipulate, edit and present information in such a way that it suits political needs or a political agenda *UK, 2003*. **2** in circus and carnival usage, to speak a language or dialect fluently *US, 1981*. **3** to search *UK, 1972*. **4** to play a record, especially on the radio *US, 1965*. **5** in the language surrounding the Grateful Dead, to tape a concert *US, 1994*. **6** to turn back a car's odometer (mileometer) *US, 1952*. **7** to deceive *US, 1952*. **8** to leave *US, 1989*. ▶ **spin a dit** in nautical use, to tell a story, especially a tall story. From DIT (a tale) *AUSTRALIA, 1943*. ▶ **spin a drum; spin** to search a private premises *UK, 1977*. ▶ **spin the shit** to discuss something *UK, 1995*

spinal *noun* a paraplegic *US, 1998*

spinal tap *noun* falling over backwards while snowboarding *US, 1990*

spinbin *noun* a residential facility for psychiatric treatment *UK: SCOTLAND, 1988*

spindle-man *noun* a game operator in a carnival *US, 1969*

spinebash *noun* a period resting rather than working *AUSTRALIA, 1968*

spine-bash *verb* to loaf *AUSTRALIA, 1958*

spinebasher *noun* a loafer *AUSTRALIA, 1945*

spinebashing *noun* loafing *AUSTRALIA, 1941*

spinmeister *noun* an acknowledged expert in the art of spin. A combination of SPIN and German *meister* (master) *US, 1986*

spinnable *adjective* open to persuasion by manipulated information; also, used of information that is suitable for biased interpretation *UK, 2003*

spinnaker *noun* a five-pound note; the sum of £5 *AUSTRALIA, 1898*

spinner *noun* **1** in the used car business, a person who is adept at reducing the mileage on a car's odometer (mileometer) *US, 1975*. **2** in hot rodding, a showy hubcap *US, 1958*. **3** a radio disc jockey *US, 1950*. **4** a person who is mentally unstable after extensive medication *US, 1989*. **5** in the gambling game two-up, the person who tosses the coins *AUSTRALIA, 1911*. **6** in air-traffic control, a shift of employment covering absent workers' responsibilities *UK, 1981*. **7** in dominoes, a double that may be played on both ends *US, 1959*. **8** in poker, a streak of good luck *US, 1988*

spinny *adjective* crazy, insane *CANADA, 1992*

spin on it!; spin! a derisive invitation that accompanies the offensive gesture of a raised middle finger *UK, 2003*

spin out *verb* in the gambling game two-up, to throw a pair of tails and hence lose the right to continue spinning *AUSTRALIA, 1951*

spins *noun* the heightened state of dizziness you feel when you lie down very drunk *US, 1993*

spin up *verb* to roll a cigarette with tobacco or marijuana *UK, 2003*

spit *noun* **1** an exact, or near-exact, likeness of someone *UK, 1825*. **2** something of no value *US, 1987*. **3** a small sum of money *US, 1985*. **4** the payout in coins from a computer poker game *AUSTRALIA, 1989*. **5** in some games of poker, a card turned face-up in the centre of the table which may be used by all players' hands. Also called a 'spit in the ocean' *US, 1961*

spit *verb* to perform a rap lyric *US, 2001*. ► **spit beef** to vomit *US, 1978*. ► **spit blood** to be very angry, especially in the phrase 'could spit blood' *UK, 1963*. ► **spit bricks** to be furious *UK, 2002*. ► **spit chips** to vent anger verbally *AUSTRALIA, 1947*. ► **spit cotton** to salivate while under the influence of heroin *US, 1953*. ► **spit lead** to fire a gun *US, 1949*. ► **spit the dummy; spit the dummy out** to become furious; to throw a tantrum. From the image of an upset baby spitting out its dummy and crying *AUSTRALIA, 1984*

spit! be quiet! *US, 1950*

spit and drag; spit and a drag *noun* a cigarette; a cigarette being smoked, especially when the act of smoking is clandestine. Rhyming slang for FAG *UK, 1960*

spit and git *verb* to accomplish a task quickly *US, 1972*

spit and image *noun* an exact likeness of someone or something. The surviving form of 'spit and fetch' (image, picture), in which 'spit' is surely the substance of a body, or perhaps its corrupted 'spirit' and the noun with which it is combined represents an outer-appearance, ('fetch' is defined by the *Oxford English Dictionary* as 'the apparition, double or wraith of a living person'); 'spit and' has varied in dialect use to *spitten* leading, ultimately, to the conventional synonym: 'spitting image' *UK, 1895*

spit-back *noun* a technique of spitting a drink back into a glass to give the appearance of consuming more alcohol than you are *US, 1964*

spitball *verb* in the entertainment industry, to offer up a suggestion for discussion; to brainstorm *US, 1955*

spit black *noun* mascara. Because water is needed to apply *UK, 1952*

spit box *noun* in horse racing, the barn where horses are taken after a race to have their saliva tested for the presence of illegal drugs or their metabolites *US, 1997*

spit fuck *verb* to penetrate a rectum or vagina using only saliva as a lubricant *US, 1979*

spit kit *noun* in the US submarine corps, an anti-submarine vessel *US, 1948*

spit out *verb* to say something that is emotionally difficult to say *UK, 1855*

spit-roast *noun* a sexual position in which a woman (or a man) performs oral sex on one man whilst being penetrated by another from behind; the woman (or man) receiving such attention. The two erect penises necessary for this activity create the illusory image of a single spit going in one end and out the other. Mainly heterosexual usage *UK, 1998*

spit-roast *verb* to have sex as an active participant in the spit-roast position *UK, 2003*

spits *noun* sunflower seeds *CANADA, 1987*

spit spiders *verb* to be furious *UK, 2001*

spitter *noun* **1** a person who spits out semen after oral sex *AUSTRALIA, 1987*. **2** a killer *US, 1975*. **3** a wave that sprays from its end as it collapses *US, 1964*

spitting feathers *adjective* **1** very thirsty *UK, 1997*. **2** furiously angry *UK, 2003*

spittin' time *noun* the bleed period of a woman's menstrual cycle *US, 1954*

spiv *noun* a sharply dressed individual who lives by his wits – within the law for preference, and not too far outside the law whenever possible. Several possible etymologies vie for credence: an acronym from police records 'Suspected Persons and Itinerant Vagrants'; back slang of the acronym for 'Very Important Persons' (VIPs); dialect *spif* or *spiff* (neat, smart, dandified), which also leads to SPIFFING (excellent); *spivic*, an apparently obsolete Romany word for 'sparrow', used to describe those who followed the gypsies and picked up their leavings *UK, 1934*

spivias *noun* amphetamines; MDMA, the recreational drug best known as ecstasy *UK, 2003*

spivvery *noun* petty crime and other behaviour associated with a spiv *UK, 1956*

spizz *noun* a hypodermic needle *US, 1961*

SP joint *noun* an establishment operating starting price bookmaking *AUSTRALIA, 1945*

splack *noun* sex *US, 1994*

splack *verb* **1** to steal a car, especially by shattering the steering column *US, 1993*. **2** to ejaculate in sexual climax *US, 2001*

splaff *noun* a marijuana cigarette laced with LSD. 'A' for ACID substitutes the 'i' in SPLIFF (a marijuana cigarette) *UK, 2003*

splash *noun* **1** an amphetamine or other central nervous system stimulant *US, 1966*. **2** a small amount of water added to an alcoholic drink *US, 1996*. **3** tea (the beverage) *UK, 1960*. **4** a bath *US, 1972*

splash *verb* **1** to take a bath *US, 1972*. **2** to ejaculate *US, 1970*. ► **splash the boots** to urinate *AUSTRALIA, 1968*. ► **splash the pot** in a game of poker, to throw betting tokens directly into the pile of chips in the centre of the table instead of lining them up for other players to see before adding them to the pot *US, 1961*

splashing *noun* in a prostitute's advertising, semen, urine and other fluids secreted at orgasm *UK, 2003*

splash move *noun* in cheating at dice, a switch of the dice *US, 1997*

splash out *verb* to spend money extravagantly *UK, 1934*

splashover *noun* a signal leaking from one citizens' band radio channel to another *US, 1976*

splash shot *noun* a scene in a pornographic film or photograph depicting a man ejaculating *US, 1997*

splat *noun* **1** any food not subject to ready identification. From the sound made when it hits the mess kit *US, 1968*. **2** the * character on a computer keyboard *US, 1983*

splat *verb* to be killed bungee jumping *US, 1992*

splat hat *noun* a motorcycle crash helmet *UK, 1981*

splendiferous; splendacious; splendidious; spledidous *adjective* excellent; very splendid *US, 1843*

splib *noun* a black person. Offensive. *US, 1964*

splice *verb* to marry someone *UK, 1710*

spliced *adjective* married *US, 1997*

spliff *noun* **1** a marijuana cigarette *JAMAICA, 1936*. **2** marijuana. Also used in the variant 'splif' *UK, 1967*. **3** a cigarette adulterated with crack cocaine *UK, 2002*. **4** a hand-rolled cigarette *UK, 1984*. ▶ **on the spliff** a state of marijuana intoxication *UK, 2001*

spliff *verb* to smoke marijuana and be under its influence *UK, 1977*

spliffed; spliffed out; spliffed up *adjective* in a state of intoxication as a result of smoking marijuana *UK, 1994*

spliff up *verb* to prepare a marijuana cigarette; to smoke marijuana in cigarette form *UK, 2000*

spliff wine *noun* marijuana wine *UK, 2002*

spliffy *noun* a marijuana cigarette *UK, 2000*

spliffy *adjective* in a state of gentle intoxication as a result of smoking marijuana; in a manner that suggests the smoking of marijuana. Playing on SQUIFFY (drunk) *UK, 2001*

splifted *adjective* marijuana-intoxicated; exhilarated *US, 1995*

splim *noun* marijuana. A misreading or simple variation of SPLIFF *US, 1982*

splinky *noun* the penis. A term apparently coined by the writers of *Mad About You*, a US situation comedy (NBC, 1992–99); repeated with referential humour *US, 1999*

splint *noun* a marijuana cigarette *US, 1992*

splinters *noun* adversity *US, 1954*

split *noun* **1** the vagina *US, 1967*. **2** a share of mutual property or profits *UK, 1889*. **3** a tranquillizer or other central nervous system depressant *US, 1969*. **4** a decongestant tablet sold as MDMA, the recreational drug best known as ecstasy *US, 1996*

split *verb* **1** to leave. Each night, during the 1960s, Philadelphia rock 'n' roll disc jockey Hy Lit ended his broadcast with the mantra, 'Nuff said Ted, solid ahead, time to split the scene and leave it clean' *US, 1956*. **2** from a male perspective, to have sex. Probably more to do with bragging than as a considered threat of violence *UK, 1937*. ▶ **split a gut** to exert yourself to the extreme, especially laughing *US, 1958*. ▶ **split on someone** to inform on or betray someone *UK, 1795*. ▶ **split the breeze** to drive fast *US, 1976*. ▶ **split the difference** from a male perspective, to have sex. A punning elaboration of SPLIT *UK, 1974*. ▶ **split the scene** to leave *US, 1990*. ▶ **split the sheets** to divorce *US, 1976*. ▶ **split the whiskers** (of a woman) to urinate *AUSTRALIA, 1992*. ▶ **split your sides** to laugh heartily *UK, 1704*

split-arse *noun* a woman. Noted as current in the northeast of England by Chris Lewis, *The Dictionary of Playground Slang*, 2003 *UK, 1998*

split beaver; spread beaver *noun* the vagina displayed with lips parted. A familiar cliché of pornography *US, 1969*

split C-note *noun* a fifty-dollar note *US, 1954*

splith *noun* marijuana prepared and smoked in the fashion of a cigarette. A jocular variation of SPLIFF *US, 2000*

split knish *noun* the vagina. A conventional 'knish' is a baked or fried turnover of Russian Jewish origins; 'split' describes the nature of the vagina and exposes the savoury filling *US, 1998*

split-tail *noun* a female *US, 1950*

split-whisker *noun* a woman *AUSTRALIA, 1945*

splivins *noun* amphetamines *US, 1970*

splo *noun* inexpensive, low quality whisky *US, 1974*

splonk *noun* in horse race betting, the favourite *UK, 1967*

splooge *noun* semen *US, 1989*

splooge *verb* to ejaculate *US, 1989*

splosher *noun* a drunk *UK, 2000*

splow *noun* palms slapped in greeting *US, 1976*

splurge *verb* to spend money extravagantly; to recklessly use an expensive resource *US, 1934*

SP man *noun* a starting price bookmaker *AUSTRALIA, 1932*

Spock *noun* used as a term of address for anyone who is coming across as intellectual or superior. From the intellectual and superior character on *Star Trek US, 1978*

spock *verb* to examine something or someone *US, 1991*

spod *noun* a student whose devotion to study excludes all other interests or society, hence an unpopular student; someone who is considered too studious; someone obsessed with computers *UK, 1998*

spoddy *adjective* obsessively studious and unstylish *UK, 2001*

spodiodi *noun* **1** a mixture of cheap port and whisky. Used (and drunk) by jazz-lovers and musicians *CANADA, 1959*. **2** wine *US, 1975*

spoggie; spoggy *noun* (chiefly in south Australia) the common house sparrow, *passer domesticus AUSTRALIA, 1975*

spoiled water *noun* any non-alcoholic beverage *US, 1962*

spoiler *noun* a team that has no chance of winning a championship but which takes pride if not pleasure in defeating teams that are vying for a championship *US, 1962*

spokadocious; spankadocious *adjective* attractive; fashionable *BAHAMAS, 1982*

spoke *adjective* spoken. Especially of language, in the construction 'as she is spoke' *UK, 1937*

spon *verb* to tell a lie *UK, 1999*

spondonicles; spondonicals; spongs *noun* a pair of metal tongs for lifting a hot cooking utensil off a fire *AUSTRALIA, 2003*

spondooli *noun* money. Variation of SPONDULICS *UK, 1997*

spondulics; spondulix; sponds; spondos *noun* money *US, 1857*

sponge *noun* **1** a group, notional or real, opposed to the gains of the civil rights movement. The vocalised abbreviation stood for 'Society for the Prevention of Negroes Getting Everything'. The group was more notional than real, but, for example, in 1965 the Student Council of the University of Virginia was petitioned by an organisation calling itself SPONGE for status as an independent organisation eligible to receive Student Council funds *US, 1965*. **2** a boogie boarder, who rides waves on a small foam board. Used in a disparaging manner by surfers *US, 1991*

sponge *verb* **1** to obtain something in a parasitic manner *UK, 1673*. **2** in horse racing, to insert a sponge into a horse's nostril just before a race, impeding its breathing during the race *US, 1951*

spongelled *adjective* drunk *UK, 2002*

sponger *noun* a person who obtains things in a parasitic manner *UK, 1677*

sponge-worthy *adjective* used of a man, so sexually desirable as to warrant the use of a contraceptive sponge. Coined and popularised on an episode of Jerry Seinfeld's television comedy show ('The Sponge') that first aired on 7th December 1995 *US, 1995*

spongies *noun* in the usage of youthful model road racers (slot car racers), smooth, soft tyres *US, 1997*

sponk *noun* semen. A variation of SPUNK *UK, 2001*

spoo *noun* semen. Variant pronunciation of SPEW (semen), from SPEW/SPOO (to ejaculate) *US, 1989*

spoo *verb* to ejaculate. Variant pronunciation of SPEW (to ejaculate), from conventional 'spew' (to vomit), the suggestion therefore is of a copious quantity of semen *US, 2005*

spoof *noun* **1** a hoax, a bluff; an act of hoaxing *UK, 1889*. **2** a parody *UK, 1958*. **3** semen. Rhymes with 'hoof' *AUSTRALIA, 1916*

spoof *verb* **1** to hoax; to fool *UK, 1889*. **2** to make a parodic version of something *UK, 1927*. **3** to ejaculate *AUSTRALIA, 1992*

spoof *adjective* parodic; fake; bogus *UK, 1884*

spoofed *adjective* used of an electronic message, of a suspect origin *US, 1997*

spoofer *noun* **1** in carnival usage, a large stuffed dog offered as a game prize *US, 1985*. **2** a hoaxer; a bluffer *UK, 2001*

spoofing *noun* **1** the sending of e-mail that claims to come from one organisation but in fact comes from another. Known more fully as 'IP spoofing' *US, 1989*. **2** the creation of a false website that looks exactly like a real site. More fully known as 'web spoofing'. The attacher can lure an Internet user to the false site, can see everything that the user is doing, and can modify traffic from the user to any web server *US, 2004*

spoof tube *noun* a cardboard tube filled with scented cloth that masks the smell of exhaled marijuana smoke *US, 2003*

spoofy *adjective* spermy *AUSTRALIA, 1998*

spooge *noun* **1** semen *US, 1987*. **2** any viscous matter of unknown origin *US, 1995*. **3** in computing, code or output which cannot be understood *US, 1991*

spooge booth *noun* a private booth in a pornography arcade *US, 2001*

spook *noun* **1** a black person. Derogatory and offensive *US, 1945*. **2** a ghost *US, 1801*. **3** a spy *US, 1942*. **4** a drug-addict. From the addict's ghostly pallor *UK, 1958*. **5** a psychiatrist *US, 1961*. **6** in casino blackjack, a player who can spot the dealer's down card *US, 1991*. **7** in drag racing, a car that crosses the starting line too soon *US, 1960s*

spook *verb* **1** to frighten or startle someone. Also variant 'spook out' *US, 1935*. **2** to drive a car without a destination, merely for the pleasure of driving and the social aspects of being seen *US, 1958*. **3** in blackjack, to peak and see the dealer's down card *US, 1985*

spooked *adjective* used of playing cards, marked for cheating *US, 1963*

spooky *adjective* **1** in surfing, difficult or unpredictable *US, 1963*. **2** fine, good. West Indian and UK black usage, recorded August 2002 *UK, 2002*

spool of pipe thread *noun* used as a mythical task assigned to a newly hired helper *US, 1963*

spoon *noun* **1** the amount of a drug needed for a single dose. A measure of heroin, sufficient for a single injection, approximately equal to a standard teaspoon *US, 1973*. **2** the handle of a hand grenade. From its curved, spoon-like shape *US, 1977*. **3** an army cook *US, 1991*. **4** the dip up at the front nose of a surfboard *US, 1963*. **5** a dolt *NEW ZEALAND, 1982*

spoon *verb* **1** to lie behind someone, your face towards their back *US, 1887*. **2** to tongue a woman's vagina and clitoris *US, 1971*

spoondoolie *noun* the penis *UK, 2001*

spooney *noun* an effeminate male who may or may not be homosexual *US, 1978*

sport *noun* used as a term of address, usually male-to-male. In Australia an everyday usage. In the US, a self-conscious term that conveys a jocular feeling *AUSTRALIA, 1935*

sport *verb* to wear something in order to display it *UK, 1778*

sport fucking *noun* sex without any pretence of a relationship, although with a competitive edge *US, 1986*

sporting girl *noun* a prostitute *US, 1938*

sporting house *noun* a brothel *US, 1894*

sporting lady *noun* a prostitute *US, 1972*

sporting life *noun* **1** the business and lifestyle of prostitution and pimping *US, 1973*. **2** a wife. Rhyming slang *UK, 1992*. **3** cocaine. From *Porgy and Bess*, in which the character Sportin' Life sells cocaine. Retro and rare. The shortened form is 'sporting' *US, 1978*

sportsman *noun* a pimp. In the mid-C19, the term referred to a gambler. By mid-C20 it was a somewhat grandiose euphemism for 'pimp' *US, 1967*

sportsman's paradise *noun* a bar favoured by pimps *US, 1978*

sporty *adjective* excellent *BERMUDA, 1985*

s'pose; 'spose *verb* suppose.*UK, 1852*

spot *noun* **1** a difficult or dangerous position. Usually in phrases: 'in a spot' and 'in a bit of a spot' *UK, 1936*. **2** a venue, especially a place of entertainment *UK, 1936*. **3** an apartment or house *US, 2001*. **4** a place in a programme of entertainment, or an item of entertainment performed in such a programme *US, 2001*. **5** a large party, a convention or other event that is a promising source for swindle victims *US, 1977*. **6** of food, a portion or meal that should not be described as extravagant; of abstracts like work, rest and pleasure, a small amount *UK, 1932*. **7** a small measure of drink *UK, 1885*.

8 money *US, 1947*. **9** a one-hundred-pound note; the sum of £100. After the introduction of decimal currency in 1966, used for $100 *AUSTRALIA, 1945*. **10** a prison term, often prefixed with a numeral that denotes the number of years *US, 1901*. **11** any of the large suit symbols printed on the face of a playing card *US, 1967*. **12** in a deck of playing cards, an ace *US, 1988*. **13** in poolroom betting, a handicap given in a bet-upon game *US, 1967*. ▶ **put someone to the spot** to kill someone who has been lured to a rendezvous *US, 1948*

spot *verb* **1** to recognise, discover or detect someone or something. Colloquial *US, 1848*. **2** to rain in a few scattered drops. Originally dialect; 'spotting with rain' is a constant and current feature of UK weather reports *UK, 1849*. **3** in trucking, to park a truck *US, 1946*

spot card *noun* in a deck of playing cards, any card other than an ace or face card *US, 1967*

spot on *adverb* absolutely accurate, exact; precisely *UK, 1920*

spot play *noun* in horse racing, an approach to betting in which the bettor only bets in situations where the odds seem advantageous *US, 1975*

spots *noun* **1** dice *UK, 2000*. **2** in circus usage, leopards *US, 1981*

spotted dick *adjective* ill. Rhyming slang for 'sick', formed on a great British pudding *UK, 1992*

spotter *noun* **1** a spy hired by an employer to observe and report on employees' activities *US, 1876*. **2** a criminal who finds or identifies a likely victim for robbery *UK, 1937*. **3** a look out in a drug-selling operation *US, 1990*. **4** a train*spotter*, a plane*spotter*, a bus-*spotter* or a similar type of hobbyist. *Spotter's Guides* have been published by Mayflower Books of New York since 1979 *US, 2003*

spotters *noun* the eyes *US, 1945*

spotters and skinners *noun* childlike, scratchy handwriting *BARBADOS, 1992*

spotting it a method of consuming cannabis resin: pieces of hash, cut to the approximate size of matcheads, are picked up on the end of a lit cigarette; once the drug is burning the smoke given off is inhaled by means of a hollow tube, such as the empty body of a ballpoint pen *UK, 2000*

spotty dog; spotty *noun* a foreigner. Rhyming slang for **WOG** *UK, 1979*

spout *noun* ▶ **up the spout 1** in trouble; close to ruin; bankrupt. From the earlier sense (to pawn) *UK, 1829*. **2** of a bullet, in the rifle barrel and ready to fire. Often as 'one up the spout' *UK, 1931*. **3** pregnant. From the earlier sense (ruined) *UK, 1937*

spout *verb* to speak. A broadening of conventional sense (1750s), 'to declaim' *UK, 1964*

spraddle *verb* to step awkwardly around something or someone. A blend of 'sprawl' and 'straddle' *BARBADOS, 1965*

sprag *noun* **1** in school, an informer, a tell-tale. Commented on by the Plain English Campaign in October 2003 *UK, 2003*. **2** chiefly in Queensland, the common house sparrow, *passer domesticus* *AUSTRALIA, 1981*

spranksious *adjective* energetic, playful *BARBADOS, 1965*

sprassey; spraser; sprazey; sprowsie; sprouse *noun* sixpence or 6d; a coin of that value. Many variations, ultimately from Shelta *sprazi*. Inflation has rendered the conversion from 6d to 2½p meaningless *UK, 1931*

spraunce *verb* to lie; to tell a trivial lie *UK, 1998*

sprauncy *adjective* ostentatious, showy *UK, 1980*

spray *noun* an aerosol used when inhaling solvents *UK, 1996*

spray *verb* **1** to ejaculate semen onto a sexual partner *UK, 2001*. **2** to fart *US, 2002*

spray and pray *verb* in a military engagement, to shoot wildly then run *US, 2003*

spread *noun* **1** an assortment of food laid out on a table or served at a social event *US, 1822*. **2** in sports betting, the margin of victory incorporated into a bet *US, 1973*. **3** a photograph of a naked woman exposing her genitals *US, 1969*. **4** in pool, the first shot of the game *US, 1990*

spread *verb* to share information or cards while engaging in a cheating scheme *US, 1968*. ▶ **spread a game** to start a card game *US, 1977*. ▶ **spread for someone** of a woman, to dispose herself for sex with someone *UK, 1978*. ▶ **spread the eagle** to escape from prison or jail *US, 1950*. ▶ **spread your shot** to speak honestly and directly *US, 1976*

spread-bet *noun* a type of gamble against predicted odds *US, 1992*

spread-betting *noun* a form of gambling against a bookmaker's predicted result (see citation) *US, 2001*

spread-eagle *verb* to spread and stretch out a person's arms and legs *UK, 1826*

spreadhead *noun* a devoted follower of the band Widespread Panic. An evolution of 'deadhead' (a follower of the Grateful Dead) *US, 2001*

spreading broads *noun* an act of playing or cheating at cards, especially the manipulating of cards in the three-card trick *UK, 1886*

spread shot *noun* a photograph or scene in a pornographic film showing a woman's spread vagina *US, 1971*

spreck up *verb* (of a male) to orgasm. A possible pun on 'ejaculate' based on German *sprechen* (to speak) *UK, 2002*

spree boy *noun* a person who loves fun but not work *BARBADOS, 1965*

sprigs *noun* sparse facial hair *BAHAMAS, 1982*

spring *verb* to escape, or effect someone's escape or release, from prison or detention *US, 1904*

spring buster *noun* a hole in a road, jarring to the driver when encountered *US, 1962*

springbutt *noun* a person who is eager to please *US, 1962*

spring chicken *noun* a youthful, attractive boy as the object of sexual desire of an older homosexual man *US, 1979*

springer *noun* **1** any person in the position to get you out of jail, from a bail bondsman to a lawyer to a judge *US, 1950*. **2** in horse racing, a horse that becomes the betting favourite or nearly the favourite after betting opens on a race *UK, 1948*

springy *noun* a wetsuit covering the body, neck and limbs to the elbows and knees *AUSTRALIA, 1992*

springy thingy *noun* in drag racing, a car with a light structure and thus maximum flexibility *US, 1965*

sprinkle *verb* to urinate *UK, 1992*

spritz *verb* to squirt, especially a mist *US, 1917*

spritzer *noun* a fuel injector *US, 1992*

sprog *noun* **1** a baby; a child. From obsolete 'sprag' (a lively young fellow) *UK, 1706*. **2** a recruit. Royal Air Force originally, then Royal Navy, now police. Probably derives from obsolete 'sprag' (1706) 'a lively young fellow' but etymological theories abound: a reversal of 'frog spawn' – because it's so very green; a confusion of 'cog and sprocket' – a metaphor with the recruit just a cog (a sprocket) in a wheel; a distortion of 'sprout'; it has also been claimed that a 'sprog' is 'a young gannet' *UK, 1941*. **3** semen *AUSTRALIA, 1992*

sprog *verb* to parent a child *UK, 2000*

sprogged *adjective* pregnant *NEW ZEALAND, 1984*

sprogie *adjective* stylish; fashionable *BAHAMAS, 1982*

spronce *verb* to show off, especially by your choice of clothes *UK, 1991*

sproncy; sprauntsy; sprauncy *adjective* showily dressed; fashionable; showy *UK, 1957*

spruik *verb* to declaim; to hold forth; to make a speech like a showman. Exact origin unknown, but no doubt related to the Germanic, such as Dutch *spreken* (to speak) or Yiddish *shpruch* (a saying, a charm) *AUSTRALIA, 1902*

spruiker *noun* a speaker employed to attract a crowd to a venue, show or demonstration of a product; a barker *AUSTRALIA, 1902*

sprung *adjective* addicted *US, 1992*

sprung on *adjective* infatuated with *US, 1995*

SP shop *noun* an establishment operating starting price bookmaking *AUSTRALIA, 1948*

spud *noun* **1** a potato *NEW ZEALAND, 1845*. **2** a trainee *UK, 2001*. **3** a SCUD missile. An obvious rhyme that belittles the enemy's weaponry *US, 1993*

spud and onion gang *noun* a group of wharf workers who load or unload produce *AUSTRALIA, 1995*

spud-bashing *noun* potato peeling; hence, kitchen fatigues. Military, combining SPUD (a potato) with the suffix -BASHING (vigorous compulsory activity) *UK, 1940*

spud cocky *noun* a potato farmer *AUSTRALIA, 1950*

spudge *verb* to poke a fire's logs, making the fire blaze up *CANADA, 1984*

spud juice *noun* a potent homemade alcoholic beverage produced by fermenting potatoes *US, 1977*

spun *noun* in the television and film industries, a light diffuser made with synthetic materials. Originally an abbreviation of 'spun glass', the term was retained when the material changed *US, 1990*

spun *adjective* **1** crazy; disoriented *US, 1997*. **2** very drug-intoxicated *US, 1997*. **3** excited, enthusiastic *US, 1984*

spunk *noun* **1** mettle, courage. A word forever associated in the US with actress Mary Tyler Moore; in the initial episode of *The Mary Tyler Moore Show* in 1970, Moore's boss Lou Grant assesses her – 'You've got spunk. I hate spunk!' *UK, 1774*. **2** semen *UK, 1888*. **3** a very attractive person *AUSTRALIA, 1978*

spunk *verb* **1** (of a male) to ejaculate. Also used in the variants 'spunk off' and 'spunk up' *AUSTRALIA, 1974*. **2** to spend or waste money or time. From 'spunk' (to ejaculate semen), punning on 'spend' *UK, 2000*

spunk bin *noun* the vagina *UK, 2001*

spunkbubble *noun* **1** used between men as a term of abuse *UK, 1984*. **2** a sexually attractive person *AUSTRALIA, 1992*

spunk dust *noun* used between men as a term of abuse *UK, 1984*

spunker *noun* used by adolescent girls as a derisive term for any boy of similar maturity. Demonstrates a very basic grasp of biology: only males produce SPUNK (semen) *UK, 1997*

spunkette *noun* a sexually attractive young woman *AUSTRALIA, 1994*

spunkiness *noun* good looks *AUSTRALIA, 1981*

spunkrat *noun* a sexually attractive person *AUSTRALIA, 1987*

spunky *noun* a sexually attractive person *AUSTRALIA, 1967*

spunky *adjective* **1** brave; spirited; plucky. From SPUNK (courage) *UK, 1786*. **2** sexually attractive *AUSTRALIA, 1973*

spun out *adjective* crazy *UK, 2000*

sputnik *noun* a mixture of marijuana from Pakistan and opium; marijuana. From 'sputnik' (the Russian satellites, first launched in 1957), hence its use here as something else to take you out of this world *US, 1998*

squab *noun* a young girl or woman. From the standard sense (a newly hatched or very young bird) *US, 1948*

squab *verb* to fight *US, 1986*

squab job *noun* a sexually attractive girl below the legal age of consent *US, 1964*

squack *noun* a woman; sex with a woman *US, 1972*

squack *verb* to ejaculate *US, 1993*

squad *noun* a police car. Known conventionally as a 'squad car' *US, 1965*

Squad *noun* ▶ **the Squad** the Flying *Squad* (a unit of the Metropolitan Police, known as the Flying Squad since 1921) *UK, 1996*

squaddie; squaddy *noun* a soldier, usually ranked private. From a new recruit's placement in a squad *UK, 1933*

square *noun* **1** a person with a conventional job and lifestyle; an old-fashioned person *US, 1944*. **2** a heterosexual *AUSTRALIA, 1960*. **3** a filling meal *US, 1882*. **4** a factory-manufactured cigarette *US, 1958*. **5** a one-dollar note *US, 1993*. ▶ **on the square 1** honest, truthful, trustworthy. Possibly from Masonic symbolism and jargon *UK, 1872*. **2** in a faithful monogamous relationship with someone *AUSTRALIA, 1944*.

3 being a freemason. From symbolism that is employed in freemasonry *UK, 1984*

square *verb* to satisfactorily settle matters or resolve a problem, generally by the use of power and influence, bribery or threat. From 'square' (to balance the books) *UK, 1853*. ▶ **square it away** to settle matters *AUSTRALIA, 1985*

square *adjective* **1** old fashioned; decent and honest; conventional *US, 1946*. **2** heterosexual *AUSTRALIA, 1944*. **3** in cricket, used to describe fielding positions along an imaginary line extending to the left and right of the batsman's wicket *UK, 1851*. ▶ **live square** to conduct your life as an honest citizen *AUSTRALIA, 1975*

square as a bear *adjective* extremely conventional. The bear appears for the rhyming value, nothing else *US, 1957*

square away *verb* to put in order, to tidy away; hence, to learn *UK, 1909*

square-bashing *noun* military parade drill. From the 'parade *square*' *UK, 1943*

square bitch *noun* any woman who is not a prostitute *US, 1972*

square box *noun* in court, a witness box *UK, 1996*

squared *adjective* craving drugs *US, 1958*

square dancing ticket *noun* a dose of LSD on a square of blotting paper *US, 2003*

square-eyed *adjective* applied contemptuously to someone who watches 'too much' television *UK, 1984*

square from Delaware *noun* an exceptionally naive, conventional person. Delaware exists for the rhyme; it is no more or less square than any other state. In the 1930s and 40s, there was a cottage industry in inventing terms along the line of this construction – a 'clown from Allenton', a 'pester from Chester' and so on. The 'square from Delaware' was one of the few that truly worked itself into speech *US, 1938*

square grouper *noun* a brick of compressed marijuana. The name of a notional fish, alluding to the presence of marijuana smugglers in south Florida waters *US, 1989*

squarehead *noun* **1** a German, especially a German soldier in World Wars 1 and 2. A derogatory term that has lingered, perhaps, through films retelling how we won the war *US, 1999*. **2** any Scandanavian. Left from the language of the logging camps of the early C20 *US, 1975*. **3** in Quebec, an anglophone *US, 1978*. **4** a non-criminal *AUSTRALIA, 1890*

square Jane *noun* an exceptionally conventional woman *US, 1986*

square John *noun* a decent and law-abiding, if naive, person *US, 1934*

square joint *noun* a tobacco cigarette *US, 1971*

square mackerel *noun* marijuana. From the shape of packages smuggled by sea *US, 1998*

square monicker *noun* a person's legal, given name *US, 1959*

square name *noun* a person's legal name, sometimes unknown to his associates who know him only by a nickname *US, 1955*

square-off *noun* something that puts matters right; an apology *AUSTRALIA, 1941*

square off *verb* to settle matters; to make everything right *AUSTRALIA, 1950*

square pair *noun* in craps, an eight rolled with a pair of fours *US, 1985*

squarer *noun* in circus and carnival usage, a claims adjuster and mender of legal problems *US, 1981*

square rigger *noun* a black person. Rhyming slang for NIGGER. Offensive *UK, 1992*

square Sam *noun* an exceedingly honest, upright, conventional person *US, 1953*

square shooter *noun* a truthful, direct, honourable person *US, 1914*

square time bob *noun* crack cocaine *UK, 1998*

square up *verb* to return to the path of righteousness after a sojourn in sin *US, 1968*

square weed *noun* tobacco *US, 1959*

square-wheeled *adjective* parked. Citizens' band radio slang *UK, 1981*

square wife *noun* in law enforcement, a wife in the literal sense of the word, as opposed to the sense of work partner *US, 1988*

square woman *noun* a woman who is not a prostitute *US, 1967*

squarie *noun* **1** especially in nautical parlance, a young woman *AUSTRALIA, 1917*. **2** a non-criminal *AUSTRALIA, 1950*

squash *noun* **1** a kiss. Circus and carnival usage *US, 1981*. **2** the skull or brain *US, 1985*

squash it! forget it! *US, 1993*

squash rot *noun* the medical condition suffered by severe stroke victims *US, 1983*

squat *noun* **1** nothing. A shortened form of DOODLY-SQUAT. Often found in double negative constructions *US, 1967*. **2** an act of defecation *NEW ZEALAND, 2002*. **3** a seat; a chair *US, 1973*

squat *verb* **1** to execute someone by electrocution in the electric chair *US, 1950*. **2** to assemble to discuss and mediate disagreements among prisoners *US, 1976*

squat team *noun* in prison (especially HMP Holloway), a unit of prison officers trained to discover drugs and other contraband *UK, 1996*

squatter *noun* a chair *US, 1945*

squat through *verb* to lower your stance to a squat to maintain control of your surfboard while a wave is cresting over you *US, 1965*

squatum *noun* in Newfoundland, homemade berry wine *CANADA, 1964*

squawk *noun* a complaint, especially a vociferous and indignant one *US, 1909*

squawk *verb* **1** to complain *US, 1970*. **2** (of an aircraft) to transmit an identification and location signal. Used among air-traffic controllers *US, 1956*

squawk book *noun* a book in which complaints are registered *US, 1955*

squawk box *noun* **1** a low-fidelity public address system *US, 1945*. **2** a citizens' band radio *US, 1976*. **3** a child hospital patient who persistently cries or complains *US, 1994*

squaw money *noun* a two-dollar note *CANADA, 1987*

squaw pee *noun* ginger beer *CANADA, 1992*

squaw piss *noun* beer with a low alcohol content *US, 1968*

squaw winter *noun* the first snowstorm or cold snap, just before Indian summer *CANADA, 2001*

squeak *noun* **1** a police informer *US, 1950*. **2** a cheapskate *US, 1963*

squeak *verb* to complain *UK, 2003*

squeaker *noun* a very close score in any athletic contest. Often used with irony to describe a large margin of victory *US, 1977*

squeal *noun* in police work, a person who reports a crime; the call reporting the crime *UK, 1977*

squeal *verb* **1** to inform on someone; to betray someone *US, 1846*. **2** from a standstill, to accelerate a car suddenly, squealing the tyres on the road *US, 1951*

squealer *noun* **1** a police informer *UK, 1865*. **2** in trucking, a device that records time and speed data, used by company officials to assure compliance with laws and regulations. Known conventionally as a 'tachograph' *US, 1971*. **3** a baby, especially an illegitimate one *UK, 1865*

squealers *noun* bacon *US, 1996*

squeegee cop *noun* in Burnaby, British Columbia, a police undercover officer posing as someone offering to clean windscreens in stopped traffic in order to catch seat-belt violators *CANADA, 2002*

squeegee man *noun* a street-corner hawker of car windscreen washing services *UK, 2002*

squeegie *noun* a young person who is hopelessly out of touch with current fashions and trends. Youth usage *US, 1949*

squeeze *noun* **1** a partner in romance. A shortening of MAIN SQUEEZE (a man's primary romantic partner) *US, 1980*. **2** a benefit; an advantage *UK, 2000*. **3** in prison, a prisoner's application or request which is favourably dealt with *UK, 1996*. **4** a light sentence of imprisonment

UK, 1996. **5** extortion or graft *US, 1949*. ► **put the squeeze on someone** to exert influence on someone *US, 1941*. ► **the squeeze** permission to enter *UK, 1996*

squeeze *verb* **1** to recount or tell something *US, 1947*. **2** in poker, to surround a player with two confederates whose collusive betting tactics relieve the middle player of his bankroll and drive him from the game *US, 1949*. **3** while playing cards, to look only at the very edge of a card *US, 1967*. ► **squeeze (her) easy** to slow down a truck *US, 1976*. ► **squeeze a lemon; squeeze the lemon** to drive through a traffic light as it changes from yellow to red *US, 1993*. ► **squeeze one out** to fart; to defecate; of a male, to masturbate *UK, 2005*. ► **squeeze the breeze** to close a car window *US, 1991*. ► **squeeze the cheese** to fart *US, 1993*. ► **squeeze the lemon** to urinate *UK, 1984*. ► **squeeze your head; squeeze** to defecate *UK, 1984*

squeeze box *noun* **1** an accordion or concertina. Musicians' slang *UK, 1936*. **2** in greyhound racing, the number five starting position (the yellow box) *AUSTRALIA, 1989*

squeeze cheese *noun* a pasteurised processed cheese product, semi-solid, sold in a plastic bottle. A clever name for a vile thing *US, 1986*

squeeze off *verb* to fire a shot from a gun *US, 1956*

squeezers *noun* dice that have been squeezed out of shape in a vice for use by cheats *US, 1950*

squeeze up *verb* to ejaculate *UK, 1974*

squeezings *noun* a gel formed with liquid ethanol and saturated calcium acetate solution; when ignited, the alcohol in the gel burns. Used as a source of fuel in portable cooking stoves and as a source of alcohol for truly desperate derelicts who squeeze the gel through sponges and collect the liquid *US, 1980*

squib *noun* **1** a coward *AUSTRALIA, 1908*. **2** in the television and film industries, a small explosive charge that simulates being struck by a bullet *US, 1990*. **3** in target shooting, a hand-loaded cartridge that does not fully detonate *US, 1957*. **4** a slow racehorse *AUSTRALIA, 1915*

squib *verb* **1** to act the coward *AUSTRALIA, 1918*. **2** to fire a gun to frighten rather than to wound *CANADA, 1999*

squid *noun* **1** a serious, dedicated, diligent student *US, 1987*. **2** a despicable, spineless person *US, 1974*. **3** an inexperienced, unskilled motorcyclist. Perhaps from the image of flailing arms *US, 2002*. **4** a US Navy sailor. From the perspective of the US Marines *US, 1991*. **5** a fisherman *US, 1991*. **6** a Japanese person who is lacking in all social skills. Hawaiian youth usage; highly insulting *US, 1982*. **7** one pound sterling (£1). A play on QUID *UK, 1997*

squid *verb* to study hard *US, 1981*

squidge *verb* **1** to squeeze; to squelch together so as to make a sucking noise. Originally Isle of Wight dialect *UK: ENGLAND, 1881*. **2** in tiddlywinks, to shoot a wink with an oversized wink *US, 1977*

squidgy black *noun* a variety of marijuana *UK, 1996*

squidjigger *noun* in Canada, any resident of the Maritime Provinces *CANADA, 1978*

squiffed off *adjective* annoyed; angry *US, 1952*

squiff out *verb* to lose consciousness as a result of excessive consumption of alcohol *US, 1953*

squiffy *adjective* drunk. Probably from SKEW-WHIFF (at the wrong angle) *UK, 1855*

squigg *noun* a prank *US, 1988*

squiggle *noun* a tilde (~) on a computer keyboard *US, 1991*

squiggles *noun* during the 1991 US war against Iraq, any writing in the Arabic script *US, 1991*

squiggly *noun* a sexually attractive woman *BERMUDA, 1985*

squillionaire *noun* a multi-millionaire *UK, 1978*

squinch-eyed *adjective* with eyes half closed *US, 1946*

squinchy *adjective* very small *BAHAMAS, 1982*

squint *noun* **1** a look; a glance. Generally phrased 'have a squint at' *UK, 1673*. **2** in the car sales business, tinted glass *US, 1953*. **3** a person

lacking in social skills, fashion or both *US, 1978*. ► **on the squint** on the look-out for something *US, 1970*

squire *noun* used as a familiar form of address to a man *UK, 1961*

squirm seat *noun* the chair in which witnesses sit in a courtroom *US, 1962*

squirrel *noun* **1** a reckless driver who weaves in and out of traffic *US, 1962*. **2** a drug addict who hides drug portions for future use *US, 1957*

squirrel *verb* **1** to smoke cocaine, marijuana and phencyclidine, the recreational drug known as PCP or angel dust. It makes you nuts; squirrels like nuts *UK, 1999*. **2** on the railways, to climb up the side of a coach *US, 1977*

squirrel away *verb* to hide something; to conceal something for later use; to store something away. Like the squirrel and his nuts *UK, 1977*

squirrel cage *noun* in electric line work, a pole-mounted steel bracket used for supporting a conductor *US, 1980*

squirrel trap *noun* the vagina *UK, 2001*

squirrely *adjective* **1** completely obsessed with acquiring and hoarding amphetamine *US, 1989*. **2** in motorcyle racing, difficult to control or out of control *US, 1973*

squirt *noun* **1** a person who is small in stature, character or both *US, 1848*. **2** twenty-five cents or twenty-five dollars *US, 1951*. **3** in the car sales business, windscreen cleaner *US, 1953*

squirt *verb* in pool, to strike the cue ball off centre producing a course in the opposite direction proportional to the degree to which the ball is hit off centre *US, 1978*. ► **squirt it into the air** to test an idea by bringing it up before a group and asking for comments *US, 1974*

squirt brakes *noun* hydraulic brakes *US, 1965*

squirter *noun* a scene in a pornographic film or photograph depicting a man ejaculating *US, 1995*

squirt racing *noun* drag racing *US, 1993*

squishy *adjective* forgetful. Teen slang *US, 1951*

squit *noun* an insignificant person. Probably cognate with SQUIRT *UK, 1825*

squits; the squits *noun* diarrhoea. A shortening of SQUITTERS *UK, 1841*

squitters *noun* diarrhoea. From obsolete dialect *squitter* (to squirt) *UK, 1664*

squiz; squizz *noun* a brief look; a peek *AUSTRALIA, 1913*

squiz; squizz *verb* to have a brief look. From British dialect (Devon) *AUSTRALIA, 1941*

squulch *verb* to crush *BARBADOS, 1965*

Sri Lanka *noun* a contemptible individual. Rhyming slang for WANKER, apparently inspired by the Sri Lankan cricket team *UK, 1998*

SRO standing room only; completely sold-out *US, 1890*

SS *noun* **1** an injection of drugs into the skin, avoiding a vein. An initialism of 'skin shot' *US, 1938*. **2** the Department of Social Security (DSS, previously DHSS). An obvious, hard to resist pun on Nazi stormtroopers *UK, 1988*

ssss... *noun* an informer. From the hissing sound of a SNAKE (an informer) *UK, 1996*

ssstoned *adjective* intoxicated with marijuana. Extends STONED to demonstrate the effects of marijuana *UK, 1999*

stab *noun* **1** a short and sudden type of scratch (a manipulation of a record to create a musical effect) *UK, 2002*. **2** a victim of a knife fight *US, 1985*. ► **have a stab; make a stab at** to attempt; to guess *US, 1895*

stab *verb* **1** to disparage someone with profanity *US, 2001*. **2** in pool, to hit the cue ball with enough backspin so that it stops immediately after striking the object ball *UK, 1873*

stable *noun* **1** a group of prostitutes working for a single pimp or madam *US, 1937*. **2** a group of 'slaves' in the control of, or at the disposal of, a dominatrix; a collection of masochists in the control of, a sadist *US, 1989*. **3** by extension, a group of people working for someone *UK, 1942*. **4** a house or apartment *US, 2000*

stable *verb* (used of a pimp) to induce a prostitute to join other prostitutes working for him *US, 1969*

stable boy's favourite *noun* a controlled throw of dice onto a dirt surface *US, 1974*

stable of lace *noun* the prostitutes associated with one pimp *US, 1976*

stable sister *noun* one prostitute in relation to the other prostitutes in a pimp's stable *US, 1972*

'stache *noun* a moustache *US, 1989*

stack *noun* **1** in rock music, an assemblage of loudspeakers *UK, 1996*. **2** in pool, the balls assembled inside the rack before a game *US, 1977*. **3** in pool, the clustered pack of balls left at the foot of the table after the first shot of the game *US, 1990*. **4** a package of marijuana cigarettes *US, 1955*. **5** one thousand dollars *US, 2002*. **6** money *US, 1997*. **7** in trucking, a smokestack from the truck engine *US, 1971*. **8** a large amount of something *US, 1870*

stack *verb* **1** to crash a vehicle *AUSTRALIA, 1971*. **2** to earn a lot of money *US, 1997*. ▶ **stack on a blue** to begin a fight *AUSTRALIA, 1944*. ▶ **stack on a turn** to kick up a fuss *AUSTRALIA, 1971*. ▶ **stack on an act** to kick up a fuss *AUSTRALIA, 1962*

stack away *verb* to eat or drink heartily *AUSTRALIA, 1960*

stacked *adjective* **1** possessing large breasts. Sometimes intensified with phrases such as 'stone to the bone' or rhymed as in 'stacked and packed' (the name of a photographic calendar produced by former Nixon operative G. Gordon Liddy, featuring nearly naked women holding guns) *US, 1942*. **2** muscular *US, 2002*. **3** used of prison sentences, consecutive, not concurrent *US, 1998*. **4** well-provided; wealthy *UK, 2001*

stackhat *noun* a crash helmet *AUSTRALIA, 1985*

stack it *verb* to brag or boast. Prison usage *NEW ZEALAND, 1999*

stacks *noun* **1** a large amount *US, 1892*. **2** a lot of intimate activity with the opposite sex *UK, 1987*. **3** in hot rodding, an exhaust system *US, 1948*

stackup *noun* a group of waves; a group of surfers on a single wave *US, 1977*

stack up *verb* on the railways, to have a collision *US, 1977*

staff *noun* ▶ **go to work without a staff** (of a female) to masturbate *US, 2001*. ▶ **meet the staff** to have sex. Punning on 'staff' (a long stick/weapon/personnel) as 'penis' *US, 2001*

stag *noun* **1** at a social function, a man without a date *US, 1905*. **2** a male at a stag party. A back-formation from STAG PARTY (a party for men only) *UK, 2003*. **3** a pornographic film. An elliptical form of STAG MOVIE *US, 1966*. **4** guard duty. Military *US, 1943*. **5** amyl or butyl nitrite. Possibly derived from a brand marketing the drug as a male sex-aid *UK, 1998*. **6** the butt end of a cigarette *US, 2002*

stag dinner *noun* a males-only dinner featuring sexual entertainment in the form of pornographic films, dancers and/or prostitutes *US, 1889*

stag do; stag night; stag *noun* a social event for men only. After STAG PARTY *UK, 1965*

stage *verb* **1** to single someone out in front of a crowd *US, 2004*. **2** in drag racing, to bring the front wheels of a car to the starting line preparatory to starting the race *US, 1973*

stage door Johnny *noun* a man waiting outside the stage door for an actress *US, 1912*

stage fright *noun* a *light* ale. Rhyming slang *UK, 1977*

stage mother *noun* in hospital usage, a mother who coaches their child in answering questions from a doctor and who has a preconceived notion of the diagnosis and appropriate treatment *US, 1978*

stage name *noun* a criminal's alias *US, 1950*

stage stop *noun* a truck stop. A jocular comparison to the days of stage coaches *US, 1976*

stag fight *noun* an amateur, extra-legally staged boxing match *US, 1955*

stag film *noun* a pornographic film *US, 1967*

stag flick *noun* a pornographic film *US, 1966*

stagged-off pants *noun* among loggers in British Columbia, trousers cut off short *CANADA, 1989*

stagger soup *noun* whisky *US, 1977*

stagger-through; stagger *noun* an early and rough attempt at rehearsing an entire piece of work. Theatrical *UK, 1964*

stag line *noun* at a dance, a line of men without dates, waiting to dance *US, 1934*

stag movie *noun* a pornographic film made for and enjoyed by men *US, 1960*

stag party *noun* a party for men only, usually organised to view pornography, tell sexual jokes and/or be entertained by strippers or prostitutes *US, 1856*

stain *noun* a contemptible person. Shortened from WANK-STAIN *UK, 1997*

staining *noun* the bleed period of the menstrual cycle *UK, 1951*

stair-dancer *noun* a thief whose speciality is office buildings with multiple floors *NEW ZEALAND, 1953*

stake *noun* **1** money needed to finance an enterprise or to contribute as a share to finance an enterprise *US, 1738*. **2** in gambling circles, money *US, 1963*

stake *verb* to provide someone with money or other needed resources *US, 1853*

staked out *adjective* tired of a necessary but tedious task *BARBADOS, 1992*

stake driver *noun* on the railways, an engineer in the engineering department *US, 1946*

stakehorse *noun* in pool, a person who financially backs the wagers of a professional player *US, 1990*

stake-out *noun* an act of covert surveillance on a stationary target *US, 1942*

stake out *verb* to carry out surveillance of a building or other place. Extends the imagery of a goat tethered to a stake to bait a trap *US, 1951*

stakey *adjective* anxious; jumpy; ready to leave *US, 1965*

stal; stallie *noun* a stalactite formation and/or stalagmite formation. A cavers' and pot-holers' term *UK, 1980*

Stalin Hill *noun* a hill within the punch bowl basin, occupied by North Korean and Chinese troops during the Korean war. Also refers to hills in North Vietnam and Prague (the site of a statue of Stalin from 1955 to 62) *US, 1989*

stalk *noun* **1** the penis, especially when in a state of erection *UK, 1961*. **2** man's obvious sexual appetite; courage; impudence. Extended from the previous sense *UK, 1977*. **3** a plastic sheath used for medical examination of the rectum *IRELAND, 1994*

stalks *noun* the legs *US, 1972*

stall *noun* a pickpocket's confederate who distracts the victim *UK, 1591*

stall *verb* **1** to make excuses; to play for time *UK, 1829*. **2** in pool, to intentionally miss a shot or lose a game *US, 1967*

stallion *noun* an attractive, sensual woman, especially a tall one *US, 1970*

stall the ball! stop! *IRELAND, 1999*

stall the digger! stop! *IRELAND, 1997*

stall walker *noun* in horse racing, a nervous jockey who paces before a race. A term originally for a racehorse pacing in the stall *US, 1953*

Stamford Hill cowboy *noun* an orthodox Jewish resident in the Stamford Hill/Stoke Newington area of north London. From the wide-brimmed black hat that is conventionally worn and the consequent image created by a group with the sun behind them *UK, 2002*

stammer and stutter *noun* butter. Rhyming slang *UK, 1937*

stamper *noun* a shoe *UK, 1565*

stamping ground *noun* a territory; an area of responsibility *UK, 1821*

stamp on *verb* to adulterate an illegal drug *UK, 1983*

Stan and Ollie *noun* an umbrella. Rhyming slang for BROLLY, formed on the names of film comedians Stan Laurel and Oliver Hardy *UK, 1998*

stand *verb* in blackjack, to accept your hand without any further cards *US, 1980*. ▶ **stand for** to endure or tolerate something *US, 1896*

stand-about *noun* a idler. A variation of 'layabout', but so literal as to be almost conventional *INDIA, 2002*

stand-at-ease *noun* cheese. Rhyming slang, originally military, current during Word War 1 *UK, 1979*

stand by for a ramming! used as a jocular prediction that trouble is impending *US, 1994*

stand from under *noun* thunder. Rhyming slang *UK, 1960*

stand on it to accelerate a car to full speed *US, 1970*

stand on me believe me *UK, 1933*

stand-over *noun* intimidation. Used attributively *AUSTRALIA, 1956*

standover *verb* to intimidate someone with the threat of violence *AUSTRALIA, 1939*

standover man *noun* a criminal who uses intimidation; a thug *AUSTRALIA, 1939*

standover merchant *noun* a criminal who uses intimidation; a thug *AUSTRALIA, 1944*

stand-read *noun* an act of *stand*ing and *read*ing magazines, newspapers, etc where they are displayed on a vendor's shelves. A subtle form of theft *UK, 1999*

stand-to-attention *noun* a pension. Rhyming slang, originally military, probably from the early part of C20 and used exclusively of a military pension; now in wider use *UK, 1961*

stand up *verb* **1** to fail to keep a social appointment or romantic engagement with someone *US, 1902*. **2** to refuse to co-operate when questioned by the police; to withstand pressure to confess *US, 1971*

stand-up *adjective* **1** loyal to the end, devoted and dependable. Perhaps from boxing, where a stand-up fight was one in which the fighters stood up to each without flinching or evasion. The ultimate praise in the world of organised crime *US, 1971*. **2** solid; pure *US, 1973*

stand-up *adverb* describing someone's play in pool, at your true skill level, not below it *US, 1993*

standy-up *adjective* used of an on-your-feet position or posture *UK, 2002*

stang *noun* prospective goods to be stolen *US, 1965*

Stang *noun* a Ford Mustang car *US, 1993*

stank *noun* the vagina; sex. Usually said unkindly *US, 1980*. ▶ **get your stank on** (from a female perspective) to have sex. Reclaiming STANK (the vagina) for women *UK, 2002*

stanky *adjective* bad-smelling *US, 1980*

Stanley *noun* **1** a Pole or Polish-American. Coined in Chicago *US, 1982*. **2** an industrial knife with a retractable blade, often used as a discreet weapon. Although similar tools are manufactured by many other companies, the Stanley brand provides the generic identity *UK, 1997*

stanley knife *noun* a wife. Rhyming slang, formed from a proprietary cutting tool that is a generic for such tools *UK, 1998*

stanza *noun* in horse racing, a single race *US, 1951*

star *noun* **1** cocaine. Possibly from shortening STARDUST (cocaine) *US, 2003*. **2** methcathinone *UK, 2003*. **3** a prisoner serving a first custodial sentence *UK, 1996*. **4** an asterisk sign (*) on a computer keyboard *US, 1991*. **5** man; used as a general form of address. West Indian, hence UK black. Also spelt 'starr' *JAMAICA, 1995*

starch *noun* semen *US, 1967*

stardust *noun* **1** cocaine *US, 1967*. **2** phencyclidine. Recorded as a 'current PCP alias' *US, 1977*

starfish *noun* the anus. A visual pun *UK, 2001*

starfish trooper *noun* a male homosexual. An allusion to anal sex based on STARFISH (the anus), playing on the popular science fiction image of a starship trooper *NEW ZEALAND, 2002*

starfucker *noun* anyone who seeks to provide free sexual services to the famous; hence, an ingratiating hanger-on of anyone with celebrity status *UK, 1970*

star gazer *noun* **1** on the railways, a brakeman who has misread oncoming signals *US, 1975*. **2** in horse racing, a horse that holds its head too high *UK, 1948*

star grade *noun* in the US military, the rank of general *US, 1982*

stark bollock naked *adjective* absolutely naked. An amended spelling of earlier 'stark ballock naked', 1922 *UK, 1984*

stark bollocky; stark bollocky naked; stark ballocky *adjective* totally naked *AUSTRALIA, 1972*

starkers *adjective* totally naked *NEW ZEALAND, 1923*

stark mother naked *adjective* totally naked *AUSTRALIA, 1967*

stark staring bonkers *adjective* utterly mad *UK, 2001*

starlight hotel *noun* sleeping in the open air at night *NEW ZEALAND, 1998*

stars *noun* LSD. From the design printed on the dose *UK, 1998*

Starship Enterprise *noun* a marijuana cigarette. In the cult televison series *Star Trek* (1966–69) and sequels, the Starship Enterprise is a means 'to boldly go' exploring space – simply a ROCKET for the next generation *UK, 2001*

Starsky and Hutch; starsky *noun* the crotch. Rhyming slang, formed from a US television police-action-adventure series, 1976–81 *UK, 1998*

star's nap *verb* to borrow something, especially money. Rhyming slang for TAP *UK, 1961*

star-spangled powder *noun* cocaine *UK, 1998*

start *verb* **1** to start your menstrual period *US, 2001*. **2** to act as if you want a fight *IRELAND, 1998*

starter *noun* a gambler hired by a casino to gamble and thereby create interest in a game *US, 1977*

starter cap *noun* a condom. To stop anything starting *US, 1996*

starters *noun* any lubricant used to facilitate anal sex *UK, 2002*. ▶ **for starters** to begin with *UK, 1969*

starting juice *noun* pressurised ether in a spray can, used to spray in the carburettor to help start a car that is not inclined to start *US, 1992*

startler *noun* in typography, an exclamation mark (!) *UK, 2003*

star up *verb* (used of a young prisoner, on turning 21) to be transferred to an adult prison *UK, 1996*

starver *noun* a saveloy *AUSTRALIA, 1941*

starve the crows! used for expressing great surprise *AUSTRALIA, 1918*

starve the lizards! used for expressing great surprise *AUSTRALIA, 1927*

starve the mice! used for expressing great surprise *AUSTRALIA, 1962*

starving Armenians *noun* used as an example when parents urge children to finish their dinner. There are endless variations on the theme *US, 1979*

starving days *noun* the first few, unproductive days of a project. A logger term that survived the end of mass logging *US, 1975*

stash *noun* **1** a hidden supply of drugs, usually marijuana; the hiding place itself *US, 1942*. **2** in the illegal production of alcohol, a cache of alcohol *US, 1974*. **3** ill-gotten or illicit goods kept in a hidden store *UK, 1914*. **4** a person's hiding place *US, 1927*. **5** a room, apartment or house *US, 1946*

stash *verb* **1** to hide something, especially drugs *US, 1914*. **2** (used of a prostitute) to retain some of your earnings and not turn them over to your pimp *US, 1989*

stash apartment *noun* an apartment where drugs are hidden *US, 1992*

stash catcher *noun* an employee of a drug dealer whose job it is to retrieve supplies of drugs that are jettisoned in the event of a police raid *US, 1992*

stash pad *noun* the room, apartment or house where someone hides their drugs *UK, 1983*

stat *noun* **1** a statistic. Usually used in the plural *US, 1961*. **2** a *statut*ory tenant *UK, 1963*. **3** methcathinone *US, 2003*

statch *adjective* statutory *US, 1994*

state *noun* **1** a dirty, ill-kempt or poorly preserved condition *UK, 1879*. **2** a condition of excitement; agitation; anxiety; a state of drunkenness *UK, 1837*. **3** a state prison *US, 1991*

State and Perversion *nickname* in Chicago, the intersection of State and Division Streets *US, 1958*

state college *noun* a state prison *US, 1949*

state electrician *noun* the executioner in a state using electrocution in the electric chair for capital punishment *US, 1982*

stateful *adjective* in a nervous or excited condition, 'in a state'. Teen slang *UK, 2003*

State of Maine bankroll *noun* a bankroll made from a real note folded around paper cut to the shape of currency *US, 1975*

state-of-the-monte *adjective* state of the art, using up-to-date technology. Formed with the FULL MONTE (everything) *UK, 1999*

state-raised *adjective* said of a prisoner who has spent most of his life incarcerated *US, 1992*

States *noun* ▶ **the States** in Alaska, all states except Alaska *US, 1984*

stateside *adjective* of the US; American *US, 1943*

state time *noun* a prison sentence served in a state prison. More serious than time in COUNTY, and within the state jurisdiction as opposed to federal jurisdiction *US, 1995*

statey *noun* a state highway trooper *US, 1985*

static *noun* harassment; trouble; complications *US, 1926*

stationery *noun* free tickets to an athletic or entertainment event *UK, 1952*

stations of the cross a police tactic in which a person who has been arrested is moved from one precinct to another in rapid succession, making it impossible for him to be located and bailed out by his friends and family *US, 1992*

stave *noun* a drinking session *IRELAND, 1984*

staving drunk *adjective* very drunk. This phrase has lasted past the time when alcohol came only in barrels (although SWISH still does) *CANADA, 1999*

stay *verb* to reside *US, 1973*. ▶ **stay awake** to use amphetamines or methamphetamine continuously. A vague euphemism *US, 1989*: ▶ **stay loose** to remain calm *US, 1959*

stay and pray *verb* in poker, to stay in a hand with a large amount of money bet, hoping for a particular card to be drawn to improve your hand *US, 1988*

stay-awake *noun* amphetamine sulphate or any other central nervous system stimulant *US, 1993*

stay-behind *adjective* left to operate in enemy territory. CIA Director Allen Dulles formed 'Operation Stay Behind' shortly after World War 2, building a wide network of anti-communist guerrillas – including many former Nazis – who would fight behind the lines in the event of a Soviet invasion of Europe *US, 1982*

stayer *noun* **1** in poker, a hand that warrants staying in the game but not raising the bet *US, 1949*. **2** in horse racing, a horse that performs well in longer distance races *US, 1976*

stay-home sauce *noun* food or drink made with ingredients believed to instil sexual fidelity or attraction *GUYANA, 1992*

stay-out *noun* in prison, a confrontational tactic in which prisoners refuse to return to their cells *US, 1976*

stay out of the Koolaid! mind your own business! *US, 1995*

stay put to remain in place, to stay where you are *US, 1843*

stay up used as a farewell *US, 1998*

stay-wag *noun* a station wagon *US, 1991*

St Cat's *noun* in Montreal, Rue St Catherine *CANADA, 2002*

STD grab bag *noun* a person who has had many sexual partners and is likely, therefore, to be a source of sexually transmitted disease *UK, 2003*

steady *noun* a steady boyfriend or girlfriend *US, 1897*

steady Eddie *noun* a reliable, dependable, trustworthy person *US, 2003*

Steak and Kidney *noun* Sydney. Rhyming slang *AUSTRALIA, 1905*

steak and kidney pie *noun* the eye. Rhyming slang *UK, 1960*

steak drapes *noun* the vaginal labia. A play on BEEF CURTAINS *UK, 1998*

steal *noun* something cheap or made available at a cheaper cost *US, 1944*

steal *verb* in poker, to win a hand with an inferior hand either through superior bluffing skills or poor estimation by other players *US, 1979*. ▶ **steal someone blind** to rob someone of everything. An illiterate variation of 'rob someone blind' *US, 1976*. ▶ **steal the ante** in poker, to bet aggressively early in a hand, driving out other players and leaving a pot consisting mostly of the buy-in antes *US, 1975*. ▶ **steal the show** in a public display, to outshine other performers, to gain most applause *US, 1928*

stealth bomber *nickname* Stella Artois™ lager. Named after the nickname of the US Air Force's B2 Spirit, which is used here to imply invisible strength and a great power to inflict damage *UK, 2002*

steam *noun* **1** alcohol *AUSTRALIA, 1941*. **2** hashish *CANADA, 2002*. **3** in sports betting, a flurry of betting on one side of a bet *US, 1991*. ▶ **not give the steam off your turds; not give the steam of your piss** expresses an absolute refusal to give or be generous. The predominate style is 'off', rather than 'of'. The term employed for appropriate bodily excretions may be as varied as the user's vocabulary: 'steam off your shit' is a familiar example *UK, 2000*

steam *verb* in gambling, to bet increasingly larger amounts of money in a losing effort to recoup recurring losses *US, 1985*

steam and cream; steam job *noun* during the Vietnam war, a bath and sex with a prostitute *US, 1969*

steamboat *noun* a cardboard tube or box with a hole for a marijuana cigarette and a hole for inhaling, used to trap the smoke *US, 1967*

steamboats *adjective* **1** foolish, silly. Probably derives as rhyming slang from *Steamboat Willie*, the 1928 animated film that introduced Mickey Mouse *UK, 2000*. **2** drunk *UK: SCOTLAND, 1996*

steame *noun* a steamed hot dog *CANADA, 2001*

steamer *noun* **1** a member of a youth gang taking part in a steaming attack *UK, 1987*. **2** in horse racing, a horse that attracts heavy betting on the morning of a race, at a time before the odds being offered by bookmakers are reduced *UK, 1991*. **3** an act of oral sex performed on a man *UK, 2003*. **4** a homosexual man, especially one who seeks passive partners. Ultimately from STEAM TUG (a MUG) *UK, 1958*. **5** a prostitute's client *UK, 2002*. **6** a gambler who increases the size of his bets after losing *US, 1968*. **7** a drinking session *UK: SCOTLAND, 1988*. **8** a full wetsuit covering the torso, legs and arms *AUSTRALIA, 1985*

steam in *verb* to engage in an activity, especially fighting, with absolute commitment *UK, 1961*

steaming *noun* youth gang activity involving robbing and escaping en masse *UK, 1987*

steaming *adjective* **1** used as an intensifier *UK, 1962*. **2** drunk *UK, 2002*

steaming demon *noun* any large American car *UK, 1981*

steam packet *noun* a jacket. Rhyming slang *UK, 1857*

steampigged *adjective* drunk *UK, 2002*

steam-powered *adjective* obsolete *US, 1991*

steamroller *noun* **1** a thick hand-rolled cigarette *NEW ZEALAND, 1953*. **2** a bowler hat. Rhyming slang. Glossed as: 'A dying piece simply because the headwear of the typical city gent is a thing of the past' by Ray Puxley, *Cockney Rabbit*, 1992 *UK, 1992*

steam tug; steamer *noun* a fool; a victim. Rhyming slang for MUG *UK, 1932*

steeazick *noun* a marijuana cigarette *US, 1947*

steel *noun* a pistol. A variation of the more common 'iron' *US, 1993*. ▶ **off the steel** not engaged in railway work *US, 1977*

steel and concrete cure *noun* the sudden and complete deprivation of drugs to a jailed drug addict, who suffers intensely *US, 1950*

steel beach *noun* the deck of an aircraft carrier or other warship when used for recreational purposes *US, 1982*

steel door *noun* a hospital-admitting physician who admits only the sickest patients *US, 1994*

steelie *noun* a ball bearing used in a game of marbles *US, 1978*

steelies *noun* steel-toed boots, especially those made by Doc Marten *US, 2000*

steel pot *noun* the US military standard-issue M-1 helmet. Vietnam war usage *US, 1968*

steely *noun* **1** a steel guitar *UK, 1967*. **2** in trucking, a brake made with a magnesium-steel brake shoe in a steel drum *US, 1971*

steen *noun* an imaginary large number *US, 1900*

steep *adjective* **1** excessively expensive; over-priced *US, 1856*. **2** sought by the police; wanted *US, 1995*

steer *noun* ▶ **all a steer can do is try** said to justify, humbly, an attempt to do the seemingly impossible *CANADA, 1987*

steer *verb* in confidence swindles, to direct the confederate(s) who will swindle the victim *US, 1889*

steerage *noun* economy class on a commercial airliner *US, 2002*

steerer *noun* a person who directs potential customers to an illegal enterprise *US, 1989*

steerman *noun* **1** a member of a swindling enterprise who identifies potential victims and directs them into the swindle *US, 1993*. **2** in tandem surfing, the person towards the rear of the surfboard *US, 1957*

steeze *noun* a person's image or style *US, 2003*

Steffi Graf; Steffi *noun* **1** a laugh. Rhyming slang, formed from the name of the German tennis champion (b.1969) *UK, 1998*. **2** a bath. Rhyming slang, based on the name of the German tennis player Steffi Graf (b.1969) *UK, 1998*. **3** *half* an ounce, especially of drugs. Rhyming slang *UK, 2003*

steggies *noun* steroids *UK, 2002*

Steinie *noun* a bottle of Steinlager™ beer *NEW ZEALAND, 1998*

stella blue *noun* a variety of marijuana. Possibly named after a 1973 song by the Grateful Dead: 'It seems like all this life / Was just a dream / Stella Blue / Stella Blue' *UK, 1995*

stellar *adjective* very good. A conventional adjective rendered slangy through attitude, pronunciation and application to objects such as hamburgers *US, 1986*

Stella the Steno *noun* used as a personification of the stereotypical female office worker *US, 1946*

stem *noun* **1** a main street or boulevard, especially one frequented by tramps, prostitutes, pimps, and their ilk *US, 1914*. **2** the dominant culture in a society. An abbreviation of 'system' *US, 1995*. **3** the penis *US, 1972*. **4** a railway track *US, 1946*. **5** a laboratory pipette used to smoke crack cocaine *US, 1992*. ▶ **on the stem** performing or inclined to perform oral sex on a man *US, 1976*. ▶ **up against the stem** addicted to smoking marijuana. From 'stem' (the non-smokeable part of the marijuana plant) *UK, 1998*

stem *verb* to beg on the street *US, 1958*

stemmer *noun* a beggar *US, 1962*

stems *noun* **1** the legs *UK, 1860*. **2** marijuana. An example of BAD meaning 'good'; the non-smokeable part of the plant is here adopted as a name for the good *UK, 2003*

stenchel *noun* molasses, water and ground ginger, to go on porridge or as a drink in the field *CANADA, 1988*

stench trench *noun* the vagina *UK, 1997*

stencil *noun* a thin and long marijuana cigarette *US, 1980*

stenked *adjective* drunk *UK: SCOTLAND, 1996*

steno *noun* a stenographer *US, 1906*

stenographer *noun* in a deck of playing cards, a queen *US, 1988*

step *verb* ▶ **step on** to dilute a powdered drug *US, 1971*. ▶ **step on the gas; step on it** to hurry; to accelerate; often used as an imperative. Originally applied just to motor vehicles; the 'it' is the accelerator pedal *US, 1920*. ▶ **step on your dick** to commit

a self-damaging act *US, 1980*. ▶ **step on your meat** to engage in self-defeating conduct *US, 1981*. ▶ **step up to the plate** to rise to a challenge. From the image of a batter in baseball coming up to bat *US, 1919*

Stephenson's rocket *noun* a pocket. Rhyming slang, formed from the early locomotive *UK, 1998*

Stepin Fetchit *noun* an black person who curries favour with whites through obsequious behaviour. After the stage name of Lincoln Theodore Monroe Perry (1902–85), a black actor known for his film portrayal of stereotypical black minstrel characters *US, 1940*

step off *verb* to go away *US, 1993*

stepper *noun* **1** a prostitute; a promiscuous woman *US, 1953*. **2** a gunman *JAMAICA, 2000*. ▶ **up the steps; up the stairs** on trial. The accused goes up the steps/stairs from the cells into the court *UK, 1931*

step to *verb* to get into a fight *US, 1995*

step up *verb* to start a fight *US, 2001*

stern-wheeler *noun* the passive participant in anal sex *US, 1979*

Steve Canyon *noun* any fighter pilot. Vietnam war usage, alluding to the name of a comic strip popular in the US in the 1950s and 60s *US, 1968*

Steve McQueen's *noun* jeans. Rhyming slang *UK, 2002*

Stevie Wonder *noun* thunder. Rhyming slang, formed from the name of the US singer and musician (b.1950) *UK, 1998*

stew *noun* **1** an awkward position; an agitated condition *UK, 1806*. **2** a state of alcohol intoxication *US, 1965*. **3** a drunkard *US, 1950*. **4** nitroglycerin used to blow open a safe *US, 1949*. **5** an airline flight attendant. A shortened form of 'stewardess' *US, 1969*

stew *verb* ▶ **stew in your own juice** to endure the consequences of your actions *UK, 1885*

stewards'; steward's *noun* an informal investigation of any situation. Reduced from 'stewards' inquiry' (an authorised investigation by the officials who control horse racing) *UK, 1999*

Stewart Granger *noun* danger. Rhyming slang, formed from the name of the British film actor *UK, 1992*

stew bum; stewbum *noun* an alcoholic derelict *US, 1902*

stewed *adjective* drunk. Another drunk synonym, first recorded by Benjamin Franklin *US, 1737*

stewed prune *noun* a tune. Rhyming slang *UK, 1979*

stewie *noun* an alcoholic *US, 1945*

St. Gapour *noun* in Quebec, the alcoholic mixed drink best known as a Singapore Sling *CANADA, 1992*

stick *noun* **1** ability in pool *US, 1970*. **2** a cigarette. Indian English *INDIA, 1979*. **3** marijuana *UK, 2003*. **4** phencyclidine, the recreational drug known as PCP or angel dust *UK, 2001*. **5** a truncheon; a riot baton. In police and prison-service use; narrowing but continuing the sense as 'cudgel', which has been in recorded use since 1377 *US, 1929*. **6** a burglar's pry-bar *UK, 1879*. **7** a clarinet. A shortened form of LIQUORICE STICK *US, 1946*. **8** a handgun. Recorded in use August 2002 *UK, 1781*. **9** a surfboard *US, 1964*. **10** a skateboard *US, 1984*. **11** in horse racing, the whip used by jockeys *US, 1976*. **12** a pool player *US, 1990*. **13** the game of pool *US, 1966*. **14** a set of rules for a game of pool *US, 1990*. **15** criticism, especially harsh criticism. A softening of the sense 'to beat with a stick' *UK, 1942*. **16** violent punishment; a severe reprimand. Originally 'the stick' (a beating with a stick) *UK, 1856*. **17** harsh or extreme demands made of a motor engine. Usually as 'give it (some) stick'; derives from the sense of the 'cane', as 'punishment' *UK, 1978*. **18** a manually operated car transmission. A shortened form of 'stick shift' *US, 1960*. **19** in drag and motor racing, tyre traction *US, 1980*. **20** a prisoner's personal influence or power *US, 1992*. **21** a person of a type described *UK, 1784*. **22** a fighter pilot *US, 1986*. **23** a prostitute *US, 1972*. **24** one thousand dollars. Probably an evolution of YARD *US, 1978*. **25** in circus or carnival, a person playing a game or concession with the house's money in an attempt to attract other patrons to play *US, 1980* ▷ *see:* BELLY-STICK. ▶ **give it stick; give it some stick** to enjoy something noisily, and to the utmost *UK, 1984*. ▶ **give stick; give some stick** to energetically criticise someone; to inflict physical damage on something or someone *UK, 2000*. ▶ **had the stick** to be ruined or irreparably broken; to be finished *AUSTRALIA, 1953*. ▶ **up the stick** pregnant *AUSTRALIA, 1941*

stick *verb* **1** to stab someone with a knife *US, 1975*. **2** to inject a drug *US, 1992*. **3** to punch or hit someone *US, 2003*. **4** (from the male perspective) to have sex *US, 1972*. **5** to tolerate or endure someone or something *UK, 1899*. **6** to burden someone *UK, 1851*. ▶ **stick a hit** in snowboarding, to achieve impressive height when jumping *US, 1995*. ▶ **stick beef** (used of a male) to have sex *BAHAMAS, 1982*. ▶ **stick fat** to remain loyal. Prison usage *NEW ZEALAND, 1997*. ▶ **stick in promise land for** to threaten someone with a prison sentence. Prison use *UK, 1959*. ▶ **stick it up** to treat someone unfairly *AUSTRALIA, 1974*. ▶ **stick like shit to a blanket** to adhere tenaciously *UK, 1956*. ▶ **stick one on someone** to hit someone *UK, 1960*. ▶ **stick to your knitting** to limit your efforts to doing what you know how to do; in the business world, to avoid the temptation to diversify beyond your company's expertise *US, 1991*. ▶ **stick with** to persevere with something; to endure; to remain faithful to someone or something *UK, 1882*. ▶ **stick your neck out** to take a risk *US, 1926*

stick ▶ **stick your bib in** to interfere; to meddle *AUSTRALIA, 1952*

stickability *noun* perseverance *US, 1888*

stick and stone; stick *noun* a bone. Rhyming slang, generally plural *UK, 1992*

stick book *noun* a pornographic book or magazine *AUSTRALIA, 1967*

stick bun *noun* a son. Rhyming slang *UK, 1992*

sticker *noun* **1** a knife *UK, 1896*. **2** a warrant or bill of detainer *US, 1976*. **3** a prisoner who is remanded in custody pending a court appearance *UK, 1977*

stick for *verb* to charge too much for something *UK, 1961*

stick hall *noun* a pool room *US, 1958*

stick horse *noun* in horse racing, a horse that runs best with some encouragement from the jockey and whip *US, 1976*

stickie *nickname* a member of the 'official' IRA and Sinn Fein *IRELAND, 1972*

stick Indian *noun* a backwoods Indian *CANADA, 1956*

sticking out *adjective* good; fashionable *UK, 1983*

stick-in-the-mud *noun* someone who resists change *UK, 1733*

stick it up your arse!; stick it in your ear!; stick it up your jumper! expressions of contemptuous rejection *US, 1960*

stick mag *noun* a pornographic magazine *AUSTRALIA, 1992*

stickman *noun* **1** a pickpocket, shoplifter or other petty criminal's accomplice who is passed the stolen goods, and also impedes any pursuit. West Indian slang *UK, 1861*. **2** a marijuana smoker *US, 1966*. **3** a sexually active heterosexual male who prides himself on his skill and prowess *UK, 1975*

stick me with a fork – I'm done! used for expressing submission in the face of a challenge *US, 2000*

stick of rock *noun* the penis. Rhyming slang for COCK; a visual pun on a long pink sweet that is made to be sucked *UK, 1992*

stick of tea *noun* marijuana prepared and smoked in the fashion of a cigarette. Combines STICK (a cigarette) with TEA (marijuana) *US, 1940*

stick out *verb* to be conspicuous or obvious. From 'stick out a mile'. Originally in conventional use, colloquial or slang since mid-C19 *UK, 1638*. ▶ **stick out like dog's balls** to be obvious; to stand out prominently *AUSTRALIA, 1971*

sticks *noun* **1** the countryside *US, 1905*. **2** goalposts. Examples include football (soccer) and Australian Rules football *AUSTRALIA, 1876*. **3** skis; ski poles *US, 1963*. **4** furniture *US, 1956*. **5** good quality marijuana *UK, 2000*

sticks and stones *noun* the game of pool *US, 1990*

sticksing *noun* pickpocketing. West Indian slang *UK, 1977*

stick sister *noun* a woman who shares a sexual partner with another woman *AUSTRALIA, 1987*

stickspin *noun* a scene in a pornographic film in which a woman changes positions without losing her vaginal grip on the man's penis *US, 1995*

stick up *verb* to rob someone at gunpoint; to hold up a place *AUSTRALIA, 1843*

stick-up *adjective* engaged in sex *TRINIDAD AND TOBAGO, 1974*

stickup; stick-up *noun* **1** an armed hold-up *US, 1904*. **2** glue used in solvent abuse. A play on the conventional use of glue *UK, 1996*

stick up for *verb* to champion or defend someone or something *UK, 1837*

stick-up merchant *noun* an armed robber *AUSTRALIA, 2001*

sticky *noun* an inquisitive look. Short for STICKYBEAK *AUSTRALIA, 1974*

sticky *adjective* **1** of a situation, incident, work, etc, unpleasant, very difficult, dangerous *UK, 1915*. **2** in trouble *BARBADOS, 1965*. **3** of a website, successful at attracting repeated or extended visits from Internet users *UK, 2003*. **4** in volleyball, said of a ball that is briefly, and illegally, held *US, 1972*

stickybeak; sticky-beak *noun* **1** an overly inqusitive person *AUSTRALIA, 1920*. **2** an inquisitive look *AUSTRALIA, 1971*

stickybeak; sticky-beak *verb* to pry *AUSTRALIA, 1933*

sticky book *noun* a pornographic book or magazine *UK, 2000*

sticky buns; the stickys *noun* diarrhoea. Rhyming slang for THE RUNS *UK, 2003*

sticky dog *noun* in cricket, a rain-soaked pitch which the sun is drying *UK, 1933*

sticky end *noun* ▶ **come to a sticky end 1** (of a person) to end up in prison, or to die an unpleasant (and unnatural) death; (thus, of an abstract or physical thing) to cease to exist, to be destroyed *UK, 1961*. **2** to masturbate. A pleasing pun *AUSTRALIA, 1984*

sticky end of the stick the least desirable part *TRINIDAD AND TOBAGO, 1987*

sticky finger *verb* to shoplift *US, 1970*

sticky-fingered *adjective* inclined to thievery *UK, 1890*

sticky fingers *noun* **1** an inclination to steal *US, 1939*. **2** a shoplifter *US, 1982*

sticky-icky *noun* marijuana *US, 2002*

sticky toffee *noun* coffee *UK, 1979*

sticky wicket *noun* **1** a tricky or uncertain situation. From the game of cricket; the ball bounces unpredictably on a pitch that is drying out *UK, 1882*. **2** in croquet, a difficult shot *US, 1977*

stiff *noun* **1** a corpse *US, 1859*. **2** an ordinary person; a person who conforms *US, 1998*. **3** in any endeavour, a disappointing, poor performer *US, 1978*. **4** a non-player in a gambling establishment *US, 1979*. **5** a poor tipper *US, 1974*. **6** a disagreeable person who is likely to try to cheat *US, 1882*. **7** a tramp; a hobo *UK, 1899*. **8** in an illegal betting operation, a person who has agreed to pose as the head of the operation to protect the actual head in the event of a police raid and arrest *US, 1952*. **9** an unskilled pool player *US, 1993*. **10** in horse racing, a horse that is favoured to win but is not ridden in an effort to win *US, 1947*. **11** in pool, the cue ball left with no easy shot *US, 1993*. **12** a worthless cheque *US, 1950*. **13** in the usage of telephone swindlers, a payment by cheque *US, 1959*. **14** a clandestine letter; in prison, a letter smuggled into, out of, or between prisons *UK, 1900*. **15** in blackjack, a card with a value of two, three, four, five or six. Combined with a ten-point card, a card that leaves the player in limbo *US, 1975*. ▶ **the stiff** money or correspondence to the benefit of a prisoner passed to a prison warder by a prisoner's friend or relative *US, 1875*

stiff *verb* **1** to cheat someone; to rob someone; to refuse to pay someone *US, 1950*. **2** to extort from someone *UK, 1978*. **3** to kill someone *UK, 1977*. **4** to fail miserably *US, 1996*. **5** (of a male) to have sex. Used in both the passive and active forms *UK, 1977*

stiff *adjective* **1** of alcoholic liquor, potent or undiluted *UK, 1813*. **2** drunk *US, 1737*. **3** excellent *BERMUDA, 1985*. **4** frustrated; out of luck. From earlier sense as 'broke, penniless', 1898 (*Australian National Dictionary*) *AUSTRALIA, 1917*

stiff *adverb* greatly; used to intensify, especially 'bore' and 'scare'. From 'stiff' (dead) hence, here, 'to death'; always after the verb it modifies *UK, 1905*

stiff! tough luck! *AUSTRALIA, 1985*

stiff-assed; stiff-arsed *adjective* used of a person who behaves in a superior manner and doesn't mix with others *US, 1937*

stiff bikkies! used for expressing a lack of sympathy with a bad turn of events *NEW ZEALAND, 1992*

stiff cheddar! tough luck! *AUSTRALIA, 1979*

stiff cheese! tough luck! *AUSTRALIA, 1979*

stiffen the crows! heavens above! *AUSTRALIA, 1932*

stiffen the wombats! heavens above! *AUSTRALIA, 1962*

stiff-eye *verb* to look at someone without establishing eye contact *US, 1964*

stiffie *noun* an erection *NEW ZEALAND, 1995*

stiff luck *noun* bad luck *AUSTRALIA, 1919*

stiff one *noun* any strong alcoholic drink *UK, 1813*

stiff shit! tough luck! *AUSTRALIA, 1969*

stiff-toe gang *noun* the dead *BAHAMAS, 1995*

stiff turps *noun* bad luck *AUSTRALIA, 1960*

stiff upper lip *noun* a personal quality characterised as repressed emotion or quiet courage, and regarded as typically British. In early use you would 'carry' or 'keep' a stiff upper lip; later use is mainly jocular or derisory. Although widely considered a stereotypical British characteristic, actually of US origin *US, 1815*

stiff with *adjective* closely packed, densely crowded. Hyperbole; originally (from C17) a conventional use of 'stiff' *UK, 1907*

stiffy *noun* **1** an erection. Also variants 'stiffie' and 'stiff'. *UK, 1980.* **2** in snowboarding, a stiff-legged jumping manoeuvre *US, 1995.* **3** an engraved invitation card. Upper-class society use; from the unbending quality of the card and the (stiff) formality of the occasion *UK, 1982.* **4** a computer disc. From the packaging *SOUTH AFRICA, 1993*

stifle *verb* to silence yourself. A verb popularised by the Archie Bunker character on the television series *All in the Family US, 1971*

still *nickname* a Falkland Islander *UK, 2002*

still game *noun* a card game held on a regular basis with regular players *US, 1977*

stillies *noun* stiletto shoes *UK, 2005*

stilt person; stilt people *noun* a celebrity *NEW ZEALAND, 2003*

stilts *noun* the legs *US, 1945*

stim *noun* an empty bottle with a refundable deposit *UK, 1995*

stimey *noun* ten dollars' worth of drugs. From the synonymous DIME BAG; a contraction of 'it's a dimey' *US, 2001*

stimp *noun* the leg *UK, 2002*

stimp cover *noun* a nylon stocking. Based on STIMP (the leg) *UK, 2002*

sting *noun* **1** any crime that achieves its purpose by fraud or deception *US, 1930.* **2** a robbery *US, 1940.* **3** a short, sharp chord played to make or disssolve a sense of suspense *US, 1973*

sting *verb* **1** to swindle someone; to cheat, to rob someone *UK, 1812.* **2** in horse racing, to shock a horse with an electrical device during a race *US, 1951.* ▶ **sting between the toes** (from a male perspective) to have sex *AUSTRALIA, 1971*

stinger *noun* **1** a pinched nerve *US, 1999.* **2** the penis *US, 1967.* **4** a high velocity, hollow-nose, expanding bullet *US, 1981.* **4** in poker, a sequence of five cards. Known conventionally as a 'straight' *US, 1988.* **5** a railway brakesman *US, 1977.* **6** an improvised heating element consisting of exposed wires attached to a small metal plate, used for heating water *US, 1989.* **7** an illegal vote. Chicago Mayor Richard Daley was given credit for delivering Chicago and the state of Illinois to John Kennedy in the 1960 presidential election through extensive use of 'stingers'. Subsequent research dispelled most of these rumours, but Daley enjoyed the power the stories gave him *US, 1982.* **8** a radio antenna *US, 1976*

stingo *noun* strong, illegally manufactured whisky *US, 1999*

stingy brim *noun* a hat with a thin brim *US, 1949*

stink *noun* a commotion; a loud complaint *UK, 1812.* ▶ **like stink** desperately hard, extremely fast, very much, etc *UK, 1929*

stink *verb* to be aesthetically or morally offensive *US, 1934*

stink bomb *noun* in the used car business, a car that won't sell because of a lingering, nauseating smell *US, 1992*

stinker *noun* **1** an offensive or despicable person or thing *US, 1911.* **2** a corpse that has begun to decompose and, as a result, smell *US, 1996.* **3** an onion *US, 1962.* **4** a cigar. So known because of the offensive smell the cigar emits *US, 1907.* **5** in dominoes, a player who forces the next player to draw by cutting him off *US, 1959.* **6** a strongly worded letter *UK, 1912*

stinkeroo *noun* a complete failure. Coined by Damon Runyon *US, 1934*

stinker squad *noun* a police homicide investigative department *US, 1981*

stink-eye *noun* a hateful glare. Hawaiian youth usage *US, 1981*

stink-finger *noun* **1** the insertion of a finger or fingers into a woman's vagina *UK, 1903.* **2** the middle finger. From the vaginal odour occasioned by the finger's predominant use in sexual foreplay *UK, 1984*

stink-finger *verb* to insert a finger or fingers into a woman's vagina *US, 1992*

stinking *adjective* **1** disgusting, contemptible. In conventional use for centuries, but now considered vulgar *UK, 1961.* **2** drunk, very drunk. This sense is recorded earlier than STINKING DRUNK *US, 1887*

stinking drunk *adjective* very drunk. A combination of two adjectives with the same sense *UK, 1926*

stinkingly *adverb* excessively *UK, 1906*

stinking rich; stinking *adjective* very wealthy. First recorded as 'stinking' in 1940; with 'rich' in 1945 *US, 2003*

stinking thinking *noun* the rationalisation of an addiction as 'not that bad' or as something short of an addiction. Used in twelve-step recovery programmes such as Alcoholics Anonymous *US, 1998*

stinking with money; stinking with it *adjective* very wealthy. A variation of STINKING RICH *UK, 1961*

stinko *noun* alcohol, especially wine *AUSTRALIA, 1958*

stinko *adjective* exceedingly drunk *US, 1927*

stinkoed *adjective* drunk. A variation of STINKO *UK, 1997*

stinkout *noun* a prank in which bad-smelling material is put in a room, making it uninhabitable *US, 1967*

stink pot *noun* the vagina *US, 1980*

stink stiff *noun* a badly decomposed and smelly corpse *US, 1984*

stinkum *noun* any bad-smelling substance *US, 1972*

stinkweed; stink weed *noun* marijuana *US, 1950*

stinky *noun* **1** a promiscuous woman *BERMUDA, 1985.* **2** a female member of the Royal Air Force. In Royal Air Force use, 2002 *UK, 2002.* ▶ **go stinky** to defecate *US, 1979*

stinky pinky *noun* **1** a finger enriched with the aroma of vagina *US, 1993.* **2** a party game based on rhymes. An overworked prostitute is a 'sore whore', excretory humour is 'shit wit', etc *US, 1949*

stipe *noun* a stipendiary steward at a racecourse *AUSTRALIA, 1902*

stir *noun* **1** a prison or jail. Derives from Romany *stariben, steripen* thus Welsh gispy *star* (to be imprisoned), *stardo* (imprisoned) *UK, 1851.* **2** a party *NEW ZEALAND, 1998.* **3** teasing *AUSTRALIA, 1985.* ▶ **do stir** to serve time in prison *UK, 1994*

stir *verb* **1** to have sex *US, 1973.* **2** to tease someone *AUSTRALIA, 1969.* ▶ **stir the porridge** (of a man) to have sex with a woman whose vagina is newly awash with the semen of her previous partner(s), especially if the final man in the line; to have sex with a woman who is in a sexual relationship with another man. The appearance of mixed ejaculate put the coiner in mind of porridge *AUSTRALIA, 1970.* ▶ **stir the shit** to cause trouble, especially by gossiping or telling tales *UK, 1984*

stir bug *noun* a prisoner crazed by years of incarceration *US, 1950*

stir-crazy *adjective* deranged by incarceration *US, 1908*

stir-happy *adjective* adversely affected by imprisonment *UK, 1959*

Stirling Moss; stirling *noun* a thing of little or no value. Rhyming slang for TOSS, formed from the champion racing driver, Stirling Moss (b.1929) *UK, 1992*

stirrer *noun* a teaser; a troublemaker *AUSTRALIA, 1966*

stirrup *noun* **1** in trucking, any device that provides help for climbing up into the cab *US, 1971*. **2** on the railways, the lowest step on a freight wagon *US, 1946*

stir-simple *adjective* mentally unstable because of incarceration *US, 1952*

stitch *noun* a confidence trick, often good-natured rather than criminal *UK, 1995*

stitch and bitch *noun* the (Canadian) Officer's Wives Club at an air base *CANADA, 1995*

stitch queen *noun* a male homosexual wardrobe assistant *US, 1973*

stitch that!; stitch this! said at the moment of physical attack with a knife or similar weapon, usually as the climax to a catchphrase threat such as 'Can your wife do first aid? Stitch that!' or 'Are you any good at sewing? Stitch this!' *UK, 1992*

stitch-up *noun* an act that unjustly places criminal, financial or moral responsibility on someone else *UK, 1984*

stitch up *verb* **1** (of the police) to incriminate someone, especially by planting false evidence *UK, 1977*. **2** to deliberately take unfair advantage of someone *UK, 1970*

stitchy *noun* in circus and carnival usage, a tailor *US, 1981*

stivver *verb* to stagger *CANADA, 1953*

STL *adjective* said of a hospital patient who is in a persistent vegetative state, who is similar to lettuce. *US, 1994*

St. Louis *noun* in circus and carnival usage, second helpings of food. According to Wilmeth, an allusion to the fact that circus engagements in St. Louis played in two sections *US, 1981*

St Louis blues; St Louis *noun* **1** shoes. Rhyming slang, formed from 'St Louis Blues', a song by William Christopher Handy, published in 1914, and now a jazz classic *UK, 1980*. **2** news; the news. Glasgow rhyming slang *UK: SCOTLAND, 1985*

St. Louis stop *noun* a rolling stop at a traffic signal or stop sign *US, 1999*

St. Martins-le-Grand; St Martin; Martin-le-Grand; martin *noun* the hand. Rhyming slang *UK, 1857*

stoat *verb* (of a bet) to win *UK: SCOTLAND, 1988*

stoat down *verb* to rain very heavily. Formed on Scots *stot* (to bounce) *UK: SCOTLAND, 1996*

stoated *adjective* drunk *UK, 1999*

stoater *noun* something excellent; a particularly good-looking person, especially a woman *UK: SCOTLAND, 1911*

stoating *adjective* excellent. From STOATER (a good thing) *UK: SCOTLAND, 1988*

stoat-the-baw; stoater *noun* a paedophile; a child-molester. From Scots for 'bounce-the-ball', possibly an image of a child's head being patted as if bouncing a ball *UK: SCOTLAND, 1988*

stocious; stotious *adjective* drunk. Of Anglo-Irish origins *UK, 1937*

stock *noun* the prizes in a carnival midway game concession *US, 1985*. ▶ **throw stock** to distribute prizes in a carnival game *US, 1966*

-stock *suffix* used in combination with an entertainer's name (or part thereof) to create a name for a musical festival. The second syllable of legendary music festival Woodstock, 1969, is taken to lend quality and scale to a current music event. In August 1992, the group Madness reformed after eight years, and hosted and headlined a weekend-long open-air concert called Madstock in London's Finsbury Park. Officially titled 'Big Beach Boutique', Normstock is, or was, a one-day festival of dance music hosted on Brighton beach by DJ Fatboy Slim, real name: Norman Cook. When the crowds in attendance proved to be greater than the authorities expected the parallel to Woodstock was drawn *UK, 1992*

stockbroker's Tudor; stockbroker Tudor *noun* faux-Tudor architecture *UK, 1938*

stockholder *noun* on the railways, any employee who appears to be more concerned about the company than his fellow workers *US, 1977*

stockings *noun* female legs *US, 1971*

stocking stuffer *noun* **1** in poker, money bet by a player who has withdrawn from the hand *US, 1996*. **2** cash *US, 2003*

stocks and bonds a slogan used by prostitutes to advertise bondage services. A punning euphemism *UK, 2001*

stocks and shares *noun* stairs. Rhyming slang *UK, 1992*

stocky *noun* a habitual user of cocaine. Recorded as 'cokehead' by a Jamaican inmate in a UK prison *UK, 2002*

stogie *noun* **1** a cigar *US, 1873*. **2** an extra-large marijuana cigarette. Derives ultimately from Conestoga, a town in Pennsylvania, and the name given to a horse-drawn freight wagon originating in that region in the C18. Conestoga (the town and the wagon) abbreviated to 'Stogy'; 'Stogy drivers', apparently, smoked a coarse cigar which became known as a 'stogie', and by the late C19 a 'stogie' was a generic cheap or roughly made cigar *US, 1980*. **3** a cigarette *US, 1995*

stokaboka *adjective* extremely enthusiastic *US, 1991*

stoke *verb* (from a male perspective) to have sex. Coined for the pun illustrated in the following citation *UK, 2001*. ▶ **stoke the boiler** in a swindle operated by telephone, to telephone a prospective victim *US, 1988*

stoked *adjective* **1** excited. A major word of the surf lexicon, it was the title and only word in the lyric of a 1963 Beach Boys song written by Brian Wilson *US, 1963*. **2** drug-intoxicated *US, 1986*. **3** drunk *US, 1964*

Stoke-on-Trent *adjective* homosexual. Rhyming slang for BENT, formed from the Staffordshire town *UK, 1992*

stoker *noun* a wave that excites surfers *US, 1977*

Stokey *noun* Stoke Newington, in north London *UK: ENGLAND, 1998*

Stolly; Stoli; Stoly *nickname* Stolichnaya™, vodka *UK, 1998*

stomach *noun* ▶ **stomach thinks your throat has been cut** to be extremely hungry *AUSTRALIA, 1950*

stomach Steinway *noun* the accordion *US, 1994*

stomp *verb* in computing, to mistakenly overwrite something *US, 1991*

stomp-down *adjective* excellent, admirable *US, 1968*

stomper *noun* **1** an aggressive, 'mannish' lesbian *US, 1967*. **2** the foot; a shoe, especially a heavy shoe. Also used in the variant 'stomp' *US, 1960*

stompie *noun* a cigarette butt, especially one saved for smoking later *SOUTH AFRICA, 1947*

stomping *noun* an attack, especially by kicking *UK, 1971*

stomp pad *noun* on a snowboard, the pad between the bindings *US, 1993*

stomps *noun* shoes *US, 1970*

stone *noun* **1** a diamond or other precious stone *SOUTH AFRICA, 1884*. **2** an Opel car. Citizens' band radio slang; pun on 'opal' *UK, 1981*. **3** crack cocaine; a piece of crack cocaine. A recurring rock metaphor *UK, 1996*. **4** a state of drug intoxication *US, 1980*. **5** a billiard ball *US, 1990*. **6** in motorcycle racing, a very slow racer *US, 1965*. **7** in the usage of youthful model road racers (slot car racers), a slow car *US, 1997*

stone *verb* **1** to render a drug user intoxicated, especially of marijuana *US, 1952*. **2** by extension, to amaze or impress someone *US, 1950*

stone *adverb* completely, utterly *UK, 1928*

Stone Age *noun* in computing, the years from 1943 until the mid-1950s *US, 1991*

stonebonker *noun* in horse racing, a horse sure to win a race. Popularised by radio race caller Cliff Caller, a fixture in Australia beginning in the mid-1960s *AUSTRALIA, 1989*

stoned *adjective* **1** intoxicated on a drug, usually marijuana *US, 1952*. **2** very drunk *US, 1952*. **3** exhilarated, unrelated to drugs *US, 1971*

stoned out *adjective* in a state of drug intoxication. An elaboration of STONED *US, 1952*

stoned out of your playpen *adjective* highly drug-intoxicated *UK, 2000*

stone ginger *adjective* absolutely certain. From the name of a horse that won virtually every race it ran *NEW ZEALAND, 1936*

stonehead *noun* a regular user of marijuana. A combination of STONED (drug-intoxicated) and HEAD (a user) *UK, 2002*

stone John *noun* a jail or prison *US, 1962*

stone jug *noun* a gullible fool; an easy dupe. Rhyming slang for 'mug' *UK, 1998*

stone me! used for registering surprise or exasperation. Execution by stoning was current in biblical times, which lends this innocent expletive a mildly blasphemous feel; the inspiration, however, could just as likely be STONES (testicles). However obscene the original intention, from the mid-1950s its popularity (and innocence) was spread by comedian Tony Hancock (1924–68) and the BBC *UK, 1958*

stone motherless *adjective* in horse racing, used for describing a horse running a distant last *AUSTRALIA, 1989*

stoner *noun* a regular or habitual user of marijuana; a drug user *US, 1988*

stoner moment *noun* a short interval in which a marijuana user succumbs to a mental or physical lack of energy or consistency. After SENIOR MOMENT *UK, 2004*

stones *noun* **1** the testicles *UK, 1154*. **2** courage. From 'stones' as 'testicles' and 'testicles' as 'courage' *US, 1990*. **3** crack cocaine *US, 1994*. **4** dominoes *US, 1959*

stone the crows! *verb* heavens above! *AUSTRALIA, 1927*

Stonewall Jackson *noun* used as a soubriquet for an extremely frugal person. Thomas 'Stonewall' Jackson was a general in the Confederate Army, killed by 'friendly fire' in 1863 *US, 1962*

stone work *noun* a jewellery robbery *US, 1949*

stoney *adjective* of drugs, capable of causing intoxication. From STONED (drug-intoxicated). Also known as 'stoney weed' *UK, 2003*

stoney weed *noun* marijuana. A combination of STONEY (capable of intoxicating) and conventional 'weed' or 'weed' as marijuana *UK, 2003*

stonker *noun* **1** anything impressive in its field *UK, 1997*. **2** the erect penis. A personal specialisation of something impressive *UK, 2001*

stonker *verb* **1** to make someone drunk *AUSTRALIA, 1947*. **2** to bring a halt to someone or something; to thwart, overcome or stop something *AUSTRALIA, 1964*

stonkered *adjective* **1** drunk *AUSTRALIA, 1918*. **2** very tired *NEW ZEALAND, 1984*

stonking *adjective* **1** excellent, great; used generally to add positive emphasis to adjectives of size or quality *UK, 1980*. **2** drunk. After the previous sense *UK, 2002*

stonk-on *noun* the erect penis *UK, 2003*

stony *adjective* **1** without money. A shortened form of STONY-BROKE *UK, 1886*. **2** used of a golf ball, extremely close to the hole, such that the making of the putt is a foregone conclusion. From the more conventional but still slangy 'stone dead' *US, 1985*

stony-broke; stone-broke *adjective* without money *UK, 1886*

stony lonesome *noun* prison *US, 1993*

stooge *noun* **1** a performer whose role in an entertainment is as the butt of a leading character's jokes, or straight man or feed *US, 1913*. **2** a person in a subservient position *UK, 1937*. **3** a petty criminal who confesses falsely to a crime committed by a more powerful villain and takes the rap for him *UK, 1999*

stooge *verb* to act as someone's lackey *US, 1939*

stookie *noun* a stiffly formal person; a fool; a stupid person. Extends from STOOKY (a plastercast) *UK: SCOTLAND, 1911*

stooky *noun* a plastercast on a broken arm or leg. From 'stucco' (a type of plaster) *UK: SCOTLAND, 1985*

stool *noun* a police informer. A shortened version of STOOL PIGEON *US, 1906*

stool *verb* to inform on *US, 1911*

stoolie; stooly *noun* a police informer. A shortened form of STOOL PIGEON *US, 1924*

stool magnet *noun* a person with bad luck *US, 1994*

stool pigeon *noun* a police informer *US, 1906*

stoop *adjective* used of work, usually agricultural, requiring the worker to bend at the waist to work near the ground *US, 1953*

stooper *noun* in horse racing, a bettor who examines discarded tickets on the ground in the hope of finding a winning bet *US, 1947*

stoosh *adjective* pretentious *JAMAICA, 2003*

stooshie; stushie; stushy *noun* an uproar. Scottish dialect *stushie UK: SCOTLAND, 2000*

stop *noun* sufficient marijuana for a single joint or pipe; hence, marijuana *SOUTH AFRICA, 1949*

stop-and-go *noun* **1** a traffic signal. Michigan Upper Peninsula Usage *US, 2003*. **2** the toe. Rhyming slang. Can be shortened to 'stop' *UK, 1992*

stop and start *noun* the heart. Rhyming slang *UK, 1992*

stop-at-a-winner *noun* in gambling, a conditional bet: an instruction to the bookmaker to halt a series of bets when a winning result is recorded *UK, 2001*

stop gun *noun* on the railways, a torpedo placed on the track to warn a train operator of a problem ahead *US, 1977*

stop it – I like it! used for registering a guilty pleasure, especially as a pretence that a partner's caresses are unwanted *US, 1970*

stop-over *noun* a short jail sentence, either empirically or in proportion to the crime involved *US, 1962*

stopper *noun* **1** a central nervous system depressant; a barbiturate *US, 1977*. **2** air or artillery fire used to prevent enemy ground troops from escaping *US, 1990*

stoppo driver *noun* a getaway driver *UK, 1996*

store *noun* **1** a betting operation *US, 1951*. **2** any rigged game or attraction in a carnival *US, 1985*. **3** in a big con swindle, the fake office, poolroom or betting establishment created for the swindle *US, 1940*. ▶ **your store is open** a catchphrase used to advise that your (trouser) fly is undone *CANADA, 1968*

store-bought *adjective* factory-manufactured cigarettes, as opposed to hand-rolled *US, 1969*

store choppers *noun* false teeth *US, 1975*

store dice *noun* inexpensive store-bought dice, not milled to casino-level tolerances *US, 1962*

store dick *noun* a department store's private detective *US, 1960*

stork bite *noun* a flat pink birthmark or capillary hemangioma *US, 1991*

storked *adjective* pregnant *US, 1945*

storm *verb* **1** in hot rodding, to perform very well *US, 1965*. **2** to attend a party to which you are not invited *TRINIDAD AND TOBAGO, 1969*

storm carpenter *noun* an untrained, unskilled, incompetent carpenter. The formation of storm-CRAFT is used with other crafts as well, such as 'storm mason' *TRINIDAD AND TOBAGO, 1831*

storm damage *noun* applied to a person of limited intelligence *UK: SCOTLAND, 1988*

stormer *noun* **1** any excellent thing *UK: SCOTLAND, 1985*. **2** an excellent performance in a sports match (hurling, soccer, Gaelic football) *IRELAND, 1996*. **3** a theatrical success *UK, 2001*. **4** in hot rodding, a fast car *US, 1958*

storming *adjective* excellent; exciting *UK, 2003*

Stormin' Norman *nickname* **1** US Army General H. Norman Schwarzkopf, commander of the anti-Iraq forces in the Persian Gulf war *US, 1991*. **2** Norm Van Brocklin (1926–83), quarterback for the Los Angeles Rams during their glory days (1949–57) and then for the Philadelphia Eagles (1958–60) *US, 1960*

storm-stayed *adjective* prevented from reaching home by a storm *CANADA, 1989*

stoush *noun* a fight; a brawl; fighting. Possibly a variant of Scottish dialect *stashie* (a commotion, disturbance, quarrel) which was recorded in C19 Aberdeen as 'stash' without the '-ie' suffix. During both World Wars used by servicemen to refer to the war, with a touch of jocular or ironic bravado *AUSTRALIA, 1893*. ▶ **deal out a stoush** to assault with violence *AUSTRALIA, 1900*

stoush *verb* to punch, to hit; to struggle, to battle *AUSTRALIA, 1893*

stove *noun* a truck or car heater *US, 1971*

stovebolt *noun* a Chevrolet or Chevrolet engine *US, 1965*

stovepipe *noun* **1** a distended, gaping anus produced by recent anal intercourse *US, 1995*. **2** a revolver *US, 1957*. **3** a jet aircraft *US, 1956*. **4** gossip. From the image of railwaymen gathered around a stove gossiping *US, 1977*. **5** a three-part bet in an illegal numbers gambling lottery, in which the bettor must correctly guess two of the three digits in the winning number and have the third digit be one of eight bet on *US, 1949*

stove up *adjective* injured, ill or exhausted *US, 1901*

stow *verb* ▶ **stow your chant** to stop talking *US, 1964*

STP *noun* a type of synthetic hallucinogen. Probably coined as an abbreviation of 'serotonin triphosphate' and as an allusion to the trademark name of an motor oil additive, and later de-abbreviated to 'serenity, tranquility and peace' *US, 1967*

St Pete *noun* in shuffleboard, a disc hidden midway on your opponent's side of the court *US, 1967*

str8 *adjective* straight, in all its senses *US, 1993*

str8 draw *noun* a move in an on-line game of hold 'em poker, when the player gambles on making a straight with the final card. A variant spelling of a conventional term *UK, 2003*

strack; strac *adjective* professional; neat; clean. Military slang *US, 1982*

Strad *noun* a *Strad*ivarius violin *UK, 1884*

straddle *noun* in poker, an increased bet made without looking at your cards *US, 1988*

straggler *noun* in horse racing, a winning bet that is not cashed in immediately after a race but, unlike an out ticket, is cashed in before the end of the day *US, 1982*

straight *noun* **1** a conventional person, blind to the values of a counter-culture *US, 1967*. **2** a factory-made cigarette *US, 1951*. **3** a house dweller. Used by late-1980s–early 90s counterculture travellers *UK, 1999*. **4** a heterosexual *US, 1941*. **5** simple vaginal intercourse *US, 1961*. **6** unadulterated tobacco *UK, 1978*. **7** in horse racing, a bet that a horse will win a race *US, 1976*

straight *adjective* **1** heterosexual *US, 1941*. **2** conventional, not part of the counterculture *US, 1960*. **3** not currently drug-intoxicated; no longer using drugs *UK, 1967*. **4** under the influence of drugs, or at least not suffering from withdrawal symptoms *US, 1946*. **5** correct *US, 1996*. **6** good, pleasing, acceptable *US, 1993*. **7** of an utterance, outspoken, straightforward *UK, 1894*. **8** honest, honourable, frank *UK, 1864*. **9** of alcoholic drinks, undiluted *US, 1874*. **10** without a 'minus' or 'plus' attached to a grade *US, 1968*. ▶ **go straight** to abandon a criminal lifestyle in favour of honesty *UK, 1940*

straight! honestly! it's a fact! *UK, 1897*

straight and narrow; straight *noun* an honest, conventional or virtuous way of life, especially when temptation is resisted. Always with 'the'; a shortening of 'the straight and narrow path' *UK, 1930*

straight arrow *noun* an honest or honourable person. From the proverbial expression, 'straight as an arrow' *US, 1969*

straight as a monk's cock *adjective* very honest *UK, 1999*

straight as a stiff *adjective* very honest or honourable. An elaboration of STRAIGHT (honest); punning the final posture of a STIFF (a dead body) with the impossibility of the dead being anything

other than honest. An interesting comparison with STIFF (to cheat) *UK, 2001*

straight as a string *adjective* used of a racehorse, fully exerting itself *US, 1976*

straight date *noun* conventional vaginal sex with a prostitute *US, 1972*

straight-down-the-line *adjective* very honest; used to describe someone who sticks to the rules. An elaboration of STRAIGHT *UK, 2001*

straight down the line *adverb* honestly *UK, 1996*

straight edge *adjective* reflecting a philosophy that promotes hardcore rock music, abstinence from drugs and abstinence from promiscuous sex. Probably coined by Ian Mackaye in the self-titled song 'Straight Edge' while Mackaye was the singer of the Washington D.C. band Minor Threat *US, 1983*

straighten *verb* **1** to bribe someone *US, 1923*. **2** to avenge someone. A part of TEDDY BOY culture *UK, 1959*. **3** to produce drug intoxication in someone *US, 1958*. ▶ **straighten out a curve** to enter a curve driving too fast and leave the road *US, 1962*

straightener *noun* a fist fight to settle an argument, to *straighten* matters out; a fair fight. A TEDDY BOY term *UK, 1956*

straighten out *verb* **1** to correct someone; to put someone right *UK, 1956*. **2** (of a drug addict) to cease drug use *UK, 2001*. **3** to feel the effects of a drug, relieving any pangs of withdrawal *US, 1966*. **4** to bring someone up to date *US, 1946*

straight face *noun* an facial expression that is hiding amusement or successfully restraining laughter *UK, 1897*

straight-faced *adjective* displaying a facial expression devoid of humour *UK, 1975*

straight flush wannabe *noun* in poker, a sequenced hand comprised of all red or all black suits, but not a flush. Impressive looking, but worth no more than any non-flush straight *US, 1996*

straight-goer *noun* a dependable, honest person *AUSTRALIA, 1899*

straight-leg *noun* an infantry soldier, unattached to a mechanised or airborne unit *US, 1951*

straight moniker *noun* a person's legal name *US, 1966*

straight puda *noun* the complete, whole truth *US, 1968*

straights *noun* straight pool or continuous pocket billiards *US, 1984*

straight shooter *noun* a glass or metal device used to smoke crack cocaine *US, 1995*

straight trade *noun* homosexual sex with a man who considers himself heterosexual *US, 1972*

straight trick *noun* vaginal sex between a prostitute and customer *US, 1972*

straight up *adjective* **1** used of an alcoholic drink or a drug, undiluted *US, 1973*. **2** a prison sentence, without reduction for good behaviour or other factors *US, 1969*. **3** pure, unadulterated *US, 1995*. **4** used of a person, especially a girl, thin *US, 1947*

straight up! honestly; used for emphasis *UK, 1959*

straight up and down *adverb* entirely *US, 1999*

straight up the platform *adverb* absolutely, completely, entirely *UK, 1999*

straight wire *noun* the whole truth *NEW ZEALAND, 1998*

strain *verb* ▶ **strain at the leash** to demonstrate a great eagerness. From the characteristic behaviour of a dog *UK, 1910*. ▶ **strain the potatoes; strain the spuds; strain your taters** to urinate *AUSTRALIA, 1965*

strange *noun* a new and unknown sexual partner *US, 1967*

strange *adjective* new, fresh, unknown, especially sexually *US, 1957*. ▶ **don't be strange** don't resist; don't hesitate. A polari catchphrase, always in the imperative *UK, 1967*

strangely weird; strangely *noun* a beard. Rhyming slang *UK, 1992*

stranger *noun* **1** used as a form of address emphasising the fact that the two people have not seen each other for a while *US, 1996*. **2** in poker, any card added to a hand by draw *US, 1988*

strangers *noun* in gin, cards in a hand that do not and cannot form a sequence *US, 1965*

strange stuff *noun* a new and different sex-partner *US, 1950*

strangle *verb* **1** to turn something off; to deactivate something *US, 1963*. **2** to prevent a horse from winning a race. Strictly, and originally, by pulling back on the reins so strongly that the horse is almost strangled *AUSTRALIA, 1949*. ▶ **strangle a darkie** to defecate *UK, 1985*

strap *noun* **1** a naughty or lascivious girl *IRELAND, 2000*. **2** a handgun. Recorded in UK prison use, August 2002 *US, 1991*

strap *verb* **1** to interrogate someone in a severe manner *UK, 1996*. **2** to have sex. Also used in the variant 'strap on' *US, 1971*

strap-hanger *noun* **1** a passenger on public transport who stands supported by an overhead strap (or other type of grip) *UK, 1905*. **2** a member of the armed forces, stationed well away from combat, accompanying troops into the field without having a specific role to play *US, 1986*

strap-on *noun* a dildo that is harnessed to a person's body *UK, 1999*

strapped *adjective* **1** armed, especially with a gun. From STRAP (a handgun) *US, 1993*. **2** short of money. Also appears as 'cash-strapped'. *US, 1857*

straps *noun* suspenders *US, 1945*

strap up *verb* to carry a pistol *US, 1998*

strat *noun* a cigarette *UK, 1996*

Strat *noun* a Fender '*Strat*ocaster' guitar, first manufactured in 1954 *US, 2004*

strat *verb* to deceive someone *BARBADOS, 1965*

straw *noun* **1** marijuana; a marijuana cigarette. Playing on GRASS or HAY *US, 1971*. **2** a hat *US, 1976*

strawb *noun* a strawberry *AUSTRALIA, 1985*

strawberries *noun* LSD bearing a strawberry design *UK, 1998*

strawberries and cream *noun* a variety of MDMA, the recreational drug best known as ecstasy, identified by the pink and white colours of a pill *UK, 2002*

strawberry *noun* **1** a woman who trades sex for crack cocaine *US, 1989*. **2** the female nipple. Usually in the plural *US, 1982*. **3** a tablet of mescaline. From the colour of the tablet *US, 1971*. **4** a bruise or scrape *CANADA, 1921*

strawberry fields; fields; strawberries *noun* LSD. Named after the drug-inspired imagery that is the Beatles song 'Strawberry Fields Forever', 1966. Strawberry Fields is an area of Liverpool *US, 1986*

strawberry jam *noun* **1** the corpse of a person who has died with massive injuries *US, 1987*. **2** an unspecified flammable substance *US, 1987*

strawberry patch *noun* a brakevan (caboose) seen from the rear at night. From the red lights *US, 1946*

strawberry ripple *noun* a cripple. Rhyming slang, from an ice-cream variety *UK, 1982*

strawberry shortcake *noun* amphetamine; MDMA, the recreational drug best known as ecstasy *US, 1970*

strawberry tablet; strawberry *noun* a variety of MDMA, the recreational drug best known as ecstasy. From the pink colour of the tablet *UK, 1996*

strawberry tart; strawberry *noun* the heart. Rhyming slang *UK, 1984*

straw boss *noun* an assistant foreman *US, 1894*

strawboss *verb* to work as an assistant foreman *US, 1977*

straw hat *noun* in the car sales business, a convertible top *US, 1953*

strawny *verb* to figure something out *CANADA, 1999*

straws *noun* strawberries. Greengrocers' abbreviation, both spoken and used in signage *UK, 1961*

stray *noun* a solitary enemy soldier. Borrowed from the lexicon of the cowhand, referring to stray cattle *US, 1991*

streak *noun* a thin person. Usually qualified (LONG STREAK OF MISERY; LONG STREAK OF PISS); in its unqualified form it is more often used in Australia and New Zealand but not exclusively so *AUSTRALIA, 1941*. ▶ **put a streak in it** to hurry *UK, 1968*

streak *verb* **1** to move at great speed *UK, 1768*. **2** to run naked through a crowd, especially at public events, either as a protest or out of exhibitionism. Adapted from the sense 'to go very fast' *US, 1966*

streak of misery *noun* a tall, thin, morose person *AUSTRALIA, 1961*

streak of pelican shit *noun* a tall, thin person *AUSTRALIA, 1969*

streak of piss *noun* an inconsequential or weak person. Adapted from LONG STREAK OF PISS (a tall, thin person) *UK, 2001*

streak of rust *noun* a railway *US, 1946*

streak of the squeak *noun* cowardice *UK, 2000*

streaky weather *noun* a changing weather situation *CANADA, 1990*

street *noun* **1** the essence of modern urban life for the poor, with suggestions of the underworld or the shadows between the underworld and the legitimate mainstream *US, 1967*. **2** in stud poker, a card. For example, the fifth card dealt is known as 'fifth street' *US, 1988*. ▶ **on the street** not imprisoned; released from prison *US, 1935*

street *adjective* **1** experienced in or possessing the necessary qualities for urban survival *US, 1980*. **2** having an admired-as-fashionable quality of being understood by or of urban youth. Abbreviated from STREETCRED in turn shortened from 'street-credibility', but also informed by STREET (the essence of modern urban life) *UK, 2001*

street bookie *noun* a bookmaker who takes bets on the street, without an established place of business *US, 1972*

street cat *noun* a man, especially a young black man, who spends his life on the edges of crime *US, 1976*

street cred *noun* an admired-as-fashionable quality of being understood by or of urban youth. Abbreviated from 'street-credibility' (late 1970s) *UK, 1981*

street divorce *noun* a domestic quarrel that ends in one spouse murdering the other *US, 2001*

street doctor *noun* a drug dealer *US, 1998*

streeter *noun* a person who spends his time fraternising and carousing on the street *US, 1968*

street-legal *adjective* used of a motor vehicle, in compliance with all motor vehicle laws *US, 1993*

street machine *noun* a car made for street driving *US, 1970*

street name *noun* a nickname by which you are known by acquaintances *US, 1983*

street person; street people *noun* a person living, or spending most of their time, on the street. A semi-voluntary, semi-political state that preceded 'homelessness' as a label *US, 1968*

streets ahead *adjective* absolutely superior *UK, 1898*

streets behind *adjective* greatly inferior. The natural opposite of STREETS AHEAD *UK, 1984*

streets better *adjective* greatly superior. A variation of STREETS AHEAD *UK, 1917*

street-smart *adjective* familiar with the human condition as played out in an urban setting *US, 1976*

street smarts *noun* an intuitive understanding of human nature as played out in urban reality *US, 1990*

street squirrel *noun* a person who rides a moped or small motorcycle with an attitude and style befitting a large motorcycle *US, 1992*

street sweeper *noun* a taxi driver who solicits customers on the street *US, 2004*

streetsy *adjective* of a manner of speech or vocabulary, having a contemporary urban quality *US, 1997*

street tax *noun* in an illegal drug-selling enterprise, the share of an individual's earnings paid to his gang *US, 1997*

streetwalker *noun* **1** a prostitute who seeks customers on the street *UK, 1592*. **2** in oil drilling, an operator who does not have an office *US, 1954*

street-wise *adjective* experienced in or possessing the necessary qualities for urban survival *US, 1981*

-strel *suffix* when combined with a music style, a singer in that style. From 'minstrel'. 'Teen angstrel' (a teen singer affecting angst) and 'popstrel' are noted by Susie Dent, *The Language Report*, 2003 *UK, 2003*

strength *noun* the essential facts; the pertinent details *AUSTRALIA, 1908*. ▶ **on the strength** used to signify agreement, import or sincerity *US, 1995*

stress-head *noun* a person who is habitually stressed; a constant worrier *AUSTRALIA, 1996*

stretch *noun* **1** a prison sentence; one year's imprisonment. A prison sentence of a number of years is given with the number of years preceding 'stretch' *US, 1821*. **2** a longer-than-normal limousine with extended seating. From 'stretch limousine' *US, 1982*. **3** the penis *UK, 2001*. **4** in poker, a hand consisting of a sequence of five cards. Known conventionally as a 'straight' *US, 1988*. ▶ **to do a stretch** to shoplift *NEW ZEALAND, 1985*

stretch *verb* **1** to serve time in prison. From STRETCH (a prison sentence) *US, 2002*. **2** to put someone to death by hanging *US, 1962*

stretched out *adjective* in trucking, travelling fast *US, 1971*

stretcher *noun* **1** a lie *UK, 1674*. **2** a substance added to a drug for the simple purpose of diluting it for increased profit when sold *US, 1970*

stretcher-case *noun* a person who is exhausted *UK, 2002*

stretchers *noun* shoe laces *US, 1962*

stretches *noun* years; a very long time. From STRETCH (a year's imprisonment) *UK, 2000*

strewth!; struth! used as an oath. A shortening of 'God's truth!' *UK, 1892*

strides *noun* **1** trousers. Being the tailored articles in which you 'stride' *UK, 1889*. **2** trousers that are reserved for messy jobs, especially in car customising *US, 1960*

strike! used as an expression of shock, surprise or astonishment. Short for STRIKE ME BLIND! or STRIKE A LIGHT! *AUSTRALIA, 1915*

strike a light! used as an expression of shock, surprise or astonishment *AUSTRALIA, 1922*

strike me! used for expressing great surprise *AUSTRALIA, 1874*

strike me blind!; strike me dumb!; strike me lucky! used for registering shock, surprise or astonishment. Other variations include calls on God to strike the speaker 'bountiful', 'vulgar', 'ugly' or 'pink'. The earliest variation recorded is 'strike me dumb' in Vanbrugh's *The Relapse*, 1696 and 'strike me blind!' appears in 1704; 'strike me lucky!' from 1849, was a popular catchphrase in Australia in the 1930s. Other Australian examples are listed below *UK, 1971*

strike me dead; strike me *noun* bread. Rhyming slang *UK, 1992*

strike me dead! used for expressing great surprise *AUSTRALIA, 1932*

strike me fat! used for expressing great surprise *AUSTRALIA, 1895*

strike me handsome! used for expressing great surprise *AUSTRALIA, 1955*

strike me pink! used for expressing great surprise *AUSTRALIA, 1892*

strike me purple! used for expressing great surprise *AUSTRALIA, 1915*

strike me roan! used for expressing great surprise *AUSTRALIA, 1917*

strike me up a gum-tree! used for expressing great surprise *AUSTRALIA, 1960*

strike-out *noun* a hospital patient who has died or lapsed into a neurologically depressed state *US, 1977*

Strike U *nickname* the US Naval Strike Warfare Center, Fallon, Nevada *US, 1991*

strillers; strill; strills *noun* a musical instrument, especially a piano; a musician. Polari; possibly from Italian *strillare* (to shriek).

Thus, for a pianist: 'strill homey' or 'strillers omee' (a piano man), or 'strill polone' (a piano woman) *UK, 1967*

Strine *noun* broad Australian English, specifically that form of Australian English which appeared in the books of Alastair Morrison. 'Strine' is supposedly how the word 'Australian' is said in the Australian accent. It is not a separate language or dialect, but rather a jocular celebration of the Australian accent utilising respelling, shifting word boundaries and much elision to give the impression that other words are being spoken, e.g. *sly drool* is Strine for 'slide rule', *Emma Chisit* for 'how much is it?', *laze and gem* for 'ladies and gentlemen', *let stalk Strine* for 'let's talk Australian' *AUSTRALIA, 1964*

string *noun* **1** being hoaxed; being kept under control *UK, 1958*. **2** the group of prostitutes working for a particular pimp *US, 1913*

string *verb* to manipulate a wire into a slot machine to trigger the free-play mechanism *US, 1985*

string bean *noun* a tall, thin person *UK, 2003*

string beans; strings *noun* jeans. Rhyming slang *UK, 1992*

stringer *noun* **1** in poker, an instalment bet or the person making it *US, 1988*. **2** in poker, a hand of five cards in sequence. Conventionally known as a 'straight' *US, 1967*. **3** a railway brakeman *US, 1977*. **4** a narrow strip of laminated wood on a surfboard *US, 1979*

stringie *noun* a string bag *AUSTRALIA, 1968*

strings *noun* **1** the female legs *US, 1963*. **2** spaghetti *US, 1956*

string up *verb* to execute someone by hanging *UK, 1964*

string vest *noun* a *pest*, a nuisance. Rhyming slang *UK, 1998*

strip *noun* **1** in a striptease show, the portion of the show in which the dancer removes her last garments *US, 1945*. **2** a neighbourhood *BAHAMAS, 1982*. **3** a thoroughfare in a town or city lined with bars, nightclubs, off-licences and restaurants *US, 1939*. **4** a Benzedrine™-soaked strip of paper from an inhaler, removed from the inhaler and ingested as a central nervous system stimulant *US, 1951*. ▶ **the Strip 1** the portion of Sunset Boulevard between Crescent Heights Boulevard and Doheny Drive, Los Angeles, California *US, 1951*. **2** Las Vegas Boulevard south of central Las Vegas, Nevada, lined with neon-signed hotels and casinos *US, 1971*. **3** a section of Yonge Street, between Dundas and Bloor, in central Toronto, Ontario. A flashy, noisy part of town *US, 1987*

stripe *noun* **1** a scar, usually the result of a razor slash. Hence the adjective 'striped' *UK, 1958*. **2** in the military, a promotion *US, 1968*

stripe *verb* to slash someone with a blade. Descriptive of the scar that is made *UK, 1958*

stripe me! used as a register of surprise or exasperation *UK, 1997*

striper *noun* in prison, an improvised cutting weapon *UK, 1996*

stripes *noun* **1** a referee in an athletic contest *US, 1997*. **2** in pool, the striped balls numbered 9 to 15 *US, 1984*. **3** in circus usage, tigers *US, 1981*

stripes and solids *noun* in pool, the game of eight-ball *US, 1974*

striping *noun* a severe reprimand. From STRIPE (to slash with a blade) *UK, 2000*

stripper *noun* **1** a striptease dancer (usually female), a performer who undresses creatively for the purpose of entertainment. Gypsy Rose Lee (Rose Louise Hovick, 1914–70) was, perhaps, the most famous of all strippers; in *Gypsy*, the musical biography (1962) by Stephen Sondheim, she discovers the word 'ecdysiast' to give her job description a veneer of respectability *US, 1981*. **2** a pickpocket *US, 1950*. **3** a car thief who targets newer cars that will be stripped for parts *US, 1962*. **4** a playing card that has been altered in a manner that facilitates its extraction from a full deck *US, 1962*

stripping hole; stripping pit *noun* a strip mine *US, 1997*

strippy *noun* in prison, a strip search *UK, 1996*

strips *noun* in prison, a segregation unit *UK, 1996*

stroke *noun* **1** an underhand, immoral or illegal trick *UK, 1970*. **2** praise or flattery. Almost always in the plural *US, 1964*. **3** appetite *IRELAND, 2000*

stroke *verb* **1** to flatter someone *US, 1979*. **2** to masturbate. Also 'stroke off' *US, 1986*. ▶ **stroke it 1** in car racing, to drive with care and caution *US, 1965*. **2** to perform badly on purpose *US, 1989*. ▶ **stroke the lizard** (of a male) to masturbate *US, 1971*

stroke book *noun* a magazine or book viewed while masturbating *US, 1967*

stroke mag *noun* a pornographic magazine. The 'stroke' thus inspired is a direct reference to masturbatory technique *UK, 1995*

stroke-me-off *noun* used as a humorous nickname for stroganoff, as in 'beef stroganoff' *US, 1985*

stroker *noun* **1** a petty thief *IRELAND, 1996*. **2** a hospital patient who has suffered a stroke *US, 1961*

stroll *noun* ▶ **the stroll** the collective activities on a street, mostly illegal, some involving sauntering as if innocently strolling *US, 1946*. ▶ **The Stroll** Seventh Avenue, New York *US, 1946*

stroller *noun* **1** a car *US, 1960*. **2** a stone on the surface of the field *CANADA, 1987*

stroll on! used for registering disbelief or surprise *UK, 1959*

strong *noun* alcohol *TRINIDAD AND TOBAGO, 1989*. ▶ **the strong of** the essential facts; the pertinent details *AUSTRALIA, 1908*

strong *verb* ▶ **strong it** to behave in an aggressive manner, or to take things to an extreme. A variation of COME ON STRONG *UK, 1964*

strong *adjective* **1** of a theatrical performance, very sexual *US, 1962*. **2** well-funded at the moment. Teen slang *US, 1958*. **3** flush with money *US, 1954*. ▶ **be going strong** to be prosperous, or enjoying continuing success, or full of energy and vigour *UK, 1898*. ▶ **come it strong** to behave with boldness; to overstate something *UK, 1837*. ▶ **come on strong** to behave aggressively or exhibit aggressive behaviour; to have a success *US, 1970*. ▶ **go strong on** to support or follow a particular course with great energy or investment *UK, 1844*

strongarm *noun* **1** a crime involving brute physical violence; a violent criminal *US, 1901*. **2** a person who lends physicality and a capacity for brutal physical force to the moment. Also called 'strongarm man' *US, 1907*

strong-arm *verb* to rob a place roughly or violently *US, 1903*

strong as a Mallee bull *adjective* physically strong *AUSTRALIA, 1990*

strong-back *adjective* sexually aggressive; virile *TRINIDAD AND TOBAGO, 2003*

strong box *noun* a prison cell, usually windowless; designed for disruptive prisoners *UK, 1996*

strong like moose *adjective* used humorously with a literal meaning. A catchphrase of US television in the 1950s and 60s, first from the Uncle Tenoose character on *The Danny Thomas Show* and then from Boris Bandanov of the *Rocky and Bullwinkle Show*; spoken with a thick Russian accent *US, 1968*

strong move to the hole *noun* a direct approach to seducing a girl. Application of a basketball term to sexual relations, punning on HOLE as 'the basket' in the basketball term and 'the vagina' in this usage *US, 1992*

stronk *noun* male and female sexual secretions. Recorded in the song 'The Ballad of Kirriemuir' in Martin Page's collection of World War 2 songs and balads, 'For Gawdsake Don't Take Me', 1976 *UK: SCOTLAND, 1976*

strop *noun* **1** a display of bad temper. From STROPPY (bad-tempered), ultimately from 'obstreperous' *UK, 1970*. **2** male masturbation. From the conventional action. Also variant 'stropping' *UK, 1992*

strop *verb* ▶ **strop the Mulligan** (of a male) to masturbate. Also variant 'stropping' *AUSTRALIA, 1971*

stroppy *adjective* **1** bad-tempered. Conventional 'obstreperous' wrongly abbreviated and understood *UK, 1951*. **2** stubborn, defiant *NEW ZEALAND, 1984*

struck *noun* a girl's steady boyfriend *US, 1963*

struck; struck by; struck with *adjective* charmed, attracted to or delighted by someone or something. From an older sense as 'bewitched' *UK, 1839*

structural engineering *noun* a well-constructed foundation garment, or garments; also applied to the uplifting effect that a well-designed and well-fitted brassiere can have on a woman's shape *AUSTRALIA, 1984*

structure *noun* the human body *JAMAICA, 2000*

struddle *verb* to fool with something you shouldn't. The word is from the German *strudeln* (boil, spout, proceed rashly) *CANADA, 1999*

strudel *noun* the 'at' sign (@) on a computer keyboard *US, 1991*

struggle *verb* **1** to dance *US, 1960*. **2** to experience a hangover *US, 2001*

struggle and strain *noun* a train *UK, 1931*

struggle and strain *verb* to train; to exercise. Rhyming slang *UK, 1992*

struggle and strainer; struggle *noun* a trainer (shoe). Rhyming slang, extended from STRUGGLE AND STRAIN (to train) *UK, 1992*

struggle-and-strife; struggle *noun* **1** a wife. Rhyming slang *UK, 1959*. **2** life; a life. Rhyming slang *UK, 1992*

struggle-buggy *noun* a broken-down car *US, 1946*

struggling *adjective* worn out; neglected *US, 2000*

strum *verb* to masturbate. Also variant 'strum off'. From the up and down stroking action that is strumming a guitar *UK, 1999*. ▶ **strum heads** to fight *US, 1990*. ▶ **strum the banjo** (of a woman) to masturbate. A surreal elaboration of STRUM (to masturbate) *UK, 2001*

strummed up *adjective* stimulated by drugs *US, 1972*

strung out *adjective* **1** addicted to a drug; in a poor state of physical and mental health as a result of drug addiction. Used as a participial adjective *US, 1958*. **2** obsessed with or overly concerned about an activity or condition; emotionally disturbed *US, 1973*. **3** extended *UK, 2001*. **4** in love; infatuated *US, 1968*

strunt *verb* to sulk *CANADA, 1990*

strychnine *noun* in craps, the point and number nine *US, 1950*

stub *verb* to kick, particularly a ball, especially in rugby *UK, 1947*

stubbie; stubby *noun* a small, squat beer bottle, now 385 ml; the contents of a stubbie. From the noun use of 'stubby' (short and squat) *AUSTRALIA, 1966*

stubbie guts *noun* a game in which frisbees are used to knock over stubbies *AUSTRALIA, 1993*

stubbie holder *noun* an insulating container for keeping a stubbie of beer cool whilst being held *AUSTRALIA, 1981*

stubble jumper *noun* a prairie farmer *CANADA, 1961*

stub down *verb* in the language surrounding the Grateful Dead, to move to better seats at a concert using ticket stubs for the better sections smuggled up by friends *US, 1994*

stube *noun* a tavern *US, 1950*

stuck *adjective* of a player in a game of poker or other gambling game, losing *US, 1974*. ▶ **get stuck in** to initiate or become vigorously involved in an activity *AUSTRALIA, 1941*. ▶ **get stuck into** to attack a task or a person vigorously *AUSTRALIA, 1941*

stuck on *adjective* infatuated by, or enamoured of, someone *US, 1886*

stuck-up *adjective* conceited; pretentious *UK, 1829*

stud *noun* **1** a man, especially a manly man *UK, 1895*. **2** used as a jocular term of address to a man *US, 1999*. **3** in homosexual usage, a person who plays the 'masculine' role sexually and emotionally in a relationship *US, 1961*. **4** amyl or butyl nitrite. Possibly derived from a brand marketed as a male sex-aid *UK, 1998*. **5** loose tobacco *US, 2002*

stud broad *noun* a lesbian *US, 1968*

stud duck *noun* in oil drilling, an important company official *US, 1954*

student *noun* an inexperienced drug user *US, 1952*

student tobacco *noun* marijuana. From a perception that those undergoing higher and further education are drug users *UK: SCOTLAND, 1996*

stud hustler *noun* a male homosexual prostitute who projects a tough, masculine image *US, 1963*

Studie *noun* a Studebaker car *US, 1950*

studio-fuel *noun* cocaine. Probably coined by cocaine-fuelled musicians *UK, 2003*

studly *adjective* **1** describes a man who is considered to be above average in his sexual adventuring *US, 1999*. **2** admirable *US, 1966*. **3** unpleasant; unpopular *US, 1960*

stud muffin *noun* a handsome, well-built man *US, 1992*

stud puppy *noun* an attractive person. A variation of STUD MUFFIN *US, 1989*

stud up *noun* in prison, a prisoner who attempts to abandon homosexual activity and return to his previous state of heterosexual celibacy *US, 1990*

study bunny *noun* a serious and diligent student *US, 1987*

stuff *noun* **1** a drug, especially heroin *US, 1929*. **2** used for any noun that the user cannot or does not wish to specify *UK, 1889*. **3** anything at all. Used as a euphemism for FUCK in constructions such 'I don't give a stuff about it' *NEW ZEALAND, 1969*. **4** in prison, anything of value *US, 1967*. **5** the female genitals *US, 1982*. **6** a woman as a sexual object *US, 1967*. **7** the male genitals *US, 1966*. **8** an effeminate homosexual man *US, 1976*. **9** in pool, spin imparted on the cue ball to affect the course of the object ball or the cue ball after striking the object ball *US, 1993*

stuff *verb* **1** used as an emphatic rejection; and euphemistically for 'fuck' in all senses *UK, 1955*. **2** to have sex from the male point of view *NEW ZEALAND, 1984*. **3** to block the pay chute of a casino slot machine with the expectation of returning later, unblocking the chute and retrieving the interim earnings *US, 1999*. **4** to persuade someone to buy something that they did not know they wanted to buy *US, 1997*. ▶ **stuff your face** to overeat; to eat greedily; to eat. An unconventional and over-active digestion would be required if this simple description of the apparent action was as accurate as the imagery *US, 1996*

stuffed *adjective* very tired *NEW ZEALAND, 2002*

stuffed shirt *noun* a person who is overly formal, aloof, and out of touch *US, 1913*

stuffer *noun* **1** a male homosexual who plays the active role in anal sex *US, 1949*. **2** a parachute rigger *US, 1991*. **3** in hot rodding, a supercharger *US, 1968*

stuffy *adjective* conservative; very conventional; straitlaced. Derives from STUFFED SHIRT *UK, 1895*

stugots; stugats *noun* the penis. From southern Italian dialect, adapted/corrupted by Italian-American immigrants *US, 1962*

stuk; stukkie *noun* a woman sexually objectified *SOUTH AFRICA, 1946*

stulper *verb* to stumble *CANADA, 1999*

stum *noun* any central nervous system depressant *US, 1980*

stumble biscuit *noun* a tablet of the recreational drug methaqualone, best known as Quaaludes™. From the lack of coordination associated with the drug *US, 1993*

stumblebum *noun* a poor and foolish drunk *US, 1932*

stumbler *noun* any barbiturate or central nervous system depressant *US, 1977*

stumbles *noun* a loss of coordination, especially as the result of drug or alcohol intoxication *US, 1971*

stumer *noun* **1** a fool. The spelling 'stumor' is also used *UK: SCOTLAND, 1985*. **2** a forged or bad cheque *UK, 1890*. **3** a mistake; a blunder; a mess *UK, 1983*

stump *noun* **1** the leg. Survives mainly in the phrase 'stir your stumps!' (start doing something!, get moving!) *UK, 1460*. **2** the penis. In a world where size matters, often but not always applied to a short penis *US, 1993*. **3** a shoe *US, 1973*

stump *verb* to challenge or dare someone *CANADA, 1959*

stump-broke *adjective* unconditionally obedient. From the quaint notion of a mule trained to step forward and then backwards for sex with a man standing on a stump *US, 1967*

stumpers *noun* shoes *US, 1971*

stump-floater *noun* heavy rain *CANADA, 2002*

stumphole whiskey *noun* strong, homemade whisky *US, 1971*

stump-jumper *noun* an infantry soldier *US, 1991*

stump ranch *noun* in the Canadian west, a poorly run farm *CANADA, 1989*

stump up; stump *verb* to pay *UK, 1833*

stumpy *noun* a short person. Often used as a term of address *US, 1997*

stunned *adjective* drunk *US, 1982*

stunned mullet *noun* used as the epitome of one who is dazed, stupid, foolish *AUSTRALIA, 1953*

stunner *noun* **1** an exceedingly attractive woman *UK, 1848*. **2** a person or thing of extraordinary excellence *UK, 1855*. **3** a pin-up, topless or soft-porn model. Adapted by the tabloid press from the earlier, and continuing use, as 'a good looking woman'. Often combined with 'Page 3', in reference to the *Sun* newspaper's daily placing of naked female breasts. The spellings 'stunna' and 'stunnah' also exist *UK, 1999*

stunning *adjective* **1** excellent; extremely good looking *UK, 1847*. **2** in computing, incomprehensibly stupid *US, 1991*

stunt *noun* in advertising, marketing, etc, an event contrived to attract attention and gain publicity. Still regarded as colloquial by those who keep up our standards *UK, 1878*

stunt *verb* to wear expensive clothes and jewellery as a display of conspicuous consumption; to show off *US, 2001*

stunt cock; stunt dick; stunt *noun* a male pornography performer who fills in for another performer who is unable to maintain an erection or ejaculate when needed *US, 2000*

stunt pussy *noun* a female pornography performer who fills in for another performer for the purposes of genital filming only *US, 2000*

stunts *noun* sex *US, 1994*

stupe; stoop *noun* a stupid person. Often, not always, used affectionately *UK, 1762*

stupid *adjective* **1** used to describe a 'smart' weapon that fails to function properly *US, 2003*. **2** good. The spelling 'stoopid' is also used *US, 1989*. ▶ **get your stupid on** to drink to the point of intoxication *US, 2003*

stupid *adverb* extremely *US, 1992*

stupid badge *noun* a temporary identification card worn by a worker who has lost or left his identification at home *US, 1955*

stupid-baker *noun* a Studebaker car *US, 1992*

stupidee *noun* a stupid or insignificant person *TRINIDAD AND TOBAGO, 1959*

stupid labour *noun* public labour *CANADA, 1987*

stupidness! used for expressing scorn *CAYMAN ISLANDS, 1985*

stupid, stupid used as an expression of utter disapproval. From the cry of 'stupid, stupid rat creatures!' in the *Bone* comic book *US, 1997*

sturgeon *noun* a surgeon *US, 1994*

stutter and stammer; stutter *noun* a hammer. Rhyming slang *UK, 1992*

stuvac *noun* especially in New South Wales, student holidays from school or university. From 'student vacation' *AUSTRALIA, 1970*

style *noun* graffiti *US, 1997*

style *verb* to conduct or carry yourself in a stylish manner, especially in an exaggerated, showy way *US, 1972*

stylee *noun* a style, determined by the cultural category that precedes it. A fashionable elaboration of 'style' *UK, 1997*

stylie *noun* a white person with dreadlocks *US, 1994*

stylin' and profilin' *adjective* very fashionable *US, 1988*

stylo milo *adjective* very fashionable *SINGAPORE, 2002*

sub *noun* **1** a submarine *UK, 1917*. **2** a subscription *UK, 1833*. **3** in publishing, a sub-editor *UK, 1859*. **4** a sexual submissive, a willing slave in a sado-masochistic relationship *US, 1987*. **5** the submissive performer in a pornographic sex scene *US, 2000*. **6** in prison, a subversive *UK, 1996*. **7** on an athletic team, a reserve player who may enter the game as a substitute for a starter *UK, 1849*. **8** a loan. An abbreviation of 'subsistence', with the loan characterised as a 'subsistence advance' *AUSTRALIA, 1989*. **9** a financial advance, especially when given against wages or salary *UK, 1866*. **10** a concealed pocket, used by a casino employee to hide stolen chips *US, 1980*

sub *verb* **1** to give or receive a financial advance *UK, 1874*. **2** to serve as a *sub*stitute *US, 1853*

sub *adjective* mentally *sub*-normal *UK, 1963*

subby *noun* a *sub*contractor *AUSTRALIA, 1978*

sub-deb *noun* a girl in her mid-teens *US, 1917*

sublime *adjective* ▶ **from the sublime to the gorblimey; from the sublime to the ridiculous** from one extreme to another *UK, 1984*

submarine *noun* **1** a marijuana cigarette, especially a large one *SOUTH AFRICA, 1946*. **2** a surfboard that is too small for the person using it. So named because the person forces the board under water *US, 1964*. **3** in the used car business, a car that has spent time submerged in water *US, 1975*. **4** a gambling casino scheme in which a stolen chip is slipped into the thief's trousers *US, 1977*. **5** an after-hours drinking session in a Rugby club *UK, 1984*

submarine *verb* **1** in tiddlywinks, to shoot a wink under another *US, 1977*. **2** to ride through tall grass *AUSTRALIA, 1951*

submarine belt *noun* in motor racing, a safety belt that clips onto the buckle of a lap belt and is attached to the chassis under the driver's seat *US, 1980*

submarine races *noun* used as a euphemism for foreplay in a car at a remote spot *US, 1967*

subway *noun* in roller derby, contact between skaters who are eligible to score before they reach the back of the pack of blocking skaters, taking them to the floor of the track *US, 1999*

subway dealer *noun* in a card game, a dealer who cheats by dealing some cards off the bottom of the deck *US, 1962*

Subway Sam *noun* a man who is partial to sex in subway toilets *US, 1966*

Subway silver *noun* ▷ *see:* MANHATTAN SILVER

subway tickets *noun* in a card game, cards that did not come off the top of the deck because of cheating in the dealing *US, 1988*

sub-Z *nickname* a Sub-Zero™ freezer. Collected in Berkeley, California, in 2000 *US, 2000*

such a bitter experience never again; such a bloody experience never again *nickname* the former Belgian airline 'Sabena'. Most airlines attract jocular mnemonics of their names *US, 2002*

such-a-much *noun* an important or self-important person *US, 1968*

suck *noun* **1** an act of oral sex *US, 1870*. **2** a sycophant *US, 1977*

suck *verb* **1** to be useless, unpopular, distasteful, of no worth. When the term came into currency in the US in the 1960s, sexual connotations made it a vulgar, taboo-ridden term. By the mid-1990s, all sense of taboo had vanished in the US except for older speakers for whom the sexual connotation remained inescapable. In UK English, the term, first used as a noun (1913) expressing contempt, never enjoyed the sexual implications found in the US. If anything, there was long an upper-class air to the term thanks in part to the 'Yah boo, sucks to you' catchphrase associated with Billy Bunter, a fat upper-crust schoolboy created by author Frank Richards *US, 1965*. **2** to perform oral sex *US, 1881*. **3** to consume alcoholic drinks *AUSTRALIA, 1960*. **4** in pool, to hit the cue ball with backspin that appears to draw or suck the cue ball backwards after it strikes the object ball *US, 1990*. ▶ **it sucks to be you** used for expressing a trace of commiseration in a situation that might call for a bit more *US, 1999*. ▶ **suck ass; suck arse** to behave subserviently. A variation of KISS ARSE/ASS *US, 1956*. ▶ **suck butt** to curry favour *US, 1997*. ▶ **suck cock** to perform oral sex on a man *US, 1941*. ▶ **suck diesel** to make rapid progress; to move rapidly, especially in a motor vehicle *IRELAND, 1997*. ▶ **suck face** to kiss, especially in a prolonged fashion. Hawaiian youth usage *US, 1982*. ▶ **suck milk** to be knocked off your surfboard and then be thrashed by a wave *US, 1991*. ▶ **suck out loud** to be very bad *US, 1994*. ▶ **suck salt** to experience difficulties *TRINIDAD AND TOBAGO, 1966*. ▶ **suck suds** to drink beer *US, 1947*. ▶ **suck the arse out of a durry** to smoke a hand-rolled cigarette to the very end *NEW ZEALAND, 1998*. ▶ **suck the big one** to be terrible *US, 1999*. ▶ **suck to the bulls** to act friendly with police *US, 1992*. ▶ **suck tubes** to

smoke marijuana *US, 1998*. ▶ **suck weight** to drink large amounts of liquids in a short period in order to gain weight to qualify for a sporting event *US, 2001*. ▶ **suck wind** to fail; to lose out. Hawaiian youth usage *US, 1972*. ▶ **suck your flavour; suck your flava** to copy your style *US, 1993*

sucka *noun* a fool; a dupe. Misspelling of SUCKER (a gullible individual) *US, 2000*

suck-ass *noun* a sycophant who curries favour in a self-demeaning fashion *US, 1980*

suck-ass *adjective* subservient; sycophantic; obsequious *US, 1985*

suck back *verb* to drink something *US, 1980*

sucked up *adjective* **1** weak; undeveloped physically *US, 2001*. **2** angry *US, 1989*

suckee-suckee *noun* oral sex performed on a man. From the patois of Vietnamese prostitutes during the war, embraced by soldiers *US, 1987*

sucker *noun* **1** a gullible individual *US, 1838*. **2** a fellow. Neutral but informal *US, 1980*. **3** someone who is unable to resist a stated temptation or addiction; an enthusiast *US, 1957*. **4** a thing *US, 1987*. **5** in caving and pot-holing, a caver who uses another's equipment while the owner is otherwise engaged. Examples of use include 'chair-sucker', 'rope-sucker', 'stove-sucker', etc *US, 2004*. **6** the buttocks *NEW ZEALAND, 1999*

sucker *verb* to deceive or trick someone *US, 1939*

sucker life *noun* conventional life, with a conventional job and conventional lifestyle *US, 1977*

sucker pocket *noun* the hip pocket, an easy pocket to pick *US, 1982*

sucker-punch *verb* to hit someone without warning, especially in the face *US, 1947*

sucker weed *noun* faked, adulterated or poor quality marijuana. WEED (marijuana) that can be sold to a SUCKER (someone gullible) *US, 1980*

sucker wild *adjective* completely unrestrained and uninhibited *US, 1969*

suck gas to breath nitrous oxide for pleasure *US, late 1960s*

suck-happy *adjective* obsessed with oral sex *AUSTRALIA, 1975*

suckhole *noun* **1** a sycophant; a flatterer; a toady; an unpleasant person *AUSTRALIA, 1943*. **2** a hole between private video booths in a pornography arcade or between stalls in a public toilet, designed for anonymous oral sex between men *US, 1987*

suckhole *verb* to behave in an ingratiatingly sycophantic manner *CANADA, 1961*

suck-holer *noun* a sycophant *NEW ZEALAND, 1998*

Suckie *nickname* Sauchiehall Street, Glasgow *UK: SCOTLAND, 1988*

suckie fuckie *verb* to perform oral sex on a man followed by sexual intercourse. Vietnam war usage *US, 1973*

sucking *noun* an act of oral sex *UK, 1869*

sucking wind *adjective* in firefighter usage, said of extremely smoky conditions *US, 1954*

suck job *noun* an act of oral sex *US, 1969*

suck-off *noun* an act of oral sex *US, 1995*

suck off *verb* to perform oral sex on either a man or woman, especially to the point of orgasm *UK, 1909*

suckout *noun* in surfing, a wave that is breaking fast in front of itself, creating a tunnel or tube *US, 1977*

suck out *verb* **1** to speed past a parked police car, drawing it into a chase *US, 1962*. **2** in poker, to win in the face of every known convention and probability *US, 1996*

suck points *noun* imaginary credits earned by obsequious ingratiation *US, 1994*

suck-up *noun* a sycophant *US, 2001*

suck up *verb* to seek favour through obsequious behaviour *UK, 1860*

suck wind! leave me alone! Hawaiian youth usage *US, 1981*

sucky *noun* a hollow wave *AUSTRALIA, 1985*

sucky *adjective* awful *US, 1984*

sucky face *noun* kissing *US, 2000*

sucrose *noun* money *US, 1951*

sudden death *noun* in sports, games and recreations, as diverse as league football and television quiz shows, a period of extra time during which the first to score or achieve a specified target wins. Originally 'a single toss of the dice' *UK, 1834*

suds *noun* **1** beer *US, 1904*. **2** a large amount of money *US, 1945*

suds artist *noun* a habitual beer drinker *AUSTRALIA, 1972*

sue *verb* ▶ **sue the ass off someone; sue someone's arse off** to take a legal action against somebody in pursuit of punitive damages *US, 2002*

suede *noun* a black person *US, 1973*

suedehead; suede *noun* a member of a late 1960s youth fashion and gang movement, characterised by a close-cropped scalp and smart utilitarian wear, associated with football hooliganism, racist violence and neo-Nazism. This lexicographic development matches exactly the SKINHEAD fashion's further growth; 'suede' is the velvety surface of leather and thus describes the soft nap on a previously shaven head *UK, 1982*

sufferation *noun* hard times *TRINIDAD AND TOBAGO, 2003*

sufferin' sheepdip! used for expressing disapproval. A signature line of the Colonel Sherman Potter on *M*A*S*H* (CBS, 1972–83). Repeated with referential humour *US, 1983*

sug *noun* used as an affectionate term of address. A shortened form of SUGAR *US, 1947*

sugar *noun* **1** used as a term of endearment. A distinct southern ring. Variation include 'sugar-pie', 'sugar-babe', 'sugar-baby', etc *US, 1930*. **2** diabetes *US, 1968*. **3** a type of snow suitable for skiing *UK, 1968*. **4** heroin; powdered heroin adulterated with sugar. From the appearance *US, 1977*. **5** cocaine. A white powder *UK, 1998*. **6** sand *US, 1977*. **7** money *US, 1951* ▷*see:* SUGAR LUMP

sugar! used an all-purpose euphemism for 'shit', especially as an exclamation. Pronunciation often hesitates over the 'sh' before committing itself to 'shit' or 'sugar', possibly from a combination of 'shit' and BUGGER!, RECORDED IN 1901 AS 'I'll be sugared!' *UK, 1995*

sugar and honey; sugar *noun* money. Rhyming slang *UK, 1859*

sugar and spice *noun* ice, especially as served with a drink. Rhyming slang *UK, 1992*

sugar and spice; sugar *adjective* nice. Rhyming slang; not especially sarcastic in use *UK, 1992*

sugarbeeter *noun* a resident of the Lower Peninsula of Michigan. Michigan Upper Peninsula usage *US, 2003*

sugar block *noun* crack cocaine *UK, 1998*

sugar candy *noun* brandy. Rhyming slang *UK, 1992*

sugar candy *adjective* useful, generally in a negative context. Rhyming slang for 'handy' *UK, 1992*

sugar cube *noun* LSD. From the method of ingesting a dose of the drug dripped onto a sugar cube *US, 1967*

sugar daddy *noun* an older man who supports or helps support a young lover. With occasional playful variants *UK, 1926*

sugar dish *noun* the vagina. A variation of C19 obsolete 'sugar basin' (the vagina) *US, 1998*

sugar down *verb* to dilute powder narcotics, especially with powdered milk sugar (lactose) *US, 1970*

sugarhead *noun* strong, homemade whisky *US, 1999*

sugar hill *noun* a brothel *US, 1987*

sugaring-off *noun* in Canadian maple syrup making, the process of boiling the maple sap down to syrup or sugar *CANADA, 1995*

sugar lips *noun* a smooth talker *AUSTRALIA, 1989*

sugar lump; sugar *noun* LSD. Probably from 'sugar cubes' which are sometimes used as a medium for taking the drug *UK, 1973*

sugar pimp *noun* a pimp who controls his prostitutes through charm and attention *US, 1972*

sugar report *noun* during war, a letter from home, especially from a girlfriend *US, 1991*

sugar shack *noun* a small hut built for boiling down maple sap to make maple syrup *CANADA, 1998*

sugar stick *noun* the penis. Rhyming slang for PRICK *UK, 1992*

sugar tit *noun* any cherished object or habit *US, 1971*

sugar up *verb* to curry favour *US, 1964*

sugar weed *noun* marijuana which has been adulterated and bulked-out with sugar water or honey *US, 1969*

suicide alley *noun* in shuffleboard, a quarter of the opponent's side of the court *US, 1967*

suicide axle *noun* in hot rodding and drag racing, a special axle assembly that allows a lower front end *US, 1965*

suicide blonde *noun* a girl or woman who has dyed her hair blonde at home. From the pun: 'dyed by her own hand' *US, 1962*

suicide box *noun* in trucking, a sleeper added to a conventional cab. So named because of the danger presented to anyone sleeping in the box should the truck jackknife *US, 1971*

suicide club *noun* a mythical group of jockeys who ride in steeplechase races *US, 1951*

suicide clutch *noun* a foot-operated clutch on a motorcycle. If your foot slips off when stopped, it engaged the clutch *US, 1966*

suicide door *noun* on a car, a door that hinges at the back and opens towards the rear *US, 1993*

suicide jockey *noun* **1** the driver of a vehicle hauling dangerous cargo *US, 1976*. **2** a dangerous driver *UK, 1981*

suicide king *noun* in a deck of cards, the king of hearts. It appears that he is plunging a knife into his head *US, 1988*

suicide season *noun* the few months leading up to the wet season in Australia's tropical north *AUSTRALIA, 1975*

suicide seat *noun* the front, passenger seat in a car *US, 1992*

suicide stew *noun* a combination of central nervous system depressants and alcohol *US, 1966*

suit *noun* **1** an executive; a person of authority but no creativity. The term usually suggests a them-against-us mentality, with 'them' being the executives who wear suits; pejorative *US, 1979*. **2** in prison, an official non-uniformed visitor *UK, 1996*

suitcase *noun* the rectum *US, 1992*

suitcase *verb* to conceal drugs inside a condom or balloon inside a body orifice *US, 1987*

suitcase farmer *noun* a farmer who also works in the town *CANADA, 1959*

suitcase pimp; suitcase *noun* a boyfriend, agent or other male who accompanies a female pornography performer to the set. Not flattering *US, 1995*

suited and booted *adjective* well-dressed *UK, 1998*

suit up *verb* to place a condom on a penis *US, 2000*

sulker *noun* in horse racing, a moody horse *US, 1951*

sulphate; sulph *noun* amphetamine *sulphate UK, 1996*

Sumatran red *noun* a variety of marijuana *UK, 1996*

sumbitch; sombitch *noun* a son of a bitch. A southern corruption *US, 1972*

summat *noun* something. A phonetic slovening *UK, 1984*

Summerland Donkey Cock *noun* a variety of marijuana from British Columbia *CANADA, 2002*

summer sausage *noun* the female partner of a boy in a summer romance at camp *CANADA, 1997*

SUMO shut up and move on. An acronym from the world of office jargon *UK, 2005*

sun *noun* ▶ **the sun shines out of someone's arse** said of a person who is considered perfect *UK, 2000*. ▶ **the sun's drawing her backstays; the sun's got her backstays down** lines in the sky coming down from the sun, predicting rain or bad weather *CANADA, 1968*

sunbathers *noun* in poker, a pair of queens dealt face-up *US, 1988*

sunbeam *noun* a piece of cutlery or crockery that was not used during a meal and thus needs no washing up *AUSTRALIA, 1981*

sun belt *noun* the southern states in the US *US, 1969*

sunburnt *adjective* used for describing playing cards that have been left in the sun to discolour slightly to aid a cheat in identifying them in another player's hand *US, 1988*

Sunday *noun* a surprise blow from the blind side *US, 1967*

Sunday *verb* to hit someone from their blind side *US, 1993*

Sunday best *noun* **1** your smartest clothes. Such clothes were originally reserved for Sunday wear *UK, 1846*. **2** a vest. Rhyming slang, with a fine sense of irony *UK, 1992*

Sunday-go-to-meeting *adjective* used of clothes, suitable for wearing to church. Intentionally rural *US, 1831*

Sunday morn *noun* an erection (of the penis). Rhyming slang for HORN *UK, 1992*

Sunday popper *noun* an occasional user of an addictive drug *US, 1966*

Sunday punch *noun* a blow from a person's blind side *US, 1968*

Sunday run *noun* in circus and carnival usage, a long trip between engagements *US, 1981*

Sunday school show; Sunday school *noun* a circus or carnival with no crooked games and no performances with sexual content *US, 1980*

Sunday science lecture *noun* any presentation made with a captive audience *ANTARCTICA, 1997*

Sunday suit *noun* no clothes at all *US, 1976*

sundowner *noun* **1** an itinerant traveller. So-called from their habit of arriving at a country property just on sundown so that they can ask for sustenance without being given any manual labour *AUSTRALIA, 1868*. **2** a senile patient who is quiet during the day but becomes agitated at dark *US, 1983*. **3** any alcoholic drink enjoyed at the end of the day. Recorded in India, Singapore, the East Indies and Australia; also in south and east Africa *UK, 1938*. **4** a VF-111 combat aircraft. The plane was first deployed in 1942 in the Pacific with the mission of shooting down Japanese 'Suns'. Deployed in Korea and Vietnam *US, 1990*

sun gonna shine *noun* a type of bet in an illegal numbers game lottery *US, 1957*

sun gun *noun* in the television and film industries, a portable, intense light *US, 1990*

sunker *noun* in Newfoundland, a rock or reef just underwater *CANADA, 1962*

sun kink *noun* an expansion of railway track caused by hot weather conditions *US, 1975*

sunner *noun* a thief who snatches a chain from the wearer's neck. Recorded by a Jamaican inmate of a UK prison, August 2002 *UK, 2002*

sunnies *noun* sunglasses *AUSTRALIA, 1981*

sunny side up *adjective* of eggs, fried, with the yolk on top *US, 1901*

sun parlour *noun* a brakevan (caboose) cupola *US, 1977*

sunrise *noun* a Toyota car. Citizens' band radio slang; plays on SUNSET (a Datsun car); also of Japanese manufacture, and Japan's identity is 'the land of the rising sun' *UK, 1981*

sunset *noun* a Datsun car. A weakly derogative play on Sunny, a late-1960s Datsun brand *UK, 1981*

sunshine *noun* **1** used as a form of address, often patronising with an underlying note of disapproval or threat *UK, 1972*. **2** LSD *US, 1971*

Sunshine Coast *noun* **1** Vancouver, British Columbia *CANADA, 1965*. **2** Brisbane, Australia *AUSTRALIA, 1999*

sunspots *noun* in computing, the purported reason for an unanticipated error *US, 1991*

suntans *noun* a summer-weight tan military uniform *US, 1937*

sup *noun* supper *US, 1969*

s'up? used as a greeting. A very slurred 'what's up?' *US, 1981*

super *noun* **1** a *super*intendent, especially of an apartment building *AUSTRALIA, 1857*. **2** a *super*numerary *UK, 1838*. **3** high-octane or top-grade petrol *UK, 1967*. **4** in carnival usage, a handsome watch displayed as a prize *US, 1981*

super *adjective* excellent *UK, 1895*

super- *adjective* in combination with a person, animal or thing, well above the usual standard of its type. Under the influence of Nietzsche's philosophical concept, expanded by George Bernard Shaw's play *Man and Superman*, 1903, and made most familiar by *Super*man, a US comic strip *super*hero first seen in 1938 *UK, 2003*

super *adverb* very. Adds a melodramatic, gushing flavour to the intensification *US, 1968*

superbissimo *adjective* excellent; superb. A decorative elaboration of 'superb' formed, loosely, with an Italian suffix *UK, 2003*

superblush *noun* in poker, a sequence of cards in a red suit – diamonds or hearts *US, 1996*

super C *noun* ketamine hydrochloride, an anaesthetic used as a hallucinogen *US, 1994*

supercalifragilisticexpialidocious used in various contexts with various meanings by children fascinated with the size of the word. Popularised, but apparently not coined, in the 1964 film *Mary Poppins*. The term did not appear in the book, and so some credit must be given to Robert B. Sherman, who wrote the lyrics of the song. According to *The Straight Dope* (6th August 2002), songwriters Barney Young and Gloria Parker brought a copyright infringement suit, claiming that they had written a song with a variant spelling of the term in 1949. In the 1960s, the term replaced 'antidisestablishmentarianism' in US youth 'longest word' contests *US, 1964*

super chicken *noun* in trucking, a truck owned by Yellow Freight Systems *US, 1976*

super citral *noun* an especially narcotic variety of marijuana *UK, 2003*

super dope *noun* marijuana with formaldehyde added *US, 1982*

superduper; super *noun* a hydrogen bomb *US, 1951*

super-duper *adjective* exceptionally good. Childish, or intentionally evocative of childishness *US, 1940*

superfly *noun* **1** a drug dealer. From the film *Superfly*, 1972 *US, 1973*. **2** a curly hairstyle popular with black men and women in the mid-1970s *US, 1975*

superfly *adjective* extremely fashionable, attractive, and appealing *US, 1974*

supergrass *noun* **1** an informer who gives the police substantial amounts of information, or who informs on a major crime or terrorist operation. Bertie Smalls, a notorious or legendary (depending on your point of view) small-time robber turned police informer became, in 1973, the original 'supergrass' *UK, 1978*. **2** good quality marijuana; phencyclidine, the recreational drug known as PCP or angel dust; a combination of the two *US, 1977*

super hopper *noun* a Citroen car. Citizens' band radio slang *UK, 1981*

super joint *noun* phencyclidine, the recreational drug known as PCP or angel dust *US, 1982*

super Ketama *noun* a superior grade of hashish from the Ketama region of Morocco *UK, 2003*

super kools *noun* phencyclidine, the recreational drug known as PCP or angel dust. Because the addition of PCP makes Kools™, a brand name cigarette and hence any cigarette, 'superior' *US, 1997*

superman *noun* **1** a variety of MDMA, the recreational drug best known as ecstasy, identified by the embossed Superman shield-shaped 'S' motif *UK, 2002*. **2** a variety of LSD identified by a cartoon graphic of the comic book and film superhero *UK, 1996*

Super Mario *noun* a variety of MDMA, the recreational drug best known as ecstasy, identified by the embossed Super Mario™ motif *UK, 2002*

Supermax *noun* the Penitentiary Administrative Maximum facility (the highest security prison in US) *US, 1994*

super pot *noun* marijuana which has been soused in alcohol then dried *US, 1967*

Super Scooper *noun* a water bomber, with a huge scoop for filling at speed from a lake or waterway, to dump on fires CANADA, 1994

superskunk *noun* an extremely potent marijuana UK, 1999

superslab *noun* a major road. Citizens' band radio slang, elaboration of SLAB US, 1976

super-snooper *noun* a special inspector employed by the former Department of Health & Social Services to uncover fraudulent claims UK, 1983

super-snoopy *noun* a helicopter with a camera that has the capability to take close-up pictures from a kilometre's distance UK, 1980

superstud *noun* a man with superior sexual prowess, or one reputed to be so lucky. Enhancement of STUD UK, 1997

supersweet *adjective* excellent US, 2002

Super T *noun* Tennants Super™, a super strength lager UK, 1997

super Thai *noun* an 'everyday' variety of marijuana UK, 2003

superweed *noun* marijuana, especially if of extra strength UK, 1996

super-yankee *noun* a multiple bet, gambling on 5 different horses in a specific combination of 26 win stakes or 52 each-way. Also known as a CANADIAN UK, 2001

supes *noun* a superior; a respectful form of address. Black usage UK, 2000

supon *noun* cornmeal mush CANADA, 1955

supremo *adjective* excellent; extreme US, 1979

sure *adjective* ▶ **be sure and** take care, don't fail to do something UK, 1892

sure as Christmas certain UK, 1959

sure as eggs is eggs absolutely certain, without a doubt. Early usage recorded as 'as sure as eggs be eggs' this idiom is now so familiar that even the shortening to 'sure as eggs' is understood UK, 1699

sure as God made little apples; sure as God made little green apples very certain. The earliest form is 'little apples'; the second form appears to derive from the song by Bobby Russell, 'Little Green Apples', 1968, in which it is likely that 'green' is added for the scansion of the lyric UK, 1874

sure as shit and taxes very certain US, 1957

surefire; sure shot *adjective* certain to succeed or prevail US, 1901

Sure. I knew you could. used as a sarcastic expression of great doubt. A borrowing from the children's television programme *Mr Rogers* US, 1981

sure off *verb* in an illegal numbers gambling lottery, to insure numbers that are the object of heavy betting US, 1949

sure pops *noun* dice that have been heavily weighted and are likely to produce the desired results US, 1950

sure thing certainly. From the conventional sense (a certainty) US, 1896

sure-thing man *noun* in carnival usage, a confederate who is hired to play and win a game in order to generate business US, 1981

surf *verb* ▶ **surf the crimson tide** to experience the bleed period of the menstrual cycle US, 1995

surface *verb* **1** to wake up; to get up; to get up and start the business of the day. Probably of Naval origins, from a submarine surfacing UK, 1963. **2** to come out of hiding; to leave a surreptitious existence and become more public US, 1971

surfboard Suzie *noun* a stereotypical woman who spends time at the beach admiring male surfers US, 1990

surf bum *noun* a surfing enthusiast who haunts popular beaches UK, 1958

surf bunny *noun* a woman who spends a great deal of time at the beach, associating with surfers and/or surfing US, 1980

surf dog *noun* an avid, veteran surfer US, 1991

surfie *noun* a surfer AUSTRALIA, 1962

surfie chick *noun* a young woman companion of a surfer AUSTRALIA, 1979

surfing knobs; surfing bumps *noun* calcium deposits near the knees and feet caused by extended contact with a hard surfboard US, 1964

surf nazi *noun* a zealous, devoted surfer US, 1988

surf-o *adjective* obsessed with surfing US, 1991

surf rat *noun* a beginner surfer US, 1990

surf safari *noun* a trip in search of good surfing conditions US, 1964

surf's down used for expressing dismay at poor surf conditions US, 1977

surf silks *noun* silk or nylon swimming trunks worn under a wetsuit US, 1977

surge *noun* surgical spirit as an alcoholic drink UK, 2000

surgical truss *noun* a bus. Rhyming slang UK, 1998

surprise party *noun* in poker, a hand that should not win, that is not expected by its holder to win, but that wins US, 1996

surprise! surprise! with heavy irony or sarcasm, used as an expression of disappointment, or resignation that the expected worst has happened UK, 1964

Surrey Docks *noun* syphilis; hence any sexually transmitted infection. Rhyming slang for POX, formed on a famous south-of-the-river location UK, 1974

sus; suss *noun* **1** suspicion UK, 1936. **2** an arrest on suspicion; a person being arrested for loitering with suspicion UK, 1977

sus; suss *adjective* suspicious; suspect UK, 1958

Susie College *noun* a stereotypical female college student US, 1970

suspense *noun* the time allotted to complete an action US, 1986

suspicion *verb* to suspect someone US, 1834

suss *noun* common sense UK, 1977

suss *verb* to suspect, or discover the truth about, someone or something. A shortened form of 'suspect' UK, 1953

sussed *adjective* **1** having knowledge about something; well informed UK, 1984. **2** arrested as a suspected person loitering UK, 1977

sussies *noun* suspenders UK, 1995

susso *noun* **1** government sustenance provided during the depression of the 1930s AUSTRALIA, 1941. **2** a person receiving government sustenance AUSTRALIA, 1947

suss out; suss; suss on *verb* to work out, discover, find, ascertain or understand something. Extended from various senses of SUS and SUSS UK, 1962

sussy *adjective* suspicious, in both active and passive senses UK, 1965

suzie *noun* a Suzuki motorcycle (manufactured since 1936 but only popular in the UK from about 1960) UK, 1979

Suzie Wong; suzie *noun* **1** a song UK, 1998. **2** an unpleasant smell. Rhyming slang for PONG, formed from the film *The World of Suzie Wong*, 1960 UK, 1998

Suzy Robincrotch; Suzy Rottencrotch; Suzy *noun* during the Vietnam war, the generic girlfriend back home US, 1991

Suzy Sorority *noun* a stereotypical sorority member who looks, dresses, talks and lives the part US, 1974

swa *noun* southwest Asia US, 1998

swab *noun* a roll of money US, 1965

swab *verb* ▶ **swab the deck** to perform oral sex on a woman US, 1964

swabbie; swabby *noun* a sailor US, 1944

swab jockey *noun* a marine US, 1958

swacked *adjective* drunk or drug-intoxicated US, 1945

swag *noun* **1** stolen goods; loot; bounty. Derives from the earlier sense 'a shop' hence the contents seen as the object of theft; originally, especially linens and clothes rather than precious metals and stones UK, 1794. **2** contraband. Used both as an adjective and a noun US, 1951. **3** free merchandise or tickets to concerts handed out by music recording companies US, 1997. **4** the possessions of an itinerant traveller rolled up in a blanket and carried from place to place. The 'swag' and the 'swagman/swaggie' are Australian cultural icons *AUSTRALIA, 1841*. **5** a person's possessions when travelling light. Metaphoric use of the swagman's swag *AUSTRALIA, 1987*. **6** a bedroll *AUSTRALIA, 1865*. **7** clothes. The best known meaning of 'swag' (stolen property) originally referred especially to linens and clothes. Here the sense narrows to the type of goods with no suggestion of theft *UK, 1999*. **8** money *US, 1976*. **9** a large amount of something *AUSTRALIA, 1882*. **10** inferior quality marijuana. It seems unlikely that this usage should derive from the C19, now obsolete adjective 'swag' (worthless) but stranger etymologies have happened *US, 2001*. ▶ **on the swag** carrying a swag and travelling as an itinerant *AUSTRALIA, 1982*

SWAG *noun* a joking and derogatory prediction or estimate. A 'scientific wild-assed guess' *CANADA, 1995*

swag *verb* **1** to move articles in a hurried manner. Extends from the sense 'to hustle' *UK, 1956*. **2** to hustle or hurry someone *UK, 1958*

swag *adjective* **1** stolen *US, 1979*. **2** inferior *UK, 2004*

swag bag *noun* a bag for loot or special contraband *US, 1974*

swaggie *noun* a swagman *AUSTRALIA, 1891*

swagman *noun* an itinerant man looking for work; a tramp *AUSTRALIA, 1859*

swag off *verb* to lock a prisoner's possessions away *UK, 1996*

SWAK; SWALK; SWANK written on an envelope, or at the foot of a lover's letter, as lovers' code for 'sealed with *a* kiss'. Embellishments included a 'loving' kiss and a 'nice' kiss. Widely known, and well used by servicemen, then a nearly mandatory sign-off line in any American teenage love letter of the 1950s and 60s, now a part of the coded vocabulary of texting *UK, 1925*

swallow *noun* a drink of alcohol *UK, 1822*

swallow *verb* **1** to easily accept something as true *UK, 1594*. **2** to accept something that has happened without complaint or acknowledgement. A shortening of 'swallow your pride' *UK, 2000*. ▶ **swallow a dictionary** to be loquacious or sesquipedalian; to habitually use long or erudite words *AUSTRALIA, 1957*. ▶ **swallow a gun** to commit suicide by gunshot to the mouth *US, 1981*. ▶ **swallow spit** to stop talking; to be quiet *US, 1993*. ▶ **swallow the olive** to lose your composure and concentration *US, 1961*

swallow and sigh *noun* a collar and tie. Rhyming slang *UK, 1938*

swallower *noun* a person who swallows semen during oral sex *AUSTRALIA, 1987*

swally *noun* a drink; a drinking session. Glasgow slang from 'swallow' *UK: SCOTLAND, 1985*

swami *noun* a poker player with the annoying habit of coaching other players *US, 1996*

swamp *verb* to drink an alcoholic beverage after eating *UK, 1983*

swamp-donkey *noun* a particularly unattractive woman *UK, 1998*

swamped *adjective* drunk *US, 1945*

swamper *noun* **1** a labourer who loads or unloads cargo *US, 1981*. **2** rubber boots worn during mud season. Michigan Upper Peninsula usage *US, 2003*.

swamp rat *noun* any person living near or coming from near the great swamps of the southern US *US, 1978*

swampy *noun* a rural New Englander who is thoroughly and steadfastly rural. An abbreviation of SWAMP YANKEE *US, 1963*

swamp Yankee *noun* a rural New Englander who is thoroughly and steadfastly rural *US, 1939*

swan *verb* ▶ **swan about; swan around; swan off** to move idly or with no apparent purpose (although pleasure is often presumed). The imagery of swans gliding on water; originally military, of armoured vehicles (perhaps sliding over mud) *UK, 1942*

swan dive *noun* to pretend to be injured or fouled while playing a team sport *CANADA, 2002*

Swanee river *noun* the liver. Rhyming slang *UK, 1992*

swank *noun* a drink of sweetened water *BARBADOS, 1965*

swank and wank *verb* to preen in a self-satisfied manner. A neat, rhyming combination of 'swank' (to behave in a pretentious manner) and WANK (to masturbate) *UK, 2002*

swanky *adjective* showy; conceited; pretentious; pretentiously grand. First recorded as Wiltshire dialect *UK, 1842*

Swan Lake; swan *noun* a cake. Rhyming slang, formed from the ballet by Tchaikovsky *UK, 1992*

swannie *noun* a bush shirt. From the branded Swanndri™ shirt *NEW ZEALAND, 1998*

swanson *noun* a coward *US, 2004*

swap *verb* ▶ **swap cans** (used of a male homosexual couple) to take turns as the active participant in anal sex *US, 1965*. ▶ **swap lies and swat flies** to engage in prolonged, aimless conversation *US, 1962*. ▶ **swap slop** to kiss *US, 1947*. ▶ **swap spit** to kiss long and hard *US, 1952*

swap out *verb* to exchange roles in homosexual sex after one partner achieves satisfaction *US, 2002*

swapper *noun* a married person who engages in spouse swapping at sex parties *US, 1967*

swarming *noun* a gathering swiftly formed as the result of a snowball-effect proliferation of instant text message communication *UK, 2003*

swash *noun* foaming water after a wave breaks on shore *US, 1963*

swass *noun* sweaty buttocks. A contraction of 'sweaty' and 'ass' *CANADA, 2003*

swatch *noun* a quick look *UK: SCOTLAND, 1911*

swatty-blouse *noun* an effeminate intellectual *NEW ZEALAND, 1995*

swave and blaze *adjective* suave and blasé. An intentional mispronunciation, meant to be humorous *US, 1967*

swear *verb* ▶ **swear and cuss** a bus. Rhyming slang *UK, 1938*. ▶ **swear by** to have a great confidence in something *UK, 1815*

sweat *noun* a worry or difficulty. Usually used in the negative, most often as 'no sweat!' *US, 1979*

sweat *verb* **1** to coerce someone through intense pressure, usually not involving physical force *US, 1947*. **2** to admire or desire someone or something *US, 1999*. **3** to disclose that a pool player is in fact a skilled betting professional *US, 1990*. **4** to gamble nervously and cautiously *US, 1991*. ▶ **sweat blood 1** to make an unsparing effort *UK, 1911*. **2** to be very afraid *UK, 1924*. ▶ **sweat bullets** to experience a high degree of nervous tension, usually sweating profusely *US, 1977*. ▶ **sweat cobs** to perspire heavily *UK, 1978*. ▶ **sweat it** to worry *UK, 1998*. ▶ **sweat like a glassblower's arse** to perspire heavily *UK, 2003*. ▶ **sweat on** to wait with nervous expectation *UK, 1917*. ▶ **sweat the brass** in horse racing, to race a horse day after day, without giving it a rest period *US, 1951*. ▶ **sweat your guts out** to labour extremely hard; to make the utmost effort *UK, 1890*

sweatback *noun* an illegal immigrant to the US who is working. A WETBACK who is working, and thus sweating *US, 1962*

sweat box *noun* **1** a police interview room *UK, 1971*. **2** the waiting area outside the room in which a parole hearing is to take place *US, 1962*. **3** a vehicle for transporting prisoners in small individual cubicles *UK, 1996*. **4** in trucking, a sleeping compartment behind the seat *US, 1971*

sweat chovey *noun* a gymnasium or weights room. A combination of 'chovey' (an otherwise obsolete term for a shop) with a product of working-out *UK, 2002*

sweater *noun* **1** a casino employee or executive who cheats gamblers *US, 1977*. **2** in a casino or other gambling establishment, a person who observes but does not participate in a game *US, 1968*. **3** a person who worries *US, 1966*

sweater meat *noun* the female breasts *US, 2004*

sweater puppies *noun* the female breasts *US, 1995*

sweater queen *noun* a neatly and nicely dressed homosexual male *US, 1997*

sweat room *noun* a small room in a police station where suspects are interrogated or 'sweated' *UK, 1974*

Sweatshop *noun* ▶ **the Sweatshop** the Apollo Theatre, New York *US, 1949*

sweaty sock; sweaty *noun* a Scot. Rhyming slang for JOCK (a Scot); derogatory, both in its own imagery and as demonstrated in the usage by football supporters to taunt rivals. Certainly in use in the Newcastle-upon-Tyne area in 1990 *UK, 2002*

swede *noun* **1** the head; hence, the hair on the head. From the shape of the vegetable *UK, 1999*. **2** a potentially naive provincial police officer investigating complaints in London. A nuance used by the Metropolitan Police *UK, 1999*

swede-basher; swede *noun* a person from the countryside; an unsophisticated type. Derives from the root vegetable *UK, 1943*

swedeland *noun* the countryside as seen from the town. Derogatory. From SWEDE-BASHER (a person from the countryside; an unsophisticated type) *UK, 1967*

swedey *noun* ▶ **the swedey** the provincial police of 'Operation Countryman' drafted to London, from 1978 to the early 1980s to investigate alleged corruption in the Metropolitan Police, particularly in the Flying Squad. Derisive; formed on SWEDE (a provincial police officer), punning on THE SWEENEY (the Flying Squad) *UK, 1980*

swedge *verb* to fight *UK: SCOTLAND, 1999*

Swedish *adjective* sexually permissive. From the Swedish attitude to pornography *UK, 2000*

Swedish fiddle *noun* among loggers, a cross-cut saw. The reference to Sweden likely alludes to the 'Swedish saw' *CANADA, 1942*

Swedish headache *noun* an aching in the testicles from sexual activity that does not culminate in ejaculation *US, 1932*

Swedish massage *noun* ejaculation achieved with the man's penis between the woman's breasts *UK, 1973*

sweedie *noun* a friend, an acquaintance; recognised as a form of address with shallow sincerity. An ironic mid-Atlantic approximation of SWEETIE; identified and popularised in BBC television comedy *Absolutely Fabulous* (1992–2001) *UK, 2002*

Sweeney *noun* ▶ **on your Sweeney** on your own *IRELAND, 1996*. ▶ **the Sweeney** the Flying Squad, Metropolitan Police branch C1 (1921–48), subsequently C8; a member of the Flying Squad. Rhyming slang formed from 'Sweeney Todd' for 'Flying Squad'. Sweeney Todd was the legendary 'Demon Barber of Fleet Street'. Brought to widespread popular attention by television police drama series *The Sweeney*, originally broadcast from 1974–78, which gave the impression that all police work was about guns and fast cars *UK, 1938*

sweep *noun* **1** in combat, a search and destroy mission or a concerted search through an area *US, 1977*. **2** a concerted effort to find someone or something illegal *US, 1974*

sweep *verb* to systematically search for surveillance devices *US, 1985*. ▶ **sweep the leaves** to drive at the back of a group of trucks travelling together, watching for police from the rear *US, 1976*

sweeper *noun* **1** in mountain biking, a tree limb overhanging the trail at approximately face height *US, 1992*. **2** an expert hired to search for and locate surveillance devices *US, 1985*

sweet *noun* **1** an effeminate male homosexual *US, 1990*. **2** an amphetamine tablet *US, 1994*

sweet *adjective* **1** all right *UK, 1890*. **2** excellent; in style; admirable *US, 1982*. **3** amenable. A shift in the earlier (C18–19) sense as 'gullible, unsuspicious' *UK, 1999*. **4** when combined in phrases meaning nothing, absolute *UK, 1958*. **5** homosexual *US, 1972*. **6** drunk *BARBADOS, 1965*

sweet! used to express approval *UK, 2003*

sweet-arse *adjective* used for describing someone or something with approval. A variation of SWEET *UK, 1998*

sweet as *adjective* satisfying and easy, especially of a crime. A shortening of the familiar SWEET AS A NUT *UK, 2001*

sweet as a nut *adjective* satisfying and easy, especially of a crime *UK, 1937*

sweet BA *noun* nothing whatsoever. A euphemistic variation of SWEET BUGGER ALL *UK, 1958*

sweet bugger all *noun* absolutely nothing at all. A sarcastic or emphatic variation of BUGGER ALL *UK, 1918*

sweet chat *noun* flattery *TRINIDAD AND TOBAGO, 1977*

sweet cop *noun* an easy job *AUSTRALIA, 1918*

sweet count *noun* in dominoes, a good hand *US, 1997*

sweet daddy *noun* a pimp *US, 1957*

sweet deedee *noun* in horse racing, a combination wager conventionally known as the 'daily double' *US, 1968*

sweet dreams *noun* heroin *UK, 1998*

sweet dying Jesus an affectionate exclamatory oath *CANADA, 1985*

sweeten *verb* **1** in poker, to increase the amount bet *US, 1963*. **2** in the television and film industries, to make subtle improvements in the soundtrack *US, 1990*

sweetened air *noun* candy floss *US, 1981*

sweetener *noun* **1** a bribe *UK, 1996*. **2** cash *US, 2003*

Sweet evening breeze *noun* ▷*see:* EVENING BREEZE

sweet Fanny Adams; sweet FA *noun* ▷*see:* FANNY ADAMS

sweet fuck all *noun* absolutely nothing at all. A sarcastic or emphatic variation of FUCK ALL *UK, 1969*

sweethead *noun* a marijuana user *US, 1997*

sweetheart *noun* **1** used as an endearment or what is intended to be an endearing form of address. Often patronising *UK, 1290*. **2** used as a menacing form of address. An ironic variation of the genuine endearment *UK, 1977*

sweetheart *adjective* used of a trade union overly sympathetic to, if not controlled by, management *US, 1959*

sweet Heaven! used as a mild expletive, or register of shock, surprise, etc *UK, 2002*

sweetie *noun* **1** a sweetheart *US, 1925*. **2** used as a wheedling, patronising form of address *US, 1971*. **3** an effeminate man, usually an effeminate homosexual. A pejorative, adopted by gays as an ironic endearment *US, 1972*. **4** a sweet (an individual chocolate- or sugar-based item of confectionary). From 'sweetmeat', but now considered a childish extension of 'sweet'; generally heard in the plural *UK, 1860*. **5** tablets for medication or recreation. From the sense as 'confectionary' *UK, 2000*. **6** the drug Preludin™, a stimulant that suppresses the appetite *US, 1970*. **7** an amphetamine or MDMA tablet *UK, 1994*

sweetie-pie *noun* a sweetheart; a dear friend; a CAMP form of address. An extension of all variants of SWEETIE as an endearment. In 1947 the animated cartoon *Tweety Pie* won an Oscar *UK, 1928*

sweet Jesus *noun* morphine; heroin *US, 1967*

sweet Jesus! used as a mild expletive, or register of shock, surprise, etc *UK, 2002*

sweet leaf *noun* marijuana *US, 2001*

sweet limburger! used for expressing disapproval. A signature line of Colonel Sherman Potter on *M*A*S*H* (CBS, 1972–83). Repeated with referential humour *US, 1983*

sweet Lucy *noun* **1** muscatel wine *US, 1973*. **2** any cheap wine *US, 1997*. **3** a solution of hashish and wine *US, 1948*. **4** marijuana *US, 1969*

sweet mack *noun* a pimp who controls his prostitutes through charm and attention *US, 1972*

sweetman *noun* a man who is supported by his lover; a pimp *TRINIDAD AND TOBAGO, 1939*

sweet Miss Adams *noun* ▷*see:* FANNY ADAMS

sweet name *noun* any affectionate nickname *TRINIDAD AND TOBAGO, 1971*

sweetness *noun* used as an endearment *UK, 1992*

sweet on infatuated by someone or something *UK, 1740*

sweet shit in a bucket! used for registering anger, frustration or despair *US, 1970*

sweet spot *noun* in surfing, the forward position on the surfboard that maximises speed and the back position that maximises the ability to manoeuver *AUSTRALIA, 2003*

sweet stuff *noun* powdered drugs; cocaine, heroin or morphine *US, 1936*

sweet-talk *verb* to flatter someone, to convince someone through kind words *US, 1936*

sweet thing *noun* an attractive young woman *US, 1971*

sweet tooth *noun* an addiction to morphine *US, 1961*

swell *noun* a well-dressed, fashionable man *UK, 1786*

swell *adjective* good; attractive; stylish. A key piece of slang for more than a century, eventually displaced by COOL *UK, 1812*

swellbow *noun* a swollen elbow. Skateboarders' and scooter-riders' slang; an elision of 'swell' and 'elbow' *UK, 1998*

swell pipes *noun* in circus and carnival usage, a good singing voice *US, 1981*

swell-up *noun* crack cocaine *UK, 1998*

swerve *noun* **1** a deception, practical joke or false report *US, 1997*. **2** intoxication *US, 2001*. ▶ **get your swerve on** to drink to the point of intoxication *US, 1998*

swerve *verb* **1** to avoid someone or something. From the conventional sense (to change direction abruptly); probably a shortening of BODY-SWERVE *UK: SCOTLAND, 1985*. **2** to make a late change in your plans. Teen slang *UK, 2003*

swerve past *verb* to visit a place briefly; to go out of your way *UK, 1999*

swift *adjective* **1** good, clever *US, 1970*. **2** of police, corrupt *UK, 1977*

swiftie *noun* **1** a deceitful trick; a con *AUSTRALIA, 1945*. **2** an alcoholic drink quickly drunk, a '*swift* drink'. The spelling 'swifty' is also used *UK, 2001*

swifting *noun* in the police, an action of making a quick arrest when it may not be clear that all elements of the offence can be proved. From 'swift 'un' (a quick, possibly unfair arrest) *UK, 1999*

swig *noun* an act of drinking deeply, especially of intoxicating liquor *UK, 1621*

swig *verb* to drink, especially deeply, and especially of intoxicating liquor. From SWIG (a drink) *UK, 1654*

swill *noun* a drink *UK, 2001*

swill cup *noun* a combination of leftover alcoholic beverages *US, 2003*

swiller *noun* a public house *UK, 2001*

swim *noun* ▶ **in the swim** active socially, up to date with trends and fashions *UK, 1869*

swim *verb* **1** to parade ostentatiously. A variation of SWAN (to move with no purpose) *UK, 1952*. **2** to move through a stadium or auditorium, experiencing a concert from different perspectives *US, 1994*

swimmer *noun* **1** a car that has been driven or fallen into a body of water *US, 1962*. **2** in horse racing, a horse that peforms very well on wet track conditions *AUSTRALIA, 1989*

swimmers *noun* a swimming costume *AUSTRALIA, 1967*

swimmies *noun* swimwear; a swimming costume *UK: SCOTLAND, 1988*

swindle sheet *noun* **1** a record of reimbursable business expenses that is completed by a travelling sales representative or business executive. An implicit suggestion that these records are not always entirely honest *US, 1949*. **2** in trucking, a trucker's daily log book *US, 1971*

swine *noun* **1** an unpleasant person, especially a coarse or degraded person; a sensualist *UK, 1842*. **2** a police officer; the police *US, 1997*. **3** a prison guard *US, 1976*. **4** a difficult or awkward thing. From the sense as 'an unpleasant person' *UK, 1933*. **5** leather, especially leather car upholstery *US, 2002*

swing *noun* **1** a bag (or similar receptacle) that is used to transfer contraband items between prison cells by being attached to a length of string (or similar) and swung from one cell window to another. Also called a 'swinger' *UK, 1996*. **2** a punch delivered with a wide sweep of the arm, especially in the phrase: take a swing at *UK, 1910*. **3** an employee's rest period in a shift system; a pattern of working that incorporates such rest periods; hence, time off work *US, 1917*. **4** a consensual orgy *US, 1969*

swing *verb* **1** to enjoy frequent casual sex with different partners *UK, 1964*. **2** to have fun, especially in a currently fashionable or unconventional activity; hence, to be fashionable *US, 1957*. **3** to accomplish something, especially something that is difficult *UK, 1933*. **4** to be executed by hanging. Hanging has been the principal form of execution in the British Isles since the C5; the death penalty was abolished in the UK in 1965 (except for crimes of treason, piracy with violence and arson in the Royal Dockyards) *UK, 1542*. **5** to play jazz with feeling and a basic understanding of the medium *US, 1933*. **6** to cheat or swindle someone *US, 1952*. **7** to steal something. Casino usage *US, 1980*. **8** in high-low poker, to declare for both high and low *US, 1979*. ▶ **swing both ways** to be bisexual *UK, 1972*. ▶ **swing it 1** to malinger; to shirk responsibility; to evade duty. Variation of SWING THE LEAD *UK, 1959*. **2** to achieve something by trickery or influence *UK, 1959*. ▶ **swing the lead** to malinger; to shirk responsibility; to evade duty. Popular etymology holds this to be the 'sounding-lead' with which the depth of water is measured; in practice 'heaving the lead' is a skilled task. The term certainly has naval origins *US, 1917*

swing by *verb* to visit briefly; to go out of your way *UK, 2001*

swingdom *noun* a culture of casual sexual interaction *US, 1997*

swinger *noun* **1** a person who freely enjoys life's pleasures *US, 1959*. **2** someone who engages in spouse or partner swapping *US, 1964*. **3** a person who has died by hanging *US, 1987*. **4** a prisoner who has attempted suicide by hanging *UK, 1996*. **5** in trucking, a large load *US, 1971*

swing gang *noun* in the television and film industries, the crew that prepares and dismantles the set *US, 1990*

swinging *noun* consensual swapping of sexual partners as a deliberate activity *UK, 1976*

swinging *adjective* **1** lively and alert and progressive; uninhibited; fashionable *UK, 1967*. **2** of a court case, adjourned until a later date *AUSTRALIA, 1975*

swinging dick *noun* an ordinary fellow. Sometimes euphemised (barely) as 'swinging Richard' *US, 1966*

swingle *noun* an unmarried person in search of a sexual partner *US, 1968*

swing oil *noun* to a golfer, beer or alcohol *US, 2000*

swing-out *noun* a fight between youth gangs *US, 1972*

swings and roundabouts the rough and the smooth; used of a fluctuating situation where the average outcome remains constant whatever action is taken. A reduction of the proverb 'what you lose on the swings you gain on the roundabouts' *UK, 1983*

swing shift *noun* a work schedule that begins late in the afternoon and continues until the middle of the night, traditionally from 4 pm until midnight *US, 1943*

swipe *noun* **1** a heavy blow delivered with a swinging motion (may be applied to a bat addressing a ball, or a hand hitting flesh) *UK, 1807*. **2** an instance of adverse criticism. Extended from the previous sense *UK, 1932*. **3** an objectionable person *UK, 1929*. **4** the penis *US, 1969*. **5** potent, homemade pineapple-based alcohol. Hawaiian usage *US, 1982*. **6** to drink great amounts of kava, a tranquillity-inducing herbal beverage *FIJI, 1997*

swipe *verb* **1** to hit someone. From an earlier sense, 'to swing the arms in a circular motion' *UK, 1851*. **2** to steal something *US, 1889*. **3** to take something, but not necessarily to steal it *UK, 1947*

swipe me! a euphemistic cry of surprise, replacing 'fuck me!'. A slight variant of the obsolete and hence euphemistic 'swive' (to have sex) *UK, 1955*

swipes *noun* **1** in horse racing, a groom *US, 1947*. **2** beer. Originally (1786) 'a small beer' *UK, 1805*

swish *noun* **1** a homosexual male, especially of the dramatically effeminate type *US, 1941*. **2** weak alcohol made by letting water stand in old screech barrels *CANADA, 2001*

swish *verb* **1** (of a homosexual male) to behave in a flamboyant, camp or effeminate manner *US, 1960*. **2** (among drug users) to distribute drugs, especially hallucinogenic drugs *NEW ZEALAND, 1982*

swish *adjective* **1** fashionable; elegant. Colloquial, from Devonshire dialect *UK, 1879*. **2** blatantly homosexual. Also variant 'swishy' *US, 1941*

swish Alps *noun* the Hollywood Hills, Los Angeles, California. A homosexual enclave *US, 1983*

swisher *noun* a hollowed-out cigar refilled with marijuana *US, 1999*

swish faggot *noun* an effeminate, melodramatic homosexual man *US, 1980*

swish tank *noun* a holding cell in a jail where homosexual suspects and prisoners are kept *US, 1992*

Swiss Army knife; swiss army *noun* a wife. Rhyming slang, formed on a commercial tool that is marketed in a wide range of variations *UK, 1998*

Swiss banker *noun* used as an all-purpose form of abuse. Rhyming slang for WANKER *UK, 2003*

Swiss-cheeze up *verb* to shoot a person or place full of holes. The image of a piece of cheese such as Emmental *US, 2002*

switch *noun* **1** a switchblade knife that opens with a button-operated spring *US, 1949*. **2** in a sexually oriented massage parlour, a massage given to the masseuse by the customer *US, 1982*. **3** the buttocks *US, 1949*

switch *verb* to act upon bisexual impulses *US, 1970*. ▶ **switch lanes** to change allegiance. Used by teenage gang members *UK, 2003*

switchable *noun* a person who is willing to play either the sadist or masochist role in a sado-masochism encounter *US, 1979*

switchboard jockey *noun* a telephone operator *US, 1957*

switched on *adjective* **1** in fashion, up-to-date and well-informed *UK, 1964*. **2** drug-intoxicated *US, 1972*. **3** excited by music; aroused by a sexual opportunity. Electrical imagery *UK, 1977*

switcher *noun* a bisexual *US, 1966*

switcheroo *noun* a swapping; an exchange *US, 1933*

switchfoot *noun* a surfer who can surf with either foot forward, depending on the conditions *US, 1964*

switch hitter *noun* **1** a bisexual *US, 1960*. **2** a person who masturbates with first one hand and then the other *US, 2002*

switchies *noun* sex involving more than two people *US, 1983*

switch list *noun* on the railways, a menu *US, 1977*

switch monkey *noun* a railway pointsman *US, 1977*

switch off *verb* **1** to stop paying attention; to lose interest *UK, 1921*. **2** to knock someone out. Electrical imagery *UK, 2000*

swizzle; swiz; swizz *noun* a swindle; a disappointment half-jokingly described as a 'swindle' *UK, 1913*

swole *adjective* upset; provoked; angry *US, 1998*

swoles *noun* muscles. From 'swollen' *US, 2004*

swoll *adjective* muscular *US, 1997*

swollen-headed *adjective* conceited *UK, 1928*

swonked *adjective* exhausted by heavy work *CANADA, 1953*

swoon *verb* to seduce or romance someone *UK, 2003*

swoonie *nickname* the contemporary dollar coin. In 2002, with the Canadian dollar dropping in value, this parody nickname is derived from LOONY *CANADA, 2002*

swoontime *noun* the approximate time when young people congregate somewhere to socialise *US, 1953*

swooper *noun* a prisoner who collects discarded cigarette-ends (to roll new ones). The swooper *swoops* on his prey *UK, 1996*

swoop squad; swoop team *noun* a unit of prison officers detailed to discover drugs and other contraband *UK, 1996*

swoosh *noun* the name given to the tick-shaped logo of Nike™, the sports shoe manufacturer *US, 2001*

S-word *noun* **1** the word 'shit' *US, 1999*. **2** the word 'sex' *US, 1988*. **3** the word 'socialism' *US, 1987*

sword fighting *noun* a sexual act in which two erect penises compete for or share the attention of a single person performing oral sex *UK, 2002*

swordsman *noun* **1** a man with an impressive reputation for his sexual prowess *UK, 1998*. **2** a male homosexual *UK, 1983*

sword swallower *noun* a person who performs oral sex on a man. The working title of the 1970s pornographic classic *Deep Throat* was *Sword Swallower US, 1964*

swot *verb* to study, especially at the last possible moment before an examination *NEW ZEALAND, 1984*

swot; swat *noun* an extra-studious student *UK, 1850*

swot vac *noun* student holidays from school or university *AUSTRALIA, 1983*

swy *noun* **1** the gambling game two-up. Ultimately from German *zwei* (two), possibly via Yiddish *AUSTRALIA, 1913*. **2** two; a two-year prison sentence; two shillings; two pounds; two ounces of tobacco. From German *zwei* (two). The spelling 'swi' is also used *AUSTRALIA, 1921*

swy game *noun* the gambling game two-up *AUSTRALIA, 1946*

swy school *noun* a group of people playing the gambling game two-up *AUSTRALIA, 1944*

sXe *noun* used as an identifying word by members of the Straight Edge youth culture. The 's' and 'e' are, obviously, the initials of 'Straight Edge', while the 'X' represents the rubber stamp marked on the hands of under-age patrons at youth clubs *US, 2000*

Sydney Harbour *noun* a barber. Rhyming slang *AUSTRALIA, 1942*

Sydney or the bush all or nothing *AUSTRALIA, 1915*

Sylvester Stallone; sylvester *adjective* alone. Rhyming slang, formed on the US film actor (b.1950) *UK, 1998*

synch *noun* ▶ **in synch; in sync** in accord with. Figurative use of the abbreviated *in synch*ronization (working together) *US, 1961*

syndicat *noun* in Quebec, a trade union *CANADA, 2002*

syndicate *noun* **1** a criminal organisation *US, 1929*. **2** a small group of close friends. Joining CREW and POSSE as crime terms applied to friends *US, 1993*

synergy *noun* 4-bromo-2, 5-dimethoxyphenethylamine, a mild hallucinogen *US, 1995*

syph *noun* syphilis *US, 1914*

syrup *noun* prescription cough syrup, used recreationally *US, 1995*

syrup head *noun* a person who abuses for non-medicinal purposes non-prescription medication containing dextromethorphan (DXM) *US, 2003*

syrup of fig; syrup of figs; syrup *noun* a wig. Rhyming slang. Syrup of figs is used as a laxative. Noted in use among criminals by David Powis, *The Signs of Crime*, 1977; as a showbusiness term by Red Daniells, 1980, and in wide and general use by Ray Puxley, *Cockney Rabbit*, 1992 *UK, 1977*

syrupped up *adjective* intoxicated by cough syrup taken for non-medicinal purposes *US, 1970*

system *noun* **1** the criminal justice system; jail *US, 1995*. **2** an audio system, especially a loud car audio system *US, 1993*

systems kicker *noun* in prison, a rebellious inmate. One who kicks against the system *UK, 1996*

SYT *noun* a youthful, attractive homosexual male; a *sweet young thing US, 1979*

Tt

T *noun* **1** marijuana. The simplest abbreviation of TEA *UK, 1950*. **2** cocaine. Probably an abbreviation of another slang term for 'cocaine' such as TOOT *UK, 2003*. **3** a tee shirt *UK, 2003*. ▶ **to a T** precisely, exactly *UK, 1693*

T *nickname* the local rail system serving urban and suburban Boston, Massachusetts. used with 'the'. From the official designation 'Boston Transport' *US, 1987*

ta thank you. An abbreviation of 'thanks' or 'thank you'; originally childish or juvenile, now widespread *UK, 1772*

tab *noun* **1** a tablet, usually one taken as a recreational drug; a single dose of LSD. Originally medical and pharmaceutical jargon, added to the vocabulary of drugs users in the 1950s *UK, 1961*. **2** a tabloid newspaper *US, 1951*. **3** a bill, especially in a restaurant or bar *US, 1946*. **4** a cigarette. Originally northern dialect, spread with media usage *UK, 1934*. **5** a walk or march across country *UK, 1982*. **6** an enterprise, an activity *US, 1946*. ▶ **run a tab** to order drinks without paying for each one, paying instead the entire bill at the end of the session *US, 1995*

tab *verb* **1** to march or otherwise travel on foot across country. Military *UK, 1982*. **2** to make a drug into tablet form *US, 1967*

tabasco *noun* napalm *US, 1991*

tabbed *adjective* dressed stylishly *US, 1980*

tabla *noun* a surfboard. Spanish, imported to the US from Mexico by American surfers *US, 1977*

table *noun* a pinball machine *UK, 1977*

table dance *noun* in a strip-club, a semi-private sexual performance near or on a customer's table *US, 1992*

table grade *adjective* used of a woman, sexually appealing. A clear suggestion of oral sex, or eating *US, 1972*

table-hopper; table-topper *noun* a necrophile *US, 1987*

table manners *noun* in poker, a player's mannerisms, which may provide clues as to the relative strength of his hand *US, 1981*

table muscle *noun* the stomach *US, 1984*

table pussy *noun* a woman with good looks and manners *US, 1970*

tablescore *verb* to take food left on restaurant tables *US, 1997*

table talk *noun* in poker, idle chatter that does not rise to the level of intentionally distracting talk *US, 1979*

table time *noun* a time-based charge for playing pool *US, 1993*

table zamboni *noun* a cleaning rag used by a bartender. Zamboni is an ice resurfacer used on ice rinks *US, 1987*

tab out *verb* to pay a bar bill and leave the bar *US, 1992*

tabs *noun* the ears *US, 1970*

tacit *noun* ▶ **take a tacit** to stop talking *US, 1947*

tack *noun* **1** anything that demonstrates a quality of vulgarity, bad taste or kitsch *US, 1986*. **2** a tattoo *US, 1992*. **3** marijuana *UK, 1996*

tacked *adjective* drunk or drug-intoxicated *US, 2004*

tacked back *adjective* covered with tattoos *US, 1989*

tacked out *adjective* in trucking, running at full speed. A construction from 'tachometer' *US, 1971*

tacker *noun* a child. From British dialect (Devon and Cornwall) *AUSTRALIA, 1942*

tackety bit; tackety *noun* the female breast. Glasgow rhyming slang for TIT from the local pronunciation of 'tackety' (steel-tipped and -heeled) boots *UK: SCOTLAND, 1988*

tackie *noun* a tyre *SOUTH AFRICA, 1978*

tackies *noun* running shoes, trainers *SOUTH AFRICA, 1913*

tackiness *noun* a state of unrefined vulgarity *US, 1977*

tackle *noun* **1** the male genitalia. Originally 'a man's tackle' subsequent familiarity reduced the necessity for 'a man's' *UK, 1788*. **2** food and drink; 'stuff'; more recently, drugs *UK, 1857*

tackle *verb* to court; to flirt *TRINIDAD AND TOBAGO, 1987*

tacky *adjective* vulgar, unrefined, unattractive, aesthetically unappealling; 'cheap and nasty' *US, 1862*

taco *adjective* Mexican. Offensive. From the Mexican street food *US, 1990*

taco bender *noun* a Mexican or Mexican-American. Offensive *US, 1992*

Taco Hell *nickname* a Taco Bell™ fast-food restaurant *US, 1990*

tacoland *noun* a Mexican or Mexican-American neighbourhood. Offensive *US, 1981*

taco wagon *noun* a car embellished with bright colours, chrome and other accessories associated with Mexican-American car enthusiasts *US, 1960*

tad *adjective* little; a small amount. Perhaps from dialect *tad* (toad) *UK, 1940*

tadger *noun* the penis. Originally dialect; survives in rhyming slang FOX AND BADGER *UK, 1961*

tadpole *noun* an OH-6 light observation military helicopter. From its shape *US, 1991*

tadpole factory *noun* the testicles *UK, 2003*

ta ever so thank you. An elaboration of TA and variation of THANKS EVER SO *UK, 1970*

Taffia; Tafia *noun* a notional conspiracy of influential Welsh people, especially Welsh-speakers, that control many areas of Welsh life for its own benefit. A blend of TAFF (Welsh) and 'mafia' (a criminal association) *UK: WALES, 1980*

Taffy; Taff *noun* a native of Wales. From Welsh *Dafydd* (David – the Welsh patron saint and everyday christian name) as heard by English ears. Taffy since about 1700; Taff since 1929 *UK, 1964*

tag *noun* **1** the stylised signature of a graffiti artist. From 'tag' (a label) *US, 1998*. **2** a stylised signature often confused with graffiti *US, 1997*. **3** a nickname, or popular designation *US, 1950*. **4** a number plate *US, 1972*. **5** a planned murder *US, 1982*. **6** in the television and film industries, a very short final scene *US, 1990*

tag *verb* **1** to shoot and hit someone or something *US, 1992*. **2** to strike or hit someone or something *US, 1975*. **3** to catch or arrest someone, or convict someone of a crime *US, 1966*. **4** to spray-paint graffiti in a signature styling *US, 1980*. **5** to tattoo part of the body *US, 1993*. **6** to bestow a nickname on someone *US, 1960*. **7** to identify someone or something *US, 1951*

tag-along *noun* someone who joins an activity without invitation *US, 1961*

tag and bag *verb* to put a name tag on a corpse and place the body in a body bag. Vietnam war usage *US, 1981*

tagger *noun* a person who writes his signature in a stylised fashion on public walls, subways, etc *US, 1997*

tagging crew *noun* a group of graffiti artists *US, 1989*

tag plant *noun* a prison number plate manufacturing shop *US, 2000*

tag shop *noun* the area in a prison where number plates are manufactured *US, 1958*

Taig; Teague *nickname* a Catholic. From the anglicised spelling of the Irish name/nickname *Tadhg* *UK, 1971*

tail *noun* **1** the backside, buttocks and/or anus *UK, 1303*. **2** a woman, regarded as a sexual object; women, collectively, categorised with the same regard *UK, 1846*. **3** an act of sexual intercourse or sexual intercourse in a general sense. The earlier, obsolete, senses of 'penis' and 'vagina' come together in a logical consequence *UK, 1933*.

4 a person who is following someone else closely and secretly US, 1914. **5** in prison, an informer US, 1990. **6** the term of a prisoner's parole US, 1992. **7** in hot rodding, a fox tail or racoon tail tied to the car US, 1960. ▶ **bust your tail** to give the maximum effort US, 1996

tail verb to follow someone closely and secretly US, 1907. ▶ **tail 'em** in the gambling game two-up, to throw a pair of tails AUSTRALIA, 1911

tail-better noun in the gambling game two-up, a player who bets on tails AUSTRALIA, 1963

tail-end Charlie noun someone at the rear of any group or expedition. Originally the name given to the rear gunner on a Royal Air Force bomber, hence 'the man at the back' UK, 1941

tailgate verb **1** to walk very closely behind another person. A variation of the conventional sense UK, 2003. **2** to eat and drink clustered in parking lot before a sports event US, 1995

tailgunner noun a homosexual male NEW ZEALAND, 1998

tailie noun in the gambling game two-up, a player who bets on tails AUSTRALIA, 1919

tail lights noun LSD UK, 1998

tailor noun in gin, a win without the opponent scoring US, 1950

tailor-made; tailor; taylor noun a factory-made cigarette US, 1924

tail pain noun anal pain TRINIDAD AND TOBAGO, 2003

taily noun the penis US, 1982

taima noun marijuana. Possibly an elision of Spanish Tailandés (Thai) and marijuana UK, 1998

taint noun the perineum US, 1955

t'aint no crack, but a solid fact what I am saying is the truth US, 1973

Taj Mahal noun a dome covering radar antennae at NORAD air defence radar stations CANADA, 1995

take noun **1** an opinion; a view. Possibly from television and film jargon, 'take' (a recorded scene), suggesting a point of view UK, 2001. **2** stolen property, especially money US, 1888. **3** a theft AUSTRALIA, 1975. ▶ **on the take** accepting bribes US, 1930

take verb **1** (of a male) to have sex with someone UK, 1915. **2** to defeat someone UK, 1939. **3** to successfully swindle someone UK, 1946. ▶ **take advantage** (of a man) to seduce someone, to have sex with someone, to force sex upon someone. Euphemistic, but often jocular US, 1928. ▶ **take back water** to back down on a brag or dare; to refuse a challenge. This phrase is derived from rowing CANADA, 1972. ▶ **take care of someone** to kill someone; to kill one or more, especially as an expedient solution to a problem UK, 1984. ▶ **take in laundry** to wear underwear internally UK, 2001. ▶ **take it in the shorts** to be abused or defeated US, 1994. ▶ **take it lying down** to submit tamely UK, 1961. ▶ **take it Nelson** to relax UK, 1996. ▶ **take on for the team** to accept responsibility for an unpleasant task for the greater good of a group. Originally a baseball team, used as an ex post facto explanation of a batter advancing to first base after being hit with a pitch US, 2001. ▶ **take one** to be open to bribery UK, 1970. ▶ **take one for the team** in a social situation, to pay attention to the less attractive of a pair of friends in the hope that your friend will have success with the more attractive member of the pair US, 2002. ▶ **take someone apart** to absolutely defeat someone in a fight; to reprimand someone severely UK, 1984. ▶ **take someone for a ride 1** to swindle or deceive someone US, 1925. **2** in a car, to take a planned victim to a convenient spot for murder US, 1927. ▶ **take stoppo** to escape. Based on 'stoppo' (a getaway) UK, 1956. ▶ **take the biscuit** used in the context of surprise or annoyance at something which is remarkable or extraordinary UK, 1907. ▶ **take the cake** used in the context of surprise or annoyance at something that is startlingly improbable US, 1900. ▶ **take the cheese** to be considered in the most negative manner; in a figurative sense, to take the prize for being worst UK, 1997. ▶ **take the micky; take the mickey; take the mick; take the michael** to make fun of someone; to pull someone's leg. All variations of rhyming slang MIKE BLISS; MICKY BLISS (PISS); literal and euphemistic translations of TAKE THE PISS. The variations on 'mickey', 'mick' etc. may be given an initial capital UK, 1935. ▶ **take the piss; take the piss out of someone 1** to make a

fool of someone; to pull someone's leg. To PISS and hence deflate a bladder gives the central idea of deflation, in this case by making a fool of; perhaps coincidentally an inflated bladder (on a stick) is the mediaeval comedy prop associated with a fool UK, 1984. **2** to implement a urine test. A literal pun on the sense 'to tease someone' UK, 1996. ▶ **take the ta-ta kiss; take the ta-ta** to make a fool of someone; to pull someone's leg. Rhyming slang for TAKE THE PISS, formed on a goodbye kiss UK, 1992. ▶ **take yourself in hand** (of a male) to masturbate UK, 1953

take a little, leave a little used as a description of the standing orders that carnival workers have for cheating customers US, 1985

take a running jump!; take a running jump at yourself! used as a contemptuous expression of dismissal UK, 1933

take a train! used as an all-purpose insult US, 1951

takedown noun the amount earned US, 1990

take down verb to arrest and convict someone US, 1997. ▶ **take someone down a peg** to reduce a person's self-esteem; to force a brash or bumptious person to conform US, 1959

take-down brights noun the very bright lights on a police car used when ordering a driver to pull over US, 1992

take-homes noun a several-day supply of methadone US, 1989

take it away! commence the entertainment!; start the music! UK, 1984

take-man noun the member of a criminal gang who actually steals the money AUSTRALIA, 1975

take money noun the proceeds of a robbery or other illegal scheme US, 1975

take night to make day used for describing an all-out effort TRINIDAD AND TOBAGO, 1986

taken short adjective desperate to urinate or defecate UK, 1890

take-off noun **1** in a gambling operation, the amount of the bet money taken by the house US, 1950. **2** a mimicking impression; a parody US, 1846. **3** in surfing, the catching of a wave and start of a ride US, 1970

take off verb **1** to use a drug, especially to inject a drug US, 1952. **2** to bring someone to orgasm US, 1975. **3** to go; to leave UK, 1959. **4** in surfing, to catch the momentum of a wave and begin a ride US, 1970. **5** to rob a place; to steal something US, 1960. **6** to mimic or parody someone or something UK, 1766. ▶ **take off a piece of work** to masturbate US, 2002

take-off artist noun an escaped prisoner UK, 1996

take on verb to have sex with someone US, 1972

take-out noun in poker, the minimum number of chips that a player can buy from the bank at once US, 1967

take out verb **1** to kill someone US, 1939. **2** to win a game, an award a prize or the like AUSTRALIA, 1976

taker noun a thief who snatches a chain from the wearer's neck. Recorded by a Jamaican inmate of a UK prison, August 2002 UK, 2002

takey-ah-ways noun take-away food. Pronounced with a mock Maori accent NEW ZEALAND, 1998

take you everywhere twice – the second time to apologise used as a jocular reprimand to a companion who has just said or done something contrary to the accepted social code; or (replacing you with him or her) to the company at large, as a humorous acknowledgement of such a faux pas UK, 2002

take your pick adjective stupid. Rhyming slang for THICK, possibly formed from the title of a television quiz show broadcast between 1955 and 68 UK, 1998

takkies noun running shoes SOUTH AFRICA, 2001

takkouri noun hashish. A corruption of Tunisian takrouri (hashish) UK, 1998

talala noun the vulva and vagina TRINIDAD AND TOBAGO, 1959

talc; talco noun cocaine. Another white powder as a metaphor US, 1984

talent noun **1** a categorisation of sexually attractive people (within a given area), usually by heterosexual men of women and by

homosexual men of men; occasional use by women increased in the 1990s *UK, 1947*. **2** an intelligent, resourceful criminal *US, 1962*.
▶ **the talent** in the entertainment industry, the actors, the performers *US, 1991*

talented *adjective* attractive *US, 1996*

Tale of Two Cities; tale o' twos *adjective* the female breasts. Rhyming slang for TITTIE(S), formed from the title of Charles Dickens' novel, 1859. Often spoonerised as 'Sale of Two Titties' *UK, 1960*

Taliban *adjective* given as a nickname to any eccentric or unconventional student, especially one of Arab ethnicity. Teen slang, post 11th September 2001; from the Muslim fundamentalist government. The words 'terrorist' and 'fundamentalist' are also current as nicknames *US, 2002*

talk *verb* **1** to betray someone; to inform on someone *US, 1924*. **2** to have a sexual relationship in prison *US, 1982*. **3** (used of a truck) to emit a clear sound from the smokestack *US, 1971*. ▶ **talk game** to analyse the business of prostitution *US, 1972*. ▶ **talk noise** to exaggerate; to lie *US, 1986*. ▶ **talk shit 1** to disparage someone or something; to exaggerate *US, 1965*. **2** to talk nonsense *US, mid-C20*. ▶ **talk smack** to disparage someone or something *US, 1993*. ▶ **talk stink** to malign someone or something. Hawaiian youth usage *US, 1981*. ▶ **talk story** to gossip; to engage in idle conversation. Hawaiian youth usage *US, 1981*. ▶ **talk the hind legs off a donkey** to talk until a listener is distracted; to talk persuasively. The surviving variation of many de-legged creatures: 'bird' (1929), 'cow' or 'dog' (1887), 'horse' (mainly dialect), 'jackal', etc *UK, 1915*. ▶ **talk though your neck** to talk nonsense *UK, 1899*. ▶ **talk through your arse; talk through your ass; talk out of your arse** to talk nonsense *UK, 1985*. ▶ **talk through your hat** to talk (ill-informed) nonsense *US, 1888*. ▶ **talk to Ralph Beukler** to vomit *CANADA, 2002*. ▶ **talk to Ralph on the big white phone** to vomit *US, 1986*. ▶ **talk to the canoe driver** to perform oral sex on a woman *US, 1971*. ▶ **talk to the seals** to vomit. Surfer usage *US, 1997*. ▶ **talk trash** to engage in aggressive verbal sparring; to speak offensively *US, 1967*. ▶ **talk turkey** to speak candidly and openly about an important issue *US, 1903*

talk and walk *noun* the practice of professing psychological improvement in a prison therapeutic setting to improve your chances of parole *US, 1971*

talk at *verb* to talk to someone. The 'at' is a folksy affectation that decreases the formality of the statement *US, 1999*

talkdown *noun* the conversational technique used to guide an LSD user who is having a difficult time back to reality *US, 1994*

talker *noun* in the circus or carnival, a person who entices customers into the side show *US, 1960*

talkie *noun* a film with sound; a film. Mainly historical, as an opposite to silent films *US, 1913*

talking handbag *noun* a portable radio *UK, 1996*

talking head *noun* an expert guest on a television or radio news show *US, 1977*

talking woman *noun* a female performer who banters with the audience as she strips off her clothes *US, 1950*

talkman *noun* an electrical torture device attached to a prisoner's face. Gulf war usage, punning on the Walkman™ portable music device *US, 1991*

talk of the devil! said of a person who, while being spoken of, arrives unexpectedly; hence, an ungracious, though not necessarily unfriendly, greeting to that person. A shortening of the proverb 'Talk of the Devil, and he's presently at your elbow' *UK, 1666*

talk powder *noun* any central nervous system stimulant *US, 1988*

talk to the hand; tell it to the hand (because the face isn't listening); speak to the hand used for expressing a complete lack of interest in what is being said. Usually followed with 'because the face don't give a damn' or something in a similar vein, accompanied by a gesture of a raised hand, palm facing the other person *US, 1995*

talk-up *noun* in sales and marketing, a raising of awareness and expectations. A jargon-like variation of 'praise' *UK, 1999*

tall *adjective* **1** used of a jail sentence, lengthy *US, 1992*. **2** drug-intoxicated. A play on HIGH *US, 1946*

tallboy *noun* a 16-ounce can of beer *US, 1984*

tall grass *noun* in circus and carnival usage, an extremely remote location *US, 1981*

tallie; tally *noun* chiefly in Queensland, a tall, 750 ml bottle of beer *AUSTRALIA, 2003*

tall order *noun* an excessive demand, a difficult thing to achieve *US, 1893*

tall poppy *noun* an eminent, wealthy or successful person when viewed as needing deflation *AUSTRALIA, 1902*

tall poppy syndrome *noun* the habit of denigrating successful people. An outgrowth of the Australian's strong sense of egalitarianism and habit of siding with the underdog *AUSTRALIA, 1983*

tall story; tall tale *noun* an elaborate lie; an (enjoyable) exaggeration *UK, 1846*

tall wine *noun* sex in which the woman below the man moves and keeps her buttocks up off the bed *TRINIDAD AND TOBAGO, 1986*

Tally *adjective* Italian *UK: SCOTLAND, 1985*

tallywhacker; tallywacker *noun* the penis *US, 1966*

tam *noun* a knitted hat used by a Rastafarian to contain his dreadlocks. An abbreviation of conventional 'tam o'shanter' *JAMAICA, 2002*

tamale *noun* the vagina. The imagery is of a savoury dish (originally from Mexico): a rolled pancake with a spicy filling *US, 1998*

tamboo bamboo *noun* the penis. An allusion to a musical instrument made from a length of bamboo *TRINIDAD AND TOBAGO, 1980*

Tammie *noun* a capsule of Temazepam™, a branded sleeping pill *US, 1997*

tammy *noun* a *tampon UK, 2001*

tamp *verb* to walk *US, 1953*

Tampa; Tampa pilot *noun* in shuffleboard, a hide disc on your side of the court near the apex of the ten *US, 1967*

tampax *noun* filter-tipped cigarette(s). From the similarity in appearance between the white tubes of manufactured cigarettes and Tampax™, a well-known brand of tampons *UK, 1984*

tampi; tampee *noun* marijuana *JAMAICA, 1975*

tamping *noun* a beating *US, 1967*

tampon *noun* **1** a snobbish, unpleasant person. An allusion to the nature of tampons in the sense that they are all 'stuck up cunts', punning on 'stuck-up' (snobbish) and CUNT (an unpleasant person) *UK, 2001*. **2** a fat marijuana cigarette *US, 1997*. ▶ **maybe your tampon will be flushed** perhaps you will be feeling better; maybe your mood will have improved. Note south Wales dialect *tamping* (angry) *US, 1988*

tampon dick *noun* a contemptible man *UK, 1997*

tamp up *verb* to beat someone physically *US, 1962*

tampy *noun* marijuana *BAHAMAS, 1982*

ta muchly thank you very much. A deliberate solecism used for humorous effect *UK, 1969*

tan *verb* **1** to consume something voraciously; to do something briskly or with urgency *UK: SCOTLAND, 1988*. **2** to burgle somewhere *UK: SCOTLAND, 1988*. ▶ **tan someone's hide; tan someone's arse** to beat someone on the buttocks (as a punishment) *UK, 1670*

T and A *noun* visual depictions of sexually provocative females. From TITS AND ASS; TITS AND ARSE *US, 1993*

T and T *verb* to tape record and trace the origin of a phone call *US, 2001*

tangerine dream *noun* a type of MDMA, the recreational drug best known as ecstasy. Named for the colour of the tablet and after a German group that plays electronic, synthesized music *UK, 1996*

Tangier tiger *noun* a low grade variety of hashish from the foothills of the Rif Mountains *UK, 2003*

tangle *noun* ▶ **on the tangle** drinking; on an alcohol binge *NEW ZEALAND, 1966*

tangle *verb* to fight *US, 1990*. ▶ **tangle ass** to brawl *US, 1950*.
▶ **tangle assholes** to become involved in a confrontation *US, 1985*

tanglefoot *noun* **1** strong, homemade whisky *US, 1860*. **2** barbed wire staked to the ground as a defensive perimeter around a military camp or base *US, 1990*

tango *noun* a type of MDMA, the recreational drug best known as ecstasy. From the colour of the tablet; possibly an abbreviation of TANGERINE DREAM, or named after Tango™, a branded carbonated orange drink that, according to the product's advertising, has a surreal effect on all who drink it *UK, 1996*

tango boat *noun* an armoured landing craft *US, 1971*

tango november *noun* a token black soldier in an otherwise white unit or corps, especially the officer corps. From the military phonetic alphabet 'TN', short for 'token nigger' *US, 1990*

tank *noun* **1** a jail cell, especially one in a local police station *US, 1912*. **2** an intentional loss in a competition. Originally boxing slang. Also called a 'tank job' *US, 1955*. **3** a room in the Pentagon where the Joint Chiefs and Staff meet jointly with the Operations Deputies *US, 1986*. **4** a safe *NEW ZEALAND, 1937*. **5** a safe burglary. Prison slang. *NEW ZEALAND, 1999*. **6** of money, all you have with you *UK: SCOTLAND, 1988*. **7** an old and heavy surfboard *US, 1988*. **8** a heavy-set woman *TRINIDAD AND TOBAGO, 1964*. **9** an ugly girl *US, 1966*. **10** money. Probably evolves from TANKER (a prizefighter who accepts payment to throw a fight in a fixed boxing match) *UK, 1991*. ▶ **go in the tank** used of an athletic contest, lost on purpose *US, 1955*. ▶ **in the tank** drunk *US, 1975*

tank-ass *noun* buttocks that are disproportionately large *US, 2001*

tanked *adjective* **1** drunk or drug-intoxicated. Also used as 'tanked up' *UK, 1893*. **2** in computing, not operating *US, 1991*

tanker *noun* **1** a hired thug *UK, 2003*. **2** a heavy drinker. From TANK UP (to drink) *CANADA, 1984*. **3** a boxing match or other athletic contest that has been fixed *US, 1955*

tanker wanker *noun* someone who flies in air-to-air refuellers. A Royal Air Force term, formed by rhyming the airborne 'tanker' with an all-purpose pejorative; reported by Squadron Leader G.D. Wilson, 1979 *UK, 1979*

tankman *noun* a safe-blower *AUSTRALIA, 1972*

tank money *noun* funds that are employed to give a fraudulent impression of substance or wealth *UK, 2000*

tank town *noun* a small, unimportant town. A possible railway etymology *US, 1906*

tank tracks *noun* in the Canadian military, folds that develop along the top of the official beret *CANADA, 1995*

tank-up *noun* a drinking binge *NEW ZEALAND, 1959*

tank up *verb* **1** to administer fluids to a dehydrated hospital patient *US, 1994*. **2** to consume large quantities of something, especially alcohol *US, 1902*

tanner *noun* in pre-decimalisation currency, sixpence, 6d; a coin of that value. Inflation has rendered the conversion from 6d to 2½p meaningless *UK, 1811*

tanorexia *noun* an addiction to sunbathing, especially by means of sunbeds. A punning combination of 'tan' and 'anorexia' which sacrifices the meaning of anorexia for a journalistic tag *UK, 1997*

tanorexic *noun* a person who is addicted to sunbathing, especially by means of sunbeds *US, 1998*

tans *noun* the standard US Army summer khaki uniform *US, 1990*

Tans *noun* the Black and Tans *IRELAND, 1992*

tantie *noun* ▶ **tantie come to town** to experience the bleed period of your menstrual cycle *TRINIDAD AND TOBAGO, 2003*

tanty *noun* a tantrum *AUSTRALIA, 1987*

tan valise *noun* a blonde prostitute *US, 1960*

tap *noun* **1** a blow given or received in a fight *UK, 1996*. **2** a murder *US, 1963*. **3** in circus and carnival usage, the admission price *US, 1981*

tap *verb* **1** to borrow something, especially money *UK, 1953*. **2** to ask f or, or imply readiness to accept, a tip. Used by ships' stewards *UK, 1961*.

3 to successfully attract a partner for sexual intimacy *UK, 2002*. **4** to have sex *US, 1949*. **5** to kill someone *US, 1963*. **6** to intercept a telephone communication. From an earlier sense of intercepting a telegraphic message *UK, 1869*. **7** in poker, to bet all of your chips, or an amount equal to an opponent's bet, depending on context *US, 1947*. ▶ **tap a kidney** to urinate *US, 1997*. ▶ **tap the pot** in bar dice games, to bet the total amount of the pot *US, 1971*

tap city *noun* when gambling, the position of being out of funds *US, 1976*

tap code *noun* a method of cell-to-cell communication in a prison where talking is forbidden *US, 1982*

tap dancer *noun* **1** a black person who curries favour from white people with obsequious conduct *US, 1974*. **2** a delivery truck driver *US, 1971*

tape and tuck *verb* (used of a male) to tape your penis and testicles between your legs in an effort to pass as a woman *AUSTRALIA, 1985*

tape dance *verb* to buy a block of stock at a price slightly higher than the last price on the tape for that stock *US, 1988*

tapioca *noun* **1** semen; an urgent need to ejaculate semen. The unsettling image of a hot milk-pudding *UK, 1980*. **2** a joker (the playing card). Rhyming slang *UK, 1992*

tapo *noun* an inadvertent error in a taped message *US, 1982*

tap-out *noun* a complete depletion of funds, especially in gambling *US, 1979*

tap out *verb* **1** to run out of money, usually as a result of gambling *US, 1939*. **2** in a casino, to relieve a dealer from duty *US, 1961*

tapped *adjective* ▷ *see:* DOOLALLY

tapped-out *adjective* having been emptied. A figurative use of 'tap' (to draw off liquid) *UK, 2001*

tapper *noun* **1** a persistent borrower *UK, 1981*. **2** a boy who persists in asking a girl for a date when reason would dictate a strategic retreat. Teen slang *US, 1951*. **3** someone who sells the police false or useless information in return for a small sum *UK, 1959*

tappers *noun* dice that have been loaded with mercury that shifts when the dice are tapped *US, 1962*

tap up *verb* to approach someone with a proposal *UK, 2001*

tar *noun* **1** coffee. Citizens' band radio slang, from the colour rather than the consistency *US, 1976*. **2** crude, dark, gummy heroin, usually from Mexico *US, 1992*. **3** opium. From the colour and consistency of raw opium *US, 1936*. **4** crack cocaine and heroin mixed and smoked together *UK, 2002*. **5** rum *TRINIDAD AND TOBAGO, 2003*. **6** a sailor. Probably a shortening of obsolete 'tarpaulin' *UK, 1676*

tara; ta-ra; tarra; tra goodbye. Originally northern, now more widespread through the agency of *Coronation Street* and other television programmes; possibly a slovening of TA-TA *UK, 1958*

tar and feather; tar *noun* a *leather* jacket. Rhyming slang *UK, 1992*

Tara Palmer-Tomkinson; Tara Palmer; tara *noun* a drama. Rhyming slang, formed from the name of a celebrity-socialite; generally applied to a minor inconvenience *UK, 2000*

tararabit goodbye. A Liverpudlian elaboration of TARA (goodbye), thus 'goodbye [for] a bit' *UK, 1984*

tar baby *noun* a black person. Offensive. From the *Br'er Rabbit* stories by Joel Chandler Harris *US, 1962*

tar beach *noun* a flat urban rooftop, used for sleeping or drug use *US, 1970*

tardust *noun* cocaine. A pun on STARDUST (cocaine) *UK, 2003*

tariff *noun* **1** the portion of a life-sentence to be served in custody. A nuance of the conventional sense *UK, 2002*. **2** the fee charged by a prostitute *TRINIDAD AND TOBAGO, 2003*

Tarka *verb* to have anal intercourse. Rhyming slang, based on the novel by Henry Williamson (1895–1977), *Tarka the Otter*, rhyming with 'DOT her' (to have anal sex) *UK, 2002*

tarmac *noun* in Canadian military aviation, the ramp section of an air base hangar line *CANADA, 1995*

tarnation *noun* used as a euphemism for 'damnation' *US, 1790*

tarred *adjective* drunk *BARBADOS, 1965*

Tarrier *noun* a Catholic, especially of Irish descent *UK, 2002*

tart *noun* **1** a woman *AUSTRALIA, 1903*. **2** a promiscuous woman *UK, 1887*. **3** a prostitute *UK, 1894*. **4** a girlfriend or sweetheart *UK, 1864*. **5** a wife or female partner. Rhyming slang for 'sweetheart' *UK, 1864*. **6** a weak, ineffectual man. A term of abuse, used to call a man a woman; a wider gender-only sense of 'tart' than when applied to a woman *UK, 1999*

tartan *noun* cocaïne. Etymology unknown *UK, 2001*

tartan banner *noun* a sixpenny coin; sixpence. Rhyming slang for TANNER that dropped out of circulation after decimalisation in 1971 *UK, 1960*

tartanize *verb* to adapt an English product for Scottish use or sale; hence, the adjective: tartanized *UK, 2004*

tarted-up *adjective* **1** dressed like a prostitute; dressed smartly *UK, 1947*. **2** of a thing, business, building, etc, having a new image or presentation. Often derogatory in tone *UK, 1984*

tart fuel *noun* bottled alcopop (branded alcoholic beverage with the characteristics of a soft drink) or other alcoholic drinks deemed to be for feminine consumption. A fashionable drink amongst young women who will, when inebriated, it is suggested/hoped by the coiner of this term, relax their moral standards and behave promiscuously *UK, 2002*

tart's delight *noun* a frilly, fussy, looped-up way of hanging lace curtains at windows *UK, 1980*

tart's fart *noun* used as a comparitive measure of little or negligible worth *UK, 2002*

tart up *verb* to dress someone up or decorate something smartly. Often with the implication of tastelessness or tawdriness *UK, 1952*

tarty *adjective* like a prostitute *UK, 1918*

Tarzan *noun* **1** sex outdoors *US, 1966*. **2** a soldier who is overly anxious to take the highly visible and dangerous point position on a combat march *US, 1991*. ▶ **like ten Tarzan** quickly; loudly *TRINIDAD AND TOBAGO, 1984*

tash; tache *noun* a moustache *UK, 1893*

tashered *adjective* drunk *UK, 2002*

tash test *noun* a man's moustache seen as an indicator of homosexuality and, hence, predictive of HIV status. Formed from TASH (a moustache). A medical observation that, hopefully, was more witty than practical *UK, 2002*

task *noun* in prison, an act of masturbation *UK, 1996*

Tasmaniac *noun* a person from Tasmania *AUSTRALIA, 1867*

Tasmanian Tiger *noun* a strain of marijuana, known elsewhere as New Zealand green, Thai Buddha and Hawaiian head *AUSTRALIA, 2002*

Tasmanian yawn *noun* vomiting, especially when experienced crossing the Tasmanian Sea *AUSTRALIA, 1995*

tassel dance *noun* a sexual dance focused on the woman's breasts and the tassels worn attached thereto *US, 1977*

tassie *noun* an intaglio (an engraved figure or design). Used by antique dealers *UK, 1977*

Tassie *noun* **1** Tasmania *AUSTRALIA, 1892*. **2** a Tasmanian *AUSTRALIA, 1914*

taste *noun* **1** an alcoholic drink *US, 1919*. **2** a sample *US, 1990*. **3** a small sample of drugs, especially heroin *US, 1952*

taste-face *noun* a heroin user who lends his syringe to others in return for small amounts of heroin *US, 1978*

-tastic *suffix* used as an intensifier. On the model of POPTASTIC *US, 2003*

tasty *adjective* **1** attractive, sexually appealing *UK, 1899*. **2** worthwhile; valuable; exhibiting strength *UK, 1975*. **3** competent; polished. The term can be applied to either the work or the person who did it *IRELAND, 1999*. **4** used of a known, especially well-respected criminal; capable of physical violence *UK, 1975*. **5** having a pleasing flavour; appetising. In conventional use from the early 1600s; by mid-C19 considered colloquial *UK, 1617*

Taswegian *nickname* a person from Tasmania. Blend of *Tas*mania and Nor*wegian AUSTRALIA, 1961*

tat *noun* **1** an article, or collection of articles, of inferior or rubbishy quality; odds and ends of material. The spelling 'tatt' is also used *UK, 1951*. **2** a tattoo *US, 1994*. **3** a swindle featuring dice and doubled bets *US, 1963*

tata *noun* nonsense *TRINIDAD AND TOBAGO, 1990*

ta-ta goodbye. At first chiefly nursery, now (in the US) simply highly affected *UK, 1823*

ta-tas *noun* the shakes *AUSTRALIA, 1977*

tatas *noun* the female breasts *US, 1995*

Tate and Lyle *noun* style. Rhyming slang, formed from the company that describes itself as 'world leader in carbohydrate ingredients' *UK, 1992*

tater; tatur; tottie *noun* a potato *UK, 1759*

tatered *adjective* drunk *US, 1993*

taters *noun* the buttocks *US, 1999*

taters in the mould; potatoes in the mould; taters *adjective* cold. Rhyming slang, most commonly used as 'taters' *UK, 1934*

tats *noun* dice, especially loaded dice or dice marked for cheating *UK, 1688*

TATT (in doctors' shorthand) tired all the time *UK, 2002*

tatted *adjective* tatooed *US, 1990*

tatting down *noun* an act of tidying away possessions and making ready for travel. Used by late 1980s – early 90s counterculture travellers *UK, 1999*

tattletale *noun* **1** in trucking, a device that records time and speed data, used by company officials to assure compliance with laws and regulations. Known conventionally as a 'tachograph' *US, 1962*. **2** in motor racing, a specially designed tachometer that measures and records the engine's highest speed during a run or lap *US, 1965*. **3** in trucking, a dangling chain that shows the approximate weight of the load by its distance from the axle *US, 1961*

Tatts *nickname* **1** Tattersalls (a racecourse enclosure) *UK, 1991*. **2** a lottery originally run from Tattersall's Hotel, Sydney *AUSTRALIA, 1916*

tatty *adjective* shabby, tawdry *UK, 1933*

tatty-bye goodbye. Probably a conflation of TA-TA and 'bye!'. Popularised by Liverpool comedian Ken Dodd (b.1929); in widespread use by the mid-1970s *UK, 1980*

taury rope *noun* the Pope. Glasgow rhyming slang, formed on Scottish dialect for 'tarry rope' *UK: SCOTLAND, 1988*

taw; toy *noun* in marbles, a marble used for shooting *UK, 1709*

tawny *adjective* excellent *US, 1993*

tax; taxing *noun* the fee paid to enter a crack house *US, 1992*

tax *verb* **1** to steal something; to rob somewhere *UK, 1994*. **2** to steal valuables from vehicles that are waiting at traffic lights *UK, 1996*. **3** in Montreal, to forcibly confront and force someone to hand over money, jewellery or clothes *CANADA, 2002*. **4** in prison, to extort money or other payment such as tobacco from a weaker prisoner by threat of violence *UK, 1996*. **5** to tease or berate someone *US, 2001*

taxi *noun* a call girl. Glossed as 'Colloquialism used in the appropriate urban circles for a prostitute who operates at a place required by her clients[.]' by Nigel Hankin, *Hanklyn-Janklyn*, 2003 *INDIA, 2003*

taxi bit *noun* a prison sentence of between five and fifteen years *US, 1950*

taxi-cab *noun* a crab; crab meat. Rhyming slang *UK, 1992*

taxi-cabs; taxis *noun* pubic lice. Rhyming slang for CRABS *UK, 1959*

taxi dance *verb* to work as a taxi dancer *US, 1973*

taxi dancer; taxi girl *noun* a woman who will dance and talk with bar patrons, but stops short of prostitution; a prostitute *US, 1930*

taxing *noun* **1** the theft of high-price training shoes being worn by the victim *UK, 1992*. **2** the robbery of drug dealers by drug dealers *UK, 2002*

taxi rank; taxi *noun* **1** an act of masturbation. Rhyming slang for WANK *UK, 1992*. **2** a bank. Rhyming slang *UK, 1998*

taxi-rank; taxi *verb* to masturbate. Rhyming slang for WANK *UK, 1984*

taxpayer *noun* a building that generates enough rental income to pay the taxes on it *US, 1921*

taylaylay *noun* the vagina *TRINIDAD AND TOBAGO, 2003*

TB *noun* **1** tuberculosis *US, 1912.* **2** in circus and carnival usage, a dull town where business is poor. An abbreviation of TOTAL BLANK *US, 1981*

TB *adjective* loyal, *true* blue *US, 1997*

TBF *noun* severe morbidity, usually terminal. A *'total body failure' US, 1989*

TBH *adjective* potentially available for gay sex. Acronym of *'to be had' UK, 1970*

T-bird *noun* **1** a Ford Thunderbird. First sold in October 1954, the Thunderbird became an American cultural icon *US, 1994.* **2** Thunderbird™ wine *US, 1973.* **3** a T-33 jet trainer aircraft *US, 1956.* **4** a capsule of amobarbital sodium and secobarbital sodium (trade name Tuinal™), a combination of central nervous system depressants *US, 1993*

T-bone *noun* a Model T Ford car, first built in 1908 *US, 1970*

T-bone *verb* while driving a car, to drive into the side of another car *US, 1991*

T bowl *noun* a toilet *US, 1982*

TBP in doctors' shorthand *total body pain UK, 2002*

TCB *verb* to take care of business. Coined by the black community and then spread into widespread use *US, 1964*

T-dot *nickname* Toronto, Ontario. From the proliferation of high-tech businesses in the city *CANADA, 2004*

tea *noun* **1** marijuana *US, 1935.* **2** in horse racing, a drug (especially cocaine or strychnine) which will stimulate a horse *US, 1951.* ► **not for all the tea in China!** certainly not!; not at any price *AUSTRALIA, 1937*

tea and cocoa *verb* to say so. Rhyming slang *UK, 1992*

tea and toast *noun* the mail, the *post.* Rhyming slang *UK, 1992*

teabag *noun* **1** a contemptible person. Rhyming slang for SLAG *UK, 2000.* **2** a marijuana cigarette *US, 1982*

tea-bag *verb* in the pursuit of sexual pleasure, to take a man's scrotum completely into the mouth, sucking and tonguing it *US, 1998*

tea-bagger *noun* in motor racing, a lover of British sports cars *US, 1965*

teabagging *noun* the sucking of a man's entire scrotum *US, 1998*

teabags *verb* to steal something. Rhyming prison slang: from TEALEAF (a thief), punning on 'bag' (to steal) *NEW ZEALAND, 1999*

tea boat *noun* in prison, a financial alliance between several prisoners to pay for tea *UK, 1996*

tea boy *noun* a person who runs errands and performs other menial tasks *UK, 1968*

tea, breakfast and dinner *noun* everything *TRINIDAD AND TOBAGO, 1990*

tea caddy *noun* an Irish person. Rhyming slang for PADDY *UK, 2000*

teach *noun* a teacher *UK, 1958*

teacher *noun* a traffic police officer who lectures violators instead of issuing citations *US, 1962*

teacher arms *noun* the flabby arms of an overweight person *AUSTRALIA, 2000*

teacup queer *noun* an effeminate homosexual man *US, 1957*

tea'd up *adjective* marijuana-intoxicated *US, 1959*

tea for two; teafer *noun* a Jewish person. Rhyming slang for 'Jew' *UK, 1992*

tea girl *noun* a quasi-prostitute in a Vietnamese bar who cadges US servicemen into buying her drinks, especially of Saigon tea *US, 1966*

tea grout *noun* a Boy Scout. Rhyming slang *UK, 1961*

tea head *noun* a user of marijuana *US, 1949*

tea hound *noun* a marijuana user *US, 1951*

tea-leaf *verb* to rob someone; to steal something. Rhyming slang; from the noun sense *UK, 2000*

tealeaf; tea-leaf *noun* **1** a thief. Rhyming slang *UK, 1903.* **2** a small penis. A small, limp, black visual metaphor *JAMAICA, 2002*

tea-leafing *adjective* inclined to thievery. Rhyming slang for THIEVING extended from TEALEAF (a thief) *UK, 1960*

team *noun* a criminal gang *UK, 1950.* ► **on the team** homosexual, from the homosexual point of view *UK, 1993*

team *adjective* dressing in a style that identifies you with a particular group *US, 1989*

team cream *noun* an orgy *US, 1970*

team-handed *adjective* working together as a gang. From TEAM (a criminal gang) *UK, 1996*

team Jesus *noun* a group of zealous, proselytising Christian students *US, 2004*

tea pad *noun* an apartment, house or room where marijuana is smoked *US, 1938*

tea party *noun* a social party where marijuana is smoked *US, 1968*

teapot *noun* **1** a heavy user of marijuana *UK, 1983.* **2** standing with your hands on your hips *NEW ZEALAND, 1998*

teapot lid; teapot *noun* **1** a Jewish person. Rhyming slang for YID *UK, 1960.* **2** a child. Rhyming slang for KID *UK, 1960.* **3** a pound sterling. Rhyming slang for QUID *UK, 1960*

teapot lid; teapot *verb* to fool, to pretend. Rhyming slang for KID *UK, 1934*

tear *noun* **1** a spree, a period of self-indulgent enjoyment *UK: SCOTLAND, 1985.* **2** an expedition to deface advertising billboards *US, 2001.* **3** a manipulation of a record to create a musical effect that plays a sample in two sections with a jolt-effect in the middle, *2002.* ► **on the tear** engaged in a drinking session *IRELAND, 2003*

tear *verb* **1** to leave, especially in a hurry *US, 1951.* **2** to surf aggressively and with skill *US, 1988.* ► **tear a passion to tatters** in a dramatic performance, to over-act *US, 1973.* ► **tear a strip off someone; tear someone off a strip** to reprimand someone *UK, 1941.* ► **tear it** to frustrate or thwart someone's intentions, usually in the phrase 'that's torn it' *UK, 1909.* ► **tear off a chunk** to have sex *US, 1973.* ► **tear off a tab; tear off a scab** to open a can of beer *NEW ZEALAND, 1984.* ► **tear off; tear off a piece** to have sex *US, 1964.* ► **tear someone a new asshole** to thrash someone; to abuse someone verbally *US, 1968.* ► **tear the arse out of** to destroy or spoil something *UK, 1999.* ► **tear the roof off** to create or intensify mass excitement through the agency of loud music. A refinement of 'raise the roof' (to make a great noise) *UK, 2001.* ► **tear them apart; tear them up** to delight an audience *UK, 1933.* ► **tear your pants** to commit a social gaffe *US, 1947*

tear-arse around; tear-arse about; tear ass *verb* to race about wildly. Elaboration of 'tear' (to rush) *UK, 1999*

tearaway *noun* a minor criminal, one who tends towards violence at the slightest excuse. Originally a 'ladies' tearaway', a criminal specialising in snatching (tearing away) women's handbags *UK, 1958*

teardrop *noun* **1** a dose of crack cocaine, packaged in the corner of a plastic bag *US, 1994.* **2** a surfboard that is wide at the rear and narrow at the nose *AUSTRALIA, 1963*

tearjerker *noun* a melodramatic or sentimental and sad story or song *US, 1921*

tear-off *noun* a minor criminal, one who tends towards violence at the slightest excuse. A variation of TEARAWAY *UK, 1966*

tearoom; t-room *noun* a public toilet. From an era when a great deal of homosexual contact was in public toilets; probably an abbreviation of 'toilet room', a term used in reported criminal prosecutions of homosexuals in the late C19. A public toilet in Illinois was the focus of Laud Humphrey's famous sociological study *Tearoom Trade US, 1941*

tea-room cruiser *noun* a male homosexual prostitute who frequents public toilets *US, 1982*

tea-room trade *noun* a sexual partner found in a public toilet *US, 1980*

tear-up *noun* **1** a gang fight; a brawl. From conventional 'tear-up' (a commotion) *US, 1964.* **2** in jazz use, a period of wild, inspired music-making *US, 1958.* **3** any valueless letter addressed to Scotland Yard. Officially filed in the Metropolitan Police's General Registry as GM [General Matters]51 *UK, 1999*

tease and please *noun* sexual arousal after which satisfaction is delayed under the pretence that such gratification is denied, especially when advertised as a service offered by a prostitute *UK, 2003*

teaser *noun* **1** in horse breeding, a horse used to test a mare's readiness for breeding *US, 1976*. **2** in sports betting, a bet that ties two or more games together *US, 1975*

teaspoon *noun* a measure of heroin or other narcotic drug *UK, 1996*

tea strainer *noun* a trainer (a shoe). Rhyming slang *UK, 1992*

tea-towel head *noun* an offensive term for an Arabic person *AUSTRALIA, 1981*

tea-towel holder *noun* the anus. A resemblance in shape and detail *UK, 2002*

tea wagon *noun* in the television and film industries, the console used by the sound mixer *US, 1977*

tec *noun* a detective *UK, 1879*

tecate; tecatos *noun* heroin. Directly from Mexican Spanish *US, 1982*

tecato *noun* a heroin or morphine addict. Directly from Mexican Spanish *US, 1970*

tech *noun* **1** a technical college, an institution that provides further and higher education. Often 'the Tech' is used for your local one *UK, 2000*. **2** a technician; someone employed to deal with technological devices, especially in a creative milieu. Also called a 'techie' *US, 1942*. **3** a nine-millimetre handgun *US, 1995*

tech dog *noun* in foot-propelled scootering, a rider with strong technical skills *UK, 2000*

technical; tech *noun* in foot-powered scootering, any trick that is performed on a flat surface or ledge and requires a good deal of technical skill *UK, 2000*

technicolour laugh *noun* an act of vomiting; vomit *AUSTRALIA, 1964*

technicolour yawn *noun* an act of vomiting *AUSTRALIA, 1964*

techno *adjective* as a combining form, denotes intrinsic technological expertise or inspiration, especially in relation to computing, gadgetry or music fashions *US, 1989*

technobabble *noun* pretentious scientific chatter. Modelled on 'psychobabble' *US, 1981*

technodolt *noun* a person who is completely technologically illiterate *US, 1990*

technodweeb *noun* a person who is passionately interested in technology *US, 1990*

technosavvy *noun* someone who understands technology *US, 1996*

technowords *noun* a scientific vocabulary *US, 1996*

teddy *noun* a bottle of alcohol, legal or otherwise *CANADA, 1986*

teddy bear *noun* **1** a dose of LSD identified by the printed picture of a teddy bear *UK, 2003*. **2** a person who dresses and behaves in a showy manner. Rhyming slang for LAIR *AUSTRALIA, 1944*. **3** a pear. Rhyming slang, formed from a cuddly toy *UK, 1992*

teddy bear suit *noun* heavy winter garments issued to US troops during World War 2 and later in Korea *US, 1982*

Teddy Boy; Teddy; Ted *noun* a member of a youth cult of the mid-to late 1950s, characterised by a style of dress loosely inspired by fashions of the Edwardian era (1901–10). Edward abbreviates to Teddy and Ted. Teddy boys referred to themselves as Teds *UK, 1954*

Ted Frazer *noun* a cut-throat razor. Rhyming slang *UK, 1997*

Ted Heath *noun* a thief. Rhyming slang, formed (satirically) on Edward Heath (1916–2005), Conservative Prime Minister 1970–74 *UK, 1972*

Ted Ray *adjective* homosexual. Rhyming slang for FAY; probably formed from the British comedian and actor (1905–77); however, Bodmin Dark, *Dirty Cockney Rhyming Slang*, 2003, suggests an American jazz musician of the same name *UK, 2003*

Teds *noun* ▷*see:* EDWARD HEALTH

teedle-ee *noun* a urination. Glasgow rhyming slang for PEE *UK: SCOTLAND, 1988*

teed off *adjective* angry *US, 1950*

teef *verb* to steal something. A mispronunciation of 'thieve' or an elision of TEA-LEAF (to thieve) *UK, 1997*

teem *noun* team. Fashionable misspelling *UK, 2002*

teenager *noun* **1** a person aged between 13 and 19. Originally 'teen-ager'. Since about 1955 has usually been written as one word, and since about 1960 has been regarded as standard English *US, 1935*. **2** cocaine *UK, 2002*

teener *noun* one sixteenth of an ounce *US, 1993*

teen-flick *noun* a film intended for teenagers *UK, 2003*

teenie *noun* **1** a younger teenager *US, 1968*. **2** one-sixteenth of a dollar. Trader usage *US, 1992*

teensy *adjective* tiny. A childish corruption *US, 1899*

teensy-weensy *adjective* very small *US, 1906*

teenth *noun* a six*teenth* of an ounce (of drugs) *UK, 2001*

teeny *adjective* very small *UK, 1825*

teenybop *adjective* of or for teenyboppers *US, 1967*

teenybopper *noun* a young teenager, especially a girl *US, 1965*

teenyhooker *noun* a young female prostitute *US, 1982*

teeny weeny *adjective* tiny. 'Teeny' came from 'tiny', and then the reduplicative 'teeny weeny', which is often found in the same breath as 'itsy bitsy' *US, 1931*

tee off *verb* **1** to annoy or to irritate someone *US, 1961*. **2** to fart *UK, 1998*

tees *noun* dice on which some numbers are repeated, usually made with identical numbers on opposite sides *US, 1950*

teeth *noun* cocaine; crack cocaine. From the resemblance of the drug to small teeth *US, 1994*. ▶ **my back teeth are floating** I am desperate to urinate *UK, 2001*

TEETH (in doctors' shorthand) *t*ried *e*verything *e*lse, *t*ry *h*omeopathy. Medical slang *UK, 2003*

teeth and tits used to remind dancers that an attractive smile and a distracting display will stop an audience noticing the footwork. Theatrical *UK, 2005*

teething troubles *noun* initial problems with any new device, invention, enterprise, technology, etc *UK, 1937*

teev *noun* a television *AUSTRALIA, 1982*

teflon *adjective* describes a person to whom blame doesn't stick. From the non-stick properties of polytetrafluoroethylene, trademarked as Teflon™ *US, 2004*

tekno *noun* the recreational drug ketamine. Back slang for 'on ket' *UK, 2004*

tele *noun* a television set; television. Early use mainly US (as television itself), adopted enthusistically in the UK in the mid-50s *US, 1940*

telegram *noun* **1** a message designed for mass distribution from prisoner to prisoner, passed from one cell to the next *US, 1992*. **2** in prison, a written notice given to an inmate who has been placed on report for an offence *UK, 1996*

telegraph *verb* to inadvertently disclose or reveal your intentions to an opponent *UK, 1925*

telephone *noun* a bilingual Canadian who serves as a go-between for English and French speakers *CANADA, 1979*

telephone booth *noun* in poker, a player who regularly 'calls' (matches the bet of the previous player) *US, 1988*

telephone number *noun* a long prison sentence *US, 1950*

telephone numbers *noun* **1** a large sum of money *US, 1979*. **2** in horse racing, a winning bet at high odds *US, 1934*

telephone pole *noun* ▷*see:* FLYING TELEPHONE POLE

telephone tag *noun* the serial leaving of messages when two people who are trying to talk by telephone can never reach each other *US, 1979*

telescope *noun* the penis. A jocular euphemism *US, 1968*

teletubby; telletubby *noun* a husband. Rhyming slang for HUBBY, formed on *Teletubbies*, a BBC television programme for young children, first seen in 1996 *UK, 1998*

tell *noun* **1** an unintentionally honest reaction; a revealing piece of body-language. Adopted from gambling jargon *UK, 1999*. **2** in gambling, any mannerism that reveals the relative value of the player's hand *US, 1991*

tell *verb* ▶ **I'll tell you what; tell you what** I'll tell you something; this is how it is; often as the introduction to a suggestion *UK, 1596*. ▶ **tell it like it is 1** to speak directly, candidly and with a self-righteous conviction of access to a great truth *US, 1965*. **2** to tell the whole truth. In black usage originally *US, 1964*. ▶ **tell on someone** to inform on someone *UK, 1539*. ▶ **tell someone where to get off** to severely rebuke someone; to scold someone *US, 1900*. ▶ **tell the tale** in a swindle, to explain to the victim just how he will profit from the arrangement being proposed *US, 1989*

tell ▶ **tell someone where to stick it** to emphatically reject. A variation of 'stick it up your arse' *UK, 1999*

teller *noun* a skateboarder whose tales of accomplishments are exaggerated *US, 1984*

telling-off *noun* a scolding, a reprimand. From TELL OFF *UK, 1911*

tell it to the marines! used for registering disbelief. Formed, apparently, from an inter-service jibe against the credulity of the marines *UK, 1806*

tell me another one used for registering disbelief *UK, 1914*

tell off *verb* to scold or reprimand someone *UK, 1919*

telltale *noun* in the language of wind surfing, a streamer on the mast used to determine wind direction *US, 1985*

tell-tale-tit *noun* someone who tells tales. A nursery term, featured in children's playground rhymes *UK, 1841*

telly *noun* television *US, 1940*. ▶ **off the telly** as seen on television *UK, 2000*

Telly *nickname* Telegraph Avenue, Berkeley, California *US, 1966*

telly- *prefix* telephone. Used for constructions such as 'tellypole' or 'tellywires' *US, 1970*

temazzies; temazies; temmies; temazes; tems *noun* Temazepam™, a branded tranquillizer *UK, 1998*

temp *noun* a temporary worker *US, 1980*

temp *verb* to work as a temporary worker *US, 1980*

temper *noun* a restaurant customer who leaves a 10% tip *US, 1995*

temperance punch *noun* a non-alcoholic fruit punch drink *US, 1957*

temple balls; temple bells; temple hash *noun* potent hashish shaped as small balls, claimed to originate in Nepal *US, 1971*

temple du vin *noun* Le Clos Jordan, a winery to be designed by Frank Gehry on the Jordan Bench, on Ontario's Niagara Peninsula, Canada's main wine-producing area *CANADA, 2002*

ten *noun* **1** a perfectly beautiful woman. Based on a grading scale of one to ten, popularised in the 1979 film *10* starring Bo Derek *US, 1979*. **2** a tablet of MDMA, the recreational drug best known as ecstasy *US, 2003*

ten *adjective* very good. Teen slang, from the marking of schoolwork *UK, 1977*

ten-bob twist *noun* a drug sale involving drugs, usually marijuana, costing ten shillings *UK, 1983*

ten-cent line *noun* in an illegal betting operation, the ten percent charge for making a bet *US, 1973*

ten-cent pistol *noun* a dose of heroin that is either adulterated with a poison or contains a more pure heroin than usual, sold or given to someone with the intent of injuring or killing them *US, 1966*

ten-cent rock *noun* ten dollars' worth of crack cocaine *US, 1991*

ten commandments *noun* bare feet. As Long John Silver said, it is good to have ten toes *TRINIDAD AND TOBAGO, 2003*

tend *verb* to mind your own business *US, 1995*

ten-days *noun* any temporary job *TRINIDAD AND TOBAGO, 2003*

ten-day sweat *noun* treatment for a sexually transmitted infection, involving heat therapy and sulpha-based drugs *US, 1949*

tender *adjective* **1** in poker, said of a hand that is probably unplayable *US, 1988*. **2** weakened by oxidation; rusty *CANADA, 1992*

tenement *noun* in hold 'em poker, a ten and nine *US, 1996*

ten F *noun* a gall bladder patient. Often a fat, fair, fecund, fortyish, flatulent, female with foul, frothy, floating faeces *US, 1985*

ten-man job *noun* a very tough man, a very hard man to arrest *UK, 1998*

Tennant Creek *noun* a Greek person. Rhyming slang, from the name of a goldmining town in the Northern Territory *AUSTRALIA, 1977*

tenner *noun* **1** a ten-pound note; the value of £10; a ten-dollar note *UK, 1845*. **2** a prison sentence of ten years *US, 1950*. **3** in the television and film industries, a 10,000-watt spotlight *US, 1990*

Tennessee top hat *noun* a hairstyle in which the hair is worn short at the front and long at the back. Better known, perhaps, as a MULLET *US, 2000*

tennies *noun* tennis shoes; trainers *US, 1965*

tennis, anyone? used for humorously suggesting an activity. Seen as quintessentially British and enormously witty in its many variant forms *US, 1951*

tennis racket; tennis *noun* a jacket. Rhyming slang *UK, 1992*

tennis shoes *noun* tyres *US, 1976*

ten one hundred *noun* the act of urination *US, 1976*

ten over *noun* a surfing stance in which the surfer's ten toes extend over the nose or front of the board *US, 1991*

ten percenter *noun* a person who buys and resells stolen goods *US, 1976*

tens *noun* amphetamine *UK, 2003*

tense *adjective* used of a computer program, smart and economical *US, 1983*

tension *noun* crack cocaine *US, 1993*

tensky *noun* a ten-dollar note. The 'sky' is a meaningless decorative embellishment *US, 1962*

ten-spot *noun* **1** a ten-dollar note *US, 1954*. **2** a ten-pound note. Adopted directly from the previous sense *UK, 1984*. **3** a ten-year prison sentence *US, 1965*

Tenth Street *noun* a ten-dollar note *US, 1946*

'tention *noun* in poker, a ten *US, 1951*

tent peg *noun* an egg. Rhyming slang *UK, 1949*

tent pole *noun* an erect penis. From the image of an erect penis pushing up against a sheet *US, 1992*

tent squirrel *noun* in circus and carnival usage, a performer *US, 1981*

tenuc; teenuc *noun* the vagina; an unpleasant or despicable person. Back slang for CUNT *UK, 1904*

termination dust *noun* the first snow of the winter. Because it terminates construction in the north *US, 1957*

termite *noun* a carpenter *US, 1963*

terper *noun* a professional dancer. An abbreviation of Terpischore, daughter of Jupiter and Mnemosyne, the muse of dancing *US, 1973*

terps; turps *noun* a cough syrup containing elixir of terpin hydrate and codeine, abused for non-medicinal purposes *US, 1971*

terr; ter; terro; terry *noun* a guerilla soldier; a terrorist. Originally Rhodesian military slang *SOUTH AFRICA, 1978*

terra-poo *noun* a crossbreed of terrier and poodle *US, 2001*

terrible *adjective* excellent *US, 1960*

terrible Turk *noun* work. Rhyming slang *UK, 1992*

terribly *adverb* used as a positive intensifier with the meaning exceedingly, greatly, very *UK, 1833*

terrier *noun* a railway track worker *US, 1977*

terrif *adjective* terrific. Not a lot of thought goes into clipped adjectives, and with a few exceptions they do not last long *US, 1951*

Territory rig *noun* any of various adaptations of formal attire worn by men in far northern Australia *AUSTRALIA, 1964*

terrorist *noun* a teacher who intimidates his pupils into learning. Teen slang, post 11th September 2001 *US, 2002*

terrorize *verb* to cover something with graffiti *US, 1997*

terror track *noun* in cricket, a wicket best suited to fast bowlers *UK, 1996*

Terry toon *noun* a prostitute's pimp. Rhyming slang for HOON *AUSTRALIA, 1973*

Terry Waite *adjective* late. Rhyming slang, formed (surely with irony) on the church envoy and hostage negotiator (b.1939) who was held hostage in Beirut for 1,760 days between January 1987 and November 1991 *UK, 1998*

tess *noun* a young man *TRINIDAD AND TOBAGO, 1960*

test *verb* ▶ **test the shocks** to have sex in a car *US, 1997*

tester *noun* a sample of drugs *UK, 2000*

testicules *noun* the testicles *UK, 2003*

test-tube baby *noun* a poker player whose experience is largely limited to simulated computer poker games *US, 1996*

test-tube wallah *noun* a forensic scientist. Police use *UK, 1971*

tete *noun* the female breast *TRINIDAD AND TOBAGO, 2003*

Texas Cadillac *noun* a Chevrolet Suburban sports utility vehicle *CANADA, 1991*

Texas gate *noun* a cattleguard *CANADA, 1997*

Texas mickey *noun* a very large bottle of alcohol *CANADA, 2001*

Texas pot *noun* marijuana cultivated in Texas *US, 2003*

Texas Ranger; TR *noun* danger. Glasgow rhyming slang *UK: SCOTLAND, 1988*

Texas rat *noun* in the used car business, a car previously owned by a salesman or other long-distance driver *US, 1968*

Texas stop *noun* slowing down but not fully stopping as required by law at a stop sign *US, 1962*

Texas sunflowers *noun* in craps, a roll of two fives *US, 1983*

Texas tea *noun* **1** marijuana *US, 1938*. **2** oil *US, 1984*

Texas toothbrush *noun* the penis. In Texas, known as an 'Oklahoma toothbrush' *US, 1994*

Texas Volkswagen *noun* a Cadillac *US, 1956*

Texican *noun* a Texan *US, 1984*

Tex-Mex *noun* marijuana, of *Texan-Mexican* origin *UK, 1998*

Tex Ritter; tex *noun* bitter (beer). Rhyming slang, formed from the US cowboy film actor, 1907–74 *UK, 1992*

text *verb* to send a text message on a mobile phone *UK, 2001*

textile *noun* among naturists, a person who wears clothes *UK, 1995*

textile *adjective* clothed, as distinct from nude. From the noun sense *UK, 1995*

tezzers *noun* the testicles *UK, 2003*

TFB *too fucking bad US, 1996*

TFTF an after-dinner bloated condition unsuited to the advancement of romance. A coded message: 'too fat to fuck' *UK, 2002*

TG *noun* a young member of a youth gang *US, 2001*

TGIF *Thank God it's Friday*. Notable variations: the restaurant chain 'T.G.I. Friday's', established in New York in 1965, now worldwide; and the controversial UK television programme *TFI Friday*, 1996–2000 *US, 1941*

T-grams *noun* a grandmother *US, 1998*

TH *noun* in betting, odds of 8–1 *UK, 1991*

Thai Buddha *noun* a strain of marijuana, known elsewhere as New Zealand green, Tasmanian tiger and Hawaiian head *AUSTRALIA, 2002*

Thai green *noun* a strain of marijuana originating in Thailand *UK, 2002*

Thai stick *noun* marijuana cultivated in Thailand, soaked in hashish oil, wound on short thin sticks of bamboo which are bundled for sale; a cigarette rolled from marijuana cultivated in Thailand *US, 1975*

Thai weed; Thai *noun* marijuana cultivated in Thailand; marijuana from Thailand soaked in hashish oil *UK, 1997*

Thames trout; trout *noun* a condom. Appears to be a London coinage, probably after the rare appearance of a condom floating down the River Thames; remembered by a correspondent from Sheffield as a 1970s usage *UK, 2004*

thang *noun* thing. Slang by vowel exchange *US, 1977*

thanie *noun* heroin *UK, 2003*

thank fuck used in relief when others may be grateful to God. Euphemistic use of 'fuck' for what might otherwise border on blasphemy *UK, 1999*

thank goodness used as a register of heartfelt or exaggerated gratitude *UK, 1872*

thanks a bunch used as an insincere or derisory declaration of gratitude *UK, 2003*

thanks a bundle used as an insincere or derisory declaration of gratitude *UK, 1990*

thanks a million thank you very much indeed. Usually sincere, but occasionally derisory *UK, 1984*

thanks awfully thank you! Quintessentially English middle- and upper-class *UK, 1890*

thanks but no thanks used when declining an offer *UK, 1979*

thanks ever so thank you! *UK, 1914*

thank you and good night! used in final dismissal of a foolish suggestion, or in surrender to overwhelming misfortune. A valedictory phrase that became a broadcasting cliché which inspired a catchphrase *UK, 1975*

thank-you-m'am *noun* a bump or dip in a road which produces a moment of slight uneasiness in the stomach *US, 1960*

that *adjective* used as a mildly derogatory prefix to a (usually proper) noun *UK, 1976*

that *adverb* to such a degree; so; very. In conventional use from the mid-C15, but by C20 considered colloquial or dialect *UK, 1999*

that *pronoun* used persuasively in anticipated commendation *UK, 1849*

that and this *noun* urine; an act of urination. Rhyming slang, PISS, also employed as a verb *UK, 1961*

Thatcher *noun* a type of MDMA, the recreational drug best known as ecstasy. From Margaret Thatcher (b.1925), former UK Prime Minister 1979–90, later Baroness Thatcher of Kesteven; her name is used here by an illicit drug manufacturer, perhaps as a tribute to her commitment to free enterprise *UK, 1996*

Thatcher wagon *noun* a car with the back cut away *CANADA, 1987*

that had to hurt! used as a humorous if not particularly sympathetic observation of a painful event *US, 1992*

that'll be the day! used of something that is not very likely to occur or be done *AUSTRALIA, 1941*

that'll happen used as a humorous comment on something that should not happen or never happens. Coined and popularised by ESPN's Keith Olberman *US, 1997*

that plays used for expressing approval *US, 1966*

that's chalk! that's great! *BAHAMAS, 1982*

that's close used for expressing doubt about a statement or request *US, 1973*

that's dead! used for expressing a strong negative *US, 1991*

that's that used in final emphasis of a preceding statement: that's all there is, there is no more *UK, 1872*

that's the name of that tune used for summing up or signalling the end of an explanation. A signature line of actor Robert Blake on the television police drama *Baretta* (ABC, 1975–78). Repeated with referential humour, especially after Blake's arrest in the early 2000s for the murder of his wife *US, 1978*

that's the ticket! used as a humorous expression of assent. From a skit on *Saturday Night Live* featuring Jon Lovitz as a pathological liar *US, 1986*

that's what I'm talking about! I agree strongly! Almost a cliché *US, 2002*

that's word! used for expressing strong assent *US, 1992*

that time *noun* the bleed period of a woman's menstrual cycle *US, 1954*

that way *adjective* homosexual. Shortened from the euphemistic phrase 'that way inclined' *UK, 1956*

thaw shay *noun* a spendthrift *IRELAND, 2000*

THC *noun* marijuana. The psychoactive chemical in marijuana is delta-9-tetrahydrocannabinol, or THC *US, 1971*

THC doctors' shorthand for what the homeless require from a day and night's hospitalisation: *three hots and a cot* (three meals and a bed) *UK, 2002*

the *adjective* **1** my. Colloquial *UK, 1838.* **2** used in the formation of colloquial nicknames for places. Thus Alice Springs becomes 'the Alice'; Mount Isa becomes 'the Isa'; Cloncurry becomes 'the Curry'; Wollongong becomes 'the Gong' *AUSTRALIA, 1883*

theatrical *noun* an actor. Generally seen in the plural *UK, 1859*

Thelma Ritter; the thelma *noun* a toilet; the anus. Rhyming slang for SHITTER, formed from the name of the US film actress, 1905–69 *UK, 1998*

Thelonius Monk; thelonius *noun* semen. Rhyming slang for SPUNK, formed from the name of the US jazz pianist, 1917–82 *UK, 1992*

them's my orders used as an apology for acting in accordance with orders *US, 1973*

them's the breaks used as a world-wise expression of resigned acceptance of a misfortune *US, 1988*

them's the rules used as a humorous deference to protocol or rules *US, 1997*

them things *noun* marijuana cigarettes *US, 1992*

the nerve of the scurve! used as a humorous exclamation, half admiring *US, 1975*

there *adverb* ▶ **be there** to be alert and alive to your situation *UK, 1890.* ▶ **have been there; have been there before** to have experienced something *UK, 1877.* ▶ **have someone there** to cause someone to be at a loss; to nonplus someone *UK, 1937*

there it is used as a common form of assent by US soldiers in Vietnam *US, 1991*

there I was with Davey Crockett... used as a humorous introduction to a story. A signature line used by the Trooper Duffy character played by Bob Steele on the television comedy *F Troop* (ABC, 1965–67). Repeated with referential humour *US, 1967*

Theresa Truncheon; Theresa *noun* a police officer; the police. An example of CAMP trans-gender assignment, in this case an assonant play on 'truncheon' as stereotypical police equipment *UK, 1992*

there's no answer to that! used in answer to a question, implying an innuendo within the question which renders an answer unnecessary. A catchphrase of British comedian Eric Morecambe, 1926–84, widely adopted as a useful face-saver *UK, 1975*

there you are *noun* tea (a drink). Rhyming slang for CHAR *UK, 1992*

there you are then!; there you are! used as the (triumphant) last words in an argument as a point is proved. Often preceded by 'so' or 'well' *UK, 1907*

there you go! used for expressing approval *US, 1970*

thermos bottle *noun* a tanker lorry. From the shape *US, 1976*

these and those *noun* **1** the toes. Rhyming slang *UK, 1960.* **2** the nose. Rhyming slang *AUSTRALIA, 1960.* **3** clothes. Rhyming slang *UK, 1992*

the shot heard 'round the world *noun* the homerun hit by New York Giants Bobby Thompson to defeat the Brooklyn Dodgers in the final game of a three-game playoff series for the National League Championship in 1951. An allusion to the first skirmish of the American Revolution on the village green in Lexington, Massachusetts, on 19th April 1775 *US, 1951*

thesp *noun* an actor. An abbreviation of the conventional 'thespian' *UK, 1962*

thews *noun* muscles; the thighs; the forearms. A variation of the conventional sense as 'vigour'; only recorded in the plural *UK, 1966*

They *noun* the mysterious authority over all authority, the power behind the throne. Beloved in the political culture of the 1960s *US, 1968*

Theydon Bois *noun* noise. Rhyming slang, formed from the name of an Essex village *UK, 1992*

thick *adjective* **1** in close association, familiar, intimate. Often elaborated as THICK AS THIEVES *UK, 1756.* **2** stupid, dense *UK, 1935.* **3** sexually appealing, attractive, well built *US, 1998.* **4** of a bet, large *UK, 1991*

thick-a *adjective* very dense. Used in Maine, as in 'thick-a-fog', 'thick-a-snow' or 'thick-a-vapor' *US, 1978*

thick and thin *noun* **1** the chin. Rhyming slang *UK, 1992.* **2** gin. Rhyming slang *UK, 1992*

thick as a docker's sandwich *adjective* very stupid. 'Thick as' is used as the basis for many similes *UK, 1998*

thick as a plank *adjective* very stupid. The simplified variation of THICK AS TWO SHORT PLANKS *UK, 1980*

thick as a pudding *adjective* very stupid. A north of England variation on a theme; the 'pudding' is a Yorkshire pudding *UK: ENGLAND, 2003*

thick as pigshit *adjective* very stupid *UK, 1999*

thick as thieves *adjective* in close association, familiar, intimate, inseparable *UK, 1833*

thick as two short planks *adjective* very stupid. Originally military; one of the best-known modern variations on a Shakespearean theme *UK, 1984*

thick dick; thick Dick *noun* a stupid person. Teen slang *UK, 1982*

thick ear *noun* a blow round the head. From the swelling of the ear – if the blow is accurate *UK, 1909*

thick end of the stick *noun* an unfair position to be in, or inequitable treatment *UK, 1957*

thick head *noun* a headache, especially one that results from drinking alcohol *UK, 1991*

thickhead *adjective* idiotic, foolish, stupid. From the noun sense *UK, 1999*

thickie; thicky; thicko *noun* a fool. Variations of THICK *UK, 1968*

thick on the ground *adjective* abundant, numerous, crowded *UK, 1893*

thick piss *noun* semen *NEW ZEALAND, 1998*

thief *noun* in horse racing, a horse that runs worst when its chances seem best *US, 1976*

Thief Row *noun* London Heathrow airport. Jocular but telling *UK, 1999*

thieve *noun* ▶ **on the thieve** engaged in the occupation or act of stealing *UK, 2001*

thieving *adjective* inclined to thievery. Originally in conventional use *UK, 1598*

thighbrows *noun* female pubic hair that escapes the confines of underwear or swimwear *UK, 2002*

thigh-highs *noun* stockings worn up the middle of the thigh *US, 1995*

thigh opener *noun* a vodka gimlet *US, 1985*

thighslapper *noun* in pantomime, the role of principal boy. From the traditional gesture by which an attractive actress convinces an audience of her manhood *UK, 2003*

T. Hill *noun* Tommy Hilfiger™ clothing *US, 1998*

thimble and thumb; thimble *noun* rum. Rhyming slang *UK, 1992*

thimble-titted *adjective* small breasted *US, 1994*

thin *noun* in prison, a key *UK, 1996*

thin blue line *noun* the police. From the image of, and originally recorded as, a line of police holding back a crowd *UK, 1984*

thing *noun* **1** used to replace any noun that the user cannot or does not wish to specify. Also called a 'thingy' *US, 1968.* **2** the penis. Since Chaucer, and still *UK, 1386.* **3** the vagina. Euphemism. Early use implied in obsolete 'thingstable' (1785) where 'thing' replaces CUNT in a policeman's title *US, 1970*. **4** an interest, obsession, attraction *US, 1841*. **5** a romantic affair *US, 1974*. **6** an instinctive or irrational dislike of, or aversion to, someone or something *UK, 1936*. **7** heroin; a capsule of heroin *US, 1958*. **8** cocaine *UK, 2002*. ▶ **do your own thing; do your thing** to behave according to your own self-centred philosophy, appetites and idiosyncracies. Originally a black coinage, adopted by the hippies in the 1960s *US, 1967*. ▶ **have a thing for; have a thing about** to be attracted, perhaps obsessively so, to someone or something *UK, 1936*. ▶ **the Thing** an M-50A1 Ontos antitank tracked vehicle, heavily armed *US, 1990*. ▶ **the thing** the requisite, notable or special point *UK, 1850*

thingamajig; thingumajig; thingummyjig *noun* used as a psuedo-term for something the name of which is unknown, forgotten or not important *UK, 1824*

thingamerry; thingumbobsy *noun* an object the name of which escapes the speaker *BARBADOS, 1965*

thingie; thingy *noun* **1** a thing *UK, 1933*. **2** the penis *UK, 1977*

thingio *noun* used as a vague replacement for an unremembered or unnamed person, object or action. A variation of THINGIE (a replacement noun) *UK, 2001*

thingio *verb* used as a vague replacement for an unremembered or unnamed verb *UK, 2002*

thingo *noun* an unnamed, or temporarily unnameable, person or thing *AUSTRALIA, 1966*

things *noun* **1** possessions, personal effects carried with you at a given time *UK, 1290*. **2** garments, clothing *UK, 1634*. ▶ **do things to someone** to excite someone, especially sexually; to arouse a passion, whether deep or momentary *UK, 1951*

things are crook in Tallarook things are very bad. Tallarook is a town in central Victoria *AUSTRALIA, 1963*

things-on-the-springs *noun* a military inspection of a soldier's gear displayed on his bed *US, 1991*

thing-thing *noun* an object the name of which escapes or is unimportant to the speaker *US, 1976*

thingumabob; thingummybob *noun* used as a replacement for any noun that the user cannot or does not wish to specify *UK, 1832*

thingummy *noun* used as a replacement for any noun that the user cannot or does not wish to specify *UK, 1796*

thingummy-whatsit *noun* used as a euphemistic replacement for any noun that the user cannot or does not wish to specify *UK, 2002*

thingy *noun* in drag racing, a car that has been modified and enhanced for speed *US, 1960* ▷ *see:* THINGIE

thin hairs *noun* ▶ **have someone by the thin hairs** to hold someone at a disadvantage; to exercise complete control over someone *US, 1946*

think *verb* ▶ **think outside the box** to reject standard assumptions and strive for a creative solution to a problem. From a brain-teaser puzzle which can be solved only if you reject the boundaries of a box. It vaulted into cliché use quickly, and provided the inspiration for author Jim Tompkins' 2001 book *Think Outside the Box: The Most Trite, Generic, Hokey, Overused, Cliched or Unmotivating Motivational Slogans US, 1999*. ▶ **think your shit doesn't stink** to be very conceited *UK, 1961*. ▶ **you're not paid to think** a catchphrase admonition in response to any excuse that begins 'but I thought...'. Originally a military truism *UK, 1971*

think again, dearie used for humorously expressing the negative *US, 1987*

think it ain't? used for expressing affirmation *US, 1992*

thinko *noun* a momentary loss of memory or disruption in a thought process. A play on 'typo' *US, 1991*

think-piece *noun* a serious article of journalism *UK, 1960*

think tank *noun* a toilet. Punning on the term usually applied to non-governmental organisations that analyse policy *US, 1997*

thin man *noun* a person who does not exist who is placed on a payroll as a bookkeeping fiction *US, 1973*

thinny *noun* a very thin hand-rolled cigarette or joint *UK, 2000*

thin one *noun* a dime, or ten-cent piece *US, 1962*

thin on the ground *adjective* sparse, scarce. The natural opposite of THICK ON THE GROUND (abundant) *UK, 1942*

thin-out *verb* to depart *UK, 1987*

third base *noun* in casino blackjack, the seat immediately to the dealer's right *US, 1985*

third degree *noun* an intense level of interrogation *US, 1880*

third hat *noun* an assistant drill instructor in the US Marine Corps. Generally the drill instructor who hands out physical discipline – Physical Incentive Training *US, 2004*

third leg *noun* the penis *US, 1994*

third rail *noun* **1** a bill, especially in a restaurant. A term of the 1940s music industry *US, 1950*. **2** an extremely controversial political issue. Like the third rail in an electric railway system, it is to be avoided *US, 2000*. **3** inexpensive, potent alcohol *US, 1962*

third sex *noun* homosexuals as a group *US, 1896*

third-world botherer *noun* a person who acts upon the need to do good in less fortunate areas of the world *UK, 2000*

third world briefcase *noun* a large portable stereo system associated, stereotypically, with black youth culture *US, 1987*

thirst monster *noun* a crack cocaine user *US, 2002*

thirsty *adjective* intensely craving crack cocaine *US, 1992*

thirteen *noun* **1** marijuana; a marijuana cigarette. Because 'M' is the 13th letter of the alphabet *US, 1966*. **2** in a deck of playing cards, any king *US, 1996* ▷ *see:* 13

thirteen *nickname* the Mexican Mafia prison gang *US, 2000*

thirteenth gear *noun* in trucking, neutral gear, used to coast down hills *US, 1971*

thirty days *noun* in poker, a hand with three tens *US, 1963*

thirty dirty miles *noun* in a game of poker, a hand with three tens *US, 1963*

thirty miles of railroad track *noun* in poker, a hand consisting of three tens *US, 1988*

thirtysomething *adjective* describing the age of the generation of baby boomers as they moved into their thirties. From the name of a television drama (1987–91) focusing on YUPPIE angst *US, 1990*

thirty-thirty *noun* a central nervous system stimulant other than amphetamine packaged to look like and sold as amphetamine *US, 1993*

thirty-weight *noun* strong coffee. Inviting a comparison with motor oil *US, 1976*

this and that *noun* a hat. Rhyming slang *AUSTRALIA, 1937*

this and that *verb* in cricket, to bat. Rhyming slang *UK, 1961*

thisavvy *noun* this afternoon. A Liverpool slurring *UK, 2001*

this is it used when something that has been talked about happens or is happening *UK, 1942*

this is me used in place of 'hello' when answering the telephone *US, 1978*

this time it's personal used as a humorous assertion that an issue is being taken personally. A moderately popular catchphrase from *Jaws: The Revenge* (1987) *US, 1999*

this will separate the men from the boys; this will sort the men from the boys this task, event, crisis or activity will only be successfully managed by someone of sufficient experience or maturity. The original use, 'this is where the men are separated from the boys' or 'this is where they separate the men from the boys', is attributed to US film actress Mae West, in which case this dates to the late 1930s and is laden with sexual innuendo *UK, 1974*

T.H. Lowry *noun* a Maori. Prison rhyming slang, formed from a famed horse-breeder *NEW ZEALAND, 1997*

Thomas Cook *noun* a look. Rhyming slang, invented by the advertisers for travel company Thomas Cook in the slogan 'Take a Thomas Cook at our Prices!' and now in limited circulation. *UK, 1998*

Thomas More *noun* a whore. Rhyming slang, probably formed from the renaissance writer and Catholic martyr (1478–1535) *UK, 2003*

thong feminism *noun* contemporary forms of feminism CANADA, 2002

thook *verb* to spit UK, 2006

thooleramawn *noun* a contemptible, incompetent person IRELAND, 1989

Thora Hird; Thora *noun* **1** a third-class university degree. Rhyming slang, based on British stage and screen actress Dame Thora Hird (1911–2003) UK, 1998. **2** a turd, hence an act of defecation. Rhyming slang, based on the name of British stage and screen actress Dame Thora Hird (1911–2003) UK, 2002

thorazine shuffle *noun* the slow, dragging walk of a patient being medicated with thorazine US, 1994

thorn *noun* **1** a nail. Used by workers in the building trade in Glasgow UK: SCOTLAND, 1988. **2** a knife US, 1993

thoroughbred *noun* a drug dealer who sells high quality, pure drugs US, 1970

those days *noun* the bleed period of a woman's menstrual cycle US, 1954

thou *noun* **1** a thousand US, 1867. **2** a thousandth of an inch UK, 1902

though used, after a question or statement, as an intensifier; truly. A colloquial term UK, 1905

thousand miler *noun* a sateen shirt worn by railway workers US, 1946

thousand percent *adverb* completely. The most famous use of the term in the US came in 1972 when Democratic presidential nominee Senator George McGovern announced that he was 'one thousand percent' in support of his running mate, Thomas Eagleton, despite revelations that Eagleton had once received shock treatment; McGovern dropped Eagleton from the ticket several days after this endorsement US, 1963

thousand-yard stare; thousand-metre stare *noun* a lost, unfocused look, especially as the result of brutal combat US, 1986

thou shalt not be found out; thou shalt not get found out propounded as the Eleventh Commandment UK, 1974

thrap *verb* (of a male) to masturbate UK, 2001

thrash *noun* **1** a high-spirited party UK, 1967. **2** a style of hard rock music that appeals to disaffected suburban adolescent boys – fast, relentlessly loud and heavy US, 1994

thrash *verb* **1** to surf aggressively and with skill US, 1988. **2** to skateboard aggressively and with skill US, 1989. **3** in drag racing, to work on a car hurriedly if not frantically in the hours just before a race US, 2003

thrashed *adjective* tired, worn-down, exhausted, especially as a result of excessive indulgence in hedonistic pleasures; dishevelled US, 1999

thrasher *noun* **1** a party where guests bring bottles of alcohol that are poured into a rubbish bin for all to share. Michigan Upper Peninsula practice and usage US, 2003. **2** a person who violently responds to the pricks of a tattoo needle US, 1997. **3** a skilled and fearless skateboarder US, 1984

threaders *adjective* fed-up; being ready to lose your temper. Royal Navy, especially marine, slang; an abbreviation of 'threadbare', suggesting patience worn thin UK, 1989

threads *noun* clothes US, 1926

three *noun* a three-dollar bag of heroin US, 1976. ▶ **or three** either by exaggeration or understatement, used for emphasis of an amount UK, 1976

three; three up *verb* in prison, to share a cell with two other inmates UK, 1996

three and a half *noun* in Quebec, an apartment with a living room, kitchen, bedroom and bathroom. Similarly, in Quebec, a 'two-and-a-half' is an apartment with a living-dining room, bedroom and bathroom; a 'four-and a half' has two bedrooms; and so forth up to 'seven-and-a-half' CANADA, 2002

three and four *noun* a whore. Rhyming slang UK, 2003

three-bagger *noun* **1** an unattractive girl. From the tease that she is so ugly that you have to put two bags over her head and one over yours US, 1987. **2** a train pulled by three engines US, 1946

three-balls *noun* a Jewish person. An allusion to the historical signage outside a pawn shop US, 1980

three blind mice *noun* rice. Rhyming slang, formed from a nursery rhyme UK, 1992

three-bug *noun* in horse racing, an inexperienced jockey given a weight allowance of ten pounds US, 1990

three-cents people *noun* a poor family. When the colonial British Guyana dollar was based on the British pound sterling, 'three cents' was used to indicate cheapness. The term survives as a metaphorical relic GUYANA, 1998

three-D *adjective* said of a school that recruits basketball players but does not prepare them for life after college. It is said that the college that does not teach players to play *d*efense, does not instill *d*iscipline, and in the end does not award *d*iplomas to many of its student athletes US, 1983

three day chop *noun* a period of partial or absolute withdrawal from drugs or a drug-substitute UK, 1996

three days by canoe *adjective* a long distance US, 1993

three days' delay *noun* in Quebec, three days' notice CANADA, 2002

three days older than dirt *adjective* very old indeed US, 1994

three-decker *noun* a three-storey house. Coined and primarily used by Irish immigrants and then Irish-Americans in Boston US, 1990

three deuces *noun* in hot rodding, three two-barrel carburettors US, 1992

three-dollar bill *noun* **1** used for comparisons of something that is rare or odd US, 1942. **2** a homosexual. From the expression 'as strange as a three-dollar bill' US, 1965

three drags and a spit *noun* a cigarette. Gay use; a deliberate reversal of rhyming slang SPIT AND DRAG (a cigarette) thereby avoiding the rhyme on FAG and its derogatory homosexual connotations UK, 2002

three Ds *noun* ▷ *see:* DERRY-DOWN-DERRY

three'd up *adjective* in prison, used of three inmates sharing a single cell UK, 1974

three fates *noun* in poker, three queens US, 1988

three fifty-seven; three fifty-seven Magnum *noun* a central nervous system stimulant, the exact nature of which is unknown, sold as amphetamine on the street US, 1993

three-fingered salute *noun* when operating a computer, the keyed-combination of the characters Ctrl-Alt-Delete used to restart the machine US, 2004

three-finger fuck around *noun* a disorganised activity with no apparent purpose US, 1991

three-for-two *noun* fifty percent interest US, 1967

three-hairs *noun* a Vietnamese woman. From the perception of the US soldier that the pubic hair of Vietnamese women is very sparse US, 1991

three H enema *noun* in hospital usage, an aggressive enema – high, hot and a hell of a lot US, 1980

three-holer *nickname* an aircraft with three engines, especially the Boeing 727 US, 1985

three hots and a cot *noun* room and board. From the sense of HOT as 'a meal' US, 1930

three-hundred club *noun* a notional association of those who experience a temperature swing of three hundred degrees farenheit, usually by rolling naked in the Antarctic night and then entering a sauna ANTARCTICA, 2003

three-legged beaver *noun* a homosexual man. Two legs and an erect penis make the three legs, feminised by BEAVER (a woman/vagina) UK, 1981

three-martini lunch *noun* a leisurely business lunch paid for from an expense account, often centred around alcohol US, 1972

three minutes *noun* a gang punishment in which the offending member must fight another gang member for three minutes US, 2001

three moon *noun* a three-month prison sentence. A multiple of MOON, included here for the singular nature of the plural UK, 1950

three on the tree *noun* a three speed manual transmission with the gear shift mounted on the steering column *US, 1993*

threepenny bits; thrupennies; threepennies; thrups *noun* **1** the female breasts. Rhyming slang for, (TIT(S)) , based on a small coin (3d) that ceased to be legal tender with decimalisation in 1971; when this slang was coined, you got 80 threepenny bits to the pound *UK, 1961*. **2** an urgent need to defecate; diarrhoea. Rhyming slang for THE SHITS *AUSTRALIA, 1971*

three-phase set *noun* in electric line work, a set of three shovels: a cup-shaped spoon, a spade and a shovel *US, 1980*

three-point c and b *noun* a painful parachute landing. The three points were the head, heels and buttocks, while the 'c and b' was a 'crash and burn' *US, 1991*

three-rounder *noun* a petty criminal, a small operator. From the three-round bouts of junior and novice boxing *UK, 1961*

threes *noun* **1** the third landing or floor level in a prison *UK, 1978*. **2** in poker, three cards of the same rank in a hand *US, 1967*. ▶ **all the threes** thirty-three. In Bingo, House or Housey-Housey calling, the formula 'all the' announces a double number *UK, 1943*

three-sheet *verb* to wear theatrical makeup in public *US, 1971*

three sheets in the wind *adjective* very drunk *UK, 1821*

three-sixty *noun* a complete, 360-degree turn; in the UK, especially while joyriding *US, 1927*

three-skinner *noun* a marijuana- or hashish-filled cigarette fashioned out of three cigarette papers *UK, 2003*

threesome *noun* group sex with three participants *US, 1972*

three squares *noun* three square meals a day *US, 1922*

three-time loser *noun* a criminal who has been convicted of a third serious crime, probably guaranteeing life imprisonment *US, 1966*

three-toed sloth *noun* a slow-thinking, slow-talking, slow-acting hospital patient *US, 1985*

three-toke killer *noun* extremely potent marijuana. Derived from the perception that the marijuana will produce extreme intoxication after only three inhalations *US, 1993*

three-tone *noun* of a car, badly repaired after an accident. A play on the advertising of 'two-tone' cars (cars painted in two colours) *UK, 1981*

three-two-hundred out, one-six-hundred in *adjective* completely confused. From the standard 6400-mil circular artillery chart *US, 1968*

three up and three down *noun* a master sergeant in the US Army. From the stripe configuration *US, 1991*

three up and two down *noun* a sergeant first-class or platoon sergeant in the US Army. From the stripe configuration *US, 1991*

three-way *noun* sex involving three people simultaneously *US, 1985*

three-way *adjective* (used of a woman) willing to engage in vaginal, anal and oral sex *US, 1967*

three-way freeway *noun* a woman who consents to vaginal, anal and oral sex *US, 2001*

three wheel trike; three-wheeler *noun* a lesbian. Rhyming slang for DYKE *UK, 2003*

thrift *verb* to live a frugal, if attractive, lifestyle *US, 1997*

thrift shop *noun* any low-limit, low-ante poker game *US, 1996*

Thrilla in Manilla *nickname* the heavyweight boxing championship fight between Muhammed Ali and Joe Frazier on 1st October 1975 in Manilla, won by Ali when Frazier's manager Eddie Futch threw in the towel before the 15th round *US, 1998*

thrilled *adjective* pleased, delighted *UK, 1937*

thrilled to bits *adjective* utterly delighted; very pleased *UK, 1964*

thriller *noun* a sensational (adventure) story told as a play, film or novel; such a form of entertainment. A narrow sense of the general meaning *UK, 1889*

thrill pill *noun* a central nervous system stimulant in tablet form. A reduplication that never really caught on; too true for a euphemism and too euphemistic for the street *US, 1953*

throat *noun* ▶ **have someone by the throat** to have someone completely under control *AUSTRALIA, 1947*

thrombo *noun* a fit of rage. From 'thrombosis', suggesting a rush of blood to the head *UK, 2002*

throne *noun* **1** a toilet seat; a pedestal lavatory (as a place on which you sit) *UK, 1922*. **2** the most coveted position for a bookmaker at the track *AUSTRALIA, 1989*

throttle artist; throttle jerker; throttle puller *noun* a train engineer *US, 1977*

throttle jockey *noun* a combat jet pilot *US, 1956*

throttling pit *noun* a lavatory *AUSTRALIA, 1971*

through-the-card *noun* a wager that bets on all the races at a meeting. Commonly used when gambling on greyhound racing *UK, 2001*

through-ticket *noun* in pool, a player who continues to play and to lose money until he has lost his entire bankroll *US, 1993*

throw *noun* **1** the cost of an item or action, usually preceded by a specific amount. Probably from the old side shows of the fair *US, 1898*. **2** an act of vomiting; vomit *AUSTRALIA, 1967*

throw *verb* **1** to disconcert, to confuse *US, 1844*. **2** to deliberately lose a contest *US, 1868*. **3** to break an addiction *US, 1952*. ▶ **throw a fin; throw the fin** while surfing, to reach the top of a wave and expose to the air the surfboard's fin(s) *US, 1987*. ▶ **throw a fit** to become very angry or agitated *US, 1926*. ▶ **throw a party** to lose heavily when gambling *US, 1982*. ▶ **throw a shape** to make an impression, *1999*. ▶ **throw a shine** to ignore someone. Usage by Mexican-American youth (Pachucos) in the southwestern US *US, 1947*. ▶ **throw a shoe** to suffer a tyre blowout or flat tyre *US, 1963*. ▶ **throw blows** to fight *US, 1965*. ▶ **throw flame** in trucking, to show an actual flame or a red glow suggesting a flame on a smokestack *US, 1971*. ▶ **throw forty fits** to become very angry or agitated. An occasional intensification of THROW A FIT *UK, 1984*. ▶ **throw gravel** to accelerate briskly from a dirt road shoulder *US, 1962*. ▶ **throw hands** to fight *US, 2002*. ▶ **throw it to someone** from a male perspective, to have sex *US, 1969*. ▶ **throw off at** to deride someone or something *AUSTRALIA, 1812*. ▶ **throw one** from the male perspective, to have sex *US, 1954*. ▶ **throw shade** to project a defiant attitude *US, 1995*. ▶ **throw shapes** to box *IRELAND, 1995*. ▶ **throw signs** to flash hand signals, almost always gang-related *US, 2001*. ▶ **throw teddy out of the pram** to throw a tantrum; to lose your temper. An allusion to childish behaviour *UK, 1998*. ▶ **throw the bald-headed champ** to perform oral sex on a man *US, 1972*. ▶ **throw the book at someone** to discipline or penalise someone severely. Making maximum use of the rulebook that inspires the punishment *US, 1960*. ▶ **throw the head** to lose one's temper *IRELAND, 1995*. ▶ **throw the knockwurst** from the male perspective, to have sex *US, 1973*. ▶ **throw the latch** in a hotel, to activate a mechnical device advising hotel employees to carefully watch activity in a particular room *US, 1954*. ▶ **throw the leg over** to mount a racehorse *AUSTRALIA, 1989*. ▶ **throw the voice; throw your voice** to vomit *AUSTRALIA, 1962*. ▶ **throw up your set** to flash gang hand signals *US, 1995*. ▶ **throw waist** to thrust with vigour during sex *TRINIDAD AND TOBAGO, 2003*. ▶ **throw your weight about; throw your weight around** to 'show off' in an unpleasant, domineering way; to bully people *UK, 1917*

throwaway *noun* an outer garment quickly discarded by a criminal after a crime to thwart easy identification *US, 1987*

throw away *verb* to abort a foetus *TRINIDAD AND TOBAGO, 1939*

throwaway *adjective* used of a gun unregistered and not capable of being traced, and thus used to place in the vicinity of someone whom the police have shot to justify the shooting *US, 1981*

throwdown *noun* a large party *US, 1996*

throw down *verb* **1** to threaten someone with a weapon *US, 1972*. **2** to kill *US, 1963*. **3** in basketball, to forcefully drive the ball down through the basket *US, 1997*. **4** to dance. Sometimes embellished with 'some happy feet' as a direct object *US, 1983*

throw-down gun; throwdown *noun* a gun that is not registered and not capable of being traced, and thus placed by the police in the vicinity of someone whom they have shot to justify the shooting *US, 1983*

throw off *verb* to perform at a skill level below your capability *US, 1965*

throw-out *noun* **1** the prize that a carnival game operator arranges for a player to win to entice more customers to play *US, 1985*. **2** a trinket thrown by a parader to spectators *US, 1951*

throw-up *noun* a large, simple piece of graffiti art *US, 1994*

throw up *verb* **1** to vomit. Abbreviated from the elaborately elegant 'throw up your accounts' (C18) *UK, 1793*. **2** to create large graffiti pieces (especially on trains, walls, etc) *US, 1994*

thrush *noun* **1** a female singer *US, 1940*. **2** an attractive young woman *AUSTRALIA, 1960*

thrust *noun* amyl, butyl or isobutyl nitrite. A definite suggestion of sexual vigour and therefore, probably, derives from brand marketing as a male sex-aid *UK, 1996*

thruster *noun* **1** an amphetamine or other central nervous system stimulant *US, 1969*. **2** a modern surfboard with three fins *AUSTRALIA, 1985*

thrutch *noun* a difficult challenge *ANTARCTICA, 2003*

thud *nickname* an F-105 Thunderchief aircraft. From the fact that many were shot down during the Vietnam war. A two-seated F-105 was known as a 'double thud' *US, 1965*

thug *noun* a youth gang member *UK, 2003*

thugged-out *adjective* in hip-hop culture, self-sufficient and dangerous. From conventional 'thug' (a violent person) which has been adopted by some urban blacks as an honourable term and condition *US, 2002*

th-uh, th-uh, that's all folks used as a humorous farewell. Used as the sign off on Looney Toon cartoons produced by Warner Brothers by a stuttering Porky the Pig. Repeated with referential humour *US, 1955*

thumb *noun* marijuana; a marijuana cigarette. Probably because you suck your thumb for comfort in much the same way as you suck on a cigarette *US, 1960*. ▶ **on the thumb** hitchhiking *UK, 2004*. ▶ **with the thumb** in betting, used for indicating that the current odds will not continue to be offered for long. From the TICK-TACK signal used by bookmakers *UK, 1991*

thumb *verb* to hitchhike *US, 1932*. ▶ **thumb your nose** to treat someone or something contemptuously *US, 1973*

thumb buster *noun* **1** a knob attached to a car or truck's steering wheel to help the driver make turns quickly. When the steering wheel returns to its normal position, the knob can injure the hand of a driver who is not careful *US, 1971*. **2** a railway mechanic *US, 1977*

thumb-check *noun* a cursory examination of a long document or packet of documents. US naval aviator usage *US, 1986*

thumb job *noun* a hitchthiker; the act of hitchhiking. Citizens' band radio slang *US, 1976*

thumb merchant *noun* a hitchhiker *US, 1976*

thumbs down *noun* a rejection or refusal. From the gesture famously used to signal 'no mercy' for gladiators in the arenas of ancient Rome and Hollywood *UK, 1929*

thumbsucker *noun* a long and complex piece of journalism; a writer of such articles *US, 2003*

thumbs up *noun* approval; positive news. After the gesture that spared the life of Roman gladiators *UK, 1951*

thump *noun* a fight *US, 1971*

thump *verb* to defeat someone soundly *UK, 1594*

thumper *noun* **1** a hand grenade launcher *US, 1990*. **2** a drummer *US, 1981*. **3** a piece of rope used by dog handlers to discipline sled dogs *ANTARCTICA, 1982*. **4** in electric line work, an underground fault locator *US, 1980*

thumper bumper *noun* in pinball, a bumper that upon impact with a ball scores and then propels the ball back into play *US, 1977*

thump gun *noun* an M79 grenade launcher. Vietnam war usage *US, 1982*

thumping *adjective* unusually large or heavy; of an untruth, outrageous *UK, 1576*

thumping *adverb* used as an intensifier of adjectives of large size *UK, 1961*

thunder *noun* **1** male sexual prowess *TRINIDAD AND TOBAGO, 1989*. **2** heroin *UK, 2002*. ▶ **do a thunder** to defecate *IRELAND, 1994*

thunder *verb* to excel *US, 1989*

thunderbags *noun* underpants *AUSTRALIA, 1971*

thunderbirds *noun* the female breasts. From the mammaric and lexicographic symbolism of the science fiction Thunderbirds, especially Thunderbird 2, in cult television supermarionation puppet-series *Thunderbirds* by Gerry Anderson, from 1965, and relaunched in the 1990s *UK, 2001*

Thunderbirds are go used for denoting or announcing that something is proceeding. A catchphrase from *Thunderbirds*, a cult science fiction puppet series, first broadcast on television in 1965 *UK, 2001*

thunderbowl *noun* a lavatory *UK, 1982*

thunderbox *noun* a lavatory. Originally coined for a 'portable commode' *UK, 1939*

thunderbumper *noun* a cumulonimbus cloud *CANADA, 1995*

thunderdome *noun* a variety of MDMA, the recreational drug best known as ecstasy. A reference to the film *Mad Max: Beyond The Thunderdome*, 1985 *UK, 1999*

thundering *adjective* forcible, violent; hence, as an intensifier: great, excessive *UK, 1618*

thundering *adverb* excessively *UK, 1809*

thunderingly *adverb* violently, forcibly, powerfully, energetically; greatly; excessively *UK, 1680*

Thunder Road *noun* Highway 13, north of Saigon, South Vietnam. So named because of the US Army's frequent THUNDER RUNS on Highway 13 *US, 1971*

thunder run *noun* **1** during the Vietnam war, a tactic of having a small armoured convoy drive at high speeds shooting at both sides of the road to thwart ambushes by the Viet Cong; in Iraq in 2003, used by soldiers of a death or glory incursion into Baghdad. Possibly originating in the Korean war, 1950–53, where it was used figuratively for a final bar crawl before leaving a posting *US, 1983*. **2** in white-water rafting, the most treacherous rapids or the act of negotiating them *US, 2003*

thunder thighs *noun* large, heavy thighs, especially on a woman *US, 1977*

thunk *noun* in computing, code that supplies an address *US, 1991*

thunk *verb* used as an alternative past tense of 'think' in place of 'thought'. Intentionally jocular or rural *UK, 1876*

TI *nickname* the federal correctional institution, Terminal Island, California *US, 1981*

tia *noun* marijuana. A Spanish aunt such as AUNT MARY (marijuana) *UK, 2003*

TIA used as Internet shorthand to mean 'thanks in advance' *US, 1997*

Tibb's Day *noun* the day after Resurrection, Judgment Day etc, i.e. a day that will never come in this lifetime. C. L. Apperson, in *English Proverbs and Proverbial Phrases*, calls it 'a day neither before nor after Christmas'. Brewer's *Dictionary of Phrase and Fable* (1870) points out that there never was such a saint as St Tibb, hence the use of the term as a synonym for 'never' *CANADA, 1999*

tic *noun* phencyclidine *US, 1977*

TIC *noun* when a criminal is on trial, a crime which does not form a part of the case being heard but which the defendant may request to have taken into account during sentencing. A partial acronym of 'taken into account' *UK, 1996*

tical *noun* marijuana. A coinage claimed by rap artist Methodman; usage spread with his adoption of 'tical' as one of many drug-related aliases *US, 1998*

tick *noun* **1** a moment; a second, a minute *UK, 1879*. **2** credit, deferred payment. Generally in the phrase 'on tick' (on credit) *UK, 1642*. **3** in spread-betting, a tenth *UK, 2001*. **4** in basketball, a shot *US, 1986*. **5** in a hospital, an intern *US, 1994*

tick *verb* ▶ **tick along nicely** to make satisfactory progress Ireland *IRELAND, 2003*

tick *adjective* sexually attractive *UK, 1950*

ticked off *adjective* angry *US, 1959*

ticker *noun* **1** a clock, especially a pocket watch *US, 1964*. **2** the heart. Analogised to a clock ticking *US, 1930*. **3** courage *AUSTRALIA, 1977*

ticket *noun* **1** an ordinary person. Used generally in Glasgow and MOD culture *UK, 1985*. **2** an amusing or charming person *IRELAND, 1992*. **3** a follower (not an originator) of Mod fashion *UK, 1964*. **4** a professional licence; a certificate of qualification. Originally military *US, 1951*. **5** a warrant or bill of detainer *US, 2002*. **6** an official misconduct report in prison *US, 1976*. **7** an order to be locked in solitary confinement *US, 1965*. **8** in prison, a contract for a killing or beating *US, 1974*. **9** in horse racing, a betting receipt *US, 1951*. **10** a playing card. As in the expression 'I held some good tickets' *US, 1961*. **11** LSD; a dose of LSD. Another LSD-as-travel metaphor *US, 1969*. ▶ **just the ticket; that's the ticket** exactly what is required *UK, 1838*

ticket agent *noun* an LSD dealer. Premised on a TRIP metaphor *US, 1974*

Ticket Bastard *nickname* the Ticketmaster ticket service *US, 1994*

ticket of leave man *noun* a parolee *UK, 1998*

ticket-punching *noun* in the military, nearly automatic promotion from rank to rank with short periods in combat to justify the promotion *US, 1988*

tickets *noun* the female breasts. A term from the coarse sector of the entertainment industry, recognising the selling power of sex *US, 1977*. ▶ **have tickets on yourself** to be conceited *AUSTRALIA, 1918*

tickety-boo *adjective* fine, correct, in order, satisfactory. Originally military; a variation of 'ticket', as in JUST THE TICKET (correct), with Hindu *tikai babu* (it's all right, sir') *UK, 1939*

tick-hunter *noun* an ardent bird-watcher, usually one who is excitable. From a bird-watcher's habit of ticking-off observations in a note book *UK, 1977*

tick in cow's arse *noun* something or someone who is very close to something or someone else *TRINIDAD AND TOBAGO, 1982*

ticking-off *noun* a reprimand *UK, 1984*

tickle *noun* **1** a robbery or other profitable criminal enterprise. Probably derives from the image of a poacher 'tickling a trout', an activity for the 'light-fingered' *UK, 1938*. **2** in the sport of polo, a weak hit on the ball *UK, 2003*. **3** a pleasurable sensation caused by drug use *UK, 2000*. **4** a deep v-bottom on a boat; also, especially in Newfoundland, a narrow strait between mainland and an island *CANADA, 1947*

tickle *verb* **1** to prime an engine. To start the cold engine of a motorcycle, it is sometimes necessary to prime the carburettor, or 'tickle the pot' *US, 2003*. **2** to administer oral sex to a male pornographer performer before or between scenes to help him maintain an erection *US, 2000*. **3** to rob *NEW ZEALAND, 1998*. ▶ **tickle a bug** in computing, to activate a normally inactive malfunction *US, 1991*. ▶ **tickle the peter** to steal from a till or cashbox *AUSTRALIA, 1941*. ▶ **tickle the pickle** from the male perspective, to have sex *US, 1964*

ticklebelly *noun* the queasy feeling experienced when a car crests a poorly graded hill too fast *CANADA, 2002*

tickled; tickled to death; tickled pink *adjective* very pleased *UK, 1907*

tickler *noun* **1** an office system that serves to remind of impending deadlines *US, 1905*. **2** anything worn on the penis that is designed to stimulate the vagina or the clitoris during sex *UK, 1974*

tickle your fancy *noun* a homosexual. Rhyming slang, NANCY (BOY), noted as a post-World War 2 term by Ray Puxley, *Cockney Rabbit*, 1992, who suggests a corruption of the children's song 'Billy Boy' as a possible source *UK, 1992*

ticklish *adjective* difficult, awkward *UK, 1591*

tick off *verb* to reprimand someone *UK, 1915*

tick-tack; tic-tac *noun* **1** a system of hand signalling used by racecourse bookmakers *UK, 1899*. **2** a signal of any kind. From race track use *UK, 1992*

tick-tack; tic-tac *verb* to signal betting information by tick-tack *AUSTRALIA, 1956*

tick-tacker *noun* a person who signals betting information by tick-tack *AUSTRALIA, 1897*

tick-tacking *noun* an illegal system of sign language used between bookmakers and touts on a racecourse *AUSTRALIA, 1899*

tick-tack man *noun* a tick-tacker *AUSTRALIA, 1939*

tick-tick *noun* a bicycle with three gears *TRINIDAD AND TOBAGO, 2003*

tick-tock *noun* a clock. A children's colloquialism, from the conventional imitation of the ticking of a clock *UK, 1984*

tick-tock used to mark the passing of an instant. From the ticking of a clock *UK, 1959*

tick twenty *noun* ten o'clock *US, 1946*

ticky *adjective* old-fashioned, out-of-date *US, 1960*

tic-tac *noun* **1** a person who signals betting information by tick-tack *UK, 1990*. **2** a fact. Rhyming slang, from the race track signalling system *UK, 1992*. **3** phencyclidine, the recreational drug known as PCP or angel dust *US, 1994*

tid-bit *noun* an appetising and toothsome woman *US, 1973*

tiddie; tiddy *noun* the female breast. A variation of TITTY *UK, 2003*

tiddle *verb* to urinate. A children's colloquialism *UK, 1961*

tiddled off *adjective* annoyed, cross. After TIDDLE (to urinate), thus a variation of PISSED OFF *UK, 1977*

tiddler *noun* **1** any small fish. Originally applied to a stickleback *UK, 1885*. **2** anything small; a child, a small animal, a small drink, etc *UK, 1927*. **3** any small coin (of size rather than denomination) *UK, 1966*. **4** a player of tiddleywinks *US, 1958*

tiddler's bait; tiddley bait; tiddley; Tilly Bates *adjective* late. Rhyming slang *UK, 1960*

tiddly; tiddley *adjective* mildly drunk *UK, 1905*

tiddlywink; tiddly-wink; tiddleywink; tiddly; tid *noun* **1** an alcoholic drink. Rhyming slang *UK, 1859*. **2** a Chinese person. Rhyming slang for CHINK (a Chinese person) *UK, 1977*

tidemark *noun* a dirty mark that is left by, and marks the extent of, a child's neck-washing regime *UK, 1961*

tide's in *adjective* experiencing the bleed period of the menstrual cycle *US, 1999*

tide's out *adjective* experiencing the bleed period of the menstrual cycle *US, 1999*

tidy *adjective* **1** large, considerable. As in the song sung by Boy Scouts: 'The great meat pie was a tidy size, / And it took a week to make it, / A day to carry it to the shop, / And just a week to bake it' *UK, 1838*. **2** satisfactory; good; decent; correct. Widely exampled by John Edwards, *Talk Tidy!* (the title is defined in the book as 'speak properly!'), 1985 *UK, 1844*. **3** sexually attractive; sexy *UK, 2000*

tidy! in South Wales, used as a positive affirmation *UK: WALES, 1985*

tidy; tidy up *verb* **1** to make something orderly, clean, etc *UK, 1821*. **2** to wash the vulva and vagina *TRINIDAD AND TOBAGO, 1978*

tidy and neat; tidy *verb* to eat. Rhyming slang *UK, 1992*

tidy away *verb* to clear up for tidiness' sake *UK, 1867*

tidy whities *noun* white, boxer-style men's underpants *US, 1994*

tie *verb* to inject with a drug *UK, 2003*. ▶ **tie on one** to get very drunk *US, 1996*. ▶ **tie the knot** to marry *UK, 1605*. ▶ **tie them down** on the railways, to apply hand brakes *US, 1946*

tie a knot in it! addressed to someone (usually a male) who needs to urinate but is having to control the urge; also, said to someone who is whistling tunelessly *UK, 2001*

tie and tease *noun* sexual bondage alternating pleasurable stimulation and deliberate frustration, especially when advertised as a service offered by a prostitute *UK, 2003*

tie-eye *noun* a commotion or ruckus *CANADA, 1999*

tie off *verb* to restrict the flow of blood in a vein in preparation for an injection of narcotic drugs *US, 1996*

tie-tongued *adjective* suffering from a speaking disability such as a lisp *BARBADOS, 1965*

tie-up *noun* the rope or cord used to restrict the flow of blood in a vein in preparation for an injection of drugs *UK, 1996*

tie up *verb* to apply an improvised tourniquet, usually on the arm, preparatory to injecting a drug *US, 1990*

tiff *noun* a petty quarrel; a brief peevish disagreement *UK, 1754*

tiger *noun* **1** a person who is keen for or enthusiastic about something *AUSTRALIA, 1896*. **2** a male homosexual *UK, 1983*. **3** a wife. A Cockney endearment *UK, 1980*. **4** an outstanding sportsman; a confident climber; a formidable sporting opponent *UK, 1929*. ▶ **take a tiger for a walk** (used of a food addict) to eat in moderation. A term in twelve-step recovery programmes such as Alcoholics Anonymous *US, 1998*

tiger cage *noun* an underground, high security jail cell *US, 1992*

tiger country *noun* **1** rough, uncultivated country or terrain *AUSTRALIA, 1945*. **2** any challenging situation. From World War 2, referring to territory patrolled by German Tiger tanks *NEW ZEALAND, 1945*. **3** in hospital operating theatre usage, any part of the body where surgery is high risk *US, 1994*

tiger in the tank *noun* a linear amplifier for a citizens' band radio. From the 1960's Esso advertising slogan 'Put a tiger in your tank' *US, 1976*

tiger lady *noun* a female Vietnamese civilian building worker at a US facility during the war *US, 1990*

tiger piss *noun* Tiger Paw™ beer. A south Vietnamese speciality, made with formaldehyde *US, 1991*

tiger stripe *noun* a scar from intravenous drug injections *US, 1958*

tiger stripes *noun* camouflage worn in the jungle *US, 1971*

tiger suit *noun* jungle camouflage uniforms worn by soldiers in the South Vietnamese Army *US, 1990*

tiger sweat *noun* strong, illegally manufactured whisky *CANADA, 1999*

tiger tank *noun* a thing of little worth. Rhyming slang for, WANK (rubbish), usually phrased 'not worth a tiger tank'; from the advertising slogan 'put a tiger in your tank' *UK, 1980*

Tiggerish; tiggerish *adjective* energetically enthusiastic and cheerful. From the character of Tigger, created by A.A. Milne, 1882–1956, especially as filtered through the Disney animations of Winnie the Pooh's adventures *UK, 2003*

tight *noun* **1** a close friend *BAHAMAS, 1982*. **2** in poker, a hand consisting of three cards of the same rank and a pair. Known conventionally as a 'full house' *CANADA, 1988*. ▶ **in a tight** in serious trouble *US, 1984*

tight *adjective* **1** tipsy; drunk *US, 1830*. **2** lacking generosity, mean *UK, 2000*. **3** aggressive; cruel; unpleasant. From the previous sense as 'mean' as 'cruel' *UK, 1999*. **4** hard; severe; difficult *UK, 1764*. **5** of a slot machine, disadvantageous to the gambler in terms of the frequency of payouts *US, 1984*. **6** used of a hard bargain *US, 1828*. **7** of money; hard to come by; in short-circulation *UK, 1846*. **8** used of a player in poker extremely conservative in play and betting *US, 1990*. **9** of a contest, close, evenly matched *US, 1848*. **10** friendly *US, 1956*. **11** good; fashionable; in style *US, 1998*

tight-arse *noun* a person who is mean with money *UK, 1999*

tight-arsed *adjective* **1** mean, close-fisted, ungenerous *UK, 1966*. **2** puritanical; very restrained; self-centred *UK, 1990*

tight as a crab's arse *adjective* miserly *UK, 1999*

tight as a gnat's twat *adjective* miserly *UK, 2001*

tight-ass *noun* a highly strung, nervous person *US, 1971*

tight-assed *adjective* highly strung, nervous *US, 1970*

tighten *verb* ▶ **tighten the wig** to smoke marijuana *US, 2001*. ▶ **tighten up someone's game** to educate or coach someone *US, 1972*

tightener *noun* **1** any alcoholic drink *US, 1969*. **2** in horse racing, a race seen as preparation for the next race *US, 1994*

tighter than a camel's arse in a sand storm *adjective* miserly. An elaboration of TIGHT (mean) *UK, 1999*

tighter than bark to a tree *adjective* miserly *CANADA, 1992*

tight fight with a short stick *noun* a difficult job with poor equipment to do it *US, 1954*

tight hole *noun* an oil well whose discovery and location have not been reported *US, 1997*

tight laces *noun* commerically manufactured cigarettes, especially with filters *US, 1990*

tight-roll *noun* a manufactured cigarette *US, 1984*

tightwad *noun* a miserly person *US, 1906*

tighty-whities *noun* form-fitting men's jockey shorts *US, 1985*

tig ol' bitties *noun* large breasts. An intentional Spoonerism of 'big old titties' *US, 2001*

tigre; tigre blanco; tigre del norte *noun* heroin. Possibly 'branded' types of heroin, from Spanish for 'tiger', white 'tiger' and 'northern tiger' *UK, 2003*

Tijuana 12 *noun* a cigarette made with tobacco and marijuana *US, 1982*

Tijuana Bible *noun* a pornographic comic book *US, 1979*

Tijuana chrome *noun* silver spray paint. Tijuana is just across the border from California in the Mexican state of Baja California. Californian youth often took their customised cars to Tijuana, where much of the best and some of the shoddiest customising work was done *US, 1993*

Tijuana taxi *noun* a well marked police car *US, 1976*

tik *noun* a potential victim. West Indian and UK black *UK, 1996*

Tilbury Docks; the Tilburys *noun* any sexually transmitted infection. Rhyming slang for POX, formed on a part of the Port of London. An earlier, now obsolete sense for this rhyme was 'socks' *UK, 1992*

tiles *noun* dominoes *US, 1959*. ▶ **on the tiles** partying *NEW ZEALAND, 1984*

till-tap *verb* to steal money from a cash till *US, 1970*

till tapper *noun* in a casino, a person who steals coins or tokens from a slot machine being played by someone else *US, 1999*

till tapping *noun* theft from a cash register when the cashier is distracted *US, 1964*

tilly *noun* (especially in Queensland and northern New South Wales) a utility truck *AUSTRALIA, 1957*

Tilly *noun* used as a personification of the police *US, 1970*

Tilly Bates *adjective* ▷*see:* TIDDLER'S BAIT

tilly-tallied *adjective* drunk. Possibly from obsolete 'tilly-vally' (nonsense), which is what tends to be spoken when drunk *UK, 1999*

tilt *noun* **1** especially in the Maritime Provinces, a crude shelter, open on one side and with its back to the wind *CANADA, 1958*. **2** in pinball, a mechanism on the machine that ends a game when the player moves the machine too forcefully *US, 1979*. ▶ **on tilt** used of a poker player's playing, exceptionally poor *US, 1979*

Tim *noun* a Roman Catholic. Who the original Tim is or was is unknown *UK: SCOTLAND, 2000*

timber *noun* **1** a toothpick *US, 1948*. **2** in horse racing, a hurdle in a steeplechase race *US, 1976*. **3** in poker, the cards that have been discarded *US, 1951*. **4** in the circus or carnival, a person playing a game or concession with the house's money in an attempt to attract other patrons to play *US, 1968*

timber nigger *noun* a Native American Indian. Offensive. Used by sporting enthusiasts and those in the tourist industry to describe Native American Indians involved in the fishing/hunting rights debate *US, 1993*

timber rider *noun* in horse racing, a jockey in a steeplechase event *US, 1976*

timbit *noun* a rendezvous for coffee and snack proposed by one police officer to another. A doughnut hole from Tim Horton's™;

refers to the dough that is punched out of a ring doughnut, fried, and sold as a 'hole' CANADA, 2000

time noun time in prison; a jail sentence UK, 1837. ▶ **(he) wouldn't give you the time of day; too mean to give you the time of day** applied to a notoriously mean person UK, 1984. ▶ **do time** **1** to serve a prison sentence, especially in a manner that preserves the prisoner's sanity UK, 1865. **2** to stay after school in detention US, 1954. ▶ **for the time** in poolroom betting, playing with the loser paying for the use of the table US, 1967. ▶ **have no time for someone** to have no respect for someone AUSTRALIA, 1911. ▶ **in no time; in less than no time** immediately UK, 1822. ▶ **make time; make time with someone** to have sex with someone; to make sexual advances towards someone US, 1934

time-and-a-half noun in blackjack, the payout to a player of one and a half times their bet when the player is dealt a natural 21. A pun using a term usually applied to an overtime rate of pay US, 1977

time of the month noun the bleed period of a woman's menstrual cycle. Barely euphemistic UK, 1931

time out! used for warning others of approaching police US, 2000

timer noun father. An abbreviation of 'old-timer' CANADA, 1993

time-stretcher noun a prisoner whose attitude and actions serve to make the time served by others seem longer than it is US, 2002

time through the gate noun the on-the-job experience of a prison officer UK, 1996

Timmy noun a Tristar aircraft. In Royal Air Force use UK, 2002

timothy noun a brothel. A shortening of 'Timothy Titmouse', rhyming slang for 'house' AUSTRALIA, 1950

timps noun timpani (kettle-drums); timpanists. An abbreviation of 'timpani' UK, 1934

Timshop noun a Roman Catholic chapel UK: SCOTLAND, 1996

tim tam noun a tampon. Abbreviation and reduplication AUSTRALIA, 2001

tin noun **1** a police badge US, 1958. **2** a police officer US, 1950. **3** a gun US, 1986. **4** a safe US, 1970. **5** one ounce of marijuana. Probably from a pipe tobacco tin as a measured container US, 1946. **6** beer in any quantity or container US, 1980. **7** in drag racing, a trophy, especially one awarded without a cash prize US, 1965. ▶ **does what it says on the tin; does exactly what it says on the tin** used as an assurance that whatever is so described will be, or behave, as expected. From a catchphrase-slogan for Ronseal™ wood-treatments; first introduced in the early 1990s, the phrase is now part of the company's registered trademarking, and widely applied in the sense recorded here UK, 2001

tin-arse; tin-bum noun a lucky person. Derives, perhaps, from a play on 'copper-bottomed' AUSTRALIA, 1953

tin arse; tin arsed adjective lucky AUSTRALIA, 1919

Tina Turner; tina noun **1** a profitable activity. Rhyming slang for, 'earner'; formed from the popular US singer and actress (b.1938) UK, 2001. **2** Rhyming slang for GURNER (a person intoxicated by MDMA) UK

tin bath; tin noun **1** a laugh. Rhyming slang UK, 2002. **2** a scarf. Rhyming slang UK, 1992

tin can noun **1** a safe that is easily broken into by criminals US, 1949. **2** an older ship in disrepair US, 1970. **3** a citizens' band radio set. From one of the most primitive technical means of communi-cation: two tin cans joined by a piece of string US, 1976

tinchy adjective petty; small BAHAMAS, 1982

Tin City noun a sheet metal barracks in Guam used to house Vietnamese refugees after the North Vietnamese conquest in 1975 US, 1990

tin collector noun a police officer or prosecutor involved in investi-gating police misconduct US, 2001

tincture noun **1** an alcoholic drink. Popularised, if not inspired by the 'Dear Bill' letters in Private Eye UK, 1980. **2** a light drug in liquid form. A jocular euphemism UK, 1968

tin dog noun a snowmobile NEW ZEALAND, 1969

tin ear noun tone deafness US, 1935

Tin-Ear Alley noun the boxing world. A journalists' pun on 'Tin-Pan Alley' (the world of music) UK, 1961

tin flute noun a suit. A variation of WHISTLE AND FLUTE in Glasgow rhyming slang UK: SCOTLAND, 1988

t'ing noun thing. West Indian and UK black pronunciation UK, 1994

ting noun money; a payment, especially in an illegal context TRINIDAD AND TOBAGO, 1989

ting-a-ling noun **1** the penis BAHAMAS, 1982. **2** a ring (jewellery). Rhyming slang UK, 1992. **3** in playing cards, a king. Rhyming slang UK, 1992

tin grin noun any person with orthodontia US, 1977

tings noun the testicles. West Indian pronunciation of 'things' UK, 2000

tingum noun a person or thing the name of which escapes the speaker BAHAMAS, 1995

tin hat noun **1** a fool, an idiot. Rhyming slang for PRAT UK, 1998. **2** on the railways, a company official US, 1977. ▶ **put the tin hat on it; put the tin hat on something** to bring an unfortunate sequence to an unwelcome climax; to finish something off UK, 1919

tinhorn noun a cheap and offensive person US, 1887

tinhorn adjective shoddy; inconsequential; inferior US, 1886

tin Indian noun a Pontiac car US, 1993

tinker noun **1** a member of the travelling community. Conventionally 'an (itinerant) mender of pots, pans, kettles etc.', but now more generally applied IRELAND, 1997. **2** a child, especially a mischievous child. Remembered in use in New Zealand in 1904 and in Australia in 1910 NEW ZEALAND, 1996. **3** a piece of scrap from wreckage CANADA, 1983

tinker's cuss; tinker's damn; tinker's toss noun something of no value UK, 1824

tinkle noun urine, the act of urination US, 1960. ▶ **give a tinkle** to telephone someone. From the ringing bell of original telephones UK, 1938

tinkle verb to urinate. Children's vocabulary, used coyly by adults US, 1960

tinklebox noun a piano US, 1946

tin lid noun **1** a Jewish person. Rhyming slang for YID UK, 1992. **2** a child. Rhyming slang for KID AUSTRALIA, 1905

tinned dog noun canned meat AUSTRALIA, 1895

tinnie; tinny noun a can of beer AUSTRALIA, 1964

tinny noun **1** an imprecise measure of marijuana wrapped in tinfoil, usually enough for about three cigarettes NEW ZEALAND, 1995. **2** a small aluminium boat AUSTRALIA, 1979. **3** a station wagon with a steel body and no wood trim US, 1993

tinny adjective lucky AUSTRALIA, 1919

tinny house noun a place where marijuana tinnies are sold NEW ZEALAND, 1999

tin plate noun **1** a mate. Rhyming slang NEW ZEALAND, 1992. **2** in circus and carnival usage, a law enforcement official in a small town US, 1981

tin sandwich noun a harmonica; a mouth organ. Used as the title of an album of harmonica music by Tommy Basker, 'The Tin Sandwich', 1994 US, 1999

tinsel-teeth noun **1** any person with orthodontia US, 1979. **2** orthodontic braces US, 1971

Tinsel Town nickname Hollywood US, 1939

tins of beans; tins noun jeans (denim trousers). Rhyming slang UK, 1992

tin soldier noun a prostitute's client who pays not for conventional sex, but to act as a prostitute's 'slave'. Noted as a 'voyeur-type male, usually of middle- or upper-class background' by David Powis, The Signs of Crime, 1977 UK, 1977

tin tack noun **1** dismissal from employment. Rhyming slang for SACK. Recorded in 1932 but believed to be late C19 UK, 1932. **2** a fact. Rhyming slang based on BRASS TACKS, generally plural UK, 1999

tin tank noun a bank. Rhyming slang UK, 1932

tin termites *noun* rust *UK, 1972*

tints *noun* **1** sunglasses *US, 1972*. **2** tinted car windows *US, 1980*

tiny *noun* **1** a child *AUSTRALIA, 1961*. **2** a very young member of a youth gang *US, 1981*

tiny gangster *noun* a young member of a youth gang *US, 1989*

tiny mind *noun* ▶ **out of your tiny mind; out of your tiny** you are crazy, foolish, mad *UK, 1970*

Tiny Tim *noun* a five-pound note; the sum of £5. Rhyming slang for FLIM, formed on a character in Charles Dickens' *A Christmas Carol*, 1843 *UK, 1992*

Tio Taco *noun* a Mexican-American who curries favour with the dominant white culture. Literally 'Uncle Taco', referring to a Mexican dish made with a fried corn tortilla *US, 1969*

tip *noun* **1** a point of view, an aspect or perspective; a concentration upon an aspect *UK, 1994*. **2** special information conveyed by an expert or insider; a piece of professional advice; private knowledge, especially in connection with investment or gambling *UK, 1845*. **3** that which is 'tipped' to win; the probable winner in a race *UK, 1873*. **4** a dirty or chaotically untidy place. Especially applied, apparently, to teenagers' bedrooms; from a community site where rubbish is tipped *UK, 1983*. **5** a small group with specific economic functions, such as a drug-selling enterprise *US, 1995*. **6** a gang *US, 1990*. **7** a rubber thong sandal *CAYMAN ISLANDS, 1985*. **8** a crowd gathered in front of a carnival game or show *US, 1968*. **9** a steady, repeating player in a carnival midway game *US, 1985*

tip *verb* **1** to convey expert, inside or specialist information, especially about a profitable investment or a probable winner *UK, 1883*. **2** to give a gratuity *UK, 1706*. **3** to behave foolishly. Gulf war usage *US, 1991*. **4** to reckon that something will occur *AUSTRALIA, 1955*. **5** to perform oral sex. A shortening of TIP THE VELVET (to kiss with the tongue) *UK, 2002*. **6** to become aware of a swindle *US, 1963*. ▶ **tip it** in trucking, to drive fast *US, 1946*. ▶ **tip someone the wink** to warn someone; to privately signal to someone *UK, 1676*. ▶ **tip the brandy** to lick, suck and tongue another's anus. A combination of TIP (to perform oral sex) and BRANDY AND RUM (the buttocks) *UK, 2002*. ▶ **tip the bucket on someone** to denigrate or criticise someone *AUSTRALIA, 1986*. ▶ **tip the gas** in drag racing, to fill the petrol tank *US, 1968*. ▶ **tip the ivy** to lick, suck and tongue another's anus *UK, 2002*. ▶ **tip the load** to go to confession *AUSTRALIA, 1989*. ▶ **tip the velvet 1** to kiss with the tongue, especially to 'tongue a woman'. Based on obsolete 'velvet' (the tongue) *UK, 1699*. **2** to perform oral sex *UK, 2002*. **3** in homosexual sex, to lick, suck and tongue another's anus *UK, 1997*

tip-fiddle *noun* a military deployment list. Back-formation from TPFDL (time-phased forces deployment list) *US, 2003*

tip-off *noun* a warning; an item of private information. A variation of TIP *UK, 1901*

tip off *verb* to give information to someone, especially about an impending crime *US, 1891*

tipper *noun* a dump truck *US, 1971*

tippety-run *noun* a form of cricket played by children in which the person batting has to run every time the ball is hit. Also with great variation as 'tip-and-go', 'tip-and-run', 'tippety', 'tippety-cricket', 'tippety-runs', 'tippy-cricket', 'tippy-go', 'tippy-go-run', 'tippy-runs', 'tipsy and tipsy-runs' – and that's ignoring vast spelling variation *AUSTRALIA, 1983*

tipple *noun* **1** alcohol; especially a drink of regular choice. From the conventional verb *UK, 1581*. **2** by extension, a recreational drug of choice *UK, 2000*

tippy-toe *verb* to walk on tiptoe. Childish variation of conventional 'tiptoe' *UK, 1901*

tips *noun* in betting, odds of 11–10 *UK, 1991*

tip-slinger *noun* a person who offers racecourse tips *AUSTRALIA, 1915*

tipster *noun* in horse racing, someone who gives his opinions on various horses and their chances in a race *US, 1951*

tip-toe *verb* in motor racing, to manoeuvre carefully through or past an obstruction or dangerous condition *US, 1980*

tip-top *adjective* excellent *UK, 1755*

tip up *verb* to join a gang, especially a prison gang *US, 2000*

tip-up town *noun* a collection of ice fishing shanties on a lake's frozen surface. The 'tip-up' is the small fishing pole used for ice fishing. Michigan Upper Peninsula usage *US, 2003*

tire *noun* an apron worn by a young girl to keep her dress clean. This very old word – Shakespeare often used it – is still in use in Nova Scotia *CANADA, 1988*

tire billy *noun* a short stick with a weighted head used by truck drivers to test the air pressure of their tyres *US, 1971*

tired *adjective* boring *UK, 1987*

tired and emotional *adjective* drunk. A barbed journalistic euphemism thought to have been coined, or noted in political use and gleefully adopted, by satirical magazine *Private Eye UK, 1981*

tire-kicker; tyre-kicker *noun* in the used car business, a customer who studiously inspects the cars for sale, seemingly at the expense of ever getting around to buying a car. Reported by sales assistants in a UK electrical goods retail chain in August 2002 as meaning 'a customer who spends a long time looking and fails to make a purchase' *US, 1997*

tish note *noun* in circus and carnival usage, counterfeit money, especially when used to pay a prostitute *US, 1981*

tissue *noun* **1** crack cocaine. The variant 'tisher' is also used *UK, 1998*. **2** (especially in Tasmania) a cigarette paper *AUSTRALIA, 1966*

tissue odds; tissue *noun* a betting forecast used by bookmakers. From the flimsy paper originally used for this purpose *UK, 1942*

tiswas; tizwas; tizz-wozz *noun* a state of excitement or confusion. Originally Royal Air Force use; possibly a blend of 'it is/it was' as a variation of 'not know if you are coming or going' or a variation of TIZZ (an emotional state). From 1974–82 *Tiswas* was a popular Saturday morning television programme that demonstrated the qualities of excitement and confusion *UK, 1960*

tit *noun* **1** the female breast *UK, 1928*. **2** any finger-touch button such as on an electric bell; thus any button-like or knobby protruberance that vaguely resembles a nipple. Originally military *UK, 1943*. **3** a police officer's helmet. From the shape *UK, 2002*. **4** a fool. Often as 'look a right tit' or 'an absolute tit', and the amusing popular favourite 'feel a right tit' *UK, 1947*. **5** a small raised bump on a computer keyboard key, most commonly the f and j keys, to provide orientation for the user's fingers *US, 1991*. ▶ **a tit full of Wild Turkey** used for describing an alcoholic's fondest sexual fantasy *US, 1994*. ▶ **get tit** to succeed in the goal of touching or fondling a girl's breasts *US, 1974*. ▶ **on the tit** enjoying charity, or quasi-charity, in the form of undemanding work *US, 1957*

tit *adjective* undemanding, easy *US, 1990*

tit about *verb* to waste time; to play about; to be engaged in trivial activity *UK, 1999*

tit and clit chain *noun* a decorative chain that connects a woman's pierced nipples and clitoris *US, 1996*

titanic *noun* someone who performs oral sex on first acquaintance. A jokey reference to 'going down' (performing oral sex) first time out; the RMS Titanic famously sunk on her maiden voyage *UK, 2002*

titbag *noun* **1** a brassiere *US, 1994*. **2** a fool. An elaboration of TIT (a fool) *UK, 2001*

titch *nickname* applied to a person of small stature or a little child. Derives, via the earlier spelling 'tich', from music hall entertainer Little Tich (diminutive comedian Harry Relph, 1868–1928), who took as his stage name the nickname he was given as a child from his resemblance to Arthur Orton, the man who claimed to be the missing heir to an English baronetcy, Richard Tichborne *UK, 1934*

titchy *adjective* small, of small stature, insignificant. From TITCH *UK, 1950*

tit-clamp *noun* a device, designed to cause discomfort or pain for sexual stimulation, that is attached to a breast or nipple *UK, 1995*

tit-for-tat *noun* **1** a reaction equal and opposite to the action *UK, 1556*. **2** a hat. Rhyming slang. Can be shortend to 'titfer', 'titfa' or 'tit-for' *UK, 1930*. **3** a trade union traitor. Rhyming slang for RAT *AUSTRALIA, 2002*

tit-fuck *noun* an act of rubbing the penis in the compressed cleavage between a woman's breasts *US, 1972*

tit-fuck *verb* to rub the penis in the compressed cleavage between a woman's breasts *US, 1986*

tit-hammock *noun* a brassiere *UK, 1961*

tithead *noun* an idiot. Elaboration of TIT (an idiot) on the pattern of DICKHEAD (an idiot) *UK, 1999*

titi *noun* the female breast *TRINIDAD AND TOBAGO, 2003*

tit joint *noun* a bar or club featuring bare-breasted women servers *US, 1984*

tit-kisser *noun* a man sexually obsessed with women *US, 1977*

tit lift *noun* a procedure in cosmetic surgery to enhance the female breast *UK, 1992*

tit mag *noun* a magazine that features pictures of half-naked or naked women in erotic poses *UK, 1976*

tit magazine *noun* a magazine featuring photographs of naked women *US, 1972*

tit-man; tits-man *noun* a male with a (declared) primary interest in a woman's breasts as a point of attraction *US, 1974*

tito *noun* a rand (unit of currency). Teen slang, after South African Reserve Bank Governor Tito Mboweni *SOUTH AFRICA, 2003*

tit off *verb* to annoy or to aggravate someone *UK, 1997*

tit ring *noun* a ring that passes through a pierced nipple *US, 1984*

tit run *noun* a walk through a crowd in search of attractive female breasts *US, 1995*

tits *noun* **1** when preceded by a characteristic or adjective, a person (of either gender) of the type defined by that characteristic or adjective *UK, 1997.* **2** heroin. Probably from TITS (exceptionally good) *UK, 2002.* ▶ **get on someone's tits** to annoy or irritate someone. Used by either gender *UK, 1945.* ▶ **off your tits** drunk or drug-intoxicated *UK, 2000.* ▶ **the tits** the best; absolute perfection, *mid-C20*

tits *adjective* exceptionally good *US, 1966*

tits! used for expressing excitement *US, 1992*

tits and ass; tits and arse *adjective* said of a film, television programme, or magazine featuring nudity *US, 1965*

tits out *adverb* in an uncompromising fashion, determinedly. Office jargon with a non-gender specific application *UK, 2005*

tits up *adjective* dead; out of operation. A coarser BELLY-UP, of military (possibly Royal Air Force) origin *UK, 1981*

tittie twister *noun* a pinch and twist of the breast, especially the nipple *US, 1997*

tit tip *noun* a female nipple *US, 1982*

tittle-tattle *verb* to inform on someone. A nuance of the conventional sense (to chat, to gossip), perhaps influenced by 'tell-tale' *UK, 2003*

titty; tittie *noun* the female breast *IRELAND, 1922*

titty bar; tittie bar *noun* a bar featuring bare-breasted female servers and/or dancers *US, 1991*

titty-deep *adjective* used of a fox hole shallow *US, 1990*

titty-fuck *noun* an act of rubbing the penis in the compressed cleavage between a woman's breasts. Elaboration of TIT-FUCK *US, 1988*

titty-fuck *verb* to rub the penis in the compressed cleavage between a woman's breasts *US, 1998*

titty hard-ons *noun* erect nipples *AUSTRALIA, 1996*

titty pink *adjective* a bright pink shade of lipstick. Thought to resemble the colour of a nipple *US, 1982*

tittytainment *noun* television programming that exploits sex. Used in the German media *US, 1998*

tit-wank *noun* an act of sexual gratification in which the penis is rubbed between a female partner's breasts *UK, 2002*

tit willow *noun* a pillow. Rhyming slang; playing on the pillowing effect of a TIT (the female breast) *UK, 1932*

tizz *verb* to frizz something up *AUSTRALIA, 1967*

tizz; tiz; tizzy *noun* a state of panic or confused excitement *US, 1935*

tizzic *noun* a lingering, throaty cough *BARBADOS, 1998*

tizz up *verb* to dress up *AUSTRALIA, 1977*

tizzy *adjective* ostentatiously dressed *AUSTRALIA, 1953*

tizzy up *verb* to smarten or spruce something up *AUSTRALIA, 1960*

TJ *nickname* Tijuana, Baja California, Mexico. On the California-Mexico border, just south of San Diego, California *US, 1981*

T-Jones *noun* a mother *US, 1988*

tjorrie *noun* ▷ *see:* CHORRIE

TL *noun* a sycophant. From the Yiddish *tuchus leker* (ass licker) *US, 1972*

TLC *noun* tender, loving care *US, 1973*

TM *noun* **1** a commerically rolled cigarette. A shortened form of TAILOR-MADE *US, 1976.* **2** transcendental meditation *US, 1979*

TMB doctors' shorthand applied to an elderly patient. An initialism of 'too many birthdays' *UK, 2002*

TMI used for expressing the sentiment that a conversation has become too personal, that the speaker is imparting *too much information US, 1997*

TMT used to designate the person who will feature in your immediate masturbatory fantasies *UK, 2002*

TNT *noun* **1** heroin. A play on DYNAMITE (a powerful drug) *UK, 1977.* **2** amyl or butyl nitrite *UK, 1998.* **3** a variety of MDMA, the recreational drug best known as ecstasy. A pun on TNT (the explosive trinitrotulene), suggesting that the ecstasy experience is explosive *UK, 1999.* **4** fentanyl, a synthetic narcotic analgesic that is used as a recreational drug, *2004*

TNX used as Internet discussion group shorthand to mean 'thanks' *US, 1997*

to *preposition* at. In conventional use from C10 to mid-C19; now in regional and dialect use in the UK, and colloquial use in the US *UK, 1985*

toad *noun* **1** an unattractive, older male homosexual *US, 1985.* **2** a very sick, derelict hospital patient. An initialism for a 'trashy old alcoholic derelict' *US, 1977.* **3** a black prisoner *US, 1989.* **4** a used car that is in very poor condition *US, 1980*

TOAD used for describing what happens when a surfer catches a big wave and almost immediately falls from his board. An abbreviation of 'take off and die' *US, 1988*

toadie *noun* the vagina *US, 1998*

toadskins *noun* money. A play on FROGSKIN *CANADA, 1912*

toad-stabber; toad-sticker *noun* a knife *US, 1945*

to and fro *noun* snow. Rhyming slang *UK, 1992*

to-and-fro'ing; to'ing-and-fro'ing *noun* a constant moving about *UK, 1961*

to and from *noun* an English person. Rhyming slang for POM *AUSTRALIA, 1946*

toast *noun* **1** something that is completely broken or inoperable *US, 1991.* **2** a forest that has been burnt by a forest fire *US, 1991.* **3** a narrative poem *US, 1976.* **4** an amusing story told as part of a rap performance. Adopted from a West Indian DJ's 'toast' (to perform a lyric) *US, 2000*

toast *verb* to heat a powdered drug such as heroin for injection *CANADA, 1966*

toast *adjective* dead *US, 1983*

toasted *adjective* **1** drunk *US, 1980.* **2** emotionally unstable *ANTARCTICA, 1997*

toasted bread *adjective* dead. A variation of the familiar rhyming slang 'brown bread'; *UK, 1998*

toast rack *noun* a very thin cow *NEW ZEALAND, 2002*

tobacco juice; tobacco stain *noun* faecal stains in the underwear or on a toilet bowl *US, 1966*

tobaccy *noun* tobacco *US, 1935*

Tobago love *noun* a relationship in which there is little or no display of affection *TRINIDAD AND TOBAGO, 1993*

Tobago sugar *noun* wood waste left by termites *TRINIDAD AND TOBAGO, 2003*

tober *noun* a field or other site recognised as the temporary home and responsibility of a circus, fair or market. Shelta *UK, 1890*

Tobermory *noun* a story. Rhyming slang, from the main village on the Isle of Mull, Scotland *UK, 2001*

tober omee *noun* a toll collector, a rent collector; a landlord *UK, 1934*

tober showman *noun* a travelling musician *UK, 2002*

Toblerone; tobler *noun* alone; on my own. Rhyming slang, formed from a branded chocolate confection. Often as 'on my tobler' *IRELAND, 2003*

to buggery *adverb* used to intensify an adjective. In phrases like 'blown to buggery' *UK, 2002*

toby *noun* the road, the highway. From Shelta *tobar* or *tober UK, 1958*

toby jug *noun* the ear. Rhyming slang for, LUG. *UK, 1992*

tochis; tuckus; tochas *noun* the buttocks. Yiddish *US, 1934*

tochis-over-teakettle *adverb* head-over-heels *US, 1991*

tockley *noun* the penis *AUSTRALIA, 1992*

to coin a phrase used as an ironic acknowledgement or apology for an immediately preceding or ensuing triteness *US, 1951*

toddie *noun* a potato *UK, 1984*

toddle *verb* to go; to leave *UK, 1812*

toddy *noun* an alcoholic beverage made with the alcohol of choice, hot water and sugar *UK, 1991*

todge omee-palone *noun* the passive partner in homosexual anal sex *UK, 2002*

todger *noun* the penis. From the obsolete verb 'todge' (to smash to a pulp), the penis seen as a smashing tool *UK, 2001*

todger dodger *noun* a lesbian. Literally 'someone who avoids a TODGER' (the penis) *UK, 2002*

to-do *noun* a social function or party. Extending the more general sense of 'to-do' (a fuss) creates this slightly critical variation of DO (a party) *UK, 2001*

Tod Sloan; tod *noun* alone. Rhyming slang for 'alone' although usage suggests a rhyme on 'own': 'on your tod' (on your own). Tod Sloan (1874–1933) was a US jockey who raced in the UK, under royal colours, from 1896. In 1901 he was banned by the English Jockey Club; by 1906 he was ruled off the turf everywhere. Coined originally for his fame, continued ironically with his infamy when he was truly 'on his tod'. Still used though the man is forgotten *UK, 1934*

toe *noun* ▶ **on the toe** nervous, anxious *AUSTRALIA, 1989*

toe-ender *noun* a kick *UK: SCOTLAND, 1985*

toefoot *noun* a numbing of the feet in cold water, creating the sensation of having no toes, only a foot. Surfing usage *US, 2004*

toe-jam *noun* the amalgam of dirt and sweat that gathers between the toes of unwashed feet *US, 1999*

toe nails in the radiator; toes on the radiator; toe nails on the front bumper; toes on the bumper *adjective* describing a vehicle being driven at top speed, or the driver of that vehicle. Citizens' band radio slang; the image of a driver's foot pressing the accelerator pedal through the floor *US, 1976*

toe-popper *noun* a small antipersonnel mine powerful enough to blow off a hand or foot *US, 1990*

toe-rag *noun* **1** a person who is disliked, usually with good reason. Ultimately from the rags worn on a tramp's feet, hence a beggar, and hence this term of contempt which is the only sense that survives *UK, 1875*. **2** a slut. Rhyming slang for SLAG *UK, 1992*

toes *noun* ▶ **on your toes** on the run *UK, 1996*

toes over *adjective* said when a surfer has any number of toes extended over the front end of the surfboard *US, 1964*

toes-up *adjective* sleeping. Prison usage *NEW ZEALAND, 1997*

toe ticket *noun* the name tag affixed to the toe of a corpse in a morgue *US, 1962*

toe-to-toe *noun* a fight *UK, 2000*

toe toucher *noun* a male homosexual, especially the passive partner in anal sex *UK, 1983*

toe up *adjective* drunk. A corruption of 'torn up' *US, 2001*

toey *adjective* **1** fast, fleet-footed *AUSTRALIA, 1971*. **2** restless; uneasy. From an earlier sense of 'a racehorse keen to run' (1930) *AUSTRALIA, 1959*. **3** anxious for sex *NEW ZEALAND, 1995*

toff *noun* **1** a person who is, or appears to be, of a superior social status or well-to-do. From 'tuft' which, in 1670, was a gold tassel worn by titled undergraduates at Oxford and Cambridge, and, by 1755, was university slang for a person of rank and title and hence down the social scale to 'swell' and 'nob'. In 1865 there was a music hall song entitled 'The Shoreditch Toff' by Arthur Lloyd *UK, 1851*. **2** a completely reliable and dependable person *AUSTRALIA, 1989*

toffee *noun* **1** nonsense or flattery *UK, 1967*. **2** (a stick of) gelignite. From its appearance *UK, 1964*. ▶ **not for toffee** of a person's ability to do something, not at all, by no means, not in any circumstances *UK, 1914*

toffee-nose *noun* a snob; a supercilious individual. A play on TOFF (a well-to-do person) as the sort of person who would look down their nose at a lesser individual *UK, 1964*

toffee-nosed *adjective* supercilious, snobbish *UK, 1925*

toffee wrapper; toffee *noun* the head. Rhyming slang for NAPPER *UK, 1998*

toff omee *noun* a wealthy older male homosexual lover; a homosexual sugar daddy. After the obsolete sense as 'a very well-to-do gentleman' *UK, 2002*

tog *noun* a men's suit *CANADA, 1965*

tog *verb* to dress. Conventional English reincarnated as slang in black vernacular *US, 1946*

together *adjective* having your life, career or emotions under control; self-assured *US, 1969*. ▶ **get it together** to take control of your personal condition; to get your mind and emotions under control; to become organised *US, 1975*

togged out *adjective* dressed *UK, 1793*

togged up *adjective* dressed up, usually for a special occasion. From TOGS (clothes) *UK, 1793*

toggle jockey *noun* in the US Air Force, a co-pilot *US, 1946*

togs *noun* **1** clothing. Conventional English starting in the late C18, resurrected as slang in the C20 *UK, 1779*. **2** especially on the eastern mainland, a swimming costume *AUSTRALIA, 1918*

toilet *noun* **1** an inferior venue *UK, 2002*. **2** in the used car business, a used car with serious hygiene issues *US, 1992*. **3** a person as a sex object *US, 1980*. **4** fat buttocks *BAHAMAS, 1982*. **5** a casino. An insider term *US, 1980*. ▶ **in the toilet 1** lost, wasted *US, 1987*. **2** in serious trouble *US, 2001*

toilet-bowl *adjective* having an inferior location or very low status *US, 1995*

toilet-bowl woman *noun* a prostitute who operates on Main Street in downtown Los Angeles. Another name for a 'comfort lady' *US, 2000*

toilet mouth *noun* a person who employs a vocabulary that is considered foul or obscene *US, 1976*

toilet queen *noun* a homosexual male who loiters around public toilets in search of sex-partners *US, 1967*

toilet roll; toilet *noun* unemployment benefit. Rhyming slang for THE DOLE *UK, 1992*

toilet seat *noun* in electric line work, an insulator retainer *US, 1980*

toilet-seat flying *noun* short run commercial flying, with lots of stops *CANADA, 1996*

toilet services *noun* in a prostitute's advertising, the act of urination, or defecation, by one person on another for fetishistic gratification *UK, 2003*

toilet snipe *noun* a thief who robs homosexuals at public toilets, often after posing as a homosexual himself *UK, 1983*

toilet talk *noun* speech that is considered obscenely offensive *US, 1971*

Toiling Tillie *noun* used as a personification of the stereotypical female office worker *US, 1955*

to'ing-and-fro'ing *noun* ▷*see:* TO-AND-FRO'ING

toke *noun* **1** an inhalation of marijuana smoke *US, 1962.* **2** marijuana *UK, 2001.* **3** a dose of a drug *US, 1994.* **4** cocaine *UK, 2003.* **5** in casino gambling, a gratuity either in the form of betting chips or in the form of a bet made in the name of the dealer. An abbreviation of 'token of gratitude' *US, 1981*

toke *verb* **1** to inhale smoke from a tobacco cigarette, a marijuana cigarette, a crack cocaine pipe or other drug *US, 1952.* **2** to sniff up and inhale cocaine *UK, 2001.* **3** to tip someone. Almost exclusively casino usage *US, 1983*

toke pipe *noun* a short-stemmed pipe used for smoking marijuana *US, 1982*

toker *noun* **1** a marijuana smoker *US, 1973.* **2** in a casino, a tipper. Because tips in casinos are most often in the form of gambling tokens or 'tokes' *US, 1974*

toke up *verb* to smoke marijuana *US, 1959*

to kill for *adjective* extremely desirable *UK, 2001*

Tokyo toughies *noun* inexpensive tennis shoes *US, 1991*

tol'able used as a response to the query of how you are. A youth-slurred 'tolerable' *US, 1981*

toley; toly *noun* excrement, especially a turd. From Scottish dialect *toalie* or *tolie* (a small cake) *UK: SCOTLAND, 1967*

toller *noun* a carved wooden duck decoy *CANADA, 1946*

tolley *noun* toluene, a paint solvent inhaled by the truly desperate abuser *US, 1997*

tolly mug *noun* a tooth mug or glass *UK, 1947*

tom *noun* **1** a prostitute. Thus a police unit that targets prostitution may be dubbed 'tom squad' or 'tom patrol' *UK, 1948.* **2** a resident of Toronto, Ottawa, and Montreal, the power elite of Canada *CANADA, 1979.* **3** in a casino, a poor tipper *US, 1993.* **4** money *SOUTH AFRICA, 1975.* **5** a British private soldier. A shortening of TOMMY *US, 1995*

Tom *noun* a black person who curries favour with white people by obsequious and servile behaviour. A shortened form of UNCLE TOM *US, 1959*

tom *verb* to work as a prostitute. From TOM (a prostitute) *UK, 1964* ▷*see:* TOMORROW

Tom *verb* to curry favour by acting obsequiously and in a servile manner *US, 1967*

Tom *adjective* shoddy, inferior *US, 1989*

Tom and Dick; Tom, Harry and Dick; Harry, Tom and Dick; Tom Harry *adjective* sick. Rhyming slang *UK, 1954*

tomato *noun* an attractive woman, especially a young one *US, 1929*

tomato can *noun* a mediocre boxer *US, 1955*

tomato puree; tomato *noun* a jury. Rhyming slang *UK, 1998*

tomato sauce *noun* a racehorse. Rhyming slang *UK, 1992*

tombowler; tombola *noun* a large marble; a highly prized marble *AUSTRALIA, 1977*

Tombs *nickname* the Manhattan Detention Complex or city jail. Named when built in the mid-C19 because it was modelled on an Egyptian-style mausoleum. The present facility bears no resemblance to the original structure but still carries the sobriquet *US, 1840*

tombstone disposition *noun* a surly, graceless, fearless character *US, 1970*

tom cat *noun* **1** a sewing machine needle converted to use for injecting drugs *US, 1949.* **2** a mat. Rhyming slang *UK, 1961*

tom-cat; tomcat *verb* to pursue women for the purpose of fleeting sexual encounters *US, 1927*

Tom Cruise *noun* alcohol. Rhyming slang for BOOZE, formed on the name of the US film actor (b.1962) *UK, 1998*

Tom, Dick and Harrilal *noun* used as the Trinidadian version of the common man Tom, Dick and Harry *TRINIDAD AND TOBAGO, 1990*

Tom, Dick and Harry *noun* any man – by random example. From C16, obsolete variations abound, not the least of which is Shakespeare's 'Tom, Dick and Francis'; 'Tom Dick and Harry' is not recorded until 1865 *UK, 1865*

Tom Dooleys *noun* the testicles. Rhyming slang for GOOLIES (the testicles), formed from a folk song character who, fittingly, was hung *UK, 1992*

Tom Finney *adjective* skinny. Rhyming slang, formed from the name of Preston and England footballer, Tom Finney (b.1922) *UK, 1998*

tomfoolery; tom *noun* jewellery. Rhyming slang. The abbreviated form is first recorded in 1955 *UK, 1931*

tomming *noun* prostitution *UK, 2002*

Tom Mix; tom *noun* an injection of a drug. Rhyming slang for FIX, formed on the name of US film actor Tom Mix, 1880–1940 *UK, 1978*

tommy *noun* the penis *BAHAMAS, 1982*

Tommy *noun* a British private soldier. The name Tommy Atkins was used as a specimen signature on official forms *UK, 1884*

Tommy Dodd *noun* **1** God. Rhyming slang *UK, 1960.* **2** a gun. Rhyming slang for ROD *US, 1944*

Tommy Dodd *adjective* odd. Rhyming slang *UK, 1992*

Tommy Dodds *noun* betting odds. Rhyming slang, extended from TOMMY DODD (odd) used from the mid-C19 in relation to coin tossing *UK, 1960*

Tommy Farr *noun* a (drinks) bar. Rhyming slang formed on the name of the Welsh champion boxer, 1914–86 *UK, 1992*

Tommy Guns *noun* diarrhoea. Rhyming slang for THE RUNS *UK, 1998*

Tommy Rollocks; rollocks; rollicks *noun* the testicles; nonsense, especially as an exclamation. Rhyming slang for BOLLOCKS *UK, 1961*

tommyrot *noun* nonsense *UK, 1884*

tommy squeaker *noun* a fart *UK, 2003*

Tommy Trinder *noun* a window. Rhyming slang, formed from the name of the popular Cockney comedian, 1909–89 *UK, 1998*

Tommy Tripe; tommy *verb* to look at someone or something. Rhyming slang for PIPE *UK, 1992*

Tommy Trotter *noun* a lump of nasal mucus. Glasgow rhyming slang for SNOTTER *UK: SCOTLAND, 1988*

Tommy Tucker *noun* **1** the penis, especially when erect. Possibly rhyming slang for 'fucker' *UK, 1966.* **2** a spirited person. Rhyming slang for FUCKER, formed from a nursery rhyme character. Normally said without malice *UK, 1998.* **3** a gullible individual. Rhyming slang for SUCKER *UK, 1998*

tomo *noun* a subterranean stream. From the Maori term for 'cave' *NEW ZEALAND, 1972*

tomorrow *noun* ▶ **like there was no tomorrow; as if there was no tomorrow** with desperate vigour, urgently *UK, 1980*

tomorrow; tom *verb* to borrow. Rhyming slang *UK, 1992*

tomorrow next day *noun* among Nova Scotians of German descent, the indefinite future *CANADA, 1999*

toms *noun* a fit of annoyance. Short for TOM TITS *AUSTRALIA, 1960*

Tom Sawyer *noun* a lawyer. Rhyming slang, formed from Mark Twain's eponymous hero *UK, 1961*

Tom Tank *noun* an act of male masturbation. Rhyming slang for WANK (an act of masturbation) *UK, 2003*

Tom Terrific *nickname* Tom Seaver (b.1944), a pitcher who almost single-handedly carried the New York Mets from last place in 1967 to the World Series champions in 1969. From a television cartoon show popular in the late 1950s and early 60s *US, 1969*

Tom Thumb *noun* rum. Rhyming slang *AUSTRALIA, 1905*

tom tit; tom *noun* an act of defecation. Rhyming slang for SHIT *UK, 1943*

tom tits; toms *noun* **1** diarrhoea. Rhyming slang for THE SHITS *AUSTRALIA, 1943.* **2** a fit of annoyance. Rhyming slang for SHITS *AUSTRALIA, 1944*

Tom Tug noun a bug. Rhyming slang UK, 1998

ton noun **1** a large amount. Often in the plural UK, 1770. **2** in any miscellaneous context, one hundred UK, 1962. **3** one hundred miles per hour UK, 1954. **4** one hundred pounds sterling UK, 1946. **5** one hundred Australian dollars AUSTRALIA, 1989

ton verb ▶ **ton it** to drive at 100 miles per hour UK, 2000

tone noun rude or disparaging talk TRINIDAD AND TOBAGO, 1957

tone on tone noun a car with the same colour interior and exterior US, 1997

toney adjective ▷ see: TONY

tongs noun heroin. Possibly in reference to the Chinese 'tongs' (criminal organisations) responsible in part for the import and distribution of the drug UK, 2002

tongue noun **1** the clitoris TRINIDAD AND TOBAGO, 2003. **2** an attorney US, 1962. ▶ **get tongue** in the categorisation of sexual activity by teenage boys, to kiss with tongue contact US, 1986

tongue job noun oral sex on a woman UK, 1984

tongue-pash verb to kiss with open mouths AUSTRALIA, 2000

tongue-trooper noun a Quebec inspector of signs, commissioned to enforce Bill 101, the language law making French primary in the province. Mordecai Richler is widely credited with having invented this popular nickname for the 'language police' in his controversial New Yorker essay 'Oh Canada! Oh Quebec!' (1992) CANADA, 2000

tongue wash noun oral sex, especially on a woman US, 1981

tonguey; tonguie noun a tongue-kiss AUSTRALIA, 1995

tonk noun **1** a homosexual male. From 'tonka bean', rhyming slang for QUEEN NEW ZEALAND, 1946. **2** the penis AUSTRALIA, 1972

tonk verb **1** to have sex. Euphemistic for FUCK UK, 1974. **2** in sport, to defeat someone resoundingly. Noted as 'imitative of a powerful blow having reached its target' by Susie Dent, The Language Report, 2003 UK, 1997

tonking noun a humiliating beating. From TONK UK, 1999

tonking adjective used as an intensifier UK, 1974

tonky noun the genitals, male or female BAHAMAS, 1982

tonky adjective fashionable. A possible blend of French ton (style) and SWANKY (showy) NEW ZEALAND, 1998

Tonky; tonkie noun a member of the Batonka tribe; an unsophisticated person or thing; someone who has 'gone native'. Derogatory ZIMBABWE, 2000

tonsil hockey noun passionate kissing US, 1986

tonsil juice noun saliva US, 1946

tonsil paint noun whisky US, 1977

tonsil test noun a film or theatre audition UK, 1952

tonsil-tickling noun intensive kissing. Slang for those who don't let it get too serious UK, 1990s

tonto adjective crazy, silly, foolish, eccentric. From Spanish tonto (stupid) US, 1973

ton-up noun a speed of 100 miles per hour, especially with reference to motorcycles UK, 1961

ton-up boy noun a motorcyclist who has driven at 100 miles per hour; generically, a member of a motorcycle gang. From TON (100) UK, 1983

tony; toney adjective up-market, sophisticated, stylish; snobbish, swanky. Conventionally meaning 'style'. Also used in Australia and New Zealand since 1900 US, 2001

Tony Benn noun ten. Rhyming slang, formed from the name of popular socialist politician Tony Benn (b.1925) UK, 1998

Tony Benner noun ten pounds. Rhyming slang for TENNER, extended on the name of Tony Benn (b.1925), a popular socialist politician UK, 1998

Tony Blair; tony noun hair. Rhyming slang, based on prime minister Tony Blair (b.1953), probably inspired by the new hairstyle he adopted (with widespread media attention) in 1996 UK, 1998

Tony Blairs noun flared trousers. Rhyming slang for 'flares' UK, 1998

Tony Hatch noun a match. Rhyming slang, formed from the name of the British tunesmith (b.1939) UK, 1998

tony's noun dice that have been marked to have two identical faces US, 1950

toodlembuck; toodle-em-buck; doodle-em-buck noun any of various gambling games played by children utilising a spinning device with the names of horses in a race written on it. From a 'toodle/doodle' frequentative formation expressive of spinning, 'em' (them) and 'buck' (a gambling marker) AUSTRALIA, 1924

toodle-oo goodbye. Cute. In the US, quite affected in a British sort of way UK, 1907

toodle-pip; tootle-pip goodbye. Very dated; contemporary usage is generally ironic, denoting a certain type of foolish upper-class speaker UK, 1907

toodles goodbye. Affected; an American corruption of TOODLE-OO, perceived in the US as quaintly and quintessentially British. A signature line of the Francine 'Gidget' Lawrence character played by Sally Fields on Gidget (ABC, 1965–66). Repeated with referential humour US, 1966

toody-hoo used as a greeting US, 1983

too fool adjective lacking common sense CAYMAN ISLANDS, 1985

tooie; tuie; tooey; toolie; toole noun a capsule of amobarbital sodium and secobarbital sodium (trade name Tuinal™), a combination of central nervous system depressants US, 1966

tool noun **1** the penis. Conventional English at first – found in Shakespeare's Henry VIII – and then rediscovered in the C20 as handy slang UK, 1553. **2** an objectionable idiot, a fool UK, 2001. **3** a diligent student US, 1965. **4** a weapon, generally a gun or a knife UK, 1942. **5** a skilled pickpocket US, 1950. **6** in pool, a player's cue stick US, 1993. **7** a surfboard US, 1987

tool verb **1** to drive, to go, to travel, usually in a carefree manner. Originally of horse-drawn transports, applied in the C20 to motor vehicles, boats and aircraft US, 1948. **2** to wander aimlessly; to do nothing in particular. The variant 'tool around' is also used US, 1932. **3** to have sex US, 1993. **4** to slash a person with a razor UK, 1959. **5** to work hard US, 1997

toolbox noun **1** the male genitals US, 1964. **2** the vagina US, 1967

tool check noun an inspection by a military doctor or medic of male recruits for signs of sexually transmitted disease US, 1967

tooled up adjective **1** in possession of a weapon. From TOOL (a gun or knife); popularised in such 1970s television crime dramas as The Sweeney UK, 1959. **2** carrying cocaine. A self-important adoption of an earlier gangster cliché UK, 2001. **3** in possession of house-breaking implements UK, 1959

tooler noun a show-off US, 1965

tooley bird noun in oil drilling, a loud squeak caused by poorly lubricated equipment US, 1954

toolie noun **1** in oil drilling, a driller's helper US, 1954. **2** a man who, in a quest for sex, joins a group of young people during the Schoolies Week holiday AUSTRALIA, 2003

toolies noun a pair of men's close-fitting and revealing nylon swimming trunks. From TOOL (the penis) AUSTRALIA, 2003 ▷ see: TULES

toolio noun a social outcast US, 1997

tools noun **1** the syringe and other equipment used to prepare and inject drugs US, 1966. **2** the jewellery, cars, clothing and material flourishes that support a pimp's image US, 1972. **3** a racecourse bookmaker's equipment UK, 2001

tools of the trade noun any objects used in sado-masochistic activities, especially when advertised by a prostitute UK, 2003

tool up verb (of a man) to ready yourself for sexual intercourse, by erecting the penis UK, 1984

too much adjective great, wonderful, excellent US, 1969

too much! used as a humorous commentary, suggesting that someone has gone too far US, 1963

too much perspective; too much fucking perspective used for expressing the sentiment that too much information is being shared.

A catchphrase from *Spinal Tap*, used with humour and referentially *US, 1984*

toonie *noun* a two-dollar coin. An alternative to 'doubl00nie', both nicknames derived from the LOONY *CANADA, 1987*

toonkins *noun* used as an endearing term of address to a child *BARBADOS, 1965*

too right yes indeed!, absolutely! *AUSTRALIA, 1919*

tooroo goodbye. Variant of 'too-ra-loo' *AUSTRALIA, 1927*

too serious *adjective* very good *US, 1980*

toot *noun* 1 a dose of a drug, especially cocaine to be snorted *US, 1971*. 2 an inhalation of marijuana smoke *UK, 2004*. 3 cocaine; heroin *UK, 1977*. 4 butyl nitrite *US, 1984*. 5 a drinking spree *US, 1891*. 6 the toilet. Rhymes with 'foot'. Perhaps a euphemistic alteration of 'toilet'. The suggestion in the *Australian National Dictionary* that it derives from British dialect *tut* (a small seat or hassock), recorded in C19, fails to impress as it doesn't take into account the fact that the dialect word was pronounced to rhyme with 'putt' *AUSTRALIA, 1965*. 7 a prostitute *US, 2001* ▷ *see:* WHISTLE AND TOOT

toot *verb* 1 to inhale a powdered drug, such as cocaine *US, 1975*. 2 to inhale crack cocaine vapours *UK, 1996*. 3 to fart *US, 1978*

toot; tute *nickname* in Canadian military aviation, the Tutor one-engine jet trainer *CANADA, 1995*

tooter *noun* a (improvised) tube for inhaling cocaine into the nose *US, 1981*

toothbrush day *noun* after a guilty verdict, the day when sentencing is announced *US, 1985*

toothing *noun* anonymous casual sexual activity with any partner arranged over Bluetooth™ radio technology enabled mobile phones *UK, 2004*

toothless gibbon *noun* the vagina. A visual pun, evocative of, if not inspired by, The Goodies 'Funky Gibbon', 1970 *UK, 1999*

toothpick *noun* 1 a thinly rolled marijuana cigarette. Collected during an extensive survey of New Zealand prison slang, 1996–2000 *NEW ZEALAND, 2000*. 2 a long, thin, old-fashioned surfboard *AUSTRALIA, 1985*. 3 a railway tie *US, 1977*. 4 a pool cue stick that is lighter than average *US, 1990*. 5 a sharp knife *US, 1945*

tooth-to-tail ratio *noun* the ratio of combat troops (tooth) to rear-echelon support personnel (tail) *US, 1991*

tootie *adjective* homosexual *US, 1999*

tooting *adverb* completely, absolutely. Usually further intensified with a preceding adverb *US, 1932*

Tooting Bec *noun* 1 food; a little to eat. Rhyming slang for PECK formed from an area of south London *UK, 1937*. 2 a kiss. Rhyming slang for 'peck' *UK, 1992*

tootle; tootle around; tootle along; tootle off *verb* to go; to wander; to travel *UK, 1959*

too true used as a stressed affirmative *UK, 1969*

toots *noun* used as an affectionate term of address, usually to a girl or woman *US, 1936*

tootsie *noun* 1 a woman, a girlfriend; often used as a form of address, either humourous or affectionate *US, 1895*. 2 a child's foot; a woman's foot. A baby-talk coinage; playful or affectionate usage *US, 1999*. 3 a capsule of secobarbital sodium and amobarbital sodium (trade name Tuinal™), a combination of central nervous system depressants. Also variant 'tootie' *US, 1977*

tootsie roll *noun* distilled and concentrated heroin *US, 1987*

tootsie trade *noun* a sexual coupling of two effeminate homosexual men *UK, 2002*

toov *noun* cigarettes, tobacco. English gypsy use *UK, 2000*

too wet to plow *adjective* experiencing the bleed period of the menstrual cycle *US, 1999*

top *noun* 1 the dominant partner in a homosexual or sado-masochistic relationship *US, 1961*. 2 a maximum prison sentence *US, 1968*. 3 a first sergeant. Variants include 'topper' and 'tap kick' *US, 1991*. ▶ **be on top** to be discovered in a criminal enterprise; to be arrested. Presumably from the exposed and conspicuous position

that is normally meant by 'on top' *UK, 1970*. ▶ **over the top** said of a score in pinball when the score exceeds the capacity of the scoring device and thus returns to zero *US, 1977*. ▶ **the top** 1 the beginning of something, often in the phrase 'from the top' *UK, 1976*. 2 the northern parts of Australia *AUSTRALIA, 1951*

top *verb* 1 to execute someone especially by hanging or beheading; hence, to kill someone *UK, 1718*. 2 to take the dominant, controlling role in a sado-masochistic relationship *US, 1997*. ▶ **top from the bottom; top from below** (of a sexual submissive in a sado-masochistic relationship), to take, or attempt to take, the dominant, controlling role *UK, 1996*. ▶ **top the hills and pop the pills** used as a stock description of a trucker's work *US, 1976*. ▶ **top yourself** to commit suicide. A specific variant of TOP (to kill deliberately) *UK, 1718*

top *adjective* great; excellent *US, 1935*

top banana *noun* the headliner in a vaudeville show; by figurative extension, the leading figure in any enterprise *US, 1953*

top bitch *noun* in a group of prostitutes working for a pimp, the latest addition to the group *US, 1967*

top bollocks; top ballocks *noun* the female breasts *UK, 1961*

top brass; brass *noun* high-ranking police officers. Adopted from military usage, preceded by 'big brass' and 'high brass' *UK, 1949*

top dog *noun* 1 a very important person *UK, 1900*. 2 in poker, the highest pair in a hand *US, 1996*

top dog *adjective* of a person, important *UK, 1998*

top dollar *noun* a high price or the best price; or rate of pay *US, 1994*

top dollar *adjective* first-rate, genuine *UK, 2001*

top-drawer *adjective* well-bred, high-class, the best *UK, 1920*

top dresser drawer *noun* the uppermost berth in a brakevan (caboose) *US, 1946*

toped *verb* drunk. From the conventional, if rarely used, verb 'tope' *UK, 2003*

Top End; top end *noun* the northern parts of the Northern Territory *AUSTRALIA, 1933*

Top Ender *noun* a person from the Top End *AUSTRALIA, 1941*

top-flight *adjective* first rate *US, 1939*

top gun *noun* 1 crack cocaine *US, 1994*. 2 one hundred pounds. Rhyming slang for TON, formed from the title of a 1986 film *UK, 1998*

top hat *noun* 1 the vagina. Rhyming slang for PRAT *UK, 1998*. 2 a fool. Rhyming slang for PRAT *UK, 1998*. 3 in the television and film industries, a device used to enable shooting very low angles *UK, 1960*

top hats *noun* erect nipples *US, 1997*

top-hole *adjective* excellent. Arch and dated but still used without irony *UK, 1908*

topless *noun* in the used car business, a convertible *US, 1992*

top mag *noun* a fast-talking criminal. Possibly an elaboration on earlier sense of 'mag' (a chatterer) *AUSTRALIA, 1975*

top man *noun* in a homosexual couple, the partner who plays the active role during sex *US, 1941*

top notch *noun* a gang member with high standing within the gang *JAMAICA, 1989*

top-notch *adjective* of the best quality. Figurative use of a 'top notch' representing the highest point achievable *UK, 1984*

top-notcher *noun* an outstanding person *AUSTRALIA, 1947*

topo *noun* crack cocaine *UK, 2003*

top-off *noun* a police informer *AUSTRALIA, 1940*

top-off merchant *noun* a police informer *AUSTRALIA, 1944*

top of the head *noun* in betting, odds of 9–4. From the TICK-TACK signal used by bookmakers *UK, 1991*

top of the pops *noun* the police. Rhyming slang for COPS, formed on the title of UK television's longest-running popular music show (BBC television, 1964–2006) *UK, 2005*

top of the shop *adjective* excellent. An elaboration of TOP (excellent) *UK, 1999*

top of the world *noun* a feeling of elation, good health or prosperity *US, 1920*

top one *noun* the best of times *UK, 1999*

topper *noun* **1** a remark or action that serves as the *coup de grace* of a conversation or series of events *US, 1939.* **2** a criminal who represents the interests of a cheque forger *UK, 1956.* **3** in circus and carnival usage, a featured act *US, 1981*

topping *adjective* excellent *UK, 1822*

topping shed *noun* in prison, a place of execution *UK, 1950*

tops *noun* dice that have been marked to have two identical faces *US, 1962*

tops *adjective* topmost in quality, the best *US, 1935*

tops *adverb* at the most *US, 1987*

tops and bottoms *noun* **1** in poker, a hand consisting of a pair of aces (the highest card) and a pair of twos (the lowest card) *US, 1951.* **2** a roll of trimmed paper 'topped' and 'bottomed' with a genuine banknote to give the impression of a weighty roll of money *UK, 1959.* **3** a combination of Taluin™, a painkiller, and the antihistamine Pyribenzamine™, abused for non-medicinal purposes *US, 1989*

top-shelf *adjective* excellent or the best *US, 1892*

top stick *noun* the best regular player in a pool hall *US, 1990*

topsy *noun* a chamber pot *BARBADOS, 1965*

topsy-turvy *adjective* **1** disordered, in a chaotic state, very untidy *UK, 1528.* **2** upside down; in reverse order *UK, 1530*

top totty *noun* an especially desirable or sexually available woman or women *UK, 2001*

top 'uns *noun* a woman's breasts *UK, 1958*

top whack; top wack *noun* the most expensive price. Derives from WHACK (a share of money) *UK, 1974*

top willow! in cricket, used for registering enthusiastic approval of a batman's performance. A cricket bat is traditionally made of willow. Displayed on a placard at the England v West Indies 2nd Test, Edgbaston, 31st July 2004 *UK, 2004*

toque; tuque *noun* a knitted cap made from wool *CANADA, 1871*

torch *noun* **1** an arsonist *US, 1938.* **2** an act of arson *US, 1981.* **3** a cigarette lighter *US, 1972.* **4** a handgun *US, 1962.* **5** marijuana; a marijuana cigarette. A conical shape holding fire at the flared end *US, 1977.* **6** a love song or ballad *US, 1948*

torch *verb* to light a fire, especially an arson fire *US, 1931*

torched *adjective* drunk *US, 1990*

torch job *noun* an enema containing a heat-inducing agent such as Vicks Vaporub™, Ben-Gay™, Heet™, or Tabasco™ sauce *US, 1972*

torch up *noun* to smoke marijuana; to light up a joint *US, 1955*

tore down *adjective* very disoriented, usually because of drug intoxication *UK, 1983*

toreeon *noun* a variety of marijuana *UK, 1980*

tore up *adjective* distressed *US, 1960*

tornado bait *noun* a mobile home or trailer, especially in a tornado zone *US, 1992*

torn up *adjective* hurt; upset *US, 1968*

Toronto the Good *nickname* the city of Toronto, considered with reference to its longtime (into the 1980s) strict rectitude in law and custom. Also nicknamed Hogtown, Toronto continues to carry both terms though money and a cosmopolitan and international flavour have replaced slaughterhouses and the former moral stiffness *CANADA, 2001*

torpecker *noun* a torpedo *US, 1948*

torpedo *noun* **1** a hired gunman or killer *US, 1929.* **2** the penis *US, 2003.* **3** a marijuana cigarette *SOUTH AFRICA, 1946.* **4** a marijuana and crack cocaine cigarette *US, 1994.* **5** in trucking, a large, bullet-shaped light on a cab *US, 1971*

torpedo juice *noun* any improvised liquor on board a submarine *US, 1948*

torpedos *noun* beans *US, 1977*

torqued *adjective* angered, annoyed *US, 1968*

tortoise head *noun* the erect penis *UK, 2001*

torture chamber *noun* a jail or prison where illegal drugs are not available *US, 1982*

Torvill and Dean *noun* a homosexual. Rhyming slang for QUEEN, formed from ice-dancing champions and Olympic gold medal winners 1984, Jayne Torvill and Christopher Dean *UK, 2003*

Toryglental *adjective* insane, crazy. Glasgow rhyming slang for 'mental', contrived on the Toryglen area of Glasgow *UK: SCOTLAND, 1988*

tosh *noun* **1** nonsense. A compound of synonyms 'bosh' and 'trash' *UK, 1892.* **2** used as a form of male address. Possibly Scottish in origin. In 1990, car manufacturer Toshiba created a new slogan 'Ullo Tosh! Gotta Toshiba?' based on the song 'Ullo John! Gotta New Motor?', Alexei Sayle, 1983 *UK, 1954.* **3** a bath. School slang *UK, 1881*

tosheroon; tusheroon; 'roon *noun* in pre-decimalisation currency, a half-crown coin; two shillings and sixpence *UK, 1859*

toshing *verb* painting and decorating *UK, 1998*

tosh up *verb* to make something look as good as new. Car dealers' term *UK, 1983*

toss *noun* **1** nonsense, especially if self-indulgent *UK, 1990.* **2** something of little or no value *UK, 1994.* **3** an act of masturbation *UK, 1785.* **4** a search of a person or place *US, 1973.* **5** an armed robbery *US, 1950.* ▶ **not give a toss; not care a toss** to not care one way or another; to reject. Two suggested etymologies prevail, either 'to not care enough to toss a coin' or 'to toss (masturbate) yourself'; on balance, probably 'to toss a coin' as it takes a deal less effort and therefore the rejection is greater *UK, 2001*

toss *verb* **1** (of a male) to masturbate. Often used with 'off' *UK, 1879.* **2** to get the better of someone; to overcome someone or something *AUSTRALIA, 1949.* **3** to search a room, apartment, house, office or person without regard to the condition in which the premises or person are left *US, 1939.* **4** to rob a place *US, 1950.* **5** to gulp a drink down, *1992.* ▶ **toss a grind** to eat *US, 1992.* ▶ **toss chow** to eat quickly and voraciously *US, 1993.* ▶ **toss it in** stop doing something *AUSTRALIA, 1954.* ▶ **toss it to someone** to have sex with a woman *US, 1964.* ▶ **toss salad** to engage in oral stimulation of the anus *US, 2001.* ▶ **toss the boards** to play three card molly, a street swindle in which the object is to identify a given card among three cards that are quickly moved around *US, 1972.* ▶ **toss the tiger** to vomit. A visual allusion to multi-coloured vomit *NEW ZEALAND, 1960.* ▶ **toss your cookies** to vomit. Children's vocabulary *US, 1941.* ▶ **toss your lollies** to vomit *NEW ZEALAND, 1998*

tossbag *noun* a contemptible individual *UK, 1977*

tossed salad *noun* any of several sexual practices involving oral-anal stimulation *US, 1997*

tosser *noun* **1** someone who is considered worthless or despicable. A synonym of WANKER *UK, 1977.* **2** nothing at all; something of very little value. From the meaning as 'a penny' (a coin of little value) *UK: SCOTLAND, 1988.* **3** a penny. From the low value coin used in games of pitch-and-toss. Still current in Northen Ireland *UK, 1934*

tossily *adverb* self-indulgently, hence pretentiously. From TOSS (to masturbate) *UK, 2000*

tossle; tossel *noun* the penis. Variant of 'tassle' (something that dangles) *AUSTRALIA, 1945*

tosspot *noun* a fool; a generally abusive term for a person; in Australia, used as an affectionate form of address. Derives originally (C16) from the conventional sense as 'drunkard'. The more abusive sense combines 'fool' and TOSSER, a synonym for WANKER (a despicable person) *UK, 1983*

toss-up *noun* **1** an even chance; anything dependant on chance. From the tossing of a coin *UK, 1809.* **2** a person who will trade sex for crack cocaine *US, 1989.* **3** a promiscuous female *US, 1995*

toss-ups *noun* crack cocaine. From 'toss-up' (a person who trades sex for crack) *UK, 2003*

tossy *adjective* pathetic *UK, 2001*

tot *verb* to collect rubbish *UK, 1884*

TOT used for suggesting that it is time to tell the complete truth. From the Yiddish for 'buttocks on the table' *US, 1989*

total *verb* to wreck something beyond repair. Originally and chiefly applied to a car *US, 1954*

total *adjective* utter; out-and-out; complete; used as an all-purpose intensifier *US, 1999*

total bang up *noun* in prison, a regime under which inmates are locked in their cells for 24 hours a day *UK, 1996*

total blank *noun* in circus and carnival usage, a dull town where business is poor *US, 1981*

totalled; totalled out *adjective* drunk *US, 1966*

totally *adverb* completely. Very close to standard English, but with the right attitude quite slangy *US, 1982*

totally! used as an enthusiastic expression of agreement *US, 1982*

total out *adjective* to an extreme; to excess. Hawaiian youth usage *US, 1982*

total wreck *noun* a cheque. Rhyming slang *UK, 1996*

tote *noun* in horse racing, a pari-mutuel betting machine. An abbreviation of 'totalisator' *AUSTRALIA, 1890*

tote *verb* to carry a pistol *US, 1998*

tote! used for expressing assent. An abbreviation of TOTALLY! *US, 2000*

to the bad of time, late *UK, 2000*

to the good *adverb* of time, early *UK, 2000*

to the nth degree *adjective* to an extent beyond any reasonable measurement. Uses 'n' (a mathematical symbol for an indefinite number) to create a quasi-scientific sounding approximation *UK, 2001*

to the rack! used by pool players for expressing dismay and utter defeat. The player has no choice in this situation but to return his cue to the rack *US, 1993*

tothersider *noun* in Western Australia, a person from an eastern state *AUSTRALIA, 1872*

toto *noun* the penis *TRINIDAD AND TOBAGO, 1987*

toto-ed *adjective* in a state of drug-induced exhilaration. Inspired by *The Wizard of Oz*, 1939, in which Judy Garland (1922–69) as Dorothy, says to her dog: 'Toto, I don't think we're in Kansas anymore' *UK, 2001*

totonol *noun* frequent, regular sex as a cure for a woman's ailments *TRINIDAD AND TOBAGO, 2003*

tottie; totty; tot *noun* a person who is not white, especially a 'coloured' person; originally and particularly, one of the Khoikhoi race. Derivies from Hottentot; now considered derogatory and offensive *SOUTH AFRICA, 1832* ▷*see:* TATER

tottita *noun* the vagina *US, 1998*

tot-tots *noun* the female breasts *TRINIDAD AND TOBAGO, 1974*

totty; tottie; tott *noun* a sexually available or desirable young woman or women *UK, 1890*

totty *adjective* attractive, desirable *UK, 2002*

tot up *verb* to amount to; to add up; to calculate. Ultimately from 'total'. An older variant, 'tot together', is still familiar *UK, 2004*

touch *noun* **1** a sum of money obtained at one time, especially by cadging or theft *US, 1846*. **2** a satisfying result. Derives from the 'something-for-nothing' senses *UK, 2000*. **3** in pool, finesse *US, 1895*. **4** a resemblance or evocative quality. When combined with a pluralised proper noun, it is used to suggest characteristics associated with that noun, as 'a touch of the Prince Edwards', 'a touch of the Bob Dylans' or 'a touch of the Hollywoods' *UK, 1388*. ▶ **put the touch on someone** to attempt to extract money from someone with glib or coercive talk *US, 1956*

touch *verb* **1** to borrow from someone *US, 1955*. **2** to subject someone to extortion or bribery *UK, 1654*. **3** to finance someone *UK, 1999*. **4** to have sex with someone *IRELAND, 1984*. ▶ **I wouldn't touch it with yours** used by one male to another as an expression of distaste or contempt for a female. Here 'it' is 'a woman' and 'yours' is 'a penis' *UK, 1984*. ▶ **not touch it with a bargepole** used as an

indication of extreme distaste or contempt. In many minor variations *UK, 1984*. ▶ **touch home** to communicate a feeling; to make sense *US, 1959*. ▶ **touching cloth; touching cotton** having an urgent need to defecate *UK, 2002*

touch and go *adjective* of uncertain outcome, unsure *UK, 1815*

touch and tap *noun* a cap (hat). Rhyming slang *UK, 1992*

touched; touched in the head *adjective* mentally impaired; insane *UK, 1893*

touched by the moon *adjective* (slightly) insane. An elaboration of TOUCHED (insane), in the form of rhyming slang on LOON (a madman) *UK, 1992*

touche eclat *verb* to conceal something. From French, where, if the construction were used, it would mean (very loosely) 'a brilliant or acclaimed touch'. A contemporary gay usage *UK, 2003*

touchhead *noun* a convert to the musical cult of the Grateful Dead after the 1987 release of the song 'Touch of Grey'. A play on the common DEADHEAD (a Grateful Dead follower) *US, 1995*

touching *adjective* used of playing cards adjacent in rank *US, 1996*

touch man *noun* a criminal who specialises in breaking into safes by manipulating the combinations until they open *US, 1970*

touch off *verb* to light a fire, especially if arson *US, 1979*

touch'ole *noun* a cow's anus *CANADA, 1992*

touch-on *noun* an erection *UK, 2001*

touchous *adjective* irritable, easily upset *TRINIDAD AND TOBAGO, 1956*

touch the dog's arse *noun* car theft. Prison slang for the initialism TDA (taking and driving away) *UK: ENGLAND, 1998*

touch up *verb* **1** to caress and fondle someone in a sexual manner *UK, 1903*. **2** to steal something *US, 1997*

touch wood used superstitiously as a precaution against bad luck, spoken to accompany the action of touching wood (often humorously tapping your own *wooden* head); or to replace the need for the action; or by rote, without superstition, as a general way of saying 'with luck'. After a Christian belief in the benefit of touching the cross, hence the proverbial 'Touch wood, it's sure to come good' *UK, 1908*

touchy-feely *adjective* overly sensitive, caring or emotional. Originating in psycho-therapy, now generally used dismissively to describe every state between tactile and lecherous *US, 1968*

touch you! used for conveying surprise and admiration *US, 1997*

tough *verb* to inject a drug into a vein on the underside of the tongue. It is not particularly difficult to guess why this practice is so named *US, 1986*. ▶ **tough it out; tough** to bear hardship; to determinedly face up to a difficulty *2000*

tough! 'hard luck!'; unfair *UK, 1929*

tough; tuff *adjective* good, admirable *US, 1937*

tough biccies! used for expressing a profound lack of sympathy for a bad turn of events *NEW ZEALAND, 1977*

tough cheeko used for expressing a lack of sympathy *US, 1969*

tough darts too bad *US, 1968*

tougher *noun* in poker, an increased bet *US, 1951*

tough guys *noun* in craps, the proposition bets (bets that a number will be rolled in a pair) *US, 1983*

toughie; toughy *noun* a tough person or situation *US, 1929*

toughies *noun* in craps, the proposition bets (bets that a number will be rolled in a pair) *US, 1983*

tough love *noun* a mixture of compassion and strictness designed to affect change in destructive behaviour *US, 1981*

tough nut; tough nut to crack; hard nut; hard nut to crack *noun* someone who is difficult to deal with, especially one with a tendency to violence *US, 1999*

tough shit who cares?, so what? An unsympathetic variation of 'tough luck': 'tough' (unfortunate, unpleasant) and SHIT (an abstract form) for 'luck' *US, 1934*

tough shitski used as a humorous embellishment of tough shit, or too bad. A mock Slav or Russian suffix *US, 1961*

tough titty; tough titties; tough tit used for conveying a lack of sympathy with a difficult turn of events *US, 1934*

toup *noun* a man's hairpiece *US, 1985*

tour ball *noun* in pinball, a ball that stays in play for a relatively long period without scoring many points *US, 1977*

tour crud *noun* in the language surrounding the Grateful Dead, a bacterial or viral infection that quickly spreads among those following the band on tour *US, 1994*

tourist *noun* **1** in relation to a specified subject area, a person who takes a temporary interest *UK, 2002.* **2** a summer worker in Antarctica *ANTARCTICA, 1966*

Tourist Annie *noun* the stereotypical female tourist in Port of Spain, dressed in what she perceives as traditional island clothing *TRINIDAD AND TOBAGO, 1971*

tourist disc *noun* in shuffleboard, a shot that passes through without hitting a target disc or discs *US, 1967*

tourist trap *noun* a place that attracts and makes unreasonable profits from tourists *UK, 1939*

touristy *adjective* full of tourists; designed or developed to appeal to tourists; characteristic of tourists. Often with derogatory connotations *UK, 1906*

tourniquet *noun* an engagement or wedding ring *US, 1961*

tour rat *noun* in the language surrounding the Grateful Dead, a fan who follows the band on tour at all costs *US, 1994*

tout *noun* **1** an informer, especially one who works for the IRA *UK: NORTHERN IRELAND, 1979.* **2** in horse racing, someone who sells generally worthless advice with the promise of inside information bound to help bettors win *UK, 1865.* **3** a horse racing enthusiast who closely watches workouts and is generally disliked by those on the inside of the sport *AUSTRALIA, 1989.* **4** in a confidence swindle or sales scheme, an agent who for a commission locates potential victims *US, 1988.* **5** in a whe-whe lottery game, a person who records and collects bets, takes the bets to the banker and pays off winners *TRINIDAD AND TOBAGO, 1996*

tow *verb* ▶ **I'll tow that one alongside for a bit before I bring it aboard** among Nova Scotia fishermen, used for expressing doubt about the truth or reliability of an idea or project *CANADA, 1992*

towel *noun* ▶ **chuck in the towel; throw in the towel; toss in the towel** to admit or concede defeat. From boxing *UK, 1915*

towelhead; towel-head *noun* an Arab; also a Sikh or other turban-wearer. An offensive or derogatory term; from the traditional headwear of the various races and creeds *US, 1979*

towel up *verb* to beat someone up *AUSTRALIA, 1919*

tower bird *noun* in oil drilling, a worker on a derrick *US, 1954*

Tower Bridge, tower *noun* a refrigerator. Rhyming slang for 'fridge' *UK, 1992*

Tower Hill *verb* to kill. Rhyming slang, formed on an area of London *UK, 1998*

towie *noun* a tow-truck driver *AUSTRALIA, 1975*

town *noun* **1** London. Used by Charles Dickens, Oscar Wilde and present-day commuters *UK, 1837.* **2** city. A coy term that harkens back *US, 1999.* ▶ **go to town** to make the utmost effort; to tackle something with zest and vigour *UK, 1933.* ▶ **go to town on** to attack excessively either verbally or physically *IRELAND, 1992.* ▶ **in town** in horse racing, on major metropolitan tracks. The opposite of the 'bushes' *AUSTRALIA, 1989.* ▶ **out of town** in jail or prison *US, 1982*

town bike *noun* a promiscuous female. Everybody has, it seems, 'taken a ride' *AUSTRALIA, 1945*

town clown *noun* in carnival usage, a local police officer *US, 1989*

town crier *noun* a liar. Rhyming slang *UK, 1992*

town dollars *noun* in horse racing, money bet at a betting operation away from the track *US, 1951*

towner *noun* a local resident. Circus and carnival usage *US, 1980*

town hall drapes *noun* the foreskin of an uncircumcised penis *UK, 2002*

townie *noun* **1** a townsperson, contrasted with a visiting student or summer visitor *US, 1852.* **2** any member of a subcultural urban adolescent grouping that seems to be defined by a hip-hop dress and jewellery sense *UK, 2004*

town punch *noun* an extremely promiscuous girl or woman *US, 1975*

towns *noun* the testicles. Rhyming slang on 'town hall' for BALL(S); appears to originate in Liverpool *UK, 2001*

towns and cities *noun* the female breasts. Rhyming slang for TITTIE(S), recorded as obsolete by Julian Franklyn, *A Dictionary of Rhyming Slang*, 1960, but noted as a variant of BRISTOL CITY by Ray Puxley, *Cockney Rabbit*, 1992 *UK, 1960*

toxic *adjective* **1** of a situation, unhealthy, poisonous. Figurative application of the conventional sense *UK, 1998.* **2** amazing, powerful *US, 1987*

Toxic Hell *noun* a Taco Bell™ restaurant (a Mexican fast-food chain in the US) *US, 1993*

toy *noun* **1** a can in which opium is stored, whether the can is tin, tinned iron or another metal; a small amount of opium *US, 1934.* **2** any object that is used for sexual stimulation during masturbation, foreplay, sexual intercourse or fetish-play *US, 1977.* **3** a desk with an attached bookcase *UK, 1947.* **4** a computer system *US, 1991.* **5** an inexperienced or incompetent graffiti artist *US, 1990.* **6** in drag racing, a dragster (a car designed specifically and exclusively for drag racing) *US, 1965* ▷ *see:* TAW

toy boy *noun* a younger male lover *UK, 1981*

toy dolls *noun* the testicles. A vaguely assonant euphemism *UK: SCOTLAND, 1988*

Toyko Rose; tokyo *noun* the nose. Rhyming slang, formed from the name given by the US administration and soldiers in World War 2 to the many female voices that broadcast Japanese propaganda, but especially associated with Iva Ikuko Toguri (b.1916), a Japanese-American, who actually broadcast under the name Orphan Ann. *UK, 1992*

toy otter *noun* in car repair, a Toyota car *US, 1992*

toys *noun* heroin *UK, 2003*

TP *noun* **1** a scene in a pornographic film or a photograph depicting a woman having simultaneous oral, vaginal and anal sex. An abbreviation of 'triple penetration' *US, 2000.* **2** a woman with large breasts and large buttocks. A 'total package' *US, 2000*

TR-6 *noun* an amphetamine. Possibly from a Triumph TR-6, the legendary sports car manufactured from the late 1960s to the mid-70s, used here as an allegory for SPEED (amphetamine) *UK, 1998*

trac *noun* an intractable prisoner *AUSTRALIA, 1967*

track *noun* **1** the street or area where prostitutes solicit customers *US, 1969.* **2** the open road as used by itinerant travellers. Commonly in the phrase 'on the track' *AUSTRALIA, 1873.* **3** the course of an event; the course of time *AUSTRALIA, 1945.* **4** an armoured personnel carrier, especially the M-113 *US, 1971.* **5** a warder who carries contraband for prisoners. An earlier variant 'track-in' has been recorded from 1939 *AUSTRALIA, 1950.* ▶ **the track** the Savoy ballroom, New York. A major night spot on Lenox Avenue between 140th and 141st Streets in New York from 1927 until the 50s *US, 1946*

track *verb* to inject drugs *UK, 1996*

track-basher *noun* a specialist trainspotter who travels (and so 'collects') little-used sections of the rail network *UK, 2003*

tracked up *adjective* scarred from regular intravenous drug injection *US, 1971*

tracker *noun* in the television and film industries, a low-level development executive *US, 1997*

trackie; tracky *noun* a tracksuit. Also in the plural form 'trackies' *AUSTRALIA, 1987*

trackie-bottoms *noun* tracksuit trousers *UK: SCOTLAND, 1996*

trackie daks *noun* tracksuit trousers *AUSTRALIA, 2000*

track lawyer *noun* in horse racing, someone who constantly resorts to claims of technical rule violations, the pettier the better *US, 1947*

track record *noun* the known facts about relevant history *US, 1951*

tracks *noun* bruises, punctures and sores visible on the skin of an intravenous drug user *US, 1960*. ▶ **across the tracks; wrong side of the tracks** the socially inferior area of town. The railway often separated the better-off part of an American town from the poorer quarters. Duke Ellington's 'Across the Tracks Blues' dates to 1943 *US, 1943*. ▶ **make tracks** to leave *US, 1945*

traction *noun* in confidence games, an amount of money used to begin an increasingly larger series of swindles *US, 1997*

traddie *noun* a traditional jazz enthusiast *UK, 1983*

trade *noun* **1** a man, self-identified as heterosexual, who engages in active anal homosexual sex or passive oral homosexual sex but will not reciprocate *US, 1927*. **2** heterosexual or homosexual prostitution; customers of that prostitution, especially homosexual. Originally 'the trade' *UK, 1680*

trade *verb* ▶ **trade numbers** to bid for a job based on an estimated cost *US, 1989*. ▶ **trade paint** to be involved in a car accident with another car *US, 1997*

trade queen *noun* a homosexual man who prefers sex with a seemingly heterosexual man who consents to homosexual sex in the 'male' role, receiving orally or giving anally *US, 1970*

trade-rage *noun* an outburst of enraged hostility within a business environment *UK, 2003*

trades *noun* the trade journals of the US entertainment industry *US, 1984*

tradesman's entrance; tradesman's *noun* the anus, designated as an entry suitable for sex. In the grand houses of polite society the tradesman's entrance is traditionally round the back *UK, 2001*

trade up *verb* to escape criminal prosecution or lessen the charges against you by providing the police with information about other criminals *US, 1981*

Tradies *noun* a tradesmen's club *AUSTRALIA, 1987*

traditional discipline *noun* corporal punishment, especially when used in a prostitute's advertising matter *UK, 2003*

trad jazz; trad *noun* traditional jazz *UK, 1956*

traf *verb* to fart. Back slang *AUSTRALIA, 1998*

Trafalgar Square; trafalgar *noun* a chair. Rhyming slang *UK, 1998*

tragic *noun* an inferior or pathetic person. From the adjective *UK, 2005*

tragic *adjective* inferior, pathetic, no good. Used, especially in a sporting context, as an opposite of MAGIC (excellent). 'Liverpool are magic... Everton are tragic' is legendarily ascribed to footballer Emlyn Hughes (1947–2004) *UK, 1984*

tragic magic *noun* **1** heroin *US, 1990*. **2** crack cocaine dipped in phencyclidine, the recreational drug known as PCP or angel dust *UK, 1998*

trailer *noun* in a striptease performance, the preliminary march across the stage that precedes the removal of any piece of clothing *US, 1981*. ▶ **pull a trailer** to possess large buttocks *US, 1988*

trailer *verb* to pull a dragster onto its carrying trailer after it has been eliminated from an event. A car that has lost is referred to as 'being trailered' *US, 1970*

trail hog *noun* a skier who is inconsiderate of other skiers, monopolising a narrow trail *US, 1963*

trail marker *noun* an unappetising piece of food, the identity of which is uncertain *US, 1991*

trail mix *noun* a recreational drug cocktail of MDMA, the recreational drug best known as ecstasy, and Viagra™, a branded drug that enables a male erection *US, 2003*

trails *noun* **1** cocaine *UK, 2003*. **2** while under the influence of LSD or another hallucinogen, sequences of repeating after-images trailing a moving object *US, 1999*

train *noun* **1** cocaine *US, 1993*. **2** heroin *UK, 2003*. **3** in prison, drugs. To say 'the train has arrived' is to say that illegal drugs have arrived at the prison *US, 1982*. **4** a series of waves *US, 1963*. **5** multiple orgasms *US, 1985*. ▶ **pull a train; run a train** to engage in serial sex with

multiple partners, homosexual or heterosexual, usually consensual *US, 1965*

train *verb* ▶ **train Thomas at the Terracotta; train Terrence/Terence at the terracotta** (of a male) to urinate *AUSTRALIA, 1971*

trainies *noun* trainers, sports shoes *UK, 2001*

training beer *noun* low alcohol beer *CANADA, 1995*

training wheels *noun* a learner's driving permit *US, 1976*

train smash *noun* **1** fried or tinned tomatoes; tomato sauce. Military black humour; an especially unappetising example of visual imagery *UK, 1941*. **2** a hastily prepared savoury dish of tomatoes with onions, eggs, sausages, etc *AUSTRALIA, 1960*

trainspotter *noun* anyone with a pedantic interest in and an obsessive knowledge of a specific topic. Genuine trainspotters, of the variety that stand on railway platforms, are the stereotypical arch-hobbyists *UK, 1995*

train-surfing; urban surfing; roof-riding *noun* riding illegally on the roof of a train (or car, bus, etc) for the thrills. A ten-year craze from the early 1980s *US, 1993*

train wreck *noun* a horribly wounded soldier or casualty department patient. Used by medical corpsmen in Vietnam *US, 1978*

tram *noun* ▶ **wouldn't know if a tram was up you** to be docilely unaware *AUSTRALIA, 1972*

trammie *noun* a tram driver or conductor *AUSTRALIA, 1919*

tramp *noun* **1** a promiscuous man or woman *US, 1922*. **2** a worker who moves from job to job, city to city *UK, 1808*

Trance Canada *nickname* the Trans-Canada highway. This nickname is either a reference to 'highway hypnosis' (on boring sections like the 401 from Montreal to Toronto) or to the 'spellbinding scenery' on such parts as the Rocky Mountain crossing or the Maritime sections *CANADA, 2001*

tranced out; tranced *adjective* in a state of extreme distraction *UK, 1997*

trancey *adjective* of trance music *UK, 1998*

Trane *nickname* John Coltrane (1926–67). A jazz titan *US, 1985*

trank *noun* **1** any central nervous system depressant. Variant spelling include 'trang' and 'tranx' *US, 1971*. **2** a person who takes the excitement out of something; a killjoy. A figurative use of 'a tranquillizer' *US, 1979*

tranked *adjective* sedated; under the influence of tranquillizers *US, 1991*

trannie *adjective* transsexual *US, 1999*

trannie; tranny *noun* **1** a transvestite *UK, 1984*. **2** a transsexual *US, 1997*. **3** a transistor radio *UK, 1969*. **4** in a car or truck, a transmission *US, 1993*. **5** any surface used for skating or foot-propelled scootering that is not totally horizontal. From 'transition' *UK, 2000*

trans *noun* **1** a car *US, 1995*. **2** transport *BAHAMAS, 1982*

transcend *verb* to smoke marijuana *US, 1974*

transformer *noun* **1** a transsexual *US, 1991*. **2** a stuttering type of manipulation of a record to create a musical effect *2002*

transfusion *noun* a replenishment of cash *AUSTRALIA, 1989*. ▶ **get a transfusion** to fill a vehicle with petrol or diesel *US, 1976*

transit *noun* ▶ **in transit** experiencing the effects of LSD *US, 1971*

transvesty; transvestie *noun* a transvestite *US, 1987*

transy *noun* a transsexual *US, 1987*

trap *noun* **1** the mouth *UK, 1776*. **2** a police officer. Now only historical *AUSTRALIA, 1812*. **3** a prostitute's earnings. A shortened form of TRAP MONEY *US, 1973*. **4** an electronic device that records the originating telephone number of all incoming calls. A term and practice made obsolete with the advent of the 'caller ID' feature on telephones in the late 1990s *US, 1991*. **5** a hiding place for illegal drugs *US, 1967*. **6** a residence *US, 1957*. **7** a timing light at the finish line of a drag race *US, 1970*. **8** in poker, a deceptive bet *US, 1979*

trap *verb* **1** to have success attracting members of the opposite sex. Royal Navy slang *UK, 1989*. **2** to install an electronic trap on a telephone line *US, 1996*. **3** to land safely and accurately on an aircraft carrier *US, 1991*

trap door *noun* **1** a scab under which a drug addict injects drugs *US, 1992*. **2** a computing function that is easily performed but difficult to perform in the inverse. Extremely useful in cryptography *US, 1991*

trapeze artist *noun* a person engaged in simultaneous anal and oral sex *US, 1979*

trap money *noun* **1** a prostitute's gross earnings *US, 1974*. **2** money containing tear gas and/or dye kept in a bank to be given to bank robbers. An abbreviation of 'booby-trap money' *US, 2004*

trap off *verb* to deceive or manipulate someone *US, 2002*

trapper *noun* a person who can open envelopes and reseal them without a trace *US, 1982*

trappy *adjective* loud and boastful, possibly insulting. TRAP is 'mouth', therefore 'trappy' is MOUTHY *UK, 1999*

traps *noun* **1** drums and other items of percussion, collectively. Musicians' slang *US, 1903*. **2** the trapezius muscles connecting the neck and shoulder *US, 1984*. **3** your usual haunts *AUSTRALIA, 1933*

trap smasher *noun* in lobstering, a severe storm *US, 1978*

trap two; trap number two *noun* the anus. From greyhound racing *UK, 1998*

trash *noun* **1** contemptible people; a contemptible person *UK, 1604*. **2** military decorations, awards and patches *US, 1990*. **3** marijuana *US, 2001*. **4** heroin *UK, 2003*. **5** waves that collapse before they break, making poor surfing conditions *US, 1977*

trash *verb* **1** to destroy something *UK, 1970*. **2** to criticise or malign someone or something *US, 1975*. **3** to frighten someone. Market traders' term; directly from Romany *UK, 1979*

trashed *adjective* very drunk or drug-intoxicated *US, 1966*

trash hand *noun* in poker, an unplayable hand *US, 1992*

trash hauler *noun* during the Vietnam war, a cargo transport pilot *US, 1988*

trashing *noun* looting from shops *US, 1975*

trash time *noun* a short jail sentence, especially one spent on a litter cleaning duty *US, 1987*

traumatic *adjective* very exciting; excellent *US, 1990*

travel *verb* ▶ **travel on a tie pass** to walk along a train track *US, 1977*

travel agent *noun* an LSD dealer. A euphemism based on a TRIP metaphor *US, 1966*

traveller *noun* alcohol taken in a car on the way to a party or concert *US, 2004*

traveller's check *noun* in poker or other gambling, a betting token that rolls across the table or floor. From the insider slang term CHECK (a gambling token) *US, 1996*

traveller's marrow *noun* an erection brought on while travelling, especially while sleeping *UK, 1985*

travelling agent *noun* in a whe-whe lottery game, a person who collects and records bets, brings the bets and money to the banker and pays off winners *TRINIDAD AND TOBAGO, 1996*

tray *noun* a bunch of vials containing crack cocaine *US, 1994*

tray *adjective* three. A variation of TREY *UK, 2002*

treacle *noun* used as an endearment. Probably, simply, a simile for 'sweet'; possibly, rhyming slang 'treacle tart', for 'sweetheart' *UK, 2001*

treacle *verb* to flatter someone; to behave in an obsequious manner *UK, 1943*

treacle tart; treacle *noun* a fart. Rhyming slang *UK, 1998*

tread *noun* a shoe *UK, 1959*

treaders *noun* shoes *US, 1970*

treadhead *noun* a member of a combat tank crew *US, 1987*

treadly *noun* a bicycle *AUSTRALIA, 1990*

treash; treas *noun* a term of affectionate address. A shortening of 'treasure' *UK, 2002*

treasure *noun* a highly valued person. Often applied to people who provide a service *UK, 1810*

treasure chest *noun* a brakevan (caboose) *US, 1977*

Treasure Coast *noun* that portion of Florida between Cape Kennedy and West Palm Beach. After the sunken treasure believed to lie off the coast *US, 1965*

treasure hunt *noun* **1** the search in a gambling establishment or cardroom for someone from whom to borrow money *US, 1982*. **2** the vagina; a fool; a despicable person. Rhyming slang, CUNT. Can be shortened to 'treasure' *UK, 1998*

treat *noun* ▶ **a treat** beautifully, enjoyably, extremely *UK, 1964*. ▶ **do a treat; do someone a treat** to suit someone admirably *UK, 1904*. ▶ **do someone a treat; do someone up a treat** to thrash someone. An elaboration of DO (to beat) or DO UP (to beat up), possibly a deliberate pun on 'do someone a treat' (to suit someone very well) *UK, 1975*

treat *verb* ▶ **treat a J** to add another drug or drugs to a marijuana cigarette *US, 1982*

treat 'n' street *verb* in a hospital's casualty department, to tend to a patient's needs and discharge him or her as swiftly as possible *UK, 2002*

treble chance *noun* a dance. Rhyming slang *UK, 1992*

tree; trees *noun* marijuana. An exaggerated BUSH *US, 1995*. ▶ **out of your tree** drunk or drug-intoxicated *IRELAND, 1991*. ▶ **out of your tree; off your tree** crazed; mentally deranged *US, 1966*. ▶ **out yer tree** drunk *UK, 2002*

tree-eater *noun* a member of the US Special Service Forces. Because of the constant survival training the special forces undergo *US, 1993*

tree-fucker *noun* a stereotyped enviromentalist. A variant of TREE-HUGGER *UK, 2000*

tree-hugger *noun* an environmental activist *US, 1977*

tree-hugging *adjective* environmentally aware; active in environmental protection *US, 1999*

tree-jumper *noun* a chronic sex offender *US, 1992*

trees *noun* broccoli *US, 1966*. ▶ **put in the trees** to overcharge someone *US, 1980*

treetop level and all engines out *adjective* near death *US, 1994*

tree up *verb* when parachuting, to land and become entangled in a tree *US, 1959*

treeware *noun* books, magazines, newspapers, etc, as opposed to all alternate forms of providing such texts. Computer hacker slang, deriding the fact that paper is made from pulped wood *US, 1997*

Trekker *noun* a zealous fan of *Star Trek*. Preferred by the fans over the term 'TREKKIE' *US, 1978*

Trekkie *noun* a devoted fan of *Star Trek*, the original science fiction television programme (which started in 1966) and subsequent films and spin-offs *US, 1978*

trekky *adjective* in the style of *Star Trek*, the cult science-fiction television programme first seen in 1966 *UK, 2001*

trenches *noun* ▶ **in the trenches** involved in the hard, dirty aspect of an enterprise *US, 1970*

trendy *noun* **1** a follower of fashion *UK, 1968*. **2** a youth defined by a skateboarders' particular sense of fashion *UK, 2002*

trendy *adjective* fashionable *UK, 1962*

tres *noun* in betting, odds of 3–1. A variation of TREY *UK, 1991*

tres *adverb* very. Directly from the French *UK, 2000*

trev *nickname* a person whose prime characteristic is vanity; a person who wears nothing but designer-label clothes. Presumably derives from an unknown but especially well-groomed Trevor. Usually derogatory *UK, 2003*

trey *noun* **1** three *UK, 1859*. **2** a prison sentence of three years *US, 1983*. **3** a threepence. Shortening of TREY BIT *AUSTRALIA, 1896*. **4** three dollars' worth of a drug *US, 1966*

trey bit *noun* a threepence *AUSTRALIA, 1898*

trey eight *noun* a .38 calibre handgun *US, 1992*

treyer *noun* three years or three dollars *US, 1950*

trial-size *adjective* used of a person, very short *US, 1988*

triantelope *noun* the Australian tarantula, any of various large spiders of the genus *Isopoda*. Seems to be a blend of 'tarantula' and 'antelope' *AUSTRALIA, 1845*

triantiwontigongolope; triantiwontigong *noun* a mythical insect or monster; also, a name for something unknown. From a poem for children about a non-existent creature so named by C.J. Dennis in *A Book for Kids*, 1921 *AUSTRALIA, 1965*

Tribe *nickname* the Cleveland Indians professional baseball team. References to native American Indians in US professional sports teams (Indians, Braves, Redskins) persist in an era when many other stereotypes have withered *US, 1950*

tribe *adjective* contemptibly unfashionable. Collected on the 17th June 2005 from teenage girls (who described themselves as 'townies') in Swansea, south Wales: 'You don't want to go there – it's tribe.' *UK: WALES, 2005*

Tri-Chevy *noun* a Chevrolet car or truck manufactured in 1955, 1956 or 1957 *US, 1993*

trick *noun* **1** a prostitute's customer *US, 1925*. **2** an act of sex between a prostitute and customer *US, 1926*. **3** a short-term homosexual sexual partner, not paying *US, 1963*. **4** a casual sexual partner *US, 1968*. **5** a prostitute *UK, 1999*. **6** any dupe *US, 1865*. **7** a swindle. Far less common in this sense, but not unheard *UK, 1865*. **8** on the railways, a work shift *US, 1946*. ▶ **can't take a trick** to be consistently unsuccessful. From card games *AUSTRALIA, 1944*. ▶ **do the trick** to achieve your object *UK, 1812*

trick *verb* **1** to engage in sex with a paying customer, usually in an expeditious fashion *US, 1960*. **2** to have sex with a short-term partner, without emotion or money passed *US, 1968*

trick *adjective* **1** excellent *US, 1988*. **2** in hot rodding and drag racing, abnormal, unusual *US, 1968*

trickact *verb* to play about mischievously *IRELAND, 1992*

trick baby *noun* the offspring of a prostitute and an unknown customer, often of mixed race *US, 1969*

trick bag *noun* **1** a bag used by a prostitute to carry tools of the trade. A search warrant issued by the Sausalito (California) Police Department in its investigation of a massage parlour/brothel defines a trick bag as 'a large woman's handbag, which will generally enclose the following items which are used in the practice of prostitution: clothing, especially a change of undergarments such as panties, bras, camisoles and negligees, wet wipes, paper tissues, Vaseline and personal lubricants, bottles of mouth wash, rubbing alcohol, baby oil, various kinds and numbers of condoms, douches and other forms of feminine hygiene, and various cosmetics, small hand towels which are normally used in the practice of prostitution to wipe the ejaculatory excretions from the bodies of the prostitute and the customers[.]' *US, 2003*. **2** a dilemma with no clear solution *US, 1992*

trick book *noun* a prostitute's list of customers *US, 1972*

trick bunk *noun* in prison, a bed used for sexual encounters *US, 1990*

trick-cyclist *noun* a psychiatrist. Originally military *UK, 1930*

trick day *noun* an agreed time when homosexuals in long-term relationships may have sex outside the relationship *US, 1964*

trick dress; trick suit *noun* a dress that a prostitute can remove easily *US, 1963*

trick flick *noun* a pornographic film, usually homosexual *US, 1970*

trick house *noun* a house or apartment where prostitutes take their customers for sex *US, 1972*

Trickidadian *noun* a Trinidadian. A term that can be used with admiration or as disparagement *TRINIDAD AND TOBAGO, 1982*

trick name *noun* a prostitute's business alias *US, 1991*

trick off *verb* to perform oral sex on a man *US, 1997*

trick out *verb* to decorate something, or dress somebody, elaborately *US, 1727*

trick pad *noun* an apartment or room which a prostitute uses only for sex with customers *US, 1970*

trick pants *noun* pants that are easily removed, favoured by prostitutes *US, 1967*

trick rig *noun* a sexually attractive body *US, 1997*

trick room *noun* a room where a prostitute takes customers *US, 1969*

tricks *noun* ▶ **on the tricks** working as a prostitute *US, 1961*

trick seat *noun* the passenger seat on a motorcycle *US, 1984*

trickster *noun* a prostitute *US, 1976*

trick towel *noun* a towel or wash rag used to clean up after sex *US, 1970*

Trick Wiley *noun* used as a generic term for any gullible victim of a swindle *US, 1965*

tricky *adjective* needing careful handling or cautious action; difficult; risky *UK, 1887*

tricky Dick *noun* the penis *US, 1984*

Tricky Dick; Tricky Dickie *nickname* Richard Nixon. President of the US from 1969 until 1974, not known for his honesty or fair play *US, 1970*

tricon *noun* in poker, a hand with three cards of the same rank *US, 1967*

trier *noun* a racehorse genuinely being run to win *AUSTRALIA, 1915*

trife *adjective* possessing low or no moral character *US, 2002*

trifecta *noun* in US horse racing, a bet on the first three in the correct order *US, 1991*

triff *adjective* great, marvellous, superlative. A shortening of TRIFFIC *UK, 1982*

triffic *adjective* great, marvellous, superlative – often used with heavy irony. A slovening of 'terrific' (genuinely great) *UK, 1984*

trigger *noun* **1** in a shooting, the shooter *US, 1980*. **2** any prison guard carrying a gun *US, 1992*

trigger-happy *adjective* too eager to shoot a gun *US, 1945*

trigger time *noun* time spent in combat *US, 1987*

trike *noun* a three-wheeled motorcycle such as the Harley-Davidson Servi-Car. Biker (motorcycle) usage, referring to a child's tricycle *US, 2003*

trilby hat; trilby *noun* a fool. Rhyming slang for PRAT *UK, 1992*

trill *verb* **1** to idle with friends, especially with drugs and/or alcohol enlightening the idling *US, 2004*. **2** to stroll, to strut; to leave. Also 'trilly'. The heroine of Du Maurier's 1894 novel *Trilby* was noted for her beautiful feet; Trilbys came to mean 'feet', and then 'to stroll' *US, 1945*

triller *noun* an attractive young woman. West Indian patois variation of 'thriller', recorded by a Jamaican inmate in a UK prison, August 2002 *JAMAICA, 2002*

trim *noun* **1** the vagina; a woman as a sex object; sex with a woman *US, 1949*. **2** in the television and film industries, sections of scene cut by an editor *US, 1990*

trim *verb* **1** to cheat, defraud or swindle someone *UK, 1600*. **2** to have sex with a woman *US, 1972*

trimmer *noun* **1** an outstanding person or thing *AUSTRALIA, 1878*. **2** in cricket, 'a fast ball of exceptional quality, especially one that narrowly misses the stumps' *UK, 1959*

trims *noun* playing cards altered for cheating by slightly trimming off the edges of certain cards *US, 1979*

Trini *adjective* Trinidadian *TRINIDAD AND TOBAGO, 1973*

Trini by boat *noun* a long-standing immigrant in Trinidad *TRINIDAD AND TOBAGO, 1987*

Trinidad time; Trini time *noun* used for expressing an expected and accepted lack of punctuality *TRINIDAD AND TOBAGO, 1990*

trinity *noun* a style of three-storey terraced house consisting of three rooms stacked vertically *US, 1996*

trio *noun* in poker, a hand with three cards of the same rank *US, 1967*

trip *noun* **1** a hallucinatory drug experience. Uncertainty surrounds the first slang usage of the term. US slang lexicographer Peter Tamony argued in *American Speech* (Summer 1981) that the term was first used in a slang sense by Jack Gelber in *The Connection*, a 1957 play dealing with heroin addicts. Tamony privately conceded that the usage was not 'a smoking gun', and in retrospect it appears more figurative than slang. The *Oxford English Dictionary* points to Norman Mailer's 1959 *Advertisements for Myself*, in which Mailer wrote of taking mescaline and of 'a long and private trip', but there is no evidence that Mailer's use reflected a colloquial understanding and was not simply literary metaphor. Similarly, in a 1963 article about LSD in *Playboy*, Allan Harrington used the term 'trip', but again the context suggests metaphor, not slang. The slang sense of the word is indelibly associated with Ken Kesey and his LSD-taking Merry Pranksters. In 1964, Ken Kesey bought a soon-to-be-famous International Harvester school bus in the name of Intrepid Trips, Inc., suggesting an already current, if private, slang sense. In September 1999, Kesey wrote about his recollection of the first use of the term: 'I think it came from our bus trip in 1964, when Cassady said "This trip is a trip"' *US, 1966*. **2** any profound experience *US, 1966*. **3** a state of mind. Used in an extremely vague and amorphous way, usually suggesting something profound *US, 1966*. **4** interest *US, 1967*. **5** a personal or sexual experience, especially if non-conventional *US, 1971*. **6** a dose of LSD, usually in the form of a blotting paper tab. Derived from the sense as 'a hallucinogenic experience' that follows ingestion *UK, 2000*. **7** a prison sentence *US, 1952*

trip *verb* **1** to experience a drug-induced hallucinogenic euphoria. Also 'trip out' *US, 1966*. **2** to engage in flights of fancy, especially while in prison *US, 1967*. **3** to get angry, to lose control because of anger *US, 1990s*. **4** to insult *US, 1995*

tripe *noun* **1** utter nonsense; anything worthless or of poor quality, rubbish. Derives from 'tripe' as a source of inferior food *UK, 1676*. **2** in the theatre, electrical lines dangling from overhead fixtures *UK, 1952*. **3** a tripod. Used by travelling salesmen and itinerant swindlers to support a suitcase full of merchandise *US, 1981*

trip grass *noun* marijuana enhanced with amphetamine *US, 1982*

triple *noun* sex involving three people *US, 1988*

triple crown *noun* oral, vaginal and anal sex in the same session *US, 2004*

triple C's *noun* dextromethorphan (DXM), an active ingredient in non-prescription cold and cough medication, often abused for non-medicinal purposes *US, 2003*

triple jet ace *noun* a fighter pilot who shoots down three aircraft in a single day *US, 1964*

triple m *noun* mutual manual masturbation *US, 1985*

triple-nickels *noun* the 555th Parachute Infantry Battalion, US Army. The US Army's first all-black parachute infantry test platoon, company and battalion *US, 1991*

triplets *noun* in poker, three of a kind *US, 1963*

triple W *noun* a woman as the provider of good sex. The W's are 'warm', 'wet' and 'womb' *US, 1970*

triple X *noun* **1** a tablet of MDBA that also contains the analogues MDA and MDEA *UK, 1996*. **2** someone who abstains from sex, alcohol and drugs. Reminiscent of the slang term for a decaffeinated espresso drink made with non-fat milk – why bother? *US, 1996*

trip out *verb* **1** to undergo an hallucinogenic experience as a result of drug-intoxication *US, 1967*. **2** to upset someone; to confuse someone; to disturb someone *US, 1960s*. **3** to amaze someone; to enlighten someone *US, 1968*. **4** to become involved in something in a focused and intense manner *US, 1966*

tripped out *adjective* hallucinogen-intoxicated *US, 1973*

tripper *noun* **1** a person using LSD or another hallucinogenic drug *US, 1999*. **2** LSD. From TRIP (a period of LSD intoxication) *UK, 1998*. **3** a train passenger *US, 1977*

tripple-dipper *noun* a veteran of World War 2, Korea and Vietnam *US, 1966*

trippy *adjective* **1** hallucinatory *UK, 2001*. **2** of psychedelic design. From TRIP (an LSD experience) and the psychedelic imagery inspired by such drug usage *US, 1993*. **3** excellent *US, 1988*. **4** extremely committed to the hippie life, especially the drug aspects of it *US, 1968*

trips *noun* **1** LSD *US, 1969*. **2** in poker, a hand with three cards of the same rank. An abbreviation of 'triplets' *US, 1997*. **3** dice with intentionally rounded edges used for cheating *US, 1974*

trisaurus *noun* a Boeing 727 aircraft. From its three jet engines; the plane was produced from the late 1960s to 1984 *UK, 1994*

trisexual; trysexual *adjective* willing to try anything sexually; open to any sexual experience. Borrowing from 'bisexual', punning 'tri' with 'try' *US, 1988*

triss *noun* a male homosexual *AUSTRALIA, 1953*

trissy *adjective* homosexual *AUSTRALIA, 1982*

triumphant *adjective* excellent *US, 1991*

trivet *noun* in poker, a three-dollar bet *US, 1996*

trivial *adjective* in computing, too simple to bother explaining *US, 1997*

trixie *noun* a multiple bet, gambling on three horses in four combined bets *UK, 1991*

trizz *noun* a prostitute's customer *US, 1973*

trog *noun* **1** a stuffy, old-fashioned person. From 'troglodyte' (an ancient cave-dweller) *UK, 1965*. **2** a slow, careful, trundling driver. Probably extends from the previous sense *UK, 1972*. **3** a visiting surfer *AUSTRALIA, 1977*

trog *verb* to walk; to depart; to drive without urgency. Military *UK, 1995*

troglodyte *noun* a computer enthusiast who has abandoned all contact with life outside his computer *US, 1991*

trog off *verb* to go, especially if it means making an effort *UK, 2004*

trog up *verb* to dress and equip yourself for caving and pot-holing. Probably derives from 'troglodyte' *UK, 2004*

trojan *noun* a condom, Trojan™ brand or otherwise *US, 1997*

Trojan *noun* an AT-28 aircraft, used as a ground-attack aircraft and then a fighter bomber in the Vietnam war *US, 1985*

Trojan horse *noun* **1** in computing, an intentionally destructive program disguised and sent in benevolent form *US, 1991*. **2** in poker, an unexpectedly strong hand held by another player whose betting has successfully masked its strength *US*

troll *noun* **1** a resident of the Lower Peninsula of Michigan. Because they live below the Mackinac Bridge that connects the peninsulas. Upper Peninsula usage *US, 2003*. **2** a message posted on an Internet discussion group with the hope of attracting vitriolic response *US, 1997*

troll *verb* (of a homosexual man) to walk the streets in search of sexual adventure; (of a homosexual man) to walk, to wander. Familiarity of usage has resulted in the original, conventional sense being re-derived, here from the specifically sexual sense *UK, 1967*

trolley *noun* a line used by prisoners to exchange notes *US, 1950*.
▶ **off your trolley 1** mentally disordered; crazed. A 'trolley' is an electric powered tram that runs on rails, hence 'to be off your trolley' is to not follow an ordered course *UK, 1896*. **2** drunk *UK, 2000*

trolley and tram; trolley *noun* ham. Rhyming slang *UK, 1992*

trolley and truck *noun* an act of sexual intercouse. Rhyming slang for FUCK *UK, 1992*

trolleyed; trollied *adjective* drunk or drug-intoxicated. Derives from 'OFF YOUR TROLLET'. *UK, 1996*

trolley jockey *noun* a tram operator *US, 1954*

trolley man *noun* a man engaged in the racing of horses and ponies in trotting matches *UK, 2000*

trolley off *verb* to go away; to leave *UK, 1974*

trollies; trolleys; trollys *noun* underpants; trousers. Originally dialect, adopted by the Royal Navy and from there into more general use; it is interesting to note that polari speakers claim the word for gay society, probably from its relationship with TROLL (to walk with the purpose of attracting sexual interest) *UK, 2002*

trombone *noun* **1** a telephone. Rhyming slang; generally used as 'the old trombone' *UK, 1961*. **2** in the television and film industries, a hanger that can be extended from a wall to support lighting *US, 1977*

trombone *verb* **1** in the sport of clayshooting, to slide the hand back along the barrel of the gun whilst swinging upwards to aim and fire. Imitative of the sliding-action when involved in playing a trombone *UK, 1983*. **2** to lick the anus of a male partner while caressing his erect penis. The actions involved mimic the playing of a trombone *UK, 2001*

tromp and stomp *noun* a marching drill *US, 1957*

troop *noun* **1** a single soldier; used as a term of address to a soldier *US, 1986*. **2** crack cocaine *UK, 1998*

trooper *noun* a person who is the ultimately stalwart good sport *US, 1951*

troopie-groupie *noun* **1** a girl who freely offers her sexual availability to soldiers. Military *UK, 2001*. **2** a war correspondent, or like-minded civilian, who is enthusiastically supportive of the military. From GROUPIE (a follower) *UK, 1982*

troops *noun* collectively, the mechanics in a car repair shop *US, 1992*

trophy *adjective* used of a wife or girlfriend, young and beautiful to an extent that would not be expected with the man *US, 1998*

trophy fuck *verb* to have sex with a famous person because of that person's celebrity, *2001*

tropical *adjective* **1** extremely eccentric or mildly insane *US, 1946*. **2** of goods, stolen. Synonym of HOT *AUSTRALIA, 1950*

tropical fish; tropie *noun* an act of urination. Rhyming slang for PISH (a Scottish variation of PISS) *UK, 2002*

Tropic Lightning *nickname* the 25th Infantry Division, US Army *US, 1979*

troppo *adjective* **1** insane, mad, crazy. Of military origins; an abbreviation of 'tropical' or 'tropics' as a reference to mental or nervous instability caused by war service in the tropics *AUSTRALIA, 1941*. **2** sunburnt, suffering from too much exposure to the sun and wind *AUSTRALIA, 1991*. **3** especially in Queensland, of a building designed for tropical weather *AUSTRALIA, 2003*

trot *noun* **1** a period of time considered in terms of how you fared during it *AUSTRALIA, 1911*. **2** a line-by-line translation of a work in a foreign language *US, 1891*. ▶ **on the trot 1** in succession *UK, 1956*. **2** engaged in evading discovery or capture by the police *UK, 2000*

Trot *noun* a *Trot*skyist; thus *Trot*skyite; hence used of or applied to anyone or anything associated with political views from the extreme left *UK, 1962*

trots *noun* **1** diarrhoea. Used with 'the' *US, 1904*. **2** a horse race meeting for trotting and pacing; such meetings collectively *AUSTRALIA, 1890*

trotter *noun* **1** a deserter from the military; an escaped prisoner; anyone on the run from the police. Originally military *UK, 1950*. **2** pork *US, 1976*

trotters *noun* the feet *UK, 1775*

trou *noun* trousers; pants *US, 1968*

trouble *noun* a type of bet in an illegal numbers game lottery *US, 1957*

trouble and fuss *noun* bus. Rhyming slang *UK, 1992*

trouble and strife; trouble *noun* **1** a wife. Rhyming slang *UK, 1908*. **2** life. Rhyming slang *UK, 1998*

troubled *adjective* drunk *UK, 2002*

trough *noun* **1** a place where you (regularly) eat or drink *UK, 2001*. **2** a bar, especially at a horse racetrack *AUSTRALIA, 1989*

trough *verb* to eat. Armed services' slang; adapted from conventional 'trough' (a receptacle for feeding domestic animals) *UK, 1987*

trouncer *noun* an attractive girl *UK: NORTHERN IRELAND, 1996*

troused *adjective* drunk *US, 1997*

trouser *noun* a man or men objectified sexually. Probably derived in response to SKIRT (a woman, women) *UK, 1995*

trouser *verb* to pocket something; to earn money. Extended from a 'trouser pocket' *UK, 1892*

trouser cough *noun* a fart *UK, 1978*

trousered *adjective* drunk *UK, 2002*

trousers *noun* ▶ **with your trousers down** being taken by surprise; in a state of unreadiness. Generally prefaced with the verb 'catch/caught' *UK, 1966*

trousers and skirts *adjective* bisexual *UK, 1981*

trouser snake *noun* the penis *US, 1976*

trouser trout *noun* the penis *UK, 1998*

trout *noun* an unattractive (older or old) woman *UK, 1897* ▷ *see:* THAMES TROUT. ▶ **all about trout** alert, watchful *UK, 1962*

trout pout *noun* unnaturally inflated lips as a result of collagen implants. An unfortunate similarity to the freshwater fish *UK, 2003*

truck *verb* to stroll; to stride *US, 1938*

truck driver *noun* **1** an aggressive, 'mannish' lesbian *US, 1967*. **2** in prison, a prisoner or guard who delivers messages *US, 1976*. **3** an amphetamine or other central nervous system stimulant *US, 1967*

trucker's powder *noun* amphetamine. A variation on TRUCK DRIVER (amphetamines), this plays on SPEED and the need to stay awake *UK, 2001*

truckie *noun* a truck driver *AUSTRALIA, 1919*

truck stop Annie *noun* a prostitute working at a truck stop *US, 1977*

truck stop cowboy *noun* a person who looks the part of a trucker, plays the part of a trucker, but is not a trucker *US, 1976*

Trudeau acre *noun* a hectare. As the Canadian French measure of land is in the hectare (a metric unit equivalent to 2.471 acres), and the English is in the acre unit, 1970s anti-Trudeau feeling took parodic form here as much as in opposition to the Prime Minister's promotion of bilingualism and biculturalism nationwide *CANADA, 1987*

true *adverb* especially in Aboriginal English, is it true?, really? *AUSTRALIA, 1959*

true bull; true bool *noun* a tested and proven leader. Hawaiian youth usage *US, 1982*

true love *noun* a type of bet in an illegal numbers game lottery *US, 1957*

True North *noun* Canada. 'The True North, strong and free' is a line from the Canadian national anthem. In its patriotic connotation, this expression suggests pride and strength, but it may also suggest the extreme cold, snow and ice which Canadians endure *CANADA, 2001*

true's God! used for affirming the truth of what has been said *FIJI, 1976*

true that!; true dat! used for expressing strong agreement *US, 1998*

true-true *adjective* authentic *BAHAMAS, 1982*

true virgins make dull company the air navigation system: True heading plus/minus Variation gives you Magnetic heading plus/minus Deviation gives you Compass heading. The reverse mnemonic is 'Can Dead Men Vote Twice?' *CANADA, 1995*

truggy *noun* an off-road vehicle that combines features of a truck and a tubular buggy. Collected by John Thompson of Hendersonville, North Carolina, 2004 *US, 2004*

Trujillo's revenge *noun* diarrhoea. Homage to Dominican dictator Rafael Trujillo *US, 1982*

trull *noun* a prostitute, a concubine, a loose-moralled woman. A generally obsolete conventional English term *UK, 1519*

Truman's folly *noun* the Korean war. Another Republican party coining *US, 1968*

trummus *noun* the buttocks, the posterior *UK, 2002*

trump *noun* a fart. From the sound of a trumpet *UK, 1903*

trump *verb* to fart. From C15; from the sound of a trumpet *UK, 1425*

trumpet *noun* **1** a telephone *UK, 1977*. **2** a stethoscope *TRINIDAD AND TOBAGO, 1987*. **3** a fart. Juvenile use, extending the more familiar

TRUMP (a fart) back to its origins *UK, 1997*. **4** in hot rodding, a tailpipe extension *US, 1958*. **5** cocaine *UK, 1999*

trumpets *noun* MDMA, the recreational drug best known as ecstasy. Specifically used of any MDMA tablet stamped with the stylised image of a horn-player (possibly an angel) *UK, 2004*

trump of the dump *noun* the person in charge of an enterprise *NEW ZEALAND, 1998*

trunch *noun* a blow or a beating with a *trunch*eon *UK, 1980*

trundling-cheat *noun* a car; originally any wheeled vehicle *UK, 1630*

trunk *noun* the human nose. Derisory, emphasising the size of someone's nose or, figuratively, the intrusive quality of that person's nosiness *UK, 2000*

trunk and tree *noun* the knee. Rhyming slang *UK, 1998*

trunk job *noun* a corpse, especially a badly decomposed corpse, found in a car boot (trunk) *US, 1993*

trupence bag *noun* marijuana *UK, 2003*

trust *verb* ▶ **I wouldn't trust you as far as I can throw you** used as an expression of deep mistrust in someone *UK, 1961*

trustafarian *noun* a young person who lives a counterculture life-style on the proceeds of a trust fund *US, 1992*

trust you! used as an ironic register of predictable behaviour. Also with other nouns or names *UK, 1834*

truth chamber *noun* a police interview room *UK, 1971*

try *verb* ▶ **try it on; try it on with** to make an attempt to outwit or impose upon someone *UK, 1811*. ▶ **try this on for size; try this for size** to consider a notion; to try something out; also used in horseplay as a battle-cry *US, 1956*

trying! you are trying too hard to be something you are not! Hawaiian youth usage *US, 1981*

try-on *noun* an attempt to deceive. From TRY IT ON *UK, 1874*

try-out *noun* a selective trial *US, 1903*

try walking across US airline company Trans World Airlines (TWA). An ironic play on the famous initials. Most airlines attract jocular variations of their names; TWA seems to have more than most, including: 'Travel Without Arrival'; 'Try Walking, Asshole'; 'Try Walking Again'; 'The Worst Airline'; 'Took Wrong Airline'; 'Take Weapons Aboard'; 'Thieves, Whores and Alcoholics'; and so on *US, 1995*

TS too bad. An abbreviation of TOUGH SHIT *US, 1957*

T's and blues *noun* a combination of Taluin™, a painkiller, and the antihistamine Pyribenzamine™, abused for non-medicinal purposes *US, 1989*

tsatske *noun* a pretty, sexy, brainless woman. Yiddish, with the Yiddish diminutive of *tsatskeleh US, 1961*

TS card *noun* a notional card that is punched when a person complains. An abbreviation of the sympathy-lacking TOUGH SHIT *US, 1948*

tsk tsk *verb* to express commiseration, or disappointment or irri-tation by making the sound 'tsk tsk' *UK, 1966*

tsk tsk used for expressing commiseration, or disappointment, or irritation. An attempted written representation of the sound of this non-verbal exclamation that is somewhere between 'tut tut' and a sucking of the teeth *UK, 1947*

tsotsies *noun* non-white adolescent criminals *SOUTH AFRICA, 1968*

tsuris; tzuris; tszoris *noun* troubles, problems, suffering. Yiddish *US, 1970*

TTFN goodbye. An initialism of 'ta-ta for now', which served as a catchphrase first in the BBC radio programme *ITMA*, 1941–49, and was picked-up by popular BBC radio broadcaster Jimmy Young (b.1921) who began broadcasting in 1949 *UK, 1948*

TTFO (in doctors' shorthand) *told to fuck off* (go away). Medical slang *UK, 2003*

T-timers *noun* dark glasses worn by marijuana smokers *US, 1952*

tub *noun* **1** a drum *US, 1958*. **2** a seat on an amusement ride *US, 1980*. **3** a small crap table *US, 1983*. **4** in electric line work, an overhead transformer *US, 1980*

tubby *adjective* **1** emphasising low frequencies, producing poorly defined sound. Used in describing a location's sound quality in television and film-making *US, 1987*. **2** overweight *UK, 1835*

tubby; tubs *noun* an overweight person. Both variants serve as nickname and derogatory term; 'tubs' is the abbreviation of 'tubby' *UK, 1999*

tube *noun* **1** a fool, an idiot; a despicable or contemptible person. Probably from an earlier sense as 'penis', thus PRICK *UK: SCOTLAND, 1985*. **2** a person *UK: SCOTLAND, 1988*. **3** a marijuana cigarette *US, 1937*. **4** a telephone *US, 1960*. **5** a prison officer who listens to inmates' conversation and for information from informers *UK, 1950*. **6** a can of beer *AUSTRALIA, 1964*. **7** the concave face of a wave *US, 1963*. **8** a shotgun *US, 1994*. **9** in a casino, the rack where betting tokens are stored at a gambling table *US, 1996*. **10** a totally unnecessary breast examination *UK, 1999*. ▶ **down the tubes** ruined with no chances left; done-for; lost; wasted. A variation of 'down the drain' or 'down the pan'; literally 'down the toilet' *US, 1963*. ▶ **lay tube** from the male point of view, to have sex *US, 1983*. ▶ **the tube** a television; television. Originally applied to the telephone, but then much more widely to television *US, 1959*

Tube *noun* ▶ **the Tube** the London Underground transport system. Originally, in this context, the tunnel in which an underground electric train runs (late C19), hence this abbreviation of 'tube-railway'. The Central London Railway, which opened in 1900, was known as 'The Twopenny Tube' for its fixed-price fee. The cost of a journey has been going up ever since *US, 1902*

tube *verb* **1** to watch television *US, 1979*. **2** to surf below and inside the crest of the wave *US, 1979*. **3** to insert an endotracheal tube into a patient. Medical use *UK, 1980*. **4** to fail, to do poorly *US, 1966*

tube lube *noun* oral sex on a man *US, 1970*

tuber *noun* a person who spends too much of the day on a sofa watching television. From the dominant term COUCH POTATO and punning on THE TUBE (television) *US, 1986*

tubes *noun* the London Underground transport system. A variation of THE TUBE *UK, 1996*

tube steak *noun* **1** a frankfurter, a hot dog *US, 1963*. **2** by visual extension, the penis *US, 1980*

tube top *noun* a woman's garment, elasticised, stretching from the waist to under the arms *US, 1974*

tub of lard *noun* a fat person. A neat combination of a pun on TUBBY (fat) and 'lard' (a soft white fat). When Roy Hattersley MP, an overweight politician, declined to guest on the satirical BBC television quiz *Have I Got News For You* he was replaced, to great hilarity, with an actual tub of lard *UK, 1993*

tubs *noun* drums *US, 1946*. ▶ **the tubs** a gay bath house; the gay bath house scene collectively *US, 1964*

tubular *adjective* **1** used of a wave, hollow as it breaks, creating a chamber which can be surfed through *US, 1988*. **2** spectacular *US, 1982*

tuck *noun* **1** food, especially snacks and delicacies. Mainly school slang *UK, 1857*. **2** a cosmetic operation to remove fat or skin *US, 1993*

tuck *verb* in transsexual usage, to tape your penis onto your groin to avoid any telltale bulge which might tip off someone as to your genetic sex *US, 1987*. ▶ **tuck in; tuck into; tuck away** to eat heartily; to start eating. 'Tuck away' is first recorded in 1861 *UK, 1810*

tuck and roll; tucked and rolled *adjective* descriptive of a highly stylised car upholstery design, popular with hot rodders and low riders *US, 1963*

tucked and rolled *adjective* medically transformed from a male to a female *US, 1990*

tucked up *adjective* arrested *UK, 1996*

tucker *noun* food *AUSTRALIA, 1850*

tucker *verb* to provide someone with food; to feed someone *AUSTRALIA, 1891*

tuckerbag *noun* a bag for carrying food *AUSTRALIA, 1885*

tucker box *noun* a box used to store and transport food; a lunch box AUSTRALIA, 1897

tuckered; tuckered out *adjective* tired, exhausted US, 1840

tucker fucker *noun* a cook AUSTRALIA, 1983

tuckerless *adjective* without food AUSTRALIA, 1910

tuckers *noun* a tuck shop UK, 1947

tucker time *noun* meal time AUSTRALIA, 1902

tuck in *noun* a meal AUSTRALIA, 1889

tuck shop *noun* a school's purveyor of snacks UK, 1857

tud *noun* a totally unnecessary drink that causes you to vomit US, 2001

'tude *noun* a bad attitude US, 1987

tudge boy *noun* a criminal hired to enforce criminal rules on other criminals US, 2002

tuft *noun* the female pubic hair UK, 1980

tug *noun* **1** an act of masturbation AUSTRALIA, 2001. **2** an arrest. A pun on PULL (an arrest) UK, 1999. **3** a warning of imminent danger given from one criminal to another, or beggar to beggar, etc. Often in the phrase 'give you the tug' AUSTRALIA, 1975. ▶ **give someone a tug** to arrest someone UK, 2000

tug *verb* **1** (from criminal to criminal, or beggar to beggar, etc) to give a warning of imminent danger. Often in the phrase 'tug your coat' AUSTRALIA, 1975. **2** to masturbate NEW ZEALAND, 1998. ▶ **tug on 1** to inhale smoke from a cigarette UK, 2000. **2** to think about something. Figurative use of conventional 'tug' (to pull) UK, 2001

tug and rub *noun* an erotic massage CANADA, 2001

tug o' war *noun* a whore. Rhyming slang UK, 1992

tules; toolies *noun* a remote rural area. An extension of the name of a type of cattail that grows in the very rural San Joaquin Valley of California US, 1974

tulip *noun* someone whose looks or behaviour mark them as abnormal IRELAND, 1991

tulips *noun* a variety of MDMA, the recreational drug best known as ecstasy UK, 2001

tum *noun* the stomach. A shortening of TUMMY UK, 1869

tumble *noun* **1** an act of sexual intercourse; an invitation to engage in sexual intercourse UK, 1903. **2** recognition by the police or the interruption of a crime US, 1950. **3** a fight, especially a gang fight US, 1960. ▶ **come a tumble** to be noticed US, 1958

tumble *verb* **1** to discover, to understand, to notice, to realise, to become aware of UK, 1846. **2** to have sex with someone. Found in Shakespeare and understood in context if not used heavily today UK, 1602. **3** to get married US, 1970

tumble and trip; tumble *noun* a collection from a group of people. Rhyming slang for WHIP-ROUND UK, 1992

tumble down the sink; tumble *noun* a drink. Rhyming slang; first recorded in *Songs and Slang of the British Soldier: 1914–1918*, John Brophy and Eric Partridge, 1930 UK, 1979

tumblers *noun* **1** the female breasts UK, 2003. **2** dice with rounded edges US, 1950

tummy *noun* the stomach UK, 1869

tummy banana *noun* the penis AUSTRALIA, 1968

tummy tuck *noun* cosmetic surgery designed to reduce the fat around a person's waist US, 1977

tum-tum *noun* the stomach. A variation of TUMMY or, more likely, the first babyish variation of 'stomach' from which 'tummy' derives UK, 1864

tuna *noun* **1** the vagina. Fish, as an allusion to what some claim to be the natural odour of a woman US, 1986. **2** a female US, 1971. **3** a young sailor as the object of desire of a homosexual man US, 1985

tunage *noun* music US, 1996

tuna party *noun* a party where girls far outnumber boys US, 2004

tuna snuffling *noun* the act of oral sex on a woman. Combines TUNA (the vagina) with a reasonably conventional usage of 'snuffle' US, 2001

tune *noun* **1** a recorded song. Deviating from the literal meaning to embrace not just the tune, but all that goes into the song US, 1993. **2** a tablet of Tuinal™, a branded barbiturate. An approximate abbreviation, usually in the plural; probably also as a pun on Tunes™, a branded medicated sweet UK, 1996

tune *verb* **1** to talk; to say something SOUTH AFRICA, 1976. **2** to beat somone physically. Also used with 'up' UK, 1788

tune-and-toe show *noun* a musical-theatre entertainment. A play on 'song and dance' UK, 1979

tune grief *verb* to verbally abuse someone SOUTH AFRICA, 1972

tuner *noun* in the television and film industries, a musical composer US, 1977

tune up *verb* to beat a better attitude into a fellow prisoner with a poor attitude US, 1989

tuning *noun* an instance of sexual intercourse which the female partner finds satisfying. Automotive imagery UK, 1959

tunnel of love *noun* the vagina US, 2001

tunnel rat *noun* **1** a US soldier who explored Viet Cong tunnels and underground networks US, 1977. **2** a police officer working for the New York Transit Bureau. New York police slang US, 1997

tunnel shot *noun* a photograph or shot in a film focusing on a woman's vagina US, 1970

tuntun *noun* the vagina TRINIDAD AND TOBAGO, 2003

tuppence *noun* two pence; hence, in later use, a notional sum of negligible value UK, 1857

tuppenceworth *noun* a small contribution. Literally, 'two-penny-worth' UK, 2000

tuppenny fuck *noun* a thing of no worth UK, 2003

tuppenny ha'penny; tuppenny halfpenny; twopenny-halfpenny *adjective* of little worth; insignificant UK, 1909

tupperware *noun* in electric line work, plastic protective covering for a conductor US, 1980

tuppy *noun* the vagina. Borrowed from an Aboriginal language AUSTRALIA, 1985

turbo *noun* **1** marijuana UK, 2003. **2** marijuana mixed with crack cocaine US, 1994. **3** a fast driver US, 1997

turbo-gobbed *adjective* describes someone who talks endlessly and without pause UK, 2002

turd *noun* **1** a piece of excrement. In conventional use since about the year 1000, it is described in the *Oxford English Dictionary* as not now in polite use UK, 1766. **2** a contemptible person, a shit. The earliest meaning (a length of excrement) redirected UK, 1936. **3** a negative comment in a personnel file US, 1967

turd bird *noun* a Ford Thunderbird US, 1992

turd burglar *noun* a male homosexual UK, 1983

turd-burgling *adjective* anal sex UK, 2002

turdcutter *noun* the buttocks. Imprecise and crude physiology US, 1977

turd-floater *noun* a heavy rain CANADA, 2002

turdhead *noun* a despicable person US, 1953

turd herder *noun* a plumber US, 1963

turdpacker *noun* in anal sex, the active partner US, 1940s

turdtapper *noun* a male homosexual. An allusion to anal sex CANADA, 2003

turf *noun* **1** the territory controlled by a gang; a sphere of influence US, 1952. **2** a job, responsibility, obligation US, 1970. **3** the place where a whe-whe lottery game is operated TRINIDAD AND TOBAGO, 1986. **4** the street US, 1978

turf *verb* in hospital usage, to transfer a patient to another's responsibility US, 1994

turf consultant *noun* in horse racing, someone who makes a living selling tips to bettors US, 1947

turf dance *noun* a stylised dance developed and performed by an urban youth gang US, 2002

turistas; touristas *noun* diarrhoea *US, 1972*

Turk *noun* **1** a homosexual man who assumes the active role in anal sex *US, 1950*. **2** a strong and aggressive young man *US, 1949*

Turk *verb* (of a male) to have sex, especially in a brutal fashion *UK, 1966*

turkey *noun* **1** in films and showbusiness, an absolute failure or disaster, critical or financial; hence, in wider usage, a failure or disaster. Why the turkey, a native of America, is the symbol of spectacular failure is a mystery *US, 1927*. **2** an incompetent, ineffective or disliked person. May be used with affection *US, 1951*. **3** a member of a youth gang who is reluctant or unwilling to join in gang fights *US, 1949*. **4** an Irishman or a person of Irish descent *US, 1982*. **5** a patient who has been mishandled medically *US, 1961*. **6** in hospital usage, a patient with a petty medical complaint *US, 1978*. **7** a planespotter who is new to the hobby, or does not have good equipment, or does not take the hobby seriously *UK, 2003*. **8** in motorcycle racing, an old and/or heavy and bulky motorcycle *US, 1973*. **9** amphetamine *UK, 1998*. **10** cocaine *UK, 1998*. **11** poor quality, adulterated or counterfeit drugs *US, 1958*. **12** a tip of fifty cents *US, 1977*. ▶ **the turkey** an act of withdrawing from addictive drugs; the time period of that withdrawal (without direct reference to the symptoms). A variation of COLD TURKEY *UK, 2002*

turkey *verb* **1** to withdraw from a habit or addiction suddenly and without any tapering off. An abbreviation of 'cold turkey' *UK, 1996*. **2** to inhale marijuana smoke nasally *US, 1970*

turkeyhead *noun* a dolt *US, 1955*

turkey line *noun* in the language of hang gliding, a line used by an instructor to prevent the nose from dipping during landing or take-off *US, 1977*

turkey neck *noun* the penis. The similarity between a penis with shaved surround and a plucked turkey's neck hanging down *US, 1997*

turkey shoot *noun* an overwhelming slaughter of helpless victims. From the C19 'sport' of a shooting match in which the target was a live turkey *US, 1970*

Turkey trot *noun* diarrhoea suffered by tourists *US, 1960*

Turkish bath; Turkish *noun* a laugh, especially at someone else's expense. Rhyming slang *UK, 1998*

Turkish culture *noun* anal sex *US, 1972*

Turkish delight *noun* in homosexual usage, anal sex *US, 1987*

Turkish delight; Turkish *adjective* **1** miserly. Rhyming slang for TIGHT; no racial slur is intended *UK, 1998*. **2** of poor quality. Rhyming slang for SHITE; here the racial slur seems deliberate *UK, 2002*

Turkish rope *noun* a heavy gold necklace *US, 1995*

Turk McGurk *noun* any unethical, vindictive person *US, 1977*

turn *noun* **1** a histrionic display *AUSTRALIA, 1971*. **2** a (theatrical) performer *UK, 1715*. **3** a party *AUSTRALIA, 1953*. **4** in trucking, a return trip *US, 1976*. **5** a jail sentence *US, 1995*. ▶ **do a turn** to have sex. A play on a theatrical act *UK, 2002*

turn *verb* **1** in trucking, to make a round trip to and from the specified destination *US, 1971*. **2** to sell something, especially stolen goods *US, 1972*. **3** to convert a man to homosexuality *US, 1991*. **4** in drag racing, to register a speed *US, 1960*. ▶ **turn 'em and burn 'em** to quickly service a fighter plane and return it to combat. Gulf war usage *US, 1991*. ▶ **turn a film** in Quebec, to shoot a film. The French origin of this English phrase is *tourner un film CANADA, 2001*. ▶ **turn in** to retire to bed *UK, 1695*. ▶ **turn into a pumpkin** in transsexual usage, to dress in keeping with your genetic sex *US, 1987*. ▶ **turn it on 1** to make an all-out effort at some task *AUSTRALIA, 1944*. **2** (of a woman) to perform sexually *AUSTRALIA, 1944*. **3** to enliven something *UK, 1983*. **4** to provide for a party or celebration *AUSTRALIA, 1941*. ▶ **turn it up** to consent to sex *NEW ZEALAND, 1973*. ▶ **turn Japanese** to masturbate. From the perceived resemblance between a stereotypical Japanese face and the facial expression that accompanies a quest for orgasm *UK, 1980*. ▶ **turn over the covers** to examine the other side of an issue *US, 1974*. ▶ **turn state** to become a witness for the prosecuting authorities. From the term 'state witness' *US, 1990*. ▶ **turn the corner** to begin to improve; to change your attitude for the better *UK, 2003*. ▶ **turn the duke** in circus and carnival usage, to shortchange someone

US, 1981. ▶ **turn the mit** to shortchange *US, 1980*. ▶ **turn tricks** to work as a prostitute. *1996*. ▶ **turn turtle** (of a surfer) to pass through a wave coming at them by rolling under their surfboard *US, 1977*. ▶ **turn up trumps** to succeed, to turn out well *UK, 1862*. ▶ **turn up your nose** to view or treat with contempt *UK, 1818*. ▶ **turn your key** to make you angry. A variation of WOUND UP *UK, 2001*

turnaround *noun* **1** in trucking, a return trip *US, 1976*. **2** training time for navy pilots between aircraft carrier cruises *US, 1990*

turn around *verb* in criminal or police usage, to persuade someone to inform or otherwise betray *US, 1975*

turned on *adjective* **1** sexually aroused *UK, 1977*. **2** able to comprehend, especially as a result of drug use *US, 1978*. **3** stimulated and inspired by some music *UK, 1977*

turn it in! stop doing that!; stop talking! A variation of TURN IT UP! *UK, 1999*

turn it up! stop! Originally 'turn up' (to renounce), 'turn it up' (to move home or, otherwise, change your life), hence the current meaning *AUSTRALIA, 1927*

turn-off *noun* something that disgusts or creates antipathy *US, 1983*

turn-off *verb* **1** to create antipathy in someone, to disillusion someone *US, 1970*. **2** to disgust someone *US, 1970*

turn-on *noun* **1** something that excites or arouses someone sexually *AUSTRALIA, 1969*. **2** a sharing or gifting of drugs *US, 1995*. **3** a single instance of drug-intoxication. Also known as a 'turning-on' *UK, 1978*

turn on *verb* **1** to use a drug *US, 1953*. **2** to introduce someone to something, especially drugs *US, 1961*. **3** to arouse an interest, sexual or abstract in someone; to stimulate someone; to thrill someone *US, 1965*

turn on, tune in (and) drop out used as a slogan for, and invitation to join, the hippy counterculture. Credited to Timothy Leary (1920–96) the self-styled high priest of LSD, this pocket-philosophy combined TURN ON (to use drugs), 'tune in' (to become culturally aware) and DROP OUT (to cease to be part of a conventional society) in a catchphrase that seemed to be more than the sum of its parts *US, 1968*

turnout *noun* **1** a novice prostitute; a prostitute working in a particular brothel for the first time *US, 1973*. **2** in the illegal production of alcohol, the yield of whisky compared to the amount of raw materials *US, 1974*

turn out *verb* **1** to recruit and convert someone to prostitution *US, 1960*. **2** to engage a woman in serial sex with multiple partners *US, 1966*. **3** to convert someone to homosexuality *US, 1952*

turnover *noun* **1** a robbery of stolen goods from a criminal accomplice *UK, 1959*. **2** a search of a prison cell. The abbreviated form 'TO' is also used *UK, 1940*

turn over *verb* **1** (of the police) to search a property or to stop and search a person; in criminal use, to burgle a property or rob a person *UK, 1859*. **2** to set upon someone and beat them up *UK, 1962*

turn round and used as an embellishment between to and do. An unnecessary formula used in north London *UK, 1999*

turntablism *noun* the creation of music and rhythmic patterns by manipulation of record turntables. A mid-1990s coinage credited to DJ Babu of the Beat Junkies *US, 2002*

turntablist *noun* a DJ who uses turntables as instruments to create and manipulate sound. From the turntable 'decks' the DJ manipulates *US, 2002*

turn-up *noun* an outcome, especially a surprise. An abbreviation, with a slightly narrower sense, of TURN-UP FOR THE BOOKS *UK, 1964*

turn-up for the books; turn-up *noun* an unexpected happening, usually positive. Originally racecourse and gambling use *UK, 1873*

turpentine; the turps *noun* the Serpentine (a lake in London's Hyde Park). Rhyming slang *UK, 1960*

turps *noun* **1** turpentine *UK, 1823*. **2** alcohol. An abbreviation of 'turpentine' *AUSTRALIA, 1865* ▷ *see:* TERPS

turtle *noun* **1** a variety of LSD. Named after, and identified by a depiction of, the *Teenage Mutant Ninja Turtles*, a cult comic and television programme from the 1980s *UK, 2001*. **2** the replacement for a combat soldier who is due to return home. Like the turtle, the replacement seems never to get there quickly enough *US, 1968*

turtle *verb* (used of a boat) to turn over completely in the water, exposing the bottom of the hull to the sky *US, 1966*

turtle dove *noun* **1** love, as a term of address. Very old-fashioned rhyming slang *UK, 1974*. **2** a glove. The short form 'turtle' is also used *UK, 1857*

turtlehead; turtle's head *noun* a piece of faeces semi-emerged from the rectum *UK, 1997*

turtleneck *noun* the foreskin on an uncircumsised penis *US, 1983*

tush; tushie; tushy *noun* the backside, the buttocks. Yiddish *US, 1962*

tush hog *noun* **1** a strong and powerful man who extorts money from others *US, 1946*. **2** a person with a short temper *US, 1972*

tusker *noun* an all-in-all unattractive girl *US, 1968*

tuskie; tuskee *noun* a marijuana cigarette *US, 1977*

tuss *verb* to abuse for non-medicinal purposes non-prescription medication containing dextromethorphan (DXM) *US, 2003*

tussin *noun* dextromethorphan (DXM), an active ingredient in non-prescription cold and cough medication, often abused for non-medicinal purposes. From the branded cough syrup Robitussin™ *US, 2003*

tustin *noun* marijuana originating, perhaps, in Tustin, California *UK, 2003*

tutae *noun* faeces. From the Maori *NEW ZEALAND, 1985*

tutti *noun* a latrine *TRINIDAD AND TOBAGO, 2003*

tutti frutti *noun* lemon extract *CANADA, 1999*

tut-tuts *noun* the female breasts *TRINIDAD AND TOBAGO, 1956*

tutty *noun* makeup *UK, 1999*

tutty *adjective* pathetic. British Indian (Hindi) urban youth slang *UK, 2006*

tutu *noun* **1** a tablet of MDMA, the recreational drug best known as ecstasy *UK, 2003*. **2** in craps, a roll of four. A homophonic pun – two, two *US, 1999*

tuxedo; tux *noun* a strait jacket *US, 1949*

TV *noun* a transvestite *UK, 2003*

TV parking *noun* the chance of finding a car parking space exactly where you need it *US, 1998*

TV rental *noun* a Ford 'Granada' car. A reference to high street business Granada Television Rentals *UK, 1981*

TV-style *noun* anal sex from behind a person on their hands and knees. An allusion to the fact that both participants are facing the same way and can watch television during sex *US, 1979*

TWA *noun* a teeny-weeny aircraft or helicopter *US, 1991*

twack *verb* to go window-shopping, look, ask about cost, but buy nothing *CANADA, 1955*

twaddle *noun* nonsense *UK, 1782*

twak *noun* **1** rubbish *SOUTH AFRICA, 1953*. **2** tobacco *SOUTH AFRICA, 1844*

twally *noun* an idiot, a fool. Glasgow slang *UK: SCOTLAND, 1996*

twang *verb* ► **twang the wire** (of a male) to masturbate *AUSTRALIA, 1971*

twanger *noun* **1** the penis *FIJI, 1994*. **2** a citizens' band radio antenna *US, 1976*

twangie boy *noun* a young male prostitute. A term coined by novelist Robert Campbell *US, 1987*

twat *noun* **1** the vagina *UK, 1656*. **2** a woman *UK, 1929*. **3** a promiscuous homosexual man *US, 1987*. **4** used as an abusive epithet for someone you would otherwise call a cunt. From the sense as 'the vagina' *UK, 1929*. **5** an unfortunate or difficult situation; an unpleasant task; a problem. A logical extension of the previous sense TWAT *UK, 2001*

twat *verb* to hit someone *UK, 1999*

twat 'there *we are* then', used to (reluctantly) acknowledge an occurrence. Acronym in use by south Wales police *UK, 2001*

TWAT The War Against Terrorism. An unfortunate acronym, highlighted on BBC Radio 4 panel game *The News Quiz*, October 2001. Subsequently, some broadcasters began using 'The War On Terrorism', inviting TWOT. TWAT (the vagina) and 'twot' are synonymous *UK, 2001*

twat around *verb* to play the fool, to waste time; to make a mess of something; to inconvenience someone *UK, 2002*

twat bubble *noun* a contemptible person. Offensive and insulting *UK, 2005*

twatch *verb* to do emergency sewing repairs crudely *CANADA, 1999*

twat chat *noun* talking about sex from the female perspective; also used as a nickname for *The Vagina Monologues* by Eve Ensler, 2001 *UK, 2001*

twat-hooks *noun* the fingers; the hands. From an image based on TWAT (the vagina). Heard by Partridge on the BBC, 18th January 1973 *UK, 1973*

twat mag *noun* a pornographic magazine that features naked women. A combination of TWAT (the vagina), probably not TWAT (a fool), with MAG (a magazine) *UK, 1996*

twat off! go away! *UK, 2000*

twatted *adjective* drunk or drug-intoxicated *UK, 1999*

twattery *noun* foolishness; nonsense *UK, 2002*

twatting *adjective* used as an intensifier *UK, 2000*

twattoo *noun* a tattoo on the female pubis; a tattoo of unfashionable design *UK, 1995*

twatty *adjective* **1** foolish, idiotic *UK, 2000*. **2** unpleasant *UK, 2002*

tweak *noun* in mountain biking, any low, destabilising contact with a rock, root or stump *US, 1992*

tweak *verb* **1** to bend *US, 1990*. **2** in computing or electronics, to make a minor adjustment *US, 1983*. **3** to use methamphetamines. The spelling 'tweek' is also used *US, 1996*

tweak and freak *verb* to engage in kinky sex after injecting methamphetamine *US, 1989*

tweaker; tweeker *noun* a user of methamphetamine or amphetamines *US, 1989*

tweaks *noun* crack cocaine *UK, 2003*

twee *adjective* affectedly dainty, over-refined *UK, 1905*

tweed; tweeds *noun* marijuana. Contraction of 'the WEED', thus 't'weed', 'tweed' *US, 1995*

Tweed Curtain *noun* an invisible barrier between Oak Bay and Greater Victoria, British Columbia *CANADA, 1989*

tweedle *noun* a confidence trick in which a counterfeit such as fake jewellery or, in the 'whisky tweedle', a 30-gallon barrel containing only a quart of alcohol is sold in the stead of a genuine purchase *UK, 1890*

tweedle *verb* to operate the tweedle confidence trick, exchanging a genuine purchase for a fake *UK, 1956*

tweedler *noun* **1** a stolen vehicle offered for an honest sale *UK, 1977*. **2** a very minor or petty confidence trickster *UK, 1959*

tweeds *noun* **1** trousers *AUSTRALIA, 1954*. **2** clothing, especially a suit *US, 1968*

tweek *verb* ► **to get tweeked** to be knocked from your surfboard and then be pummelled by the ocean *US, 1988*

tweeker *noun* methcathinone *US, 2003*

tweetie *noun* an effeminate male. An imitation of a lisped 'sweetie' and an allusion to Tweetie Pie, a cartoon character of the 1950s and 60s *US, 1968*

Tweety Bird *noun* a tablet of MDMA, the recreational drug best known as ecstasy, identified by an embossed icon of Warner Bros' animated character Tweety Pie *UK, 2003*

twelve *noun* in a deck of playing cards, any queen *US, 1996*

twelve inch rule *noun* a fool. Rhyming slang *UK, 1992*

twelve-ounce curls *noun* drinking beer *US, 1985*

twelver *noun* a twelve-pack of beer *US, 1997*

twennie *noun* a twenty-dollar dose of crack cocaine *US, 1989*

twenties *noun* a swindle featuring a twenty-dollar note *US, 1952*

twenty; 20 *noun* **1** a twenty-pound note *UK, 1999*. **2** a location. Citizens' band radio slang *US, 1975*

twenty-cent bag *noun* twenty dollars' worth of a drug *US, 1972*

twenty-cent rock *noun* crack cocaine worth $20 *US, 1991*

twenty-five *noun* LSD. From the slightly more formal LSD-25, from the most formal D-Lysergic Acid Diethlamide *US, 1966*

twenty-four hours *noun* a homemade alcoholic beverage made with sugar, yeast, water and flavouring *FIJI, 1997*

twenty-four seven *adverb* ▷ *see*: 24/7

twenty-nine *noun* ► **she's a twenty-nine this morning** usually of a wife, very angry or upset *CANADA, 1999*

twenty-one days in the county jail *noun* in poker, a hand consisting of three sevens *US, 1988*

twenty rock *noun* crack cocaine *UK, 2003*

twenty spot; twenty spotter *noun* a twenty-pound note. Adopted directly from US currency *UK, 1976*

twenty stretch *noun* a twenty-year prison sentence *UK, 2001*

twenty-twenty *adjective* good-looking; attractive. Punning, leaping from 'seeing well' to 'good-looking' *US, 1947*

twenty-twenty hindsight *noun* the ability to see clearly what should have been done *US, 1962*

twenty-two carat; twenty-four carat *adjective* genuine, first-class. Figurative application of gold standards; 'twenty-four carat' from 1900, 'twenty-two carat' since 1962 *UK, 1962*

twerp; twirp *noun* an idiot, a fool, a despicable person *UK, 1874*

twerpy *adjective* idiotic, foolish *US, 1971*

twice-and-a-half truck *noun* a 2.5 ton truck *US, 1968*

twice as cold as zero *adjective* very cold. The arithmetic impossibility lends an ironic charm to the expression *US, 1975*

twice pipes *noun* in hot rodding, a dual exhaust system *US, 1993*

twicer *noun* a two-year prison sentence *UK, 1974*

twicicles-as-nicicles *noun* the testicles. Based on an advertising slogan and a vague aural similarity *UK, 2002*

twiddle *noun* **1** the tilde character (~) on a computer keyboard *US, 1983*. **2** in fencing, a circular parry *UK, 1988*

twig *noun* **1** a radio aerial. Probably of military origin *UK, 1981*. **2** a match (usually in the plural). Used by borstal boys *UK, 1958*. **3** marijuana *US, 1970*. **4** cocaine, amphetamines or any other central nervous system stimulant *US, 1993*. **5** in sports betting, a half-point increment in the pointspread *US, 1984*. ► **drop off the twig; fall off the twig** to die *AUSTRALIA, 1974*

twig *verb* **1** to realise something. From the obsolete sense (to watch); ultimately from English dialect *twick* (to pinch), especially in the sense 'to arrest' *UK, 1815*. **2** to probe your eye or your anus to relieve an irritation *UK, 1992*

twilight *verb* to lose yourself in a daydream *US, 1974*

twilight zone *noun* **1** in drag racing, the state of travelling at extremely high speeds *US, 1965*. **2** in railway employment, the period of waiting for promotion from fireman to driver *UK, 1970*

twilly *noun* a woman, especially an attractive or promiscuous one *US, 1934*

twin *noun* in hot rodding, an engine with two cylinders *US, 1965*

twin caper *noun* a double date *US, 1960*

twin fin *noun* a surfboard with two fins *AUSTRALIA, 1985*

twin fins *noun* in craps, two fives *US, 1983*

twink *noun* **1** an effeminate, young, handsome homosexual male *US, 1968*. **2** a new military recruit *US, 1983*. **3** a coward *US, 1982*. **4** a moment, the merest measure of time. Originally, 'a wink of the eye', a 'twinkling' *UK, 1754*

twinkie *noun* **1** an eccentric; someone who doesn't conform to peer-group expectations *US, 1998*. **2** a person who is profoundly out of touch with reality *US, 1982*. **3** an Asian-American who embraces the dominant white culture in an attempt to curry favour. An allusion to a Hostess™ dessert cake that is yellow on the outside and white on the inside *US, 1998*. **4** a youthful, sexually inexperienced male who is the object of an older homosexual's desire. The spelling 'twinky' is also used *US, 1979*

twinkies *noun* car wheel rims *US, 2003*

twinkles used as a verbal talisman when two people say the same thing at the same time *US, 1993*

twinkle star *noun* in trucking, an International Harvester Transtar model truck *US, 1986*

twinkle-toes *noun* **1** a dancer; often used as a nickname or term of endearment *US, 1975*. **2** a youthful, effeminate homosexual man *US, 1979*

twinkling *noun* silent applause: raising both hands and wiggling your fingers, with your open palms facing the recipient of the gesture *UK, 2003*

twins *noun* **1** two women having sex with one man or with each other for the pleasure of the man *US, 1977*. **2** a woman's breasts *US, 2001*. **3** the fists *US, 1998*

twins *adverb* ► **go twins** to go on a double date *US, 1959*

twirl *noun* **1** a key, especially a skeleton key. Because a burglar twirls it as he uses it *UK, 1879*. **2** a prison officer. From the sense as 'a key' *UK, 1933*

twirling *noun* the dishonest substitution of a winning betting slip for a losing one. In use among bookmakers *UK, 1960*

twirly *noun* an elderly bus passenger. An elision of 'too early', from the high incidence of such passengers wishing to use their free bus-passes too early *UK, 1980*

twist *noun* **1** a girl *AUSTRALIA, 1924*. **2** the passive, 'feminine' member of a lesbian relationship *US, 1970*. **3** a marijuana cigarette. The paper end is *twisted* to prevent the loss of its contents *US, 1920*. **4** a small bag or paper wrap of heroin *UK, 2002*. **5** a turn to buy drinks in a group of people drinking *IRELAND, 1991*. **6** severe pressure or coercion to do something, *1996*. **7** a multiple bet, gambling on three different horses in separate races in a total of seven bets. More popularly known as a **PATENT** *UK, 2001*. ► **around the twist** eccentric, crazy *NEW ZEALAND, 2002*

twist *verb* **1** to cheat or swindle someone *AUSTRALIA, 1956*. **2** to arrest someone *US, 1953*. **3** to spend time in jail or prison *US, 1971*. **4** to roll a marijuana cigarette *US, 1958*. **5** in pool, to apply spin to a shot to affect the course of the object ball or the cue ball after it hits the object ball *US, 1990*. ► **twist a braid** to say goodbye *US, 1993*. ► **twist a dream** to roll a marijuana cigarette *US, 1949*. ► **twist her tail** to start a car or to accelerate suddenly *US, 1962*. ► **twist your arm** to persuade someone; strictly, to persuade someone by force or threat, but often jocular *UK, 1953*

twist! a derisive suggestion that accompanies the offensive gesture of a raised middle finger *UK, 2001*

twist 'n' go *adjective* used of a motor-scooter. From the handlebar throttle on such machines *UK, 2004*

twist and twirl; twist *noun* a girl. Rhyming slang *US, 1928*

twisted *adjective* **1** perverted *US, 1900*. **2** drunk or drug-intoxicated *US, 1958*

twister *noun* **1** a key *US, 1940*. **2** an individual who prepares marijuana cigarettes *US, 1936*. **3** a strong drug injection, especially a combination of heroin and cocaine *US, 1959*

twistie *noun* a bottle of beer with a screw top *AUSTRALIA, 1993*

twistum *noun* a marijuana cigarette. An elaboration of **TWIST** *US, 1998*

twist up *verb* to roll a marijuana cigarette *US, 1997*

twisty *noun* a devious, even dishonest, practice *NEW ZEALAND, 1997*

twisty *adjective* odd, strange *UK, 1957*

twit *noun* an inept and ineffectual person. Widely popularised by UK radio comedy *The Goons* (1951–60) and celebrated by *Monty Python's Flying Circus* in 'The Upper-Class Twit of the Year' sketch (1970) *UK, 1934*

twit *verb* to tease or taunt someone *UK, 1530*

twitch *noun* **1** a prostitute *US, 1962*. **2** a personal pleasure *US, 1981*. **3** a bird-watching trip. Bird-watchers' slang, from the observation that many bird-watchers do twitch with excitement *UK, 1977*. **4** in hospital usage, a hypochondriac *US, 1994*

twitcher *noun* **1** a bird-watcher. Bird-watchers' slang. Originally from the observation that many bird-watchers do twitch with excitement and applied only to excitable members of the bird-watching community, now well known and applied generally *UK, 1977*. **2** anyone with a pedantic interest in, and an obsessive knowledge of, a specific topic. Extended from its sense in the bird-watching world *UK, 2003*

twitching; twitchin' *adjective* excellent *US, 1993*

twitchy *adjective* **1** agitated, nervously restless, anxious *UK, 1874*. **2** in motor racing, moving in a jerky or sudden fashion *US, 1980*

twittering *adjective* experiencing the bleed period of the menstrual cycle. A schoolgirl term *UK, 1958*

twitting *adjective* inept; unfashionable *US, 1959*

twizzle; twizzle-about *verb* to rotate; to twirl; to twist something into a twirl shape *UK, 1788*

two *noun* an act of defecation. An abbreviation of NUMBER TWO *TRINIDAD AND TOBAGO, 2003* ▷*see:* TWO SHOT, TWO STRETCH. ▶ **giz a two** used to request a *two*-way share *UK, 1996*. ▶ **in two** in bar dice games, to make a hand in two rolls of the dice *US, 1971*. ▶ **in two-twos** instantly *TRINIDAD AND TOBAGO, 1990*

two; two up *verb* to share a cell with one other prisoner *UK, 1996*

two-0 *noun* a twenty-dollar note *US, 1982*

two and a juice *noun* two beers and a tomato juice *CANADA, 1987*

two and eight *noun* a confusion; an attack of nerves; an emotional state; drunk. Rhyming slang for STATE *UK, 1938*

two and two *noun* cocaine *US, 1974*

two bad boys from Illinois *noun* in craps, a roll of two *US, 1985*

two-bit *adjective* inconsequential; of no note. 'Two bits' represented a quarter of a dollar, a small sum; most younger speakers who use the term would not be familiar with its monetary roots *US, 1932*

two bits *noun* **1** a small amount *US, 1989*. **2** twenty-five dollars. An example of the 'cent = dollar' mechanism in drug slang *US, 1968*. **3** twenty-five thousand dollars *US, 1986*

two bob *noun* the sum of two shillings. After decimal currency was introduced in 1966, used for the sum of twenty cents *AUSTRALIA, 1934*. ▶ **have two bob each way** to have all contingencies working for you; to hedge your bets *AUSTRALIA, 1973*

two bob *adjective* inferior, rubbishy, useless. Derives from Australian similes such as 'as silly as a two bob watch'; explained by G.A. Wilkes in *A Dictionary of Australian Colloquialisms*, 1978, as the sum of money most often used in derogatory expressions of worth. A BOB is 'a shilling' in pre-decimal currency (5p for what it's worth, 5c in Australia). It compares with US TWO BIT and UK 'two penny' *AUSTRALIA, 1944*

two bob bit *noun* a fart; as a plural, diarrhoea. Rhyming slang for THE SHITS *UK, 1992*

two-bob lair *noun* a person who dresses flashily but cheaply *AUSTRALIA, 1944*

two-bob piece; two-bob bit *noun* a two-shilling coin. After the introduction of decimal currency in 1966, used for a 20-cent piece *AUSTRALIA, 1956*

two-bob watch *noun* a cheap, poorly made watch. Used metaphorically *AUSTRALIA, 1954*. ▶ **go off like a two-bob watch** (of a woman) to be an astoundingly good sexual partner *AUSTRALIA, 1971*

two-bottle jump; two-quart jump *noun* a relatively long move between performances *US, 1973*

two-bug *noun* in horse racing, an inexperienced jockey with a weight allowance of seven pounds *US, 1990*

two bulb *noun* a police squad car *IRELAND, 2005*

two-by-four *noun* a small house *BARBADOS, 1965*

two-carbon abuser *noun* a drunkard. Hospital usage. Alcohol has two carbon atoms *US, 1978*

two cents' worth; two cents *noun* a personal opinion, advice or point of view *US, 1970*

twocker; twok; twoc *noun* a criminal who *takes* (usually a vehicle) without owner's consent; occasionally, someone who is suspected of dishonesty *UK, 1996*

twocking *noun* the criminal act of taking (usually a vehicle) without owner's consent *UK, 1996*

two dots and a dash *noun* the male genitals *US, 1964*

two'd up *adjective* applied to two inmates in a prison cell *UK, 1978*

twoer *noun* **1** anything comprised by, or reckoned as, two *UK, 1899*. **2** two hundred pounds *UK, 1970*

twofer *noun* **1** any situation in which you obtain two of something when only one is expected or paid for. A shortening and corruption of 'two-for-one'; originally applied to a pair of theatre tickets sold for the price of one, and then picked up in more general use *US, 1936*. **2** in American casinos, a chip worth $2.50 *US, 1985*

two-fingered *adjective* anti-social. A reference to the offensive V-SIGN gesture *UK, 1999*

two foot table eater *noun* an active participant in oral sex. West Indian and UK use, recorded in August 2002 *JAMAICA, 2002*

two-for-one *noun* **1** double credit for time served in prison by inmates with jobs or positions as prison trustees *US, 1972*. **2** 100% interest *UK, 1996*

two-four *noun* a case of beer containing 24 bottles. This term is the universal Canadian designator for the item, though 'case' may sometimes mean 'the box of 12' *US, 1993*

two-four-seven *adverb* at all times – twenty-four hours a day, seven days a week. A variation of 24/7 *UK, 2000*

TWOG *noun* someone who travels to underdeveloped countries and seeks to become a part of meanest level of local society. An imperfect acronym for 'Third World Groupie', used by white Zimbabweans *ZIMBABWE, 2000*

two-in-one *noun* cocaine and heroin mixed for injection together *US, 1964*

two in the glue *noun* in a car or truck, a two-speed automatic transmission *US, 1993*

two lamps burning and no ship at sea used for describing the ultimate in wastefulness *US, 1963*

two man *noun* second degree manslaughter *US, 1982*

two men and a dog a very small crowd *NEW ZEALAND, 2002*

two minutes *noun* a small amount of time *UK, 2002*

twomp *noun* twenty dollars *US, 2001*

twomp *adjective* costing twenty dollars *US, 2001*

twomping *noun* a beating, a thumping *UK, 1998*

twonk *noun* a fool *UK, 2003*

two-o *noun* a twenty-dollar chunk of crack cocaine *US, 1989*

two-o-eight *noun* a military discharge for mental unfitness *US, 1968*

twopenny-farthing *adjective* of little worth, unimportant. A devaluation of TUPPENNY HA'PENNY *UK, 1959*

two pennyworth; twopenneth *noun* an opinion. From conventional sense (a small amount, hence a small contribution) *UK, 1965*

two-percenter *noun* ▷*see:* ONE-PERCENTER

two pi *noun* the number of years consumed completing a doctoral thesis *US, 1991*

two-pipe *noun* a double-barrel shotgun *US, 1949*

two-pot screamer *noun* a person who gets drunk on very little alcohol *AUSTRALIA, 1959*

two-pump chump *noun* a male who ejaculates without much stimulation *US, 2004*

two rolls and no coffee *noun* in craps, a roll of seven on the first roll after establishing your point. A pun on 'roll', with the player here losing after two rolls *US, 1949*

twos *noun* **1** the second landing or floor level in a prison *UK, 1996*. **2** a share *UK, 1996*. ▶ **all the twos** twenty-two. In Bingo, House or

Housey-Housey calling, the formula 'all the' announces a double number *UK, 1943*

twos and blues *noun* a two-tone horn and flashing blue light used to signal a police vehicle travelling urgently *UK, 2002*

twos and fews *noun* small-denomination notes or loose change *US, 1973*

two-seater *noun* an outdoor privy which accomodates two people at once *US, 1966*

twosey *noun* an act of defecation *AUSTRALIA, 1995*

Two Shades of Soul *noun* the 173rd Airborne Brigade, US Army. So named because of the amicable relations between black and white soldiers in the unit, the first major US combat unit sent to Vietnam *US, 1988*

two shot; two *noun* in the television and film industries, a shot of two actors facing each other, each taking up half the screen *US, 1977*

twosky *noun* two hundred dollars. The 'sky' suffix is purely decorative *US, 1994*

two snaps up! used for expressing approval. A catchphrase from the television programme *In Living Color US, 1990*

two-spirited *adjective* applied to homosexual, lesbian, bisexual or transgendered Native Americans. First used among Native Americans of transgendered people only, it has also been offensively applied to half-breeds and those who have adopted white culture *CANADA, 1996*

two-step *noun* the highly venomous bamboo viper, found and feared in Vietnam. So named because of the belief – false but vivid – that the venom is so toxic that it kills a person before they can take two steps after being bitten *US, 1991*

two stretch; two *noun* a two-year sentence of imprisonment. A multiple of STRETCH (a year's sentence) *UK, 1950*

two's up *adjective* sharing, especially a cigarette. Used in borstals and detention centres *UK, 1978*

twot *noun* an abusive epithet for someone you would otherwise call a cunt. A variant spelling (originally pronunced in a similar manner) of TWAT (the vagina). As time has passed the pronunciations have separated *UK, 1999*

two-thirds of five-eighths of fuck all *noun* almost nothing. From the final line of 'The young man of Bengal' limerick. A recorded song based on the variation 'two thirds of four fifths of fuck all' was released in the UK in 2005 by Ivor Biggun *NEW ZEALAND, 1998*

two-thirty *adjective* grimy, dirty. Rhyming slang for 'dirty' *UK, 1960*

two-time *verb* to be seeing more than one sexual partner without the knowledge of the partner(s); to be unfaithful *US, 1924*

two-timer *noun* a person who is unfaithful to another person or a cause *US, 1927*

two-timing woman *noun* a type of bet in an illegal numbers game lottery *US, 1957*

two-toilet *adjective* used of an Irish immigrant, relatively well-off economically and straying from the Irish cultural ties that bind. A term coined in Boston and rarely used elsewhere *US, 1990*

two-two *noun* a prostitute *CANADA, 1993*

two-two *adverb* in pairs *INDIA, 1979*

two-up *noun* **1** a gesture that is used to insult or otherwise cause offence. The forefinger and the middle finger are extended to form a V shape, with the palm turned in towards the gesturer *UK: SCOTLAND, 1985*. **2** a gambling game in which two pennies are tossed from a small flat bat *AUSTRALIA, 1884*

two-up school *noun* a place at which a two-up game is held; a group of people playing two-up *AUSTRALIA, 1897*

two-way *noun* a position for mutual, simultaneous oral sex between two people, or the act itself, especially when advertised as a service offered by a prostitute *UK, 2003*

two-way *adjective* said of a carnival game or attraction that can be operated either legitimately or in a crooked fashion *US, 1989*

two-way bondage *noun* a restriction of movement to facilitate an erotic encounter or sexual intercourse, especially when advertised as a service offered and received by a prostitute *UK, 2003*

two-way man *noun* a male prostitute who is available for both anal and oral sex *US, 1941*

two-way watersports *noun* when used in a prostitute's advertising, indicates that the prostitute is willing both to urinate over the client, and be urinated upon. A specification of WATER SPORTS (the practice of urophilia and uralgnia) *UK, 2003*

two-wire *noun* an electronic technician. US Navy usage *US, 1998*

two words, three effs fuck off. If the intention is euphemistic why spell it out? *UK, 2000*

twozee *verb* to defecate. Children's vocabulary *TRINIDAD AND TOBAGO, 1986*

twunt *noun* a despicable person, an idiot. A blend of CUNT and TWAT *UK, 2005*

TX in on-line poker playing, thanks *UK, 2003*

txt *verb* to send a text message. A new vocabulary of abbreviations, of which this is probably the most recognisable, has grown rapidly as texting becomes evermore popular and mobile phone companies limit the number of characters subscribers may use *UK, 2000*

tyke *noun* **1** a child, especially one who is disobedient, impudent or mischievous; a youth. Probably from the sense as 'a dog' *UK, 1400*. **2** a Yorkshireman. Originally pejorative, ultimately from the sense as 'a dog'; now in general use, and adopted with pride by yorkshire people: Barnsley football club is nicknamed 'The Tykes' *UK, about 1700*. **3** a rough, ill-mannered fellow *UK: NORTHERN IRELAND, 1996*. **4** a Roman Catholic. Probably Northern Ireland English *Taig AUSTRALIA, 1902*. **5** a scruffy dog; a mongrel. Now widely used as a pet name *UK, about 1400*

type *noun* a person, especially one of a stated or implied character. Colloquial *UK, 1922*

typer *noun* a typewriter *US, 1982*

typewriter *noun* **1** a machine gun *UK, 1915*. **2** a fighter; a boxer. Rhyming slang *UK, 1931*. **3** the push-button automatic transmission on a Dodge car *US, 1968*

typewriter commando *noun* a soldier assigned to clerical support duty far from combat *US, 1947*

typewriter jockey *noun* a stenographer or typist *US, 1960*

typist *noun* in a deck of playing cards, a queen *US, 1988*

typo *noun* a *typo*graphical error *UK, 1945*

tyrannosaurus rex; tyrannosaurus *noun* sex. Rhyming slang *UK, 1998*

Tyrone *noun* a potent strain of marijuana *US, 1995*

Uu

Ubangi *noun* a black person. Offensive *US, 1979*

U-barrel *noun* a large steel drum used for collecting urine where there is no plumbing *ANTARCTICA, 2003*

über-; uber- *prefix* super-high in quality or degree. Adopted directly from German preposition *über* (over, above), combines to form words that exceed the norm *US, 1992*

UBI doctors' shorthand for the facetious diagnosis: *u*nexplained *b*eer *i*njury. Medical slang *UK, 2003*

uc dai loi; ouc-dai-loi *noun* (during the Vietnam conflict) an Australian soldier. From Vietnamese. Spelt with much variation *AUSTRALIA, 1975*

u cunt *nickname* *Uncut* magazine (since 1997). Originally a cut and paste by disgruntled employees, then adopted by the magazine's competition *UK, 2001*

udder *noun* **1** the female breast. Originally (about 1708) in conventional or poetic use *UK, 1933*. **2** a despised, disrespected or foolish woman. Possibly a variation of COW; more likely to derive from 'udder' (the female breast) hence used here as a synonym for TIT *UK, 2001*. **3** a protruding paunch produced by too much beer drinking. Recorded as a contemporary gay usage *UK, 2003*

u-ey; u-ee; yewie; you-ee *noun* a u-turn *US, 1969*

uggies *noun* a pair of Ugg™ boots *AUSTRALIA, 2003*

ughly *adjective* uglier than ugly *US, 1966*

ugly as a hatful of arseholes *adjective* especially ugly *AUSTRALIA, 1971*

ugly as fuck *adjective* very ugly *US, 1989*

ugly Australian *noun* a rough, loutish Australian; an Australian yobbo *AUSTRALIA, 1974*

ugly sister *noun* a blister. Rhyming slang *UK, 1992*

ugly stick *noun* a notional stick with which a person has been beaten in order to make them ugly *US, 1969*

ugs *noun* ▷*see:* HUGS AND KISSES

uh-oh used in recognition of trouble *US, 2001*

uh-uh *adverb* no *US, 1924*

UIC ski team *noun* unemployed winter skiers *CANADA, 1989*

uke *noun* a ukulele *US, 1915*

ukelele *noun* on the railways, a short-handled shovel *US, 1977*

UKG *noun* British gangsta music and culture. An abbreviation of *U*nited *K*ingdom *G*angsta *UK, 2002*

Ukrainian peanut *noun* a sunflower seed *CANADA, 1987*

ultimate *noun* in the coded terminology used in advertising for sexual contact, full sexual intercourse *UK, 2006*

ultimate xphoria *noun* MDMA, the recreational drug best known as ecstasy *UK, 2003*

ulysses *noun* a u-turn *US, 1968*

-um *suffix* added to words to give the impression of English as spoken by an American Indian *US, 1946*

um and ah *verb* to hesitate; to be uncertain. From the vocal sounds that may accompany hesitation *UK, 2000*

umbrella *noun* **1** a fellow, especially a husband or boyfriend. Rhyming slang for FELLAH; FELLA *UK, 1998*. **2** in the television and film industries, a reflector used to bounce light onto a subject *US, 1990*

umpteen *noun* an imprecise, large number *UK, 1918*

umpteenhundred *noun* a point in the yet-to-be-determined, indefinite future *US, 1988*

umpteenth; unteenth *adjective* used of a great but unspecific number or amount *UK, 1918*

una *adjective* one. From Italian *uno* *UK, 1996*

unass *verb* **1** to stand up; to remove yourself from your immediate location *US, 1967*. **2** to knock someone out of a sitting position *US, 1991*

unbling *noun* cheap, shoddy, unimpressive jewellery. The opposite of BLING *UK, 2005*

unbutton *verb* to force or rip open a safe *US, 1949*. ▶ **unbutton the mutton** to undo clothing and liberate the penis *AUSTRALIA, 1971*

unc *noun* an uncle, especially as a term of address *AUSTRALIA, 1946*

uncle *noun* **1** a pawnbroker *UK, 1756*. **2** a person who buys stolen goods from criminals *US, 1950*. ▶ **cry uncle; say uncle; holler uncle** to admit defeat; to beg for mercy. From Irish *anacol* (mercy) *US, 1918*

uncle *verb* to act in a passive or subservient fashion. From UNCLE TOM *US, 1969*

uncle and aunt *noun* a plant. Rhyming slang *UK, 1992*

unclear on the concept *adjective* completely and dramatically ignorant about a particular subject *US, 1988*

Uncle Bert *noun* a shirt. Rhyming slang *UK, 1961*

Uncle Bertie *adjective* angry, especially if only temporarily; characteristically ill-tempered. Rhyming slang for SHIRTY; extended from UNCLE BERT (a shirt) *UK, 1992*

Uncle Bill *noun* the police. A variation of 'old Bill' *UK, 1962*

Uncle Bloody *noun* the bleed period of the menstrual cycle *US, 2001*

Uncle Bob *noun* **1** a police officer *UK, 1965*. **2** the penis. Rhyming slang for KNOB *UK, 1992*

Uncle Charles; Uncle C *noun* cocaine *UK, 2002*

Uncle Charlie *noun* **1** used as a representation of the dominant white culture in the US *US, 1963*. **2** among truckers using citizens' band radio, the Federal Communications Commission *US, 1976*. **3** the Viet Cong *US, 1985*

Uncle Charlie is visiting; my Uncle Charlie is visiting I am experiencing menstruation *US, 2001*

Uncle Daniel *noun* in hot rodding, a deceptively normal-looking car that has been modified and enhanced for speed *US, 1958*

Uncle Dick *noun* the penis. Rhyming slang for PRICK *UK, 1960*

Uncle Dick; dickey; dickie *adjective* sick. Rhyming slang *UK, 1960*

Uncle Fred *noun* bread. Rhyming slang, generally childish *UK, 1932*

Uncle Ho *noun* Ho Chi Minh *US, 1976*

Uncle Joe *noun* Joseph Stalin *UK, 1943*

Uncle Junk *noun* heroin. Elaboration of JUNK (heroin) *US, 1985*

Uncle Lester *noun* a child molester. Rhyming slang *UK, 2002*

Uncle Mac *noun* **1** a smack. Rhyming slang, formed from 'Children's Favourites' radio presenter Uncle Mac (Derek McCulloch), *BBC Light Programme*, 1954–67 *UK, 1992*. **2** heroin. Rhyming slang for SMACK, extended from the earlier, more innocent use as 'a smack' *UK, 1992*

Uncle Miltie *nickname* Milton Berle, US comedian of vaudeville, radio and television (1908–2002). Berle was also known as Mr Television *US, 1968*

Uncle Milty *noun* *Milt*own™, a branded tranquilliser *US, 1998*

Uncle Ned *noun* a bed. Rhyming slang *UK, 1925*

Uncle Sam *noun* the US federal government *US, 1950*

Uncle Sid *noun* LSD. A play on the second syllable of ACID (LSD) *UK, 2003*

Uncle Tom *noun* a black person who curries favour from whites through obsequious, fawning behaviour. In recent US history,

Supreme Court Justice Clarence Thomas has attracted the 'Uncle Tom' label more than any other black American, in part due to the irresistible Tom-Thomas pun *US, 1922*

Uncle Tom *verb* (used of a black person) to try to curry favour with white people by obsequious behaviour *US, 1937*

Uncle Willie *adjective* **1** silly. Rhyming slang *UK, 1932*. **2** chilly. Rhyming slang *UK, 1961*

unco *adjective* **1** clumsy; awkward. Short for '*unco*ordinated' *AUSTRALIA, 1996*. **2** weird *AUSTRALIA, 1996*

uncommon horn *noun* an unusually urgent sexual appetite *UK, 2001*

uncool *adjective* unpleasant, aggressive, dangerous; excitable; tending to show your feelings more than is prudent or advisable *US, 1953*

un-cred *adjective* unfashionable. The antonym of CRED (acceptible to your peers) *UK, 2001*

uncunt *verb* to withdraw the penis from a woman's vagina *US, 1961*

uncut *adjective* not circumcised *US, 1957*

under *noun* sexual intercourse. The location of the sexual organs: 'under a body' or, perhaps, 'under a skirt' *UK, 1936*

under *adjective* a state of sobriety when measured against drug-intoxication *UK, 2003*

underage *adjective* in snowboarding, used to describe the not-yet-perfected performance of a trick or manoeuvre *US, 1995*

under-arm *adjective* pornographic *UK, 1979*

underchunders *noun* underpants. From '*under*wear' and CHUNDER (vomit), because they are revolting *AUSTRALIA, 1966*

undercover *adjective* used of a racehorse, trained in secret *US, 1951*

undercrackers *noun* underpants *UK, 1997*

underdaks *noun* underpants *AUSTRALIA, 1966*

underdungers *noun* underpants *NEW ZEALAND, 1981*

under four eyes; under two eyes *adjective* face to face *TRINIDAD AND TOBAGO, 1990*

underground *noun* a hidden counter culture. Usually in a political context, although in the 1960s also in a cultural context *US, 1935*

underground mutton *noun* rabbit meat *AUSTRALIA, 1919*

undergunned *adjective* having too small a surfboard for the surf conditions *AUSTRALIA, 1989*

underlook *verb* to look at someone or something with grave doubt *BARBADOS, 1965*

underpass *noun* the posterior; the buttocks, the anus. Rhyming slang for ARSE and appropriate imagery *UK, 2003*

under-stain *noun* the bleed period of the menstrual cycle. A euphemism *UK, 1980*

under starter's orders *adjective* arrested. Criminal and police slang, from horse racing *UK, 1959*

undertaker *noun* a bookmaker who will only accept bets at odds under those offered by his competition *AUSTRALIA, 1989*

under the affluence of incohol drunk. A deliberate spoonerism, probably Australian but post-war UK comedians are worthy of consideration *AUSTRALIA, 1984*

under-the-arm *adjective* no good; inferior; loathsome. Implies that the object described is a STINKER *UK, 1930s to 1960s*

underwhelm *verb* to arouse little or no interest in someone. Jocular. Now included in the *Oxford English Dictionary UK, 1956*

under yonder *noun* the anus *US, 1972*

undies *noun* underwear. Abbreviated 'underwear'. In the UK, applied most commonly to women's underwear; in Australia to men's; in the US to children's *UK, 1906*

undressed *adjective* used of a citizens' band radio operated without a linear amplifier *US, 1976*

unemployed *noun* the penis. Especially in the phrase SHAKE HANDS WITH THE UNEMPLOYED *AUSTRALIA, 1971*

unforgettable *noun* a combination of cocaine, heroin and valium *US, 1993*

unfragged *adjective* not listed on the daily frag order specifying the military objectives of the day. Vietnam war usage *US, 1986*

unfuckable *adjective* too ugly to be considered as a sexual partner *AUSTRALIA, 1979*

unfucked *adjective* re-ordered; having order brought out of chaos *US, 1997*

unglue *verb* in drag racing and hot rodding, to blow up an engine *US, 1968*

unglued *adjective* out of control *US, 1962*

ungodly *adjective* **1** of time, unpleasantly early in the day *UK, 1889*. **2** superlative *US, 1974*

ungowa; ungowa bwana yes, affirmative, OK. Citizens' band radio slang *US, 1976*

ungrateful *adjective* said of a hospital patient who dies after heroic efforts to save his life *US, 1989*

unhinged *adjective* angry; emotionally unsettled *UK, 1719*

unholy *adjective* awful; outrageous *UK, 1842*

unhook *verb* to remove handcuffs *US, 1982*

unhook the U-haul! 'hurry up!'. The image is of unhooking a rental trailer that is slowing you down *US, 1993*

uni *noun* **1** university; a university *AUSTRALIA, 1898*. **2** a school uniform. Pronounced 'unny' *UK, 1947*

uniboob *noun* a woman's chest clothed in a manner that presents the two breasts as a single entity *US, 2001*

uniform *noun* **1** a uniformed police officer, as distinguished from a detective in street clothes *US, 1969*. **2** a member of the armed forces *US, 1941*

uniform tango *noun* an UNCLE TOM. From the military phonetic alphabet, UT *US, 1991*

uninteresting *adjective* used of a computer problem, subject to being solved with enough time, not requiring creative problem-solving skills *US, 1991*

Union Jack *noun* **1** a multiple bet on 9 selections. Named after the Union Jack flag which a schemata of the wager resembles *UK, 2001*. **2** the back. Rhyming slang. The short form 'union' is also used *UK, 1992*

Union Pacific *noun* in poker, a hand consisting of three sixes and a pair. The sixes are known as 'boxcars', hence the railway company name *US, 1988*

unit *noun* **1** the penis. The slang sense of the word gives special meaning to the nickname 'The Big Unit' given to baseball pitcher Randy Johnson *US, 1985*. **2** the vagina *US, 1978*

United Parcel Service *noun* any amphetamine, methamphetamine or other central nervous system stimulant. A forced formation: the initials UPS represent stimulants as 'ups' (see UPPER) *US, 1976*

units *noun* parents. An abbreviation of 'parental *units*' *US, 1987*

University of a Billion Chinks *nickname* the University of British Columbia, in racist reference to the large student population of immigrants from South Asia *CANADA, 2001*

University of Freebies *noun* the University of Florida. Back-formation from the initials FU, playing on the role of athletics at the university *US, 2004*

university of hard knocks *noun* experience, especially when valued against a university education. An admixture of the clichés UNIVERSITY OF LIFE and SCHOOL OF HARD KNOCKS *UK, 1984*

university of life *noun* experience, especially when valued against a university education *UK, 1959*

unk-unk *noun* an unknown that is unknown or not even suspected. Aerospace usage *US, 1974*

unleaded *adjective* caffeine-free. Borrowing from the language of car fuel for application to the world of coffee drinks and, to a lesser extent, soft drinks *US, 1996*

unload *verb* **1** (of a male) to ejaculate. Originally in gay use *US, 1995*. **2** to punch someone; to beat someone. Probably from an earlier sense (to drop bombs) *UK, 1998*. **3** in air combat, to accelerate *US, 1990*.

4 on the railways, to end a work shift or to jump off a moving train *US, 1977*

unotque *noun* marijuana *UK, 2003*

unpack *verb* to vomit *UK, 1983*

unprofessional, that's what you are used as a humorous if pointed insult. Coined by ESPN's Keith Olberman to describe the level of play of strike-breaking, 'replacement' baseball players in 1995 *US, 1997*

unreal *adjective* excellent; exceptionally bad. Depends on context and tone *US, 1965*

unrool *adjective* great; terrific. Representing a pronunciation of UNREAL *AUSTRALIA, 1990*

unscrewed *adjective* out of control *US, 1962*

unsliced *adjective* not circumcised *US, 1988*

unteenth *adjective* ▷*see:* UMPTEENTH

until the wheels fall off *adjective* until a prison clique disbands; ultimately loyal. Back-formation from a CAR (a clique) *US, 1989*

untogether *adjective* not in control of your personal condition; unable to get your mind and emotions under control; disorganised *UK, 1969*

untold *adjective* excellent; terrific; wonderful *AUSTRALIA, 1979*

untolds *noun* lots; heaps *AUSTRALIA, 1987*

unwind *verb* to relax after a period of tension or stress *UK, 1958*

up *noun* **1** a tablet of amphetamine, methamphetamine or other central nervous system stimulant *US, 1979*. **2** an inspiration; an elevated mood *US, 1966*. **3** in the used car business, a potential customer who has walked on to the sales forecourt *US, 1975*. ▶ **on the up and up** legitimate, honest *US, 1863*

up *verb* **1** to start suddenly or boldly; to rise abruptly *UK, 1831*. **2** to arouse or aggravate someone *UK, 2000*. **3** to increase a bet in cards *US, 1942*. ▶ **up it** to pay off a debt *US, 1980*. ▶ **up sticks** to pack up and go; to move. Originally nautical, from raising the mast prior to setting sail *UK, 1877*

up *adjective* **1** happening; going on *UK, 1838*. **2** wrong; amiss *UK, 1849*. **3** successful *US, 1990*. **4** under the influence of a drug, especially LSD and, later, MDMA, the recreational drug best known as ecstasy *US, 1966*. **5** pregnant *TRINIDAD AND TOBAGO, 1991*. **6** used of waves, large. Giving rise to the cry, 'Surf's up!' *US, 1964*. **7** imprisoned *US, 1975*. **8** of food or drink, made, cooked, ready, served *UK, 1961*. **9** in the used car business, next on the salesmen's rotation list to approach a potential customer who has walked onto the sales forecourt *US, 1975*. **10** used of an actor in the television and film industries, unable to remember lines *US, 1977*. **11** of a male, having sexual intercourse with someone *UK, 1937*

up *adverb* **1** each; equal in quantity *UK, 1809*. **2** up to or up at *AUSTRALIA, 1884*

-up *suffix* **1** used to form adjectives and verbs with the meaning 'to be under, or put someone under, the influence of a drug'. *2000*. **2** having adopted a stated style or characteristic. Formed in combination with a participial adjective *UK, 2004*

up against *adjective* confronted by a difficulty *US, 1896*

up against it in a difficult position, in trouble *US, 1896*

up against the wall helpless, dominated by another; used for expressing power over others. A catch-phrase of the politically active in the US 1960s, echoing a police command *US, 1960s*

up-and-down *noun* **1** an order of Kessler ale and Stroh's beer *US, 1981*. **2** sex *US, 1993*. **3** in gambling, a type of conditional bet: a single-stakes-about or a double-stakes-about *UK, 2001*

up and down *adjective* brown, especially applied to brown ale. Rhyming slang *UK, 1992*

up-and-downer; upper-and-downer *noun* a violent quarrel; a fight *UK, 1927*

up and down of it *noun* the gist of something; the whole thing; the outcome of a situation *UK, 1994*

up and under *noun* thunder. Rhyming slang, formed from a rugby manoeuvre that became a popular catchphrase for BBC rugby league commentator Eddie Waring, 1910–86 *UK, 1998*

upchuck *noun* ground beef. Playing on 'ground chuck' for the beef as well as the slang for 'vomit' *US, 1996*

upchuck *verb* to vomit *US, 1936*

up country *adjective* South Vietnam north of Saigon *US, 1977*

up for it *adjective* ready to party *UK, 1999*

upfront *adjective* honest, open, frank *US, 1970*

upful *adjective* happy, positive. Mainly West Indian and UK black usage *UK, 1997*

uphill gardening *noun* anal intercourse *UK, 1997*

uphills *noun* dice that have been altered in a fashion that produces high numbers when rolled *US, 1962*

upholstered *adjective* suffering from a sexually transmitted infection *US, 1949*

Upjohn *noun* a tablet of Dexedrine™, Benzedrine™ or other central nervous system stimulant *US, 1971*

up jumped the devil! used for expressing dismay at the toss of a seven by a craps player trying to make his point *US, 1950*

up north *adverb* to prison *US, 1989*

up on one *adjective* of a police officer, on a charge, standing accused *UK, 1974*

upper *noun* an amphetamine or other central nervous system stimulant *US, 1973*

upper-class snob *noun* an act of oral sex, especially performed on a man. Rhyming slang for BLOW JOB *UK, 2003*

upper-crust *noun* the upper classes; the higher circles of society *UK, 1843*

upper deck *noun* the female breasts *US, 1967*

upper persuasion for lower invasion *noun* foreplay *US, 1968*

uppie *noun* an amphetamine or other central nervous system stimulant. A variation of UPPER *US, 1982*

Uppie *noun* a student of the University of Port Elizabeth. Formed on the initialism, by which the university is known, UPE; Radio Uppie is the UPE student radio station *SOUTH AFRICA, 1972*

uppity; uppidy *adjective* brash; arrogant; refusing to accept one's place in society. Originally coined by southern blacks, now widely used *US, 1880*

uprights *noun* the legs *US, 1970*

upsidaisy!; upsadaisy!; oops-a-daisy! used to comfort a child who has fallen over and to lightly encourage a recovery *UK, 1862*

upside *preposition* against *US, 1959*

upskirt *noun* a type of voyeurism devoted to seeing what is beneath a woman's skirt *US, 1995*

upslice *noun* the vagina; a disagreeable woman *US, 2001*

upstairs *adverb* in poker, in the form of a raised bet *US, 1996*. ▶ **not right upstairs; short of a few rooms upstairs** not completely sane *UK, 1931*

upstate *adjective* **1** in prison *US, 1934*. **2** murdered *US, 2003*

upta *adjective* no good; hopeless; worthless. Originally short for UP TO PUTTY, but now conceived of as short for UP TO SHIT *AUSTRALIA, 1918*

up the aisle *noun* a sexual position in which the woman kneels and the man enters her from behind. Rhyming slang for DOG-STYLE, combining a pun on 'a narrow passage' with an implication of marriage *UK, 2003*

up the in and out *adjective* ruined; pregnant. Rhyming slang for UP THE SPOUT *UK, 1998*

up the Irons! used as a greeting, especially between Iron Maiden fans. Collected from fans of heavy metal music by Seamus O'Reilly, January 1995 *US, 1995*

up there Cazaly come on! Used as a cry of encouragement. Originally a cry of support for Ron Cazaly (1893–1963), Australian Rules football player *AUSTRALIA, 1943*

up there for thinking, down there for dancing; up here for thinking, down there for dancing a catchphrase used as a jocular demonstration of the speaker's grasp on anatomy *UK, 1999*

uptight *adjective* **1** nervous, anxious *US, 1934*. **2** inhibited; narrow-minded; very correct and straightlaced *US, 1968*

up top *noun* **1** a person's intelligence *UK, 1961*. **2** a woman's breasts, or the area of the breasts *UK, 2003*

uptown *noun* **1** cocaine. Uptown is expensive and glamorous, as is cocaine *US, 1980*. **2** in pool, the area at the head of the table *US, 1993*

uptown *adjective* upscale, prosperous *US, 1946*

up west; up West *noun* the West End of London. Originally as viewed from the East End, subsequently used throughout suburbia regardless of the compass *UK, 1979*

up you! used as an exclamation of contempt, derision or defiance; a euphemism for 'fuck you!'. Often accompanied by, or used instead of, the raised middle finger gesture which carries the same meaning. Apparently not recorded before 1984 but, surely, much earlier *UK, 1984*

up you for the rent! damn you! *AUSTRALIA, 1955*

up your alley! used as a dismissive retort. A euphemism for UP YOUR ASS/ARSE! *UK, 1976*

up your giggy! used as an expression of contemptuous rejection. After GIGGY (the anus) *CANADA, 1961*

up your nose with a rubber hose used as a general-purpose, nonsensical insult. A signature line of Vinnie Barbarino, played by John Travolta, on the television comedy *Welcome Back, Kotter* (ABC, 1975–79). Repeated with referential humour *US, 1979*

up yours! used as an expression of contempt, rejection, or derision. A shortening of UP YOUR ASS/ARSE! *UK, 1956*

urban surfing *verb* ▷ *see:* TRAIN-SURFING

urger *noun* a racecourse tipster *AUSTRALIA, 1919*

Uriah Heep *noun* an objectionable or unpleasant person; a dull or insignificant person. Rhyming slang for CREEP, formed from a character in Charles Dickens' *David Copperfield*, 1849 *UK, 1992*

urine express *noun* an elevator in a public housing development. New York police slang *US, 1997*

urine-stained *adjective* not good enough; not socially acceptable *US, 1996*

us *adjective* my. Too widely used to be simply a dialect of northern England *UK, 1999*

US *adjective* not in working order. A military abbreviation of 'unserviceable', 'useless', and/or UP TO SHIT *UK, 1942*

us *pronoun* me. Queen Elizabeth II is often derided for referring to herself as 'we' (known as the 'royal we'); this is the 'working-class us' *UK, 1828*

use *verb* **1** to use drugs, especially addictive drugs such as heroin. Used without an object. A euphemism, but one which is crystal clear in slang context *US, 1971*. **2** to enjoy something (if only you could get the something that is wished for) *UK, 1956*. ▶ **use your loaf** to act intelligently, think. Often as an imperative *UK, 1997*. ▶ **use yourself** **1** to masturbate *BAHAMAS, 1982*. **2** to use physical violence; to fight. By elision from 'use yourself as a weapon' *UK, 1962*

used beer department *noun* a toilet. Modified to 'used coffee department' and the like for office settings *US, 1995*

useful *adjective* **1** good; capable; effective; satisfactory *UK, 1955*. **2** competitive *IRELAND, 1991*

useful as an ashtray on a motorbike *adjective* useless *AUSTRALIA, 1986*

useless as tits on a boar; useless as tits on a boar hog; useless as tits on a bull *adjective* ineffectual, serving no useful purpose *CANADA, 1981*

useless smile *noun* used for describing the happy, vacant facial expression of someone under the influence of LSD *US, 1994*

user *noun* **1** a drug addict *UK, 1935*. **2** a person who exploits others for their own gain *AUSTRALIA, 1978*

ush *verb* to work as an usher in a theatre *US, 1981*

US of A *noun* the United States of America. A variation of the conventional abbreviations US and USA *US, 1973*

USP *noun* amphetamines; MDMA, the recreational drug best known as ecstasy *UK, 2003*

UTA *adjective* in abundance *US, 1986*

ute *noun* a utility truck *AUSTRALIA, 1943*

utensil *noun* a chamberpot *TRINIDAD AND TOBAGO, 1909*

utilities *noun* US Marines' combat fatigues *US, 1991*

U-turn *noun* a reversal of political policy. From motorists' jargon *UK, 1984*

UVs *noun* sun rays. An abbreviation of 'ultra-violet sun rays' *US, 1968*

UYB *noun* an uppity yankee bitch. The southern US view of some northern US women *US, 1986*

Uzi *noun* a pipe used for smoking crack cocaine *US, 1994*

uzzfay *noun* a police officer. Pig Latin for FUZZ *US, 1955*

Vv

V *noun* **1** Valium™ *US, 1984*. **2** sildenafil citrate marketed as Viagra™, an anti-impotence drug taken recreationally for performance enhancement, in combination with other chemicals that stimulate the sexual appetites *UK, 2000*. **3** a V-sign *UK, 2002*. **4** a visit *US, 2002*. **5** a five year prison sentence. From the Roman numeral for five *US, 1945*. **6** five dollars *US, 1962*. **7** marijuana *US, 1979*

V *adjective* very. Upper-class society origins (perhaps from abbreviation use in school) into wider middle-class usage *UK, 1982*

V-8 gang *noun* a youth gang that uses large American cars *NEW ZEALAND, 1984*

V-8s *noun* men's shorts *US, 1972*

VA *noun* the vagina. Adopted from the standard abbreviation for the state of Virginia, punning the phonetic similarity *US, 1998*

Vaalie; Valie *noun* an inhabitant of the region formerly known as Transvaal. Often derogatory or patronising *SOUTH AFRICA, 1976*

vac *noun* a vacation *UK, 1709*

vacation *noun* time spent in jail or prison *US, 1971*

vacaya *noun* **1** any mechanical or electrical device that produces sound; a jukebox; a record player *UK, 2002*. **2** a mobile phone. From the earlier, more general sense (a device that produces sound) *UK, 2002*

vada; varda; vardi; vardo; vardy *verb* to see; to look; to observe. Polari *UK, 1859*

vadavision; vardavision *noun* a television *UK, 2002*

VAF! (when first noticing an attractive person) 'look!'. Polari; an acronym for '*VADA* absolutely *FANTABULOSA!*' *UK, 2002*

vag *noun* **1** a vagrant *US, 1868*. **2** vagrancy; a criminal charge of vagrancy *US, 1859*

vag *verb* to charge someone with vagrancy *US, 1859*

vage; vag; vadge; vaj *noun* the vagina *US, 1986*

vaggerie; vagary; vagarie *verb* to go; to leave; to travel. Probably from Italian *vagare* (to roam) *UK, 2002*

vagina vandal *noun* a rapist *US, 1962*

val *noun* **1** a tablet of diazepam (trade name Valium™), an anti-anxiety agent *US, 1986*. **2** value *UK, 2000*. **3** a resident of the San Fernando Valley, Los Angeles County, California *US, 1982*

valentine *noun* a very short jail sentence *US, 1949*

Valentine *noun* in college, a notification of academic deficiency *US, 1968*

Valentine Dyalls; valentines *noun* haemorrhoids. Rhyming slang for *PILES*, formed on the actor Valentine Dyall, 1908–85 *UK, 1998*

valet *noun* in a deck of playing cards, a jack or knave *US, 1988*

vali; vallie; vally *noun* Valium™, a branded tranquillizer *UK, 1996*

valley *noun* the antecubital vein at the inside of the elbow, a prime site for intravenous drug injections *US, 1970*

Valley *noun* ▶ **the Valley 1** the San Fernando Valley, Los Angeles County, California *US, 1994*. **2** a low-lying area east of Seventh Avenue in Harlem, New York *US, 1966*

valley dolls *noun* LSD *UK, 2003*

Valleyite *noun* a resident of the San Fernando Valley, Los Angeles *US, 1985*

valve job *noun* sex in a car *US, 1997*

vamoose *verb* to go; to leave. Spanish *vamanos* (let us go) *US, 1834*

vamp *noun* a woman that makes it her habit or business to captivate men by an unscrupulous employment of her sexual charms *UK, 1911*

vamp *verb* **1** (of a woman) to flirt, and otherwise employ an obvious sexuality to attract a mate *UK, 1927*. **2** to smell bad *TRINIDAD AND TOBAGO, 1973*

vampire *noun* a medical operative who draws off a patient's or donor's blood; a member of any National Blood Transfusion collecting team. Jocular and affectionate, usually *UK, 1961*. ▶ **take the vampire's kiss; take the vampires** to tease someone, to pull someone's leg. Rhyming slang for TAKE THE PISS *UK, 1998*

van *noun* a brakevan (caboose) *US, 1977*

Van *nickname* the city of Vancouver, British Columbia *CANADA, 2002*

V and A *nickname* Victoria and Albert Museum *UK, 1937*

vandoo *noun* in the Canadian Forces, a member of the Royal 22nd Regiment, the francophone army unit *CANADA, 1995*

V and T *noun* vodka and tonic *UK, 1997*

V and X *noun* in carnival usage, a five-and-ten cent store *US, 1981*

Van Gogh *noun* a trucker operating with a citizens' band radio. A trucker without a citizens' band radio is said to be driving 'without ears', and hence the artistic allusion *US, 1976*

Vangroovy *noun* Vancouver, British Columbia *CANADA, 2002*

vanilla *adjective* **1** white-skinned, Caucasian. Originally black usage, now widespread *US, 1994*. **2** ordinary, simple, basic. Derives from the plainest ice-cream variety *US, 1977*. **3** of sex, conventional; of homosexual sex, gentle, traditional, emotional *US, 1984*. **4** used of pornography, relatively high-brow, designed for couples and first-time viewers *US, 2000*

vanilla fudge *noun* a judge. Rhyming slang *UK, 2004*

Vanity Fair *noun* a chair. Rhyming slang, formed from the title of Thackeray's novel *UK, 1961*

Vanna *noun* used as a term of address between homosexual males. From Vanna White, of television game show fame *US, 1990*

Vanouver *noun* any vacuum cleaner. Rhyming slang for HOOVER *UK, 1992*

vap *verb* when throwing dice, to snap your fingers *BARBADOS, 1965*

vap; vaps *noun* an impulse; a sudden urge *TRINIDAD AND TOBAGO, 1957*

vapour lock *noun* a temporary loss of common sense or memory. An allusion to a mechanical problem with the carburettor of an internal combustion engine *US, 1996*

vapourware *noun* in computing, a program that is announced well before it is completed and released *US, 1991*

varda d'amour *noun* the look of love. A combination of polari and French *UK, 1992*

varder; varda *noun* a look. Polari *UK, 1996*

vardo *noun* in gypsy or traveller use, a trailer, a wagon, a caravan *UK, 1934*

varicose alley *noun* the platform that extends from a stage used by strippers out into the audience *US, 1945*

varicose vein *noun* a baby; a child. Glasgow rhyming slang on Scottish dialect *wean* (pronounced 'wayne') *UK: SCOTLAND, 1996*

vark *noun* used as a term of abuse, especially applied to a police officer. A contemptuous term, from Afrikaans *vark* (pig) *SOUTH AFRICA, 1975*

varnish *noun* on the railways, a passenger train *US, 1946*

varnish *verb* ▶ **varnish the cane** (from the male perspective) to have sex *US, 1968*

vasso *noun* vaseline *AUSTRALIA, 1998*

VAT *noun* vodka and tonic. Initialism, punning on value added tax; made popular by 1980s television series *Minder UK, 1994*

Vatican roulette *noun* birth control by the rhythm method *US, 1979*

vato; bato *noun* a guy. Border Spanish used in English conversation by Mexican-Americans *US, 1950*

vato loco; bato loco *noun* a wild guy *US, 1965*

vault *noun* a hotel baggage checkroom *US, 1954*

va va voom *noun* style; a powerful or seductive style. Used as a song title by Cinerama 'Va Va Voom', 1998, and as an advertising strap line for Renault's Clio™ (2001+) *US, 1996*

VC *noun* the Viet Cong; a member of the Viet Cong *US, 1966* ▷ *see:* VICTORIA CROSS

V-card *noun* a person's virginity *US, 2001*

VCR *noun* a vicious campus rumour *US, 1966*

VD bonnet *noun* a condom. A reference to the prevention of venereal disease *US, 1972*

V-Dub; Vee-Dub *noun* a Volkswagen motor vehicle. Shortening of *vee double-u*, that is, Volkswagen *AUSTRALIA, 1970*

veal cutlet *noun* in gambling cheating schemes, a victim *US, 1962*

veal of the sea *noun* the green sea turtle *BAHAMAS, 1982*

veddy *adverb* very. A jocular pronunciation, approximating a child's, or an American's (attempting a 'British' accent), rendering of 'very' *UK, 1859*

vee *noun* sex involving three people, two of whom are focused on the pleasure of the third *US, 1995*

veeblefetzer *noun* a corporate manager. Not a term of endearment *US, 1997*

vee dub *noun* a completely depillated female pubis. Also as a verb and, thus, an adjectival participle. From a similarity in shape and finish to the bonnet of a Volkswagen Beetle *US, 2003*

veep *noun* a vice president *US, 1949* ▷ *see:* VIP

vee wee *noun* a Volkswagen motor vehicle *UK, 1984*

veg *noun* vegetables *UK, 1898*

Vegemite-driller *noun* a male homosexual *AUSTRALIA, 1985*

Vegemite valley *noun* the anus and rectal passage. Use is often suggestive of homosexual activity. Vegemite™ is a dark brown foodstuff *AUSTRALIA, 2003*

vegetable *noun* **1** a person who is mentally and physically incapacitated to a degree that renders the comparison with a plant organism fair if cruel *UK, 1921*. **2** a person with an inactive, undemanding lifestyle. A derogatory use arising from the semi-conventional medical sense above *UK, 2001*

vegetable garden *noun* a group of neurologically depressed hospital patients *US, 1978*

vegetation *noun* relaxation *US, 1986*

vegged out *adjective* relaxed and inactive *US, 2001*

veggie *noun* **1** a vegetable *US, 1955*. **2** a vegetarian. The variant spelling 'veggy' is also used *UK, 1975*

vegie *adjective* of school subjects, of the easiest grade *AUSTRALIA, 1992*

vego *noun* a vegetarian *AUSTRALIA, 1996*

vego *adjective* vegetarian *AUSTRALIA, 1988*

veg out *verb* to relax and do nothing *US, 1995*

veins *noun* ▶ **get veins** in bodybuilding, to achieve definition, or well-developed and sculpted muscles *US, 1984*

velcro *noun* a lesbian. Figurative use of Velcro™, from the French *velours croché* (hooked velvet), a branded material fastener *UK, 2000*

velvet *noun* **1** gambling winnings *US, 1974*. **2** a passenger train carriage *US, 1977*. ▶ **on velvet** in good shape *US, 1997*

velvet fog *nickname* singer Mel Tormé (1925–99) *US, 2000*

vendor *noun* a juke box *US, 1965*

vendor's *noun* a commercial bottled beer, even when obtained from a bootlegger *CANADA, 1999*

vengeance *noun* ▶ **with a vengeance** to a great degree, very much *UK, 1568*

vent *verb* to express frustrations in larger-than-life dimensions. What an earlier generation would have called 'let off some steam' *US, 1996*

vent; vent act *noun* a ventriloquist *UK, 1893*. ▶ **take it to the vent** to commit suicide *US, 1989*

ventilate *verb* to shoot someone. From the image of bullet holes ventilating the body *US, 1947*. ▶ **ventilate the block** in hot rodding and drag racing, to blow a rod out through the engine *US, 1960s*

ventilator *noun* a machine gun *US, 1962*

Vera Lynn; Vera *noun* **1** gin. Rhyming slang, based on the name of singer Vera Lynn (b.1917) known from World War 2 as 'the forces' sweetheart' *UK, 1952*. **2** a cigarette paper. Rhyming slang for SKIN (a cigarette paper) *UK, 1992*

verandah over the toy shop *noun* a paunch or beer-belly *AUSTRALIA, 1987*

vera vice; victoria vice; veras *noun* the police vice squad. A CAMP elaboration *UK, 1996*

verbal; verbals *noun* **1** a conversation, a talk *UK, 1997*. **2** a verbal statement given to the police, often self-incriminatory *UK, 1963*

verbal; verbal up *verb* to fake a confession of criminal guilt *UK, 1979*

verbal diarrhoea *noun* unwarranted verbosity *UK, 1823*

verballing *noun* the act of faking a criminal confession *UK, 1974*

vergla *noun* freezing rain. The word is borrowed, modified but pronounced fairly correctly, from the French *verglas*, which means the same thing *CANADA, 2002*

Veronica Lake *noun* steak. Rhyming slang, formed from the name of the US film actress, 1919–73 *UK, 1992*

verrrry in-ter-est-ing; very interesting, but stupid used as a humorous comment on a remark or event; used for humorously dismissing what has just been said. A signature line on *Rowan and Martin's Laugh-In* (NBC, 1968–73), uttered by Arte Johnson while playing a wacky Nazi soldier. Repeated with referential humour *US, 1969*

versatile *adjective* bisexual *UK, 2002*

versing *preposition* ▶ **be versing** to compete against. A corruption of the preposition 'versus', almost always heard in the progressive form *US, 1984*

versioning *noun* a technique in hip-hop music of blending different periods and styles of recorded music *US, 2000*

vert *noun* in skateboarding, an almost *vertical* ramp *UK, 2003*

vertical bacon sandwich *noun* the vagina. From the resemblance *UK, 2002*

vertical jockey *noun* an elevator operator *US, 1953*

very *adjective* excellent *US, 1989*

very *adverb* very much, absolutely *UK, 2002*

very à la *adjective* absolutely in fashion. Generally contemptuous, disparaging or ironic in tone *UK, 1984*

vest *noun* a show-off *US, 1965*

vestibules *noun* the testicles *UK, 2003*

vestige *noun* a brassiere. Recorded as a contemporary gay usage *UK, 2003*

vest out *verb* to retire from police service after vesting in the pension plan with 15 years of service. New York police slang *US, 1997*

vet *noun* **1** an ex-member of the military *US, 1848*. **2** a prison doctor *SOUTH AFRICA, 1974*

veterano *noun* an experienced, respected gang member. Spanish used by English-speakers *US, 1975*

veterinarian *noun* a physician who regards his patients as of animal intelligence *US, 1978*

Vette *noun* a Corvette car *US, 1994*

vex *verb* to engage someone in an abusive verbal attack *UK, 2001*

VG *adjective* very good. Abbreviation *UK, 1982*

V girl *noun* a woman who is attracted to men in military uniform *US,* *1960*

Viaggy *noun* a Viagra™ tablet *UK, 2002*

vibe *verb* to create and enjoy a good atmosphere *UK, 2001*

vibe; vibes *noun* the atmosphere generated by any event; mood; nuances intimately related to all senses. An abbreviation of 'vibration', which has the same meaning *US, 1960*

vibed up *adjective* excited; in the mood *UK, 1983*

vibe off *verb* to take inspiration from someone or something *UK, 1999*

vibe out *verb* to intimidate someone *UK, 1983*

vibes *noun* a vibraphone *UK, 1940*

vibey *adjective* fashionably atmospheric; in tune with the zeitgeist. From the 1990s; a positive sense of VIBE (the atmosphere of an event) *UK, 1999*

vibrations *noun* the atmosphere generated by any event; mood; nuances intimately related to all senses *US, 1966*

vibrator *noun* a motorcyle *US, 1962*

vic *noun* **1** a victim *US, 1968*. **2** a sucker or an easy target for crime *US, 1969*

Vic *nickname* Victoria, a southern state of Australia *AUSTRALIA, 1902*

Vicar of Bray *noun* **1** a tray. Rhyming slang, formed from a C18 song *UK, 1960*. **2** the number three; three. Rhyming slang for TREY *UK, 1960*

vice *noun* a police vice squad. Usually used with 'the' *UK, 1966*

vice president *noun* in poker, the player with the second best hand *US, 1988*

vice versa *noun* reciprocal oral sex between two lesbians. The earliest known lesbian periodical in the US (1947) was named *Vice Versa US, 1963*

vicey *adjective* sinful; depraved *TRINIDAD AND TOBAGO, 1993*

vicious *adjective* handsome *US, 1982*

vick *verb* to steal. Probably an evolution from 'victim' *US, 1993*

Vicky *noun* a Ford Victoria sedan, first built in the 1930s and then revived in the 1950s *US, 1965*

vicky; vick *noun* a two-fingered gesture that is used to insult or otherwise cause offence. Glasgow slang; the forefinger and the middle finger are extended to form a V shape, with the palm turned in towards the gesturer *UK· SCOTLAND, 1985*

vicky-verky vice-versa. Used as a song title by Squeeze, 1981 *UK, 1961*

Victor Charlie *nickname* the Viet Cong *US, 1966*

Victoria *noun* used of a person otherwise described as *nouveau riche*. After singer and footballer's wife Victoria Beckham (b.1975); recorded as a contemporary gay usage *UK, 2003*

Victoria Cross; VC *noun* something of little or no value. Rhyming slang for TOSS, formed from the highest military honour for valour *UK, 1992*

Victoria Monk *noun* semen. Rhyming slang for SPUNK, after the music hall singer, best remembered for 'Won't You Come Home, Bill Bailey?', Victoria Monks, 1884–1972 *UK, 1960*

Victory V *noun* **1** urine; an act of urination. Rhyming slang for PEE or WEE, formed from the Churchillian gesture or Victory V branded medicinal-confectionery *UK, 1998*. **2** a Triumph car. Citizens' band radio slang; 'victory' as a synonym for 'triumph' *UK, 1981*

vid *noun* **1** a video cassette, a video recording *UK, 2000*. **2** a music video *US, 1985*

video-nasty *noun* an exceptionally unpleasant horror film, available on video *UK, 1982*

vidrio *noun* heroin. The Spanish for GLASS (heroin) *UK, 2003*

Viet *noun* a Vietnamese person *US, 1966*

Vietnam rose *noun* any sexually transmitted infection *AUSTRALIA, 1988*

Viet shits *noun* diarrhoea *US, 1991*

vig *noun* **1** interest owed on an illegal loan. A shortened form of VIGORISH *US, 1990*. **2** profit. Freely adapted from VIGORISH (interest on a loan) *UK, 2001*

vigorish *noun* the interest owed on an illegal loan. Yiddish slang from the Russian *vyigrysh* (winnings-out-to-pay) *US, 1966*

vikes *noun* the prescription drug Vicodin™ *US, 1996*

Viking queen *noun* in homosexual usage, a muscular, blonde man *US, 1987*

vill *noun* a village or town. Found in the poetry of the early C18, but not particularly thereafter until the war in Vietnam *US, 1976*

village *noun* a notional community of racecourse bookmakers *UK, 1991*

Village *noun* ► **the Village** Greenwich Village, New York, a small neighbourhood below 14th Street and west of Broadway, haven to Bohemians *US, 1952*

village *adjective* unsophisticated, out of touch with trends *US, 2002*

village bike *noun* **1** a promiscuous woman. As with the TOWN BIKE, 'everyone has ridden her' *UK, 1995*. **2** a lesbian. Rhyming slang for DYKE *UK, 2003*

village pump *noun* a girl who is free and easy sexually *CANADA, 1992*

village ram *noun* a sexually aggressive male *TRINIDAD AND TOBAGO, 1964*

villain *noun* a professional criminal; someone with a criminal record *UK, 1945*

Ville *noun* ► **the Ville** Penton*ville* prison, London *UK, 1903*

-ville *suffix* used for making or emphasising an adjective; used in combination with a characteristic to describe a place or a condition. Modern usage began with the US beats and travelled back to the UK. By the mid-1970s the US form was presumed obsolete having been replaced by '-city'. It survives in the UK without obvious irony *US, 1891*

Vincent *nickname* the Viet Cong; a member of the Viet Cong *US, 1965*

Vincent Price; vincent *noun* ice. Rhyming slang, formed from the US actor, 1911–93, particularly famed for his roles in horror films *UK, 1992*

Vincent Van Gogh; vincent *noun* a cough. Rhyming slang, based on the predominant UK pronunciation of impressionist artist Vincent Van Gogh (1853–90) *UK, 2002*

vine *noun* **1** a men's suit; clothing *US, 1932*. **2** the penis *US, 1972*

vine down *verb* to dress up *US, 1969*

vinegar stroke; vinegar *noun* the final penile thrust culminating in ejaculation when copulating or masturbating. Alluding to the facial expression of the male. Also, in the plural, 'the final thrusts preceding ejaculation'. UK comedian Phill Jupitus, who uses this term to describe the closing moments of his act, explains: 'Just before a bloke comes he looks like you've popped a teaspoon of vinegar into his mouth' *AUSTRALIA, 1961*

viney bones *noun* rubber bands. Used by motorcyclists. Douglas Dunford, of the Beaulieu Motor Museum, gives the following etymology: 'Originated with the famous [motorcycle] trials rider Hugh Viney of the '30s who used to cut up old inner-tubes and supply his mates with bands to fix their riding numbers.' *UK, 1984*

Vinnies; St Vinnies *nickname* a St Vincent de Paul charity store *AUSTRALIA, 1970*

vino *noun* **1** wine, especially cheap wine. From Spanish and Italian *vino* (wine) *AUSTRALIA, 1919*. **2** a drinker of doctored cheap wine *UK, 1966*

vinyl *noun* used generically for musical recordings produced on such material *UK, 1976*

violet *noun* ► **come up smelling of violets** to emerge unscathed from a difficult or troublesome situation, used especially of someone who is consistently and remarkably lucky. Probably somewhat dated by the time it was recorded. The form survives as 'come up smelling of roses' *UK, 1981*

violin cases *noun* large, heavy shoes *US, 1946*

vip; veep *noun* a *v*ery *i*mportant *p*erson *US, 1945*

viper *noun* **1** a marijuana dealer *US, 1958*. **2** a marijuana user. A term of the 1930s with some lingering use until the 1960s *US, 1938*

viper's weed; viper's drag *noun* marijuana; a marijuana cigarette *US, 1938*

VIP massage *noun* a sexual service offered in some massage parlours, in which a hand-massage includes masturbation of the client *UK, 2003*

VIP services *noun* sexual intercourse, as distinct from masturbation, when advertised as a service offered by a prostitute *UK, 2003*

viral marketing *noun* word-of-mouth as a deliberate marketing tactic *US, 2000*

virgin *noun* **1** a person who has not contracted a sexually transmitted infection *US, 1947*. **2** a letter which has not been postmarked *US, 1977*

virgin *adjective* used of a green on a par-3 hole, untouched by any ball of a foursome *US, 2000*

virgin bride; virgin *noun* a ride, especially in the sense an act of sexual intercourse. Rhyming slang, now rare *AUSTRALIA, 1902*

virgin ears *noun* used, usually in the first person, for a claim of innocence in matters sexual *US, 1970*

Virgin for short – but not for long applied to girls named Virginia. Part-catchphrase, part-nickname; often irresistible, always hilarious *UK, 1984*

virginia *noun* the vagina *BAHAMAS, 1982*

Virginia vitamin *noun* any central nervous system stimulant *US, 1977*

virginity curtain *noun* a canvas screen secured to the underside of a warship's accommodation to preserve the modesty of those who go up and down the gangway from those who look up. Similar in purpose and design to a CUNT SCREEN *UK, 1969*

Virgin Mary *noun* a non-alcoholic version of the Bloody Mary, made with tomato juice, horseradish, Worcestershire and/or Tabasco sauce, celery, salt and black pepper; unadulterated tomato juice. A tasty pun, using 'virgin' as 'non-alcoholic' *US, 1993*

virgin pie *noun* cherry pie *US, 1952*

virgin principle *noun* the belief among gamblers that a beginner will have good luck *US, 1993*

virgin state *noun* the period when a person has started using an addictive drug but is not yet fully addicted *US, 1970*

virtual Friday *noun* the last day in a working week shortened by a holiday at the end of the week *US, 1991*

virus *noun* **1** HIV, the human immunodeficiency virus *US, 1992*. **2** in computing, a program that duplicates itself maliciously when it finds a host, often with a mechanism that enables it then to spread to new hosts *US, 1990*

visit *verb* ▶ **to visit Aunt Lillian** to experience the bleed period of the menstrual cycle *US, 1968*

visitations *noun* ▶ **the visitations** the bleed period of the menstrual cycle *US, 1999*

visit from the cardinal *noun* the bleed period of the menstrual cycle. Playing on the colour of a cardinal's robes *US, 2000*

visit from the French lady *noun* the bleed period of the menstrual cycle. Euphemism, credited to Stella Tilyard, *Aristocrats*, 1994 *US, 1994*

visiting card *noun* an act of defecation at the scene of the crime by the criminal *US, 1945*

visitor *noun* the bleed period of the menstrual cycle *US, 1949*

visuals *noun* hallucinations experienced under the influence of psychoactive mushrooms or peyote *US, 1992*

vitamin A *noun* LSD. From the common term ACID *US, 1997*

vitamin B *noun* beer *US, 1990*

vitamin C *noun* cocaine *US, 1984*

vitamin D *noun* dextromethorphan (DXM), an active ingredient in non-prescription cold and cough medication, often abused for non-medicinal purposes *US, 2003*

vitamin DB *noun* Dominion Breweries draught bitter *NEW ZEALAND, 1998*

vitamin E *noun* MDMA, the recreational drug best known as ecstasy. An elaboration of E *UK, 1998*

vitamin H *noun* haloperidol, a potent tranquillizer *US, 1989*

vitamin K; vit K *noun* ketamine hydrochloride, an anaesthetic used as a hallucinogen *US, 1989*

vitamin M *noun* Motrin™ *US, 1994*

vitamin N *noun* nicotine; a cigarette *US, 2004*

vitamin P *noun* **1** sex. 'P' is for PUSSY *US, 1989*. **2** the game of poker *US, 1996*

vitamin Q *noun* the recreational drug methaqualone, best known as Quaalude™ *US, 1982*

vitamins *noun* **1** drugs in tablet or capsule form *UK, 1996*. **2** any central nervous system stimulant *US, 1977*

vitamin T *noun* marijuana *US, 1997*

vitamin V *noun* valium *US, 1994*

vittles *noun* food. An American corruption of the C14 'victual' *US, 1946*

vizzo *noun* in prison, a visit *UK, 1996*

VJ; veejay *noun* a video jockey, a television presenter of music videos; a visual artist who mixes lights and images in a club environment. Initialism, on the model of DJ *US, 1982*

VO *noun* a beautiful woman. An abbreviation of 'visual orgasm' *US, 1997*

voce; votch; voche *noun* the voice, especially a singing voice; a singer. Theatrical, polari; from Italian *voce* *UK, 1989*

vod *noun* vodka *US, 1986*

vodders *noun* vodka *UK, 2002*

voddie; voddy *noun* vodka *UK, 1988*

vodka acid *noun* LSD *UK, 2003*

vogue *noun* **1** a posture that implies, or is part of, a fashion-style *US, 2003*. **2** a cigarette. Polari *UK, 1992*. **3** a wheel rim *US, 2001*

vogue *verb* **1** to engage in a style competition that values posturing *US, 1995*. **2** to light a cigarette. From VOGUE (a cigarette) *UK, 1993*

voice *verb* to telephone *US, 1991*

vol *noun* in prison, a *vol*unteer *UK, 1996*

volcano *noun* the bleed period of the menstrual cycle *CANADA, 2001*

Volks *noun* a *Volks*wagen car *US, 1964*

Volksie *noun* a Volkswagen car, especially the 'Beetle' *SOUTH AFRICA, 1962*

volley *noun* an abusive verbal attack *UK, 1996*

volley *verb* to hit someone. Tennis jargon, 'volley' (to strike a ball before it bounces) adopted for a less sporting use *UK, 1999*

volley dolly *noun* a woman attracted to male volleyball players *US, 1990*

volley off *verb* to engage in an abusive verbal attack *UK, 2001*

vom *verb* to vomit *CANADA, 1993*

vomatose *adjective* extremely disgusting *US, 1983*

vomit comet *noun* **1** any late-night public transport used by drunken passengers. From the probable outcome of movement and alcohol *UK, 2003*. **2** the modified KC-135A reduced-gravity aircraft. The aircraft flies parabolas in order to investigate the effects of zero gravity; passengers are often sick to their stomachs *US, 1999*

vomiting viper *noun* the penis *UK, 1984*

vonce *noun* **1** marijuana *US, 1960*. **2** the butt of a marijuana cigarette *US, 1965*

vonka *noun* the nose *UK, 2002*

Von Trapp *noun* excrement; nonsense, rubbish. Rhyming slang for CRAP, formed from the family whose story is told in *The Sound of Music* *UK, 2003*

vote *verb* to propose something that you want *UK, 1814*

voyou *noun* in Quebec, a hoodlum, or more specifically a striker who commits vandalism against the company. The French word here used in English carries the sense of 'outside the law' CANADA, 2002

VP *noun* a sex offender. An initialism of 'vulnerable prisoner' UK, 1996

VPL a visible panty line, the most heinous of fashion crimes. Popularised by Paul Simon in Woody Allen's *Annie Hall* US, 1967

VRB *noun* vodka and Red Bull™. Initialism for a popular cocktail (Red Bull is a brand name 'energy' drink) UK, 2001

vroom *verb* to leave noisily US, 1967

vrot *adjective* rotten; hence, drunk. From Afrikaans SOUTH AFRICA, 1910

VS *noun* an injection of drugs into a vein. Initialism of a 'vein SHOT' US, 1938

V-sign *noun* a gesture that is used to insult or otherwise cause offence, especially when made in conjunction with threatening or abusive language, e.g. 'fuck off!' or 'up yours!' with which the sign may be considered synonymous. The forefinger and the middle finger are extended to form a V shape, the palm turned in towards the gesturer; as an obscene gesture it is confined almost entirely to the UK. There is a legend that French archers, when captured by the British at the Battle of Agincourt (1415), had their middle and forefingers – those necessary to draw the bowstring – chopped off. The Welsh bowmen are said to have waggled their two fingers, taunting the French. The earliest written description of a v-sign as both threat and insult is French: '[Pangurge]

stretched out the forefinger, and middle finger or medical of his right hand, holding them asunder as much as he could, and thrusting them towards Thaumast' (François Rabelais, 1532). Further derivations abound: 1) Farmer and Henley's *Slang and its Analogues* (1890) suggests a representation of cuckold's horns, however this is traditionally made with the first and fourth fingers. 2) Symbolic of the phallus; the raised middle finger (FLIP THE BIRD) has been known since Roman times and, it is suggested, the v-sign enlarges the penis or doubles the quotient; or disguises the single finger insult. 3) The fingers represent themselves inserted in the vagina – though why this should be insulting is not explained. 4) Symbolic of female legs or labia spread wide; or represents the triangular shape of female pubic hair. 5) A corrupted victory sign – however the Churchillian symbol is first recorded in 1941, contrived by a Belgian Lawyer named Victor De Lavelaye. Probably more than one of the above, except 5, is the truth UK, 1948

V spot *noun* a five-dollar note US, 1949

Vulcan nerve pinch *noun* when operating a computer, the keyed-combination of the characters Ctrl-Alt-Delete used to restart the machine. A figurative application of a fictional technique used in the television science fiction series, *Star Trek* US, 2004

vulture *noun* in trucking, a police plane used for spotting speeders US, 1971

VW *noun* a variety of MDMA, the recreational drug best known as ecstasy, identified by VW embossed on the tablet UK, 2002

Ww

w *noun* a toilet. An abbreviation of the common WC *NEW ZEALAND, 1916*

W *noun* **1** a police *w*arrant for search or arrest *UK, 1956.* **2** in sports, a win *US, 1970*

wac; wack *noun* **1** phencyclidine, the recreational drug known as PCP or angel dust *US, 1981.* **2** marijuana mixed with phencyclidine, the recreational drug known as PCP or angel dust *UK, 1998*

wack *adjective* inferior, unacceptable, very bad *US, 1984*

wacked *adjective* **1** excited *US, 1959.* **2** beyond repair. Extends WACK (inferior) *UK, 1997*

wacked out *adjective* crazy, eccentric, mad *US, 1968*

wacked up *adjective* crazy, odd, irrational *US, 1947*

wackelass *noun* a cat that is a troublesome, clumsy creature *CANADA, 1999*

wacker; wack; whacker *noun* used as a term of address to a man. Liverpudlian *UK, 1768*

wacker *adjective* worse. From WACK (bad) *US, 1999*

wackie; wacky *noun* a stereotypical member of the working-class; a conformist. Teen slang *UK, 1982*

wack job; whack job *noun* a person who is mentally ill *US, 1979*

wacko; whacko *adjective* a person who is crazy, eccentric or mentally imbalanced *US, 1977*

wackoid *adjective* odd, eccentric *UK, 1999*

wacktic *adjective* very bad *UK, 1983*

wacky *adjective* odd, eccentric, crazy *US, 1935*

wacky baccy; wacky backy *noun* marijuana. From WACKY as 'eccentric'. Many variants exist, including 'whacky baccy/backy', 'whackatabachy', 'wacky tobaccy/tobacky' and 'whacky weed' *US, 1975*

wacky for khaki *adjective* infatuated with men in military uniform *US, 1967*

wac-wac *noun* phencyclidine, the recreational drug known as PCP or angel dust *US, 1995*

wad *noun* **1** the semen ejaculated at orgasm. From 'wad' (a large quantity) *US, 1969.* **2** expectorated sputum *US, 1989.* **3** a rag saturated with glue or any volatile solvent that is inhaled for the intoxicating effect *US, 1970.* **4** a sandwich; a bun; a cake *UK, 1919.* **5** a roll of money; a great deal of money *US, 1951*

wad *verb* (of a male) to reach orgasm. After WAD (semen) *UK, 2003*

wad cutter *noun* a flat-nosed bullet *US, 1962*

wadded *adjective* well-off, rich. From WAD (a great deal of money) *UK, 2002*

waddy *noun* a club; a hefty piece of wood suitable for a club. From the name of an Australian Aboriginal weapon in the extinct language Dharug, Sydney region *AUSTRALIA, 1809*

waders *noun* shoes *US, 1945*

wadge *noun* ▷*see:* WODGE

wafer *noun* **1** a tablet of MDMA, the recreational drug best known as ecstasy. If dance is seen as a new religion, then MDMA is as important a part of the ritual as the wafer is in conventional church rites *UK, 2003.* **2** a cigarette paper *UK, 1996*

waffle *noun* **1** nonsense; incessant or unfocused talk *UK, 1900.* **2** in trucking, a non-skid tyre *US, 1971*

Waffle *noun* a movement in Canada's New Democratic Party to change somewhat its left-wing policies *CANADA, 2001*

waffle *verb* **1** to vacillate; to take both sides of an issue *UK, 1803.* **2** to talk nonsense; to talk incessantly or in an unfocused way *UK, 1937*

waffy *adjective* comfortable. Hip-hop, urban slang. A compound of 'warm' and 'fluffy' noted in connection with a legal dispute over rap lyrics by *BBC News*, 6th June 2003 *US, 2003*

wag *noun* a social outcast, especially a non-surfer *US, 1991*

WAG *noun* **1** the female partner of a footballer, especially an England team player. WAGs, the acronym for *w*ives *a*nd *g*irlfriends, was applied to the players' partners during the 2006 World Cup. The collective usage was soon individualised *UK, 2006.* **2** Welsh Assembly Government. Initialism *UK: WALES, 1999*

wag *verb* to play truant *UK, 1848.* ▶ **wag wienie; wag your wienie** to commit indecent exposure of the male masturbatory variety *US, 1984*

wage slave *noun* anyone reliant on the income generated by regular employment *UK, 1964*

waggle *verb* in pool, to make practice shots before actually hitting the cue ball *US, 1993*

wagon *noun* **1** a woman, especially a pushy one, or one capable of invective *IRELAND, 2003.* **2** abstention from drug use. Extending previous sense *UK, 1997.* **3** an old, worn-out, beat-up car *US, 1959.* ▶ **on the wagon** abstaining from drinking alcohol *US, 1906*

wagon burner *noun* a native American Indian. Offensive *US, 1995*

wagon-chasing *adjective* used of a lawyer, unscrupulous, inclined to solicit business from those in trouble with the law *US, 1953*

wagons ho! used as a humorous signal that a venture is about to begin. From cowboy films *US, 1994*

wagon-spotter *noun* a trainspotter who specialises in 'collecting' freight wagons *UK, 2003*

wagwon? 'what's going on?'. Either directly from, or in imitation of, West Indian speech *UK, 2003*

wahey! used for registering a feeling of exuberance *UK, 2003*

wahini *noun* a female surfer. From the Hawaiian *US, 1963*

wail *verb* **1** in jazz, to perform with great feeling *US, 1955.* **2** in pinball, to score a large number of points in a short period of time *US, 1977.* ▶ **wail down the place** to dance with enthusiasm that borders on vulgarity *TRINIDAD AND TOBAGO, 1990*

wailer *noun* in drag racing, a very fast car *US, 1970*

wailing *adjective* exciting *US, 1965*

Waiouru blonde *noun* a Maori woman. Waiouru is a remote North Island military base *NEW ZEALAND, 1997*

waist *noun* ▶ **make waist** to make pelvic thrusts and gyrations during sex *TRINIDAD AND TOBAGO, 2003*

wait-a-minute vine; wait-a-minute bush *noun* a heavy, thorny vine found in the jungles of Vietnam. When it snagged you, you had to wait a minute to disentangle yourself *US, 1976*

wait and linger *noun* the finger. Rhyming slang, applied only in an anatomical sense *UK, 1992*

waiter's delight *noun* in poker, a hand consisting of three threes and a pair. A 'three' is a TREY, the hand is conventionally known as a 'full house', hence 'treys full', the waiter pun *US, 1988*

waiting room *noun* in surfing, the area beyond the breakers where surfers wait to catch waves *ISRAEL, 1977*

wait up! 'wait for me!' *US, 1944*

wake; wake up *verb* to become aware of something *AUSTRALIA, 1910*

'wake; wake up' *verb* ▶ **wake your ideas up** to concentrate; to use your wits. Often as an imperative *UK, 1961.* ▶ **wouldn't wake if...** to be generally unaware of what's what *AUSTRALIA, 1961*

wake and bake; wake-n-bake *verb* to smoke marijuana as one of the first acts of the day *US, 1997*

waker-upper *noun* a heroin addict's first injection of the morning *US, 1982*

wake-up *noun* **1** the day's first dose of a drug taken by an addict *US, 1954*. **2** any amphetamine or central nervous system stimulant *US, 1972*. **3** a short time remaining on a jail sentence or term of military service, especially the last morning *US, 1950*

wake up *verb* **1** to make someone aware; to inform someone *AUSTRALIA, 1859*. **2** to become aware that you are being swindled *US, 1969*. **3** in horse racing, to stimulate a horse illegally by electric shock or drugs *US, 1947*

wake-up *adjective* used of an addictive substance taken upon waking up *US, 1981*

wake-up pill *noun* an amphetamine or other central nervous system stimulant *US, 1979*

wake you *verb* to make you aware of something *US, 1953*

wakey-wakey *noun* a wake-up call. Adapted from the exclamation, 'wakey, wakey!' *UK, 2001*

wakey, wakey! 'wake up!'. Probably of military origin; widespread once adopted as the catchphrase of bandleader Billy Cotton (1899–1969) in his 1949–68 BBC radio Sunday lunchtime variety programme, *The Billy Cotton Bandshow UK, 1959*

wakey, wakey, eggs and bakey! used for calling someone from sleep to breakfast. Used with great comic effect by Quentin Tarantino in *Kill Bill Volume 2* (2004) as Bill's brother Budd awakens The Bride to bury her alive *US, 2000*

wakey, wakey, hands off snakie! used for humorously waking up a male *AUSTRALIA, 1985*

Waldorf-Astoria *noun* an especially spartan solitary confinement cell *US, 1976*

walk *noun* **1** a release from jail *US, 1965*. **2** during the Vietnam war, a 30-day patrol in which contact with the enemy is expected *US, 1991*

walk *verb* **1** to win something easily *UK, 1903*. **2** to escape unpunished *US, 1979*. **3** to quit a job or commitment *US, 1999*. **4** (of objects) to disappear, presumed borrowed or stolen *UK, 1898*. **5** to move a boat sideways *US, 1989*. **6** (used of a military aviator) to suit up for battle. From the vocabulary of fighter pilots *US, 2001*. ► **walk a cat back** to trace a missile back to its launch site. Gulf war usage *US, 1991*. ► **walk back the cat** to reconstruct events in order to understand what went wrong *US, 1997*. ► **walk in tall corn** to make a great deal of money *US, 1997*. ► **walk out on** to abandon someone or something. Of theatrical origin *UK, 1937*. ► **walk the dog 1** while surfing, to move frontwards and backwards on the surfboard to affect its speed *US, 1987*. **2** on the railways, to operate a freight train at such a high speed that the wagons sway *US, 1977*. ► **walk the nose** while surfing, to advance to the front of the board *US, 1962*. ► **walk the plank** to move forward on a surfboard, increasing the speed of the ride *AUSTRALIA, 1963*. ► **walk the twelve steps** to go to court *CAYMAN ISLANDS, 1985*. ► **walk the walk of the trollop** to convey sexuality while walking. Another catchphrase from the 'Wayne's World' sketch on *Saturday Night Live US, 1991*. ► **walk the walk; walk the walk and talk the talk** to be (or behave as if) totally familiar with, and a part of, a given circumstance *UK, 2004*. ► **walk the yard** to methodically walk in a prison open space *US, 1981*. ► **walk with your Lucy** to inject a drug *US, 1981*. ► **walk your dog** to use the toilet *US, 1968*

walkabout; walk-about *noun* a journey on foot taken by an Aboriginal, especially when withdrawing from white society for a period *AUSTRALIA, 1910*. ► **go walkabout 1** (of an aboriginal) to go on a walkabout *AUSTRALIA, 1927*. **2** (of a person) to go off somewhere else *AUSTRALIA, 1969*. **3** (of an important person) to make an informal tour on foot. Variants include 'do a walkabout' *UK, 1984*

walkaway *noun* **1** a type of theft in which the thief walks away with a suitcase in a public place, leaving behind his suitcase as an alibi if apprehended *US, 1954*. **2** the final step in a confidence swindle, in which the swindlers walk away with the victim's money *US, 1981*

walk-back *noun* an apartment in the rear of a building *US, 1970*

walkboards *noun* a platform outside a carnival show or attraction *US, 1966*

walk-buddy *noun* in prison, a close friend and steady companion *US, 1976*

walker *noun* **1** a prisoner who constantly paces in his cell *US, 1984*. **2** a striptease dancer who disrobes while walking *US, 1981*. **3** in dominoes, the highest piece of its suit that is not a double and has been played *US, 1964*

walkers *noun* the legs *US, 1992*

walkie *noun* a close and dependable friend. A term that suggests 'talkie', which in turn suggests friendship *US, 1991*

walkies *noun* a walk with a small child or a dog. A childish or jocular term addressed to, and understood by, that child or dog *US, 1923*

walkie-talkie *noun* **1** an able-bodied person (from the perspective of a disabled person) *UK, 2003*. **2** a portable two-way radio *US, 1939*. **3** a prisoner who associates with guards *US, 1992*

walk-in *noun* a thief who steals from unlocked hotel rooms *US, 1954*

walking *adjective* used of an order for food at a restaurant, to be taken from the restaurant *US, 1952*

walking crab *noun* in electric line work, a lever lift *US, 1980*

walking disaster area *noun* an especially inept or accident-prone person *UK, 1984*

walking man's special *noun* in the used car business, a run-down car that is not much to look at but still runs, in a fashion *US, 1993*

walking money *noun* in gambling, a small amount of money given by the house or other players to someone who has just lost all of his money *US, 1961*

walking tree *noun* in a criminal enterprise, a watchman or lookout *US, 1956*

walking writer *noun* in an illegal numbers gambling lottery, a person who collects and records bets *US, 1949*

walk in the park *noun* an easy thing to do *UK, 1998*

walk in the sun *noun* a combat march without a significant chance of engaging the enemy *US, 1991*

walk of fame *noun* the walk home or to work after spending the night with a beautiful and popular woman *US, 2001*

walk of shame *noun* the walk home or to work after spending the night with a date, still wearing yesterday's clothes *US, 2002*

walk-on *noun* in sports, an athlete who gets chosen for a team having appeared at practice unsolicited and unexpected *US, 1978*

walkover *noun* in horse racing, a race in which all but one of the entries are withdrawn. The lone horse starting the race can win the purse simply by walking the distance of the race *US, 1965*

walk-up *noun* a brothel *US, 1950*

wall *noun* ► **behind the wall** imprisoned *US, 1989*. ► **go over the wall** to escape from prison *US, 1934*. ► **go to the wall** to lose money in stock investments *US, 1988*. ► **off the wall** in auction fraud, where non-existent bids are said to come from *UK, 2003*. ► **the wall** a maximum security prison *US, 2002*. ► **up the wall** crazy; crazed by circumstances; angry *UK, 1951*

wall *verb* to lean against the wall at a party or other social gathering *US, 1997*

wallaby *noun* ► **on the wallaby** wandering around. Originally 'Tramping the outback in search of work (as though following the track made by wallabies)', G.A. Wilkes, *A Dictionary of Australian Colloquialisms*, 1978 *AUSTRALIA, 1861*

Wallace and Gromit; wallace *verb* to vomit. Rhyming slang, based on Oscar-winning (1990) animated characters *UK, 1998*

Wallace Beery; wallace *noun* in a betting shop, a dispute over the sum due. Rhyming slang for 'query', formed from the name of the US film actor (1885–1949) *UK, 1998*

wallah; walla *noun* **1** a man identified by relation to the activity, occupation or philosophy to which it is properly affixed. Adopted directly by Anglo-Indians, hence military, from Hindu *wālā* ('a person connected in some way with the thing expressed in the first word', George Clifford Whitworth, *An Anglo-Indian Dictionary*, 1885) *INDIA, 1785*. **2** in the television and film industries, indistinguishable background voices *US, 1990*

wallbanger *noun* a person whose impairment with central nervous system depressants has produced a marked lack of coordination *US, 1977*

wallet *noun* **1** a person who finances a (criminal) project *UK, 2003*. **2** a generous person *US, 1997*

wallet lane *noun* the passing lane of a motorway. Trucker use, with a reference to a 'wallet' because of the likelihood of having to pay a ticket if caught using the passing lane *US, 1977*

walleyed *adjective* drunk *US, 1992*

wallflower week *noun* the bleed period of the menstrual cycle *US, 1954*

wallie *noun* in skateboarding, any jumping manoeuvre performed from a wall. A combination of 'wall' and OLLY; OLLIE (a jumping manoeuvre) *UK, 2004* ▷*see:* WALLY

wallies *noun* nothing, zero *UK, 2000*

wallin' *noun* the act or habit of sitting or standing against a wall at a party. Teen slang *UK, 2003*

wall job *noun* sex with one of the participants standing against a wall *US, 2001*

wallop *noun* **1** a heavy blow *UK, 1823*. **2** an attempt, a go. A pun on BASH (a try) *UK, 2001*. **3** the strength to deliver a heavy blow. Boxing slang *UK, 1914*. **4** beer *UK, 1933*

wallop *verb* **1** to hit someone *UK, 1825*. **2** to get the better of someone. A figurative application of the previous sense *UK, 1865*. **3** to dance *UK, 1992*

walloped *adjective* drunk or drug-intoxicated *UK, 2002*

walloper *noun* **1** the penis *UK: SCOTLAND, 2002*. **2** a male who masturbates to excess *NEW ZEALAND, 1998*. **3** a police officer *AUSTRALIA, 1945*. **4** a dancer, especially a professional dancer. Theatrical slang *UK, 1937*

wallopies *noun* large female breasts *US, 1975*

walloping *noun* a beating, a thrashing; a win by a more than convincing margin *UK, 1871*

walloping *adjective* large, great *UK, 1847*

wallops *noun* choreography. From WALLOP (to dance) *UK, 1992*

wallpaper *noun* **1** a background pattern or photograph for a computer display screen *US, 1991*. **2** counterfeit money *US, 1949*. **3** a postcard acknowledging receipt of a citizens' band or ham radio message *US, 1976*

wall-stretcher *noun* an imaginary tool for which a building trades apprentice may be sent to fetch *UK, 1961*

wall ticket *noun* in Keno, a big win. Casinos often post large winning tickets on the wall of the Keno lounge as an enticement to bettors *US, 1987*

wall time *noun* the time as shown on wall clocks, as contrasted with GMT or another common time used on computers *ANTARCTICA, 1991*

wall-to-wall *adjective* abundant; appearing everywhere. From wall-to-wall carpets that cover the entire floor *UK, 1967*

wall-to-waller *noun* a pornographic film shot in one day on a very low budget *US, 2000*

Wally ▶ **call it Wally** to agree that a matter is settled *GUYANA, 1962*

wally; wallie; wolly *noun* **1** an unfashionable individual; someone who is innocent, or foolish; a fool. Possibly originates in the name Wally, however Scottish dialect *wally-draigle* (a feeble, ill-grown person) may well have had an influence *UK, 1969*. **2** in CID slang, a uniformed police officer, especially a constable; more generally, a trainee or an incompetent police officer. 'Woolly' is also recorded by the *Oxford English Dictionary* in 1965 *UK, 1970*

wallyo; wal-yo *noun* a young man, usually an Italian-American *US, 1975*

Wally Pipp *noun* any athlete who misses a game and is thereafter replaced by a better player. On 1st June, 1925, the New York Yankees first baseman Wally Pipp did not play because he was sick; his place was taken by Lou Gehrig, who played for the next 2130 games *US, 1967*

walnut storage disease *noun* any unspecified mental problem. A play on NUTTY (crazy) *US, 1983*

walnut whip; walnut *noun* **1** sleep. Rhyming slang for KIP, formed on a chocolate confection *UK, 1998*. **2** a vasectomy. Rhyming slang for THE SNIP *UK, 2002*

Walter Mitty *noun* **1** a person who poses as a heroic ex-soldier. From Walter Mitty, the title character of James Thurber's short story *The Secret Life of Walter Mitty* (1939) and successful film of the same title starring Danny Kaye (1947) *AUSTRALIA, 2002*. **2** the female breast. Rhyming slang for TITTY. The short form 'walter' can also be used *UK, 2003*

Walts *noun* 14 Int (an undercover intelligence unit of the British Army). Abbreviated from Walter Mitty, the name of a character, created in 1941 by James Thurber, who has become a cultural reference for a person who leads a dual existence *UK, 1995*

waltz *noun* intense warfare, be it a fire fight or hand-to-hand combat *US, 1991*

waltz *verb* to move in a nonchalant manner *US, 1887*. ▶ **waltz matilda** to travel as a swagman. From 'Matilda' (a swag) and 'waltz' (to lead in a waltz), here punning on the female name. Now of course obsolete, except in the well-known Australian song. Most singers are entirely unaware of the literal meaning of the phrase *AUSTRALIA, 1893*

waltz off *verb* to leave in a nonchalant or cavalier manner *US, 1989*

wamper *noun* a sandal made with pieces of tyre and tied with thatch string *CAYMAN ISLANDS, 1985*

wampum *noun* money. An imitation of Native American Indian language *US, 1950*

wampy *adjective* crazy *NEW ZEALAND, 1950*

wand *noun* **1** the penis. The magic stick that you wave in your hand *UK, 2001*. **2** in pool, a player's cue stick *US, 1993*

wandering hands brigade *noun* a male's hands exploring a female's body *NEW ZEALAND, 1984*

wandwaver *noun* a male exhibitionist *US, 1980*

wang; whang *noun* the penis *US, 1935*

wangbar *noun* an electric guitar's tremolo arm *US, 1980*

wanger *noun* ▷*see:* WHANGER

wangle *noun* a swindle; a convenient arrangement. The successful outcome of the verb WANGLE *UK, 1915*

wangle *verb* to arrange something to suit yourself; to contrive or obtain something with sly cunning; to manipulate something. Widely used, especially in the military, as 'wangle a job', 'wangling leave (of absence)', etc *UK, 1888*

wang-wang *noun* the penis *US, 1980*

wank *noun* **1** an act of masturbation; hence, an act of self-indulgence. An earlier spelling 'whank' has given way to 'wank' *UK, 1948*. **2** a waste of time *UK, 1998*. **3** a fool; a despicable person *UK, 2002*. **4** nonsense; rubbish. As in the expression 'that's a load of old wank' and the exclamation (current in the armed services, especially army, 1960–70s) 'wank! wank!' (pronounced almost as if quacked) greeting any announcement or declaration considered to be rubbish *UK, 1979*

wank *verb* **1** to masturbate. The Scots dialect word *whank* (to beat) was the usual spelling until the 1970s. Also used with 'off' *UK, 1950*. **2** to party with zeal and a lack of inhibition *CANADA, 1993*

wank *adjective* of poor quality; pathetic; self-indulgent *UK, 2002*

wank about; wank around *verb* to waste time *UK, 2001*

wank-bank *noun* a personal collection of inspirational erotic images. Formed on WANK (an act of masturbation) *UK, 2003*

wanked-out *adjective* drained of life *UK, 2000*

wanker *noun* **1** a masturbator. The earlier spelling 'whanker' has given way to 'wanker' *UK, 1978*. **2** a despicable person; an all-purpose form of abuse. From the sense as 'a masturbator'; some commentators suggest late C19 dialect *wanker* (a simpleton) *UK, 1972*

wankered *adjective* drunk or drug-intoxicated, *2001*

wanker's doom *noun* the mythological disease that is the inevitable result of excessive masturbation *US, 1977*

wanker tank *noun* a large 4WD vehicle that never gets used for off-road driving *AUSTRALIA, 2003*

wanking-spanner *noun* the hand. A masturbatory tool that loosens nuts *UK, 1961*

wank mag *noun* a pornographic magazine. Combines WANK (to masturbate) with MAG (a magazine) *UK, 1998*

wank-off *adjective* self-indulgent. A figurative application for 'an act of masturbation' *UK, 2000*

wank-pit; wanking-pit *noun* a man's (unshared) bed. Military slang, formed on WANK (masturbation) *UK, 1961*

wank shaft *noun* **1** the vagina *UK, 2001*. **2** the penis; also used as a term of abuse. Formed on the word WANK (masturbation) *UK, 2003*

wank sock *noun* an item of (men's) footwear used to contain the penis during masturbation *UK, 2003*

wanksta *noun* someone, especially a white person, who postures as a gangsta rapper. A derisory play on WANKER (a despised person) *US, 2002*

wank-stain *noun* a contemptible person *UK, 1997*

wank tanks *noun* the testicles. Celebrating the testicles as no more than a source of semen for masturbation *UK, 2002*

wank trade *noun* the pornography industry *US, 1997*

wankware *noun* software on compact disc intended for sexual stimulation *CANADA, 1995*

wanky *adjective* **1** of poor quality; pathetic. Original printer's use cognisant with WONKY; survives into a modern use which presumes WANK as the inspiration *UK, 1890*. **2** pretentious *AUSTRALIA, 1979*

wannabe *noun* someone who wants to be and pretends to be that which he is not. Deemed potentially offensive by Multicultural Management Program Fellows, *Dictionary of Cautionary Words and Phrases*, 1989 *US, 1980*

wanna-bet shirt *noun* in a rowing competition, a team's shirt which is the object of a wager between competing teams, where the winner claims the opposing team's shirts which are worn as a badge of victory *US, 2001*

Wanno *nickname* Wandsworth Prison *UK, 2004*

wan singer, wan song ▷*see:* ONE SINGER, ONE SONG

want *noun* a notification that a person is wanted by the police *US, 1958*

want *verb* ▶ **want in** to wish to enter; to desire to be a part of something. Originally a colloquial term in Scotland, Northern Ireland and the US *UK, 1836*. ▶ **want out** to wish to exit; to desire a complete change of circumstances *UK: SCOTLAND, 1870*

wap *noun* ▷*see:* WASP

wappy *adjective* idealistic, sentimental. Perhaps as a blend of WET (weak, lacking in effectiveness) and SOPPY (foolishly sentimental, naive) *UK, 1959*

war *noun* ▶ **go to war** to fight *US, 2002*

war and strife *noun* a wife. Rhyming slang; a less-used variation of TROUBLE AND STRIFE *UK, 1931*

warb *noun* a decrepit, unclean or otherwise disgusting person. Perhaps from 'warble' (a type of maggot) *AUSTRALIA, 1933*

warby *adjective* decrepit; unkempt; filthy; disgusting *AUSTRALIA, 1923*

warchalk *verb* to chalk icons on walls, etc, to indicate an area where a wireless Internet connection may be made for free. Derived as a back-formation from WARCHALKING *UK, 2002*

warchalker *noun* a computer user who chalks icons on walls, etc, to indicate to other computer users an area where a wireless Internet connection may be made for free *UK, 2002*

warchalking *noun* the practice of chalking icons on walls, etc, to indicate an area where a wireless Internet connection may be made for free. Coined in June 2002 by Matt Jones, a London-based 'information architect', as a play on 'wardialing' (a computer-directed assault by telephone). 'Warchalking' is based on the system of symbols used by UK tramps and beggars, first recorded in 1849, and developed by US hobos during the Depression. The three basic symbols are

✗ (open node), ◯ (closed node) and ⓦ (wep [wired equivalent privacy] node) *UK, 2002*

warden *noun* **1** a parent *US, 1968*. **2** a spouse. Usually a spouse of the female persuasion as perceived by the spouse of the male persuasion *US, 1976*. **3** a school principal *US, 1954*. **4** a teacher. Teen slang *US, 1951*. **5** on the railways, the supervisor of a track crew *US, 1977*

war department *noun* someone's wife or girlfriend *US, 1984*

war dialer *noun* a computer program that dials a given range of telephone connections in order to hack into computer or telecommunications systems *US, 1989*

warehoused *adjective* used of a prisoner who is neither educated nor trained during a period of imprisonment but simply contained *UK, 1996*

warez *noun* pirated computer software offered over the Internet. A deliberate respelling of 'wares' *UK, 2003*

warhead *noun* in cricket, a fast bowler *UK, 1996*

warlord *noun* a high-level member of a political organisation *US, 1991*

warm *noun* an act of warming; an act of becoming warm. Colloquial *UK, 1768*

warm *adjective* good *UK, 1996*

warm for someone's form *adjective* sexually attracted to someone *US, 1964*

warm fuzzies *noun* the feeling when praised by a superior *US, 1986*

warm one *noun* a bullet *US, 1998*

warmup *noun* a loose-fitting, athletic warmup suit *US, 1999*

warm up *verb* to refill a cup of coffee *US, 1996*

warn't *verb* was not; were not *US, 1970*

warp *noun* a bent card used by a card cheat to identify the value of the card *US, 1996*

war paint *noun* makeup, cosmetics. Originally theatrical *US, 1869*

warped *adjective* **1** perverted *US, 1993*. **2** drug-intoxicated *US, 1979*. **3** drunk *UK, 2002*

warp one *noun* a high speed. Figurative US naval aviator usage *US, 1986*

warp seven *adverb* very quickly *US, 1992*

warrior *noun* a fearless, violent member of a youth gang *US, 1995*

warrior bold *noun* a cold *UK, 1961*

wars *noun* ▶ **have been in the wars** to show signs of injury. especially the trivial wounds that afflict children *UK, 1850*

warthog *noun* a US Air Force attack plane formally known as an A-10 Thunderbolt. Gulf war usage *US, 1991*

warts and all with all blemishes or imperfections unconcealed *UK, 1930*

war wagon *noun* a vehicle carrying weapons on a motorcycle gang outing when trouble is expected *US, 1992*

Warwick Farm; warwick *noun* the arm. Rhyming slang, after the name of a racecourse in Sydney *AUSTRALIA, 1944*

war zone *noun* an area in Washington D.C. infamous for drug sales and other crime *US, 1984*

wash *noun* **1** crack cocaine. A shortened form of 'readywash'. To manufacture crack cocaine, hydrachloride is *washed* in a solution of baking soda and water *UK, 1996*. **2** the effect of a drug *US, 1974*. **3** a large number of things or people *BARBADOS, 1965*. ▶ **the wash** theft of money in public lavatories while the owner is washing *UK, 1977*

wash *verb* **1** to kill *US, 1941*. **2** to purge or expunge something *US, 1983*. **3** to give money obtained illegally the appearance of legitimacy through accounting and banking schemes *US, 1997*. **4** to shuffle a deck of cards *US, 1965*. **5** to receive favourable consideration *US, 1986*. **6** to be credible *UK, 1849*. ▶ **not a child in the house washed** nothing done, no progress made *IRELAND, 1996*. ▶ **wash mouth** to criticise someone or something without concern for the consequences *TRINIDAD AND TOBAGO, 1986*. ▶ **wash your face** when selling a lot by auction, to break even *UK, 2004*. ▶ **wash your mouth out; wash out your mouth** addressed to someone using *filthy* language or *dirty* words. Often as an imperative, and occasionally elaborated with 'soap', or 'soap and water' *UK, 1961*

wash away *verb* to kill someone *US, 1941*

washboard *noun* in mountain biking, an area of hard, rippled earth *US, 1996*

washboard *adjective* of an abdomen, trim, muscular, defined. From the appearance – solid and rippled *US, 1992*

washdown *noun* beer. Especially in the context of drinking after a session of drinking the tranquillizing herbal beverage kava *FIJI, 1991*

washed-up *adjective* no longer successful, finished *US, 1923*

washer *noun* ▶ **put a washer on** to urinate. A Lancashire term *UK, 1967*

washer-dryer *noun* a douche bag and towel *US, 1980*

wash-foot-and-come *noun* a noisy, rowdy party *ANTIGUA AND BARBUDA, 1998*

washicongs *noun* trainers, sneakers *TRINIDAD AND TOBAGO, 1992*

washing machine *noun* **1** in computing, an obsolete large hard disk found in a large floor cabinet *US, 1991*. **2** a wave as it breaks over and thrashes a surfer *US, 1991*

Washington *noun* a one-dollar note. From the portrait of George Washington on the note *US, 1959*

Washington Monument *noun* in poker, a hand with three fives. A rather esoteric allusion to the fact that the Washington Monument is 555 feet high *US, 1988*

washout *noun* **1** a failure (a thing or a person); a disappointment; a cancellation *UK, 1902*. **2** in motorcyle racing, the condition that occurs when the front wheel begins to slide in soft dirt; also used in mountain biking *US, 1973*

wash out *verb* **1** to fail and expel someone from a course or training *US, 1970*. **2** in motor racing, to suffer a loss or decrease in steering responsiveness *US, 1980*. **3** in mountain-biking, to lose front-wheel traction *US, 1996*. **4** to process cocaine into crack cocaine *UK, 1996*

wash-pot *noun* something or someone easily obtained *TRINIDAD AND TOBAGO, 1971*

wash rock *noun* crack cocaine. Combines two separate terms for CRACK *UK, 1997*

wash-up *noun* a post-event analytical discussion. Originally Royal Navy, then the wider military, and from there into corporate and political jargon *UK, 1965*

wash up *verb* in heterosexual intercourse, to enter the vagina from behind *UK, 2001*

washwoman's gig *noun* in an illegal numbers gambling lottery, a bet on 4, 11 and 44 *US, 1949*

washy *adjective* used of a racehorse sweating, especially with anxiety *US, 1976*

wasp; wap *noun* **1** a white Anglo-Saxon Protestant. The term is applied to whites without particular regard to the religious component *US, 1957*. **2** a white *Appalachian southern Protestant US, 1981*. **3** a traffic warden. From the yellow band on the uniform hat and sleeves (no doubt influenced by a characteristic intent to 'sting' a harmless motorist) *UK, 1966*

waspishness *noun* the state of being distinctly white, Anglo-Saxon and Protestant *US, 1957*

WASS *verb* ▷*see:* WAZ

wassock; wazzock; wazzuck *noun* a fool; an annoying or stupid individual *UK, 1983*

wassup?; whas up?; wassuuup? used as a greeting. A slurred 'what's up?' with dozens of variant spellings. Wildly popular pop speak in the US (and, to a degree, UK) in 2000 in response to a series of television advertisements for Budweiser™ beer *US, 1990*

wassy *adjective* ostentatious, especially in a sexually provocative way *TRINIDAD AND TOBAGO, 1987*

waste *verb* **1** to kill someone *US, 1964*. **2** to smoke marijuana *US, 1967*. **3** (used of a jockey in horse racing) to lose weight *AUSTRALIA, 1989*. ▶ **waste babies** (of a male) to masturbate *US, 2001*. ▶ **waste groceries** to vomit *US, 1987*

wastebasket *noun* in pool, a pocket that seems receptive to balls dropping *US, 1993*

waste-case *noun* a drunkard *US, 1987*

wasted *adjective* **1** drunk or drug-intoxicated *US, 1964*. **2** absolutely exhausted. From earlier uses as 'intoxicated' *UK, 1995*

Waste Island *nickname* the West Island of Montreal. Likely nicknamed with this derogatory term by teenagers, the West Island area of the city is heavily residential and suburban, meaning that under-age citizens have to be transported around by their parents or use the bus, and by contrast with central Montreal, it is boring *CANADA, 2002*

waster *noun* a lazy, unambitious person *IRELAND, 1991*

waste-time *adjective* dull, boring, uninteresting. Hawaiian youth usage *US, 1972*

wastoid *noun* a worthless, dim-witted person; a person whose drug or alcohol use is ruining their life *US, 1985*

wastry *noun* rubbish (trash) *JAMAICA, 2003*

watch *verb* ▶ **watch your lip; watch your mouth; watch your trap** to talk politely; to mind your manners; to not speak out of turn. Often exclamatory *UK, 1997*. ▶ **watch your step** to be careful; to be cautious in a current or planned activity. Often as a warning *UK, 1959*

Watcha ▷*see:* WOTCHER

watch and chain; watch *noun* the brain. Rhyming slang *UK, 1992*

watchie *noun* a watchman *UK: SCOTLAND, 1996*

watch it *verb* used as a (sometimes threatening) warning to be careful. Always imperative, often exclamatory *UK, 1916*

watch queen *noun* **1** a homosexual man who derives sexual pleasure from watching other men having sex *US, 1970*. **2** a lookout during anonymous homosexual sex in public places *US, 1975*

watch this space used as an announcement that further developments may be expected. Originally, and still, used of space in a newspaper, etc *UK, 1917*

watch works *noun* the brain. Teen slang, reported by a Toronto newspaper in 1946, although reportedly 'obsolescent or obsolete' by 1959 *CANADA, 1946*

water *noun* **1** methamphetamine or another central nervous system stimulant *US, 1989*. **2** phencyclidine, the recreational drug known as PCP or angel dust *US, 1989*. **3** semen *TRINIDAD AND TOBAGO, 1983* ▷*see:* WATERCRESS, WATER HEN. ▶ **go in the water** to lose an athletic contest or other competition intentionally *US, 1955*. ▶ **go to water** to be overcome with fear; to fail to maintain a resolve *AUSTRALIA, 1950*. ▶ **in the water; out in the water** in debt *US, 1992*. ▶ **over the water** Northern Ireland. A British armed services' view of the world *UK, 1995*

water *verb* ▶ **water her garden** (of a man) to have sex with a woman *JAMAICA, 1998*. ▶ **water the garden** to change the bottles of intravenous fluid that feed a neurologically depressed hospital patient *US, 1978*. ▶ **water the horses** to urinate *AUSTRALIA, 1971*. ▶ **water the vegetables** to administer intravenous fluids to a hospital's neurologically depressed patients *US, 1985*

water black *noun* mascara. Because water is needed for application *UK, 1952*

waterbomber *noun* an aircraft for fighting fires. Most of the world's waterbombers are made by Canadair in Montreal, and are known in Europe as 'le Canadair' and 'le pelican' *CANADA, 1965* ▷ FIREBOMBER

water box *noun* in drag racing, the area where cars heat and clean their tyres before a race *US, 1997*

waterboy *noun* a truck with a water tank used to spray water or other liquids on the ground *US, 1971*

water burner *noun* a cook. The form 'water scorcher' has been recorded as early as 1916 *AUSTRALIA, 1982*

watercooler moment *noun* a televisual moment that is expected to get people talking the next day. The discussions about such a moment are envisaged to happen when office workers meet at a watercooler *US, 2003*

watercress; water *noun* a dress. Rhyming slang *UK, 1998*

watercress; water *verb* to dress. Rhyming slang *UK, 1998*

water dog *noun* **1** in circus and carnival usage, a seal *US, 1981*. **2** in trucking, a truck with leaking water lines *US, 1971*

waterfall *verb* to drink from a can or bottle by cascading the liquid into your mouth without touching the can or bottle with your lips. Collected from a 13-year-old in Irvine, California, April 2003 *US, 2003*

Waterford *adjective* easily understood; perfectly clear. Puns the synonymous 'crystal clear' with well-known Irish glass manufacturers Waterford Crystal *UK, 2001*

waterhead *noun* a person with mental problems *US, 2002*

water hen; water *noun* ten. Rhyming slang, especially in horse racing *UK, 1969*

waterhole; water hole *noun* **1** a public hotel *AUSTRALIA, 1968*. **2** a truck stop *US, 1976*

watering hole; watering spot *noun* a bar or club where alcohol is served; a public hotel *US, 1955*

Waterloo *noun* a stew. Rhyming slang, from the area of London *UK, 1992*

watermelons *noun* female breasts of generous dimensions. From the all-too-obvious resemblance *US, 1995*

water sports *noun* **1** sexual activity involving the giving and getting of an enema *US, 1969*. **2** sexual activity that includes urination *US, 1969*

water-walker *noun* a fellow aviator whose accomplishments approach the miraculous. US naval aviator usage *US, 1986*

water-water *noun* marijuana *UK, 2003*

water works *noun* **1** tears *UK, 1647*. **2** the urinary system *US, 1961*

wave *noun* **1** the semi-erect penis *US, 1987*. **2** crack cocaine *UK, 1998*

wave *verb* to bend the edge of a playing card for later cheating *US, 1979*. ► **wave a dead chicken** to knowingly make a futile attempt to resolve a problem. Possibly an allusion to voodoo *US, 1996*. ► **wave your wig** to comb your hair. High school student usage *US, 1961*

wavelength *noun* ► **on your wavelength; on the same wavelength** to comprehend (and agree with) another's point of view or approach. Figurative application of a clear radio signal *US, 1927*

waves *noun* ► **make waves** to stir up trouble; to upset an established or accepted routine *US, 1962*

wax *noun* phonograph records. Recordings were originally made on wax cylinders or discs; the term applied to shellac discs and, subsequently, vinyl, but is not used to refer to newer technologies such as CD, tape, etc *US, 1932*. ► **put the wax on the tracks** to get ready and start out *UK, 2003*

wax *verb* **1** to shoot or kill someone *US, 1960*. **2** to excel; to perform well *US, 2001*. **3** in children's games, to share turns at bat, kicking or the like *AUSTRALIA, 1990*. ► **wax the carrot** (of a male) to masturbate *US, 2001*. ► **wax the dolphin** (of a male) to masturbate *US, 1987*. ► **wax the weezer** (of a male) to masturbate *US, 2001*

waxa *adjective* good, excellent *UK, 2003*

waxhead *noun* a surfer. From the wax used on surfboards *AUSTRALIA, 1981*

wax me used as an injunction or request to be given a marijuana cigarette *UK, 1996*

wax up *verb* to conceal contraband in a small container in readiness for hiding the container in the anus *UK, 1996*

waxy *noun* in horse racing, an enthusiast who can't help shouting in the ears of those near him *AUSTRALIA, 1989*

way *noun* a familiar neighbourhood; your home territory *US, 1987*. ► **in a big way** to an extreme *US, 1987*. ► **on the way out** of a person, approaching retirement or likely to be dismissed; of a thing, coming to the end of its useful existence *UK, 1961*. ► **that's the way (something does something)** that's how things turn out. Used in a formulaic construction of 'that's the way the NOUN VERBs' *US, 1952*. ► **the other way** diverging from a stated condition *UK, 1858*

way *adverb* extremely; without doubt *US, 1982*

wayback *adjective* in remote areas *AUSTRALIA, 1899*

way enough! in team rowing, used as a command by the coxswain to the rowers to stop rowing *US, 2003*

Wayne Fontanas *adjective* mad. Rhyming slang for BANANAS; formed from British singer Wayne Fontana (Glyn Ellis) (b.1945) who, with Wayne Fontana & The Mindbenders, came to prominence in the mid-1960s *UK, 2004*

wayout *noun* a person who is dressed in an extraordinary, unconventional fashion. From WAY OUT (unconventional) *US, 1969*

way out *adjective* extreme; unconventional; experimental or innovative; good *US, 1958*

way past *adverb* extremely *US, 1992*

way to go! used for registering approval; 'well done!'. Abbreviated from 'that's the way to go!' *US, 1972*

way up *adjective* drunk *US, 1955*

waz; wazz; wass *verb* to urinate *UK, 1984*

waz; wazz; whaz *noun* an act of urination *UK, 1999*

wazoo *noun* the anus and/or rectum *US, 1965*

wazz *verb* to rain. A figurative use of the sense 'to urinate' *UK, 1980*. ► **wazz on your bonfire** to spoil your fun, to ruin something good. Combines WAZ; WAZZ (urination) with a symbol of celebration *UK, 1998*

wazzed *adjective* drunk. A variation of PISSED. The Batfinks 'Wazzed 'n' Blasted' was recorded in the 1980s but not released until 1998 *UK, 1996*

wazzer; wazz *adjective* wonderful *UK, 1983*

wazzock; wazzuck *noun* ▷*see:* WASSOCK

WC *noun* a lavatory. Abbreviated from 'water closet' *UK, 1815*

weak! used as a prompt and short expression of disagreement with what has just been said *US, 1986*

weakheart *noun* a police officer; a representative of the establishment or authority. Used by West Indians, and intended to be offensive *UK, 1977*

weakie *noun* a poker player who lacks courage *US, 1996*

weak sister *noun* **1** a weak, ineffective person *US, 1857*. **2** an investor who buys a stock as an investment but sells it as soon as the price rises *US, 1988*

weaky-weaky *adjective* frail *TRINIDAD AND TOBAGO, 1987*

weapon *noun* **1** the penis. First recorded around the year 1000; and ever thus *UK, 1000*. **2** in pool, a player's cue stick *US, 1993*. ► **spit shine the weapon** to perform oral sex on a man. Perhaps this phrase has military origins *US, 2001*

weapons *noun* an actor's arsenal of make up *UK, 1952*

weapons-grade *adjective* very strong. Teen slang, post 11th September 2001 *US, 2002*

wear *verb* **1** to tolerate or accept something. Originally military *UK, 1925*. **2** to use a name *US, 1968*. ► **wear American gloves** among Canadian military personnel, to have your hands in your pockets *CANADA, 1995*. ► **wear buttons** to be extremely gullible *US, 1976*. ► **wear it** to take the blame, and punishment, for another's crime *UK, 1996*. ► **wear stripes** to serve a prison sentence *US, 1949*. ► **wear the face off someone** to vigorously French kiss someone *IRELAND, 2003*

we are not worthy used as a humorous recognition of accomplishment *US, 1992*

wearing the smalls *noun* the testicles. Rhyming slang for BALLS *UK, 2003*

Weary Willie *noun* a person who is perpetually tired, sad and pessimistic. From the character portrayed by circus clown Emmett Kelly (1898–1979) *US, 1947*

Weary Winny *noun* a prostitute who seeks customers on the street. From the title of a 1927 film *US, 1951*

weasel *noun* a tip, a gratuity. Used by railway porters; probably derived from WEASELING (extracting tips) *UK, 1965*

weasel *verb* **1** to use ambiguous language in an attempt to equivocate on the meaning *US, 1956*. **2** to use cunning to achieve your end; to cheat *UK, 1975*. ▶ **weasel out; weasel your way out** to avoid a responsibility or obligation, especially in a sly or underhand manner *UK, 1962*

weasel and stoat; weasel *noun* a coat. Rhyming slang *UK, 1971*

weaseling; weaselling *noun* extracting gratuities. Used by railway porters *UK, 1970*

We, as official Video Rangers, hereby promise... used with humour as an oath or pledge. From the US children's television programme *Captain Video and his Video Rangers* (1947–57), in which the viewers were asked to join with Captain Video in promising to 'support forever the causes of freedom, truth and justice throughout the universe'. Used with irony in later years by those who as children had been warped by television *US, 1957*

weather *noun* ▶ **under the weather 1** ill, unwell *US, 1850*. **2** experiencing the bleed period of the menstrual cycle. A narrowing of the general sense of 'vaguely unwell' *CANADA, 1961*. **3** tipsy, drunk. From the conventional sense as 'unwell' *AUSTRALIA, 1942*

weather guesser *noun* a meteorologist *ANTARCTICA, 2003*

weather in; weather out *verb* (of bad weather) to confine pilots in Canada's west to the airport until conditions improve. This term was used in alternation with, or perhaps more often than, 'storm-stayed', in western Canada winters *CANADA, 1989*

weave *noun* **1** real and synthetic hair woven into existing hair to hide baldness or thinning hair *US, 1993*. **2** clothes *US, 1972*

weave *verb* ▶ **get weaving** to start (immediately). Originally Royal Air Force slang *UK, 1942*

web *noun* a television network *US, 1990*

webbed up *adjective* involved, entangled; addicted *UK, 2000*

webfoot *noun* **1** a dairy farmer *NEW ZEALAND, 2002*. **2** a racehorse that performs well on a muddy track *US, 1951*

weblish *noun* the informally coded and abbreviated form of English that is used in text messaging, chat rooms, etc *UK, 2001*

web rage *noun* an outburst of enraged hostility within a cyber-environment *US, 1996*

wedding *noun* a one-on-one battle between fighter pilots *US, 1986*

wedding bells *noun* morning glory seeds, eaten for their purported hallucinogenic effect *US, 1970*

wedding bells acid; wedding bells *noun* LSD *US, 1971*

wedding kit *noun* the genitals *US, 1964*

wedding night *noun* the first occasion on which two homosexual men have sex with each other *UK, 2002*

wedding tackle *noun* the male genitals *UK, 1961*

wedge *noun* **1** a thick fold of currency notes; money in general. In the C18 and C19 'wedge' meant both 'money' and 'silver'; however, these senses were obsolete long before the current usages. The modern derivation comes from folded banknotes which form a wedge shape; hence the coincidental generic usage *UK, 1977*. **2** one hundred pounds *UK, 2000*. **3** a dose of LSD; LSD *US, 1971*. **4** in drag racing, an engine with a combustion chamber that is shaped like a wedge *US, 1999*. **5** a car. Teen slang *US, 1951*

wedged *adjective* in computing, suspended in mid-operation and unable to proceed *US, 1983*

wedged up *adjective* having money to spend *UK, 2000*

wedger *noun* someone who pushes into a queue *US, 1994*

wedgie *noun* a wedge-tailed eagle *AUSTRALIA, 1941*

wedgies *noun* wedge-heeled shoes *UK, 1959*

wedginald *noun* money. Disguising WEDGE (money) with a play on the name Reginald *UK, 1999*

wedgy; wedgie *noun* **1** the condition that exists when someone pulls your trousers or underpants forcefully upward, forming a wedge between buttock cheeks *US, 1988*. **2** a sandal, the thong of which wedges between the toes *US, 1981*

wee; wee wee *noun* urine; an act of urination. Juvenile or jocular in the main *UK, 1937*

wee *verb* to urinate *IRELAND, 1934*.

weebles *noun* an ill-defined or undefined illness *US, 1947*

weed *noun* **1** marijuana. The preferred slang term for marijuana until the 1950s, and despite the popularity of its successors it has never completely vanished from the lexicon *US, 1928*. **2** a marijuana cigarette *US, 1958*. **3** a cigarette *US, 1951*. **4** tobacco *UK, 1606*. **5** a thin, unhealthily delicate and weak person *UK, 1869*. **6** in horse racing, an undersized thoroughbred *UK, 1948*. **7** an expert *BARBADOS, 1965*. **8** a beginner surfer *US, 1990*. ▶ **get into the weeds** to micro-manage the smallest details *US, 1991*

weed *verb* **1** in a gambling establishment, to provide an employee with money to gamble in the hopes of building up business *US, 1947*. **2** to pilfer. Survives as WEEDING *UK, 1811*. ▶ **weed a poke** to remove all money and valuable items from a stolen wallet *US, 1962*

weedburner *noun* in drag racing, exhaust pipes that extend downward and to the rear of the car, terminating near the ground *US, 1993*

weeder *noun* on the railways, the supervisor of a track crew *US, 1977*

weed head *noun* a marijuana smoker *US, 1945*

weeding *noun* stealing, especially from an employer, or at the scene of a crime already committed. From WEED (to pilfer) *UK, 1977*

weedly *noun* a female marijuana smoker *US, 1955*

weed monkey; weed mule *noun* an old car or truck used to haul raw materials used in the illegal production of alcohol *US, 1974*

weedo *noun* a marijuana user *US, 1958*

weed of wisdom *noun* marijuana *UK, 1994*

weeds *noun* clothes *US, 1961*

weed tea *noun* a narcotic drink made by the infusion of marijuana leaves. A combination of WEED (marijuana) and 'tea' in the conventional sense *US, 1960*

weedwacker team *noun* in law enforcement, a surveillance team *US, 1997*

weedy *adjective* lacking in physical, moral or emotional strength *UK, 1852*

Wee Georgie Wood; wee georgie *adjective* good. Rhyming slang, formed on music hall entertainer Wee Georgie Wood (1894–1979), perhaps via the Tasmanian Wee Georgie Wood Steam Railway (named after a locomotive presumably named, in turn, after the entertainer); especially in the phrase 'any wee georgie wood?' *AUSTRALIA, 1942*

wee hammock *noun* a sanitary towel. From the similarity of appearance; in usage while such capacious reinforcement was the popular choice; certainly in use during the mid-to late 1960s *UK, 2001*

wee heavy *noun* a nip-sized bottle of strong ale or barley wine. First used for Fowler's Wee Heavy™, then generic. Recorded by Brian Glover, *CAMRA Dictionary of Beer*, 1985 *UK, 1985*

wee hours *noun* very early in the morning; the hours just after midnight *US, 1973*

weekend *noun* any short term of imprisonment *UK, 1950*

weekend *adjective* used derisively for indicating a part-time or casual dedication to a stated activity. Not restricted to weekend usage *UK, 1935*

weekender *noun* a person serving a jail sentence for a minor offence on weekends *US, 1971*

weekend habit *noun* a sporadic use of recreational drugs *UK, 1996*

weekend hippie *noun* a person with a conventional lifestyle who at the weekend adopts a counterculture persona *US, 1968*

weekend pass *noun* a glass. Rhyming slang, probably of military origin *UK, 2002*

weekend root *noun* a sexual partner with no illusions of a sustained relationship *NEW ZEALAND, 1998*

weekend warrior *noun* **1** a member of the National Guard. Members of reserve units must typically devote one weekend a month to refresher training *US, 1976*. **2** in drag racing, a hobbyist/enthusiast who confines his passion to weekend events *US, 1965*

weenie; weeny *adjective* small, tiny *UK, 1790*

weenie; weeny; wienie *noun* **1** a hot dog. From the German *wienerwurst US, 1906*. **2** the penis *US, 1978*

weenie bin *noun* a library carrel *US, 1987*

weenie wagger; weenie waver *noun* a male sexual exhibitionist *US, 1970*

weeny; weenie; wienie *noun* an unlikeable, weak person *US, 1963*

weeny-bopper *noun* a young girl, not yet a teenager but with a teenager's tastes. After TEENYBOPPER (a young teenager, especially a girl) *UK, 1972*

weep and wail *noun* a sob story told by a beggar. Rhyming slang for 'tale' *UK, 1960*

weep and wait *verb* to serve a prison sentence while awaiting news on the outcome of an appeal *US, 1962*

weeper *noun* a prisoner who cannot manage his incarceration and constantly complains *US, 1976*

weepie *noun* a film, novel, play, song, etc, with a sentimental narrative or emotional effect *UK, 1952*

weeping willow *noun* a pillow. Rhyming slang *UK, 1880*

weeping womb *noun* the bleed period of the menstrual cycle *US, 1999*

weeps *noun* tears *US, 1946*

wees *noun* an act of urination *NEW ZEALAND, 1984*

weevil *noun* in oil drilling, a new and inexperienced worker *US, 1954*

wee-wee *noun* **1** the penis *US, 1969*. **2** the vagina *US, 1998* ▷*see:* WEE

wee-wee *verb* to urinate. Children's vocabulary *UK, 1937*

wee-wee *adjective* very small *BARBADOS, 1965*

weezee *verb* to urinate. Children's vocabulary *TRINIDAD AND TOBAGO, 1986*

we go! 'let's leave!'. Hawaiian youth usage *US, 1981*

we gone goodbye. Originally used for signing off on a citizens' band radio transmission, but too good to stay there *US, 1976*

We Ho *noun* West Hollywood, California *US, 2001*

weigh *verb* ▶ **weigh in** to bring influence to bear; to make a forceful contribution to a topic under discussion *UK, 1909*. ▶ **weigh in with** to produce something additional; to introduce something extra or unexpected; to contribute *UK, 1885*. ▶ **weigh into someone 1** to attack someone *AUSTRALIA, 1941*. **2** to ensnare someone in a swindle *US, 1965*. ▶ **weigh on** to pay or repay someone. English Gypsy use *UK, 2000*

weigh off *verb* **1** to sentence someone to imprisonment or other judicial punishment. In a wider sense 'to weigh up' is 'to consider'; this usage is originally military *UK, 1925*. **2** to take revenge. To redress the balance by adjusting the weight *UK, 1977*

weight *noun* **1** large quantities of a drug *US, 1964*. **2** a large amount of money *US, 1964*. **3** blame, responsibility *US, 1960*. **4** difficulties, problems *US, 1997*. **5** the handicap that a skilled pool player will allow an opponent *US, 1984*. ▶ **do the weight** to slim, to lose weight *UK, 1999*. ▶ **put on weight** to undergo breast enhancement surgery *US, 1997*

weight house *noun* in an illegal drug enterprise, any place where a dealer hides his major supply of drugs *US, 2002*

weightless *adjective* drug-intoxicated, especially by crack cocaine *UK, 1998*

weight pile *noun* the area where weightlifting equipment is kept. Prison terminology *US, 1990*

weights *noun* loaded dice *US, 1977*

weight watcher *noun* a Department of Transportation employee at a roadside weigh station for trucks *US, 1976*

weigh up *verb* to consider or appraise something *UK, 1894*

weiner *noun* ▷*see:* WIENER

weird and wonderful *adjective* remarkably eccentric; peculiar; unfathomable. A colloquial coupling; usually ironic or derogatory, always clichéd *UK, 1859*

weirdo *noun* a weird person *US, 1955*

weird out *verb* **1** to begin to act weirdly *US, 1980*. **2** to frighten someone; to cause someone emotional turmoil *US, 1993*

weirdy; weirdie *noun* **1** an eccentric; a very odd person *UK, 1894*. **2** a homosexual, usually male *UK, 1969*

welch *verb* ▷*see:* WELSH

welcome aboard! a catchphrase used in greeting to a newcomer to any organisation, institution or closed group *US, 1962*

welcome to my world used for expressing limited sympathy when someone is complaining about something that happens to you regularly *US, 1999*

welcome to the club! used for expressing faint sympathy for someone who is complaining about something that others suffer *US, 1993*

weld *verb* to have sex *JAMAICA, 1992*

welder *noun* a male pornography performer *US, 1995*

well *noun* to a pickpocket, an inside jacket pocket *US, 1979*. ▶ **the Well** Bridewell Jail, Chicago *US, 1976*

well *adjective* used of a drug addict, unaffected by withdrawal symptoms *US, 1969*

well *adverb* used generally to add positive emphasis to adjectives *UK, 1986*

well and truly *adverb* utterly, beyond doubt, to an unarguable degree *UK, 1948*

well away *adjective* **1** sound asleep *UK, 1927*. **2** tipsy *UK, 1931*. ▶ **be well away** to prosper, to be doing very well. As in the example: 'He's well away with that girl' *UK, 1937*

well-endowed *adjective* **1** of a man, having impressively proportioned genitals *UK, 1951*. **2** of a woman, having generously proportioned breasts *UK, 1984*

well-gone *adjective* drunk *UK, 2000*

well-hard *adjective* very tough *UK, 1995*

well-heeled *adjective* rich; having more than sufficient money *US, 1897*

well hung *adjective* **1** of a man, having generously proportioned genitals *UK, 1685*. **2** young. Rhyming slang *UK, 1992*

wellie *verb* **1** to smash something or defeat someone. Used by the Royal Marines in the Falklands war, made familiar in the SAS fictions of Chris Ryan and Andy McNab *UK, 1982*. **2** to kick someone or something *UK, 1966*

wellie; welly *noun* **1** a Wellington boot (rubberised or plastic waterproof footware). In the 1970s, it began to be used in phrases where 'boot' occurred, e.g. 'The welly's on the other foot now'; 'he's getting too big for his wellies'. Perhaps started by *The Great Northern Welly Boot Show* put on by Billy Connolly at the Edinburgh Festival in the early 1970s. 'Well boot' is also a variant *UK, 1961*. **2** power, energy, especially when harnessed as acceleration *UK, 1980*. ▶ **give it some wellie; give it some welly** to vigorously attack someone or something; hence, to put all your effort into something. After WELLIE (Wellington boot), hence a play on STICK THE BOOT IN *UK, 1990*

wellied *adjective* drunk *UK, 2002*

wellie-whanging *noun* Wellington boot hurling as an unconventional competitive sport *UK, 1984*

well, I'll be a blue-nosed gopher! used for expressing surprise. A signature line of the Ollie character in the 'Spin and Marty' segment of the *Mickey Mouse Club* in the 1950s. Repeated with referential humour *US, 1955*

well, I'll be a dirty bird! used for expressing surprise humorously. A signature line of George Gobel on the television comedy *The George Gobel Showcase* (CBS, 1954–60). Repeated widely with referential humour *US, 1960*

well, I'm damned! ▷*see:* I'LL BE DAMNED

well I never!; well I never did! used for registering surprise *UK, 1848*

wellington *noun* a condom. A figurative application of waterproof footwear. 'Welly boot' is also a variant *UK, 2003*

wellington boot; wellington *noun* an act of sexual intercourse. Rhyming slang for ROOT *AUSTRALIA, 1970*

well-lined *adjective* reasonably wealthy *UK, 1999*

well-oiled *adjective* drunk. An intensification of OILED that now stands alone *UK, 1937*

welnaw *no US, 1993*

welsh; welch *verb* to swindle someone out of money wagered. Originates in the supposed untrustworthiness of the Welsh, possibly as speakers of a language few other mainland Britons understand (and such private communication is, after all, the intention of most criminal slang) *UK, 1857*

Welshie; Welshy *noun* a Welsh person *UK, 1951*

Welsh Wales *noun* Wales. If this referred specifically to the parts of Wales where Welsh is the predominant language this could well be considered as a correct usage; however, this is used generally and patronisingly, often in a faux-Welsh accent, of Wales as a whole *UK, 2004*

Welsh Windbag *nickname* politician Neil Kinnock (b.1942); hence, any loquacious Welsh person. A happy alliteration given to Kinnock from his weakness for big speeches that (unhappily) undermined his credibility with the electorate; the tag dates from his time as leader of the Labour party from 1983–92 *UK, 1984*

wendy *noun* a white homosexual male. Gay slang, formed on the name Wendy, probably elaborating the initial 'w' for *white*, and originating among Cape coloureds *SOUTH AFRICA, 2000*

Wendy house *noun* **1** in prison, a time when prisoners are permitted to associate with each other. From a child's Wendy house, thus an allusion to playtime and the possibility for discreet association *UK, 1996.* **2** the Duty Chief Inspector's office in the Information Room at New Scotland Yard. From the conventional sense as 'a children's playhouse' *UK, 1999*

Werris *noun* a Greek person *AUSTRALIA, 1977*

Werris Creek *noun* **1** a Greek person. Rhyming slang. From the name of a New South Wales town *AUSTRALIA, 1977.* **2** an act of urination. Rhyming slang for LEAK *AUSTRALIA, 2002*

wert' *noun* worthless. Hawaiian youth usage *US, 1982*

Wesson party *noun* group sex enhanced by spreading vegetable oil on the participants' bodies. An allusion and tribute to Wesson™ vegetable oil *US, 1971*

west coaster *noun* in trucking, a large, rectangular rear view mirror *US, 1971*

west coast turnaround *noun* any strong central nervous system stimulant. Powerful enough to keep a truck driver awake for a trip to the west coast and back *US, 1971*

West End show *noun* heroin. London's West End is known as 'Theatreland'; this jocular term in use amongst musicians suggests that heroin is a popular entertainment that will, in the words of a critical cliché, 'run and run' *UK, 2001*

West End thespian *noun* a lesbian. Rhyming slang *UK, 2003*

western grip *noun* used of a male when masturbating, gripping your penis with your thumb facing your body. From the grip used on the reins by those riding Western style *US, 2004*

western style *adjective* used of coffee, stale and lukewarm. Punning on the observation that the coffee has 'been on the range all day' *US, 1976*

West Ham reserves; west hams *noun* the nerves. Rhyming slang, formed from the football club *UK, 1961*

westie *noun* a young tough person. Originally referring to people from the western suburbs of Sydney, it now has spread to other parts of the country. In Sydney it was used as a derogatory sobriquet to refer to inhabitants of suburbs west of one's own, which meant that everyone except those people living in the eastern beach suburbs was liable to be called a 'westie' by someone. Similarly, in New Zealand, applied to those from the suburbs west of Auckland *AUSTRALIA, 1977*

Westminster Abbey *noun* a cab driver. Rhyming slang for CABBY *UK, 1992*

Westminster Abbey *adjective* shabby. Rhyming slang; originally theatrical, nicely ironic *UK, 1961*

Westralia *noun* Western Australia. Hence 'someone or something of Western Australia' is 'Westralian' *AUSTRALIA, 1893*

west side passkeys *noun* burglary tools. Coined in Chicago *US, 1982*

Westy *noun* US Army General William Childs Westmoreland (b.1914), US commander in Vietnam 1964–68 *US, 1991*

wet *noun* **1** a politician with middle-of-the-road views on controversial issues, especially (during the 1980s) a Conservative not entirely supportive of Margaret Thatcher's monetarist policies *UK, 1931.* **2** in motor racing, a tyre designed for racing in the rain *US, 1992.* **3** a drink of an alcoholic beverage. C10 *wœt*, first recorded in slang as 'heavy-wet' (malt liquor) *UK, 1982.* **4** alcoholic beverages. Gulf war usage *UK, 1991.* **5** an act of urination *UK, 1925.* **6** a conventional cigarette infused with embalming fluid *US, 2001.* **7** rain; wet weather *US, 1945.* **8** a Mexican national illegally present in the US. Shortened form of WETBACK, from the Spanish *mojado*, drawn from the image of swimming across the Rio Grande River from Mexico into Texas. Derogatory *US, 1979.* ▶ **the wet** the wet season in Australia's tropical north *AUSTRALIA, 1908*

wet *verb* ▶ **wet the baby's head** to drink to celebrate the birth (and christening) of a child *UK, 1885.* ▶ **wet the elbow** to enjoy a few drinks *NEW ZEALAND, 1994.* ▶ **wet your whistle** to have a drink, especially an alcoholic drink *US, 1720.* ▶ **wet yourself** to laugh uproariously *US, 1970*

wet *adjective* **1** of a woman, sexually excited; ready for sex. Not recorded before 1937 but surely in use much earlier *UK, 1937.* **2** in politics, willing to compromise. Adopted from the sense 'weak, lacking in effectiveness'; in this context often as Tory 'wet' (see following citation) *UK, 1980.* **3** weak, lacking in effectiveness. Upper-class society use *UK, 1916.* **4** foolish *NEW ZEALAND, 2002.* **5** excellent *US, 2000.* **6** pertaining to killing *US, 1992.* **7** permitting the purchase and consumption of alcoholic beverages *US, 1950*

wetback *noun* **1** an illegal immigrant to the US from Mexico. An offensive and figurative term deriving from the crossing of the Rio Grande River between Mexico and the US. Displaying a candour endemic to the time, the US Border Patrol launched 'Operation Wetback' in 1954 to stem the tide of illegal immigration from Mexico *US, 1929.* **2** in surfing, a large wave *US, 1957*

wet behind the ears *adjective* inexperienced *UK, 1931*

wet blanket *noun* a killjoy, a spoilsport *UK, 1857*

wet bum *noun* a weak individual. Derogatory; the image of a baby with a wet bottom, punning on WET (weak) *UK, 1997*

wetcoast *noun* the strip of British Columbia along the Pacific Ocean *CANADA, 1989*

Wetcoast Samsonite *noun* a green rubbish bag used for luggage *CANADA, 1989*

wet decks *noun* a woman who has recently had sex with several men *US, 1972*

wet dream *noun* **1** among men, a sleeping fantasy that triggers orgasm *UK, 1851.* **2** a dream come true. A figurative application of the unconsious fantasy that triggers an orgasm *UK, 1971*

wet dreamer *noun* an exciting experience *UK, 1999*

wet fart *adjective* ineffectual, pointless *UK, 2000*

wet-finger *noun* ▶ **get wet-finger** in the categorisation of sexual activity by teenage boys, to insert a finger into a girl's vagina *US, 1986*

Wet Nelly *noun* used as a generic name for any form of bread pudding. There is anecdotal evidence of Wet Nelly being enjoyed during World War 1 *UK, 2000*

wet paper could cut you used for describing a person who can't do anything right *TRINIDAD AND TOBAGO, 1989*

wet rag *noun* an unpopular, socially inept person *US, 1955*

wet road block *noun* the Yalu River, Korea. US troops were prohibited from crossing the Yalu, even in pursuit of enemy soldiers *US, 1982*

wet season *noun* the bleed period of the menstrual cycle *AUSTRALIA, 1988*

wet shot *noun* a scene in a pornographic film or photograph depicting a man ejaculating *US, 1991*

wet smack *noun* a sexually frigid woman *US, 1977*

wet stuff *noun* explicit violence or sex in a television programme or film *US, 1997*

wetsuit *noun* a condom *US, 1993*

wettie *noun* especially among surfers, a wetsuit *AUSTRALIA, 1987*

wettie rash *noun* a rash caused by wearing a wetsuit *AUSTRALIA, 1996*

wetware *noun* a human being; the human brain *US, 1991*

wet week; wet weekend *noun* ▶ **like a wet week; like a wet weekend** miserable, wretched *UK, 1984*

wet willie *noun* an act in which a spit-moistened finger is forced into a victim's ear and twisted *US, 1992*

WFO *adjective* used of a throttle, all the way open. An abbreviation of 'wide fucking open' *US, 2001*

whack *noun* **1** a heavy, resounding blow; a blow with a stick, often as corporal punishment *UK, 1737*. **2** a share, a portion, a part, a measure *AUSTRALIA, 1889*. **3** heroin *UK, 2003*. **4** crack cocaine *UK, 2003*. **5** a poorly executed piece of graffiti art *US, 1997*. ▶ **have a whack at; take a whack at** to attempt something; to attack someone *US, 1904*. ▶ **out of whack** not in proper shape or order *US, 1885*

whack *verb* **1** to kill someone, especially by gunshot. Also used with 'out' *US, 1977*. **2** to strike someone vigorously *UK, 1721*. ▶ **whack plaque** in a dentist's office, to clean teeth. Collected from an orthodontist in Bangor, Maine, in April 2001 *US, 2001*. ▶ **whack your doodle** (of a male) to masturbate *US, 1970*

whack! in the language of hang gliding, used for commenting on a poor landing *US, 1992*

whackadoo *noun* a crazy person *US, 1979*

whack attack *noun* **1** in the language of hang gliding, a string of bad landings *US, 1992*. **2** an irrational and violent reaction to hallucinogenic drugs *US, 2001*

whacked *adjective* **1** exhausted *UK, 1919*. **2** drunk or drug-intoxicated. Also used with 'out' *US, 1967*. **3** out of control *UK, 1995*

whacker; wacker *noun* a fool; a jerk *AUSTRALIA, 1966*

whacking *noun* **1** a beating; a defeat. The figurative, sporting sense is not recorded before 1951 *UK, 1862*. **2** a killing. From WHACK (to murder) *US, 2001*

whacking *adverb* used to intensify adjectives of largeness *UK, 1853*

whacko *adjective* **1** terrific; wonderful *AUSTRALIA, 1953*. **2** crazy; eccentric *US, 1957*

whacko! used for expressing shock *AUSTRALIA, 1937*

whack-off *noun* an act of masturbation *US, 1969*

whack off *verb* to masturbate *US, 1969*

whack off with *verb* to steal something *AUSTRALIA, 1977*

whacko Jacko *adjective* crazy. A catchphrase formed from the nickname of entertainer Michael Jackson, whose well-publicised eccentricities give rise to this usage *UK, 1989*

whacko the chook! used for expressing shock *AUSTRALIA, 1981*

whacko-the-diddle-oh used for expressing shock *AUSTRALIA, 1966*

whack out *verb* to kill someone *US, 1979*

whack-silly *adjective* obsessed with masturbation *US, 1962*

whack up *verb* to divide something, especially a quantity of illegal drugs, into portions *US, 1973*

whaddup? used as a greeting *US, 1994*

whaddya hear?; whaddya say? used as a greeting. The trademark greeting of James Cagney ('Rocky' Sullivan) in the 1938 Warner Brothers film *Angels With Dirty Faces* *US, 1938*

wha happen?; what happenin? used as a greeting *TRINIDAD AND TOBAGO, 1993*

whaka blonde *noun* a Maori woman. A coinage from the Whakarewarewa Thermal Village in Rotora, a Maori tourist attraction *NEW ZEALAND, 1950*

whale *noun* a gambler who places large bets *US, 1995*

whale *verb* **1** to beat someone *UK, 1790*. **2** to have sex *US, 1967*. **3** to play music with passion and gusto *US, 1958*

whale belly *noun* on the railways, a coal tender with a drop bottom *US, 1946*

whale in the bay *noun* someone looking for payment of a gambling debt *AUSTRALIA, 1989*

whale kisser *noun* an environmentalist *US, 2003*

whale of a time *noun* a good time *US, 1913*

whale sperm *noun* a plexiglas cleaning agent *US, 1991*

whale tail *noun* that portion of the 'T' at the rear of a thong that becomes exposed during wear *UK, 2005*

wham *noun* a striptease act in which the dancer ends her performance completely naked *US, 1981*

wham! used for registering the suddenness of an occurrence. Figurative use of 'wham' (to hit) *UK, 1999*

wham bag *noun* a bag full of explosives *US, 1988*

wham, bam, thank you m'am used for describing anything done in very short order, especially sex. Sometimes abbreviated, and sometimes embellished with other rhymes *US, 1942*

whammer *noun* the penis *US, 1989*

whammy *noun* **1** a curse or hex. *US, 1940*. **2** something that is upsetting or sets you back *US, 1961*

whammy bar *noun* a floating bridge on an electric guitar that makes tremolos, vibrators, dives, bends and other effects possible *US, 1992*

wham-wham *noun* in prison, store-bought snacks *US, 1981*

whandoodles *noun* in poker, a temporary increase in the betting limit after a player wins a hand with a rare hand *US, 1967*

whangdoodle *noun* on the railways, a remote telephone *US, 1977*

whanger; wanger *noun* the penis *US, 1939*

wha'ppen(?) 'what's happening?'; used as a greeting. West Indian and UK Black usage *UK, 1981*

whapp'n used as a greeting. Derived from 'what's happening?' but not used as an interrogative *UK, 2003*

wharfie *noun* a wharf labourer *AUSTRALIA, 1911*

wharf rat *noun* in the language surrounding the Grateful Dead, a follower of the band who abstains from alcohol and drugs. From the title of a Grateful Dead song *US, 1994*

whark *verb* to vomit *UK, 1985*

whassname *noun* used to refer to a name that is unknown, forgotten, to be avoided or hardly worth mentioning. Slovening of WHATS-HIS-NAME *UK, 2000*

what *noun* ▶ **or what?** used as a final (often the only), wholly indefinite choice *UK, 1766*

what a gay day! used as a conversation starter or filler; also as an indicator of homosexual company. The catchphrase of CAMP comedian and television compere Larry Grayson (1923–95) it caught the public imagination in the mid-1970s and was adopted into popular use *UK, 2004*

what a loss used for expressing sympathy for a difficult situation *US, 1983*

what am I going to do with you? said to someone you know well as an expression of tolerance and forgiveness *UK, 1984*

what a revolting development this is used for expressing displeasure. A signature line of working-class hero Chester A. Riley on the television comedy *The Life of Riley* (NBC, 1949–58). Repeated with referential humour *US, 1958*

what are you like? an exclamation directed at someone whose behaviour is unacceptable *IRELAND, 1995*

what can I do you for? 'how can I help?', 'what can I do for you?'. A jocular suggestion *UK, 1961*

whatcha' thinking? used as a greeting *US, 1986*

what'chu talkin' about, Willis? used for humorously expressing a lack of understanding or belief. A stock line on the television comedy *Diff'rent Strokes* (1978–86), uttered by the Arnold Jackson character played by Gary Coleman. Repeated with referential humour *US, 1986*

what did your last slave die of? used as an expression of discontent to someone who is demanding that too much be done *UK, 1976*

whatdja; whatdya; whaddya 'what do you'. A phonetic recording of general slurring *UK, 1999*

what-do-you-call-it; what-d'ye-call-it *noun* used as a replacement for any noun that the user cannot or does not wish to specify *UK, 1600*

what do you know?; whaddya know? used as a register of surprise *US, 1914*

what do you know, Joe? used as a greeting *US, 1947*

what do you think of the show so far? – rubbish! a question and answer catchphrase widely used and often without an appropriate context. Comedian Eric Morecambe (1926–84) introduced this catchphrase in the early 1970s. The response was usually voiced by Morecambe in the manner of a ventriloquist: 'ruggish!' *UK, 1981*

what else did you get for Christmas? directed at a person showing-off with a new 'toy'; often addressed to the tail of a disappearing vehicle *UK, 1975*

whatever *adverb* used for registering self-pitying acceptance *US, 2003*

whatever *pronoun* used as an emphatic form of 'what?'. In conventional use from C14–C19, then colloquial *UK, 1974*

whatever! used as a dismissing retort to what has just been said. Said with attitude, with a pause after 'what', and sometimes with thumbs and forefingers shaped like a 'W' *US, 1989*

whatever's fair used as a non-responsive, vague answer to a direct question *US, 1969*

whatever turns you on your individual tastes, foibles, hobbies, interests, etc. Generally spoken to indicate a tolerance of tastes that do not coincide with your own *US, 1978*

what for a thing is that? among Nova Scotians of German descent, used as a query to mean 'what kind of a thing is that?' *CANADA, 1999*

what goes up must come down a Cockney catchphrase that comments generally on the inevitability of things happening, and, specifically, on the nature of a pregnancy *UK, 1969*

what-have-you *noun* used in place of any other item or items in a category *UK, 1999*

what is it with you? why are you behaving in such a manner? *UK, 1996*

what it is used as a greeting *US, 1974*

what kind? what's the matter with you? *US, 1963*

what makes you tick the inner-workings of your mind. As if by clockwork *UK, 1999*

whatnot *noun* anything and everything. Usually a characteristic of individual speakers, not a group, and often used with an annoying regularity *UK, 1540*

what price NOUN? consider the worth of… something!; what do you think of… something? Occasionally admiring, but generally sarcastic, in reference to a declared or well-understood value *UK, 1893*

what say? 1 what do you think?; what do you say to the proposal?, etc *UK, 1895*. **2** used as a greeting *US, 1965*

what's-er-name; what's-her-name *noun* used to refer to a name that is unknown, forgotten, to be avoided or hardly worth mentioning *UK, 1978*

what's-his-face; what's-her-face *noun* used to refer to a name that is unknown, forgotten, to be avoided or hardly worth mentioning *UK, 1995*

what's-his-name; what's-his-namey *noun* used to refer to a person whose name is unknown, forgotten, to be avoided or hardly worth mentioning *UK, 1697*

whatsit; whatsis; whatzis *noun* used to refer to a name that is unknown, forgotten, to be avoided or hardly worth mentioning *US, 1882*

what's it to you? used (often aggressively) as the rhetorical response to a question, the answer to which is thus signalled to be none of the questioner's business *UK, 1959*

what's kicking? used as a greeting, along the lines of 'what is new?' *US, 1949*

what's my name? used as a taunt while beating someone. In 1967, boxer Muhammed Ali fought Ernie Terrell, who insisted on calling Ali 'Cassius Clay'; as Ali pounded Terrell, Ali taunted 'What's my name, fool? What's my name?' *US, 1997*

what's poppin? used as a peer-to-peer greeting *US, 1995*

what's shaking?; what's shakin'? used as a greeting *US, 1951*

what's that when it's at home? used as an expression of contempt or derision for something. Any person, people or object may, of course, substitute for 'that' *UK, 1932*

what's the damage? how much do I owe?; what is the cost? Formed on DAMAGE (expense) *UK, 1984*

what's the dealio?; what's the dillio? what is new?, what is going on? Popularised by rapper Busta Rhymes in the late 1990s *US, 2002*

what's the difference between NOUN and NOUN? a well-worn joke-telling formula that is only usually half answered (a more vulgar or scandalous response to the question is implied) *US, 1851*

what's the drill? what are the arrangements, or usual procedures? Originally military, now general *UK, 1961*

what's the score? what is the latest information, situation, etc? Originally Royal Air Force, then more general *UK, 1961*

what's the story, morning glory? used as a cheerful greeting *US, 1959*

what's up? used as a greeting *US, 1993*

whatsup? used as a greeting *US, 1990*

what's up, Doc? used as an all-purpose enquiry. The catchphrase of Loony Tunes cartoon hero Bugs Bunny, who, from his third outing, in July 1940 (and much repeated), would inquire 'Mnyeh… what's up, Doc?' as a taunt to pursuers. Also used cinematically, this time without specific context, as the title of a 1972 Hollywood film. Popular with sub-editors as a headline for any number of articles on the National Health *US, 1940*

what's up with that? used for expressing interest in more facts *US, 1994*

what's with you? what's amiss with you?; why are you behaving in such a way?; what has happened to you?; explain yourself!; why? Also applied to inanimate objects *US, 1940*

what's your damage? what's your problem?; what's the matter? *US, 1988*

what's your song, King Kong? used as a greeting *US, 1947*

what the fuck! used for registering annoyance, resignation or surprise. Possibly a shortening of 'what the fucking hell!', in turn an elaboration of WHAT THE HELL! *UK, 1999*

what the heck! used as an exclamation of surprise, indignation, etc; also used dismissively and as an expression of resignation *UK, 1887*

what-the-hell *adjective* indifferent, uncaring *UK, 1968*

what the hell! used in annoyance, resignation or surprise *UK, 1872*

what the hellfire! used for registering annoyance or surprise. A variation of WHAT THE HELL! *UK, 1997*

what the hey! used as a humorous declaration of surprise, bemusement or dismissal. Popularised by Milton Berle in the early days of US television; an early television catchphrase that swept the nation *US, 1957*

what up? used as a greeting *US, 1990*

what up, love one? used as a greeting. Used as a coded greeting by members of the Black Guerrilla Family prison gang *US, 2000*

what/which part of no don't you understand? used for humourously emphasizing a previous negative answer. Wildly popular, and over-used, in the 1990s; an instant favourite of US parents scolding children. First made famous by Lorrie Morgan in a 1991 song 'What Part of No', written by Wayne Perry and Gerald Smith – 'I'll be glad to explain it / If it's too hard to comprehend / So tell me what part of no / Don't you understand?' *US, 1991*

whatyoucallit *noun* used as a replacement for any noun that the user cannot or does not wish to specify *UK, 2002*

what-you-may-call-it; whatchamacallit *noun* used in place of a word that is temporarily forgotten or not important for the context *UK, 1598*

wheat *noun* marijuana. A play on GRASS and an assonant pun on WEED *US, 1969*

wheech *verb* to move swiftly; to move something swiftly away. Probably derived, in some way, from Scots dialect *wheech* (a stink) *UK: SCOTLAND, 1911*

wheel *noun* **1** a leader; an important person *US, 1933.* **2** a mid-level employee in an illegal lottery *US, 1978.* **3** the game of roulette *US, 1993.* **4** a tablet of MDMA, the recreational drug best known as ecstasy *UK, 2003.* **5** in a carnival, any ride that is in the form of a wheel *US, 1960.* **6** a life prison sentence *US, 1991.* **7** in lowball poker, the lowest possible straight (five to ace) *US, 1981.* **8** the ankle *US, 1986*

wheel *verb* **1** to travel; to drive *US, 1721.* **2** (used of a racehorse) to turn around suddenly *US, 1968*

wheel and deal *verb* to engage in profit-making in a flamboyant manner *US, 1961*

wheeler-dealer *noun* a scheming, contriving deal-maker with many connections. The reduplication of the vowel sound serves to intensify *US, 1960*

wheeler-dealing; wheeling-and-dealing *noun* scheming business practice *US, 1984*

wheel horse *noun* in oil drilling, the best worker on a crew *US, 1954*

wheelie; wheely *noun* **1** a wheelstand, the lifting of the front wheels of a car or front wheel of a motorcyle, bicycle or skateboard off the ground due to sudden acceleration *US, 1966.* **2** a wheelchair *UK, 1999.* ▶ **pop a wheelie** to perform a wheelie *US, 1995*

wheelie-bin *noun* a large, wheeled rubbish bin *AUSTRALIA, 1984*

wheel jockey *noun* a military convoy truck driver *US, 1991*

wheel man *noun* **1** in a criminal operation, the getaway driver *US, 1935.* **2** a person who brings together pool players who are willing to play for money *US, 1993*

wheels *noun* **1** a car *US, 1959.* **2** a record turntable or turntables used by DJs. From the circular shape and revolving motion. Variants include 'wheels of steel' and the singular 'wheel' *US, 1999.* **3** shoes or boots *US, 1990.* **4** the legs, especially a woman's legs *US, 1966.* ▶ **on wheels** to the extreme *US, 1943.* ▶ **put wheels on it** used in restaurants to note that the order is a take-away *CANADA, 1993.* ▶ **the wheels are coming off** to be getting out of control; to not be going as planned *UK, 1998*

wheels man *noun* a good driver *IRELAND, 1996*

wheesht! be quiet! From Scots dialect *wheesh* (a hush) *UK: SCOTLAND, 1985*

wheeze *noun* **1** a piece of comedic business; a trick; a clever idea. Originally theatrical, used by clowns and comedians; then

especially popular with schoolchildren *UK, 1864.* **2** a false belief *US, 1965*

wheezy Anna *noun* a spanner. Rhyming slang, formed from the title of a 1930s comic song *UK, 1992*

when *adverb* now. The natural response to the conventionally polite enquiry 'Say when?' *UK, 1976*

when fowl have teet; when cock have teet used for expressing an impossibility *TRINIDAD AND TOBAGO, 1945*

when it's at home used to intensify any question of identity. A derisive tag implying contempt or incredulity, suffixed to 'what is a....?'. The earliest usages of this scornful device were grammatically correct: '[W]here your friends are when they're at home?' (Rudyard Kipling, *Plain Tales from the Hills*, 1888). Current usage, however, will occasionally reform a sentence that should commence correctly with 'who is...?' by converting the proper noun to object status, e.g. 'What is a John Smith when it's at home?' *UK, 1957*

when push comes to shove when there is no longer any choice but to proceed; when worse comes to worst *US, 1958*

when-shee *noun* heroin. A variation of YEN-SHEE (heroin) *2003*

when you've got to go, you've got to go; when you gotta go, you gotta go applied philosophically to death, prosaically to responsibility ('duty calls') and trivially to a visit to the toilet. Popularised by Hollywood films *US, 1975*

where it is at; where it's at 1 the centre of a situation, a place where something important is happening *US, 1965.* **2** in touch *UK, 1965*

where someone is at the person's point of view or opinion *US, 1968*

where's the fire? used for expressing a lack of shared concern *US, 2003*

where the big nobs hang out *noun* a toilet (as used by men), especially a public convenience. A self-serving pun *AUSTRALIA, 1971*

where the sun don't shine in your rectum *US, 1992*

wherever? *adverb* used as an emphatic variation of 'where?'. In conventional use from the C10 to C19; now colloquial *UK, 2002*

where were you when the shit hit the fan? used as a greeting between US Marines in Korea *US, 1986*

where you're coming from your point of view or opinion *US, 1975*

which foot you kick with your personal preference of politics, religion or sexuality. Left or right, Catholic or Protestant, hetero- or homosexual *UK: SCOTLAND, 2000*

whickerbill *noun* a railway brakesman *US, 1946*

whif *adjective* what-if. Used in 'what if...?' exercises projecting possible contingencies and developing reactions to them *US, 1974*

whiff *noun* **1** an unpleasant smell. From WHIFFY (bad-smelling) *UK, 1899.* **2** cocaine *US, 1983*

whiff *verb* **1** to give off an unpleasant smell *UK, 1899.* **2** to inhale a powdered drug through the nose *US, 1981*

whiffle dust *noun* **1** amphetamine powder. From the imaginary magic powder used by conjurors, manufacturers, marketing professionals and others to enhance their product or presentation *UK, 2003.* **2** MDMA, the recreational drug best known as ecstasy *UK, 2003* ▷ *see:* MUMMY DUST

whiffler *noun* an auction house employee who moves and displays the items for sale *UK, 2003*

whiffy *adjective* having an unpleasant odour, smelly *UK, 1849*

whiler *noun* a man with more than one girlfriend. In West Indian and UK black use, August 2002 *UK, 2002*

whim-whams *noun* a feeling of dread or anxiety; a state of anxiety or nervousness; the jitters *US, 1950*

whiney gyny club *noun* complaining hospital patients recovering from gynecological surgery *US, 1985*

whinge *noun* a moaning complaint. From the verb *UK, 1984*

whinge; winge *verb* to complain; to whine *AUSTRALIA, 1938*

whinge bag *noun* a complainer. Formed on WHINGE (a moaning complaint) *UK, 2003*

whingeing pom *noun* an English person viewed as a habitual complainer. A stock Australian stereotype *AUSTRALIA, 1962*

whinger *noun* a person who whinges; a habitual complainer *AUSTRALIA, 1934*

whip *noun* **1** a car. Used by urban black youths *UK, 2004*. **2** a long radio antenna *US, 1976*. **3** a boss or supervisor *US, 1984*. **4** a close friend *BAHAMAS, 1982*. **5** rum *AUSTRALIA, 1953* ▷*see:* WHIP-ROUND

whip *verb* to arrest someone *US, 1971*. ▶ **whip it in, whip it out** a catchphrase that celebrates a male approach to sexual relations. From the lyric of a rugby song: 'Whip it in, whip it out, quit fucking about Yo ho, yo ho, yo ho'. Sometimes further extended with: 'wipe it off, walk away' *UK, 1998*. ▶ **whip it out** to release the penis from the confines of the trousers, a bold genital display *US, 1997*. ▶ **whip the cat** to feel remorse; to regret something *AUSTRALIA, 1847*. ▶ **whip up on skippy** (used of a male) to masturbate, *2001*. ▶ **whip your wang** (used of a male) to masturbate *US, 1969*

whip and lash; whip *noun* a moustache. Rhyming slang for TASH *UK, 1992*

whip and top; whip *verb* to masturbate. Rhyming slang for STROP *UK, 1992*

whiplash *noun* a rash. Rhyming slang; perhaps, also, a sexual innuendo *UK, 1998*

whip off *verb* (used of a male) to masturbate *US, 1975*

whip-out *noun* **1** a bankroll designed to impress when whipped out of the pocket *US, 1972*. **2** a regular payment *US, 1981*

whip o'will *noun* an act of vomiting; vomit. Possibly rhyming slang for '*spill* your guts' *AUSTRALIA, 1967*

whipped *adjective* dominated by a girlfriend or wife. A shortened form of PUSSY-WHIPPED *US, 1965*

whipper *noun* **1** a small cartridge of nitrous oxide. Designed for use in making whipped cream, but often abused for the psychoactive effects of the gas *US, 1986*. **2** a person who enjoys being whipped in a sado-masochistic encounter *US, 1970*

whippersnapper; snapper *noun* a young, impertinent person unmindful of his station in life. Still heard, but used with the effect of dating the speaker *UK, 1700*

whippet *noun* a shotgun with both barrel and stock sawn off for hiding on the body *US, 1982*

whippets; whippits *noun* capsules of nitrous oxide used as a recreational drug *US, 1980*

Whippins and Lashins *noun* the Irish Girl Guides *IRELAND, 1995*

whippy *noun* **1** a place used for the home base in children's game hide-and-seek *AUSTRALIA, 1964*. **2** a pocket in which money is kept; hence, the money kept there *AUSTRALIA, 1973*

whippy *adjective* clever *US, 1969*

whip-round; whip-around; whip *noun* an informal fund collected from a group of people. Originally military 'whip' (a collection for more wine in the mess) *UK, 1874*

whips *noun* a great deal of. A play on LASHINGS *AUSTRALIA, 1890*

whips and jingles *noun* symptoms of heroin withdrawal. Referring to the physical pain and frayed nerves suffered *US, 1973*

whipsaw *verb* **1** in poker, to surround a player with two confederates whose collusive betting tactics relieve the middle player of his bankroll and drive him from the game *US, 1949*. **2** in horse racing, to correctly pick both the winner and second-place finisher in a race *US, 1947*

whip shot *noun* a type of controlled toss of the dice, effective by a skilled cheat *US, 1963*

whipster *noun* an untrustworthy individual *IRELAND, 1997*

whip-whap *adverb* quickly, without second thought *TRINIDAD AND TOBAGO, 2003*

whirl *noun* an attempt *US, 1884*

whirl bet *noun* in craps, a one-roll bet on 2, 3, 7, 11 and 12 *US, 1961*

whirlies *noun* extreme dizziness experienced when drunk *US, 1966*

whirligig *noun* a revolver *US, 1957*

whirlpooling; whirlpool *noun* the assault of a girl by a group of males in a swimming pool who grope her while churning water around her *US, 1993*

whirly *noun* **1** in the television and film industries, a hydraulic lift used for shooting scenes from above *US, 1990*. **2** a small, localised whirlwind. The variant spelling 'whirlie' is sometimes used *AUSTRALIA, 1894*

whirlybird *noun* a helicopter *US, 1951*

whirlygigs *noun* ▶ **having the whirlygigs** drunk *UK, 2002*

whirly pig *noun* a helicopter-borne police officer. Quoted as a term used by residents of Berkeley, California, to describe police in helicopters *US, 1970*

whirly-whirly *noun* a small, localised whirlwind. From 'whirl', but modelled on WILLY-WILLY *AUSTRALIA, 1926*

whirly wind *noun* especially in Queensland, a small, localised whirlwind *AUSTRALIA, 1969*

whisker *noun* usually in comparisons, a narrow margin, a small amount *US, 1913*

whiskers *noun* **1** seniority or tenure on a job *US, 1973*. **2** pubic hair *US, 1967*

whiskey *noun* a type of bet in an illegal numbers game lottery *US, 1957*

whiskey dent *noun* a dent on your car that you don't remember incurring while driving drunk *US, 1984*

whiskeyleg *noun* a drunkard *US, 1957*

whiskey papa *noun* a white phosphorous flare or grenade. From the military phonetic alphabet – WP *US, 1990*

whiskey-rot *noun* any unspecified illness *US, 1970*

whisper *noun* **1** a rumour *UK, 1596*. **2** the very end of a prison sentence *US, 1976*

whistle *noun* in the sport of polo, energy *UK, 2003*. ▶ **wet your whistle** to take a drink; to quench a thirst *UK, 1530*

whistle *verb* ▶ **whistle in the dark** to perform oral sex on a woman *US, 1967*. ▶ **whistle through the wheatfield** to engage in oral sex on a woman, especially a blonde woman *US, 2001*

whistle and flute; whistle *noun* **1** a suit (of clothes). Rhyming slang *UK, 1931*. **2** cocaine. Rhyming slang for TOOT *UK, 2000*

whistle and flute; whistle *verb* to inhale drugs or drug smoke. Rhyming slang for TOOT *UK, 1996*

whistle and toot; whistle and flute; toot *noun* money. Rhyming slang for LOOT, used mainly in the reduced form *UK, 1950*

whistlebait *noun* an attractive woman or girl *US, 1947*

whistlecock *noun* amongst Australian Aboriginals, a penis that has had a small slit made in the base of the urethra as a means of birth control; a man who has had this operation *AUSTRALIA, 1945*

whistle for *verb* to wait for, or expect, something in vain *UK, 1882*

whistler *noun* a police car *US, 1971*

whistlers *noun* pieces of metal scrap packed in an artillery shell that makes a screaming sound as the shell moves through the air *US, 1990*

whistlestop *noun* a small town. From the image of a train making a brief stop at the town *US, 1947*

whistling gear *noun* in trucking, the highest gear. May have been named for the whistling sound older tractors made when in overdrive gear, or for the possibility that a rig travelling in this gear could attract the attention of a 'whistler' – a police car *US, 1971*

white *noun* **1** a capsule of Benzedrine™ (amphetamine sulphate) or any other central nervous system stimulant *US, 1966*. **2** heroin, cocaine or morphine. From the colour of the powdered drug *US, 1914*. **3** crack cocaine. A derivative of the previous sense *US, 1995*. **4** a five-pound note. From the colour of the large five-pound notes, which were withdrawn from circulation in 1957 *UK, 1946*. **5** platinum jewellery *UK, 1950*. **6** in American casinos, a white betting token worth one dollar US, 1985. **7** in American casinos, a white betting token worth $500 US, 1961. **8** a day; daytime US, 1975. **9** 'silver' coins. Variants include 'whites' and 'white money' UK, 1887. ▶ **like white on rice** entirely, utterly, completely US, 1987. ▶ **the white** surgical spirit as an alcoholic drink. The liquid is clear but 'white' differentiates this from BLUE (methylated spirits) UK, 2000. ▶ **white-boy shuffle** an uncoordinated, ungraceful, counter-rhythmic dancing style US, 1993

white adjective decent. Usually used sarcastically and as a conscious rejection of the racism that once would have inspired the saying US, 1913

white-ant verb to undermine someone or something. From 'white ant' (a termite) AUSTRALIA, 1922

white-ass; white-assed adjective bland; insipid; lacking creativity. A reciprocal in formation to the common 'black-ass'; not praise US, 1995

white ball noun crack cocaine UK, 1998

white boy noun heroin. An embellishment of BOY (heroin), from the colour of the powdered drug US, 1986

white-bread adjective everyday, unexciting, respectable; representing the epitome of white middle-class values and style US, 1991

white burger noun a tablet of MDMA, the recreational drug best known as ecstasy UK, 1996

white Cali; white Cally noun a variety of MDMA, the recreational drug best known as ecstasy; an antihistamine tablet sold as MDMA. From the colour combined with an abbreviation of California, the presumed place of origin UK, 1996

white cliffs of Dover; white cliffs adjective over. Rhyming slang, formed from the famous landmark, celebrated in song and geography UK, 1998

white cloud noun crack cocaine US, 1989

white cockroach noun a white person TRINIDAD AND TOBAGO, 1838

white crinkle noun a five-pound note. A combination of CRINKLE (paper money) and the colour of five pound notes, which were withdrawn from circulation in 1957 UK, 1957

white cross noun an amphetamine or methamphetamine tablet, sectioned with an X US, 1965

white cylinder week noun the bleed period of the menstrual cycle. Refers to a tampon applicator US, 1999

white devil noun cocaine US, 1972

white drugs noun heroin, cocaine, morphine, etc. From the colour of the refined powder US, 1961

white dust noun powdered amphetamine UK, 1996

white eye noun illegal alcohol smuggled from the French islands of Saint-Pierre and Miquelon. This term appears in Tom Dalzell's The Slang of Sin to mean 'whisky' CANADA, 1998

white-eyes noun a white person US, 1978

whitefellow; whitefella noun a white person as opposed to a native Australian Aboriginal AUSTRALIA, 1826

white fever noun used of people of colour, a strong attraction towards white people. The opposite of JUNGLE FEVER US, 1969

white fingers noun cocaine US, 2002

white fluff noun LSD UK, 2003

white ghost noun crack cocaine UK, 1998

white girl noun **1** cocaine US, 1971. **2** heroin UK, 1998

white goods noun cocaine. From the colour; adopts the retailing term for 'large white electrical goods' (refrigerators etc.) UK, 2001

white-haired lady noun marijuana. Possibly derives as a simile for something considered to be as dangerous as marijuana UK, 1998

white hat noun **1** an officer in a firefighting company US, 1954. **2** a computer hacker who acts with a legal or moral justification US, 2001

white horse noun **1** heroin. An elaboration of HORSE (heroin) UK, 2003. **2** cocaine. A play on HORSE (heroin) which is mostly brown US, 1977

white junk noun heroin, possibly of the finest quality. An embellishment of JUNK (heroin) from the colour of the powdered drug US, 1977

white kaffir noun a white person who associates with black people. Racist and abusive SOUTH AFRICA, 1846

white knight noun a night spent under the influence of cocaine. The colour of cocaine and a pun on 'night' UK, 2001

white-knuckle verb to persevere on courage alone, especially in the quitting of an addictive drug US, 1974

white-knuckle adjective anxiety-making; frightening; thrilling. From the effect of holding-on tightly UK, 1988

white lady noun **1** any strong white spirit such as gin or methylated spirits AUSTRALIA, 1935. **2** a powdered narcotic, especially cocaine or heroin. The shortened form 'lady' is also used US, 1968

white light noun LSD. Possibly a reference to The Velvet Underground's 1967 album 'White Light/White Heat' UK, 1969

white lightning noun **1** strong, if inferior, homemade whisky US, 1921. **2** LSD; LSD mixed with methamphetamine or similar US, 1970

whiteline fever noun an addiction to cocaine. The white powder is shaped in a LINE for inhalation UK, 1996

white man noun an honourable man US, 1865

white man's time noun used for denoting punctuality US, 1963

white meat noun a white person as a sex object; the genitals of a white person; sex with a white person US, 1957

white mice noun **1** during the conflict in Vietnam, the South Vietnamese civilian police. From their white helmets and gloves US, 1977. **2** dice. Rhyming slang UK, 1954

white missy noun a glass of cheap white rum BARBADOS, 1965

white money noun in prison, actual currency. Required for major purchases, such as drugs US, 1976

white mosquitoes; white mosquito noun cocaine. Probably from the 'sting' of an injection US, 1949

white mule noun an illegally manufactured whisky, colourless and powerful US, 1921

white nigger noun a French-Canadian. Offensive CANADA, 1971

white nurse; nurse noun powdered drugs; cocaine; heroin; morphine US, 1936

white-on-white noun a white shirt that was deemed fashionable in the 1940s US, 1976

white-out; whitey noun an instance of paling as a symptom of imminent faintness, dizziness or vomiting. From the draining of colour from the face UK: SCOTLAND, 1988

White Owl noun a branded White Owl™ cigar re-made to contain marijuana US, 2003

white Owsley noun a type of high quality LSD. From the name of legendary LSD manufacturer Augustus Owsley Stanley III US, 1974

white pipe noun a mixture of marijuana and crushed Mandrax™ (a branded tranquilizer in tablet form) smoked or ingested orally. A tablet of Mandrax, also known as a 'white', enhances the effect of the marijuana. When 'white pipe' is smoked it is usually in a pipe improvised with a broken bottle SOUTH AFRICA, 1998

white policeman's roll noun in an illegal numbers gambling lottery, a bet on 13, 37 and 70 US, 1949

white powder noun a narcotic in white powder form, that is, heroin, cocaine or morphine US, 1908

white-powder bar noun lawyers who defend drug dealers UK, 1998

white robin noun a variety of MDMA, the recreational drug best known as ecstasy. From the colour of the tablet and the embossed motif UK, 2002

white rock noun high quality methamphetamine in rock form US, 1989

white Russian noun in homosexual usage, the passing of semen from one mouth to another US, 1987

white shirt *noun* in roller derby, a skater who plays honourably and is seen as the 'good guy', usually from the team designated as the home team *US, 1999*

whiteshirt *noun* a senior prison officer. From the uniform *UK, 1996*

white shit *noun* cocaine *UK, 1996*

white shoes *noun* white-wall tyres *US, 1978*

white sidewalls *noun* the visible scalp on the side of the head after a short haircut, especially a military haircut *US, 1968*

whiteskin *noun* in poker, any card ranked ten or lower *US, 1943*

white slave *noun* a woman engaged in enforced prostitution *UK, 1857*

whitesocks *noun* a ferocious if tiny mosquito *US, 1965*

white stuff *noun* any powdered drug – morphine, heroin or cocaine *US, 1914*

white sugar *noun* crack cocaine. From the appearance *UK, 1998*

white telephone *noun* ▶ **speak on the great white telephone; talk into the big white telephone; talk to God on the big white telephone** to vomit into a lavatory bowl. From the image of a sick person leaning over a white lavatory bowl and crying 'God!' in despair *US, 1978*

white tornado *noun* freebase cocaine *US, 1979*

white trash *noun* an impoverished or anti-social white person or persons; originally, and still, the poverty-stricken white population of the southern US. Originally black usage; derogatory; abbreviates to 'trash' (rubbish) *US, 1831*

white turtle-neck brigade *noun* male homosexuals. From a type of jumper that was in vogue, and, perhaps intended as a discreet signal between gay men *UK, 1969*

white van man *noun* the average tabloid-reader-in-the-street, the man-in-the-street. It is a statistical probability that the driver constructively criticising your driving is behind the wheel of a white van. Coined in 1997 by BBC Radio 2 DJ Sarah Kennedy *UK, 1997*

whitewash *noun* in sports, a victory in which the opponent does not score at all *US, 1867*

whitewash *verb* to win a game without your opponent scoring *US, 1971*

white widow *noun* a variety of marijuana, *2002*

white wog *noun* a Welsh person. Usually jocular, from WOG (any person of non-white ethnicity) and a recognition of the Welsh as a race apart within the British Isles; it is, perhaps, interesting to note that a Welsh accent attempted by an English person has a pronounced tendency to sound Indian *UK, 1984*

white worm *noun* an uninfected appendix removed in surgery based on an incorrect diagnosis *US, 1994*

whitey *noun* **1** a white person or white people collectively. Insulting; a gesture of resistance *US, 1942*. **2** an amphetamine pill *US, 1982*. **3** in pool, the cue ball *US, 1983* ▷*see:* **WHITE-OUT**

Whitney dressed as Britney applied to an older person dressed in a younger fashion. A modern variation of the popular idiom, 'mutton dressed as lamb'; formed on the US entertainers Whitney Houston (b.1963) and Britney Spears (b.1981) *UK, 2004*

whittle *verb* ▶ **whittle the gut stick** (of a male) to masturbate *UK, 2003*

whiz *noun* ▶ **the whiz** pick pocketing *UK, 1937*

whiz *verb* to urinate *US, 1971*

whiz; whizz *noun* **1** a genius; somebody who is extremely proficient at a given activity. An abbreviation of 'wizard' *US, 1914*. **2** an act of urinating. Often in a construction such as 'take a whiz' *US, 1971*. **3** whisky *US, 1953*. **4** on the railways, the pressurised air that operates the brake system *US, 1977*. ▶ **on the whiz** operating as a pickpocket *US, 1950*

whizbang *verb* to travel fast *US, 1966*

whizbang; whizz-bang *noun* an injected mixture of cocaine and heroin; cocaine; heroin *US, 1933*

whizbox *noun* a global positioning system device. Gulf war usage *US, 1991*

whiz-kid; whizz-kid *noun* a precociously bright child; hence a young person advancing in business faster than expectations *US, 1960*

whizo *noun* a weapons system officer *US, 1991*

whizz *verb* to use amphetamines *UK, 2000*

whizz; wizz; whiz *noun* amphetamine. A pun on SPEED *UK, 1993*

whizzbang *noun* a pretty girl *US, 1947*

whizzer *noun* **1** an excellent thing; also used as a nickname for a person who excels *UK, 1888*. **2** the penis *US, 1999*. **3** a pickpocket. Variants include 'whiz' and 'whizz' *US, 1925*. **4** in poker, a successful play of an inferior hand, or the person playing it *US, 1988*. **5** a drinking bout *CANADA, 1975* ▷*see:* **WYSSA**

whizzhead *noun* a habitual amphetamine user *UK, 2000*

whizz kid *noun* a habitual amphetamine user *UK, 1999*

whizz-kids *noun* in police use, forensic scientists or a forensic science department. Usually used with 'the'. Formed on 'whizz-kid' (a precociously bright child) *UK, 1971*

whizz mob *noun* a gang of pickpockets *UK, 1929*

whizzo; wizzo *noun* in the US military, a weapons system operator or officer. From a vocalisation of the abbreviation WSO *US, 1993*

whizzo!; wizzo! splendid! *UK, 1905*

whizzo; wizzo *adjective* excellent. After WHIZZO! (an exclamation of delight) *UK, 1948*

whizzy *adjective* used of a computer program, well-designed and attractive *US, 1991*

whoa! used for urging a serious reconsideration of the direction that the conversation is taking. From the C19 command to a horse or ox to stop, and still evocative of a simple, rural world *US, 1981*

whoady *noun* a close friend or family member *US, 2004*

who are you looking at? used aggressively as an offensive challenge *UK, 1999*

Who ate all the pies? You fat bastard, You fat bastard a call and response chant used to taunt anyone who is overweight. A chant from the football terraces that has spread wider *UK, 2001*

who-began-it *noun* an admonishment or a threatened beating *IRELAND, 2000*

who cares? expresses a dismissive lack of concern or interest *US, 1844*

whodunnit; whodunit *noun* **1** a murder mystery novel, film or other entertainment; a detective novel. Adopted in the UK in 1942 from the US *US, 1930*. **2** in prison, a meat pie. A body has been discovered under the pastry! *UK, 1950*

who he? usually used for jocular or dismissive effect *UK, 1981*

who knows it? used as a ritualistic questioning of the veracity of a statement *US, 1963*

whole ball of wax *noun* everything *US, 1953*

whole box and dice *noun* everything *AUSTRALIA, 1888*

whole hog *noun* ▶ **go the whole hog** to do something in a thorough way *US, 1828*

whole lot; whole lotta *adverb* a great deal; very much *US, 1907*

who loves ya, baby? used for expressing affection in a humorous fashion. The signature line of the police captain played by Telly Savalas on the television police drama *Kojak* (CBS, 1973–78). Repeated with referential humour *US, 1978*

whomp back *verb* to drink. A play on KNOCK BACK (to drink) *US, 1973*

whomper *noun* a powerful, hard-breaking wave *US, 1964*

whoof *verb* to fart *UK, 1966*

whoof back *verb* to eat or drink greedily *UK, 2000*

whoo-hoo! used as a humorous expression of happiness, usually ironic. From the television cartoon *The Simpsons US, 1996*

whoop; woop *noun* a bit; a small amount *US, 1904*

whoop *verb* ▶ **whoop it up** to make a great deal of rowdy noise *US, 1884*

whoop; woop *noun* ▶ **give a whoop in hell** to care, generally in a negative context *US, 1970*

whoop and holler *noun* an indeterminate, relatively small distance *US, 1964*

whoop and holler *verb* to shout; to carry on loudly *US, 1969*

whoop-de-do *noun* **1** in horse racing, a style of racing based on the premise of establishing an early lead and then running as fast as possible with maximum whip and heel encouragement *US, 1959*. **2** in motorcycle racing, a closely spaced sequence of hills or rises *US, 1973*. **3** a loud and rowdy event or gathering *US, 1929*

whoop-de-do *adjective* **1** in horse racing, employing the strategy of riding all-out from the start of the race *US, 1948*. **2** celebratory, uproarious. Variants include 'whoop-de-doodle' and 'whoopidy-do' *US, 1932*

whoop-de-doo!; woop-tee-doo! used as an expression of strong support or celebration. Often ironic *US, 2000*

whoopee *noun* ▶ **make whoopee 1** to have sex. A forced and silly euphemism, but one sanctioned by television censors; it was used with annoying regularity by Bob Eubanks, host of *The Newlywed Game* television programme (ABC, 1966–90) *US, 1928*. **2** to indulge in, and take pleasure in, boisterous or rowdy merry-making *UK, 1933*

whoopee! used for expressing great excitement *UK, 1862*

whoopee card *noun* a computer punch card with all the holes punched out *US, 1991*

whoopeedoo! used as an, often ironic, expression of celebration. An elaboration of WHOOPEE! *UK, 2001*

whoops! used as a hurried expression of regret *US, 1937*

whoopsie *noun* a male homosexual *US, 1961*

whoopsie-daisy!; whoops-a-daisy! used for registering dismay or surprise, often implying clumsiness *US, 1925*

whoop-up trail *noun* the terrain over which men and boys ride horses fast *CANADA, 1987*

Whoor's melt *noun* ▷ *see:* HOOR'S MELT

whop *verb* to strike someone with heavy blows *UK, 1575*

whopper *noun* **1** something that is extremely and unusually large. The best known Whopper in the US is a hamburger sandwich introduced by the original Burger King™ restaurant in Miami in 1957 *UK, 1785*. **2** a big lie *US, 1984*

whopper with cheese *noun* a fat woman with thrush. Medical slang, punning on a well-advertised burger *UK, 2002*

whopping *adjective* enormous, powerful *UK, 1706*

whop stick *noun* a hammer *US, 1992*

who pulled your chain? who asked for your opinion?; what has upset you? *UK, 1937*

who rattled your cage? who asked for your opinion?; what has upset you? *UK, 1985*

whore *noun* **1** a girl. Used with sarcasm in reference to a girl who is definitely neither a prostitute nor even apparently promiscuous *US, 1981*. **2** in a deck of playing cards, a queen *US, 1967*. **3** used as a semi-affectionate term for a man *IRELAND, 1959*

whore *verb* to work as a prostitute *UK, 1583*

whore-dog *noun* a promiscuous woman *US, 1980*

whore-hopper *noun* a frequent customer of prostitutes *US, 1977*

whore house cut *noun* cutting a deck of cards by removing a section from the middle of the deck and moving it to the top or bottom *US, 1951*

whore note *noun* a two-dollar note *US, 1970*

whore of Babylon *noun* an extremely promiscuous woman. Originally a disparaging sobriquet for the Church of Rome, in allusion to the Book of Revelations, Chapter XVII, where she is one of several mysterious Christian allegorical figures of evil *US, 1992*

whore's bath; whore splash *noun* an impromptu and quick cleaning of the body at a sink, with special attention to cleaning the genitals *US, 1950*

whore scars *noun* puncture wounds and bruises from needle use *US, 1970*

whore's egg *noun* in lobstering, a sea urchin (*Strongylocentrotus drobachiensis*) *CANADA, 1829*

whoreshop *noun* a brothel *UK, 1938*

whore's melt *noun* ▷ *see:* HOOR'S MELT

whore-style *adverb* said when a woman has sex with her underpants still around one leg *US, 1973*

whoretel *noun* a hotel or motel that caters for prostitutes *US, 1973*

whore wagon *noun* a police van used for sweeps to arrest prostitutes *US, 1970*

Whorez *nickname* Juarez, Mexico. The phonics work and Juarez has something of a reputation for its prostitutes *US, 1970*

who-shot-John *noun* a reproach or interrogation *US, 1969*

whosis *noun* used in place of a person's name which the speaker cannot remember or doesn't think is important *US, 1953*

whosit; whoosit; whozit; whoozit *noun* used to refer to a name (usually of a person, sometimes a thing) that is unknown, forgotten, to be avoided or hardly worth mentioning *UK, 1948*

who smelt it dealt it used for attributing the source of a fart. A childish rhyme, sometimes with formulaic responses *UK, 1998*

who's robbing this coach? mind your own business. This comes from an old joke about Ned Kelly (a famous Australian bushranger) robbing a coach. He declares he's going to 'rob all the men and rape all the women'. A gentlemen attempts to intervene on behalf of the women, when one of the ladies pipes up and says 'Who's robbing this coach, you or Mr Kelly?' *AUSTRALIA, 1945*

who's up who who is in charge?; what's going on here? Supplied to Baker in a notebook of World War 2 slang. Sometimes used literally as regards the interpersonal relationships of a group of people, but often metaphorically. Also elaborated to 'who's up who and who's paying the rent' *AUSTRALIA, 1966*

who's your daddy?; who's the daddy? who is in charge (of this situation)? *US, 2001*

who threw you nuts? who excited your interest?; who asked for your opinion? By implication the person addressed is being called a monkey *UK, 1999*

Whovian *noun* a dedicated fan of BBC cult science fiction television programme *Dr Who* *UK, 1998*

whup *verb* to beat someone *US, 1945*

why-for *noun* the reason or cause *US, 1954*

Whykickamoocow *noun* a notional remote town *NEW ZEALAND, 1984*

wibbly-wobbly *adjective* very wobbly; unsteady *UK, 1984*

wick *noun* **1** the penis. A reduced form of HAMPTON WICK (PRICK) *UK, 1960*. **2** an irritating or bad-tempered person *UK: SCOTLAND, 1988*. **3** in bowls, a glancing blow which (generally more by luck than judgement) brings a bowl into contention. Not a very polite term *UK, 1990*. ▶ **get on your wick** to get on your nerves; to exasperate you. Based on rhyming slang for PRICK (the penis) *UK, 1945*

wick! used for registering firm approval. Abbreviated from WICKED! but extended to two syllables as spoken 'wee-ick!' by 10-year-old children in Cardiff, south Wales, 16th October 2001 *UK, 2001*

wick-dipper *noun* a man objectified sexually. From WICK (the penis) and DIP YOUR WICK (to have sex) *UK, 1994*

wicked *noun* especially pure heroin *UK, 2002*

wicked *adjective* excellent *US, 1920*

wicked *adverb* extremely. A rare instance of late C20 American slang that has stayed regional; a common term in New England ('wicked hot', 'wicked cold' etc.) rarely heard elsewhere *US, 1984*

wicked witch *noun* a woman, especially a malicious or contemptible woman. Rhyming slang for BITCH *UK, 1998*

wicker-head *noun* a Vietnamese peasant. From their straw hats *US, 1991*

wick off *verb* to exasperate or aggravate someone. A variation of GET ON YOUR WICK *UK, 2002*

wicky *noun* the buttocks *BAHAMAS, 1982*

wid *preposition* with. Colloquial pronunciation *UK, 1869*

widder; widda; widdy *noun* a widow *UK, 1837*

widdle *verb* to urinate *UK, 1961*

wide *noun* ▶ **give a wide** to avoid something or someone *UK, 2000*

wide *adjective* **1** immoral *UK, 1594*. **2** knowing, informed, aware *IRELAND, 1991*

wide boy *noun* a man living by his wits, often a petty criminal *UK, 1937*

wide brown land *noun* Australia. Made famous by the poem *My Country* by Dorothea Mackellar, 1914 *AUSTRALIA, 1908*

wide girl *noun* a woman living by her wits, often a petty criminal *UK, 1956*

wide load *noun* someone with a broad backside. From a common road sign indicating that ahead of the escorting vehicle is a truck with a wide load *US, 1990*

wide-on *noun* a state of sexual excitement in a woman. A jocular riposte to HARD-ON (an erect penis) *AUSTRALIA, 1987*

wide open *adjective* unrestrained by authority; unrestricted by the police; wild *US, 1950*

wide ride *noun* a heavy woman *US, 1994*

widger *noun* **1** a small boy. Noted originally as a Royal Navy usage, probably from the late 1950s; an elaboration of 'wee' (small) *UK, 1984*. **2** the penis, especially a relatively small penis. Probably direct from the sense as 'a small boy' on the model of LITTLE MAN (the penis) *UK, 1997*

widget *noun* used generally for a small gadget; specifically a small device for making beer foam as the can is opened. In the 1990s, UK brewers John Smith's advertisers sold canned beer with a 'widget' – an easier option than to explain the chemistry and technology that creates the beery froth *US, 1931*

widgie *noun* a female teenage delinquent of the 'bodgie and widgie' subculture of the 1950s and 60s. Noted for their promiscuity, wild behaviour and revealing clothing. Perhaps a blend of BODGIE with 'wi-', the first syllable of 'women' *AUSTRALIA, 1950*

wido; wide-oh *noun* a villain, a petty criminal, a rogue. Probably a variation of WIDE BOY (a petty criminal) *UK: SCOTLAND, 1988*

widow *noun* **1** a single word, or two, set on a new line at the end of a paragraph, especially when set on a new page *UK, 1925*. **2** in some poker games, an extra card dealt to the table for all players to use in their hands *US, 1967*. **3** in electric line work, a cable grip *US, 1980*. ▶ **the widow** Veuve Clicquot™ champagne; champagne. From French *veuve* (widow) *UK, 1781*

widow Jones *noun* a toilet *US, 1949*

widow-maker *noun* **1** the M-16 rifle, introduced as the standard US Army infantry rifle in 1967. Early versions of the rifle were prone to jamming, thus 'making widows' *US, 1990*. **2** in Vietnam, a Viet Cong booby trap *US, 1990*. **3** in trucking, any long haul truck *US, 1971*

widow's mite; widow's *noun* a light, especially of the type required by a smoker. Rhyming slang *UK, 1931*

widow's wink; widow's *noun* a Chinese person. Rhyming slang for CHINK (a Chinese person) *UK, 1979*

Widow Twankey; widow *noun* **1** a handkerchief. Rhyming slang for HANKY, formed on the pantomime 'dame' who is Aladdin's mother *UK, 1992*. **2** an American. Rhyming slang for YANKEE *UK, 1992*

wiener; weiner *noun* the penis. The phallic connotations of the food item lead to this usage *US, 1960*

wiener roast *noun* a picnic featuring hot dogs *US, 1920*

wienie *noun* in drag racing, a slick racing tyre *US, 1965* ▷ *see:* WEENIE, WEENY

wienie roaster *noun* in drag racing, a jet-powered car *US, 1993*

wife *noun* **1** in a homosexual relationship, the more passive or 'feminine' partner *US, 1883* ▷ *see:* WEENIE, WEENY. **2** in law enforcement, a work partner *US, 1988*. ▶ **the wife** your wife. Folksy, potentially annoying, and almost inevitably patronising *US, 1989*

wife-beater *noun* **1** a sleeveless tee-shirt or undershirt *US, 1994*. **2** any alcoholic drink, especially beer *UK: WALES, 2004*

wifed up *adjective* of a male, in a serious relationship with a female who appears to dominate him *US, 2004*

wife duty *noun* a promise or obligation to spend time with your wife or girlfriend *US, 2000*

wife-in-law *noun* one prostitute in relation to another prostitute working for the same pimp *US, 1957*

wife's best friend *noun* the penis *AUSTRALIA, 1971*

wife starver *noun* a man who defaults on maintenance payments *AUSTRALIA, 1950*

wifey; wifie *noun* a wife. A slightly patronising term *UK, 1996*

wifey *adjective* used of a female, dowdy, mature and proper *US, 2001*

wifie *noun* an old woman *UK, 2002*

wig *noun* **1** the head; the mind *US, 1944*. **2** a judge; a barrister *UK, 1956*. ▶ **tighten your wig** to use drugs and become intoxicated *US, 1986*. ▶ **with a wig** owing; to pay. A shameless pun on 'toupee' and 'to pay' *AUSTRALIA, 1989*

wig; wig out *verb* to lose control of your emotions; to become angry *US, 1955*

wig-chop *noun* a haircut. Teen slang *US, 1955*

wig city *noun* a medical institution for the mentally ill. Extended from the adjective sense *US, 2001*

wig city *adjective* mentally unbalanced, eccentric (usually when the latter is thought to be the former) *US, 1998*

wigged *adjective* confused, disoriented, especially as a result of drug use; drug-intoxicated *US, 1951*

wigged out *adjective* in an extreme state of drug intoxication, excitement or rage; dissociated from reality *US, 1968*

wigger; wigga; whigger *noun* a white youth who affects the speech patterns, fashion and other mannerisms of black youth. An elision of 'white NIGGER' *US, 1988*

wiggle *noun* in electric line work, a secondary voltage tester with a glow-light indicator *US, 1980*. ▶ **get a wiggle on** to hurry *US, 1896*

wiggle *verb* to wriggle; to walk with a sinuous swaying of the hips. A colloquial variation; in conventional use from the C13 to C19 *UK, 2002*

wiggle room *noun* scope for freedom of thought or action; room for political manoeuvring and compromise *US, 1941*

wigglers *noun* the fingers *US, 1970*

wiggly; wiggly-waggly *adjective* of movement, wriggly; of form, irregularly undulated *UK, 1907*

wiggy *adjective* crazy; outstanding; wild; creative *US, 1961*

wigit *noun* MDMA, the recreational drug best known as ecstasy *UK, 2003*

wig-out *noun* a period of controlled craziness *UK, 2001*

wig out *verb* to become angry, to lose your temper *UK, 1955*

wig-out *adjective* crazed *UK, 2001*

wig picker *noun* a psychiatrist *US, 1961*

wig-trig *noun* an idea *US, 1946*

wigwag *noun* in the television and film industries, a light outside a sound stage indicating that shooting is in process *US, 1990*

wigwam *noun* in a deck of cards, an ace. From the visual similarity between an 'A' and a wigwam *US, 1988*

wigwam for a goose's bridle *noun* used as a nonsense answer to a question *AUSTRALIA, 1960*

Wilbur Wright; wilbur *noun* a flight (air travel). Rhyming slang, formed from the elder of the US aviation pioneers, the Wright Brothers *UK, 1992*

Wilcannia shower *noun* a dust storm. Wilcannia is an inland town in New South Wales. Other locations similarly used by nature, weather and irony: Bedourie, Bogan, Bourke, Cobar, Darling and Wimmera *AUSTRALIA, 1945*

wilco; willco (I) *will c*omply!; generally, used as a signal of assent. Originally used as military communications, often to complement ROGER (message understood). *UK, 1946*

wild *adjective* **1** used of film in the television and film industries, shot without sound *US, 1990*. **2** of prison sentences, served consecutively *US, 1972*. ▶ **go wild in the bush** (used of a white person) to have sex with a black person *BAHAMAS, 1982*

wild about *adjective* enthusiastic about; having a strong liking for; sexually infatuated with *UK, 1868*

wild card *noun* **1** an unpredictable factor; an unknown. From card playing jargon where it represents a card of no predetermined value *US, 2002*. **2** a dangerously unpredictable person *UK, 2001*. **3** an enemy fighter plane *US, 1986*

wildcat *noun* **1** strong, illegally manufactured whisky *US, 1999*. **2** methcathinone mixed with cocaine. An elaboration of CAT (methcathinone) *US, 1998*. **3** in oil drilling, a well drilled in unproven land *US, 1954*

wildcat *adjective* **1** unauthorised, unlicensed, unsanctioned *US, 1870*. **2** characterised by high risk and unsound business planning *US, 1877*

wildcatter *noun* **1** an independent, risk-taking oil driller who drills wildcat wells *US, 1883*. **2** in trucking, an owner-operator who works independently *US, 1946*

wild colonial boy *noun* an uninhibited, free-living man. Originally meaning 'a bushranger'. From the title of a popular folk song and still often used allusively *AUSTRALIA, 1881*

wild duck *noun* a person who has failed to pay a debt and is not seen as likely to do so *AUSTRALIA, 1989*

wild flower *noun* a variety of MDMA, the recreational drug best known as ecstasy *UK, 2002*

wild hair *noun* an impulsive notion. A shortened form of WILD HAIR UP YOUR ASS without the full connotation of annoyance *US, 1989*

wild hair up your ass; wild hair up your butt *noun* the notional cause of irrational, obsessive behaviour *US, 1981*

wild horse *noun* a Ford 'Mustang' car. Citizens' band radio slang *UK, 1981*

wilding *noun* violent youth gang activity directed towards random victims. A term popularised by the 'Central Park Jogger' case in 1989 *US, 1989*

wildo *noun* a person behaving in a wild or crazy manner *UK, 1966*

wild-out *noun* a gang fight *US, 1999*

wild thing *noun* ▶ **do the wild thing** to have sex *US, 1990*

wild up *verb* to agitate someone; to make someone nervous *US, 2003*

Wilfred *noun* the penis. A variation of WILLY (the penis) *UK, 2001*

Wilhemina *noun* a female customer, especially of discreet or illegal services. A feminisation of BILLY BUNTER (a customer) *UK, 2002*

Wilkie Bard *noun* a card; a business card; a playing card; a race card, etc. Rhyming slang, formed from a music hall comedian, 1874–1944 *UK, 1960*

Wilkinson Sword *noun* bald. Rhyming slang, formed from the name of a razor manufacturer *UK, 1998*

will do used as an expression of assent to carry out an action. By ellipsis of the personal pronoun, possibly influenced by WILCO *UK, 1955*

willets *noun* the female breasts *UK, 1998*

william *noun* a piece of currency. A pun on 'bill' *US, 1983*

William Hague *adjective* vague. Rhyming slang, formed from the politician who led the Conservative party, 1997–2001 *UK, 1998*

William Pitt *noun* excrement. Rhyming slang for SHIT, formed from the British Prime Minister known, historically, as 'Pitt the Elder', 1708–78, or his son, also Prime Minister, 'Pitt the Younger', 1759–1806 *UK, 1998*

William Powell *noun* a towel. Rhyming slang, formed from the US film actor, 1874–1944 *UK, 1961*

William Tell *verb* to give off an unpleasant *smell*. Rhyming slang, formed from a legendary Swiss hero *UK, 1992*

William the Third *noun* a piece of excrement. Rhyming slang for 'turd' *AUSTRALIA, 1968*

willie *noun* **1** a piece of currency. A pun on 'bill' *US, 1983*. **2** a gambler's wallet or financial resources *AUSTRALIA, 1949*

Willie Peter; Wilie Peter grenade *noun* an M-34 white phosphorous anti-personnel hand grenade. Another use of the military phonetic alphabet *US, 1977*

willies *noun* a condition of fear or nervousness *US, 1896*

Willie the Shit Burner *noun* used as a generic term for the poor soul assigned to collect and burn solid human waste collected in latrines at US military bases in Vietnam *US, 1990*

willie weaver *noun* a drunk driver *US, 1976*

willing *adjective* gutsy; courageous; unwavering; aggressive *AUSTRALIA, 1899*

will o' the wisp; willer *noun* a potato crisp. Rhyming slang *UK, 1992*

Will's Whiff *noun* *syph*ilis. Rhyming slang, formed from a brand of small cigar *UK, 1992*

willy *noun* **1** the penis. Originally northern English, not dialect, for 'a child's penis' or a childish name for any penis. Adopted by adults as a jocular reference, now widely used as a non-offensive and broadcastable term. The spelling 'willie' is also used *UK, 1905*. **2** a tantrum. Generally in the phrases 'chuck' or 'throw a willy' *AUSTRALIA, 1941*. **3** a supply of money for gambling *AUSTRALIA, 1949*. **4** a wallet *AUSTRALIA, 1967*

willy-nilly *adverb* here and there, haphazardly. Not particularly related to the C17 sense of the phrase meaning 'willingly or unwillingly' *US, 1934*

willy warmer *noun* the vagina *UK, 2001*

willy-waving *noun* macho behaviour that is especially unnecessary or foolish. Formed on WILLY (the penis) *UK, 1997*

willy-willy *noun* a small, localised whirlwind. From the Australian Aboriginal language Yindjibarndi *AUSTRALIA, 1894*

Willy Wonka *noun* a fool. Rhyming slang for PLONKER (a fool *and* the penis), that may be an elaborate play on WILLY (the penis) *UK, 1998*

willy woofter *noun* a homosexual man. Elaboration of WOOFTER (a male homosexual) *UK, 2000*

Wilma *noun* a Protestant female, especially one who is a supporter of Glasgow Rangers football club. A female form of William, and the female equivalent of BILLY-BOY *UK: SCOTLAND, 1996*

wilma *adjective* meek. A personification of uncertain pedigree, recorded as a contemporary gay usage *UK, 2003*

Wilson *noun* in skateboarding, a fall producing serious injury *US, 1984*

Wilson Pickett *noun* **1** a white phosphorous flare or grenade. From the initials WP; Pickett was a popular American rhythm and blues singer *US, 1991*. **2** a ticket. Rhyming slang, formed from the name of the US soul singer (b.1941) *UK, 1992*

Wimmera shower *noun* a dust storm. Wimmera is an inland town in Victoria. Other locations similarly used by nature, weather and irony: Bedourie, Bogan, Bourke, Cobar, Darling and Wilcannia *AUSTRALIA, 1945*

wimmin; wimmen *noun* women. The first variation was adopted and promoted by politically aware feminists to avoid ending with 'men'; the second variation is a phonetic accident *UK, 1910*

wimmos *noun* women. A variation of pronounced 'wimmin', used by cricketers *UK, 2003*

wimp *noun* a weak and timid person. A thorough treatment of the word may be found in 'Wimp', Reinhold Aman, *Maledicta*, Volume VIII, p. 43–56, 1984–1985. The word played a major role in the US presidential election of 1988, in which President George H.W. Bush had to overcome a widely held perception that he was 'a wimp' *US, 1920*

wimpish *adjective* weak, ineffectual *US, 1925*

wimp out *verb* to give way to timidity or fear *US, 1981*

wimpy *adjective* feeble; afraid. From WIMP (a weak and timid person). Although the adjective was not recorded until the late 1960s, the *Popeye the Sailor* radio programme gave the US J. Wellington Wimpy, known simply as Wimpy, in 1936 *US, 1967*

win *verb* ▶ **are you winning?** used as a rhetorical greeting *UK, 1984*. ▶ **win hands down** to win with great ease. From horse racing, when a jockey may relax the hold on the reins when victory seems certain *UK, 1882*. ▶ **would win doing hand-springs; would win with its head in its chest; would win shelling peas** of a racehorse, certain to win. Also used as 'could win' *UK, 1994*. ▶ **you can't win** used for expressing the futility of action, or the inevitability of failure *UK, 1926*

winch *verb* **1** to date a member of the opposite sex; to court; to go steady. Probably from 'wench' (a girl) *UK: SCOTLAND, 1985*. **2** to kiss and cuddle. Extends from the sense 'to date, to court' *UK: SCOTLAND, 1985*

winchell *noun* a trusting, unsophisticated person *US, 1972*

winco *noun* a *wing* commander in the Royal Air Force *UK, 1941*

wind *noun* ▶ **a wind so sharp it cuts the whiskers right off your face** a cold, hard wind *CANADA, 1988*. ▶ **get in the wind** to run quickly; to depart *US, 1965*. ▶ **get the wind** to smoke marijuana *UK, 1998*. ▶ **get the wind up; have the wind up** to be nervous or scared *UK, 1916*. ▶ **in the wind** free from prison *US, 1992*. ▶ **put the wind up someone** to make someone afraid *UK, 1916*. ▶ **take someone's wind** to kill someone *US, 1974*

wind *verb* ▷*see:* WINE

wind and kite *noun* a website. Rhyming slang *UK, 2002*

windbag *noun* a habitually verbose talker *UK, 1827*

windball *noun* intestinal pain *US, 2003*

winded *adjective* hungover *US, 1992*

winder *noun* a drug addict who regularly enters and leaves treatment programmes *US, 1970*

windie *noun* a wind surfer *NEW ZEALAND, 1994*

Windies *nickname* the West Indies international cricket team *AUSTRALIA, 1964*

windjammer *noun* **1** a person who talks too much *US, 1949*. **2** a citizens' band radio user who monopolises conversation *US, 1976*. **3** in drag racing and hot rodding, a supercharger *US, 1968*. **4** a railway air brake *US, 1946*. **5** a hammer. Rhyming slang *UK, 1992*

windmill *noun* in hot rodding and drag racing, a supercharger *US, 1965*

window *noun* **1** in card games, the card at the end of a player's hand *US, 1967*. **2** in American casinos, the space through which the careful observer can see the blackjack dealer's down-card as he deals *US, 1985*. ▶ **out the window; out of the window** out of the question *US, 1983*. ▶ **pick a window – you're leaving!** used as a jocular threat of violence *UK, 1995*. ▶ **window's open** used for describing obvious and inept cheating *US, 1979*

window dress *verb* in poker, accidentally on purpose to let other players see the end card in your hand *US, 1967*

window hop *verb* to move from window to window inside a house at night, waiting for a substance-addicted spouse to come home *US, 1998*

window-licker *noun* a severely disabled person. Offensive. Derived, apparently, from the attitude of such a person when seen travelling on a bus *UK, 2003*

window music *noun* on the railways, scenery *US, 1977*

windowpane; window *noun* a dose of LSD on a tiny, clear piece of gelatin *US, 1975*

window party *noun* an act of vengeful vandalism, in which the aggrieved party breaks all the glass in his victim's boat *CANADA, 1999*

window rattler *noun* someone who snores with great resonance *UK, 1964*

window washer *noun* a heavy rain storm *US, 1976*

Windoze *noun* Microsoft Windows™. Not praise *US, 1997*

wind pie *noun* nothing to eat *FIJI, 1994*

windshield time *noun* time spent driving; paid travel time between a reporting location and the job site, or between job sites *US, 1978*

wind, skin and ice *noun* as specifications for a car, air conditioning, leather upholstery and *in*-car entertainment. Motor trade slang *UK, 2004*

Windsor ballet *nickname* collectively, the strip and sex clubs in Windsor, Ontario, Canada *US, 1997*

Windsor Castle; windsor; brown windsor *noun* the anus. Rhyming slang for ARSEHOLE, formed from a royal residence; shortened to 'windsor' and then punningly elaborated to 'brown windsor' as a type of soup *UK, 1992*

windsucker *noun* in horse racing, a horse that swallows air when running *US, 1947*

wind trap *noun* strands of hair that a semi-bald man may cultivate and style to lay over his naked pate. Rhyming slang for FLAP *UK, 1992*

wind tunnel *noun* in homosexual usage, a loose anus and rectum *US, 1981*

wind-up *noun* **1** a practical joke; a send-up *UK, 1984*. **2** a person who teases *UK, 1977*

wind up *verb* **1** to make fun of someone; to play a practical joke on someone. The image of the mainspring in a clockwork motor getting more and more tightly wound *UK, 1979*. **2** to arrive; to arrive eventually; to settle in a final position *US, 1918*

windy *noun* **1** a windproof jacket and over-trousers *ANTARCTICA, 2003*. **2** in pool, a shot that passes the object ball without touching it. Based on the image of the cue ball breezing by the object ball *US, 1993*

Windy *noun* ▶ **the Windy** Chicago, Illinois. From the winds that sweep the city; a short form of WINDY CITY *US, 1969*

windy *adjective* afraid; very nervous; ill at ease *UK, 1916*

Windy City *nickname* **1** Chicago, Illinois. New York slang lexicographer Barry Popik has relentlessly worked to debunk the myth that the term was coined in conjunction with the 1893 World's Fair. Popik has traced the term to Cincinnati newspapers in 1876. Wide usage still *US, 1876*. **2** Port Elizabeth *SOUTH AFRICA, 1989*. **3** Wellington, New Zealand *NEW ZEALAND, 2004*

wind your neck in! 'be quiet!' *UK, 1943*

Windypeg *nickname* Winnipeg, Manitoba *CANADA, 2002*

wine; wind *verb* while dancing, to gyrate the pelvis in a sexual manner *TRINIDAD AND TOBAGO, 1916*

wine and dine *verb* to entertain someone with wine and food. Earlier as 'dine and wine' *UK, 1916*

wine grape *noun* a Roman Catholic. Glasgow rhyming slang for PAPE *UK: SCOTLAND, 1985*

wine head *noun* a drunkard who favours wine *US, 1962*

wine shed *noun* a bar *US, 1984*

winfly *noun* a flight made during winter from New Zealand to Antarctica *ANTARCTICA, 1969*

wing *noun* **1** the arm *UK, 1823*. **2** a winning streak in poker *US, 1988*

wing *verb* **1** to shoot at someone and wound them but not seriously *UK, 1802*. **2** to discipline someone *UK, 1996*. ▶ **wing it** to improvise; to do something with little preparation. Originally from the theatre, indicating the necessity of learning a part at short notice, standing in the wings of a stage *US, 1970*

wing and a prayer *noun* a very narrow margin of automotive power or control; hence, a slender hope or chance. Originally applied to the minimum requirement for an aircraft's emergency landing *UK, 1943*

wingding; wing-ding *noun* **1** a party, a celebration *US, 1949*. **3** in motorcyle racing, a brief loss of control for which the rider compensates *US, 1965*. **2** a fit, especially one feigned by a drug addict; a person feigning such a fit *US, 1927*

winge *verb* ▷*see:* WHINGE

winging *adjective* drunk or drug-intoxicated *US, 1970*

wingnut *noun* a person who is easily angered or flustered. As a piece of hardware, a 'wingnut' is easily tightened – the basis for its application to a person *US, 1990*

wings *noun* **1** any powdered drug, especially cocaine, heroin or morphine. Because wings give you the lift that gets you HIGH *US, 1953*. **2** insignia worn by motorcycle gang members signifying sexual conquests *US, 1966*. ▶ **get your wings** to use heroin for the first time. A nod to aviation terminology *US, 1989*

wing-wang *noun* the rectum *US, 1970*

wing wipe *noun* a crew member of a military jet aircraft. A term used by the infantry *US, 1990*

wingy *noun* a person with one arm *US, 1980*

wingy *adjective* very loose-fitting, giving the appearance of extreme thinness *TRINIDAD AND TOBAGO, 2003*

wink *noun* the penis *UK, 2001*

winker *noun* the vagina. The imagery of an eye that opens and closes *UK, 1970*

winkie *noun* **1** the vagina *UK, 2001*. **2** a sideways punctuation face indicating laughter, generally formed as ;-) *US, 1995*

winking *noun* ▶ **like winking; like eyes-a-winking** very quickly *UK, 1827*

winkle *noun* a boy's penis; a small penis *US, 1966*. ▶ **have on the winkle** to be obsessed by something *UK, 1969*

winkle-trip *noun* a male striptease act performed for an all-female audience on a Thames pleasure boat *UK, 1980*

winky; winkie *noun* the penis; a small penis; a boy's penis. Usually juvenile, occasionally derisory; probably a variation of WINKLE *UK, 1984*

winner *noun* a loser socially. Sardonic, cruel *US, 1964*

winners *noun* dice that have been altered so as to roll numbers other than seven, useful to the shooter in craps *US, 1950*

winners and losers *noun* trousers. Glasgow rhyming slang on 'troosers' *UK: SCOTLAND, 1985*

winny-popper *noun* the penis. A schoolchildren's term *CANADA, 1968*

wino *noun* **1** a lowly drunk *US, 1913*. **2** a wine connoisseur *NEW ZEALAND, 1997*

win or lose *noun* any and all alcoholic drinks. Rhyming slang for BOOZE *UK, 1992*

wino time *noun* a short jail sentence *US, 1992*

winter *noun* any period between carnival seasons, regardless of the actual time of year *US, 1966*

winter blossoms *noun* the older, female, winter residents of a hotel *UK, 1977*

winterer; winteroverer *noun* a person who spends the winter in Antarctica *ANTARCTICA, 1958*

Winterpeg *nickname* Winnipeg, Manitoba *CANADA, 2002*

winter wear *noun* the foreskin on an uncircumcised penis *US, 1983*

win-win *adjective* said of a situation in which the parties involved all feel that they have done well *US, 1977*

wipe *noun* a handkerchief *US, 1981*

wipe *verb* **1** to dismiss or reject a person; to wash your hands of someone *AUSTRALIA, 1941*. **2** in drag racing, to defeat another car. Created by back-formation; when a car is defeated, the name of the driver is wiped from the list of those competing, so the driver is 'wiped' *US, 2003*. ▶ **wipe the clock** to set a train's air brake valve at the position used for full emergency application. An allusion to the sudden drop of the pressure needle on the air gauge to zero *US, 1975*. ▶ **wipe the floor with; wipe up the floor with; wipe the earth with; wipe the ground with** to inflict an absolute defeat on someone; to surpass someone *UK, 1896*

wiped *adjective* **1** infatuated *UK, 2004*. **2** drunk *US, 1968*. **3** exhausted *US, 1996*

wiped out *adjective* very drug-intoxicated *US, 1974*

wipe-off *noun* **1** a cursory washing of the body using little water *US, 1953*. **2** a total wreck; a write-off *AUSTRALIA, 1945*

wipe off *verb* to wreck or ruin something *AUSTRALIA, 1962*

wipe-out *noun* a fall from a surfboard, usually caused by a wave. A major word of the surfer's lexicon; it was the title and one-word lyric of the 1963 'surf instrumental' by the Surfaris that featured a drum solo practised on the school desk of many an early 1960s schoolboy *AUSTRALIA, 1962*

wipe out *verb* **1** to destroy something; to kill or wound someone *US, 1968*. **2** to remove someone from their position *UK, 1969*

wire *noun* **1** a telegraph message; a telegram *UK, 1876*. **2** a report; information. A vestigial term from the era of telegraphy *UK, 1925*. **3** news transmitted privately *TRINIDAD AND TOBAGO, 1938*. **4** a bookmaking operation *US, 1981*. **5** a small microphone and transmitting device worn on the person as part of law enforcement interception of oral communications *US, 1973*. **6** the penis *IRELAND, 1991*. **7** the buttocks *TRINIDAD AND TOBAGO, 1968*. **8** in a pickpocketing team, the thief who actually picks the victim's pocket *UK, 1851*. **9** in horse racing, the finish line *US, 1974*. **10** amphetamines *UK, 2003*. **11** in pool, the score string *US, 1993*. ▶ **have your wires crossed; get your wires crossed** to be at cross purposes; to be affected by a mutual misunderstanding *UK, 2001*. ▶ **on the wire** in pool, having scored or having been awarded a score as part of the handicapping of a game *US, 1993*

wire *verb* **1** to send a telegraph message *UK, 1859*. **2** to use a small microphone or transmitting device to intercept oral communications *US, 1973*. **3** in skateboarding, to analyse and plan a difficult manoeuvre or trick *US, 1976*

wired *adjective* **1** intoxicated on amphetamines or cocaine. Also used with 'up' *US, 1966*. **2** tense, anxious *UK, 1979*. **3** well-rehearsed *US, 1995*. **4** used of a pair in stud poker, dealt in the first two cards of a hand *US, 1981*

wired to the moon *adjective* extremely drug-intoxicated. An elaboration of WIRED (drug-intoxicated) *UK, 1995*

wired up *adjective* **1** intoxicated on central nervous system depressants *US, 1979*. **2** available for homosexual relations *US, 1961*

wire-fu *noun* a technique that employs wires and pulleys to create choreographed martial art fights. Formed on 'kung fu' *US, 1997*

wirehead *noun* a computer hardware specialist *US, 1991*

wire room *noun* an illegal betting establishment's telephone office *US, 1950*

wires *noun* any central nervous system stimulant *US, 1977*

wire store *noun* a big con based on a supposedly corrupt telegraph official who claims he can delay the reporting of race results to the benefit of the victim *US, 1969*

wire to wire *noun* in horse racing, the entire distance of the race, from start to finish *US, 1951*

wise *verb* to inform or educate someone; to explain something *US, 1905*. ▶ **wise up; wise up to** to learn, realise or understand something *US, 1919*

wise *adjective* ▶ **be wise; be wise to; get wise; get wise to** to be aware of something; to be warned about something *US, 1896*. ▶ **put wise; put wise to** to make someone aware of something; to warn someone about something *US, 1913*

-wise *suffix* in the manner of, or to do with, a conjoined subject *US, 1942*

wiseacre *noun* a smart alec *UK, 1595*

wiseass *noun* an obnoxious person with delusions of cleverness *US, 1971*

wisecrack *noun* a smart, humorous, sometimes cruel remark *US, 1924*

wisecrack *verb* to make smart, humorous and sometimes cruel remarks *US, 1946*

wisecracker *noun* someone who makes smart, humorous and sometimes cruel remarks *US, 1923*

wisecracking *adjective* given to making smart, humorous and sometimes cruel remarks *US, 1915*

wise guy *noun* a recognised member of an organised crime enterprise *US, 1975*

wise monkey *noun* a condom. Rhyming slang for DUNKY, influenced perhaps by the usual number of wise monkeys and a PACKET OF THREE *UK, 1992*

wisenheimer *noun* a smart alec, a wise guy *UK, 1904*

wisepuss *noun* an obnoxious person with delusions of cleverness. A variation of WISEASS *US, 1971*

wish *verb* to greet someone *INDIA, 1979*

wishbone *noun* in hot rodding, a triangular suspension control device *US, 1993*

wishing book *noun* a mail-order catalogue *US, 1975*

wish-was *noun* someone who wishes that he were something that he is not *US, 1991*

wishy-washy *adjective* **1** weak; uncertain *UK, 1703*. **2** in poor condition *TRINIDAD AND TOBAGO, 1993*

wiss *noun* a urination. Glasgow slang *UK, 1996*

wisteria *adjective* clingy. From the characteristics of the plant; a contemporary gay usage *UK, 2003*

wit *noun* a witness *US, 1999*

wit! 'what was just said is not funny!' *US, 1986*

witch *noun* ▶ **the witch** any powdered drug; cocaine, heroin, etc *US, 1949*

witch doctor *noun* a doctor who specialises in internal medicine *US, 1985*

witches' knickers *noun* plastic bags caught up in trees or shrubs *IRELAND, 2000*

witch hazel *noun* heroin *US, 1959*

witch's brew *noun* LSD enhanced with botanical drugs from plants such as deadly nightshade or jimsonweed *US, 1970*

witch's cackle *noun* the male genitals. Rhyming slang for WEDDING TACKLE *UK, 2003*

with authority! used as a humorous comment on a remark made or action taken without hesitation and boldly. Coined on ESPN's Sports Center while narrating footage showing a basketball slam dunk *US, 1997*

with it *adjective* aware of all that is happening; stylish; part of a subculture *US, 1945*

without *adjective* clueless; out of touch; out of style *US, 1999*

wiwi *noun* a French person. A Maori approximation of the French 'oui, oui' *NEW ZEALAND, 1998*

wix *adjective* excellent. Urban youth slang. Probably a reduction of WICKED *UK, 2005*

wizard *noun* **1** an expertly skilled person *UK, 1620*. **2** in computing, a person who has specific and detailed expertise *US, 1983*. **3** in pinball, an expert player *US, 1977*

wizard *adjective* excellent, marvellous. Magical origins; mainly used by the privileged and officer classes until after World War 2, then widespread. Of upper-class society use: '[...] still used, though almost always in inverted commas' (Ann Barr and Peter York, *The Official Sloane Ranger Handbook, p.159, 1982*) *UK, 1922*

wizard! used for expressing approval *UK, 1933*

wizard's sleeve *noun* a capacious vagina. Coined for humorous magazine Viz *UK, 1999*

wizz *noun* ▷*see:* WHIZZ, WHIZZO

wizzard; wizzard of oz *noun* an ounce of marijuana. This plays on the conventional abbreviation 'oz' (ounce) and, by association with the film *The Wizard of Oz*, 1939, which contains the song 'Somewhere Over The Rainbow', suggesting where this measure of marijuana might take you. The misspelling 'wizzard', if deliberate, may be punning on WHIZZ (amphetamine) *UK, 2001*

wizzo *noun* the weapons officer on a military aircraft *US, 1998*

wizzy *adjective* excellent, exciting, wonderful; used for registering general approval. A variation of WIZARD *UK, 1998*

wizzy-wizzy *verb* to whisper *BARBADOS, 1965*

wobble *verb* ▶ **wobble the job** to cause trouble among workers on a unionised worksite *CANADA, 1989*

wobble board *noun* a simple musical instrument made of a sheet of stiff material that is wobbled rhythmically. Invention of the instrument and its name is credited to Australian artist and entertainer Rolf Harris (b.1930) *AUSTRALIA, 1957*

wobbler *noun* **1** an outburst of temper *UK, 1983*. **2** in trucking, a spoke wheel *US, 1971*. ▶ **throw a wobbler** to have a fit of bad temper or anger *US, 2003*

wobblestick *noun* a gear lever on a truck or car *US, 1971*

wobblies; wobs *noun* a powerful and deep vibration of the board while skateboarding fast *US, 1976*

wobbly *noun* a fit of anger *UK, 1977*. ▶ **throw a wobbly** to have a fit of bad temper or anger *NEW ZEALAND, 1984*

Wobbly *noun* a member of the anarchist trade union the International Workers of the World *US, 1914*

wobbly *adjective* uncertain; undecided; risky *UK, 1884*

wobbly egg; wobbly; egg *noun* a capsule of Temazepam™, a branded tranquillizer; any central nervous system depressant; in the plural it refers to the drug in general. From the characteristic nature of gelatine, the original method of manufacturing the capsules *UK, 1996*

wobbly hole *noun* in trucking, the neutral gear *US, 1971*

wobbly orange *noun* a warrant officer in the Royal Air Force. A ludicrous re-use of the initials *UK, 2002*

wodge; wadge *noun* a large amount. Originally used of a bulky mass *UK, 1860*

wog *noun* **1** any person of non-white ethnicity; a native of the Indian subcontinent; an Arab; any (non-British) foreigner, as in 'the wogs begin at Calais'. Derogatory, patronising. Derives possibly from an abbreviation of 'golliwog' (a caricature, black-faced, curly-haired doll) but the widest usage is in reference to Asians and not black people. Popular, unproven etymology has 'wog' as an acronym of 'Western(ised) [or] Wily Oriental Gentleman' *UK, 1929*. **2** any language that isn't English *AUSTRALIA, 1988*. **3** a germ that causes an illness *AUSTRALIA, 1941*

wog *adjective* **1** foreign *UK, 1956*. **2** of non-Anglo-Celtic origin *AUSTRALIA, 1944*

wogball *noun* soccer *AUSTRALIA, 1984*

wog box *noun* a large portable stereo system associated, stereotypically, with black youth culture *UK, 1990*

woggy *adjective* **1** characteristic of a non-white person *AUSTRALIA, 1988*. **2** of non-Anglo-Celtic background *AUSTRALIA, 1968*

wojus *adjective* inferior; of poor quality *IRELAND, 2004*

woke-up *adjective* informed; up-to-date *US, 1968*

wolf *noun* **1** a sexually aggressive man *US, 1945*. **2** in prison, an aggressive, predatory homosexual *US, 1952*. **3** in homosexual anal sex, the active participant *US, 1940*. **4** a prison sentence of 15 years *US, 1990s*

wolf *verb* to act in a sexually aggressive manner *US, 1974*

wolf bait *noun* an attractive young woman *US, 1960*

Wolfhounds *noun* the 27th Infantry Regiment of the 25th Division. Formed in 1901, named by the White Russians in World War 1, distinguished fighters in World War 2, Korea and Vietnam *US, 1968*

wolf in the pack *noun* a traffic police car in the midst of other cars *US, 1962*

wolf pack *noun* a group of friends who play poker at cardrooms, taking advantage of unskilled strangers *US, 1996*

wolf-pack *verb* **1** to engage in criminal gang activity *US, 1982*. **2** to congregate with other teenagers around their cars at shopping centre carparks, drinking beer and idling *US, 1989*

wolf ticket *noun* a threat or other act of intimidation used to coerce *US, 1974*

wolf whistle *noun* a distinctive whistle (generally, a sharply terminated rising note, followed by one that rises briefly before descending and fading) used as a declaration of appreciation for a sexually attractive person. After WOLF (a sexually aggressive man), and generally, but not exclusively, in the vocabulary of men *US, 1952*

wolf-whistle *verb* to whistle in a distinctive declaration of appreciation for a sexually attractive person. From the noun *US, 1955*

wollie; woolah *noun* crack cocaine added to a marijuana cigarette or cigar *US, 1989*

wolly *noun* ▷*see:* WALLY

wollyback *noun* anyone living in a rural area *IRELAND, 1995*

wolver *noun* the penis. Rhyming slang, formed from Midlands' town Wolverhampton as an elaboration of 'hampton', the shortened form of HAMPTON WICK (PRICK) *UK, 1967*

woman in the sun *noun* heroin. Collected in private correspondence with certain musicians *UK, 2001*

womb *noun* the rectum *US, 1983*

wombat *noun* **1** a dull, uninteresting or stupid person. From the name of a stocky native nocturnal marsupial *AUSTRALIA, 1905*. **2** in computing, a *waste of money, brains and time US, 1991*

wombat-headed *adjective* stupid; fat-headed. First used by the bushranger Ned Kelly in his famous 'Jerilderie Letter' in 1879 *AUSTRALIA, 1971*

womb broom *noun* the penis *US, 1973*

womb duster *noun* the penis *US, 1977*

womble *noun* **1** in prison, an inmate detailed as a litter collector. After the children's characters created by Elizabeth Beresford, and in a BBC television series launched in 1973 *UK, 2003*. **2** a fool *UK, 1986*

womble *verb* to pick up litter. From the *raison d'être* of children's television characters in *The Wombles*, who collected litter in the 70s from 1973, and again from 1998 *UK, 1996*

womb sweeper *noun* the penis *US, 1978*

womb-trembler *noun* something that causes great excitement *UK, 2001*

women and children off the street! in shuffleboard, used as a humorous commentary on a hard shooter *US, 1967*

womp; whomp *verb* to beat someone *US, 1964*

wonder star *noun* methcathinone *UK, 1998*

wonder veg *noun* any mushroom with a hallucinogenic effect *UK, 1996*

wonder wand *noun* the penis. An elaboration of WAND (the penis) *US, 2001*

wong *verb* in casino blackjack, to play several hands at a table where the count of cards played favours the player, and then to move on to another table. Named after Stanford Wong, a blackjack expert *US, 1991*

wonga *noun* **1** money. From Romany *wanger* or *wonger*, defined by George Borrow in *Romano Lavo-Lil*, 1907, as 'Coal. Also a term for money; probably because Coal in the cant [criminal] language signifies money'. Romany 'wongar-camming miser' is literally 'one who loves coal'. (Now obsolete 'coal', also 'cole', meant 'money' from the mid-C17, and all but faded away by C20). Variants include 'wong' and 'wonger' *UK, 1953*. **2** marijuana *UK, 1985*

wonk *noun* a student who studies harder than contemporaries consider necessary; a political professional who is studious and therefore well informed. Derogatory *US, 1962*

wonkey; wonky *adjective* broken *US, 2001*

wonk out *verb* to study excessively *US, 1987*

wonky *adjective* **1** unbalanced; out-of-true. Variation of obsolete sense of 'wanky' (inferior, damaged) *UK, 1919*. **2** unsound or unreliable *UK, 1925*. **3** intellectual; out of touch with reality *US, 1970*

won't do itself used before tackling any task as an expression of resigned determination. A very clichéd truism if not a catchphrase *UK, 1999*

woo *noun* sexual foreplay *NEW ZEALAND, 1998*

wood *noun* **1** the fully erect penis *US, 1991*. **2** the penis *TRINIDAD AND TOBAGO, 1950*. **3** in a casino or other gambling establishment, a person who watches without playing. An abbreviation of

DEADWOOD *US, 1950*. ▶ **have the wood on someone** to have an advantage over someone *AUSTRALIA, 1949*. ▶ **on the wood 1** in horse racing, racing along the rail *US, 1994*. **2** in hot rodding and motor racing, throttled to the maximum *US, 1993*

Woodbine; woodie; woody; wood *noun* any cheap cigarette. From branded 'Wild Woodbine'™ cigarettes, manufactured by WD & HO Wills and among the cheapest to be had *UK, 1916*

wood burner *noun* an attractive female. A suggestion that the woman consumes WOOD in the 'erect' sense of the word *US, 1990*

wooden *verb* to beat someone with a club of some sort *AUSTRALIA, 1905*

wooden *adjective* in poker, said of a hand that is unplayable *US, 1951*

wooden aspro *noun* a blow to the head with a police baton *NEW ZEALAND, 1980*

wooden cat *noun* a Morris Traveller car. Citizens' band radio slang; OLD CAT is a Morris Minor; this 'cat' is amended for the wooden bars in the model's design *UK, 1981*

woodener *noun* a sentence of imprisonment for 30 days. Rhyming slang, WOODEN SPOON for MOON (a month's imprisonment) *UK, 1950*

wooden hill; little wooden hill *noun* the stairs. Nursery use, especially in the phrase CLIMB THE WOODEN HILL TO BEDFORDSHIRE (to go upstairs to bed) *UK, 1961*

wooden horses *noun* a carousel *BARBADOS, 1965*

wooden Indian *noun* a poker player who does not talk or display emotion *US, 1996*

wooden leg *noun* an egg. Rhyming slang *UK, 1998*

wooden overcoat *noun* a coffin. A bleakly cynical euphemism, since 1903. Later variations are 'wooden kimono', 1926 and 'wooden suit', 1968 *UK, 1903*

wooden plank *noun* an American, especially an American in the UK. Rhyming slang for YANK *UK, 1992*

wooden spoon *noun* **1** a notional trophy awarded to an individual or a team placed last in a competition. From an actual wooden spoon that was customarily presented to the lowest on the Mathematical Tripos list at Cambridge University *UK, 1858*. **2** a month's imprisonment. Rhyming slang for MOON *UK, 1998*

wooden-spooner *noun* in a sporting competition, an individual or team that comes last. From WOODEN SPOON *UK, 1954*

wooden-spoonist *noun* in a competition, an individual or team that comes last. From WOODEN SPOON *UK, 1927*

woodentop *noun* **1** a uniformed police officer. After the children's television puppet show *The Woodentops* (1955–58). The variant 'woody' is also used *UK, 1982*. **2** a fool; also attributed as an adjective. After the sense 'a police officer' *UK, 1983*

Wood family *noun* used as a humorous description of empty seats in a theatre *UK, 1952*

woodfoot *noun* numbing of the foot in cold water. Surfing usage *US, 2004*

woodie *noun* **1** a Wills Woodbine™ cigarette *UK, 1931*. **2** a wooden powerboat, especially one built between the 1920s and 60s *US, 2001*

wooding *noun* among vagrant alcoholics, a task of collecting firewood *UK, 1966*

woodpecker *noun* a machinegun *AUSTRALIA, 1898*

woodpile *noun* **1** a xylophone *US, 1945*. **2** the area in a prison yard where white prisoners exercise. Formed from PECKERWOOD (a white person) and IRON PILE (weightlifting equipment) *US, 1989*

woodpile cousin *noun* an actual, if distant, blood relative *US, 1975*

wood rash *noun* any injury, especially grazing, sustained when riding a skateboard on a wooden ramp. A combination of location and appearance; ironically modest *US, 2001*

woods *noun* the vulva; a woman's pubic hair. Usually used with 'the' *US, 1968*

woods French *noun* a limited ability in French *CANADA, 1980*

woodshed *verb* to rehearse, especially in private *US, 1936*

woodsman *noun* a male pornography performer who can be counted upon to maintain an erection as long as needed and to ejaculate more or less on demand *US, 1995*

woodster *noun* a male pornography performer whose erections can be counted on *US, 2000*

woodsy *noun* a party held in the country *US, 1967*

woodwork *noun* ▶ **come out of the woodwork; crawl out of the woodwork; creep out of the woodwork** (of someone or something unpleasant) to appear; to arrive on the scene; to emerge. Usage is often with humorous intent but the allusion is to insects normally found in the woodwork – woodworm, deathwatch beetle, cockroach, etc *UK, 1973*

woody; woodie *noun* **1** an erection. US pornographer Joey Silvera is given credit for coining this term, which did not stay within the confines of pornography for long *US, 1985*. **2** a car with wood or synthetic wood paneling on its body *US, 1962* ▷*see:* WOODBINE

woody pill *noun* a genuine or a generic Viagra™ tablet. Based on WOODY (an erection) *UK, 2002*

Woody Woodpecker *noun* a tablet of MDMA, the recreational drug best known as ecstasy, embossed with a representation of the popular animation character *UK, 1999*

woof *verb* **1** to vomit *US, 1978*. **2** to eat very quickly. Possibly from 'wolf down' *UK, 1943*. **3** to threaten or intimidate someone; to engage someone in ritualistic, quasi-friendly insulting *US, 1967*

woof! used as a shout of approval, especially as a male declaration of appreciation for a sexually desirable female. Originated by television talk show host Arsenio Hall in 1989; the barking is accompanied by a pumped raised hand, fist clenched *US, 1992*

woofer *noun* an unattractive woman or man. A variation of DOG *UK, 1995*

woofter *noun* a homosexual man. A variation of POOFTER (a male homosexual) *UK, 1977*

woofterish *adjective* ineffecutal *NEW ZEALAND, 1993*

wook *noun* a quintessential rural hippie. From the Wookie character in the George Lucas *Star Wars* films *US, 2004*

wool *noun* **1** pubic hair; by extension, sex *US, 1972*. **2** used derogatively of someone who is not from the city; a stereotypical country-dweller; a YOKEL. From WOOLLY BACK *UK, 2001*

woola; woolas; wooly; wool *noun* crack cocaine or phencyclidine sprinkled over marijuana which is then smoked in a cigarette; a hollowed-out cigar filled with marijuana and phencyclidine *US, 1995*

woolah *noun* ▷*see:* WOLLIE

woolie *noun* a female's pubic hair *NEW ZEALAND, 1994*

woolies *noun* winter clothing *US, 1945*

Woolies *nickname* high street shop FW Woolworth's, later Woolworth's *AUSTRALIA, 1944*

woollies *noun* marijuana and crack cocaine mixture; marijuana and phencyclidine, the recreational drug known as PCP or angel dust *UK, 1998*

Woolloomooloo Yank *noun* an Australian who puts on an American accent *AUSTRALIA, 1945*

woolly *noun* **1** a black person. Variants include 'wooley head' *US, 1969*. **2** in CID slang, a uniformed police officer *UK, 1965*

woolly back *noun* **1** a stereotype of the unsophisticated country-dweller. An allusion to the intelligence and appearance of sheep *UK, 1981*. **2** a Welsh person *US, 2003*

woollyback breaker *noun* a citizens' band radio user from North Wales. Citizens' band radio slang BREAKER (a citizens' band user) with an allusion to sheep *UK, 1981*

woolly mitten *noun* a kitten. Rhyming slang *UK, 1998*

woolly nose *noun* a railway fettler *AUSTRALIA, 1969*

woolly-pully *noun* a military-issue heavy jumper. A customised *wool*len *pull*over *UK, 1984*

woolly vest *noun* a pest. Rhyming slang *UK, 1998*

woolly woofter; woolly *noun* a male homosexual. Rhyming slang with POOFTER *AUSTRALIA, 1988*

Woolwich and Greenwich *noun* spinach. Rhyming slang, formed from two London locations for crossing over the Thames *UK, 1992*

Woolwich Ferry *noun* sherry. Rhyming slang, formed from a transport across the Thames *UK, 1992*

Woolworth *noun* in hold 'em poker, a five and a ten as the first two cards dealt to a player. Woolworth's was the most famous five and dime store in the US *US, 1981*

Woolworth's finest *noun* in shuffleboard, a ten *US, 1967*

wooly bear *noun* in caving and pot-holing, a fibre-pile undersuit *US, 1997*

wooly blunt; woolly blunt *noun* a marijuana and crack cocaine cigarette *UK, 2003*

woop *noun* ▷*see:* WHOOP

Woop Woop *noun* an imaginary remote place *AUSTRALIA, 1918*

wooshed up *adjective* having been whisked to a froth (as of a milkshake); figuratively of anything having been subjected to random inflation (see citation) *UK, 1999*

wooter *noun* the penis *US, 1981*

wooz *noun* marijuana. From WOOZY (intoxicated) *UK, 2003*

wooziness *noun* a fuddled state, muzziness; often used to describe a morning-after-the-night-before feeling *US, 1977*

woozy *adjective* unsteady; dizzy; disoriented; intoxicated with drugs or drink. Anglicised by Conan Doyle in 1917 *US, 1897*

wop *noun* an Italian immigrant or Italian-American *US, 1914*. ▶ **up the wop 1** pregnant *NEW ZEALAND, 1981*. **2** broken; unsound *NEW ZEALAND, 2001*

wop *adjective* Italian *US, 1961*

wopcacker *noun* a superlative example of something *AUSTRALIA, 1941*

wop-jawed *adjective* in circus and carnival usage, amazed by an act or demonstration *US, 1981*

wop-wops *noun* remote back country *NEW ZEALAND, 1984*

word *noun* ▶ **get a word in edgeways** to contribute to a conversation. Generally in a negative form *UK, 1984*. ▶ **put the word on someone** to proposition someone *AUSTRALIA, 1975*. ▶ **take the word** in the illegal production of alcohol, to warn someone about a pending law enforcement raid *US, 1974*. ▶ **the word 1** gossip, rumours *US, 1961*. **2** an order *US, 1962*

word *verb* to speak to someone *AUSTRALIA, 1905*

word! used for expressing assent *US, 1987*

word in your shell-like *noun* a brief and discreet (one-sided) conversation. variation of 'word in your ear'; 'shell-like', which does not appear outside of this phrase until later, derives from a similarity of shape between the ear and some (delicate, pink) shells *UK, 1985*

words *noun* a quarrel (of violent words not actions). A refinement of a sense that has served since 1462 *UK, 1862*

word up *verb* to speak to someone in a flattering manner *AUSTRALIA, 1985*

word up 1 used for expressing agreement *US, 1986*. **2** used as a greeting. Used in the hip-hop community *US, 2003*

work *noun* **1** the betting slips in an illegal lottery or gambling operation *US, 1972*. **2** cheating in gambling, especially in craps. The statement 'There's work down' means that altered dice or cards are in play *US, 1950*. **3** dice or cards that have been altered for the purpose of cheating *US, 1963*. **4** crack cocaine *US, 1989*. **5** sex *US, 1959*. ▶ **do the work on someone** to kill someone *US, 1994*. ▶ **have your work cut out; have your work cut out for you; have all your work cut out** to have enough, or all you can manage, to do – anything more would be too much. From an earlier sense (to have your work prepared for you) *UK, 1856*

work *verb* **1** to cheat at gambling *US, 1963*. **2** to have sex with someone *US, 1957*. **3** to sell drugs *US, 1993*. **4** to dilute a powdered drug *US, 1989*. ▶ **to get worked** to be knocked from your surfboard and pummelled by the ocean *US, 1987*. ▶ **work a**

ginger (of a prostitute) to rob a client. From GINGER *AUSTRALIA, 1953.*
▶ **work for Standard Oil** to drive a truck that burns excessive amounts of fuel or oil *US, 1971.* ▶ **work like a charm** to achieve a purpose with absolute ease. From the idea of a magic charm influencing the action *UK, 1882.* ▶ **work like a nigger** to work very hard. Praise and contempt in equal parts *US, 1836.* ▶ **work the cuts** (used of a prostitute) to solicit customers on the streets *US, 1987.* ▶ **work the glory rode** to affect religious conversion while in prison in the hope of receiving an early parole *US, 1976.* ▶ **work the hole** to rob drunks sleeping on underground platforms or in the carriages *US, 1953.* ▶ **work the kerb** (of a prostitute) to ply for trade from passing motorists *UK, 2002.* ▶ **work the nuts** to operate a shell game in a circus midway or carnival *US, 1980.* ▶ **work the other side of the street** to be on opposing sides of a bipolar situation; to make a living as a criminal *US, 1982.* ▶ **work your bollocks off** to work very hard *UK, 2002.* ▶ **work your ticket** to obtain a discharge from employment on the grounds of physical injury or ill health; originally military but in the prevailing compensation culture applied to any employment situation where benefits of discharge are considerable, and thus fraudulent endeavour is often implied *UK, 1899*

workaround *noun* in computing, a temporary fix of a problem *US, 1991*

worker *noun* **1** a professional wrestler who puts on a good performance *US, 1999.* **2** a member of a drug-selling enterprise who sells drugs on the street *US, 1995.* **3** a gambling cheat *US, 1962.* **4** in the circus or carnival, a large blown-up balloon shown by the concession selling packages of balloons *US, 1980*

workie *noun* a worker *UK, 2002*

working *adjective* in craps, said of a bet that will be in effect on the next roll *US, 1981*

working boy *noun* a male prostitute *US, 1987*

working class *noun* a glass. Rhyming slang *UK, 1992*

working classes *noun* spectacles, glasses. Rhyming slang *UK, 1992*

working end *noun* the dangerous end of a tool or weapon *US, 1992*

working fifty *noun* a large piece of crack cocaine bought at a wholesale price *US, 1990*

working girl *noun* a prostitute *US, 1968*

working john *noun* an honest, hard-working man *US, 1957*

workingman's weed *noun* marijuana. An allusion to the 1970 album 'Workingman's Dead' by the Grateful Dead, a band well known for the use of recreational drugs *UK, 2000*

working-over *noun* a beating-up, a thrashing *UK, 1984*

working parts *noun* the genitals *UK, 1995*

working stiff *noun* a hard-working labourer *US, 1966*

work is the curse of the drinking classes a catchphrase that reverses a popular cliché. Attributed to Oscar Wilde *UK, 1946*

work out *verb* to masturbate *US, 2002*

work over *verb* to beat someone up; to thrash someone (both physically and figuratively) *UK, 1927*

works *noun* the equipment used to prepare and inject drugs *US, 1934.*
▶ **get on someone's works** to annoy someone *AUSTRALIA, 1956.*
▶ **in the works** already in progress, due to happen *CANADA, 1973.*
▶ **the works** the complete treatment *US, 1899*

works *adjective* in motor racing, supported by the car manufacturer *US, 1965*

works for me! used for expressing agreement. A signature line of Los Angeles Police Department Detective Sergeant Rick Hunter on the television police drama *Hunter* (NBC, 1984–91). Repeated with referential humour *US, 1991*

world *noun* ▶ **the world** during the war in Vietnam, back home, the US, life outside the military *US, 1970*

world of shit *noun* a very dangerous situation *US, 1984*

worlds *noun* commerically manufactured cigarettes *US, 1990*

worm *noun* **1** a computer program that maliciously duplicates itself repeatedly in a host computer until it clogs and crashes the system *US, 1990.* **2** a coiled condenser used in the illegal production of alcohol *US, 1974.* **3** a facial blemish *BARBADOS, 1965.* **4** phencyclidine, the recreational drug known as PCP or angel dust *US, 1981.* **5** an inexperienced oil field worker *US, 1984.* ▶ **wet down the worm** to perfom oral sex on a man *US, 2001*

worm and snail; worm *noun* a finger*nail*. Rhyming slang *UK, 1992*

worm dirt *noun* chewing tobacco. An obvious visual comparison *US, 2001*

worms *noun* ▶ **are you keeping it for the worms?; are you saving it for the worms?** said, probably in frustration, to a female rejecting sexual advances or to one who is presumed to be a virgin. 'It' being a state of virginity, 'the worms' signifying death *US, 1977*

Wormtown *nickname* Worcester, Massachusetts *US, 1997*

wormy *adjective* nervous or anxious, especially when manifested in the stomach *NORFOLK ISLAND, 1992*

worra laff! what a laugh! A phonetic slovening, probably of Liverpool origin *UK, 1999*

worry *verb* **1** to steal something *CAYMAN ISLANDS, 1985.* **2** (said of a jockey in horse racing) to ride a horse *US, 1951*

worse for wear *adjective* **1** somewhat drunk *UK, 1984.* **2** hung over *US, 1979*

worse luck! more's the pity! *UK, 1861*

worth *adjective* ▶ **not worth two cents to jingle on a tombstone** of a person, without any redeeming qualities *CANADA, 1988.* ▶ **worth a few bob; worth a bob or two** of people, fairly wealthy; of things, fairly valuable. From BOB (a shilling, now equivalent to 5p but not of equal value) *UK, 1981*

wossface *noun* a person whose name is unknown, forgotten, to be avoided, or hardly worth mentioning. A slurring of WHAT'S-HIS-FACE *UK, 2001*

wossie *noun* ▷*see:* WUSSIE

wot *pronoun* what *UK, 1829*

wotcher; watcha; what yer used as a greeting. Elision of the C16 greeting 'what cheer'. Stereotypically Cockney but in wider use. The earliest recorded use is '"Wot cher!" all the neighbours cried, / "Who're yer goin' to meet, Bill? Have you bought the street, Bill?"' (Albert Chevalier, 'Wot Cher!' or 'Knocked 'em in the Old Kent Road', 1891) *UK, 1953*

wot no...? used humorously for registering an absence or a shortage. A misspelling of 'what' provides this endlessly variable graffiti catchphrase, presented in a speech-bubble, or as a caption to a drawing of Chad, or Mr Chad looking over a wall, this used to highlight or protest about another World War 2 shortage. The formula has lingered in speech but Chad slowly faded from view *UK, 1945*

wotsit *noun* an unnamed thing. Reduction of the phrase 'what is it?', usually seen as WHATSIT; this variation is possibly inspired by Golden Wonder's Wotsits™, a popular cheesy flavour snack *UK, 1997*

wotsit in a sock *noun* the penis. A specific variation of WHATSIT (an unspecified object) *UK, 2005*

wouldn't it? used for expressing exasperation. Elliptical for such phrases as 'wouldn't it make you sick', though mostly euphemistically so for such phrases containing profanity, such as 'wouldn't it give you the shits' or 'wouldn't it root you' *AUSTRALIA, 1940*

wouldn't it rip you? used for expressing exasperation *AUSTRALIA, 1941*

wouldn't it root you? used for expressing exasperation. Also WOULDN'T IT RIP/ ROTATE YOU? both of which are presumably euphemisms for the 'root' form, even though the earliest recorded form is 'rip' (1941, Australian National Dictionary). Also, 'wouldn't it root your boot' *AUSTRALIA, 1945*

wouldn't it rotate you? used for expressing exasperation. Euphemistic for WOULDN'T IT ROOT YOU *AUSTRALIA, 1944*

wouldn't it rot your socks? used for expressing exasperation *AUSTRALIA, 1982*

wouldn't say no used for registering acceptance of something, sometimes as a suggestion that something would be accepted if it were offered *UK, 1939*

wouldn't work in an iron lung to be extremely lazy *AUSTRALIA, 1971*

would you believe...? used for humorously probing for a statement that can be believed. The signature line of spy Maxwell Smart, played by Don Adams, on the television comedy *Get Smart* (1965–70). Adams had used the line earlier on *The Bill Dana Show* (NBC, 1963–65). Repeated with referential humour *US, 1965*

wounded soldier *noun* a bottle or can of beer that has been partly consumed. Playing on DEAD SOLDIER as 'an empty bottle' *US, 1991*

wound up *adjective* angry, annoyed. The image is of a clock's mainspring wound too tight and ready to lose control *UK, 2001*

wow *noun* **1** a thing of wonder; a sensational success. From the exclamation 'wow!' *US, 1920.* **2** an exclamation mark (!) *US, 1983*

Wow *nickname* the psychiatric hospital in Auckland. The hospital is near the Whau River *NEW ZEALAND, 1998*

wowser *noun* a spoilsport of the worst kind; a moral crusader; a prude. Claimed by John Norton, editor of the Sydney *Truth* (1891–1916) as his own coinage and an acronym from the phrase '*we only want social evils remedied*', a supposed catchcry of 'the wowsers'. This story has sadly never been corroborated, and its derivation must be sought elsewhere. *The Australian National Dictionary* suggests British dialect *wow* (to howl or bark as a dog, to complain), which seems to fit well, but one correspondent to the *Truth* in 1910, after denying the word as Norton's invention, goes on to say 'a false sense of public decency forbids the publication of the derivation and true meaning', which suggests some profane origin *AUSTRALIA, 1900*

wowserish *adjective* prudish; puritanical *AUSTRALIA, 1906*

wowserism *noun* the characteristic behaviour of a WOWSER; prudishness *AUSTRALIA, 1904*

wowseristic *adjective* prudish; puritanical *AUSTRALIA, 1907*

woz *was.* A deliberate misspelling, especially in graffiti *UK, 1984*

woza *noun* a person who used to be successful or well known. From 'was a' *UK, 2001*

wozzed *adjective* exhausted *NEW ZEALAND, 1998*

wrap *noun* **1** a small paper-wrapping containing powdered drugs *UK, 1996.* **2** a wrapped roll of coins *US, 1977.* **3** the end of a session. Originally from the entertainment industry, extended to general situations *US, 1972.* **4** praise; a compliment or commendation. Variants include 'wrap-up', 'rap' and 'rap-up' *AUSTRALIA, 1939*

wrap; wrap up *noun* ▶ **wrap yourself around** to eat or consume something *AUSTRALIA, 1965*

wrap; wrap up *verb* to roll a marijuana cigarette *UK, 1999.* ▶ **wrap round; wrap around** to crash a vehicle into an immovable object *UK, 1950*

wrap-head *noun* a follower of the Pocomania Afro-Christian religion *JAMAICA, 1987*

wrapped; wrapped up *adjective* pleased; overjoyed; enamoured *AUSTRALIA, 1963*

wrapper *noun* **1** a motor vehicle. Citizens' band radio' slang *US, 1976.* **2** an unmarked police vehicle. Originally citizens' band radio slang. Variants include 'plain wrapper' and 'plain wrap' *US, 1976.* ▶ **in the wrapper 1** drunk *US, 1985.* **2** in bed *US, 1997*

wraps *noun* cigarette rolling papers *US, 1994.* ▶ **under wraps** kept in secret *UK, 1939*

wrap-up *noun* a female sex-partner who, by a vague yet firm understanding, is regularly available *UK, 1970*

wrap up *verb* **1** to cease talking; to stop making a noise. Usually in the imperative, often as a two word exclamation *UK, 1958.* **2** to complete the final days of a prison sentence *US, 1976*

wreck *verb* ▶ **wreck my head** to agitate me to an extreme degree *IRELAND, 2003*

wrecked *adjective* very drunk or drug-intoxicated *US, 1968*

wrecking crew *noun* **1** theatre insiders who watch a show's early performances and spread negative comments about the show *US, 1973.* **2** crack cocaine *UK, 1998.* **3** on the railways, a relief crew *US, 1946*

wren *noun* a woman *US, 1920*

wrench *noun* in drag and motor racing, a mechanic *US, 1980*

wrench *verb* **1** to go *US, 2002.* **2** to disrupt or upset someone *US, 1976.* **3** in motor racing and hot rodding, to perform mechanical work on a car, whether it literally involves using a wrench or not *US, 2004*

wrench artist *noun* a railway mechanic *US, 1977*

wrencher *noun* a car enthusiast with considerable mechanical ability *US, 2003*

wrestle; rassle *verb* to play a game of bar dice *US, 1971*

wretch *verb* to vomit *US, 1966*

wriggle *noun* ▶ **get a wriggle on** to hurry. A variation of GET A WIGGLE ON *AUSTRALIA, 1971*

wriggle out *verb* to avoid a responsibility or duty *UK, 1848*

wriggly *adjective* out of the ordinary; suspiciously different *UK, 1995*

wring *verb* ▶ **wring out your mule** to urinate *US, 1974.* ▶ **wring out your sock** to urinate *US, 1988.* ▶ **wring the rattlesnake** to urinate *AUSTRALIA, 1971*

wringer *noun* a bankruptcy petition *US, 1954*

wrinkle *noun* a clever device, trick or method *UK, 1817*

wrinkleneck *noun* in horse racing, a seasoned and experienced horse handler *US, 1951*

wrinkle room *noun* a bar frequented by older homosexual men *US, 1985*

wrinkly *noun* an old person. A reference to the wrinkled skin of advanced years. Partridge qualified the definition: 'as applied to anyone over the venerable age of thirty' *UK, 1972*

wrist *noun* **1** a contemptible person. From WRIST JOB (an act of masturbation) – or similar term – hence, this is synonymous with WANKER *UK, 1998.* **2** in betting, odds of 5–4. From the TICK-TACK signal used by bookmakers *UK, 1991*

wristers *noun* in lobstering, knitted gloves with no fingers *US, 1978*

wrist job *noun* **1** an act of masturbation. Used as a song title by Humble Pie in 1969 *UK, 1969.* **2** used as an all-purpose form of abuse; a substitute form of wanker *UK, 2000*

wristy *adjective* having the characteristics of a masturbator; hence, inferior or unpleasant. From WRIST (a contemptible person) *UK, 2000*

write *verb* **1** to write a prescription for a narcotic which will not be used for medicinal purposes *US, 1953.* **2** to create graffiti art *US, 1997.* ▶ **write numbers** to take bets on an illegal policy game (numbers lottery) *US, 1975*

write-off *noun* any motor vehicle damaged beyond economic repair; any thing (physical or abstract) or person considered to be beyond saving. Originally Royal Air Force slang for 'a wrecked aircraft', now thought of as the language of insurance *UK, 1918*

write off *verb* to destroy something; to damage something beyond repair, generally a vehicle. From the conventional use 'to write off the value or the investment' *UK, 1991*

writer *noun* **1** a graffiti artist *US, 1997.* **2** in a casino, employee who accepts and records bets on Keno *US, 1972* ▷ *see:* SHEET WRITER

wrong *noun* in craps, a bet against the shooter *US, 1974*

wrong *adjective* known to inform the police *US, 1953*

wrongle *noun* in craps, someone who bets against the shooter *US, 1974*

wrong number *noun* an untrustworthy person *US, 1972*

wrong-o *noun* a bad person *US, 1970*

wrong side of *noun* used of an age that is greater than a stated number *UK, 1663*

wrong time *noun* a woman's menstrual period *US, 1954*

wrong 'un *noun* **1** a lawbreaker; someone on the wrong side of the law *AUSTRALIA, 1985.* **2** a police informer. English gypsy use *UK, 2000.*

3 in prison, a sex offender or convicted paedophile; an informer *UK, 1996*

wrong-way English *noun* in pool, spin imparted on the cue ball such that the angle of refraction off a cushion is different, if not opposite, from what would be expected *US, 1993*

WS *noun* a sado-masochist encounter involving enemas or urination. An abbreviation for WATERSPORTS *US, 1979*

WTF used in computer message shorthand to mean 'what the fuck?' or 'who the fuck?' *US, 1991*

WUCIWUG what you see is what you get. Quasi-initialism used for text messaging *UK, 2001*

wudja? 'would you?'. Apparently coined by television production company Brighter Pictures but rapidly gained wider use *UK, 2002*

wuffo; whuffo *noun* in the language of hang gliding and parachuting, anyone other than a fellow expert. Purportedly derived from the question, 'Wuffo they do that?' *US, 1978*

wumpers *noun* a rubber-soled sandal, especially one made from a car tyre *BAHAMAS, 1982*

wunch *noun* a group of bankers. Collective noun. A jokey Spoonerism of 'bunch of wankers' *UK, 2002*

wunzee *verb* to urinate. An evolution of the children's vocabulary of NUMBER ONE and NUMBER TWO *TRINIDAD AND TOBAGO, 2003*

wurley *noun* a hut. Originally an Aboriginal dwelling *AUSTRALIA, 1839*

wurzel *noun* a person from the countryside. Derogatory; most probably from the television series *Wurzel Gummidge*, 1979–81, based on the stories about the 'scarecrow of Scatterbrook' created by Barbara Euphan Todd *UK, 2000*

wuss *noun* a weak, timid person. A blend of WIMP and PUSSY, both meaning 'a weak and timid person' *US, 1982*

wussie; wussy; wossie *noun* a weak, timid, passive person *US, 1982*

wuss out *verb* to back down; to fail to do as promised *US, 1977*

wussy *adjective* weak, timid, passive *US, 1995*

wuwoo *noun* a mixture of marijuana and cocaine; marijuana. Possibly adapted from a celebratory reaction to the drugs' effects *UK, 2001*

wuzzy *noun* a female. A corruption of the French *oiseau*, or BIRD (a young woman) *UK, 1983*

Wyamine *noun* a Benzedrine™ inhaler. The Wyamine™ inhaler was manufactured by Wyeth Laboratories; it became a generic name for any inhaler with Benzedrine-infused cotton strips, valued by amphetamine users *US, 1967*

Wyatt *nickname* sometimes applied to a person who burps loudly and for comic effect. From rhyming slang WYATT EARP (a burp) *UK, 1992*

Wyatt Earp *noun* **1** the penis. Rhyming slang for CURP (the penis), formed on the name of the legendary US lawman (1848–1929), possibly informed by the film-myth of Wyatt Earp as a heroic shootist *UK, 1980*. **2** a belch. Rhyming slang for BURP, based on the name of hero of countless films, Wyatt Earp *UK, 1992*

wyman *noun* ▷*see:* BILL WYMAN

Wynona Ryder; wynona *noun* cider. Rhyming slang, based on the name of the popular film actress (b.1971) *UK, 2002*

wyssa; whizzer; wyzza *noun* a personal message sent or received in the Antarctic or sub-Antarctic. Derives from the Australian Antarctic Division telex code for 'with all my/our love darling' *AUSTRALIA, 1959*

Wythenshawe white man *noun* a black man with the manners and standards of contemporary white society. Wythenshawe is a suburb of Manchester *UK, 2002*

Xx

X *noun* an empty railway wagon *US, 1946*

X *noun* **1** MDMA, the recreational drug best known as ecstasy. Generally an abbreviated 'ecstasy' specifically used of any MDMA tablet stamped with a symbol that may be read as an X *US, 1988*. **2** marijuana *UK, 2003*. **3** in blackjack, any card worth ten points. A Roman numeral used by card counters *US, 1991*. **4** a cross-breed of a dog *CANADA, 1997*. **5** a grip on all illegal gambling *US, 1974* ▷*see:* **GENERATION XER**. ▶ **the X** in the circus or carnival, exclusive rights for an item or concession *US, 1980*

X *verb* to take MDMA, the recreational drug best known as ecstasy *US, 1985*

X *adjective* **1** annoyed, irritated, angry. A pun on 'cross' *UK, 1962*. **2** in drag racing, experimental. The designation FX means an experimental car from a factory; MX means an experimental component from a manufacturer *US, 1970*

x-double-minus *adjective* very bad. Alluding to a non-existent grading scale *US, 1968*

x-dressing *noun* cross-dressing *UK, 2003*

Xer *noun* ▷*see:* **GENERATION XER**

X-Files *noun* haemorrhoids. Rhyming slang for PILES, formed on US television science-fiction/conspiracy drama *The X-Files* first broadcast in 1993 *UK, 1998*

X-Files E *noun* a tablet of MDMA, the recreational drug best known as ecstasy, branded with a borrowed logo. After *The X Files*, a cult science fiction televison programme from the mid-1990s, playing on X (E) *UK, 1996*

x-ing *noun* MDMA, the recreational drug best known as ecstasy *UK, 1998*

X marks the spot used as a caption or legend to a specific location (marked with a cross) on a map or in a photograph. Of catchphrase status although rarely spoken. Familiar uses include: the scene of the crime, a hotel window on a postcard and pirate treasure maps *UK, 1968*

Xmas *noun* Christmas. Pronounced 'Exmas'. Originally pronounced as 'Christmas', derived from Greek, the initial letter of *Christos*, yet is generally presumed to be a coinage of modern marketing and, while widely recognised, remains an unconventional usage *UK, 1755*

X queen *noun* a homosexual male who is a frequent user of MDMA, the recreational drug best known as ecstasy *US, 1994*

x-ray eyes *noun* the sense of intuition of a poker player who can ascertain the hands held by other players *US, 1988*

X-row *noun* the area in a prison housing inmates condemned to death *US, 1992*

xs and os *noun* the basic elements of a plan. From play diagrams in basketball, football or other sports, in which the xs represent the players of one team, and the os represent players of the other *US, 1984*

XTC *noun* MDMA, the recreational drug best known as ecstasy. Pronounced 'ecstasy' *US, 1985*

X vid *noun* a sexually explicit video *US, 1992*

XX *noun* a twenty-dollar note *US, 1982*

XY *noun* a spouse. A mutual abbreviation from XYL (a wife) and XYM (a husband) *US, 1976*

XYL *noun* a wife. A partial acronym: '*ex-young lady*' *US, 1976*

XYM *noun* a husband. A partial acronym: '*ex-young-man*' *US, 1976*

XYZ *noun* a citizens' band radio user of undiscovered gender; hence, a homosexual. By extension from XYL (a wife) and XYM (a husband) *US, 1976*

XYZ used to alert someone that their fly zipper is open. A partial acronym: '*examine your zippers US, 1999*

Yy

Y *noun* ▶ **the Y** a premises of the Young Men's Christian Association (YMCA) or Young Women's Christian Association (YWCA); also the YMCA or YWCA organisation *US, 1915*

Y2K *noun* **1** the year 2000; the first second of the year 2000. Y (year) plus 2κ (2000) *CANADA, 1995*. **2** used as the first three characters for any year between 2001 and 2009 *INDIA, 2004*

yaba *noun* paramethoxyamphetamine, PMA. A phonetic approximation (perhaps Thai or Burmese), literally 'crazy medicine', by which name it is also known, *2002*

yabba *noun* methamphetamine in pill form when taken as a recreational drug *UK, 2001*

yabba-dabba doo! used as a cry of exultation. *The Flintstones*, a US television animation-comedy, first broadcast in 1960, introduced 'yabba-dabba-doo!' as a catchphrase. 'A yabba-dabba doo time' (an excellent time) comes directly from the theme song, 'The Flintstones: Rise and Shine', written by William Hanna and Joseph Barbera, the show's creators. As a noun, 'yabba-dabba doo' means 'exuberance' *US, 1998*

yabber *noun* a conversation; a chat *AUSTRALIA, 1855*

yabber *verb* to talk, converse, chat, now especially used of unintelligible language that is annoying; hence, to chatter, blabber, be noisy. Originally used in Australian pidgin. From an Australian Aboriginal language, possibly the Wuywurung language of the Melbourne region *AUSTRALIA, 1841*

yabbering *noun* talk, conversation *AUSTRALIA, 1847*

yabby *noun* an Australian freshwater crayfish, found throughout eastern Australia and introduced into Western Australia, commonly caught for food; later applied to various other similar freshwater crayfish. From Wemba, an Australian Aboriginal language of Victoria *AUSTRALIA, 1894*

yabby *verb* to fish for freshwater crayfish. After the noun sense *AUSTRALIA, 1934*

yabbying *noun* the act of fishing for yabbies, usually with a bit of meat on a string *AUSTRALIA, 1934*

yack *adjective* sick *UK, 2001*

yack; yak *noun* **1** voluble talk. Echoic of idle chatter *US, 1952*. **2** a joke *US, 1951*. **3** a telephone sales solicitor, either for a legitimate business or for a confidence swindle *US, 1985*. **4** a watch. Possibly derived from Welsh gypsy *yåkengeri* (a clock, literally 'a thing of the eyes'). Still current, in second spelling, among market traders *UK, 1812*

yack; yak *verb* **1** to talk volubly and either idly or stupidly or both *US, 1949*. **2** to vomit *US, 1992*

yacker *noun* a swindler working on a phony investment scam by telephone *US, 1988* ▷ *see:* YAKKA

yacker *verb* to talk *AUSTRALIA, 1882*

yackety-yack *noun* inconsequential talk *UK, 1958*

yadda yadda yadda used for suggesting meaningless conversation *US, 1993*

yaffle *verb* **1** to eat hurriedly or greedily. Originally, 'to eat or drink'; still current in Royal Navy slang but only as 'to eat' *UK, 1788*. **2** to engage in oral sex. From the sense 'to eat' *UK, 1998*

yaffler *noun* a person who talks too much *AUSTRALIA, 1995*

yag *noun* yttrium aluminium garnet. Used in the diamond trade *UK, 1975*

yage *noun* *ayahuasca* also known as *yajé*, a psychedelic drink from South America *US, 1999*

yah boo! used as an expression of scorn or derision. A childish use *UK, 1921*

yah boo sucks! used as an expression of defiance, scorn or derision. Originally used by children, now childish; an elaboration of YAH BOO! *UK, 1980*

yahoo *noun* **1** an unrefined, loutish, uncultured person. An imaginary race of brutes created by Swift in *Gulliver's Travels UK, 1726*. **2** crack cocaine *US, 1994*

yahoo! used as an exuberant expression of excitement or delight *UK, 1976*

yahoos *noun* the female breasts. Perhaps from 'yahoo!' as a celebratory cry *US, 2001*

yahso *adverb* here; in or to this place *JAMAICA, 1995*

yak *noun* during the Korean war, an enemy aircraft. Coined as an allusion to North Korea's YAK-9 fighter jet *US, 1991* ▷ *see:* YACK

yakenal *noun* a capsule of phentobarbital sodium (trade name Nembutal™), a central nervous system depressant *US, 1982*

yakka; yacker *noun* work. From the now defunct verb 'yacker' (to work), from the Australian Aboriginal language Yagara, Brisbane region. Connection with the Ulster word 'yokkin' (a spell of work) is untenable. Now usually in the phrase HARD YAKKA *AUSTRALIA, 1888*

yakker *noun* **1** talk *AUSTRALIA, 1961*. **2** food. From Australian pidgin; possibly equating YAKKA (work) with food. Variants include 'yack' *AUSTRALIA, 1942*

yale *noun* crack cocaine *UK, 2003*

Yale *noun* a commerical hypodermic needle, whether or not it is manufactured by Yale *US, 1973*

Yalie *noun* a student or alumnus of Yale University *US, 1952*

yam *verb* **1** to talk too much *US, 1951*. **2** to eat as if famished *BARBADOS, 1965*

yam foot *noun* a foot that is broad and splayed out *TRINIDAD AND TOBAGO, 2003*

yammagi; yamidgee *noun* an Aboriginal, especially an Aboriginal male. A Western Australian Aboriginal (Watjari) term, *yamaji*, used generically. Variant spellings include: 'yamagee', 'yamagi', 'yammagee' and 'yammogee' *AUSTRALIA, 1925*

Yammie; Yammy *noun* a Yamaha motorcycle, in production since 1954 *UK, 1999*

yandy *noun* a shallow dish used for separating seeds from other matter *AUSTRALIA, 1903*

yandy *verb* to separate seeds from surrounding matter in a YANDY; hence, in tin-mining, to pan. Such work is done by a 'yandier' *AUSTRALIA, 1914*

yang *noun* **1** the penis. From the masculine principle in the Chinese philosophy of yin-yang *US, 1983*. **2** the rectum *US, 1974*

yang-yang *adjective* of a horse, lively or spirited *AUSTRALIA, 1976*

Yank *noun* **1** an American. Originally a New Englander or someone from the northern states of America. An abbreviation of YANKEE; often derogatory *UK, 1778*. **2** an American bird. Bird-watching slang *UK, 1977*

yank *verb* to tug something with sudden energy; to remove something *US, 1848*

yank and bank *verb* to execute a turn in a fighter plane *US, 1986*

yankee *noun* a multiple bet, gambling on four different horses in a specific combination of eleven bets *UK, 1967*

Yankee *noun* **1** a native or inhabitant of New England; hence, more generally, of the northern states of America. The most likely derivation is from Dutch *Janke*, a diminutive of *Jan* (John) as a pejorative nickname; also possible is a North American Indian corruption of 'English'; or Cherokee *eankke* (a slave, a coward). Used by the Confederates of the Federal army during the

American Civil War, 1861–65, and since by the south of the north *US, 1765*. **2** a tool used by car thieves to pull out the cyclinder of the ignition lock *UK, 1977*

Yankee *adjective* American *UK, 1781*

Yankee-bashing *noun* an act of engaging US servicemen in sexual activity. Well-used by members of the Women's Royal Army Corps in Hong Kong during the 1960s *UK, 1984*

Yankee clipper *noun* a North American moving van *US, 1976*

yankee dime *noun* a kiss *US, 1900*

Yankeeland *noun* the United States of America *UK, 2000*

Yankee shout *noun* a social outing where everyone pays for themselves *AUSTRALIA, 1945*

Yankee tournament *noun* a sporting contest in which everyone plays everyone else. An Australian nuance of YANKEE (American) as 'equal for all' *AUSTRALIA, 1961*

Yanking *noun* an act of engaging US servicemen in sexual activity. Formed on YANK (an American) *UK, 1950*

Yank tank *noun* a large car, especially one manufactured in the US *AUSTRALIA, 1981*

ya-o *noun* crack cocaine *US, 1995*

yaoh *noun* cocaine *UK, 1999*

yap *noun* **1** the mouth *US, 1900*. **2** inconsequential talk *US, 1907*. **3** in circus and carnival usage, a naive, gullible local resident *US, 1981*

yap *verb* to talk incessantly. The term existed in this sense in C19 English dialect, and then independently arose in the US in the 1920s *UK, 1886*

yapper, snapper, and crapper *noun* oral, vaginal and anal sex with a woman. A clever phrase heard in jokes but rarely in real life *US, 2004*

yappies *noun* ▶ **the yappies** greyhound racing or coursing. A play on THE DOGS *AUSTRALIA, 1984*

yappy; yappified *adjective* idiotic *UK, 1979*

yar! used as a general-purpose interjection, usually conveying excitement about something *US, 1989*

yarco; yark *noun* a member of a subcultural urban adolescent grouping in Yarmouth, Norfolk, that seems to be defined by a hip-hop dress and jewellery sense *UK, 2005*

yard *noun* **1** one hundred dollars *US, 1926*. **2** one thousand dollars *US, 1932*. **3** a prison sentence of 100 years *US, 1969*. **4** a prison sentence of one year *US, 1950*. **5** your country, especially Jamaica *UK, 1994*. **6** your home, your house; in prison, your cell. West Indian and UK black *JAMAICA, 1950*. **7** a member of the Montagnard tribe, the aborigine hill tribes of Vietnam's Central Highlands *US, 1991*

Yard *noun* ▶ **the Yard** Scotland Yard, subsequently New Scotland Yard, headquarters of the Metropolitan police. Originally, since 1888, used of the location of London's Metropolitan Police; the familiar name stayed when the headquarters moved to new premises in 1967 *UK, 1888*

yard *verb* **1** to be sexually unfaithful *US, 1960*. **2** to get hold of someone *CANADA, 1984*

yardage *noun* a big penis *US, 1970s*

yard-and-a-half *noun* one hundred and fifty dollars *US, 1962*

yardbird *noun* **1** a chicken *US, 1956*. **2** a prisoner, a convict *US, 1965*. **3** a newly arrived military recruit *US, 1945*. **4** in trucking, a terminal employee who moves trucks around the yard *US, 1971*. **5** on the railways, an injured employee assigned to limited duty in a railway yard *US, 1968*

Yardbird *nickname* Charlie Parker, jazz saxophonist *US, 1949*

yard buddy *noun* a close friend in prison *US, 1974*

yard bull; yard dick *noun* a railway detective *US, 1958*. a railway detective *US, 1950*

yard dog *noun* an unsophisticated, uncouth person *US, 1973*

yard goose *noun* a railway pointsman *US, 1977*

yardie *noun* **1** a member of a violent gang culture rooted in the West Indies, especially Jamaica. Yardies have an international repu-

tation for drug-related crime *JAMAICA, 1986*. **2** a person from your neighbourhood; a friend *JAMAICA, 2003*. **3** a yardman *AUSTRALIA, 1990*

yard man *noun* a Jamaican *JAMAICA, 1994*

yardney *noun* a manner of speech combining West Indian and London accents and vocabularies. Combining YARDIE (a Jamaican gangster) and 'Cockney' (a stereotypical Londoner) *UK, 1999*

yard out *verb* to exercise in a prison yard *US, 1984*

yard sale *noun* in snow-based sports, the result of an accident in which equipment is deposited over a wide area *US, 1995*

yardstick *noun* a road mile marker *US, 1976*

yarn *noun* **1** a story, an adventure story, especially a long, marvellous or incredible story. Of nautical origin; from 'spin a yarn' (to tell such a story) *UK, 1812*. **2** a chat, a talk, a conversation *AUSTRALIA, 1852*

yarn *verb* **1** to tell a story *UK, 1812*. **2** to talk; to have a chat *AUSTRALIA, 1847*

yarpie *noun* ▷ *see:* JAPIE

yarra *adjective* mad, stupid, eccentric. From the mental asylum at Yarra Bend, Victoria *AUSTRALIA, 1943*

Yarra-banker *noun* a loafer or vagrant idling on the banks of the Yarra River, Melbourne; a Melbourne soap box orator *AUSTRALIA, 1895*

Yarra – stinking Yarra! used as an offensive catchphrase addressed by Sydneyites to Melbournites. Melbourne sits on the banks of the Yarra River *AUSTRALIA, 1984*

yassoo! used as a greeting among troops who have served in Cyprus. From Greek *giasou!* (an all-purpose word for 'hello', 'goodbye', 'cheers!'). Sometimes elaborated in mock-Scots as 'yassoo the noo!' *UK, 1984*

yattie *noun* a girl *UK, 2003*

yawn *noun* anything which induces boredom *UK, 1974*

yawn *verb* ▶ **yawn in technicolor** to vomit *US, 1981*

yawn said to register the speaker's boredom, instead of actually yawning *UK, 2000*

yay! used as an exclamation of delight *UK, 1963*

yay; yayoo; yeah-O; yeyo; yeo *noun* crack cocaine *US, 1995*

Y-bone *noun* the vulva and vagina as an object of oral sex *NEW ZEALAND, 1998*

Y Dub *noun* a premises of the YWCA (the Young Women's Christian Association), or the organisation itself. Short for YW. Later use seems to be predominantly in New Zealand *US, 1984*

yea; yay *adverb* when describing size, and combined with an appropriate gesture: this, so *US, 1960*

yeah *noun* yes, used as a signal of assent *US, 1905*

yeah-yeah no. Said dismissively; a rare instance of a double affirmative producing a negative *UK, 2000*

year *noun* a one-hundred dollar note *US, 1997*

year blob *noun* a notional date that, within context, was a very long time ago. A variation of YEAR DOT *UK, 1997*

year dot *noun* a notional date long ago; time immemorial *UK, 1895*

yeast *verb* to exaggerate *US, 1973*

yee yes *US, 1980*

yegg *noun* a criminal, especially a burglar or safecracker. Anglicised by 1932 *US, 1900*

ye gods!; ye gods and little fishes! used as a mild oath, especially to express exasperation or indignation. The former dates from 1807; and elaborated with 'little fishes' since the 1850s. Original use was no doubt sincere but from the 1960s usage has been derisory or jocular *UK, 2002*

yeh *noun* marijuana *UK, 1998*

Yekke; Yekkie *noun* a German Jew. Derogatory. From Yiddish, but of uncertain origin *UK, 1950*

yeller feller; yellow feller; yellow fellow *noun* a person of mixed Aboriginal and white parentage *AUSTRALIA, 1913*

yellow *noun* **1** a capsule of pentobarbital sodium (trade name Nembutal™), a central nervous system depressant; any barbiturate *US, 1944.* **2** LSD *US, 1977*

yellow *adjective* **1** cowardly, afraid *US, 1856.* **2** used to describe that section of the printed news media which tends towards the sensational, the unscrupulous and the tawdry. Derives from an 1895 experiment by the *New York World* in the use of colour-printing with the intent to attract more readers; a cartoon of a young girl in a yellow dress known as 'The Yellow Kid' *US, 1898.* **3** light-skinned; of mixed race *US, 1934*

yellow and white earth *noun* money *CANADA, 1983*

yellow bam *noun* **1** a capsule of pentobarbital sodium (trade name Nembutal™), a central nervous system depressant *US, 1986.* **2** methamphetamine hydrochloride, a powerful central nervous system stimulant *US, 1994*

yellow-bellied *adjective* cowardly *US, 1924*

yellow-belly *noun* **1** a coward *US, 1930.* **2** a person of mixed Asian and white parentage. A derogatory and racist reference to skin-tone. An earlier use, from 1842, was by Americans of Mexicans *UK, 1867*

yellow-belly bird *noun* a coward *TRINIDAD AND TOBAGO, 1960*

yellow bullet *noun* a capsule of pentobarbital sodium (trade name Nembutal™), a central nervous system depressant *US, 1977*

yellow canary *noun* in trucking, a Yellow Transit Freight Lines truck *US, 1976*

yellow dimple; yellow dimples *noun* LSD, especially in combination with another drug *US, 1982*

yellow doll *noun* a capsule of phentobarbital sodium (trade name Nembutal™), a central nervous system depressant *US, 1977*

yellow egg *noun* Temazapam™, a branded tranquillizer *UK, 1998*

yellow jacket *noun* **1** a barbiturate or other central nervous system depressant, especially Nembutal™ *US, 1952.* **2** a high-velocity, hollow-nose, expanding bullet *US, 1981*

yellow legs *noun* the US Marines. Korean war usage; coined by the North Koreans alluding to the marine leggings *US, 1968*

Yellow Legs *noun* the Royal Canadian Mounted Police *CANADA, 1974*

yellow pages *noun* in poker, a play or a bet made strictly for the purpose of creating an impression *US, 1996*

yellow peril *noun* **1** a danger (real or imagined) that armies of any and all Asiatic peoples will overrun the West. From the conventional use of 'yellow' to convey an Asiatic or Oriental complexion. Usage is mainly historical but paranoia and the Internet keeps the phrase alive *UK, 1900.* **2** used as a collective noun for all sorts of things with a yellow connection. Mainly jocular. Used by motorcyclists of traffic wardens (from the yellow flashes on their uniforms) *UK, 1943.* **3** hepatitis. A peril of shared needles by drug addicts; their usage, with a pun on the fear of Asians and the skin discolouration associated with hepatitis *UK, 1985.* **4** in prison, school, or any canteen in any institution, a bright yellow cake favoured by the caterers. Originally services *UK, 1961*

Yellow Peril *nickname* in Canadian military aviation, the Harvard training aircraft *CANADA, 1995*

yellow rock *noun* methamphetamine in rock form, yellow in colour either because of incomplete processing or the presence of adulterants *US, 1989*

yellow sheet *noun* a criminal record. A generic in UK use, from the colour of the New York Police Department document at the time of coining *US, 1992*

yellow streak *noun* a trait of cowardice *UK, 1911*

yellow submarine *noun* marijuana. A fanciful similarity in shape between a JOINT and The Beatles' musical cartoon creation 'Yellow Submarine', 1969; however, both promise a colourful journey *UK, 2003*

yellow sunshine; yellow cap; yellow dot *noun* LSD *US, 1972*

yells, bells and knells *noun* newspaper announcements of births, marriages and deaths. A journalistic summation of life; a variation of HATCH, MATCH AND DISPATCH *AUSTRALIA, 1984*

yen *noun* an intense craving, especially for a drug; an addiction *UK, 1876*

yen *verb* to crave a drug intensely. From the Chinese; originally applied to opium users *US, 1919*

yenems; yenams; yenhams *noun* free cigarettes; anything belonging to someone else. Adopted from Yiddish, possibly as early as the mid-1920s *UK, 1984*

yennep; yennap; yenep *noun* a penny. Back slang *UK, 1851*

yen pock *noun* an opium pellet *US, 1934*

yen pop *noun* marijuana *US, 1950*

yen pox *noun* opium ash *US, 1957*

yen-shee *noun* heroin. From an earlier generalised sense as 'opium' (which included heroin in its definition) *US, 1960*

Yenshee baby *noun* an extremely constipated bowel movement that is the product of opiate addiction. *Yenshee* is Chinese for 'opium residue' *US, 1938*

yen-shee-suey *noun* opium or heroin dissolved in wine *US, 1949*

yen sleep *noun* a drowsiness encountered by many LSD users after the effects of the drug have worn off *US, 1972*

yenta *noun* a gossip; a busybody; a scold. Yiddish *US, 1923*

yeola *noun* marijuana *UK, 2003*

yep yes. A variation of 'yes'; the final plosive stresses the affirmative and gives it a semi-interjection or exclamatory sense *US, 1891*

yerba *noun* marijuana. A Mexican Spanish word that means 'herb' or 'grass', thus HERB (marijuana) or GRASS (marijuana) *US, 1967*

yerba mala *noun* poor quality marijuana; phencyclidine. Adopted from Mexican Spanish, the literal meaning is 'bad/evil grass'; *yerba beuna* (good grass) is probably also used *US, 1986*

yerhia *noun* marijuana *UK, 2003*

yer man *noun* an unnamed male *IRELAND, 1997*

yer one *noun* an unnamed female *IRELAND, 1997*

yers *pronoun* a variant spelling of YOUSE *AUSTRALIA, 1923*

yesca; yesco *noun* marijuana. Directly from Spanish *yesca* (tinder), 'a fuel that is burnt' *US, 1949*

yes, if you've got the inclination; yes, but not the inclination used as a catchphrase response to: 'Have you got the time?'. Also, 'yes, if you've got the money' *UK, 1977*

yes man; yes-man *noun* an obsequious subordinate; a person who agrees with everything a superior says or does *UK, 1912*

yessir! yes indeed *US, 1913*

yes siree (Bob) yes indeed *US, 1846*

yes sir, we're pals, and pals stick together used as a humorous affirmation of agreement. Used as the sign-off by Ed McConnell on the *Smilin' Ed's Gang* (1950–55) children's television programme. Repeated with referential humour *US, 1955*

yes sir, yes sir, three bags full used for mocking unquestioning, blind obedience. US naval aviator usage, from the children's song 'Ba Ba Black Sheep' *US, 1986*

yessus!; yesus!; yissus! used for expressing anger, frustration, shock, surprise, etc. From the Afrikaans pronunciation of 'Jesus' as an oath or exclamation *SOUTH AFRICA, 1942*

yesterday *adjective* out-dated; unaware of current fashions and trends *US, 1968*

Yes way! used for humorously rebutting someone who has just said 'No way!' *US, 1989*

yes-woman; yes-girl *noun* an obsequious female subordinate; a person who agrees with everything her superior says or does. A consequence of YES MAN; originally 'yes-girl' had primacy but current use favours 'yes-woman' *US, 1930*

yettie *noun* a successful person who is young, entrepreurial and technical *UK, 2000*

yet to be *adjective* free, gratis. Rhyming slang *UK, 1961*

yew *noun* the eye. Usually in the plural *UK, 2002*

yeyo; jejo *noun* cocaine. Adopted directly from Spanish *UK, 1998*

yez *pronoun* you (plural). Originally only in representations of Irish speakers, but later as the typical Australian pronunciation with an unstressed vowel *IRELAND, 1828*

Yid *noun* a Jewish person. Offensive *US, 1874*

yiddel; yiddle *noun* a Jewish person *US, 1946*

Yiddish highway *noun* US Highway 301, which runs between New York and Miami, Florida *US, 1979*

Yid kid *noun* a young Jewish person *US, 1978*

Yidsbury *nickname* Finsbury, an area of north London with (traditionally) a large Jewish population. A combination with YID (a Jewish person) *UK, 1981*

yike *noun* a fight; an altercation *AUSTRALIA, 1940*

yikes! used in surprise, pain or shock. Possibly a variant of conventional 'yoicks!' or 'crikey!' (Christ!) *US, 1971*

Yim, Yoe and Yesus *noun* in poker, three jacks. A play on 'Jim, Joe and Jesus' (instead of Jack), but the reason why is unknown *AUSTRALIA, 1953*

yimyom *noun* crack cocaine *UK, 1998*

yin *noun* one, indicating a single person or thing. Often in nicknames, such as 'Big yin' (Billy Connolly), 'wee yin', etc *UK: SCOTLAND, 1911*

ying *noun* marijuana. This word seems to derive from the combination of two facts lodged in a vaguely HIPPIE philosophy: 1) the female cannabis plant is considered superior; 2) in Eastern philosophy, the concept of two complementary forces that make life is *yin yang*. 'Yin', mispronounced here as 'ying', represents the female *UK, 2003*

ying yang *noun* **1** the anus and/or rectum *US, 1968.* **2** the penis *US, 1981.* **3** a variety of LSD identified by the ying yang (yin yang) symbol *UK, 1996.* ▶ **up the ying yang** to excess. The suggestion of 'ying-yang' is 'the rectum' *US, 1976*

yin-yang *noun* a well-known variety of MDMA, the recreational drug best known as ecstasy, identified by the yin and yang symbols embossed on the tablet *UK, 2002*

yip *verb* to bark in a piercing and shrill manner *US, 1907*

yipes!; yipe! used in shock, pain or surprise. Synonymous variations of YIKES! *US, 1998*

yippee!; yippy! used as a declaration of excitement and assent *US, 1920*

yippie *noun* a member of, or adherent (knowing or not) to, the principles of the Youth International Party, a short-lived blend of 1960s counterculture values and New Left politics *US, 1967*

YL *noun* an unmarried woman; a girlfriend. An abbreviation of 'young *lady' US, 1976*

YM *noun* **1** a premises of the YMCA (the Young Men's Christian Association), or the organisation itself. Pronounced 'wy em' *US, 1937.* **2** a boyfriend. Acronym of 'young *man': US, 1976*

YMCA dinner *noun* a meal made from leftovers. Standing for 'yesterday's muck cooked again' *AUSTRALIA, 2003*

yo; Yolanda *noun* in craps, a roll of eleven *US, 1999*

yo! 1 used as a greeting. Both Italian-American and black communities lay claim to 'yo!'. First recorded in 1944 among Philadelphia's Italian-Americans and popularised by Sylvester Stallone in the 1976 film *Rocky US, 1944.* **2** used as an expression of surprise, contempt, dismay, etc *SOUTH AFRICA, 1871*

yob *noun* an uncultured, boorish person. Ultimately back slang, from 'boy' *AUSTRALIA, 1938*

yobbery *noun* hooliganism *UK, 1974*

yobbish *adjective* loutish, characteristic of a YOB *UK, 1972*

yobbo; yobo; yobboe *noun* a lout. A variation of YOB *UK, 1938*

yobby *adjective* characteristic of a yob *UK, 1955*

yo-bo *noun* a member of the Korean Service Corps. Korean war usage *US, 1957*

yochie *noun* in the language surrounding the Grateful Dead, a follower of the band who has lost all touch with reality *US, 1994*

yock *noun* a laugh *US, 1938*

yock *verb* **1** to laugh *US, 1938.* **2** to expel nasal mucus *UK, 2001*

yockele *noun* a Christian. Slightly derogatory East End Yiddish; perhaps an elaborate back slang variation of GOY. 'Yog' is recorded for 'a Gentile' in 1939 *UK, 1977*

yocks *noun* the eyes. English Gypsy use *UK, 1936*

yodel *noun* an act of vomiting *NEW ZEALAND, 1995*

yodel *verb* **1** to vomit *AUSTRALIA, 1965.* **2** to perform oral sex on a woman *US, 1941.* ▶ **yodel up the valley** to perform oral sex on a woman. An elaboration of conventional 'yodel' *AUSTRALIA, 1971*

yodeller *noun* a Chrysler car. Citizens' band radio slang *1981*

yog; yogg *noun* a fire in the hearth. Market traders' use, directly from Romany *UK, 1979*

yogga *noun* a gun. English Gypsy use, perhaps from YOG (a fire) *UK, 2000*

yoghurt cannon *noun* the penis. An image formed on an ejaculating penis *UK, 1998*

yogi *noun* **1** a member of the uniformed personnel (commissionaire, security, etc) at Nottingham University in the early 1970s. Derives, apparently, from US animated cartoon series *Yogi Bear*, first broadcast in 1958 *UK, 1984.* **2** a poker player with the annoying habit of coaching other players *US, 1996*

yoink *verb* to steal *US, 2002*

yoinks! used for registering surprise *UK, 1997*

yoke *noun* **1** a tablet of MDMA, the recreational drug best known as ecstasy. This usage is an extension of the Hiberno-English use of the term for 'something whose name does not spring immediately to mind' *IRELAND, 1998.* **2** a choke hold. Originally military slang embraced by the police *US, 1987.* **3** robbery by force *US, 1951*

yoked; yolked *adjective* muscular *US, 1993*

yokel *noun* an unsophisticated, gullible person, especially one with a rural background *UK, 1812*

yola *noun* a light-skinned black female *US, 1947*

yomo; yom *noun* a person, a fellow *US, 1977*

yomp *verb* to cross rough country on foot, especially when fully laden with equipment. A Royal Marines term from the Falklands/Malvinas war *UK, 1982*

Yonge and Eligible *noun* the Yonge and Eglinton street area *CANADA, 2002*

yoni *noun* the vagina. From the Sanskrit term, which is an object of Hindu veneration *TRINIDAD AND TOBAGO, 2003*

yonks *noun* an indefinitely long time *UK, 1968*

yonnie *noun* a small stone suitable for throwing. Probably from an Australian Aboriginal language *AUSTRALIA, 1941*

yoof *adjective* used to describe any product (especially of the media) for the youth-market that may be characterised as high on fashionable content and criticised as low-culture. A deliberate misspelling of 'youth', mocking the pronunciation of stereotypical 'yoof' television presenters, emphasising the critical view *UK, 2000*

yoof; yufe *noun* a young person; the period of youth. A deliberate mispronunciation of 'youth', used by Leicestershire teenagers *UK, 1977*

yoofsploitation *noun* the exploitation of youth culture and imagery for commercial gain, especially in films *UK, 2002*

yoo-hoo *noun* a poker player who engages in excessive needless table talk *US, 1996*

yoo-hoo *verb* to try to get someone's attention by calling 'yoo-hoo' *US, 1948*

yoot; yut; yout *noun* a youth; a youth gang member. West Indian *US, 1949*

yop *verb* to inform on someone. School slang, recorded in Glasgow *UK: SCOTLAND, 1985*

york *verb* to vomit *US, 1966*

Yorkie; Yorky *noun* a Yorkshireman or -woman *UK: ENGLAND, 1818*

Yorkshire Penny Bank *noun* an act of masturbation; more usually, something of little or no value. Rhyming slang for WANK (an act of masturbation) *UK, 1980*

Yorkshire Ripper *noun* a slipper. Rhyming slang, formed on the nickname of mass murderer Peter Sutcliffe who was at large in the 1970s *UK, 1992*

Yorkshire tyke *noun* a microphone. Rhyming slang for MIKE *UK, 1957*

you ain't said nothing used for expressing contempt for what has just been said *US, 1968*

you and me *noun* **1** a flea. Rhyming slang. A C19 term recorded as current *UK, 1998*. **2** tea. Rhyming slang *UK, 1925*. **3** urine; urination. Rhyming slang for WEE or PEE *UK, 1998*. **4** a pea. Rhyming slang *UK, 1998*

you beaut *adjective* great; excellent *AUSTRALIA, 1974*

you beaut!; you beauty!; you bewdy! excellent, terrific, hooray! *AUSTRALIA, 1943*

you beautery *noun* excellence *AUSTRALIA, 1965*

you betcha! used for expressing emphatic affirmation *US, 1983*

you better believe it a catchphrase used for expressing emphatic agreement *US, 1969*

you can go off some people, you know used as a (usually jocular) response to offence or imagined offence *UK, 1984*

you can have it!; you can keep it! 'I want nothing to do with it!' *UK, 1930*

you cannot be serious! 'that is preposterous!'. A stock phrase of US tennis star John McEnroe whose questioning of officials' calls was as legendary as his genius at the game. Of all his rants against tennis officialdom, this one spread into mainstream catchphrase status *US, 2002*

you can say that again used as an expression of heartfelt agreement *US, 1942*

you can say that in spades used as an expression of heartfelt agreement. Card playing imagery *UK, 1961*

you can't stop him, you can only hope to contain him used as a humorous comment on a high achiever. Popularised by ESPN's Dan Patrick *US, 1997*

you can't take it with you! directed at someone who, in saving money, loses happiness *UK, 1847*

you could have knocked me down with a feather used for expressing astonishment at something that has happened *UK, 1741*

you don't even know used as an intensifier when words fail *US, 1984*

you don't know the half of it! used, as a catchphrase, to imply so much more *US, 2002*

you don't say! used for expressing astonishment at a statement *US, 1912*

you don't say so! used for expressing astonishment at a statement *UK, 1779*

you for coffee? an unambiguous invitation to drink coffee pronounced 'you fuck-offee!' *UK, 1984*

you go, girl! used as an encouragement or exhortation. Popularised by several black entertainers relatively simultaneously in the 1990s, and widely repeated, usually in a woman-to-woman context *US, 1993*

you haven't got the brains you were born with used as a derisive catchphrase *UK, 1961*

you have some explaining to do used for humour when there is in fact some explanation owed. A catchphrase from the *I Love Lucy* television series (1951- 61), with the 'explaining' often butchered with a pseudo Desi Arnaz Cuban accent to 'splaining' *US, 1996*

you heard! 'you heard me all right, so don't pretend you didn't!' or 'Oh, you understand, so stop pretending!' *US, 1960*

you know *noun* cocaine. Rhyming slang for SNOW (or, possibly, BLOW) *UK, 1998*

you know used as a verbal pause for indicating that the speaker assumes that the listener is listening, understanding and agreeing. An annoying discourse marker if ever there was one *UK, 1599*

you know what an unnamed (but strongly implied) activity or thing. The ultimate multi-purpose euphemism *UK, 1845*

you know what you can do!; you know what you can do with it!; you know what to do with it! used as a very definite expression of rejection of someone or something. A barely euphemistic catchphrase *UK, 1945*

you like? used as a humorous mock pidgin version of 'do you like this?' *US, 1990*

you little beaut; you little beauty used as praise *AUSTRALIA, 1945*

you'll be a long time dead! a catchphrase offered as an excuse for indulgent behaviour *UK, 1957*

you'll do yourself out of a job used as a jocular catchphrase addressed to someone working hard *UK, 1977*

you look marrrrvelous used for humorous praise. Popularised by comedian Billy Crystal on NBC's *Saturday Night Live* in the 1980s; uttered by a Crystal character, Fernando. Repeated with referential humour *US, 1984*

you make a better door than a window addressed to a person getting in the light, or blocking a view *NEW ZEALAND, 1941*

you never get a satisfied cock without a wet pussy used for expressing the principle of symbiosis *UK, 1967*

you never know something unexpected may well happen *UK, 1924*

young *adjective* ▶ **not so young as I was; not as young as he used to be** getting or being old *UK, 1852*. ▶ **the night is young; the night is yet young** it is still early *UK, 1937*

youngblood *noun* a young man, especially a young black man and especially an impetuous one; used as a term of address to a young man *US, 1946*

young, dumb, and full of come *adjective* used for describing a young man with great hopes and little experience *US, 1966*

young fellow-me-lad; young feller-me-lad *noun* used as a semi-jocular form of address *UK, 1926*

young fogey *noun* a young person with out-dated ideas and values. Coinage is claimed by Australian writer and wit Clive James *UK, 2001*

youngie *noun* a young woman; a young person. The natural corollary of OLDIE *AUSTRALIA, 1965*

young lady *noun* a female sweetheart *UK, 1896*

young man *noun* a male sweetheart *UK, 1851*

young one *noun* an attractive young girl who is sexually of age *IRELAND, 1991*

young stir *noun* a reformatory for junvenile offenders. A pun on 'youngster' *US, 1982*

young 'un *noun* a child, a young or younger person *UK, 1810*

young volunteer *noun* a youthful male homosexual prostitute *US, 1982*

young woman *noun* a female sweetheart *UK, 1858*

you now what?; you know what! used as an introductory catchphrase *UK, 1961*

your actual; yer actual *adjective* used to emphasise a noun *UK, 1966*

you rang? used as a humorous line when entering a room. A signature line of the hipster character Maynard G. Krebs on the television situation comedy *The Many Loves of Dobie Gillis* (CBS, 1959–63). Repeated with referential humour *US, 1963*

your arse! used as an expression of contempt, rejection, disbelief or derision *UK, 1988*

your arse in parsley! you are talking nonsense! An elaborated form of (UP) YOUR ARSE! *UK: SCOTLAND, 1985*

you're right, you fox used as a tease when someone has finally stumbled over the obvious *US, 1966*

you're sharing used as an admonition that the speaker is straying into personal matters that should be kept private *US, 1995*

you're telling me used for concurring with another speaker *UK, 1932*

you're the boss you decide, you make the choice. Used among equals, or even to a child, with no real superiority involved *AUSTRALIA, 1984*

you're the doctor! whatever you say; you are the authority, or the expert, or the one in charge; the responsibility is yours *US, 1907*

your man *noun* a specific male individual. An idiomatic phrase used in Hiberno-English *IRELAND, 1991*

your one *noun* a specific female individual. An idiomatic phrase used in Hiberno-English *IRELAND, 1995*

yours and ours *noun* flowers. Rhyming slang; noted as current among Covent Garden porters *UK, 1960*

yourself *pronoun* ▶ **up yourself** smugly self-satisfied; self-involved *AUSTRALIA, 1987*

yours truly *pronoun* used for 'me' or 'I'; a reference to yourself. Adopted from the formal subscription to a letter; usage is generally jocular in tone *UK, 1866*

youse; yous; youze; yers; yez *noun* you, both singular and plural *AUSTRALIA, 1885*

you shot who? I didn't hear you – what did you just say? *US, 1988*

you tell me! used for expressing a complete lack of understanding of the subject under discussion *UK, 1969*

you the man used for registering the personal superiority of a man so addressed; hence, used to encourage and to champion someone *US, 1997*

you've said it! 'yes, indeed!', I entirely agree with you *US, 1931*

you were born stupid – you've learnt nothing – and you've forgotten that a catchphrase addressed to someone who has said or done something foolish. Probably of military origin *AUSTRALIA, 1984*

you weren't born – you were pissed up against the wall and hatched in the sun a catchphrase used in response to such assertions as 'before I was born', 'when I was born', etc *UK, 1977*

you what?; y'what? what did you say? Often challenging, disbelieving or truculent *UK, 1964*

you won't know yourself a catchphrase used as encouragement to diet or exercise or to try a change of style (clothes, hair, etc) *UK, 1961*

you wouldn't want to know you would be terribly amazed, disappointed, disgusted; you would not believe it! *AUSTRALIA, 1975*

yow! 1 watch out! Used as a warning to people engaged in some criminal activity *AUSTRALIA, 1950*. **2** used as an expression of surprise. Popularised in the *Zippie the Pinhead* cartoon *US, 1991*

yowge *adjective* emphatically huge. Liverpool dialect echoes the stressed pronunciation *UK, 2001*

yowl *noun* the exhaust note of a twin two-stroke motorcycle engine *UK, 1979*

yoy *noun* an editorial rant likely to contain the phrase 'why oh why'. An acronym in journalistic use *UK, 2005*

yo-yo *noun* **1** a fool *US, 1955*. **2** a bisexual *US, 1986*. **3** a hot rod enthusiast who races illegally *US, 1956*. **4** in air combat, a steep climb and dive in an attempt to gain a more favourable position *US, 1989*. ▶ **up and down like a yo-yo** used of a person whose moods alternate rapidly between optimism and despair *UK, 1984*

yoyo *verb* to perform a tactic in aerial combat resembling a roller coaster ride *US, 1983*

yoyo children *noun* children who become pawns in a violent matrimonial battle and are constantly changing home *UK, 1977*

yoyo mouth *noun* a citizens' band radio user who talks too much *US, 1976*

yoyo nickers; yo-yo knickers *noun* a woman who (allegedly) exhibits a casual readiness for sexual encounters. The image is drawn of panties going up and down, up and down *UK, 1999*

YP *noun* in prison, used insultingly of an inmate who is not behaving in an adult manner. An initialism of 'young prisoner' *UK, 1996*

Y's *noun* male underpants. Presumably this term is restricted to pants with a Y-shaped opening *UK: SCOTLAND, 1985*

YT yours truly, me *UK, 2001*

yuck *noun* **1** a laugh *US, 1971*. **2** a fool *US, 1943*. **3** in gambling cheating schemes, a victim *US, 1962*. **4** crack cocaine *US, 1993*

yuck!; yech!; yuk! used as an indication of disgust. Echoic of vomiting *UK, 1966*

yuck; yuk; yuk-yuk *verb* to laugh. Echoic *US, 1974*. ▶ **yuck it** to stop doing something *UK: SCOTLAND, 1985*. ▶ **yuck it up; yuk it up** to behave in a foolish, time-wasting way *US, 1964*

yucky; yukky; yukkie *adjective* disgusting *US, 1970*

yug *noun* a deviation from an intended flight-path. In Royal Air Force use *UK, 1979*

yuk *verb* to vomit *US, 1997*

yuletide log; yuletide *noun* a dog, especially a racing greyhound. Rhyming slang; a variation of CHRISTMAS LOG *UK, 1974*

yuletide logs; yuletides *noun* greyhound racing. Rhyming slang for THE DOGS *UK, 1974*

yum!; yum-yum! used for registering pleasurable anticipation, especially with regard to your personal appetites *UK, 1878*

yumlicious *adjective* of a young man, sexually attractive. Teenage girls' usage, or foisted upon them by the magazines they read. Elision of YUMMY (tasty, attractive) and 'delicious'; literally 'good enough to eat' *UK, 1998*

yummy *noun* an attractive woman who is not easily seduced. Often embellished to KANSAS YUMMY *US, 1985*

yummy *adjective* tasty, delicious, attractive *UK, 1899*

yummy mummy *noun* a sexually desirable mother. Not to be confused with the branded breakfast cereal which probably lent its name to this breed *IRELAND, 2001*

yum-yums *noun* any illegal drug in capsule form *US, 1980*

yup *noun* a yuppie (young upwardly mobile professional). A sneering abbreviation of a sneering initialism *US, 1984*

yup yes, absolutely. A variation of YEP, the final plosive stresses the intention and gives it a semi-exclamatory sense *US, 1906*

yuppie *noun* an individual socially categorised as a young upwardly mobile professional. An acronym, often used derogatively, probably coined by several people independently. Variations include: BUPPIE/BUPPY (black upwardly mobile professional), 'chuppy' (Chinese etc.), 'puppy' (Punjabi etc.). These social groupings are the stuff of personal ads where you can find new, evermore contrived acronyms including, according to David Rowan, *A Glossary for the 90s*, 1998: SINBAD (single income, no boyfriend and absolutely desperate), SITCOM (single income, two children and an oppressive mortgage) and YAPPIE (young affluent parent) *US, 1982*

yuppie scum *noun* an arrogant young professional. A favourite epithet of the 1980s *US, 1992*

yuppification *noun* the change that is made in order that something or somewhere becomes attractive to the yuppie market; gentrification. Derogatory in tone *UK, 1999*

yuppify *verb* to style or remodel something in a manner characteristic of, or suitable for, yuppy life *UK, 1984*

yupster *noun* a young upwardly mobile professional. A variation of YUPPIE *US, 1986*

yutz *noun* a fool. From Yiddish *yutz* (the penis) *US, 1991*

Zz

z noun **1** in hip-hop culture, used for replacing the letter 's' when creating plurals US, 2002. **2** an outcast; a despised person US, 1963

Z noun an ounce of narcotics US, 1975. ▶ **the Z** the demilitarised zone US, 1976

-z suffix used in the abbreviating of a forename, by truncating the given name to its first open syllable which is then closed with -z. Examples: Gary or Gareth becomes Gaz; Jeremy, Jez; Terry or Terence, Tez; Sharon, Shaz UK, 1984

za noun pizza US, 1996

zac noun a six-month or six-year prison sentence. From ZACK (six pence) AUSTRALIA, 1919

Zacatecas purple noun a potent variety of marijuana originating in Mexico. Named after the location and the colour of the buds US, 1974

Zachary Scotts; Zacharys noun diarrhoea. Rhyming slang for TROTS; formed on the name of US film actor Zachary Scott (1914–65) UK, 1992

zack; zac noun a sixpence; the sum of six pence. Origin unknown. Perhaps from Scottish dialect saxpence (sixpence), or possibly Yiddish from German sechs (six). After the introduction of decimal currency in 1966, it came to mean 'a five-cent piece', or its value, a similar coin with about the same comparative value; dying out from the 1980s, now seldom heard AUSTRALIA, 1898. ▶ **not have a zack** to be broke AUSTRALIA, 1989. ▶ **not worth a zack** worthless AUSTRALIA, 1962

zaftig; zoftig adjective sexy; buxom. From German/Yiddish for 'juicy' US, 1932

zag verb when faced with two courses of action, to take the right one. Most commonly used in variations of 'I zigged when I should have zagged' US, 1948

zags noun thin papers used for rolling cigarettes. From the branded name Zig Zag™, the dominant rolling papers during the hippie years US, 1970

zambi noun marijuana presumed to originate in the Republic of Zambia US, 1998

zambuck noun a member of St John Ambulance Brigade. From a proprietary name of an antiseptic ointment commonly used by them AUSTRALIA, 1918

zami noun a lesbian. From a misplaced juncture of the French les amies (women friends) TRINIDAD AND TOBAGO, 2003

Zanussi noun ▶ **on Zanussi** drug-intoxicated; wildly excited or distracted. A variant of ON ANOTHER PLANET, from the advertising for Zanussi, a manufacturer of domestic electrical appliances UK, 1995

zap noun **1** amyl nitrite UK, 1996. **2** an electrical shock US, 1994

zap verb **1** to kill someone. A major piece of slang from the Vietnam war US, 1942. **2** to shoot someone. A Royal Navy variation on the previous sense UK, 1989. **3** to finish something off. A figurative variation of the sense 'to kill' UK, 1999. **4** to defeat someone heavily US, 1968. **5** to give someone an electrical shock; to administer electric shock treatment to someone. Recorded as 'administering shock treatment' in 'The language of nursing', Philip C. Kolin, American Speech, p. 209, Fall–Winter 1973 US, 1995. **6** to operate electronically, often by remote-control, 2001. **7** to overwhelm someone US, 1967. **8** to move quickly US, 1974. **9** to have sex US, 1985. **10** to present, to give US, 1967. **11** to steal something UK, 2002. **12** to use the (remote) fast-forward facility on video playback to pass advertising; to use a remote control to switch between television channels (to avoid advertising, or simply to find a programme that engages you) US, 1983. **13** to send a text message UK, 2003. **14** to heat something up in a microwave oven US, 1999. **15** to give a student in college a notification of academic deficiency US, 1968. **16** in Canadian military aviation, to affix a sticker on which is the badge of a military unit onto an aircraft of another service CANADA, 1982

zap over verb to change your mind UK, 1972

zapped adjective **1** drug-intoxicated US, 1979. **2** spicy US, 1983

zapper noun any remote-control device used with domestic entertainment equipment – television, stereo, video, DVD player, etc US, 1981

zappy adjective lively, energetic UK, 1983

zap up verb to enliven something UK, 1988

Zat? ▷ see: OWZAT?

zatch noun the genitals of either gender. Originally used of female genitals UK, 1950

Zazu Pitts noun diarrhoea. Rhyming slang for THE SHITS, formed on the name of the US film actress, 1914–65 UK, 1992

zazzy adjective ostentatious, showy US, 1961

Z-bag noun the bed US, 1968

Z-bars noun in motorcycle racing, handlebars each shaped like the letter Z, facing each other US, 1973

zebbled adjective circumcised UK, 2003

zebra noun a cadet officer in the US Air Force. An allusion to how conscious the officer is of his stripes US, 1946

zebra adjective racially mixed US, 1971

Zec noun an area in Quebec where logging and hunting are controlled or prohibited CANADA, 1992

zeds noun **1** sleep. Royal Navy slang; echoic, based on UK pronunciation of 'z', from the strip-cartoon legend 'zzzz' as an indicator of sleep. Used in phrases such as 'racking (or piling) up the zeds' (sleeping) and 'zeds merchant' (someone who likes to sleep) UK, 1989. **2** central nervous system depressants UK, 1983

zeek freak noun a person who greatly enjoys sex while under the influence of crack cocaine US, 1989

zeke noun in circus usage, a hyena US, 1981

Zelda noun **1** a girl or a woman, especially if dull or uninteresting. Possibly after Zelda Fitzgerald (1900–48) with the suggestion that the name is dull and old-fashioned; Zelda Fitzgerald was herself named after the character of a gypsy queen in a romantic novel US, 2002. **2** a high school girl who is a socially inept outcast US, 1961. **3** a witch. Perhaps from the character Aunt Zelda, a 2000-year-old witch in Sabrina, The Teenage Witch, from a 1962 comic book creation, subsequently in animated and live-action television series UK, 2002

zeller noun an over-devoted surfer US, 1988

zen noun LSD. From the other-worldly state sought by Zen Buddhism UK, 1978

Zen noun MDMA, the recreational drug best known as ecstasy US, 1989

zen in verb to grasp completely through intuition US, 1967

zenith noun ketamine hydrochloride, an anaesthetic used as a hallucinogen US, 2002

zeppelin noun a poker player who contemplates long and hard before every bet or play US, 1996

zero noun **1** a person of no significance; a nobody US, 1979. **2** a gambler who is a chronic loser US, 1996

zero verb **1** to kill someone US, 1990. **2** to identify or locate someone or something US, 1955

zero-dark-thirty noun very early in the morning US, 1991

zero out verb **1** to kill someone. Korean war usage US, 1989. **2** to be killed US, 1992

zero week noun the orientation week preceding eight weeks of basic military training US, 1968

Z-game *noun* the game with the lowest betting limits in a gambling operation or cardroom. There need not be 26 tables to arrive at the Z-game; it is the lowest-stakes table in the place *US, 1988*

zhoosh; jhoosh *noun* **1** ornamentation *UK, 2002*. **2** clothing *UK, 1968*

zhoosh; jhoosh *verb* **1** to swallow something *UK, 2002*. **2** to tidy the appearance of something; to tittivate, to trim, to ornament *UK, 1997*

zhooshing *noun* shop-lifting *UK, 1995*

zhoosh off; jhoosh off *verb* to leave; to go *UK, 2002*

zhooshy *adjective* showy, ornate *UK, 2002*

ziff *noun* a beard. Origin unknown. Now all but obsolete *AUSTRALIA, 1917*

ziffed; be-ziffed *adjective* bearded. From ZIFF (a beard) *AUSTRALIA, 1973*

zig *noun* ▶ **get the zig** to become annoyed or angry with someone *UK, 2000*

zig *verb* **1** when faced with two courses of action, to take the wrong one. Most commonly used in some variation of 'I zigged when I should have zagged' *US, 1948*. **2** to shoot down an enemy fighter plane *US, 1986*

Zig and Zag *noun* **1** a variety of LSD identified by a picture of television puppets Zig and Zag *UK, 1996*. **2** an act of sexual intercourse. Rhyming slang for SHAG, formed from a double act of television puppets, in turn named from an in-and-out movement *UK, 2003*

ziggerboo *noun* an eccentric or crazy person *US, 1947*

zig-zag *noun* **1** cigarette rolling papers. A brand name that acquired a generic meaning *US, 1968*. **2** sex with a prostitute *US, 1954*

zig-zag *adjective* unreliable; dishonest *TRINIDAD AND TOBAGO, 1960*

zigzag man *noun* **1** marijuana *UK, 2003*. **2** LSD. Perhaps from a icon printed on the drug *UK, 2003*

zig-zig *noun* sexual intercourse. Familiar pidgin in the Far, Near and Middle East and Mediterranean, originally military; a variation of JIG-A-JIG. Used by US soldiers in the South Pacific *UK, 1918*

zig-zig *verb* to have sex. Familiar pidgin in the Far, Near and Middle East and Mediterranean, originally military; a variation of JIG-A-JIG *US, 1918*

zilch *noun* **1** nothing *US, 1940*. **2** a socially inept outcast *US, 1965*

zillion *noun* an almost unimaginably large number. One of several invented numbers used to convey a large number; probably coined by Damon Runyon *US, 1944*

zillionaire *noun* a multi-millionaire *US, 1946*

Zimbo *noun* a person from Zimbabwe *NEW ZEALAND, 1995*

zimmer *noun* a girl *US, 1990*

zinc *noun* an obviously unfashionable child or youth. Pejorative. Commented on by the Plain English Campaign in October 2003 *UK, 2003*

zine *noun* an inexpensively self-published magazine devoted to such topics as hobbies, music, film and politics. An abbreviation of FANZINE, ultimately 'magazine' *US, 1978*

zined *noun* a fan magazine editor *US, 1976*

zinfandel *noun* serious trouble. Zinfandel is a wine from California that seems not to have travelled well *CANADA, 1970*

zing *noun* **1** energy, vigour *US, 1918*. **2** sex appeal. A nuance of the previous sense *US, 1961*. **3** an amphetamine tablet *US, 1997*

Z-ing *noun* the practice of targeting tourists as victims of crime by the 'Z' as the first letter on the car number plate, designating a rental car *US, 1994*

zing *verb* **1** (of a bullet) to ricochet *US, 2001*. **2** to travel quickly *US, 1920*. **3** to affect someone suddenly and forcefully *US, 1975*. **4** to feel pleasurable sensations resulting from drug use *UK, 1971*. ▶ **zing it in** to bet heavily *US, 1979*

zing! used to represent a sudden change in circumstance or emotion *UK, 1919*

zingaro *noun* in circus and carnival usage, a gypsy *US, 1981*

zinger *noun* **1** the punch-line of a joke; the last word *US, 1964*. **2** an arranged ending to a competition *US, 1959*. **3** a surprise, an awkward or unexpected turn of events *US, 1973*. **4** an exceptionally good example of something *UK, 1955*. **5** a very attractive woman *US, 1959*. **6** an amphetamine tablet *US, 1993*. **7** a hot pepper *US, 1996*. **8** a hard stare that is intended to impart bad luck on the recipient *US, 1979*

zingy *adjective* exciting, energetic *US, 1948*

zip *noun* **1** an Italian or Sicilian criminal brought to the US for criminal purposes, especially murder *US, 1993*. **2** a Viet Cong; a Vietnamese; any South Asian person *US, 1970*. **3** energy *UK, 1900*. **4** methamphetamine *US, 1997*. **5** cocaine. Probably from ZIPPED (drug-intoxicated) *US, 1998*. **6** used for representing the sharp sound of, for instance, a bullet or a mosquito as it moves through the air; specifically of bullets, it is often reduplicated: 'zip-zip' or 'zip, zip' *UK, 1875*. **7** nothing at all; zero *US, 1900*. **8** a hand-made gun, a zip gun *US, 1967*

zip *verb* **1** to move quickly *US, 1852*. **2** to kill someone *US, 1982*. ▶ **zip it** to stop talking. From the image of zipping your mouth shut *US, 1999*. ▶ **zip your lip; zip your mouth** to stop talking. The image of a zip fastener (zipper) sealing your lips; may be mimed rather than spoken; often as an imperative *US, 1942*

zip ball *noun* in pinball, a ball that leaves play without having scored *US, 1977*

zip-five *noun* a prison sentence of a maximum of five years *US, 1964*

zip gun *noun* an inexpensive, homemade gun, usually consisting of a tube, a grip and a rudimentary striking device *US, 1950*

zipped *noun* drug-intoxicated *US, 1973*

zipper *noun* **1** a scar *US, 1978*. **2** an electronic display of news or publicity which is scrolled across a screen fixed to a building *US, 2003*. **3** a short but well-formed wave *US, 1988*. **4** a trap play in poker *US, 1996*

zipperhead *noun* **1** a Vietnamese person. Offensive *US, 1987*. **2** a stupid person *US, 1989*

zipper ripper *noun* in craps, a roll of ten. Evolved from the more common BIG DICK (a roll of ten) *US, 1999*

zippily *adverb* energetically, swiftly *UK, 1983*

zippiness *noun* an energetic quality, speediness *UK, 1924*

zippity-doo-dah *noun* nothing at all. An elaboration of ZIP (zero) *US, 1977*

zippity-doo-dah! used as a nonsensical, all-purpose utterance. From the lyrics of a song in the 1946 Walt Disney film *Song of the South US, 1992*

zippo *noun* **1** nothing. An embellished form of ZIP *US, 1993*. **2** energy *US, 1981*. **3** a tank-mounted flame thrower. An allusion to the branded cigarette lighter *US, 1966*

zippo *verb* to set something on fire and burn it. An allusion to the branded cigarette lighter *US, 1966*

zippo job *noun* the burning of a village as part of a military sweep through the area *US, 1988*

zippola *noun* nothing at all *US, 1994*

zippy *noun* someone whose lifestyle mixes hippy ideals and modern technology. An acronym of 'zen-inspired professional pagan' *UK, 1990s*

zippy *adjective* lively, bright, energetic, vigorous; fast, speedy *US, 1904*

zips *noun* the first decade of the 21st century *UK, 2003*

zip squat *noun* a very small amount. Two words that mean 'nothing' *US, 1990*

zip top *noun* A Jewish person. Offensive *US, 1987*

zip up *verb* to stop talking. The image of a zip fastener sealing the lips *UK, 1999*

zirconia flush *noun* in poker, four diamonds. Named after the synthetic diamond *US, 1996*

zit *noun* an acne pimple *US, 1966*

zitfarm *noun* a teenager. From the adolescent tendency towards ZIT (a pimple, a spot)-production in agricultural quantities *US, 1981*

zizz *noun* a snooze, a brief sleep; sleep. Military usage; echoic in as much as the cartoon-strip legend 'zzzz' is an accurate indicator of sleep *UK, 1941*

zizz *verb* **1** to sleep. Military usage; echoic in as much as the cartoon-strip legend 'zzzz' is an accurate indicator of sleep *UK, 1942.* **2** to prepare food in a blender *UK, 2002*

zizzy *adjective* fancy, showy *US, 1954*

Z-list *noun* denotes all that is associated with a level of minor-celebrity so despised that obscurity is almost achieved. A notional social grouping that contrasts with A-LIST (top-rank celebrity); 'Z-list' inclusion is a matter of derogatory opinion *US, 1979*

zloty *noun* in poker, low-stakes betting. Named after the lowest value coin in the Polish monetary system *US, 1996*

zob *noun* an unlikeable, despicable person *US, 1911* .

zobbit *noun* an officer. Royal Air Force lower ranks' usage, from Arabic *dabat* (an officer) *UK, 1967*

zod *noun* someone who is socially inept to the extreme *US, 1982*

zog *noun* the US federal government. A basic piece of racist, right-wing political vocabulary in the US *US, 2000*

zoinks! used for expressing fear or surprise. Popularised as a signature line of the character Shaggy, voiced by Casey Kasem, on the television cartoon *Scooby Doo, Where are You?* (CBS, 1969–72). Repeated with referential humour *US, 1972*

zol *noun* a marijuana cigarette *US, 1955*

Zola Budd *noun* a police vehicle, especially a slow-moving armoured vehicle; a small bus, especially a Toyota. Township slang; after the South African-born British Athlete (b.1966) who was involved in a controversial incident in the 1984 Olympic 3,000 metres race. *SOUTH AFRICA, 1985*

zombie *noun* **1** a dull, personality-free person. From the belief of certain west African religions that corpses can be revived to walk the earth without souls *US, 1941.* **2** in poker, an expert player who shows no emotion, no matter how good or bad his hand is *US, 1979.* **3** a policewoman. Usually in the plural *UK, 1956.* **4** among air-traffic controllers, a suspicious unidentified flying object *UK, 1982*

zombie *verb* to put someone into an apathetic condition. From a belief in soulless corpses that walk the earth (and film sets) having been revived by voodoo *UK, 1990*

zombied *adjective* very drunk. In a condition generally seen among the undead *UK, 2002*

zombie job *noun* during the Korean war, a night patrol *US, 1957*

zombie medicine *noun* tranquillizers. From the desired effect of the medication *UK, 1996*

zombie weed *noun* phencyclidine, the recreational drug known as PCP or angel dust *US, 1981*

zone *noun* a state of such concentration that consequent action seems instinctual. Often in the phrase 'in the zone' *US, 1995.* ▶ **on the zone** lost in a daydream *US, 1974.* ▶ **the zone** a state of being qualified for, and meeting all other parameters for, a promotion in rank. Originally Royal Navy, then army use *UK, 1962*

zoned out *adjective* mentally absent *US, 1971*

zone out; zone off; zone *verb* to absent yourself mentally, with or without the aid of drugs *US, 1992*

zoner; zonie *noun* someone from Arizona *US, 1991*

zonk *verb* **1** to fall asleep, especially as a result of drugs or drink. Also used with 'out' *US, 1970.* **2** to hit or strike, literally or figuratively *US, 1969*

zonked *noun* the recreational drug GHB. From the drug-intoxicated sense of ZONKED *US, 2000*

zonked *adjective* **1** intoxicated on a drug, especially marijuana; drunk. Also used with 'out' *US, 1958.* **2** exhilarated; intoxicated by an abstract thought *UK, 1980.* **3** exhausted *US, 1968*

zonker *noun* a drug user who indulges to excess. A cartoon strip by Garry Trudeau has had a laid-back marijuana-smoking character called Zonker since 1972 *US, 1996*

zonkers *noun* the female breasts. An abbreviation of BAZONKAS *US, 1995*

zonking *adverb* used as an intensifier of adjectives that convey positivity or largeness *UK, 1958*

zonks *noun* an indefinitely long time. A variation of YONKS *UK, 1982*

zoo *noun* **1** the section of a prison where 'vulnerable prisoners' are kept for their own safety. In *Prison Patter*, 1996, Angela Devlin notes that an ANIMAL is 'a sex offender', and animals are kept in a zoo *UK, 1996.* **2** a police station. Citizens' band radio slang *US, 1976.* **3** in motor racing, the pit area where cars stop for fuelling and repairs *US, 1980.* **4** a brakevan (caboose) *US, 1977.* **5** a notional or actual grouping or assemblage of people; the place where they are assembled. Often mildly contemptuous *UK, 1924.* **6** a zoophile, a person with a sexual interest in animals *UK, 2002*

zoob *noun* a large penis *AUSTRALIA, 1985*

zoo book *noun* a student directory with photographs of each student *US, 1968*

zoobs *noun* the female breasts. A blend of BOOB(S) and BAZOOMS *US, 1968*

zoo doo *noun* compost made from multi-species faeces *US, 1981*

zooed *adjective* **1** drunk *US, 1979.* **2** crowded. Surfer usage *US, 1988*

zooie *noun* a cylindrical implement that holds the butt of a marijuana joint *2001*

zook *noun* a marijuana and tobacco cigarette; may also contain crack cocaine *UK, 2000*

zookeeper *noun* in motor racing, the official in charge of the pit area *US, 1980*

zoom *noun* **1** phencyclidine, the recreational drug known as PCP or angel dust *US, 1994.* **2** marijuana laced with phencyclidine, the recreational drug known as PCP or angel dust. 'Zoom!' is a comic book caption for the drugs' combined effect *US, 1982*

zoom *verb* **1** to move very quickly. From aviation slang *US, 1946.* **2** to induce someone to commit a crime that they were not otherwise inclined to commit *US, 1970*

zoom bag *noun* a military flier's flight suit *US, 1991*

zoomer *noun* **1** an energetic fool. From ZOOM (to move quickly) *UK, 2000.* **2** a person who sells fake crack cocaine and then quickly disappears *US, 2002*

zoomers *noun* the female breasts *US, 1968*

zoomie *noun* **1** a graduate of the United States Air Force Academy *US, 1991.* **2** in drag racing cars, an exhaust pipe that curves upward directing some of the exhaust gases to heat the tyres *US, 1968.* **3** a crew member of a military jet aircraft. A term used by the infantry and navy *US, 1948*

zooms *noun* the female breasts. A shortened form of BAZOOMS *US, 1968*

zoo-only *adjective* applied to the sexual predilection of a zoophile with no other interests *UK, 2002*

zoot *noun* **1** a ZOOT SUIT *US, 1947.* **2** a marijuana cigarette. Also called a 'zut' or 'zootie' *UK, 1996.* **3** a cigarette butt *TRINIDAD AND TOBAGO, 1956*

zoot canary *noun* a fashion model. Beatniks' use, therefore late 1950s *UK, 1984*

zooted; zooted up *adjective* drug-intoxicated *US, 1986*

zooter *noun* **1** in cricket, a non-spinning ball bowled by a spin-bowler. Coinage credited to Australian cricketers Shane Warne (b.1969) and Terry Jenner (b.1944) to describe a style that they developed *AUSTRALIA, 2002.* **2** a ZOOT SUITER *US, 1994*

zootie *adjective* emotionally unbalanced or drug-intoxicated *US, 1990*

zootied *adjective* very marijuana-intoxicated *US, 1982*

zoot suit *noun* a type of man's suit characterised by its exaggerated style: padded shoulders, long jacket, high-waisted trousers, bright colours. Perhaps by reduplication of 'suit' *US, 1942*

zoot suiter *noun* a member of an identifiable group of zoot-suit-wearing young men, characterised by fashion and as flashy and vulgar *US, 1943*

zoot up *verb* to dress in a zoot suit and accessories *US, 1947*

zooty *adjective* fashionable, stylish. Derived from, and an allusion to, ZOOT SUIT *US, 1946*

zoo-zoo; zuu-zuu *noun* in prison, sweets, snacks, soda or any other special treat *US, 1981*

zoquete *noun* heroin. Directly from Spanish for 'block' or 'chunk' *UK, 2003*

Zorba the Greek; Zorba *verb* to urinate; an act of urination. Also used as a noun. Rhyming slang for LEAK, formed on the title of a 1946 novel by Nikos Kazantzakis and 1964 film *UK, 1992*

zorch *verb* in computing, to move or process quickly *US, 1983*

zorries *noun* inexpensive, practical foam rubber thong sandals *US, 1990*

zot *noun* zero; nothing *US, 1965*

zot *verb* to move suddenly or swiftly. Perhaps from the nonsense, all-purpose word – especially used as a substitute for God – coined by US cartoonist Johnny Hart (b.1931) *US, 1974*

zotz *noun* a planned murder; an assassination *US, 1988*

zotz *verb* to kill someone *US, 1982*

zotzed *adjective* drunk or drug-intoxicated *US, 1992*

zounds! used for registering a strong reaction. Compounded from 'God's wounds!', modern usage is often ironic *UK, 1616*

zowie! used as a vocal representation of an instantaneous happening *UK, 1913*

z's *noun* sleep. From Z's as the representation of snoring in comic strips used with a verb such as 'catch', 'cop', 'cut', get', 'grab' or 'rip' *US, 1963*. ▶ **stack z's** to sleep *US, 1975*

zubrick; zoob *noun* the penis. Mainly in soldiers' Arabic *shufti zubrick* or *shufti zoob* (let's see/show the penis), possibly enhanced by the rhyme on PRICK but not rhyming slang *UK, 1958*

zucchini *noun* an extended fibreglass field hut *ANTARCTICA, 1991*

zug up *verb* to cut hair unevenly *TRINIDAD AND TOBAGO, 1959*

zuke *noun* in American casinos, a gratuity *US, 1985*

Zulu *noun* **1** a black person. Offensive *US, 1960*. **2** a large marijuana cigarette *US, 1973*

Zulu princess *noun* in homosexual usage, a young and attractive black man *US, 1987*

zulu time *noun* Greenwich Mean Time *US, 1960*

'zup? used as a greeting. A slurred 'what's up?' *US, 1990*

zut *adjective* stupid *TRINIDAD AND TOBAGO, 1984*

zymotic; zymy *adjective* contemptible. A figurative application of the conventional senses relating to infectious disease and containing putrefactive germs, thus creating a synonym for LOUSY. Noted in use amongst teenagers *UK, 1965*

0-9

10 – 1; ten-one *adjective* broken. Teen slang taken from citizens' band radio jargon *UK, 1982*

10 – 4; ten-four used as an acknowledgement that a message has been received *US, 1976*

11 *noun* the loudest possible amplification. From a comic conceit in the film *This Is Spinal Tap US, 1984*

110 per cent *adverb* absolutely, utterly *UK, 2001*

12 *noun* a recording available on twelve-inch vinyl disc *UK, 2002*

125 *noun* cocaine. Rhyming slang, from the Inter-City 125, the nearest thing the UK has to a high-speed *train UK, 2001*

12-er *noun* a twelve-pack of beer *US, 2003*

14 *nickname* **1** used as an indication that a person is a member of a northern California Mexican-American gang. 'N' for Norteno (the name of a gang) is the fourteenth letter of the alphabet *US, 1985*. **2** a member of the Nuestra Familia prison gang. 'N' is the fourteenth letter of the alphabet *US, 2000*

151; one-fifty-one; fifty-one *noun* crack cocaine *US, 1998*

187; one-eight-seven *noun* **1** a homicide. From the California penal code number used by the police as radio shorthand for a homicide. Adopted into the lyrics of GANGSTA RAP(S) from Los Angeles Police Department usage *US, 1992*. **2** no possibility; no chance. A figurative use of the previous sense, hence 'any possibility is dead'. *US, 1996*

1984 *adjective* oppressively authoritarian. Directly from the novel *Nineteen Eighty-Four* by George Orwell, 1949 *US, 1970*

21 *nickname* Newquay, Cornwall. Puns 'new key': 'He's got the key of the door, never been twenty-one before' *UK, 1981*

24/7; twenty-four seven *adverb* at all times – twenty-four hours a day, seven days a week *US, 1989*

24-hour hootch *noun* a beverage of apple juice, yeast and aspirins *CANADA, 1989*

276 *nickname* the prison gang more commonly known as the Black Guerrilla Family *US, 2000*

288; two eighty-eight *adjective* too disgusting, too gross. An excruciating pun on 288 as 'two gross' (2 x 144 = 288) *US, 1995*

28 cheeks *noun* girls who are not romantically or sexually faithful to one partner; two timers. Teen slang, of uncertain origin. This may well also apply in the singular *SOUTH AFRICA, 2003*

2C-B *noun* 4-bromo-2, 5-dimethoxyphenethylamine, a mild hallucinogen used recreationally *US, 1995*

364; three-sixty-four *noun* a 364-day jail sentence in the US, the maximum jail term for misdemeanours, served in county jail *US, 1992*

365; three-six-five *noun* a mutton chop. So named because it is served for breakfast every day of the year *NEW ZEALAND, 2001*

365; three-sixty-five *adverb* all the time. Every day of the year *US, 1990*

37461 *noun* crack cocaine *UK, 2003*

3750 *noun* marijuana *UK, 2003*

3-m *noun* (1) mutual (2) manual (3) masturbation *US, 1985*

3-peat; three-peat *verb* to win a sports championship three times consecutively. When he was the coach of the Los Angeles Lakers basketball team, Pat Riley sought and obtained a trademark for the term *US, 1992*

40 *noun* **1** a forty-ounce bottle of malt liquor. Also spelt out as 'forty' or 'forty-ounce' *US, 1990*. **2** a 40-milligram dose of the synthetic opiate oxycodone used recreationally *US, 2001*

404; four-o-four *adjective* mentally lost, very unaware. From the Internet message '404, URL not found' *US, 1997*

411; four-one-one *noun* gossip, information. 411 is the universal telephone number for directory enquiries – known commonly as 'information' in the US *US, 1991*

415 *noun* a prison gang with black members *US, 2000*

420 man; four-twenty man *noun* a cheat; a fraudster. A reference to the Indian Penal Code *INDIA, 2003*

45 *noun* a single song recording on vinyl. From the rpm (revolutions per minute) *UK, 1950*

5000; five thousand goodbye. An abbreviation of AUDI 5000! *US, 1996*

50 Cent *adjective* homosexual. Rhyming slang for bent, formed on the stage name of New York rapper Curtis Jackson (b.1977) *UK, 2005*

5318008 *noun* a numerical sequence that displays boobies (the female breasts) upside down in the window of a calculator or mobile phone. Probably first seen in the 1970s, still in use, *2003*

5-H-1-T *noun* shit. A euphemism employed by some doctors *UK, 2002*

5 watter; five watter a fool. A play on the dimmest unit of electric lighting and a person who is not very bright; in Royal Air Force use, 2002 *UK, 2002*

6 – 10 *verb* to have sex *UK, 1981*

64; six-four; six-fo' *noun* a 1964 Chevrolet Impala, an ultimate prize of car customisers and lowriders *US, 1997*

650 lifer *noun* in Michigan, a prisoner sentenced to life in prison for possession of more than 650 grams of cocaine *US, 1997*

69; sixty-nine *verb* to engage in simultaneous, mutual oral sex with someone *US, 1971*

69; sixty-nine; sixty-niner *noun* mutual, simultaneous oral sex between two people (used of both the position and the act) *UK, 1888*

6-up; six-up *noun* a police officer *US, 2003*

79 *noun* an M79 grenade launcher. Vietnam war usage. It is a single-shot, break-open, breech-loading, shoulder-fired weapon *US, 1992*

7-up *noun* in casinos, a wire bent in the shape of a seven that is slipped into slot machines to trigger a payout *US, 1997*

8; number 8; number eight; eight *noun* heroin. H (heroin) is the eighth letter of the alphabet *US, 1994*

80's bush *noun* a bushy female hairstyle, popular in the 1980s and mocked thereafter *US, 2001*

88 used as a symbol of fascist and racist beliefs. 'H' is the eighth letter of the alphabet, and so 88 translates into HH, or 'Heil Hitler' *US, 2000*

8th; eighth *noun* an eighth of an ounce, especially of a drug *UK, 1989*

9; nine *noun* **1** a 9mm pistol *US, 1990*. **2** a nine-gallon keg of beer *AUSTRALIA, 1943*

900 *noun* in skateboarding, a jumping manoeuvre of two and a half revolutions *UK, 2004*

98; ninety-eight *noun* any classic car, especially an Oldsmobile 98 *US, 1997*

99s used euphemistically to avoid swearing in citizens' band radio transmissions *UK, 1981*

Related titles from Routledge

Sex Slang
Tom Dalzell and Terry Victor

Are you a beaver cleaver or the office bike? Would you rather pack fudge or munch carpet? Do you content yourself with paddling the pickle as you're still a cherry boy?

Sex Slang will not only give you 3,000 words to talk about your favourite pastimes, but also open your eyes to practices you didn't even know existed.

All words are illustrated by a reference from a variety of sources to prove their existence. This naughty book will give you a spectacular sexual vocabulary from all over the English speaking world, as well as hours of reading pleasure.

ISBN10: 0-415-37180-5

ISBN13: 978-0-415-37180-3

Available at all good bookshops
For ordering and further information please visit:
www.routledge.com

Related titles from Routledge

Vice Slang
Tom Dalzell and Terry Victor

Are you a bit of a chairwarmer? Do you use the wins from a country straight to get scudded on snakebite in a blind tiger? Do you ride the waves on puddle or death drop?

Vice Slang gently eases you into the language of gambling, drugs and alcohol, providing you with 3,000 words to establish yourself firmly in the world of corruption and wickedness.

All words are illustrated by a reference from a variety of sources to prove their existence in alleys and dives throughout the English speaking world. This entertaining book will give you hours of reading pleasure.

ISBN10: 0-415-37181-3
ISBN13: 978-0-415-37181-0

Available at all good bookshops
For ordering and further information please visit:
www.routledge.com